S0-AHC-976

Great Britain

&

Ireland

2009

Contents

Sommaire
Sommario
Inhaltsverzeichnis

How to use this guide

TOURIST INFORMATION

Distances from
the main towns,
tourist offices,
local tourist
attractions,
means of transport,
golf courses and
leisure activities...

HOTELS

From 🏨🏨🏨 to 🏠, ↑:
categories of comfort.
In red 🏨🏨🏨... 🏠, ↑:
the most pleasant.

RESTAURANTS AND PUBS

From XXXXX to X, ⏸: categories
of comfort.
In red XXXXX... X, ⏸:
the most pleasant.

STARS

❀❀❀ Worth a special journey.
❀❀ Worth a detour.
❀ A very good restaurant.

GOOD FOOD AND ACCOMMODATION AT MODERATE PRICES

⊛ Bib Gourmand

⊠ Bib Hotel

CAMBRIDGE – Cambs – **504** U27 – **pop. 117 717** – ◼ Great

◻ London 55 – Coventry 88 – Ipswich 54 – Leicest
Nottingham 88 – Oxford 100
🛬 Cambridge Airport : ℰ (01223) 373737, E: 2 m o
🚂 The Old Library, Wheeleer St, ℰ (01223) 45758
🏨 Cambridgeshire Moat House Hotel, Bar Hill, (
◉ Town : St John's College ACY – King's
Fitzwilliam Museumy Z **M1** – Trinity College
College AC Z
◔ Audley End, S: 13m by A1309 – Imperi
on M11

Hotel Gloria ⏵
Whitehouse lane, Huntington Rd, CB3 OLX,
– ℰ (01223) 277985 – help@hotelgloria.co
Rest The Melrose – Menu £16 (lunch) – ⏛ £7.50
52 rm – †£136 ††£168/255 – ⏛ £7.50
• Built as a private house in 1852, now
contemporary rooms include state of
garden and terrace.

Alexander House (Johns)
Midsummer Common, CB4 1HA – ℰ
– resa@alexanderhouse.co.uk – Fa
– closed 2 weeks Christmas, 2 wee
Rest – Menu (dinner only and lu
Spec. Salad of smoked eel, pig's
nuts and pistachios and aspara
des bois and mint.
• A river Cam idyll. Chic con
terrace with blissful views o

The Roasted Pepper
35 Chesterton Rd,CB4 3AX
– Fax (01223) 351873 – clo
Rest (booking essential)
• Personally run Victori
Italian dishes with mild

at Histon North : 3 m on B10

Blue House Farm
44 High St, CB3 7HV
– Fax (01223) 2621€
22 rm ⏛ – †£38 †
• Red-brick 18C li
house overlooks
bread and pres

4

A **3**

OTHER MICHELIN PUBLICATIONS

References for the Michelin map and Green Guide which cover the area.

LOCATING THE TOWN

Locate the town on the map at the end of the guide (map number and coordinates).

orwich 61 –

X
m@cambridge.gov.uk
249988 X
e Z – The Backs YZ –
e's Yardx Y **M2** – Queen's

Museumx, Duxford, S: 9m

QUIET HOTELS

⌂ Quiet hotel.
⌂ Very quiet hotel.

Z **d**

st: 1,5 m by A1307
(01223) 277986
20/35.50

DESCRIPTION OF THE ESTABLISHMENT

Atmosphere, style, character and specialities.

dern and stylish public areas. The
acilities. Sleek restaurant overlooks

Y **a**

69 245
369246
, 1 week spring, Sunday and Monday
-Saturday) £30/50
nd apple purée. Braised turbot with pea-
nelloni of apricot, Strawberry sorbet, fraises

LOCATING THE ESTABLISHMENT

Located on the town plan (coordinates and letters giving the location).

dining room with smart first floor bar and
ver.

FACILITIES AND SERVICES

Y **c**

3) 351872 – seancarter@roastedpepper.co.uk
xmas-New Year and Sunday
nly) Menu £25
ouse with smartly clad tables. Classic French and
uences, served at reasonable prices.

PRICES

Cambridge

rest
23) 262164 – reservations@bluehousefarm.uk.co
d 2 weeks Christmas-New Year

house on a working farm... with beautiful blue windows;
. Sunny garden room for breakfast, including home-made
naculate rooms.

A **12**

R29 – **pop. 47 123 (inc. Frimley)** – ▌ *Great Britain*
ton 76 – Dover 15 – Maidstone 28 – Margate 17
(0870) 400 8245

off Portsmouth Rd (A325) – ℰ (0870) 400 8245
Fax (0870) 4008246

bedrooms; some
dern. 19C

5

Commitments

*"This volume was created at the turn of the century
and will last at least as long".*

This foreword to the very first edition of the MICHELIN guide, written in 1900, has become famous over the years and the guide has lived up to the prediction. It is read across the world and the key to its popularity is the consistency of its commitment to its readers, which is based on the following promises.

The Michelin Guide's commitments :

Anonymous inspections: our inspectors make regular and anonymous visits to hotels and restaurants to gauge the quality of products and services offered to an ordinary customer. They settle their own bill and may then introduce themselves and ask for more information about the establishment. Our readers' comments are also a valuable source of information, which we can then follow up with another visit of our own.

Independence: Our choice of establishments is a completely independent one, made for the benefit of our readers alone. The decisions to be taken are discussed around the table by the inspectors and the editor. The most important awards are decided at a European level. Inclusion in the guide is completely free of charge.

Selection and choice: The guide offers a selection of the best hotels and restaurants in every category of comfort and price. This is only possible because all the inspectors rigorously apply the same methods.

Annual updates: All the practical information, the classifications and awards are revised and updated every single year to give the most reliable information possible.

Consistency: The criteria for the classifications are the same in every country covered by the Michelin guide.

… and our aim: to do everything possible to make travel, holidays and eating out a pleasure, as part of Michelin's ongoing commitment to improving travel and mobility.

Dear reader

Dear reader,

We are delighted to introduce the 36th edition of The Michelin guide Great Britain & Ireland.

This selection of the best hotels and restaurants in every price category is chosen by a team of full-time inspectors with a professional background in the industry. They cover every corner of the country, visiting new establishments and testing the quality and consistency of the hotels and restaurants already listed in the Guide.

Every year we pick out the best restaurants by awarding them from ✿ to ✿ ✿ ✿. Stars are awarded for cuisine of the highest standards and reflect the quality of the ingredients, the skill in their preparation, the combination of flavours, the levels of creativity and value for money, and the ability to combine all these qualities not just once, but time and time again.

This year again, a number of restaurants have been newly awarded stars for the quality of their cuisine. ´N´ highlights the new promotions for this new 2009 edition, announcing their arrival with one, two or three stars.

In addition, we have continued to pick out a selection of « *Rising Stars* ». These establishments, listed in red, are the best in their present category. They have the potential to rise further, and already have an element of superior quality; as soon as they produce this quality consistently, and in all aspects of their cuisine, they will be hot tips for a higher award. We've highlighted these promising restaurants so you can try them for yourselves; we think they offer a foretaste of the gastronomy of the future.

We're very interested to hear what you think of our selection, particularly the " *Rising Stars* ", so please continue to send us your comments. Your opinions and suggestions help to shape your guide, and help us to keep improving it, year after year. Thank you for your support. We hope you enjoy travelling with the Michelin guide 2009.

Consult the Michelin guide at www.ViaMichelin.com
and write to us at:
themichelinguide-gbirl@uk.michelin.com

Classification
& awards

CATEGORIES OF COMFORT

The Michelin guide selection lists the best hotels and restaurants in each category of comfort and price. The establishments we choose are classified according to their levels of comfort and, within each category, are listed in order of preference.

🏨🏨🏨	XXXXX	Luxury in the traditional style
🏨🏨🏨	XXXX	Top class comfort
🏨🏨	XXX	Very comfortable
🏨	XX	Comfortable
🏠	X	Quite comfortable
	🍴	Pubs serving good food
⌂		Other recommended accommodation (Guesthouses, farmhouses and private homes)
without rest.		This hotel has no restaurant
with rm		This restaurant also offers accommodation

THE AWARDS

To help you make the best choice, some exceptional establishments have been given an award in this year's Guide. They are marked ✿ or 🐷 and **Rest**.

THE BEST CUISINE

Michelin stars are awarded to establishments serving cuisine, of whatever style, which is of the highest quality. The cuisine is judged on the quality of ingredients, the skill in their preparation, the combination of flavours, the levels of creativity, the value for money and the consistency of culinary standards.

✿✿✿	**Exceptional cuisine, worth a special journey** One always eats extremely well here, sometimes superbly.
✿✿	**Excellent cooking, worth a detour**
✿	**Very good cooking in its category**

GOOD FOOD AND ACCOMMODATION AT MODERATE PRICES

🐷	**Bib Gourmand** Establishment offering good quality cuisine for under £28 or €40 in the Republic of Ireland (price of a 3 course meal not including drinks).
🛏	**Bib Hotel** Establishment offering good levels of comfort and service, with most rooms priced at under £80 or under €105 in the Republic of Ireland (price of a room for 2 people, including breakfast).

PLEASANT HOTELS AND RESTAURANTS

Symbols shown in red indicate particularly pleasant or restful establishments: the character of the building, its décor, the setting, the welcome and services offered may all contribute to this special appeal.

⌂, 🏠 to 🏠🏠🏠   **Pleasant hotels**

🍴, 🍴 to 🍴🍴🍴🍴🍴   **Pleasant restaurants**

OTHER SPECIAL FEATURES

As well as the categories and awards given to the establishment, Michelin inspectors also make special note of other criteria which can be important when choosing an establishment.

LOCATION

If you are looking for a particularly restful establishment, or one with a special view, look out for the following symbols:

     🦢   **Quiet hotel**

     🦢   **Very quiet hotel**

     ⋵   **Interesting view**

     ⋵   **Exceptional view**

WINE LIST

If you are looking for an establishment with a particularly interesting wine list, look out for the following symbol:

     🍷   **Particularly interesting wine list**

               This symbol might cover the list presented by a sommelier in a luxury restaurant or that of a simple pub or restaurant where the owner has a passion for wine. The two lists will offer something exceptional but very different, so beware of comparing them by each other's standards.

SMOKING

In Great Britain and the Republic of Ireland the law prohibits smoking in all pubs, restaurants and hotel public areas.

Facilities
& services

30 rm	Number of rooms
	Lift (elevator)
AC	Air conditioning (in all or part of the establishment)
	Fast Internet access in bedrooms
	Wi-fi Internet access in bedrooms
	Establishment at least partly accessible to those of restricted mobility
	Special facilities for children
	Meals served in garden or on terrace
Spa	An extensive facility for relaxation and well-being
	Sauna – Exercise room
	Swimming pool: outdoor or indoor
	Garden – Park
	Tennis court – Golf course and number of holes
	Fishing available to hotel guests. A charge may be made
	Equipped conference room
	Private dining rooms
	Hotel garage (additional charge in most cases)
P	Car park for customers only
	No dogs allowed (in all or part of the establishment)
	Nearest Underground station (in London)
May-October	Dates when open, as indicated by the hotelier

Prices

Prices quoted in this guide were supplied in autumn 2008 and apply to low and high seasons. They are subject to alteration if goods and service costs are revised. By supplying the information, hotels and restaurants have undertaken to maintain these rates for our readers.

In some towns, when commercial, cultural or sporting events are taking place the hotel rates are likely to be considerably higher.

Prices are given in £ sterling, except for the Republic of Ireland where euros are quoted.

All accommodation prices include both service and V.A.T. All restaurant prices include V.A.T. Service is also included when an **s** appears after the prices.

Where no **s** is shown, prices may be subject to the addition of a variable service charge which is usually between 10 % - 15 %.

(V.A.T. does not apply in the Channel Islands).

Out of season, certain establishments offer special rates. Ask when booking.

RESERVATION AND DEPOSITS

Some hotels will require a deposit which confirms the commitment of both the customer and the hotelier. Ask the hotelier to provide you with all the terms and conditions applicable to your reservation in their written confirmation.

CREDIT CARDS

Credit cards accepted by the establishment:

AE ⑩ ⑯ *VISA* American Express – Diners Club – MasterCard – Visa

ROOMS

rm 🛉 50.00/90.00 Lowest price 50.00 and highest price 90.00 for a comfortable single room

rm 🛉🛉 70.00/120.00 Lowest price 70.00 and highest price 120.00 for a double or twin room for 2 people

rm ⌣ 55.00/85.00 Full cooked breakfast (whether taken or not) is included in the price of the room

⌣ 6.00 Price of breakfast

SHORT BREAKS

Many hotels offer a special rate for a stay of two or more nights which comprises dinner, room and breakfast usually for a minimum of two people. Please enquire at hotel for rates.

RESTAURANT

Set meals: lowest price £13.00, highest price £28.00, usually for a 3 course meal. The lowest priced set menu is often only available at lunchtimes.

A la carte meals: the prices represent the range of charges from a simple to an elaborate 3 course meal.

s Service included

🎭 Restaurants offering lower priced pre and/or post theatre menus

🏠 : Dinner in this category of establishment will generally be offered from a fixed price menu of limited choice, served at a set time to residents only. Lunch is rarely offered. Many will not be licensed to sell alcohol.

Towns

GENERAL INFORMATION

✉ **York**	Postal address
501 M27, ⑩	Michelin map and co-ordinates or fold
▌*Great Britain*	See the Michelin Green Guide Great Britain
pop. 1057	Population
	Source: 2001 Census (Key Statistics for Urban Areas)
	Crown copyright 2004
BX **a**	Letters giving the location of a place on a town plan
🏌18	Golf course and number of holes (handicap sometimes required, telephone reservation strongly advised)
※ ≤	Panoramic view, viewpoint
✈	Airport
⛴	Shipping line (passengers & cars)
⛴	Passenger transport only
🛈	Tourist Information Centre

STANDARD TIME

In winter, standard time throughout the British Isles is Greenwich Mean Time (GMT). In summer, British clocks are advanced by one hour to give British Summer Time (BST). The actual dates are announced annually but always occur over weekends in March and October.

TOURIST INFORMATION

STAR-RATING

★★★	Highly recommended
★★	Recommended
★	Interesting
AC	Admission charge

LOCATION

👁	Sights in town
🅖	On the outskirts
N, S, E, W	The sight lies North, South, East or West of the town
A 22	Take road A 22, indicated by the same symbol on the Guide map
2m.	Distance in miles (In the Republic of Ireland kilometres are quoted).

Town plans

⊖●a   Hotels – restaurants

SIGHTS

Place of interest
Interesting place of worship

ROADS

Motorway
Numbered junctions: complete, limited
Dual carriageway with motorway characteristics
Main traffic artery
Primary route (GB) and National route (IRL)
One-way street – Unsuitable for traffic or street subject to restrictions
Pedestrian street – Tramway
Piccadilly   P   R   Shopping street – Car park – Park and Ride
Gateway – Street passing under arch – Tunnel
Low headroom (16'6" max.) on major through routes
Station and railway
Funicular – Cable-car
Lever bridge – Car ferry

VARIOUS SIGNS

Tourist Information Centre
Church/Place of worship - Mosque – Synagogue
Communications tower or mast – Ruins
Garden, park, wood – Cemetery
Stadium - Racecourse - Golf course
Golf course (with restrictions for visitors) – Skating rink
Outdoor or indoor swimming pool
View – Panorama
Monument – Fountain – Hospital – Covered market
Pleasure boat harbour – Lighthouse
Airport – Underground station – Coach station
Ferry services: passengers and cars
Main post office
Public buildings located by letter:
C   H   J   - County Council Offices – Town Hall – Law Courts
M   T   U   - Museum – Theatre – University, College
POL.   - Police (in large towns police headquarters)

LONDON

BRENT WEMBLEY   Borough – Area
Borough boundary
Congestion Zone – Charge applies Monday-Friday 07.00-18.00
⊖   Nearest Underground station to the hotel or restaurant

13

Mode d'emploi

INFORMATIONS TOURISTIQUES

Distances depuis les villes principales,
offices de tourisme, sites touristiques locaux,
moyens de transports,
golfs et loisirs...

CAMBRIDGE – Cambs – **504** U27 – **pop. 117 717** – ▯ Great F

▶ London 55 – Coventry 88 – Ipswich 54 – Leiceste
Nottingham 88 – Oxford 100

🛧 Cambridge Airport : ℰ (01223) 373737, E: 2 m or
, ℰ (01223) 45758

🔢 The Old Library, Wheeleer St,

🏨 Cambridgeshire Moat House Hotel, Bar Hill,

◻ Town : St John's College AC Y – King's A
Fitzwilliam Museumy Z **M1** – Trinity College
College AC Z

◸ Audley End, S: 13m by A1309 – Imperi
on M11

L'HÉBERGEMENT

De 🏠🏠🏠🏠 à 🏠, ↑ :
catégories de confort.
En rouge 🏠🏠🏠 ... 🏠, ↑ :
les plus agréables.

🏠 **Hotel Gloria** 🌣
Whitehouse lane, Huntington Rd, CB3 OLX,
– ℰ (01223) 277985 – help@hotelgloria.co.
Rest The Melrose – Menu £16 (lunch) – ⌑ £7.50
52 rm – ♦£136 ♦♦£168/255 –
♦ Built as a private house in 1852, now
contemporary rooms include state of
garden and terrace.

LES RESTAURANTS ET LES PUBS

De 𝗫𝗫𝗫𝗫𝗫 à 𝗫, 🍽 :
catégories de confort.
En rouge 𝗫𝗫𝗫𝗫𝗫... 𝗫, 🍽 :
les plus agréables.

𝗫𝗫𝗫 **Alexander House** (Johns)
❀ Midsummer Common, CB4 1HA – ℰ
– resa@alexanderhouse.co.uk – Fax
– closed 2 weeks Christmas, 2 week
Rest – Menu (dinner only and lu
Spec. Salad of smoked eel, pig's
nuts and pistachios and asparag
des bois and mint.
♦ A river Cam idyll. Chic cons
terrace with blissful views ov

LES TABLES ÉTOILÉES

❀❀❀ Vaut le voyage.
❀❀ Mérite un détour.
❀ Très bonne cuisine.

𝗫𝗫 **The Roasted Pepper**
🌣 35 Chesterton Rd,CB4 3AX –clos
– Fax (01223) 351873 – clos
Rest (booking essential) (
♦ Personally run Victoria
Italian dishes with mild

LES MEILLEURES ADRESSES À PETITS PRIX

🅑 Bib Gourmand.
🍽 Bib Hôtel.

at Histon North : 3 m on B10

🏠 **Blue House Farm**
🍽 44 High St, CB3 7HV
– Fax (01223) 26216
22 rm – ♦£38 ♦
♦ Red-brick 18C li
house overlooks
bread and prese

▾ – Ken

14

**AUTRES
PUBLICATIONS MICHELIN**

Références de la carte Michelin et du Guide Vert
où vous retrouverez la localité.

LOCALISER LA VILLE

Repérage de la localité
sur la carte régionale en fin de guide
(n° de la carte et coordonnées).

**LES HÔTELS
TRANQUILLES**

Hôtel tranquille.
Hôtel très tranquille.

**DESCRIPTION
DE L'ÉTABLISSEMENT**

Atmosphère, style,
caractère et spécialités.

**LOCALISER
L'ÉTABLISSEMENT**

Localisation sur le plan de ville
(coordonnées et indice).

**ÉQUIPEMENTS
ET SERVICES**

PRIX

A 3

Norwich 61 –

X
m@cambridge.gov.uk
4) 249988 X
ge Z – The Backs YZ –
tle's Yardx Y M2 – Queen's

Museumx, Duxford, S: 9m

Z d

est: 1,5 m by A1307
x (01223) 277986
5.20/35.50

odern and stylish public areas. The
facilities. Sleek restaurant overlooks

Y a

369 245
369246
st, 1 week spring, Sunday and Monday
ay-Saturday) £30/50
and apple purée. Braised turbot with pea-
nelloni of apricot, Strawberry sorbet, fraises

y dining room with smart first floor bar and
river.

Y c

23) 351872 – seancarter@roastedpepper.co.uk
stmas-New Year and Sunday
only) Menu £25
house with smartly clad tables. Classic French and
fluences, served at reasonable prices.

Cambridge

ut rest
23) 262164 – reservations@bluehousefarm.uk.co
ed 2 weeks Christmas-New Year

mhouse on a working farm... with beautiful blue windows;
w. Sunny garden room for breakfast, including home-made
maculate rooms.

A 12

R29 – **pop. 47 123 (inc. Frimley)** – Great Britain
hton 76 – Dover 15 – Maidstone 28 – Margate 17
(0870) 400 8245
off Portsmouth Rd (A325) – (0870) 4008246
Fax (0870) 4008246
edrooms; some
ern. 19C

15

Engagements

« Ce guide est né avec le siècle et il durera autant que lui. »

Cet avant-propos de la première édition du guide MICHELIN 1900 est devenu célèbre au fil des années et s'est révélé prémonitoire. Si le guide est aujourd'hui autant lu à travers le monde, c'est notamment grâce à la constance de son engagement vis-à-vis de ses lecteurs.

Nous voulons ici le réaffirmer.

Les engagements du Guide Michelin :

La visite anonyme : les inspecteurs testent de façon anonyme et régulière les tables et les chambres afin d'apprécier le niveau des prestations offertes à tout client. Ils paient leurs additions et peuvent se présenter pour obtenir des renseignements supplémentaires sur les établissements. Le courrier des lecteurs nous fournit par ailleurs une information précieuse pour orienter nos visites.

L'indépendance : la sélection des établissements s'effectue en toute indépendance, dans le seul intérêt du lecteur. Les décisions sont discutées collégialement par les inspecteurs et le rédacteur en chef. Les plus hautes distinctions sont décidées à un niveau européen. L'inscription des établissements dans le guide est totalement gratuite.

La sélection : le guide offre une sélection des meilleurs hôtels et restaurants dans toutes les catégories de confort et de prix. Celle-ci résulte de l'application rigoureuse d'une même méthode par tous les inspecteurs.

La mise à jour annuelle : chaque année toutes les informations pratiques, les classements et les distinctions sont revus et mis à jour afin d'offrir l'information la plus fiable.

L'homogénéité de la sélection : les critères de classification sont identiques pour tous les pays couverts par le guide Michelin.

... et un seul objectif : tout mettre en œuvre pour aider le lecteur à faire de chaque sortie un moment de plaisir, conformément à la mission que s'est donnée Michelin : contribuer à une meilleure mobilité.

Édito

Cher lecteur,

Nous avons le plaisir de vous proposer notre 36ᵉ édition du guide Michelin Great Britain & Ireland. Cette sélection des meilleurs hôtels et restaurants dans chaque catégorie de prix est effectuée par une équipe d'inspecteurs professionnels, de formation hôtelière. Tous les ans, ils sillonnent le pays pour visiter de nouveaux établissements et vérifier le niveau des prestations de ceux déjà cités dans le Guide.

Au sein de la sélection, nous reconnaissons également chaque année les meilleures tables en leur décernant de ✿ a ✿✿✿. Les étoiles distinguent les établissements qui proposent la meilleure qualité de cuisine, dans tous les styles, en tenant compte des choix de produits, de la créativité, de la maîtrise des cuissons et des saveurs, du rapport qualité/prix ainsi que de la régularité.

Cette année encore, de nombreuses tables ont été remarquées pour l'évolution de leur cuisine. Un « **N** » accompagne les nouveaux promus de ce millésime 2009, annonçant leur arrivée parmi les établissements ayant une, deux ou trois étoiles.

De plus, nous souhaitons indiquer les établissements « *espoirs* » pour la catégorie supérieure. Ces établissements, mentionnés en rouge dans notre liste, sont les meilleurs de leur catégorie. Ils pourront accéder à la distinction supérieure dès lors que la régularité de leurs prestations, dans le temps et sur l'ensemble de la carte, aura progressé. Par cette mention spéciale, nous entendons vous faire connaître les tables qui constituent à nos yeux, les espoirs de la gastronomie de demain.

Votre avis nous intéresse, en particulier sur ces « espoirs » ; n'hésitez pas à nous écrire. Votre participation est importante pour orienter nos visites et améliorer sans cesse votre guide. Merci encore de votre fidélité. Nous vous souhaitons de bons voyages avec le guide Michelin 2009.

Consultez le guide Michelin sur **www.ViaMichelin.com**
Et écrivez-nous à : **themichelinguide-gbirl@uk.michelin.com**

Classement & distinctions

LES CATÉGORIES DE CONFORT

Le guide Michelin retient dans sa sélection les meilleures adresses dans chaque catégorie de confort et de prix. Les établissements sélectionnés sont classés selon leur confort et cités par ordre de préférence dans chaque catégorie.

🏨🏨🏨	XxXxX	Grand luxe et tradition
🏨🏨🏨	XxxX	Grand confort
🏨🏨	XxX	Très confortable
🏨	XX	De bon confort
🏠	X	Assez confortable
	🍴	Pub servant des repas
🏠		Autres formes d'hébergement conseillées (b&b, logis à la ferme et cottages)
without rest.		L'hôtel n'a pas de restaurant
with rm		Le restaurant possède des chambres

LES DISTINCTIONS

Pour vous aider à faire le meilleur choix, certaines adresses particulièrement remarquables ont reçu une distinction : étoiles ou Bib Gourmand. Elles sont repérables dans la marge par ✿ ou 😋 et dans le texte par **Rest.**

LES ÉTOILES : LES MEILLEURES TABLES

Les étoiles distinguent les établissements, tous les styles de cuisine confondus, qui proposent la meilleure qualité de cuisine. Les critères retenus sont : le choix des produits, la créativité, la maîtrise des cuissons et des saveurs, le rapport qualité/prix ainsi que la régularité.

✿✿✿	**Cuisine remarquable, cette table vaut le voyage** On y mange toujours très bien, parfois merveilleusement.
✿✿	**Cuisine excellente, cette table mérite un détour**
✿	**Une très bonne cuisine dans sa catégorie**

LES BIB : LES MEILLEURES ADRESSES À PETIT PRIX

😋	**Bib Gourmand** Établissement proposant une cuisine de qualité à moins de £28 ou €40 en République d'Irlande (repas composé de 3 plats, hors boisson).
🛏️	**Bib Hôtel** Établissement offrant une prestation de qualité avec une majorité des chambres à moins de £80 ou moins de €105 en République d'Irlande (prix d'une chambre double, petit-déjeuner compris).

LES ADRESSES LES PLUS AGRÉABLES

Le rouge signale les établissements particulièrement agréables. Cela peut tenir
au caractère de l'édifice, à l'originalité du décor, au site, à l'accueil ou aux services
proposés.

⌂, ⌂ to ⌂⌂⌂⌂   **Hôtels agréables**

🍴, X to XXXXX   **Restaurants agréables**

LES MENTIONS PARTICULIÈRES

En dehors des distinctions décernées aux établissements, les inspecteurs Michelin
apprécient d'autres critères souvent importants dans le choix d'un établissement.

SITUATION

Vous cherchez un établissement tranquille ou offrant une vue attractive ?
Suivez les symboles suivants :

      🐾   **Hôtel tranquille**

      🐾   **Hôtel très tranquille**

      ≼   **Vue intéressante**

      ≼   **Vue exceptionnelle**

CARTE DES VINS

Vous cherchez un restaurant dont la carte des vins offre un choix particulièrement
intéressant ? Suivez le symbole suivant :

      🍷   **Carte des vins particulièrement attractive**
                  Toutefois, ne comparez pas la carte présentée par le sommelier d'un
                  grand restaurant avec celle d'un pub ou d'un restaurant beaucoup
                  plus simple. Les deux cartes vous offriront de l'exceptionnel, mais
                  de niveau très différent.

FUMEUR

En Grande Bretagne et République d'Irlande il est formellement interdit de
fumer dans les pubs, restaurants et hotels.

Équipements & services

30 rm	Nombre de chambres
	Ascenseur
[AC]	Air conditionné (dans tout ou partie de l'établissement)
	Connexion Internet à haut débit dans la chambre
	Connection Internet « Wireless Lan » dans la chambre
	Établissement en partie accessible aux personnes à mobilité réduite.
	Équipements d'accueil pour les enfants
	Repas servi au jardin ou en terrasse
	Bel espace de bien-être et de relaxation
	Sauna - Salle de remise en forme
	Piscine : de plein air ou couverte
	Jardin – Parc
	Court de tennis, golf et nombre de trous
	Pêche ouverte aux clients de l'hôtel (éventuellement payant)
	Salles de conférences
	Salon privé
	Garage dans l'hôtel (généralement payant)
[P]	Parking réservé à la clientèle
	Accès interdit au chiens (dans tout ou partie de l'établissement)
	Station de métro à proximité (Londres)
May-October	Période d'ouverture (ou fermeture), communiquée par l'hôtelier

Prix

Les prix indiqués dans ce guide ont été établis à l'automne 2008 et s'appliquent en basse et haute saisons. Ils sont susceptibles de modifications, notamment en cas de variation des prix des biens et des services. Les hôteliers et restaurateurs se sont engagés, sous leur propre responsabilité, à appliquer ces prix aux clients. Dans certaines villes, à l'occasion de manifestations commerciales ou touristiques, les prix demandés par les hôteliers risquent d'être considérablement majorés. Les prix sont indiqués en livres sterling sauf en République d'Irlande où ils sont donnés en euros. Les tarifs de l'hébergement comprennent le service et la T.V.A. La T.V.A. est également incluse dans les prix des repas. Toutefois, le service est uniquement compris dans les repas si la mention « s » apparaît après le prix. Dans le cas contraire, une charge supplémentaire variant de 10 à 15% du montant de l'addition est demandée. (La T.V.A. n'est pas appliquée dans les Channel Islands). Hors saison, certains établissements proposent des conditions avantageuses, renseignez-vous dès votre réservation.

LES ARRHES
Certains hôteliers demandent le versement d'arrhes. Il s'agit d'un dépôt-garantie qui engage l'hôtelier comme le client. Bien demander à l'hôtelier de vous fournir dans sa lettre d'accord toutes les précisions utiles sur la réservation et les conditions de séjour.

CARTES DE PAIEMENT
Carte de paiement acceptées :
AE ⊙ ⊛ⓒ VISA   American Express –Diners Club – Mastercard – Visa.

CHAMBRES
rm ♦ 50.00/90.00   Prix minimum/maximum pour une chambre confortable d'une personne
rm ♦♦ 70.00/120.00   Prix minimum/maximum pour une chambre de deux personnes
rm ⌕ 55.00/85.00   Prix de la chambre petit-déjeuner compris
⌕ 6.00   Prix du petit-déjeuner si non inclus

SHORT BREAKS
Certains hôtels proposent des conditions avantageuses pour un séjour de deux ou trois nuits. Ce forfait, calculé par personne pour 2 personnes au minimum, comprend le dîner, la chambre et le petit-déjeuner. Se renseigner auprès de l'hôtelier.

RESTAURANT
Menu à prix fixe : minimum £13, maximum £28 comprenant généralement 3 plats. Le prix minimum correspond souvent à celui d'un déjeuner.

Repas à la carte : le 1er prix correspond à un repas simple comprenant une entrée, un plat du jour et un dessert. Le 2e prix concerne un repas plus complet (avec spécialité) comprenant un hors d'œuvre, un plat principal, fromage ou dessert

s   Service compris
🎭   Restaurants proposant des menus à prix attractifs servis avant ou après le théâtre

↑: Dans les établissements de cette catégorie, le dîner est servi à heure fixe exclusivement aux personnes résidentes. Le menu à prix unique offre un choix limité de plats. Le déjeuner est rarement proposé. Beaucoup de ces établissements ne sont pas autorisés à vendre des boissons alcoolisées.

Villes

GÉNÉRALITÉS

✉ **York**	Numéro de code postal et nom du bureau distributeur du courrier
501 M27, ⑩	Numéro des cartes Michelin et carroyage ou numéro du pli
📗 *Great Britain*	Voir le Guide Vert Michelin Grande-Bretagne
pop. 1057	Population (d'après le recensement de 2001)
BX **a**	Lettre repérant un emplacement sur le plan
🏌18	Golf et nombre de trous (handicap parfois demandé, réservation par téléphone vivement recommandée)
✳ ≼	Panorama, point de vue
✈	Aéroport
⛴	Transports maritimes
⛴	Transports maritimes (pour passagers seulement)
🛈	Information touristique

HEURE LÉGALE

Les visiteurs devront tenir compte de l'heure officielle en Grande-Bretagne : une heure de retard sur l'heure française.

INFORMATIONS TOURISTIQUES

INTÉRÊT TOURISTIQUE

★★★	Vaut le voyage
★★	Mérite un détour
★	Intéressant
AC	Entrée payante

SITUATION

👁	Dans la ville
👁	Aux environs de la ville
N, S, E, W	La curiosité est située : au Nord, au Sud, à l'Est, à l'Ouest
A 22	On s'y rend par la route A 22, repérée par le même signe que sur le plan du Guide
2m.	Distance en miles (calculée en kilomètre pour la République d'Irlande)

Plans

� ● a   Hôtels – Restaurants

CURIOSITÉS

Bâtiment intéressant
Édifice religieux intéressant

VOIRIE

M 1	Autoroute
4 4	Numéro d'échangeur : complet, partiel
	Route à chaussées séparées de type autoroutier
	Grande voie de circulation
A 2	Itinéraire principal (GB) - Route nationale (IRL)
◄ =====	Sens unique – Rue impraticable, réglementée
	Rue piétonne – Tramway
Piccadilly P R	Rue commerçante – Parking – Parking Relais
÷ ⊣⊢ ⊣⊢	Porte – Passage sous voûte – Tunnel
15'5	Passage bas (inférieur à 16'6'') sur les grandes voies de circulation
	Gare et voie ferrée
o+++++o o-●-●-o	Funiculaire – Téléphérique, télécabine
⊿ B	Pont mobile – Bac pour autos

SIGNES DIVERS

Information touristique
Église/édifice religieux – Mosquée – Synagogue
Tour ou pylône de télécommunication – Ruines
Jardin, parc, bois – Cimetière
Stade – Hippodrome – Golf
Golf (réservé) – Patinoire
Piscine de plein air, couverte
Vue – Panorama
Monument – Fontaine – Hôpital – Marché couvert
Port de plaisance – Phare
Aéroport – Station de métro – Gare routière
Transport par bateau :
  – passagers et voitures
Bureau principal
Bâtiment public repéré par une lettre :
C H   - Bureau de l'Administration du comté – Hôtel de ville
J   Palais de justice
M T U   - Musée - Théâtre - Université, grande école
POL.   - Police (Commissariat central)

LONDRES

BRENT WEMBLEY	Nom d'arrondissement (borough) - de quartier (area)	
	Limite de « borough »	
	Zone à péage du centre-ville lundi-vendredi 7h-18h	
⊖	Station de métro à proximité de l'hôtel ou du restaurant	

23

Come leggere la guida

INFORMAZIONI TURISTICHE

Distanza dalle città di riferimento, uffici turismo, siti turistici locali, mezzi di trasporto, golfs e tempo libero...

L'ALLOGGIO

Da 🏨🏨🏨🏨 a 🏠, ↟:
categorie di confort.
In rosso 🏨🏨🏨🏨 ... 🏠, ↟:
I più ameni.

I RISTORANTI E I PUBS

Da 🏵🏵🏵🏵🏵 a 🏵, 🍴:
categorie di confort.
In rosso 🏵🏵🏵🏵🏵 ... 🏵, 🍴: i più ameni.

LE TAVOLE STELLATE

🏵🏵🏵	Vale il viaggio.
🏵🏵	Merita una deviazione.
🏵	Ottima cucina.

I MIGLIORI ESERCIZI A PREZZI CONTENUTI

🏵 Bib Gourmand.
🏩 Bib Hotel.

24

CAMBRIDGE – Cambs – **504** U27 – pop. **117 717** – ▮ Grea
London 55 – Coventry 88 – Ipswich 54 – Leices
Nottingham 88 – Oxford 100
⊠ Cambridge Airport : ℰ (01223) 373737, E: 2 m
⊠ The Old Library, Wheeleer St, ℰ (01223) 4575
ℹ Cambridgeshire Moat House Hotel, Bar Hill,
⊠ Town : St John's College AC Y – King's
Fitzwilliam Museumy Z **M1** – Trinity Colleg
College AC Z
Audley End, S: 13m by A1309 – Impe
on M11

🏨🏨 **Hotel Gloria** 🏵
Whitehouse lane, Huntington Rd, CB3 OLX
– ℰ (01223) 277985 – help@hotelgloria.cc
Rest The Melrose – Menu £16 (lunch) – 🍴 £7.50
52 rm – ✝£136 ✝✝£168/255 – ☷ £7.50
• Built as a private house in 1852, now
contemporary rooms include state of
garden and terrace.

🏵🏵🏵 **Alexander House** (Johns) – ℰ
🏵 Midsummer Common, CB4 1HA – ℰ
– resa@alexanderhouse.co.uk – Fo
– closed 2 weeks Christmas, 2 wee
Rest – Menu (dinner only and lu
Spec. Salad of smoked eel, pig'
nuts and pistachios and aspara
des bois and mint.
• A river Cam idyll. Chic con
terrace with blissful views o

🏵🏵 **The Roasted Pepper**
🏵 35 Chesterton Rd,CB4 3AX
– Fax (01223) 351873 – clo
Rest (booking essential)
• Personally run Victori
Italian dishes with mild

at Histon North : 3 m on B10

🏠 **Blue House Farm**
🏩 44 High St, CB3 7HV
– Fax (01223) 2621
22 rm ☷ – ✝£38 ✝
• Red-brick 18C l
house overlooks
bread and pres
ENGLAND

RY – Ke

A **3**

Norwich 61 –

3 X
sm@cambridge.gov.uk
4) 249988 X
ege Z – The Backs YZ –
ttle's Yardx Y **M2** – Queen's

Museumx, Duxford, S: 9m

Z **d**

est: 1,5 m by A1307
x (01223) 277986
25.20/35.50

odern and stylish public areas. The
facilities. Sleek restaurant overlooks

Y **a**

369 245
3) 369246
st, 1 week spring, Sunday and Monday
ay-Saturday) £30/50
and apple purée. Braised turbot with pea-
nnelloni of apricot, Strawberry sorbet, fraises
ry dining room with smart first floor bar and
river.

Y **c**

223) 351872 – seancarter@roastedpepper.co.uk
stmas-New Year and Sunday
only) Menu £25
house with smartly clad tables. Classic French and
nfluences, served at reasonable prices.

Cambridge

ut rest
223) 262164 – reservations@bluehousefarm.uk.co
ed 2 weeks Christmas-New Year

mhouse on a working farm... with beautiful blue windows;
w. Sunny garden room for breakfast, including home-made
nmaculate rooms.

A **12**

4 R29 – **pop. 47 123 (inc. Frimley)** – Great Britain
ghton 76 – Dover 15 – Maidstone 28 – Margate 17
off Portsmouth Rd (A325) – (0870) 400 8245
ax (0870) 4008246
edrooms; some
orn, 19C

ALTRE PUBBLICAZIONI MICHELIN

Riferimento alla carta Michelin
ed alla Guida Verde in cui figura la località..

LOCALIZZARE LA CITTÀ

Posizione della località
sulla carta regionale alla fine della guida
(n° della carta e coordinate).

GLI ALBERGHI TRANQUILLI

Albergo tranquillo.
Albergo molto tranquillo.

DESCRIZIONE DELL'ESERCIZIO

Atmosfera, stile,
carattere e spécialità.

LOCALIZZARE L'ESERCIZIO

Localizzazione sulla pianta
di città (coordinate ed indice).

INSTALLAZIONI E SERVIZI

PREZZI

Principi

« *Quest'opera nasce col secolo e durerà quanto esso.* »

La prefazione della prima Edizione della guida MICHELIN 1900, divenuta famosa nel corso degli anni, si è rivelata profetica. Se la guida viene oggi consultata in tutto il mondo è grazie al suo costante impegno nei confronti dei lettori.

Desideriamo qui ribadirlo.

I principi della Guida Michelin:

La visita anonima: per poter apprezzare il livello delle prestazioni offerte ad ogni cliente, gli ispettori verificano regolarmente ristoranti ed alberghi mantenendo l'anonimato. Questi pagano il conto e possono presentarsi per ottenere ulteriori informazioni sugli esercizi. La posta dei lettori fornisce peraltro preziosi suggerimenti che permettono di orientare le nostre visite.

L'indipendenza: la selezione degli esercizi viene effettuata in totale indipendenza, nel solo interesse del lettore. Gli ispettori e il caporedattore discutono collegialmente le scelte. Le massime decisioni vengono prese a livello europeo. La segnalazione degli esercizi all'interno della Guida è interamente gratuita.

La selezione: la guida offre una selezione dei migliori alberghi e ristoranti per ogni categoria di confort e di prezzo. Tale selezione è il frutto di uno stesso metodo, applicato con rigorosità da tutti gli ispettori.

L'aggiornamento annuale: ogni anno viene riveduto e aggiornato l'insieme dei consigli pratici, delle classifiche e della simbologia al fine di garantire le informazioni più attendibili.

L'omogeneità della selezione: i criteri di valutazione sono gli stessi per tutti i paesi presi in considerazione dalla guida Michelin.

... e un unico obiettivo: prodigarsi per aiutare il lettore a fare di ogni spostamento e di ogni uscita un momento di piacere, conformemente alla missione che la Michelin si è prefissata: contribuire ad una miglior mobilità.

Caro lettore,

Abbiamo il piacere di presentarle la nostra 36a edizione della guida Michelin Gran Bretagna & Irlanda.

Questa selezione, che comprende i migliori alberghi e ristoranti per ogni categoria di prezzo, viene effettuata da un'équipe di ispettori professionisti di formazione alberghiera. Ogni anno, percorrono l'intero paese per visitare nuovi esercizi e verificare il livello delle prestazioni di quelli già inseriti nella Guida.

All'interno della selezione, vengono inoltre assegnate ogni anno da ❀ a ❀❀❀ alle migliori tavole. Le stelle contraddistinguono gli esercizi che propongono la miglior cucina, in tutti gli stili, tenendo conto della scelta dei prodotti, della creatività, dell'abilità nel raggiungimento della giusta cottura e nell'abbinamento dei sapori, del rapporto qualità/prezzo, nonché della costanza.

Anche quest'anno diversi ristoranti hanno ricevuto la stella per la qualità della loro cucina. Una « N » evidenzia le nuove promozioni per questa edizione del 2009 annuniciandone il loro inserimento con una, due o tre stelle.

Abbiano inoltre continuato a selezionare le « *promesse* » per la categoria superiore. Questi esercizi, evidenziati in rosso nella nostra lista, sono i migliori della loro categoria e potranno accedere alla categoria superiore non appena le loro prestazioni avranno raggiunto un livello costante nel tempo, e nelle proposte della carta. Con questa segnalazione speciale, è nostra intenzione farvi conoscere le tavole che costituiscono, dal nostro punto di vista, le principali promesse della gastronomia di domani.

Il vostro parere ci interessa, specialmente riguardo a queste « *promesse* ». Non esitate quindi a scriverci, la vostra partecipazione è importante per orientare le nostre visite e migliorare costantemente la vostra guida. Grazie ancora per la vostra fedeltà e vi auguriamo buon viaggio con la guida Michelin 2009.

Consultate la guida Michelin su
www.ViaMichelin.com
e scriveteci a:
themichelinguide-gbirl@uk.michelin.com

Categorie
& simboli distintivi

LE CATEGORIE DI CONFORT

Nella selezione della guida Michelin vengono segnalati i migliori indirizzi per ogni categoria di confort e di prezzo.Gli esercizi selezionati sono classificati in base al confort che offrono e vengono citati in ordine di preferenza per ogni categoria.

🏨🏨🏨	XXXXX	Gran lusso e tradizione
🏨🏨	XXXX	Gran confort
🏨🏨	XXX	Molto confortevole
🏨🏨	XX	Di buon confort
🏨	X	Abbastanza confortevole
	🍴	Pub con cucina
⬆		Pensione, fattorie, case private (forme alternative di ospitalità)
without rest.		L'albergo non ha ristorante
with rm		Il ristorante dispone di camere

I SIMBOLI DISTINTIVI

Per aiutarvi ad effettuare la scelta migliore, segnaliamo gli esercizi che si distinguono in modo particolare. Questi ristoranti sono evidenziati nel testo con ✿ o 🅐 e **Rest.**

LE MIGLIORI TAVOLE

Le stelle distinguono gli esercizi che propongono la miglior qualità in campo gastro-nomico, indipendentemente dagli stili di cucina. I criteri presi in considerazione sono: la scelta dei prodotti, l'abilità nel raggiungimento della giusta cottura e nell'abbina-mento dei sapori, il rapporto qualità/prezzo nonché la costanza.

✿✿✿	**Una delle migliori cucine, questa tavola vale il viaggio** Vi si mangia sempre molto bene, a volte meravigliosamente.
✿✿	**Cucina eccellente, questa tavola merita una deviazione**
✿	**Un'ottima cucina nella sua categoria**

I MIGLIORI ESERCIZI A PREZZI CONTENUTI

🅐	**Bib Gourmand** Esercizio che offre una cucina di qualità a meno di £28 (€40 per l'Ir-landa). Prezzo di un pasto, bevanda esclusa.
🏠	**Bib Hotel** Esercizio che offre un soggiorno di qualità a meno di £80 (€105 per l'Irlanda) per la maggior parte delle camere. Prezzi per 2 persone, prima colazione esclusa.

GLI ESERCIZI AMENI

Il rosso indica gli esercizi particolarmente ameni. Questo per le caratteristiche dell'edificio, le decorazioni non comuni, la sua posizione ed il servizio offerto.

⭑, 🏠 to 🏨🏨🏨   **Alberghi ameni**

🍴, 🍴 to 🍴🍴🍴🍴🍴   **Ristoranti ameni**

LE SEGNALAZIONI PARTICOLARI

Oltre alle distinzioni conferite agli esercizi, gli ispettori Michelin apprezzano altri criteri spesso importanti nella scelta di un esercizio.

POSIZIONE

Cercate un esercizio tranquillo o che offre una vista piacevole ? Seguite i simboli seguenti:

     🐾   **Albergo tranquillo**

     🐾   **Albergo molto tranquillo**

     ←   **Vista interessante**

     ←   **Vista eccezionale**

CARTA DEI VINI

Cercate un ristorante la cui carta dei vini offre una scelta particolarmente interessante ? Seguite il simbolo seguente:

     🍷   **Carta dei vini particolarmente interessante**

                Attenzione a non confrontare la carta presentata da un sommelier in un grande ristorante con quella di un pub o di un ristorante più semplice. Le due carte vi offriranno degli ottimi vini di diverso livello.

FUMARE

In Gran Bretagna & Irlanda la legge vieta il fumo in tutti pub, Ristoranti e le zone comuni degli alberghi.

Installazioni & servizi

30 rm	Numero di camere
	Ascensore
AIC	Aria condizionata (in tutto o in parte dell'esercizio)
	Connessione Internet ad alta velocità in camera
	Connessione Internet « Wireless Lan » in camera
	Esercizio accessibile in parte alle persone con difficoltà motorie
	Attrezzatura per accoglienza e ricreazione dei bambini
	Pasti serviti in giardino o in terrazza
Spa	Centro attrezzato per il benessere ed il relax
	Sauna - Palestra
	Piscina: all'aperto, coperta
	Giardino – Parco
	Campo di tennis – Golf e numero di buche
	Pesca aperta ai clienti dell'albergo (eventualmente a pagamento)
	Sale per conferenze
	Saloni particolari
	Garage nell'albergo (generalmente a pagamento)
P	Parcheggio riservato alla clientela
	Accesso vietato ai cani (in tutto o in parte dell'esercizio)
	Stazione della metropolitana più vicina (a Londra)
May-October	Periodo di apertura, comunicato dall'albergatore

Prezzi

I prezzi riportati nella guida ci sono stati forniti nell'autunno del 2008 e si applicano alla bassa e all'alta stagione. Potranno subire delle variazioni in relazione ai cambiamenti dei prezzi di beni e servizi. Gli albergatori e i ristoratori si sono impegnati, sotto la propria responsabilità, a praticare questi prezzi ai clienti. In occasione di alcune manifestazioni commerciali o turistiche i prezzi richiesti dagli albergatori potrebbero subire un sensibile aumento nelle località interessate e nei loro dintorni. I prezzi sono indicati in lire sterline (1 £ = 100 pence) ad eccezione per la Repubblica d'Irlanda dove sono indicati in euro. Tutte le tariffe per il soggiorno includono sia servizio che I.V.A. Tutti i prezzi dei ristoranti includono l'I.V.A., il servizio è incluso quando dopo il prezzo appare « **s** ». Quando non compare « **s** », il prezzo può essere soggetto ad un aumento per il servizio solitamente compreso tra il 10 % e il 15 %. In bassa stagione, alcuni esercizi applicano condizioni più vantaggiose, informatevi al momento della prenotazione. Entrate nell'albergo o nel ristorante con la guida in mano, dismostrando in tal modo la fiducia in chi vi ha indirizzato.

LA CAPARRA

Alcuni albergatori chiedono il versamento di una caparra. Si tratta di un deposito-garanzia che impegna sia l'albergatore che il cliente. Vi consigliamo di farvi precisare le norme riguardanti la reciproca garanzia di tale caparra.

CARTE DI CREDITO

Carte di credito accettate:
AE ⑩ ⓂⓈ VISA   American Express – Diners Club – MasterCard – Visa

CAMERE

rm ♉ 50.00/90.00   Prezzo minimo e massimo per una camera singola di buon confort
rm ♉♉ 70.00/120.00 Prezzo minimo e massimo per una camera doppia per due persone
rm ⌒ 55.00/85.00   Prezzo della camera compresa la prima colazione
⌒ 6.00   Prezzo della prima colazione

SHORT BREAKS

Alcuni alberghi propongono delle condizioni particolarmente vantaggiose o short break per un soggiorno minimo di due notti. Questo prezzo, calcolato per persona e per un minimo di due persone, comprende: camera, cena e prima colazione. Informarsi presso l'albergatore.

RISTORANTE

Menu a prezzo fisso: prezzo minimo £13 e massimo £28 comprendente generalmente 3 piatti. Il menu a prezzo minimo è spesso disponibile solo a pranzo.
Pasto alla carta: il primo prezzo corrisponde ad un pasto semplice comprendente: primo, piatto del giorno e dessert. Il secondo prezzo corrisponde ad un pasto più completo (con specialità) comprendente: due piatti e dessert.

s   Servizio compreso
🎭   Ristoranti che offrono menu a prezzi ridotti prima e/o dopo gli spettacoli teatrali

⚡: Negli alberghi di questa categoria, la cena viene servita, ad un'ora stabilita, esclusivamente a chi vi alloggia. Il menu, a prezzo fisso, offre una scelta limitata di piatti. Raramente viene servito anche il pranzo. Molti di questi esercizi non hanno l'autorizzazione a vendere alcolici.

Città

GENERALITÀ

⊠ **York**	Codice di avviamento postale
501 M27, ⑩	Numero della carta Michelin e del riquadro
▌ *Great Britain*	Vedere la Guida Verde Michelin Gran Bretagna
pop. 1057	Popolazione residente
BX **a**	Lettere indicanti l'ubicazione sulla pianta
🏌18	Golf e numero di buche (handicap generalmente richiesto, prenotazione telefonica vivamente consigliata)
❋ ≼	Panorama, vista
🛪	Aeroporto
⛴	Trasporti marittimi
⛴	Trasporti marittimi (solo passeggeri)
🛈	Ufficio informazioni turistiche

ORA LEGALE

I visitatori dovranno tenere in considerazione l'ora ufficiale nelle Isole Britanniche: un'ora di ritardo sull'ora italiana.

INFORMAZIONI TURISTICHE

INTERESSE TURISTICO

★★★	Vale il viaggio
★★	Merita una deviazione
★	Interessante
AC	Entrata a pagamento

UBICAZIONE

◉	Nella città
⟳	Nei dintorni della città
N, S, E, W	Il luogo si trova a Nord, a Sud, a Est, a Ovest della località
A 22	Ci si va per la strada A 22 indicata con lo stesso segno sulla pianta
2m.	Distanza in miglia (solo per la Gran Bretagna)

Piante

⊖ ● a   Alberghi – Ristoranti

CURIOSITÀ

Edificio interessante
Costruzione religiosa interessante

VIABILITÀ

Autostrada
numero dello svincolo: completo, parziale
Strada a carreggiate separate
Grande via di circolazione
Itinerario principale: Primary route (GB) o National route (IRL)
Senso unico – Via impraticabile, a circolazione regolamentata
Via pedonale – Tranvia
Piccadilly 🅿 🅿   Via commerciale – Parcheggio – Parcheggio Ristoro
Porta – Sottopassaggio – Galleria
Sottopassaggio (altezza inferiore a 15'5) sulle grandi vie di circolazione
Stazione e ferrovia
Funicolare – Funivia, cabinovia
Ponte mobile – Traghetto per auto

SIMBOLI VARI

Ufficio informazioni turistiche
Chiesa – Moschea – Sinagoga
Torre o pilone per telecomunicazioni – Ruderi
Giardino, parco, bosco – Cimitero
Stadio – Ippodromo – Golf
Golf riservato – Pattinaggio
Piscina: all'aperto, coperta
Vista – Panorama
Monumento – Fontana – Ospedale – Mercato coperto
Porto turistico – Faro
Aeroporto – Stazione della metropolitana – Autostazione
Trasporto con traghetto: passeggeri ed autovetture
Ufficio postale centrale
Edificio pubblico indicato con lettera:
C H J   Sede dell'Amministrazione di Contea – Municipio – Palazzo di Giustizia
M T U   Museo – Teatro – Università, Scuola superiore
POL.   Polizia (Questura, nelle grandi città)

LONDRA

BRENT WEMBLEY Distretto amministrativo (Borough) – Quartiere (Area)
Limite del Borough
Area con circolazione a pagamento Lunedì-Venerdì 07.00-18.00
⊖   Stazione della metropolitana più vicina all'albergo o al ristorante

Hinweise zur Benutzung

TOURISTISCHE INFORMATIONEN

Entfernungen
zu größeren
Städten,
Informationsstellen,
Sehenswürdigkeiten,
Verkehrsmittel,
Golfplätze und lokale
Veranstaltungen...

DIE UNTERBRINGUNG

Von 🏨🏨🏨🏨 bis 🏨, 🛏:
Komfortkategorien.
In rot 🏨🏨🏨🏨... 🏨, 🛏:
Besonders angenehme Häuser.

DIE RESTAURANTS UND DIE PUBS

Von XXXXX bis X, 🍴:
Komfortkategorien.
In rot XXXXX... X, 🍴: Besonders
angenehme Häuser.

DIE STERNE-RESTAURANTS

🕸🕸🕸 Eine Reise wert.
🕸🕸 Verdient einen Umweg.
🕸 Eine sehr gute Küche.

DIE BESTEN PREISWERTEN ADRESSEN

🔵 Bib Gourmand.
🔷 Bib Hotel.

CAMBRIDGE – Cambs – **504** U27 – pop. **117717** – ▮ Great
London 55 – Coventry 88 – Ipswich 54 – Leiceste
Nottingham 88 – Oxford 100
✈ Cambridge Airport : ℘ (01223) 373737, E: 2 m o
🅰 The Old Library, Wheeleer St, ℘ (01223) 45758
🅱 Cambridgeshire Moat House Hotel, Bar Hill, A
🅲 Town : St John's College AC Y – King's A
Fitzwilliam Museumy Z **M1** – Trinity College
College AC Z
🅶 Audley End, S: 13m by A1309 – Imperi
on M11

Hotel Gloria
Whitehouse lane, Huntington Rd, CB3 OLX,
– ℘ (01223) 277985 – help@hotelgloria.co.
Rest The Melrose – Menu £16 (lunch) – C
52 rm – ✝£136 ✝✝£168/255 – ☕ £7.50
♦ Built as a private house in 1852, now
contemporary rooms include state of ▮
garden and terrace.

Alexander House (Johns)
Midsummer Common, CB4 1HA – ℘
– resa@alexanderhouse.co.uk – Fax
– closed 2 weeks Christmas, 2 week
Rest – Menu (dinner only and lu
Spec. Salad of smoked eel, pig's
nuts and pistachios and asparag
des bois and mint.
♦ A river Cam idyll. Chic cons
terrace with blissful views ov

The Roasted Pepper
35 Chesterton Rd,CB4 3AX –
– Fax (01223) 351873 – clos
Rest (booking essential) (
♦ Personally run Victoria
Italian dishes with mild ▮

at Histon North : 3 m on B10

Blue House Farm
44 High St, CB3 7HV –
– Fax (01223) 26216
22 rm – ☕ ✝£38 ✝
♦ Red-brick 18C lis
house overlooks
bread and prese

▮ – Ken

34

ANDERE MICHELIN-PUBLIKATIONEN

Angabe der Michelin-Karte und des Grünen Michelin-Reiseführers, wo der Ort zu finden ist.

LAGE DER STADT

Markierung des Ortes auf der Regionalkarte am Ende des Buchs (Nr. der Karte und Koordinaten).

RUHIGE HOTELS

  Ruhiges Hotel.
  Sehr ruhiges Hotel.

BESCHREIBUNG DES HAUSES

Atmosphäre, Stil, Charakter und Spezialitäten.

LAGE DES HAUSES

Markierung auf dem Stadtplan (Planquadrat und Koordinate).

EINRICHTUNG UND SERVICE

PREISE

Norwich 61 –

3 X
ism@cambridge.gov.uk
54) 249988 X
ege Z – The Backs YZ –
ettle's Yardx Y **M2** – Queen's

: Museumx, Duxford, S: 9m

Z d

west: 1,5 m by A1307
x (01223) 277986
25.20/35.50

modern and stylish public areas. The
c facilities. Sleek restaurant overlooks

Y a

) 369 245
) 369246
ust, 1 week spring, Sunday and Monday
day-Saturday) £30/50
er and apple purée. Braised turbot with pea-
annelloni of apricot, Strawberry sorbet, fraises

ory dining room with smart first floor bar and
e river.

Y c

223) 351872 – seancarter@roastedpepper.co.uk
ristmas-New Year and Sunday
r only) Menu £25
n house with smartly clad tables. Classic French and
nfluences, served at reasonable prices.

☒ **Cambridge**

out rest
1223) 262164 – reservations@bluehousefarm.uk.co
sed 2 weeks Christmas-New Year
armhouse on a working farm... with beautiful blue windows;
ow. Sunny garden room for breakfast, including home-made
mmaculate rooms.

A 12

04 R29 – **pop. 47 123 (inc. Frimley)** – *Great Britain*
ghton 76 – Dover 15 – Maidstone 28 – Margate 17
off Portsmouth Rd (A325) – ℰ (0870) 400 8245
Fax (0870) 4008246

bedrooms; some
dern. 19C

Grundsätze

„Dieses Werk hat zugleich mit dem Jahrhundert das Licht der Welt erblickt, und es wird ihm ein ebenso langes Leben beschieden sein."

Das Vorwort der ersten Ausgabe des MICHELIN-Führers von 1900 wurde im Laufe der Jahre berühmt und hat sich inzwischen durch den Erfolg dieses Ratgebers bestätigt. Der MICHELIN-Führer wird heute auf der ganzen Welt gelesen. Den Erfolg verdankt er seiner konstanten Qualität, die einzig den Lesern verpflichtet ist und auf festen Grundsätzen beruht.

Die Grundsätze des Michelin-Führers:

Anonymer Besuch: Die Inspektoren testen regelmäßig und anonym die Restaurants und Hotels, um deren Leistungsniveau zu beurteilen. Sie bezahlen alle in Anspruch genommenen Leistungen und geben sich nur zu erkennen, um ergänzende Auskünfte zu den Häusern zu erhalten. Für die Reiseplanung der Inspektoren sind die Briefe der Leser im Übrigen eine wertvolle Hilfe.

Unabhängigkeit: Die Auswahl der Häuser erfolgt völlig unabhängig und ist einzig am Nutzen für den Leser orientiert. Die Entscheidungen werden von den Inspektoren und dem Chefredakteur gemeinsam getroffen. Über die höchsten Auszeichnungen wird sogar auf europäischer Ebene entschieden. Die Empfehlung der Häuser im Michelin-Führer ist völlig kostenlos.

Objektivität der Auswahl: Der Michelin-Führer bietet eine Auswahl der besten Hotels und Restaurants in allen Komfort- und Preiskategorien. Diese Auswahl erfolgt unter strikter Anwendung eines an objektiven Maßstäben ausgerichteten Bewertungssystems durch alle Inspektoren.

Einheitlichkeit der Auswahl: Die Klassifizierungskriterien sind für alle vom Michelin-Führer abgedeckten Länder identisch.

Jährliche Aktualisierung: Jedes Jahr werden alle praktischen Hinweise, Klassifizierungen und Auszeichnungen überprüft und aktualisiert, um ein Höchstmaß an Zuverlässigkeit zu gewährleisten.

... und sein einziges Ziel – dem Leser bestmöglich behilflich zu sein, damit jede Reise und jeder Restaurantbesuch zu einem Vergnügen werden, entsprechend der Aufgabe, die sich Michelin gesetzt hat: die Mobilität in den Vordergrund zu stellen.

Lieber Leser

Lieber Leser,

Wir freuen uns, Ihnen die 36. Ausgabe des Michelin-Führers Great Britain & Ireland vorstellen zu dürfen. Diese Auswahl der besten Hotels und Restaurants in allen Preiskategorien wird von einem Team von Inspektoren mit Ausbildung in der Hotellerie erstellt. Sie bereisen das ganze Jahr hindurch das Land. Ihre Aufgabe ist es, die Qualität und Leistung der bereits empfohlenen und der neu hinzu kommenden Hotels und Restaurants kritisch zu prüfen. In unserer Auswahl weisen wir jedes Jahr auf die besten Restaurants hin, die wir mit ✿ bis ✿✿✿ kennzeichnen. Die Sterne zeichnen die Häuser mit der besten Küche aus, wobei untersc-hiedliche Küchenstilrichtungen vertreten sind. Als Kriterien dienen die Wahl der Produkte, die fachgerechte Zubereitung, der Geschmack der Gerichte, die Kreativität und das Preis-Leistungs-Verhältnis, sowie die Beständigkeit der Küchenleistung. Auch in diesem Jahr werden einige Restaurants erstmals für die Qualität ihrer Küche ausgezeichnet. Um diese neuen Ein-, Zwei- oder Drei-Sterne-Häuser zu präsentieren, haben wir sie in der Sterneliste mit einem "N" gekennzeichnet.

Außerdem haben wir wieder eine Auswahl an *"Hoffnungsträger"* für die nächsthöheren Kategorien getroffen. Diese Häuser, die in der Liste in Rot aufgeführt sind, sind die besten ihrer Kategorie und könnten in Zukunft aufsteigen, wenn sich die Qualität ihrer Leistungen dauerhaft und auf die gesamte Karte bezogen bestätigt hat. Mit dieser besonderen Kennzeichnung möchten wir Ihnen die Restaurants aufzeigen, die in unseren Augen die Hoffnung für die Gastronomie von morgen sind. Ihre Meinung interessiert uns! Bitte teilen Sie uns diese mit, insbesondere hinsichtlich dieser *"Hoffnungsträger"*. Ihre Mitarbeit ist für die Planung unserer Besuche und für die ständige Verbesserung des Michelin-Führers von großer Bedeutung.

Wir danken Ihnen für Ihre Treue und wünschen Ihnen angenehme Reisen mit dem Michelin-Führer 2009.

Den Michelin-Führer finden Sie auch im Internet unter
www.ViaMichelin.com
oder schreiben Sie uns eine E-Mail:
themichelinguide-gbirl@uk.michelin.com

Kategorien
& Auszeichnungen

KOMFORTKATEGORIEN

Der Michelin-Führer bietet in seiner Auswahl die besten Adressen jeder Komfort- und Preiskategorie. Die ausgewählten Häuser sind nach dem gebotenen Komfort geordnet; die Reihenfolge innerhalb jeder Kategorie drückt eine weitere Rangordnung aus.

⛫⛫⛫	XXXXX	Großer Luxus und Tradition
⛫⛫⛫	XXXX	Großer Komfort
⛫⛫	XXX	Sehr komfortabel
⛫	XX	Mit gutem Komfort
⛫	X	Mit Standard-Komfort
	🍴	Pubs, die Speisen anbieten
↑		Andere empfohlene Übernachtungsmöglichkeiten (Gästehäuser, Bauernhäuser und private Übernachtungsmöglichkeiten)
without rest.		Hotel ohne Restaurant
with rm		Restaurant vermietet auch Zimmer

AUSZEICHNUNGEN

Um ihnen behilflich zu sein, die bestmögliche Wahl zu treffen, haben einige besonders bemerkenswerte Adressen dieses Jahr eine Auszeichnung erhalten. Die Sterne bzw. „Bib Gourmand" sind durch das entsprechende Symbol ۞ bzw. ⊛ und **Rest** gekennzeichnet.

DIE BESTEN RESTAURANTS

Die Häuser, die eine überdurchschnittlich gute Küche bieten, wobei alle Stilrichtungen vertreten sind, wurden mit einem Stern ausgezeichnet. Die Kriterien sind: die Wahl der Produkte, die Kreativität, die fachgerechte Zubereitung und der Geschmack, sowie das Preis-Leistungs-Verhältnis und die immer gleich bleibende Qualität.

۞ ۞ ۞	**Eine der besten Küchen: eine Reise wert**
	Man isst hier immer sehr gut, öfters auch exzellent.
۞ ۞	**Eine hervorragende Küche: verdient einen Umweg**
۞	**Ein sehr gutes Restaurant in seiner Kategorie**

DIE BESTEN PREISWERTEN HÄUSER

⊛	**Bib Gourmand**
	Häuser, die eine gute Küche für weniger als £28 (GB) bzw. €40 (IRE) bieten (Preis für eine dreigängige Mahlzeit ohne Getränke).
🏠	**Bib Hotel**
	Häuser, die eine Mehrzahl ihrer komfortablen Zimmer für weniger als £80 (GB) bzw. €105 (IRE) anbieten (Preis für 2 Personen inkl. Frühstück).

DIE ANGENEHMSTEN ADRESSEN

Die rote Kennzeichnung weist auf besonders angenehme Häuser hin. Dies kann sich auf den besonderen Charakter des Gebäudes, die nicht alltägliche Einrichtung, die Lage, den Empfang oder den gebotenen Service beziehen.

🏠, 🏠 to 🏠🏠🏠🏠 **Angenehme Hotels**

🍴, 🍴 to 🍴🍴🍴🍴🍴 **Angenehme Restaurants**

BESONDERE ANGABEN

Neben den Auszeichnungen, die den Häusern verliehen werden, legen die Michelin-Inspektoren auch Wert auf andere Kriterien, die bei der Wahl einer Adresse oft von Bedeutung sind.

LAGE

Wenn Sie eine ruhige Adresse oder ein Haus mit einer schönen Aussicht suchen, achten Sie auf diese Symbole:

> 🌿 Ruhiges Hotel
>
> 🌿 Sehr ruhiges Hotel
>
> ⇐ Interessante Sicht
>
> ⇐ Besonders schöne Aussicht

WEINKARTE

Wenn Sie ein Restaurant mit einer besonders interessanten Weinauswahl suchen, achten Sie auf dieses Symbol:

> 🍇 Weinkarte mit besonders attraktivem Angebot
>
> Aber vergleichen Sie bitte nicht die Weinkarte, die Ihnen vom Sommelier eines großen Hauses präsentiert wird, mit der Auswahl eines Gasthauses, dessen Besitzer die Weine der Region mit Sorgfalt zusammenstellt.

RAUCHEND
In GroBritannien und der Republik Irland ist Rauchen per Gesetz verboten: In allen Pubs, Restaurants und in den offentlichen Bereichen der Hotels.

Einrichtung & Service

30 rm	Anzahl der Zimmer
	Fahrstuhl
A/C	Klimaanlage (im ganzen Haus bzw. in den Zimmern oder im Restaurant)
	High-Speed Internetzugang in den Zimmern möglich
	Internetzugang mit W-Lan in den Zimmern möglich
	Für Körperbehinderte leicht zugängliches Haus
	Spezielle Angebote für Kinder
	Terrasse mit Speisenservice
	Wellnessbereich
	Sauna - Fitnessraum
	Freibad oder Hallenbad
	Liegewiese, Garten – Park
	Tennisplatz – Golfplatz und Lochzahl
	Angelmöglichkeit für Hotelgäste, evtl. gegen Gebühr
	Konferenzraum
	Veranstaltungsraum
	Hotelgarage (wird gewöhnlich berechnet)
P	Parkplatz reserviert für Gäste
	Hunde sind unerwünscht (im ganzen Haus bzw. in den Zimmern oder im Restaurant)
	Nächstgelegene U-Bahnstation (in London)
May-October	Öffnungszeit, vom Hotelier mitgeteilt

Preise

Die in diesem Führer genannten Preise wurden uns im Herbst 2008. Der erste Preis ist der Mindestpreis in der Nebensaison, der zweite Preis der Höchstpreis in der Hauptsaison. Sie können sich mit den Preisen von Waren und Dienstleistungen ändern. Die Häuser haben sich verpflichtet, die von den Hoteliers selbst angegebenen Preise den Kunden zu berechnen. Anlässlich größerer Veranstaltungen, Messen und Ausstellungen werden von den Hotels in manchen Städten und deren Umgebung erhöhte Preise verlangt. Die Preise sind in Pfund Sterling angegeben (1 £ = 100 pence) mit Ausnahme der Republik Irland, wo sie in Euro angegeben sind. Alle Übernachtungspreise enthalten Bedienung und MWSt. Die Restaurantpreise enthalten die MWSt., Bedienung ist enthalten, wenn ein **s** nach dem Preis steht. Wo kein **s** angegeben ist, können unterschiedliche Zuschläge erhoben wer-den, normalerweise zwischen 10%-15% (keine MWSt. auf den Kanalinseln). Erkundigen Sie sich bei den Hoteliers nach eventuellen Sonderbedingungen.

RESERVIERUNG UND ANZAHLUNG

Einige Hoteliers verlangen zur Bestätigung der Reservierung eine Anzahlung. Dies ist als Garantie sowohl für den Hotelier als auch für den Gast anzusehen. Bitten Sie den Hotelier, dass er Ihnen in seinem Bestätigungsschreiben alle seine Bedingungen mitteilt.

KREDITKARTEN

Akzeptierte Kreditkarten:

[AE] [D] [MC] [VISA] American Express – Diners Club – Mastercard – Visa

ZIMMER

rm ♥ 50.00/90.00 Mindestpreis 50.00 und Höchstpreis 90.00 für ein Einzelzimmer
rm ♥♥ 70.00/120.00 Mindestpreis 70.00 und Höchstpreis 120.00 für ein Doppelzimmer
rm ☞ 55.00/85.00 Zimmerpreis inkl. Frühstück (selbst wenn dieses nicht eingenommen wird)
☞ 6.00 Preis des Frühstücks

SHORT BREAKS

Einige Hotels bieten Vorzugskonditionen für einen Mindestaufenthalt von zwei Nächten oder mehr (Short break). Der Preis ist pro Person kalkuliert, bei einer Mindestbeteiligung von zwei Personen und schließt das Zimmer, Abendessen und Frühstück ein. Bitte fragen Sie im Hotel nach dieser Rate.

RESTAURANT

Menupreise: mindestens £13.00, höchstens £28.00 für eine dreigängige Mahlzeit. Das Menu mit dem niedrigen Preis ist oft nur mittags erhältlich.
Mahlzeiten "à la carte": Die Preise entsprechen einer dreigängigen Mahlzeit.
s Bedienung inkl.
☺☺ Restaurants mit preiswerten Menus vor oder nach dem Theaterbesuch
↑ : In dieser Hotelkategorie wird ein Abendessen normalerweise nur zu bestimmten Zeiten für Hotelgäste angeboten. Es besteht aus einem Menu mit begrenzter Auswahl zu festgesetztem Preis. Mittagessen wird selten angeboten. Viele dieser Hotels sind nicht berechtigt, alkoholische Getränke auszuschenken.

Städte

ALLGEMEINES

✉ **York**	Postadresse
501 M27, ⑩	Nummer der Michelin-Karte mit Koordinaten
▮ *Great Britain*	Siehe Grünen Michelin-Reiseführer Großbritannien
pop. 1057	Einwohnerzahl
BX **a**	Markierung auf dem Stadtplan
▮18	Golfplatz mit Lochzahl (Handicap manchmal erforderlich, telefonische Reservierung empfehlenswert)
✳ ⩔	Rundblick, Aussichtspunkt
✈	Flughafen
⛴	Autofähre
⛴	Personenfähre
ℹ	Informationsstelle

UHRZEIT

In Großbritannien ist eine Zeitverschiebung zu beachten und die Uhr gegen-über der deutschen Zeit um 1 Stunde zurückzustellen.

SEHENSWÜRDIGKEITEN

BEWERTUNG

★★★	Eine Reise wert
★★	Verdient einen Umweg
★	Sehenswert
AC	Eintrittspreis

LAGE

◉	In der Stadt
◐	In der Umgebung der Stadt
N, S, E, W	Im Norden, Süden, Osten, Westen der Stadt
A 22	Zu erreichen über die Straße A 22
2m.	Entfernung in Meilen (in der Republik Irland in Kilometern)

Stadtpläne

⊚ ● a   Hotels – Restaurants

SEHENSWÜRDIGKEITEN

Sehenswertes Gebäude
Sehenswerte Kirche

STRASSEN

Autobahn
Nummern der Anschlussstellen: Autobahnein - und/oder - ausfahrt
Schnellstraße
Hauptverkehrsstraße
Fernverkehrsstraße (Primary route: GB – National route: IRL))
Einbahnstraße – Gesperrte Straße, mit Verkehrsbeschränkungen
Fußgängerzone – Straßenbahn
Piccadilly Einkaufsstraße – Parkplatz, Parkhaus – Park -and-Ride-Plätze
Tor – Passage – Tunnel
Unterführung (Höhe bis 16'6'') auf Hauptverkehrsstraßen
Bahnhof und Bahnlinie
Standseilbahn – Cable Car
Bewegliche Brücke – Autofähre

SONSTIGE ZEICHEN

Informationsstelle
Kirche/Gebetshaus – Moschee – Synagoge
Funk-, Fernsehturm – Ruine
Garten, Park, Wäldchen – Friedhof
Stadion – Pferderennbahn – Golfplatz
Golfplatz (Zutritt bedingt erlaubt) – Eisbahn
Freibad – Hallenbad
Aussicht – Rundblick
Denkmal – Brunnen – Krankenhaus – Markthalle
Jachthafen – Leuchtturm
Flughafen – U-Bahnstation – Autobusbahnhof
Schiffsverbindungen: Autofähre – Personenfähre
Hauptpostamt
Öffentliches Gebäude, durch einen Buchstaben gekennzeichnet:
C H J – Sitz der Grafschaftsverwaltung – Rathaus-Gerichtsgebäude
M T U – Museum – Theater – Universität, Hochschule
POL. – Polizei (in größeren Städten Polizeipräsidium)

LONDON

BRENT WEMBLEY – Name des Stadtteils (borough) – Name des Viertels (area)
– Grenze des «borough»
– Gebührenpflichtiger Innenstadtbereich (Mo-Fr 7-18 Uhr)
⊖ – Dem Hotel oder Restaurant nächstgelegene U-Bahnstation

Awards 2009

Distinctions 2009
Le distinzioni 2009
Auszeichnungen 2009

Starred establishments 2009

Lochinver
Achiltibuie

The colour corresponds to the establishment
with the most stars in this location.

London	This location has at least one 3 star restaurant	✱✱✱
Dublin	This location has at least one 2 star restaurant	✱✱
Belfast	This location has at least one 1 star restaurant	✱

Fort William
Ballachulish

Dalry

NORTHERN
IRELAND

Portpatrick

Belfast

Dublin · Malahide
Ranelagh

REPUBLIC
OF IRELAND

GUERNSEY
· Fermain Bay
JERSEY
La Pulente · · St Helier

ISLES OF SCILLY

Fowey

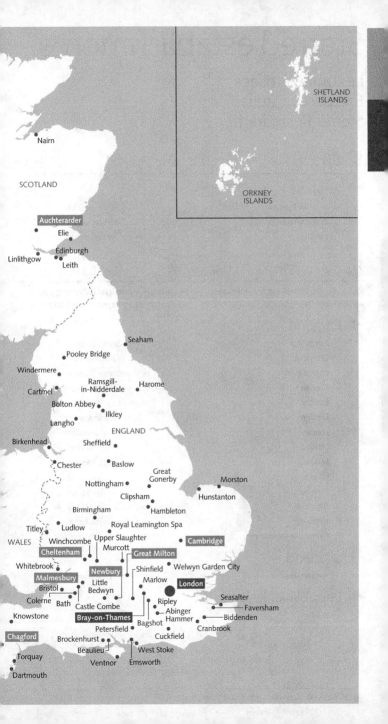

SHETLAND
ISLANDS

ORKNEY
ISLANDS

Nairn

SCOTLAND

Auchterarder
Elie
Edinburgh
Linlithgow
Leith

Seaham

Pooley Bridge

Windermere
Ramsgill-
in-Nidderdale
Harome
Cartmel
Bolton Abbey
Ilkley
Langho

Birkenhead
Sheffield

ENGLAND

Chester
Baslow
Nottingham
Great
Gonerby
Morston

Clipsham
Hunstanton
Birmingham
Hambleton
Royal Leamington Spa
Titley
Ludlow
Upper Slaughter
Cambridge

WALES
Winchcombe
Cheltenham
Murcott
Great Milton

Whitebrook
Shinfield
Welwyn Garden City
Newbury
Malmesbury
Little
Bedwyn
Marlow
London
Bristol
Colerne
Bath
Castle Combe
Ripley
Seasalter
Knowstone
Bray-on-Thames
Abinger
Hammer
Faversham
Biddenden
Petersfield
Bagshot
Cranbrook
Chagford
Brockenhurst
Cuckfield
Torquay
Beaulieu
West Stoke
Ventnor
Emsworth
Dartmouth

Starred establishments

Les tables étoilées
Esercizi con stelle
Sterne-Restaurants

✿✿✿

→ England

Bray-on-Thames	Fat Duck
Bray-on-Thames	The Waterside Inn
London	Gordon Ramsay

✿✿

→ In red the 2009 Rising Stars for ✿✿✿
→ En rouge les espoirs 2009 pour ✿✿✿
→ In rosso le promesse 2009 per ✿✿✿
→ In rote die Hoffnungsträger 2009 fur ✿✿✿

→ England

Cambridge	Midsummer House
Chagford	Gidleigh Park
Cheltenham	Le Champignon Sauvage
London	Alain Ducasse at The Dorchester **N**
London	L'Atelier de Joël Robuchon **N**
London	The Capital Restaurant
London	Le Gavroche
London	Hibiscus **N**
London	Marcus Wareing at The Berkeley
London	Pied à Terre
London	The Square
Malmesbury	The Dining Room (at Whatley Manor) **N**
Newbury	The Vineyard at Stockcross
Oxford / Great Milton	Le Manoir aux Quat' Saisons

→ Scotland

Auchterarder	Andrew Fairlie at Gleneagles

→ Republic of Ireland

Dublin	Patrick Guilbaud

→ **N** New → Nouveau → Nuovo → Neu

→ *In red* the 2009 Rising Stars for ✿✿   → *In rosso* le promesse 2009 per ✿✿
→ *En rouge* les espoirs 2009 pour ✿✿   → *In rote* die Hoffnungsträger 2009 fur ✿✿

→ England

Abinger Hammer	Drakes on the Pond
Bagshot	Michael Wignall at The Latymer **N**
Baslow	Fischer's at Baslow Hall
Bath / Colerne	The Park (at Lucknam Park)
Bath	Bath Priory
Beaulieu	The Terrace (at Montagu Arms) **N**
Biddenden	The West House
Birkenhead	Fraiche **N**
Birmingham	Purnell's **N**
Birmingham	Simpsons
Birmingham	Turners **N**
Blackburn / Langho	Northcote
Blakeney / Morston	Morston Hall
Bolton Abbey	The Burlington (at The Devonshire Arms Country House) **N**
Bourton-on-the-Water / Upper Slaughter	Lords of the Manor **N**
Bristol	Casamia **N**
Brockenhurst	Le Poussin at Whitley Ridge
Castle Combe	Manor House H. and Golf Club **N**
Chester	Simon Radley at The Chester Grosvenor
Chichester / West Stoke	West Stoke House
Cranbrook	Apicius
Cuckfield	Ockenden Manor
Dartmouth	The New Angel
Emsworth	36 on the Quay
Faversham	Read's
Fowey	Nathan Outlaw (at Marina Villa)
Grange-over-Sands / Cartmel	L'Enclume
Grantham / Great Gonerby	Harry's Place
Guernsey / Fermain Bay	Christophe
Helmsley / Harome	The Star Inn
Hunstanton	The Neptune **N**
Ilkley	Box Tree
Jersey / La Pulente	Atlantic
Jersey / St Helier	Bohemia
Kington / Titley	The Stagg Inn
London	Ambassade de L'Ile **N**
London	Amaya
London	Arbutus
London	Assaggi
London	Aubergine

London	L'Autre Pied	**N**
London	Benares	
London	Chapter One	**N**
London	Chez Bruce	
London	Club Gascon	
London	Foliage (at Mandarin Oriental Hyde Park)	
London	The Glasshouse	
London	Gordon Ramsay at Claridge's	
London	The Greenhouse	
London	Hakkasan	
London	Hélène Darroze at The Connaught	**N**
London	Kai	**N**
London	The Ledbury	
London	Locanda Locatelli	
London	Maze	
London	Murano	**N**
London	Nahm (at The Halkin)	
London	Nobu (at The Metropolitan)	
London	Nobu Berkeley St	
London	Quilon (at Crowne Plaza London - St James)	
London	Rasoi	
London	Rhodes Twenty Four	
London	Rhodes W1 (Restaurant) (at The Cumberland)	
London	Richard Corrigan at Lindsay House	
London	River Café	
London	Roussillon	
London	St John	**N**
London	Semplice	**N**
London	Sketch (The Lecture Room and Library)	
London	Tom Aikens	
London	La Trompette	
London	Umu	
London	Wild Honey	
London	Yauatcha	
London	Zafferano	
Ludlow	La Bécasse	**N**
Ludlow	Mr Underhill's at Dinham Weir	
Marlborough / Little Bedwyn	The Harrow at Little Bedwyn	
Marlow	The Hand and Flowers	
Murcott	The Nut Tree	**N**
Nottingham	Restaurant Sat Bains	
Oakham / Hambleton	Hambleton Hall	
Pateley Bridge / Ramsgill-in-Nidderdale	The Yorke Arms	
Petersfield	JSW	
Reading / Shinfield	L'Ortolan	

Ripley	Drake's
Royal Leamington Spa	The Dining Room (at Mallory Court)
Seaham	Seaham Hall
Sheffield	Old Vicarage
South Molton / Knowstone	The Masons Arms
Stamford / Clipsham	The Olive Branch & Beech House
Torquay	The Room in the Elephant
Ullswater / Pooley Bridge	Sharrow Bay Country House
Welwyn Garden City	Auberge du Lac **N**
Whitstable / Seasalter	The Sportsman
Wight (Isle of) / Ventnor	The Hambrough **N**
Winchcombe	5 North St
Windermere	Holbeck Ghyll

→ Scotland

Achiltibuie	Summer Isles
Ballachulish	Ballachulish House
Dalry	Braidwoods
Edinburgh / Leith	The Kitchin
Edinburgh / Leith	Martin Wishart
Edinburgh / Leith	Plumed Horse **N**
Edinburgh	Number One (at The Balmoral)
Elie	Sangster's **N**
Fort William	Inverlochy Castle
Linlithgow	Champany Inn
Lochinver	The Albannach **N**
Nairn	Boath House **N**
Portpatrick	Knockinaam Lodge

→ Wales

Monmouth / Whitebrook	The Crown at Whitebrook

→ Northern Ireland

Belfast	Deanes

→ Republic of Ireland

Dublin / Ranelagh	Mint
Dublin	Chapter One
Dublin	L'Ecrivain
Dublin	Thornton's (at The Fitzwilliam)
Malahide	Bon Appétit

The 2009 Bib Gourmands

- Places with at least one Bib Gourmand establishment.

Kilberry

NORTHERN IRELAND
Holywood
Belfast

Warrenpoint

REPUBLIC OF IRELAND

Dublin

Clonegall

Cashel

Dingle

Duncannon

Kenmare

Durrus
Kinsale
Kilbrittain
Baltimore

GUERNSEY
St Saviour

JERSEY

Gorey

Padstow

Summercourt
Freathy

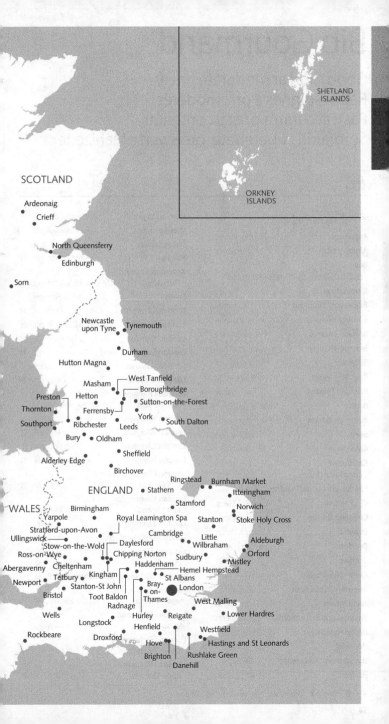

SHETLAND
ISLANDS

ORKNEY
ISLANDS

SCOTLAND

Ardeonaig
Crieff

North Queensferry
Edinburgh

Sorn

Newcastle
upon Tyne   Tynemouth

Durham

Hutton Magna

Masham   West Tanfield
Hetton   Boroughbridge
Preston   Ferrensby   Sutton-on-the-Forest
Thornton
Southport   Ribchester   York   South Dalton
Bury   Oldham   Leeds

Alderley Edge

Sheffield

Birchover

Ringstead   Burnham Market
ENGLAND   Stathern   Itteringham
Stamford   Norwich
WALES   Birmingham   Stanton   Stoke Holy Cross
Yarpole   Royal Leamington Spa
Stratford-upon-Avon   Cambridge   Aldeburgh
Ullingswick   Stow-on-the-Wold   Daylesford   Little   Orford
Ross-on-Wye   Chipping Norton   Wilbraham
Abergavenny   Cheltenham   Haddenham   Sudbury   Mistley
Newport   Tetbury   Kingham   Hemel Hempstead
Bristol   Stanton-St John   Bray-   St Albans
Toot Baldon   on-   London
Radnage   Thames
Wells   West Malling
Longstock   Hurley   Reigate   Lower Hardres
Rockbeare   Henfield   Westfield
Droxford   Hove   Hastings and St Leonards
Brighton   Rushlake Green
Danehill

Bib Gourmand

Good food at moderate prices
Repas soignés à prix modérés
Pasti accurati a prezzi contenuti
Sorgfältig zubereitete, preiswerte Mahlzeiten

→ England

Aldeburgh	The Lighthouse	
Alderley Edge	The Wizard	
Beverley / South Dalton	The Pipe and Glass Inn	
Birmingham	Pascal's	
Blackpool / Thornton	Twelve	
Boroughbridge	thediningroom	
Bray-on-Thames	The Hinds Head	
Bray-on-Thames	The Royal Oak	
Brighton	Terre à Terre	
Brighton / Hove	The Ginger Pig	
Brighton / Hove	The Meadow	N
Bristol	Greens' Dining Room	N
Burnham Market	The Hoste Arms	
Bury	The Waggon	
Cambridge	22 Chesterton Road	
Cambridge / Little Wilbraham	The Hole in the Wall	
Canterbury / Lower Hardres	The Granville	
Cheltenham	Royal Well Tavern	N
Chipping Norton	The Masons Arms	
Danehill	Coach & Horses	
Droxford	The Bakers Arms	N
Durham	Bistro 21	
Exeter / Rockbeare	Jack in the Green Inn	
Guernsey / St Saviour	The Pavilion	
Haddenham	The Green Dragon	
Hastings and St. Leonards	St Clements	
Hemel Hempstead	Restaurant 65	
Henfield	The Ginger Fox	N
Hunstanton / Ringstead	The Gin Trap Inn	
Hurley	Black Boys Inn	
Hutton Magna	The Oak Tree Inn	
Itteringham	The Walpole Arms	
Jersey / Gorey	Village Bistro	
Kingham	The Kingham Plough	N
Knaresborough / Ferrensby	The General Tarleton Inn	
Leeds	Anthony's at Flannels	
London/Camden	Bradley's	N
London/Camden	Giaconda Dining Room	N
London/Camden	Great Queen Street	
London/Camden	Market	N
London/Camden	Salt Yard	
London/Croydon	Le Cassoulet	N
London / Hammersmith and Fulham	The Havelock Tavern	
London/Islington	Comptoir Gascon	
London/Islington	Medcalf	N
London/Islington	Metrogusto	
London/Islington	The Modern Pantry	N
London / Kensington and Chelsea	Foxtrot Oscar	N
London / Kensington and Chelsea	Malabar	
London/Lambeth	Upstairs	
London/Lewisham	Chapters	
London / Richmond-upon-Thames	The Brown Dog	
London / Richmond-upon-Thames	Brula	
London / Richmond-upon-Thames	Ma Cuisine (Barnes)	
London / Richmond-upon-Thames	Ma Cuisine (Twickenham)	
London / Richmond-upon-Thames	Ma Cuisine (Kew)	
London / Richmond-upon-Thames	Mango and Silk	N

London / Richmond-upon-Thames	Tangawizi
London / Southwark	The Anchor and Hope
London / Tower Hamlets	Cafe Spice Namaste
London / Tower Hamlets	The Narrow
London Wandsworth	Kastoori
London / City of Westminster	L'Accento
London / City of Westminster	Al Duca
London / City of Westminster	Benja
London / City of Westminster	Dehesa N
London / City of Westminster	Galvin Bistrot de Luxe
London / City of Westminster	Hereford Road N
London / City of Westminster	Via Condotti
Masham	Vennell's
Matlock / Birchover	The Druid Inn
Melton Mowbray / Stathern	Red Lion Inn
Millbrook / Freathy	The View
Mistley	The Mistley Thorn
Newcastle upon Tyne	Amer's
Norwich / Stoke Holy Cross	Wildebeest Arms
Norwich	1 Up at the Mad Moose Arms
Oldham	The White Hart Inn
Orford	The Trinity
Oxford / Stanton St John	The Talkhouse
Oxford / Toot Baldon	The Mole Inn
Padstow	Rick Stein's Café
Preston	Winckley Square Chop House
Reigate	The Westerly
Ribchester	The White Bull
Ross-on-Wye	The Lough Pool at Sellack
Royal Leamington Spa	Oscar's
Rushlake Green	Stone House
St Albans	Sukiyaki
Sheffield	Artisan
Skipton / Hetton	The Angel Inn
Southport	Warehouse Brasserie
Stamford	Jim's Yard
Stanton	The Leaping Hare
Stockbridge / Longstock	The Peat Spade Inn N
Stokenchurch / Radnage	The Three Horseshoes Inn
Stow-on-the-Wold / Daylesford	The Cafe at Daylesford Organic N

Stow-on-the-Wold	The Old Butchers
Stratford-upon-Avon	Malbec
Sudbury	Hitchcock's
Summercourt	Viners
Sutton-on-the-Forest	Rose & Crown
Tetbury	The Gumstool Inn
Tynemouth	Sidney's
Ullingswick	Three Crowns Inn
Wells	The Old Spot
Westfield	The Wild Mushroom
West Malling	The Swan
West Tanfield	The Bruce Arms N
Yarpole	The Bell Inn N
York	J. Baker's

→ Scotland

Crieff	The Bank
Edinburgh	Atrium
Edinburgh	Duck's at Le Marche Noir
Edinburgh	The Dogs N
Killin / Ardeonaig	The Restaurant (at Ardeonaig)
Kintyre (Peninsula) / Kilberry	The Kilberry Inn
North Queensferry	The Wee Restaurant
Sorn	The Sorn Inn

→ Wales

Abergavenny	The Hardwick
Newport	The Chandlery

→ Northern Ireland

Belfast	Cayenne
Holywood	Fontana
Warrenpoint	Restaurant 23

→ Republic of Ireland

Baltimore	Customs House
Cashel (Tipperary)	Cafe Hans
Clonegall	Sha Roe Bistro
Dingle	The Chart House
Dublin	Bang Café
Dublin	La Maison des Gourmets
Dublin	The Winding Stair
Duncannon	Aldridge Lodge
Durrus	Good Things Cafe
Kenmare	The Lime Tree
Kilbrittain	Casino House
Kinsale	Fishy Fishy Cafe

Bib Hotel

Good accommodation at moderate prices
Bonnes nuits à petits prix
Buona sistemazione a prezzo contenuto
Hier übernachten Sie gut und preiswert

→ England

Armscote	Willow Corner
Askrigg	The Apothecary's House
Barnard Castle	Greta House
Barnard Castle	Homelands **N**
Battle	Fox Hole Farm
Belford	Market Cross
Biddenden	Barclay Farmhouse
Bishop's Stortford / Stansted Mountfitchet	Chimneys
Bledlow	The Old Station
Bodmin	Bokiddick Farm
Bourton-on-the-Water	Coombe House **N**
Bovey Tracey	Brookfield House
Bury St Edmunds / Beyton	Manorhouse
Cheddleton	Choir Cottage
Devizes / Potterne	Blounts Court Farm
Eastbourne	Brayscroft
Ely / Little Thetford	Springfields
Enstone	Swan Lodge
Harrogate / Kettlesing	Knabbs Ash
Hartland	Golden Park
Henfield / Wineham	Frylands
Hexham	West Close House
Holbeach	Pipwell Manor
Iron Bridge	Bridge House
Longtown	Bessiestown Farm
Morpeth / Longhorsley	Thistleyhaugh Farm
North Bovey	The Gate House
Oxhill	Oxbourne House
Penrith / Newbiggin	The Old School
Pickering	Bramwood
Ripon / Aldfield	Bay Tree Farm
Ripon	Sharow Cross House
Ross-on-Wye / Kerne Bridge	Lumleys
Rothbury	Farm Cottage
Rothbury	Thropton Demesne Farmhouse
St Just	Boscean Country House
Salisbury / Little Langford	Little Langford Farmhouse **N**
Scarborough	Alexander **N**
Southend-on-Sea	Beaches
South Molton	Kerscott Farm
Stow-on-the-Wold	Number Nine
Telford	Dovecote Grange
Tewkesbury	Alstone Fields Farm **N**
Torquay	Colindale
Upton-upon-Severn / Hanley Swan	Yew Tree House
Wallingford	North Moreton House
Wareham	Gold Court House
Warwick	Park Cottage
Wells / Easton	Beaconsfield Farm
Whitby / Briggswath	The Lawns
Windermere	Newstead
Woodstock	The Laurels

→ **N** *New* → *Nouveau* → *Nuovo* → *Neu*

→ Scotland

Aberdeen	Penny Meadow
Anstruther	The Spindrift
Auchencairn	Balcary Mews
Aultbea	Mellondale **N**
Aviemore	The Old Minister's Guest House
Ayr	Coila
Ayr	No.26 The Crescent
Ballater	Moorside House
Banchory	The Old West Manse
Blairgowrie	Gilmore House
Brora	Glenaveron
Carnoustie	The Old Manor
Crieff	Merlindale
Dunkeld	Letter Farm
Duror	Bealach House
Edinburgh	The Beverley
Forres / Dyke	The Old Kirk
Killin	Breadalbane House
Kingussie	Hermitage
Linlithgow	Arden House
Lochearnhead	Mansewood Country House
Montrose	36 The Mall **N**
Nairn	Bracadale House
North Berwick	Beach Lodge
Oban	The Barriemore
Perth	Taythorpe
Skye (Isle of) / Broadford	Tigh an Dochais
Strathpeffer	Craigvar
Thornhill	Gillbank House
Ullapool	Point Cottage

→ Wales

Betws Garmon	Betws Inn
Betws-y-Coed	Bryn Bella
Brecon	Canal Bank
Dolgellau	Tyddyn Mawr
Llandrindod Wells / Crossgates	Guidfa House
Llangrannog	The Grange
Llanuwchllyn	Eifionydd
Ruthin	Firgrove

→ Northern Ireland

Bangor	Cairn Bay Lodge
Bangor	Hebron House
Belfast	Ravenhill House
Crumlin	Caldhame Lodge
Downpatrick	Pheasants' Hill Farm
Dundrum (Down)	The Carriage House

→ Republic of Ireland

Ballynamult	Sliabh gCua Farmhouse
Ballyvaughan	Drumcreehy House
Carlingford	Beaufort House
Cashel (Tipperary)	Aulber House
Castlegregory	The Shores Country House
Donegal	Ardeevin
Dundalk	Rosemount
Dungarvan	An Bohreen
Killarney	Kingfisher Lodge
Oughterard	Railway Lodge
Oughterard	Waterfall Lodge
Toormore	Fortview House
Tramore	Glenorney

Particularly pleasant hotels

Hôtels agréables
Alberghi ameni
Angenehme Hotels

🏨🏨🏨

→ **England**

Dogmersfield	Four Seasons
London	The Berkeley
London	Claridge's
London	The Connaught
London	Dorchester
London	Mandarin Oriental Hyde Park
London	The Ritz
New Milton	Chewton Glen
Oxford /	
Great Milton	Le Manoir aux Quat' Saisons
Taplow	Cliveden

→ **Republic of Ireland**

Straffan	The K Club

🏨🏨🏨

→ **England**

Aylesbury	Hartwell House
Bath / Colerne	Lucknam Park
Bath	The Royal Crescent
Chagford	Gidleigh Park
Jersey / St Saviour	Longueville Manor
London	The Goring
London	One Aldwych
London	The Soho
Malmesbury	Whatley Manor
Newbury	The Vineyard at Stockcross
North Bovey	Bovey Castle

→ **Scotland**

Ballantrae	Glenapp Castle
Bishopton	Mar Hall
Dunkeld	Kinnaird
Eriska	Isle of Eriska
Fort William	Inverlochy Castle

→ **Republic of Ireland**

Dublin	The Merrion
Kenmare	Park
Kenmare	Sheen Falls Lodge
Killarney	Killarney Park

→ **England**

Abberley	The Elms
Amberley	Amberley Castle
Bath	Bath Priory
Bolton Abbey	The Devonshire Arms Country House
Bourton-on-the-Water /	
Lower Slaughter	Lower Slaughter Manor
Bourton-on-the-Water /	
Upper Slaughter	Lords of the Manor
Broadway / Buckland	Buckland Manor
Castle Combe	Manor House H. and Golf Club

Dedham	Maison Talbooth
East Grinstead	Gravetye Manor
Evershot	Summer Lodge
Gillingham	Stock Hill Country House
Jersey / La Pulente	Atlantic
Littlehampton	Bailiffscourt & Spa
London	Blakes
London	Capital
London	Charlotte Street
London	Covent Garden
London	Draycott
London	Dukes
London	The Halkin
London	The Milestone
London	The Pelham
London	Stafford
Oakham / Hambleton	Hambleton Hall
Reading	The Forbury
Royal Leamington Spa	Mallory Court
Scilly Isles / St Martin's	St Martin's on the Isle
Scilly Isles / Tresco	The Island
Seaham	Seaham Hall
Tetbury	Calcot Manor

Ullswater / Pooley Bridge	Sharrow Bay Country House
Winchester / Sparsholt	Lainston House
Windermere / Bowness-on-Windermere	Gilpin Lodge
York	Middlethorpe Hall

→ Scotland

Blairgowrie	Kinloch House
Edinburgh	The Howard
Edinburgh	Prestonfield
Peebles	Cringletie House
Torridon	The Torridon

→ Wales

Llandudno	Bodysgallen Hall
Llangammarch Wells	Lake Country House and Spa

→ Northern Ireland

Belfast	The Merchant

→ Republic of Ireland

Dublin	Dylan
Galway	The G
Mallow	Longueville House

→ England

Ambleside	The Samling
Bath	Queensberry
Bigbury-on-Sea	Burgh Island
Blakeney / Morston	Morston Hall
Brampton / Gilsland	Farlam Hall
Burnham Market	The Hoste Arms
Cheltenham	Hotel on the Park
Chester	Green Bough
Cirencester / Barnsley	Barnsley House
Cuckfield	Ockenden Manor
Frome	Babington House
Helmsley	Feversham Arms
Horley	Langshott Manor
Kingsbridge / Goveton	Buckland-Tout-Saints
King's Lynn / Grimston	Congham Hall

Lewdown	Lewtrenchard Manor
London	Dorset Square
London	Egerton House
London	Knightsbridge
London	The Levin
London	Number Sixteen
North Walsham	Beechwood
Orford	The Crown and Castle
Rushlake Green	Stone House
St Mawes	Tresanton
Southampton / Netley Marsh	Hotel TerraVina
Tavistock / Milton Abbot	Hotel Endsleigh
Torquay / Maidencombe	Orestone Manor
Wareham	The Priory
Windermere	Holbeck Ghyll
Woodstock	Feathers

→ Scotland

Achiltibuie	Summer Isles
Arran (Isle of)	Kilmichael Country House
Port Appin	Airds
Portpatrick	Knockinaam Lodge
Skye (Isle of) / Kinloch	Kinloch Lodge

→ Wales

Llandudno	Osborne House
Machynlleth	Ynyshir Hall
Swansea / Llanrhidian	Fairyhill
Talsarnau	Maes-y-Neuadd

→ Republic of Ireland

Arthurstown	Dunbrody Country House
Ballingarry	Mustard Seed at Echo Lodge
Glin	Glin Castle
Kinsale	Perryville House

→ England

Ashwater	Blagdon Manor
Askrigg	Yorebridge House
Bourton-on-the-Water	The Dial House
Burnham Market	Vine House
Chillington	Whitehouse
Coln St Aldwyns	New Inn At Coln
Dartmouth / Kingswear	Nonsuch House
Helmsley / Harome	Cross House Lodge at The Star Inn
Keswick / Portinscale	Swinside Lodge
Ludlow	De Grey's Town House
Lynton / Martinhoe	Old Rectory
Lynton	Hewitt's - Villa Spaldi
Porlock	Oaks
Portscatho	Driftwood
St Ives	Blue Hayes
Salisbury / Teffont Magna	Howard's House
Staverton	Kingston House

→ Scotland

Annbank	Enterkine
Glamis	Castleton House
Kelso / Ednam	Edenwater House
Killin / Ardeonaig	Ardeonaig
Maybole	Ladyburn
Muir of Ord	Dower House
Mull (Isle of) / Tiroran	Tiroran House
Nairn	Boath House
Tain / Hilton of Cadboll	Glenmorangie House

→ Wales

Betws-y-Coed	Tan-y-Foel Country House
Conwy / Llansanffraid Glan Conwy	Old Rectory Country House

→ Republic of Ireland

Bagenalstown	Kilgraney Country House
Dingle	Emlagh Country House
Lahinch	Moy House

→ England

Ash	Great Weddington
Austwick	Austwick Hall
Billingshurst	Old Wharf
Blackpool	Number One St Lukes
Bridport / Burton Bradstock	Norburton Hall
Broad Oak	Fairacres
Budleigh Salterton	Downderry House
Cheltenham	Thirty Two

Chipping Campden / Broad Campden	Malt House
Clun	Birches Mill
Crackington Haven	Manor Farm
Cranbrook	Cloth Hall Oast
East Hoathly	Old Whyly
Grange-over-Sands / Cartmel	Hill Farm
Hawkshead / Far Sawrey	West Vale
Haworth	Ashmount Country House
Helmsley / Byland Abbey	Oldstead Grange
Honiton / Payhembury	Cokesputt House
Ivychurch	Olde Moat House
Kendal	Beech House
Lavenham	Lavenham Priory
Ledbury / Kynaston	Hall End
Lizard	Landewednack House
Ludlow	Bromley Court
Man (Isle of) / Port St Mary	Aaron House
Marazion / Perranuthnoe	Ednovean Farm
Moreton-in-Marsh	The Old School
North Bovey	The Gate House
Petworth	Old Railway Station
Pickering / Levisham	The Moorlands Country House
Pickering	17 Burgate
Ripon	Sharow Cross House
St Austell / Tregrehan	Anchorage House
St Blazey	Nanscawen Manor House
Shrewsbury	Pinewood House
Stow-on-the-Wold / Lower Swell	Rectory Farmhouse
Stratford-upon-Avon / Pillerton Priors	Fulready Manor
Tavistock / Chillaton	Tor Cottage
Teignmouth	Thomas Luny House
Thursford Green	Holly Lodge
Wareham	Gold Court House
Willesley	Beaufort House
Wold Newton	Wold Cottage
York	Alexander House

→ Scotland

Ballantrae	Cosses Country House
Bute (Isle of) / Ascog	Balmory Hall
Connel	Ards House
Edinburgh	Davenport House
Fortrose	Water's Edge
Fort William	Crolinnhe
Fort William	The Grange
Islay (Isle of) / Ballygrant	Kilmeny
Linlithgow	Arden House
Lochinver	Ruddyglow Park Country House
Orkney Islands / Loch of Harray	Holland House
Mull (Isle of) / Gruline	Gruline Home Farm
Skirling	Skirling House
Strathpeffer	Craigvar

→ Wales

Betws-y-Coed / Penmachno	Penmachno Hall
Colwyn Bay	Rathlin Country House
Dolfor	Old Vicarage
Menai Bridge	Neuadd Lwyd
Pwllheli / Boduan	The Old Rectory
St Clears	Coedllys Country House

→ Northern Ireland

Dungannon	Grange Lodge
Holywood	Beech Hill

→ Republic of Ireland

Castlegregory	The Shores Country House
Castlelyons	Ballyvolane House
Cong	Ballywarren House
Fethard	Mobarnane House
Kanturk	Glenlohane
Kenmare	Sallyport House
Kilkenny	Blanchville House
Portlaoise	Ivyleigh House

Particularly pleasant restaurants

Restaurants agréables
Ristoranti ameni
Angenehme Restaurants

XXXXX

→ England

London	The Ritz Restaurant

XXXX

→ England

Bath / Colerne	The Park (at Lucknam Park)
Bolton Abbey	The Burlington (at The Devonshire Arms Country House)
Bray-on-Thames	The Waterside Inn
London	Hélène Darroze at The Connaught
London	Marcus Wareing at The Berkeley
Malmesbury	The Dining Room (at Whatley Manor)
Winteringham	Winteringham Fields

→ Republic of Ireland

Dublin	Patrick Guilbaud

XXX

→ England

Baslow	Fischer's at Baslow Hall
Birmingham	Simpsons
Blackburn / Langho	Northcote
Brockenhurst	Le Poussin at Whitley Ridge
Cambridge	Midsummer House
Dedham	Le Talbooth
Emsworth	36 on the Quay
Grange-over-Sands / Cartmel	L'Enclume
Ilkley	Box Tree
Lavenham	The Great House
London	Bibendum
London	The Capital Restaurant
London	Cecconi's
London	Quo Vadis
London	Scott's
London	The Wolseley
Newcastle upon Tyne	Fisherman's Lodge
Royal Leamington Spa	The Dining room (at Mallory Court)
Skipton / Hetton	Angel Inn and Barn Lodgings
Tavistock / Gulworthy	The Horn of Plenty
Welwyn Garden City	Auberge du Lac

→ Wales

Llandrillo	Tyddyn Llan

✗✗

→ England

Arlingham	The Old Passage Inn
Derby / Darley Abbey	Darleys
Fowey	Nathan Outlaw (at Marina Villa)
Goring	Leatherne Bottel
Grantham / Great Gonerby	Harry's Place
Grantham / Hough-on-the-Hill	The Brownlow Arms
Jersey / Gorey	Suma's
Kirkby Lonsdale / Cowan Bridge	Hipping Hall
London	Le Café Anglais
London	Le Caprice
London	J. Sheekey
London	Mon Plaisir
London	Rules
London	Wild Honey
Ludlow	Mr Underhill's at Dinham Weir
Malmesbury	Le Mazot
Padstow	The Seafood
Pateley Bridge / Ramsgill-in-Nidderdale	The Yorke Arms
Stanton	The Leaping Hare
Windermere	Miller Howe
Yeovil / Barwick	Little Barwick House

→ Scotland

Kingussie	The Cross at Kingussie
Lochearnhead / Balquhidder	Monachyle Mhor
Lochinver	The Albannach
Skye (Isle of) / Dunvegan	The Three Chimneys & The House Over-By

→ Wales

Pwllheli	Plas Bodegroes

→ Republic of Ireland

Clogheen	Old Convent
Dunfanaghy	The Mill
Kenmare	The Lime Tree
Kilbrittain	Casino House

✗

→ England

Bray-on-Thames / Bray Marina	Riverside Brasserie
Jersey / Green Island	Green Island
London	L'Atelier de Joël Robuchon
London	Oxo Tower Brasserie
London	Petersham Nurseries Café
Mousehole	Cornish Range
Stow-on-the-Wold / Daylesford	The Cafe at Daylesford Organic
Studland	Shell Bay

→ Scotland

Thurso / Scrabster	The Captain's Galley

→ Republic of Ireland

Dingle	The Chart House

##

→ England

Alton / Lower Froyle	The Anchor Inn
Ambleside	Drunken Duck Inn
Barnard Castle / Romaldkirk	Rose and Crown
Bath / Combe Hay	The Wheatsheaf
Baughurst	The Wellington Arms
Biggleswade / Old Warden	Hare & Hounds
Bildeston	The Bildeston Crown
Broadhembury	The Drewe Arms

Burnham Market	The Hoste Arms
Chichester / East Lavant	The Royal Oak Inn
Cirencester / Sapperton	The Bell
Devizes / Marden	The Millstream
Helmsley / Harome	The Star Inn
High Ongar	The Wheatsheaf
Ilmington	The Howard Arms
Kendal / Crosthwaite	The Punch Bowl Inn
Keyston	The Pheasant
Kingham	The Kingham Plough
Lydford	The Dartmoor Inn
Milton Keynes / Newton Longville	The Crooked Billet
Shefford	The Black Horse
Skipton / Hetton	The Angel Inn
South Molton / Knowstone	The Masons Arms
Stamford / Clipsham	The Olive Branch & Beech House
Stockbridge / Longstock	The Peat Spade Inn
Stokenchurch / Radnage	The Three Horseshoes Inn
Stow-on-the-Wold / Lower Oddington	The Fox Inn
Summercourt	Viners
Sutton-on-the-Forest	Rose & Crown
Tarr Steps	Tarr Farm Inn
Woburn	The Birch

→ Wales

Aberaeron	Harbourmaster
Brecon	The Felin Fach Griffin
Caersws / Pontdolgoch	The Talkhouse
Skenfrith	The Bell at Skenfrith

Further information

Pour en savoir plus

Per saperne di piú

Gut zu wissen

Beer

Beer is one of the oldest and most popular alcoholic drinks in the world. Traditional draught beer is made by grinding malted barley, heating it with water and adding hops which add the familiar aroma and bitterness. Beers in Britain can be divided into 2 principal types: Ales and Lagers which differ principally in their respective warm and cool fermentations. In terms of sales the split between the two is approximately equal. Beer can also be divided into keg or cask.

Kàg beer – is filtered, pasteurised and chilled and then packed into pressurised containers from which it gets its name.

Cask beer – or `Real Ale' as it is often referred to, is not filtered, pasteurised or chilled and is served from casks using simple pumps. It is considered by some to be a more characterful, flavoursome and natural beer.

There are several different beer styles in Britain and Ireland:

Bitter – whilst it is the most popular traditional beer in England and Wales it is now outsold by lager. Although no precise definition exists it is usually paler and dryer than Mild with a high hop content and slightly bitter taste.

Mild – is largely found in Wales, the West Midlands and the North West of England. The name refers to the hop character as it is gentle, sweetish and full flavoured beer. It is generally lower in alcohol and sometimes darker in colour, caused by the addition of caramel or by using dark malt.

Stout – the great dry stouts are brewed in Ireland and are instantly recognisable by their black colour and creamy head. They have a pronounced roast flavour with plenty of hop bitterness.

In Scotland the beers produced are full bodied and malty and are often known simply as Light, Heavy, or Export which refers to the body and strength of the beer.

Although Ireland is most famous for its stouts, it also makes a range of beers which have variously been described as malty, buttery, rounded and fruity with a reddish tinge.

Whisky

The term whisky is derived from the Scottish Gaelic *uisage beatha* and the Irish Gaelic *uisce beathadh*, both meaning "water of life". When spelt without an e it usually refers to Scotch Whisky which can only be produced in Scotland by the distillation of malted and unmalted barley, maize, rye, and mixtures of two or more of these. Often simply referred to as Scotch it can be divided into 2 basic types: malt whisky and grain whisky.

Malt whisky – is made only from malted barley which is traditionally dried over peat fires. The malt is then milled and mixed with hot water before mashing turns the starches into sugars and the resulting liquid, called wort, is filtered out. Yeast is added and fermentation takes place followed by two distilling processes using a pot still. The whisky is matured in oak, ideally sherry casks, for at least three years which affects both its colour and flavour. All malts have a more distinctive smell and intense flavour than grain whiskies and each distillery will produce a completely individual whisky of great complexity. A single malt is the product of an individual distillery. There are approximately 100 malt whisky distilleries in Scotland.

Grain whisky – is made from a mixture of any malted or unmalted cereal such as maize or wheat and is distilled in the Coffey, or patent still, by a continuous process. Very little grain whisky is ever drunk unblended.

Blended whisky – is a mix of more than one malt whisky or a mix of malt and grain whiskies to produce a soft, smooth and consistent drink. There are over 2,000 such blends which form the vast majority of Scottish whisky production.

Irish Whiskey – differs from Scotch whisky both in its spelling and method of production. It is traditionally made from cereals, distilled three times and matured for at least 7 years. The different brands are as individual as straight malt and considered by some to be gentler in character.

La bière

La bière est l'une des plus anciennes et populaires boissons alcoolisées dans le monde. Pour produire la bière pression traditionnelle, on écrase l'orge maltée que l'on chauffe ensuite avec de l'eau à laquelle on ajoute le houblon. C'est ce qui lui donne son arôme et son goût amer bien connus. Deux types de bières sont principalement vendues en Grande-Bretagne : les Ales fermentées à chaud et les Lagers fermentées à froid. Elles se divisent en « keg beer » et en « cask beer ».

Bière en keg : elle est filtrée, pasteurisée et refroidie, puis versée dans des tonnelets pressurisés appelés kegs.

Bière en cask ou « Real Ale » : elle n'est ni filtrée, ni pasteurisée, ni refroidie mais tirée directement du tonneau à l'aide d'une simple pompe. Selon certains, cette bière, de qualité bien distincte, a plus de saveur et est plus naturelle.

Types de bières vendues au Royaume-Uni et en Irlande :

Bitter – C'est la bière traditionnelle la plus populaire en Angleterre et au pays de Galles mais ses ventes diminuent au profit des lagers. La Bitter est généralement plus pâle et son goût plus sec que la Mild. Son contenu en houblon est élevé et elle a un goût légèrement amer.

La Mild se consomme surtout au pays de Galles, dans le Midlands de l'Ouest et dans le Nord-Ouest de l'Angleterre. On l'appelle ainsi en raison de son goût moelleux légèrement douceâtre conféré par le houblon. Cette bière, généralement moins alcoolisée, est plus foncée par le caramel qui lui est ajouté ou par l'utilisation de malt plus brun.

Stout – les grandes marques de bières brunes sont brassées en Irlande et sont reconnaissables par leur couleur noire rehaussée de mousse crémeuse. Elles ont un goût prononcé de houblon grillé et une saveur amère.

Celles produites en Écosse sont maltées ; elles ont du corps et se dénomment le plus souvent Light, Heavy ou Export en référence au corps et à leur teneur en alcool.

Whisky

Le mot whisky est un dérivé du gaélique écossais *uisage beatha* et du gaélique irlandais *uisce beathadh* signifiant tous deux « eau de vie ». Quand il est écrit sans e, il se réfère au whisky écossais qui ne peut être produit qu'en Écosse par la distillation de céréales maltées ou non comme l'orge, le maïs, le seigle ou d'un mélange de deux ou plus de ces céréales. Souvent appelé tout simplement Scotch il se réfère à deux types de whiskies : whisky pur malt ou whisky de grain.

Le **whisky pur malt** est fait seulement à partir d'orge maltée qui est traditionnellement séchée au-dessus de feux de tourbe. Le malt est moulu et mélangé avec de l'eau chaude, puis le brassage transforme l'amidon en sucre ; le moût est ensuite filtré. On y ajoute de la levure et après la fermentation on fait distiller deux fois dans un alambic. Le whisky est alors vieilli pendant au moins trois ans dans des fûts de chêne, ayant contenu de préférence du sherry, ce qui transforme son goût et sa couleur. Tous les whiskies pur malt ont un arôme particulier et une saveur plus intense que les whiskies de grain et chaque distillerie produit son propre whisky avec des qualités bien distinctes. Il y a environ une centaine de distilleries de whiskies pur malt en Écosse.

Le **whisky de grain** est fait d'un mélange de céréales, maltées ou non, comme le maïs ou le froment et est distillé dans un alambic de type Coffey suivant un procédé continu. Très peu de whiskies de grain sont consommés à l'état pur. On procède à des mélanges pour la consommation.

Blended whisky est le mélange d'un ou de plusieurs whiskies pur malt et de whiskies de grain afin de produire un alcool léger, moelleux et de qualité. Il existe plus de 2 000 marques de blended whiskies qui forment la majeure partie de la production écossaise.

Le **whisky irlandais**, différent du whisky écossais par sa fabrication, est traditionnellement produit à partir de céréales ; il est ensuite distillé trois fois et vieilli pendant au moins sept ans. Certains le trouvent plus moelleux.

La Birra

La birra è una delle bevande alcoliche più antiche e popolari. La tradizionale birra alla spina si ottiene macinando l'orzo, riscaldandolo con l'acqua e aggiungendo il luppolo, che le conferisce l'aroma e il tipico sapore amaro.

Le birre britanniche si dividono in due tipi principali: Ales e Lagers, che differiscono essenzialmente per la fermentazione, rispettivamente calda e fredda. In termini di vendita, i due tipi approssimativamente si equivalgono. La birra può anche dividersi in keg (lett, barilotto), e cask (lett botte).

La keg beer è filtrata, pastorizzata e raffreddata, e poi messa in contenitori pressurizzati, da cui deriva il nome.

La cask beer, o Real Ale, come viene comunemente indicata, non è filtrata, pastorizzata o raffeddata, ed è servita dalle botti, usando semplici pompe. Alcuni la considerano una birra più ricca di carattere e di gusto e più naturale.

In Gran Bretagna e Irlanda, le birre si caratterizzano anche in base a « stili » diversi.

Le bitter costituisce la birra tradizionalmente più popolare in Inghilterra e nel Galles, ma è ora « superata » dalla lager. Non esiste definizione specifica per la birra bitter, ma si può dire che si tratta in genere di una birra più pallida e secca della mild, dall'alto contenuto di luppolo e dal gusto leggermente amaro.

La mild è diffusa in Galles, West Midlands e Inghilterra nord-occidentale. Il nome richiama il carattere del luppolo, essendo delicata, dolce e dal gusto pieno. Contiene solitamente una limitata quantità di alcol ed è talvolta scura per l'aggiunta di caramello e per l'impiego di malto scuro.

La secche stouts vengono prodotte in Irlanda e sono immediatamente riconoscibili dal colore nero e dalla schiuma cremosa. Hanno una decisa fragranza di tostatura e un gusto amaro di luppolo.

Whisky

Il termine whisky deriva dal gealico scozzese *uisage beatha* e dal gaelico irlandese *uisce beathadh*, che significano « acqua di vita ». Se scritto senza la e, indica di solito lo Scotch Whisky, che può essere unicamente prodotto in Scozia dalla distillazione di malto e orzo, granturco e segale, e dall'unione di due o più di questi ingredienti. Spesso chiamato semplicemente Scoveri, si divide in due tipi: malt whisky e grain whisky.

Il malt whisky viene prodotto unicamente con malto, tradizionalmente seccato su fuochi alimentati con torba. Il malto viene poi macinato e gli viene aggiunta acqua bollente prima che l'impasto muti gli amidi in zuccheri e il liquido che ne deriva, chiamato wort (mosto di malto), venga filtrato. Si amalgama poi il lievito e avviene la fermentazione, seguita da due processi di distillazione nell'alambicco. Il whisky è lasciato invecchiare in legno di quercia, idealmente in botti di sherry, per almeno tre anni, perchè acquisti colore e sapore. Ogni tipo di malt whisky ha un profumo più distintivo e un gusto più intenso del grain whisky. Ogni distilleria produce un whisky dal carattere individuale, che richiede un processo di grande complessità. Un solo malt whisky è il prodotto di una specifica distilleria. In Scozia, esistono circa 100 distillerie di malt whisky.

Il grain whisky è il risultato della fusione di qualsiasi cereale con o senza malto, come il granturco o il frumento, es viene distillato nel Coffey, o alambicco brevettato, grazie ad un processo continuo. È molto scarsa la quantità di grain whisky che si beve puro.

Il blended whisky nasce dalla fusione di più di un malt whisky, o da quella di *malt* e grain whiskies. Il risultato è una bevanda dal gusto delicato, dolce e pieno. Esistono più di 2000 whisky di questo tipo, che costituiscono la parte più consistente della produzione scozzese.

Bier

Bier ist eines der ältesten und beliebtesten alkoholischen Getränke der Welt. Das traditionelle Fassbier wird aus gemahlener und gemalzter Gerste hergestellt, die in Wasser erhitzt wird. Durch Beigabe von Hopfen werden das bekannte Aroma und der typische bittere Geschmack erzeugt.

Die Biersorten in Großbritannien unterteilen sich in zwei Hauptgruppen: Ales und Lagers, wobei die Art der Gärung – im einen Fall warm, im anderen kalt – ausschlaggebend für das Endresultat ist. Beide Sorten haben hierzulande einen ungefähr gleichen Marktanteil. Da sich die meisten Brauvorgänge anfangs gleichen, entscheiden erst die Endphasen des Brauens, welche der verschiedenen Biersorten entsteht.

Darüber hinaus kann das englische Bier auch nach der Art seiner Abfüllung in Keg- bzw. Cask-Bier unterschieden werden:

Keg beer wird gefiltert, pasteurisiert, abgekühlt und anschließend in luftdichte, unter Druck gesetzte Metallbehälter gefüllt, von denen das Bier auch seinen Namen erhält.

Cask beer, gewöhnlich Real Ale genannt, wird weder gefiltert, noch pasteurisiert oder gekühlt, sondern mit einfachen (zumeist Hand-) Pumpen vom Faß gezapft.

Es gibt folgende Biersorten in Großbritannien und Irland: Bitter ist das meistbekannte traditionelle Bier in England und Wales. Eine genaue Definition, was ein Bitter ausmacht, sucht man vergeblich; es ist gewöhnlich heller und trockener als das Mild, hat einen hohen Hopfenanteil und einen leicht bitteren Geschmack. In den letzten Jahren hat das – meist importierte oder in Lizenz gebraute – Lager ihm jedoch den Rang abgelaufen.

Mild ist übergewiegend in Wales, in den westlichen Midlands und Nordwestengland zu finden. Der Name bezieht sich auf den Hopfenanteil, der es zu einem milden, etwas süßlichen und vollmundigen Bier macht. Es hat einen geringeren Alkoholgehalt und besitzt wegen der Zugabe von Karamel oder dunklem Malz bisweilen eine dunklere Farbe.

Stouts von hervorragendem trockenem Geschmack werden in Irland gebraut und sind unmittelbar an ihrer schwarzen Farbe und der cremigen Blume erkennbar. Sie haben einen ausgesprochen starken Geschmack nach bitterem Hopfen.

In Schottland hergestellte Biere sind alkoholstark und malzig; sie sind oft einfach bekannt als: Light, Heavy oder Export – Bezeichnungen, die auf Körper und Stärke des Bieres hinweisen.

Whisky

Die Bezeichnung Whisky entstammt dem Gälischen, wo im Schottischen der Ausdruck *uisage beatha*, im Irischen des Ausdruck *uisce beathadh* jeweils « Wasser des Lebens » bedeuten. Wird Whisky ohne ein e am Ende geschrieben, ist Scotch Whisky gemeint, der nur in Schottland aus gemalzter und ungemalzter Gerste, Mais, Roggen oder aus Mischungen zweier oder mehrerer dieser Zutaten gebrannt werden darf. Oft auch nur als Scotch bezeichnet, kann dieser in zwei Grundarten unterschieden werden: malt whisky und grain whisky.

Malt (Malz) whisky wird nur aus gemalzter Gerste hergestellt, die traditionell über Torffeuern getrocknet wird. Danach wird das Malz gemahlen und mit heißem Wasser vermischt, wonach in der Maische die Stärke in Zucker umgewandelt wird. Die dadurch entstandene Flüssigkeit, « wort » genannt, wird gefiltert und mit Hefe versetzt, was den Gärungsprozess einleitet. Anschließend folgen zwei Destillierungen im herkömmlichen Topf über offenem Feuer. Der Whisky reift danach mindestens drei Jahre lang in Eichenholz, idealerweise in Sherry-Fässern, was sich sowohl auf Farbe wie auf Geschmack des Whiskys auswirkt. Alle malts haben einen ausgeprägteren Geruch und intensiveren Geschmack als die grain-Whiskies; und jede Destillerie erzeugt einen völlig eigenen Whisky mit individueller Geschmacksnote und großer Komplexität. Ein sogenannter single malt entstammt aus einer einzigen Destillerie. Es gibt ungefähr 100 Malt Whisky-Destillerien in Schottland.

Grain (Korn) whisky wird aus Mischungen von gemalzten und ungemalzten Getreidesorten, wie Mais oder Weizen, hergestellt und wird in einem kontinuierlichen Prozeß in dem sogenannten « Coffey » destilliert. Nur sehr wenige Kornwhisky-Sorten sind nicht das Ergebnis von blending, dem Abstimmen des Geschmacks durch Mischung.

Blended whisky wird aus mehr als einer Sorte Malt Whisky oder aus Malt und Grain Whiskies gemischt, um ein weiches, geschmacklich harmonisches Getränk von beständiger Güte zu garantieren. Die über 2000 im Handel zu findenden blends stellen den Großteil der schottischen Whiskyerzeugung dar.

Irish Whiskey unterscheidet sich vom Scotch Whisky sowohl in der Schreibweise wie auch dem Herstellungsverfahren. Er wird traditionell aus Getreide hergestellt, wird dreifach destilliert und reift mindestens sieben Jahre lang. Die verschiedenen Sorten sind so individuell ausgeprägt wie reine Malt Whiskies und werden oft als weicher und gefälliger empfunden.

C. Labonne/MICHELIN

Great Britain

Towns
from A to Z

Villes
de A à Z

Città
de A a Z

Städte
von A bis Z

England
Channel Islands
Isle of Man

ABBERLEY – Worcestershire – 503 M 27 – pop. 654 – ⊠ Worcester   18 **B2**
▶ London 137 mi – Birmingham 27 mi – Worcester 13 mi

🏠🏠🏠 The Elms   ← 🍴 🐾 📺 ✻ 🎿 ⚒ ❝ 🏐 P **VISA** ⓪ **AE**
West : 2 m. on A 443 ⊠ *WR6 6AT* – ℰ *(01299) 896 666*
– www.theelmshotel.co.uk – info@theelmshotel.co.uk – Fax (01299) 896 804
23 rm ⌆ – †£ 130/230 ††£ 145/245   **Rest** – Menu £ 18/50
◆ Impressive Queen Anne mansion in well-kept grounds, with countryside views
from most bedrooms. Stylishly refurbished interior with contemporary style. Special
facilities for children. Restaurant serving classically based dishes with modern
touches.

ABBOTSBURY – Dorset – 503 M 32 – pop. 422   3 **B3**
▶ London 146 mi – Bournemouth 44 mi – Exeter 50 mi – Weymouth 10 mi
◎ Town★★ - Chesil Beach★★ - Swannery★ **AC** – Sub-Tropical Gardens★ **AC**
◉ St Catherine's Chapel★, ½ m. uphill (30 mn rtn on foot). Maiden Castle★★
(← ★) NE : 7½ m

🏠 Abbey House *without rest* ⌂   🍴 ✻ P
Church St ⊠ *DT3 4JJ* – ℰ *(01305) 871 330* – *www.theabbeyhouse.co.uk*
– Fax (01305) 871 088
5 rm ⌆ – †£ 85 ††£ 100
◆ Historic stone house, part 15C abbey infirmary. Garden holds a unique Benedictine
water mill. Breakfast room with low beamed ceiling and fireplace. Cosy bedrooms.

ABINGDON – Oxfordshire – 503 Q 28 – pop. 36 010 📖 *Great Britain*   10 **B2**
▶ London 64 mi – Oxford 6 mi – Reading 25 mi
🚢 from Abingdon Bridge to Oxford (Salter Bros. Ltd) 2 daily (summer only)
🛈 25 Bridge Street ℰ (01235) 522711, abingdontic@btconnect.com
🏁 Drayton Park Drayton Steventon Rd, ℰ (01235) 550 607
◎ Town★ – County Hall★

🏠🏠 Upper Reaches   ✻ 📞 ♨ P **VISA** ⓪ **AE**
Thames St ⊠ *OX14 3JA* – ℰ *(01235) 522 536*
– www.upperreaches-abingdon.co.uk – info@upperreaches-abingdon.co.uk
– Fax (01235) 555 182
31 rm ⌆ – †£ 100/140 ††£ 150/180   **Rest** – Menu £ 15/26 – Carte £ 24/30
◆ Former corn mill on island on River Thames accessed via small bridge. Period
buildings, traditional décor. Bedrooms in modern block are the most spacious and
have river views. Open plan restaurant houses revolving mill wheel and millrace.

ABINGER COMMON – Surrey – 504 S 30 – see Dorking

ABINGER HAMMER – Surrey – 504 S 30   7 **C2**
▶ London 35 mi – Brighton 40 mi – Dover 91 mi – Portsmouth 50 mi
– Reading 33 mi

✂✂ Drakes on the Pond (John Morris)   🔳 P **VISA** ⓪
✂ *Dorking Rd, on A 25* ⊠ *RH5 6SA* – ℰ *(01306) 731 174*
*– www.drakesonthepond.com – Fax (01306) 731 174 – Closed 2 weeks Christmas,
2 weeks late August, Saturday lunch, Sunday and Monday*
Rest – Menu £ 24 (lunch) – Carte £ 44/54
Spec. Smoked haddock and ventreche ham beignets, pea and ham panna
cotta. Canon of lamb with potato and celeriac Dauphinoise, red wine jus. Trio
of crème brûlée, chocolate brownie and black cherry ice cream.
◆ Friendly neighbourhood restaurant in long, simply furnished room; a former cow-
shed! Selection of simply-presented, classical dishes. Appealing, confident and flavourful cooking.

ACTON GREEN – Worcs. – 503 M 27 – see Great Malvern

ACTON BURNELL – Shrops. – 503 L 26 – see Shrewsbury

ADDINGHAM – West Yorkshire – **502** O 22 – pop. **3 215** ▮ *Great Britain*　22 **B2**

　　▶ London 225 mi – Bradford 16 mi – Ilkley 4 mi
　　◖ Bolton Priory **AC**, N : 3.5 m. on B 6160

⫯◻　**The Fleece**　　　　　　　　　　　　　　**P** *VISA* ◍◐ **AE**
　　152-154 Main St ✉ *LS29 0LY* – ☎ *(01943) 830 491 – www.fleeceaddingham.com*
　　Rest – Carte £ 21/30
　　♦ Personally run pub on village main street. Open fires, solid stone floor, rustic walls
　　filled with country prints. Wide ranging menu with good use of seasonal ingredients.

ALBRIGHTON – Shrops. – **502** L 25 – see Shrewsbury

ALDEBURGH – Suffolk – **504** Y 27 – pop. **2 654**　　　　　　　　　　15 **D3**

　　▶ London 97 mi – Ipswich 24 mi – Norwich 41 mi
　　🄓 152 High St ☎ (01728) 453637, atic@suffolkcoastal.gov.uk
　　🄳 Thorpeness Golf Hotel Thorpeness, ☎ (01728) 452 890

🏠🏠🏠　**Wentworth**　　　　⟨ 🛋 🞸 ⅗ **P** *VISA* ◍◐ **AE** ⑩
　　Wentworth Rd ✉ *IP15 5BD* – ☎ *(01728) 452 312*
　　– www.wentworth-aldeburgh.com – stay@wentworth-aldeburgh.co.uk
　　– Fax (01728) 454 343
　　35 rm ⊆ – †£ 93/104 ††£ 205/225
　　Rest – Menu £ 21 (dinner) – Carte £ 20/24
　　♦ Carefully furnished, traditional seaside hotel; coast view bedrooms are equipped
　　with binoculars and all have a copy of "Orlando the Marmalade Cat", a story set in the
　　area. Formal dining room offers mix of brasserie and classic dishes.

✗　　**The Lighthouse**　　　　　　　　🞸 **AC** *VISA* ◍◐ **AE**
☺　　*77 High St* ✉ *IP15 5AU* – ☎ *(01728) 453 377*
　　– www.thelighthouserestaurant.co.uk – sarafox@diron.co.uk – Fax (01728)
　　454 38 31
　　Rest – (booking essential) Carte £ 21/33
　　♦ Busy, unpretentious bistro boasts a wealth of Suffolk produce from local meats to
　　Aldeburgh cod and potted shrimps. Good choice of wines; amiable service.

✗　　**152**　　　　　　　　　　　　　　🞸 *VISA* ◍◐ **AE**
　　152 High St ✉ *IP15 5AX* – ☎ *(01728) 454 594 – www.152aldeburgh.co.uk*
　　– info@152aldeburgh.co.uk – Fax (01502) 731 099
　　Rest – Menu £ 20 (dinner) – Carte £ 22/29
　　♦ Choose between the bright, informal restaurant or the courtyard terrace on sum-
　　mer days to enjoy the keenly priced menu that features a wide variety of local
　　produce.

✗　　**Regatta**　　　　　　　　　　　**AC** *VISA* ◍◐ **AE**
　　171-173 High St ✉ *IP15 5AN* – ☎ *(01728) 452 011 – www.regattaaldeburgh.com*
　　– Fax (01728) 453 324 – Closed 24-26 December, 31 December and 1 January
　　Rest – Carte £ 19/30
　　♦ Maritime murals on the walls and cheerful décor make this fish-inspired eatery a
　　good catch. Local seafood's a speciality: it's good quality and prepared in a sure-
　　footed way.

at Friston Northwest : 4 m. by A 1094 on B 1121 – ✉ **Aldeburgh**

🏠　　**The Old School** without rest　　　　　　🛋 🞸 **P**
　　✉ *IP17 1NP* – ☎ *(01728) 688 173 – www.fristonoldschool.com*
　　– fristonoldschool@btinternet.com
　　3 rm ⊆ – †£ 64 ††£ 72
　　♦ Redbrick former school house in pleasant garden. Good breakfast served family
　　style in spacious room. Comfortable modern rooms with good amenities in the house
　　or annexe.

　Look out for red symbols, indicating particularly pleasant establishments.

▶ London 187 mi – Chester 34 mi – Manchester 14 mi – Stoke-on-Trent 25 mi
⌖ Wilmslow Mobberley Great Warford, ℰ (01565) 872 148

Alderley Edge   🍴 🐴 ⅌ 📶 🏊 **P.** **VISA** **☞** **AE** **①**
Macclesfield Rd ⊠ *SK9 7BJ –* ℰ *(01625) 583 033 – www.alderleyedgehotel.com*
– sales@alderleyedgehotel.com – Fax (01625) 586 343 – Closed 25 December
50 rm – ♦£73/130 ♦♦£110/145, ⊆ £15 – 1 suite
Rest *The Alderley* – see restaurant listing
♦ A substantial late Victorian house with an easy-going style. Relaxing lounges furnished with cushion-clad easy chairs. Well-furnished, comfortable bedrooms, some with views.

The Alderley – at Alderley Edge H.   🍴 **AC** **P.** **VISA** **☞** **AE** **①**
Macclesfield Rd ⊠ *SK9 7BJ –* ℰ *(01625) 583 033 – www.alderleyedgehotel.com*
– sales@alderleyedgehotel.com – Fax (01625) 586 343 – Closed 25 December
Rest – (Closed Sunday dinner to non-residents) Menu £19/30 – Carte £37/43
♦ Conservatory dining room; comfortably spaced tables. The cuisine, served by dinner-suited staff, is modern British. Particularly proud of 500 wine list and 100 Champagnes.

London Road Restaurant and Wine Bar   🍴 **AC** ✧
46 London Rd ⊠ *SK9 7DZ –* ℰ *(01625) 584 163*   **VISA** **☞** **AE**
– www.heathcotes.co.uk – Closed 1 January
Rest – Menu £14 (lunch) – Carte £27/41
♦ Sleek, modern brasserie with bar, basement, private dining room and terrace. Large menus offer modern European dishes with Northern influences; cooking is clean and unfussy.

The Wizard   🍴 🏡 ⅌ **P.** **VISA** **☞** **AE**
Macclesfield Rd, Southeast : 1 ¼ m. on B 5087 ⊠ *SK10 4UB –* ℰ *(01625) 584 000*
– www.wizardrestaurant.googlepages.com – wizardrestaurant@googlemail.com
– Fax (01625) 585 105 – Closed Christmas-New Year
Rest – (Closed Sunday dinner and Monday) Menu £10/15 – Carte £20/40
♦ Located in a National Trust area, this 200-year old pub restaurant serves up-to-date dishes at reasonable prices. Sticky puddings of chocolate, toffee or caramel feature.

> Your opinions are important to us:
> please write and let us know about your discoveries and experiences –
> good and bad!

▶ London 189 mi – Chester 6 mi – Liverpool 25 mi

The Grosvenor Arms   🍴 🏡 **P.** **VISA** **☞** **AE**
Chester Rd ⊠ *CH3 6HJ –* ℰ *(01244) 620 228*
– www.grosvenorarms-aldford.co.uk – grosvenor-arms@brunningandprice.co.uk
– Fax (01224) 620 247 – Closed 25-26 December dinner and 1 January dinner
Rest – Carte £18/30
♦ Spacious 19C red brick pub, with several eating areas indoors and out. Daily changing menu features generous and tasty British pub classics, with a few more sophisticated choices.

ENGLAND

ALDRIDGE – West Midlands – 502 O 26 – pop. 15 659 – ⊠ Walsall   19 C2

> ▶ London 130 mi – Birmingham 12 mi – Derby 32 mi – Leicester 40 mi – Stoke-on-Trent 38 mi

Plan : see Birmingham p. 5

🏠 Fairlawns   🚗 🖥 🌐 🍸 ⅃⅄ ✗ ఉ rm, ⯑ rest, ⑪ 🕍 🅿 VISA 🐵 AE ⓪
178 Little Aston Rd, East : 1 m. on A 454 ⊠ WS9 0NU – ℰ (01922) 455 122
– www.fairlawns.co.uk – welcome@fairlawns.co.uk – Fax (01922) 743 148
– Restricted opening 24 December-2 January   CT**n**
55 rm ⌾ – †£80/175 ††£110/195 – 6 suites
Rest – (closed Saturday lunch and Bank Holidays) Menu £19/25
– Carte £25/39
♦ Privately owned hotel with well-equipped leisure facility. A choice range of rooms from budget to superior, all comfy and spacious, some with good views over open countryside. Restaurant gains from its rural ambience.

ALFRISTON – East Sussex – 504 U 31 – pop. 1 721 – ⊠ Polegate   8 A3

> ▶ London 66 mi – Eastbourne 9 mi – Lewes 10 mi – Newhaven 8 mi

🏠 Star Inn   🕍 🅿 VISA 🐵
High St ⊠ BN26 5TA – ℰ (01323) 870 495 – www.thestaralfriston.com
– bookings@thestaralfriston.com – Fax (01323) 870 922
37 rm ⌾ – †£99/110 ††£140/150
Rest – (bar lunch Monday-Saturday) Menu £29
♦ 14C coaching inn with original half-timbered façade where smugglers once met. Décor includes flagstone floor and beamed ceilings; bar serves real ale. Well-kept bedrooms. Atmospheric Tudor style restaurant.

✗✗ Moonrakers   🚗 VISA 🐵 AE
High St. ⊠ BN2 5TD – ℰ (01323) 871 199 – Closed 2 weeks February, 1 week October, Sunday dinner, Monday and Tuesday
Rest – Carte £25/33
♦ Attractive 600 year old cottage in pleasant village with low beams, log burner and pretty terrace. Concise modern menu of local, seasonal produce displays precise, flavoursome cooking.

🍷 The George Inn with rm   🚗 🚗 ⯑ rm, VISA 🐵 ⓪
High St ⊠ BN26 5SY – ℰ (01323) 870 319 – www.thegeorge-alfriston.com
– info@thegeorge-alfriston.com – Closed 25-26 December
6 rm ⌾ – †£60 ††£130   **Rest** – (booking advisable) Carte £21/28
♦ Charming stone and timber building in delightful South Downs village, with hanging hops, inglenook fireplaces and large rear garden. Wide range of international dishes. Characterful antique-furnished bedrooms retain oak beams.

ALNWICK – Northumberland – 501 O 17 – pop. 7 767 ▌ Great Britain   24 B2

> ▶ London 320 mi – Edinburgh 86 mi – Newcastle upon Tyne 34 mi
> 🆔 2 The Shambles ℰ (01665) 511 333, alnwicktic@alnwick.gov.uk
> 🖼 Swansfield Park, ℰ (01665) 602 632
> ◎ Town ★ - Castle ★★ AC
> ◎ Dunstanburgh Castle ★ AC, NE : 8 m. by B 1340 and Dunstan rd (last 2½ m. on foot)

🏠 Aln House without rest   🚗 ✗ 🅿 VISA 🐵
South Rd, Southeast : ¾ m. by B 6346 on Newcastle rd ⊠ NE66 2NZ – ℰ (01665) 602 265 – www.alnhouse.co.uk – enquiries@alnhouse.co.uk
6 rm ⌾ – †£40/70 ††£70/80
♦ Semi detached Edwardian house with mature front and rear gardens, an easy walk from castle. Homely lounge enhanced by personal touches. Individually appointed rooms.

at North Charlton North : 6 ¾ m. by A 1 – ⊠ Alnwick

⌂   **North Charlton Farm** without rest ॐ   ⟨ 🚗 ⏰ 🌀 **P**
⊠ NE67 5HP – ⟨° (01665) 579 443 – www.northcharltonfarm.co.uk
– stay@northcharltonfarm.co.uk – Fax (01665) 579 407 – Easter-October
3 rm 😊 – ♦£70/80 ♦♦£70/80
♦ Attractive house on working farm with agricultural museum. Offers traditional accommodation. Each bedroom is individually decorated and has countryside views.

ALSTON – Cumbria – 501 M 19 – pop. 2 065   21 **B2**
▶ London 309 mi – Carlisle 28 mi – Newcastle upon Tyne 45 mi
🄸 Alston Moor Tourist Information Centre, Town Hall ⟨° (01434) 382244,
   alston.tic@eden.gov.uk
🄶 Alston Moor The Hermitage, ⟨° (01434) 381 675

🏠   **Lovelady Shield Country House** ॐ   ⟨ 🚗 📶 **P** 𝗩𝗜𝗦𝗔 ⓜⓞ 𝗔𝗘
Nenthead Rd, East : 2½ m. on A 689 ⊠ CA9 3LF – ⟨° (01434) 381 203
– www.lovelady.co.uk – enquiries@lovelady.co.uk – Fax (01434) 381 515
– Weekends only in January
12 rm 😊 – ♦£100 ♦♦£200
Rest – (dinner only and Sunday lunch) (booking essential for non-residents)
Menu £43
♦ Victorian country house in beautiful countryside location with peaceful garden and view to River Nent. Traditional bar and cosy lounge with open fire. Refurbished bedrooms. Ambitious menus served in dining room.

ALTON – Hampshire – 504 R 30 – pop. 16 051   6 **B2**
▶ London 53 mi – Reading 24 mi – Southampton 29 mi – Winchester 18 mi
🄸 7 Cross and Pillory Lane ⟨° (01420) 88448, altoninfo@btconnect.com
🄶 Old Odiham Rd, ⟨° (01420) 82 042

🏠   **Alton Grange**   🚗 🌀 📶 🛁 **P** 𝗩𝗜𝗦𝗔 ⓜⓞ 𝗔𝗘 ⓞ
London Rd, Northeast : 1 m. on B 3004 ⊠ GU34 4EG – ⟨° (01420) 86 565
– www.altongrange.co.uk – info@altongrange.co.uk – Fax (01420) 541 346
– Closed 25-26 December and 1 January
34 rm 😊 – ♦£90/110 ♦♦£120/170
Rest *Truffles* – (Closed Saturday lunch) Menu £23/32 – Carte £23/32
♦ Hotel set in well-kept, oriental inspired gardens. The bar serves bistro-style snacks. Bedrooms are individually decorated, particularly junior suites and Saxon room. Dining room boasts myriad of Tiffany lamps and fusion cuisine.

at Beech Northwest : 2 ¼ m by A339

⌂   **Beech Barns** without rest   🚗 ዸ 📶 **P** 𝗩𝗜𝗦𝗔 ⓜⓞ
61 Wellhouse Rd ⊠ GU34 4AQ – ⟨° (01420) 85 575 – www.beechbarns.co.uk
– timandnikki@beechbarns.co.uk
8 rm 😊 – ♦£60/80 ♦♦£90/120
♦ An early 18C barn conversion in a wooded area. Welcoming young owners. The house has an attractively understated and stylish quality. Breakfast is free range and organic.

at Lower Froyle Northeast : 4 ½ m. by A31

🍴   **The Anchor Inn** with rm   🚗 🖙 📶 **P** 𝗩𝗜𝗦𝗔 ⓜⓞ 𝗔𝗘
⊠ GU34 4NA – ⟨° (01420) 23 261 – www.anchorinnatlowerfroyle.co.uk
– info@anchorinnatlowerfroyle.co.uk – Closed 25 December
5 rm – ♦♦£130/170, 😊 £11   **Rest** – Carte £15/30
♦ 14C inn boasting cosy, low beamed bar and more formal candlelit drawing room. Traditional British dishes, simply served and precisely crafted from well sourced local ingredients. Well equipped, comfortable bedrooms.

ALTRINCHAM – Greater Manchester – 502 N 23 – pop. 40 695

- ▶ London 191 mi – Chester 30 mi – Liverpool 30 mi – Manchester 8 mi
- 🖬 20 Stamford New Rd ℰ (0161) 912 5931,
  tourist.information@trafford.gov.uk
- 🖭 Altrincham Municipal Timperley Stockport Rd, ℰ (0161) 928 0761
- 🖭 Dunham Forest Oldfield Lane, ℰ (0161) 928 2605
- 🖭 Ringway Hale Barns Hale Mount, ℰ (0161) 980 2630

XX Dilli   AC VISA ◯◯ AE
60 Stamford New Rd ⊠ WA14 1EE – ℰ (0161) 929 7484 – www.dilli.co.uk
– info@dilli.co.uk – Fax (0161) 929 1213 – Closed 25 December
Rest – Indian – Menu £ 15 (lunch) – Carte £ 15/24
♦ Intriguing interior: the décor is a mix of Indian wooden fretwork and minimalism.
Totally authentic Indian dishes use quality ingredients. Lunches are particularly good
value.

X The Fat Loaf   ⬜ ⬭ VISA ◯◯
28-32 Greenwood Street – ℰ (0161) 929 6700 – www.thefatloaf.co.uk
– fatloaf@aol.com – Closed 25-26 December, 1 January and Sunday
Rest – Menu £ 18 (lunch) **s** – Carte £ 22/32 **s**
♦ Relaxed, stylish eatery with high ceilings and bold patterned wallpapers. Wide
ranging menu of local, seasonal produce features simple dishes, clear flavours and
generous portions.

🏠 The Victoria   VISA ◯◯ AE
29 Stamford Street ⊠ WA14 1EX – ℰ (0161) 613 1855
– the.victoria@yahoo.co.uk – Closed 26 December, 1-2 January and Sunday
dinner
Rest – Carte £ 21/30
♦ Traditional pub on a quiet road in the town centre. Using local produce, menus
feature tasty, generous portions of interesting dishes. Battered butties available in
the bar.

at Little Bollington Southwest : 3 ¼ m. on A 56 – ⊠ Altrincham

🏠 Ash Farm without rest ⅘   🚗 ⅗ 📶 P. VISA ◯◯ AE ◑
Park Lane ⊠ WA14 4TJ – ℰ (0161) 929 9290 – www.ashfarm.co.uk
– ashfarm66@yahoo.co.uk
4 rm ⌂ – ♦£ 58 ♦♦£ 82
♦ Attractive, creeper-clad 18C former farmhouse in quiet location, being modernised
by the son - the new owner. Pretty stone-flagged breakfast room; cosy, individually
styled bedrooms.

ALVELEY – Shrops. – 502 M 26 – see Bridgnorth

ALVESTON – Warks. – see Stratford-upon-Avon

AMBERLEY – West Sussex – 504 S 31 – pop. 525 – ⊠ Arundel   7 C2
📗 Great Britain

- ▶ London 56 mi – Brighton 24 mi – Portsmouth 31 mi
- 🄲 Bignor Roman Villa (mosaics★) **AC**, NW : 3 ½ m. by B 2139 via Bury

🏰 Amberley Castle ⅘   🚗 🎱 ☆ ※ ⅗ 👶 P. VISA ◯◯ AE
Southwest : ½ m. on B 2139 ⊠ BN18 9LT – ℰ (01798) 831 992
– www.amberleycastle.co.uk – info@amberleycastle.co.uk – Fax (01798) 831 998
13 rm – ♦£ 400/450 ♦♦£ 400/450, ⌂ £ 18.50 – 6 suites
Rest *Queen's Room* – (booking essential) Menu £ 28/55
♦ Enchanting 12C castle with serene gardens, majestic battlements, intimate sitting
rooms and sumptuous, characterful bedrooms with luxurious jacuzzi bathrooms. Formal dining, with professional, attentive service. Barrel-vaulted ceiling and mural.

ENGLAND

▷ London 278 mi – Carlisle 47 mi – Kendal 14 mi
🛈 Central Buildings, Market Cross ℰ (015394) 32582 AZ, amblesidetic@southlakeland.gov.ukMain Car Park, Waterhead ℰ (015394) 32729 (summer only) BY
◲ Lake Windermere★★ – Dove Cottage, Grasmere★ **AC** AY **A** – Brockhole National Park Centre★ **AC**, SE : 3 m. by A 591 AZ. Wrynose Pass★★, W : 7 ½ m. by A 593 AY – Hard Knott Pass★★, W : 10 m. by A 593 AY

Plan opposite

The Samling ⌂   ← ⇘ ◐ ℅ 🄿 VISA ⓿ AE
Ambleside Rd, South : 1 ½ m. on A 591 ⊠ LA23 1LR – ℰ (015394) 31 922 – www.thesamling.co.uk – info@thesamling.co.uk – Fax (015394) 30 400
9 rm (dinner included) � – ♛£475 ♛♛£520 – 2 suites
Rest – (booking essential for non-residents) Menu £ 34/55 – Carte £ 55/67
♦ Traditional manor house appearance belies boutique interior; stylish lounge and highly individual bedrooms; two with stunning lake views. Marvellous garden with croquet lawn. Traditional linen-laid dining room; cooking has a classic base and an inventive edge.

The Waterhead   ← ⇘ 👓 sá 🄿 VISA ⓿ AE ①
Lake Rd ⊠ LA22 0ER – ℰ (015394) 32 566 – www.elh.co.uk – waterhead@elhmail.co.uk – Fax (015394) 31 255   BY**x**
41 rm ⊐ – ♛£128/256 ♛♛£128/256
Rest *The Bay* – (light lunch Monday-Saturday) Carte £ 24/36 **s**
♦ Traditional lakeside house boasting modern interior. Bright, contemporary bedrooms and stylish en suites with heated floors; Luxury rooms have the best lake views. European menu served under purple-hued lighting in The Bay restaurant.

Rothay Manor   ⇘ & rm, ℅ 🄿 VISA ⓿ AE ①
Rothay Bridge, South : ½ m. on A 593 ⊠ LA22 0EH – ℰ (015394) 33 605 – www.rothaymanor.co.uk – hotel@rothaymanor.co.uk – Fax (015394) 33 607 – Closed 3-24 January   BY**r**
16 rm ⊐ – ♛£95/155 ♛♛£145/200 – 3 suites
Rest – Menu £ 20/38 – Carte lunch £ 16/21
♦ Elegant Regency house boasting modern, stylish interior. Contemporary drawing room decorated in warm tones. Finely-kept bedrooms; 'Superior' rooms at the front have balconies. Mixture of modern and classic dishes with a distinct French flavour served in formal dining room.

Brathay Lodge without rest   📶 🄿 VISA ⓿ AE
Rothay Rd ⊠ LA22 0EE – ℰ (01539) 432 000 – www.brathay-lodge.com – info@brathay-lodge.com   AZ**e**
21 rm – ♛£65/99 ♛♛£70/129
♦ Stylish accommodation in the heart of Ambleside. Unfussy, bright and warm décor. Continental breakfast only. All bedrooms have spa baths and some boast four posters.

Lakes Lodge without rest   ℅ 📶 🄿 VISA ⓿
Lake Rd ⊠ LA22 0DB – ℰ (015394) 33 240 – www.lakeslodge.co.uk – info@lakeslodge.co.uk – Fax (015394) 33 240 – Closed 19-27 December   AZ**s**
12 rm – ♛£75 ♛♛£65/160
♦ Imposing traditional stone house with relaxed, laid back feel. Contemporary bedrooms in white; 10 has the best view. Continental breakfast plus homemade pastries and muffins.

Elder Grove without rest   ℅ 📶 🄿 VISA ⓿
Lake Rd ⊠ LA22 0DB – ℰ (015394) 32 504 – www.eldergrove.co.uk – info@eldergrove.co.uk – Fax (015394) 32251 – Closed 24-26 December   AZ**a**
10 rm ⊐ – ♛£30/110 ♛♛£60/120
♦ Ivy-clad stone house with cosy lounge bar full of firemen's memorabilia and bright, traditionally-furnished bedrooms. Locally sourced produce served in neat breakfast room.

ENGLAND

AMBLESIDE

Borrans Rd .... **BY** 2
Cheapside .... **AZ** 4
Church St .... **AZ** 6
Compston St .... **AZ** 8
Kelsick Rd .... **AZ** 12

King St. .... **AZ** 13
Lake Rd .... **AZ**
Market Pl. .... **AZ** 14
North Rd .... **AZ** 17
Old Lake Rd .... **AZ** 20
St Mary's
  Lane .... **AZ** 22

Smithy Brow .... **AZ** 23

GRASMERE

Broadgate .... **BZ** 3
Easedale Rd .... **BZ** 10
Swan Lane .... **AY** 24

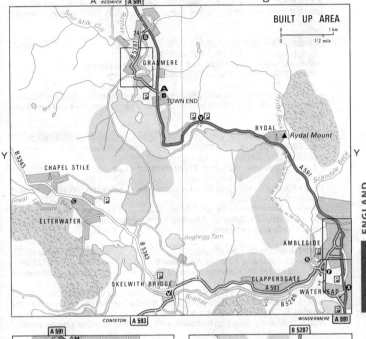

BUILT UP AREA

ENGLAND

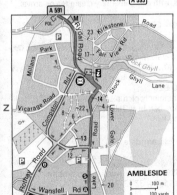

AMBLESIDE

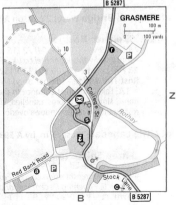

GRASMERE

If breakfast is included the ⌑ symbol appears after the number of rooms.

81

AMBLESIDE

ENGLAND

⌂ **Red Bank** without rest 🚗 🛜 📶 🅿
Wansfell Rd ⌂ LA22 0EG – ℰ (015394) 34637 – www.red-bank.co.uk
– info@redbank.co.uk – Closed 24-26 December   AZr
3 rm ⥮ – †£60/90 ††£78/90
♦ Edwardian house, a minute's walk from town. Cosy central lounge and pleasant
breakfast room overlooking garden. Immaculate, tastefully furnished rooms; room 2
is most popular.

⌂ **Riverside** without rest ⌂ ≤ 🚗 🛜 🅿 VISA ⓜⓞ
Under Loughrigg ⌂ LA22 9LJ – ℰ (015394) 32395
– www.riverside-at-ambleside.co.uk – info@riverside-ambleside.co.uk
– Fax (015394) 32240 – Closed 14 December-28 January   BYs
6 rm ⥮ – †£88 ††£104
♦ Stone house beside river with delightful sun deck and garden. Light, airy breakfast
room. Individually-styled bedrooms, immaculately kept; room 2 has four poster and
spa bath.

✕✕ **The Log House** with rm 🚗 🛜 📶 VISA ⓜⓞ AE
Lake Rd ⌂ LA22 0DN – ℰ (015394) 31077 – www.loghouse.co.uk
– nicola@loghouse.co.uk
– Closed 7 January - 1 February, 25 December and 1 January   BYv
3 rm ⥮ – †£60/90 ††£80/90
Rest – (Closed Sunday and Monday September-1 February) (booking essential
in winter) Carte £30/34
♦ Imported from Norway by artist Alfred Heaton Cooper to use as a studio, this is
now a characterful restaurant, with a flower-filled terrace and a modern, international
menu. Comfortable bedrooms.

⌂ **Drunken Duck Inn** with rm ≤ 🚗 🛏 🛜 📶 🅿 VISA ⓜⓞ AE
Barngates, Southwest : 3 m. by A 593 and B 5286 on Tarn Hows rd ⌂ LA22 0NG
– ℰ (01539) 436347 – www.drunkenduckinn.co.uk – info@drunkenduckinn.co.uk
– Fax (01539) 436781
17 rm ⥮ – †£95/120 ††£220/250   **Rest** – (booking essential) Carte £35/50
♦ Busy 16C pub with on-site brewery; cross the road and admire the view from the
benches. Eat in the cosy, firelit bar or at linen-laid tables in one of the beamed dining
rooms. Individually decorated bedrooms, with complimentary cream tea on arrival.

at Skelwith Bridge West : 2½ m. on A 593 – ⌂ **Ambleside**

🏨 **Skelwith Bridge** ♿ rm, 🆑 rest, 🅿 VISA ⓜⓞ
⌂ LA22 9NJ – ℰ (015394) 32115 – www.skelwithbridgehotel.co.uk
– info@skelwithbridgehotel.co.uk – Fax (015394) 34254   AYv
28 rm ⥮ – †£45/106 ††£110/152
Rest The Bridge – (dinner only) Menu £28
♦ 17C Lakeland inn at entrance to the stunningly picturesque Langdale Valley. Traditional, simple bedrooms; panelled, clubby bar; busy Talbot Bar for walkers. Popular
restaurant has large windows overlooking fells.

at Little Langdale West : 5 m. by A 593 – ⌂ **Langdale**

🏠 **Three Shires Inn** ⌂ ≤ 🚗 🛜 📶 🅿 VISA ⓜⓞ
Little Langdale ⌂ LA22 9NZ – ℰ (015394) 37215 – www.threeshiresinn.co.uk
– enquiry@threeshiresinn.co.uk – Fax (015394) 37127
– Restricted opening December-January   AYc
10 rm ⥮ – †£40/90 ††£80/110   **Rest** – (bar lunch) Carte £18/28
♦ Traditional family-owned lakeland inn in prime walking country. Homely front
lounge and busy back bar. Neat, floral bedrooms; those at front have countryside
views. Homemade fare served in cloth-clad dining room. Plenty of whiskies and
wines.

 Look out for red symbols, indicating particularly pleasant establishments.

82

AMERSHAM (Old Town) – Buckinghamshire – 504 S 29
– pop. 21 470
> ▶ London 29 mi – Aylesbury 16 mi – Oxford 33 mi
> ▣ Little Chalfont Lodge Lane, ℰ (01494) 764 877

✕✕ Artichoke   *VISA* ◍◉
9 Market Sq. ⊠ HP7 0DF – ℰ (01494) 726 611
– www.theartichokerestaurant.co.uk – info@theartichokerestaurant.co.uk
– Closed 2 weeks late August, 1 week Christmas, Sunday and Monday
Rest – Menu £ 23/38 – Carte lunch approx. £ 38
♦ 16C brick house with smart façade; an artichoke etched on its window. Narrow room with stylish, modern look but retaining period detail. Accomplished, well-presented cooking.

✕ Gilbey's   ᚛ AC *VISA* ◍◉ AE ◍
1 Market Sq. ⊠ HP7 0DF – ℰ (01494) 727 242 – www.gilbeygroup.com
– oldamersham@gilbeygroup.com – Fax (01494) 431 243
– Closed 24-28 December and 1 January
Rest – (booking essential) Menu £ 20 (lunch) – Carte £ 30/33
♦ Part of a former 17C school, this busy neighbourhood restaurant is cosy and informal with modern artwork on walls. Eclectic range of British cooking with global influences.

AMESBURY – Wiltshire – 503 O 30 – pop. 8 312   4 D2
> ▶ London 87 mi – Bristol 52 mi – Southampton 32 mi – Taunton 66 mi
> 🛈 Amesbury Libary, Smithfield St ℰ (01980) 622833,
>   amesburytic@salisbury.gov.uk
> ⓖ Stonehenge★★★ **AC**, W : 2 m. by A 303. Wilton Village★ Wilton House★★
>   **AC**, Wilton Carpet Factory★ **AC**), SW : 13 m. by A 303, B 3083 and A 36

ENGLAND

⌂ Mandalay without rest   ᚛ ✿ P. *VISA* ◍◉ AE ◍
15 Stonehenge Rd, via Church St ⊠ SP4 7BA – ℰ (01980) 623 733
– nick.ramplin@btinternet.com – Fax (01980) 626 642
5 rm ⊡ – †£ 45/55 ††£ 65/70
♦ Only two minutes' drive from Stonehenge, this brick-built house boasts a bygone style and pleasant garden. Varied breakfasts. Individual rooms, named after famous authors.

AMPLEFORTH – N. Yorks. – 502 Q 21 – see Helmsley

APPLEBY-IN-WESTMORLAND – Cumbria – 502 M 20 – pop. 2 862   21 B2
> ▶ London 285 mi – Carlisle 33 mi – Kendal 24 mi – Middlesbrough 58 mi
> 🛈 Moot Hall, Boroughgate ℰ (017683) 51177, tic@applebytown.org.uk
> ▣ Appleby Brackenber Moor, ℰ (017683) 51 432

🏠 Appleby Manor Country House ⌖   ᚛ ᚛ ᚛ ✿ ᛨ ⚓ P.
Roman Rd, East : 1 m. by B 6542 and Station Rd ⊠ CA16   *VISA* ◍◉ AE ◍
6JB – ℰ (017683) 51 571 – www.applebymanor.co.uk
– reception@applebymanor.co.uk – Fax (017683) 52 888 – Closed 24-26 December
31 rm ⊡ – †£ 120/130 ††£ 140/150   **Rest** – Carte £ 26/36
♦ Wooded grounds and good views of Appleby Castle at this elevated 19C pink sandstone country manor. Traditional bedrooms in extension; those in main house are more contemporary. Conservatory restaurant serves classic menu.

🏠 Tufton Arms   ᚛ ᛨ ⚓ P. *VISA* ◍◉ AE ◍
Market Sq ⊠ CA16 6XA – ℰ (017683) 51 593 – www.tuftonarmshotel.co.uk
– info@tuftonarmshotel.co.uk – Fax (017683) 52 761 – Closed 25-26 December
20 rm ⊡ – †£ 72/112 ††£ 160 – 2 suites   **Rest** – Carte £ 19/34
♦ 16C former coaching inn in traditional market town boasts new contemporary interior; chic, comfortable bedrooms in bold colours. Fishing, shooting and stalking can be arranged. Easy-going menu served in modern dining room.

APPLEDORE – Devon – 503 H 30 – pop. 2 187   2 C1

▶ London 228 mi – Barnstaple 12 mi – Exeter 46 mi – Plymouth 61 mi
– Taunton 63 mi
◉ Town ★

    West Farm without rest   
Irsha St, West : ¼ m. ✉ EX39 1RY – ✆ (01237) 425 269
– westfarm@appledore-devon.co.uk – Closed Christmas and New Year
3 rm ☑ – †£64 ††£98
♦ 17C house, boasting particularly pleasant garden at the back, in a charming little coastal village. Delightfully appointed sitting room. Bedrooms feel comfortable and homely.

APPLETREEWICK – North Yorkshire – 502 O 21   22 B2

▶ London 236 mi – Harrogate 25 mi – Skipton 11 mi

⌂   **Knowles Lodge** without rest ॐ   ⊞ 🔟 ➚ ✿ ⁽ᵗ⁾ **P** **VISA** **◑**
South : 1 m. on Bolton Abbey rd ✉ BD23 6DQ – ✆ (01756) 720 228
– www.knowleslodge.com – pam@knowleslodge.com – Fax (01756) 720 381
4 rm ☑ – †£55 ††£90
♦ Unusual Canadian ranch-house style guesthouse, clad in timber and sited in quiet dales location. Large sitting room with fine outlook. Cosy bedrooms have garden views.

> A good night's sleep without spending a fortune?
> Look for a Bib Hotel 🏨

ARDENS GRAFTON – Warks. – see Stratford-upon-Avon

ARLINGHAM – Gloucestershire – 503 M 28 – pop. 377 – ✉ Gloucester   4 C1

▶ London 120 mi – Birmingham 69 mi – Bristol 34 mi – Gloucester 16 mi

XX   **The Old Passage Inn** with rm ॐ   ≤ ☷ **AK** ✿ ⁽ᵗ⁾ **P** **VISA** **◑** **AE**
Passage Rd, West : ¾ m ✉ GL2 7JR – ✆ (01452) 740 547
– www.fishattheoldpassageinn.co.uk – oldpassage@ukonline.co.uk – Fax (01452) 741 871 – Closed 25 December, Sunday dinner and Monday
3 rm – †£60/130 ††£80/130, ☑ £7.50
Rest – Seafood – Menu £15 (weekday lunch) – Carte £31/61 ❀
♦ Eye-catching, former inn with bright yellow interior and colourful local artwork. Appealing seafood menus; unfussy cooking relies on the quality of the produce. Smart rooms with river views.

ARMSCOTE – Warwickshire – 504 P 27   19 C3

▶ London 91 mi – Birmingham 36 mi – Oxford 38 mi

⌂   **Willow Corner** without rest   ⊞ ✿ **P**
🏨   ✉ CV37 8DE – ✆ (01608) 682 391 – www.willowcorner.co.uk
– trishandalan@willowcorner.co.uk – Closed two weeks Christmas-New Year
3 rm ☑ – †£55 ††£80
♦ Lovely thatched property in quaint village with stable door, mullioned windows and low ceilings. Pretty bedrooms with thoughtful extras; homemade biscuits and tea on arrival.

🍴   **The Fox & Goose Inn** with rm   ⊞ **P** **VISA** **◑**
Front St ✉ CV37 8DD – ✆ (01608) 682 293 – www.foxandgoose.co.uk
– mail@foxandgoose.co.uk – Fax (01608) 682 293
4 rm ☑ – †£45/65 ††£75/115   **Rest** – Menu £12 (lunch) – Carte £24/40
♦ Creeper-clad red brick inn with modern interior; bright open-plan bar and dining room. Mix of fairly-priced pub and restaurant dishes. Bright, buzzy service. Bedrooms named after Cluedo characters.

ENGLAND

ARNCLIFFE – North Yorkshire – **502** N 21 – **pop. 79** – ⊠ Skipton   22 **A2**

  ▶ London 232 mi – Kendal 41 mi – Leeds 41 mi – Preston 50 mi
    – York 52 mi

XX   **Amerdale House** with rm ⤸   ≤ 🛋 🎥 ⅏ **P** VISA 🐵 AE
     ⊠ BD23 5QE – 𝒞 (01756) 770 250 – www.amerdalehouse.co.uk
     – info@amerdalehouse.co.uk – Closed January
     10 rm ⯐ – ♦£130 ♦♦£200
     Rest – (dinner only and Sunday lunch) (booking essential) Carte £22/28
     ♦ Rurally located 17C house. The classical menu changes weekly and the seasonal
     ingredients come from within 5 miles, with eggs from the chickens and fruit from the
     garden. Comfortable bedrooms, immaculately kept.

ARUNDEL – West Sussex – **504** S 31 – **pop. 3 297** 📗 Great Britain   7 **C2**

  ▶ London 58 – Brighton 21 – Southampton 41 – Worthing 9
  🖪 61 High St 𝒞 (01903) 882268, arundel.vic@arun.gov.uk
  ◎ Castle★★ AC

XX   **The Town House** with rm   VISA 🐵 AE ①
     65 High St – 𝒞 (01903) 883 847 – www.thetownhouse.co.uk
     – enquiries@thetownhouse.co.uk – Closed 2 weeks January, 2 weeks October,
     25-26 December
     4 rm – ♦£75 ♦♦£120
     Rest – (closed Sunday and Monday) Menu £18/28
     ♦ Grade II listed house at top of town. Beautiful Renaissance ceiling with gilded
     walnut panels. Cooking is rich, classic, unfussy and skilled, and uses local, seasonal
     produce. Simple, traditional bedrooms. Best are at front facing castle.

XX   **Arundel House** with rm   ♫ⁱ⁰ VISA 🐵 AE
     11 High St – 𝒞 (01903) 882 136 – www.arundelhouseonline.co.uk – Fax (01903)
     881 177 – Closed 6-16 April, 19-29 October, 21-27 December,
     Sunday and Bank Holidays
     5 rm ⯐ – ♦£80/100 ♦♦£140/160   **Rest** – Menu £20/30
     ♦ Bow fronted high street property with courtyard. Contemporary bedrooms boast
     mod cons, ipod docking stations and good bathrooms; 1 split level room. Restaurant
     offers monthly menu of well proportioned, highly seasonal dishes; priced per course.

at Burpham Northeast : 3 m. by A 27 – ⊠ Arundel

🏠   **Burpham Country House** ⤸   ≤ 🛋 ⅏ ♫ⁱ⁰ **P** VISA 🐵
     The Street ⊠ BN18 9RJ – 𝒞 (01903) 882 160 – www.burphamcountryhouse.com
     – info@burphamcountryhouse.com – Fax (01903) 884 627 – Closed 25 December
     and 12-31 January
     10 rm ⯐ – ♦£30/120 ♦♦£140
     Rest – (booking essential dinner only) (Wednesday - Saturday) Menu £27
     ♦ Reputedly a hunting lodge for the Duke of Norfolk, this quiet hotel constitutes the
     ideal "stress remedy break". Calm, pastel coloured bedrooms overlook exquisite gar-
     dens.

🏠   **George and Dragon**   **P** VISA 🐵 ①
     Main St ⊠ BN18 9RR – 𝒞 (01903) 883 131
     – www.georgeanddragonburpham.com – sara.cheney@btinternet.com
     – Fax (01903) 883 341 – Closed 25 December and Sunday dinner
     Rest – Menu £16 – Carte £16/28
     ♦ Welcoming pub in picturesque village. Seasonal offerings from local suppliers,
     including game from the Duke of Norfolk's estate served in bar or more formal dining
     room.

ENGLAND

at Walberton West : 3 m. by A 27 off B 2132 – ⊠ Arundel

🏨 **Hilton Avisford Park** ≤ 🏊 🛏 🍸 🔟 🏊 £6 ✗ 📺 � rm, 🎾 🐾
Yapton Lane, on B 2132 ⊠ BN18 0LS – ✆ (01243) 🅿 VISA ◉◉ AE ⓪
558 300 – www.hilton.co.uk/arundel – general.manager@hilton.com
– Fax (01243) 552 485
134 rm ☲ – ♦£ 109/199 ♦♦£ 119/209 – 5 suites
Rest – (bar lunch Monday-Saturday) Menu £ 26 – Carte £ 26/41
♦ Former school and one-time home of Baronet Montagu, Nelson's admiral; retains a
stately air with grand façade and 62-acre grounds. Generous drapes and furnishings
in rooms. Dining room features honours board listing prefects of yesteryear.

ASCOT – Windsor and Maidenhead – **504** R 29 – **pop. 15 761**　　　　　11 **D3**
　🚇 London 36 mi – Reading 15 mi
　🏌 Mill Ride Ascot, ✆ (01344) 886 777

🏨 **Berystede** 🏊 🔟 ⊛ 🏊 £6 ♨ 🎾 rm, ⓐⓒ 📶 ☝ 🅿 VISA ◉◉ AE ⓪
Bagshot Rd, Sunninghill, South : 1½ m. on A 330 ⊠ SL5 9JH – ✆ (0844) 87 991
– www.berystede.com – general.berystede@macdonald-hotels.co.uk
– Fax (01344) 873 061
121 rm ☲ – ♦£ 80/200 ♦♦£ 100/250 – 5 suites
Rest *Hyperion* – ✆ (0870) 400 81 11 (closed Saturday lunch) Menu £ 30/41
♦ Turreted red brick Victorian house in mature gardens, boasts classically-styled
lounge, panelled bar with terrace and variously-sized bedrooms, with warm, contemporary feel. Formal dining at Hyperion, with classic menus and countryside outlook.

✗✗ **Ascot Oriental** 🍴 ⓐⓒ ⇔ 🅿 VISA ◉◉ AE
East : 2¼ m. on A 329 ⊠ SL5 0PU – ✆ (01344) 621 877
– www.ascotoriental.com – info@ascotoriental.com – Fax (01344) 621 885
– Closed 25-26 December
Rest – Chinese – Menu £ 28 – Carte £ 29/44
♦ Stylish modern restaurant with a vibrantly hued interior. Private dining in attractive
conservatory. An interesting menu of Chinese dishes prepared with originality and
verve.

at Sunninghill South : 1½ m. by A 329 on B 3020 – ⊠ Ascot

✗✗ **Jade Fountain** ⓐⓒ VISA ◉◉ AE ⓪
38 High St ⊠ SL5 9NE – ✆ (01344) 627 070 – www.jadefountainrestaurant.com
– jadefountain-restaurant.co.uk – Fax (01344) 627 070 – Closed 24-28 December
Rest – Chinese – Menu £ 27 (dinner) – Carte £ 20/27
♦ Chinese restaurant specialising in sizzling dishes from Sichuan and Beijing - Peking
duck, spring rolls and noodles amongst them. Also some Thai specialities.

ASENBY – N. Yorks. – see Thirsk

ASH – Kent – **504** X 30　　　　　　　　　　　　　　　　9 **D2**
　🚇 London 70 mi – Canterbury 9 mi – Dover 15 mi

🏠 **Great Weddington** 🍴 🎾 📶 🅿 VISA ◉◉ AE
Northeast : ½ m. by A 257 on Weddington rd ⊠ CT3 2AR – ✆ (01304) 813 407
– www.greatweddington.co.uk – greatweddington@hotmail.com – Fax (01304)
812 531 – Closed Chistmas and New Year
4 rm ☲ – ♦£ 72/80 ♦♦£ 90/110
Rest – (by arrangement, communal dining) Menu £ 33
♦ Charming Regency country house, ideally located for Canterbury and Dover. Well
appointed drawing room and terrace. Thoughtfully furnished, carefully co-ordinated
rooms. Communal dining room; owner an avid cook.

ENGLAND

ASHBOURNE – Derbyshire – 502 O 24 – pop. 5 020 📗 *Great Britain* 16 **A2**

> ▶ London 146 mi – Birmingham 47 mi – Manchester 48 mi
> – Nottingham 33 mi – Sheffield 44 mi
> 🛈 13 Market Pl 𝒞 (01335) 343666, ashbourneinfo@derbyshiredales.gov.uk
> 🗺 Dovedale★★ (Ilam Rock★) NW : 6 m. by A 515

🏠 Callow Hall ⌂   ⟨ 🍴 🕙 🐕 ♐ 🤸 👃 P̲ VISA ⓪⑤ 🅰🅴 ⓪
Mappleton Rd, West : ¾ m. by Union St (off Market Pl) ⊠ DE6 2AA – 𝒞 (01335)
300 900 – www.callowhall.co.uk – reservations@callowhall.co.uk – Fax (01335)
300 512 – Closed 25-26 December and 1 week Februrary
15 rm ⌲ – ♦£105/140 ♦♦£150/195 – 1 suite
Rest – (closed Sunday dinner to non residents) (dinner only and Sunday
lunch) Menu £29/42 – Carte dinner £33/40
♦ Victorian country house in 42 acres. Cosy period bar lounge. Spacious bedrooms in
main house have views of parkland; those in former servants' wing recently refurbished. Modern European menu; home-smoked salmon.

✗✗ the dining room   VISA ⓪⑤
33 St Johns St ⊠ DE6 1GP – 𝒞 (01335) 300 666
*– www.thediningroomashbourne.co.uk – Closed 1 week March, 1 week August,
26 December-9 January, Sunday and Monday*
Rest – (booking essential) Menu £29 (lunch) – Carte dinner £37/45
♦ Modern, stylish décor blends agreeably with period features including exposed
beams and cast iron range. Well sourced, seasonal ingredients inform intricate modern dishes.

at Marston Montgomery South : 7½ m. by A 515 – ⊠ Ashbourne

ENGLAND

🏠 The Crown Inn with rm   🍴 🤸 P̲ VISA ⓪⑤ 🅰🅴
Riggs Lane ⊠ DE6 2FF – 𝒞 (01889) 590 541
*– www.thecrowninn-derbyshire.co.uk – info@thecrowninn-derbyshire.co.uk
– Fax (01889) 591 576 – Closed 25 December, 1 January*
7 rm ⌲ – ♦£60 ♦♦£80
Rest – (Restaurant closed Sunday dinner) Menu £18 – Carte £24/34
♦ Traditional creeper-clad pub in a peaceful hamlet. Menus change weekly and
include an à la carte and good value set lunch menu; fish often features on the daily
specials. Simple bedrooms.

> The red ⌂ symbol?
> This denotes the very essence of peace
> – only the sound of birdsong first thing in the morning…

ASHBURTON – Devon – 503 I 32 – pop. 3 309 2 **C2**

> ▶ London 220 mi – Exeter 20 mi – Plymouth 25 mi
> 🗺 Dartmoor National Park★★

✗ Agaric with rm   🤸 🤸 VISA ⓪⑤
30 and 36 North St ⊠ TQ13 7QD – 𝒞 (01364) 654 478
*– www.agaricrestaurant.co.uk – eat@agaricrestaurant.co.uk – Closed last 2 weeks
Christmas, 2 weeks August, Sunday, Monday and Tuesday*
5 rm – ♦£50/65 ♦♦£125   **Rest** – (booking essential) Carte £29/39
♦ 200 year-old house, selling home-made jams, fudge and olives. Relaxed neighbourhood restaurant using a blend of cooking styles. Very stylish, individually themed
bedrooms.

ASHFORD – Kent – 504 W 30 9 **C2**

> ▶ London 56 mi – Canterbury 14 mi – Dover 24 mi – Hastings 30 mi
> – Maidstone 19 mi
> **Access** Channel Tunnel : Eurostar information and reservations 𝒞 (08705)
> 186186
> 🛈 18 The Churchyard 𝒞 (01233) 629165, tourism@ashford.gov.uk

Eastwell Manor ⌖   ← 🚗 🏊 🔲 🍸 🐕 🏠 ♨ 🐾 ✕ 🍴 🏋 ♨ **P**

Eastwell Park, Boughton Lees, North : 3 m. by A 28 on A   VISA ⓒ AE ①
251 ⊠ TN25 4HR – ℰ (01233) 213 000 – www.eastwellmanor.co.uk
– enquiries@eastwellmanor.co.uk – Fax (01233) 213 175
20 rm ⊇ – †£160/235 ††£190/265 – 42 suites
Rest *Manor* – Menu £18/38 – Carte £32/70
Rest *Brasserie* – Menu £15 (lunch) – Carte £21/37
♦ Mansion house in formal gardens, replete with interesting detail including carved panelled rooms and stone fireplaces. Smart individual bedrooms. Manor offers seasonal menus. Swish brasserie in luxury spa with marbled entrance hall.

Ashford International   🏠 🔲 ⓦ 🐕 🏋 🍸 🖆 ⅋ rm, 🍴 ♨ **P** VISA ⓒ AE

Simone Weil Ave, North : 1½ m. by A 20 ⊠ TN24 8UX – ℰ (01233) 219 988
– www.qhotels.co.uk – ashford@qhotels.co.uk – Fax (01233) 647 743
179 rm ⊇ – †£133/143 ††£143
Rest *Horizon* – Carte £22/30
♦ Enormous corporate oriented hotel, benefiting from a recent top-to-toe refurbishment. Modern, comfortable bedrooms with good level of facilities. Contemporary cooking at Horizon.

ASHFORD-IN-THE-WATER – Derbs. – **502** O 24 – **see Bakewell**

ASHURST – W. Sussex – **504** T 31 – **see Steyning**

ASHWATER – Devon   2 **C2**

▶ London 218 mi – Bude 16 mi – Virginstow 3 mi

Blagdon Manor ⌖   ← 🚗 🏠 🐕 **P** VISA ⓒ

Beaworthy, Northwest : 2 m. by Holsworthy rd on Blagdon rd ⊠ EX21 5DF
– ℰ (01409) 211 224 – www.blagdon.com – stay@blagdon.com – Fax (01409)
211 634 – Closed January, and 10 days in Autumn
8 rm ⊇ – ††£135/180
Rest – (closed lunch Monday and Tuesday) (booking essential) (residents only Monday and Sunday dinner) Menu £24/35
♦ Proudly run former farmhouse in peaceful, rural location. Modern country house bedrooms, spotlessly kept, named after surrounding villages. Library, lounges and flag-floored bar. Classically-based cooking with a modern touch, served in dining room with conservatory extension.

ASKRIGG – North Yorkshire – **502** N 21 – **pop. 1 002** – ⊠ Leyburn   22 **A1**

▶ London 251 mi – Kendal 32 mi – Leeds 70 mi – Newcastle upon Tyne 70 mi
– York 63 mi

Yorebridge House   🚗 ✕ **P** VISA ⓒ

⊠ DL8 3EE – ℰ (01969) 652 060 – www.yorebridgehouse.com
– enquiries@yorebridgehouse.com – Fax (01969) 650 258
11 rm ⊇ – †£205/235 ††£235   **Rest** – Menu £35
♦ A fine period house, with warm and hospitable owners. Modern, stylish and comfortable interior. Mod cons include lots of Bang & Olufsen. Some rooms have hot tubs. Locally sourced produce in relaxing dining room.

The Apothecary's House without rest   ✕ 📞 **P**

 Market Pl ⊠ DL8 3HT – ℰ (01969) 650 626 – www.apothecaryhouse.co.uk
– bookings@apothecaryhouse.co.uk – Closed 24-26 December, 31 December and
1 January
3 rm ⊇ – †£45 ††£75
♦ Built in 1756 by the local apothecary in centre of village; overlooks church. Combined lounge and breakfast room has fresh, modern feel. Rear bedroom boasts exposed timbers.

ENGLAND

The Kings Arms   VISA ⓒⓞ
Market Place – ℰ (01969) 650817 – thekingsarms@yahoo.co.uk – Fax (01969) 650856 – Closed one week early January
Rest – Carte £ 21/30 **s**
♦ Characterful pub built in mid-18C by racehorse owner; what is now the bar area was once the tack room. Huge open fire, beamed ceilings and games room. Rustic, hearty cooking.

ASTON CANTLOW – Warwickshire – 503 O 27 📗 *Great Britain*   19 **C3**
🚩 London 106 mi – Birmingham 20 mi – Stratford-upon-Avon 5 mi
🅖 Mary Arden's House★ **AC**, SE : 2 m. by Wilmcote Lane and Aston Cantlow Rd

The King's Head   🚗 🏠 **P** VISA ⓒⓞ
21 Bearley Rd ⊠ B95 6HY – ℰ (01789) 488242 – www.thekh.co.uk – info@thekh.co.uk – Fax (01789) 488137 – Closed 25 December
Rest – Menu £ 15 – Carte £ 20/30
♦ Pretty 15C pub in idyllic village. Chic, French farmhouse style restaurant. Heavily beamed lounge bar with large stone fireplaces. Regularly held duck suppers.

Red = Pleasant. Look for the red 🍴 and 🏠 symbols.

ENGLAND

ASTON CLINTON – Buckinghamshire – 504 R 28 – pop. 4 038   11 **C2**
– ⊠ Aylesbury
🚩 London 42 mi – Aylesbury 4 mi – Oxford 26 mi

West Lodge   🚗 🏠 🏊 ⁽ʸ⁾ **P** VISA ⓒⓞ AE
45 London Rd ⊠ HP22 5HL – ℰ (01296) 630362 – www.westlodge.co.uk – jibwl@westlodge.co.uk – Fax (01296) 630151
9 rm ⌷ – ♦£62/75 ♦♦£90
Rest – (dinner only) (residents only) Menu £ 23 – Carte £ 23/30
♦ 19C former hunting lodge for Rothschild estate with walled Victorian garden. Bedrooms in converted outbuilding are largest/quietest. Balloon theme throughout adds interest. Conservatory dining room serving residents only.

ASTON TIRROLD – Oxfordshire   10 **B3**
🚩 London 58 mi – Reading 16 mi – Streatley 4 mi

The Sweet Olive at The Chequers Inn   🏠 **P** VISA ⓒⓞ AE
Baker St ⊠ OX11 9DD – ℰ (01235) 851272 – www.sweet-olive.com – Closed February and 1 week in July
Rest – (Closed Wednesday) (booking essential) Carte £ 23/30
♦ British on the outside, French on the inside; it's cosy, friendly and popular with the locals. Blackboard menus feature interesting French, British and European dishes.

ATCHAM – Shrops. – 503 L 25 – see Shrewsbury

AUSTWICK – North Yorkshire – 502 M 21 – pop. 467 – ⊠ Lancaster   22 **A2**
(Lancs.)
🚩 London 259 mi – Kendal 28 mi – Lancaster 20 mi – Leeds 46 mi

Austwick Traddock 🌿   🚗 ⁽ʸ⁾ **P** VISA ⓒⓞ
⊠ LA2 8BY – ℰ (015242) 51224 – www.thetraddock.co.uk
– info@austwicktraddock.co.uk – Fax (015242) 51796 – Closed 5-14 January
10 rm ⌷ – ♦£85/125 ♦♦£180
Rest – (dinner only and Saturday and Sunday lunch) (booking essential for non-residents) Carte £ 24/38
♦ A Georgian country house decorated with both English and Asian antiques. Bedrooms are individually styled to a high standard and overlook the secluded gardens. Dining room split into two rooms and lit by candlelight.

⌂ **Austwick Hall**   🚗 💥 🛜 **P** 𝖵𝖨𝖲𝖠 ⦿Ⓞ AE
Southeast : ½ m on Townend Lane ⊠ *LA2 8BS –* ℰ *(015242) 51 794*
– www.austwickhall.co.uk – austwickhall@austwick.org
5 rm ⌣ – †£85/140 ††£95/155   **Rest** – Menu £ 30
♦ Spacious and comfortable house with open fires and welcoming atmosphere.
Located in a delightful village on the edge of the dales. Very much a family concern.
A strong organic base to the cooking.

⌂ **Wood View** without rest   🚗 **P** 𝖵𝖨𝖲𝖠 ⦿Ⓞ
The Green ⊠ *LA2 8BB –* ℰ *(015242) 51 190 – www.woodviewbandb.com*
– woodview@austwick.org – Fax (015242) 51 190
5 rm ⌣ – †£40 ††£76
♦ In a charming spot on the village green, the cottage dates back to 17C with many
of the original features still in place including exposed rafters in several bedrooms.

AVONWICK – Devon   2 **C2**
▶ London 202 mi – Plymouth 17 mi – Totnes 8 mi

🍴 **The Turtley Corn Mill**   🚗 🍸 **P** 𝖵𝖨𝖲𝖠 ⦿Ⓞ
Northwest : 1 m. on Plymouth rd ⊠ *TQ10 9ES –* ℰ *(01364) 646 100*
– www.avonwick.net – mill@avonwick.net – Fax (01364) 646 101
– Closed 25 December
Rest – Carte £ 20/31
♦ Refurbished 18C mill in six acres, with original beams and pillars in situ. A clean,
light and airy feel helps enhance the enjoyment of dishes ranging from classics to
modern.

🍴 **The Avon Inn**   🚗 🍸 **P** 𝖵𝖨𝖲𝖠 ⦿Ⓞ
⊠ *TQ10 9NB –* ℰ *(01364) 73 475 – www.eatoutdevon.co.uk*
– rosec@beeb.net
Rest – French Mediterranean – (Closed Sunday dinner and Monday lunch)
Carte £ 15/28
♦ Homely pub with an interior of beams and hop bines. French owner/chef serves
accomplished dishes with classic Gallic base and plenty of local seafood and
fish.

AXBRIDGE – Somerset – 503 L 30 – pop. 2 025   3 **B2**
▶ London 142 mi – Bristol 17 mi – Taunton 27 mi – Weston-Super-Mare 11 mi

⌂ **The Parsonage** without rest   ⩽ 🚗 💥 🛜 **P**
Parsonage Lane, Cheddar Rd, East : ¾ m. on A 371 ⊠ *BS26 2DN*
– ℰ *(01934) 733 078 – www.the-parsonage-axbridge.co.uk*
– Fax (01934) 733 078
3 rm ⌣ – †£49 ††£60
♦ Former Victorian parsonage nestling in the southern slopes of the Mendip Hills
overlooking the Somerset Levels. The comfortable bedrooms are tastefully furnished.

AXFORD – Wiltshire – pop. 1 717 – ⊠ Marlborough   4 **D2**
▶ London 74 mi – Marlborough 3 mi – Swindon 15 mi

🍴 **The Red Lion Inn**   🚗 🍸 ⇔ **P** 𝖵𝖨𝖲𝖠 ⦿Ⓞ
⊠ *SN8 2HA –* ℰ *(01672) 520 271 – www.redlionaxford.com*
– info@redlionaxford.com – Closed 25 December
Rest – (Closed Sunday dinner) Carte £ 20/28
♦ Early Victorian-fronted flint and red-brick pub run by convivial patron and his loyal
team. Good blackboard choices and classic, unfussy cooking, with fish and game
specialities.

AXMINSTER – Devon – **503** L 31 – pop. 4 952　　　　　　　　2 **D2**

　　🚘 London 156 mi – Exeter 27 mi – Lyme Regis 5 mi – Taunton 22 mi
　　　– Yeovil 24 mi
　　🛈 The Old Courthouse, Church St 𝒞 (01297) 34386,
　　　axminstertic@btopenworld.com
　　🅖 Lyme Regis★ - The Cobb★, SE : 5½ m. by A 35 and A 3070

 Fairwater Head ⬙　　　　　　　　≤ 🚃 🛋 **P** 💳 ⦿
Hawkchurch, Northeast : 5¼ m. by B 3261 and A 35 off B 3165 ✉ *EX13 5TX*
– 𝒞 (01297) 678 349 – www.fairwaterheadhotel.co.uk
– info@fairwaterheadhotel.co.uk – Fax (01297) 678 459 – Closed 3-30 January
18 rm ⤓ – 🛉£95/110 🛉🛉£150/180
Rest – (Closed lunch Monday-Tuesday) Menu £18/29 (Light lunch) **s**
◆ Edwardian hotel in flower-filled gardens. Tea and fresh cakes served in the afternoon. Many rooms have Axe Valley views. Attractive outlook over garden and countryside accompanies diners enjoying locally sourced cooking.

 Kerrington House without rest　　　　🚃 ⅏ ⦇ **P** 💳 ⦿
Musbury Rd, Southwest : ½ m. ✉ *EX13 5JR – 𝒞 (01297) 35 333*
– www.kerringtonhouse.com – enquiries@kerringtonhouse.com
6 rm ⤓ – 🛉£75 🛉🛉£110
◆ Pleasantly converted Victorian house with original tiles and homely character; close to town centre. Warm, welcoming owners. Spacious sitting room. Large, comfy bedrooms.

Don't confuse 🕇 with 🕸!
🕇 defines comfort, while stars are awarded for the best cuisine,
across all categories of comfort.

ENGLAND

AYLESBURY – Buckinghamshire – **504** R 28 – pop. 69 021　　　　11 **C2**
📗 *Great Britain*

　　🚘 London 46 mi – Birmingham 72 mi – Northampton 37 mi – Oxford 22 mi
　　🛈 The Kings Head, Kings Head Passage off Market Square 𝒞 (01296) 330559,
　　　tic@aylesburyvaledc.gov.uk
　　🏌 Weston Turville New Rd, 𝒞 (01296) 424 084
　　🏌 Aylesbury Golf Centre Bierton Hulcott Lane, 𝒞 (01296) 393 644
　　🅖 Waddesdon Manor★★, NW : 5½ m. by A 41 – Chiltern Hills★

Hartwell House ⬙　　≤ 🚃 🐾 ⏛ 🔲 ⊛ 🐾 ⅃♨ ✕ 🕮 ⅏ ⁙ 🏌 **P**
Oxford Rd, Southwest : 2 m. on A 418 ✉ *HP17 8NL*　　　💳 ⦿ 🆎
– 𝒞 (01296) 747 444 – www.hartwell-house.com – info@hartwell-house.com
– Fax (01296) 747 450
38 rm – 🛉£160/200 🛉🛉£260, ⤓ £7.50 – 10 suites
Rest *The Soane* – Menu £30/39 **s** – Carte £36/50 **s**
◆ Stunning stately home in beautiful grounds; elegant rooms, portraits and antique furniture. Magnificent Gothic staircase leading to luxurious bedrooms, some with four posters. Neo-classical dining room serves elaborate cooking.

AYLESFORD – Kent – **504** V 30　　　　　　　　　　　　8 **B1**
　　🚘 London 37 mi – Maidstone 3 mi – Rochester 8 mi

✕✕✕ **Hengist**　　　　　　　　　　　　🆎 ⇔ 💳 ⦿ 🆎
7-9 High St ✉ *ME20 7AX – 𝒞 (01622) 719 273 – www.hengistrestaurant.co.uk*
– restaurant@thehengist.co.uk – Fax (01622) 715 027
– Closed Sunday dinner and Monday
Rest – Menu £13/20 – Carte £28/40
◆ Converted 16C town house, elegantly appointed throughout, with bonus of exposed rafters and smart private dining room upstairs. Accomplished modern cooking with seasonal base.

AYLESHAM – Kent – 504 X 30
9 D2

◘ London 69 mi – Maidstone 37 mi – Ashford 23 mi – Margate 18 mi

at Barfreston Southwest 4m. by B2046 and then east following signs for Womenswold, Woolage and Barfreston

🏠 **The Yew Tree** ⚲ ✿ **P** *VISA* **◍ ◐**
✉ CT15 7JH – ✆ (01304) 831 000 – www.yewtree.info – yew.tree@live.co.uk
– Closed 26-27 December and Sunday dinner
Rest – (booking advisable) Carte £ 23/31
♦ This is a small pub with only eight tables, in a tiny hamlet, where the focus is on the food. It is prepared with care, using much of the produce brought to the door by the locals.

AYLMERTON – Norfolk – 504 X 25
15 D1

◘ London 138 mi – Norwich 25 mi – East Dereham 26 mi – Taverham 23 mi

🏠 **Eiders** without rest 🛏 🌲 ❲❳ **P**
Holt Rd ✉ NR11 8QA – ✆ (01263) 837 280 – www.eiders.co.uk
– eidersnorfolk@aol.com – Closed mid December- mid February
6 rm ⌑ – ♦£50 ♦♦£100
♦ Whitewashed house with large lawned gardens, ornamental pond and swimming pool. Modern, spacious, ground floor bedrooms, 3 with balconies and pond views; excellent bathrooms.

AYSGARTH – North Yorkshire – 502 O 21
22 A1

◘ London 249 mi – Ripon 28 mi – York 56 mi

🏠 **George and Dragon Inn** with rm ⚲ **P** *VISA* **◍ ◐**
✉ DL8 3AD – ✆ (01969) 663 358 – www.georgeanddragonaysgarth.co.uk
– info@georgeanddragonaysgarth.co.uk – Fax (01969) 663 773 – Closed 2 weeks January
7 rm ⌑ – ♦£40/55 ♦♦£72/85   **Rest** – Menu £13/16 – Carte £ 20/30
♦ Traditional pub near Aysgarth falls. Smart terrace with thatched umbrellas. Local ales dominate welcoming bar. Wide range of fresh fare: local produce to fore. Comfy rooms.

BABCARY – Somerset – 403 M 30
4 C2

◘ London 128 mi – Glastonbury 12 mi – Yeovil 12 mi

🏠 **The Red Lion Inn** 🛏 ⚲ **P** *VISA* **◍ AE**
✉ TA11 7ED – ✆ (01458) 223 230 – www.redlionbabcary.co.uk – Fax (01458) 224 510 – Closed 25 December
Rest – (Closed Sunday dinner) Carte £ 16/22
♦ Attractive stone-built thatched pub; a tasteful blend of old and new. Soft sofas, locally sourced produce and homemade cuisine. Modern dishes with some Asian influences.

BADINGHAM Suffolk – 504 Y 27 – see Framlingham

BAGSHOT – Surrey – 504 R 29 – pop. 5 247
7 C1

◘ London 37 mi – Reading 17 mi – Southampton 49 mi
⛳ Windlesham Grove End, ✆ (01276) 452 220

🏨 **Pennyhill Park** ⚘ ← 🛏 ⓘ ⚲ 🌲 🔲 ⊕ 🛁 ✕ 🖪 ❧ rm, ❲❳ 🏋
London Rd, Southwest : 1 m. on A 30 ✉ GU19 5EU **P** *VISA* **◍ AE**
– ✆ (01276) 471 774 – www.exclusivehotels.co.uk
– enquiries@pennyhillpark.co.uk – Fax (01276) 473 217
113 rm – ♦£ 295 ♦♦£ 295, ⌑ £20 – 11 suites
Rest *Michael Wignall at The Latymer* – see restaurant listing
Rest *Brasserie* – (buffet lunch) Menu £ 30 (lunch midweek) – Carte £ 33/47
♦ Sympathetically extended ivy-clad 19C manor house in wooded parkland. Intimate lounges. Outstanding spa. Rooms with fine antique furniture share a relaxing period elegance. Marble and stained glass enhanced restaurant overlooks garden.

XXX **Michael Wignall at The Latymer** – at Pennyhill Park Hotel   🚗 🈯 AC
🏵 *London Rd, Southwest : 1 m. on A 30 ⊠ GU19 5EU*   P. VISA ⬥◉ AE
– ℰ *(01276) 486 156 – www.exclusivehotels.co.uk*
– *enquiries@pennyhillpark.co.uk – Fax (01276) 473 217 – Closed 1-12 January,
Monday and lunch Saturday and Sunday*
Rest – (booking essential) Menu £ 32/58
Spec. Cumin scented tuna with langoustines and smoked eel. Suckling pig
with asparagus, consommé and Jerez jus. Dark chocolate negus, baileys can-
nelloni, salted caramel and cardamom ice cream.
♦ Fine dining at this recently refurbished restaurant, courtesy of the eponymous new
chef. Get closer to the action with a seat at the chef's table. Elaborate, original cooking.

BAKEWELL – Derbyshire – **502** O 24 – **pop. 3 676** 📖 *Great Britain*   16 **A1**
- 🚊 London 160 mi – Derby 26 mi – Manchester 37 mi – Nottingham 33 mi
  – Sheffield 17 mi
- 🛈 Old Market Hall, Bridge St ℰ (01629) 816558,
  bakewell@peakdistrict.gov.uk
- 🟢 Chatsworth ★★★ (Park and Garden ★★★) AC, NE : 2 ½ m. by A 619 –
  Haddon Hall ★★ AC, SE : 2 m. by A 6

at Ashford-in-the-Water Northwest : 1 ¾ m. by A 6 and A 6020 – ⊠ Bakewell

🏨 **Riverside House**   🚗 🈯 P. VISA ⬥◉ AE
Fennel St ⊠ DE45 1QF – ℰ (01629) 814 275 – www.riversidehouse.co.uk
– *riversidehouse@enta.net – Fax (01629) 812 873*
14 rm ⊇ – †£ 165/200 ††£ 295
Rest *The Riverside Room* – see restaurant listing
♦ Delightful former shooting lodge by River Wye. Comfortable, tastefully decorated
rooms boast period features. Ground floor bedrooms in newer wing open onto
garden.

XX **The Riverside Room** – at Riverside House   P. VISA ⬥◉ AE ◉
Fennel St ⊠ DE45 1QF – ℰ (01629) 814 275 – Fax (01629) 812 873
Rest – Menu £ 23/45 – Carte lunch £ 20/22
♦ Popular restaurant serving classic French cooking; comprises Regency Room, Gar-
den Room, Range Room and Conservatory.

BALSALL COMMON – W. Mids. – see Coventry

BAMBURGH – Northumberland – **501** O 17 📖 *Great Britain*   24 **B1**
- 🚊 London 337 mi – Edinburgh 77 mi – Newcastle upon Tyne 51 mi
- 🟢 Castle ★ AC

🏠 **Lord Crewe Arms**   P. VISA ⬥◉
Front Street ⊠ NE69 7BL – ℰ (01668) 214 243 – www.lordcrewe.co.uk
– *lordcrewebamburgh@tiscali.co.uk – Fax (01668) 214 273 – Closed December
and January*
17 rm ⊇ – †£ 65/110 ††£ 100/170   **Rest** – (bar lunch) Carte £ 19/30
♦ In the shadow of the Norman castle, a neat and traditional market town hotel, still
in private hands. Smartly fitted bedrooms; spacious, comfy lounge. Characterful
beamed bar. Alluring timber and stone restaurant.

at Waren Mill West : 2 ¾ m. on B 1342 – ⊠ Belford

🏨 **Waren House** 🌿   ⇐ 🚗 🕊 🛁 P. VISA ⬥◉ AE ◉
⊠ *NE70 7EE – ℰ (01668) 214 581 – www.warenhousehotel.co.uk*
– *enquiries@warenhousehotel.co.uk – Fax (01668) 214 484*
11 rm ⊇ – †£ 116/143 ††£ 138/175 – 2 suites
Rest – (dinner only) Menu £ 32
♦ A Georgian country house in attractive grounds and formal gardens, with views to
Lindisfarne. Individually decorated bedrooms with themes ranging from Oriental to
Edwardian. Classical dining room overlooking gardens.

BAMPTON – Devon – 503 J 31 – pop. 1 617

2 **D1**

■ London 189 mi – Exeter 18 mi – Minehead 21 mi – Taunton 15 mi

Bark House

🖼 **P** VISA ◑◐ AE

Oakfordbridge, West : 3. m. by B 3227 on A 396 ⊠ EX16 9HZ – 𝒞 (01398) 351 236 – www.thebarkhouse.co.uk – bark.house.hotel@btconnect.com
6 rm ⚏ – ♦£69/77 ♦♦£118/136
Rest – (Closed Sunday - Tuesday) (dinner only) (booking essential for non-residents) (set menu only) Menu £ 30
♦ Neat, personally run stone cottages which once stored wood from Exmoor forest. Bright bedrooms of different sizes are decorated in pretty floral fabrics. Terraced rear garden. Home-cooking proudly served in neat dining room.

The Quarrymans Rest with rm

🖼 **P** VISA ◑◐

Briton St, Bampton ⊠ EX16 9LN – 𝒞 (01398) 331 480 – www.thequarrymansrest.co.uk – info@thequarrymansrest.co.uk
3 rm ⚏ – ♦£40 ♦♦£80   **Rest** – (Closed Sunday dinner) Carte £ 16/23
♦ Honest 17C village pub with traditional interior. Appealing, classical menu featuring local produce, regional influences and knowledgeable cooking. Simple, good value bedrooms.

BANBURY – Oxfordshire – 503 P 27 – pop. 43 867 ▮ Great Britain

10 **B1**

■ London 76 mi – Birmingham 40 mi – Coventry 25 mi – Oxford 23 mi
🛈 Spiceball Park Rd 𝒞 (01295) 259855, banbury.tic@cherwell-dc.gov.uk
🖼 Cherwell Edge Chacombe, 𝒞 (01295) 711 591
◉ Upton House★ **AC**, NW : 7 m. by A 422

Mercure Whately Hall

🖼 🛈 ♿ **P** VISA ◑◐ AE ⓞ

Horsefair, by Banbury Cross ⊠ OX16 0AN – 𝒞 (01295) 253 261 – www.mercure-uk.com – h6633@accor.com – Fax (01295) 271 736
64 rm – ♦£60/135 ♦♦£60/135, ⚏ £13.95 – 5 suites   **Rest** – Carte £ 20/29
♦ Imposing 17C hotel known for its secret passages, hidden staircases and resident ghost, Father Bernard. Panelled bar and lounge; well-appointed bedrooms - some in extension.   Breakfast room overlooks rear garden. Smaller side room offers formal dining.

Banbury House

♿ rm, 🖼 rest, ⌘ 🛈 ♿ **P** VISA ◑◐ AE ⓞ

Oxford Rd ⊠ OX16 9AH – 𝒞 (01295) 259 361 – www.banburyhouse.co.uk – sales@banburyhouse.co.uk – Fax (01295) 270 954
– Closed 24 December-2 January
64 rm – ♦£50/145 ♦♦£90/250, ⚏ £15   **Rest** – (bar lunch) Menu £ 25 **s**
♦ Georgian property combining the traditional with the more modern. Well-maintained bedrooms in contemporary styles. Uptons restaurant offering contemporary British menu. Bar 29 popular for lunchtime snacks.

at Milton South : 5½ m. by A 4260 – ⊠ Banbury

The Black Boy Inn

🖼 **P** VISA ◑◐

⊠ OX15 4HH – 𝒞 (01295) 722 111 – www.blackboyinn.com – info@blackboyinn.com
Rest – Menu £ 15 – Carte £ 20/30
♦ Popular dining destination. Enthusiastic, confident kitchen sources local produce, serving modern menu with French edge. Keen service. Candles and fresh flowers decorate.

at Wigginton Southwest : 7 m. by A 361 – ⊠ Banbury

Pretty Bush Barn without rest

⌘ **P**

⊠ OX15 4LD – 𝒞 (01608) 738 262 – trev@prettybushbarn.wanadoo.co.uk – Fax (01608) 738 263 – Closed 12 December-18 January
3 rm ⚏ – ♦£40/45 ♦♦£60/65
♦ Barn conversion dating from 1827 situated in middle of village. Good value bedrooms with up-to-date furnishings; rustic breakfast room with communal table.

at North Newington West : 2 ¼ m. by B 4035 – ⊠ Banbury

⌂   **The Mill House** without rest ☜   ⬚ ❄ ♨ **P** *VISA* ⓿
⊠ OX15 6AA – 𝒞 (01295) 730 212 – www.themillhousebanbury.co.uk
– lamadonett@aol.com – Fax (01295) 730 363 – Closed Christmas and New Year
6 rm ⊿ – ♦£69 ♦♦£120
♦ Keenly run 17C manor house and converted cottages set in tranquil location, with
lawned garden to front and 15C mill and stream behind. Comfy bedrooms include
one four poster.

at Sibford Gower West : 8 m. by B 4035 – ⊠ Banbury

⍟   **The Wykham Arms**   ⬚ ☜ **P** *VISA* ⓿
Temple Mill Road ⊠ OX15 5RX – 𝒞 (01295) 788 808 – www.wykhamarms.co.uk
– info@wykhamarms.co.uk – Fax (01295) 788 806 – Closed 1 January
Rest – Menu £ 20 (lunch) – Carte £ 19/30
♦ Thatched 17C inn in picturesque village. Modernised interior retains rural character
with exposed beams, flag floors and glass-covered well. Local suppliers listed on
board.

BANSTEAD   **7 D1**
   🄳 London 17 – Reading 49 – Portsmouth 71 – Luton 64

⍟⍟   **Tony Tobin @ Post**   **AC** *VISA* ⓿ **AE** ⓞ
28 High St – 𝒞 (01737) 372 839 – www.postrestaurant.co.uk
– enquiries@postrestaurant.co.uk – Closed 26 December
Rest – (closed Saturday lunch, Sunday dinner and Monday) Menu £ 20
– Carte £ 30/72
Rest *Brasserie* – 𝒞 (01737) 373 839 – Carte £ 18/34
♦ Restaurant, brasserie and deli in former post office, owned by celebrity chef Tony
Tobin; a piece of London brought to the suburbs. Informal dining upstairs in restau-
rant. Vast choice on menu in airy brasserie.

BARFRESTON – Kent – **504** X 30 – **see Aylesham**

BAR HILL – Cambs. – **504** U 27 – **see Cambridge**

BARNARD CASTLE – Durham – **502** O 20 – pop. 6 714 📗 *Great Britain*   24 **A3**
   🄳 London 258 mi – Carlisle 63 mi – Leeds 68 mi – Middlesbrough 31 mi
      – Newcastle upon Tyne 39 mi
   🄸 Woodleigh, Flatts Rd 𝒞 (01833) 690909, tourism@teesdale.gov.uk
   🅸🅱 Harmire Rd, 𝒞 (01833) 638 355
   ◉ Bowes Museum★ **AC**
   🄶 Raby Castle★ **AC**, NE : 6 ½ m. by A 688

⌂   **Greta House** without rest   ⬚ ❄
🄰   89 Galgate ⊠ DL12 8ES – 𝒞 (01833) 631 193 – www.gretahouse.co.uk
– kathchesman@btinternet.com – Fax (01833) 631 193
3 rm ⊿ – ♦£45/50 ♦♦£65/70
♦ Part of a Victorian terrace with leafy garden. Bedrooms are spacious and individually decorated. Evening snacks may be taken in your room; plenty of books to browse
through.

⌂   **Homelands** without rest   ⬚ ❄ *VISA* ⓿
🄰   85 Galgate ⊠ DL12 8ES – 𝒞 (01833) 638 757
– www.homelandsguesthouse.co.uk – enquiries@homelandsguesthouse.co.uk
– Closed 23 December-2 January
5 rm ⊿ – ♦£47/50 ♦♦£68/75
♦ Immaculately maintained 19C terraced house on main road. Cosy lounge and
compact but pleasantly furnished, well-priced rooms, some overlooking the long
mature rear garden.

at Greta Bridge Southeast : 4½ m. off A 66 – ⊠ Barnard Castle

The Morritt   ⛵ 🍴 ⛄ ♨️ **P** *VISA* ⚫
⊠ DL12 9SE – ✆ (01833) 627 232 – www.themorritt.co.uk
– relax@themorritt.co.uk – Fax (01833) 627 392
27 rm ☕ – †£170 ††£170
Rest *The Morritt* – Carte £27/39
Rest *Bistro/Bar* – Carte £27/39
♦ 19C coaching inn where Charles Dickens stayed in 1839. The Dickens bar has murals by John Gilroy, historian of the Guinness firm. All rooms individually designed. The Morritt is oak panelled restaurant. Informal warmth at Bistro/Bar.

at Romaldkirk Northwest : 6 m. by A 67 on B 6277 – ⊠ Barnard Castle

Rose and Crown with rm   🍴 **P** *VISA* ⚫
⊠ DL12 9EB – ✆ (01833) 650 213 – www.rose-and-crown.co.uk
– hotel@rose-and-crown.co.uk – Fax (01833) 650 828 – Closed 24-26 December
12 rm ☕ – †£85/115 ††£135/165
Rest *The Brasserie and Bar* – Menu £18/30 – Carte £15/28
Rest *The Restaurant* – (dinner only and Sunday lunch) Menu £26 ⚜
♦ Ivy-clad former 18C coaching inn overlooking village green. Characterful, snug bar with open fires. Comfortable bedrooms. Rustic restaurant and polite organised service.

at Whorlton East: 4 3/4m. by A67

The Bridge Inn   🍴 🍴 **P** *VISA* ⚫
⊠ DL12 8XD – ✆ (01833) 627 341 – www.thebridgeinnrestaurant.co.uk
– info@thebridgeinnrestaurant.co.uk – Fax (01833) 627 995
– Closed 25-26 December, 1 January
Rest – (Closed Sunday dinner, Monday and Tuesday) Menu £14
– Carte £16/40
♦ Situated in a pleasant country location. Menu combines big city sophistication with fresh, country ingredients to create modern, precise dishes and well-executed combinations.

BARNARD GATE – Oxon. – **503** P 28 – see Witney

BARNSLEY – Glos. – **503** O 28 – see Cirencester

BARNSLEY – South Yorkshire – **502** P 23 – pop. 71 599   22 **B3**
🚗 London 177 mi – Leeds 21 mi – Manchester 36 mi – Sheffield 15 mi
🛈 Cooper Gallery, Church St ✆ (01226) 206757, barnsley@ytbtic.co.uk
🔟 Staincross Wakefield Rd, ✆ (01226) 382 856
🔟 Silkstone Elmhirst Lane, Field Head, ✆ (01226) 790 328
🔟 Wombwell Hillies Wombwell Wentworth View, ✆ (01226) 754 433

Tankersley Manor   ⛵ 🔟 ♨️ ♨️ 🏊 ♨️ 🍴 rm, 🅰️🅲 rest, ♨️ 🔆 **P** *VISA* ⚫ 🅰️🅴 ①
Church Lane, South : 6¼ m. on A 61 ⊠ S75 3DQ – ✆ (01226) 744 700
– www.marstonhotels.com – tankersleymanor@qhotels.co.uk – Fax (01226) 745 405
98 rm ☕ – †£135 ††£145 – 2 suites
Rest – (closed Saturday lunch) Carte £30/41
♦ Part 17C house, sympathetically enlarged to cater for corporate functions and weddings. Low-beamed lounge and bar with Regency-style furniture. Rooms have useful mod cons. Formal or informal option: characterful pub or stone-walled dining room.

BARNSTAPLE – Devon – **503** H 30 – pop. 30 765   2 **C1**
🚗 London 222 mi – Exeter 40 mi – Taunton 51 mi
🛈 36 Boutport St ✆ (01271) 375000
🔟 Chulmleigh Leigh Rd, ✆ (01769) 580 519
◻ Town★ – Long Bridge★
◼ Arlington Court★★ (Carriage Collection★) **AC**, NE : 6 m. by A 39

ENGLAND

Imperial [icons] rest, [icons] [VISA] [MC] [①]
Taw Vale Parade ⊠ EX32 8NB – ℰ (01271) 345 861 – www.brend-imperial.co.uk
– info@brend-imperial.co.uk – Fax (01271) 324 448
63 rm – ♦£90/175 ♦♦£100/175, ☲ £13 **Rest** – Menu £15/35
♦ Attractive riverside hotel dating from the turn of 20C. Convivial bar and smart accommodation: deluxe front bedrooms have balconies overlooking the Taw. Grand, bay-windowed dining room.

BARROWDEN – Rutland   17 **C2**
▶ London 94 mi – Peterborough 17 mi – Stamford 8 mi

Exeter Arms with rm   [icons] **P** [VISA] [MC] [①]
28 Main St ⊠ LE15 8EQ – ℰ (01572) 747 247 – www.exeterarms.com
– info@exeterarms.com – Fax (01572) 747 247 – Closed Sunday dinner and
November-April Monday lunch
3 rm ☲ – ♦£75 ♦♦£75 **Rest** – (residents only) Menu £17 – Carte £18/24
♦ Stone-built, family owned 17C inn overlooking green and duck pond. Ales from pub's own micro brewery. Accomplished cuisine proffers modernity with Asian undercurrent.

BARSTON – West Midlands – 504 O 26   19 **C2**
▶ London 110 mi – Birmingham 17 mi – Coventry 11 mi

The Malt Shovel   [icons] [AC] **P** [VISA] [MC] [AE]
Barston Lane, West : ¾ m ⊠ B92 0JP – ℰ (01675) 443 223
– www.themaltshovelatbarston.com – Fax (01675) 443 223 – Closed 25 December
Rest – (Closed Sunday dinner) (lunch bookings not accepted) Menu £26 (dinner) – Carte £21/34
♦ Modern dining pub, an oasis in a rustic hideaway, with large garden and patio. Good sized menus: noteworthy seafood specials. Busy at lunchtimes - you can't book so go early!

BARTON – Lancashire – 502 L 22 – see Preston

BARTON-ON-SEA – Hampshire – 503 P 31   6 **A3**
▶ London 108 mi – Bournemouth 11 mi – Southampton 24 mi
– Winchester 35 mi

Pebble Beach with rm   [icons] [AC] **P** [VISA] [MC] [AE]
Marine Drive ⊠ BH25 7DZ – ℰ (01425) 627 777 – www.pebblebeach-uk.com
– email@pebblebeach-uk.com – Fax (01425) 610 689
3 rm – ♦£60 ♦♦£80, ☲ £7 **Rest** – Seafood – Carte £29/49
♦ Cliff-top position: striking terrace views over Solent and The Needles. Bright, modish interior with large windows. Wide range of choice on modern menus. Well-equipped rooms.

BARWICK – Somerset – 503 M 31 – see Yeovil

BASHALL EAVES – Lancashire – see Clitheroe

BASILDON – Essex – 504 V 29 – pop. 99 876   13 **C3**
▶ London 30 mi – Chelmsford 17 mi – Southend-on-Sea 13 mi
Clayhill Lane, Kingswood, ℰ (01268) 533 297
Langdon Hills Bulphan Lower Dunton Rd, ℰ (01268) 548 444

at Wickford North : 5 ¼ m. by A 132 – ⊠ Basildon

Chichester   [icons] &rm, [AC] rest, [icons] **P** [VISA] [MC] [①]
Old London Rd, Rawreth, East : 2 ¾ m. by A 129 ⊠ SS11 8UE – ℰ (01268)
560 555 – www.chichesterhotel.com – reception@thechichesterhotel.com
– Fax (01268) 560 580
35 rm – ♦£70 ♦♦£70, ☲ £9.50
Rest – (dinner only and Sunday lunch) Carte £19/25 **s**
♦ Traditional, family-run hotel surrounded by farmland. Open lounge and immaculately-kept bedrooms set around central courtyard. Simply furnished restaurant serves tried-and-tested dishes.

BASINGSTOKE - Hampshire - 503 Q 30 - pop. 90 171 6 B1

London 55 mi – Reading 17 mi – Southampton 31 mi – Winchester 18 mi
Willis Museum, Old Town Hall, Market Pl ✆ (01256) 817618
Test Valley Overton Micheldever Rd, ✆ (01256) 771 737
Weybrook Park Basingstoke Rooksdown Lane, ✆ (01256) 320 347

BASINGSTOKE

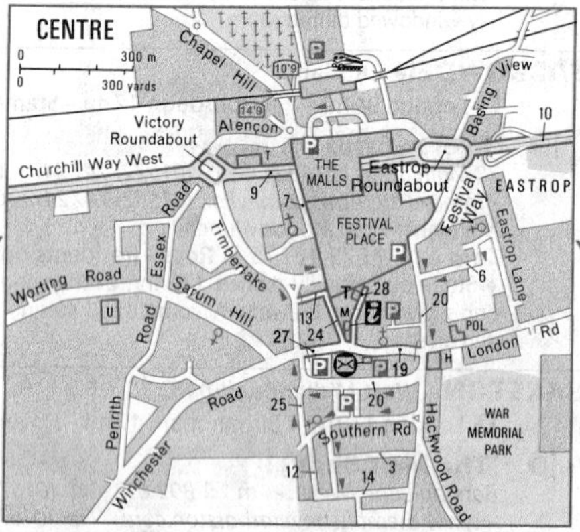

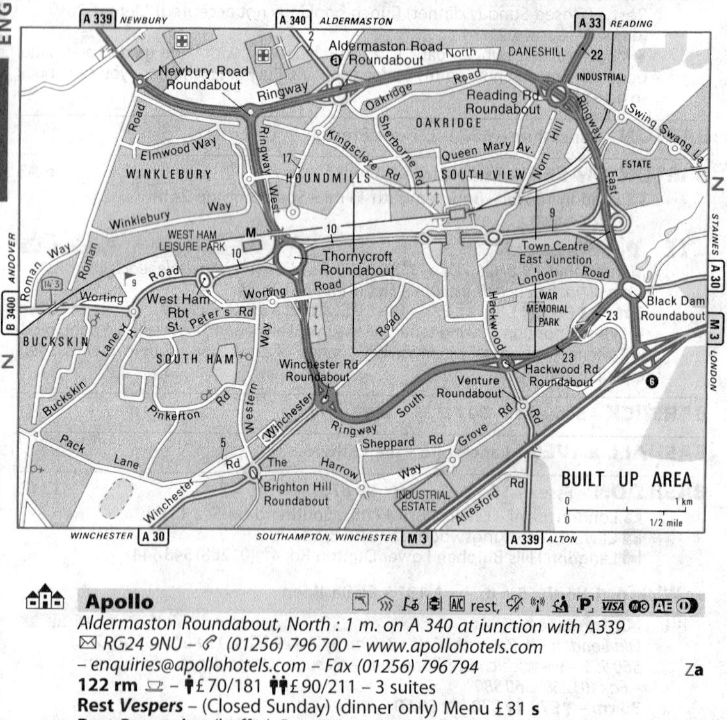

Apollo

rest,

Aldermaston Roundabout, North : 1 m. on A 340 at junction with A339
RG24 9NU – ✆ (01256) 796 700 – www.apollohotels.com
– enquiries@apollohotels.com – Fax (01256) 796 794 Za

122 rm – £70/181 £90/211 – 3 suites

Rest *Vespers* – (Closed Sunday) (dinner only) Menu £31 **s**

Rest *Brasserie* – (buffet) Carte £21/33 **s**

◆ Smart, modern hotel aimed at business clients; well situated on Basingstoke ring road. Extensive conference and leisure facilities. Modern, well equipped rooms. Vespers is an intimate fine dining room. Large, modern Brasserie with centre servery.

▶ London 161 mi – Derby 27 mi – Manchester 35 mi – Sheffield 13 mi
◉ Chatsworth ★★★ (Park and Garden ★★★) **AC**

🏨🏨🏨 **The Cavendish**   ⟨ 🛏 ⟲ ⟲ 🖋 ⁂ 🖎 **P** **VISA** **◍◎** **AE** **①**
Church Lane, on A 619 ✉ *DE45 1SP* – ℰ *(01246) 582 311* – *www.cavendish-*
hotel.net – *info@cavendish-hotel.net* – *Fax (01246) 582 312* – *Closed 25 December*
23 rm – ♦£131/168 ♦♦£169/210, ⌑ £15 – 1 suite
Rest *The Gallery* – Menu £40
Rest *Garden Room* – Carte £24/34
♦ Well established, elegant hotel; handsomely decorated, with antiques, oil paintings
and log fires. Individually furnished, country house style bedrooms. Classical cooking
served in The Gallery, with table in kitchen for watching chefs. Conservatory Garden
Room with views of Chatsworth Estate.

✗✗✗ **Fischer's at Baslow Hall** with rm   ⌸ ⁂ ⁑ **P** **VISA** **◍◎** **AE**
❀ *Calver Rd, on A 623* ✉ *DE45 1RR* – ℰ *(01246) 583 259*
– *www.fischers-baslowhall.co.uk* – *reservations@fischers-baslowhall.co.uk*
– *Fax (01246) 583 818* – *Closed 25-26 and 31 December*
10 rm – ♦£100/140 ♦♦£140/195, ⌑ £10 – 1 suite
Rest – (closed Sunday dinner to non-residents and Monday lunch) (booking
essential) Menu £27/63⌛
Spec. Textures of foie gras with spiced cherries and pigeon carpaccio. Derbyshire Lamb with pommes boulangère and rosemary jus. Lemon chiboust
with gingerbread and bay leaf ice cream.
♦ Edwardian manor house with impressive formal gardens and walled vegetable garden. Elaborate modern cooking uses local produce. Adventurous à la carte and good
value lunch menu. Comfortable bedrooms in main house and newer garden house.

✗ **Rowley's**   **P** **VISA** **◍◎**
Church Street ✉ *DE45 1RY* – ℰ *(01246) 583 880* – *www.rowleysrestaurant.co.uk*
– *info@rowleysrestaurant.co.uk*
Rest – (closed 1-5 January and Sunday dinner) Carte £27/43
♦ Contemporary restaurant and bar set over two floors; downstairs with view of open
plan kitchen. Modern menu, with produce sourced from in and around Peak District.

▶ London 300 mi – Carlisle 24 mi – Keswick 7 mi

🏨🏨🏨 **Armathwaite Hall** ⌖   ⟨ ⌸ ⟲ ⟲ 🖸 ⁙ ⌰ ⁂ 🖎 ⁑ 🖋 **P**
West : 1½ m. on B 5291, ✉ *Keswick* ✉ *CA12 4RE*   **VISA** **◍◎** **AE** **①**
– ℰ *(017687) 76 551* – *www.armathwaite-hall.com*
– *reservations@armathwaite-hall.com* – *Fax (017687) 76 220*
42 rm ⌑ – ♦£130/160 ♦♦£210/350   **Rest** – Menu £24/44
♦ Lakeside mansion dominates tranquil 400-acre woods and deer park. Rooms, some
in rebuilt stables, vary in size and, like the panelled hall, marry modern and period
fittings. 'Old-World' restaurant with carved oak ceiling and fireplace.

🏨🏨 **The Pheasant**   ⌸ ⟲ ⁂ ⟲ **P** **VISA** **◍◎**
Southwest : 3¼ m. by B 5291 on Wythop Mill rd, ✉ *Cockermouth* ✉ *CA13 9YE*
– ℰ *(017687) 76 234* – *www.the-pheasant.co.uk* – *info@the-pheasant.co.uk*
– *Fax (017687) 76 002* – *Closed 25 December*
15 rm ⌑ – ♦£85/105 ♦♦£160/210   **Rest** – Menu £28/32
♦ Bright bedrooms, sensitively and individually updated, in a rural 16C coaching inn.
Firelit bar with oak settles, local prints and game fish trophies serves regional ales.
Charmingly simple restaurant decorated with chinaware.

▶ London 130 mi – Bournemouth 50 mi – Bristol 24 mi – Salisbury 40 mi
– Taunton 40 mi

🏠 **The Three Horseshoes Inn** with rm   ⌸ 🈝 **P** **VISA** **◍◎**
✉ *BA4 6HE* – ℰ *(01749) 850 359* – *www.thethreehorseshoesinn.co.uk*
– *Fax (01749) 850 615*
3 rm ⌑ – ♦♦£   **Rest** – (Closed Sunday dinner and Monday) Carte £18/30
♦ Characterful, low beamed pub with rustic bar, intimate snug and more formal restaurant. Chickens roam in neat garden and local, organic produce features highly on
menu. Neat, simply decorated bedrooms.

ENGLAND

H. Champollion/MICHELIN

BATH

County: Bath and North East Somerset
Michelin REGIONAL map: n° **503** M 29
▶ London 119 mi – Bristol 13 mi
– Southampton 63 mi – Taunton 49 mi

Population: 90 144   4 C2
▌ *Great Britain*

PRACTICAL INFORMATION

🔲 Tourist Information
Abbey Chambers, Abbey Church Yard ✆ (0906) 711 2000, tourism@bathnes.gov.uk

Golf Courses
🔲 Tracy Park Wick Bath Rd, ✆ (0771) 737 2251

🔲 Lansdown, ✆ (01225) 422 138

🔲 Entry Hill, ✆ (01225) 834 248

🔲 SIGHTS

IN TOWN

City★★★ - Royal Crescent★★★ AV
(No.1 Royal Crescent★★ **AC**AV **A**)
– The Circus★★★ AV – Museum of
Costume★★★ **AC**AV **M7** – Roman
Baths★★ **AC**BX **D** – Holburne Museum
and Crafts Study Centre★★ **AC**Y **M5**
– Pump Room★ BX **B** - Assembly
Rooms★ AV – Bath Abbey★ BX
– Pulteney Bridge★ BV – Bath
Industrial Heritage Centre★ **AC**AV **M1**
– Lansdown Crescent★★ (Somerset
Place★) Y – Camden Crescent★ Y

– Beckford Tower and Museum **AC**
(prospect★) Y **M6** – Museum of East
Asian Art★ AV **M9** – Orange Grove★ BX

ON THE OUTSKIRTS

Claverton (American Museum★★ **AC**,
Claverton Pumping Station★ **AC**)
E: 3 m. by A 36 Y

IN THE SURROUNDING AREA

Corsham Court★★ **AC**, NE: 8 ½ m.
by A 4 – Dyrham Park★ **AC**, N: 6 ½ m.
by A 4 and A 46

ENGLAND

BATH

0 ———— 1 km
0 ———— 1 mile

🏛🏛🏛 **The Royal Crescent** ⟨ symbols ⟩ *VISA* *MC* *AE* ①

16 Royal Crescent ✉ *BA1 2LS* – ☎ *(01225) 823 333* – *www.royalcrescent.co.uk*
– info@royalcrescent.co.uk – *Fax (01225) 339 401*   AV**a**
35 rm ⌂ – ♦£335 ♦♦£335 – 13 suites
Rest *The Dower House* – see restaurant listing
♦ Meticulously restored historic town house in sweeping Georgian crescent. Classically
styled bedrooms and drawing rooms; period furniture. Stylish spa. Professional service.

🏛🏛🏛 **Bath Spa** ⟨ symbols ⟩ *VISA* *MC* *AE* ①

Sydney Rd ✉ *BA2 6JF* – ☎ *(0870) 400 8 22* – *www.bathspahotel.com*
– sales.bathspa@macdonald-hotels.co.uk – *Fax (01225) 444 006*   Y**z**
118 rm – ♦£339 ♦♦£339, ⌂ £22 – 11 suites
Rest *Vellore* – (dinner only and Sunday lunch) (booking essential) Menu £38
– Carte £43/51
Rest *Alfresco* – (closed Sunday lunch) Carte £22/38
♦ Impressive 19C mansion in mature gardens; refurbished, with new wing of rooms.
Period lounges and contemporary bedrooms; full butler service in Imperial Suites.
Superb spa. Vellore is smart with intimate lounge and terrace. Alfresco more informal,
with Mediterranean menus.

🏛🏛🏛 **Bath Priory** ⟨ symbols ⟩ *VISA* *MC* *AE* ①
⁂

Weston Rd ✉ *BA1 2XT* – ☎ *(01225) 331 922* – *www.thebathpriory.co.uk*
– mail@thebathpriory.co.uk – *Fax (01225) 448 276*   Y**c**
26 rm ⌂ – ♦£215/380 ♦♦£380/415   **Rest** – Menu £30/65 **s** 🍴
Spec. Pigeon cured with birch sap, sweet potato and seeds. Dab with lime
pastille and crayfish. Cocoa shot. Strawberry brûlée and basil ice cream
with vanilla.
♦ Attractive Georgian property with mature gardens. Stylish, recently refurbished
interior, with fine art collection. Comfortable bedrooms with contemporary touches.
Two dining rooms; the smaller more romantic, the larger more modern. Accomplished modern cooking with kitchens now under the direction of Michael Caines.

102

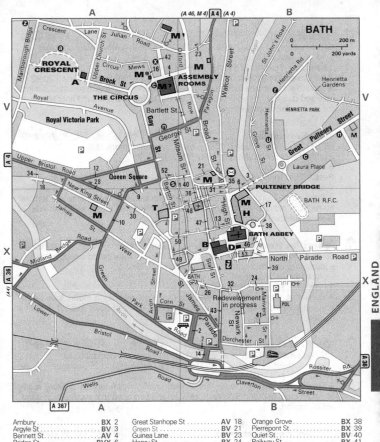

BATH

Homewood Park

Abbey Lane, Hinton Charterhouse, Southeast : 6½ m. on A 36 ⊠ BA2 7TB
– 𝒞 (01225) 723 731 – www.homewoodpark.co.uk – info@homewoodpark.co.uk
– Fax (01225) 723 820
19 rm ⌂ – †£120/160 ††£265/305   **Rest** – Menu £19/44
♦ Well-proportioned bedrooms, with views of the idyllic wooded gardens and cro-
quet lawn, and cosy country house drawing rooms retain strong elements of the
Georgian interior. Ask for dining room window table when garden is in full bloom.

Queensberry

Russell St ⊠ BA1 2QF – 𝒞 (01225) 447 928 – www.thequeensberry.co.uk
– reservations@thequeensberry.co.uk – Fax (01225) 446 065   AV**x**
29 rm – †£120/170 ††£120/230, ⌂ £15
Rest *Olive Tree* – see restaurant listing
♦ Classy boutique merger of Georgian town house décor with contemporary furnishing,
understated style and well-chosen detail. Ample, unfussy rooms; pretty courtyard garden.

ENGLAND

ENGLAND

Dukes   🛆 ⅏ ⅏ VISA ⓪ AE

Great Pulteney St ⊠ BA2 4DN – ℰ (01225) 787960 – www.dukesbath.co.uk
– info@dukesbath.co.uk – Fax (01225) 787961   BV**n**
13 rm ⌑ – ♦£100/152 ♦♦£152/189 – 4 suites
Rest *Cavendish* – (Closed Monday lunch) Menu £13 (lunch) – Carte £20/42
♦ Attractive townhouse in fine Georgian street. Paved terrace with parasols. Comfortable and classically styled bedrooms boast rich décor. Lower ground floor restaurant for modern British cuisine.

The Residence   🛆 🛆 🛆 ⅏ ⅏ P VISA ⓪ AE

⊠ BA1 2XZ – ℰ (01225) 750180 – www.theresidencebath.com
– info@theresidencebath.com – Fax (01225) 430283   Y**n**
6 rm ⌑ – ♦♦£350
Rest – (light lunch/dinner) (booking essential residents only) Carte approx.
£28 **s**
♦ Restored, 18C property. Beautiful garden with terraced seating area and summer house. Rich red-coloured lounges. Individually decorated rooms with high level of facilities. Informal dining; seasonal, modern cooking.

Paradise House without rest   ⇐ 🛆 ⅏ ⅏ P 🛆 VISA ⓪ AE

86-88 Holloway ⊠ BA2 4PX – ℰ (01225) 317723 – www.paradise-house.co.uk
– info@paradise-house.co.uk – Fax (01225) 482005
– Closed 24-25 December   Z**c**
11 rm – ♦£65/165 ♦♦£75/195
♦ Elegant yet homely hotel on Beechen Cliff. Most rear-facing rooms have exceptional city views; all reflect 18C origins in their décor and boast Jacuzzis. Beautiful garden.

Oldfields without rest   🛆 ⅏ ⅏ P VISA ⓪ AE

102 Wells Rd ⊠ BA2 3AL – ℰ (01225) 317984 – www.oldfields.co.uk
– info@oldfields.co.uk – Fax (01225) 444471 – Closed 24 and 25 December   Z**u**
16 rm ⌑ – ♦£49/120 ♦♦£69/150
♦ Spaciously elegant Victorian house with comfy, well-furnished drawing room, breakfast room boasting 'Bath rooftops' view and bedrooms that exude a high standard of comfort.

Apsley House without rest   🛆 ⅏ ⅏ P VISA ⓪ AE

141 Newbridge Hill ⊠ BA1 3PT – ℰ (01225) 336966 – www.apsley-house.co.uk
– info@apsley-house.co.uk – Fax (01225) 425462 – Closed 24-26 December   Y**x**
12 rm ⌑ – ♦£55/150 ♦♦£70/160
♦ Built for the Duke of Wellington and staffed with the unobtrusive calm of an English private house. Spacious individual rooms; two open on to a peaceful, mature rear garden.

Kennard without rest   🛆 ⅏ ⅏ P VISA ⓪ AE

11 Henrietta St ⊠ BA2 6LL – ℰ (01225) 310472 – www.kennard.co.uk
– reception@kennard.co.uk – Fax (01225) 460054
– Closed Christmas and New Year   BV**u**
12 rm ⌑ – ♦£58/99 ♦♦£118/140
♦ Classic Georgian town house with tranquil garden and charming breakfast room. Bedrooms vary in style; some classic, some contemporary.

Cheriton House without rest   🛆 ⅏ ⅏ P VISA ⓪ AE

9 Upper Oldfield Park ⊠ BA2 3JX – ℰ (01225) 429862
– www.cheritonhouse.co.uk – info@cheritonhouse.co.uk
– Fax (01225) 428403   Z**u**
12 rm ⌑ – ♦£55/95 ♦♦£85/120
♦ Immaculately kept house with 19C origins, run by very charming hosts. Comfortable, sizeable rooms and lounge, with some fine tiled fireplaces. Breakfast in the conservatory.

Dorian House without rest   ⇐ 🚗 🛇 📶 **P** **VISA** **◎** **AE**
1 Upper Oldfield Park ⊠ BA2 3JX – ℰ (01225) 426 336 – www.dorianhouse.co.uk
– info@dorianhouse.co.uk – Fax (01225) 444 699   Z**u**
11 rm ⌂ – †£55/95 ††£89/165
◆ Charming 19C house preserves original tiling and stained glass; attic rooms are refreshingly modern, others Victorian. Breakfast to recordings of owner's cello performances.

Tasburgh House without rest   ⇐ 🚗 🛇 📶 **P** **VISA** **◎**
Warminster Rd, East : 1 m. on A 36 ⊠ BA2 6SH – ℰ (01225) 425 096
– www.bathtasburgh.co.uk – hotel@bathtasburgh.co.uk – Fax (01225) 463 842
– Closed 21 December-16 January   Y**a**
12 rm – †£70/95 ††£110/130, ⌂ £7.50
◆ Personally run by charming owner and recently much improved. Bedrooms are spotless, pastel and named after British authors. Conservatory breakfast. Lovely garden and great views of Bath.

Villa Magdala without rest   🚗 🛇 📶 **P** **VISA** **◎**
Henrietta Rd ⊠ BA2 6LX – ℰ (01225) 466 329 – www.villamagdala.co.uk
– office@villamagdala.co.uk – Fax (01225) 483 207
– Closed 25-26 December and 1 January   BV**r**
18 rm – †£85/110 ††£130
◆ Named after Napier's 1868 victory. Well-equipped rooms, floral furnishings; carefully preserved ornate balustrade and showpiece bedroom with four-poster and chaise longue.

Harington's   🛇 📶 **P** **VISA** **◎** **AE**
8-10 Queen St ⊠ BA1 1HE – ℰ (01225) 461 728 – www.haringtonshotel.co.uk
– post@haringtonshotel.co.uk – Fax (01225) 444 804 – Closed Christmas   AV**s**
13 rm ⌂ – †£140 ††£150   **Rest** – (residents only) Carte £22/30
◆ 18C houses on a cobbled street in the heart of the city and perfectly located for the shops. Simply styled but diligently maintained accommodation on offer. Easygoing bistro with menu to match.

One Three Nine without rest   ⇐ 🚗 **AC** 📶 **VISA** **◎**
139 Wells Rd ⊠ BA2 3AL – ℰ (01225) 314 769 – www.139bath.co.uk
– info@139bath.co.uk – Fax (01225) 443 079 – Closed 24-25 December   Z**r**
10 rm ⌂ – †£65/110 ††£75/165
◆ Unassuming Victorian building conceals the chic, bold décor of a stylish boutique hotel. Individually styled bedrooms may include four-posters or spa baths. Excellent terrace breakfast.

The Windsor without rest   🛇 📶 **P** **VISA** **◎**
69 Great Pulteney St ⊠ BA2 4DL – ℰ (01225) 422 100
– www.bathwindsorguesthouse.com – sales@bathwindsorguesthouse.com
– Fax (01225) 422 550 – Closed 2 weeks Christmas - New Year   BV**c**
13 rm – †£75/85 ††£150/220, ⌂ £6
◆ Grade I listed building in Georgian boulevard. Fine furniture and tastefully co-ordinated floral fabrics in individually styled bedrooms.

The Town House without rest   📶 **VISA** **◎** **AE**
7 Bennett St ⊠ BA1 2QJ – ℰ (01225) 422 505 – www.thetownhousebath.co.uk
– stay@thetownhousebath.co.uk – Fax (01225) 422 505 – Closed January   AV**c**
3 rm ⌂ – †£120 ††£125
◆ Welcoming 18C house in excellent location, designed by John Wood and rebuilt after war damage. Spacious bedrooms with South African wildlife décor. Communal breakfast.

Lavender House without rest   🚗 🛇 📶 **P** 🚭 **VISA** **◎**
17 Bloomfield Park, (off Bloomfield Rd) ⊠ BA2 2BY – ℰ (01225) 314 500
– www.lavenderhouse-bath.com – post@lavenderhouse-bath.com   Z**s**
5 rm ⌂ – †£55/65 ††£100/120
◆ New owners have made a major investment in this Edwardian house. Rooms have plenty of antiques but also boast a modern, clean feel. Breakfast is served family-style.

ENGLAND

ENGLAND

⌂ **Meadowland** without rest   🛋 ⚇ **P** VISA ⓪
36 Bloomfield Park, off Bloomfield Rd ⊠ *BA2 2BX –* ℰ *(01225) 311 079*
– www.meadowlandbath.co.uk – stay@meadowlandbath.co.uk
– Closed Christmas   Z**e**
3 rm �byₓ – †£55/65 ††£105/115
♦ Small suburban guesthouse with a welcoming ambience; comfortably furnished and immaculately maintained accommodation. A neat breakfast room gives onto a lawned garden.

⌂ **Athole** without rest   🛋 ⚇ 🛜 **P** VISA ⓪ AE
33 Upper Oldfield Park ⊠ *BA2 3JX –* ℰ *(01225) 320 000*
– www.atholehouse.co.uk – info@atholehouse.co.uk – Fax (01225) 320 009
– Closed 24 December - 1 January   Z**i**
4 rm ⊐ – †£58 ††£93
♦ Spacious, bay windowed Victorian guesthouse with large garden, away from city centre. Bright breakfast room; conservatory lounge. Light, airy, contemporary bedrooms.

⌂ **Cranleigh** without rest   🛋 ⚇ 🛜 **P** VISA ⓪
159 Newbridge Hill ⊠ *BA1 3PX –* ℰ *(01225) 310 197*
– www.cranleighguesthouse.com – cranleigh@btinternet.com – Fax (01225) 423 143 – Closed 25-26 December   Y**e**
9 rm ⊐ – †£55/75 ††£95
♦ Airy, high-ceilinged bedrooms, the largest ideal for families, with brightly patterned fabrics. Pleasant south-facing garden. Smoked salmon and eggs a breakfast speciality.

XXXX **The Dower House** – at The Royal Crescent H.   🛋 🏛 AK ⇔
16 Royal Crescent ⊠ *BA1 2LS –* ℰ *(01225) 823 333 – www.royalcrescent.co.uk*
– info@royalcrescent.co.uk   AV**a**
Rest – Menu £35/60 ⅋⅋
♦ Impressive restaurant with striking green and brown décor and seaweed art feature. Intimate feel. Attentive service. Flavourful, well-presented, classically-based cooking.

XX **Olive Tree** – at Queensberry H.   AK ⇔ VISA ⓪ AE
Russell St ⊠ *BA1 2QF –* ℰ *(01225) 447 928 – reservations@thequeensberry.co.uk*
– Fax (01225) 446 065 – Closed Monday lunch   AV**x**
Rest – Menu £18 (lunch) – Carte £34/44
♦ Up-to-date restaurant with a classy, stylish and contemporary ambience. Modern artworks adorn the split-level basement. Modern British cooking. Helpful staff.

X **Hole in the Wall**   🍴 ⇔ VISA ⓪ AE
16 George St ⊠ *BA1 2EH –* ℰ *(01225) 425 242 – www.theholeinthewall.co.uk*
– info@theholeinthewall.co.uk – Sunday lunch   AV**n**
Rest – Menu £14 (lunch) – Carte £14/28
♦ Once a starting point of British culinary renaissance; former coal hole mixes whitewashed walls, antique chairs and a relaxed mood. Slightly eclectic cuisine.

ⓘ **The Marlborough Tavern**   🏛 VISA ⓪
35 Marlborough Buildings ⊠ *BA1 2LY –* ℰ *(01225) 423 731*
– www.marlborough-tavern.com – info@marlborough-tavern.com
– Closed 25 December   AV**z**
Rest – (Closed Sunday dinner) (booking advisable) Carte £22/32
♦ Spacious, modern pub near the Royal Crescent and Royal Victoria Park. Unfussy, seasonal and local cooking; big on flavour and big of portion. Friendly, attentive service.

ⓘ **White Hart**   🏛 VISA ⓪
Widcombe Hill ⊠ *BA2 6AA –* ℰ *(01225) 338 053 – www.whitehartbath.co.uk*
– enquiries@whitehartbath.co.uk – Fax (01225) 338 053 – Closed 25-26 December, 1 January and Bank Holidays   Z**o**
Rest – (Closed Sunday dinner) (booking essential at dinner) Carte £25/31
♦ 'Keep it simple', the chef's motto says it all; quality, local produce and unfussy presentation create a concise but hearty British menu. Eat at worn tables or on the attractive terrace.

BATH

at **Box** Northeast : 4 ¾ m. on A 4 - Y – ⊠ Corsham

🏠 **The Northey**   🛋 🛋 **P** **VISA** **CO** **AE**
Bath Road ⊠ SN13 8AE – ✆ (01225) 742 333 – www.ohhcompany.co.uk
– office@ohhcompany.co.uk – *Closed 25 December*
Rest – Carte £ 20/35
♦ Traditional exterior belies modern Mediterranean-styled interior, mostly set for dining. Tasty mix of Mediterranean and British cooking on menu. Live jazz every other week.

at **Colerne** Northeast : 6 ½ m. by A 4 - Y - Batheaston rd and Bannerdown Rd
– ⊠ Chippenham

🏠🏠🏠 **Lucknam Park** 🐾   ≤ 🛋 🏊 🖵 ⊕ ☎ ♨ ⅃♂ ✗ ✗ ៕ ㊙ **P**
North :½ m. on Marshfield rd ⊠ SN14 8AZ – ✆ (01225)   **VISA** **CO** **AE** ①
742 777 – www.lucknampark.co.uk – reservations@lucknampark.co.uk
– Fax (01225) 743 536
36 rm – ♦£ 280 ♦♦£ 280/460, ⚍ £18.50 – 5 suites
Rest *The Park* and *The Garden Brasserie* – see restaurant listing
♦ Imposing Palladian mansion with tree lined drive. Grand and luxurious throughout with rich décor, antique furniture and sumptuous fabrics. Full range of top class facilities and services; renowned equestrian centre.

✗✗✗✗ **The Park** – at Lucknam Park Hotel   ≤ 🛋 🏊 **P** **VISA** **CO** **AE** ①
❀   ⊠ SN14 8AZ – ✆ (01225) 742 777 – www.lucknampark.co.uk
– reservations@lucknampark.co.uk – Fax (01225) 743 536 – *Closed Sunday dinner and Monday*
Rest – (dinner only and Sunday lunch) (booking essential) Menu £ 70
Spec. Roast scallops with brandade fritters, tomato and cumin vinaigrette. Loin and shoulder of lamb, sweetbread dumplings and crushed peas. Exotic fruit ravioli with rum and raisin financier and coconut ice cream.
♦ Lavish, formal dining with a contemporary undertone. Crafted from local and farm sourced ingredients, classically based menus display modern European influences. Skilled, amiable service.

✗✗ **The Garden Brasserie** – at Lucknam Park Hotel   **P** **VISA** **CO** **AE** ①
North :½ m. on Marshfield rd ⊠ SN14 8AZ – ✆ (01225) 742 777
– www.lucknampark.co.uk – reservations@lucknampark.co.uk – Fax (01225)
743 536 – *Closed 25-26 December and 1 January*
Rest – Carte £ 25/40
♦ Part of the recently opened spa complex, the all day Brasserie carries through the wellbeing theme, offering a broad range of light and healthy dishes in an informal atmosphere.

at **Combe Hay** Southwest : 5 m. by A 367 – ⊠ Bath

🏠 **The Wheatsheaf** – at Lucknam Park Hotel   🛋 🛋 **P** **VISA** **CO** **AE**
⊠ BA2 7EG – ✆ (01225) 833 504 – www.wheatsheafcombehay.com
– info@wheatsheafcombehay.com – Fax (01225) 836 123 – *Closed 25 December and first 2 weeks in January*
3 rm ⚍ – ♦♦£ 95/140
Rest – (Closed Sunday dinner and Monday) Menu £ 22 (lunch) – Carte £ 22/55
♦ Picture perfect pub with a stylish interior. French and British influences inform the concise, contemporary menu, which displays refined, seasonal and flavoursome cooking. Chic bedrooms feature luxury showers; breakfast times are flexible.

at **Monkton Combe** Southeast : 4 ½ m. by A 36 - Y – ⊠ Bath

🏠 **Wheelwrights Arms** with rm   🛋 ㊙ ៕ **P** **VISA** **CO**
Church Lane, Monkton Combe ⊠ BA2 7HB – ✆ (01225) 722 287
– www.wheelwrightsarms.co.uk – bookings@wheelwrightsarms.co.uk
– Fax (01225) 722 259
7 rm – ♦£ 95 ♦♦£ 145   **Rest** – Carte £ 19/26
♦ Intimate 18C pub with regularly-stoked log fire and cosy snug, where honest, hearty cooking comes in portions large enough to revive the most exhausted of walkers. Luxurious bedrooms in converted workshop.

107

BATTLE – East Sussex – 504 V 31 – pop. 5 190 ▮ *Great Britain* 8 **B3**

🚗 London 55 mi – Brighton 34 mi – Folkestone 43 mi – Maidstone 30 mi
ℹ High St ℰ (01424) 773721, battletic@rother.gov.uk
◎ Town★ – Abbey and Site of the Battle of Hastings★ **AC**

Powder Mills ⌖ ≤ 🚗 🏊 🐕 🛏 🎣 🏋 ♔ 🖧 **P** 🆅🆂🅰 ◐◐ 🅰🅴 ①
Powdermill Lane, South : 1½ m. by A 2100 on Catsfield rd ✉ TN33 0SP
– ℰ (01424) 775 511 – www.powdermillshotel.com – powdc@aol.com
– Fax (01424) 774 540
40 rm � – ♗£115 ♗♗£170
Rest *Orangery* – Menu £ 20/35
◆ Part Georgian gunpowder mill in 150 acres of woods and lakes. Individually decorated rooms - more sizable in annex and with better views - combine antiques and modern pieces. Dining room terrace overlooks pool.

Fox Hole Farm *without rest* ⌖ 🚗 🖧 **P** 🆅🆂🅰 ◐◐
Kane Hythe Rd, Northwest : 2½ m. by A 2100 and A 271 on B 2096 (Netherfield rd)
✉ TN33 9QU – ℰ (01424) 772 053
– foxholefarm@kanehythe.orangehome.co.uk – Fax (01424) 772 053
– Closed 24 December - 1 February
3 rm ⊃ – ♗£45/53 ♗♗£69/75
◆ Peaceful 18C woodcutters cottage by 1000 acres of protected forest. Simple pine furnished bedrooms with sea-grass matting. Timbered lounge centred around a log stove.

Nobles 🖧 🆅🆂🅰 ◐◐ 🅰🅴
17 High St ✉ TN33 0AE – ℰ (01424) 774 422 – www.noblesrestaurant.co.uk
– debbie@noblesrestaurant.co.uk – Closed Sunday and most Bank Holidays
Rest – Carte £ 27/34
◆ Simple, tasteful eatery with terrace, in heart of historical high street. Regularly changing menus offer unfussy classical dishes of local seasonal produce, with the occasional twist.

BAUGHURST – Hampshire 6 **B1**

🚗 London 61 mi – Camberley 28 mi – Farnborough 27 mi

The Wellington Arms 🚗 🏋 **P** 🆅🆂🅰 ◐◐ ①
Baughurst Rd, Southwest : ¾ m. ✉ RG26 5LP – ℰ (0118) 982 0110
– www.thewellingtonarms.com – info@thewellingtonarms.com – Closed Sunday dinner, Monday and lunch Tuesday
Rest – (booking essential) Menu £ 18 (lunch) – Carte £ 18/32
◆ Cosy, characterful former hunting lodge. Blackboard menu features flavoursome, modern British cooking, with pub favourites at lunch. They keep chickens and bees, and grow their own veg.

BAWBURGH – Norfolk – 504 X 26 – *see Norwich*

BEACONSFIELD – Buckinghamshire – 504 S 29 – pop. 12 292 11 **D3**

🚗 London 26 mi – Aylesbury 19 mi – Oxford 32 mi
⛳ Beaconsfield Seer Green, ℰ (01494) 676 545

at Wooburn Common Southwest : 3½ m. by A 40 – ✉ Beaconsfield

Chequers Inn *with rm* ⌖ 🚗 🏋 ♘ ♔ **P** 🆅🆂🅰 ◐◐ 🅰🅴 ①
Kiln Lane, Southwest : 1 m. on Bourne End rd ✉ HP10 0JQ – ℰ (01628) 529 575
– www.chequers-inn.com – info@chequers-inn.com – Fax (01628) 850 124
17 rm – ♗£100 ♗♗£108, ⊃ £9.95
Rest – Menu £ 19 (weekdays)/28 – Carte £ 27/30
◆ Formal restaurant serves modern English dishes. Attractive red brick 17C inn with cosy beamed bar and spacious, stylish lounge. Good-sized bedrooms; one with four poster.

ENGLAND

BEADNELL – Northumberland – 501 P 17
24 **B1**

🚩 London 341 mi – Edinburgh 81 mi – Newcastle upon Tyne 47 mi

⛺ **Beach Court** without rest ⟨ ⁿ⁰ **P** _VISA_ **CO**
Harbour Rd ✉ *NE67 5BJ* – ☎ *(01665) 720225 – www.beachcourt.com*
– info@beachcourt.com – Fax (01665) 721499 – Closed Christmas-New Year
3 rm ⌂ – †£75 ††£99/159
♦ Turreted house enjoys fine views of Beadnell Bay. Simple, traditional en suite rooms; leafy little conservatory. Hospitable owners with a real enthusiasm for entertaining.

BEAMHURST – Staffs. – see Uttoxeter

BEAMINSTER – Dorset – 503 L 31 – pop. 2 791
3 **B3**

🚩 London 154 mi – Exeter 45 mi – Taunton 30 mi – Weymouth 29 mi
 Chedington Court South Perrott, ☎ (01935) 891 413

🏨 **Bridge House** 🚗 ⁿ⁰ **P** _VISA_ **CO** **AE** **①**
3 Prout Bridge ✉ *DT8 3AY* – ☎ *(01308) 862200 – www.bridge-house.co.uk*
– enquiries@bridge-house.co.uk – Fax (01308) 863700
14 rm ⌂ – †£190/210 ††£230/250
Rest – (residents only Sunday and Monday dinner) Carte £19/36
♦ Priest's house reputed to date back to the 1200s. Large bedrooms, in the new block, with cheerful floral fabrics. Firelit lounge, charming walled garden, informal, rural feel. Oak beamed restaurant with conservatory.

ENGLAND

Hotels and restaurants change every year,
so change your Michelin guide every year!

BEARSTED – Kent – 504 V 30 – see Maidstone

BEAULIEU – Hampshire – 503 P 31 – ✉ Brockenhurst ▌ *Great Britain*
6 **B2**

🚩 London 102 mi – Bournemouth 24 mi – Southampton 13 mi
– Winchester 23 mi
◉ Town★★ - National Motor Museum★★ **AC**
◎ Buckler's Hard★ (Maritime Museum★ **AC**) SE : 2 m

🏨 **Montagu Arms** 🚗 ⁿ⁰ ⁿ⁰ ⛉ **P** _VISA_ **CO** **AE**
Palace Lane ✉ *SO42 7ZL* – ☎ *(01590) 612324 – www.montaguarmshotel.co.uk*
– reservations@montaguarmshotel.co.uk – Fax (01590) 612188
18 rm ⌂ – †£139 ††£178 – 4 suites
Rest *The Terrace* – see restaurant listing
Rest *Monty's Brasserie* – Carte £23/29
♦ Ivy-covered 18C inn. Bedrooms, in various shapes and sizes, can't quite match the warmth of the inviting panelled lounge with log fires, but are tidy with useful mod cons. Monty's is bright, warm brasserie.

XXX **The Terrace** – at Montagu Arms Hotel 🚗 🍴 ⛉ **P** _VISA_ **CO** **①**
ॐ *Palace Lane* ✉ *SO42 7ZL* – ☎ *(01590) 612324 – www.montaguarmshotel.co.uk*
– reservations@montaguarmshotel.co.uk – Fax (01590) 612188
Rest – Menu £25/48
Spec. Grilled red mullet with spiced lentil salad and cauliflower purée. Rump and braised shoulder tartlet of lamb, spinach and rosemary oil. Glazed lemon tart with blackcurrant ice cream.
♦ Formal but friendly restaurant overlooking the garden. The cooking reflects the chef's classical background and is executed with precision; flavours are bold and distinct.

BEAUMONT – 503 P 33 – see Channel Islands (Jersey)

BEDFORD

ENGLAND

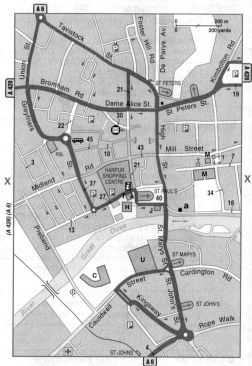

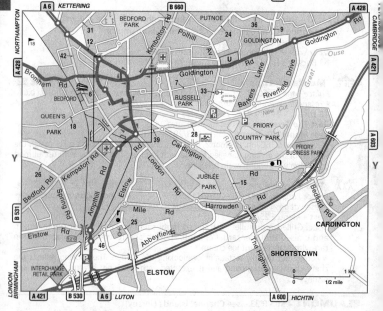

BEDFORD – Bedfordshire – 504 S 27 – pop. 82 488

12 **A1**

▶ London 59 mi – Cambridge 31 mi – Colchester 70 mi – Leicester 51 mi
– Lincoln 95 mi – Luton 20 mi – Oxford 52 mi – Southend-on-Sea 85 mi
🛈 Town Hall, St Paul's Sq ℰ (01234) 221 712, touristinfo@bedford.gov.uk
🏌 Bedfordshire Biddenham Bromham Rd, ℰ (01234) 261 669
🏌 Mowsbury Kimbolton Rd, ℰ (01234) 772 700

Plan opposite

The Barns
&rm, ℅ ℌ 🖧 **P** VISA ⓶ AE ①
Cardington Rd, East : 2 m. on A 603 ⊠ MK44 3SA – ℰ (0844) 600 8701
– www.foliohotels.com – reservations.barns@foliohotels.com
– Fax (01234) 273 102   Y**n**
49 rm – ♦£89/120 ♦♦£89/120, �£13.95
Rest – (Closed Saturday lunch) Menu £15/19 – Carte dinner £20/31
♦ Hotel set in three acres of gardens with spacious bedrooms and a delightful 13C tithe barn conversion; now a function room. Semi-split level dining room with views of the Great Ouse. Fish-based menu.

Bedford Swan
🖧 🖥 🖢 Ⓚ rest, ℅ ℌ 🖧 **P** VISA ⓶ AE
The Embankment ⊠ MK40 1RW – ℰ (01234) 346 565
– www.bedfordswanhotel.co.uk – info@bedfordswanhotel.co.uk
– Fax (01234) 212 009   X**a**
113 rm – ♦£60/99 ♦♦£60/119, ⊠£11.95   **Rest** – Carte £27/30 **s**
♦ Impressive Georgian house built in 1794 for the 5th Duke of Bedford. Bedrooms split between main house and more modern in adjacent block. Beautiful Roman style indoor pool. Long, narrow dining room and pleasant terrace.

at Elstow South : 2 m. by A 6 – ⊠ Bedford

St Helena
🖧 **P** VISA ⓶ AE
High St ⊠ MK42 9XP – ℰ (01234) 344 848 – www.sqintHelenas.co.uk – Closed
Christmas-New Year, Saturday lunch, Sunday and Monday   Y**r**
Rest – Menu £22/35
♦ Delightful 16C house in mature gardens with intimate, personally-furnished bar, homely dining room and conservatory extension. Seasonally based menus and appetising specials.

at Houghton Conquest South : 6½ m. by A 6 - Y – ⊠ Bedford

Knife and Cleaver with rm
🖧 🖧 Ⓚ ℅ rest, **P** VISA ⓶ AE ①
The Grove ⊠ MK45 3LA – ℰ (01234) 740 387 – www.knifeandcleaver.com
– info@knifeandcleaver.com – Fax (01234) 740 900 – Closed 27-31 December
9 rm ⊠ – ♦£75 ♦♦£89   **Rest** – Menu £17/24 – Carte £22/38
♦ Spacious conservatory overlooking garden. Seasonal, daily-changing menus with the emphasis on fresh fish. Personally-run by long-established owners. Snug bar with Jacobean panelling and a relaxing feel; homely bedrooms in converted stables.

BEECH – Hampshire – 504 R 30 – See Alton

BEELEY – Derbyshire – pop. 165

16 **B1**

▶ London 160 mi – Derby 26 mi – Matlock 5 mi

The Devonshire Arms with rm
🖧 **P** VISA ⓶ AE
Devonshire Square ⊠ DE4 2NR – ℰ (01629) 733 259
– www.devonshirebeeley.co.uk – enquiries@devonshirebeeley.co.uk
– Fax (01629) 733 259
8 rm – ♦£145 ♦♦£165   **Rest** – Carte £30/45 🍴
♦ Low ceilings, oak beams and inglenook fireplace, plus a brightly furnished modern extension. Dishes' seasonal ingredients come from the Chatsworth Estate. Stylish bedrooms.

BEESTON – Notts. – 502 Q 25 – see Nottingham

ENGLAND

BELCHFORD – Lincolnshire – **502** T 24 – ⊠ **Horncastle**   17 **C1**
▶ London 169 mi – Horncastle 5 mi – Lincoln 28 mi

🍺   **The Blue Bell Inn**   🛋 **P** VISA ⓜⓞ
1 Main Rd ⊠ LN9 6LQ – ℰ (01507) 533 602 – Closed 2nd and 3rd weeks in January
Rest – Carte £ 18/30
♦ A traditionally styled whitewashed pub, popular with walkers on the Viking Way. Numerous blackboard menus list sandwiches, pub favourites and more ambitious choices.

BELFORD – Northumberland – **501** O 17   24 **A1**
▶ London 335 mi – Edinburgh 71 mi – Newcastle upon Tyne 49 mi
🏌 Belford South Rd, ℰ (01668) 213 323

🏠   **Market Cross** without rest   🚗 ⁘ VISA ⓜⓞ
1 Church St ⊠ NE70 7LS – ℰ (01668) 213 013 – www.marketcross.net – info@marketcross.net
4 rm � – †£ 40/90 ††£ 80/100
♦ 200 year-old stone house in rural town centre. Warmly decorated lounge, homely touches in tasteful bedrooms. Wide, locally inspired breakfast choice in cosy pine surroundings.

BELPER – Derbyshire – **502** P 24 – pop. 21 938   16 **B2**
▶ London 141 mi – Birmingham 59 mi – Leicester 40 mi – Manchester 55 mi – Nottingham 17 mi

🏨   **Shottle Hall** 🅎   ⟨ 🚗 🕭 😣 ⁘ 🝓 **P** VISA ⓜⓞ
White Lane, West : 4 m. by A 517 and B 5023 on Shottle rd ⊠ DE56 2EB – ℰ (01773) 550 577 – www.shottlehall.co.uk – info@shottlehall.co.uk
8 rm � – †£ 95/110 ††£ 210
Rest – (closed Sunday dinner, Monday and Bank Holidays) Carte dinner £ 21/30
♦ Attractive country house offering high levels of comfort. Light, airy lounge; library and bar. Bedrooms are individually styled; some traditional, others more contemporary. The Orangery restaurant serves traditional as well as more adventurous dishes. Celestial décor.

at Shottle Northwest : 4 m. by A 517 – ⊠ Belper

🏠   **Dannah Farm** without rest 🅎   🚗 🕭 😣 ⁘ **P** VISA ⓜⓞ
Bowmans Lane, North : ¼ m. by Alport rd ⊠ DE56 2DR – ℰ (01773) 550 273 – www.dannah.co.uk – reservations@dannah.co.uk – Fax (01773) 550 590 – Closed 24-26 December
6 rm ⊋ – †£ 75/95 ††£ 110/190 – 4 suites
♦ Family-run converted farmhouse - part of a working farm. Spacious, contemporary bedrooms are diverse in style; the two level Studio suite includes hot tub and spiral staircase.

BELTON – Leics. – see Loughborough

BEPTON – W. Sussex – see Midhurst

BERKHAMSTED – Hertfordshire – **504** S 28 – pop. 18 800   12 **A2**
📗 Great Britain
▶ London 34 mi – Aylesbury 14 mi – St Albans 11 mi
🎡 Whipsnade Wild Animal Park ★ **AC**, N : 9½ m. on A 4251, B 4506 and B 4540

🍴   **Eatfish**   🛋 🄰🄲 ⇔ VISA ⓜⓞ 🄰🄴
163-165 The High St ⊠ HP4 3HB – ℰ (01442) 879 988 – www.eatfish.co.uk – info@eatfish.co.uk – Fax (01442) 879 977 – Closed 25-26 December
Rest – Seafood – Carte £ 25/47
♦ Well-run seafood restaurant with characterful, rustic feel; photos of Scottish produce and its suppliers on walls. Flexible menu, with large/smaller portions. Summer terrace.

ENGLAND

BERWICK-UPON-TWEED – Northumberland – 501 O 16

– pop. 12 870 ▌ *Great Britain*

> ▶ London 349 mi – Edinburgh 57 mi – Newcastle upon Tyne 63 mi
> 🖪 106 Marygate 🕿 (01289) 330733, tourism@berwick-upon-tweed.gov.uk
> 🖼 Goswick, 🕿 (01289) 387 256
> 🖼 Magdalene Fields, 🕿 (01289) 306 130
> 🔘 Town★★ - Walls★
> 🅖 Foulden★, NW : 5 m. - Paxton House (Chippendale furniture★) **AC**, W : 5 m. by A 6105, A 1 and B 6461. St Abb's Head★★ (≤★), NW : 12 m. by A 1, A 1107 and B 6438 - SW : Tweed Valley★★ – Eyemouth Museum★ **AC**, N : 7½ m. by A 1 and A 1107 – Holy Island★ (Priory ruins★ **AC**, Lindisfarne Castle★ **AC**), SE : 9 m. by A 1167 and A 1 – Manderston★ (stables★), W : 13 m. by A 6105 - Ladykirk (Kirk o'Steil★), SW : 8½ m. by A 698 and B 6470

⌂ Sallyport
🎧 VISA ◉◉

1 Sallyport, off Bridge St ✉ TD15 1EZ – 🕿 (01289) 308 827
– www.sallyport.co.uk – info@sallyport.co.uk
6 rm ☕ – ♦£110/170 ♦♦£110/170 **Rest** – (communal dining) Menu £40
♦ 17C Grade II listed house on cobbled alley. The bedrooms are a strong point: they boast a boutique style, with a high standard of facilities, and lots of homely extra touches. Characterful farmhouse kitchen style dining room.

⌂ West Coates
🚌 🖾 🌣 🎧 P VISA ◉◉

30 Castle Terrace, North : ¾ m. by Castlegate on Kelso rd ✉ TD15 1NZ
– 🕿 (01289) 309 666 – www.westcoates.co.uk
– karenbrownwestcoates@yahoo.com – Fax (01289) 309 666
– Closed 12 December - 9 January
3 rm ☕ – ♦£70/150 ♦♦£100/120
Rest – (dinner only) (by arrangement, communal dining) Menu £35
♦ Step off the train and you're practically at the front door of this personally run 19C house set in mature garden and grounds. Welcoming lounge; annex boasts pool and hot tub. Communal dining table; fine border ingredients are sourced.

BEVERLEY – East Riding of Yorkshire – 502 S 22 – pop. 29 110

– ✉ Kingston-upon-Hull ▌ *Great Britain*

> ▶ London 188 mi – Kingston-upon-Hull 8 mi – Leeds 52 mi – York 29 mi
> 🖪 34 Butcher Row 🕿 (01482) 867430, beverley.tic@eastriding.gov.uk
> 🖼 The Westwood, 🕿 (01482) 868 757
> 🔘 Town★ - Minster★★ – St Mary's Church★

⌂ Burton Mount
🚌 P VISA ◉◉

Malton Rd, Northwest : 2¾ m by A164, B1248 on Leconfield rd ✉ HU17 7RA
– 🕿 (01964) 550 541 – www.burtonmount.co.uk – pg@burtonmount.co.uk
– Fax (01964) 551 955
3 rm ☕ – ♦£115 ♦♦£140 **Rest** – (dinner by arrangement) Menu £35
♦ Homely red brick house overlooking large, mature gardens. Dining room boasts French windows opening onto the terrace. Comfy bedrooms display heavy fabrics and dark wood furniture. Good breakfasts; dinners of well sourced local produce cooked on the Aga.

at Tickton Northeast : 3½ m. by A 1035 – ✉ Kingston-upon-Hull

🏠 Tickton Grange
🚌 🕭 🌣 🎧 ⓢ P VISA ◉◉ AE ①

Tickton, on A 1035 ✉ HU17 9SH – 🕿 (01964) 543 666
– www.ticktongrange.co.uk – info@ticktongrange.co.uk – Fax (01964) 542 556
20 rm ☕ – ♦£93 ♦♦£125
Rest *The Champagne Restaurant* – (Closed 25-26 December) Menu £22/40
– Carte £23/40
♦ Carefully renovated bedrooms blend Georgian and contemporary architecture, antique and period-inspired furniture. Richly swagged fabrics and open fires in an inviting lounge. Dine in the Georgian style; large bay windows look out onto the lawn.

BEVERLEY

at South Dalton Northwest : 5 m. by A 164 and B 1248 – ✉ Beverley

The Pipe and Glass Inn

West End ✉ *HU17 7PN –* ℰ *(01430) 810246 – www.pipeandglass.co.uk*
– email@pipeandglass.co.uk – Fax (01430) 810246 – Closed 25 December and
2 weeks January
Rest – (Closed Sunday dinner and Monday) Carte £ 22/32
♦ Friendly, bustling pub whose hearty cooking makes good use of Yorkshire produce. Well priced menu. Comfortable lounge area with leather Chesterfields and
wood burning stove.

BEYTON – Suffolk – 504 W 27 – see Bury St Edmunds

BIBURY – Gloucestershire – 503 O 28 – ✉ Cirencester ▯ Great Britain   4 **D1**
  ▯ London 86 mi – Gloucester 26 mi – Oxford 30 mi
  ◙ Village★

The Swan

✉ *GL7 5NW –* ℰ *(01285) 740695 – www.cotswold-inns-hotels.co.uk*
– info@swanhotel.co.uk – Fax (01285) 740473 – Closed 25 December
19 rm ⌑ – ♥£ 119 ♥♥£ 165 – 3 suites
Rest *Gallery* – (closed 25 and 31 December to non residents) (dinner only
and Sunday lunch) Menu £ 19/33
Rest *Café Swan* – Menu £ 19/33
♦ Ivy-clad 17C coaching inn with private gardens; idyllic village location by a trout
stream. Comfortable rooms with a contemporary edge. Gallery is formally stylish and
spacious. Café Swan is a brasserie with stone-flagged courtyard.

Cotteswold House without rest

Arlington, on B 4425 ✉ *GL7 5ND –* ℰ *(01285) 740609*
– www.cotteswoldhouse.org.uk – enquiries@cotteswoldhouse.org.uk
– Fax (01285) 740609
3 rm ⌑ – ♥£ 48 ♥♥£ 68
♦ Set in a manicured garden outside the picturesque village. Homely, spotless and
modestly priced bedrooms, comprehensively remodelled behind a Victorian façade.

BIDDENDEN – Kent – 504 V 30 – pop. 2 205 ▯ Great Britain   9 **C2**
  ▯ London 52 mi – Ashford 13 mi – Maidstone 16 mi
  ◙ Bodiam Castle★★, S : 10 m. by A 262, A 229 and B 2244 – Sissinghurst
  Garden★, W : 3 m. by A 262 – Battle Abbey★, S : 20 m. by A 262, A 229,
  A 21 and A 2100

Barclay Farmhouse without rest

Woolpack Corner, South :½ m. by A 262 on Benenden rd ✉ *TN27 8BQ*
– ℰ *(01580) 292626 – www.barclayfarmhouse.co.uk*
– info@barclayfarmhouse.co.uk – Fax (01580) 292288
3 rm ⌑ – ♥£ 60/65 ♥♥£ 75/90
♦ Set in an acre of pleasant garden: well-priced, very comfortable accommodation
with fine French oak flooring and furniture. Inventive breakfasts in granary or barn
conversion.

Bishopsdale Oast ⌂

South : 3 m. by A 262 and Benenden rd on Tenterden rd ✉ *TN27 8DR*
– ℰ *(01580) 291027 – www.bishopsdaleoast.co.uk*
– drysdale@bishopsdaleoast.co.uk – Closed Christmas
5 rm ⌑ – ♥£ 50 ♥♥£ 82
Rest – (by arrangement, communal dining) Menu £ 29
♦ Extended oast house in four acres of mature grounds with wild flower garden.
Comfy lounge with log fire; plenty of trinkets and books in bright, clean, good sized
rooms. Family size dining table; interesting meals employ home-grown, organic produce.

ENGLAND

X **The West House** (Graham Garrett) [P] [VISA] [MO]
£3 28 High St ⊠ TN27 8AH – ℰ (01580) 291 341
– www.thewesthouserestaurant.co.uk – thewesthouse@btconnect.com
– Fax (01580) 291 341 – Closed Christmas-New Year, 2 weeks in summer,
Saturday lunch, Sunday dinner and Monday
Rest – Menu £ 25/38
Spec. Carpaccio of smoked haddock with pickled samphire and pea shoots.
Shoulder and breast of lamb with ewe's cheese and broad beans. Cappuccino
and coffee panna cotta with liquorice ice cream.
♦ Pretty part 16C former weavers' cottages in picturesque village. Charming beamed
interior with inglenook and modern artwork. Concise seasonal menu; assured, precise
cooking.

🍴 **The Three Chimneys** 🍺 🍽 [P] [VISA] [MO]
Hareplain Road, West : 1½ m. off A 262 ⊠ TN27 8LW – ℰ (01580) 291 472
– Closed 25 and 31 December
Rest – (booking essential) Carte £ 20/33
♦ Hugely characterful, low-ceilinged 15C pub with cask ales, rear restaurant and
pleasant garden. Hearty portions of seasonal produce, with nursery puddings like
Bakewell tart.

BIDEFORD – Devon – 503 H 30 – pop. 16 262 2 **C1**
🚆 London 231 mi – Exeter 43 mi – Plymouth 58 mi – Taunton 60 mi
🚢 to Lundy Island (Lundy Co. Ltd) (1 h 45 mn)
🛈 Victoria Park, The Quay ℰ (01237) 477676, bidefordtic@torridge.gov.uk
🏌 Royal North Devon Westward Ho Golf Links Rd, ℰ (01237) 473 824
🏌 Torrington Weare Trees, ℰ (01805) 622 229
◎ Bridge★★ – Burton Art Gallery★ **AC**
🔲 Appledore★, N : 2 m. Clovelly★★, W : 11 m. by A 39 and B 3237 – Lundy
Island★★, NW : by ferry - Rosemoor★ – Great Torrington (Dartington
Crystal★ **AC**) SE : 7½ m. by A 386

🏠 **Yeoldon House** ⌘ ← 🍽 ⁙ [P] [VISA] [MO] [AE]
Durrant Lane, Northam, North : 1½ m. by B 3235 off A 386 ⊠ EX39 2RL
– ℰ (01237) 474 400 – www.yeoldonhousehotel.co.uk – yeoldonhouse@aol.com
– Fax (01237) 476 618 – Closed Christmas
10 rm ⌂ – †£ 80 ††£ 135
Rest – (closed Sunday) (dinner only) (booking essential for non-residents)
(Light lunch Monday-Friday) Carte Dinner approx. £ 33
♦ Privately run 19C house with lovely gardens overlooking the Torridge. Comfortable
lounge bar with books, dried flowers and curios. Period-style rooms, some with
balconies. Smart restaurant overlooking river.

XX **Memories** [AC] [VISA] [AE] [O]
8 Fore St, Northam, North : 2 m. by B 3235 off A 386 ⊠ EX39 1AW – ℰ (01237)
473 419 – Fax (01237) 473 419 – Closed 1 week May, 1 week September,
Sunday-Tuesday and Bank Holidays
Rest – (dinner only) Menu £ 23 (weekdays) – Carte weekends £ 23/27
♦ Simple, blue and white painted restaurant with vibrant local ambience. Enthusiastic owners serve well-prepared, traditional menus at a reasonable price.

at Instow North : 3 m. by A 386 on B 3233 – ⊠ Bideford

XX **Decks** ← 🍽 [AC] [VISA] [MO] [AE]
Marine Parade ⊠ EX39 4JJ – ℰ (01271) 860 671 – www.decksrestaurant.co.uk
– decks@instow.net – Closed 1 week November, 25-26 December, Sunday and
Monday
Rest – (dinner only) Menu £ 24 – Carte £ 25/34
♦ Sit on the outside deck and watch the sun go down over Appledore. Enjoy accom-
plished modern dishes while contemplating the wacky murals. Superb views from all
vantage points.

ENGLAND

BIGBURY – Devon – **503** I 33

2 **C3**

> 🚇 London 195 mi – Exeter 41 mi – Plymouth 22 mi
> 🚾 Kingsbridge★, E : 13 m. by B 3392 and A 379

⚇ **The Oyster Shack**   🛋 **P** **VISA** **◎** **AE**

Milburn Orchard Farm, Stakes Hill, East : 1 m. on Easton rd ⊠ TQ7 4BE
– 𝒞 (01548) 810876 – www.oystershack.co.uk – bigbury@oystershack.co.uk
– Closed 25 December and Monday-Tuesday November to March
Rest – Seafood – (booking essential) Carte £ 23/28
♦ Eccentric venue, half a lovely covered terrace, decorated with fishing nets. Seafood, particularly local oyster dishes; classic and modern dishes using the freshest produce.

BIGBURY-ON-SEA – Devon – **503** I 33 – ⊠ Kingsbridge

2 **C3**

> 🚇 London 196 mi – Exeter 42 mi – Plymouth 23 mi

🏨 **Burgh Island** 🅂   ≼ 🚗 ᴆ 🛋 🐎 🏋 🎿 🏄 ⛴ **P** **VISA** **◎**

South : ½ m. by sea tractor ⊠ TQ7 4BG – 𝒞 (01548) 810514
– www.burghisland.com – reception@burghisland.com – Fax (01548) 810243
– Closed 2 weeks January
14 rm ⌛ – †£ 280 ††£ 385 – 11 suites – ††£ 440/606
Rest – (dinner only and Sunday lunch) (booking essential for non-residents)
Menu £ 55
♦ Unique Grade II listed 1930s country house in private island setting: stylishly romantic Art Deco interior. Charmingly individual rooms with views: some have fantastic style. Ballroom dining: dress in black tie. Owners pride themselves on accomplished cooking.

🏠 **Henley** 🅂   ≼ 🚗 🍷 **P** **VISA** **◎** **AE**

Folly Hill ⊠ TQ7 4AR – 𝒞 (01548) 810240 – www.thehenleyhotel.co.uk
– thehenleyhotel@btconnect.com – Fax (01548) 810240 – March-October
5 rm ⌛ – †£ 65/72 ††£ 127/136
Rest – (dinner only) (booking essential for non-residents) Menu £ 33
♦ Personally run cottage of 16C origin. Stunning views of the bay and Bolt Tail from modern conservatory with deep wicker chairs and pleasant, individual rooms in pastel tones. Homely dining room with magnificent sea views.

BIGGLESWADE – Bedfordshire – **504** T 27 – pop. 15 383

12 **B1**

> 🚇 London 46 mi – Bedford 12 mi – Luton 24 mi

at Old Warden West : 3 ½ m. by A 6001 off B 658 – ⊠ Biggleswade

🏠 **Hare & Hounds**   🚗 🛋 **P** **VISA** **◎**

The Village ⊠ SG18 9HQ – 𝒞 (01767) 627225
– www.hareandhoundsoldwarden.co.uk – thehareandhounds@hotmail.co.uk
– Fax (01767) 627588 – Closed 25 December
Rest – (Closed Mondays except Bank Holidays) Carte £ 20/28
♦ Picture postcard village pub with mature gardens, warm atmosphere and immense charm and style. Locally sourced ingredients. Regularly changing British menu. Attentive service.

BILBROOK – Somerset – **503** J 30

3 **A2**

> 🚇 London 179 mi – Cardiff 92 mi – Weston-super-Mare 42 mi – Taunton 19 mi

🏠 **Dragon House**   🚗 🛋 **P** **VISA** **◎**

on A39 ⊠ TA24 6HQ – 𝒞 (01984) 640215 – www.dragonhouse.co.uk
– info@dragonhouse.co.uk
10 rm ⌛ – †£ 50 ††£ 90   **Rest** – Carte £ 25/35
♦ Small hotel with comfy lounge, leather sofas and central burner, pleasant bar, conservatory and terrace. Clean, modern bedrooms – ask for those newly refurbished. Smart oak panelled restaurant with modern menu of local, seasonal fare; veg being grown in garden.

BILBROUGH – North Yorkshire – **502** Q 22   23 **C2**

▶ London 204 mi – Leeds 25 mi – Bradford 37 mi – York 8 mi

🛏️   **The Three Hares Country Inn**   🖼️ 🕯️ ⚙️ **P** **VISA** **OO** **AE** **①**
Main St ⊠ *YO23 3PH* – ℰ *(01937) 832 128* – *www.thethreehares.co.uk*
– info@thethreehares.co.uk – Fax (01937) 836 186
– Closed Monday and Bank Holidays
Rest – Carte £ 23/30
♦ Characterful whitewashed pub in a sleepy village. Frequently-changing menu displays hearty, tasty dishes with a classical Yorkshire base and a focus on local, seasonal produce.

BILDESTON – Suffolk – **504** W 27   15 **C3**

▶ London 85 mi – Bury St Edmunds 18 mi – Ipswich 15 mi

🛏️   **The Bildeston Crown** with rm   🖼️ 🕯️ ♿ rm, 📶 **P** **VISA** **OO** **AE**
104 High Street ⊠ *IP7 7EB* – ℰ *(01449) 740 510* – *www.thebildestoncrown.co.uk*
– info@thebildestoncrown.co.uk – Fax (01449) 741 843
12 rm � – ♦£80 ♦♦£220   **Rest** – Menu £ 20 – Carte £ 28/38
♦ Stylishly modernised pub with 15C roots, typified by beamed bar and inglenook. Dining room merges period and modern decor. Elaborate or classic dishes. Delightful bedrooms.

BILLESLEY – Warks. – see Stratford-upon-Avon

BILLINGSHURST – West Sussex – **504** S 30 – pop. 5 465   7 **C2**

▶ London 44 mi – Brighton 24 mi – Guildford 25 mi – Portsmouth 40 mi

🏠   **Old Wharf** without rest ⊗   ⩽ 🖼️ 🕯️ ⚙️ 📶 **P**
Wharf Farm, Newbridge, Wisborough Green, West : 1¾ m. on A 272 ⊠ *RH14 OJG*
– ℰ (01403) 784 096 – david.mitchell@farming.co.uk – Fax (01403) 784 096
– Closed 2 weeks Christmas-New Year
3 rm ⊏ – ♦£70/100 ♦♦£150
♦ Charming touches to former 19C canalside warehouse: antiques, dried flowers and brimming bookshelves. Breakfast in farmhouse kitchen; cosy country house rooms overlook water.

BINGHAM – Nottinghamshire – **502** R 25 – pop. 8 685   16 **B2**

▶ London 125 mi – Leicester 26 mi – Lincoln 28 mi – Nottingham 11 mi
– Sheffield 35 mi

✕✕   **Yeung Sing**   🄰🄲 ⇔ **P** **VISA** **OO** **AE** **①**
Market St ⊠ *NG13 8AB* – ℰ *(01949) 831 222* – *www.yeungsing.com*
– info@yeungsing.com – Fax (01949) 838 833 – Closed 25-26 December
Rest – Chinese – (closed lunch Monday-Wednesday) Menu £ 15 (dinner)/19
– Carte £ 18/27
♦ Long-standing, family-owned restaurant with lounge and bar, serving authentic Cantonese and regional Chinese cuisine. Deep red décor, carved wood and huge 3D dragons on walls.

BINGLEY – West Yorkshire – **502** O 22 – pop. 19 884 – ⊠ Bradford   22 **B2**

▶ London 204 mi – Bradford 6 mi – Leeds 15 mi – Skipton 13 mi
🗺️ St Ives Est., ℰ (01274) 562 436

🏠   **Five Rise Locks**   🖼️ 🕯️ 📶 **P** **VISA** **OO** **AE** **①**
Beck Lane, via Park Rd ⊠ *BD16 4DD* – ℰ *(01274) 565 296*
– www.five-rise-locks.co.uk – info@five-rise-locks.co.uk – Fax (01274) 568 828
– Closed 27 December - 2 January
9 rm ⊏ – ♦£60/70 ♦♦£75/105
Rest – (dinner only and Sunday lunch) (residents only Sunday and Monday)
Carte £ 19/26
♦ Neat mid-Victorian house named after the locks on the nearby Leeds-Liverpool canal. Cheerful, modern, individuallly styled rooms, some with views of the distant dales. Well-kept dining room employs local produce on menus.

BINLEY – W. Mids. – see Coventry

BIRCHOVER – Derbs. – see Matlock

BIRKENHEAD – Merseyside – 502 K 23 – pop. 83 729 — 20 A3

London 222 mi – Liverpool 2 mi
Access Mersey Tunnels (toll)
to Liverpool and Wallasey (Mersey Ferries) frequent services daily
Woodside Ferry Terminal ✆ (0151) 647 6780, touristinfo@wirral.gov.uk
Arrowe Park Woodchurch, ✆ (0151) 677 1527
Prenton Golf Links Rd, ✆ (0151) 609 3426

Plan : see Liverpool p. 3

River Hill

Talbot Rd, Oxton, Southwest : 2 ¼ m. by A 552 on B 5151 ✉ CH43 2HJ – ✆ (0151) 653 3773 – www.theriverhill.co.uk – reception@theriverhill.co.uk – Fax (0151) 653 7162 – Closed 26 December
14 rm – †£ 70/90 ††£ 90, ☕ £ 7.95
Rest – (dinner only and Sunday lunch) Menu £ 19 – Carte £ 25/29
◆ Imposing redbrick Victorian house with substantial purpose-built extension. Sizeable lounge and bar. Spacious, characterful bedrooms now more modern, following redecoration. Carefully tended garden adjoins restaurant.

ENGLAND

Fraiche (Marc Wilkinson)

11 Rose Mount, Oxton, Southwest : 2 ¼ m. by A 552 and B 5151 ✉ CH43 5SG – ✆ (0151) 652 2914 – www.restaurantfraiche.com – contact@restaurantfraiche.com – Closed 1 week January, 25 December, Monday, Tuesday and lunch Friday and Saturday
Rest – (booking essential) Menu £ 24/55
Spec. Scallops, tarragon infused grapes and sweetcorn purée. Fillet of rose veal with celery heart and pea cream. "Textures of orange".
◆ Smart, intimate restaurant enhanced by modern artwork and coloured glassware. Innovative flavour combinations and eye-catching presentation. Attentive, well-paced service.

K. Blackwell/MICHELIN

BIRMINGHAM

County: W. Mids.
Michelin REGIONAL map: n° **503** O 26
▶ London 122 m – Bristol 91 m –
Liverpool 103 m – Manchester 86 m –
Nottingham 50 m

Population: 970 892   19 **C2**
Great Britain

Birmingham   pp. 3-9

PRACTICAL INFORMATION

🛈 Tourist Information
The Rotunda, 150 New St ℘ (0870) 225 0127, (0121) 616 1038

Tourism Centre, National Exhibition Centre ℘ (0121) 202 5099

Airport
✈ Birmingham International Airport: ℘ (08707) 335511, E: 6 ½ m. by A 45 DU

Golf Courses
▣ Edgbaston Church Rd, ℘ (0121) 454 1736 ;

▣ Hilltop Handsworth Park Lane, ℘ (0121) 554 4463 ;

▣ Hatchford Brook Sheldon Coventry Rd, ℘ (0121) 743 9821 ;

▣ Brandhall Warley Heron Rd, Oldbury, ℘ (0121) 552 2195 ;

▣ Harborne Church Farm Harborne Vicarage Rd, ℘ (0121) 427 1204.

🖸 SIGHTS

IN TOWN

City★ – Museum and Art Gallery★★
LY **M2** – Barber Institute of Fine Arts★★
(at Birmingham University) EX **U**
– Cathedral of St Philip (stained glass
portrayals★) LMY – Millennium Point
FV

ON THE OUTSKIRTS

Aston Hall★★ FV **M**

IN THE SURROUNDING AREA

Black Country Museum★ , Dudley,
NW: 10 m. by A 456 and A 4123 AU
– Bournville★ , SW: 4 m. on A 38 and
A 441

ENGLAND

(M 54)
STAFFORD A 449   CANNOCK (M 54.M 6) A 460   MANCHESTER STOKE-ON-T. M 6 A 462 (M 6) CANNOCK A 34   BROWNHIL A 412

A
B

A 41 WHITCHURCH

Wergs

18

Stafford Rd

Cannock Road

B 4156

BUSHBURY

A 4210

BLOXWICH

Lichfield Road

A 4124

WEDNESFIELD

Canal

A 462

M 6

Green Lane

A 34

Can

TETTENHALL

Compton Rd

A 454 BRIDGNORTH

Willenhall Rd

WILLENHALL

19

Walsall Rd

B 4464

10 A 454

Pleck Rd

See
WOLVERHAMPTON

29

BLAKENHALL

A 4039

BILSTON

A 454

3

A 451

DARLASTON

A 4038

A 452

A 481

M 6

9 A 4148

27

T

Penn

A 449

A 4123

Birmingham Rd

Oxford St

A 463

Holyhead Rd

A 41

WEDNESBURY

A 4037

A 4098

Canal

SEDGLEY

A 463

Wolverhampton Rd

A 457

New Rd

COSELEY

WEST BROMWICH

A 41

A 4035

12

Church Lane

A 4031

HIMLEY PARK

9

A 459

DUDLEY ZOO

M

A 491

Dudley Road

A 457

SANDWELL

HIMLEY

B 4176

B 4588

A 4123

A 4182

B 4175

DUDLEY

A 4101

A 461

2

Oldbury Rd

Thimblemill

B 4182

A 449 KIDDERMINSTER

A 491

KINGSWINFORD

18

OLDBURY

B 4171

A 4034

WARLEY

9

Wolverhampton Rd

BRIERLEY HILL

B 4180

MERRY HILL

A 459

ROWLEY REGIS

A 4036

A 4100

A 4034

U

AMBLECOTE

A 461

Canal

A 458 BRIDGNORTH

Stour

A 458

A 458

HALESOWEN

3

STOURBRIDGE

B 4183

A 456

KIDDERMINSTER

A 491

HAGLEY

B 4187

HAGLEY PARK

HAGLEY WOOD

UFFMOOR WOOD

BARTLEY RESERVOIR

A 451

KIDDERMINSTER A 456   A 491 BROMSGROVE A   (A 491) B 4551   B   M 5 BRISTOL

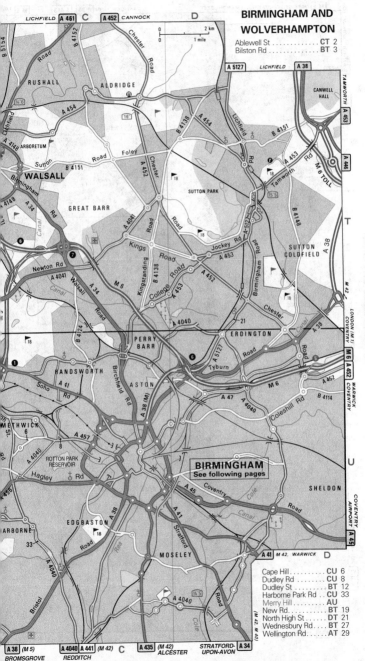

BIRMINGHAM AND
WOLVERHAMPTON

ENGLAND

M 5 (M6), STOKE-ON-TRENT, MANCHESTER   E   CANNOCK. (M6) A 34 A 453 F M 6 TRE

0 1 km
0 1/2 mile

M 5
A 41 WOLVERHAMPTON
BRISTOL
M 5
A 457 High

PERRY BARR

Aldridge Road
Brookvale Rd

Oxhill Rd
Rookery Rd
Church Lane
Wellington Road A 4040
Birchfield Road
Aston Lane
Witton

Island
Holyhead Rd
HANDSWORTH
Hamstead Road
Witton

Booth St.
Soho Rd
Villa Rd
Lozells Rd
High St
ASTON
Victoria
Aston Expressway Rd.
Lichfie

Rolfe St
Hockley Circus
New John St West
54
13
50

SMETHWICK
Heath St
Green Rd
Lodge Rd
A 4540
A 41
A 34
22
A 47
15
U

Cape Hill
Dudley Rd
Spring Hill
Icknield Port Rd
A 4540
Icknield
A 457
36
40
MILLENNIUM POINT

Rotton Rd
Park Rd
A 4040 Portland Rd
ROTTON PARK RESERVOIR
Middleway
Broad St.
24
85
17

Beakwood
Sandon Rd
City Rd
A 4030

Hagley Rd A 456
Rd
14
42
Bristol St
A 4540
High St
15
19

Westfield Rd
Norfolk Rd
55
Harborne
Rd
Church Rd
A 38
A 441
2
1
Highgate

Court Oak Rd
HARBORNE
High St
Matchley Lane
Harborne Park Rd
EDGBASTON
Priory Rd
Edgbaston Rd
Haden Way
Moseley Rd A 435

9
Canal
U
P
Bristol Rd
Pershore Rd
Salisbury Rd
MOSELEY

Harborne La.
Rea
Alcester Rd
Wake Gree
KING'S HEATH

Oak Tree La.
Linden Road
Bristol Road
Rd
High St
Addison Rd

ENGLAND
A 456 (M 5), KIDDERMINSTER
A 4040
V
X
A 4123 WOLVERHAMPTON

Fordhouse Lane
Pershore
Vicarage Rd
Rd
Alcester

(M 5) A 38 BROMSGROVE   E   REDDITCH A4040 A 441 REDDITCH   F   A 435 ALCESTER

ENGLAND

BIRMINGHAM

ENGLAND

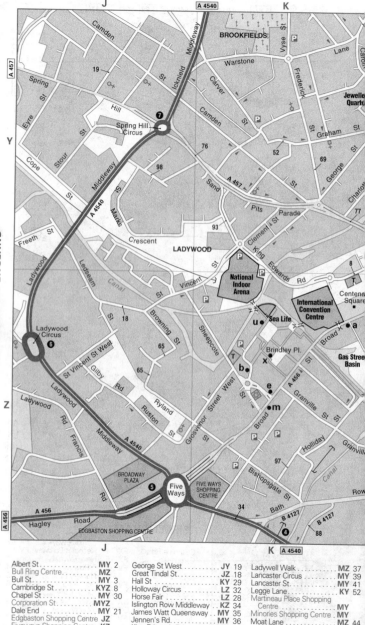

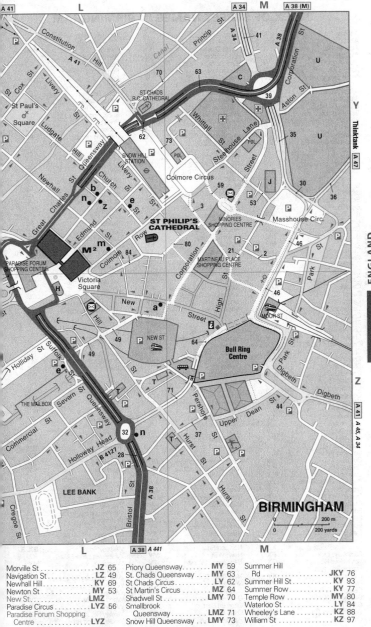

ENGLAND

Thinktank **A 47**

BIRMINGHAM

0   200 m
0   200 yards

INDEX OF STREET NAMES IN BIRMINGHAM

ENGLAND

⚞ Radisson SAS ⚞ 🏬 ⚹ rm, 🖾 ⚹ 🐾 🖾 VISA ⚭ AE ①

12 Holloway Circus ⊠ *B1 1BT –* ℰ *(0121) 654 6000*
– www.birmingham.radissonsas.com – info.birmingham@radissonsas.com
– Fax (0161) 654 6001   LZ**n**
204 rm – ♥£99/205 ♥♥£99/205, ⚏ £14.95 – 7 suites
Rest *Filini* – Italian – (Closed Saturday lunch and Sunday) Carte £20/48
◆ Occupies 18 uber-modern floors of a city centre skyscraper. Well-equipped business facilities; ultra stylish bedrooms in three distinctly slinky themes. Modern bar leads to airy, easy-going Italian restaurant, Filini.

⚞ Hyatt Regency ⚞ 🖾 🌐 🏬 ⅃⅃ ⚹ ⚹ rm, 🖾 ⚹ 🐾 ⚹ 🚗 VISA ⚭ AE ①

2 Bridge St ⊠ *B1 2JZ –* ℰ *(0121) 643 1234 – www.birmingham.hyatt.com*
– Fax (0121) 616 2323   KZ**a**
315 rm – ♥£199 ♥♥£199, ⚏ £15.25 – 4 suites
Rest *Aria* – British – Menu £14/17 – Carte £25/41
◆ Striking mirrored exterior. Glass enclosed lifts offer panoramic views. Sizeable rooms with floor to ceiling windows. Covered link with International Convention Centre. Contemporary style restaurant in central atrium; modish cooking.

⚞ Malmaison 🏬 ⅃⅃ ⚹ ⚹ rm, 🖾 ⚹ 🐾 ⚹ VISA ⚭ AE

Mailbox, 1 Wharfside St ⊠ *B1 1RD –* ℰ *(0121) 246 5000 – www.malmaison.com*
– birmingham@malmaison.com – Fax (0121) 246 5002   LZ**e**
184 rm – ♥£170 ♥♥£495, ⚏ £13.95 – 5 suites
Rest *Brasserie* – British – Menu £16 (dinner) – Carte £26/33
◆ Stylish, modern boutique hotel, forms centrepiece of Mailbox development. Stylish bar. Spacious contemporary bedrooms with every modern facility; superb petit spa. Brasserie serving contemporary French influenced cooking at reasonable prices.

⚞ Hotel Du Vin 🚗 🏬 ⅃⅃ ⚹ ⚹ rm, 🖾 rm, ⚹ 🐾 ⚹ VISA ⚭ AE

25 Church St ⊠ *B3 2NR –* ℰ *(0121) 200 0600 – www.hotelduvin.com*
– info.birmingham@hotelduvin.com – Fax (0121) 236 0889   LY**e**
66 rm – ♥£150/185 ♥♥£150/185, ⚏ £13.50
Rest *Bistro* – French – Carte £25/35 ⚶
◆ Former 19C eye hospital in heart of shopping centre; has relaxed, individual, boutique style. Low lighting in rooms of muted tones: Egyptian cotton and superb bathrooms. Champagne in "bubble lounge"; Parisian style brasserie.

⚞ The Burlington 🏬 ⅃⅃ ⚹ ⚹ rm, 🖾 ⚹ 🚗 VISA ⚭ AE ①

Burlington Arcade, 126 New St ⊠ *B2 4JQ –* ℰ *(0844) 879 9019*
– www.macdonaldhotels.co.uk – general.burlington@macdonald-hotels.co.uk
– Fax (0121) 628 5005 – Closed 25-26 December   LZ**a**
110 rm – ♥£175 ♥♥£195, ⚏ £17.50 – 2 suites
Rest *Berlioz* – Mediterranean – ℰ *(0121) 643 9191* (dinner only) Carte £20/35
◆ Approached by a period arcade. Restored Victorian former railway hotel retains much of its original charm. Period décor to bedrooms yet with fax, modem and voice mail. Elegant dining room: ornate ceiling, chandeliers and vast mirrors.

⚞ City Inn 🚗 ⅃⅃ ⚹ ⚹ rm, 🖾 ⚹ 🚗 VISA ⚭ AE ①

1 Brunswick Sq, Brindley Pl ⊠ *B1 2HW –* ℰ *(0121) 643 1003 – www.cityinn.com*
– birmingham.reservations@cityinn.com – Fax (0121) 643 1005   KZ**b**
238 rm – ♥£89/225 ♥♥£89/225, ⚏ £12.50
Rest *City Café* – British – Menu £15/17 – Carte £19/48
◆ In heart of vibrant Brindley Place; the spacious atrium with bright rugs and blond wood sets the tone for equally stylish rooms. Corporate friendly with many meeting rooms. Eat in restaurant, terrace or bar.

⚞ TOTEL without rest 🅿 VISA ⚭ AE

19 Portland Rd, Edgbaston ⊠ *B16 9HN –* ℰ *(0121) 454 5282 – www.toteluk.com*
– info@toteluk.com – Fax (0121) 456 4668   EX**c**
1 rm – 10 suites – ♥♥£75/105
◆ 19C house converted into comfortable, spacious fully-serviced apartments, individually styled with modern facilities. Friendly service. Continental breakfast served in room.

ENGLAND

ENGLAND

Novotel

▒ 🎐 🖿 🕭 rm, ¶ 🍴 🚗 VISA 🐼 AE ①

70 Broad St ⊠ B1 2HT – ℰ (0121) 643 2000 – www.novotel.com
– h1077@accor.com – Fax (0121) 643 9786

KZe

148 rm – ♥£152 ♥♥£152, ☑£12.50

Rest – Mediterranean – (meals in bar) Menu £20 **s** – Carte £21/28 **s**

♦ Well located for the increasingly popular Brindleyplace development. Underground parking. Modern, well-kept, branded bedrooms suitable for families. Modern, open-plan restaurant.

Simpsons (Andreas Antona) with rm

🚗 🍴 AC rest, P. VISA 🐼 AE ①

✿

20 Highfield Rd, Edgbaston ⊠ B15 3DU – ℰ (0121) 454 3434
– www.simpsonsrestaurant.co.uk – info@simpsonsrestaurant.co.uk – Fax (0121)
454 3399 – Closed 24-27 and 31 December-1 January

EXe

4 rm – ♥♥£160/225

Rest – Innovative – (closed Sunday dinner and Bank Holidays) Menu £28/33
– Carte £45/53 ▒

Spec. Ravioli of scallops with baby vegetables, ginger and lemon grass sauce. Confit of rabbit with pancetta and sweet and sour sauce. Chocolate and passion fruit délice with coconut ice cream.

♦ Impressive Georgian mansion with blend of contemporary furnishings and period touches. L-shaped dining room set around terrace. Classically based menus with a personal twist. Large, individually themed bedrooms.

Pascal's

VISA 🐼

🕭

1 Montague Rd ⊠ B16 9HN – ℰ (0121) 455 0999 – www.pascalsrestaurant.co.uk
– info@pascalsrestaurant.co.uk – Fax (0121) 455 0999
– Closed 1 week Easter, last 2 weeks July, 1 week Christmas, Saturday lunch,
Sunday and Monday

EXc

Rest – French – Menu £20/29 – Carte £20/29

♦ Two main rooms; a darker inner hall and lighter, more airy conservatory with views of the small rear garden. Classical, carefully priced cooking with strong French overtones.

Purnell's (Glynn Purnell)

VISA 🐼 AE

✿

55 Cornwall St ⊠ B3 2DH – ℰ (0121) 212 9799 – www.purnellsrestaurant.com
– Closed 1 week Easter, last week July, 1st week August, 1 week Christmas,
Saturday lunch, Sunday and Monday

LYb

Rest – Innovative – Menu £20/40

Spec. Salad of crab with smoked paprika and honeycomb. Slow cooked ox cheek with monkfish and spiced lentils. Raspberry pavlova with lavender and raspberry sorbet.

♦ Red brick Victorian building in heart of city, boasting large arched floor to ceiling windows and central bar. Well-priced, modern and innovative food uses quality ingredients.

Opus

AC ⟷ VISA 🐼 AE

54 Cornwall St ⊠ B3 2DE – ℰ (0121) 200 2323 – www.opusrestaurant.co.uk
– restaurant@opusrestaurant.co.uk – Fax (0121) 200 2090
– Closed 25 December-4 January, Saturday lunch, Sunday and Bank Holidays

Rest – Modern – Menu £20 – Carte £30/38

LYz

♦ Restaurant of floor-to-ceiling glass in evolving area of city. Seafood and shellfish bar for diners on the move. Assured cooking underpins modern menus with traditional base.

Asha's

VISA 🐼 AE

12-22 Newhall St – ℰ (0121) 200 2767 – www.ashasrestaurants.co.uk
– info@ashasrestaurant.co.uk – Closed 25 December, 1 January and lunch
Saturday, Sunday and Bank Holidays

LYm

Rest – Indian – Carte £20/28

♦ Smart restaurant with delightful décor and vivid artwork. Owned by renowned artiste/gourmet Asha Bhosle. Authentic North West Indian cuisine cooked by chefs originally from that region.

XXX **Edmunds**   *VISA* **MC** **AE**
6 Brindley Place ⊠ B1 2JB – ℰ (0121) 633 4944
– www.edmundsbirmingham.com – info@edmundsbirmingham.com
– Fax (0121) 497 49 74 – Closed 1 week per season, Saturday lunch, Sunday and
Bank Holidays   KZ**x**
Rest – Menu £ 20/40
♦ Formal restaurant in heart of city. Smart interior with neutral décor and modern lighting. Immaculately laid tables boast fine china and glassware. Smart, attentive staff.

XX **Turners** Richard Turner   *VISA* **MC**
☆ *69 High Street, Harborne ⊠ B17 9NS – ℰ (0121) 426 4440 – Closed Saturday*
lunch, Sunday dinner and Monday   EX**a**
Rest – (booking advisable) Menu £ 18 (lunch) – Carte £ 35/50
Spec. Roast and confit quail with soft boiled egg, and walnut vinaigrette. Assiette of lamb, shallot purée and thyme sauce. Raspberry sablé Breton with basil ice cream.
♦ Unlikely venue in a parade of shops; simple, crisp interior. The cooking reflects the experienced chef's classical background; flavours are clean and dishes well balanced.

XX **Lasan**   *VISA* **MC** **AE**
3-4 Dakota Buildings, James St ⊠ B3 1SD – ℰ (0121) 212 3664
– www.lasan.co.uk – info@lasan.co.uk – Fax (0121) 212 3665
– Closed 25-26 December and Saturday lunch   KY**a**
Rest – Indian – Carte £ 26/40 **s**
♦ Jewellery quarter restaurant of sophistication and style; good quality ingredients allow the clarity of the spices to shine through in this well-run Indian establishment.

XX **Bank**   🖼 **AC** 🗄 ⇔ *VISA* **MC** **AE** **①**
4 Brindleyplace ⊠ B1 2JB – ℰ (0121) 633 4466 – www.bankrestaurants.com
– birmres@bankrestaurants.com – Fax (0121) 633 4465   KZ**u**
Rest – Modern – Menu £ 15 – Carte approx. £ 29
♦ Capacious, modern and busy bar-restaurant where chefs can be watched through a glass wall preparing the tasty modern dishes. Pleasant terrace area.

XX **Metro Bar and Grill**   **AC** *VISA* **MC** **AE**
73 Cornwall St ⊠ B3 2DF – ℰ (0121) 200 1911 – www.metrobarandgrill.co.uk
– birmingham@metrobarandgrill.co.uk – Fax (0121) 200 1611
– Closed 25 December-2 January, Sunday and Bank Holidays   LY**n**
Rest – Modern – (booking essential) Menu £ 18 (dinner) – Carte £ 22/32
♦ Gleaming chrome and mirrors in a bright, contemporary basement restaurant. Modern cooking with rotisserie specialities. Spacious, ever-lively bar serves lighter meals.

XX **Shimla Pinks**   **AC** *VISA* **MC** **AE** **①**
214 Broad St ⊠ B15 1AY – ℰ (0121) 633 0366 – www.shimlapinks.com
– info@shimlapinks.com – Fax (0121) 643 3325   KZ**m**
Rest – Indian – (dinner only) Menu £ 25 – Carte £ 20/30
♦ A vast establishment In a street full of restaurants. Buzzy ambience prevails: open-plan kitchen adds to atmosphere. Authentic, modern Indian cuisine; impressive set menus.

at Hall Green Southeast : 5 ¾ m. by A 41 on A 34 – ⊠ Birmingham

XX **Liaison**   *VISA* **MC**
1558 Stratford Rd ⊠ B28 9HA – ℰ (0121) 733 7336
– www.liaisonrestaurant.co.uk – Fax (0121) 733 1677 – Closed 2 weeks
September, 1 week Christmas, Saturday lunch, Sunday and Monday   GX**i**
Rest – Menu £ 18/29
♦ Pleasant restaurant with understated décor in residential location. Linen table cloths and friendly service. Classically based modern eclectic cooking.

ENGLAND

at Birmingham Airport Southeast : 9 m. by A 45 - DU – ✉ Birmingham

Novotel Birmingham Airport 🍴 &. rm, ⁽ᵗ⁾ 🄰 VISA ⓪ AE ⓪
Terminal 1 ✉ B26 3QL – ℰ (0121) 782 7000 – www.novotel.com
– h1058@accor.com – Fax (0121) 782 0445
195 rm – ♦£139 ♦♦£139, 🖵 £14.50
Rest – Mediterranean – (bar lunch Saturday, Sunday and Bank Holidays)
Menu £17 (lunch) – Carte £23/35
♦ Opposite main terminal building: modern hotel benefits from sound proofed doors and double glazing. Mini bars and power showers provided in spacious with sofa beds. Open-plan garden brasserie.

at National Exhibition Centre Southeast : 9½ m. on A 45 - DU
– ✉ Birmingham

Crowne Plaza ⁂ 📶 🍴 &. rm, 🄼 ⅋ ⁽ᵗ⁾ 🄰 🄿 VISA ⓪ AE ⓪
Pendigo Way ✉ B40 1PS – ℰ (0870) 400 9160 – www.crowneplaza.co.uk
– Fax (0121) 781 4321 – Closed 21 December-4 January
242 rm 🖵 – ♦£89/269 ♦♦£89/269
Rest – Classic – (closed Sunday lunch) Menu £15/25 – Carte £22/35
♦ Modern hotel adjacent to NEC. Small terrace area overlooks lake. Extensive conference facilities. State-of-the-art bedrooms with a host of extras. Basement dining room: food with a Yorkshire twist.

BIRMINGHAM AIRPORT – W. Mids. – **503** O 26 – see Birmingham

BISHOP'S STORTFORD – Hertfordshire – **504** U 28 – pop. 35 325   12 **B2**
📖 Great Britain

🖸 London 34 mi – Cambridge 27 mi – Chelmsford 19 mi – Colchester 33 mi
🛦 Stansted Airport : ℰ (0870) 0000303, NE : 3½ m
🅸 The Old Monastery, Windhill ℰ (0871) 7162529, tic@bishopsstortford.org
🄶 Audley End★★ AC, N : 11 m. by B 1383

The Cottage without rest ⊗ 🖼 ⅋ ⁽ᵗ⁾ 🄿 VISA ⓪ AE ⓪
71 Birchanger Lane, Northeast : 2¼ m. by B 1383 on Birchanger rd ✉ CM23 5QA
– ℰ (01279) 812 349 – www.thecottagebirchanger.co.uk
– bookings@thecottagebirchanger.co.uk – Fax (01279) 815 045
– Closed Christmas and New Year
14 rm 🖵 – ♦£50/65 ♦♦£80/90
♦ Rurally-set part 17/18C cottages - yet close to airport. Cosy reception rooms with oak panelling and exposed beams. Conservatory style breakfast room and homely bedrooms.

The Lemon Tree 🄰 ✿ VISA ⓪ AE ⓪
14-16 Water Lane ✉ CM23 2LB – ℰ (01279) 757 788 – www.lemontree.co.uk
– mail@lemontree.co.uk – Fax (01279) 757 766
– Closed 25-26 December, 1 January, and Sunday dinner
Rest – Carte £21/32
♦ Cosy, vibrant restaurant in centre of town. Light and airy dining rooms, open bar; spacious private dining room on first floor. Wide-ranging menu, locally sourced ingredients.

Host 🖼 🄰 VISA ⓪ AE ⓪
4 The Corn Exchange, Market Sq ✉ CM23 3UU – ℰ (01279) 657 000
– www.hostrestaurant.co.uk – bar@hostrestaurant.co.uk – Fax (01279) 655 566
– Closed 25-26 December and Sunday dinner
Rest – Carte £15/30
♦ Grade I listed building with unique roof terrace. Main restaurant has industrial feel, with modern bar and open kitchen. Oft-changing menu incorporates global influences.

at Stansted Mountfitchet Northeast : 3 ½ m. by B 1383 on B 1051 – ⊠ Bishop's Stortford

⌂ **Chimneys** without rest 『P』『VISA』『MO』
44 Lower St, on B 1351 ⊠ CM24 8LR – ℰ (01279) 813 388
– www.chimneysguesthouse.co.uk – info@chimneysguesthouse.co.uk
– Fax (01376) 310 169
4 rm ⌂ – ┇£55/60 ┇┇£78
♦ Charming 17C house with friendly hosts, beamed ceilings, snug breakfast room and homely lounge. Comfy bedrooms - single has largest bathroom. Usefully located for airport.

at Hatfield Heath Southeast : 6 m. on A 1060 – ⊠ Bishop's Stortford

🏨 **Down Hall Country House** ⊗ ← 🚗 🏊 📺 ⌘ ✕ 🛗 ᴬᴄ rest,
South : 1 ½ m. by Matching Lane ⊠ CM22 7AS 『P』 ᴋᴀ 『P』 『VISA』『MO』『AE』『①』
– ℰ (01279) 731 441 – www.downhall.co.uk – reservations@downhall.co.uk
– Fax (01279) 730 416
99 rm ⌂ – ┇£105/155 ┇┇£135/155
Rest *Ibbetsons* – (dinner only Thursday-Saturday) (booking essential for non-residents) Carte £39/51
Rest *The Grill Room* – (closed lunch Saturday and Bank Holidays) Carte £27/37
♦ Ornate 19C Italianate mansion house in delightful grounds. Period style bedrooms; the most characterful in the old part of the house. Fine dining in traditional Ibbetsons restaurant. The contemporary Grill Room is less formal.

Undecided between two equivalent establishments?
Within each category, establishments are classified
in our order of preference.

BISHOPSTONE – Swindon – **503** P 29 – see Swindon

BISPHAM GREEN – Lancashire

🍴 **Eagle & Child** 🚗 🏡 『P』『VISA』『MO』
⊠ L40 3SG – ℰ (01257) 462 297 – www.ainscoughs.co.uk
– eagle@ainscoughs.co.uk – Fax (01257) 464 718
Rest – Carte £17/26
♦ Traditional 200 year old pub with a warm, cosy feel. Hearty, tasty cooking includes simple British classics and more ambitious daily specials. Up to 12 real ales available.

BLACKAWTON – see DARTMOUTH

BLACKBURN – Blackburn with Darwen – **502** M 22 – pop. 105 085 20 **B2**
🚗 London 228 mi – Leeds 47 mi – Liverpool 39 mi – Manchester 24 mi
– Preston 11 mi
🗺 50-54 Church St ℰ (01254) 53277, visit@blackburn.gov.uk
🏌 Pleasington, ℰ (01254) 202 177
🏌 Wilpshire 72 Whalley Rd, ℰ (01254) 248 260
🏌 Great Harwood Harwood Bar, Whalley Rd, ℰ (01254) 884 391

🍴 **The Clog & Billycock** 🏡 『P』『VISA』『MO』『AE』
Billinge End Rd, West : 2 m. by A 677 ⊠ BB2 6QB – ℰ (01254) 201 163
– www.theclogandbillycock.com – enquiries@theclogandbillycock.com
– Closed 25 December
Rest – Carte £18/32
♦ Recently modernised stone pub in pleasant rural suburb. Open plan with flag floors and plain wall adorned with pictures. Huge menu offers rustic, generous dishes with a Lancastrian slant.

ENGLAND

at Langho North : 4½ m. on A 666 – ✉ Whalley

XXX   **Northcote** (Nigel Haworth) with rm   🚗 &. rm, 🎐 ℣ **P** **VISA** ⦿⦿ **AE**
⊗   *Northcote Rd, North : ½ m. on A 59 at junction with A 666 ✉ BB6 8BE*
   – ℰ (01254) 240 555 – www.northcote.com – reservations@northcote.com
   – Fax (01254) 246 568 – Closed 25 December
   14 rm �Ⓩ – 🛉£ 195 🛉🛉£ 225   **Rest** – Menu £ 25 (lunch) – Carte £ 40/55 ⅜
   Spec. Black pudding and buttered pink trout with mustard and nettle sauce.
   Lamb in puff pastry, pear purée and caramelised shallot. Apple crumble soufflé
   with Lancashire cheese ice cream.
   ♦ Red brick Victorian house with welcoming fire-lit lounges. Passionate kitchen
   serves modern dishes with emphasis on Lancashire produce. Window tables most
   popular. Smart and comfortable bedrooms, recently refurbished.

at Mellor Northwest : 3 ¼ m. by A 677 – ✉ Blackburn

🏨   **Stanley House**   🚗 ℀ ⊠ 🅰🅲 🎐 ℣ 🕸 **P** **VISA** ⦿⦿ **AE**
   Southwest : ¾ m. by A 677 and Further Lane ✉ BB2 7NP – ℰ (01254) 769 200
   – www.stanleyhouse.co.uk – info@stanleyhouse.co.uk – Fax (01254) 769 206
   12 rm �Ⓩ – 🛉£ 185/210 🛉🛉£ 185/210
   Rest *Cassis* – see restaurant listing
   ♦ 17C manor with superb rural views houses elegantly proportioned rooms defined
   by wonderfully rich colours. Bar and conference facilities in converted farmhouse.

🏨   **Millstone**   🎐 **P** **VISA** ⦿⦿ **AE** ①
   Church Lane ✉ BB2 7JR – ℰ (01254) 813 333 – www.shirehotels.com
   – info@millstonehotel.co.uk – Fax (01254) 812 628
   22 rm �Ⓩ – 🛉£ 109 🛉🛉£ 125 – 1 suite
   Rest – (bar lunch) Menu £ 30 (dinner) **s** – Carte £ 30 **s**
   ♦ Attractive little sandstone former coaching inn in quiet village. Lounge bar with log
   fire and comfy sofas. Cosy bedrooms: matching floral patterns, botanical prints. Elegant wood panelled dining room warmed by fire.

XXX   **Cassis** – at Stanley House Hotel   🅰🅲 **P** **VISA** ⦿⦿ **AE**
   Southwest : ¾ m. by A 677 and Further Lane ✉ BB2 7NP – ℰ (01254) 769 200
   – www.stanleyhouse.co.uk – cassis@stanleyhouse.co.uk – Fax (01254) 769 206
   – Closed Saturday and Tuesday lunch, Sunday dinner and Monday
   Rest – Menu £ 21/36 – Carte dinner £ 32/50 ⅜
   ♦ Independent from main hotel. Name derives from rich blackcurrant theme
   throughout! Vast raised mezzanine for apéritifs. Weekly evolving menus with vibrant
   Lancashire accent.

BLACKMORE – Essex   13 **C2**

🖪 London 26 mi – Brentwood 7 mi – Chelmsford 8 mi

🍺   **The Leather Bottle**   🚗 **VISA** ⦿⦿
   The Green ✉ CM4 0RL – ℰ (01277) 823 538 – www.theleatherbottle.net
   – leatherbottle@tiscali.co.uk
   Rest – (Closed Sunday dinner) Menu £ 10 – Carte £ 19/26
   ♦ Pub dating from 1750s, overlooking village green. Cosy, flagstoned bar; dining area
   and airy conservatory. All-encompassing seasonal menu includes European and Asian
   flavours.

BLACKPOOL – Blackpool – 502 K 22 – pop. 142 283 ▌ Great Britain   20 **A2**

🖪 London 246 mi – Leeds 88 mi – Liverpool 56 mi – Manchester 51 mi
   – Middlesbrough 123 mi

🛧 Blackpool Airport : ℰ (0871) 8556868, S : 3 m. by A 584

🛈 1 Clifton St ℰ (01253) 478222, tic@blackpool.gov.uk

🏌 Blackpool Park North Park Drive, ℰ (01253) 397 916

🏌 Poulton-le-Fylde Breck Rd, Myrtle Farm, ℰ (01253) 892 444

◎ Tower★ **AC** AY **A**

Plan opposite

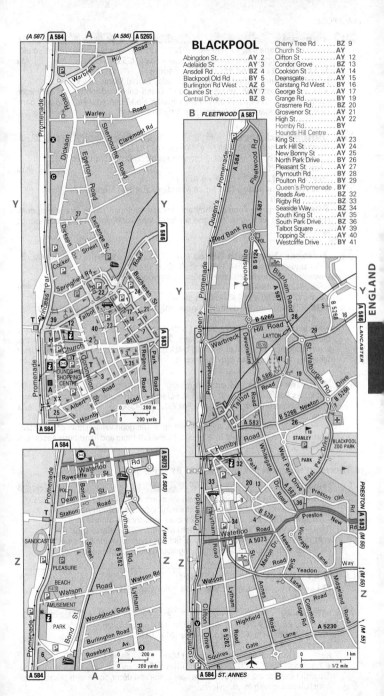

BLACKPOOL

Abingdon St.	AY	2
Adelaide St	AY	3
Ansdell Rd	BZ	4
Blackpool Old Rd	BY	5
Burlington Rd West	AZ	6
Caunce St	AY	7
Central Drive	BZ	8
Cherry Tree Rd	BZ	9
Church St.	AY	
Clifton St	AY	12
Condor Grove	BZ	13
Cookson St	AY	14
Deansgate	AY	15
Garstang Rd West	BY	16
George St	AY	17
Grange Rd	BY	19
Grasmere Rd	BZ	20
Grosvenor St.	AY	21
High St	AY	22
Hornby Rd	BY	
Hounds Hill Centre	AY	
King St	AY	23
Lark Hill St	AY	24
New Bonny St	AY	25
North Park Drive	BY	26
Pleasant St	AY	27
Plymouth Rd	BZ	28
Poulton Rd	BY	29
Queen's Promenade	BY	
Reads Ave	BZ	32
Rigby Rd	BZ	33
Seaside Way	BZ	34
South King St	AY	35
South Park Drive	BZ	36
Talbot Square	AY	39
Topping St	AY	40
Westcliffe Drive	BY	41

ENGLAND

135

ENGLAND

🏨 Imperial ⟨ 🖼 🐕 🖥 ⚡ ♨ 🛁 ℙ VISA ⬤ AE ①
North Promenade ⊠ *FY1 2HB* – ℰ *(01253) 623 971* – *www.barcelo-hotels.co.uk*
– *imperialblackpool@barcelo-hotels.co.uk* – *Fax (01253) 751 784*   AY**c**
173 rm ⌑ – †£64/168 ††£84/178 – 7 suites
Rest *Palm Court* – (dinner only and Sunday lunch) Menu £23 **s**
♦ Imposing, classic 19C promenade hotel. Grand columned lobby, well-appointed rooms, many with views. Photos in the convivial No.10 bar recall PMs and past party conferences. Elegant restaurant with smartly liveried staff.

🏨 Hilton Blackpool ⟨ 🖼 🐕 🖥 ⚡ 🛁 rm, AC rest, ♨ 🛁 ℙ VISA ⬤ AE ①
North Promenade ⊠ *FY1 2JQ* – ℰ *(01253) 623 434*
– *www.hilton.co.uk/blackpool* – *reservations.blackpool@hilton.com*
– *Fax (01253) 294 371*   AY**x**
268 rm ⌑ – †£260 ††£270 – 6 suites
Rest *The Promenade* – (bar lunch Monday-Saturday) Menu £22
– Carte £21/30
♦ Open-plan, marble-floored lobby and smartly equipped rooms in contemporary style, almost all with views over the sea-front. Informal dining after cocktail lounge aperitifs.

🏨 Number One South Beach 🖥 🛁 rm, 🕯 ℙ VISA ⬤ ①
4 Harrowside West ⊠ *FY4 1NW* – ℰ *(01253) 343 900*
– *www.numberonehotels.com* – *info@numberonesouthbeach.com*
– *Fax (01253) 343 906*   BZ**v**
14 rm ⌑ – †£80 ††£145/150 – 1 suite
Rest – (Closed Sunday dinner) (dinner only and Sunday lunch) Menu £20
– Carte £23/31
♦ Modernised hotel on promenade. Contemporary interior with stylish, individually themed bedrooms; two with 4 posters. Superb bathrooms with whirlpool baths, luxury tiling and TVs. Restaurant with black runners on wood tables and vivid colour schemes; monthly menus provide interest.

🏠 Number One St Lukes without rest 🚗 ⚡ 🕯 ℙ VISA ⬤ ①
1 St Lukes Rd ⊠ *FY4 2EL* – ℰ *(01253) 343 901* – *www.numberoneblackpool.com*
– *info@numberoneblackpool.com* – *Fax (01253) 343 901*   AZ**a**
3 rm ⌑ – †£80/100 ††£125/130
♦ Engagingly run, enticingly stylish guesthouse. The good value nature of the establishment is further enhanced by an elegant breakfast room and luxuriously appointed bedrooms.

at Thornton Northeast : 5½ m. by A 584 - BY - on B 5412 – ⊠ **Blackpool**

✗✗ Twelve VISA ⬤ AE
Marsh Mill, Fleetwood Rd South, North :½ m. on A 585 ⊠ *FY5 4JZ* – ℰ *(01253)*
821 212 – *www.twelve-restaurant.co.uk* – *info@twelve-restaurant.co.uk*
– *Fax (01253) 821 212* – *Closed first 2 weeks January and Monday*
Rest – (dinner only and Sunday lunch) Menu £19/26 – Carte £29/42
♦ Attractively located in the shadow of famous restored windmill. Interesting, original dishes with a modern flair, employing abundance of local produce.

BLAKENEY – **Norfolk** – **504** X 25 – ⊠ **Holt**   15 **C1**
▶ London 127 mi – King's Lynn 37 mi – Norwich 28 mi

🏨 Blakeney ⟨ 🚗 🖼 🐕 🖥 🛁 🛁 ℙ VISA ⬤ AE ①
The Quay ⊠ *NR25 7NE* – ℰ *(01263) 740 797* – *www.blakeney-hotel.co.uk*
– *reception@blakeney-hotel.co.uk* – *Fax (01263) 740 795*
63 rm ⌑ – †£138/212 ††£276/304
Rest – (light lunch Monday-Saturday) Menu £28 – Carte £28/42
♦ Traditional hotel on the quayside with views of estuary and a big sky! Sun lounge a delightful spot for the vista. Bedrooms vary in size and décor, some with private patio. Armchair dining with estuary views.

XX **The Moorings**   VISA 𝕄𝕆
High St ⊠ NR25 7NA – ℰ (01263) 740 054 – www.blakeney-moorings.co.uk
– reservations@blakeney-moorings.co.uk
– Closed 10 days January and Sunday dinner
Rest – (booking essential) Carte £ 25/32
♦ Bright village bistro near the estuary, offering popular light lunches. Classical
dinner menu boasts unfussy, seasonal dishes, including game and local seafood.
Good puddings.

🏠 **The White Horse** with rm   🗺 🍴 **P** VISA 𝕄𝕆
4 High St ⊠ NR25 7AL – ℰ (01263) 740 574 – www.blakeneywhitehorse.co.uk
– info@blakeneywhitehorse.co.uk – Fax (01263) 741 303 – Closed 25 December
9 rm ☐ – †£80 ††£140   **Rest** – Menu £ 20/32 – Carte £ 18/30
♦ Part 17C brick-and-flint coaching inn near the harbour. Friendly, real ale bar and
small dining room to the front, with appealing, seasonal cooking. Cosy rooms.

at Cley next the Sea East : 1½ m. on A 149 – ⊠ Holt

🏠 **Cley Windmill** ⌂   ⩽ 🗺 🍴 **P** VISA 𝕄𝕆
The Quay ⊠ NR25 7RP – ℰ (01263) 740 209 – www.cleywindmill.co.uk
– info@cleywindmill.co.uk
10 rm ☐ – ††£92/145
Rest – (by arrangement, communal dining) Menu £ 25 (dinner)
♦ Restored 18C redbrick windmill in salt marshes with a viewing gallery: a bird-
watcher's paradise. Neatly kept rooms, full of character, in the mill, stable and
boatshed. Flagstoned dining room; communal table.

🏠 **Old Town Hall House** without rest   🍴 VISA 𝕄𝕆
Coast Rd ⊠ NR25 7RB – ℰ (01263) 740 284 – www.oldtownhallhouse.co.uk
– March - mid December
3 rm ☐ – †£75 ††£95
♦ Victorian house in small, coastal village, with relaxed, bohemian style. Modern,
unfussy bedrooms with simple facilities; no TV. Neat, compact shower rooms. Local/
homemade breakfast.

🏠 **The George** with rm   🗺 🗺 **P** VISA 𝕄𝕆
High St ⊠ NR25 7RN – ℰ (01263) 740 652 – www.thegeorgehotelatcley.co.uk
– info@thegeorgehotelatcley.co.uk – Fax (01263) 741 275 – Closed 25 December
12 rm ☐ – †£40/70 ††£50/130 – 1 suite   **Rest** – Carte £ 15/25
♦ Imposing, stalwart Victorian/Edwardian pub. Warmly hued bar and restaurant. Rustic British cuisine to fore; lots of local seafood. Book top floor bedrooms for best views.

at Morston West : 1½ m. on A 149 – ⊠ Holt

🏠🏠 **Morston Hall** (Galton Blackiston) ⌂   🗺 🍴 **P** VISA 𝕄𝕆 AE ⓪
⍟ The Street ⊠ NR25 7AA – ℰ (01263) 741 041 – www.morstonhall.com
– reception@morstonhall.com – Fax (01263) 740 419 – Closed 2 days Christmas
and 1-30 January
13 rm ☐ – †£230 ††£300/340
Rest – (dinner only and Sunday lunch) (booking essential) (set menu only)
Menu £ 42 **s**
Spec. Pea mousse with slow poached pullet egg and crispy bacon. Roast loin
and confit shoulder of lamb with parmentier new potatoes and Paloise sauce.
Feuillatine of berries, lemon balm ice cream and champagne sabayon.
♦ Attractive, ivy covered country house in quiet village, very personally run by husband and wife team. Modern bedrooms. Accomplished menu offers balanced, sea-
sonal dishes made from fine, locally sourced ingredients. Pleasant conservatory.

at Wiveton South : 1m by A149 on Wiveton Rd

🏠 **The Wiveton Bell** with rm   🗺 🍴 **P** VISA 𝕄𝕆
Blakeney Rd ⊠ NR25 7TL – ℰ (01263) 740 101 – www.wivetonbell.com
2 rm ☐ – †£82/85 ††£130
Rest – (Closed Sunday dinner in winter) (booking advisable) Carte £ 19/28
♦ Charming pub in an attractive spot. Traditional à la carte menu offers mainly Brit-
ish dishes with some international influence; salads and light meals also available.
Charming, comfortable bedrooms.

ENGLAND

BLANDFORD FORUM – Dorset – 503 N 31 – pop. 9 854 — 4 C3

- London 124 mi – Bournemouth 17 mi – Dorchester 17 mi – Salisbury 24 mi
- 1 Greyhound Yard ℰ (01258) 454770, blandfordtic@north-dorset.gov.uk
- Ashley Wood Wimborne Rd, ℰ (01258) 452 253
- Town ★
- Kingston Lacy ★★ **AC**, SE : 5 ½ m. by B 3082 – Royal Signals Museum ★, NE : 2 m. by B 3082. Milton Abbas ★, SW : 8 m. by A 354 – Sturminster Newton ★, NW : 8 m. by A 357

⌂ **Portman Lodge** without rest ⁽ᵗ⁾ **P** VISA ⬤⬤
Whitecliff Mill Street ⊠ DT11 7BP – ℰ (01258) 453 727
– www.portmanlodge.co.uk – enquiries@portmanlodge.co.uk
– Closed 23 December - 15 January
3 rm ⊡ – ♦£50 ♦♦£70
♦ Red brick Victorian house close to Georgian town centre; many original features. All rooms crammed with artefacts; individually decorated bedrooms with unique identities and styles.

at Farnham Northeast : 7 ½ m. by A 354 – ⊠ Blandford Forum

⌂ **Farnham Farm House** without rest ⌕ ≤ 🖙 ♨ ⊃ **P** VISA ⬤⬤ AE
North : 1m. by Shaftesbury rd ⊠ DT11 8DG – ℰ (01725) 516 254
– www.farnhamfarmhouse.co.uk – info@farnhamfarmhouse.co.uk – Fax (01725) 516 306 – Closed 25-26 December
3 rm ⊡ – ♦£60 ♦♦£80
♦ Attractive farmhouse in peaceful location. Simple, individually furnished bedrooms with country views. Swimming pool and therapy centre on site. Breakfast features local produce; picnics available.

⏠ **The Museum Inn** with rm 🖙 **P** VISA ⬤⬤
⊠ DT11 8DE – ℰ (01725) 516 261 – www.museuminn.co.uk
– enquiries@museuminn.co.uk – Fax (01725) 516 988 – Closed 25 December, dinner 31 December and 1 January
8 rm ⊡ – ♦£95 ♦♦£120   **Rest** – (bookings not accepted) Carte £ 25/35
♦ Part thatched 17C country pub, in a picture postcard village. Menu offers British classics with a Mediterranean edge; cooking is seasonal, unfussy and local. Bedrooms range from small and cottagey, to spacious with four-posters.

at Chettle Northeast : 7 ¼ m. by A 354 – ⊠ Blandford Forum

XX **Castleman** with rm ⌕ ≤ 🖙 ♨ **P** VISA ⬤⬤
⊠ DT11 8DB – ℰ (01258) 830 096 – www.castlemanhotel.co.uk
– enquiry@castlemanhotel.co.uk – Fax (01258) 830 051
– Closed February and 25-26 and 31 December
8 rm ⊡ – ♦£50 ♦♦£80/90
Rest – (dinner only and Sunday lunch) Menu £ 21 (lunch) – Carte £ 20/27
♦ Traditional feel to this part 16C dower house with Victorian extensions. Classical cooking with ingredients sourced from small local producers; game from their own estate. Spacious, traditionally-styled bedrooms.

at Iwerne Minster North : 6 m. on A 350

⏠ **The Talbot** with rm 🖙 ⁽ᵗ⁾ **P** VISA ⬤⬤
Iwerne Minster ⊠ DT11 8QN – ℰ (01747) 811 269 – www.the-talbot.com
– enquiries@the-talbot.com – Fax (01747) 811 269
5 rm ⊡ – ♦£65/75 ♦♦£80/95   **Rest** – Carte £ 18/26
♦ Pleasant and unfussy mock-Elizabethan inn. Hearty and generous cooking features British classics at lunch and substantial, regularly-changing dishes in the evening. Rooms are comfortable, well-appointed and up-to-date.

BLEDINGTON – Oxon. – 503 P 28 – see Stow-on-the-Wold

 Look out for red symbols, indicating particularly pleasant establishments.

BLEDLOW – Buckinghamshire – pop. 2 249 – ⊠ **Princes Risborough**   11 **C2**
 ▶ London 43 mi – High Wycombe 9 mi – Oxford 21 mi

⌂
⌂◻   **The Old Station** without rest ⌂
    Sandpit Lane ⊠ HP27 9QQ – ℰ (01844) 345 086
    – www.theoldstation-bledlow.co.uk – ianmackinson@hotmail.com
    4 rm – ♦£49/60 ♦♦£69/70
    ♦ A station until 1994 - the owner's relations used to be station masters. Now a
    comfortable guest house, the breakfast room was once the station waiting room.
    Homely bedrooms.

BLOCKLEY – Gloucestershire – 503 O 27 – ⊠ **Moreton-in-Marsh**   4 **D1**
 ▶ London 91 mi – Birmingham 39 mi – Oxford 34 mi

⌂   **Lower Brook House**   P. VISA ◐ AE
    Lower St ⊠ GL56 9DS – ℰ (01386) 700 286 – www.lowerbrookhouse.com
    – info@lowerbrookhouse.com – Fax (01386) 701 400 – Closed Christmas
    6 rm ⌂ – ♦£80/175 ♦♦£95/175
    Rest – (closed Sunday) (dinner only) (booking essential for non-residents)
    Menu £25
    ♦ Personally run, adjoining 17C Cotswold stone cottages with huge inglenooks,
    beams and flagged floors. Characterful and stylish from every aspect. Individually
    appointed rooms. Imaginative evening menus of local Cotswold produce.

BLUNDELLSANDS – Mersey. – 502 L 23 – **see Liverpool**

BLUNSDON – Wilts. – 503 O 29 – **see Swindon**

BLYTH – Nottinghamshire – 502 Q 23 – ⊠ **Worksop**   16 **B1**
 ▶ London 166 mi – Doncaster 13 mi – Lincoln 30 mi – Nottingham 32 mi
   – Sheffield 20 mi

⌂⌂⌂   **Charnwood**   ▦ ⌂ AC rest, ⌂ ⌂ ⌂ P. VISA ◐ AE ◐
    Sheffield Rd, West : ¾ m. on A 634 ⊠ S81 8HF – ℰ (01909) 591 610
    – www.bw-charnwood-hotel.co.uk – charnwood@bestwestern.co.uk
    – Fax (01909) 591 427
    45 rm ⌂ – ♦£65/95 ♦♦£105/145
    Rest – (Closed Sunday dinner) Menu £18 (lunch) – Carte £27/44
    ♦ Well suited to the business traveller, this hotel offers consistently well-kept bed-
    rooms. Its most recent additions are spacious, stylish, well-equipped and overlook the
    garden. A lounge bar offers informal dining; the large restaurant is smart with up-to-
    date décor.

BODMIN – Cornwall – 503 F 32 – pop. 12 778   1 **B2**
 ▶ London 270 mi – Newquay 18 mi – Plymouth 32 mi – Truro 23 mi
 ⓘ Shire Hall, Mount Folly ℰ (01208) 76616, bodmintic@visit.org.uk
 ◉ St Petroc Church★
 ◖ Bodmin Moor★★ - Lanhydrock★★, S : 3 m. by B 3269 – Blisland★
   (Church★), N : 5½ m. by A 30 and minor roads – Pencarrow★, NW : 4 m.
   by A 389 and minor roads – Cardinham (Church★), NE : 4 m. by A 30 and
   minor rd – St Mabyn (Church★), N : 5½ m. by A 389, B 3266 and minor rd.
   St Tudy★, N : 7 m. by A 389, B 3266 and minor rd

⌂   **Trehellas House**   ▦ ⌂ ⌂ P. VISA ◐ AE
    Washaway, Northwest: 3 m. on A 389 ⊠ PL30 3AD – ℰ (01208) 72 700
    – www.trehellashouse.co.uk – trehellashouse@btconnect.com
    – Fax (01208) 73 336
    12 rm ⌂ – ♦£50/72 ♦♦£80/130
    Rest – Menu £15/25 – Carte dinner £32/47 **s**
    ♦ Relaxed, personally run country house with keen owners. Bedrooms divided be-
    tween main house and converted stable. Cosy and cottagey feel without being
    chintzy. Traditional cooking; venison a speciality.

ENGLAND

⌂ **Bokiddick Farm** without rest ⌖   🚗 🕪 🍴 **P** **VISA** **①**

Lanivet, South : 5 m. by A 30 following signs for Lanhydrock and Bokiddick
✉ PL30 5HP – ✆ (01208) 831 481 – www.bokiddickfarm.co.uk
– gillhugo@bokiddickfarm.co.uk – Fax (01208) 831 481 – Closed Christmas and
New Year

5 rm ⌂ – †£45/50 ††£62/76

♦ Sizeable house on dairy farm: do take a quick tour. Warm welcome assured. Neat,
well priced rooms with added amenities in old house; smart stable conversion for
more rooms.

BODSHAM – Kent   9 **C2**

▶ London 65 mi – Ashford 10 mi – Canterbury 10 mi

🍴 **Froggies at the Timber Batts**   🚗 **P** **VISA** **①** **AE**

School Lane ✉ TN25 5JQ – ✆ (01223) 750 237 – www.thetimberbatts.co.uk
– post@thetimberbatts.co.uk – Fax (01223) 750 176 – Closed one week at
Christmas

Rest – French – (closed Monday and Tuesday after Bank Holidays) Menu 26
– Carte £30/38

♦ All things ranine are celebrated at this 15C pub, thanks to the jolly French owner
with a sense of irony. Traditional beamed bar. Authentic French dishes and classic
desserts.

BOLNHURST – Bedfordshire   12 **A1**

▶ London 64 mi – Bedford 8 mi – St Neots 7 mi

🍴 **The Plough at Bolnhurst**   🚗 🛋 **P** **VISA** **①**

Kimbolton Rd, South : ½ m. on B 660 ✉ MK44 2EX – ✆ (01234) 376 274
– www.bolnhurst.com – theplough@bolnhurst.com
– Closed 31 December and 2 weeks in January

Rest – (Closed Sunday dinner and Monday) Menu £17 – Carte £26/35

♦ Restored, whitewashed pub with spacious, rustic interior, smart terrace and pleasant gardens. Assured service from smartly dressed staff. Wide-ranging, seasonal
menu.

BOLTON ABBEY – North Yorkshire – **502** O 22 – ✉ Skipton   22 **B2**

📗 *Great Britain*

▶ London 216 mi – Harrogate 18 mi – Leeds 23 mi – Skipton 6 mi
◉ Bolton Priory ★ **AC**

🏨 **The Devonshire Arms Country House** ⌖   ⟨ 🚗 🕪 🔸 🔲

✉ BD23 6AJ – ✆ (01756) 710 441   🏊 🛖 🏋 🍴 🏌 🔸 **P** **VISA** **①** **AE** **①**
– www.devonshirehotels.co.uk – res@devonshirehotels.co.uk
– Fax (01756) 710 564

38 rm ⌂ – †£180 ††£370 – 2 suites

Rest *The Burlington* **and** *The Brasserie* – see restaurant listing

♦ Sympathetically restored period coaching inn. Bar and comfy sitting rooms filled
with antiques, open fires and curios aplenty. Pleasant, floral themed bedrooms boast
quality furnishings.

𝕏𝕏𝕏𝕏 **The Burlington** – at The Devonshire Arms Country House Hotel   ⟨ 🚗 🕪

✉ BD23 6AJ – ✆ (01756) 710 441   🍴 **P** **VISA** **①** **AE** **①**
– www.devonshirehotels.co.uk – res@devonshirehotels.co.uk
– Fax (01756) 710 564

Rest – (closed Monday) (dinner only and Sunday lunch) Menu £58

Spec. Foie gras terrine with fig purée and red wine jelly. Halibut with clams,
cèpe gnocchi and tonka bean foam. 'Chocolate mayhem', passion fruit purée
and peanut ice cream.

♦ Elegant formal dining room filled with antiques. Precise and appealingly presented
seasonal cooking; game and fish from local Bolton Abbey Estate, herbs and veg from
the kitchen garden.

ENGLAND

XX **The Brasserie** – at The Devonshire Arms Country House Hotel   VISA ⓒⓞ AE ①
⊠ BD23 6AJ – ℰ (01756) 710 441 – www.devonshirehotels.co.uk
– res@devonshirehotels.co.uk – Fax (01756) 710 564
Rest – Carte approx. £ 22
♦ A contrast to the restaurant in atmosphere and design. This is a modern, vividly decorated brasserie; the kitchen produces carefully prepared, satisfying brasserie favourites.

BOLTON-BY-BOWLAND – Lancashire – **502** M/N 22 ▌ Great Britain   20 **B2**
▶ London 246 mi – Blackburn 17 mi – Skipton 15 mi
◖ Skipton - Castle ★, E : 12 m. by A 59 – Bolton Priory ★, E : 17 m. by A 59

↑ **Middle Flass Lodge** ⌂   🗏 ☆ P VISA ⓒⓞ
Settle Rd, North : 2 ½ m. by Clitheroe rd on Settle rd ⊠ BB7 4NY – ℰ (01200)
447 259 – www.middleflasslodge.co.uk – middleflasslodge@btconnect.com
– Fax (01200) 447 300
7 rm ⌑ – ♥£ 44/54 ♥♥£ 60/75   **Rest** – (by arrangement) Carte £ 26/35
♦ Friendly, welcoming owners in a delightfully located barn conversion. Plenty of
beams add to rustic effect. Pleasantly decorated, comfy rooms with countryside
outlook. Blackboard's eclectic menu boasts local, seasonal backbone.

BONCHURCH – Isle of Wight – **504** P 32 – see Wight (Isle of)

BOROUGHBRIDGE – North Yorkshire – **502** P 21 – pop. 3 311   22 **B2**
▶ London 215 mi – Leeds 19 mi – Middlesbrough 36 mi – York 16 mi
🖪 2 Fishergate ℰ (01423) 323 373

XX **thediningroom**   VISA ⓒⓞ
☺ 20 St James's Sq ⊠ YO51 9AR – ℰ (01423) 326 426
– www.thediningroomonline.co.uk – Fax (01423) 326 426 – Closed 26 December,
1 January, Sunday dinner and Monday
Rest – (dinner only and Sunday lunch) (booking essential) Menu £ 28 (dinner)
– Carte lunch £ 25/28
♦ Characterful cottage with beamed dining room. Vivid fireside sofas and Impressionist oils, as modern as the well-prepared dishes: duck on rocket and pesto features.

at Roecliffe

🍴 **The Crown Inn**   P VISA ⓒⓞ
⊠ YO5 9LY – ℰ (01423) 322 300 – www.crowninnroecliffe.com
– info@crowninnroecliffe.com – Fax (01423) 322 035
Rest – Carte £ 20/40
♦ 16C coaching inn with flagstones, beams and open fires. Locally sourced produce
used in classical, carefully-crafted cooking, served in the bar and elegant restaurant.

BORROWDALE – Cumbria – **502** K 20 – see Keswick

BOSCASTLE – Cornwall – **503** F 31   1 **B2**
▶ London 260 mi – Bude 14 mi – Exeter 59 mi – Plymouth 43 mi
◎ Village ★
◖ Poundstock Church ★ – Tintagel Old Post Office ★

↑ **Trerosewill Farm** without rest ⌂   ≪ 🗏 🕭 ☆ ⟨⟨ P VISA ⓒⓞ
Paradise, South : 1 m. off B 3263 ⊠ PL35 0BL – ℰ (01840) 250 545
– www.trerosewill.co.uk – cheryl@trerosewill.co.uk – Fax (01840) 250 727 – Closed
mid December-mid January
8 rm ⌑ – ♥£ 50/85 ♥♥£ 80/95
♦ Modern house on 50-acre working farm: fine views of the coast and good clifftop
walks. Lovely conservatory breakfast room. Bedrooms in matching patterns, some
with Jacuzzis.

ENGLAND

BOSCASTLE

↑↑ **Old Rectory** without rest ⑤   📠 ❝ 🅿 VISA ⊕
St Juliot, Northeast : 2 1/2 m. by B 3263 ⊠ PL35 0BT – ℰ (01840) 250 225
– www.stjuliot.com – sally@stjuliot.com – Fax (01840) 250 225 – Closed December
and January
4 rm ⌑ – ❢£45/60 ❢❢£80/90
♦ Communal breakfast room, with views of Victorian walled garden, from whence
much of the produce comes. Characterful bedrooms; one in converted stables.
Thomas Hardy stayed here.

BOSHAM – W. Sussex – **504** R 31 – see Chichester

BOSTON SPA – West Yorkshire – **502** P 22 – pop. 5 952   22 **B2**
▶ London 127 mi – Harrogate 12 mi – Leeds 12 mi – York 16 mi

↑↑ **Four Gables** without rest ⑤   📠 ❝ 🅿
Oaks Lane, West : ¼ m. by A 659 ⊠ LS23 6DS – ℰ (01937) 845 592
– www.fourgables.co.uk – info@fourgables.co.uk – Closed Christmas and January
4 rm ⌑ – ❢£50/60 ❢❢£78/88
♦ Down a quiet private road, a 1900 house, after Lutyens: period fireplaces, stripped
oak and terracotta tile floors. Traditional, individually decorated rooms. Mature garden.

BOUGHTON MONCHELSEA Kent – Kent – pop. 2 863   8 **B2**
▶ London 46 mi – Southend-on-Sea 60 mi – Basildon 48 mi – Maidstone 4 mi

✗ **The Mulberry Tree**   📠 ☕ 🅿 VISA ⊕
Hermitage Lane, South : 1½ m. by Park Lane and East Hall Hill ⊠ ME17 4DA
– ℰ (01622) 749 082 – www.themulberrytreekent.co.uk
– info@themulberrytreekent.co.uk – Fax (01622) 741 058
Rest – (closed Sunday dinner) Menu £16 (weekday lunch) – Carte £21/26
♦ Remotely situated, stylishly decorated, family-owned restaurant with enclosed gar-
den. Daily-changing menus offer modern, tasty dishes, homemade using the best lo-
cal produce.

BOULEY BAY – **503** L 33 – see Channel Islands (Jersey)

BOURNEMOUTH – Bournemouth – **503** – pop. 167 527   4 **D3**
▶ London 114 mi – Bristol 76 mi – Southampton 34 mi
✈ Bournemouth (Hurn) Airport : ℰ (01202) 364000, N : 5 m. by Hurn - DV
🛈 Westover Rd ℰ (0845) 0511700, info@bournemouth.gov.uk
⛳ Queens Park Queens Park West Drive, ℰ (01202) 302 611
⛳ Meyrick Park Central Drive, ℰ (01202) 786 000
🏛 Compton Acres★★ (English Garden ≤★★★) AC AX – Russell-Cotes Art
Gallery and Museum★★ AC DZ M1 - Shelley Rooms AC EX M2
🏞 Poole★, W : 4 m. by A 338 – Brownsea Island★ (Baden-Powell Stone ≤★★)
AC, by boat from Sandbanks BX or Poole Quay – Christchurch★ (Priory
Church★) E : 4½ m. on A 35. Corfe Castle★, SW : 18 m. by A 35 and A 351
– Lulworth Cove★ (Blue Pool★) W : 8 m. of Corfe Castle by B 3070 –
Swanage★, E : 5 m. of Corfe Castle by A 351

Plans on following pages

🏨 **Bournemouth Highcliff Marriott**   ≤ 📠 🔥 ⋢ 🖵 ♨ 💆 ✗
St Michael's Rd, West Cliff ⊠ BH2   📶 ⅃ rm, 🅼 ❄ ☕ 💪 🅿 VISA ⊕ AE ⊕
5DU – ℰ (0870) 400 72 11 – www.bournemouthhighcliffmarriott.co.uk
– Fax (01202) 293 155   CZ**z**
157 rm ⌑ – ❢£150/270 ❢❢£160/280 – 3 suites
Rest – (buffet lunch) Carte £25/36
♦ Imposing white clifftop landmark, linked by funicular to the beach. Elegant drawing rooms; bedrooms, in the grand tradition, and leisure centre are comprehensively
equipped. Secure a bay view table in elegant formal restaurant.

142

Norfolk Royale 　　🔲 📺 🏠 🛗 ⅙ rm, 🅰🅲 rest, ⚡ 📞 ♨ 🚗 🏧 _VISA_ 🆔 ①
Richmond Hill ⊠ *BH2 6EN* – ℰ *(01202) 551 521* – *www.englishrosehotels.co.uk*
– *sales@englishrosehotels.co.uk*
– *Fax (01202) 294 031*　　　　　　　　　　　　　　　　　　　　　CY**u**
91 rm ⌿ – ♥£129/159 ♥♥£179 – 4 suites
Rest *Echoes* – Menu £30 – Carte £30/45
♦ Edwardian hotel, once the summer retreat of the Duke of Norfolk. Bold, modern colours brighten the neat bedrooms; the lobby, with its deep sofas, has a more clubby feel. Spacious candlelit conservatory dining room.

 The Chine 　　⟨ ☕ 🔲 📺 🏠 ⅙ 🛗 ♨ 🅿 _VISA_ 🆀 🅰🅴
Boscombe Spa Rd ⊠ *BH5 1AX* – ℰ *(01202) 396 234* – *www.fjbhotels.co.uk*
– *reservations@chinehotel.co.uk* – *Fax (01202) 391 737*　　　　　　DX**e**
88 rm ⌿ – ♥£45/85 ♥♥£150/170
Rest – (closed Saturday lunch) (buffet lunch) Menu £26
♦ Extended former spa takes its name from the chine or ravine that runs down to the sea. Bedrooms vary in shape and size; those in west wing slightly more up to date. Restaurant with sweeping views over the treetops.

Miramar 　　⟨ ☕ 🛗 ⅙ rm, 🔥 🅿 _VISA_ 🆀 🅰🅴
19 Grove Rd, East Overcliff ⊠ *BH1 3AL* – ℰ *(01202) 556 581*
– *www.miramar-bournemouth.com* – *sales@miramar-bournemouth.com*
– *Fax (01202) 291 242*　　　　　　　　　　　　　　　　　　　　　DZ**u**
43 rm ⌿ – ♥£37/87 ♥♥£74/164
Rest – (closed Saturday lunch) Menu £15/26
♦ Along the handsome lines of a grand Edwardian villa. Large, well cared for rooms, a few with curved balconies, in floral patterns. Library and a sun terrace facing the sea. Traditional menu.

Urban Beach 　　📶 ⁽ᵗ⁾ _VISA_ 🆀 🅰🅴
23 Argyll Road ⊠ *BH5 1EB* – ℰ *(01202) 301 509* – *www.urbanbeachhotel.co.uk*
– *info@urbanbeachhotel.co.uk*　　　　　　　　　　　　　　　　　DEX**r**
12 rm ⌿ – ♥£70/145 ♥♥£135/145　　**Rest** – Carte £20/31
♦ Close to the beach and town, with large decked terrace; small reception in trendy bar/bistro. Unremarkable exterior hides spacious designer bedrooms and stylish, luxury bathrooms. Large menu of modern classics and steaks.

XX **Noble House** 　　🅰🅲 _VISA_ 🆀 🅰🅴 ①
3-5 Lansdowne Rd ⊠ *BH1 1RZ* – ℰ *(01202) 291 277* – *www.noble-house.co.uk*
– *Fax (01202) 291 312* – *Closed 25-26 December and Sunday*　　　DEY**i**
Rest – Chinese – Menu £6/12 – Carte £13/22
♦ A hospitable family team are behind a comprehensive menu of authentic Chinese cuisine, carefully prepared from fresh ingredients. Smoothly run; handy town centre location.

X **West Beach** 　　📶 _VISA_ 🆀 🅰🅴
Pier Approach ⊠ *BH2 5AA* – ℰ *(01202) 587 785*
– *www.west-beach.co.uk*　　　　　　　　　　　　　　　　　　　DZ**c**
Rest – Seafood – (booking essential at lunch) Carte £26/55
♦ Seafood restaurant on the beach, with folding glass doors and a decked terrace. Busy - particularly at lunch. Fish and shellfish caught locally; some in front of restaurant.

ENGLAND

Your opinions are important to us:
please write and let us know about your discoveries and experiences – good and bad!

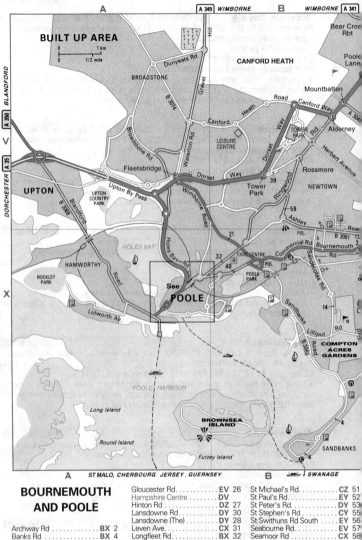

BOURNEMOUTH AND POOLE

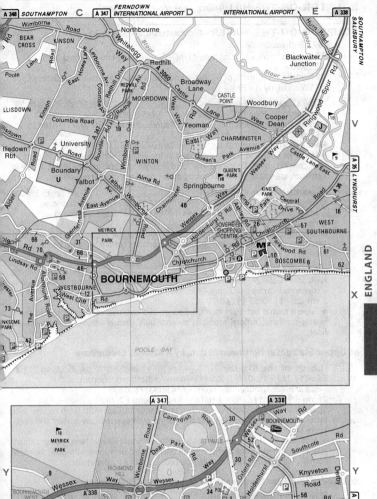

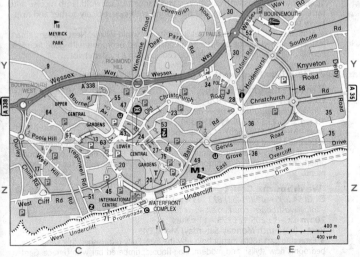

BOURTON-ON-THE-WATER – Gloucestershire – **503** O 28   4 **D1**
– pop. 3 093 ▌ *Great Britain*

▶ London 91 mi – Birmingham 47 mi – Gloucester 24 mi – Oxford 36 mi
◉ Town ★
◎ Northleach (Church of SS. Peter and Paul ★, Wool Merchants' Brasses ★),
SW : 5 m. by A 429

The Dial House
The Chestnuts, High St ✉ *GL54 2AG* – ✆ *(01451) 822 244*
– *www.dialhousehotel.com* – *info@dialhousehotel.com* – *Fax (01451) 810 126*
13 rm ⌂ – †£160/200 ††£180/240
Rest – (booking essential for non-residents) Carte £27/40
♦ House of Cotswold stone - the oldest in the village - with lovely lawned gardens
and drawing room. Bedrooms mix of the contemporary and the floral; those in
extension are smaller. Refined cooking makes good use of local ingredients.

Coombe House without rest
Rissington Rd ✉ *GL54 2DT* – ✆ *(01451) 821 966* – *www.coombehouse.net*
– *info@coombehouse.net* – *Fax (01451) 810 477* – *Restricted opening in winter*
6 rm ⌂ – †£50/60 ††£70/80
♦ Creeper-clad 1920s house on the quiet outskirts of the village, near the local bird
sanctuary. Homely lounge and spotless, comfortable, cottage style bedrooms in soft
chintz.

Manor Close without rest
High St ✉ *GL54 2AP* – ✆ *(01451) 820 339* – *www.manorclosedbandb.com*
– *sheenamanorclose@aol.com* – *Closed 25 December*
3 rm ⌂ – †£50/55 ††£60/70
♦ Superb central but quiet location. Lounge and breakfast room in Cotswold stone
house; comfortable floral rooms in purpose-built garden annexe, one on ground
floor.

at Upper Slaughter Northwest : 2 ½ m. by A 429 – ✉ Cheltenham

Lords of the Manor ⌘
✉ *GL54 2JD* – ✆ *(01451) 820 243* – *www.lordsofthemanor.com*
– *enquiries@lordsofthemanor.com* – *Fax (01451) 820 696*
26 rm – †£195 ††£380 – 1 suite   **Rest** – Menu £26/49
Spec. Roast scallops with cauliflower and pancetta. Cotswold lamb niçoise and
tapenade jus. Vanilla parfait and nougatine with sweet cicely sorbet and raspberry soup.
♦ Attractive 17C former rectory set in pretty Cotswold village. Neat gardens; smart
leather furnished lounge and bar; traditionally styled bedrooms with good facilities.
Formal dining room; confident, classical cooking with a modern twist.

at Lower Slaughter Northwest : 1 ¾ m. by A 429 – ✉ Cheltenham

Lower Slaughter Manor ⌘
✉ *GL54 2HP* – ✆ *(01451) 820 456* – *www.lowerslaughter.co.uk*
– *info@lowerslaughter.co.uk* – *Fax (01451) 822 150*
19 rm ⌂ – †£175/215 ††£310/390
Rest – Menu £31 (lunch) – Carte dinner £37/61
♦ Beautiful listed part 17C manor in warm Cotswold stone with lovely garden. Open
fires and period detail throughout; furnishings and fabrics rich yet contemporary.
Smart, boldly coloured bedrooms. Elegant dining room with French-influenced
menu.

Washbourne Court
✉ *GL54 2HS* – ✆ *(01451) 822 143* – *www.washbournecourt.co.uk*
– *info@washbournecourt.co.uk* – *Fax (01451) 821 045*
20 rm ⌂ – †£205 ††£375 – 11 suites
Rest – (bar lunch Monday-Saturday) Menu £45
♦ Extended part 1800s manor house by the Eyre. Fully refurbished following a flood;
bedrooms now stylish and modern. Flag-floored, timbered bar with terrace. Garden
and local produce used in the restaurant.

ENGLAND

BOVEY TRACEY – Devon – 503 I 32 – ⊠ Newton Abbot

- ▶ London 214 mi – Exeter 14 mi – Plymouth 32 mi
- ▦ Newton Abbot, ℰ (01626) 52 460
- ◎ St Peter, St Paul and St Thomas of Canterbury Church★
- ◉ Dartmoor National Park★★

🏠 Edgemoor   🚗 ᵴ P VISA ⲟⲟ
Haytor Rd, West : 1 m. on B 3387 ⊠ TQ13 9LE – ℰ (01626) 832 466
– www.edgemoor.co.uk – reservations@edgemoor.co.uk – Fax (01626) 834 760
– Closed 2-15 January
16 rm ⊑ – ♦£95/125 ♦♦£160 **Rest** – (bar lunch) Menu £35 – Carte £26/37
♦ Country style, creeper-clad former school house. Lofty beamed, firelit lounge has deep chintz armchairs. Smart rooms - in main house or ex-schoolrooms - in floral prints. Elegantly proportioned dining room.

🏠 Brookfield House without rest ⑤   🚗 ⁒ P VISA ⲟⲟ
Challabrook Lane, Southwest : ¾ m. by Brimley rd ⊠ TQ13 9DF – ℰ (01626)
836 181 – www.brookfield-house.com – enquiries@brookfield-house.com – Closed
December-January
3 rm ⊑ – ♦£50/54 ♦♦£70/78
♦ Well-kept early Edwardian house in two acres of attractive gardens surrounded by Dartmoor. The three large bedrooms have expansive windows and are immaculately appointed.

at Haytor Vale West : 3½ m. by B 3387 – ⊠ Newton Abbot

🏠 The Rock Inn with rm   🚗 ⁒ ⁒ ⑨ P VISA ⲟⲟ
⊠ TQ13 9XP – ℰ (01364) 661 305 – www.rock-inn.co.uk – cg@rock-inn.co.uk
– Fax (01364) 661 242 – Closed 25-26 December
9 rm ⊑ – ♦£67/88 ♦♦£117 **Rest** – Menu £21 (dinner) – Carte £22/33
♦ Attractive 18C former coaching inn. Rustic charm aplenty with log fires, beams and sloping floors. Simple bar menu; more elaborate restaurant menu. Bedrooms named after Grand National winners.

BOWNESS-ON-WINDERMERE – Cumbria – 502 L 20 – see Windermere

BOX – Bath & North East Somerset – 503 N 29 – see Bath

BRADFORD – West Yorkshire – 502 O 22 – pop. 293 717 🏛 *Great Britain*   22 **B2**
- ▶ London 212 mi – Leeds 9 mi – Manchester 39 mi – Middlesbrough 75 mi
  – Sheffield 45 mi
- ✈ Leeds and Bradford Airport : ℰ (0113) 250 9696, NE : 6 m. by A 658 BX
- 🛈 City Hall ℰ (01274) 433678, tourist.information@bradford.gov.uk
- ▦ West Bowling Rooley Lane, Newall Hall, ℰ (01274) 728 036
- ▦ Woodhall Hills Pudsley Woodhall Rd, Calverley, ℰ (0113) 256 4771
- ▥ Bradford Moor Pollard Lane Scarr Hall, ℰ (01274) 771 716
- ▥ East Brierley South View Rd, ℰ (01274) 681 023
- ▥ Queensbury Brighouse Rd, ℰ (01274) 882 155
- ◎ City★ – National Media Museum★ AZ **M**

Plan of Enlarged Area : see Leeds

Plan on next page

🏨 Hilton Bradford   📶 ᵹ rm, 🅰🅒 rest, ⁒ ᵴ VISA ⲟⲟ AE ①
Hall Ings ⊠ BD1 5SH – ℰ (01274) 734 734 – www.hilton.co.uk
– Fax (01274) 306 146
116 rm ⊑ – ♦£65/105 ♦♦£75/115 – 5 suites
Rest *City 3* – Menu £15/19 – Carte £26/32
♦ City centre hotel, convenient for rail travellers. Don't be put off by dated 60s exterior. Well-equipped rooms; some look over City Hall. Comfortable cocktail lounge. Easy informality is the by-word in restaurant.

ENGLAND

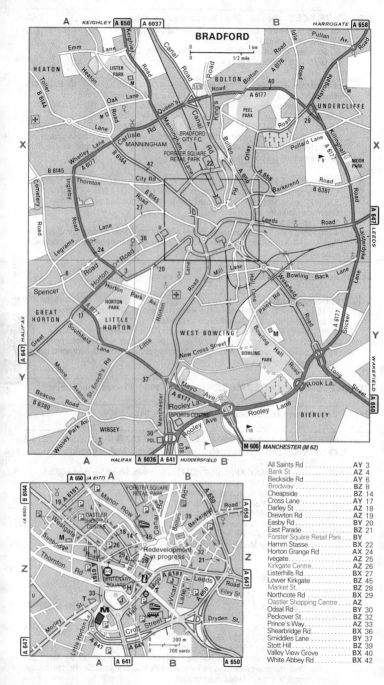

BRADFORD

BRADFORD-ON-AVON – Wiltshire – 503 N 29 – pop. 9 072 4 C2

- ▶ London 118 mi – Bristol 24 mi – Salisbury 35 mi – Swindon 33 mi
- 🖪 The Greenhouse 🖋 (01225) 865797, tic@bradfordonavon.co.uk
- 🔘 Town★★ - Saxon Church of St Lawrence★★ - Tithe Barn★ - Bridge★
- 🔘 Great Chalfield Manor★ (All Saints★) AC, NE : 3 m. by B 3109 – Westwood Manor★ AC, S : 1 ½ m. by B 3109 – Top Rank Tory (≤★). Bath★★★, NW : 7 ½ m. by A 363 and A 4 – Corsham Court★★ AC, NE : 6 ½ m. by B 3109 and A 4

🏠 Woolley Grange 🔲 🕭 🗇 🔄 🕂 🔄 P VISA ⅏ AE
Woolley Green, Northeast : ¾ m. by B 3107 on Woolley St ⊠ BA15 1TX
– 🖋 (01225) 864 705 – www.woolleygrangehotel.co.uk
– info@woolleygrangehotel.co.uk – Fax (01225) 864 059
19 rm – ♦£ 200/220 ♦♦£ 210/260 – 7 suites
Rest – Menu £ 40 (dinner) – Carte lunch £ 20/29
♦ Modern art, period furniture: innumerable charming details spread through the rooms of a beautiful Jacobean manor. This is an hotel very much geared to families. Classic British cooking in restaurant, conservatory or terrace.

🏠 Swan 🗇 ⒳ 🔄 P VISA ⅏
1 Church St ⊠ BA15 1LN – 🖋 (01225) 868 686 – www.theswan-hotel.com
– theswan-hotel@btconnect.com
13 rm ⌑ – ♦£ 75/110 ♦♦£ 95/140
Rest – (Closed dinner Sunday and Monday) Carte £ 18/30
♦ Smart former 16C coaching inn refurbished in modern browns and creams, with rear dining terrace. Stylish bedrooms have contemporary touches and up-to-date facilities. Large, wood furnished dining room.

🏠 Bradford Old Windmill ≤ 🗇 🕅 P VISA ⅏
4 Masons Lane, on A 363 ⊠ BA15 1QN – 🖋 (01225) 866 842
– www.bradfordoldwindmill.co.uk – michelin@bradfordoldwindmill.co.uk
– Fax (01225) 866 648 – March-October
3 rm ⌑ – ♦£ 59/99 ♦♦£ 99/109
Rest – (by arrangement, communal dining) Menu £ 25
♦ 1807 windmill in redressed local stone; Gothic windows and restored bridge. Rooms and circular lounge, stacked with books and curios, share a homely, un-affected quirkiness. Flavourful vegetarian menus.

at Holt East : 2 m. on B 3107 – ⊠ Trowbridge

🏠 The Tollgate Inn with rm 🗇 🗇 P VISA ⅏
Ham Green ⊠ BA14 6PX – 🖋 (01225) 782 326 – www.tollgateholt.co.uk
– alison@tollgateholt.co.uk – Fax (01225) 782 805
– Closed 25 December and 1 January
4 rm ⌑ – ♦£ 50/100 ♦♦£ 80/100
Rest – (Closed Sunday dinner and Monday) (booking essential) Menu £ 14 (lunch) – Carte £ 23/30
♦ Warm, friendly pub with traditional décor. Classic cooking, well-honed recipes and local produce create tried and tested 'light bites' at lunch and hearty, meaty dishes at dinner. Bedrooms are cosy and thoughtfully appointed.

BRAITHWAITE – Cumbria – 502 K 20 – see Keswick

BRAMFIELD – Suffolk – 504 Y 27 – pop. 1 778 – ⊠ Ipswich 15 D2
- ▶ London 215 mi – Ipswich 27 mi – Norwich 28 mi

🏠 Queen's Head 🗇 P VISA ⅏ AE
The Street ⊠ IP19 9HT – 🖋 (01986) 784 214 – www.queensheadbramfield.co.uk
– qhbfield@aol.com – Closed 26 December
Rest – Carte £ 16/26
♦ Roadside pub in heart of village. Characterful beamed interior with flagstone floors and small conservatory. Eclectic menu uses locally sourced food and organic farm produce.

BRAMHOPE – W. Yorks. – **502** P 22 – see Leeds

BRAMLEY S. Yorks – **502** P 23 – see Rotherham

BRAMPTON – Cumbria – **501** L 19 – pop. 3 965 ▯ *Great Britain*   21 **B1**

▪ London 317 mi – Carlisle 9 mi – Newcastle upon Tyne 49 mi
▪ Moot Hall, Market Pl ✆ (016977) 3433
▪ Talkin Tarn, ✆ (016977) 2255
  Brampton Park Huntingdon Buckden Road, ✆ (01480) 434 700
▪ Hadrian's Wall★★, NW : by A 6077

at Gilsland Northeast : 9 m. by A 6071 and A 69 on B 6318 – ⌧ Brampton

🄷🄷 **Farlam Hall** ॐ   ≤ ☞ **P** *VISA* **©© AE**
Southeast : 2 ¾ m. on A 689 ⌧ *CA8 2NG* – ✆ (016977) 46 234
– www.farlamhall.co.uk – Fax (016977) 46 683 – Closed 23-30 December
12 rm ⌑ – ♦£ 160/185 ♦♦£ 350
Rest – (dinner only) (booking essential for non-residents) Menu £ 42
(midweek)/44 (Saturday)ॐ
♦ Long-standing, family-owned Victorian country house. Comfortable guest areas
overlook ornamental gardens and lake. Traditional bedrooms in bold florals. Resident
llamas. Fine, formal dining in sumptuous dining room. Attentive, pristine service.

⌂ **The Hill on the Wall** without rest ॐ   ≤ ☞ ॐ ⁇ **P**
West : ½ m. on Kirkcambeck rd ⌧ *CA8 7DA* – ✆ (016977) 47 214
– www.hadrians-wallbedandbreakfast.com
– info@hadrians-wallbedandbreakfast.com – Fax (016977) 47 214
– Closed December-January
3 rm ⌑ – ♦£ 50 ♦♦£ 75
♦ Spacious 16C guest house in fabulous elevated location overlooking the Irthing
Valley, with terrific views from the garden and the lounge. Comfortable bedrooms.

at Castle Carrock South : 4 m. on B 6413 – ⌧ Brampton

🄳 **The Weary at Castle Carrock** with rm   ⁇ ॐ **P** *VISA* **©© AE**
⌧ *CA8 9LU* – ✆ (01228) 670 230 – www.theweary.com – relax@theweary.com
– Fax (01228) 670 089 – Closed 25-26 December, 1 January
5 rm ⌑ – ♦£ 79/85 ♦♦£ 105/125
Rest – (Closed Mondays except for residents) Carte £ 14/32
♦ Conservatory, terrace and relaxed candlelit bar. Seasonal food with international
flavours. Friendly service. Striking, contemporary bedrooms equipped with latest
technology.

> The ॐ award is the crème de la crème.
> This is awarded to restaurants
> which are really worth travelling miles for!

BRANCASTER STAITHE – Norfolk   15 **C1**

▪ London 131 mi – King's Lynn 25 mi – Boston 57 mi – East Dereham 27 mi

🄳 **The White Horse** with rm   ≤ ⁇ ☏ **P** *VISA* **©© ①**
⌧ *PE31 8BY* – ✆ (01485) 210 262 – www.whitehorsebrancaster.co.uk
– reception@whitehorsebrancaster.co.uk – Fax (01485) 210 930
15 rm ⌑ – ♦£ 75/89 ♦♦£ 100/128   **Rest** – (booking essential) Carte £ 25/36
♦ Elevated position affords beautiful coastal views from rear conservatory and terrace, while landscaped front terrace boasts parasols, heaters and lights. Varied menu
with local seafood. Up-to-date, comfortable bedrooms.

ENGLAND

BRANDESBURTON – East Riding of Yorkshire – 502 T 22 – pop. 1 835   23 **D2**
– ✉ Great Driffield

> **▶** London 197 mi – Kingston-upon-Hull 16 mi – York 37 mi

 Burton Lodge   ⟲ ※ 🖼 ⁽ᵗ⁾ 🅿 💳 ◍ 🄰🄴
Southwest : ½ m. on Leven rd ✉ YO25 8RU – ℰ (01964) 542847
– www.burton-lodge.co.uk – enquiries@burton-lodge.co.uk – Fax (01964) 544771
– Closed 25-26 December
9 rm ☷ – ♥£42 ♥♥£50   **Rest** – (dinner only) (residents only) Menu £18
♦ Personally run, extended 1930s house. Neat, modern bedrooms in soft pastels, some overlooking the golf course - perfect for an early round. A short drive to Beverley Minster. Neat dining room overlooks grounds.

BRANDS HATCH – Kent – 504 U 29 – ✉ Dartford   8 **B1**

> **▶** London 22 mi – Maidstone 18 mi
> **🖸** Fawkham Valley Dartford Fawkham, Gay Dawn Farm, ℰ (01474) 707 144

at Fawkham Green East : 1½ m. by A 20 – ✉ Ash Green

 Brands Hatch Place   ⟲ 🄰 🖾 ◍ 🕥 ⌨ ※ ✿ rm, 🛖 🄰🄲 rest, ※
✉ DA3 8NQ – ℰ (01474) 875 000   🕻 🄰 🅿 💳 ◍ 🄰🄴 🄾
– www.handpicked.co.uk/brandshatchplace
– brandshatchplace@handpicked.co.uk – Fax (01474) 879 652
38 rm ☷ – ♥£95/155 ♥♥£160/260   **Rest** – Carte £30/39 **s**
♦ Sensitively extended Georgian house in 12 acres offering smart bedrooms, some in the annexe, with hi-tech facilities. Also, a range of conference and entertainment packages. Smart, contemporary restaurant.

> The red ⬈ symbol?
> This denotes the very essence of peace
> – only the sound of birdsong first thing in the morning…

BRANSCOMBE – Devon – 503 K 31 – ✉ Seaton   2 **D2**

> **▶** London 167 mi – Exeter 20 mi – Lyme Regis 11 mi
> **◙** Village ★
> **🄶** Seaton (≤★★), NW : 3 m – Colyton ★

 Masons Arms with rm   🕴 🕻 🅿 💳 ◍
✉ EX12 3DJ – ℰ (01297) 680 300 – www.masonsarms.co.uk
– reception@masonsarms.co.uk – Fax (01297) 680 500
21 rm ☷ – ♥£85 ♥♥£170
Rest – Menu £28 (dinner) – Carte £19/27
♦ Dine in the populous bar with its dressed stone interior and huge open fire. Family run 14C inn; cosy, unspoilt bar with slate floors and ships' timbers, popular with locals. Bedrooms in the inn have more character; those in the annex are much larger.

BRANSFORD – Worcs. – see Worcester

BRANSTON – Lincs. – 502 S 24 – see Lincoln

BRATTON – Wrekin – see Telford

BRAYE – 503 Q 33 – see Channel Islands (Alderney)

BRAY MARINA – Windsor & Maidenhead – see Bray-on-Thames

ENGLAND

▶ London 34 mi – Reading 13 mi

Plan : see Maidenhead

XXXX   **The Waterside Inn** (Alain Roux) with rm   ≤ AC ⅝ (•)) P VISA ◯◯ AE ◯
❀❀❀   *Ferry Rd ✉ SL6 2AT – ℰ (01628) 620 691 – www.waterside-inn.co.uk*
   – reservations@waterside-inn.co.uk – Fax (01628) 784 710
   – Closed 26 December-7 April   Xs
   8 rm � – †£ 180/280 ††£ 180/280 – 3 suites
   Rest – French – (closed Tuesday except dinner June-August and Monday)
   (booking essential) Menu £ 48/96 – Carte £ 87/132 ⅛
   Spec. Tronçonnettes de homard poëlées minute au Porto blanc. Filets de
   lapereau grillés aux marrons glacés. Péché Gourmand selon "Alain" et "Michel".
   ♦ Ever delightful Thames idyll: sip an aperitif on the terrace overlooking the river.
   Exquisite French cuisine and exemplary service.   Luxurious bedrooms are spacious
   and classically chic.

XXX   **Fat Duck** (Heston Blumenthal)   VISA ◯◯ AE ◯
❀❀❀   *High St ✉ SL6 2AQ – ℰ (01628) 580 333 – www.fatduck.co.uk – Fax (01628)*
   776 188 – Closed 2 weeks Christmas and Monday   Xe
   Rest – (booking essential 2 months in advance) Menu £ 95/125 ⅛
   Spec. Mock Turtle soup, Madhatter tea. "Sound of the sea". Flaming sorbet.
   ♦ Low-beamed, converted pub where history and science combine in an exciting,
   innovative alchemy of contrasting flavours and textures. Colourful artwork, stylish
   milieu; attentive, formal service.

XX   **Caldesi in Campagna**   �── VISA ◯◯ AE
   Old Mill Lane ✉ SL6 2BG – ℰ (01628) 788 502 – www.caldesi.com
   – campagna@caldesi.com – Closed Sunday dinner and Monday
   Rest – Italian – Menu £ 25 (lunch) – Carte dinner £ 36/46
   ♦ Welcoming roadside pub with smart interior, conservatory and decked garden with
   wood fired oven. Flavoursome Italian cooking displays Ligurian, Tuscan and Sicilian
   influences.

🍴   **The Hinds Head**   ⬦ P VISA ◯◯ AE
(◉)   *High St ✉ SL6 2AB – ℰ (01628) 626 151 – www.hindsheadhotel.co.uk*
   – info@hindsheadhotel.co.uk – Fax (01628) 623 394
   – Closed 25-26 December   Xe
   Rest – (Closed Sunday dinner) (booking essential) Carte £ 18/32
   ♦ Charming pub in the heart of the village, with dark wood panelling, log fires and
   flag floors. Heart-warming traditional British dishes; some dating back to Tudor
   times.

🍴   **The Royal Oak**   �── ⅝ P VISA ◯◯
(◉)   *Paley Street, Southwest : 3½ m. by A 308, A 330 on B 3024 ✉ SL6 3JN*
   – ℰ (01628) 620 541 – www.theroyaloakpaleystreet.com
   – royaloakmail@aol.com – Closed 26 December
   Rest – Carte £ 24/35
   ♦ Characterful roadside pub with beamed ceilings, comfy leather sofas and a pretty
   patio. Seasonally-changing menus offer satisfying homemade food. Relaxed, friendly
   atmosphere.

at Bray Marina Southeast : 2 m. by B 3208, A 308 - X - on Monkey Island Lane
– ✉ Bray-on-Thames

X   **Riverside Brasserie**   �── P VISA ◯◯ AE ◯
   (follow road through the marina) ✉ SL6 2EB – ℰ (01628) 780 553
   – www.riversidebrasserie.co.uk – April-September
   Rest – (booking essential) Carte £ 30/37
   ♦ Marina boathouse, idyllically set on the banks of the Thames. Very simply appointed
   interior and decked terrace. Inventive cooking in informal, busy and buzzy surroundings.

ENGLAND

BREEDON ON THE HILL – Leics. – see Castle Donington

BREENTWOOD – Essex – 504 V 29 – pop. 47 593
13 **C2**

> ▣ London 22 mi – Chelmsford 11 mi – Southend-on-Sea 21 mi
> 🛈 44 High St 𝒞 (01277) 200300, tic@brentwood.gov.uk
> 🏌 Bentley G. & C.C. Ongar Rd, 𝒞 (01277) 373 179
> 🏌 Warley Park Little Warley Magpie Lane, 𝒞 (01277) 224 891

🏠 Marygreen Manor
🛋 👈 ㏂ ⚇ 🛅 P VISA ⓸⓹ AE ①

London Rd, Southwest : 1 ¼ m. on A 1023 ⊠ CM14 4NR – 𝒞 (01277) 225 252
– www.marygreenmanor.co.uk – info@marygreenmanor.co.uk – Fax (01277)
262 809
55 rm – ♦£135 ♦♦£150, � £14.50 – 1 suite
Rest *Tudors* – see restaurant listing
♦ Charming Tudor building with wood panelled rooms and open fires. Bedrooms split between main house and courtyard - some named after Henry VIII's wives. Professionally run.

XXX Tudors – at Marygreen Manor Hotel
㏂ P

London Rd, Southwest : 1 ¼ m. on A 1023 ⊠ CM14 4NR – 𝒞 (01277) 225 252
– info@marygreenmanor.co.uk – Fax (01277) 262 809
Rest – (Closed dinner Sunday and Bank Holidays) Menu £20/30
– Carte £20/40
♦ Spacious Tudor-style dining room with stained glass, wood beams and tapestries. Well-spaced, dressed tables and formal service. Appealing, modern food with a seasonal base.

at Great Warley Southwest : 2 m. on B 186 – ⊠ Brentwood

🍴 The Headley
㏂ ⚇ P VISA ⓸⓹ ①

The Common, Northeast : ½ m. off B 186 ⊠ CM13 3HS – 𝒞 (01277) 216 104
– www.theheadley.co.uk – reservations@theheadley.co.uk
Rest – (Closed Sunday dinner and Monday) Carte £22/26
♦ Spacious two floor pub, with a small terrace. Menu features local, seasonal produce and plenty of fish; Tues-Fri sees a good value set lunch that comes with a glass of wine.

BRIDGNORTH – Shropshire – 502 M 26 – pop. 11 891 📗 *Great Britain*
18 **B2**

> ▣ London 146 mi – Birmingham 26 mi – Shrewsbury 20 mi – Worcester 29 mi
> 🛈 The Library, Listley St 𝒞 (01746) 763257,
>   bridgnorth.tourism@shropshire-cc.gov.uk
> 🏌 Stanley Lane, 𝒞 (01746) 763 315
> 🄲 Ironbridge Gorge Museum★★ **AC** (The Iron Bridge★★ - Coalport China Museum★★ - Blists Hill Open Air Museum★★ - Museum of the Gorge and Visitor Centre★) NW : 8 m. by B 4373

at Worfield Northeast : 4 m. by A 454 – ⊠ Bridgnorth

🏠 The Old Vicarage 🌿
🛋 ㏂ 👈 rm, 🛎 P VISA ⓸⓹

⊠ WV15 5JZ – 𝒞 (01746) 716 497 – www.theoldvicarageworfield.com
– admin@the-old-vicarage.demon.co.uk – Fax (01746) 716 552
13 rm ⊒ – ♦£80 ♦♦£100 – 1 suite **Rest** – (booking essential) Menu £26/43
♦ Antiques, rare prints and rustic pottery: a personally run Edwardian parsonage in a rural setting with thoughtfully appointed bedrooms, some in the coach house. Delightful orangery dining room overlooking garden; modern British cooking.

at Alveley Southeast : 7 m. by A 442 – ⊠ Bridgnorth

🏠 Mill
🛋 🏋 ⚇ 🛅 P VISA ⓸⓹ AE

Birdsgreen, Northeast : ¾ m. ⊠ WV15 6HL – 𝒞 (01746) 780437
– www.themill-hotel.co.uk – info@themill-hotel.co.uk – Fax (01746) 780850
41 rm – ♦£88 ♦♦£95, ⊒ £8.50
Rest *Waterside* – Menu £15/27 – Carte £28/39
♦ Hugely extended water mill. Below traditionally styled rooms in flowery patterns, ducks paddle around the pond and fountain. Popular wedding venue. Capacious restaurant, busy at weekends, overlooks garden and duck pond.

ENGLAND

BRIDGWATER – Somerset – 503 L 30 – pop. 36 563   3 **B2**

> ▣ London 160 mi – Bristol 39 mi – Taunton 11 mi
> 🛈 King Sq ℰ (01278) 436438, bridgwater.tic@sedgemoor.gov.uk
> 🔟 Enmore Park Enmore, ℰ (01278) 672 108
> ◉ Town★ – Castle Street★ – St Mary's★ – Admiral Blake Museum★ **AC**
> ⓒ Westonzoyland (St Mary's Church★★) SE : 4 m. by A 372 – North Petherton (Church Tower★★) S : 3½ m. by A 38. Stogursey Priory Church★★, NW : 14 m. by A 39

at Woolavington Northeast : 5 m. by A 39 on B 3141 – ⊠ Bridgwater

⌂ **Chestnut House** without rest   🖅 ⁗ P. VISA ⓸
Hectors Stones Lower Road ⊠ *TA7 8EF* – ℰ *(01278) 683 658*
– www.chestnuthousehotel.com – paul@chestnuthousehotel.com – Fax (01278) 684 333 – Closed Christmas-New Year
7 rm ⌧ – †£68/70 ††£90/92
♦ Converted farmhouse, personally run; the exposed stone and beams in the homely lounge testify to its 16C origins. Rooms are neat, comfortable. Informal suppers on request.

at Cannington Northwest : 3½ m. by A 39 – ⊠ Bridgwater

⌂ **Blackmore Farm** without rest   🖅 ⓘ ⅙ ⁒ P. VISA ⓸ AE ①
Southwest : 1½ m. by A 39 on Bradley Green rd ⊠ *TA5 2NE* – ℰ *(01278) 653 442*
– www.dyerfarm.co.uk – dyerfarm@aol.com – Fax (01278) 653 427
6 rm ⌧ – †£45/55 ††£75/90
♦ Part 15C manor, now a working dairy farm, with great hall and chapel, set against a backdrop of the Quantocks. Bedrooms in the main house have the greater character.

BRIDPORT – Dorset – 503 L 31 – pop. 12 977   3 **B3**

> ▣ London 150 mi – Exeter 38 mi – Taunton 33 mi – Weymouth 19 mi
> 🛈 47 South St ℰ (01308) 424901, bridport.tic@westdorset-dc.gov.uk
> 🔟 Bridport and West Dorset West Bay East Cliff, ℰ (01308) 422 597
> ⓒ Mapperton Gardens★, N : 4 m. by A 3066 and minor rd. Lyme Regis★ – The Cobb★, W : 11 m. by A 35 and A 3052

⌂ **Roundham House** without rest   🖅 P. VISA ⓸
Roundham Gdns, West Bay Rd, South : 1 m. by B 3157 ⊠ *DT6 4BD* – ℰ *(01308) 422 753 – www.roundhamhouse.co.uk – cyprencom@compuserve.com*
– Fax (01308) 421 500 – April-October
8 rm ⌧ – †£49/85 ††£85/118
♦ Elegant 1903 house with trim, spacious bedrooms, their broad windows overlooking woods, fields and a lawned garden. Coffee in the smart lounge with its marble fireplace.

⌂ **Britmead House** without rest   🖅 P. VISA ⓸
West Bay Rd, South : 1 m. on B 3157 ⊠ *DT6 4EG* – ℰ *(01308) 422 941*
– www.britmeadhouse.co.uk – britmead@talk21.com – Fax (01308) 422 516
– Closed 24 -26 December and 31 December
8 rm – †£40/52 ††£64/76
♦ On the road to West Bay and the Dorset Coast Path, a neat, redbrick Edwardian house with well-proportioned rooms and a comfortable lounge leading out to the garden.

✗ **Riverside**   ⩽ ⌁ VISA ⓸ AE
West Bay, South : 1¾ m. by B 3157 ⊠ *DT6 4EZ* – ℰ *(01308) 422 011*
– www.thefishrestaurant-westbay.co.uk – Fax (01308) 458 808 – 14 February-29 November, closed Sunday dinner and Monday except Bank Holidays
Rest – Seafood – (booking essential) Menu £ 23 (lunch weekdays)
– Carte £ 33/38
♦ Follow the footbridge across the river to this popular seafood café overlooking the harbour, renowned for its extensive choice of specials and its friendly service.

ENGLAND

🛏️ **The Bull** with rm   🛜 📞 **P** *VISA* 𝕄𝕆 AE
34 East St ✉ *DT6 3LF* – ℰ *(01308) 422 878* – *www.thebullhotel.co.uk*
– *info@thebullhotel.co.uk* – *Fax (01308) 426 872*
14 rm ☐ – 🛏£ 60/100 🛏🛏£ 140/180   **Rest** – Carte £ 25/45
♦ Boutique inn displaying a mix of period features and contemporary chic. Local fish and meat make up a mix of classic English and Mediterranean brasserie dishes. Uniquely styled, modern bedrooms boast feature walls and stylish bathrooms.

at Shipton Gorge Southeast : 3 m. by A 35 – ✉ Bridport

🏠 **Innsacre Farmhouse** without rest ♨   🚘 🐕 **P** *VISA* 𝕄𝕆
Shipton Lane, North : 1 m. ✉ *DT6 4LJ* – ℰ *(01308) 456 137* – *www.innsacre.com*
– *innsacre.farmhouse@btinternet.com* – *Closed Christmas and New Year*
4 rm ☐ – 🛏£ 80/95 🛏🛏£ 80/95
♦ 17C farmhouse in acres of lawns and orchards. Simple comfortable lounge centred on old fireplace. Sizeable rooms in bold colours.

at Burton Bradstock Southeast : 2 m. by B 3157

🏠 **Norburton Hall** without rest ♨   ⩽ 🚘 📶 **P**
Shipton Lane ✉ *DT6 4NQ* – ℰ *(01308) 897 007* – *www.norburtonhall.com*
– *info@norburtonhall.com*
3 rm ☐ – 🛏£ 180/200 🛏🛏£ 200/220
♦ Spacious Edwardian Arts and Crafts house with coastal views and 6 acres of mature grounds. Woodwork, ornate carvings and period furniture abound; classical bedrooms, modern shower rooms.

ENGLAND

BRIGGSWATH – N. Yorks. – **502** S 20 – see Whitby

BRIGHOUSE – West Yorkshire – **502** O 22 – pop. 32 360   22 **B2**
▶ London 213 mi – Bradford 12 mi – Burnley 28 mi – Leeds 15 mi
    – Manchester 35 mi – Sheffield 39 mi
🟥 Crow Nest Park Hove Edge Coach Rd, ℰ (01484) 401 121

🍴🍴 **Brook's**   ⇧ *VISA* 𝕄𝕆
6 Bradford Rd ✉ *HD6 1RW* – ℰ *(01484) 715 284* – *www.brooks-restaurant.co.uk*
– *info@brooks-restaurant.co.uk* – *Fax (01484) 712 641*
– *Closed 10 days January, 2 weeks summer and Sunday*
Rest – (dinner only) Carte approx. £ 29
♦ Eclectic art collection fills the walls of this informal restaurant and wine bar with its vaguely Edwardian upstairs lounge. Robust, tasty cooking with 'Spam' on the menu!

BRIGHSTONE – Isle of Wight – **504** P 32 – see Wight (Isle of)

BRIGHTON AND HOVE – Brighton and Hove – **504** T 31   8 **A3**
– pop. 134 293 📗 *Great Britain*
▶ London 53 mi – Portsmouth 48 mi – Southampton 61 mi
✈ Shoreham Airport : ℰ (01273) 467373, W : 8 m. by A 27 AV
🛈 Royal Pavilion Shops ℰ (01273) 292595,
   brighton-tourism@brighton-hove.gov.uk
🟥 East Brighton Roedean Rd, ℰ (01273) 604838
🟥 The Dyke Devil's Dyke Rd, Devil's Dyke, ℰ (01273) 857 296
🟥 Hollingbury Park Ditchling Rd, ℰ (01273) 552 010
🟥 Waterhall Waterhall Rd, ℰ (01273) 508 658
◎ Town★★ - Royal Pavilion★★★ **AC** CZ – Seafront★★ – The Lanes★ BCZ –
   St Bartholomew's★ **AC** CX B
🟢 Devil's Dyke (⩽★) NW : 5 m. by Dyke Rd (B 2121) BY

Plan on next page

BRIGHTON AND HOVE

BUILT UP AREA

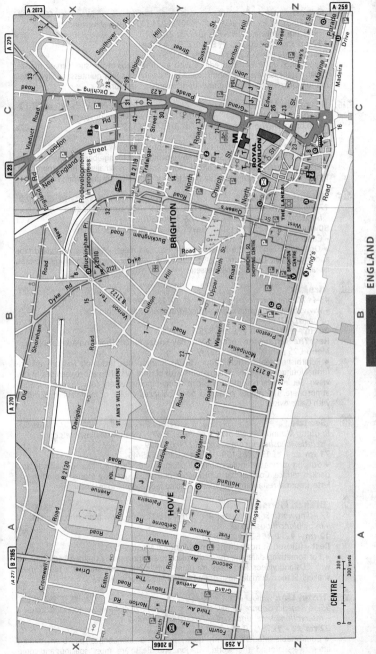

ENGLAND

BRIGHTON

HOVE

ROYAL PAVILION

ST. ANN'S WELL GARDENS

THE LANES

THE BRIGHTON CENTRE

CHURCHILL SQ. SHOPPING CENTRE

King's Road

Kingsway

CENTRE

0   300 m
0   300 yards

157

ENGLAND

Grand
≤ 🖼 🏊 ₤₆ 🖭 🕹 rm, 🕻 🏤 🚗 𝘝𝘐𝘚𝘈 ⓜⓞ 🅰🅴 🄾
97-99 Kings Rd ⊠ BN1 2FW – ☎ (01273) 224300 – www.devere-hotels.co.uk
– bookings@devere.co.uk – Fax (01273) 224321   BZv
197 rm ⌸ – †₤100/260 ††₤130/270 – 4 suites
Rest Kings – Menu £25/32 – Carte £41/54
◆ Imposing, white Victorian edifice with a prime place in the sun. Ornate marble,
striking staircase, elegant rooms, indulgent cream teas in a quintessentially English
lounge. Discreet, traditional grandeur distinguishes restaurant.

Hotel du Vin
🄰🄲 🍴 🕯 🏤 🚗 𝘝𝘐𝘚𝘈 ⓜⓞ 🅰🅴 🄾
2-6 Ship St ⊠ BN1 1AD – ☎ (01273) 718588 – www.hotelduvin.com
– info.brighton@hotelduvin.com – Fax (01273) 718599   CZa
37 rm – †₤180 ††₤180, ⌸ £13.50
Rest Bistro – (booking essential) Carte approx. £35 ⑱
◆ 19C part Gothic building. Style is the keyword here: lounge bar full of wine books;
mezzanine cigar gallery has billiard table. Striking, minimalist rooms, some with
terraces. Bistro with bohemian slant: cellar stocks predictably huge wine selection.

Myhotel Brighton
🖼 🖭 🕯 🚗 𝘝𝘐𝘚𝘈 ⓜⓞ 🅰🅴 🄾
17 Jubilee St ⊠ BN1 1GE – ☎ (01273) 900300 – www.myhotels.com
– brighton@myhotels.com – Fax (01273) 900301   CYz
80 rm ⌸ – †₤125 ††₤140   **Rest** – Italian – Menu £25 (lunch)
– Carte £25/42
◆ Opened in 2008, in the heart of town. Has East-meets-West theme; relaxed vibe
and stylish bar. Quirky, minimalist bedrooms with the latest technological extras.
Italian specialities in informal brasserie.

drakes
≤ 🄰🄲 🕯 𝘝𝘐𝘚𝘈 ⓜⓞ 🅰🅴
43-44 Marine Parade ⊠ BN2 1PE – ☎ (01273) 696934
– www.drakesofbrighton.com – info@drakesofbrighton.com
– Fax (01273) 684805   CZu
20 rm – †₤100/150 ††₤250/325, ⌸ £12.50
Rest The Restaurant – (closed Monday-Friday lunch) (booking advisable)
Menu £25 (lunch) – Carte £32/37
◆ Refurbished seaside hotel, now with Asian ambience, including Thai artwork. Informal lounge/reception. Stylish rooms with plasma TVs: choose between sea or city
views. Set in hotel basement, this cool, contemporary eatery conveys a soft, moody
atmosphere. The menus present a good balanced choice of modern British dishes
with Gallic twists.

Seattle
≤ 🕯 🖭 ₤₆ rm, 🄰🄲 rest, 🕯 🏤 🄿 𝘝𝘐𝘚𝘈 ⓜⓞ 🅰🅴
Brighton Marina ⊠ BN2 5WA – ☎ (01273) 679799 – www.aliashotels.com
– seattle@aliashotels.com – Fax (01273) 679899   CVc
71 rm ⌸ – †₤139 ††₤159   **Rest** – Carte £25/45
◆ Striking marina setting: exploits its position with delightful "Saloon" lounge and
decked terrace. Cocktail bar with Beatles portraits. Light, airy rooms in modish palette. Informal restaurant with totally relaxed feel; absorbing marina views.

Blanch House
🕯 𝘝𝘐𝘚𝘈 ⓜⓞ 🅰🅴
17 Atlingworth St ⊠ BN2 1PL – ☎ (01273) 603504 – www.blanchhouse.co.uk
– info@blanchhouse.co.uk   CZo
12 rm – †₤80 ††₤230, ⌸ £8.50
Rest – (Closed Sunday dinner and Monday) Menu £22/32
◆ For something different, this is the place to be. Individually themed bedrooms, all
with CDs and videos. Red roses are pinned up in one room; another is full of snow
shakers. Stark, minimalist restaurant beyond famed cocktail bar.

Hotel Una without rest
🖭 🕯 𝘝𝘐𝘚𝘈 ⓜⓞ 🅰🅴
55-56 Regency Square ⊠ BN2 2FF – ☎ (01273) 820464 – www.hotel-una.co.uk
– reservation@hotel-una.co.uk – Fax (01273) 724895   BZa
22 rm ⌸ – †₤75/110 ††₤290/375
◆ Comfortable, modern, slightly quirky hotel with alphabetical bedrooms named
after rivers around the world. Aragon and Belise are most spacious and come
with sauna and jacuzzi.

↑ **Brighton Pavilions** without rest   VISA CO AE
7 Charlotte St ⊠ BN2 1AG – ℰ (01273) 621 750 – www.brightonpavilions.com
– brightonpavilions@tiscali.co.uk – Fax (01273) 622 477   CVe
10 rm ⊡ – †£46/70 ††£100/105
♦ Terraced house yards from seafront with something a little different - bedrooms all
have individual themes: for example, Titanic Room has clock set at time it hit iceberg!

↑ **Brighton House** without rest   ⁒ (ⁱ) VISA CO ①
52 Regency Sq ⊠ BN1 2FF – ℰ (01273) 323 282 – www.brighton-house.co.uk
– info@brighton-house.co.uk – Fax (01273) 773 307   BZc
16 rm ⊡ – †£45/80 ††£100/130
♦ Beautiful Regency house on four floors in charming square. Clean, classic décor
throughout. Rooms benefit from period detail such as high ceilings and plenty of
space.

↑ **Paskins** without rest   (ⁱ) VISA CO AE ①
18-19 Charlotte St ⊠ BN2 1AG – ℰ (01273) 601 203 – www.paskins.co.uk
– welcome@paskins.co.uk – Fax (01273) 621 973   CVe
19 rm ⊡ – †£50/75 ††£80/120
♦ Highly eco-friendly hotel. Small, modern bedrooms are simply furnished and well
kept. Showers only – to save water – and eco-toiletries. Organic breakfast features
homemade sausages and several specials.

XX **The Gingerman**   AC VISA CO AE
21A Norfolk Sq ⊠ BN1 2PD – ℰ (01273) 326 688
– www.gingermanrestaurants.com – info@gingermanrestaurants.com
– Fax (01273) 326 688 – Closed 1 week Christmas-New Year and Monday   BZi
Rest – (booking essential) Menu £18/30
♦ Tucked away off the promenade; French and Mediterranean flavours to the fore in
a confident, affordable, modern repertoire: genuine neighbourhood feel.

X **Sevendials**   🖙 ⇆ VISA CO AE
1 Buckingham Pl ⊠ BN1 3TD – ℰ (01273) 885 555
– www.sevendialsrestaurant.co.uk – sam@sevendialsrestaurant.co.uk
– Fax (0870) 912 74 08
– Closed 25-26 December, 1 January and Sunday dinner   BXa
Rest – Carte £22/35
♦ Former bank on street corner: the vault now acts as function room. Light, airy feel
with high ceiling. Modern menus with local ingredients admirably to fore. Good value
lunch.

X **Terre à Terre**   🖙 AC VISA CO AE ①
⊛ 71 East St ⊠ BN1 1HQ – ℰ (01273) 729 051 – www.terreaterre.co.uk
– mail@terreaterre.co.uk – Fax (01273) 327 561
– Closed 24-26 December and Monday   CZe
Rest – Vegetarian – Menu £32 (dinner) – Carte £23/32
♦ Hearty helpings of bold, original vegetarian cuisine lyrically evoked on an eclectic
menu. Despite its popularity, still friendly, hip and suitably down-to-earth.

X **Havana**   AC VISA CO AE
32 Duke St ⊠ BN1 1AG – ℰ (01273) 773 388 – www.havana.uk.com
– Fax (01273) 748 923   CZc
Rest – Menu £22/35 – Carte £24/47
♦ 1790s theatre, now a busy, spacious, two-tiered restaurant, its pediments and
balustrades combined with mock-colonial styling. International dishes and exotic
combinations.

X **Due South**   🖙 AC ⇆ VISA CO AE
139 King's Rd Arches ⊠ BN1 2FN – ℰ (01273) 821 218 – www.duesouth.co.uk
– info@duesouth.co.uk – Closed 25 December and 1 January   BZx
Rest – Menu £35 (dinner) – Carte £23/36
♦ Beside the beach, with lovely arch interior: best tables upstairs facing half-moon
window overlooking sea. Organic prominence in modern menus using distinctly local
produce.

ENGLAND

ENGLAND

✗ **Sam's of Brighton** `VISA` `MO` `AE` `①`
1 Paston Place ⊠ *BN2 1HA – ℰ (01273) 676 222 – www.samsofbrighton.co.uk*
– Closed 25-27 December, 1 January, Monday lunch and Sunday dinner CV**a**
Rest – Menu £ 15 (lunch) – Carte £ 20/30
♦ Simple neighbourhood eatery boasting large bar and 3 enormous candelabras. Simple menu of classical, seasonal dishes. Early brunch on offer at weekends and concise à la carte at noon.

at Hove

🏠 **The Claremont** without rest `VISA` `MO`
13 Second Ave ⊠ *BN3 2LL – ℰ (01273) 735 161 – www.theclaremont.eu*
– info@theclaremont.eu – Fax (01273) 736 836 AY**c**
11 rm ⊒ – ♥£ 75/100 ♥♥£ 150
♦ Personally run Victorian town house with a neat garden; its tall windows and high ceilings lend a sense of space to the spotlessly kept, traditionally decorated bed-rooms.

✗ **The Meadow** `VISA` `MO`
64 Western Rd ⊠ *BN2 2JQ – ℰ (01273) 721 182*
– www.themeadowrestaurant.co.uk – info@themeadowrestaurant.co.uk
– Fax (01273) 326 871
– Closed 25-26 December, Sunday dinner and Monday AY**o**
Rest – Menu £ 15 (midweek) – Carte £ 22/29
♦ Name symbolises local producer relationships – the 'grass roots' needed for their 'Meadow'. Simple, classical cooking with the odd French/Italian influence; tasty, un-fussy dishes.

✗ **Graze** `VISA` `MO` `AE`
42 Western Road ⊠ *BN3 1JD – ℰ (01273) 823 707*
– www.graze-restaurant.co.uk – info@graze-restaurant.co.uk
– Closed 25-26 December, 1 January, Sunday dinner and Monday AY**z**
Rest – Menu £ 14 (lunch) – Carte £ 23/42
♦ Modern restaurant with fresh, funky feel and clever details. Simply prepared, fla-voursome 'English Tapas' dishes; create your own or choose a set menu. Some larger dishes available.

✗ **The Real Eating Company** `VISA` `MO` `AE` `①`
86-87 Western Rd ⊠ *BN3 1JB – ℰ (01273) 221 444 – www.real-eating.co.uk*
– hove@real-eating.co.uk – Fax (01273) 221 442 – Closed 25-26 December AY**x**
Rest – (booking essential at dinner) Carte £ 20/28
♦ Unique food store, bursting with speciality foods and 'food to go'. Ground floor dining area exudes buzzy ambience: superb in-house cooking using produce sold in the shop.

🍴 **The Ginger Pig** `VISA` `MO` `AE`
3 Hove Street ⊠ *BN3 2TR – ℰ (01273) 736 123*
– www.gingermanrestaurants.com – Closed 25 December AV**c**
Rest – (bookings not accepted) Carte £ 21/31
♦ Striking pub just off seafront. Contemporary interior with sofas and bold artwork. Spacious dining area and terrace. Keen service. Appealing menu; flavourful, filling food.

BRIGSTEER – Cumbria – see Kendal

BRIMFIELD – Herefordshire – **503** L 27 – see Ludlow

BRIMSCOMBE – Glos. – **503** N 28 – see Stroud

Y. Duhamel/MICHELIN

BRISTOL

County: City of Bristol
Michelin REGIONAL map: n° **503** M 29
▶ London 121 mi – Birmingham 91 mi

Population: 420 556   4 **C2**
▌ *Great Britain*

Access Severn Bridge (toll)

PRACTICAL INFORMATION

🛈 Tourist Information
Explore-at-Bristol, Harbourside, ℰ (0906) 711 2191, information@at-bristol.org.uk

Airport
✈ Bristol Airport: ℰ (0871) 334 4444, SW: 7 m. by A 38 AX

Bridge
Severn Bridge (toll)

Golf Courses
🏌 Mangotsfield Carsons Rd, ℰ (0117) 956 5501

🏌 Clifton Beggar Clifton Bush Lane, Failand, ℰ (01275) 393 474

🏌 Knowle, Fairway Brislington West Town Lane, ℰ (0117) 977 0660

🏌 Long Ashton Clarken Coombe, ℰ (01275) 392 229

🏌 Stockwood Vale Keynsham Stockwood Lane, ℰ (0117) 986 0509

👁 SIGHTS

IN TOWN

City★★ – St Mary Redcliffe★★ DZ
- At-Bristol★★ CZ - Brandon Hill★★
AX - Georgian House★★ AX **K** – Bristol
Museum★★ CZ **M3** - Brunel's ss Great
Britain and Maritime Heritage Centre★
ACAX **S2** – The Old City★ CYZ : Theatre
Royal★★ CZ **T** - Merchant Seamen's
Almshouses★ CZ **Q** – St Stephen's
City★ CY **S1** - St John the Baptist★
CY – College Green★ CYZ (Bristol
Cathedral★, Lord Mayor's Chapel★)
– City Museum and Art Gallery★
AX **M1**

ON THE OUTSKIRTS

Clifton★★ AX (Clifton Suspension
Bridge★★ (toll), RC Cathedral of
St Peter and St Paul★★ **F1**, Bristol
Zoological Gardens★★ **AC**, Village★)
– Blaise Hamlet★★ - Blaise Castle
House Museum★, NW: 5 m. by A 4018
and B 4057 AV

IN THE SURROUNDING AREA

Bath★★★ , SE: 13 m. by A 4 BX – Chew Ma-
gna★ (Stanton Drew Stone Circles★ **AC**) S:
8 m. by A 37 - BX - and B 3130 – Clevedon★
(Clevedon Court★ **AC**, ≼ ★) W: 11 ½ m. by
A 370, B 3128 - AX - and B 3130

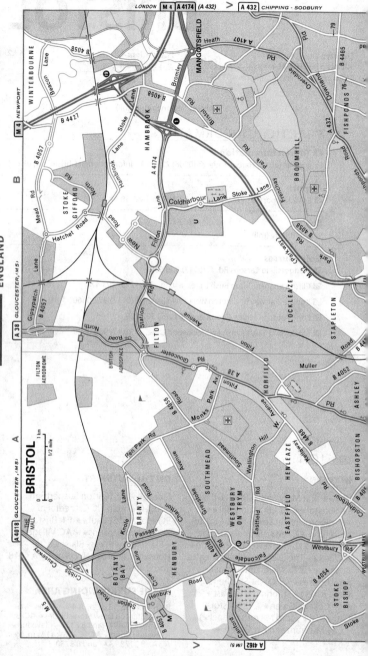

ENGLAND

BRISTOL

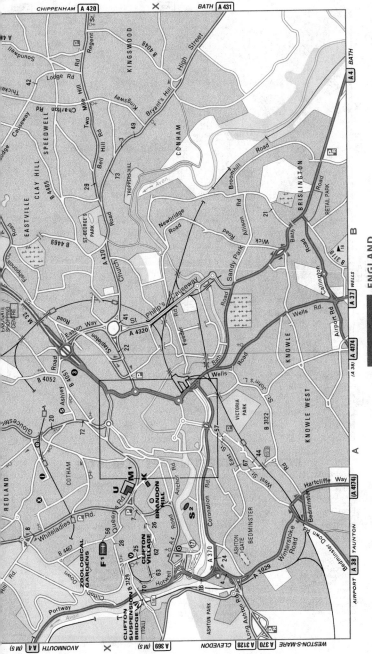

165

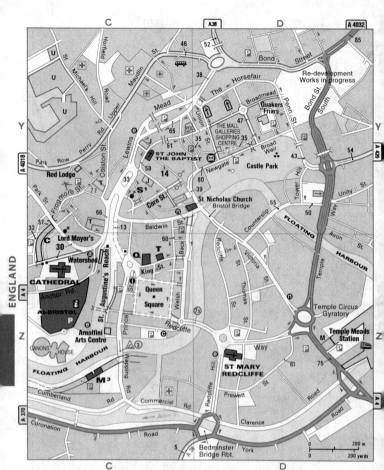

INDEX OF STREET NAMES IN BRISTOL

Bristol Marriott Royal 🔲 ⟐ 𝔦₆ 🕯 & rm, 🕸 ⅏ ⸙ 🗚 ⌂
College Green ⊠ BS1 5TA – 𝒞 (0117) 925 5100 VISA ⱺ AE ⑪
– www.bristolmarriottroyal.co.uk – Fax (0117) 251 515 CZ**a**
230 rm – †👬£159/169, 🖵£14.95 – 12 suites
Rest *Palm Court* – (bar lunch) Carte approx. £38 **s**
♦ Striking Victorian building next to the cathedral and facing College Green. Bedrooms, classic and individual, combine period styling and an array of modern facilities. Classic style at Terrace: wide variety of dishes to suit all tastes.

Hotel du Vin 🕯 🗚 rm, ⅏ 🗚 🄿 ⌂ VISA ⱺ AE
The Sugar House, Narrow Lewins Mead ⊠ BS1 2NU – 𝒞 (0117) 925 5577
– www.hotelduvin.com – info.bristol@hotelduvin.com
– Fax (0117) 925 1199 CY**e**
40 rm – †£145/150 👬£145/150, 🖵£13.50
Rest *Bistro* – (booking essential) Menu £18 (lunch) – Carte £27/34 ⌘
♦ A massive chimney towers over the 18C sugar refinery; stylish loft rooms in minimalist tones: dark leather and wood, low-slung beds, Egyptian linen and subtle wine curios. Noisy, bustling bar and bistro; plenty of classics. Good wine list.

Mercure Brigstow Bristol ⩽ 🕯 & rm, 🗚 🕸 ⅏ 🗚 VISA ⱺ AE ⑪
5-7 Welsh Back ⊠ BS1 4SP – 𝒞 (0117) 929 1030 – www.mercure.com
– H6548@accor.com – Fax (0117) 929 2030 CY**n**
115 rm 🖵 – †£142/152 👬£165 – 1 suite
Rest *Ellipse* – Carte £24/34
♦ Smart city centre hotel with charming riverside position. Stylish public areas typified by lounges and mezzanine. 21C rooms, full of curves, bright colours and plasma TVs. Modern brasserie and bar overlooking river.

Mercure Holland House H. & Spa 🔲 ⊕ 𝔦₆ 🕯 & 🗚 ⅏ 🗚
Redcliffe Hill ⊠ BS1 6SQ – 𝒞 (01179) 689 900 🄿 VISA ⱺ AE
– www.mercure-uk.com – H6698-re@accor.com – Fax (01179) 689 812 DZ**e**
271 rm – †£180 👬£200, 🖵£13.95 – 4 suites **Rest** – Carte £26/31
♦ Large, stylish hotel in city centre, with modern, comfortable bedrooms and free wi-fi. Special children's rooms with toys/games available. Complimentary bicycles. Impressive 14 room spa. Contemporary restaurant serves international cuisine.

Novotel 𝔦₆ 🕯 & rm, 🗚 ⅏ ⅏ ⌂ VISA ⱺ AE ⑪
Victoria St ⊠ BS1 6HY – 𝒞 (0117) 976 9988 – www.novotel.com
– h5622@accor.com – Fax (0117) 925 5040 DZ**n**
130 rm – †£139 👬£139, 🖵£12 – 1 suite
Rest – (meals in bar Saturday-Sunday) Carte £21/33
♦ Purpose-built hotel in heart of business district, close to Temple Meads station. Ample conference facilities. Bedrooms are spacious and up-to-date. Open-plan lounge bar and restaurant catering for many tastes.

XX **Casamia** (Jonray and Peter Sanchez-Iglesias) 🕯 VISA ⱺ
❀ *38 High St, Westbury-on-Trym, Northwest : 2 m. by A 4018 ⊠ BS9 3DZ*
– 𝒞 (0117) 959 2884 – www.casamiarestaurant.co.uk – Fax (0117) 959 3658
– Closed Monday (except Bank Holidays), 25-26 December,
1 week January and 1 week summer AV**e**
Rest – Italian – Menu £20 (lunch) – Carte £26/33
Spec. Beetroot risotto with pistachio and pickled fennel. Roast loin of lamb with pesto and Mediterranean vegetables. "Deconstructed tiramisu".
♦ Seek out this hidden family-run restaurant. Aperitifs in cosy bar; innovative and balanced Italian cooking from the brothers shows a high level of skill and is full of flavour.

XX **Bordeaux Quay (The Restaurant)** ⇔ VISA ⱺ AE
First Floor, V-Shed, Canons Way ⊠ BS1 5UH – 𝒞 (0117) 943 1200
– www.bordeaux-quay.co.uk – info@bordeaux-quay.co.uk – Fax (0117) 906 5567
– Closed 25-26 December and Sunday dinner CZ**e**
Rest – Menu £23 (lunch) – Carte dinner £24/30
♦ Former dockside warehouse for Bordeaux wine, now a deli and vast restaurant with concrete ceiling, good quayside views and frequently changing menus with strong ethical base.

ENGLAND

ENGLAND

�×× Bell's Diner
`VISA ⦿ AE`
1 York Rd, Montpelier ⊠ BS6 5QB – ℰ (0117) 924 0357 – www.bellsdiner.co.uk
– info@bellsdiner.co.uk – Fax (0117) 924 4280 – Closed 24-30 December, Saturday
and Monday lunch and Sunday   AX**s**
Rest – (booking essential at dinner) Menu £ 45 – Carte £ 26/33
♦ Two-roomed restaurant; rear more modern; front more characterful. Small lounge.
Innovative menus with clever combinations of taste, flavours and texture. Precise
cooking.

× Riverstation
`⇔ VISA ⦿ ◐`
The Grove, Harbourside ⊠ BS1 4RB – ℰ (0117) 914 4434
– www.riverstation.co.uk – relax@riverstation.co.uk – Fax (0117) 934 9990
– Closed 24-26 December, 1 January and Sunday dinner   CZ**c**
Rest – Menu £ 15 – Carte £ 25/36
♦ Striking first floor restaurant, and ground floor café, with great views of harbour
activity. Open plan with lots of glass. Full-flavoured mains; good value lunches, too.

× Culinaria
`VISA ⦿`
1 Chandos Rd, Redland ⊠ BS6 6PG – ℰ (0117) 973 7999
– www.culinariabristol.co.uk – Closed Sunday-Wednesday   AX**x**
Rest – (dinner only and lunch Friday and Saturday) Carte £ 29/32
♦ Combined deli and eatery; the personally run diner is informal with lots of light
and space. Sound cooking behind a collection of Mediterranean, English and French
dishes.

× Greens' Dining Room
`VISA ⦿`
25 Zetland Rd ⊠ BS6 7AH – ℰ (0117) 924 64 37 – www.greensdiningroom.com
– Closed mid-August - early September, 1 week Christmas,
Sunday and Monday   AX**e**
Rest – (booking essential) Menu 28 – Carte £ 20/25
♦ Family run neighbourhood eatery, with intimate retro interior and convivial atmos-
phere. Unfussy British/Med dishes rely on natural flavours and carefully sourced
produce.

ᵢ◱ Queen Square Dining Room and Bar
`⇔ ℣ VISA ⦿ AE`
63 Queen Square ⊠ BS1 4JZ – ℰ (0117) 929 0700 – www.queen-square.com
– info@queen-square.com – Closed 25-30 December   AV**v**
Rest – (Closed Sunday and Monday dinner) Carte £ 19/30
♦ Contemporary, open plan pub with leather sofas and lively atmosphere. More
formal restaurant serving precisely cooked modern dishes made with local produce.
Polite service.

ᵢ◱ The Albion Public House and Dining Rooms
`⇔`
Boyces Avenue, Clifton Village ⊠ BS8 4AA
– ℰ (0117) 973 3522 – www.thealbionclifton.co.uk – info@thealbionclifton.co.uk `VISA ⦿ AE`
– Fax (0117) 973 9768 – Closed 25-26 December, 1 January   AX**v**
Rest – (Closed Sunday dinner and Monday) (booking essential) Carte £ 20/38
♦ Grade II listed 17C inn hidden away in Clifton. Loads of character: settles, beams
and roaring fire lend a suitably rustic feel for the enjoyment of tasty West Country
fare.

ᵢ◱ The Kensington Arms
`VISA ⦿ AE`
35-37 Stanley Rd ⊠ BS6 6NP – ℰ (0117) 944 6444
– www.thekensingtonarms.co.uk – info@thekensingtonarms.co.uk – Fax (0117)
924 8095 – Closed 25 December, 1 January   AX**i**
Rest – (Closed Sunday dinner) Carte £ 23/40
♦ Neglected boozer turned gastropub, with high ceilings and quirky décor. Modern,
no-nonsense approach to food means that recreated pub classics come exactly as
described.

The Pump House   P. VISA ◑◐ AE
Merchants Rd ⊠ B58 4PZ – ℰ (0117) 927 2229 – www.the-pumphouse.com
– info@the-pumphouse.com – Fax (0117) 227 9557
– Closed 25 December, 1 January   AXo
Rest – Menu £ 19 (lunch) – Carte £ 18/30
♦ Converted Victorian pumping station; stylish and modern after extensive refurbishment, with mezzanine restaurant and outside terrace. Menus offer an imaginative twist on classic dishes.

Robin Hood's Retreat   ⅍ VISA ◑◐ AE
197 Gloucester Rd ⊠ BS7 8BG – ℰ (0845) 202 50 91
– www.robinhoodsretreat.co.uk – Closed 25 December   AXa
Rest – (Closed Sunday dinner) (booking advisable at dinner) Carte £ 21/40
♦ Red-brick Victorian pub offering a good value daily-changing menu of original and interesting British classics, created using French techniques. Eight real ales available on tap.

at Chew Magna South : 8 ¼ m. by A 37 - BX - on B 3130 – ⊠ Bristol

Bear & Swan   P. VISA ◑◐
13 South Parade ⊠ BS40 8SL – ℰ (01275) 331 100 – www.bearandswan.co.uk
– enquiries@bearandswan.co.uk – Fax (01275) 331 204 – Closed 25 December
Rest – (Closed Sunday dinner) Carte £ 25/30
♦ A combination of good food, real ales, friendly staff and a warm, genuine ambience attracts a loyal local following. Eat from the bar menu or in the candlelit restaurant.

BRITWELL SALOME – Oxfordshire   11 **C2**
◪ London 75 mi – Oxford 21 mi – Reading 19 mi

ⅩⅩ **The Goose**   P. VISA ◑◐ AE
⊠ OX49 5LG – ℰ (01491) 612 304 – www.thegooserestaurant.co.uk
– info@thegooserestaurant.com – Fax (01491) 613 945
– Closed late summer, 1 week early January, Sunday dinner and Monday
Rest – Menu £ 18 (lunch)/24 (midweek dinner) – Carte £ 30/40
♦ Relaxed and snug, its cosy bar lit by tea lights. Intimate main dining room for balanced cooking that adds modern touches to classical combinations. Decent value lunch.

BROAD CAMPDEN – Glos. – see Chipping Campden

BROADHEMBURY – Devon – 503 K 31 – ⊠ Honiton   2 **D2**
◪ London 191 mi – Exeter 17 mi – Honiton 5 mi – Taunton 23 mi

The Drewe Arms   P. VISA ◑◐
⊠ EX14 3NF – ℰ (01404) 841 267 – drewe.arms@btconnect.com
– Closed 25 December
Rest – Seafood – (Closed Sunday dinner) (booking essential) Carte £ 15/30 ⅌
♦ At heart of a historic cob and thatch village; snug bar, rustic dining areas and marine theme. Prime local fish, simply prepared with quality ingredients. Relaxed atmosphere.

BROAD OAK – Kent   9 **D1**
◪ London 62 mi – Hastings 8 mi – Rye 7 mi

⌂ **Fairacres** without rest   P.
Udimore Rd, on B 2089 ⊠ TN31 6DG – ℰ (01424) 883 236
– john-shelagh@fairacres.fsworld.co.uk – Fax (01424) 883 236 – Closed Christmas - New Year
3 rm ⌷ – ♰£ 60 ♰♰£ 100
♦ Listed 17C cottage in picture-postcard pink. Big breakfasts under low beams. Individual rooms: one overlooks superb magnolia tree in garden. All have many thoughtful extras.

169

> ▶ London 93 mi – Birmingham 36 mi – Cheltenham 15 mi – Oxford 38 mi
> – Worcester 22 mi
> 🔢 1 Cotswold Court ℰ (01386) 852937
> ◉ Town ★
> 🟢 Country Park (Broadway Tower ❋ ★★★), SE : 2 m. by A 44 – Snowshill
> Manor ★ (Terrace Garden ★) **AC**, S : 2½ m

ENGLAND

🏨 **The Lygon Arms**
High St ⊠ WR12 7DU – ℰ (01386) 852 255
– www.barcelo-hotels.co.uk/lygonarms
– thelygonarms.information@barcelo-hotels.co.uk – Fax (01386) 854 470
77 rm ☲ – ✝£121/241 ✝✝£133/253 – 6 suites
Rest *Goblets* – see restaurant listing
Rest *The Great Hall* – (dinner only and Sunday lunch) Menu £43
♦ Superbly enticing, quintessentially English coaching inn with many 16C architectural details in its panelled, beamed interiors and rooms Charles I and Cromwell once stayed in. Refined dining and baronial splendours: heraldic friezes and minstrels' gallery.

🏨 **Dormy House**
Willersey Hill, East : 3¼ m. by A 44 and Broadway Golf Club rd ⊠ WR12 7LF
– ℰ (01386) 852 711 – www.dormyhouse.co.uk – david.field@dormyhouse.co.uk
– Fax (01386) 858 636 – Closed 25-26 December
42 rm ☲ – ✝£132 ✝✝£215 – 3 suites
Rest *The Dining Room* – (dinner only and Sunday lunch) Menu £36 (dinner)
– Carte £23/43
Rest *Barn Owl* – Carte £20/31
♦ Creeper-clad 17C farmhouse and outbuildings. Sizeable rooms and comfortable lounge: open fires, wing armchairs and a warm country house palette. Dine in cosy, rustic rooms or conservatory. Barn Owl is an A-framed hall with flagged floors.

🏨 **The Broadway**
The Green ⊠ WR12 7AA – ℰ (01386) 852 401 – www.cotswold-inns-hotels.co.uk
– info@broadwayhotel.info – Fax (01386) 853 879
19 rm ☲ – ✝£100/105 ✝✝£165/175
Rest *The Courtyard* – Menu £16/26
♦ A 16C inn on the green, built as an abbot's retreat; sympathetically updated rooms in a pretty mix of rural patterns with an atmospheric, horse racing themed, timbered bar. Half-timbered restaurant with leaded windows.

🏠 **The Olive Branch** without rest
78 High St ⊠ WR12 7AJ – ℰ (01386) 853 440
– www.theolivebranch-broadway.com
– davidpam@theolivebranch-broadway.com
8 rm ☲ – ✝£50/70 ✝✝£92/102
♦ A 1590s former staging post on the high street run by a friendly husband and wife team. Flagged floors, sandstone walls and compact bedrooms with a few charming touches.

🏠 **Windrush House** without rest
Station Rd ⊠ WR12 7DE – ℰ (01386) 853 577 – www.broadway-windrush.co.uk
– evan@broadway-windrush.co.uk – Fax (01386) 852 850
5 rm ☲ – ✝£75/80 ✝✝£85/90
♦ Personally run guesthouse and landscaped garden with an updated Edwardian elegance and subtle period style. Tastefully individual rooms; pleasant views to front and rear.

🏠 **Whiteacres** without rest
Station Rd ⊠ WR12 7DE – ℰ (01386) 852 320 – www.broadwaybandb.com
– whiteacres@btinternet.com
5 rm ☲ – ✝£55/65 ✝✝£70/80
♦ Spacious accommodation - homely, pleasantly updated and modestly priced - in a personally owned Victorian house, a short walk from the village centre.

XX **Russell's** with rm   🕭 AC 🕭 P VISA ⚫ AE
20 High St ⊠ WR12 7DT – ℰ (01386) 853 555
– www.russellsofbroadway.co.uk – info@russellsofbroadway.co.uk
– Fax (01386) 853 964
7 rm ⌷ – †£85 ††£205/245
Rest – (closed Sunday dinner and Bank Holiday Monday dinner) Menu £17/18
– Carte £27/43
♦ Behind the splendid Cotswold stone façade lies a stylish modern restaurant with
terrace front and rear. Seasonally influenced, regularly changing menus. Smart, comfy
bedrooms.

X **Goblets** – at The Lygon Arms   P VISA ⚫ AE ①
High St ⊠ WR12 7DU – ℰ (01386) 854 418
– www.barcleo-hotels.co.uk/lygonarms.co.uk
– thelygonarms.information@barcelo-hotels.co.uk
– Fax (01386) 858 611
Rest – (booking essential) Carte £25/30
♦ Charactefully firelit in rustic dark oak. Modern dining room at front more atmos-
pheric than one to rear. Menus of light, tasty, seasonal dishes offered.

at Buckland Southwest : 2 ¼ m. by B 4632 – ⊠ Broadway

🏠 **Buckland Manor** ⚶   ≤ 🗂 ❀ ⚴ 🕭 P VISA ⚫ AE
⊠ WR12 7LY – ℰ (01386) 852 626 – www.bucklandmanor.com
– info@bucklandmanor.co.uk – Fax (01386) 853 557
14 rm ⌷ – †£265 ††£470
Rest – (booking essential for non-residents) Menu £23 (lunch)
– Carte £46/52🍽
♦ Secluded part 13C country house with beautiful gardens. Individually furnished
bedrooms boast high degree of luxury. Fine service throughout as old-world serenity
prevails. Restaurant boasts elegant crystal, fine china and smooth service.

BROCKDISH – Norfolk – **504** X 26 – see Diss

BROCKENHURST – Hampshire – **503** P 31 – pop. 2 865 ▌ *Great Britain*   6 **A2**
🚗 London 99 mi – Bournemouth 17 mi – Southampton 14 mi
  – Winchester 27 mi
🏌 Brockenhurst Manor Sway Rd, ℰ (01590) 623 332
🗺 New Forest★★ (Rhinefield Ornamental Drive★★, Bolderwood Ornamental
  Drive★★)

🏠 **Rhinefield House** ⚶   🗂 🕭 ⚚ 🛏 ❀ & ⚴ 🕭 🛁 P VISA ⚫ AE ①
Rhinefield Rd, Northwest : 3 m. ⊠ SO42 7QB – ℰ (01590) 622 922
– www.rhinefieldhousehotel.co.uk – rhinefieldhouse@handpicked.co.uk
– Fax (01590) 622 800
50 rm ⌷ – †£175/240 ††£185/250 – 1 suite
Rest *Armada* – Menu £20/45 – Carte approx. £38
Rest *The Brasserie* – Carte £25/34
♦ A long ornamental pond reflects this imposing 19C New Forest mansion, surveying
parterres and a yew maze. Panelled drawing room. Handsomely appointed bedrooms
in 21C wing. Dining room in gleaming oak with forest views.

🏠 **New Park Manor** ⚶   ≤ 🗂 ⚚ 🛏 🍳 ⊚ ❀ 🛏 🍴 🛁 P VISA ⚫ AE ①
Lyndhurst Rd, North : 1½ m. on A 337 ⊠ SO42 7QH – ℰ (01590) 623 467
– www.newparkmanorhotel.co.uk – info@newparkmanorhotel.co.uk
– Fax (01590) 622 268
24 rm ⌷ – †£108/118 ††£135/155
Rest *The Stag* – Menu £42 (dinner) – Carte £35/42
♦ Extended, elegantly proportioned hunting lodge with equestrian centre for guided
forest treks. Rooms, some in former servants' quarters, have four posters and parkland views. Candlelit fine dining.

ENGLAND

The Cloud
       🏠 ⚑ 🕯 ⚑ P VISA ⚫⚫

Meerut Rd ⊠ SO42 7TD – ℰ (01590) 622 165 – www.cloudhotel.co.uk
– enquiries@cloudhotel.co.uk – Fax (01590) 622818
– Closed 2 weeks December-January
18 rm (dinner included) � – ♥£103/190 ♥♥£206/230
Rest – Menu £16/32 **s**

♦ Well-kept, comfortable and personally owned, with something of a country cottage character. Simple, pine furnished accommodation; views over the wooded countryside. Intimate little restaurant with pleasant covered terrace.

Cottage Lodge without rest
       ⚑ & ✿ P VISA ⚫⚫ ①

Sway Rd ⊠ SO42 7SH – ℰ (01590) 622 296 – www.cottagehotel.org
– chris@cottagehotel.org – Fax (01590) 623 014 – Closed Christmas - mid-January
12 rm ⊻ – ♥£50/160 ♥♥£55/165

♦ 300-year old former forester's cottage in the heart of the village: family run and faultlessly kept. Low oak beamed ceiling, cosy snug bar and large, neatly appointed rooms.

Le Poussin at Whitley Ridge (Alex Aitken) with rm ✎
       ⟵ ⚑

Beaulieu Rd, East : 1 m. on B 3055 ⊠ SO42 7QL   🍴 ⚑ ✿ P VISA ⚫⚫
– ℰ (01590) 622 354 – www.whitleyridge.com – info@whitleyridge.co.uk
– Fax (01590) 622 856
16 rm (dinner included) ⊻ – ♥£144/232 ♥♥£198/350 – 1 suite
Rest – Menu £23/45 – Carte approx. £45
Spec. Salad of watermelon and summer vegetables with mixed herb vinaigrette. Roasted monkfish, shellfish broth and baby vegetables. Passion fruit soufflé.

♦ Attractive, wisteria-clad Georgian house located in 14 acres of mature gardens in the New Forest. Stylish, individually decorated bedrooms. Attractive dining room overlooking front lawn; well-dressed tables and formal service. Extensive use of local/wild ingredients and touches of individuality in the cooking.

Simply Poussin
       VISA ⚫⚫

The Courtyard, rear of 49-51 Brookley Rd ⊠ SO42 7FZ – ℰ (01590) 623 063
– www.simplypoussin.co.uk – simply@lepoussin.co.uk – Fax (01590) 623 144
– Closed Sunday-Monday
Rest – (booking essential) Menu £18 (lunch)/18 (midweek dinner)
– Carte £23/35

♦ Intimate little mews restaurant, tucked away off the village centre, with well-spaced, subtly spotlit tables. Capable, flavourful modern British menu; unobtrusive service.

Thatched Cottage with rm
       ⚑ P VISA ⚫⚫ AE

16 Brookley Rd ⊠ SO42 7RR – ℰ (01590) 623 090 – www.thatchedcottage.co.uk
– sales@thatchedcottage.co.uk – Fax (01590) 623 479
5 rm ⊻ – ♥£70/160 ♥♥£80/170
Rest – (closed Monday and Tuesday) (booking essential) Menu £20/50

♦ 17C farmhouse and one-off rooms with a touch of eccentricity to their blend of curios, pictures and bright flowers. Open kitchen; elaborate, locally sourced menu.

at Sway Southwest : 3 m. by B 3055 – ⊠ Lymington

The Nurse's Cottage with rm
       AC rest, ⚑ P VISA ⚫⚫ AE

Station Rd ⊠ SO41 6BA – ℰ (01590) 683 402 – www.nursescottage.co.uk
– nurses.cottage@lineone.net – Closed 3 weeks February-March and 3 weeks November
5 rm ⊻ – ♥£90/110 ♥♥£170/190
Rest – (dinner only) (booking essential) Menu £25

♦ Personally run, welcoming conservatory restaurant with an intimate charm. Traditional menus make good use of Hampshire's larder. Pristine, comfy rooms with pretty details.

BROCKTON – Shrops. – see Much Wenlock

BROCKWORTH – Glos. – **504** N 28 – **see Cheltenham**

BROME – Suffolk – **504** X 26 – **see Diss (Norfolk)**

BROMFIELD – Shrops. – **503** L 26 – **see Ludlow**

BROOK – Hampshire – **503** P 31 – ✉ **Lyndhurst**   6 **A2**
> ◻ London 92 mi – Bournemouth 24 mi – Southampton 14 mi

🏨 **Bell Inn**   🖨 🖼 ⚄ 🕍 **P** _VISA_ ⓪ 🆎 ①
✉ SO43 7HE – ☎ (023) 8081 2214 – www.bellinnbramshaw.co.uk
– bell@bramshaw.co.uk – Fax (023) 8081 3958
27 rm ☲ – ♥£ 95/140 ♥♥£ 140/200
Rest – (bar lunch Monday-Saturday) Menu £ 35
♦ 400 year old former coaching inn in the heart of the New Forest where most of the
guests come for one of the golf courses. Bedrooms being modernised and updated.
Pub classics in bar; more sophisticated offerings in restaurant.

BROXTON – Cheshire – **502** L 24   20 **A3**
> ◻ London 197 mi – Birmingham 68 mi – Chester 12 mi – Manchester 44 mi
> – Stoke-on-Trent 29 mi

🏨 **De Vere Carden Park**   🖨 🕭 🈂 🖼 🕎 🏤 ⒧ ✕ 🖼 🖻 ⅍ rm,
West : 1½ m. on A 534 ✉ CH3 9DQ   🏃 🖹 rest, ⚟ 🕍 **P** _VISA_ ⓪ 🆎 ①
– ☎ (01829) 731 000 – www.devere.co.uk – stephanie.booth@devere-hotels.co.uk
– Fax (01829) 731 599
189 rm ☲ – ♥£ 190 ♥♥£ 200 – 4 suites
Rest _Redmonds_ – (dinner only) Carte £ 23/46
Rest _The Brasserie_ – Carte £ 17/28
♦ Very well equipped and up-to-date leisure hotel with extensive grounds in a rural
location. Golf breaks a speciality. Main house or courtyard rooms are equally comfort-
able. Formal Redmonds Restaurant with Carden estate wines. Smart Brasserie.

🍴🍴 **Cock O Barton**   🖨 🈂 🖼 ⇆ **P** _VISA_ ⓪
Barton Rd, Barton, West : 2 m. on a 534 ✉ SY14 7HU – ☎ (01829) 782 277
– www.thecockobarton.co.uk – info@thecockobarton.co.uk – Fax (01829) 782 888
– Closed Monday
Rest – Carte £ 20/32
♦ Stylishly furnished restaurant; delightful dining room featuring antler chandeliers.
Local, traceable ingredients and regional meats and cheeses. Sharing plates a speciality.

BRUNDALL – Norfolk – **504** Y 26   15 **D2**
> ◻ London 118 mi – Great Yarmouth 15 mi – Norwich 8 mi

🍴🍴 **The Lavender House**   **P** _VISA_ ⓪
39 The Street ✉ NR13 5AA – ☎ (01603) 712 215 – www.thelavenderhouse.co.uk
– Closed 4-16 January, Monday and Sunday dinner
Rest – (dinner only) (booking essential) Menu £ 40
♦ Locally renowned restaurant with pleasant lounge for pre-prandials. Intimate,
beamed dining room. Proudly local menus with the suppliers listed; ingredients are
in season.

BRUNTINGTHORPE – Leicestershire ▌ _Great Britain_   16 **B3**
> ◻ London 96 mi – Leicester 10 mi – Market Harborough 15 mi
> ◰ Leicester - Museum and Art Gallery★, Guildhall★ and St Mary de Castro
> Church★, N : 11 m. by minor rd and A 5199

🍴 **Joiners Arms**   **P** _VISA_ ⓪
Church Walk ✉ LE17 5QH – ☎ (0116) 247 8258 – www.thejoinersarms.co.uk
– stephenjoiners@btconnect.com – Closed 25-26 December
Rest – (Closed Sunday dinner and Monday) (booking essential) Menu £ 14
– Carte £ 24/29
♦ A charming 18C with small front terrace, large main bar and chatty service. Hearty,
classical dishes are homemade using locally sourced ingredients.

ENGLAND

BRUSHFORD – Somerset – **503** J 30 – **see Dulverton**

BRUTON – Somerset – **503** M 30 – **pop. 2 982**   4 **C2**
- London 118 mi – Bristol 27 mi – Bournemouth 44 mi – Salisbury 35 mi
  – Taunton 36 mi
- Stourhead ★★★ **AC**, W : 8 m. by B 3081

XX   **Bruton House** with rm   *VISA* *◯◯* *AE*
2-4 High St ⊠ BA10 0AA – ℰ (01749) 813 395 – www.brutonhouse.co.uk
– info@brutonhouse.co.uk – Closed 2 weeks January, Sunday and Monday
2 rm – †£45 ††£70, ⊆ £7.50   **Rest** – Menu £39 (dinner) **s** – Carte £20/39 **s**
♦ Comfy lounge for canapés and drinks. Intimate dining room with dark beams and
contemporary artwork. Classic British dishes with modern touches, cooked using local
produce. Simple bedrooms – rear one is quieter.

XX   **Truffles**   *AE* *VISA* *◯◯*
95 High St ⊠ BA10 0AR – ℰ (01749) 812 255 – www.trufflesbruton.co.uk
– deborah@trufflesbruton.co.uk – Closed Sunday dinner and Monday
Rest – (dinner only and Sunday lunch) Menu £30
♦ Cottagey façade; intimate and cosy two-level interior. Personally run, the husband
and wife team take pride in a small, well prepared menu rich in market fresh local
produce.

BRYHER – Cornwall – **503** A/B 34 – **see Scilly (Isles of)**

BUCKDEN – Cambridgeshire – **504** T 27 – **pop. 2 385** – ⊠ **Huntingdon**   14 **A2**
- London 65 mi – Bedford 15 mi – Cambridge 20 mi – Northampton 31 mi

🏨   **The George**   ⬆ ⚘ ℂ 🐾 **P** *VISA* *◯◯* *AE* *◯*
High St ⊠ PE19 5XA – ℰ (01480) 812 300 – www.thegeorgebuckden.com
– manager@thegeorgebuckden.com – Fax (01480) 813 920
12 rm – †£80/130 ††£130
Rest *Brasserie* – see restaurant listing
♦ Delightfully restored former 19C coaching inn with stylish, contemporary look,
typified by leather tub chairs and sofas. Smart bedrooms are all named after famous
Georges.

🏠   **Lion**   ⚘ 🐾 **P** *VISA* *◯◯* *AE*
High St ⊠ PE19 5XA – ℰ (01480) 810 313 – www.lionhotel.co.uk
– reception@thelionbuckden.co.uk – Fax (01480) 811 070
15 rm ⊆ – †£71/91 ††£81/101   **Rest** – Carte £18/32 **s**
♦ Charming 15C inn with panelled bar, period fireplace and beautifully ornate ceiling. Individually decorated bedrooms, some with four posters. Resident ghost: the
Lady in Grey. Dining room with stained glass windows.

X   **Brasserie** – at The George Hotel   🖼 ⚘ **P** *VISA* *◯◯* *AE* *◯*
High St ⊠ PE19 5XA – ℰ (01480) 812 300 – www.thegeorgebuckden.com
– mail@thegeorgebuckden.com – Fax (01480) 813 920
Rest – Carte £24/40
♦ Spacious, modern brasserie serving a range from traditional English game to Mediterranean and Moroccan influenced dishes. French windows lead to courtyard, creating airy feel.

BUCKHORN WESTON – Dorset   4 **C3**
- London 117 mi – Poole 36 mi – Bath 33 mi – Weymouth 37 mi

🏠   **The Stapleton Arms** with rm   🖼 🖼 **P** *VISA* *◯◯* *AE*
Church Hill ⊠ SP8 5HS – ℰ (01963) 370 396 – www.thestapletonarms.com
– relax@thestapletonarms.com – Fax (01963) 370 396
4 rm ⊆ – †£72/96 ††£100/120   **Rest** – Carte £20/25
♦ Smart, stylish pub with elegant dining room; muddy boots, dogs and children all
welcome. Wide-ranging menu offers traditional choices with some Mediterranean
touches. Spacious, contemporary bedrooms, some with underfloor heating.

BUCKINGHAM – Buckinghamshire – 503 Q 27 ▌Great Britain   11 C1

D London 64 mi – Birmingham 61 mi – Northampton 20 mi – Oxford 25 mi
Tra Silverstone Stowe Silverstone Rd, *☎* (01280) 850 005
Tra Tingewick Rd, *☎* (01280) 815 566
G Stowe Gardens★★, NW : 3 m. by minor rd. Claydon House★ **AC**, S : 8 m. by A 413

🏨 Villiers   🛗 📶 rest, ⚄ ⭐ 🔊 🅿 VISA ⑳ 🆎

3 Castle St ⊠ MK18 1BS – ☎ (01280) 822 444 – www.oxfordshire-hotels.co.uk
– villiers@oxfordshire-hotels.co.uk – Fax (01280) 822 113
43 rm � – †£70/150 ††£85/160 – 3 suites
Rest *Villiers* – Carte £24/32
♦ 17C former coaching inn at centre of town opposite old town hall. Attractive cobbled courtyard for al fresco dining. Traditionally furnished lounge and bedrooms. Modern restaurant serves inspired dishes with Mediterranean influences.

BUCKLAND – Glos. – 503 O 27 – see Broadway (Worcs.)

BUCKLAND – Oxfordshire – 503 P 28 – ⊠ Faringdon   10 A2

D London 78 mi – Oxford 16 mi – Swindon 15 mi

🍺 The Lamb at Buckland   🏡 🏞 ⭐ 🅿 VISA ⑳

Lamb Lane ⊠ SN7 8QN – ☎ (01367) 870 484 – www.thelambatbuckland.co.uk
– enquiries@thelambatbuckland.co.uk – Fax (01367) 870 675
– Closed from 24 December for 2 weeks
Rest – (Closed Sunday dinner and Monday) Carte £16/35
♦ Family-owned 17C pub decorated with ovine-inspired curios. Rear garden and sunken terrace. Heavily beamed restaurant; tasty traditional British cooking on blackboard menu.

BUCKLAND MARSH – Oxfordshire – pop. 2 243   10 A2

D London 76 mi – Faringdon 4 mi – Oxford 15 mi

🍺 The Trout at Tadpole Bridge with rm   🏡 🏞 📞 🅿 VISA ⑳

⊠ SN7 8RF – ☎ (01367) 870 382 – www.troutinn.co.uk – info@troutinn.co.uk
– Fax (01367) 870 912 – Closed 25-26 December
6 rm ⊠ – †£75 ††£110   **Rest** – (Closed Sunday dinner) Carte £23/30
♦ Pretty stone pub with gardens leading to River Thames. Own moorings. Open plan bar with log burners. Quality cooking using local produce. Comfortable, well-furnished bedrooms.

BUCKLERS HARD – Hants. – 503 P 31 – see Beaulieu

BUDE – Cornwall – 503 G 31 – pop. 3 681   1 B2

D London 252 mi – Exeter 51 mi – Plymouth 50 mi – Truro 53 mi
i Visitor Centre, The Crescent *☎* (01288) 354240, budetic@visitbude.info
Tra Burn View, *☎* (01288) 352 006
◎ The Breakwater★★ – Compass Point (≤★)
G Poughill★ (church★★), N : 2½ m. - E : Tamar River★★ – Kilkhampton (Church★), NE : 5½ m. by A 39 – Stratton (Church★), E : 1½ m. – Launcells (Church★), E : 3 m. by A 3072 – Marhamchurch (St Morwenne's Church★), SE : 2½ m. by A 39 – Poundstock★ (≤★★, church★, guildhouse★), S : 4½ m. by A 39. Morwenstow (cliffs★★, church★), N : 8½ m. by A 39 and minor roads - Jacobstow (Church★), S : 7 m. by A 39

🏨 Falcon   ≤ 🏡 🛗 ⭐ 🔊 🔊 🅿 VISA ⑳

Breakwater Rd ⊠ EX23 8SD – ☎ (01288) 352 005 – www.falconhotel.com
– reception@falconhotel.com – Fax (01288) 356 359 – Closed 25 December
29 rm ⊠ – †£60/75 ††£120/125 – 1 suite   **Rest** – Carte £19/27 **s**
♦ An imposing, personally run hotel with the proudly traditional character of a bygone age. Contemporary and classic blend in bedrooms. Separate private garden. Formal dining.

BUDLEIGH SALTERTON – Devon – 503 K 32 – pop. 4 801   2 D2

▶ London 182 mi – Exeter 16 mi – Plymouth 55 mi
🚹 Fore St ℰ (01395) 445275, budleigh.tic@btconnect.com
🛏 East Devon Links Rd, Budleigh Salterton, ℰ (01395) 443 370
◙ East Budleigh (Church★), N : 2½ m. by A 376 – Bicton★ (Gardens★) **AC**, N : 3 m. by A 376

⌂ **Downderry House** without rest   🖼 📶 **P** VISA ⑩
10 Exmouth Rd, Northwest : 1 m. on B 3178 ⊠ EX9 6AQ – ℰ (01395) 442 663
– www.downderryhouse.co.uk – info@downderryhouse.co.uk
5 rm – ♦£65/89 ♦♦£89/99
♦ Comfortable guest house where charming owners extend warm welcome. Breakfast room overlooks lawned garden. Modern, individually decorated bedrooms named after local villages.

⌂ **The Long Range**   🖼 📶 📶 **P** VISA ⑩
5 Vales Rd, by Raleigh Rd ⊠ EX9 6HS – ℰ (01395) 443 321
– www.thelongrangehotel.co.uk – info@thelongrangehotel.co.uk – Fax (01395) 442 132
7 rm � – ♦£45/75 ♦♦£100/112
Rest – (by arrangement) Menu £25
♦ Homely and unassuming guesthouse, personally run in quiet residential street. Sun lounge with bright aspect, overlooking broad lawn and neat borders. Simple, unfussy rooms. Tasty, locally sourced dishes in a comfy dining room.

If breakfast is included the ☲ symbol appears after the number of rooms.

ENGLAND

BUNBURY – Ches. – 502 M 24 – see Tarporley

BUNGAY – Suffolk – 504 Y 26 – pop. 4 895 ▌ Great Britain   15 D2

▶ London 108 mi – Beccles 6 mi – Ipswich 38 mi
◙ Norwich★★ - Cathedral★★, Castle Museum★, Market Place★, NW : 15 m. by B 1332 and A 146

at Earsham Southwest : 3 m. by A 144 and A 143 – ⊠ Bungay

⌂ **Earsham Park Farm** without rest ≫   ≼ 🖼 📶 📶 **P** VISA ⑩
Old Railway Rd, on A 143 ⊠ NR35 2AQ – ℰ (01986) 892 180
– www.earsham-parkfarm.co.uk – bobbie@earsham-parkfarm.co.uk
– Fax (01986) 894 796
3 rm ☲ – ♦£48/52 ♦♦£75/80
♦ Isolated red-brick Victorian farmhouse, surrounded by working farm which supplies the produce for breakfast. Well appointed rooms with rural names.

BURCOMBE – Wilts. – see Salisbury

BURFORD – Oxfordshire – 503 P 28   10 A2

▶ London 76 mi – Birmingham 55 mi – Gloucester 32 mi – Oxford 20 mi
🚹 The Brewery, Sheep St ℰ (01993) 823558, burford.vic@westoxon.gov.uk
🛏 , ℰ (01993) 822 583

🏨 **Bay Tree**   🖼 🍽 🖼 **P** VISA ⑩ AE ①
12-14 Sheep St ⊠ OX18 4LW – ℰ (01993) 822 791
– www.cotswold-inns-hotels.co.uk/bay-tree – info@baytreehotel.info
– Fax (01993) 823 008
21 rm ☲ – ♦£119/129 ♦♦£240/250   **Rest** – Menu £16/28 – Carte £22/27
♦ Characterful, creeper-clad 16C house with coaching inn style, antique furnishings and original features. Two front lounges with vast stone fireplaces. Comfortable bedrooms. Light, airy restaurant overlooking beautiful landscaped garden.

🏠 **Burford House** 🚐 🌴 ✑ VISA ⓞⓞ AE
99 High St ✉ *OX18 4QA* – ✆ *(01993) 823 151 – www.burfordhouse.co.uk*
– stay@burfordhouse.co.uk – Fax (01993) 823 240
– Closed 25-26 December
8 rm ⊃ – †£110 ††£185
Rest – (Closed Monday-Wednesday dinner and Sunday) Carte £19/38
◆ 17C town house. Welcoming lounge with honesty bar. Individually decorated bedrooms with contemporary touches are named after local villages – four poster Southrop is the best.

🍴 **The Lamb Inn** with rm 🚐 🍴 🕊 P VISA ⓞⓞ AE ①
✉ *OX18 4LR* – ✆ *(01993) 823 155 – www.cotswold-inns-hotel.co.uk*
– info@lambinn-burford.co.uk – Fax (01993) 822 228
17 rm ⊃ – ††£145/255
Rest – (bar lunch Monday-Saturday) Menu £33 – Carte £20/33
◆ Restaurant has glass skylight and dressed tables. Attractive 14C Cotswold stone inn with deep sofas, open fires and uneven flag floors. Cosy bedrooms named after flowers.

at Swinbrook East : 2¾ m. by A 40 – ✉ Burford

🍴 **The Swan Inn** 🚐 🍴 P VISA ⓞⓞ
✉ *OX18 4DY* – ✆ *(01993) 823 339 – www.theswanswinbrook.co.uk*
– swanninnswinbrook@btconnect.com – Closed 25 December
Rest – (Closed 26 December, Sunday dinner and Monday dinner in winter)
Carte £20/30
◆ English country pub on a lane next to the river. Menus balance traditional and modern British dishes, using local, seasonal produce as their base; game is from the nearby Estate.

 Look out for red symbols, indicating particularly pleasant establishments.

BURGHCLERE – Hampshire – **503** Q 29   6 **B1**
🄳 London 67 mi – Newbury 4 mi – Reading 30 mi

🍴 **Carnarvon Arms** with rm 🍴 🏧 rm, 🕊 P VISA ⓞⓞ AE
Winchester Rd, Whitway, South : 1½ m. by Highclere rd on Whitway rd
✉ *RG20 9LE* – ✆ *(01635) 278 222 – www.carnarvonarms.com*
– infoc@carnarvonarms.com – Fax (01635) 278 444
23 rm ⊃ – †£70/90 ††£80/100
Rest – Menu £15 (lunch) – Carte £25/35
◆ Spacious modern dining pub serving up-to-date British cooking. Comfy sofas in bar; more formal dining area in converted barn with hieroglyphics on the walls. Compact, modern bedrooms.

BURLEYDAM – Ches. – see Whitchurch (Shrops.)

BURLTON – Shropshire – ✉ Shrewsbury   18 **B1**
🄳 London 235 mi – Shrewsbury 10 mi – Wrexham 20 mi

🍴 **The Burlton Inn** with rm 🍴 P VISA ⓞⓞ
✉ *SY4 5TB* – ✆ *(01939) 270 284 – www.burltoninn.co.uk*
– robertlesterrc@yahoo.com – Closed 25 December and 1 January
6 rm ⊃ – †£50 ††£80
Rest – (restricted lunch Monday) Carte £25/30
◆ Bustling, family run pub with a characterful, wood furnished interior. Extensive menus of traditional fare. Bedrooms in contemporary style. Four Poster bed available.

ENGLAND

█ London 128 mi – Cambridge 71 mi – Norwich 36 mi
▦ Lambourne Dropmore Rd, ✆ (01628) 666 755
⬡ Holkham Hall★★ **AC**, E : 3 m. by B 1155

The Hoste Arms   ⬚ ⟨⟩ ⅍ **P** VISA ⓶

The Green ✉ *PE31 8HD* – ✆ *(01328) 738 777 – www.hostearms.co.uk*
– reception@hostearms.co.uk – Fax (01328) 730 103
35 rm ⌖ – ♦£95/220 ♦♦£166/270 – 1 suite
Rest *The Restaurant* – see restaurant listing
♦ Renowned and restored 17C inn in this pretty village. Intriguing wing in Zulu style. Individually designed rooms provide a high level of comfort. Informal ambience.

Vine House without rest   ⒜ ⅍ ⟨⟩ **P** VISA ⓶

The Green ✉ *PE31 8HD* – ✆ *(01328) 738 777*
– www.vinehouseboutiquehotel.com
7 rm ⌖ – ♦£125/220 ♦♦£180/280
♦ Stylish, comfortable and elegant rooms with great bathrooms at this extended Georgian house. Evening butler service for drinks. Reception and meals at Hoste Arms opposite.

Railway Inn without rest   ⅍ ⟨⟩ **P** VISA ⓶

Creake Rd ✉ *PE31 8HD* – ✆ *(01328) 738 777 – www.hostearms.co.uk*
– reception@hostearms.co.uk
6 rm ⌖ – ♦£62/125 ♦♦£74/140
♦ Former station house with derelict platform and carriage to rear. Stylish, contemporary bedrooms boast bold feature walls, modern furniture, retro fittings and good facilities.

Fishes with rm   ⒜ ⟨⟩ VISA ⓶

Market Pl ✉ *PE31 8HE* – ✆ *(01328) 738 588 – www.fishescafe.co.uk*
– info@fishescafe.co.uk – Fax (01328) 730 534 – Closed 1 week Christmas and Sunday
2 rm ⌖ – ♦£70/90 ♦♦£95/130   **Rest** – Seafood – (lunch only) Carte £ 23/28
♦ Owners have changed the restaurant into a much simpler operation. The service remains friendly and locally caught seafood is still the highlight of the menu. Two elegant new bedrooms overlook the village green.

The Hoste Arms   ⬚ ⒜ ⬩ **P** VISA ⓶

The Green ✉ *PE31 8HD* – ✆ *(01328) 738 777 – www.hostearms.co.uk*
– reception@hostearms.co.uk – Fax (01328) 730 103
Rest – (booking essential) Carte £ 23/34 **s**⬚
♦ North Sea fish features in an Anglo-European and oriental fusion menu. Delightful terrace with Moroccan theme for summer dining. Invariably friendly staff.

at Burnham Thorpe Southeast : 1 ¼ m. by B 1355 – ✉ Burnham Market

The Lord Nelson   ⬚ ⬚ **P** VISA ⓶

Walsingham Rd ✉ *PE31 8HL* – ✆ *(01328) 738 241 – www.nelsonslocal.co.uk*
– enquiries@nelsonslocal.co.uk – Fax (01328) 738 241 – Closed Monday (except school holidays and half term holidays)
Rest – Menu £ 20 (dinner) – Carte £ 19/34
♦ Cosy, characterful pub in small village - Nelson was indeed born here: much memorabilia to remind you. Flagged floors, beams and a tiny bar. Good value, tasty dishes.

BURNHAM THORPE – Norfolk – **504** W 25 – see Burnham Market

BURNLEY – Lancashire – **502** N 22 – pop. 73 021   20 **B2**

█ London 236 mi – Bradford 32 mi – Leeds 37 mi – Liverpool 55 mi
– Manchester 25 mi – Middlesbrough 104 mi – Preston 22 mi
– Sheffield 68 mi
🛈 Bus Station, Croft St ✆ (01282) 664421, tic@burnley.gov.uk
▦ Towneley Todmorden Rd, Towneley Park, ✆ (01282) 451 636
▦ Glen View, ✆ (0870) 330 66 55

ENGLAND

Rosehill House 🗗 ⚉ ᵗⁱ P VISA ⦿ AE ①

Rosehill Ave, Manchester Rd, South : 1¼ m. by A 56 ✉ *BB11 2PW* – ℰ *(01282) 453 931* – *www.rosehillhousehotel.com* – *rhhotel@provider.co.uk* – *Fax (01282) 455 628*

29 rm � – †£55/70 ††£75 – 2 suites

Rest *Dugdales* – Carte £16/26

♦ Turreted 19C house in wooded grounds; residentially set. Airy lounge with long leather Chesterfields. Carefully repaired ornate ceilings a particular feature of various rooms. Imposing, elegantly panelled Dugdales evokes period charm.

BURNSALL – **North Yorkshire** – **502** O 21 – ✉ **Skipton**   22 **A2**

  ◘ London 223 mi – Bradford 26 mi – Leeds 29 mi

The Red Lion   ⇐ 🗗 ⚲ ᵗⁱ ⚐ P VISA ⦿ AE

✉ *BD23 6BU* – ℰ *(01756) 720 204* – *www.redlion.co.uk* – *redlion@daelnet.co.uk* – *Fax (01756) 720 292*

14 rm ⊃ – †£65/110 ††£83/150 – 3 suites

Rest *The Restaurant* – see restaurant listing

♦ Part 16C inn on the River Wharfe, ideal for walks, fishing and shooting. Cosy bedrooms, some in adjacent cottage: all have 19C brass beds or overlook the village green.

Devonshire Fell   ⇐ 🗗 ⚐ P VISA ⦿ AE ①

✉ *BD23 6BT* – ℰ *(01756) 729 000* – *www.devonshirefell.co.uk* – *res@devonshirehotels.co.uk* – *Fax (01756) 729 009*

10 rm ⊃ – †£95 ††£145/195 – 2 suites   **Rest** – Carte £25/30

♦ Once a club for 19C mill owners; strikingly updated by Lady Hartington with vivid colours and Hockney prints. Wide-ranging modern menu. Stylish rooms with Dales views.

✗✗ **The Red Lion**   🗗 P VISA ⦿ AE

✉ *BD23 6BU* – ℰ *(01756) 720 204* – *www.redlion.co.uk* – *redlion@daelnet.co.uk* – *Fax (01756) 720 292*

Rest – (bar lunch Monday-Saturday) Menu £32 (dinner) – Carte £19/34

♦ Dales meat, game and local cheeses in robust, seasonal menu. Eat in the firelit, oak-panelled bar or the dining room with mullioned windows facing the green. Keen staff.

BURPHAM – **W. Sussex** – **504** S 30 – **see Arundel**

BURRINGTON – **Devon** – **503** I 31   2 **C1**

  ◘ London 260 mi – Barnstaple 14 mi – Exeter 28 mi – Taunton 50 mi

Northcote Manor ⑤   ⇐ 🗗 ⚆ ✗ ᵗⁱ ⚐ P VISA ⦿ AE

Northwest : 2 m. on A 377 ✉ *EX37 9LZ* – ℰ *(01769) 560 501* – *www.northcotemanor.co.uk* – *rest@northcotemanor.co.uk* – *Fax (01769) 560 770*

10 rm ⊃ – †£170 ††£215 – 1 suite

Rest – (booking essential) (lunch by arrangement) Menu £15/38 **s**

♦ Creeper-clad hall above River Tew dating from 1716. Fine fabrics and antiques in elegant, individually styled rooms; attention to well-judged detail lends air of idyllic calm. Country house restaurant features eye-catching murals.

BURTON BRADSTOCK – **Dorset** – **503** L 31 – **See Bridport**

BURTON-UPON-TRENT – **Staffordshire** – **502** O 25 – **pop. 43 784**   19 **C1**

  ◘ London 128 mi – Birmingham 29 mi – Leicester 27 mi – Nottingham 27 mi – Stafford 27 mi

  🖪 Coors Visitor Centre, Horninglow St ℰ (01283) 508111, tic@eaststaffsbc.gov.uk

  🖪 Branston G. & C.C. Burton Rd, ℰ (01283) 528 320

  🖪 Craythorne Stretton Craythorne Rd, ℰ (01283) 564 329

ENGLAND

at Stretton North : 3 ¼ m. by A 5121 (A 38 Derby) – ⊠ Burton-upon-Trent

Dovecliff Hall ❧ ⟨⟩ ⟨⟩ ⟨⟩ ⟨⟩ AC rest, ⟨⟩ ⟨⟩ P VISA ⟨⟩ AE
Dovecliff Rd ⊠ DE13 0DJ – ℰ (01283) 531818 – www.dovecliffhallhotel.co.uk
– enquiries@dovecliffhallhotel.co.uk – Fax (01283) 516546
15 rm ⌨ – †£95/105 ††£225
Rest – (closed Sunday dinner) Menu £18 (lunch) – Carte £31/44
◆ Imposing, listed 1790s house with lovely gardens and spacious rooms, nestling in an elevated position above the Trent. Airy bedrooms, most boasting garden vistas. Formal dining rooms in restaurant and delightful orangery.

BURY – Greater Manchester – **502** N 23 – pop. 60 718   20 **B2**
🚩 London 211 mi – Leeds 45 mi – Liverpool 35 mi – Manchester 9 mi
🛈 The Met Art Centre, Market St ℰ (0161) 253 5111, touristinformation@bury.gov.uk
🖼 Greenmount, ℰ (01204) 883712

The Waggon ⟨⟩ P VISA ⟨⟩ AE
131 Bury and Rochdale Old Rd, Birtle, East : 2 m. on B 6222 ⊠ BL9 6UE
– ℰ (01706) 622955 – www.thewaggonatbirtle.co.uk
– Closed 26 December - 9 January, Sunday dinner and 2 weeks in August
Rest – Menu £16 (midweek) – Carte £20/28
◆ Unprepossessing façade hides a pleasantly decorated eatery with good value, no-nonsense cooking featuring a decidedly strong Lancashire base and the famous Bury Black Pudding.

BURY ST EDMUNDS – Suffolk – **504** W 27 – pop. 36 218   15 **C2**
Great Britain
🚩 London 79 mi – Cambridge 27 mi – Ipswich 26 mi – Norwich 41 mi
🛈 6 Angel Hill ℰ (01284) 764667, tic@stedsbc.gov.uk
🖼 The Swallow Suffolk Hotel G. & C.C. Fornham St Genevieve, ℰ (01284) 706777
⦿ Town ★ - Abbey and Cathedral ★
⦿ Ickworth House ★ **AC**, SW : 3 m. by A 143

Angel ⟨⟩ ⟨⟩ rm, AC rm, ⟨⟩ ⟨⟩ P VISA ⟨⟩ AE ⟨⟩
3 Angel Hill ⊠ IP33 1LT – ℰ (01284) 714000 – www.theangel.co.uk
– staying@theangel.co.uk – Fax (01284) 714001
74 rm ⌨ – †£99/140 ††£109/159 – 2 suites
Rest *The Eatery* – Menu £15 (lunch) s – Carte £24/34 s
◆ 15C inn near the Abbey Gardens with a fine Georgian façade. Rooms offer a bright, modern take on classic style: a few, named after famous visitors, have four poster beds. The Eatery is in atmospheric 12C cellars.

Ravenwood Hall ⟨⟩ ⟨⟩ ⟨⟩ ⟨⟩ ⟨⟩ P VISA ⟨⟩ AE ⟨⟩
East : 4 m. by A 14 ⊠ IP30 9JA – ℰ (01359) 270345 – www.ravenwoodhall.co.uk
– enquiries@ravenwood.co.uk – Fax (01359) 270788
14 rm ⌨ – †£100/133 ††£153/199
Rest – (Dinner only and Sunday lunch) Menu £37 – Carte £23/43
◆ Tudor dower house set in seven acres of calm lawns and woods. Welcoming lounge and individually designed bedrooms, more compact in the mews, are furnished with antiques. Restaurant with old wooden beams and inglenook fireplace.

Ounce House without rest ⟨⟩ ⟨⟩ ⟨⟩ P VISA ⟨⟩ ⟨⟩
Northgate St ⊠ IP33 1HP – ℰ (01284) 761779 – www.ouncehouse.co.uk
– enquiries@ouncehouse.co.uk – Fax (01284) 768315
5 rm ⌨ – †£80/95 ††£120/135
◆ Two 1870s houses knocked together; well furnished with Victorian elegance. Spacious, individually styled bedrooms; well-chosen antiques contribute to a characterful interior.

✗✗ **Maison Bleue** `VISA` ⓪⓪
30-31 Churchgate St ✉ *IP33 1RG –* 🕾 *(01284) 760623*
– www.maisonbleue.co.uk – info@maisonbleue.co.uk – Fax (01284) 761611
– Closed January, 2 weeks summer, Sunday and Monday
Rest – Seafood – Menu £ 17/26 – Carte £ 27/43
♦ 17C house with attractive façade and window boxes. Timbered interior with maritime memorabilia. A number of different rooms to eat in; predominantly seafood menu.

at Ixworth Northeast : 7 m. by A 143 – ✉ Bury St Edmunds

✗✗ **Theobalds** `VISA` ⓪⓪
68 High St ✉ *IP31 2HJ –* 🕾 *(01359) 231707 – www.theobaldsrestaurant.co.uk*
– Fax (01359) 231707 – Closed 10 days spring, Sunday dinner and Monday
Rest – (dinner only and lunch Sunday, Wednesday and Friday) Menu £ 28 (lunch) – Carte (dinner) £ 31/35
♦ Beamed part 16C cottage with a cosy firelit lounge. Friendly service and well-judged seasonal menus combine heartwarming favourites and contemporary dishes.

at Beyton East : 6 m. by A 14 – ✉ Bury St Edmunds

⌂ **Manorhouse** without rest
The Green ✉ *IP30 9AF –* 🕾 *(01359) 270960 – www.beyton.com*
– manorhouse@beyton.com – Closed Christmas
4 rm ⌷ – ♦£50/55 ♦♦£70/74
♦ Part 15C Suffolk longhouse with mature garden in idyllic spot overlooking village green. Two rooms are in converted barn; all have a rustic feel to them. Personally run.

at Horringer Southwest : 3 m. on A 143 – ✉ Bury St Edmunds

🏨 **The Ickworth** ⌖ `VISA` ⓪⓪ `AE` ⓪
✉ *IP29 5QE –* 🕾 *(01284) 735350 – www.lckworthhotel.com*
– info@lckworthhotel.co.uk – Fax (01284) 736300
29 rm ⌷ – ♦£200 ♦♦£310/440 – 11 suites
Rest *Fredericks* – (dinner only) Menu £ 40
Rest *Conservatory* – Carte approx. £ 30
♦ Ickworth House's east wing mixes modern and country house styles. Three airy drawing rooms; conservatory breakfasts. Comfy rooms with views. A favourite with young families. Smart Fredericks overlooks gardens. informal family dining in Conservatory.

🍴 **The Beehive** `VISA` ⓪⓪
The Street ✉ *IP29 5SN –* 🕾 *(01284) 735260 – Fax (01284) 735532 – Closed 25-26 December*
Rest – (Closed dinner Sunday) Carte £ 20/28
♦ Rustic, low-ceilinged, brick-and-flint pub near Ickworth House. Tasty daily specials like scallops in garlic butter affably served at pine tables or on a sheltered terrace.

BUSHEY – Hertfordshire – **504** S 29
12 A2

🚇 London 18 mi – Luton 21 mi – Watford 3 mi
🚉 Bushey Hall Bushey Hall Drive, 🕾 (01923) 222253
🚉 Bushey G. & C.C. High St, 🕾 (020) 8950 2283

Plan : see Greater London (North-West) 1

✗✗ **st James** `AC` `VISA` ⓪⓪ `AE`
30 High St ✉ *WD23 3HL –* 🕾 *(020) 8950 2480 – www.stjamesrestaurant.co.uk*
– info@stjamesresturant.co.uk – Fax (020) 8950 4107 – Closed 25 December, Sunday and Bank Holidays
BT**c**
Rest – Carte £ 23/30
♦ Long-standing, likeable restaurant with wood floored front room and bar, plus rear room for large parties. Appealing British menu shows real understanding of what guests want.

ENGLAND

BUTTERMERE – Cumbria – 502 K 20 – ⊠ Cockermouth

21 **A2**

🚄 London 306 mi – Carlisle 35 mi – Kendal 43 mi

介 | **Wood House** 🖉   ⇐ 🚗 ⤻ ⤼ **P**
Northwest : ½ m. on B 5289 ⊠ CA13 9XA – 🖋 (017687) 70208
– www.wdhse.co.uk – woodhouse.guest@virgin.net – Fax (017687) 70241
– April - October
3 rm ⌑ – 🛏£65 🛏🛏£100
Rest – (by arrangement, communal dining) Menu £29
♦ 16C guest house with wonderfully serene lakeside setting and stunning views.
Well-appointed lounge; antique furnished bedrooms. Meals cooked on the Aga using
fresh seasonal, local ingredients and served family-style around an antique table.

BUXHALL Suffolk – Suffolk – see Stowmarket

BUXTON – Derbyshire – 502 O 24 – pop. 20 836

16 **A1**

🚄 London 172 mi – Derby 38 mi – Manchester 25 mi – Stoke-on-Trent 24 mi
🅸 The Crescent 🖋 (01298) 25106, tourism@highpeak.gov.uk
🅶 Buxton and High Peak Townend, 🖋 (01298) 26263

🏨 | **Lee Wood**   🚗 🛗 🍴 🆚 **P** VISA ◯◯ AE ◑
The Park, on A 5004 ⊠ SK17 6TQ – 🖋 (01298) 23002 – www.leewoodhotel.co.uk
– reservations@leewoodhotel.co.uk – Fax (01298) 23228
– Closed 22-25 December
40 rm ⌑ – 🛏£70/110 🛏🛏£95/140
Rest *Elements* – Carte £25/37
♦ Family-owned hotel - a popular wedding venue - with contemporary, leather-furnished bar. Bedrooms come in standard or executive grades - the front ones are
the best. Large conservatory restaurant serves classical dishes.

介 | **Buxton's Victorian** without rest   🦠 **P** VISA ◯◯ AE
3A Broad Walk ⊠ SK17 6JE – 🖋 (01298) 78759 – www.buxtonvictorian.co.uk
– buxtonvictorian@btconnect.com – Fax (01298) 74732 – Closed Christmas
7 rm ⌑ – 🛏£58/78 🛏🛏£88/148
♦ Charming Victorian house built in 1860 for the Duke of Devonshire. Cosy lounge
and breakfast room with views over boating lake and bandstand. Bedrooms boast
period furniture.

介 | **Grendon** without rest   🚗 🍴 **P** VISA ◯◯
Bishops Lane ⊠ SK17 6UN – 🖋 (01298) 78831 – www.grendonguesthouse.co.uk
– grendonguesthouse@hotmail.com – Closed January - mid February
5 rm ⌑ – 🛏£45/70 🛏🛏£80/90
♦ Cosy Edwardian house on edge of town, built for a wealthy mill owner in the
1900s, with period features and pleasant gardens. Comfortable, traditionally furnished bedrooms.

BYFORD – Herefordshire – 503 L 27 – see Hereford

BYLAND ABBEY – N. Yorks. – 502 Q 21 – see Helmsley

CALLINGTON – Cornwall – 503 H 32

2 **C2**

🚄 London 237 mi – Exeter 53 mi – Plymouth 15 mi – Truro 46 mi

XX | **Langmans**   VISA ◯◯
3 Church St ⊠ PL17 7RE – 🖋 (01579) 384933 – www.langmansrestaurant.co.uk
– dine@langmansrestaurant.co.uk – Closed Sunday-Wednesday
Rest – (dinner only) (booking essential) (set tasting menu only) Menu £36
♦ Truly individual establishment: seven course tasting menus change monthly, employing skilful cooking with finesse; ingredients from small local suppliers. Booking
essential.

ENGLAND

CALLOW HILL – Worcestershire – 503

> ▶ London 120 mi – Birmingham 26 mi – Coventry 35 mi
>   – Wolverhampton 27 mi

🍺 **The Royal Forester**   🏡 🌿 **P** VISA ⓜ AE
  ✉ DY14 9XW – ☎ (01299) 266 286 – www.royalforesterinn.co.uk
  – contact@royalforesterinn.co.uk
  Rest – Menu £ 13 – Carte £ 20/30
  ♦ Traditional 15C pub that's undergone a sympathetic refurbishment. Appealing, down-to-earth menus feature a good value set meal or more wide-ranging à la carte. Modern, comfortable bedrooms, designed after foodstuffs.

CAMBER – E. Sussex – 504 W 31 – see Rye

CAMBERLEY – Surrey – 504 R 29 – pop. 46 120

> ▶ London 40 mi – Reading 13 mi – Southampton 48 mi
> 🏌 Camberley Heath Golf Drive, ☎ (01276) 23 258

🏨 **Frimley Hall H & Spa** ॐ 🍴 🔲 🕸 🕸 🖊 🔊 ⁽ᵞ⁾ ⅏ **P** VISA ⓜ AE ⓞ
  Lime Ave via Conifer Drive, East : ¾ m. off Portsmouth Rd (A 325) ✉ GU15 2BG
  – ☎ (0870) 400 8224 – www.macdonald-hotels.com
  – sales.frimleyhall@macdonald-hotels.co.uk – Fax (01276) 691 253
  98 rm ⊇ – ♦£239 ♦♦£239
  Rest *Linden* – Menu £ 24 (lunch) – Carte (dinner) £ 30/44
  ♦ Ivy-clad Victorian manor. A carved wooden staircase leads to the bedrooms; some are traditional with inlaid mahogany furniture, others are bright and modern. 19C restaurant with contemporary furnishings.

CAMBOURNE – Cambs. – see Cambridge

CAMBRIDGE – Cambridgeshire – 504 U 27 – pop. 117 717

📗 Great Britain

> ▶ London 55 mi – Coventry 88 mi – Ipswich 54 mi
>   – Kingston-upon-Hull 137 mi – Leicester 74 mi – Norwich 61 mi
>   – Nottingham 88 mi – Oxford 100 mi
> ✈ Cambridge City Airport : ☎ (01223) 373765, E : 2 m. on A 1303 X
> 🚩 The Old Library, Wheeler St ☎ (0871) 2268006, tourism@cambridge.gov.uk
> 🏌 Cambridge Menzies Hotel Bar Hill, ☎ (01954) 780 098
> 🔘 Town★★★ – St John's College★★★ **AC** Y – King's College★★ (King's College Chapel★★★) Z The Backs★★YZ – Fitzwilliam Museum★★Z **M1** – Trinity College★★Y – Clare College★Z **B** – Kettle's Yard★Y **M2** – Queen's College★ **AC** Z
> 🔲 Audley End★★, S : 13 m. on Trumpington Rd, A 1309, A 1301 and B 1383 – Imperial War Museum★, Duxford, S : 9 m. on M 11

Plan on next page

🏨 **Hotel du Vin** 🍴 🏢 ㅑ rm, 🖊 ⁽ᵞ⁾ ⅏ **P** VISA ⓜ AE
  15-19 Trumpington St ✉ CB2 1QA – ☎ (01223) 227 330 – www.hotelduvin.com
  – info.cambridge@hotelduvin.com – Fax (01223) 227 331 Ze
  41 rm – ♦£150 ♦♦£450, ⊇ £13.50
  Rest *Bistro* – Menu £ 18 (lunch) – Carte £ 27/36 ⊗
  ♦ A row of period houses converted into a smart and contemporary hotel. Lots of nooks and crannies; delightful library and cellar bar. Wine themed rooms with good extras. Relaxed bistro; classic dishes with French undertones.

🏨 **Hotel Felix** ॐ 🍴 🏡 🏢 ㅑ rm, ⁽ᵞ⁾ ⅏ **P** VISA ⓜ AE ⓞ
  Whitehouse Lane, Huntingdon Rd, Northwest : 1½ m. by A 1307 ✉ CB3 0LX
  – ☎ (01223) 277 977 – www.hotelfelix.co.uk – help@hotelfelix.co.uk
  – Fax (01223) 277 973
  52 rm – ♦£205 ♦♦£300, ⊇ £7.50
  Rest *Graffiti* – Menu £ 17 (lunch) – Carte dinner £ 28/39
  ♦ Privately owned Victorian mansion set in 3 acres of gardens with contemporary interior. Majority of bedrooms in extension; spacious and luxurious. Modern artwork decorates. Graffiti restaurant overlooks terrace and gardens.

ENGLAND

CAMBRIDGE

COLLEGES

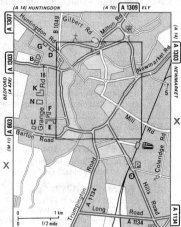

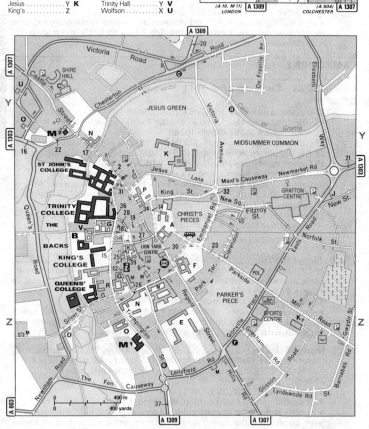

University Arms
🛗 ⅙ rm, 🄰🄲 ♍ 🐕 🄿 𝘝𝘐𝘚𝘈 ⓦ🄰🄴 ⓞ

Regent St ⊠ CB2 1AD – ℰ (01223) 273 000 – www.devere.co.uk
– dua.sales@devere-hotels.com – Fax (01223) 273 037
119 rm ⚏ – ♦£200/215 ♦♦£220 – 1 suite
Rest *Restaurant 17* – (dinner only) Menu £24 – Carte £26/35
♦ Charming Victorian hotel overlooking Parker's Piece. Dramatic atrium. Bedrooms are a mix of older period rooms and more modern; some with balconies and views over the green. Stylish, contemporary restaurant.

Gonville
🛗 ⅙ rm, 🄰🄲 rest, ♍ 🐕 🄿 𝘝𝘐𝘚𝘈 ⓦ🄰🄴

Gonville Pl ⊠ CB1 1LY – ℰ (01223) 366 611 – www.gonvillehotel.co.uk
– info@gonvillehotel.co.uk – Fax (01223) 315 470   **Zr**
73 rm – ♦£110/160 ♦♦£140/160, ⚏£12.75
Rest – (Closed 27-30 December) (bar lunch) Carte £18/26
♦ Popular family-owned, personally-run hotel with spacious, traditional interior. Newer bedrooms at rear of hotel. International menu served in the relaxed Atrium. Formal main dining room used only at weekends.

XXX Midsummer House (Daniel Clifford)
🚗 ⇔ 𝘝𝘐𝘚𝘈 ⓦ🄰🄴
❀❀

Midsummer Common ⊠ CB4 1HA – ℰ (01223) 369 299
– www.midsummerhouse.co.uk – reservations@midsummerhouse.co.uk
– Fax (01223) 302 672
– Closed 2 weeks Christmas, 2 weeks August, 1 week Easter, Tuesday lunch,
Sunday and Monday   **Ya**
Rest – (dinner only and lunch Friday-Saturday) Menu £33/65 🍷
Spec. Caramelised sweetbreads with ox tongue and maple jelly. Braised turbot with scallops and asparagus. Roasted pineapple and coconut gateau with lime sorbet.
♦ Idyllic location beside the River Cam, with conservatory dining. Mediterranean menus offer inventive, precise and detailed cooking. Smooth, formal service.

XXX Alimentum
🄰🄲 🕭 ⇔ 𝘝𝘐𝘚𝘈 ⓦ🄰🄴

152-154 Hills Rd ⊠ CB2 8PB – ℰ (01223) 413 000
– www.restaurantalimentum.co.uk – info@restaurantalimentum.co.uk
– Closed Chriustmas, Sunday dinner and Bank Holidays   **Xa**
Rest – Menu £16 (lunch) – Carte £31/42
♦ Sleek, stylish restaurant with striking red and black décor and spacious cocktail bar. Modern menu has French base; dishes are clean and unfussy with some innovative touches.

XX 22 Chesterton Road
🄰🄲 𝘝𝘐𝘚𝘈 ⓦ🄰🄴
🙂

22 Chesterton Rd ⊠ CB4 3AX – ℰ (01223) 351 880 – www.restaurant22.co.uk
– a&stommaso@restaurant22.co.uk – Fax (01223) 323 814
– Closed 1 week Christmas-New Year, Sunday and Monday   **Yc**
Rest – (dinner only) (booking essential) Menu £28
♦ Converted Victorian house with distinctive dining room decorated in rich colours. Monthly-changing classical menu; tasty, good value French-influenced dishes. Formal service.

at Histon North : 3 m. on B 1049 - X – ⊠ Cambridge

XX Phoenix
🄰🄲 🄿 𝘝𝘐𝘚𝘈 ⓦ

20 The Green ⊠ CB4 9JA – ℰ (01223) 233 766
– Closed 25-27 December
Rest – Chinese – (dinner only and Sunday lunch) Menu £25 – Carte £60/90
♦ Popular Chinese restaurant in former pub on village green. Comfortable, homely inner. Polite, smartly attired staff. Vast menu with plenty of Peking and Sichuan favourites.

ENGLAND

at Horningsea Northeast : 4 m. by A 1303 - X - and B 1047 on Horningsea rd – ⊠ **Cambridge**

🍴 **Crown and Punchbowl** with rm   🚗 ⅍ **P** 𝒱𝐼𝑆𝐴 ⓶ⓞ **AE**
High St ⊠ CB25 9JG – ℰ (01223) 860643 – www.thecrownandpunchbowl.co.uk – info@the crownandpunchbowl.co.uk – Fax (01223) 441814
5 rm – ♥£75 ♥♥£95
Rest – (Closed dinner Sunday and dinner Bank Holiday Monday) Carte £15/40
♦ Pub noteable for its lack of a bar. Snug, charming and rustic, with open fires and low beamed ceilings. Two main dining areas serving appealing seasonal and local food. Modern, spacious and relaxing bedrooms.

at Madingley West : 4½ m. by A 1303 - X – ⊠ **Cambridge**

🍴 **The Three Horseshoes**   🚗 ⅍ **P** 𝒱𝐼𝑆𝐴 ⓶ⓞ **AE**
High St ⊠ CB4 8SA – ℰ (01954) 210221 – www.thethreehorseshoesmadingley.com – 3hs@btconnect.com – Fax (01954) 212043 – Closed 1-2 January
Rest – Menu £20 – Carte £18/40 ❀
♦ Thatched inn with snug, fire-warmed bar and dressed tables in more formal dining room. Seasonal, Italian food made with best local produce. Professional, unobtrusive service.

at Hardwick West : 5 m. by A 1303 - X – ⊠ **Cambridge**

🏠 **Wallis Farmhouse** without rest   🚗 🕭 ⅍ ♔ **P** 𝒱𝐼𝑆𝐴 ⓶ⓞ **AE**
98 Main St ⊠ CB23 7QU – ℰ (01954) 210347 – www.wallisfarmhouse.co.uk – enquiries@wallisfarmhouse.co.uk – Fax (01954) 210988
4 rm ⊇ – ♥£50/55 ♥♥£68/75
♦ Remotely set Georgian house in picturesque village. Immaculately kept bedrooms in a converted barn across courtyard. Breakfast served in main house. Spacious rear garden.

at Cambourne West : 7 m. by A 428 - X – ⊠ **Cambridge**

🏨 **The Cambridge Belfry**   🚗 🖭 ✆ 🐾 ♨ ₤₅ 🖥 𝐀𝐂 rest, ⅍ ☏ 🕭 **P** 𝒱𝐼𝑆𝐴 ⓶ⓞ **AE** ①
Back Lane ⊠ CB23 6BW – ℰ (01954) 714600 – www.qhotels.co.uk – cambridgebelfry@qhotels.co.uk – Fax (01954) 714998
110 rm ⊇ – ♥£90/130 ♥♥£100/140 – 10 suites
Rest *Bridge* – (Closed Sunday lunch) (bar lunch Sunday) Carte £29/40
♦ Brick-built hotel in centre of new town. Large, well-equipped gym and spa facilities; several conference rooms. Refurbished, high quality bedrooms. Formal dining in the spacious Bridge.

at Bar Hill Northwest : 5½ m. by A 1307 - X - off A 14 – ⊠ **Cambridge**

🏨 **Menzies Cambridge**   🚗 🖭 🐾 ₤₅ ✕ 🖪 🖥 ⅁ rm, 𝐀𝐂 rest, ⍩ 🕭 **P** 𝒱𝐼𝑆𝐴 ⓶ⓞ **AE** ①
Bar Hill ⊠ CB23 8EU – ℰ (01954) 249988 – www.menzieshotels.co.uk – lisa.porter@menzieshotels.co.uk – Fax (01954) 780010
136 rm – ♥£120 ♥♥£140, ⊇ £9.95
Rest – ℰ (0871) 4720002 (dinner only) Carte £24/38
♦ Well-located, tastefully refurbished hotel with high quality bedrooms; ideal for tourists as well as the business traveller. Up-to-the-minute conference rooms; golf course and spa. Family-friendly dining in Brasserie restaurant.

at Little Shelford South : 5½ m. by A 1309 - X - off A 10 – ⊠ **Cambridge**

✕✕ **Sycamore House**   **P** 𝒱𝐼𝑆𝐴 ⓶ⓞ
1 Church St ⊠ CB22 5HG – ℰ (01223) 843396 – Closed Christmas-New Year and Sunday-Tuesday
Rest – (dinner only) (booking essential) Menu £25
♦ Converted 16C cottage in a sleepy hamlet. Long narrow dining room with thick walls, low ceiling and open fire. Frequently-changing, seasonal menu with hearty base.

at Little Wilbraham East : 7 ¼ m. by A 1303 - X – ✉ **Cambridge**

The Hole in the Wall
*2 High St ✉ CB21 5JY – ℰ (01223) 812 282 – www.the-holeinthewall.com
– Closed 25 December and 2 weeks in January*
Rest – (Closed Monday (except bank holidays for lunch), dinner Sunday)
Carte £ 21/30
◆ Remotely set 15C pub with plenty of charm. The confident kitchen produces good value, flavoursome British dishes and tasty puddings, using seasonal ingredients in classical ways.

CANNINGTON – Somerset – **503** K 30 – **see Bridgwater**

CANTERBURY – Kent – **504** X 30 – **pop. 43 552** ▌ *Great Britain*   9 **D2**
▶ London 59 mi – Brighton 76 mi – Dover 15 mi – Maidstone 28 mi
– Margate 17 mi
🛈 12-13 Sun St, Buttermarket ℰ (01227) 378100,
canterburyinformation@canterbury.gov.uk
◉ City★★★ - Cathedral★★★ Y - St Augustine's Abbey★★ **AC** YZ **K** – King's
School★ Y – Mercery Lane★ Y **12** - Christ Church Gate★ Y **D** – Museum of
Canterbury★ **AC** Y **M1** – St Martin's Church★ Y **N** – West Gate Towers★ **AC**
Y **R**

Plan on next page

ENGLAND

Abode Canterbury
*High St ✉ CT1 2RX – ℰ (01227) 766 266 – www.abodehotels.co.uk
– reservationscanterbury@abodehotels.co.uk – Fax (01227) 784874*   Y**a**
72 rm – †£ 89/190 ††£ 89/295, ☑ £ 13.50
Rest Michael Caines – see restaurant listing
◆ Centrally located, this smart hotel has undergone a vast top-to-toe transformation. A distinctive modern feel pertains, typified by sleek, airy bedrooms.

Ebury
*65-67 New Dover Rd ✉ CT1 3DX – ℰ (01227) 768 433 – www.ebury-hotel.co.uk
– info@ebury-hotel.co.uk – Fax (01227) 459 187
– Closed 24 December-12 January*   Z**r**
15 rm ☑ – †£ 70/100 ††£ 90/120
Rest – (closed Sunday) (dinner only) Menu £ 25 **s**
◆ 1850s redbrick hotel where drinks are served in a lounge holding a collection of Bulls Eye clocks. Bedrooms are all spacious and comfortable. Restaurant ambience reflects age of hotel.

Magnolia House
*36 St Dunstan's Terrace ✉ CT2 8AX – ℰ (01227) 765 121
– www.magnoliahousecanterbury.co.uk – info@magnoliahousecanterbury.co.uk
– Fax (01227) 765 121 – Closed 25-26 December*   Y**s**
6 rm ☑ – †£ 55/70 ††£ 95/125   **Rest** – (by arrangement) Menu £ 35
◆ Gracious Georgian house with calm, sunny interior and plush bedrooms including four-poster suite. Breakfast room offers good choice, and boasts charming garden outlook. Home-cooked dinners.

Michael Caines – at Abode Canterbury Hotel
*High St ✉ CT1 2RX – ℰ (01227) 826 684 – www.michaelcaines.com
– reservationscanterbury@abodehotels.co.uk – Fax (01227) 784874*   Y**a**
Rest – (Closed Sunday dinner) Menu £ 20/25 – Carte £ 36/44
◆ Enjoy a glass of Champagne in smart bar before repairing to the upmarket restaurant to enjoy modern British cooking utilising a variety of styles and classical techniques.

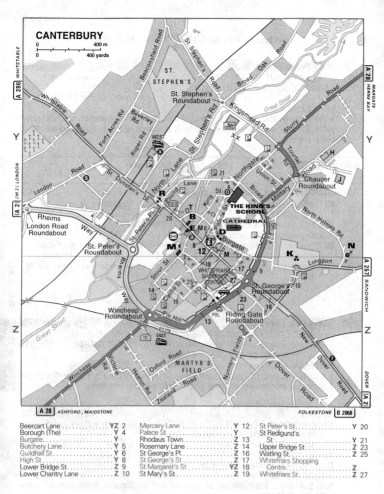

CANTERBURY

0 ———— 400 m
0 ———— 400 yards

✗ **The Goods Shed**   ℙ VISA 🅜🅞 AE ①

Station Rd West, St Dunstans ✉ *CT2 8AN* – ℰ *(01227) 459153*
– Closed Sunday dinner and Monday   Y**x**

Rest – Carte £ 22/31

◆ Once derelict railway shed, now a farmers' market that's open all day. Its eating area offers superbly fresh produce with no frills and real flavours very much to the fore.

---

at Tyler Hill North West 4.5 m by A28 and A290 turning right into Tyler Hill rd in Blean

---

🏠 **The Ivy House**   ℙ VISA 🅜🅞

27 Hackington Rd ✉ *CT2 9NE* – ℰ *(01227) 472200* – *Closed Sunday dinner and Monday*

Rest – Carte £ 24/33

◆ Owners came from Dove at Dargate and have given this traditional village pub a lick of paint. Simpler lunch menu; dinner showcases confident, seasonal cooking in substantial portions.

188

at Lower Hardres South : 3 m. on B 2068 - Z – ⊠ Canterbury

🏠 **The Granville**   🚗 🕭 AC P VISA ◍◉ AE
😊 Street End ⊠ CT4 7AL – ✆ (01227) 700402 – Fax (01227) 700925
– Closed 25-26 December
Rest – Carte £ 23/36
♦ Open plan Scandinavian-style rooms, with exposed beams, leather sofas and a central fire. A concise menu keeps things commendably simple, with the focus on local produce.

CARBIS BAY – Cornwall – **503** D 33 – **see St Ives**

CARLISLE – Cumbria – **501** L 19 – **pop. 71 773** 📗 Great Britain   21 **B1**
🚗 London 317 mi – Blackpool 95 mi – Edinburgh 101 mi – Glasgow 100 mi – Leeds 124 mi – Liverpool 127 mi – Manchester 122 mi – Newcastle upon Tyne 59 mi
✈ Carlisle Airport ✆ (01228) 573641, NW : 5 ½ m. by A 7 - BY - and B 6264
🛈 Old Town Hall, Green Market ✆ (01228) 625600, tourism@carlisle-city.gov.uk
🏌 Aglionby, ✆ (01228) 513029
🏌 Stony Holme St Aidan's Rd, ✆ (01228) 625511
🏌 Dalston Hall Dalston, ✆ (01228) 710165
👁 Town ★ - Cathedral ★ (Painted Ceiling ★) AY E – Tithe Barn ★ BY A
🖸 Hadrian's Wall ★★, N : by A 7 AY

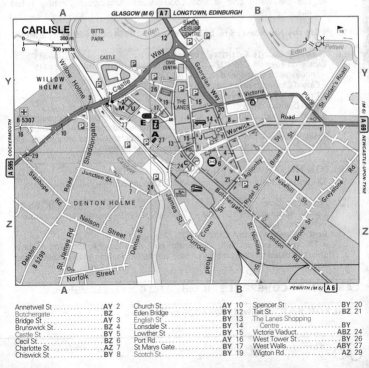

ENGLAND

Cumbria Park
32 Scotland Rd, North : 1 m. on A 7 ⊠ CA3 9DG
– ℰ (01228) 522887
– www.cumbriaparkhotel.co.uk
– cumbriaparkhotel@wightcablenorth.net
– Fax (01228) 514796
– Closed 25-26 December
47 rm ⊊ – ✝£78 ✝✝£150
Rest – (bar lunch) Carte £15/29 **s**
♦ Traditional hotel with well kept bedrooms; some with jacuzzi baths. Corridor walls filled with postcards and posters from owner's travels. Bottle green restaurant with Roman theme serves classic menu. Bar meals among the fishtanks in lounge/bar.

Number Thirty One
31 Howard Place ⊠ CA1 1HR – ℰ (01228) 597 080 – www.number31.co.uk
– pruirving@aol.com – Fax (01228) 597 080   BY**a**
4 rm ⊊ – ✝£65 ✝✝£90
Rest – (dinner only) (by arrangement) Menu £20
♦ Well-appointed Victorian townhouse with sumptuous lounge and immaculately-kept bedrooms. Richly decorated dining room with window onto plant-filled terrace.

Gallo Rosso
Parkhouse Rd, Kingstown, Northwest : 2 ¾ m. by A 7 ⊠ CA6 4BY – ℰ (01228) 526 037 – www.gallorosso.co.uk – Fax (01228) 550 074
– Closed 23 December -14 February and Tuesday
Rest – Italian – Carte £18/30
♦ Busy Italian restaurant with cosy lounge, linen-laid tables and a large open kitchen so you can watch chef at work. Good value cooking including freshly baked bread.

at High Crosby Northeast : 5 m. by A 7 - BY - and B 6264 off A 689 – ⊠ **Carlisle**

Crosby Lodge Country House
Crosby-on-Eden ⊠ CA6 4QZ – ℰ (01228) 573 618 – www.crosbylodge.co.uk
– enquiries@crosbylodge.co.uk – Fax (01228) 573 428
– Closed Christmas-mid January
11 rm ⊊ – ✝£90/98 ✝✝£160/170
Rest – (Sunday dinner residents only) Menu £40 (dinner) – Carte £37/57
♦ Grade II listed, castellated house built in 1802. Warm ambience and welcoming hostess. Traditionally furnished lounge. Comfortable bedrooms with pleasant countryside outlook. Richly coloured dining room with polished brass around fireplace. Classic, homecooked food includes renowned sweet trolley.

CARLTON HUSTHWAITE – North Yorkshire – 502 Q 21   22 B2
◘ London 230 mi – Leeds 51 mi – Middlesbrough 32 mi – York 20 mi

Carlton Bore
Carlton Husthwaite ⊠ YO7 2BU – ℰ (01845) 501 265 – www.carltonbore.co.uk
– chefhessel@aol.com
Rest – (Closed Monday) Carte £17/25
♦ 17C inn set in a delightful village with rural views. Diverse, appealing menu of Yorkshire based produce; worthy of note are the Deli Platters and Yorkshire cheese selection.

CARLTON-IN-COVERDALE – N. Yorks. – 502 O 21 – see Middleham

CARLYON BAY – Cornwall – 503 F 33 – see St Austell

> If breakfast is included the ⊊ symbol appears after the number of rooms.

CARTERWAY HEADS – Northumberland – **501** O 19 – ⊠ **Shotley**
Bridge

> ▶ London 272 mi – Carlisle 59 mi – Newcastle upon Tyne 21 mi

🍴🛏 **Manor House Inn** with rm   **P** 𝒱𝒾𝒮𝒜 **◑◐** **AE**
on A 68 ⊠ *DH8 9LX* – ✆ *(01207) 255 268* – *www.manorhouse-a68.co.uk*
– Closed dinner 25 December
4 rm ⊆ – †£46 ††£79   **Rest** – Carte £18/20
♦ 18C inn with views over the moors; whet your whistle in the bar or dine in the
smartly refurbished restaurant. Tasty dishes and home-made desserts. Smart rooms
with views.

> The 🏵 award is the crème de la crème.
> This is awarded to restaurants
> which are really worth travelling miles for!

CARTHORPE – North Yorkshire   22 **B1**

> ▶ London 228 mi – Leeds 49 mi – Middlesbrough 40 mi – York 34 mi

🍴🛏 **Fox and Hounds**   🎭 **P** 𝒱𝒾𝒮𝒜 **◑◐**
⊠ *DL8 2LG* – ✆ *(01845) 567433* – *www.foxandhoundscarthorpe.co.uk*
– helenjt36@btinternet.com – Fax (01845) 567155
– Closed 25 December, 26 December dinner and first week in January
Rest – (Closed Monday) Menu £16 (weekdays) – Carte £18/28
♦ Former village smithy; forge and water pump still in restaurant. Walls and shelves
stacked with ornaments, plates, photos and old farm equipment. Classic homemade
pub dishes.

CARTMEL – Cumbria – **502** L 21 – **see Grange-over-Sands**

CASTLE CARROCK – Cumbria – **502** L 19 – **see Brampton**

CASTLE CARY – Somerset – **503** M 30 – **pop. 3 056**   4 **C2**

> ▶ London 127 mi – Bristol 28 mi – Wells 13 mi

🏠 **Clanville Manor** without rest   🛏 🜂 ⚓ 🎭 📶 **P** 𝒱𝒾𝒮𝒜 **◑◐**
West : 2 m. by B 3152 and A 371 on B 3153 ⊠ *BA7 7PJ* – ✆ *(01963) 350124*
– www.clanvillemanor.co.uk – info@clanvillemanor.co.uk – Fax (01963) 350719
– Closed Christmas and New Year
4 rm ⊆ – †£35/80 ††£70/90
♦ 18C house, charmingly cluttered. Heirlooms and antiques abound. Breakfasts
served from the Aga. Walled garden boasts heated pool. Individual bedrooms, including four-poster.

at Lovington West : 4 m. by B 3152 and A 371 on B 3153 – ⊠ **Castle Cary**

🍴🛏 **The Pilgrims at Lovington** with rm   🎭 🛏 rm, 📞 **P** 𝒱𝒾𝒮𝒜 **◑◐** **AE**
Lovington ⊠ *BA7 7PT* – ✆ *(01963) 240 597*
– www.thepilgrimsatlovington.co.uk
– jools@thepilgrimsatlovington.co.uk
5 rm ⊆ – ††£110
Rest – (Closed Sunday dinner, Monday and Tuesday lunch)
Carte £17/38
♦ Unremarkable appearance masks charming interior. British/Mediterranean menu
uses local and homemade produce. Comfortable, contemporary bedrooms, luxurious
bathrooms and substantial breakfasts.

ENGLAND

> ◗ London 110 mi – Bristol 23 mi – Chippenham 6 mi
> ◉ Village ★★

Manor House H. and Golf Club ⅋   🎎 🕭 🗟 🍴 🔣 🛠

⊠ SN14 7HR – ℰ (01249) 782 206   **P** VISA ⓶ AE ⓪
– www.exclusivehotels.co.uk – enquiries@manor-housecc.co.uk
– Fax (01249) 783 100
44 rm ⊡ – ♦£ 180 ♦♦£ 235 – 4 suites
Rest *The Bybrook* – Menu £ 19/52 **s**
Spec. Seared scallops with sautéed potatoes and creamed truffle. Fillet of beef
with cauliflower soubise and wild mushroom ravioli. Pineapple parfait and carpaccio with coconut sorbet.
♦ Particularly peaceful manor in a sweeping green with trout in the river. Fine fabrics
and oak panelling exude history. Luxurious bedrooms in mews cottages or main
house. Smart restaurant; cooking is exact and confident.

Castle Inn   🕭 🍴 VISA ⓶ AE

⊠ SN14 7HN – ℰ (01249) 783 030 – www.castle-inn.info
– enquiries@castle-inn.info – Fax (01249) 782 315 – Closed 25 December
11 rm ⊡ – ♦£ 80/150 ♦♦£ 175   **Rest** – Carte £ 19/31
♦ A hostelry dating back to the 12C in the middle of a delightful and historic village.
Wooden beams and much character throughout. Breakfast in conservatory. Large
and varied menu served in rustic bar.

at Nettleton Shrub West : 2 m. by B 4039 on Nettleton rd (Fosse Way)
– ⊠ Chippenham

Fosse Farmhouse ⅋   🎐 🕈 **P** VISA ⓶

⊠ SN14 7NJ – ℰ (01249) 782 286 – www.fossefarmhouse.com
– caron@fossefarmhouse.com – Fax (01249) 783 066
3 rm ⊡ – ♦£ 65/85 ♦♦£ 90/130   **Rest** – (by arrangement) Menu £ 28
♦ 18C Cotswold Stone farmhouse personally run by enthusiastic owner. Cream teas
served in the garden in summer. Welcoming bedrooms with French artefacts and
Gallic style.

> ◗ London 123 mi – Birmingham 38 mi – Leicester 23 mi – Nottingham 13 mi
> ✈ Nottingham East Midlands Airport : ℰ (0871) 919 9000, S : by B 6540 and
>   A 453

Priest House on the River ⅋   ≤ 🕭 🗟 🕭 🍴 🕈 🛁 **P** VISA ⓶ AE ⓪

Kings Mills, West : 1 ¾ m. by Park Lane ⊠ DE74 2RR – ℰ (01332) 810649
– www.handpicked.co.uk/thepriesthouse – enquiries@thepriesthouse.co.uk
– Fax (01332) 815 334
39 rm ⊡ – ♦£ 80/140 ♦♦£ 100/165 – 3 suites
Rest *Brasserie* – Carte £ 25/40
♦ Stylish, contemporary hotel in tranquil riverside setting. Comfortable bedrooms -
some with views of the river - decorated in neutral shades, with giant plasma screen
TVs. Brasserie has bar as well as tables laid with starched linen.

at Breedon on the Hill Southwest : 4 m. by Breedon rd off A 453 – ⊠ Castle
Donington

The Three Horseshoes Inn   🕭 **P** VISA ⓶

Main St ⊠ DE73 8AN – ℰ (01332) 695 129 – www.thehorseshoes.com
– ian@thehorseshoes.com – Closed 25 and 31 December, 1 January
Rest – (Closed Sunday dinner) Carte £ 25/32
♦ Welcoming pub with open fire and interesting artefacts. Menu features local, seasonal produce and simple, honest dishes with an international edge; homemade
classical puddings.

ENGLAND

CATEL – **503** P 33 – see Channel Islands (Guernsey)

CAUNTON – Notts. – **502** R 24 – see Newark-on-Trent

CHADDESLEY CORBETT – Worcs. – **503** N 26 – see Kidderminster

CHADWICK END – West Midlands – **503** O 26   19 **C2**
▪ London 106 mi – Birmingham 13 mi – Leicester 40 mi
  – Stratford-upon-Avon 16 mi

The Orange Tree   🖼 🕯 **P** *VISA* **◎ ①**
Warwick Road, on A 4141 ✉ *B93 0BN* – 𝒞 *(01564) 785 364*
– *www.lovelypubs.co.uk* – *Fax (01564) 782 988* – *Closed 25 December and Sunday dinner*
Rest – (booking essential) Menu £15 (lunch) – Carte £15/22
♦ Modern roadside dining pub with attractive exterior and stylish interior. The menu of modish classics is good value and has an appealing, flexible range.

> We try to be as accurate as possible when giving room rates
> but prices are susceptible to change.
> Please check rates when booking.

ENGLAND

CHAGFORD – Devon – **503** I 31   2 **C2**
▪ London 218 mi – Exeter 17 mi – Plymouth 27 mi
⑥ Dartmoor National Park★★

Gidleigh Park (Michael Caines) ⌂   ⟨ 🖼 🏊 🎾 ॐ ⅙ rm, ☝ **P**
❀❀ *Northwest : 2 m. by Gidleigh Rd* ✉ *TQ13 8HH*   *VISA* **◎ AE ①**
– 𝒞 *(01647) 432 367* – *www.gidleigh.com* – *gidleighpark@gidleigh.co.uk*
– *Fax (01647) 432 574*
23 rm � – ♦£240 ♦♦£480 – 1 suite
Rest – (booking essential) Menu £48/95 🕮
Spec. Roast quail with ravioli of spinach and pea purée. Slow roast veal with lettuce and broad beans. Strawberry mousse and jelly with a black olive and basil purée.
♦ Smart, stylish and beautifully situated in 45 Dartmoor acres; sumptuous rooms the epitome of style, with fine English fabrics and antiques; those to the front have best views. Classically based cooking, prepared with skill and flair, proudly showcases local produce. Excellent choice of wines.

22 Mill Street with rm   *VISA* **◎ AE ①**
22 Mill Street ✉ *TQ13 8AW* – 𝒞 *(01647) 432 244* – *www.22millst.com*
– *enquiries@22millst.com*
2 rm – ♦£99/119 ♦♦£99/119, ⊆ £12.50
Rest – (Closed Sunday dinner and Monday) (booking essential) Menu £35/45
♦ Smart, intimate restaurant on high street of scenic village; immaculately laid tables. Modern menu displays a strong French base and relies on locally sourced ingredients. Pleasant, contemporary bedrooms.

at Easton Northeast : 1 ½ m. on A 382 – ✉ Chagford

Easton Court without rest   🖼 ☝ **P** *VISA* **◎**
Easton Cross ✉ *TQ13 8JL* – 𝒞 *(01647) 433 469* – *www.easton.co.uk*
– *stay@easton.co.uk*
5 rm ⊆ – ♦£60/65 ♦♦£75/80
♦ Well appointed accommodation and a high ceilinged lounge overlooking the immaculate gardens. Home made marmalade a speciality. Friendly atmosphere.

at Sandypark Northeast : 2 ¼ m. on A 382 – ⊠ Chagford

Mill End   🚗 🗫 📶 **P.** *VISA* **MC**
on A 382 ⊠ *TQ13 8JN – ℰ (01647) 432 282 – www.millendhotel.com*
– info@millendhotel.com – Fax (01647) 433 106 – Closed 1-14 January
14 rm ☲ – **†**£90/140 **††**£90/240 – 2 suites
Rest – (light lunch Monday-Saturday) Menu £42
♦ Country house with mill wheel; river Teign runs through garden. Framed pictures, curios grace interiors. Upstairs bedrooms have views; those downstairs have private patios. Pretty restaurant, bright and comfortable.

Parford Well without rest 🌫   🚗 🎇 📶
on Drewsteignton rd ⊠ *TQ13 8JW – ℰ (01647) 433 353*
– www.parfordwell.co.uk – tim@parfordwell.co.uk – Closed Christmas and New Year
3 rm ☲ – **†**£85 **††**£95
♦ Tastefully maintained with superbly tended gardens. Elegant sitting room has plenty of books and French windows to garden. Two breakfast rooms. Homely, immaculate rooms.

The Sandy Park Inn with rm   🚗 🗫 🍴 *VISA* **MC** **AE** **①**
⊠ *TQ13 8JW – ℰ (01647) 433 267 – www.sandyparkinn.co.uk*
– enquiries@sandyparkinn.co.uk
5 rm ☲ – **†**£55 **††**£92   **Rest** – Carte £20/28
♦ Small but characterful 17C thatched inn with flagged floors, heavy beams and open fires. Delightful hillside garden. Modern, sophisticated cooking. Cosy bedrooms have flat screen TVs.

CHANNEL ISLANDS

503 KLM 33

ALDERNEY – Alderney – **503** M 32 – **pop. 2 400**   5 **B1**

- Aurigny Air Services ℰ (0871) 871 0717
- States Office, Queen Elizabeth II St ℰ (01481) 822994, tourism@alderney.net
- Braye Bay★ – Mannez Garenne (≤★ from Quesnard Lighthouse) – Telegraph Bay★ – Vallee des Trois Vaux★ – Clonque Bay★

Braye – Alderney   5 **B1**

Braye Beach ⌂   ≤ 🕮 📶 🖥 AC rest, 🛜 ⁀ ✿ P. VISA ⓪ AE

✉ GY9 3XT – ℰ (01481) 824 300 – www.brayebeach.com
– reception@brayebeach.com – Fax (01481) 824 301
27 rm ⌷ – †£ 60/120 ††£ 120/180
Rest – Carte £ 23/36 **s**

♦ Smart, contemporary hotel set on edge of beach. Vaulted basement houses a series of lounges, dining room and a 19-seat cinema. Modern European cooking with a subtle seafood slant.

First and Last   ≤ VISA ⓪ AE ①

✉ GY9 3TH – ℰ (01481) 823 162
– Easter-October
Rest – Seafood – (Closed Monday) (dinner only) Carte £ 21/33

♦ Positioned by the harbour with scenic views. Simple pine furniture, blue gingham tablecloths. Nautical theme prevails. Keen use of island produce with seafood base.

St Anne – Alderney   5 **B1**

Farm Court without rest   🚗 🛜 ⁀ VISA ⓪ ①

Le Petit Val ✉ GY9 3UX – ℰ (01481) 822 075 – www.farmcourt-alderney.co.uk
– relax@farmcourt-alderney.co.uk – Fax (01481) 822 075 – Closed Christmas and New Year
11 rm ⌷ – †£ 39/60 ††£ 78/98

♦ Converted stone farm buildings around cobbled courtyard and garden. Sitting room and breakfast room. Spacious well-appointed bedrooms with contemporary and antique furniture.

Your opinions are important to us:
please write and let us know about your discoveries and experiences –
good and bad!

ENGLAND

GUERNSEY – Guernsey – 503 L 32 – pop. 58 867   5 **A2**

🛧 Guernsey Airport 𝒞 (01481) 237766, Aurigny Air 𝒞 (0871) 871 0717

🚢 from St Peter Port to France (St Malo) and Jersey (St Helier) (Condor Ferries Ltd) 2 weekly – from St Peter Port to France (Dielette) (Manche Iles Express) (summer only) (60 mn) – from St Peter Port to Herm (Herm Seaway) (25 mn) – from St Peter Port to Sark (Isle of Sark Shipping Co. Ltd) (45 mn) – from St Peter Port to Jersey (St Helier) (HD Ferries) (1hr) – from St Peter Port to Jersey (St Helier) (Condor Ferries Ltd) daily

🚢 from St Peter Port to France (St Malo) and Jersey (St Helier) (Condor Ferries Ltd) – from St Peter Port to Jersey (St Helier) and Weymouth (Condor Ferries Ltd)

🛈 P.O. Box 23, North Esplanade 𝒞 (01481) 723552 Passenger Terminal, New Jetty 𝒞 (01481) 715885, enquiries@guernseytourist board.com

◎ Island★ – Pezeries Point★★ – Icart Point★★ – Côbo Bay★★ – St Martin's Point★★ – St Apolline's Chapel★ – Vale Castle★ – Fort Doyle★ – La Gran'mere du Chimquiere★ – Rocquaine Bay★ – Jerbourg Point★

Catel/Castel – pop. 8 975   5 **A2**

🏨 | **Cobo Bay**   ≼ 🕏 📶 🗚 rest, ✗ ♈ 🄿 𝓥𝓘𝓢𝓐 ⦿ 🄰🄴
Cobo Coast Rd ✉ GY5 7HB – 𝒞 (01481) 257 102 – www.cobobayhotel.com
– reservations@cobobayhotel.com – Fax (01481) 254 542
– Closed 4 January - 1 March
36 rm ⌂ – ♈£49/120 ♈♈£99/150
Rest – (dinner only and Sunday lunch) Menu £ 25
♦ Modern hotel on peaceful, sandy Cobo Bay; an ideal location for families. The rooms are pleasant with bright décor and some have the delightful addition of seaview balconies. Romantic dining with views of sunsets.

Fermain Bay – Guernsey   5 **A2**

🏨 | **Fermain Valley** ⌂   ≼ 🚗 🕏 🗖 🕏 📶 ॑ & rm, 🗚 rest, ♈ 🄿 𝓥𝓘𝓢𝓐 ⦿ 🄰🄴
Fermain Lane ✉ GY11ZZ – 𝒞 (01481) 235 666 – www.fermainvalley.com
– info@fermainvalley.com – Fax (01481) 235 413
45 rm ⌂ – ♈£ 110/140 ♈♈£ 180/220
Rest Restaurant – (dinner only and Sunday lunch) Carte £ 21/33 **s**
Rest Valley Brasserie – Carte £ 20/30 **s**
♦ Fine sea views through the trees. Smart contemporary country house theme prevails: sleek lounges, decked terrace, library, and fresh, carefully appointed rooms with balconies. Fine dining in comfortable Restaurant. Fresh fish and simple grills at the Brasserie.

✗✗✗ | **Christophe** (Christophe Vincent)   ≼ 🚗 🕏 ⇔ 🄿 𝓥𝓘𝓢𝓐 ⦿ 🄰🄴
🕸 | Fort Rd ✉ GY1 1ZP – 𝒞 (01481) 230 725 – www.christophe-restaurant.co.uk
– christophe@fermainvalley.com – Fax (01481) 230 726 – Closed Sunday dinner and Monday
Rest – Menu £ 20 (lunch) – Carte £ 32/49
Spec. Crab in gazpacho with coriander chantilly. Guernsey beef hindquarter. Raspberry soufflé with white chocolate sorbet.
♦ Contemporary and seriously stylish restaurant with superb sea views, serving good value, boldly flavoured, seasonal dishes using quality French produce. Personable service.

Forest – Guernsey – pop. 1 549   5 **A2**

✗ | **Cafe d'Escalier**   🕏 🄿 𝓥𝓘𝓢𝓐 ⦿
Le Gouffre, Southwest : 2 m. ✉ GY8 0BN – 𝒞 (01481) 264 121
– armelleanddean@hotmail.com – Fax (01481) 263 319
Rest – Carte £ 15/30
♦ Lively eatery with easy going style. Wide menu offers homemade produce with Mediterranean influences; from breakfast and snacks through to afternoon tea and dinner. Buzzy, alert service.

Vazon Bay – Guernsey – ⊠ Catel   5 **A2**

La Grande Mare   ⪡ 🚗 🕭 🔍 🍴 🍽 🎣 📺 🛏 🎾 📶 ⛳

Vazon Coast Rd ⊠ GY5 7LL – ℰ *(01481) 256 576*   **P** **VISA** **◉◉** **AE** **①**
– www.lagrandemare.com – reservations@lagrandemare.com
– Fax (01481) 256 532
12 rm ⌂ – †£95/105 ††£95/110
– 13 suites – ††£109/130
Rest – Menu £15/24 **s** – Carte £20/32 **s**
◆ Resort complex, constantly evolving. Bedrooms are a good size, are well kept and
boast every mod con; some have balconies. Family friendly, with indoor/outdoor
activities. Formal dining room overlooks golf course.

Kings Mills – Guernsey   5 **A2**

Fleur du Jardin   🚗 🕭 🔍 📶 **P** **VISA** **◉◉** **AE** **①**

Castel ⊠ GY5 7JT – ℰ *(01481) 257 996 – www.fleurdujardin.com*
– info@fleurdujardin.com – Fax (01481) 256 834
15 rm ⌂ – †£50 ††£128
Rest – Menu £13 (lunch) – Carte £15/25
◆ Characterful 15C inn. A few traditional bedrooms remain but most are fresh and
modern, displaying neutral colours and a New England style; luxury bathrooms.
Traditional bar with modern dining rooms and contemporary terrace offers local
produce and good fish.

St Martin – Guernsey – pop. 6 267   5 **A2**

▶ St Peter Port 2 mi

Bon Port ⌖   ⪡ 🚗 🕭 🔍 📶 **P** **VISA** **◉◉**

Moulin Huet Bay ⊠ GY4 6EW – ℰ *(01481) 239 249 – www.bonport.com*
– mail@bonport.com – Fax (01481) 239 596
– Closed January-February
23 rm ⌂ – †£104/159 ††£115/199
– 1 suite
Rest *Bon Port* – (bar lunch Monday-Saturday) Menu £29
– Carte £20/36
◆ Perched on the top of the cliff, with a commanding view of the bay, this hotel is
very keenly and personally run. Improving rooms vary in size and style and some
have balconies. Relaxed dining in large, redecorated bistro.

Jerbourg ⌖   ⪡ 🚗 🕭 🔍 🄰🄲 rest, 📶 **P** **VISA** **◉◉**

Jerbourg Point ⊠ GY4 6BJ – ℰ *(01481) 238 826 – www.hoteljerboug.com*
– stay@hoteljerbourg.com – Fax (01481) 238 238
– Closed 5 January-1 March
29 rm ⌂ – †£42/92 ††£82/117
– 1 suite
Rest – Menu £22 (dinner) – Carte £16/44
◆ In a prime position for walks to sandy bays. Popular terrace for afternoon teas.
Equipped with solar heated outdoor pool and garden patio. Most rooms have pleasant sea views. Finely presented, fish based cuisine.

La Barbarie ⌖   🚗 🕭 🔍 📶 📶 **P** **VISA** **◉◉**

Saints Bay ⊠ GY4 6ES – ℰ *(01481) 235 217 – www.labarbariehotel.com*
– reservations@labarbariehotel.com – Fax (01481) 235 208
– March-October
21 rm ⌂ – †£57/74 ††£74/108
– 1 suite
Rest – (residents only bar lunch) Menu £22 – Carte £19/29
◆ Stone-built former farmhouse with a welcoming, cottagey style. Characterful bar;
well-kept pool and terrace. Bedrooms are traditional and comfortable. Seafood a
speciality.

ENGLAND

ENGLAND

Saints Bay ⌖ ⛋ 🍴 🦢 ⚒ ⛟ 🅿 VISA ⓒⓞ AE ⓞ
Icart ✉ GY4 6JG – ℰ *(01481) 238 888* – www.saintsbayhotel.com
– *info@saintsbayhotel.com* – Fax *(01481) 235 558*
– *Closed 3 January-7 March*
35 rm ⊡ – �£39/72 ♦♦£58/124
Rest – (bar lunch Monday-Saturday) Menu £19 – Carte approx. £16 **s**
◆ Located on Icart Point, close to Fisherman's Harbour, the southern tip of the island and perfect for cliff top walks. Multilingual staff; neat bedrooms with all amenities. Broad choice of menus.

La Michele ⌖ 🦢 🍴 🦢 🅿 VISA ⓒⓞ AE
Les Hubits ✉ GY4 6NB – ℰ *(01481) 238 065* – www.lamichelehotel.com
– *info@lamichelehotel.com* – Fax *(01481) 239 492*
– *April-October*
16 rm ⊡ – ♦£44/65 ♦♦£88/130
Rest – (dinner only) (residents only) Menu £16
◆ Painted and canopied façade with conservatory lounge and secluded garden. Lovely seating area around the pool. Fermain bay is nearby; pleasant, unfussy bedrooms.

Sunnydene Country ⌖ 🦢 🍴 🦢 🅿 VISA ⓒⓞ AE
Rue des Marettes ✉ GY4 6JH – ℰ *(01481) 236 870*
– www.sunnydenecountryhotel.com – *info@sunnydenecountryhotel.com*
– Fax *(01481) 237 468* – *Closed 6 October - 1 April*
20 rm ⊡ – ♦£37/67 ♦♦£64/94
Rest – (dinner only) Menu £18 – Carte £14/21
◆ Neat and tidy hotel with pitch and putt to rear of garden! Comfortable, homely lounge; linen-laid dining room. Pretty pool and terrace area. Rooms in house or garden.

The Auberge ⚒ ⛟ 🍴 🅿 VISA ⓒⓞ AE ⓞ
Jerbourg Rd ✉ GY4 6BH – ℰ *(01481) 238 485* – www.theauberge.gg
– *dine@theauberge.gg* – Fax *(01481) 710 936*
– *Closed 25-26 and 31 December-5 February and Sunday dinner in winter*
Rest – (booking essential) Carte approx. £34
◆ A splendid spot to sample contemporary brasserie-style dishes. Modern informal style, attractive terrace and excellent views of sea and islands.

St Peter Port – Guernsey – pop. 16 648   5 **A2**
🏌 Rohais St Pierre Park, ℰ *(01481) 727 039*
◉ Town★★ – St Peter's Church★ Z – Hauteville House★ **AC** Z – Castle Cornet★ (≤★) **AC** Z
◷ Saumarez Park★ (Guernsey Folk Museum★), W : 2 m. by road to Catel Z – Little Chapel★, SW : 2¼ m. by Mount Durand road Z

Plan opposite

Old Government House H. & Spa ⚒ ⛟ 🍴 🦢 ⊕ 🦢 ♨ 🎱
St Ann's Pl ✉ GY1 2NU – ℰ *(01481)*   ♿ rm, 🦢 ⚒ 🧖 🅿 VISA ⓒⓞ AE ⓞ
724 921 – www.theoghhotel.com – *ogh@theoghhotel.com*
– Fax *(01481) 724 429*   **Ya**
60 rm ⊡ – ♦£135/160 ♦♦£160/320
Rest *Governors* – (Closed Monday and lunch Saturday-Sunday) (booking essential) Menu £43 (lunch) – Carte £36/43
Rest *The Brasserie* – Carte £27/39
◆ Now owned by Red Carnation Hotels with plans to improve this 18C house, first built for island governors. Already sitting room and leisure have been upgraded. Bedrooms planned next. Fine-dining in Governors. Informal Brasserie with local produce.

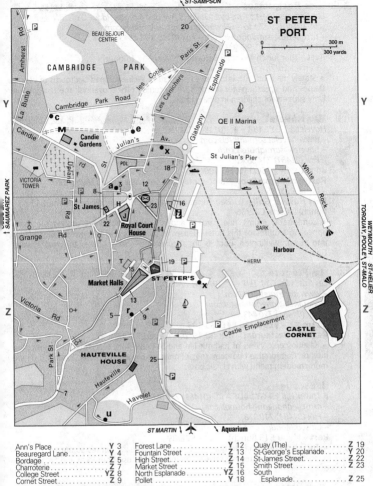

ST PETER PORT

L'ANCRESSE ST-SAMPSON

0   300 m
0   300 yards

CAMBRIDGE PARK

BEAU SEJOUR CENTRE

Paris St.
les Cotils
Les Canichers
Glategny
Esplanade
Amherst Rd
La Burte
Candie
Cambridge Park Road
Candie Gardens
Julian's Av.
Upland rd
St James
Grange Rd
Victoria Rd
Park St.
Victoria Tower
Royal Court House
Market Halls
ST PETER'S
HAUTEVILLE HOUSE
Hauteville
Havelet

QE II Marina
St Julian's Pier
White Rock
SARK
HERM
Harbour
Castle Emplacement
CASTLE CORNET

SALMAREZ PARK
WEYMOUTH/TOROUAY/POOLE
ST-HELIER
ST-MALO

ST MARTIN   Aquarium

Duke of Richmond

⟨ 🛋 🏊 🛎 🍴 🛜 🦼 *VISA* ⊙ **AE** ①

Cambridge Park ✉ *GY1 1UY –* ☎ *(01481) 726 221*
– www.dukeofrichmond.com
– reception@dukeofrichmond.com
– Fax (01481) 728 945

Yc

74 rm ☕ – ♦£65/88 ♦♦£95/145
– 1 suite
Rest – (bar lunch Monday-Friday) Menu £21 – Carte £22/34
♦ Boasts views over Candie Gardens. Refurbished bedrooms are nicely coordinated and have good amenities; those at the rear overlook the terrace. Large dining room; local seafood the speciality.

199

Les Rocquettes　　　🚗 🌿 🖼 🛅 📶 🛊 ⚕ 🍴 ♨ 👗 🅿 VISA ⓜ AE ⓘ

Les Gravees, West : 1 m. by St Julian's Ave and Grange Rd ✉ *GY1 1RN*
– ℰ *(01481) 722 146 – www.rocquettes.sarniahotels.com*
– *rocquettes@sarniahotels.com – Fax (01481) 714 543*
51 rm 🍽 – ♦£50/95 ♦♦£100/140
Rest – (bar lunch Monday-Saturday) Menu £17 (dinner)
– Carte £16/28

♦ Stately mansion with impressive health suite. Well-equipped bedrooms of various shapes and sizes. Superior rooms have balconies; others overlook the rear garden. Early suppers for children in dining room.

De Havelet　　　🚗 🖼 ♨ 🅰 rest, ⚕ 🍴 🅿 VISA ⓜ AE ⓘ

Havelet ✉ *GY1 1BA* – ℰ *(01481) 722 199*
– *www.havelet.sarniahotels.com*
– *havelet@sarniahotels.com*
– *Fax (01481) 714 057*　　　　　　　　　　　　　　　　　　Zu
34 rm 🍽 – ♦£50/110 ♦♦£100/150
Rest *Wellington Boot* – (dinner only and Saturday lunch) Menu £20
– Carte £25/36
Rest *Havelet Grill* – (closed Sunday lunch and Monday dinner) Menu £15
(lunch) – Carte £22/36

♦ Comfortable rooms, fine gardens and a hilltop location are among the many appealing features of this hotel. Elegant indoor pool and a courtesy bus for trips into town. Wellington Boot is in a converted coach house. Informal Havelet Grill.

La Frégate ♨　　　🚗 🌿 🅰 🍴 👗 🅿 VISA ⓜ AE ⓘ

Les Cotils ✉ *GY1 1UT* – ℰ *(01481) 724 624*
– *www.lafregatehotel.com*
– *enquiries@lafregatehotel.com*
– *Fax (01481) 720 443*　　　　　　　　　　　　　　　　　　Ye
22 rm 🍽 – ♦£90/180 ♦♦£180/195
Rest *The Restaurant* – Menu £19/28 – Carte £24/37

♦ Kaleidoscopic views of harbour life and St Peter Port. Peaceful location; modern interior. Comfortable bedrooms; newer ones are bigger and better. Extended dining room; modern menu with classic base.

L'Escalier　　　🌿 🅰 VISA ⓜ

6 Tower Hill ✉ *GY1 1DF* – ℰ *(01481) 710 088*
– *armelleanddean@hotmail.com*
– *Fax (01481) 710 878*
– *Closed Monday and Saturday lunch*　　　　　　　　　　　　　Zr
Rest – Menu £15 (lunch) – Carte £25/39

♦ Tucked away in the old quarter of town, a personally run restaurant with a sheltered terrace and attentive service. Complex dishes use both local and French produce.

Saltwater　　　🍴 🌿 🅰 VISA ⓜ AE

Albert Pier ✉ *GY1 1AD* – ℰ *(01481) 720 823 – www.saltwater.gg*
– *Fax (01481) 722 702 – Closed 2 weeks Christmas-New Year, Saturday lunch
and Sunday*　　　　　　　　　　　　　　　　　　　　　　　　Zx
Rest – Seafood – Carte approx. £40

♦ Warmly run restaurant in impressive location at end of historic pier overlooking harbour near large marina. Modern feel. Extensive menus have a solid seafood slant.

The Swan Inn　　　VISA ⓜ AE ⓘ

St Julian's Avenue ✉ *GY1 1WA* – ℰ *(01481) 728 655*
– *www.christiesleisuregroup.com – Fax (01481) 728 655*
– *Closed Sunday in summer*　　　　　　　　　　　　　　　　Yx
Rest – Menu £15 (dinner) – Carte £16/25

♦ Traditional Victorian pub with green façade and cosy wood burners; a popular stop off after work. More sedate dining upstairs. Generous classic dishes of hearty, satisfying food.

ENGLAND

St Saviour – Guernsey – pop. 2 696

5 **A2**

▶ St Peter Port 4 mi

🖪 The Farmhouse

🚗 🎋 ⃛ AC ⃛ 👍 P VISA ⓜ AE

Route des Bas Courtils ⊠ *GY7 9YF –* ℰ *(01481) 264 181 – www.thefarmhouse.gg*
– enquiries@thefarmhouse.gg – Fax (01481) 266 272
14 rm ⊆ – ♀£ 120/150 ♀♀£ 120/250   **Rest** – Carte £ 24/31
♦ Former farm restyled in boutique vein. Stylish, sumptuous bedrooms with high-tech amenities; bathrooms with heated floors. Pleasant garden and pool; terrace and kitchen garden to follow. Contemporary cooking with international edge uses Island's finest produce in eclectic ways.

✂ The Pavilion

🚗 🎋 P VISA ⓜ

😊 *Le Gron* ⊠ *GY9 9RN –* ℰ *(01481) 264 165 – lecknleck@cwgsy.net – Closed*
Christmas-mid January, and Mondays in winter
Rest – (Lunch only and Saturday dinner in summer) Carte £ 21/28
♦ Located in grounds of jewellers Bruce Russell and Son. Pleasant interior of exposed stone and beams. Excellent value, well executed dishes using good quality local produce.

HERM – Herm – 503 M 33 – pop. 60

🚢 to Guernsey (St Peter Port) (Herm Seaway) (20 mn)
◎ Le Grand Monceau★

🖪 White House ⌂

≤ 🚗 ⃛ 🎋 ⃛ ✻ ✻ VISA ⓜ

⊠ *GY1 3HR –* ℰ *(01481) 722 159 – www.herm-island.com*
– hotel@herm-island.com – Fax (01481) 710 066 – 20 March-6 October
40 rm (dinner included) ⊆ – ♀£ 85/115 ♀♀£ 260
Rest *Conservatory* – (booking essential) Menu £ 26 (dinner) – Carte lunch
£ 21/27
Rest *Ship Inn* – (booking advisable) Carte approx. £ 19
♦ Hotel with real country house feel: offset by verdant hills, the beach extends to the door. Guernsey and Jethou can be viewed from the hushed lounge. Attractive rooms. Formal Conservatory with seafood emphasis. Relaxed Ship Inn.

JERSEY – C.I. – 503 L 33 – pop. 85 150

5 **B2**

🛬 States of Jersey Airport : ℰ (01534) 445 500
🚢 from St Helier to France (St Malo) (Condor Ferries Ltd) (summer only) –
from St Helier to France (St Malo) (Condor Ferries Ltd) 3 weekly - from
Gorey to France (Carteret) (Manche Iles Express) (summer only) (60mn) –
from St Helier to Guernsey (St Peter Port) (Condor Ferries Ltd) (50 mn) –
from St Helier to Guernsey (St Peter Port) (Condor Ferries Ltd) daily
🚢 from St Helier to France (St Malo) and Guernsey (St Peter Port) (Condor
Ferries Ltd) – from St Helier to Sark (Condor Ferries Ltd) (50 mn) – from
St Helier to Guernsey (St Peter Port) and Weymouth (Condor Ferries Ltd)
🖪 Liberation Sq, St Helier ℰ (01534) 448877, info@jersey.com
◎ Island★★ - Jersey Zoo★★ AC – Jersey Museum★ - Eric Young Orchid
Foundation★ – St Catherine's Bay★ (≤★★) – Grosnez Point★ - Devil's
Hole★ – St Matthews Church, Millbrook (glasswork★) – La Hougue Bie★
(Neolithic tomb★ AC) - Waterworks Valley - Hamptonne Country Life
Museum★ – St Catherine's Bay★ (≤★★) – Noirmont Point★

Beaumont – Saint Peter

5 **B2**

✂ Bistro Soleil

≤ 🎋 P VISA ⓜ AE

La Route de la Haule ⊠ *JE3 7BA –* ℰ *(01534) 720 249*
– www.aboutjersey.net/eat/bistro_soleil – bistrosoleil@aboutjersey.net
– Fax (01534) 625 621 – Closed 25-26 December, 1 January, Sunday dinner,
Monday and Bank Holidays
Rest – Menu £ 15/25 – Carte £ 24/30
♦ Series of connected rooms with superb views over St Aubins Bay. Minimalist style: just a couple of modern pictures. Freshly prepared, bold menus with Mediterranean accent.

ENGLAND

Bouley Bay – Trinity   5 **B2**

▶ St Helier 6 mi

🏨 **The Water's Edge**   ← 🚗 🏊 🛁 ⚡ 🎿 **P** *VISA* **◍**
✉ *JE3 5AS* – ✆ *(01534) 862 777* – *www.watersedgehotel.co.je*
– *mail@watersedgehotel.co.je* – *Early April-mid October*
47 rm ⌸ – †£43/97 ††£110/168 – 3 suites
Rest *Waterside* – (dinner only) Menu £26 **s**
Rest *Black Dog Bar* – Carte £18/21 **s**
♦ A long standing hotel that boasts breathtaking bay views. Secluded garden with
well-manicured lawns. Comfortable, well-appointed accommodation. Formal Waterside for tables-with-a-view. Black Dog Bar with quarterdeck al fresco area.

Gorey – Saint Martin – ✉ **St Martin**   5 **B2**

▶ St Helier 4 mi
◉ Mont Orgueil Castle★ (≤★★) **AC** – Jersey Pottery★

🏨 **Moorings**   **AC** rest, 📶 *VISA* **◍** **AE**
Gorey Pier ✉ *JE3 6EW* – ✆ *(01534) 853 633* – *www.themooringshotel.com*
– *reservations@themooringshotel.com* – *Fax (01534) 857 618*
15 rm ⌸ – †£56/102 ††£112/144
Rest – Menu £16/22 – Carte £30/58 **s**
♦ Located at the base of Gorey Castle, overlooking the waterfront, once the heart of
the oyster fishing industry. Well-priced; the first floor bedrooms have terraces. Pleasant decked area at front of restaurant.

🍴🍴 **Suma's**   ← 🏞 **AC** *VISA* **◍** **AE** **◑**
Gorey Hill ✉ *JE3 6ET* – ✆ *(01534) 853 291* – *www.sumasrestaurant .com*
– *Fax (01534) 851 913* – *Closed 23 December- 22 January*
Rest – (booking essential) Menu £19 (lunch) – Carte £28/46 **s** 🍷
♦ Cheerful and contemporary; fine terrace views of Gorey Castle and harbour. Dishes
are carefully prepared and innovatively presented; pleasant service enhances the
enjoyment.

🍴 **Village Bistro**   🏞 *VISA* **◍**
☺ *Gorey Village* ✉ *JE3 9EP* – ✆ *(01534) 853 429* – *www.village-bistro.com*
– *thevillagebistro@yahoo.co.uk* – *Closed Sunday dinner and Monday*
Rest – Menu £14/19 – Carte £24/30
♦ Local produce sourced daily from small suppliers. Unpretentious feel; interesting
choices to be made, particularly of seafood dishes.

Green Island – Saint Clement   5 **B2**

🍴 **Green Island**   🏞 *VISA* **◍**
St Clement ✉ *JE2 6LS* – ✆ *(01534) 857 787* – *www.greenislandrestaurant.com*
– *greenislandrestaurant@jerseymail.co.uk* – *Closed 21 December - early February,*
Sunday dinner and Monday
Rest – Seafood – (booking essential) Carte £30/42
♦ Relaxed, intimate restaurant with seafront terrace. Internationally influenced menu
relies on island produce to create well-judged flavoursome dishes; mainly seafood
specials.

Grouville – Grouville   5 **B2**

▶ St Helier 3 mi

🍴 **Cafe Poste**   🏞 **P** *VISA* **◍** **◑**
La Rue de la ville ES Renauds ✉ *JE3 9FY* – ✆ *(01534) 859696 – Closed 1 week*
early January, 1 week June and 2 weeks November, Monday and Tuesday
Rest – Carte £21/39
♦ Former post office and general store with hidden decked area for outdoor dining.
Very much a neighbourhood favourite. Strong use of island produce on eclectic,
modish menus.

La Haule – Saint Peter – ✉ St Brelade

🏠 **La Haule Manor** without rest ← 🚗 🏊 ⁱ⁰ 🅟 VISA ◐ 🖭
St Aubin's Bay ✉ JE3 8BS – ℰ (01534) 746 013 – www.lahaulemanor.com
– lahaulemanor@jerseymail.co.uk – Fax (01534) 745 501
– April-14 October
10 rm – ♦£ 54/85 ♦♦£ 90/122
♦ Attractive, extended Georgian house with fine coastal outlook. Period style sitting room; stylish breakfast room; large basement bar. Airy, well-kept bedrooms with good view.

🏠 **Au Caprice** 🏊 VISA ◐
Route de la Haule, on A 1 ✉ JE3 8BA – ℰ (01534) 722 083
– www.aucapricejersey.ie – aucaprice@jerseymail.co.uk – Fax (01534) 280 058
– 15 March-October
12 rm ⌑ – ♦£ 33/50 ♦♦£ 50/70   **Rest** – (by arrangement) Menu £ 12
♦ Clean-lined white guesthouse with French windows; light and airy, providing homely good value rooms: two of them share large balcony at the front. Close to large sandy beach. Each morning, guests told dining room menu.

La Pulente – Saint Brelade – ✉ St Brelade

5 **B2**

▶ St Helier 7 mi
🏌 Les Mielles G. & C.C. St Ouens Bay, ℰ (01534) 482 787

🏠🏠 **Atlantic** 🐾 ← 🚗 🏖 🏊 🔳 🍴 ⅄₆ 🍽 🏥 🏊 ⁱ⁰ 🛁 🅟 VISA ◐ AE ◑
🏵 *Le Mont de la Pulente, on B 35 ✉ JE3 8HE – ℰ (01534) 744 101*
– www.theatlantichotel.com – info@theatlantichotel.com – Fax (01534) 744 102
– Closed 4 January-5 February
49 rm ⌑ – ♦£ 150/175 ♦♦£ 200/300 – 1 suite
Rest *Ocean* – (booking essential) Menu £ 23/45
Spec. Langoustine with pork belly and asparagus. Sea bass with cabbage, borlotti beans and a cep infusion. Kaffir lime parfait and jelly with chocolate tortellini.
♦ Striking hotel with contemporary style overlooking La Pulente Bay. Bedrooms are spacious; Garden suites have own terrace; others have balconies. Elegant restaurant serving precise, unfussy cooking; chef an ambassador of Jersey's fine larder. High calibre service.

La Rocque – Grouville

5 **B2**

▶ St Helier 8 mi

🍴🍴 **Borsalino Rocque** 🏖 🅟 VISA ◐ AE
✉ JE3 9FF – ℰ (01534) 852 111 – reservations@borsalinorocque.com
– Fax (01534) 856 404 – Closed 25-26 December and Tuesday
Rest – Seafood – Menu £ 11/16 – Carte £ 26/33
♦ Well-spaced tables in large conservatory and dining room filled with curios. A long-established family business, popular with island residents. Wide choice in menus.

Rozel Bay – Saint Martin – ✉ St Martin

5 **B2**

▶ St Helier 6 mi

🏠🏠 **Chateau La Chaire** 🐾 🚗 🏖 🏊 ⁱ⁰ 🅟 VISA ◐ AE
Rozel Valley ✉ JE3 6AJ – ℰ (01534) 863 354 – www.chateau-la-chaire.co.uk
– res@chateau-la-chaire.co.uk – Fax (01534) 865 137
12 rm ⌑ – ♦£ 85/120 ♦♦£ 170/245 – 2 suites
Rest – Menu £ 15/25 – Carte £ 36/44
♦ Imposing chateau dated 1843, rich in paintings and antiques: individually decorated bedrooms overlook the quiet wooded grounds. Ornate sitting room. Conservatory dining room; terrace popular in summer.

St Aubin – Saint Brelade – ⊠ St Brelade   5 **B2**
> ▶ St Helier 4 mi

🔓🔓 Somerville   ≪ 🚗 ⌘ ⬧ 🔟 rest, ⍋ ⬩⬩ **P.** *VISA* **⬧⬧** **AE**
Mont du Boulevard, South :¾ m. via harbour ⊠ *JE3 8AD* – ℰ *(01534) 741 226*
– www.dolanhotels.com – somerville@dolanhotels.com – Fax (01534) 746 621
56 rm ⌁ – †£65/145 ††£109/219
Rest *Tides* – Menu £16/30 **s** – Carte approx. £38 **s**
♦ Delightful views of the harbour, bay and village. Evening entertainment laid on. Cheerful rooms, some in superior style. Cloth clad, classic dining room.

🏠 Panorama without rest   ≪ 🚗 ⍋ ⬩⬩ *VISA* **⬧⬧** **AE**
La Rue du Crocquet ⊠ *JE3 8BZ* – ℰ *(01534) 742 429*
– www.panoramajersey.com – info@panoramajersey.com – Fax (01534) 745 940
– Early April-October
14 rm ⌁ – †£55/102 ††£109/135
♦ Personally run hotel with conservatory, garden and bay views. Also boasts a teapot collection. The superior style bedrooms are very pleasant. All rooms boast good amenities.

🏠 Sabots d'or   ⍋ ⬩⬩ *VISA* **⬧⬧** **AE**
High St ⊠ *JE3 8BZ* – ℰ *(01534) 743 732* – *mail@sabotsdor.com* – *Fax (01534) 490 142* – *Closed 22 December-7 January*
12 rm ⌁ – †£25/42 ††£54/64   **Rest** – (by arrangement) Menu £14
♦ Floral furnishings in homely and cosy bedrooms. Well located for shops, watersports; its cobbled high street position not far from picturesque harbour. Traditional cooking.

✕ Salty Dog Bar and Bistro   🏠 *VISA* **⬧⬧**
Le Boulevard ⊠ *JE3 8AB* – ℰ *(01534) 742 760* – *www.saltydogbistro.com*
– info@saltydogbistro.com – Fax (01534) 742 932
– Closed 2 weeks from 24 December
Rest – Asian influences – (Closed lunch Monday-Thursday except in Summer) Menu £22/30 – Carte £25/40
♦ Wood panelled walls and church pews create rustic feel in quirky, informal restaurant in St. Aubin's harbour. Menus blend local produce with New World and Asian influences.

🏠 Old Court House Inn with rm   ≪ 🏠 *VISA* **⬧⬧** **AE** **①**
St Aubin's Harbour ⊠ *JE3 8AB* – ℰ *(01534) 746 433*
– www.oldcourthousejersey.com – info@oldcourthousejersey.com – Fax (01534) 745 103 – Closed 25 December
9 rm ⌁ – †£40 ††£120   **Rest** – Menu £13 (lunch) – Carte £30/50
♦ Atmospheric quayside inn, once a courthouse and merchant's house, dating from 15C. Bar featured in Bergerac TV series. Cosmopolitan menu with seafood emphasis. Neat bedrooms.

St Brelade's Bay – Saint Brelade – pop. 9 560 – ⊠ St Brelade   5 **B2**
> ▶ St Helier 6 mi
> ◉ Fishermen's Chapel (frescoes ★)

🏠🏠🏠 L'Horizon   ≪ 🏠 🔟 🛳 🐾 ⌆ ⬧ ⬧ rm, 🏃 🔟 rest, ⍋ ⬩⬩ 🔥 **P.**
⊠ *JE3 8EF* – ℰ *(01534) 743 101*   *VISA* **⬧⬧** **AE** **①**
– www.handpicked.co.uk/lhorizon – lhorizon@handpicked.co.uk – Fax (01534) 746 269 – Closed 2 weeks Christmas and New Year
99 rm ⌁ – †£85/190 ††£170/320 – 7 suites
Rest *The Grill* – see restaurant listing
Rest *Brasserie* – (Closed Sunday) Menu £34 (dinner) – Carte £28/41
♦ Period hotel right on the beach and consequently popular for its stunning views from the terrace and some of its tastefully decorated front bedrooms. Serene indoor pool. Informal brasserie adjacent to the sea.

St Brelade's Bay

La Route de la Baie ⊠ *JE3 8EF* – ℰ *(01534) 746 141*
– www.stbreladesbayhotel.com – info@stbreladesbayhotel.com – Fax (01534)
747 278 – 3 April-2 October
88 rm ⊑ – †£88/212 ††£206/304 – 3 suites
Rest – Menu £15/30 – Carte £28/39

♦ Traditional seafront hotel with mouth-watering views of bay and resplendent gardens with pool. Rattan furnished sitting room and spacious bedrooms. Friendly and family run. Front, sea-facing restaurant.

Golden Sands

La Route de la Baie ⊠ *JE3 8EF* – ℰ *(01534) 741 241 – www.dolanhotels.com*
– goldensands@dolanhotels.com – Fax (01534) 499 366 – April-October
62 rm ⊑ – †£46/156 ††£72/182
Rest – (bar lunch) Menu £24 (dinner) **s** – Carte £19/30 **s**

♦ With adjacent sweep of a sandy bay and many of the bedrooms south-facing with balconies, this hotel is a popular spot. Within easy reach of the airport and St Helier. Seasonal menus.

The Grill – at L'Horizon Hotel

⊠ *JE3 8EF* – ℰ *(01534) 490 082 – www.handpicked.co.uk/lhorizon*
– lhorizon@handpicked.co.uk – Fax (01534) 746 269 – Closed Sunday and
Monday
Rest – (dinner only) Menu £43

♦ Intimately styled grill room with tasteful cream and brown banquettes and framed photos of film stars. Seafood stars but faces competition from a strong suit of meat dishes.

Oyster Box

La Route de la Baie ⊠ *JE3 8EF* – ℰ *(01534) 743 311 – www.oysterbox.co.uk*
– eat@oysterbox.co.uk – Closed 25-26 December and 1 January
Rest – Carte £20/45

♦ Cool, modern restaurant on the beach with al fresco dining. Flexible menu ranges from sandwiches to 3 courses, featuring quality ingredients prepared in a fresh, simple manner.

St Helier – Saint Helier – pop. 28 310   5 **B2**

🖻 Jersey Museum★ **AC** Z - Elizabeth Castle (≤★) **AC** Z – Fort Regent (≤★ **AC**) Z
🖸 St Peter's Valley - German Underground Hospital★ **AC**, NW : 4 m. by A 1,
A 11 St Peter's Valley rd and C 112

Plan opposite

Royal Yacht

Weighbridge ⊠ *JE2 3NF* – ℰ *(01534) 720 511 – www.theroyalyacht.com*
– reception@theroyalyacht.com – Fax (01534) 767 729   Zb
108 rm ⊑ – †£125 ††£205 – 2 suites
Rest *Sirocco* – (Closed Saturday lunch, Monday and Tuesday) Menu £28/34
– Carte £45/65
Rest *Cafe Zephyr* – Carte £26/32
Rest *The Grill* – Carte £20/29

♦ Striking hotel with contemporary interior and stunning spa. The most spacious bedrooms look towards harbour; the quietest over inner courtyard. Two stunning suites with hot tubs. Lively brasserie with pavement terrace. More formal dining in Sirocco restaurant. The Grill retains traditional feel.

Radisson SAS Waterfront

Rue de l'Etau ⊠ *JE2 4HE* – ℰ *(01534) 769 744*
– www.jerseyradissonsas.com – info.jersey@radissonsas.com   Zc
181 rm ⊑ – †£99/135 ††£165/205 – 14 suites
Rest – Menu £23 (dinner) – Carte £26/44

♦ Fantastic location overlooking the harbour. Very spacious bedrooms, light and contemporary in style; most of them with views. Vast fish tank in reception. Waterfront terrace. Contemporary brasserie style restaurant.

ENGLAND

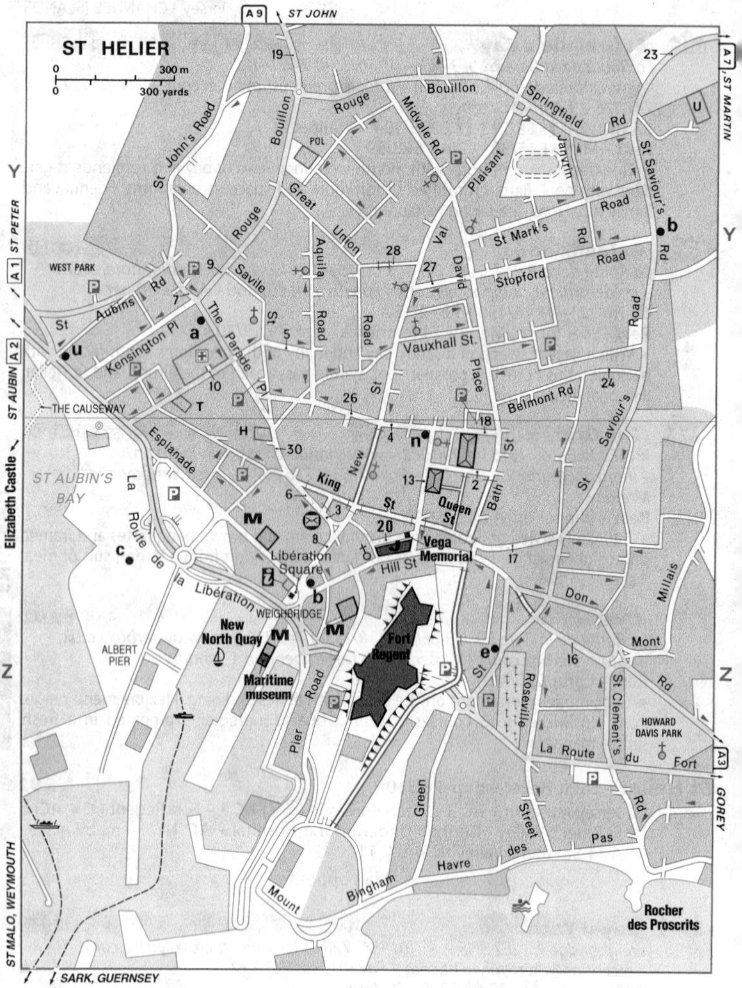

Beresford Street	Z 2	Gloucester Street	Y 10	Royal Square	Z 20
Broad Street	Z 3	Halkett Place	Z 13	St-Saviours Hill	Y 23
Burrard Street	Z 4	King Street	Z	Simon Place	Y 24
Cannon Street	Y 5	La Colomberie	Z 16	Union Street	Y 26
Charing Cross	Z 6	La Motte Street	Z 17	Victoria Street	Y 27
Cheapside	Y 7	Minden Place	Z 18	Windsor Road	Y 28
Conway Street	Z 8	Queen Street	Z	York Street	Y 30
Elizabeth Place	Y 9	Queen's Road	Y 19		

The Club Hotel & Spa

Green St ✉ JE2 4UH – ✆ (01534) 876 500 – www.theclubjersey.com
– reservations@theclubjersey.com – Fax (01534) 720 371 Ze

42 rm – 🚹£ 155/215 🚹🚹£ 155/215, ☕ £11.95 – 4 suites

Rest *Bohemia* – see restaurant listing

Rest – (Saturday brunch) Carte £ 24/37

◆ Above the Bohemia restaurant, a town house hotel of contemporary luxury with particularly pleasant roof terrace; the cosy bedrooms are fitted with many stylish mod cons. Small New York café style restaurant.

Hotel de France

St Saviours Rd ✉ *JE1 7XP* – ✆ *(01534) 614 000* – *www.defrance.co.uk*
– *general@defrance.co.uk* – *Fax (01534) 614 999*
– *Closed Christmas*   Y**b**
276 rm ☲ – †£115/120 ††£150/160 – 8 suites
Rest *Saffrons* – (Closed Sunday) (dinner only) Carte £35/50
Rest *Café Aroma* – ✆ (01534) 614 178 – Carte £17/30
♦ A well-located grand hotel with sweeping balustraded staircase leading to neatly furnished rooms. Cinema on complex and extensive range of business facilities. Saffrons restaurant boasts intimate, fine dining experience. Informal Café Aroma.

Grand

The Esplanade ✉ *JE4 8WD* – ✆ *(01534) 722 301* – *www.grandjersey.com*
– *dining@grand.jersey.com* – *Fax (01534) 737 815*   Y**u**
117 rm ☲ – †£110/175 ††£190/225 – 6 suites
Rest *Tassili* – (closed Sunday and Monday) (dinner only)
Menu £47
Rest *Victoria's* – (Closed Saturday lunch) Menu £26 (dinner)
– Carte £26/40
♦ Impressive Victorian hotel with pitched white façade overlooking St Aubins Bay, given contemporary makeover. Strong leisure facilities and comfortable bedrooms. Tassili for formal dining. Brasserie style in Victoria's.

Eulah Country House *without rest*

Mont Cochon, Northwest : 2 m. by A 1 on B 27 ✉ *JE2 3JA* – ✆ *(01534) 626 626*
– *www.eulah.co.uk* – *eulah@jerseymail.co.uk*
– *Fax (01534) 626 000*
9 rm ☲ – †£105/185 ††£150/230
♦ Informally run Edwardian country house proves pleasantly unconventional. Stylish combined lounge and breakfast room, luxurious bedrooms and superb views of St Aubin's Bay.

ENGLAND

XXX Bohemia – at The Club Hotel & Spa Hotel

Green St ✉ *JE2 4UH* – ✆ *(01534) 880 588* – *www.bohemiajersey.com*
– *bohemia@huggler.com* – *Fax (01534) 875 054*
– *Closed Sunday*   Z**e**
Rest – (Saturday brunch) Menu £22/53 – Carte £53/74
Spec. Oysters with caviar, saffron noodles and lemon butter. Belly pork and cheek with langoustine and a quince and butternut ice cream. Lavender scented panna cotta with strawberries.
♦ Elegant restaurant serving precise, confident cooking which makes use of seasonal Jersey produce. Meticulous service. Wide-ranging wine list, with decent selection by the glass.

XX La Capannina

65-67 Halkett Pl ✉ *JE2 4WG* – ✆ *(01534) 734 602* – *Fax (01534) 877 628*
– *Closed Sunday and Bank Holidays*   Z**n**
Rest – Italian – Menu £16/25 – Carte £21/52
♦ A buffet display of seafood and Parma ham preside over airy dining room with prints of Venice and Pisa. Choose between Jersey fish and Italian pasta. Dessert from the trolley.

X Ad-Lib

2 Edward Place, The Parade ✉ *JE2 3QP* – ✆ *(01534) 615 639*
– *www.adlibrestaurant.weebly.com* – *adlibrestaurant@hotmail.com*
– *Closed 2 weeks Spring, 2 weeks November and Sunday*   Y**a**
Rest – Menu £16 (lunch) – Carte £20/30
♦ Unassuming former pub just off sea front. Bar with banquettes leads into barrel-vaulted cellar restaurant with informal feel. Fresh, seasonal homemade cooking. Keen service.

ENGLAND

St Lawrence – Saint Lawrence   5 **B2**

🔐 **Cristina**   ← 🚗 ⅃ ⚙ **P** 𝖵𝖨𝖲𝖠 ⦾ 𝖠𝖤
Mont Felard ⊠ JE3 1JA – ℰ (01534) 758024 – www.dolanhotels.com
– cristina@dolanhotels.com – Fax (01534) 758028 – March-October
63 rm ⊇ – †£62/140 ††£135/180
Rest Indigo – Menu £26 (dinner) – Carte £32/43
♦ Traditional, white painted hotel in elevated position. Well-kept pool and garden terrace area. Spacious bar and wicker furnished lounge. Modern, pristine bedrooms. Tiled floors, suede fabrics add character to restaurant.

St Peter – Saint Peter – pop. 4 293   5 **B2**

▶ St Helier 5 mi
◉ Living Legend ★

🔐 **Greenhill's Country H.** ⌖   🚗 ⅃ 🆑 rest, ⚙ ⚟ **P** 𝖵𝖨𝖲𝖠 ⦾ 𝖠𝖤
Mont de l'Ecole, Coin Varin, on C 112 ⊠ JE3 7EL – ℰ (01534) 481042
– www.greenhillshotel.com – greenhills@messages.co.uk – Fax (01534) 485322
– Closed 19 December- 4 February
30 rm ⊇ – †£58/113 ††£115/165 – 1 suite
Rest – Menu £16/30 – Carte £32/46
♦ Very popular with regular guests, this part 17C stone farmhouse is a fine place to settle down in, with flower-filled gardens, country style rooms and wood panelled lounge. Floral, cream restaurant.

St Saviour – Saint Saviour – pop. 12 491   5 **B2**

▶ St Helier 1 mi

🔐 **Longueville Manor**   🚗 ⚙ 🏠 ⅃ ⚙ 📶 ⚟ **P** 𝖵𝖨𝖲𝖠 ⦾ 𝖠𝖤 ⓪
Longueville Rd, on A 3 ⊠ JE2 7WF – ℰ (01534) 725501
– www.longuevillemanor.com – longuevillemanor@relaischateaux.com
– Fax (01534) 731613
28 rm ⊇ – †£185/248 ††£315/440 – 2 suites
Rest – Menu £21/75 – Carte approx. £55 s⚬
♦ Exemplary part 14C manor for a special stay; every detail from furnishings to service is considered. Sumptuous rooms, delightful garden, poolside terrace. Panelled restaurant and terrace room overlooking garden; locally-inspired classics with modern twists.

SARK – Sark – 503 L 33 – pop. 550

⛴ to Guernsey (St Peter Port) (Isle of Sark Shipping Co. Ltd) (summer only) (45 mn)
⛴ to Jersey (St Helier) (Condor Ferries Ltd) (50 mn)
🏛 Sark Island ℰ (01481) 832345
◉ Island ★★ - La Coupáe ★★★ – Port du Moulin ★★ - Creux Harbour ★ – La Seigneurie ★ **AC** – Pilcher Monument ★ - Hog's Back ★

🔐 **Aval du Creux** ⌖   🚗 🏠 ⅃ ⚙ ⚟ 𝖵𝖨𝖲𝖠 ⦾ 𝖠𝖤
Harbour Hill ⊠ GY9 0SB – ℰ (01481) 832036 – www.avalducreux.co.uk
– reservations@avalducreux.co.uk – Fax (01481) 832368
20 rm ⊇ – †£45/90 ††£90/140
Rest The Restaurant – Menu £24 (dinner) – Carte £25/44
♦ Secluded stone built hotel - the closest to the harbour - with 21C extensions. South facing mature gardens. Comfortable modern bedrooms. Dining room and terrace overlook garden and port.

🔐 **Stocks Island** ⌖   🚗 🏠 ⅃ 𝖵𝖨𝖲𝖠 ⦾ 𝖠𝖤 ⓪
⊠ GY9 0SD – ℰ (01481) 832001 – www.stockshotel.com
– enquiries@stockshotel.com – Fax (01481) 832130 – 5 April-September
18 rm ⊇ – †£40/110 ††£80/180 s
Rest – (bar lunch) Menu £25/28 s – Carte £20/30 s
♦ A mellow granite former farmhouse built in 1741, family owned and very personally run. Quiet location facing wooded valley. Well-kept bedrooms and period beamed bar. Organic produce to fore in charming restaurant.

ENGLAND

Petit Champ ⌂ ⚶ 〈 ⊞ ⊠ ⊃ ♨ **VISA 🆗 AE ①**
⊠ GY9 0SF – ℰ (01481) 832 046 – www.hotelpetitchamp.co.uk
– info@hotelpetitchamp.co.uk – Fax (01481) 832 469 – 22 April- 3 October
10 rm (dinner included) ⌂ – †£66/76 ††£129/149
Rest – Menu £23 (dinner) – Carte £15/30
♦ Ideal for views of neighbouring islands, with three sun lounges to enjoy them from; neat, trim rooms. Quarry, from which hotel's stone comes, is site of solar heated pool. Dining room features Sark specialities.

XX **La Sablonnerie** with rm ⚶ ⊞ ⊠ **VISA 🆗**
Little Sark ⊠ GY9 0SD – ℰ (01481) 832 061 – www.lasablonnerie.com
– lasablonnerie@cwgsy.net – Fax (01481) 832 408 – Easter-mid October
21 rm ⌂ – †£60/146 ††£135/195 – 1 suite
Rest – Menu £25/29 – Carte £22/35
♦ Immaculately whitewashed 16C former farmhouse: a long low building. Diners greeted from jetty by Victorian horse and carriage. Home-produced ingredients to fore. Smart rooms.

"Rest" appears in red for establishments with a 🅮 (star) or 🅮 (Bib Gourmand).

CHANNEL TUNNEL – Kent – **504** X 30 – **see Folkestone**

CHAPEL-EN-LE-FRITH – Derbyshire – **504** O24   16 **A1**
▣ London 175 mi – Sheffield 27 mi – Manchester 21 mi – Stoke-on-Trent 34 mi

⌂ **High Croft** without rest   〈 ⊞ **P**
Manchester Rd, West : ¾ m. on B 5470 ⊠ SK23 9UH – ℰ (01298) 814 843
– www.highcroft-guesthouse.co.uk – elaine@highcroft-guesthouse.co.uk
4 rm ⌂ – †£70 ††£100
♦ Edwardian house with period features and lovely mature garden. Comfortable bedrooms overlook surrounding hills and valleys; Atholl suite - a four poster with tub - is best.

CHAPELTOWN – N. Yorks. – **502** P 23 – **see Sheffield**

CHARD – Somerset – **503** L 31 – **pop. 12 008**   3 **B3**
▣ London 157 mi – Exeter 32 mi – Lyme Regis 12 mi – Taunton 18 mi
 – Yeovil 17 mi
🛈 The Guildhall, Fore St ℰ (01460) 65710, chardtic@chard.gov.uk

⌂ **Bellplot House**   ⊞ ♨ 🁢 **P VISA 🆗 AE**
High St ⊠ TA20 1QB – ℰ (01460) 62 600 – www.bellplothouse.co.uk
– info@bellplothouse.co.uk – Fax (01460) 62 600
7 rm – †£70/80 ††£80, ⌂ £7.75
Rest – (closed Sunday) (dinner only) Menu £25 – Carte £25/33
♦ Impressive mid-Georgian house named after shape of original plot of land. Lounge with plush sofas and fitted bar. Bedrooms stylishly modern with bright yellow décor. Locally renowned restaurant where local, seasonal produce is very much centre stage.

CHARLESTOWN – Cornwall – **503** F 32 – **see St Austell**

CHARLTON – W. Sussex – **504** R 31 – **see Chichester**

CHARLTON – Wilts. – **503** N 29 – **see Malmesbury**

CHARLWOOD – Surrey – 504 T 30 – ⊠ Horley 7 **D2**
▶ London 30 mi – Brighton 29 mi – Royal Tunbridge Wells 28 mi

🏨 **Stanhill Court** ⟫ ◁ 🚗 🏊 ⚿ 📶 🛁 **P** VISA ⓞⓞ AE ⓞ
Stan Hill, Northwest : 1 m. by Norwood Hill Rd ⊠ RH6 0EP – ℰ (01293) 862 166
– www.stanhillcourthotel.co.uk – enquiries@stanhillcourthotel.co.uk
– Fax (01293) 862 773
34 rm ⊑ – †£ 85/115 ††£ 105/165
Rest – (booking essential for non-residents) Menu £ 18/25 – Carte dinner
£ 35/40
♦ Attractive Victorian country house in 30 acres of parkland. Striking panelled baronial hall with stained glass. Huge conservatory. Bedrooms retain some original features. Pleasant dining room in classic style.

CHARMOUTH – Dorset – 503 L 31 – ⊠ Bridport 3 **B3**
▶ London 157 mi – Dorchester 22 mi – Exeter 31 mi – Taunton 27 mi

🏠 **White House** ⚿ 📶 **P** VISA ⓞⓞ
2 Hillside, The Street ⊠ DT6 6PJ – ℰ (01297) 560 411
– www.whitehousehotel.com – ian@whitehousehotel.com – Restricted opening in winter
6 rm ⊑ – †£ 90/120 ††£ 120
Rest – (closed Sunday and Monday) (dinner only) Menu £ 33
♦ Gleaming white Regency hotel a stone's throw from magnificent coastal scenery; popular with fossil hunters. Tasteful rooms, with pretty furnishings. Garden herbs and fruit used in home-cooked meals.

CHEDDAR – Somerset – 503 L 30 3 **B2**
▶ London 157 mi – Bristol 20 mi – Caerdydd / Cardiff 70 mi – Casnewydd / Newport 57 mi

🏠 **Batts Farm** without rest ⟫ ◁ 🚗 ⚿ **P** VISA ⓞⓞ
Latches Lane, South East : 2½ m by A371 on Nyland Rd ⊠ BS27 3UD
– ℰ (01934) 741 469 – www.batts-farm.co.uk – clare@batts-farm.co.uk
4 rm ⊑ – †£ 55 ††£ 90
♦ Friendly and welcoming – drinks on arrival and homemade biscuits in rooms. Pristine bedrooms offer thoughtful extras. Summer house looks onto peaceful garden. Excellent breakfast.

CHEDDLETON – Staffordshire – 502 N 24 – pop. 2 719 – ⊠ Leek 19 **C1**
▶ London 125 mi – Birmingham 48 mi – Derby 33 mi – Manchester 42 mi – Stoke-on-Trent 11 mi

🏠 **Choir Cottage** without rest 🚗 ⚿ 📶 **P**
Ostlers Lane, via Hollow Lane (opposite Red Lion on A 520) ⊠ ST13 7HS
– ℰ (01538) 360 561 – www.choircottage.co.uk – enquiries@choircottage.co.uk
3 rm ⊑ – †£ 45/59 ††£ 70/75
♦ Personally run 17C stone cottage, formerly church owned, and let to the poor, rent used to buy choir gowns. Individually furnished bedrooms with four-posters.

CHELMSFORD – Essex – 504 V 28 – pop. 99 962 13 **C2**
▶ London 33 mi – Cambridge 46 mi – Ipswich 40 mi – Southend-on-Sea 19 mi
🛈 Unit 3, Dukes Way, Duke St ℰ (01245) 283400, tic@cheltenham.gov.uk

✗✗ **Barda** 🍴 AC VISA ⓞⓞ AE ⓞ
30-32 Broomfield Rd ⊠ CM1 1SW – ℰ (01245) 357 799
– www.barda-restaurant.com – Fax (01245) 350 333
– Closed 25 December - 2 January, Sunday dinner, Monday and Bank Holidays
Rest – Menu £ 17 – Carte £ 26/36
♦ Modern restaurant with spacious interior, decked terrace, banquette seating and contemporary art on walls. Precise, modern menu offers seasonal dishes with a French flavour.

ENGLAND

The Alma
37 Arbour Lane, Northeast : 1 m. by B 1137 (Springfield Rd) ✉ CM1 7RG – ✆ (01245) 256 783 – www.eyho.co.uk/alma – alma@eyho.co.uk – Fax (01245) 256 793
Rest – Carte £ 18/26
◆ Smart, contemporary bar with bright yellow exterior and pleasant terrace. Wide ranging menu displays a mix of British and European dishes, as well as hearty pub favourites.

at Great Baddow **Southeast : 3 m. by A 1114 – ✉ Chelmsford**

Pontlands Park
West Hanningfield Rd ✉ CM2 8HR – ✆ (01245) 476 444 – www.heritageleisure.co.uk – sales@pontlandsparkhotel.co.uk – Fax (01245) 478 393 – Closed 24-31 December
31 rm – †£ 115 ††£ 135/170, ☕ £ 12 – 4 suites
Rest – (Closed Saturday lunch, Sunday dinner and Bank Holidays)
Carte £ 33/37
◆ Charming, extended Victorian house with comfortable, individually-furnished bedrooms, well run leisure facilities and popular meeting rooms. Formal linen-clad dining room.

CHELTENHAM – **Gloucestershire** – **503** N 28 – **pop. 98 875** 4 **C1**
Great Britain

London 99 mi – Birmingham 48 mi – Bristol 40 mi – Gloucester 9 mi – Oxford 43 mi
Municipal Offices, 77 Promenade ✆ (01242) 522878, info@cheltenham.gov.uk
Cleeve Hill, ✆ (01242) 672 025
Cotswold Hills Ullenwood, ✆ (01242) 515 264
Town★
Sudeley Castle★ (Paintings★) **AC**, NE : 7 m. by B 4632 A

Plan on next page

Hotel du Vin
Parabola Rd ✉ GL50 3AQ – ✆ (01242) 588 450 – www.hotelduvin.com – info.cheltenham@hotelduvin.com – Fax (01242) 588 455 BY**c**
48 rm – †£ 155/300 ††£ 155/300, ☕ £ 9.95 – 1 suite
Rest *Bistro* – Menu £ 16 (lunch) – Carte £ 24/35
◆ Stylish Regency house in smart area: lounge features chandelier made from wine glasses; bedrooms named after wines boast contemporary furnishings and wine-themed artwork. Bistro restaurant with paved terrace offers classic menus with French influences.

The Queen's
Promenade ✉ GL50 1NN – ✆ (01242) 514 754 – www.thequeens-cheltenham.co.uk – h6632@accor.com – Fax (01242) 224 145 BZ**n**
79 rm ☕ – †£ 120/170 ††£ 130/170
Rest *Napier* – Menu £ 25/35 – Carte £ 22/35
◆ A white columned neo-classical 1898 building with views over Imperial Square and the Ladies College. Grand reception and wood panelled bar. Individually styled bedrooms. Restaurant has conservatory extension.

Hotel on the Park
38 Evesham Rd ✉ GL52 2AH – ✆ (01242) 518 898 – www.hotelonthepark.com – stay@hotelonthepark.com – Fax (01242) 511 526 CY**r**
12 rm – †£ 155/395 ††£ 155/395, ☕ £ 15
Rest *Parkers* – see restaurant listing
◆ Regency town house of distinction. Bedrooms are named after dukes and dignitaries; individually decorated with paintings, antiques, mirrors and lamps. Stately library.

ENGLAND

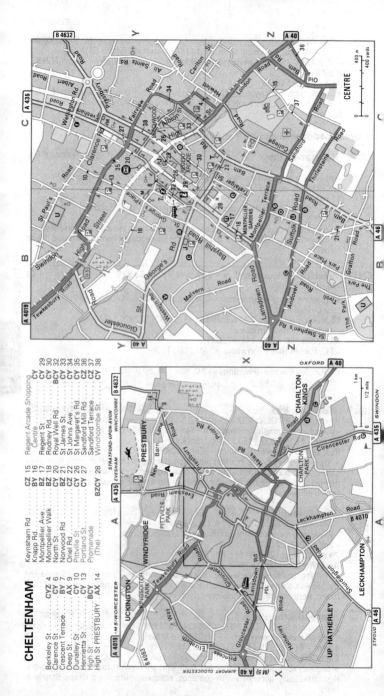

CHELTENHAM

The George 🔼 rest, 🍽 📶 ⚑ **P** **VISA** **◑◐** **AE** **①**
St George's Rd ⊠ GL50 3DZ – ℰ (01242) 235 751 – www.stayatthegeorge.co.uk
– hotel@stayatthegeorge.co.uk – Fax (01242) 224 359
– Closed 25-26 December   BY**a**
31 rm ⌂ – †£115 ††£125 – 1 suite
Rest Monty's – Carte £27/44
♦ In a good central location amongst other Regency town houses. Bright, modern, well-equipped bedrooms; larger variety boasts extra facilities. Two rooms called 'Monty's' serve brasserie style food and seafood respectively.

Beaumont House without rest 🚗 🍽 📶 **P** **VISA** **◑◐** **AE** **①**
56 Shurdington Rd ⊠ GL53 0JE – ℰ (01242) 223 311 – www.bhhotel.co.uk
– reservations@bhhotel.co.uk – Fax (01242) 520 044   AX**u**
16 rm ⌂ – †£66/73 ††£164/201
♦ Keenly run Georgian house with comfy drawing room and bar; breakfast room overlooks lawned garden. Refurbished bedrooms are stylish and contemporary with excellent bathrooms.

Lypiatt House without rest 🚗 🍽 📶 **P** **VISA** **◑◐** **AE**
Lypiatt Rd ⊠ GL50 2QW – ℰ (01242) 224 994 – www.staylypiatt.co.uk
– stay@lypiatt.co.uk – Fax (01242) 224 996   BZ**c**
10 rm ⌂ – †£70/90 ††£80/120
♦ A privately owned, serene Victorian house with friendly service. Rooms on top floor with dormer roof tend to be smaller than those on the ground floor. Soft, pale colours.

Butlers without rest 🚗 📶 **P** **VISA** **◑◐**
Western Rd ⊠ GL50 3RN – ℰ (01242) 570 771 – www.butlers-hotel.co.uk
– info@butlers-hotel.co.uk – Fax (01242) 528 724   BY**v**
9 rm ⌂ – †£55/60 ††£85/95
♦ Personally managed hotel where bedrooms constitute a peaceful haven with stylish drapes and canopies. Rooms named after famous butlers; some overlook wooded garden to rear.

Charlton Kings 🚗 📶 **P** **VISA** **◑◐** **AE**
London Rd, Charlton Kings ⊠ GL52 6UU – ℰ (01242) 231 061
– www.charltonkingshotel.co.uk – enquiries@charltonkingshotel.co.uk
– Fax (01242) 241 900   AX**c**
13 rm ⌂ – †£65/85 ††£125
Rest – (bar lunch Monday-Saturday) Carte £21/29
♦ A cream washed, purpose-built hotel with unfussy pastel interiors. Pristine, plainly painted bedrooms with light wood furniture. The rural setting bestows tranquillity. Dining room enhanced by a simple, modern design.

Hilden Lodge without rest 🚗 📶 **P** **VISA** **◑◐** **AE** **①**
271 London Rd, Charlton Kings ⊠ GL52 6YG – ℰ (01242) 583 242
– www.hildenlodge.co.uk – info@hildenlodge.co.uk – Fax (01242) 263 511   AX**a**
9 rm ⌂ – †£49/69 ††£69/79
♦ Cream washed Regency house with small garden/terrace. Bedrooms are half light, half dark wood furnished, with smart, compact bathrooms and good facilities. Breakfast cooked to order.

Thirty Two without rest 📶 **P** **VISA** **◑◐**
32 Imperial Sq ⊠ GL50 1QZ – ℰ (01242) 771 110 – www.thirtytwoltd.com
– info@thirtytwoltd.com – Fax (01242) 771 119
– 25-26 December   BZ**e**
4 rm ⌂ – †£149 ††£198
♦ Immaculate Regency house overlooking grassy city square. Stylish, beautifully appointed bedrooms with furniture designed by owner; superb bathrooms. Excellent facilities and extra touches.

ENGLAND

213

⚐ **Georgian House** without rest   🍴 📶 **P** **VISA** **⦿** **AE** **①**
77 Montpellier Terrace ⊠ *GL50 1XA* – *𝒞 (01242) 515 577*
– www.georgianhouse.net – penny@georgianhouse.net – Fax (01242) 545 929
– Closed Christmas and New Year   BZ**s**
3 rm ⌑ – ✚£65/80 ✚✚£85/105
♦ Smart, terraced Georgian house, hospitably run, in sought-after Montpelier area. Good-sized bedrooms decorated in authentic period style. Comfy, elegant communal rooms.

XXX **Le Champignon Sauvage** (David Everitt-Matthias)   **AC** **VISA** **⦿** **AE** **①**
❄ ❄ *24-28 Suffolk Rd* ⊠ *GL50 2AQ* – *𝒞 (01242) 573 449*
– www.lechampignonsauvage.com – mail@lechampignonsauvage.com
– Fax (01242) 234 365 – Closed Easter, 3 weeks June, 10 days Christmas,
Sunday and Monday.   BZ**a**
Rest – Menu £30/50
Spec. Seared scallops with artichokes and liquorice root. Zander fillet with cauliflower purée, bladder campion and hibiscus sauce. Bitter chocolate and olive tart with fennel ice cream.
♦ Professionally run restaurant stylishly decorated in blue and cream, with modern art on walls. Confident, accomplished cooking uses excellent produce; some original touches.

XX **Lumière**   **AC** **VISA** **⦿**
Clarence Parade ⊠ *GL50 3PA* – *𝒞 (01242) 222 200 – www.lumiere.cc*
– dinner@lumiere.cc – Closed first 2 weeks January, 2 weeks summer,
Sunday and Monday   BCY**z**
Rest – (dinner only) Menu £39
♦ Personally run, intimate glass fronted restaurant decked out in chic browns and leather. Original colourful artwork. Skilfully concocted cooking covering a modern range.

XX **Parkers** – at On the Park H.   🍴 **P** **VISA** **⦿** **AE**
38 Evesham Rd ⊠ *GL52 2AH* – *𝒞 (01242) 518 898 – www.hotelonthepark.com*
– stay@hotelonthepark.com – Fax (01242) 511 526 – Closed Monday lunch   CY**r**
Rest – Carte £28/42
♦ A carefully decorated restaurant with mirrors, high ceilings, hand painted cornices and murals. Modern British cooking with classical undertones and a good range of wine.

XX **The Daffodil**   **AC** **VISA** **⦿** **AE**
18-20 Suffolk Parade ⊠ *GL50 2AE* – *𝒞 (01242) 700 055 – www.thedaffodil.com*
– eat@thedaffodil.com – Fax (01242) 700 088 – Closed 25 December, first 2 weeks
January and Sunday   BZ**u**
Rest – Menu £15 (lunch) – Carte £25/34
♦ Move from the art of film to the art of food in this 1920s converted cinema. The open-plan kitchen occupies the original screen area. Modern cooking with generous puddings.

X **Royal Well Tavern**   **AC** **VISA** **⦿** **AE**
☺ *5 Royal Well Pl. Cheltenham* – *𝒞 (01242) 221 212 – www.theroyalwelltavern.com*
– info@theroyalwelltavern.com – Closed Christmas - New Year and Sunday
Rest – Menu £15 (lunch) – Carte £17/30
♦ Tucked away in side street close to theatre. Bustling contemporary eatery; fusion of gentleman's club/brasserie. Rustic modern menu of carefully prepared dishes; many available in 2 sizes.

X **Brosh**   **VISA** **⦿**
8 Suffolk Parade, Montpellier ⊠ *GL50 2AB* – *𝒞 (01242) 227 277*
– www.broshrestaurant.co.uk – info@broshrestaurant.co.uk – Fax (01242)
227 277 – Closed 2 weeks Christmas - New Year, and Sunday-Tuesday   BZ**o**
Rest – Mediterranean – (dinner only) Carte £20/31
♦ Cosy restaurant with atmospheric Moroccan-styled interior: evening candles and dimmed lights make for a great atmosphere. Specialist 'east' Mediterranean cooking with mezze.

❌ **Vanilla**   `VISA` `OO`
9-10 Cambray Pl ✉ GL50 1JS – ☎ (01242) 228 228 – www.vanillainc.co.uk
– info@vanillainc.co.uk – Fax (01242) 228 228
– Closed 25-26 December, 1 January, and Sunday   CYe
Rest – Carte £ 16/29
◆ Centrally located, in Regency house basement; discreet, soft spot lighting, wooden floors, scoopback chairs. Staff serve light, modern dishes garnished with home-made sauces.

at Cleeve Hill Northeast : 4 m. on B 4632 - AX – ✉ **Cheltenham**

🏠 **Cleeve Hill** without rest   ← 🚊 🛜 **P** `VISA` `OO` `AE`
✉ GL52 3PR – ☎ (01242) 672 052 – www.cleevehill-hotel.co.uk
– info@cleevehill-hotel.co.uk – Fax (01242) 679 969
6 rm ⛄ – ♦£ 55/75 ♦♦£ 85/110
◆ Edwardian house in elevated spot; most bedrooms have views across Cleeve Common and the Malvern Hills. Breakfast room is in the conservatory; admire the landscape over coffee.

❌❌ **Hacketts** with rm   ← 🚊 🛜 **P** `VISA` `OO` `①`
✉ GL52 3PR – ☎ (01242) 672 017 – www.malvernviewhotel.co.uk
– paul.hackett@btconnect.com – Closed first 3 weeks January and last week October
6 rm ⛄ – ♦£ 55/75 ♦♦£ 90/110
Rest – (Closed Tuesday lunch, Sunday dinner and Monday) Menu £ 16/25
– Carte £ 25/34
◆ Pleasant, personally run restaurant up a hill with views to distant Malverns. Classically styled lounges; modern British cooking with good value choice. Well-appointed rooms.

at Shurdington Southwest : 3 ¾ m. on A 46 - AX – ✉ **Cheltenham**

🏠🏠 **The Greenway** ⚘   🚊 🍴 🛜 ♨ **P** `VISA` `OO` `AE`
✉ GL51 4UG – ☎ (01242) 862 352 – www.thegreenway.co.uk
– info@thegreenway.co.uk – Fax (01242) 862 780
20 rm ⛄ – ♦£ 140/385 ♦♦£ 180/465 – 1 suite   **Rest** – Menu £ 23/45
◆ Ivy-clad Elizabethan manor house set in large grounds and peaceful lawned gardens. Spacious, classically styled lounges and drawing rooms. Bedrooms have country house feel. Garden and lily pond on view from formal restaurant.

at Brockworth Southwest : 5 ½ m. on A 46 - AX – ✉ **Cheltenham**

🏠🏠 **Cheltenham Chase**   🚊 🍴 🏊 🛁 🎮 🛜 rm, 🎦 🍴 🛜 ♨ **P** `VISA` `OO` `AE` `①`
Shurdington Rd, on A 46 ✉ GL3 4PB – ☎ (01452) 519 988 – www.qhotels.co.uk
– cheltenham@qhotels.co.uk – Fax (01452) 519 977
120 rm – ♦£ 114/144 ♦♦£ 124/154 – 2 suites
Rest – (closed 27-28 November and December) (bar lunch) Carte £ 30/41
◆ A modern corporate hotel located in landscaped grounds on the edge of the Cotswolds. Good leisure and conference facilities, relaxing bar and lounge and spacious bedrooms. Contemporary restaurant.

at Little Witcombe Southwest : 6 m. by A 46 - AX - and Bentham rd
– ✉ **Cheltenham**

🏠 **Crickley Court** without rest   🚊 🛜 🛜 **P** `VISA` `OO` `AE` `①`
Dog Lane ✉ GL3 4UF – ☎ (01452) 863 634 – www.crickleycourt.co.uk
– lispilgrimmorris@yahoo.co.uk
4 rm ⛄ – ♦£ 40 ♦♦£ 75
◆ Old inn dating from 16C. Lounge provided with an array of books. Family style breakfast. Outdoor pool. Spacious, bright and clean rooms with modern amenities.

If breakfast is included the ⛄ symbol appears after the number of rooms.

ENGLAND

CHENIES – Buckinghamshire – **504** S 28 – ⊠ Rickmansworth (Herts.)   11 **D2**
▶ London 30 mi – Aylesbury 18 mi – Watford 7 mi

 Bedford Arms   🛋 🛜 ☕ rm, ⟨ℹ⟩ **P** 𝗩𝗜𝗦𝗔 ◉◉ 𝗔𝗘 ◍

⊠ WD3 6EQ – *ℰ (01923) 283 301* – *www.bedfordarms.co.uk*
– *contact@bedfordarms.co.uk* – Fax *(01923) 284 825*
– *Closed 26 December - 5 January*
18 rm ⊇ – ♦£ 90/110 ♦♦£ 130
Rest – (Closed Sunday dinner) Carte £ 25/35

♦ A homely hotel, pub-like in character. Well proportioned rooms, some with views of a pretty garden. Country house style bars and a meeting room for business guests. Oak panelled dining room; adjacent cocktail bar.

CHESTER – Cheshire – **502** L 24 – **pop. 80 121** ▌ *Great Britain*   20 **A3**
▶ London 207 mi – Birkenhead 7 mi – Birmingham 91 mi – Liverpool 21 mi
– Manchester 40 mi – Preston 52 mi – Sheffield 76 mi – Stoke-on-Trent 38 mi
ℹ Chester Visitor Centre, Vicars Lane *ℰ (01244) 402111, tis@chester.gov.uk*
🏌 Upton-by-Chester Upton Lane, *ℰ (01244) 381 183*
🏌 Curzon Park, *ℰ (01244) 675 130*
◉ City★★ - The Rows★★B – Cathedral★B – City Walls★B
◉ Chester Zoo★ **AC**, N : 3 m. by A 5116

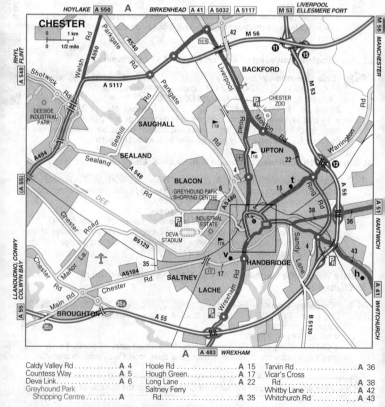

146 YEARS OF EXPERIENCE, 27 HERBS AND SPICES, 1 PERFECT BLEND

BÉNÉDICTINE
Liqueur

DOM BÉNÉDICTINE. A TRADITION OF TASTE.

INTERNATIONAL WINE & SPIRIT COMPETITION BEST IN CLASS:
2005, 2007, 2008

ViaMichelin

Click...make your choice, Click...place your booking

HOTEL BOOKING AT

www.ViaMichelin.com

Plan your route on-line with ViaMichelin to make the most of all your trips. You can compare routes, select your stops at recommended restaurants and learn more about any not-to-be-missed tourist sites along your route. And...for peace of mind, you can check real-time availability in 60,000 hotels across Europe (independents and chains). Simply specify your preferences (parking, restaurant, etc) and place your booking on-line.

- **No booking fee**
- **No cancellation fee**
- **No credit card fee**
- **Best available prices**
- **The option to filter and select hotels from The Michelin Guide**

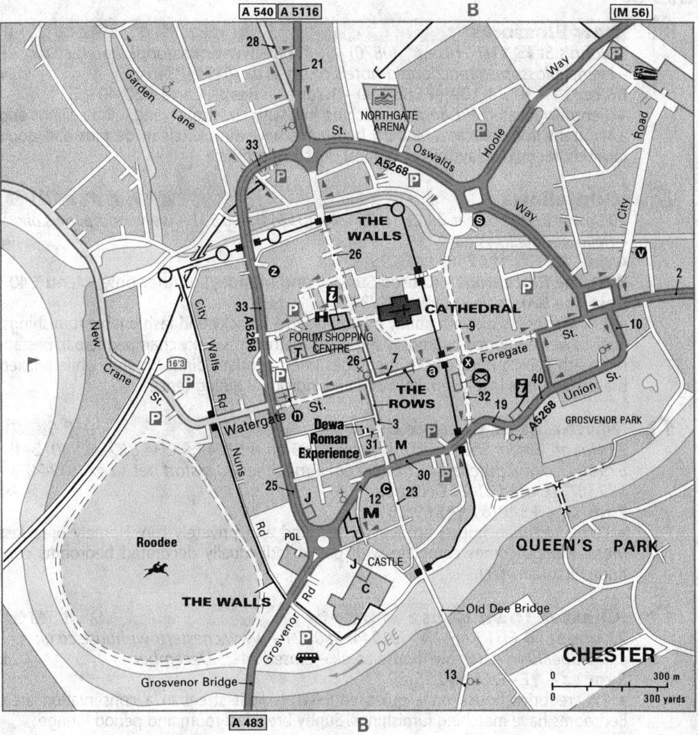

Boughton	B	2	Handbridge	B	13	Pepper St	B	30
Bridge St	B	3	Little St John St	B	19	Pierpoint Lane	B	31
Eastgate St	B	7	Liverpool Rd	B	21	St John St	B	32
Forum Shopping centre	B		Lower Bridge St	B	23	St Martins Way	B	33
Frodsham St	B	9	Nicholas St	B	25	Vicar's Lane	B	40
Grosvenor Park Rd	B	10	Northgate St	B	26	Watergate St	B	
Grosvenor St	B	12	Parkgate Rd	B	28			

The Chester Grosvenor and Spa

Eastgate ✉ CH1 1LT – ✆ (01244) 324 024 – www.chestergrosvenor.com – restaurants@chestergrosvenor.com – Fax (01244) 313 246 – Closed 25-26 December Ba

76 rm – †£ 195 ††£ 285, ☕ £19 – 4 suites

Rest *Simon Radley at The Chester Grosvenor* and ***La Brasserie*** – see restaurant listing

◆ 19C coaching inn in heart of city. Lavishly furnished with antiques and oil paintings. Superb spa facilities. Luxuriously appointed, individually styled bedrooms.

Green Bough

60 Hoole Rd, on A 56 ✉ CH2 3NL – ✆ (01244) 326 241 – www.greenbough.co.uk – luxury@greenbough.co.uk – Fax (01244) 326 265 – Closed 25 December-1 January At

13 rm ☕ – †£ 105/170 ††£ 245 – 2 suites

Rest *Olive Tree* – Menu £ 25 – Carte £ 32/46

◆ Personally run and very comfortable, boasting high quality decor; owner pays notable attention to detail. Individually styled, generously sized rooms with wrought iron beds. Dine formally in attractive surroundings.

ENGLAND

New Blossoms 🏨

St John's St ⌂ CH1 1HL – ℰ (0870) 400 81 08 – www.macdonaldhotels.co.uk
– events.blossoms@macdonald-hotels.co.uk – Fax (01244) 346 433   B**x**
66 rm ⌂ – ♦£74/109 ♦♦£88/180 – 1 suite   **Rest** – Carte £20/40
♦ Centrally located 17C former coaching inn, with classical styling, high ceilings and a wrought iron staircase. Modern bedrooms have simple, clean designs and good facilities. Menu displays plenty of local, seasonal produce.

Oddfellows 🏨

20 Lower Bridge Street ⌂ CH1 1RS – ℰ (01244) 400 001 – www.oddfellows.biz
– hello@oddfellows.biz   B**c**
4 rm – ♦£175 ♦♦£250, ⌂ £8.95
Rest *The Restaurant* – (Closed Sunday and Monday) (dinner only) Menu £40
Rest *The Brasserie* – Carte £20/31
♦ 17C Manor House with quirky mix off bizarre, whacky and fashionable furnishings. Stylish, well equipped bedrooms with great bathrooms. Sexy champagne bar. Restaurant with ceiling hung photo montages offers modern dinner menu, while relaxed brasserie boasts lovely terrace, pond and individual dining tents.

Mitchell's of Chester without rest ↑

28 Hough Green, Southwest : 1 m. by A 483 on A 5104 ⌂ CH4 8JQ – ℰ (01244)
679 004 – www.mitchellsofchester.com – mitoches@dialstart.net – Fax (01244)
659 567 – Closed 21-29 December   A**v**
7 rm ⌂ – ♦£40/69 ♦♦£69/78
♦ Large Victorian house, attractively restored and privately run. Homely breakfast room; lounge comes complete with parrot. Individually decorated bedrooms continue Victoriana feel.

Chester Town House without rest ↑

23 King St ⌂ CH1 2AH – ℰ (01244) 350 021 – www.chestertownhouse.co.uk
– davidbellis@chestertownhouse.co.uk – Closed 24-25 December   B**z**
5 rm ⌂ – ♦£45/65 ♦♦£75/80
♦ 17C redbrick house on a quiet, cobbled, lamplit street in a conservation area. Bedrooms have matching furnishings. Sunny breakfast room and period lounge.

Simon Radley at The Chester Grosvenor 𝕏𝕏𝕏𝕏

Eastgate ⌂ CH1 1LT – ℰ (01244) 324 024 – www.chestergrosvenor.com
– restaurants@chestergrosvenor.com – Fax (01244) 313 246
– Closed 25-27 December, 1-9 January, 1 week August,
Sunday and Monday   B**a**
Rest – (dinner only) Menu £59 ⊛
Spec. Dressed crab with cucumber jelly and caviar wafer. Canon and pastilla of mutton with green sauce and candied shallot. Vanilla and lime risotto with iced butternut and chocolate parmesan.
♦ Formerly Arkle; now with a softer, warmer and more stylish feel. Classically based, sophisticated cooking with some innovative touches. Strong service.

Upstairs at the Grill 𝕏𝕏

70 Watergate St ⌂ CH1 2LA – ℰ (01244) 344 883 – www.upstairsatthegrill.co.uk
– katie.hearse@upstairsatthegrill.co.uk – Fax (01244) 329 720
– Closed lunch Monday - Friday   B**n**
Rest – Beef specialities – Carte £24/40
♦ Door bell entry to 19C building; sumptuous first floor bar has leather sofas and roulette table. Cow theme predominates. Prime quality Welsh steaks chargrilled to perfection.

Brasserie 10-16 𝕏𝕏

Brookdale Pl ⌂ CH1 3DY – ℰ (01244) 322 288 – www.brasserie1016.com
– info@brasserie1016.com – Fax (01244) 322 325 – Closed 25-26 December   B**s**
Rest – Carte £20/32
♦ Contemporary brasserie on two levels. Open plan kitchen on ground floor. Large modern British menu with Mediterranean touches, including plenty for the more adventurous.

XX **La Brasserie** – at The Chester Grosvenor and Spa Hotel   AC P VISA ☎ AE ⓞ
Eastgate ⊠ CH1 1LT – ℰ (01244) 324 024 – www.chestergrosvenor.com
– restaurant@chestergrosvenor.com – Fax (01244) 313 246
– Closed 25-26 December   B**a**
Rest – Carte £ 32/52
◆ Burnished interior, Parisian-style eatery with mirrors and glass frontage. Eclectic
menu with classic French and Italian staples of pasta and meat dishes. Weekend live
music.

🏮 **The Old Harkers Arms**   VISA ☎ AE
1 Russell St ⊠ CH3 5AL – ℰ (01244) 344 525 – www.brunningandprice.co.uk
– harkers.arms@brunningandprice.co.uk – Fax (01244) 344 814
– Closed 25 December   B**v**
Rest – Carte £ 20/30
◆ Characterful canalside pub in a Victorian warehouse. Cooking is rustic, unfussy and
generous, and the daily-changing menu displays plenty of classics; over 100 whiskies
are on offer.

at Rowton Southeast : 3 m. on A 41 – ⊠ Chester

🏨 **Rowton Hall H. & Spa**   🚗 �іiⁱ 📺 📶 ℎ ⓜ 🎾 AC rest, ¶ ⅃ P
Whitchurch Rd ⊠ CH3 6AD – ℰ (01244) 335 262   VISA ☎ AE ⓞ
– www.rowtonhallhotel.co.uk – reception@rowtonhallhotelandspa.co.uk
– Fax (01244) 335 464   A**h**
36 rm ⊑ – ♥£ 125/145 ♥♥£ 145/165 – 2 suites
Rest Langdale – Menu £ 20 (dinner) – Carte £ 29/42
◆ Gracious 18C sandstone hotel with many original features: hand-carved staircase,
Robert Adam fireplace, range of bedrooms. Business facilities offered. Country house
style. Colonial style restaurant with wooden blinds and rattan furniture.

at Pulford Southwest : 5 m. by A 483 - A - and B 5445 – ⊠ Chester

🏨 **The Grosvenor Pulford**   🚗 🌀 📺 📶 ℎ ℎ 🎾 ┃ ⅃ ᗕ rm, ¶ ⅃
Wrexham Rd, on B 5445 ⊠ CH4 9DG – ℰ (01244)   P VISA ☎ AE ⓞ
570 560 – www.grosvenorpulfordhotel.co.uk
– reservations@grosvenorpulfordhotel.co.uk – Fax (01244) 570 809
73 rm ⊑ – ♥£ 75/95 ♥♥£ 80/160
Rest Ciro's – Mediterranean – (Closed Saturday lunch) Carte £ 25/31
◆ Family owned hotel 10 minutes' drive from city. Popular business and wedding
venue. Pleasant gardens; spacious gym and pool. Diverse range of individualistic
rooms.

CHESTER-LE-STREET – Durham – 501   24 B2

▶ London 275 mi – Durham 7 mi – Newcastle upon Tyne 8 mi
🏌 Lumley Park, ℰ (0191) 388 3218
🏌 Roseberry Grange Grange Villa, ℰ (0191) 370 0660

🏨 **Lumley Castle** ⌾   🚗 🎾 ¶ ⅃ P VISA ☎ AE ⓞ
East : 1 m. on B 1284 ⊠ DH3 4NX – ℰ (0191) 389 1111 – www.lumleycastle.com
– reception@lumleycastle.com – Fax (0191) 389 1881 – Closed 24-26 December
and 1 January
73 rm – ♥£ 93/156 ♥♥£ 229/315, ⊑ £ 14.95 – 1 suite
Rest Black Knight – (Closed Saturday lunch) Menu £ 22/34 – Carte dinner
£ 27/46
◆ Norman castle, without additions, underscoring its uniqueness. Rich, gothic interiors of carved wood, chandeliers, statues, tapestries, rugs. Rooms imbued with
atmosphere. Restaurant offers classical dishes with an original twist.

CHETNOLE – Dorset – see Sherborne

CHETTLE – Dorset – see Blandford Forum

CHEW MAGNA – Somerset – 503 M 29 – see Bristol

CHEWTON MENDIP – Somerset – **503** M 30   4 **C2**

▶ London 134 mi – Bristol 15 mi – Casnewydd / Newport 46 mi – Bath 18 mi

The Kings Arms   🚙 🛖 ⇔ **P.** **VISA** **ᗧᗧ** **AE** **⓪**
Litton ☒ *BA3 4PW* – 𝒞 *(01761) 241 301* – *www.thekingsarmslitton.co.uk*
– *info@thekingsarmslitton.co.uk* – *Fax (01761) 241 301*
Rest – Carte £ 20/35
♦ Stylish rustic/chic décor and cheery service. Confident, unfussy and generous cooking, ranges from flavoursome British classics to sharing platters; excellent homemade bread.

CHICHESTER – West Sussex – **504** R 31 – pop. 27 477 📗 *Great Britain*   7 **C2**

▶ London 69 mi – Brighton 31 mi – Portsmouth 18 mi – Southampton 30 mi
🛈 29a South St 𝒞 (01243) 775888, chitic@chichester.gov.uk
🏌 Goodwood Kennel Hill, 𝒞 (01243) 755 133
🏌 Chichester Golf Centre Hunston Village, 𝒞 (01243) 533 833
◎ City ★★ – Cathedral ★★ BZ **A** – St Mary's Hospital ★ BY **D** – Pallant House ★ **AC** BZ **M**
◎ Fishbourne Roman Palace ★★ (mosaics ★) **AC** AZ **R**. Weald and Downland Open Air Museum ★★ **AC**, N : 6 m. by A 286 AY

Plan opposite

Crouchers Country H.   🚙 ৬ rm, 🍴 **P.** **VISA** **ᗧᗧ** **AE**
Birdham Rd, Apuldram, Southwest : 2½ m. on A 286 ☒ *PO20 7EH* – 𝒞 *(01243) 784 995* – *www.croucherscountryhotel.com* – *info@crouchersbottom.com*
– *Fax (01243) 539 797*
26 rm ☒ – †£ 75/95 ††£ 120/140   **Rest** – Menu £ 20/24 – Carte £ 26/38
♦ 1900s farmhouse surrounded by fields. Bedrooms are in a separate coach house, some on ground floor; furnished with matching floral fabrics. Admire waterfowl in nearby pond. Bright, modern dining room.

The Ship   🛏 ❄ ੴ ৫৯ **P.** **VISA** **ᗧᗧ** **AE**
North St ☒ *PO19 1NH* – 𝒞 *(01243) 778 000* – *www.shiphotelchichester.co.uk*
– *enquiries@chichester.theplacehotels.co.uk* – *Fax (01243) 788 000*   BY**s**
36 rm ☒ – †£ 95 ††£ 120   **Rest** – Menu £ 15 – Carte £ 20/35
♦ Grade II listed building, formerly home to one of Nelson's men. Georgian and Regency features remain, including a cantilevered wrought iron staircase. Modern bedrooms display original cornices and fireplaces. Light, airy brasserie with modern menu; meat and game from nearby Goodwood Estate.

𝗫𝗫 Comme ça   🚙 🛖 ੴ ⇔ **P.** **VISA** **ᗧᗧ** **AE** **⓪**
67 Broyle Rd, on A 286 ☒ *PO19 6BD* – 𝒞 *(01243) 788 724*
– *www.commeca.co.uk* – *comme.ca@commeca.co.uk* – *Fax (01243) 530 052*
– *Closed Christmas - New Year, Monday, Tuesday lunch and Sunday dinner*   AY**c**
Rest – French – Menu £ 21 (lunch) – Carte dinner £ 28/39
♦ Strong French cooking ministered by Normand chef; generous à la carte, set menus and French family lunch on Sundays. Festoons of hops on exposed beams complete the décor.

𝗫𝗫 The Dining Room at Purchases   🛖 **VISA** **ᗧᗧ** **AE**
31 North St ☒ *PO19 1LY* – 𝒞 *(01243) 537 352* – *www.thediningroom.biz*
– *info@thediningroom.biz* – *Fax (01243) 780 773* – *Closed 25-26 December, 31 December, 2 January, Sunday and Bank Holiday Mondays*   BY**c**
Rest – Carte £ 27/37
♦ Charming Georgian house owned by country's oldest wine merchant; garden terrace, new wine bar, deep red hued restaurant serving shellfish and game menus. Great wine selection.

at Charlton North : 6¼ m. by A 286 - AY – ☒ **Chichester**

Woodstock House *without rest*   🚙 🍴 **P.** **VISA** **ᗧᗧ**
☒ *PO18 0HU* – 𝒞 *(01243) 811 666* – *www.woodstockhousehotel.co.uk*
– *info@woodstockhousehotel.co.uk* – *Fax (01243) 811 666*
13 rm ☒ – †£ 65/90 ††£ 98/125
♦ A row of flint and whitewashed cottages close to Goodwood Racecourse. Indoors, relax in the mulberry coloured, cottage style lounge or the floral furnished bedrooms.

ENGLAND

CHICHESTER

The Fox Goes Free with rm — rm, P VISA MC AE
⊠ PO18 0HU – ℰ (01243) 811 461 – www.thefoxgoesfree.com
– thefoxgoesfree-always@virgin.net – Fax (01243) 811 712 – Closed 25 December
5 rm ⊇ – †£60/100 ††£85/140   **Rest** – Carte £ 20/30
♦ Flint 17C inn retaining its character in the form of exposed stone walls, tile floors, beams and inglenook. Short, seasonal menus have a strong reliance on local produce. Comfortable, well-equipped bedrooms.

at Halnaker Northeast : 3 ¼ m. on A 285 - BY – ⊠ Chichester

The Old Store without rest — ⊒ ⅍ P VISA MC
Stane St, on A 285 ⊠ PO18 0QL – ℰ (01243) 531 977
– www.theoldstoreguesthouse.com – theoldstore4@aol.com
– 19 March - 20 December
7 rm ⊇ – †£35/75 ††£65/90
♦ An 18C listed building, originally belonging to the Goodwood Estate and used as a village store and bakery. Floral bedrooms. Well placed for Goodwood events and Chichester.

at Mid Lavant North 2m. on A286

Rooks Hill without rest — ⊒ ⅍ P VISA MC AE
Lavant Rd ⊠ PO18 0BQ – ℰ (01243) 528 400 – www.rookshill.co.uk
– enquires@rookshill.co.uk – Closed 22 December - 5 January
6 rm ⊇ – †£105 ††£150
♦ Charming Grade II listed guesthouse with mix of contemporary styling and original features. Breakfast room opens into lovely terrace/garden. Well appointed bedrooms with attractive bathrooms. Large buffet breakfast.

The Earl of March — P VISA MC ①
Mid Lavant ⊠ PO18 0BQ – ℰ (01243) 533 993 – www.theearlofmarch.com
– gt@theearlofmarch.com – Fax (01243) 783 991
Rest – (Closed Sunday dinner) Carte £ 21/29
♦ Modern pub situated at the edge of the Goodwood Estate. Classic British à la carte menu, with daily-changing specials of game in winter and fish in summer; hearty, flavoursome cooking.

ENGLAND

at Tangmere East : 2 m. by A 27 - AY – ⊠ Chichester

XX **Cassons** 🗋 **P** VISA ⓞⓞ AE
Arundel Rd, Northwest : ¼ m. off A 27 (westbound) ⊠ PO15 0DU – ℰ (01243)
773 294 – www.cassonsrestaurant.co.uk – cassonsresto@aol.com – Fax (01243)
778 148 – Closed 25-26 December, Tuesday lunch, Sunday dinner and Monday
Rest – Menu £ 19/27 (midweek) – Carte £ 35/49
♦ Eponymous owners run a homely and appealing neighbourhood restaurant where
theme evenings (eg, India, New Zealand) gel with the locally renowned classical,
seasonal cooking.

at Bosham West : 4 m. by A 259 – AZ – ⊠ Chichester

🏨 **Millstream** 🗋 ఉ rm, 🅐🅒 rest, ఞ ꜞꜞ **P** VISA ⓞⓞ AE ⓞ
Bosham Lane ⊠ PO18 8HL – ℰ (01243) 573 234 – www.millstream-hotel.co.uk
– info@millstream-hotel.co.uk – Fax (01243) 573 459
32 rm ☑ – ♦£85/125 ♦♦£ 145/165 – 3 suites
Rest – Menu £ 23 (lunch) – Carte £ 27/35
♦ Pretty hotel with garden that backs onto stream bobbing with ducks. Cosy bedrooms, individually co-ordinated fabric furnishings, sandwash fitted furniture and
large windows. Seasonal, daily changing menus.

at West Stoke Northwest : 2 ¾ m. by B 2178 – AY - off B 2146 – ⊠ Chichester

XX **West Stoke House** with rm 🌿 ≼ 🗋 🗈 ꜞꜞ **P** VISA ⓞⓞ AE ⓞ
❀ *Downs Rd* ⊠ PO18 9BN – ℰ (01243) 575 226 – www.weststokehouse.co.uk
– info@weststokehouse.co.uk – Fax (01243) 574 655 – Closed 25-26 December
8 rm ☑ – ♦£95 ♦♦£215
Rest – (Closed Sunday dinner Monday and Tuesday) (booking essential)
Menu £ 25/45 **s**
Spec. Turbot with spring onion beignets and chive foam. Rump of lamb
with sweetbreads and garlic. Milk chocolate crunch with walnut nougatine
and milk sorbet.
♦ Charmingly peaceful part 17C manor, set in very pleasant gardens. Reception with
log burner seamlessly blends subtle elegance to modern art; strikingly understated
rooms. Ambitious, skilled kitchen; local produce and seasonality to the fore. Personable service.

at Funtington Northwest : 4 ¾ m. by B 2178 – AY – on B 2146 – ⊠ Chichester

XX **Hallidays** **P** VISA ⓞⓞ
Watery Lane ⊠ PO18 9LF – ℰ (01243) 575 331 – www.hallidays.info
– Closed 2 weeks March, 1 week August, Monday, Tuesday, Saturday lunch and
Sunday dinner
Rest – Menu £ 35 (dinner) – Carte lunch £ 22/33
♦ A row of part 13C thatched cottages; confident and keen chef delivers a lively
medley of frequently changing set menus and à la carte. Modern meals sit alongside
classics.

at Sidlesham South : 5 m. on B 2145 - AZ

🏠 **Landseer House** without rest 🗋 ꜞꜞ **P** VISA ⓞⓞ
Cow Lane, South : 1½m. by B2145 and Keynor Lane. ⊠ PO20 7LN – ℰ (01243)
641 525 – www.landseerhouse.co.uk – enq@landseerhouse.co.uk
6 rm ☑ – ♦£85/110 ♦♦£95/195
♦ Delightful, simply furnished family house with large conservatory and unusual
furniture. Set in 4½ acres of gardens by a Nature Reserve and harbour; views to the
Isle of Wight.

🍴 **Crab & Lobster** with rm 🗋 ఞ ꜞꜞ **P** ⓞⓞ AE
Mill Lane, South : 1 m. by B 2145, then turn right onto Rookery Lane ⊠ PO20 7NB
– ℰ (01243) 641 233 – www.thesussexpub.co.uk – enquiries@crab-lobster.co.uk
4 rm – ♦£75 ♦♦£140   **Rest** – (booking advisable) Carte £ 24/36
♦ 18C pub situated on a nature reserve not far from the beach. British/Mediterranean
menu features simply constructed, cleanly presented dishes and plenty of seafood.
Spacious, contemporary rooms with sea or rural views.

at East Lavant North : 2½ m. off A 286 - AY – ⊠ Chichester

The Royal Oak Inn with rm   😩 **P.** VISA ⓦ AE
Pook Lane ⊠ *PO18 0AX* – ℰ *(01243) 527434* – *www.royaloakeastlavant.co.uk*
– info@royaloakeastlavant.co.uk – *Closed 25-26 December*
8 rm ☑ – ♦£75/95 ♦♦£95/180   **Rest** – Carte £25/35
◆ 18C inn with warm, rustic atmosphere combines the contemporary with the more traditional. Seasonal, modern cooking with game from the Goodwood Estate. Bedrooms – some above the bar, others in cottages and a barn – are furnished to a high standard.

CHIDDINGFOLD – Surrey – 504 S 30   7 C2
▶ London 47 mi – Guildford 10 mi – Haslemere 5 mi

The Swan Inn with rm   😩 AC **P.** VISA ⓦ AE
Petworth Rd ⊠ *GU8 4TY* – ℰ *(01428) 682073* – *www.theswaninn.biz*
– enquiries@theswaninn.biz – *Fax (01428) 683259*
11 rm – ♦£75/100 ♦♦£150   **Rest** – Carte £26/35
◆ Majestic pub with a modern, stylish interior and popular terrace. Food is simple, unfussy and classical; specials change twice a day in line with the latest seasonal produce. Contemporary bedrooms with good bathrooms and mod cons.

CHIEVELEY – West Berkshire – 503 Q 29   10 B3
▶ London 60 mi – Newbury 5 mi – Swindon 25 mi

The Crab at Chieveley with rm   😩 📞 **P.** VISA ⓦ AE ①
Wantage Rd, West : 2½ m. by School Rd on B 4494 ⊠ *RG20 8UE* – ℰ *(01635) 247550* – *www.crabatchieveley.com* – *info@crabatchieveley.com* – *Fax (01635) 248440*
14 rm ☑ – ♦♦£120/160   **Rest** – Menu £20 (lunch) – Carte £28/57
◆ Thatched former inn, a lively venue, on a country road with wheat fields. Choice of bistro or restaurant for seafood menu. Highly original bedrooms themed as famous hotels.

CHILLATON – Devon – 503 H 32 – see Tavistock

CHILLINGTON – Devon – 503 I 33   2 C3
▶ London 217 mi – Plymouth 26 mi – Torbay 20 mi – Torquay 22 mi

Whitehouse   🚗 📞 **P.** VISA ⓦ AE ①
⊠ *TQ7 2JX* – ℰ *(01548) 580505* – *www.whitehousedevon.com*
– frontofhouse@whitehousedevon.com
5 rm ☑ – ♦£180 ♦♦£200   **Rest** – Carte £24/39
◆ Sizeable Georgian house with modern furnishings, relaxed atmosphere and beautiful gardens. Sumptuous, well appointed bedrooms, with large baths and handmade toiletries. Lovely dining room with casual, airy feel and appealing menu.

CHINNOR – Oxfordshire – 504 R 28 – pop. 5 407 ▌ Great Britain   11 C2
▶ London 45 mi – Oxford 19 mi
◪ Ridgeway Path★★

at Sprigg's Alley Southeast : 2½ m. by Bledlow Ridge rd – ⊠ Chinnor

Sir Charles Napier   🚗 😩 **P.** VISA ⓦ
⊠ *OX39 4BX* – ℰ *(01494) 483011* – *www.sircharlesnapier.co.uk*
– info@sircharlesnapier.co.uk – *Fax (01494) 485311* – *Closed 3 days at Christmas*
Rest – (Closed Sunday dinner and Monday) Carte £32/45 ⊛
◆ Early 18C inn serving modern British food with French influences. Quarry-tiled bar with sofas; beamed dining rooms; beautiful rear garden and vine-covered terrace. Sculptures.

at Kingston Blount Southwest : 1 ¾ m. on B 4009 – ⊠ Chinnor

Lakeside Town Farm without rest   📠 ⁂ 📶 **P** *VISA* 🆗 ⓪
Brook St, (off Sydenham rd) ⊠ *OX39 4RZ* – 𝒞 *(01844) 352 152*
– www.townfarmcottage.co.uk – townfarmcottage@oxfree.com – Fax (01844)
352 152 – Closed Christmas
4 rm ⊃⊂ – †£60 ††£100
♦ Modern building, on a working farm, in a sympathetic style that engenders a traditional, old-fashioned ambience. Charming, Victorian-style bedrooms. Attractive gardens.

CHIPPENHAM – Wiltshire – 503 N 29 – pop. 33 189   4 **C2**
🚗 London 106 mi – Bristol 27 mi – Southampton 64 mi – Swindon 21 mi
🇮 Yelde Hall, Market Place 𝒞 (01249) 665970, tourism@chippenham.gov.uk
🏌 Monkton Park (Par Three), 𝒞 (01249) 653 928
◉ Yelde Hall★
🖼 Corsham Court★★ **AC**, SW : 4 m. by A 4 – Sheldon Manor★ **AC**, W : 1 ½ m.
by A 420 – Biddestone★, W : 3 ½ m. – Bowood House★ **AC** (Library ≤★) SE :
5 m. by A 4 and A 342. Castle Combe★★, NW : 6 m. by A 420 and B 4039

at Stanton St Quintin North : 5 m. by A 429 – ⊠ Chippenham

Stanton Manor ⑳   📠 🕪 🈂 ¶⁙ 🛎 🚲 **P** *VISA* 🆗 AE
⊠ *SN14 6DQ* – 𝒞 *(01666) 837 552 – www.stantonmanor.co.uk*
– reception@stantonmanor.co.uk – Fax (01666) 837 022
23 rm ⊃⊂ – †£190 ††£220   **Rest** – Carte £30/37
♦ Extended 19C manor in formal gardens; popular as a wedding venue. Appealing range of bedrooms, geared to corporate market; the deluxe rooms considerably better than the standards. Elegant restaurant uses produce from the garden.

CHIPPING – Lancashire – 502 M 22 – ⊠ Preston   20 **B2**
🚗 London 233 mi – Lancaster 30 mi – Leeds 54 mi – Manchester 40 mi
– Preston 12 mi

Gibbon Bridge ⑳   📠 🕪 🎴 ⁙ 🈐 & rm, Ⓐ rest, ⁂ ¶⁙ 🚲 **P**
East : 1 m. on Clitheroe rd ⊠ *PR3 2TQ* – 𝒞 *(01995) 61456*   *VISA* 🆗 AE ⓪
– www.gibbon-bridge.co.uk – reception@gibbon-bridge.co.uk – Fax (01995)
61 277 – Closed 1 week January
11 rm ⊃⊂ – †£90/100 ††£130/230 – 18 suites
Rest – Menu £18 (lunch) – Carte dinner £28/34
♦ Converted stone farm buildings set in the heart of the Trough of Bowland. Bedrooms, all of which are very comfy and individual, include split-level suites with four-posters. Own bakery produce in restaurant, which overlooks delightful gardens.

CHIPPING CAMPDEN – Gloucestershire – 503 O 27 – pop. 1 943   4 **D1**
📗 Great Britain
🚗 London 93 mi – Cheltenham 21 mi – Oxford 37 mi
– Stratford-upon-Avon 12 mi
🇮 Old Police Station 𝒞 (01386) 841206, visitchippingcampden@lineone.net
◉ Town★
🖼 Hidcote Manor Garden★★ **AC**, NE : 2 ½ m

Cotswold House   📠 🈂 Ⓐ rest, 📶 🚲 **P** *VISA* 🆗 AE
The Square ⊠ *GL55 6AN* – 𝒞 *(01386) 840 330 – www.cotswoldhouse.com*
– reception@cotswoldhouse.com – Fax (01386) 840 310
27 rm ⊃⊂ – †£150/275 ††£500 – 3 suites
Rest *Hicks'* – see restaurant listing
Rest *Juliana's* – (Closed Sunday and Monday) (dinner only) Menu £50
♦ Enviably stylish Regency town house with graceful spiral staircase winding upwards to luxurious rooms, some very modern, boasting every mod con imaginable. Impressive service. Formal though stylish Juliana's for accomplished cooking with an original style.

ENGLAND

XX **The Kings** with rm   🚗 🌣 ⁽¹⁾ P. VISA ⓒ AE
The Square ⊠ *GL55 6AW* – *ℰ (01386) 840 256* – *www.kingscampden.co.uk*
– info@kingscampden.co.uk – *Fax (01386) 841 598*
14 rm � – ♦£85/95 ♦♦£95/175   **Rest** – Menu £17/21 – Carte £25/30
♦ Attractive red brick house in centre of town; modernised but retaining period
character. Intimate dining room serves well-presented, quality cooking. Garden and
rear terrace. Stylish bedrooms on upper two floors.

X **Hicks'** – at Cotswold House Hotel   P. VISA ⓒ AE
The Square ⊠ *GL55 6AN* – *ℰ (01386) 840 330* – *www.cotswoldhouse.com*
– reception@cotswoldhouse.com – *Fax (01386) 840 310*
Rest – (booking essential) Menu £20 (lunch midweek) – Carte £24/31
♦ Named after local benefactor. Booking advised; open all day serving locals and
residents with modern varied menu. Morning coffees, afternoon teas, home-made
cake available.

⁑ **Eight Bells Inn** with rm   🌣 VISA ⓒ
Church St ⊠ *GL55 6JG* – *ℰ (01386) 840 371* – *www.eightbellsinn.co.uk*
– neilhargreaves@bellinn.fsnet.co.uk – *Fax (01386) 841 669* – *Closed 25 December*
7 rm ⊐ – ♦£55/85 ♦♦£85/125   **Rest** – Carte £20/30
♦ Atmospheric 14C pub with bustling bar and terraced garden. Menu offers an
appealing blend of traditional and contemporary dishes, with specials chalked on the
board. Bedrooms are warmly decorated and well looked after; room 7 has beams.

at Mickleton North : 3¼ m. by B 4035 and B 4081 on B 4632 – ⊠ Chipping
Campden

🏨 **Three Ways House**   🚗 ⎢⭤⎢ AC rest, ⁽¹⁾ ⅍ P. VISA ⓒ AE ①
⊠ *GL55 6SB* – *ℰ (01386) 438 429* – *www.puddingclub.com*
– reception@puddingclub.com – *Fax (01386) 438 118*
48 rm ⊐ – ♦£80/110 ♦♦£139/220
Rest – (dinner only and Sunday lunch) Menu £35
♦ Built in 1870; renowned as home of the "Pudding Club". Two types of room, in
original house and modern block, all very comfy and modern. Bar with antique tiled
floor. Arcaded dining room; Pudding Club meets here to vote after tastings.

⌂ **Nineveh Farm** without rest   🚗 ⅍ P. VISA ⓒ
Southwest : ¾ m. by B4632 on B4081 ⊠ *GL55 6PS* – *ℰ (01386) 438 923*
– www.ninevehfarm.co.uk – *ninevehfarm@hotmail.com*
5 rm ⊐ – ♦£55/75 ♦♦£65/85
♦ Georgian farmhouse in pleasant garden. Warm welcome; local information in resident's lounge. Comfortable rooms with view in house or with French windows in
garden house.

⌂ **Myrtle House** without rest   🚗 ⁽¹⁾ P. VISA ⓒ
⊠ *GL55 6SA* – *ℰ (01386) 430 032* – *www.myrtlehouse.co.uk*
– louanne@myrtlehouse.co.uk
5 rm ⊐ – ♦£45/55 ♦♦£65/85
♦ Part Georgian house with large lawned garden. Bedrooms named and styled after
flowers and plants, those on top floor most characterful.

at Broad Campden South : 1¼ m. by B 4081 – ⊠ Chipping Campden

⌂ **Malt House** without rest ⤸   🚗 P. VISA ⓒ
⊠ *GL55 6UU* – *ℰ (01386) 840 295* – *www.malt-house.co.uk*
– info@malt-house.co.uk – *Fax (01386) 841 334* – *Closed 1 week Christmas*
7 rm ⊐ – ♦£85 ♦♦£143/160
♦ For a rare experience of the countryside idyll, this 16C malting house is a must. Cut
flowers from the gardens on view in bedrooms decked out in fabrics to delight the
eye.

Red = Pleasant. Look for the red X and 🏨 symbols.

225

ENGLAND

CHIPPING NORTON – Oxfordshire – **503** P 28 – **pop. 5 688**   10 **A1**

▶ London 77 mi – Oxford 22 mi – Stow-on-the-Wold 9 mi

🍺 ⊕   **The Masons Arms**   🎄 🏠 ✗ **P** **VISA** **⦿⦿** **AE** **①**

Banbury Rd, Swerford, Northeast : 5 m. on A 361 ✉ OX7 4AP – ✆ (01608)
683 212 – www.masons-arms.com – themasonschef@hotmail.com – Fax (01608)
683 105 – Closed 25-26 December
Rest – (Closed Sunday dinner) Menu £ 15/20 – Carte £ 24/29
♦ Rurally-set modernised dining pub with countryside views. Various menus provide
plenty of choice. Well-presented, flavoursome dishes; including British classics with a
modern slant.

CHISELDON – Wilts. – **503** O 29 – see Swindon

CHORLEY – Lancashire – **502** M 23 – **pop. 33 424**   20 **A2**

▶ London 222 – Blackpool 30 – Liverpool 33 – Manchester 26
🏌 Duxbury Park Duxbury Hall Rd, ✆ (01257) 265 380
🏌 Shaw Hill Hotel G. & C.C. Whittle-le-Woods Preston Rd, ✆ (01257) 269 221

✗✗   **The Red Cat**   **P** **VISA** **⦿⦿** **AE**

Blackburn Rd, Whittle-Le-Woods, Northeast : 2½ m on A 674 – ✆ (01257) 263 966
– www.theredcat.co.uk – enquiries@theredcat.co.uk – Closed Tuesday lunch and
Monday
Rest – Menu £ 17 (lunch) **s** – Carte dinner £ 26/39 **s**
♦ Restored pub with original beams, stone walls and brick fireplaces. Unfussy, modern dishes display good ingredients and sound cooking in well presented, classic
combinations.

CHORLTON-CUM-HARDY – Gtr Manchester – **502** N 23 – see Manchester

---

CHRISHALL – Essex

▶ London 58 mi – Barnet 44 mi – Enfield 51 mi – Luton 36 mi

🍺   **The Red Cow**   🎄 🏠 **P** **VISA** **⦿⦿**

11 High St ✉ SG8 8RN – ✆ (01763) 838 792 – www.theredcow.com – Closed
Monday lunch and Sunday dinner
Rest – Carte £ 19/30
♦ Hugely characterful part 14C thatched pub, set in small village off the beaten track.
Cosy interior with plenty of beams and open fires. Simple menu of British dishes
reflects the seasons.

CHRISTCHURCH – Dorset – **503** O 31 – **pop. 40 208**   4 **D3**

▶ London 111 mi – Bournemouth 6 mi – Salisbury 26 mi – Southampton 24 mi
   – Winchester 39 mi
ℹ 49 High St ✆ (01202) 471 780, enquiries@christchurchtourism.info
🏌 Highcliffe Castle Highcliffe-on-Sea 107 Lymington Rd, ✆ (01425) 272 953
🏌 Riverside Ave, ✆ (01202) 436 436
◎ Town★ - Priory★
◉ Hengistbury Head★ (≤★★) SW : 4½ m. by A 35 and B 3059

🏨   **Captain's Club**   ≤ 🌐 🏠 🛗 & 🅰 🎙 🛁 **P** **VISA** **⦿⦿** **AE** **①**

Wick Ferry, Wick Lane ✉ BH23 1HU – ✆ (01202) 475 111
– www.captainsclubhotel.com – enquiries@captainsclubhotel.com – Fax (01202)
490 111
17 rm – †£ 169/185 ††£ 169/269, ☕ £ 15 – 12 suites
Rest Tides – see restaurant listing
♦ Trendy hotel displaying striking art deco and nautical influences. Floor to ceiling
windows throughout; attractive river views. Smart, simply furnished bedrooms/suites.
Stylish spa.

ENGLAND

ENGLAND

↑ **Druid House** without rest
26 Sopers Lane ⊠ BH23 1JE – ℰ (01202) 485 615 – www.druid-house.co.uk
– reservations@druid-house.co.uk – Fax (01202) 473 484
10 rm ⊡ – †£ 35/70 ††£ 70/84
♦ Bright, fresh interior in contrast to exterior. Cottagey breakfast room; light and airy conservatory sitting room, smart bar. Spacious bedrooms, two with balconies.

XX **Splinters**
12 Church St ⊠ BH23 1BW – ℰ (01202) 483 454 – www.splinters.uk.com
– eating@splinters.uk.com – Fax (01202) 480 180 – Closed 1-10 January, Sunday and Monday
Rest – Menu £ 14/26 – Carte £ 26/39
♦ Brasserie-like exterior; two dining areas inside: one has intimate pine booths; upstairs more formal with high-backed chairs. French-influenced cuisine.

XX **Tides** – at Captain's Club Hotel
Wick Ferry, Wick Lane ⊠ BH23 1HU – ℰ (01202) 475 111
– www.captainsclubhotel.com – enquiries@captainsclubhotel.com – Fax (01202) 490 111
Rest – Menu £ 16 (lunch) – Carte £ 26/35
♦ Stylish restaurant with water feature wall, oversized windows and river views. Modern, well judged cooking offers a wide choice, good combinations and some unusual formats.

CHURCH ENSTONE – Oxfordshire – ⊠ Chipping Norton   10 **B1**
  ▣ London 72 mi – Banbury 13 mi – Oxford 38 mi

↑ **The Crown Inn**
Mill Lane ⊠ OX7 4NN – ℰ (01608) 677 262 – www.crowninnenstone.co.uk
– Closed 26 December, 1 January
Rest – Menu £ 18 (lunch) – Carte £ 18/27
♦ Pretty, well-run inn with homely feel and good mix of drinkers and diners. Light and airy conservatory. Display of handcrafted walking sticks in hall. Unfussy, honest cooking.

CHURCHILL – Oxfordshire – **503** P 28 – ⊠ Chipping Norton   10 **A1**
  ▣ London 79 mi – Birmingham 46 mi – Cheltenham 29 mi – Oxford 23 mi
    – Swindon 31 mi

↑ **The Chequers**
Church Rd ⊠ OX7 6NJ – ℰ (01608) 659 393 – Closed 25 December for food
Rest – Carte £ 20/29
♦ Popular, open plan pub built of Cotswold stone, with high-ceilings, inglenook fireplace and warm, welcoming atmosphere. Traditional dishes made with local ingredients.

CHURCH STRETTON – Shropshire – **502** L 26 – pop. 3 841   18 **B2**
🖫 Great Britain
  ▣ London 166 mi – Birmingham 46 mi – Hereford 39 mi – Shrewsbury 14 mi
  🖫 Trevor Hill, ℰ (01694) 722 281
  🖫 Wenlock Edge★, E : by B 4371

↑ **Jinlye** without rest
Castle Hill, All Stretton, North : 2 ¼ m. by B 4370 turning left beside telephone box in All Stretton ⊠ SY6 6JP – ℰ (01694) 723 243 – www.jinlye.co.uk
– info@jinlye.co.uk – Fax (01694) 723 243
6 rm ⊡ – †£ 50/65 ††£ 60/90
♦ Enjoy wonderful views of Long Mynd from this characterful crofter's cottage high in the hills, run by charming owner and daughter. Grandiose breakfast room. 19C conservatory.

ΧΧ **The Studio** 🖵 🖫 *VISA* 🖭
59 High St ⊠ SY6 6BY – 𝒞 (01694) 722672 – www.thestudiorestaurant.net
– info@thestudiorestaurant.net – Closed Christmas and New Year,
3 weeks January, 1 week Spring, 1 week Autumn, Sunday and Monday
Rest – (dinner only) Menu £28

◆ Personally run former art studio; walls enhanced by local artwork. Pleasant rear terrace for sunny lunches. Tried-and-tested dishes: much care taken over local produce.

CIRENCESTER – Gloucestershire – 503 O 28 – pop. 15 861   4 **D1**

▌ *Great Britain*

🗗 London 97 mi – Bristol 37 mi – Gloucester 19 mi – Oxford 37 mi
🗗 Corn Hall, Market Pl 𝒞 (01285) 654180, cirencesterservic@cotswold.gov.uk
🗓 Bagendon Cheltenham Rd, 𝒞 (01285) 652465
🗗 Town★ – Church of St John the Baptist★ – Corinium Museum★ (Mosaic pavements★) **AC**
🗗 Fairford : Church of St Mary★ (stained glass windows★★) E : 7 m. by A 417

🏠 **No 12** without rest 🖵 🕉 📞 *VISA* 🖭
12 Park St ⊠ GL7 2BW – 𝒞 (01285) 640232 – www.no12cirencester.co.uk
– enquiries@no12cirencester.co.uk
4 rm ☲ – †£65 ††£85/100

◆ 16C property with Georgian façade, hidden away in the old alleyways. Delightful rear walled garden. Excellent organic breakfast. Stylish rooms charmingly blend old and new.

🏠 **The Old Brewhouse** without rest 🕭 🕉 📞 **P** *VISA* 🖭 **AE**
7 London Rd ⊠ GL7 2PU – 𝒞 (01285) 656099 – www.theoldbrewhouse.com
– info@theoldbrewhouse.com – Fax (01285) 656099 – Closed 5 days Christmas
10 rm ☲ – †£55/65 ††£65/75

◆ Former 17C brewhouse with a cosy, cottagey ambience. Exposed stone in two breakfast rooms. Cast iron bedsteads adorn some of the rooms, all of which boast period character.

at Barnsley Northeast : 4 m. by A 429 on B 4425 – ⊠ Cirencester

🏨 **Barnsley House** ॐ   ← 🖵 🕭 🎇 🖭 🕸 ΧΧ 📞 🛦 **P** *VISA* 🖭
⊠ GL7 5EE – 𝒞 (01285) 740000 – www.barnsleyhouse.com
– info@barnsleyhouse.com – Fax (01285) 740925
11 rm – †£325/355 ††£495/545, ☲ £12 – 7 suites
Rest – (booking essential for non-residents at dinner) Menu £26/40
– Carte £22/43

◆ Impressive 17C Cotswold manor house. Contemporary interior, with hi tech bedrooms; largest and most modern in annexed courtyard. Well kept gardens, hydrotherapy pool, cinema. Dining room has pleasant outlook. Modern, interesting menus.

🍴 **Village Pub** with rm 🖫 **P** *VISA* 🖭
⊠ GL7 5EE – 𝒞 (01285) 740421 – www.thevillagepub.co.uk
– rec@barnsleyhouse.com – Fax (01285) 740925
7 rm – †£95 ††£225, ☲ £5   **Rest** – Carte £20/29

◆ Characterful stone pub in a charming village. Dishes vary in style between pub and restaurant, rustic and refined; changing daily and even between services. Bedrooms feature beams, antique furniture and Victorian or four poster beds.

at Ewen Southwest : 3 ¼ m. by A 429 – ⊠ Cirencester

🍴 **The Wild Duck Inn** with rm 🖫 📞 **P** *VISA* 🖭 **AE**
Drake's Island ⊠ GL7 6BY – 𝒞 (01285) 770310 – www.thewildduckinn.co.uk
– wduckinn@aol.com – Fax (01285) 770924 – Closed 25 December for food
12 rm ☲ – †£80 ††£180   **Rest** – Carte £25/40

◆ 16C stone pub with original features and plenty of character. Traditional menu features pub classics and old British favourites. Bedrooms in the original building are large and characterful, with high ceilings and a period feel.

ENGLAND

at Sapperton West : 5 m. by A 419 – ⊠ Cirencester

🛏️ **The Bell** 　　　　　　🍴 🛋️ ⇔ 🅿️ VISA ⚫️
⊠ GL7 6LE – ℰ (01285) 760 298 – www.foodatthebell.co.uk
– thebell@sapperton66.freeserve.co.uk – Fax (01285) 760 761
– Closed 25 December
Rest – Carte £ 23/35 🍷
♦ Charming pub in a pretty village. Wide-ranging monthly menu and daily seafood specials take on a refined yet rustic style, relying on regional produce. Interesting wine list.

CLANFIELD – Oxfordshire – 503 P 28 – pop. 1 709　　　10 **A2**
　▶ London 75 mi – Oxford 24 mi – Swindon 16 mi

🏠 **Plough at Clanfield** 　　　🍴 🛋️ ♿ rm, 🛜 🅿️ VISA ⚫️
Bourton Rd, on A 4095 ⊠ OX18 2RB – ℰ (01367) 810 222
– www.theploughclanfield.co.uk – info@theploughclanfield.co.uk
12 rm � – ♦£75 ♦♦£110　**Rest** – Carte £ 17/36
♦ Restored Elizabethan manor (1560), sitting in pretty gardens. Serene lounge with original fireplace; choice of rooms with character in main house and larger, newer rooms. Intimate restaurant.

CLAVERING – Essex – 504 U 28 – pop. 1 663 – ⊠ Saffron Walden　12 **B2**
　▶ London 44 mi – Cambridge 25 mi – Colchester 44 mi – Luton 29 mi

🛏️ **The Cricketers** with rm 　　🍴 🛋️ ♿ rm, 🛜 🅿️ VISA ⚫️ AE
⊠ CB11 4QT – ℰ (01799) 550 442 – www.thecricketers.co.uk
– info@thecricketers.co.uk – Fax (01799) 550 882 – Closed 25-26 December
14 rm ⊒ – ♦£65/75 ♦♦£90/110　**Rest** – Menu £ 30 – Carte £ 20/30
♦ 16C pub where Jamie Oliver first learned to chop an onion - still run by his parents. Traditional feel; low beamed ceilings. Choice of cottagey or more modern bedrooms.

CLAYTON-LE-WOODS – Lancashire – 502 M 24 – pop. 14 173　20 **A2**
– ⊠ Chorley
　▶ London 220 mi – Liverpool 34 mi – Manchester 26 mi – Preston 5 mi

🏠 **The Pines** 　　🍴 🛋️ 🏊 🛜 🧖 🅿️ VISA ⚫️
570 Preston Rd, on A 6 at junction with B 5256 ⊠ PR6 7ED – ℰ (01772) 338 551
– www.thepineshotel.co.uk – mail@thepineshotel.co.uk – Fax (01772) 629 002
33 rm ⊒ – ♦£75 ♦♦£105 – 2 suites
Rest Haworths – Menu £ 19 (except Saturday dinner)/30 – Carte £ 21/33
♦ Prospering on a heady round of weddings and cabarets, this redbrick Victorian hotel boasts two fashionable lounges and a smart set of bedrooms, all individually decorated. Restaurant with unique stained glass roof and modern, assured cooking.

CLEETHORPES – North East Lincolnshire – 502 U 23 – pop. 31 853　23 **D3**
　▶ London 171 mi – Lincoln 38 mi – Sheffield 77 mi
　✈ Humberside Airport : ℰ (01652) 688 456, W : 16 m. by A 46 and A 18 Y
　🛈 42-43 Alexandra Rd ℰ (01472) 323 111, cleetic@nelc.gov.uk

🍴🍴 **Riverside Bar and Restaurant** 　　　AC ⇔ VISA ⚫️
2 Alexandra Rd ⊠ DN35 8LQ – ℰ (01472) 600 515
– www.theriversidebarandrestaurant.com
– enquiries@theriversidebarandrestaurant.com – Fax (01472) 290 270
– Closed 25-26 December, 1 January, Monday and Sunday in winter
Rest – Carte £ 23/31
♦ Actually looking out to sea, this 19C terraced property has a modern interior with a ground floor bar and smart restaurant upstairs where modern classics take centre stage.

CLEEVE HILL – Glos. – 503 N 28 – see Cheltenham

> ▶ London 127 mi – Birmingham 12 mi – Hagley 2 mi
> 🄶 Black Country Museum★, N : 7 m. by A 491 and A 4036 – Birmingham★ - Museum and Art Gallery★★, Aston Hall★★, NE : 10 m. by A 491 and A 456

🍴 Bell & Cross 🚗 🔲 **P** VISA 🌑

Holy Cross, West :½ m. off A 491 (northbound carriageway) (Bromsgrove rd)
✉ DY9 9QL – ✆ (01562) 730 319 – www.bellandcrossclent.co.uk
– *Closed 25 December*
Rest – Carte £ 20/28

♦ Early 19C village pub with gardens and dining terrace. Traditional public bar and five intimate dining rooms. Friendly service; blackboard specials and seasonal produce.

CLEY NEXT THE SEA – **Norfolk** – **504** X 25 – **see Blakeney**

CLIPSHAM – **Rutland** – **see Stamford**

CLITHEROE – **Lancashire** – **502** M 22 – **pop. 14 697** 20 **B2**

> ▶ London 64 mi – Blackpool 35 mi – Manchester 31 mi
> 🄸 12-14 Market Pl ✆ (01200) 425566,tourism@ribblevalley.gov.uk
> 🄷 Whalley Rd, ✆ (01200) 422 618

⌂ Brooklyn without rest 🚭

32 Pimlico Rd ✉ BB7 2AH – ✆ (01200) 428 268
– www.brooklynguesthouse.co.uk – Fax (01200) 428 699
5 rm ☲ – †£ 35/45 ††£ 65

♦ Stone 19C house, two minutes' walk from town, with floral furnished rooms, quieter at the rear. Good base from which to explore the Trough of Bowland and Clitheroe Castle.

---

at Bashall Eaves Northwest : 3 m. by B6243

🍴 The Red Pump Inn with rm 🚗 🚭 **P** VISA 🌑

Clitheroe Road ✉ BB7 3DA – ✆ (01254) 826 227 – www.theredpumpinn.co.uk
– info@theredpumpinn.co.uk – Fax (01254) 826 750 – *Closed 1 week mid February*
3 rm ☲ – †£ 45/55 ††£ 70/90
Rest – (Closed Monday except Bank Holidays) Carte approx. £ 30

♦ One of the oldest inns in the Ribble Valley. The traditional menu is hearty and generous, featuring regional produce, including a variety of game dishes in season. Spacious, modern bedrooms with handmade furniture and oversized beds.

---

at Grindleton Northeast : 3 m. by A 671

🍴 Duke of York Inn 🚗 **P** VISA 🌑 AE

Brow Top ✉ BB7 4QR – ✆ (01200) 441 266 – www.dukeofyorkgrindleton.com
– duke-ofyork@btconnect.com – Fax (01200) 441 250 – *Closed Monday*
Rest – Menu £ 13 (lunch) – Carte £ 19/29

♦ Ivy clad pub in a pleasant hamlet, with large decked terrace. Great value lunch/ early evening set menu and wide-ranging à la carte. Carefully prepared, tasty, seasonal cooking.

CLOVELLY – **Devon** – **503** G 31 – **pop. 439** – ✉ **Bideford** 1 **B1**

> ▶ London 241 mi – Barnstaple 18 mi – Exeter 52 mi – Penzance 92 mi
> 🄾 Village★★
> 🄶 SW : Tamar River★★. Hartland : Hartland Church★ - Hartland Quay★ (viewpoint★★) - Hartland Point ≤★★★, W : 6½ m. by B 3237 and B 3248 – Morwenstow (Church★, cliffs★★), SW : 11½ m. by A 39

🏠 Red Lion ≤ 🚭 🛜 **P** VISA 🌑 AE

The Quay ✉ EX39 5TF – ✆ (01237) 431 237 – www.clovelly.co.uk
– redlion@clovelly.co.uk – Fax (01237) 431 044
11 rm ☲ – †£ 62/77 ††£ 124/134 **Rest** – (bar lunch) Menu £ 30

♦ Cosy little hotel/inn on the quayside; a superb location. All rooms enjoy sea and harbour views and are dressed in soft, understated colours, providing a smart resting place. Simple dining room looks out to harbour.

ENGLAND

CLOWS TOP – Worcestershire – pop. 1 164

18 **B2**

▶ London 141 mi – Bewdley 6 mi – Stourport-on-Seven 10 mi

The Colliers Arms 🛏 🗓 **P** *VISA* **◐◐**
Tenbury Road, East : ½ m. on A 456 ⊠ DY14 9HA – ℰ (01299) 832 242
– www.colliersarms.com – thecolliersarms@aol.com
Rest – Carte £ 18/25
♦ Snug, traditional bar; open main bar with log fire and fishy wallpaper; airy rear dining room with views of garden. Hearty British classics - all fresh, seasonal and homemade.

CLUN – Shropshire – 503 K 26

18 **A2**

▶ London 173 mi – Church Stretton 16 mi – Ludlow 16 mi

Birches Mill without rest ⌂ 🛏 ⚘ **P** *VISA* **◐◐**
Northwest : 3 m. by A 488, Bicton rd, Mainstone rd and Burlow rd ⊠ SY7 8NL
– ℰ (01588) 640 409 – www.birchesmill.co.uk – gill@birchesmill.fsnet.co.uk
– Fax (01588) 640 409 – April-October
3 rm ⌂ – †£66/70 ††£84
♦ High quality comforts in remote former corn mill: interior has characterful 17C/18C structures. Flagged lounge with lovely inglenook. Simple but tastefully decorated rooms.

> Your opinions are important to us:
> please write and let us know about your discoveries and experiences – good and bad!

ENGLAND

COBHAM – Surrey – 504 S 30 – pop. 1 586

7 **D1**

▶ London 24 mi – Guildford 10 mi

Plan : see Greater London (South-West) 5

at Stoke D'Abernon Southeast : 1½ m. on A 245 – ⊠ Cobham

Woodlands Park 🛏 🕪 ※ 🖥 ᴅ rm, ※ 🕿 🖄 **P** *VISA* **◐◐** **AE** **①**
Woodlands Lane, on A 245 ⊠ KT11 3QB – ℰ (01372) 843 933
– www.handpicked.co.uk/woodlandspark – woodlandspark@handpicked.co.uk
– Fax (01372) 842 704
57 rm ⌂ – †£115/175 ††£130/205
Rest *Oak Room* – (Closed Sunday dinner and Monday) (dinner only and Sunday lunch) Carte £44/50
Rest *Bensons Brasserie* – Carte £ 21/41
♦ Designed in 1885 for son of founder of Bryant and May match company; one of first houses with electricity. Frequented by Prince of Wales and Lillie Langtry. Modish rooms. Appealingly welcoming Oak Room restaurant; also brasserie.

COCKERMOUTH – Cumbria – 501 J 20 – pop. 7 446

21 **A2**

▶ London 306 mi – Carlisle 25 mi – Keswick 13 mi
🛈 Town Hall, Market St ℰ (01900) 822634, cockermouthtic@co-net.com
🖭 Embleton, ℰ (017687) 76 223

Trout 🛏 🕿 🖙 🖄 **P** *VISA* **◐◐** **AE**
Crown St ⊠ CA13 0EJ – ℰ (01900) 823 591 – www.trouthotel.co.uk
– enquiries@trouthotel.co.uk – Fax (01900) 827 514
47 rm ⌂ – †£60/99 ††£135
Rest *The Restaurant* – (Dinner only and Sunday lunch) Carte £ 26/41
Rest *The Terrace* – Carte £ 18/26
♦ Well run, extended hotel on banks of River Derwent. Refurbished, contemporary lounges and classically styled bedrooms; some in main house have original beams. The linen-laid Restaurant offers a daily set menu. The Terrace Bar and Bistro offers informal and al fresco dining, with a modern, international choice.

at Lorton Southeast : 4 ¼ m. by B 5292 – ⊠ Cockermouth

🏠 **Winder Hall Country House** ⤸ ≤ 🚗 🎾 📞 **P** 🆅🅸🆂🅰 ⓜⓞ 🅰🅴
on B 5289 ⊠ CA13 9UP – ℘ (01900) 85 107 – www.winderhall.co.uk
– nick@winderhall.co.uk – Fax (01900) 85 479
– Closed 20 December- 12 February
7 rm ⌤ – ♦£ 99/104 ♦♦£ 138/148
Rest – (dinner only) (booking essential for non-residents)
Menu £ 39 **s**

♦ Part-Jacobean manor house with mullioned windows and tranquil garden.Comfortable lounge and high quality bedrooms retain rich history of house and include two four posters. Oak panelled dining room overlooks garden. Local produce well-used in homemade dishes. Relaxed, friendly service.

🏠 **New House Farm** ≤ 🚗 🐾 📞 **P** 🆅🅸🆂🅰 ⓜⓞ
South : 1¼ m. on B 5289 ⊠ CA13 9UU – ℘ (01900) 85 404
– www.newhouse-farm.com – hazel@newhouse-farm.co.uk
– Fax (01900) 85 478
5 rm ⌤ – ♦£ 80 ♦♦£ 150/160
Rest – Menu £ 24

♦ Very well appointed, richly decorated guest house. Hot tub in garden, sumptuous bedrooms; one with double jacuzzi, two with four posters. Fine furnishings, roll top baths. Aga-cooked breakfasts and evenings meals.

🏠 **The Old Vicarage** 🚗 🎾 📞 **P** 🆅🅸🆂🅰 ⓜⓞ
Church Lane, North :¼ m. on Lorton Church rd ⊠ CA13 9UN
– ℘ (01900) 85 656
– www.oldvicarage.co.uk
– enquiries@oldvicarage.co.uk
8 rm ⌤ – ♦£ 75/80 ♦♦£ 120
Rest – (by arrangement) Menu £ 27

♦ Well kept Victorian house in beautiful countryside spot. Comfortable lounge. Hospitable owners. Sympathetically modernised bedrooms; four-postered Room 1 is the best. Cosy dining room; homecooked meals made with local produce.

COCKLEFORD – Gloucestershire – ⊠ Cheltenham 4 **C1**
🚹 London 95 mi – Bristol 48 mi – Cheltenham 7 mi

🍺 **The Green Dragon Inn** with rm 🚗 🌳 ⅃ **P** 🆅🅸🆂🅰 ⓜⓞ 🅰🅴
⊠ GL53 9NW – ℘ (01242) 870 271 – www.green-dragon-inn.co.uk
– green-dragon@buccaneer.co.uk – Fax (01242) 870 171
– Closed dinner 25-26 December and 1 January
9 rm ⌤ – ♦£ ♦♦£
Rest – (booking essential) Carte £ 20/30

♦ 17C country inn of old Cotswold stone with beams, log fire and large outside terrace. Tasty meals employing good use of local ingredients. Smart rooms.

CODFORD ST MARY – Wiltshire – **504** N 30 📗 Great Britain 4 **C2**
🚹 London 101 mi – Bristol 38 mi – Warminster 8 mi
🄶 Stonehenge★★★ **AC**, E : 10½ m. by A 36 and A 303

🍺 **The George** 🌳 🎾 **P** 🆅🅸🆂🅰 ⓜⓞ
High St ⊠ BA12 0NG – ℘ (01985) 850 270
– www.thegeorgecodford.co.uk
Rest – (Closed Sunday dinner and Tuesday) Carte £ 20/34

♦ Unspectacular in outward appearance but spot-on with the cooking. The established chef has expertly mastered both British pub classics and more interesting, ambitious dishes.

ENGLAND

COGGESHALL – Essex – **504** W 28 – pop. 3 919 – ⊠ Colchester

▶ London 49 mi – Braintree 6 mi – Chelmsford 16 mi – Colchester 9 mi

🏠 White Hart
`P. VISA ⦿ AE`

Market End ⊠ CO6 1NH – ℰ (01376) 561 654 – www.whitehart-coggeshall.com
– whitehart.coggeshall@greeneking.co.uk
– Fax (01376) 561 789
18 rm ⌑ – †£75/85 ††£95/135
Rest – (in bar Sunday dinner) Carte £25/34

♦ Part 15C guildhall in centre of this historic market town, boasting solid stone floor and walls and warmed by open fires. Characterful bedrooms with exposed timbers. Formal rear dining room serves cooking with an Italian emphasis.

🍴🍴 Baumanns Brasserie
`VISA ⦿ AE`

4-6 Stoneham St ⊠ CO6 1TT – ℰ (01376) 561 453
– www.baumannsbrasserie.co.uk – food@baumanns.brasserie.co.uk
– Fax (01376) 563 762 – Closed first 2 weeks January, Monday and Tuesday
Rest – Menu £22 (dinner) – Carte £28/35

♦ Characterful 16C building, its walls packed with pictures and prints. Tasty cooking, made using local produce, brings out classic flavour combinations. Speedy service.

at Pattiswick Northwest : 3 m. by A 120 (Braintree Rd) – ⊠ Coggeshall

🍴 The Compasses at Pattiswick
`🛏 🛋 ⇔ P. VISA ⦿`

Compasses Rd ⊠ CM77 8BG – ℰ (01376) 561 322
– www.thecompassesatpattiswick.co.uk – info@thecompassesatpattiswick.co.uk
– Fax (01376) 564 343
Rest – Carte £19/30

♦ Country pub with modernised interior, terrace and extensive gardens. Menus feature simple, hearty dishes of local produce; game comes courtesy of the nearby Holifield Estate.

COLCHESTER – Essex – **504** W 28 – pop. 104 390 ▌ Great Britain

▶ London 52 mi – Cambridge 48 mi – Ipswich 18 mi – Luton 76 mi
– Southend-on-Sea 41 mi
🛈 Visitor Information Centre, Tymperleys Clock Museum ℰ (01206) 282 920,
vic@colchester.gov.uk
⛳ Birch Grove Layer Rd, ℰ (01206) 734 276
◉ Castle and Museum★ **AC** BZ

Plan on next page

🏠 Rose and Crown
`& rm, 🍴 🛜 ⅍ P. VISA ⦿ AE ⓘ`

East St, Eastgates ⊠ CO1 2TZ – ℰ (01206) 866 677
– www.rose-and-crown.com
– info@rose-and-crown.com
– Fax (01206) 866 616
CZd
39 rm – †£55/120 ††£75/180, ⌑ £10.95
Rest – (Dinner only and Sunday lunch) Carte £18/29

♦ Part 15C black and white inn boasting original stained glass and exposed beams. Characterful four posters in the main house; larger rooms in lodge better suit business needs. Formal dining room with open feel. Wide-ranging menu features fusion cooking with a strong Indian base.

🏠 Red House without rest
`🛏 🍴 🛜`

29 Wimpole Rd ⊠ CO1 2DL – ℰ (01206) 509 005
– theredhousecolchester@hotmail.com
CZa
3 rm ⌑ – †£35/40 ††£65/70

♦ Red-brick Victorian house away from main centre. Original fittings include stained glass and ornate plasterwork on ceiling in sitting room. Ample bedrooms; personal touches.

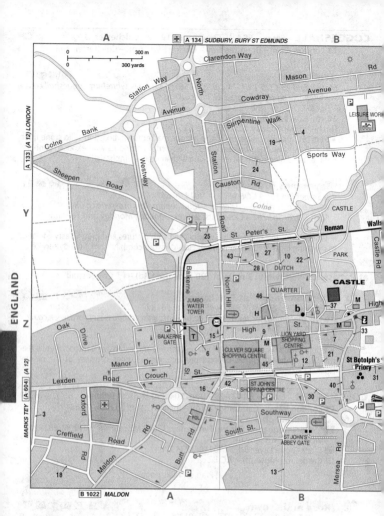

A 134 *SUDBURY, BURY ST EDMUNDS*

COLERNE – Wilts. – **503** M 29 – see Bath (Bath & North East Somerset)

COLESBOURNE – Gloucestershire – **503** N 28   4 **C-D1**
    ▶ London 104 mi – Swindon 27 mi – Gloucester 16 mi – Cheltenham 7 mi

The Colesbourne Inn with rm   🛏 🏠 **P** VISA **①③**
    ✉ GL53 9NP – 𝒞 (01242) 870 376 – www.thecolesbourneinn.co.uk
    – info@thecolesbourneinn.co.uk
    9 rm ⚌ – †£ 55/65 ††£ 75/85
    Rest – Carte £ 18/32
    ♦ Early 19C coaching inn, halfway between Cirencester and Cheltenham, featuring
    open fires, flagged floors and hanging hops and tankards. Unfussy bar menu; more
    elaborate à la carte. Antique-furnished bedrooms in former stables.

COLLYWESTON – Northants. – **502** S 26 – see Stamford

234

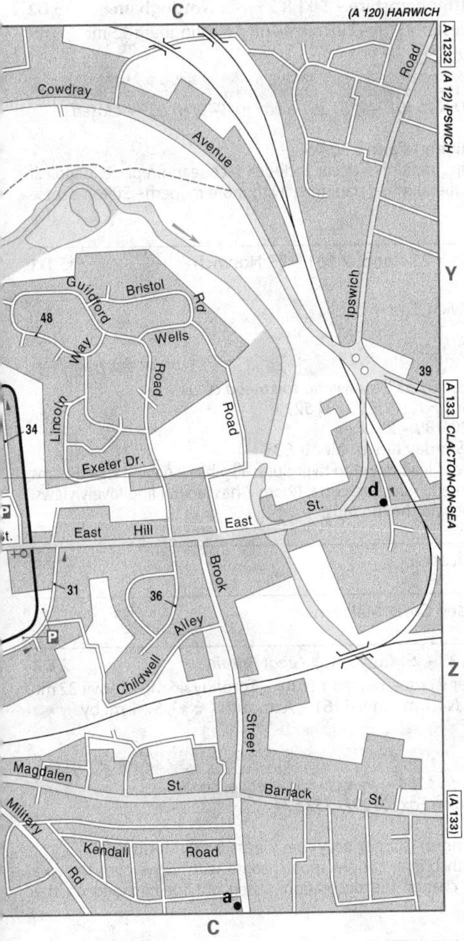

COLCHESTER

Beverley Rd	AZ	3
Catchpool Rd	BY	4
Church St	AZ	6
Culver Square Shopping Centre	BZ	
Culver St East	BZ	7
Culver St West	BZ	9
East Stockwell St	BYZ	10
Eld Lane	BZ	12
Flagstaff Rd	BZ	13
Headgate	ABZ	16
Head St	BZ	15
High St	BZ	
Inglis Rd	AZ	18
Kings Meadow Rd	BY	19
Lion Yard Shopping Centre	BZ	
Long Wyre St	BZ	21
Maidenburgh St	BYZ	22
Margaret Rd	BY	24
Middleborough	AY	25
Northgate St	BY	27
Nunn's Rd	BY	28
Osborne St	BZ	30
Priory St	BCZ	31
Queen St	BZ	33
Roman Rd	CY	34
Rosebery Ave	CY	36
Ryegate Rd	BYZ	37
St Andrews Ave	CY	39
St Botolph's St	BZ	40
St John's Shopping Centre	BZ	
St John's St	BZ	42
Short Cut Rd	BY	43
Trinity St	BZ	45
West Stockwell St	BYZ	46
Worcester Rd	CY	48

COLN ST ALDWYNS – Gloucestershire – 503 O 28 – ✉ Cirencester 4 D1

London 101 mi – Bristol 53 mi – Gloucester 20 mi – Oxford 28 mi – Swindon 15 mi

New Inn At Coln

✉ *GL7 5AN* – *(01285) 750 651* – *www.new-inn.co.uk* – *info@thenewinnatcoln.co.uk* – *Fax (01285) 750 657*

13 rm – £75 £90/180

Rest – (Closed Sunday dinner) (bar lunch) (booking essential for non-residents) Carte £24/35

◆ Pretty 16C Cotswold coaching inn. New owner has refurbished throughout; bedrooms are now bold and colourful and are either in main building or dovecote to rear. Stylish dining room with modern menu.

Look out for red symbols, indicating particularly pleasant establishments.

COLSTON BASSETT – Nottinghamshire – 502 R 25 – ⊠ Nottingham   16 B2

> ▣ London 129 mi – Leicester 23 mi – Lincoln 40 mi – Nottingham 15 mi
> – Sheffield 51 mi

The Martins Arms   🚗 ☂ ❄ **P** *VISA* **⊚** **AE**
*School Lane ⊠ NG12 3FD – 𝒞 (01949) 81 361 – Fax (01949) 81 039 – Closed
25-26 December dinner*
Rest – (Closed Sunday dinner) Carte £ 30/45
♦ Welcoming and well run; traditional décor includes Jacobean fireplace. Candlelit
snug, formal dining room; menu mixes traditional with more modern - Stilton cheese
features.

COLTISHALL – Norfolk – 504 Y 25 – pop. 2 161 – ⊠ Norwich   15 D1
Great Britain

> ▣ London 133 mi – Norwich 8 mi
> ⃝ Norfolk Broads★

Norfolk Mead ⬙   ≤ 🚗 ◑ ➘ ⫝ ⁇ **P** *VISA* **⊚** **AE** **①**
*⊠ NR12 7DN – 𝒞 (01603) 737 531 – www.norfolkmead.co.uk
– info@norfolkmead.co.uk – Fax (01603) 737 521*
13 rm ⌂ – †£ 95 ††£ 120/180 – 2 suites
Rest – (dinner only and Sunday lunch) Menu £ 35
♦ Restful 18C manor; gardens lead down to river Bure; also has a fishing lake. Rooms
are individually colour themed: blue, terracotta. Room 7 has jacuzzi and lovely views.
Candlelit restaurant overlooking the grounds.

COLTON – N. Yorks. – see Tadcaster

COLWALL – Herefordshire – see Great Malvern

COLYFORD – Devon – 503 K 31 – ⊠ Colyton *Great Britain*   2 D2

> ▣ London 168 mi – Exeter 21 mi – Taunton 30 mi – Torquay 46 mi – Yeovil 32 mi
> ⃝ Colyton★ (Church★), N : 1 m. on B 3161 – Axmouth (≤★), S : 1 m. by
> A 3052 and B 3172

Swallows Eaves   🚗 ❄ ⁇ **P** *VISA* **⊚**
*⊠ EX24 6QJ – 𝒞 (01297) 553 184 – www.swallowseaves.co.uk
– info@swallowseaves.co.uk – Fax (01297) 553 574*
8 rm ⌂ – †£ 62/79 ††£ 112/118
Rest – (Closed Sunday dinner) (dinner only) (residents only) Menu £ 26
♦ Pristine 1920s house with bright, spright rooms, some with views over the Axe
Valley. New owner set to change the decoration. Listen out for birdsong on the
marshes. Home-cooking.

COMBE HAY – Bath & North East Somerset – see Bath

CONEYTHORPE – North Yorkshire – see Knaresborough

CONGLETON – Cheshire – 502 N 24 – pop. 25 400 *Great Britain*   20 B3

> ▣ London 183 mi – Liverpool 50 mi – Manchester 25 mi – Sheffield 46 mi
> – Stoke-on-Trent 13 mi
> 🛈 Town Hall, High St 𝒞 (01260) 271095, tourism@congleton.gov.uk
> ⃝ Biddulph Rd, 𝒞 (01260) 273 540
> ⃝ Little Moreton Hall★★ **AC**, SW : 3 m. by A 34

Sandhole Farm *without rest* ⬙   🚗 ◑ ❄ ⁇ **P** *VISA* **⊚** **①**
*Hulme Walfield, North : 2¼ m. on A 34 ⊠ CW12 2JH – 𝒞 (01260) 224 419
– www.sandholefarm.co.uk – veronica@sandholefarm.co.uk – Fax (01260) 224 766*
15 rm ⌂ – †£ 70 ††£ 80
♦ Former farm with its stable block converted into comfy, well-equipped bedrooms
with a rustic feel. Breakfast taken in the farmhouse's conservatory overlooking the
countryside.

XX Pecks   AC ⇔ P VISA ☻ AE
Newcastle Rd, Moreton, South : 2 ¾ m. on A 34 ⊠ *CW12 4SB –* ℰ *(01260)*
275 161 – www.pecksrest.co.uk – info@pecksrest.co.uk – Fax (01260) 299 640
– Closed 25-30 December, Sunday dinner and Monday
Rest – Menu £ 18/43 – Carte £ 20/26
♦ Airy, modish restaurant with jaunty yellow décor: well regarded locally. 5 or 7 course
dinners served sharp at 8pm. Dishes are an interesting mix of modern and traditional.

X L'Endroit   🍴 VISA ☻ ①
70-72 Lawton St ⊠ *CW12 1RS –* ℰ *(01260) 299 548 – www.lendroit.co.uk*
– Fax (01260) 299 548 – Closed 2 weeks February/March, 1 week end June,
1 week end September, Saturday lunch, Sunday and Monday
Rest – French – Carte £ 21/32
♦ Relaxing eatery, away from town centre, boasting the tangible feel of a bistro: vivid
walls with foodie prints, chunky wood tables. Tasty French dishes with seasonal
specials.

CONGRESBURY – 503 L29   3 B2
🚇 London 145 mi – Bristol 13 mi – Cardiff 56 mi – Swansea 95 mi

🏨 Cadbury House H. & Spa   ≤ 🛏 🖥 ⑳ 🔊 🖐 🛗 ᖴ AC ✂ ¶
Frost Hill, North : 1/2m. on B3133 ⊠ *BS49 5AD*   🛗 P VISA ☻ AE
– ℰ *(01934) 834 343 – www.cadbury.com – info@cadburyhouse.com*
– Fax (01934) 834 390
72 rm – †£ 115/135 ††£ 155/350, � £12.50
Rest *The Restaurant* – (dinner only and Sunday lunch) Menu £ 30
– Carte £ 31/40 **s**
Rest *The Lounge* – Carte £ 15/23 **s**
♦ 18C country house and 5 storey extension, plus impressive leisure club. Modern,
stylish bedrooms with smart bathrooms; Executive rooms are larger with good norther-
ly views. Large restaurant offers seasonal à la carte. The Lounge offers popular all
day dining menu and has pleasant balcony terrace.

CONISTON – Cumbria – 502 K 20 – pop. 1 304 📖 *Great Britain*   21 A2
🚇 London 285 mi – Carlisle 55 mi – Kendal 22 mi – Lancaster 42 mi
🛈 Ruskin Ave ℰ (015394) 41533, mail@conistontic.org
📷 Coniston Water★ – Brantwood★ **AC**, SE : 2 m. on east side of Coniston
    Water. Hard Knott Pass★★, Wrynose Pass★★, NW : 10 m. by A 593 and
    minor road

↑ Coniston Lodge without rest   ✂ ¶ P VISA ☻
Station Rd ⊠ *LA21 8HH –* ℰ *(015394) 41 201 – www.coniston-lodge.com*
– info@coniston-lodge.com – Fax (015394) 41 201 – Closed 25 December
6 rm ⊒ – †£ 57/69 ††£ 108
♦ Personally run hotel; Donald Campbell's Bluebird memorabilia adorns lounge.
Home-made jams for sale - and for breakfast. Rooms named after tarns; some overlook garden.

at Torver Southwest : 2 ¼ m. on A 593 – ⊠ Coniston

↑ Old Rectory 🌣   ≤ 🛏 P VISA ☻
Northeast : ¼ m. by A 593 ⊠ *LA21 8AX –* ℰ *(015394) 41 353*
– www.theoldrectoryhotel.com – enquiries@theoldrectoryhotel.com
– February-November
9 rm ⊒ – †£ 55 ††£ 72/90   **Rest** – (dinner only) (residents only) Menu £ 25 **s**
♦ Beneath the Coniston Old Man, close to Coniston Water stands this country house
built in 1868 for the Rev Thomas Ellwood. Snug bedrooms afford panoramic views of
landscape. Fine meadow vistas from conservatory style dining room.

CONSTABLE BURTON – N. Yorks. – 502 O 21 – see Leyburn

CONSTANTINE BAY – Cornwall – 503 E 32 – see Padstow

ENGLAND

COOKHAM DEAN – Windsor and Maidenhead █ Great Britain   11 **C3**

🄳 London 32 mi – High Wycombe 7 mi – Oxford 31 mi – Reading 16 mi
🄶 Windsor Castle★★★, Eton★★ and Windsor★, S : 5 m. by B 4447, A 4 (westbound) and A 308

XX   **The Inn on the Green** with rm   🗔 ⛭ **P** VISA ◍ AE
The Old Cricket Common ⊠ *SL6 9NZ –* ℰ *(01628) 482638*
– www.theinnonthegreen.com – reception@theinnonthegreen.com – Fax (01628) 487474 – Closed Sunday dinner and Monday
9 rm � – †£95/115 ††£130/150   **Rest** – (booking essential) Carte £26/45
♦ Part timbered inn with delightful patio terrace. Rustic bar; two dining rooms and conservatory: modern British cooking. Individually furnished rooms in the inn or annex.

CORBRIDGE – Northumberland – **501** N 19 – pop. 2 800 █ Great Britain   24 **A2**

🄳 London 300 mi – Hexham 3 mi – Newcastle upon Tyne 18 mi
🄸 Hill St ℰ (01434) 632815, corbridgetic@btconnect.com
🄶 Hadrian's Wall★★, N : 3 m. by A 68 – Corstopitum★ **AC**, NW : ½ m

↑   **Riggsacre** without rest   🗔 ⅍ **P**
Appletree Lane, by B 6321 (Aydon rd) ⊠ *NE45 5DN –* ℰ *(01434) 632617*
– www.riggsacrebandb.co.uk – atclive@supanet.com – Closed Christmas and New Year
3 rm – †£46 ††£76
♦ Charming owners run an immaculate, well-priced guesthouse in a peaceful area. Mature gardens; communal breakfast room. Thoughtful extras enhance delightful, good sized rooms.

🄸📭   **The Angel of Corbridge** with rm   🕾 ⅍ **P** VISA ◍
Main St ⊠ *NE45 5LA –* ℰ *(01434) 632119 – Fax (01434) 633796*
15 rm � – †£65 ††£120   **Rest** – Carte £15/25
♦ 18C cream-washed village centre coaching inn. Wood-panelled lounge with leather Chesterfield. Tasty, Northumbrian dishes in bar or restaurant. Smart rooms with quality decor.

at Great Whittington North : 5½ m. by A 68 off B 6318 – ⊠ Corbridge

🄸📭   **Queens Head Inn**   **P** VISA ◍
⊠ *NE19 2HP –* ℰ *(01434) 672267 – www.the-queens-head-inn.co.uk*
– Fax (01434) 672267
Rest – (Closed 25 December and Monday January-March) Carte £20/35
♦ 17C coaching inn in sleepy village serving classic, regionally-influenced cooking. Characterful, timbered bar, open fire and stone walls. Friendly staff, informal atmosphere.

CORFE CASTLE – Dorset – **503** N 32 – ⊠ Wareham   4 **C3**

🄳 London 129 mi – Bournemouth 18 mi – Weymouth 23 mi
🄶 Castle★ (≤★★) **AC**

🏠   **Mortons House**   🗔 🕾 ᴅ ⅍ 🍴 **P** VISA ◍
45 East St ⊠ *BH20 5EE –* ℰ *(01929) 480988 – www.mortonshouse.co.uk*
– stay@mortonshouse.co.uk – Fax (01929) 480820
18 rm � – †£75/179 ††£159/179 – 2 suites   **Rest** – Carte £25/50
♦ Elizabethan manor built in the shape of an "E" in Queen's honour. Wood panelled drawing room; range of bedrooms, some themed: the Victoria room has original Victorian bath. Colourful dining room with views over courtyard.

Good food and accommodation at moderate prices?
Look for the Bib symbols:
red Bib Gourmand ⊛ for food, blue Bib Hotel 🛏 for hotels

▶ London 345 mi – Edinburgh 49 mi – Newcastle upon Tyne 59 mi
© Ladykirk (Kirk o'Steil★), NE : 6 m. by A 698 and B 6470

🏨 **Tillmouth Park** ⬩   ⬩ 🚗 🔥 🅿️ 𝖵𝖨𝖲𝖠 ⬤
Northeast : 2½ m. on A 698 ✉ *TD12 4UU* – ℰ *(01890) 882 255*
– www.tillmouthpark.co.uk – reception@tillmouthpark.f9.co.uk – Fax (01890)
882 540 – Closed 6 January - 3 April
14 rm ⬷ – †£75/100 ††£120/140
Rest *The Library* – (bar lunch Monday-Saturday) Menu £15/35 – Carte £26/40
Rest *Bistro* – Menu £15/35 – Carte £26/40
♦ In an area renowned for its fishing, a 19C country house in mature grounds and woodland. Inside one finds stained glass windows, grand staircases and antique furniture. Light meals in bistro. Large, panelled Library restaurant has good views of grounds.

🏠 **Coach House**   🚗 ⅊ rm, 🅿️ 𝖵𝖨𝖲𝖠 ⬤
Crookham, East : 4 m. on A 697 ✉ *TD12 4TD* – ℰ *(01890) 820 293*
– www.coachhousecrookham.com – stay@coachhousecrookham.com
– Fax (01890) 820 284 – Closed December
10 rm ⬷ – †£38/82 ††£86/104
Rest – (dinner only) (booking essential for non-residents) Menu £23
♦ Converted from a collection of farm buildings, including a 1680s dower house, and set around a courtyard. Recently modernised, comfortable rooms with character.

CORSE LAWN – **Worcs.** – see Tewkesbury (Glos.)

▶ London 107 mi – Bristol 22 mi – Chippenham 5 mi

🏠 **Heatherly Cottage** without rest ⬩   ⬩ 🚗 ⅊ 🅿️
Ladbrook Lane, Gastard, Southeast : 1¼ m. by B 3353 ✉ *SN13 9PE* – ℰ *(01249)*
701 402 – www.heatherlycottage.co.uk – pandj@heatherly.plus.com
– Fax (01249) 701 412 – Closed December and January
3 rm ⬷ – †£55 ††£68/72
♦ Part 17C stone cottage set down a quiet country road close to small village. Three very good value rooms: spacious, individually furnished and with good facilities.

▶ London 123 mi – Bath 40 mi – Taunton 36 mi – Weymouth 33 mi

🍴 **The Queen's Arms** with rm   🚗 ⅊ rm, 🅿️ 𝖵𝖨𝖲𝖠 ⬤ 𝖠𝖤
✉ *DT9 4LR* – ℰ *(01963) 220 317 – www.thequeensarms.com*
– relax@thequeensarms.com
5 rm ⬷ – †£60/90 ††£75/120   **Rest** – Carte £19/26
♦ A comfy, firelit bar is at the hub of this 18C inn, which serves hearty, flavoursome cooking in big bowls. They keep their own pigs and chickens, with the focus on local, seasonal produce. Modern, stylish bedrooms with flat screen TVs and smart bathrooms.

▶ London 46 mi – Luton 24 mi – Cambridge 29 mi – Watford 43 mi

🍴 **The Bull of Cottered**   🚗 ⅊ 🅿️ 𝖵𝖨𝖲𝖠 ⬤
✉ *SG9 9QP* – ℰ *(01763) 281 243 – cordell39@btinternet.com*
Rest – Carte £17/33
♦ Traditional, homely pub with flower baskets, polished horse brasses and log fires - a popular stop off point on way to Stansted Airport. Traditional menu offers eclectic mix.

ENGLAND

ENGLAND

COVENTRY

Bayley Lane	AV	3
Bishop St.	AV	5
Broadgate	AV	6
Burges (The)	AV	7
Central Six Retail Park Shopping	AV	
Corporation St.	AV	
Earl St.	AV	10
Fairfax St.	AV	12
Far Gosford St.	AV	13

Gallagher Retail Park	BX	
Gosford St.	AV	15
Greyfriars Lane	AV	16
Hales St.	AV	17
Hearsall Lane	AV	21
High St.	AV	22
Ironmonger Rd	AV	23
Jordan Well	AV	26
Leicester Row	AV	29
Light Lane	AV	30
Little Park St.	AV	31
Precincts Shopping	AV	
Primrose Hill St.	AV	34

Queen Victoria Rd	AV	35
St Johns (Ringway)	AV	38
St Nicholas (Ringway)	AV	39
Swanswell (Ringway)	AV	40
Trinity St.	AV	41
Upper Well St.	AV	43
Vecqueray St.	AV	45
Victoria St.	AV	46
Warwick Rd.	AV	49
White Friars (Ringway)	AV	54
White St.	AV	51
Windsor St.	AV	52

BUILT UP AREA

CENTRE

240

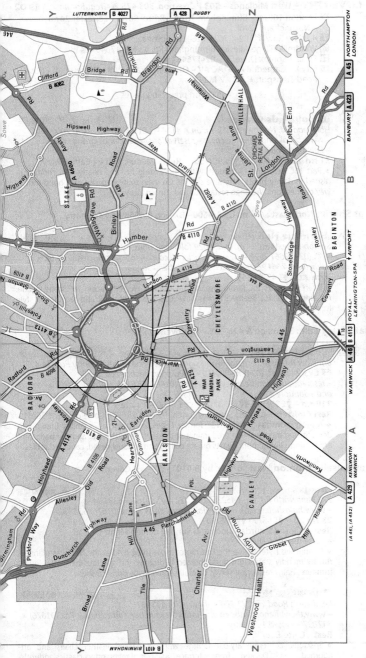

ENGLAND

▶ London 100 mi – Birmingham 18 mi – Bristol 96 mi – Leicester 24 mi
– Nottingham 52 mi

🆔 4 Priory Row ℰ (024) 7622 7264, tic@cvone.co.uk

🏧 Windmill Village Allesley Birmingham Rd, ℰ (024) 7640 4041

🏌 Sphinx Sphinx Drive, ℰ (024) 7645 1361

🅾 City★ - Cathedral★★★ **AC** AV - Old Cathedral★ AV **B** – Museum of British
Road Transport★ **AC** AV **M2**

Plans on preceding pages

🔠 Brooklands Grange   🚗 &rm, ⁽ŗ⁾ **P** **VISA** **◉◉** **AE**

Holyhead Rd, Northwest : 2½ m. on A 4114 ⊠ CV5 8HX – ℰ (024) 7660 1601
– www.brooklands-grange.co.uk – reservations@brooklands-grange.co.uk
– Fax (024) 7660 1277   AYe
31 rm ⊇ – †£60/120 ††£90/150   **Rest** – Menu £17/24 – Carte £21/36
♦ Part 16C yeoman's farmhouse with comfy, snug bar and neatly kept rooms furnished in dainty prints. Attentive service. On main route into city with good motorway connections. Victorian restaurant and conservatory.

at Shilton Northeast: 6 ¾ m. by A 4600 - BX - on B 4065 – ⊠ Coventry

⌂ Barnacle Hall without rest   🚗 ⅚ **P**

Shilton Lane, West : 1 m. by B 4029 following signs for garden centre ⊠ CV7 9LH
– ℰ (024) 7661 2629 – www.barnaclehall.co.uk – rose@barnaclehall.co.uk
– Fax (024) 7661 2629 – Closed 24 December-1 January
3 rm ⊇ – †£45 ††£45
♦ Interesting part 16C farmhouse in rural location. Westerly facing 18C stone façade;
remainder 16/17C. Beamed rooms have countryside outlook and farmhouse style
furnishings.

at Binley East : 3 ½ m. on A 428 - BY – ⊠ Coventry

🏨 Coombe Abbey ⌂   ← 🚗 🕭 🖹 &rm, ⅚ ⁽ŗ⁾ 🛦 **P** **VISA** **◉◉** **AE** **①**

Brinklow Rd, East : 2 m. following signs for Coombe Abbey Country Park (A 427)
⊠ CV3 2AB – ℰ (024) 7645 0450 – www.coombeabbey.com
– reservations@coombeabbey.com – Fax (024) 7663 5101 – Closed 24-26 December
and 1 January
118 rm – †£95/165 ††£115/185, ⊇ £14.50 – 1 suite
Rest *Cloisters* – (Closed Saturday lunch) Menu £25/30 – Carte dinner £36/51
♦ A most individually styled 12C former Cistercian abbey in Capability Brown gardens. Strong medieval feel predominates: the staff are costumed, and the bedrooms
are striking. Dining room boasts ornate ceiling and unusual raised, canopied tables.

at Balsall Common West : 6 ¾ m. by B 4101 - AY – ⊠ Coventry

🏠 Haigs   🚗 ⁽ŗ⁾ **P** **VISA** **◉◉** **AE**

273 Kenilworth Rd, on A 452 ⊠ CV7 7EL – ℰ (01676) 533 004
– www.haigshotel.co.uk – info@haigsemail.co.uk – Fax (01676) 535 132
23 rm ⊇ – †£55/90 ††£65/90
Rest – (Closed Saturday lunch and Sunday dinner) Menu £12/18
– Carte dinner £18/26
♦ Established hotel where the first motor show to be held at the NEC was planned;
run by friendly staff. Light floral themed bedrooms and spacious bar with elegant
furniture. Haigs restaurant serves carefully home-made British dishes.

🏠 The White Horse   🚗 **P** **VISA** **◉◉** **AE** **①**

Kenilworth Road ⊠ CV7 7DT – ℰ (01676) 533 207
– www.thewhitehorseatbc.co.uk – info@thewhitehorseatbc.co.uk – Fax (01676)
532 827 – Closed 1 January
Rest – Carte £18/28
♦ Spacious, contemporary bar lounge with low backed leather chairs and art-
adorned walls. Decked front terrace. Universal menu offers classics and rotisserie. Generous portions.

ENGLAND

at Meriden Northwest : 6 m. by A 45 - AX - on B 4104 - ⊠ Coventry

Manor 🚗 🛗 AK rest, 📞 🔊 P VISA ⓪ AE ①
Main Rd ⊠ *CV7 7NH –* 𝒞 *(01676) 522 735 – www.manorhotelmeriden.co.uk*
– reservations@manorhotelmeriden.co.uk
– Fax (01676) 522 186
108 rm ⌓ – †£140 ††£150 – 2 suites
Rest *Regency* – (closed Saturday lunch) (booking essential at lunch)
Menu £28 **s** – Carte £29/34 **s**
Rest *Houstons* – Carte £17/26
♦ Convenient for the NEC, a Georgian manor converted to an hotel in the 1950s. Triumph motorbike themed bar. Sweeping wooden staircase leads to sizable rooms, quieter at rear. Smart, formal restaurant.

COVERACK – Cornwall – **503** E 33   1 **A3**
 ▣ London 300 mi – Penzance 25 mi – Truro 27 mi

🏠 **The Bay** ≤ 🚗 ⛵ P VISA ⓪
North Corner ⊠ *TR12 6TF –* 𝒞 *(01326) 280 464 – www.thebayhotel.co.uk*
– enquiries@thebayhotel.co.uk – March - 1 January
13 rm (dinner included) ⌓ – †£84/143 ††£170/228 – 1 suite
Rest – (bar lunch) Menu £25
♦ New experienced owners have given this hotel a new lease of life. Located in pretty fishing village. Now all very contemporary in style with spacious bedrooms. Dining room has conservatory extension.

> Don't confuse X with ✿!
> X defines comfort, while stars are awarded for the best cuisine,
> across all categories of comfort.

COWAN BRIDGE – Lancs. – **502** M 21 – **see Kirkby Lonsdale**

COWLEY – Gloucestershire – **504** N 28   4 **C1**
 ▣ London 105 mi – Swindon 28 mi – Gloucester 14 mi – Cheltenham 6 mi

Cowley Manor ⤳ 🚗 🏌 ⚓ ❄ 🌐 🏋 👜 🛗 📞 🔊 P VISA ⓪ AE
⊠ *GL53 9NL –* 𝒞 *(01242) 870 900 – www.cowleymanor.com*
– stay@cowleymanor.com – Fax (01242) 870 901
22 rm ⌓ – ††£250/470 – 8 suites
Rest – Menu £20 (lunch) – Carte dinner £31/43
♦ Impressive Regency house. 55 acres; beautiful gardens. Retro interior, bold colours, obscure fittings, excellent mod cons. Stylish bedrooms, some with balconies/lake views, most with huge bathrooms. Spa, 2 pools and sun terrace. Semi-formal restaurant with paved terrace serves classic British dishes.

COWSHILL – Durham – **502** N 19   24 **A3**
 ▣ London 295 mi – Newcastle upon Tyne 42 mi – Stanhope 10 mi
 – Wolsingham 16 mi

⌂ **Low Cornriggs Farm** ⤳ ≤ 🚗 🏌 🍴 P VISA ⓪
Weardale, Northwest : ¾ m. on A 689 ⊠ *DL13 1AQ –* 𝒞 *(01388) 537 600*
– www.britnett.net/lowcornriggsfarm – cornriggsfarm@btconnect.com
– Fax (01388) 537 777 – Closed 20 December - 3 January
3 rm ⌓ – †£38/40 ††£58/60
Rest – (by arrangement) Menu £17
♦ Stone-built 300 year-old farmhouse boasting some superb views over Teesdale. Conservatory dining room for summer use. Cosy, pine-furnished bedrooms. Beamed dining room offers hearty, home-cooked, organic dishes.

ENGLAND

CRACKINGTON HAVEN – Cornwall – 503 G 31 – ✉ Bude 1 B2

London 262 mi – Bude 11 mi – Plymouth 44 mi – Truro 42 mi

Poundstock★ (≤★★, church★, guildhouse★), NE : 5½ m. by A 39 – Jacobstow (Church★), E : 3½ m

Manor Farm without rest

Southeast : 1¼ m. by Boscastle rd taking left turn onto Church Park Rd after 1m. then taking first right onto unmarked lane ✉ EX23 0JW – ✆ (01840) 230 304 – Closed Christmas

3 rm – ♦£ 50 ♦♦£ 80/90

♦ Appears in the Domesday Book and belonged to William the Conqueror's half brother. A lovely manor in beautifully manicured grounds. Affable owner and comfortable rooms.

CRANBROOK – Kent – 504 V 30 – pop. 4 225 *Great Britain* 8 B2

London 53 mi – Hastings 19 mi – Maidstone 15 mi

Vestry Hall, Stone St ✆ (01580) 712538 (summer only)

Sissinghurst Castle★ **AC**, NE : 2½ m. by A 229 and A 262

Cloth Hall Oast

Coursehorn Lane, East : 1 m. by Tenterden rd ✉ TN17 3NR – ✆ (01580) 712 220 – clothhalloast@aol.com – Fax (01580) 712 220 – Closed Christmas

3 rm – ♦£ 70 ♦♦£ 125

Rest – (by arrangement, communal dining) Menu £ 25

♦ Run by former owner of Old Cloth Hall, with well-tended garden, rhododendrons lining the drive. Peaceful spot. Charming sitting room. Immaculate bedrooms exude personal style.

Apicius (Tim Johnson)

23 Stone St ✉ TN17 3HE – ✆ (01580) 714 666 – www.restaurant-apicius.co.uk – Closed 2 weeks Christmas-New Year, Sunday dinner, Monday, Tuesday and Saturday lunch

Rest – Menu £ 26/30

Spec. Roast scallop and bacon brochette with vanilla linguini. Braised shoulder of veal and truffle macaroni cheese. Apple tart with apple sorbet and crème Anglaise.

♦ Named after Roman author of world's first cookbook. Cosy interior mixes original features with modern style. Passionate, well balanced, precise cooking uses local ingredients.

at Sissinghurst Northeast : 1¾ m. by B 2189 on A 262 – ✉ Cranbrook

Rankins

The Street, on A 262 ✉ TN17 2JH – ✆ (01580) 713 964 – www.rankinsrestaurant.com – rankins@btconnect.com – Closed Sunday dinner, Monday, Tuesday and Bank Holidays

Rest – (dinner only and Sunday lunch) (booking essential) Menu £ 34

♦ A friendly, well-established, family run bistro-style restaurant, not far from Sissinghurst Castle. The set menu has an international focus.

CRAWLEY – West Sussex – 504 T 30 – pop. 100 547 7 D2

London 33 mi – Brighton 21 mi – Lewes 23 mi – Royal Tunbridge Wells 23 mi

County Mall ✆ (01293) 846968, vip@countymall.co.uk

36 Cottesmore Pease Pottage Buchan Hill, ✆ (01293) 528 256

27 Tilgate Forest Tilgate Titmus Drive, ✆ (01293) 530 103

9 Gatwick Manor Lowfield Heath London Rd, ✆ (01293) 538 587

9 Pease Pottage Horsham Rd, ✆ (01293) 521 706

Plan of enlarged Area : see Gatwick Z

Plan opposite

ENGLAND

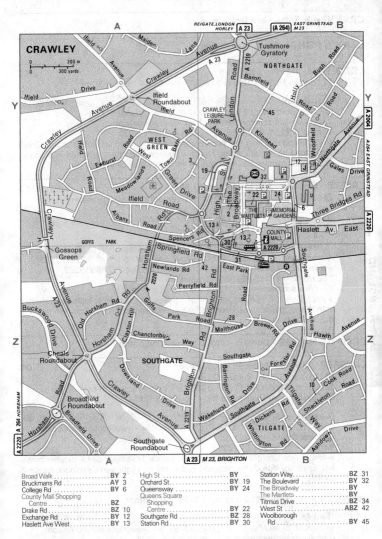

CRAWLEY

300 m
300 yards

REIGATE, LONDON HORLEY **A 23** — (A 264) EAST GRINSTEAD M 23

Arora International 🖧 |🖳| ⚐ rm, 🅰️ ⚐ 🕻 🛁 🅿️ VISA ⑩ AE ①

Southgate Ave, Southgate ⊠ RH10 6LW – ☎ (01293) 530000
– www.arorainternational.com – gatwickreservations@arorainternational.com
– Fax (01293) 555112

BZ**a**

431 rm – ♦£75/165 ♦♦£75/165, ⌑ £13 – 1 suite
Rest Gallucci – Italian – Menu £17 (lunch) – Carte £20/33

♦ Futuristically designed, business oriented hotel with airport rail access. Calming water features and striking open-plan atrium. Impressive leisure facilities and bedrooms. A taste of Italy at Gallucci.

If breakfast is included the ⌑ symbol appears after the number of rooms.

245

CRAYKE – N. Yorks. – see Easingwold

CRAY'S POND – Oxon. – see Goring

CREDITON – Devon – **503** J 31   2 **C2**
> London 187 mi – Torbay 32 mi – Exeter 9 mi – Torquay 30 mi

📙   **Lamb Inn** with rm   🚗 🍴 VISA ⬥◎ AE
Crediton, Northwest : 1 ¾ m. ⊠ EX17 4LW – ✆ (01363) 773 676
– www.lambinnsandford.co.uk – thelambinn@gmail.com
3 rm � – †£ 59/85 ††£ 65/89   **Rest** – Carte £ 16/20
♦ 16C period coaching inn; picturesque, pleasantly dated and full of charm. Classically based menu with strong French influences and dishes prepared in a simple, unassuming manner. Very spacious, recently converted bedrooms.

CREWE – Cheshire – **502** M 24 – pop. 67 683   20 **B3**
> London 174 mi – Chester 24 mi – Liverpool 49 mi – Manchester 36 mi
> – Stoke-on-Trent 15 mi
🏛 Queen's Park Queen's Park Drive, ✆ (01270) 662 378
🏞 Haslington Fields Rd, ✆ (01270) 584 227

🏨🏨🏨   **Crewe Hall**   🚗 🔲 ◎ 🌀 ⅃₆ ℀ ⌹ ⅂ rm, ℀ ⌨ ╇ P VISA ⬥◎ AE ①
Weston Road, Southeast : 1 ¾ m. on A 5020 ⊠ CW1 6UZ – ✆ (01270) 253 333
– www.qhotels.co.uk – crewehall@qhotels.co.uk – Fax (01270) 253 322
112 rm ⊂ – †£ 155 ††£ 165 – 5 suites
Rest *Ilrá Brasserie* – ✆ (01270) 259 319 – Carte £ 24/37
♦ Impressive 17C mansion with formal gardens. Victorian décor featuring alabaster, marble and stained glass. Rooms offer luxurious comfort. Popular modern menu in the chic Brasserie.

CROFT-ON-TEES – Durham – **502** P 20 – see Darlington

CROMER – Norfolk – **504** X 25 – pop. 8 836   15 **D1**
> London 132 mi – Norwich 23 mi
🛈 Prince of Wales Rd ✆ (0871) 2003071, cromertic@north-norfolk.gov.uk
🏞 Royal Cromer Overstrand Rd, ✆ (01263) 512 884

⌂   **Captains House** without rest   ⇐ ℀ ⌨ P VISA ⬥◎
5 The Crescent ⊠ NR27 9EX – ✆ (01263) 515 434 – www.captains-house.co.uk
– captainshouse@aol.com
4 rm ⊂ – †£ 60 ††£ 140/200
♦ Immaculate Georgian house in seafront parade; tables outside for summer breakfast. Spacious, individually designed bedrooms with light seaside colours; excellent bathrooms.

at Overstrand Southeast : 2 ½ m. by B 1159 – ⊠ Cromer

🏛   **Sea Marge**   ⇐ 🚗 ╇ ⌨ P VISA ⬥◎
16 High St ⊠ NR27 0AB – ✆ (01263) 579 579 – www.mackenziehotels.com
– info@mackenziehotels.com – Fax (01263) 579 524
25 rm ⊂ – †£ 87 ††£ 134/166 – 3 suites
Rest – (bar lunch) Menu £ 21 – Carte £ 19/28
♦ Mock Elizabethan house built in 1908; gardens lead down to beach. Interior features panelled bar, minstrel gallery. Most bedrooms have sea views; newer ones with colonial feel. Restaurant offers views from a large leaded window.

at Northrepps Southeast : 3 m. by A 149 and Northrepps rd – ⊠ Cromer

⌂   **Shrublands Farm** without rest   🚗 ℀ ⌨ P VISA ⬥◎
⊠ NR27 0AA – ✆ (01263) 579 297 – www.shrublandsfarm.com
– youngman@farming.co.uk – Fax (01263) 579 297 – Closed 25-26 December
3 rm ⊂ – †£ 45 ††£ 70
♦ Part 18C arable farm in wooded gardens. Conservatory, lounge, neat rooms with cut flowers and garden views. Guests are encouraged to explore the farm.

ENGLAND

CROSTHWAITE – Cumbria – **502** L 21 – see Kendal

CROYDE – Devon – **503** H 30 – ⊠ Braunton   2 **C1**
▶ London 232 mi – Barnstaple 10 mi – Exeter 50 mi – Taunton 61 mi

⌂   **Whiteleaf**   �</> **P** *VISA* **⬤⬤**
Hobbs Hill ⊠ EX33 1PN – ℰ (01271) 890 266 – www.thewhiteleaf.co.uk – Closed
24-28 December
5 rm ☲ – †£55/65 ††£72/125   **Rest** – (by arrangement) Carte £ 23/34
♦ Homely guesthouse close to North Devon and Somerset coastal path; views of
Baggy Point, Lundy Island. Co-ordinated accommodation with mini-bars: choose the
four-poster room. Restaurant looks out onto garden.

CRUDWELL – Wilts. – **503** N 29 – see Malmesbury

CUCKFIELD – West Sussex – **504** T 30 – pop. 3 266   7 **D2**
▶ London 40 mi – Brighton 15 mi

🏨   **Ockenden Manor** ⌘   🚒 🐾 ⑀ 🐾 🕰 **P** *VISA* **⬤⬤** **AE** **①**
❀   Ockenden Lane ⊠ RH17 5LD – ℰ (01444) 416 111
– www.ockenden-manor.co.uk – reservations@ockenden-manor.com
– Fax (01444) 415 549
19 rm ☲ – †£110/120 ††£365 – 3 suites
Rest – (booking essential at lunch) Menu £ 27/50 – Carte £ 49/68
Spec. Ballotine of sea trout, fromage blanc and oyster beignet. Lamb with
confit fennel, courgette provençale, smoked bacon and kidney brochette. Earl
Grey crème brûlée, dark chocolate, lemon sorbet.
♦ Secluded part 16C manor; heritage is on display in antique furnished bedrooms,
many named after previous owners. Ideal for golfers, historians and the romantic.
Wood panelled dining room offers some of Sussex's finest cooking.

CUDDINGTON – Buckinghamshire – **503** M 24 ▮ *Great Britain*   11 **C2**
▶ London 48 mi – Aylesbury 6 mi – Oxford 17 mi
◖ Waddesdon Manor ★★ **AC**, NE : 6 m. via Cuddington Hill, Cannon's Hill,
Waddesdon Hill and A 41

🍴   **The Crown**   ⑀ **P** *VISA* **⬤⬤** **AE**
Aylesbury Rd ⊠ HP18 0BB – ℰ (01844) 292 222
– www.thecrowncuddington.co.uk – david@thecrowncuddington.co.uk
Rest – Menu £ 13/24 – Carte £ 23/29
♦ Thatched 16C pub with traditional décor, low beamed ceilings and huge inglenooks featuring beehive chimneys. Tasty, modern dishes made with an eclectic range
of ingredients.

CULLINGWORTH – W. Yorks. – **502** O 22 – see Haworth

CURY – Cornwall – **503** E 33 – see Helston

CUTNALL GREEN – Worcs. – **503** N 27 – see Droitwich Spa

CUXHAM – Oxfordshire – **504** Q 29   11 **C2**
▶ London 49 mi – Hillingdon 32 mi – Reading 18 mi – Milton Keynes 61 mi

🍴   **The Half Moon**   **P** *VISA* **⬤⬤**
Cuxham ⊠ 0X49 5NF – ℰ (01491) 614 151 – www.thehalf-moon.com
– info@thehalf-moon.com
Rest – (Closed Sunday dinner in winter) Carte £ 19/30
♦ Sympathetically restored 17C whitewashed pub in a sleepy village. Twice-daily
blackboard menu features local, ethical produce: veg from the kitchen garden and
plenty of offal.

ENGLAND

DALTON – N. Yorks. – **502** O 20 – see Richmond

DANEHILL – East Sussex ▌ *Great Britain*   8 **A2**
> ▶ London 53 mi – Brighton 21 mi – East Grinstead 7 mi
> ◪ Sheffield Park Garden★, S : 3 m. on A 275

🍴   **Coach & Horses**   🚗 🌣 **P** *VISA* **◐◉** **AE**
(🙂) *School Lane, Northeast : ¾ m. on Chelwood Common rd ⊠ RH17 7JF*
– ℰ (01825) 740369 – www.coachandhorses.danehill.biz
– coachandhorses@danehill.biz – Fax (01825) 740369 – Closed 25 December
dinner, 26 December and 1 January dinner
Rest – Carte £ 21/27
♦ Charming firelit locals bar and more formal dining area in converted stables. Traditional menus utilise locally sourced ingredients and often include offal as well as more unusual cuts of meat.

DARLEY – North Yorkshire   22 **B2**
> ▶ London 217 mi – Harrogate 8 mi – Ripon 16 mi

🏠   **Cold Cotes** ⌖   🚗 🌣 **P** *VISA* **◐◉**
Cold Cotes Rd, Felliscliffe, South : 2 m. by Kettlesing rd, going straight over
crossroads and on Harrogate rd ⊠ HG3 2LW – ℰ (01423) 770937
– www.coldcotes.com – info@coldcotes.com
– Restricted opening in January
6 rm ⌂ – †£90 ††£90/95
Rest – (by arrangement) Menu £ 25
♦ Victorian farmhouse in five acres of lovely gardens. Cosy lounge with open fire. Communal breakfasts overlooking grounds. Extra touches adorn the pleasant, well-priced rooms.

DARLEY ABBEY – Derbs. – **502** P 25 – see Derby

DARLINGTON – Darlington – **502** P 20 – pop. 86 082   22 **B1**
> ▶ London 251 mi – Leeds 61 mi – Middlesbrough 14 mi – Newcastle upon
> Tyne 35 mi
> ✈ Teesside Airport : ℰ (01325) 332811, E : 6 m. by A 67
> ⓲ 13 Horsemarket ℰ (01325) 388666, tic@darlington.gov.uk
> ◪ Blackwell Grange Briar Close, ℰ (01325) 464458
> ◪ Stressholme Snipe Lane, ℰ (01325) 461002

at Croft-on-Tees South : 3½ m. on A 167 – ⊠ Darlington

🏠   **Clow Beck House** ⌖   🍃 🚗 🅚 🐾 🅫 rm, 🌣 🎵 **P** *VISA* **◐◉** **AE**
Monk End Farm, West : ¾ m. by A 167 off Barton rd ⊠ DL2 2SW – ℰ (01325)
721075 – www.clowbeckhouse.co.uk – heather@clowbeckhouse.co.uk
– Fax (01325) 720419 – Closed 24 December-2 January
13 rm ⌂ – †£85 ††£135
Rest – (dinner only) (residents only) Carte £ 24/37 s
♦ Collection of stone houses styled on an old farm building. The residence has a friendly, homely atmosphere. Spacious rooms with individual character. Tasty, home-cooked meals.

at Headlam Northwest : 8 m. by A 67 – ⊠ Gainford

🏠🅗   **Headlam Hall** ⌖   🍃 🚗 🅚 🐾 🖵 🅫 ⅃⑤ 🌣 🖂 🅫 rm, 🎵 🚴 **P**
⊠ DL2 3HA – ℰ (01325) 730238 – www.headlamhall.co.uk   *VISA* **◐◉** **AE**
– admin@headlamhall.co.uk – Fax (01325) 730790 – Closed 24-26 December
40 rm ⌂ – †£90 ††£140 – 1 suite
Rest – Menu £ 15 (lunch) – Carte £ 26/34 s
♦ Part Georgian, part Jacobean manor house in delightful, secluded countryside with charming walled gardens. Period interior furnishings and antiques. Good leisure facilities. Country house restaurant in four distinctively decorated rooms.

at Redworth Northwest : 7 m. by A 68 on A 6072 – ⊠ Bishop Auckland

Redworth Hall 🚗 🕭 🖳 🕭 🕭 ↳ ✕ 🖪 ㄴ rm, 🕭 🔏 🅿 𝘷𝘪𝘴𝘢 ⓿ AE ⓪
⊠ DL5 6NL – ℰ (01388) 770600 – www.barcelo-hotels.co.uk
– redworthhall@barcelo-hotels.co.uk – Fax (01388) 770654
135 rm – ♦£69/150 ♦♦£69/150, 🖙 £13.95 – 4 suites
Rest *The Restaurant* – Menu £25 – Carte £25/48 **s**
♦ 17C manor house of Elizabethan origins with a tranquil ambience. Original features include a period banqueting hall. Comfortable, modern bedrooms. Good leisure. Conservatory restaurant has light, open atmosphere.

DARTFORD – Kent – 504 U 29 – pop. 56 818   8 **B1**
🚇 London 20 mi – Hastings 51 mi – Maidstone 22 mi
Access Dartford Tunnel and Bridge (toll)

at Wilmington Southwest : 1 ½ m. A 225 on B 258 – ⊠ Dartford

Rowhill Grange 🕭 🚗 🕭 🖳 🕭 🕭 ↳ 🖪 🖪 ㄴ rm, ✕ 🕭 🔏 🅿
Southwest : 2 m. on Hextable rd (B 258) ⊠ DA2 7QH   𝘷𝘪𝘴𝘢 ⓿ AE ⓪
– ℰ (01322) 615136 – www.rowhillgrange.com – admin@rowhillgrange.com
– Fax (01322) 615137
37 rm 🖙 – ♦£175/260 ♦♦£200/370 – 1 suite
Rest *Truffles* – (Closed Saturday lunch) Menu £20/35 – Carte £35/46
Rest *Elements* – Carte £22/28
♦ Extended 19C thatched house set in pretty, fifteen-acre gardens. Bold-coloured rooms with teak beds, eight in the converted clockhouse. Smart, up-to-date leisure club. Kentish ingredients to fore in modern Truffles. Flag-floored Elements next to leisure club.

ENGLAND

We try to be as accurate as possible when giving room rates but prices are susceptible to change.
Please check rates when booking.

DARTMOUTH – Devon – 503 J 32 – pop. 5 512   2 **C3**
🚇 London 236 mi – Exeter 36 mi – Plymouth 35 mi
🅳 The Engine House, Mayor's Ave ℰ (01803) 834224,
Holidays@DiscoverDartmouth.com
🅾 Town★★ (≤★) - Old Town - Butterwalk★ - Dartmouth Castle (≤★★★) **AC**
🅶 Start Point (≤★), S : 13 m. (including 1 m. on foot)

Dart Marina ≤ 🚗 🖳 ↳ 🖪 ㄴ rm, 🔟 rest, 🅿 𝘷𝘪𝘴𝘢 ⓿ AE
Sandquay ⊠ TQ6 9PH – ℰ (01803) 832580 – www.dartmarina.com
– reservations@dartmarina.com – Fax (01803) 835040
47 rm 🖙 – ♦£95/185 ♦♦£125/195 – 2 suites
Rest *River Restaurant* – (Dinner only and Saturday lunch)
Menu £32
Rest *Wildfire* – Carte £30/40
♦ Lovely location with excellent views over the Dart Marina. The hotel has smart, comfy bedrooms, many with balconies. Welcoming, bright, modern public areas. Stylish River Restaurant; terrace overlooks river. Modern, informal Wildfire offers eclectic menus.

Royal Castle ≤ 🕭 🅿 𝘷𝘪𝘴𝘢 ⓿ AE
11 The Quay ⊠ TQ6 9PS – ℰ (01803) 833033 – www.royalcastle.co.uk
– enquiry@royalcastle.co.uk – Fax (01803) 835445
25 rm 🖙 – ♦£90/95 ♦♦£175/199   **Rest** – Carte £23/36
♦ Harbour views and 18C origins enhance this smart hotel with its cosy bar and open log fires. Each of the comfortable rooms is individually styled, some boast four-poster beds. Harbour-facing restaurant particularly proud of sourcing fresh fish.

ENGLAND

Brown's Hotel
VISA ◎◎ AE
27-29 Victoria Rd ⊠ *TQ6 9RT* – ℰ *(01803) 832 572*
– www.brownshoteldartmouth.co.uk – enquiries@brownshoteldartmouth.co.uk
– Closed 26-28 December
10 rm ☲ – †£65/85 ††£175
Rest – (dinner only Thursday-Saturday) Carte £20/28
♦ Georgian charm, in a personally run hotel, close to the harbour, with a chic modern townhouse style. Bedrooms are individually appointed with clean modern lines. Informal tapas-style dining; great original art.

New Angel Rooms
🕏 🕈 P VISA ◎◎ ①
51 Victoria Rd ⊠ *TQ6 9RT* – ℰ *(01803) 839 425* – *www.thenewangel.co.uk*
– info@thenewangel.co.uk – Fax (01803) 839 505 – Closed January
6 rm ☲ – †£130/150 ††£140/200
Rest *The New Angel* – see restaurant listing
♦ Townhouse tucked away from quayside towards rear of town. Good quality breakfasts amongst oak wood and rattan. Stylish, bold and designery bedrooms.

Broome Court without rest ⌂
≤ 🚗 P
Broomhill, West : 2 . m. by A 3122 and Venn Lane ⊠ *TQ6 0LD* – ℰ *(01803) 834 275 – boughtontml@aol.com – Fax (01803) 833 260*
3 rm ☲ – †£60/80 ††£100/120
♦ Pretty house in a stunning, secluded location. Two sitting rooms: one for winter, one for summer. Breakfast "en famille" in huge kitchen, complete with Aga. Cottagey bedrooms.

The New Angel (John Burton-Race)
≤ ⇔ VISA ◎◎ ①
❀
2 South Embankment ⊠ *TQ6 9BH* – ℰ *(01803) 839 425*
– www.thenewangel.co.uk – info@thenewangel.co.uk – Fax (01803) 839 505
– Closed January, Sunday dinner and Monday in winter
Rest – (booking essential) Menu £30/35 – Carte £40/54
Spec. Dartmouth crab with avocado and young salad leaves. Pan-fried fillets of John Dory with cocotte potatoes and mussel butter. Chocolate fondant with pistachio ice cream.
♦ Busy, modern restaurant with open kitchen; first floor is quieter, with the best views over the Dart Estuary. Classically-based cooking concentrates on quality local produce.

The Seahorse
🍴 VISA ◎◎ AE ①
5 South Embankment ⊠ *TQ6 9BH* – ℰ *(01803) 835 147*
– www.seahorserestaurant.co.uk – enquiries@seahorserestaurant.co.uk
– Closed 7 January - 14 February, Sunday dinner and lunch Monday-Wednesday
Rest – Seafood – (booking essential) Carte £26/47
♦ Picturesque location overlooking estuary/harbour; some al fresco tables. Classic bistro dishes with strong seafood slant; cooked in charcoal oven. Twice daily menu; simplicity is key.

Jan and Freddies Brasserie
VISA ◎◎ AE ①
10 Fairfax Place ⊠ *TQ6 9AD* – ℰ *(01803) 832 491*
– www.janandfreddiesbrasserie.co.uk – info@janandfreddiesbrasserie.co.uk
– Closed Monday October to May and Sunday
Rest – (booking advisable) Menu £30 (dinner) – Carte £26/36
♦ Bright, stylish brasserie in the town centre, with welcoming service and a personal touch. Menus are classically based, with dishes crafted from local, seasonal produce.

The Floating Bridge
P VISA ◎◎ AE
By Lower Ferry ⊠ *TQ6 9PH* – ℰ *(01803) 832 354 – www.dartmarina.com*
– amf46@btinternet.com – Closed November-March Monday-Tuesday
Rest – Carte £18/28
♦ Unusually situated on a ferry slip road. Traditional, predominantly local menu features tasty, wholesome fare, with greater variety and fish specials available in the summer.

at Kingswear East : via lower ferry – ✉ Dartmouth

Nonsuch House
                               ⪦ 🚗 ⅙ (ꞇ) *VISA* ◍◍
Church Hill, from lower ferry take first right onto Church Hill before Steam Packet Inn ✉ *TQ6 0BX* – ℰ *(01803) 752 829 – www.nonsuch-house.co.uk*
– enquiries@nonsuch-house.co.uk – Fax (01803) 752 357
4 rm � – ††£80/110 †††£105/135
Rest – (closed Tuesday, Wednesday and Saturday) (dinner only) (residents only, set menu only, unlicensed) Menu £35 **s**
♦ Charming, personally run Edwardian house stunningly sited above the river town. Smart conservatory terrace and large, well appointed bedrooms. Good, homely breakfasts. Fresh, local, seasonal cooking.

at Strete Southwest : 4 m. on A 379 – ✉ Dartmouth

The Kings Arms
                             🚗 🏡 ⅙ **P** *VISA* ◍◍
Dartmouth Rd ✉ *TQ6 0RW* – ℰ *(01803) 770 377*
– www.kingsarms-dartmouth.co.uk
Rest – (Closed in winter, Sunday dinner and Monday) Carte £28/36
♦ Mid-18C pub with rear terrace that looks to sea. Smart restaurant is where serious, accomplished cooking takes place: local, seasonal produce well utilised on modern menus.

at Blackawton West : 6 m. by B 3122

Woodside Cottage without rest ⌂
                     🚗 ⅙ (ꞇ) **P** *VISA* ◍◍
Blackawton, Northeast :½ m. on Dartmouth rd ✉ *TQ9 7BL* – ℰ *(01803) 898 164*
– www.woodsidedartmouth.co.uk – Fax (0870) 687 417 – Closed 25-26 December
3 rm ⊇ – ††£70 †††£75/90
♦ Pleasant former farmhouse/cottage in pretty rural setting. Attractive landscaped gardens lead into well-furnished sitting room and conservatory. Simple, bright and airy rooms.

The Normandy Arms
                                 🏡 *VISA* ◍◍
Chapel St ✉ *TQ9 7BN* – ℰ *(01803) 712 884 – www.thenormandyarms.co.uk*
– peter.alcroft@btconnect.com – Fax (01830) 712 374 – Closed 25 December and 1 week in October
Rest – (Closed Sunday dinner in winter and Monday) (dinner only lunch Friday-Sunday) Carte £19/30
♦ Refurbished village pub, popular with locals and simple in style with comfy leather seats and two distinct dining areas. Straightforward cooking, homemade using local produce.

> Undecided between two equivalent establishments?
> Within each category, establishments are classified
> in our order of preference.

DARWEN – Blackburn with Darwen – **502** M 22   **20 B2**

    ◨ London 222 mi – Blackburn 5 mi – Blackpool 34 mi – Leeds 59 mi
       – Liverpool 43 mi – Manchester 24 mi
    ▨ Winter Hill, ℰ (01254) 701 287

Astley Bank
                    🚗 ⅙ (ꞇ) 🛁 **P** *VISA* ◍◍ **AE**
Bolton Rd, South :¾ m. on A 666 ✉ *BB3 2QB* – ℰ *(01254) 777 700*
– www.astleybank.co.uk – sales@astleybank.co.uk – Fax (01254) 777 707 – Closed 25 December and 1 January
37 rm ⊇ – ††£86/96 †††£116/136   **Rest** – Menu £19/26 – Carte £22/36
♦ Part Georgian, part Victorian privately owned hotel in elevated position above town. Varied rooms overlook the pleasant gardens. Well-equipped conference rooms. Conservatory dining is elegantly semi-split.

ENGLAND

🚗 London 31 mi – Luton 15 mi – Stevenage 6 mi

🏨 **Coltsfoot Country Retreat** ⬦   ⬦ 🍴 👌 rm, 🌿 📶 **P** **VISA** 🌐 **AE** ①
Coltsfoot Lane, Bulls Green, South : ¾ m. by Bramfield Rd ⊠ *SG3 6SB*
– 𝒞 (01438) 212 800 – www.coltsfoot.com – info@coltsfoot.com – Fax (01438)
212 840 – Closed 25, 26 and 31 December
15 rm ⊆ – †£135 ††£160
Rest – (closed Sunday) (dinner only) (booking essential) Menu £30
– Carte £25/33

♦ Stylish hotel, once a working farm, in 40 rural acres. Lounge bar with log-burning stove. Highly individual rooms around courtyard have vaulted ceilings and rich furnishings. Main barn houses restaurant: concise modern menus employ good seasonal produce.

🏠 **The Tilbury**   🍴 ⬦ 🌿 **P** **VISA** 🌐 **AE**
Watton Rd ⊠ *SG3 6TB – 𝒞 (01438) 815 550 – www.thetilbury.co.uk*
– info@thetilbury.co.uk – Fax (01438) 718 340
– Closed 25-26 December, 1 January and some Bank Holidays
Rest – Menu £16 (lunch) – Carte £18/33
♦ Red brick pub with flower baskets, terrace, garden and fresh, contemporary interior. Modern European menu offers honest, locally sourced food. Cookery school spans the globe.

🚗 London 79 mi – Coventry 23 mi – Leicester 31 mi – Northampton 13 mi
– Oxford 46 mi
🏛 Moot Hall, Market Sq 𝒞 (01327) 300277
⛳ Norton Rd, 𝒞 (01327) 702 829
⛳ Hellidon Lakes H. & C.C. Hellidon, 𝒞 (01327) 262 550
⛳ Staverton Park Staverton, 𝒞 (01327) 302 000

🏨 **Fawsley Hall** ⬦   ≤ 🍴 🍳 🐉 ⊕ 🏛 ⅃ぅ 🌿 📶 ⅃ **P** **VISA** 🌐 **AE** ①
Fawsley, South : 6½ m. by A 45 off A 361 ⊠ *NN11 3BA – 𝒞 (01327) 892 000*
– www.fawsleyhall.com – reservations@fawsleyhall.com – Fax (01327) 892 001
47 rm – †£170 ††£305/325, ⊆ £8 – 5 suites – ††£389/459
Rest *Equilibrium* – (Closed Sunday and Monday) (booking essential)
Menu £59 (dinner only)
♦ Impressive Tudor Manor house set in 2000 acres. Spacious, individually styled bedrooms display original features, heavy fabrics and plenty of luxury. Georgian and Victorian wings. Restaurant offers ambitious cooking and unusual combinations.

🏨 **Barcelo Daventry**   🔲 🐉 ⅃ぅ 👌 rm, 🅼 rest, 🌿 📶 ⅃ **P** **VISA** 🌐 **AE**
Sedgemoor Way, off Ashby Rd, North : 2 m. on A 361 ⊠ *NN11 0SG – 𝒞 (01327)*
307 000 – www.barcelo-hotels.co.uk – daventry@barcelo-hotels.co.uk
– Fax (01327) 706 313
155 rm – †£135/155 ††£135/255, ⊆ £12   **Rest** – Carte £20/40
♦ A large and spacious modern hotel with comprehensive conference facilities and a well equipped leisure centre. Contemporary, comfy rooms, some with "study areas". Restaurant has pleasant views over Drayton Water.

at Staverton Southwest : 2¾ m. by A 45 off A 425 – ⊠ Daventry

🏠 **Colledges House**   🍴 🌿 **P** **VISA** 🌐
Oakham Lane, off Glebe Lane ⊠ *NN11 6JQ – 𝒞 (01327) 702 737*
– www.colledgeshouse.co.uk – lizjarrett@colledgeshouse.co.uk
– Closed 25 December
4 rm ⊆ – †£68 ††£106
Rest – (by arrangement, communal dining) Menu £32
♦ Part 17C house in a quiet village. Full of charm with antiques, curios, portraits and an inglenook fireplace. Homely rooms are in the main house and an adjacent cottage. Evening meals served at elegant oak table.

ENGLAND

DAWLISH – Devon – **503** J 32

➤ London 184 mi – Exeter 13 mi – Teignmouth 3 mi

⌂ **Lammas Park House**   ≼ ☞ ⅍ 🛜 **P** **VISA** **⃝⃝** **AE**
3 Priory Rd, via High St and Strand Hill ✉ *EX7 9JF –* ✆ *(01626) 888 064*
– www.lammasparkhouse.co.uk – lammaspark@hotmail.com – Fax (01626)
888 064
3 rm ⌵ – ♦£70 ♦♦£90
Rest – (by arrangement, communal dining) Menu £20
♦ Lovely early 19C townhouse boasting a superb secluded rear terrace garden and
handsome period details in situ. Clean, uncluttered rooms. Sit and admire views from
observatory. Dinners served in communal style; owners are experiened restaurateurs.

DAYLESFORD Glos – **503** O28 – See Stow-on-the-Wold

DEAL – Kent – **504** Y 30 – pop. 29 248

➤ London 78 mi – Canterbury 19 mi – Dover 8 mi – Margate 16 mi
🛈 The Landmark Centre, 129 High St ✆ (01304) 369576, info@deal.gov.uk
🖥 Walmer & Kingsdown Kingsdown The Leas, ✆ (01304) 373 256

🏠 **Dunkerley's**   ≼ ⅍ 🛜 **VISA** **⃝⃝** **AE** **⃝**
19 Beach St ✉ *CT14 7AH –* ✆ *(01304) 375 016 – www.dunkerleys.co.uk*
– ddunkerley@btconnect.com – Fax (01304) 380 187
16 rm ⌵ – ♦£70 ♦♦£100/130
Rest *Restaurant* – see restaurant listing
♦ The hotel faces the beach and the Channel. Bedrooms are comfortably furnished
and the principal rooms have jacuzzis. Comfortable bar offers a lighter menu than the
restaurant.

⌂ **Sutherland House**   ☞ ⅍ **P** **VISA** **⃝⃝** **AE** **⃝**
186 London Rd ✉ *CT14 9PT –* ✆ *(01304) 362 853*
– www.sutherlandhousehotel.co.uk – info@sutherlandhouse.fsnet.co.uk
– Fax (01304) 381 146
4 rm ⌵ – ♦£57/65 ♦♦£67/75   **Rest** – (by arrangement) Menu £27
♦ An Edwardian house with garden in a quiet residential area. Stylish, welcoming
bedrooms are individually decorated. Friendly, relaxed atmosphere. Refined dining
room with homely ambience.

✗✗ **Restaurant** – at Dunkerley's Hotel   ☞ **AK** **VISA** **⃝⃝** **AE** **⃝**
19 Beach St ✉ *CT14 7AH –* ✆ *(01304) 375 016 – www.dunkerleys.co.uk*
– ddunkerley@btconnect.com – Fax (01304) 380 187 – Closed Sunday and
Monday
Rest – Seafood – Menu £15/27
♦ With views of the Channel, the restaurant is best known for preparing locally
caught seafood, although non-seafood options are also available. Wide ranging wine
list.

at Worth

⌂ **Solley Farm House** without rest   ☞ ⅍ 🛜 **P** **VISA** **⃝⃝**
The Street ✉ *CT14 0DG –* ✆ *(01304) 613 701 – www.solleyfarmhouse.co.uk*
– sollyfarmhouse@tiscali.co.uk – Fax (01304) 613 701 – Closed 25-26 December
3 rm ⌵ – ♦£80 ♦♦£100
♦ 300 year old house, overlooking the village pond and church. Full of character and
charm, with a very welcoming owner. Organic breakfasts served on the terrace in
summer.

ENGLAND

Your opinions are important to us:
please write and let us know about your discoveries and experiences –
good and bad!

DEDDINGTON – Oxfordshire – **503** Q 28 – **pop. 1 595**   10 **B1**
> London 72 mi – Birmingham 46 mi – Coventry 33 mi – Oxford 18 mi

Deddington Arms   AC rest, ⚡ 🛁 P VISA ⓜⓞ AE
Horsefair ⊠ *OX15 0SH –* ℰ *(01869) 338 364 – www.oxfordshire-hotels.com*
– deddarms@oxfordshire-hotels.co.uk – Fax (01869) 337 010
27 rm ⊊ – ♦£90 ♦♦£110/130   **Rest** – Carte £28/32
♦ Traditional coaching inn with a smart, modish ambience, on the market place.
Spacious modern bedrooms in rear extension. Stylish rooms, two four-postered, in
the main house. The restaurant is decorated in a warm and contemporary style.

Otters   VISA ⓜⓞ AE ①
Market Place ⊠ *OX15 0SA –* ℰ *(01869) 338 813*
*– ottersrestaurant@hotmail.co.uk – Fax (01295) 273 205 – Closed 2 weeks in
August, 1 week Christmas, Monday and Sunday dinner*
Rest – Menu £11/15 – Carte £16/30
♦ Cosy restaurant set over two floors; low ceilinged and heavily beamed, but with a
light airy feel. Traditional menu; well presented dishes.

DEDHAM – Essex – **504** W 28 – ⊠ **Colchester** ‖ *Great Britain*   13 **D2**
> London 63 mi – Chelmsford 30 mi – Colchester 8 mi – Ipswich 12 mi
ⓖ Stour Valley★ – Flatford Mill★, E : 6 m. by B 1029, A 12 and B 1070

Maison Talbooth ॐ   ⇐ 🖃 ⒥ ⊛ ⚙ ⚙ ⛟ P VISA ⓜⓞ AE ①
Stratford Rd, West : ½ m. ⊠ *CO7 6HN –* ℰ *(01206) 322 367*
– www.milsomhotels.com – maison@milsomhotels.com – Fax (01206) 322 752
12 rm ⊊ – ♦£150 ♦♦£375
Rest *Le Talbooth* – see restaurant listing
♦ Quiet, Victorian country house with intimate atmosphere, lawned gardens and
views over river valley. Some rooms are smart and contemporary, others more traditional in style.

Milsoms   🖃 🍽 ⅙ rm, AC rest, P VISA ⓜⓞ AE
Stratford Rd, West : ¾ m. ⊠ *CO7 6HW –* ℰ *(01206) 323 689*
– www.milsomhotels.com – milsoms@milsomhotels.co.uk – Fax (01206) 323 689
15 rm – ♦£175 ♦♦£175, ⊊ £15
Rest – (bookings not accepted) Carte £19/35
♦ Modern hotel overlooking Constable's Dedham Vale with attractive garden and
stylish lounge. Bright, airy and welcoming rooms feature unfussy décor and modern
colours. Likeably modish, wood-floored bistro.

Le Talbooth   🖃 🍽 P VISA ⓜⓞ AE ①
Gun Hill, West : 1 m. ⊠ *CO7 6HP –* ℰ *(01206) 323 150 – www.milsomhotels.com*
*– talbooth@milsomhotels.com – Fax (01206) 322 309 – Closed Sunday dinner
September-May*
Rest – Menu £28 (lunch) – Carte £34/52 🍷
♦ Part Tudor house in attractive riverside setting, with exposed beams and real fires
contributing to the traditional atmosphere. Menus combine the classic with the more
modern. Well chosen wine list.

Fountain House & Dedham Hall with rm ॐ   🖃 ⅙ P
Brook St ⊠ *CO7 6AD –* ℰ *(01206) 323 027*   VISA ⓜⓞ
*– www.dedhamhall.demon.co.uk – sarton@dedhamhall.demon.co.uk
– Fax (01206) 323 293 – Closed Christmas-New Year*
5 rm ⊊ – ♦£55 ♦♦£95
Rest – (Closed Sunday-Monday) (dinner only) (booking essential) Menu £31
♦ In a quiet, country house dating back to 15C with traditional, uncluttered ambience. Weekly changing traditionally based set menu. Comfortable rooms also available.

The Sun Inn with rm   🖃 P VISA ⓜⓞ
High St ⊠ *CO7 6DF –* ℰ *(01206) 323 351 – www.thesuninndedham.com*
– office@thesuninndedham.com – Closed 25, 26, 31 December
5 rm ⊊ – ♦£65 ♦♦£130   **Rest** – Menu £25/25 – Carte £22/27
♦ Modernised 15C coaching inn in heart of village. Welcoming sunny yellow façade;
spacious interior. Interesting, original Mediterranean style menus. Boutique bedrooms.

DENHAM – Buckinghamshire – **504** S 29 – pop. 2 269 ▌ *Great Britain*   11 **D3**
- 🄳 London 20 mi – Buckingham 42 mi – Oxford 41 mi
- 🄶 Windsor Castle ★★★, Eton ★★ and Windsor ★, S : 10 m. by A 412

🍺 **The Swan Inn**   🍴 ☂ **P** *VISA* **◑** **AE**
Village Rd ✉ *UB9 5BH* – ℰ *(01895) 832 085* – *www.swaninndenham.co.uk*
– *info@swaninndenham.co.uk* – *Fax (01895) 835 516* – *Closed 25-26 December*
Rest – (booking essential) Carte £ 20/30
♦ Ivy-covered inn; part bar, part restaurant leading through to pleasant terrace and spacious garden. Good modern dishes with blackboard specials changing daily.

DENMEAD – Hampshire – **503** Q 31 – pop. 5 788   6 **B2**
- 🄳 London 70 mi – Portsmouth 11 mi – Southampton 27 mi

🍴🍴 **Barnard's**   ☂ *VISA* **◑** **AE**
Hambledon Rd ✉ *PO7 6NU* – ℰ *(023) 9225 7788* – *www.barnardsrestaurant.co.uk*
– *mail@barnardsrestaurant.co.uk* – *Fax (023) 9225 7788* – *Closed 1 week Christmas,
1 week summer, Saturday lunch, Sunday, Monday and Bank Holidays*
Rest – (light lunch) Menu £ 20 – Carte £ 23/33
♦ Friendly village centre shop conversion; bright and airy with a small bar area. Classic and modern dishes: ricotta and basil gnocchi, chorizo salad or pork in mustard sauce.

DERBY – Derby – **502** P 25 – pop. 229 407 ▌ *Great Britain*   16 **B2**
- 🄳 London 132 mi – Birmingham 40 mi – Coventry 49 mi – Leicester 29 mi
  – Manchester 62 mi – Nottingham 16 mi – Sheffield 47 mi
  – Stoke-on-Trent 35 mi
- 🄰 Nottingham East Midlands Airport, Castle Donington : ℰ *(0871) 919 9000*,
  SE : 12 m. by A 6 X
- 🄸 Assembly Rooms, Market Pl ℰ *(01332) 255802, tourism@derby.gov.uk*
- 🄸🄸 Sinfin Wilmore Rd, ℰ *(01332) 766 323*
- 🄸🄸 Mickleover Uttoxeter Rd, ℰ *(01332) 516 011*
- 🄸🄸 Kedleston Park Quardon Kedlston, ℰ *(01332) 840 035*
- 🄸🄸 Breadsall Priory H. & C.C. Morley Moor Rd, ℰ *(01332) 836 106*
- 🄸🄸 Allestree Park Allestree Allestree Hall, ℰ *(01332) 550 616*
- 🄾 City ★ – Museum and Art Gallery ★ (Collection of Derby Porcelain ★) YZ **M1**
  – Royal Crown Derby Museum ★ **AC** Z **M2**
- 🄶 Kedleston Hall ★★ **AC**, NW : 4½ m. by Kedleston Rd X

Plan on next page

🏨 **Midland**   🍴 ☂ 🛎 ⚷ 🍽 ♨ **P** *VISA* **◑** **AE** **◍**
Midland Rd ✉ *DE1 2SQ* – ℰ *(01332) 345 894* – *www.midland-derby.co.uk*
– *sales@midland-derby.co.uk* – *Fax (01332) 293 522*   Zi
94 rm – †£ 106/114 ††£ 114, ⚏ £ 14.50 – 1 suite   **Rest** – Menu £ 25
♦ A pleasant, early-Victorian railway hotel with good sized modern rooms and traditionally decorated public areas. Wide array of conference rooms. Pretty dining room in the Victorian style of the hotel.

at Darley Abbey North : 2½ m. off A 6 - X – ✉ Derby

🍴🍴 **Darleys**   **AC** **P** *VISA* **◑**
Darley Abbey Mill ✉ *DE22 1DZ* – ℰ *(01332) 364 987* – *www.darleys.com*
– *info@darleys.com* – *Fax (01332) 364 987* – *Closed 25 December-8 January,
Sunday dinner and Bank Holidays*
Rest – Menu £ 17 (lunch) – Carte (dinner) £ 31/36
♦ A converted cotton mill in an attractive riverside setting. The interior is modern, stylish and comfortable. High quality British cuisine of satisfying, classical character.

at Weston Underwood Northwest : 5½ m. by A 52 - X - and Kedleston Rd
– ✉ Derby

🏠 **Park View Farm** without rest   ≤ 🍴 ⚷ **P**
✉ *DE6 4PA* – ℰ *(01335) 360 352* – *www.parkviewfarm.co.uk*
– *enquiries@parkviewfarm.co.uk* – *Fax (01335) 360 352* – *Closed Christmas*
3 rm ⚏ – †£ 60 ††£ 80/85
♦ Friendly couple run this elegant house on a working farm, in sight of Kedleston Hall. Antique-filled lounge with oils and a Victorian fireplace. Simple rooms in stripped pine.

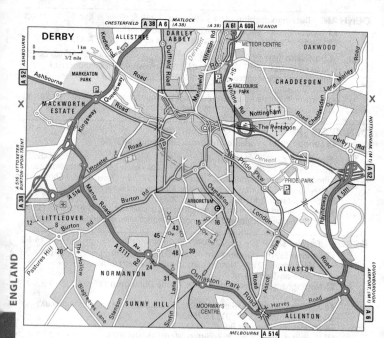

DERBY

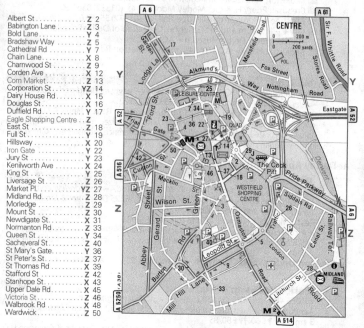

DEVIZES – Wiltshire – **503** O 29 – pop. 14 379

- ▶ London 98 mi – Bristol 38 mi – Salisbury 25 mi – Southampton 50 mi – Swindon 19 mi
- 🛈 Cromwell House, Market Pl 𝒞 (01380) 729408, all.tics@kennet.go.uk
- 🔢 Erlestoke, 𝒞 (01380) 831 069
- ◎ St John's Church★★ – Market Place★ – Wiltshire Heritage Museum★ **AC**
- ◎ Potterne (Porch House★★) S : 2½ m. by A 360 – E : Vale of Pewsey★. Stonehenge★★★ **AC**, SE : 16 m. by A 360 and A 344 – Avebury★★ (The Stones★, Church★) NE : 7 m. by A 361

at Marden Southeast : 6½ m. by A 342 – ✉ Devizes

🍴 **The Millstream** 🍺 ⛲ **P.** *VISA* **⬤⬤**
✉ SN10 3RH – 𝒞 (01380) 848 308 – www.the-millstream.net
– info@the-millstream.net – Fax (01380) 848 337 – Closed Monday except Bank Holidays and Sunday
Rest – Menu £ 16 (lunch) – Carte £ 25/36
◆ Charming pub with chic country interior and delightfully eye-catching décor. Traditional pub dishes use local, seasonal ingredients, with contemporary influences and a French edge.

at Potterne South : 2¼ m. on A 360 – ✉ Devizes

🏠 **Blounts Court Farm** without rest 🐾 🍺 🕭 ⚘ 📶 **P.** *VISA* **⬤⬤**
Coxhill Lane ✉ SN10 5PH – 𝒞 (01380) 727 180 – www.blountscourtfarm.co.uk
– caroline@blountscourtfarm.co.uk
3 rm 🍽 – †£38/72 ††£68/72
◆ Working farm personally run by charming owner: good value accommodation in blissful spot. Cosy rooms in converted barn are handsomely furnished with interesting artefacts.

at Rowde Northwest : 2 m. by A 361 on A 342 – ✉ Devizes

🍴 **The George & Dragon** with rm 🍺 ⛲ ⚘ **P.** *VISA* **⬤⬤**
High Street, Rowde ✉ SN10 2PN – 𝒞 (01380) 723 053
– www.thegeorgeanddragonrowde.co.uk – thegandd@tiscali.co.uk – Closed 25-26 December
3 rm 🍽 – †£85 ††£105
Rest – Seafood – (Closed Sunday dinner) (booking essential) Menu £ 16 (lunch) – Carte £ 24/45
◆ Unspectacular from the outside but warm and characterful inside. Excellent fish specials created from the daily catch accompany a menu of comforting British classics. Well-equipped, trendy-meets-old-world bedrooms.

The 😳 award is the crème de la crème.
This is awarded to restaurants
which are really worth travelling miles for!

DICKLEBURGH – Norfolk – **504** X 26 – see Diss

DIDSBURY – Gtr Manchester – **502** N 23 – see Manchester

DIPTFORD – Devon – **503** I 32 – ✉ Totnes

- ▶ London 202 mi – Plymouth 20 mi – Torbay 16 mi – Exeter 31 mi

🏠 **The Old Rectory** 🐾 ≤ 🍺 **P.** *VISA* **⬤⬤**
✉ TQ9 7NY – 𝒞 (01548) 821 575 – www.oldrectorydiptford.co.uk
– hitchins@oldrectorydiptford.co.uk – Closed Christmas, minimum 2 night stay
5 rm 🍽 – †£65/85 ††£110 **Rest** – (by arrangement) Menu £ 28
◆ Classic Georgian house of cavernous proportions with a three-acre garden. The lounge, though, is small and cosy. Airy rooms benefit from rural views; luxurious bathrooms. Food taken seriously: fine home-cooked meals served with pride.

ENGLAND

DISS – Norfolk – **504** X 26 – **pop. 7 444**

    🛆 London 98 mi – Ipswich 25 mi – Norwich 21 mi – Thetford 17 mi
    🛈 Meres Mouth, Mere St ℰ (01379) 650523, dtic@s-norfolk.gov.uk

at Dickleburgh Northeast : 4½ m. by A 1066 off A 140 – ✉ Diss

⚲   **Dickleburgh Hall Country House** without rest   🚗 🍸 📷₁₈ 🌿 **P**
    Semere Green Lane, North : 1 m. ✉ *IP21 4NT* – ℰ *(01379) 741 259*
    – www.dickhall.co.uk – johntaylor05@btinternet.com – March-October
    3 rm ⌂ – 🛏£45/55 🛏🛏£65/90
    ♦ 16C house still in private hands. Trim rooms in traditional patterns, beamed lounge with an inglenook fireplace; snooker room and golf course.

at Brockdish East : 7 m. by A 1066, A 140 and A 143 – ✉ Diss

⚲   **Grove Thorpe** without rest ⟐   🚗 🍸 🞕 🐟 🌿 **P**
    Grove Rd, North : ¾ m. ✉ *IP21 4JR* – ℰ *(01379) 668 305*
    – www.grovethorpe.co.uk – grovethorpe@btinternet.com – March-November
    3 rm ⌂ – 🛏£65/70 🛏🛏£90/95
    ♦ Pretty 17C bailiff's house in peaceful pastureland with fishing; very welcoming owners. Cosy ambience. Characterful interior with oak beams, inglenook and antique furniture.

at Brome Southeast : 2 ¾ m. by A 1066 on B 1077 – ✉ Eye

🏨   **The Cornwallis** ⟐   🚗 🍸 🞕 🌿 🏋 **P** 𝘝𝘐𝘚𝘈 ⓜⓞ 🅐🅔
    ✉ *IP23 8AJ* – ℰ *(01379) 870 326 – www.thecornwallis.com*
    – reservations.cornwallis@ohiml.com – Fax (01379) 870 051
    16 rm ⌂ – 🛏£90 🛏🛏£120/175
    Rest – (Closed Sunday dinner) (booking essential) Carte £25/35
    ♦ Part 16C dower house with quiet topiary gardens. Spacious, individually decorated timbered rooms with antique furniture. 40ft well in very characterful bar dating from 1561. Dining room with delightful conservatory lounge overlooking gardens.

> The red ⟐ symbol?
> This denotes the very essence of peace
> – only the sound of birdsong first thing in the morning…

DITCHEAT – Somerset

    🛆 London 124 mi – Bath 29 mi

🛏   **The Manor House Inn** with rm   🚗 🞕 🌿 📞 **P** 𝘝𝘐𝘚𝘈 ⓜⓞ
    ✉ *BA4 6RB* – ℰ *(01749) 860 276 – www.manorhouseinn.co.uk*
    – info@manorhouseinn.co.uk – Closed 25 December
    3 rm ⌂ – 🛏£50 🛏🛏£90
    Rest – (Closed Sunday dinner) Menu £17 – Carte £18/28
    ♦ Watch the horses on their way to the gallops from this characterful 17C pub. Drink at flag-floored or sports bars. Dishes are satisfyingly rustic. Pleasant rooms in annex.

DOGMERSFIELD – Hampshire

    🛆 London 44 mi – Farnham 6 mi – Fleet 2 mi

🏨🏨🏨 **Four Seasons** ⟐   ≤ 🚗 🍸 🞕 🞖 🗳 ⑳ 🞖 𝄞 ✕ 🞖 🞖 rm, 🚶 🄰🄲
    Dogmersfield Park, Chalky Lane ✉ *RG27 8TD*   📞 🗳 **P** 𝘝𝘐𝘚𝘈 ⓜⓞ 🅐🅔 ①
    – ℰ (01252) 853 000 – www.fourseasons.com/hampshire
    – reservations.hampshire@fourseasons.com – Fax (01252) 853 010
    111 rm – 🛏£229/264 🛏🛏£222/264, ⌂ £24 – 21 suites
    Rest *Seasons* – Menu £55 (dinner) – Carte £38/58
    ♦ Part Georgian splendour in extensive woodlands; many original features in situ. Superb spa facilities: vast selection of leisure pursuits. Luxurious, highly equipped bedrooms. Restaurant has thoroughly modish, relaxing feel.

DONCASTER – South Yorkshire – **502** Q 23 – **pop. 67 977** 23 **C3**

London 173 mi – Kingston-upon-Hull 46 mi – Leeds 30 mi – Nottingham 46 mi – Sheffield 19 mi

Robin Hood Airport : ✆ (08708) 332210, SE : 7m off A638

38-40 High St ✆ (01302) 734309, touristi.nformation@doncaster.gov.uk

18 Doncaster Town Moor Belle Vue Bawtry Rd, ✆ (01302) 533 778

18 Crookhill Park Conisborough, ✆ (01709) 862 979

18 Wheatley Amthorpe Rd, ✆ (01302) 831 655

9 Owston Park Owston Owston Lane, Carcroft, ✆ (01302) 330 821

DONCASTER

Albion Pl. . . . . . C 3
Apley Rd . . . . . . C 5
Balby Rd . . . . . . C 8
Broxholme Lane C
Carr House Rd. C
Chequer Ave . . . . . . C 12
Chequer Rd C
Christ Church Rd. C
Church Way. C
Cleveland St C
Colonnades Shopping Centre C
Cunningham Rd . . . . . . C 17
East Laith Gate . . . . . . C 24
Frenchgate Shopping Centre C
Grey Friars Rd C
Hall Gate C
Highfield Rd. C
High St. . . . . . C 36
Milton Walk . . . . . . C 40
Nether Hall Rd. . . . . . C 43
North Bridge Rd . . . . . . C 44
Queen's Rd . . . . . . C 46
St George's Bridge C
St Jame's Bridge. . . . . . C 48
St Jame's St C
Silver St C
South Parade. C
Thorne Rd C
Trafford Way C
Waterdale C
Waterdale Shopping Centre C
White Rose Way. . . . . . C 70
Wood St. C

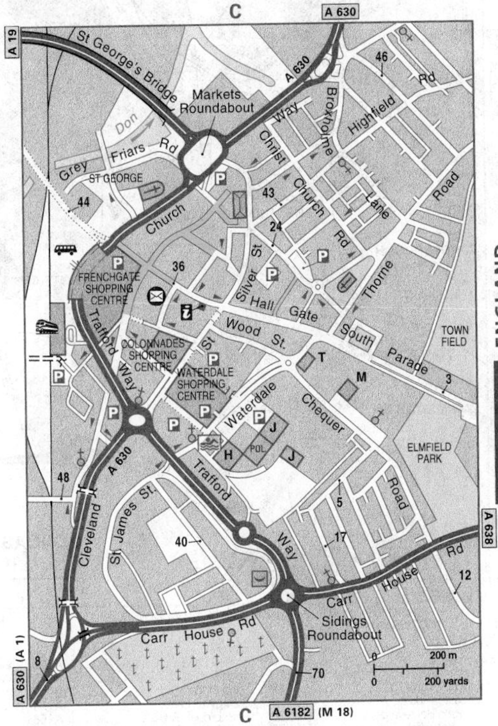

Mount Pleasant rm, rest, VISA

Great North Rd, Southeast : 6 m. on A 638 ✉ DN11 0HW – ✆ (01302) 868 696 – www.mountpleasant.co.uk – reception@mountpleasant.co.uk – Fax (01302) 865 130 – Closed 25 December

54 rm – †£ 60/95 ††£ 125/160 – 2 suites

Rest *Garden* – Carte dinner £ 26/40

♦ Stone-built farmhouse with sympathetic extension. Traditionally styled throughout: wood panelled lounges and a small bar. Well-kept bedrooms, including one with a five-poster! Restaurant with garden views.

Red = Pleasant. Look for the red and symbols.

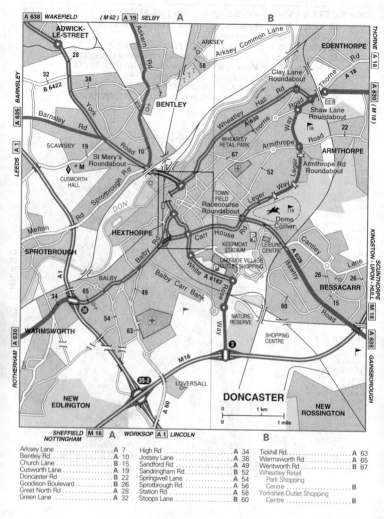

Arksey Lane	A 7	High Rd	A 34
Bentley Rd.	A 10	Jossey Lane	A 38
Church Lane	B 15	Sandford Rd	A 49
Cusworth Lane	A 19	Sandringham Rd	B 52
Doncaster Rd	B 22	Springwell Lane	A 54
Goodison Boulevard	B 26	Sprotbrough Rd.	A 56
Great North Rd	A 28	Station Rd	A 58
Green Lane	A 32	Stoops Lane	B 60

Tickhill Rd.	A 63
Warmsworth Rd.	A 65
Wentworth Rd	B 67
Wheatley Retail Park Shopping Centre	B
Yorkshire Outlet Shopping Centre	B

Look out for red symbols, indicating particularly pleasant establishments.

DONHEAD-ST-ANDREW – Wiltshire – 503 N 30

4 C3

🄳 London 115 mi – Bournemouth 34 mi – Poole 32 mi – Bath 37 mi

Forester Inn

Lower Street, ✉ SP7 9EE – ℰ (01747) 828 038
– possums1@btinternet.com – Fax (01747) 828 038
Rest – (Closed Sunday dinner) Menu £ 17 (lunch) – Carte £ 17/30
♦ Thatched 13C stone pub with low beams and inglenooks. Modern British cooking, with Mediterranean/Asian influences: plenty of fish and seafood; locally sourced artisan cheeses.

DORCHESTER – Dorset – **503** M 31 – pop. **16 171**   4 **C3**

> ▶ London 135 mi – Bournemouth 27 mi – Exeter 53 mi – Southampton 53 mi
> 🛈 11 Antelope Walk ℰ (01305) 267992, dorchester.tic@westdorset-dc.gov.uk
> 🏌 Came Down, ℰ (01305) 813 494
> 👁 Town★ - Dorset County Museum★ **AC**
> 🔲 Maiden Castle★★ (≤★) SW : 2½ m. – Puddletown Church★, NE : 5½ m. by
> A 35. Moreton Church★★, E : 7½ m. – Bere Regis★ (St John the Baptist
> Church★ - Roof★★) NE : 11 m. by A 35 – Athelhampton House★ **AC**,
> NE : 6½ m. by A 35 - Cerne Abbas★, N : 7 m. by A 352 – Milton Abbas★,
> NE : 12 m. on A 354 and by-road

🏠 **Casterbridge** without rest   ⅍ 🛜 **VISA** **CO** **AE**
49 High East St ⊠ *DT1 1HU – ℰ (01305) 264 043 – www.casterbridgehotel.co.uk*
– reception@casterbridgehotel.co.uk – Fax (01305) 260 884 – Closed Christmas
15 rm ⊡ – †£60/90 ††£110/135
◆ A Georgian town house with courtyard and conservatory at the bottom of the high
street. Well decorated throughout in a comfortable, traditional style. Bar and quiet
lounge.

🏠 **Yalbury Cottage**   🛏 🛜 **P** **VISA** **CO** **AE**
(Lower Bockhampton), East; 3¾ m by the A35 ⊠ *DT2 8PZ – ℰ (01305) 262 382*
– www.yalburycottage.com – enquiries@yalburycottage.com – Closed 1 week
Christmas and first 3 weeks in January
8 rm ⊡ – †£85 ††£120   **Rest** – (Closed Monday lunch) Menu £21/36 **s**
◆ Attractive 300 year old thatched cottage set in a quiet hamlet. Lounge and dining
room boast heavy beams and inglenooks. Bedrooms are simple and comfortable.
Interesting fixed price menu features local produce.

🏠 **Westwood House** without rest   ⅍ 🛜 **VISA** **CO** **①**
29 High West St ⊠ *DT1 1UP – ℰ (01305) 268 018 – www.westwoodhouse.co.uk*
– reservations@westwoodhouse.co.uk
7 rm ⊡ – †£50/55 ††£85/90
◆ Georgian town house on the high street with a welcoming atmosphere. Breakfast
served in the conservatory. Rooms are decorated in bold colours and are well kept
and spacious.

🏠 **Little Court** without rest   🛏 🏊 ⅍ 🛜 **P** **VISA** **CO** **AE**
5 Westleaze, Charminster , North : 1m by A 37, turning right at Loders garage
⊠ *DT2 9PZ – ℰ (01305) 261 576 – www.littlecourt.net – info@littlecourt.net*
– Fax (01305) 261 359 – Closed 24 December - 2 January
8 rm ⊡ – †£69/89 ††£79/129
◆ Attractive Lutyens style Edwardian house with tennis court, pool and 5 acres of
gardens. Original wood, brickwork and leaded windows. Comfortable bedrooms;
modern bathrooms.

✕✕ **Sienna**   **AC** **VISA** **CO**
36 High West St ⊠ *DT1 1UP – ℰ (01305) 250 022 – www.siennarestaurant.co.uk*
– browns@siennarestaurant.co.uk – Closed 2 weeks spring, 2 weeks Autumn,
Sunday and Monday
Rest – (booking essential) Menu £25/39
◆ Charming, intimate restaurant at top of high street. Cheerful yellow walls with
modern artwork and banquette seating on one side. Modern British dishes using local
produce.

at Winterbourne Steepleton West : 4¾ m. by B 3150 and A 35 on B 3159
– ⊠ Dorchester

🏠 **Old Rectory** without rest   🛏 ⅍ **P**
⊠ *DT2 9LG – ℰ (01305) 889 468 – www.theoldrectorybandb.co.uk*
– caroline@theoldrectorybandb.co.uk – Closed Christmas
4 rm – †£60 ††£100
◆ Built in 1850 and having a characterful exterior. Situated in the middle of a charming village. Well kept, good sized rooms overlook the pleasant garden.

ENGLAND

DORCHESTER-ON-THAMES – Oxfordshire – **503** Q 29 – **pop. 2 256**   10 **B2**

🛈 *Great Britain*

> ▶ London 51 mi – Abingdon 6 mi – Oxford 8 mi – Reading 17 mi
> ◎ Town ★
> ⓒ Ridgeway Path ★★

🏠   **White Hart**   🛆 rm, ⅍ 🌢 🛀 **P.** 🆅🅸🆂🅰 ⓪ 🅰🅴

26 High St ⊠ OX10 7HN – ℰ (01865) 340 074 – www.oxfordshire-hotels.co.uk
– whitehart@oxfordshire-hotels.co.uk – Fax (01865) 341 082
26 rm ⊃ – †£95 ††£95/105 – 2 suites
Rest – Menu £14 (lunch) – Carte £23/29
♦ 17C coaching inn with charm and character. The comfortable bar has large leather
armchairs. Well-kept pretty bedrooms with smart bathrooms. Striking beamed dining
room.

DORKING – Surrey – **504** T 30 – **pop. 16 071**   7 **D2**

> ▶ London 26 mi – Brighton 39 mi – Guildford 12 mi – Worthing 33 mi
> 🏌 Betchworth Park Reigate Rd, ℰ (01306) 882 052

🏨   **Burford Bridge**   🚊 🏊 ⅍ 🌢 🛀 **P.** 🆅🅸🆂🅰 ⓪ 🅰🅴 ⓪

Box Hill, North : 1½ m. on A 24 ⊠ RH5 6BX – ℰ (01306) 884 561
– www.mercure.com – h6635@accor.com – Fax (01306) 880 386
57 rm ⊃ – †£135/185 ††£145/195   **Rest** – Menu £32
♦ Wordsworth and Sheridan frequented this part 16C hotel. Well run, high quality
feel throughout. Antique paintings in public areas, embossed wallpaper in bedrooms.
The dining room has a smart, well kept air.

at Abinger Common Southwest : 4½ m. by A 25 – ⊠ Dorking

🍴   **Stephan Langton Inn**   🏡 **P.** 🆅🅸🆂🅰 ⓪ 🅰🅴 ⓪

Friday St, Abinger Common ⊠ RH5 6JR – ℰ (01306) 730 775
– www.stephan-langton.co.uk – chris@stephan-langton.co.uk
Rest – (Closed Sunday-Tuesday dinner and Monday lunch) Carte £18/28
♦ Simply-furnished pub with wood floors and open fires, in the heart of the privately
owned Wooton Estate. Concise, seasonal, daily-changing menu offers tasty homemade fare.

DORRIDGE – West Midlands – **503** O 26 – ⊠ Birmingham   19 **C2**

> ▶ London 109 mi – Birmingham 11 mi – Warwick 11 mi

🍴🍴   **The Forest** with rm   🏡 🅺 rest, 🌢 🛀 **P.** 🆅🅸🆂🅰 ⓪ 🅰🅴

25 Station Approach ⊠ B93 8JA – ℰ (01564) 772 120 – www.forest-hotel.com
– info@forest-hotel.com – Fax (01564) 732 680 – Closed 25 December
12 rm – †£95/130 ††£110/140, ⊃ £10
Rest – (closed Sunday dinner) Menu £16 (midweek) – Carte £20/31
♦ Attractive red-brick and timber former pub with a busy ambience. Food is its
backbone: modern classics served in stylish bar and restaurant. Cool, modern bedrooms.

DOUGLAS – Isle of Man – **502** G 21 – see Man (Isle of)

DOVER – Kent – **504** Y 30 – **pop. 34 087** 🛈 *Great Britain*   9 **D2**

> ▶ London 76 mi – Brighton 84 mi
> 🚢 to France (Calais) (P & O Stena Line) frequent services daily (1 h 15 mn) –
> to France (Calais) (SeaFrance S.A.) frequent services daily (1 h 30 mn) –
> to France (Boulogne) (SpeedFerries) 3-5 daily (50 mn)
> 🛈 The Old Town Gaol, Biggin ℰ (01304) 205108, tic@doveruk.com
> ◎ Castle ★★ **AC** Y
> ⓒ White Cliffs, Langdon Cliffs, NE : 1 m. on A 2 Z and A 258

Plan opposite

ENGLAND

DOVER

ENGLAND

at St Margaret's at Cliffe Northeast : 4 m. by A 258 - Z – ⊠ Dover

Wallett's Court Country House　🚗 🖥 🕸 ⅙ ⚒ ⚒ **P** *VISA* ⚫⚫ AE ⓪
West Cliffe, Northwest : ¾ m. on Dover rd ⊠ CT15 6EW – ℰ (01304) 852424
– www.wallettscourt.com – mail@wallettscourt.com – Fax (01304) 853 430
– Closed 24 and 26 December
17 rm ⌂ – †£109/129 ††£129/199
Rest *The Restaurant* – see restaurant listing
♦ With origins dating back to the Doomsday Book, a wealth of Jacobean features remain in this relaxed country house. Most characterful rooms in main house; luxurious spa rooms.

263

ENGLAND

XX **The Restaurant** – at Wallett's Court Hotel 🚗 **P** **VISA** **◍** **AE** **◍**
West Cliffe, Northwest : ¾ m. on Dover rd ☒ CT15 6EW – ℰ (01304) 852 424
– ww.wallettscourt.com – mail@wallettscourt.com – Fax (01304) 853 430 – Closed
24-26 December
Rest – (dinner only and Sunday lunch) Menu £ 40 ⅋
♦ Local produce dominates the imaginative, monthly changing, seasonal menu. Dine
by candlelight in the beamed restaurant after drinks are taken by the open fire.

DOWNTON – Hants. – **503** P 31 – **see Lymington**

DRIFT – Cornwall – **see Penzance**

DROITWICH SPA – Worcestershire – **503** N 27 – **pop. 22 585**   19 **C3**
🔼 London 129 mi – Birmingham 20 mi – Bristol 66 mi – Worcester 6 mi
𝖎 St Richard's House, Victoria Sq ℰ (01905) 774312,
heritage@droitwichspa.gov.uk
🔟 Droitwich G. & C.C. Ford Lane, ℰ (01905) 774 344

at Cutnall Green North : 3 m. on A 442 – ☒ **Droitwich Spa**

🍺 **The Chequers** 🚗 **P** **VISA** **◍**
Kidderminster Rd ☒ WR9 0PJ – ℰ (01299) 851 292
– www.chequerscutnallgreen.co.uk – Fax (01299) 851 744 – Closed 25 December
and 1 January
Rest – Carte £ 21/27
♦ Half-timbered roadside pub, comprising main bar with beams and fire or cosy
garden room. Impressively wide range of highly interesting dishes, firmly traditional
or modern.

at Hadley Heath Southwest : 4 m. by Ombersley Way, A 4133 and Ladywood rd
– ☒ **Droitwich Spa**

⌂ **Old Farmhouse** without rest 🚗 � ✗ **P**
☒ WR9 0AR – ℰ (01905) 620837 – www.theoldfarmhouse.uk.com
– judylambe@theoldfarmhouse.uk.com – Fax (01905) 621 722 – Closed
Christmas-New Year
5 rm ⊑ – ♦ £ 45/50 ♦♦ £ 75
♦ Converted farmhouse in quiet and rural location. Spacious comfortable rooms,
three in the main house and two, more private and perhaps suited to families, in the
annex.

DROXFORD – Hampshire – **504** Q 31   6 **B2**
🔼 London 79 mi – Southampton 21 mi – Portsmouth 16 mi
– Basingstoke 37 mi

🍺 **The Bakers Arms** ☂ **P** **VISA** **◍**
⊛ *High St, Droxford ☒ SO32 3PA – ℰ (01489) 877 533*
– www.thebakersarmsdroxford.com – info@thebakersarmsdroxford.com – Closed
Bank Holiday Mondays
Rest – (Closed Sunday dinner, Monday) Carte £ 20/24
♦ Characterful pub with keen owners and a friendly team. Cooking is simple and
unfussy, featuring British classics with a French/Mediterranean touch. Much of the
produce is local.

DULVERTON – Somerset – **503** J 30   3 **A2**
🔼 London 198 mi – Barnstaple 27 mi – Exeter 26 mi – Minehead 18 mi
– Taunton 27 mi
◉ Village ★
◨ Exmoor National Park ★★ - Tarr Steps ★★, NW : 6 m. by B 3223

Ashwick House ⓢ   ⟨ 🍴 🌅 ⚄ P. VISA ⚫

Northwest : 4¼ m. by B 3223 turning left after second cattle grid ⊠ *TA22 9QD*
– ℰ (01398) 323 868 – www.ashwickhouse.com
– reservations@ashwickhouse.com – Fax (01398) 323 868
8 rm ⌧ – ♦£84/94 ♦♦£138/158
Rest – (booking essential for non-residents, dinner only) Carte £ 30/40
♦ Delightful, peaceful and secluded Edwardian country house in extensive gardens
with pheasants and rabbits. Smartly appointed, airy rooms with thoughtful touches.
Classic cuisine with strong local flavour in elegant dining room.

Woods   🌅 VISA ⚫

4 Banks Square ⊠ *TA22 9BU – ℰ (01398) 324 007 – Fax (01398) 323 366*
Rest – Carte £ 20/30
♦ Converted bakery with charming décor and hand-made furniture. Cooking is classical with a French slant and uses local, traceable produce. Meat comes from the
owner's farm.

at Brushford South : 1 ¾ m. on B 3222 – ⊠ **Dulverton**

Three Acres Country House *without rest*   🛋 ⁽ʸ⁾ P. VISA ⚫ AE

⊠ *TA22 9AR – ℰ (01398) 323 730 – www.threeacrescountryhouse.co.uk*
– enquiries@threeacrescountryhouse.co.uk
6 rm ⌧ – ♦£60 ♦♦£120
♦ Keenly run and friendly 20C guesthouse. Super-comfy bedrooms are the strong
point. There's an airy lounge, cosy bar and breakfasts are locally sourced.

DUNSLEY – N. Yorks. – see Whitby

DUNSTER – Somerset – **503** J 30   3 **A2**

🚗 London 185 mi – Minehead 3 mi – Taunton 23 mi
◎ Town★★ - Castle★★ **AC** (upper rooms ⩽★) - Water Mill★ **AC** - St George's
Church★ - Dovecote★

Exmoor House *without rest*   ⚄ VISA ⚫

12 West St ⊠ *TA24 6SN – ℰ (01643) 821 268 – www.exmoorhousedunster.co.uk*
– stay@exmoorhousedunster.co.uk – Closed 25-26 December, January and
February
6 rm ⌧ – ♦£45 ♦♦£75
♦ Georgian terraced house with cream exterior, enhanced by colourful window
boxes. Spacious, comfy lounge and welcoming breakfast room. Chintz rooms with
pleasing extra touches.

No 7 West Street   🌅 VISA ⚫

7 West St ⊠ *TA24 6SN – ℰ (01643) 821 064 – www.no7weststreet.co.uk*
– info@no7weststreet.co.uk – Closed 20-31 December
3 rm ⌧ – ♦£50/55 ♦♦£80/85   **Rest** – (by arrangement) Menu £ 33
♦ Passionately run 17C guest house in village centre, with bedrooms decorated in
classic English style and beamed ceilings throughout. Open plan lounge; open fire,
comfy sofas. Local Exmoor produce used in French-influenced cooking, including
7 course tasting menu.

DURHAM – Durham – **501** P 19 – pop. 42 939 ▐ *Great Britain*   24 **B3**

🚗 London 267 mi – Leeds 77 mi – Middlesbrough 23 mi – Newcastle upon
Tyne 20 mi – Sunderland 12 mi
🛈 2 Millennium Pl ℰ (0191) 384 3720, touristinfo@durhamcity.gov.uk
🏌 Mount Oswald South Rd, ℰ (0191) 386 7527
◎ City★★★ - Cathedral★★★ (Nave★★★, Chapel of the Nine Altars★★★,
Sanctuary Knocker★) B – Oriental Museum★★ **AC** (at Durham University
by A 167) B – City and Riverside (Prebends' Bridge ⩽★★★A , Framwellgate
Bridge ⩽★★B) – Monastic Buildings (Cathedral Treasury★, Central
Tower ⩽★) B – Castle★ (Norman chapel★) **AC** B
◎ Hartlepool Historic Quay★, SE : 14 m. by A 181, A 19 and A 179

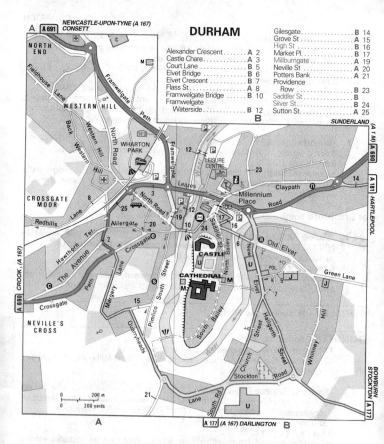

DURHAM

🛏🛏🛏 **Durham Marriott H. Royal County** 🖥 ⏱ 🏖 ⁄ᷓ 🛏 rm, 📞
Old Elvet ⊠ *DH1 3JN* – 🕭 *(0191) 386 6821*   🛎 🅿 VISA ⬤⬤ AE
– *www.durhammarriottroyalcounty.co.uk* – *mhrsvudm.frontdesk@marriott.com*
– *Fax (0191) 386 0704*   B**a**
147 rm – †£130/195 ††£130/195, ⚏ £14.95 – 3 suites
Rest *County* – (dinner only and Sunday lunch) Carte £25/44
Rest *Cruz* – Menu £13 (lunch) **s** – Carte dinner £19/29 **s**
♦ Scene of miners' rallies in the 1950s and 60s. The quality of accommodation at this
town centre hotel is of a comfortable, refined, modern standard. Good leisure facilities. County has elegant décor and linen settings. Bright, relaxed Cruz brasserie.

🏠 **Grafton House** ⟨ 🛁 📞 VISA ⬤⬤
40 South St ⊠ *DH1 4QP* – 🕭 *(0191) 375 67 90*
– *www.grafton-house.co.uk*
– *stay@grafton-house.co.uk*
– *Fax (0191) 375 67 91*   A**s**
9 rm ⚏ – †£125 ††£225
Rest – Menu £25
♦ Comfortable boutique-style hotel. Contemporary décor includes good quality furnishings and flat-screen tvs. Largest bedrooms to the front of the house boast Cathedral views. Formal dining with traditional menu.

Farnley Tower

🔲 **P** VISA ⓜⓞ

The Avenue ⊠ DH1 4DX – 𝒞 (0191) 375 0011 – www.farnley-tower.co.uk
– enquiries@farnley-tower.co.uk – Fax (0191) 383 9694   A**c**

13 rm ⌷ – ♦£60/75 ♦♦£85/95

Rest *Gourmet Spot* – (Closed Sunday and Monday) (dinner only)
Carte £27/48 **s**

♦ Spacious Victorian house in quiet residential area close to city centre. Modern, airy,
well-equipped bedrooms with a good degree of comfort. Gourmet Spot, stylish and
slick in black granite and leather, specialises in molecular gastronomy.

Cathedral View Town House *without rest*

🔲 🖐 ⁽ᵖⁱ⁾ VISA ⓜⓞ

212 Lower Gilesgate ⊠ DH1 1QN – 𝒞 (0191) 386 9566
– www.cathedralview.com – cathedralview@hotmail.com   B**n**

6 rm ⌷ – ♦£60/90 ♦♦£80/90

♦ Alluring Georgian townhouse with terraced garden in older part of the city near
the centre. Attractive breakfast room with good views. Spacious, individually named
rooms.

Castle View *without rest*

🖐 ⁽ᵖⁱ⁾ VISA ⓜⓞ ⓞ

4 Crossgate ⊠ DH1 4PS – 𝒞 (0191) 386 8852 – www.castle-view.co.uk
– castle_view@hotmail.com – Closed 2 weeks Christmas and New Year   A**e**

6 rm ⌷ – ♦£55/70 ♦♦£80/90

♦ Attractive Georgian townhouse off steep cobbled hill, reputedly once the vicarage
to adjacent church. Breakfast on terrace in summer. Individually furnished bedrooms.

Bistro 21

🔲 ⇔ **P** VISA ⓜⓞ AE

Aykley Heads House, Aykley Heads, Northwest : 1½ m. by A 691 and B 6532
⊠ DH1 5TS – 𝒞 (0191) 384 4354 – www.bistrotwentyone.co.uk
– admin@bistrotwentyone.co.uk – Fax (0191) 384 1149 – Closed 25-26 December,
1 January and Sunday dinner

Rest – Menu £18 (lunch and weekday dinner) – Carte £26/41

♦ Part 17C villa with an interior modelled on a simple, Mediterranean style. Good
modern British food, with some rustic tone, served in a beamed room or an enclosed
courtyard.

DUXFORD – **Cambridgeshire** – **504** U 27 – **pop. 1 836** – ⊠ **Cambridge**   14 **B3**

🖪 London 50 mi – Cambridge 11 mi – Colchester 45 mi – Peterborough 45 mi

Duxford Lodge

🔲 ⁽ᵖⁱ⁾ 🏛 **P** VISA ⓜⓞ AE

Ickleton Rd ⊠ CB22 4RT – 𝒞 (01223) 836 444 – www.duxfordlodgehotel.co.uk
– admin@duxfordlodgehotel.co.uk – Fax (01223) 832 271
– Closed 24 December-2 January

15 rm ⌷ – ♦£89 ♦♦£119

Rest *Le Paradis* – Menu £28 – Carte approx. £41

♦ Large, smart, redbrick building set in an acre of garden in a quiet village. Public
areas and bedrooms, which are tidy and well proportioned, have co-ordinated chintz
décor. Themed dining room overlooks garden.

EAGLESCLIFFE Stockton-on-Tees – **502** P 20 – **see Stockton-on-Tees**

EARL STONHAM – **Suffolk** – **504** X 27   15 **C3**

🖪 London 91 mi – Ipswich 12 mi – Colchester 33 mi – Clacton-on-Sea 38 mi

Bays Farm *without rest* ♨

🔲 ⁽ᵖⁱ⁾ **P** VISA ⓜⓞ AE

Forward Green, Northwest : 1 m. by A1120 on Broad Green rd ⊠ IP14 5HU
– 𝒞 (01449) 711 286 – www.baysfarmsuffolk.co.uk – info@baysfarmsuffolk.co.uk

3 rm ⌷ – ♦£75 ♦♦£85

♦ 17C former farmhouse in 4 acres of lawned gardens. Comfortable bedrooms with a
country feel, 2 with garden views. Traditional, wood-filled guest areas. Breakfast
outside in summer.

EARSHAM – **Norfolk** – **504** Y 26 – **see Bungay**

ENGLAND

EASINGWOLD – North Yorkshire – 502 Q 21 – pop. 3 975 – ⊠ York 23 **C2**

🚗 London 217 mi – Leeds 38 mi – Middlesbrough 37 mi – York 14 mi
ℹ️ Chapel Lane ℰ (01347) 821530
⛳ Stillington Rd, ℰ (01347) 821 486

⌂ **Old Vicarage** without rest 🍽 ⚙ 📶 **P**
Market Pl ⊠ YO61 3AL – ℰ (01347) 821015
– www.oldvicarage-easingwold.co.uk – info@oldvicarage-easingwold.co.uk
– Fax (01347) 823465 – Closed December and January
4 rm ⊇ – ♦£75 ♦♦£95
♦ Spacious, part Georgian country house with walled rose garden and adjacent croquet lawn. Immaculately kept throughout with fine period antiques in the elegant sitting room.

at Crayke East : 2 m. on Helmsley Rd – ⊠ York

🍺 **The Durham Ox** with rm 🍽 ⚙ **P** VISA ⓜ AE
Westway ⊠ YO61 4TE – ℰ (01347) 821 506 – www.thedurhamox.com
– enquiries@thedurhamox.com – Fax (01347) 823 326 – Closed 25 December
4 rm ⊇ – ♦£60 ♦♦£120 **Rest** – (booking essential) Carte £ 16/26
♦ Open fires, finest English oak bar panelling and exposed beams create a great country pub atmosphere. Hearty dishes from local ingredients. Well-kept rooms.

EAST ALLINGTON 2 **C3**

🚗 London 210 mi – Plymouth 24 mi – Torbay 18 mi – Exeter 38 mi

🍺 **Fortescue Arms** with rm 🍽 🍽 **P** VISA ⓜ
⊠ TQ9 7RA – ℰ (01548) 521 215 – www.fortescue-arms.co.uk
– info@fortescue-arms.co.uk
3 rm ⊇ – ♦£40 ♦♦£60 **Rest** – (Closed Monday lunch) Carte £ 25/30
♦ Ivy-clad pub with decked terrace, set in rural village. Beamed bar serves rustic pub dishes and warm organic bread, while focus is on more refined dishes in smart dining room. Simple bedrooms.

EASTBOURNE – East Sussex – 504 U 31 – pop. 106 562 ▌*Great Britain* 8 **B3**

🚗 London 68 mi – Brighton 25 mi – Dover 61 mi – Maidstone 49 mi
ℹ️ Cornfield Rd ℰ (01323) 415450, tic@eastbourne.gov.uk
⛳ Royal Eastbourne Paradise Drive, ℰ (01323) 729 738
⛳ Eastbourne Downs East Dean Rd, ℰ (01323) 720 827
⛳ Eastbourne Golfing Park Lottbridge Drove, ℰ (01323) 520 400
◎ Seafront★
◎ Beachy Head★★★, SW : 3 m. by B 2103 Z

Plan opposite

🏨 **Grand** ⇐ 🍽 🏊 📺 🛎 🅛 🍽 & rm, ⚙ AC rest, 🕿 🎫 **P** VISA ⓜ AE ①
King Edward's Parade ⊠ BN21 4EQ – ℰ (01323) 412345
– www.grandeastbourne.com – reservations@grandeastbourne.co.uk
– Fax (01323) 412 233
Z**x**
131 rm ⊇ – ♦£160/505 ♦♦£190/535 – 21 suites
Rest *Mirabelle* – see restaurant listing
Rest *Garden Restaurant* – Menu £ 19/35 **s** – Carte £ 38/57 **s**
♦ Huge, pillared lobby with ornate plasterwork sets the tone of this opulently refurbished, Victorian hotel in prime seafront location. High levels of comfort throughout. Garden Restaurant exudes a light, comfy atmosphere.

🏨 **Lansdowne** ⇐ 🛎 & rm, 🍽 🎫 🔒 VISA ⓜ AE ①
King Edward's Parade ⊠ BN21 4EE – ℰ (01323) 725 174
– www.bw-lansdownehotel.co.uk – reception@lansdowne-hotel.co.uk
– Fax (01323) 739 721 – Closed 2-13 January
Z**z**
102 rm ⊇ – ♦£53/80 ♦♦£99/151
Rest – (bar lunch Monday-Saturday) Menu £ 24 – Carte £ 23/27
♦ Traditional seaside hotel in the same family since 1912. Bedrooms are a mix of décor, either traditional or modern, some with sea views. Dining room has classic feel.

ENGLAND

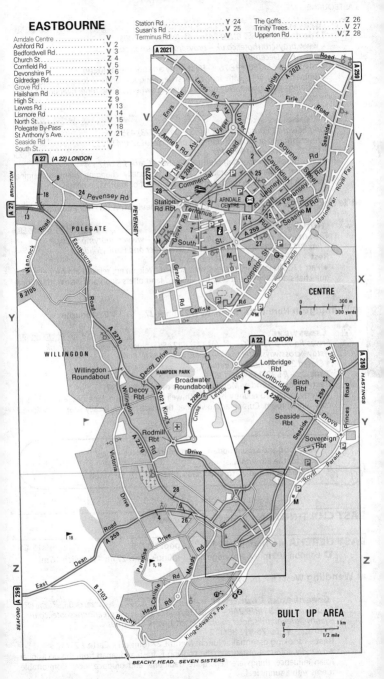

EASTBOURNE

CENTRE

0   300 m
0   300 yards

BUILT UP AREA

0   1 km
0   1/2 mile

BEACHY HEAD, SEVEN SISTERS

269

Brayscroft

🏠 🍴

⚽ 📶 VISA ⓪ AE

13 South Cliff Ave ⊠ BN20 7AH – ℰ (01323) 647005
– www.brayscrofthotel.co.uk – brayscroft@hotmail.com
– Closed 25 December

Zn

6 rm ⊒ – ♦£38/50 ♦♦£76   **Rest** – (by arrangement) Menu £15
♦ Immaculately kept with individual style, antiques, original local art and comfy furnishings throughout. Well run by charming owners. Dining room overlooks a smart terrace.

Mirabelle – at Grand Hotel

🍴🍴🍴🍴

AC P VISA ⓪ AE ⓪

King Edward's Parade ⊠ BN21 4EQ – ℰ (01323) 435066
– reservations@grandeastbourne.co.uk – Fax (01323) 412233
– Closed Sunday and Monday

Zx

Rest – (booking essential) Menu £22/38 **s** – Carte £51/62 **s** 🈴
♦ Elegant, comfortable restaurant with a seasonally changing menu of original dishes. A bar lounge in the basement and wine list of impressive names.

at Jevington Northwest : 6 m. by A 259 - Z - on Jevington Rd – ⊠ Polegate

Hungry Monk

🍴🍴

AC ⇦ P VISA ⓪ AE

The Street ⊠ BN26 5QF – ℰ (01323) 482178 – www.hungrymonk.co.uk
– Fax (01323) 483989 – Closed 24-25 December and Bank Holidays
Rest – (booking essential) Menu £31/34
♦ Part 17C Elizabethan cottages with garden. Welcoming, relaxed atmosphere; antique chairs and log fires add to the charm. Menu offers good and hearty, traditional fare.

at Wilmington Northwest : 6½ m. by A 22 on A 27 - Y – ⊠ Eastbourne

Crossways

🏠

🚗 ⚽ 📶 P VISA ⓪ AE

Lewes Rd ⊠ BN26 5SG – ℰ (01323) 482455 – www.crosswayshotel.co.uk
– stay@crosswayshotel.co.uk – Fax (01323) 487811
– Closed 23 December-23 January
7 rm ⊒ – ♦£72/115 ♦♦£135
Rest – (closed Sunday-Monday) (dinner only) Menu £37
♦ Pretty, detached country house with well tended garden. Linen covered tables in cosy dining room. Cuisine acknowledges the classics with locally sourced, seasonal dishes.

Good food and accommodation at moderate prices?
Look for the Bib symbols:
red Bib Gourmand 🈴 for food, blue Bib Hotel 🍴🏠 for hotels

EAST CHILTINGTON – E. Sussex – see Lewes

EAST DEREHAM – Norfolk – 504 W 25 – pop. 17 779   15 C1
🖪 London 109 mi – Cambridge 57 mi – King's Lynn 27 mi – Norwich 16 mi

at Wendling West : 5½ m. by A 47

Greenbanks Country H. with rm

🍴

🚗 🐾 📺 ⌂ ♿ rm, P VISA ⓪

Swaffham Rd ⊠ NR19 2AB – ℰ (01362) 687742 – www.greenbankshotel.co.uk
– jenny@greenbanks.hotel.co.uk – Closed 1 week Christmas
9 rm ⊒ – ♦£60/75 ♦♦£86/112
Rest – (booking essential at lunch) Menu £27 (dinner) – Carte £21/32 **s**
♦ Friendly, informal restaurant. The cooking is fresh and, apart from the occasional Asian influence, things are kept quite traditional and produce local. Comfortable rooms with a sunny feel.

ENGLAND

EASTGATE – Durham – **502** N 19

▶ London 288 mi – Bishop Auckland 20 mi – Newcastle upon Tyne 35 mi
– Stanhope 3 mi

Horsley Hall ⌂
Southeast : 1 m. by A 689 ⊠ DL13 2LJ – 🖉 *(01388) 517239
– www.horsleyhall.co.uk – info@horsleyhall.co.uk – Fax (01388) 517608*
7 rm ⌂ – ♦£70/85 ♦♦£130/140
Rest – (closed Sunday dinner to non-residents) (booking essential for
non-residents) (lunch by arrangement) Menu £15/25 – Carte £24/33
♦ Ivy-clad 17C former shooting lodge, built for Bishop of Durham, in exquisitely
tranquil setting. Country house style lounge. Spacious bedrooms with telling extra
touches. Baronial style dining room with ornate ceiling: homecooked local produce.

EAST GRINSTEAD – West Sussex – **504** T 30 – pop. 26 222

▶ London 48 mi – Brighton 30 mi – Eastbourne 32 mi – Lewes 21 mi
– Maidstone 37 mi
🏠 Copthorne Borers Arm Rd, 🖉 (01342) 712 508

Gravetye Manor ⌂
*Vowels Lane, Southwest 4½m.by B2110 taking second turn left towards West
Hoathly ⊠ RH19 4LJ –* 🖉 *(01342) 810 567 – www.gravetyemanor.co.uk
– info@gravetyemanor.co.uk – Fax (01342) 810 080*
18 rm – ♦£115/345 ♦♦£175/345, ⌂ £20
Rest – (closed dinner 25 December to non-residents) (booking essential)
Menu £25 – Carte £25/52 s ⌘
♦ Beautiful 16C manor house featuring polished oak, fine English fabrics, antiques
and charming log fires. Beautiful grounds house gazebo for al fresco dining.
Luxurious bedrooms, some with fine views. Classically based cooking; professional
service.

Felbridge H & Spa
London Rd, West 2m. on A264 ⊠ RH19 2BH – 🖉 *(01342) 337 700
– www.felbridgehotel.co.uk – info@felbridgehotel.co.uk – Fax (01342) 337 715*
120 rm – ♦£160 ♦♦£220
Rest *Anise* – Menu £35
Rest *Bay Tree* – Carte £22/34
♦ Semi-circular shaped hotel recently transformed. Now a smart, contemporary corporate hotel with a number of lounges. The better bedrooms look out over the
gardens. Compact Anise for "fine dining". Bay Tree is the main hotel dining room.

EAST HOATHLY – East Sussex – **504** U 31

▶ London 60 mi – Brighton 16 mi – Eastbourne 13 mi – Hastings 25 mi
– Maidstone 32 mi

Old Whyly ⌂
*London Rd, West :½ m., turning right after post box on right, taking centre
gravel drive after approx. 400 metres ⊠ BN8 6EL –* 🖉 *(01825) 840 216
– www.oldwhyly.co.uk – stay@oldwhyly.co.uk – Fax (01825) 840 738*
3 rm ⌂ – ♦£70/85 ♦♦£90/140
Rest – (by arrangement, communal dining) Menu £30
♦ Charming, secluded Georgian manor house decorated with antiques, oils and watercolours. Airy bedrooms individually styled. Delightful owner. Warm, informal dining room.

EAST LAVANT – W. Sussex – see Chichester

EASTON – Devon – **503** I 31 – see Chagford

EASTON – Hants. – see Winchester

EASTON – Somerset – see Wells

ENGLAND

EAST WITTON – North Yorkshire – 502 O 21 – ⊠ Leyburn 22 **B1**
▣ London 238 mi – Leeds 45 mi – Middlesbrough 30 mi – York 39 mi

⌂ **The Blue Lion** with rm 🛋 🕮 **P** **VISA** ⬤⬤
⊠ DL8 4SN – ✆ (01969) 624 273 – www.thebluelion.co.uk
– bluelion@breathe.net – Fax (01969) 624 189
15 rm ⬛ – ✝£68 ✝✝£120/135
Rest – (closed 25 December and Sunday lunch) (booking essential)
Carte £ 21/35
♦ Charming, characterful countryside pub. Daily-changing menu features a tasty mix of classic and modern dishes, all with seasonality and traceability at their core. Bedrooms – in the pub and outbuildings – are warm and cosy.

ECCLESTON – Lancashire – 502 L 23 – pop. 4 708 20 **A2**
▣ London 219 mi – Birmingham 103 mi – Liverpool 29 mi – Preston 11 mi

⌂ **Parr Hall Farm** without rest 🛋 🌿 📶 **P** **VISA** ⬤⬤
Parr Lane ⊠ PR7 5SL – ✆ (01257) 451 917 – www.parrhallfarm.com
– enquiries@parrhallfarm.com – Fax (01257) 453 749
10 rm ⬛ – ✝£40 ✝✝£70
♦ Part 18C former farmhouse with neat lawned gardens in small, pleasant town. Bedrooms all in a converted barn; decorated with matching pine furniture and good bathrooms.

EDENBRIDGE – Kent – 504 U 30 – pop. 7 123 ▌ Great Britain 8 **A2**
▣ London 35 mi – Brighton 36 mi – Maidstone 29 mi
🏌 The Kent & Surrey G & C.C. Crouch House Rd, ✆ (01732) 867 381
🆉 Hever Castle ★ AC, E : 2½ m. – Chartwell ★ AC, N : 3 m. by B 2026

✗ **Haxted Mill** 🛋 🕮 **P** **VISA** ⬤⬤
Haxted Rd, West : 2¼ m. on Haxted Rd ⊠ TN8 6PU – ✆ (01732) 862 914
– www.haxtedmill.co.uk – david@haxtedmill.co.uk – Closed 3 weeks
from 23 December, Tuesday following Bank Holidays, Sunday dinner and Monday
Rest – Menu £ 23/28 – Carte £ 26/41
♦ Converted 17C clapboard stables located next to the watermill with large terrace overlooking the river Eden. Seasonally changing menu with emphasis on seafood in the summer.

EGHAM – Surrey – 504 S 29 – pop. 27 666 7 **C1**
▣ London 29 mi – Reading 21 mi

⌂⌂⌂ **Great Fosters** ⬤ 🌀 ✗ 🌿 📶 ♨ **P** **VISA** ⬤⬤ **AE** **⓪**
Stroude Rd, South : 1¼ m. by B 388 ⊠ TW20 9UR – ✆ (01784) 433 822
– www.greatfosters.co.uk – enquiries@greatfosters.co.uk – Fax (01784) 472 455
41 rm – ✝£125/170 ✝✝£165, ⬛ £19 – 3 suites
Rest – (closed Saturday lunch) Menu £ 25/37 – Carte £ 41/50
♦ Elizabethan mansion with magnificent gardens. Delightfully original interior has tapestries, oak panelling and antiques. Bedrooms in the main house especially notable. Two historic dining rooms: one an ancient tithe barn, the other in 16C French style.

✗✗ **Monsoon** **AC** **VISA** ⬤⬤ **AE**
20 High St ⊠ TW20 9DT – ✆ (01784) 432 141 – www.monsoonrestaurant.co.uk
– Fax (01784) 432 194
Rest – Indian – Menu £ 15 – Carte £ 16/25
♦ Smart, stylish restaurant that prides itself on immaculate upkeep and personable service. Contemporary artwork enlivens the walls. Freshly cooked, authentic Indian dishes.

ELDERSFIELD – Worcestershire – see Tewkesbury

ELLAND – West Yorkshire – **502** O 22 – **pop. 14 554** – ✉ **Halifax**   22 **B3**
- 🚗 London 204 mi – Bradford 12 mi – Burnley 29 mi – Leeds 17 mi – Manchester 30 mi
- 🏌 Hullen Edge Hammerstones Leach Lane, ℰ (01422) 372 505

✗ **La Cachette**   AC VISA ◉◉
31 Huddersfield Rd ✉ HX5 9AW – ℰ (01422) 378 833
– www.lacachette-elland.com – Fax (01422) 327 567
– Closed 2 weeks August, 1 week January, Sunday and most Bank Holidays
Rest – Menu £ 20 (dinner) – Carte £ 21/32
♦ A busy, bustling brasserie-style restaurant with sprinkling of French panache. Menu of eclectically blended interpretations served in the dining room or well-stocked wine bar.

ELSLACK – North Yorkshire – **see SKIPTON**

ELSTED – W. Sussex – **504** R 31 – **see Midhurst**

ELSTOW – Beds. – **504** S 27 – **see Bedford**

ELTISLEY – Cambridgeshire – **504** T 27   14 **A3**
- 🚗 London 63 mi – Luton 36 mi – Peterborough 32 mi – Cambridge 15 mi

🏠 **The Eltisley**   🛋 ⚘ P VISA ◉◉
2 The Green ✉ PE19 6TG – ℰ (01480) 880 308 – www.theeltisley.co.uk
– theeltisley@btconnect.com
Rest – (Closed Monday (except Bank Holiday Monday) and Sunday dinner) Carte £ 20/30
♦ Chic and stylish gastropub beside a village green. Simple, unfussy cooking relies on quality, local produce to speak for itself; everything from starters to desserts is homemade.

ELTON – Cambridgeshire – **504** S 26   14 **A2**
- 🚗 London 84 mi – Peterborough 11 mi – Bedford 40 mi – Kettering 24 mi

🏠 **The Crown Inn** with rm   🛋 P VISA ◉◉ AE
8 Duck St ✉ PE8 6RQ – ℰ (01832) 280 232 – www.thecrowninn.org
– inncrown@googlemail.com – Closed 10 days from 1 January
4 rm ⚏ – †£ 60 ††£ 90
Rest – (Closed Sunday dinner, Monday except Bank Holiday Mondays when closed Tuesday) Carte £ 20/33
♦ 17C thatched inn with a conservatory, terrace and plenty of character. Cooking is traditional and generous, with a touch of Italian influence; lunch sees lighter dishes. Smart, individually-styled bedrooms with spacious bathrooms.

ELY – Cambridgeshire – **504** U 26 – **pop. 13 954** ▌ *Great Britain*   14 **B2**
- 🚗 London 74 mi – Cambridge 16 mi – Norwich 60 mi
- 🅸 Oliver Cromwell's House, 29 St Mary's St ℰ (01353) 662062, tic@eastcambs.gov.uk
- 🏌 107 Cambridge Rd, ℰ (01353) 662 751
- ◎ Cathedral★★ AC
- ◉ Wicken Fen★, SE : 9 m. by A 10 and A 1123

✗ **The Boathouse**   ⬉ 🛋 AC VISA ◉◉
5-5A Annesdale ✉ CB7 4BN – ℰ (01353) 664 388 – www.cambscuisine.com
– boathouse@cambscuisine.com – Fax (01353) 666 688
Rest – (booking essential) Menu £ 15 (lunch excluding Sunday) – Carte £ 22/30
♦ A riverside setting makes for a charming ambience: bag a terrace table if you can. Airy, dark wood interior where worldwide menus benefit from numerous creative touches.

at Little Thetford South : 2 ¾ m. off A 10 – ⊠ Ely

⌂ **Springfields** without rest ⚄ ⚙ 🛜 **P**
Ely Road, North : ½ m. on A 10 ⊠ CB6 3HJ – ℰ (01353) 663637
– www.baileysatspringfields.co.uk – springfields@talk21.com – Fax (01353)
663130 – Closed 2 weeks Christmas and New Year
3 rm ⌷ – †£60 ††£75
♦ Spotlessly kept guesthouse and gardens. Breakfast served at communal table.
Chintz bedrooms with bric-a-brac and extras such as perfume, fresh flowers and
sweets.

at Sutton Gault West : 8 m. by A 142 off B 1381 – ⊠ Ely

⌂ **The Anchor Inn** with rm ⚙ **P** **VISA** **◍◍** **AE**
⊠ CB6 2BD – ℰ (01353) 778537 – www.anchor-inn-restaurant.co.uk
– anchorinn@popmail.bta.com – Fax (01353) 776180
4 rm ⌷ – †£60 ††£130/155   **Rest** – Menu £16 (lunch) – Carte £20/30
♦ Part 17C inn on the western edge of the Isle of Ely, enhanced by open fires.
Balanced à la carte menu of traditional British food from the blackboard. Comfortable
bedrooms.

EMSWORTH – Hampshire – 504 R 31 – pop. 18 310   6 **B2**
🚩 London 75 mi – Brighton 37 mi – Portsmouth 10 mi – Southampton 22 mi

XXX **36 on the Quay** (Ramon Farthing) with rm ⟵ **VISA** **◍◍** **◍**
✿ 47 South St, The Quay ⊠ PO10 7EG – ℰ (01243) 375592
– www.36onthequay.co.uk – 36@onthequay.plus.com – Closed first 3 weeks
January, 1 week October, 1 week Christmas
4 rm – †£70/90 ††£95/110 – 1 suite
Rest – (closed Sunday-Monday) (booking essential) Menu £26/47
Spec. Quail with parsnip cream and honey madeira reduction. Lamb with
courgettes, confit tomato and Dauphinoise potatoes. Iced peanut parfait with
butterscotch doughnuts and coffee foam.
♦ A delightful quayside restaurant with smart, slinky cream and brown interior and
comfortable, contemporary bedrooms; Vanilla is the most luxurious, with the best
view. Well presented, flavourful international dishes. Informal, friendly service.

X **Fat Olives** **VISA** **◍◍**
30 South St ⊠ PO10 7EH – ℰ (01243) 377914 – www.fatolives.co.uk
– info@fatolives.co.uk – Closed 2 weeks June-July, 2 weeks Christmas, Sunday and
Monday
Rest – (booking essential) Menu £19 (lunch) – Carte £26/38
♦ Small terraced house with a welcoming ambience. Simply decorated with wood
floor and rough plaster walls. Tasty modern British menu and, yes, fat olives are
available!

ENSTONE – Oxfordshire – 503 P 28 – ⊠ Chipping Norton   10 **B1**
🚩 London 73 mi – Birmingham 48 mi – Gloucester 32 mi – Oxford 18 mi

⌂ **Swan Lodge** without rest ⚄ ⚙ **P**
on A 44 ⊠ OX7 4NE – ℰ (01608) 678736 – Fax (01608) 678736
– Closed 25-27 December
3 rm ⌷ – †£55/65 ††£70/85
♦ 18C former coaching inn ideally situated for the Cotswolds. Well kept and furnished with antiques and log fires. Sizeable, comfy, mahogany furnished bedrooms.

EPSOM – Surrey – 504 T 30 – pop. 64 493   7 **D1**
🚩 London 17 mi – Guildford 16 mi
🏙 Longdown Lane South Epsom Downs, ℰ (01372) 721666
🏙 Horton Park G & C.C. Hook Rd, ℰ (020) 8393 8400

Chalk Lane
Chalk Lane, Southwest : ½ m. by A 24 and Woodcote Rd ✉ *KT18 7BB*
– ℰ (01372) 721 179 – www.chalklanehotel.com
– smcgregor@chalklanehotel.com – Fax (01372) 727 878
22 rm ☲ – **†**£95/180 **††**£130/180 **Rest** – Menu £18 (lunch) – Carte £30/43
◆ At the foot of the Epsom Downs and near to the racecourse. Quality furnishings throughout; the neatly kept bedrooms are most comfortable. Smart, modern dining room.

Le Raj
211 Fir Tree Rd, Epsom Downs, Southeast : 2¼ m. by B 289 and B 284 on B 291
✉ *KT17 3LB – ℰ (01737) 371 371 – www.lerajrestaurant.co.uk*
– bookings@lerajrestaurant.co.uk – Fax (01737) 211 903
Rest – Bangladeshi – Menu £30 (lunch) – Carte £26/41
◆ Original, interesting menu makes good use of fresh ingredients and brings a modern style to traditional Bangladeshi cuisine. Smart, vibrant, contemporary interior décor.

ERMINGTON – Devon
2 **C2**
▶ London 216 mi – Plymouth 11 mi – Salcombe 15 mi

Plantation House with rm
Totnes Rd, Southwest : ½ m. on A 3121 ✉ *PL21 9NS – ℰ (01548) 831 100*
– www.plantationhousehotel.co.uk – info@plantationhousehotel.co.uk
9 rm ☲ – **†**£59/79 **††**£130
Rest – (closed Sunday and Monday to non-residents) (dinner only) (booking essential for non-residents) Menu £36
◆ Appealing, converted Georgian rectory with smart gardens and terraced seating area. Personally run. Sound cooking of locally sourced ingredients. Individually styled bedrooms.

ERPINGHAM – Norfolk – 504 X 25
15 **D1**
▶ London 123 mi – Cromer 8 mi – King's Lynn 46 mi – Norwich 16 mi

The Saracen's Head with rm
Wolterton, West : 1½ m. on Itteringham rd ✉ *NR11 7LX – ℰ (01263) 768 909*
– www.saracenshead-norfolk.co.uk – saracenshead@wolterton.freeserve.co.uk
– Fax (01263) 768 993 – Closed 25 December and dinner 26 December
6 rm ☲ – **†**£50 **††**£90
Rest – (booking essential) Menu £10 (lunch) – Carte £24/32
◆ Personally run 19C coaching inn with courtyard and walled garden. Log fires, stone floors and bright en suite rooms. Blackboard menu of unpretentious, country dishes.

ESCRICK – N. Yorks. – 502 Q 22 – see York

ESHER – Surrey – 504 S 29 – pop. 46 599
7 **D1**
▶ London 20 mi – Portsmouth 58 mi
🔘 Thames Ditton & Esher Portsmouth Rd, ℰ (020) 8398 1551
🔘 Moore Place Portsmouth Rd, ℰ (01372) 463 533
🔘 Cranfield Golf at Sandown More Lane, ℰ (01372) 468 093

Plan : see Greater London (South-West) 5

George
104 High St ✉ *KT10 9QJ – ℰ (01372) 471 500 – www.george-esher.com*
– reservations@george-esher.com – Fax (01372) 471 500 – Closed
25-26 December, 1 January, lunch Saturday, lunch Monday and Sunday dinner
Rest – Menu £25/43
◆ Elegant and understated restaurant with added refinement of airy cocktail bar. Immaculately laid tables lend a formal air to modern dishes that change with the seasons.

ENGLAND

ENGLAND

XX Good Earth
AC VISA ⓜⓞ AE

14-18 High St ⊠ KT10 9RT – 𝒸 *(01372) 462 489 – Fax (01372) 460 668
– Closed 23-30 December*

BZ**e**

Rest – Chinese – Menu £ 30/36 – Carte £ 30/60

♦ A large Chinese restaurant with a smart, smooth style in décor and service. Well presented menu with much choice including vegetarian sections.

ESHOTT – Northd. – see Morpeth

EVERSHOT – Dorset – 503 M 31 – ⊠ Dorchester
4 **C3**

D London 149 mi – Bournemouth 39 mi – Dorchester 12 mi – Salisbury 53 mi – Taunton 30 mi – Yeovil 10 mi

🏠🏠 Summer Lodge ⌁
🚗 ⌂ 🔲 🅿 🚽 ♨ ⅃⌂ ℀ ⌖ rm, AC ⌖ P.

9 Fore St ⊠ DT2 0JR – 𝒸 (01935) 482 000

VISA ⓜⓞ AE ⓞ

– www.summerlodgehotel.com – summer@relaischateaux.com – Fax (01935) 482 040

20 rm ⌁ – ♦£ 195/515 ♦♦£ 225/500 – 4 suites

Rest *The Restaurant* – (booking essential to non residents) Menu £ 25
– Carte dinner £ 48/64 ⌂

♦ Part Georgian dower house in quiet village, in the best tradition of stylish, English country hotels. Boasts a range of sleek, smart, up-to-date bedrooms. Elegant restaurant overlooking walled garden; excellent wine list.

🛏 The Acorn Inn with rm
🚗 P. VISA ⓜⓞ AE ⓞ

*28 Fore St ⊠ DT2 0JW – 𝒸 (01935) 83 228 – www.acorn-inn.co.uk
– stay@acorn-inn.co.uk – Fax (01935) 83 707*

10 rm ⌁ – ♦£ 95 ♦♦£ 135/160   **Rest** – Carte £ 25/30

♦ Quintessentially English coaching inn referenced in 'Tess of the d'Urbervilles'. Menu displays traditional pub classics at lunch, with more interest and sophistication in the evening. Traditional English country bedrooms.

Don't confuse X with ❀!
X defines comfort, while stars are awarded for the best cuisine, across all categories of comfort.

EVESHAM – Worcestershire – 503 O 27 – pop. 22 179
19 **C3**

D London 99 mi – Birmingham 30 mi – Cheltenham 16 mi – Coventry 32 mi

i The Almonry, Abbey Gate 𝒸 (01386) 446944

🏠🏠 Wood Norton Hall
🚗 ⌂ ℀ ⌖ rm, ⌂ ⌂⌂ P. VISA ⓜⓞ AE

*Northwest : 2¼ m. on A 4538 ⊠ WR11 4YB – 𝒸 (01386) 425 780
– www.wnhall.co.uk – info@wnhall.co.uk – Fax (01386) 425 781*

44 rm ⌁ – ♦£ 95 ♦♦£ 95 – 1 suite

Rest *Le Duc's* – (booking essential) Carte £ 33/40

♦ Superbly wood-panelled 19C Vale of Evesham country house. Built by a French duke, and once a BBC training centre. Antiques, original fittings and a library. Large, airy rooms. Formal elements define restaurant.

🏠 Evesham
🚗 🔲 ⌂ ⌖ rm, ⌖⌖ P. VISA ⓜⓞ AE ⓞ

*Coopers Lane, off Waterside ⊠ WR11 1DA – 𝒸 (01386) 765 566
– www.eveshamhotel.com – reception@eveshamhotel.com – Fax (01386) 765 443
– Closed 25-26 December*

40 rm ⌁ – ♦£ 73/86 ♦♦£ 117/140

Rest *Cedar* – Carte £ 26/35 **s**

♦ Idiosyncratic family run hotel in a quiet location. Guest families well catered for, with jolly japes at every turn. Individual rooms with cottage décor and eclectic themes. Unconventional menus in keeping with hotel style.

EWEN – Glos. – 503 O 28 – see Cirencester

- ► London 201 mi – Bournemouth 83 mi – Bristol 83 mi – Plymouth 46 mi – Southampton 110 mi
- ✈ Exeter Airport : ℰ (01392) 367433, E : 5 m. by A 30 V
- 🛈 Princesshay Development, Dixs Field ℰ (01392) 665700, evit@exeter.gov.uk
- 🔞 Downes Crediton Hookway, ℰ (01363) 773 025
- ◉ City★★ - Cathedral★★ Z – Royal Albert Memorial Museum★ Y
- ⒢ Killerton★★ **AC**, NE : 7 m. by B 3181 V – Ottery St Mary★ (St Mary's★) E : 12 m. by B 3183 - Y - A 30 and B 3174 – Crediton (Holy Cross Church★), NW : 9 m. by A 377

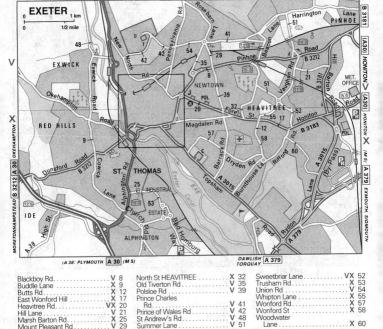

Blackboy Rd.	V 8	North St HEAVITREE	X 32	Sweetbriar Lane	VX 52
Buddle Lane	X 9	Old Tiverton Rd	V 35	Trusham Rd	X 53
Butts Rd	X 12	Polsloe Rd	V 39	Union Rd	V 54
East Wonford Hill	X 17	Prince Charles		Whipton Lane	V 55
Heavitree Rd.	VX 20	Prince of Wales Rd	V 42	Wonford Rd	X 57
Hill Lane	V 21	Prince of Wales Rd	V 42	Wonford St	X 58
Marsh Barton Rd.	X 25	St Andrew's Rd	V 48	Woodwater	
Mount Pleasant Rd	V 29	Summer Lane	V 51	Lane	X 60

Abode Exeter

🗖 📶 🔥 🔠 rest, 🛇 ☏ ⅍ 🆅🅸🆂🅰 ⚫⚫ 🅰🅴 ⓪

The Royal Clarence, Cathedral Yard ⊠ EX1 1HD – ℰ (01392) 319 955
– www.abodehotels.co.uk – info@abodehotels.co.uk – Fax (01392) 439 423   Y**z**
52 rm – ♦£125/145 ♦♦£285, ☑ £13.50 – 1 suite
Rest *Michael Caines* – see restaurant listing

◆ Georgian-style frontage; located on the doorstep of the cathedral. Boutique style hotel with a very modern, stylish interior. Understated bedrooms feature good mod cons.

Barcelona

📶 📶 🎶 ⅍ 🅿 🆅🅸🆂🅰 ⚫⚫ 🅰🅴 ⓪

Magdalen St ⊠ EX2 4HY – ℰ (01392) 281 000 – www.aliashotels.com
– barcelona@aliashotels.com – Fax (01392) 281 001   Z**s**
46 rm – ♦£99/110 ♦♦£115/130, ☑ £12.95
Rest *Café Paradiso* – Menu £15 (lunch) – Carte £24/33

◆ Trendy hotel located in Victorian former infirmary. Informal atmosphere. Two fashionable lounges with contemporary furniture. Autumnal coloured rooms with modern facilities. Informality marks dining room style and menus.

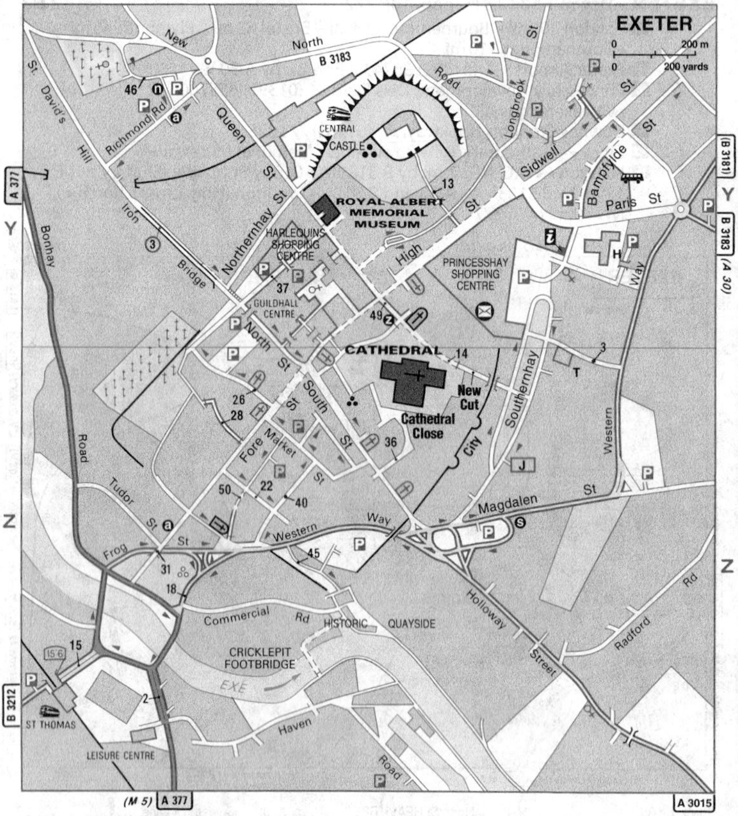

Alphington Rd . . . . Z 2	Harlequins Shopping Centre . . . . Y	Paul St . . . . Y 37
Barnfield Rd . . . . Z 3	High St . . . . Y	Preston St . . . . Z 40
Castle St. . . . . Y 13	King St . . . . Z 22	Princesshay Shopping Centre . . . . Y
Cathedral Close Walk . . . . YZ 14	Mary Arches St . . . . Z 26	Quay Hill . . . . Z 45
Cowick St. . . . . Z 15	Mint (The) . . . . Z 28	Queen's Terrace . . . . Y 46
Edmund St. . . . . Z 18	New Bridge St . . . . Z 31	St Martin's Lane . . . . Y 49
Fore St . . . . Z	Palace Gate . . . . Z 36	Stepcote Hill. . . . . Z 50
Guildhall Shopping Centre . . . . . Y		

The Queens Court

Bystock Terrace ✉ EX4 4HY – ✆ (01392) 272 709 – www.queenscourt-hotel.co.uk – enquiries@queenscourt-hotel.co.uk – Fax (01392) 491 390 – Closed 25-26 December Y**n**

18 rm – †£ 87/97 ††£ 97

Rest *Olive Tree* – (dinner only) (residents only) Menu £ 25 – Carte £ 22/30

♦ A town house hotel located close to Central train station. Bright public areas decorated in a clean, modern style. Well-equipped, tidily furnished and co-ordinated bedrooms. Brightly painted, clean-lined restaurant.

The Edwardian without rest

30-32 Heavitree Rd ✉ EX1 2LQ – ✆ (01392) 276 102 – www.edwardianexeter.co.uk – michael@edwardianexeter.co.uk V**a**

13 rm – †£ 55/65 ††£ 75/105

♦ Personally run hotel with a welcoming ambience. Edwardian themed lounge. Rooms vary between the modern and the traditional and some have four-poster beds.

↑ **Silversprings** without rest ⸱ 📶 **P.** **VISA** **⊙⊙**
12 Richmond Rd ⊠ *EX4 4JA –* ℰ *(01392) 494 040 – www.silversprings.co.uk*
– reservations@silversprings.co.uk – Fax (01392) 494 040
– Closed Christmas to New Year Y**a**
12 rm ⌑ – ♥£55/80 ♥♥£80/120
♦ Cream coloured Georgian terraced house in Roman part of town. Warm and
friendly, with immaculately kept public areas. Varied palettes and cathedral views
distinguish rooms.

↑ **The Grange** without rest ⸱ 🚗 **J** **%** **P.**
Stoke Hill, Northeast : 1 ¾ m. by Old Tiverton Rd ⊠ *EX4 7JH –* ℰ *(01392)*
259 723 – dudleythegrange@aol.com
4 rm ⌑ – ♥£34/38 ♥♥£54/58
♦ Quiet, detached, 1930s country house set in three acres of woodland yet conveniently located for the city. Accommodation is simple and homely.

✗✗ **Michael Caines** – at Abode Exeter Hotel **AC** **VISA** **⊙⊙** **AE** **①**
The Royal Clarence, Cathedral Yard ⊠ *EX1 1HD –* ℰ *(01392) 223 638*
– www.michaelcaines.com – tablesexeter@michaelcaines.com
– Closed Sunday Y**z**
Rest – Menu £15 (lunch) – Carte £40/49
♦ Comfortable, contemporarily stylish restaurant overlooking Cathedral. Menu has
good choice of well-balanced and confident modern British cooking. Pleasant, effi-
cient service.

✗✗ **Angela's** **VISA** **⊙⊙**
38 New Bridge Street ⊠ *EX4 3AH –* ℰ *(01392) 499 038*
– www.angelasrestaurant.co.uk – richardvalder@hotmail.com – Closed 1 week
spring, 1 week winter, Tuesday lunch, Sunday dinner and Monday Z**a**
Rest – Menu £16 (lunch) – Carte £28/37
♦ Neighbourhood restaurant with welcoming feel. Plain décor with oils and prints;
large well spaced tables. Extensive menu of local, seasonal fare; plenty of meat, fish
and vegetarian choices.

at Rockbeare East : 7 1/2 m. by A 30 - V – ⊠ Exeter

🍴 **Jack in the Green Inn** 🚗 🏠 **AC** **%** **P.** **VISA** **⊙⊙**
London Rd ⊠ *EX5 2EE –* ℰ *(01404) 822 240 – www.jackinthegreen.uk.com*
– info@jackinthegreen.uk.com – Fax (01404) 823 540
– Closed 25 December-6 January
Rest – Menu £25 – Carte £30/40
♦ Characterful pub near Exeter airport, with leather-furnished lounge and beamed
dining rooms. Unfussy, seasonal dishes, with good use of local ingredients. Friendly
service.

at Kenton Southeast : 7 m. by A 3015 - X - on A 379 – ⊠ Exeter

✗✗ **Rodean** **VISA** **⊙⊙**
The Triangle ⊠ *EX6 8LS –* ℰ *(01626) 890 195 – www.rodeanrestaurant.co.uk*
– excellence@rodeanrestaurant.co.uk – Closed 1 week January, 2 weeks Autumn,
Sunday dinner and Monday
Rest – (dinner only and Sunday lunch) Carte £28/37
♦ Family run early 20C butchers shop in pretty spot. Bar area for pre-prandials.
Restaurant in two rooms with beams and local photos. Menus employ good use of
local ingredients.

EXFORD – Somerset – **503** J 30 3 **A2**
🄳 London 193 mi – Exeter 41 mi – Minehead 14 mi – Taunton 33 mi
🄲 Church★
🄶 Exmoor National Park★★

🏨 **The Crown** 🚗 🔧 📶 **P.** **VISA** **⊙⊙**
⊠ *TA24 7PP –* ℰ *(01643) 831 554 – www.crownhotelexmoor.co.uk*
– info@crownhotelexmoor.co.uk – Fax (01643) 831 665
17 rm ⌑ – ♥£70/90 ♥♥£140 **Rest** – (bar lunch) Carte £21/38
♦ Pretty 17C coaching inn with a delightful rear water garden. Open fires and country
prints. Comfy, individualistic rooms, some retaining period features.

ENGLAND

EXMOUTH – Devon – 503 J 32 – pop. 32 972   2 **D2**

> ▶ London 210 mi – Exeter 11 mi
> ℹ️ Alexandra Terr 𝒞 (01395) 222299, info@exmouthtourism.co.uk
> ◉ A la Ronde★ **AC**, N : 2 m. by B 3180

🏠 **The Barn** without rest ॐ   ≤ ⌂ ℤ ⁒ **P** 𝘝𝘐𝘚𝘈 ⓐⓔ
Foxholes Hill, East : 1 m. via Esplanade and Queens Drive ⊠ EX8 2DF
– 𝒞 (01395) 224411 – www.barnhotel.co.uk – info@barnhotel.co.uk
– Fax (01395) 225445 – Closed 22 December - 8 January
11 rm � – ♦£35/70 ♦♦£88/104
♦ Grade II listed Arts and Crafts house in a peacefully elevated position offering sea views from many bedrooms. Personal and friendly service.

EXTON – Devon   2 **D2**

> ▶ London 176 mi – Exmouth 4 mi – Topsham 3 mi

🍽 **The Puffing Billy**   ⌂ **AC** ⁒ **P** 𝘝𝘐𝘚𝘈 ⓐⓔ
Station Rd ⊠ EX3 0PR – 𝒞 (01392) 877888 – www.eatoutdevon.com
– Closed 8 days from Christmas to New Year
Rest – Carte £ 19/32
♦ Modernised pub with barn-like extension. Relaxed ambience: comfy leather seating in lounge bar. Menus designed to please all, from informal favourites to fine dining.

> We try to be as accurate as possible when giving room rates but prices are susceptible to change.
> Please check rates when booking.

FADMOOR – N. Yorks. – see Kirkbymoorside

FAIRFORD – Gloucestershire – 503 O 28 – pop. 2 960 ▌ *Great Britain*   4 **D1**

> ▶ London 88 mi – Cirencester 9 mi – Oxford 29 mi
> ◉ Church of St Mary★ (Stained glass windows★★)
> ◉ Cirencester - Church of St John the Baptist★ - Corinium Museum★ (Mosaic Pavements★), W : 9 m. on A 429, A 435, Spitalgate Lane and Dollar St – Swindon - Great Railway Museum★ **AC** - Railway Village Museum★ **AC**, S : 17 m. on A 419, A 4312, A 4259 and B 4289

🍽🍽🍽 **Allium**   𝘝𝘐𝘚𝘈 ⓐⓔ
1 London St, Market Pl ⊠ GL7 4AH – 𝒞 (01285) 712200 – www.allium.uk.net
– restaurant@allium.uk.net – Closed 2 weeks Christmas, 2 weeks August, Sunday dinner, Monday and Tuesday
Rest – Menu £ 20/39
♦ Pair of Cotswold stone cottages on a main road. Squashy sofas in lounge and bar. Food's a serious matter here: modern dishes are prepared with skill and care. Personally run.

FALMOUTH – Cornwall – 503 E 33 – pop. 21 635   1 **A3**

> ▶ London 308 mi – Penzance 26 mi – Plymouth 65 mi – Truro 11 mi
> ℹ️ 11 Market Strand, Prince of Wales Pier 𝒞 (01326) 312300, falmouthtic@yahoo.co.uk
> 🏌 Swanpool Rd, 𝒞 (01326) 311 262
> 🏌 Budock Vean Hotel Mawnan Smith, 𝒞 (01326) 252 102
> ◉ Town★ – Pendennis Castle★ (≤★★) **AC** B
> ◉ Glendurgan Garden★★ **AC** - Trebah Garden★, SW : 4½ m. by Swanpool Rd A – Mawnan Parish Church★ (≤★★) S : 4 m. by Swanpool Rd A – Cruise along Helford River★. Trelissick★★ (≤★★) NW : 13 m. by A 39 and B 3289 A – Carn Brea (≤★★) NW : 10 m. by A 393 A – Gweek (Setting★, Seal Sanctuary★) SW : 8 m. by A 39 and Treverva rd – Wendron (Poldark Mine★) **AC**, SW : 12½ m. by A 39 - A - and A 394

Plan opposite

ENGLAND

FALMOUTH

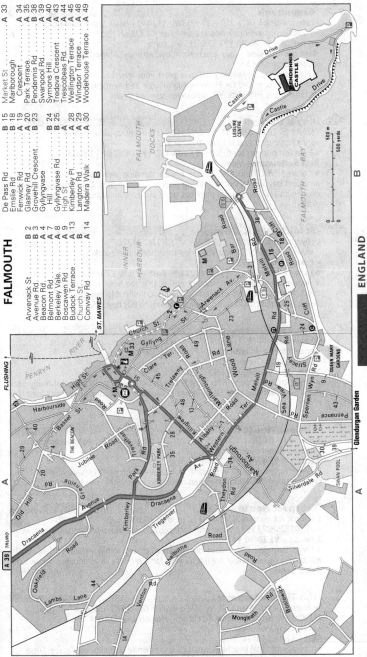

ENGLAND

Greenbank

Harbourside ⊠ *TR11 2SR –* ℰ *(01326) 312 440 – www.greenbank-hotel.co.uk*
– reception@greenbank-hotel.co.uk – Fax (01326) 211 362 **Aa**
58 rm ⊃ – †£70/80 ††£175/215 – 1 suite
Rest *Harbourside* – (bar lunch Monday-Saturday) Menu £17 (lunch)
– Carte approx. £33
• Flagstones and sweeping staircase greet your arrival in this ex-17C coaching inn,
just as they once did for Florence Nightingale and Kenneth Grahame. Rooms with
harbour views. Fine vista of bay from modern restaurant.

Royal Duchy

Cliff Rd ⊠ *TR11 4NX –* ℰ *(01326) 313 042 – www.royalduchy.com*
– info@royalduchy.com – Fax (01326) 319 420 **Ba**
42 rm (dinner included) ⊃ – †£108/135 ††£140/240 – 1 suite
Rest – Menu £35
• Located on clifftop next to beach with stunning views of Pendennis Castle on
headland beyond. Indoor swimming pool and leisure area. Comfortable bedrooms,
many with sea views. Restaurant has good choice menus promoting local, seasonal
dishes.

St Michael's H & Spa

Gyllyngvase Beach ⊠ *TR11 4NB –* ℰ *(01326) 312 707*
– www.stmichaelshotel.co.uk – info@stmichaelshotel.co.uk
– Fax (01326) 211 772 **Bc**
61 rm ⊃ – †£65/107 ††£130/214   **Rest** – Carte £24/35 **s**
• Reinvestment and refurbishment ensure that the hotel remains fresh, bright and
contemporary. Nautical theme throughout. Comfortable bedrooms, many with sea
views. Restaurant looks down sloping gardens to bay beyond.

Dolvean House without rest

50 Melvill Rd ⊠ *TR11 4DQ –* ℰ *(01326) 313 658 – www.dolvean.co.uk*
– reservations@dolvean.co.uk – Fax (01326) 313 995
– Closed 24-26 December **Bn**
10 rm ⊃ – †£35/60 ††£90
• Smart cream property with local books and guides in parlour: exceptionally good
detail wherever you look. Elegant, neatly laid breakfast room. Bright, well-kept bedrooms.

Chelsea House without rest

2 Emslie Rd ⊠ *TR11 4BG –* ℰ *(01326) 212 230 – www.chelseahousehotel.com*
– info@chelseahousehotel.com **Be**
8 rm ⊃ – †£42/47 ††£78/90
• Large Victorian house in quiet residential area with partial sea-view at front. Neat
breakfast room; well-appointed bedrooms, three with their own balconies.

Prospect House without rest

1 Church Rd, Penryn, Northwest : 2 m. by A 39 on B 3292 ⊠ *TR10 8DA*
– ℰ *(01326) 373 198 – www.prospecthouse.co.uk – stay@prospecthouse.co.uk*
3 rm ⊃ – †£28/40 ††£70
• Large Georgian guesthouse on Penryn river, set within walled garden, run by
welcoming owner. Super breakfasts with local produce in abundance. Individually
styled rooms.

✗ The Three Mackerel

Swanpool Beach, South : ¾ m. off Pennance Rd ⊠ *TR11 5BG –* ℰ *(01326)*
311 886 – www.thethreemackerel.com – Fax (01326) 316 014
– Closed 25 December **An**
Rest – Carte £18/31
• Casually informal beachside restaurant with white clapperboard façade. Super ter-
race or light interior. Seasonal, local ingredients provide the core of modern menus.

✗ **Bistro de la Mer**   VISA ⓜⓞ AE ①
28 Arwenack St – ℰ (01326) 316 509 – www.bistrodelamer.com
– bistrodelamer@aol.com – Closed 2 weeks early November, 1 week March,
25-26 December, 1 January, Sunday and Monday except dinner May-October   B**r**
Rest – Menu £16 (lunch) – Carte £25/38
♦ Modest bistro with a subtle Mediterranean feel, set over two floors and decorated in sunny seaside colours of yellow and blue. Extensive seafood-oriented menu; honest cooking.

at Mylor Bridge North : 4½ m. by A 39 - A - and B 3292 on Mylor rd
– ✉ Falmouth

🍴 **Pandora Inn**   ≤ 🏠 ⇔ **P** VISA ⓜⓞ AE
Restronguet Creek, Northeast : 1 m. by Passage Hill off Restronguet Hill
✉ *TR11 5ST – ℰ (01326) 372 678 – www.pandorainn.co.uk*
– pandorainn@yahoo.co.uk – Fax (01326) 378 958
Rest – Carte £21/28
♦ A very characterful thatched inn of 13C origins in stunning location next to harbour. Flagstone flooring, low ceilings, exposed beams. Dining room has more formal style.

at Mawnan Smith Southwest : 5 m. by Trescobeas Rd - A - ✉ Falmouth

🏨 **Meudon** ⟡   🚲 🕊 ⁽ᵗⁱ⁾ **P** VISA ⓜⓞ AE ①
East : ½ m. by Carwinion Rd ✉ *TR11 5HT – ℰ (01326) 250 541*
– www.meudon.co.uk – wecare@meudon.co.uk – Fax (01326) 250 543
– Closed January
27 rm ☲ – ♦£86/140 ♦♦£172/280 – 2 suites
Rest – Menu £40 (dinner) **s** – Carte £30/40 **s**
♦ Landscaped sub-tropical gardens are the abiding allure of this elegant hotel. Antiques, oil paintings, log fires and fresh flowers abound. Comfy rooms, many with views. Conservatory restaurant highlighted by fruiting vine.

at Maenporth Beach South : 3¾ m. by Pennance Rd

✗ **The Cove**   ≤ 🏠 AC **P** VISA ⓜⓞ
Maenporth Beach ✉ *TR11 5HN – ℰ (01326) 251 136*
– www.thecovemaenporth.co.uk – info@thecovemaenporth.co.uk
Rest – Carte £24/31
♦ Within a modern building overlooking the beach and cove. Concise menu with daily specials; bright, unfussy cooking, with the occasional Asian note. Young, enthusiastic service.

If breakfast is included the ☲ symbol appears after the number of rooms.

FAREHAM – Hampshire – **503** Q 31 – **pop. 54 866** 📖 *Great Britain*   6 **B2**
　🚗 London 77 mi – Portsmouth 9 mi – Southampton 13 mi – Winchester 19 mi
　🛈 Westbury Manor, 84 West St ℰ (01329) 221342,
　　touristinfo@fareham.gov.uk
　⊙ Portchester castle ★ **AC**, SE : 2½ m. by A 27

✗ **Lauro's brasserie**   AC VISA ⓜⓞ AE
8 High St ✉ *PO16 7AN – ℰ (01329) 234 179 – www.laurosbrasserie.co.uk*
– lauros@laurosbrasserie.co.uk. – Fax (01329) 822 776
– Closed 25 December, 1 January, Sunday dinner and Monday
Rest – Menu £13 (midweek)/26 – Carte £28/36
♦ Picture-window façade; long narrow interior with red hued walls and open-plan kitchen. The unpretentious cooking has influences ranging from the Mediterranean to Japan.

FARNHAM – Dorset – **503** N 31 – see Blandford Forum

ENGLAND

FARNHAM ROYAL – Buckinghamshire – **503** S 29

11 **D3**

▶ London 27 mi – Burnham 2 mi – Windsor 5 mi

The King of Prussia   🛋 😋 ℅ **P.** *VISA* 💳

Blackpond Lane, Northwest : ¾ m. by A 355 off Cherry Tree Rd ✉ *SL2 3EG*
– ℰ (01753) 643 006 – www.thekingofprussia.com – gm@tkop.co.uk
– Closed 25 December and 1 January
Rest – (Closed Sunday dinner) Carte £ 20/35

♦ Youthful pub with bucket chairs, low tables and modern décor. In contrast, cooking
is classical, seasonal and simple. Everything is homemade, with pies being the speciality.

FARNINGHAM – Kent – **504** U 29

8 **B1**

▶ London 22 mi – Dartford 7 mi – Maidstone 20 mi

⌂   **Beesfield Farm** *without rest* 🌿   🛋 ℅ ⁽ᵗ⁾ **P.**

Beesfield Lane, off A 225 ✉ *DA4 0LA – ℰ (01322) 863 900*
– www.beesfieldfarm.co.uk – kim.vingoe@btinternet.com – Fax (01322) 863 900
– Closed 14 December-14 January
3 rm ☷ – †£ 65/70 ††£ 80/90

♦ Peaceful valley setting, with attractive garden. Exudes character: oldest part is
400 year-old Kentish longhouse. Comfy sitting room; bedrooms boast beams and
garden outlook.

FAR SAWREY – Cumbria – **502** L 20 – see Hawkshead

FAVERSHAM – Kent – **504** W 30 – pop. 18 222

9 **C1**

▶ London 52 mi – Dover 26 mi – Maidstone 21 mi – Margate 25 mi
🛈 Fleur de Lis Heritage Centre, 13 Preston St ℰ (01795) 534542,
ticfaversham@btconnect.com

XXX   **Read's** (David Pitchford) *with rm*   🛋 😋 ℅ ⁽ᵗ⁾ **P.** *VISA* 💳 **AE** ①
❀   *Macknade Manor, Canterbury Rd, East : 1 m. on A 2* ✉ *ME13 8XE – ℰ (01795)*
535 344 – www.reads.com – enquiries@reads.com – Fax (01795) 591 200
– Closed 25-26 December, first week January, 2 weeks September,
Sunday and Monday
6 rm ☷ – †£ 125/185 ††£ 165/195
Rest – Menu £ 24/52 🏵

Spec. Cheddar cheese and smoked haddock soufflé. Fillet of beef with foie
gras and red wine jus. Milk chocolate mousse with an orange and hazelnut ice
cream.

♦ Elegant red brick house with beautiful grounds. Confident, classically based dishes
make the best of local produce, including fruit, vegetables and herbs from the walled
garden. Comfortable bedrooms in country house style.

FAWKHAM GREEN – Kent – **504** U 29 – see Brands Hatch

FENCE – Blackburn – **502** N 22 – see Padiham

FERMAIN BAY – **503** L 33 – see Channel Islands (Guernsey)

FERRENSBY – N. Yorks. – see Knaresborough

Undecided between two equivalent establishments?
Within each category, establishments are classified
in our order of preference.

ENGLAND

FINDON – West Sussex – **504** S 31 – pop. 1 720 – ⊠ **Worthing**   7 **C2**
    ◘ London 49 mi – Brighton 13 mi – Southampton 50 mi – Worthing 4 mi

🏠   **Findon Manor**   🛏 🏊 📶 🖧 **P** **VISA** **©©** **AE** **①**
High St, off A 24 ⊠ BN14 0TA – ℰ (01903) 872 733 – www.findonmanor.com
– hotel@findonmanor.com – Fax (01903) 877 473
– Closed Christmas-New Year
11 rm ⌚ – †£80 ††£110/150
Rest – (bar lunch Monday-Saturday) Menu £30 **s**
♦ Flint-built former rectory dating from the 16C. Characterful lounge with heavy
drapes, real fire and flagstones. Spacious, country house bedrooms. Elegant restaurant opening onto secluded gardens.

FLAUNDEN – Hertfordshire – pop. 5 468   12 **A2**
    ◘ London 35 mi – Reading 43 mi – Luton 23 mi – Milton Keynes 42 mi

🍴   **The Bricklayers Arms**   🛏 🏡 **P** **VISA** **©©** **AE**
Hogpits Bottom ⊠ HP3 0PH – ℰ (01442) 833 322 – www.bricklayersarms.com
– goodfood@bricklayersarms.com – Fax (01442) 834 841
Rest – (Closed 25 December) Carte £23/34
♦ Charming 18C pub with slate roof, wooden beams and low ceilings. Spacious main
bar, with country-style prints and exposed brick walls. Emphasis on French classics.

FLETCHING – East Sussex – **504** U 30/31   8 **A2**
    ◘ London 45 mi – Brighton 20 mi – Eastbourne 24 mi – Maidstone 20 mi

🍴   **The Griffin Inn** with rm   🛏 🏡 **P** **VISA** **©©** **AE** **①**
⊠ TN22 3SS – ℰ (01825) 722 890 – www.thegriffininn.co.uk
– info@thegriffininn.co.uk – Fax (01825) 722 810
– Closed 25 December, 1 January dinner
13 rm ⌚ – †£70 ††£110/145
Rest – (meals in bar Sunday dinner) Menu £30 (Sunday lunch) – Carte £21/35
♦ 16C red and white brick pub with terrace and large garden. Daily-changing menu
offers modern British dishes with some Italian influences; produce is locally sourced.
Beamed bedrooms feature four-posters, rushmat flooring and hand-painted murals.

FLITWICK – Bedfordshire – **504** S 27 – pop. 12 700   12 **A1**
    ◘ London 45 mi – Bedford 13 mi – Luton 12 mi – Northampton 28 mi

🏠   **Flitwick Manor** ⌖   ≤ 🛏 🕭 ⚡ **P** **VISA** **©©** **AE** **①**
Church Rd, off Dunstable Rd ⊠ MK45 1AE – ℰ (0871) 472 4016
– www.bookmenzies.com – flitwick@menzies-hotels.co.uk – Fax (01525) 718 753
18 rm – †£125/175 ††£145/195, ⌚ £19   **Rest** – Menu £25/50
♦ Georgian manor house set in 27 acres. Elegant lounge. Individually decorated
rooms: those on ground floor have garden seating areas, others overlook 300-year
old cedar tree. Formal restaurant in Georgian house style.

FOLKESTONE – Kent – **504** X 30 – pop. 45 273 ▌ Great Britain   9 **D2**
    ◘ London 76 mi – Brighton 76 mi – Dover 8 mi – Maidstone 33 mi
    Access Channel Tunnel : Eurotunnel information and reservations ℰ (08705)
353535
    🄸 Harbour St ℰ (01303) 258594, tourism@folkestone.org.uk
    ◙ The Leas★ (≤★) Z

Plan on next page

🏠   **The Relish** without rest   🏊 📶 **VISA** **©©** **AE**
4 Augusta Gardens ⊠ CT20 2RR – ℰ (01303) 850 952 – www.hotelrelish.co.uk
– reservations@hotelrelish.co.uk – Fax (01303) 850 958
– Closed 22 December-2 January, minimum 2 night stay at weekends   **Z n**
10 rm ⌚ – †£65/90 ††£90/140
♦ Large Regency townhouse overlooking private parkland. Stylish black canopy to
entrance; modish furnishings. Handy food and drink area at foot of stairs. Light, airy
rooms.

FOLKESTONE

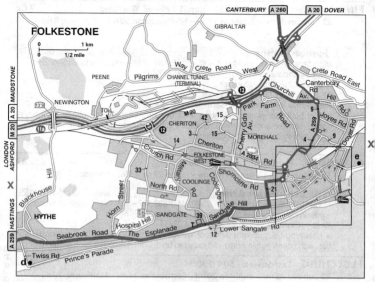

FOLKESTONE

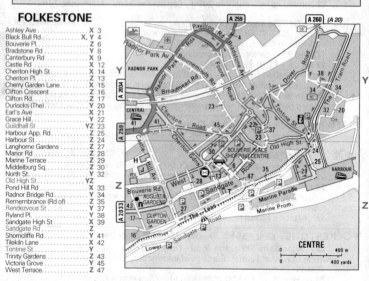

 Look out for red symbols, indicating particularly pleasant establishments.

FORDINGBRIDGE – Hampshire – **503** O 31 – pop. 5 755   6 **A2**

  🛈 London 101 mi – Bournemouth 17 mi – Salisbury 11 mi
    – Southampton 22 mi – Winchester 30 mi
  🛈 Kings Yard, Salisbury St ✆ (01425) 654560,
    fordingbridgetic@tourismse.com

at Stuckton Southeast : 1 m. by B 3078 – ⊠ Fordingbridge

Three Lions with rm
Stuckton Rd ⊠ SP6 2HF – ℰ (01425) 652 489 – www.thethreelionsrestaurant.co.uk
– the3lions@btinternet.com – Fax (01425) 656 144 – Closed last 2 weeks February
4 rm – ♦£69/79 ♦♦£80/125, ☲ £7.75
Rest – (Closed Sunday dinner and Monday) Menu £20 (lunch) – Carte £32/43
♦ Personally run former farmhouse. Impressive blackboard menu includes local produce like wild New Forest mushrooms or venison. Bright, cosy rooms with thoughtful extras.

FOREST – 503 P 33 – see Channel Islands (Guernsey)

FOREST GREEN – Surrey – pop. 1 843 – ⊠ Dorking   7 **D2**
🔹 London 34 mi – Guildford 13 mi – Horsham 10 mi

Parrot Inn
⊠ RH5 5RZ – ℰ (01306) 621 339 – www.the parrot.co.uk
– drinks@the parrot.co.uk – Closed 25 December for food
Rest – (Closed Sunday dinner) Carte £20/28
♦ Characterful 17C pub overlooking a village green. The menu features plenty of meat from the owners' farm, as well as quality, local ingredients; cooking is unfussy and generous.

FOREST ROW – East Sussex – 504 U 30 – pop. 3 623   8 **A2**
🔹 London 35 mi – Brighton 26 mi – Eastbourne 30 mi – Maidstone 32 mi
🔹 Royal Ashdown Forest Forest Row, Chapel Lane, ℰ (01342) 822 018

at Wych Cross South : 2½ m. on A 22 – ⊠ Forest Row

Ashdown Park
East : ¾ m. on Hartfield rd ⊠ RH18 5JR – ℰ (01342) 824 988
– www.ashdownpark.com – reservations@ashdownpark.com – Fax (01342) 826 206
94 rm ☲ – ♦£160 ♦♦£190 – 2 suites
Rest *Anderida* – Menu £24/38 **s** – Carte £50/70
♦ Part 19C manor in landscaped woodland with antiques, real fires. Former convent. Extensive leisure facilities. Immaculate rooms in two wings boast writing desks, armchairs. Ornate ceiling dominates formal restaurant.

FORTON – Staffordshire – 502 M 25 – ⊠ Lancaster ▌ Great Britain   18 **B1**
🔹 London 236 mi – Blackpool 18 mi – Manchester 45 mi
🔹 Lancaster - Castle★, N : 5½ m. by A 6

The Bay Horse Inn with rm
Bay Horse Lane, North : 1¼ m. by A 6 on Quernmore rd ⊠ LA2 0HR – ℰ (01524)
791 204 – www.bayhorseinn.com – bayhorseinfo@aol.com – Fax (01524) 791 204
– Closed 25-26 December, Tuesday after Bank Holiday Monday
3 rm ☲ – ♦£79/89 ♦♦£79/89
Rest – (Closed Sunday dinner and Monday except Bank Holiday Monday)
Menu £20 (lunch) – Carte £17/30
♦ Rurally set inn dating from 18C with open fires, exposed beams and enthusiastic owners. Good selection of real ales. Tasty, well-prepared, home-made dishes.

FOTHERINGHAY Northants – 504 S 26 – see Oundle

FOWEY – Cornwall – 503 G 32 – pop. 2 064   1 **B2**
🔹 London 277 mi – Newquay 24 mi – Plymouth 34 mi – Truro 22 mi
🔹 5 South St ℰ (01726) 833616, info@fowey.co.uk
🔹 Town★★
🔹 Gribbin Head (≤★★) 6 m. rtn on foot – Bodinnick (≤★★) - Lanteglos Church★, E : 5 m. by ferry – Polruan (≤★★) SE : 6 m. by ferry – Polkerris★, W : 2 m. by A 3082

ENGLAND

🛖🛖🛖 Fowey Hall   ≤ 🚗 🛜 ▢ 🚶 🛁 P VISA ⓜ AE
Hanson Drive, West : ½ m. off A 3082 ⊠ *PL23 1ET –* ℰ *(01726) 833 866*
– www.foyehallhotel.co.uk – info@foyehallhotel.co.uk – Fax (01726) 834 100
24 rm (dinner included) ⥬ – **♦**£180/250 **♦♦**£200/275 – 12 suites
Rest – (light lunch Monday-Saturday) Carte approx. £40
♦ Imposing 19C country house within walled garden. Two spacious lounges with real fires, wicker furnished garden room. Smart, plush rooms. Special facilities for children. Impressive oak-panelled restaurant.

🏠 Marina Villa   ≤ 🛜 🚗 VISA ⓜ AE
17 The Esplanade ⊠ *PL23 1HY –* ℰ *(01726) 833 315*
– www.themarinahotel.co.uk – enquiries@themarinahotel.co.uk – Fax (01726)
832 779 – Closed 3 weeks January
17 rm ⥬ – **♦**£100/120 **♦♦**£224/280 – 1 suite
Rest *Nathan Outlaw* – see restaurant listing
♦ Small house in tiny street with splendid views of river and quay. Attractive interior with well-kept lounge, and rooms of varying size with a contemporary, individual feel.

🏠 Old Quay House   ≤ 🛜 🌿 🛜 VISA ⓜ AE
28 Fore St ⊠ *PL23 1AQ –* ℰ *(01726) 833 302 – www.theoldquayhouse.com*
– info@theoldquayhouse.com – Fax (01726) 833 668
11 rm ⥬ – **♦**£100 **♦♦**£130/230
Rest – (Closed lunch midweek in winter) Menu £35 (dinner) – Carte lunch £21/37
♦ Former Victorian seamen's mission idyllically set on the waterfront. Stylish, contemporary lounge. Rear terrace overlooks the river. Smart, individually decorated bedrooms. Spacious restaurant with wicker and wood furniture, serving modern British dishes.

✗✗ Nathan Outlaw – at Marina Villa Hotel   ≤ 🛜 VISA ⓜ AE
❀ *17 The Esplanade* ⊠ *PL23 1HY –* ℰ *(01726) 833 315*
– www.themarinahotel.co.uk – enquiries@themarinahotel.co.uk – Fax (01726)
832 779 – Closed 3 weeks January, Monday in low season and Sunday
Rest – Menu £35 (lunch) – Carte £46/65
Spec. Pigeon with chocolate, cherries and potato cake. Rose veal, with artichoke, sage and broad beans. Lemon curd with poached meringue and yoghurt ice cream.
♦ Restaurant with feel of ship's cabin. Understated menu descriptions belie inherent understanding of first class ingredients. Accomplished cooking; perfectly balanced dishes.

at Golant North : 3 m. by B 3269 – ⊠ *Fowey*

🏠 Cormorant ⌂   ≤ 🚗 🛜 ▢ 🛜 P VISA ⓜ AE
⊠ *PL23 1LL –* ℰ *(01726) 833 426 – www.cormoranthotel.co.uk*
– relax@cormoranthotel.co.uk – Fax (01726) 833 219
14 rm – **♦**£95/150 **♦♦**£125/180
Rest – (Dinner only and Sunday lunch and Wednesday, Friday and Saturday lunch in summer) (booking essential at lunch) Carte £25/43
♦ Stunningly located with wonderful views. All bedrooms have river vista, flatscreen TVs, fridges and large beds; several also have balconies. Comfortable lounge with fireplace. Pretty dining room with balcony terrace. Appealing menus.

FRAMLINGHAM – Suffolk – **504** Y 27 – pop. 2 839 – ⊠ *Woodbridge*   15 **D3**
🅳 London 92 mi – Ipswich 19 mi – Norwich 42 mi

✗ Off the Square   VISA ⓜ AE
3 Church St ⊠ *IP13 9BE –* ℰ *(01728) 621 232 – www.otsframltd.co.uk*
– greatfood@otsframltd.co.uk – Closed Sunday dinner and Monday
Rest – Carte £21/33
♦ Modern, keenly run, brasserie style restaurant with spacious, open plan interior and buzzy, informal atmosphere. Good value, neat cooking with a touch of the Mediterranean.

at Badingham Northeast : 3 ¼ m. by B 1120 on A 1120 – ⊠ Woodbridge

⚏ **Colston Hall** without rest ⚭   🚗 🍸 🕯 P. VISA ⚫◯
Badingham, North : 4 ¼ m. by B 1120 off A 1120 ⊠ IP13 8LB – ℰ (01728)
638 375 – www.colstonhall.com – lizjohn@colstonhall.com – Fax (01728) 638 084
6 rm ⌑ – †£50/85 ††£85/95
◆ Part Elizabethan farmhouse in rural location with lakes and garden. Comfy rooms -
three of which are in stables - with character: plenty of timbers and small sitting
areas.

FREATHY – Cornwall – see Millbrook

FRESSINGFIELD – Suffolk – **504** X 26   15 **D2**
🚉 London 104 mi – Ipswich 34 mi – Lowestoft 27 mi

XX **The Fox & Goose Inn**   🕯 P. VISA ⚫◯
Church Rd ⊠ IP21 5PB – ℰ (01379) 586 247 – www.foxandgoose.net
– foxandgoose@uk2.net – Fax (01379) 586 106
– Closed 6-20 January, 27-31 December and Monday
Rest – (booking essential) Menu £ 16 (lunch) – Carte £ 26/32
◆ Spacious black and white inn with leaded panes. Beams and wooden floor in
dining room. Extensive menu of traditional dishes with modern influence; some use
of local produce.

FRILSHAM – Newbury – see Yattendon

FRISTON – Suffolk – see Aldeburgh

FRITHSDEN – Herts. – see Hemel Hempstead

FRITTON – Norfolk   1 **D2**
🚉 London 133 mi – Great Yarmouth 8 mi – Norwich 19 mi

⚏ **Fritton House** ⚭   ⪡ 🚗 🍸 P. VISA ⚫◯
Church Lane ⊠ NR31 9HA – ℰ (01493) 484 008 – www.frittonhouse.co
– frittonhouse@somerleyton.co.uk
7 rm ⌑ – †£ 150/160 ††£ 150/160 – 1 suite   **Rest** – Carte £ 25/32
◆ Successful meeting point of 18C charm and contemporary boutique style. Elegant
drawing room with sumptuous sofas and fresh flowers. Comfortable, sleek bedrooms.
Dine on intriguing 21C dishes in relaxed, raftered surroundings.

FROGGATT EDGE – Derbyshire – **502** P 24   16 **A1**
🚉 London 167 mi – Bakewell 6 mi – Sheffield 11 mi

⚏ **The Chequers Inn** with rm   🕯 P. VISA ⚫◯ AE
Froggatt Edge, on A 625 ⊠ S32 3ZJ – ℰ (01433) 630 231
– www.chequers-froggatt.com – info@chequers-froggatt.com – Fax (01433)
631 072 – Closed 25 December
5 rm ⌑ – ††£75/95   **Rest** – Carte £ 21/28
◆ Refurbished 16C Grade II listed building, retaining many period features. Wide-
ranging, modern menus enhanced by accomplished cooking. Pleasant, cosy bedrooms.

FROME – Somerset – **503** M/N 30   4 **C2**
🚉 London 118 mi – Bristol 24 mi – Southampton 52 mi – Swindon 44 mi

⚏ **Babington House** ⚭   🚗 🍸 ♨ 🏊 📺 💻 👶 Ġ 🍽 🎾 🐾 🗻 ⚴
Babington, Northwest : 6 ½ m. by A 362 on Vobster rd   P. VISA ⚫◯ AE ①
⊠ BA11 3RW – ℰ (01373) 812 266 – www.babingtonhouse.co.uk
– enquiries@babingtonhouse.co.uk – Fax (01373) 813 866
32 rm – †£ 260/600 ††£ 260/600, ⌑ £14.50
Rest *The Orangery* – (residents and members only) Carte £ 25/45
◆ Country house with vivid difference: Georgian exterior; cool, trendy interior. Good
health club, even a cinema. Modern, understated and recently refurbished bedrooms.
Relaxed dining with modern menu.

ENGLAND

※※ **The Settle**   VISA ◯◯ AE
16 Cheap St, off Market Pl ⊠ BA11 1BN – 𝒞 (01373) 465 975 – Fax (01373)
465 975 – Closed 2 weeks Christmas-New Year, 1 week Spring, 1 week Summer
and Sunday-Wednesday
Rest – (dinner only) Menu £ 27
♦ First-floor restaurant above tea shop in town centre. Vivid red and blue linen colour
scheme adds panache to compact dining area. Well-prepared dishes using local
produce.

FUNTINGTON – W. Sussex – **504** R 31 – **see Chichester**

FYFIELD – Oxfordshire – pop. 540 – ⊠ Abingdon   10 **B2**
🔁 London 70 mi – Abingdon 6 mi – Oxford 9 mi

🏚 **The White Hart**   ◱ ⌂ **P** VISA ◯◯
Main Road ⊠ OX13 5LW – 𝒞 (01865) 390 585 – www.whitehart-fyfield.com
– info@whitehart-fyfield.com
Rest – (Closed Sunday dinner and Monday) Menu £ 17 – Carte £ 24/32
♦ 15C former chantry house complete with minstrels' gallery and cellar room. Glob-
ally influenced menu; fresh, flavoursome food. Uplit terrace and large garden.

GATESHEAD – Tyne and Wear – **501** P 19 – pop. 78 403 ▌Great Britain 24 **B2**
🔁 London 282 mi – Durham 16 mi – Middlesbrough 38 mi – Newcastle upon
   Tyne 1 mi – Sunderland 11 mi
Access Tyne Tunnel (toll)
🛈 Central Library, Prince Consort Rd 𝒞 (0191) 433 8420 BX - [Metrocentre,
   Portcullis, 7 The Arcade] Old Town Hall 𝒞 (0191) 478 4222 AX
🖩 Ravensworth Wrekenton Angel View, Long Bank, 𝒞 (0191) 487 6014
🖩 Heworth Gingling Gate, 𝒞 (0191) 469 9832
⧠ Beamish : North of England Open Air Museum★★ AC, SW : 6 m. by A 692
   and A 6076 BX

Plan : see Newcastle upon Tyne

at Low Fell South : 2 m. on A 167 - BX - ⊠ Gateshead

🏨 **Eslington Villa**   ◱ ⚒ 🗣 ⚐ **P** VISA ◯◯ AE
8 Station Rd, West : ¾ m. by Belle Vue Bank, turning left at T junction, right at
roundabout then taking first turn right ⊠ NE9 6DR – 𝒞 (0191) 487 6017
– www.eslingtonvilla.co.uk – home@eslingtonvilla.co.uk – Fax (0191) 420 0667
– Closed 25-26 December
18 rm ⊇ – ♦£ 70/75 ♦♦£ 90/95
Rest The Restaurant – see restaurant listing
♦ Well-run, stylish, privately owned hotel 10 minutes' drive from city centre. Nicely
furnished lounge bar leads from smart reception. Attractively styled, modern bedrooms.

※※ **The Restaurant** – at Eslington Villa Hotel   ◱ **P** VISA ◯◯ AE
8 Station Rd, West : ¾ by Belle Vue Bank, turning left at T junction, right at
roundabout then taking first turn right ⊠ NE9 6DR – 𝒞 (0191) 487 6017
– www.eslingtonvillahotel.co.uk – home@eslingtonvilla.co.uk – Fax (0191)
420 0667 – Closed 25-26 December
Rest – (Closed Saturday lunch, Sunday dinner and Bank Holidays)
Menu £ 16/20 – Carte £ 28/33
♦ Two separate dining areas, one of which is a conservatory. Both are classically
decorated and serve good range of traditionally based dishes with modern twists.

at Whickham West : 4 m. by A 184, A 1, A 692 on B 6317 – ⊠ Newcastle upon Tyne

🏨 **Gibside**   ⅋ rm, 🎞 rest, 🗣 ⚐ 🚗 VISA ◯◯ AE
Front St ⊠ NE16 4JG – 𝒞 (0191) 488 9292 – www.gibside-hotel.co.uk
– reception@gibside-hotel.co.uk – Fax (0191) 488 8000   AX**s**
45 rm – ♦£ 63 ♦♦£ 73/95, ⊇ £ 8.95
Rest – (bar lunch Monday-Saturday) Carte £ 25/34 **s**
♦ Purpose-built hotel in small town near Gateshead with views over Tyne Valley. Set
on hill, so its up to date facilities are on different levels. Cosy, unfussy rooms. Newly
refurbished modern restaurant.

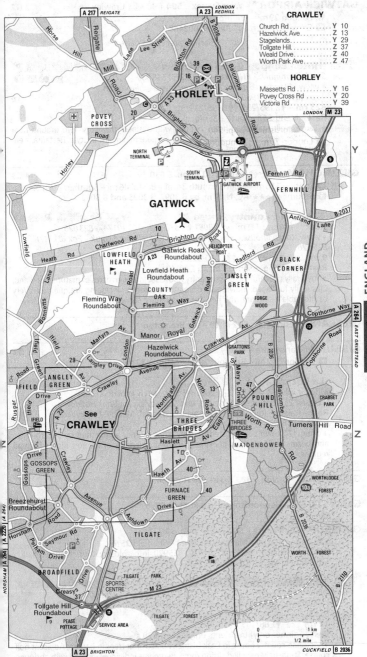

ENGLAND

GATWICK AIRPORT – West Sussex – **504** T 30 – ⊠ Crawley   7 **D2**
- ▶ London 29 mi – Brighton 28 mi
- ✈ Gatwick Airport : 𝒞 (0870) 0002468

Plan on preceding page

🏨🏨 **Hilton London Gatwick Airport**   𝓕𝓫 ⧈ 𝓫 rm, 𝔸�ℂ 🛜 📞 🦽 🅿
South Terminal ⊠ RH6 0LL – 𝒞 (01293) 518 080   𝓥𝓘𝓢𝓐 ⦿ AE ⓪
– www.hilton.co.uk/gatwick – londongatwick@hilton.com
– Fax (01293) 528 980   Y**u**
823 rm – ♦£195/239 ♦♦£195/239, ⇆ £18.50
Rest – Menu £18 – Carte £35/40
♦ Large, well-established hotel, popular with business travellers. Two ground floor bars. Older rooms co-ordinated, newer ones more minimalist in style. Restaurant enlivened by floral profusions.

GILLINGHAM – Dorset – **503** N 30 – pop. 8 630   4 **C3**
- ▶ London 116 mi – Bournemouth 34 mi – Bristol 46 mi – Southampton 52 mi
- 🖾 Stourhead ★★★ AC, N : 9 m. by B 3092, B 3095 and B 3092

🏠 **Stock Hill Country House** 🍃   🚗 🐾 🖥 ✗ 🍽 🗠 🅿 𝓥𝓘𝓢𝓐 ⦿
Stock Hill, West : 1½ m. on B 3081 ⊠ SP8 5NR – 𝒞 (01747) 823 626
– www.stockhillhouse.co.uk – reception@stockhillhouse.co.uk – Fax (01747)
825 628
9 rm ⇆ – ♦£125/165 ♦♦£280/320
Rest – (booking essential) Menu £30/40 🍴
♦ Idyllically peaceful Victorian country house set in eleven acres of mature woodland. Classically furnished. Individually decorated bedrooms, including antique beds. Very comfortable restaurant with rich drapes, attentive service.

GILSLAND – Cumbria – **502** M 19 – see Brampton

GISBURN – Lancashire – **502** N 22   20 **B2**
- ▶ London 242 mi – Bradford 28 mi – Skipton 12 mi

✗ **La Locanda**   𝓥𝓘𝓢𝓐 ⦿ AE
Main St ⊠ BB7 4HH – 𝒞 (01200) 445 303 – www.lalocanda.co.uk
– Closed 25 December - 1 January and Monday except Bank Holidays
Rest – Italian – (dinner only) (booking essential) Menu £14 (weekdays)
– Carte £18/27
♦ Snug 17C town centre osteria. Lovely stone interior augmented by superb joists and beams. Italian 'nonna' cooking of the first order: lots of comfort dishes from all regions.

GITTISHAM – Devon – **503** K 31 – see Honiton

GLEWSTONE – Herefordshire – see Ross-on-Wye

GLOSSOP – Derbyshire – **502** O 23 – pop. 30 771   16 **A1**
- ▶ London 194 mi – Manchester 18 mi – Sheffield 25 mi
- 🖹 Bank House, Henry St 𝒞 (01457) 855920, info@glossoptouristcentre.co.uk
- 🖾 Sheffield Rd, 𝒞 (01457) 865 247

🏠 **The Wind in the Willows** 🍃   🚗 ✗ 📶 🦽 🅿 𝓥𝓘𝓢𝓐 ⦿ AE ⓪
Derbyshire Level, East : 1 m. by A 57 ⊠ SK13 7PT – 𝒞 (01457) 868 001
– www.windinthewillows.co.uk – info@windinthewillows.co.uk – Fax (01457)
853 354
12 rm ⇆ – ♦£88/105 ♦♦£130/155
Rest – (dinner only) (residents only) Menu £29 **s**
♦ Victorian country house in Peak District, named after trees in garden. Adjacent golf course. Snug, fully-panelled sitting room. Bedrooms individually styled with antiques. Eat on carved chairs at gleaming wooden tables.

GOATHLAND – North Yorkshire – **502** R 20 – ⊠ Whitby 23 **C1**
▶ London 248 mi – Middlesbrough 36 mi – York 38 mi

 Heatherdene 🦢 ≤ 🚗 🌦 **P** VISA ⚫Ⓞ AE
The Common ⊠ Y022 5AN – 𝒸 *(01947) 896 334 – www.heatherdenehotel.com*
– info@heatherdenehotel.com – Fax (01947) 896 334
– Closed January and 1 week Christmas-New Year
7 rm ☲ – †£40/65 ††£95
Rest – (dinner only) (booking essential for non residents) Menu £20
♦ Country house hotel in converted vicarage with good village views. Sitting room
has contemporary styling, which is reflected to slightly lesser degree in the bedrooms. Hearty, home-cooked meals in modern dining room.

GOLANT Cornwall – **503** G 32 – see Fowey

GOLCAR – W. Yorks. – see Huddersfield

GOLDSBOROUGH – North Yorkshire – see Whitby

GOODNESTONE – Kent – see Wingham

GOREY – **503** P 33 – see Channel Islands (Jersey)

GORING – Oxfordshire – **503** Q 29 – **pop. 4 193** ▌ *Great Britain* 10 **B3**
▶ London 56 mi – Oxford 16 mi – Reading 12 mi
🅖 Ridgeway Path ★★

✕✕ **Leatherne Bottel** ≤ 🍽 **P** VISA ⚫Ⓞ AE
The Bridleway, North : 1½ m. by B 4009 ⊠ RG8 0HS – 𝒸 *(01491) 872 667*
– www.leathernebottel.co.uk – leathernebottel@aol.com – Fax (01491) 875 308
– Closed 5-21 January and Sunday dinner - Monday February-March and
October-November
Rest – (booking essential) Menu £25/30 – Carte £37/45 🍷
♦ Charming Thames-side restaurant; idyllic views of Berkshire Downs. Neat, linen-
clad round tables, sparkling windows, travel photos on walls. Imaginative interna-
tional menu.

at Cray's Pond East : 2 m. on B 4526 – ⊠ Goring

🍴 **The White Lion** 🚗 🍽 **P** VISA ⚫Ⓞ
Goring Rd, Goring Heath, Cray's Pond ⊠ RG8 7SH – 𝒸 *(01491) 680 471*
– www.thewhitelioncrayspond.com – reservations@thewhitelioncrayspond.com
Rest – (Closed Monday) Carte £20/30
♦ Part 18C pub sporting 21C appearance. Front terrace for summer dining. Stylish
interior: mix of old beams, low ceilings and soft lights. Eclectic dishes and British
staples.

GOSFORTH – Tyne and Wear – **501** P 18 – see Newcastle upon Tyne

GOUDHURST – Kent – **504** V 30 8 **B2**
▶ London 50 mi – Hastings 25 mi – Maidstone 17 mi

↑ **West Winchet** without rest 🦢 🚗 **P**
Winchet Hill, North : 2½ m. on B 2079 ⊠ TN17 1JX – 𝒸 *(01580) 212 024*
– annieparker@jpa-ltd.co.uk – Fax (01580) 212 250 – Closed 26-30 December
3 rm ☲ – †£50/55 ††£75/80
♦ Victorian house with large, attractive rear garden. Breakfast taken in vast and
attractively decorated drawing room. Traditional bedrooms offer country style décor.

GOVETON Devon – **503** I 33 – see Kingsbridge

GRANGE-OVER-SANDS – Cumbria – **502** L 21 – pop. 4 835 21 **A3**

Great Britain

London 268 mi – Kendal 13 mi – Lancaster 24 mi
Victoria Hall, Main St ✆ (015395) 34026, grangetic@southlakeland.gov.uk
Meathop Rd, ✆ (015395) 33 180
Cartmel Priory★, NW : 3 m

Netherwood
rm, rest, P VISA MC

Lindale Rd ✉ LA11 6ET – ✆ (015395) 32 552 – www.netherwood-hotel.co.uk – enquiries@netherwood-hotel.co.uk – Fax (015395) 34 121

32 rm – †£ 110/120 ††£ 180/200 **Rest** – Menu £ 18/32 **s**

◆ Unusual, castellated late 18C hotel offering fine view of Morecambe Bay. Atmospheric wood-panelled lounges, each boasting open log fire. Comfy rooms with good mod cons. Dine formally and enjoy superb bay vistas.

Clare House
P VISA MC

Park Rd ✉ LA11 7HQ – ✆ (015395) 33 026 – www.clarehousehotel.co.uk – info@clarehousehotel.co.uk – Fax (015395) 34 310 – Mid March-early November

18 rm – †£ 80/140 ††£ 160

Rest – (dinner only) (booking essential for non-residents) Menu £ 30

◆ Longstanding family run hotel, its lovely lawned garden looking over Morecambe Bay. Two smartly furnished lounges. Traditionally styled rooms, most with bay views. Two pleasant dining rooms; daily changing five-course menus show care and interest.

ENGLAND

at Cartmel Northwest : 3 m – ✉ Grange-over-Sands

Aynsome Manor
P VISA MC AE

North : ¾ m. by Cartmel Priory rd on Wood Broughton rd ✉ LA11 6HH – ✆ (015395) 36 653 – www.aynsomemanorhotel.co.uk – aynsomemanor@btinternet.com – Fax (015395) 36 016 – Closed 25-26 December and 2-28 January

12 rm – †£ 95 ††£ 130/170

Rest – (Closed Sunday dinner to non-residents) (dinner only and Sunday lunch) Menu £ 26

◆ Country house, personally run by two generations of the same family. Open fired snug bar and lounge with fine clocks. Sitting room has Priory view. Airy, traditional rooms. Dine on candle-lit, polished wood tables with silver.

Hill Farm without rest
P

Northwest : 1½ m. bearing to right of village shop in Market Square then left onto Cul-de-Sac rd after the racecourse ✉ LA11 7SS – ✆ (015395) 36 477 – www.hillfarmbb.co.uk – patfoulerton@btinternet.com – Fax (015395) 36 477 – February-October

3 rm – †£ 45/50 ††£ 45/50

◆ Superb hospitality a feature of this 16C farmhouse with cottagey interior and lovely gardens: a peaceful setting. Individual colour schemes enhance the pretty bedrooms.

L'Enclume (Simon Rogan) with rm
P VISA MC AE

Cavendish St ✉ LA11 6PZ – ✆ (015395) 36 362 – www.lenclume.co.uk – info@lenclume.co.uk – Fax (015395) 38 907

12 rm – †£ 68 ††£ 198, £ 18.95

Rest – (dinner only and lunch Saturday-Sunday) (booking essential) Menu £ 50/90

Spec. Sea scallop, beetroot and sea fennel. Rump of lamb with chenopodiums and hyssop. Chocolate, praline, milk and blood orange.

◆ Converted smithy in quaint village with polished tables and owner's artwork on walls. Displaying innovation and creativity, menus are well balanced with clean, clear flavours. Wide selection of cosy, individually styled bedrooms.

Rogan and Company
VISA MC

The Square ✉ LA11 6QD – ✆ (015395) 35 917 – www.roganandcompany.co.uk – reservations@roganandcompany.co.uk

Rest – Carte £ 27/39

◆ Converted cottages in heart of rustic village. Modern interior with relaxed atmosphere low level seating, raised stools and some antiques. Appealing menu offers real choice.

▶ London 113 mi – Leicester 31 mi – Lincoln 29 mi – Nottingham 24 mi

🛈 The Guildhall Centre, St Peter's Hill 𝒞 (01476) 406166, granthamtic@southkesteven.gov.uk

🏞 Belton Park Londonthorpe Rd, Belton Lane, 𝒞 (01476) 567 399

🏌 De Vere Belton Woods H., 𝒞 (01476) 593 200

◎ St Wulfram's Church★

◎ Belton House★ **AC**, N : 2½ m. by A 607. Belvoir Castle★★ **AC**, W : 6 m. by A 607

🏨🏨🏨 **Belton Woods**   🍴 🐾 🏠 🖼 ⊙ 🏠 ℉ ⅃ ✕ 🖼 🛗 ♿ rm, ⚶ ⌇ 🏊

Belton, North : 2 m. on A 607 ⊠ NG32 2LN   **P VISA ✪ AE ⓵**
– 𝒞 (01476) 593 200 – www.devereonline.co.uk
– belton.woods@devere-hotels.com – Fax (01476) 574 547
132 rm ⊇ – ♦£165 ♦♦£175/275 – 4 suites
Rest *Stantons Brasserie* – Carte £ 25/50
♦ Set in acres of countryside, this modern hotel offers impressive leisure facilities, including three golf courses. Range of conference suites. Spacious bedrooms. Light, modern décor in Stantons Brasserie.

---

at Hough-on-the-Hill North : 6 ¾ m. by A 607 – ⊠ Grantham

✕✕ **The Brownlow Arms** with rm   🏠 **AC** rest, ✕ **P VISA ✪**

High Rd ⊠ NG32 2AZ – 𝒞 (01400) 250 234 – armsinn@yahoo.co.uk
– Closed 3 weeks January and 25-26 December
4 rm ⊇ – ♦£65 ♦♦£96
Rest – (closed Sunday dinner and Monday) (dinner only and Sunday lunch) Carte £ 28/41
♦ Attractive part 17/19C inn in heart of rural Lincolnshire. Wood-panelled bar with deep armchairs. Formal dining: well executed modern British dishes. Very tasteful rooms.

---

at Woolsthorpe-by-Belvoir West : 7 ½ m. by A 607 – ⊠ Grantham

🍴 **The Chequers** with rm   🍴 🏠 **P VISA ✪ AE**

Main Street ⊠ NG32 1LU – 𝒞 (01476) 870 701 – www.chequersinn.net
– justinnabar@yahoo.co.uk – Closed 25-26 December dinner, 1 January dinner
4 rm ⊇ – ♦£49 ♦♦£59   **Rest** – Menu £ 15/17 – Carte £ 21/32
♦ Attractive pub, orignally built as 17C farmhouse. Various nooks, crannies, exposed bricks and beams. Traditional English cuisine with emphasis on game. Simple, clean rooms.

---

at Harlaxton Southwest : 2 ½ m. on A 607 – ⊠ Grantham

🍴 **The Gregory**   🏠 **P VISA ✪**

The Drift ⊠ NG32 1AD – 𝒞 (01476) 577 076 – www.thegregory.co.uk – Closed 25-26 December
Rest – (Closed Sunday dinner and Monday) Carte £ 18/25 **s**
♦ Whitewashed, ivy-clad pub that's had an extensive refurbishment. Modern menu displays a selection of classic pub favourites, with the odd ambitious dish appearing at dinner.

---

at Great Gonerby Northwest : 2 m. on B 1174 – ⊠ Grantham

✕✕ **Harry's Place** (Harry Hallam)   **P VISA ✪**

❀ 17 High St ⊠ NG31 8JS – 𝒞 (01476) 561 780 – Closed Christmas-New Year, Sunday, Monday and Bank Holidays
Rest – (booking essential) Carte £ 52/62
Spec. Terrine of wild Scottish salmon. Loin of Gascony black pork and foie gras. Hot apricot soufflé.
♦ Just three tables, bedecked with flowers, candles and antique cutlery. Husband and wife team present handwritten, daily-changing menu; exquisite, classically based cooking.

🛈 London 282 mi – Carlisle 43 mi – Kendal 18 mi
🛈 Redbank Rd ℰ (015394) 35245 (summer only) BZ
◎ Dove Cottage★ **AC** AY **A**
◎ Lake Windermere★★, SE : by A 591 AZ

Plans : see Ambleside

🏨 Gold Rill   ≤ 🛋 Ⓐ rest, ॐ P VISA ⬤

Red Bank Rd ⊠ LA22 9PU – ℰ (015394) 35 486 – www.gold-rill.com – reception@
gold-rill.com – Fax (015394) 85 486 – Closed 2 weeks January and 2 weeks December
31 rm – ♦£60/86 ♦♦£120/172 – 1 suite   BZ**a**
Rest – (bar lunch) Menu £ 27 – Carte approx. £ 29
♦ Liberally proportioned, privately owned hotel in quiet part of town. Good views,
open fires, slate based walls, traditional décor. Large bar with fine ales. Homely
bedrooms. Quiet rear dining room overlooking lake.

🏠 Moss Grove Organic without rest   ¶¹ P VISA ⬤

⊠ LA22 9SW – ℰ (015394) 35 251 – www.mossgrove.com – enquiries@
mossgrove.com – Fax (015394) 35 306 – Closed 24-25 December   BZ**s**
11 rm – ♦£110/180 ♦♦£125/325
♦ Uniquely organic hotel whose bedrooms offer top comforts; all have spa baths,
some have four posters or balconies with rocking chairs. Mediterranean buffet in
breakfast room.

🏠 Grasmere   🛋 ¶¹ P VISA ⬤

Broadgate ⊠ LA22 9TA – ℰ (015394) 35 277 – www.grasmerehotel.co.uk
– enquiries@grasmerehotel.co.uk – Fax (015394) 35 277
– Closed 2 January-early February   BZ**r**
13 rm ⊇ – ♦£60/110 ♦♦£120/150 – 1 suite
Rest – (dinner only) (booking essential for non-residents) Menu £ 30
♦ Small Victorian country house with pleasant acre of garden through which River
Rothay flows. Snug, open-fired bar with good malt whisky selection. Individually
styled rooms. Pleasant pine roofed rear dining room.

🏠 Lake View Country House without rest ॐ   ≤ 🛋 P VISA ⬤

Lake View Drive ⊠ LA22 9TD – ℰ (015394) 35 384
– www.lakeview-grasmere.com – info@lake-view.grasmere.com   BZ
4 rm ⊇ – ♦♦£85/110
♦ Country house whose large garden boasts views of lake and a badger sett. Comfy
bedrooms, two with spa baths. Breakfast includes homemade yoghurt, compotes and
fruit platters.

🏠 Riversdale   ¶¹ P VISA ⬤

White Bridge, North : 1/2 m. on B 5287 ⊠ LA22 9RH – ℰ (015394) 35 619
– www.riversdalegrasmere.co.uk – info@riversdalegrasmere.co.uk   AY**s**
3 rm ⊇ – ♦£55/70 ♦♦£90/95   **Rest** – (by arrangement) Menu £ 23 **s**
♦ Immaculately kept lakeland guest house run by friendly couple who offer tea and
cake on arrival and on the patio in good weather. Comfy bedrooms offer every conceivable extra. Homecooked meals served in neat dining room; wide choice available
on breakfast menu.

🛈 London 240 mi – Bradford 30 mi – Burnley 28 mi – Leeds 37 mi
🛈 National Park Centre, Colvend, Hebden Rd ℰ (01756) 751690,
grassington@yorkshiredales.org.uk

🏠 Ashfield House   🛋 ॐ ¶¹ P VISA ⬤ AE

Summers Fold, off Main St ⊠ BD23 5AE – ℰ (01756) 752 584
– www.ashfieldhouse.co.uk – sales@ashfieldhouse.co.uk – Closed 2 weeks March
and 24-26 December
8 rm ⊇ – ♦£68/128 ♦♦£97/123
Rest – (closed Sunday and Wednesday) (dinner only) (booking essential for
non-residents) Menu £ 34 **s**
♦ Sturdy 17C small stone hotel with beams and flagged floors: oozes period charm.
Individually decorated, cottagey bedrooms with occasional exposed timber. Delightful garden. Tasty, locally-inspired dishes.

ENGLAND

🏠 **Grassington House**   📞 P VISA ⓂⓈ
5 The Square ⊠ *BD23 5AQ* – ℰ *(01756) 752 406*
– www.grassingtonhousehotel.co.uk – bookings@grassingtonhousehotel.co.uk
– Closed 25-26 December
11 rm ⌸ – ♦£90 ♦♦£110
Rest *No 5 The Square* – Menu £19/28
♦ Refurbished Georgian house on cobbled street in busy village centre. Contemporary bar; terrace with smart cushioned furniture. Smart, modern bedrooms with good facilities. Restaurant offers large menu of classic British dishes with some worldwide influences.

🏠 **Grassington Lodge** without rest   ⫶ ⁕ P VISA ⓂⓈ
8 Wood Lane ⊠ *BD23 5LU* – ℰ *(01756) 752 518* – *www.grassingtonlodge.co.uk*
– relax@grassingtonlodge.co.uk
11 rm ⌸ – ♦£80 ♦♦£80/150
♦ Modern guesthouse at gateway to Yorkshire Dales. Built over 100 years ago as home of village doctor. Gallery of local photos on display around the house. Stylish, smart rooms.

GREAT BADDOW – Essex – **504** V 28 – see Chelmsford

GREAT BIRCHAM – Norfolk – **502** V 25   14 **B1**
▶ London 115 mi – Hunstanton 10 mi – King's Lynn 15 mi

🏠 **King's Head**   🏠 AC rest, ⁕ P VISA ⓂⓈ
⊠ *PE31 6RJ* – ℰ *(01485) 578 265* – *www.the-kings-head-bircham.co.uk*
– welcome@the-kings-head-bircham.co.uk – *Fax (01485) 578 635*
12 rm ⌸ – ♦£75/115 ♦♦£165/185   **Rest** – Carte £25/35
♦ Victorian inn with purpose-built extensions. Smart interior: relaxed bar and stylish residents lounge with big leather chairs. Bedrooms have contemporary feel. Modern menus in restaurant with sheltered courtyard terrace.

GREAT DUNMOW – Essex – **504** V 28 – pop. 5 943   13 **C2**
▶ London 42 mi – Cambridge 27 mi – Chelmsford 13 mi – Colchester 24 mi

XXX **The Starr** with rm   ⫶ ⁕ ♨ P VISA ⓂⓈ AE ①
Market Place ⊠ *CM6 1AX* – ℰ *(01371) 874 321* – *www.the-starr.co.uk*
– starrestaurant@btinternet.com – *Fax (01371) 876 337*
– Closed 27 December-5 January
8 rm ⌸ – ♦£90 ♦♦£160
Rest – (closed Sunday dinner) Menu £49 (dinner) – Carte approx. £34
♦ Former 15C pub with rustic bar and fire. Characterful restaurant has exposed beams and conservatory. Strong, interesting cooking, traditionally inspired. Smart bedrooms.

X **Square 1**   VISA ⓂⓈ
15 High St ⊠ *CM6 1AB* – ℰ *(01371) 859 922* – *www.square1restaurant.co.uk*
– square1restaurant@yahoo.co.uk – *Closed 25-26 December, 1 January and
Sunday dinner*
Rest – Menu £16 (lunch) – Carte dinner £25/32
♦ Modern family-run restaurant in 14C monastic reading room. Stylish interior with vibrant artwork and open plan kitchen. Contemporary menu with subtle Mediterranean feel.

GREAT GONERBY – Lincs. – **502** S 25 – see Grantham

GREAT HENNY – Essex – pop. 126   13 **C2**
▶ London 64 mi – Braintree 14 mi – Sudbury 4 mi

🏠 **Henny Swan**   ▱ 🏠 P VISA ⓂⓈ
Henny St ⊠ *CO10 7LS* – ℰ *(01787) 269 238* – *www.hennyswan.com*
– harry@hennyswan.com – *Closed Monday and Sunday November-April dinner*
Rest – Menu £11 – Carte £19/26
♦ Spacious pub set over two floors boasts comfy leather furniture and open fires. Oft-changing menus; confident, flavoursome cooking uses locally produced, seasonal ingredients.

ENGLAND

▶ London 127 mi – Birmingham 34 mi – Cardiff 66 mi – Gloucester 24 mi
🏢 21 Church St 𝒞 (01684) 892289, malvern.tic@malvernhills.gov.uk B

Plan opposite

🏠 **Bredon House** without rest   ≤ 🚗 ⁛ P VISA ◑◐
34 Worcester Rd ✉ WR14 4AA – 𝒞 (01684) 566 990 – www.bredonhouse.co.uk
– enquiries@bredonhouse.co.uk – Fax (01684) 577 530   B**a**
10 rm 🍽 – ✝£55/75 ✝✝£95/110
♦ Elegant, Grade II listed Regency house with spectacular views. Personable owners make breakfast a special event. Most of the individually styled rooms enjoy the fine vista.

🏠 **The Cotford**   🚗 ⁛ P VISA ◑◐
51 Graham Street ✉ WR14 2HU – 𝒞 (01684) 572 427 – www.cotfordhotel.co.uk
– reservations@cotfordhotel.co.uk – Fax (01684) 572 952
15 rm 🍽 – ✝£65/79 ✝✝£115
Rest – (dinner only and Sunday lunch)) Menu £28
♦ Recently refurbished Victorian gothic stone building in landscaped gardens; built in 1851 for the Bishop of Worcester. Modern but homely guest areas; cosy bedrooms. Modern dining room with garden views; seasonal menu of local, organic produce.

at Guarlford East : 2 1/2 m. on B 4211

🍴 **Plough and Harrow**   🚗 🌳 P VISA ◑◐
Rhydd Rd, East 3/4 m. on B 4211 ✉ WR13 6NY – 𝒞 (01684) 310 453
– www.theploughandharrow.co.uk – info@theploughandharrow.co.uk – Closed first 2 weeks November, 25 December, 1 January
Rest – (Closed Sunday dinner and Monday) Carte £15/30
♦ Modernised country pub with low-beamed bar and open fire; more formal dining room and large lawned garden. Unfussy cooking uses good quality produce, some from kitchen garden.

at Malvern Wells South : 2 m. on A 449 – ✉ Malvern

🏠🏠 **Cottage in the Wood** 🌿   ≤ 🚗 🌳 AK rest, ⁛ P VISA ◑◐ AE
Holywell Rd ✉ WR14 4LG – 𝒞 (01684) 575 859 – www.cottageinthewood.co.uk
– reception@cottageinthewood.co.uk – Fax (01684) 560 662   A**z**
30 rm 🍽 – ✝£79/112 ✝✝£99/185   **Rest** – Carte £23/37 s ⁂
♦ Early Victorian house, family owned and run, with superb view over surrounding vales. Very comfortable sitting room and bar. Individually furnished rooms in traditional style. Lovely restaurant with Oriental silk prints and Vale views.

at Colwall Southwest : 3 m. on B 4218 – ✉ Great Malvern

🏠🏠 **Colwall Park**   🚗 ⁛ 🏌 P VISA ◑◐
✉ WR13 6QG – 𝒞 (01684) 540 000 – www.colwall.co.uk – hotel@colwall.com
– Fax (01684) 540 847   A**v**
21 rm 🍽 – ✝£80 ✝✝£120 – 1 suite
Rest Seasons – see restaurant listing
♦ Built in 1903, this personally run hotel has a distinct Edwardian feel. Play croquet in the garden or wander into the nearby Malvern Hills. Individually decorated bedrooms.

✕✕ **Seasons** – at Colwall Park Hotel   🚗 P VISA ◑◐
✉ WR13 6QG – 𝒞 (01684) 540 000 – www.colwall.co.uk – hotel@colwall.com
– Fax (01684) 540 847   A**v**
Rest – (booking essential at lunch) Menu £20 (lunch) – Carte dinner £32/37 s
♦ Predominant oak panelling merges seamlessly with modern styling in a spacious location for formal dining. Accomplished and interesting modern British cooking.

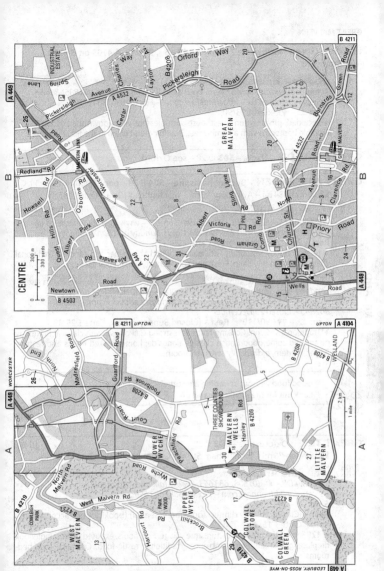

GREAT MALVERN

at Acton Green Northwest : 7 m. by A 449 - B -, B 4219, A 4103 on B 4220
– ✉ Bromyard

↑ **Hidelow House** without rest ⌂　　　　　　🖥 ⚒ 📶 **P** _VISA_ ⓪ **AE**
Acton Beauchamp, South : ¾ m. on B 4220 ✉ *WR6 5AH –* ℰ *(01886) 884 547*
– www.hidelow.co.uk – info@hidelow.co.uk – Fax (01886) 884658
3 rm ⌷ – ♦£45 ♦♦£73/90
♦ Secluded, privately run guesthouse with pleasant views down the Leadon Valley.
Sizeable bedrooms with a homely feel. Boudoir grand piano in the firelit lounge.

GREAT MILTON – Oxon. – **503** Q 28 – **see Oxford**

GREAT MISSENDEN – Buckinghamshire – **504** R 28 – **pop. 7 980**　　11 **C2**
🚊 London 34 mi – Aylesbury 10 mi – Maidenhead 19 mi – Oxford 35 mi

✗✗ **La Petite Auberge**　　　　　　　　　　　　　　　　_VISA_ ⓪
107 High St ✉ *HP16 0BB –* ℰ *(01494) 865 370 – www.lapetiteauberge.co.uk*
– Closed 2 weeks Easter, 2 weeks Christmas, Sunday and Bank Holidays
Rest – French – (dinner only) Carte £ 29/37
♦ Neat, cottagey restaurant with painted wood chip paper and candles. Traditional
chairs, crisp and tidy linen. Fresh and confident style of French cooking.

🍴 **The Nags Head** with rm　　　　　　　　　　🖥 **P** _VISA_ ⓪ **AE**
London Road, Southeast : 1m ✉ *HP16 0DG –* ℰ *(01494) 862 200*
– www.nagsheadbucks.com – goodfood@nagsheadbucks.com – Fax (01494)
862 945 – Closed 25 December
6 rm ⌷ – ♦♦£90/110　　**Rest** – (Closed Sunday dinner) Carte £ 25/38
♦ Traditional 15C inn. Cooking features a strong Gallic base, with classical Burgundy
dishes and some good British classics alongside; home-smoked meats also feature.
Bright, modern, individually styled bedrooms.

> Good food without spending a fortune?
> Look out for the Bib Gourmand 🐵

GREAT TEW – Oxfordshire – **503** P 28　　　　　　　　　　　10 **B1**
🚊 London 75 mi – Birmingham 50 mi – Gloucester 42 mi – Oxford 21 mi

🍴 **Falkland Arms** with rm　　　　　　　🖥 🍴 ⚒ _VISA_ ⓪ **AE**
✉ *OX7 4DB –* ℰ *(01608) 683 653 – www.falklandarms.org.uk*
– sjcourage@btconnect.com – Fax (01608) 683 656
5 rm ⌷ – ♦♦£110
Rest – (Closed Sunday dinner) (booking essential) (bookings not accepted at
lunch) Carte £ 15/30
♦ 17C inn on the green in picturesque village. Flag floors, exposed beams, inglenook
fireplace guarantee warm ambience. Traditional, rustic food. Compact, cosy bedrooms.

GREAT WHITTINGTON – Northd. – **501** O 18 – **see Corbridge**

GREAT WOLFORD – Warwickshire – **503** P 27　　　　　　　19 **C3**
🚊 London 84 mi – Birmingham 37 mi – Cheltenham 26 mi

🍴 **The Fox & Hounds Inn** with rm　　　　　　　🍴 **P** _VISA_ ⓪
✉ *CV36 5NQ –* ℰ *(01608) 674 220 – www.thefoxandhoundsinn.com*
– enquiries@thefoxandhoundsinn.com
3 rm ⌷ – ♦£55 ♦♦£90　　**Rest** – Carte £ 20/40
♦ Warm and welcoming, family-run pub with dried hops, log burner and cosy atmosphere. Concise blackboard menu; bold flavoursome cooking made from locally-
sourced ingredients. Simple, neat, spacious bedrooms.

ENGLAND

GREAT YARMOUTH – Norfolk – 504 Z 26 – pop. 58 032　　　15 D2

 Great Britain

- London 126 mi – Cambridge 81 mi – Ipswich 53 mi – Norwich 20 mi
- 25 Marine Parade, ℰ (01493) 846345, tourism@great-yarmouth.gov.uk
- Gorleston Warren Rd, ℰ (01493) 661 911
- Beach House Caister-on-Sea, Great Yarmouth & Caister, ℰ (01493) 728 699
- Norfolk Broads ★

Imperial　　　⇐ 🏬 AK rest, 📶 🖥 🅿 VISA ⓒ AE ①
*North Drive ⊠ NR30 1EQ – ℰ (01493) 842 000 – www.imperialhotel.co.uk
– reception@imperialhotel.co.uk – Fax (01493) 852 229*
39 rm �),– ♦£80/90 ♦♦£90/110 – 1 suite
Rest *Cafe Cru* – (closed Sunday dinner) (dinner only and Sunday lunch)
Menu £18 – Carte £19/35 **s**
◆ Turn of 20C classic promenade hotel, still privately owned, with imposing exterior.
Pleasant bedrooms in light fabrics include four wine-themed rooms. Front rooms
with sea and beach outlook. French feel pervades basement restaurant.

No 78 without rest　　　📞 VISA ⓒ
*78 Marine Par – ℰ (01493) 850 001 – www.no78.co.uk – info@no78.co.uk
– Fax (01493) 850 001*
8 rm �), – ♦£35 ♦♦£85
◆ Late Victorian house overlooking bowling green and pier. Modern, airy bedrooms
with original sash windows and smart bathrooms. Lounge with sea views; large
basement breakfast room.

Seafood　　　AK VISA ⓒ AE ①
*85 North Quay ⊠ NR30 1JF – ℰ (01493) 856 009 – seafood01@btconnect.com
– Fax (01493) 332 256 – Closed 2 weeks Christmas, 2 weeks May, Saturday lunch,
Sunday and Bank Holidays*
Rest – Seafood – Carte £36/49
◆ Run by a husband and wife team, a long-standing neighbourhood restaurant.
Lobster tank, fish display, fresh, generous seafood, attentive service and home-made
chocolates!

GREEN ISLAND – 503 P 33 – **see Channel Islands (Jersey)**

GRETA BRIDGE – Durham – 502 O 20 – **see Barnard Castle**

GRIMSTON – Norfolk – 504 V 25 – **see King's Lynn**

GRINDLETON – Lancashire – 502 M 22 – **see Clitheroe**

GRINSHILL – Shrops. – 503 L 25 – **see Shrewsbury**

GROUVILLE – 503 M 33 – **see Channel Islands (Jersey)**

GUARLFORD Worcs – 503 N 27 – **see Great Malvern**

GUERNSEY – 503 OP 33 – **see Channel Islands**

GUILDFORD – Surrey – 504 S 30 – **pop. 69 400** 📗 *Great Britain*　　　7 C1
- London 33 mi – Brighton 43 mi – Reading 27 mi – Southampton 49 mi
- 14 Tunsgate ℰ (01483) 444333, tic@guildford.gov.uk Y
- Clandon Park ★★, E : 3 m. by A 246 Z – Hatchlands Park ★, E : 6 m. by A 246
Z. Painshill ★★, Cobham, NE : 10 m – Polesden Lacey ★, E : 13 m. by A 246 Z
and minor rd

Plan on next page

ENGLAND

GUILDFORD

ENGLAND

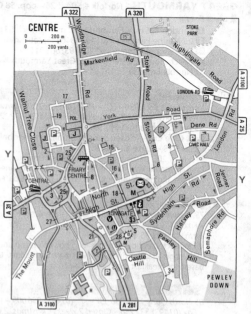

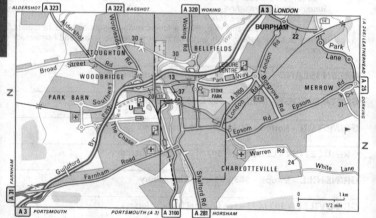

✕✕ **Café de Paris**   🔓 🗄 VISA 🅼🅲 AE
35 Castle St ✉ GU1 3UQ – ✆ (01483) 534896 – www.cafedeparisguildford.co.uk
– Fax (01483) 300411
– Closed Sunday and Bank Holidays (except Good Friday)   **Yu**
Rest – French – (booking essential) Carte £22/38
♦ French-style backstreet eatery. Take your pick of brasserie in front or restaurant at
back. Prix fixe or à la carte dishes with traditional twist and seasonal changes.

X **Zinfandel** 🏧 🎬 VISA ⚫️ AE
*4-5 Chapel St ⊠ GU1 3UH – ℰ (01483) 455 155 – www.zinfandel.org.uk
– mail@zinfandel.org.uk – Closed 25 December, 1 January, and dinner Sunday
and Monday* Y**v**
Rest – Carte £ 18/31

♦ Welcoming, modern and irresistibly laid back; Napa Valley cuisine mixes grills, Pacific Rim salads, full-flavoured, wood-fired pizzas and picket-fence classics like pecan pie.

at Shere East : 6 ¾ m. by A 246 off A 25 - Z - ⊠ **Guildford**

XX **Kinghams** 🅿️ VISA ⚫️ AE ①
*Gomshall Lane ⊠ GU5 9HE – ℰ (01483) 202 168
– www.kinghams-restaurant.co.uk – paul.baker@googlemail.com
– Closed 25 December-6 January, Sunday dinner and Monday*
Rest – (booking essential) Menu £ 23 – Carte £ 32/37

♦ Popular restaurant in 17C cottage in appealing village. Daily blackboard and fish specials are particularly good value. Adventurous modern menus with bold combinations.

> Look out for red symbols, indicating particularly pleasant establishments.

ENGLAND

GUITING POWER – Gloucestershire – **503** O 28 – ⊠ **Cheltenham** **4 D1**
🚇 London 95 mi – Birmingham 47 mi – Gloucester 30 mi – Oxford 39 mi

⌂ **Guiting Guest House** VISA ⚫️ ①
*Post Office Lane ⊠ GL54 5TZ – ℰ (01451) 850 470
– www.guitingguesthouse.com – info@guitingguesthouse.com*
7 rm ⌴ – †£45/56 ††£85 **Rest** – (by arrangement) Menu £ 35

♦ 16C stone-built former Cotswold farmhouse in centre of charming village. Cosy lounge, wood floors and original open fire. Two particularly comfortable converted cottage rooms. Intimate, low-beamed 'hop-strung' dining-room.

GULWORTHY – Devon – **503** H 32 – **see Tavistock**

GUNNERSIDE – North Yorkshire – **502** N 20 – ⊠ **Darlington** **22 A1**
🚇 London 268 mi – Newcastle upon Tyne 60 mi – Richmond 17 mi

⌂ **Oxnop Hall** without rest ⟡ ⩓ ⟁ ⁑ 🅿️
*Low Oxnop, West : 1 ½ m. on B 6270 ⊠ DL11 6JJ – ℰ (01748) 886 253
– www.oxnophall.com – Fax (01748) 886 253 – March-October*
5 rm ⌴ – †£34/49 ††£66/76

♦ Pleasant stone-built 17C farmhouse and working sheep farm in agreeable hillside position. Cosy little lounge. Bedrooms feature beams, mullion windows and rural views.

GUNWALLOE – Cornwall – **503** E 33 – **see Helston**

HADDENHAM – Buckinghamshire – **504** R 28 – pop. **4 720** **11 C2**
🚇 London 54 mi – Aylesbury 8 mi – Oxford 21 mi

🍴 **The Green Dragon** ⩃ ⁑ 🅿️ VISA ⚫️
ⓐ *8 Churchway ⊠ HP17 8AA – ℰ (01844) 291 403
– www.greendragonhaddenham.co.uk – enquiries@oaktreeinns.co.uk
– Fax (01844) 299 532 – Closed 25 December and Sunday dinner*
Rest – (booking essential) Carte £ 24/32

♦ Warmly decorated, modern-style pub-restaurant with a friendly atmosphere and pleasant service. Very good value, from simple pub food to more elaborate restaurant-style dishes.

HADLEIGH – Suffolk – 504 W 27 – pop. 7 124   15 **C3**

▶ London 72 mi – Cambridge 49 mi – Colchester 17 mi – Ipswich 10 mi
🚹 Hadleigh Library, 29 High St 𝒸 (01473) 823778

↑ **Edge Hall** without rest   🚗 **P**
2 High St ✉ *IP7 5AP –* 𝒸 *(01473) 822 458 – www.edgehall.co.uk*
– r.rolfe@edgehall.co.uk
6 rm ☲ – †£68/100 ††£90/150
◆ One of the oldest houses in the town (1590), with a Georgian façade. Spacious, comfy bedrooms are traditionally furnished, as are the communal areas. Very well-kept gardens.

HADLEY HEATH – Worcs. – see Droitwich Spa

HAILSHAM – East Sussex – 504 U 31 – pop. 19 177   8 **B3**

▶ London 57 mi – Brighton 23 mi – Eastbourne 7 mi – Hastings 20 mi
📷 Wellshurst G. & C.C. Hellingly North St, 𝒸 (01435) 813 636

at Magham Down Northeast : 2 m. by A 295 on A 271 – ✉ Hailsham

🏠 **Olde Forge**   📶 **P** 𝗩𝗜𝗦𝗔 ⓪⓪
✉ *BN27 1PN –* 𝒸 *(01323) 842 893 – www.theoldeforgehotel.co.uk*
– theoldeforgehotel@tesco.net – Fax (01323) 842 893
6 rm ☲ – †£48 ††£90   **Rest** – (dinner only) Menu £27
◆ Privately owned timbered house with cottage feel, charmingly run by helpful, friendly owners. Rooms are individually furnished in elegant pine; one boasts a four-poster bed. Beamed restaurant with carefully compiled menu.

> If breakfast is included the ☲ symbol appears after the number of rooms.

HALAM – Nottinghamshire ▌*Great Britain*   16 **B1**

▶ London 134 mi – Derby 8 mi – Nottingham 8 mi
📷 Southwell Minster★★ **AC**, E : 2 m. on Mansfield Rd, Halam Hill, Market Pl and A 612

🍴 **Waggon and Horses**   🚭 **P** 𝗩𝗜𝗦𝗔 ⓪⓪
The Turnpike, Mansfield Rd ✉ *NG22 8AE –* 𝒸 *(01636) 813 109*
– www.thewaggonathalam.co.uk – info@thewaggonathalam.co.uk – Fax (01636) 816 228
Rest – (Closed Sunday dinner) Menu £15 – Carte £20/35
◆ A bright and up-to-date pub. Daily blackboard menu features lots of fish and local meat dishes: sides of veg are free. Good value set menu at lunch, with OAP discount Tues-Sun.

HALFORD – Warwickshire – 503 P 27 – pop. 301   19 **C3**

▶ London 94 mi – Oxford 43 mi – Stratford-upon-Avon 8 mi

↑ **Old Manor House** ⌂   🚗 ⚓ ✗ **P** 𝗩𝗜𝗦𝗔 ⓪⓪ 𝗔𝗘
Queens St ✉ *CV36 5BT –* 𝒸 *(01789) 740 264 – www.oldmanor-halford.co.uk*
– info@oldmanor.halford.fsnet.co.uk – Fax (01789) 740 609 – Closed Christmas and New Year
3 rm – †£50/60 ††£90/100
Rest – (by arrangement, communal dining) Menu £25
◆ Characterful house in quiet residential area, well located for Stratford and the Cotswolds. Spacious garden next to River Stour. Well appointed drawing room and atmospheric bedrooms with rich fabrics. Family style dining; fine tableware; good use of local produce.

HALFWAY BRIDGE – W. Sussex – 504 R 31 – see Petworth

HALIFAX – West Yorkshire – **502** O 22 – pop. 83 570   22 **B2**

> ▣ London 205 mi – Bradford 8 mi – Burnley 21 mi – Leeds 15 mi
>   – Manchester 28 mi
> 🄸 Piece Hall ℰ (01422) 368725, halifax@ytbtic.co.uk
> 🄶 Halifax Bradley Hall Holywell Green, ℰ (01422) 374 108
> 🄶 Halifax West End Highroad Well Paddock Lane, ℰ (01422) 341 878
> 🄶 Ryburn Sowerby Bridge Norland, ℰ (01422) 831 355
> 🄶 Lightcliffe Knowle Top Rd, ℰ (01422) 202 459
> 🄶 Ogden Union Lane, ℰ (01422) 244 171

🏠🏠🏠 **Holdsworth House** ❧   🚗 🛖 & rm, ☏ 🔏 **P** 𝚟𝚒𝚜𝚊 ⓞⓞ 𝔸𝔼 ⓞ
Holmfield, North : 3 m. by A 629 and Shay Lane ✉ *HX2 9TG – ℰ (01422)*
240 024 – www.holdsworthhouse.co.uk – info@holdsworthhouse.co.uk
– Fax (01422) 245 174 – Closed 24 December-3 January
36 rm ☑ – †£105/125 ††£150 – 4 suites
Rest – (closed Saturday lunch and Sunday) Carte £25/42
♦ Characterful and extended part 17C manor house in a quiet location. Comfortable,
traditionally decorated rooms with wood furniture. Country house-style throughout.
Three-roomed, wood-panelled restaurant overlooks garden.

XX **Design House**   🄰🄲 ⇔ **P** 𝚟𝚒𝚜𝚊 ⓞⓞ 𝔸𝔼 ⓞ
Dean Clough (Gate 5) ✉ *HX3 5AX – ℰ (01422) 383 242*
– www.designhouserestaurant.co.uk – enquiries@designhouserestaurant.co.uk
– Fax (01422) 322 732 – Closed 26 December-8 January, Saturday lunch, Sunday
and Bank Holidays
Rest – Menu £21 (dinner) – Carte £30/41
♦ Located within converted mill on outskirts of town, an impressively stylish and
modern restaurant with Philippe Starck furniture. Varied menu of contemporary British cooking.

🄸▢ **Shibden Mill Inn** with rm   🚗 🛖 **P** 𝚟𝚒𝚜𝚊 ⓞⓞ 𝔸𝔼
Shibden Mill Fold, Northeast : 2¼ m. by A 58 and Kell Lane (turning left at Stump
Cross public house) on Blake Hill Rd ✉ *HX3 7UL – ℰ (01422) 365 840*
– www.shibdenmillinn.com – simonheaton@shibdenmillinn.com – Fax (01422)
362 971 – Closed 25 and 31 December dinner
11 rm ☑ – †£68/75 ††£100/136   **Rest** – Menu £18 (lunch) – Carte £22/32
♦ A sense of historic charm inhabits the cosy, cluttered rooms of this inn. Menus are
wide-ranging, offering mainly traditional British dishes, with a few influences from
the Med. Bedrooms have good facilities, the 5 newest are most modern.

HALL GREEN – W. Mids. – **502** O 26 – see Birmingham

HALNAKER – W. Sussex – see Chichester

HALTWHISTLE – Northumberland – **501** M 19 – pop. 3 811   24 **A2**

▮ Great Britain

> ▣ London 335 mi – Carlisle 22 mi – Newcastle upon Tyne 37 mi
> 🄸 Railway Station, Station Rd ℰ (01434) 322002,
>   haltwhistletic@btconnect.com
> 🄶 Wallend Farm Greenhead, ℰ (01697) 747 367
> 🄶 Hadrian's Wall★★, N : 4½ m. by A 6079 – Housesteads★★ **AC**, NE : 6 m. by
>   B 6318 – Roman Army Museum★ **AC**, NW : 5 m. by A 69 and B 6318 –
>   Vindolanda (Museum★) **AC**, NE : 5 m. by A 69 – Steel Rig (≼★) NE : 5½ m.
>   by B 6318

🏠🄷 **Centre of Britain**   ☏ 🔏 **P** 𝚟𝚒𝚜𝚊 ⓞⓞ 𝔸𝔼 ⓞ
Main St ✉ *NE49 0BH – ℰ (01434) 322 422 – www.centre-of-britain.org.uk*
– enquiries@centre-of-britain.org.uk – Fax (01434) 322 655
– Closed 25-26 December
12 rm ☑ – †£50 ††£110   **Rest** – (dinner only) Menu £20
♦ Attractive hotel on busy main street. Oldest part, a pele tower, dates from 15C.
Comfortable modern décor, including bedrooms, incorporates original architectural
features. Glass-roofed restaurant with light, airy feel.

ENGLAND

Ashcroft without rest
Lantys Lonnen ✉ NE49 0DA – ℰ (01434) 320213
– www.ashcroftguesthouse.co.uk – info@ashcroftguesthouse.co.uk – Fax (01434)
321641 – Closed 25 December
8 rm ☲ – ♦£36/55 ♦♦£84/90
♦ Imposing Victorian house, formerly a vicarage, with beautifully kept gardens. Family run and attractively furnished throughout creating a welcoming atmosphere. Large bedrooms.

HAMBLE-LE-RICE – Southampton – **503** Q 31 – see Southampton

---

HAMBLETON – Rutland – see Oakham

HANLEY SWAN – Worcs. – **503** N 27 – see Upton-upon-Severn

HARDWICK – Cambs. – see Cambridge

Your opinions are important to us:
please write and let us know about your discoveries and experiences –
good and bad!

ENGLAND

HARLAXTON – Lincs. – **502** S 25 – see Grantham

HAROME – N. Yorks. – see Helmsley

HARPENDEN – Hertfordshire – **504** S 28 – pop. 28 452   12 **A2**
🖪 London 32 mi – Luton 6 mi
🖪 Harpenden Common East Common, ℰ (01582) 711320
🖪 Hammonds End, ℰ (01582) 712580

The Bean Tree
20A Leyton Rd ✉ AL5 2HU – ℰ (01582) 460901 – www.thebeantree.com
– enquiries@thebeantree.com – Fax (01582) 460826 – Closed Saturday lunch,
Sunday dinner and Monday
Rest – Menu £17/27 – Carte £28/53 ⏸
♦ Converted red-brick cottage with bean tree and smart terrace. Intimate, softly lit restaurant with sage green palette. Carefully sought ingredients; precise modern cooking.

The White Horse
Hatching Green, Southwest : 1 m. by A 1081 on B 487 ✉ AL5 2JW – ℰ (01582)
469290 – www.atouchofnovelli.com – twh@atouchofnovelli.com
– Closed 25 December
Rest – (Closed Sunday dinner) (booking essential) Menu £20 – Carte £24/33
♦ Appealing 17C whitewashed pub with a cosy bar, formal restaurant and large terrace. Part-owned by Jean-Christophe Novelli, his influences can clearly be seen on the menu.

The Fox
469 Luton Rd, Kinsbourne Green, Northwest : 2 m. on A 1081 ✉ AL5 3QE
– ℰ (01582) 713817 – www.thefoxharpenden.co.uk
Rest – Carte £19/34
♦ Cosy country pub with a decked terrace and friendly atmosphere. With a wide ranging menu, popular rotisserie and list of daily specials, there's something for everyone.

▶ London 211 mi – Bradford 18 mi – Leeds 15 mi – Newcastle upon
  Tyne 76 mi – York 22 mi
🏛 Royal Baths, Crescent Rd 🕾 (01423) 537300, tic@harrogate.gov.uk
🏠 Forest Lane Head, 🕾 (01423) 863 158
🏠 Pannal Follifoot Rd, 🕾 (01423) 872 628
🏠 Oakdale, 🕾 (01423) 567 162
🏠 Crimple Valley Hookstone Wood Rd, 🕾 (01423) 883 485
🔲 Town★
🏛 Fountains Abbey★★★ **AC** :- Studley Royal **AC** (≤★ from Anne Boleyn's
  Seat) - Fountains Hall (Fa½ade★), N : 13 m. by A 61 and B 6265 AY –
  Harewood House★★ (The Gallery★) **AC**, S : 7½ m. by A 61 BZ

Plan on next page

🏨 Rudding Park   📶 🕭 🎧 🖻 🎱 ⅏ rm, 🅰 rest, 🕼 🕯 🌢 **P** 🆚 ⊕⊚ 🅰🅴 ⓪
*Rudding Park, Follifoot, Southeast : 3 ¾ m. by A 661 ⊠ HG3 1JH – 🕾 (01423)
871 350 – www.ruddingpark.co.uk – sales@ruddingpark.com – Fax (01423)
872 286*
46 rm ⌺ – †£ 165 ††£ 195 – 3 suites
Rest *The Clocktower* – Menu £ 32 – Carte £ 31/40 **s**
♦ Grade I listed Georgian house in rural location with modern extension. Comfortable, elegant style throughout. Rooms are simple and classical with modern, colourful
fabrics. Smart, contemporary brasserie with oak floors.

🏨 Hotel du Vin   🎱 ⅏ 🕼 🌢 **P** 🆚 ⊕⊚ 🅰🅴
*Prospect Pl ⊠ HG1 1LB – 🕾 (01423) 856 800 – www.hotelduvin.com
– info.harrogate@hotelduvin.com – Fax (01423) 856 801*   BZ**a**
48 rm – †£ 125/170 ††£ 125/170, ⌺ £ 13.50
Rest *Bistro* – French – (light lunch) Carte £ 30/40 🕸
♦ Terrace of Georgian houses overlooking pleasant green. Individually appointed
bedrooms with wine-theme decor and modern facilities. Buzzy, modern, stylish
French bistro and private dining rooms. Good menu of Gallic influenced dishes.

🏨 The Balmoral   🅰 rest, 🕼 **P** 🆚 ⊕⊚
*Franklin Mount ⊠ HG1 5EJ – 🕾 (01423) 508 208 – www.balmoralhotel.co.uk
– info@balmoralhotel.co.uk – Fax (01423) 530 652*   BY**v**
20 rm – †£ 80/99 ††£ 135/150, ⌺ £ 10 – 3 suites
Rest *Harrogate Grille* – (dinner only) Menu £ 14 (lunch) – Carte £ 25/33
♦ Privately run, Gothic-style, Victorian property; charm accentuated by antique fur-
nishings and individually decorated rooms. Bar with Harry Houdini memorabilia.
Bustling informality in restaurant, where modern minimalism prevails.

🏠 Alexa House without rest   📶 🕼 **P** 🆚 ⊕⊚ 🅰🅴
*26 Ripon Rd ⊠ HG1 2JJ – 🕾 (01423) 501 988 – www.alexa-house.co.uk
– enquires@alexa-house.co.uk – Fax (01423) 504 086
– Closed last 2 weeks December*   AY**n**
13 rm ⌺ – †£ 55/70 ††£ 85/90
♦ Georgian house built in 1830 for Baron-de-Ferrier: contemporary interior touches
provide a seamless contrast. Bedrooms in two buildings: more characterful in main
house.

🏠 Alexandra Court without rest   📶 🕼 **P** 🆚 ⊕⊚ 🅰🅴
*8 Alexandra Rd ⊠ HG1 5JS – 🕾 (01423) 502 764
– www.alexandracourt.co.uk
– office@alexandracourt.co.uk
– Fax (01423) 850 383*   BY**o**
12 rm ⌺ – †£ 57/58 ††£ 82
♦ Detached, family owned Victorian house, retaining original features, in quiet residential area. Bedrooms and communal areas have a simple elegance in décor and
ambience.

ENGLAND

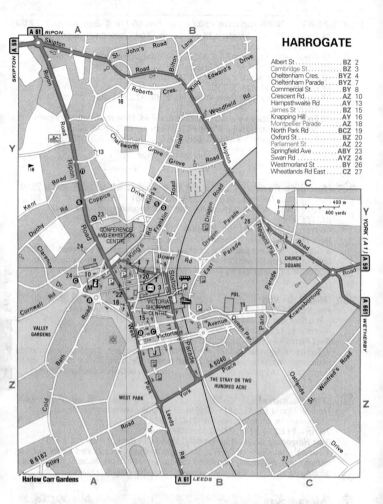

HARROGATE

↑ **Brookfield House** without rest ❧ 🛇 🄿 VISA ⑳ AE ①

5 Alexandra Rd ⊠ HG1 5JS – 𝒞 (01423) 506 646
– www.brookfieldhousehotel.co.uk – office@brookfieldhousehotel.co.uk
– Closed Christmas and New Year BY**s**
6 rm ⊇ – †£65/75 ††£75/85

♦ Family owned Victorian property in a quiet, residential location close to the town centre. Homely feel in communal areas and comfortable bedrooms with a mix of styles.

↑ **The Bijou** without rest 🖨 🄿 VISA ⑳ AE ①

17 Ripon Road ⊠ HG1 2JL – 𝒞 (01423) 567 974 – www.thebijou.co.uk
– info@thebijou.co.uk – Fax (01423) 566 200 AY**s**
10 rm ⊇ – †£85 ††£95

♦ As the name suggests, a small period house, in the centre of town close to the Convention Centre. Immaculately kept bedrooms; elegantly set breakfast room.

↥ **Acacia** without rest   ⚥ ⁌ P
3 Springfield Ave ⊠ *HG1 2HR* – ℰ *(01423) 560752*
– *www.acaciaharrogate.co.uk* – *dee@acaciaharrogate.co.uk*
– *Closed Christmas to New Year and restricted opening November-March,
minimum stay 2 nights*   AY**o**
4 rm ⌑ – ✝£55/85 ✝✝£75/85
♦ Centrally located Victorian solid stone guesthouse, within a few minutes' walk of
the shops; very personably run. Immaculately kept throughout. Attractive, pine-clad
bedrooms.

XX **Quantro**   AC 🅗 VISA ◍ AE
3 Royal Par ⊠ *HG1 2SZ* – ℰ *(01423) 503034* – *www.quantro.co.uk*
– *info@quantro.co.uk* – *Fax (01423) 503034* – *Closed 25-26 December, 1 January
and Sunday*   AZ**a**
Rest – Mediterranean – Menu £14 – Carte £24/29
♦ Modern art murals and mirrors adorn this smart restaurant. Comfy banquettes and
black tables. Good value mix of interesting dishes with Mediterranean underpinnings.

XX **Orchid**   AC ⬦ P VISA ◍ AE ◉
28 Swan Rd ⊠ *HG1 2SE* – ℰ *(01423) 560425* – *www.orchidrestaurant.co.uk*
– *info@orchidrestaurant.co.uk* – *Fax (01423) 530967*
– *Closed Saturday lunch*   AZ**c**
Rest – South East Asian – Menu £13/22 – Carte £22/38
♦ Unfussy, uncluttered restaurant with Asian styling. Polite, friendly service adds to
the enjoyment of richly authentic dishes from a wide range of south-east Asian
countries.

X **Sasso**   VISA ◍ AE
8-10 Princes Sq ⊠ *HG1 1LX* – ℰ *(01423) 508838* – *Fax (01423) 508838*
– *Closed 25 December, Sunday and Bank Holidays*   BZ**c**
Rest – Italian – Carte £22/36
♦ In the basement of a 19C property. Antiques, ceramics and modern art embellish
the interior. The menu offers a good choice of authentic Italian dishes with modern
influences.

at Kettlesing West : 6½ m. by A 59 – AY – ⊠ Harrogate

↥ **Knabbs Ash** without rest   ⩻ 🖛 🕭 ⚥ P
Skipton Rd, on A 59 ⊠ *HG3 2LT* – ℰ *(01423) 771040* – *www.knabbsash.co.uk*
– *sheila@knabbsash.co.uk* – *Closed 25-26 December*
3 rm ⌑ – ✝£50/60 ✝✝£70/75
♦ Stone built cottage with spacious gardens and grounds. Cosy lounge; pine furnished breakfast room. Homely and simple, largely floral interior; rooms individually
decorated.

The ❀ award is the crème de la crème.
This is awarded to restaurants
which are really worth travelling miles for!

HARTINGTON – Derbyshire – **502** O 24 – ⊠ Buxton   16 **A1**
🖸 London 168 mi – Derby 36 mi – Manchester 40 mi – Sheffield 34 mi
– Stoke-on-Trent 22 mi

🏠 **Biggin Hall** ⚘   ⩻ 🖛 P VISA ◍ AE
Biggin, Southeast : 2 m. by B 5054 ⊠ *SK17 0DH* – ℰ *(01298) 84451*
– *www.bigginhall.co.uk* – *enquiries@bigginhall.co.uk* – *Fax (01298) 84681*
20 rm ⌑ – ✝£50/70 ✝✝£120/140
Rest – (booking essential) Menu £11/19 **s**
♦ Charming house with much rustic personality and individuality. Stone floored
lounges and open fires. Antique furnished bedrooms vary in size and shape. Elegant
dining room with low beams.

ENGLAND

HARTLAND – Devon – **503** G 31   1 **B1**

▣ London 221 mi – Bude 15 mi – Clovelly 4 mi

⌂   **Golden Park** without rest ⌖   🚗 🕦 ℛ 🖐 **P**
Southwest : 5 m. following signs for Elmscott and Bude ✉ EX39 6EP
– ℰ (01237) 441 254 – www.goldenpark.co.uk – lynda@goldenpark.co.uk
– Closed 25 December and restricted opening in winter
3 rm ⌷ – †£60 ††£65/90

♦ Walk to the North Devon coast from this delightfully set part 17C farmhouse. Style and character prevail, particularly in guests' lounge and beamed, smartly decorated rooms.

🍴   **The Hart Inn**   🚗 🕦 **P** **VISA** **⚫** **AE**
The Square ✉ EX39 6BL – ℰ (01237) 441 474 – www.thehartinn.com
– bjornmoen@hotmail.com – Closed 25 December and first two weeks in February
Rest – (Closed Sunday dinner and Monday lunch) Carte £11/16

♦ Part 14 and 16C coaching inn with rustic, homely interior. Regularly changing menu features some Scandinavian influences but produce remains seasonal and local; generous portions.

HARWELL – Oxfordshire – **503** Q 29 – pop. 2 015   10 **B3**

▣ London 64 mi – Oxford 16 mi – Reading 18 mi – Swindon 22 mi

🏨   **Kingswell**   ⅙ rm, 🕦 🖐 🔊 **P** **VISA** **⚫** **AE** **①**
Reading Rd, East : ¾ m. on A 417 ✉ OX11 0LZ – ℰ (01235) 833 043
– www.kingswell-hotel.com – kingswell@breathemail.net – Fax (01235) 833 193
– Closed 24-30 December
20 rm ⌷ – †£98 ††£115   **Rest** – Menu £21/25 – Carte £19/40 **s**

♦ Large redbrick hotel located on the south Oxfordshire Downs. Convenient for Didcot rail and Oxford. Spacious, uniform, traditional bedrooms and pubby public areas. Classic menus served in traditional dining room.

HARWICH and DOVERCOURT – Essex – **504** X 28 – pop. 20 130   13 **D2**

▣ London 78 mi – Chelmsford 41 mi – Colchester 20 mi – Ipswich 23 mi
⛴ to Denmark (Esbjerg) (DFDS Seaways A/S) 3-4 weekly (20 h) – to The Netherlands (Hook of Holland) (Stena Line) 2 daily (3 h 30 mn)
🛈 Iconfield Park, Parkeston ℰ (01255) 506139, harwichtic@btconnect.com
🖼 Parkeston Station Rd, ℰ (01255) 503 616

🏨   **Pier at Harwich**   ⇐ 🕦 🖐 **P** **VISA** **⚫** **AE** **①**
The Quay ✉ CO12 3HH – ℰ (01255) 241 212 – www.milsomhotels.com
– pier@milsomhotels.com – Fax (01255) 551 922
14 rm ⌷ – †£80 ††£185
Rest *Harbourside* – Seafood – Menu £25 (lunch) – Carte £26/43
Rest *Ha'Penny* – Carte £20/27

♦ Bright Victorian building located on the quayside giving many bedrooms views of the area's busy sea lanes. Décor is comfortably stylish and contemporary with a nautical theme. Seafood restaurant with North Sea outlook. Informal bistro.

HASTINGS and ST LEONARDS – East Sussex – **504** V 31   8 **B3**
– pop. 85 828

▣ London 65 mi – Brighton 37 mi – Folkestone 37 mi – Maidstone 34 mi
🛈 Town Hall, Queen's Sq, Priory Meadow -The Stade, Old Town ℰ (0845) 2741001, hic@hastings.gov.uk
🖼 Hastings G & CC St Leonards-on-Sea Battle Rd, Beauport Park, ℰ (01424) 854 243

Plan opposite

🏠   **Tower House 1066** without rest   🚗 🕦 🖐 **VISA** **⚫** **①**
26-28 Tower Road West ✉ TN38 0RG – ℰ (01424) 427 217
– www.towerhouse1066.co.uk – reservations@towerhousehotel.com
– Fax (01424) 430 165 – Closed 1-14 January   **AYc**
10 rm ⌷ – †£45/65 ††£90/99

♦ Friendly and well run, a redbrick Victorian house in a residential area. Comfortably furnished with individually decorated bedrooms and a conservatory bar lounge area.

HASTINGS ST. LEONARDS

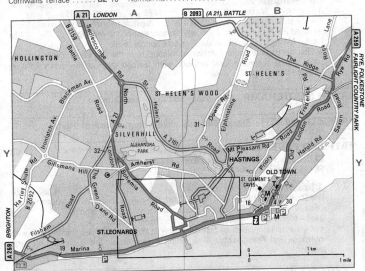

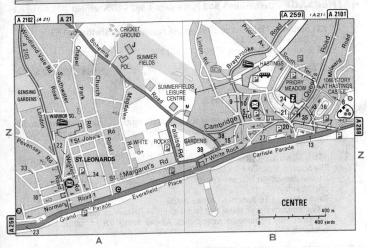

 If breakfast is included the ⌂ symbol appears after the number of rooms.

⌂ **Zanzibar** without rest ⁣ 📶 VISA ⓶ AE ①
9 Eversfield Place ⊠ TN34 6BY – ℰ (01424) 460 109 – www.zanzibarhotel.co.uk
– info@zanzibarhotel.co.uk AZc
9 rm – ♦£170/215 ♦♦£170/215
♦ Contemporary guest house with slightly unusual design. Bedrooms are named after countries and continents; South America is largest, with feature whirlpool bath and seaview.

X **St Clements** VISA ⓶ ①
🐭 *3 Mercatoria, St Leonards on Sea ⊠ TN38 0EB – ℰ (01424) 200 355*
– www.stclementsrestaurant.co.uk – enquiries@stclementsrestaurant.co.uk
– Closed 25-26 December, 1 January, Sunday dinner and Monday AZa
Rest – Menu £17 (weekdays)/22 – Carte approx. £28
♦ Charming, contemporary restaurant minutes from the sea. Classically based, seasonal menus showcase local produce, with seafood fresh off the boats. Relaxed, intimate mood.

HATCH BEAUCHAMP – Somerset – **503** K 30 – **see Taunton**

HATFIELD HEATH – Essex – **504** U 28 – **see Bishop's Stortford (Herts.)**

HATFIELD PEVEREL – Essex – **504** V 28 – **pop. 3 258** Great Britain 13 **C2**
🖸 London 39 mi – Chelmsford 8 mi – Maldon 12 mi
🖸 Colchester - Castle and Museum★, E : 13 m. by A 12

XX **Blue Strawberry Bistrot** 🍴 P VISA ⓶ AE
The Street ⊠ CM3 2DW – ℰ (01245) 381 333 – www.bluestrawberrybistrot.co.uk
– Fax (01245) 340 498 – Closed Saturday lunch and Sunday dinner
Rest – Menu £15 (weekdays)/21 – Carte dinner £21/33
♦ Make your reservation by first name only in this characterful converted pub with inglenook and Victorian style. Rear dining terrace. Classic British cooking off large menus.

HATHERSAGE – Derbyshire – **502** P 24 – **pop. 1 582** – ⊠ **Sheffield** 16 **A1**
(S. Yorks.)
🖸 London 177 mi – Derby 39 mi – Manchester 34 mi – Sheffield 11 mi
– Stoke-on-Trent 44 mi
🖸 Sickleholme Bamford, ℰ (01433) 651 306

🏠 **The George** ⁣ 📶 ♨ P VISA ⓶ AE ①
⊠ *S32 1BB – ℰ (01433) 650 436 – www.george-hotel.net*
– info@george-hotel.net – Fax (01433) 650 099
22 rm ⊑ – ♦£88/97 ♦♦£165
Rest *George's* – Menu £40
♦ Built in 14C as an inn to serve the packhorse route. Sympathetically restored in rustic style, with oak beams and stone walls. Bedrooms have a bright, more modern feel. Rustically decorated, vibrant-hued dining room.

XX **The Walnut Club** 🍴 AC P VISA ⓶
The Square, Main Rd ⊠ S32 1BB – ℰ (01433) 651 155
– www.thewalnutclub.com – craig@thewalnutclub.com – Closed Sunday dinner and Monday
Rest – Menu £16 (lunch) – Carte £20/30
♦ Contemporary style restaurant found deep in Derbyshire walking country, serving generously portioned organic dishes. All day dining. Varied menus. Live jazz at weekends.

HAWES – North Yorkshire – **502** N 21 22 **A1**
🖸 London 253 mi – Kendal 27 mi – Leeds 72 mi – Newcastle upon Tyne 76 mi
– York 65 mi
🖸 Dales Countryside Museum, Station Yard ℰ (01969) 666210.
hawes@ytbtic.co.uk

Simonstone Hall ⚜

Simonstone, North : 1½ m. on Muker rd ⌧ *DL8 3LY –* ✆ *(01969) 667 255*
– www.simonstonehall.co.uk – email@simonstonehall.demon.co.uk – Fax (01969)
667 741

18 rm ⌷ – **†**£160/190 **††**£220/240 – 1 suite
Rest – (bar lunch) Menu £ 30 – Carte £ 21/30
♦ Part 18C country house, with historic feel, amidst lovely countryside. Individually furnished bedrooms, many of which enjoy pleasant views from the front of the building. Dining room or tavern eating options.

Stone House ⚜

Sedbusk, North : 1 m. by Muker rd ⌧ *DL8 3PT –* ✆ *(01969) 667 571*
– www.stonehousehotel.com – daleshotel@aol.com – Fax (01969) 667 720
– Closed January and mid week in December
23 rm ⌷ – **†**£49/138 **††**£138 **Rest** – (dinner only) Menu £ 35
♦ Built in 1908 as a family home. Interior decorated in traditional style; public areas include billiard room and oak panelled lounge. Some rooms with private conservatories. Dining room has exposed beams and wooden tables.

Rookhurst Country House ⚜

Gayle, South : ½ m. by Gayle rd ⌧ *DL8 3RT –* ✆ *(01969) 667 454*
– www.rookhurst.co.uk – enquiries@rookhurst.co.uk – Closed Christmas and New Year
5 rm ⌷ – **†**£55 **††**£110/130
Rest – (dinner only) (booking essential) (residents only) Menu £ 20 **s**
♦ Spacious yet cosy country house with a very comfortable, smart, traditional atmosphere that's friendly and informal. Convenient for the Pennine Way. Uncluttered bedrooms.

Cockett's

Market Pl ⌧ *DL8 3RD –* ✆ *(01969) 667 312 – www.cocketts.co.uk*
– enquiries@cocketts.co.uk – Fax (01969) 667 162
– Closed 25-26 December and 3 January - 1 February
10 rm ⌷ – **†**£45/50 **††**£69/89
Rest – (closed Tuesday) (dinner only) Menu £ 20 – Carte £ 19/28
♦ Grade II listed building with a historic inscribed door lintel - reputedly the most photographed doorway in the country. Cosy, traditional atmosphere throughout. Dining room with enticing, age-old ambience.

Red = Pleasant. Look for the red ⚜ and 🏠 symbols.

HAWKSHEAD – Cumbria – **502** L 20 – **pop. 570** – ⌧ **Ambleside** 21 **A2**
🔲 *Great Britain*

🔼 London 283 mi – Carlisle 52 mi – Kendal 19 mi
🔼 Main Street ✆ (015394) 36946 (summer only), enquiries@hawksheadtouristinfo.org.uk
◉ Village★
🔳 Lake Windermere★★ – Coniston Water★ (Brantwood★, on east side), SW : by B 5285

at Near Sawrey Southeast : 2 m. on B 5285 – ⌧ Ambleside

Ees Wyke Country House ⚜

⌧ *LA22 0JZ –* ✆ *(015394) 36 393 – www.eeswyke.co.uk – mail@eeswyke.co.uk*
– Restricted opening in winter
8 rm ⌷ – **†**£50/80 **††**£100/130
Rest – (dinner only) (booking essential) Menu £ 34
♦ Panoramic views of Esthwaite Water and Grizedale Forest from this large, impressive Georgian house. Good sized bedrooms with distinctive, homely charm. Dining room's large windows afford lovely views.

ENGLAND

at Far Sawrey Southeast : 2½ m. on B 5285 – ⊠ Ambleside

⤂

West Vale   ⇐ ⌘ ⁏ P VISA ⊚⊙
⊠ LA22 0LQ – ℰ (015394) 42817 – www.westvalecountryhouse.co.uk
– enquiries@westvalecountryhouse.co.uk – Fax (015394) 45302
– Closed 25-26 December
7 rm ⌕ – ♦£75/110 ♦♦£120/170   **Rest** – (by arrangement) Menu £36
♦ Victorian house on edge of hamlet with attractive country views. A warm welcome
to an interior with open-fired, stone-floored sitting room and snug bedrooms. Meals
locally sourced, proudly home cooked.

HAWNBY – North Yorkshire – **502** Q 21 – ⊠ Helmsley   23 **C1**
🚘 London 245 mi – Middlesbrough 27 mi – Newcastle upon Tyne 69 mi
– York 30 mi

🏠

Hawnby ❧   ⇐ ⌗ ⚲ ⌘ ⁏ P VISA ⊚⊙
⊠ YO62 5QS – ℰ (01439) 798202 – www.hawnbyhotel.co.uk
– info@hawnbyhotel.co.uk – Fax (01439) 798344
9 rm ⌕ – ♦£69 ♦♦£89   **Rest** – Carte £18/29
♦ Personally run small hotel in a very rural location with commanding views of
nearby countryside – ideal for walking in the Dales. Snug bedrooms with a cottage
feel. Tried-and-tested menus.

at Laskill Northeast : 2¼ m. by Osmotherley rd – ⊠ Hawnby

⤂

Laskill Grange without rest   ⌗ ⚵ P VISA ⊚⊙
Easterside ⊠ YO62 5NB – ℰ (01439) 798268 – www.laskillgrange.co.uk
– laskillgrange@tiscali.co.uk
7 rm ⌕ – ♦£38/80 ♦♦£80/120
♦ A working farm with four cottagey bedrooms set in two converted Victorian stable
blocks, surrounded by 1000 acres of rolling farmland. Breakfast served in sunny
conservatory.

HAWORTH – West Yorkshire – **502** O 22 – **pop. 6 078** – ⊠ Keighley   22 **A2**
▌ Great Britain
🚘 London 213 mi – Burnley 22 mi – Leeds 22 mi – Manchester 34 mi
🛈 2-4 West Lane ℰ (01535) 642329, haworth@ytbtic.co.uk
◉ Brontë Parsonage Museum **AC**

⤂

Ashmount Country House without rest   ⌗ ⁏ P VISA ⊚⊙
Mytholmes Lane ⊠ BD22 8EZ – ℰ (01535) 645726
– www.ashmounthaworth.co.uk – info@ashmounthaworth.co.uk – Fax (01535)
642550
10 rm ⌕ – ♦£60 ♦♦£145/160
♦ Built in 1870 by the physician to the Brontë sisters, this refurbished house has extremely comfortable bedrooms with period furniture and state-of-the-art bathrooms.

⤂

Old Registry without rest   ⁏ VISA ⊚⊙ AE
4 Main St ⊠ BD22 8DA – ℰ (01535) 646503 – www.theoldregistryhaworth.co.uk
– enquiries@theoldregistryhaworth.co.uk – Closed 24-27 December
10 rm ⌕ – ♦£85 ♦♦£100
♦ Stone house – a former registrar's office – on the cobbled main street. Bedrooms
are individually themed, featuring rich fabrics and antique furniture. Breakfast of local
produce.

⤂

Rosebud Cottage   ⌗ ⌘ ⁏ P VISA ⊚⊙ AE
1 Belle Isle Rd ⊠ BD22 8QQ – ℰ (01535) 640321 – www.rosebudcottage.co.uk
– info@rosebudcottage.co.uk – Closed 25-26 December
5 rm ⌕ – ♦£35/45 ♦♦£75/80   **Rest** – (by arrangement) Menu £16
♦ Compact, cosy sandstone end-of-terrace cottage built in 1752, next to station on
preserved railway line. The homely bedrooms are all very different with individual
themes. Pine-furnished dining room overlooks conservatory; home-cooked dishes.

ENGLAND

XX **Weaver's** with rm   AC rest, ✗ ((p)) VISA OO AE ①
15 West Lane ✉ *BD22 8DU* – ☎ *(01535) 643 822* – *www.weaversmallhotel.co.uk*
– *weaversltd@btconnect.com* – *Fax (01535) 644 832* – *Closed 24 December-
10 January*
3 rm ☲ – †£60 ††£100
Rest – (Closed Sunday and Monday) Menu £18 (lunch) – Carte £23/35
♦ Former weavers cottages with an informal atmosphere and some charm. Characterful cluttered lounge with ornaments and artefacts. Homely cooking, surroundings
and bedrooms.

at Cullingworth Southeast : 3 m. by B 6144 – ✉ Haworth

↑ **The Manor** without rest   🚗 ((p)) P VISA OO AE ①
Sutton Drive ✉ *BD13 5BQ* – ☎ *(01535) 274 374* – *www.cullingworthmanor.co.uk*
– *info@cullingworthmanor.co.uk* – *Fax (01535) 274 374*
3 rm ☲ – †£55/65 ††£65/75
♦ Modernised former manor house with formal gardens and spacious, tastefully converted bedrooms. Breakfast room/lounge with leather sofas and French windows
onto decking.

HAYDON BRIDGE – Northd. – **501** N 19 – see Hexham

HAYLING ISLAND – Hampshire – **504** R 31 – pop. 14 842   **6 B3**
◻ London 77 mi – Brighton 45 mi – Southampton 28 mi
🅱 Beachlands, Seafront ☎ (023) 9246 7111, tourism@havant.gov.uk
🖼 Links Lane, ☎ (023) 9246 4446

↑ **Cockle Warren Cottage** without rest   🚗 ⊐ ((p)) P VISA OO
36 Seafront ✉ *PO11 9HL* – ☎ *(023) 9246 4961* – *www.cocklewarren.co.uk*
– *cockle-warren@amserve.com* – *Fax (023) 9243 3518*
6 rm ☲ – †£45/55 ††£65/85
♦ A pleasant cottage just across the road from the beach. Conservatory breakfast
room overlooks pool. Comfortable, well-kept bedrooms. Families particularly welcome.

HAYTOR VALE – Devon – see Bovey Tracey

HAYWARDS HEATH – West Sussex – **504** T 31 – pop. 29 110   **7 D2**
📗 Great Britain
◻ London 41 mi – Brighton 16 mi
🖼 Lindfield East Mascalls Lane, ☎ (01444) 484 467
🅶 Sheffield Park Garden★, E : 5 m. on A 272 and A 275

XX **Jeremy's at Borde Hill**   🚗 🏡 P VISA OO AE ①
Borde Hill Gdns, North : 1 ¾ m. by B 2028 on Balcombe Rd ✉ *RH16 1XP*
– ☎ *(01444) 441 102* – *www.jeremysrestaurant.com*
– *reservations@jeremysrestaurant.com* – *Fax (01494) 441 355*
Closed 1-11 January, Sunday dinner and Monday - except Bank Holidays
Rest – Carte £23/40
♦ Converted 19C stables with delightful views to Victorian walled garden. Contemporary interior with modern art. Confident, vibrant cooking in a light Mediterranean
style.

HEACHAM – Norfolk – **504** V 25   **14 B1**
◻ London 116 mi – Hunstanton 2 mi – King's Lynn 15 mi

↑ **The Grove** without rest   🚗 ✗ P
17 Collins Lane ✉ *PE31 7DZ* – ☎ *(01485) 570 513*
– *www.thegroveandoldbarn.co.uk* – *tm.shannon@tiscali.co.uk*
3 rm ☲ – †£45/60 ††£70
♦ Victorian house set on high street continuation. Cosy, book-strewn guest lounge.
Communal breakfasts. Two rooms homely and spotless; secluded stable room.

HEADLAM – Durham – **502** O 20 – see Darlington

HEATHROW AIRPORT – Middx. – **504** S 29 – see Hillingdon (Greater London)

HEBDEN BRIDGE – West Yorkshire – **502** N 22 – pop. 4 086   22 **A2**
   ◻ London 218 mi – Leeds 29 mi – Manchester 31 mi – Bradford 17 mi

⌂ **Holme House** without rest   P VISA ❿ AE
   New Road ⊠ HX7 8AD – 𝒞 (01422) 847 588
   – www.holmehousehebdenbridge.co.uk – mail@holmehousehebdenbridge.co.uk
   – Fax (01422) 847 354
   3 rm ⌓ – †£55 ††£70
   ♦ Late Georgian house in town centre with gated parking and neat garden. Smart,
   comfortable, well furnished rooms. Bedrooms boast excellent facilities and spacious
   bathrooms.

HEDDON ON THE WALL – Northumberland   24 **A2**
   ◻ London 288 mi – Blaydon 7 mi – Newcastle upon Tyne 8 mi

🏛 **Close House** ❦   ⇐ ⌂ ⒦ 📶 ※ ¶ 💆 P VISA ❿ AE ⓞ
   Southwest : 2¼ m. by B 6528 ⊠ NE15 0HT – 𝒞 (01661) 852 255
   – www.closehouse.co.uk – events@closehouse.co.uk – Fax (01661) 853 322
   – Closed 1-16 January
   19 rm ⌓ – †£123/195 ††£170/195
   Rest – (Closed Sunday dinner) Menu £20 (lunch) – Carte dinner £25/40
   ♦ Wedding oriented Georgian manor house in 300 acres of grounds in Hadrian's Wall
   country. Marble-floored reception leads to comfy lounge and bar. Stylish Regency
   rooms. Dining room in warm burgundy serves modern menus.

HEDLEY ON THE HILL – Northumberland   24 **A2**
   ◻ London 293 mi – Newcastle upon Tyne 16 mi – Sunderland 26 mi – South
      Shields 26 mi

🍴 **The Feathers Inn**   ⇧ ※ P VISA ❿
   ⊠ NE43 7SW – 𝒞 (01661) 843 607 – www.thefeathers.net – info@thefeathers.net
   Rest – (Closed Monday lunch) Carte £15/20
   ♦ Attractive stone pub on a steep hill. Carefully sourced produce and straightforward
   British cooking produces tasty combinations of hearty, wholesome fare and good
   clear flavours.

HELMSLEY – North Yorkshire – **502** Q 21 – pop. 1 559 📖 Great Britain   23 **C1**
   ◻ London 239 mi – Leeds 51 mi – Middlesbrough 28 mi – York 24 mi
   🛈 Helmsley Castle, Castlegate 𝒞 (01439) 770173, helmsley@ytbtic.co.uk
   🖿 Ampleforth College Castle Drive, Gilling East, 𝒞 (01439) 788 212
   ◩ Rievaulx Abbey★★ AC, NW : 2½ m. by B 1257

🏨 **The Black Swan**   ⌂ P VISA ❿ AE ⓞ
   Market Pl ⊠ YO62 5BJ – 𝒞 (01439) 770 466 – www.blackswan-helmsley.co.uk
   – enquiries@blackswan-helmsley.co.uk – Fax (01439) 770 174
   45 rm ⌓ – †£190/205 ††£240/270
   Rest The Rutland Room – (dinner only and Sunday lunch) Menu £30
   – Carte £37/44
   ♦ Part 16C coaching inn in a historic market town; indeed it overlooks the market.
   Charming rustic interior with exposed beams. Many bedrooms with period fittings
   and features. Formal dining in classically furnished restaurant.

🏛 **Feversham Arms**   ⌂ ⇧ ⓩ ※ ¶ 💆 P VISA ❿ AE
   on B 1257 ⊠ YO62 5AG – 𝒞 (01439) 770 766 – www.fevershamarmshotel.com
   – info@fevershamarmshotel.com – Fax (01439) 770 346
   33 rm (dinner included) ⌓ – †£160 ††£200/395
   Rest The Restaurant – Menu £33 – Carte £40/43
   ♦ A former coaching inn; its stone façade conceals surprisingly modern rooms of a
   quiet restful nature: walls, floors in muted colours, spot lighting, quality fabrics. Range
   of dining locations, including around the pool.

ENGLAND

↑ **No.54** without rest 🚲 **P** VISA ⓪③
54 Bondgate ⊠ YO62 5EZ – ℰ (01439) 771 533 – www.no54.co.uk
– lizzie@no54.co.uk – Fax (01439) 771 533 – Closed Christmas and New Year
4 rm ⌂ – ♦£40/55 ♦♦£100
• Victorian terraced cottage, formerly the village vet's. Charming owner. Bedrooms
are strong point: set around flagged courtyard, they're airy, bright and very well-
equipped.

↑ **Carlton Lodge** without rest ((¶)) **P** VISA ⓪③
Bondgate ⊠ YO62 5EY – ℰ (01439) 770 557 – www.carlton-lodge.com
– enquiries@carlton-lodge.com – Fax (01439) 772 378
8 rm ⌂ – ♦£45/65 ♦♦£80/90
• Late 19C house set just out of town. Homely and traditional air to the décor in the
communal areas and the bedrooms, some of which have period features. Cosy breakfast room.

at Nawton East : 3¼ m. on A 170 – ⊠ York

↑ **Plumpton Court** without rest 🚲 ⅍ **P** VISA ⓪③ AE ⓪
High St ⊠ YO62 7TT – ℰ (01439) 771 223 – www.plumptoncourt.com
– mail@plumptoncourt.com – February-November
7 rm ⌂ – ♦£45 ♦♦£65
• The emphasis here is on homeliness; this is well provided by cottage-style traditional décor, open fires and a friendly welcome. Top floor bedrooms have modern
style.

at Harome Southeast : 2¾ m. by A 170 – ⊠ York

🏠 **The Pheasant** 🚲 ▢ **P** VISA ⓪③
⊠ YO62 5JG – ℰ (01439) 771 241 – www.@thepheasanthotel.com
*– reservations@thepheasanthotel.com – Fax (01439) 771 744 – Closed Christmas
and New Year*
12 rm (dinner included) ⌂ – ♦£85/98 ♦♦£170/190 – 2 suites
Rest – (Closed December and January) (bar lunch) Menu £30
• Family run and hidden away in picturesque hamlet with a duck pond and mill
stream close by. Open fires and beams in traditionally styled building with modern
furniture. Conservatory dining room.

🏠 **Cross House Lodge at The Star Inn** 🚲 **P** VISA ⓪③
⊠ YO62 5JE – ℰ (01439) 770 397 – www.thestaratharome.co.uk
*– jpern@thestarinnatharome.co.uk – Fax (01439) 771 833 – Closed 25-26
December*
14 rm ⌂ – ♦£140 ♦♦£230
Rest *The Star Inn* – see restaurant listing
Rest *The Piggery* – (booking essential) (residents only, set menu only)
Menu £45
• Converted farm building set opposite pub in pretty village. Open-plan, split-level
lounge. Ultra-stylish, super-smart bedrooms in either main building, annex or local
cottages. Communal dining and breakfast for residents in The Piggery.

▢ **The Star Inn** (Andrew Pern) 🚲 ⅍ ⅍ ↻ **P** VISA ⓪③
ⵣ *High St ⊠ YO62 5JE – ℰ (01439) 770 397 – www.thestaratharome.co.uk*
– jpern@thestaratharome.co.uk – Fax (01439) 771 833
– Closed 25 December
Rest – (booking essential) Carte £25/40 s ⅍
Spec. Black pudding with foie gras and watercress salad. John Dory with broad
beans, lovage and truffle. Yorkshire curd tart with prune ice cream.
• 700 year old inn with herb garden, butcher's shop and deli. Very appealing cooking
combines traditional Northern flavours with more up-to-date nuances, using local
farm and estate produce.

ENGLAND

at Ampleforth Southwest : 4½ m. by A 170 off B 1257 – ✉ Helmsley

⌂ Shallowdale House without rest ⌖ ⪡ 🚗 🛝 P̲ *VISA* ⬤⬤
West : ½ m. ✉ YO62 4DY – ☎ (01439) 788 325 – www.shallowdalehouse.co.uk
– stay@shallowdalehouse.co.uk – Fax (01439) 788 885
– Closed Christmas - New Year
3 rm ⌂ – ♥£75/85 ♥♥£95/115
♦ Modern guesthouse with spectacular views of the Howardian Hills; an area of outstanding beauty. Spacious rooms with large picture windows for the scenery. Warm and relaxed.

at Byland Abbey Southwest : 6½ m. by A 170 – ✉ Helmsley

⌂ Oldstead Grange without rest ⌖ 🚗 ⓘ 🛝 P̲ *VISA* ⬤⬤
Oldstead, Northwest : 1¼ m. on Oldstead rd ✉ YO61 4BJ – ☎ (01347) 868 634
– www.yorkshireuk.com – oldsteadgrange@yorkshireuk.com – Closed 2 weeks January
3 rm ⌂ – ♥£60/80 ♥♥£80/100
♦ Comfort is paramount in this part 17C farmhouse on working farm. Cosy, warm lounge with real fire. Hand-made oak furniture adorns bedrooms which benefit from rural outlook.

🍴 The Abbey Inn with rm 🚗 ⌂ 🛝 P̲ *VISA* ⬤⬤
✉ YO61 4BD – ☎ (01347) 868 204 – www.bylandabbeyinn.com
– abbeyinn@english-heritage.org.uk – Fax (01347) 868 678 – Closed 24 December dinner, 25-26 December, 31 December dinner, 1 January
3 rm ⌂ – ♥£95 ♥♥£199
Rest – (Closed Sunday dinner, Monday and Tuesday) (booking essential)
Menu £17 (lunch) – Carte £17/28
♦ Delightful, sympathetically restored period pub, in a breathtaking location. Local, seasonal cooking uses simple techniques and relies on natural flavours to show through. Charming bedrooms, two with Abbey views; luxurious bathrooms.

at Oldstead West : 6 m. by A 170

🍴 The Black Swan 🚗 ⌂ 🛝 P̲ *VISA* ⬤⬤
✉ YO61 4BL – ☎ (01347) 868 387 – www.blackswanoldstead.co.uk
– enquiries@blackswanoldstead.co.uk
Rest – (Closed Monday) Carte £20/28
♦ 16C house lovingly converted into cosy pub with open fires, stone floors and antique furniture. Spacious dining room, tasty homemade dishes and simpler menu for children.

at Scawton West 8½ m. by A 170 – ✉ Helmsley

🍴 The Hare Inn 🛝 P̲ *VISA* ⬤⬤ AE
Scawton ✉ YO7 2HG – ☎ (01845) 597 769 – www.thehareinn.co.uk
– geoff@brucearms.com – Closed Sunday dinner and Monday
Rest – Carte £20/30
♦ Smart yellow façade. Delightful bar with open fired stove. Spacious main dining room. Satisfying, seasonal cooking with a classical base, freshly prepared with local ingredients.

HELSTON – Cornwall – 503 E 33 – pop. 10 578   1 A3
🚾 London 306 mi – Falmouth 13 mi – Penzance 14 mi – Truro 17 mi
◉ The Flora Day Furry Dance★★
◐ Lizard Peninsula★ - Gunwalloe Fishing Cove★, S : 4 m. by A 3083 and minor rd - Culdrose (Flambards Village Theme Park★), SE : 1 m. - Wendron (Poldark Mine★), NE : 2½ m. by B 3297 – Gweek (Seal Sanctuary★), E : 4 m. by A 394 and minor rd

ENGLAND

at Trelowarren Southeast : 4 m. by A 394 and A 3083 on B 3293 – ⊠ Helston

✗ **New Yard** – at Trelowarren Estate   🛗 **P** *VISA* **OO**
⊠ TR12 6AF – 𝒞 (01326) 221 595 – www.trelowarren.com
– newyardrestaurant@trelowarren.com – Fax (01326) 221 595
– Closed 26 December, 1 January and Monday October-Whitsun
Rest – (booking advisable at dinner) Menu £ 15/22 – Carte £ 21/32
♦ Converted country house stable yard adjoining craft gallery. Terrace view from modern tables and chairs. Dinner offers full menus of locally inspired dishes; lunch is simpler.

at Gunwalloe South : 5 m. by A 394 off A 3083 – ⊠ Helston

🏠 **The Halzephron Inn** with rm 🐾   ⇐ 🛗 ⅏ **P** *VISA* **OO** **AE**
⊠ TR12 7QB – 𝒞 (01326) 240 406 – www.halzephron-inn.co.uk
– halzephroninn@gunwalloe1.fsnet.co.uk – Fax (01326) 241 442
– Closed 25 December
2 rm ⊇ – †£ 50/52 ††£ 90/94   **Rest** – Carte £ 19/35
♦ Country pub in pretty coastal setting. Gleaming copper, original paintings. Adventurous or traditional dishes using local produce. Selection of Cornish cheeses. Neat rooms.

at Cury South : 5m by A394 and A3083

🏠 **Colvennor Farmhouse** without rest   ⊿ ⅏ **P** *VISA* **OO**
Cury, West 1m following sign for Poldu off A3083 and then sign for Nantithet
⊠ TR12 7BJ – 𝒞 (01326) 241 208 – www.colvennorfarmhouse.com
– colvennor@aol.com – Closed Christmas and New Year, restricted opening in winter
3 rm ⊇ – †£ 36/40 ††£ 60/66
♦ The farmer has moved out into one of the barns and the farmhouse now provides spotless, simple accommodation. There's a pretty and colourful garden. Breakfast is a hearty affair.

HEMEL HEMPSTEAD – Hertfordshire – **504** S 28 – pop. 83 118   12 **A2**
📗 Great Britain
▶ London 30 mi – Aylesbury 16 mi – Luton 10 mi – Northampton 46 mi
🄳 Dacorum Information Centre, Marlowes 𝒞 (01442) 234222
🅼 Little Hay Golf Complex Bovingdon Box Lane, 𝒞 (01442) 833 798
🄶 Boxmoor 18 Box Lane, 𝒞 (01442) 242 434
🄶 Whipsnade Wild Animal Park★

✗ **Restaurant 65**   *VISA* **OO** **AE**
😊 65 High St (Old Town) ⊠ HP1 5AL – 𝒞 (01442) 239 010
– www.restaurant65.com – enquiries@restaurant65.com – Closed 1-5 January, last week July, Saturday lunch, Sunday dinner and Monday
Rest – Menu £ 20/28
♦ Charming 17C building in old part of town; snug restaurant with white walls, black beams and homely, relaxed feel. Well executed modern British cooking with a classical base.

at Frithsden Northwest : 4 ½ m. by A 4146 – ⊠ Hemel Hempstead

🏠 **The Alford Arms**   🛗 **P** *VISA* **OO** **AE**
⊠ HP1 3DD – 𝒞 (01442) 864 480 – www.alfordarmsfrithsden.co.uk
– info@alfordarmsfrithsden.co.uk – Fax (01442) 876 893 – Closed 25-26 December
Rest – Carte £ 20/29
♦ Tucked away in a small hamlet, popular with cyclists and walkers. A pleasant, modern interior of terracotta and cream hues; stylish dishes with interesting combinations.

HEMINGFORD GREY – Cambs. – **504** T 27 – see Huntingdon

ENGLAND

HENFIELD – West Sussex – **504** T 31 – pop. 4 527   7 **D2**

🔼 London 47 mi – Brighton 10 mi – Worthing 11 mi

The Ginger Fox   🛋 🏠 ⇄ **P** ⓜⓞ **AE** **①**

Albourne, Southwest 3 m. on A281 ✉ *BN6 9EA* – ℰ *(01273) 857 888*
– www.gingermanrestaurants.com – info@gingermanrestaurants.com – Closed
25 December
Rest – Carte £ 21/26

♦ Whitewashed thatched pub. Daily changing à la carte and specials, with straight-forward descriptions and rich, deep flavours; traditional and satisfying cooking with a twist.

at Wineham Northeast : 3 ½ m. by A 281, B 2116 and Wineham Lane
– ✉ **Henfield**

🔼 **Frylands** without rest ⌂   ⇐ 🛋 🌐 🔌 ⚒ ⚙ ⚓ **P**

West : ¼ m. taking left turn at telephone box ✉ *BN5 9BP* – ℰ *(01403) 710 214*
– www.frylands.co.uk – b+b@frylands.co.uk – Fax (01403) 711 449
– Closed 20 December - 1 January
3 rm ⌂ – †£ 30 ††£ 60

♦ Part Elizabethan farmhouse in 250 acres with woodlands and fishing. Fresh home-cooked breakfasts. Bedrooms exude charm and character with homely furnishings, original features.

HENLEY-IN-ARDEN – Warwickshire – **503** O 27 – pop. 2 803   19 **C3**

🔼 London 104 mi – Birmingham 15 mi – Stratford-upon-Avon 8 mi
– Warwick 8 mi

🏢 **Ardencote Manor H. & Country Club and Spa** ⌂   🛋 🌐

Lye Green Rd,   🏠 🖧 🌐 ♨ 🏋 ⚒ 📺 🎛 ᰥ & rm, Ⓚ ⚙ ᯤ **P** **VISA** ⓜⓞ **AE** **①**
Claverdon, East : 3 ¾ m. by A 4189 on Shrewley rd ✉ *CV35 8LT* – ℰ *(01926)*
843 111 – www.ardencote.com – hotel@ardencote.com – Fax (01926) 842 646
76 rm ⌂ – †£ 90/105 ††£ 90/165
Rest *The Lodge* – Menu £ 30 (dinner) – Carte £ 27/42

♦ Secluded manor house with modern extension and spacious leisure facilities, in formal gardens and grounds. Bedrooms are generally large and traditionally furnished. Informal dining room.

The Crabmill   🛋 🏠 **P** **VISA** ⓜⓞ

Claverdon, East : 1 m. on A 4189 ✉ *B95 5EE* – ℰ *(01926) 843 342*
– www.lovelypubs.co.uk – thecrabmill@lovelypubs.co.uk – Fax (01926) 843 989
– Closed 25 December
Rest – (Closed Sunday dinner) (booking essential) Carte £ 20/30

♦ Charming mix of the old and new; ancient beams blending with contemporary chocolate and pink décor. Relaxing summer room; summer terrace and garden. Modern Mediterranean menu.

at Tanworth-in-Arden Northwest : 4 ½ m. by A 3400 and Tanworth Rd
– ✉ **Henley-in-Arden**

The Bell Inn with rm   ⚙ **P** **VISA** ⓜⓞ **AE**

The Green ✉ *B94 5AL* – ℰ *(01564) 742 212*
– www.thebellattanworthinarden.co.uk – thebell@realcoolbars.com
9 rm ⌂ – †£ 60 ††£ 120   **Rest** – (Closed Sunday dinner) Carte £ 18/28

♦ Very pleasant modern pub with rustic tones in pretty village; spacious bar. Intimate dining room serving good food with modish twists. Stylish rooms with designer touches.

HENLEY-ON-THAMES – Oxfordshire – **504** R 29 – pop. 10 513   11 **C3**

🔼 London 40 mi – Oxford 23 mi – Reading 9 mi
🚢 to Reading (Salter Bros. Ltd) (summer only) daily (2 h 15 mn) – to Marlow
(Salter Bros. Ltd) (summer only) daily (2 h 15 mn)
🅹 Kings Arms Barn, Kings Rd ℰ (01491) 578034
🔟 Huntercombe Nuffield, ℰ (01491) 641 207

Hotel du Vin
🛏 ⏰ rm, Ⓚ rm, ⁗ 🄰 🄿 VISA ⓪ AE ⓪

New St ⊠ RG9 2BP – ✆ (01491) 848 400 – www.hotelduvin.com
– info@henley.hotelduvin.com – Fax (01491) 848 401
38 rm – ♦£145/445 ♦♦£145/445, ⌷£13.50 – 2 suites
Rest *Bistro* – Menu £15 (lunch) – Carte approx. £35 ⌀

♦ Former brewery premises; now an easy-going, designer styled boutique hotel. Stunning rooms: studios with outdoor terrace and bath tub or airy doubles with great amenities. Bistro with resolutely Gallic style, French influenced menus and excellent wine list.

Red Lion
< 🕸 ⁗ 🄰 🄿 VISA ⓪ AE

Hart St ⊠ RG9 2AR – ✆ (01491) 572 161 – www.redlionhenley.co.uk
– reservations@redlionhenley.co.uk – Fax (01491) 410 039
34 rm – ♦£115/135 ♦♦£125/165, ⌷£13.50
Rest – Menu £17 (lunch) – Carte £25/31

♦ Hostelry since 15C; has accommodated three kings and overlooks the regatta course. Rooms are well furnished with antiques; an elegant, traditional style pervades throughout. Dining room exudes crisp, light feel.

Lenwade without rest
🚗 🕸 ⁗ 🄿

3 Western Rd (off St Andrews Rd) ⊠ RG9 1JL – ✆ (01491) 573 468
– www.lenwade.com – jacquie@lenwade.com – Fax (01491) 411 664
– Closed 25 -26 December
3 rm ⌷ – ♦£55/60 ♦♦£70/75

♦ Late 19C home in a quiet residential area. Neatly kept throughout with modern appointments. Bedrooms are of a good size and pine furnished.

Alushta without rest
🕸 ⁗ 🄿

23 Queen St ⊠ RG9 1AR – ✆ (01491) 636 041 – www.alushta.co.uk
– sdr@alushta.co.uk – Fax (01491) 636 042
5 rm ⌷ – ♦£40/65 ♦♦£65/85

♦ Centrally located guesthouse, built in late 18C. Very pleasant breakfast room: display shelves boast Russian china. Well-appointed bedrooms with thoughtful extras.

ENGLAND

HEREFORD – County of Herefordshire – 503 L 27 – pop. 56 373   18 B3
📗 Great Britain

🔟 London 133 mi – Birmingham 51 mi – Cardiff 56 mi
🅳 1 King St ✆ (01432) 268430, tic-hereford@herefordshire.gov.uk
🔟 Raven's Causeway Wormsley, ✆ (01432) 830 219
🔟 Belmont Lodge Belmont Ruckhall Lane, ✆ (01432) 352 666
🔟 Hereford Municipal Holmer Rd, ✆ (01432) 344 376
🔟 Burghill Valley Burghill Tillington Rd, ✆ (01432) 760 456
🔘 City★ - Cathedral★★ (Mappa Mundi★) A **A** – Old House★A **B**
🔘 Kilpeck (Church of SS. Mary and David★★) SW : 8 m. by A 465 B

Plan on next page

Castle House
🚗 🛏 🛗 ⏰ rm, Ⓚ rest, 📞 🄿 VISA ⓪ AE

Castle St ⊠ HR1 2NW – ✆ (01432) 356 321 – www.castlehse.co.uk
– info@castlehse.co.uk – Fax (01432) 365 909   A**e**
15 rm ⌷ – ♦£120/140 ♦♦£175
Rest *La Rive* – Carte £22/34 ⌀

♦ Stylish and exclusive air to this contemporarily furnished, classically proportioned Georgian house, near the cathedral. Excellent quality and attention to detail throughout. Smart restaurant overlooks gardens and Wye.

Brandon Lodge without rest
🚗 ⁗ 🄿 VISA ⓪

Ross Rd, South : 1 ¾ m. on A 49 ⊠ HR2 8BH – ✆ (01432) 355 621
– www.brandonlodge.co.uk – info@brandonlodge.co.uk – Fax (01432) 355 621
10 rm ⌷ – ♦£45/50 ♦♦£60/68

♦ A good value hotel with 18C origins, charmingly overseen by owner. Bedrooms in main building or adjacent annex: all are spacious, boasting a cheery warmth and good facilities.

HEREFORD

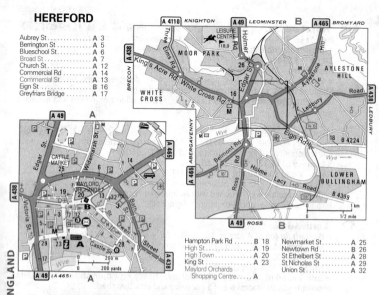

ENGLAND

✗ The Stewing Pot   VISA ⬤⬤
17 Church St ✉ HR1 2LR – ℰ (01432) 265 233 – www.stewingpot.co.uk
– info@stewingpot.co.uk – Closed 2 weeks Christmas, Sunday and Monday   **Aa**
Rest – Menu £ 15 (lunch) – Carte £ 24/35
♦ Neighbourhood eatery tucked away down a narrow street, with plain décor and simple, homely furnishings. Taking on a bistro style, cooking is classical and reliably tasty.

at Byford West : 7 ½ m. by A 438 - B – ✉ Hereford

⭡ Old Rectory without rest   🚗 ⅍ P
✉ HR4 7LD – ℰ (01981) 590 218 – www.theoldrectory.uk.com
– info@theoldrectory.uk.com – March-October
3 rm ⏛ – †£50/65 ††£79
♦ Rurally set Georgian-style 19C rectory with pleasant gardens. Spacious yet homely atmosphere and décor; the bedrooms are furnished in a simple, traditional style.

at Winforton Northwest : 15 m. on A 438 – ✉ Hereford

⭡ Winforton Court without rest   🚗 ⟨⟩ P
✉ HR3 6EA – ℰ (01544) 328 498 – www.winfortoncourt.co.uk – Fax (01544)
328 498 – Closed 24-29 December
3 rm ⏛ – †£55/65 ††£80/95
♦ Wonderfully characterful 16C house used as a circuit court by "Hanging" Judge Jeffries. Exudes personality with exposed beams, thick walls and uneven floors. Rustic rooms.

HERM – **503** P 33 – **see Channel Islands**

HERMITAGE – **Dorset** – **see Sherborne**

> Luxury pad or humble abode?
> 🏰🏰 and ⭡ denote categories of comfort.

▸ London 63 mi – Eastbourne 12 mi – Hastings 14 mi – Lewes 16 mi

XXX **Sundial**   ⬚ **P** **VISA** **⑳** **①**
Gardner St ✉ *BN27 4LA* – ℰ *(01323) 832 217* – *www.sundialrestaurant.co.uk*
– sundialrestaurant@hotmail.com – *Fax (01323) 832 909* – *Closed Sunday dinner
and Monday*
Rest – French – Menu £ 23 – Carte £ 34/45
♦ Converted 16C cottage retaining leaded windows and a beamed ceiling. Comfortable chairs in a well spaced dining room. Menu is French with a classic, familiar style.

at Wartling Southeast : 3 ¾ m. by A 271 and Wartling rd – ✉ **Herstmonceux**

⌂ **Wartling Place** without rest   ⬚ ⚘ 📶 **P** **VISA** **⑳** **AE**
✉ *BN27 1RY* – ℰ *(01323) 832 590* – *www.countryhouseaccommodation.co.uk*
– accom@wartlingplace.prestel.co.uk
4 rm 😑 – †£ 75/105 ††£ 130/175
♦ Part Georgian house with three acres of gardens, sited in the village. Pleasantly furnished, with some antiques; two of the rooms have four-poster beds.

🍺 **The Lamb Inn**   ⬚ **P** **VISA** **⑳** **AE**
Wartling Rd ✉ *BN27 1RY* – ℰ *(01323) 832 116* – *www.lambinnwartling.co.uk*
– alison.farncombe@virgin.net – *Fax (01323) 832 637* – *Closed Sunday dinner*
Rest – Carte £ 18/30
♦ Popular with locals, this early 16C pub offers a friendly welcome. Steeped in character with flag floors, fires and beams. Robust cooking uses quality, traceable ingredients.

▸ London 304 mi – Carlisle 37 mi – Newcastle upon Tyne 21 mi
🇮 Wentworth Car Park ℰ (01434) 652 220, hexham.tic@tynedale.gov.uk
🔸 Spital Park, ℰ (01434) 603 072
🔸 De Vere Slaley Hall Slaley, ℰ (01434) 673 154
🔹 Tynedale Tyne Green, ℰ (01434) 608 154
◉ Abbey★ (Saxon Crypt★★, Leschman chantry★)
🄲 Hadrian's Wall★★, N : 4½ m. by A 6079. Housesteads★★, NW : 12½ m. by
    A 6079 and B 6318

🏨 **Beaumont**   🖺 ᴊ rm, ⚘ 📶 ♨ **P** **VISA** **⑳** **AE**
Beaumont St ✉ *NE46 3LT* – ℰ *(01434) 602 331* – *www.bw-beaumonthotel.co.uk*
– reservations@beaumonthotel.eclipse.co.uk – *Fax (01434) 606 184*
35 rm 😑 – †£ 70/90 ††£ 98/120
Rest *The Park* – Menu £ 13/21 **s**
♦ Victorian building of local stone overlooking park and the town's ancient abbey - which is visible from some of the comfortable rooms. Personally run with a warm atmosphere. Park restaurant on the first floor with views of the abbey.

⌂ **Hallbank**   ⚘ 📶 **P** **VISA** **⑳** **①**
Hallgate ✉ *NE46 1XA* – ℰ *(01434) 606 656* – *www.hallbankguesthouse.com*
– hallbank@freenetname.co.uk – *Fax (01434) 605 567*
8 rm 😑 – †£ 60/90 ††£ 90/110   **Rest** – (by arrangement) Menu £ 18
♦ Red-brick Georgian house close to market square, set in the shadow of the old gaol. Fully refurbished rooms exhibit a warm, classic style with good modern facilities. Dine in adjacent, informal café/bistro.

⌂ **West Close House** without rest ⌖   ⬚ ⚘ **P**
Hextol Terrace, Southwest : ½ m. off B 6305 ✉ *NE46 2AD* – ℰ *(01434) 603 307*
– Closed Christmas - New Year and January
3 rm 😑 – †£ 28/40 ††£ 55
♦ Detached house in a residential area providing a high standard of simple, good value accommodation. Polished wood floors and immaculately kept.

ENGLAND

⌂ **Dene House** without rest ♨   🍽 🍴 **P**
Juniper, South : 3¾ m. by B 6306 following signs for Dye House ⊠ NE46 1SJ
– ℰ (01434) 673 413 – www.denehouse-hexham.co.uk
– margaret@denehouse-hexham.co.uk – Closed December
3 rm – 🛏£30/40 🛏🛏£60
♦ Attractive stone cottage in a quiet spot with pleasant views, numerous country walks in the environs. Cosy feel throughout. Simple, homely rooms.

✗✗ **Valley Connection 301**   *VISA* **MO** **AE**
Market Pl ⊠ NE46 3NX – ℰ (01434) 601 234 – www.valleyrestaurants.co.uk
– Fax (01434) 606 629 – Closed 25 December, 1 January and Mondays except Bank Holidays
Rest – Indian – (dinner only) Carte £18/22
♦ Near Hexham Abbey; views of the market place from both floors. Old favourites interspersed with modern dishes in a tasty Indian menu.

🍴 **The Rat Inn**   🍽 🍴 **P** *VISA* **MO** **AE**
Anick ⊠ NE46 4LN – ℰ (01434) 602 814 – www.theratinn.com
– info@theratinn.com
Rest – (Closed Sunday dinner and Monday) Carte £15/30
♦ Traditional pub with an open range and pleasant garden views. Daily-changing blackboard menu features wholesome cooking, with classic pub and more ambitious dishes – including some for two.

at Slaley Southeast : 5½ m. by B 6306 – ⊠ Hexham

🏨 **Slaley Hall** ♨   ← 🚗 🌀 🍴 🖥 ⏰ ♨ ⅃⅃ 🎬 🖥 ⅃ 🔥 rm, 🏃 **AK** 📞 🛁
Southeast : 2¼ m. ⊠ NE47 0BY – ℰ (01434) 673 350   **P** *VISA* **MO** **AE** ⓪
– www.devere.co.uk – slaley.hall@deverehotels.com – Fax (01434) 673 962
132 rm ⊊ – 🛏£175/195 🛏🛏£210/235 – 10 suites
Rest – (bar lunch Monday-Saturday) Carte £29/50
♦ Extended Edwardian manor house, now a leisure oriented hotel, grounds with woodland and two golf courses. Spacious bedrooms with up-to-date facilities and country views. Formal restaurant offering menus based on a modern English style.

at Haydon Bridge West : 7½ m. on A 69 – ⊠ Hexham

🏨 **Langley Castle** ♨   🚗 🌀 🔥 rm, 🍴 🛁 **P** *VISA* **MO** **AE**
Langley-on-Tyne, South : 2 m. by A 69 on A 686 ⊠ NE47 5LU – ℰ (01434)
688 888 – www.langleycastle.com – manager@langleycastle.com – Fax (01434)
684 019
19 rm ⊊ – 🛏£115/206 🛏🛏£140/265 – 1 suite   **Rest** – Menu £20/35
♦ Turreted stone castle in 12 acres. Tapestry style fabrics, heraldic themed ornaments, open fire. Spacious rooms in castle or converted stables. Formal restaurant with beams and stone floor; classic dishes using local produce.

 Look out for red symbols, indicating particularly pleasant establishments.

HEYTESBURY – Wilts. – **503** N 30 – see Warminster

HIGH ONGAR – Essex   12 **B2**
  ⬛ London 24 mi – Brentwood 11 mi – Chelmsford 10 mi

🍴 **The Wheatsheaf**   🚗 🍽 🍴 **P** *VISA* **MO** **AE** ⓪
King St, East : 2 m. by A 414 on Blackmore rd ⊠ CM5 9NS – ℰ (01277) 822 220
– www.thewheatsheafbrasserie.co.uk – Closed 26-30 December, Sunday dinner and Monday
Rest – (booking essential) Carte £23/33
♦ Pretty, converted pub with large garden and terrace. Dine in four different rooms with open fires and homely ornamentation. Good value, accomplished British cuisine.

ENGLAND

HIGH WYCOMBE – Buckinghamshire – **504** R 29 – pop. **77 178**

Great Britain

- ▶ London 34 mi – Aylesbury 17 mi – Oxford 26 mi – Reading 18 mi
- 🛈 Paul's Row ✆ (01494) 421892, tourism_enquiries@wycombe.gov.uk
- 🏌 Hazlemere G & C.C. Hazlemere Penn Rd, ✆ (01494) 719 300
- 🏌 Wycombe Heights Loudwater Rayners Ave, ✆ (01494) 816 686
- ◎ Chiltern Hills ★

※※ **Eat-Thai** 　　　　　　　　　　　　　　　　　　 🏧 ⇄ 𝗩𝗜𝗦𝗔 ⦿⦿ 𝗔𝗘

14-15 Easton St ✉ HP11 1NT – ✆ (01494) 532 888 – www.eat-thai.co.uk
– eatthai@eat-thai.co.uk – Fax (01494) 532 889 – Closed 25-28 December
Rest – Thai – Menu £ 12/25 – Carte £ 22/32 **s**

♦ Modern restaurant with wood floors and well-spaced tables. Three distinct areas serving fresh, tasty dishes with ingredients flown regularly from Thailand. Attentive service.

HIGHCLERE – Hampshire – **503** P 29 – pop. **2 409** – ✉ Newbury

6 **B1**

- ▶ London 69 mi – Newbury 5 mi – Reading 25 mi

🏠 **The Yew Tree** with rm 　　　　　　　　　　　　 ☕ **P** 𝗩𝗜𝗦𝗔 ⦿⦿ 𝗔𝗘

Hollington Cross, Andover Road, South : 1 m. on A 343 ✉ RG20 9SE – ✆ (01635) 253 360 – www.theyewtree.net – info@theyewtree.net – Fax (01635) 255 035
6 rm ⊆ – ♥ £ 100 　　**Rest** – Menu £ 19 (lunch) – Carte £ 38/55

♦ Smart 17C pub with a marble topped bar, owned by Marco Pierre White. Menu blends British frankness with French sophistication, ranging from pub classics to restaurant style dishes. Modern bedrooms with personality.

Good food and accommodation at moderate prices?
Look for the Bib symbols:
red Bib Gourmand 🅑 for food, blue Bib Hotel 🏨 for hotels

ENGLAND

HIGHCLIFFE – Dorset – **503** O 31

4 **D3**

- ▶ London 112 mi – Bournemouth 10 mi – Salisbury 21 mi
  – Southampton 26 mi – Winchester 37 mi

🏠 **Lord Bute** 　　　　　　　　　　　 🏧 📶 🧖 **P** 𝗩𝗜𝗦𝗔 ⦿⦿ 𝗔𝗘

*Lymington Rd ✉ BH23 4JS – ✆ (01425) 278 884 – www.lordbute.co.uk
– mail@lordbute.co.uk – Fax (01425) 279 258*
11 rm ⊆ – ♥ £ 98/108 ♥♥ £ 108/225 – 2 suites
Rest – (Closed Sunday dinner and Monday) Menu £ 17/32 – Carte £ 19/40

♦ Modern property with a traditional style. Well designed, light, airy lounge. Bedrooms are well appointed and include safes and spa baths. Formal dining room adjacent to Orangery lounge.

HIGH CROSBY – Cumbria – see Carlisle

HIGHER BURWARDSLEY – Ches. – see Tattenhall

HIGHWORTH – Swindon – **503** O 29 – pop. **7 996**

4 **D1**

- ▶ London 85 mi – Oxford 26 mi – Swindon 6 mi

※※ **Jesmonds of Highworth** with rm 　　　 ☕ 🏧 rest, 📞 **P** 𝗩𝗜𝗦𝗔 ⦿⦿

*Jesmond House ✉ SN6 7HJ – ✆ (01793) 762 364
– www.jesmondsofhighworth.com – info@jesmondsofhighworth.com
– Fax (01793) 861 201*
10 rm – ♥ £ 100 ♥♥ £ 125/180 　　**Rest** – Menu £ 20/36 – Carte £ 25/36

♦ Grade II listed red brick building; two modern dining rooms, one with glass atrium and paved terrace. Constantly evolving menus; modern, quite creative cooking. Stylishly refurbished and comfortable bedrooms with contemporary fabrics and a high level of facilities.

HINCKLEY – Leicestershire – 502 P 26 – pop. 43 246   16 B2

▶ London 103 mi – Birmingham 31 mi – Coventry 12 mi – Leicester 14 mi
🔎 Hinckley Library, Lancaster Rd ℰ (01455) 635106, hinckleytic@leics.gov.uk

Sketchley Grange   🚗 ⛱ 🖥 ⊛ 🏊 ♨ 🖐 🧖 AK rest, ⚑ 🏋 **P**
Sketchley Lane, South : 1½ m. by B 4109 (Rugby Rd)   **VISA** **CO** **AE** **①**
⊠ LE10 3HU – ℰ (01455) 251 133 – www.sketchleygrange.co.uk
– reservations@sketchleygrange.co.uk – Fax (01455) 631 384
51 rm – ♦£130 ♦♦£130, ⚏ £12.50 – 1 suite
Rest *The Willow* – (Closed Sunday dinner and Monday) (dinner only and
Sunday lunch) Carte £27/41
Rest *The Terrace Bistro* – Menu £19 – Carte £19/30
♦ Privately owned, spacious hotel with good leisure and an array of conference
facilities. Bedrooms are well proportioned, and furniture is comfortable and well
chosen. The Willow exudes elegance and garden views. The Terrace Bistro is bright
and spacious.

HINDON – Wiltshire – 503 N 30   4 C2

▶ London 103 mi – Shaftesbury 7 mi – Warminster 10 mi

The Lamb Inn with rm   🚗 ⛱ **P** **VISA** **CO** **AE**
High St ⊠ SP3 6DP – ℰ (01747) 820 573 – info@lambathindon.co.uk
– Fax (01747) 820 605
17 rm ⚏ – ♦£70 ♦♦£135   **Rest** – Carte £25/30
♦ Scottish-themed bar with red décor and dark wood tables. Produce is predominantly local, with some Scottish contributions; dishes are a mix of British and Mediterranean. Traditional country bedrooms and furnishings.

HINDRINGHAM – Norfolk   15 C1

▶ London 118 mi – Fakenham 8 mi – Holt 8 mi

Field House without rest   🚗 ⚙ ⚑ **P**
Moorgate Rd ⊠ NR21 0PT – ℰ (01328) 878 726
– www.fieldhousehindringham.co.uk – stay@fieldhousehindringham.co.uk
– Closed Christmas and New Year
3 rm ⚏ – ♦£70/75 ♦♦£90/110
♦ Well-kept flint stone house with pretty garden and summer house. Pristine lounge
with books and magazines. Extensive breakfast menus. Carefully co-ordinated rooms
with extras.

HINTLESHAM – Suffolk – 504 X 27 – see Ipswich

HINTON ST GEORGE – Somerset   3 B3

▶ London 138 mi – Taunton 21 mi – Weymouth 41 mi – Yeovil 13 mi

Lord Poulett Arms with rm   ⛱ **P** **VISA** **CO**
High St ⊠ TA17 8SE – ℰ (01460) 73 149 – www.lordpoulettarms.com
– steveandmichelle@lordpoulettarms.com – Closed 26 December and 1 January
4 rm ⚏ – ♦£59/88 ♦♦£88   **Rest** – Carte £19/28
♦ Beautifully restored 17C inn on delightful high street. Immense charm and character: stone floors, exposed brickwork. Accomplished, classical cooking. Immaculate
rooms.

HISTON – Cambs. – 504 U 27 – see Cambridge

HOCKLEY HEATH – West Midlands – 503 – pop. 1 525 – ⊠ Solihull   19 C2

▶ London 117 mi – Birmingham 11 mi – Coventry 17 mi

Nuthurst Grange Country House   🚗 ⚙ ⚑ 🏋 **P** **VISA** **CO** **AE** **①**
Nuthurst Grange Lane, South : ¾ m. by A 3400 ⊠ B94 5NL – ℰ (01564) 783 972
– www.nuthurst-grange.com – info@nuthurst-grange.co.uk – Fax (01564) 783 919
19 rm ⚏ – ♦£95/139 ♦♦£165/195
Rest *The Restaurant* – see restaurant listing
♦ Part Edwardian manor house, overlooking M40 and convenient for Birmingham
airport. Classic English country décor throughout. Spacious rooms with high level of
comfort.

XXX **The Restaurant** – at Nuthurst Grange Country House Hotel
Nuthurst Grange Lane, South : ¾ m. by A 3400 ⊠ B94 5NL
– ℰ (01564) 783 972 – Fax (01564) 783 919
Rest – (closed Sunday dinner) Menu £ 19/30 **s**
♦ Thoroughly traditional tone in the dining room's décor which contributes to a formal ambience. Seasonal menu draws on British and French traditions.

at Lapworth Southeast : 2 m. on B 4439 – ⊠ Warwick

🛏 **The Boot Inn** 🎢 🏚 ⅏ **P** **VISA** **⚫⚫** **AE**
Old Warwick Rd, on B 4439 ⊠ B94 6JU – ℰ (01564) 782 464
– www.thebootatlapworth.co.uk – bootinn@hotmail.com – Fax (01564) 784 989
– Closed 25 December
Rest – (booking essential) Carte £ 22/30
♦ Bustling modern dining pub, with traditional bucolic character at the front and spacious dining room to rear. Appealing rustic dishes supplemented by daily changing specials.

HOLBEACH – Lincolnshire – **502** U 25 – pop. 7 247   17 **D2**
◘ London 117 mi – Kingston-upon-Hull 81 mi – Norwich 62 mi
– Nottingham 60 mi – Peterborough 25 mi

⌂ **Pipwell Manor** without rest 🎢 ⅏ **P**
🏠 *Washway Rd, Saracen's Head, Northwest : 1½ m. by A 17 ⊠ PE12 8AY*
– ℰ (01406) 423 119 – honnor@pipwellmanor.freeserve.co.uk – Fax (01406) 423 119
3 rm ⊇ – ♦£ 40 ♦♦£ 56
♦ Georgian manor built on site of Cisterian Grange, close to solitude of the Wash. Garden railway for train spotters. Complimentary tea, cake on arrival. Country style rooms.

HOLFORD – Somerset – **503** K 30 – ⊠ Bridgwater 🔖 *Great Britain*   3 **B2**
◘ London 171 mi – Bristol 48 mi – Minehead 15 mi – Taunton 22 mi
🔲 Stogursey Priory Church★★, W : 4½ m.

🏨 **Combe House** 🏖 🎢 🐾 ⅏ 🐕 **P** **VISA** **⚫⚫**
Southwest : ¾ m. by Youth Hostel rd ⊠ TA5 1RZ – ℰ (01278) 741 382
– www.combehouse.co.uk – enquiries@combehouse.co.uk – Fax (01278) 741 322
19 rm ⊇ – ♦£ 75/115 ♦♦£ 130/180   **Rest** – Carte £ 26/48
♦ Fresh and modern look being added by the new owners. Swish bathrooms and stylish bedrooms with all mod cons. Delightful setting, with lovely garden and waterwheel. Well run restaurant with a modern menu.

HOLKHAM – Norfolk – **504** W 25   15 **C1**
◘ London 124 mi – King's Lynn 32 mi – Norwich 39 mi

🏨 **The Victoria** ≤ 🎢 㐂 ⅏ **P** **VISA** **⚫⚫** **AE**
Park Rd ⊠ NR23 1RG – ℰ (01328) 711 008 – www.victoriaatholkham.co.uk
– victoria@holkham.co.uk – Fax (01328) 711 009
9 rm ⊇ – ♦£ 100/140 ♦♦£ 120/170
Rest *The Restaurant* – see restaurant listing
♦ Shabby chic hotel, built in 1838, overlooking Holkham nature reserve. Bedrooms are individually styled with much of the furniture sourced from Rajasthan.

XX **The Restaurant** – at The Victoria Hotel
Park Rd ⊠ NR23 1RG – ℰ (01328) 711 008 – www.victoriaatholkham.co.uk
– victoria@holkham.co.uk – Fax (01328) 711 009
Rest – Carte £ 30/35
♦ Extensive dining areas, now including conservatory option, specialise in modish menus as well as fine fish and seafood dishes. The bar offers a buzzy alternative.

ENGLAND

HOLMFIRTH – West Yorkshire – 502 O 23 – pop. 21 979

22 **B3**

🔁 London 187 mi – Leeds 35 mi – Sheffield 32 mi – Manchester 25 mi

⛫ **Sunnybank** without rest ⌖   🛋 ⌦ 🕪 **P** **VISA** **©©**
78 Upperthong Lane, West : ½ m by A6024 ⊠ HD9 3BQ – ℰ (01484) 684 065
– www.sunnybankguesthouse.co.uk – info@sunnybankguesthouse.co.uk
3 rm ⌸ – ♦£60/65 ♦♦£90/100
♦ Attractive Victorian house in mature gardens with smart bedrooms, good facilities
and a modern edge; 2 rooms have great country views. Breakfast room boasts cushioned window seats.

HOLT – Norfolk – 504 X 25 – pop. 3 550

15 **C1**

🔁 London 124 mi – King's Lynn 34 mi – Norwich 22 mi

⌂ **Byfords**   🛋 & ⌦ **P** **VISA** **©©**
Shirehall Plain ⊠ NR25 6BG – ℰ (01263) 711 400 – www.byfords.org.uk
– queries@byfords.org.uk – Fax (01263) 713 520
16 rm ⌸ – ♦£95/105 ♦♦£130/150
Rest – Menu £15 (dinner) – Carte £21/27
♦ Flint-fronted Grade II listed house that boasts something different: a well-stocked
deli; rustic cellar café; and stunning rooms, with great bathrooms and under-floor
heating.

⛫ **Plantation House** without rest   🛋 ⌦ 🕪 **P** **VISA** **©©** **AE**
Old Cromer Rd, East 1¼ m. by A148 on Kelling Hospital rd ⊠ NR25 6AJ
– ℰ (01263) 710 121 – www.plantation-house.net – info@plantation-house.net
– Closed 22 December- 4 January
4 rm ⌸ – ♦£60/75 ♦♦£80/95
♦ Red brick house just out of town, in exceptional mature gardens. Colonial style
with heavy fabrics and objets d'art. Individually styled bedrooms with extra touches;
most overlook garden.

✗ **Butlers**   🍴 **AC** **VISA** **©©** **①**
9 Appleyard ⊠ NR25 6BN – ℰ (01263) 710 790 – www.butlersofholt.com
– eat@butlersofholt.com – Closed 25 December, Sunday dinner and Bank
Holidays
Rest – Carte £19/24
♦ Set in a pedestrianised area, with small terraces front and back. Classical menu
displays a good mix of tasty, unfussy dishes, with regional produce and fresh local
fish to the fore.

HOLT – Wilts. – 503 – see Bradford-on-Avon

HOLYWELL GREEN – West Yorkshire – 502 O 22

22 **B3**

🔁 London 208 mi – Leeds 19 mi – Sheffield 53 mi – Manchester 28 mi

🔢 **The Rock**   🛋 🏠 & ⌦ 🕪 🏊 **P** **VISA** **©©** **AE** **①**
⊠ HX4 9BS – ℰ (01422) 379 721 – www.therockhotel.biz
– enquiries@therockhotel.biz – Fax (01422) 379 110
27 rm ⌸ – ♦£48 ♦♦£90/120   **Rest** – Menu £10/21
♦ Spacious, open plan stone building set in the village centre – formerly an inn.
Bedrooms split between compact standard rooms and larger executive rooms which
come with extras. Upper floor restaurant serves modern, tasty dishes.

HONITON – Devon – 503 K 31 – pop. 11 213

2 **D2**

🔁 London 186 mi – Exeter 17 mi – Southampton 93 mi – Taunton 18 mi
ℹ Lace Walk Car Park ℰ (01404) 43716, honitontic@btconnect.com
🗺 All Hallows Museum★ **AC**
🗺 Ottery St Mary★ (St Mary's★) SW : 5 m. by A 30 and B 3177. Faraway
Countryside Park (≤★) **AC**, SE : 6½ m. by A 375 and B 3174

ENGLAND

The Holt `AE ①`
178 High St, Honiton ⊠ EX14 1LA – ℰ (01404) 47707
– www.theholt-honiton.com – enquiries@theholt-honiton.com
– Closed 25-26 December
Rest – (Closed Sunday-Monday) Carte £ 15/28
♦ Rustic family-run pub providing a 'distinctive and sustainable taste of Devon'. Regularly changing menu of regional and homemade produce; local ales from the family brewery.

at Yarcombe Northeast : 8 m. on A 30 – ⊠ Honiton

Belfry Country H. `≤ ⚘ P VISA ⍟⍟ AE`
on A 30 ⊠ EX14 9BD – ℰ (01404) 861234 – www.thebelfrycountryhotel.com
– stay@thebelfrycountryhotel.com – Fax (01404) 861579 – Closed Christmas-New Year
6 rm ⊆ – †£ 55/65 ††£ 85/95
Rest – (Closed Tuesday) (dinner only) (booking essential for non-residents) Menu £ 28 **s**
♦ Pretty cottage, formerly the village school, opposite 14C church. Personally run and hospitable, with light, cosy bedrooms, named after poets, featuring stained glass windows. Comfy restaurant decorated with owner's world travel photos.

at Gittisham Southwest : 3 m. by A 30 – ⊠ Honiton

Combe House ⍟ `≤ ⚘ ⍤ ⍟ 🍽 🖧 P VISA ⍟⍟`
⊠ EX14 3AD – ℰ (01404) 540400 – www.thishotel.com – stay@thishotel.com
– Fax (01404) 46004 – Closed 2 weeks January
13 rm ⊆ – †£ 150/175 ††£ 170/185 – 3 suites
Rest – (booking essential for non-residents) Menu £ 29/44
♦ Listed Elizabethan mansion set in glorious Devon countryside. Impressive Great Hall. Individually designed, stylish bedrooms with fine antiques and roaring fires. Unfussy cooking makes good use of local produce. Friendly service.

at Payhembury Northwest : 7 m. by A 373 – ⊠ Honiton

Cokesputt House ⍟ `≤ ⚘ ⍟ P VISA ⍟⍟`
West : ¼ m. on Tale rd ⊠ EX14 3HD – ℰ (01404) 841289
– aeac.forbes@virgin.net – Closed Christmas and New Year
3 rm ⊆ – †£ 42/55 ††£ 84
Rest – (booking essential) (communal dining) Menu £ 30
♦ Part 17C and 18C house with gardens. Elegant antique furnished interior, in the best traditions of English country style. Charming bedrooms. Home-grown meals at welcoming communal table.

Don't confuse ✗ with ✿!
✗ defines comfort, while stars are awarded for the best cuisine, across all categories of comfort.

HOOK – Hampshire – **504** R 30 – pop. 6 471 – ⊠ Basingstoke   6 **B1**
D London 47 mi – Oxford 39 mi – Reading 13 mi – Southampton 31 mi

Tylney Hall ⍟ `⚘ ⍤ ⍗ ⍟ 🏊 ♨ ✗ ⅋ ⍟ 🍽 🖧 P VISA ⍟⍟ AE ①`
Rotherwick , Northwest : 2½ m. by A30 and Newnham rd on Ridge Lane
⊠ RG27 9AZ – ℰ (01256) 764881 – www.tylneyhall.com – sales@tylneyhall.com
– Fax (01256) 768141
103 rm ⊆ – †£ 160 ††£ 350/510 – 14 suites
Rest *Oak Room* – Menu £ 25/38 **s** – Carte £ 38/48 **s**
♦ Grand and beautifully restored 19C mansion in delightful, extensive Gertrude Jekyll gardens. Country house rooms, some with private conservatories or suites over two floors. Classically English dining room with oak panelling and garden views.

ENGLAND

HOPE – Derbyshire – **502** O 23 – ⊠ Sheffield

▶ London 180 mi – Derby 50 mi – Manchester 31 mi – Sheffield 15 mi – Stoke-on-Trent 40 mi

⌂ **Underleigh House** without rest ⟨ ⟩ ⟨ ⟩ ⟨ ⟩ **P** ⟨VISA⟩ ⟨OO⟩
Hope Valley, North : 1 m. by Edale Rd ⊠ S33 6RF – ℰ (01433) 621 372
– www.underleighhouse.co.uk – underleigh.house@btconnect.com – Fax (01433)
621 324 – Closed Christmas, New Year and January
5 rm � – †£60 ††£85

♦ Converted Victorian property, rurally located and personally run, well located for the Peak District. Countryside views and a welcoming country ambience.

HOPE COVE – Devon – **503** I 33 – see Salcombe

HORLEY – Surrey – **504** T 30 – pop. 22 582

▶ London 27 mi – Brighton 26 mi – Royal Tunbridge Wells 22 mi

Plan : see Gatwick

🏨 **Langshott Manor** ⟨ ⟩ ⟨ ⟩ ⟨ ⟩ ⟨ ⟩ **P** ⟨VISA⟩ ⟨OO⟩ ⟨AE⟩ ⟨O⟩
Langshott, North : by A 23 turning right at Thistle Gatwick H. onto Ladbroke Rd
⊠ RH6 9LN – ℰ (01293) 786 680 – www.langshottmanor.com
– admin@langshottmanor.com – Fax (01293) 825 872
21 rm � – †£130/150 ††£290/320 – 1 suite
Rest *Mulberry* – (booking essential) Menu £20/42

♦ Part Elizabethan manor house set amidst gardens of roses, vines and ponds. For centuries the home of aristocrats, now a refined and harmonious country house hotel. Country house-style dining room with intimate ambience.

HORNCASTLE – Lincolnshire – **502** T 24 – pop. 6 090

▶ London 143 mi – Lincoln 22 mi – Nottingham 62 mi
🛈 14 Bull Ring ℰ (01507) 526636, horncastleinfo@e-lindsey.gov.uk

✗✗ **Magpies** ⟨AC⟩ ⟨VISA⟩ ⟨OO⟩
71-75 East St ⊠ LN9 6AA – ℰ (01507) 527 004 – www.eatatthemagpies.co.uk
– Fax (01507) 525 068 – Closed 2-21 January, and Monday-Tuesday
Rest – Menu £25/36

♦ Renowned, family run restaurant in a converted 18C house. Snug, comfortable, beamed interior. Local ingredients used in accomplished, refined dishes in a modern style.

HORNDON-ON-THE-HILL – Thurrock – **504** V 29

▶ London 25 mi – Chelmsford 22 mi – Maidstone 34 mi – Southend-on-Sea 16 mi

🏠 **The Bell** with rm ⟨ ⟩ **P** ⟨VISA⟩ ⟨OO⟩ ⟨AE⟩
High Rd ⊠ SS17 8LD – ℰ (01375) 642 463 – www.bell-inn.co.uk
– joanne@bell-inn.co.uk – Fax (01375) 361 611 – Closed 25-26 December and
Bank Holiday Mondays
15 rm – ††£65/104, ⊆ £9.50 **Rest** – Carte £22/31

♦ 16C part timbered coaching inn. Log fire in bar and beamed ceiling in restaurant. Eclectically influenced range of menus. Comfortable, individually furnished bedrooms.

HORNINGSEA – Cambs. – see Cambridge

HORNINGSHAM – Wiltshire – **504** N 30 – see Warminster

HORN'S CROSS – Devon – **503** H 31 – ⊠ Bideford ▌ *Great Britain*

▶ London 222 mi – Barnstaple 15 mi – Exeter 46 mi
🅖 Clovelly ★★, W : 6½ m. on A 39 and B 3237 – Bideford : Bridge ★★ – Burton Art Gallery ★ **AC** - Lundy Island ★★ (by ferry), NE : 7 m. on a 39 and B 3235 – Hartland : Hartland Church ★ - Hartland Quay ★ (⟨※ ★★⟩) - Hartland Point ⟨≤ ★★★⟩, W : 9 m. on A 39 and B 3248 – Great Torrington (Dartington Crystal ★ **AC**), SE : 15 m. on A 39 and A 386 – Rosemoor ★, SE : 16 m. on A 39, A 386 and B 3220

⛺ **The Roundhouse** without rest   🚲 **P** 𝗩𝗜𝗦𝗔 ⓜⓞ ①
West : 1 m. on A 39 ✉ *EX39 5DN* – ℰ *(01237) 451 687*
– www.theroundhouse.co.uk – enquiries@the-round-house.co.uk – Fax (01237)
451 924 – Closed 25 and 26 December
3 rm ⬲ – †£40 ††£65
♦ Located on site of 13C corn mill, this friendly guesthouse offers cream teas on
arrival! Spacious lounge and good quality breakfasts. Comfy, clean, well-kept bedrooms.

🍺 **The Hoops Inn** with rm   🚲 🛜 **P** 𝗩𝗜𝗦𝗔 ⓜⓞ 𝗔𝗘
West :½ m. on A 39 ✉ *EX39 5DL* – ℰ *(01237) 451 222 – www.hoopsinn.co.uk*
– sales@hoopsinn.co.uk – Fax (01237) 451 247
13 rm ⬲ – †£65 ††£95   **Rest** – Menu £25 (dinner) – Carte £20/35
♦ Dating from 13C, this archetypal thatched Devonshire inn has timbers, thick cob
walls and oak panels. Menus feature quality local produce. Comfortable rooms.

HORRINGER – Suffolk – **504** W 27 – see Bury St Edmunds

We try to be as accurate as possible when giving room rates
but prices are susceptible to change.
Please check rates when booking.

HORSHAM – West Sussex – **504** T 30 – pop. 47 804   **7 D2**
🚹 London 39 mi – Brighton 23 mi – Guildford 20 mi – Lewes 25 mi
   – Worthing 20 mi
🛈 9 Causeway ℰ (01403) 211661, tourist.information@horsham.gov.uk
🏌 Mannings Heath Fullers, Hammerpond Rd, Mannings Heath,
  ℰ (01403) 210 228

🏨 **South Lodge** ⌂   ≤ 🚲 🕙 🛜 ⅄ ✗ �ⓐ 🍴 🗖 **P** 𝗩𝗜𝗦𝗔 ⓜⓞ 𝗔𝗘
Brighton Rd, Lower Beeding, Southeast : 5 m. on A 281 ✉ *RH13 6PS* – ℰ *(01403)*
891 711 – www.exclusivehotel.co.uk – enquiries@southlodgehotel.co.uk
– Fax (01403) 892 289
83 rm – †£195 ††£195, ⬲ £16 – 3 suites
Rest *Camellia* – (booking essential for non-residents) Menu £19 (lunch)
– Carte dinner £35/55
Rest *The Pass* – (Closed Monday-Tuesday) Menu £28/68
♦ Victorian mansion in 93 acres of immaculate gardens and parkland, overlooking
South Downs. Opulent yet relaxed antique furnished public areas. Charming indi-
vidual bedrooms. Camellia opens onto terrace; traditional menus. The Pass for
creative and innovative cooking.

✗✗ **Restaurant Tristan**   𝗩𝗜𝗦𝗔 ⓜⓞ
Stans Way ✉ *RH12 1HU* – ℰ *(01403) 255 688 – www.restauranttristan.co.uk*
– info@restauranttristan.co.uk – Closed first 2 weeks January, first 2 weeks
August, 25-26 December, Sunday and Monday
Rest – Menu £20/32
♦ The dining happens in the beamed upstairs room of this period house. The cook-
ing is seasonal but also elaborate in style; the kitchen is a fan of modern techniques.
Service is quite formal.

at Rowhook Northwest : 4 m. by A 264 and A 281 off A 29 – ✉ Horsham

🍺 **The Chequers Inn**   🚲 **P** 𝗩𝗜𝗦𝗔 ⓜⓞ
✉ *RH12 3PY* – ℰ *(01403) 790 480 – nealsrestaurants.biz*
– thechequers1@aol.com – Closed 25 December
Rest – Carte £23/30
♦ Delightful 18C inn with low beams, formal restaurant and relaxed atmosphere.
Menus showcase local produce – including game from nearby estates – and fresh
homemade puddings.

ENGLAND

HORWICH – Greater Manchester – **502** M 23 – ⊠ Bolton   20 **B2**
> ▶ London 217 mi – Liverpool 35 mi – Manchester 21 mi – Preston 16 mi

🏨 **Whites**   ▣ ⊛ ㊙ ゟ 🗃 ㋡ rm, Ⅻ rest, ℅ ㏗ ㏈ 🅿 ⅦⅩⅣ ⅭⅤ ⅭⅤ
The Reebok Stadium, (Car Park A), De Havilland Way, Southeast : 2½ m. by A 673 on A 6027 ⊠ BL6 6SF – ℰ (01204) 667 788 – www.devere.co.uk – whites@devere-hotels.com – Fax (01204) 673 721
119 rm ⊇ – ♦£75/150 ♦♦£110/160 – 6 suites
Rest *Brasserie at Whites* – Menu £20 (dinner) – Carte £25/39
♦ Modern business hotel, uniquely part of Bolton Wanderers' football stadium. Well equipped all round with good, modern bedrooms. Corporate clients can use stadium facilities. Brasserie at Whites is a "must" for Wanderers fans.

HOUGH-ON-THE-HILL – Lincs. – see Grantham

HOUGHTON – Cambs. – see Huntingdon

> If breakfast is included the ⊇ symbol appears after the number of rooms.

HOUGHTON CONQUEST – Beds. – **504** S 27 – see Bedford

HOVE – Brighton and Hove – **504** T 31 – see Brighton and Hove

HOVINGHAM – North Yorkshire – **502** R 21 – ⊠ York   23 **C2**
> ▶ London 235 mi – Leeds 47 mi – Middlesbrough 36 mi – York 25 mi

🏨 **Worsley Arms**   ⤬ ℅ ㏈ 🅿 ⅦⅩⅣ ⅭⅤ ①
High St ⊠ YO62 4LA – ℰ (01653) 628 234 – www.worsleyarms.co.uk – enquiries@worsleyarms.co.uk – Fax (01653) 628 130
19 rm ⊇ – ♦£85/115 ♦♦£120/140
Rest *Cricketer's Bistro* – (dinner only and Sunday lunch) Carte £20/32
Rest *Worsley Arms* – (dinner only and Sunday lunch) Carte £20/32
♦ Part 19C coaching inn set in delightful Yorkshire stone village. Charm and character throughout the classically traditional public rooms. Comfortable individual bedrooms. Same menu served in informal Cricketer's Bistro and more refined Worsley Arms restaurant.

HUDDERSFIELD – West Yorkshire – **502** O 23 – pop. 146 234   22 **B3**
> ▶ London 191 mi – Bradford 11 mi – Leeds 15 mi – Manchester 25 mi – Sheffield 26 mi
> 🛈 3 Albion St ℰ (01484) 223200, huddersfield.tic@kirklees.gov.uk
> 🏌 Bradley Park Bradley Rd, ℰ (01484) 223 772
> 🏌 Woodsome Hall Fenay Bridge, ℰ (01484) 602 971
> 🏌 Outlane Slack Lane, Off New Hey Rd, ℰ (01422) 374 762
> 🏌 Meltham Thick Hollins Hall, ℰ (01484) 850 227
> 🏌 Fixby Hall Lightridge Rd, ℰ (01484) 426 203
> 🏌 Crosland Heath Felks Stile Rd, ℰ (01484) 653 216

Plan opposite

at Thunder Bridge Southeast : 5¾ m. by A 629 – B – ⊠ Huddersfield

🍺 **Woodman Inn** with rm   🅿 ⅦⅩⅣ ⅭⅤ
⊠ HD8 0PX – ℰ (01484) 605 778 – www.woodman-inn.co.uk – thewoodman@connectfree.co.uk – Fax (01484) 604 110 – Closed 25 December dinner
12 rm ⊇ – ♦£45/454 ♦♦£68/78   **Rest** – Carte £14/27
♦ Traditional 19C pub set in a small hamlet in the valley. The classic British menus are extensive and change with the seasons. Lunch is simple and hearty, dinner more ambitious. Nearby cottage bedrooms are simple but well-kept.

ENGLAND

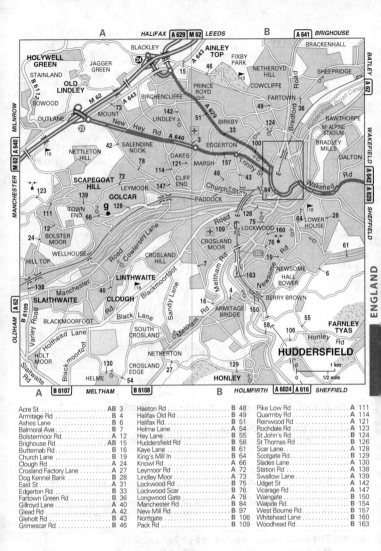

Acre St	AB 3	Haeton Rd	B 48	Pike Low Rd	A 111
Armitage Rd	B 4	Halifax Old Rd	B 49	Quarmby Rd	A 114
Ashes Lane	B 6	Halifax Rd	B 51	Reinwood Rd	A 121
Balmoral Ave	B 7	Helme Lane	A 54	Rochdale Rd	A 123
Bolstermoor Rd	A 12	Hey Lane	B 55	St John's Rd	B 124
Brighouse Rd	AB 15	Huddersfield Rd	B 58	St Thomas Rd	B 126
Butternab Rd	B 16	Kaye Lane	B 61	Scar Lane	A 128
Church Lane	B 19	King's Mill In	B 64	Scotgate Rd	B 129
Clough Rd	A 24	Knowl Rd	A 66	Slades Lane	B 130
Crosland Factory Lane	A 27	Leymoor Rd	A 72	Station Rd	A 138
Dog Kennel Bank	A 31	Lindley Moor	A 73	Swallow Lane	A 139
East St	A 33	Lockwood Rd	B 75	Udget St	A 142
Edgerton Rd	B 36	Lockwood Scar	B 76	Vicarage Rd	A 147
Fartown Green Rd	A 40	Longwood Gate	A 78	Waingate	B 150
Gillroyd Lane	B 42	Manchester Rd	B 84	Walpde Rd	B 154
Glead Rd	B 43	New Mill Rd	B 97	West Bourne Rd	B 157
Gleholt Rd	B 43	Norttgate	B 106	Whitehead Lane	B 160
Grimescar Rd	B 46	Pack Rd	B 109	Woodhead Rd	B 163

at Shelley Southeast : 6 ¼ m. by A 629 - B - on B 6116 – ⊠ Huddersfield

🏠 **The Three Acres**   🍴 🍴 🖭 rest, 🌣 🅿 *VISA* 🐵 🖭
Roydhouse, Northeast : 1½ m. on Flockton rd ⊠ HD8 8LR – 𝒞 (01484) 602 606
– www.3acres.com – 3acres@globalnet.co.uk – Fax (01484) 608 411
– Closed 25 December, 26 December, 1st January
16 rm ⌿ – ♦£80/100 ♦♦£120 – 1 suite
Rest – (closed Saturday lunch) (booking essential) Carte £27/44
♦ Well-established stone inn in rural location. Annex rooms more spacious and quiet;
those in main house closer to the bar and dining room; all warm, modern and
comfortable. Agreeably busy restaurant with open fires: fish dishes prepared at open
seafood bar.

HUDDERSFIELD

Chapel Hill . . . . C 18
Claremont St . . . . C 21
Fitzwilliam St . . . . C 37
Gaswoors St . . . . C 39
Great Northern St . . . . C 45
Imperial Arcade . . . . C 60
Kingsgate Shopping
Centre C
King St . . . . C 63
Lower Fitzwilliam St . . . . . C 79
Manchester Rd . . . . C 84
Market Pl. . . . . C 85
Market St. . . . . C 87
Merton St. . . . . C 91
New North Rd . . . . C 100
Northumberland St . . . . . . C 105
Outcote Bank . . . . C 108
Piazza Shopping Centre . . C
Portland St . . . . C 112
Queen St . . . . C 115
Queen St South. . . . . C 117
Railway St . . . . C 120
St Peter's St. . . . . C 125
Springwood Ave . . . . C 136
Spring St . . . . C 133
Trinity St. . . . . C 141
Venn St. . . . . C 145
Victoria Lane . . . . C 148
Wakefield Rd . . . . C 151
Water St. . . . . C 156

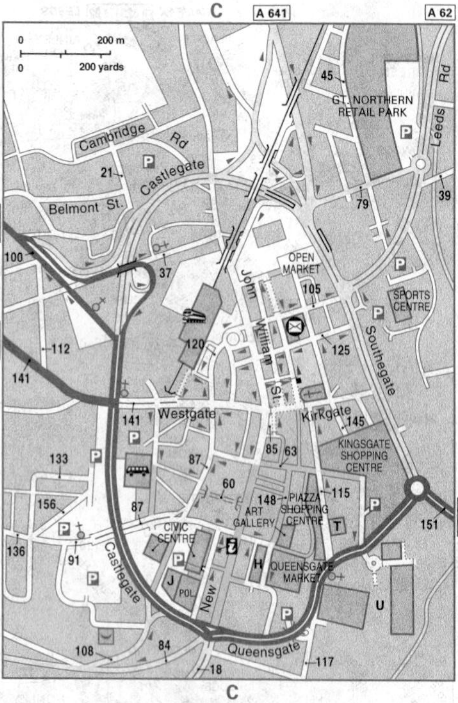

ENGLAND

at Golcar West : 3 ½ m. by A 62 on B 6111 – ✉ Huddersfield

XXX **The Weavers Shed** with rm
88 Knowl Rd, via Scar Lane ✉ HD7 4AN – ✆ (01484) 654 284
– www.weaversshed.co.uk – info@weaversshed.co.uk – Fax (01484) 650 980
– Closed Christmas- First week January Ag
5 rm – †£ 90 ††£ 110
Rest – (closed Saturday lunch, Sunday and Monday) Menu £ 18 (lunch)
– Carte £ 35/53
♦ Converted 18C cloth finishing mill with stone floored dining area. Modern British menu supplied by an extensive kitchen garden and allotment. Smart bedrooms.

HUNGERFORD – West Berkshire – **503** P 29 – **pop. 4 938** 10 **A3**
London 74 mi – Bristol 57 mi – Oxford 28 mi – Reading 26 mi
– Southampton 46 mi
Savernake Forest★★ (Grand Avenue★★★), W : 7 m. by A 4 – Crofton Beam Engines★, SW : 8 m. by A 338 and minor roads

Fishers Farm without rest
Shefford Woodlands, North : 4 m. by A 4 and A 338 on B 4000 ✉ RG17 7AB
– ✆ (01488) 648 466 – www.fishersfarm.co.uk – mail@fishersfarm.co.uk
– Fax (01488) 648 706
3 rm – †£ 50/60 ††£ 65/80
♦ Attractive redbrick farmhouse in a rural spot on a working farm. Well-appointed sitting room. Breakfast served family style. Individually styled rooms with country views.

at Lambourn Woodlands North : 6 m. by A 338 on B 4000 – ✉ Hungerford

XX **The Hare** 🚗 🌳 **P** **VISA** **MO**
✉ RG17 7SD – 📞 (01488) 71 386 – www.theharerestaurant.co.uk
– cuisine@theharerestaurant.co.uk – Fax (01488) 71 186 – Closed 2 weeks Winter,
1 week Spring, 2 weeks Summer, 25-26 December, 1 January, Sunday dinner and
Monday
Rest – (booking essential) Menu £ 23 (midweek)/26 – Carte (dinner) approx.
£ 40
♦ Contemporary pub conversion with modish interior of three dining rooms and
original beams. Building a strong local reputation based on innovative cooking of a
high standard.

at Kintbury Southeast : 3 ¾ m. by A 4 – ✉ Hungerford

🍴 **The Dundas Arms** with rm 🌳 🌿 **P** **VISA** **MO**
Station Rd ✉ RG17 9UT – 📞 (01488) 658 263 – www.dundasarms.co.uk
– info@dundasarms.co.uk – Closed 25 December, 31 December dinner
5 rm ☲ – †£ 80 ††£ 90 **Rest** – (Closed Sunday) Carte £ 22/27
♦ Set on tiny island between river and canal. Unexceptional interior: the food's the
thing here - tasty, accomplished, homecooked dishes. Bedrooms with small riverside
terraces.

Undecided between two equivalent establishments?
Within each category, establishments are classified
in our order of preference.

ENGLAND

HUNSDON – Hertfordshire 12 **B2**
🚩 London 26 mi – Bishop's Stortford 8 mi – Harlow 7 mi

🍴 **Fox and Hounds** 🚗 🌳 **P** **VISA** **MO**
2 High St ✉ SG12 8NH – 📞 (01279) 843 999
– www.foxandhounds-hunsdon.co.uk – info@foxandhounds-hunsdon.co.uk
– Fax (01279) 841 092 – Closed Sunday dinner and Monday (except Bank Holiday
lunch)
Rest – Menu £ 16/18 – Carte £ 21/30
♦ Spacious pub featuring a rustic bar, smart dining room, large garden and terrace.
Daily-changing menu displays a wide range of local seasonal produce, cooked simply
and stylishly.

HUNSTANTON – Norfolk – **502** V 25 – pop. 4 505 14 **B1**
🚩 London 120 mi – Cambridge 60 mi – Norwich 45 mi
ℹ️ Town Hall, The Green 📞 (01485) 532610,
hunstanton.tic@west-norfolk.gov.uk
⛳ Golf Course Rd, 📞 (01485) 532 811

🏠 **Shellbrooke** without rest 🌿 📶 **P** **VISA** **MO** **AE**
9 Cliff Terrace ✉ PE36 6DY – 📞 (01485) 532 289 – www.theshellbrooke.co.uk
– info@theshellbrooke.co.uk
12 rm ☲ – †£ 55 ††£ 72
♦ Recently refurbished seaside hotel with terrace. Comfy lounge and modern breakfast room. Good sized bedrooms with good facilities and modern bathrooms. Front
rooms have partial sea views.

🏠 **Claremont** without rest
35 Greevegate ✉ PE36 6AF – 📞 (01485) 533 171 – claremontgh@tiscali.co.uk
– April-October
7 rm ☲ – †£ 35/45 ††£ 70
♦ Classic seaside guesthouse in a Victorian building close to beach, shops and
gardens. Well-kept, traditional interior and a toaster on each table at breakfast.

✗✗ ✿ The Neptune (Kevin Mangeolles) with rm 📞 P VISA 🅭

85 Old Hunstanton Rd, Old Hunstanton, Northeast : 1 1/2 m. on A 149
✉ PE36 6HZ – ℰ (01485) 532122 – www.theneptune.co.uk
– reservations@theneptune.co.uk – Closed 26 December, 5-22 January, 1 week
November and Monday in winter
7 rm – �£65/95 ♟♟£110
Rest – (dinner only and Sunday lunch) (lunch midweek by arrangement)
Menu £21 – Carte £34/44
Spec. Mackerel, watermelon and crab salad. Aberdeen Angus beef with spi-
nach purée, pickled onion and beef tea. Lemon custard with lemon grass ice
cream and vanilla lemonade.
♦ Ivy-clad, red brick 19C former coaching inn; New England style prevails throughout.
Concise menu delivers refined, unfussy and flavoursome cooking. Simple bedrooms.

at Ringstead East : 3 ¾ m. by A 149 – ✉ Hunstanton

🛏 The Gin Trap Inn with rm 🍴 🌳 📞 P VISA 🅭 AE

6 High St ✉ PE36 5JU – ℰ (01485) 525264 – www.gintrapinn.co.uk
– thegintrap@hotmail.co.uk
3 rm – ♟£49/70 ♟♟£78/140   **Rest** – Carte £19/27
♦ Attractive whitewashed inn with cosy front bar and spacious, wood-floored conservatory. Well-presented, value-for-money dishes mix the traditional and the more
modern. Bedrooms boast wrought iron beds and roll top baths.

HUNSTRETE – Bath & North East Somerset – **503** M 29 – **see Bristol**

HUNTINGDON – Cambridgeshire – **504** T 26 – **pop. 20 600**   14 **A2**

🔼 London 69 mi – Bedford 21 mi – Cambridge 16 mi
🔼 The Library, Princes St ℰ (01480) 388588, hunts.tic@huntsdc.gov.uk
🔼 Hemingford Abbots Cambridge Rd, New Farm Lodge, ℰ (01480) 495000

🏨 Huntingdon Marriott 📺 🏊 ℱ♠ 🖥 ♿ rm, 🔃 📞 ♠ P VISA 🅭 AE ①

Kingfisher Way, Hinchingbrooke Business Park, West : 1½ m. by A 141 at junction
with A 14 ✉ PE29 6FL – ℰ (01480) 446000 – www.huntingdonmarriott.co.uk
– reservations.huntingdon@marriotthotels.co.uk – Fax (01480) 451111
146 rm – ♟£120/139 ♟♟£120/139, ⌑ £15.95 – 4 suites
Rest – (buffet lunch) Carte £23/38
♦ Purpose-built 1990s hotel, well geared to the modern business traveller. Good
standard of brand furniture in public areas and well-equipped rooms which include
data ports. Smart, airy dining room.

🏨 Old Bridge 🔃 ♠ P VISA 🅭 AE ①

1 High St ✉ PE29 3TQ – ℰ (01480) 424300 – www.huntsbridge.com
– oldbridge@huntsbridge.co.uk – Fax (01480) 411017
24 rm ⌑ – ♟£95/110 ♟♟£190
Rest *Terrace* – see restaurant listing
♦ 18C former private bank overlooking the river. All bedrooms, some very contemporary, are decorated to a good standard and bathrooms often have deep Victorian-style baths.

✗✗ Terrace – at Old Bridge Hotel 🍴 🌳 P VISA 🅭 AE ①

1 High St ✉ PE29 3TQ – ℰ (01480) 424300 – Fax (01480) 411017
Rest – Menu £19 (lunch) – Carte £28/37 🍴
♦ Two dining areas: a formal wood panelled room and a more casual conservatory
with terrace. Hearty rustic Italian dishes provide the basis for menus.

at Hemingford Grey Southeast : 5 m. by A 1198 off A 14 – ✉ Huntingdon

🏠 The Willow without rest 📶 📞 P VISA 🅭

45 High St ✉ PE28 9BJ – ℰ (01480) 494748 – www.thewillowguesthouse.co.uk
– Fax (01480) 464456
7 rm ⌑ – ♟£45/70 ♟♟£70
♦ Very personally run guesthouse in picturesque village location: its vivid yellow
exterior makes it easy to spot. Good value, and close to The Cock. Immaculately kept
bedrooms.

🏠 **The Cock**   🅿 VISA ⓪
47 High St ⊠ PE28 9BJ – ☏ (01480) 463 609 – www.cambscuisine.com
– cock@cambscuisine.com – Fax (01480) 461 747
Rest – Menu £ 15 – Carte £ 21/25
♦ Real ale pub with spacious dining area that features a wood-burning stove and oil paintings for sale. Good choice of dishes: fresh fish or sausage selections are a speciality.

at Spaldwick West : 7½ m. by A 141 off A 14 – ⊠ Huntingdon

🏠 **The George Inn**   🆔 🏧 ❀ ⇔ 🅿 VISA ⓪
5 High St ⊠ PE28 0TD – ☏ (01480) 890 293 – www.georgeofspaldwick.co.uk
– info@georgeofspaldwick.co.uk – Fax (01480) 896 847
Rest – Carte £ 23/33
♦ Built in the early 1500s, now sporting lilac and aubergine walls and an imposing fireplace. Characterful beamed restaurant: menus mix modern European with home-grown classics.

HUNWORTH – Norfolk   15 **C1**
🄳 London 129 mi – Norwich 25 mi – East Dereham 17 mi – Taverham 19 mi

🏠 **The Hunny Bell**   🅿 VISA ⓪
The Green ⊠ NR24 2AA – ☏ (01263) 712 300 – www.thehunnybell.co.uk
– hunnybell@animalinns.co.uk
Rest – Carte £ 15/29
♦ Renovated whitewashed pub with a smart country interior. Cooking is modern-European meets traditional pub and is local, seasonal and keenly priced. Much of the food is homemade.

HURLEY – Windsor and Maidenhead   11 **C3**
🄳 London 35 mi – Maidenhead 5 mi – Reading 18 mi

🏠 **Black Boys Inn** with rm   ❀ 🖤 👝 VISA ⓪ 🅰🅴
🉐   Henley Rd, Southwest : 1½ m. on A 4130 ⊠ SL6 5NQ – ☏ (01628) 824 212
– www.blackboysinn.co.uk – info@blackboysinn.co.uk – Closed 2 weeks at
Christmas, 2 weeks in August
8 rm ⌂ – ♦£95/120   **Rest** – (Closed Sunday dinner, Monday) Carte £ 24/37
♦ 16C pub with stylish modern interior, comfy lounge and wood burning stove. Cooking is well-crafted and flavoursome, with restaurant-style dishes. Friendly, knowledgeable service. Individually-styled bedrooms with excellent en suites.

HURST – Berks. – **503** Q 29 – **see Reading**

HURSTBOURNE TARRANT – Hampshire – **503** P 30 – ⊠ Andover   6 **B1**
🄳 London 77 mi – Bristol 77 mi – Oxford 38 mi – Southampton 33 mi

🏨 **Esseborne Manor** ⌖   ❀ 🖤 👝 🅿 VISA ⓪ 🅰🅴 ⓪
Northeast : 1½ m. on A 343 ⊠ SP11 0ER – ☏ (01264) 736 444
– www.esseborne-manor.co.uk – info@esseborne-manor.co.uk – Fax (01264)
736 725
19 rm ⌂ – ♦£98/110 ♦♦£150/240   **Rest** – Menu £15/20 **s** – Carte £29/50 **s**
♦ 100 year old country house in attractive grounds with herb garden. Smart, well-appointed bedrooms, three in garden cottages. Ferndown room boasts a spa bath and private patio. Long, narrow dining room with large windows.

HUTTON-LE-HOLE – North Yorkshire – **502** R 21   23 **C1**
🄳 London 244 mi – Scarborough 27 mi – York 33 mi

🏠 **Burnley House** without rest   🅿
⊠ YO62 6UA – ☏ (01751) 417 548 – www.burnleyhouse.co.uk
– info@burnleyhouse.co.uk
7 rm ⌂ – ♦£60 ♦♦£90/95
♦ Attractive part 16C, part Georgian house, Grade II listed in a picturesque Moors village. Brown trout in beck winding through garden. Simple, individually styled bedrooms.

ENGLAND

HUTTON MAGNA – Durham – pop. 86 ▮ Great Britain 24 **A3**

- ▶ London 258 mi – Darlington 17 mi – Newcastle upon Tyne 53 mi – Scarborough 75 mi
- ⌖ Raby Castle★, N : 5 m. by B 6274. Richmond★, S : 8 m. by B 6274 – Bowes Museum★, W : 8 m. by A 66

🍴 ⊛ **The Oak Tree Inn** **P** **VISA** ◉◉
⊠ DL11 7HH – ℰ (01833) 627371 – www.elevation-it.co.uk/oaktree – Closed 24-26 and 31 December, 1-2 January and Monday
Rest – (dinner only) Carte £ 26/33
♦ Part 18C inn in an unspoilt rural location. Interior beams and stone walls with homely décor. Blackboard menus offering a good range of modern pub dishes.

HYTHE – Kent – 504 X 30 – pop. 14 766 9 **D2**

- ▶ London 68 mi – Folkestone 6 mi – Hastings 33 mi – Maidstone 31 mi
- 🛈 Railway Station, Scanlons Bridge Rd ℰ (01303) 266421
- 🏌 Sene Valley Folkestone Sene, ℰ (01303) 268 513

Plan : see Folkestone

🏨 **Hythe Imperial** ≤ 🚗 🏊 🏕 🖥 ☒ 🍴 ℎ ℱℴ ✗ 🔲 🛗 ⅗ rm, ✗ 🛜
Prince's Parade ⊠ CT21 6AE – ℰ (01303) 267441 ♨ **P** **VISA** ◉◉ **AE** ◉
– www.mercure-uk.com – h6862@accor.com – Fax (01303) 264 610 **Xd**
100 rm – †£ 80/145 ††£ 80/185, ⌷ £ 12.95
Rest The Princes Room – (bar lunch Monday -Saturday) Menu 27
♦ Set in a 50 acre estate, this classic Victorian hotel retains the elegance of a former age. Wide range of bedrooms cater for everyone from families to business travellers. Spacious restaurant with classic style and menus to match.

🍴 **Hythe Bay** ≤ 🏕 **P** **VISA** ◉◉ **AE** ◉
Marine Parade ⊠ CT21 6AW – ℰ (01303) 233 844 – www.thehythebay.co.uk
– enquiries@thehythebay.co.uk – Fax (01303) 233 845
Rest – Seafood – (buffet lunch Sunday) Carte £ 25/38
♦ Originally built as tea rooms and in a great position just feet from the beach. Bright, airy room with views out to Channel. Seafood menus - ideal for lunch on a summer's day.

ICKLESHAM – East Sussex – 504 V/W 31 9 **C3**

- ▶ London 66 mi – Brighton 42 mi – Hastings 7 mi

🏠 **Manor Farm Oast** ⌖ 🚗 ✗ 🛜 **P** **VISA** ◉◉ ◉
Windmill Lane, South : ½ m. ⊠ TN36 4WL – ℰ (01424) 813 787
– www.manorfarmoast.co.uk – manor.farm.oast@lineone.net – Fax (01424)
813 787 – Closed 23 December-2 January and 10 January-12 February
3 rm ⌷ – †£ 88/98 ††£ 88/98 **Rest** – (by arrangement) Menu £ 30
♦ 19C former oast house retaining original features and surrounded by orchards. Welcoming beamed lounge with open fire. One of the comfy bedrooms is completely in the round! Home-cooked menus in circular dining room.

IGHTHAM COMMON – Kent – 504 U 30 – see Sevenoaks

ILFRACOMBE – Devon – 503 H 30 ▮ Great Britain 2 **C1**

- ▶ London 218 mi – Barnstaple 13 mi – Exeter 53 mi
- ⌖ Mortehoe★★ : St Mary's Church - Morte Point★, SW : 5½ m. on B 3343 – Lundy Island★★ (by ferry). Braunton : St Brannock's Church★, Braunton Burrows★, S : 8 m. on A 361 – Barnstaple★ : Bridge★, S : 12 m. on A 3123, B 3230, A 39, A 361 and B 3233

🍴🍴 **The Quay** ≤ 🏕 **VISA** ◉◉ **AE** ◉
11 The Quay ⊠ EX34 9EQ – ℰ (01271) 868 090 – www.11thequay.com
– info@11thequay.com – Fax (01271) 865 599
– Closed 25-26 December and 3 weeks January
Rest – Carte £ 26/36
♦ Handsome 18C brick harbourside building, part owned by Damien Hirst. Cool, modish interior, typified by plethora of Hirst artworks.

ENGLAND

ILKLEY – West Yorkshire – 502 O 22 – pop. 13 472   22 B2

▶ London 210 mi – Bradford 13 mi – Harrogate 17 mi – Leeds 16 mi
– Preston 46 mi

🛈 Town Hall, Station Rd ℰ (01943) 602319, ilkleytic@bradford.gov.uk

🏠 Myddleton, ℰ (01943) 607 277

Rombalds   🛄 ⚓ P. VISA ⦵ AE ①
11 West View, Wells Rd ✉ LS29 9JG – ℰ (01943) 603 201 – www.rombalds.co.uk
– reception@rombalds.demon.co.uk – Fax (01943) 816 586 – Closed 27 December
- early New Year
15 rm – ♦£85/105 ♦♦£120/135, ☐ £11.95 – 4 suites
Rest – Menu £15 (lunch) – Carte £25/35
♦ Privately owned Georgian town house on edge of Moor. Elegant fixtures and
fittings adorn its sitting room. Individually styled bedrooms have matching fabrics
and drapes. Yorkshire produce to fore in cool blue restaurant.

Box Tree (Simon Gueller)   AC ⇄ VISA ⦵
37 Church St, on A 65 ✉ LS29 9DR – ℰ (01943) 608 484 – www.theboxtree.co.uk
– info@theboxtree.co.uk – Fax (01943) 607 186 – Closed 27-30 December and first
week January
Rest – (dinner only lunch Friday-Sunday) Menu £28/30 – Carte £51/58
Spec. Warm salad of ham with smoked eel and duck liver. Fillet and daube of
beef, pomme purée and glazed vegetables. Strawberry soufflé and sauce.
♦ Characterful 18C sandstone cottage, adorned with antiques, paintings and ornaments. Clearly defined, flavourful modern cooking served in generous portions.
Charming service.

ILLOGAN – Cornwall – 503 E 33 – ✉ Redruth   1 A3

▶ London 305 mi – Falmouth 14 mi – Penzance 17 mi – Truro 11 mi

◙ Portreath★, NW : 2 m. by B 3300 – Hell's Mouth★, SW : 5 m. by B 3301

Aviary Court ⦵   🚗 ✗ ✗ P. VISA ⦵
Mary's Well, Northwest : ¾ m. by Alexandra Rd ✉ TR16 4QZ – ℰ (01209)
842 256 – www.aviarycourthotel.co.uk – info@aviarycourthotel.co.uk
– Fax (01209) 843 744
6 rm ☐ – ♦£53/84 ♦♦£84/89
Rest – (dinner only) (residents only) Menu £20
♦ Tranquillity reigns at this cosy Cornish hotel with its neat, well-kept gardens. Tradi-
tional ambience prevails throughout with colourful furnishings and traditional rooms.
Cornish ingredients dominate cuisine.

ILMINGTON – Warwickshire – 504 O 27 📗 Great Britain   19 C3

▶ London 91 mi – Birmingham 31 mi – Oxford 34 mi
– Stratford-upon-Avon 9 mi

◙ Hidcote Manor Garden★★, SW : 2 m. by minor rd – Chipping Campden★★,
SW : 4 m. by minor rd

Folly Farm Cottage   🚗 ✗ 🛄 P. VISA ⦵ AE
Back St ✉ CV36 4LJ – ℰ (01608) 682 425 – www.follyfarm.co.uk
– bruceandpam@follyfarm.co.uk – Fax (01608) 682 425
3 rm ☐ – ♦£55 ♦♦£84   **Rest** – (dinner only) Menu £19
♦ Welcoming, cosy guesthouse with snug interior. Notable, sunny seating area in rear
garden. Spacious breakfast room. Immaculate bedrooms, where breakfast may also
be taken. A la carte served at dinner.

The Howard Arms with rm   🚗 🏠 AC rest, ✗ P. VISA ⦵ AE
Lower Green ✉ CV36 4LT – ℰ (01608) 682 226 – www.howardarms.com
– info@howardarms.com – Fax (01608) 682 226 – Closed 25 December
8 rm ☐ – ♦£88/95 ♦♦£150   **Rest** – Carte £15/25
♦ Gold stone English country inn, with a terrace, set on a peaceful village green.
Wide-ranging, weekly changing menu is informed by seasonal produce from local
farms and Estates. Cosy bedrooms with antique furniture.

ENGLAND

INGLETON – North Yorkshire – **502** M 21 – **pop. 1 641** – ⊠ Carnforth   22 **A2**
(Lancs.)

🚘 London 266 mi – Kendal 21 mi – Lancaster 18 mi – Leeds 53 mi
🛈 The Community Centre ℰ (015242) 41049, ingleton@ytbtic.co.uk

⚲ **Riverside Lodge**   ⟨ 🚘 🐾 ⚇ **P.** ⟨VISA⟩ ⟨⟩
24 Main St ⊠ LA6 3HJ – ℰ (015242) 41 359 – www.riversideingleton.co.uk
– info@riversideingleton.co.uk – Closed 24-25 December and mid week
January-February
7 rm ⌕ – †£41 ††£62   **Rest** – (by arrangement) Menu £16
♦ Pleasant 19C house close to famous pot-holing caves. Conservatory dining room
with great views across Yorkshire Dales. Informal gardens. Cosy sitting room and
homely bedrooms.

INSTOW – Devon – **503** H 30 – **see Bideford**

IPSWICH – Suffolk – **504** X 27 – **pop. 138 718** 📖 Great Britain   15 **C3**
🚘 London 76 mi – Norwich 43 mi
🛈 St Stephens Church, St Stephens Lane ℰ (01473) 258070,
tourist@ipswich.gov.uk
🏌 Rushmere Rushmere Heath, ℰ (01473) 725 648
🏌 Purdis Heath Bucklesham Rd, ℰ (01473) 728 941
🏌 Fynn Valley Witnesham, ℰ (01473) 785 267
🏰 Sutton Hoo★, NE : 12 m. by A 12 Y and B 1083 from Woodbridge

Plan opposite

🏨 **Salthouse Harbour**   ⟨ 🐾 📶 ⅙ rm, **P.** ⟨VISA⟩ ⟨⟩ ⟨AE⟩ ⟨①⟩
1 Neptune Quay ⊠ IP4 1AX – ℰ (01473) 226 789
– www.salthouseharbour.co.uk
– staying@salthouseharbour.co.uk
– Fax (01473) 226 927   X**a**
41 rm ⌕ – †£120/170 ††£120/170 – 2 suites
Rest *The Eaterie* – Menu £15 (lunch) – Carte £22/35
♦ Converted 6-storey former salt house overlooking the marina. Lounge with sea-
grass seats. Designer style bedrooms with modern facilities; some with good views;
two penthouse suites. Modern brasserie with a Mediterranean touch.

🏨 **Kesgrave Hall**   🚘 🕭 🐾 ⅙ 📶 **P.** ⟨VISA⟩ ⟨⟩ ⟨AE⟩ ⟨①⟩
Hall Rd, East : 4¾ m. by A1214 on Bealings rd ⊠ IP5 2PU – ℰ (01473) 333 471
– www.kesgravehall.com – reception@kesgravehall.com
– Fax (01473) 617 614
15 rm – †£165 ††£165, ⌕ £15   **Rest** – Carte £24/35
♦ Characterful Georgian mansion with large terrace, set in mature grounds. Stylish
bedrooms display bold décor and a mix of furniture; some even have baths in the
room. Seasonally-changing modern European menus feature local, organic produce.

🍴🍴 **The Dining Room**   ⟨VISA⟩ ⟨⟩ ⟨AE⟩
14-20 Fore St ⊠ IP4 1JU – ℰ (01473) 225 888 – www.the-diningroom.co.uk
– enquiries@the-diningroom.co.uk – Closed Monday   X**z**
Rest – Menu £16/20 – Carte £22/24
♦ Spacious glass-fronted restaurant in city centre, with striking black and white décor. Unfussy, flavoursome dishes take their influences from modern Britain, Europe
and the Med.

⚲ **Sidegate Guest House** without rest   🚘 📶 **P.**
121 Sidegate Lane ⊠ IP4 4JB – ℰ (01473) 728 714
– www.sidegateguesthouse.co.uk – bookings@sidegateguesthouse.co.uk   Y**a**
6 rm ⌕ – †£51/61 ††£71
♦ Compact, friendly guesthouse in residential area. Comfy lounge with terraced
doors onto garden. Neatly laid breakfast room. Bright, refurbished bedrooms.

IPSWICH

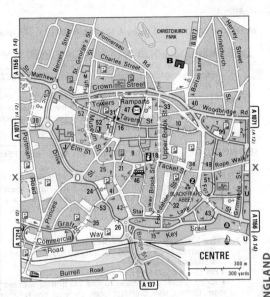

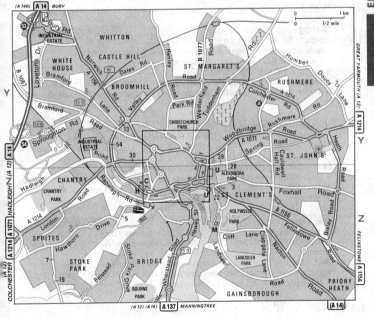

ENGLAND

Look out for red symbols, indicating particularly pleasant establishments.

at **Hintlesham** West : 5 m. by A 1214 on A 1071 - Y - ✉ Ipswich

Hintlesham Hall 🕭 ← 🚗 ▨ ⌇ 🖭 ⅃⌂ ⚒ 🖼 🛈 ⚙ 🅿 VISA ⓜⓞ AE
✉ IP8 3NS – ✆ (01473) 652 334 – www.hintleshamhall.com
– reservations@hintleshamhall.com – Fax (01473) 652 463
31 rm ⌂ – ♦£285 ♦♦£285 – 2 suites
Rest – (closed Saturday lunch) Menu £33 (lunch) – Carte £45/62
♦ Grand and impressive Georgian manor house of 16C origins set in parkland with golf course. Stuart carved oak staircase. Ornate wedding room. Individually decorated rooms. Opulent room for fine dining.

IRONBRIDGE – Telford and Wrekin – **503** M 26 – pop. 1 560   18 **B2**

Great Britain

▶ London 135 mi – Birmingham 36 mi – Shrewsbury 18 mi
🛈 The Wharfage ✆ (01952) 432166, info@ironbridge.org.uk
◉ Ironbridge Gorge Museum★★ **AC** (The Iron Bridge★★, Coalport China Museum★★, Blists Hill Open Air Museum★★, Museum of the Gorge and Visitor Centre★)

The Library House without rest   🚗 ⚒ 🛈 VISA ⓜⓞ
11 Severn Bank ✉ TF8 7AN – ✆ (01952) 432 299 – www.libraryhouse.com
– info@libraryhouse.com
4 rm ⌂ – ♦£65/75 ♦♦£95
♦ Nicely hidden, albeit tricky to find, guesthouse with rear terrace. Homely sitting room. Cottage style breakfast room. Compact, comfy rooms, with a touch of style about them.

Bridge House without rest   🚗 ⚒ 🅿 VISA ⓜⓞ
Buildwas Rd, West : 2 m. on B 4380 ✉ TF8 7BN – ✆ (01952) 432 105
– www.BridgehouseShropshire.co.uk – janet.hedges@btconnect.com
– Fax (01952) 432 105 – March-November
4 rm ⌂ – ♦£50/55 ♦♦£75/80
♦ Characterful 17C cottage with interesting turn of 20C machines in garden. Comfy reception room, fine collection of local objects and photos. Individually decorated rooms.

Restaurant Severn   VISA ⓜⓞ AE
33 High Street – ✆ (01952) 432 233 – www.restaurantseven.co.uk
– ericbruce@talktalk.net – Fax (01952) 510086 – Closed Sunday dinner, Monday and Tuesday
Rest – (booking essential) Menu £25 (midweek)/28
♦ Close to the Severn and world heritage site 'Ironbridge'. Pleasant, light and airy dining room with a real family feel. Experienced owners cook tasty, classically based dishes.

da Vinci   VISA ⓜⓞ
26 High St ✉ TF8 7AD – ✆ (01952) 432 250 – www.davincisironbridge.co.uk
– Davincis1996@aol.com – Closed 2 weeks Christmas and New Year, Sunday and Monday
Rest – Italian – (dinner only) (booking essential) Carte £17/37
♦ Buzzy, personally run town centre restaurant with its rustic interior, painted boards, exposed brickwork and framed Leonardo prints. Tasty, authentic Italian cooking.

ISLE OF MAN – I.O.M. – **502** FG 21 – see Man (Isle of)

Your opinions are important to us:
please write and let us know about your discoveries and experiences – good and bad!

ITTERINGHAM – Norfolk – ✉ Aylsham
15 **C1**

▶ London 126 mi – Cromer 11 mi – Norwich 17 mi

The Walpole Arms
🍴 📶 P VISA ⓪⓪

The Common ✉ *NR11 7AR –* ✆ *(01263) 587258 – www.thewalpolearms.co.uk – goodfood@thewalpolearms.co.uk – Fax (01263) 587074 – Closed 25 December and Sunday dinner*

Rest – Carte £ 20/28

♦ Charming, friendly, part 18C inn. Seasonal British menu draws intelligently on global ideas: dine at linen-clad parlour tables or in inviting, oak-beamed bar. Regional ale.

IVYCHURCH – Kent – 504 W 30 ▌ *Great Britain*
9 **C2**

▶ London 67 mi – Ashford 11 mi – Rye 10 mi

◉ Rye Old Town★★ : Mermaid St★ - St Mary's Church (≤★), SW : 9 m. on A 2070 and A 259

Olde Moat House without rest ≫
📶 📡 P VISA ⓪⓪

Northwest : ¾ m. on B 2070 ✉ *TN29 0AZ –* ✆ *(01797) 344700 – www.oldemoathouse.co.uk – oldemoathouse@hotmail.com*

3 rm ☲ – †£40/60 ††£60/80

♦ Blissfully characterful guesthouse with 15C origins, set in over three acres, encircled by small moat. Beamed sitting room with inglenook. Individual, homely styled rooms.

IWERNE MINSTER – Dorset – see Blandford Forum

IXWORTH – Suffolk – 504 W 27 – see Bury St Edmunds

JERSEY – 503 OP 33 – see Channel Islands

JEVINGTON – E. Sussex – 504 U 31 – see Eastbourne

KEGWORTH – Leicestershire – 502 Q 25 ▌ *Great Britain*
16 **B2**

▶ London 123 mi – Leicester 18 mi – Loughborough 6 mi – Nottingham 13 mi

◉ Calke Abbey★, SW : 7 m. by A 6 (northbound) and A 453 (southbound) – Derby★ - Museum and Art Gallery★, Royal Crown Derby Museum★, NW : 9 m. by A 50 – Nottingham Castle Museum★, N : 11 m. by A 453 and A 52

Kegworth House
📶 📡 P VISA ⓪⓪ AE

42 High St ✉ *DE74 2DA –* ✆ *(01509) 672575 – www.kegworthhouse.co.uk – info@kegworthhouse.co.uk – Fax (01509) 670645 – Closed Christmas-early January*

11 rm ☲ – †£65/100 ††£75/195

Rest – (dinner only) (residents only, communal dining) Menu £ 25

♦ Georgian manor house in village, secluded in walled garden. Fine interior with original decorative features. Individually-decorated bedrooms of charm and character. Home cooking by arrangement.

KELSALE – Suffolk – 504 Y 27 – ✉ Saxmundham
15 **D3**

▶ London 103 mi – Cambridge 68 mi – Ipswich 23 mi – Norwich 37 mi

Mile Hill Barn without rest
📶 📡 P

North Green, North : 1½ m. on (main) A 12 ✉ *IP17 2RG –* ✆ *(01728) 668519 – www.mile-hill-barn.co.uk – mail@mile-hill-barn.co.uk – Closed December*

3 rm ☲ – †£60/80 ††£90/110

♦ Converted 16C barn well placed for glorious Suffolk countryside. Timbered ceiling invokes rustic feel in pleasant lounge. Comfy bedrooms with pine and chintz furnishings.

KENDAL – Cumbria – **502** L 21 – **pop. 28 030** 📖 *Great Britain*   21 **B2**

▶ London 270 mi – Bradford 64 mi – Burnley 63 mi – Carlisle 49 mi
– Lancaster 22 mi – Leeds 72 mi – Middlesbrough 77 mi – Newcastle upon
Tyne 104 mi

🅩 Town Hall, Highgate 𝒞 (01539) 725758, kendaltic@southlakeland.gov.uk

🅩 The Heights, 𝒞 (01539) 723 499

🅖 Levens Hall and Garden★ **AC**, S : 4½ m. by A 591, A 590 and A 6. Lake
Windermere★★, NW : 8 m. by A 5284 and A 591

⌂ **Beech House** without rest   🚗 🕏 📶 **P** **VISA** **⬤** **①**
40 Greenside, by All Hallows Lane ✉ *LA9 4LD* – 𝒞 *(01539) 720 385*
– www.beechhouse-kendal.co.uk – stay@beechhouse-kendal.co.uk – Fax (01539)
724 082 – Closed 1 week Christmas
6 rm ⚌ – ▮£50/75 ▮▮£80/90
♦ Tasteful and stylish semi-detached Georgian villa. Open-plan lounge; communal
breakfasts. Individually decorated rooms are particularly tasteful and comfortable.

✕✕ **Bridge Street Restaurant**   **VISA** **⬤** **①**
1 Bridge St ✉ *LA9 7DD* – 𝒞 *(01539) 738 855 – www.bridgestreetkendal.co.uk*
– Closed 25-26 December, 1 January, Sunday and Monday
Rest – Menu £13/27
♦ Sited within a Georgian building by the River Kent. Modern ground-floor lounge;
dining upstairs in two rooms. Menus boast a distinct local accent.

at Sizergh Southwest : 3 m. by A 591 – ✉ **Kendal**

🍴 **The Strickland Arms**   🚗 🕏 **P** **VISA** **⬤**
✉ *LA8 8DZ* – 𝒞 *(01539) 561 010 – thestricklandarms@yahoo.co.uk*
– Fax (01539) 561 067 – Closed 25 December
Rest – Carte £20/30
♦ Imposing grey pub with a large garden; neighbour to Sizergh Castle. Hearty home-
made dishes arrive in huge portions and there's a good selection of real ales and
wines by the glass.

at Brigsteer Southwest : 3¾ m. by All Hallows Lane – ✉ **Kendal**

🍴 **The Wheatsheaf** with rm   📞 **P** **VISA** **⬤** **AE** **①**
✉ *LA8 8AN* – 𝒞 *(015395) 68 254 – www.brigsteer.gb.com*
– wheatsheaf@brigsteer.gb.com
3 rm – ▮▮£85   **Rest** – (booking essential) Menu £17 – Carte £15/25
♦ Refurbished 18C pub with a light, airy, contemporary feel. The seasonal menu is
proudly Cumbrian with smoked salmon from Cartmel Valley and shrimps from More-
combe Bay. Classically-styled, pine-furnished bedrooms.

at Crosthwaite West : 5¼ m. by All Hallows Lane – ✉ **Kendal**

🍴 **The Punch Bowl Inn** with rm   ≤ 🕏 **P** **VISA** **⬤** **AE**
✉ *LA8 8HR Crosthwaite* – 𝒞 *(01539) 568 237 – www.the-punchbowl.co.uk*
– info@the-punchbowl.co.uk – Fax (01539) 568 875
9 rm ⚌ – ▮£83/109 ▮▮£245/310   **Rest** – Carte £25/35
♦ Our Pub of the Year 2009, with glorious valley views and richly furnished, appealingly informal bar and restaurant. Tasty, classically created dishes make good use of
local, seasonal ingredients. Luxurious bedrooms show great attention to detail.

KENILWORTH – Warwickshire – **503** P 26 – **pop. 22 218** 📖 *Great Britain*   19 **C2**

▶ London 102 mi – Birmingham 19 mi – Coventry 5 mi – Leicester 32 mi
– Warwick 5 mi

🅩 The Library, 11 Smalley Pl 𝒞 (01926) 748900,
kenilworthlibrary@warwickshire.gov.uk

🅖 Castle★ **AC**

Chesford Grange

Chesford Bridge, Southeast : 1¾ m. by A 452 on B 4115 ⊠ *CV8 2LD –* ℰ *(01926) 859331 – www.qhotels.co.uk – chesfordreservations@qhotels.co.uk – Fax (01926) 855272*

209 rm � – †£130/160 ††£140/170

Rest – (carvery lunch) Menu £15/25 – Carte dinner £23/38 **s**

♦ Sizeable hotel in 17 acres of private gardens near Warwick Castle. Characterful foyer and staircase of oak. Extensive meeting facilities and leisure club. Spacious bedrooms. Smart dining room exudes comfy air.

Castle Laurels without rest

22 Castle Rd, North : ½ m. on Stonebridge rd ⊠ *CV8 1NG –* ℰ *(01926) 856179 – www.castlelaurels.co.uk – reception@castlelaurels.co.uk – Fax (01926) 854954*

12 rm ⊂ – †£45/75 ††£75/85

♦ Characterful Victorian house adjacent to Kenilworth Castle. Semi-panelled entrance, stained glass windows, original tiled floor. Homely sitting room and ample sized rooms.

Victoria Lodge without rest

180 Warwick Rd ⊠ *CV8 1HU –* ℰ *(01926) 512020 – www.victorialodgehotel.co.uk – info@victorialodgehotel.co.uk – Fax (01926) 858703 – Closed 2 weeks Christmas to Easter*

10 rm ⊂ – †£49/62 ††£75

♦ Personally run hotel situated close to town centre. Small sitting room with adjacent bar. Simple and homely breakfast room. Immaculately kept, ample sized rooms.

✗✗ Petit Gourmand

101-103 Warwick Rd ⊠ *CV8 1HL –* ℰ *(01926) 864567 – www.petit-gourmand.co.uk – info@petit-gourmand.co.uk – Fax (01926) 864510 – Closed 25-26 and 31 December, last two weeks August, Bank Holidays, Sunday and Monday*

Rest – Menu £18 (lunch) – Carte £25/32

♦ Boasts contemporary feel, typified by striking mirrors and artwork. Good value, hearty, robust classically based dishes supplemented by tried-and-tested daily specials.

✗✗ Bosquet

97a Warwick Rd ⊠ *CV8 1HP –* ℰ *(01926) 852463 – www.restaurantbosquet.co.uk – rest.bosquet@aol.com – Fax (01926) 852463 – Closed 2 weeks August and 1 week Christmas,*

Rest – French – (dinner only) (lunch by arrangement) Menu £32 (midweek) – Carte £34/40

♦ Established restaurant near town centre, with wooden floors, well-spaced tables and stylish leather chairs. Rich, well-informed cooking displays a classical French base.

Red = Pleasant. Look for the red ✗ and 🏠 symbols.

ENGLAND

KENTON – Exeter – **503** J 31 – see Exeter

KERNE BRIDGE – Herefordshire – **503** M 28 – see Ross-on-Wye

---

KESWICK – Cumbria – **502** K 20 – pop. 4 984 ▌ *Great Britain*   21 **A2**

▷ London 294 mi – Carlisle 31 mi – Kendal 30 mi

ℹ Moot Hall, Market Sq. ℰ (017687) 72645, keswicktic@lake-district.gov.uk - at Seatoller, Seatoller Barn, Borrowdale ℰ (017687) 77294, seatolleric@lake-district.gov.uk

🏁 Threlkeld Hall, ℰ (017687) 79324

🟩 Derwentwater★X – Thirlmere (Castlerigg Stone Circle★), E : 1½ m. X **A**

Plan on next page

KESWICK

ENGLAND

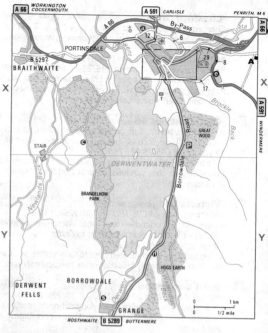

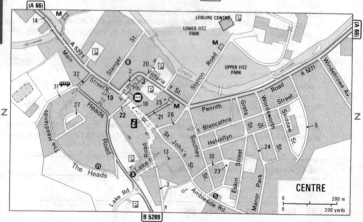

CENTRE

 Underscar Manor ⚿ ← 🚗 🐕 ⌨ 🏔 ⅃⑥ ⚘ 🛜 🅿 *VISA* ⑩⊙ AE
Applethwaite, North : 1 ¾ m. by A 591 on Underscar rd ⊠ *CA12 4PH*
– 🕾 (017687) 75 000 – www.underscarmanor.co.uk
– reception@underscarmanor.co.uk – Fax (017687) 74 904 – Closed 5-7 January
11 rm ⚍ – †£ 125 ††£ 250/325
Rest *The Restaurant* – see restaurant listing
◆ Blissfully located Victorian Italianate manor with commanding views of Derwent
Water and Fells. Two comfortable sitting rooms. Modern leisure centre. Large, well
kept rooms.

346

Dale Head Hall Lakeside ⌖   ⬅ 🚗 🏊 🐾 🖐 **P** *VISA* **⑩** **AE**
Thirlmere, Southeast : 5 ¾ m. on A 591 ⌧ *CA12 4TN* – ℰ *(017687) 72 478*
– www.daleheadhall.co.uk – onthelakeside@daleheadhall.co.uk
– Closed January
12 rm (dinner included) ⌕ – ♦£130/145 ♦♦£280/300
Rest – (booking essential for non-residents) Menu £20/45 **s**
♦ Wonderfully set 18C house on Lake Thirlmere. The family run friendliness lends a rich country house ambience. Log fired lounges, smart rooms. Daily changing dinner menu shows a careful touch; choose lake views or a rustic 16C dining room.

Highfield ⬅ 🚗 **K** rest, 🏊 🐾 **P** *VISA* **⑩** **AE**
The Heads ⌧ *CA12 5ER* – ℰ *(017687) 72 508 – www.highfieldkeswick.co.uk*
– info@highfieldkeswick.co.uk – Fax (017687) 80 234 – Closed Christmas
and January - mid February   **Z n**
18 rm ⌕ – ♦£80/110 ♦♦£180   **Rest** – (dinner only) Menu £40
♦ Substantial, keenly run 19C house with fine views across Derwent Water to Borrowdale Valley. Most bedrooms offer the vista; all are spacious and individually decorated. Traditional restaurant has big windows and imaginatively created dishes.

Lairbeck ⌖ 🚗 🏊 🖐 **P** *VISA* **⑩**
Vicarage Hill ⌧ *CA12 5QB* – ℰ *(017687) 73 373*
– www.lairbeckhotel-keswick.co.uk – info@lairbeckhotel-keswick.co.uk
– Fax (017687) 73 144   **X a**
14 rm ⌕ – ♦£46/80 ♦♦£120/130
Rest – (dinner only) (residents only) Menu £25
♦ Victorian house tucked away on north side of town, traditional in style, with immaculately-kept bedrooms. Room 4 is largest; four poster in room 7. Warm ambience in bar. Honest country cooking served in richly coloured dining room.

Abacourt House without rest   🏊 **P**
26 Stanger St ⌧ *CA12 5JU* – ℰ *(017687) 72 967 – www.abacourt.co.uk*
– abacourt@btinternet.com – Closed 20-27 December   **Z e**
5 rm ⌕ – ♦£60 ♦♦£60
♦ Converted Victorian town house close to town centre. Boasts original features such as pitch pine doors and staircase. Simple, cosy breakfast room. Immaculately kept bedrooms.

Claremont House without rest   ⬅ 🚗 🏊 **P**
Chestnut Hill ⌧ *CA12 4LT* – ℰ *(017687) 72 089*
– www.claremonthousekeswick.co.uk – claremonthouse@btinternet.com
– Closed 24-26 December   **X e**
6 rm ⌕ – ♦£45/70 ♦♦£60/75
♦ Built 150 years ago, this former lodge house has good views over Keswick. Lounge filled with lovely prints and lithographs. Extensive breakfast menu. Spotless, homely rooms.

Acorn House without rest   🏊 **P** *VISA* **⑩**
Ambleside Rd ⌧ *CA12 4DL* – ℰ *(017687) 72 553 – www.acornhousehotel.co.uk*
– info@acornhousehotel.co.uk – Closed first 3 weeks December   **Z s**
9 rm ⌕ – ♦£50/65 ♦♦£84
♦ Characterful Georgian house in residential part of town. Well cared for gardens are a step away from elegant, comfortable lounge. Very bright, traditional, spacious bedrooms.

XXX   **The Restaurant** – at Underscar Manor Hotel   ⬅ 🚗 🍴 **P** *VISA* **⑩** **AE**
Applethwaite, North : 1 ¾ m. by A 591 on Underscar rd ⌧ *CA12 4PH*
– ℰ (017687) 75 000 – www.keswickrestaurant.co.uk
– reception@underscarmanor.co.uk – Fax (017687) 74 904 – Closed 5-7 January
Rest – Menu £28/38 – Carte £40/49
♦ Conservatory dining room of impressive height. Formal ambience with lace clothed tables and elegant glassware. Traditional menus: à la carte with classic base.

ENGLAND

✗✗ Morrel's

34 Lake Rd ⊠ CA12 5AQ – ℰ (017687) 72 666 – www.morrels.co.uk
– info@morrels.co.uk
– Closed 24-26 December, 1 week January and Monday

Rest – (dinner only) Carte £ 20/32

Zx

♦ Pleasingly refurbished and personally run. Etched glass and vivid artwork dominate interior. Menus designed to appeal to all: an agreeable blend of traditional and modern.

at Threlkeld East : 4 m. by A 66 – X – ⊠ Keswick

⌂ Scales Farm without rest

Northeast : 1½ m. off A 66 on Scales rd ⊠ CA12 4SY – ℰ (017687) 79 660
– www.scalesfarm.com – scales@scalesfarm.com – Fax (017687) 79 510
– April-October

6 rm ⊇ – ♦£72 ♦♦£72

♦ Converted 17C farmhouse with much rustic charm. It boasts open stove, exposed beams and solid interior walls. Comfortable, homely sitting room. Spacious cottage style rooms.

at Borrowdale South : on B 5289 – ⊠ Keswick

🏨 The Lodore Falls

⊠ CA12 5UX – ℰ (017687) 77 285
– www.lakedistricthotels.net – lodorefalls@lakedistricthotels.net
– Fax (017687) 77 343

Yn

64 rm ⊇ – ♦£83/113 ♦♦£176 – 5 suites   **Rest** – Menu £ 17/34

♦ Swiss-styled exterior, in wonderfully commanding position overlooking Derwent Water; Lodore waterfalls in grounds. Leisure oriented. Choose west facing rooms overlooking lake. Linen-clad dining room with classic Lakeland views.

at Rosthwaite South : 6 m. on B 5289 - Y – ⊠ Keswick

🏨 Hazel Bank Country House

⊠ CA12 5XB – ℰ (017687) 77 248 – www.hazelbankhotel.co.uk
– enquiries@hazelbankhotel.co.uk – Fax (017687) 77 373 – Closed Christmas and restricted opening in winter

8 rm – ♦£65/95 ♦♦£130/190

Rest – (dinner only) (booking essential for non-residents) (set menu only) Menu £ 33

♦ Panoramic fell views accentuate the isolated appeal of this very personally run 19C country house. Original fittings; stained glass windows. Rooms have stamp of individuality. Accomplished cuisine with daily changing set menus.

at Portinscale West : 1½ m. by A 66 – ⊠ Keswick

🏨 Swinside Lodge

Newlands, South : 1½ m. on Grange Rd ⊠ CA12 5UE – ℰ (017687) 72 948
– www.swinsidelodge-hotel.co.uk – info@swinsidelodge-hotel.co.uk
– Fax (017687) 73 312 – Closed 24-26 December

Xc

7 rm ⊇ – ♦£128 ♦♦£236

Rest – (dinner only) (booking essential for non-residents) (set menu only) Menu £ 40 s

♦ Personally run 19C country house in beguilingly tranquil position close to extensive walks with mountain views. Two comfortable lounges; well furnished, traditional rooms. Intimate Victorian style dining room with large antique dresser.

at Braithwaite West : 2 m. by A 66 – X – on B 5292 – ⊠ Keswick

🏨 Cottage in the Wood

Whinlatter Forest, Northwest : 1¾ m. on B 5292 ⊠ CA12 5TW – ℰ (017687) 78 409 – www.thecottageinthewood.co.uk – relax@thecottageinthewood.co.uk
– Fax (017687) 78 064 – Closed 2 January-1 February

9 rm ⊇ – ♦£70 ♦♦£75/120

Rest – (Closed Sunday and Monday) (dinner only) Carte £ 25/29

♦ Dramatically set 17C former coaching inn high up in large pine forest. Comfy, beamed lounge with fire. Smart, updated bedrooms look out over Skiddaw or the forest. Proudly local ingredients sourced for modern British cooking; mountain views.

ENGLAND

KETTERING – Northamptonshire – **504** R 26 – **pop. 51 063** 17 **C3**

❱ London 88 mi – Birmingham 54 mi – Leicester 16 mi – Northampton 24 mi
❚ The Coach House, Sheep St ✆ (01536) 410266, tic@kettering.gov.uk

at Rushton Northwest : 3½ m. by A 14 and Rushton Rd – ✉ Kettering

fiiii Rushton Hall ⚓ 🖙 🕪 🗞 🏊 🅿 🕭 🏊 🎾 🏐 ⚓ 🛎 🥂 🅿 VISA ⓞⓞ ᴀᴇ
✉ NN14 1RR – ✆ (01536) 713001 – www.rushtonhall.com
– enquiries@rushtonhall.com – Fax (01536) 713010
41 rm ⬚ – **♗**£170 **♗♗**£170/350 – 3 suites
Rest – Menu £25 (lunch) **s** – Carte dinner £36/53 **s**
♦ Hugely imposing 15C house in quadrangle boasting delightful grounds, baronial style sitting room of incredible proportions and immaculate bedrooms appointed most luxuriously. Spacious, formal dining room serving classical, wide-ranging menus.

KETTLESING – N. Yorks. – **502** P 21 – **see Harrogate**

KETTLEWELL – North Yorkshire – **502** N 21 22 **A2**

❱ London 246 mi – Darlington 42 mi – Harrogate 30 mi – Lancaster 42 mi

⌂ Littlebeck without rest 🎾 🅿 VISA ⓞⓞ
The Green, take turning at the Old Smithy shop by the bridge ✉ BD23 5RD
– ✆ (01756) 760378 – www.little-beck.co.uk – stay@little-beck.co.uk – Closed
25-26 December, restricted opening in winter
3 rm ⬚ – **♗**£45/50 **♗♗**£68/75
♦ Characterful stone house from 13C with Georgian façade overlooking village may-pole. Cosy lounge; extensive dales breakfast served. Attractively decorated bedrooms.

KEYSTON – Cambridgeshire – **504** S 26 – ✉ Huntingdon 14 **A2**

❱ London 75 mi – Cambridge 29 mi – Northampton 24 mi

⌱ The Pheasant 🏠 🅿 VISA ⓞⓞ ᴀᴇ
Village Loop Road ✉ PE28 0RE – ✆ (01832) 710241
– www.thepheasant-keyston.co.uk – info@thepheasant-keyston.co.uk
Rest – (booking essential) Menu £18 – Carte £24/42⟐
♦ Charming thatched inn with a delightful garden, hidden in a sleepy hamlet. Daily changing menu provides a good choice of dishes made from local, seasonal ingredients.

KIBWORTH BEAUCHAMP – Leicestershire – **504** QR 26 – **pop. 3 550** 16 **B2**
– ✉ Leicester

❱ London 85 mi – Birmingham 49 mi – Leicester 6 mi – Northampton 17 mi

XX Firenze VISA ⓞⓞ
9 Station St ✉ LE8 0LN – ✆ (0116) 2796260 – www.firenze.co.uk
– info@firenze.co.uk – Fax (0116) 2793646 – Closed 1 week Christmas-New Year, Sunday and Bank Holidays
Rest – Italian – (booking essential) Menu £27 (dinner midweek)
– Carte £30/45
♦ Modern Italian restaurant in village centre. Beamed interior; contemporary décor. Highback wood-framed chairs. Expect king prawns with pancetta or quail with sage and garlic.

KIBWORTH HARCOURT Leics. – **504** R 26 16 **B2**

❱ London 101 mi – Leicester 9 mi – Coventry 36 mi – Nottingham 41 mi

X Boboli 🏠 ᴀᴄ 🅿 VISA ⓞⓞ
88 Main St ✉ LE8 0NQ – ✆ (0116) 2793303 – www.bobolirestaurant.co.uk
– info@firenze.co.uk – Fax (0116) 2793646 – Closed 25-26 December, 1 week January, Monday and Bank Holidays
Rest – Italian – Carte £17/30
♦ Stylish Italian restaurant named after gardens in Florence. Fresh, simple and seasonally-changing cooking with bold flavours. Affordable wines and cheery, prompt service.

ENGLAND

KIDDERMINSTER – Worcestershire – **503** N 26 – **pop. 55 348**   18 **B2**
▶ London 139 mi – Birmingham 17 mi – Shrewsbury 34 mi – Worcester 15 mi

at Chaddesley Corbett Southeast : 4½ m. by A 448 – ⊠ **Kidderminster**

🏠🏠   **Brockencote Hall** 🌳   ⟨ 🌿 💧 🍴 ⚘ 👌 ⚘ ⚘ 🚗 **P** **VISA** **CO** **AE** **①**
on A 448 ⊠ DY10 4PY – 🕿 (01562) 777876 – www.brockencotehall.com
– info@brockencotehall.com – Fax (01562) 777872
17 rm � – ♦£96/120 ♦♦£150/190
Rest *The Restaurant* – see restaurant listing
♦ Reminiscent of a French château, a 19C mansion in extensive parkland. Pine and maple library, boldy decorated conservatory. Good-sized rooms, all unique in style and décor.

XXX   **The Restaurant** – at Brockencote Hall Hotel   🚗 **P** **VISA** **CO** **AE** **①**
on A 448 ⊠ DY10 4PY – 🕿 (01562) 777876 – www.brockencotehall.com
– info@brockencotehall.com – Fax (01562) 777872
Rest – French – Menu £21/38 **s** – Carte £34/54 **s**
♦ Two adjacent dining rooms: impressive high ceilings, fine oak panelled walls, a formal but discreet and relaxed atmosphere and fine modern dishes from local produce.

KIDMORE END – Oxon. – **see Reading**

KIMMERIDGE – Dorset – **503** N32 – **see Wareham**

KINGHAM – Oxfordshire – **503** P 28   10 **A1**
▶ London 81 mi – Gloucester 32 mi – Oxford 25 mi

🏠   **Mill House** 🌳   🚗 🌿 👌 **P** **VISA** **CO** **AE** **①**
⊠ OX7 6UH – 🕿 (01608) 658188 – www.millhousehotel.co.uk
– stay@millhousehotel.co.uk – Fax (01608) 658492
23 rm ⊟ – ♦£95 ♦♦£140   **Rest** – Menu £15/32 – Carte £24/32
♦ Privately run house in 10 acres of lawned gardens with brook flowing through grounds. Spacious lounge with comfortable armchairs and books. Country house style bedrooms. Modern décor suffuses restaurant.

🍴   **The Kingham Plough** with rm   🚗 🏡 **P**
The Green ⊠ OX7 6YD – 🕿 (01608) 658327 – www.thekinghamplough.co.uk
– book@thekinghamplough.co.uk – Fax (01608) 658327 – Closed 25 December
7 rm ⊟ – ♦£70/80 ♦♦£85/110   **Rest** – Carte £20/35
♦ Quintessentially British pub overlooking the village green and serving carefully-prepared, gutsy pub food firmly rooted in the region. Stylish bedrooms boast pocket sprung beds and crisp Egyptian linen.

🍴   **The Tollgate Inn** with rm   🏡 🕿 **P** **VISA** **CO** **AE**
Church St ⊠ OX7 6YA – 🕿 (01608) 658389 – www.thetollgate.com
– info@thetollgate.com – Closed first week January, Sunday dinner and Monday
9 rm ⊟ – ♦£60 ♦♦£100
Rest – Menu £16 – Carte £20/30
♦ Grade II listed Georgian farmhouse, sympathetically refurbished to combine old and new. Traditional snacks and blackboard specials lie alongside a more ambitious à la carte. Bedrooms are simple, light and airy.

KINGSBRIDGE – Devon – **503** I 33 – **pop. 5 521**   2 **C3**
▶ London 236 mi – Exeter 36 mi – Plymouth 24 mi – Torquay 21 mi
🛈 The Quay 🕿 (01548) 853195, advice@kingsbridgeinfo.co.uk
🏌 Thurlestone, 🕿 (01548) 560405
◎ Town★ – Boat Trip to Salcombe★★ **AC**
◎ Prawle Point (⟨★★★) SE : 10 m. around coast by A 379

at Goveton Northeast : 2 ½ m. by A 381 – ⊠ **Kingsbridge**

Buckland-Tout-Saints ⟨icons⟩
Goveton, Northeast : 2 ½ m. by A 381 ⊠ TQ7 2DS – ℰ *(01548) 853 055*
– www.tout-saints.co.uk – buckland@tout-saints.co.uk – Fax (01548) 856 261
14 rm ⊡ – ❚£ 90/105 ❚❚£ 120/140 – 2 suites
Rest – Menu £ 20/37 – Carte £ 23/35
♦ Immaculate, impressive Queen Anne mansion with neat lawned gardens in rural location. Wood panelled lounge; all other areas full of antiques. Well-furnished bedrooms. Accomplished cooking in beautiful wood-panelled country house restaurant.

KINGSKERSWELL – Devon – **503** J 32 – ⊠ **Torquay**   2 **C2**
▷ London 199 mi – Exeter 18 mi – Torquay 4 mi

Bickley Mill with rm
Stoneycombe, West : 2 m. ⊠ TQ12 5LN – ℰ *(01803) 873 201*
– www.bickleymill.co.uk – info@bickleymill.co.uk – Fax (01803) 875 129 – Closed 27-28 December and 1 January
9 rm ⊡ – ❚£ 55 ❚❚£ 70   **Rest** – Carte £ 24/35
♦ Converted flour mill dating back to 13C boasts pleasant garden and decked terrace. Modernised interior retains rustic stone walls and exposed beams. Modern British cooking. Contemporary bedrooms.

KING'S LYNN – Norfolk – **502** V 25 – pop. 40 921 ▮ *Great Britain*   14 **B1**
▷ London 103 mi – Cambridge 45 mi – Leicester 75 mi – Norwich 44 mi
🄸 The Custom House, Purfleet Quay ℰ (01553) 763044, kings-lynn.tic@west-norfolk.gov.uk
🄶 Eagles Tilney All Saints School Rd, ℰ (01553) 827 147
🄶 Houghton Hall★★ **AC**, NE : 14 ½ m. by A 148 – Four Fenland Churches★ (Terrington St Clement, Walpole St Peter, West Walton, Walsoken) SW : by A 47

at Grimston East : 6 ¼ m. by A 148 – ⊠ **King's Lynn**

Congham Hall ⟨icons⟩
Lynn Rd ⊠ PE32 1AH – ℰ *(01485) 600 250 – www.conghamhallhotel.co.uk*
– info@conghamhallhotel.co.uk – Fax (01485) 601 191
12 rm ⊡ – ❚£ 100/179 ❚❚£ 195/245 – 2 suites
Rest *Orangery* – Menu £ 21/49
♦ Immaculately peaceful cream-washed part Georgian house with formal flower garden. Classic country house style lounges with many antiques. Elegant bedrooms of varying sizes. Pleasant, classic restaurant using herb garden produce.

KINGS MILLS – see Channel Islands (Guernsey)

KINGSTON BAGPUIZE – Oxon. – **503** P 28 – see Oxford

KINGSTON BLOUNT – Oxon. – see Chinnor

KINGSTON-UPON-HULL – City of Kingston upon Hull – **502** S 22   23 **D2**
– pop. 301 416 ▮ *Great Britain*
▷ London 183 mi – Leeds 61 mi – Nottingham 94 mi – Sheffield 68 mi
Access Humber Bridge (toll)
🄰 Humberside Airport : ℰ (01652) 688456, S : 19 m. by A 63
🄴 to The Netherlands (Rotterdam) (P & O North Sea Ferries) daily (11 h) – to Belgium (Zeebrugge) (P & O North Sea Ferries) 3-4 weekly (13 h 45 mn)
🄸 1 Paragon St ℰ (01482) 223559, tourist.information@hullcc.gov.uk
🄶 Springhead Park Willerby Rd, ℰ (01482) 656 309
🄶 Sutton Park Salthouse Rd, ℰ (01482) 374 242
🄶 Burton Constable★ **AC**, NE : 9 m. by A 165 and B 1238 Z

KINGSTON-UPON-HULL

ENGLAND

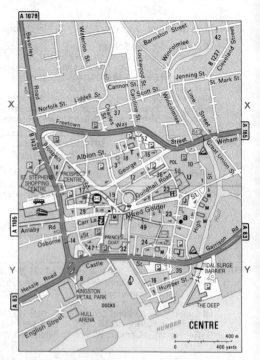

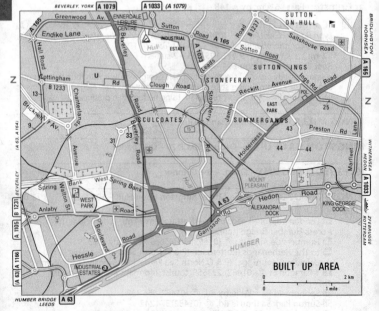

352

ᵭ**Village**   🔲 ☺ 🏠 Ⅰ🛣 ⅰ 🅰🆆 rest, 🍴 ⅕ **P** 🆅🆂🅰 🆖 🅰🅴 🆔

Henry Boot Way, Priory Park East, Southwest : 2 m. by A 63 ⊠ *HU4 7DY*
– 𝒞 (0844) 847 29 75 – village.hull@village-hotels.com
– Fax (0870) 421 57 43   Z**a**
116 rm ☲ – **†**£ 149 **††**£ 149
Rest *Verve* – (Bar lunch Monday-Saturday) Carte £ 18/30 **s**
♦ Five minutes' drive from the Humber Bridge. Spacious, modern interior. Sports themed pub for snacks. Impressive state-of-the-art gym and pool area. Airy, functional rooms. Traditional British cooking in boothed restaurant.

⊠ **Boars Nest**   🆅🆂🅰 🆖 🅰🅴

22-24 Princes Ave, Northwest : 1 m. by Ferensway off West Spring Bank Rd
⊠ *HU5 3QA – 𝒞 (01482) 445 577 – www.theboarsnesthull.com*
– boarsnest@boarsnest.co.uk – Fax (01482) 445 577 – Closed 1 January
Rest – Menu £ 10/20 – Carte dinner £ 23/38
♦ Early 20C butchers, with original tiles and carcass rails in situ. Comfy, cluttered first-floor lounge. Eat hearty English dishes downstairs at mismatched tables and chairs.

at Hessle Southwest : 2 m. by A 63 – ⊠ Kingston-upon-Hull

⊠⊠ **Artisan**   🆅🆂🅰 🆖 🅰🅴 🆔

22 The Weir ⊠ *HU13 0RU – 𝒞 (01482) 644 906 – www.artisanrestaurant.com*
– eat@artisanrestaurant.com – Closed 10 days Christmas, 1 week summer
Rest – (dinner only) (booking essential) Menu £ 35
♦ Homely, neighbourhood restaurant with vivid artwork on the walls. Formal tableware offset by cheerful, enthusiastic owner. Classical cooking utilising regional ingredients.

KINGSWEAR – Devon – **503** J 32 – see Dartmouth

KINGTON – County of Herefordshire – **503** K 27 – pop. 2 597   18 **A3**
🄳 London 152 mi – Birmingham 61 mi – Hereford 19 mi – Shrewsbury 54 mi

at Titley Northeast : 3 ½ m. on B 4355 – ⊠ Kington

🄳 **The Stagg Inn** (Steve Reynolds) with rm   🚃 🏠 **P** 🆅🆂🅰 🆖
☸ ⊠ *HR5 3RL – 𝒞 (01544) 230 221 – www.thestagg.co.uk*
– reservations@thestagg.co.uk
6 rm ☲ – **†**£ 70/90 **††**£ 85/120
Rest – (Closed Sunday dinner and Monday) (booking essential) Carte £ 21/29
Spec. Scallops on parsnip purée with black pepper oil. Fillet of beef with set wild mushroom cream and dauphinoise potato. Trio of crème brûlée.
♦ Rustic dining pub offers seasonally-changing menu featuring quality local produce, including the inn's own pigs and vegetables from the garden. Comfy rooms split between the pub and the old vicarage, two minutes walk down the road.

KINTBURY – Newbury – **503** P 29 – see Hungerford

KIRKBY LONSDALE – Cumbria – **502** M 21 – pop. 2 076   21 **B3**
– ⊠ Carnforth (Lancs.)
🄳 London 259 mi – Carlisle 62 mi – Kendal 13 mi – Lancaster 17 mi – Leeds 58 mi
🄸 24 Main St 𝒞 (015242) 71437, kltic@southlakeland.gov.uk
🄸🄱 Scaleber Lane Barbon, 𝒞 (015242) 76 365
🄶 Casterton Sedbergh Rd, 𝒞 (015242) 71 592

at Cowan Bridge Southeast : 2 m. on A 65 – ⊠ Carnforth (Lancs.)

⊠⊠ **Hipping Hall** with rm   🚃 ⅖ rm, **P** 🆅🆂🅰 🆖 🅰🅴 🆔
Southeast : ½ m. on A 65 ⊠ *LA6 2JJ – 𝒞 (015242) 71 187 – www.hippinghall.com*
– info@hippinghall.com – Fax (015242) 72 452 – Closed 3 weeks January
9 rm (dinner included) ☲ – **†**£ 175 **††**£ 250
Rest – (dinner only and Saturday lunch) Menu £ 30/50
♦ Charming part 15/16C house in mature grounds with stream and flagged terrace. Modern, inventive cooking does justice to characterful hall dining room. Distinctly modish rooms.

ENGLAND

at Nether Burrow South : 2 m. by A 65 and on a 683 – ⊠ Kirkby Lonsdale

The Highwayman   🛜 **P** VISA ⓪⓪ AE
⊠ LA6 2RJ – ℰ (01524) 826 888 – www.highwaymaninn.co.uk
– enquiries@highwaymaninn.co.uk – Closed 25 December
Rest – Carte £ 17/28
♦ Spacious, refurbished inn with open fires, friendly service and stone terrace. Owners passionate about local, traceable produce, serving hearty, wholesome fayre.

at Tunstall South : 3 ½ m. by A 65 on A 683 – ⊠ Kirkby Lonsdale

The Lunesdale Arms   🛜 **P** VISA ⓪⓪
⊠ LA6 2QN – ℰ (01524) 274 203 – www.thelunesdale.co.uk
– info@thelunesdale.co.uk – Fax (01524) 274 229
– Closed 25-26 December, 1 January
Rest – (Closed Monday except Bank Holidays) Carte £ 20/25
♦ Relaxed atmosphere and enthusiastic, friendly staff. Blackboard menu of tasty, honest cooking, with staples like pies, steak and sausages, as well as delicious home-made puds

---

KIRKBYMOORSIDE – North Yorkshire – 502 R 21 – pop. 2 595   23 C1
🖪 London 244 mi – Leeds 61 mi – Scarborough 26 mi – York 33 mi
🛏 Manor Vale, ℰ (01751) 431 525

Brickfields Farm without rest ⌂   🖼 🦅 **P** VISA ⓪⓪
Kirby Mills, East : ¾ m. by A 170 on Kirby Mills Industrial Estate rd ⊠ YO62 6NS
– ℰ (01751) 433 074 – www.brickfieldsfarm.co.uk – janet@brickfieldsfarm.co.uk
6 rm ⊡ – †£ 50/100 ††£ 80/120
♦ Personally run 1850s red-brick former farmhouse set down private driveway. Rooms are very comfortably appointed in rustic style with thoughtful extra touches.

The Cornmill   🖼 ⑂ ⅙ rm, 🦅 **P** VISA ⓪⓪
Kirby Mills, East : ½ m. by A 170 ⊠ YO62 6NP – ℰ (01751) 432 000
– www.kirbymills.demon.co.uk – cornmill@kirbymills.demon.co.uk – Fax (01751) 432 300
5 rm ⊡ – †£ 65/68 ††£ 99/105   **Rest** – (by arrangement) Menu £ 28
♦ Converted 18C cornmill, its millrace still visible through the glass floor of a beamed and flagged dining room. Individually decorated bedrooms in the Victorian farm-house.

at Fadmoor Northwest : 2 ¼ m. – ⊠ Kirkbymoorside

The Plough Inn   🖼 🛜 ⅙ **P** VISA ⓪⓪
Main Street ⊠ YO62 7HY – ℰ (01751) 431 515
– enquiries@theploughfadmoor.co.uk – Fax (01751) 432 492
– Closed 25-26 December and 1 January
Rest – Menu £ 13 – Carte £ 18/31
♦ Pleasant rural pub with original tiled floor, rustic walls, scrubbed tables and real ales. Blackboard menu changes daily: traditional cooking with a modern twist.

KIRKBY STEPHEN – Cumbria – 502 M 20 – pop. 1 832   21 B2
🖪 London 296 mi – Carlisle 46 mi – Darlington 37 mi – Kendal 28 mi

Augill Castle ⌂   ⩽ 🖼 🕙 ⅙ ⅙ **P** VISA ⓪⓪
Northeast : 4 ½ m. by A 685 ⊠ CA17 4DE – ℰ (01768) 341 937
– www.stayinacastle.com – enquiries@augillcastle.co.uk – Fax (01768) 342 287
– Closed Christmas
12 rm ⊡ – †£ 80 ††£ 160
Rest – (Closed Sunday and Tuesday) (dinner only) (residents only, communal dining, set menu only) Menu £ 35 **s**
♦ Carefully restored Victorian folly in neo-Gothic style with extensive gardens; fine antiques and curios abound. Comfy music room and library. Individually decorated rooms. Expansive dining room with ornate ceiling and Spode tableware.

KIRKWHELPINGTON – Northumberland – **501** N/O 18 – ⊠ Morpeth   24 **A2**

🔲 *Great Britain*

> ▶ London 305 mi – Carlisle 46 mi – Newcastle upon Tyne 20 mi
> ◨ Wallington House ★ **AC**, E : 3 ½ m. by A 696 and B 6342

⛰ **Shieldhall** ⍋   🚗 🐾 **P** *VISA* ⦿⦿
Wallington, Southeast : 2 ½ m. by A 696 on B 6342 ⊠ NE61 4AQ – ℰ (01830)
540 387 – www.shieldhallguesthouse.co.uk – stay@shieldhallguesthouse.co.uk
– Fax (01830) 540490 – Closed December and January
4 rm � – †£50/60 ††£80   **Rest** – (by arrangement) Menu £ 25
♦ Converted 18C farm buildings with gardens. Well-furnished lounge/library. Spotless rooms in former stable block: furniture constructed by cabinet-making owner!

KIRTLINGTON – Oxfordshire – **503** Q 28   10 **B2**

> ▶ London 70 mi – Bicester 11 mi – Oxford 16 mi

🏠 **The Dashwood**   🚗 🐾 ఈ rm, 🕉 ⍟ **P** *VISA* ⦿⦿ **AE**
South Green, Heyford Rd ⊠ OX5 3HJ – ℰ (01869) 352 707
– www.thedashwood.co.uk – reservations@thedashwood.co.uk – Fax (01869)
351432 – Closed last week December and first week January
12 rm ⍁ – †£85 ††£110/150
Rest – (closed Sunday dinner to non-residents) Menu £ 15 (lunch)
– Carte dinner £ 22/36
♦ Grade II listed 16C building in local soft stone. Lounge with comfy leather armchairs. Bedrooms, boasting super contemporary décor, divided between main building and barn. Exposed stone dining room: impressive menus with modern European slant.

KNARESBOROUGH – North Yorkshire – **502** P 21 – pop. 13 380   22 **B2**

> ▶ London 217 mi – Bradford 21 mi – Harrogate 3 mi – Leeds 18 mi
> – York 18 mi
> 🄸 9 Castle Courtyard, Market Pl ℰ (01423) 866886 (summer only),
> kntic@harrogate.gov.uk
> ◨ Boroughbridge Rd, ℰ (01423) 862 690

🏨 **Dower House**   🚗 🖥 🕉 ఓ6 ఈ rm, 🍴 ⍟ **P** *VISA* ⦿⦿ **AE**
Bond End ⊠ HG5 9AL – ℰ (01423) 863 302 – www.dowerhouse-hotel.co.uk
– enquiries@dowerhouse-hotel.co.uk – Fax (01423) 867 665
31 rm ⍁ – †£70/85 ††£110/124
Rest – Menu £ 17/26 **s** – Carte dinner £ 23/36 **s**
♦ Part 15C, ivy clad, red brick house near town centre. Stone-floored reception and cosy bar. Small, well-equipped leisure centre. Good-sized, traditional bedrooms. Warmly toned restaurant overlooks the garden.

🏠 **Newton House** without rest   ⍟ **P** *VISA* ⦿⦿ **AE**
5-7 York Place – ℰ (01423) 863 539 – www.newtonhouseyorkshire.com
– newtonhouse@btinternet.com – Closed 1 week at Christmas
11 rm – †£50/85 ††£100
♦ Extended mid-18C house boasts homely lounge with soft suites and smart, comfortable, individually decorated bedrooms; those on the first floor and in the annexe are larger.

at Ferrensby Northeast : 3 m. on A 6055

🍴 **The General Tarleton Inn** with rm   ⍟ ⍟ **P** *VISA* ⦿⦿ **AE**
Boroughbridge Rd ⊠ HG5 0PZ – ℰ (01423) 340 284
– www.generaltarleton.co.uk – gti@generaltarleton.co.uk – Fax (01423) 340 288
14 rm ⍁ – †£ 108 ††£120
Rest – Menu £ 33 – Carte £ 22/33
♦ 18C coaching inn with several dining areas inside and out. Menu has a strong seasonal Yorkshire base, featuring tasty, warming dishes and classics aplenty. Bedrooms are comfortable and luxurious.

ENGLAND

at Coneythorpe Northeast : 4 ¾ m. by A 59

🛏 **The Tiger Inn**   �"🖳 **P** VISA ⲙⲟ AE
✉ HG5 0RY – ℰ (01423) 330 439 – www.tiger-inn.co.uk – ifgill@btinternet.com
– Fax (01423) 331 095 – Closed 25 December
Rest – (Closed Sunday dinner, Monday) Menu £ 15 – Carte £ 20/25
♦ Traditional red brick pub overlooking the green with formal rear dining room.
Hearty, robust menu offers a modern take on classic British favourites; blackboard of
mainly fish specials.

KNIPTON – Leicestershire   17 **C2**
🔼 London 125 mi – Leicester 28 mi – Melton Mowbray 10 mi

🏨 **Manners Arms**   🚗 🖳 **P** VISA ⲙⲟ AE
Croxton Rd ✉ NG32 1RH – ℰ (01476) 879 222 – www.mannersarms.com
– info@mannersarms.com – Fax (01476) 879 228
– Accommodation closed 24-26 December and 1 January
10 rm ☞ – ♦£ 65/80 ♦♦£ 120   **Rest** – Menu £ 18/25 – Carte £ 21/34
♦ Refurbished former hunting lodge originally built for sixth Duke of Rutland; a
relaxing feel pervades. Locals gather round bar's roaring fire. Individually styled bedrooms. Spacious dining room offers hearty rustic cooking.

ENGLAND

Look out for red symbols, indicating particularly pleasant establishments.

KNOWLE GREEN – Lancs. – see Longridge

KNOWSTONE – Devon – see South Molton

KNUTSFORD – Cheshire – **502** M 24 – pop. 12 656   20 **B3**
🔼 London 187 mi – Chester 25 mi – Liverpool 33 mi – Manchester 18 mi
– Stoke-on-Trent 30 mi
🛈 Council Offices, Toft Rd ℰ (01565) 632611

🏠 **Longview**   &.rm, ⁽ⁱ⁾ **P** VISA ⲙⲟ AE
55 Manchester Rd, on A 50 ✉ WA16 0LX – ℰ (01565) 632 119
– www.longviewhotel.com – enquiries@longviewhotel.com – Fax (01565) 652 402
– Closed Christmas and New Year
29 rm ☞ – ♦£ 89/99 ♦♦£ 122 – 3 suites
Rest – (closed Sunday) (dinner only) Carte £ 21/29 **s**
♦ Bay-windowed Victorian house, family run. Open log fire in reception. At foot of
stone staircase lies cellar bar with soft lighting and low ceiling. Pleasant, comfy
bedrooms. Mahogany furniture and chandeliers make for relaxed dining.

🍴🍴 **Belle Epoque Brasserie** with rm   🚗 ⁓ ⁽ⁱ⁾ VISA ⲙⲟ AE ①
60 King St ✉ WA16 6DT – ℰ (01565) 633 060 – www.thebelleepoque.com
– info@thebelleepoque.com – Fax (01565) 634 150 – Closed 25-26 December
6 rm – ♦£ 95 ♦♦£ 115, ☞ £ 9.95   **Rest** – (closed Sunday dinner) Carte £ 25/34
♦ Bustling brasserie with Art Nouveau décor. Traditional and modern dishes with
international touches using local produce. Contemporary style bedrooms with modern facilities.

---

at Mobberley Northeast : 2 ½ m. by A 537 on B 5085 – ✉ Knutsford

🏠 **Hinton**   🚗 ⁓ ⁽ⁱ⁾ **P** VISA ⲙⲟ AE ①
Town Lane, on B 5085 ✉ WA16 7HH – ℰ (01565) 873 484
– the.hinton@virgin.net
6 rm ☞ – ♦£ 48 ♦♦£ 62   **Rest** – (by arrangement) Menu £ 18
♦ Bay-windowed guesthouse with rear garden. Homely lounge; simple, uncluttered
bedrooms with floral theme. Friendly owners. Local produce used in the kitchen.

🍴 **The Frozen Mop**   ☂ ⅀ 🅿 VISA 🐵 AE ⓪
Faulkeners Lane ⊠ WA16 7AL – ℰ (01565) 873 234 – www.thefrozenmop.co.uk
Rest – Carte £ 18/23
♦ Stylish, modern gastropub with an upmarket clientele. The modern menu features something for everyone, ranging from salads and sharing platters to pizzas, pastas and grills.

at Lach Dennis Southwest : 7 m. by A 50, B 5081 and B 5082 – ⊠ **Knutsford**

🍴 **Duke of Portland**   ☲ ☂ ⅀ 🅿 VISA 🐵 AE
Penny's Lane ⊠ CW9 7SY – ℰ (01606) 46 264 – www.dukeofportland.com
– info@dukeofportland.com – Fax (01606) 41 724
Rest – Carte £ 20/40
♦ Airy, rural pub, its rustic ambience balanced by two lounges with a contemporary feel. Personally run by long-standing restaurant owners. Tasty, well-priced home-made dishes.

KYNASTON – Herefordshire – see Ledbury

LACH DENNIS – Ches. – see Knutsford

LACOCK – Wiltshire – **503** N 29 – ⊠ **Chippenham**   4 **C2**

ENGLAND

▶ London 109 mi – Bath 16 mi – Bristol 30 mi – Chippenham 3 mi
◎ Village ★★ - Lacock Abbey ★ **AC** – High St ★, St Cyriac ★, Fox Talbot Museum of Photography ★ **AC**

🏠 **At The Sign of the Angel**   ☲ ☂ 📶 🅿 VISA 🐵 AE ⓪
6 Church St ⊠ SN15 2LB – ℰ (01249) 730 230 – www.lacock.co.uk
– angel@lacock.co.uk – Fax (01249) 730 527 – Closed Christmas
10 rm ⌂ – ♦£82 ♦♦£145
Rest – (closed Monday lunch except Bank Holidays) Carte £ 24/36
♦ Part 14C and 15C former wool merchant's house in charming National Trust village. Relaxed and historic atmosphere. Antique furnished rooms, four in the garden cottage. Tremendously characterful dining room of hotel's vintage: traditional English dishes served.

LADOCK – Cornwall – **503** F 33   1 **B2**

▶ London 268 mi – Exeter 84 mi – Newquay 12 mi – Penzance 37 mi
– Plymouth 51 mi – Truro 13 mi

🏠 **Bissick Old Mill** without rest   ⅀ 📶 🅿 VISA 🐵 AE
off B 3275 ⊠ TR2 4PG – ℰ (01726) 882 557 – www.bissickoldmill.co.uk
– enquiries@bissickoldmill.plus.com
4 rm ⌂ – ♦£58/60 ♦♦£75/90
♦ Charming stone-built 17C former mill. Much historic character with low beamed ceilings and stone fireplaces. Comfortable bedrooms. Breakfast room has much period charm.

LA HAULE – **503** L 33 – see Channel Islands (Jersey)

LAMBOURN WOODLANDS – Berks. – see Hungerford

LANCASTER – Lancashire – **502** L 21 – **pop. 45 952** ▐ *Great Britain*   20 **A1**

▶ London 252 mi – Blackpool 26 mi – Bradford 62 mi – Burnley 44 mi
– Leeds 71 mi – Middlesbrough 97 mi – Preston 26 mi
🛈 29 Castle Hill ℰ (01524) 32878, lancastertic@lancaster.gov.uk
🏌 Ashton Hall Ashton-with-Stodday, ℰ (01524) 752 090
🏌 Lansil Caton Rd, ℰ (01524) 39 269
◎ Castle ★ **AC**

🍴 **The Borough**   🖼 AC VISA ⓪
3 Dalton Sq ⊠ LA1 1PP – ℰ (01524) 64 170 – www.theboroughlancaster.co.uk
– info@theboroughlancaster.co.uk – Closed 25 December and 1 January
Rest – Carte £ 16/35

♦ Victorian-fronted Georgian building with period flooring and leaded windows. Generous, regional dishes and 'create-your-own' Deli Boards use local, traceable produce.

LANCING – West Sussex – **504** S 31 – pop. 29 575   7 **D3**
▶ London 59 mi – Brighton 4 mi – Southampton 53 mi

🏨 **Sussex Pad**   🖼 ⒤ P. VISA ⓪ AE ⓪
Old Shoreham Rd, East : 1 m. off A 27 ⊠ BN15 0RH – ℰ (01273) 454647
– www.sussexpadhotel.co.uk – reception@sussexpadhotel.co.uk – Fax (01273) 453010
18 rm ⌂ – ♦£80 ♦♦£120   **Rest** – Carte £21/31

♦ Pubby modern hotel against the formidable backdrop of Lancing College. Co-ordinated rooms named after grand marque Champagnes: their namesakes in plentiful supply in the bar. Dine on seafood from nearby Brighton market.

LANGAR – Nottinghamshire – **502** R 25   16 **B2**
▶ London 132 mi – Boston 45 mi – Leicester 25 mi – Lincoln 37 mi
    – Nottingham 14 mi

🏨 **Langar Hall** ◈   ⟨ 🖼 ⒤ ⟩ 🎐 ⒤ P. VISA ⓪
⊠ *NG13 9HG – ℰ (01949) 860 559 – www.langarhall.co.uk*
– info@langarhall.co.uk – Fax (01949) 861 045
11 rm ⌂ – ♦£80/125 ♦♦£210 – 1 suite
Rest – Menu £18 (lunch) – Carte dinner £27/46

♦ Georgian manor in pastoral setting, next to early English church; overlooks park, medieval fishponds. Antique filled rooms named after people featuring in house's history. Elegant, candle-lit, pillared dining room.

LANGHO – Lancs. – **502** M 22 – see Blackburn

LANGPORT – Somerset – **503** L 30   3 **B3**
▶ London 134 mi – Weston-super-Mare 31 mi – Taunton 15 mi – Yeovil 16 mi

🏠 **The Parsonage**   🖼 ⒤ ⒤ P. VISA ⓪ AE
Mulchelney, South : 2m on Muchelney Pottery rd ⊠ TA10 0DL – ℰ (01458) 259058 – www.parsonagesomerset.co.uk – valerie@parsonagesomerset.co.uk
– Closed Christmas and New Year
3 rm ⌂ – ♦£53 ♦♦£95
Rest – ((communal dining) (by arrangement)) Carte approx. £29

♦ Traditional Somerset longhouse in charming setting with airy, well-kept country bedrooms and lovely rear garden. Delightful hosts dine with their guests at family style meals crafted from fresh, local ingredients. Al fresco breakfast in summer.

LANGTHWAITE – N. Yorks. – **502** O 20 – see Reeth

LA PULENTE – **503** P 33 – see Channel Islands (Jersey)

LAPWORTH – Warks. – see Hockley Heath

LA ROCQUE – **503** P 33 – see Channel Islands (Jersey)

LASKILL N. Yorks – **502** Q 21 – see Hawnby

LASTINGHAM – North Yorkshire – 502 R 21 – pop. 87 – ⊠ York 23 **C1**
▶ London 244 mi – Scarborough 26 mi – York 32 mi

Lastingham Grange ⌖ 🛋 🕼 🎧 ⚫ P VISA ⚫⚫
⊠ YO62 6TH – ℰ (01751) 417345 – www.lastinghamgrange.com
– reservations@lastinghamgrange.com – Fax (01751) 417358 – March-November
11 rm ⌂ – †£100/140 ††£160/199
Rest – (light lunch Monday-Saturday) Menu 38 – Carte £16/26
♦ A delightfully traditional country house atmosphere prevails throughout this extended, pleasantly old-fashioned, 17C farmhouse. Lovely gardens; well-appointed bedrooms. Dining room with rustic fare and rose garden view.

LAUNCESTON – Cornwall – 503 G 32 1 **B2**
▶ London 228 mi – Bude 23 mi – Exeter 47 mi – Plymouth 27 mi
🖸 Trethorne Kennards House, ℰ (01566) 86324

Springer Spaniel 🎧 P VISA ⚫⚫
Treburley ⊠ PL15 9NS – ℰ (01579) 370424 – www.thespringerspaniel.org.uk
– enquiries@thespringerspaniel.org.uk
Rest – Carte £20/36
♦ Sizeable 18C former coaching inn with a friendly, informal atmosphere. Wide-ranging classical menu uses local, traceable produce, including meat from the owners' nearby farm.

LAVENHAM – Suffolk – 504 W 27 – ⊠ Sudbury ⃞ Great Britain 15 **C3**
▶ London 66 mi – Cambridge 39 mi – Colchester 22 mi – Ipswich 19 mi
🖥 Lady St ℰ (01787) 248207, lavenhamtic@babergh.gov.uk
◎ Town★★ – Church of St Peter and St Paul★

ENGLAND

Swan 🛋 🎧 🎧 ♨ P VISA ⚫⚫ AE
High St ⊠ CO10 9QA – ℰ (01787) 247477 – www.theswanatlavenham.co.uk
– info@theswanatlavenham.co.uk – Fax (01787) 248286
43 rm (dinner included) ⌂ – †£95/155 ††£220 – 2 suites
Rest – Menu £16/32 – Carte £22/32
♦ Well-restored, part 14C, half timbered house with an engaging historical ambience. Each atmospheric bedroom is individually and stylishly decorated. Dining room has impressive timbered ceiling verging on the cavernous.

Lavenham Priory without rest 🛋 ⌾ 🎧 P VISA ⚫⚫
Water St ⊠ CO10 9RW – ℰ (01787) 247404 – www.lavenhampriory.co.uk
– mail@lavenhampriory.co.uk – Fax (01787) 248472
– Closed Christmas-New Year
6 rm ⌂ – †£75/85 ††£120/165
♦ A Jacobean oak staircase and Elizabethan wall paintings are just two elements of this part 13C former priory, bursting with character. Bedrooms stylishly furnished with antiques.

The Great House with rm 🎧 🎧 VISA ⚫⚫
Market Pl ⊠ CO10 9QZ – ℰ (01787) 247431 – www.greathouse.co.uk
– info@greathouse.co.uk – Fax (01787) 248007
– Closed 3 weeks January and 2 weeks summer
3 rm – †£90 ††£120/180, ⌂£12.50
Rest – French – (closed Monday, Sunday dinner and Tuesday lunch)
Menu £18/27 – Carte £23/44
♦ Georgian façade at the front, timbered house dating from 14C at the rear. Smart, refurbished dining room; classically based French cooking with some modern twists. Contemporary bedrooms but with original features.

The Angel with rm 🛋 🎧 P VISA ⚫⚫
Market Pl ⊠ CO10 9QZ – ℰ (01787) 247388 – www.maypolehotels.com
– angel@maypolehotels.com – Fax (01787) 248344 – Closed 25-26 December
8 rm – †£60/70 ††£85/120, ⌂£6 **Rest** – Carte £16/25
♦ 15C inn on the market square. Residents' lounge has original early 17C ceiling. Comfortable, well-kept rooms are individually furnished and some are heavily timbered.

LEDBURY – County of Herefordshire – **503** M 27 – pop. 8 491   18 **B3**

> London 119 mi – Hereford 14 mi – Newport 46 mi – Worcester 16 mi

🛏🛏   **The Feathers**   🍴 🔲 ♨ ℃ 🏋 **P** VISA ◉◎ AE ⓪
High St ⊠ HR8 1DS – ℰ (01531) 635 266 – www.feathers-ledbury.co.uk
– mary@feathers-ledbury.co.uk – Fax (01531) 638 955
22 rm ☕ – ♦£88/129 ♦♦£130/220
Rest *Quills* – (dinner only Friday-Saturday and Sunday lunch) Carte £23/31
Rest *Fuggles* – Carte £23/31
♦ Impressive timbered 16C inn in centre of town. Much character with open fires and
antique furnishings. Rooms vary in design, though they all lay claim to a stylish
modernity. Intimate dining in Quills restaurant. Fuggles is decorated with hops.

✗   **The Malthouse**   🍴 VISA ◉◎
Church Lane ⊠ HR8 1DW – ℰ (01531) 634 443
– Closed first week January, 1 autumn, 25 December, Sunday and Monday
Rest – (dinner only and Saturday lunch) Carte £22/33
♦ Tucked away behind the butter market; rustic décor and attractive courtyard lend
a classic country cottage aura. Monthly menu of carefully prepared dishes using local
produce.

at Kynaston West : 6½ m. by A 449, A 4172, Aylton Rd, on Fownhope Rd
– ⊠ Ledbury

🏠   **Hall End** ⤫   ⬅ 🚗 🌀 ⅃ 🍴 🐾 **P**
⊠ HR8 2PD – ℰ (01531) 670 225 – www.hallendhouse.com
– khjefferson@hallend91.freeserve.co.uk – Fax (01531) 670 747 – Closed Christmas
and New Year
3 rm ☕ – ♦♦£95/120
Rest – (booking essential) (communal dining, by arrangement) Menu £28
♦ Lovingly restored, personally run, part Georgian home and livery stable in the
countryside. Relax in the orangery and, suitably reposed, retire to lavishly furnished
bedrooms.

at Trumpet Northwest : 3¼ m. on A 438 – ⊠ Ledbury

🛏🛏   **Verzon House**   ⬅ 🚗 🌀 🐾 🎧 **P** VISA ◉◎ AE ⓪
Hereford Rd ⊠ HR8 2PZ – ℰ (01531) 670 381 – www.verzonhouse.com
– info@verzonhouse.com – Fax (01531) 670 830
8 rm ☕ – ♦£105/155 ♦♦£145/185   **Rest** – Menu £20 (lunch) – Carte £30/39
♦ Extended Georgian redbrick house with stylish lounge bar, contemporary artwork and comfy seats. Modern bedrooms are named after cider apples; most
have view over courtyard. Modern dishes served in restaurant, with decking for al
fresco dining.

ENGLAND

Cécile Labonne/MICHELIN

LEEDS

County: West Yorkshire
Michelin REGIONAL map: n° **502** P 22
▶ London 204 mi – Liverpool 75 mi – Manchester 43 mi – Newcastle upon Tyne 95 mi – Nottingham 74 mi

Population: 443 247   22 **B2**
▌ *Great Britain*

PRACTICAL INFORMATION

🛈 Tourist Information
The Arcade, City Station ☎ (0113) 242 5242, tourinfo@leeds.gov.uk

Airport
✈ Leeds-Bradford Airport: ☎ (0113) 250 9696, NW: 8 m. by A 65 and A 658 BT

Golf Courses
🏌 Temple Newsam Halton Temple Newsam Rd, ☎ (0113) 264 5624

🏌 Gotts Park Armley Armley Ridge Rd, ☎ (0113) 234 2019

🏌 Middleton Park Middleton Ring Rd, Beeston Park, ☎ (0113) 270 0449

🏌 Moor Allerton Wike Coal Rd, ☎ (0113) 266 1154

🏌 Howley Hall Morley Scotchman Lane, ☎ (01924) 350 100

🏌 Roundhay Park Lane, ☎ (0113) 266 2695

👁 SIGHTS

IN TOWN

City★ - Royal Armouries Museum★★★ GZ - City Art Gallery★ **AC**GY **M**

ON THE OUTSKIRTS

Kirkstall Abbey★ **AC**, NW: 3 m. by A 65 GY – Temple Newsam★ (decorative arts★) **AC**, E: 5 m. by A 64 and A 63 CU **D**

IN THE SURROUNDING AREA

Harewood House★★ (The Gallery★) **AC**, N: 8 m. by A 61 CT – Nostell Priory★ , SE: 18 m. by A 61 and A 638 – Yorkshire Sculpture Park★ , S: 20 m. by M 1 to junction 38 and 1 m. north off A 637 – Brodsworth Hall★ , SE: 25 m. by M 1 to junction 40, A 638 and minor rd (right) in Upton

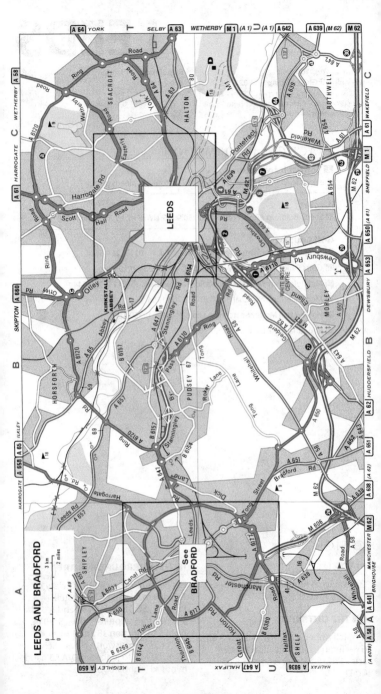

LEEDS AND BRADFORD

See BRADFORD

LEEDS

KIRKSTALL ABBEY

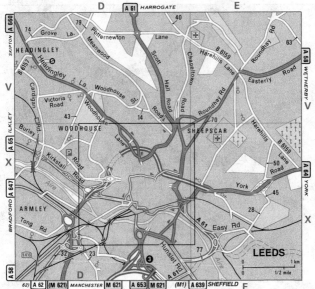

Bradford Rd. . . . . **AT** 9	Huddersfield Rd. . . . . **AU** 41	Roseville Rd . . . . **EVX** 70
Cambridge Rd . . . . **DV** 14	Hyde Park Rd . . . . **AV** 43	Shaw Lane . . . . **DV** 74
Cleckheaton Rd . . . . **AU** 16	Ivy St . . . . **EX** 45	South Accommodation
Commercial Rd. . . . . **BT** 17	Lupton Ave . . . . **EX** 51	Rd . . . . **EX** 77
Domestic St . . . . **DX** 23	New Rd Side . . . . **BT** 59	Stainbeck Rd . . . . **DV** 79
East Park Parade . . . . **EX** 28	Oakwood Lane . . . . **EV** 63	Templenewsam
Gelderd Rd . . . . **DX** 32	Pudsey Rd. . . . . **BT** 67	Rd . . . . **CT** 80
Harrogate Rd . . . . **DV** 40	Rodley Lane . . . . **BV** 69	White Rose Centre . . . . **CU**

ENGLAND

Thorpe Park H. and Spa   🔒 📺 🌐 🏊 ♨ ♨ 🔊 ♿ rm, 🅐🅒 ⚡ ⁽ᵖ⁾ ♨

1150 Century Way, Thorpe Park, East : 6 m. by A 64 and   **P**, *VISA* **⦿⦿** **AE**
A 63 off B 6120 ⊠ *LS15 8ZB –* ℰ *(0113) 264 1000 – www.shirehotels.co.uk*
– thorpepark@shirehotels.com – Fax (0113) 264 1010 – Closed 24-30 December
117 rm ⬄ – ♦£ 160 ♦♦£ 185   **Rest** – (bar lunch) Carte approx. £ 30

♦ Smart, modish hotel, close to motorways. Open-fired reception and richly toned central atrium. Fully equipped leisure centre with spa. Immaculate rooms with host of extras. Spacious, modern restaurant.

The Queens   ♿ 🅐🅒 ⁽ᵖ⁾ ♨ 🚗 *VISA* **⦿⦿** **AE** **①**

City Sq ⊠ *LS1 1PJ –* ℰ *(0113) 243 1323 – www.qhotels.co.uk*
– queensreception@qhotels.co.uk – Fax (0113) 243 5315   **FGZg**
187 rm ⬄ – ♦£ 175 ♦♦£ 175 – 30 suites
Rest *Grill* – Carte £ 30/45

♦ Fully restored to stunning proportions, this 30s Art Deco hotel has many original features in situ, including ballroom and splendid bar. Impressive rooms with period fittings. Basement dining room.

Radisson SAS   🔊 ♿ rm, 🅐🅒 ⚡ ⁽ᵖ⁾ ♨ *VISA* **⦿⦿** **AE** **①**

No.1 The Light, The Headrow ⊠ *LS1 8TL –* ℰ *(0113) 236 6000*
– www.leeds.radissonsas.com – info.leeds@radissonsas.com
– Fax (0113) 236 6100   **GYa**
147 rm – ♦£ 139 ♦♦£ 139, ⬄ £ 13.95
Rest – (in lounge) Menu £ 20 – Carte £ 29/39

♦ Grade II listed building with Art Deco facia. Open atrium and individually styled furnishings throughout. State-of-art meeting rooms. Ultra modern, very well appointed rooms.

365

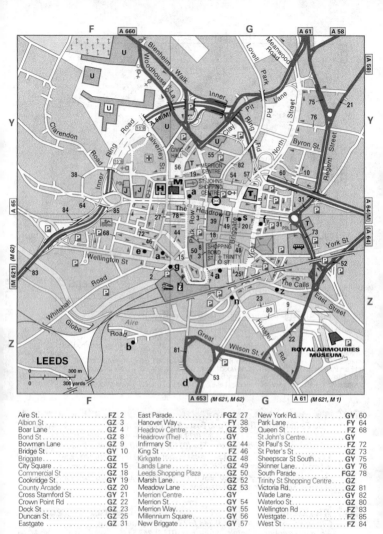

LEEDS

300 m
300 yards

Malmaison
ᵘⁿⁱᵗ 🛏 📶 ⎰ rm, 🏧 🛜 🏊 💳 ⑩ 🅰🅴 ①

1 Swinegate ⊠ *LS1 4AG –* ℰ *(0113) 398 1000 – www.malmaison.com*
– leeds@malmaison.com – Fax (0113) 398 1002   GZ**n**
100 rm – 🛏£125/160 🛏🛏£160/375, ⌷ £13.95 – 1 suite   **Rest** – Carte £ 28/35
♦ Relaxed, contemporary hotel hides behind imposing Victorian exterior. Vibrantly
and individually decorated rooms are stylishly furnished, with modern facilities to the
fore. Dine in modern interpretation of a French brasserie.

Quebecs without rest
🛜 ⎰ 🏧 ⚒ 🛜 💳 ⑩ 🅰🅴 ①

9 Quebec St ⊠ *LS1 2HA –* ℰ *(0113) 244 8989 – www.theetoncollection.com*
– resquebecs@theetoncollection.com – Fax (0113) 244 9090
– Closed 24-27 December   FZ**a**
43 rm – 🛏£75/105 🛏🛏£95/115, ⌷ £15.75 – 2 suites
♦ 19C former Liberal Club, now a modish, intimate boutique hotel. Original features
include oak staircase and stained glass window depicting Yorkshire cities. Stylish rooms.

42 The Calls ⌂⌂⌂ ⟨ 📶 ⏰ 👤 📺 VISA 🄌 AE ⓪

42 The Calls ⊠ LS2 7EW – 𝒞 (0113) 244 0099 – www.42thecalls.co.uk
– reservations@42thecalls.co.uk – Fax (0113) 234 4100
– Closed 3 days Christmas   GZ**z**
38 rm – †£ 89/180 ††£ 125/225, ⊆ £ 14.50 – 3 suites
Rest *Brasserie Forty Four* – see restaurant listing
♦ Stylish, contemporary converted quayside grain mill retaining many of the original workings. Rooms facing river have best views; all well equipped with a host of extras.

Haley's ⌂⌂ 🚗 📺 rest, ❄ 📶 👤 🅿 VISA 🄌 AE ⓪

8 Shire Oak Rd, Headingley, Northwest : 2 m. by A 660 ⊠ LS6 2DE – 𝒞 (0113)
278 4446 – www.haleys.co.uk – info@haleys.co.uk – Fax (0113) 275 3342
– Closed 2 weeks December   DV**s**
22 rm ⊆ **– †£ 70 ††£ 105/110**
Rest – Menu £ 22 (lunch) – Carte dinner approx. £ 27
♦ Named after a prominent stonemason, this part 19C country house in a quiet area is handy for cricket fans. Antique furnished public areas. Individually styled bedrooms. Elegant, relaxed dining room with collection of original local artwork.

Bewley's ⌂⌂ 📶 ⏰ rm, 📺 rest, ❄ 📞 🚗 VISA 🄌 AE ⓪

City Walk, Sweet St ⊠ LS11 9AT – 𝒞 (0113) 234 2340 – www.bewleyshotels.com
– leeds@bewleyshotels.com – Fax (0113) 234 2349
– Closed 24-30 December   GZ**d**
334 rm – †£ 79 ††£ 79, ⊆ £ 7.95
Rest *The Brasserie* – (dinner only) Carte £ 14/27 **s**
♦ This competitively priced hotel boasts a very spacious, stylishly furnished lounge, and is ideal for both tourists or business travellers. Well-kept rooms. Bright, informal brasserie with classically based menus.

Anthony's XXX 🄰🄲 VISA 🄌

19 Boar Lane ⊠ LS1 6EA – 𝒞 (0113) 245 5922 – www.anthonysrestaurant.co.uk
– reservations@anthonysrestaurant.co.uk
– Closed Christmas-New Year, Sunday and Monday   GZ**a**
Rest – (booking essential) Menu £ 24/42
♦ Converted 19C property; ground floor lounge with Chesterfield sofas; minimalist basement dining room offers innovative menus with some intriguing combinations.

No.3 York Place XX 🄰🄲 VISA 🄌 AE

3 York Pl ⊠ LS1 2DR – 𝒞 (0113) 245 9922 – www.no3yorkplace.co.uk
– dine@no3yorkplace.co.uk – Fax (0113) 245 9965 – Closed 25 December-
6 January, Saturday lunch, Sunday and Bank Holidays   FZ**e**
Rest – Menu £ 19 (lunch) – Carte £ 24/33
♦ A minimalist and discreet environment keeps the spotlight on the appealing cuisine. Classic flavours reinterpreted in a tasty range of brasserie style dishes.

The Foundry XX 🚗 🄰🄲 VISA 🄌 ⓪

1 Saw Mill Yard, Round Foundry ⊠ LS11 5WH – 𝒞 (0113) 245 0390
– www.thefoundrywinebar.co.uk – Fax (0113) 243 8934
– Closed Saturday lunch and Sunday   FZ**b**
Rest – Carte £ 25/32
♦ Located in Industrial Revolution's cradle, this converted brick vaulted warehouse has a snug interior, offering unfussy seasonal cooking with a wide variety of daily specials.

Fourth Floor – at Harvey Nichols XX 🚗 🄰🄲 📞 VISA 🄌 AE ⓪

107-111 Briggate ⊠ LS1 6AZ – 𝒞 (0113) 204 8000 – www.harveynichols.com
– leedsreservations@harveynicholls.com – Fax (0113) 204 8080 – Closed
25-26 December, 1 January, Easter Sunday and dinner Sunday-Wednesday   GZ**s**
Rest – (lunch bookings not accepted on Saturday) Menu £ 18/20
– Carte £ 31/36
♦ Watch the chefs prepare the modern food with world-wide influences in these bright, stylish, buzzy, contemporary surroundings. Advisable to get here early at lunch.

ENGLAND

XX **Brasserie Forty Four** – at 42 The Calls Hotel   🈶 🎟 🐕 ⇄ 𝘝𝘐𝘚𝘈 ⬤◑ 🎟 ⬤
44 The Calls ⊠ LS2 7EW – ℰ (0113) 234 3232 – www.brasserie44.com
– info@brasserie44.com – Fax (0113) 234 3332 – Closed Sunday and Bank
Holidays, except Good Friday   GZ**z**
Rest – Menu £ 22 (dinner) – Carte £ 25/30
♦ Former riverside warehouse with stylish bar; exudes atmosphere of buzzy informality. Smokehouse and char-grilled options in an eclectic range of menu dishes.

XX **Anthony's at Flannels**   🎟 𝘝𝘐𝘚𝘈 ⬤◑
😊 *Third Floor, 68 Vicar Lane ⊠ LS1 7JH – ℰ (0113) 242 8732*
– www.anthonysatflannels.co.uk – reservations@anthonysatflannels.co.uk
– Closed Monday   GZ**f**
Rest – (lunch only and dinner Friday-Saturday) Menu £ 18 (lunch)
– Carte £ 24/35
♦ Go to third floor of upmarket clothing store to find this sunny, stylish restaurant, adjacent to an art gallery. Friendly family service of good value, tasty, seasonal dishes.

LEICESTER – Leicester – **502** Q 26 – **pop. 330 574** ▌ *Great Britain*   16 **B2**

▶ London 107 mi – Birmingham 43 mi – Coventry 24 mi – Nottingham 26 mi
🛧 East Midlands Airport, Castle Donington : ℰ (0871) 9199000 NW : 22 m. by
   A 50 - AX - and M 1
🖸 7-9 Every St, Town Hall Sq ℰ (0906) 294 1113 (calls charged),
   info@goleicestershire.com
🖥 Leicestershire Evington Lane, ℰ (0116) 273 8825
🖥 Western Park Scudamore Rd, ℰ (0116) 287 5211
🖥 Humberstone Heights Gipsy Lane, ℰ (0116) 299 5570
🖥 Oadby Leicester Road Racecourse, ℰ (0116) 270 0215
🖸 Blaby Lutterworth Rd, ℰ (0116) 278 4804
◎ Guildhall ★ BY **B** – Museum and Art Gallery ★ CY **M3** – St Mary de Castro
   Church ★ BY **D**
🅖 National Space Centre ★ N : 2 m. by A 6 - AX - turning east into
   Corporation Rd and right into Exploration Drive

Plan opposite

🏨🏨 **Leicester Marriott**   🖭 🕉 🕭 🖩 🔌 rm, 🎟 🕻 🔏 🄿 𝘝𝘐𝘚𝘈 ⬤◑ 🎟 ⬤
Smith Way, Grove Park, Enderby, Southwest : 4 m. by A 5460 off A 563 at
junction 21 of M 1 ⊠ LE19 1SW – ℰ (0116) 282 01 000
– www.leicestermarriott.co.uk – Fax (0116) 282 0101   AY**z**
226 rm – 🕴£ 129 🕴🕴£ 129, � £ 15.50 – 1 suite
Rest – Menu £ 16/21 **s** – Carte approx. £ 32 **s**
♦ Sleekly designed, comfortable hotel in useful location by junction 21 of M1. Coffee shop and bar. State-of-the-art gym. Standard and executive bedrooms.   East meets west in contemporary restaurant; choice of buffet and eclectic à la carte.

🏨🏨 **Belmont House**   🖩 🔌 rm, 🕻 🔏 🄿 𝘝𝘐𝘚𝘈 ⬤◑ 🎟 ⬤
De Montfort St ⊠ LE1 7GR – ℰ (0116) 254 4773 – www.belmonthotel.co.uk
– info@belmonthotel.co.uk – Fax (0116) 247 0804   CY**c**
76 rm – 🕴£ 60/130 🕴🕴£ 80/135, � £ 12.95 – 1 suite
Rest *Cherry's* – (closed Saturday lunch and Sunday dinner) Carte £ 22/32
♦ Privately owned, centrally located and adjacent to a conservation area. Enlarged to provide a large bar and several function rooms. Spacious, comfortable bedrooms. Conservatory restaurant with formal air.

🏨🏨 **Holiday Inn Leicester City**   🖭 🕉 🕭 🖩 🎟 🕻 🔏 🄿 𝘝𝘐𝘚𝘈 ⬤◑ 🎟 ⬤
129 St Nicholas Circle ⊠ LE1 5LX – ℰ (0870) 400 90 48 – www.holiday-inn.co.uk
– leicestercity.reservations@ihg.com – Fax (0116) 251 3169   BY**c**
187 rm ⊆ – 🕴£ 149/179 🕴🕴£ 159/189 – 1 suite
Rest – Menu £ 20 (dinner) – Carte £ 25/30
♦ Centrally located, imposing modern hotel convenient for the ring road. Comfortable brand style bedrooms with fitted furniture and particularly good Executive rooms. Stylish modern restaurant and bar with American style menus.

LEICESTER

✗✗ Watsons
`AC` `VISA` `MC`

5-9 Upper Brown St ⊠ LE1 5TE – ℰ (0116) 222 7770
– www.watsons-restaurant.com – watsons.restaurant@virgin.net – Fax (0116)
222 7771 – Closed Sunday and Bank Holidays   BY**x**
Rest – Menu £17 (lunch) – Carte £21/30

◆ Converted Victorian cotton mill in the centre of town. Vivid modern interior replete with chrome, glass and a cosmopolitan ambience. Wide ranging, competent, modern menu.

✗✗ The Tiffin
`AC` `⇔` `VISA` `MC` `AE` `①`

1 De Montfort St ⊠ LE1 7GE – ℰ (0116) 247 0420 – www.the-tiffin.co.uk
– thetiffin@msn.com
– Closed 24-26 December, 1 January, Saturday lunch and Sunday   CY**r**
Rest – Indian – (booking essential) Menu £23 (dinner) – Carte £26/37

◆ Busy, spacious and comfortable with a gentle Eastern theme to the décor. Tasty, authentic flavour in carefully prepared Indian dishes.

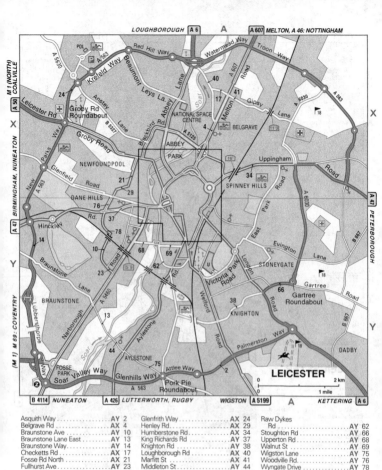

✗✗ **The Case** ⟷ 𝘝𝘐𝘚𝘈 ⬤⬤ 𝗔𝗘 ①

4-6 Hotel St, St Martin's ✉ LE1 5AW – ✆ (0116) 251 7675 – www.thecase.co.uk
– thecase@btconnect.com – Fax (0116) 251 7675
– Closed Sunday and Bank Holidays   BY**n**
Rest – Menu £ 13 (lunch) – Carte £ 16/29

♦ Stylish modern restaurant in a converted Victorian luggage factory. Open main dining area and a small bar. Large, modern, seasonal menu. Champagne bar adjacent.

LEIGH-ON-SEA – Southend-on-Sea – **504** W 29   13 **C3**

🄳 London 37 mi – Brighton 85 mi – Dover 86 mi – Ipswich 57 mi

✗✗ **Boatyard** ⟵ 𝗔𝗖 ⟷ 𝗣 𝘝𝘐𝘚𝘈 ⬤⬤

8-13 High St ✉ SS9 2EN – ✆ (01702) 475 588
– www.theboatyardrestaurant.co.uk – info@theboatyardrestaurant.co.uk
– Fax (01702) 477 392 – Closed Sunday dinner, Monday and Tuesday lunch
Rest – Menu £ 17 (lunch) – Carte £ 28/48

♦ Locally renowned, within a former boatyard by the Thames Estuary. Strikingly modern with floor to ceiling windows, deck terrace, oyster bar. Dishes have wide eclectic base.

XX **The Bank** 🍴 AC ⇔ VISA ⓦ AE
1470 London Rd ⊠ SS9 2UR – ℰ (01702) 719 000 – www.thebankonline.co.uk
– info@thebankonline.co.uk – Closed Sunday dinner and Monday
Rest – Menu £20 (lunch) – Carte £30/37
♦ Former bank set in parade of shops. Spacious restaurant with small terrace and bar,
high ceilings and intimate lighting. Wide menu of classic 80's cooking displays fresh,
neat flavours.

X **The Sandbar & Seafood Co. Ltd** VISA ⓦ AE
71 Broadway ⊠ SS9 1PE – ℰ (01702) 480 067 – www.sandbarandseafood.co.uk
– thesandbar@btconnect.com – Closed 25-26 December, 31 December, 1 January
and Sunday dinner
Rest – (booking essential) Carte £19/32
♦ Family-run restaurant on main street offering wide seafood menu with classic
French base. Sleek black décor. Upstairs lounge with open fireplace. Photos of
chefs on walls.

LEINTWARDINE – County of Herefordshire – **503** L 26 – ⊠ **Craven**   18 **A2**
Arms

▣ London 156 mi – Birmingham 55 mi – Hereford 24 mi – Worcester 40 mi

⌂ **Upper Buckton Farm** ⏚ ≤ 🚗 🕭 ⚘ P
Buckton, West : 2 m. by A 4113 and Buckton rd ⊠ SY7 0JU – ℰ (01547) 540 634
– ghlloydco@btconnect.com – Fax (01547) 540 634 – Closed 25 December
3 rm ⊑ – ✝£60 ✝✝£90
Rest – (by arrangement, communal dining) Menu £30
♦ Fine Georgian farmhouse, part of a working farm, surrounded by countryside.
Comfortable, simple, country feel with open fires in the lounge and characterful
bedrooms. Traditional dining; local produce.

LENHAM – Kent – **504** W 30 – pop. 2 191 – ⊠ **Maidstone**   9 **C2**
▣ London 45 mi – Folkestone 28 mi – Maidstone 9 mi

🏨 **Chilston Park** ≤ 🚗 🕭 ⚘ 🖼 ⅙ rm, ⚘ 🕾 🛁 P VISA ⓦ AE ①
Sandway, South : 1¾ m. off Broughton Malherbe rd ⊠ ME17 2BE – ℰ (01622)
859 803 – www.handpicked.co.uk/chilstonpark – chilstonpark@handpicked.co.uk
– Fax (01622) 858 588
53 rm ⊑ – ✝£85/160 ✝✝£95/170 – 4 suites
Rest – (Closed Saturday lunch) Menu £21 (lunch) **s** – Carte dinner £37/50 **s**
♦ Part 17C mansion, set in parkland and furnished with antiques. Bedrooms are very
individual and comfortable. Old stable conference facilities retain original stalls!
Smart dining room and well-appointed sitting room.

LEOMINSTER – County of Herefordshire – **503** L 27 – pop. 10 440   18 **B3**
▌ Great Britain
▣ London 141 mi – Birmingham 47 mi – Hereford 13 mi – Worcester 26 mi
🛈 1 Corn Sq ℰ (01568) 616460, tic-leominster@herefordshire.gov.uk
🖼 Ford Bridge, ℰ (01568) 612 863
🖼 Berrington Hall★ **AC**, N : 3 m. by A 49

at Leysters Northeast : 5 m. by A 49 on A 4112 – ⊠ **Leominster**

⌂ **The Hills Farm** without rest ⏚ ≤ 🚗 🕭 ⚘ P VISA ⓦ
⊠ HR6 0HP – ℰ (01568) 750 205 – www.thehillsfarm.co.uk
– jconolly@btconnect.com – March-October
3 rm ⊑ – ✝£35/39 ✝✝£70/78
♦ An attractive ivy-clad farmhouse on a working farm. The interior is delightfully
comfortable, from the cosy lounge to the country-cottage rooms, three in the converted barns.

ENGLAND

LETCHWORTH – Hertfordshire – 504 T 28

12 B2

🖪 London 39 mi – Luton 18 mi – Stevenage 7 mi

at Willian South : 1 ¾ m. by A 6141 – ⊠ Letchworth

🏠 **The Fox**　　　　　　　　　　　　　　　🚗 **P** VISA ⓪⓪
⊠ SG6 2AE – 𝒞 (01462) 480 233 – www.foxatwillian.co.uk
– info@foxatwillian.co.uk – Fax (01462) 676 966
Rest – (Closed Sunday dinner) Carte £ 25/50
♦ 18C pub with smart, modern bar, spacious dining room and small terrace. Regularly-changing menu has a seafood base, featuring fresh Norfolk fish and local meat and veg.

LEVINGTON – Suffolk

15 **D3**

🖪 London 75 mi – Ipswich 5 mi – Woodbridge 8 mi

🏠 **The Ship Inn**　　　　　　　　　　　🚗 ⅍ **P** VISA ⓪⓪
Church Lane ⊠ IP10 0LQ – 𝒞 (01473) 659 573 – Closed 25-26 December, dinner 31 December
Rest – Carte £ 18/25
♦ Characterful, part 14C thatched and beamed pub with plenty of maritime curios and rustic charm. Fish a key element of dishes which range from traditional to rather innovative.

LEVISHAM – N. Yorks. – 502 R 21 – see Pickering

LEWDOWN – Devon – 503 H 32

2 **C2**

🖪 London 238 mi – Exeter 37 mi – Plymouth 29 mi
🅖 Lydford★★, E : 4 m. Launceston★ - Castle★ (≼★) St Mary Magdalene★, W : 8 m. by A 30 and A 388

🏨 **Lewtrenchard Manor** ⊗　　　　🚗 ◑ ⌐ ᵞᵞ ⅍ **P** VISA ⓪⓪ AE
South : ¾ m. by Lewtrenchard rd ⊠ EX20 4PN – 𝒞 (01566) 783 222
– www.lewtrenchard.co.uk – info@lewtrenchard.co.uk – Fax (01566) 783 332
13 rm � – †£ 165/245 ††£ 195/275 – 1 suite
Rest – (Closed Monday lunch) (booking essential for non-residents)
Menu £ 19/45 **s**
♦ A grand historical atmosphere pervades this delightfully secluded 17C manor house. Plenty of personality with antiques, artworks, ornate ceilings and panelling throughout. Two elegant dining rooms with stained glass windows.

LEWES – East Sussex – 504 U 31 – pop. 15 988 ▌ Great Britain

8 **A3**

🖪 London 53 mi – Brighton 8 mi – Hastings 29 mi – Maidstone 43 mi
�ℹ 187 High St 𝒞 (01273) 483448, lewes.tic@lewes.gov.uk
🏴 Chapel Hill, 𝒞 (01273) 473 245
🅞 Town★ (High St★, Keere St★) – Castle (≼★) **AC**
🅖 Sheffield Park Garden★ **AC**, N : 9 ½ m. by A 275

🏨 **Shelleys**　　　　　　　　　　🚗 🚗 ᵞᵞ ⅍ **P** VISA ⓪⓪ AE
High St ⊠ BN7 1XS – 𝒞 (01273) 472 361 – www.shelleys-hotel.com
– info@shelleys-hotel-lewes.com – Fax (01273) 483 152
18 rm ⊇ – †£ 115/155 ††£ 220/300 – 1 suite
Rest – Carte £ 30/40
♦ The great poet's family once owned this Georgian former inn. It has spacious bedrooms which are furnished and decorated in keeping with its historical connections. Smart restaurant exudes Georgian panache.

🏠 **Millers** without rest　　　　　　　　　　　　🚗 ⅍
134 High St ⊠ BN7 1XS – 𝒞 (01273) 475 631
– www.millersbedandbreakfast.com – millers134@aol.com – Closed 20 December - 5 January and 5 November
3 rm ⊇ – †£ 70/80 ††£ 85/90
♦ Characterful, small family home in a row of 16C houses that lead to the high street. Appealing personal feel in the individual bedrooms with books, trinkets and knickknacks.

ENGLAND

at East Chiltington Northwest : 5½ m. by A 275 and B 2116 off Novington Lane – ✉ Lewes

🍴 **The Jolly Sportsman**   🅿 VISA ◍◎

Chapel Lane ✉ BN7 3BA – ✆ (01273) 890 400 – www.thejollysportsman.com
– info@thejollysportsman.com – Fax (01273) 890 400
– Closed 25-27 December

Rest – (Closed Sunday dinner and Monday) Menu £ 16 – Carte £ 23/30

♦ Creeper-clad pub with raised rear garden and paved terrace. Menu displays simple dishes made from quality ingredients, with a subtle Mediterranean influence; fish is a strength.

LEYBURN – North Yorkshire – **502** O 21 – pop. 1 844   **22 B1**

🔁 London 251 mi – Darlington 25 mi – Kendal 43 mi – Leeds 53 mi
 – Newcastle upon Tyne 62 mi – York 49 mi
🔏 4 Central Chambers, Railway St ✆ (01748) 828747, leyburn@ytbtic.co.uk

🏠 **Clyde House** without rest   ⚙ 🤟 VISA ◍◎ AE

5 Railway St ✉ DL8 5AY – ✆ (01969) 623 941 – www.clydehouseleyburn.co.uk
– lucia.fisher1@btinternet.com – Closed 2-31 January

6 rm ☲ – ♦ £ 40/45 ♦♦ £ 70/75

♦ Recently refurbished to a high standard, this former coaching inn dates from mid-18C and is one of the oldest buildings in town. Hearty Yorkshire breakfasts to start the day.

🏠 **The Dales Haven** without rest   ⚙ 🅿 VISA ◍◎

Market Pl ✉ DL8 5BJ – ✆ (01969) 623 814 – www.daleshaven.co.uk
– info@daleshaven.co.uk

6 rm ☲ – ♦ £ 45/49 ♦♦ £ 65/69

♦ Neat and tidy house in village centre. Pleasant rural views from breakfast room, which also displays artwork from local gallery. Colourful rooms include DVD and CD players.

🍴 **The Sandpiper Inn** with rm   🙿 🅿 VISA ◍◎

Market Pl ✉ DL8 5AT – ✆ (01969) 622 206 – www.sandpiperinn.co.uk
– hsandpiper99@aol.com – Fax (01969) 625 367
– Closed 25 December and 1 January

2 rm ☲ – ♦ £ 65 ♦♦ £ 80

Rest – (Closed Tuesday in winter) Carte £ 24/33

♦ Converted 16C stone house off market square. Rustic and simple with daily changing blackboard menu of tasty Yorkshire fare; good local ales. Pleasant pine furnished rooms.

at Constable Burton East : 3½ m. on A 684 – ✉ Leyburn

🍴 **Wyvill Arms** with rm   🍴 🙿 🅿 VISA ◍◎

✉ DL8 5LH – ✆ (01677) 450 581

2 rm ☲ – ♦ £ 55 ♦♦ £ 75   **Rest** – (Closed Monday) Carte £ 24/36

♦ A classic Yorkshire pub with stone bar area and good choice of ales. Seasonally changing menu with steaks a speciality: eat in bar or formal dining room. Neat, tidy bedrooms.

LEYSTERS – Herefordshire – **503** M 27 – see Leominster

LICHFIELD – Staffordshire – **502** O 25 – pop. 28 435 ▮ *Great Britain*   **19 C2**

🔁 London 128 mi – Birmingham 16 mi – Derby 23 mi – Stoke-on-Trent 30 mi
🔏 Lichfield Garrick, Castle Dyke ✆ (01543) 412112
🔷 Seedy Mill Elmhurst, ✆ (01543) 417 333
◉ City★ - Cathedral★★ AC

ENGLAND

LICHFIELD

🏠 Swinfen Hall   🍴 ❄ 🎿 ♪ 🛎 🅿 VISA ⓪ AE

Southeast : 2¼ m. by A 5206 on A 38 ⊠ WS14 9RE – ℰ *(01543) 481 494*
– www.swinfenhallhotel.co.uk – info@swinfenhallhotel.co.uk – Fax (01543)
480 341 – Restricted opening between Christmas and New Year
17 rm ⌕ – ♦£145/160 ♦♦£170/200 – 1 suite
Rest *Four Seasons* – (closed Saturday lunch and Sunday dinner to
non-residents) Menu £23/42
♦ Very fine 18C house in 100 acres with beautiful façade, impressive stucco ceilings
and elegant lounges furnished with taste and style. Bedrooms offer high levels of
comfort. Modern menus served in superb oak-panelled restaurant with Grinling Gibbons carvings.

🍴 Chandlers Grande Brasserie   AC VISA ⓪ AE

Corn Exchange, Conduit St ⊠ WS13 6JU – ℰ *(01543) 416 688*
– www.chandlersrestaurant.co.uk – info@chandlersrestaurant.co.uk – Fax (01543)
417 887 – Closed Sunday dinner and Bank Holidays
Rest – Menu £14/18 (midweek) – Carte £18/30
♦ On two floors in old cornmarket building. Tiled floors, prints and pin lights; a
pleasant, relaxed atmosphere in which to enjoy a brasserie menu with good value
lunch options.

LICKFOLD – W. Sussex – see Petworth

LIDGATE – Suffolk – **504** V 27 – see Newmarket

LIFTON – Devon – **503** H 32 – pop. 964   2 **C2**
🄳 London 238 mi – Bude 24 mi – Exeter 37 mi – Launceston 4 mi
   – Plymouth 26 mi
🄶 Launceston★ - Castle★ (≤★) St Mary Magdalene★, W : 4½ m. by A 30 and
   A 388

🏠 Arundell Arms   🍴 ♫ 🎿 ♪ 🛎 🅿 VISA ⓪ AE ⓪

Fore St ⊠ PL16 0AA – ℰ *(01566) 784 666 – www.arundellarms.com*
– reservations@arundellarms.com – Fax (01566) 784 494 – Accommodation
closed 24-26 December
21 rm ⌕ – ♦£115 ♦♦£190/218   **Rest** – Menu £25/46 s🍴
♦ Coaching inn, in a valley of five rivers, dating back to Saxon times. True English
sporting hotel - popular with shooting parties and fishermen. Good country lodge
style. English and French cuisine in opulently grand dining room.

🍴 Tinhay Mill with rm   🍴 🅿 VISA ⓪

Tinhay ⊠ PL16 0AJ – ℰ *(01566) 784 201 – www.tinhaymillrestaurant.co.uk*
– tinhay.mill@talk21.com – Fax (01566) 784 201
– Closed 2 weeks Christmas - New Year
5 rm ⌕ – ♦£60/65 ♦♦£85/90
Rest – (closed Sunday-Monday) (dinner only) Menu £31 – Carte £26/41
♦ Small converted mill: furnishings a mix of rustic and traditional, creating a cosy feel.
Locally based, tasty cuisine from renowned Devonian owner/cook. Cottagey bed-
rooms.

LINCOLN – Lincolnshire – **502** S 24 – pop. 85 963 📗 *Great Britain*   17 **C1**
🄳 London 140 mi – Bradford 81 mi – Cambridge 94 mi
   – Kingston-upon-Hull 44 mi – Leeds 73 mi – Leicester 53 mi
   – Norwich 104 mi – Nottingham 38 mi
🛫 Humberside Airport : ℰ (01652) 688456, N : 32 m. by A 15 - Y - M 180 and
   A 18
🄸 9 Castle Hill ℰ (01522) 873213
🄶 Carholme Carholme Rd, ℰ (01522) 523 725
◉ City★★ - Cathedral and Precincts★★★ AC Y – High Bridge★★Z 9 – Usher
   Gallery★ AC YZ M1 – Jew's House★Y – Castle★ AC Y
🄶 Doddington Hall★ AC, W : 6 m. by B 1003 - Z - and B 1190. Gainsborough
   Old Hall★ AC, NW : 19 m. by A 57 - Z - and A 156
Plan opposite

ENGLAND

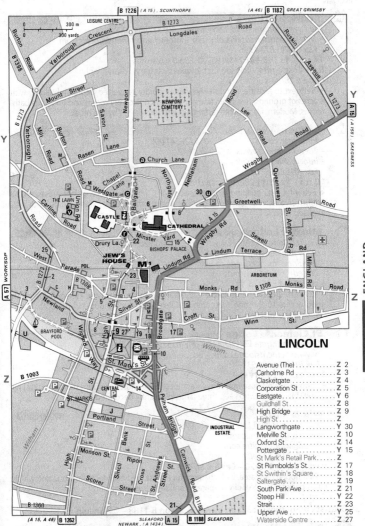

LINCOLN

ENGLAND

🏠 Bentley 🔟 ⅏ ⌗ ⌷ ⌧ rm, ⒶⒸ rest, ⅌ ⅍ 🅿 *VISA* ⓪ ⒶⒺ ①
Newark Rd, South Hykeham, Southwest : 5¾ m. by A 15 on B 1434 at junction
with A 46 ⊠ LN6 9NH – ℰ *(01522) 878 000 – www.thebentleyhotel.uk.com*
– info the bentleyhotel@btconnect.com – Fax (01522) 878 001
80 rm ⊒ – ♥£90/100 ♥♥£105/115
Rest – (carvery lunch) Menu £14/20 **s** – Carte dinner £21/37 **s**
♦ New purpose-built hotel. Smart, modern feel with traditional touches throughout.
Well kept bedrooms including Executive and more traditional styles. Well-run leisure
club. Formal or relaxed dining alternatives.

ENGLAND

Charlotte House

🛋 🏠 Ⓚ rest, ⚒ ᵗⁿ 👗 🅿 VISA ⯍ AE ①

The Lawns, Union Rd ✉ *LN1 3BJ* – ℰ *(01522) 541 000*
– www.charlottehouselincoln.com – info@charlottehouselincoln.com
– Fax (0871) 872 43 96   Yv
14 rm – ♦£145 ♦♦£145/195, ⌣£9.50 – 6 suites
Rest *Castlegate* – (closed first 2 weeks January) (dinner only)
Carte £28/37 **s**
♦ Set next to a castle, a stylish and contemporary converted Georgian building with 8 acres of grounds; free town transfers. Super-cool, comfy rooms and luxurious bathrooms. Modern, fashionable restaurant with terrace, set by the moat.

Bailhouse without rest

🛋 ⚒ ᵗⁿ 🅿 VISA ⯍ AE

34 Bailgate ✉ *LN1 3AP* – ℰ *(01522) 541 000*
– www.bailhouse.co.uk
– info@bailhouse.co.uk
– Fax (01522) 521 829   Yc
10 rm – ♦£75 ♦♦£89/175, ⌣£9.50
♦ Beautiful 14C building with 19C additions. Intimate, relaxing feel enhanced by unobtrusive service, enclosed garden, and rooms oozing charm, some with 14C exposed beams.

Minster Lodge without rest

⚒ ᵗⁿ 🅿 VISA ⯍ AE

3 Church Lane ✉ *LN2 1QJ* – ℰ *(01522) 513 220*
– www.minsterlodge.co.uk
– enquiries@minsterlodge.co.uk
– Closed 1 week Christmas   Ya
6 rm ⌣ – ♦£65/75 ♦♦£75/85
♦ Converted house, close to the cathedral and castle, just by 3C Newport Arch with good access to the ring road. Immaculately kept throughout and run with a professional touch.

St Clements Lodge without rest

⚒ ᵗⁿ 🅿

21 Langworthgate ✉ *LN2 4AD* – ℰ *(01522) 521 532*
– www.stclementslodge.co.uk – enquiries@stclementslodge.co.uk
– Fax (01522) 521 532   Yu
3 rm ⌣ – ♦£45 ♦♦£60
♦ A good value house in a convenient location, a short walk from the sights. Run by hospitable owners who keep three large, pleasantly decorated bedrooms.

Wig & Mitre

VISA ⯍ AE ①

30-32 Steep Hill ✉ *LN2 1LU* – ℰ *(01522) 535 190*
– www.wigandmitre.com
– email@wigandmitre.com
– Fax (01522) 532 402   Yr
Rest – Menu £15/20 – Carte £21/38
♦ First floor dining area, with characterful almost medieval decor, in a building which dates back to 14C. Skilfully prepared, confident, classic cooking.

at Branston Southeast : 3½ m. by A 15 - Z - on B 1188 – ✉ **Lincoln**

Branston Hall

🛋 ⚑ 📺 ⌂ 📶 ⛲ 👗 rm, ⚒ ᵗⁿ 👗 🅿 VISA ⯍ AE ①

Lincoln Road ✉ *LN4 1PD* – ℰ *(01522) 793 305*
– www.branstonhall.com
– info@branstonhall.com
– Fax (01522) 790 734
50 rm ⌣ – ♦£80/90 ♦♦£180
Rest – Menu £17/27 – Carte dinner £27/36
♦ Privately owned hall built in 1736, with additions. Stands in impressive grounds with lake. Bags of period charm, such as original wood panelling. Homely, comfortable rooms. Huge dining room has a formal feel and classical menus.

If breakfast is included the ⌣ symbol appears after the number of rooms.

LISKEARD – Cornwall – **503** G 32 – **pop. 8 478**

> ▶ London 261 mi – Exeter 59 mi – Plymouth 19 mi – Truro 37 mi
>
> ◎ Church★
>
> ⒢ Lanhydrock★★, W : 11½ m. by A 38 and A 390 – NW : Bodmin Moor★★ -
> St Endellion Church★★ - Altarnun Church★ - St Breward Church★ -
> Blisland★ (church★) - Camelford★ - Cardinham Church★ - Michaelstow
> Church★ - St Kew★ (church★) - St Mabyn Church★ – St Neot★ (Parish
> Church★★) - St Sidwell's, Laneast★ - St Teath Church★ - St Tudy★ –
> Launceston★ - Castle★ (≤★) St Mary Magdalene★, NE : 19 m. by A 390
> and A 388

  The Well House ☞   ← 🚗 🍴 ✂ 🐾 📞 **P** **VISA** **◍◍** **①**
St Keyne, South : 3½ m. by B 3254 on St Keyne Well rd ⊠ *PL14 4RN –* ℰ *(01579)*
342 001 – www.wellhouse.co.uk – enquiries@wellhouse.co.uk
– Fax (01579) 343 891
9 rm ⌫ – †£ 139/193 ††£ 155/215
Rest – (dinner only) (booking essential for non-residents)
Menu £ 38
◆ Large 19C country house surrounded by extensive grounds; personally run by
friendly owner. Individual rooms have winning outlooks; those by the garden have
private patios. Stylish, modern country house restaurant looks out over the countryside.

  Pencubitt Country House ☞   🚗 ✂ 🐾 📞 **P** **VISA** **◍◍**
Station Rd, South :½ m. by B 3254 on Lamellion rd ⊠ *PL14 4EB*
– ℰ *(01579) 342 694 – www.pencubitt.com*
– hotel@pencubitt.com – Fax (01579) 342 694
– Closed 22 December - 30 January
9 rm ⌫ – †£ 60/75 ††£ 110/120
Rest – (dinner only) (booking essential) Menu £ 30 **s**
◆ Late Victorian mansion, with fine views of East Looe Valley. Spacious drawing room
with open fire, plus sitting room, bar and veranda. Comfy rooms, most with rural
views. Attractive, candlelit dining room.

> Your opinions are important to us:
> please write and let us know about your discoveries and experiences –
> good and bad!

LITTLE BEDWYN – Newbury – **503** P 29 – **see Marlborough**

LITTLE BOLLINGTON – Gtr Manchester – **see Altrincham**

LITTLE BUDWORTH – Ches. – **502** M 24 – **see Tarporley**

LITTLE CHALFONT – Buckinghamshire – **504** S 29   **11 D2**

> ▶ London 33 mi – Amersham 2 mi – Watford 11 mi

🍽 **The Sugar Loaf Inn**   ☂ **P** **VISA** **◍◍**
Station Road ⊠ *HP7 9PN –* ℰ *(01494) 765 579*
– www.thesugarloafinn.com
– info@thesugarloafinn.com
– Closed 25-26 December and 1 January
Rest – Menu £ 10 (lunch) – Carte £ 20/26
◆ Restored 1930s roadside pub in heart of Chilterns village. Characterful interior with
oak panelled walls and mood lighting. Fresh, unfussy cooking with modern British
edge.

ENGLAND

LITTLEHAMPTON – West Sussex – **504** S 31 – pop. 55 716

> ▶ London 64 mi – Brighton 18 mi – Portsmouth 31 mi
> 🔎 The Look and Sea Centre, 63-65 Surrey St ✆ (01903) 721866, littlehampton.vic@arun.gov.uk

🏠 **Bailiffscourt & Spa** 🌾   🚗 🕴 🛋 ⚒ 🖎 ⊛ ♨ ⒣ ✕ 🕭 🛍 **P**
Climbing St, Climping, West : 2 ¾ m. by A 259 ⊠ BN17 5RW   VISA ⓜⓞ AE ①
– ✆ (01903) 723 511 – www.hshotels.co.uk – bailiffscourt@hshotels.co.uk
– Fax (01903) 723 107
39 rm ⌒ – †£170 ††£250   **Rest** – Menu £19/46
♦ Alluring reconstructed medieval house basking in acres of utterly peaceful grounds. Rich antiques and fine period features in an enchanting medieval ambience. Superb spa. Split-room dining area nestling amidst warmly tapestried walls.

🏠 **Amberley Court** without rest 🌾   🚗 ✕ **P**
Crookthorn Lane, Climping, West : 1 ¾ m. by B 2187 off A 259 ⊠ BN17 5SN
– ✆ (01903) 725 131 – msimmonds06@aol.com – Fax (01903) 725 131 – Closed
Christmas, January and February
5 rm ⌒ – †£50/55 ††£89
♦ Converted farm barn with a tidy, homely atmosphere. Exposed beams, flourishing plants and a warm welcome. Simply decorated rooms, some in grounds, with traditional chintz.

LITTLE LANGDALE – Cumbria – **502** K 20 – see Ambleside

LITTLE LANGFORD – Wilts. – see Salisbury

LITTLE PETHERICK – Cornwall – **503** F 32 – see Padstow

LITTLE SHELFORD – Cambs. – **504** U 27 – see Cambridge

LITTLE THETFORD – Cambs. – see Ely

LITTLE WILBRAHAM – Cambs. – see Cambridge

LITTLE WITCOMBE – Gloucestershire – see Cheltenham

Cécile Labonne/MICHELIN

LIVERPOOL

County: Merseyside
Michelin REGIONAL map: n° **502** L 23
▶ London 219 mi – Birmingham 103 mi
– Leeds 75 mi – Manchester 35 mi

Population: 469 017   20 **A2**
🛡 *Great Britain*

Liverpool   pp. 3-7

PRACTICAL INFORMATION

🚾 Tourist Information
08 Place, 36-38 Whitechapel, 𝒫 (0151) 233 2459, 08place@liverpool.gov.uk

Airport
🛫 Liverpool John Lennon Airport: 𝒫 (0871) 521 8484, SE: 6 m. by A 561 BX

Ferries and Shipping Lines
🚢 to Birkenhead and Wallasey (Mersey Ferries) frequent services daily

🚢 to Isle of Man (Douglas) (Isle of Man Steam Packet Co. Ltd) (2 h 30

mn/4 h) – to Northern Ireland (Belfast) (Norfolkline Irish Sea Ltd) 1-2 daily (11 h) – to
Dublin (NorseMerchant Ferries Ltd) 2 daily (approx. 7 h 45 mn) – to Dublin (P & O Irish
Sea) daily (8 h) – to Dublin (P & O Irish Sea) daily February-November (3 h 45 mn)

Tunnel
Mersey Tunnels (toll) AX

Golf Courses
⛳ Allerton Municipal Allerton Rd, 𝒫 (0151) 428 1046

⛳ Liverpool Municipal Kirby Ingoe Lane, 𝒫 (0151) 546 5435

⛳ Bowring Roby Rd, Bowring Park, 𝒫 (0151) 489 1901

📷 SIGHTS

IN TOWN

City★ – The Walker★★ DY **M3** –
Liverpool Cathedral★★ (Lady Chapel★)
EZ – Metropolitan Cathedral of Christ
the King★★ EY – Albert Dock★ CZ
(Merseyside Maritime Museum★
AC M2 - Tate Liverpool★)

IN THE SURROUNDING AREA

Speke Hall★ **AC**, SE: 8 m. by A 561 BX

ENGLAND

(M 57)

A 580 MANCHESTER,(M 57, M 6)

PRESTON **A 59** (M 57, M 58)

PRESTON **A 5036**

(A 59, M 57, M 58)

A 565 CROSBY

LIVERPOOL

SEFTON

LITHERLAND

BOOTLE

WATERLOO

SEAFORTH

CROSBY

MERSEY

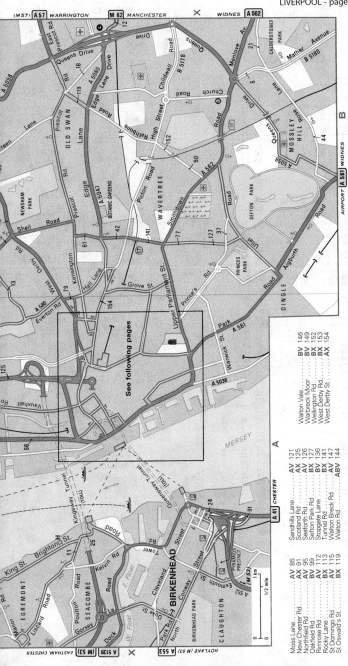

ENGLAND

ENGLAND

LIVERPOOL

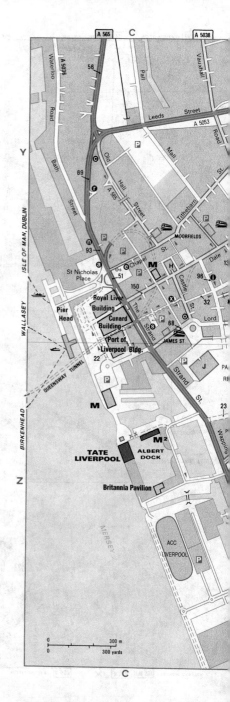

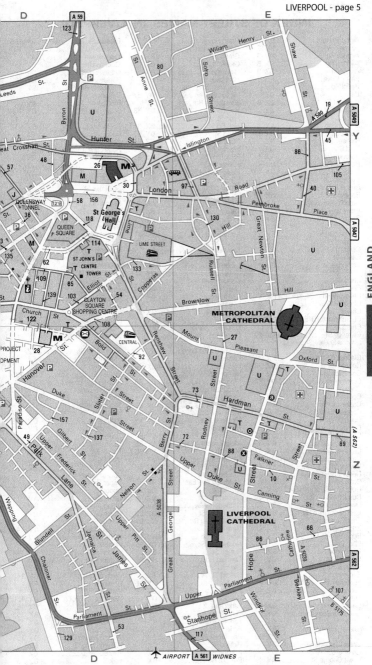

ENGLAND

INDEX OF STREET NAMES IN LIVERPOOL

Radisson SAS 🗔 🕸 ₤6 🗍 & rm, 🔃 ⑪ ₥ 🆅🆂🅰 🆎

107 Old Hall St ⊠ L3 9BD – ℰ (0151) 966 1500 – www.radissonsas.com
– info.liverpool@radissonsas.com – Fax (0151) 966 1501   CY**c**
189 rm – †£99/160 ††£99/160, ⊊ £15.95 – 5 suites
Rest *Filini* – (Closed Sunday) Menu £16 (lunch) – Carte £16/40
♦ Waterfront style: sleek meeting rooms and very well equipped leisure facilities. Chic bar in two Grade II listed cottages. Modern bedrooms themed "ocean" or "urban". Spacious dining room with Italian influenced menus.

Crowne Plaza Liverpool 🗔 🕸 ₤6 🗍 & rm, 🔃 ⑫ ⑪ ₥ 🅿

St Nicholas Pl, Princes Dock, Pier Head ⊠ L3 1QW   🆅🆂🅰 🆎 🅞
– ℰ (0151) 243 8000 – www.cpliverpool.com – sales@cpliverpool.com
– Fax (0151) 243 8070   CY**a**
155 rm ⊊ – †£129 ††£149 – 4 suites
Rest *Plaza Brasserie* – (closed lunch Saturday and Sunday) Menu £19 – Carte £28/40
♦ A busy conference venue within the popular dockside development. Enjoys views of the Mersey and the Liver Building. Well-appointed and very comfortable rooms. Spacious, informal ground floor brasserie.

Malmaison ₤6 🗍 & rm, 🔃 ⑪ ₥ 🆅🆂🅰 🆎 🅞

7 William Jessop Way, Princes Dock ⊠ L3 1QZ – ℰ (0151) 229 5000
– www.malmaison-liverpool.com – liverpool@malmaison.com
– Fax (0151) 229 5002   CY**n**
129 rm – †£99/150 ††£99/150, ⊊ £13.95 – 2 suites
Rest *Brasserie* – Menu £20 (dinner) – Carte £27/32
♦ Eye-catching building in redeveloped area of city. Smart, up-to-date bedrooms; those on the waterside have best outlook. Plum evening lounge. Look out for Beatles memorabilia. Stylish brasserie with glass-fronted wine cellar serves extensive menu of classic French dishes.

Hope Street 🗍 & ⑪ ₥ 🆅🆂🅰 🆎

40 Hope St ⊠ L1 9DA – ℰ (0151) 709 3000 – www.hopestreethotel.co.uk
– sleep@hopestreethotel.co.uk – Fax (0151) 709 2454   EZ**o**
41 rm – †£140 ††£165, ⊊ £15 – 6 suites
Rest *The London Carriage Works* – see restaurant listing
♦ Converted 19C city centre property with modern, stylish interior: leather furniture prominent. Contemporary bedrooms boast state-of-the-art facilities.

Hard Days Night 🗍 & rm, 🔃 ⑫ ⑪ ₥ 🆅🆂🅰 🆎

Central buildings, North John Street ⊠ L2 6RR – ℰ (0151) 236 1964
– www.harddaysnighthotel.com – info@harddaysnighthotel.com
– Fax (0151) 243 2154   CY**i**
110 rm – †£275 ††£275, ⊊ £15.95 – 2 suites
Rest *Blakes* – (closed 1 January and Sunday dinner) Menu £20 (lunch) – Carte £27/42
♦ Unique Beatles themed hotel; their story recounted in artwork from doorstep to rooftop, with every room featuring original works. Suites styled around Lennon and McCartney. Blakes restaurant features modern style brasserie menu.

62 Castle Street 🗍 ⑪ ₥ 🆅🆂🅰 🆎 🅞

62 Castle St ⊠ L2 7LQ – ℰ (0151) 702 7898 – www.62castlest.com
– reservations@62castlest.com – Fax (0151) 702 7899   CY**o**
20 rm – †£125 ††£125, ⊊ £10   **Rest** – Carte approx. £25
♦ Grade II listed Victorian building in city centre combines contemporary and period styles. Smart, spacious bedrooms, with high levels of comfort and facilities. Informal dining room serves extensive menus of international dishes.

Racquet Club 🕸 ₤6 🗍 🆅🆂🅰 🆎

Hargreaves Buildings, 5 Chapel St ⊠ L3 9AG – ℰ (0151) 236 6676
– www.racquetclub.org – info@racquetclub.org.uk – Fax (0151) 236 6870
– Closed Christmas and Bank Holidays   CY**e**
8 rm – †£140/180 ††£140/180, ⊊ £12
Rest *Ziba* – see restaurant listing
♦ Ornate Victorian city centre building converted into club offering unusual accommodation. Leisure facilities are a particularly strong point. Simple, well-equipped rooms.

ENGLAND

ENGLAND

XXX Panoramic ≤ AC VISA ⓜ AE ①

34th floor, West Tower, ⊠ L3 9PJ – ℰ (0151) 236 55 34
– www.panoramicliverpool.com – info@panoramicliverpool.com – Fax (0151)
227 43 96 – Closed lunch Saturday, Sunday and Bank Holidays   CYr
Rest – Menu £ 18 (lunch) – Carte £ 28/46
♦ Highest restaurant in the UK, with 360° views towards Wales, the coast, Liverpool
and the Mersey below. Cooking is creative, ambitious and well executed; good value
lunch.

XX 60 Hope Street AC ⓖ ⇔ VISA ⓜ AE

60 Hope St ⊠ L1 9BZ – ℰ (0151) 707 6060 – www.60hopestreet.com
– info@60hopestreet.com – Fax (0151) 707 6016
– Closed Saturday lunch, Sunday and Bank Holidays   EZx
Rest – Menu £ 18 (lunch) – Carte £ 32/48
♦ Modern restaurant within an attractive Grade II Georgian house. Informal base-
ment café-bar, brightly decorated dining room and private room above. Modern
European cooking.

XX The London Carriage Works – at Hope Street Hotel AC ⓖ VISA ⓜ AE ①

40 Hope St ⊠ L1 9DA – ℰ (0151) 705 2222 – www.hopestreethotel.co.uk
– eat@hopestreethotel.co.uk – Fax (0151) 709 2454   EZo
Rest – Menu £ 25 s – Carte £ 42/60 s
♦ Stylish twin dining options in eponymous venue: an informal brasserie and bar, or
impressive restaurant with strikingly prominent glass feature, and ambitious, seasonal menus.

XX Simply Heathcotes ⸜⸝ AC ⓖ ⇔ VISA ⓜ AE

Beetham Plaza, 25 The Strand ⊠ L2 0XL – ℰ (0151) 236 3536
– www.heathcotes.co.uk – liverpool@heathcotes.co.uk – Fax (0151) 236 3534
– Closed 25-26 December, 1 January and Bank Holidays   CYs
Rest – Carte £ 20/35
♦ Behind a sloping glass façade is a modish dining room where staff in emblemed
shirts serve variations on the classics: hash brown of black pudding. Views of water
sculpture.

XX The Restaurant bar and grill AC ⇔ VISA ⓜ AE ①

Halifax House, Brunswick Street ⊠ L2 0UU – ℰ (0151) 236 67 03
– www.therestaurantbarandgrill.co.uk – liverpool@ircplc.co.uk – Fax (0151)
236 67 21 – Closed 25 December and 1 January   CYr
Rest – Carte £ 21/39
♦ Spacious former banking hall, divided by huge glass wine racks. Large menu of
homemade produce; mainly modern European fare, with some British classics and
influences from Asia.

XX Ziba – at Racquet Club Hotel AC ⇔ VISA ⓜ AE

Hargreaves Buildings, 5 Chapel St ⊠ L3 9AG – ℰ (0151) 236 6676
– www.racquetclub.org – info@racquetclub.org.uk – Fax (0151) 236 6870 – Closed
Christmas, Saturday lunch, Sunday and Bank Holidays   CYe
Rest – Menu £ 18/22 s – Carte £ 30/46 s
♦ Modern restaurant in old Victorian building with huge windows and artwork on
walls. Small lunch menus, more extensive dinner menus, offering classic-based modern dishes.

XX Spire AC VISA ⓜ AE ①

1 Church Rd ⊠ L15 9EA – ℰ (0151) 734 5040 – www.spirerestaurant.co.uk
– spirerestaurant@btinternet.com – Fax (0151) 735 0058 – Closed Sunday and
lunch Monday and Saturday   BXa
Rest – Menu £ 12/15 – Carte £ 25/32
♦ Glass-fronted restaurant in residential area; large mirror, abstract modern art. First
floor best place to sit; window tables most popular. Unfussy modern British cooking.

X **The Side Door**   AC 🕸 VISA ⓪
*29a Hope St ⊠ L1 9BQ – ℰ (0151) 707 7888 – www.thesidedoor.co.uk
– Fax (0151) 707 7888*
– Closed 25-26 December, 1 January, Sunday and Bank Holidays   EZ**a**
Rest – Menu £ 18 (dinner) – Carte £ 19/28
♦ Victorian end of terrace ground floor and basement eatery with green painted brick and wood floors. Good value dishes are supplemented by a concise wine list.

at Blundellsands North : 7½ m. by A 565 - CY – ⊠ Liverpool

⌂ **The Blundellsands** without rest   🕸 📶 P VISA ⓪
*9 Elton Ave ⊠ L23 8UN – ℰ (0151) 924 6947 – www.bundellsands.info
– bsbb@blueyonder.co.uk – Fax (0151) 924 6947*
4 rm ⌑ – †£ 45/65 ††£ 79/85
♦ Large semi-detached guesthouse with residential setting. Comfortable guests' lounge; the bedrooms, chintz in style, are clean, well-kept and have lots of extra touches.

at Speke Southeast : 8¾ m. by A 561 - BX – ⊠ Liverpool

🏨 **Crowne Plaza Liverpool John Lennon Airport**   ▨ ⊛ 🏠
Speke Aerodrome, Speke   ƒ♦ ℀ 🍴 ♿ rm, AC 🕸 📶 ♨ P VISA ⓪ AE ⓪
*Rd, West : 1¾ m. on A 561 ⊠ L24 8QD – ℰ (0151) 494 5000
– www.crowneplaza.com/liverpoolarpt – events@liverpool.kewgreen.co.uk
– Fax (0151) 494 5050*
163 rm – †£ 104 ††£ 195, ⌑ £ 14.95 – 135 suites
Rest *Starways* – Menu £ 17 (lunch) – Carte £ 22/35
♦ Converted Art Deco airport terminal building, built 1937. Aviation and 1930s era the prevailing themes throughout. The modern, well-equipped bedrooms have a stylish appeal. Smart brasserie within original airport terminal; in keeping with hotel's style.

ENGLAND

LIZARD – Cornwall – 503 E 34   1 **A3**

▶ London 326 mi – Penzance 24 mi – Truro 29 mi
◧ Lizard Peninsula★ - Mullion Cove★★ (Church★) - Kynance Cove★★ - Cadgwith★ - Coverack★ - Cury★ (Church★) - Gunwalloe Fishing Cove★ - St Keverne (Church★) - Landewednack★ (Church★) – Mawgan-in-Meneage (Church★) - Ruan Minor (Church★) - St Anthony-in-Meneage★

⌂ **Housel Bay** ৩   ≤ 🖃 🍴 📶 P VISA ⓪ AE
*Housel Bay ⊠ TR12 7PG – ℰ (01326) 290 417 – www.houselbay.com
– info@houselbay.com – Fax (01326) 290 359 – Closed 2-16 January*
21 rm ⌑ – †£ 50/60 ††£ 80/140
Rest – (bar lunch Monday-Saturday) Carte £ 24/30
♦ Britain's most southerly mainland hotel, with spectacular views of Atlantic and Channel: the Cornish coastal path runs through its gardens. Comfortable bedrooms. Dining room affords dramatic sea and lighthouse views.

⌂ **Landewednack House** ৩   🖃 ⅂ 📶 P VISA ⓪ ⓪
*Church Cove, East : 1 m. by A 3083 ⊠ TR12 7PQ – ℰ (01326) 290 877
– www.landewednackhouse.com – luxurybandb@landewednackhouse.com
– Fax (01326) 290 192*
4 rm ⌑ – †£ 110/150 ††£ 130/190   **Rest** – (communal dining) Menu 38
♦ Part 17C former rectory and garden, overlooking Church Cove. Smart interiors stylishly furnished with antiques. Diners encouraged to discuss menus: best local produce to hand.

⌂ **Tregullas House** without rest ৩   ≤ 🖃 P
Housel Bay ⊠ TR12 7PF – ℰ (01326) 290 351 – March-November
3 rm ⌑ – †£ 28/45 ††£ 60
♦ Simple guesthouse in a charming location with mature garden and sea vista. Spotlessly kept with a cottage style. Uncluttered bedrooms. At breakfast, take in the garden view.

MICHELIN

LONDON

PRACTICAL INFORMATION

🛈 Tourist Information
Britain & London Visitor Centre, 1 Regent St, W1 ☏ (020) 8846 9000, bvlcenquiry@visitlondon.com

Airports
🛧 **Heathrow** ☏ 0870 000 0123 **12 AX** Terminal: Airbus (A1) from Victoria, Airbus (A2) from Paddington Underground (Piccadilly line) frequent service daily.

🛧 **Gatwick** ☏ 08700 002468 **13**: by A23 EZ and M23 - Terminal: Coach service from Victoria Coach Station (Flightline 777, hourly service) - Railink (Gatwick Express) from Victoria (24 h service).

🛧 **London City Airport** ☏ (020) 7646 0088 **11 HV**

🛧 **Stansted**, at Bishop's Stortford ☏ 08700 000303, NE: 34m **11** by M11 JT and A12O.

Banks
Open, generally 9.30 am to 4.30 pm weekdays (except public holidays). You need ID (passport) for cashing cheques. Banks levy smaller commissions than hotels. Many `Bureaux de Change` around Piccadilly open 7 days.

Medical Emergencies
To contact a doctor for first aid, emergency medical advice and chemists night service: ☏ 07000 372255.

Accident & Emergency: dial 999 for Ambulance, Police or Fire Services.

Post Offices
Open Monday to Friday 9am to 5.30 pm. Late collections made from Leicester Square.

Shopping
Most stores are found in Oxford Street (Selfridges, M & S), Regent Street (Hamleys, Libertys) and Knightsbridge (Harrods, Harvey Nichols). Open usually Monday to Saturday 9 am to 6 pm. Some open later (8 pm) once a week; Knightsbridge Wednesday, Oxford Street and Regent Street Thursday. Other areas worth visiting include Jermyn Street and Savile Row (mens outfitters), Bond Street (jewellers and haute couture).

Theatres
The «West End» has many major theatre performances and can generally be found around Shaftesbury Avenue. Most daily newspapers give details of performances. A half-price ticket booth is located in Leicester Square and is open Monday to Saturday 1 pm to 6.30 pm, Sunday and matinée days 12 noon to 6.30 pm. Restrictions apply.

Tipping
When a service charge is included in a bill it is not necessary to tip extra. If service is not included between 10-15% is normal.

Travel
As driving in London is difficult, it is advisable to take the Underground, a bus or taxi. Taxis can be hailed when the amber light is illuminated.

Congestion Charging

The congestion charge is £8 per day on all vehicles (except motor cycles and exempt vehicles) entering the central zone between 7.00 am and 6.00 pm - Monday to Friday except on Bank Holldays.

Payment can be made in advance, on the day, by post, on the Internet, by telephone (0845 900 1234) or at retail outlets.

A charge of up to £100 will be made for non-payment.

Further information is available on the Transport for London website - www.cclondon.com

Localities outside the Greater London limits are listed alphabetically throughout the guide.

Les localités situées en dehors des limites de Greater London se trouvent à leur place alphabetique dans le guide.

Alle Städte und Gemeinden außerhalb von Greater London sind in alphabetischer Reihenfolge aufgelistet.

Le località situate al di fuori dei confini della Greater London sono ordinate alfabeticamente all'interno della Guida.

◉ SIGHTS

HISTORICAL BUILDINGS AND MONUMENTS

Palace of Westminster ★★★: House of Lords ★★, Westminster Hall ★ (hammerbeam roof ★★★), Robing Room ★, Central Lobby ★, House of Commons ★, Big Ben ★, Victoria Tower ★ 39 ALX - Tower of London ★★★ (Crown Jewels ★★★, White Tower or Keep ★★★, St John's Chapel ★★) - British Airways London Eye (views ★★★) 32 AMV.
Banqueting House ★★ 31 ALV - Buckingham Palace ★★ (Changing of the Guard, Royal Mews ★★, Queen's Gallery ★★) 38 AIX - Kensington Palace ★★ 27 ABV - Lincoln's Inn ★★ 32 AMT - Lloyds Building ★★ 34 ARU - Royal Hospital Chelsea ★★ 37 AGZ - St James`s Palace ★★ 30 AJV - Somerset House ★★ 32 AMU - South Bank Arts Centre ★★ (Royal Festival Hall ★, National Theatre Royal ★, County Hall ★) 32 AMV - Spencer House ★★ 30 AIV - The Temple ★★ (Middle Temple Hall ★★) 32 ANU - Tower Bridge ★★ 34 ASV.

Albert Memorial ★ 36 ADX - Apsley House ★ 30 AHV - Burlington House ★ 30 AIV - Charterhouse ★ 19 UZD - George Inn ★, Southwark 33 AQV - Gray's Inn ★ 32 AMV - Guildhall ★ (Lord Mayor's Show) 33 AQT - Shakespeare`s Globe ★ 33 APV - Dr Johnson's House ★ 32 ANT - Leighton House ★ 35 AAX - Linley Sambourne House ★ 35 AAX - London Bridge ★ 34 ARV - Mansion House ★ (plate and insignia ★★) 33 AQV - The Monument ★ (❋ ★) 34 ARU - Old Admiralty ★ 31 AKV - Royal Albert Hall ★ 36 ADX - Royal Exchange ★ 34 ARU - Royal Opera House ★ (Covent Garden) 31 ALU - Staple Inn ★ 32 ANT - Theatre Royal ★ (Haymarket) 31 AKV - Westminster Bridge ★ 39 ALX.

CHURCHES

The City Churches
St Paul's Cathedral ★★★ (Dome ≤ ★★★) 33 APU.
St Bartholomew the Great ★★ (choir ★) 33 APT - St Dunstan-in-the-East ★ (Tower ★) 34 ARU - St Mary-at-Hill ★★ (plan ★) 34 ARU - Temple Church ★★ 32 ANU.

All Hallows-by-the-Tower (font cover★★, brasses★) **34 ARU** - Christ Church★ **33 APT** - Cole Abbey Presbyterian Church (spire★) **33 APU** - St Andrew Undershaft (monuments★) **34 ARU** - St Bride★ (steeple★★) **32 ANU** - St Clement Eastcheap (pulpit★) **34 ARU** - St Edmund the King and Martyr (spire★) **34 ARU** - St Giles Cripplegate★ **33 AQT** - St Helen Bishopsgate★ (monuments★★) **34 ART** - St James Garlickhythe (spire★, sword rests★) **33 AQU** - St Magnus the Martyr (tower★, sword rest★) **34 ARU** - St Margaret Lothbury★ (spire★, woodwork★, screen★, font★) **33 AQT** - St Margaret Pattens (spire★, woodwork★) **34 ARU** - St Martin-within-Ludgate (spire★, door cases★) **33 APU** - St Mary Abchurch★ (reredos★, spire★, dome★) **33 AQU** - St Mary-le-Bow (steeple★★) **33 AQU** - St Michael Paternoster Royal (spire★) **35 AQU** - St Olave★ **34 ARU** - St Peter upon Cornhill (screen★) **34 ARU** - St Stephen Walbrook★ (steeple★, dome★) **33 AQU**.

Other Churches

Westminster Abbey★★★ (Henry VII Chapel★★★, Chapel of Edward the Confessor★★, Chapter House★★, Poets'Corner★) **39 ALX**. Southwark Cathedral★★ **33 AQV**. Queen's Chapel★ **39 AJV** - St Clement Danes★ **32 AMU** - St James's★ **30 AJV** - St Margaret's★ **39 ALX** - St Martin-in-the-Fields★ **31 ALV** - St Paul's★ (Covent Garden) **31 ALU** - Westminster Roman Catholic Cathedral★ **39 ALX**.

PARKS

Regent's Park★★★ (terraces★★, Zoo★★) **11 QZC**. Hyde Park **29 AFV** - Kensington Gardens★★ **28 ACV** (Orangery★) **27 ABV** - St James's Park★★ **31 AKV**.

STREETS AND SQUARES

The City★★★ **33 AQT**. Bedford Square★★ **31 AKT** - Belgrave Square★★ **37 AGX** - Burlington Arcade★ **30 AIV** - Covent Garden★★ (The Piazza★★) **31 ALU** - The Mall★★ **31 AKV** - Piccadilly★ **30 AIV** - Trafalgar Square★★ **31 AKV** - Whitehall★★ (Horse Guards★) **31 ALV**. Barbican★ **33 AQT** - Bond Street★ **30 AIU** - Canonbury Square★ **13 UZB** - Carlton House Terrace★ **31 AKV** - Cheyne Walk★ **23 PZG** - Fitzroy Square★ **18 RZD** - Jermyn Street★ **30 AJV** - Leicester Square★ **31 AKU** - Merrick Square★ **19 VZE** - Montpelier Square★ **37 AFX** - Neal's Yard★ **31 ALU** - Piccadilly Arcade★ **30 AIV** - Piccadilly Circus★ **31 AKU** - Portman Square★ **29 AGT** - Regent Street★ **30 AIU** - Royal Opera Arcade★ **31 AKV** - St James's Square★ **31 AJV** - St James's Street★ **30 AIV** - Shepherd Market★ **30 AHV** - Trinity Church Square★ **19 VZE** - Victoria Emban kment Gardens★ **31 ALV** - Waterloo Place★ **31 AKV**.

MUSEUMS

British Museum★★★ **31 AKL** - Imperial War Museum★★★ **40 ANY** - National Gallery★★★ **31 AKV** - Science Museum★★★ **36 ADX** - Tate Britain★★★ **39 ALY** - Victoria and Albert Museum★★★ **36 ADY** - Wallace Collection★★★ **29 AGT**. Courtauld Institute Galleries★★ (Somerset House) **32 AMU** - Gilbert Collection★★ (Somerset House) **32 AMU** - Museum of London★★ **33 APT** - National Portrait Gallery★★ **31 AKU** - Natural History Museum★★ **36 ADY** - Sir John Soane's Museum★★ **32 AMT** - Tate Modern★★ (views★★★ from top floors) **33 APV**. Clock Museum★ (Guildhall) **33 AQT** - London`s Transport Museum★ **31 ALU** - Madame Tussaud's Waxworks★ **17 QZD** - National Army Museum★ **37 AGZ** - Percival David Foundation of Chinese Art★ **18 SZD** - Wellington Museum★ (Apsley House) **30 AHV**.

393

OUTER LONDON

Blackheath 8 HX terraces and houses★, Eltham Palace★ **A**
Brentford 5 BX Syon Park★★, gardens★
Bromley 7 GXY The Crystal Palace Park★
Chiswick 6 CV Chiswick Mall★★, Chiswick House★ **D**, Hogarth's House★ **E**
Dulwich 11 Picture Gallery★ F**X**X
Greenwich 7 and 8 GHV Cutty Sark★★ GV**F**, Footway Tunnel (⬅ ★★), Fan Museum★ 10 GV**A**, National Maritime Museum★★ (Queen's House★★) GV**M²** Royal Naval College★★ (Painted Hall★, the Chapel★) GV**G**, The Park and Old Royal Observatory★ (Meridian Building: collection★★) HV**K**, Ranger's House★ (Wernher Collection) GX**N**
Hampstead Kenwood House★★ (Adam Library★★, paintings★★) 2 EU**P**, Fenton House★★ 11 PZ**A**
Hampton Court 5 BY (The Palace★★★, gardens★★★, Fountain Court★, The Great Vine★)

Kew 6 CX Royal Botanic Gardens★★★: Palm House★★, Temperate House★, Kew Palace or Dutch House★★, Orangery★, Pagoda★, Japanese Gateway★
Hendon★ 2 Royal Air Force Museum★★ CT**M³**
Hounslow 5 BV Osterley Park★★
Lewisham 7 GX Horniman Museum★ **M⁴**
Richmond 5 and 6 CX Richmond Park★★, ⚜ ★★★ CX, Richmond Hill ⚜ ★★ CX, Richmond Bridge★★ BX**R**, Richmond Green★★ BX**S**, (Maids of Honour Row★★, Trumpeter's House★), Asgill House★ BX**B**, Ham House★★ BX**V**
Shoreditch 14 XZ Beffrye Museum★ **M**
Tower Hamlets 7 GV Canary Wharf★★ **B**, Isle of Dogs★ St Katharine Dock★ 34 AS**V**
Twickenham 5 BX Marble Hill House★ **Z**, Strawberry Hill★ **A**

The maps in this section of the Guide are based upon the Ordnance Survey of Great Britain with the permission of the Controller of Her Majesty's Stationery Office. © Crown Copyright 100000247

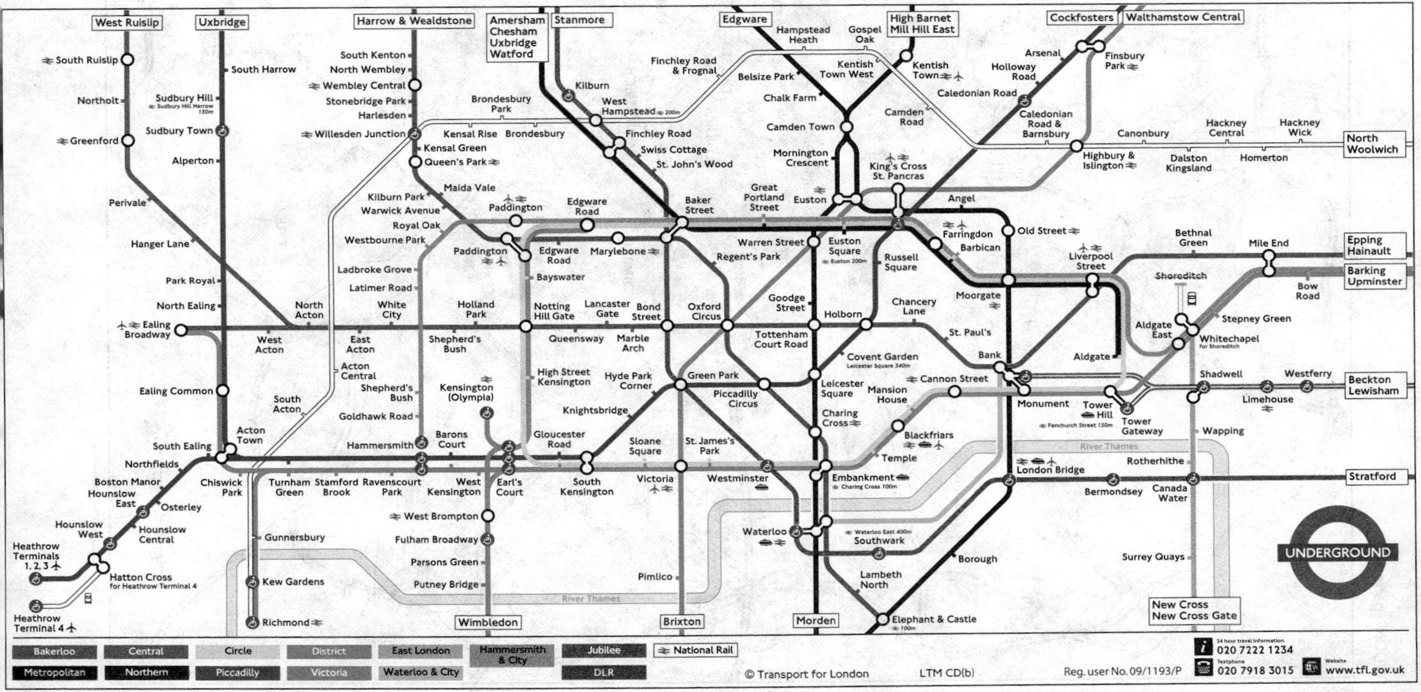

West Ruislip
Uxbridge
Harrow & Wealdstone
Amersham Chesham Uxbridge Watford
Stanmore
Edgware
High Barnet Mill Hill East
Cockfosters
Walthamstow Central
North Woolwich
Epping Hainault
Barking Upminster
Beckton Lewisham
Stratford
New Cross New Cross Gate
Wimbledon
Brixton
Morden
South Ruislip
Northolt
Greenford
South Harrow
Sudbury Hill
Sudbury Hill Harrow 150m
Sudbury Town
Alperton
Perivale
Hanger Lane
Park Royal
North Ealing
Ealing Broadway
Ealing Common
South Ealing
Northfields
Boston Manor
Osterley
Hounslow East
Hounslow Central
Hounslow West
Hatton Cross
for Heathrow Terminal 4
Heathrow Terminals 1, 2, 3
Heathrow Terminal 4
Acton Town
Chiswick Park
Turnham Green
Stamford Brook
Ravenscourt Park
Hammersmith
Barons Court
West Kensington
Earl's Court
Gunnersbury
Kew Gardens
Richmond
West Brompton
Fulham Broadway
Parsons Green
Putney Bridge
South Acton
Acton Central
Shepherd's Bush
Goldhawk Road
Kensington (Olympia)
West Acton
North Acton
East Acton
White City
Holland Park
Notting Hill Gate
Queensway
Lancaster Gate
Marble Arch
Bond Street
Oxford Circus
Tottenham Court Road
Holborn
Chancery Lane
St. Paul's
Bank
Liverpool Street
Bethnal Green
Mile End
South Kenton
North Wembley
Wembley Central
Stonebridge Park
Harlesden
Willesden Junction
Kensal Green
Queen's Park
Kilburn Park
Maida Vale
Warwick Avenue
Paddington
Edgware Road
Marylebone
Baker Street
Regent's Park
Oxford Circus
Piccadilly Circus
Charing Cross
Embankment
Waterloo
Lambeth North
Elephant & Castle
Elephant & Castle 100m
Royal Oak
Westbourne Park
Ladbroke Grove
Latimer Road
Bayswater
High Street Kensington
Gloucester Road
South Kensington
Sloane Square
Victoria
St. James's Park
Westminster
Temple
Blackfriars
Mansion House
Cannon Street
Monument
Fenchurch Street 150m
Tower Hill
Tower Gateway
Aldgate
Aldgate East
Whitechapel
for Shoreditch
Shoreditch
Stepney Green
Bow Road
Shadwell
Wapping
Rotherhithe
Canada Water
Surrey Quays
Limehouse
Westferry
Kensal Rise
Brondesbury Park
Brondesbury
West Hampstead
West Hampstead 200m
Finchley Road & Frognal
Hampstead Heath
Gospel Oak
Kentish Town West
Kentish Town
Camden Road
Caledonian Road & Barnsbury
Highbury & Islington
Canonbury
Dalston Kingsland
Hackney Central
Homerton
Hackney Wick
Kilburn
Finchley Road
Swiss Cottage
St. John's Wood
Belsize Park
Chalk Farm
Camden Town
Mornington Crescent
Euston
King's Cross St. Pancras
Great Portland Street
Euston Square
Euston 200m
Warren Street
Goodge Street
Russell Square
Angel
Old Street
Farringdon
Barbican
Moorgate
Arsenal
Holloway Road
Caledonian Road
Finsbury Park
Hyde Park Corner
Green Park
Knightsbridge
Leicester Square
Covent Garden
Leicester Square 340m
Charing Cross 100m
Waterloo East 400m
Southwark
Borough
London Bridge
Bermondsey
Pimlico
River Thames
UNDERGROUND
Bakerloo
Central
Circle
District
East London
Hammersmith & City
Jubilee
National Rail
Metropolitan
Northern
Piccadilly
Victoria
Waterloo & City
DLR
© Transport for London
LTM CD(b)
Reg. user No. 09/1193/P
24 hour travel information
020 7222 1234
Textphone
020 7918 3015
Website
www.tfl.gov.uk

LONDON

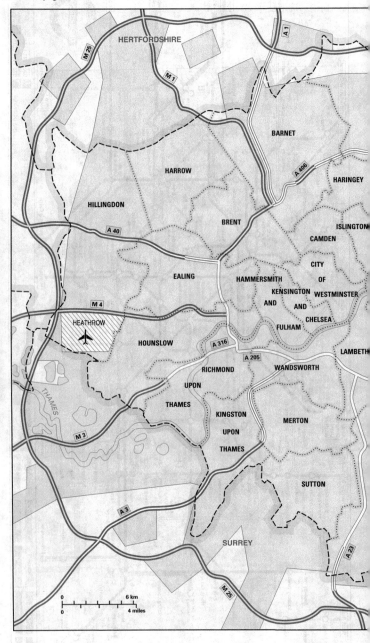

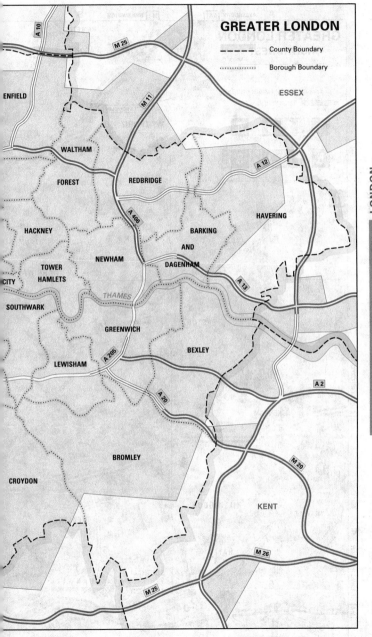

GREATER LONDON

- - - - County Boundary
· · · · · · · Borough Boundary

ESSEX

ENFIELD

WALTHAM

FOREST

REDBRIDGE

HAVERING

HACKNEY

BARKING

AND

NEWHAM

DAGENHAM

TOWER

HAMLETS

CITY

SOUTHWARK

THAMES

GREENWICH

BEXLEY

LEWISHAM

BROMLEY

CROYDON

KENT

A 10

M 25

M 11

A 12

A 406

A 13

A 205

A 20

A 2

M 20

M 26

M 25

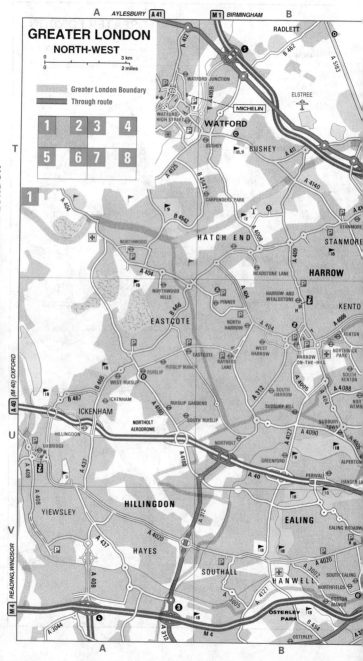

GREATER LONDON
NORTH-WEST

3 km
2 miles

Greater London Boundary
Through route

| 1 | 2 | 3 | 4 |
| 5 | 6 | 7 | 8 |

AYLESBURY A 41 M 1 BIRMINGHAM

RADLETT

B 462

A 5183

A 412

WATFORD JUNCTION

ELSTREE

A 4008

MICHELIN

WATFORD HIGH STREET

WATFORD

BUSHEY

BUSHEY A 411

A 4140

A 4125

B 4542

CARPENDERS PARK

HATCH END

A 4008

STANMORE

A 404

NORTHWOOD

A 404

HEADSTONE LANE

A 409

HARROW

NORTHWOOD HILLS

PINNER

A 404

HARROW AND WEALDSTONE

KENTON

B 466

EASTCOTE

NORTH HARROW

A 404

KENTON

A 4006

WEST HARROW

HARROW ON-THE-HILL

NORTHWICK PARK

SOUTH KENTON

EASTCOTE

RAYNERS LANE

A 4005

A 4088

RUISLIP MANOR

A 312

SOUTH HARROW

A 404

NORTH WEMB

B 467

WEST RUISLIP

RUISLIP

ICKENHAM

SUDBURY HILL

SUDBURY TOWN

A 4127

A 4090

A 400

B 467

ICKENHAM

A 4180

RUISLIP GARDENS

SOUTH RUISLIP

NORTHOLT AERODROME

HILLINGDON

UXBRIDGE

A 437

NORTHOLT

A 4180

GREENFORD

A 40

PERIVALE

ALPERTON

HANGER LA

A 408

YIEWSLEY

A 437

HILLINGDON

A 4020

HAYES

A 312

EALING

EALING BROADW

A 408

SOUTHALL

HANWELL

A 4020

SOUTH EALING

NORTHFIELDS

BOSTON MANOR

M 4

READING, WINDSOR

A 3044

A 408

A 3005

A 4127

A 3002

OSTERLEY PARK

B 454

M 4

OSTERLEY

A 40 (M 40) OXFORD

A 40

LONDON

398

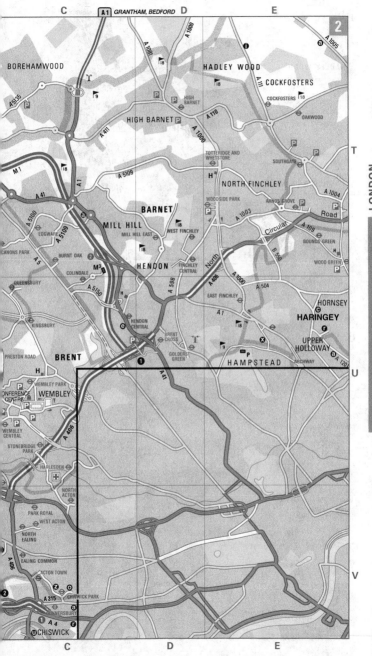

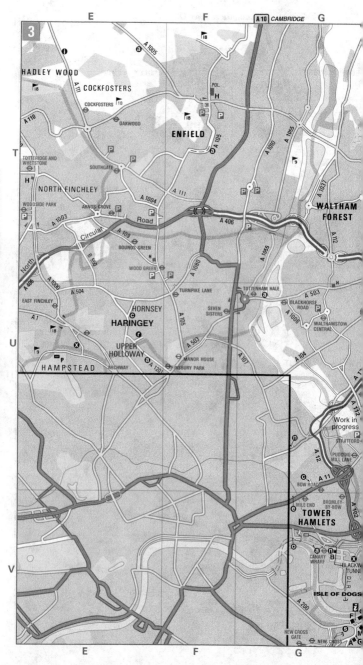

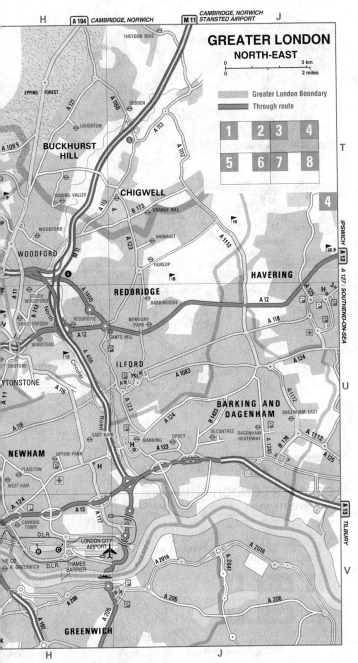

GREATER LONDON
NORTH-EAST

0 ——— 3 km
0 ——— 2 miles

Greater London Boundary
Through route

| 1 | 2 | 3 | 4 |
| 5 | 6 | 7 | 8 |

LONDON

Map labels:

A 104 CAMBRIDGE, NORWICH
M 11 CAMBRIDGE, NORWICH STANSTED AIRPORT

THEYDON BOIS
EPPING FOREST
A 121
A 1168
DEBDEN
LOUGHTON
A 1069
BUCKHURST HILL
A 113
RODING VALLEY
CHIGWELL
A 1112
B 173
GRANGE HILL
WOODFORD
A 123
HAINAULT
WOODFORD
FAIRLOP
M 11
HAVERING
SOUTH WOODFORD
A 1400
REDBRIDGE
A 125
A 12
J
BARKINGSIDE
REDBRIDGE
NEWBURY PARK
A 118
A 11 North
A 13
A 12
GANTS HILL
SNARESBROOK
WANSTEAD
A 406
IPSWICH A 12
A 127: SOUTHEND-ON-SEA
LEYTONSTONE
LEYTONSTONE
A 11
A 116
ILFORD
A 1083
A 124
Circular
POL
A 123
BARKING AND DAGENHAM
DAGENHAM EAST
A 1112
Road
A 118
EAST HAM
A 124
B 1335
BECONTREE
DAGENHAM HEATHWAY
B 178
A 1240
A 1112
NEWHAM
UPTON PARK
BARKING
UPNEY
A 125
A 123
PLAISTOW
WEST HAM
A 124
A 13
A 13 TILBURY
CANNING TOWN
D.L.R.
A 117
THE O2
N. GREENWICH D.L.R.
LONDON CITY AIRPORT
A 2016
A 2016
A 2041
THAMES BARRIER
A 206
A 206
A 206
A 102
A 205
GREENWICH

H   J

401

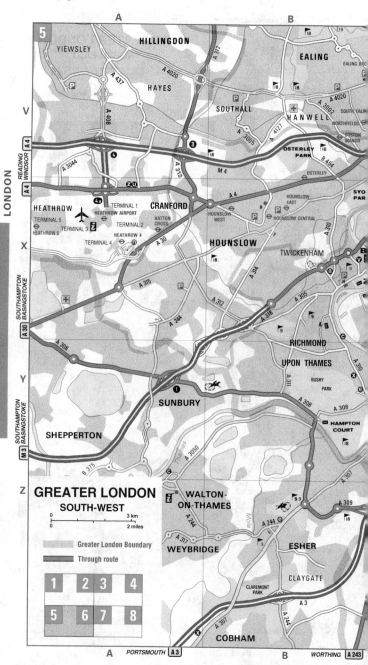

LONDON

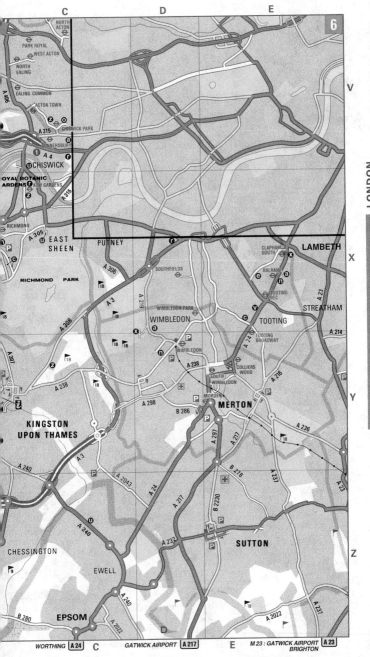

6

C   D   E

V

X

Y

Z

NORTH ACTON
PARK ROYAL
WEST ACTON
NORTH EALING
A 406
EALING COMMON
ACTON TOWN
A 315
GUNNERSBURY
CHISWICK PARK
A 4
CHISWICK
ROYAL BOTANIC GARDENS
KEW GARDENS
A 316
RICHMOND
A 305
EAST SHEEN
PUTNEY
LAMBETH
CLAPHAM SOUTH
RICHMOND PARK
A 306
SOUTHFIELDS
BALHAM
STREATHAM
TOOTING BEC
A 23
A 3
A 219
WIMBLEDON PARK
WIMBLEDON
TOOTING
A 214
A 308
A 307
18
18
18
18
WIMBLEDON
TOOTING BROADWAY
A 238
A 238
A 298
SOUTH WIMBLEDON
COLLIERS WOOD
A 24
A 216
MORDEN
MERTON
A 236
KINGSTON UPON THAMES
B 286
A 297
A 217
18
A 240
A 3
A 2043
A 24
A 217
B 278
B 2230
A 231
A 23
A 240
CHESSINGTON
EWELL
A 232
SUTTON
9
A 240
A 2022
18
EPSOM
B 280
A 2022
A 2022
18

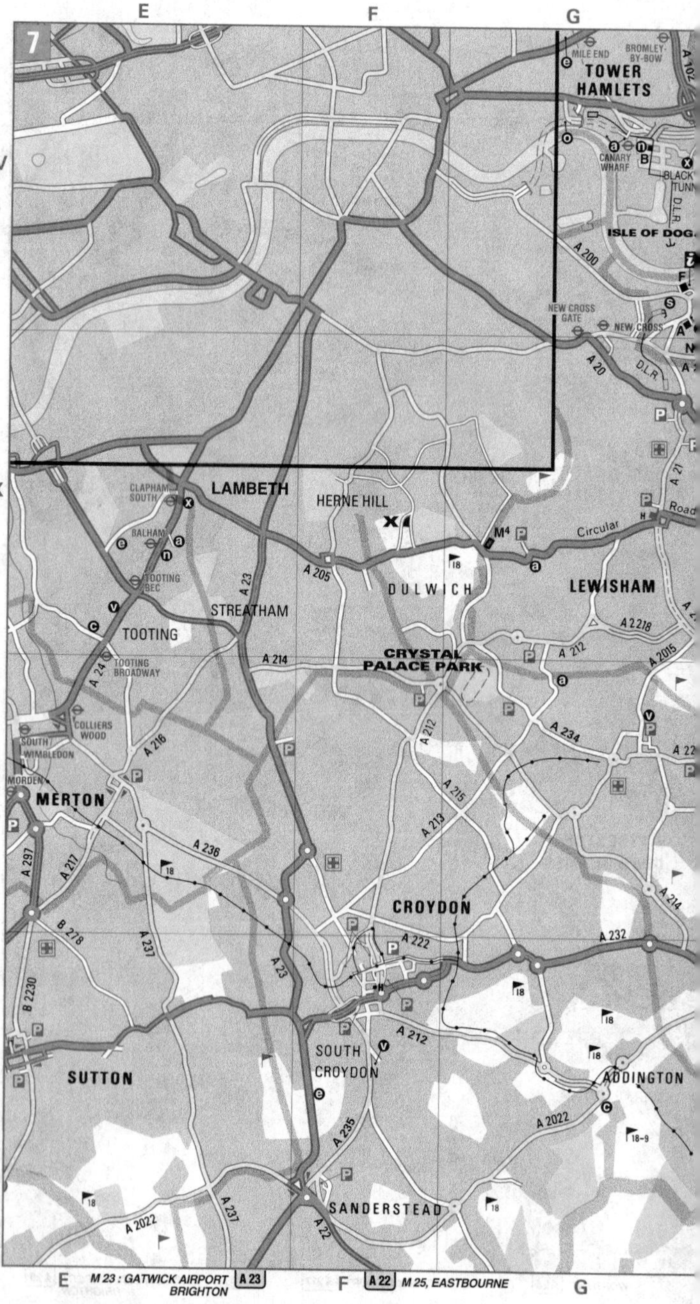

LONDON

7

E   F   G

V

X

Y

Z

MILE END

BROMLEY BY-BOW

TOWER HAMLETS

A 701

A 702

CANARY WHARF

BLACK TUN

ISLE OF DOG.

A 200

NEW CROSS GATE

NEW CROSS

DLR

A 20

A 21

Road

Circular

LEWISHAM

A 2218

A 205

A 212

CLAPHAM SOUTH

LAMBETH

HERNE HILL

M 4

BALHAM

TOOTING BEC

STREATHAM

A 23

DULWICH

A 18

TOOTING

TOOTING BROADWAY

A 24

A 214

CRYSTAL PALACE PARK

A 212

A 234

A 22

COLLIERS WOOD

SOUTH WIMBLEDON

A 216

A 212

A 215

MORDEN

MERTON

A 297

A 217

A 236

A 213

A 214

B 278

A 18

A 23

CROYDON

A 222

A 232

B 2230

A 237

A 212

SUTTON

SOUTH CROYDON

A 212

ADDINGTON

A 18

A 235

A 2022

A 18-9

A 18

A 2022

A 237

SANDERSTEAD

A 22

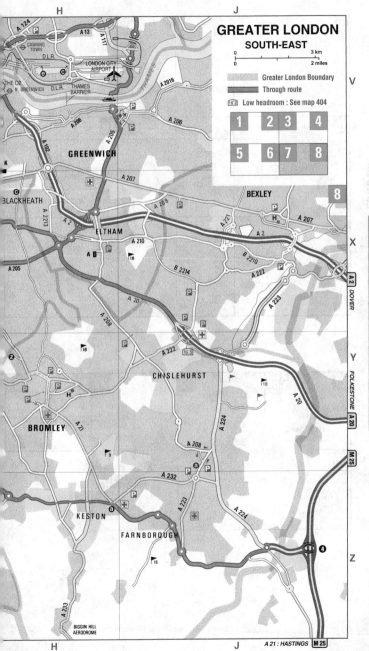

GREATER LONDON
SOUTH-EAST

| 0 | | 3 km |
| 0 | | 2 miles |

Greater London Boundary

Through route

16.2 Low headroom : See map 404

| 1 | 2 | 3 | 4 |
| 5 | 6 | 7 | 8 |

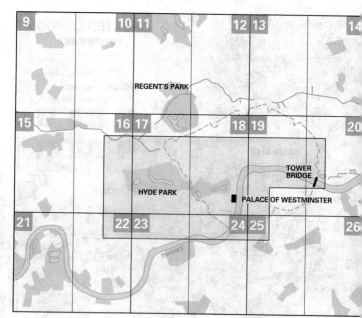

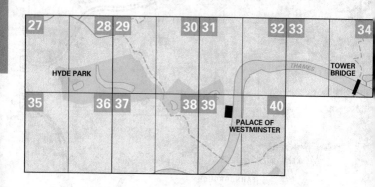

INDEX OF STREET NAMES IN LONDON CENTRE

LONDON

LONDON

409

LONDON

LONDON

LONDON

LONDON

LONDON

9

LONDON

Brent Reservoir

A 406

North Circular Road

Crest Avenue

Coles Green Rd

Edgware Rd

A 5

Brook Rd

Lane

Cricklewood

Tanfield

Dollis Hill

NEASDEN JUNCTION

ZA

A 4088

Dudden

Neasden

Neasden

GLADSTONE PARK

BRENT

Mora Rd

Sneyd Rd

Kendal Rd

Park Ave North

Anson Road

Hill

Burnley Road

Sherrick Green Rd

Dollis Hill

15.3

Denzil Road

Chapter Road

Willesden Green

High Road

Lane

Pound

WILLESDEN GREEN

e

High Road

a

Walm

Road

482

Roundwood Road

WILLESDEN CEMETERY

A 407

357

P

Brondesbury

Rd

Church

Peter Ave

KILBURN

Sidmouth

Mount Pleasant

ZB

351

196

ROUNDWOOD PARK

Harlesden Road

Donnington Road

Chamberlayne

A 404

352

Manor Park Rd

Doyle

Avenue

Hardinge Rd

480

Road

Acton Lane

P

High Street

Wrottesley

Road

All Souls Gdns

College

Clifford Gdns

KEN RIS

Harley Road

Furness Road

Bathurst Gdns

Rd

ZC

Oak Lane

Willesden Junction

Harrow Road

Mortime

A 404

Kensal Grê

Harrow

K

15

L

10

M N O

0   500 m
0   500 yards

CHILD'S HILL

Vale

Hendon Way

A 41

Claremont

The

475

BARNET

476

Cricklewood La.

Lyndale Ave

Finchley Rd

Hermitage La.

West Heath Road

477

● c

Platt's La.

FENTON HOUS

Road

Lane

CRICKLEWOOD

Cricklewood

A 407

Lichfield Rd

Redington Road

Frognal

ZA LONDON

U

Finchley

Heath Drive

Anson Rd

Shoot

Westbere Rd

Mill

West End

Road

Frognal Lane

Palm Lane

Up

Hill

Lane

Crediton Hill

Finchley

A 41

Arkwrig

gnmouth Road

Road

● a

Lane

FINCHLEY ROAD AND FROGNAL

Chatsworth

Kilburn

Road

Iverson

Rd

WEST HAMPSTEAD

Finchl Road

Willesden

Mapesbury

Cavendish

Ave

● a

14.9

West Hampstead

West End Lane

Broadhurst Gdns

Park

A 4003

Lane

Avenue

BRONDESBURY

15.9

Dyne Rd

Kilburn

A 5

Gascony Ave

478

Fairhazel

Canfield

Greencroft

FINCHLEY ROAD

stone Rd

Christchurch

The

Salusbury

Willesden

Lane

High

479

Abbey

Quex

Priory

Rd

Road

Road

Belsize

ZB

Tiverton

Avenue

BRONDESBURY PARK

Rd

Kingswood

PADDINGTON CEMETERY

Road

Brondesbury

Villas

Road

Road

Bound

Chevening

Milman

Rd

● b

QUEEN'S PARK

POL

Brondesbury

335

KILBURN HIGH ROAD

● c

Greville Pl.

● a

Abb

Carlton

Maida

Hamilton

Chamberlayne

Ave

Harvist

Road

Queen's Park

Lane

Kilburn

Carlton

Kilburn Park

336

Randolph

Vale

● a

Rd

Brayington

Fernhead

Kilburn Park

Ave

Avenue

ZC

Maida Vale

Randol

Elgin

● X

Road

Shir

16

M N O

417

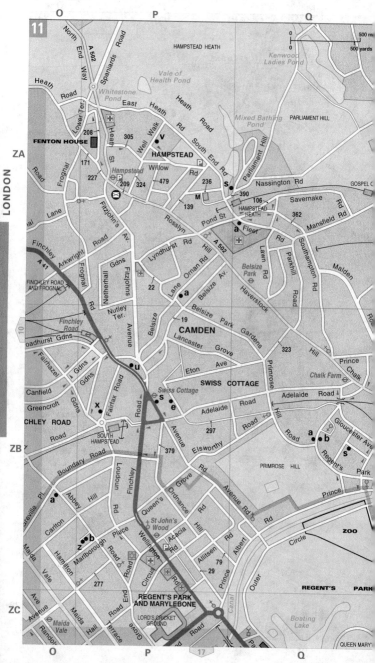

R
S
T
12
Archway
Holloway
Road
UPPER
HOLLOWAY
A 1
Hornsey
Tollington
Park
Tollington Way
Sisters
DARTMOUTH
PARK
Dartmouth
Park
Hill
Junction
Lane
Chetwynd Road
Tufnell
Park
Tufnell Park Road
Holloway
Seven
Hornsey
A 503
ZA
Dalmeny Rd
Dalmeny Ave
Carleton Rd
Parkhurst Road
Caledonian
Road
Highgate
Rd
Fortess Road
Lady Margaret Rd
Leighton Rd
Kentish Town
A 400
Islip Street
Busby Place
Gaisford Street
Patshull Road
Spring Place
Willes Road
KENTISH TOWN
Wales Road
16
Torriano Ave
Camden Road
Hillmarton Road
Hungerford Road
North Road
Caledonian Road
Mackenzie
Roman
ISLING
A 503
York Way
Market Road
Brewery Road
A 5200
A 5203
CALEDONIAN AND BARNSB
13
Town
St Pancras
Camden
Agar Grove
Farm
CAMDEN ROAD
366
Way
Offord
Richmo
ZB
Road
Kentish
Camden Town
Camden Rd
Royal
Camden
St
Pancras Way
College
Pratt St
Parkway
Camden High St
Street
Rd
Delancey St
York
Copenhagen St
Road
Outer
Park Village East
Albany
Crowndale Rd
Pancras Rd
Mornington Crescent
Hampstead
Eversholt
M
455
Caledonian
Calshot St
Pentonville
KING'S CROSS
ST PANCRAS
BRITISH LIBRARY
Midland Rd
Ossulston St
Street
Pancras Rd
Way
King's
417
ZC
TERRACES
REGENT'S PARK
Circle
Robert Street
Chester Rd
St
Road
EUSTON
Euston
Judd
H
Cross
18
LONDON

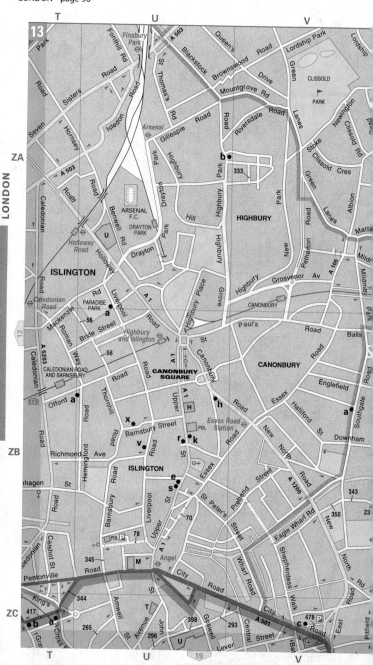

LONDON

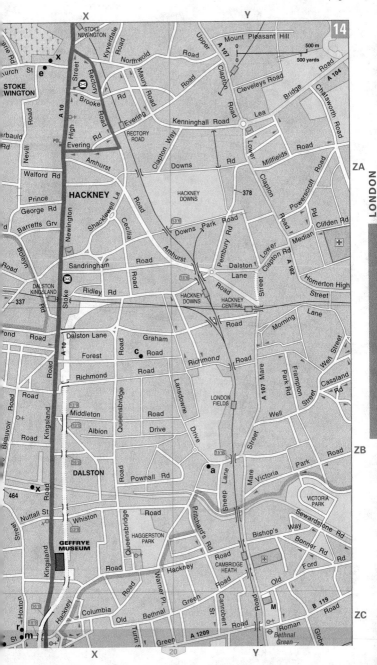

14

ZA

ZB

ZC

X

Y

500 m
500 yards

421

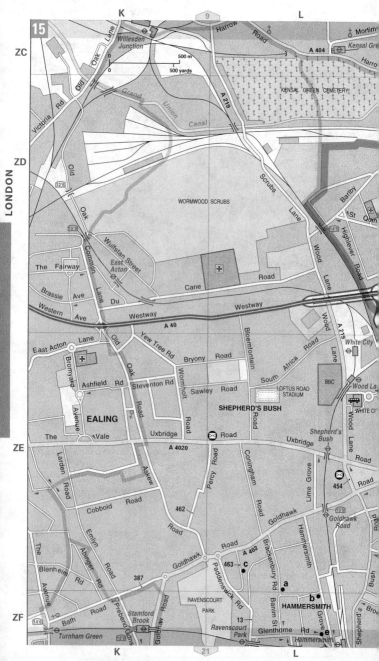

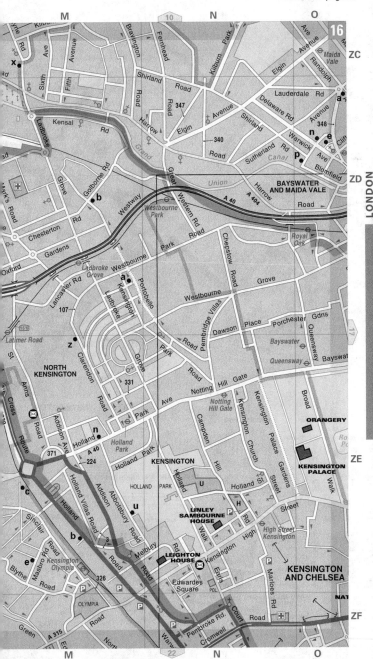

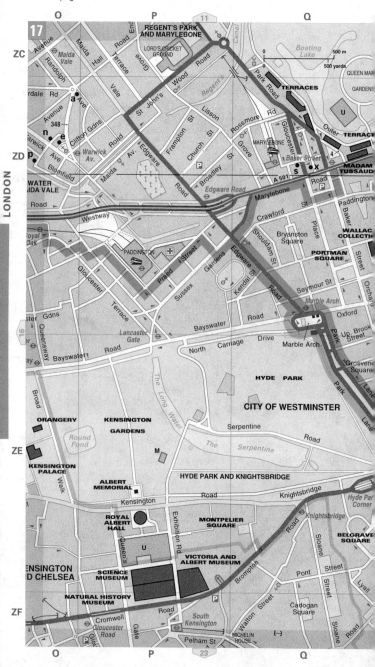

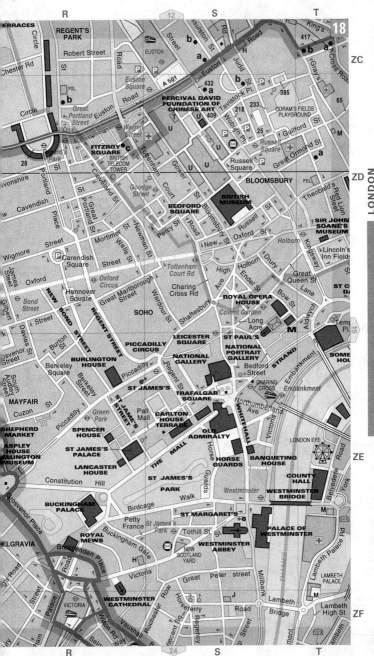

18

R S T

12

ZC
ZD
ZE
ZF

19

24

Map labels:

TERRACES
REGENT'S PARK
Robert Street
Chester Rd
Circle
St
EUSTON
Euston Square
Great Portland Street
Warren Street
Euston Road
A 501
POL
Circle
28
Regent's Park
St
devonshire
Portland
W Cavendish
Wigmore
James Steet
Oxford
Bond Street
Gilbert
K
Gosvenor St Street
Davies St
South Audley Street
MAYFAIR
Cuzon St
Piccadilly
SHEPHERD MARKET
APSLEY HOUSE WELLINGTON MUSEUM
Constitution Hill
Grosvenor Place
ELGRAVIA
BUCKINGHAM PALACE
ROYAL MEWS
Buckingham Gate
Bressenden Place
VICTORIA
WESTMINSTER CATHEDRAL

FITZROY SQUARE
BRITISH TELECOM TOWER
Cleveland Street
Goodge Street
Mortimer St
Newman St
Percy St
Tottenham Court Rd
Charing Cross Rd
Great Marlborough Street
Wardour St
SOHO
Shaftesbury
LEICESTER SQUARE
PICCADILLY CIRCUS
NATIONAL GALLERY
Regent Street
ST JAMES'S
BURLINGTON HOUSE
Berkeley Square
Berkeley St
Piccadilly
ST JAMES'S STREET
Pall Mall
CARLTON HOUSE TERRACE
SPENCER HOUSE
ST JAMES'S PALACE
LANCASTER HOUSE
THE MALL
ST JAMES'S PARK
Birdcage Walk
Petty France
Tothill St
NEW SCOTLAND YARD
WESTMINSTER ABBEY
ST MARGARET'S
PALACE OF WESTMINSTER
Great Peter street
Horseferry
Regency
Lambeth

PERCIVAL DAVID FOUNDATION OF CHINESE ART
Tavistock Pl
Woburn Pl
Russell Square
CORAM'S FIELDS PLAYGROUND
Guilford St
Great Ormond St
BLOOMSBURY
Theobald's Road
Red Lion Street
BRITISH MUSEUM
New Oxford St
Holborn
SIR JOHN SOANE'S MUSEUM
Lincoln's Inn Fields
High Holborn
Kingsway
Drury
Endel St
Great Queen St
Bow St
ROYAL OPERA HOUSE
Covent Garden
Long Acre
ST PAUL'S
NATIONAL PORTRAIT GALLERY
Bedford Street
STRAND
Aldwych
Temple Pl
CHARING CROSS
Embankment
TRAFALGAR SQUARE
Northumberland Ave
WHITEHALL
OLD ADMIRALTY
HORSE GUARDS
Horse Guards
BANQUETING HOUSE
LONDON EYE
COUNTY HALL
WESTMINSTER BRIDGE
Belvedere Road
York Road
Westminster
THAMES
Millbank
LAMBETH PALACE
Lambeth Palace Rd
Lambeth Bridge
Lambeth High St

King's
Cross Road
Gray's
417
65
385
432
409
218
233
25
12

425

LONDON

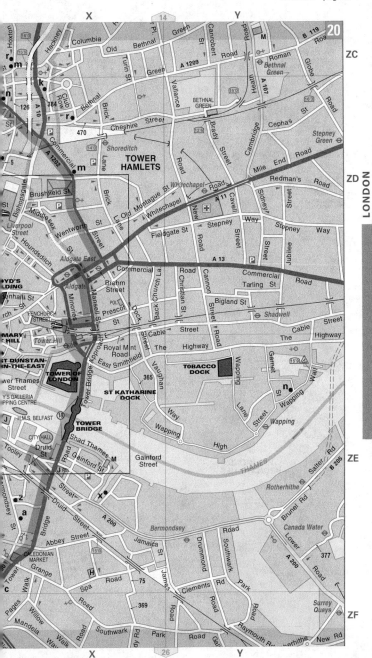

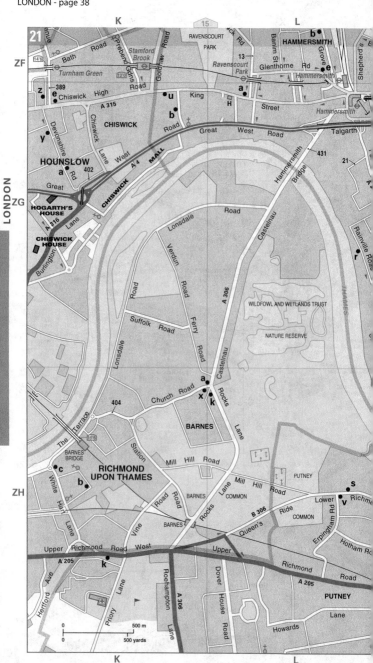

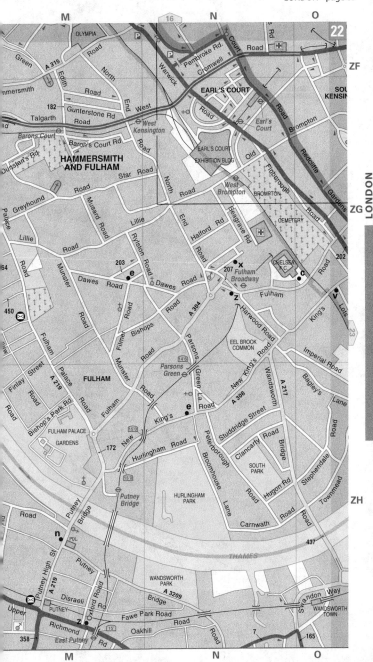

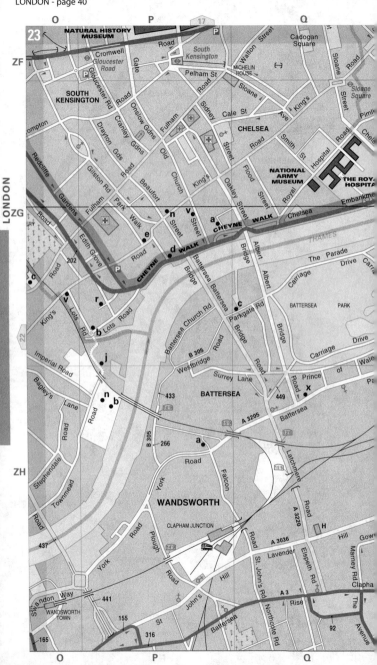

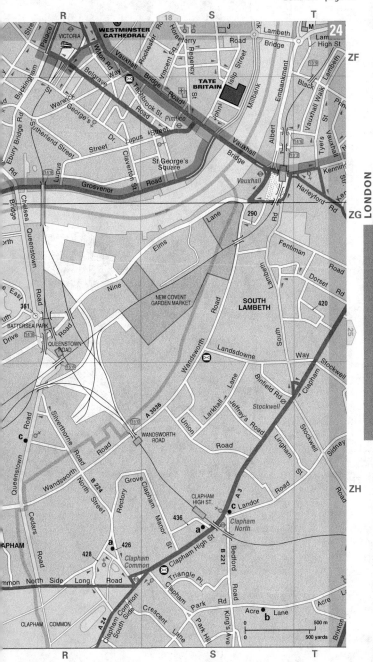

431

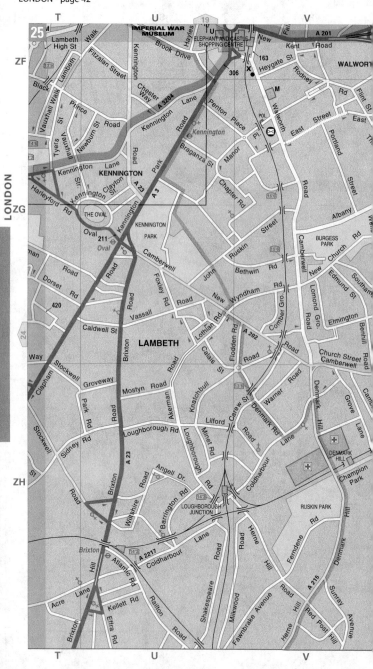

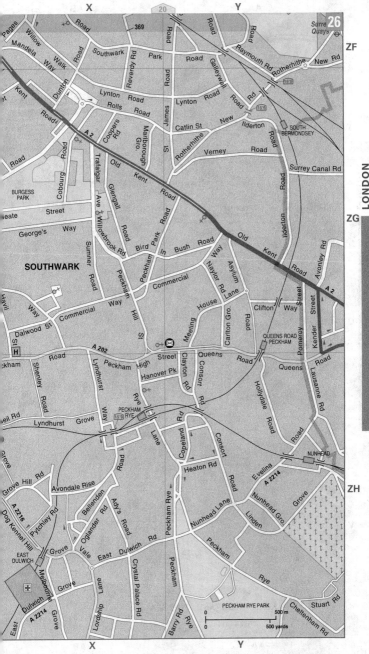

433

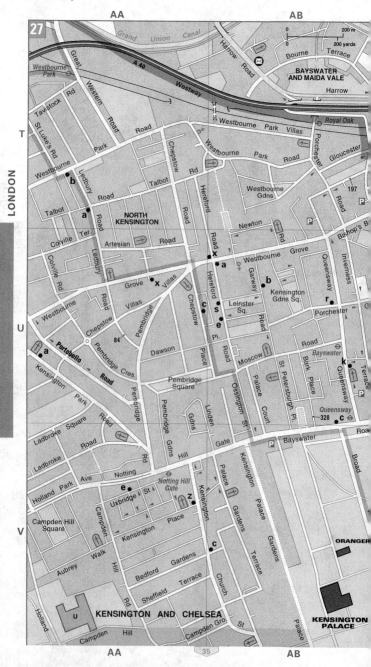

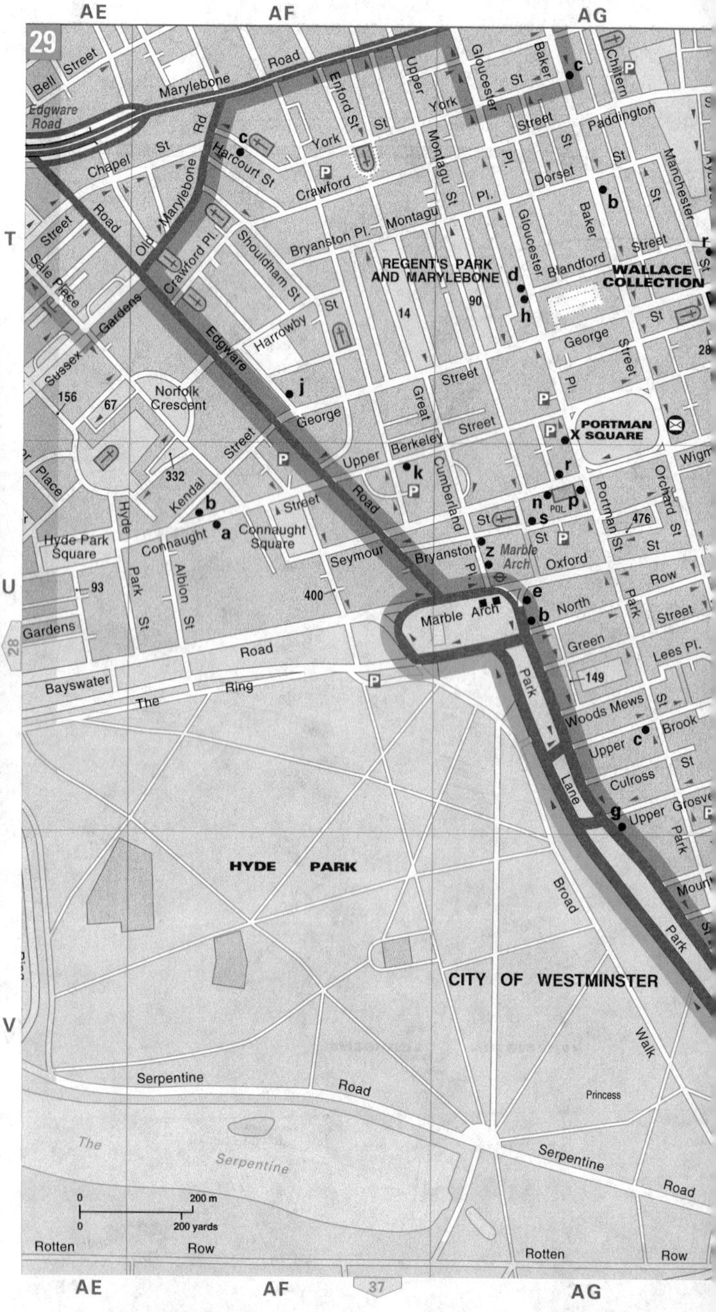
AE
AF
AG
29
T
U
V
Bell Street
Marylebone Road
Edgware Road
Chapel St
Harcourt St
Old Marylebone Rd
Enford St
Upper York St
York St
Gloucester Pl.
Baker St
Chiltern
Paddington St
Manchester St
Crawford St
Montagu St
Montagu Pl.
Dorset St
Bryanston Pl.
Sale Place
Crawford Pl.
Shouldham St
REGENT'S PARK AND MARYLEBONE
WALLACE COLLECTION
Blandford Street
Sussex Gardens
Harrowby St
George St
Norfolk Crescent
156
67
14
90
28
Great Cumberland Pl.
Upper Berkeley Street
Kendal Street
332
Hyde Park Square
Connaught St
Connaught Square
Seymour St
Bryanston St
Marble Arch
PORTMAN SQUARE
Portman St
Orchard St
Wigm
POL
476
Oxford St
Hyde Park St
Albion St
93
400
Gardens
North Row
Park Street
North Row
Green St
Lees Pl.
149
Bayswater Road
The Ring
Park Lane
Woods Mews
Upper Brook St
Culross St
Upper Grosvenor
Mount
Broad Walk
Park Lane
HYDE PARK
CITY OF WESTMINSTER
Serpentine Road
The Serpentine
Princess
0 200 m
0 200 yards
Rotten Row
37

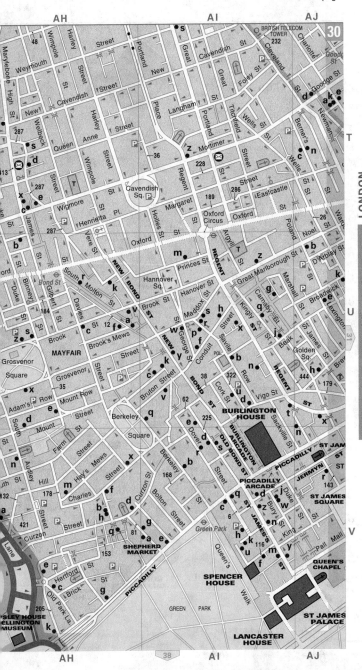

AH AI AJ

30

232

BRITISH TELECOM TOWER

Goodge St

Marylebone High St
Weymouth Street
Wimpole Street
Harley Street
Portland Place
New Cavendish St
Great Cavendish St
Cleveland
Charlotte
48

New Cavendish Street
Harley Street
Queen Anne
Langham Place
Titchfield
Portland
Foley St
Wells St
Berner's
Goodge St
Newman
d a k e
287

s
d
Wigmore
Welbeck
Street
Wimpole Street
Queen
Anne
Street
Mortimer Street
Wells
n
T
13

x e
c 287
Cavendish Sq.
36
z
228
286
Eastcastle St
Ward
T

b
287
Henrietta Pl.
Holles St
Margaret
189
Oxford Circus
Oxford St
Poland
Noel St
b
26

James St
Vere St
Oxford
Oxford St
Argyll St
T
z
D'Arblay St
ford
Bond St
South Molton
r
New Bond St
Princes St
REGENT
Great Marlborough St
Marshall
Broadwick
k

m
Hannover Sq.
Hanover St
g
Carnaby St
e
Lexington St

Binney
Gilbert St
Davies St
k
Brook St
NEW BOND ST
Magdox St
s h
Kingly St
q
Beak
j
St James

184
v
a
George St
w
p r
x
Golden Sq.
h
Brew

Duke St
S
Z
c
12 f
NEW BOND ST
y
Conduit
Savile
Regent St
444
179

MAYFAIR
Brook's Mews
Street
k
George St
c
b
n
St

Grosvenor Square
Grosvenor St
v
Bruton Street
BOND ST
38
322
Vigo St
ST
t
x

Adam's Row
35
e
Mount Row
q
Berkeley Square
62
Cork St
p u d
BURLINGTON HOUSE
n

d
Mount St
Farm St
e
225
Dover St
BURLINGTON ARCADE
Sackville St
PICCADILLY
ST JAM
ST

n
Audley
Hill
m
Hay's Mews
x
b r
OLD BOND ST
s
PICCADILLY ARCADE
JERMYN
ST
ST JAMES
r
143
ST JAMES SQUARE

132
178
Charles
f
168
Berkeley St
Green Park
q e d
j w
Bury St
ST JAMES'S
z
Duke St
V

a
421
d
h
Curzon St
Bolton Street
81
g
SHEPHERD MARKET
q
6
c
Green Park
h
k
n
116
m y
Pall Mall
QUEEN'S CHAPEL

e
153
a e
PICCADILLY
u
f
ST

c
Brick St
g
Old Park La
Queen's Walk
SPENCER HOUSE
ST JAMES PALACE

SLEY HOUSE
ELLINGTON MUSEUM
205
k
GREEN PARK
LANCASTER HOUSE

AH 38 AI AJ

437

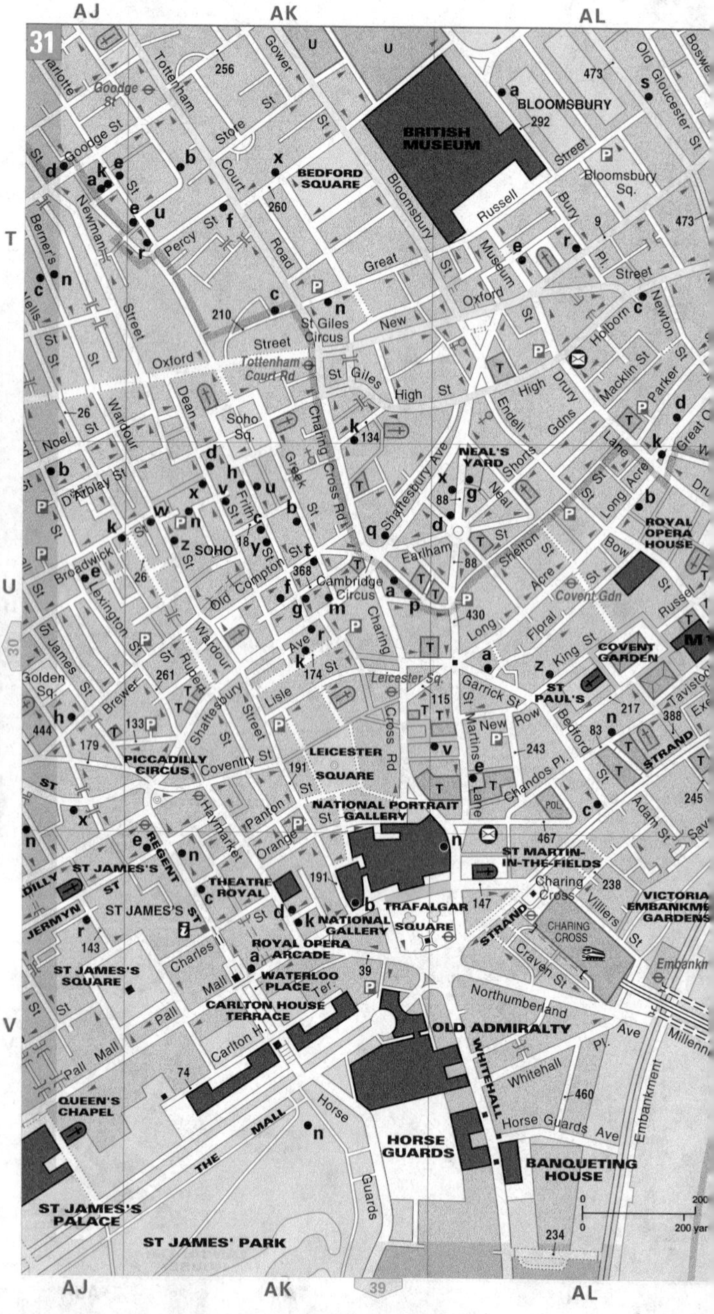
AJ
AK
AL
31
T
U
V
30
39
BRITISH MUSEUM
BLOOMSBURY
Bloomsbury Sq.
BEDFORD SQUARE
Goodge St
Tottenham Court Rd
St Giles Circus
Oxford Street
New Oxford St
Great Russell Street
Bloomsbury St
Gower St
Store St
Charlotte St
Newman St
Berner's St
Percy St
Dean St
Wardour St
Soho Sq.
SOHO
Frith St
Greek St
Old Compton St
Charing Cross Rd
Cambridge Circus
Shaftesbury Ave
St Giles High St
NEAL'S YARD
Neal St
Endell St
Earlham St
Shelton St
Long Acre
Floral St
Covent Gdn
ROYAL OPERA HOUSE
Bow St
Drury Lane
High Holborn
COVENT GARDEN
ST PAUL'S
King St
Garrick St
St Martin's Lane
New Row
Bedford St
Chandos Pl.
Tavistock St
Exeter St
Wellington St
STRAND
Lisle St
Leicester Sq.
LEICESTER SQUARE
Coventry St
PICCADILLY CIRCUS
Panton St
Orange St
NATIONAL PORTRAIT GALLERY
ST MARTIN-IN-THE-FIELDS
TRAFALGAR SQUARE
NATIONAL GALLERY
Charing Cross
CHARING CROSS
Villiers St
Craven St
VICTORIA EMBANKMENT GARDENS
Embankment
Northumberland Ave
Whitehall Pl.
WHITEHALL
Horse Guards Ave
HORSE GUARDS
BANQUETING HOUSE
OLD ADMIRALTY
Haymarket
REGENT ST
THEATRE ROYAL
ROYAL OPERA ARCADE
WATERLOO PLACE
CARLTON HOUSE TERRACE
Carlton H. Ter.
Pall Mall
Charles II St
ST JAMES'S ST
JERMYN ST
ST JAMES'S SQUARE
QUEEN'S CHAPEL
ST JAMES'S PALACE
THE MALL
ST JAMES' PARK
Horse Guards
Brewer St
Golden Sq.
Broadwick St
Lexington St
D'Arblay St
Noel St
Poland St
Rupert St
Great Windmill St
Museum St
Bury Pl.
Newton St
Macklin St
Parker St
Great Queen St
Shorts Gdns
Old Gloucester St
Boswell St
Millennium
0
200
200 yards

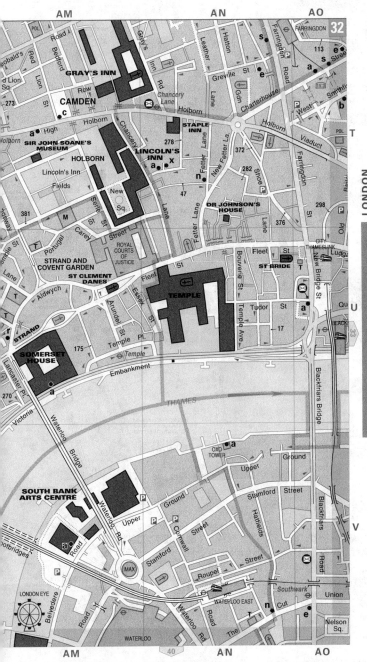

AO AP AQ

33

NGDON p a c
299
113
s e
a Street
Smithfield
ST BARTHOLOMEW
THE GREAT
b
West
Viaduct
POL
St BARTHOLOMEW'S
Farringdon
298
Old
ST MARTIN
LUDGATE
X Paternoster
CITY
THAMESLINK
New Bridge St
Ludgate
a
Queen
BLACKFRIARS
Blackfriars Bridge
und
eet
Blackfriars
Road
ark
Union
e
Nelson Sq.

Barbican Lane
475
Long Lane
Aldersgate
Z M
264
292
264 London
247
CHRIST
CHURCH
Newgate
J St
294
380
St Paul's
ST VEDAST
St PAUL'S
CATHEDRAL
Hill St. Paul's Churchyard
Queen Victoria St.
COLE ABBEY
PRESBYTERIAN
Mansion
House
ST JAMES
GARRICKHYTHE
Upper
Millennium Bridge

BARBICAN CENTRE
P
Silk St
ST GILES
CRIPPLEGATE
Fore St
Moor
MUSEUM
OF LONDON
BARBICAN
Wall
Wood
London Wall
Basinghall
GUILDHALL
Gresham Street
Foster La
S
Wood St
CITY OF
LONDON
Cheapside
ST MARY-
LE-BOW
Bow La
King St
Cannon
Victoria St
c
MANSION
HOUSE
304
ST STEPHEN
WALBROOK
Queen
D
Mansion
House
301
Thames
Moorgate
ST MARGAR
LOTHBURY
Lothbury
PRINCES St
BANK OF
ENGLAN
Poultry
Bank
308
ST MARY
ABCHURCH
Cannon Stre
CANNON
STREET
Street

Ropemaker S
31
Moo
Moorgate
Lon

INTERNATIONAL
SHAKESPEARE
GLOBE CENTRE
TATE
MODERN
s
291
Park St
c
169
SOUTHWARK
Southwark Street
Great
Suffolk St
Southwark
BRAMAH MUSEUM
OF TEA AND COFFEE
Ewer St
Guildford
Union Street
Great Suffolk St
Street
Southwark Bridge Road
Southwark Bridge
Road
Stoney
M
Z
h
m
e
m
k
SOUTHWARK
CATHEDRAL
London
Bridge
GEORGE
INN
Borough High Street
Southwark Street
Redcross Way
Borough
Newcomen St
GUY'S AN
ST THOMA

AO AP AQ

440

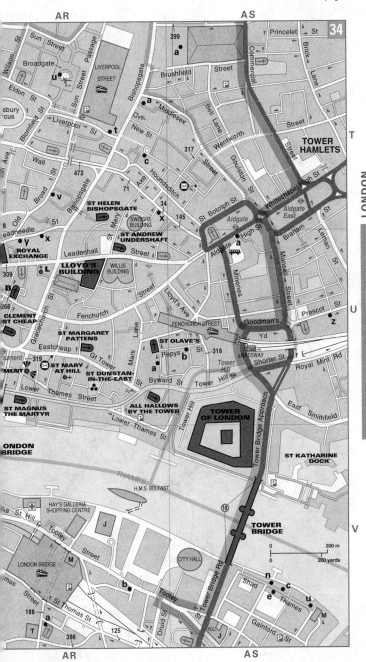

35

27

LONDON

0   200 m
0   200 yards

KENSINGTON

U

Campden

Walk

Holland

Hornton

St

Kensington Church St

Green

c P Kensing

r

u

241

HOLLAND

PARK

Argyll

Hill

H

Road

Phillimore

Holland

Gdns

Street

High

Street

Kensington

P

High

n

Young Street

Street

241

LINLEY SAMBOURNE HOUSE

High Street Kensington

242

Kensington Square

Kensington

Walk

X

Melbury

Street

High

LEIGHTON HOUSE

x

a

d

Abingdon

Earls

St Alban's Gro

c

Road

Kensington

Villas

Marloes

P

Edwardes Square

v

c

POL

Court

Scarsdale

Rd

Road

Cornwall

Cornwall

342

Lexham

Gardens

Lexham Gdns

Cromwell

Warwick

Gardens

Road

Place

Cromwell

Road

b

Knaresborough Pl

Courtfield Gdns

101

Y

Warwick

Pembroke

Logan

119

Kenway

Rd

r

Courtfield Gdt

Longridge

Road

Neverm

Pl

Court

Earls Court Gdns

Barkston

Gdns

99

s

410

a

c

Road

Road

x

Bramham

Gdns

Cromwell

Road

Warwick

Nevern Square

u

Earl's Court

EARL'S COURT

Earls

Court

Rd

Bolton

Gardens

Philbeach

Gardens

Road

Trebovir

Penywern

Rd

Earl's Court Sq.

e

Road

Redcliffe

Road

O

EARL'S COURT EXHIBITION BLDG

151

Z

Finborough

Square

WEST KENSINGTON

North

End

Road

Old

Brompton

Redcliffe

Gardens

Lillie

Seagrave

Rd

West Brompton

BROMPTON CEMETERY

a

Ifield

Road

Road

P

442

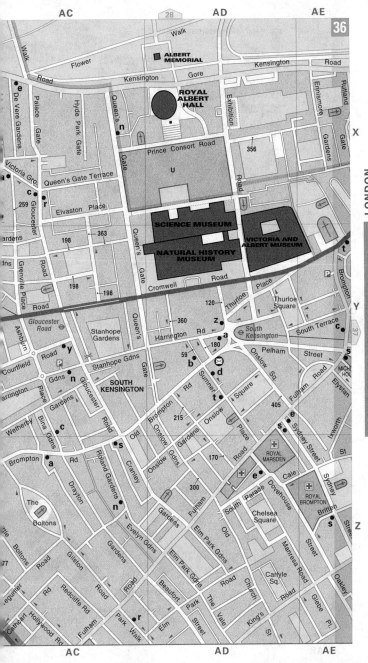

Walk

Flower

Road

Kensington

Gore

ALBERT
MEMORIAL

Kensington

Road

e

De Vere Gardens

Palace Gate

Hyde Park Gate

Queen's Gate

ROYAL
ALBERT
HALL

n

Exhibition

Rutland

Ennismore

Road

Victoria Gro.

Queen's Gate Terrace

Prince Consort Road

356

Gate

Gardens

X

a

c

r

259

Gloucester

Elvaston Place

Queen's Gate

U

198

363

SCIENCE MUSEUM

VICTORIA AND
ALBERT MUSEUM

t

Road

Brompton

Y

ardens

Grenville Place

Road

198

198

NATURAL HISTORY
MUSEUM

dns

Gloucester
Road

Cromwell

Road

Place

P

Ashburn

Stanhope
Gardens

Queen's Gate

360

120

Thurloe

Thurloe
Square

South Terrace

c

37

Harrington Rd

z

a

South
Kensington

S

MICH
HOU

Courtfield

Road

y

P

Stanhope Gdns

180

59

b

Pelham

Street

e

Britten

Onslow Sq.

Fulham Road

Elysian

Gdns

n

Gloucester

SOUTH
KENSINGTON

Sumner

d

Onslow

Square

405

e

arrington Place

Gardens

Rd

t

Place

S

Sydney Street

Ixworth

St

Wetherby

Bina Gdns

c

Brompton

Old

Onslow Gdns

215

Onslow

Gardens

Road

S

e

Brompton

a

Rd

Roland Gardens

Cranley

Onslow Gdns

170

ROYAL
MARSDEN

Cale

Sydney

The

Boltons

Drayton

Gardens

Fulham

300

Old

South Parade

e

ROYAL
BROMPTON

S

Z

Boltons

Road

Gilston

Evelyn Gdns

Gardens

Elm Park Gdns

Road

Chelsea
Square

Street

Manresa Road

Street

77

egurtler

Rd

Redcliffe Rd

Road

Road

Beaufort

Elm Park Gdns

Park

The Vale

Church

Carlyle
Sq.

Globe Pl.

Oakley

Cathcart

Hollywood Rd

Fulham

r

Park Walk

Elm

Street

King's

St

AC

AD

AE

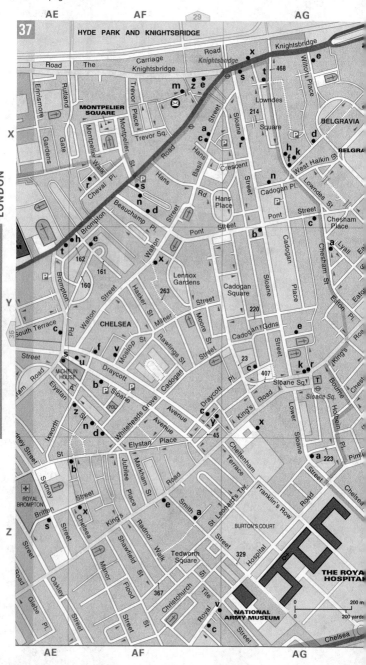

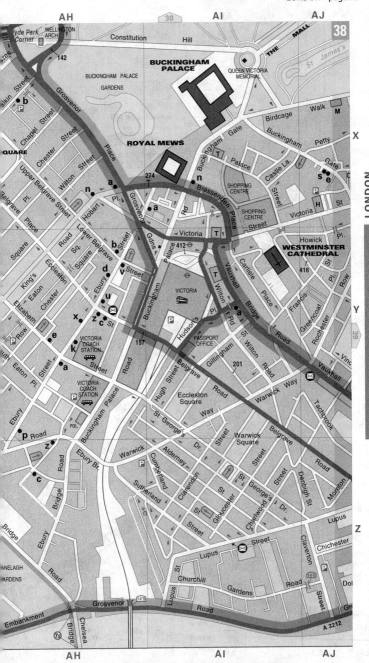

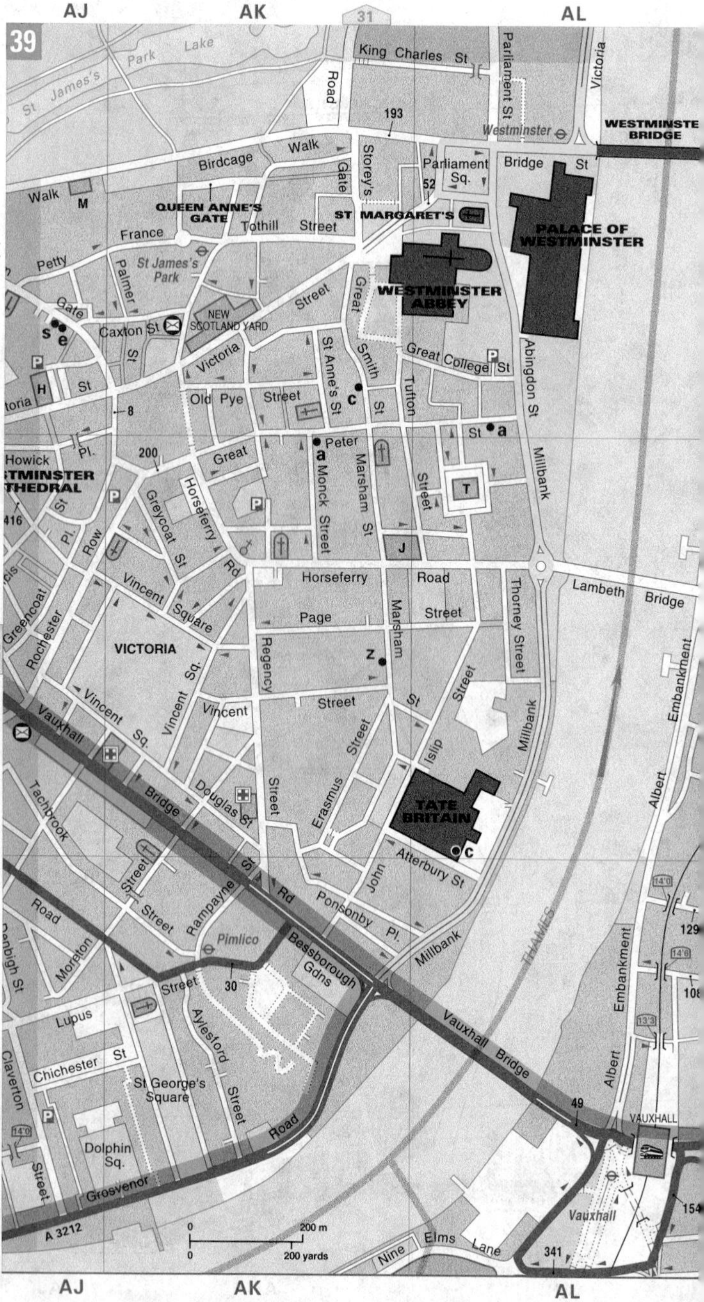

AJ
AK
AL
31
39
X
Y
Z
38
St James's Park Lake
King Charles St
Parliament St
Victoria
Road
193
Westminster
WESTMINSTER BRIDGE
Birdcage Walk
Storey's Gate
Parliament Sq.
52
Bridge St
M
QUEEN ANNE'S GATE
Tothill Street
ST MARGARET'S
PALACE OF WESTMINSTER
France
Petty
Palmer
St James's Park
Great
WESTMINSTER ABBEY
Gate
NEW SCOTLAND YARD
Caxton St
Street
s
e
Victoria
St Anne's St
Smith
Great College St
P
H
St
Old Pye Street
c
Tufton
Abingdon St
8
St
a
Howick Pl.
200
Great Peter
Marsham St
Millbank
WESTMINSTER CATHEDRAL
Horseferry
Greycoat St
Monck Street
Street
T
416
Row
Pl.
J
Rd
Horseferry Road
Lambeth Bridge
Vincent Square
Page Street
Thorney Street
Greencoat
Rochester
VICTORIA
Regency
Marsham
z
Vincent Sq.
Vincent Street
St
Street
Embankment
Vauxhall
Millbank
Islip
Street
Erasmus
Albert
Tachbrook
Bridge
Douglas St
TATE BRITAIN
c
Atterbury St
John
14'0
Road
Street
Street
Rampayne St
Rd
Ponsonby Pl.
129
Denbigh St
Moreton
Pimlico
Bessborough Gdns
Millbank
THAMES
14'6
108
Embankment
Street
30
Vauxhall Bridge
Lupus
13'3
Aylesford
Claverton
Chichester St
St George's Square
Albert
Street
49
P
VAUXHALL
Road
Dolphin Sq.
Street
Grosvenor
Vauxhall
154
A 3212
0
200 m
0
200 yards
Nine Elms Lane
341

AM
AN
AO

32

40

York

Webber

Blackfriars

COUNTY
HALL

Waterloo

Street

Westminster

M

Bridge

Lower

Marsh

Rd

St

Road

Road

Bayliss

Pearman

Road

Lambeth
North

X

ST THOMAS'S

Palace

Hercules

Kennington

Westminster

Bridge

Road

London

Rd

St

Road

LAMBETH
PALACE GARDENS

POL

George's

173

LAMBETH PALACE

Road

Lambeth

IMPERIAL
WAR MUSEUM

Road

M

Lambeth

Road

GERALDINE MARY
HARMSWORTH
PARK

West
Sq.

St

Hayles

LAMBETH

Brook

Walk

Juxon

St

Walnut Tree Walk

Walcot

Square

Drive

Y

Lambeth High St

Fitzalan

Kennington

Wincott

Renfrew

Dante Rd

Black

Prince Rd

Street

Street

Rd

Lambeth

e

Walk

Street

Chester

Way

Lane

Vauxhall

Johnathan St

Black

Prince

Rd

Kennington

Road

Tyers

Sancroft

St

Newburn

Courtenay

St

Street

Kennington

Park

Kennington

SPRING
GARDENS

Street

Cleaver

Street

J

Brabanza

St

Z

Tyers

St

219

St

Kennington

De

Laune

Kennington

Lane

Vauxhall

St

Lane

Stannary

St

Cooks

Rd

Harleyford

150

Kennington

Road

Clayton

St

Oval

THE OVAL

Road

KENNINGTON PARK

AM
AN
AO

LONDON

447

ALPHABETICAL LIST OF HOTELS
LISTE ALPHABÉTIQUE DES HÔTELS
ELENCO ALFABETICO DEGLI ALBERGHI
ALPHABETISCHES HOTELVERZEICHNIS

ALPHABETICAL LIST OF RESTAURANTS
LISTE ALPHABÉTIQUE DES RESTAURANTS
ELENCO ALFABETICO DEGLI RISTORANTI
ALPHABETISCHES RESTAURANTVERZEICHNIS

LONDON

LONDON

STARRED ESTABLISHMENTS
LES TABLES ÉTOILÉES
ESERCIZI CON STELLE
DIE STERNE-RESTAURANTS

✿✿✿		Page
Gordon Ramsay	XxxX	503

✿✿		Page
Alain Ducasse at The Dorchester	XxXxX	540 N
The Capital Restaurant	XxX	503
Le Gavroche	XxxX	541
Hibiscus	XxX	542 N
L'Atelier de Joël Robuchon	X	564 N
Marcus Wareing at The Berkeley	XxxX	536
Pied à Terre	XxX	474
The Square	XxxX	541

✿		Page			Page
Amaya	XxX	536	Nahm	XX	536
Ambassade de L'Ile	XxX	516 N	Nobu	XX	545
Arbutus	X	561	Nobu Berkeley St	XX	546
Assaggi	X	533	Quilon	XxX	566
Aubergine	XxX	504	Rasoi	XX	505
L'Autre Pied	XX	552 N	Rhodes Twenty Four	XxX	482
Benares	XxX	543	Rhodes W1		
Chapter One	XxX	472 N	(Restaurant)	XxxX	551
Chez Bruce	XX	531	Richard Corrigan		
Club Gascon	XX	482	at Lindsay House	XxX	559
Foliage	XxX	537	River Café	XX	490
The Glasshouse	XX	521	Roussillon	XxX	566
Gordon Ramsay			St John	X	496 N
at Claridge's	XxxX	541	Semplice	XX	544 N
The Greenhouse	XxX	542	Sketch (The Lecture Room		
Hakkasan	XX	474	and Library)	XxxX	541
Hélène Darroze			Tom Aikens	XxX	504
at The Connaught	XxxX	540 N	La Trompette	XxX	494
Kai	XxX	543 N	Umu	XxX	543
The Ledbury	XxX	513	Wild Honey	XX	544
Locanda Locatelli	XxX	551	Yauatcha	XX	560
Maze	XxX	542	Zafferano	XxX	536
Murano	XxX	542 N			

GOOD FOOD AT MODERATE PRICES
REPAS SOIGNÉS À PRIX MODÉRÉS
PASTI ACCURATI A PREZZI CONTENUTI
SORGFÄLTIG ZUBEREITETE, PREISWERTE MAHLZEITEN

PARTICULARLY PLEASANT HOTELS
HÔTELS AGRÉABLES
ALBERGHI AMENI
ANGENEHME HOTELS

LONDON

459

PARTICULARLY PLEASANT RESTAURANTS
RESTAURANTS AGRÉABLES
RISTORANTI AMENI
ANGENEHME RESTAURANTS

RESTAURANTS CLASSIFIED ACCORDING TO TYPE
RESTAURANTS CLASSÉS SUIVANT LEUR GENRE
RISTORANTI CLASSIFICATI SECONDO IL LORO GENERE
RESTAURANTS NACH ART UND EINRICHTUNG GEORDNET

American
		Page
Automat	X	548

Asian
		Page
Champor-Champor	X	525
Cicada	X	499
Cocoon	XX	547
Crazy Bear	XX	475
E & O	XX	514
Eight over Eight	XX	507
Great Eastern Dining Room	XX	487
Haiku	XX	547
Kiasu	X	534
Singapore Garden	XX	480
Taman Gang	XX	546
XO	XX	472

Beef specialities
		Page
Barnes Grill	X	520
The Grill Room	X	523
Kew Grill	XX	521
Maze Grill	XX	545
Notting Grill	X	514

British
		Page
Bedford and Strand	X	564
Bentley's (Grill)	XXX	543
Bluebird	XX	506
Butlers Wharf Chop House	X	525
Canteen (Southbank)	X	518
Canteen (Spitalfields)	X	529
Cat and Mutton	ID	487
The Fat Badger	ID	514
Great Queen Street	X ❀	478
Hereford Road	X ❀	534
Hix Oyster and Chop House	X	497
Inn the Park	X	558
Magdalen	X	524
Market	X ❀	476
Medcalf	X ❀	498
The Narrow	ID ❀	528
The National Dining Rooms	X	558
The Only Running Footman	ID	548
Paternoster Chop House	X	484
Quality Chop House	X	498
Quo Vadis	XXX	559

Rex Whistler	XX	567
Rhodes Twenty Four	XXX ✿	482
Rhodes W1 Brasserie	XX	552
Rivington (Greenwich)	X	486
Rivington (Shoreditch)	X	488
Roast	XX	526
Rules	XX	563
St John	X ✿	496
St John Bread and Wine	X	528
Shepherd's	XXX	567
Tate Modern (Restaurant)	X	526

Chinese Page

Bar Shu	X	562
China Tang	XXXX	541
Chinese Experience	X	562
Dragon Castle	XX	525
Good Earth (Mill Hill)	XX	470
Good Earth (Chelsea)	XX	507
Hakkasan	XX ✿	474
Haozhan	XX	560
Kai	XXX ✿	543
Ken Lo's Memories of China	XX	567
Mao Tai	XX	490
Maxim	XX	485
Memories of China	XX	512
Min Jiang	XXX	511
Mr Chow	XX	537
Pearl Liang	XX	533
Phoenix Palace	XX	553
Snazz Sichuan	XX	477
Xian	XX	472
Yauatcha	XX ✿	560
Yi-Ban	XX	489

Eastern european Page

Baltic	XX	526

French Page

L'Absinthe	X	479
Admiralty	XX	564
Alain Ducasse at The Dorchester	XXXXX ✿ ✿ ✿	540
Almeida	XX	499
Ambassade de L'Ile	XXX ✿	516
Angelus	XX	533
L'Atelier de Joël Robuchon	X ✿ ✿	564
Aubaine	X	508
L'Auberge	XX	530
Aubergine	XXX ✿	504
L'Aventure	XX	553
Belvedere	XXX	511
Bibendum	XXX	503
Bistro Aix	X	492
Bleeding Heart	XX	477
Le Boudin Blanc	X	548

LONDON

LONDON

Greek

		Page
Real Greek Mezedopolio	X	488

Indian

		Page
Amaya	XxX ✿	536
Benares	XxX ✿	543
Bengal Clipper	XX	524
Bombay Brasserie	XxX	516
Café Lazeez	XX	561
Cafe Spice Namaste	XX ⊛	529
Chor Bizarre	XX	546
Chutney Mary	XxX	505
The Cinnamon Club	XxX	566
Eriki	XX	480
Imli	X	562
Indian Zing	XX	490
Jamuna	XX	532
Kastoori	X ⊛	531
Khan's of Kensington	XX	516
Malabar	X ⊛	513
Mango and Silk	X ⊛	521
Memories of India on the River	XxX	489
Mint Leaf	XX	557
Mint Leaf Lounge	XX	483
Moti Mahal	XX	478
Painted Heron	XX	506
Planet Spice	XX	484
La Porte des Indes	XX	552
Quilon	XxX ✿	566
Rasa	X	489
Rasa Samudra	XX	553
Rasa Travancore	X	489
Rasoi	XX ✿	505
Red Fort	XxX	560
Tamarind	XxX	543
Tangawizi	X ⊛	523
Urban Turban	X	534
Vama	XX	507
Veeraswamy	XX	547
Zaika	XX	512

Innovative

		Page
Archipelago	XX	475
L'Etranger	XX	516
Foliage	XxX ✿	537
The Greenhouse	XxX ✿	542
Hibiscus	XxX ✿ ✿	542
Maze	XxX ✿	542
Pied à Terre	XxX	474
The Providores	XX	552
Texture	XX	551
Tom Aikens	XxX ✿	504
Trinity	XX	517

LONDON

International

		Page
Aquasia	XxX	504
Cantina Vinopolis	X	526
The Ivy	XXX	563
Light House	X	519
Mews of Mayfair	XX	546
Michael Moore	X	554
The Modern Pantry	X ⊛	499
Ottolenghi	X	500
Silk	XX	560
Sketch (The Gallery)	XX	547
Union Café	X	554

Italian

		Page
L'Accento	X ⊛	534
A Cena	XX	523
Al Duca	X ⊛	558
Alloro	XX	545
L'Anima	XxX	488
Arturo	X	534
Assaggi	X ✿	533
Avista	XxX	544
Caffé Caldesi	X	554
Caldesi	XX	553
Camerino	XX	475
Cantina Del Ponte	X	525
Caraffini	XX	507
Carpaccio	XX	507
Cecconi's	XXX	543
Cibo	X	513
Il Convivio	XX	567
Daphne's	XX	505
Edera	XX	514
Enoteca Turi	XX	530
Fifteen London	X	488
Franco's	XX	557
Incanto	XX	493
Latium	XXX	551
Locanda Locatelli	XxX ✿	551
Luciano	XXX	557
Manicomio (City of London)	XX	484
Manicomio (Chelsea)	X	508
Metrogusto	XX ⊛	500
Olivo	X	568
Osteria Emilia	X	472
Osteria Stecca	XX	554
Passione	X	475
Pellicano	XX	506
Quadrato	XxX	527
Quirinale	XX	568
Riva	X	520
River Café	XX ✿	490
Santini	XxX	567
Sardo	XX	474
Sardo Canale	XX	479
Sartoria	XXX	544

LONDON

465

LONDON

LONDON

467

Moroccan

North african

Polish

Scottish

Seafood

LONDON

Boroughs and areas

Greater London *is divided, for adminitrative purposes, into 32 boroughs plus the City: these sub-divide naturally into minor areas, usually grouped around former villages or quarters, which often maintain a distinctive character.*

BARNET – Greater London   12 **B2**

LONDON

Child's Hill – Greater London – ⊠ NW2

XX **Philpott's Mezzaluna**   AC VISA ⓐⓞ
    424 Finchley Rd ⊠ NW2 2HY – ℰ (020) 7794 0455
    – www.philpotts-mezzaluna.com – Fax (020) 7794 0452
    – Closed 25-26 December, 1 January, Saturday lunch and Monday   10NZA**c**
    Rest – Italian influences – Menu £ 20/28
    ♦ Homely Italian restaurant run by owners, with loyal local following. Monthly changing menus offer satisfying and unpretentious cuisine, with influences from across Italy.

Hendon – Greater London – ⊠ NW1

XX **Gallery**   AC VISA ⓐⓞ AE
    407-411 Hendon Way ⊠ NW4 3LH⊖ Hendon Central – ℰ (020) 8202 4000
    – www.galleryhendon.com – reservations@galleryhendon.com – Fax (020)
    8202 4433 – Closed Sunday dinner and Monday   2CU**e**
    Rest – Modern European – (dinner only and Sunday lunch) Menu £ 25
    – Carte £ 23/39
    ♦ A touch of opulence on Hendon Way courtesy of quality artworks ranging from pastels to lithographs and seascapes to portraits. British ingredients prepared with French flair.

Mill Hill – Greater London – ⊠ NW7
    🔝 100 Barnet Way Mill Hill, ℰ (020) 8959 2339

XX **Good Earth**   AC VISA ⓐⓞ AE
    143 The Broadway ⊠ NW7 4RN – ℰ (020) 8959 7011
    – www.goodearthgroup@aol.com – Closed 23-30 December   2CT**a**
    Rest – Chinese – Carte £ 27/37
    ♦ Smart, well-kept Chinese restaurant set slightly back from the busy A1 outside. Spacious and comfortable with efficient staff. Authentic menu; extensive vegetarian choice.

BRENT – Greater London   12 **A3**

Kensal Green – ⊠ NW10/W10

🍴 **The Greyhound**   🔝 AC VISA ⓐⓞ AE
    64-66 Chamberlayne Road ⊠ NW10 3JJ⊖ Kensal Green – ℰ (020) 8969 8080
    – thegreyhound@needtoeat.co.uk – Fax (020) 8969 8081 – Closed 25 December
    and 1 January   10MZB**a**
    Rest – Menu £ 18 – Carte £ 20/25
    ♦ Trendy gastropub, popular with locals. On one side: bar with leather sofas; on other: restaurant with reclaimed furniture, black oak floors and modern British cooking.

🍺 **Paradise by way of Kensal Green**   AK ⇔ VISA ⬤ AE
19 Kilburn Lane ⊠ W10 4AE⊖ Kensal Green – ℰ *(020) 8969 0098*
– www.theparadise.co.uk – Fax (020) 8969 8830
– Closed 25-26 December, 1 January and lunch Monday-Friday   1MZC**x**
Rest – Carte £ 23/30
♦ Decorated in a bohemian style with mismatched furniture, portraits and Murano chandeliers. Lighter lunch in bar, generously-sized portions of seasonal British fare in the rear restaurant.

Kilburn – Greater London – ⊠ NW6
🔁 London 7 mi – Luton 31 mi – Watford 16 mi – Slough 28 mi

🍺 **North London Tavern**   VISA ⬤
375 Kilburn High Rd ⊠ NW6 7QB⊖ Kilburn – ℰ *(020) 7625 6634*
– www.realpubs.co.uk – northlondontavern@realpubs.co.uk – Fax (020) 7372 2723 – Closed 25 December   10NZB**a**
Rest – (Closed Monday lunch) Carte £ 23/27
♦ Black exterior, popular bar for locals and a separate rear dining room with slight gothic feel. Appetising and gutsy gastropub staples with a wine list offering most bottles under £20.

Queen's Park – Greater London – ⊠ NW6

🍺 **The Salusbury**   VISA ⬤ ⓘ
50-52 Salusbury Road ⊠ NW6 6NN – ℰ *(020) 7328 3286*
– thesalusbury@london.com – Closed 25 December, 1 January and Monday lunch except Bank Holidays   10MZB**b**
Rest – Carte £ 22/29
♦ Half pub, half dining room with its own food store a few doors down. Italian influenced cooking with pronounced flavours and quality ingredients comes in generous portions.

Willesden Green – Greater London – ⊠ NW2/NW10

🍴 **Sushi-Say**   VISA ⬤
33B Walm Lane ⊠ NW2 5SH⊖ Willesden Green – ℰ *(020) 8459 2971*
– Fax (020) 8907 3229 – Closed 25-26 December, 1 January, 2 weeks August, Monday and Tuesday following Bank Holiday Monday   9LZB**a**
Rest – Japanese – Menu £ 10/21 – Carte £ 15/40
♦ Friendly service provided by the owner in traditional dress. From bare wooden tables, watch her husband in the open-plan kitchen carefully prepare authentic Japanese food.

Your opinions are important to us:
please write and let us know about your discoveries and experiences –
good and bad!

BROMLEY – Greater London   12 **B3**
🏌 Cray Valley Sandy Lane, St Paul's Cray, ℰ (01689) 837 909

Beckenham – Greater London – ⊠ BR3

🍴🍴 **Mello**   AK P VISA ⬤ AE
2 Southend Rd ⊠ BR3 1SD – ℰ *(020) 8663 0994 – www.mello.uk.com*
– info@mello.uk.com – Fax (020) 8663 3674   7GY**v**
Rest – Modern European – Carte £ 21/37
♦ Unassuming and welcomingly run neighbourhood restaurant; walls hung with multi-coloured modern oils. Good value, seasonally sensitive dishes enhanced by precise execution.

Bromley – Greater London – ✉   12 **B3**

    🖬 Magpie Hall Lane Magpie Hall Lane, ☏ (020) 8462 7014

🏠 **Bromley Court**   🚗 🍽 🔥 ❄ 🆔 ⚶ 🏊 **P** 🏦 *VISA* 🇲🇴 **AE** ⓪

Bromley Hill ✉ BR1 4JD – ☏ (020) 8461 8600
– www.bw-bromleycourthotel.co.uk – enquiries@bromleycourthotel.co.uk
– Fax (020) 8460 0899   8HY**z**
112 rm 🍽 – †£89/109 ††£105/120
Rest – (closed Saturday lunch) Menu £20/23

♦ A grand neo-Gothic mansion in three acres of well-tended garden. Popular with corporate guests for the large conference space. Constant redecoration ensures bedrooms remain bright. Conservatory or terrace dining available.

Farnborough – Greater London – ✉ BR6   12 **B3**

XXX **Chapter One**   🆔 ✥ **P** *VISA* 🇲🇴 **AE** ⓪
😊 *Farnborough Common, Locksbottom ✉ BR6 8NF – ☏ (01689) 854 848*
– www.chaptersrestaurants.com – info@chaptersrestaurants.com – Fax (01689)
858 439 – Closed first week January   8HZ**a**
Rest – Modern European – Menu £19 (lunch) – Carte approx. £30
Spec. Rabbit and foie gras terrine with cranberries, truffle mayonnaise and roasted apples. Roast rump and braised navarin of lamb, artichoke, tomato and bagna cauda. Blood orange trifle with warm blood orange espuma.

♦ The revitalised kitchen produces precisely executed, modern European cooking at a fair price. The mock Tudor exterior belies the contemporary styling of the restaurant and bar within.

Orpington – Greater London – ✉ BR6

    🖬 High Elms High Elms Rd, Downe, ☏ (01689) 858 175

XX **Xian**   🆔 *VISA* 🇲🇴 **AE** ⓪
324 High St ✉ BR6 0NG – ☏ (01689) 871 881 – Fax (01689) 829 437
– Closed 1 week September and 25-26 December   8JY**a**
Rest – Chinese – Menu £10/16 – Carte £16/22

♦ Modern, marbled interior with oriental artefacts make this personally run Chinese restaurant a firm favourite with locals. Look out for the Peking specialities.

Look out for red symbols, indicating particularly pleasant establishments.

CAMDEN – Greater London   12 **B3**

Belsize Park – Greater London – ✉ NW3

    🅳 London 5 mi – Luton 33 mi – Watford 18 mi – Slough 28 mi

XX **XO**   🆔 *VISA* 🇲🇴 **AE** ⓪
29 Belsize Lane ✉ NW3 5AS⊖ Belsize Park – ☏ (020) 7433 0888
– www.rickerrestaurants.com – xo@rickerrestaurant.com – Fax (020) 7794 3474
– Closed 25-26 December and 1 January   11PZA**a**
Rest – Asian – Carte £24/33

♦ Stylish dining room with banquettes, revolving lights and mirrors. Vibrant atmosphere; popular with locals. Japanese, Korean, Thai and Chinese cooking; dishes are best shared.

X **Osteria Emilia**   🆔 *VISA* 🇲🇴 **AE**
85b Fleet Road ✉ NW3 2QY⊖ Belsize Park – ☏ (020) 7433 3317 – info@oe.com
– Closed Sunday, Saturday lunch and Monday lunch   11QZA**a**
Rest – Italian – Carte £24/36

♦ The name refers to Emilia-Romagna whose influences inform the cooking at this neighbourhood Italian. Spread over 2 floors, with bright, pared-down décor. The family also own the deli opposite.

Bloomsbury – Greater London – ⊠ W1/WC1/WC2

Covent Garden
     Ló ☰ AC 🦢 '¶' *ḾA* VISA ○○ AE ①

10 Monmouth St ⊠ WC2H 9HB⊖ Covent Garden – 𝒞 (020) 7806 1000
– www.coventgardenhotel.co.uk – covent@firmdale.com
– Fax (020) 7806 1100
             31ALU**x**

56 rm – ♦£264/323 ♦♦£376, ⊇ £19.50 – 2 suites

Rest *Brasserie Max* – (closed Sunday lunch) (booking essential) Carte £30/46

♦ Individually designed and stylish bedrooms, with CDs and VCRs discreetly concealed. Boasts a very relaxing first floor oak-panelled drawing room with its own honesty bar. Informal restaurant.

Montague on the Gardens
     🗐 🍴 ☷ *Ló* ☰ & rm, AC '¶' *ḾA*
                    VISA ○○ AE ①

15 Montague St ⊠ WC1B 5BJ⊖ Holborn – 𝒞 (020)
7637 1001 – www.montaguehotel.com – bookmt@rchmail.com
– Fax (020) 7637 2516
             31ALT**a**

93 rm – ♦£123/217 ♦♦£159/247, ⊇ £16.50 – 6 suites

Rest *The Chef's Table* – Menu £25 (dinner) – Carte £35/53

♦ A period townhouse with pretty hanging baskets outside. The hushed conservatory overlooks a secluded garden. The clubby bar has a Scottish golfing theme. Rich bedroom décor. Restaurant divided into two small, pretty rooms.

Mountbatten
     Ló ☰ AC 🦢 '¶' *ḾA* VISA ○○ AE ①

20 Monmouth St ⊠ WC2H 9HD⊖ Covent Garden – 𝒞 (020) 7836 4300
– www.radissonedwardian.com – dial@radisson.com
– Fax (020) 7240 3540
             31ALU**d**

149 rm ⊇ – ♦£90/227 ♦♦£140/249 – 3 suites

Rest *Dial* – (Closed Saturday lunch, Sunday and Bank Holidays) Menu £25 – Carte £28/34

♦ Photographs and memorabilia of the eponymous Lord Louis adorn the walls and corridors. Ideally located in the heart of Covent Garden. Compact but comfortable bedrooms. Bright, stylish restaurant.

Jurys Gt Russell St
     ☰ & rm, AC 🦢 ⛯ *ḾA* VISA ○○ AE ①

16-22 Gt Russell St ⊠ WC1B 3NN⊖ Tottenham Court Road – 𝒞 (020) 7347 1000
– www.jurysdoyle.com – gtrussellstreet@jurysdoyle.com
– Fax (020) 7347 1001
             31AKT**n**

169 rm – ♦£245 ♦♦£245, ⊇ £16 – 1 suite

Rest *Landseer* – (bar lunch) Carte £34/45 **s**

♦ Neo-Georgian building by Edward Lutyens, built for YMCA in 1929. Smart comfortable interior decoration from the lounge to the bedrooms. Facilities include a business centre. Restaurant has understated traditional style.

Myhotel Bloomsbury
     Ló ☰ AC 🦢 ⛯ *ḾA* VISA ○○ AE ①

11-13 Bayley St, Bedford Sq ⊠ WC1B 3HD⊖ Tottenham Court Road – 𝒞 (020)
3004 6000 – www.myhotels.com – bloomsbury@myhotels.com
– Fax (020) 3004 6044
             31AKT**x**

78 rm – ♦£128/240 ♦♦£151/276, ⊇ £18

Rest *Yo! Sushi* – 𝒞 (020) 7667 6000 – Menu £16 (lunch) – Carte £22/33

♦ The minimalist interior is designed on the principles of feng shui; even the smaller bedrooms are stylish and uncluttered. Mybar is a fashionable meeting point. Diners can enjoy Japanese food from conveyor belt.

Ambassadors
     ☰ AC 🦢 ⛯ *ḾA* VISA ○○ AE ①

12 Upper Woburn Place ⊠ WC1H 0HX⊖ Euston – 𝒞 (020) 7693 5400
– www.ambassadors.co.uk – reservations@ambassadors.co.uk
– Fax (020) 7388 9930
             18SZC**a**

100 rm – ♦£169/255 ♦♦£189/325, ⊇ £16

Rest *Number Twelve* – Menu £16/23 – Carte £26/31

♦ Contemporary hotel near to Euston Station. Six floors of cleverly designed bedrooms with all mod. cons; Premier rooms the most spacious. Several well-equipped meeting rooms. Ground floor restaurant has relaxed style and offers Italian menu.

LONDON

XXX Pied à Terre (Shane Osborn)   AC ⇔ VISA ◍ AE
ಬಿಬಿ 34 Charlotte St ⊠ W1T 2NH⊖ Goodge Street – ℰ (020) 7636 1178
– www.pied-a-terre.co.uk – reservations@pied-a-terre.co.uk – Fax (020) 7916 1171
– Closed first week January, Saturday lunch and Sunday   31AJTe
Rest – Innovative – Menu £ 32/69🕮
Spec. Crayfish and garlic gnocchi, broccoli, Lardo di Colonnata and grapefruit.
Suckling pig with beetroot, girolles and apple cider sauce. Bitter sweet choco-
late tart, stout ice cream and macadamia nut cream.
♦ Smart, low-key exterior; stylish but compact interior with intimately-set tables and
well-structured service. Elaborate, expertly-crafted classical dishes, artfully presented.

XX Mon Plaisir   ⏄ VISA ◍ AE ①
21 Monmouth St ⊠ WC2H 9DD⊖ Covent Garden – ℰ (020) 7836 7243
– www.monplaisir.co.uk – monplaisirrestaurant@googlemail.com – Fax (020)
7240 4774 – Closed 25 December-2 January, Saturday lunch,
Sunday and Bank Holidays   31ALUg
Rest – French – Menu £ 17 (lunch) – Carte £ 28/41
♦ London's oldest French restaurant and family-run for over fifty years. Divided into
four rooms, all with a different feel but all proudly Gallic in their decoration.

XX Incognico   AC ⇔ VISA ◍ AE ①
117 Shaftesbury Ave ⊠ WC2H 8AD⊖ Tottenham Court Road
– ℰ (020) 7836 8866 – www.incognico.com
– incognicorestaurant@gmail.com – Fax (020) 7240 9525
– Closed 1 week Christmas, Sunday and Bank Holidays   31AKUq
Rest – French – Menu £ 33 (lunch) – Carte £ 30/35
♦ Firmly established with robust décor of wood panelling and brown leather chairs.
Downstairs bar has a window into the kitchen, from where French and English
classics derive.

XX Hakkasan   AC VISA ◍ AE
ಬಿ 8 Hanway Place ⊠ W1T 1HD⊖ Tottenham Court Road – ℰ (020) 7927 7000
– www.hakkasan.com – reservations@hakkasan.com – Fax (020) 7907 1889
– Closed 24-25 December   31AKTc
Rest – Chinese – Menu £ 40/55 – Carte £ 37/110
Spec. Roasted mango duck with lemon sauce. Stir-fried ostrich in yellow bean
sauce. Rum and caramel banana cookie crumble.
♦ Contemporary basement restaurant, with sexy, sophisticated styling and bustling
atmosphere. Well-organised staff serve expertly crafted and innovative Chinese cooking. Dim sum at lunch.

XX Sardo   AC VISA ◍ AE ①
45 Grafton Way ⊠ W1T 5DQ⊖ Warren Street – ℰ (020) 7387 2521
– www.sardo-restaurant.com – info@sardo-restaurant.com – Fax (020) 7387 2559
– Closed 24-29 December, 1 January, Saturday lunch and Sunday   18RZDc
Rest – Italian – Carte £ 23/32
♦ Simple, stylish interior run in a very warm and welcoming manner with very efficient service. Rustic Italian cooking with a Sardinian character and a modern tone.

XX Fino   VISA ◍ AE
33 Charlotte St (entrance on Rathbone St) ⊠ W1T 1RR⊖ Goodge Street
– ℰ (020) 7813 8010 – www.finorestaurant.com – reception@finorestaurant.com
– Fax (020) 7813 8011
– Closed 25 December, Saturday lunch, Sunday and Bank Holidays   31AJTa
Rest – Spanish – Carte approx. £ 30
♦ Spanish-run basement bar with modern style décor and banquette seating. Wide-
ranging menu of authentic dishes; 2 set-price selections offering an introduction to
tapas.

XX **Crazy Bear**
26-28 Whitfield St ⊠ W1T 2RG⊖ Goodge Street – ℰ (020) 7631 0088
– www.crazybeargroup.co.uk – enquiries@crazybear-london.co.uk – Fax (020)
7631 1188 – Closed Saturday lunch, Sunday and Bank Holidays   31AKT**b**
Rest – Asian – Carte £ 29/41
♦ Exotic destination: downstairs bar geared to fashionable set; ground floor dining
room is art deco inspired. Asian flavoured menus, with predominance towards Thai
dishes.

XX **Camerino**
16 Percy St ⊠ W1T 1DT⊖ Tottenham Court Road – ℰ (020) 7637 9900
– www.camerinorestaurant.com – info@camerinorestaurant.com
– Fax (020) 7637 9696
– Closed 24 -26 December, Saturday lunch, Sunday and Bank Holidays   31AKT**f**
Rest – Italian – Menu £ 17 – Carte £ 20/28
♦ Personally run, wood floored restaurant where bold red drapes contrast with crisp
white linen-clad tables. Menus take the authentic taste of Italy's regions for inspiration.

XX **Archipelago**
110 Whitfield St ⊠ W1T 5ED⊖ Goodge Street – ℰ (020) 7383 3346
– www.archipelago-restaurant.co.uk – info@archipelago-restaurant.co.uk
– Fax (020) 7383 7181
– Closed Christmas -New Year, Saturday lunch and Sunday   18RZD**c**
Rest – Innovative – Carte £ 27/37
♦ Eccentric in both menu and décor and not for the faint hearted. Crammed with
knick-knacks from cages to Buddhas. Menu an eclectic mix of influences from around
the world.

X **Passione**
10 Charlotte St ⊠ W1T 2LT⊖ Tottenham Court Road – ℰ (020) 7636 2833
– www.passione.co.uk – liz@passione.co.uk – Fax (020) 7636 2889 – Closed
Christmas-New Year, Bank Holidays, Saturday lunch and Sunday   31AKT**u**
Rest – Italian – (booking essential) Carte £ 40/47
♦ Compact but light and airy. Modern Italian cooking served in informal surroundings, with friendly and affable service. Particularly busy at lunchtime.

X **Cigala**
54 Lamb's Conduit St ⊠ WC1N 3LW⊖ Russell Square – ℰ (020) 7405 1717
– www.cigala.co.uk – tasty@cigala.co.uk – Fax (020) 7242 9949
– Closed 24-26 December, 1 January and Easter   19TZD**a**
Rest – Spanish – (booking essential) Menu £ 18 (lunch) – Carte £ 24/35
♦ Spanish restaurant on corner of attractive street. Simply furnished; open-plan
kitchen. Robust Iberian cooking, with some dishes designed for sharing; interesting
drinks list.

X **Giaconda Dining Room**
9 Denmark Street London ⊖ Tottenham Court Road – ℰ (020) 7240 3334
– www.giacondadining.com – paulmerrony@gmail.com – Closed Saturday,
Sunday, August and 1 week between Christmas and New Year   31AKT**k**
Rest – Modern European – (booking essential) Carte £ 22/27
♦ Aussie owners run a small, fun and very busy place in an unpromising location. The
very well priced menu offers an appealing mix of gutsy, confident, no-nonsense food,
with French and Italian influences.

X **Salt Yard**
54 Goodge St ⊠ W1T 4NA⊖ Goodge Street – ℰ (020) 7637 0657
– www.saltyard.co.uk – info@saltyard.co.uk – Fax (020) 7580 7435 – Closed
24 December -3 January, Sunday, Saturday lunch and Bank Holidays   31AJT**d**
Rest – Mediterranean – Carte £ 20/37
♦ Vogue destination with buzzy downstairs restaurant specialising in inexpensive
sharing plates of tasty Italian and Spanish dishes: try the freshly cut hams. Super wine
list.

475

LONDON

※ **Acorn House**   AC VISA ⓒ AE ①
69 Swinton St ⊠ WC1X 9NT⊖ King's Cross – ℰ (020) 7812 1842
– www.acornhouserestaurant.com – info@acornhouserestaurant.com – Closed
24-28 December, Sunday and Bank Holidays   18TZC**b**
Rest – Italian influences – Carte £ 27/44
♦ London's first eco-friendly training restaurant, with bright earthy interior and chirpy staff. Modern European food with largely Italian influences. Fresh, natural flavours.

※ **Abeno**   AC VISA ⓒ
47 Museum St ⊠ WC1A 1LY⊖ Tottenham Court Road – ℰ (020) 7405 3211
– www.abeno.co.uk – okonomi@abeno.co.uk – Fax (020) 7405 3212 – Closed
24-26 December and 1 January   31ALT**e**
Rest – Japanese – Menu £ 11 (lunch) – Carte £ 16/39
♦ Specialises in okonomi-yaki: little Japanese 'pancakes' cooked on a hotplate on each table. Choose your own filling and the size of your pancake.

Camden Town – Greater London – ⊠ NW1

※※ **York & Albany** with rm   ⚘ 🖻 📶 VISA ⓒ AE ①
127-129 Parkway ⊠ NW1 7PS⊖ Camden Town – ℰ (020) 7388 3344
– www.gordonramsay.com – y&a@gordonramsay.com   12RZB**s**
10 rm ⊇ – ♦£ 155 ♦♦£ 205
Rest – Modern European – (booking essential) Carte £ 26/33
♦ Gordon Ramsay's first hotel, with the restaurant as focal point. Dishes are comforting, straightforward but still deftly prepared. Lower level for views of the kitchen. Cosy bedrooms combine antiques with mod cons.

※ **Market**   AC VISA ⓒ AE ①
43 Parkway ⊠ NW1 7PN⊖ Camden Town – ℰ (020) 7267 9700
– www.marketrestaurant.co.uk – primrose.gourmet@btconnect.com – Closed
Christmas-New Year, Sunday dinner and Bank Holidays   12RZB**x**
Rest – British – (booking essential) Menu £ 15 (lunch) – Carte £ 20/30
♦ The highlights of the well-priced, daily menu are the classic British dishes, using market fresh ingredients. Simple comforts of exposed brick walls, zinc-topped tables and school chairs work well.

🍽 **Prince Albert**   ⚘ VISA ⓒ AE ①
163 Royal College St ⊠ NW1 0SG⊖ Camden Town – ℰ (020) 7485 0270
– www.princealbertcamden.com – info@princealbertcamden.com – Fax (020)
7713 5994 – Closed 25-26 December   12RZB**c**
Rest – (Closed Sunday dinner) (booking essential) Menu £ 17/22
– Carte £ 23/33
♦ Light, airy pub with welcoming neighbourhood feel. Simply prepared, satisfying dishes, with emphasis on freshness and traceability. Upstairs restaurant has own menu in evening.

Euston – Greater London – ⊠ NW1/WC1

🏨 **Novotel London St. Pancras**   🛅 ⅃ 🖻 ⅃ rm, AC 🕸 🐾 ⅃
100-110 Euston Rd ⊠ NW1 2AJ⊖ Euston – ℰ (020)   VISA ⓒ AE ①
7666 9000 – www.novotel.com – h5309@accor.com
– Fax (020) 7666 9025   18SZC**a**
309 rm – ♦£ 229 ♦♦£ 229, ⊇ £ 14.50 – 3 suites
Rest – (bar lunch Saturday and Sunday) Menu £ 20/25 – Carte £ 27/35
♦ Halfway between Euston and Kings Cross, this hotel has good-sized bedrooms for a London hotel and those on the higher floors enjoy views over the city. Good business amenities. International menu and buffet breakfast offered in Mirrors restaurant.

XX **Snazz Sichuan**   ⇔ VISA ⓜⓞ ①
37 Chalton St ⊠ NW1 1JD⊖ Euston – ℰ (020) 7388 0808
– www.newchinaclub.co.uk   12SZC**b**
Rest – Chinese – Menu £ 19/39 – Carte £ 10/50
♦ Authentic Sichuan atmosphere and cooking, with gallery and traditional tea room. Menu split into hot and cold dishes; the fiery Sichuan pepper helps heat you from inside out.

Hampstead – Greater London – ⊠ NW3

⬛ Hampstead Winnington Rd, ℰ (020) 8455 0203

⌂ **Langorf** without rest   ⬛ ⌗ 📶 VISA ⓜⓞ AE ①
20 Frognal ⊠ NW3 6AG⊖ Finchley Road – ℰ (020) 7794 4483
– www.langorfhotel.com – info@langorfhotel.com
– Fax (020) 7435 9055   11PZA**c**
41 rm – ♦£ 82/98 ♦♦£ 95/98, ⌷ £ 6 – 5 suites
♦ Converted Edwardian house in a quiet residential area. Bright breakfast room overlooks secluded walled garden. Fresh bedrooms, many of which have high ceilings.

⍮ **The Wells**   ⌗ AC VISA ⓜⓞ
30 Well Walk ⊠ NW3 1BX⊖ Hampstead – ℰ (020) 7794 3785
– www.thewellshampstead.co.uk – info@thewellshampstead.co.uk
– Fax (020) 7794 6817   11PZA**v**
Rest – Carte £ 25/35
♦ Bustling pub, equi-distant from the Heath and the High Street, with a less frenetic upstairs dining area. Menu offers muscular gastropub dishes, as well some from the Med.

⍮ **The Magdala**   ⌗ ⇔ VISA ⓜⓞ
2A South Hill Park ⊠ NW3 2SB⊖ Belsize Park – ℰ (020) 7435 2503
– www.the-magdala.com – themagdala@hotmail.co.uk
– Fax (020) 7435 6167   11PZA**s**
Rest – Carte £ 18/26
♦ Friendly pub on edge of Heath; turn right for drinking, left for eating. Concise but balanced menu with interesting snacks and sharing plates. Upstairs room used at weekends.

Hatton Garden – Greater London – ⊠ EC1

XX **Bleeding Heart**   ⌗ ⇔ VISA ⓜⓞ AE ①
Bleeding Heart Yard, off Greville St ⊠ EC1N 8SJ⊖ Farringdon – ℰ (020)
7242 8238 – www.bleedingheart.co.uk – bookings@bleedingheart.co.uk
– Fax (020) 7831 1402
– Closed Christmas-New Year, Sunday and Bank Holidays   32ANT**e**
Rest – French – (booking essential) Carte £ 25/39 ⌘
♦ Busy downstairs restaurant, popular with City suits. Fast-paced service, terrific wine list and well-practised cooking. Seasonally-changing French menu with traditional core.

Holborn – Greater London – ⊠ WC1/WC2

🏨🏨 **Renaissance Chancery Court**   ⑩ 🎭 ♨ ⬛ 👥 AC ⌗ 📶 🛁
252 High Holborn ⊠ WC1V 7EN⊖ Holborn – ℰ (020)   VISA ⓜⓞ AE ①
7829 9888 – www.renaissancechancerycourt.com
– sales.chancerycourt@renaissancehotels.com – Fax (020) 7829 9889   32AMT**a**
356 rm – ♦£ 282/411 ♦♦£ 282/411, ⌷ £ 24.50 – 2 suites
Rest *Pearl* – see restaurant listing
♦ Striking building built in 1914, now an imposing place to stay. Impressive marbled lobby and grand central courtyard. Very large bedrooms with comprehensive modern facilities.

LONDON

Kingsway Hall

Ló 🖼 ஞ rm, 🆎 ⚡ (ᵗ) 🔊 VISA ⍉ AE ①

Great Queen St ⊠ WC2B 5BX⊖ Holborn – ℰ (020) 7309 0909
– www.kingswayhall.co.uk – sales@kingswayhall.co.uk
– Fax (020) 7309 9129   31ALT**b**
168 rm – †£223/340, ††£223/340, ⊆ £15.95 – 2 suites
Rest – Menu £20 – Carte £28/35

♦ Large, corporate-minded hotel. Striking glass-framed and marbled lobby. Stylish ground floor bar. Well-appointed bedrooms with an extensive array of mod cons. European menus in smart, minimalist restaurant.

XXX Pearl – at Renaissance Chancery Court Hotel

🆎 ⇄ VISA ⍉ AE ①

252 High Holborn ⊠ WC1V 7EN⊖ Holborn – ℰ (020) 7829 7000
– www.pearl-restaurant.com – info@pearl-restaurant.com – Fax (020) 7829 9889
– Closed last 2 weeks August, 25-26 December,
Saturday lunch and Sunday   32AMT**a**
Rest – French – Menu £29/54 ⅋⅋

♦ Impressive dining room with walls clad in Italian marble; Corinthian columns. Waiters provide efficient service at well-spaced tables; original menus.

XX Matsuri - High Holborn

VISA ⍉ AE ①

Mid City Pl, 71 High Holborn ⊠ WC1V 6EA⊖ Holborn – ℰ (020) 7430 1970
– www.matsuri-restaurant.com – eat@matsuri-restaurant.com
– Fax (020) 7430 1971
– Closed 25 December,1 January, Sunday and Bank Holidays   32AMT**c**
Rest – Japanese – Menu £27/47 – Carte £19/75

♦ Spacious, airy Japanese restaurant. Authentic menu served in main dining room, in basement teppan-yaki bar and at large sushi counter, where chefs demonstrate their skills.

XX Asadal

🆎 VISA ⍉ AE

227 High Holborn ⊠ WC1V 7DA⊖ Holborn – ℰ (020) 7430 9006
– www.asadal.co.uk – info@asadal.co.uk – Closed 25-26 December, 1 January
and Sunday lunch   31ALT**n**
Rest – Korean – Menu £10 (lunch) – Carte £10/18

♦ A hectic, unprepossessing location, but delivers the authenticity of a modest Korean café with the comfort and service of a proper restaurant. Good quality Korean cooking.

XX Moti Mahal

🆎 ⇄ VISA ⍉ AE ①

45 Great Queen St ⊠ WC2B 5AA⊖ Holborn – ℰ (020) 7240 9329
– www.motimahal.com – reservations@motimahal-uk.com – Fax (020)
7836 0790 – Closed 24-29 December and Sunday   31ALU**k**
Rest – Indian – Menu £15/20 – Carte £35/51

♦ Bright and contemporary Indian restaurant spread over two floors. Chefs on view behind glass, with the tandoor oven the star of the show. Innovative and ambitious specialities. Keen service.

X Great Queen Street

🍴 ▒⊘ VISA ⍉

32 Great Queen St ⊠ WC2B 5AA⊖ Holborn – ℰ (020) 7242 0622 – Fax (020)
7404 9582 – Closed Christmas-New Year, Monday lunch, Sunday dinner and Bank
Holiday weekends   31ALT**d**
Rest – British – (booking essential) Carte £24/38

♦ Simply decorated, with ruby red walls. The menu is a model of British understatement; the cooking, confident and satisfying with laudably low prices and generous portions.

Primrose Hill – Greater London – ✉ NW1

※※ Odette's   🗦 AC ⟷ VISA ⓜⓞ AE

130 Regent's Park Rd ✉ NW1 8XL ⊖ Chalk Farm
– ℰ (020) 7586 8569 – www.odettesprimrosehill.com
– info@odettesprimrosehill.com – Fax (020) 7586 8362
– Closed Christmas, Sunday dinner and Monday   11QZB**b**
Rest – Modern European – Menu £22 (lunch) – Carte approx. £40
♦ Warm and inviting local institution, with enclosed rear terrace. Elaborate and sophisticated cooking which brings a little bit of the Welsh owner-chef's homeland to NW London.

※※ Sardo Canale   🗦 AC VISA ⓜⓞ AE ⓞ

42 Gloucester Ave ✉ NW1 8JD ⊖ Chalk Farm – ℰ (020) 7722 2800
– www.sardocanale.com – info@sardocanale.com – Fax (020) 7722 0802
– Closed Christmas and Sunday lunch   12RZB**a**
Rest – Italian – Carte £25/32
♦ A series of five snug but individual dining rooms in conservatory style; delightful terrace with 200 year old olive tree. Appealing Italian menus with strong Sardinian accent.

※ L'Absinthe   AC VISA ⓜⓞ AE

40 Chalcot Road ✉ NW18LS ⊖ Chalk Farm – ℰ (020) 7483 4848 – Closed
Christmas, August and Monday   11QZB**s**
Rest – French – Carte £21/32 ⅋
♦ Lively and enthusiastically run French bistro, with tightly packed tables, spread over two floors. All the favourites, from Lyonnais salad to duck confit. Commendably priced French wine list.

⫿🅳 The Queens   🗦 VISA AE

49 Regent's Park Rd ✉ NW1 8XD ⊖ Chalk Farm – ℰ (020) 7586 0408
– www.geronimo-inns.co.uk – thequeens@geronimo-inns.co.uk – Fax (020)
7586 5677 – Closed 25 December   11QZB**a**
Rest – Carte £18/29
♦ Popular neighbourhood pub – one of the pioneers of the 'gastropub' movement. Cooking is commendably classical, straightforward and generous, with interesting side dishes.

⫿🅳 The Engineer   🗦 P, VISA ⓜⓞ

65 Gloucester Ave ✉ NW1 8JH ⊖ Chalk Farm – ℰ (020) 7722 0950
– www.the-engineer.com – info@the-engineer.com – Fax (020) 7483 0592
– Closed 25-28 December   11QZB**z**
Rest – Carte £30/60
♦ Busy pub that boasts a warm, neighbourhood feel. Dining room, decorated with modern pictures, has modish appeal. Informal, chatty service. Modern cuisine.

St Pancras – Greater London – ✉ WC1

🄳 London 3 mi – Luton 35 mi – Watford 20 mi – Slough 29 mi

⫿🅳 Norfolk Arms   ⟷ VISA ⓜⓞ AE

28 Leigh Street ✉ WC1H 9EP ⊖ Russell Square – ℰ (020) 7388 3937
– www.norfolkarms.co.uk – info@norfolkarms.co.uk
– Closed 25-26 December, 1 January   18SZD**b**
Rest – Carte £19/22
♦ Charming gastropub with ornate ceiling squares and raw plaster walls, where dried peppers, chillies and onions hang from the walls. Mediterranean menu, dominated by tapas.

Swiss Cottage – **Greater London** – ✉ NW3

✗✗ **Bradley's**   🄰🄲 🖼 🆅🅸🆂🄰 🄼🄾 🄰🄴 🄾

25 Winchester Rd ✉ NW3 3NR⊖ Swiss Cottage – ☎ (020) 7722 3457
– www.bradleysnw3.co.uk – bradleysnw3@btinternet.com – Fax (020) 7435 1392
– Closed 1 week Christmas and Sunday dinner   11PZB**e**
Rest – Modern European – Menu £ 17/23 – Carte £ 30/36
♦ Warm pastel colours and modern artwork add a Mediterranean touch to this neighbourhood restaurant. Good value set menu; ingredients from across the British Isles.

✗✗ **Eriki**   🄰🄲 🆅🅸🆂🄰 🄼🄾 🄰🄴

4-6 Northways Parade, Finchley Rd ✉ NW3 5EN⊖ Swiss Cottage – ☎ (020)
7722 0606 – www.eriki.co.uk – info@eriki.co.uk – Fax (020) 7722 8866
– Closed 24-25 December, 1 January, lunch Saturday
and Bank Holidays   11PZB**u**
Rest – Indian – Carte £ 28/30
♦ A calm and relaxing venue, in spite of the bright interior set off by vivid red walls. Obliging service of carefully presented, flavoursome dishes from southern India.

✗✗ **Singapore Garden**   🄰🄲 🆅🅸🆂🄰 🄼🄾 🄰🄴

83 Fairfax Road ✉ NW6 4DY⊖ Swiss Cottage – ☎ (020) 7328 5314
– www.singaporegarden.co.uk – Fax (020) 7624 0656
– Closed 5 days Christmas   11PZB**x**
Rest – Asian – Menu £ 20/29 – Carte £ 26/46
♦ A smart, bright and comfortable room, with endearingly enthusiastic service. Your best bet is to pick vibrant and zesty dishes from the list of Singaporean and Malaysian specialities.

Tufnell Park – **Greater London** – ✉ NW5

🏠 **Junction Tavern**   🄰 🆅🅸🆂🄰 🄼🄾

101 Fortess Rd ✉ NW5 1AG⊖ Tufnell Park – ☎ (020) 7485 9400
– www.junctiontavern.co.uk – Fax (020) 7485 9401
– Closed 24-26 December and 1 January   12RZA**x**
Rest – Carte £ 22/30
♦ Typical Victorian pub with wood panelling. Eat in the bar or in view of the open plan kitchen. Robust cooking using good fresh ingredients, served in generous portions.

West Hampstead – **Greater London** – ✉ NW6

✗ **Walnut**   🄰🄲 🆅🅸🆂🄰 🄼🄾 🄰🄴 🄾

280 West End Lane ✉ NW6 1LJ⊖ West Hampstead – ☎ (020) 7794 7772
– www.walnutwalnut.com – info@walnutwalnut.com – Closed 1 week Christmas
and 1 week late August   10NZA**a**
Rest – Traditional – (dinner only) Menu £ 24/35
♦ Eco-aware chef-owner in his raised, open kitchen offers classical cooking, where game and fish are the specialities. Relaxed and informal corner restaurant, with plenty of local regulars.

> The ✿ award is the crème de la crème.
> This is awarded to restaurants
> which are really worth travelling miles for!

CITY OF LONDON – Greater London – ⊠ E1/EC1/EC2/EC3/EC4   12 **B3**

LONDON

Andaz Liverpool Street   Ⅰ6 ⅼ6 ⅼ rm, 🅰🅲 ❄ 🎵 🔊 VISA 🆑 AE ⓘ
Liverpool St ⊠ EC2M 7QN⊖ Liverpool Street – ℰ (020) 7961 1234
– www.london.liverpoolstreet.andaz.com – info.londonliv@andaz.com
– Fax (020) 7961 1235   34ART**t**
264 rm ⌂ – ♦£428 ♦♦£605 – 3 suites
Rest *1901* – ℰ (020) 7618 7000 (closed Saturday lunch and Sunday)
Carte approx. £44⅍
Rest *Catch* – ℰ (020) 7618 7200 (closed Saturday and Sunday) Carte £37/40
Rest *Miyako* – ℰ (020) 7618 7100 (closed Saturday lunch and Sunday)
(booking essential) Carte £21/41
♦ A contemporary and stylish interior hides behind the classic Victorian façade. Part of Hyatt group. Bright and spacious bedrooms with state-of-the-art facilities. European cooking on offer in Grade II listed 1901. Seafood at Catch, based within original hotel lobby. Miyako is a compact Japanese restaurant.

Crowne Plaza London - The City   🎵 Ⅰ6 ⅼ ⅼ rm, 🅰🅲 ❄ 🎵 🔊
19 New Bridge St ⊠ EC4V 6DB⊖ Blackfriars – ℰ (0870)   VISA 🆑 AE ⓘ
400 91 90 – www.crowneplaza.com – loncy.info@ihg.com
– Fax (020) 7438 8080   32AOU**a**
201 rm – ♦£347/423 ♦♦£347/423, ⌂ £19.50 – 2 suites
Rest *Refettorio* – ℰ (020) 7438 8052 (Closed Saturday lunch, Sunday and Bank Holidays) Menu £23 (dinner) – Carte £31/39
Rest *Spicers* – ℰ (020) 7438 8051 (lunch only Monday - Saturday) Menu £15
– Carte £25/30
♦ Art deco façade by the river; interior enhanced by funky chocolate, cream and brown palette. Compact meeting room; well equipped fitness centre. Sizable, stylish rooms. Modish Refettorio for Italian cuisine. British dishes with a modern twist at Spicers.

Threadneedles   ⅼ ⅼ 🅰🅲 ❄ 🎵 🔊 VISA 🆑 AE ⓘ
5 Threadneedle St ⊠ EC2R 8AY⊖ Bank – ℰ (020) 7657 8080
– www.theetoncollection.com – restthreadneedles@theetoncollection.com
– Fax (020) 7657 8100   34ARU**y**
68 rm – ♦£264/394 ♦♦£264/394, ⌂ £19 – 1 suite
Rest *Bonds* – see restaurant listing
♦ A converted bank, dating from 1856, with a stunning stained-glass cupola in the lounge. Rooms are very stylish and individual featuring CD players and Egyptian cotton sheets.

Apex City of London   🎵 Ⅰ6 ⅼ ⅼ rm, 🅰🅲 ❄ 🎵 🔊 VISA 🆑 AE ⓘ
No 1, Seething Lane ⊠ EC3N 4AX⊖ Fenchurch Street – ℰ (020) 7702 2020
– www.apexhotels.co.uk – london.guestrelations@apexhotels.co.uk
– Fax (020) 7702 2217   34ARU**a**
129 rm – ♦£311 ♦♦£311, ⌂ £10 – 1 suite
Rest *Addendum* – Modern European – ℰ (020) 7977 9500 (closed Saturday and Sunday) Menu £22 (lunch) – Carte £33/42
Rest *Addendum Bar* – Carte £23/31
♦ Tucked away behind Tower of London, overlooking leafy square. Smart meeting facilities, well-equipped gym and treatment rooms. Bedrooms are super sleek with bespoke extras. Bar opens out in summer.

Novotel London Tower Bridge   🎵 Ⅰ6 ⅼ ⅼ rm, 🅰🅲 rest, 🎵 🔊
10 Pepys St ⊠ EC3N 2NR⊖ Tower Hill – ℰ (020)   VISA 🆑 AE ⓘ
7265 6000 – www.accorhotels.com – h3107@accor.com
– Fax (020) 7265 6060   34ASU**b**
199 rm – ♦£280 ♦♦£300, ⌂ £13.95 – 4 suites
Rest *The Garden Brasserie* – (buffet lunch, bar lunch Saturday-Sunday)
Menu £20/25 – Carte £23/36 **s**
♦ Modern, purpose-built hotel with carefully planned, comfortable bedrooms. Useful City location and close to Tower of London which is visible from some of the higher rooms. Informally styled brasserie.

LONDON

XXX **Rhodes Twenty Four** ◁ AC ⇔ VISA ⦿ AE ①
❀ *24th floor, Tower 42, 25 Old Broad St* ✉ *EC2N 1HQ*⊖ *Liverpool Street* – ℰ *(020) 7877 7703 – www.rhodes24.co.uk – reservations@rhodes24.co.uk – Fax (020) 7877 7788*
– *Closed Christmas-New Year, Saturday, Sunday and Bank Holidays*   34ARTv
Rest – British – Carte £ 37/55
Spec. Seared scallops, mashed potato and shallot mustard sauce. Steamed mutton and onion suet pudding with buttered carrots. Bread and butter pudding.
♦ Panoramic views are afforded from this contemporary restaurant, set on the 24th floor of Tower 42; the former Natwest building. Well balanced British dishes, appetisingly presented.

XXX **Coq d'Argent** 🌿 AC 🐕 VISA ⦿ AE ①
✉ *EC2R 8EJ*⊖ *Bank* – ℰ *(020) 7395 5000 – www.danddlondon.com – coqd-argent@danddlondon.com – Fax (020) 7395 5050 – Closed Christmas, Easter, Saturday lunch and Bank Holidays*   33AQUc
Rest – French – (booking essential) Menu £ 29 – Carte £ 34/50
♦ Take the dedicated lift to the top of this modern office block. Tables on the rooftop terrace have city views; busy bar. Gallic menus highlighted by popular shellfish dishes.

XXX **1 Lombard Street** AC ⇔ VISA ⦿ AE
1 Lombard St ✉ *EC3V 9AA*⊖ *Bank* – ℰ *(020) 7929 6611*
– *www.1lombardstreet.com – hb@1lombardstreet.com – Fax (020) 7929 6622*
– *Closed 25 December- 6 January, Saturday, Sunday and Bank Holidays*   33AQUr
Rest – French – (booking essential at lunch) Menu £ 44/45 – Carte £ 52/62
♦ Grade II listed banking hall; rear room for elaborately presented, classical cooking using luxury ingredients. Bustling front brasserie and bar.

XXX **Bonds** – at Threadneedles H. AC 🐕 ⇔ VISA ⦿ AE ①
5 Threadneedle St ✉ *EC2R 8AY*⊖ *Bank* – ℰ *(020) 7657 8088*
– *www.theetoncollection.com – bonds@theetongroup.com – Fax (020) 7657 8089*
– *Closed Saturday, Sunday and Bank Holidays*   34ARUy
Rest – Modern European – Menu £ 18 (lunch) – Carte £ 28/46
♦ Modern interior juxtaposed with the grandeur of a listed city building. Vast dining room with high ceiling and tall pillars. Attentive service of hearty, contemporary food.

XX **Club Gascon** (Pascal Aussignac) AC VISA ⦿ AE
❀ *57 West Smithfield* ✉ *EC1A 9DS*⊖ *Barbican* – ℰ *(020) 7796 0600*
– *www.clubgascon.com – info@clubgascon.com – Fax (020) 7796 0601*
– *Closed January, Saturday lunch, Sunday and Bank Holidays*   33APTz
Rest – French – (booking essential) Menu £ 28/42 – Carte £ 34/48 ⭐
Spec. Abalone and razor clams à la plancha, parsnip and seaweed tartare. Cappuccino of black pudding and lobster. Rhubarb and champagne sorbet, rose Chantilly.
♦ Former bank; its marble walls now softened by big floral displays and mirrors. Elegantly crafted 'petits plats' are a paean to Gascony and the gastronomy of South West France.

XX **The Chancery** AC VISA ⦿ AE ①
9 Cursitor St ✉ *EC4A 1LL*⊖ *Chancery Lane* – ℰ *(020) 7831 4000*
– *www.thechancery.co.uk – reservations@thechancery.co.uk – Fax (020) 7831 4002 – Closed 25 December, Saturday and Sunday*   32ANTa
Rest – Modern European – Menu £ 34
♦ Near Law Courts, a small restaurant with basement bar. Contemporary interior with intimate style. Quality ingredients put to good use in accomplished, modern dishes.

XX **Mint Leaf Lounge**   AC VISA ⓜⓞ AE ⓞ
12 Angel Court, Lothbury ⊠ *EC2R 7HB*⊖ *Bank –* ℰ *(020) 7600 0992*
– www.mintleaflounge.com – reservations@mintleaflounge.com
– Fax (020) 7600 6628
– Closed 22 December-3 January, Saturday lunch and Sunday   33AQT**b**
Rest – Indian – Menu £ 23 (lunch) – Carte £ 28/44
♦ Sister branch to the original in St James's. Slick and stylish, with busy bar. Well paced service of carefully prepared contemporary Indian food, with many of the influences from the south.

XX **Vanilla Black**   AC VISA ⓜⓞ AE
17-18 Tooks Court ⊠ *EC4A 1LB*⊖ *Chancery Lane –* ℰ *(020) 7242 2622*
– www.vanillablack.co.uk
– Closed Saturday, Sunday and 2 weeks Christmas   32ANT**x**
Rest – Vegetarian – Menu £ 23/30
♦ Proving that vegetarian food can be flavoursome and satisfying, with a menu that is varied and imaginative. This is a well run, friendly restaurant with understated décor, run by a husband and wife team.

XX **Kenza**   AC ⇔ VISA ⓜⓞ AE ⓞ
10 Devonshire Square ⊠ *EC2M 4YP*⊖ *Liverpool Street –* ℰ *(020) 7929 5533*
– www.kenza-restaurant.com – info@kenza-restaurant.com – Fax (020)
7929 0303 – Closed Saturday lunch and Sunday   34ART**c**
Rest – Lebanese – Carte approx. £ 35
♦ Exotic basement restaurant, with lamps, carvings, pumping music and nightly belly dancing. Lebanese and Moroccan cooking are the menu influences and the cooking is authentic and accurate.

XX **Devonshire Terrace**   🍴 AC ⇔ VISA ⓜⓞ AE
Devonshire Sq ⊠ *EC2M 4YY*⊖ *Liverpool Street –* ℰ *(020) 7256 3233*
– www.devonshireterrace.co.uk – info@devonshireterrace.co.uk – Fax (020)
7256 3244 – Closed Christmas-New Year, Saturday and Sunday   34ART**c**
Rest – Modern European – Carte £ 22/34
♦ Brasserie-style cooking, where you choose the sauce and side dish to accompany your main course. Bright and busy restaurant with open kitchen and choice of two terraces, one within large atrium.

XX **The Mercer**   AC VISA ⓜⓞ AE
34 Threadneedle St ⊠ *EC2R 8AY*⊖ *Bank –* ℰ *(020) 7628 0001*
– www.themercer.co.uk – info@themercer.co.uk – Fax (020) 7588 2822 – Closed
25 December - 1 January, Saturday, Sunday and Bank Holidays   34ARU**x**
Rest – Modern European – Carte £ 29/50 🍷
♦ Converted bank, with airy feels thanks to high ceilings and large windows. Brasserie style menu with appealing mix of classics and comfort food. Huge choice of wines available by glass or carafe.

XX **Sauterelle**   AC ⇔ VISA ⓜⓞ AE ⓞ
The Royal Exchange ⊠ *EC3V 3LR*⊖ *Bank –* ℰ *(020) 7618 2483*
– www.restaurantsauterelle.com – Closed Saturday and Sunday   33AQU**a**
Rest – French – Menu £ 21 (dinner) – Carte £ 33/56
♦ Located on mezzanine level of Royal Exchange, a stunning 16C property with ornate columns and pillars. Appealing and rustic French menus attract plenty of lunchtime diners.

XX **Boisdale of Bishopsgate**   AC VISA ⓜⓞ AE
Swedeland Court, 202 Bishopsgate ⊠ *EC2M 4NR*⊖ *Liverpool Street –* ℰ *(020)*
7283 1763 – www.boisdale.co.uk – info@boisdale-city.co.uk – Fax (020) 7283 1664
– Closed 25 December - 3 January, Saturday, Sunday
and Bank Holidays   34ART**a**
Rest – Scottish – Carte £ 25/59
♦ Through ground floor bar, serving oysters and champagne, to brick vaulted basement with red and tartan décor. Menu featuring Scottish produce. Live jazz most evenings.

LONDON

XX **Bevis Marks** 🍴 VISA ⓪ AE

Bevis Marks ⊠ EC3A 5DQ⊖ Aldgate – ℰ *(020) 7283 2220*
– www.bevismarkstherestaurant.com – enquiries@bevismarkstherestaurant.com
– Fax (020) 7283 2221 – Closed Saturday, Sunday and Jewish Holidays   34ART**x**
Rest – Kosher – Carte £ 32/39
♦ Glass-roofed extension to city's oldest synagogue: limestone flooring, modern murals on wall. Regularly changing Kosher menus; influences from Mediterranean and Middle East.

XX **Tatsuso** AC ⇔ VISA ⓪ AE ⓪

32 Broadgate Circle ⊠ EC2M 2QS⊖ Liverpool Street – ℰ *(020) 7638 5863*
– info.tatsuso@btinternet.com – Fax (020) 7638 5864 – Closed Christmas, New
Year, Saturday, Sunday and Bank Holidays   34ART**u**
Rest – Japanese – (booking essential) Carte £ 35/80
♦ Dine in the busy teppan-yaki bar or in the more formal restaurant. Approachable staff in traditional costume provide attentive service of authentic and precise dishes.

XX **Manicomio** AC VISA ⓪ AE

6 Gutter Lane ⊠ EC2V 7AD⊖ St Paul's – ℰ *(020) 726 50 10*
– www.manicomio.co.uk – gutterlane@manicomio.co.uk – Fax (020) 726 50 11
– Closed Christmas-New Year, Saturday and Sunday   33APT**s**
Rest – Italian – Carte £ 22/35
♦ Second branch to follow the first in Chelsea. Regional Italian fare, with top-notch ingredients. Bright and fresh first floor restaurant, with deli-café on the ground floor and bar on top floor.

XX **The White Swan** AC ℅ VISA ⓪ AE

108 Fetter Lane ⊠ EC4A 1ES⊖ Temple – ℰ *(020) 7242 9696*
– www.thewhiteswanlondon.com – info@thewhiteswanlondon.com
– Fax (020) 7404 2250 – Closed Christmas, Saturday, Sunday,
Monday dinner and Bank Holidays   32ANT**n**
Rest – Modern European – Menu £ 28 (lunch) – Carte £ 26/30
♦ Smart dining room above pub just off Fleet Street: mirrored ceilings, colourful paintings on wall. Modern, daily changing menus, are good value for the heart of London.

X **Paternoster Chop House** 🍴 AC VISA ⓪ AE ⓪

Warwick Court, Paternoster Square ⊠ EC4N 7DX⊖ St Paul's – ℰ *(020)*
7029 9400 – www.paternosterchophouse.com – Fax (020) 7029 9409 – Closed 10
days Christmas, dinner Sunday, Saturday and Bank Holidays   33APT**x**
Rest – British – Carte £ 31/41
♦ On ground floor of office block, with large terrace. Classic and robust British cooking; menu a mix of traditional favourites, shellfish and comfort food. Busy and noisy.

CROYDON – Greater London   12 **B3**

Addington – Greater London – ⊠ CR2

🏌 Addington Court Featherbed Lane, ℰ (020) 8657 0281
🏌 The Addington 205 Shirley Church Rd, ℰ (020) 8777 1055

XX **Planet Spice** AC P VISA ⓪ AE

88 Selsdon Park Rd ⊠ CR2 8JT – ℰ *(020) 8651 3300 – www.planet-spice.com*
– emdad@planet-spice.com – Fax (020) 8651 4400 – Closed 26 December   7GZ**c**
Rest – Indian – Menu £ 20 (lunch) **s** – Carte £ 22/29 **s**
♦ Brasserie style Indian restaurant with fresh, vibrant décor and a modern feel. Attentive and helpful service. Traditional cooking with some innovative touches.

The 🏵 award is the crème de la crème.
This is awarded to restaurants
which are really worth travelling miles for!

Croydon – **Greater London** – ⊠ **CR9**   12 **B3**

🔢 Croydon Clocktower, Katharine St ☎ (020) 8253 1009

🏨🏨🏨 **Hilton Croydon**   🔲 𝔫 ƒ⅙ 🛗 ₲ rm, 𝕂 ⅍ ⁾⁾ 🛎 🅿 𝕍𝕊𝔸 ⓜⓞ 𝔸𝔼 ⓪

Waddon Way, Purley Way ⊠ *CR9 4HH* – ☎ *(020) 8680 3000*
– www.hilton.co.uk/croydon – reservations.croydon@hilton.com – Fax (020)
86816171 – Closed Christmas   7FZ**e**
168 rm – ⸙£70/129 ⸙⸙£81/139, ⌕ £15.95
Rest – (dinner only) Carte approx. £20
♦ A modern hotel where the relaxing café in the open-plan lobby is open all day.
Internet access is available in all bedrooms, which are decorated to a good standard.
Open-plan dining room; informal char-grill concept.

South Croydon – **Greater London** – ⊠ **CR2**

XX **Le Cassoulet**   𝕂 𝕍𝕊𝔸 ⓜⓞ 𝔸𝔼

🙂 ⊠ *CR2 6PA* – ☎ *(020) 8633 1818* – *www.lecassoulet.com* – *info@lecassoulet.com*
– Fax (020) 8633 1815   7FZ**v**
Rest – French – Menu £17/20 **s** – Carte £26/40 **s**
♦ Good value, traditional French fare, with a more elaborate menu at dinner. Chic
and elegant interior; carefully run, with attentive service. Same ownership as Le
Vacherin in South Ealing.

EALING – **Greater London**   12 **A3**

Acton Green – **Greater London** – ⊠ **W4**   18 **B3**

🍺 **The Bollo**   ⛱ 𝕍𝕊𝔸 ⓜⓞ 𝔸𝔼
13-15 Bollo Lane ⊠ *W4 5LR*⊖ *Chiswick Park* – ☎ *(020) 8994 6037*
– www.thebollohouse.co.uk – thebollohouse@btconnect.com
– Closed 25 December   6CV**z**
Rest – Carte £20/35
♦ Early Victorian corner pub with a bona fide London feel and a rough and ready
vibe. Daily blackboard menu displays full-bodied, satisfying dishes, often using local
market produce.

🍺 **Duke of Sussex**   ⛱ 𝕍𝕊𝔸 ⓜⓞ
75 South Parade ⊠ *W4 5LF*⊖ *Chiswick Park* – ☎ *(020) 8742 8801*
– michael-buurman@yahoo.co.uk   6CV**o**
Rest – (Closed Monday lunch except bank holidays) Carte £21/24
♦ A grand Victorian pub with ornate décor. Appealingly rustic Spanish influences in
the daily changing menu, with stews and cured meats a speciality; some dishes
designed for sharing.

Ealing – **Greater London** – ⊠ **W13**   12 **A3**

🏌 West Middlesex Southall Greenford Rd, ☎ (020) 8574 3450
🏌 Horsenden Hill Greenford Woodland Rise, ☎ (020) 8902 4555

XX **Maxim**   𝕂 𝕍𝕊𝔸 ⓜⓞ 𝔸𝔼
153-155 Northfield Ave ⊠ *W13 9QT*⊖ *Northfields* – ☎ *(020) 8567 1719*
– Fax (020) 8932 0717 – Closed 25-28 December and Sunday lunch   1BV**a**
Rest – Chinese – Menu £15/20 – Carte £18/30
♦ Decorated with assorted oriental ornaments and pictures. Well-organised service
from smartly attired staff. Authentic Chinese cooking from the extensive menu.

X **Charlotte's Place**   𝕍𝕊𝔸 ⓜⓞ
16 St Matthew's Rd ⊠ *W5 3JT*⊖ *Ealing Common* – ☎ *(020) 8567 7541*
– www.charlottes.co.uk – restaurant@charlottes.co.uk
– Closed 1-2 January, 26-30 December and lunch Monday   2CV**c**
Rest – Modern European – Menu £15 (lunch) – Carte £24/32
♦ Friendly neighbourhood restaurant whose large windows and mirror ensure plenty
of light. Modern European dishes and some brasserie classics come in decently-sized
portions.

LONDON

ENFIELD – Greater London
12 **B2**

🏌 Leaside GC Edmonton Picketts Lock Lane, Lee Valley Leisure,
𝒞 (020) 8803 3611

Enfield – Greater London – ✉ EN1
12 **B2**

🏌 Whitewebbs Clay Hill Beggars Hollow, N : 1 m., 𝒞 (020) 8363 2951

🏠 **Oak Lodge** without rest 　　　　🚗 ఉ ⁇ *VISA* ⚫⚫ ⓘ
80 Village Rd, Bush Hill Park ✉ EN1 2EU – 𝒞 (020) 8360 7082
– www.oaklodgehotel-enfield.co.uk – info@oaklodgehotel-enfield.co.uk 　3FT**a**
8 rm – ⁑£80 ⁑⁑£90
◆ An Edwardian house located in a residential area. Individually decorated bedrooms
are compact but well equipped; the ideal antidote to faceless corporate hotels.

Hadley Wood – Greater London – ✉ EN4

🏨 **West Lodge Park** 🌿　　　≼ 🚗 🏊 🎣 ▣ ఉ rm, ⁇ ⁇ 🕸 **P**
off Cockfosters Rd ✉ EN4 0PY – 𝒞 (020) 8216 3900 　　　　*VISA* ⚫⚫ Æ
– www.bealeshotels.co.uk – westlodgepark@bealeshotels.co.uk
– Fax (020) 8216 3937 　3ET**i**
59 rm – ⁑£90/140 ⁑⁑£185, � £15
Rest *The Cedar* – Menu £20/25 – Carte £29/44
◆ Family owned for over half a century, a country house in sweeping grounds with
arboretum. Comfortable sitting rooms; neat, spacious bedrooms. Use of nearby leisure centre. Dining room boasts large windows and exposed brick walls.

GREENWICH – Greater London
12 **B3**

Greenwich – Greater London – ✉ SE10
12 **B3**

ⅩⅩ **Spread Eagle** 　　　　　　　　🄰🄲 *VISA* ⚫⚫ ⓘ
1-2 Stockwell St ✉ SE10 9FN ⊖ Greenwich (DLR) – 𝒞 (020) 8853 2333
– www.spreadeaglerestaurant.co.uk – Fax (020) 8293 1024 　7GV**c**
Rest – French – Menu £20 (lunch) **s** – Carte £21/41 **s**
◆ This converted pub is something of an institution. Cosy booth seating, wood
panelling and a further upstairs room. Traditional French-influenced menu with attentive service.

Ⅹ **Rivington** 　　　　　　　　🄰🄲 *VISA* ⚫⚫ Æ
178 Greenwich High Rd ✉ SE10 8NN ⊖ Greenwich (DLR) – 𝒞 (020) 8293 9270
– www.rivingtongrill.co.uk – office@rivingtongrill.co.uk – Closed 25-26 December,
Monday, lunch Tuesday and Wednesday 　7GV**s**
Rest – British – Carte £21/39
◆ Part of the Picturehouse complex; 21C rustic interior with closely set tables. Firmly
English menus in bar and galleried restaurant. Banquets and market breakfasts on
offer.

HACKNEY – Greater London
12 **B3**

Hackney – Greater London – ✉ E8/E9
12 **B3**

🍴 **The Empress of India** 　　　　　　🏠 *VISA* ⚫⚫ Æ ⓘ
130 Lauriston Road, Victoria Park ✉ E9 7LH ⊖ Mile End – 𝒞 (020) 8533 5123
– www.theempressofindia.com – info@theempressofindia.com – Fax (020)
7404 2250 – Closed 25-26 December 　3GU**n**
Rest – Menu £25 – Carte £19/33
◆ Smart open-plan pub boasting mosaic floors and Indian murals. Classically based,
seasonally-evolving menu blends the robust with the refined, using only the best rare
breeds.

Cat & Mutton
VISA **CO** *AE*

76 Broadway Market ⊠ E8 4QJ⊖ *Bethnal Green* – 𝒞 (020) 7254 5599
– www.catandmutton.co.uk – catandmutton@yahoo.co.uk – Fax (020) 7254 2797
– *Closed 25-26 December, 1 January, Sunday dinner
and Monday lunch* 14YZB**a**
Rest – British – Menu £15 (weekday dinner) – Carte £21/33
♦ Early Victorian drinking pub that serves decent food; upstairs room used at week-ends. Blackboard menu offers full-bodied, satisfying dishes; many ingredients from the local market.

Prince Arthur
VISA **CO** *①*

95 Forest Road ⊠ E8 3BH⊖ *Bethnal Green* – 𝒞 (020) 7249 9996
– www.theprincearthurlondonfields.com – info@theprincearthurlondonfields.com
– Fax (020) 7249 7074 14XZB**c**
Rest – (Closed Monday-Thursday lunch) Carte £20/27
♦ An intimate local pub for local people, with plenty of character. Unpretentious and heart-warming menu, with classics like a pint of prawns and cottage pie; filling puddings.

Hoxton – Greater London – ⊠ E1/EC1/EC2/N1

Crowne Plaza
𝄞 ⌕ 📺 ⅏ ⁣ ⒮ ☎ *VISA* **CO** *AE* *①*

100 Shoreditch High St ⊠ E1 6JQ⊖ *Shoreditch* – 𝒞 (020) 7613 9800
– www.cplondon.com – marketing@cplondon.com
– Fax (020) 7613 9811 20XZD**k**
196 rm – ♦£116/243 ♦♦£159/293, � £16.95
Rest – Menu £15/25 – Carte approx. £34
♦ Purpose-built hotel on the edge of the Square Mile. Clean-lined, co-ordinated rooms with smart mod cons and king-size beds. Stylish 'Saints' bar. The Globe bar and restaurant has great views over The City.

The Hoxton
𝄞 ⌕ & rm, 📺 ⅏ ⁣ ⒮ *VISA* **CO** *AE* *①*

81 Great Eastern St ⊠ EC2A 3HU⊖ *Old Street* – 𝒞 (020) 7550 1000
– www.hoxtonhotels.com – info@hoxtonhotels.com
– Fax (020) 7550 1090 20XZD**x**
205 rm – ♦£59/199 ♦♦£59/199, ⊆ £8.50
Rest *Hoxton Grille* – Carte £19/31
♦ Urban lodge: industrial styled, clean lined modernism. "No ripoffs" mantra: cheap phone rate, free internet, complimentary 'lite pret' breakfast. Carefully considered rooms. Cooking style: New York deli meets French brasserie.

Great Eastern Dining Room
📺 *VISA* **CO** *AE* *①*

54 Great Eastern St ⊠ EC2A 3QR⊖ *Old Street* – 𝒞 (020) 7613 4545
– www.rickerrestaurants.com – greateastern@rickerrestaurants.com – Fax (020)
7613 4137 – *Closed Saturday lunch and Sunday* 20XZD**n**
Rest – Asian – Menu £30/45 – Carte £23/29
♦ Half the place is a bar that's heaving in the evening. Dining area has candle-lit tables, contemporary chandeliers, and carefully prepared, seriously tasty pan-Asian cooking.

Water House
𝄞 *VISA* **CO** *AE*

10 Orsman Road ⊠ N1 5QJ⊖ *Essex Road Station* – 𝒞 (020) 7033 0123
– www.waterhouserestaurant – eat@waterhouserestaurant.co.uk
– *Closed Sunday dinner* 14XZB**x**
Rest – Italian influences – Carte £23/36
♦ Sister to Acorn House, it shares its eco-friendly credentials and commitment to training local people. The menu is concise and seasonal; cooking has an Italian accent and flavours are natural.

LONDON

X **Fifteen London** ⛾ 🗹🖭 🗹🗷🗗 🆎
13 Westland Pl ⊠ *N1 7LP*⊖ *Old Street* – ☏ *(0871) 330 1515 – www.fifteen.net*
– Fax (020) 7251 2749 – Closed 25-26 December and 1 January 13VZC**c**
Rest – Italian – Menu £ 30 (weekday lunch) – Carte £ 39/44
♦ Original branch of Jamie Oliver's charitable restaurants; run by trainees alongside full-time staff. Buzzy ground floor trattoria; more formal basement restaurant. Tasty, seasonal Italian food.

X **Hoxton Apprentice** 🖼 🖭 ⇔ 🗹🗷🗗 🆎
16 Hoxton Sq ⊠ *N1 6NT*⊖ *Old Street* – ☏ *(020) 7749 2828*
– www.hoxtonapprentice.com – info@hoxtonapprentice.com
– Closed Monday 20XZC**r**
Rest – Modern European – Menu £ 13 (lunch) – Carte £ 18/31
♦ Set up as charitable enterprise in 19C former primary school; now stands on its own as accomplished restaurant where apprentices and pros cook interesting, seasonal dishes.

X **Real Greek Mezedopolio** 🗷🗗 🆎 🆔
15 Hoxton Market ⊠ *N1 6HG*⊖ *Old Street* – ☏ *(020) 7739 8212*
– www.therealgreek.co.uk – hoxton@therealgreek.com – Fax (020) 7739 4910
– Closed 25-26 December and 1 January 20XZC**v**
Rest – Greek – Carte £ 15/20
♦ Very relaxed restaurant with emphasis on unstructured, shared eating experience. Fresh, healthy menu divided into cold and hot meze, souvlaki and large plates for 'sharers'.

Shoreditch – Greater London – ⊠ **EC2**

XXX **L'Anima** 🗹🗷🗗 🆎
1 Snowden Street ⊠ *EC2 2DA*⊖ *Liverpool St* – ☏ *(0207) 422 7000*
– www.lanima.co.uk – enquiries@lanima.co.uk – Fax (0207) 422 7077 – Closed
Saturday, Sunday, Christmas and Bank Holidays 20XZD**a**
Rest – Italian – Menu £ 24 (lunch) – Carte £ 34/51
♦ Strikingly elegant room, with brown stone, limestone, marble and leather adding to the luxury. Flavoursome Italian food using top quality ingredients; influences from Sardinia and the south.

X **Rivington** 🖼 🗹🗷🗗 🆎
28-30 Rivington St ⊠ *EC2A 3DZ*⊖ *Old Street* – ☏ *(020) 7729 7053*
– www.rivingtongrill.co.uk – shoreditch@rivingtongrill.co.uk
– Closed 25-26 December 20XZD**e**
Rest – British – Carte £ 21/39
♦ Ex-button factory with a local buzz. Airy main restaurant has school chairs, well worn floor. There's also a comfy lounge and an intimate front area. Solidly British cooking.

🍴 **The Princess** ⛾ 🗹🗷🗗 🆎
76-78 Paul St ⊠ *EC2A 4NE*⊖ *Old Street* – ☏ *(020) 7729 9270*
– princesspub@gmail.com
– Closed 24 December-1 January and Bank Holidays 19VZD**a**
Rest – (Closed Saturday lunch) Carte £ 25/30
♦ Traditional corner pub given a gastro makeover. Dining room, above busy bar, has a stylish appeal matched by interesting international dishes underpinned by strong cooking.

🍴 **The Fox** 🗹🗷🗗
28 Paul St ⊠ *EC2A 4LB*⊖ *Old Street* – ☏ *(020) 7729 5708*
– www.thefoxpublichouse.com – thefoxpublichouse@thefoxpublichouse.com
– Closed one week Christmas to New Year 19VZD**c**
Rest – (booking essential) Carte £ 19/25
♦ Rough and ready pub with a great menu: this is found upstairs in the rather serene, but Gothic, restaurant. No nonsense dishes with bold, seasonal, unfussy, fresh flavours.

Stoke Newington – Greater London – ✉ N16

ℵ Rasa   🅰🅲 💳 ⚪ 🅰🅴

55 Stoke Newington Church St ✉ N16 0AR – ☏ (020) 7249 0344
– www.rasarestaurants.com – Fax (020) 7637 0224
– Closed 24-26 December, and 1 January   14XZA**e**
Rest – Indian – (dinner only and lunch Saturday and Sunday) (booking
essential) Menu £16 – Carte £9/13
♦ Busy Indian restaurant, an unpretentious environment in which to sample authentic, sometimes unusual, dishes. The "Feast" offers a taste of the range of foods on offer.

ℵ Rasa Travancore   🅰🅲 💳 ⚪ 🅰🅴 ①

56 Stoke Newington Church St ✉ N16 0NB – ☏ (020) 7249 1340
– www.rasarestaurants.com – Closed 23-30 December   14XZA**x**
Rest – Indian – (dinner only) Carte approx. £12
♦ Friendly, knowledgable service a distinct bonus to diners getting to know Keralan cooking. Good value dishes: 'feast' menu recommended by staff offers the full experience.

HAMMERSMITH and FULHAM – Greater London   12 **B3**

Fulham – Greater London – ✉ SW6

ℵℵℵ Saran Rom   🍴 🅰🅲 ⇔ 💳 ⚪ 🅰🅴

The Boulevard, Imperial Wharf, Townmead Rd ✉ SW6 2UB⊖ Fulham Broadway
– ☏ (020) 7751 3111 – www.blueelephant.com/river
– river@blueelephant.com   23PZH**b**
Rest – Thai – Menu £39 – Carte £42/43
♦ Terrific riverside terrace and elegantly decorated interior; based on Thai Royal summer palace. Now owned by Blue Elephant group. Slight seafood bias to the appealing and concise menu.

ℵℵℵ Memories of India on the River   🍴 🅰🅲 💳 ⚪ 🅰🅴 ①

7 The Boulevard, Imperial Wharf ✉ SW6 2UB⊖ Fulham Broadway – ☏ (020)
7736 0077 – www.memoriesofindiaontheriver.co.uk – Fax (020) 7731 5222
– Closed 25 December   23PZH**n**
Rest – Indian – Menu £25 (lunch) – Carte £32/43
♦ Indian fabrics adorn this slinky restaurant in a spanking new wharf complex. Vast palm useful for getting your bearings: interesting, original, well-presented Indian dishes.

ℵℵ Yi-Ban   🅰🅲 💳 ⚪ 🅰🅴

5 The Boulevard, Imperial Rd, Imperial Wharf ✉ SW6 2SX⊖ Fulham Broadway
– ☏ (020) 7731 6606 – www.yi-ban.co.uk – chelsea@yi-ban.co.uk – Fax (020)
7731 7584 – Closed Sunday and Bank Holidays   23PZH**n**
Rest – Chinese – (dinner only) Carte approx. £21
♦ Very stylish and contemporary with dark, seductice interior divided by opaque nets; cocktail bar adds to the mix. Modern Chinese dishes meet tried-and-tested favourites.

ℵℵ Deep   🍴 🅰🅲 💳 ⚪ 🅰🅴

The Boulevard, Imperial Wharf ✉ SW6 2UB⊖ Fulham Broadway – ☏ (020)
7736 3337 – www.deeplondon.co.uk – info@deeplondon.co.uk – Fax (020)
7736 7578 – Closed 2 weeks Christmas - New Year, 1 week August, Monday,
Sunday dinner, Saturday lunch and Bank Holidays   23PZH**n**
Rest – Seafood – Carte £25/43
♦ Slick, modern restaurant on rejuvenated riverside wharf. Linen-clad tables; floor-to-ceiling windows. Modern seafood dishes with Scandinavian feel; large aquavit selection.

XX **Blue Elephant** `AC` `VISA` `MO` `AE` `①`
4-6 Fulham Broadway ⊠ SW6 1AA⊖ Fulham Broadway – ℰ (020) 7385 6595
– www.blueelephant.com – london@blueelephant.com – Fax (020) 7386 7665
– Closed Christmas and Saturday lunch   22NZG**z**
Rest – Thai – (booking essential) Menu £ 15/35 – Carte £ 30/50
♦ Elaborately ornate, unrestrained décor: fountains, bridges, orchids and ponds with
carp. Authentic Thai food served by attentive staff in national costumes.

XX **Mao Tai** `AC` `VISA` `MO` `AE` `①`
58 New Kings Rd, Parsons Green ⊠ SW6 4LS⊖ Parsons Green – ℰ (020)
7731 2520 – www.maotai.co.uk – mark.maotai@googlemail.com
– Closed 24-25 December   22NZH**e**
Rest – Chinese – (dinner only and Sunday lunch) Carte £ 33/47
♦ A light and modern interior with wood flooring and framed artwork with an eastern theme. Well organised service. Chinese cuisine with Szechuan specialities.

🗓 **The Farm** `AC` `VISA` `MO` `AE`
18 Farm Lane ⊠ SW6 1PP⊖ Fulham Broadway – ℰ (020) 7381 3331
– www.thefarmfulham.co.uk – info@thefarmfulham.co.uk
– Closed 25 December   22NZG**x**
Rest – Menu £ 25/29 – Carte £ 25/40
♦ Somewhat austere looking façade but welcoming fireplaces within. Ambitious
menu displays international influences alongside more traditionally British dishes;
beef is especially tender.

Hammersmith – Greater London – ⊠ W6/W14

XX **River Café** (Ruth Rogers & Rose Gray) `🌳` `✦` `VISA` `MO` `AE` `①`
🕄 Thames Wharf, Rainville Rd ⊠ W6 9HA⊖ Barons Court – ℰ (020) 7386 4200
– www.rivercafe.co.uk – info@rivercafe.co.uk – Fax (020) 7386 4201
– Closed Christmas-New Year, Bank Holidays and Sunday dinner   21LZG**r**
Rest – Italian – (booking essential) Carte £ 42/56
Spec. Tagliarini with red mullet and tomato. Veal shin, white wine, cannellini
beans and Summer Savory. Apricot and almond tart
♦ Changes in 2008 include a new cheese-room, a more open-plan kitchen and bigger
billing given to the wood-fired oven. Cooking remains earthy, seasonal, full of flavour
and satisfying.

XX **Chez Kristof** `🌳` `AC` `✦` `VISA` `MO` `AE`
111 Hammersmith Grove, Brook Green ⊠ W6 0NQ⊖ Hammersmith – ℰ (020)
8741 1177 – www.chezkristof.co.uk – info@chezkristof.co.uk
– Closed Christmas   21LZF**b**
Rest – French – Menu £ 18 – Carte £ 23/30
♦ Well worth seeking out in Brook Green: there's a deli, delightful terrace, and a
menu of satisfying classics. Influences are mostly from within Europe, particularly
France.

XX **Indian Zing** `🌳` `AC` `VISA` `MO` `AE` `①`
236 King St ⊠ W6 0RF⊖ Ravenscourt Park – ℰ (020) 8748 5959
– www.indianzing.co.uk – indianzing@aol.com – Fax (020) 8748 2332   21LZG**a**
Rest – Indian – Menu £ 15/22 – Carte £ 22/36
♦ Sophisticated, modern restaurant with crisp white walls adorned with photos of
life on the subcontinent. Traditional Indian menus are jettisoned for modish, original
dishes.

X **The Brackenbury** `🌳` `VISA` `MO` `AE`
129-131 Brackenbury Rd ⊠ W6 0BQ⊖ Ravenscourt Park – ℰ (020) 8748 0107
– www.thebrackenbury.co.uk – info@thebrackenbury.com – Fax (020) 8748 6159
– Closed 25-26 December, 1 January, Saturday lunch and Sunday dinner   15LZE**a**
Rest – Modern European – Menu £ 15/18 – Carte £ 25/34
♦ The closely set wooden tables, pavement terrace and relaxed service add to the
cosy, neighbourhood feel. Cooking is equally unfussy; modern yet robust.

Azou

375 King St ✉ W6 9NJ ⊖ Stamford Brook – ✆ (020) 8563 7266 – www.azou.co.uk – info@azou.co.uk – Closed 25 December, Bank Holidays and lunch Saturday and Sunday 21KZG**u**

Rest – North African – Carte £ 17/25

◆ The North African theme is not confined to the menu; the room is decorated with hanging lanterns, screens and assorted knick-knacks. Friendly service and well priced dishes.

Anglesea Arms

35 Wingate Rd ✉ W6 0UR ⊖ Ravenscourt Park – ✆ (020) 8749 1291 – www.angleseaarms.co.uk – anglesea.events@gmail.com – Fax (020) 8749 1254 – Closed 23-27 December 15LZE**c**

Rest – (bookings not accepted) Carte £ 15/35

◆ The twice daily changing menu of gutsy, wholesome food is served in both the glass-roofed restaurant with the open kitchen and the dark panelled bar. Good selection of wines by the glass

The Havelock Tavern

57 Masbro Rd, Brook Green ✉ W14 0LS ⊖ Kensington Olympia – ✆ (020) 7603 5374 – www.thehavelocktavern.co.uk – info@thehavelocktavern.co.uk – Closed 25 December 16MZE**e**

Rest – (bookings not accepted) Carte £ 19/28

◆ True and honest community pub that isn't afraid to hold onto its roots. Great value blackboard menu features modern, seasonal, gutsy dishes and proper heart-warming puddings.

Carpenter's Arms

91 Black Lion Lane ✉ W6 9BG ⊖ Stamford Brook – ✆ (020) 8741 8386 – info@carpentersarms-info – Fax (020) 8741 6437 – Closed 25 December and 1 January 21KZG**b**

Rest – (booking essential) Carte £ 22/35

◆ May not look like a pub but is a busy place with smart service. Good British ingredients to the fore, particularly the seasonal vegetables, in rustic and satisfying dishes.

The Dartmouth Castle

26 Glenthorne Road ✉ W6 0LS ⊖ Hammersmith – ✆ (020) 8748 3614 – www.thedartmouthcastle.co.uk – dartmouth.castle@btconnect.com – Fax (020) 8748 3619 – Closed 24 December to 1 January, first Monday in August 21LZF**e**

Rest – Carte £ 18/27

◆ Busy, hospitable pub serving monthly-changing, Mediterranean-influenced menu. Cheery staff, regularly-changing cask ales and board games encourage the locals to linger.

Shepherd's Bush – Greater London – ✉ W14

K West

Richmond Way ✉ W14 0AX ⊖ Kensington Olympia – ✆ (020) 8008 6600 – www.k-west.co.uk – bookit@k-west.co.uk – Fax (020) 8008 6650 16MZE**c**

214 rm – †£ 229 ††£ 412, ☕ £ 17 – 6 suites

Rest *Kanteen* – ✆ (020) 8008 6631 – Carte £ 19/30

◆ Former BBC offices, the interior is decorated in a smart, contemporary fashion. Bedrooms in understated modern style, deluxe rooms with work desks and DVD and CD facilities. Modish menus in trendy dining room.

Good food and accommodation at moderate prices?
Look for the Bib symbols:
red Bib Gourmand for food, blue Bib Hotel for hotels

LONDON

HARINGEY – Greater London 12 **B3**

Crouch End – Greater London – ✉ N4/N8

⚐ **Mountview** without rest 🔌 🕸 🕪 *VISA* 🅒🅞
31 Mount View Rd ✉ N4 4SS – ✆ (020) 8340 9222
– www.mountviewguesthouse.com – info@mountviewguesthouse.com 3EU**r**
3 rm ⌑ – †£55/60 ††£90
♦ Redbrick Victorian house with a warm and stylish ambience engendered by the homely décor. One bedroom features an original fireplace and two overlook the quiet rear garden.

🍴 **Bistro Aix** *VISA* 🅒🅞 🅰🅔 🅞
54 Topsfield Parade, Tottenham Lane ✉ N8 8PT – ✆ (020) 8340 6346
– www.bistroaix.co.uk – bistroaix@hotmail.co.uk – Fax (020) 8348 7236
– Closed Monday 3EU**v**
Rest – French – (dinner only and lunch Saturday-Sunday) Menu £15
– Carte £19/35
♦ The simple wood furniture is complemented by plants and pictures. The owner chef's experience in France is reflected in the menu and the robust and hearty cooking.

🍺 **The Queens Pub and Dining Room** 🌇 🅰🅒 *VISA* 🅒🅞 🅰🅔
26 Broadway Parade ✉ N8 9DE – ✆ (020) 8340 2031
– www.thequeenscrouchend.co.uk – queens@foodandfuel.co.uk 3EU**c**
Rest – Carte £15/28
♦ Classic Victorian pub with shimmering chandeliers, mahogany panelling and ornate ceilings. Menu offers a mix of modern British dishes with plenty of Mediterranean influence.

Highgate – Greater London – ✉ N6

🍺 **The Bull** 🌇 ⇔ **P** *VISA* 🅒🅞 🅰🅔
13 North Hill ✉ N6 4AB ⊖ Highgate – ✆ (0845) 456 5033
– www.themeredithgroup.co.uk – info@inthebull.biz – Closed 26 December,
1 January and Monday lunch except Bank Holidays 2EU**x**
Rest – Menu £18 (lunch) – Carte £28/35
♦ Not your typical pub, The Bull offers seasonal and carefully prepared European food with a dominant French gene. Good breads. A bright room, clued-up service; more family-orientated at weekends.

Stroud Green – Greater London – ✉ N4

🍺 **The Old Dairy** 🅰🅒 *VISA* 🅒🅞
1-3 Crouch Hill ✉ N4 4AP – ✆ (020) 7263 3337 – www.realpubs.co.uk
– theolddairy@realpubs.co.uk – Fax (020) 7561 1851 3EU**a**
Rest – (Closed Monday-Thursday lunch) Carte £20/25
♦ Picture panels illustrate this listed building's former use as a dairy. Now serving modern British cooking with a hint of Europe; bold and honest, with well judged portions.

Tottenham – Greater London – ✉ N17

🍴🍴 **The Lock** **P** *VISA* 🅒🅞 🅰🅔
Heron House, Hale Wharf, Ferry Lane ✉ N17 9NF ⊖ Tottenham Hale – ✆ (020)
8885 2829 – www.thelockrestaurant.com – thelock06@btconnect.com – Fax (020)
8885 1618 – Closed Monday 3GU**a**
Rest – Modern European – Menu £19 – Carte £20/33
♦ An oasis of cool in N17. By the side of a lock, there's a long bar with sofas, and restaurant with wood or mosaic tables. Original touches enhance tasty French/Italian mix.

HARROW – Greater London 12 **A3**

Harrow on the Hill – Greater London – ⊠ HA1

XX **Incanto** 🔤 *VISA* 🆀 AE

41 High St ⊠ HA1 3HT⊖ Harrow on the Hill – ℰ (020) 8426 6767
– www.incanto.co.uk – dtaylor@incanto.co.uk – Fax (020) 8423 5087
– Closed 25 December, 1 January, Sunday dinner and Monday 1BU**z**
Rest – Italian – Menu £22 (lunch) – Carte £24/28
♦ Within Grade II former post office; split-level restaurant to rear of well stocked deli. Well paced service; Southern Italian bias to the rustic cooking, with quality produce to the fore.

Harrow Weald – Greater London – ⊠ HA3

🔠 **Grim's Dyke** 🌳 🕪 ᇰ rm, 🖋 P, *VISA* 🆀 AE ①

Old Redding ⊠ HA3 6SH – ℰ (020) 8385 3100 – www.grimsdyke.com
– reservations@grimsdyke.com – Fax (020) 8954 4560 1BT**a**
46 rm ☑ – †£85/95 ††£95/130
Rest *Gilberts* – (closed Saturday lunch) Carte £24/50
♦ Victorian mansion, former country residence of W.S.Gilbert. Rooms divided between main house and lodge, the former more characterful. Over 40 acres of garden and woodland. Restaurant with ornately carved fireplace.

Pinner – Greater London – ⊠ HA5

XX **Friends** 🔤 *VISA* 🆀 AE

11 High St ⊠ HA5 5PJ⊖ Pinner – ℰ (020) 8866 0286
– www.friendsrestaurant.co.uk – info@friendsrestaurant.co.uk – Fax (020)
8866 0286 – Closed 2 weeks July-August, 25-26 December,
Sunday dinner and Monday 1BU**a**
Rest – Modern European – Menu £22/30
♦ Pretty beamed cottage, with some parts dating back 400 years. Inside, a welcoming glow from the log fire; personal service from owners and a fresh, regularly-changing menu.

If breakfast is included the ☑ symbol appears after the number of rooms.

HILLINGDON – Greater London 12 **A3**

🔟 Haste Hill Northwood The Drive, ℰ (01923) 825 224

Heathrow Airport – Greater London

🔠 **London Heathrow Marriott** 🔲 🕉 Ӻᴓ 🖹 ᇰ rm, 🔤 🕸 🕪 ᇲ P
Bath Rd, Hayes ⊠ UB3 5AN – ℰ (020) 8990 1100 *VISA* 🆀 AE ①
– www.londonheathrowmarriott.co.uk – Fax (020) 8990 1110 5AX**z**
391 rm – †£182 ††£182, ☑ £16.95 – 2 suites
Rest *Tuscany* – Italian – ℰ (0870) 400 7250 (Closed Sunday) (dinner only)
Menu £39 – Carte £33/46
Rest *Allie's grille* – ℰ (0870) 400 7250 – Carte £21/38
♦ Built at the end of 20C, this modern, comfortable hotel is centred around a large atrium, with comprehensive business facilities: there is an exclusive Executive floor. Italian cuisine at bright and convivial Tuscany. Grill favourites at Allie's.

🔠 **Sheraton Skyline** 🔲 Ӻᴓ 🖹 ᇰ rm, 🔤 🕪 ᇲ P, *VISA* 🆀 AE ①
Bath Rd, Hayes ⊠ UB3 5BP – ℰ (020) 8759 2535 – www.sheraton.com/skyline
– res268-skyline@sheraton.com – Fax (020) 8750 9151 5AX**u**
348 rm – †£69/245 ††£349, ☑ £17
Rest *Al Dente* – Carte £21/30
♦ Well known for its unique indoor swimming pool surrounded by a tropical garden which is overlooked by many of the bedrooms. Business centre available. Italian dining in Al Dente.

Hilton London Heathrow Airport

☑ ⋙ 𝐿₆ 🛗 ᴷ rm, Ꮶ 🕻

Terminal 4 ⊠ TW6 3AF – ℰ (020) 8759 7755

🏧 P̶ VISA ᴹᴼ ᴬᴱ ①

– www.hilton.co.uk/heathrow – gm-heathrow@hilton.com

– Fax (020) 8759 7579

5AXn

390 rm – ♦£292 ♦♦£292, ☑ £20.50 – 5 suites

Rest *Brasserie* – Modern – (closed lunch Saturday and Sunday) (buffet lunch)
Menu £28/35 – Carte dinner £33/50

Rest *Zen Oriental* – Chinese – (closed Bank Holidays) Carte £23/24

♦ Group hotel with a striking modern exterior and linked to Terminal 4 by a covered walkway. Good sized bedrooms, with contemporary styled suites. Spacious Brasserie in vast atrium. Zen Oriental offers formal Chinese experience.

Ruislip – Greater London

Hawtrey's – at The Barn Hotel

🚊 Ꮶ ⇔ P̶ VISA ᴹᴼ ᴬᴱ ①

West End Rd ⊠ HA4 6JB⊖ Ruislip – ℰ (01895) 679 999

– www.thebarnhotel.co.uk – info@thebarnhotel.co.uk – Fax (01895) 638 379

– Closed Saturday lunch Sunday dinner

1AUe

Rest – Modern European – Menu £16/29 **s** – Carte £29/43 **s**

♦ Jacobean styled baronial hall: an extension to 16C Barn Hotel. Cloth clad tables, bright chandeliers. Fine dining - modern cooking that's confident and assured.

Don't confuse ※ with ۞!
※ defines comfort, while stars are awarded for the best cuisine, across all categories of comfort.

HOUNSLOW – Greater London

12 **A3**

🛈 The Treaty Centre, High St ℰ (0845) 456 2929 (closed Sunday), tic@cip.org.uk

🏌 Wyke Green Isleworth Syon Lane, ℰ (020) 8560 8777

🏌 Airlinks Southall Lane, ℰ (020) 8561 1418

🏌 Hounslow HeathStaines Rd, ℰ (020) 8570 5271

Chiswick – Greater London – ⊠ W4

12 **A3**

High Road House

🛗 Ꮶ 📶 VISA ᴹᴼ ᴬᴱ

162 Chiswick High Rd ⊠ W4 1PR⊖ Turnham Green – ℰ (020) 8742 1717

– www.highroadhouse.co.uk – reservation@highroadhouse.co.uk

– Fax (020) 8987 8762

21KZGf

14 rm – ♦£140 ♦♦£140, ☑ £10

♦ Cool, sleek hotel and club, the latter a slick place to lounge around or play games. Light, bright bedrooms with crisp linen. A carefully appointed, fair-priced destination.

La Trompette

۞

🍴 Ꮶ VISA ᴹᴼ ᴬᴱ

5-7 Devonshire Rd ⊠ W4 2EU⊖ Turnham Green – ℰ (020) 8747 1836

– www.latrompette.co.uk – reception@latrompette.co.uk – Fax (020) 8995 8097

– Closed 24-27 December and 1 January

21KZGy

Rest – Modern European – (booking essential) Menu £24/38 ⅋

Spec. Sea trout, crab and cucumber with vichyssoise. Poulet noir, leeks, vin Jaune and tarragon. Chocolate marquise with milk sorbet, chicory and praline.

♦ Genuine neighbourhood restaurant with pretty front terrace. Classical, flavoursome French cooking makes vibrant use of the freshest of ingredients. Exceptional wine list.

High Road Brasserie

🍴 Ꮶ VISA ᴹᴼ ᴬᴱ

162 Chiswick High Rd ⊠ W4 1PR⊖ Turnham Green – ℰ (020) 8742 7474

– www.highroadhouse.co.uk

21KZGf

Rest – Traditional – Carte £34/38

♦ Confidently stylish place to eat. Marble-topped bar and Belgian tiled dining area provide sleek backdrop to well-priced, satisfying menus full of interesting brasserie dishes.

XX Le Vacherin [AK]

76-77 South Par. ⊠ W4 5LF⊖ *Chiswick Park* – ℰ (020) 8742 2121
– www.levacherin.co.uk – info@levacherin.co.uk – Fax (020) 8742 0799
– Closed 1-2 January, Monday lunch and Bank Holidays   6CV**o**
Rest – French – Carte £ 26/45
♦ Smart and authentic French brasserie, complete with belle époque prints. Satisfying menu of carefully prepared classics, from snails to cassoulet, including baked Vacherin. All French wine list.

X Fish Hook [AK] [VISA] [CO] [AE]

6-8 Elliott Rd ⊠ W4 1PE⊖ *Turnham Green* – ℰ (020) 8742 0766
– www.fishhook.co.uk – info@fishhook.co.uk – Fax (020) 8742 3374
– Closed 25 December   21KZG**z**
Rest – Seafood – Menu £ 15 (lunch) – Carte £ 35/49
♦ Chef-owner sources most of his fish from around British Isles. Simple room with convivial atmosphere. Confident cooking from open-plan kitchen, with the occasional Asian note.

X Sam's Brasserie [AK] [VISA] [CO] [AE]

11 Barley Mow Passage ⊠ W4 4PH⊖ *Turnham Green* – ℰ (020) 8987 0555
– www.samsbrasserie.co.uk – info@samsbrasserie.co.uk – Fax (020) 8987 7389
– Closed 25-26 December   2CV**a**
Rest – Mediterranean – Menu £ 15 (lunch) – Carte £ 25/32
♦ Former paper mill by Turnham Green. 'Industrial', open plan feel with concrete and stainless steel. Robust brasserie dishes seem to be in keeping with the surroundings.

🏠 The Devonshire [VISA] [CO] [AE]

126 Devonshire Rd ⊠ W4 2JJ⊖ *Turnham Green* – ℰ (020) 7592 7962
– www.gordonramsay.com – thedevonshire@gordonramsay.com
– Fax (020) 7592 1603   21KZG**a**
Rest – Menu £ 17 (lunch) – Carte £ 25/28
♦ The second member of Gordon Ramsay's burgeoning pub group. Appealing snacks like cockles and scotch eggs in the bar; pub classics, pies, soups and more elaborate dishes in the neat restaurant.

We try to be as accurate as possible when giving room rates but prices are susceptible to change.
Please check rates when booking.

ISLINGTON – Greater London   12 **B3**

Archway – ⊠ N19

🏠 St John's [VISA] [CO] [AE]

91 Junction Rd ⊠ N19 5QU⊖ *Archway* – ℰ (020) 7272 1587
– st.johns@virgin.net – Closed 25-26 December and 1 January   12RZA**s**
Rest – (dinner only and lunch Friday-Sunday) Carte £ 20/32
♦ Busy front bar enjoys a lively atmosphere; dining room in a large rear room. Log fire at one end, open hatch into kitchen the other. Blackboard menu; rustic cooking.

Barnsbury – Greater London – ⊠ N1/N7

XX Morgan M [AK] [VISA] [CO] [①]

489 Liverpool Rd ⊠ N7 8NS⊖ *Highbury and Islington* – ℰ (020) 7609 3560
– www.morganm.com – Fax (020) 8292 5699 – Closed 24-30 December, lunch Tuesday and Saturday, Sunday dinner and Monday   13UZA**a**
Rest – French – Menu £ 26/39 – Carte £ 39/45
♦ Simple restaurant in a converted pub. Smartly-laid tables complemented by formal service. Modern dishes based on classical French combinations.

✗ Fig 🏠 VISA 🐵 AE

169 Hemingford Rd ✉ *N1 1DA*⊖ *Caledonian Road –* ☏ *(020) 7609 3009*
– www.fig-restaurant.co.uk – figrestaurant@btconnect.com
– Closed 2 weeks Christmas   13UZB**a**
Rest – Modern European – (dinner only) Carte £ 25/35
♦ Attractive and cosy neighbourhood restaurant with fig tree leaning over garden terrace. Original combinations move the weekly changing menu away from the modern European norm.

Canonbury – Greater London – ✉ N1

🍺 The House 🏠 VISA 🐵 AE

63-69 Canonbury Rd ✉ *N1 2DG*⊖ *Highbury and Islington –* ☏ *(020) 7704 7410*
– www.themeredithgroup.co.uk – info@inthehouse.biz
– Fax (020) 7704 9388   13UZB**h**
Rest – (Closed Monday lunch) Menu £ 18 (lunch) – Carte £ 26/35
♦ This pleasant pub, on a street corner and popular with locals, has a restaurant with linen-covered tables, ceiling fans, art for sale, and modern menus with a classical base.

Clerkenwell – Greater London – ✉ EC1

🏨 Malmaison 🔥 🎣 🛁 rm, 🅰️🅲 🕙 🎵 🛁 VISA 🐵 AE ①

18-21 Charterhouse Sq ✉ *EC1M 6AH*⊖ *Barbican –* ☏ *(020) 7012 3700*
– www.malmaison.com – london@malmaison.com
– Fax (020) 7012 3702   19UZD**o**
97 rm – �{£ 252 �{�{£ 276/580, ⌂ £17.95
Rest *Brasserie* – (closed Saturday lunch) Menu £ 18 (weekdays)
– Carte £ 24/40
♦ Striking early 20C redbrick building overlooking pleasant square. Stylish, comfy public areas. Bedrooms in vivid, bold colours, with extras such as stereo and free broadband. Modern brasserie employing meats from Smithfield.

🏠 The Rookery without rest 🅰️🅲 🎣 🎵 🛁 VISA 🐵 AE ①

12 Peters Lane, Cowcross St ✉ *EC1M 6DS*⊖ *Barbican –* ☏ *(020) 7336 0931*
– www.rookeryhotel.com – reservations@rookery.co.uk
– Fax (020) 7336 0931   33AOT**p**
32 rm – �{£ 206/241 �{�{£ 259/347, ⌂ £9.95 – 1 suite
♦ A row of charmingly restored 18C houses. Wood panelling, stone-flagged flooring, open fires and antique furniture. Highly individual bedrooms, with Victorian bathrooms.

✗✗ Smiths of Smithfield ≤ 🏠 🅰️🅲 VISA 🐵 AE ①

Top Floor, 67-77 Charterhouse St ✉ *EC1M 6HJ*⊖ *Barbican –* ☏ *(020) 7251 7950*
– www.smithsofsmithfield.co.uk – reservations@smithsofsmithfield.co.uk
– Fax (020) 7236 5666
– Closed 24 December - 2 January and Saturday lunch   33AOT**s**
Rest – Modern European – Carte £ 34/47
Rest *The Dining Room* – (closed Saturday lunch, Sunday and Bank Holidays)
Carte £ 22/28
♦ On three floors where the higher you go the more formal it becomes. Busy, bustling atmosphere and modern menu. Good views of the market from the top floor terrace. The Dining Room with mirrors and dark blue walls.

✗ St John 🅰️🅲 ⇔ VISA 🐵 AE ①

☼3 *26 St John St* ✉ *EC1M 4AY*⊖ *Barbican –* ☏ *(020) 7251 0848*
– www.stjohnrestaurant.com – reservations@stjohnrestaurant.com
– Fax (020) 7251 4090 – Closed Christmas, Easter, Saturday lunch,
Sunday and Bank Holidays   33APT**c**
Rest – British – (booking essential) Carte £ 26/39
Spec. Brown shrimps and white cabbage. Venison liver and lentils. Eccles cake and Lancashire cheese.
♦ 'Nose to tail eating' is how they describe their cooking at this busy, bright, converted 19C smokehouse. Strong on offal, game and unusual cuts; gloriously British, appealingly simple and very satisfying.

✗ **Hix Oyster and Chop House** 🛜 VISA ⬥ AE ⓘ
36-37 Greenhill Rents ✉ EC1M 6BN⊖ Farringdon – ℰ (0207) 0171930
– www.restaurantsetcltd.com – chophouse@restaurantsetcltd.co.uk – Fax (0207)
0171931 – Closed Saturday lunch and Sunday dinner   33AOT**e**
Rest – British – Carte £24/62
♦ Appropriately utilitarian surroundings put the focus on seasonal and often under-
used British ingredients. Cooking is satisfying and unfussy, with plenty of oysters and
aged beef served on the bone.

✗ **Vinoteca** VISA ⬥
7 St John St ✉ EC1M 4AA⊖ Farringdon – ℰ (020) 72538786
– www.vinoteca.co.uk – enquiries@vinoteca.co.uk – Closed Christmas-New Year,
Sunday and Bank Holidays   33APT**a**
Rest – Modern European – (booking essential at lunch) Carte £25/30
♦ Bold, modern dishes with perfect wine pairing in this thoroughly informal 'wine
bar' eatery. Well-stocked shelves a great attraction: take out your favourite or drink
within.

✗ **Comptoir Gascon** AK VISA ⬥ AE
61-63 Charterhouse St ✉ EC1M 6HJ⊖ Barbican – ℰ (020) 76080851
– www.comptoirgascon.com – info@comptoirgascon.com – Fax (020) 76080871
– Closed Christmas-New Year, Sunday and Monday   33AOT**a**
Rest – French – Carte £20/32
♦ Half restaurant, half deli, opposite Smithfield. Rustic notions enhanced by exposed
brick. Well priced, comforting specialities from south west France. Same owners as
Club Gascon.

✗ **Flâneur** VISA ⬥ AE ⓘ
41 Farringdon Rd ✉ EC1M 3JB⊖ Farringdon – ℰ (020) 74044422
– www.flaneur.com – mail@flaneur.com – Fax (020) 78314532
– Closed 24 December-2 January and Sunday   32ANT**s**
Rest – Modern European – (Sunday brunch) Menu £26 – Carte approx. £27
♦ Pleasant food store and eatery: the former has immaculately lined shelves of deli
products, the latter is surrounded by succulent aromas; cooking is robust modern
European.

🍴 **The Coach & Horses** 🛜 VISA ⬥ AE
26-28 Ray St ✉ EC1R 3DJ⊖ Farringdon – ℰ (020) 72788990
– www.thecoachandhorses.com – info@thecoachandhorses.com
– Fax (020) 72781478
– Closed Christmas to New Year, Easter weekend, Bank Holidays   19UZD**a**
Rest – Italian influences – Carte £22/28
♦ Characterful Victorian pub, recently refurbished and moving with the times. Pleas-
ant and well run dining room with strong Mediterranean influence on the menu.
Appealing snack menu in the bar.

Finsbury – Greater London – ✉ EC1

🏠 **The Zetter** 🛜 🖥 ᴗ rm, AK 📶 ᴣ VISA ⬥ AE
St John's Square, 86-88 Clerkenwell Rd ✉ EC1M 5RJ⊖ Farringdon – ℰ (020)
73244444 – www.thezetter.com – info@thezetter.com
– Fax (020) 73244456   19UZD**s**
59 rm – †£194 ††£194, � £16.50
Rest – (closed 25-26 December) Carte £21/37
♦ Discreetly trendy modern design in the well-equipped bedrooms and rooftop
studios of a converted 19C warehouse:pleasant extras from old paperbacks to flat-
screen TV/DVDs. Light, informal restaurant serves modern Mediterranean dishes and
weekend brunches.

XX The Clerkenwell Dining Room   AC ⇔ VISA ⊕⊖ AE ⓪

69-73 St John St ⊠ EC1M 4AN⊖ Farringdon – ℰ (020) 7253 9000
– www.theclerkenwell.com – reservations@theclerkenwell.com – Fax (020)
7253 3322 – Closed Saturday lunch and Sunday   19UZD**h**
Rest – French – Menu £ 20 – Carte £ 30/40

♦ Former pub, now a stylish modern restaurant with etched glass façade. Three adjoining dining areas with bar provide setting for contemporary cooking with its roots in France.

XX Portal   AC ⇔ VISA ⊕⊖ AE

88 St John St ⊠ EC1M 4EH⊖ Farringdon – ℰ (020) 7253 6950
– www.portalrestaurant.com – reservations@portalrestaurant.com – Fax (020)
7490 5836 – Closed Saturday lunch, Sunday and Bank Holidays   19UZD**r**
Rest – Mediterranean – Carte £ 34/56

♦ Portugal and Southern Europe are the main influences, with fish and pork dishes the house specialities. Busy front bar and a chic, semi-industrial feel to the rear restaurant. Helpful service.

XX The Larder   AC ⇔ VISA ⊕⊖ AE

91-93 St John St ⊠ EC1M 4NU⊖ Farringdon – ℰ (020) 7608 1558
– www.thelarderrestaurant.com – info@thelarderrestaurant.com – Fax (120)
7253 9285 – Closed 23 December - 5 January, Saturday lunch,
Sunday and Bank Holidays   19UZD**f**
Rest – Modern European – Carte £ 24/35

♦ Large, glass-fronted restaurant with stark, noisy, industrial feel and own bakery selling breads and pastries. Unfussy food has an English accent with some European influences.

X Quality Chop House   AC VISA ⊕⊖ AE

94 Farringdon Rd ⊠ EC1R 3EA⊖ Farringdon – ℰ (020) 7837 5093
– www.qualitychophouse.co.uk – enquiries@qualitychophouse.co.uk – Fax (020)
7833 8748 – Closed 25-26 December, 1 January and Saturday lunch   19UZD**n**
Rest – British – Carte £ 21/38

♦ On the window is etched "Progressive working class caterers". This is borne out with the individual café-style booths and a menu ranging from jellied eels to caviar.

X Moro   AC VISA ⊕⊖ AE ⓪

34-36 Exmouth Market ⊠ EC1R 4QE⊖ Farringdon – ℰ (020) 7833 8336
– www.moro.co.uk – info@moro.co.uk – Fax (020) 7833 9338 – Closed Easter,
Christmas, Sunday and Bank Holidays   19UZD**b**
Rest – Mediterranean – (booking essential) Carte £ 29/35

♦ Daily changing menu an eclectic mix of Mediterranean, Moroccan and Spanish. Friendly T-shirted staff. Informal surroundings with bare tables and a large zinc bar.

X The Ambassador   VISA ⊕⊖ AE

55 Exmouth Market ⊠ EC1R 4QL⊖ Farringdon – ℰ (020) 7837 0009
– www.theambassadorcafe.co.uk – clive@theambassadorcafe.co.uk
– Closed 24 December-2 January, Sunday dinner and Bank Holidays   19UZD**c**
Rest – Traditional – Menu £ 16 (lunch) – Carte £ 19/31

♦ Lino and melamine give a refreshing retro appeal to this cool, buzzy diner. Seasonal, honest, earthy ingredients inform all-day Eurocentric menus that tend towards the Gallic.

X Medcalf   🍴 VISA ⊕⊖

40 Exmouth Market ⊠ EC1R 4QE⊖ Farringdon – ℰ (020) 7833 3533
– www.medcalfbar.co.uk – mail@medcalfbar.co.uk – Fax (020) 7833 1321
– Closed 24 December-2 January, Sunday dinner and Bank Holidays   19UZD**b**
Rest – British – (booking essential) Carte £ 26/35

♦ Bustling, no-frills former butcher's shop with lively atmosphere. Satisfying robust cooking, with the emphasis on seasonal, British ingredients. Good range of beer and wine by the glass.

✗ **Cicada**   ⇔ VISA ⓞⓞ AE ⓞ
132-136 St John St ✉ *EC1V 4JT*⊖ *Farringdon –* ✆ *(020) 7608 1550*
– www.rickerrestaurants.com – cicada@rickerrestaurants.com – Fax (020)
8608 1551 – Closed 23 December-3 January, Saturday lunch,
Sunday and Bank Holidays   19UZD**d**
Rest – Asian – Menu £ 15 (lunch) – Carte £ 15/30
♦ Set in a culinary hotbed, this buzzy restaurant and vibrant bar is spacious, lively
and popular for its South East Asian dishes: pop in for one course and a beer if you
like.

✗ **The Modern Pantry**   ㄘ AC ⇔ VISA ⓞⓞ AE
⊛ *47-48 St John's Sq* ✉ *EC1V 4JJ*⊖ *Farringdon –* ✆ *(020) 7250 0833*
– www.themodernpantry.co.uk – enquiries@themodernpantry.co.uk
– Closed Christmas-New Year and Bank Holidays   19UZD**k**
Rest – International – (booking advisable) Carte £ 25/32
♦ Zesty, vivacious, cooking stars at Anna Hansen's restaurant, housed within a Georgian building. Café-style ground floor more fun than upstairs. Good value menu;
fusion without being convoluted.

⒤ **The Peasant**   VISA ⓞⓞ AE
240 St John St ✉ *EC1V 4PH*⊖ *Farringdon –* ✆ *(020) 7336 7726*
– www.thepeasant.co.uk – gapsbairs@aol.com – Fax (020) 7490 1089
– Closed 25 December to 3 January   19UZD**e**
Rest – (booking essential) Carte £ 25/40
♦ Classic Victorian pub involved in the vanguard of the original gastro-pub movement. Robust, hearty fare downstairs and more original dishes in the formal upstairs
restaurant.

⒤ **The Well**   VISA ⓞⓞ AE ⓞ
180 St John St ✉ *EC1V 4JY*⊖ *Farringdon –* ✆ *(020) 7251 9363*
– www.downthewell.co.uk – drink@downthewell.co.uk – Fax (020) 7253 9683
– Closed 25-26 December   19UZD**x**
Rest – Carte £ 23/30
♦ Rather predictable looking pub distinguished by big black canopies. Food lifts it
above the average: everything from 'pie of the week' to sophisticated modern British
dishes.

Highbury – Greater London – ✉ N5

✗ **Au Lac**   AC VISA ⓞⓞ
82 Highbury Park ✉ *N5 2XE*⊖ *Arsenal –* ✆ *(020) 7704 9187*
– Fax (020) 7704 9187   13VZA**b**
Rest – Vietnamese – (dinner only and lunch Thursday and Friday) Carte £ 8/21
♦ Cosy Vietnamese restaurant, with brightly coloured walls and painted fans. Large
menus with authentic dishes usefully highlighted. Fresh flavours; good value.

Islington – Greater London – ✉ N1   12 **B3**

🏨 **Hilton London Islington**   ㄘ ℼ Ⓕⓢ 阝 ⓡ rm, AC ℀ ℻ 㐅 P
53 Upper St ✉ *N1 0UY*⊖ *Angel –* ✆ *(020) 7354 7700*   VISA ⓞⓞ AE ⓞ
– www.hilton.co.uk/islington – reservations.islington@hilton.com
– Fax (020) 7354 7711   13UZB**s**
184 rm – ∲£ 140/234 ∲∲£ 140/234, ⌑ £ 17.95 **Rest** – Carte £ 21/34
♦ Benefits from its location adjacent to the Business Design Centre. A purpose-built
hotel with all bedrooms enjoying the appropriate creature comforts. Open-plan brasserie with small bar.

✗✗ **Almeida**   AC ℀ ⇔ VISA ⓞⓞ AE
30 Almeida St ✉ *N1 1AD*⊖ *Angel –* ✆ *(020) 7354 4777*
– www.almeida-restaurant.co.uk – sharonw@danddlondon.com
– Fax (020) 7354 2777   13UZB**r**
Rest – French – Menu £ 18 – Carte £ 18/30
♦ Spacious, open plan restaurant with pleasant contemporary styling adjacent to
Almeida Theatre. Large à la carte: a collection of classic French dishes.

LONDON - page 110 - Islington

XX Metrogusto   🄰🄲 ⊗ VISA ⓜⓞ 🄰🄴

13 Theberton St ⊠ N1 0QY ⊖ Angel – ✆ (020) 7226 9400
– www.metrogusto.co.uk – ambroianeselli@btconnect.com – Fax (020) 7226 9400
– Closed 25-26 December and lunch Monday-Tuesday   13UZB**e**
Rest – Italian – Menu £ 19 (dinner) – Carte £ 24/36
♦ Relaxed neighbourhood Italian set over two rooms, with eye-catching artwork and slightly bohemian feel. Proudly run by Italian owner. Modern, carefully prepared Italian food.

X Ottolenghi   🄰🄲 VISA ⓜⓞ 🄰🄴 ⓞ

287 Upper St ⊠ N1 2TZ ⊖ Highbury and Islington – ✆ (020) 7288 1454
– www.ottolenghi.co.uk – upper@ottolenghi.co.uk – Fax (020) 7704 1456
– Closed 25-26 December, 1 January and Sunday dinner   13UZB**k**
Rest – International – Carte £ 24/45
♦ Cool, contemporary restaurant behind a smart deli. Two long tables accommodate most diners. Grazing style dishes are fresh, vibrant and tasty with a subtle Eastern spicing.

🍴 The Drapers Arms   🍴 VISA ⓜⓞ 🄰🄴

44 Barnsbury St ⊠ N1 1ER ⊖ Highbury and Islington – ✆ (020) 7619 0348
– www.thedrapersarms.co.uk – info@thedrapersarms.co.uk
– Fax (020) 7619 0413   13UZB**x**
Rest – Carte £ 22/28
♦ Battleship grey pub in leafy residential road. Lively bar; more formal upstairs dining room. Earthy menu features British dishes with Mediterranean influences.

🍴 The Northgate   🍴 VISA ⓜⓞ

113 Southgate Rd ⊠ N1 3JS ⊖ Old Street – ✆ (020) 7359 7392
– thenorthgate@hotmail.co.uk – Fax (020) 7359 7393   13VZB**a**
Rest – (dinner only and lunch Saturday and Sunday) Carte £ 20/30
♦ Corner pub with wood flooring and modern art on display. Rear dining area with a large blackboard menu offering a cross section of internationally influenced modern dishes.

🍴 The Barnsbury   🍴 VISA ⓜⓞ

209-211 Liverpool Rd ⊠ N1 1LX ⊖ Highbury and Islington – ✆ (020) 7607 5519
– www.thebarnsbury.co.uk – info@thebarnsbury.co.uk – Fax (020) 7607 3256
– Closed 25-26 December, 1 January   13UZB**v**
Rest – Carte £ 35/45
♦ Former public house with pine tables and chairs arranged round central counter bar; art work for sale on the walls. Robust and hearty food in generous portions.

King's Cross – Greater London – ⊠ WC1

X Konstam at the Prince Albert   ⇔ VISA ⓜⓞ 🄰🄴

2 Acton St ⊠ WC1X 9NA ⊖ King's Cross St Pancras – ✆ (020) 7833 5040
– www.konstam.co.uk – princealbert@konstam.co.uk – Fax (020) 7833 5045
– Closed 25 December-3 January, Saturday lunch,
Sunday and Bank Holidays   18TZC**a**
Rest – Traditional – Carte £ 25/36
♦ Avert your gaze from the hugely wondrous light display to enjoy interesting dishes sourced totally from within boundaries of London Transport network! Chef has own allotment.

Undecided between two equivalent establishments?
Within each category, establishments are classified
in our order of preference.

KENSINGTON and CHELSEA (Royal Borough of) – **Greater London**   12 **B3**

Chelsea – Greater London – ⊠ SW1/SW3/SW7/SW10

🏠🏠🏠 Jumeirah Carlton Tower   ≤ 🗐 🖥 🖨 🛏 ⅙ ✕ 🛎 ⅙ rm, 🗚

Cadogan Pl ⊠ SW1X 9PY ⊖ Knightsbridge   ⅙ 🛉 🗖 🚭 ₩ 🔥 🖂 🗭 ⅙
– 𝒞 (020) 7235 1234 – www.jumeirah.com – jctinfo@jumeirah.com
– Fax (020) 7235 9129   37AGX**n**
190 rm – ∮£288/550 ∮∮£288/550, ⊑£30 – 30 suites
Rest *Rib Room* – Carte £40/68

♦ Imposing international hotel overlooking a leafy square. Well-equipped roof-top health club has funky views. Generously proportioned rooms boast every conceivable facility. Rib Room restaurant has a clubby atmosphere.

🏠🏠🏠 Wyndham Grand   ≤ 🗐 🖥 🖨 🛏 🛎 ⅙ 🗚 🕻 🗖 🚭

Chelsea Harbour ⊠ SW10 0XG ⊖ Fulham Broadway   🚭 🗭 ⅙ 🖂 🗭 ⅙
– 𝒞 (020) 7823 3000 – www.wyndhamgrandlondon.co.uk
– wyndhamlondon@wyndham.com – Fax (020) 7352 8174   23PZG**j**
160 suites – ∮∮£558, ⊑£20
Rest *Aquasia* – see restaurant listing

♦ Modern, all-suite hotel within an exclusive marina and retail development. Many of the spacious and well-appointed rooms have balconies and views across the Thames.

🏠🏠🏠 Sheraton Park Tower   ≤ 🛏 🛎 ⅙ 🗚 🗭 🗖 🚭 🖂 🗭 ⅙

101 Knightsbridge ⊠ SW1X 7RN ⊖ Knightsbridge – 𝒞 (020) 7235 8050
– www.luxurycollection.com/parktowerlondon
– central.london.reservations@sheraton.com – Fax (020) 7235 8231   37AGX**t**
275 rm – ∮£505 ∮∮£705, ⊑£25 – 5 suites
Rest *One-O-One* – see restaurant listing

♦ Built in the 1970s in a unique cylindrical shape. Well-equipped bedrooms are all identical in size. Top floor executive rooms have commanding views of Hyde Park and City.

🏠🏠 Capital   🛎 🗚 🚭 🗭 🗖 🚭 🖂 🗭 ⅙

22-24 Basil St ⊠ SW3 1AT ⊖ Knightsbridge – 𝒞 (020) 7589 5171
– www.capitalhotel.co.uk – reservations@capitalhotel.co.uk
– Fax (020) 7225 0011   37AFX**a**
49 rm – ∮£253 ∮∮£345/523, ⊑£18.50
Rest *The Capital Restaurant* – see restaurant listing

♦ Discreet and privately owned town house with distinct English charm. Individually decorated rooms with plenty of thoughtful touches.

🏠🏠 Draycott without rest   🗖 🛎 🗚 🗭 🖂 🗭 🖂 🗭 ⅙

26 Cadogan Gdns ⊠ SW3 2RP ⊖ Sloane Square – 𝒞 (020) 7730 6466
– www.draycotthotel.com – reservations@draycotthotel.com
– Fax (020) 7730 0236   37AGY**c**
31 rm – ∮£158/183 ∮∮£233/370, ⊑£21.95 – 4 suites

♦ Charmingly discreet 19C house with elegant sitting room overlooking tranquil garden, for afternoon tea. Individual rooms in a country house style, named after writers or actors.

🏠🏠 The Cadogan   🗖 🛏 ✕ 🛎 🗚 🚭 🗭 🗖 🖂 🗭 ⅙

75 Sloane St ⊠ SW1X 9SG ⊖ Knightsbridge – 𝒞 (020) 7235 7141
– www.cadogan.com – info@thesteingroup.com
– Fax (020) 7245 0994   37AGY**b**
63 rm – ∮£300/347 ∮∮£347, ⊑£24 – 2 suites
Rest *Langtry's* – (Closed Sunday dinner and Bank Holidays) Menu £20
– Carte £27/35

♦ An Edwardian town house, where Oscar Wilde was arrested; modernised and refurbished with a French accent. Contemporary drawing room. Stylish bedrooms; latest facilities. Discreet, stylish restaurant.

Millennium Knightsbridge ⌖ & rm, AC ⚡ 📞 ⅏
🏨⌖
17-25 Sloane St ⊠ SW1X 9NU⊖ Knightsbridge – ℰ (020) VISA ⚬⚬ AE ①
7235 4377 – www.millenniumhotels.co.uk/knightsbridge
– reservations.knightsbridge@mill-cop.com – Fax (020) 7235 3705 37AGX**r**
218 rm – ⛨£176/323 ⛨⛨£265/393, ⊆£25.75 – 4 suites
Rest *MU* – Menu £23/27 – Carte £31/39
♦ Modern, corporate hotel in the heart of London's most fashionable shopping district. Club bedrooms are well-appointed and equipped with the latest technology.

Knightsbridge 🏨 & rm, AC ⚡ 📶 VISA ⚬⚬ AE ①
🏨
10 Beaufort Gdns ⊠ SW3 1PT⊖ Knightsbridge – ℰ (020) 7584 6300
– www.knightsbridgehotel.com – knightsbridge@firmdale.com
– Fax (020) 7584 6355 37AFX**s**
44 rm – ⛨£200/247 ⛨⛨£345/405, ⊆£17.50
Rest – (room service only) (room service only)
♦ Attractively furnished town house with a very stylish, discreet feel. Every bedroom is immaculately appointed and has an individuality of its own; fine detailing throughout.

San Domenico House 🛁 🏨 AC ⚡ 📞 VISA ⚬⚬ AE ①
🏨
29-31 Draycott Pl ⊠ SW3 2SH⊖ Sloane Square – ℰ (020) 7581 5757
– www.sandomenicohouse.com – info@sandomenicohouse.com
– Fax (020) 7584 1348 37AFY**c**
15 rm – ⛨£210/246 ⛨⛨£255/299, ⊆£22 **Rest** – (room service only)
♦ Intimate and discreet Victorian town house with an attractive rooftop terrace. Individually styled and generally spacious rooms with antique furniture and rich fabrics.

Egerton House 🏨 AC ⚡ 📶 VISA ⚬⚬ AE
🏨
17-19 Egerton Terrace ⊠ SW3 2BX⊖ South Kensington – ℰ (020) 7589 2412
– www.egertonhousehotel.com – bookeg@rchmail.com
– Fax (020) 7584 6540 37AFY**e**
27 rm – ⛨£300 ⛨⛨£370, ⊆£24.50 – 1 suite **Rest** – (room service only)
♦ Discreet, compact but comfortable townhouse in a good location, recently refurbished throughout and owned by Red Carnation group. High levels of personal service make the hotel stand out.

Beaufort without rest 🏨 AC ⚡ 📶 VISA ⚬⚬ AE ①
🏨
33 Beaufort Gdns ⊠ SW3 1PP⊖ Knightsbridge – ℰ (020) 7584 5252
– www.thebeaufort.co.uk – reservations@thebeaufort.co.uk
– Fax (020) 7589 2834 37AFX**n**
29 rm – ⛨£141/241 ⛨⛨£270/382, ⊆£12.50
♦ World's largest collection of English floral watercolours adorn this 19C town house. Modern and co-ordinated rooms. Tariff includes all drinks and afternoon tea.

Myhotel Chelsea 🛁 🏨 AC ⚡ 📶 ⅏ VISA ⚬⚬ AE ①
🏨
35 Ixworth Pl ⊠ SW3 3QX⊖ South Kensington – ℰ (020) 7225 7500
– www.myhotels.com – mychelsea@myhotels.com
– Fax (020) 7225 7555 37AFY**z**
44 rm – ⛨£128/276 ⛨⛨£151/276, ⊆£18 – 1 suite
Rest – Menu £16 (lunch) – Carte £21/34
♦ Restored Victorian property in a fairly quiet and smart side street. Modern and well-equipped rooms are ideal for the corporate traveller. Smart dining room for modern menus.

Sydney House 🏨 AC ⚡ 📶 VISA ⚬⚬ AE ①
🏨
9-11 Sydney St ⊠ SW3 6PU⊖ South Kensington – ℰ (020) 7376 7711
– www.sydneyhousechelsea.com – info@sydneyhousechelsea.com – Fax (020)
7376 4233 – Closed 24-29 December 36ADY**s**
21 rm – ⛨£125/195 ⛨⛨£145/225, ⊆£9.95 **Rest** – Carte £18/29
♦ Two usefully located Victorian town houses. Basement breakfast room; small lounge near entrance. Compact contemporary style bedrooms; one on top floor with own roof terrace.

The Sloane Square H. 📶 & 🅰️ ✄ ⟨⟩ VISA ⓒⓢ AE

Sloane Sq ⊠ SW1W 8EG⊖ Sloane Square – ℰ *(020) 7896 9988*
– www.sloanesquarehotel.co.uk – reservations@sloanesquarehotel.co.uk
– Fax (020) 7751 4211 37AGY**k**
102 rm – †£125/168 ††£175/245, ⌑ £10.75
Rest Chelsea Brasserie – see restaurant listing
♦ Redbrick hotel opened in 2007, boasts bright, contemporary décor. Stylish, coordinated bedrooms, with laptops; library of DVDs and games available. Rooms at back slightly quieter.

The Levin 📶 🅰️ ✄ ⟨⟩ VISA ⓒⓢ AE ⓞ

28 Basil St ⊠ SW3 1AS⊖ Knightsbridge – ℰ *(020) 7589 6286*
– www.thelevinhotel.co.uk – reservations@thelevinhotel.co.uk
– Fax (020) 7823 7826 37AFX**c**
12 rm – ††£300/535, ⌑ £16.50
Rest Le Metro – (Closed Sunday dinner) Carte £27/37
♦ Impressive façade, contemporary interior and comfortable bedrooms in subtle art deco style, boasting marvellous champagne mini bars. Sister to The Capital hotel. Informal brasserie offers classic bistro fare; includes blackboard menu and pies of the week.

Eleven Cadogan Gardens 🍴 📺 📶 🅰️ ✄ ⟨⟩ VISA ⓒⓢ AE ⓞ

11 Cadogan Gardens ⊠ SW3 2RJ⊖ Sloane Square – ℰ *(020) 7730 7000*
– www.no11london.com – info@no11london.com
– Fax (020) 7730 5217 37AGY**u**
60 rm – †£194/553 ††£294/617, ⌑ £20   **Rest** – Carte £31/45
♦ Made up of four Victorian houses; decorated in a flamboyant style, particularly the richly furnished lounge. Bedrooms currently more traditional in style. Concise menu in basement dining room.

Gordon Ramsay 🅰️ ⟨⟩ VISA ⓒⓢ AE ⓞ
✿✿✿
68-69 Royal Hospital Rd ⊠ SW3 4HP⊖ Sloane Square – ℰ *(020) 7352 4441*
– www.gordonramsay.com – Fax (020) 7352 3334
– Closed 1 week Christmas - New Year, Saturday and Sunday 37AFZ**c**
Rest – French – (booking essential) Menu £45/90 🏵
Spec. Roasted Scottish lobster tail, bouillabaisse sauce, cabbage and ratatouille. Best end of lamb and confit shoulder, provençale vegetables, spinach, thyme jus. Prune and armagnac soufflé with chocolate sorbet.
♦ Discreetly located, with meticulous service; its best tables by the windows. Luxury ingredients employed in perfectly balanced classical dishes. Book 2 months in advance.

The Capital Restaurant – at Capital Hotel 🅰️ ⟨⟩ VISA ⓒⓢ AE ⓞ
✿✿
22-24 Basil St ⊖ Knightsbridge – ℰ *(020) 7589 5171 – www.capitalhotel.co.uk*
– reservations@capitalhotel.co.uk – Fax (020) 7225 0011 37AFX**a**
Rest – French – (booking essential) Menu £38/58 🏵
Spec. Crab lasagne with langoustine cappuccino. Saddle of rabbit provençale with seared calamari. Iced coffee parfait with chocolate fondant.
♦ Hotel restaurant imbued with an understated elegance. Confident, precise cooking; classical dishes come with impishly ingenious touches. Enthusiastic and knowledgeable staff.

Bibendum 🅰️ ⟨⟩ VISA ⓒⓢ AE ⓞ
Michelin House, 81 Fulham Rd ⊠ SW3 6RD⊖ South Kensington – ℰ *(020)*
7581 5817 – www.bibendum.co.uk – reservations@bibendum.co.uk – Fax (020)
7823 7925 – Closed 25-26 December and 1 January 37AEY**s**
Rest – French – Menu £30 (lunch and Sunday dinner) – Carte £41/60 🏵
♦ A fine example of Art Nouveau architecture; a London landmark. 1st floor restaurant with striking stained glass 'Michelin Man'. Attentive service of modern British cooking.

LONDON

LONDON

XXX **Tom Aikens**   AC VISA ◐◐ AE
❀

43 Elystan St ⊠ SW3 3NT⊖ South Kensington – ℰ (020) 7584 2003
– www.tomaikens.co.uk – info@tomaikens.co.uk – Fax (020) 7584 2001
– Closed last two weeks August, 10 days Christmas-New Year, Saturday, Sunday
and Bank Holidays   37AFY**n**
Rest – Innovative – Menu £ 29/65 ❀

Spec. Lobster and rabbit roasted in vanilla butter with cannelloni. Cutlet and belly of pork with squid. Truffle and vanilla panna cotta with truffle mousse.
♦ Minimalist in style, with a warm feel. Classically based French cooking features original touches, with the focus firmly on seasonal, traceable ingredients. Attentive service.

XXX **Aubergine** (William Drabble)   AC VISA ◐◐ AE ◑
❀

11 Park Walk ⊠ SW10 0AJ⊖ South Kensington – ℰ (020) 7352 3449
– www.auberginerestaurant.co.uk – info@auberginerestaurant.co.uk
– Fax (020) 7351 1770 – Closed 2 weeks Christmas, Easter, Saturday lunch,
Sunday and Bank Holidays   36ACZ**r**
Rest – French – (booking essential) Menu £ 34 (lunch)/64

Spec. Assiette of foie gras. Baked fillets of sole, apple, mussels and chives. Iced clementine mousse with rhubarb.
♦ Longstanding restaurant in heart of Chelsea, serving classic French cooking which shows off the kitchen's considerable skill. Elegant, intimate feel; immaculately laid tables.

XXX **Aquasia** – at Wyndham Grand Hotel   ⇐ 🍴 AC P VISA ◐◐ AE ◑

Chelsea Harbour ⊠ SW10 0XG⊖ Fulham Broadway – ℰ (020) 7300 8443
– www.wyndhamlondon.com   23PZG**j**
Rest – International – Carte £ 34/47

♦ Modern restaurant located within Wyndham Grand hotel. Views over Chelsea Harbour. Cuisine captures the essence of the Mediterranean and Asia.

XXX **Drones**   AC ⇔ VISA ◐◐ AE ◑

1 Pont St ⊠ SW1X 9EJ⊖ Knightsbridge – ℰ (020) 7235 9555
– www.whitestarline.org.uk – sales@whitestarline.org.uk – Fax (020) 7235 9566
– Closed 26 December, 1 January, Saturday lunch and Sunday dinner   37AGX**c**
Rest – Modern European – Menu £ 19 (lunch) – Carte £ 32/45

♦ Smart exterior with etched plate-glass window. U-shaped interior with moody film star photos on walls. French and classically inspired tone to dishes.

XXX **Fifth Floor** – at Harvey Nichols   AC 🍴 VISA ◐◐ AE ◑

Knightsbridge ⊠ SW1X 7RJ⊖ Knightsbridge – ℰ (020) 7235 5250
– www.harveynichols.com – reception@harveynicols.com – Fax (0870) 191 60 19
– Closed Christmas and Sunday dinner   37AGX**s**
Rest – Modern European – Menu £ 20 – Carte £ 29/47 ❀

♦ Stylish, colour-changing surroundings on Harvey Nichols' fifth floor, reached via its own lift. Modern cooking with some originality and the emphasis on France. Good wine list.

XXX **Toto's**   🍴 VISA ◐◐ AE

Walton House, Walton St ⊠ SW3 2JH⊖ Knightsbridge – ℰ (020) 7589 0075
– Fax (020) 7581 9668 – Closed 3 days Christmas   37AFY**x**
Rest – Italian – (booking essential at dinner) Menu £ 27 (lunch) – Carte £ 49/54
♦ Old-fashioned in the best sense, with caring service. Ground floor has the better atmosphere. Earthy and rustic Italian cooking, with handmade pasta a speciality.

XXX **Awana**   AC VISA ◐◐ AE ◑

85 Sloane Ave ⊠ SW3 3DX⊖ South Kensington – ℰ (020) 7584 8880
– www.awana.co.uk – info@awana.co.uk – Fax (020) 7584 6188
– Closed 25-26 December and 1 January   37AFY**b**
Rest – Malaysian – (booking essential) Menu £ 15 (lunch) – Carte £ 26/43
♦ Enter into stylish cocktail bar. Traditional Malay elements adorn restaurant. Satay chef cooks to order. Malaysian dishes authentically prepared and smartly presented.

THE ARTISTRY OF CHAMPAGNE

You've got
the right address !

From palaces to bed and breakfasts, from fine restaurants to small bistrot, th
MICHELIN guide collection includes 45,000 hotels and restaurants selected b
our inspectors in Europe and beyond. Wherever you may be, whatever yo
budget, you can be sure you have the right address!

www.michelin.co.uk

MICHELIN
A better way forward

XXX **Chutney Mary** 🖪 ⇔ 𝘝𝘐𝘚𝘈 ⓒⓞ 𝗔𝗘 ⓞ
535 King's Rd ⊠ SW10 0SZ⊖ Fulham Broadway – ✆ (020) 7351 3113
– www.realindianfood – chutneymary@realindianfood.com
– Fax (020) 7351 7694   22OZG**v**
Rest – Indian – (dinner only and lunch Saturday and Sunday) Carte £ 34/45
♦ Soft lighting and sepia etchings hold sway at this forever popular restaurant. Extensive menu of specialities from all corners of India. Complementary wine list.

XXX **One-O-One** – at Sheraton Park Tower H. 🖪 𝘝𝘐𝘚𝘈 ⓒⓞ 𝗔𝗘 ⓞ
101 Knightsbridge ⊠ SW1X 7RN⊖ Knightsbridge – ✆ (020) 7290 7101
– www.onetoonerestaurant.com – Fax (020) 7235 6196   37AGX**t**
Rest – Seafood – (closed 25-26 December and 1 January) Menu £ 19
– Carte £ 19/69
♦ Brittany-born chef focuses primarily on seafood, especially Norwegian, served either in standard sizes or 'petits plats' for a more flexible eating experience.

XX **Chelsea Brasserie** – at The Sloane Square Hotel 🖪 🕰 𝘝𝘐𝘚𝘈 ⓒⓞ 𝗔𝗘 ⓞ
7-12 Sloane Sq. ⊠ SW1W 8EG⊖ Sloane Square – ✆ (020) 7881 5999
– www.sloanesquarehotel.co.uk – robert@chelsea-brasserie.co.uk
– Closed 25 December   37AGY**k**
Rest – French – (closed Sunday dinner) Carte £ 24/42
♦ Glass doors open into roomy brasserie-style restaurant, with smoky green lamps and brick walls inlaid with mirror tiles. A European menu includes some classic French dishes.

XX **Daphne's** 🖪 ⇔ 𝘝𝘐𝘚𝘈 ⓒⓞ 𝗔𝗘 ⓞ
112 Draycott Ave ⊠ SW3 3AE⊖ South Kensington – ✆ (020) 7589 4257
– www.daphnes-restaurant.co.uk – reservations@daphnes-restaurant.co.uk
– Fax (020) 7225 2766 – Closed 25-26 December   37AFY**j**
Rest – Italian – (booking essential) Menu £ 17 (lunch) – Carte £ 33/49
♦ Positively buzzes in the evening, the Chelsea set gelling smoothly and seamlessly with the welcoming Tuscan interior ambience. A modern twist updates classic Italian dishes.

XX **Rasoi** (Vineet Bhatia) 🖪 ⇔ 𝘝𝘐𝘚𝘈 ⓒⓞ 𝗔𝗘 ⓞ
✿
10 Lincoln St ⊠ SW3 2TS⊖ Sloane Square – ✆ (020) 7225 1881
– www.rasoirestaurant.co.uk – info@rasoirestaurant.co.uk – Fax (020) 7581 0220
– Closed 25 -26 December, Saturday lunch, and Sunday   37AFY**y**
Rest – Indian – Menu £ 26 (lunch) – Carte £ 55/80
Spec. Mustard infused chicken tikka with milk fritter and chilli chutney. Lamb shank and morels with saffron mash, rosemary naan. Rose petal sandwich with saffron yoghurt and fruit jelly.
♦ L-shaped dining room and conservatory decorated with Indian trinkets; intimate upstairs rooms. Contemporary Indian cooking with subtle spicing and innovative flavour combinations.

XX **Racine** 🖪 🕰 𝘝𝘐𝘚𝘈 ⓒⓞ 𝗔𝗘
239 Brompton Rd ⊠ SW3 2EP⊖ South Kensington – ✆ (020) 7584 4477
– Fax (020) 7584 4900 – Closed 25 December   37AEY**t**
Rest – French – Menu £ 20 – Carte £ 31/47
♦ Dark leather banquettes, large mirrors and wood floors create the atmosphere of a genuine Parisienne brasserie. Tasty, well crafted, regional French fare.

XX **Papillon** 🖪 ⇔ 𝘝𝘐𝘚𝘈 ⓒⓞ 𝗔𝗘
96 Draycott Ave ⊠ SW3 3AD⊖ South Kensington – ✆ (020) 7225 2555
– www.papillonchelsea.co.uk – info@papillonchelsea.co.uk – Fax (020) 7225 2554
– Closed 24-26 December and 1January   37AFY**f**
Rest – French – (closed Sunday dinner) Menu £ 17 (lunch) **s** – Carte £ 33/51 **s**
♦ Classic French regional fare, from fish soup to Chateaubriand, all feature at this well run brasserie. French windows, lamps and a fleur-de-lys motif add to the authenticity.

LONDON

LONDON

XX **Nozomi**   AC ⇔ VISA ⓜ AE
15 Beauchamp Pl ⊠ SW3 1NQ⊖ Knightsbridge – ℰ *(020) 7838 1500*
– www.nozomi.co.uk – marios@nozomi.co.uk – Fax (020) 7838 1001
– Closed Sunday   37AFX**d**
Rest – Japanese – Carte £ 50/80
♦ DJ mixes lounge music at the front bar; up the stairs in the restaurant the feeling is
minimal with soft lighting. Innovative Japanese menus provide an interesting choice.

XX **Bluebird**   AC ⓥ ⇔ VISA ⓜ AE ⓞ
350 King's Rd ⊠ SW3 5UU⊖ Sloane Square – ℰ *(020) 7559 1000*
– www.bluebird-restaurant.com – enquiries@bluebird-restaurant.co.uk
– Fax (020) 7559 1115   23PZG**n**
Rest – British – Menu £ 19 – Carte £ 32/52
♦ A foodstore, café and homeware shop also feature at this impressive skylit restaurant. Much of the modern British food is cooked in wood-fired ovens. Lively atmosphere.

XX **Poissonnerie de l'Avenue**   AC ⇔ VISA ⓜ AE ⓞ
82 Sloane Ave ⊠ SW3 3DZ⊖ South Kensington – ℰ *(020) 7589 2457*
– www.poissonneriedelavenue.co.uk – peterr@poissoneire.co.uk – Fax (020)
7581 3360 – Closed 24-26 December and Sunday   37AFY**u**
Rest – French – Menu £ 24 (lunch) – Carte £ 29/45
♦ A Chelsea institution with a loyal following. Classically decorated and comfortable.
Emphasis on well-sourced and very fresh seafood, in dishes with a Mediterranean
accent.

XX **Le Cercle**   AC VISA ⓜ AE
1 Wilbraham Pl ⊠ SW1X 9AE⊖ Sloane Square – ℰ *(020) 7901 9999*
– www.lecercle.co.uk – info@lecercle.co.uk – Fax (020) 7901 9111 – Closed
Christmas - New Year, Sunday, Monday and Bank Holidays   37AGY**e**
Rest – French – Menu £ 15 (lunch) – Carte £ 18/31
♦ Discreetly signed basement restaurant down residential side street. High, spacious
room with chocolate banquettes. Tapas style French menus; accomplished cooking.

XX **Le Colombier**   ⓥ ⇔ VISA ⓜ AE
145 Dovehouse St ⊠ SW3 6LB⊖ South Kensington – ℰ *(020) 7351 1155*
– www.lecolombier-sw3.co.uk – lecolombier1998@aol.com
– Fax (020) 7351 5124   36ADZ**e**
Rest – French – Carte £ 30/40
♦ Proudly Gallic corner restaurant in an affluent residential area. Attractive enclosed
terrace. Bright and cheerful surroundings and service of traditional French cooking.

XX **Painted Heron**   ㊟ AC VISA ⓜ AE
112 Cheyne Walk ⊠ SW10 0DJ⊖ Gloucester Road – ℰ *(020) 7351 5232*
– www.thepaintedheron.com
– Closed 25 December, 1 January and Saturday lunch   40PZG**s**
Rest – Indian – Menu £ 32 – Carte £ 33/40
♦ Just off Cheyne Walk near the river. Contemporary in style, exemplified by oil
paintings. Modern Indian dishes with eclectic ingredients drawn from around the
sub-continent.

XX **Pellicano**   ㊟ AC ⇔ VISA ⓜ AE ⓞ
19-21 Elystan St ⊠ SW3 3NT⊖ South Kensington – ℰ *(020) 7589 3718*
– www.pellicanorestaurant.co.uk – pellicano@btconnect.com – Fax (020)
7584 1789 – Closed Christmas and New Year   37AFY**d**
Rest – Italian – Menu £ 20 (lunch) – Carte £ 25/41
♦ Dark blue canopy announces attractive neighbourhood restaurant. Contemporary
interior with wood floors. Tasty and interesting modern Italian dishes; Sardinian
specialities.

XX **Caraffini**   🍴 AC VISA ⓪ AE

61-63 Lower Sloane St ✉ SW1W 8DH⊖ Sloane Square – ℰ (020) 7259 0235
– www.caraffini.co.uk – info@caraffini.co.uk – Fax (020) 7259 0236
– Closed 25 December, Easter, Sunday and Bank Holidays   37AGZa
Rest – Italian – (booking essential) Carte £ 27/38

♦ The omnipresent and ebullient owner oversees the friendly service in this attractive neighbourhood restaurant. Authentic and robust Italian cooking; informal atmosphere.

XX **Vama**   VISA ⓪ AE ⓪

438 King's Rd ✉ SW10 0LJ⊖ Sloane Square – ℰ (020) 7565 8500
– www.vama.co.uk – vamakingsroad@tiffinbites.com – Fax (020) 7565 8501
– Closed 25-26 December and 1 January   23PZGe
Rest – Indian – (closed Monday) (dinner only and lunch Saturday-Sunday) (booking essential) Carte £ 35/45 **s**

♦ Adorned with traditional artefacts, a modern and bright restaurant. Keen and eager service of an elaborate and seasonally changing menu of Northwest Indian specialities.

XX **Marco**   VISA ⓪ AE

Stamford Bridge, Fulham Rd ✉ SW6 1HS⊖ Fulham Broadway – ℰ (020) 7915 2929 – www.marcorestaurant.co.uk – info@marcorestaurant.co.uk
– Fax (020) 7915 2931 – Closed Sunday and Monday   22OZGc
Rest – Traditional – (dinner only) Carte £ 34/59

♦ Marco Pierre White's restaurant at Chelsea Football Club offers an appealing range of classics, from British favourites to satisfying French and Italian fare. Comfortable and well run room.

XX **Carpaccio**   AC ⇔ VISA ⓪ AE

4 Sydney St ✉ SW3 6PP⊖ South Kensington – ℰ (020) 7352 3335
– www.carpacciorestaurant.co.uk – carpacciorest@aol.com – Fax (020) 7622 8304
– closed 25 December, Easter, last 2 weeks August,
Sunday and Bank Holidays   36ADYe
Rest – Italian – Carte £ 23/35

♦ Fine Georgian exterior housing James Bond stills, 1920s silent Italian comedies, Ayrton Senna's Honda cockpit, witty waiters, and enjoyable, classical Trattoria style cooking.

XX **Eight over Eight**   AC ⇔ VISA ⓪ AE ⓪

392 King's Rd ✉ SW3 5UZ⊖ Gloucester Road – ℰ (020) 7349 9934
– www.rickerrestaurants.com – Fax (020) 7351 5157
– Closed 25 December, 1 January and lunch Sunday   23PZGn
Rest – Asian – Carte £ 27/43

♦ Lively modern restaurant in converted theatre pub; bar in front and dining room at rear. Enthusiastic service. Eclectic Asian menu: strong flavours and unusual combinations.

XX **Good Earth**   AC VISA ⓪ AE

233 Brompton Rd ✉ SW3 2EP⊖ Knightsbridge – ℰ (020) 7584 3658
– www.goodearthgroup.co.uk – goodearthgroup@aol.com – Fax (020) 7823 8769
– Closed 22-31 December   37AFYh
Rest – Chinese – Carte £ 24/50

♦ Ornately decorated, long-established and comfortable restaurant. Polite and efficient service. Extensive and traditional Chinese menu.

XX **The Botanist**   AC VISA ⓪ AE

7 Sloane Square ✉ SW1W 8EE⊖ Sloane Square – ℰ (020) 7730 0077
– www.thebotanistonsloanesquare.com – info@thebotanistonsloanesquare.com
– Fax (020) 7730 7177   37AGYr
Rest – Modern European – Carte £ 26/43

♦ Busy bar, popular with after-work crowd; the swish and stylish restaurant occupies the other half of this corner site. Crisp and clean cooking, with influences kept within Europe.

507

LONDON

X
Foxtrot Oscar   AC VISA ⚫⚫ AE ⓪
79 Royal Hospital Rd ⊠ SW3 4HN⊖ Sloane Square – ℰ (020) 7349 9595
– www.gordonramsay.com – foxtrotoscar@gordonramsay.com
– Fax (020) 7592 1603   37AFZv
Rest – Traditional – (booking essential) Carte £ 20/30
♦ A real Chelsea institution, now under the ownership of the Gordon Ramsay group.
Expect authentic comfort food from cassoulet and coq au vin to burgers and eggs
Benedict and all at sensible prices.

X
Bibendum Oyster Bar   VISA ⚫⚫ AE ⓪
Michelin House, 81 Fulham Rd ⊠ SW3 6RD⊖ South Kensington – ℰ (020)
7823 7925 – www.bibendum.co.uk – reservations@bibendum.co.uk – Fax (020)
7823 7148 – Closed 25-26 December and 1 January   37AEYs
Rest – Seafood – (bookings not accepted) Carte £ 25/35
♦ Dine in either the busy bar, or in the light and relaxed foyer of this striking
landmark. Concise menu of mainly cold dishes focusing on fresh seafood and shellfish.

X
Manicomio   🌡 AC VISA ⚫⚫ AE ⓪
85 Duke of York Sq, King's Rd ⊠ SW3 4LY⊖ Sloane Square – ℰ (020) 7730 3366
– www.manicomio.co.uk – Fax (020) 7730 3377
– Closed 25-26 December and 1 January   37AGYx
Rest – Italian – Carte £ 28/41
♦ Outside, a delightful terrace overlooks the trendy Square. Inside, a clean, modern,
informal style prevails. Rustic Italian menus. Next door, a café and superbly stocked
deli.

X
Aubaine   AC VISA ⚫⚫ AE
260-262 Brompton Rd ⊠ SW3 2AS⊖ South Kensington – ℰ (020) 7052 0100
– www.aubaine.co.uk – info@aubaine.co.uk – Fax (020) 7052 0622   37AEYc
Rest – French – Carte £ 22/44
♦ 'Boulangerie, patisserie, restaurant'. Pass the bakery aromas to an all-day eatery
with 'distressed' country feel. Well-judged menus range from croque monsieur to coq
au vin.

X
Tom's Kitchen   VISA ⚫⚫ AE
27 Cale St ⊖ South Kensington – ℰ (020) 7349 0202 – www.tomskitchen.co.uk
– info@tomskitchen.co.uk – Fax (020) 7823 3652
– Closed 25 Decmeber and 1 January   37AFZb
Rest – French – Carte £ 29/51
♦ A converted pub, whose white tiles and mirrors help to give it an industrial feel.
Appealing and wholesome dishes come in man-sized portions. The eponymous Tom
is Tom Aikens.

⧄
The Admiral Codrington   🌡 AC ⇔ VISA ⚫⚫ AE ⓪
17 Mossop St ⊠ SW3 2LY⊖ South Kensington – ℰ (020) 7581 0005
– www.theadmiralcodrington.com – admiral-codrington@333holdingsltd.com
– Fax (020) 7589 2452 – Closed 24-27 December   37AFYv
Rest – Carte £ 25/32
♦ Local landmark pub, with separate dining room complete with retractable roof.
Menu is an appealing mix of satisfying British and European classics. The bar gets
busy in the evenings.

⧄
Chelsea Ram   AC VISA ⚫⚫
32 Burnaby St ⊠ SW10 0PL⊖ Fulham Broadway – ℰ (020) 7351 4008
– bookings@chelsearam.co.uk   23PZGr
Rest – Carte £ 20/27
♦ A stalwart of the London pub scene. Full table service of honest home-cooking and
comforting classics, from lamb chops to cottage pies and heart-warming puddings.
Over 20 wines by the glass.

Swag and Tails   🍴 VISA ⓞⓞ AE
10-11 Fairholt St, Knightsbridge ⊠ SW7 1EG⊖ Knightsbridge – ℰ (020)
7584 6926 – www.swagandtails.com – theswag@swagandtails.com
– Fax (020) 7581 9935 – Closed Christmas-New Year, Saturday,
Sunday and Bank Holidays   37AFX**r**
Rest – Carte £ 22/32
◆ Attractive Victorian pub close to Harrods and the fashionable Knightsbridge shops.
Polite and approachable service of a blackboard menu of light snacks and seasonal
dishes.

Builders Arms   AC VISA ⓞⓞ AE
13 Britten St ⊠ SW3 3TY⊖ South Kensington – ℰ (020) 7349 9040
– www.geronimo-inns.co.uk – buildersarms@geronimo-inns.co.uk
– Closed 25-26 December   37AFZ**x**
Rest – (bookings not accepted) Carte £ 20/35
◆ Extremely busy modern 'gastropub' favoured by the locals. Eclectic menu of contemporary dishes with blackboard specials. Polite service from a young and eager
team.

The Pig's Ear   VISA ⓞⓞ AE
35 Old Church St ⊠ SW3 5BS⊖ Sloane Square – ℰ (020) 7352 2908
– www.thepigsear.co.uk – thepigsear@hotmail.co.uk – Fax (020) 7352 9321
– Closed 10 days Christmas to New Year   23PZG**v**
Rest – Carte £ 30/50
◆ Busy bar, romantic panelled dining room and cosy, curtained-off Blue Room with
fire. Modern British meets Mediterranean menu; dishes like beef marrow or lamb stew
and dumplings.

The Phoenix   AC VISA ⓞⓞ AE
23 Smith St ⊠ SW3 4EE⊖ Sloane Square – ℰ (020) 7730 9182
– www.geronimo-inns.co.uk – thephoenix@geronimo-inns.co.uk
– Closed 25-26 December   37AFZ**a**
Rest – Carte £ 15/25
◆ The main bar is popular with locals but go through to the dining room at the back
which was redecorated in 2008. Expect proper pub food with interesting and seasonal daily specials.

The Cross Keys   AC VISA ⓞⓞ AE
1 Lawrence St ⊠ SW3 5NB⊖ South Kensington – ℰ (020) 7349 9111
– www.thexkeys.net – xkeys.nicole@hotmail.co.uk – Fax (020) 7349 9333 – Closed
24-25 December, 1 January, Bank Holidays   23PZG**a**
Rest – Carte £ 25/30
◆ Hidden away near the Embankment, this 18C pub has period furniture and impressive carved stone fireplaces. Interesting, modern menus include blackboard of
daily specials.

Lots Road Pub & Dining Room   AC VISA ⓞⓞ AE
114 Lots Rd ⊠ SW10 0RJ⊖ Fulham Broadway – ℰ (020) 7352 6645
– www.lotsroadpub.com – lotsroad@foodandfuel.co.uk   23PZG**b**
Rest – (Closed Sunday) Carte £ 20/26
◆ Traditional corner pub with an open-plan kitchen, flowers at each table and large
modern pictures on the walls. Contemporary menus change daily.

Earl's Court – Greater London – ⊠ SW5

K + K George   🚗 🛗 AC ⁽ᵗ⁾ ⅍ P VISA ⓞⓞ AE ⓞ
1-15 Templeton Pl ⊠ SW5 9NB⊖ Earl's Court – ℰ (020) 7598 8700
– www.kkhotels.com – hotelgeorge@kkhotels.co.uk
– Fax (020) 7370 2285   35AAY**s**
154 rm � – †£ 259 ††£ 294   **Rest** – Carte £ 20/32
◆ Five converted 19C houses overlooking large rear garden. Scandinavian style to
rooms with low beds, white walls and light wood furniture. Breakfast room has the
garden view. Informal dining in the bar.

LONDON

⌂ **Twenty Nevern Square** without rest   📶 ❄ 📶 **P** *VISA* ⓪ AE
20 Nevern Sq ⌂ SW5 9PD⊖ Earl's Court – ℰ (020) 7565 9555
– www.twentyneversquare.co.uk – hotel@twentyneversquare.co.uk
– Fax (020) 7565 9444   35AAY**u**
20 rm – ♦£85/115 ♦♦£110/150, ⊇ £9
◆ In an attractive Victorian garden square, an individually designed, privately owned town house. Original pieces of furniture and some rooms with their own terrace.

⌂ **Mayflower** without rest   📶 ❄ 📶 *VISA* ⓪ AE
26-28 Trebovir Rd ⌂ SW5 9NJ⊖ Earl's Court – ℰ (020) 7370 0991
– www.mayflowerhotel.co.uk – info@mayflower-group.co.uk
– Fax (020) 7370 0994   35ABY**x**
46 rm – ♦£79/109 ♦♦£99/145, ⊇ £9
◆ Conveniently placed, friendly establishment with a secluded rear breakfast terrace and basement breakfast room. Individually styled rooms with Asian influence.

⌂ **Amsterdam** without rest   🚗 📶 ❄ 📶 *VISA* ⓪ AE ⓪
7 and 9 Trebovir Rd ⌂ SW5 9LS⊖ Earl's Court – ℰ (020) 7370 2814
– www.amsterdam-hotel.com – reservations@amsterdam-hotel.com
– Fax (020) 7244 7608   35ABY**c**
19 rm – ♦£70/90 ♦♦£94/125, ⊇ £2 – 8 suites
◆ Basement breakfast room and a small secluded garden. The brightly decorated bedrooms are light and airy. Some have smart wood floors; some boast their own balcony.

⌂ **Rushmore** without rest   ❄ 📶 *VISA* ⓪ AE ⓪
11 Trebovir Rd ⌂ SW5 9LS⊖ Earl's Court – ℰ (020) 7370 3839
– www.rushmore-hotel.co.uk – rushmore-reservations@london.com
– Fax (020) 7370 0274   35ABY**a**
22 rm ⊇ – ♦£69/84 ♦♦£89/99
◆ Behind its Victorian façade lies an hotel popular with tourists. Individually decorated bedrooms in a variety of shapes and sizes. Piazza-styled conservatory breakfast room.

✕✕ **Langan's Coq d'Or**   🌳 AC *VISA* ⓪ AE ⓪
254-260 Old Brompton Rd ⌂ SW5 9HR⊖ Earl's Court – ℰ (020) 7259 2599
– www.langansrestaurants.co.uk – admin@langansrestaurant.co.uk – Fax (020)
7370 7735 – Closed 25-26 December   35ABZ**e**
Rest – Traditional – Menu £24 – Carte approx. £28
◆ Classic, buzzy brasserie and excellent-value menu to match. Walls adorned with pictures of celebrities: look out for more from the enclosed pavement terrace. Smooth service.

Kensington – Greater London – ⌂ SW7/W8/W11/W14

🏠🏠🏠 **Royal Garden**   ← 🍴 ſå 📶 ᗴ rm, AC ❄ 📶 🛁 **P** *VISA* ⓪ AE ⓪
2-24 Kensington High St ⌂ W8 4PT⊖ High Street Kensington – ℰ (020)
7937 8000 – www.royalgardenhotel.co.uk – sales@royalgardenhotel.co.uk
– Fax (020) 7361 1991   35ABX**c**
376 rm – ♦£175/388 ♦♦£175/388, ⊇ £19
– 20 suites
Rest Min Jiang – see restaurant listing
Rest Park Terrace – Menu £18/30
◆ A tall, modern hotel with many of its rooms enjoying enviable views over the adjacent Kensington Gardens. All the modern amenities and services, with well-drilled staff. Bright, spacious Park Terrace offers British, Asian and modern European cuisine.

The Milestone · 🏠 £₅ 📶 🔊 🛜 💳 🟰 🅰🅴 🛈

1-2 Kensington Court ⊠ W8 5DL⊖ High Street Kensington – ℰ (020) 7917 1000
– www.milestonehotel.com – bookms@rchmail.com
– Fax (020) 7917 1010   35ABX**u**
57 rm – ⍦£276/311 ⍦⍦£370/405, ☑ £25
– 6 suites
Rest – (booking essential for non-residents) Menu £27 (lunch) – Carte £42/67
♦ Elegant hotel with decorative Victorian façade and English feel. Charming oak
panelled lounge and snug bar. Meticulously decorated bedrooms with period detail.
Panelled dining room with charming little oratory for privacy seekers.

Baglioni · 🏡 🏠 £₅ 🔊 📶 💥 📞 🧖 💳 🟰 🅰🅴 🛈

60 Hyde Park Gate ⊠ SW7 5BB⊖ High Street Kensington – ℰ (020) 7368 5700
– www.baglionihotels.com – info@baglionihotellondon.com
– Fax (020) 7368 5701   36ACX**e**
52 rm – ⍦£423 ⍦⍦£423, ☑ £25
– 15 suites
Rest *Brunello* – ℰ (020) 7368 5900 – Menu £24 (lunch) – Carte £37/51
♦ Opposite Kensington Palace: ornate interior, trendy basement bar. Impressively
high levels of service. Small gym/sauna. Superb rooms in cool shades boast striking
facilities. Restaurant specialises in rustic Italian cooking.

Launceston Place · 📶 ⇄ 💳 🟰 🅰🅴 🛈

1a Launceston Pl ⊠ W8 5RL⊖ Gloucester Road – ℰ (020) 7937 6912
– www.launcestonplace-restaurant.co.uk – lpr-res@danddlondon.com – Fax (020)
7938 2412 – Closed Christmas and New Year and Monday lunch   35ACX**a**
Rest – Modern European – Menu £24/38 – Carte £35/48
♦ Re-launched and reinvigorated, with dark walls and moody lighting, but still with
that local feel. Cooking is original and deftly executed and uses ingredients largely
from the British Isles.

Belvedere · 🚪 🏡 📶 🥂 ⇄ 💳 🟰 🅰🅴 🛈

Holland House, off Abbotsbury Rd ⊠ W8 6LU⊖ Holland Park – ℰ (020)
7602 1238 – www.belvedererestaurant.co.uk – info@belvedererestaurant.co.uk
– Fax (020) 7610 4382
– Closed 26 December, 1 January and Sunday dinner   16MZE**u**
Rest – French – Menu £18 (lunch) – Carte £28/53
♦ Former 19C orangery in a delightful position in the middle of the Park. On two
floors with a bar and balcony terrace. Huge vases of flowers. Modern take on classic
dishes.

Min Jiang – at Royal Garden Hotel · ≤ 📶 💳 🟰 🅰🅴 🛈

10th Floor, 2-24 Kensington High St ⊠ W8 4PT⊖ High Street Kensington
– ℰ (020) 7361 1988 – www.minjiang.co.uk – reservations@minjiang.co.uk
– Fax (020) 7361 1987   35ABX**c**
Rest – Chinese – Carte £30/50
♦ Stylish and comfortable Chinese restaurant on the 10th floor of the hotel, with
terrific views. Lunchtime dim sum a strength; the Beijing duck is a speciality and
comes roasted in a wood-fired oven.

Babylon – at The Roof Gardens · ≤ 🏡 📶 ⇄ 💳 🟰 🅰🅴

99 Kensington High St (entrance on Derry St) ⊠ W8 5SA⊖ High Street
Kensington – ℰ (020) 7368 3993 – www.roofgardens.com
– babylon@roofgardens.virgin.co.uk – Fax (020) 7368 3995
– Closed Christmas-New Year and Sunday dinner   35ABX**n**
Rest – Modern European – Menu £20 (lunch) – Carte £39/55
♦ Situated on the roof of this pleasant London building affording attractive views of
the London skyline. Stylish modern décor in keeping with the contemporary, British
cooking.

LONDON

XX **Clarke's**   AC VISA ⓜ AE ①
124 Kensington Church St ⊠ W8 4BH⊖ Notting Hill Gate – ℰ (020) 7221 9225
– www.sallyclarke.com – restaurant@sallyclarke.com – Fax (020) 7229 4564
– Closed 2 weeks Christmas - New Year and Bank Holidays   27ABV**c**
Rest – Modern European – Menu £ 47 (dinner) – Carte lunch £ 29/32
♦ Forever popular restaurant, now serving a choice of dishes boasting trademark fresh, seasonal ingredients and famed lightness of touch. Loyal following for over 20 years.

XX **Zaika**   AC VISA ⓜ AE ①
1 Kensington High St ⊠ W8 5NP⊖ High Street Kensington – ℰ (020) 7795 6533
– www.zaika-restaurant.co.uk – info@zaika-restaurant.co.uk
– Fax (020) 7937 8854
– Closed Saturday lunch, Christmas, New Year and Bank Holidays   35ABX**r**
Rest – Indian – Menu £ 20 (lunch) – Carte £ 29/43
♦ A converted bank, sympathetically restored, with original features and Indian artefacts. Well organised service of modern Indian dishes.

XX **Whits**   AC VISA ⓜ AE
21 Abingdon Rd ⊠ W8 6AH⊖ High Street Kensington – ℰ (020) 7938 1122
– www.whits.co.uk – eva@whits.co.uk – Fax (020) 7937 6121 – Closed Christmas -
New Year, Easter, Saturday lunch, Sunday dinner and Monday   35AAX**d**
Rest – Modern European – (dinner only and Sunday lunch) Menu £ 19/24
– Carte £ 29/37
♦ Run by friendly owner. Bar runs length of lower level. Most diners migrate upstairs with its modish art work and intimate tables. Modern cooking with generous portions.

XX **Memories of China**   AC VISA ⓜ AE
353 Kensington High St ⊖ High Street Kensington – ℰ (020) 7603 6951
– www.memories-of-china.co.uk – Fax (020) 7603 0848
– Closed Christmas-New Year   35AAY**v**
Rest – Chinese – (booking essential) Carte £ 25/50
♦ Subtle lighting and brightly coloured high-back chairs add to the modern feel of this Chinese restaurant. Screens separate the tables. Plenty of choice from extensive menu.

XX **Timo**   AC VISA ⓜ AE
343 Kensington High St ⊠ W8 6NW⊖ High Street Kensington – ℰ (020)
7603 3888 – www.timorestaurant.co.uk – timorestaurant@fsmail.net – Fax (020)
7603 8111 – Closed 25 December, Sunday and Bank Holidays   35AAY**c**
Rest – Italian – Menu £ 14 (lunch) – Carte dinner £ 28/44
♦ Modern, personally run restaurant with unadorned walls and comfortable seating in brown suede banquettes. Italian menus of contemporary dishes and daily changing specials.

XX **11 Abingdon Road**   AC VISA ⓜ AE
11 Abingdon Rd ⊠ W8 6AH⊖ High Street Kensington – ℰ (020) 7937 0120
– www.abingdonroad.co.uk – eleven@abingdonroad.co.uk
– Closed Bank Holidays   35AAX**a**
Rest – Mediterranean – Carte £ 26/33
♦ Part of a little 'eating oasis' off Ken High Street. Stylish frosted glass façade with a clean, white interior. Cooking's from the modern British stable with Euro accents.

XX **L Restaurant & Bar**   AC ⟷ VISA ⓜ AE
2 Abingdon Rd ⊠ W8 6AF⊖ High Street Kensington – ℰ (020) 7795 6969
– www.l-restaurant.co.uk – info@l-restaurant.co.uk – Fax (020) 7795 6699
– Closed 25 December and Monday lunch   35AAX**x**
Rest – Spanish – Carte £ 26/36
♦ Wonderfully airy glass-roofed dining room with tastefully designed wood work and mirrors. Authentic Iberian menus with an emphasis on tapas matched by good-value wine list.

X **Kensington Place** 　　　　　　　　　　　　AC VISA ⓪ AE ⓪
201 Kensington Church St ⊠ W8 7LX⊖ Notting Hill Gate – 𝒞 (020) 7727 3184
– www.kensingtonplace-restaurant.co.uk – kprreservations@danddlondon.com
– Fax (020) 7792 9388　　　　　　　　　　　　27AAV**z**
Rest – Modern European – (booking essential) Menu £ 20/25 – Carte £ 22/46
♦ A cosmopolitan crowd still head for this establishment that set the trend for large, bustling and informal restaurants. Professionally run with skilled modern cooking.

X **Cibo** 　　　　　　　　　　　　　　　VISA ⓪ AE
3 Russell Gdns ⊠ W14 8EZ⊖ Kensington Olympia – 𝒞 (020) 7371 6271
– www.ciborestaurant.net – ciborestaurant@aol.com – Fax (020) 7602 1371
– Closed Christmas-New Year, Saturday lunch and Sunday dinner　　16MZE**b**
Rest – Italian – Carte £ 25/39
♦ Smoothly run Italian restaurant that combines style with the atmosphere of a neighbourhood favourite. Unaffected service with robust and tasty food.

X **Malabar** 　　　　　　　　　　　　AC VISA ⓪ AE
（㊟）*27 Uxbridge St ⊠ W8 7TQ⊖ Notting Hill Gate – 𝒞 (020) 7727 8800*
– www.malabar-restaurant.co.uk – feedback@malabar-restaurant.co.uk
– Closed 23-27 December　　　　　　　　　　　27AAV**e**
Rest – Indian – (buffet lunch Sunday) Menu £ 23 – Carte £ 21/28 **s**
♦ Indian restaurant in a residential street. Three rooms with individual personalities and informal service. Extensive range of good value dishes, particularly vegetarian.

X **Wódka** 　　　　　　　　　　　　　⟳ VISA ⓪ AE
12 St Albans Grove ⊠ W8 5PN⊖ High Street Kensington – 𝒞 (020) 7937 6513
– www.wodka.co.uk – info@wodka.co.uk – Fax (020) 7937 8621
– Closed 25-26 December, 1 January, Easter Sunday,
Monday lunch and Saturday lunch　　　　　　　35ABX**c**
Rest – Polish – Menu £ 15 (lunch) – Carte £ 29/34
♦ Unpretentious Polish restaurant with rustic, authentic menu. Assorted blinis and flavoured vodkas a speciality. Simply decorated, with wooden tables and paper napkins.

North Kensington – ⊠ W2/W11

⌂⌂ **The Portobello** without rest 　　　　　📶 ⁋ VISA ⓪ AE
22 Stanley Gdns ⊠ W11 2NG⊖ Notting Hill Gate – 𝒞 (020) 7727 2777
– www.portobello-hotel.co.uk – info@portobello-hotel.co.uk – Fax (020)
7792 9641 – Closed 23-29 December　　　　　　16NZE**n**
21 rm – ♦£ 150/180 ♦♦£ 355, ⊇ £ 17
♦ An attractive Victorian town house in an elegant terrace. Original and theatrical décor. Circular beds, half-testers, Victorian baths: no two bedrooms are the same.

⌂ **Guesthouse West** 　　　　　🏠 AC ❄ ⁋ VISA ⓪ AE
163-165 Westbourne Grove ⊠ W11 2RS⊖ Notting Hill Gate – 𝒞 (020)
7792 9800 – www.guesthousewest.com – reception@guesthousewest.com
– Fax (020) 7792 9797　　　　　　　　　　　27AAU**x**
20 rm – ♦£ 194 ♦♦£ 229, ⊇ £ 15　　**Rest** – Carte £ 27/37
♦ Attractive Edwardian house in the heart of Notting Hill, close to its shops and restaurants. Contemporary bedrooms boast the latest in audio visual gadgetry. Chic Parlour Bar for all-day light dishes in a tapas style.

XXX **The Ledbury** 　　　　　　　　　🏠 AC VISA ⓪ AE
☼ *127 Ledbury Rd ⊠ W11 2AQ⊖ Notting Hill Gate – 𝒞 (020) 7792 9090*
– www.theledbury.com – info@theledbury.com – Fax (020) 7792 9191 – Closed
24-26 December and August Bank Holiday　　　　　27AAT**a**
Rest – French – Menu £ 60 (dinner) – Carte lunch £ 38/50🕸
Spec. Flame-grilled mackerel with a mackerel tartare, avocado and shiso. Breast and confit of pigeon, sweetcorn, almond and girolles. Date and vanilla tart with cardamom and orange ice cream.
♦ Former pub with elegant, minimalist décor. Seasonal menu with innovative edge; flavours are pronounced and well judged; ingredients are superbly sourced.

XX **Notting Hill Brasserie**　　　　　　　　　　　AC ⇔ VISA ⚈ AE
92 Kensington Park Rd ⊠ W11 2PN⊖ Notting Hill Gate – ℰ (020) 7229 4481
– www.nottinghillbrasserie.com – enquiries@nottinghillbrasserie.com – Fax (020)
7221 1246 – Closed Bank Holidays and lunch Monday and Tuesday　　　27AAU**a**
Rest – French – Menu £ 23 (lunch) – Carte £ 40/48
♦ Modern, comfortable restaurant with quiet, formal atmosphere set over four small
rooms. Authentic African artwork on walls. Contemporary dishes with European influence.

XX **Edera**　　　　　　　　　　　　　　　　　AC ⇔ VISA ⚈ AE
148 Holland Park Ave ⊠ W11 4UE⊖ Holland Park – ℰ (020) 7221 6090
– Fax (020) 7313 9700 – Closed Bank Holidays　　　　　　　　　　16MZE**n**
Rest – Italian – Carte £ 32/49
♦ Split level restaurant with outdoor tables. Modern Italian cooking with some
unusual ingredients and combinations. Sardinian specialities include Bottarga and
homemade pastas.

XX **E&O**　　　　　　　　　　　　　　　AC ⇔ VISA ⚈ AE ①
14 Blenheim Crescent ⊠ W11 1NN⊖ Ladbroke Grove – ℰ (020) 7229 5454
– www.rickerrestaurants.com – eando@rickerrestaurants.com – Fax (020)
7229 5522 – Closed Christmas, New Year and August Bank Holiday　　16MZD**a**
Rest – Asian – Carte £ 31/42
♦ Mean, dark and moody: never mind the exterior, we're talking about the A-list
diners. Minimalist chic meets high sound levels. Menus scour Far East: cutlery/chopstick choice.

X **Notting Grill**　　　　　　　　　　　　　🍴 VISA ⚈ AE ①
123A Clarendon Rd ⊠ W11 4JG⊖ Holland Park – ℰ (020) 7229 1500
– www.awt.com – nottinggrill@awtrestaurants.com – Fax (020) 7229 8889
– Closed 25-26 December and Monday-Friday lunch except December　　16MZE**z**
Rest – Beef specialities – Carte £ 32/35
♦ Converted pub that retains a rustic feel, with bare brick walls and wooden tables.
Specialises in well sourced, quality meats.

X **Bumpkin**　　　　　　　　　　　　　　AC ⇔ VISA ⚈ AE
209 Westbourne Park Rd ⊠ W11 1EA⊖ Westbourne Park – ℰ (020) 7243 9818
– www.bumpkinuk.com – Fax (020) 7229 1826
– Closed 25-26 December and 1 January　　　　　　　　　　　　27AAT**b**
Rest – Modern European – (closed Sunday dinner and Monday) (dinner only
and Sunday lunch) Carte £ 27/40
Rest *Brasserie* – Carte £ 27/40
♦ Converted pea-green pub with casual, clubby feel and wholesome philosophy of
cooking seasonal, carefully-sourced and organic food. Whisky tasting and private
dining on top floors. First floor restaurant offers modern Mediterranean menu.

🍺 **The Fat Badger**　　　　　　　　　　　　　VISA ⚈ AE ①
310 Portobello Road ⊠ W10 5TA⊖ Ladbroke Grove. – ℰ (020) 8969 4500
– www.thefatbadger.com – rupert@thefatbadger.com
– Closed 25-26 December　　　　　　　　　　　　　　　　　16MZD**b**
Rest – British – Menu £ 15 – Carte £ 30/50
♦ Large rustic pub with old sofas, chandeliers, upstairs dining room and some intriguing wallpaper. Seasonal and earthy British food, with whole beasts delivered to
the kitchen.

South Kensington – Greater London – ⊠ SW5/SW7

🏨 **The Pelham**　　　　　　Lᔕ 📶 AC ⅍ 📶 VISA ⚈ AE ①
15 Cromwell Pl ⊠ SW7 2LA⊖ South Kensington – ℰ (020) 7589 8288
– www.pelhamhotel.co.uk – reservations@pelhamhotel.co.uk
– Fax (020) 7584 8444　　　　　　　　　　　　　　　　36ADY**z**
51 rm – ♦£ 212/235 ♦♦£ 341, ⊇ £ 17.50 – 1 suite
Rest *Kemps* – Menu £ 18 – Carte £ 29/41
♦ Attractive Victorian town house with a discreet and comfortable feel. Wood panelled drawing room and individually decorated bedrooms with marble bathrooms.
Detailed service. Warm basement dining room.

Blakes
Ló | ☆ | AC rest, ※ 🖤 VISA ⚫ AE ①

33 Roland Gdns ⊠ SW7 3PF ⊖ Gloucester Road – ℰ (020) 7370 6701
– www.blakeshotels.com – blakes@blakeshotels.com
– Fax (020) 7373 0442
36ACZ**n**

40 rm – ♦£176/311 ♦♦£382/441, ⊇ £25 – 8 suites **Rest** – Carte £60/90

♦ Behind the Victorian façade lies one of London's first 'boutique' hotels. Dramatic, bold and eclectic décor, with oriental influences and antiques from around the globe. Fashionable restaurant with bamboo and black walls.

The Bentley
⋒ *Ló* | ☆ | AC ※ 🕻 ⠵ VISA ⚫ AE ①

27-33 Harrington Gdns ⊠ SW7 4JX ⊖ Gloucester Road – ℰ (020) 7244 5555
– www.thebentley-hotel.com – info@thebentley-hotel.com
– Fax (020) 7244 5566
36ACY**k**

52 rm – ♦£353 ♦♦£470, ⊇ £22.50 – 12 suites
Rest *1880* – (closed Sunday-Monday) (dinner only) Menu £26/32
– Carte £34/53

♦ A number of stucco-fronted 19C houses were joined to create this opulent, lavish hotel decorated with marble, mosaics and ornate gold leaf. Bedrooms with gorgeous silk fabrics. 1880 for formal dining and ambitious cooking.

NH Harrington Hall
⋒ *Ló* | ☆ | AC ※ 🖤 ⠵ VISA ⚫ AE ①

5-25 Harrington Gdns ⊠ SW7 4JB ⊖ Gloucester Road – ℰ (020) 7396 9696
– www.nh-hotels.com – nhharringtonhall@nh-hotels.com
– Fax (020) 7396 1719
36ACY**n**

200 rm – ♦£210 ♦♦£270, ⊇ £18

Rest *Wetherby's* – Menu £16 – Carte £26/35

♦ A series of adjoined terraced houses, with an attractive period façade that belies the size. Tastefully furnished bedrooms, with an extensive array of facilities. Classically decorated dining room.

Number Sixteen without rest
⇗ | ☆ | AC ※ 🕻 VISA ⚫ AE

16 Sumner Pl ⊠ SW7 3EG ⊖ South Kensington – ℰ (020) 7589 5232
– www.numbersixteenhotel.co.uk – sixteen@firmdale.com
– Fax (020) 7584 8615
36ADY**d**

42 rm – ♦£141/235 ♦♦£317, ⊇ £17.50

♦ Enticingly refurbished 19C town houses in smart area. Discreet entrance, comfy sitting room and charming breakfast terrace. Bedrooms in English country house style.

The Cranley without rest
| ☆ | AC ※ 🕻 VISA ⚫ AE ①

10 Bina Gardens ⊠ SW5 0LA ⊖ Gloucester Road – ℰ (020) 7373 0123
– www.thecranley.com – info@thecranley.com – Fax (020) 7373 9497   36ACY**c**

38 rm – ♦£264/294 ♦♦£294, ⊇ £19.50 – 1 suite

♦ Delightful Regency town house combines charm and period details with modern comforts and technology. Individually styled bedrooms; some with four-posters. Room service available.

The Rockwell
🔓 | ☆ | AC 🕻 VISA ⚫ AE

181-183 Cromwell Rd ⊠ SW5 0SF ⊖ Earl's Court – ℰ (020) 7244 2000
– www.therockwell.com – enquiries@therockwell.com
– Fax (020) 7244 2001
35ABY**b**

40 rm – ♦£120/180 ♦♦£180/200, ⊇ £12.50   **Rest** – Carte £23/34

♦ Two Victorian houses with open, modern lobby and secluded, south-facing garden terrace. Bedrooms come in bold warm colours; 'Garden rooms' come with their own patios. Small dining room offers easy menu of modern European staples.

The Gore
| ☆ | AC ※ 🕻 ⠵ VISA ⚫ AE ①

190 Queen's Gate ⊠ SW7 5EX ⊖ Gloucester Road – ℰ (020) 7584 6601
– www.gorehotel.com – reservations@gorehotel.com
– Fax (020) 7589 8127
36ACX**n**

50 rm – ♦£212/269 ♦♦£269, ⊇ £16.95

Rest *190 Queensgate* – (booking essential) Carte £27/39

♦ Idiosyncratic Victorian house, with lobby covered with pictures and prints. Individually styled bedrooms have discreet mod cons and charming bathrooms. Informal bistro with European menu.

LONDON

Aster House *without rest* 🚱 AC 🚫 🕯 VISA 🐵

3 Sumner Pl ⊠ SW7 3EE⊖ South Kensington – ℰ *(020) 7581 5888*
– www.asterhouse.com – asterhouse@btinternet.com
– Fax (020) 7584 4925 36ADY**t**
13 rm ⫘ – ♦£80/135 ♦♦£120/180
♦ End of terrace Victorian house with a pretty little rear garden and first floor conservatory. Ground floor rooms available. A wholly non-smoking establishment.

Ambassade de L'Ile (Jean-Christophe Ansanay-Alex) AC ✿

🛱 *117-119 Old Brompton Rd ⊠ SW7 3RN London ⊖ Gloucester* VISA 🐵 AE
Road – ℰ *(020) 7373 7774 – www.ambassadedelile.com*
– direction@ambassadedelile.com – Fax (020) 7373 4472
– Closed Sunday 36ACZ**s**
Rest – French – Menu £65 – Carte £63/88
Spec. Watermelon gazpacho, avocado and langoustines. Rib of milk fed veal with girolles, spinach and potato gnocchi. White peach soufflé.
♦ Eccentric 1970s retro décor of shag-pile carpet and white leather. This is the London outpost of the Lyonnais restaurant L'Auberge de L'Ile. The French cooking is original, detailed and ambitious.

Bombay Brasserie AC VISA 🐵 AE ①

Courtfield Rd ⊠ SW7 4QH⊖ Gloucester Road – ℰ *(020) 7370 4040*
– www.bombaybrasserielondon.com – bombay1brasserie@aol.com – Fax (020)
7835 1669 – Closed 25-26 December 36ACY**y**
Rest – Indian – Menu £19 (weekday lunch buffet) – Carte £42/52
♦ Something of a London institution: an ever busy Indian restaurant with Raj-style décor. Ask to sit in the brighter plant-filled conservatory. Popular lunchtime buffet.

L'Etranger AC 🐾 VISA 🐵 AE ①

36 Gloucester Rd ⊠ SW7 4QT⊖ Gloucester Road – ℰ *(020) 7584 1118*
– www.circagroupltd.co.uk – etranger@etranger.co.uk – Fax (020) 7584 8886
– Closed 25-26 December and Saturday lunch 35ACX**c**
Rest – Innovative – (booking essential) Menu £20 (lunch) – Carte £31/86⅜
♦ Corner restaurant with mosaic entrance floor and bay window. Modern décor. Tables extend into adjoining wine shop. French based cooking with Asian influences.

Pasha AC ✿ VISA 🐵 AE ①

1 Gloucester Rd ⊠ SW7 4PP⊖ Gloucester Road – ℰ *(020) 7589 7969*
– www.pasha-restaurant.co.uk – info@pasha-restaurant.co.uk – Fax (020)
7581 9996 – Closed 24-25 December and 1 January 36ACX**r**
Rest – Moroccan – Menu £15/37 – Carte £24/42
♦ Relax over ground floor cocktails, then descend to mosaic floored restaurant where the rose-petal strewn tables are the ideal accompaniment to tasty Moroccan home cooking.

Khan's of Kensington AC VISA 🐵 AE

3 Harrington Rd ⊠ SW7 3ES⊖ South Kensington – ℰ *(020) 7584 4114*
– www.khansofkensington.co.uk – info@khansofkensington.co.uk
– Fax (020) 7581 2900 36ADY**a**
Rest – Indian – Carte £18/29
♦ Bright room with wood flooring and a large mural depicting scenes from old India. Basement bar in a colonial style. Authentic Indian cooking with attentive service.

Cambio de Tercio AC ✿ VISA 🐵 AE ①

163 Old Brompton Rd ⊠ SW5 0LJ⊖ Gloucester Road – ℰ *(020) 7244 8970*
– www.cambiodetercio.co.uk – alusa@btconnect.com – Fax (020) 7373 2359
– Closed 2 weeks Christmas 36ACZ**a**
Rest – Spanish – Carte £27/39
♦ The keen young owners have created a vibrant destination offering a mix of traditional and sophisticated Spanish cooking complemented by a well-sourced regional wine list.

X **Bangkok**   AC VISA ◉◉

*9 Bute St ⊠ SW7 3EY⊖ South Kensington – ℰ (020) 7584 8529
– www.bankokrestaurant.co.uk – Closed Christmas-New Year, Sunday and Bank
Holidays*   36ADY**b**

Rest – Thai – Carte £ 20/28

♦ This simple Thai bistro has been a popular local haunt for many years. Guests can
watch the chefs at work, preparing inexpensive dishes from the succinct menu.

KINGSTON UPON THAMES – Greater London   12 **A3**

⛳ Hampton Court Palace Hampton Wick, ℰ (020) 8977 2423

Surbiton – Greater London – ⊠ Surrey

XX **The French Table**   AC VISA ◉◉ AE

*85 Maple Rd ⊠ KT6 4AW – ℰ (020) 8399 2365 – www.thefrenchtable.co.uk
– Fax (020) 8390 5353 – Closed 2 weeks August, 1-6 January,
Sunday dinner and Monday*   6CY**a**

Rest – Mediterranean – Menu £ 23 (lunch) – Carte dinner £ 30/38

♦ Run by a husband and wife team; a narrow room with a lively, local atmosphere.
Gutsy and satisfying French-Mediterranean cooking. Saturday morning cookery les-
sons.

> Your opinions are important to us:
> please write and let us know about your discoveries and experiences –
> good and bad!

LAMBETH – Greater London   12 **B3**

Brixton – Greater London – ⊠ SW2   12 **B3**

▶ London 3 mi – Watford 24 mi – Slough 27 mi – Basildon 36 mi

XX **Upstairs**   VISA ◉◉ AE
🏠
*89b Acre Lane ⊠ SW2 5TN⊖ Clapham North – ℰ (020) 7733 8855
– www.upstairslondon.com – Closed 18-31 August, 22 December - 4 January,
Sunday and Monday*   24SZH**b**

Rest – Modern European – (dinner only) Menu £ 25

♦ Entrance buzzer, then narrow stairs to first floor bar and second floor restaurant.
Cosy, with simple, stylish décor. A mix of French and English cooking; neat and accurate.

Clapham Common – Greater London – ⊠ SW4

XX **Trinity**   AC

*4 The Polygon ⊠ SW4 0JG⊖ Clapham Common – ℰ (020) 7622 1199
– www.trinityrestaurant.co.uk – dine@trinityrestaurant.co.uk – Fax (020)
7622 1166 – Closed 25-26 December, 1 January and Monday lunch*   24RZH**a**

Rest – Innovative – Menu £ 20 (lunch) – Carte dinner £ 31/42

♦ Contemporary, stylish and bright restaurant with abstract art, crisp linen tablecloths and relaxed atmosphere. Original menu offers precise, artfully presented modern cooking.

XX **Four O Nine**   AC VISA ◉◉ AE

*entrance on Landor Rd, 409 Clapham Rd ⊠ SW9 9BT⊖ Clapham North
– ℰ (020) 7737 0722 – www.fouronine.co.uk
– reservations@fouronine.co.uk*   24SZH**c**

Rest – Modern European – (dinner only and Sunday lunch) Carte £ 31/38

♦ Intimate, stylish first floor restaurant with secretive entrance. Crisp, unfussy, appe-
tisingly-presented food, with natural flavours to the fore. French/Italian influences.

LONDON

✗ Tsunami
AC VISA ◑ AE

Unit 3, 5-7 Voltaire Rd ⊠ SW4 6DQ⊖ Clapham North – ℰ (020) 7978 1610
– www.tsunamijapaneserestaurant.co.uk – Fax (020) 7978 1591
– Closed 25-26 December and Easter 24SZH**a**
Rest – Japanese – (dinner only and Saturday-Sunday lunch) Carte £ 23/54
♦ Trendy, mininalist-style restaurant. Interesting Japanese menu with many dishes designed for sharing and plenty of original options. Good Sushi and Sashimi selection.

Kennington – Greater London – ⊠ SE11

✗ Lobster Pot
AC VISA ◑ AE ◑

3 Kennington Lane ⊠ SE11 4RG⊖ Kennington – ℰ (020) 7582 5556
– www.lobsterpotrestaurant.co.uk
– Closed 2 weeks Christmas, Sunday and Monday 40AOY**e**
Rest – French – Carte £ 34/45
♦ A nautical theme so bold you'll need your sea legs: fishing nets, shells, aquariums, portholes, even the sound of seagulls. Classic French seafood menu is more restrained.

Southbank – Greater London – ⊠ SE1

🏨 London Marriott H. County Hall
⇐ 🔲 ⊕ 🏊 Ⅰ₅ 🏋 ᕈ rm, AC
🍴 ⸙ 🛁 VISA ◑ AE ◑

Westminster Bridge Rd ⊠ SE1
7PB⊖ Westminster – ℰ (020) 7928 5200 – www.marriott.countyhall.com
– Fax (020) 7928 5300 40AMX**a**
195 rm – †£ 328 ††£ 363, ⸞ £21.95 – 5 suites
Rest *County Hall* – Menu £ 26 – Carte £ 33/45
♦ Occupying the historic County Hall building. Many of the spacious and comfortable bedrooms enjoy river and Parliament outlook. Impressive leisure facilities. World famous views from restaurant.

✗✗✗ Skylon
⇐ AC VISA ◑ AE ◑

1 Southbank Centre, Belvedere Rd ⊠ SE1 8XX⊖ Waterloo – ℰ (020) 7654 7800
– www.skylonrestaurant.co.uk – skylon@danddlondon.com
– Fax (020) 7654 7801 32AMV**a**
Rest – Modern European – Menu £ 27 (lunch) – Carte £ 29/40 ⅏
♦ 1950s style dining flagship in Royal Festival Hall. Grill with bar, river views and easy-to-eat menu. Restaurant offers more ambitious dishes, which means higher prices.

✗ Canteen
🍴 AC VISA ◑ AE

Southbank Centre, Belvedere Rd ⊠ SE1 8XX⊖ Waterloo – ℰ (0845) 686 1122
– www.canteen.co.uk – rth@canteen.co.uk
– Closed 25 December and 1 January 32AMV**a**
Rest – British – Carte £ 35/40
♦ On ground floor of Royal Festival Hall, with booths and refectory style tables plus large outdoor terrace area. Extensive menu offers classic British food at reasonable prices.

West Dulwich

🏠 The Rosendale
🍴 AC 🍴 ⇔ VISA ◑

65 Rosendale Rd West Dulwich ⊖ West Dulwich (rail) – ℰ (020) 8670 0812
– www.therosendale.co.uk – dine@therosendale.co.uk – Fax (020) 8671 9008
– Closed 1 January 7FX**a**
Rest – Menu £ 20 (lunch) – Carte £ 20/28 ⅏
♦ Huge, high-ceilinged former coaching inn with buzzy atmosphere and smart rear terrace. Local produce well-used; even the bread and butter are homemade. Outstanding wine list.

 Red = Pleasant. Look for the red ✗ and 🏠 symbols.

LEWISHAM – Greater London   12 **B3**

Blackheath – Greater London – ⊠ SE3   12 **B3**

XX   **Chapters**   🍴 AC VISA ⓶ AE ①
43-45 Montpelier Vale ⊠ SE3 0TJ – ℰ (020) 8333 2666
– www.chapterrestaurants.com – info@chaptersrestaurants.com
– Fax (020) 8355 8399   8HX**c**
Rest – Modern European – Menu £ 19/24 – Carte approx. £ 24
♦ Formerly Chapter Two, now a contemporary and bustling all-day brasserie and bar. Large, appealingly priced menu with British and Mediterranean influences, with meats cooked over charcoal a speciality.

Forest Hill – Greater London – ⊠ SE23

🏠   **The Dartmouth Arms**   🍴 ⅍ P VISA ⓶ AE
7 Dartmouth Road ⊠ SE23 3HN – ℰ (020) 8488 3117
– www.thedartmoutharms.com – info@thedartmoutharms.com – Fax (020)
7771 7230 – Closed 25-26 December, 1 January   7GX**a**
Rest – Menu £ 15/18 – Carte £ 23/31
♦ Across the road from the train station, offering an appealing mix of dishes, commendable in their Britishness and inventiveness, and with a healthy regard for seasonality.

LONDON HEATHROW AIRPORT – see Hillingdon, London p. 87

MERTON – Greater London   12 **B3**

Wimbledon – Greater London – ⊠ SW19

🏨   **Cannizaro House** ⊛   ≤ 🐎 ⅍ 🛏 ⅏ ⅍ P VISA ⓶ AE ①
West Side, Wimbledon Common ⊠ SW19 4UE ⊖ Wimbledon – ℰ (020)
8879 1464 – www.cannizarohouse.com – info@cannizarohouse.com
– Fax (020) 8879 7338   6DXY**x**
44 rm ☲ – †£ 395 ††£ 485 – 2 suites
Rest – Menu £ 23/27 – Carte £ 33/42
♦ Part Georgian mansion in a charming spot on the Common. Appealing drawing room popular for afternoon tea. Rooms in original house are antique furnished, some with balconies. Refined restaurant overlooks splendid formal garden.

X   **Light House**   VISA ⓶ AE
75-77 Ridgway ⊠ SW19 4ST ⊖ Wimbledon – ℰ (020) 8944 6338
– www.lighthousewimbledon.com – info@lighthousewimbledon.com
– Fax (020) 8946 4440
– Closed 25-26 December, 1 January, Easter Day and Sunday dinner   6DY**n**
Rest – International – Menu £ 17 (midweek lunch) – Carte £ 23/33
♦ Bright and modern neighbourhood restaurant with open plan kitchen. Informal service of a weekly changing and diverse menu of progressive Italian/fusion dishes.

🏠   **The Fire Stables**   AC ⅍ VISA ⓶ AE ①
27-29 Church Rd ⊠ SW19 5DQ ⊖ Wimbledon – ℰ (020) 8946 3197
– www.firestableswimbledon.co.uk – thefirestables@youngs.co.uk
– Fax (020) 8946 1101   6DX**a**
Rest – Menu £ 16/25 – Carte £ 20/30
♦ Modern gastropub in village centre. Open-plan kitchen. Polished wood tables and banquettes. Varied modern British dishes. Expect fishcakes, duck confit salad or risotto.

NEWHAM – Greater London 12 B3

ExCel – Greater London – ✉ E16

Crowne Plaza Docklands
Royal Victoria Dock, Western Gateway ✉ E16 1AL ⊖ Royal Victoria – ✆ (0870) 990 96 92 – www.crownplazadocklands.co.uk – sales@crowneplazadocklands.co.uk – Fax (0870) 990 96 93 8HVa
205 rm – †£ 288 ††£ 300, ☕ £ 16.95 – 5 suites
Rest *Docklands Bar & Grill* – (bar lunch) Carte £ 20/26
◆ Spacious and stylish hotel with emphasis on the business traveller. State-of-the-art meeting rooms; snazzy, compact leisure centre. Ultra-smart, well-equipped rooms. Modish dining room with funky bar.

RICHMOND-UPON-THAMES – Greater London

Old Town Hall, Whittaker Ave 020 8940 9125, info@visitrichmond.co.uk

Barnes – Greater London – ✉ SW13 12 B3

Sonny's
94 Church Rd ✉ SW13 0DQ – ✆ (020) 8748 0393 – www.sonnys.co.uk – manager@sonnys.co.uk – Fax (020) 8748 2698 – Closed Sunday dinner and Bank Holidays 21KZHx
Rest – Modern European – Carte £ 26/34
◆ Bright, modern and informal neighbourhood restaurant. Balanced set menu, with good choice of easy-to-eat dishes with European influences. Plenty of wines by the glass.

Riva
169 Church Rd ✉ SW13 9HR – ✆ (020) 8748 0434 – Fax (020) 8748 0434 – Closed last 2 weeks August, 1 week Christmas, Saturday lunch and Bank Holidays 21LZHa
Rest – Italian – Carte £ 32/44
◆ The eponymous owner manages the polite service in this unassuming restaurant. Rustic and robust cooking uses some of Italy's finest produce. Extensive all-Italian wine list.

Barnes Grill
2-3 Rocks Lane ✉ SW13 0DB – ✆ (020) 8878 4488 – www.awtrestaurants.com – barnesgrill@awtrestaurants.com – Closed 25-26 December 21LZHk
Rest – Beef specialities – (dinner only and lunch at weekends) (booking essential) Carte £ 26/42
◆ Popular neighbourhood addition: eye-catching wall-mounted feather displays and mounted bull's head. Steaks, hung for 35 days, typify the heartily old-fashioned British dishes.

Ma Cuisine
7 White Hart Lane ✉ SW13 0PX – ✆ (020) 8878 4092 – www.macuisinebarnes.co.uk – info@macuisinebarnes.co.uk 21KZHc
Rest – French – Menu £ 16 (lunch) – Carte £ 21/29
◆ Neighbourhood restaurant with long narrow room split in two. Earthy, satisfying French classics made with quality ingredients, at philanthropic prices. Warm, welcoming service.

The Brown Dog
28 Cross Street ✉ SW13 0AP – ✆ (020) 8392 2200 – www.thebrowndog.co.uk – Fax (020) 8392 2200 – Closed 25-26 December and 1 January 21KZHB
Rest – Carte £ 22/33
◆ Horseshoe bar, snug lounge and separate dining room; charming décor includes cast iron fireplaces, antique furniture and space age lamps. Seasonal menu; tasty, moreish food.

East Sheen – Greater London – ✉ SW14

※ Mango & Silk
VISA ◯◯ AE
199 Upper Richmond Rd West ✉ SW14 4 QT – ✆ (020) 8876 6220
– www.mangoandsilk.co.uk – Closed Monday 21KZHk
Rest – Indian – (dinner only and lunch Saturday and Sunday) Carte £14/16
♦ An air of calm pervades the restaurant, thanks to the charming owner. Udit Sarkhel is the chef and his cooking is as expertly crafted as ever. The generous prices make over-ordering the easy option.

🍴 The Victoria
P VISA ◯◯ AE
✉ SW14 7RT – ✆ (020) 8876 4238 – www.thevictoria.net
– bookings@thevictoria.net – Fax (020) 8878 3464
– Closed 24-27 December 6CXu
Rest – Carte £22/38
♦ Comfy, minimalist pub in residential street. All day bar snacks and concise menu of modern, interesting dishes. Large terrace with flat-topped range and rotisserie for summer weekends.

Hampton Wick – Greater London – ✉ KT1

🏠 Chase Lodge *without rest*
VISA ◯◯ AE
10 Park Rd ✉ KT1 4AS – ✆ (020) 8943 1862 – www.chaselodgehotel.com
– info@chaselodgehotel.com – Fax (020) 8943 9363 5BYe
13 rm – †£55/98 ††£98/185
♦ Personally-run small hotel in mid-terrace Victorian property in an area of outstanding architectural and historical interest. Individually furnished, comfortable rooms.

Kew – Greater London – ✉ TW9 12 A3

※※ The Glasshouse
AC VISA ◯◯ AE
14 Station Parade ✉ TW9 3PZ⊖ Kew Gardens – ✆ (020) 8940 6777
– www.glasshouserestaurant.co.uk – info@glasshouserestaurant.co.uk
– Fax (020) 8940 3833 – Closed 24-26 December and 1 January 6CXz
Rest – Modern European – Menu £36/48
Spec. Spaghetti of rabbit, girolles, tarragon and parmesan. Sea bass and king prawn with fennel purée. Peaches with rice pudding Chantilly.
♦ Relaxed contemporary neighbourhood restaurant featuring two walls of glass. The comprehensive menu offers modern European dishes; cooking is honest, earthy and well-priced.

※※ Kew Grill
AC VISA ◯◯ AE
10b Kew Green ✉ TW9 3BH⊖ Kew Gardens – ✆ (020) 8948 4433
– www.awtrestaurants.com – kewgrill@awtrestaurants.com – Fax (020) 8605 3532 – Closed 24-26 December and Monday lunch 6CXu
Rest – Beef specialities – (booking essential) Menu £15 (lunch) – Carte approx. £31
♦ Just off Kew Green, this long, narrow restaurant has a Mediterranean style and feel. Grilled specialities employing top-rate ingredients: the beef is hung for 35 days.

※ Ma Cuisine
VISA ◯◯
The Old Post Office, 9 Station Approach ✉ TW9 3QB⊖ Kew Gardens
– ✆ (020) 8332 1923 – www.macuisinekew.co.uk
– info@macuisinekew.co.uk 6CXr
Rest – French – Menu £16 (lunch) – Carte £21/29
♦ Formerly Kew's post office building; features tables on the pavement, arched roof and red gingham tablecloths. Good value, classic French dishes. Truly, "le petit bistrot".

Richmond – Greater London – ✉ TW9/TW10   12 **A3**

🛈 Old Town Hall, Whittaker Ave ✆ (020) 8940 9125
📷 Richmond Park Roehampton Gate, ✆ (020) 8876 3205
📷 Sudbrook Park, ✆ (020) 8940 4351

Petersham   ⪦ 🚗 🛗 ✄ ⸙ ♨ 🏊 P VISA MO AE ⓘ
Nightingale Lane ✉ *TW10 6UZ* – ✆ *(020) 8940 7471*
– *www.petershamhotel.co.uk* – *enq@petershamhotel.co.uk*
– *Fax (020) 8939 1098*   6CX**c**
60 rm ⌣ – †£95/160 ††£150/170 – 1 suite
Rest *Restaurant* – see restaurant listing
♦ Extended over the years, a fine example of Victorian Gothic architecture. Impressive Portland stone, self-supporting staircase. Most comfortable rooms overlook the Thames.

Richmond Gate   🚗 🖥 🕸 🛁 ⸙ ♨ 🏊 P VISA MO AE
158 Richmond Hill ✉ *TW10 6RP* – ✆ *(020) 8940 0061*
– *www.foliohotels.com/richmondgate*
– *reservations.richmondgate@foliohotels.com* – *Fax (020) 8332 0354*   6CX**c**
68 rm – †£119/215 ††£129/235, ⌣ £16.50 – 1 suite
Rest *Gates On The Park* – Classic – (Closed lunch Saturday and Bank Holidays) Menu £22 (lunch)/33 – Carte dinner £24/40 **s**
♦ Originally four elegant Georgian town houses and now a very comfortable corporate hotel. Cosy lounges have a period charm. Well-appointed deluxe rooms have thoughtful extras. Comfortable restaurant has intimate feel.

XXX The Restaurant at The Petersham – at Petersham Hotel   ⪦
Nightingale Lane ✉ *TW10 6UZ* – ✆ *(020)*   🚗 AK ⟷ P VISA MO AE ⓘ
8939 1084 – *www.petershamhotel.co.uk* – *restaurant@petershamhotel.co.uk*
– *Fax (020) 8939 1002*   6CX**c**
Rest – French – Carte £38/44 ▨
♦ Tables by the window have spectacular views across royal parkland and the winding Thames. Formal surroundings in which to enjoy classic and modern cooking. See the cellars.

X Matsuba   AK VISA MO AE
10 Red Lion St ✉ *TW9 1RW* – ✆ *(020) 8605 3513* – *www.matsuba.co.uk*
– *matsuba10@hotmail.com*
– *Closed 25-26 December, 1 January and Sunday*   6CX**n**
Rest – Japanese – Menu £35/45 – Carte £15/24
♦ Family-run restaurant with slick, contemporary interior featuring a rear sushi bar and authentic, market fresh, super value Japanese menus. Gets packed in the evenings!

X Petersham Nurseries Café   🍴 VISA MO AE ⓘ
Church Lane (off Petersham Rd) ✉ *TW10 7AG* – ✆ *(020) 8605 3627*
– *www.petershamnurseries.com* – *cafe@petershamnurseries.com*
– *Closed Monday*   6CX**x**
Rest – Italian influences – (lunch only) Carte £36/48
♦ Uniquely set in glasshouse (or outside, if sunny), with earthy implements and romantic Indian artefacts. Flavourful cooking with Italian influences; friendly service from welly-shod staff.

Teddington – Greater London – ✉ TW11

XX The Wharf   ⪦ 🍴 AK P VISA MO AE
22 Manor Rd ✉ *TW11 8BG* – ✆ *(020) 8977 6333*
– *www.thewharfteddington.com* – *team@thewharfteddington.com* – *Fax (020)*
8977 9444 – *Closed Monday and Bank Holidays*   5BX**c**
Rest – Modern European – Menu £16 (lunch) – Carte £28/40
♦ Riverside restaurant with large heated terrace opposite Teddington lock. Modern menu of good value dishes; fixed price menu in the week; modern music.

X **Simply Thai**   AC VISA ☺☺
196 Kingston Rd ⊠ TW11 9JD – ℰ (020) 8943 9747
– www.simplythai-restaurant.co.uk – simplythai1@yahoo.co.uk – Closed Easter
Sunday, 25 December and Sunday lunch   5BY**x**
Rest – Thai – (booking essential at lunch) Menu £ 17 – Carte £ 20/26
♦ Friendly Thai restaurant with popular local following. Extensive menus offer flavourful dishes proudly made with the best ingredients; seafood a speciality. Polite service.

Twickenham – Greater London – ⊠ TW1   12 **A3**

XX **A Cena**   AC VISA ☺☺ AE
418 Richmond Rd ⊠ TW1 2EB⊖ Richmond – ℰ (020) 8288 0108
– www.acena.co.uk – Fax (020) 8940 5346
– Closed Christmas, Sunday dinner and Monday lunch   5BX**e**
Rest – Italian – Carte £ 20/37
♦ Smart, neighbourhood style restaurant with pleasant bar boasting extensive cocktail list and dining room festooned with mirrors. Accomplished dishes from all regions of Italy.

X **The Grill Room**   AC VISA ☺☺ AE
2 Whitton Rd – ℰ (020) 8891 0803 – www.thegrillroomtw1.co.uk
– johnmac21@aol.com – Closed Sunday dinner   5BA**x**
Rest – Beef specialities – Carte £ 19/33
♦ Classic steakhouse menu, with cuts sourced from across the UK and all hung on the premises for between 32 and 42 days. Other favourite British dishes available. Try reserving one of the booths.

X **Tangawizi**   AC VISA ☺☺ AE
⌂ *406 Richmond Rd, Richmond Bridge ⊠ TW1 2EB⊖ Richmond – ℰ (020)*
8891 3737 – www.tangawizi.co.uk – tangawizi_richmond@hotmail.com
– Fax (020) 8891 3737 – Closed 25 December   5BX**e**
Rest – Indian – (dinner only) Carte £ 14/28
♦ Name means Ginger in Swahili. Sleek décor in warm purple with subtle Indian touches. Well priced, nicely balanced, slowly evolving menus take their influence from North India.

X **Brula**   ⟺ VISA ☺☺ AE
⌂ *43 Crown Rd, St Margarets ⊠ TW1 3EJ – ℰ (020) 8892 0602 – www.brula.co.uk*
– lawrence@brula.co.uk – Fax (020) 8892 7727 – Closed 1 week Christmas 5BX**v**
Rest – French – (booking essential) Menu £ 20/29 – Carte £ 20/36
♦ French brasserie in look, with mirrors and chandeliers. Good value, well crafted cooking is largely French but now comes with other European influences. Friendly service and popular with locals.

X **Ma Cuisine**   VISA ☺☺
⌂ *6 Whitton Rd ⊠ TW1 1BJ – ℰ (020) 8607 9849 – www.macuisinetw1.co.uk*
– info@macuisinetw1.co.uk – Closed 1 January and Sunday   5BX**a**
Rest – French – Menu £ 16 (lunch) – Carte £ 21/29
♦ Small neighbourhood bistro style restaurant offering good value. Classic French country cooking with blackboard specials; concise wine list.

X **Tapas y Vino**   VISA ☺☺
111 London Rd ⊠ TW1 1EE – ℰ (020) 8892 5417 – www.tapasyvino.co.uk
– info@tapasyvino.co.uk
– Closed Sunday, Monday and restricted opening July-August   5BX**a**
Rest – Mediterranean – Carte £ 15/20
♦ Simply furnished in Spanish style and serving carefully judged, satisfying tapas with influences from France, Morocco and Greece; four plates per person should be sufficient.

SOUTHWARK – Greater London · · · 12 **B3**

🛈 Level 2, Tate Modern, Bankside ✆ (020) 7401 5266, tourisminfo@southwark.gov.uk

Bermondsey – Greater London – ✉ SE1

🏠 **London Bridge** · · · *La* 🏨 & rm, 🖳 ⚡ 🔊 💰 🟦 🟠 🟦 🟦

8-18 London Bridge St ✉ SE1 9SG ⊖ London Bridge – ✆ (020) 7855 2200
– www.londonbridgehotel.com – sales@londonbridgehotel.com
– Fax (020) 7855 2233 · · · 33AQV**a**
135 rm – ♦£229 ♦♦£229, � £14.95 – 3 suites
Rest *Georgetown* – (dinner only) Carte £26/33
♦ In one of the oldest parts of London, independently owned with an ornate façade dating from 1915. Modern interior with classically decorated bedrooms and an impressive gym. Restaurant echoing the colonial style serving Malaysian dishes.

XXX **Le Pont de la Tour** · · · ⩽ 🏨 ⟳ 🟦 🟠 🟦

36d Shad Thames, Butlers Wharf ✉ SE1 2YE ⊖ London Bridge – ✆ (020)
7403 8403 – www.danddlondon.com – lepontdelatour@danddlondon.com
– Fax (020) 7940 1835 · · · 34ASV**c**
Rest – French – Menu £25 (lunch) – Carte £37/52 🏵
♦ Elegant and stylish room commanding spectacular views of the Thames and Tower Bridge. Formal and detailed service. Modern menu with an informal bar attached.

XX **Bengal Clipper** · · · 🖳 🟦 🟠 🟦

Cardamom Building, Shad Thames, Butlers Wharf ✉ SE1 2YR ⊖ London Bridge
– ✆ (020) 7357 9001 – www.bengalclipper.co.uk – mail@bengalclipper.co.uk
– Fax (020) 7357 9002 · · · 34ASV**e**
Rest – Indian – Carte £14/20
♦ Housed in a Thames-side converted warehouse, a smart Indian restaurant with original brickwork and steel supports. Menu features Bengali and Goan dishes. Evening pianist.

X **Blueprint Café** · · · ⩽ 🟦 🟠 🟦 🟦

Design Museum, Shad Thames, Butlers Wharf ✉ SE1 2YD ⊖ London Bridge
– ✆ (020) 7378 7031 – www.danddlondon.com
– blueprintcafe@danddlondon.com – Fax (020) 7357 8810
– Closed 24-27 December and Sunday dinner · · · 34ASV**u**
Rest – Modern European – Menu £20 – Carte £29/43
♦ Above the Design Museum, with impressive views of the river and bridge: handy binoculars on tables. Eager and energetic service, modern British menus: robust and rustic.

X **Magdalen** · · · 🖳 🟦 🟠 🟦

152 Tooley St ✉ SE1 2TU ⊖ London Bridge – ✆ (020) 7403 1342
– www.magdalenrestaurant.co.uk – info@magdalenrestaurant.co.uk – Fax (020)
7403 9950 – Closed last 2 weeks August, 1 week Christmas,
Saturday lunch and Sunday · · · 34ARV**b**
Rest – British – Menu £19 (lunch) – Carte £28/45
♦ Appealing bistro style restaurant set over two floors, with aubergine-coloured walls and chandeliers. Seasonal menus offer precise, well-executed and simply presented cooking.

X **Village East** · · · 🖳 ⟳ 🟦 🟠 🟦

171 Bermondsey St ✉ SE1 3UW ⊖ London Bridge – ✆ (020) 7357 6082
– www.villageeast.co.uk – info@villageeast.co.uk – Fax (020) 7403 3360
– Closed 25-26 December · · · 20XZE**a**
Rest – Modern European – Carte £23/34
♦ In a glass fronted block sandwiched by Georgian townhouses, this trendy restaurant has two loud, buzzy bars and dining areas serving ample portions of modern British fare.

X **Cantina Del Ponte**   ⟨ ⌂ VISA ⊕ AE ①
36c Shad Thames, Butlers Wharf ⊠ SE1 2YE⊖ London Bridge – ℰ (020)
7403 5403 – www.conran.com – cantina@danddlondon.com – Fax (020)
7940 1845 – Closed 24-26 December
34ASV**c**
Rest – Italian – Menu £ 18 (lunch) – Carte £ 22/36
♦ An Italian stalwart, refurbished late in 2007. Simple menu offers an appealing mix of classic dishes, with a good value set menu until 7pm. Riverside setting with pleasant terrace.

X **Butlers Wharf Chop House**   ⟨ ⌂ VISA ⊕ AE ①
36e Shad Thames, Butlers Wharf ⊠ SE1 2YE⊖ London Bridge – ℰ (020)
7403 3403 – www.danddlondon.com – bwchophouse@danddlondon.com
– Fax (020) 7940 1855 – Closed 1-2 January
34ASV**n**
Rest – British – Menu £ 26 – Carte £ 26/38
♦ Book the terrace in summer and dine in the shadow of Tower Bridge. Rustic feel to the interior, with obliging service. Menu focuses on traditional English dishes.

X **Champor-Champor**   AC ⟷ VISA ⊕ AE
62-64 Weston St ⊠ SE1 3QJ⊖ London Bridge – ℰ (020) 7403 4600
– www.champor-champor.com – mail@champor-champor.com – Closed
Easter, 1 week Christmas and Sunday
34ARV**a**
Rest – Asian – (dinner only and lunch Thursday-Friday) (booking essential)
Menu £ 24/30 – Carte £ 28/36
♦ Brims over with colourful Asian décor and artefacts including serene Buddha and sacred cow. Two intimate dining rooms: tasty, appealing mix of Malay, Chinese and Thai cuisine.

⌂ **The Hartley**   AC VISA ⊕ AE ①
64 Tower Bridge Road ⊠ SE1 4TR⊖ Borough. – ℰ (020) 7394 7023
– www.thehartley.com – enquries@thehartley.com – Closed 25-26 December and
Bank Holidays
20XZE**c**
Rest – (Closed Sunday dinner) Carte £ 20/27
♦ Classic 19C red brick pub, named after former Hartley jam factory opposite: jam jars even adorn the walls! Interesting menus offer five daily changing blackboard specials.

⌂ **The Garrison**   AC ⌗ ⟷
99-101 Bermondsey St ⊠ SE1 3XB⊖ London Bridge – ℰ (020) 7089 9355
– www.thegarrison.co.uk – info@thegarrison.co.uk
– Closed 25-26 December, 1 January
20XZE**z**
Rest – (booking essential at dinner) Carte £ 28/45
♦ Part-shabby-chic gastropub, part boho brasserie, with booths, bustling vibe and mini cinema for private dining. Wholesome, homemade, no-nonsense cooking and organic ales.

Elephant and Castle – Greater London – ⊠ SE17   12 **B3**

XX **Dragon Castle**   AC VISA ⊕ AE
114 Walworth Rd ⊠ SE17 1JL⊖ Elephant and Castle – ℰ (020) 7277 3388
– www.dragoncastle.eu – dragoncastle@hotmail.com
– Closed 25-26 December
25VZF**x**
Rest – Chinese – Carte £ 15/30
♦ Large blue building with red studded door and decoratively understated interior. Generous plates of authentic Cantonese food plus popular dim sum menu. Attentive service.

Southwark – Greater London – ⊠ SE1   12 **B3**

⌂ **Southwark Rose**   🛗 ⅙ rm, AC ⌗ 🌐 🛉 P VISA ⊕ AE
43-47 Southwark Bridge Rd ⊠ SE1 9HH⊖ London Bridge – ℰ (020) 7015 1480
– www.southwarkrosehotel.co.uk – info@southwarkrosehotel.co.uk
– Fax (020) 7015 1481
34AQV**c**
78 rm – †£ 105/190 ††£ 105/190, � £ 12.95 – 6 suites
Rest – (dinner only) Carte £ 14/22
♦ Purpose built budget hotel south of the City, near the Globe Theatre. Top floor dining room with bar. Uniform style, reasonably spacious bedrooms with writing desks.

LONDON

XXX Oxo Tower
⟨ 🔲 AK VISA ◎ AE ①

(8th floor), Oxo Tower Wharf, Barge House St ⊠ SE1 9PH⊖ Southwark
– 𝒞 (020) 7803 3888 – www.harveynichols.com
– oxo.reservations@harveynichols.com – Fax (020) 7803 3838
– Closed 24-26 December   32ANV**a**

Rest – Modern European – Menu £ 33 – Carte £ 45/61🕮
Rest*Oxo Tower Brasserie* – see restaurant listing
♦ Top of a converted factory, providing stunning views of the Thames and beyond. Stylish, minimalist interior with huge windows. Modern, mostly European, cuisine.

XX Roast
AK 🕮 VISA ◎ AE

The Floral Hall, Borough Market ⊠ SE1 1TL⊖ London Bridge – 𝒞 (020)
7940 1300 – www.roast-restaurant.com – info@roast-restaurant.com – Fax (020)
7655 2079 – Closed 25 December and Sunday dinner   33AQV**e**

Rest – English – (booking essential) Carte £ 33/48
♦ Set into the roof of Borough Market's Floral Hall. Extensive cocktail list in bar; split-level restaurant has views to St. Paul's. Robust English cooking using market produce.

XX Baltic
VISA ◎ AE ①

74 Blackfriars Rd ⊠ SE1 8HA⊖ Southwark – 𝒞 (020) 7928 1111
– www.balticrestaurant.co.uk – info@balticrestaurant.co.uk – Fax (020) 7928 8487
– Closed 24-26 December and 1 January   33AOV**e**

Rest – Eastern European – Menu £ 18 (lunch) – Carte £ 25/30
♦ Set in a Grade II listed 18C former coach house. Enjoy authentic and hearty east European and Baltic influenced food. Interesting vodka selection and live jazz on Sundays.

X Oxo Tower Brasserie
⟨ 🔲 AK VISA ◎ AE ①

(8th floor), Oxo Tower Wharf, Barge House St ⊠ SE1 9PH⊖ Southwark
– 𝒞 (020) 7803 3888 – www.harveynichols.com
– oxo.reservations@harveynichols.com – Fax (020) 7803 3838
– Closed 24-26 December   32ANV**a**

Rest – Modern European – Menu £ 25 (lunch) – Carte £ 39/50
♦ Same views but less formal than the restaurant. Open-plan kitchen, relaxed service, the modern menu is slightly lighter. In summer, try to secure a table on the terrace.

X Cantina Vinopolis
AK VISA ◎ AE ①

No.1 Bank End ⊠ SE1 9BU⊖ London Bridge – 𝒞 (020) 7940 8333
– www.cantinavinopolis.com – cantina@vinopolis.co.uk – Fax (020) 7089 9339
– Closed Sunday dinner and Bank Holidays   33AQV**z**

Rest – International – Menu £ 30 – Carte £ 23/34🕮
♦ Large, solid brick vaulted room under Victorian railway arches, with an adjacent wine museum. Modern menu with a huge selection of wines by the glass.

X Tate Modern (Restaurant)
⟨ VISA ◎

7th Floor, Tate Modern, Bankside ⊠ SE1 9LS⊖ Southwark – 𝒞 (020) 7401 5020
– www.tate.org.uk/modern/information/eating.htm
– tate.modernrestaurant@tztc.org – Closed 25 December   33APV**s**

Rest – British – (lunch only and dinner Friday-Saturday) Carte £ 24/35
♦ 7th floor restaurant with floor to ceilings windows on two sides and large mural. Appealing mix of light and zesty dishes, with seasonal produce. Good choice of wines and non-alcoholic drinks.

X Tapas Brindisa
VISA ◎ AE

18-20 Southwark St, Borough Market ⊠ SE1 1TJ⊖ London Bridge – 𝒞 (020)
7357 8880 – www.brindisa.com – office@tapasbrindisa.com
– Closed 25-26 December, 1 January, Sunday and Bank Holidays   33AQV**k**

Rest – Spanish – (bookings not accepted) Carte £ 12/37
♦ Primary quality Spanish produce sold in owner's shops and this bustling eatery on edge of Borough Market. Freshly prepared, tasty tapas: waiters will assist with your choice.

✗ Wright Brothers VISA ⓴ AE

11 Stoney St, Borough Market ⊠ *SE1 9AD* ⊖ *London Bridge –* ℰ *(020) 7403 9554 – www.wrightbros.eu.com – reservations@wrightbros.eu.com – Fax (020) 7403 9558 – Closed Sunday, Christmas and Bank Holidays* 33AQV**m**

Rest – Seafood – Carte £ 22/35

♦ Classic style oyster and porter house - a large number of porter ales on offer. Simple settings afford a welcoming ambience to enjoy huge range of oysters and prime shellfish.

✗ Brew Wharf ☆ AC VISA ⓴ AE ⓘ

Brew Wharf Yard, Stoney St ⊠ *SE1 9AD* ⊖ *London Bridge –* ℰ *(020) 7378 6601 – www.brewwharf.com – brewwharf@vinopolis.co.uk – Fax (020) 7940 5997 – Closed Christmas-New Year and Sunday dinner* 33AQV**h**

Rest – Traditional – Menu £ 26 – Carte £ 19/29

♦ Bustling market eatery and micro-brewery housed in three huge railway arches. The beers and concise wine list are the reasons most people come here; menus are quite simple.

🍽 The Anchor & Hope VISA ⓴ ⓘ

36 The Cut ⊠ *SE1 8LP* ⊖ *Southwark. –* ℰ *(020) 7928 9898 – anchorandhope@btconnect.com – Fax (020) 7928 4595 – Closed 2 weeks at Christmas, Easter, May Bank Holidays, last 2 weeks in August* 32ANV**n**

Rest – (Closed Sunday dinner and Monday lunch) (bookings not accepted) Carte £ 20/35

♦ Close to Waterloo, the distinctive dark green exterior lures visitors in droves. Bare floorboards, simple wooden furniture. Seriously original cooking with rustic French base.

TOWER HAMLETS – Greater London 12 **B3**

Bow – Greater London – ⊠ E3

🚊 London 7 mi – Luton 53 mi – Watford 44 mi – Slough 33 mi

🍽 The Morgan Arms ☆ AC VISA ⓴ AE

43 Morgan St ⊠ *E3 5AA* ⊖ *Bow Road. –* ℰ *(020) 8980 6389 – www.geronimo-inns.co.uk – themorgan@geronimo-inns.co.uk – Closed 24-26 December, 1 January* 3GU**c**

Rest – (Closed Sunday dinner) (bookings not accepted) Carte £ 20/31

♦ Characterful pub with mismatch of furniture and shabby chic appeal. Constantly evolving menu offers robust cooking, using some unusual and sometimes unfamiliar ingredients.

Canary Wharf – Greater London – ⊠ E14

🏨 Four Seasons ← 🔲 🐾 🛁 🚻 ⑤ AC 🖳 🏊 🚗 VISA ⓴ AE ⓘ

Westferry Circus ⊠ *E14 8RS* ⊖ *Canary Wharf –* ℰ *(020) 7510 1999 – www.fourseasons.com/canarywharf – sales.caw@fourseasons.com – Fax (020) 7510 1998* 3GV**a**

128 rm – ✝£ 252/434 ✝✝£ 270/494, ⌑ £ 25 – 14 suites

Rest *Quadrato* – see restaurant listing

♦ Sleek and stylish with striking river and city views. Atrium lobby leading to modern bedrooms boasting every conceivable extra. Detailed service.

✗✗✗ Quadrato – at Four Seasons Hotel ☆ AC VISA ⓴ AE ⓘ

Westferry Circus ⊠ *E14 8RS* ⊖ *Canary Wharf –* ℰ *(020) 7510 1999 – Fax (020) 7510 1998* 3GV**a**

Rest – Italian – Menu £ 40/45 – Carte £ 45/56

♦ Striking, modern restaurant with terrace overlooking river. Sleek, stylish dining room with glass-fronted open-plan kitchen. Menu of northern Italian dishes; swift service.

LONDON

LONDON

XX **Plateau**   🔊 AC 🔄 VISA 🅿️ AE ①
(4th floor) Canada Place, Canada Square ⊠ E14 5ER⊖ Canary Wharf – 𝒞 (020)
7715 7100 – www.plateaurestaurant.com
– plateaureservations@danddlondon.com – Fax (020) 7715 7110
– Closed 25-26 December, 1 January, Sunday and Bank Holidays   3GV**n**
Rest – Modern European – Menu £ 35 – Carte £ 21/35
◆ Impressive open plan space with dramatic glass walls and ceilings and striking 1970s design. Rotisserie meats in the Grill; globally-influenced dishes in formal restaurant.

🍺 **The Gun**   🔊 🌂 🔄 VISA 🆗 AE
27 Coldharbour ⊠ E14 9NS⊖ Blackwall (DLR) – 𝒞 (020) 7515 5222
– www.thegundocklands.com – info@thegundocklands.com
– Closed 25-26 December   7GV**x**
Rest – Carte £ 27/32
◆ A restored 18C pub in cobbled street with proud history and views of the O2 Arena. European influences to dishes and daily fish from Billingsgate the best choice. Professional service.

Limehouse – Greater London – ⊠ E14   12 **B3**
▶ London 3 mi – Watford 24 mi – Slough 30 mi – Basildon 28 mi

🍺 **The Narrow**   🔊 AC 🔄 🅿️ VISA 🆗 AE
🕊 Narrow Street ⊠ E14 8DP⊖ Limehouse (DLR) – 𝒞 (020) 7592 7950
– www.gordonramsay.com – thenarrow@gordonramsay.com
– Fax (020) 7265 9503   3GV**o**
Rest – British – (booking essential) Carte £ 35/45
◆ Gordon Ramsay's Grade II listed former dockmaster's house on the edge of the Thames, restyled and serving good value old school British favourites. Spacious terrace.

Mile End – Greater London – ⊠ E1

🍺 **L'Oasis**   AC 🌂 VISA 🆗 AE
237 Mile End Rd ⊠ E1 4AA⊖ Stepney Green. – 𝒞 (020) 7702 7051
– www.loasisstepney.co.uk – info@loasisstepney.co.uk – Fax (020) 7265 9850
– Closed Monday and Bank Holidays   3GVU**e**
Rest – Carte £ 20/33
◆ Narrow, cavernous and bright, its original features include ornamental Victorian ceiling. Concise menus offer hearty, rustic cooking with influences from all over the world.

Spitalfields – Greater London – ⊠ E1

XX **Les Trois Garcons**   AC 🔄 VISA 🆗 AE ①
1 Club Row ⊠ E1 6JX⊖ Shoreditch – 𝒞 (020) 7613 1924
– www.lestroisgarcons.com – info@lestroisgarcons.com – Fax (020) 7012 1236
– Closed 2 weeks late August - early September,
Christmas-New Year and Sunday   20XZD**r**
Rest – French – (dinner only and lunch in December) Menu £ 50
◆ Extraordinarily eccentric, with stuffed animals, twinkling beads, assorted chandeliers and ceiling handbags. The French food is more traditional and governed by the seasons.

X **St John Bread and Wine**   AC VISA 🆗 AE ①
94-96 Commercial St ⊠ E1 6LZ⊖ Shoreditch – 𝒞 (020) 7251 0848
– www.stjohnbreadandwine.com – reservations@stjohnbreadandwine.com
– Fax (020) 7247 8924
– Closed Christmas-New Year and Bank Holidays   20XZD**m**
Rest – British – Carte £ 23/27
◆ Very popular neighbourhood bakery providing wide variety of home-made breads. Appealing, intimate dining section: all day menus that offer continually changing dishes.

X **Canteen** `AC VISA CO AE ①`
2 Crispin Pl ⊠ E1 6DW⊖ Liverpool Street – ℰ (07957) 216 444
– www.canteen.co.uk – lisa.ispani@canteen.co.uk
– Closed 25 December 34AST**a**
Rest – British – Carte approx. £ 23
♦ All-glass modernist restaurant in 'new' Spitalfields. Sit on blond wood benches at communal refectory tables and enjoy well-sourced, well-priced classic British options.

Wapping – Greater London – ⊠ E1

X **Wapping Food** `P VISA CO AE`
Wapping Wall ⊠ E1W 3SG⊖ Wapping – ℰ (020) 7680 2080
– www.thewappingproject.com – Closed Christmas-New Year, Sunday dinner and Bank Holidays 20YZE**n**
Rest – Modern European – Carte £ 25/45
♦ Something a little unusual; a combination of restaurant and gallery in a converted hydraulic power station. Enjoy the unfussy, modern menu surrounded by turbines and art.

Whitechapel – Greater London – ⊠ E1

XX **Cafe Spice Namaste** `AC VISA CO AE ①`
☺ *16 Prescot St ⊠ E1 8AZ⊖ Tower Hill – ℰ (020) 7488 9242*
– www.cafespice.co.uk – info@cafespice.co.uk – Fax (020) 7481 0508 – Closed Christmas-New Year, Saturday lunch, Sunday and Bank Holidays 34ASU**z**
Rest – Indian – Menu £ 30 – Carte £ 23/29
♦ A riot of colour from the brightly painted walls to the flowing drapes. Sweet-natured service adds to the engaging feel. Fragrant and competitively priced Indian cooking.

WANDSWORTH – Greater London 12 **B3**

Balham – Greater London – ⊠ SW12

X **Harrison's** `VISA CO AE`
15-19 Bedford Hill ⊠ SW12 9EX⊖ Balham – ℰ (020) 8675 6900
– www.harrisonsbalham.co.uk – info@harrisonsbalham.co.uk
– Fax (020) 8673 3965 6EX**a**
Rest – Mediterranean – Menu £ 16/18 (lunch midweek) – Carte £ 26/36
♦ Sister to Sam's Brasserie in Chiswick. Open all day, with an appealing menu of favourites, from fishcakes to Cumberland sausages. Weekend brunches; kids' menu; good value weekday set menus.

X **Lamberts** `VISA CO`
2 Station Parade ⊠ SW12 9AZ⊖ Balham – ℰ (020) 8675 2233
– www.lambertsrestaurant.com – bookings@lambertsrestaurant.com – Closed Sunday dinner and Monday 6EX**n**
Rest – Traditional – (dinner only and lunch Saturday-Sunday) Menu £ 20 (midweek) – Carte £ 28/35
♦ Simple restaurant offering unfussy, generous dishes of quality produce in a casual environment. Good value set menus or seasonal à la carte. Classical cooking, modern presentation.

X **Brasserie James** `VISA CO AE`
47 Balham Hill ⊠ SW12 9DR ⊖ Clapham South – ℰ (020) 8772 0057
– www.brasseriejames.com – info@brasseriejames.com
– Closed 24 December - 4 January 6EX**x**
Rest – Modern European – Menu £ 14 (lunch) – Carte £ 19/32
♦ Crisp and neat brasserie owned and run by former Conran/D&D chef. Something for everyone on the seasonal menu, from moules to pasta. Weekend brunches; good value set menus; wines by carafe.

LONDON

Battersea – **Greater London** – ✉ SW8/SW11/SW18   12 **B3**

XX **Chada**   AC VISA ⦿⦿ AE ⦿
208-210 Battersea Park Rd ✉ *SW11 4ND* – ✆ *(020) 7622 2209*
*– www.chadathai.com – enquiry@chadathai.com – Fax (020) 7924 2791 – Closed
Sunday and Bank Holidays*   23QZH**x**
Rest – Thai – (dinner only) Carte £ 21/37
♦ Weather notwithstanding, the Thai ornaments and charming staff in traditional silk
costumes transport you to Bangkok. Carefully prepared and authentic dishes.

X **Ransome's Dock**   🍴 VISA ⦿⦿ AE ⦿
35-37 Parkgate Rd ✉ *SW11 4NP* – ✆ *(020) 7223 1611*
*– www.ransomesdock.co.uk – chef@ransomesdock.co.uk – Fax (020) 7924 2614
– Closed Christmas, August Bank Holiday and Sunday dinner*   23QZG**c**
Rest – Modern European – Carte £ 25/38 ⊞
♦ Secreted in a warehouse development, with a dock-side terrace in summer. Vivid
blue interior, crowded with pictures. Chef patron produces reliable brasserie-style
cuisine.

X **Tom Ilić**   AC VISA ⦿⦿ AE
123 Queenstown Rd ✉ *SW8 3RH* – ✆ *(020) 7622 0555 – www.tomilic.com*
*– info@tomilic.com – Closed 1 week August, 1 week Christmas, Tuesday lunch,
Saturday lunch, Sunday dinner and Monday*   24RZH**c**
Rest – Traditional – (booking essential) Menu £ 15 (lunch) – Carte dinner
£ 24/29
♦ Bold flavours, plenty of offal and quite a lot of pork are features of this popular,
neighbourhood restaurant. Simply decorated with closely set tables and a semi-open
kitchen.

X **The Butcher & Grill**   🍴 AC VISA ⦿⦿ AE
39-41 Parkgate Rd ✉ *SW11 4NP* – ✆ *(020) 7924 3999*
*– www.thebutcherandgrill.com – info@thebutcherandgrill.com – Fax (020)
7223 7977 – Closed 26 December and Sunday dinner*   23QZG**c**
Rest – Traditional – Menu £ 15 (midweek lunch) – Carte £ 21/42
♦ Shop at the master butcher for prime cuts; or dine at former riverside warehouse
with rear terrace. Industrial interior matched by hearty, traditional, unfussy meat
dishes.

🍺 **The Greyhound at Battersea**   🍴 ⇔ VISA ⦿⦿ AE
136 Battersea High St ✉ *SW11 3JR* – ✆ *(020) 7978 7021*
– www.thegreyhoundatbattersea.co.uk – eddie@savpubs.com
– Fax (020) 7978 0599
– Closed 24 December - 1 January, Sunday dinner and Monday   23PZH**a**
Rest – Menu £ 21 (lunch) – Carte £ 21/33 ⊞
♦ Popular pub serving simply presented, flavourful dishes, with slight Italian accent
and ingredients sourced from artisan producers. Some unusual wines available by the
glass.

Putney – ✉ SW15

XX **Enoteca Turi**   AC VISA ⦿⦿ AE ⦿
28 Putney High St ✉ *SW15 1SQ* ⊖ *Putney Bridge* – ✆ *(020) 8785 4449*
*– www.enotecaturi.com – enoteca@tiscali.co.uk – Fax (020) 8780 5409 – Closed
25-26 December, 1 January, Sunday and lunch Bank Holidays*   22MZH**n**
Rest – Italian – Menu £ 18 (lunch) – Carte £ 31/39
♦ A long-standing owner-run Italian restaurant. Earthy cooking focuses on the north-
erly regions of Italy. Interesting wine list, with plenty by the glass and carafe.

XX **L'Auberge**   VISA ⦿⦿
22 Upper Richmond Rd ✉ *SW15 2RX* – ✆ *(020) 8874 3593 – www.ardillys.com*
– Closed 2 weeks Summer, 1 week Winter, Sunday and Monday   6DX**r**
Rest – French – (dinner only) Menu £ 17 – Carte £ 24/31
♦ Locally renowned neighbourhood restaurant. Art Nouveau prints of famous Champagne houses set tone for frequently changing, authentic French dishes; personable
service assured.

The Phoenix
🛠 🎔 AC VISA ⓜⓢ AE

Pentlow St ⊠ SW15 1LY – ℰ (020) 8780 3131 – www.sonnys.co.uk
– thephoenix@sonnys.co.uk – Closed Bank Holidays
21LZH**s**
Rest – Italian influences – Menu £16 (lunch) – Carte £19/35
♦ Light and bright interior with French windows leading out on to a spacious terrace. Unfussy and considerate service. An eclectic element to the modern Mediterranean menu.

The Spencer Arms
🏮 AC VISA ⓜⓢ

237 Lower Richmond Road ⊠ SW15 1HJ⊖ East Putney. – ℰ (020) 8788 0640
– www.thespencerarms.co.uk – info@thespencerarms.co.uk – Fax (020) 8788 2216
– Closed 25 December, 1 January
21LZH**V**
Rest – Carte £22/32
♦ Attractive Victorian corner pub on Putney Common. Library area with books, games and leather sofas. Rustic bar/restaurant serves concise, seasonal, daily changing menus.

Prince of Wales
🏮 VISA ⓜⓢ

138 Upper Richmond Rd ⊠ SW15 2SP⊖ East Putney – ℰ (020) 8788 1552
– www.princeofwalesputney.co.uk – info@princeofwalesputney.co.uk – Fax (020) 8180 0191 – Closed 25-26 December
22MZH**z**
Rest – Carte £22/30
♦ Scottish owner aims to make it a 'country pub in the city'. Robust and largely British cooking, with plenty of game in season, usual cuts, stews and terrines. Sunday night is quiz night.

Tooting – Greater London – ⊠ SW17
12 **B3**

Kastoori
🛠 ⊛ AC VISA ⓜⓢ

188 Upper Tooting Rd ⊠ SW17 7EJ⊖ Tooting Bec – ℰ (020) 8767 7027 – Closed 25-26 December and lunch Monday and Tuesday
6EX**v**
Rest – Indian – Carte £14/18
♦ Specialising in Indian vegetarian cooking with a subtle East African influence. Family-run for many years, a warm and welcoming establishment with helpful service.

Wandsworth – Greater London – ⊠SW17/SW18
12 **B3**

Chez Bruce (Bruce Poole)
🛠🛠 ❀ AC VISA ⓜⓢ AE ⓞ

2 Bellevue Rd ⊠ SW17 7EG⊖ Tooting Bec – ℰ (020) 8672 0114
– www.chezbruce.co.uk – enquiries@chezbruce.co.uk – Fax (020) 8767 6648
– Closed 24-26 December, January and first 2 weeks February
6EX**e**
Rest – French – (booking essential) Menu £26/40 ❀
Spec. Foie gras and chicken liver parfait, brioche. Fillet of bream, risotto nero, squid and provençale vegetables. Roast spiced pineapple, pain d'épice, coconut sorbet.
♦ Simply decorated neighbourhood restaurant serving confident classical French cooking with a touch of the Mediterranean. Animated, informal atmosphere; well organised service.

WESTMINSTER (City of) – Greater London
12 **B3**

Bayswater and Maida Vale – Greater London – ⊠ NW6/W2/W9

Hilton London Paddington
🏨 ৷♨ 🛗 & rm, AC ⚚ 🤵 🎿 VISA ⓜⓢ AE ⓞ

146 Praed St ⊠ W2 1EE⊖ Paddington – ℰ (020) 7850 0500
– www.hilton.co.uk/paddington – sales.paddington@hilton.com – Fax (020) 7850 0600
28ADU**a**
344 rm – †£328 ††£328, � £19.95 – 20 suites
Rest *The Brasserie* – Carte £29/46
♦ Early Victorian railway hotel, sympathetically restored in contemporary style with Art Deco details. Co-ordinated bedrooms with high tech facilities continue the modern style. Contemporarily styled brasserie offering a modern menu.

LONDON

🏨🏨🏨 Royal Lancaster   ⇐ 🗐 � ℔ ⍺ ⌾ 🛈 🛉 🅿 🆅🆂🅰 ⓶ 🅰🅴 ⓞ
Lancaster Terrace ⊠ W2 2TY ⊖ Lancaster Gate – 𝒞 (020) 7262 6737
– www.royallancaster.com – sales@royallancaster.com
– Fax (020) 7724 3191   28ADU**e**
394 rm – 🛉£304 🛉🛉£304, ⌷ £19 – 22 suites
Rest Island and **Nipa** – see restaurant listing
♦ Imposing 1960s purpose-built hotel overlooking Hyde Park. Some of London's most extensive conference facilities. Well-equipped bedrooms are decorated in traditional style.

🏨🏨 The Hempel 🕭   ⬚ ᶠ⌀ 🗐 ℔ rm, ⍺ ⌾ 🛈 🆅🆂🅰 ⓶ 🅰🅴 ⓞ
31-35 Craven Hill Gdns ⊠ W2 3EA ⊖ Queensway – 𝒞 (020) 7298 9000
– www.the-hempel.co.uk – hotel@the-hempel.co.uk – Fax (020) 7402 4666
– Closed 24-28 December   28ACU**a**
46 rm – 🛉£210/304 🛉🛉£210/304, ⌷ £21.50 – 4 suites
Rest – (closed Sunday and Bank Holidays) (dinner only) Carte £33/54
♦ A striking example of minimalist design. Individually appointed bedrooms are understated yet very comfortable. Relaxed ambience. Modern basement restaurant.

🏨🏨 London Marriott H. Maida Vale   ⬚ ᶠ⌀ ᶠ⌀ ℔ 🗐 ℔ rm, ⍺ ⌾ 🛈
Plaza Parade ⊠ NW6 5RP ⊖ Kilburn Park   🛉 🆎 🆅🆂🅰 ⓶ 🅰🅴 ⓞ
– 𝒞 (020) 7543 6000 – www.londonmarriottmaidavale.co.uk
– mhrs.lonwh.reservations@marriotthotels.com – Fax (020) 7543 2100   10NZB**c**
226 rm – 🛉£182/347 🛉🛉£182/347, ⌷ £16.95 – 11 suites
Rest Fratelli – (closed Sunday) (dinner only) Menu £24 – Carte £26/31
♦ A capacious hotel, away from the busier city centre streets. Well equipped with both business and leisure facilities including 12m pool. Suites have small kitchens. Informal Italian restaurant and brasserie.

🏨🏨 Colonnade Town House without rest   🗐 ⍺ ⌾ ☎ 🆅🆂🅰 ⓶ 🅰🅴 ⓞ
2 Warrington Crescent ⊠ W9 1ER ⊖ Warwick Avenue – 𝒞 (020) 7286 1052
– www.theetoncollection.com – rescolonnade@theetoncollection.com
– Fax (020) 7286 1057   17OZD**e**
43 rm – 🛉£116/182 🛉🛉£135/264, ⌷ £15
♦ Two Victorian townhouses with comfortable well-furnished communal rooms decorated with fresh flowers. Stylish and comfortable bedrooms with many extra touches.

🏨🏨 New Linden without rest   🗐 ⌾ 🛈 🆅🆂🅰 ⓶ 🅰🅴
58-60 Leinster Sq ⊠ W2 4PS ⊖ Bayswater – 𝒞 (020) 7221 4321
– www.newlinden.co.uk – newlindenhotel@mayflower-group.co.uk
– Fax (020) 7727 3156   27ABU**e**
50 rm – 🛉£79/109 🛉🛉£115/145
♦ Smart four storey white stucco façade. Basement breakfast room with sunny aspect. Bedrooms are its strength: flat screen TVs and wooden floors; two split level family rooms.

🏨 Miller's without rest   ⌾ 🛈 🆅🆂🅰 ⓶ 🅰🅴
111A Westbourne Grove (entrance on Hereford Rd) ⊠ W2 4UW ⊖ Bayswater
– 𝒞 (020) 7243 1024 – www.millershotel.com – enquiries@millershotel.com
– Fax (020) 7243 1064   27ABU**a**
8 rm – 🛉£176 🛉🛉£217/270
♦ Victorian house brimming with antiques and knick-knacks. Charming sitting room provides the setting for a relaxed breakfast. Individual, theatrical rooms named after poets.

🍴🍴 Jamuna   ⍺ 🆅🆂🅰 ⓶ 🅰🅴
38A Southwick St ⊠ W2 1JQ ⊖ Edgware Road – 𝒞 (020) 7723 5056
– www.jamuna.co.uk – info@jamuna.co.uk – Fax (020) 7706 1870
– Closed 25-26 December   28ADT**x**
Rest – Indian – (dinner only) Menu £30 – Carte £37/60
♦ Don't be put off by the unprepossessing nature of the area: this is a modern out of the ordinary Indian restaurant with cooking that's well presented, refined and flavoursome.

XX **Island** – at Royal Lancaster Hotel 🔟 VISA ⓪ AE ①
Lancaster Terrace ✉ *W2 2TY* ⊖ *Lancaster Gate* – 𝒞 *(020) 7551 6070*
– www.islandrestaurant.co.uk – eat@islandrestaurant.co.uk
– Fax (020) 7551 6071   28ADU**e**
Rest – Modern European – Carte £ 28/43
♦ Modern, stylish restaurant with buzzy open kitchen. Full length windows allow good views of adjacent Hyde Park. Seasonally based, modern menus with wide range of dishes.

XX **Trenta** 🔟 VISA ⓪ AE
30 Connaught St ✉ *W2 2AF* ⊖ *Marble Arch* – 𝒞 *(020) 7262 9623 – Fax (020) 7262 9636 – Closed Christmas-New Year, Sunday and Bank Holidays*   29AFU**b**
Rest – Italian – (dinner only and lunch Thursday and Friday) Carte £ 23/31
♦ Only 7 tables on ground floor and 5 more downstairs; red and cream with comfy leather seats. Uncomplicated Italian cooking on constantly changing menu.

XX **Pearl Liang** 🔟 ⟷ VISA ⓪
8 Sheldon Sq., Paddington Central ✉ *W2 6EZ* ⊖ *Paddington* – 𝒞 *(020) 7289 7000 – www.pearlliang.co.uk – Closed 25-26 December*   28ACT**b**
Rest – Chinese – Menu £ 15 (lunch) – Carte £ 25/65 **s**
♦ Large Chinese restaurant in new development. Comfy and airy with eye-catching painting on one wall. Dim sum available until 5p.m.; extensive choice of authentic specialities.

XX **Nipa** – at Royal Lancaster Hotel 🔟 ℙ VISA ⓪ AE ①
Lancaster Terrace ✉ *W2 2TY* ⊖ *Lancaster Gate* – 𝒞 *(020) 7551 6039*
– www.niparestaurant.co.uk – Fax (020) 7724 3191 – Closed 24-30 December, 1-4 January, Saturday lunch, Sunday and Bank Holidays   28ADU**e**
Rest – Thai – Menu £ 27 – Carte £ 23/32
♦ On the 1st floor and overlooking Hyde Park. Authentic and ornately decorated restaurant offers subtly spiced Thai cuisine. Keen to please staff in traditional silk costumes.

XX **Angelus** 🔟 ⟷ VISA ⓪ AE
4 Bathurst St ✉ *W2 2SD* ⊖ *Lancaster Gate* – 𝒞 *(020) 7402 0083*
– www.angelusrestaurant.co.uk – info@angelusrestaurant.co.uk – Fax (020) 7402 5383 – Closed Christmas-New Year and Monday   28ADU**c**
Rest – French – Menu £ 36 (lunch) – Carte £ 39/55
♦ In the style of a French brasserie, with studded leather banquettes, huge art nouveau mirror, Murano chandeliers and lounge bar. Unfussy, French dishes; clean, precise cooking.

XX **Le Café Anglais** 🔟 VISA ⓪ AE
8 Porchester Gardens ✉ *W2 4BD* ⊖ *Bayswater* – 𝒞 *(020) 7221 1415*
– www.lecafeanglais.co.uk – info@lecafeanglais.co.uk
– Closed 26 December   27ABU**r**
Rest – Modern European – Menu £ 20 (lunch midweek) – Carte £ 23/47
♦ Opened in late 2007, a large, modern brasserie with art deco styling within Whiteley's shopping centre. Large and very appealing selection of classic brasserie food; the rotisserie is the centrepiece.

X **Assaggi** (Nino Sassu) 🔟 VISA ⓪ ①
🕸 *39 Chepstow Pl, (above Chepstow pub)* ✉ *W2 4TS* ⊖ *Bayswater* – 𝒞 *(020) 7792 5501 – www.assaggi.com – nipi@assaggi.demon.co.uk*
– Closed 2 weeks Christmas and Sunday   27AAU**c**
Rest – Italian – (booking essential) Carte £ 31/46
Spec. Pecorino con San Daniele e Rucola. Pan-fried calf's liver with balsamic vinegar. Bitter chocolate tart with pastry cream.
♦ Tall windows add to the brightness of this room above a pub. High quality ingredients are used to create appetisingly rustic dishes with more than a hint of Sardinia.

533

LONDON

✗ **Hereford Road**

AK VISA ⓜ AE

3 Hereford Rd ⊠ W2 4AB⊖ Bayswater – ℰ (020) 7727 1144
– www.herefordroad.org – info@herefordroad.org
– Closed 25-30 December   27ABU**s**
Rest – British – (booking essential) Carte £ 24/32

♦ Converted butcher's shop now specialises in classic British dishes and recipes, with first rate, seasonal ingredients. Booths for six people are the prize seats. Friendly and relaxed feel.

✗ **L'Accento**

VISA ⓜ AE

16 Garway Rd ⊠ W2 4NH⊖ Bayswater – ℰ (020) 7243 2201
– www.laccentorestaurant.co.uk – laccentorest@aol.com – Fax (020) 7243 2201
– Closed Sunday and Bank Holidays   27ABU**b**
Rest – Italian – Menu £ 24 – Carte £ 27/33

♦ Rustic surroundings and provincial, well priced, Italian cooking. Menu specialises in tasty pasta, made on the premises, and shellfish. Rear conservatory for the summer.

✗ **Arturo**

AK VISA ⓜ AE

23 Connaught St ⊠ W2 2AY⊖ Marble Arch – ℰ (020) 7706 3388
– www.arturorestaurant.co.uk – enquiries@arturorestaurant.co.uk
– Fax (020) 7402 9195 – Closed 25-26 December, 1 January, Good Friday and
Easter Sunday   29AFU**a**
Rest – Italian – Menu £ 17 (lunch) – Carte £ 22/30

♦ On a smart street near Hyde Park: sleek, modish feel imbues interior with intimate, elegant informality. Tuscan and Sicilian dishes cooked with confidence and originality.

✗ **Kiasu**

AK VISA ⓜ

48 Queensway ⊠ W2 3RY⊖ Bayswater – ℰ (020) 7727 8810 – www.kiasu.co.uk
– info@kiasu.co.uk – Fax (020) 7727 7220   27ABU**k**
Rest – Asian – Carte £ 12/26

♦ Its name means 'afraid to be second best.' Malaysian owner; some dishes are hot and spicy, others light and fragrant; all designed for sharing. Brightly decorated; good fun.

✗ **Urban Turban**

AK ⇔ VISA ⓜ AE

98 Westbourne Grove ⊠ W2 5RU⊖ Bayswater – ℰ (020) 7243 4200
– www.urbanturban.uk.com – info@urbanturban.uk.com
– Fax (020) 7243 4080   27ABU**x**
Rest – Indian – Carte £ 24/26

♦ Mumbai street food is the inspiration behind this venture from Vineet Bhatia. Order a number of dishes to share. Ground floor for the bustle and bar; the downstairs area is calmer.

🍺 **Prince Alfred & Formosa Dining Room**

AK VISA ⓜ

5A Formosa St ⊠ W9 1EE⊖ Warwick Avenue – ℰ (020) 7286 3287
– www.princealfred.co.uk – princealfred@youngs.co.uk   17OZD**n**
Rest – Carte £ 23/33

♦ Traditional pub appearance and a relaxed dining experience on offer behind the elegant main bar. Contemporary style of cooking.

🍺 **The Warrington**

AK ⅙ ⇔ VISA ⓜ AE

93 Warrington Crescent ⊠ W9 1EH⊖ Maida Vale. – ℰ (020) 7592 7960
– www.gordonramsay.com – thewarrington@gordonramsay.com
– Fax (020) 7592 1603   17OZD**a**
Rest – Carte £ 25/35

♦ Imposing Victorian pub, now owned by Gordon Ramsay, with traditional feel to the ground floor bar. Upstairs is the smarter dining room with appealing menu of French and British classics.

The Waterway

54 Formosa St ✉ W9 2JU ⊖ Warwick Avenue – ✆ (020) 7266 3557 – www.thewaterway.co.uk – info@thewaterway.co.uk – Fax (020) 7266 3547 17OZD**p**

Rest – Carte £ 30/40

◆ Pub with a thoroughly modern, metropolitan ambience. Spacious bar and large decked terrace overlooking canal. Concise, well-balanced menu served in open plan dining room.

Belgravia – Greater London – ✉ SW1

The Berkeley

Wilton Pl ✉ SW1X 7RL ⊖ Knightsbridge – ✆ (020) 7235 6000 – www.the-berkeley.co.uk – info@the-berkeley.co.uk – Fax (020) 7235 4330 37AGX**e**

189 rm – 🚹£ 552/658 🚹🚹£ 658, ☕ £ 26 – 25 suites

Rest *Marcus Wareing at The Berkeley* – see restaurant listing

Rest *Boxwood café* – ✆ (020) 7235 1010 – Menu £ 28 – Carte £ 31/47

◆ Discreet and rejuvenated hotel with roof-top pool and opulently decorated bedrooms. Relax in the gilded and panelled Caramel Room or have a drink in the cool Blue Bar. Modern cooking in glitzy Boxwood Café.

LONDON

The Lanesborough

Hyde Park Corner ✉ SW1X 7TA ⊖ Hyde Park Corner – ✆ (020) 7259 5599 – www.lanesborough.com – info@lanesborough.com – Fax (020) 7259 5606 37AGX**a**

86 rm – 🚹£ 441/582 🚹🚹£ 582, ☕ £ 30 – 9 suites

Rest *Apsleys* – Italian – Carte £ 41/61

◆ Converted in the 1990s from 18C St George's Hospital. Butler service offered. Regency-era decorated, lavishly appointed rooms with impressive technological extras. Opulent, glass-roofed Italian restaurant with rustic food.

The Halkin

5 Halkin St ✉ SW1X 7DJ ⊖ Hyde Park Corner – ✆ (020) 7333 1000 – www.halkin.como.bz – res@halkin.como.bz – Fax (020) 7333 1100 38AHX**b**

35 rm – 🚹£ 458 🚹🚹£ 458, ☕ £ 26 – 6 suites

Rest *Nahm* – see restaurant listing

◆ One of London's first minimalist hotels. The cool, marbled reception and bar have an understated charm. Spacious rooms have every conceivable facility.

Jumeirah Lowndes

21 Lowndes St ✉ SW1X 9ES ⊖ Knightsbridge – ✆ (020) 7823 1234 – www.jumeirahlowndeshotel.com – jlhinfo@jumeirah.com – Fax (020) 7235 1154 37AGX**h**

81 rm – 🚹🚹£ 570, ☕ £ 27 – 5 suites

Rest *Mimosa* – Menu £ 18 (lunch) – Carte approx. £ 43

◆ Compact yet friendly modern corporate hotel within this exclusive residential area. Good levels of personal service offered. Close to the famous shops of Knightsbridge. Modern restaurant opens onto street terrace.

Diplomat without rest

2 Chesham St ✉ SW1X 8DT ⊖ Sloane Square – ✆ (020) 7235 1544 – www.btinternet.com/~diplomat.hotel – diplomat.hotel@btinternet.com – Fax (020) 7259 6153 37AGY**a**

26 rm ☕ – 🚹£ 98/120 🚹🚹£ 180

◆ Imposing Victorian corner house built in 1882 by Thomas Cubitt. Attractive glass-domed stairwell and sweeping staircase. Good value accommodation considering location.

LONDON

XXXX **Marcus Wareing at The Berkeley**   AC ⇔ VISA 🌕 AE ⓘ

ε3 ε3 *Wilton Pl ⊠ SW1X 7RL⊖ Knightsbridge – ℰ (020) 7235 1200*
– www.marcuswareing.com – marcuswareing@the-berkeley.co.uk – Fax (020)
7235 1266 – Closed 25-26 December, Saturday lunch and Sunday   37AGX**e**
Rest – French – Menu £ 35/75 🌶

Spec. Poached lobster with braised trotters, vanilla butter and roasted salsify.
Roasted veal, fricassee of snails, wild garlic and bacon. Lemon crème, salted
caramel popcorn and milk ice cream.
♦ Intimate, richly-appointed restaurant serving exceptionally well-crafted, classically-
inspired cuisine. Watch the kitchen at work from the chef's table. Polished, graceful
service.

XXX **Amaya**   AC ⇔ VISA 🌕 AE ⓘ

ε3 *Halkin Arcade, 19 Motcomb St ⊠ SW1X 8JT⊖ Knightsbridge – ℰ (020)*
7823 1166 – www.realindianfood.com – amaya@realindianfood.com – Fax (020)
7259 6464 – Closed 25 December   37AGX**k**
Rest – Indian – Menu £ 22/40 – Carte approx. £ 34

Spec. Tandoori ocean wild prawns, tomato and ginger. Grilled lamb chops
with lime and coriander. Whipped chocolate and yoghurt.
♦ Light, piquant and aromatic Indian cooking specialising in kebabs from a tawa
skillet, sigri grill or tandoor oven. Chic comfortable surroundings, modern and subtly
exotic.

XXX **Zafferano**   AC ⇔ VISA 🌕 AE ⓘ

ε3 *15 Lowndes St ⊠ SW1X 9EY⊖ Knightsbridge – ℰ (020) 7235 5800*
– www.zafferanorestaurant.com – info@zafferanorestaurant.com – Fax (020)
7235 1100 – Closed 2 weeks Christmas-New Year   37AGX**f**
Rest – Italian – (booking essential) Menu £ 35/45 🌶

Spec. Sliced cured beef, rocket and goat's cheese. Grilled monkfish with courgettes and sweet chilli. Chocolate fondant with gianduia ice cream.
♦ Busy, three–roomed restaurant decorated in Mediterranean colours. Classic, unfussy, flavoursome Italian cooking, where the quality of the ingredients shines
through.

XX **Nahm** – at The Halkin Hotel   AC ⇔ VISA 🌕 AE ⓘ

ε3 *5 Halkin St ⊠ SW1X 7DJ⊖ Hyde Park Corner – ℰ (020) 7333 1234*
– www.halkin.como.bz – res@nahm.como.bz – Fax (020) 7333 1100   38AHX**b**
Rest – Thai – (closed 25 December, 1 January, Easter, Saturday lunch, Sunday
lunch and Bank Holidays) (booking advisable) Menu £ 26 (lunch)
– Carte £ 40/46

Spec. Salted chicken wafers, longans and Thai basil. Pork belly braised with
peanuts. Coconut cake with rambutans and perfumed syrup.
♦ Discreet, comfortable dining room; sleek understated décor. Sophisticated cooking
showcases the harmony of Thai cooking achieved through careful combinations of
textures and flavours.

XX **Mango Tree**   AC 🐾 VISA 🌕 AE ⓘ

46 Grosvenor Pl ⊠ SW1X 7EQ⊖ Victoria – ℰ (020) 7823 1888
– www.mangotree.org.uk – info@mangotree.org.uk – Fax (020) 7838 9275
– Closed 24-25 December and 1 January   38AHX**a**
Rest – Thai – Menu £ 18 (lunch) – Carte approx. £ 25
♦ Thai staff in regional dress in contemporarily styled dining room of refined yet
minimalist furnishings sums up the cuisine: authentic Thai dishes with modern presentation.

XX **Noura Brasserie**   AC VISA 🌕 AE ⓘ

16 Hobart Pl ⊠ SW1W 0HH⊖ Victoria – ℰ (020) 7235 9444 – www.noura.co.uk
– noura@noura.co.uk – Fax (020) 7235 9244   38AHX**n**
Rest – Lebanese – Menu £ 18/40 – Carte £ 24/39
♦ Dine in either the bright bar or the comfortable, contemporary restaurant. Authentic, modern Lebanese cooking specialises in char-grilled meats and mezzes.

🛏 **The Pantechnicon Rooms** `VISA` `OO` `AE` `O`
10 Motcomb St ⊠ SW1X 8LA⊖ Knightsbridge – ℰ (020) 77306074
– www.thepantechnicon.com – reservations@thepantechnicon.com – Fax (020)
77306055 – Closed 25 December and Good Friday 37AGX**d**
Rest – Menu £25 (lunch) – Carte £25/50
♦ Same owners as the nearby Thomas Cubitt; a smart pub with more formal dining room upstairs. Shellfish and seafood a speciality. Bright, comfortable surroundings with enthusiastic service.

Hyde Park and Knightsbridge – Greater London – ⊠ SW1/SW7

🏨🏨 **Mandarin Oriental Hyde Park** ⪕ ⑱ 🕭 ℔ 🛗 ↧ rm, 🄰 ⅗ ⟨⟨)⟩
66 Knightsbridge ⊠ SW1X 7LA⊖ Knightsbridge 🧖 `VISA` `OO` `AE` `O`
– ℰ (020) 72352000 – www.mandarinoriental.com/london
– molon-dine@mohg.com – Fax (020) 72352001 37AGX**x**
173 rm – �$£452/652 �$�$£593/652, � £29 – 25 suites
Rest *Foliage* – see restaurant listing
Rest *The Park* – Menu £33 – Carte £35/57
♦ Built in 1889 this classic hotel, with striking façade, remains one of London's grandest. Many of the luxurious bedrooms enjoy Park views. Immaculate and detailed service. Smart ambience in The Park.

🏨 **Knightsbridge Green** without rest 🛗 🄰 ⅗ ⟨⟨)⟩ `VISA` `OO` `AE` `O`
159 Knightsbridge ⊠ SW1X 7PD⊖ Knightsbridge – ℰ (020) 75846274
– www.thekghotel.com – reservations@thekghotel.com – Fax (020) 72251635
– Closed 25-26 December 37AFX**z**
16 rm – �$£150/180 �$�$£200/250 – 12 suites
♦ Just yards from Hyde Park and all the smartest shops. Small lounge; breakfast served in the well-proportioned bedrooms spread over six floors. Privately owned.

🍴🍴🍴 **Foliage** – at Mandarin Oriental Hyde Park Hotel 🄰 `VISA` `OO` `AE` `O`
😋 *66 Knightsbridge ⊠ SW1X 7LA⊖ Knightsbridge*
– ℰ (020) 72013723
– www.mandarinoriental.com/london
– molon-dine@mohg.com – Fax (020) 72354552
– Closed 26 December and 1 January 37AGX**x**
Rest – Innovative – Menu £35/40
Spec. Sweetbreads, glazed leeks and morels. Pigeon, red cabbage, endive tart tatin. Calvados soufflé, iced apple parfait, sea salt caramel.
♦ Sophisticated, modern cooking features experimental combinations and unexpected flavours. View of the park through the windows reflected by earthy colours and foliage motif.

🍴🍴 **Zuma** 🄰 `VISA` `OO` `AE`
5 Raphael St ⊠ SW7 1DL⊖ Knightsbridge – ℰ (020) 75841010
– www.zumarestaurant.com – info@zumarestaurant.com
– Closed 25 December and 1 January 37AFX**m**
Rest – Japanese – Carte approx. £26
♦ Eye-catching design that blends east with west. Bustling atmosphere; fashionable clientele; popular sushi bar. Varied and interesting contemporary Japanese food.

🍴🍴 **Mr Chow** 🄰 `VISA` `OO` `AE` `O`
151 Knightsbridge ⊠ SW1X 7PA⊖ Knightsbridge – ℰ (020) 75897347
– www.mrchow.com – mrchowuk@aol.com – Fax (020) 75845780
– Closed 24-26 December and 1 January 37AFX**e**
Rest – Chinese – Menu £27/38 – Carte dinner £39/48
♦ Long-standing Chinese restaurant, opened in 1968. Smart clientele, stylish and comfortable surroundings and prompt service from Italian waiters. Carefully prepared and satisfying food.

Mayfair – Greater London – ⊠ W1

ⓕⓕⓕⓕ Dorchester ☺ 🕅 🕽 🗲 🖾 🗟 rm, 🖫 ⅋ 🖤 🏊 ⌂ 🗾 ⓪ 🗚 ⓪
Park Lane ⊠ *W1K 1QA⊖ Hyde Park Corner –* ℰ *(020) 7629 8888*
– www.thedorchester.com – info@thedorchester.com
– Fax (020) 7629 8080   30AHVa
200 rm – †£335/699 ††£652/828 – 49 suites
Rest Alain Ducasse at The Dorchester and **China Tang** – see restaurant
listing
Rest The Grill – Menu £28 – Carte £51/68
♦ A sumptuously decorated, luxury hotel offering every possible facility. Impressive
marbled and pillared promenade. Rooms quintessentially English in style. Faultless
service. Exuberant tartan décor in The Grill.

ⓕⓕⓕⓕ Claridge's 🕽 🗟 🗲 🖫 ⅋ 🖤 🏊 🗾 ⓪ 🗚 ⓪
Brook St ⊠ *W1K 4HR⊖ Bond Street –* ℰ *(020) 7629 8860 – www.claridges.co.uk*
– guest@claridges.co.uk – Fax (020) 7499 2210   30AHUc
143 rm – †£576/658 ††£776, ⌑ £28 – 60 suites
Rest Gordon Ramsay at Claridge's – see restaurant listing
♦ The epitome of English grandeur, celebrated for its Art Deco. Exceptionally well-
appointed and sumptuous bedrooms, all with butler service. Magnificently restored
foyer.

ⓕⓕⓕⓕ The Connaught 🕽 🗟 🖫 ⅋ 🖤 🏊 🗾 ⓪ 🗚 ⓪
Carlos Place ⊠ *W1K 2AL⊖ Bond St –* ℰ *(020) 7499 7070*
– www.the-connaught.co.uk – info@theconnaught.co.uk
– Fax (020) 7495 3262   30AHUe
95 rm – †£387/717 ††£434/717, ⌑ £28 – 27 suites
Rest Hélène Darroze at The Connaught – see restaurant listing
Rest Espelette – Carte £44/63
♦ This famous hotel reopened in 2008 after a major renovation. Luxury bedrooms
updated in style and mod cons while retaining that elegant British feel. Choice of two
stylish bars. Espelette for all-day, informal dining.

ⓕⓕⓕⓕ InterContinental ≤ ☺ 🕅 🕽 🗟 🖾 rm, 🖫 ⅋ 🖤 🏊 ⌂
1 Hamilton Place, Park Lane ⊠ *W1J 7QY⊖ Hyde Park*   🗾 ⓪ 🗚 ⓪
Corner – ℰ *(020) 7409 3131 – www.london.intercontinental.com*
– london@ihg.com – Fax (020) 7493 3476   30AHVk
399 rm – †£282/388 ††£282/388, ⌑ £27 – 48 suites
Rest Theo Randall – see restaurant listing
Rest Cookbook Café – Carte £30/44
♦ International hotel relaunched in 2007 after major refit. English style bedrooms
with high tech equipment and large, open plan lobby. Cookbook Café invites visiting
chefs to showcase their talents.

ⓕⓕⓕⓕ London Hilton ≤ 🕅 🕽 🗟 🖾 rm, 🖫 ⅋ 🖤 🏊 🗾 ⓪ 🗚
22 Park Lane ⊠ *W1K 1BE⊖ Hyde Park Corner –* ℰ *(020) 7493 8000*
– www.hilton.co.uk/londonparklane – reservations.parklane@hilton.com
– Fax (020) 7208 4142   30AHVe
395 rm – †£234/516 ††£328/563, ⌑ £27 – 56 suites
Rest Galvin at Windows – see restaurant listing
Rest Trader Vics – (closed lunch Saturday and Sunday) Carte £32/47
Rest Podium – Menu £22/30 – Carte £29/40
♦ This 28 storey tower is one of the city's tallest hotels, providing impressive views
from the upper floors. Club floor bedrooms are particularly comfortable. Exotic Trader
Vics with bamboo and plants. Modern European food in Podium.

LONDON

Grosvenor House   *£ó* 🛗 🔊 &, rm, 📶 ❄ 🐾 ♨ 🍸 🚗 VISA ⑩ AE ①

Park Lane ⊠ *W1K 7TN*⊖ *Marble Arch –* ℰ *(020) 7499 6363*
– www.grosvenorhouse.co.uk – grosvenor.house@marriotthotels.com
– Fax (020) 7493 3341   29AGU**g**
378 rm – ♦£ 299/399 ♦♦£ 299/399, ☲ £ 21.50 – 55 suites
Rest *Bord'eaux* – French – Menu £ 26 – Carte £ 27/44
♦ Refurbished hotel in commanding position by Hyde Park. Uniform, comfortable bedrooms in classic Marriott styling. Boasts the largest ballroom in Europe. Brasserie specialises in SW France.

Brown's   *£ó* &, rm, 📶 ❄ 🐾 VISA ⑩ AE ①

Albemarle St ⊠ *W1S 4BP*⊖ *Green Park –* ℰ *(020) 7493 6020*
– www.roccofortecollection.com – reservations.browns@roccofortecollection.com
– Fax (020) 7493 9381   30AIV**d**
105 rm – ♦£ 415/575 ♦♦£ 540/725, ☲ £ 27 – 12 suites
Rest *The Albemarle* – British – ℰ *(020) 7518 4004* – Carte £ 28/52
♦ After a major refit, this urbane hotel offers a swish bar featuring Terence Donovan prints, up-to-the-minute rooms and a quintessentially English sitting room for tea. Wood panelled dining room with traditional British cooking.

London Marriott H. Park Lane   🔲 *£ó* 🛗 &, rm, 📶 ❄ 🐾 🍸

140 Park Lane ⊠ *W1K 7AA*⊖ *Marble Arch –* ℰ *(020)*   VISA ⑩ AE ①
7493 7000 – www.marriott.com/lonpl – Fax (020) 7493 8333   29AGU**b**
148 rm – ♦♦£ 347/370, ☲ £ 18.95 – 9 suites
Rest *140 Park Lane* – Menu £ 19 – Carte £ 23/39
♦ Superbly located 'boutique' style hotel at intersection of Park Lane and Oxford Street. Attractive basement health club. Spacious, well-equipped rooms with luxurious elements. Attractive restaurant overlooking Marble Arch.

Westbury   *£ó* 🛗 &, rm, 📶 ❄ 🍸 🍸 VISA ⑩ AE ①

Bond St ⊠ *W1S 2YF*⊖ *Bond Street –* ℰ *(020) 7629 7755*
– www.westburymayfair.com – sales@westburymayfair.com
– Fax (020) 7495 1163   30AIU**a**
232 rm – ♦£ 504/539 ♦♦£ 539, ☲ £ 22.50 – 17 suites
Rest – (Closed Sunday and Bank Holidays) Menu £ 25 – Carte £ 47/56
♦ Surrounded by London's most fashionable shops; the renowned Polo bar and lounge provide soothing sanctuary. Some suites have their own terrace. Bright, fresh restaurant enhanced by modern art.

The Metropolitan   ⟨ *£ó* 🛗 📶 ❄ 🍸 🚗 VISA ⑩ AE ①

Old Park Lane ⊠ *W1K 1LB*⊖ *Hyde Park Corner –* ℰ *(020) 7447 1000*
– www.metropolitan.como.bz – res.lon@metropolitan.como.bz
– Fax (020) 7447 1100   30AHV**c**
147 rm – ♦£ 763 ♦♦£ 763, ☲ £ 26 – 3 suites
Rest *Nobu* – see restaurant listing
♦ Minimalist interior and a voguish reputation make this the favoured hotel of pop stars and celebrities. Sleek design and fashionably attired staff set it apart.

Athenaeum   ⟫ *£ó* 🛗 📶 🍸 🍸 VISA ⑩ AE ①

116 Piccadilly ⊠ *W1J 7BJ*⊖ *Hyde Park Corner –* ℰ *(020) 7499 3464*
– www.athenaeumhotel.com – info@athenaeumhotel.com
– Fax (020) 7493 1860   30AHV**g**
145 rm – ♦♦£ 176/411, ☲ £ 27 – 12 suites
Rest *Damask* – Menu £ 21/26 – Carte £ 36/46
♦ Built in 1925 as a luxury apartment block. Comfortable bedrooms with video and CD players. Individually designed suites are in an adjacent Edwardian townhouse. Conservatory roofed dining room renowned for its mosaics and malt whiskies.

Chesterfield
🖳 ⅏ rm, 🅰🅺 ⁽¹⁾ 🛝 🆅🅸🆂🅰 ⓦⓢ 🅰🅴 ⓘ

35 Charles St ⊠ *W1J 5EB*⊖ *Green Park* – ✆ *(020) 7491 2622*
– www.chesterfieldmayfair.com – bookch@rchmail.com
– Fax (020) 7491 4793
30AHV**f**
103 rm – ♦£135/382 ♦♦£170/405, � £22 – 4 suites
Rest – (Closed Saturday lunch) Menu £20 (lunch) – Carte £33/61
♦ An assuredly English feel to this Georgian house. Discreet lobby leads to a clubby bar and wood panelled library. Individually decorated bedrooms, with some antique pieces. Classically decorated restaurant.

Washington Mayfair
🖙 🖳 ⅏ rm, 🅰🅺 🛜 ⁽¹⁾ 🛝 🆅🅸🆂🅰 ⓦⓢ 🅰🅴 ⓘ

5-7 Curzon St ⊠ *W1J 5HE*⊖ *Green Park* – ✆ *(020) 7499 7000*
– www.washington-mayfair.co.uk – info@washington-mayfair.co.uk
– Fax (020) 7495 6172
30AHV**d**
166 rm – ♦£176/382 ♦♦£176/382, ⊏⊐ £19.50 – 5 suites
Rest – Menu £23 – Carte £28/39
♦ Successfully blends a classical style with modern amenities. Relaxing lounge with traditional English furniture and bedrooms with polished, burred oak. Piano bar annex to formal dining room.

London Marriott H. Grosvenor Square
🖙 🖳 ⅏ 🅰🅺 🛜 ⁽¹⁾

Grosvenor Sq ⊠ *W1K 6JP*⊖ *Bond Street* – ✆ *(020)*
🛝 🆅🅸🆂🅰 ⓦⓢ 🅰🅴 ⓘ
7493 1232 – www.marriottgrosvenorsquare.com
– london.regional.reservations@marriott.com – Fax (020) 7491 3201
30AHU**s**
224 rm – ♦£281/351 ♦♦£281/351, ⊏⊐ £22 – 12 suites
Rest *Maze Grill* – see restaurant listing
♦ A well-appointed international group hotel that benefits from an excellent location. Many of the bedrooms specifically equipped for the business traveller.

Hilton London Green Park
🖳 ⅏ rm, 🅰🅺 rest, 🛜 ⁽¹⁾ 🛝 🆅🅸🆂🅰 ⓦⓢ 🅰🅴 ⓘ

Half Moon St ⊠ *W1J 7BN*⊖ *Green Park* – ✆ *(020) 7629 7522*
– www.hilton.co.uk/greenpark – reservations.greenpark@hilton.com – Fax (020)
7491 8971
30AIV**a**
162 rm – ♦£140/311 ♦♦£152/311, ⊏⊐ £19.50
Rest – (bar lunch) Carte £31/37
♦ A row of sympathetically adjoined townhouses, dating from the 1730s. Well maintained bedrooms share the same décor but vary in size and shape. Monet prints decorate light, airy dining room.

XXXXX Alain Ducasse at The Dorchester
⇔ 🆅🅸🆂🅰 ⓦⓢ 🅰🅴 ⓘ
❀ ❀
Park Lane ⊠ *W1K 1QA*⊖ *Hyde Park Corner* – ✆ *(020) 7629 8866*
– www.alainducasse-dorchester.com – alainducasse@thedorchester.com
– Fax (020) 7629 8686 – Closed 3 weeks summer, 5 days early January, Saturday lunch, Sunday and Monday
30AHV**a**
Rest – French – Menu £45/75 ❀
Spec. Soft-boiled egg, crayfish, wild mushrooms and Nantua sauce. Fillet of beef and seared foie gras Rossini, "sacristain potatoes" and Périgueux sauce. "Baba like in Monte-Carlo".
♦ Luxury and extravagance are the hallmarks of this Alain Ducasse outpost. Dining room is elegant without being staid; food is modern and refined yet satisfying and balanced. Service is formal and well organised.

XXXX Hélène Darroze at The Connaught
🆅🅸🆂🅰 ⓦⓢ 🅰🅴 ⓘ
❀
Carlos Place ⊠ *W1K 2AL*⊖ *Bond St* – ✆ *(020) 3147 7200*
– www.the-connaught.co.uk – info@theconnaught.co.uk
30AHU**e**
Rest – French – (closed Saturday and Sunday) (booking essential)
Menu £39/75 ❀
Spec. Lobster ravioli with spices, citrus and carrot mousseline. Irish wild salmon, puy lentils, carrots and spring onions. Peach, pistachio ice cream and sponge.
♦ With influences from Landes and SW of France; the accomplished cooking is creative and flavours are bold and confident. Formal and elegant room; original mahogany panelling.

XXXX **Le Gavroche** (Michel Roux)   AC VISA ⓪⓪ AE ⓪

✿✿ 43 Upper Brook St ⊠ W1K 7QR⊖ Marble Arch – ℰ (020) 7408 0881
– www.le-gavroche.co.uk – bookings@le-gavroche.com – Fax (020) 7491 4387
– Closed Christmas-New Year, Sunday, Saturday lunch
and Bank Holidays   29AGU**c**
Rest – French – (booking essential) Menu £ 48 (lunch) – Carte £ 58/137 ⅏
Spec. Hot duck foie gras, grapes, and crispy duck pancake flavoured with cinnamon. Roast saddle of rabbit with crispy potatoes and parmesan. Bitter chocolate and praline 'indulgence'.
♦ Long-standing, renowned restaurant with a clubby, formal atmosphere. Accomplished classical French cuisine, served by smartly attired and well-drilled staff.

XXXX **The Square** (Philip Howard)   AC ⇆ VISA ⓪⓪ AE ⓪

✿✿ 6-10 Bruton St ⊠ W1J 6PU⊖ Green Park – ℰ (020) 7495 7100
– www.squarerestaurant.com – reception@squarerestaurant.com
– Fax (020) 7495 7150 – Closed 25 December, 1 January and Saturday lunch,
Sunday and Bank Holidays   30AIU**v**
Rest – French – Menu £ 35/75 ⅏
Spec. Crab lasagne, cappuccino of shellfish, champagne foam. Herb crusted
saddle of lamb, rosemary and shallot purée. Assiette of chocolate.
♦ Smart, busy restaurant; comfortable and never overformal. Cooking is thoughtful
and honest, with a dextrous balance of flavours and textures. Prompt, efficient serv-
ice.

XXXX **Sketch (The Lecture Room & Library)**   AC VISA ⓪⓪ AE ⓪

✿ First Floor, 9 Conduit St ⊠ W1S 2XG⊖ Oxford Street – ℰ (020) 7659 4500
– www.sketch.uk.com – info@sketch.uk.com – Fax (020) 7629 1683
– Closed 25-30 December, 2 weeks summer, Saturday lunch, Sunday,
Monday and Bank Holidays   30AIU**h**
Rest – French – (booking essential) Menu £ 35/65 – Carte £ 65/94 ⅏
Spec. Langoustines 'addressed in five ways'. Fillet of Simmental beef, pancake
and truffle. Caraïbe chocolate and ground nuts.
♦ A work of animated art, full of energy, vitality and colour; an experience of true
sensory stimulation. Ambitious, highly elaborate and skilled cooking; try the tasting
menu.

XXXX **China Tang** – at Dorchester Hotel   AC ⇆ VISA ⓪⓪ AE ⓪

Park Lane ⊠ W1A 2HJ⊖ Hyde Park Corner – ℰ (020) 7629 9988
– www.thedorchester.com – chinatang@dorchesterhotel.com
– Fax (020) 7629 9595 – Closed 25 December   30AHV**a**
Rest – Chinese – Menu £ 15 (lunch) – Carte £ 40/100
♦ A striking mix of Art Deco, Oriental motifs, hand-painted fabrics, mirrors and marbled table tops. Carefully prepared, traditional Cantonese dishes using quality ingredients.

XXXX **Galvin at Windows** – at London Hilton Hotel   ≤ AC VISA ⓪⓪ AE ⓪

22 Park Lane ⊠ W1K 1BE⊖ Hyde Park Corner – ℰ (020) 7208 4021
– www.galvinatwindows.com – reservations@galvinatwindows.com – Fax (020)
7208 4144 – Closed Saturday lunch and Bank Holidays   30AHV**e**
Rest – French – Menu £ 29/58 – Carte £ 60/75
♦ On the 28th floor, so the views are spectacular. Contemporary styling includes silk
curtains and opulent gold leaf effect sculpture on ceiling. Detailed and elaborate
cooking.

XXXX **Gordon Ramsay at Claridge's**   AC VISA ⓪⓪ AE ⓪

✿ Brook St ⊠ W1K 4HR⊖ Bond St – ℰ (020) 7499 0099
– www.gordonramsay.com – reservations@gordonramsay.com
– Fax (020) 7499 3099   30AHU**c**
Rest – Modern European – (booking essential) Menu £ 30/70 ⅏
Spec. Salad of crab with carrot à la grecque, ginger and carrot dressing. Roast
rib of beef with cep relish and smoked potato purée. Valrhona chocolate and
honeycomb fondant with orange yoghurt sorbet.
♦ A thoroughly comfortable dining room with a charming and gracious atmosphere.
Serves classically-inspired food executed with a high degree of finesse.

LONDON

LONDON

XXX   Scott's   AK ⇔ VISA ◐◐ AE ◑

20 Mount St ⊠ W1K 2HE⊖ Bond St – ℰ (020) 7495 7309
– www.scotts-restaurant.com – Fax (020) 7647 6327
– Closed 25-26 December, 1 January and August Bank holiday   30AHU**d**
Rest – Seafood – Carte £ 38/87
♦ A landmark London institution reborn. Stylish yet traditional; oak panelling juxtaposed with vibrant artwork from young British artists. Top quality seafood, kept simple.

XXX   The Greenhouse   AK ⇔ VISA ◐◐ AE ◑
❀
27a Hay's Mews ⊠ W1J 5NY⊖ Hyde Park Corner
– ℰ (020) 7499 3331 – www.greenhouserestaurant.co.uk
– reservations@greenhouserestaurant.co.uk – Fax (020) 7499 5368
– Closed 24 December - 6 January, Saturday lunch, Sunday
and Bank Holidays   30AHV**m**
Rest – Innovative – Menu £ 29/65 ❀
Spec. Foie gras glazed with lemon, honey, apricot and begonia flowers. Veal rump with asparagus and tamarind reduction. "Snix" - chocolate, salted caramel and peanuts.
♦ Smart, elegant restaurant broken up into sections by glass screens. Innovative selection of elaborately presented dishes, underpinned with sound French culinary techniques.

XXX   Hibiscus (Claude Bosi)   AK ⇔ VISA ◐◐ AE
❀ ❀
29 Maddox St ⊠ W1S 2PA⊖ Oxford Circus
– ℰ (020) 7629 2999 – www.hibiscusrestaurant.co.uk
– enquiries@hibiscusrestaurant.co.uk – Fax (020) 7514 9552
– Closed 2 weeks summer, 2 weeks Christmas, Saturday except dinner
1 November - 20 December and Sunday   30AIU**s**
Rest – Innovative – Menu £ 25 (lunch)/60
Spec. Sweetbeads, oak smoked goat's cheese, onion fondue. Chicken stuffed with crayfish, girolles and green mango. Tart of sweet peas, mint and sheep's whey with coconut ice cream.
♦ French oak wood panelling and Welsh slate walls reminiscent of its previous incarnation in Ludlow. Shropshire ingredients feature; cooking is accomplished and bold.

XXX   Murano   VISA ◐◐ AE ◑
❀
20 Queen St ⊠ W1J 5PR ⊖ Green Park – ℰ (020) 7592 1222
– www.angelahartnett.com – murano@gordonramsay.com – Fax (020) 7592 1213
– Closed Sunday   30AHV**b**
Rest – Italian influences – Menu £ 25/55
Spec. Scallop, watermelon and Joselito ham salad. Duck breast and confit of leg with mustard fruits and potato cakes. Apricot soufflé with Amaretto di Saronno ice cream.
♦ Angela Hartnett's bright and stylish restaurant, in collaboration with Gordon Ramsay, provides a luminous setting for her refined and balanced cooking, with its strong Italian influences.

XXX   Maze   AK ⇔ VISA ◐◐ AE
❀
10-13 Grosvenor Sq ⊠ W1K 6JP⊖ Bond Street – ℰ (020) 7107 0000
– www.gordonramsay.com – maze@gordonramsay.com
– Fax (020) 7107 0001   30AHU**z**
Rest – Innovative – Carte approx. £ 57 **s** ❀
Spec. Crab salad with mooli and apple jelly. Red mullet and sardine with saffron rice and pimento purée. Pineapple carpaccio with seaweed croquette and Malibu lime jelly.
♦ Choose between a variety of small dishes at this sleek, contemporary restaurant. Innovative, balanced and precise, cooking has a French base and the occasional Asian influence.

XXX
ⓔ **Benares** (Atul Kochhar)   🗚 ⇦ 𝚅𝙸𝚂𝙰 ⑳ 𝙰𝙴 ⓞ
12a Berkeley Square House ✉ W1J 6BS⊖ Green Park – ℰ *(020) 76298886*
– www.benaresrestaurant.com – reservations@benaresrestaurant.com
– Fax (020) 74992430
– Closed 25-26 December, 1 January, and Bank Holidays   30AIU**q**
Rest – Indian – Menu £ 30 (lunch) – Carte £ 39/61
Spec. Tandoori roasted quails' with red chilli and yoghurt marinade. Tiger
prawns with curry leaf, onion and tomato sauce. Saffron and mango jelly with
coconut.
♦ A smart and stylish, first floor Indian restaurant. Many of the regional dishes are
given innovative twists but flavours remain authentic. Convivial atmosphere and
pleasant service.

XXX
ⓔ **Umu**   🗚 𝚅𝙸𝚂𝙰 ⑳ 𝙰𝙴 ⓞ
14-16 Bruton Pl ✉ W1J 6LX⊖ Bond Street – ℰ *(020) 74998881*
– www.umurestaurant.com – reception@umurestaurant.com – Fax (020)
70165120 – Closed 24 December - 7 January, Saturday lunch,
Sunday and Bank Holidays   30AIU**k**
Rest – Japanese – Menu £ 21 (lunch) – Carte £ 34/73 𝕊
Spec. Sweet shrimp with sake jelly and caviar. Grilled skill fish teriyaki, yuzu
and citrus flavoured grated radish. Black bean ice cream.
♦ Stylish, discreet interior using natural materials, with central sushi bar. Japanese
dishes, specialising in Kyoto cuisine; choose one of the Kaiseki menus. Over 160
different labels of sake.

XXX **Cecconi's**   🗚 𝚅𝙸𝚂𝙰 ⑳ 𝙰𝙴
5a Burlington Gdns ✉ W1S 3EP⊖ Green Park – ℰ *(020) 74341500*
– www.cecconis.com – giacomo@cecconis.co.uk – Fax (020) 74342020
– Closed 25 December   30AIU**d**
Rest – Italian – (booking essential) Carte £ 28/46
♦ A chic bar and a stylish, modern dining venue, invariably busy; the menus call on
the Italian classics with unusual touches.

XXX **Tamarind**   🗚 𝚅𝙸𝚂𝙰 ⑳ 𝙰𝙴 ⓞ
20 Queen St ✉ W1J 5PR⊖ Green Park – ℰ *(020) 76293561*
– www.tamarindrestaurant.com – manager@tamarindrestaurant.com
– Fax (020) 74995034 – Closed 25-26 December, 1 January and lunch Saturday
and Bank Holidays   30AHV**h**
Rest – Indian – Menu £ 22/52 – Carte £ 39/61
♦ The starting point is the Moghul cooking of the North West and the use of the
tandoor oven – kebabs are a speciality. The spacious and stylish basement restaurant
is popular with the smart set.

XXX **Bentley's (Grill)**   🗚 ⇦ 𝚅𝙸𝚂𝙰 ⑳ 𝙰𝙴
11-15 Swallow St ✉ W1B 4DG⊖ Piccadilly Circus – ℰ *(020) 77344756*
– www.bentleysoysterbarandgrill.co.uk – reservations@bentleys.org – Closed
25-26 December, 1 January, Saturday lunch and Sunday   30AJU**n**
Rest – British – Menu £ 22 (lunch) – Carte £ 36/62
♦ Entrance into striking bar; panelled staircase to richly decorated restaurant. Carefully sourced seafood or meat dishes enhanced by clean, crisp cooking. Unruffled
service.

XXX
ⓔ **Kai**   🗚 ⇦ 𝚅𝙸𝚂𝙰 ⑳ 𝙰𝙴 ⓞ
65 South Audley St ✉ W1K 2QU⊖ Hyde Park Corner – ℰ *(020) 74938988*
– www.kaimayfair.com – kai@kaimayfair.com – Fax (020) 74931456
– Closed 25-26 December and 1 January   30AHV**n**
Rest – Chinese – (booking essential) Menu £ 24 (lunch) – Carte £ 34/84
Spec. Pan-fried prawns with mustard greens and buttered lettuce. Lamb
with Sichuan peppercorns, flower mushroom and bamboo shoot. 'Pumpkin
Cream' with purple rice, coconut ice cream.
♦ Stylish and slick surroundings spread over two floors, with unobtrusive and sweet
natured service. Highly skilled cooking blends the traditional with the modern to
good effect on extensive menu.

LONDON

LONDON

XXX Theo Randall – at InterContinental Hotel   AC ⇄ VISA ◑◐ AE ◍
1 Hamilton Place, Park Lane ⊠ W1J 7QY⊖ Hyde Park Corner – ℰ (020)
73188747 – www.theorandall.com – Closed 25-26 December, Saturday lunch,
Sunday and Bank Holidays   30AHVk
Rest – Italian – Menu £ 25 (weekday lunch) – Carte £ 43/50
♦ Stylish and spacious ground floor restaurant; helpful and chatty service. Rustic,
seasonal Italian dishes focus on the best ingredients; wood oven the speciality.

XXX Avista   AC ⇄ VISA ◑◐ AE ◍
Millennium Mayfair H, 39 Grosvenor Sq ⊠ W1K 2HP⊖ Bond Street – ℰ (020)
7596 3444 – www.avistarestaurant.com – reservations@avistarestaurant.com
– Fax (020) 7596 3443 – Closed 25 December and 1 January   30AHUx
Rest – Italian – Menu £ 24 (lunch) – Carte £ 26/46
♦ A large room, softened by neutral shades, within the Millennium Hotel. The menu
traverses Italy and the cooking marries the rustic with the more refined. Pasta dishes
are a highlight.

XXX Sartoria   AC 🄿 ⇄ VISA ◑◐ AE
20 Savile Row ⊠ W1S 3PR⊖ Green Park – ℰ (020) 7534 7000
– www.danddlondon.com – sartoriareservations@danddlondon.com
– Fax (020) 7534 7070
– Closed 25-26 December, 1 January, Sunday and Bank Holidays   30AIUb
Rest – Italian – Menu £ 25 – Carte £ 35/46
♦ In the street renowned for English tailoring, a coolly sophisticated restaurant to
suit those looking for classic Italian cooking with modern touches.

XXX Embassy   🄿 AC VISA ◑◐ AE
29 Old Burlington St ⊠ W1S 3AN⊖ Green Park – ℰ (020) 7851 0956
– www.embassylondon.com – embassy@embassylondon.com
– Fax (020) 7434 3074
– Closed Saturday lunch, Sunday, Monday and Bank Holidays   30AIUu
Rest – Modern European – Menu £ 25 (lunch) – Carte £ 24/45
♦ Marble floors, ornate cornicing and a long bar create a characterful, moody dining
room. Tables are smartly laid and menus offer accomplished, classic dishes.

XX Semplice (Marco Torri)   AC VISA ◑◐ AE
£3
9-10 Blenheim St ⊠ W1S 1LJ⊖ Bond Street – ℰ (020) 7495 1509
– www.ristorantesemplice.com – info@ristorantesemplice.com
– Fax (020) 7493 7074 – Closed Christmas, Easter, Saturday lunch,
Sunday and Bank Holidays   30AHUk
Rest – Italian – (booking essential at dinner) Menu £ 19 (lunch)
– Carte £ 31/47 🕸
Spec. Pan-fried goat's cheese with beetroot and balsamic vinegar. Fassone
beef with spiced French beans and salad. Domori chocolate fondant and pista-
chio ice cream.
♦ Comfortable and stylish with custom laquered ebony, wavy gold walls and leather
seating. Owners' passion about produce evident on the plate; northern Italy influences.

J XX Wild Honey   AC 🄿 VISA ◑◐ AE
£3
12 St George St ⊠ W1S 2FB⊖ Oxford Circus – ℰ (020) 7758 9160
– www.wildhoneyrestaurant.co.uk – info@wildhoneyrestaurant.co.uk – Fax (020)
7493 4549 – Closed 25-26 December and 1 January   30AIUw
Rest – Modern European – Menu £ 17 (lunch) – Carte £ 23/37
Spec. Dorset crab, salad of peas and young shoots. Saddle and shoulder of
rabbit, gnocchi, olives and tomatoes. Rum 'Baba' , raspberries, Chantilly cream.
♦ High-ceilinged, oak-panelled restaurant, with banquette and booth seating; sister
to Arbutus in Soho. Easy to eat, gimmick-free food with flavoursome and seasonal ingredients.

XX **Maze Grill** – at London Marriott H. Grosvenor Square   🔥 rm, AC ✻
Grosvenor Sq ⊠ W1K 6JP⊖ Bond Street – 𝒞 (020)   VISA ◍ AE ①
7493 1232 – www.marriottgrosvenorsquare.com
– london.regional.reservations@marriott.com – Fax (020) 7514 1528   30AHU**s**
Rest – Beef specialities – Carte £ 28/31
♦ Opened in 2008 as an addendum to Maze. Menu specialises in steaks, from Hereford grass-fed to Wagyu 9th grade, with a variety of sauces and side dishes available as accompaniments.

XX **Bellamy's**   AC VISA ◍ AE
18 Bruton Pl ⊠ W1J 6LY⊖ Bond Street – 𝒞 (020) 7491 2727
– www.bellamysrestaurant.co.uk – info@bellamysrestaurant.co.uk
– Fax (020) 7491 9990 – Closed Saturday lunch, Sunday, Christmas, Easter and
Bank Holidays   30AIU**c**
Rest – Traditional – Menu £ 29 – Carte £ 36/54
♦ French deli/brasserie tucked down a smart mews. Go past the caviar and cheeses into the restaurant proper for a very traditional, but well-executed, range of Gallic classics.

XX **Patterson's**   AC ⟷ VISA ◍ AE
4 Mill St ⊠ W1S 2AX⊖ Oxford Street – 𝒞 (020) 7499 1308
– www.pattersonsrestaurant.co.uk – info@pattersonsrestaurant.co.uk – Fax (020)
7491 2122 – Closed Saturday lunch, Sunday and Bank Holidays   30AIU**p**
Rest – Modern European – Menu £ 25 (lunch) – Carte £ 20/45
♦ Stylish modern interior in black and white. Elegant tables and attentive service. Modern British cooking with concise wine list and sensible prices.

XX **Alloro**   AC ⟷ VISA ◍ AE ①
19-20 Dover St ⊠ W1S 4LU⊖ Green Park – 𝒞 (020) 7495 4768
– www.londonfinedininggroup.com – alloro@finedininggroup.com
– Fax (020) 7629 5348 – Closed Easter, 25 December, 1 January,
Saturday lunch and Sunday   30AIV**r**
Rest – Italian – Menu £ 32/35 – Carte £ 40/60
♦ One of the new breed of stylish Italian restaurants with contemporary art and leather seating. A separate, bustling bar. Smoothly run with modern cooking.

XX **Hush**   🍽 AC ⟷ VISA ◍ AE
8 Lancashire Court, Brook St ⊠ W1S 1EY⊖ Bond Street – 𝒞 (020) 7659 1500
– www.hush.co.uk – info@hush.co.uk – Fax (020) 7659 1501   30AHU**v**
Rest – Modern European – (Closed 25 December, 31 December, 1 January and Sunday except lunch April-September) (booking essential) Carte £ 23/49
Rest *The Silver Room* – (Closed Saturday lunch and Sunday) (booking essential) Carte £ 27/57
♦ Tucked away down a delightful mews courtyard, this brasserie - with sunny courtyard terrace - is an informal and lively little place to eat rustic Mediterranean fare. Upstairs, The Silver Room serves slightly more refined dining menus.

XX **Fakhreldine**   AC VISA ◍ AE
85 Piccadilly ⊠ W1J 7NB⊖ Green Park – 𝒞 (020) 7493 3424
– www.fakhreldine.co.uk – info@fakhreldine.co.uk – Fax (020) 7495 1977
– Closed 24 to 26 December   30AIV**e**
Rest – Lebanese – Menu £ 19 (lunch) – Carte £ 28/48
♦ Long-standing Lebanese restaurant with great view of Green Park. Large selection of classic mezze dishes and more modern European styled menu of original Lebanese dishes.

XX **Nobu** – at The Metropolitan Hotel   ≤ AC ⟷ VISA ◍ AE
🕄 19 Old Park Lane ⊠ W1Y 1LB⊖ Hyde Park Corner – 𝒞 (020) 7447 4747
– www.noburestaurants.com – london@noburestaurants.com – Fax (020)
7447 4749 – Closed 25-26 December and 1 January   30AHV**c**
Rest – Japanese – (booking essential) Menu £ 50/90 – Carte £ 32/50
Spec. Tuna sashimi salad with matsuhiza dressing. Black cod with miso. Suntory whisky cappuccino.
♦ Its celebrity clientele has made this one of the most glamorous spots. Staff are fully conversant in the unique menu that adds South American influences to Japanese cooking.

LONDON

XX **Via Condotti**   AC 🐕 ⇔ VISA ⦿ AE

23 Conduit St ✉ *W1S 2XS*⊖ *Oxford Circus –* ℰ *(020) 7493 7050*
– www.viacondotti.co.uk – info@viacondotti.co.uk – Fax (020) 7409 7985 – Closed
Christmas, New Year, Sunday and Bank Holidays   30AIU**f**
Rest – Italian – Menu £ 19/28

♦ Reliable and keenly run Italian, as warm and welcoming as the pretty façade suggests. Balanced and appetising cooking, using influences from the north of Italy, and all fairly priced.

XX **Taman Gang**   AC VISA ⦿ AE

141 Park Lane ✉ *W1K 7AA*⊖ *Marble Arch –* ℰ *(020) 7518 3160*
– www.tamangang.com – info@tamangang.com – Fax (020) 7518 3161 – Closed
Sunday and Bank Holidays   29AGU**e**
Rest – Asian – (dinner only) Carte £ 28/73

♦ Basement restaurant with largish bar and lounge area. Stylish but intimate décor. Informal and intelligent service. Pan-Asian dishes presented in exciting modern manner.

XX **Nobu Berkeley St**   AC VISA ⦿ AE
ॐ
15 Berkeley St ✉ *W1J 8DY*⊖ *Green Park –* ℰ *(020) 7290 9222*
– www.noburestaurants.com – nobuberkeleyst@noburestaurants.com – Fax (020)
7290 9223 – Closed 25-26 December, Saturday lunch, Sunday lunch
and Bank Holidays   30AIV**b**
Rest – Japanese – Menu £ 28/85 – Carte £ 33/49
Spec. Octopus carpaccio with botarga. Duck breast with wasabi salsa. Chocolate santandagi with pistachios.

♦ In a prime position off Berkeley Square: downstairs 'destination' bar and above, a top quality, soft-hued restaurant. Innovative Japanese dishes with original combinations.

XX **Sumosan**   AC VISA ⦿ AE ➀

26 Albemarle St ✉ *W1S 4HY*⊖ *Green Park –* ℰ *(020) 7495 5999*
– www.sumosan.com – info@sumosan.co.uk – Fax (020) 7355 1247
– Closed 25-26 December, New Year, Saturday lunch, Sunday lunch
and Bank Holidays   30AIU**e**
Rest – Japanese – Menu £ 23 (lunch) – Carte approx. £ 70

♦ A very smart interior in which diners sit in comfy banquettes and armchairs. Sushi bar to the rear with some semi-private booths. Extensive menus of Sushi and Sashimi.

XX **Mews of Mayfair**   VISA ⦿ AE ➀

10-11 Lancashire Court, Brook St (first floor) ✉ *W1S 1EY*⊖ *Bond Street*
– ℰ *(020) 7518 9388 – www.mewsofmayfair.com*
– info@mewsofmayfair.com
– Fax (020) 7518 9389
– Closed 25-26 December and Sunday   30AHU**a**
Rest – International – Menu £ 23 (lunch) – Carte £ 36/48

♦ Converted mews houses once used as storage rooms for Savile Row. Ground floor bar with French windows. Pretty first floor restaurant where eclectic modern menus are served.

XX **Chor Bizarre**   AC VISA ⦿ AE ➀

16 Albemarle St ✉ *W1S 4HW*⊖ *Green Park –* ℰ *(020) 7629 9802*
– www.chorbizarre.com – chorbizarrelondon@oldworldhospitality.com
– Fax (020) 7493 7756
– Closed 25-26 December, 1 January, and Sunday lunch   30AIV**s**
Rest – Indian – Menu £ 17 (lunch) – Carte £ 24/38

♦ Translates as 'thieves market' and the décor is equally vibrant; antiques, curios, carvings and ornaments abound. Cooking and recipes chiefly from North India and Kashmir.

XX Sketch (The Gallery)

AC VISA ◑ AE ①

9 Conduit St ⊠ *W1S 2XG* ⊖ *Oxford Street* – ℰ *(020) 7659 4500*
– *www.sketch.uk.com* – *info@sketch.uk.com* – *Fax (020) 7629 1683*
– *Closed 25-26 December Sunday and Bank Holidays*
30AIU**h**
Rest – International – (dinner only) (booking essential) Carte £ 32/52
♦ On the ground floor of the Sketch building: daytime video art gallery metamorphoses into evening brasserie with ambient wall projections and light menus with eclectic range.

XX Cocoon

AC ஜ ⇔ VISA ◑ AE

65 Regent St ⊠ *W1B 4EA* ⊖ *Piccadilly Circus* – ℰ *(020) 7494 7600*
– *www.cocoon-restaurants.com* – *reservations@cocoon-restaurants.com*
– *Fax (020) 7494 7607*
– *Closed 25-27 December, Saturday lunch and Sunday*
30AJU**x**
Rest – Asian – Menu £ 15 (lunch) – Carte £ 28/51
♦ Trendy restaurant, based on a prime Regent Street site. Silk nets cleverly divide long, winding room. Bold, eclectic menus cover a wide spectrum of Asian dishes.

XX Momo

🍴 AC VISA ◑ AE ①

25 Heddon St ⊠ *W1B 4BH* ⊖ *Oxford Circus* – ℰ *(020) 7434 4040*
– *www.momoresto.com* – *info@momoresto.com* – *Fax (020) 7287 0404*
– *Closed Sunday lunch*
30AIU**n**
Rest – Moroccan – Menu £ 24/40 – Carte £ 30/43
♦ Elaborate adornment of rugs, drapes and ornaments mixed with Arabic music lend an authentic feel to this busy Moroccan restaurant. Helpful service. Popular basement bar.

XX Veeraswamy

AC ஜ ⇔ VISA ◑ AE ①

Victory House, 99 Regent St, entrance on Swallow St ⊠ *W1B 4RS* ⊖ *Piccadilly Circus* – ℰ *(020) 7734 1401* – *www.realindianfood.com*
– *veeraswamy@realindianfood.com* – *Fax (020) 7439 8434*
– *Closed dinner 25 December*
30AIU**t**
Rest – Indian – Menu £ 20 (lunch) – Carte £ 36/44
♦ The country's oldest Indian restaurant enlivened by vivid coloured walls and glass screens. The menu also combines the familiar with some modern twists.

XX Kiku

AC VISA ◑ AE ①

17 Half Moon St ⊠ *W1J 7BE* ⊖ *Green Park* – ℰ *(020) 7499 4208*
– *www.kikurestaurant.co.uk* – *Fax (020) 7409 3259* – *Closed 25 December,*
1 January, lunch Sunday and Bank Holidays
30AIV**g**
Rest – Japanese – Menu £ 18/46 – Carte £ 33/55
♦ Bright and fresh feel thanks to minimalistic décor of stone and natural wood. A plethora of menus, a fierce adherence to seasonality and an authentic emphasis on presentation.

XX Haiku

AC VISA ◑ AE

15 New Burlington Place ⊠ *W1S 2HX* ⊖ *Oxford Circus* – ℰ *(020) 7494 4777*
– *www.haikurestaurant.com*
30AIU**x**
Rest – Asian – Menu £ 22/40 – Carte £ 40/50
♦ Elegant, moodily lit and set over three floors with open kitchen, the unusual theme here is 'Asian tapas,' and the menu features dishes from Japan, India, China and Thailand.

XX La Petite Maison

🍴 AC VISA ◑ AE

54 Brooks Mews ⊠ *W1K 4EG* ⊖ *Bond Street* – ℰ *(020) 7495 4774*
– *www.lpmlondon.co.uk* – *info@lpmlondon.co.uk*
– *Closed Sunday dinner*
30AHU**f**
Rest – French – Carte £ 31/64
♦ Open plan restaurant; sister to the eponymous Nice original. Healthy French Mediterranean cooking with a seafood slant. 20 starters to choose from; sharing is encouraged.

Chisou
4 Princes St ✉ W1B 2LE ⊖ Oxford Circus – ✆ (020) 7629 3931
– www.chisou.co.uk – chisou@xln.co.uk – Fax (020) 7629 5255
– Closed Sunday 30AIU**m**
Rest – Japanese – Menu £ 17 (lunch) – Carte £ 24/43
♦ In Mayfair's Japanese quarter; simple slate flooring and polished wood tables. Cosy sushi bar to rear. Elaborate menus of modern/classic Japanese dishes. Gets very busy.

Bentley's (Oyster Bar)
11-15 Swallow St ✉ W1B 4DG ⊖ Piccadilly Circus – ✆ (020) 7734 4756
– www.bentleysoysterbarand grill.co.uk – reservations@bentleys.org – Fax (020) 7758 4140 – Closed 24-26 December and 1 January 30AJU**n**
Rest – Seafood – Carte £ 28/64
♦ Ground floor location, behind the busy bar. White-jacketed staff open oysters by the bucket load. Interesting seafood menus feature tasty fish pies. Hearty Sunday roasts.

Automat
33 Dover St ✉ W1S 4NF ⊖ Green Park – ✆ (020) 7499 3033
– www.automat-london.com – info@automat-london.com – Fax (020) 7499 2682
– Closed 25 December and 1 January 30AIV**r**
Rest – American – Carte £ 39/52
♦ Buzzing New York style brasserie in three areas: a café, a 'dining car' with deep leather banquettes, and actual brasserie itself. Classic dishes from burgers to cheesecake.

The Cafe at Sotheby's
34-35 New Bond St ✉ W1A 2AA ⊖ Bond Street – ✆ (020) 7293 5077
– www.sothebys.com – ken.hall@sothebys.com – Fax (020) 7293 6993
– Closed 24 December-4 January, Saturday and Sunday 30AIU**y**
Rest – Modern European – (lunch only) (booking essential) Carte £ 25/33 **s**
♦ A velvet rope separates this simple room from the main lobby of this famous auction house. Pleasant service from staff in aprons. Menu is short but well-chosen and light.

Le Boudin Blanc
5 Trebeck St ⊖ Green Park – ✆ (020) 7499 3292 – www.boudinblanc.co.uk
– reservations@boudinblanc.co.uk – Fax (020) 7495 6973
– Closed 25 December 30AHV**q**
Rest – French – Menu £ 15 (lunch) – Carte £ 28/48
♦ Very busy restaurant with a simple bistro style; the first floor is marginally less frantic than the ground floor. Robust and satisfying French classics have authentic flavour.

The Only Running Footman
5 Charles St. ✉ W1J 5DF ⊖ Green Park – ✆ (020) 7499 2988
– www.therunningfootman.biz – info@therunningfootman.biz
– Fax (020) 7491 8162 30AHV**x**
Rest – British – Carte £ 29/39
♦ Charming, historic pub whose small, atmospheric ground floor is always busy, with a first-come-first-served rule. Upstairs you can book, it's plush and the menu more ambitious.

Regent's Park and Marylebone – Greater London – ✉ NW1/NW8/W1

Landmark London
222 Marylebone Rd ✉ NW1 6JQ ⊖ Edgware Rd – ✆ (020) 7631 8000 – www.landmarklondon.co.uk – reservations@thelandmark.co.uk
– Fax (020) 7631 8080 29AFT**a**
290 rm – †£ 329/535 ††£ 364/535, ☕ £ 28 – 9 suites
Rest *Winter Garden* – Menu £ 35 (lunch) – Carte £ 40/68
♦ Imposing Victorian Gothic building with a vast glass enclosed atrium, overlooked by many of the modern, well-equipped bedrooms. Winter Garden popular for afternoon tea.

Langham

1c Portland Pl, Regent St ✉ W1B 1JA ⊖ Oxford Circus – ✆ (020) 7636 1000 – www.langhamhotels.com – loninfo@langhamhotels.com – Fax (020) 7323 2340 30AITe

365 rm – †£ 476 ††£ 476, ☕ £27.50 – 17 suites

Rest *The Landau* – ✆ (020) 7965 0165 – Menu £ 33/45 – Carte £ 49/62

◆ A classic Victorian hotel with a long history, opposite the BBC. Currently undergoing a major refurbishment to be completed by early 2009. The Landau is an impressively ornate, circular room, with elaborate and ambitious cooking.

The Cumberland

Great Cumberland Place ✉ W1H 4DL ⊖ Marble Arch – ✆ (0870) 333 92 80 – www.guoman.com – enquiries@thecumberland.co.uk – Fax (0870) 333 92 81 29AGUz

1010 rm ☕ – †£ 358 ††£ 366

Rest *Rhodes W1 Restaurant* and ***Rhodes W1 Brasserie*** – see restaurant listing

◆ Fully refurbished, conference oriented hotel whose vast lobby boasts modern art, sculpture and running water panels. Distinctive bedrooms with a host of impressive extras.

Hyatt Regency London-The Churchill

30 Portman Sq ✉ W1H 7BH ⊖ Marble Arch – ✆ (020) 7486 5800 – www.london.churchill.hyatt.com – london.churchill@hyatt.com – Fax (020) 7486 1255 29AGTx

404 rm – †£ 194/447 ††£ 217/470, ☕ £25 – 40 suites

Rest *The Montagu* – Menu £ 22/25 – Carte £ 35/47

◆ Smart property overlooking attractive square. Elegant marbled lobby. Well-appointed and recently refurbished rooms have the international traveller in mind. Restaurant provides popular Sunday brunch entertainment.

Charlotte Street

15 Charlotte St ✉ W1T 1RJ ⊖ Goodge Street – ✆ (020) 7806 2000 – www.charlottestreethotel.co.uk – charlotte@firmdale.com – Fax (020) 7806 2002 31AKTe

48 rm – †£ 259/294 ††£ 364, ☕ £19 – 4 suites

Rest *Oscar* – see restaurant listing

◆ Interior designed with a charming and understated English feel. Welcoming lobby laden with floral displays. Individually decorated rooms with CDs and mobile phones.

Sanderson

50 Berners St ✉ W1T 3NG ⊖ Oxford Circus – ✆ (020) 7300 1400 – www.morganshotelgroup.com – sanderson@morganshotelgroup.com – Fax (020) 7300 1401 31AJTc

150 rm – †£ 282/423 ††£ 282/423, ☕ £25

Rest *Suka* – Menu £ 24 – Carte £ 27/55

◆ Designed by Philipe Starck: the height of contemporary design. Bar is the place to see and be seen. Bedrooms with minimalistic white décor have DVDs and striking bathrooms. Malaysian dishes designed for sharing in Suka.

The Leonard

15 Seymour St ✉ W1H 7JW ⊖ Marble Arch – ✆ (020) 7935 2010 – www.theleonard.com – reservations@theleonard.com – Fax (020) 7935 6700 29AGUn

32 rm – †£ 153 ††£ 293, ☕ £19.50 – 16 suites

Rest – (Closed Sunday dinner) Carte £ 21/27

◆ Around the corner from Selfridges, an attractive Georgian townhouse: antiques and oil paintings abound. Well-appointed rooms in classic country house style. Intimate front dining room.

LONDON

London Marriott H. Marble Arch 🗖 🕅 ⅃ゟ 🖢 ᇯ rm, ㎢ ※

134 George St ⊠ *W1H 5DN*⊖ *Marble Arch* ℡ ⅏ 🄿 ᴠɪꜱᴀ 🐵 ᴀᴇ
– ℰ *(020) 7723 1277 – www.marriott.com/lonma*
– *mhrs.lonma.salesadmin@marriott.com – Fax (020) 7725 5924* 29AFT**j**
240 rm – ✝£ 304/351 ✝✝£ 304/351, ☑ £18.95
Rest *Mediterrano* – (dinner only) Carte £ 35/45

♦ Centrally located and modern. Offers comprehensive conference facilities. Leisure centre underground. An ideal base for both corporate and leisure guests. Mediterranean-influenced cooking.

Dorset Square 🚄 🖢 ㎢ ※ ⅌ ᴠɪꜱᴀ 🐵 ᴀᴇ ①

39-40 Dorset Sq ⊠ *NW1 6QN*⊖ *Marylebone* – ℰ *(020) 7723 7874*
– *www.dorsetsquare.co.uk – reservations@dorsetsquare.co.uk – Fax (020)*
7724 3328 – Closed 1 week Christmas 17QZD**s**
37 rm – ✝£ 165/282 ✝✝£ 206/329, ☑ £14.50
Rest *The Potting Shed* – (Closed Saturday lunch and Sunday dinner) (booking essential) Menu £ 23

♦ Converted Regency townhouses in a charming square and the site of the original Lord's cricket ground. A relaxed country house in the city. Individually decorated rooms. The Potting Shed features modern cuisine and a set business menu.

Durrants 🖢 ㎢ rest, ※ ⅌ ᴕ᷍ ᴠɪꜱᴀ 🐵 ᴀᴇ

26-32 George St ⊠ *W1H 5BJ*⊖ *Bond Street* – ℰ *(020) 7935 8131*
– *www.durrantshotel.co.uk – enquiries@durrantshotel.co.uk*
– *Fax (020) 7487 3510* 29AGT**e**
89 rm – ✝£ 125 ✝✝£ 175, ☑ £14.50 – 3 suites
Rest – Menu £ 22 – Carte £ 30/43

♦ Traditional, privately owned hotel with friendly, long-standing staff. Newly refurbished bedrooms are brighter in style but still English in character. Clubby dining room for mix of British classics and lighter, European dishes.

The Mandeville 🖢 ᇯ rm, ㎢ ※ ᴕ᷍ ᴕ᷍ ᴠɪꜱᴀ 🐵 ᴀᴇ ①

Mandeville Pl ⊠ *W1U 2BE*⊖ *Bond Street* – ℰ *(020) 7935 5599*
– *www.mandeville.co.uk – info@mandeville.co.uk*
– *Fax (020) 7935 9588* 30AHT**x**
140 rm – ✝£ 340/363 ✝✝£ 363, ☑ £22.50 – 2 suites
Rest *de Ville* – (Closed Sunday) Menu £ 25 – Carte £ 37/44

♦ Fashionably located hotel, refurbished in 2005 with marbled reception and strikingly colourful bar. Stylish rooms have flatscreen TVs and make good use of the space available. Modern British cuisine served in splendid de Ville restaurant.

The Sumner without rest 🖢 ᇯ ㎢ ※ ᴕ᷍ ᴠɪꜱᴀ 🐵 ᴀᴇ ①

54 Upper Berkeley St ⊠ *W1H 7QR*⊖ *Marble Arch* – ℰ *(020) 7723 2244*
– *www.thesumner.com – hotel@thesumner.com*
– *Fax (0870) 705 8767* 29AFU**k**
20 rm ☑ – ✝£ 165 ✝✝£ 188

♦ Two Georgian terrace houses in developing area of town. Comfy, stylish sitting room; basement breakfast room. Largest bedrooms, 101 and 201, have sunny, full-length windows.

Park Plaza Sherlock Holmes London 🕅 ⅃ゟ 🖢 ㎢ ᴕ᷍ ⅏

108 Baker St ⊠ *W1U 6LJ*⊖ *Baker Street* – ℰ *(020)* ᴠɪꜱᴀ 🐵 ᴀᴇ ①
7486 6161 – www.sherlockholmeshotel.com – info@sherlockholmeshotel.com
– *Fax (020) 7958 5211* 29AGT**c**
116 rm – ✝£ 305 ✝✝£ 317, ☑ £16.50 – 3 suites
Rest – (closed Monday) Menu £ 17 – Carte £ 27/34

♦ A stylish building with a relaxed contemporary feel. Comfortable guests' lounge with Holmes pictures on the walls. Bedrooms welcoming and smart, some with wood floors. Brasserie style dining.

Hart House without rest   🛜 📶 VISA 🔵

51 Gloucester Pl ⊠ W1U 8JF⊖ Marble Arch – 𝒞 (020) 7935 2288
– www.harthouse.co.uk – reservations@harthouse.co.uk
– Fax (020) 7935 8516   29AGT**d**
15 rm ⬛ – **†**£75/125 **††**£98/135

♦ Within an attractive Georgian terrace. Run by the same family for over 35 years. Warm and welcoming service; well kept, competitively priced bedrooms over three floors.

St George without rest   🛜 📶 VISA 🔵 AE

49 Gloucester Pl ⊠ W1U 8JE⊖ Marble Arch – 𝒞 (020) 7486 8586
– www.stgeorge-hotel.net – reservations@stgeorge-hotel.net
– Fax (020) 7486 6567   29AGT**h**
19 rm ⬛ – **†**£85/105 **††**£110/125

♦ Terraced house on a busy street, usefully located within walking distance of many attractions. Offers a warm welcome and comfortable bedrooms which are spotlessly maintained.

Rhodes W1 (Restaurant) – at The Cumberland Hotel   VISA 🔵 AE
☾
Great Cumberland Place ⊠ W1H 7DL⊖ Marble Arch – 𝒞 (020) 7616 5930
– www.rhodesw1.com – restaurant@rhodesw1.com – Fax (020) 7479 3888
– Closed Christmas - New Year, 1 week August, Saturday lunch,
Sunday and Monday   29AGU**z**
Rest – French – (booking advisable) Menu £32/65 – Carte £65/83 ⬛
Spec. Crispy pork belly, langoustine, caramelised apple and vanilla. Roast pigeon, pig's trotter, navet and chutney sauce. Hot chocolate moelleux, salted chocolate mousse, crème fraîche sorbet.

♦ Just 12 tables in a warm and textured room designed by Kelly Hoppen. Influences are more European than usual for a Gary Rhodes restaurant but with the same emphasis on clear, uncluttered flavours.

Locanda Locatelli   AC VISA 🔵 AE
☾
8 Seymour St ⊠ W1H 7JZ⊖ Marble Arch – 𝒞 (020) 7935 9088
– www.locandalocatelli.com – info@locandalocatelli.com – Fax (020) 7935 1149
– Closed 25 December   29AGU**r**
Rest – Italian – Carte £41/58 ⬛
Spec. Deep fried calf's foot salad and mustard fruit. Veal with Parma ham, sage and aubergine. Tasting of "Amedei" chocolate.

♦ Forever popular restaurant serving authentic, seasonal Italian cooking of outstanding quality, complemented by a comprehensive wine list. Best tables are the corner booths.

Latium   AC VISA 🔵 AE ⓪

21 Berners St, Fitzrovia ⊠ W1T 3LP⊖ Oxford Circus – 𝒞 (020) 7323 9123
– www.latiumrestaurant.com – info@latiumrestaurant.com – Fax (020) 7323 3205
– Closed Christmas, New Year, Saturday lunch, Sunday and Bank
Holidays   31AJT**n**
Rest – Italian – Menu £20/30

♦ Welcoming restaurant owned by affable chef. Smart feel with well-spaced linen-clad tables, tiled floors and rural pictures. Italian country cooking in the heart of town.

Texture   AC VISA 🔵 AE

34 Portman Square ⊠ W1H 7BY⊖ Marble Arch – 𝒞 (020) 7224 0028
– www.texture-restaurant.co.uk – info@texture-restaurant.co.uk
– Closed 2 weeks Christmas - New Year, 2 weeks August,
Sunday and Monday   29AGU**p**
Rest – Innovative – Menu £22 – Carte £48/59 ⬛

♦ The champagne bar occupies the window space; the restaurant is in the rear. Highly skilled cooking with contrasting textures, in which the chef's Icelandic roots are evident.

LONDON

551

XX L'Autre Pied (Marcus Eaves)   AC VISA ◎ AE
⟨⟩
5-7 Blandford Street ⊠ W1U 3DB⊖ Bond Street – ℰ (020) 7486 9696
– www.lautrepied.co.uk – info@lautrepied.co.uk – Fax (020) 7486 5067
– Closed 23-29 December   30AHT**k**
Rest – Modern European – Menu £20 (lunch) – Carte £35/46 ∰
Spec. Seared foie gras, artichokes and pineapple sorbet. Saddle of rabbit,
courgette, polenta with chorizo and black olive jus. Black Forest millefeuille.
♦ A more informal sibling to Pied à Terre, with red leather seating, closely set tables
and relaxed atmosphere. But cooking is just as ambitious: it is original, creative and
technically adroit.

XX Galvin Bistrot de Luxe   AC ☜ VISA ◎ AE
⟨☺⟩
66 Baker St ⊠ W1U 7DJ⊖ Baker Street – ℰ (020) 7935 4007
– www.galvinuk.com – info@galvinuk.com – Fax (020) 7486 1735
– Closed 25-26 December and 1 January   29AGT**b**
Rest – French – Menu £16 (lunch) – Carte £24/35
♦ A modern take on the classic Gallic bistro with ceiling fans, globe lights, rich wood
panelled walls and French influenced dishes where precision and good value are
paramount.

XX Roka   AC VISA ◎ AE ①
37 Charlotte St ⊠ W1T 1RR⊖ Tottenham Court Road – ℰ (020) 7580 6464
– www.rokarestaurant.com – info@rokarestaurant.com – Fax (020) 7580 0220
– Closed 25 December and 1 January   31AJT**k**
Rest – Japanese – Carte approx. £29
♦ Striking glass and steel frontage. Airy, atmospheric interior of teak, oak and paper
wall screens. Authentic, flavoursome Japanese cuisine with variety of grill dishes.

XX Rhodes W1 Brasserie – at The Cumberland Hotel   AC VISA ◎ AE
Great Cumberland Pl ⊠ W1A 4RF⊖ Marble Arch – ℰ (020) 7616 5930
– www.garyrhodes.com – brasserie@rhodesw1.com
– Fax (020) 7479 3888   29AGU**z**
Rest – British – Carte £25/42
♦ In the heart of the Cumberland Hotel, a very stylish dining experience with im-
pressively high ceiling and classical Gary Rhodes dishes bringing out the best of the
seasons.

XX Oscar – at Charlotte Street Hotel   AC VISA ◎ AE ①
15 Charlotte St ⊠ W1T 1RJ⊖ Goodge Street – ℰ (020) 7907 4005
– www.charlottestreethotel.co.uk – charlotte@firmdale.com – Fax (020)
7806 2002 – Closed Sunday lunch   31AKT**e**
Rest – Modern European – (booking essential) Carte £31/46
♦ Bright room with busy bar at the front and dominated by a large, vivid mural. Sunny Mediterranean-influenced dishes, served by attentive staff.

XX The Providores   AC VISA ◎ AE
109 Marylebone High St ⊠ W1U 4RX⊖ Bond Street – ℰ (020) 7935 6175
– www.theprovidores.co.uk – anyone@theprovidores.co.uk – Fax (020) 7935 6877
– Closed 25-26 December and 1-2 January   30AHT**y**
Rest – Innovative – Menu £44 (dinner) – Carte £19/61
♦ Packed ground floor for tapas; upstairs for innovative fusion cooking, with spices
and ingredients from around the world, including Australasia. Starter-size dishes at
dinner allow for greater choice.

XX La Porte des Indes   AC ⇔ VISA ◎ AE ①
32 Bryanston St ⊠ W1H 7EG⊖ Marble Arch – ℰ (020) 7224 0055
– www.laportedesindes.com – london.reservation@laportedesindes.com
– Fax (020) 7224 1144 – Closed 25-26 December, 1 January and Saturday 29AGU**s**
Rest – Indian – Menu £15/28 – Carte £27/42
♦ Don't be fooled by the discreet entrance: inside there is a spectacularly unrestrained display of palm trees, murals and waterfalls. French influenced Indian cuisine.

XX Ozer

AC 🦃 VISA 🚳 AE ①

4-5 Langham Pl, Regent St ⊠ W1B 3DG⊖ Oxford Circus – ℰ (020) 7323 0505
– www.sofra.co.uk – info@sofra.co.uk – Fax (020) 7323 0111
30AITz

Rest – Turkish – Menu £ 21 – Carte £ 17/25

♦ Behind the busy and vibrantly decorated bar you'll find a smart modern restaurant. Lively atmosphere and efficient service of modern, light and aromatic Turkish cooking.

XX Rasa Samudra

VISA 🚳 AE

5 Charlotte St ⊠ W1T 1RE⊖ Goodge Street – ℰ (020) 7637 0222
– www.rasarestaurants.com – Fax (020) 7637 0224 – Closed 24 December-
1 January and lunch Sunday and Bank Holidays
31AKTr

Rest – Indian – Menu £ 23/30 – Carte £ 13/24

♦ Comfortably appointed, richly decorated Indian restaurant with silks and ornaments. Back room more inviting. Authentic Keralan seafood and vegetarian specialities.

XX Levant

AC VISA 🚳 AE ①

Jason Court, 76 Wigmore St ⊠ W1U 2SJ⊖ Bond Street – ℰ (020) 7224 1111
– www.levant.co.uk – reservations@levant.co.uk
– Fax (020) 7486 1216
30AHTc

Rest – Lebanese – Menu £ 37 (dinner) – Carte £ 35/40

♦ Belly dancing, lanterns and a low slung bar all add up to an exotic dining experience. The Lebanese food is satisfying and authentic, carefully prepared and ideal for sharing in groups.

XX Caldesi

AC ⇔ VISA 🚳 AE

15-17 Marylebone Lane ⊠ W1U 2NE⊖ Bond Street – ℰ (020) 7935 9226
– www.caldesi.com – tuscan@caldesi.com – Fax (020) 7935 9228
– Closed Saturday lunch, Sunday and Bank Holidays
30AHTe

Rest – Italian – Carte approx. £ 53

♦ A traditional Italian restaurant that continues to attract a loyal clientele. Robust and authentic dishes with Tuscan specialities. Attentive service by established team.

XX Villandry

AC VISA 🚳 AE ①

170 Great Portland St ⊠ W1W 5QB⊖ Regent's Park – ℰ (020) 7631 3131
– www.villandry.com – contactus@villandry.com – Fax (020) 7631 3030
– Closed 25-26 and 31 December, 1 January and Sunday dinner
30AITs

Rest – French – Menu £ 30/35 – Carte £ 27/43

♦ The senses are heightened by passing through the well-stocked deli to the dining room behind. Bare walls, wooden tables and a menu offering simple, tasty dishes.

XX L'Aventure

🍴 VISA 🚳 AE

3 Blenheim Terrace ⊠ NW8 0EH⊖ St John's Wood – ℰ (020) 7624 6232
– Fax (020) 7625 5548 – Closed 2 weeks August, 1 week January, Saturday lunch,
Sunday and Bank Holidays
11PZBb

Rest – French – Menu £ 19/35

♦ Behind the pretty tree lined entrance you'll find a charming neighbourhood restaurant. Relaxed atmosphere and service by personable owner. Authentic French cuisine.

XX Phoenix Palace

AC ⇔ VISA 🚳 AE

3-5 Glentworth St ⊠ NW1 5PG⊖ Baker Street – ℰ (020) 7486 3515
– www.phoenixpalace.uk.com – info@phoenixpalace.uk.com
– Fax (020) 7486 3401
17QZDx

Rest – Chinese – Menu £ 25 (dinner) – Carte approx. £ 20

♦ Tucked away near Baker Street; lots of photos of celebrities who've eaten here. Huge room for 200 diners where authentic, fresh, well prepared Chinese dishes are served.

LONDON

XX Osteria Stecca
🛆 AC VISA ☻☻ AE ①

1 Blenheim Terrace ⊠ NW8 0EH⊖ St John's Wood – ℰ (020) 7328 5014
– www.osteriastecca.com – info@osteriastecca.com
– Closed Monday lunch 11PZB**z**
Rest – Italian – Menu £16 (lunch) – Carte dinner approx. £40
♦ Terrace, conservatory and brilliant white walls ensure a bright atmosphere. Reopened in 2008, with a former chef back as owner. Undemanding menu of fully garnished dishes covers all parts of Italy.

X Michael Moore
⟷ VISA ☻☻ AE ①

19 Blandford St ⊠ W1U 3DH⊖ Baker Street – ℰ (020) 7224 1898
– www.michaelmoorerestaurant.com – info@michaelmoorerestaurant.com
– Fax (020) 7224 0970 – Closed Christmas-New Year, Saturday lunch,
Sunday and Bank Holidays 29AGT**r**
Rest – International – Menu £19 (lunch) – Carte £33/49
♦ Warm glow emanates not just from mustard façade but also effusive welcome within. Cosy, locally renowned favourite, with global cuisine served by friendly, efficient staff.

X The Wallace
VISA ☻☻ AE

Hertford House, Manchester Sq ⊠ W1U 3BN⊖ Bond St – ℰ (020) 7563 9505
– www.thewallacerestaurant.com – reservations@thewallacerestaurant.com
– Closed 25 December 29AGT**k**
Rest – French – (lunch only and dinner Friday-Saturday) Menu £25
– Carte £30/41
♦ Situated in the Wallace Collection's delightful glass-roofed courtyard, divided by Japanese maple trees. Comprehensive selection of classic French fare; terrines a speciality.

X Union Café
AC VISA ☻☻ AE

96 Marylebone Lane ⊠ W1U 2QA⊖ Bond Street – ℰ (020) 7486 4860
– www.brinkleys.com – Fax (020) 7935 1537
– Closed Sunday dinner and Bank Holidays 30AHT**d**
Rest – International – Carte £31/38
♦ A quasi-industrial feel, with exposed ducts, open kitchen and bustling atmosphere. Menu full of global influences, so expect anything from dim sum to risotto, burgers to pork belly.

X Caffé Caldesi
AC VISA ☻☻ AE

1st Floor, 118 Marylebone Lane ⊠ W1U 2QF⊖ Bond Street – ℰ (020) 7935 1144
– www.caldesi.com – caffe@caldesi.com – Fax (020) 7935 8832
– Closed Sunday dinner 30AHT**s**
Rest – Italian – Carte £21/42
♦ Converted pub with a simple modern interior in which to enjoy tasty, uncomplicated Italian dishes. Downstairs is a lively bar with a deli counter serving pizzas and pastas.

X Dinings
VISA ☻☻ AE ①

22 Harcourt St. ⊠ W1H 4HH⊖ Marylebone – ℰ (020) 7723 0666 – Fax (020)
7723 3222 – Closed Sunday and Bank Holidays 29AFT**c**
Rest – Japanese – (booking essential) Carte £24/62
♦ Resembles an after-work Japanese izakaya, or pub, with chummy atmosphere and loud music. Food is a mix of small plates of delicate dishes; a mix of modern and more traditional.

X Chada Chada
AC VISA ☻☻ AE ①

16-17 Picton Pl ⊠ W1U 1BP⊖ Bond Street – ℰ (020) 7935 8212
– www.chadathai.com – enquiry@chadathai.com – Fax (020) 7924 2791
– Closed Sunday and Bank Holidays 30AHU**b**
Rest – Thai – Menu £14 (lunch) – Carte approx. £37
♦ Authentic and fragrant Thai cooking; the good value menu offers some interesting departures from the norm. Service is eager to please in the compact and cosy rooms.

The Salt House

63 Abbey Road, St John's Wood ✉ NW8 0AE ⊖ St John's Wood.
– ✆ (020) 7328 6626 – www.thesalthouse.co.uk
– salthousemail@majol.co.uk 11OZB**a**

Rest – Carte £ 20/36

◆ Grand Victorian pub appearance in bottle green. Busy bar at the front; main dining room, in calm duck egg blue, to the rear. Modern menus boast a distinct Mediterranean style.

Queen's Head & Artichoke

30-32 Albany St ✉ NW1 4EA ⊖ Great Portland Street. – ✆ (020) 7916 6206
– www.theartichoke.net – info@theartichoke.net 18RZD**b**

Rest – Carte £ 19/25

◆ Busy, wood-panelled bar and eccentrially-styled upstairs restaurant. Modern, European influenced food mixed with a large selection of all-day international 'tapas.'

LONDON

St James's – Greater London – ✉ NW1/W1/SW1

The Ritz

150 Piccadilly ✉ W1J 9BR ⊖ Green Park – ✆ (020) 7493 8181
– www.theritzlondon.com – enquire@theritzlondon.com
– Fax (020) 7493 2687 30AIV**c**

116 rm – †£ 294/552 ††£ 458/552, ☕ £30 – 17 suites

Rest *The Ritz Restaurant* – see restaurant listing

◆ Opened 1906, a fine example of Louis XVI architecture and decoration. Elegant Palm Court famed for afternoon tea. Many of the lavishly appointed rooms overlook the park.

Sofitel St James London

6 Waterloo Pl ✉ SW1Y 4AN ⊖ Piccadilly Circus – ✆ (020) 7747 2200
– www.sofitelstjames.com – H3144@accor.com
– Fax (020) 7747 2210 31AKV**a**

179 rm – †£ 382/441 ††£ 441, ☕ £21 – 6 suites

Rest *Brasserie Roux* – see restaurant listing

◆ Grade II listed building in smart Pall Mall location. Classically English interiors include floral Rose Lounge and club-style St. James bar. Comfortable, well-fitted bedrooms.

Haymarket

rm,

1 Suffolk Place ✉ SW1Y 4BP ⊖ Piccadilly Circus – ✆ (020) 7470 4000
– www.haymarkethotel.com – haymarket@firmdale.com
– Fax (020) 7470 4004 31AKV**d**

47 rm – †£ 294 ††£ 382, ☕ £18.50 – 3 suites

Rest *Brumus* – ✆ (020) 7451 1012 – Carte £ 25/45

◆ Smart, spacious hotel in John Nash Regency building, with stylish blend of modern and antique furnishings. Large, comfortable bedrooms in soothing colours. Impressive pool. Brumus bar and restaurant puts focus on Italian cooking.

Stafford

16-18 St James's Pl ✉ SW1A 1NJ ⊖ Green Park – ✆ (020) 7493 0111
– www.thestaffordhotel.co.uk – information@thestaffordhotel.co.uk
– Fax (020) 7493 7121 30AIV**u**

73 rm – †£ 353/494 ††£ 623/682, ☕ £24 – 32 suites

Rest – (Closed Saturday lunch) Menu £ 30 (lunch) **s** – Carte dinner £ 28/62 **s**

◆ A genteel atmosphere prevails in this discreet country house in the city. Bedrooms divided between main house, converted 18C stables and newer Mews. Refined, elegant, intimate dining room.

LONDON

Dukes 🕭

      🌿 🖫 AC 🛇 🖤 ℥ VISA ⓜ AE ①

35 St James's Pl ⊠ SW1A 1NY⊖ Green Park – 𝒞 (020) 7491 4840
– www.dukeshotel.com – bookings@dukeshotel.com
– Fax (020) 7493 1264
                                           30AIV**f**
83 rm – ♦£282/376 ♦♦£323/417, ⚏ £22 – 7 suites
Rest – Menu £18/28 – Carte £29/41

♦ Refurbished fully in 2008 but still retaining that discreet, traditionally British quality. Central but quiet location. Dukes bar famous for its martinis. Elegant bedrooms with country house feel. Discreet dining room.

St James's Hotel and Club 🕭

      🖫 AC 🛇 🖤 ℥ VISA ⓜ AE

7-8 Park Place ⊠ SW1A 1LP⊖ Green Park – 𝒞 (020) 7725 0274
– www.stjameshotelandclub.com – reservation@stjameshotelandclub.com
– Fax (020) 7725 0301
                                           30AIV**k**
50 rm – ♦£288/405 ♦♦£347/441, ⚏ £26 – 10 suites
Rest *Andaman by Dieter Müller* – (booking essential) Menu £55
– Carte £41/60

♦ 1890s house in cul-de-sac, formerly a private club, reopened as a hotel in 2008. Modern, boutique–style interior with over 400 paintings. Fine finish to compact, but well-equipped bedrooms. Small restaurant blends with bar; original and ambitious tasting plates.

22 Jermyn Street without rest

      🖫 AC 🖤 VISA ⓜ AE ①

22 Jermyn St ⊠ SW1Y 6HL⊖ Piccadilly Circus – 𝒞 (020) 7734 2353
– www.22jermyn.com – office@22jermyn.com – Fax (020) 7734 0750   31AKV**e**
5 rm – ♦£259 ♦♦£259 – 14 suites

♦ Exclusive boutique hotel with entrance amid famous shirt-makers' shops. Stylishly decorated bedrooms more than compensate for the lack of lounge space. Room service available.

The Ritz Restaurant – at The Ritz Hotel

      🖭 AC VISA ⓜ AE ①

150 Piccadilly ⊠ W1J 9BR⊖ Green Park – 𝒞 (020) 7493 8181
– www.theritzlondon.com – enquire@theritzlondon.com
– Fax (020) 7493 2687
                                           30AIV**c**
Rest – Traditional – Menu £36/45 – Carte £46/88 **s**

♦ The height of opulence: magnificent Louis XVI décor with trompe l'oeil and ornate gilding. Delightful terrace over Green Park. Refined service, classic and modern menu.

The Wolseley

      AC VISA ⓜ AE ①

160 Piccadilly ⊠ W1J 9EB⊖ Green Park – 𝒞 (020) 7499 6996
– www.thewolseley.com – Fax (020) 7499 6888 – Closed 25 December,
1 January, August Bank Holiday and dinner 24 and 31 December
                                         30AIV**q**
Rest – Modern European – (booking essential) Carte £26/53

♦ Has the feel of a grand European coffee house: pillars, high vaulted ceiling, mezzanine tables. Menus range from caviar to a hot dog. Also open for breakfast and tea.

Sake No Hana

      AC ⇔ VISA ⓜ AE

23 St James's St ⊠ SW1A 1HA⊖ Green Park – 𝒞 (020) 7925 8988
– www.sakenohana.com – reservations@sakenohana.com – Fax (020) 7925 8999
– Closed 24-25 December
                                         30AIV**n**
Rest – Japanese – Carte £20/85

♦ Reached via elevator, a stylish room with striking cedar wood décor. 8 page menu mixes new-style Japanese with more traditional kaiseki, with sharing the best option. Large sake list and separate sushi bar.

St Alban

      AC ℥ VISA ⓜ AE ①

4-12 Regent St ⊠ SW1Y 4PE⊖ Piccadilly Circus – 𝒞 (020) 7499 8558
– www.stalban.net – info@stalban.net – Fax (020) 7499 6888
– Closed 25-26 December and 1 January
                                         31AKV**c**
Rest – Mediterranean – Menu £20 (lunch weekends) – Carte £22/39

♦ Light, airy restaurant with colourful booth seating and feeling of space. Weekly-changing southern European menu; specialities from the wood-fired oven and charcoal grill.

XXX **Luciano**   AC ✦ VISA ⓪ AE
72-73 St James's St ⊠ *SW1A 1PH*⊖ *Green Park –* ℰ *(020) 7408 1440*
– www.lucianorestaurant.co.uk – info@lucianorestaurant.co.uk – Fax (020)
7493 6670 – Closed 25-26 December and Sunday   30AIV**m**
Rest – Italian – Menu £22 (lunch) – Carte £30/46
♦ Art Deco, David Collins styled bar leads to restaurant sympathetic to its early 19C
heritage. Mix of Italian and English dishes cooked in rustic, wholesome and earthy
manner.

XX **Le Caprice**   AC VISA ⓪ AE ⓪
Arlington House, Arlington St ⊠ *SW1A 1RJ*⊖ *Green Park –* ℰ *(020) 7629 2239*
– www.le-caprice.co.uk – reservation@le-caprice.co.uk – Fax (020) 7493 9040
– Closed 24-26 December, 1 January and 31 August   30AIV**h**
Rest – Modern European – (Sunday brunch) Carte £37/50
♦ Still attracting a fashionable clientele and as busy as ever. Dine at the bar or in the
smoothly run restaurant. Food combines timeless classics with modern dishes.

XX **Quaglino's**   AC 🕾 ✦ VISA ⓪ AE ⓪
16 Bury St ⊠ *SW1Y 6AL* ⊖ *Green Park –* ℰ *(020) 7930 6767*
– www.quaglinos.co.uk – quags-res@danddlondon.com – Fax (020) 7930 2732
– Closed 25-26 December   30AIV**j**
Rest – Modern European – (booking essential) Menu £20 (lunch)
– Carte £25/46
♦ Descend the sweeping staircase into the capacious room where a busy and buzzy
atmosphere prevails. Watch the chefs prepare everything from osso bucco to fish and
chips.

XX **Mint Leaf**   AC 🕾 VISA ⓪ AE ⓪
Suffolk Pl ⊠ *SW1Y 4HX*⊖ *Piccadilly Circus –* ℰ *(020) 7930 9020*
– www.mintleafrestaurant.com – reservations@mintleafrestaurant.com
– Fax (020) 7930 6205 – Closed Saturday lunch and Sunday   31AKV**k**
Rest – Indian – Carte £27/37
♦ Basement restaurant in theatreland. Cavernous dining room incorporating busy,
trendy bar with unique cocktail list and loud music. Helpful service. Contemporary
Indian dishes.

XX **Brasserie St Jacques**   AC ✦ VISA ⓪ AE ⓪
33 St James's Street ⊠ *SW1A 1HD*⊖ *Green Park –* ℰ *(020) 7839 1007*   ℮
– www.brasseriestjacques.co.uk – info@brasseriestjacques.co.uk – Fax (020)
7839 3204 – Closed Christmas and New Year   30AIV**z**
Rest – French – Carte £26/38
♦ With its high ceiling and narrow layout, it may lack the buzz one finds in a typical
French brasserie, but is nearer the mark with a menu that features all the classic
brasserie favourites.

XX **Franco's**   AC 🕾 VISA ⓪ AE
61 Jermyn St ⊠ *SW1Y 6LX*⊖ *Green Park –* ℰ *(020) 7499 2211*
– www.francoslondon.com – reserve@francoslondon.com – Fax (020) 7495 1375
– Closed Christmas- New Year and Sunday   30AIV**d**
Rest – Italian – (booking essential) Menu £30 (lunch) – Carte £34/49
♦ Great all-day menu at 'the café'. Further in, regulars have taken to smart refurbishment. Classic/modern Italian cooking allows bold but refined flavours to shine
through.

XX **The Avenue**   AC 🕾 VISA ⓪ AE ⓪
7-9 St James's St ⊠ *SW1A 1EE*⊖ *Green Park –* ℰ *(020) 7321 2111*
– www.theavenue-restaurant.co.uk – avenuereservations@danddlondon.com
– Fax (020) 7321 2500
– Closed 25-26 December, Saturday lunch and Sunday   30AIV**y**
Rest – Modern European – Menu £23 – Carte £20/43
♦ The attractive and stylish bar is a local favourite. Behind is a striking, modern and
busy restaurant. Appealing and contemporary food. Pre-theatre menu available.

LONDON

Matsuri - St James's   `AC` `E&` `⇄` `VISA` `OO` `AE` `O`
15 Bury St ✉ *SW1Y 6AL* ⊖ *Green Park* – ✆ *(020) 7839 1101*
– www.matsuri-restaurant.com – dine@matsuri-restaurant.com – Fax (020)
79307010 – Closed Christmas and New Year   30AIV**w**
Rest – Japanese – Carte £28/60

♦ Specialising in theatrical and precise teppan-yaki cooking. Separate restaurant offers sushi delicacies. Charming service by traditionally dressed staff.

Noura Central   `AC` `VISA` `OO` `AE` `O`
22 Lower Regent St ✉ *SW1Y 4UJ* ⊖ *Piccadilly Circus* – ✆ *(020) 7839 2020*
– www.noura.co.uk – nouracentral@noura.co.uk
– Fax (020) 7839 7700   31AKV**d**
Rest – Lebanese – Menu £18/40 – Carte £20/39

♦ Eye-catching Lebanese façade, matched by sleek interior design. Buzzy atmosphere enhanced by amplified background music. Large menus cover all aspects of Lebanese cuisine.

Brasserie Roux   `AC` `E&` `VISA` `OO` `AE` `O`
8 Pall Mall ✉ *SW1Y 5NG* ⊖ *Piccadilly Circus* – ✆ *(020) 7968 2900*
– www.sofitelstjames.com – h3144@accor.com
– Fax (020) 7747 2251   31AKV**a**
Rest – French – Menu £20 – Carte £32/55

♦ Informal, smart, classic brasserie style with large windows making the most of the location. Large menu of French classics with many daily specials; comprehensive wine list.

Al Duca   `AC` `E&` `VISA` `OO` `AE` `O`
4-5 Duke of York St ✉ *SW1Y 6LA* ⊖ *Piccadilly Circus* – ✆ *(020) 7839 3090*
– www.alduca-restaurant.co.uk – info@alduca-restaurants.co.uk – Fax (020)
78394050 – Closed Christmas, New Year, Sunday and Bank Holidays   31AJV**r**
Rest – Italian – Menu £27/28

♦ Relaxed, modern, stylish restaurant. Friendly and approachable service of robust and rustic Italian dishes. Set priced menu is good value. ✓

Inn the Park   `⇐` `🍴` `VISA` `OO` `AE`
St James's Park ✉ *SW1A 2BJ* ⊖ *Charing Cross* – ✆ *(020) 7451 9999*
– www.innthepark.com – info@innthepark.com – Fax (020) 7451 9998
– Closed 25 December and dinner January-February and
October-November   31AKV**n**
Rest – British – Carte £28/32

♦ Eco-friendly restaurant with grass covered roof; pleasant views across park and lakes. Super-heated dining terrace. Modern British menus of tasty, wholesome dishes.

Portrait   `⇐` `AC` `E&` `VISA` `OO` `AE`
3rd Floor, National Portrait Gallery, St Martin's Pl ✉ *WC2H 0HE* ⊖ *Charing Cross*
– ✆ (020) 7312 2490 – www.searcys.co.uk – portrait.restaurant@searcys.co.uk
– Fax (020) 7925 0244 – Closed 25-26 December   31ALV**n**
Rest – Modern European – (lunch only and dinner Thursday and Friday)
(booking essential) Carte £23/32

♦ On the top floor of National Portrait Gallery with rooftop local landmark views: a charming spot for lunch. Modern British/European dishes; weekend brunch.

The National Dining Rooms   `AC` `VISA` `OO` `AE`
Sainsbury Wing, The National Gallery, Trafalgar Sq ✉ *WC2N 5DN* ⊖ *Charing*
Cross – ✆ *(020) 7747 2525 – www.thenationaldiningrooms.co.uk*
– enquiries@thenationaldiningrooms.co.uk – Closed Christmas   31AKV**b**
Rest – British – (lunch only and dinner Wednesday) Carte £28/45

♦ Set on the East Wing's first floor, you can tuck into cakes in the bakery or grab a prime corner table in the restaurant for great views and proudly seasonal British menus.

Soho – Greater London – ⊠ **W1/WC2**

🏠🏠🏠 **The Soho** 🛏️ 🖃 🕭 rm, AC ⚡ 📶 🐾 VISA ⓜⓞ AE ⓘ
4 Richmond Mews ⊠ W1D 3DH⊖ Tottenham Court Road – ℰ (020) 7559 3000
– www.sohohotel.com – soho@firmdale.com – Fax (020) 7559 3003   31AKU**n**
89 rm – ♦£329 ♦♦£411, � £18.50 – 2 suites
Rest *Refuel* – Carte £23/34
♦ Opened in autumn 2004: stylish hotel with two screening rooms, comfy drawing
room and up-to-the-minute bedrooms, some vivid, others more muted, all boasting
hi-tec extras. Contemporary bar and restaurant.

🏠🏠🏠 **Courthouse Kempinski** 🖻 🍴 🛏️ 🖃 🕭 rm, AC 📶 🐾 VISA ⓜⓞ AE ⓘ
19-21 Great Marlborough St ⊠ W1F 7HL⊖ Oxford Circus – ℰ (020) 7297 5555
– www.courthouse-hotel.com – info@courthouse-hotel.com
– Fax (020) 7297 5566   30AIU**z**
108 rm – ♦£235/353 ♦♦£235/470, � £22.50 – 4 suites
Rest *Silk* – see restaurant listing
Rest *The Carnaby* – Menu £15/20 – Carte £19/25
♦ Striking Grade II listed ex magistrates' court: interior fused imaginatively with original features; for example, the bar incorporates three former cells. Stylish rooms. Informal Carnaby offers extensive French, modern and British menu.

🏠 **Hazlitt's** without rest AC 📶 VISA ⓜⓞ AE ⓘ
6 Frith St ⊠ W1D 3JA⊖ Tottenham Court Road – ℰ (020) 7434 1771
– www.hazlittshotel.com – reservations@hazlitts.co.uk – Fax (020) 7439 1524
– Closed 25-26 December   31AKU**u**
29 rm – ♦£206/259 ♦♦£259, � £10.95 – 1 suite
♦ A row of three adjoining early 18C town houses and former home of the eponymous essayist. Individual and charming bedrooms, many with antique furniture and
Victorian baths.

XXX **Quo Vadis** AC ⇔ VISA ⓜⓞ AE
26-29 Dean St ⊠ W1D 3LL⊖ Tottenham Court Road – ℰ (020) 7437 9585
– www.quovadis.co.uk – info@quovadissoho.co.uk – Fax (020) 7734 7593
– Closed Christmas and Sunday   31AKU**v**
Rest – British – Menu £18 (lunch) – Carte £27/54
♦ A Soho institution re-launched in 2008. Striking façade matched by a refreshed and
comfortable Art Deco inspired interior. Appealing and extensive menu in the style of
classic British Grill restaurants.

XXX **Richard Corrigan at Lindsay House** AC 🍴 ⇔ VISA ⓜⓞ AE ⓘ
❀ 21 Romilly St ⊠ W1D 5AF⊖ Leicester Square – ℰ (020) 7439 0450
– www.lindsayhouse.co.uk – richardcorrigan@lindsayhouse.co.uk – Fax (020)
7437 7349 – Closed 24-27 December and Sunday   31AKU**f**
Rest – Modern European – Menu £59
Spec. Carpaccio of octopus and scallop with orange purée. Roast loin of venison, pickled red cabbage, bacon and onion. Rhubarb mousse, ginger sablé
and horseradish ice cream.
♦ Handsome four storey house; ring the doorbell before being welcomed into one of
two cosy, fabric-clad dining rooms. Modern, confidently-presented cooking boasts
bold flavours.

XXX **L'Escargot** AC 🍴 ⇔ VISA ⓜⓞ AE ⓘ
48 Greek St ⊠ W1D 4EF⊖ Tottenham Court Road – ℰ (020) 7437 2679
– www.lescargotrestaurant.co.uk – sales@whitestarline.org.uk
– Fax (020) 7437 0790   31AKU**b**
Rest – French – (Closed 25-26 December, 1 January, Sunday and Saturday
lunch) Menu £18 (lunch) – Carte £30/33
Rest *Picasso Room* – French – (Closed August, 25-26 December,
1 January, Saturday lunch, Sunday and Monday) Menu £26/48
♦ Soho institution. Ground Floor is vibrant brasserie with early-evening buzz of thea-
tre-goers and classic dishes. Intimate and more formal upstairs Picasso Room, with
more elaborate cooking.

LONDON

XXX **Red Fort**   AC 🐾 VISA ⓪ AE

77 Dean St ✉ W1D 3SH⊖ Tottenham Court Road – ℰ (020) 7437 2525
– www.redfort.co.uk – info@redfort.co.uk – Fax (020) 7434 0721 – Closed lunch
Saturday, Sunday and Bank Holidays   31AKU**x**
Rest – Indian – Menu £ 25/35 – Carte £ 26/46
♦ Smart, stylish restaurant with modern water feature and glass ceiling to rear. Seasonally changing menus of authentic dishes handed down over generations.

XX **Aaya**   AC VISA ⓪ AE

66 Brewer St ✉ W1F 9TR⊖ Piccadilly Circus – ℰ (0207) 319 38 88
– info@aaya.com – Fax (0207) 319 38 89 – Closed 25 December   30AJU**h**
Rest – Japanese – Carte £ 25/60
♦ Big, glitzy and very stylish Japanese restaurant, opened in 2008. Long, mesmerising bar and extended basement sushi counter. Sushi and sashimi the strengths of the varied, if pricey, menu.

XX **Floridita**   AC ⬦ VISA ⓪ AE ⓿

100 Wardour St ✉ W1F 0TN⊖ Tottenham Court Road – ℰ (020) 7314 4000
– www.floriditalondon.com – Fax (020) 7314 4040
– Closed 24-26 December, 1 January and Sunday   31AKU**z**
Rest – Latin American – (dinner only and lunch mid November-December) Carte £ 45/62
♦ Mediterranean tapas on the ground floor; the huge downstairs for live music, dancing and Latin American specialities, from Cuban spice to Argentinean beef. Great cocktails and a party atmosphere.

XX **Alastair Little**   AC ⬦ VISA ⓪ AE ⓿

49 Frith St ✉ W1D 5SG⊖ Tottenham Court Road – ℰ (020) 7734 5183
– Fax (020) 7734 5206 – Closed Sunday and Bank Holidays   31AKU**y**
Rest – Modern European – (booking essential) Menu £ 23/40
♦ The eponymous owner was at the vanguard of Soho's culinary renaissance. Tasty, daily changing British based cuisine; the compact room is rustic and simple.

XX **Yauatcha**   AC VISA ⓪ AE

❀ *15 Broadwick St ✉ W1F 0DL⊖ Tottenham Court Road – ℰ (020) 7494 8888*
– mail@yauatcha.com – Fax (020) 7494 8889 – Closed 24-25 December   31AJU**k**
Rest – Chinese – Carte £ 20/78
Spec. Chilean sea bass mooli roll. Crispy aromatic duck with Thai spring onion and cucumber. Coconut soufflé with lime sorbet.
♦ Choose between darker, more atmospheric basement or lighter, brighter ground floor. Refined and delicate modern Chinese dim sum served on both levels; ideal for sharing.

XX **Haozhan**   AC VISA ⓪ AE

8 Gerrard St ✉ W1D 5PJ⊖ Leicester Square – ℰ (0207) 434 38 38
– www.haozhan.co.uk – info@haozhan.co.uk – Fax (0207) 434 99 91   31AKU**k**
Rest – Chinese – Menu £ 11 (lunch) – Carte £ 17/33
♦ It bucks the trend of Chinatown mediocrity by offering well-judged, original and balanced Cantonese dishes, with Taiwanese and Malaysian specialities. Contemporary, stylish décor and helpful service.

XX **Silk** – at Courthouse Kempinski Hotel   AC VISA ⓪ AE

19-21 Great Marlborough St ✉ W1F 7HL⊖ Oxford Circus – ℰ (020) 7297 5567
– www.courthouse-hotel.com – info@courthouse-hotel.com – Fax (020)
7297 5599 – Closed 22 December-1 January, Sunday and Monday   30AIU**z**
Rest – International – (dinner only) Menu £ 25 – Carte £ 23/38
♦ Former magistrate's court with original panelling. Menu follows the journey of the Silk Route: this translates as mostly Indian flavours with some Thai; desserts more European.

XX Café Lazeez `AC VISA MC AE ①`
21 Dean St ⊠ W1D 3TN⊖ Tottenham Court Road – ℰ (020) 7434 9393
– www.lazeez.sohocom – reservations@lazeezsoho.com – Fax (020) 7434 0022
– Closed Sunday 31AKU**d**
Rest – Indian – Carte £ 27/35
♦ In the same building as Soho Theatre; the bar hums before shows, restaurant is popular for pre- and post-theatre meals of modern Indian fare. Refined décor; private booths.

XX Benja `AC VISA MC AE`
17 Beak St ⊠ W1F 9RW⊖ Oxford Circus – ℰ (020) 7287 0555
– www.benjarestaurant.com – info@krua.co.uk – Fax (020) 7287 0056 – Closed 24-25 December and Sunday 31AIU**i**
Rest – Thai – Carte approx. £ 34
♦ Soho townhouse, seductively and colourfully styled; first floor is the most appealing. Go for the interesting and unusual specialities in among the more familiar classics.

XX Vasco and Piero's Pavilion `AC VISA MC AE ①`
15 Poland St ⊠ W1F 8QE⊖ Tottenham Court Road – ℰ (020) 7437 8774
– www.vascosfood.com – eat@vascosfood.com – Fax (020) 7437 0467 – Closed Saturday lunch, Sunday and Bank Holidays 31AJU**b**
Rest – Italian – (booking essential at lunch) Menu £ 30 (dinner) – Carte lunch £ 29/38
♦ A long standing, family run Italian restaurant with a loyal local following. Pleasant service under the owners' guidance. Warm décor and traditional cooking.

XX La Trouvaille `VISA MC AE`
12A Newburgh St ⊠ W1F 7RR⊖ Oxford Circus – ℰ (020) 7287 8488
– www.latrouvaille.co.uk – Fax (020) 7434 4170 – Closed 25 December, Sunday and Bank Holidays 30AIU**g**
Rest – French – Menu £ 20/35
♦ Atmospheric restaurant located just off Carnaby Street. Hearty, robust French cooking with a rustic character. French wine list with the emphasis on southern regions.

XX Stanza `AC VISA MC AE ①`
97-107 Shaftesbury Ave ⊠ W1D 5DY⊖ Leicester Square – ℰ (020) 7494 3020
– www.stanzalondon.com – reception@stanzalondon.com – Fax (020) 7494 3050
– Closed Saturday lunch and Sunday 31AKU**m**
Rest – Modern European – Menu £ 14 (lunch) – Carte £ 28/64
♦ On the first floor in the heart of theatre-land, with a large and glitzy bar attached. Good value pre-theatre menu; à la carte name-checks key suppliers and kitchen displays a degree of originality.

X Arbutus (Anthony Demetre) `AC VISA MC AE`
63-64 Frith St ⊠ W1D 3JW⊖ Tottenham Court Road – ℰ (020) 7734 4545
– www.arbutusrestaurant.co.uk – info@arbutusrestaurant.co.uk – Fax (020) 7287 8624 – Closed 25-26 December and 1 January 31AKU**n**
Rest – Modern European – Menu £ 16 (lunch) – Carte £ 31/36
Spec. Smoked eel, beetroot and horseradish cream. Saddle of rabbit, cottage pie and peas. Doughnuts, pistachio, honey and lemon thyme ice cream.
♦ Dining room and bar that's bright and stylish without trying too hard. Bistro classics turned on their head: poised, carefully crafted cooking - but dishes still pack a punch.

X Dehesa `AC VISA MC AE`
25 Ganton St ⊠ W1F 9BP⊖ Oxford Circus – ℰ (020) 7494 4170
– www.dehesa.co.uk – info@dehesa.co.uk – Fax (020) 7494 4175
– Closed 1 week Christmas and Sunday dinner 30AIU**i**
Rest – Mediterranean – Carte £ 20/40
♦ Repeats the success of its sister restaurant, Salt Yard, by offering tasty, good value Spanish and Italian tapas. Unhurried atmosphere in appealing corner location. Terrific drinks list too.

LONDON

☆ **Cafe Boheme**   🚗 🅴🅶 *VISA* 🅼🅾 🅰🅴
13 Old Compton St ⊠ W1D 5GQ⊖ Leicester Square – ℰ (020) 7734 0623
– www.cafeboheme.co.uk – info@cafeboheme.co.uk – Fax (020) 7434 3775
– Closed 25 December   31AKU**t**
Rest – French – Carte £ 24/36
♦ Expect classic Gallic comfort-food and a zinc-topped bar surrounded by wine
drinkers. Remade as a Parisian brasserie in 2008, ideal for pre/post theatre meals.
Open from dawn to the wee small hours.

☆ **Bar Shu**   🅰🅒 ⟷ *VISA* 🅼🅾 🅰🅴
28 Frith St ⊠ W1D 5LF⊖ Leicester Square – ℰ (020) 7287 8822 – Fax (020)
7287 8858 – Closed 25-26 December   31AKU**g**
Rest – Chinese – (booking advisable) Carte £ 20/25
♦ The fiery flavours of authentic Sichuan cooking are the draw here; dishes have
some unusual names but help is at hand as menu has pictures. Best atmosphere is on
the ground floor.

☆ **Chinese Experience**   🅰🅒 *VISA* 🅼🅾
118 Shaftesbury Ave ⊠ W1D 5EP⊖ Leicester Square – ℰ (020) 7437 0377
– www.chineseexperience.com – info@chineseexperience.com
– Closed 25 December   31AKU**r**
Rest – Chinese – Menu £ 15 – Carte approx. £ 19
♦ Bright, buzzy restaurant: sit at long bench or chunky wood tables. Large, sensibly
priced menus with a wide range of Chinese dishes; good dim sum. Knowledgable
service.

☆ **Imli**   🅰🅒 *VISA* 🅼🅾 🅰🅴 🅞
167-169 Wardour St ⊠ W1F 8WR⊖ Tottenham Court Road – ℰ (020)
7287 4243 – www.imli.co.uk – info@imli.co.uk – Fax (020) 7287 4245 – Closed
25-28 December, 1 January and lunch Bank Holidays   31AKU**w**
Rest – Indian – Menu £ 18 (lunch) – Carte £ 15/23
♦ Long, spacious interior is a busy, buzzy place. Good value, fresh and tasty Indian
tapas style dishes prove a popular currency. Same owners as Tamarind.

☆ **Barrafina**   *VISA* 🅼🅾 🅰🅴
54 Frith St ⊠ W1D 3SL⊖ Tottenham Court Rd – ℰ (020) 7813 8016
– www.barrafina.co.uk – info@barrafina.co.uk – Fax (020) 7734 7593 – Closed
Christmas, Easter and Bank Holidays   31AKU**c**
Rest – Spanish – (bookings not accepted) Carte £ 18/37
♦ Centred around a counter with seating for 20, come here if you want authentic
Spanish tapas served in a buzzy atmosphere. Seafood is a speciality and the Jabugo
ham a must.

☆ **Aurora**   🍴 🅴🅶 ⟷ *VISA* 🅼🅾 🅰🅴
49 Lexington St ⊠ W1F 9AP⊖ Piccadilly Circus – ℰ (020) 7494 0514
– Closed Christmas and Sunday   31AJU**e**
Rest – Modern European – (booking essential) Carte approx. £ 25
♦ An informal, no-nonsense, bohemian style bistro with a small, but pretty, walled
garden terrace. Short but balanced menu; simple fresh food. Pleasant, languid atmosphere.

Strand and Covent Garden – Greater London – ⊠ WC2

🏠🏠🏠 **One Aldwych**   🔲 🌀 🖪 🕴 ⅙ rm, 🅰🅒 🌀 ⁋ 🕸 🅿 *VISA* 🅼🅾 🅰🅴 🅞
1 Aldwych ⊠ WC2B 4RH⊖ Temple – ℰ (020) 7300 1000
– www.onealdwych.com – sales@onealdwych.com
– Fax (020) 7300 1001   32AMU**r**
96 rm – †£ 223/447, ††£ 223/447, ☐ £24.75 – 9 suites
Rest *Axis* – see restaurant listing
Rest *Indigo* – Carte £ 34/43
♦ Decorative Edwardian building, former home to the Morning Post newspaper. Now
a stylish and contemporary address with modern artwork, a screening room and
hi-tech bedrooms. All-day restaurant looks down on fashionable bar.

⌂⌂⌂ Swissôtel The Howard

Temple Pl ⊠ *WC2R 2PR* ⊖ *Temple* – ℰ *(020) 7836 3555*
– www.london.swissotel.com – reservations.london@swissotel.com
– Fax (020) 7379 4547
32AMU**e**
177 rm – ♦♦£557 ♦♦♦£557, ⊆ £23.50 – 12 suites
Rest *12 Temple Place* – Menu £24 (lunch) – Carte approx. £37
♦ Discreet elegance is the order of the day at this handsomely appointed hotel. Many of the comfortable rooms enjoy balcony views of the Thames. Attentive service. Large terrace to restaurant serving modern European dishes.

⌂⌂⌂ The Waldorf Hilton

Aldwych ⊠ *WC2B 4DD* ⊖ *Covent Garden* – ℰ *(020) 7836 2400*
– www.hilton.co.uk/waldorf – enquiry.waldorflondon@hilton.com
– Fax (020) 7836 4648
32AMU**u**
293 rm – ♦£199/469 ♦♦£199/469, ⊆ £22 – 6 suites
Rest *Homage* – (Closed lunch Saturday and Sunday) Menu £20
– Carte £28/58
♦ Impressive curved and columned façade: an Edwardian landmark. Basement leisure club. Ornate meeting rooms. Two bedroom styles: one contemporary, one more traditional. Large, modish brasserie with extensive range of modern menus.

⌂⌂⌂ St Martins Lane

45 St Martin's Lane ⊠ *WC2N 4HX* ⊖ *Charing Cross* – ℰ *(020) 7300 5500*
– www.morganshotelgroup.com – stmartinslane@morganshotelgroup.com
– Fax (020) 7300 5501
31ALU**e**
202 rm – ♦£253/370 ♦♦£253/370, ⊆ £25 – 2 suites
Rest *Asia de Cuba* – Carte £50/115
♦ The unmistakable hand of Philippe Starck evident at this most contemporary of hotels. Unique and stylish, from the starkly modern lobby to the state-of-the-art rooms. 350 varieties of rum and tasty Asian dishes at fashionable Asia de Cuba.

XXX The Ivy

1-5 West St ⊠ *WC2H 9NQ* ⊖ *Leicester Square* – ℰ *(020) 7836 4751*
– www.the-ivy.co.uk – Fax (020) 7240 9333 – Closed 24-26 December, 1 January
and August Bank Holiday
31AKU**p**
Rest – International – Carte £26/50
♦ Wood panelling and stained glass combine with an unpretentious menu to create a veritable institution. A favourite of 'celebrities', so securing a table can be challenging.

XXX Axis

1 Aldwych ⊠ *WC2B 4RH* ⊖ *Temple* – ℰ *(020) 7300 0300*
– www.onealdwych.com – axis@onealdwych.com – Fax (020) 7300 0301 – Closed
Saturday lunch, Sunday and Bank Holidays
31AMU**r**
Rest – Modern European – Menu £18 (lunch) – Carte £28/37
♦ Spiral staircase down to this modern restaurant with very high ceiling; new fabrics and bamboo-effect façade in front of futuristic mural. British ingredients to the fore in carefully crafted dishes.

XX J. Sheekey

28-32 St Martin's Court ⊠ *WC2 4AL* ⊖ *Leicester Square* – ℰ *(020) 7240 2565*
– www.j-sheeky.co.uk – reservations@j-sheeky.co.uk – Fax (020) 7497 0891
– Closed 25-26 December, 1 January and August Bank Holiday
31ALU**v**
Rest – Seafood – (booking essential) Carte £31/51
♦ Festooned with photographs of actors and linked to the theatrical world since opening in 1890. Wood panels and alcove tables add famed intimacy. Accomplished seafood cooking.

XX Rules

35 Maiden Lane ⊠ *WC2E 7LB* ⊖ *Leicester Square* – ℰ *(020) 7836 5314*
– www.rules.co.uk – info@rules.co.uk – Fax (020) 7497 1081
– Closed 4 days Christmas
31ALU**n**
Rest – British – (booking essential) Carte £33/47
♦ London's oldest restaurant boasts a fine collection of antique cartoons, drawings and paintings. Tradition continues in the menu, specialising in game from its own estate.

LONDON

LONDON

XX **Clos Maggiore**   AC 🍴 ♿ VISA ◎ AE ①
33 King St ⊠ WC2E 8JD⊖ Leicester Square – ℰ (020) 7379 9696
– www.closmaggiore.com – enquiries@closmaggiore.com – Fax (020) 7379 6767
– Closed lunch Saturday and Sunday   31ALU**z**
Rest – French – Menu £ 20 (lunch) – Carte £ 35/47🍷
♦ Walls covered with flowering branches create delightful woodland feel to rear
dining area with retractable glass roof. French cooking shows flair, creativity and
ambition.

XX **Admiralty**   VISA ◎ AE ①
Somerset House, The Strand ⊠ WC2R 1LA⊖ Temple – ℰ (020) 7845 4646
– www.theadmiraltyrestaurant.com – info@theadmiraltyrestaurant.com
– Fax (020) 7845 4658 – Closed 25-26 December and Sunday   32AMU**a**
Rest – French – Menu £ 22/25 – Carte £ 27/38
♦ Within the magnificent surroundings of 18C Somerset House. Pretty dining room
divided into two rooms, both with plenty of light; the cooking ranges from regional
French to international.

XX **The Forge**   AC 🍴 VISA ◎ AE
14 Garrick Street ⊠ WC2E 9BJ⊖ Leicester Square – ℰ (020) 7379 1432
– www.theforgerestaurant.co.uk – info@theforgerestaurant.co.uk – Fax (020)
7379 1530 – Closed 24 and 25 December   31ALU**a**
Rest – Modern European – Menu £ 17 (lunch) – Carte £ 31/35
♦ Long and appealing menu, from eggs Benedict to Dover sole; good value theatre
menus and last orders at midnight. Most influences from within Europe. Large room
with downstairs bar.

XX **Le Deuxième**   AC 🍴 VISA ◎ AE
65a Long Acre ⊠ WC2E 9JH⊖ Covent Garden – ℰ (020) 7379 0033
– www.ledeuxieme.com – info@ledeuxieme.com – Fax (020) 7379 0066
– Closed 24-25 December   31ALU**b**
Rest – Modern European – Menu £ 17 (lunch) – Carte £ 28/33
♦ Caters well for theatregoers: opens early, closes late. Buzzy eatery, quietly decorated in white with subtle lighting. Varied international menu: Japanese to Mediterranean.

X **L'Atelier de Joël Robuchon**   AC 🍴 VISA ◎ AE
🕸 🕸 *13-15 West St ⊠ WC2H 9NE⊖ Leicester Square – ℰ (020) 7010 8600*
– www.joel-robuchon.com – info@joelrobuchon.co.uk
– Fax (020) 7010 8601   31AKU**a**
Rest – French – Menu £ 25 (lunch) – Carte £ 33/85
Rest *La Cuisine* – French – (dinner only) Carte £ 45/105
Spec. Pig's trotter on parmesan toast with black truffle. Langoustine with
mango and basil relish. La Boule surprise.
♦ Entrance into trendy atelier with counter seating; upstairs the more structured La
Cuisine; wonderfully delicate, precise modern French cooking. Cool top floor lounge
bar.

X **Le Café du Jardin**   AC 🍴 VISA ◎ AE ①
28 Wellington St ⊠ WC2E 7BD⊖ Covent Garden – ℰ (020) 7836 8769
– www.lecafedujardin.com – info@lecafedujardin.com – Fax (020) 7836 4123
– Closed 24-25 December   31ALU**f**
Rest – Mediterranean – Menu £ 17 (lunch) – Carte £ 25/32🍷
♦ Spread over two floors, with the bustle on the ground floor. Sunny, mostly Mediterranean cooking. Very busy early and late evening thanks to the good value theatre
menus which change weekly.

X **Bedford & Strand**   VISA ◎ AE
1a Bedford St ⊠ WC2E 9HH⊖ Charing Cross – ℰ (020) 7836 3033
– www.bedford-strand.com – hello@bedford-strand.com – Closed 25-26 and
31 December, 1 January, Saturday lunch, Sunday and Bank Holidays   31ALU**c**
Rest – British – (booking essential) Carte £ 22/35
♦ Basement bistro/wine bar with simple décor and easy-going atmosphere; kitchen
sources well and has a light touch with Italian, French and British dishes.

Victoria – Greater London – ✉ SW1
ℹ Victoria Station Forecourt ✆ (09068) 663344

The Goring
15 Beeston Pl, Grosvenor Gdns ✉ SW1W 0JW ⊖ Victoria – ✆ (020) 7396 9000 – www.goringhotel.co.uk – reception@goringhotel.co.uk – Fax (020) 7834 4393 38AIX**a**
65 rm – †£ 234/388 ††£ 246/717, ☕ £24 – 6 suites
Rest – British – (Closed Saturday lunch) Menu £ 37/49
◆ Opened in 1910 as a quintessentially English hotel. The fourth generation of Goring is now at the helm. Many of the attractive rooms overlook a peaceful garden. Elegantly appointed restaurant provides memorable dining experience.

Crowne Plaza London - St James
45 Buckingham Gate ✉ SW1E 6AF ⊖ St James's Park – ✆ (020) 7834 6655 – www.london.crowneplaza.com – sales@cplonsj.co.uk – Fax (020) 7630 7587 39AJX**e**
323 rm – †£ 323 ††£ 388, ☕ £14.25 – 19 suites
Rest Quilon and **Bank** – see restaurant listing
Rest *Bistro 51* – Menu £ 18/22 – Carte £ 32/43
◆ Built in 1897 as serviced accommodation for visiting aristocrats. Behind the impressive Edwardian façade lies an equally elegant interior. Quietest rooms overlook courtyard. Bright and informal café-style restaurant.

51 Buckingham Gate
51 Buckingham Gate ✉ SW1E 6AF ⊖ St James's Park – ✆ (020) 7769 7766 – www.51-buckinghamgate.com – info@51-buckinghamgate.co.uk – Fax (020) 7828 5909 39AJX**s**
86 suites – ††£ 452/670, ☕ £22
Rest Quilon and **Bank** – see restaurant listing
◆ Canopied entrance leads to luxurious suites: every detail considered, every mod con provided. Colour schemes echoed in plants and paintings. Butler and nanny service.

41 without rest
41 Buckingham Palace Rd ✉ SW1W 0PS ⊖ Victoria – ✆ (020) 7300 0041 – www.41hotel.com – book41@rchmail.com – Fax (020) 7300 0141 38AIX**n**
28 rm – †£ 264/382 ††£ 288/415, ☕ £25 – 1 suite
◆ Discreet appearance; exudes exclusive air. Leather armchairs; bookcases line the walls. Intimate service. State-of-the-art rooms where hi-tec and fireplace merge appealingly.

The Rubens at The Palace
39 Buckingham Palace Rd ✉ SW1W 0PS ⊖ Victoria – ✆ (020) 7834 6600 – www.rubenshotel.com – bookrb@rchmail.com – Fax (020) 7828 5401 38AIX**n**
159 rm – †£ 292/304 ††£ 304/320, ☕ £18.50 – 2 suites
Rest – (closed lunch Saturday and Sunday) Menu £ 28 – Carte dinner £ 28/45
◆ Traditional hotel with an air of understated elegance. Tastefully furnished rooms: the Royal Wing, themed after Kings and Queens, features TVs in bathrooms. Smart carvery restaurant.

Park Plaza Victoria
239 Vauxhall Bridge Rd ✉ SW1V 1EQ ⊖ Victoria – ✆ (020) 7769 9999 – www.parkplaza.com – info@vpp.com – Fax (020) 7769 9998 38AIY**a**
299 rm – †£ 116/352 ††£ 116/352, ☕ £16
Rest *J.B.'s* – (Closed lunch Saturday and Sunday) Carte £ 30/45
◆ Conveniently located for Victoria station. Spacious modern interior filled with modish artwork. State-of-the-art meeting rooms. Well-equipped rooms boast a host of facilities. Appealing dining room offers modern European cuisine.

LONDON

Tophams without rest ⬛ 🚭 📶 VISA ⚫ AE

24-32 Ebury Street ⊠ SW1W 0LU⊖ Victoria – ℰ *(020) 7730 3313*
– www.zolahotels.com/tophams – tophams.reservations@zolahotels.com
– Fax (020) 7730 0008   38AHY**d**
47 rm – ♦£160/195 ♦♦£175/195, � £11 – 1 suite
♦ Reopened in 2008, after a major refit. A row of five terraced houses, in a good spot for tourists. Neat bedrooms with large bathrooms and good mod cons. Comfortable breakfast room.

√ **B + B Belgravia** without rest 🚲 🕭 📶 VISA ⚫ AE

64-66 Ebury St ⊠ SW1W 9QD⊖ Victoria – ℰ *(020) 7259 8570*
– www.bb-belgravia.com – info@bb-belgravia.com
– Fax (020) 7259 8591   38AHY**x**
17 rm ⊇ – ♦£99 ♦♦£125/130
♦ Two houses, three floors, and, considering the location, some of the best value accommodation in town. Sleek, clean-lined rooms. Breakfast overlooking little garden terrace.

Lord Milner without rest ⬛ 🕭 VISA ⚫ AE

111 Ebury Street ⊠ SW1W 9QU⊖ Victoria – ℰ *(020) 7881 9880*
– www.lordmilner.com – info@lordmilner.com
– Fax (020) 7730 8027   38AHY**k**
11 rm – ♦£115 ♦♦£145/255, ⊇ £11.50
♦ A four storey terrace house, with individually decorated bedrooms, three with four-poster beds and all with marble bathrooms. Garden Suite the best room, with its own patio. No public areas.

XXX **Roussillon** (Alex Gauthier) AK VISA ⚫ AE
ఔ *16 St Barnabas St ⊠ SW1W 8PE⊖ Sloane Square –* ℰ *(020) 7730 5550*
– www.roussillon.co.uk – alexis@roussillon.co.uk – Fax (020) 7824 8617
– Closed 25-26 December, Easter, Saturday lunch and Sunday   38AHZ**c**
Rest – French – Menu £35/55 ❀
Spec. Sesame seed crusted langoustines with basil and tomato broth. Red deer with celeriac and truffle purée, poached pear. Louis XV crunchy praline and chocolate.
♦ Tucked away in a smart residential area. Cooking clearly focuses on the quality of the ingredients. Seasonal menu with inventive elements and a French base.

XXX **Quilon** – at Crowne Plaza London - St James Hotel AK VISA ⚫ AE
ఔ *41 Buckingham Gate ⊠ SW1 6AF⊖ St James's Park –* ℰ *(020) 7821 1899*
– www.quilon.co.uk – info@quilonrestaurant.co.uk – Fax (020) 7233 9597
– Closed Saturday lunch   39AJX**e**
Rest – Indian – Menu £20/35 – Carte £35/46
Spec. Marinated scallops grilled and served with spiced coconut cream. Lobster with mango, ginger, kokum and curry leaves. Almond delight with praline, yoghurt and almond ice cream.
♦ Original, vibrant and well balanced Indian dishes, many of which originate from the South West coast. Excellent use of spices, appealing seafood specialities and graceful service.

XXX **The Cinnamon Club** AK 🕭 ⬦ P VISA ⚫ AE ⓞ
30-32 Great Smith St ⊠ SW1P 3BU⊖ St James's Park – ℰ *(020) 7222 2555*
– www.cinnamonclub.com – info@cinnamonclub.com –
– Closed 26 December, 1 January, Sunday and Bank Holiday Mondays   39AKX**c**
Rest – Indian – Menu £22 (lunch) – Carte £34/54
♦ Housed in former Westminster Library: exterior has ornate detail, interior is stylish and modern. Walls are lined with books. New Wave Indian cooking with plenty of choice.

XXX **Santini**　　　　　　　　　　　　　　　AC VISA ⊕ AE
29 Ebury St ⊠ SW1W 0NZ⊖ Victoria – ℰ (020) 77304094
– www.santini-restaurant.com – info@santini-restaurant.com – Fax (020)
77300544 – Closed 24-27 December and Easter　　　　　　38AHY**v**
Rest – Italian – Carte £31/51
♦ Discreet, refined and elegantly contemporary Italian restaurant. Assured and professional service. Extensive selection of modern dishes from across Italy, using excellent produce.

XXX **Shepherd's**　　　　　　　　　　　AC ⇔ VISA ⊕ AE ①
Marsham Court, Marsham St ⊠ SW1P 4LA⊖ Pimlico – ℰ (020) 78349552
– www.langansrestaurants.co.uk – admin@langansrestaurants.co.uk – Fax (020)
72336047 – Closed Saturday, Sunday and Bank Holidays　　　　39AKY**z**
Rest – British – (booking essential) Menu £34
♦ A truly English restaurant where game and traditional puddings are a highlight. Popular with those from Westminster - the booths offer a degree of privacy.

XX **Atami**　　　　　　　　　　　　　　　AC VISA ⊕ AE
37 Monck St (entrance on Great Peter St) ⊠ SW1P 2BL⊖ Pimlico – ℰ (020)
72222218 – www.atami-restaurant.com – mail@atami-restaurant.com
– Fax (020) 72222788 – Closed Saturday lunch　　　　　　39AKY**a**
Rest – Japanese – Menu £23/45 – Carte approx. £35
♦ Clean, modern lines illuminated by vast ceiling orbs induce a sense of calm. Menus true to Japanese roots feature sushi and sashimi turning down interesting modern highways.

XX **Il Convivio**　　　　　　　　　　　AC ⇔ VISA ⊕ AE
143 Ebury St ⊠ SW1W 9QN⊖ Sloane Square – ℰ (020) 77304099
– www.etruscarestaurants.com – comments@etruscarestaurants.com – Fax (020)
77304103 – Closed 25-26 December, Sunday and Bank Holidays　　38AHY**a**
Rest – Italian – Menu £22 (lunch) – Carte £33/41
♦ A retractable roof provides alfresco dining to part of this comfortable and modern restaurant. Contemporary and traditional Italian menu with home-made pasta specialities.

XX **Boisdale**　　　　　　　　　　　🍴 AC ⇔ VISA ⊕ AE ①
15 Eccleston St ⊠ SW1W 9LX⊖ Victoria – ℰ (020) 77306922
– www.boisdale.co.uk – info@boisdale.co.uk – Fax (020) 77300548 – Closed
Christmas, Saturday lunch and Sunday　　　　　　　　38AHY**c**
Rest – Scottish – Carte £29/91
♦ Popular haunt of politicians; dark green, lacquer red panelled interior. Run by a Scot of Clanranald, hence modern British dishes with Scottish flavour.

XX **Rex Whistler**　　　　　　　　　🍴 AC VISA ⊕ AE ①
Tate Britain, Millbank ⊠ SW1P 4RG⊖ Pimlico – ℰ (020) 78878825
– www.tate.org.uk – britain.restaurant@tate.org.uk – Fax (020) 78874969
– Closed 24-26 December　　　　　　　　　　　　39ALY**c**
Rest – British – (lunch only) (booking essential) Carte £28/37 ♨
♦ Like upstairs, it celebrates Britain, with a daily catch from Newlyn and good fruity desserts the specialities. Comfortable room, with striking Rex Whistler mural. Exceedingly good wine list.

XX **Ken Lo's Memories of China**　　　AC ⇔ VISA ⊕ AE ①
65-69 Ebury St ⊠ SW1W 0NZ⊖ Victoria – ℰ (020) 77307734
– www.memories-of-china.co.uk – Fax (020) 77302992 – Closed 25-26 December,
Sunday lunch and Bank Holidays　　　　　　　　38AHY**u**
Rest – Chinese – Menu £20/32 – Carte £31/51
♦ An air of tranquillity pervades this traditionally furnished room. Lattice screens add extra privacy. Extensive Chinese menu: bold flavours with a clean, fresh style.

LONDON

XX **Quirinale**   VISA ⓜ AE ⓪

North Court, 1 Great Peter St ⊖ Westminster – ℰ (020) 7222 7080
– www.quirinale.co.uk – info@quirinale.co.uk – Closed August, 1 week Christmas -
New Year, Saturday, Sunday and Bank Holidays   39ALX**a**
Rest – Italian – Carte £ 34/40

♦ Light and bright Italian restaurant with contemporary, minimalist feel typified
by cream leather banquettes. Seasonally-changing menu encompasses all things Italian.

XX **Bank**   ⌂ AC ⊗ VISA ⓜ AE

45 Buckingham Gate ⊠ SW1E 6BS⊖ St James's Park – ℰ (020) 7630 0644
– www.bankrestaurants.com – reservations.westminster@bankrestaurants.com
– Fax (020) 7630 5665
– Closed Saturday lunch, Sunday and Bank Holidays   39AJX**e**
Rest – Modern European – (booking essential at lunch) Carte £ 29/45

♦ The understated entrance belies the vibrant contemporary interior. One of Europe's longest bars has a lively atmosphere. Conservatory restaurant, modern European cooking.

X **Olivo**   AC VISA ⓜ AE ⓪

21 Eccleston St ⊠ SW1W 9LX⊖ Victoria – ℰ (020) 7730 2505
– www.olivorestaurant.com – maurosanna@oliveto.fsnet.co.uk – Fax (020)
7823 5377 – Closed Bank Holidays, lunch Saturday and Sunday   38AHY**z**
Rest – Italian – Menu £ 23 (lunch) – Carte £ 25/33

♦ Rustic, informal Italian restaurant. Relaxed atmosphere provided by the friendly
staff. Simple, non-fussy cuisine with emphasis on best available fresh produce.

X **La Poule au Pot**   ⌂ AC VISA ⓜ AE ⓪

231 Ebury St ⊠ SW1W 8UT⊖ Sloane Square – ℰ (020) 7730 7763 – Fax (020)
7259 9651 – Closed 25-26 December and 1 January   38AHY**p**
Rest – French – Menu £ 18 (lunch) – Carte £ 29/42

♦ The subdued lighting and friendly informality make this one of London's more
romantic restaurants. Classic French menu with extensive plats du jour.

OutSide !!

X **Olivomare**   ⌂ AC VISA ⓜ AE ⓪

10 Lower Belgrave St ⊠ SW1W 0LJ⊖ Victoria – ℰ (020) 7730 9022
– www.olivorestaurants.com – maurosanna@oliveto.fsnet.co.uk – Fax (020)
7823 5377 – Closed Sunday and Bank Holidays   38AHY**b**
Rest – Seafood – Carte £ 28/33

♦ Chic minimalist décor with magic-eye mural of intertwined fish. The food is robust
and full-flavoured; seafood is the theme, with a subtle Sardinian subtext. Assured
service.

🍴 **The Ebury**   AC ℀ VISA ⓜ AE

11 Pimlico Rd ⊠ SW1W 8NA⊖ Sloane Square – ℰ (020) 7730 6784
– www.theebury.co.uk – info@theebury.co.uk – Fax (020) 7730 6149
– Closed 25 December   38AHZ**z**
Rest – Menu £ 20 (lunch) – Carte £ 30/45

♦ Victorian corner pub restaurant with walnut bar, simple tables and large seafood
bar. Friendly service. Wide-ranging menu from snacks to full meals.

🍴 **The Thomas Cubitt**   VISA ⓜ AE ⓪

44 Elizabeth Street ⊠ SW1W 9PA⊖ Sloane Square – ℰ (020) 7730 6060
– www.thethomascubitt.co.uk – reservations@thethomascubitt.co.uk – Fax (020)
7730 6055 – Closed 25 December, Good Friday   38AHY**e**
Rest – (booking essential) Carte £ 30/60

♦ Georgian pub refurbished and renamed after master builder. He'd approve of
elegant, formal dining room. Carefully supplied ingredients underpin tasty, seasonal
English dishes.

LONG CRENDON – Buckinghamshire – **503** – pop. 2 383   11 **C2**
– ✉ Aylesbury

🟦 London 50 mi – Aylesbury 11 mi – Oxford 15 mi

✗✗ **Angel** with rm   🗺 🌱 🐾 **P** **VISA** **①①** **①**
47 Bicester Rd ✉ HP18 9EE – 𝒞 (01844) 208 268 – angelrestaurant@aol.co.uk
– Fax (01844) 202 497 – Closed Sunday dinner
4 rm � – †£70 ††£95   **Rest** – Menu £20/25 – Carte £31/39
♦ Characterful former pub with low ceilings, leather furnished lounge bar and airy conservatory. Oft-changing menus offer tasty modern British cooking, with well-chosen wine list. Stylish bedrooms, all individually decorated. 3 is the cosiest, 4 the biggest.

LONGHORSLEY – Northd. – **501** – see Morpeth

LONG MELFORD – Suffolk – **504** W 27 – pop. 2 734 📘 Great Britain   15 **C3**
🟦 London 73 mi – Cambridge 34 mi – Colchester 18 mi – Ipswich 24 mi
◎ Melford Hall★ AC

🏨 **Black Lion**   🗺 🐾 **P** **VISA** **①①** **AE**
Church Walk, The Green ✉ CO10 9DN – 𝒞 (01787) 312 356
– www.blacklionhotel.net – enquiries@blacklionhotel.net – Fax (01787) 374 557
9 rm ⊆ – †£98 ††£165 – 1 suite   **Rest** – Carte £23/31
♦ 17C Georgian inn overlooking village green. Named after wines, bedrooms are smart, stylish and individually designed; good facilities and traditional bathrooms. Formal restaurant with enclosed rear terrace features extensive, popular menu.

✗ **Scutchers**   **AC** **VISA** **①①** **AE**
Westgate St, on A 1092 ✉ CO10 9DP – 𝒞 (01787) 310 200 – www.scutchers.com
– info@scutchers.com – Fax (01787) 375 700
– Closed Christmas, 1 week March, 1 week August, Sunday and Monday
Rest – Menu £24 – Carte £30/42
♦ Former medieval Hall House now contains an informal and unpretentious restaurant serving a range of creative modern dishes using good quality ingredients.

LONGRIDGE – Lancashire – **502** M 22 – pop. 7 491   20 **A2**
🟦 London 241 mi – Blackburn 12 mi – Burnley 18 mi

✗✗ **The Longridge Restaurant**   **AC** ⟷ **VISA** **①①** **AE** **①**
104-106 Higher Rd, Northeast : ½ m. by B 5269 following signs for Jeffrey Hill
✉ PR3 3SY – 𝒞 (01772) 784 969 – www.heathcotes.co.uk – longridge@
heathcotes.co.uk – Fax (01772) 785 713 – Closed Saturday lunch and Monday
Rest – Menu £25 (lunch) – Carte £24/51
♦ Former pub with stylish black and grey décor, sumptuous bar, comfy seats and elegant dining room. Modern, seasonal cooking boasts decidedly Lancastrian bias. Friendly service.

✗ **Thyme**   **AC** **VISA** **①①** **AE** **①**
1-3 Inglewhite Rd ✉ PR3 3JR – 𝒞 (01772) 786 888 – www.thyme-out.net
– Fax (01772) 784 138 – Closed 5-7 January and Monday
Rest – Menu £11/14 – Carte £23/35
♦ Modern restaurant near roundabout; wooden floors and modern lighting; artwork on the walls. Locally sourced produce used as much as possible. Good value, especially at lunch.

at Knowle Green East : 2 ¼ m. by A 5269 on B 6243 – ✉ Longridge

🏠 **Oak Lea** without rest   🖼 🌱 **P**
Clitheroe Rd, East : ½ m. on B 6243 ✉ PR3 2YS – 𝒞 (01254) 878 486
– tandm.mellor@hotmail.co.uk – Fax (01254) 878 486 – Closed Christmas and
New Year
3 rm ⊆ – †£32/35 ††£54/58
♦ Neat little guesthouse in the heart of the Ribble Valley with fine all-round views. Conservatory with access to mature garden. Pleasantly furnished bedrooms.

ENGLAND

LONG SUTTON – Somerset – **503** L 30 – ✉ **Langport**   3 **B3**
> ▶ London 132 mi – Bridgwater 16 mi – Yeovil 10 mi

🏠 **The Devonshire Arms** with rm   🖷 🕭 **P** **VISA 🐵**
✉ *TA10 9LP* – *℘ (01458) 241 271* – *www.thedevonshirearms.com*
– mail@thedevonshirearms.com – Fax (01458) 241 037
– Closed 25 December, 1 January
9 rm 🖙 – ♟£70/80 ♟♟£80/130
Rest – (bookings not accepted) Carte £ 21/35
♦ Spacious hunting lodge with modern décor, front terrace and garden. Mix of French and English dishes with a good value menu at lunch and a concise à la carte for dinner. Modern bedrooms with neutral shades and rattan furniture.

LONGTOWN – Cumbria – **501**   21 **A1**
> ▶ London 326 mi – Carlisle 9 mi – Newcastle upon Tyne 61 mi

🏠 **Bessiestown Farm** ॐ   🖷 🕭 🔲 🌿 **P** **VISA 🐵 AE ①**
🍴 *Catlowdy, Northeast : 8 m. by Netherby St on B 6318* ✉ *CA6 5QP* – *℘ (01228)*
577 219 – www.bessiestown.co.uk – info@bessiestown.co.uk – Fax (01228)
577019 – Closed 25 December
5 rm 🖙 – ♟£49 ♟♟£78   **Rest** – (by arrangement) Menu £ 18
♦ Comfortable, warm accommodation in homely, modern farmhouse conversion in a rural location on a working farm. Décor has a traditional British tone, well-kept throughout. Home-cooked food served in airy dining room.

LOOE – Cornwall – **503** G 32 – pop. 5 280   1 **B2**
> ▶ London 264 mi – Plymouth 23 mi – Truro 39 mi
> 🇮 The Guildhall, Fore St ℘ (01503) 262072, looetic@btconnect.com
> 🏠 Bin Down, ℘ (01503) 240 239
> 🏠 Whitsand Bay Hotel Torpoint Portwrinkle, ℘ (01503) 230 276
> ◻ Town★ – Monkey Sanctuary★ **AC**

🏨 **Barclay House**   ≤ 🖷 ユ 🏠 ᒲ 🌿 **P** **VISA 🐵 AE**
St Martins Rd, East Looe, East :½ m. by A 387 on B 3253 ✉ *PL13 1LP*
– ℘ (01503) 262 929 – www.barclayhouse.co.uk – info@barclayhouse.co.uk
– Fax (01503) 262632 – Closed 5-16 January
11 rm 🖙 – ♟£75/160 ♟♟£130/160
Rest *The Restaurant* – see restaurant listing
♦ Smart but relaxed and welcoming hotel near harbour. Gardens overlooking estuary. Snug sitting room and bar. Individually decorated bedrooms.

🏠 **Beach House** without rest   ≤ 🖷 ᵗᵞ **P** **VISA 🐵**
Hannafore, Southwest : 3/4 m. by Quay Rd ✉ *PL13 2DH* – *℘ (01503) 262 598*
– www.thebeachhouselooe.co.uk – enquiries@thebeachhouselooe.co.uk
– Fax (01503) 262 298 – Closed Christmas
5 rm – ♟£65 ♟♟£130
♦ Large detached house with front garden. Immaculate bedrooms: three have sea vistas; 'Fistral' with balcony is best. Breakfast room upstairs; arched window with views over bay.

🏠 **Bucklawren Farm** without rest ॐ   ≤ 🖷 🕭 🌿 **P** **VISA 🐵**
St Martin-by-Looe, Northeast : 3½ m. by A 387 and B 3253 turning right onto single track road signposted to Monkey Sanctuary ✉ *PL13 1NZ* – *℘ (01503)*
240738 – www.bucklawren.com – bucklawren@btopenworld.com – Fax (01503)
240481 – March-October
6 rm 🖙 – ♟£35/50 ♟♟£60/70
♦ Characterful farmhouse within 500 acre working farm. Large conservatory overlooks pleasant garden. Spotlessly kept interior with simple, country house-style bedrooms.

ENGLAND

※※ **The Restaurant** – at Barclay House ≤ 🚗 🛋 🍴 🅿 VISA ⓪ AE
St Martins Rd, East Looe, East : ½ m. by A 387 on B 3253 ⌂ PL13 1LP
– ℰ (01503) 262 929 – www.barclayhouse.co.uk – info@barclayhouse.co.uk
– Fax (01503) 262 632 – Closed 5-16 January
Rest – (dinner only) Menu £ 30 – Carte £ 25/40
♦ Extensive views of estuary. Matching mustard coloured walls and table cloths. Attentive well-informed service. Eclectic menu using fresh local produce, particularly seafood.

※ **Trawlers on the Quay** VISA ⓪ AE
The Quay, East Looe ⌂ PL13 1AH – ℰ (01503) 263 593
– www.trawlersrestaurant.co.uk – info@trawlersrestaurant.co.uk
– Closed Christmas, 1 week February, Sunday and Monday except Bank Holidays
Rest – Seafood – (dinner only) Carte £ 26/34
♦ Personally run restaurant in a pretty setting on the quay. Faux marble table tops; clean, neutral décor. Balanced menu of local seafood and meat dishes. Home-made bread, too.

at Talland Bay Southwest : 4 m. by A 387 – ⌂ Looe

🏨 **Talland Bay** ⏳ ≤ 🚗 ⌗ 🅿 VISA ⓪
⌂ PL13 2JB – ℰ (01503) 272 667 – www.tallandbayhotel.co.uk
– reception@tallandbayhotel.co.uk – Fax (01503) 272 940 – Closed January - early February
17 rm ⌂ – ♥£ 40/185 ♥♥£ 155/195 – 2 suites
Rest *Terrace* – (closed Monday lunch) Menu £ 25/37
♦ 16C house in secluded position with lovely gardens. Well chosen fabrics and furniture create a warm and comfortable environment. Many rooms with sea views. Modern fine dining from interesting menu.

LORTON – Cumbria – **502** K 20 – **see Cockermouth**

LOUGHBOROUGH – Leicestershire – **502** – **pop. 55 258** 16 **B2**
▶ London 117 mi – Birmingham 41 mi – Leicester 11 mi – Nottingham 15 mi
🛈 Town Hall, Market Pl ℰ (01509) 218113, tic@charnwoodbc.gov.uk
🏁 Lingdale Woodhouse Eaves Joe Moore's Lane, ℰ (01509) 890 703

at Belton West : 6 m. by A 6 on B 5324 – ⌂ Loughborough

🏠 **The Queen's Head** with rm 🚗 🛋 🅿 VISA ⓪
2 Long St ⌂ LE12 9TP – ℰ (01530) 222 359 – www.thequeenshead.org
– enquiries@thequeenshead.org – Fax (01530) 224 860
– Closed 25 December, 1 January
6 rm ⌂ – ♥£ 65 ♥♥£ 110
Rest – (Closed Sunday dinner) Menu £ 17 – Carte £ 22/28
♦ Stylish two-roomed restaurant and cool lounge and bar in calming cream tones, with chocolate leather furniture. Seasonally-evolving menus make proud use of local produce. Bright, contemporary bedrooms of varying sizes.

at Woodhouse Eaves South : 4½ m. by A 6 via Woodhouse – ⌂ Loughborough

※※ **The Woodhouse** ⇔ 🅿 VISA ⓪ AE
43 Maplewell Rd ⌂ LE12 8RG – ℰ (01509) 890 318 – www.thewoodhouse.co.uk
– paul@thewoodhouse.co.uk – Fax (01509) 890 718 – Closed lunch Saturday and Sunday dinner
Rest – Menu £ 16/17 **s** – Carte £ 27/42 **s**
♦ Bright, boldly coloured restaurant with exotic floral arrangements and artwork. Modern European cooking with a classic French base and innovative edge. Enthusiastic team.

ENGLAND

LOUTH – Lincolnshire – 502 – pop. 15 930   17 **D1**
▶ London 156 mi – Boston 34 mi – Great Grimsby 17 mi – Lincoln 26 mi
🖽 The New Market Hall, off Cornmarket 𝒞 (01507) 609289,
louthinfo@e-lindsey.gov.uk

Brackenborough   🛋 🕸 📶 🔊 **P** 🚾 ◍◍ AE
Cordeaux Corner, Brackenborough, North : 2 m. by A 16 ⊠ LN11 0SZ
– 𝒞 (01507) 609 169 – www.oakridgehotels.co.uk
– reception@brackenborough.co.uk – Fax (01507) 609 413
24 rm ☐ – ♦£79/95 ♦♦£149   **Rest** – Carte £20/32
♦ Family owned hotel run with a warm and personal style. Public areas have a relaxed feel and bedrooms are spacious, individually designed and boast a host of extras. Homely dining.

LOVINGTON – Somerset – 503 M 30 – see Castle Cary

LOW FELL – Tyne and Wear – see Gateshead

LOWER FROYLE – Hampshire – see Alton

LOWER HARDRES – Kent – 504 X 30 – see Canterbury

LOWER ODDINGTON – Glos. – see Stow-on-the-Wold

LOWER SLAUGHTER – Glos. – 503 – see Bourton-on-the-Water

LOWER SWELL – Glos. – see Stow-on-the-Wold

LOWER VOBSTER – Somerset – pop. 2 222 – ⊠ Radstock   4 **C2**
▶ London 119 mi – Bath 16 mi – Frome 5 mi

The Vobster Inn with rm   🛋 🕸 📶 **P** 🚾 ◍◍ ◍
⊠ BA3 5RJ – 𝒞 (01373) 812920 – www.vobsterinn.co.uk
– info@vobsterinn.co.uk – Fax (01373) 812920 – Closed 25 December
3 rm   Rest – (Closed Sunday dinner) Carte £18/26
♦ Sit on the terrace or in the restaurant to sample cooking from the regularly-changing menus. Choose from classic British or Spanish dishes, made using locally sourced produce.

LOWER WHITLEY – Cheshire – 502 M 24   20 **A3**
▶ London 199 mi – Liverpool 25 mi – Manchester 24 mi – Warrington 7 mi

Chetwode Arms   🛋 🛋 **P** 🚾 ◍◍
Street Lane ⊠ WA4 4EN – 𝒞 (01925) 730 203 – www.chetwodearms.com
– claudia.d@btinternet.com – Fax (01925) 730 203
– Closed 25 December and 1 January
Rest – Menu £10 (lunch) – Carte £20/38
♦ Cosy inn with a terrace and bowling green. Wide-ranging à la carte features British and Austrian cooking, as well as dishes cooked on hot rocks; including kudu, crocodile and zebra.

LOWESTOFT – Suffolk – 504 Z 26 – pop. 68 340 ▌ *Great Britain*   15 **D2**
▶ London 116 mi – Ipswich 43 mi – Norwich 30 mi
🖽 East Point Pavillion, Royal Plain 𝒞 (01502) 533600,
touristinfo@waveny.gov.uk
🏨 Rookery Park Carlton Colville, 𝒞 (01502) 509 190
◧ Norfolk Broads★

at Oulton Broad West : 2 m. by A 146 – ⊠ Lowestoft

Ivy House ॐ   🚗 🕩 🕭 🕪 🕯 🐾 **P** **VISA** **OO** **AE** **①**
Ivy Lane, Southwest : 1½ m. by A 146 ⊠ NR33 8HY – 🕿 *(01502) 501 353*
– www.ivyhousecountryhotel.co.uk – michelin@ivyhousecountryhotel.co.uk
– Fax (01502) 501 539 – Closed 2 weeks Christmas-New Year
19 rm � – ✝£99/118 ✝✝£175 – 1 suite
Rest *The Crooked Barn* – see restaurant listing
♦ Converted farm in rural seclusion down an unmade lane. Well kept gardens and grounds. Spacious bedrooms, in converted barns, have bright, fresh décor.

The Crooked Barn – at Ivy House   🏠 **P** **VISA** **OO** **AE** **①**
Ivy Lane, Southwest : 1½ m. by A 146 ⊠ NR33 8HY – 🕿 *(01502) 501 353*
– www.ivyhousecountryhotel.co.uk – michelin@ivyhousecountryhotel.co.uk
– Fax (01502) 501 539 – Closed 2 weeks Christmas-New Year
Rest – Menu £20/30 – Carte £31/42 **s**
♦ Thatched part 18C former hay loft, the focus of Ivy House Farm's characterful setting. Delightful crooked beamed interior. Modern British fare using fresh, local produce.

LUDLOW – Shropshire – **503** L 26 – pop. 9 548 ▌ *Great Britain*   18 **B2**

> 🚊 London 162 mi – Birmingham 39 mi – Hereford 24 mi – Shrewsbury 29 mi
> 🏛 Castle St 🕿 (01584) 875053, ludlow.tourism@shropshire.gov.uk
> ◉ Town★Z – Castle★ **AC** – Feathers Hotel★ – St Laurence's Parish Church★ (Misericords★) **s**
> 🄶 Stokesay Castle★ **AC**, NW : 6½ m. by A 49

ENGLAND

Plan on next page

Overton Grange   < 🚗 🕸 **P** **VISA** **OO**
Old Hereford Rd, South : 1¾ m. by B 4361 ⊠ SY8 4AD – 🕿 *(01584) 873 500*
– www.overtongrangehotel.com – info@overtongrangehotel.com
– Fax (01584) 873 524
14 rm � – ✝£105/140 ✝✝£140/190
Rest – (booking essential for non-residents) (lunch by arrangement) Menu £33/43
♦ Edwardian country house with good views of the surrounding countryside. Comfortable lounges. Attentive service and well-kept, individual rooms. Accomplished, inventive modern cuisine with a French base.

Dinham Hall   🚗 🐾 **P** **VISA** **OO** **AE** **①**
Dinham ⊠ SY8 1EJ – 🕿 *(01584) 876 464 – www.dinhamhall.co.uk*
– info@dinhamhall.co.uk – Fax (01584) 876 019   Z**b**
13 rm � – ✝£95/160 ✝✝£190
Rest – Menu £39 (dinner) – Carte lunch £29/34
♦ 18C manor house, with pretty walled garden, situated by Ludlow Castle in the heart of charming medieval town. Period furnishings and individual rooms. Crisp, bright décor and creative menu.

Fishmore Hall   🚗 🕭 🕪 **VISA** **OO** **AE**
Flshmore Rd, North : 1½ m via Corve Street ⊠ SY8 3DP – 🕿 *(01584) 875 148*
– www.fishmorehall.co.uk – reception@fishmorehall.co.uk
15 rm � – ✝£100/210 ✝✝£140/250   **Rest** – Menu £23/47
♦ Elegantly restored Georgian house – former girl's school – set out of town in half an acre of land. Very modern designer feel, boasting bold wallpaper and flat screen plasma TVs. Two smart dining rooms serve French based menu.

The Bringewood   🚗 🕪 **P** **VISA** **OO** **AE** **①**
Burrington, Southwest : 7½ m by B4361 and Burrington Rd – 🕿 *(01568) 770 033*
– www.thebringewood.co.uk – info@thebringewood.co.uk – Closed Christmas
11 rm ⊚ – ✝£85 ✝✝£120/126
Rest – (Closed Monday-Tuesday and Sunday dinner) Menu £27/29
– Carte £29/33
♦ Converted cow sheds/stables on remotely situated 250 acre working farm. Delightful rear terrace with countryside views and modern feel throughout; very comfy bedrooms. Open, airy dining room with weekly seasonal menus and home grown veg.

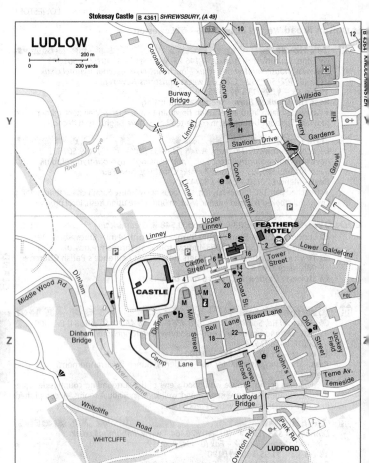

LUDLOW

Stokesay Castle B 4361 SHREWSBURY, (A 49)

0 — 200 m
0 — 200 yards

HEREFORD B 4361 (A 49)

De Grey's Town House without rest   ✦ VISA ◑◐

Broad St ⊠ SY8 1NG – ✆ (01584) 872 764 – www.degreys.co.uk
– degreys@btopenworld.com – Closed 24 December - 6 January   Z**x**
9 rm ⌁ – ♦£100 ♦♦£120/180
♦ Dating back to 1570 this building retains all its good old English style and charm.
Bedrooms are spacious, very individual and feature quality hand made oak furniture.

Bromley Court without rest   ⇌ VISA ◑◐ AE

18-20 Lower Broad St ⊠ SY8 1PQ – ✆ (01584) 876 996 – www.ludlowhotels.com
– phil@ludlowhotels.com – Minimum stay 2 nights at weekend   Z**e**
3 rm – ♦£70/115 ♦♦£80/120
♦ Delightful Tudor cottage converted to provide three well-furnished suites of bed
and living room: high quality comfort. Breakfast and check-in opposite at 73 Lower
Broad St.

XXX **La Bécasse** `VISA OO AE`
🏵 17 Corve St ⊠ SY8 1DA – 𝒞 (01584) 872 325 – www.labecasse.co.uk
– info@labecasse.co.uk – Closed 20 December - 7 January, Monday, Sunday
dinner and Tuesday lunch   Y**e**
Rest – Menu £ 24 (lunch) – Carte £ 49/60
Spec. Crab risotto with leek and truffle jelly. Poached chicken with scallops
and girolle butter sauce. Peach and lavender sugar with rice, champagne and
elderflower jelly.
♦ 17C former coaching inn; its dining room split into small rooms, with attractive listed wood panelling. Intricate and elaborate cooking using luxury ingredients. Attentive service.

XX **Mr Underhill's at Dinham Weir** (Chris Bradley) with rm   ≤ 🍴
🏵 Dinham Bridge ⊠ SY8 1EH – 𝒞 (01584) 874 431   🦃 🍴 🍸 🕯 **P** `VISA OO`
– www.mr-underhills.co.uk
– Closed 25-26 December, 1 January, Monday and Tuesday   Z**f**
6 rm ⊆ – ♥£ 110/140 ♥♥£ 130/165 – 2 suites
Rest – (dinner only) (booking essential) (set menu only) Menu £ 45/55 ⊛
Spec. Bream with spiced couscous, chorizo oil and vinaigrette. Fillet of venison, red wine and elderberry, pea purée. Hot fondant apricot tart with compote and ice cream.
♦ Yellow painted riverside house, away from town centre. Daily set menu: unfussy,
simple cooking with good flavours, prepared with skill. Smart rooms with wood and
inlay décor.

X **Koo** `VISA OO AE`
127 Old St ⊠ SY8 1NU – 𝒞 (01584) 878 462 – www.koo-ook.co.uk
– Fax (01584) 878 462
– Closed 25 December, 1 January, Sunday, Monday and Tuesday in winter   Z**a**
Rest – Japanese – (dinner only) Menu £ 26
♦ Friendly atmosphere in a simply styled interior decorated with banners and artefacts. Good value meals from a regularly changing menu of authentic and tasty
Japanese dishes.

at Woofferton South : 4 m. by B 4361 - Z - and A 49 – ⊠ Ludlow

🏠 **Ravenscourt Manor** without rest   🍴 🍸 **P**
on A 49 ⊠ SY8 4AL – 𝒞 (01584) 711 905
– elizabeth@ravenscourtmanor.plus.com – Fax (01584) 711 905 – Closed January
- March and 25 December
3 rm ⊆ – ♥£ 50 ♥♥£ 75
♦ Characterful black and white timbered 16C manor house in two and a half acres of
lawned gardens. Friendly welcome; comfy lounge. Individually decorated, period
style rooms.

at Brimfield South : 4½ m. by B 4361 - Z - and A 49 – ⊠ Ludlow

🍺 **The Roebuck Inn** with rm   🍴 **P** `VISA OO AE`
⊠ SY8 4NE – 𝒞 (01584) 711 230 – www.theroebuckinnludlow.co.uk
– info@theroebuckludlow.co.uk – Closed 25 December
3 rm ⊆ – ♥£ 65 ♥♥£ 85
Rest – (Closed Sunday dinner) (booking essential) Carte £ 13/34
♦ Country pub filled with rustic objects and curios. Well prepared, locally sourced,
traditional-style food in bar and formal dining room. Warm, homely bedrooms.

at Orleton South : 5½ m. by B 4361 - Y - ⊠ Ludlow

🏠 **Line Farm** without rest ⅏   ≤ 🍴 🕊 🍸 **P**
Tunnel Lane, Southeast : ¾ m. ⊠ SY8 4HY – 𝒞 (01568) 780 400
– www.virtual-shropshire.co.uk/linefarm – February-October
3 rm ⊆ – ♥£ 50/55 ♥♥£ 65/70
♦ Purpose-built house in a relaxing location on a working farm. Pleasant views across
a pretty garden to open countryside from each of the comfortable bedrooms.

ENGLAND

at Bromfield Northwest : 2½ m. on A 49 - Y – ⊠ Ludlow

XX **The Clive** with rm ⌂ & rm, ¶ ⅍ P VISA ⬤ AE
⊠ SY8 2JR – ℰ (01584) 856 565 – www.theclive.co.uk – info@theclive.co.uk
– Fax (01584) 856 661 – Closed 25-26 December
15 rm ☲ – †£60 ††£85 **Rest** – Carte £18/32
♦ Large converted pub with modern décor in vivid colours. Restaurant, bar, café and
bistro areas. Menu of internationally inspired traditional dishes. Very good modern
bedrooms.

LUTON – Luton – **504** S 28 – pop. 185 543 ▌ Great Britain 12 **A2**
▣ London 35 mi – Cambridge 36 mi – Ipswich 93 mi – Oxford 45 mi
– Southend-on-Sea 63 mi
▲ Luton International Airport : ℰ (01582) 405100, E : 1½ m. X
▢ Central Library, St George's Sq ℰ (01582) 401579
▤ Stockwood Park London Rd, ℰ (01582) 413 704
▣ Whipsnade Wild Animal Park★, West : 8 m. by B 489, signed from M 1
(junction 9) and M 25 (junction 21) X

▦▦▦ **Luton Hoo** ⤳ ≺ ⊞ ⌂ ▢ ⊛ ⋙ ₤ ⅔ ▤ ⬤ & ℂ ⅍ P VISA ⬤ AE ⓘ
The Mansion House, Southeast : 2½ m. by A505 and A1081 ⊠ LU1 3TQ
– ℰ (01582) 734 437 – www.lutonhoo.com – reservations@lutonhoo.com
– Fax (01582) 485 438
123 rm ☲ – †£188/235 ††£260/325 – 21 suites
Rest Wernher – (Closed Saturday lunch) Menu £30/42
Rest Adam's Brasserie – (Closed Monday, Tuesday and Sunday dinner)
Carte £29/53
♦ Stunning 18C house set in over 1,000 acres of gardens, some designed by Capabil-
ity Brown. Main mansion boasts numerous comfortable sitting rooms and character-
ful bedrooms. Formal, marble-filled Wernher restaurant offers traditional menu.
Geared towards families, Adam's brasserie is simpler.

LUXBOROUGH – Somerset – **503** J 30 – ⊠ Watchet 3 **A2**
▣ London 205 mi – Exeter 42 mi – Minehead 9 mi – Taunton 25 mi

⌂ **The Royal Oak Inn of Luxborough** with rm ⌂ P VISA ⬤
Exmoor National Park ⊠ TA23 0SH – ℰ (01984) 640 319
– www.theroyaloakinnluxborough.co.uk – info@theroyaloakinnluxborough.co.uk
– Fax (01984) 641 561 – Closed 25 December
11 rm ☲ – †£55/75 ††£75/100 **Rest** – Carte £18/28
♦ Red sandstone pub in an extremely beautiful location. Seasonal menu offers substantial dishes of classically prepared, boldly flavoured foods, with an international
edge. Bedrooms are compact but charming.

LYDDINGTON – Rutland – see Uppingham

LYDFORD – Devon – **503** H 32 – pop. 1 734 – ⊠ Okehampton 2 **C2**
▣ London 234 mi – Exeter 33 mi – Plymouth 25 mi
◉ Village★★
▣ Dartmoor National Park★★

↑ **Moor View House** ⌂ ⅍ P
Vale Down, Northeast : 1½ m. on A 386 ⊠ EX20 4BB – ℰ (01822) 820 220
– Fax (01822) 820 220 – Closed Christmas - New Year
4 rm ☲ – †£50 ††£75
Rest – (by arrangement, communal dining) Menu £25
♦ Victorian country house with attractive garden. Relaxed and friendly atmosphere
with real fires; traditionally furnished with antique pieces. Thoughtful, personal
touches. Dine with fellow guests at antique table.

L'infini pluriel

Route du Fort-de-Brégançon - 83250 La Londe-les-Maures - Tél. 33 (0)4 94 01 53 53
Fax 33 (0)4 94 01 53 54 - domaines-ott.com - ott.particuliers@domaines-ott.com

MICHELIN ATLASES
Let your imagination take you away

Get the most from your traveling with Michelin atlases
- Detailed road network coverage, updated annually
- Unique atlas format designed for the way you drive
- Route-planning made easy for business and leisure

www.michelin.co.uk

The Dartmoor Inn with rm 🅿 VISA ⬤ AE
Moorside, East : 1 m. on A 386 ⊠ EX20 4AY – ℰ *(01822) 820221*
– www.dartmoorinn.com – info@dartmoorinn.co.uk – Fax (01822) 820494
3 rm ⌂ – †£95 ††£125
Rest – (Closed Sunday dinner and Monday lunch) Menu £18 (weekdays)
– Carte £20/35
♦ Pleasant service and a relaxed ambience amidst gently rustic surroundings. Modern menu using local ingredients influenced by Mediterranean and local styles. Smart rooms.

LYME REGIS – Dorset – 503 L 31 – pop. 4 406   3 **B3**
> London 160 mi – Dorchester 25 mi – Exeter 31 mi – Taunton 27 mi
> Guildhall Cottage, Church St ℰ (01297) 442138,
> lymeregis.tic@westdorset-dc.gov.uk
> Timber Hill, ℰ (01297) 442963
> Town★ – The Cobb★

Alexandra ≤ 🚗 🏠 🅿 VISA ⬤
Pound St ⊠ DT7 3HZ – ℰ *(01297) 442010 – www.hotelalexandra.co.uk*
– enquiries@hotelalexandra.co.uk – Fax (01297) 443229 – Closed 1-23 January and Christmas
25 rm ⌂ – †£70/95 ††£180
Rest – Menu £37 (dinner) – Carte lunch £23/29
♦ A busy, family run hotel with traditional style at the top of the town. Set in manicured gardens with views of the sea. Comfortable lounge and south facing conservatory. Tasty, home-cooked menus.

Hix Oyster and Fish House ≤ 🏠 VISA ⬤ AE
Lister Gardens ⊠ DT7 3JP – ℰ *(01297) 446910 – www.restaurantsetcltd.co.uk*
– fishhouse@restaurantsetcltd.co.uk – Closed Monday
Rest – Seafood – Menu £21 (lunch midweek) – Carte £28/50
♦ Small eatery in a terrace by the new gardens; superb views over the bay and cob. Rustic, simple and understated. Daily seafood menu with real understanding of less is more.

LYMINGTON – Hampshire – 503 – pop. 14 227   6 **A3**
> London 103 mi – Bournemouth 18 mi – Southampton 19 mi
> – Winchester 32 mi
> to the Isle of Wight (Yarmouth) (Wightlink Ltd) frequent services daily (30 mn)
> St Barb Museum and Visitor Centre, New St (01590) 689000,
> information@nfdc.gov.uk

Stanwell House 🚗 ⁿ 🛁 VISA ⬤ AE
14-15 High St ⊠ SO41 9AA – ℰ *(01590) 677123 – www.stanwellhouse.com*
– enquiries@stanwellhouse.com – Fax (01590) 677756
23 rm ⌂ – †£99 ††£135 – 4 suites
Rest *Bistro* – Menu £13/27 s – Carte dinner £25/39 s
Rest *Seafood at Stanwells* – Carte £17/34
♦ Privately owned hotel with individual style in Georgian building. Rich décor verges on the gothic with sumptuous silks, crushed velvets and an eclectic mix of furniture. Atmospheric Bistro in dramatic, rich colours.

The Mill at Gordleton 🏠 AC rest, ⁿ 🅿 VISA ⬤ AE
Silver St, Hordle, Northwest : 3½ m. by A 337 and Sway Rd ⊠ SO41 6DJ
– ℰ *(01590) 682219 – www.themillatgordleton.co.uk*
– info@themillatgordleton.co.uk – Fax (01590) 683073 – Closed 25 December
6 rm ⌂ – †£90 ††£130 – 1 suite   **Rest** – Menu £16 – Carte £20/39
♦ Delightfully located quaint 17C water mill on edge of New Forest, in well-kept gardens. Comfortable, traditionally styled interior with a pubby bar and clean-lined rooms. Terrace available for alfresco dining.

ENGLAND

✗ **Egan's** 🛜 VISA ◉◉
24 Gosport St ⊠ SO41 9BG – ℰ (01590) 676 165 – johnegan@dsl.pipex.com
– Closed 25 December-8 January, Sunday and Monday
Rest – (booking essential) Menu £ 15 (lunch) – Carte dinner £ 24/32
♦ Bustling bistro style restaurant near the High Street. Warm yellow walls give it a
Mediterranean feel. Pleasant, efficient service. Fresh, simple cooking with modern
elements.

at Downton West : 3 m. on A 337 – ⊠ Lymington

⌂ **The Olde Barn** without rest ⅋ P VISA ◉◉
Christchurch Rd, East : ½ m. on A 337 ⊠ SO41 0LA – ℰ (01590) 644 939
– www.theoldebarn.co.uk – julie@theoldbarn.co.uk – Fax (01590) 644 939
3 rm ⊊ – †£50/70 ††£60/80
♦ Unsurprisingly, a converted 17C barn with large, chintzy lounge and wood burner.
Some bedrooms in barn annex: a mix of modern style and exposed brick, all spotlessly clean.

LYNMOUTH – Devon – **503** I 30 – **see Lynton**

LYNTON – Devon – **503** I 30   2 **C1**

▶ London 206 mi – Exeter 59 mi – Taunton 44 mi
🚹 Town Hall, Lee Rd ℰ (01598) 752225, info@lyntourism.co.uk
◎ Town★ (≤★)
⊙ Valley of the Rocks★, W : 1 m. – Watersmeet★, E : 1½ m. by A 39. Exmoor
National Park★★ – Doone Valley★, SE : 7½ m. by A 39 (access from Oare
on foot)

🖳 **Lynton Cottage** ⌂ ≤ 🚗 🛜 P VISA ◉◉ AE
North Walk Hill ⊠ EX35 6ED – ℰ (01598) 752 342 – www.lyntoncottage.com
– enquries@lynton-cottage.co.uk – Fax (01598) 754 016 – Closed February -
November and Christmas
16 rm ⊊ – †£68/96 ††£168/224   **Rest** – (bar lunch) Menu £ 32 **s**
♦ Stunning vistas of the bay and Countisbury Hill from this personally run, cliff top
hotel. All bedrooms to a good standard - superior rooms command the best views.
Outside the restaurant, stunning sea views. Inside, local art on the walls.

⌂ **Hewitt's - Villa Spaldi** ⌂ ≤ 🚗 ⌔ 🛜 ⌗ P VISA ◉◉ AE
North Walk ⊠ EX35 6HJ – ℰ (01598) 752 293 – www.hewittshotel.com
– hewitts.hotel@talk21.com – Fax (01598) 752 489 – 12 March-12 October
7 rm ⊊ – †£70/95 ††£ 140/180 – 1 suite
Rest – (Closed Monday and Sunday dinner) Menu £ 39 (dinner) **s**
– Carte £ 25/341 **s**
♦ Splendid 19C Arts & Crafts house in tranquil wooded cliffside setting. Stained glass
window by Burne Jones and library filled with antiques. Stylish rooms with sea views.
Oak panelled dining room; charming service.

⌂ **Highcliffe House** without rest ≤ 🚗 ⅋ ⌗ P VISA ◉◉ AE
Sinai Hill ⊠ EX35 6AR – ℰ (01598) 752 235 – www.highcliffehouse.co.uk
– info@highcliffehouse.co.uk – Mid February-mid November
7 rm ⊊ – †£90/105 ††£ 120/140
♦ Intimate, friendly atmosphere in former Victorian gentleman's residence. Authentic
period-style rooms with panoramic views and ornate antique beds.

⌂ **Victoria Lodge** without rest 🚗 ⅋ ⌗ P VISA ◉◉
30-31 Lee Rd ⊠ EX35 6BS – ℰ (01598) 753 203 – www.victorialodge.co.uk
– info@victorialodge.co.uk – Fax (01598) 753 203 – March-October
8 rm ⊊ – †£119 ††£140
♦ Large 19C house decorated with period photographs, prints and Victoriana. Traditional décor in communal areas and bedrooms which are comfortable and inviting.

ENGLAND

St Vincent 🚗 🎖️ ⁽¹⁾ VISA ⓂⓄ
Market St, Castle Hill ⊠ *EX35 6JA –* ℰ *(01598) 752 244*
– www.st-vincent-hotel.co.uk – welcome@st-vincent-hotel.co.uk – Easter-October
5 rm ⌂ *–* ♦£75 ♦♦£75/80
Rest – (Closed Monday - Tuesday) (dinner only) (booking essential for non-residents) Menu £27
♦ Grade II listed building with charming Belgian owners 200 metres from Coastal Path. Lovely Edwardian lounge with crackling fire. Neat, simple, clean bedrooms. Cloth-clad dining room: owners proud of French/Mediterranean menus.

at Lynmouth

Shelley's without rest ⩽ 🎖️ VISA ⓂⓄ AE
8 Watersmeet Rd ⊠ *EX35 6EP –* ℰ *(01598) 753 219 – www.shelleyshotel.co.uk*
– info@shelleyshotel.co.uk – Fax (01598) 753 219 – March-October
11 rm ⌂ *–* ♦£70 ♦♦£100/110
♦ Centrally located hotel named after eponymous poet who honeymooned here in 1812. Stylish public areas. Very comfortable bedrooms with good views of picturesque locale.

Bonnicott House ⩽ 🚗 🎖️ ⁽¹⁾ VISA ⓂⓄ
Watersmeet Rd ⊠ *EX35 6EP –* ℰ *(01598) 753 346 – www.bonnicott.com*
– stay@bonnicott.com
8 rm ⌂ *–* ♦£65/86 ♦♦£144/192
Rest – (Closed October-April) (dinner only) Menu £27 **s**
♦ Former 19C rectory in elevated setting. Spacious lounge with log fire: large windows offer good views to sea. Bright rooms, two with four poster, all with sherry decanter. Fresh, traditional meals cooked on the Aga.

The Heatherville 🌿 ⩽ Ⓟ VISA ⓂⓄ
Tors Park, by Tors Rd ⊠ *EX35 6NB –* ℰ *(01598) 752 327*
– www.heatherville.co.uk – Fax (01598) 752 634 – March-October
6 rm ⌂ *–* ♦£75 ♦♦£100   **Rest** – (by arrangement) Menu £25
♦ Victorian house perched above the town. Well kept throughout with bright, warm décor. Rooms with bold fabrics and woodland views: room 6 has the best outlook. Home-cooked meals employ fresh, local produce.

Sea View Villa 🚗 🎖️ ⁽¹⁾ VISA ⓂⓄ AE
6 Summer House Path ⊠ *EX35 6ES –* ℰ *(01598) 753 460*
– www.seaviewvilla.co.uk – seaviewenquiries@aol.com
– Closed 3 January-13 February and first 2 weeks November
5 rm ⌂ *–* ♦£50/80 ♦♦£110/130
Rest – (by arrangement, communal dining) Menu £32
♦ Grade II listed Georgian house a stone's throw from harbour. Luxurious interior filled with owners' mementoes. Stylish rooms furnished with taste; all boast enviable sea view. Dinner party style evening meals with fellow guests.

at Martinhoe West : 4 ¼ m. via Coast rd (toll) – ⊠ Barnstaple

Old Rectory 🌿 🚗 ⁽¹⁾ Ⓟ VISA ⓂⓄ
⊠ *EX31 4QT –* ℰ *(01598) 763 368 – www.oldrectoryhotel.co.uk*
– info@oldrectoryhotel.co.uk – Fax (01598) 763 567 – March-October
8 rm ⌂ *–* ♦♦£205   **Rest** – (dinner only) (residents only) Menu £33 **s**
♦ Built in 19C for rector of Martinhoe's 11C church. Quiet country retreat in charming three acre garden with cascading brook. Bright and co-ordinated bedrooms. Classic country house dining room.

ENGLAND

Your opinions are important to us:
please write and let us know about your discoveries and experiences – good and bad!

LYTHAM ST ANNE'S – Lancashire – **502** L 22 – pop. 41 327   20 **A2**

> ▶ London 237 mi – Blackpool 7 mi – Liverpool 44 mi – Preston 13 mi
> 🖪 67 St Annes Rd West ℰ (01253) 725610, touristinfo@flyde.gov.uk
> 🏌 Fairhaven AnsdellOakwood Avenue, ℰ (01253) 736741
> 🏌 St Annes Old Links Highbury Rd, ℰ (01253) 723597

at Lytham

🏠 **Clifton Arms**   ⇐ 🖪 ⁇ ¶ 🕍 **P** _VISA_ ◍ 🄰🄴 ➊

West Beach ⊠ *FY8 5QJ* – ℰ *(01253) 739898 – www.cliftonarms-lytham.com*
– welcome@cliftonarms-lytham.com – Fax (01253) 730657
45 rm � – ♦£140 ♦♦£160
Rest – (bar lunch Monday-Saturday) Menu £33 – Carte £20/36

♦ Former inn with strong associations with local championship golf course. Traditional country house public areas. Cottage-style rooms, front ones with great views. Restaurant's popular window tables overlook Lytham Green.

at St Anne's

🏠 **The Grand**   ⇐ 🗺 🖂 🍴 🕍 🖪 ⁇ ✆ 🕍 **P** _VISA_ ◍ 🄰🄴

South Promenade ⊠ *FY8 1NB* – ℰ *(01253) 721288 – www.the-grand.co.uk*
– book@the-grand.co.uk – Fax (01253) 714459 – Closed 24-26 December
53 rm – ♦£95 ♦♦£145, ⊇ £6.50
Rest *Café Grand* – Carte £19/32 **s**

♦ Impressive, turreted Victorian hotel on promenade. Warm, much improved interior. Spacious rooms, most with good views, turret rooms have particularly good aspect. Rich crimson restaurant overlooks the sea.

XX **Greens Bistro**   _VISA_ ◍

3-9 St Andrews Road South - Lower Ground Floor ⊠ *FY8 1SX* – ℰ *(01253)*
789990 – www.greensbistro.co.uk – info@greensbistro.co.uk – Closed 1 week
Spring, 1 week Autumn, Sunday, Monday and Bank Holidays
Rest – (dinner only) Menu £16 – Carte £22/26

♦ Worth the effort to find, this simple, pleasant bistro, hidden beneath some shops, has linen clad tables, friendly service, and good value, well executed modern British menus.

MADINGLEY – Cambs. – **504** U 27 – see Cambridge

MAENPORTH BEACH – Cornwall – see Falmouth

MAGHAM DOWN – E. Sussex – see Hailsham

MAIDENCOMBE – Devon – **503** J 32 – see Torquay

MAIDENHEAD – Windsor and Maidenhead – **504** R 29 – pop. 58 848   11 **C3**

> ▶ London 33 mi – Oxford 32 mi – Reading 13 mi
> ⛴ to Marlow, Cookham and Windsor (Salter Bros. Ltd) (summer only)
> (3 h 45 mn)
> 🖪 The Library, St Ives Rd ℰ (01628) 796502, maidenhead.tic@rbwm.gov.uk
> 🏌 Bird Hills Hawthorn Hill Drift Rd, ℰ (01628) 771030
> 🏌 Shoppenhangers Rd, ℰ (01628) 624693

Plan opposite

🏠 **Fredrick's**   🍽 🔏 🖂 ◍ 🍴 🕍 🄰🄲 ⁇ ¶ 🕍 **P** _VISA_ ◍ 🄰🄴

Shoppenhangers Rd ⊠ *SL6 2PZ* – ℰ *(01628) 581000*
– www.fredricks-hotel.co.uk – tspittles@fredricks-hotel.co.uk – Fax (01628)
771054 – Closed 24-30 December   X**c**
33 rm ⊇ – ♦£150/220 ♦♦£180/250 – 1 suite
Rest *Fredrick's* – see restaurant listing

♦ Redbrick former inn with well-equipped spa facilities. Ornate, marble reception with smoked mirrors. Conservatory with wicker chairs. Very comfy, individually styled rooms.

MAIDENHEAD

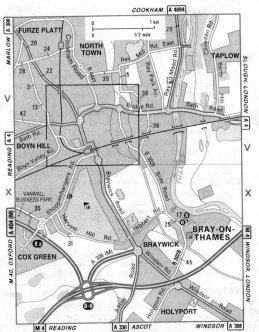

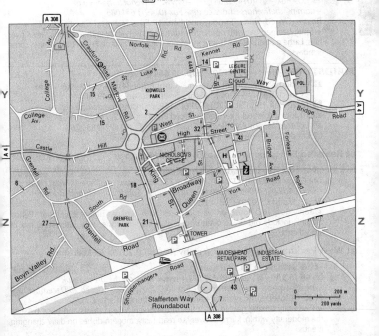

Walton Cottage 📶 ✿ 📶 ♨ P 💳 ⊕ AE ①
Marlow Rd ⊠ SL6 7LT – ℰ (01628) 624 394 – www.waltoncottagehotel.co.uk
– res@waltoncottagehotel.co.uk – Fax (01628) 773 851
– Closed 24 December-2 January Ye
69 rm � – †£110/145 ††£150/180 – 3 suites
Rest – (Closed Friday-Sunday and Bank Holidays) (dinner only) Menu £20
♦ A collection of brick built, bay-windowed houses and annexed blocks near town centre. Poet's Parlour lounge is cosy with beams and brick. Aimed at the business traveller. Restaurant prides itself in traditional home cooking.

XXX **Fredrick's** - at Fredrick's Hotel 🚗 ☆ AC ⇔ P 💳 ⊕ AE ①
Shoppenhangers Rd ⊠ SL6 2PZ – ℰ (01628) 581 000 – www.fredricks-hotel.co.uk
– tspittles@fredricks-hotel.co.uk – Fax (01628) 771 054 – Closed 24-30 December
Rest – Menu £26/39 – Carte £40/48 Xc
♦ Ornate paintings, smoked mirrors and distressed pine greet diners in this large restaurant. Chandeliers, full-length windows add to classic feel. Elaborate British menus.

MAIDEN NEWTON – Dorset – **503** M 31 4 **C3**
🖸 London 144 mi – Exeter 55 mi – Taunton 37 mi – Weymouth 16 mi

XX **Le Petit Canard** 💳 ⊕ AE
Dorchester Rd ⊠ DT2 0BE – ℰ (01300) 320 536 – www.le-petit-canard.co.uk
– craigs@le-petit-canard.co.uk – Fax (01300) 321 286 – Closed Monday and dinner Sunday
Rest – (dinner only) (Sunday lunch by arrangement) Menu £31
♦ Pleasant stone-built cottage in middle of charming village. Plenty of candles, well-spaced tables and soft music. English dishes with French and Oriental touches.

MAIDENSGROVE – Oxfordshire – pop. 1 572 – ⊠ Henley-on-Thames 11 **C3**
🖸 London 43 mi – Oxford 23 mi – Reading 15 mi

🍴 **The Five Horseshoes** 🚗 ☆ P 💳 ⊕ AE
⊠ RG9 6EX – ℰ (01491) 641 282 – www.thefivehorseshoes.co.uk
– admin@thefivehorseshoes.co.uk – Fax (01491) 641 086
Rest – (Closed dinner Sunday and Bank Holiday Monday) Carte £20/32
♦ Snug beamed bar with open fires; suntrap conservatory with southerly views over hills. Large gardens; barbeques in summer. Pie and a pint on Fridays; hog roasts some Sundays.

MAIDSTONE – Kent – **504** V 30 – pop. 89 684 📗 *Great Britain* 8 **B2**
🖸 London 36 mi – Brighton 64 mi – Cambridge 84 mi – Colchester 72 mi
– Croydon 36 mi – Dover 45 mi – Southend-on-Sea 49 mi
🛈 Town Hall, High St ℰ (01622) 602169, tourism@maidstone.gov.uk
🖈 Tudor Park Hotel Bearsted Ashford Rd, ℰ (01622) 734 334
🖈 Cobtree Manor Park Boxley Chatham Rd, ℰ (01622) 753 276
🖸 Leeds Castle ★ AC, SE : 4½ m. by A 20 and B 2163

at Bearsted East : 3 m. by A 249 off A 20 – ⊠ Maidstone

XX **Soufflé Restaurant on the Green** ☆ ⇔ P 💳 ⊕ AE
The Green ⊠ ME14 4DN – ℰ (01622) 737 065 – www.soufflerestaurant.co.uk
– Fax (01622) 737 065 – Closed Saturday lunch, Sunday dinner and Monday
Rest – Menu £15/25 – Carte £31/36
♦ Converted 16C house on village green with terrace. Timbered interior. Period features include old bread oven in one wall. Modern dishes with interesting mix of ingredients.

at West Peckham Southwest : 7 ¾ m. by A 26 off B 2016 – ⊠ Maidstone

🍴 **The Swan on the Green** ☆ P 💳 ⊕ AE ①
⊠ ME18 5JW – ℰ (01622) 812 271 – www.swan-on-the-green.co.uk
– info@swan-on-the-green.co.uk – Fax (0870) 056 0556 – Closed 25 December
Rest – (Closed Sunday dinner and Monday dinner) Carte £22/27
♦ Pleasantly ornate, gabled 16C pub on the green. Village prints and hops balance the modernity within. Micro brewery to rear. Tasty, modern dishes on daily changing menus.

▶ London 108 mi – Bristol 28 mi – Gloucester 24 mi – Swindon 19 mi
🛈 Town Hall, Market Lane ✆ (01666) 823748,
   malmesburyip@northwilts.gov.uk
◎ Town★ – Market Cross★★ – Abbey★

Whatley Manor ⟋   ⟨ 🚗 🐾 ☺ 🏠 🛁 👗 🖥 📶 🍸 **P** **VISA** **◎** **AE**
Easton Grey, West : 2¼ m. on B 4040 ⊠ SN16 0RB – ✆ (01666) 822 888
– www.whatleymanor.com – reservations@whatleymanor.com
– Fax (01666) 826 120
15 rm ⌐ – 👫£ 490 – 8 suites
Rest *The Dining Room* and *Le Mazot* – see restaurant listing
♦ Collection of Cotswold stone buildings set in beautiful, tranquil gardens. Chic,
contemporary bedrooms offer complete luxury and sumptuous bathrooms. Lavish
spa, top class business centre and new cinema.

The Old Bell   🚗 🍸 👗 **P** **VISA** **◎** **AE**
Abbey Row ⊠ SN16 0BW – ✆ (01666) 822 344 – www.oldbellhotel.com
– info@oldbellhotel.com – Fax (01666) 825 145 – Closed 2-3 January
34 rm ⌐ – 👤£ 90/99 👫£ 265/295
Rest *The Restaurant* – see restaurant listing
♦ Part 13C former abbots hostel with gardens. Elegant public areas with hugely
characterful bar and lounge. Bedrooms in main house better than those in coach-
house.

The Dining Room – at Whatley Manor Hotel   ⟨ 🚗 🐾 **P** **VISA** **◎** **AE**
Easton Grey, West : 2¼ m. on B 4040 ⊠ SN12 0RB – ✆ (01666) 822 888
– www.whatleymanor.com – reservations@whatleymanor.com
– Fax (01666) 826 120
Rest – (closed Monday-Tuesday) (dinner only) (booking essential for
non-residents) Menu £ 65/80 **s**
Spec. Smoked eel with duck and cured foie gras. Roast and braised boar
with broccoli purée and liquorice reduction. Raspberry soufflé with raspberry
'interpretations'.
♦ Subtle, chic and detailed environment, with charming service from dedicated,
personable team. Highly skilled, well established kitchen team display ambition, innovation and individual style.

Le Mazot – at Whatley Manor Hotel   **AC** **P** **VISA** **◎** **AE**
Easton Grey, West : 2¼ m. on B 4040 ⊠ SN12 0RB – ✆ (01666) 822 888
– www.whatleymanor.com – lemazot@whatleymanor.com – Fax (01666) 826 120
Rest – Menu £ 17 (lunch) **s** – Carte £ 30/36 **s**
♦ Gold wood Swiss chalet restaurant, offering casual dining on comfy banquettes.
Including some Swiss specialities, cooking is light and skilled. Polite, careful service.

The Restaurant – at The Old Bell Hotel   🌤 **P** **VISA** **◎** **AE**
Abbey Row ⊠ SN16 0BW – ✆ (01666) 822 344 – www.oldbellhotel.com
– info@oldbellhotel.com – Fax (01666) 825 145 – Closed 2-3 January
Rest – (booking essential) (light lunch) Carte £ 33/38
♦ Charming restaurant with accomplished modern cooking; local ingredients are
very much to the fore. Outside terrace with peaceful garden allows for relaxed
summer dining.

---

at Crudwell North : 4 m. on A 429 – ⊠ Malmesbury

The Rectory   🚗 🍸 🍽 🍸 **P** **VISA** **◎**
⊠ SN16 9EP – ✆ (01666) 577 194 – www.therectoryhotel.com
– info@therectoryhotel.com – Fax (01666) 577 853
11 rm ⌐ – 👤£ 95 👫£ 105/175 – 1 suite
Rest – Menu £ 19 (lunch) – Carte (dinner) £ 25/32
♦ 17C stone-built former Rectory with formal garden. A little quirky but personally
run. Comfortable, individually-styled bedrooms with many modern extras, some with
spa baths. Airy oak-panelled dining room; modern seasonal cooking.

ENGLAND

The Potting Shed ♿ **P** VISA ◑◐
The Street ✉ *SN16 9EW* – ✆ *(01666) 577833 – www.therectoryhotel.com*
Rest – (Closed Sunday dinner) Carte £ 25/40
♦ Relaxed country dining pub with gardening theme and organic herb and vegetable beds at rear. Seasonal produce and rustic, wholesome dishes served in generous portions.

at Charlton Northeast : 2 ½ m. on B 4040 – ✉ Chichester

The Horse and Groom with rm 🛋 ☏ 🛜 **P** VISA ◑◐
The Street, Charlton , on B 4040 ✉ *SN16 9DL* – ✆ *(01666) 823904*
– www.horseandgroominn.com – info@horseandgroominn.com
5 rm ⚃ – ♦£80 ♦♦£90   **Rest** – Menu £ 15 (lunch) – Carte £ 17/30
♦ 16C Cotswold stone pub with outside bar. Local, seasonal ingredients inform the wide-ranging menu of sandwiches, platters, British classics and more contemporary dishes. Beautifully appointed, stylish bedrooms with sumptuous bathrooms.

MALPAS – Cheshire – 502 20 **A3**
▶ London 177 mi – Birmingham 60 mi – Chester 15 mi – Shrewsbury 26 mi – Stoke-on-Trent 30 mi

at Tilston NW : 3 m. on Tilston Rd – ✉ Malpas

Tilston Lodge without rest 🛋 ◎ 🌿 **P**
Tilston, Northwest : 3 m. on Tilston Rd ✉ *SY14 7DR* – ✆ *(01829) 250223*
– Fax (01829) 250223 – Closed 25 December
3 rm ⚃ – ♦£48/52 ♦♦£85
♦ A former Victorian hunting lodge with delightful gardens and grounds, personally run in a very pleasant style by the charming owner. Cosy, individually appointed bedrooms.

MALVERN WELLS – Worcs. – 503 N 27 – see Great Malvern

MAN (Isle of) – I.O.M. – 502 FG 21 – pop. 80 058 📖 *Great Britain*
🚢 from Douglas to Belfast (Isle of Man Steam Packet Co. Ltd) (summer only) (2 h 45 mn) – from Douglas to Republic of Ireland (Dublin) (Isle of Man Steam Packet Co. Ltd) (2 h 45 mn/4 h) – from Douglas to Heysham (Isle of Man Steam Packet Co.) (2 h/3 h 30 mn) – from Douglas to Liverpool (Isle of Man Steam Packet Co. Ltd) (2 h 30 mn/4 h)
◎ Laxey Wheel★★ - Snaefell★ (❄★★★) - Cregneash Folk Museum★

Douglas – Douglas – pop. 26 218 20 **B1**
🛬 Ronaldsway Airport : ✆ (01624) 821600, SW : 7 m.
ℹ Sea Terminal Buildings ✆ (01624) 686766, tourism@gov.im
⛳ Douglas Pulrose Park, ✆ (01624) 675952
⛳ King Edward Bay Onchan Groudle Rd, ✆ (01624) 620430

Sefton 🖥 🕸 Ⅰ₆ 📶 ⅙ & rm, ☏ 🛜 **P** VISA ◑◐ AE
Harris Promenade ✉ *IM1 2RW* – ✆ *(01624) 645500 – www.seftonhotel.co.im*
– info@seftonhotel.co.im – Fax (01624) 676004
89 rm – ♦£95/110 ♦♦£105/110, ⚃ £10 – 3 suites
Rest *The Gallery* – (lunch residents only) Menu £ 22 (lunch) – Carte £ 30/40
♦ Victorian fronted promenade hotel, built around unique atrium water garden. Comfy, airy bedrooms may have balconies, look out to sea or have internal water garden views. Gallery restaurant with its boldly coloured Manx art, offers flambé dishes as its speciality.

The Regency ≤ 🎐 🌿 ☏ ⅙ VISA ◑◐ AE ①
Queens Promenade ✉ *IM2 4NN* – ✆ *(01624) 680680 – www.regency.im*
– mail@regency.im – Fax (01624) 680690
48 rm ⚃ – ♦£71/110 ♦♦£115/160 – 4 suites
Rest *Five Continents* – Carte £ 29/43 ⊞
♦ Perfect for business travellers: mobile phone loan, PCs with free internet in every bedroom and special office suites, combined with traditional seaside styling and Douglas Bay views. Oak panelled restaurant boasts original collection of Island pictures.

 ENGLAND

🏠 **Admiral House** without rest   📶 🛜 ♿ VISA ⓜⓞ AE
12 Loch Promenade ⊠ IM1 2LX – 🕿 (01624) 629 551 – www.admiralhouse.com
– enquiries@admiralhouse.com – Fax (01624) 675 021
23 rm ⊇ – †£ 105/155 ††£ 120/210
♦ Set on the promenade, an impressive Victorian building with turret and views over
Douglas Bay. Spacious, modern bedrooms; breakfast served in stylish coffee shop.
Close to ferry terminal.

🏠 **Penta** without rest   📶 🛜 📞 VISA ⓜⓞ AE ⓘ
Queens Promenade ⊠ IM9 4NE – 🕿 (01624) 680 680 – www.regency.im
– mail@regency.im – Fax (01624) 680 690
22 rm – †£ 49/65 ††£ 57/75
♦ Set on the promenade, with views over Douglas Bay. Large, well equipped bedrooms each have a computer with free internet access. Wine themed, Mediterranean
style breakfast room.

XXX **Ciappelli's**   VISA ⓜⓞ AE ⓘ
Admirals House, 12-13 Loch Promenade ⊠ IM1 2LX – 🕿 (01624) 677 442
– www.ciappellis.com – restaurant@ciappellis.com – Fax (01624) 671 305
– Closed Saturday lunch and Sunday
Rest – Menu £ 25 (lunch) – Carte £ 39/55
♦ Stylish, sophisticated restaurant; unique on the Island. Modern, well judged cook-
ing uses local ingredients in good combinations. Dishes arrive well presented with
clear flavours.

XX **Macfarlane's**   VISA ⓜⓞ AE
24 Duke Street ⊠ IM1 2AY – 🕿 (01624) 624 777 – dine@macfarlanes.im – Closed
2 weeks August, 1 week January, Saturday lunch, Sunday and Monday
Rest – Menu £ 15 (lunch) – Carte £ 26/40
♦ Simple, honest restaurant in heart of town, with leather topped tables and high-
sided booths. Unfussy, regularly changing menu relies on fresh local produce, with
shellfish to the fore.

Port Erin – Port Erin – pop. 3 575   20 **B1**

🏠 **Rowany Cottier** without rest   ← 🚗 🛜 🅿
Spaldrick ⊠ IM9 6PE – 🕿 (01624) 832 287 – www.rowanycottier.com
– rowanycottier@manx.net
5 rm ⊇ – †£ 45/75 ††£ 76/86
♦ Beautifully sited by peaceful Bradda Glen. Pleasant guest areas with views over
Port Erin and Calf of Man. Spacious, well kept bedrooms. Locally sourced breakfast;
homemade bread.

Port St Mary – Port Saint Mary – pop. 1 913   20 **B1**

🏠 **Aaron House** without rest   🛜
The Promenade ⊠ IM9 5DE – 🕿 (01624) 835 702 – www.aaronhouse.co.uk
– aaronhouse@manx.net – Fax (01624) 837 731 – Closed Christmas-New Year
6 rm ⊇ – †£ 49/69 ††£ 70/118
♦ Charming guesthouse with bay/harbour views. Strong Victorian feel, with period
furniture and owner in replica housemaids dress. Comfy, immaculate bedrooms.
Afternoon tea on arrival. Interesting breakfast choices.

🏠 **Ballahane House** without rest   🚗 🛜 🛜 🅿
Truggan Rd, West : ¾ m by Cregneish rd ⊠ IM9 5LD – 🕿 (01624) 834 238
– www.ballahane.co.uk – juliedavid@manx.net
3 rm ⊇ – †£ 48/55 ††£ 85/95
♦ Hidden behind farm buildings on country lane, with distant views of Bradda Head.
Individually themed bedrooms, quality furnishings, stylish bathrooms. Organic Island
breakfast produce.

Ramsey – Ramsey – pop. 7 309   20 **B1**

🏠 **The River House** without rest 🦢   🚗 🅿
North : ¼ m. turning left immediately after bridge ⊠ IM8 3DA – 🕿 (01624)
816 412 – Closed mid February - mid March
3 rm ⊇ – †£ 55/65 ††£ 79/99
♦ Attractive country house with pleasant gardens. Tastefully furnished throughout,
with comfy drawing room, antiques and objets d'art. Three stylishly furnished bedrooms with matching bathrooms.

ENGLAND

N. Boyd/Robert HARDING

MANCHESTER

County: Greater Manchester
Michelin REGIONAL map: n° **502** N 23
▶ London 202 mi – Birmingham 86 mi
– Glasgow 221 mi – Leeds 43 mi – Liver-
pool 35 mi – Nottingham 72 mi

Population: 394 269   20 **B2**
📖 *Great Britain*

PRACTICAL INFORMATION

🛈 Tourist Information

Manchester Visitor Centre, Town Hall Extension, Lloyd St 𝒫 (0871) 222 8223,
touristinformation@marketing-manchester.co.uk

Manchester Airport, International Arrivals Hall, Terminal 1 𝒫 (0161) 436 3344
- Manchester Airport, International Arrivals Hall, Terminal 2 𝒫 (0871) 222 8223
- Salford T.I.C., Pier 8, Salford Quays 𝒫 (0161) 848 8601, tic@salford.gov.uk - Portland
St 𝒫 (0845) 600 6040

Airport

✈ Manchester International Airport: 𝒫 (08712) 710 711, S: 10 m. by A 5103 - AX - and
M 56

Golf Courses

🏌 Heaton Park Prestwich, 𝒫 (0161) 654 9899

🏌 Houldsworth Park Stockport Houldsworth St, Reddish, 𝒫 (0161) 442 1712

🏌 Chorlton-cum-Hardy Barlow Hall Rd, Barlow Hall, 𝒫 (0161) 881 3139

🏌 William Wroe Flixton Pennybridge Lane, 𝒫 (0161) 748 8680

🎦 SIGHTS

SEE

City★ - Castlefield Heritage Park★ CZ
– Town Hall★ CZ – Manchester Art
Gallery★ CZ **M2** – Cathedral★ (stalls
and canopies★) CY – Museum of
Science and Industry★ CZ **M** – Urbis★
CY – Imperial War Museum North★ ,
Trafford Park AX **M**

ENV.

Whitworth Art Gallery★ , S: 1 ½ m

EXC.

Quarry Bank Mill★ , S: 10 m. off B 5166,
exit 5 from M 56

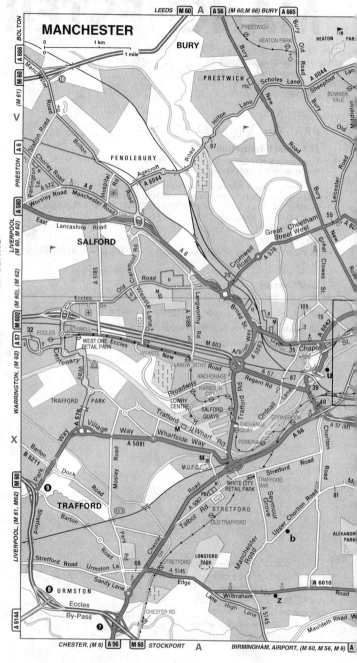

ENGLAND

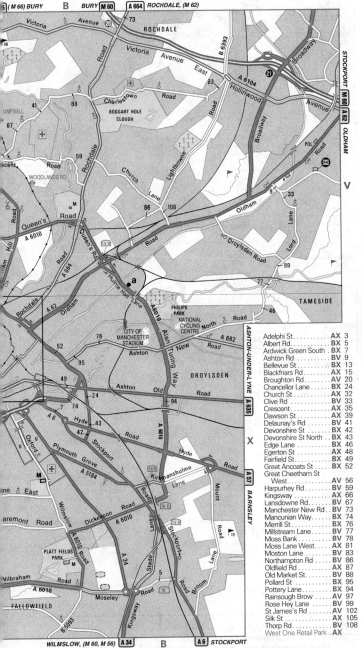

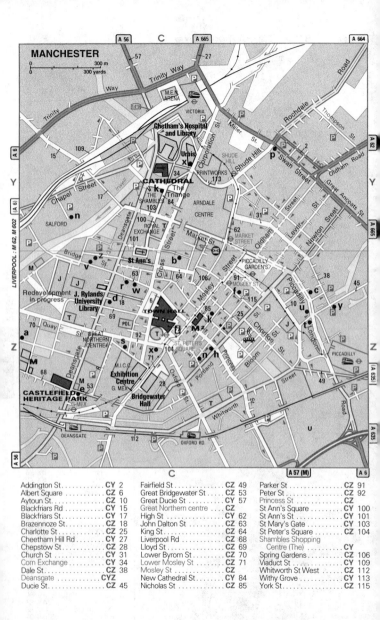

MANCHESTER

300 m
300 yards

Good food without spending a fortune?
Look out for the Bib Gourmand 😊

590

🏨🏨🏨 The Lowry
🖥 🕸 *Là* 🖢 & 🔏 🕻 🗚 **P** **VISA** ⓿ **AE** ⓞ

50 Dearmans Pl, Chapel Wharf, Salford ⊠ M3 5LH – 𝒞 *(0161) 827 4000*
– www.roccofortecollection.com – enquiries.lowry@roccofortecollection.com
– Fax (0161) 827 4001   CY**n**
158 rm – ♥£350 ♥♥£350, � £18.50 – 7 suites
Rest *The River* – see restaurant listing
♦ Stylish contemporary design with a minimalist feel. Smart spacious bedrooms have high levels of comfort and facilities; some overlook River Irwell. State-of-the-art spa.

🏨🏨🏨 The Midland
🖥 🕸 *Là* 🖢 & rm, 🔏 🕸 🕻 🗚 **VISA** ⓿ **AE** ⓞ

16 Peter St ⊠ M60 2DS – 𝒞 *(0161) 236 3333 – www.qhotels.co.uk*
– midlandsales@qhotels.co.uk – Fax (0161) 932 4100   CZ**x**
298 rm – ♥£250 ♥♥£250, ⊇ £15 – 15 suites
Rest *The French* – see restaurant listing
Rest *The Colony* – Menu £19 (lunch) – Carte dinner £23/32
♦ Edwardian splendour on a vast scale in the heart of the city. Period features and a huge open lobby combine with up-to-date facilities to create a thoroughly grand hotel. Brasserie menus take pride of place at the restaurant.

🏨🏨🏨 Radisson Edwardian
🖥 ⑯ 🕸 *Là* 🖢 & rm, 🔏 🕸 🕻 🗚 **P**
VISA ⓿ **AE** ⓞ

Free Trade Hall, Peter St ⊠ M2 5GP – 𝒞 *(0161) 835 9929*
– www.radissonedwardian.com/manchester
– reservations@radissonedwardian.com – Fax (0161) 835 9979   CZ**s**
233 rm – ♥£167/209 ♥♥£188/240 – 4 suites
Rest *Opus One* – (bar lunch) Menu £35 – Carte £27/43
♦ Smart, modern hotel incorporating impressive façade of Free Trade Hall. Grand surroundings of stone, marble and sculptures. Conference and leisure facilities. Stylish rooms. Chic fine dining, with strong Japanese influences, in Opus One.

🏨🏨🏨 Hilton
🖥 🕸 *Là* 🖢 🕻 🗚 **VISA** ⓿ **AE** ⓞ

303 Deansgate ⊠ M3 4LQ – 𝒞 *(0161) 870 1600 – www.hilton.com*
– reservations.manchesterdeansgate@hilton.com – Fax (0161) 870 1650   CZ**e**
275 rm – ♥£199/350 ♥♥£199/360, ⊇ £17.95 – 4 suites
Rest – Menu £14 – Carte £27/36
♦ 23 floors of a striking glass skyscraper. Smart atrium lobby with elevated walkways; glass bottomed pool above. Comfortable, contemporary bedrooms with views. Superb 360° outlook from Cloud bar. Stylish Podium restaurant offers modern brasserie menu of European dishes.

🏨🏨 Malmaison
⑯ 🕸 *Là* 🖢 & rm, 🔏 🕸 🗚 **VISA** ⓿ **AE** ⓞ

Piccadilly ⊠ M1 3AQ – 𝒞 *(0161) 278 1000 – www.malmaison.com*
– manchester@malmaison.com – Fax (0161) 278 1002   CZ**u**
154 rm – ♥£160 ♥♥£160, ⊇ £13.95 – 7 suites
Rest *Brasserie* – Menu £17 (dinner) – Carte £19/47
♦ A redecoration of this contemporary hotel has introduced a Moulin Rouge theme. Red and black throughout, giving hi-tech rooms seductive edge. Informal and unstuffy atmosphere. Brasserie offers plenty of classics.

🏨🏨 Abode
🖢 & 🔏 🕸 🕻 🗚 **VISA** ⓿ **AE**

107 Piccadilly ⊠ M1 2DB – 𝒞 *(0161) 247 7744 – www.abodehotels.co.uk*
– reservationsmanchester@abodehotels.co.uk – Fax (0161) 247 7747   CZ**c**
61 rm – ♥£99/130 ♥♥£149/180, ⊇ £13.50 – 1 suite
Rest Michael Caines – see restaurant listing
♦ Classic Victorian cotton merchant's warehouse with iron columns and girders still in situ. Relaxed boutique ambience with modern, trendy open plan rooms and stylish bathrooms.

🏨🏨 Yang Sing Oriental *without rest*
Là 🖢 & 🔏 🕻 **VISA** ⓿ **AE** ⓞ

36 Princess St ⊠ M1 4JY – 𝒞 *(0161) 880 0188 – www.yangsingoriental.com*
– reservations@ysoriental.com – Fax (0161) 880 0188   CZ**h**
48 rm ⊇ – ♥£179 ♥♥£569
♦ Former cotton warehouse in city centre. Modern, individual and stylish interior with original beams and steel columns. Inspired by the East, with bold colours and bespoke furniture.

ENGLAND

591

🏠 **Great John Street** without rest   *Lб ⊫ ₺ 🔳 ⁿⁱ 😗 ⚉ VISA ☺ AE*

Great John St ⊠ M3 4FD – ☏ (0161) 831 32 11 – www.greatjohnstreet.co.uk
– info@greatjohnstreet.co.uk – Fax (0161) 831 3212   CZ**a**
30 rm – †£135/235 ††£135/235, ⊡ £14.95 – 7 suites
♦ Revamped 19C school featuring many stylish, elegant touches. Rooftop terrace with hot tub, and city views. State-of-art rooms boast duplex style and vivid hues.

🏠 **Marriott Manchester Victoria and Albert**   *⊫ ₺ rm, 🔳 😗*

Water St ⊠ M3 4JB – ☏ (0161) 838 1188   *📞 ⚉ P. VISA ☺ AE ①*
– www.manchestermarriottva.co.uk – Fax (0161) 834 2484   AX**u**
144 rm – †£145/159 ††£145/159, ⊡ £16.95 – 1 suite
Rest – (bar lunch) Carte £24/32
♦ Restored 19C warehouses on the banks of the River Irwell, with exposed brick and original beams and columns. Large and well-equipped bedrooms. Restaurant proud of its timbered warehouse origins.

🏠 **City Inn**   *🏠 Lб ⊫ ₺ rm, 🔳 😗 ⁿⁱ ⚉ 🌐 VISA ☺ AE ①*

One Piccadilly Place, 1 Auburn Street ⊠ M1 3DG – ☏ (0161) 242 10 00
– www.cityinn.com – manchester.reservations@cityinn.com – Fax (0161) 242 10 01
284 rm – †£225 ††£225, ⊡ £13.95 – 1 suite   CZ**t**
Rest *Elements* – Menu £15/17 – Carte £24/43
♦ Contemporary glass building with spacious, airy interior and local art on display. Modern bedrooms boast pale hues, iMac computers and excellent entertainment facilities. Showers only. Smart, stylish restaurant with appealing, wide ranging menu.

🏠 **Novotel Manchester Centre**   *🏠 Lб ⊫ ₺ rm, 🔳 ⁿⁱ ⚉ VISA ☺ AE ①*

21 Dickinson St ⊠ M1 4LX – ☏ (0161) 235 2200 – www.novotel.com
– h3145@accor.com – Fax (0161) 235 2210   CZ**n**
164 rm – †£89/169 ††£89/169, ⊡ £12   **Rest** – (bar lunch) Carte £23/34
♦ The open-plan lobby boasts a spacious, stylish bar and residents can take advantage of an exclusive exercise area. Decently equipped, tidily appointed bedrooms. Compact dining room with grill-style menus.

XXXX **The French** – at The Midland Hotel   *🔳 P. VISA ☺ AE ①*

Peter St ⊠ M60 2DS – ☏ (0161) 236 3333 – www.qhotels.co.uk
– midlandsales@qhotels.co.uk – Fax (0161) 932 4100
– Closed 3-7 October, Sunday and Monday   CZ**x**
Rest – (dinner only) Carte £39/49
♦ As grand as the hotel in which it is housed, with gilded paintings, large mirrors and heavy drapes. Attentively formal service, classically French-based cooking.

XXX **River** – at The Lowry Hotel   *🏠 🔳 P. VISA ☺ AE ①*

50 Dearmans Pl, Chapel Wharf, Salford ⊠ M3 5LH – ☏ (0161) 827 4003
– www.roccofortecollection.com – enquiries.lowry@roccofortecollection.com
– Fax (0161) 827 4001   CY**n**
Rest – Carte £42/45 **s**
♦ Matching its surroundings, this is a stylish modern restaurant serving, in a precise manner, classic dishes that have stood the test of time. Irwell views, for good measure.

XXX **Wings**   *🔳 VISA ☺ AE*

1 Lincoln Sq ⊠ M2 5LN – ☏ (0161) 834 9000 – www.wingsrestaurant.co.uk
– wing@wingsrestaurant.co.uk   CZ**d**
Rest – Chinese (Canton) – Menu £29 **s** – Carte £27/69 **s**
♦ Chinese restaurant hidden off busy square, its smart exterior exuding an up-to-date feel. Carefully prepared, top quality dishes washed down with wide range of champagnes.

XXX **Vermilion**   *🔳 ⇔ P. VISA ☺ AE*

Hulme Hall Lane/Lord North Street ⊠ M40 8AD – ☏ (0161) 202 00 55
– www.vermilioncinnabar.com – reservations@vermilioncinnabar.com
– Fax (0161) 205 82 22 – Closed Saturday lunch   BV**a**
Rest – Asian – Menu £15/25 – Carte £22/39
♦ Destination restaurant on city fringes; rich colours and impressive furnishings. Original, interesting, and sophisticated menu features Thai, Japanese, Malaysian and Chinese influences.

XX **Michael Caines** – at Abode Hotel   AC ⌘ ⇔ VISA ◐◉ AE
107 Piccadilly ✉ *M1 2DB* – ☎ *(0161) 200 56 78*
– www.michaelcaines.com   CZ**c**
Rest – (Closed Sunday) Carte £ 38/82
♦ Stylish restaurant in hotel basement. Modern, sophisticated cooking with a well-judged French base and quality ingredients; good value 'grazing' menu of interesting tapas dishes.

XX **Ithaca**   AC VISA ◐◉ AE ◐
36 John Dalton Street ✉ *M2 6LE* – ☎ *(0161) 833 49 70*
– www.ithacamanchester.com – info@ithacamanchester.com
– Closed Sunday lunch   CZ**z**
Rest – Japanese – Menu £ 11 (lunch) – Carte £ 31/34
♦ Traditional Victorian façade masks fashionable 4 floor bar/restaurant with silver walls, black sparkly tiles and mirrored lights. Modern Japanese menu displays good use of ingredients.

XX **Second Floor - Restaurant** – at Harvey Nichols   AC VISA ◐◉ AE ◐
21 New Cathedral St ✉ *M1 1AD* – ☎ *(0161) 828 8898* – *www.harveynichols.com*
– secondfloor.reservations@harveynichols.com – Fax (0161) 828 8815 – Closed
25-26 December, 1 January, Easter and dinner Sunday and Monday   CY**k**
Rest – Menu £ 40
♦ Smart restaurant with glossy black panelling, stylish colour-changing lighting and oversized windows; city views. Elaborate modern European menu with interesting twists; good presentation.

XX **Grado**   ⌂ AC VISA ◐◉ AE
New York Street ✉ *M1 4BD* – ☎ *(0161) 238 97 90* – *www.heathcotes.co.uk*
– grado@heathcotes.co.uk – Fax (0161) 228 65 35   CZ**x**
Rest – Spanish – Menu £ 16 (weekdays) – Carte £ 21/40
♦ Set in an office block in heart of the city, with long bar for tapas dining or tables for à la carte. Menus offer classic Spanish dishes and a daily-changing charcoal oven special.

XX **Brasserie Blanc**   AC ⌘ ⇔ VISA ◐◉ AE
55 King St ✉ *M2 4LQ* – ☎ *(0161) 832 1000* – *www.brasserieblanc.co.uk*
– manchester@brasserieblanc.com – Fax (0161) 832 1001
– Closed 25-26 December and 1 January   CZ**b**
Rest – French – Menu £ 14/18 – Carte £ 20/41
♦ Busy, group-owned brasserie with large bar and polished tables. Extensive menus of classic and modern British dishes as well as regional French options. Attentive service.

XX **Pacific**   AC ⇔ VISA ◐◉ AE
58-60 George St ✉ *M1 4HF* – ☎ *(0161) 228 6668* – *www.pacificrestaurant.co.uk*
– info@pacificrestaurant.co.uk – Fax (0161) 236 0191   CZ**k**
Rest – Chinese and Thai – Menu £ 10 (lunch) – Carte £ 24/36
♦ Located in Chinatown: Chinese cuisine on first floor, Thai on the second; modern décor incorporating subtle Asian influences. Large menus boast high levels of authenticity.

XX **The Modern**   AC VISA ◐◉ AE
6th Floor, URBIS, Cathedral Gardens ✉ *M4 3BG* – ☎ *(0161) 605 8282*
– www.themodernmcr.co.uk – themodern@urbis.org.uk
– Closed 25-26 December   CY**x**
Rest – Menu £ 17 (lunch) – Carte £ 22/39
♦ Set on the 5th floor of an impressive glass building, with beautiful views. Seasonally-changing modern British menu is local and regional where possible; good value set lunch.

ENGLAND

XX **Koreana**   VISA OO AE ①

Kings House, 40a King St West ⊠ *M3 2WY – ℰ (0161) 832 4330*
– www.koreana.co.uk – alexkoreana@aol.com – Fax (0161) 832 2293
– Closed 1 week August, 25-26 December, 1 January, Sunday,
lunch Saturday and Bank Holidays   CZz
Rest – Korean – Menu £12 – Carte £13/29

♦ Authentic, family-run restaurant; Korean girls serve in traditional dresses. À la carte and set menus can be confusing; ask owners for help. Cooking is fresh, light and largely homemade.

XX **The Restaurant Bar and Grill**   AC VISA OO AE ①

14 John Dalton St ⊠ *M2 6JR – ℰ (0161) 839 1999*
– www.individualrestaurants.co.uk – manchester@ircplc.co.uk
– Fax (0161) 835 1886   CZr
Rest – Carte £33/40

♦ Striking building boasting stylish suspended staircase leading to spacious restaurant with oversized windows. Extensive menu offers modern brasserie dishes; influences from Asia/the Med.

X **Luso**   AC VISA OO AE

63 Bridge Street ⊠ *M3 3BQ – ℰ (0161) 839 55 50 – www.lusorestaurant.co.uk*
– Closed 25-28 December and Bank Holiday Mondays   CZv
Rest – Portuguese – Carte £24/35

♦ Inspired by the Roman name for Portugal – Lusitania – the owner's homeland. Large à la carte reflects this heritage and adds some international influences; tapas style 'Pesticos' at lunch.

X **Palmiro**   VISA OO AE ①

197 Upper Chorlton Rd, South : 2 m. by A 56 off Chorlton Rd ⊠ *M16 0BH*
– ℰ (0161) 860 7330 – www.palmiro.net – bookings@palmiro.net – Fax (0161)
861 7464 – Closed 25 December and 1 January   AXb
Rest – Italian – (dinner only and lunch Saturday-Sunday) Menu £12 (lunch) **s**
– Carte £21/26 **s**

♦ Spartan interior with grey mottled walls and halogen lighting: a highly regarded neighbourhood Italian eatery boasting good value rustic dishes cooked with maximum simplicity.

X **Second Floor - Brasserie** – at Harvey Nichols   AC VISA OO AE ①

21 New Cathedral St ⊠ *M1 1AD – ℰ (0161) 828 8898 – www.harveynichols.com*
– secondfloor.reservations@harveynichols.com – Fax (0161) 828 8815 – Closed
25-26 December, 1 January, Easter and dinner Sunday and Monday   CYk
Rest – Carte £25/32

♦ Relaxed brasserie and bar. Black and stainless steel furniture sits under colour-changing strip lighting. Informal menu of coffees, snacks and light meals. Popular with shoppers.

at Didsbury South : 5½ m. by 5103 - AX - on A 5145 – ⊠ **Manchester**

🏠 **Didsbury House**   Ĝ % P VISA OO AE ①

Didsbury Park, South : 1½ m. on A 5145 ⊠ *M20 5LJ – ℰ (0161) 448 2200*
– www.didsburyhouse.co.uk – info@didsburyhouse.co.uk – Fax (0161) 448 2525
23 rm – †£95/140 ††£140, ☷ £14.50 – 4 suites
Rest – (room service only)

♦ Grade II listed 19C house: grand wooden staircase, superb stained glass window. Otherwise, stylish and modern with roof-top hot tubs. Spacious, individually designed rooms.

🏠 **Eleven Didsbury Park**   ⊞ % (t) P VISA OO AE ①

11 Didsbury Park, South :½ m. by A 5145 ⊠ *M20 5LH – ℰ (0161) 448 7711*
– www.ecletic-hotel-collection.co.uk – enquiries@elevendidsburypark.com
– Fax (0161) 448 8282
20 rm – †£140 ††£140, ☷ £14.50 – 1 suite   **Rest** – (room service only)

♦ The cool contemporary design in this Victorian town house creates a serene and relaxing atmosphere. Good-sized bedrooms decorated with flair and style. Personally run.

✗ **Café Jem&I**   🥄 VISA ⓜⓞ AE
1c School Lane ✉ *M20 6SA –* ✆ *(0161) 445 3996 – jemandirestaurant.co.uk*
– jemosullivan@aol.com – Fax (0161) 448 8661
– Closed 25-26 December, 1 January, Monday lunch and Bank Holidays
Rest – Carte £ 23/36
♦ Simple, unpretentious cream coloured building tucked away off the high street.
Open-plan kitchen; homely, bistro feel. Good value, tasty modern classics.

at West Didsbury South : 5½ m. by A 5103 - AX - and A 5145 – ✉ **Manchester**

✗ **Rhubarb**   🎵 AC VISA ⓜⓞ AE
167 Burton Rd ✉ *M20 2LN –* ✆ *(0161) 448 8887 – www.rhubarbrestaurant.co.uk*
– info@rhubarbrestaurant.co.uk – Closed 25-26 December
Rest – (dinner only and Sunday lunch) Carte £ 22/28
♦ An eye-catching exterior draws in a loyal local following. Yes, there are rhubarb
walls, but the cooking, not so locally inspired, features tasty dishes from far and wide.

at Manchester Airport South : 9 m. by A 5103 - AX - off M 56 – ✉ **Manchester**

🏨 **Radisson SAS Manchester Airport**   🖼 🕸 ₤ᵦ 🛗 & rm, AC ⅏
Chicago Ave ✉ *M90 3RA –* ✆ *(0161) 490 5000*   ⁽ᵗ⁾ 🛁 P VISA ⓜⓞ AE ⓞ
– www.manchester.radissonsas.co.UK – sales.manchester@radissonsas.com
– Fax (0161) 490 5100
354 rm – †£ 143/159 ††£ 143/159, ☄ £ 17.95 – 6 suites
Rest *Phileas Fogg* – (dinner only) Carte £ 29/38
Rest *Runway Brasserie* – Carte £ 16/28
♦ Vast, modern hotel linked to airport passenger walkway. Three room styles with
many extras. Ideal for business clients or travellers. Phileas Fogg is curved restaurant
with eclectic menus and runway views. All-day Runway with arrivals/departures info.

🏨 **Hilton Manchester Airport**   ₤ᵦ 🛗 & rm, AC rest, ⁽ᵗ⁾ 🛁 P VISA ⓜⓞ AE ⓞ
Outwood Lane (Terminal One) ✉ *M90 4WP –* ✆ *(0161) 435 3000*
– www.hilton.co.uk/manchesterairport – reservations.manchester@hilton.com
– Fax (0161) 435 3040
230 rm – †£ 119 ††£ 119, ☄ £ 10
Rest – (bar lunch) Menu 30 – Carte £ 33/50 **s**
♦ Popular with corporate travellers for its business centre and location 200 metres
from the airport terminal. Comfortable, soundproofed bedrooms. Restaurant exudes
pleasant, modern style.

🏨 **Etrop Grange**   ⁽ᵗ⁾ 🛁 P VISA ⓜⓞ AE ⓞ
Thorley Lane ✉ *M90 4EG –* ✆ *(0161) 499 0500 – www.foliohotels.com*
– etropgrange@foliohotels.com – Fax (0161) 499 0790
62 rm – †£ 99/149 ††£ 99/149, ☄ £ 13.50 – 2 suites
Rest – Menu £ 25/33 – Carte £ 30/43
♦ Sympathetically extended Georgian house that retains its period feel. Refurbished
and modernised bedrooms vary in size; some boast four-posters, others cast-iron
beds. Good bathrooms. Intimate, traditionally styled dining room.

🏨 **Bewley's**   🛗 & rm, AC rest, ⅏ ⁽ᵗ⁾ 🛁 P VISA ⓜⓞ AE ⓞ
Outwood Lane, (Terminal Three) ✉ *M90 4HL –* ✆ *(0161) 498 0333*
– www.bewleyshotels.com – man@bewleyshotels.com – Fax (0161) 498 0222
365 rm – †£ 69/135 ††£ 69/135, ☄ £ 8.95   **Rest** – (bar lunch) Carte £ 16/28 **s**
♦ Competitively priced, purpose-built group hotel with large, modern and open
lobby. Brightly decorated bedrooms are a fair size and offer a decent level of comfort.
Appealing, popular dishes in restaurant or lobby café.

✗✗✗ **Moss Nook**   🚗 🥂 P VISA ⓜⓞ AE
Ringway Rd, Moss Nook, East : 1¼ m. on Cheadle rd ✉ *M22 5NA –* ✆ *(0161)*
437 4778 – www.manchesterairportrestaurant.co.uk
– enquiries@mossnookrestaurant.co.uk – Fax (0161) 498 8089 – Closed 2 weeks
Christmas, Saturday lunch, Sunday and Monday
Rest – Menu £ 20/38 – Carte £ 37/44
♦ Decorated in a combination of Art Nouveau, lace and panelling. Long-standing
owners provide polished and ceremonial service; cooking is robust and classically based.

ENGLAND

at Chorlton-Cum-Hardy Southwest : 5 m. by A 5103 - AX - on A 6010
– ✉ Manchester

⌂ Abbey Lodge without rest ♨ 📶 P VISA ◎ 匪
501 Wilbraham Rd ✉ *M21 0UJ* – ✆ *(0161) 862 9266* – *www.abbey-lodge.co.uk*
– *info@abbey-lodge.co.uk*   AX**z**
4 rm – ♦£50 ♦♦£70, ♀£6
♦ Attractive Edwardian house boasting many original features including stained glass windows. Owner provides charming hospitality and pine fitted rooms are immaculately kept.

▯ Marmalade ♨ ♨ VISA ◎ ①
60 Beech Road ✉ *M21 9EG* – ✆ *(0161) 862 9665* – *www.mymarmalade.co.uk*
– *jqmarmalade@tiscali.co.uk* – *Fax (0161) 861 7788* – *Closed 25-26 December*
Rest – (closed lunch Monday-Wednesday) Menu £12/14 – Carte £22/27
♦ Three tier cake stands, crutches and antique suitcases define this eye-catching pub. Food's a serious matter: cracking local menus. Yes, homemade marmalade's on offer, too.

MANCHESTER INTERNATIONAL AIRPORT Gtr Manchester – 503 N 23
– see Manchester

MANSFIELD – Nottinghamshire – 502 Q 24   16 B1
🔲 London 143 mi – Chesterfield 12 mi – Worksop 14 mi

✗✗ No.4 Wood Street 🅰🅲 ⇔ P VISA ◎ 匪
No.4 Wood St ✉ *NG18 1QA* – ✆ *(01623) 424 824* – *www.4woodstreet.co.uk*
– *Closed 26 December, 1 January, Monday, Sunday dinner and Saturday lunch*
Rest – Menu £19 – Carte £20/39
♦ Solid brick restaurant tucked away in town centre. Relax in lounge bar with comfy armchairs before enjoying well-executed, modern, seasonal dishes in rustic dining room.

MARAZION – Cornwall – 503 D 33 – ✉ Penzance   1 A3
🔲 London 318 mi – Penzance 3 mi – Truro 26 mi
🔲 Praa Sands Penzance, ✆ (01736) 763 445
🔲 St Michael's Mount★★ (≤★★) – Ludgvan★ (Church★) N : 2 m. by A 30 –
Chysauster Village★, N : 2 m. by A 30 – Gulval★ (Church★) W : 2½ m –
Prussia Cove★, SE : 5 ½ m. by A 30 and minor rd

⌂ Mount Haven ≤ ♨ ♨ 📶 P VISA ◎
Turnpike Rd, East : ¼ *m.* ✉ *TR17 0DQ* – ✆ *(01736) 710 249*
– *www.mounthaven.co.uk* – *reception@mounthaven.co.uk* – *Fax (01736) 711 658*
– *Closed 20 December - 10 February*
18 rm ♀ – ♦£65/90 ♦♦£120/150   **Rest** – (bar lunch) Carte £24/33 s
♦ Small hotel overlooking St Michael's Bay. Spacious bar and lounge featuring Indian crafts and fabrics. Contemporary rooms with modern amenities, some with balcony and view. Bright attractive dining room; menu mixes modern and traditional.

at St Hilary East : 2½ m. by Turnpike Rd, on B 3280 – ✉ Penzance

⌂ Ennys without rest ♨ ♨ ♪ ⅄ ✗ ♨ 📶 P VISA ◎
Trewhella Lane, St Hilary, East : 2½ m. by Turnpike Rd, on B 3280 ✉ *TR20 9BZ*
– ✆ *(01736) 740 262* – *www.ennys.co.uk* – *ennys@ennys.co.uk* – *Fax (01736)*
740 055 – *April-October*
5 rm ♀ – ♦£70/115 ♦♦£85/125
♦ Blissful 17C manor house on working farm. Spacious breakfast room and large farmhouse kitchen for afternoon tea. Redecoration has made the bedrooms brighter. Good size sitting room.

at Perranuthnoe Southeast : 1 ¾ m. by A 394 – ✉ Penzance

⌂ Ednovean Farm without rest ♨ ≤ ♨ ♪ ♨ P VISA ◎
✉ *TR20 9LZ* – ✆ *(01736) 711 883* – *www.ednoveanfarm.co.uk*
– *info@ednoveanfarm.co.uk* – *Closed Christmas - New Year*
3 rm ♀ – ♦£85/105 ♦♦£85/105
♦ Very spacious, characterful converted 17C granite barn offering peace, tranquillity and Mounts Bay views. Fine choice at breakfast on oak table. Charming, individual rooms.

🍴🛏 **Victoria Inn** with rm   🌳 **P** 𝚅𝙸𝚂𝙰 ⓜⓞ
✉ *TR20 9NP* – ✆ *(01736) 710 309* – *www.victoriainn-penzance.co.uk*
– *enquiries@victoriainn-penzance.co.uk* – *Fax (01736) 719 284* – *Closed 1 week
January and Monday in winter*
2 rm – ♦£45 ♦♦£65   **Rest** – (Closed Sunday dinner) Carte £ 19/30
♦ Rustic, country pub serving a classical menu of local, seasonal produce and very fresh
fish. Allegedly the oldest inn in Cornwall, it has simple rooms with a nautical theme.

MARDEN – Wilts. – see Devizes

MARKET DRAYTON – Shropshire – 502 M 25   18 **B1**
 ▶ London 159 mi – Nantwich 13 mi – Shrewsbury 21 mi

🏠 **Goldstone Hall** ⅏   ⩽ 🚗 🐾 🎵 **P** 𝚅𝙸𝚂𝙰 ⓜⓞ
South : 4½ m. on A 529 ✉ *TF9 2NA* – ✆ *(01630) 661 202*
– *www.goldstonehall.com* – *info@goldstonehall.com* – *Fax (01630) 661 585*
12 rm ⌨ – ♦£88 ♦♦£132/165
Rest – (closed 26-27 December) Menu £ 25/34 **s**
♦ 16C red-brick country house that's been extensively added to over the ages. Five
acres of formal garden: PG Wodehouse enjoyed its shade! Modern rooms with huge
beds. Contemporary twists on daily changing menus.

MARKET HARBOROUGH – Leicestershire – 504 R 26 – pop. 20 127   16 **B3**
 ▶ London 88 mi – Birmingham 47 mi – Leicester 15 mi – Northampton 17 mi
 🛈 Council Offices, Adam and Eve St ✆ (01858) 828282
 ⛳ Great Oxendon Rd, ✆ (01858) 463 684

at Thorpe Langton North : 3 ¾ m. by A 4304 via Great Bowden – ✉ **Market
Harborough**

🍴🛏 **The Bakers Arms**   **P** 𝚅𝙸𝚂𝙰 ⓜⓞ
Main St ✉ *LE16 7TS* – ✆ *(01858) 545 201* – *www.thebakersarms.co.uk*
– *Fax (01858) 545 924* – *Closed Monday and Sunday dinner*
Rest – (dinner only and lunch Saturday and Sunday) (booking essential)
Carte £ 22/33
♦ Atmospheric thatched pub with deep red walls, exposed timbers and pew seats.
Scrubbed wooden tables add to the relaxed feel. Tasty, well-priced, tried-and-tested
dishes.

MARLBOROUGH – Wiltshire – 503 O 29 – pop. 7 713   4 **D2**
 ▶ London 84 mi – Bristol 47 mi – Southampton 40 mi – Swindon 12 mi
 🛈 The Library, High St ✆ (01672) 513989, all.tic's@kennet.gov.uk
 ⛳ The Common, ✆ (01672) 512 147
 ◉ Town★
 🅖 Savernake Forest★★ (Grand Avenue★★★), SE : 2 m. by A 4 – Whitehorse
 (⩽★), NW : 5 m – West Kennett Long Barrow★, Silbury Hill★, W : 6 m. by
 A 4. Ridgeway Path★★ – Avebury★★ (The Stones★, Church★), W : 7 m. by
 A 4 – Crofton Beam Engines★ **AC**, SE : 9 m. by A 346 – Wilton Windmill★
 AC, SE : 9 m. by A 346, A 338 and minor rd

🍴 **Coles**   🌳 **AC** 𝚅𝙸𝚂𝙰 ⓜⓞ
27 Kingsbury Hill ✉ *SN8 1JA* – ✆ *(01672) 515 004* – *www.colesrestaurant.co.uk*
– *Fax (01672) 512 069* – *Closed Sunday and Bank Holidays*
Rest – Carte £ 25/32
♦ Shots of 70s film stars adorn a busy, bay-windowed former pub which retains its
firelit bar. Friendly staff and elaborate but robust cuisine with an array of daily specials.

at Ramsbury Northeast : 7 ¼ m. by A 346 – ✉ **Marlborough**

🍴🛏 **The Bell**   🚗 🌳 **P** 𝚅𝙸𝚂𝙰 ⓜⓞ
The Square ✉ *SN8 2PE* – ✆ *(01672) 520 230* – *www.thebellramsbury.com*
– *jeremy@thebellramsbury.com* – *Fax (01672) 520 832* – *Closed 25 December*
Rest – (Closed Sunday dinner) Menu £ 17/22 – Carte £ 20/35
♦ Black and white pub with two distinct sides: busy bar with open fire and sofas, and
long dining room featuring eye-catching abstract artwork. Classic, unfussy British
cooking.

ENGLAND

at Little Bedwyn East : 9½ m. by A 4 – ⊠ Marlborough

XX **The Harrow at Little Bedwyn** (Roger Jones)   VISA ⓪

⊠ SN8 3JP – 𝒞 (01672) 870871 – www.harrowatlittlebedwyn.co.uk
– dining@harrowinn.co.uk – Closed 2 weeks August, 2 weeks Christmas, Sunday
dinner, Monday and Tuesday
Rest – Menu £ 30/45 – Carte £ 42/55

Spec. Cured wild salmon with pea shoots and smoked salt. Fillet of line caught
turbot with English truffles. Raspberry parfait, ice cream and shortbread.
♦ Cosy former village pub, whose extensive range of menus offer accomplished,
unfussy dishes which allow the quality of the produce to shine through. An impressive wine list.

MARLDON – Devon – **503** J 32   2 **C2**

🖸 London 193 mi – Newton Abbott 7 mi – Paignton 3 mi

🝙 **Church House Inn**   P. VISA ⓪

Village Rd ⊠ TQ3 1SL – 𝒞 (01803) 558 279 – www.churchhousemarldon.com
– Fax (01803) 664 185
Rest – Carte £ 21/30

♦ Charming 18C pub displaying original Georgian windows and plenty of nooks and
crannies. Cooking is traditional and tasty, featuring quality regional produce in generous helpings.

MARLOW – Buckinghamshire – **504** R 29 – pop. 17 522   11 **C3**

🖸 London 35 mi – Aylesbury 22 mi – Oxford 29 mi – Reading 14 mi
🚋 to Henley-on-Thames (Salter Bros. Ltd) (summer only) (2 h 15 mn) – to
Maidenhead, Cookham and Windsor (Salter Bros. Ltd) (summer only)
🝙 31 High St 𝒞 (01628) 483597, tourism_enquiries@wycombe.gov.uk

Danesfield House 🏨   ⟨ 🍳 🖾 rest, 🍽

Henley Rd, Southwest : 2½ m. on A 4155   ((•)) 🕻 P. VISA ⓪ AE ⓪
⊠ SL7 2EY – 𝒞 (01628) 891 010 – www.danesfieldhouse.co.uk
– sales@danesfieldhouse.co.uk – Fax (01628) 890 408
83 rm – ♦£ 195/260 ♦♦£ 220/275, ⊆ £ 10.50 – 1 suite
Rest *Oak Room* – (Closed Christmas-New Year, Sunday, Monday, Tuesday
lunch and Bank Holidays) Menu £ 30/55
Rest *Orangery* – Carte £ 28/32

♦ Stunning house and gardens in Italian Renaissance style with breathtaking views
of Thames. Grand lounge with country house feel. Comfy rooms; state-of-art health
spa. Intimate Oak Room restaurant. Orangery is a charming terrace brasserie.

Crowne Plaza Marlow   🖾 rm, 🞳 ⟨ 🗲 🖾 🝙 ⟨ 🖾

Fieldhouse Lane, East : 2 m. by A 4155 off Parkway Rd   P. VISA ⓪ AE ⓪
⊠ SL7 1GJ – 𝒞 (0870) 444 89 40 – enquiries@crowneplazamarlow.co.uk
– Fax (0870) 444 89 50
162 rm – ♦£ 155/275 ♦♦£ 155/275, ⊆ £ 16.95 – 6 suites
Rest *Glaze* – (closed Saturday and Sunday lunch) Menu £ 28 – Carte £ 22/44
Rest *Agua* – Carte £ 19/31

♦ Purpose built business hotel near business park. Spacious lobby, leisure club and meeting
rooms. Bedrooms well equipped with large desk. Glaze with conservatory overlooking the artificial lake. More informal Agua.

Compleat Angler   ⟨ 🗲 🖾 rm, 🞳 P. VISA ⓪ AE ⓪

Marlow Bridge, Bisham Rd ⊠ SL7 1RG – 𝒞 (0870) 400 81 00
– www.macdonaldhotels.co.uk/compleatangler
– compleatangler@macdonald-hotels.co.uk – Fax (01628) 486 388
61 rm – ♦£ 170/270 ♦♦£ 170/270, ⊆ £ 17.50 – 3 suites
Rest *Aubergine at The Compleat Angler* – see restaurant listing
Rest *Bowaters* – Carte £ 31/40

♦ Picturesque riverside hotel; spectacular view of Marlow weir. Rooms are very comfortable; those on river side have four-poster beds and balcony. British cuisine in the
contemporary Bowaters, overlooking the river.

XXX **Aubergine at the Compleat Angler**   P VISA ◐◉ AE ◑
Marlow Bridge, Bisham Rd ⊠ SL7 1RG – ℰ (01628) 405 405
– www.londonfinedininggroup.com – aubergine@londonfinedininggroup.com
– Fax (01628) 486 388 – Closed Sunday dinner and Monday
Rest – Menu £ 29/55
♦ An outpost of William Drabble's Chelsea institution. Well-crafted and accomplished cooking, with a classical French base, to complement the delightful setting.

XX **The Vanilla Pod**   ⊞ AC ⇔ VISA ◐◉ AE ◑
31 West St ⊠ SL7 2LS – ℰ (01628) 898 101 – www.thevanillapod.co.uk
– contact@thevanillapod.co.uk – Fax (01628) 898 108
– Closed Easter, 23 December-6 January, Sunday and Monday
Rest – (booking essential) Menu £ 20/40
♦ Attractive townhouse – former home of T. S. Eliot – boasts refurbished restaurant with loyal following. Classic cooking with French accent makes use of seasonal ingredients.

⌂ **The Hand and Flowers** (Tom Kerridge) with rm   ⊞ ⊞ ⅍ P VISA ◐◉ AE
ॐ *126 West St ⊠ SL7 2BP – ℰ (01628) 482 277 – www.thehandandflowers.co.uk*
– theoffice@thehandandflowers.co.uk – Fax (01628) 401 913
– Closed 24-26 December
4 rm � – †£ 140 ††£ 190
Rest – (Closed Sunday dinner) (booking essential) Carte £ 28/36
Spec. Home cured anchovies with tapenade and toast. Pigeon with foie gras, girolles and boulangère potatoes. Banana soufflé with coconut sorbet.
♦ Honest pub with a smart new kitchen, where you can even shadow the chef. Dishes have depth, clarity and display an impressive command of a range of cooking techniques. Neighbouring cottages house pretty bedrooms, one with a Jacuzzi.

⌂ **The Royal Oak**   ⊞ ⊞ P VISA ◐◉ AE
Frieth Rd, Bovingdon Green, West : 1 ¼ mi. by A 4155 ⊠ SL7 2JF – ℰ (01628)
488 611 – www.royaloakmarlow.co.uk – info@royaloakmarlow.co.uk
– Fax (01628) 478 680 – Closed 25-26 December
Rest – Carte £ 20/29
♦ Characterful pub with redbrick exterior and smart interior. Full-length window area at back faces spacious garden terrace. Modern menus plus specials board.

MARPLE – Greater Manchester – **502** N 23 – pop. **18 475**   20 **B3**
 ◘ London 190 mi – Chesterfield 35 mi – Manchester 11 mi

⌂ **Springfield** without rest   ⊞ ⅍ ⅋ P VISA ◐◉ AE ◑
99 Station Rd ⊠ SK6 6PA – ℰ (0161) 449 0721
– www.springfieldhotelmarple.com – Fax (0161) 449 0766
8 rm � – †£ 55 ††£ 80
♦ Part Victorian house with sympathetic extensions and pleasant rural views. Conservatory breakfast room; individually styled bedrooms. Useful for visits to Peak District.

MARSDEN – West Yorkshire – **502** O 23 – pop. **3 499** – ⊠ Huddersfield   22 **A3**
 ◘ London 195 mi – Leeds 22 mi – Manchester 18 mi – Sheffield 30 mi

⌂ **Olive Branch** with rm   ⊞ P VISA ◐◉
Manchester Rd, Northeast : 1 m. on A 62 ⊠ HD7 6LU – ℰ (01484) 844 487
– www.olivebranch.uk.com – mail@olivebranch.uk.com – Closed 26 December
and first 2 weeks in January
3 rm – †£ 55 ††£ 70, ⊒ £ 12.50
Rest – (Closed Monday-Tuesday and lunch Saturday) Menu £ 11/19
– Carte £ 27/38
♦ Characterful drovers inn, with terrace and secluded garden. Large classical menu is split between meat and seafood, with hearty specials displayed on large post-it notes. Bedrooms are modern, comfortable and individually themed.

MARSH BENHAM – West Berks. – **see Newbury**

ENGLAND

MARSTON MONTGOMERY – Derbs. – see Ashbourne

MARTINHOE – Devon – see Lynton

MARTOCK – Somerset – 503 L 31 – pop. 4 309   3 **B3**
- London 148 mi – Taunton 19 mi – Yeovil 6 mi
- Village★ - All Saints★★
- Montacute House★★ AC, SE : 4 m. – Muchelney★★ (Parish Church★★),
  NW : 4½ m. by B 3165 – Ham Hill (≤★★), S : 2 m. by minor roads.
  Barrington Court★ AC, SW : 7½ m. by B 3165 and A 303

The Hollies   ☞ ሌ rm, ✲ ᐭ 🖧 **P** _VISA_ ⓾ **AE** ⓪
Bower Hinton, South : 1 m. on B 3165 ⊠ TA12 6LG – ℰ (01935) 822 232
– www.thehollieshotel.co.uk – info@thehollieshotel.com – Fax (01935) 822 249
51 rm ⊔ – †£95 ††£105/140 – 3 suites   **Rest** – (dinner only) Carte £25/33
♦ Impressive former 17C farmhouse in small village near grand Montacute House.
Separate annex has large, well-equipped, up-to-date bedrooms with good comforts
and facilities. Characterful oak beamed, boothed restaurant and lounge in the farmhouse.

MARTON – N. Yorks. – 502 R 21 – see Pickering

MARTON – Shropshire ▌ Great Britain   18 **A1**
- London 174 mi – Birmingham 57 mi – Shrewsbury 16 mi
- Powis Castle★★★, NW : 7 m. by B 4386 and A 490

The Sun Inn   ✲ **P** _VISA_ ⓾
⊠ SY21 8JP – ℰ (01938) 561 211 – www.suninn.org.uk
– suninnmarton@googlemail.com
Rest – (Closed Monday ,Tuesday lunch and Sunday dinner) Menu £13/16
– Carte £19/33
♦ Welcoming country pub on the English-Welsh border. A regularly changing British/
Mediterranean menu and a fresh fish board feature in the restaurant, with specials in
the bar.

MASHAM – North Yorkshire – 502 P 21 – ⊠ Ripon   22 **B1**
- London 231 mi – Leeds 38 mi – Middlesbrough 37 mi – York 32 mi

Swinton Park ৯   ≤ ☞ ᐭ ⁊ 🖬 🛗 ሌ rm, ✲ 🖧 **P** _VISA_ ⓾ **AE** ⓪
Swinton, Southwest : 1 m ⊠ HG4 4JH – ℰ (01765) 680 900
– www.swintonpark.com – enquiries@swintonpark.com – Fax (01765) 680 901
26 rm ⊔ – †£170 ††£280 – 4 suites
Rest Samuels – Menu £23/45
♦ 17C castle with Georgian and Victorian additions, on a 20,000 acre estate and deer
park. Luxurious, individually styled bed-
rooms. Grand dining room with ornate gold leaf ceiling and garden views.

Bank Villa   ☞ ✲ **P** _VISA_ ⓾
on A 6108 ⊠ HG4 4DB – ℰ (01765) 689 605 – www.bankvilla.com
– bankvilla@btopenworld.com
6 rm ⊔ – †£50/60 ††£95/105   **Rest** – (by arrangement) Carte £22/24
♦ Stone-built Georgian villa with Victorian additions. Two lounges and conservatory;
delightful, "sun-trap" stepped garden. Cosy, cottagey rooms: some are in the eaves!
Home-cooked menus in pastel dining room/tea room.

Vennell's   _VISA_ ⓾ **AE**
7 Silver St ⊠ HG4 4DX – ℰ (01765) 689 000 – www.vennellsrestaurant.co.uk
– info@vennellsrestaurant.co.uk – Closed Monday and Sunday dinner
Rest – (dinner only and Sunday lunch) (booking essential) Carte £28/40
♦ Smart restaurant with comfy basement bar; linen-clad dining room enhanced by
local artwork. Warm service of good value, seasonal dishes prepared with flair and a
flourish.

MATFEN – Northumberland – 501 O 18
24 **A2**

▶ London 309 mi – Carlisle 42 mi – Newcastle upon Tyne 24 mi

Matfen Hall 🏵   ⟨ 🚲 🏊 🚭 🌐 🐾 🏌 🎾 🖫 ⓗ rm, 💈 🏋 **P**
✉ NE20 0RH – ☎ (01661) 886 500 – www.matfenhall.com   VISA ⓜⓞ AE ⓘ
– info@matfenhall.com – Fax (01661) 886 055
53 rm ⍁ – ♦£120 ♦♦£180
Rest *Library and Print Room* – (dinner only and Sunday lunch) Carte £28/40
♦ 19C country mansion built by Thomas Ruckman, master of Gothic design. Set in 500 acres with superb Grand Hall, fine paintings, plush drawing room and mix of bedroom styles. Characterful Library dining room has display of original books.

MATLOCK – Derbyshire – 502 P 24 – pop. 11 265 📗 *Great Britain*
16 **B1**

▶ London 153 mi – Derby 17 mi – Manchester 46 mi – Nottingham 24 mi
  – Sheffield 24 mi

🖪 Crown Sq ☎ (01629) 583388, matlockinfo@derbyshiredales.gov.uk - The Pavilion, Matlock Bath ☎ (01629) 55082, matlockbathinfo@derbyshiredales.gov.uk

◉ Hardwick Hall★★ **AC**, E : 12½ m. by A 615 and B 6014 – Crich Tramway Village★ **AC**, S : 12 m. by A 6 and B 5036

at Birchover Northwest : 7½ m. by A 6 – ✉ Matlock

The Druid Inn   ☂ 🍴 **P** VISA ⓜⓞ
Main St ✉ DE4 2BL – ☎ (01629) 650 302 – www.thedruidinn.co.uk
– Closed 25 December
Rest – (Closed Sunday dinner) Menu £17 (weekdays) – Carte £25/35
♦ A rustic bar and modern, airy dining room are echoed by classic British favourites and more ambitious restaurant style dishes, including some for two; food is wholesome and tasty.

If breakfast is included the ⍁ symbol appears after the number of rooms.

MAWNAN SMITH – Cornwall – 503 E 33 – see Falmouth

MEDBOURNE – Leicestershire – 504 R 26
16 **B2**

▶ London 93 mi – Corby 9 mi – Leicester 16 mi

✗✗ **Horse & Trumpet** with rm   ☂ VISA ⓜⓞ
Old Green ✉ LE16 8DX – ☎ (01858) 565 000 – www.horseandtrumpet.com
– info@horseandtrumpet.com – Fax (01858) 565 551 – Closed 1 week January, Sunday dinner and Monday
4 rm ⍁ – ♦£75 ♦♦£75
Rest – Menu £20 (lunch)/28 (weekdays dinner) – Carte £34/40
♦ 18C thatched inn with bowling green. Stylish well-furnished bedrooms. Linen clad tables in the dining rooms; al fresco eating in courtyard. Modern menu using local produce.

MELLOR – Lancs. – see Blackburn

MELLS – Somerset – 503 M 30 – pop. 2 222
4 **C2**

▶ London 117 mi – Bath 16 mi – Frome 3 mi

The Talbot Inn with rm   VISA ⓜⓞ
Selwood St ✉ BA11 3PN – ☎ (01373) 812 254 – www.talbotinn.com
– enquiries@talbotinn.com – Fax (01373) 813 599
8 rm ⍁ – ♦♦£95   **Rest** – Menu £13 (lunch) – Carte £20/30
♦ Traditional coaching inn with a courtyard, secluded terrace and pergola. Country style cooking is hearty, robust and uses homemade produce; wide-ranging menu. Bedrooms are classical, some modest.

ENGLAND

MELTON MOWBRAY – Leicestershire – 502 R 25 – pop. 25 554   16 B2

> ◻ London 113 mi – Leicester 15 mi – Northampton 45 mi – Nottingham 18 mi
> ◻ 7 King St ℰ (01664) 480992, tic@melton.gov.uk
> ◻ Thorpe Arnold Waltham Rd, ℰ (01664) 562 118

Stapleford Park ⊗   ≤ 🚗 🐶 🔞 🖼 🍽 ♨ ♨ 🛁 ♨ 🍴 📅 ✨ 🅿
East : 5 m. by B 676 on Stapleford rd ⊠ *LE14 2EF*   VISA ⓪ AE ①
– ℰ (01572) 787 000 – www.staplefordpark.com – reservations@stapleford.co.uk
– Fax (01572) 787 001
55 rm ⊑ – †£199 ††£222/295
Rest *Grinling Gibbons Dining Room* – (Closed Saturday and Sunday dinner)
(dinner only and Sunday lunch) (booking essential) Carte £47/58
Rest *Pavilion Brasserie* – Carte approx. £15
♦ Astoundingly beautiful stately home in 500 glorious acres, exuding a grandeur
rarely surpassed. Extensive leisure facilities; uniquely designed rooms of sumptuous
elegance. Ornate rococo dining room a superb example of master craftsman's work.
Smart brasserie.

at Stathern North : 8 m. by A 607 – ⊠ Melton Mowbray

Red Lion Inn   🍴 🅿 VISA ⓪
2 Red Lion St ⊠ *LE14 4HS* – ℰ (01949) 860 868 – www.theredlioninn.co.uk
– info@theredlioninn.co.uk – Fax (01949) 861 579 – Closed 1 January
Rest – (Closed Sunday dinner and Monday) (booking essential) Menu £16
– Carte £26/33
♦ Rural pub with a predominant "country" feel: solid stone floors, wooden antiques,
rustic ornaments, solid fireplaces, skittle alley. Daily changing, modern menus.

MERIDEN – W. Mids. – 503 P 26 – see Coventry

MEVAGISSEY – Cornwall – 503 F 33 – pop. 2 221   1 B3

> ◻ London 287 mi – Newquay 21 mi – Plymouth 44 mi – Truro 20 mi
> ◻ Town ★★
> ◻ NW : Lost Gardens of Heligan ★

Trevalsa Court   ≤ 🚗 ♨ 🍴 🅿 VISA ⓪ AE
School Hill, East : ½ m. on B 3273 (St Austell rd) ⊠ *PL26 6TH* – ℰ (01726)
842 468 – www.trevalsa-hotel.co.uk – stay@trevalsa-hotel.co.uk – Fax (01726)
844 482 – Mid February- mid November
12 rm ⊑ – †£75/128 ††£100/220
Rest – (dinner only) Menu £29
♦ Charming 1930s building with lovely garden which has access to Polstreath Beach.
Homely morning room. Owners have brightened up the bedrooms and added contemporary furnishings. Oak-panelled dining room with daily menu, devised using
best available produce.

Kerryanna without rest ⊗   🚗 🐶 🍽 ♨ 🅿
Treleaven Farm ⊠ *PL26 6SA* – ℰ (01726) 843 558 – www.kerryanna.co.uk
– enquiries@kerryanna.co.uk – Fax (01726) 843 558 – May-September
3 rm ⊑ – ††£75/80
♦ Purpose-built bungalow within farm providing pleasant ambience. Useful for Lost
Gardens of Heligan. Spacious front sitting room. Immaculately kept, sizeable, chintz
bedrooms.

MICKLEHAM – Surrey – 504 T 30   7 D1

> ◻ London 21 mi – Brighton 32 mi – Guildford 14 mi – Worthing 34 mi

The King William IV   🍴 ♨ VISA ⓪ AE
Byttom Hill, North : ½ m. by A 24 ⊠ *RH5 6EL* – ℰ (01372) 372 590
– www.king-williamiv.com – iduke@another.com – Closed Sunday dinner
Rest – Carte £19/28
♦ Traditional homemade pies and simply-cooked, fresh vegetables: robust, hearty
cooking perfect for refuelling after a walk in the Surrey countryside. Lovely terraced
garden.

MICKLETON – Glos. – **503** – see Chipping Campden

MIDDLE WINTERSLOW – Wilts. – **503** O 30 – see Salisbury

MIDDLEHAM – North Yorkshire – **502** O 21   22 **B1**

▶ London 233 mi – Kendal 45 mi – Leeds 47 mi – Newcastle upon Tyne 63 mi – York 45 mi

🏠 **Waterford House**   ☞ ⚒ **P.** **VISA** ◯◉
19 Kirkgate ✉ *DL8 4PG –* ☏ *(01969) 622 090 – www.waterfordhousehotel.co.uk*
– info@waterfordhousehotel.co.uk – Fax (01969) 624 020 – Closed Christmas-New Year
4 rm � – †£75 ††£120
Rest – (Closed Sunday) (dinner only) (residents only) Menu £35 **s**
♦ Elegant Georgian house, just off cobbled market square, with neat walled garden. Drawing room boasts cluttered charm. Individually appointed rooms with thoughtful touches. Formal restaurant: home cooked menus use much local produce.

at Carlton-in-Coverdale Southwest : 4 ½ m. by Coverham rd – ✉ **Leyburn**

🏡 **Abbots Thorn** ⚐   ⟨
✉ *DL8 4AY –* ☏ *(01969) 640 620 – www.abbotsthorn.co.uk*
– abbots.thorn@virgin.net – February-November
3 rm ⊒ – †£50 ††£70
Rest – (by arrangement, communal dining) Menu £22
♦ Well priced, comfortable, quiet guesthouse in attractive rural village. Handy for visits to Moors. Cosy sitting room. Sizeable bedrooms which are homely and well-kept. Fresh, local produce to fore at dinner.

🍴 **Foresters Arms** with rm   🕿 ⚒ rest, **P.** **VISA** ◯◉
✉ *DL8 4BB –* ☏ *(01969) 640 272 – www.forestersarms-carlton.co.uk*
– chambersmic@hotmail.com – Fax (01969) 640 272 – Closed 24 December dinner, Bank Holiday dinner
3 rm ⊒ – †£65 ††£79   **Rest** – (Closed Monday) Menu £15 – Carte £20/26
♦ Compact 17C stone-built inn. Flagged floor bar with beams and open fire. Timbered restaurant where modern dishes utilise fresh, local produce. Pleasant, cottagey rooms.

MIDDLETON-IN-TEESDALE – Durham – **502** N 20 – pop. 1 143   24 **A3**

▶ London 447 mi – Carlisle 91 mi – Leeds 124 mi – Middlesbrough 70 mi – Newcastle upon Tyne 65 mi
🛈 Market Pl ☏ (01833) 641001, middletonplus@compuserve.com

🏡 **Grove Lodge**   ⟨ ☞ ⚒ **P.**
Hude, Northwest : ½ m. on B 6277 ✉ *DL12 0QW –* ☏ *(01833) 640 798*
– www.grovelodgeteesdale.co.uk
3 rm ⊒ – †£46 ††£78   **Rest** – Carte £17/29
♦ Victorian former shooting lodge perched on a hill where the two front facing rooms have the best views. Neat and friendly house, traditionally decorated. Home-cooked dinners are proudly served.

MIDHURST – West Sussex – **504** R 31 – pop. 6 120   7 **C2**

▶ London 57 mi – Brighton 38 mi – Chichester 12 mi – Southampton 41 mi
🛈 North St ☏ (01730) 817322, midtic@chichester.gov.uk

🏨 **Spread Eagle**   🖺 ◉ 🕿 ⅃⚹ 🎱 ⚙ **P.** **VISA** ◯◉ **AE** ①
South St ✉ *GU29 9NH –* ☏ *(01730) 816 911 – www.hshotels.co.uk*
– spreadeagle@hshotels.co.uk – Fax (01730) 815 668
37 rm ⊒ – †£154/163 ††£214/239 – 2 suites   **Rest** – Menu £23/40 **s**
♦ 15C hostelry boasting lovely characterful bar with uneven oak flooring and roaring fire. Many antiques. Good leisure facilities. Rooms have country house décor and style. A very traditional ambience pervades restaurant.

ENGLAND

MIDHURST

at Bepton Southwest : 2½ m. by A 286 on Bepton rd – ⊠ Midhurst

🏠 **Park House** 🕊 ⬚ 🍽 🖼 ⅙ rm, ⁿ⁾ 🖫 🅿 VISA ⬤ AE
Bepton ⊠ *GU29 0JB – 𝒞 (01730) 819000 – www.parkhousehotel.com*
– reservations@parkhousehotel.com – Fax (01730) 819099 – Closed Christmas
14 rm ⌑ – ♦£85/170 ♦♦£155/180 – 1 suite
Rest – (booking essential at lunch) Menu £27/35
♦ Comfortable, privately owned country house. Charming lounge with chintz armchairs, antique paintings, heavy drapes. Bar with honesty policy. Rooms are bright
and colourful. Classical dining room with antique tables and chairs.

at Elsted Southwest : 5 m. by A 272 on Elsted rd – ⊠ Midhurst

🏠 **Three Horseshoes** ⬚ 🅿 VISA ⬤
⊠ *GU29 0JY – 𝒞 (01730) 825746*
Rest – Carte £20/30
♦ Simply furnished, cosy beamed pub with large south-facing garden. Enormous
portions of wholesome, hearty cooking in the form of casseroles and pies; chatty,
informal service.

at Redford West : 3 m. by A272 then following signs for Redford

🏠 **Redford Cottage** without rest ⬚ 🅿
Redford ⊠ *GU29 0QF – 𝒞 (01428) 741242 – Fax (01428) 741242 – Closed 24-26*
and 31 December and 1 January
5 rm ⌑ – ♦£65 ♦♦£95
♦ Charming 15C cottage in delightful gardens. Uniquely styled, attractively furnished
bedrooms; china, books and pictures abound. Hearty breakfast from the Aga can be
taken on the terrace.

at Stedham West : 2 m. by A 272 – ⊠ Midhurst

🏠 **Nava Thai at The Hamilton Arms** 🅿 VISA ⬤ AE
School Lane ⊠ *GU29 0NZ – 𝒞 (01730) 812555 – www.thehamiltonarms.co.uk*
– hamiltonarms@hotmail.com – Fax (01730) 817459 – Closed 1-3 January
Rest – Thai – (Closed Monday except Bank Holiday Monday lunch)
Menu £20 – Carte £15/25
♦ Extensive menu of tasty Thai dishes served among authentic oriental artefacts and
incense in this traditional village inn. Fragrant, flavoursome cooking and polite serv-
ice.

at Trotton West : 3¼ m. on A 272 – ⊠ Petersfield (Hants.)

🏠 **The Keepers Arms** ⬚ 🍴 🅿 VISA ⬤ AE
Trotton ⊠ *GU31 5ER – 𝒞 (01730) 813724 – www.keepersarms.co.uk*
– info@keepersarms.co.uk – Fax (01730) 810780
– Closed 25 December dinner, 26 December
Rest – (dinner only) Carte £21/28
♦ Refurbished hillside pub set back from the main road, with cosy bar and sofas and
two feature tables. Good value, flavoursome modern British dishes on concise à la
carte menu.

MID LAVANT – West Sussex – see Chichester

MIDSOMER NORTON – Bath and North East Somerset – **503** M 30   4 **C2**
🄳 London 125mi – Bath 11mi – Wells 12mi

🍴🍴 **The Moody Goose at the Old Priory** with rm ⬚ ⁿ⁾ 🅿
Church Sq ⊠ *BA3 2HX – 𝒞 (01761) 416784* VISA ⬤ AE ⓪
– www.theoldpriory.co.uk – info@theoldpriory.co.uk – Fax (01761) 417851
– Closed 25-26 December and Sunday dinner
6 rm ⌑ – ♦£90/95 ♦♦£120/155
Rest – Menu £25 (lunch) – Carte dinner £31/44
♦ 12C former priory, by a church, with enviable walled garden. Flagged floors, beams
and vast fireplaces create impressive interior. Interesting modern cooking. Comfy
rooms.

MILFORD-ON-SEA – Hampshire – 503 P 31 – pop. 4 229   6 **A3**

– ⊠ Lymington

**�] London 109 mi – Bournemouth 15 mi – Southampton 24 mi
– Winchester 37 mi**

🏠 **Westover Hall** ⑤   ≼ 🚗 🖩 & rm, 🖐 **P** **VISA** **◉◎** **AE**
Park Lane ⊠ *SO41 0PT – ℰ (01590) 643 044 – www.westoverhallhotel.com
– info@westoverhallhotel.com – Fax (01590) 644 490*
11 rm �*** – ₸£130/165 ₸₸£230/360 – 3 suites   Rest** – Menu £25/42
♦ Characterful 19C mansion in delightful spot overlooking Christchurch Bay. Comfortable sitting room and impressive hall and minstrels gallery. Bedrooms have personality. Ornate dining room: decorative ceiling, stained glass, panelling.

MILLBROOK – Cornwall – 503 H 32   2 **C2**
▶ London 235 mi – Liskeard 16 mi – Plymouth 23 mi

at Freathy West : 3 m. by B 3247, Whitsand Bay Rd and Treninnow Cliff Rd
– ⊠ Millbrook

✗ **The View**   ≼ 🖩 **P** **VISA** **◉◎** **AE**
🙂 *East : 1 m.* ⊠ *PL10 1JY – ℰ (01752) 822 345 – www.theview-restaurant.co.uk
– Closed 3 weeks January - February, Monday except Bank Holidays and Tuesday*
Rest – Seafood – Carte £23/32
♦ Converted café: best views are from front terrace. Basic interior smartened up in evenings. Interesting, understated, seafood oriented menus: cooking is clean and delicious.

MILLOM – Cumbria – 502 K 21 – pop. 6 103 ▌ *Great Britain*   21 **A3**
▶ London 299 mi – Barrow-in-Furness 22 mi – Ulverston 17 mi
◧ Hard Knott Pass★★, N : 23 m. by A 595 and minor rd (eastbound)

🏠 **Underwood**   ≼ 🚗 🖻 ✗ ⅋ 🖐 **P** **VISA** **◉◎** **AE** **◉**
The Hill, North : 2 m. on A 5093 ⊠ *LA18 5EZ – ℰ (01229) 771 116
– www.underwoodhouse.co.uk – enquiries@underwoodhouse.co.uk – Fax (01229)
719 900 – Closed 3 weeks March, 1 week October*
5 rm ⊆ – ₸£65 ₸₸£120
Rest – (dinner only) (booking essential) (residents only) Menu £25
♦ Built in classic Lakeland grey, a Victorian former vicarage boasting two comfortable lounges and a large indoor pool. Well-kept, spacious double rooms with countryside views. Pleasant dining room overlooks gardens; tasty home cooking.

MILTON – Oxon. – see Banbury

MILTON BRYAN – Beds. – 504 S 28 – see Woburn

MILTON KEYNES – Milton Keynes – 504 R 27 – pop. 156 148   11 **C1**
**▶ London 56 mi – Bedford 16 mi – Birmingham 72 mi – Northampton 18 mi
– Oxford 37 mi**
ℹ askvic@powernet.com
🖪 Abbey Hill Two Mile Ash Monks Way, ℰ (01908) 563 845
🖪 Tattenhoe Bletchley Tattenhoe Lane, ℰ (01908) 631 113
🖪 Wavendon Golf Centre Wavendon Lower End Rd, ℰ (01908) 281 811

Plan on next page

🏨 **Holiday Inn Milton Keynes**   🖩 🖻 🛏 ⒗ 🖻 & rm, ✗ 🖐 ⚐ **P**
500 Saxon Gate West, Central Milton Keynes ⊠ *MK9 2HQ*   **VISA** **◉◎** **AE** **◉**
*– ℰ (0870) 400 9057 – www.holiday-inn.com
– reservations-miltonkeynes@ichotelsgroup.com – Fax (01908) 698 693*   EYZ**a**
164 rm ⊆ – ₸£211 ₸₸£211 – 2 suites   **Rest** – Menu £20/32 – Carte £15/25
♦ Commercial business hotel, with public areas set in modern atrium. Opposite main shopping area. Good leisure club with above average sized pool. Well-kept, clean rooms. Informal, family-friendly restaurant.

ENGLAND

HORIZONTAL ROADS

Bletcham Way (H10) . . . . **CX**
Chaffron Way (H7) . . . . **BX, CV**
Childs Way (H6) . . . . **BX, CV**
Dansteed Way (H4) . . . . **ABV**
Groveway (H9) . . . . **CVX**
Millers Way (H2) . . . . **AV**
Monks Way (H3) . . . . **ABV**
Portway (H5) . . . . **BCV**
Ridgeway (H1) . . . . **AV**
Standing Way (H8) . . . . **BX, CV**

MILTON KEYNES

Buckingham Rd . . . . **BX**
London Rd . . . . **CUV**
Manor Rd . . . . **CX**
Marsh End Rd . . . . **CU**
Newport Rd . . . . **BV**
Northampton Rd . . . . **AU**
Stoke Rd . . . . **CX**
Stratford Rd . . . . **AV**
Whaddon Way . . . . **BX**
Wolverton Rd. . . . . **BU**

VERTICAL ROADS

Brickhill St (V10) . . . . **BU, CX**
Fulmer St (V3) . . . . **ABX**
Grafton St (V6) . . . . **BVX**
Great Monks St (V5) . . . . **AV**
Marlborough St (V8) . . . . . . **BV, CX**
Overstreet (V9) . . . . **BV**
Saxon St (V7) . . . . **BVX**
Snelshall St (V1) . . . . **BX**
Tattenhoe St (V2) . . . . **ABX**
Tongwell St (V11) . . . . **CVX**
Watling St (V4) . . . . **AV, BX**

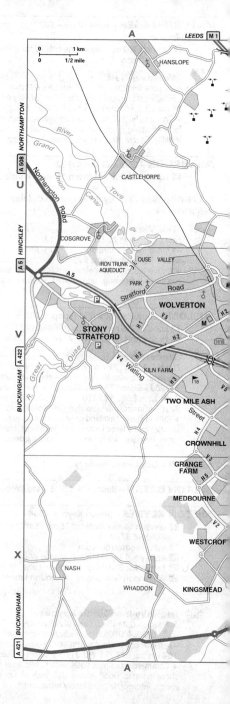

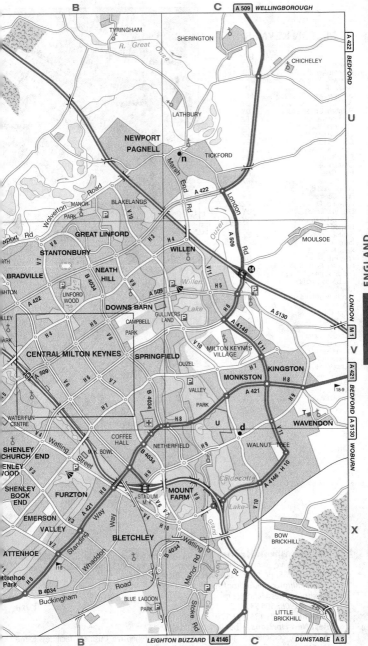

MILTON KEYNES

ENGLAND

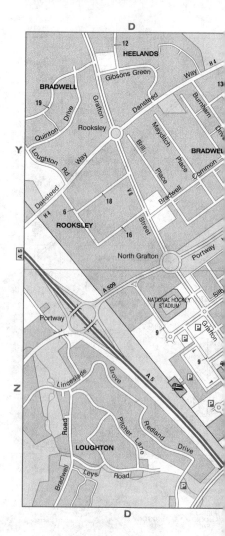

 Hilton Milton Keynes 🗐 🕉 ᵱᵤ ᵭᵤ rm, 🖾 rest, 🍴 ᶜᵘ ᶤᵤ 🅿 *VISA* ⦾ AE ⓪

Timbold Drive, Kents Hill Park, Southeast : 4 m. by B 4034 and A 421
off Brickhill St (V10) ⊠ *MK6 7AH –* ℰ *(01908) 694 433*
– www.hilton.co.uk/miltonkeynes
– miltonkeynes@hilton.com
– Fax (01908) 695 533 CVX**d**
138 rm ⊡ **– ♦**£135 **♦♦**£170
Rest *New Horizons* – (bar lunch) Carte £27/32

♦ Modern, commercial group hotel with comprehensive business facilities. Large
lounge and bar. Comfortable rooms in three different grades varying slightly by size.
Informal dining room aimed at business traveller.

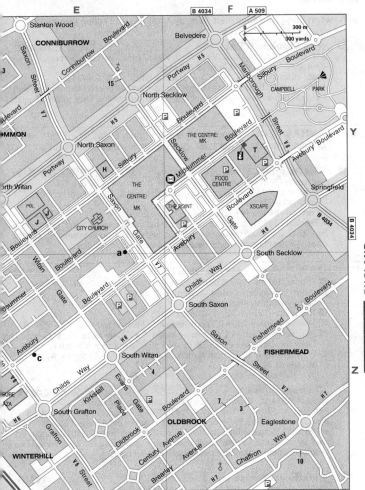

ENGLAND

✂ **Brasserie Blanc**   AC 💬 VISA ⓜⓞ AE
Chelsea House, 301 Avebury Blvd ⊠ MK9 2GA
– ℰ *(01908) 546 590*
– *www.brasserieblanc.com*
– *miltonkeynes@brasserieblanc.com – Fax (01908) 546 591*
– *Closed 25-26 December and 1 January*   EZ**c**
Rest – French – (booking essential) Menu £ 14/18
– Carte £ 20/40
◆ Striking modern building with a bustling trade – part of the Raymond Blanc chain. Menu features refined French brasserie dishes, mainly classics, with some house specialities.

at Newton Longville Southwest : 6 m. by A 421 - AX – ⊠ Milton Keynes

🍴 **The Crooked Billet**   🖼 🌳 ⌘ 🅿 *VISA* ◉◉ **AE**
2 Westbrook End ⊠ MK17 0DF – 𝒞 (01908) 373 936 – www.thebillet.co.uk
– john@thebillet.co.uk – Closed 25 December
Rest – (Closed Sunday dinner and Monday lunch) Carte £ 20/28 ⅋
♦ A pretty, thatched exterior and large front garden greet visitors to this village pub.
Dining in two areas on scrubbed pine and mahogany tables. Tasty, modern English
menus.

MINCHINHAMPTON – Gloucestershire – **503** – pop. 2 446   4 **C1**
  ▶ London 105 mi – Bristol 35 mi – Swindon 28 mi – Gloucester 25 mi

🍴 **The Ragged Cot** with rm   🖼 🌳 📶 🅿 *VISA* ◉◉ **AE** ◉
Cirencester Rd, Minchinhampton, East : 1 m. on Tetbury rd ⊠ GL6 8PE
– 𝒞 (01453) 884 643 – www.theraggedcot.co.uk – info@theraggedcot.co.uk
– Fax (01453) 731 166
10 rm ⌑ – ♱£ 120 ♱♱£ 120   **Rest** – Carte £ 20/31
♦ Refurbished 18C pub with a lovely terrace and garden booths. Rustic, robust cook-
ing with local produce sees lighter dishes at lunch and a more structured à la carte at
dinner. Pleasant bedrooms with neutral colours and modern facilities.

MINEHEAD – Somerset – **503** J 30 – pop. 11 699   3 **A2**
  ▶ London 187 mi – Bristol 64 mi – Exeter 43 mi – Taunton 25 mi
  🛈 Visitor Information Centre, Warren Rd 𝒞 (01643) 702624,
  visitor@westsomerset.gov.uk
  🖼 The Warren Warren Rd, 𝒞 (01643) 702 057
  ◉ Town★ - Higher Town (Church Steps★, St Michael's★)
  ◙ Dunster★★ - Castle★★ **AC** (upper rooms ≤★) Water Mill★ **AC**, St George's
  Church★, Dovecote★, SE : 2½ m. by A 39 – Selworthy★ (Church★, ≤★★)
  W : 4½ m. by A 39. Exmoor National Park★★ – Cleeve Abbey★★ **AC**,
  SE : 6½ m. by A 39

🏠 **Channel House** ⌂   ≤ 🖼 ⌘ 🅿 *VISA* ◉◉ ◉
⊠ TA24 5QG – 𝒞 (01643) 703 229 – www.channelhouse.co.uk
– channel.house@virgin.net – Fax (01643) 708 925 – Restricted opening in winter
8 rm ⌑ – ♱£ 88/102 ♱♱£ 146/174   **Rest** – (dinner only) Menu £ 25
♦ Pleasantly located Edwardian hotel in rural location surrounded by mature yet
carefully manicured gardens. Small, homely style lounge and fair sized, immaculate
bedrooms. Home-cooked meals using local ingredients.

🏠 **Glendower House** without rest   🖼 ⌘ 🅿 *VISA* ◉◉ **AE**
30-32 Tregonwell Rd ⊠ TA24 5DU – 𝒞 (01643) 707 144
– www.glendower-house.co.uk – info@glendower-house.co.uk – Fax (01643)
708 719 – Closed January
11 rm ⌑ – ♱£ 40/50 ♱♱£ 80
♦ Good value, warmly run guesthouse, convenient for seafront and town; boasts
original Victorian features. Immaculately kept bedrooms with a homely feel.

MISTLEY – Essex – **504** X 28   13 **D2**
  ▶ London 69 mi – Colchester 11 mi – Ipswich 14 mi

🍴 **The Mistley Thorn** with rm   🅿 *VISA* ◉◉
High Street ⊠ CO11 1HE – 𝒞 (01206) 392 821 – www.mistleythorn.com
– info@mistleythorn.com – Fax (01206) 390 122 – Closed 25 December
5 rm ⌑ – ♱£ 75/95 ♱♱£ 90/105   **Rest** – Menu £ 15 (lunch) – Carte £ 14/23
♦ Attractive yellow painted Georgian pub with modern interior: sitting area has cosy
sofas. Interesting dishes, cooked with care, full of local, organic ingredients. Neat
rooms.

ENGLAND

MITCHELL – Cornwall – **503** E 32 – ⊠ **Truro**   1 **B2**

   ▶ London 265 mi – Plymouth 47 mi – Truro 9 mi

🏠 **The Plume of Feathers** with rm   🚗 **P** *VISA* **₥**
   ⊠ TR8 5AX – ℰ (01872) 510 387 – www.theplume.info
   – enquiries@theplume.info – Fax (01872) 511 124
   8 rm ⌘ – ♦£46 ♦♦£60/70   **Rest** – Carte £18/26
   ♦ 16C pub in village centre. Rustic, beamed interior. Pleasant dining area with fresh
   flowers and small candles. Modern food with fine Cornish ingredients. Airy, modish
   rooms.

MITTON – Lancs. – **502** M 22 – **see Whalley**

MOBBERLEY – Ches. – **502** N 24 – **see Knutsford**

MOCCAS – County of Herefordshire – **503** L 27   18 **A3**

   ▶ London 171 mi – Hereford 13 mi – Cwmbrân 45 mi – Great Malvern 36 mi

🏠 **Moccas Court** ⌂   🚗 🖉 ⬥ ⌘ *VISA* **₥** **AE**
   ⊠ HR2 9LH – ℰ (01981) 500 095 – www.moccas-court.co.uk
   – info@moccas-court.co.uk – Fax (01981) 500 098 – Closed February-March
   5 rm ⌘ – ♦£126/201 ♦♦£140/224
   Rest – (dinner only) (by arrangement, communal dining, set menu only)
   Menu £35 **s**
   ♦ Breathtakingly beautiful Grade I listed Georgian house in 100 acres of grounds on
   terraced banks over the Wye. Antique filled interior; bedrooms furnished to high
   standard. Estate sourced produce served in ornate Round Room.

MONK FRYSTON – North Yorkshire – **502** Q 22 – ⊠ **Lumby**   22 **B2**

   ▶ London 190 mi – Kingston-upon-Hull 42 mi – Leeds 13 mi – York 20 mi

🏨 **Monk Fryston Hall**   🚗 🖉 ⬥ ⌘ 🅢 **P** *VISA* **₥** **AE**
   Main St ⊠ LS25 5DU – ℰ (01977) 682 369 – www.monkfryston-hotel.co.uk
   – reception@monkfrystonhallhotel.co.uk – Fax (01977) 683 544
   29 rm ⌘ – ♦£79/89 ♦♦£135
   Rest – Menu £28 (dinner) – Carte lunch £17/23
   ♦ Very characterful, possibly haunted, manor house dating from the 1300s with
   many later additions. Spacious grounds. Baronial style hall with antiques. Imposing
   rooms. Comfortable dining room with baronial touches.

MONKS ELEIGH – Suffolk – **504** W 27   15 **C3**

   ▶ London 72 mi – Cambridge 47 mi – Colchester 17 mi – Ipswich 16 mi
   – Norwich 49 mi

🏠 **The Swan**   🏡 ⌘ ⬌ **P** *VISA* **₥**
   The Street ⊠ IP7 7AU – ℰ (01449) 741 391 – www.monkseleigh.com
   – swan@monkseleigh.com
   – Closed 25-26 December and 1 January and 1 week in summer
   Rest – Menu £19 – Carte £20/35
   ♦ Attractive honey yellow pub with a thatched roof. Relying on local produce, menus
   change daily, comprising of classic and refined pub dishes with some Italian influ-
   ences.

MORECAMBE – Lancashire – **502** L 21 – pop. 49 569   20 **A1**

   ▶ London 247 mi – Preston 27 mi – Blackpool 39 mi – Blackburn 34 mi

🏨 **Midland**   ≤ 🚗 🏡 🖦 📶 🕭 👁 🅢 **P** *VISA* **₥** **AE**
   Marine Road West ⊠ LA4 4BU – ℰ (01524) 424 000
   – www.midlandmorecambe.co.uk – hello@midlandmorecambe.co.uk
   43 rm – ♦£159 ♦♦£159/229, ⌘ £12 – 1 suite   **Rest** – Carte £22/34
   ♦ Great location gives the hotel fantastic views of the bay and mountains. Fully
   restored with superb art deco stylish enhanced by modern design. Bold colours in
   the bedrooms. Terrific bay views from the restaurant.

ENGLAND

MORETONHAMPSTEAD – Devon – 503 I 32 – ⊠ Newton Abbot 　　2 **C2**
> ▶ London 213 mi – Exeter 13 mi – Plymouth 30 mi
> ▣ Bovey Castle North Bovey, ℰ (01647) 445 009
> Ⓖ Dartmoor National Park★★

🛏️ **The White Hart**　　　🛜 ⁽ᵗ⁾ ⚒ 🏊 VISA ⓶ 🆎 ⓪
Station Rd ⊠ *TQ13 8NF* – ℰ *(01647) 441 340* – *www.whitehartdartmoor.co.uk*
– enquiries@whitehartdartmoor.co.uk – Fax (01647) 441 341
28 rm ⊇ – †£70/85 ††£118/140　　**Rest** – (bar lunch) Carte £18/27
◆ 17C Grade II listed former coaching inn in the town. Charming country furnished
residents lounge. Pleasant 'locals' bar. Attractively refurbished rooms are strong
point. Clothed dining room with Glorious Devon posters on the wall.

🏠 **Moorcote** without rest　　　⩽ 🚙 ⅏ **P**
Northwest : ¼ *m. on A 382* ⊠ *TQ13 8LS* – ℰ *(01647) 440 966*
– www.moorcotehouse.co.uk – moorcote@smartone.co.uk – March-November
4 rm ⊇ – †£50 ††£60
◆ Perched on hill above Moretonhampstead, this Victorian guesthouse has mature
gardens and well-kept bedrooms with stunning views of Dartmoor. Cosy breakfast
room and lounge.

🍴 **The White Horse Inn**　　　🛜 ⓶ 🆎 ⓪
7 George Street ⊠ *TQ13 8PG* – ℰ *(01647) 440 242*
– www.whitehorse-moretonhampstead.co.uk
– info@whitehorse-moretonhampstead.co.uk – Fax (01647) 440 148
– closed 25 December
Rest – (Closed October-May weekday lunch) Carte £20/35
◆ 17C stone pub set in a busy market village. Well-balanced menu features tasty,
unfussy dishes made from local produce, ranging from British classics to more Mediterranean fare.

MORETON-IN-MARSH – Gloucestershire – 503 O 28 – pop. 3 198 　　4 **D1**
▌ *Great Britain*
> ▶ London 86 mi – Birmingham 40 mi – Gloucester 31 mi – Oxford 29 mi
> ⒼChastleton House★★, SE : 5 m. by A 44

🏨 **Manor House**　　　🚙 🛜 🖳 ⅃ Ⓚ rest, ⅏ ⁽ᵗ⁾ 🏊 **P** VISA ⓶ 🆎
High St ⊠ *GL56 0LJ* – ℰ *(01608) 650 501*
– www.cotswold-inns-hotels.co.uk/manor – info@manorhousehotel.info
– Fax (01608) 651 481
34 rm ⊇ – †£115/155 ††£145/185
Rest *Mulberry* – (light lunch) Menu £38
◆ Part 16C manor house in town centre. Walled lawns to rear. Two country house
style low-beamed lounges with open fires. Sympathetically styled rooms; luxurious
fabrics. Contemporary restaurant with bold style and cooking.

🏠 **The Old School** without rest　　　🚙 ⁽ᵗ⁾ **P** VISA ⓶
Little Compton, East : 4 *m.on A 44* ⊠ *GL56 0SL* – ℰ *(01608) 674 588*
– www.theoldschoolbedandbreakfast.com
– wendy@theoldschoolbedandbreakfast.com
4 rm ⊇ – †£60/70 ††£92/110
◆ Attractive, well kept Victorian building with large, neat garden. Period features
such as A-frame ceilings and stained glass windows are complemented by modern
furnishings.

at Bourton-on-the-Hill West : 2 m. on A 44 – ⊠ Moreton-in-Marsh

🍴 **Horse & Groom** with rm　　　🚙 🛜 ⅏ **P** VISA ⓶
⊠ *GL56 9AQ* – ℰ *(01386) 700 413* – *www.horseandgroom.info*
– greenstocks@horseandgroom.info – Fax (01386) 700 413
– Closed 25 and 31 December
5 rm ⊇ – †£70 ††£140
Rest – (Closed Sunday dinner and Monday lunch) (booking essential)
Carte £19/30
◆ Grade II listed yellow-stone building with a friendly atmosphere. Menu features
hearty, unfussy cooking and ranges from classic pub dishes to more restaurant style
offerings. Modern bedrooms, each individually styled.

MORPETH – Northumberland – **501** O 18 – pop. 13 555   24 **B2**

> ☑ London 301 mi – Edinburgh 93 mi – Newcastle upon Tyne 15 mi
> 🖼 The Chantry, Bridge St ✆ (01670) 500700, tourism@castlemorpeth.gov.uk
> 🖼 The Clubhouse, ✆ (01670) 504 942

at Eshott North : 6 m. by A 1 – ✉ Morpeth

⬆   **Eshott Hall** ≫   🚅 🕪 ⚒ 🍴 ♨ **P** 🆅🆂🅰 ⓪❾
by unmarked drive just before entering village ✉ *NE65 9EP – ✆ (01670) 787 777
– www.eshotthall.co.uk – david.sanderson@eshotthallestate.co.uk – Fax (01670)
787 999 – Closed Christmas - New Year*
7 rm ☲ – 🛏£90 🛏🛏£150
Rest – (by arrangement, communal dining) Menu £33
♦ Impressive Georgian mansion in a private drive with mature grounds. A smart
country house feel is evident all around. Popular for weddings. Rooms exude spotless
quality. Owner cooks and serves at an antique table.

at Longhorsley Northwest : 6½ m. by A 192 on A 697 – ✉ Morpeth

⬆   **Thistleyhaugh Farm** ≫   🚅 🕪 ⚒ **P** 🆅🆂🅰 ⓪❾
🍽   *Northwest : 3¾ m. by A 697 and Todburn rd taking first right turn* ✉ *NE65 8RG
– ✆ (01665) 570 629 – www.thistleyhaugh.co.uk – thistleyhaugh@hotmail.com
– Fax (01665) 570 629 – February - late December*
5 rm ☲ – 🛏£50/70 🛏🛏£75
Rest – (by arrangement, communal dining) Menu £20
♦ Attractive Georgian farmhouse on working farm in a pleasant rural area. The River
Coquet flows through the grounds. Comfortable, cosy bedrooms in traditional style.
Communal dining overlooking garden.

> The ✿ award is the crème de la crème.
> This is awarded to restaurants
> which are really worth travelling miles for!

MORSTON – Norfolk – see Blakeney

MORTEHOE – Devon – **503** H 30 – see Woolacombe

MOULSFORD – Oxfordshire   10 **B3**

> ☑ London 53 mi – Newbury 16 mi – Reading 13 mi

✗✗   **The Beetle & Wedge Boathouse**   ❮ 🏞 **P** 🆅🆂🅰 ⓪❾ 🅰🅴
Ferry Lane ✉ *OX10 9JF – ✆ (01491) 651 381 – www.beetleandwedge.co.uk
– boathouse@beetleandwedge.co.uk – Fax (01491) 651 376 – Closed 25 December*
Rest – (booking essential) Carte £28/37
♦ Beautifully located by the Thames and enhanced by lovely terrace. Two dining
options: bare-brick char-grill or conservatory dining room. Daily changing, wide-
ranging menus.

MOULTON – North Yorkshire – **502** P 20 – ✉ Richmond   22 **B1**

> ☑ London 243 mi – Leeds 53 mi – Middlesbrough 25 mi – Newcastle upon
> Tyne 43 mi

✗✗   **Black Bull Inn**   **P** 🆅🆂🅰 ⓪❾
✉ *DL10 6QJ – ✆ (01325) 377 289 – www.blackbullmoulton.com
– enquires@blackbullmoulton.com – Fax (01325) 377 422*
Rest – Seafood – (Closed Sunday dinner) Menu £19 – Carte £20/44
♦ Old country pub with variety of dining areas, including an original Brighton Belle
Pullman carriage from 1932 and conservatory with huge grapevine. Seafood a spe-
ciality.

ENGLAND

MOUSEHOLE – Cornwall – 503 D 33 – ⊠ **Penzance**   1 **A3**
- ⬛ London 321 mi – Penzance 3 mi – Truro 29 mi
- ◉ Village★
- ⓒ Penwith★★ – Lamorna (The Merry Maidens and The Pipers Standing Stone★) SW : 3 m. by B 3315. Land's End★ (cliff scenery★★★) W : 9 m. by B 3315

🏠 **The Old Coastguard**   ⟨ 🚗 🛎 ⑆ ⑉ 🅿 VISA ⑳ AE
The Parade ⊠ *TR19 6PR* – ℰ *(01736) 731 222* – *www.oldcoastguardhotel.co.uk*
– *bookings@oldcoastguardhotel.co.uk* – *Fax (01736) 731 720*
– *Closed 24-26 December*
14 rm ⌿ – †£195/225 ††£260/300   **Rest** – Carte £26/30
♦ Creamwash hotel in unspoilt village with good views of Mounts Bay. Spacious lounge has sun terrace overlooking water. Modern rooms: Premier variety are best for the vista. Watch the bay as you eat freshly caught seafood.

✗ **Cornish Range** with rm   VISA ⑳
6 Chapel St ⊠ *TR19 6SB* – ℰ *(01736) 731 488* – *www.cornishrange.co.uk*
– *info@cornishrange.co.uk*
3 rm ⌿ – ††£80/110   **Rest** – Seafood – (booking essential) Carte £20/32
♦ Converted 18C pilchard processing cottage hidden away in narrow street. Cottagey inner filled with Cornish artwork. Excellent local seafood dishes. Very comfortable rooms.

MUCH WENLOCK – Shropshire – 502 M26 – pop. 1 959 ▌*Great Britain*   18 **B2**
- ⬛ London 154 mi – Birmingham 34 mi – Shrewsbury 12 mi – Worcester 37 mi
- 🄴 The Museum, High St ℰ (01952) 727679, muchwenlock.tourism@shropshire.gov.uk
- ◉ Priory★ AC
- ⓒ Ironbridge Gorge Museum★★ AC (The Iron Bridge★★ - Coalport China Museum★★ - Blists Hill Open Air Museum★★ – Museum of the Gorge and Visitor Centre★) NE : 4½ m. by A 4169 and B 4380

🏨 **Raven**   🛎 ⑆ 🅿 VISA ⑳ AE ①
Barrow St ⊠ *TF13 6EN* – ℰ *(01952) 727 251* – *www.ravenhotel.com*
– *enquiry@ravenhotel.com* – *Fax (01952) 728416*
– *Closed 25-26 December*
20 rm ⌿ – †£85 ††£130
Rest *The Restaurant* – Menu £20/33 **s**
♦ Hotel spread across range of historic buildings with 17C coaching inn at its heart. Pleasant inner courtyard and conservatory. Good sized bedrooms with chintz fabrics. Dining room exudes homely rustic charm.

at Brockton Southwest : 5 m. on B 4378 – ⊠ **Much Wenlock**

🏠 **The Feathers at Brockton**   🛎 ⑆ 🅿 VISA ⑳
Brockton ⊠ *TF13 6JR* – ℰ *(01746) 785 202* – *www.feathersatbrockton.co.uk*
– *feathersatbrockton@googlemail.com* – *Fax (01746) 785 202* – *Closed first week in January*
Rest – (Closed Monday) Menu £15 (weekday dinner) – Carte £15/30
♦ Characterful part 16C pub near Wenlock Edge: whitewashed stone walls, beams and vast inglenooks. Constantly changing blackboard menus provide plethora of interesting dishes.

MULLION – Cornwall – 503 E 33 – pop. 1 834 – ⊠ **Helston**   1 **A3**
- ⬛ London 323 mi – Falmouth 21 mi – Penzance 21 mi – Truro 26 mi
- ◉ Mullion Cove★★ (Church★) – Lizard Peninsula★
- ⓒ Kynance Cove★★, S : 5 m. – Cury★ (Church★), N : 2 m. by minor roads. Helston (The Flora Day Furry Dance★★) (May), N : 7½ m. by A 3083 – Culdrose (Flambards Village Theme Park★) AC, N : 6 m. by A 3083 – Wendron (Poldark Mine★), N : 9½ m. by A 3083 and B 3297

Mullion Cove ← 🚗 🏞 ⚒ 🏊 🐾 ‖ P VISA ⓜ AE

Southwest : 1 m. by B 3296 ⊠ TR12 7EP – ℰ (01326) 240328
– www.mullion-cove.com – enquiries@mullion-cove.co.uk – Fax (01326) 240998
– Closed 6 January-8 February
30 rm ⊑ – †£70/210 ††£170/270
Rest *Atlantic View* – (dinner only and Sunday lunch) Menu £32
Rest *Bistro* – Carte £16/41 **s**
♦ Dramatic Victorian hotel, personally run, standing in spectacular position on cliffs above Mullion Cove. Terrific views along coastline. Comfortable, modern rooms. Cream painted, welcoming Atlantic View. Bistro with terrace perfect for lunch.

MUNSLOW – Shropshire – 503 L 26   18 B2
▷ London 166 mi – Ludlow 10 mi – Shrewsbury 21 mi

The Crown Country Inn with rm   🚗 🏞 ❀ P VISA ⓜ AE

on B 4378 ⊠ SY7 9ET – ℰ (01584) 841205 – www.crowncountry-inn.co.uk
– info@crowncountry-inn.co.uk – Fax (01584) 841255 – Closed 25 December
3 rm ⊑ – †£50 ††£70/75
Rest – (Closed Sunday dinner and Monday) Menu £18 – Carte £22/30
♦ Hugely characterful, heavily beamed bar, crackling fire and hops hanging from the rafters. Well executed dishes served here or in linen clad restaurant. Simple, comfy rooms.

MURCOTT – Oxfordshire – pop. 1 293 – ⊠ Kidlington   10 B2
▷ London 70 mi – Oxford 14 mi – Witney 20 mi

The Nut Tree (Mike North)   🚗 🏞 P VISA ⓜ

Main Street ⊠ OX5 2RE – ℰ (01865) 331253
Rest – Menu £18 – Carte £27/40
Spec. Home smoked salmon with horseradish and salmon skin biscuit. Confit of Nut Tree raised pork, celeriac purée and apple gravy. Passion fruit soufflé and sorbet with glazed cream.
♦ Traditional thatched pub, popular with locals. Nicely balanced menu displays carefully executed pub and restaurant style dishes. Flavours are fresh, clear and satisfying.

MYLOR BRIDGE – Cornwall – 503 E 33 – see Falmouth

NANTWICH – Cheshire – 502 M 24 – pop. 13 447   20 A3
▷ London 176 mi – Chester 20 mi – Liverpool 45 mi – Manchester 40 mi
– Stoke-on-Trent 17 mi
🛈 Nantwich Civic Hall, Market St ℰ (01270) 610983,
touristi@crewe-nantwich.gov.uk
🖼 Alvaston Hall Middlewich Rd, ℰ (01270) 628473

Rookery Hall ᔰ   ← 🚗 🦯 🌳 🏞 🖽 ☺ 🐾 ⛴ ‖ & rm, ☎ ⚗ P

Worleston, North : 2½ m. by A 51 on B 5074 ⊠ CW5 6DQ   VISA ⓜ AE ⓞ
– ℰ (01270) 610016 – www.handpicked.co.uk – rookery@handpicked.co.uk
– Fax (01270) 626027
68 rm ⊑ – †£95/155 ††£105/165 – 2 suites
Rest – (bar lunch Monday-Friday) (booking essential) Menu £34
– Carte £34/49 **s**
♦ Main house dates from 19C, with pleasant grounds, but with recent additions and extensions. Geared more towards corporate market. Impressive spa. Comfortable and modern bedrooms. Wood panelled restaurant.

NATIONAL EXHIBITION CENTRE – W. Mids. – 503 O 26 – see Birmingham

---

NAWTON – N. Yorks. – see Helmsley

ENGLAND

NAYLAND – Suffolk – **504** W 28

15 **C3**

> ◘ London 64 mi – Bury St Edmunds 24 mi – Cambridge 54 mi
> – Colchester 6 mi – Ipswich 19 mi

XX **The White Hart Inn** with rm   ☆ ℅ **P** **VISA** **◐◉** **AE** **◑**
11 High St ✉ *CO6 4JF* – ℰ *(01206) 263 382* – *www.whitehart-nayland.co.uk*
– nayhart@aol.com – Fax (01206) 263 638
6 rm ☞ – ♦£76/109 ♦♦£96/129
Rest – Menu £16 (lunch) – Carte dinner £21/39 **s**
♦ Satisfying French and Mediterranean influences to the cooking, served in terracotta tiled dining room of part 15C coaching inn. Floodlit cellars. Cottagey feel to the bedrooms; those in main house have original beams.

NEAR SAWREY – Cumbria – **502** L 20 – see Hawkshead

NETHER BURROW – Cumbria – see Kirkby Lonsdale

NETLEY MARSH Southampton – **503** P 31 – see Southampton

NETTLEBED – Oxfordshire – **504** R 29

11 **C3**

> ◘ London 44 mi – Oxford 20 mi – Reading 10 mi

🏠 **White Hart**   ℅ ☏ ♿ **P** **VISA** **◐◉** **AE**
28 High St ✉ *RG9 5DD* – ℰ *(01491) 641 245* – *www.whitehartnettlebed.com*
– info@whitehartnettlebed.com – Fax (01491) 649 018
12 rm ☞ – ♦£125 ♦♦£145
Rest – (Closed Sunday dinner) Menu £18 (lunch) – Carte £20/31
♦ Recently refurbished part 17C inn boasts spacious, modern bedrooms, all uniquely styled with a certain "designer" appeal, some in original hotel, others in adjacent new block. Minimalist Bistro.

NETTLETON SHRUB – Wilts. – **503** N 29 – see Castle Combe

NEWARK-ON-TRENT – Nottinghamshire – **502** R 24 – pop. 35 454

17 **C1**

▌ *Great Britain*

> ◘ London 127 mi – Lincoln 16 mi – Nottingham 20 mi – Sheffield 42 mi
> ▣ CoddingtonNewark, ℰ (01636) 626 282
> ◉ St Mary Magdalene ★

🏠 **Grange**   ☴ ☆ ℅ ☏ **P** **VISA** **◐◉** **AE** **◑**
73 London Rd, South : ½ m. on Grantham rd (B 6326) ✉ *NG24 1RZ* – ℰ *(01636) 703 399* – *www.grangenewark.co.uk* – *info@grangenewark.co.uk* – *Fax (01636) 702 328* – *Closed 2 weeks from 24 December*
19 rm ☞ – ♦£79/90 ♦♦£110
Rest *Cutlers* – (closed Sunday dinner) (dinner only and Sunday lunch) Carte £24/29
♦ Situated in a residential area but not far from town centre, this small hotel is fitted with functional, simply decorated bedrooms and miniature pulpit-style bar. Compact dining room boasts candlelit dinners.

at Caunton Northwest : 7 m. by A 616 – ✉ Newark-on-Trent

🏠 **Caunton Beck**   ☆ **P** **VISA** **◐◉** **AE** **◑**
Main St ✉ *NG23 6AB* – ℰ *(01636) 636 793* – *www.wigandmitre.com*
– email@cauntonbeck.com – Fax (01636) 636 828
Rest – Menu £14 – Carte £21/33
♦ Welcoming modern pub, with stone-floored bar, beamed ceilings, flower-filled front terrace and restaurant serving classic pub dishes. Popular weekend breakfast destination.

NEWBURY – West Berkshire – **503** Q 29 – pop. 32 675   10 **B3**

▶ London 67 mi – Bristol 66 mi – Oxford 28 mi – Reading 17 mi
  – Southampton 38 mi

ℹ️ The Wharf ℰ (01635) 30267, tourism@westberks.gov.uk

Newbury and Crookham Greenham Common Bury's Bank Rd,
  ℰ (01635) 40 035

Donnington Valley Donnington Snelsmore House, Snelsmore Common,
  ℰ (01635) 568 140

NEWBURY

Street		No.
Almond Ave	**BY**	3
Andover Rd	**BZ**	4
Bartholomew St	**BZ**	6
Bone Lane	**BZ**	10
Carnegie Rd	**BZ**	13
Castle Grove	**BY**	15
Cheap St	**BZ**	16
Chesterfield Rd	**BZ**	18
Craven Rd	**BZ**	24
Dolman Rd	**BY**	25
Donnington Link	**BY**	27
Greenham Hill	**BZ**	31
Greenham Rd	**BZ**	33
Hambridge Rd	**BZ**	36
Kennet Shopping Centre	**BZ**	
Kiln Rd	**BY**	40
Kings Rd	**BZ**	
London Rd	**BY**	
Love Lane	**BY**	
Maple Crescent	**BY**	43
Market St	**BZ**	45
Mill Lane	**BZ**	
Newtown Rd	**BZ**	48
New Rd	**BZ**	46
Northbrook St	**BYZ**	
Northcroft Lane	**BZ**	
Old Bath Rd	**BY**	
Oxford Rd	**BY**	
Park Way	**BYZ**	50
Pound St	**BZ**	
Queens Rd	**BZ**	
Racecourse Rd	**BZ**	
Rockingham Rd	**BZ**	52
St Johns Rd	**BZ**	
Sandleford Link	**BZ**	54
Shaw Hill	**BY**	
Shaw Rd	**BY**	
Station Rd	**BZ**	
Strawberry Hill	**BY**	58
Western Ave	**BY**	
West St	**BZ**	66
Wharf St	**BZ**	67

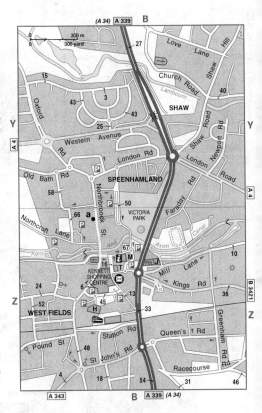

	The Vineyard at Stockcross	📠 📺 🐾 🖐️ 📶 🔟 🦽 🅿️
❀❀	*Stockcross, Northwest : 2 m. by A 4 on B 4000* ✉ *RG20 8JU*	**VISA ᐁᐂ AE**

– ℰ (01635) 528 770 – www.the-vineyard.co.uk – general@the-vineyard.co.uk
– Fax (01635) 528 398   AV**b**

34 rm – 🛏️🛏️£ 295, ☷ £15 – 15 suites   **Rest** – Menu £ 24/42 – Carte £ 24/70 ⊛

Spec. Gazpacho, crayfish and crème fraîche risotto. Rump of lamb with parsley
cous cous, olive and anchovy beignet. Passion fruit and banana with rum and
raisin panna cotta.

♦ Outside, a pool bearing bowls of fire encapsulates bright art-filled interiors. Luxurious suites with woven fabrics. Very good service. Super spa. Modern or country
house style rooms. Indulge in accomplished original cuisine and exceptional wine list.

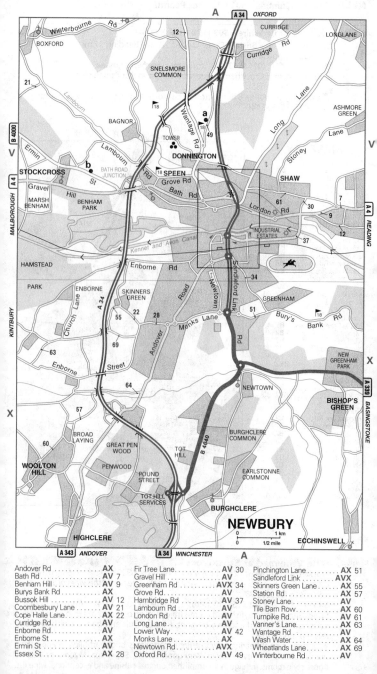

Donnington Valley H. & Spa
Old Oxford Rd, Donnington, North : 1 ¾ m. by A 4 off B 4494 ✉ *RG14 3AG – ✆ (01635) 551 199 – www.donningtonvalley.co.uk – general@donningtonvalley.co.uk – Fax (01635) 551 123* AV**a**

111 rm – †£ 129/200 ††£ 129/200, ☕ £ 14.50

Rest *Winepress* – Menu £ 23/27 – Carte £ 37/45

◆ Smart bedrooms in purpose-built country hotel with 18-hole golf course. Newer Executive rooms are the smartest. Excellent spa and leisure facilities. Large bar. Wine-themed restaurant.

The Square
5-6 Weavers Walk, Northbrook St ✉ *RG14 1AL – ✆ (01635) 44 805 – www.thesquarenewbury.co.uk – enquiries@thesquarenewbury.co.uk – Fax (01635) 523 114 – Closed 26 December, 1 January and Sunday* BZ**a**

Rest – Carte £ 20/39

◆ Tucked away in a little high street mews. French influenced artwork enlivens walls. Adventurous gastronomic excursions: expect unusual combinations with vivid presentation.

at Marsh Benham West : 3 ½ m. by A 4 - AV – ✉ Newbury

The Red House
✉ *RG20 8LY – ✆ (01635) 582 017 – www.redhousemarshbenham.co.uk – enquiries@redhousemarshbenham.co.uk – Fax (01635) 581 621 – Closed 26-27 December, 1 January*

Rest – Menu £ 17 – Carte £ 29/38

◆ Quintessentially English pub with beautiful thatched roof. Warm, inviting bar and spacious restaurant. Mediterranean à la carte and simpler set menu with good value pub classics.

The red symbol?
This denotes the very essence of peace
– only the sound of birdsong first thing in the morning…

ENGLAND

NEWBY BRIDGE – Cumbria – 502 L 21 – ✉ Ulverston *Great Britain* 21 **A3**

London 270 mi – Kendal 16 mi – Lancaster 27 mi

Lake Windermere★★

Lakeside
Lakeside, Northeast : 1 m. on Hawkshead rd ✉ *LA12 8AT – ✆ (015395) 30 001 – www.Lakesidehotel.co.uk – reservations@lakesidehotel.co.uk – Fax (015395) 31 699 – Closed 23 December-21 January*

74 rm ☕ – †£ 150/195 ††£ 170/215 – 3 suites

Rest *Lakeview* – Menu £ 29/49

Rest *John Ruskins Brasserie* – (dinner only) Menu £ 37

◆ Delightfully situated on the shores of Lake Windermere. Plenty of charm and character. Work out at the state-of-the-art leisure centre then sleep in fitted, modern bedrooms. Lakeview offers smart ambience. Bright, informal John Ruskins Brasserie.

The Knoll
Lakeside, Northeast : 1 ¼ m. on Hawkshead rd ✉ *LA12 8AU – ✆ (015395) 31 347 – www.theknoll-lakeside.co.uk – info@theknoll-lakeside.co.uk – Fax (015395) 30 850 – Closed 24-26 December*

8 rm ☕ – †£ 85/96 ††£ 120/137

Rest – (closed Sunday-Monday) (dinner only) (booking essential for non-residents) Menu £ 24 **s**

◆ Late Victorian country house close to popular lakeside, with welcoming owners, comfortable lounge and contemporary bedrooms; room 4 is the best. Extensive breakfast menu. Linen clad dining room; local produce proudly used.

NEWBY WISKE – N. Yorks. – 502 P 21 – see Northallerton

S. Vidler/Mauritius images/PHOTONONSTOP

NEWCASTLE UPON TYNE

County: Tyne and Wear
Michelin REGIONAL map: n° 501
🔼 London 276 mi – Edinburgh 105 mi
– Leeds 95 mi

Population: 189 863   24 **B2**
📗 *Great Britain*

Access Tyne Tunnel (toll)

PRACTICAL INFORMATION

🛈 Tourist Information

132 Grainger St 📞 (0191) 277 8000, tourist.info@newcastle.gov.uk

Guild Hall Visitors Centre, Quayside (0191) 277 2444

Newcastle International Airport 📞 (0191) 214 4422, niatic@hotmail.com

Airport
✈ Newcastle Airport: 📞 (0871) 882 1121, NW: 5 m. by A 696 AV

Ferries and Shipping Lines
⛴ to Norway (Bergen, Haugesund and Stavanger) (Fjord Line) (approx 26 h) – to The Netherlands (Amsterdam) (DFDS Seaways A/S) daily (15 h)

Tunnel
Tyne Tunnel (toll)

Golf Courses
🏌 Broadway East Gosforth, 📞 (0191) 285 0553

🏌 City of Newcastle Gosforth Three Mill Bridge, 📞 (0191) 285 1775

🏌 Wallsend Bigges Main Rheydt Ave,, NE: by A1058, 📞 (0191) 262 1973

🏌 Whickham Fellside Rd, Hollinside Park, 📞 (0191) 488 1576

🔲 SIGHTS

IN TOWN

City★ – Grey Street★ CZ – Quayside★ CZ : Composition★ , All Saints Church★ (interior★) – Castle Keep★ **AC**CZ – Laing Art Gallery and Museum★ **AC**CY **M1** – Museum of Antiquities★ CY **M2** – LIFE Interactive World★ CZ – Gateshead Millennium Bridge★ CZ

ON THE OUTSKIRTS

Hadrian's Wall★★ , W: by A 69 AV

IN THE SURROUNDING AREA

Beamish: North of England Open-Air Museum★★ **AC**, SW: 7 m. by A 692 and A 6076 AX – Seaton Delaval Hall★ **AC**, NE: 11 m. by A 189 - BV - and A 190

NEWCASTLE-UPON-TYNE

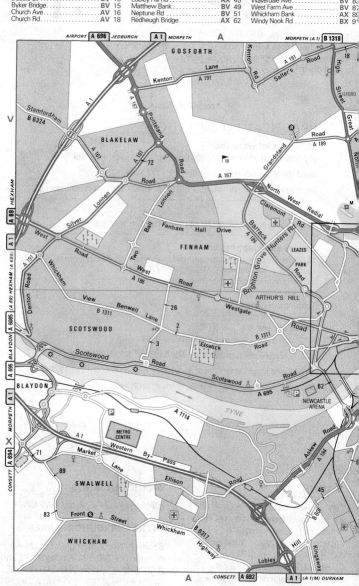

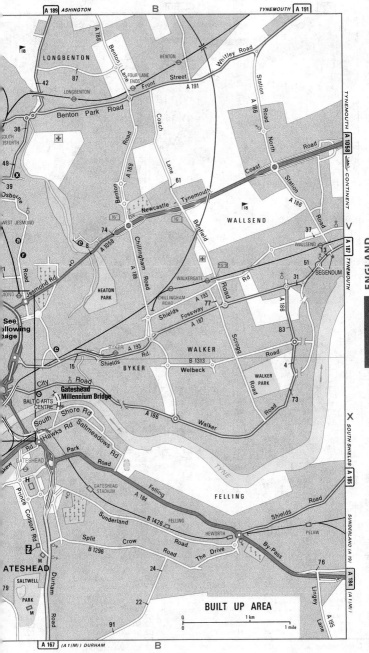

ENGLAND

LONGBENTON

BENTON

Whitley Road

Benton Lane

FOUR LANE ENDS

Front Street A 191

Coach Lane

Benton Park Road

LONGBENTON

42

87

SOUTH GOSFORTH

36

49

39

Osborne

WEST JESMOND

Road

JESMOND

See following page

Benton Road

A 188

61

Newcastle

Tynemouth

Belfield

16

16

74

8

A 1058

Chillingham Road

A 188

HEATON PARK

Station Road

A 186

North Road

Coast

Road

Station

A 186

WALLSEND

37

WALLSEND

51

SEGENDUM

31

CHILLINGHAM ROAD

WALKERGATE

Shields

Fossway

A 193

Road

Rd

A 187

77

A 186

83

BYKER A 193

Shields Rd.

BYKER

15

Road

City

Gateshead Millennium Bridge

BALTIC ARTS CENTRE

South Shore Rd

Hawks Rd

Saltmeadows Rd

Park

GATESHEAD

H

Prince Consort Rd

GATESHEAD

SALTWELL PARK

79

M

M

Durham Road

Split B 1296

Crow

Road

24

22

91

Welbeck

WALKER

B 1313

Scrogg Road

WALKER PARK

Walker

Road

73

4

A 186

Walker

GATESHEAD STADIUM

A 184

Felling

B 1426

Sunderland

Road

FELLING

Road

FELLING

HEWORTH

The Drive

By-Pass

Shields

Road

PELAW

76

Lingey Lane

TYNE

BUILT UP AREA

0   1 km

0   1 mile

TYNEMOUTH A 1058 CONTINENT

V A 187 TYNEMOUTH SEGENDUM

X SOUTH SHIELDS A 185

SUNDERLAND (A 19)

A 184 (A 1(M))

A 135

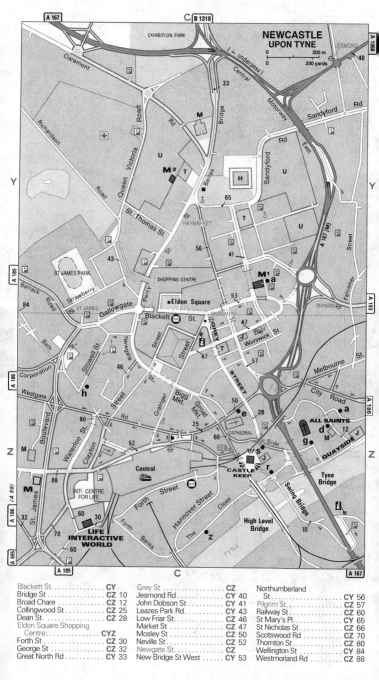

NEWCASTLE UPON TYNE

EXHIBITION PARK

ST JAMES PARK

SHOPPING CENTRE

Eldon Square

ALL SAINTS

CASTLE KEEP

CATHEDRAL

QUAYSIDE

Tyne Bridge

Swing Bridge

High Level Bridge

INT¹ CENTRE FOR LIFE

LIFE INTERACTIVE WORLD

Central Station

TYNE

Copthorne H. Newcastle $\Leftarrow$ 🍴 🔲 🕉 🖪 📶 🗵 rm, 🔟 rest, 🔝
The Close, Quayside ⊠ *NE1 3RT –* ℰ *(0191) 2220333* 🅿 *VISA* 🕡 AE ①
– www.milleniumhotels.co.uk/newcastle – sales.newcastle@milleniumhotels.co.uk
– Fax (0191) 2301111 CZz
156 rm – ♦£210 ♦♦£210, ⊑ £15.75
Rest *Quay 7* – (Closed Saturday lunch) Menu £11/22 – Carte £27/34
♦ Modern hotel beside the Tyne. Bright and airy lounges within an imposing atrium.
Well-appointed rooms have river views; ask for one with a balcony.

 Jesmond Dene House 🕸 🚿 🍴 🗵 🖧 rm, 🛱 📶 🔝 🅿 *VISA* 🕡 AE
Jesmond Dene Rd, Northeast: 1½ m. by B 1318 and A 189 ⊠ *NE2 2EY*
– ℰ (0191) 2123000 – www.jesmonddenehouse.co.uk
– info@jesmonddenehouse.co.uk – Fax (0191) 2123001 BVx
40 rm – ♦£165/175 ♦♦£250/450, ⊑ £16
Rest – Menu £25 (lunch) – Carte £40/60
♦ Stylishly refurbished 19C Grade II listed house in tranquil city dene.Two very smart
lounges, one with cocktail bar. Eclectic range of modish rooms with hi-tech feel.
Formal dining room with conservatory style extension overlooks garden.

 Malmaison 🕉 🖪 🗵 🖧 rm, 🔟 📶 🔝 🅿 *VISA* 🕡 AE ①
Quayside ⊠ *NE1 3DX –* ℰ *(0191) 245 5000 – www.malmaison.com*
– newcastle@malmaison.com – Fax (0191) 245 4545 BXe
120 rm – ♦£105/160 ♦♦£105/160, ⊑ £14 – 2 suites
Rest *Brasserie* – (bar lunch Saturday) Menu £17 (lunch) – Carte £22/41
♦ Unstuffy and contemporary hotel hides within this quayside former Co-operative
building. Vibrantly and individually decorated rooms; some overlook Millennium
Bridge. Brasserie has modern interpretation of French style.

New Northumbria 🍴 🗵 📶 🔝 *VISA* 🕡 AE
61-73 Osborne Rd, Jesmond ⊠ *NE2 2AN –* ℰ *(0191) 281 4961*
– www.newnorthumbriahotel.co.uk – reservations@newnorthumbriahotel.co.uk
– Fax (0191) 281 8588 BVa
57 rm ⊑ – ♦£85/105 ♦♦£95/105
Rest *Scalini's* – Italian – Menu £9 (lunch) **s** – Carte £14/27 **s**
Rest *Louis* – ℰ *(0191) 281 5284* (Closed Saturday lunch) Menu £14 (lunch) **s**
– Carte £20/35 **s**
♦ Welcoming hotel with bright yellow exterior and metro access to city. Bustling bar:
its lively location gives immediate access to buzzy nightspots. Well-equipped, comfy
rooms. Scalini's with Italian specialities. Smart, stylish Louis.

Waterside without rest 🗵 🛱 📶 🅿 *VISA* 🕡 AE ①
48-52 Sandhill, Quayside ⊠ *NE1 3JF –* ℰ *(0191) 2300111*
– www.watersidehotel.com – enquiries@watersidehotel.com – Fax (0191)
2301615 – Closed 1 week Christmas CZr
24 rm ⊑ – ♦£75/80 ♦♦£85
♦ Grade II listed quayside conversion close to most of the city's attractions. Compact
yet well-furnished and cosy bedrooms. Top floor rooms benefit from air-
conditioning.

XXX **Fisherman's Lodge** 🍴 ✿ 🅿 *VISA* 🕡 AE
Jesmond Dene, Jesmond ⊠ *NE7 7BQ –* ℰ *(0191) 281 3281*
– www.fishermanslodge.co.uk – info@fishermanslodge.co.uk – Fax (0191)
2816410 – Closed 25-26 December and 28-30 December, 1-2 January, Sunday
and Monday BVe
Rest – Menu £23/50
♦ Attractive Victorian house secreted in a narrow wooded valley yet close to city
centre. Series of well-appointed, stylish rooms. Modern British cooking with seafood
bias.

ENGLAND

XX **Café 21**   AC ⇄ VISA ⓜⓞ AE ①
Trinity Gardens ✉ *NE1 2HH* – ℰ *(0191) 222 0755 – www.cafetwentyone.co.uk*
– bh@cafetwentyone.co.uk – Fax (0191) 221 0761
– Closed 25-26 December and 1 January   CZ**a**
Rest – Menu £ 18 (lunch) – Carte £ 28/44
◆ Busy restaurant on ground floor of office block in redevelopment area of city. Open plan layout; warm, stylish décor. Flavoursome, bistro-style dishes have European influences.

XX **Amer's**   VISA ⓜⓞ AE
☺ *34 Osborne Rd, Jesmond* ✉ *NE2 2AJ* – ℰ *(0191) 281 5377*
– www.jesmondhotel.co.uk – jesmondhotel@aol.com – Fax (0191) 212 0783
– Closed 24-26 December, Bank Holidays, Sunday and lunch Saturday
and Monday   BV**d**
Rest – (booking essential) Menu £ 12/18 – Carte £ 18/35
◆ Popular ground floor restaurant in smart location. Cosy, stylish lounge/bar sets you up for good value dishes that are modern in style and prepared with skill and flair.

XX **Brasserie Black Door**   VISA ⓜⓞ AE
The Biscuit Factory, 16 Stoddart St ✉ *NE2 1AN* – ℰ *(0191) 260 5411*
– www.blackdoorgroup.co.uk – info@blackdoorgroup.co.uk – Fax (0191)
260 5422 – Closed 25 December, 1 January and Sunday dinner   BV**c**
Rest – Menu £ 17 (lunch) – Carte dinner £ 22/36
◆ Art gallery restaurant set in a 1930s former biscuit factory. Through modish lounge to airy dining space with industrial ambience, wall art and recognisable brasserie dishes.

XX **Grainger Rooms**   VISA ⓜⓞ AE ①
7 Higham Place ✉ *NE1 8AF* – ℰ *(0191) 232 4949 – www.graingerrooms.co.uk*
– info@graingerrooms.co.uk
– Closed 25-26 December, Sunday and Bank Holidays   CY**a**
Rest – Menu £ 15/28
◆ Red brick Georgian townhouse with first floor dining, eye-catching chandeliers and rustic photos. Hearty, flavoursome British cooking uses excellent produce. Polite service.

XX **McCoy's Brasserie**   VISA ⓜⓞ AE
32-34 Mosley St ✉ *NE1 1DF* – ℰ *(0191) 233 28 28*
– reservations@mccoysbrasserie.com – Fax (0191) 233 28 43
– Closed 25 December and Sunday dinner   CZ**e**
Rest – Menu £ 16 (lunch) – Carte £ 26/35
◆ Classic brasserie, with abstract art and bar at front for snacks. French-influenced cooking is refined in presentation but rustic and satisfying in flavour. Good value lunch.

XX **Vujon**   AC VISA ⓜⓞ AE ①
29 Queen St, Quayside ✉ *NE1 3UG* – ℰ *(0191) 221 0601 – www.vujon.com*
– mahtab@vujon.com – Fax (0191) 221 0602
– Closed 25 December, 1 January and Sunday lunch   CZ**g**
Rest – Carte £ 22/34
◆ A friendly and authentic Indian restaurant can be found behind the striking Victorian façade with modern etched windows. Menu of traditional and more contemporary dishes.

X **Caffè Vivo**   AC ✄ VISA ⓜⓞ AE
29 Broad Chare ✉ *NE1 3DQ* – ℰ *(0191) 232 13 31 – www.caffevivo.co.uk*
– enquiries@caffevivo.co.uk – Closed Sunday and Bank Holidays   CZ**d**
Rest – Italian – Menu £ 16 (lunch) – Carte £ 19/28
◆ Housed within a quayside warehouse, along with a theatre. Simpler café during the day gives way to a bustling dinner. Much of the produce imported from Italy; the cooking is simple and satisfying.

X **Blackfriars**   🔒 AK VISA ⓶ AE ①
Friars St ⊠ NE1 4XN – ℰ (0191) 261 5945 – www.blackfriarsrestaurant.co.uk
– info@blackfriarsrestaurant.co.uk
– Closed Sunday dinner and Bank Holidays   CZ**h**
Rest – Menu £ 15 (lunch) – Carte £ 22/36
♦ Late 13C stone built monks' refectory still serving food in a split level beamed restaurant. Relaxed atmosphere with friendly informal service. Interesting and original menu.

at Gosforth North : 2½ m. by B 1318 - AV – ⊠ Newcastle upon Tyne

🏨🏨🏨 **Newcastle Marriott H. Gosforth Park**   ≤ 🚗 🕭 🔲 🕭 🕭
High Gosforth Park, North :   🛁 ℀ 📶 & rm, AK ℀ 🕭 🕭 P. VISA ⓶ AE ①
2 m. on B 1318 at junction with A 1056 ⊠ NE3 5HN – ℰ (0191) 236 4111
– www.newcastlemarriottgosforthpark.co.uk
– nclgf.salesoffice.northeast@marriotthotels.com – Fax (0191) 236 8192
173 rm ⌂ – ♥£ 89/205 ♥♥£ 89/205 – 5 suites
Rest *Chats* – (dinner only and Sunday lunch) Carte approx. £ 21
Rest *The Plate* – (closed Saturday lunch) Menu £ 17 (lunch) **s** – Carte £ 27/39 **s**
♦ Ideal for both corporate and leisure guests. Extensive conference and leisure facilities. Well-equipped bedrooms with up-to-date décor. Close to the racecourse and the A1. Relaxed Park overlooks the grounds. Informal Chats for light snacks.

X **Open Kitchen**   VISA ⓶ AE ①
3rd Floor, Gosforth Squash Club, Moor Court Annexe, Southwest : 1¼ m.
by B 1318, A 189 and Kenton Rd on Westfield Rd ⊠ NE3 4YD
– ℰ (0191) 285 2909 – www.theopenkitchen.co.uk – eat@theopenkitchen.co.uk
– Closed 24-26 December and 1-2 January,   AV**a**
Rest – (dinner only) (booking essential) Carte £ 23/36
♦ Intimate restaurant on top floor of a squash club. Kitchen is, indeed, on show behind the bar. Polite, knowledgable service underpins original cooking using Fairtrade produce.

at Ponteland Northwest : 8¼ m. by A 167 on A 696 - AV – ⊠ Newcastle upon Tyne

X **Cafe Lowrey**   AK VISA ⓶ AE
33-35 Broadway, Darras Hall Estate, Southwest : 1½ m. by B 6323 and Darras
Hall Estate rd ⊠ NE20 9PW – ℰ (01661) 820 357 – www.cafelowrey.co.uk
– Fax (01661) 820 357 – Closed 25 December, 1 January, Sunday dinner and Bank Holidays
Rest – (dinner only and lunch Saturday and Sunday) (booking essential) Carte £ 25/40
♦ Small restaurant in shopping parade with wooden chairs and cloth-laid tables. Blackboard menus offering modern British cooking using local produce.

> Look out for red symbols, indicating particularly pleasant establishments.

NEWICK – East Sussex – **504** U 31 – pop. 2 129   8 **A2**
🔼 London 57 mi – Brighton 14 mi – Eastbourne 20 mi – Hastings 34 mi
– Maidstone 30 mi

🏨🏨🏨 **Newick Park** 🔊   ≤ 🚗 🕭 🕭 🕭 ℀ & rm, ℀ 🕭 P. VISA ⓶ AE
Southeast : 1½ m. following signs for Newick Park ⊠ BN8 4SB – ℰ (01825)
723 633 – www.newickpark.co.uk – bookings@newickpark.co.uk – Fax (01825) 723 969
15 rm ⌂ – ♥£ 125 ♥♥£ 165 – 1 suite
Rest – (booking essential for non-residents) Menu £ 25/43
♦ Georgian manor in 200 acres; views of Longford river and South Downs. Stately hallway and lounge. Unique rooms, some with original fireplaces, all with Egyptian cotton sheets. Dine in relaxed formality on high-back crimson chairs.

ENGLAND

XX **272**   AC P VISA OO AE
20-22 High St ⊠ BN8 4LQ – ℰ (01825) 721 272 – www.272restaurant.co.uk
– twoseventwo@hotmail.co.uk – Closed 25-26 December, Monday, Sunday dinner
and Tuesday lunch
Rest – Menu £ 17 (lunch) – Carte £ 22/38
♦ Well-run restaurant with an easy-going, relaxed feel. Chairs from Italy, modern art on walls. Frequently changing menus offer a winning blend of British and European flavours.

NEWMARKET – Suffolk – **504** V 27 – **pop. 16 947**   14 **B2**
> ◘ London 64 mi – Cambridge 13 mi – Ipswich 40 mi – Norwich 48 mi
> ◙ Palace House, Palace St ℰ (01638) 667200, tic.newmarket@forest-heath.gov.uk
> ◘ Links Cambridge Rd, ℰ (01638) 663 000

at Lidgate Southeast : 7 m. on B 1063 – ⊠ Newmarket

🏠 **The Star Inn**   ☐ ⅍ P VISA OO AE
The Street ⊠ CB8 9PP – ℰ (01638) 500 275 – Fax (01638) 500 275 – Closed 25-26 December, 1 January
Rest – Carte £ 28/32
♦ Pink washed part 16C inn, oozing charm with beams and inglenooks, in pretty village. Original, predominantly Iberian menus: local game cooked in a hearty, fresh Spanish style.

at Six Mile Bottom Southwest : 6 m. on A 1304 – ⊠ Newmarket

🏨 **Swynford Paddocks**   ≤ ☐ ☐ ☐ ⅍ P VISA OO AE ①
⊠ CB8 0UE – ℰ (01638) 570 234 – www.swynfordpaddocks.com – events@swynfordpaddocks.com – Fax (01638) 570 283
15 rm ☑ – †£ 85/165 ††£ 95/195
Rest *Silks* – Carte £ 25/40
♦ Hotel in pastures with a past: Lord Byron stayed here. Elegant bedrooms named after racehorses - their silks framed in the room. Silks brasserie an extension to main house.

NEW MILTON – Hampshire – **503** P 31 – **pop. 24 324**   6 **A3**
> ◘ London 106 mi – Bournemouth 12 mi – Southampton 21 mi – Winchester 34 mi
> ◙ Barton-on-Sea Milford Rd, ℰ (01425) 615 308

🏨🏨 **Chewton Glen** ⚘   ≤ ☐ ☐ ☐ ☐ ☐ ❀ ⅍ ⅃ᵇ ☐ ⅍ rm, AC ⅍
Christchurch Rd, West : 2 m. by A 337 and Ringwood Rd on Chewton Farm Rd ⊠ BH25 6QS – ℰ (01425) 275 341 – www.chewtonglen.com – reservations@chewtonglen.com – Fax (01425) 272 310
48 rm – †£ 299 ††£ 295/525, ☑ £ 20 – 10 suites
Rest *Marryat Room and Conservatory* – Menu £ 25/65 **s** – Carte £ 45/57 **s** ⅚
♦ A byword in luxury: 19C house where Captain Marryat wrote novels. Sherry and shortbread await in huge rooms of jewel colours; balconies overlook grounds. Scented steam room. Accomplished cooking in cool smooth conservatory and bright dining room.

NEWPORT PAGNELL – Milton Keynes – **504** R 27 – **pop. 14 739**   11 **C1**
> ◘ London 57 mi – Bedford 13 mi – Luton 21 mi – Northampton 15 mi – Oxford 46 mi

Plan : see Milton Keynes

XX **Robinsons**   VISA OO AE ①
18-20 St John St ⊠ MK16 8HJ – ℰ (01908) 611 400 – www.robinsonsrestaurant.co.uk – info@robinsonsrestaurant.co.uk – Fax (01908) 216 900 – Closed Saturday lunch, Sunday and Bank Holidays   CU**n**
Rest – Menu £ 13/21 – Carte £ 29/37
♦ A bright façade defines sunny nature of Mediterranean style cuisine. An upbeat eatery in which to sample an eclectic blend of dishes which range from modern to traditional.

ENGLAND

▶ London 148 mi – Stafford 12 mi – Telford 9 mi

The Fox   🍴 ⛱ **P** **VISA** **©©**

Pave Lane, Chetwynd Aston, South : 1½ m. by Wolverhampton rd (A 41)
✉ TF10 9LQ – ✆ (01952) 815 940 – www.fox-newport.co.uk
– fox@brunningandprice.co.uk – Fax (01952) 815 941
– Closed 25 December - 26 December

Rest – Carte £18/31

♦ Updated pub with lawned garden and terrace. Light, airy interior: walls filled with old pictures and posters. Big tables predominate for family get-togethers. Modern menus.

▶ London 291 mi – Exeter 83 mi – Penzance 34 mi – Plymouth 48 mi
– Truro 14 mi
🛧 Newquay Airport : ✆ (01637) 860600 Y
🛈 Municipal Offices, Marcus Hill ✆ (01637) 854020, info@newquay.co.uk
🏌 Tower Rd, ✆ (01637) 872 091
🏌 Treloy, ✆ (01637) 878 554
🏌 Merlin Mawgan Porth, ✆ (01841) 540 222
◨ Penhale Point and Kelsey Head★ (≤★★), SW : by A 3075 Y – Trerice★ **AC**,
SE : 3½ m. by A 392 - Y - and A 3058. St Agnes - St Agnes Beacon★★
(⁂★★), SW : 12½ m. by A 3075 - Y - and B 3285

Plan on next page

ENGLAND

The Bristol   ≤ ▣ 🍴 🛗 🎤 🛎 🏊 **P** **VISA** **©©** **AE** **①**

Narrowcliff ✉ TR7 2PQ – ✆ (01637) 870 275 – www.hotelbristol.co.uk
– info@hotelbristol.co.uk – Fax (01637) 879 347
– Closed Christmas and 2 weeks in January   Zr
73 rm ☷ – †£70/120 ††£127/147 – 1 suite
Rest – (bar lunch Monday-Saturday) Menu £16/24 **s**
– Carte dinner £25/33

♦ Classic seaside hotel built in 1933, well established and family run. Wide range of bedrooms from singles to family suites. Elements of art deco. Large conference facilities. The dining room overlooks Atlantic.

Trebarwith   ≤ 🍴 ▣ 🍴 🎤 🛎 **P** **VISA** **©©**

Trebarwith Crescent ✉ TR7 1BZ – ✆ (01637) 872 288
– www.trebarwith-hotel.co.uk – enquiry@trebarwith-hotel.co.uk
– Fax (01637) 875 431 – April-October   Za
41 rm ☷ – †£36/74 ††£72/148
Rest – (bar lunch) Menu £19 **s** – Carte £18/30

♦ Superb bay and coastline views from this renowned seaside hotel. Has its own cinema, plus evening discos and dances. You'll get the stunning vistas from traditional bedrooms. Dine by the sea beneath Wedgewood-style ceiling.

at Watergate Bay Northeast : 3 m. by A 3059 on B 3276 – ✉ **Newquay**

Fifteen Cornwall   ≤ **AC** ⇄ **VISA** **©©** **AE**

On The Beach ✉ TR8 4AA – ✆ (01637) 861 000 – www.fifteencornwall.co.uk
– restaurant@fifteencornwall.co.uk
Rest – Italian – (booking essential) Menu £26/55

♦ Phenomenally successful converted café in a golden idyll. Jamie Oliver's academy youngsters offer Cornwall-meets-Italy menus in a cavernous room bathed in West Coast hues. Dinner is 5 course tasting menu.

Good food and accommodation at moderate prices?
Look for the Bib symbols:
red Bib Gourmand 🍴 for food, blue Bib Hotel 🏨 for hotels

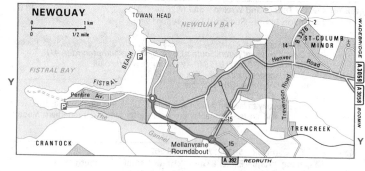

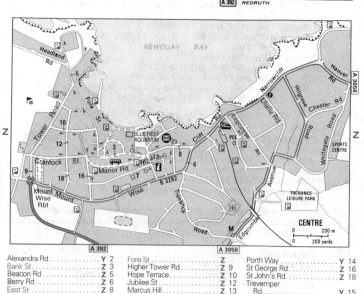

NEW ROMNEY – Kent – **504** W 31   9 **C2**

🚗 London 71 mi – Brighton 60 mi – Folkestone 17 mi – Maidstone 36 mi

🏠 **Romney Bay House** 🍃   🌿 🚗 ♨ 📶 📶 **P** *VISA* **◑◐** **AE**
   Coast Rd, Littlestone, East : 2 ¼ m. off B 2071 ✉ *TN28 8QY* – ☏ *(01797) 364 747*
   – Fax (01797) 367 156 – Closed 1 week Christmas
   10 rm 🛏 – †£95 ††£160
   Rest – (Closed Sunday, Monday and Thursday) (dinner only) (booking
   essential for non-residents) (set menu only) Menu £43
   ♦ Beach panorama for late actress Hedda Hopper's house, built by Portmeirion architect Clough Williams-Ellis. Individual rooms; sitting room with telescope and bookcases. Enjoy drinks on terrace before conservatory dining.

NEWTON LONGVILLE – Bucks. – **504** R 28 – **see Milton Keynes**

NEWTON-ON-OUSE – North Yorkshire – **502** Q 22 – **see York**

NEWTON POPPLEFORD – Devon – **503** K 31 – see Sidmouth

NITON – Isle of Wight – **504** Q 32 – see Wight (Isle of)

NOMANSLAND – Hampshire – **503** P 31   4 **D3**
> ▸ London 96 mi – Bournemouth 26 mi – Salisbury 13 mi – Southampton 14 mi
> – Winchester 25 mi

XX **Les Mirabelles**   ☞ 🏧 *VISA* ◍ AE
Forest Edge Rd ⊠ *SP5 2BN* – ℰ *(01794) 390 205* – *www.lesmirabelles.com*
– Fax (01794) 390 106 – Closed 25 December-mid January, 1 week May-June,
Sunday and Monday
Rest – French – Menu £ 20 (lunch) – Carte £ 27/54 ⅗
♦ Unpretentious little French restaurant overlooking the village common. Superb
wine list. Extensive menu of good value, classic Gallic cuisine.

NORTHALLERTON – North Yorkshire – **502** P 20 – pop. 15 517   22 **B1**
> ▸ London 238 mi – Leeds 48 mi – Middlesbrough 24 mi – Newcastle upon
> Tyne 56 mi – York 33 mi
> 🛈 Applegarth ℰ (0871) 7161924, thirsktic@hambleton.gov.uk

ENGLAND

at Staddlebridge Northeast : 7½ m. by A 684 on A 19 at junction with A 172
– ⊠ **Northallerton**

X **McCoys Bistro at The Tontine** with rm   🏧 rm, ☏ 📱 *VISA* ◍ AE ◐
on southbound carriageway (A 19) ⊠ *DL6 3JB* – ℰ *(01609) 882 671*
– www.mccoystontine.co.uk – bookings@mccoystontine.co.uk – Fax (01609)
882 660 – Closed 25-26 December and 1-3 January
6 rm ☑ – †£ 95 ††£ 120
Rest – (booking essential) Menu £ 17 (lunch) – Carte £ 28/45
♦ Yorkshire meets France in long-standing restaurant with mirrors, wood panelling,
framed memorabilia. Snug bar to plot coups in. Large bedrooms, unique in decorative style.

at Newby Wiske South : 2½ m. by A 167 – ⊠ **Northallerton**

🏨 **Solberge Hall** 🌳   ⇚ 🍴 ℐ ☞ 📱 *VISA* ◍ AE
Northwest : 1¼ m. on Warlaby rd ⊠ *DL7 9ER* – ℰ *(01609) 779 191*
– www.solbergehall.co.uk – reservations@solbergehall.co.uk – Fax (01609)
780 472
23 rm ☑ – †£ 65/95 ††£ 120 – 1 suite
Rest – Menu £ 15/28
Rest *Silks* – Carte £ 18/23
♦ Tranquil grounds surround this graceful Georgian house, situated in the heart of
the countryside. Popular for weddings; bedrooms in main house or stable block. Local
ingredients well employed in flavoursome menus.

NORTHAMPTON – Northamptonshire – **504** R 27 – pop. 189 474   16 **B3**
▌ Great Britain
> ▸ London 69 mi – Cambridge 53 mi – Coventry 34 mi – Leicester 42 mi
> – Luton 35 mi – Oxford 41 mi
> 🛈 The Royal and Derngate Theatre Foyer, Guildhall Rd ℰ (01604) 622677,
> northampton.tic@northamptonshireenterprise.ltd.uk
> 🏌 Delapre Nene Valley Way, Eagle Drive, ℰ (01604) 764 036
> 🏌 Collingtree Park Windingbrook Lane, ℰ (01604) 700 000
> 🄶 All Saints, Brixworth ★, N : 7 m. on A 508 Y

Plan on next page

NORTHAMPTON

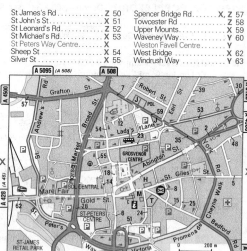

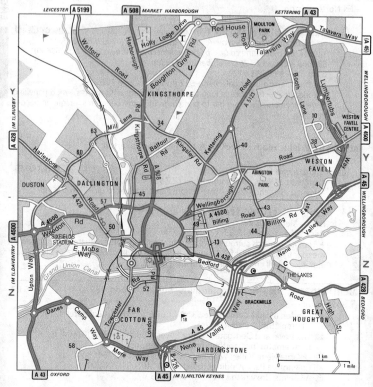

Northampton Marriott
Eagle Drive, Southeast : 2 m. by A 428 off A 45 ✉ NN4 7HW – ☎ (01604) 768 700 – www.northamptonmarriott.co.uk – Fax (01604) 769 011 Za
120 rm – £ 89/145 £ 89/155
Rest – (Closed Saturday lunch) Menu £ 16 (lunch) **s** – Carte dinner £ 23/38 **s**
◆ Modern hotel in riverside setting. Neat trim rooms, very practical, with well-lit work desks, some have disabled facilities and sofa beds. Silverstone race track is nearby. Pleasing dining room with bright brasserie feel.

Holiday Inn Northampton
Bedford Rd, Southeast : 1 ½ m. on A 428 ✉ NN4 7YF – ☎ (01604) 622 777 – Fax (01604) 604 544 Zc
104 rm – £ 110/130 £ 130/150, £13.95
Rest – Menu £ 10/18 **s** – Carte £ 20/29 **s**
◆ Purpose-built, modern hotel. Smart interior with a branded style. Comfortable bedrooms are simply appointed and well-kept. Suited to business and leisure travellers. Relaxing restaurant and adjacent lounge.

Dangs
205 Wellingborough Rd ✉ NN1 4ED – ☎ (01604) 607 060 – www.dangs.co.uk – hao@dangs.co.uk – Closed 25 December and 1 January Zx
Rest – Vietnamese – (dinner only) Menu £ 12 (weekdays) – Carte £ 15/22
◆ Immaculately furnished, contemporary Vietnamese restaurant. Passionately run, food is fresh, tasty, good value and mostly homemade. Noodle bowls are a speciality.

If breakfast is included the symbol appears after the number of rooms.

ENGLAND

NORTH BOVEY – Devon – 503 I 32 – ✉ Newton Abbot 2 C2

London 214 mi – Exeter 13 mi – Plymouth 34 mi – Torquay 21 mi
Dartmoor National Park★★

Bovey Castle
✉ TQ13 8RE – ☎ (01647) 445 000 – www.boveycastle.com – reservations.bovey@hilwoodresorts.com – Fax (01647) 445 020
59 rm – £ 135/375 £ 175/395 – 4 suites
Rest *The Mulberry* – (closed Sunday and Monday) (dinner only) (booking essential for non-residents) Menu £ 59
Rest *The Edwardian Dining Room* – (dinner only) Menu £ 43
Rest *Bistro* – Carte £ 23/39
◆ Stunningly opulent property: castle and sporting estate set in beautiful grounds with incomparable leisure facilities, awesome Cathedral Room and sumptuous, stylish bedrooms. Ambitious and elaborate cooking in The Mulberry. British fare in the Edwardian dining room. Casual, easy-going bistro.

The Gate House without rest
just off village green, past "Ring of Bells" public house ✉ TQ13 8RB – ☎ (01647) 440 479 – www.gatehouseondartmoor.com – srw.gatehouse@btinternet.com – Fax (01647) 440 479 – Closed 24-26 December
3 rm – £ 48/50 £ 76/80
◆ 15C white Devon hallhouse; picturebook pretty with thatched roof, pink climbing rose. Country style rooms; some have views of moor. Large granite fireplace in sitting room.

NORTH CHARLTON – Northd. – 501 O 17 – see Alnwick

NORTH HINKSEY – Oxon. – 504 Q 28 – see Oxford

NORTH KILWORTH – Leicestershire – 502 Q 26 16 B3

London 95 mi – Leicester 20 mi – Market Harborough 9 mi

Kilworth House ⟓   🚗 🐕 🐕 🍴 ⅃⅄ ᛫ & rm, 🍽 🌐 🛁 **P.** *VISA* **⦿** **AE**
Lutterworth Rd, West : ½ m. on A 4304 ⊠ *LE17 6JE –* ℰ *(01858) 880 058*
– www.kilworthhouse.co.uk – info@kilworthhouse.co.uk – Fax (01858) 880 349
41 rm – †£140 ††£140, ⊇ £13 – 3 suites
Rest *The Wordsworth* – (dinner only) Carte £ 28/50
Rest *The Orangery* – Carte £ 25/35
♦ 19C extended house set in 38 acres of parkland, with original staircase, stained glass windows and open air theatre. Individually appointed rooms, some with commanding views. Ornate Wordsworth with courtyard vista. Light meals in beautiful Orangery.

NORTH LOPHAM – Norfolk – 504 W 26   15 C2
🖸 London 98 mi – Norwich 34 mi – Ipswich 31 mi – Bury Saint Edmunds 20 mi

⌂   **Church Farm House**   🚗 🌐 **P.**
Church Rd ⊠ *IP22 2LP –* ℰ *(01379) 687 270 – www.churchfarmhouse.org*
– hosts@bassetts.demon.co.uk – Fax (01379) 687 270 – Closed January
3 rm ⊇ – †£45/55 ††£90   **Rest** – Menu £ 27
♦ Characterful thatched farmhouse with lovely garden, simple facilities, homely feel and personal touches. Individually styled bedrooms look to the church. Home cooked meals use local produce, with breakfast served outside in summer.

NORTH NEWINGTON – Oxon. – see Banbury

NORTHREPPS – Norfolk – 504 Y 25 – see Cromer

NORTH WALSHAM – Norfolk – 503 Y 25 – pop. 11 845 ▐ Great Britain   15 D1
🖸 London 125 mi – Norwich 16 mi
ⓖ Blicking Hall★★ AC, W : 8 ½ m. by B 1145, A 140 and B 1354

🏠   **Beechwood**   🚗 **P.** *VISA* **⦿**
20 Cromer Rd ⊠ *NR28 0HD –* ℰ *(01692) 403 231 – www.beechwood-hotel.co.uk*
– enquiries@beechwood-hotel.co.uk – Fax (01692) 407 284
17 rm ⊇ – †£75 ††£90/160
Rest – (dinner only and Sunday lunch) Menu £ 21/35 s
♦ Privately owned, peacefully set, part 19C hotel where Agatha Christie once stayed. Thoughtfully appointed bedrooms; newer ones are larger. Attentive service. Handsome dining room with flowers.

NORTON – Shrops. – see Telford

NORTON ST PHILIP – Somerset – 503 N 30 – ⊠ Bath   4 C2
🖸 London 113 mi – Bristol 22 mi – Southampton 55 mi – Swindon 40 mi

⌂   **The Plaine** without rest   🌐 **P.**
⊠ *BA2 7LT –* ℰ *(01373) 834 723 – www.theplaine.co.uk*
– enquiries@theplaine.co.uk – Fax (01373) 834 723
3 rm ⊇ – †£55/95 ††£85/125
♦ 16C stone cottages opposite George Inn on site of original market place. Beams, stone walls denote historic origins. Fresh and brighter interior, thanks to keen new owners.

NORWICH – Norfolk – 504 Y 26 – pop. 174 047 ▐ Great Britain   15 D2
🖸 London 109 mi – Kingston-upon-Hull 148 mi – Leicester 117 mi
    – Nottingham 120 mi
✈ Norwich Airport : ℰ (0844) 748 0112, N : 3 ½ m. by A 140 V
🛈 The Forum, Millennium Plain ℰ (01603) 727927, tourism@norwich.gov.uk
⛳ Royal Norwich Hellesdon Drayton High Rd, ℰ (01603) 425 712
⛳ Marriott Sprowston Manor Hotel Wroxham Rd, ℰ (0870) 400 72 29
⛳ Costessy Park Costessey, ℰ (01603) 746 333
⛳ Bawburgh Marlingford Rd, Glen Lodge, ℰ (01603) 740 404
◎ City★★ - Cathedral★★ Y – Castle (Museum and Art Gallery★ AC) Z – Market Place★ Z
ⓖ Sainsbury Centre for Visual Arts★ AC, W : 3 m. by B 1108 X. Blicking Hall★★ AC, N : 11 m. by A 140 - V - and B 1354 – NE : Norfolk Broads★

Plan opposite

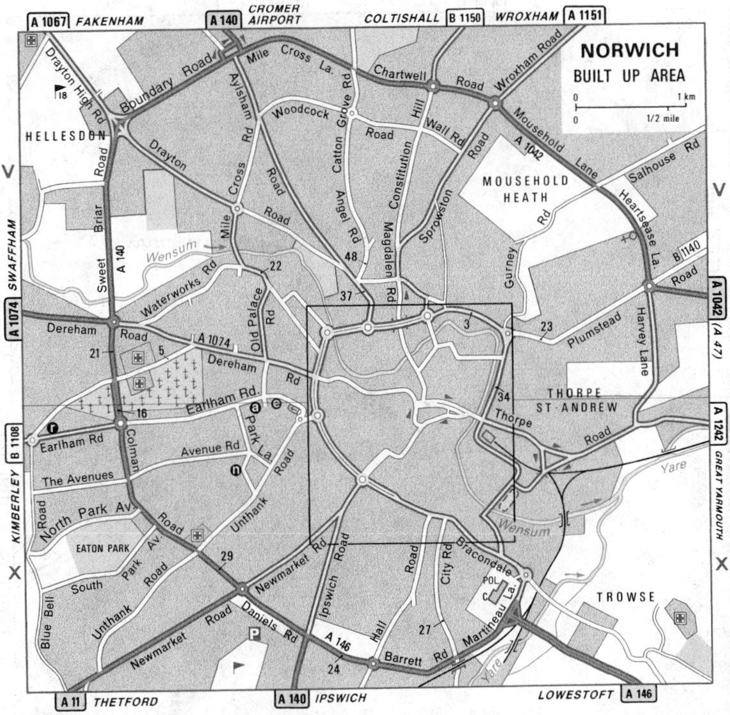

Barrack St	V 3	Heigham St	V 22	Mile End Rd	X 29
Bowthorpe Rd	V 5	Ketts Hill	V 23	Riverside Rd	V 34
Farrow Rd	V 16	Lakenham Rd	X 24	St Augustine's St	V 37
Guardian Rd	V 21	Long John Hill	X 27	Waterloo Rd	V 48

Marriott Sprowston Manor H. & Country Club

Wroxham Rd, rest, VISA AE
Northeast : 3 ¼ m. on A 1151 ✉ *NR7 8RP – ✆ (01603) 410871*
– www.marriottsprowstonmanor.co.uk – Fax (01603) 423911
93 rm – 🛉£ 200 🛉🛉£ 200/280, ☕ £14.95 – 1 suite
Rest *Manor* – (Closed Sunday dinner) (dinner only and Sunday lunch)
Menu £ 25 – Carte £ 33/41
Rest *Zest* – Carte £ 20/28

◆ Spacious 16C manor house in neat gardens and large grounds. Modern bedrooms boast quality furniture, good facilities and smart bathrooms; most have country outlooks. Good leisure club. Traditional Manor restaurant serves classical menu; more informal Zest offers brasserie fare and views over championship golf course.

St Giles House

rm, rest, VISA AE
41-45 St Giles St ✉ *NR2 1JR – ✆ (01603) 275180 – www.stgileshousehotel.com*
– info@stgileshousehotel.com – Fax (0845) 299 1905 YZ**o**
23 rm ☕ – 🛉£ 120 🛉🛉£ 220 – 1 suite
Rest – Menu £ 18 (lunch) – Carte dinner £ 25/36

◆ Boutique hotel with impressive façade in heart of old town. Superb art deco interior with open plan bar/lounge. Individually decorated bedrooms boast modern facilities. Brasserie style menu.

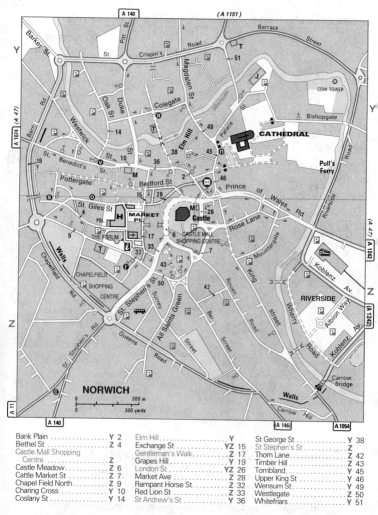

Annesley House

🛏 ✑ 👄 P VISA ⑩⑤ AE ⑥

6 Newmarket Rd ⊠ NR2 2LA – ℘ (01603) 624553
– www.bw-annesleyhouse.co.uk – annesleyhouse@bestwestern.co.uk
– Fax (01603) 621577 – Closed 22 December-3 January   Zc
26 rm – †£90/100 ††£115, ⊇ £12.50   **Rest** – (light lunch) Menu £30
♦ A relaxed atmosphere prevails at this established hotel set within three Georgian houses. Some of the generously proportioned bedrooms overlook the feature water garden. Conservatory restaurant.

Beeches without rest

🛏 ✑ P VISA ⑩⑤ AE

2-6 Earlham Rd ⊠ NR2 3DB – ℘ (01603) 621167 – www.mjbhotels.com
– beeches@mjbhotels.com – Fax (01603) 620151   VXe
42 rm ⊇ – †£74/79 ††£81/95 – 1 suite
♦ Personally run series of Grade II listed properties overlooking terraced Victorian gardens. Spacious rooms may have Cathedral views. Popular with business guests.

🏠 Catton Old Hall without rest 　　　　　 ⬚ ⬚ **P** *VISA* ⬚ **AE**
Lodge Lane, Old Catton, North : 3¼ m. by Catton Grove Rd and St Faiths Rd
✉ *NR6 7HG* – ℰ *(01603) 419 379* – *www.catton-hall.co.uk*
– *enquiries@catton-hall.co.uk* – *Fax (01603) 400 339* – *Closed 2 weeks Christmas -*
New Year
7 rm ⬚ – ⬚£75/80 ⬚⬚£120/130
◆ 17C flint fronted farmhouse in a residential area. Antique furnished lounge with log fire. Individually and attractively furnished rooms have plenty of thoughtful extras.

↑ Arbor Linden Lodge without rest 　　　　 ⬚ ⬚ ⬚ **P** *VISA* ⬚
557 Earlham Rd ✉ *NR4 7HW* – ℰ *(01603) 462 308*
– *www.guesthousenorwich.com* – *info@guesthousenorwich.com* 　　 X**r**
6 rm ⬚ – ⬚£35 ⬚⬚£55
◆ Close to both university and hospitals. Friendly and family run guesthouse. Enjoy a relaxed breakfast in the conservatory. Clean, comfortable bedrooms.

↑ Beaufort Lodge without rest 　　　　　 ⬚ ⬚ ⬚ **P**
62 Earlham Rd ✉ *NR2 3DF* – ℰ *(01603) 627 928* – *www.beaufortlodge.com*
– *beaufortlodge@aol.com* – *Fax (01603) 667 402* 　　 VX**a**
4 rm ⬚ – ⬚£50/60 ⬚⬚£65/70
◆ A large Victorian terraced house within walking distance of the city centre. Comfortable, good-sized bedrooms in modern pine. Spacious breakfast room and bright conservatory.

✗✗ Adlard's 　　　　　 *VISA* ⬚ **AE**
79 Upper St Giles St ✉ *NR2 1AB* – ℰ *(01603) 633 522* – *www.adlards.co.uk*
– *info@adlards.co.uk* – *Closed Sunday dinner and Monday lunch* 　　 YZ**s**
Rest – Menu £16 (lunch) – Carte dinner £27/33
◆ Split-level restaurant in city centre, with smart serving team dressed in waistcoats. Classically based menu makes good use of local produce; unfussy, straightforward cooking.

✗✗ By Appointment with rm 　　　　　 ⬚ **P** *VISA* ⬚
25-29 St Georges St ✉ *NR3 1AB* – ℰ *(01603) 630 730*
– *www.byappointmentnorwich.co.uk* – *puttii@tiscali.co.uk* – *Fax (01603) 630 730*
– *Closed 25 December* 　　 Y**a**
5 rm ⬚ – ⬚£80/95 ⬚⬚£140
Rest – (Closed Sunday-Monday) (dinner only) Carte £34/37
◆ Pretty, antique furnished restaurant. Interesting, traditional dishes off blackboard with theatrical service. Characterful bedrooms include a host of thoughtful extras.

✗ 1 Up at the Mad Moose Arms 　　　　 ⬚ *VISA* ⬚ **AE**
2 Warwick St, off Dover St ✉ *NR2 3LD* – ℰ *(01603) 627 687*
– *www.themadmoosearms.co.uk* – *madmoose@animalinns.co.uk* – *Fax (01603)*
633 945 – *Closed 25 December* 　　 X**n**
Rest – (dinner only) Menu 20 – Carte £23/30
◆ Enjoy the relaxed atmosphere in this converted Victorian pub. Friendly service, occasional live music. Rustic and modern food guarantees great choice in the menus.

✗ Tatler's 　　　　　 *VISA* ⬚ **AE**
21 Tombland ✉ *NR3 1RF* – ℰ *(01603) 766 670* – *www.tatlers.com*
– *info@tatlers.com* – *Fax (01603) 766 625* – *Closed Sunday dinner* 　　 Y**n**
Rest – Menu £18 – Carte £24/28
◆ Georgian townhouse near cathedral comprising small rooms on several floors set off by period detail. Relaxed atmosphere. Modern menu; inventive cooking using local produce.

✗ St Benedicts 　　　　　 ⬚ *VISA* ⬚
9 St Benedicts St ✉ *NR2 4PE* – ℰ *(01603) 765 377*
– *www.rafflesrestaurants.co.uk* – *jayner@talktalk.net* – *Fax (01603) 624 541*
– *Closed 25-31 December, Sunday and Monday* 　　 Y**v**
Rest – Menu £11/17 – Carte £17/29
◆ Informal and personally run bistro. Interesting menus of both traditional British and adventurous heart-warming dishes. Booking advisable for dinner.

✕ Mackintosh's Canteen   🛜 AC VISA ©©

Unit 410, Chapelfield Plain, (1st Floor) ⊠ NR2 1SZ – ℘ (01603) 305 280
– www.mackintoshscanteen.co.uk – info@mackintoshscanteen.co.uk
– Fax (01603) 305 281   Z**r**
Rest – Carte £ 25/30
◆ Stylish and modern; an oasis for shoppers. Bright and airy upstairs with leather banquettes, open kitchen and floor to ceiling windows. Modern cooking; interesting specials.

at Stoke Holy Cross South : 5 ¾ m. by A 140 - X – ⊠ Norwich

⃞ Wildebeest Arms   🚗 🛜 ⚙ P VISA ©© AE

82-86 Norwich Rd ⊠ NR14 8QJ – ℘ (01508) 492 497
– www.thewildebeestarms.co.uk – wildebeest@animalinns.co.uk – Fax (01508) 494 946 – Closed 25-26 December
Rest – (booking essential) Menu £ 17/19 – Carte £ 22/34
◆ Modern-rustic pub in a pretty village. Inventive, seasonal, contemporary menus served at tree-trunk tables. Garden dining recommended. Attentive service from bright staff.

NOSS MAYO – Devon   2 **C3**

◘ London 242 mi – Plymouth 12 mi – Yealmpton 3 mi
◙ Saltram House★★, NW : 7 m. by B 3186 and A 379 – Plymouth★, NW : 9 m. by B 3186 and A 379

⃞ The Ship Inn   🛜 P VISA ©© AE

⊠ PL8 1EW – ℘ (01752) 872 387 – www.nossmayo.com – ship@nossmayo.com – Fax (01752) 873 294
Rest – (Closed 25 December) Carte £ 20/30
◆ On two floors with a terrific terrace; beside the water in delightful coastal village. Oldest part dates from 1700s. Extensive menus from the simple to the adventurous.

NOTTINGHAM – City of Nottingham – **502** Q 25 – pop. 249 584   16 **B2**
▐ Great Britain

◘ London 135 mi – Birmingham 50 mi – Leeds 74 mi – Leicester 27 mi – Manchester 72 mi
🛧 Nottingham East Midlands Airport, Castle Donington : ℘ (0871) 9199000 SW : 15 m. by A 453 AZ
🛈 1-4 Smithy Row ℘ (08444) 775678, touristinfo@nottinghamcity.gov.uk
🖸 Bulwell Forest Hucknall Rd, ℘ (0115) 977 0576
🖸 Wollaton Park, ℘ (0115) 978 7574
🖸 Mapperley Central Ave, Plains Rd, ℘ (0115) 955 6672
🖸 Nottingham City Bulwell Norwich Gardens, ℘ (0115) 927 2767
🖸 Beeston Fields Beeston, ℘ (0115) 925 7062
🖸 Ruddington Grange Ruddington Wilford Rd, ℘ (0115) 984 6141
🖸 Edwalton Wellin Lane, ℘ (0115) 923 4775
🖼 Cotgrave Place G. & C.C. Stragglethorpe Cotgrave, Nr Cotgrave Village, ℘ (0115) 933 3344
◉ Castle Museum★ (alabasters★) AC, CZ **M**
◙ Wollaton Hall★ AC, W : 2½ m. by Ilkeston Rd, A 609 AZ **M**. Southwell Minster★★, NE : 14 m. by A 612 BZ - Newstead Abbey★ AC, N : 11 m. by A 60, A 611 - AY - and B 683 – Mr Straw's House★, Worksop, N : 20 m. signed from B 6045 (past Bassetlaw Hospital) – St Mary Magdalene★, Newark-on-Trent, NE : 20 m. by A 612 BZ

Plan opposite

🏨 Park Plaza   ⛉ 🖥 ♿ rm, AC ⚙ 📶 🔆 VISA ©© AE ①

41 Maid Marian Way ⊠ NG1 6GD – ℘ (0115) 947 7200
– www.parkplazanottingham.com – info@parkplazanottingham.com
– Fax (0115) 947 7300   CY**v**
177 rm – †£ 165 ††£ 165, ⌸ £ 12.95 – 1 suite
Rest Chino Latino – Pan Asian – (Closed Sunday) Carte £ 32/46 **s**
◆ Converted city centre office block with stylish and contemporary decor. Choice of meeting rooms. Spacious stylish bedrooms with many extras. Formal Chino Latino Japanese restaurant.

ENGLAND

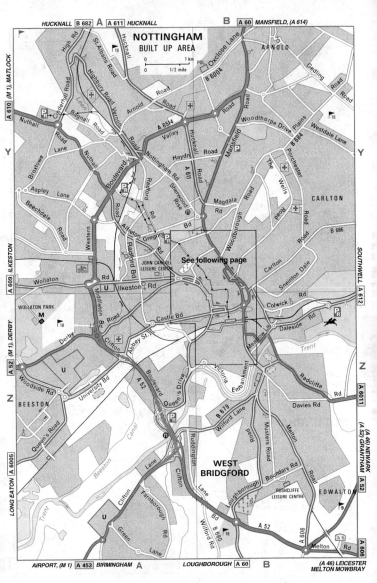

Welbeck
🛗 ⚹ rm, 🏧 ⚒ ¶¶ 🛁 🅿️ VISA ⓂⓈ AE ①

Talbot St ✉ *NG1 5GS –* ✆ *(0115) 841 1000 – www.welbeck-hotel.co.uk*
– bookings@welbeck-hotel.co.uk – Fax (0115) 841 1001
– Closed 24 December-2 January   CY**s**
96 rm – ♦£115 ♦♦£115, ☐£10.75
Rest – (Closed Sunday dinner to non-residents) Carte £23/30
♦ Bright modern hotel in city centre close to theatre. Colourful cushions and pared-down style in bedrooms. Three conference rooms for hire. Fifth floor dining room gives fine views of city.

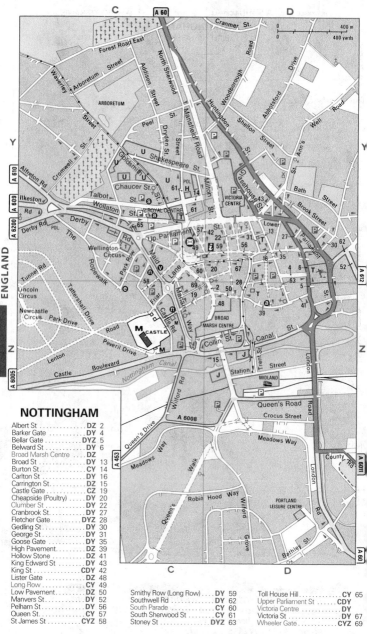

NOTTINGHAM

If breakfast is included the ⌑ symbol appears after the number of rooms.

Hart's ⟨ ⌂ 🛏 & ⌷ P VISA ⬤ AE
Standard Hill, Park Row ⊠ *NG1 6FN –* 𝒞 *(0115) 988 1900*
– www.hartsnottingham.co.uk – ask@hartsnottingham.co.uk
– Fax (0115) 947 7600   CZ**e**
30 rm – ♦£120 ♦♦£120, ☑ £13.50 – 2 suites
Rest *Harts* – see restaurant listing
♦ Stylish modern hotel. Breakfast in contemporary style bar serving light snacks. Modern bedrooms; ground floor rooms open onto patio; good views from higher floors.

Lace Market 🛏 ⌷ 🛎 VISA ⬤ AE
29-31 High Pavement ⊠ *NG1 1HE –* 𝒞 *(0115) 852 3232*
– www.lacemarkethotel.co.uk – stay@lacemarkethotel.co.uk
– Fax (0115) 852 3223   DZ**a**
42 rm ☑ – ♦£129/149 ♦♦£159
Rest *Merchants* – see restaurant listing
♦ Located in old lacemaking quarter, but nothing lacy about interiors; crisp rooms with minimalist designs, unpatterned fabrics. A stylish place to rest one's head.

Greenwood Lodge City *without rest* ⌂ 🛜 ⌷ P VISA ⬤
5 Third Ave, Sherwood Rise ⊠ *NG7 6JH –* 𝒞 *(0115) 962 1206*
– www.greenwoodlodgecityguesthouse.co.uk – pdouglas71@aol.com
– Fax (0115) 962 1206 – Closed 24-28 December   AY**n**
6 rm ☑ – ♦£48/63 ♦♦£95
♦ Regency house with elegant reception offset by paintings, antiques. Conservatory breakfast room from which to view birdlife. Period beds, lovely fabrics in pretty rooms.

XXX Restaurant Sat Bains *with rm* ⌂ AC rest, 🛜 ⌷ P VISA ⬤
☖ *Trentside, Lenton Lane* ⊠ *NG7 2SA –* 𝒞 *(0115) 986 6566*
– www.restaurantsatbains.com – info@restaurantsatbains.net – Fax (0115) 986 0343 – Closed late December-early January and 2 weeks August   AZ**n**
4 rm ☑ – ♦£114 ♦♦£129/265
Rest – (Closed Sunday-Monday) (dinner only) Menu £49 (weekdays)/67
Spec. Scallop with mussels, nuts, seeds and sprouts. Suckling lamb, sea vegetables, leek ash 'Noma'. Passion fruit with yoghurt, toffee and liquorice.
♦ Contemporary restaurant with smart staff. Precise, innovative cooking utilises excellent ingredients; go on a journey of taste, texture and temperature in the Tasting Room. Spacious bedrooms.

XX Merchants – *at Lace Market Hotel* AC VISA ⬤ AE
29-31 High Pavement, The Lace Market ⊠ *NG1 1HE –* 𝒞 *(0115) 852 3232*
– www.merchantsnottingham.co.uk – stay@lacemarkethotel.co.uk – Fax (0115) 852 3223 – Closed Sunday and Monday   DZ**a**
Rest – (dinner only) Menu £25 – Carte £29/42
♦ Located within Lace Market hotel, entered via trendy Saints bar. Stylish, modern eatery typified by deep red banquettes. Modish British cooking with a spark of originality.

XX Hart's 🍴 AC ⌷ ⇄ VISA ⬤ AE
Standard Court, Park Row ⊠ *NG1 6GN –* 𝒞 *(0115) 988 1900*
– www.hartsnottingham.co.uk – ask@hartsnottingham.co.uk – Fax (0115) 947 7600 – Closed 26 December and 1 January   CZ**e**
Rest – Menu £17 (lunch) – Carte £26/39
♦ Designer setting for vibrant cooking. Brightly coloured seats, oil paintings, impressive vases of flowers. Truffles on plates with coffee. Dashing mix of modern meals.

XX World Service 🍴 ⇄ VISA ⬤ AE
Newdigate House, Castlegate ⊠ *NG1 6AF –* 𝒞 *(0115) 847 5587*
– www.worldservicerestaurant.com – info@worldservicerestaurant.com
– Fax (0115) 847 5584 – Closed first week January   CZ**n**
Rest – Menu £17/22 – Carte £32/37
♦ Spacious Georgian mansion close to castle, with chic glass tanks containing Eastern artefacts and huge ceiling squares with vivid silks. Effective, tasty fusion food.

ENGLAND

641

ENGLAND

XX MemSaab   AC ⇔ VISA OO AE
12-14 Maid Marian Way ⊠ *NG1 6HS –* ℰ *(0115) 957 0009*
– www.mem-saab.co.uk – contact@mem-saab.co.uk
– Closed 25 December   CY**n**
Rest – Indian – (dinner only and Sunday lunch) Menu £ 17 – Carte approx. £ 25
♦ Vast city centre restaurant with smart mix of traditional Indian furnishings and
modern, contemporary styling. Authentic Indian cooking centres around the chefs'
regional backgrounds.

X 4550 Miles from Delhi   AC VISA OO AE
41 Mount St ⊠ *NG1 6HE –* ℰ *(0115) 947 5111 – www.milesfromdelhi.com*
– Fax (0115) 947 4555 – Closed Saturday lunch and Sunday lunch   CY**n**
Rest – Indian – Menu £ 20 – Carte £ 16/35
♦ Stylish, up-to-date and very spacious restaurant incorporating a three storey glazed
atrium and modish bar. Freshly prepared, skilfully cooked, authentic Indian cuisine.

🍴 Cock and Hoop   AC VISA OO AE
29-31 High Pavement ⊠ *NG1 1HE –* ℰ *(0115) 852 3232*
– www.cockandhoop.co.uk – cockandhoop@lacemarkethotel.co.uk
– Fax (0115) 852 3223   DZ**a**
Rest – Carte £ 19/45
♦ Characterful 18C pub run by the next door Lace Market Hotel. Printed and blackboard menus offer sandwiches and all the traditional pub favourites, in satisfying
portions.

at Plumtree Southeast : 5 ¾ m. by A 60 - BZ - off A 606 – ⊠ Nottingham

XX Perkins   🏡 P VISA OO AE
Old Railway Station, Station Rd ⊠ *NG12 5NA –* ℰ *(0115) 937 3695*
– www.perkinsrestaurant.co.uk – info@perkinsrestaurant.co.uk – Fax (0115)
937 6405 – Closed Sunday dinner
Rest – Menu £ 16/25 – Carte £ 28/35
♦ Longstanding restaurant named after owners; once a railway station. Dine in conservatory or relax in bar, a former waiting room. Classical cooking makes use of local
ingredients.

at Beeston Southwest : 4 ¼ m. on A 6005 - AZ – ⊠ Nottingham

🏨 Village H. & Leisure Club   🖫 🕸 ⅏ ⅃ᵴ 🖁 ᙙ rm, 🏋 AC rest, 🍴
Brailsford Way, Chilwell Meadows, Chilwell Retail   🖢 P VISA OO AE ①
Park, Southwest : 2 ¾ m. by A 6005 ⊠ *NG9 6DL –* ℰ *(0115) 946 4422*
– www.village-hotels.co.uk – village.nottingham@village-hotels.com – Fax (0115)
946 4428
135 rm ⊇ – ♦£ 79/119 ♦♦£ 89/129
Rest – (dinner only and Sunday lunch) Carte £ 19/37 **s**
♦ Modern hotel with impressive leisure facilities: large pool, toning tables, cardio
vascular area, gym, squash courts. After exercising, unwind in neat, comfortable
rooms. A couple of traditionally based restaurant alternatives.

at Sherwood Business Park Northwest : 10 m. by A 611 - AY - off A 608
– ⊠ Nottingham

🏨 Dakota   🏡 ⅃ᵴ 🖁 ᙙ rm, AC 🗱 🕸 🖢 P VISA OO AE ①
Lakeview Drive ⊠ *NG15 0DA –* ℰ *(0870) 442 27 27*
– www.dakotahotels.co.uk
– enquiries@dakotahotels.co.uk
– Fax (01623) 727 677
92 rm – ♦£ 99 ♦♦£ 99, ⊇ £ 9.95
Rest *Grill* – (bar lunch Saturday) Carte £ 25/30
♦ Hard-to-miss hotel just off the M1 - it's a big black cube! Lobby with plush sofas,
bookshelves and Dakota aircraft montage. Spacious rooms with kingsize beds and
plasma TVs. Modern British grill style menus.

at Stapleford Southwest : 5 1/2 m. by A 52 - AZ - ✉ Nottingham

XX **Crème**   AK VISA OO AE
12 Toton Lane ✉ NG9 7HA – ℰ (0115) 939 7422 – www.cremerestaurant.co.uk
– Fax (0115) 939 7453 – Closed 26 December-5 January, Monday, Saturday
lunch, Sunday dinner
Rest – Menu £ 15 (lunch) – Carte dinner £ 25/37
♦ Smart, well run restaurant offering well-presented, modern British cooking served
by friendly staff. Long lounge area with comfy sofas; airy, formally-laid dining room.

NUNEATON – Warwickshire – 503 P 26 – pop. 70 721   19 **D2**
🚄 London 102 mi – Birmingham 25 mi – Coventry 17 mi

⌂ **Leathermill Grange** ⌘   🚗 ⌘ **P.**
Leathermill Lane, Caldecote, Northwest : 3½ m. by B 4114 on B 4111 ✉ CV10 0RX
– ℰ (01827) 714 637 – www.leathermillgrange.co.uk
– davidcodd@leathermillgrange.co.uk – Fax (01827) 716 422
– Closed Christmas-New Year
3 rm ☑ – ✝£ 60 ✝✝£ 80
Rest – (by arrangement, communal dining) Menu £ 25
♦ Imposing Victorian farmhouse in peaceful rural spot. Spacious, spotless bedrooms
- one four poster. Homebaking and tea on arrival. Guest lounge and conservatory
with garden view. Meals homecooked on Aga use fruit and vegetables grown in
garden. Fine tableware.

ENGLAND

OAKHAM – Rutland – 502 R 25 – pop. 9 620 📗 Great Britain   17 **C2**
🚄 London 103 mi – Leicester 26 mi – Northampton 35 mi – Nottingham 28 mi
🛈 Rutland County Museum, Catmose St ℰ (01572) 758441,
museum@rutland.gov.uk
◉ Oakham Castle★
◧ Rutland Water★, E : by A 606 – Normanton Church★ **AC**, SE : 5 m. by A 603
and minor road East

🏠 **Barnsdale Lodge**   🚗 ⌘ rm, 📞 ⌘ **P.** VISA OO AE ①
The Avenue, Rutland Water, East : 2½ m. on A 606 ✉ LE15 8AH – ℰ (01572)
724 678 – www.barnsdalelodge.co.uk – reservations@barnsdalelodge.co.uk
– Fax (01572) 724 961
44 rm ☑ – ✝£ 85/90 ✝✝£ 125/145
Rest *Restaurant* – Menu £ 15 (lunch) – Carte £ 22/30
♦ Privately owned, converted farmhouse with mature gardens. Ample, modern
rooms, a large bar flagged in York stone and extensive meeting facilities in renovated
stables. Flavours of the season to fore in the Restaurant.

🏠 **The Whipper-In**   ⌘ ⌘ **P.** VISA OO AE
Market Pl ✉ LE15 6DT – ℰ (01572) 756 971 – www.brook-hotels.co.uk
– whipperin@brook-hotels.co.uk – Fax (01572) 757 759
24 rm – ✝£ 95 ✝✝£ 105, ☑ £ 10   **Rest** – Menu £ 20 (dinner) – Carte £ 21/33
♦ 17C inn on market square with coaching yard and traditional feel. Bedrooms in
understated country style, named after local hunts. Firelit lounge with inviting armchairs. Formal dining in restaurant.

XX **Lord Nelson's House H. and Nicks Restaurant** with rm   ⌘ ⌘
Market Pl ✉ LE15 6DT – ℰ (01572) 723 199   VISA OO AE
– www.nicksrestaurant.co.uk – simon@nicksrestaurant.co.uk – Fax (01572)
723 199 – Closed 25-26 December, 1 January, Monday and Sunday dinner
4 rm ☑ – ✝£ 60/75 ✝✝£ 70/105
Rest – Menu £ 21/22 – Carte (dinner) £ 36/44 **s**
♦ Imaginative modern interiors in 17C town house: choose nautical dark wood,
zebra-skin throws or an elegant chaise longue. Classic seasonal dishes with a flavourful flourish.

OAKHAM

at Hambleton East : 3 m. by A 606 – ⊠ Oakham

Hambleton Hall
⊠ LE15 8TH – ℰ (01572) 756 991 – www.hambletonhall.com
– hotel@hambletonhall.com – Fax (01572) 724 721
16 rm – †£ 200/240 ††£ 320/385, ⊆ £16.50 – 1 suite
Rest – Menu £ 26/39 – Carte £ 61/76
Spec. Mosaic of veal sweetbread, foie gras and chicken. Fillet of beef and baby cabbage filled with Jacob's Ladder. Chocolate truffle flavoured with olive and salted caramel.
♦ Looking over Rutland Water, a beautiful Victorian manor house with gardens, still run by its founding family. Charming period interiors and immaculate, antique filled bedrooms. Daily changing, seasonal menus offer accomplished classical dishes. Faultless service.

Finch's Arms with rm
Ketton Rd ⊠ LE15 8TL – ℰ (01572) 756 575 – www.finchsarms.co.uk
– finchsarms@talk21.com – Fax (01572) 771 142 – Closed 25 December
6 rm ⊆ – †£ 65 ††£ 75   **Rest** – Menu £ 14/19 – Carte £ 20/30
♦ Sandstone pub overlooking Rutland Water: rustic interior, flagged floors, rattan chairs. Real ales accompany tasty modern menus, brimming with Asian flavours. Cosy bedrooms.

OAKSEY – Wiltshire – **503** N 29   **4 C1**
▪ London 98 mi – Cirencester 8 mi – Stroud 20 mi

The Wheatsheaf at Oaksey
Wheatsheaf Lane ⊠ SN16 9TB – ℰ (01666) 577 348
– www.thecompletechef.co.uk – info@thecompletechef.co.uk
Rest – (Closed Sunday dinner and Monday) Carte £ 20/25
♦ Popular with the locals, this traditional Cotswold-stone pub displays a constantly evolving blackboard menu of classic, flavourful and wholesome dishes, with proper puddings to follow.

OBORNE – Dorset – **503** M 31 – **see Sherborne**

OCKLEY – Surrey – **504** S 30   **7 D2**
▪ London 31 mi – Brighton 32 mi – Guildford 23 mi – Lewes 36 mi
– Worthing 29 mi
▪ Gatton Manor Hotel G. & C.C. Standon Lane, ℰ (01306) 627 555

Bryce's
Old School House, Stane St, on A 29 ⊠ RH5 5TH – ℰ (01306) 627 430
– www.bryces.co.uk – bryces.fish@virgin.net – Fax (01306) 628 274 – Closed
25-26 December, 1 January, Sunday dinner November, January and February
Rest – Seafood – Menu £ 25/31 – Carte £ 22/28
♦ Contemporary bar and restaurant with copper-topped bar and high-backed leather chairs. Market-fresh seafood, simply cooked and full of flavour. Friendly team provide attentive service.

ODIHAM – Hampshire – **504** R 30 – pop. 2 908 – ⊠ Hook   **7 C1**
▪ London 51 mi – Reading 16 mi – Southampton 37 mi – Winchester 25 mi

St John
83 High St ⊠ RG29 1LB – ℰ (01256) 702 697 – www.stjohn-restaurant.co.uk
– info@stjohn-restaurant.co.uk – Fax (01256) 702 697 – Closed 25 December and Sunday
Rest – Menu £ 19 (lunch) – Carte £ 21/44
♦ Refurbished and stylish restaurant boasts vivid artwork, suspended arcs of wood from the ceiling and comfy leather banquettes. Eclectic menus with classical base.

OLD BURGHCLERE – Hampshire – **504** Q 29 – ⊠ **Newbury**   6 **B1**
> ■ London 77 mi – Bristol 76 mi – Newbury 10 mi – Reading 27 mi
> – Southampton 28 mi

XX **Dew Pond**   ≤ P̱ VISA ⬤⬤
⊠ *RG20 9LH* – ℰ *(01635) 278 408* – *www.dewpond.co.uk* – *Fax (01635) 278 580*
– Closed 2 weeks December-January, Sunday and Monday
Rest – (dinner only) Menu £32
♦ This traditionally decorated cottage, set in fields and parkland, overlooks Watership
Down and houses a collection of local art. Tasty Anglo-gallic menu.

OLDHAM – Greater Manchester – **502** N 23 – pop. 103 544   20 **B2**
> ■ London 212 mi – Leeds 36 mi – Manchester 7 mi – Sheffield 38 mi
> 🖪 12 Albion St ℰ (0161) 627 1024
> 🖪 Crompton and Royton Royton High Barn, ℰ (0161) 624 2154
> 🖪 Werneth Garden Suburb Green Lane, ℰ (0161) 624 1190
> 🖪 Lees New Rd, ℰ (0161) 624 4986

                          Plan : see Manchester

XX **The White Hart Inn** with rm   ⅋ ⬤ ⛵ P̱ VISA ⬤⬤ AE
51 Stockport Rd, Lydgate, East : 3 m. by A 669 on A 6050 ⊠ *OL4 4JJ*
– ℰ (01457) 872 566 – www.thewhitehart.co.uk – bookings@thewhitehart.co.uk
– Fax (01457) 875 190 – Closed 26 December, Sunday dinner and Tuesday
12 rm � – †£85/90 ††£120/130
Rest*The White Hart Pub* – see restaurant listing
Rest – (dinner only and Sunday lunch) Menu £20
♦ in a large rear extension, a smart, contemporary room. Fixed price, good value
menu feature modern British cooking, carefully prepared. Comfortable bedrooms,
named after local dignitaries, housed in the original building.

XX **Dinnerstone**   VISA ⬤⬤ ⓘ
99-101 High St, Uppermill, Saddleworth, East : 4 m. on A 669 ⊠ *OL3 6BD*
– ℰ (01457) 875 544 – www.dinnerstone.co.uk – bookings@dinnerstone.co.uk
– Fax (01457) 875 190 – Closed 26-27 December and Monday
Rest – Menu £14 (lunch) – Carte £21/30
♦ Airy modern restaurant in centre of busy village with semi-open kitchen, vibrant art
and relaxed feel. Large menu has Mediterranean base yet retains its Northern accent.

🍴 **The White Hart Inn**   ⅋ P̱ VISA ⬤⬤ AE
😊 *51 Stockport Rd, Lydgate, East : 3 m. by A 669 on A 6050* ⊠ *OL4 4JJ*
– ℰ (01457) 872 566 – www.thewhitehartinn.com
– bookings@thewhitehart.co.uk – Fax (01457) 875 190 – Closed 26 December
Rest – Carte £20/33
♦ Busy pub with old timber, open fires and exposed brick and framed photos of
owner's travels. Satisfying brasserie-style classics, featuring local produce.

OLDSTEAD – North Yorkshire – **502** Q 21 – see Helmsley

OLD WARDEN – Beds. – **504** S 27 – see Biggleswade

OLTON – W. Mids. – **502** O 26 – see Solihull

OMBERSLEY – Worcestershire – **503** N 27 – pop. 2 089   18 **B3**
> ■ London 148 mi – Birmingham 42 mi – Leominster 33 mi
> 🖪 Bishopswood Rd, ℰ (01905) 620 747

XX **The Venture In**   AC P̱ VISA ⬤⬤
Main St ⊠ *WR9 0EW* – ℰ *(01905) 620 552* – *Fax (01905) 620 552*
*– Closed 1 week Christmas, 2 weeks February, 2 weeks August, Sunday dinner and
Monday*
Rest – Menu £26/40
♦ Charming, restored Tudor inn, traditional from its broad inglenook to its fringed
Victorian lights. Modern, flavourful menu, well judged and locally sourced. Friendly
staff.

ENGLAND

ORFORD – Suffolk – 504 Y 27 – ⊠ Woodbridge

15 **D3**

🚇 London 103 mi – Ipswich 22 mi – Norwich 52 mi

The Crown and Castle

🚘 **P** VISA ⓪

⊠ IP12 2LJ – ℰ (01394) 450 205 – www.crownandcastle.co.uk
– info@crownandcastle.co.uk
19 rm (dinner included) ⌂ – †£122/152 ††£185 – 1 suite
Rest The Trinity – see restaurant listing

♦ 19C redbrick hotel standing proudly next to 12C Orford Castle. Retro-styled bar. Stylish modern rooms, some facing the Ness; best rooms are in the garden wing.

The Trinity – at The Crown and Castle Hotel

🚘 ⅍ **P** VISA ⓪

⊠ IP12 2LJ – ℰ (01394) 450 205 – www.crownandcastle.co.uk
– info@crownandcastle.co.uk
Rest – (booking essential) Carte £28/35 🕮

♦ Relaxed, stylish restaurant featuring slate fireplaces, abstract artwork and red banquettes. Classic combinations make vibrant use of local produce. Friendly service.

King's Head Inn with rm

P VISA ⓪

Front Street ⊠ IP12 2LW – ℰ (01394) 450 271
– www.kingshead-orford-suffolk.co.uk – info@crownandcastle.co.uk
4 rm ⌂ – †£54/85 ††£60/95
Rest – (Closed Sunday dinner November-January) Carte £18/24

♦ 16C pub with traditional décor of heraldic prints and banners. Wooden tables, open fired stove, large dining room. Honest, down to earth food and classic puddings. Spacious, well-furnished and comfortable bedrooms.

ORLETON – Shrops. – 503 L 23 – see Ludlow

OSMOTHERLEY – North Yorkshire – 502 Q 20 – ⊠ Northallerton

22 **B1**

🚇 London 245 mi – Darlington 25 mi – Leeds 49 mi – Middlesbrough 20 mi
– Newcastle upon Tyne 54 mi – York 36 mi

The Golden Lion with rm

⅍ VISA ⓪

6 West End ⊠ DL6 3AA – ℰ (01609) 883 526
– www.goldenlionosmotherley.co.uk – Closed 25 December, Monday lunch and Tuesday lunch after Bank Holidays
3 rm ⌂ – †£60 ††£90   **Rest** – Carte £17/24

♦ Unpretentious, beamed, firelit alehouse; plant-filled upper dining room; large menu of satisfying, full-flavoured cooking, Yorkshire beers and sprightly, engaging service.

OSWESTRY – Shropshire – 502 K 25 – pop. 16 660

18 **A1**

🚇 London 182 mi – Chester 28 mi – Shrewsbury 18 mi
🛈 Mile End Services ℰ (01691) 662488, tic@oswestry-bc.gov.uk
🏌 Aston Park, ℰ (01691) 610 535
🏌 Llanymynech Pant, ℰ (01691) 830 983

The Walls

🚗 ⇵ **P** VISA ⓪ AE

Welsh Walls ⊠ SY11 1AW – ℰ (01691) 670 970 – www.the-walls.co.uk
– info@the-walls.co.uk – Fax (01691) 653 820 – Closed first week January
Rest – Carte £19/30

♦ Built in 1841 as a school; now a buzzy restaurant. High ceiling with wooden rafters; original wood flooring. Friendly atmosphere. Varied menu offers some adventurous options.

at Trefonen Southwest : 2½ m. on Trefonen rd – ⊠ Oswestry

The Pentre ⌂

← 🚘 🕩 ⅍ **P**

Southwest : 1¾ m. by Treflach rd off New Well Lane ⊠ SY10 9EE – ℰ (01691)
653 952 – www.thepentre.com – helen@thepentre.com – Closed 1 week Christmas
3 rm ⌂ – †£40 ††£80   **Rest** – (communal dining) Menu £21

♦ Restored 16C farmhouse with superb views over Tanat Valley. Heavily timbered inglenook and wood-burning stove in lounge. Sloping floors enhance rooms of tremendous character. Home-cooked dinners served with fellow guests.

ENGLAND

at Rhydycroesau West : 3 ¼ m. on B 4580 – ⊠ Oswestry

🏠 **Pen-Y-Dyffryn Country H.** ☜ ≤ � 🎇 🛜 ℗ 𝗩𝗜𝗦𝗔 ⓪⓪
⊠ SY10 7JD – ℰ (01691) 653 700 – www.peny.co.uk – stay@peny.co.uk – Closed
1-20 January
12 rm ☲ – †£86 ††£150
Rest – (dinner only) (booking essential for non-residents) Menu £ 36
♦ Peaceful 19C listed rectory in five-acre informal gardens near Offa's Dyke. Cosy
lounge, friendly ambience; good-sized, individually styled rooms, four in the coach
house. Home-cooked dishes utilising organic ingredients.

OULTON BROAD – Suffolk – **504** Z 26 – see Lowestoft

OUNDLE – Northamptonshire – **504** S 26 – pop. 5 219   17 **C3**
– ⊠ Peterborough
  🗗 London 89 mi – Leicester 37 mi – Northampton 30 mi
  🎗 14 West St ℰ (01832) 274333, oundletic@east-northamptonshire.gov.uk
  🗺 Benefield Rd, ℰ (01832) 273 267

at Fotheringhay North : 3 ¾ m. by A 427 off A 605 – ⊠ Peterborough (Cambs.)

🏠 **Castle Farm** without rest   � 🎇 🍃 ℗
⊠ PE8 5HZ – ℰ (01832) 226 200 – Fax (01832) 226 200
5 rm ☲ – †£43/70 ††£70/72
♦ Wisteria-clad, gabled 19C house in the Nene Valley; lawned gardens beside the
river. Ample, pine furnished rooms, two in the adjacent wing; intimate lounge with
open fire.

📙 **The Falcon Inn**   🚖 🍴 ℗ 𝗩𝗜𝗦𝗔 ⓪⓪ 𝗔𝗘 ⓪
⊠ PE8 5HZ – ℰ (01832) 226 254 – www.thefalcon-inn.co.uk
– info@thefalcon-inn.co.uk – Fax (01832) 226 046
Rest – Carte £ 22/35 ⅜
♦ Popular village inn: pretty bouquets, framed prints and airy, spacious conservatory.
Mediterranean flavours to the fore in robust dishes from the modern British menu.

OVERSTRAND – Norfolk – **504** Y 25 – see Cromer

OVINGTON – Hants. – see Winchester

OXFORD – Oxfordshire – **503** Q 28 – pop. 143 016 ▌Great Britain   10 **B2**
  🗗 London 59 mi – Birmingham 63 mi – Brighton 105 mi – Bristol 73 mi
    – Cardiff 107 mi – Coventry 54 mi – Southampton 64 mi
  Access Swinford Bridge (toll)
  🚢 to Abingdon Bridge (Salter Bros. Ltd) (summer only) daily (2 h)
  🎗 15-16 Broad St ℰ (01865) 252200, tic@oxford.gov.uk
  ◉ City★★★ - Christ Church★★ (Hall★★ AC, Tom Quad★, Tom Tower★,
    Cathedral★ AC - Choir Roof★) BZ – Merton College★★ AC BZ – Magdalen
    College★★BZ – Ashmolean Museum★★BY M1 – Bodleian Library★★
    (Ceiling★★, Lierne Vaulting★) AC BZ A1 – St John's College★BY - The
    Queen's College★BZ – Lincoln College★BZ – Trinity College (Chapel★) BY
    – New College (Chapel★) AC, BZ – Radcliffe Camera★BZ P1 – Sheldonian
    Theatre★ AC, BZ T – University Museum of National History★BY M4 – Pitt
    Rivers Museum★BY M3
  ◎ Iffley Church★AZ A. Woodstock : Blenheim Palace★★★ (Park★★★) AC, NW
    : 8 m. by A 4144 and A 34 AY

Plan on next page

ENGLAND

🏨 **Randolph**   ⓪ 🐾 ♨ 🛗 & rm, 𝗔𝗖 🛜 🧖 𝗩𝗜𝗦𝗔 ⓪⓪ 𝗔𝗘 ⓪
Beaumont St ⊠ OX1 2LN – ℰ (0870) 400 82 00 – www.macdonaldhotels.co.uk
– sales.randolph@macdonald-hotels.co.uk – Fax (01865) 791 678   BYn
142 rm ☲ – †£144/290 ††£159/305 – 9 suites
Rest The Restaurant at the Randolph – Carte £ 35/50
♦ Grand Victorian edifice. Lounge bar: deep burgundy, polished wood and chandeliers. Handsome rooms in a blend of rich fabrics; some, more spacious, have half-
tester beds. Spacious, linen-clad Restaurant.

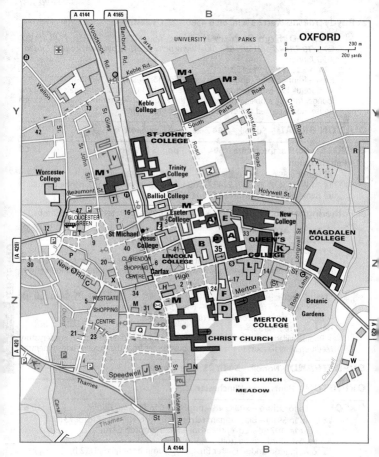

OXFORD

COLLEGES

You've got
the right address !

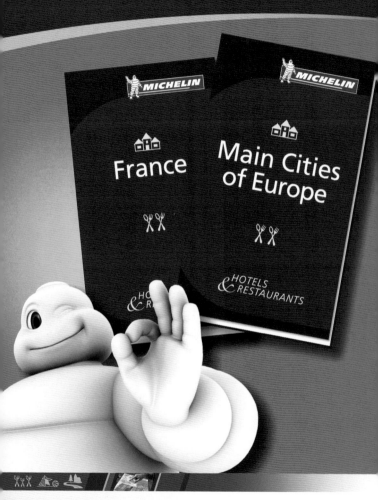

From palaces to bed and breakfast, from fine restaurants to small bistrots
the MICHELIN guide collection includes 45,000 hotels and restaurant
selected by our inspectors in Europe and beyond. Wherever you may be
whatever your budget, you are sure you have the right address!

www.michelin.co.uk

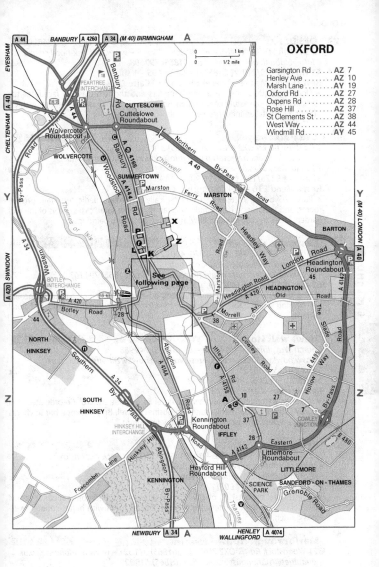

OXFORD

Malmaison   ☐ ℩⑤ 🛐 🛋 rm, Ⓜ ᵞ VISA ⑩ AE
3 Oxford Castle ⊠ OX1 1AY – ℰ (01865) 268 400 – www.malmaison.com
– oxford@malmaison.com – Fax (01865) 268 402   BZ**a**
91 rm – †£160/230 ††£160/230, ☐ £13.95 – 3 suites
Rest *Brasserie* – (Sunday brunch) Carte £23/36
◆ Unique accommodation by castle: this was a prison from 13C to 1996! Former
visitors' room now moody lounge. Stunning rooms in converted cells or former house
of correction! Brasserie in old admin area: modern British menu with fine French
edge.

ENGLAND

🏠🏠🏠 **Old Bank**
🗣 🗐 ⅙ rm, 📠 ⅍ 📶 **P** 🇻🇮🇸🇦 ⓜⓞ 🅰🅴

92-94 High St ✉ *OX1 4BN –* ℰ *(01865) 799 599 – www.oldbank-hotel.co.uk*
– info@oldbank-hotel.co.uk – Fax (01865) 799 598   BZ**s**
41 rm – †£170/210 ††£185/210, ⊊ £12.95 – 1 suite
Rest *Quod* – Menu £13 (weekday lunch) – Carte £23/34
♦ Elegantly understated, clean-lined interiors and the neo-Classical façade of the city's first bank - an astute combination. Rooms in modern wood and leather with CD players. Lively Italian-influenced brasserie.

🏠🏠 **Old Parsonage**
🚗 🗣 📠 📶 🇻🇮🇸🇦 ⓜⓞ 🅰🅴 ⓘ

1 Banbury Rd ✉ *OX2 6NN –* ℰ *(01865) 310 210*
– www.oldparsonage-hotel.co.uk – info@oldparsonage-hotel.co.uk
– Fax (01865) 311 262   BY**e**
30 rm – †£175/190 ††£175/190, ⊊ £14
Rest – Menu £16 (weekday lunch) – Carte £25/44
♦ Part 17C house, creeper-clad and typically Oxfordian; dedicated staff; pristine rooms: antiques, modern and traditional fabrics and, in some cases, views of the roof garden. Meals in cosy lounge bar with antique prints and paintings.

🏠🏠 **Eastgate** without rest
🗐 📠 ⅍ 📞 **P** 🇻🇮🇸🇦 ⓜⓞ 🅰🅴 ⓘ

73 High St ✉ *OX1 4BE –* ℰ *(0870) 400 82 01*
– www.macdonaldhotels.co.uk/eastgate
– events.eastgate@macdonald-hotels.co.uk – Fax (01865) 794 163   BZ**c**
63 rm – †£119 ††£149/159, ⊊ £13.95
♦ Near the botanical gardens and the Boathouse's punt moorings, a former coaching inn offering comfortable, traditionally styled rooms decorated in plaid and floral patterns.

🏠🏠 **Hawkwell House**
🚗 🗣 🗐 ⅙ rm, 📠 rest, ⅍ 📶 🆂🅰 **P** 🇻🇮🇸🇦 ⓜⓞ 🅰🅴 ⓘ

Church Way, Iffley ✉ *OX4 4DZ –* ℰ *(01865) 749 988*
– www.hawkwellhouse.co.uk – reservations@hawkwellhousehotel.co.uk
– Fax (01865) 748 525   AZ**c**
66 rm ⊊ **–** †£65/130 ††£85/150
Rest *Arezzo* – Carte £20/28
♦ Victorian in origin, a group-owned hotel in a quiet suburb. Co-ordinated and smartly fitted modern rooms, suited to business travel. Bright lounge bar in checks and tartans. Airy, atmospheric conservatory restaurant.

🏠 **Remont** without rest
🚗 🗐 ⅙ 📶 **P** 🇻🇮🇸🇦 ⓜⓞ

367 Banbury Rd ✉ *OX2 7PL –* ℰ *(01865) 311 020 – www.remont-oxford.co.uk*
– info@remont-oxford.co.uk – Fax (01865) 552 080
– Closed 3 weeks Christmas and New Year   AY**c**
25 rm – †£75/120 ††£97/120
♦ Stylish hotel on outskirts of city. Crisp, contemporary bedrooms; superior rooms have sofas; rear room quietest. Light, airy breakfast room with buffet counter overlooks garden.

🏠 **Marlborough House** without rest
⅍ 📶 🇻🇮🇸🇦 ⓜⓞ 🅰🅴

321 Woodstock Rd ✉ *OX2 7NY –* ℰ *(01865) 311 321 – www.marlbhouse.co.uk*
– enquiries@marlbhouse.co.uk – Fax (01865) 515 329   AY**v**
17 rm ⊊ **–** †£69/80 ††£90/98
♦ Three-storey modern house. Simple yet spacious rooms - some in bold chintz, all with a small kitchenette - in the northern suburb of Summertown.

🏠 **Burlington House** without rest
⅍ 📶 **P** 🇻🇮🇸🇦 ⓜⓞ 🅰🅴

374 Banbury Rd ✉ *OX2 7PP –* ℰ *(01865) 513 513 – www.burlington-house.co.uk*
– stay@burlington-house.co.uk – Fax (01865) 311 785
– Closed 22 December-2 January   AY**a**
12 rm ⊊ **–** †£60/75 ††£85/105
♦ Contemporary rooms, stylish and intelligently conceived, in a handsome 1889 house. Tasty breakfasts - omelettes, home-made bread and granola - presented on Delft-blue china.

⌂ **Cotswold House** without rest   ✆ ᵗᵖ **P** 𝚅𝙸𝚂𝙰 ⓪ ①
363 Banbury Rd ⊠ OX2 7PL – ℰ (01865) 310558 – www.cotswoldhouse.co.uk
– d.r.walker@talk21.com – Fax (01865) 310558   AYc
8 rm ⊆ – ♯£62/72 ♯♯£90/100
♦ Modern, Cotswold stone house, hung with baskets of flowers in summer. Affordable, spotless en suite rooms in pretty, traditional style; friendly ambience. Non smoking.

✗ **Brasserie Blanc**   𝐀𝐂 ⇔ 𝚅𝙸𝚂𝙰 ⓪ 𝐀𝐄
71-72 Walton St ⊠ OX2 6AG – ℰ (01865) 510999 – www.brasserieblanc.co.uk
– oxford@brasserieblanc.co.uk – Fax (01865) 510700
– Closed 25 December   AYz
Rest – Menu £13/18 – Carte £18/35
♦ Busy, informal brasserie; striking interior and sharp service; French regional recipes with the new-wave touch: John Dory with coriander or ribeye steak in béarnaise.

✗ **Branca**   斎 𝐀𝐂 ⇔ 𝚅𝙸𝚂𝙰 ⓪ 𝐀𝐄 ①
111 Walton St ⊠ OX2 6AJ – ℰ (01865) 556111 – www.branca-restaurants.com
– info@branca-restaurants.com – Fax (01865) 556501
– Closed 24-26 December   BYa
Rest – Italian – Carte £22/29
♦ Modern restaurant with casual, friendly feel and minimalist décor. Vibrant, simple, fresh Italian influenced dishes: antipasti taster plates, pasta and pizza are specialities.

at Stanton St John Northeast : 5½ m. by A 420 and Barton crematorium rd
on B 4027 – ⊠ Oxford

🏠 **The Talkhouse** with rm   斎 ✆ **P** 𝚅𝙸𝚂𝙰 ⓪ 𝐀𝐄 ①
🏠 *Wheatley Rd ⊠ OX33 1EX – ℰ (01865) 351648 – www.talkhouse@foyers.co.uk*
– talkhouse@fullers.co.uk – Fax (01865) 351085
4 rm – ♯£55/65 ♯♯£65/75, ⊆ £10   **Rest** – Menu £10 – Carte £15/30
♦ Attractive, partly thatched country pub. Characterful, modernised interior with open fires and heavy beams. Generous portions of classic pub dishes. Refurbished bedrooms enclose suntrap terrace.

at Sandford-on-Thames Southeast : 5 m. by A 4158 – ⊠ Oxford

🏨 **Oxford Thames Four Pillars**   🍽 ⌂ ▣ 📺 ♨ ⅃ ✗ & rm, 𝐀𝐂 rest,
Henley Rd ⊠ OX4 4GX – ℰ (01865) 334444   ✆ ᵗᵖ ♨ **P** 𝚅𝙸𝚂𝙰 ⓪ 𝐀𝐄 ①
– www.four-pillars.co.uk – thames@four-pillars.co.uk
– Fax (01865) 777372   AZv
62 rm ⊆ – ♯£125/175 ♯♯£145/209
Rest *The River Room* – Menu £15 (lunch) – Carte approx. £25
♦ Modern sandstone hotel around a 13C barn, though the pool is more reminiscent of a Roman bath; spacious lounge with medieval style chandelier, spotless, comfortable rooms. Restaurant overlooks lawned grounds and river.

at Toot Baldon Southeast : 5½ m. by B 480 - AZ – ⊠ Oxford

🏠 **The Mole Inn**   斎 ✆ **P** 𝚅𝙸𝚂𝙰 ⓪ 𝐀𝐄
🏠 *⊠ OX44 9NG – ℰ (01865) 340001 – www.themoleinn.com*
– info@themoleinn.com – Fax (01865) 343011 – Closed 25 December
Rest – Carte £20/30
♦ Much refurbished pub in tiny hamlet. Beams galore, stone tiles, cosy lounge with leather sofas, pine/oak tables. Tasty, assured menus: rustic and earthy or appealingly modish.

at Kingston Bagpuize West : 7 m. by A 415 – ⊠ Abingdon

🏨 **Fallowfields Country House** ⌕   🍽 斎 ᵗᵖ **P** 𝚅𝙸𝚂𝙰 ⓪ 𝐀𝐄
Faringdon Rd ⊠ OX13 5BH – ℰ (01865) 820416 – www.fallowfields.com
– stay@fallowfields.com – Fax (01865) 821275 – Closed 27-29 December
10 rm ⊆ – ♯£100/120 ♯♯£120/170
Rest – Menu £17/30 – Carte (dinner) £26/51
♦ Elephants are everywhere - in paintings, wood and china - in this privately run 19C manor. Cosy lounge, fireside chintz armchairs. Canopy beds in thoughtfully appointed rooms. Classically elegant restaurant views sweeping lawns.

at North Hinksey Southwest : 3 ½ m. by A 420 – ✉ Oxford

🍴 **The Fishes**   P VISA ◍ ⓪
✉ OX2 0NA – ☏ (01865) 249 796 – www.fishesoxford.co.uk
– fishes@peachpubs.com – Closed 25 December   AZ**n**
Rest – Carte £ 18/32
◆ Red brick pub with lively atmosphere, conservatory-style extension and pretty gardens for riverside picnics. Robust dishes make use of local ingredients. Well-chosen wine list.

at Wytham Northwest : 3 ¼ m. by A 420 - AY - off A 34 (northbound carriageway) – ✉ Oxford

🍴 **The White Hart** P VISA ◍
✉ OX2 8QA – ☏ (01865) 244 372 – www.thewhitehartoxford.co.uk
– enquiries@thewhitehartoxford.co.uk – Fax (01865) 248 595
Rest – (Closed dinner 25 December) Carte £ 24/37
◆ Mellow 18C inn located in a pretty hamlet. Delightful courtyard terrace; inside are roaring fires, flagged floors, scrubbed pine tables. Menus mix classics with contemporary.

at Wolvercote Northwest : 2½ m. by A 4144 (Woodstock Rd) on Godstow Rd

🍴 **Trout Inn** ⇔ P VISA ◍ AE
195 Godstow Rd, Wolvercote ✉ OX2 8PN – ☏ (01865) 302 071
– www.thetroutoxford.co.uk   AY**s**
Rest – Carte £ 20/40
◆ Modernised inn of Cotswold stone made famous by Inspector Morse, with idyllic riverside location and splendid terrace. Menu offers pastas, salads, steaks, pizzas and the like.

at Great Milton Southeast : 12 m. by A 40 off A 329 - AY - ✉ Oxford

🏨🏨🏨 **Le Manoir aux Quat' Saisons** (Raymond Blanc) ⬊   ≼ ⌿ ⬙
☸ ☸ Church Rd ✉ OX44 7PD – ☏ (01844) 278 881   AK ⅍ ⌁ P VISA ◍ AE ⓪
– www.manoir.com – lemanoir@blanc.co.uk – Fax (01844) 278 847
– Closed 1-16 January
25 rm – ♦£ 395/690 ♦♦£ 395/690, ⬚ £ 16 – 7 suites
Rest – French – Menu £ 49 (lunch) – Carte £ 87/91
Spec. Landais foie gras, Seville orange and pain d' épice. Assiette of lamb with pearl barley and Earl Grey tea sauce. Calvados soufflé, crystalline and Granny Smith sorbet.
◆ Refined elegance at every turn, resulting in picture perfect harmony. Sumptuous lounges and rooms, classic and modern, surrounded by Japanese, ornamental and kitchen gardens. Virtuoso classic French menu of precision and flair, inspired by the seasons.

OXHILL – Warwickshire – 503 P 27   19 **C3**
🚹 London 90 mi – Banbury 11 mi – Birmingham 37 mi

🏠 **Oxbourne House** ⬊   ≼ ⌿ ⅍ ⅍ P
✉ CV35 0RA – ☏ (01295) 688 202 – www.oxbournehouse.co.uk
– graememcdonald@msn.com
3 rm ⬚ – ♦£ 50/55 ♦♦£ 65/80
Rest – (by arrangement, communal dining) Menu £ 25
◆ Late 20C house oozing charm, individuality and fine rural views; splendid gardens. Antiques abound, complemented by the finest soft furnishings. Stylishly appointed bedrooms. Spacious dining room: plenty of ingredients grown in house grounds.

Don't confuse ✗ with ☸!
✗ defines comfort, while stars are awarded for the best cuisine, across all categories of comfort.

PADIHAM – Lancashire – **502** N 22   20 **B2**

▶ London 230 mi – Burnley 6 mi – Clitheroe 8 mi

at Fence Northeast : 3 m. by A 6068 – ⊠ Burnley

 Fence Gate Inn   🏠 **P.** *VISA* **©©**
Wheatley Lane Rd ⊠ BB12 9EE – ℰ (01282) 618 101 – www.fencegate.co.uk
– info@fencegate.co.uk – Fax (01282) 615 432
Rest – Carte £ 25/35
Rest *The Topiary* – Carte £ 25/33
♦ High on the moors, a cavernous 17C inn renowned for locally sourced ingredients such as tasty home-made sausages. Bar or brasserie dining: service with a sense of humour.

PADSTOW – Cornwall – **503** F 32 – pop. 2 449   1 **B2**

▶ London 288 mi – Exeter 78 mi – Plymouth 45 mi – Truro 23 mi
🛈 Red Brick Building, North Quay ℰ (01841) 533449, padstowtic@visit.org.uk
🏌 Trevose Constantine Bay, ℰ (01841) 520 208
◉ Town★ - Prideaux Place★
◉ Trevone (Cornwall Coast Path★★) W : 3 m. by B 3276 – Trevose Head★ (≼★★) W : 6 m. by B 3276. Bedruthan Steps★, SW : 7 m. by B 3276 – Pencarrow★, SE : 11 m. by A 389

ENGLAND

🏨 **The Metropole**
Station Rd ⊠ PL28 8DB – ℰ (01841) 532 486 – www.the-metropole.co.uk
– info@the-metropole.co.uk – Fax (01841) 532 867
58 rm ☲ – †£92/132 ††£184/216
Rest – (bar lunch Monday-Saturday) Menu £ 30
♦ Grand 19C hotel perched above this quaint fishing town. Exceptional views of Camel Estuary. Well-furnished sitting room. Comfortable bedrooms in smart, co-ordinated style. Traditional dining; local produce.

🏨 **Old Custom House Inn**   ≼ 🅰🅒 rest, � *VISA* **©© 🅰🅴 🅞**
South Quay ⊠ PL28 8BL – ℰ (01841) 532 359 – www.smallandfriendly.co.uk
– oldcustomhouse@smallandfriendly.co.uk – Fax (01841) 533 372
24 rm ☲ – †£75/95 ††£95/130
Rest *Pescadou* – Seafood – (booking essential) Carte £ 25/50
♦ Listed, slate-built former grain store and exciseman's house: spacious and comfortable throughout. Front and side rooms have views of the quayside and Camel Estuary. Seafood emphasis in bustling, glass-fronted restaurant.

⌂ **Woodlands Country House** without rest   ≼ 🛁 ⅙ ⅓ **P.** *VISA* **©© 🅰🅴**
Treator, West : 1 ¼ m. on B 3276 ⊠ PL28 8RU – ℰ (01841) 532 426
– www.woodlands-padstow.co.uk – info@woodlands-padstow.co.uk
– Fax (01841) 533 353 – Closed 16 December - 31 January
8 rm ☲ – †£60/66 ††£112/126
♦ Personally run Victorian country house with well-kept garden. Large lounge in classic traditional style; views sweeping down to Trevone Bay. Co-ordinated bedrooms.

⌂ **Treverbyn House** without rest   ≼ 🛁 ⅓ **P.**
Station Rd ⊠ PL28 8DA – ℰ (01841) 532 855
– www.treverbynhouse.com
– Fax (01841) 532 855
– February - November
5 rm ☲ – ††£110
♦ Something of a grand style with views of the Camel Estuary. Large rooms retain open fireplaces and have comfortable, uncluttered décor: The Turret room is the one to ask for.

ENGLAND

⟨↑⟩ **Althea Library** without rest   ℅ ⁽ᵗ⁾ **P** *VISA* **⨪⊙**
27 High St ⊠ *PL28 8BB* – ℰ *(01841) 532 717* – *www.althealibrary.co.uk*
– *enquiries@althealibrary.co.uk* – *Fax (01841) 532 717* – *Closed January, one week*
June, Christmas
3 rm ⌂ – **†**£87 **††**£92/120
♦ Grade II listed former school library with very friendly feel. Neat terrace; homely breakfast room/lounge with food cooked on the Aga. Cosy, individually styled beamed rooms.

⟨XX⟩ **The Seafood** with rm   **AK** rest, **P** *VISA* **⨪⊙**
Riverside ⊠ *PL28 8BY* – ℰ *(01841) 532 700* – *www.rickstein.com*
– *reservations@rickstein.com* – *Fax (01841) 532 942*
– *Closed dinner 24-26 December and 1 May*
20 rm ⌂ – **†**£125 **††**£260
Rest – Seafood – (booking essential) Carte approx. £60
♦ Rick Stein's buzzy converted granary and conservatory has been given a £2.5million facelift and a large sushi bar has been added. His fans come from far and wide for the local seafood. Rooms 5 and 6 have great views and balconies.

⟨XX⟩ **St Petroc's** with rm   ⌂ ⁽ᵗ⁾ ⌓ *VISA* **⨪⊙**
4 New St ⊠ *PL28 8EA* – ℰ *(01841) 532 700* – *www.rickstein.com*
– *reservations@rickstein.com* – *Fax (01841) 532 942*
– *Closed dinner 24-26 December and 1 May*
10 rm ⌂ – **††**£205 – 2 suites
Rest – Seafood – (booking essential) Carte approx. £32
♦ Handsome white-fronted house on a steep hill, where confidently prepared modern dishes with local, seasonal produce take centre stage. Stylish, individual bedrooms.

⟨XX⟩ **No.6**   ⇔ *VISA* **⨪⊙ AE**
6 Middle St ⊠ *PL28 8AP* – ℰ *(01841) 532 093* – *www.number6inpadstow.co.uk*
– *enquiries@number6inpadstow.co.uk* – *Fax (01841) 533 941* – *Closed January,*
23-27 December, Sunday and Monday except Bank Holidays
Rest – (dinner only) Carte approx. £48
♦ Targeting the top end of the market, this converted cottage has striking black and white floors, early evening as well as ambitious menus featuring elaborate, complex dishes.

⟨X⟩ **Custard**   *VISA* **⨪⊙**
1A The Strand ⊠ *PL28 8AJ* – ℰ *(08701) 700 740* – *www.custarddiner.com*
– *reservations@custarddiner.com* – *Fax (05601) 146 213*
– *Closed 25-26 December, 1 May and Tuesday*
Rest – Carte £27/35
♦ Comfortable, homely eatery. Good value menu ranges from breakfast and afternoon tea to full 3 courses; simple, flavoursome cooking features British classics with some modern twists.

⟨X⟩ **Rick Stein's Café** with rm   ⌂ *VISA* **⨪⊙**
⟨☺⟩ *10 Middle St* ⊠ *PL28 8AP* – ℰ *(01841) 532 700* – *www.rickstein.com*
– *reservations@rickstein.com* – *Fax (01841) 532 942* – *Closed 24-26 December*
and 1 May
3 rm ⌂ – **†**£90 **††**£135
Rest – (booking essential at dinner) Menu £22 – Carte £25/33
♦ Contemporary, unfussy bistro with modern, well-priced Mediterranean influenced cuisine employing the best local and seasonal ingredients. Well-appointed bedrooms.

⟨X⟩ **Margot's**   *VISA* **⨪⊙ AE ⓞ**
11 Duke St ⊠ *PL28 8AB* – ℰ *(01841) 533 441* – *www.margots.co.uk*
– *enquiries@margots.co.uk* – *Closed Sunday and Monday*
Rest – (booking essential at dinner) Menu £27 (dinner)
– Carte £29/30
♦ Informal bistro-style restaurant with a friendly welcoming atmosphere. Varied menu capitalises on finest, fresh, local ingredients and bold, characterful flavours.

at Constantine Bay West : 4 m. by B 3276 – ⊠ Padstow

🏠🏠🏠 Treglos ⑤   ← 🚗 🏠 🖂 📶 👥 ⅙ rm, 🅰 rest, 🅿 🚗 𝗩𝗜𝗦𝗔 ⓪⓪
⊠ PL28 8JH – ✆ (01841) 520 727 – www.tregloshotel.com
– stay@tregloshotel.com – Fax (01841) 521 163 – March-November
39 rm ⅏ – †£94/165 ††£188/220 – 5 suites
Rest – (bar lunch Monday-Saturday) Menu £28
♦ An extensive, family run building surrounded by garden. Facilities include games rooms, children's play area and a lounge bar. Consistently decorated, bright, neat bedrooms. Smart attire the code in very comfortable dining room.

at St Merryn West : 2½ m. by A389 on B3276

✗✗ Ripley's   𝗩𝗜𝗦𝗔 ⓪⓪
⊠ PL28 8NQ – ✆ (01841) 520 179 – Fax (01841) 521 641
Rest – (dinner only and lunch July-September) (booking essential) Menu £35 (dinner) – Carte £24/31
♦ Simply furnished with light wood chairs and tables. Daily changing menu features local, seasonal produce. Straightforward, flavoursome cooking includes excellent homemade bread.

at Little Petherick South : 3 m. on A 389 – ⊠ Wadebridge

🏠 Molesworth Manor without rest   ← 🚗 🕸 🅿
⊠ PL27 7QT – ✆ (01841) 540 292 – www.molesworth.co.uk
– molesworthmanor@aol.com – February-October
9 rm ⅏ – †£60/68 ††£92/100
♦ Part 17C and 19C former rectory. Charming individual establishment with inviting country house atmosphere amid antique furniture and curios. Rooms furnished in period style.

🏠 Old Mill House without rest   🚗 🕸 𝗩𝗜𝗦𝗔 ⓪⓪
⊠ PL27 7QT – ✆ (01841) 540 388 – www.theoldmillhouse.com
– enquiries@theoldmillhouse.com – Fax (01841) 540 406 – February - November
7 rm ⅏ – †£80/85 ††£115/120
♦ Rural curios on display in a listed, family owned 16C cornmill with working water wheel. Homely, individually decorated rooms, some overlooking the millrace and neat garden.

We try to be as accurate as possible when giving room rates but prices are susceptible to change.
Please check rates when booking.

ENGLAND (right margin)

PAIGNTON – Torbay – **503** J 32 – pop. 47 398   2 **C2**
▶ London 226 mi – Exeter 26 mi – Plymouth 29 mi
🛈 The Esplanade (01803) 211211, paignton.tic@torbay.gov.uk
◎ Torbay★ - Kirkham House★ **AC** Y **B**
⊙ Paignton Zoo★★ **AC**, SW : ½ m. by A 3022 AY (see Plan of Torbay) – Cockington★, N : 3 m. by A 3022 and minor roads

Plan of Built up Area : see Torbay

Plan on next page

🏠🏠🏠 Redcliffe   ← 🚗 🏊 🖂 🕸 ⅙ 👥 🅰 rest, 🕸 🖴 🅿 𝗩𝗜𝗦𝗔 ⓪⓪
4 Marine Drive ⊠ TQ3 2NL – ✆ (01803) 526 397 – www.redcliffehotel.co.uk
– redclfe@aol.com – Fax (01803) 528 030   Y **n**
68 rm ⅏ – †£58/120 ††£116/130
Rest – (bar lunch Monday-Saturday) Menu £20 – Carte £22/28
♦ Smoothly run family owned hotel, handily set on the seafront, a favourite of auther Dick Francis. Children's play area and putting green options. Airy, pine furnished rooms. Admire the sea views from spacious, neat restaurant.

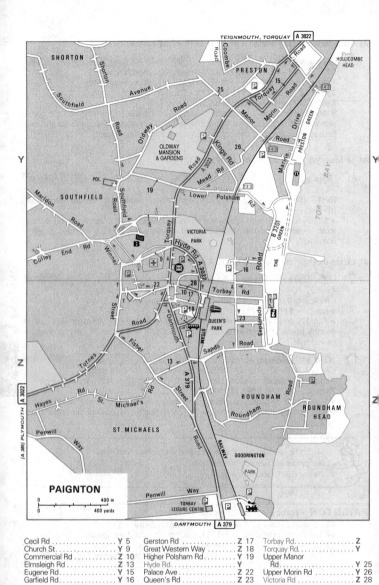

PAIGNTON

0 _____ 400 m
0 _____ 400 yards

Your opinions are important to us:
please write and let us know about your discoveries and experiences –
good and bad!

PAINSWICK – Gloucestershire – **503** N 28 – **pop. 1 666** ▌ *Great Britain*   4 **C1**
> ▶ London 107 mi – Bristol 35 mi – Cheltenham 10 mi – Gloucester 7 mi
> ◎ Town ★

🏨 **Cotswolds 88**   🚗 🏤 ॐ ⁇ **P** *VISA* **ⓒⓞ** **AE** **①**
Kemps Lane ✉ *GL6 6YB* – ℰ *(01452) 813 688* – *www.cotswolds88hotel.com*
– *reservations@cotswolds88hotel.com* – *Fax (01452) 814 059*
18 rm ☲ – 🛏£175 🛏🛏£395
Rest – (closed Monday lunch) Menu £ 20 (lunch) – Carte £ 25/35
♦ Stone Regency style house with neat garden and terrace. Bold stylish colours, quirky furnishings and striking fixtures abound. Eclectic bedrooms; modern bathrooms. Restaurant offers modern menu of organic produce.

🏠 **Cardynham House**   ॐ *VISA* **ⓒⓞ** **AE**
The Cross, by Bisley St and St Marys St ✉ *GL6 6XX* – ℰ *(01452) 814 006*
– *www.cardynham.co.uk* – *info@cardynham.co.uk* – *Fax (01452) 812 321*
9 rm ☲ – 🛏£85 🛏🛏£100   **Rest** – (by arrangement) Carte £ 19/28
♦ Part 15C house with a stylish, relaxed, even Bohemian feel to its elegant, firelit lounge. Themed, uniquely styled rooms: eight have four-poster beds, one a private pool. All day bistro with classic dishes.

PANGBOURNE – West Berkshire – **504** Q29   10 **B3**
> ▶ London 51 mi – Hillingdon 38 mi – Reading 14 mi – Oxford 23 mi

🏨 **Elephant**   🚗 🏤 🏠 ৬ ⁇ 🛁 *VISA* **ⓒⓞ** **AE**
Church Rd ✉ *RG8 7AR* – ℰ *(0118) 984 22 44* – *www.elephanthotel.co.uk*
– *reception@elephanthotel.co.uk* – *Fax (0118) 976 73 46*
22 rm ☲ – 🛏£100 🛏🛏£140   **Rest** – Carte £ 25/35
♦ Smart, stylish hotel with subtle colonial feel and pleasant rear garden. Individually decorated bedrooms have excellent facilities; some annexe rooms have terraces. Dark wood furnished restaurant boasts modern, internationally influenced brasserie menu.

PATELEY BRIDGE – North Yorkshire – **502** O 21 – **pop. 2 504**   22 **B2**
– ✉ Harrogate ▌ *Great Britain*
> ▶ London 225 mi – Leeds 28 mi – Middlesbrough 46 mi – York 32 mi
> 🄸 18 High St ℰ (01423) 711147, pbtic@harrogate.gov.uk
> ◎ Fountains Abbey ★★★ **AC** - Studley Royal **AC** (≤ ★ from Anne Boleyn's Seat) - Fountains Hall (Fa½ade ★), NE : 8 ½ m. by B 6265

at Ramsgill-in-Nidderdale Northwest : 5 m. by Low Wath Rd – ✉ Harrogate

🍴🍴 **The Yorke Arms** (Frances Atkins) with rm 🌿   🚗 🏤 **P** *VISA* **ⓒⓞ** **①**
❀❀ ✉ *HG3 5RL* – ℰ *(01423) 755 243* – *www.yorke-arms.co.uk*
– *enquiries@yorke-arms.co.uk* – *Fax (01423) 755 330*
12 rm ☲ – 🛏£100/150 🛏🛏£180/340
Rest – (Closed Sunday dinner to non-residents) Menu £ 25 (lunch)
– Carte £ 45/55 ❀
Spec. Rabbit terrine, sage and liquorice. Dales mutton with sausage, calvo nero and roasted onion skins. Grand marnier and chocolate soufflé.
♦ Creeper-clad, part 17C former shooting lodge whose antique-furnished interior features beamed ceilings and open fires. Daily specials supplement a classically-based, seasonal menu. Lavishly furnished bedrooms.

PATRICK BROMPTON – North Yorkshire – **502** P 21 – ✉ Bedale   22 **B1**
> ▶ London 242 mi – Newcastle upon Tyne 58 mi – York 43 mi

🏠 **Elmfield House** 🌿   🚗 🅚 ☜ ৬ rm, ॐ **P** *VISA* **ⓒⓞ** **AE**
Arrathorne, Northwest : 2 ¼ m. by A 684 on Richmond rd ✉ *DL8 1NE*
– ℰ *(01677) 450 558* – *www.elmfieldhouse.co.uk* – *stay@elmfieldhouse.co.uk*
– *Fax (01677) 450 557*
7 rm ☲ – 🛏£58/70 🛏🛏£85
Rest – (dinner only) (booking essential) (residents only) Menu £ 15 **s**
♦ Spacious, neatly fitted accommodation in a peaceful, personally run hotel, set in acres of gardens and open countryside. Try your luck at the adjacent fishing lake. Tasty, home-cooked meals.

ENGLAND

PATTISWICK – Essex – see Coggeshall

PAULERSPURY – Northants. – **503** R 27 – see Towcester

PAYHEMBURY – Devon – see Honiton

PEMBRIDGE – County of Herefordshire – **503** L 27   18 **A3**
> **D** London 162 mi – Hereford 15 mi – Leominster 7 mi

⌂   **Lowe Farm**   ≤ 🖭 🕪 🌱 ⁿⁱ **P** **VISA** **⦿**
West : 3 ¼ m. by A 44 following signs through Marston village ✉ *HR6 9JD*
– 𝒞 (01544) 388 395 – www.lowe-farm.co.uk – juliet@lowe-farm.co.uk
– Fax (01544) 388 395 – Closed Christmas
5 rm ⊇ – ♣£40 ♣♣£80/110   **Rest** – (by arrangement) Menu £ 23
♦ Working farm: farmhouse dates from 13C; renovated barn from 14C with pleasant lounge and countryside views. Rooms in house and barn are cosy, comfortable and of a good size. Dining room boasts chunky pine tables, exposed brick and beams.

PENN – Buckinghamshire – **504** R/S 29 – pop. 3 779   11 **D2**
> **D** London 31 mi – High Wycombe 4 mi – Oxford 36 mi

🍴   **The Old Queens Head**   🖭 🍴 **P** **VISA** **⦿** **AE**
Hammersley Lane ✉ *HP10 8EY – 𝒞 (01494) 813 371*
– www.oldqueensheadpenn.co.uk – info@oldqueensheadpenn.co.uk
– Fax (01494) 816 145 – Closed 25-26 December
Rest – Carte £ 20/29
♦ Attractive part 17C pub with flagged floors, low beams and brick fireplaces. Mix of traditional and more modern dishes served in generous portions. Garden with picnic tables.

PENRITH – Cumbria – **501** L 19 – pop. 14 471   21 **B2**
> **D** London 290 mi – Carlisle 24 mi – Kendal 31 mi – Lancaster 48 mi
> **🛈** Robinsons School, Middlegate 𝒞 (01768) 867466, pen.tic@eden.gov.uk -
>   Rheged, Redhills, Penrith 𝒞 (01768) 860034, tic@rheged.com
> **🏌** Salkeld Rd, 𝒞 (01768) 891 919

⌂   **Brooklands** without rest   🌱 ⁿⁱ **VISA** **⦿** **①**
2 Portland Place ✉ *CA11 7QN – 𝒞 (01768) 863 395*
– www.brooklandsguesthouse.com – enquiries@brooklandsguesthouse.com
– Fax (01768) 863 395 – Closed 10 days Christmas
7 rm ⊇ – ♣£35/55 ♣♣£70/80
♦ Traditonal Victorian terraced house a minute's walk from the shops: many original features restored. Pleasantly furnished breakfast room. Locally made pine enhances bedrooms.

at Temple Sowerby East : 6 ¾ m. by A 66 – ✉ Penrith

🏨   **Temple Sowerby House**   🖭 ⁿⁱ 🦮 **P** **VISA** **⦿** **AE**
✉ *CA10 1RZ – 𝒞 (01768) 361 578 – www.templesowerby.com*
– stay@templesowerby.com – Fax (01768) 361 958
– Closed 19 December - 5 January
12 rm ⊇ – ♣£90/125 ♣♣£120/175   **Rest** – (dinner only) Carte £ 29/37
♦ Listed building with Georgian frontage, run with enthusiasm and charm. Refurbished bedrooms are stylishly decorated and include spa baths and body jet showers. Dining room overlooks walled garden. Menu offers concise, modern selection, cooked using fine seasonal produce.

at Yanwath Southwest : 2 ½ m. by A 6 and B 5320 – ✉ Penrith

🍴   **The Yanwath Gate Inn**   🖭 **P** **VISA** **⦿** **AE**
✉ *CA10 2LF – 𝒞 (01768) 862 386 – www.yanwathgate.com*
– enquiries@yanwathgate.com – Closed 25 December
Rest – Carte £ 24/37
♦ Originally a toll gate, this is now a cosy pub. Cooking is carefully balanced and displays finesse, without being showy; everything is homemade and local produce is paramount.

at Newbiggin West : 3½ m. by A 66 – ⊠ Penrith

⌂ **The Old School**   🖼 **P** VISA ⚫
⌂⦿ ⊠ CA11 0HT – ℰ (01768) 483 709 – www.theold-school.com
– info@theold-school.com – Fax (01768) 483 709
– Closed 4-18 June, 21-28 December
3 rm ⊡ – ✦£35/56 ✦✦£65/70
Rest – (by arrangement, communal dining) Menu £20
◆ Well sited off two major roads, this 19C former school house has been tastefully converted with an open-fired lounge and rooms individually decorated to a high standard.

PENZANCE – Cornwall – **503** D 33 – pop. 20 255   1 **A3**
▶ London 319 mi – Exeter 113 mi – Plymouth 77 mi – Taunton 155 mi
Access Access to the Isles of Scilly by helicopter, British International Heliport (01736) 364296, Fax (01736) 363871
▬ to the Isles of Scilly (Hugh Town) (Isles of Scilly Steamship Co. Ltd) (summer only) (approx. 2 h 40 mn)
🛈 Station Rd ℰ (01736) 362207, pztic@penwith.gov.uk
◉ Town★ - Outlook★★★ – Western Promenade (≼★★★) YZ – National Lighthouse Centre★ **AC** Y – Chapel St★ Y – Maritime Museum★ **AC** Y M1 – Penlee House Gallery and Museum★, **AC**
🄶 St Buryan★★ (church tower★★), SW : 5 m. by A 30 and B 3283 - Penwith★★ – Trengwainton Garden★★, NW : 2 m. - Sancreed - Church★★ (Celtic Crosses★★) - Carn Euny★, W : 3½ m. by A 30 Z – St Michael's Mount★★ (≼★★), E : 4 m. by B 3311 - Y - and A 30 - Gulval★ (Church★), NE : 1 m. - Ludgvan★ (Church★), NE : 3½ m. by A 30 - Chysauster Village★, N : 3½ m. by A 30, B 3311 and minor rd - Newlyn★ - Pilchard Works★, SW : 1½ m. by B 3315 Z - Lanyon Quoit★, NW : 3½ m. by St Clare Street – Men-an-Tol★, NW : 5 m. by B 3312 - Madron Church★, NW : 1½ m. by St Clare Street Y. Morvah (≼★★), NW : 6½ m. by St Clare Street Y – Zennor (Church★), NW : 6 m. by B 3311 Y – Prussia Cove★, E : 8 m. by B 3311 - Y - and A 394 – Land's End★ (cliff scenery★★★), SW : 10 m. by A 30 Z – Porthcurno★, SW : 8½ m. by A 30, B 3283 and minor rd

Plan on next page

🏨 **Hotel Penzance**   ≼ 🖼 🖼 ⛉ 🄰🄲 rest, ⬱ **P** VISA ⚫ AE
Britons Hill ⊠ TR18 3AE – ℰ (01736) 363 117 – www.hotelpenzance.com
– enquiries@hotelpenzance.com – Fax (01736) 350 970   Y**c**
25 rm ⊡ – ✦£60/105 ✦✦£145/175
Rest *Bay* – (dinner only and lunch in summer) (booking essential for non-residents) Menu £16/29 – Carte £29/40
◆ Well-established hotel with modern interior in elevated spot with views to St. Michaels Mount. Comfortable lounge. Bedrooms are immaculately kept and equipped with mod cons. Bright, modern restaurant with local artwork and bar.

🏠 **The Abbey** without rest   🖼 **P** VISA ⚫ AE
Abbey St ⊠ TR18 4AR – ℰ (01736) 366 906 – www.theabbeyonline.co.uk
– hotel@theabbeyonline.co.uk – Closed 25 December   Y**u**
6 rm ⊡ – ✦£75/110 ✦✦£145/200 – 2 suites
◆ Powder blue painted 17C house with lovely Victorian gardens. Attractive antique furnishings include historical pictures. Country house atmosphere and characterful bedrooms.

🏠 **Beachfield**   ≼ VISA ⚫ AE
The Promenade ⊠ TR18 4NW – ℰ (01736) 362 067 – www.beachfield.co.uk
– office@beachfield.co.uk – Fax (01736) 331 100
– Closed Christmas-New Year   Z**a**
18 rm ⊡ – ✦£55/75 ✦✦£109/139
Rest – (bar lunch) Menu £23 **s** – Carte £20/30 **s**
◆ Classic seaside hotel with good views. Well-kept public areas include traditional lounge. Comfy bedrooms are well maintained and have a neat, bright feel. Traditional, varied menus, featuring fish specials.

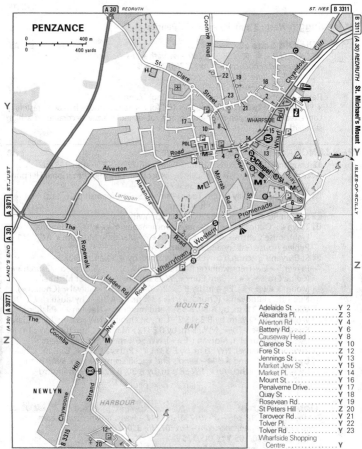

Adelaide St	Y	2
Alexandra Pl.	Z	3
Alverton Rd	Y	4
Battery Rd	Y	6
Causeway Head	Y	8
Clarence St	Y	10
Fore St	Z	12
Jennings St	Y	13
Market Jew St	Y	15
Market Pl.	Y	14
Mount St	Y	16
Penalverne Drive	Y	17
Quay St	Y	18
Rosevean Rd	Y	19
St Peters Hill	Z	20
Taroveor Rd	Y	21
Tolver Pl.	Y	22
Tolver Rd	Y	23
Wharfside Shopping Centre	Y	

Chy-An-Mor without rest

15 Regent Terrace ✉ TR18 4DW – ✆ (01736) 363 441 – www.chyanmor.co.uk – info@chyanmor.co.uk **9 rm** – †£35/40 ††£72/85 Y**e**

◆ Located on a terrace of houses overlooking the promenade. Thoroughly well kept throughout. Comfy, well-furnished bedrooms. Wake up to a good choice at breakfast.

The Abbey

Abbey St ✉ TR18 4AR – ✆ (01736) 330680 – www.theabbeyonline.com – kinga@theabbeyonline.com – Closed January-February, November-December, Sunday and Monday **Rest** – (dinner only and lunch Thursday- Saturday) Menu £25 (lunch) – Carte dinner £37/53 Y**u**

◆ Leased from the hotel next door. Vivid red bar with TV showing chefs at work. Leads upstairs to the more soberly decorated restaurant. The cooking is ambitious and quite elaborate.

Harris's

46 New St ✉ TR18 2LZ – ✆ (01736) 364408 – www.harrissrestaurant.co.uk – contact@harrissrestaurant.co.uk – Fax (01736) 333273 – Closed 2 weeks winter, 2 weeks spring, 25-26 December, Sunday and Monday except in summer Y**a**

Rest – Carte £28/37

◆ Friendly and well-established restaurant, tucked away on a cobbled street. Brightly decorated interior with smart linen clothed tables. Cornish menu with a French overlay.

XX **The Summer House** with rm 🖃 🛱 ⅗ **P** _VISA_ **©©**
Cornwall Terrace ⊠ TR18 4HL – ℰ (01736) 363 744
– www.summerhouse-cornwall.com – reception@summerhouse-cornwall.com
– Fax (01736) 360 959 – 7 April-19 October Zs
5 rm � – ♦£85/95 ♦♦£125
Rest – (closed Monday-Wednesday) (dinner only) Menu £32
♦ Listed Regency rooms and restaurant in bright blues and yellows. Relaxed, friendly ambience. Mediterranean influenced seafood; modern and flavourful. Leafy patio garden.

X **The Lime Tree** _VISA_ **©©** AE
Trevelyan House, 16 Chapel St ⊠ TR18 4AQ – ℰ (01736) 332 555
– www.the-lime-tree.co.uk – bookings@the-lime-tree.co.uk – Fax (01736) 332 555
– Closed 25 December - 2 January, Sunday, and Monday Ys
Rest – (light lunch) Carte £10/35
♦ Central three-storey Georgian townhouse comprising two dining rooms, comfy lounge and tiny lunchtime roof terrace. Adventurous dinner menus and good value lunches of interest.

X **Bakehouse** _VISA_ **©©**
Old Bakehouse Lane, Chapel St ⊠ TR18 4AE – ℰ (01736) 331 331
– www.bakehouse-penzance.co.uk – carrjasper@aol.com
– Closed 25-26 December, Sunday and Monday lunch Yz
Rest – (booking essential) Carte £21/35
♦ Penzance's original bakery, now a stylish restaurant on two floors, with old bakers oven in situ downstairs. Modern menus boast good choice of local seafood and produce.

at Drift Southwest : 2½ m. on A 30 - Z – ⊠ Penzance

↑ **Rose Farm** without rest ⌖ 🖃 **P** _VISA_ **©©** ①
Chyenhal, Buryas Bridge, Southwest : ¾ m. on Chyenhal rd ⊠ TR19 6AN
– ℰ (01736) 731 808 – www.rosefarmcornwall.co.uk
– penny@rosefarmcornwall.co.uk – Fax (01736) 731 808 – Closed 24-25 December
3 rm ⊆ – ♦£45 ♦♦£80
♦ In the heart of the countryside, a tranquil working farm. Cosy, rustic farmhouse ambience with neatly kept bedrooms including large barn room. Artist in residence and painting workshops.

PERRANUTHNOE – Cornwall – **503** D 33 – see Marazion

PERSHORE – Worcestershire – **503** N 27 – pop. 7 104 19 **C3**
🖪 London 106 mi – Birmingham 33 mi – Worcester 8 mi

↑ **The Barn** without rest ⩽ 🖃 ⅔ ⅗ **P**
Pensham Hill House, Pensham, Southeast : 1 m. by B 4084 ⊠ WR10 3HA
– ℰ (01386) 555 270 – www.pensham-barn.co.uk
– ghorton@pensham-barn.co.uk – Fax (01386) 552 894
3 rm ⊆ – ♦£50/55 ♦♦£80/90
♦ Stylish barn renovation in enviable hillside location. Attractive open-plan lounge and breakfast area with exposed roof timbers. Rooms individually styled to a high standard.

XX **Belle House** AC ⇄ _VISA_ **©©** AE ①
Bridge St ⊠ WR10 1AJ – ℰ (01386) 555 055 – www.belle-house.co.uk
– mail@belle-house.co.uk – Fax (01386) 555 377 – Closed first 2 weeks January,
1 week August, 25-26 December, Sunday and Monday
Rest – Menu £21/28
♦ 16C and 18C high street building with some very characterful parts, including heavily beamed bar. Accomplished cooking on modern menus using carefully sourced ingredients.

ENGLAND

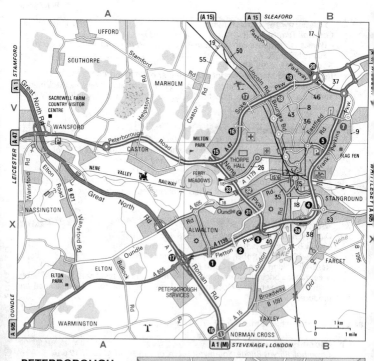

PETERBOROUGH

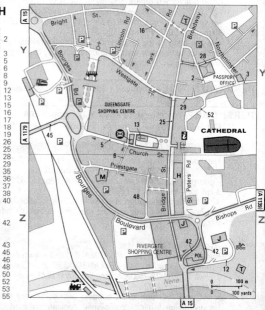

PETERBOROUGH – Peterborough – 502 T 26 – pop. 136 292   14 **A2**

 Great Britain

- ▶ London 85 mi – Cambridge 35 mi – Leicester 41 mi – Lincoln 51 mi
- 🛈 3-5 Minster Precinct – ℰ (01733) 452336, tic@peterborough.gov.uk
- ⛳ Thorpe Wood Nene Parkway, ℰ (01733) 267 701
- ⛳ Peterborough Milton Milton Ferry, ℰ (01733) 380 489
- ⛳ Orton Meadows Ham Lane, ℰ (01733) 237 478
- ◎ Cathedral★★ **AC** Y

Plan opposite

🏰 **Orton Hall**   🚗 ◐ ﹠ rm, 📞 🏖 **P** 𝗩𝗜𝗦𝗔 ⓴ 𝗔𝗘 ⓞ

The Village, Orton Longueville, Southwest : 2½ m. by Oundle Rd (A 605)
✉ PE2 7DN – ℰ (01733) 391 111 – www.abascushotels.co.uk
– reception@ortonhall.co.uk – Fax (01733) 231 912   BX**c**
72 rm – ♦£60/100 ♦♦£90/150, � £12.50
Rest *The Huntly* – (dinner only and Sunday lunch) Menu £27 **s**
◆ Smartly run, part 17C house in 20 acres, once the seat of the Marquess of Huntly. Spacious, comfortable rooms: State rooms particularly impressive. Pub in former stables. Pleasantly set dining room offers richly varied cuisine.

PETERSFIELD – Hampshire – 504 R 30   7 **C2**

- ▶ London 60 mi – Brighton 45 mi – Portsmouth 21 mi – Southampton 34 mi

🏠 **Langrish House** ⌖   🚗 ◐ 👑 🏖 **P** 𝗩𝗜𝗦𝗔 ⓴ 𝗔𝗘

Langrish, West : 3½ m. by A 272 ✉ GU32 1RN – ℰ (01730) 266 941
– www.langrishhouse.co.uk – frontdesk@langrishhouse.co.uk – Fax (01730)
260 543 – Closed 1-16 January
13 rm ⊆ – ♦£90 ♦♦£145/170
Rest – (lunch by arrangement) Menu £20/36 **s**
◆ Peaceful country house in wooded grounds, dating from 17C and family owned for seven generations. Characterful lounge in old Civil War cellars. Bright bedroom décor. Modish cuisine, proudly served.

XXX **JSW** (Jake Watkins) with rm   📶 👑 **P** 𝗩𝗜𝗦𝗔 ⓴
🍽

20 Dragon St ✉ GU31 4JJ – ℰ (01730) 262 030 – www.jswrestaurant.com
– jsw.restaurant@btconnect.com
– Closed 2 weeks January, 2 weeks July, Sunday and Monday
3 rm – ♦£75 ♦♦£110
Rest – Menu £20 (lunch) – Carte £34/50 🍴
Spec. Scallops with a cep and truffle risotto. Slow cooked lamb, wild garlic crust. Strawberry trifle with Earl Grey tea.
◆ Sympathetically restored, stylish 17C coaching inn, with attractive enclosed rear courtyard. Contemporary cooking: flavourful, well-sourced and confident. Comfortable bedrooms.

PETWORTH – West Sussex – 504 S 31 – pop. 2 298 📖 *Great Britain*   7 **C2**

- ▶ London 54 mi – Brighton 31 mi – Portsmouth 33 mi
- ⛳ Osiers Farm Petworth London Rd, ℰ (01798) 344 097
- ◎ Petworth House★★ **AC**

🏠 **Old Railway Station** without rest   🚗 🌀 **P** 𝗩𝗜𝗦𝗔 ⓴ 𝗔𝗘

South : 1½ m. off A 285 ✉ GU28 0JF – ℰ (01798) 342 346
– www.old-station.co.uk – info@old-station.co.uk – Fax (01798) 343 066 – Closed
24-26 December and 1 January
10 rm ⊆ – ♦£95/130 ♦♦£165/194
◆ As the name suggests. Waiting room with vaulted ceiling and ticket office now a lounge, Pullman carriages with marquetry now bedrooms; original features abound. Cake on arrival; breakfast on platform.

PETWORTH

XX **The Grove Inn**   🚗 🌳 **P** **VISA** **◑◐** **AE** **①**
Grove Lane, South : ½ m. by High St and Pulborough rd ⊠ *GU28 0HY*
– ℰ (01798) 343 659 – steveandvaleria@tiscali.co.uk – Closed 2 weeks January,
31 December, Sunday dinner and Monday
Rest – (light lunch) Carte £ 23/36
♦ Restored farmhouse: conservatory bar and beamed restaurant. Dinner menu with modern influence, simpler lunch menu. Attentive service.

🍴 **Badgers** with rm   🌳 **P** **VISA** **◑◐**
Coultershaw Bridge, South : 1½ m. on A 285 ⊠ *GU28 0JF – ℰ (01798) 342 651*
– Closed 25 December
3 rm ⌂ – †£ 55 ††£ 80
Rest – (Closed Sunday dinner October-April) Carte £ 22/35
♦ Lovely pub next to Old Railway Station. Beautiful oak panelled bar has old photos and 'badger and honey' theme. Log fire; intimate alcove. Eclectic, robust menus. Comfy rooms.

at Halfway Bridge West : 3 m. on A 272 – ⊠ Petworth

🍴 **The Halfway Bridge Inn** with rm   🚗 📶 **P** **VISA** **◑◐** **①**
⊠ *GU28 9BP – ℰ (01798) 861 281 – www.halfwaybridge.co.uk*
– enquiries@halfwaybridge.co.uk – Closed 25 December
6 rm ⌂ – †£ 75/95 ††£ 130/140
Rest – Carte £ 23/30
♦ Rustic pub with a contemporary edge. Honest, British cooking arrives in hearty, flavoursome portions; daily specials list pub classics and proper puddings. Comfortable, modern bedrooms with good bathrooms.

at Lickfold Northwest : 6 m. by A 272 – ⊠ Petworth

🍴 **The Lickfold Inn**   🚗 🌳 **P** **VISA** **◑◐**
⊠ *GU28 9EY – ℰ (01798) 861 285 – www.live-once-inns.co.uk*
– lickfold@live-once-inns.co.uk – Closed 25 December
Rest – Carte £ 22/33
♦ Characterful 15C red-brick pub owned by Chris Evans. Fairly ambitious restaurant style dishes and a good cheese selection. Dinner menu slightly more extensive than lunch.

Undecided between two equivalent establishments?
Within each category, establishments are classified
in our order of preference.

PICKERING – North Yorkshire – 502 R 21 – pop. 6 616   23 **C1**
🚗 London 237 mi – Middlesbrough 43 mi – Scarborough 19 mi
– York 25 mi
🚹 The Ropery ℰ (01751) 473791, pickering@ytbtic.co.uk

🏠 **White Swan Inn**   📶 **P** **VISA** **◑◐** **AE**
Market Pl ⊠ *YO18 7AA – ℰ (01751) 472 288*
– www.white-swan.co.uk
– welcome@white-swan.co.uk
– Fax (01751) 475 554
20 rm ⌂ – †£ 130 ††£ 175 – 1 suite
Rest – Carte £ 21/45
♦ Long-standing former coaching halt in a popular market town. Lovely lounge and comfortable bedrooms - the new ones in the courtyard are very stylish with contemporary touches. Traditional dining room offers lengthy menu.

ENGLAND

↑ **17 Burgate** without rest 🚗 🛜 **P** **VISA** **MO**
17 Burgate ⊠ YO18 7AU – ℰ (01751) 473 463 – www.17burgate.co.uk
– info@17-burgate.co.uk – Fax (01751) 473 463
– Closed 2 weeks February, 1 week Christmas
5 rm ⌷ – ▯£75/80 ▯▯£105
♦ Painstakingly restored 17C town house, the décor smoothly spanning 400 years. Sitting room bar; sizzling breakfasts; superbly appointed rooms, two with larger seating areas.

↑ **Bramwood** 🚗 ❄ 🛜 **P** **VISA** **MO**
19 Hall Garth ⊠ YO18 7AW – ℰ (01751) 474 066
– www.bramwoodguesthouse.co.uk – enquiries@bramwoodguesthouse.co.uk
8 rm ⌷ – ▯£40/65 ▯▯£75   **Rest** – (by arrangement) Menu £20
♦ Georgian town house with sheltered garden. Personally run with curios of rural life dotted around a firelit lounge. Cosy bedrooms in homely, cottagey style.

↑ **Old Manse** 🚗 🛜 **P** **VISA** **MO**
Middleton Rd ⊠ YO18 8AL – ℰ (01751) 476 484
– www.oldmansepickering.co.uk – info@oldmansepickering.co.uk
– Fax (01751) 477 124
10 rm ⌷ – ▯£49/65 ▯▯£85/95   **Rest** – (by arrangement) Menu £19
♦ A welcoming ambience and modestly priced rooms, spacious and spotless, make this personally run house an ideal base for touring the moors. Secluded rear garden and orchard. Informal conservatory dining room.

at Levisham Northeast : 6½ m. by A 169 – ⊠ Pickering

↑ **The Moorlands Country House** 🌳 ≤ 🚗 ❄ 🛜 **P** **VISA**
⊠ YO18 7NL – ℰ (01751) 460 229 – www.moorlandslevisham.co.uk
– ronaldoleonardo@aol.com – Fax (01751) 460 470 – March-November, minimum 2 night stay
4 rm ⌷ – ▯£65/75 ▯▯£130/150
Rest – (by arrangement) Menu £30 – Carte £16/40
♦ Restored 19C house with attractive gardens in the heart of the North York Moors National Park. There are fine views to be enjoyed here. Rooms furnished to high standard. Traditional, home-cooked meals in pretty dining room.

at Marton West : 5¼ m. by A 170 – ⊠ Pickering

🍽 **The Appletree** 🚗 🍸 ❄ **P** **VISA** **MO** **AE**
⊠ YO62 6RD – ℰ (01751) 431 457 – www.appletreeinn.co.uk
– appletreeinn@supanet.com – Fax (01751) 430 190
– Closed 25 December and 2 weeks January
Rest – (Closed Monday-Tuesday) Carte £14/28
♦ Spacious, part 18C stone-built pub. Weekly menu focuses on locality and seasonality, while careful cooking provides good natural flavours. Vegetables are from the kitchen garden.

at Sinnington Northwest : 4 m. by A 170 – ⊠ York

🍽 **Fox and Hounds** with rm 🚗 **P** **VISA** **MO**
Main St, Sinnington ⊠ YO62 6SQ – ℰ (01751) 431 577
– www.thefoxandhoundsinn.co.uk – foxhoundsinn@easynet.co.uk – Fax (01751) 432 791 – Closed 25-26 December
10 rm ⌷ – ▯£49/75 ▯▯£80/130   **Rest** – Carte £19/32
♦ At the heart of this sleepy village on the river Seven, an extended coaching house, beamed and panelled in ancient oak. Well-proportioned, cottagey rooms; hearty breakfasts. Modern restaurant or rustic bar offer dining options.

ENGLAND

Your opinions are important to us:
please write and let us know about your discoveries and experiences – good and bad!

PICKHILL – North Yorkshire – 502 P 21 – ⊠ Thirsk   22 **B1**

▶ London 229 mi – Leeds 41 mi – Middlesbrough 30 mi – York 34 mi

Nags Head Country Inn   🍴 🛋 ⁽ⁱ⁾ 🕸 **P** VISA ⓜⓞ

⊠ YO7 4JG – ☎ (01845) 567 391 – www.nagsheadpickhill.co.uk
– reservations@nagsheadpickhill.co.uk – Fax (01845) 567 212
– Closed 25 December
14 rm ⌂ – †£60/65 ††£85 – 1 suite   **Rest** – Carte £21/26
♦ Atmospheric 300 year old inn in an ancient hamlet, an easy drive to Thirsk and
Ripon races. Neat rooms in soft floral fabrics. Over 800 ties on display in the rustic bar.
Rural restaurant adorned with bookshelves and patterned rugs.

PILLERTON PRIORS – Warks. – 503 P 27 – see Stratford-upon-Avon

---

PILTDOWN – East Sussex – pop. 1 517   8 **A2**

▶ London 41 mi – Brighton 21 mi – Uckfield 3 mi

The Peacock Inn   🛋 **P** VISA ⓜⓞ

Shortbridge ⊠ TN22 3XA – ☎ (01825) 762 463 – www.peacock-inn.co.uk
– matthewarnold@aol.com – Closed 25-26 December
Rest – Carte £20/30
♦ 18C former alehouse, adorned with photos of celebrity visitors. Menu features
straightforward pub food, including steaks and grills and often fresh fish specials.

> Red = Pleasant. Look for the red 🍴 and 🏠 symbols.

PITT – Hampshire – see Winchester

PLUMTREE – Notts. – see Nottingham

PLYMOUTH – Plymouth – 503 H 32 – pop. 243 795   2 **C2**

▶ London 242 mi – Bristol 124 mi – Southampton 161 mi
Access Tamar Bridge (toll) AY
✈ Plymouth City (Roborough) Airport : ☎ (01752) 204090, N : 3½ m.
by A 386 ABY
⛴ to France (Roscoff) (Brittany Ferries) 1-3 daily (6 h) – to Spain (Santander)
(Brittany Ferries) 2 weekly (approx 24 h)
🛈 Plymouth Mayflower, 3-5 The Barbican ☎ (01752)
306330, barbicantic@plymouth.gov.uk - Plymouth Discovery Centre,
Crabtree ☎ (01752) 266030, mtic@plymouth.gov.uk
🏉 Staddon Heights Plymstock, ☎ (01752) 402 475
🏉 Elfordleigh Hotel G. & C.C. Plympton Colebrook, ☎ (01752) 348 425
◉ Town★ - Smeaton's Tower (≤★★) **AC** BZ **T1** – Plymouth Dome★ **AC** BZ –
Royal Citadel (ramparts ≤★★) **AC** BZ – City Museum and Art Gallery★
BZ **M1**
ⓒ Saltram House★★ **AC**, E : 3½ m. BY **A** - Tamar River★★ – Anthony House★
AC, W : 5 m. by A 374 – Mount Edgcumbe (≤★) **AC**, SW : 2 m. by
passenger ferry from Stonehouse AZ. NE : Dartmoor National Park★★ –
Buckland Abbey★★ **AC**, N : 7½ m. by A 386 ABY

Plan opposite

🏨 **Holiday Inn**   ≤ 🖥 🛏 🛖 🖐 👌 rm, 🔲 🕸 ⁽ⁱ⁾ 🕸 🛎 VISA ⓜⓞ 🅰 ⓞ

Armada Way ⊠ PL1 2HJ – ☎ (01752) 639 988 – www.holidayinn.co.uk
– hiplymouth@qmh-hotels.com – Fax (01752) 673 816   BZ**s**
211 rm ⌂ – †£180 ††£180
Rest – (dinner only and Sunday lunch) Menu £20 – Carte £24/38 **s**
♦ Substantial purpose-built hotel enjoys a panorama of the city skyline and the
Plymouth Sound. Neatly laid-out, well-equipped bedrooms; extensive leisure club.
Modern restaurant on top floor to make most of view.

ENGLAND

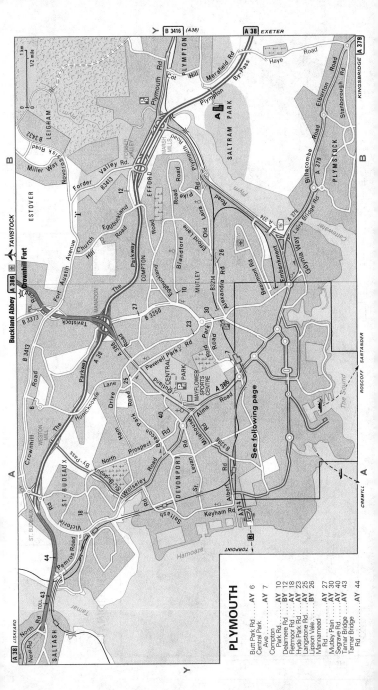

PLYMOUTH

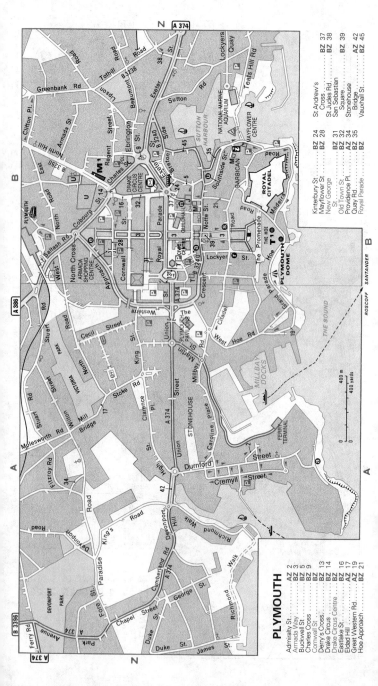

PLYMOUTH

Bowling Green *without rest*
9-10 Osborne Pl, Lockyer St, The Hoe ✉ *PL1 2PU –* ✆ *(01752) 209 090*
– www.bowlinggreenhotel.co.uk – info@bowlinggreenhotel.co.uk
– Fax (01752) 209 092   BZ**r**
12 rm ☐ – †£45/58 ††£68
♦ Georgian house, half overlooking Hoe, near site of Drake's legendary game. High-ceilinged rooms in pine and modern fabrics; some have power showers. Stroll to promenade.

XX Tanners
Prysten House, Finewell St ✉ *PL1 2AE –* ✆ *(01752) 252 001*
– www.tannersrestaurant.com – enquiries@tannersrestaurant.co.uk
– Fax (01752) 252 105 – Closed 26 and 31 December, first week January,
Sunday and Monday   BZ**n**
Rest – (booking essential) Menu £20/35 **s** – Carte £27/32 **s**
♦ Characterful 15C house, reputedly Plymouth's oldest building: mullioned windows, tapestries, exposed stone and an illuminated water well. Modern, interesting cooking.

XX Artillery Tower
Firestone Bay ✉ *PL3 3QR –* ✆ *(01752) 257 610 – www.artillerytower.co.uk*
– Closed 2 weeks in Summer, 2 weeks at Christmas, Sunday and Monday   AZ**a**
Rest – (booking essential at lunch) Menu £30/38 **s**
♦ Uniquely located in 500 year-old circular tower, built to defend the city. Courteous service of mostly well executed local dishes: blackboard fish specialities.

XX Chloe's
Gill Akaster House Princess St – ✆ *(01752) 201 523*
– www.chloesrestaurant .co.uk – chloesrestaurant@hotmail.co.uk – Fax (01752)
201 523 – Closed 2 weeks Christmas, 2 weeks August-September, 1 week late May,
Sunday and Monday   BZ**a**
Rest – Menu £17/35
♦ Airy, open plan restaurant with simple neighbourhood feel, neutral décor and hanging Hessian lights. Tasty dishes display a classical French base. Live pianist every night.

X Barbican Kitchen
Black Friars Distillery, 60 Southside St ✉ *PL1 2LQ –* ✆ *(01752) 604 448*
– www.barbicankitchen.com – info@barbicankitchen.com – Fax (01752) 604 445
– Closed 25-26 and 31 December, 1 January   BZ**u**
Rest – Carte £17/31
♦ Set within the famous Plymouth Gin Distillery, this stylish restaurant, in vivid lime green and lilac, is split between two upper rooms, offering good value brasserie fare.

at Plympton St Maurice East : 6 m. by A 374 on B 3416 - BY – ✉ **Plymouth**

St Elizabeth's House
Longbrook St – ✆ *(01752) 344 840 – www.stelizabeths.co.uk*
– enquiries@stelizabeths.co.uk – Fax (01752) 331 391
13 rm ☐ – †£99/109 ††£109/119 – 2 suites
Rest – Menu £12 (lunch) – Carte £30/43
♦ Immaculate cream-washed former convent, now a stylish boutique hotel; lounge is dressed in period décor while light bedrooms are contemporary, with up-to-date facilities. Formal dining room offers classically based cooking with a modern twist.

PLYMPTON ST MAURICE Devon – **503** H 32 – see Plymouth

The ✿ award is the crème de la crème.
This is awarded to restaurants
which are really worth travelling miles for!

POLPERRO – Cornwall – **503** G 33 – ⊠ **Looe**

   ▶ London 271 mi – Plymouth 28 mi
   ◎ Village ★

⛓   **Trenderway Farm** without rest 🏖   ≤ 🚗 🏖 🛎 ⁇ ⁇ **P** 🅥🅘🅢🅐 ⓒⓞ 🄰🄴
Northeast : 2 m. by A 387 ⊠ *PL13 2LY* – ℰ *(01503) 272 214*
– www.trenderwayfarm.co.uk – stay@trenderwayfarm@com – Fax (0870)
705 9998 – Closed Christmas and New Year
6 rm ⌸ – †£85/155 ††£85/155
♦ Charming 16C farmhouse on working farm with converted outbuildings: modish ambience in a traditional setting. Breakfast over the lake. Stylish rooms with modern fabrics.

PONTELAND – Tyne and Wear – **501** O 19 – see Newcastle upon Tyne

---

POOLE – Poole – **503** O 31 – **pop. 144 800**   4 **C3**

   ▶ London 116 mi – Bournemouth 4 mi – Dorchester 23 mi
   – Southampton 36 mi – Weymouth 28 mi
   ⛴ to France (Cherbourg) (Brittany Ferries) 1-2 daily May-October (4 h 15 mn)
   day (5 h 45 mn) night – to France (St Malo) (Brittany Ferries) daily (8 h) – to
   France (St Malo) (Condor Ferries Ltd)
   🛈 Welcome Centre, Enefco House, Poole Quay ℰ (01202) 253253,
   info@poole.gov.uk
   🏌 Parkstone Links Rd, ℰ (01202) 707 138
   🏌 Bulbury Woods Lytchett Minster Bulberry Lane, ℰ (01929) 459 574
   ◎ Town ★ (Waterfront **M1**, Scaplen's Court **M2**)
   🄶 Compton Acres ★★, (English Garden ≤★★★) **AC**, SE : 3 m. by B 3369 **BX**
   (on Bournemouth town plan) – Brownsea Island ★ (Baden-Powell Stone
   ≤★★) **AC**, by boat from Poole Quay or Sandbanks **BX** (on Bournemouth
   town plan)

Plan of Built up Area : see Bournemouth BX

Plan opposite

🏨🏨🏨   **The Haven**   ≤ 🍸 🏊 🏊 🌐 🏖 💪 ⁇ 🖳 🄰🄲 rest, ⁇ ⁇ ♨ **P** 🅥🅘🅢🅐 ⓒⓞ 🄰🄴
161 Banks Rd, Sandbanks, Southeast : 4¼ m. on B 3369 ⊠ *BH13 7QL*
– ℰ (01202) 707 333 – www.fjbhotels.co.uk – enquiries@havenhotel.co.uk
– Fax (01202) 708 796   **BXc**
76 rm ⌸ – †£95/220 ††£160/380 – 2 suites
Rest *La Roche* – Menu £24 (lunch) – Carte dinner £28/43 **s**
Rest *Seaview* – (dinner only) Menu £30 **s**
♦ Sweeping white façade and heated seawater pool. Smart modern rooms. Lounge on site of Marconi's laboratory has fireside leather wing chairs. Perched at the side of the Haven, overlooking the bay. Watch the fishing boats from wonderful adjacent terrace. Eclectic menus with seafood base and tasty local ingredients. Candlelit Seaview overlooks bay.

🏨🏨   **Harbour Heights**   ≤ 🚗 🍸 🖥 🄰🄲 ⁇ 📞 ♨ **P** 🅥🅘🅢🅐 ⓒⓞ 🄰🄴
Haven Rd, Sandbanks, Southeast : 3 m. by B 3369 ⊠ *BH13 7LW* – ℰ *(01202)*
707 272 – www.fjbhotels.co.uk – enquiries@harbourheights.net
– Fax (01202) 708 594   **BXn**
38 rm ⌸ – †£165/175 ††£310/360
Rest *harbar bistro* – Menu £27/30 – Carte £23/46
♦ 1920s hotel stylishly updated in 2003; walls decorated with vibrant modern art. Swanky, smart bedrooms boast modern interiors and all mod cons: request room with a sea view. Bistro-styled restaurant with very popular terrace.

⛓   **Cranborne House** without rest   ⁇ ⁇ **P**
45 Shaftesbury Rd ⊠ *BH15 2LU* – ℰ *(01202) 685 200*
– www.cranborne-house.co.uk   **c**
5 rm ⌸ – †£59/79 ††£69/89
♦ Victorian house with original features and pleasant, modern style. Bedrooms – in quiet rear wing of house – boast handmade pine furniture and modern bathrooms. Separate guest entrance.

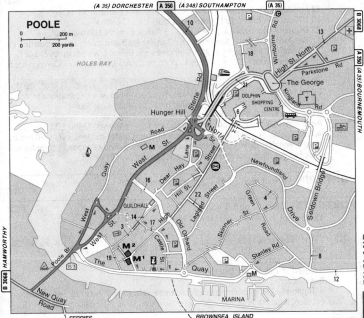

POOLE

200 m
200 yards

HOLES BAY

(A 35) DORCHESTER A 350 (A 348) SOUTHAMPTON   (A 35)

XX **Isabel's**   🍽 ❖ VISA ⦿ AE

32 Station Rd, Lower Parkstone ⊠ BH14 8UD – ℰ (01202) 747 885
– www.isabelsrestaurant.co.uk – isabels@onetel.com – Fax (01202) 747 885
– Closed 26 December, Sunday and Monday   BX**a**
Rest – (dinner only) (booking essential) Carte £ 26/36
♦ Long-established neighbourhood restaurant; old shelves recall its origins as a Victorian pharmacy. Intimate wooden booths. Classically inspired menu with a rich Gallic tone.

🍴 **The Cow**   🍽 AC ❤ ❖

58 Station Road, Ashley Cross ⊠ BH14 8UD – ℰ (01202) 749 569
– www.thecowpub.co.uk – info@thecowpub.co.uk – Fax (01202) 307 493   BX**a**
Rest – Carte £ 16/36
♦ Vibrant suburban pub with bar and bistro areas. Dishes are lighter at lunch and more ambitious in the evening: ingredients are good quality, expertly prepared and well-presented.

POOLEY BRIDGE – Cumbria – **501** L 20 – see Ullswater

The red 🌲 symbol?
This denotes the very essence of peace
– only the sound of birdsong first thing in the morning...

ENGLAND

PORLOCK – Somerset – **503** J 30 – ✉ Minehead

3 **A2**

▶ London 190 mi – Bristol 67 mi – Exeter 46 mi – Taunton 28 mi

◉ Village★ - Porlock Hill (≤★★) – St Dubricius Church★

◎ Dunkery Beacon★★★ (≤★★★), S : 5½ m. – Exmoor National Park★★ -
Selworthy★ (≤★★, Church★), E : 2 m. by A 39 and minor rd - Luccombe★
(Church★), E : 3 m. by A 39 – Culbone★ (St Beuno), W : 3½ m. by B 3225,
1½ m. on foot – Doone Valley★, W : 6 m. by A 39, access from Oare on foot

Oaks

≤ 🚗 🍴 📶 **P** **VISA** **①①**

✉ TA24 8ES – ℰ (01643) 862 265 – www.oakshotel.co.uk – info@oakshotel.co.uk
– Fax (01643) 863 131 – Easter-October and Christmas-New Year

8 rm � – ♦£103 ♦♦£145

Rest – (dinner only) (booking essential for non-residents) Menu £33

◆ Traditionally styled Edwardian country house in pretty gardens, very well run by
most hospitable owners. Stunning rural views. Cosy, individual rooms in co-ordinated
colours. Neat dining room: all land produce from a 20 mile radius.

PORT ERIN – Isle of Man – **502** F 21 – see Man (Isle of)

PORTGATE – Devon – pop. 1 453

2 **C2**

▶ London 211 mi – Launceston 8 mi – Plymouth 34 mi

The Harris Arms

🏠 **P** **VISA** **①①**

✉ EX20 4PZ – ℰ (01566) 783 331 – www.theharrisarms.co.uk
– whiteman@powernet.co.uk – Fax (01566) 783 359
– Closed 26 December, 1 January

Rest – Carte £21/29 🏵

◆ Traditional 16C pub offers friendly welcome, relaxed ambience, decked terrace and
excellent wine list. Robust, confident cooking uses local, seasonal ingredients.

PORTHLEVEN – Cornwall

1 **A3**

▶ London 284 mi – Helston 3 mi – Penzance 12 mi

Kota with rm

📶 **VISA** **①①** **AE**

Harbour Head ✉ TR13 9JA – ℰ (01326) 562 407 – www.kotarestaurant.co.uk
– kota@btinternet.com – Fax (01326) 562 407
– Closed January - 13 February, Sunday and Monday in winter

2 rm ⊇ – ♦£50/70 ♦♦£65/90

Rest – (dinner only and lunch Friday-Saturday) Menu £13 – Carte £22/32

◆ Cottagey converted 18C harbourside granary. Characterful restaurant - thick walls,
tiled floors - serves modern Asian inspired dishes with local fish specials. Simple
rooms.

PORTINSCALE – Cumbria – see Keswick

PORTLOE – Cornwall – **503** F 33 – ✉ Truro

1 **B3**

▶ London 296 mi – St Austell 15 mi – Truro 15 mi

Lugger

≤ 🚗 🍴 **P** **VISA** **①①** **AE**

✉ TR2 5RD – ℰ (01872) 501 322 – www.luggerhotel.com
– office@luggerhotel.com – Fax (01872) 501 691

22 rm ⊇ – ♦£135/190 ♦♦£220/280

Rest – (light lunch) Menu £38 – Carte £33/46

◆ Former inn in a beautiful location within pretty Cornish cove. Stylish public areas.
The bedrooms are created with a tasteful palette in strikingly contemporary vein.
Restaurant enjoys blissful outlook over the cove.

PORTSCATHO – Cornwall – **503** F 33 – ✉ Truro

1 **B3**

▶ London 298 mi – Plymouth 55 mi – Truro 16 mi

◎ St Just-in-Roseland Church★★, W : 4 m. by A 3078 – St
Anthony-in-Roseland (≤★★) S : 3½ m

Rosevine
*Rosevine, North : 2 m. by A 3078 ⊠ TR2 5EW – 𝒞 (01872) 580 206
– www.rosevine.co.uk – info@rosevine.co.uk – Fax (01872) 580 230
– Closed January*
7 rm – ♦£130/290 ♦♦£130/325, � £15 – 10 suites
Rest – (closed Sunday) (bar lunch) Carte £26/30
♦ Surrounded by attractive gardens, this family owned hotel offers traditional, homely comforts. Rooms are well looked after and a friendly air prevails. Pretty restaurant makes use of local ingredients.

Driftwood ⌂
*Rosevine, North : 2 m. by A 3078 ⊠ TR2 5EW – 𝒞 (01872) 580 644
– www.driftwoodhotel.co.uk – info@driftwoodhotel.co.uk – Fax (01872) 580 801
– Closed mid December to mid February*
15 rm ⊆ – ♦£158 ♦♦£230
Rest – (dinner only) (booking essential) Menu £42 **s**
♦ Stylish décor and a neutral, contemporary feel make this an enviable spot to lay one's head. Attractive decking affords fine sea views. Smart bedrooms with pristine style. Distinctive modern dining room with fine vistas.

PORTSMOUTH and SOUTHSEA – Portsmouth – **503** Q 31   6 **B3**
– pop. 187 056 ▌ *Great Britain*

ENGLAND

▶ London 78 mi – Brighton 48 mi – Salisbury 44 mi – Southampton 21 mi
⇆ to the Isle of Wight (Ryde) (Wightlink Ltd) frequent services daily (15 mn) – from Southsea to the Isle of Wight (Ryde) (Hovertravel Ltd) frequent services daily (10 mn)
⇆ to France (St Malo) (Brittany Ferries) daily (8 h 45 mn) day (10 h 45 mn) night – to France (Caen) (Brittany Ferries) 2-4 daily (6 h) day (6 h 45 mn) night – to France (Cherbourg) (Brittany Ferries) 2 daily (5 h) day, (7 h) night – to France (Le Havre) (LD Lines) daily (5 h 30 mn/7 h 30 mn) – to France (Cherbourg) (Brittany Ferries) 1-2 daily (2 h 45 mn) – to France (Caen) (Brittany Ferries) 2-4 daily (3 h 45 mn) – to Spain (Bilbao) (P & O European Ferries Ltd) 1-2 weekly (35 h) – to Guernsey (St Peter Port) and Jersey (St Helier) (Condor Ferries Ltd) daily except Sunday (10 hrs) – to the Isle of Wight (Fishbourne) (Wightlink Ltd) frequent services daily (35 mn)
🖪 The Hard 𝒞 (023) 9282 6722, tic@portsmouthcc.gov.uk.
🖪 Southsea Burrfields Rd, 𝒞 (023) 9266 8667
🖪 Crookhorn Lane Waterlooville Widley, 𝒞 (023) 9237 2210
🖪 Southwick Park Southwick Pinsley Drive, 𝒞 (023) 9238 0131
◎ City ★ – Naval Portsmouth BY : H.M.S. Victory ★★★ **AC**, The Mary Rose ★★, Royal Naval Museum ★★ **AC** – Old Portsmouth ★ BYZ : The Point (≤ ★★) - St Thomas Cathedral ★ – Southsea (Castle ★ **AC**) AZ – Royal Marines Museum, Eastney ★ **AC**, AZ **M1**
◎ Portchester Castle ★ **AC**, NW : 5½ m. by A 3 and A 27 AY

Plan on next page

The Retreat without rest
*35 Grove Road South, Southsea ⊠ PO5 3QS – 𝒞 (023) 9235 3701
– www.theretreatguesthouse.co.uk – theretreatguesthouse@yahoo.co.uk   CZ**e***
4 rm ⊆ – ♦£105 ♦♦£105
♦ Grade II listed Victorian corner house in residential area. Original features include terrazzo flooring and stained glass windows. Simple, spacious bedrooms; modern bathrooms.

Fortitude Cottage without rest
*51 Broad St, Old Portsmouth ⊠ PO1 2JD – 𝒞 (023) 9282 3748
– www.fortitudecottage.co.uk – info@fortitudecottage.co.uk – Fax (023) 9282 3748 – Closed December*   BY**c**
6 rm ⊆ – ♦£45/105 ♦♦£85/105
♦ Pretty little quayside townhouse named after an 18C battleship. First floor breakfast room with views of ferry terminal. Room 4 has great roof terrace. Charming owners.

673

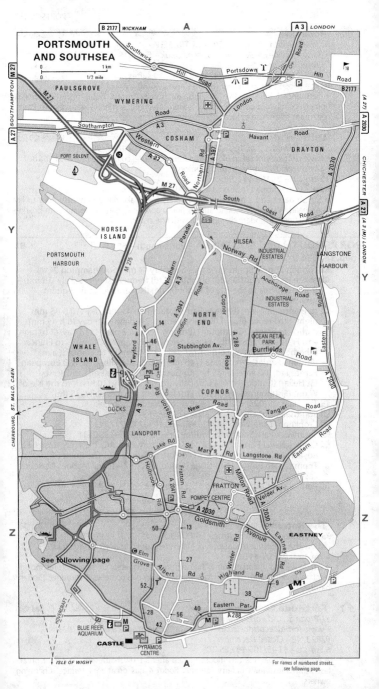

PORTSMOUTH
AND SOUTHSEA

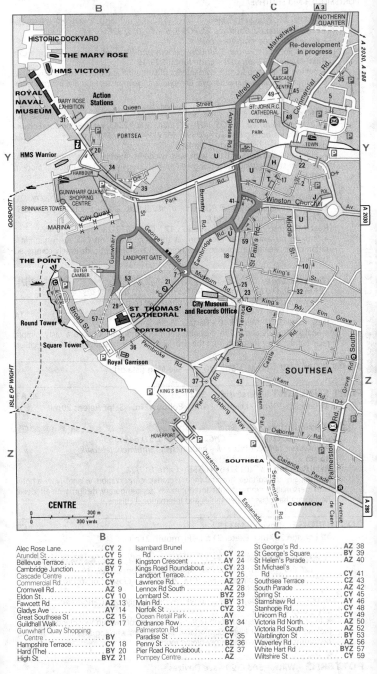

PORTSMOUTH and SOUTHSEA

XX Bistro Montparnasse   ⟡ VISA ⓞⓞ AE
103 Palmerston Rd, Southsea ⊠ PO5 3PS – ℰ (023) 9281 6754
– www.bistromontparnasse.co.uk
– Closed 25-26 December, 1 January, Sunday and Monday   CZa
Rest – Menu £ 32 (dinner) – Carte lunch £ 29/35
♦ Behind a trim shop front, a vivid interior of tangerine and blue. The menu is just as colourful: tuna, prawn and papaya, Campari orange mousse. Friendly, informal service.

XX 8 Kings Road   AC VISA ⓞⓞ ⓞ
8 Kings Rd, Southsea ⊠ PO5 3AH – ℰ (08451) 303 234 – www.8kingsroad.co.uk
– info@8kingsroad.co.uk – Fax (02392) 862 729 – Closed Monday   CZc
Rest – Menu £ 17/25 – Carte £ 28/43
♦ High ceilinged former bank with vast windows, marble floors, mezzanine and chandelier-style lighting. Quality ingredients well prepared and presented in modern French dishes.

XX Tang's   AC VISA ⓞⓞ AE
127 Elm Grove, Southsea ⊠ PO5 1LJ – ℰ (023) 9282 2722 – Fax (023) 9283 8323
– Closed 25-26 December and Monday   AZc
Rest – Chinese – (dinner only) Menu £ 17 – Carte £ 12/28
♦ Smooth presentation at every turn at this neighbourhood Chinese restaurant - rattan chairs, neat linen, impeccably attired staff and authentic, delicately composed cuisine.

X Lemon Sole   AC VISA ⓞⓞ AE
123 High St, Old Portsmouth ⊠ PO1 2HW – ℰ (023) 9281 1303
– www.lemonsole.co.uk – lemonsole@btinternet.com
– Fax (023) 9281 1345   BYa
Rest – Seafood – Menu £ 10 – Carte £ 25/35
♦ Seafood motifs abound in a bright, informal restaurant. Choose a tasty, simple recipe and market-fresh fish from the slab. Likeable, helpful staff. Part 14C wine cellar.

PORT ST MARY – I.O.M. – **502** F/G 21 – **see Man (Isle of)**

PORT SUNLIGHT – Merseyside – **502** L 23   20 **A3**
🚉 London 206 mi – Liverpool 6 mi – Bolton 42 mi – Saint Helens 20 mi

🏨 Leverhulme H. & Spa   ⌂ & ⓦ ⚘ P VISA ⓞⓞ AE
Lodge Lane, Central Rd ⊠ CH62 5EZ – ℰ (0151) 644 55 55
– www.leverhulmehotel.co.uk – enquiries@leverhulmehotel.co.uk
15 rm ⊇ – †£140 ††£395
Rest *Paesano* – ℰ (0151) 644 66 55 – Carte £ 17/28
♦ Originally the cottage hospital for a Victorian conservation village. Now a hotel with personality, whose bright interior mixes contemporary design with art deco. Restaurant has glass-topped tables and international cuisine.

POSTBRIDGE – Devon – **503** I 32   2 **C2**
🚉 London 207 mi – Exeter 21 mi – Plymouth 21 mi

🏠 Lydgate House ⌂   ⇐ ⌂ ⓛ P VISA ⓞⓞ ⓞ
⊠ PL20 6TJ – ℰ (01822) 880 209 – www.lydgatehouse.co.uk
– lydgatehouse@email.com – Fax (01822) 880 202 – Closed Christmas
7 rm ⊇ – †£45/65 ††£120
Rest – (closed Sunday and Monday) (residents only, by arrangement) Carte approx. £ 28 s
♦ In an idyllic secluded location high up on the moors within woodland and overlooking the East Dart River. Comfortable sitting room with log fires and neat, snug bedrooms. Candlelit conservatory dining room.

POTTERNE – Wilts. – **503** O 29 – **see Devizes**

676

PRESTBURY – Cheshire – **502** N 24 – **pop. 3 269**   20 **B3**

> ▶ London 184 mi – Liverpool 43 mi – Manchester 17 mi
> – Stoke-on-Trent 25 mi
> 🖼 Mottram Hall Hotel Mottram St Andrews Wilmslow Rd, ℰ (01625) 820 064

White House Manor without rest   🍽 ⅍ 🛜 **P** **VISA** **◑◐** **AE**

New Road ✉ SK10 4HP – ℰ (01625) 829 376 – www.thewhitehouse.uk.com
– info@thewhitehouse.uk.com – Fax (01625) 828 627 – Closed 25-26 December
12 rm – 🛏£55/100 🛏🛏£135/150, ⊇ £11.50
◆ Privately run 18C redbrick house with stylish, unique and individually decorated
rooms which provide every luxury. Breakfast in your room or in the conservatory.

The Bridge   🍽 🛜 &rm, ⅍ 🛜 🕸 **P** **VISA** **◑◐** **AE** **①**

The Village ✉ SK10 4DQ – ℰ (01625) 829 326 – www.bridge-hotel.co.uk
– reception@bridge-hotel.co.uk – Fax (01625) 827 557 – Closed 1-3 January
23 rm – 🛏£50/90 🛏🛏£90, ⊇ £9.75 – 1 suite
Rest – (closed Sunday dinner) Menu £14/18 – Carte £30/41
◆ Dating back to the 1600s, a sympathetically extended hotel on the river Bollin.
Classic, subtly co-ordinated décor in rooms, more characterful in the old timbered
house. Live music at weekends in the beamed, galleried hall of the restaurant.

> Look out for red symbols, indicating particularly pleasant establishments.

PRESTON – **502** L 22 – **pop. 184 836**   20 **A2**

> ▶ London 226 mi – Blackpool 18 mi – Burnley 22 mi – Liverpool 30 mi
> – Manchester 34 mi – Stoke-on-Trent 65 mi
> 🛈 The Guildhall, Lancaster Rd ℰ (01772) 253731, tourism@preston.gov.uk
> 🖼 Fulwood Fulwood Hall Lane, ℰ (01772) 700 011
> 🖼 Ingol Tanterton Hall Rd, ℰ (01772) 734 556
> 🖼 Ashton & Lea Lea Tudor Ave, Blackpool Rd, ℰ (01772) 735 282
> 🖼 Penwortham Blundell Lane, ℰ (01772) 744 630

Winckley Square Chop House   **AC** **VISA** **◑◐** **AE**

23 Winckley Sq ✉ PR1 3JJ – ℰ (01772) 252 732 – www.heathcotes.co.uk
– preston@heathcotes.co.uk – Fax (01772) 203 433
– Closed 25-26 December, 1 January and Bank Holiday Mondays
Rest – Menu £18 (lunch) – Carte £26/33
Rest *Olive Press* – Carte £17/30
◆ Chic and contemporary restaurant with a cuisine style that handsomely matches
the surroundings. Robust, balanced, classic British cooking with some regional input.
Spacious basement bar-bistro serving pizzas and pastas.

Inside Out   🍽 🛜 **P** **VISA** **◑◐** **AE**

100 Higher Walton Rd, Walton-le-Dale, Southeast : 1 ¾ m. by A 6 on A 675
✉ PR5 4HR – ℰ (01772) 251 366 – www.insideoutrestaurant.co.uk – Fax (01772)
258 918 – Closed first 2 weeks January and Monday
Rest – Menu £13 (weekday lunch)/15 – Carte £22/32
◆ Inside - a chic and stylish restaurant; 'out' - a lovely decked terrace with heaters
overlooking a garden. Well sourced, quality ingredients assembled with love and flair.

at Barton North : 5 m on A 6

The Sparling   🛜 **AC** **P** **VISA** **◑◐**

807 Garstang Road ✉ PR3 5AA – ℰ (01772) 863 789 – www.thesparling.co.uk
– info@thesparling.co.uk
Rest – Carte £21/29
◆ Unspectacular exterior, with surprisingly modern, airy styling inside. Wide-ranging
menu offers local produce and popular classics in unfussy, generous portions. Pianist
on Fri and Sat.

PULFORD – Ches. – **502** L 24 – see Chester

ENGLAND

677

PULHAM MARKET – Norfolk – **504** X 26 – **pop. 919** – ⊠ Diss   15 **C2**
   ◨ London 106 mi – Cambridge 58 mi – Ipswich 29 mi – Norwich 16 mi

⌂   **Old Bakery** without rest   ⧉ ⁕ 🌐 **P**
    Church Walk ⊠ *IP21 4SL* – ℰ *(01379) 676 492 – www.theoldbakery.net*
    – info@theoldbakery.net – Fax (01379) 676 492
    3 rm � – †£65 ††£80
    ♦ Characterful pink-hued Elizabethan house on village green. Spacious timbered
    rooms hold antiques and have plenty of personality. Pretty garden with summer
    house.

PURTON – Wiltshire – **503** O 29 – **pop. 3 328** – ⊠ Swindon   4 **D2**
   ◨ London 94 mi – Bristol 41 mi – Gloucester 31 mi – Oxford 38 mi
     – Swindon 5 mi

🏠   **Pear Tree at Purton**   ⧉ ⁕ 🔊 **P** 🟦 ⓪ 🅰 ⓪
    Church End, South : ½ m. by Church St on Lydiard Millicent rd ⊠ *SN5 4ED*
    – ℰ (01793) 772 100 – www.peartreepurton.co.uk – stay@peartreepurton.co.uk
    – Fax (01793) 772 369 – Closed 26-30 December
    15 rm ⊋ – †£120 ††£150 – 2 suites
    Rest – (closed lunch Saturday) Menu £20/35 **s**
    ♦ Personally run, extended 16C sandstone vicarage in mature seven-acre garden.
    Spacious flower-filled lounge. Rooms with traditional comforts and thoughtful extras.
    Conservatory restaurant overlooks wild flower borders.

⌂   **The Old Farmhouse** without rest ⊗   ⧉ 🔊 📷 ⁕ 🕻 **P** 🟦 ⓪ 🅰
    Bagbury Lane, Restrop, South : ¼ m. ⊠ *SN5 4LX* – ℰ *(01793) 770 130*
    – www.theoldfarmhouse.net – stay@theoldfarmhouse.net
    6 rm ⊋ – †£75 ††£160
    ♦ Late 18C former farm. Lovingly themed, luxurious bedrooms set in house and
    cowstore. Golf course, small spa, treatment room and outdoor hot-tub on site. Highly
    original breakfast.

RADNAGE – Bucks. – see Stokenchurch

RAINHAM – Medway – **504** U 29   9 **C1**
   ◨ London 14 mi – Basildon 16 mi – Dartford 9 mi

🍴🍴   **The Barn**   🅰🅲 **P** 🟦 ⓪ 🅰
    507 Lower Rainham Rd, North : 1 ¾ m. by Station Rd ⊠ *ME8 7TN* – ℰ *(01634)*
    361 363 – www.thebarnrestaurant.co.uk – info@thebarnrestaurant.co.uk – Closed
    25-26 December, Saturday lunch and Sunday dinner
    Rest – Menu £18/22 – Carte £37/54
    ♦ Rurally set, heavily beamed 17C barn with beamed dining room and cosy upstairs
    lounge. Elaborate cooking uses locally sourced, seasonal produce. Ideal for special
    occasions.

RAMSBOTTOM – Greater Manchester – **502** N 23 – **pop. 17 352**   20 **B2**
   ◨ London 223 mi – Blackpool 39 mi – Burnley 12 mi – Leeds 46 mi
     – Liverpool 39 mi – Manchester 13 mi

🍴   **ramsons**   🟦 ⓪
    18 Market Pl ⊠ *BL0 9HT* – ℰ *(01706) 825 070 – www.ramsons-restaurant.com*
    – chris@ramsons-restaurant.com – Closed one week January, 2 weeks July,
    Sunday dinner, Monday and Tuesday
    Rest – Italian influences – Menu £29 (lunch)/34 (weekday dinner)
    – Carte approx. £49 🍷
    ♦ Passionately run and slightly quirky, this well-regarded eatery offers mostly Italian
    influenced cooking utilising refined ingredients. Accompanying fine wine list.

RAMSBURY – Wilts. – **503** P 29 – see Marlborough

RAMSEY – Isle of Man – **502** G 21 – see Man (Isle of)

RAMSGILL-IN-NIDDERDALE – N. Yorks. – **502** O 21 – see Pateley Bridge

---

RANTON GREEN – Staffordshire – **502** N 25   19 **C1**

🚗 London 150 mi – Birmingham 36 mi – Stoke-on-Trent 19 mi
– Wolverhampton 32 mi

🏠 **Hand and Cleaver**   **P. ⓐ AE**
Butt Lane ⊠ *ST18 9JZ* – ℰ *(01785) 822 367* – *www.handandcleaver.co.uk*
Rest – (closed Monday) Menu £ 15 (lunch) – Carte £ 22/28
♦ Spacious 17C pub with embossed plaster walls, mid Victorian style lighting and 1970s feel throughout. Regularly changing menu of local produce ranges from nibbles to full 3 courses.

RAWTENSTALL – Lancashire – **502** N 22   20 **B2**

🚗 London 232 mi – Accrington 9 mi – Burnley 12 mi

✕✕ **The Dining Room**   **VISA ⓐ AE**
8-12 Burnley Rd ⊠ *BB4 8EW* – ℰ *(01706) 210 567*
– *www.thediningroomrestaurant.co.uk* – *thedingroom@hotmail.co.uk* – *Closed 25 December, 1 week January and Tuesday*
Rest – (booking essential) Menu £ 17 (lunch)/20 – Carte £ 36/42
♦ Bland façade hides slick, neutral interior. Semi-split level dining room hosts good value, understated, seasonal cooking where texture, balance and flavours gel seamlessly.

If breakfast is included the ⊆ symbol appears after the number of rooms.

RAYLEIGH – Essex – **504** V 29 – pop. 30 629   13 **C3**

🚗 London 35 mi – Chelmsford 13 mi – Southend-on-Sea 6 mi

at Thundersley South : 1 ¼ m. on A 129 – ⊠ Rayleigh

🏠 **The Woodmans Arms**   🍴 ✍ **P. VISA ⓐ**
Rayleigh Rd ⊠ *SS7 3TA* – ℰ *(01268) 775 799* – *www.thewoodmansarms.co.uk*
– *thewoodman@hotmail.co.uk* – *Fax (01268) 590 689*
Rest – Carte £ 18/22
♦ Updated 19C pub in gastronomic desert. Cosy lounge with comfy leather sofas. Dining areas, separated by screens, serve impressive range of dishes - eg: Thai, French, British.

READING – Reading – **503** Q 29 – pop. 232 662   11 **C3**

🚗 London 43 mi – Brighton 79 mi – Bristol 78 mi – Croydon 47 mi
– Luton 62 mi – Oxford 28 mi – Portsmouth 67 mi – Southampton 46 mi
Access Whitchurch Bridge (toll)
🚢 to Henley-on-Thames (Salter Bros. Ltd) (summer only)
🛈 Civic Centre ℰ (01189) 390900, touristinfo@reading.gov.uk
🏌 Calcot Park Calcot Bath Rd, ℰ (0118) 942 7124

Plan on next page

🏨 **Crowne Plaza Reading**   ≤ 🍴 ◻ ⓢ *L♭* 🛗 ﺕ rm, 🅰 ✍ 🕾 *sk*
Caversham Bridge, Richfield Ave ⊠ *RG1 8BD*   **P. VISA ⓐ AE ⓪**
– ℰ *(0118) 925 9988* – *www.readingholidayinn.co.uk* – *info@cp-reading.co.uk*
– *Fax (0118) 939 1665*   **Xe**
122 rm – ♦£ 179 ♦♦£ 179 – 2 suites
Rest – Menu £ 27 (dinner) – Carte £ 23/29 **s**
♦ Recently undergone a £9million refurbishment. Just out of centre on banks of Thames. Spacious public areas with large windows which look towards river. Executive rooms boast extra touches. Bright restaurant with terrace and atrium roof.

ENGLAND

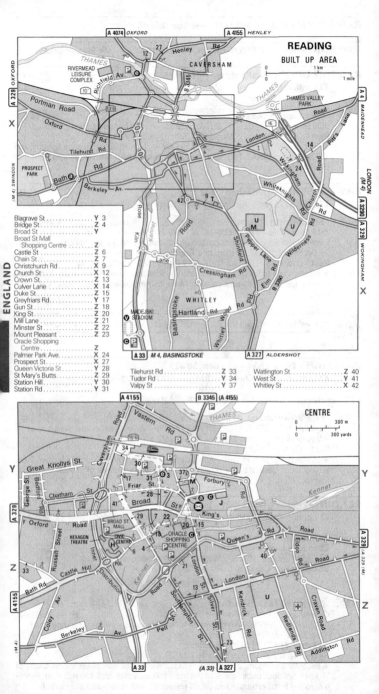

READING
BUILT UP AREA

ENGLAND

CENTRE

🏨 **Millennium Madejski** 🖥 🛏 ⅙ 🖪 ⅙ rm, 🖾 ☼ ℃ 🕍 🅿 VISA ⬤ AE ⬤
Madejski Stadium, South : 1½ m. by A 33 ⊠ RG2 0FL – ℰ (0118) 925 3500
– www.millenniumhotels.co.uk – reservations.reading@millenniumhotels.co.uk
– Fax (0118) 925 3501 X**v**
201 rm – ♦£ 200 ♦♦£ 200, ☕ £ 15.75 – 11 suites
Rest *Cilantro* – (closed 25 December - 6 January and Sunday) (dinner only)
Menu £ 50
Rest *Le Café* – (closed Saturday lunch - except match days) Menu £ 15 (lunch)
– Carte £ 25/34
♦ Purpose-built hotel, in modern retail park; part of the Madejski sports stadium.
Imposing Atrium lounge-bar and marble floored lobby. Stylish, inviting rooms. Impressively smart Cilantro. Informal Le Café is open plan to Atrium lounge.

🏨 **The Forbury** 🖪 ⅙ rm, 🖾 rest, ☼ ℃ 🕍 🅿 VISA ⬤ AE ⬤
26 The Forbury ⊠ RG1 3EJ – ℰ (0800) 078 9789 – www.theforburyhotel.co.uk
– info@theforburyhotel.co.uk – Fax (0118) 959 0806 Y**c**
23 rm – ♦£ 230/260 ♦♦£ 230/260, ☕ £ 10
Rest *Eden* – (closed Sunday, Monday and lunch Saturday and Tuesday)
– Menu £ 68
Rest *Cerise* – Carte £ 25/41
♦ Former civic hall overlooking Forbury Square Gardens; now a very stylish town
house hotel. Eye-catching artwork features in all the stunningly individualistic bedrooms. Stylish basement cocktail bar/restaurant where clean, crisp, modern cooking
holds sway.

🏨 **Malmaison** ⅙ 🖪 ⅙ rm, 🖾 ☁ VISA ⬤ AE ⬤
Great Western Rd ⊠ RG1 1JX – ℰ (0118) 956 2300 – www.malmaison.com
– Fax (0118) 956 2301 Y**e**
75 rm – ♦£ 85/160 ♦♦£ 95/180, ☕ £ 14.95
Rest *Brasserie* – (closed Saturday lunch) Menu £ 17 (dinner) – Carte £ 25/45
♦ Modernised Victorian railway hotel with contemporary furnishings, busy cafe and
smart bar. Spacious, stylish bedrooms boast high level of facilities. Railway theme
throughout. Industrial feel Brasserie serves contemporary, French influenced cooking.

🏠 **Beech House** without rest 🚲 ⅙ ℃ 🅿 VISA ⬤ AE ⬤
60 Bath Rd ⊠ RG30 2AY – ℰ (0118) 959 1901 – www.beechhousehotel.com
– relax@beechhousehotel.com – Fax (0118) 958 3200 X**a**
15 rm ☕ – ♦£ 75 ♦♦£ 85/100
♦ Red brick Victorian house with neat garden, terrace and summer house. Traditionally furnished with antiques and period ornaments. Pleasant, well equipped bedrooms with showers.

✗✗ **Forbury's** 🍴 🖾 ⇔ VISA ⬤ AE
1 Forbury Sq, The Forbury ⊠ RG1 3BB – ℰ (0118) 957 4044 – www.forburys.com
– forburys@btconnect.com – Fax (0118) 956 9191
– Closed 25-26 December, 1-2 January, and Sunday Y**a**
Rest – Menu £ 14/18 – Carte £ 32/39
♦ Modern eatery near law courts. Relaxing area of comfy leather seats. Spacious
dining room enhanced by bold prints of wine labels. Eclectic menus with Gallic
starting point.

✗✗ **LSQ2** 🍴 🖾 🅿 VISA ⬤ AE
Lime Sq., 220 South Oak Way, Green Park, South : 2 m. by A 33 ⊠ RG2 6UP
– ℰ (0118) 987 3702 – www.lsq2.co.uk – reading@lsq2.co.uk – Closed Sunday
dinner and Bank Holidays X**c**
Rest – Carte £ 25/39
♦ Head towards the wind turbine by the M4 to find this buzzy restaurant with
floor-to-ceiling glass serving 'corporate' style lunch menus and modern British dishes
for dinner.

ENGLAND

✗ **London Street Brasserie** 🏠 VISA ⓪ AE ⑩
2-4 London St ✉ RG1 4SE – ✆ (0118) 950 5036 – www.londonstbrasserie.co.uk
– paulclerehugh@l-s-b.co.uk – Fax (0118) 950 5028 Zc
Rest – (booking essential) Menu £ 15 (lunch) – Carte £ 22/34
♦ Lively and modern: a polite, friendly team serve appetising British classics and
international dishes. Deck terrace and first-floor window tables overlook the river
Kennett.

at Kidmore End North : 5 m. by A 4155 - X - off B 481 – ✉ Reading

🏠 **The New Inn** with rm 🚗 🏠 **P** VISA ⓪ AE
Chalkhouse Green Rd ✉ RG4 9AU – ✆ (0118) 972 3115
– www.thenewinnrestaurant.co.uk – thenewinn@uve.co.uk – Fax (0118) 972 4733
6 rm ⌂ – ♛♛ £ 75/220
Rest – (Closed Sunday dinner and Monday lunch) Carte £ 18/29
♦ 16C inn with rough floorboards, beams and open fires and delightful canopied
terrace. Smart, updated restaurant serves adventurous fare. Stylish, comfy, well-
equipped rooms.

at Hurst East : 5 m. by A 329 - X - on B 3030 – ✉ Reading

✗✗ **The Castle at Hurst** 🚗 🏠 ⇔ **P** VISA ⓪ AE ⑩
Church Hill ✉ RG10 0SJ – ✆ (0118) 934 0034 – www.castlerestaurant.co.uk
– info@castlerestaurant.co.uk – Fax (0118) 934 0334
Rest – Carte £ 25/34
♦ Charming 16C monk's wash-house. Part panelled dining room with wattle and
daub on display and a cosy snug. Classical French menu enhanced by modern interpretations.

at Shinfield South : 4 ¼ m. on A 327 - X – ✉ Reading

✗✗✗ **L'Ortolan** (Alan Murchison) 🚗 ⇔ **P** VISA ⓪ AE
🌸 Church Lane ✉ RG2 9BY – ✆ (0118) 988 8500 – www.lortolan.com
– info@lortolan.com – Fax (0118) 988 9338 – Closed 20 December-6 January,
Sunday and Monday except 24 November-15 December
Rest – Menu £ 26/60
Spec. Foie gras and pain d'épices sandwich. Saddle of lamb with carrot, pea
and lettuce ravioli. Crispy bitter chocolate mousse with spiced cherries and
vanilla ice cream.
♦ Pretty red brick former vicarage with lawned gardens and stylish lounge and
conservatory. Bright, comfortable dining room; classically based cooking with original
touches.

at Sonning-on-Thames Northeast : 4 ¼ m by A4 on B4446 – 504 R 29

✗✗✗ **French Horn** with rm ⩽ & rm, Ⓚ rest, **P** VISA ⓪ AE ⑩
✉ RG4 6TN – ✆ (0118) 969 22 04 – www.thefrenchhorn.co.uk
– info@thefrenchhorn.co.uk – Fax (0118) 944 22 10 – Closed 27-31 December
16 rm ⌂ – ♛ £ 125 ♛♛ £ 170 **Rest** – (booking essential) Carte £ 37/53
♦ Long-standing family owned restaurant in pretty riverside setting. Bay windowed
dining room overlooks lovely garden and offers classical French menus crafted from
seasonal ingredients. Comfy, traditional bedrooms; some in an annexe, some with
views.

REDDITCH – Worcestershire – 503 O 27 – pop. 74 803 19 **C2**
🚩 London 111 mi – Birmingham 15 mi – Cheltenham 33 mi
– Stratford-upon-Avon 15 mi
🏢 Alcester St ✆ (01527) 60806, info.centre@redditchbc.gov.uk
🏢 Abbey Hotel G. & C.C. Dagnell End Rd, ✆ (01527) 406 600
🏢 Lower Grinsty Callow Hill Green Lane, ✆ (01527) 543 079
🏢 Pitcheroak Plymouth Rd, ✆ (01527) 541 054

🏠 **Old Rectory** ⌖   🛌 📶 **P** 𝗩𝗜𝗦𝗔 ⓪⓪ 𝗔𝗘
Ipsley Lane, Ipsley ✉ *B98 0AP –* ✆ *(01527) 523 000*
– www.theoldrectory-hotel.co.uk – ipsleyoldrectory@aol.com – Fax (01527) 517003 – Closed 25 December-1 January
10 rm ⌂ – ♦£114 ♦♦£146
Rest – (closed Friday-Sunday) (dinner only) (booking essential for non-residents) Menu £25
♦ Converted early Georgian rectory surrounded by pleasant mature gardens creating a quiet and secluded haven. Smart, traditional interior décor and individually styled rooms. Charming Georgian style conservatory restaurant.

REDFORD – West Sussex – see Midhurst

REDWORTH – Durham – see Darlington

REETH – North Yorkshire – **502** O 20 – ✉ **Richmond**   22 **B1**
▶ London 253 mi – Leeds 53 mi – Middlesbrough 36 mi – Newcastle upon Tyne 61 mi
🛈 Hudson House, The Green ✆ (01748) 884059, reeth@ytbtic.co.uk

🏠🏠 **The Burgoyne**   ≤ 🛌 ⅙ rm, 📶 **P** 𝗩𝗜𝗦𝗔 ⓪⓪
On The Green ✉ *DL11 6SN –* ✆ *(01748) 884 292 – www.theburgoyne.co.uk*
– enquiries@theburgoyne.co.uk – Fax (01748) 884 292
– Closed 2 January-8 February
8 rm ⌂ – ♦£113/135 ♦♦£128/180 – 1 suite
Rest – (dinner only) (booking essential for non-residents) Menu £33
♦ Late Georgian hotel overlooking the green with views of the Dales. A charming, personally run, traditionally furnished house with well-appointed, individually styled rooms. Deep green dining room complements surrounding fells.

at Langthwaite Northwest : 3¼ m. on Langthwaite rd – ✉ Reeth

🏠 **The Charles Bathurst Inn** with rm ⌖   ≤ 🛌 **P** 𝗩𝗜𝗦𝗔 ⓪⓪
✉ *DL11 6EN –* ✆ *(01748) 884 567 – www.cbinn.co.uk – info@cbinn.co.uk*
– Fax (01748) 884 599 – Closed 25 December
19 rm ⌂ – ♦£93 ♦♦£95/120   **Rest** – Carte £20/35
♦ 18C inn sited high in the hills. Open fires provide appealing atmosphere. Fresh, locally sourced menus mixing classic with modern. Large, timbered rooms with country views.

at Low Row West : 4 m. B 6270

🏠 **The Punch Bowl Inn** with rm   🛌 📶 **P** 𝗩𝗜𝗦𝗔 ⓪⓪
✉ *DLL 6PF –* ✆ *(01748) 886 233 – www.pbinn.co.uk – info@pbinn.co.uk – Closed 25 December*
11 rm ⌂ – ♦£60/95 ♦♦£93/115   **Rest** – Carte £18/32
♦ Modernised, but retaining a wealth of rustic charm, this 17C stone inn in the heart of Swaledale is a popular stop off point for walkers. Menus have a strong sense of the seasons. Bedrooms are stylish, spacious and supremely comfortable.

REIGATE – Surrey – **504** T 30 – pop. 47 602   7 **D2**
▶ London 26 mi – Brighton 33 mi – Guildford 20 mi – Maidstone 38 mi

❌❌ **Tony Tobin @ The Dining Room**   𝗔𝗖 𝗩𝗜𝗦𝗔 ⓪⓪ 𝗔𝗘
59a High St ✉ *RH2 9AE –* ✆ *(01737) 226 650 – www.tonytobinrestaurants.co.uk*
– Fax (01737) 226 650 – Closed 23 December-3 January, Saturday lunch, Sunday dinner and Bank Holidays
Rest – Menu £20 (lunch) – Carte £36/50
♦ Top floor of a building on the High Street with a smart modern interior. Busy, bustling atmosphere. International menus with a modern style of cooking.

ENGLAND

❄ **The Westerly**   AC ⟷ VISA ◍◐ AE
😊 *2-4 London Rd ⊠ RH2 9AN – ℰ (01737) 222 733 – www.thewesterly.co.uk*
– info@thewesterly.co.uk – Closed 2 weeks summer, 2 weeks Christmas, Tuesday
lunch, Saturday lunch, Sunday and Monday
Rest – (booking essential at dinner) Menu £20 (lunch) – Carte £25/32
♦ Modern, simply decorated restaurant. Skilful kitchen, passionate about the seasons; intelligent menu and understated, wholesome cooking at honest prices. Welcoming service.

❄ **La Barbe**   AC VISA ◍◐ AE
71 Bell St ⊠ RH2 7AN – ℰ (01737) 241 966 – www.labarbe.co.uk
– restaurant@labarbe.co.uk – Fax (01737) 226 387 – Closed Christmas. Saturday
lunch, Sunday dinner and Bank Holidays
Rest – French – Menu £23/33 – Carte (Sunday lunch only) £26/31
♦ Friendly bistro with Gallic atmosphere and welcoming ambience. Regularly changing menus offer good choice of traditional French cuisine - classical and provincial in style.

RETFORD – Nottinghamshire – **502** R 24 – pop. 20 679   16 **B1**
🚇 London 148 mi – Lincoln 23 mi – Nottingham 31 mi – Sheffield 27 mi
🅩 40 Grove St (01777) 860780, retford.tourist@bassetlaw.gov.uk

⌂ **The Barns** without rest ⌘   🗐 🕳 **P** VISA ◍◐
Morton Farm, Babworth, Southwest : 2¼ m. by A 6420 ⊠ DN22 8HA
– ℰ (01777) 706 336 – www.thebarns.co.uk – enquiries@thebarns.co.uk – Closed
Christmas and New Year
6 rm ⚏ – †£42 ††£64
♦ Privately owned and run converted part 18C farmhouse on a quiet country road. Informal, old-fashioned, cottage décor throughout. Beams within and lawned gardens without.

RHYDYCROESAU – Shrops. – **502** K 25 – see Oswestry

RIBCHESTER – Lancashire – **502** M 22 – pop. 1 654   20 **B2**
🚇 London 229 mi – Blackburn 7 mi – Manchester 41 mi

📠 **The White Bull** with rm   🗐 🕳 🕳 VISA ◍◐
😊 *Church Street ⊠ PR3 3XP – ℰ (01254) 878 303 – www.whitebullrib.co.uk*
– enquiries@whitebullribchester.co.uk – Closed 2 January
3 rm ⚏ – †£55 ††£70   **Rest** – Menu £17 – Carte £17/24
♦ Stone pub dating from 1707 with spacious dining room, open fired bar and garden overlooking Roman bath remains. Hearty British pub dishes all homemade using best produce. Individually decorated, comfortable and cosy bedrooms.

RICHMOND – North Yorkshire – **502** O 20 – pop. 8 178 ▌*Great Britain*   22 **B1**
🚇 London 243 mi – Leeds 53 mi – Middlesbrough 26 mi – Newcastle upon Tyne 44 mi
🅩 Friary Gardens, Victoria Rd ℰ (01748) 850252, richmond@ytbtic.co.uk
🔟 Bend Hagg, ℰ (01748) 825 319
🔟 Catterick Leyburn Rd, ℰ (01748) 833 268
◉ Town★ - Castle★ **AC** – Georgian Theatre Royal and Museum★
◙ The Bowes Museum★, Barnard Castle, NW : 15 m. by B 6274, A 66 and minor rd (right) – Raby Castle★, NE : 6 m. of Barnard Castle by A 688

⌂ **Millgate House** without rest   🗐 🕪 **P**
3 Millgate ⊠ DL10 4JN – ℰ (01748) 823 571 – www.millgatehouse.com
– oztim@millgatehouse.demon.co.uk – Fax (01748) 850 701
4 rm ⚏ – †£85/125 ††£125
♦ Georgian townhouse with fine elevated views of river Swale and Richmond Castle. Award winning terraced garden. Antique furnished interior. Bedrooms are tastefully restrained.

ENGLAND

ENGLAND

⌂ **West End** without rest
45 Reeth Rd, West : ½ m. on A 6108 ⊠ DL10 4EX – ℰ (01748) 824 783
– www.stayatwestend.com – guesthouse@stayatwestend.com
– Closed 25 December
5 rm ⌷ – †£35/50 ††£70
♦ Pleasantly located mid 19C house with well kept gardens, close to the River Swale. Small sitting room; spacious, immaculately kept rear breakfast room. Comfortable, homely bedrooms.

at Dalton Northwest : 6 ¾ m. by Ravensworth rd and Gayles rd – ⊠ Richmond

🍴 **The Travellers Rest**
⊠ DL11 7HU – ℰ (01833) 621 225 – annebabsa@aol.com
– Closed 25-26 December, 1 January, dinner Sunday and Monday
Rest – (dinner only and Sunday lunch) Carte £ 17/30
♦ Characterful country inn in tiny hamlet. Blackboard menu offers a wide-ranging menu where traditional meets the up-to-date. Linen-laid restaurant also available.

RINGSTEAD – Norfolk – **504** V 25 – see Hunstanton

RINGWOOD – Hampshire – **503** O 31 – pop. 13 387   6 **A2**
> London 102 mi – Bournemouth 11 mi – Salisbury 17 mi
– Southampton 20 mi
🚉 The Furlong ℰ (01425) 470896, information@nfdc.gov.uk

🏠 **Moortown Lodge** without rest
244 Christchurch Rd, South : 1 m. on B 3347 ⊠ BH24 3AS – ℰ (01425) 471 404
– www.moortownlodge.co.uk – enquiries@moortownlodge.co.uk – Fax (01425) 476 527
7 rm ⌷ – †£68 ††£94
♦ House dating from the 1760s, located on the edge of the New Forest. Family run, traditional atmosphere with a cosy lounge and chintz-furnished rooms of varying sizes.

RIPLEY – North Yorkshire – **502** P 21 – ⊠ Harrogate   22 **B2**
> London 213 mi – Bradford 21 mi – Leeds 18 mi – Newcastle upon Tyne 79 mi

🏨 **The Boar's Head**
⊠ HG3 3AY – ℰ (01423) 771 888 – www.boarsheadripley.co.uk
– reservations@boarsheadripley.co.uk – Fax (01423) 771 509
25 rm ⌷ – †£105 ††£125
Rest The Restaurant – Carte £ 31/40
Rest The Bistro – Carte £ 18/27
♦ 18C coaching inn within estate village of Ripley Castle, reputedly furnished from castle's attics. Comfy, unique rooms, some in courtyard or adjacent house. The Restaurant, in deep burgundy, has period paintings. The Bistro boasts impressive flagged floors.

RIPLEY – Surrey – **504** S 30 – pop. 2 041   7 **C1**
> London 28 mi – Guildford 6 mi

🍴🍴🍴 **Drake's** (Steve Drake)
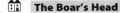
The Clock House, High St ⊠ GU23 6AQ – ℰ (01483) 224 777
– www.drakesrestaurant.co.uk – Fax (01483) 222940 – Closed Christmas, 2 weeks August, 10 days January, Saturday lunch, Sunday and Monday
Rest – Menu £ 26/46
Spec. Salad of pigeon, onion tart, beetroot and chicory vinaigrette. Sea bass, foaming vanilla and saffron butter sauce. Blueberry and ginger leather, lavender parfait and blueberry ice cream.
♦ Georgian restaurant's red brick façade dominated by large clock. Relaxing, open plan dining room with local gallery art on walls. Precise, classical cooking. Formal service.

RIPON – North Yorkshire – **502** P 21 – **pop. 16 468** ▮ *Great Britain*   22 **B2**

- ◪ London 222 mi – Leeds 26 mi – Middlesbrough 35 mi – York 23 mi
- 🄸 Minster Rd ℰ (01765) 604625, ripontic@harrogate.gov.uk
- 🛝 Ripon City Palace Rd, ℰ (01765) 603 640
- ◉ Town★ – Cathedral★★ (Saxon Crypt) **AC**
- 🄶 Fountains Abbey★★★ **AC** :- Studley Royal **AC** (⩽★ from Anne Boleyn's Seat) - Fountains Hall (Fa½ade★), SW : 2½ m. by B 6265 – Newby Hall (Tapestries★) **AC**, SE : 3½ m. by B 6265

🏠🄰 **The Old Deanery**   ⬚ 📶 🕭 🄰 **P** *VISA* **OO** **AE**

Minster Rd ⊠ *HG4 1QS – ℰ (01765) 600 003 – www.theolddeanery.co.uk*
– reception@theolddeanery.co.uk – Fax (01765) 600027 – Closed 25 December
11 rm 🖙 – †£110/120 ††£160/180
Rest – (closed Sunday dinner) Menu £16/33 – Carte lunch approx. £20
♦ Eponymously named hotel opposite cathedral. Stylish interior blends seamlessly with older charms. Afternoon tea in secluded garden. 18C oak staircase leads to modern rooms. Appealing seasonal cooking in spacious dining room.

↑ **Sharow Cross House**   ⬚ 🎨 **P**

Dishforth Rd, Sharow, Northeast : 1¾ m. by A 61 on Sharow rd ⊠ *HG4 5BQ*
– ℰ (01765) 609 866 – www.sharowcrosshouse.com
– sharowcrosshouse@btinternet.com – Closed 2 weeks Christmas and New Year
3 rm 🖙 – †£55/75 ††£75/85   **Rest** – (by arrangement) Menu £22
♦ Idyllically set 19C house, built for mill owner. Capacious hall with welcoming fire. Spacious bedrooms: the master room is huge and offers Cathedral views on clear days.

---

at Aldfield Southwest : 3¾ m. by B 6265 – ⊠ Ripon

↑ **Bay Tree Farm** 🌿   ⬚ 🕭 rm, **P** *VISA* **OO**

⊠ *HG4 3BE – ℰ (01765) 620 394 – www.baytreefarm.co.uk*
– val@btfarm.entadsl.com – Fax (01765) 620 394
6 rm 🖙 – †£40/60 ††£78   **Rest** – (by arrangement) Menu £17
♦ 18C sandstone barn with rural views, set on a working farm. Lounge with wood burning stove and French windows opening into garden; bright, spacious bedrooms with modern bathrooms. Homely food could include beef from the farm.

RISHWORTH – W. Yorks. – see Sowerby Bridge

ROADE – Northamptonshire – **504** R 27 – **pop. 2 254**   16 **B3**

- ◪ London 66 mi – Coventry 36 mi – Leicester 42 mi – Northampton 5 mi

---

✗✗ **Roade House** with rm   **AC** rest, 🎨 📶 **P** *VISA* **OO** **AE**

16 High St ⊠ *NN7 2NW – ℰ (01604) 863 372 – www.roadehousehotel.co.uk*
– info@roadehousehotel.co.uk – Fax (01604) 862 421 – Closed 1 week
Christmas-New Year
10 rm 🖙 – †£65/80 ††£75/88
Rest – (closed Saturday lunch, Sunday dinner and Bank Holidays)
Menu £25/42
♦ Personally run converted schoolhouse with comfortable bedrooms. Uncluttered, beamed dining room. Classic, seasonally based dishes with modern international elements.

ROCHDALE – Greater Manchester – **502** N 23 – **pop. 95 796**   20 **B2**

- ◪ London 224 mi – Blackpool 40 mi – Burnley 11 mi – Leeds 45 mi
  – Liverpool 40 mi – Manchester 12 mi
- 🄸 The Clock Tower, Town Hall ℰ (01706) 356592
- 🛝 Bagslate Edenfield Rd, ℰ (01706) 643 818
- 🛝 Marland Bolton Rd, Springfield Park, ℰ (01706) 649 801
- 🛝 Castle Hawk Castleton Chadwick Lane, ℰ (01706) 640 841

ENGLAND

XX **Nutters** ← ⟡ P VISA ◑◐ AE
Edenfield Rd, Norden, West : 3½ m. on A 680 ⊠ *OL12 7TT –* ℰ *(01706) 650 167*
– www.nuttersrestaurant.com – enquiries@nuttersrestaurant.com – Fax (01706)
650 167 – Closed 26-27 December, 2-3 January and Monday
Rest – Menu £17/35 – Carte £26/38
♦ Views of the lyrical gardens contrast with a menu of often complex modern British dishes with international twists and influences. Best views at either end of the room.

ROCHESTER – Medway – **504** V 29 – **pop. 27 125** – ⊠ **Chatham**   8 **B1**
▌ *Great Britain*

■ London 30 mi – Dover 45 mi – Maidstone 8 mi – Margate 46 mi
🅱 95 High St ℰ (01634) 843666, visitor.centre@medway.gov.uk
◉ Castle ★ **AC** – Cathedral ★ **AC**
ⓖ World Naval Base ★★, Chatham, NE : 2. m. of the Cathedral. Leeds Castle ★, SE : 11. m. by A 229 and M 20

🏠 **Bridgewood Manor** ▢ ◍ ⌂ ℒₔ ✗ 🛏 ⅆ rm, 🅰 rest, ✗ ⑂ 🛋
Bridgewood Roundabout, Southeast : 3. m. by A 2 and   P VISA ◑◐ AE ⓪
A 229 on Walderslade rd ⊠ *ME5 9AX –* ℰ *(01634) 201 333 – www.qhotels.co.uk*
– stay@qhotels.co.uk – Fax (01634) 201 330
96 rm ⮂ – ♦£115 ♦♦£125 – 4 suites
Rest *Squires* – Carte £27/44
♦ Purpose-built hotel with central courtyard and fitted modern interior. Bedrooms have a well-kept, comfortable feel. Geared to business travellers. Imposingly formal Squires.

ROCK – Cornwall – **503** F 32 – **pop. 4 593** – ⊠ **Wadebridge**   1 **B2**

■ London 266 mi – Newquay 24 mi – Tintagel 14 mi – Truro 32 mi
ⓖ Pencarrow ★, SE : 8½ m. by B 3314 and A 389

🏠 **St Enodoc** ← 🚗 ⌂ 🛝 ◍ ✗ ⑂ P VISA ◑◐ AE
⊠ *PL27 6LA –* ℰ *(01208) 863 394 – www.enodoc-hotel.co.uk*
– info@enodoc-hotel.co.uk – Fax (01208) 863 970
– Closed 15 December - 2 February
16 rm ⮂ – ♦£115/185 ♦♦£170/235 – 4 suites
Rest *Restaurant* – (light lunch) Carte £32/42
♦ A refreshingly modern take on the seaside hotel; neutral fabrics, sandwashed pine and contemporary oil paintings in stylish rooms, many facing the Camel Estuary.

XX **L'Estuaire** 🏠 VISA ◑◐
Rock Rd ⊠ *PL27 6JS –* ℰ *(01208) 862 622 – www.lestuairerestaurant.com*
– Fax (01208) 862 622 – Closed Christmas, 2 weeks January, 2 weeks November
and Monday-Tuesday except Bank Holidays
Rest – (booking advisable) Menu £23 (lunch) – Carte £29/55
♦ Oddly shaped building has been a dance hall and garage in its day! Now a family run restaurant, its tastefully restrained interior is matched by serious modern French menus.

---

at Trebetherick North : 1. m. by Trewint Lane – **503** F 32

🏠 **St Moritz** ← 🚗 ▢ ◍ 🛝 ℒₔ 🛏 ✗ ⑂ P VISA ◑◐ ⓪
Trebetherick ⊠ *PL27 6SD –* ℰ *(01208) 862 242 – www.stmoritzhotel.co.uk*
– reception@stmoritzhotel.co.uk – Fax (01208) 862 262
32 rm ⮂ – ♦£71/135 ♦♦£95/200 – 16 suites
Rest – (closed January-late March) Carte £24/37
♦ Art deco style hotel with leisure club, swimming pool and 6 room spa. Smartly furnished bedrooms; spacious bathrooms. Suites have a lounge, kitchen and estuary views. Restaurant displays a simple, flavoursome menu of unfussy dishes.

ROCKBEARE – Devon – see Exeter

ENGLAND

ROGATE – West Sussex – **504** R 30 – ⊠ Petersfield (Hants.)   7 **C2**

> ◻ London 63 mi – Brighton 42 mi – Guildford 29 mi – Portsmouth 23 mi
> – Southampton 36 mi

⛫ **Mizzards Farm** without rest ⌂   ≼ 🚗 🕐 ⤮ ⚑ 📶 **P**
Southwest : 1 m. by Harting rd ⊠ *GU31 5HS –* ☏ *(01730) 821656*
– francis@mizzards.co.uk – Fax (01730) 821655 – Minimum 2 night stay, closed
Christmas and New Year
3 rm ⌂ – ♦£50/55 ♦♦£88
♦ 17C farmhouse with delightful landscaped gardens, which include a lake, bordered
by river Rother. Views of woods and farmland. Fine fabrics and antiques in appealing
rooms.

ROMALDKIRK – Durham – **502** N 20 – **see Barnard Castle**

ROMSEY – Hampshire – **503** P 31 – **pop. 17 386** ▌ *Great Britain*   6 **A2**

> ◻ London 82 mi – Bournemouth 28 mi – Salisbury 16 mi – Southampton 8 mi
> – Winchester 10 mi
> 🛈 13 Church St ☏ (01794) 512987, romseytic@testvalley.gov.uk
> 🖥 Dunwood Manor Awbridge Danes Rd, ☏ (01794) 340549
> 🖥 Nursling, ☏ (023) 8073 4637
> 🖥 Wellow East Wellow Ryedown Lane, ☏ (01794) 322872
> 👁 Abbey★ (interior★★)
> ⓒ Broadlands★ **AC**, S : 1 m

⛫ **Ranvilles Farm House** without rest   🚗 **P**
Ower, Southwest : 2 m. on A 3090 (southbound carriageway) ⊠ *SO51 6AA*
– ☏ *(023) 8081 4481 – www.ranvilles.com – info@ranvilles.com – Fax (023)*
8081 4481
5 rm ⌂ – ♦£30/40 ♦♦£55/70
♦ Attractive part 16C farmhouse set within five acres of garden and fields. Welcoming
country style décor and furniture throughout, including the well-kept bedrooms.

⛫ **Highfield House** ⌂   🚗 ⚑ 📶 **P**
Newtown Rd, Awbridge, Northwest : 3½ m. by A 3090 (old A 31) and A 27
⊠ *SO51 0GG –* ☏ *(01794) 340727 – highfield_house@btinternet.com*
– Fax (01794) 340727
3 rm ⌂ – ♦£50/60 ♦♦£80
Rest – (by arrangement, communal dining) Menu £18
♦ Modern house with gardens, in a tranquil location just out of Awbridge village.
Accommodation is comfortable with good facilities. Real fires in the guest lounge.
Communal dining with garden views.

🍴 **The Three Tuns**   🍴 **P** **VISA** **◍◍** **AE**
58 Middlebridge St ⊠ *SO51 8HL –* ☏ *(01794) 512639*
– www.thethreetunsromsey.co.uk – Closed 26 December and Monday lunch
Rest – Carte £15/27
♦ Cosy period feel in thickly beamed, 300-year-old pub. Lunch menus offer pub
favourites, while the evening à la carte moves things up a notch. Friendly service and
real ales.

ROSS-ON-WYE – County of Herefordshire – **503** M 28 – **pop. 10 085**   18 **B3**
▌ *Great Britain*

> ◻ London 118 mi – Gloucester 15 mi – Hereford 15 mi – Newport 35 mi
> 🛈 Swan House, Edde Cross St ☏ (01989) 562768,
> tic-ross@herefordshire.gov.uk
> 👁 Market House★ – Yat Rock (≼★)
> ⓒ SW : Wye Valley★ – Goodrich Castle★ **AC**, SW : 3½ m. by A 40

The Chase 🛏 ⚿ 📶 ♿ 🅿 VISA ⓐ AE ⓞ
Gloucester Rd ⊠ HR9 5LH – 𝒞 (01989) 763 161 – www.chasehotel.co.uk
– res@chasehotel.co.uk – Fax (01989) 768 330 – Closed 24-27 December
36 rm ⊊ – †£90 ††£195   **Rest** – Carte £26/40
♦ Elegant Georgian country house, close to town centre. Ground floor areas have been given a contemporary makeover. Range of bedroom styles with traditional décor. Restaurant exudes airy, period feel.

Wilton Court 🛏 📶 🅿 VISA ⓐ AE
Wilton Lane, West : ¾ m. by B 4260 (A 49 Hereford) ⊠ HR9 6AQ – 𝒞 (01989) 562 569 – www.wiltoncourthotel.com – info@wiltoncourthotel.com – Fax (01989) 768 460
10 rm ⊊ – †£80/125 ††£95/145
Rest *Mulberry* – (dinner only and Sunday lunch) Menu £16 – Carte £24/35
♦ Attractive, part-Elizabethan house on the banks of the river Wye. 16C wood panelling in situ in bar and two of the bedrooms: others have a distinctly William Morris influence. Light, airy conservatory restaurant boasts Lloyd Loom furniture and garden views.

The Bridge at Wilton with rm 🛏 ⚲ 🅿 VISA ⓐ AE
Wilton ⊠ HR9 6AA – 𝒞 (01989) 562 655 – www.bridge-house-hotel.com – info@bridge-house-hotel.com – Fax (01989) 567 652
9 rm ⊊ – †£80 ††£120   **Rest** – Menu £20 (lunch) – Carte (dinner) £30/45
♦ On the banks of the Wye, boasting a kitchen garden supplying ingredients for the owners' passionate belief in home cooking. Also, a homely bar and well-maintained bedrooms.

The Lough Pool at Sellack 🛏 📶 🅿 VISA ⓐ
Sellack, Northwest : 3¼ m. by B 4260 and A 49 on Hoarwithy rd ⊠ HR9 6LX – 𝒞 (01989) 730 236 – www.loughpoolinn.co.uk – david@loughpool.co.uk – Fax (01981) 570 322 – Closed 25 December, January-March, Sunday dinner and Monday in November
Rest – Carte £18/27
♦ Characterful 16C black and white timbered inn, set in a beautiful, rural spot. Great value traditional menu changes daily, featuring fresh, local produce from just down the road.

Mill Race 🅿 VISA ⓐ AE
Walford, Ross-on-Wye ⊠ HR9 5QS – 𝒞 (01989) 562 891 – www.millrace.info – enquiries@millrace.info
Rest – Carte £20/40
♦ Spacious, modern pub with large terrace and regular events. Seasonal British menu focuses on simplicity, with the sourcing of humanely reared, sustainable produce being paramount.

at Glewstone Southwest : 3¼ m. by A 40 – ⊠ Ross-on-Wye

Glewstone Court ⇐ 🛏 📶 🅿 VISA ⓐ AE
⊠ HR9 6AW – 𝒞 (01989) 770 367 – www.glewstonecourt.com – glewstone@aol.com – Fax (01989) 770 282 – Closed 25-27 December
8 rm ⊊ – †£58/82 ††£123   **Rest** – Menu £17 (lunch) – Carte £28/35
♦ Part Georgian and Victorian country house with impressive cedar of Lebanon in grounds. Sweeping staircase leads to uncluttered rooms. Family run with charming eccentricity. Antique-strewn dining room.

at Kerne Bridge South : 3¾ m. on B 4234 – ⊠ Ross-on-Wye

Lumleys without rest 🛏 🅿
⊠ HR9 5QT – 𝒞 (01600) 890 040 – www.thelumleys.co.uk – helenmattis@tiscali.co.uk
3 rm ⊊ – †£50 ††£70
♦ Welcoming and personally run guesthouse in sympathetically converted Victorian house. Ideally located for Wye valley and Forest of Dean. Pine decorated cottage style rooms.

ENGLAND

ROSTHWAITE – Cumbria – **502** K 20 – see Keswick

ROTHBURY – Northumberland – **501** O 18 – pop. 1 963 – ✉ Morpeth   24 **A2**

Great Britain

▶ London 311 mi – Edinburgh 84 mi – Newcastle upon Tyne 29 mi

🛈 National Park Centre, Church House, Church St ☏ (01669) 620887,
tic.rothbury@nnpa.org.uk

◎ Cragside House★ (interior★) AC

⌂ **Farm Cottage** without rest   🔲 ⚞ P VISA ◍ AE
Thropton, West : 2¼ m. on B 6341 ✉ NE65 7NA – ☏ (01669) 620 831
– www.farmcottageguesthouse.co.uk – joan@farmcottageguesthouse.co.uk
– Fax (01669) 620 831 – Closed 24 December - 2 January
5 rm � – ♦£50/65 ♦♦£80/84
◆ 18C stone cottage and gardens; owner was actually born here. Two comfy lounges filled with family prints and curios. Individually styled rooms with plenty of extra touches.

⌂ **Thropton Demesne Farmhouse** 🌄   ⪡ 🔲 ⚞ P
Thropton, West : 2¼ m. on B 6341 ✉ NE65 7LT – ☏ (01669) 620 196
– www.throptondemesne.co.uk – thropton_demesne@yahoo.co.uk
– March-October
5 rm ⊆ – ♦£60 ♦♦£70   **Rest** – (by arrangement) Menu £18
◆ Early 19C stone-built former farmhouse; unbroken Coquet Valley views. Lounge defined by quality décor. Artwork on walls by owner. Individually styled rooms with lovely vistas. Home cooked dinners crafted from fresh, local ingredients.

⌂ **Lee Farm** without rest 🌄   ⪡ 🔲 ⟲ P
South : 3¼ m. by B 6342 on The Lee rd ✉ NE65 8JQ – ☏ (01665) 570 257
– www.leefarm.co.uk – enqs@leefarm.co.uk – Fax (01665) 570 257 – March -
November
3 rm ⊆ – ♦£50 ♦♦£75/80
◆ Family-run house in a peaceful valley; firelit lounge, trim, pretty rooms in pastel tones, breakfasts at a communal table. Guests are free to explore the livestock farm.

ROTHERFIELD PEPPARD – Oxfordshire – pop. 2 105   11 **C3**
– ✉ Henley-on-Thames

▶ London 41 mi – Henley-on-Thames 4 mi – Oxford 22 mi

🍴 **The Greyhound**   ⚞ P VISA ◍
Gallowstree Rd ✉ RG9 5HT – ☏ (01189) 722 227 – www.awtrestaurants.com
– greyhound@awtrestaurants.com – Fax (01189) 242 975
– Closed dinner 25-26 December and 1 January
Rest – (booking essential) Carte £35/55
◆ Characterful 17C pub on edge of picturesque village. Small bar, more formal dining and barn extension with exposed timbers and animal heads. Aberdeen Angus steak a speciality.

ROTHERHAM – South Yorkshire – **502** P 23 – pop. 117 262   22 **B3**

▶ London 166 mi – Kingston-upon-Hull 61 mi – Leeds 36 mi – Sheffield 6 mi

🛈 40 Bridgegate ☏ (01709) 835904, tic@rotherham.gov.uk

🝞 Thrybergh Park, ☏ (01709) 850 466

🝞 Grange Park Kimberworth Upper Wortley Rd, ☏ (01709) 558 884

🝞 Phoenix Brinsworth Pavilion Lane, ☏ (01709) 363 788

at Bramley East : 4½ m. by A 6021 off A 631 – ✉ Rotherham

🏨 **Elton**   ⅗ rm, 🔳 rest, ⁇ 🛎 P VISA ◍ AE ◉
Main St, Bramley ✉ S66 2SF – ☏ (01709) 545 681 – www.bw-eltonhotel.co.uk
– bestwestern.eltonhotel@btinternet.com – Fax (01709) 549 100
29 rm ⊆ – ♦£60/75 ♦♦£86/116
Rest – (closed dinner 25 December) Menu £14/21 – Carte £23/27
◆ Solid stone house with extensions, in the centre of village. Traditionally styled public areas include conservatory lounge. Extension rooms have a more modern style. Richly styled dining room with warm burgundy walls.

ENGLAND

ROUGHAM GREEN – Suffolk – see Bury St Edmunds

ROWDE – Wilts. – **503** N 29 – see Devizes

ROWHOOK – W. Sussex – see Horsham

ROWSLEY – Derbyshire – **502** P 24 – ⊠ Matlock ▌ *Great Britain*   16 **A1**
  ▶ London 157 mi – Derby 23 mi – Manchester 40 mi – Nottingham 30 mi
  ◙ Chatsworth★★★ (Park and Garden★★★) **AC**, N : by B 6012

🏠 **East Lodge** ⚘   ⬛ ⬛ ⬛ ⬛ & rm, Ⓚ rest, ❄ 🅿 🅟 VISA ⓶ⓔ ⒶⒺ
  ⊠ DE4 2EF – ℰ (01629) 734474 – www.eastlodge.com – info@eastlodge.com
  – Fax (01629) 733949
  12 rm ⊒ – ♦£120 ♦♦£250/350   **Rest** – Carte £30/43
  ◆ Elegant 17C country house set in ten acres of well kept grounds, once the lodge to
  Haddon Hall. Rooms are each individually decorated and superior rooms have garden
  views. Simple dining room with terrace.

🏠 **The Peacock**   ⬛ ⬛ ⬛ 🅿 VISA ⓶ⓔ ⒶⒺ ⓞ
  Bakewell Rd ⊠ DE4 2EB – ℰ (01629) 733518 – www.thepeacockatrowsley.com
  – reception@thepeacockatrowsley.com – Fax (01629) 732671 – Closed 24-26
  December
  16 rm – ♦£95/175 ♦♦£175/210, ⊒ £6.95   **Rest** – Carte £38/49
  ◆ Characterful, antique furnished, 17C house with gardens leading down to the river
  Derwent. Rooms, a variety of shapes and sizes, are antique or reproduction furnished.
  Restaurant divided between three smart rooms.

ROWTON – Ches. – see Chester

ROYAL LEAMINGTON SPA – Warwickshire – **503** P 27 – pop. 61595   19 **D3**
  ▶ London 99 mi – Birmingham 23 mi – Coventry 9 mi – Leicester 33 mi
    – Warwick 3 mi
  🛈 The Royal Pump Rooms, The Parade ℰ (01926) 742762
  🔟 Leamington and County Whitnash Golf Lane, ℰ (01926) 425961

ROYAL LEAMINGTON SPA

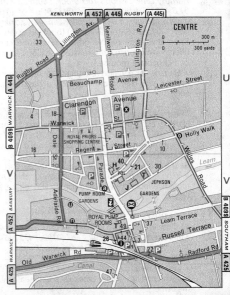

ENGLAND

Mallory Court 🕭   🚅 ※ 🗐 & ⚴ ⟨ᵗᵖ⟩ 🖒 🅿 VISA ⦿ AE ⓪

Harbury Lane, Bishop's Tachbrook, South : 2¼ m. by B 4087 (Tachbrook Rd)
✉ CV33 9QB – ℰ (01926) 330 214 – www.mallory.co.uk
– reception@mallory.co.uk – Fax (01926) 451 714
30 rm ☑ – ♔£135/145 ♔♔£365
Rest *The Dining Room* and *The Brasserie at Mallory* – see restaurant listing
♦ Part Edwardian country house in Lutyens style; extensive landscaped gardens.
Finest quality antiques and furnishings throughout public areas and individually
styled bedrooms.

Episode   🚅 ⟨ᵗᵖ⟩ 🖒 🅿 VISA ⦿ AE

64 Upper Holly Walk ✉ CV32 4JL – ℰ (01926) 883 777
– www.episodehotels.com – leamington@episodehotels.co.uk
– Fax (01926) 330 467   U**o**
32 rm ☑ – ♔£75/95 ♔♔£95/105   **Rest** – Menu £15 (lunch) – Carte £21/36
♦ Characterful Victorian house with spacious and well-decorated interior featuring
high ceilings and parquet flooring. Good comfort levels in the sizeable bedrooms.
Bistro dining room has smart, elegant, period feel.

Adams without rest   🚅 ※ ⟨ᵗᵖ⟩ 🅿 VISA ⦿

22 Avenue Rd ✉ CV31 3PQ – ℰ (01926) 450 742 – www.adams-hotel.co.uk
– bookings@adams-hotel.co.uk – Fax (01926) 313 110
– Closed 2 weeks Christmas and New Year   V**n**
14 rm ☑ – ♔£70/85 ♔♔£85/90
♦ Delightful house of the Regency period with plenty of charm and character: original features include ceiling mouldings. Immaculate and similarly attractive bedrooms.

York House without rest   ⟨ᵗᵖ⟩ VISA ⦿

9 York Rd ✉ CV31 3PR – ℰ (01926) 424 671 – www.yorkhousehotel.biz
– reservations@yorkhousehotel.biz – Fax (01926) 832 272   V**u**
8 rm ☑ – ♔£36/55 ♔♔£55/70
♦ Victorian house on a pleasant parade, retains characterful fittings such as stained
glass windows. Views of River Leam. Simply furnished rooms in period style.

XXX   The Dining Room – at Mallory Court Hotel   🚅 🛋 ※ & rm, ⇵ 🅿

❀   *Harbury Lane, Bishop's Tachbrook, South : 2¼ m.*   VISA ⦿ AE ⓪
by B 4087 (Tachbrook Rd) ✉ CV33 9QB – ℰ (01926) 330 214
– www.mallory.co.uk – reception@mallory.co.uk – Fax (01926) 451 714
Rest – (closed Saturday lunch) (booking essential) Menu £40 – Carte £40/55
Spec. Ballottine of foie gras, smoked and cured duck, pickled cherries. Cod
fillet with chorizo and roasted scallops. Caramelised banana puff pastry
and chocolate mousse.
♦ Elegant, oak panelled restaurant with terrace overlooking gardens and countryside.
Refined, well-crafted dishes display a classical base combined with an innovative
edge.

XX   The Brasserie at Mallory – at Mallory Court Hotel   🚅 🛋 AC ⇵

Harbury Lane, Bishop's Tachbrook, South : 2¼ m.   🅿 VISA ⦿ AE ⓪
by B 4087 (Tachbrook Rd) ✉ CV33 9QB – ℰ (01926) 453 939
– www.mallory.co.uk – thebrasserie@mallory.co.uk – Fax (01926) 451 714
– Closed Sunday dinner
Rest – (booking essential) Menu £20/25 – Carte £27/36
♦ In hotel annex; step into bar with eye-catching Art Deco style. Conservatory dining
room overlooks pretty walled garden and terrace. Modern British cooking in a buzzy
setting.

XX   Restaurant 23   AC VISA ⦿ AE

23 Dormer Place ✉ CV32 5AA – ℰ (01926) 422 422 – www.restaurant23.co.uk
– info@restaurant23.co.uk – Fax (01926) 422 246 – Closed 25 December, 2 weeks
January, 2 weeks August, Sunday and Monday   V**a**
Rest – Menu £20 (lunch) – Carte £36/39
♦ Ever spoken to a working chef in a restaurant? You can here, in elegantly appointed surroundings, where classically based, seasonal, modern dishes are concocted by
the owner.

Oscar's
☆☆

39 Chandos St ⊠ *CV32 4RL* – ✆ *(01926) 452 807*
– www.oscarsfrenchbistro.co.uk – enquiries@oscarsfrenchbistro.co.uk
– Closed Sunday-Monday   Ux
Rest – (booking essential) Menu £ 16/26
♦ Bustling, informal and unpretentious, set in three rooms on two floors. Good value, accomplished French bistro cooking; notable steak specialities.

The Emperors
☆☆

Bath Place ⊠ *CV31 3BP* – ✆ *(01926) 313 030* – *Fax (01926) 435 966*
– Closed 25-26 December, 1 January and Sunday   Vi
Rest – Chinese – Carte £ 16/22 **s**
♦ Large warehouse conversion adjacent to railway station. Decorated with traditional war banners and framed oriental prints. Authentic, tasty Chinese cuisine.

at Weston under Wetherley Northeast : 4 ½ m. by A 445 on B 4453 – ⊠ **Royal Leamington Spa**

Wethele Manor Farm without rest ❧
⚐

⊠ *CV33 9BZ* – ✆ *(01926) 831 772* – *www.wethelemanor.com*
– simonmoreton@wethelemanor.com – Fax (01926) 315 359
9 rm ☲ – ♦£ 65/75 ♦♦£ 80/95
♦ Lovingly restored manor house with individually furnished, characterful bedrooms, low beams and uneven boards. Breakfast room incorporates an old well. Welcoming feel.

ROYAL TUNBRIDGE WELLS – Kent – 504 U 30 – pop. 60 095   8 B2
▌ Great Britain

> ▪ London 36 mi – Brighton 33 mi – Folkestone 46 mi – Hastings 27 mi
>   – Maidstone 18 mi
> ▪ The Old Fish Market, The Pantiles ✆ (01892) 515 675,
>   touristinformationcentre@tunbridgewells.gov.uk
> ▪ Langton Rd, ✆ (01892) 523 034
> ▪ The Pantiles ★ B **26** – Calverley Park ★ B

Plan on next page

Hotel du Vin
🏨

Crescent Rd ⊠ *TN1 2LY* – ✆ *(01892) 526 455* – *www.hotelduvin.com*
– reception.tunbridgewells@hotelduvin.com – Fax (01892) 512 044   Bc
34 rm – ♦£ 120 ♦♦£ 190, ☲ £ 13.50
Rest *Bistro* – see restaurant listing
♦ Delightful Georgian house with a contemporary styled interior themed around wine; provides a stylish, comfortable feel throughout. Occasional wine-based events.

Danehurst without rest
⚐

41 Lower Green Rd, Rusthall, West : 1 ¾ m. by A 264 ⊠ *TN4 8TW* – ✆ *(01892)*
527 739 – www.danehurst.net – info@danehurst.net – Fax (01892) 514 804
– Closed 1-14 February, 25 December   Ae
5 rm ☲ – ♦£ 60/80 ♦♦£ 100
♦ Victorian family home, with koi carp in the garden, located in residential area of town. Mix of homely furniture and furnishings and a conservatory breakfast room.

Thackeray's
☆☆

85 London Rd ⊠ *TN1 1EA* – ✆ *(01892) 511 921*
– www.thackeraysrestaurant.co.uk – reservations@thackerays-restaurant.co.uk
– Fax (01892) 527 561 – Closed 26-28 December, Monday and Sunday dinner   Bn
Rest – Menu £ 18/27 – Carte £ 41/50
♦ Grade II listed 17C house with handsome Oriental terrace. Modern interior contrasts pleasingly with façade. The classically based cooking employs first rate ingredients.

ENGLAND

Benhall Mill Rd	A 3	Hall's Hole Rd	A 13	Pantiles (The)	B 26
Bishop's Down	A 4	High Rocks Lane	A 16	Prospect Rd	A 27
Calverley Rd	B	High St	B 14	Royal Victoria Pl. Shopping Centre	B
Crescent Rd	B 9	Hungershall Park Rd	A 17		
Fir Tree Rd	A 10	Lansdowne Rd	B 18	Rusthall Rd	A 28
Grosvenor Rd	B 12	Lower Green Rd	A 20	St John's Rd	B 29
		Major York's Rd	A 21	Tea Garden Lane	B 30
		Monson Rd	B 22	Vale Rd	B 33
		Mount Ephraim	A, B 23	Victoria Rd	B 34
		Mount Ephraim Rd	B 24	Warwick Park	B 35
		Mount Pleasant Rd	B 25		

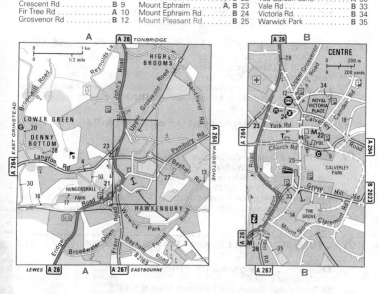

Bistro – at Hotel du Vin

TN1 2LY – ℰ (01892) 526 455 – Fax (01892) 512 044
Rest – (booking essential) Carte £ 23/39

Bc

♦ Classically styled with dark wood floors and furniture and wine memorabilia. Terrace for lunch. Interesting modern menu. Informal and efficient service.

Brasserie Blanc

Fiveways, Lime Hill Rd ⊠ TN1 1LJ – ℰ (01892) 559 170
– www.brasserieblanc.com – tunbridgewells@brasserieblanc.com – Fax (01892) 559 171 – Closed 25 December

Bx

Rest – French – Menu £ 14 – Carte £ 18/47

♦ Simple, modern décor: banquette seats and full-length glass windows. Extensive selection of menus with a French base, prepared with trademark Blanc expertise.

at Speldhurst North : 3½ m. by A 26 - A – ⊠ Royal Tunbridge Wells

George & Dragon

Speldhurst Hill ⊠ TN3 0NN – ℰ (01892) 863 125 – www.speldhurst.com
– julian@leefe-griffiths.freeserve.co.uk – Fax (01892) 863 216
– Closed 25 December, 1 January
Rest – (Closed Sunday dinner) Carte £ 20/28

♦ Warm and welcoming 13C pub with lovely terrace. Cooking is rustic and forthright, and they're proud of the range and quality of their local ingredients; heart-warming puddings.

ROZEL BAY – 503 P 33 – see Channel Islands (Jersey)

RUAN-HIGH-LANES – Cornwall – 503 F 33 – see Veryan

▶ London 285 mi – Middlesbrough 24 mi – Whitby 9 mi

Cliffemount   ⟨ 🚗 **P** _VISA_ ⓪⓪
⊠ TS13 5HU – ☏ (01947) 840 103 – www.cliffemounthotel.co.uk
– info@cliffemounthotel.co.uk – Fax (01947) 841 025
20 rm ⌂ – †£50/75 ††£135   **Rest** – Carte £18/33

♦ Enviably located hotel which has benefitted hugely from refurbishment. Cosy bar with blackboard menu. Balanced mix of luxurious or cosy bedrooms, 10 of which have balconies. Light, airy dining room boasts fantastic views of bay. Strong seafood base.

RUSHLAKE GREEN – East Sussex – **504** U 31 – ⊠ Heathfield   8 **B2**

▶ London 54 mi – Brighton 26 mi – Eastbourne 13 mi

Stone House ⌂   ⟨ 🚗 🅿 ⟩ ⟨ʷ⟩ **P** _VISA_ ⓪⓪
Northeast corner of the green ⊠ TN21 9QJ – ☏ (01435) 830 553
– www.stonehousesussex.co.uk – Fax (01435) 830 726 – Closed last week
February, first week March, 24 December-3 January
5 rm ⌂ – †£110/140 ††£199/260 – 1 suite
Rest – (dinner only lunch May-August) (residents only.) Menu £28 **s**

♦ Charming part 15C, part Georgian country house surrounded by parkland. All interiors delightfully furnished with antiques and fine art. Garden produce features on menu.

RUSHTON – Northants. – see Kettering

RYE – East Sussex – **504** W 31 – **pop. 3 708** ▯ Great Britain   9 **C2**

▶ London 61 mi – Brighton 49 mi – Folkestone 27 mi – Maidstone 33 mi
🛈 The Heritage Centre, Strand Quay ☏ (01797) 226696, ryetic@rother.gov.uk
◉ Old Town★★ : Mermaid Street★, St Mary's Church (⟨★)

The George in Rye   🏠 ⟨̷ ⟨ʷ⟩ 🧖 _VISA_ ⓪⓪ _AE_ ①
98 High St ⊠ TN31 7JT – ☏ (01797) 222 114 – www.thegeorgeinrye.com
– Fax (01797) 224 065
24 rm ⌂ – †£95 ††£175
Rest – Menu £15 (lunch) – Carte (dinner) £25/35 ▒

♦ Part 16C coaching inn; appealing mix of contemporary design and original features. Variously-sized bedrooms have state-of-the-art TVs and quality linen. Pleasant courtyard. Trendy restaurant offers Mediterranean dishes made with locally sourced produce and good choice of wines by glass.

Mermaid Inn   ⟨̷ ⟨ʷ⟩ **P** _VISA_ ⓪⓪ _AE_
Mermaid St ⊠ TN31 7EY – ☏ (01797) 223 065 – www.mermaidinn.com
– info@mermaidinn.com – Fax (01797) 225 069
31 rm ⌂ – †£68/95 ††£150/170   **Rest** – Menu £24/40 – Carte £36/56

♦ Historic inn dating from 15C. Immense character from the timbered exterior on a cobbled street to the heavily beamed, antique furnished interior warmed by roaring log fires. Two dining options: both exude age and character.

Rye Lodge   ▯ ⟨̷ ⟨ʷ⟩ **P** _VISA_ ⓪⓪ _AE_ ①
Hilders Cliff ⊠ TN31 7LD – ☏ (01797) 223 838 – www.ryelodge.co.uk
– info@ryelodge.co.uk – Fax (01797) 223 585
18 rm ⌂ – †£75/105 ††£110/220
Rest – (dinner only) Menu £30 **s** – Carte £26/35 **s**

♦ Family run house located close to historic town centre yet with Romney Marsh in sight. Welcoming guest areas and comfortable, smartly fitted rooms. Enjoy dining in candlelight.

Jeake's House without rest   **P** _VISA_ ⓪⓪
Mermaid St ⊠ TN31 7ET – ☏ (01797) 222 828 – www.jeakeshouse.com
– stay@jeakeshouse.com – Fax (01797) 222 623
11 rm ⌂ – †£70/79 ††£126

♦ Down a cobbled lane, a part 17C house, once a wool store and a Quaker meeting place. Welcoming atmosphere amid antiques, sloping floors and beams. Pretty, traditional rooms.

ENGLAND

⌂ **Oaklands** without rest ⌂   ⟨ ⧉ ✎ **P** VISA ◑◐
Udimore Rd, Southwest : 1 ¼ m. on B 2089 ✉ *TN31 6AB* – ✆ *(01797) 229 734*
– www.oaklands-rye.co.uk – info@oaklands-rye.co.uk – Fax (01797) 229 734
– Closed January
3 rm ⌒ – †£60/70 ††£84/95
♦ Restored Edwardian guest house with countryside views and welcoming hosts. Stylish breakfast room with old Arabic door as table. Spotless bedrooms include two four posters.

⌂ **Durrant House** without rest   ⧉ ✎ VISA ◑◐
2 Market St ✉ *TN31 7LA* – ✆ *(01797) 223 182 – www.durranthouse.com*
– info@durranthouse.com
5 rm ⌒ – †£78 ††£115
♦ Grade I listed house of unknown age. Neat breakfast room with daily breakfast specials. Bright lounge looks down East Street. Carefully appointed, immaculate modern rooms.

⌂ **Willow Tree House** without rest   ⧉ ✎ ⸙ **P** VISA ◑◐
113 Winchelsea Road, South ½ mile on A259 ✉ *TN31 7EL* – ✆ *(01797) 227 820*
– www.willow-tree-house.com – info@willow-tree-house.com
6 rm ⌒ – †£70/85 ††£80/120
♦ Lovingly restored 18C house close to harbour. Light colours and modern fabrics sit beside exposed brickwork and original fireplaces. Bedrooms boast excellent bathrooms with power showers. Good breakfasts.

✗✗ **Flushing Inn**   VISA ◑◐
4 Market St ✉ *TN31 7LA* – ✆ *(01797) 223 292 – www.theflushinginn.com*
– j.e.flynn@btconnect.com – Closed first two weeks January, first two weeks June, Monday and Tuesday
Rest – Seafood – Menu £ 19 (lunch) – Carte £ 21/44
♦ A neighbourhood institution, this 15C inn with heavily timbered and panelled dining area features a superb 16C fresco. The seafood oriented menu has a local, traditional tone.

✗ **Webbes at The Fish Café**   Ⓚ ⇄ VISA ◑◐ Ⓐ
17 Tower St ✉ *TN31 7AT* – ✆ *(01797) 222 226 – www.thefishcafe.com*
– info@thefishcafe.com – Fax (01797) 229 260 – Closed 3 days at Christmas
Rest – Seafood – (closed Monday November-April) (booking essential at dinner) Carte £ 27/33 **s**
♦ Large converted warehouse: terracotta painted ground floor for seafood lunches and eclectic options. Dinner upstairs features more serious piscine menus. Tangible buzziness.

🍴 **Globe Inn**   **P** VISA Ⓐ
10 Military Rd, North : 1/4 m. off A 268 ✉ *TN31 7NX* – ✆ *(01797) 227 918*
– www.theglobe-inn.com – info@theglobe-inn.com
Rest – (Closed Sunday dinner and Monday; October-June Tuesday) (booking essential) Menu £ 16 (lunch) – Carte £ 26/37
♦ Modern pub boasting leather sofas, displays of homemade goodies and quirky forties furnishings and décor. Modern British menu uses local produce. Homely puddings.

at Camber Southeast : 4 ¼ m. by A 259 – ✉ Rye

⌂ **The Place at the Beach**   ⧉ 🛏 Ⓚ rest, ✎ ⸙ ⻎ **P** VISA ◑◐ Ⓐ
New Lydd Rd, Camber Sands ✉ *TN31 7RB* – ✆ *(01797) 225 057*
– www.theplacecambersands.co.uk – enquiries@theplaceatthebeach.co.uk
– Fax (01797) 227 003 – Closed 25 December
18 rm ⌒ – †£50/110 ††£70/120   **Rest** – Carte £ 20/31
♦ Immaculately whitewashed, converted former seaside motel located over the dunes. Smart, stylish rooms with a good level of facilities and charming extra touches. Informal brasserie style restaurant with emphasis on local ingredients.

▶ London 43 mi – Bishop's Stortford 12 mi – Cambridge 18 mi

✗ **the restaurant**   *VISA* **©©** **AE**
Victoria House, 2 Church St ⊠ *CB10 1JW* – ℰ *(01799) 526 444* – *www.trocs.co.uk*
– reservations@trocs.co.uk – Closed 2 weeks Easter, Sunday and Monday
Rest – (dinner only) Menu £17 (weekdays) – Carte £22/33 **s**
◆ Stylishly converted cellar with an informal feel: candles light the brick and flint
walls and etched glass tables. Original, contemporary menu; relaxed style and service.

✗ **Dish**   *AK* *VISA* **©©**
13a King St ⊠ *CB10 1HE* – ℰ *(01799) 513 300* – *www.dishrestaurant.co.uk*
*– dishrestaurant@btinternet.com – Fax (01799) 531 699 – Closed 25-27 December
and Sunday dinner*
Rest – Menu £16 (lunch)/20 (weekday dinner) – Carte (dinner weekends)
£25/32
◆ First floor restaurant within characterful beamed house in town centre. Modern oil
paintings exude jazzy theme. Classically based dishes take on adventurous note at
dinner.

▶ London 302 mi – Newquay 12 mi – Penzance 26 mi – Truro 9 mi
🏠 Perranporth Budnic Hill, ℰ (01872) 573 701
◎ St Agnes Beacon★★ (❊★★)
◎ Portreath★, SW : 5½ m

🏨 **Rose-in-Vale Country House** ⤸   ⤤ ⅏ **P** *VISA* **©©**
Mithian, East : 2 m. by B 3285 ⊠ *TR5 0QD* – ℰ *(01872) 552 202*
– www.rose-in-vale-hotel.co.uk – reception@rose-in-vale-hotel.co.uk
– Fax (01872) 552 700
18 rm ⊑ – ♦£80/155 ♦♦£100/185 – 1 suite
Rest *The Valley* – (dinner only) Menu £30 **s**
◆ Handsome Georgian manor clad in climbing roses; outdoor pool and peaceful
gardens with summer house and dovecote. Classically styled lounge bar and library;
well-kept rooms. Neat, formal dining room with local specials.

▶ London 27 mi – Cambridge 41 mi – Luton 10 mi
🛈 Town Hall, Market Pl ℰ (01727) 864511, tic@stalbans.gov.uk
🏠 Batchwood Hall Batchwood Drive, ℰ (01727) 833 349
🏠 Redbourn Kinsbourne Green Lane, ℰ (01582) 793 493
◎ City★ - Cathedral★ BZ – Verulamium★ (Museum★ **AC** AY)
◎ Hatfield House★★ **AC**, E : 6 m. by A 1057

Plan on next page

🏨 **Sopwell House** ⤸   🛋 ⅃ 🛀 📺 ⊙ 🛋 ⅙ ♨ **AK** ❊ �📶 ⚗ **P**
Cottonmill Lane, Southeast : 1½ m. by A 1081 and   *VISA* **©©** **AE** **①**
Mile House Lane ⊠ *AL1 2HQ* – ℰ *(01727) 864 477* – *www.sopwellhouse.co.uk*
– enquiries@sopwellhouse.co.uk – Fax (01727) 844 741
127 rm ⊑ – ♦£99/129 ♦♦£169/185 – 2 suites
Rest *The Restaurant* – (Closed Monday, Saturday lunch and Sunday dinner)
Carte £24/42
Rest *The Brasserie* – Carte £23/34
◆ Smart, corporate hotel with pretty gardens. Leather furnished lounge, modern spa
with Japanese treatments, pool and gym. Modern rooms and apartments. Seasonal
modern cooking in The Restaurant. More relaxed Brasserie.

🏨 **St Michael's Manor**   ◁ ⤤ 🛀 rm, ❊ �📶 **P** *VISA* **©©** **AE** **①**
St Michael's Village, Fishpool St ⊠ *AL3 4RY* – ℰ *(01727) 864 444*
– www.stmichaelsmanor.com – reservations@stmichaelsmanor.com
– Fax (01727) 848 909   AYd
29 rm ⊑ – ♦£145 ♦♦£260 – 1 suite   **Rest** – Menu £20/25 – Carte £25/35
◆ This part 16C, part William and Mary manor house overlooks a lake. Elegant bedrooms are named after trees; some are suites with sitting rooms, all are luxurious and
stylish. Conservatory dining room with splendid vistas.

ENGLAND

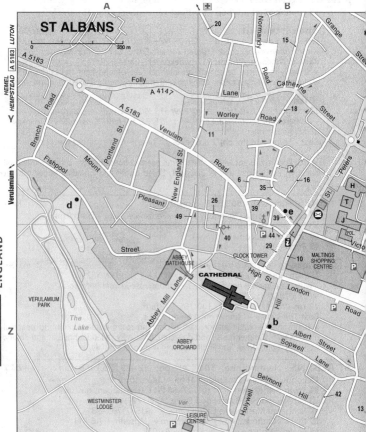

ST ALBANS

ENGLAND

WATFORD A 5183 (M1) LONDON

🏠 **Comfort** 🛗 🔥 rm, 🅺 rest, 🕻 🔊 🅿 VISA ◍◐ AE ①

Ryder House, Holywell Hill ⊠ *AL1 1HG –* 𝒞 *(01727) 848 849*
– www.comfortinnstalbans.net – admin@gb055.u-net.com
– Fax (01727) 812 210   BZ**b**
60 rm – †£79 ††£79/85, � £8.95
Rest – (Closed Sunday) (dinner only) Menu £15 – Carte £18/25
♦ Built by Samuel Ryder, donor of golf's Ryder cup. Defined by Edwardian features: stained glass dome and carved fireplace. The bedrooms, though, are of practical bent. Meals served in restaurant or your room.

🏠 **Ardmore House** 🚗 📶 🕻 🅿 VISA ◍◐ AE

54 Lemsford Rd ⊠ *AL1 3PR –* 𝒞 *(01727) 859 313*
– www.ardmorehousehotel.co.uk – info@ardmorehousehotel.co.uk
– Fax (01727) 859 313   CY**a**
40 rm ⊂ **–** †£68/70 ††£81/135
Rest *Belvedere* **–** (Closed Sunday dinner) Carte £26/38
♦ Edwardian residence with Victorian annex: this is a traditional, family owned hotel. Homely bedrooms have the feel of a lounge, boasting sofas and wall lamps. Traditional dining room with menu to match.

A 1081 *HARPENDEN, LUTON*

Abbey Mill Lane	**AZ**
Albert St.	**BZ**
Alma Rd.	**CZ**
Avenue Rd	**CY**
Beaconsfield Rd	**CYZ**
Belmont Hill	**BZ**
Branch Rd	**AY**
Bricket Rd	**BCYZ** 5
Britton Ave	**BY** 6
Carlisle Ave.	**BCY** 8
Catherine St	**BY**
Chequer St	**BZ** 10
Church Crescent	**ABY** 11
Cottonmill Lane	**BCZ** 13
Dalton St	**BY** 15
Drovers Way	**BY** 16
Etna Rd	**BY** 18
Fishpool St	**AYZ**
Folly Ave	**BY** 20
Folly Lane	**ABY**
Grange St	**BY**
Grimston Rd	**CZ** 21
Grosvenor Rd	**CZ** 22
Hall Pl. Gardens	**CY**
Hatfield Rd	**CY**
High St.	**BZ**
Hillside Rd	**CY**
Holywell Hill	**BZ**
Lattimore Rd	**CZ**
Lemsford Rd	**CY**
London Rd	**BCZ**
Lower Dagnall St	**BYZ** 26
Maltings Shopping Centre	**BZ**
Manor Rd	**CY**
Market Pl.	**BZ** 29
Marlborough Rd	**CZ** 28
Mount Pleasant	**AY**
New England St	**AY**
Normandy Rd	**BY**
Old London Rd	**CZ**
Portland St.	**AY**
Ridgemont Rd.	**CZ**
Russell Ave	**BY** 35
St Peter's Rd.	**CY** 37
St Peter's St.	**BCY**
Sopwell Lane	**BZ**
Spencer St	**BY** 39
Spicer St College	**BYZ** 40
Station Way	**CZ**
Thorpe Rd	**BZ** 42
Upper Dagnall St	**BYZ** 44
Upper Lattimore Rd	**CYZ**
Upper Marlborough Rd	**CYZ** 46
Verulam Rd	**ABY**
Victoria St	**BCZ**
Watson's Walk	**CZ** 48
Welclose St	**AYZ** 49
Worley Rd	**BY**

ENGLAND

✗ **Sukiyaki**   VISA ⓜⓞ AE ①

😊 6 Spencer St ⊠ AL3 5EG – ℘ (01727) 865 009 – Closed 2 weeks in summer,
1 week Christmas, Sunday, Monday and Tuesday lunch   BY**e**
Rest – Japanese – Menu £ 8/20 – Carte £ 15/19

♦ A pared-down style, minimally decorated restaurant with simple, precise helpings
of Japanese food. No noodles or sushi, expect instead sukiyaki (a beef dish), and
tempura.

ST ANNE – 503 Q 33 – see Channel Islands (Alderney)

ST ANNE'S – Lancs. – 502 K 22 – see Lytham St Anne's

ST AUBIN – 503 P 33 – see Channel Islands (Jersey)

Red = Pleasant. Look for the red ✗ and 🏠 symbols.

■ London 281 mi – Newquay 16 mi – Plymouth 38 mi – Truro 14 mi
🏊 Carlyon Bay, 𝒞 (01726) 814 250
◎ Holy Trinity Church★
◙ St Austell Bay★★ (Gribbin Head★★) E : by A 390 and A 3082 – Carthew : Wheal Martyn China Clay Heritage Centre★★ **AC**, N : 2 m. by A 391 – Mevagissey★★, S : 5 m. by B 3273 – Lost Gardens of Heligan★, S : 5 m. by B 3273 – Charlestown★, SE : 2 m. by A 390 – Eden Project★★, NE : 3 m. by A 390 at St Blazey Gate. Trewithen★★★ **AC**, NE : 7 m. by A 390 – Lanhydrock★★, NE : 11 m. by A 390 and B 3269 – Polkerris★, E : 7 m. by A 390 and A 3082

⚲ **Poltarrow Farm** without rest   🚪 🕭 📺 🍴 **P** VISA ◍◍
*St Mewan, Southwest : 1 ¾ m. by A 390 ✉ PL26 7DR – 𝒞 (01726) 67 111
– www.poltarrow.co.uk – enquire@poltarrow.co.uk – Fax (01726) 67 111 – Closed
Christmas and New Year*
5 rm ☲ – ♦£50 ♦♦£75
♦ Tucked away down a tree-lined drive stands this working farm equipped with indoor pool, elegant sitting room and conservatory serving Cornish breakfasts. Rooms have views.

at Tregrehan East : 2½ m. by A 390 – ✉ St Austell

⚲ **Anchorage House**   🚪 📺 🕭 𝑙⻌ 🍴 🕪 **P** VISA ◍◍ AE
*Nettles Corner, Boscundle ✉ PL25 3RH – 𝒞 (01726) 814 071
– www.anchoragehouse.co.uk – info@anchoragehouse.co.uk – Fax (01726)
813 462 – March-November*
5 rm ☲ – ♦£85/120 ♦♦£140/150
Rest – (by arrangement, communal dining) Menu £23
♦ Intriguing mix of modern and period styles in welcoming house set in peaceful position. Antique beds in spacious rooms plus extras: flowers, fruit, hot water bottles.

at Carlyon Bay East : 2½ m. by A 3601 – ✉ St Austell

🏨 **Carlyon Bay**   ⪕ 🚪 🕭 ⍟ 📺 ◍ 🕭 𝑙⻌ 🍴 📷 🛗 🕴 Ⓐ rest, 🍴 🕪
✉ PL25 3RD – 𝒞 (01726) 812 304   𝑙⻌ **P** VISA ◍◍ AE ◑
– www.carlyonbay.com – reservations@carlyonbay.com – Fax (01726) 814 938
86 rm – ♦£95/115 ♦♦£230/300, ☲ £16   **Rest** – Menu £20/35
– Carte £45/55
♦ With superb views across bay and well-positioned pool as suntrap, this family friendly hotel has golf course access and lays on programmes for children. Spacious, neat rooms. Dining room with live music and handsome vistas.

🏨 **Porth Avallen**   ⪕ 🚪 🏠 🍴 🕪 𝑙⻌ **P** VISA ◍◍ AE
*Sea Rd ✉ PL25 3SG – 𝒞 (01726) 812 802 – www.porthavallen.co.uk
– info@porthavallen.co.uk – Fax (01726) 817 097*
28 rm ☲ – ♦£64/96 ♦♦£108/120
Rest – Menu £35 (dinner) **s** – Carte £24/35 **s**
♦ Built as a family home in 1928; enjoys a commanding position overlooking Carlyon Bay. Warmly decorated interiors with wood panelling, rich coloured carpets and furnishings. Restaurant with fine sea views.

✗ **Austell's**   VISA ◍◍
*10 Beach Rd. ✉ PL25 3PH – 𝒞 (01726) 813 888 – www.austells.net
– brett@austells.net – Closed 1-14 January, 25 December, Tuesday January-Easter
and Monday*
Rest – (dinner only) Carte £27/42
♦ Light, airy eatery in modern parade of shops. Seasonal menu displays quality ingredients used with flair and imagination. Some simpler dishes, some more adventurous. Good presentation.

ENGLAND

at Charlestown Southeast : 2 m. by A 390 – ⊠ St Austell

The Beeches   🏠 ✕ 📶 P VISA ⬤
60 Charlestown Rd – ☎ (01726) 73 106 – www.thebeechescharlestown.co.uk
– info@thebeechescharlestown.co.uk – Closed 24-27 December
4 rm ⌑ – †£120/220 ††£120/220
Rest – Menu £30 (dinner) – Carte approx. £30
◆ Detached house in pleasant gardens, close to harbour. Spacious bedrooms feature heavy Oriental furniture and exude a calm, relaxing air; 1 has round bath. Numerous spa and treatment rooms downstairs. Small restaurant offers simple dishes and plenty of local seafood.

T' Gallants without rest   ✕ VISA ⬤ AE
6 Charlestown Rd ⊠ PL25 3NJ – ☎ (01726) 70 203 – www.tgallants.co.uk
– enquiries@tgallants.co.uk
8 rm ⌑ – †£45 ††£60/70
◆ Georgian house in quiet fishing port. Benches in walled garden for sunning yourself. Good value accommodation: try and book Room 5, which boasts four poster and the best view.

ST BLAZEY – Cornwall – 503 F 32 – pop. 8 837   1 B2
▶ London 276 mi – Newquay 21 mi – Plymouth 33 mi – Truro 19 mi
◉ Eden Project★★, NW; 1½ m. by A 390 and minor roads

Nanscawen Manor House without rest   ≤ 🌲 ⌿ ✕ 📶 P
Prideaux Rd, West : ¾ m. by Luxulyan rd ⊠ PL24 2SR   VISA ⬤
– ☎ (01726) 814 488 – www.nanscawen.com – keith@nanscawen.com
3 rm ⌑ – †£69/78 ††£99/122
◆ Sumptuous country house, until 1520 the home of Nanscawen family. Conservatory breakfast room set in fragrant gardens. Welcoming bedrooms; outdoor spa bath. Non smoking.

ST BRELADE'S BAY – 503 P 33 – see Channel Islands (Jersey)

ST HELIER – 503 P 33 – see Channel Islands (Jersey)

ST HILARY – Cornwall – see Marazion

ST IVES – Cornwall – 503 D 33   1 A3
▶ London 319 mi – Penzance 10 mi – Truro 25 mi
🚉 The Guildhall, Street-an-Pol ☎ (01736) 796297, ivtic@penwith.gov.uk
⛳ Tregenna Castle H., ☎ (01736) 795 254
⛳ West Cornwall Lelant, ☎ (01736) 753 401
◎ Town★★ - Barbara Hepworth Museum★★ AC Y M1 – Tate St Ives★★
(≤★★) Y – St Nicholas Chapel (≤★★) Y – Parish Church★ Y A
◉ S : Penwith★★ Y. St Michael's Mount★★ (≤★★) S : 10 m. by B 3306 - Y - B 3311, B 3309 and A 30

Plan on next page

The Garrack   ≤ 🌲 🗓 ⌂ L�ₛ P VISA ⬤ AE ⓘ
Burthallan Lane ⊠ TR26 3AA – ☎ (01736) 796 199 – www.garrack.com
– mich@garrack.com – Fax (01736) 798 955 – Closed Christmas   Ya
18 rm (dinner included) ⌑ – †£75/160 ††£180/198
Rest *The Restaurant* – (dinner only and Sunday lunch) Menu £25
– Carte £26/56
◆ Well-established hotel with pleasant gardens close to Tate. Plenty of homely touches. Spacious pool and sauna. Individually designed bedrooms, many with feature beds. Very popular dining room serves Cornish specialities.

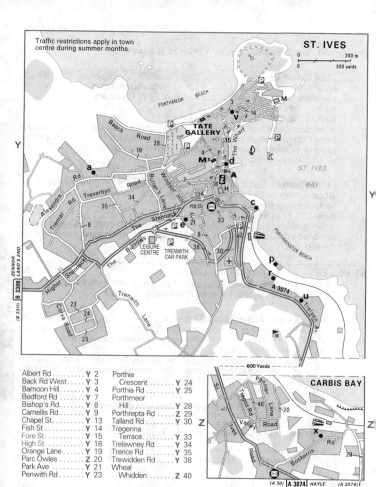

Traffic restrictions apply in town centre during summer months.

ST. IVES

CARBIS BAY

Pedn-Olva ← 🏡 🏊 ⚒ 🕊 **P** _VISA_ ⊕⊙ **AE**

West Porthminster Beach ⊠ *TR26 2EA –* ℰ *(01736) 796 222*
– www.pednolva.co.uk – pednolva@staustellbrewery.co.uk
– Fax (01736) 797 710

31 rm ⊇ **–** ♦£55/75 ♦♦£150/220

Rest *The Lookout* – (bar lunch) Carte £23/32

♦ Meaning "lookout on the headland" in Cornish; boasts commanding views of harbour and bay. Sheltered sun terrace and pool. Neutral décor typified by simple bedrooms. Restaurant offers diners splendid outlook.

Yc

Blue Hayes without rest ← 🚗 💈 🕊 **P** _VISA_ ⊕⊙ **AE**

Trelyon Ave ⊠ *TR26 2AD –* ℰ *(01736) 797 129 – www.bluehayes.co.uk*
– info@bluehayes.co.uk – Fax (01736) 799 098 – March to October

6 rm ⊇ **–** ♦£75/140 ♦♦£190/210

Yu

♦ 19C house with super view from terrace over the harbour; access to coast path from garden. Hi-tech interior. Single course supper available. Well-appointed bedrooms.

↑ **Primrose Valley** without rest ⟨ ⚿ ⓣ **P** 𝗩𝗜𝗦𝗔 ⓒⓞ
Porthminster Beach ⊠ *TR26 2ED* – ℰ *(01736) 794 939*
– www.primroseonline.co.uk – info@primroseonline.co.uk – Fax (01736) 794 939
– Closed Christmas and 3-30 January   Y**r**
10 rm – †£125/155 ††£125/155
♦ Edwardian villa with unrivalled proximity to beach. Stylish café bar and lounge; relaxing front patio. Local suppliers ensure good breakfast choice. Individually styled rooms.

↑ **Pebble** without rest ⟨ ⚿ ⓣ 𝗩𝗜𝗦𝗔 ⓒⓞ
4 Park Ave ⊠ *TR26 2DN* – ℰ *(01736) 794 168 – www.pebble-hotel.co.uk*
– info@pebble-hotel.co.uk – Restricted opening in winter   Y**e**
7 rm ⌿ – †£45/55 ††£94/110
♦ Small family run hotel; superb views of harbour and bay. Make yourself at home in lounge stocked with local information books. Refurbished, modern bedrooms.

XX **Alba** ⟨ 𝗔𝗖 𝗩𝗜𝗦𝗔 ⓒⓞ 𝗔𝗘
Old Lifeboat House, The Wharf ⊠ *TR26 1LF* – ℰ *(01736) 797 222*
– www.thealbarestaurant.com – albarestaurant@aol.co.uk – Fax (01736) 798 937
– Closed 25-26 December   Y**d**
Rest – Menu £17 – Carte £27/33
♦ Ideally situated in centre of town, on both floors of Old Lifeboat House; good harbour views. Modern feel; artwork on walls. Tasty, extensive menus with a modern slant.

X **Porthminster Cafe** ⟨ 🛋 𝗩𝗜𝗦𝗔 ⓒⓞ
Porthminster Beach ⊠ *TR26 2EB* – ℰ *(01736) 795 352*
– www.porthminstercafe.co.uk – p.minster@btconnect.com – Fax (01736) 795 352
– Closed 25 December   Y**p**
Rest – Seafood – (booking advisable) Carte £26/48
♦ 1930s beach house on Porthminster sands. Super views: large terrace for al fresco dining. Colourful local artwork on walls. Seafood oriented dishes plus eclectic dinner menus.

X **Blue Fish** ⟨ 🛋 𝗩𝗜𝗦𝗔 ⓒⓞ ⓞ
Norway Lane ⊠ *TR26 1LZ* – ℰ *(01736) 794 204 – bluefishrest@btconnect.com*
– Restricted opening in winter   Y**v**
Rest – Seafood – Carte £25/36
♦ Welcoming, family run eatery in the centre of town with a charming sunny terrace affording views of the town. Local and Mediterranean seafood in a simple, relaxed style.

at Carbis Bay South : 1¾ m. on A 3074 – ⊠ St Ives

🏠 **Boskerris** ⟨ 🚗 ⚿ ⓣ **P** 𝗩𝗜𝗦𝗔 ⓒⓞ
Boskerris Rd ⊠ *TR26 2NQ* – ℰ *(01736) 795 295 – www.boskerrishotel.co.uk*
– reservations@boskerrishotel.co.uk – Closed December and January   Z**x**
15 rm ⌿ – †£70/125 ††£95/205 **Rest** – (dinner only) Carte £24/31
♦ Ever-improving, contemporary hotel with panoramic views of Carbis Bay and coastline. Tastefully appointed bedrooms; relaxing lounge. Enthusiastic young owners. Good, honest home-cooking.

ST JUST – Cornwall – **503** C 33 – pop. 1 890   1 **A3**
▶ London 325 mi – Penzance 7 mi – Truro 35 mi
🏌 Cape Cornwall G. & C.C., ℰ (01736) 788 611
◎ Church★
⚑ Penwith★★ – Sancreed - Church★★ (Celtic Crosses★★), SE : 3 m. by
A 3071 – St Buryan★★ (Church Tower★★), SE : 5½ m. by B 3306 and
A 30 – Land's End★ (cliff scenery★★★), S : 5½ m. by B 3306 and A 30
– Cape Cornwall★ (⟨★★), W : 1½ m. - Morvah (⟨★★), NE : 4½ m.
by B 3306 – Geevor Tin Mine★ **AC**, N : 3 m. by B 3306 – Carn Euny★,
SE : 3 m. by A 3071 - Wayside Cross★ – Sennen Cove★ (⟨★), S : 5½ m.
by B 3306 and A 30. Porthcurno★, S : 9½ m. by B 3306, A 30 and B 3315

🏠 **Boscean Country House** without rest 🏡   ≤ 🖨 🛠 📶 **P** 𝚅𝙸𝚂𝙰 ⓪⓪
🍴 *Northwest : ½ m. by Boswedden Rd* ⊠ *TR19 7QP* – 𝒞 *(01736) 788 748*
– www.bosceancountryhotel.co.uk – boscean.hotel@yahoo.com – April-October
12 rm ⌕ – **†**£50/65 **††**£75/110
♦ Originally a doctor's residence; this Edwardian house is surrounded by 3 acres of walled gardens, a haven for wildlife. Wealth of oak panelling indoors; most rooms have views.

ST KEVERNE – Cornwall – 503 E 33   1 A3
🚉 London 302 mi – Penzance 26 mi – Truro 28 mi

↑ **Old Temperance House** without rest   🛠 📶 **P**
The Square ⊠ *TR12 6NA* – 𝒞 *(01326) 280 986 – www.oldtemperancehouse.co.uk*
– info@oldtemperancehouse.co.uk – April-November
4 rm ⌕ – **†**£45/50 **††**£74/80
♦ 'Roses round the door' charm, in idyllic spot on pretty square. Spotlessly neat lounge. Excellent, out-of-the-ordinary breakfasts. Fresh, bright, carefully co-ordinated rooms.

✗ **The Greenhouse**   𝚅𝙸𝚂𝙰 ⓪⓪
6 High Street ⊠ *TR12 6NN* – 𝒞 *(01326) 280 800 – www.tgor.co.uk*
– t.g.o.r@hotmail.co.uk – Closed 1 week January, Monday and Tuesday in winter
Rest – (dinner only) Carte £18/30
♦ Simple, sweet restaurant run by husband and wife, who use as much local produce as possible, from beer to salt. The cooking is tasty, wholesome and heart-warming.

ST LAWRENCE – 503 P 33 – see Channel Islands (Jersey)

ST LAWRENCE – I.O.W. – 503 Q 32 – see Wight (Isle of)

ST MARGARET'S AT CLIFFE – Kent – 504 Y 30 – see Dover

ST MARTIN – 503 P 33 – see Channel Islands (Guernsey)

ST MARTIN'S – Cornwall – 503 B 34 – see Scilly (Isles of)

ST MARY'S – Cornwall – 503 B 34 – see Scilly (Isles of)

ST MAWES – Cornwall – 503 E 33 – ⊠ Truro   1 B3
🚉 London 299 mi – Plymouth 56 mi – Truro 18 mi
◎ Town★ - Castle★ AC (≤★)
◙ St Just-in-Roseland Church★★, N : 2½ m. by A 3078

🏨 **Tresanton** 🏡   ≤ 🚗 ᴊᴊ 🛠 📶 🏊 **P** 𝚅𝙸𝚂𝙰 ⓪⓪ 🅐🅔
27 Lower Castle Rd ⊠ *TR2 5DR* – 𝒞 *(01326) 270 055 – www.tresanton.com*
– info@tresanton.com – Fax (01326) 270 053 – Closed 2 weeks early January
27 rm ⌕ – **†**£229/283 **††**£255/315 – 2 suites
Rest – (booking essential for non-residents) Menu £33/42
♦ Enduringly trendy former 1940s yachtsman's club with cinema. Watercolours on pale walls; gleaming crisp rooms with views; contemporary lounge and attentive service. Dining room boasts open terrace with harbour views and modern seafood dishes.

🏨 **Idle Rocks**   ≤ 📶 𝚅𝙸𝚂𝙰 ⓪⓪ 🅐🅔
Harbourside, 1 Tredenham Rd ⊠ *TR2 5AN* – 𝒞 *(01326) 270 771*
– www.idlerocks.co.uk – reception@idlerocks.co.uk – Fax (01326) 270 062
27 rm ⌕ – **†**£93/156 **††**£226/295
Rest *The Water's Edge* – (light lunch) Menu £33 – Carte £19/32
♦ Fine waterfront hotel with splendid views of the harbour and fishermen's cottages. Deep comfortable chairs in lounge and bright bedrooms, many with sea views. Restaurant with terrace overlooks the sea.

ENGLAND

ST MERRYN – Cornwall – **503** F 32 – see Padstow

ST PETER – **503** P 33 – see Channel Islands (Jersey)

ST PETER PORT – **503** P 33 – see Channel Islands (Guernsey)

ST SAVIOUR – **503** P 33 – see Channel Islands (Guernsey)

ST SAVIOUR – **503** P 33 – see Channel Islands (Jersey)

SALCOMBE – Devon – **503** I 33 – pop. 1 893   2 **C3**
- ▶ London 243 mi – Exeter 43 mi – Plymouth 27 mi – Torquay 28 mi
- ▪ Council Hall, Market St ℰ (01548) 843927,
  info@salcombeinformation.co.uk
- ◧ Sharpitor (Overbecks Museum and Garden★) (≤★★) **AC**, S : 2 m. by South
  Sands Z. Prawle Point (≤★★★) E : 16 m. around coast by A 381 - Y - and
  A 379

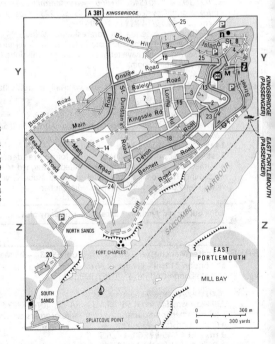

SALCOMBE

Allenhayes Rd	**Y** 2
Bonaventure Rd	**Y** 3
Buckley St	**Y** 4
Camperdown Rd	**Y** 7
Church St	**Y** 8
Coronation Rd	**Y** 9
Devon Rd	**Y** 13
Fore St	**Y**
Fortescue Rd	**Z** 14
Grenville Rd	**Y** 15
Herbert Rd	**Z** 18
Knowle Rd	**Y** 19
Moult Rd	**Z** 20
Newton Rd	**Z** 23
Sandhills Rd	**Z** 24
Shadycombe Rd	**Y** 25

🏨 **Marine**   ≤ 🏛 🖼 🛎 🗗 🖨 **P** *VISA* ⑩ 🅰🅴
Cliff Rd ⊠ *TQ8 8JH* – ℰ *(01548) 844 444* – *www.marinehotelsalcombe.com*
– *bookings@marinehotelsalcombe.com* – *Fax (01548) 843 109*
– *Closing September for major rebuild*   Y**e**
52 rm ⊇ – ♱£75/145 ♱♱£150/217 – 1 suite
Rest – (dinner only and Sunday lunch) Menu £17/35
◆ Spectacular position on water's edge overlooking the estuary. Hotel makes the
most of this; many bedrooms have balconies whilst centrally located rooms share the
best views. Bright, roomy restaurant looks onto the water.

Tides Reach
≤ 🚗 🔲 🎵 *L₆* 🏖 **P** VISA ◑◐ AE

South Sands ⊠ *TQ8 8LJ –* ✆ *(01548) 843 466 – www.tidesreach.com*
– enquire@tidesreach.com – Fax (01548) 843 954 – Mid February-November Z**x**
32 rm ⥮ – †£90/158 ††£154/350   **Rest** – (bar lunch) Menu £35 **s**

◆ Traditional, personally run hotel set in pleasant sandy cove on Salcombe Estuary. Lilac and green rooms boast floral fabrics and flowers; many have balconies and a fine view. Restaurant overlooks attractive gardens and pond.

✗ The Oyster Shack
VISA ◑◐

Hannaford's Landing, Island St – ✆ *(01548) 843 596 – www.oystershack.co.uk*
– salcombe@oystershack.co.uk Y**n**
Rest – Carte £23/28

◆ Set in modern arcade amongst chandleries and sail makers. Central bar with stools, open dining room and terrace with harbour/estuary views. Seafood menu centred around oyster dishes.

at Soar Mill Cove Southwest : 4 ¼ m. by A 381 - Y - via Malborough village
– ⊠ **Salcombe**

Soar Mill Cove ≫
≤ 🚗 🎋 ⏛ 🔲 🎵 ✗ 🏃 **P** VISA ◑◐

⊠ *TQ7 3DS –* ✆ *(01548) 561 566 – www.soarmillcove.co.uk*
– info@soarmillcove.co.uk – Fax (01548) 561 223 – Closed January
22 rm ⥮ – †£79/149 ††£99/199

Rest – (booking essential for non-residents) Menu £29 – Carte £20/32

◆ Family run local stone and slate hotel on one level in delightful and secluded coastal setting; rooms have terraces and chintz furnishings. Geared for families. Classically styled dining room.

at Hope Cove West : 4 m. by A 381 - Y - via Malborough village – ⊠ **Kingsbridge**

🏠 Lantern Lodge ≫
≤ 🚗 🔲 🎵 ✗ **P** VISA ◑◐

by Grand View Rd ⊠ *TQ7 3HE –* ✆ *(01548) 561 280 – www.lantern-lodge.co.uk*
– lanternlodge@hopecove.wanadoo.co.uk – Fax (01548) 561 736
– March-mid November
14 rm ⥮ – †£105/128 ††£140/170

Rest – (dinner only) (booking essential for non-residents) Menu £25

◆ Named after its lantern window, reputedly designed to guide sailors home, this welcoming, traditional clifftop hotel overlooks Hope Cove. Front bedrooms have views. Pretty dining room with small, adjacent bar.

Look out for red symbols, indicating particularly pleasant establishments.

SALE – Greater Manchester – **502** N 23 – **pop. 55 234** – ⊠ **Manchester**   20 **B3**
🚇 London 212 mi – Liverpool 36 mi – Manchester 6 mi – Sheffield 43 mi
🏌 Sale Lodge Golf Rd, ✆ (0161) 973 1638

🏠 Cornerstones without rest
🚗 ✗ 🛏 **P** VISA ◑◐ ①

230 Washway Rd, (on A 56) ⊠ *M33 4RA –* ✆ *(0161) 283 6909*
– www.cornerstonesguesthouse.com – info@cornerstonesguesthouse.com
– Closed Christmas-New Year
9 rm – †£42/45 ††£60, ⥮ £6.50

◆ Built in 1871 for the Lord Mayor, this restored Victorian house is personally run. A medley of rooms: spacious with varied décor and fabrics. Homely breakfast room.

✗ The Fat Loaf
🎋 VISA ◑◐

62 Green Lane, Ashton on Mersey, West : ½ m by B 5166 – ✆ *(0161) 972 0397*
– www.thefatloaf.co.uk – fatloaf@aol.com – Closed 25-26 December, 1 January and Sunday
Rest – Menu £18 (lunch) **s** – Carte £22/32 **s**

◆ Keenly run neighbourhood eatery, hidden away on a small residential parade. Good value lunch/early evening menu and wide ranging à la carte. Fresh, clean, flavoursome cooking.

ENGLAND

SALISBURY – Wiltshire – 503 O 30 – pop. 43 355   4 **D3**

▶ London 91 mi – Bournemouth 28 mi – Bristol 53 mi – Southampton 23 mi
🖼 Fish Row ℰ (01722) 334956, visitorinfo@salisbury.gov.uk
🏌 Salisbury & South Wilts. Netherhampton, ℰ (01722) 742 645
🏌 High Post Great Durnford, ℰ (01722) 782 356
◉ City ★★ - Cathedral ★★★ AC Z – Salisbury and South Wiltshire Museum ★
AC Z **M2** – Close ★ Z : Mompesson House ★ AC Z A – Sarum St Thomas
Church ★ Y **B** – Redcoats in the Wardrobe ★ Z **M1**
🅖 Wilton Village ★ (Wilton House ★★ AC, Wilton Carpet Factory ★ AC), W :
3 m. by A 30 Y – Old Sarum ★ AC, N : 2 m. by A 345 Y – Woodford (Heale
House Garden ★) AC, NW : 4½ m. by Stratford Rd Y. Stonehenge ★★★ AC,
NW : 10 m. by A 345 - Y - and A 303 – Wardour Castle ★ AC, W : 15 m. by
A 30 Y

Plan on next page

🏠 **Cricket Field House** without rest   🚗 ⅃ ⚭ ℁ ⁽ᵗⁱ⁾ ⅏ **P** 📵 **VISA** 🐵 **AE**
Wilton Rd, West : 1¼ m. on A 36 ✉ *SP2 9NS – ℰ (01722) 322 595
– www.cricketfieldhouse.co.uk – cricketfieldcottage@btinternet.com – Fax (01722)
322 595*
14 rm ⊆ – ✝£50/75 ✝✝£70/95
◆ Personally run extended house overlooking the County Cricket Ground. Bedrooms
are prettily decorated with pictures and floral touches; majority of rooms are in the
annex.

🏠 **Websters** without rest   ⅃ ⁽ᵗⁱ⁾ **P** **VISA** 🐵
11 Hartington Rd, (off A 360 Devizes Rd) ✉ *SP2 7LG – ℰ (01722) 339 779
– www.websters-bed-breakfast.com – enquiries@websters-bed-breakfast.com
– Closed Christmas and New Year*   **Yn**
5 rm ⊆ – ✝£45/58 ✝✝£60/65
◆ Secluded Victorian terrace house, with own parking, close to town centre. Friendly
owner. Cosy breakfast room. Homely style bedrooms, immaculately kept; very good
value.

🏠 **St Anns House** without rest   ℁ ⁽ᵗⁱ⁾ **VISA** 🐵
32-34 St Ann St ✉ *SP1 2DP – ℰ (01722) 335 657 – www.stannshouse.co.uk
– info@stannshouse.co.uk – Closed 22 December-7 January*   **Ze**
8 rm ⊆ – ✝£65/85 ✝✝£110
◆ Traditional Georgian townhouse with immaculate bedrooms, sash windows and
original fireplaces. Large breakfast menu offers well sourced options. Honesty bar and
private dining available.

✕✕ **Anokaa**   **AC** **VISA** 🐵 **AE**
60 Fisherton St ✉ *SP2 7RB – ℰ (01772) 414 142 – www.anokaa.com
– info@anokaa.com – Fax (01772) 414 142 – Closed 25-26 December*   **Ye**
Rest – Indian – (buffet lunch) Menu £8/25 – Carte £15/48
◆ Lives up to being "something out of the ordinary", with eye-catching interior and
staff in silky full-length gowns. Indian dishes mix modern and classical styles with
aplomb.

🍴🏠 **The Gastrobistro at the Pheasant Inn**   🏯 ℁ ⇔ **VISA** 🐵 **AE**
19 Salt Lane ✉ *SP1 1DT – ℰ (01722) 414 926 – www.gastrobistro.co.uk
– gastrobistro@googlemail.com
– Closed 25 December dinner and first 2 weeks January*   **Yo**
Rest – Carte £19/30
◆ Ivy-clad, red-brick pub with a decked terrace and neat garden. Flavoursome cooking displays honest country foundations and good combinations; excellent homemade puddings.

at Middle Winterslow Northeast : 6½ m. by A 30 - Y – ✉ **Salisbury**

🏠 **The Beadles** without rest ❧   🚗 ℁ **P** 🐵
Middleton ✉ *SP5 1QS – ℰ (01980) 862 922 – www.guestaccom.co.uk/754.htm
– winterbead@aol.com – Fax (01980) 863 565 – Restricted opening in winter*
3 rm ⊆ – ✝£40/50 ✝✝£75/80
◆ Recently built from 100-year old bricks and Georgian in style; geese clack in garden. Flower-filled rooms with extra touches: pictures, reading lamps, comfortable
chairs.

707

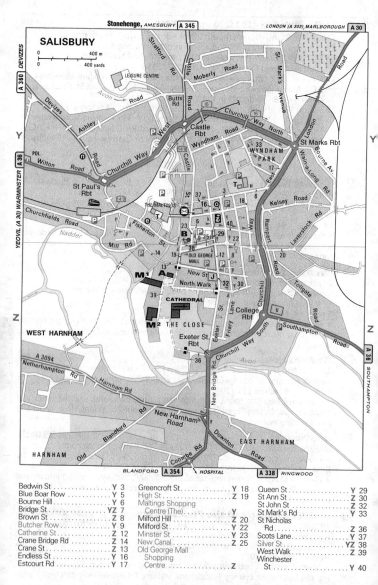

SALISBURY

Stonehenge, AMESBURY **A 345**

LONDON (A 303), MARLBOROUGH **A 30**

DEVIZES **A 360**

YEOVIL (A 30) WARMINSTER **A 36**

BLANDFORD **A 354** HOSPITAL **A 338** RINGWOOD

SOUTHAMPTON **A 36**

at Whiteparish Southeast : 7 ½ m. by A 36 - Z - on A 27 – ⊠ Salisbury

⌂ **Newton Farmhouse** without rest   🚗 �🏊 ⌗ **P** **VISA** ⓜⓒ

Southampton Rd, Southwest : 1 ½ m. on A 36 ⊠ SP5 2QL – ℰ (01794) 884 416
– www.newtonfarmhouse.com – lizzie@newtonfarmhouse.com
– Fax (01794) 884 105

9 rm ⌸ – †£ 55/80 ††£ 110

♦ Step back in time in this 16C farmhouse, gifted to Nelson's family after Battle of Trafalgar. Original bread oven in inglenook fireplace, oak beams and well. Garden rooms the nicest.

at Burcombe West : 5 ¼ m. by A 36 - Y - off A 30 – ⊠ Salisbury

🏠 **The Ship Inn**   🚗 🍴 **P** VISA ◍ AE
Burcombe Lane ⊠ SP2 0EJ – ℰ (01722) 743 182 – www.theshipburcombe.co.uk
– theshipburcombe@mail.com
Rest – Carte £ 19/30
♦ Old and new blend seamlessly, while large windows overlook a superb riverside garden. Cooking is generous and flavoursome – British and Mediterranean – with twice-daily specials.

at Teffont West : 10 ¼ m. by A 36 - Y - and A 30 on B 3089 – ⊠ Salisbury

🏠 **Howard's House** ♨   🎯 📶 **P** VISA ◍ AE
Teffont Evias ⊠ SP3 5RJ – ℰ (01722) 716 392 – www.howardshousehotel.co.uk
– enq@howardshousehotel.co.uk – Fax (01722) 716 820 – Closed Christmas
9 rm ☑ – ♦£105 ♦♦£175
Rest – (closed lunch Monday, Friday and Saturday) (booking essential for non-residents) Menu £ 27/28 – Carte (dinner) £ 28/45
♦ Personally run, part 17C dower house boasting fine gardens in a quaint, quiet village. Comfortable lounge and pleasant bedrooms with village or garden vistas. Garden herbs and vegetables grace accomplished cooking.

at Little Langford Northwest : 8 m. by A 36 - Y - and Great Wishford rd
– ⊠ Salisbury

🏠 **Little Langford Farmhouse** without rest   ≤ 🚗 🏠 ✍ **P** VISA ◍
⊠ SP3 4NP – ℰ (01722) 790 205 – www.littlelangford.co.uk
– bandb@littlelangford.co.uk – Fax (01722) 790 086 – Restricted opening in winter
3 rm ☑ – ♦£60/65 ♦♦£72/75
♦ An unusual Victorian Gothic farmhouse with turret, crenellations and lancet windows. Period style interiors throughout. Spacious, well-furnished bedrooms with rural views.

SANDFORD-ON-THAMES – Oxon. – see Oxford

SANDFORD ORCAS – Dorset – **503** M 31 – see Sherborne

SANDIWAY – Cheshire – **502** M 24 – ⊠ Northwich   20 **A3**
　▶ London 191 mi – Liverpool 34 mi – Manchester 22 mi
　– Stoke-on-Trent 26 mi

🏨 **Nunsmere Hall**   🚗 🎯 🍴 🎷 ✍ 📶 🛎 **P** VISA ◍ AE ⓪
Tarporley Rd, Southwest : 1 ½ m. by A 556 on A 49 ⊠ CW8 2ES – ℰ (01606)
889 100 – www.nunsmere.co.uk – reservations@nunsmere.co.uk – Fax (01606)
889 055
36 rm – ♦£130/160 ♦♦£160/185, ☑ £19.50
Rest *The Crystal* – Menu £ 22/30 – Carte (dinner) £ 34/50
♦ Secluded, on a wooded peninsular, originally built in 1900. Deep-seated sofas and sumptuous drawing rooms. Tasteful, individually furnished bedrooms exude quality and comfort. Dine in the classical style on imaginative and accomplished cuisine.

SANDSEND – N. Yorks. – **502** R/S 20 – see Whitby

SANDWICH – Kent – **504** Y 30 – pop. 4 398 📗 *Great Britain*   9 **D2**
　▶ London 72 mi – Canterbury 13 mi – Dover 12 mi
　🖈 Guildhall ℰ (01304) 613565, info@ticsandwich.wanadoo.co.uk
　◎ Town★

🏨 **The Bell at Sandwich**   ✍ 📶 🛎 **P** VISA ◍ AE
The Quay ⊠ CT13 9EF – ℰ (01304) 613 388 – www.bellhotelsandwich.co.uk
– reservations@bellhotelsandwich.co.uk – Fax (01304) 615 308 – Accommodation
closed 25-26 December
34 rm ☑ – ♦£95/119 ♦♦£119/199
Rest *The Place Brasserie* – Carte £ 26/32
♦ Situated by River Stour with original Victorian fittings in situ. Refurbishment has resulted in stunning transformation of bedrooms: now cool, elegant, stylish and welcoming. Pleasant brasserie with strong seafood base.

ENGLAND

SANDY – Bedfordshire – 504 T 27 – pop. 10 887   12 **A1**

- ◻ London 49 mi – Bedford 8 mi – Cambridge 24 mi – Peterborough 35 mi
- ◪ 5 Shannon Court, High St ℰ (01767) 682728, tourism@sandytowncouncil.gov.uk

⚲ **Highfield Farm** without rest   🛌 ⏤ **P** _VISA_ **◍◍**
Tempsford Rd, North : 2. m. by B 1042 on A 1 (southbound carriageway) ⊠ SG19 2AQ – ℰ (01767) 682 332 – www.highfield-farm.co.uk
– margaret@highfield-farm.co.uk
8 rm � – ♦£65/80 ♦♦£75/85
♦ Working arable farm with gardens and 300 acres of land. Light, airy breakfast room, homely lounge and immaculately kept bedrooms, three of which are outside in coach house.

SANDYPARK – Devon – 503 I 31 – see Chagford

SAPPERTON – Glos. – 503 N 28 – see Cirencester

SARK – 503 P 33 – see Channel Islands

SATWELL – Oxfordshire – pop. 1 163   11 **C3**

- ◻ London 43 mi – Oxford 24 mi – Reading 8 mi

🍴 **The Lamb**   🚗 🏡 **P** _VISA_ **◍◍**
⊠ RG9 4QZ – ℰ (01491) 628 482 – www.awtonline.co.uk
– thelamb@awtrestaurants.com – Fax (01491) 628 257 – Closed dinner 25-26 December
Rest – (bookings not accepted) Carte £ 17/26
♦ 17C timbers, low ceilings, quarry tiled floors and inglenook. Candlelight contributes to the cosy, informal ambience. Old photos decorate. Serves generous, heart-warming classics.

SAUNTON – Devon – 503 H 30 – ⊠ Braunton   2 **C1**

- ◻ London 230 mi – Barnstaple 8 mi – Exeter 48 mi
- 🗓 Saunton Braunton, ℰ (01271) 812436
- 🅖 Braunton ★ - St Brannock's Church ★, E : 2½ m. on B 3231 – Braunton Burrows ★, E : ½ m. on B 3231

🏨 **Saunton Sands**   ⬅ 🚗 ⚊ 🖥 ◍◍ ⋔ ♨ ⋇ 🖺 🏃 🖾 rest, ⋇ ⸮
⊠ EX33 1LQ – ℰ (01271) 890 212   ⚙ **P** _VISA_ **◍◍** AE ◑
– www.sauntonsands.com – reservations@sauntonsands.com – Fax (01271) 890 145
92 rm ⊇ – ♦£115/131 ♦♦£252/272   **Rest** – Menu £ 23/35 – Carte £ 27/35
♦ Imposing and busy 1930s seaside hotel in a prominent elevated position. Airy, spacious deluxe rooms have sea vistas. Families are well catered for; staffed crèche available. Classic dining room has sweeping sea views.

SAWDON – N. Yorks. – see Scarborough

SAXMUNDHAM – Suffolk – 504 Y 27 – pop. 2 712 – ⊠ Ipswich   15 **D3**

- ◻ London 95 mi – Aldeburgh 7 mi – Ipswich 20 mi

🏠 **The Bell**   _VISA_ **◍◍**
31 High St ⊠ IP17 1AF – ℰ (01728) 602 331 – thebell@saxhighstreet.fsnet.co.uk
– Fax (01728) 602 331
10 rm – ♦£50 ♦♦£80, ⊇ £5.95
Rest – (closed 1 week in spring, 1 week in autumn, Sunday and Monday except Bank Holidays) Menu £ 16/20 – Carte £ 25/30 **s**
♦ 17C former coaching inn, retaining much original visual character. Striking wall mural in hall. Local ale flows in cosy public bar. Simply furnished but spacious bedrooms Accomplished cooking in smart dining room.

ENGLAND

SCARBOROUGH – North Yorkshire – 502 S 21 – pop. 38 364 | 23 D1

Great Britain

London 253 mi – Kingston-upon-Hull 47 mi – Leeds 67 mi – Middlesbrough 52 mi

Brunswick, Westborough - Harbourside, Sandside ✆ (01723) 383636, tourismbureau@scarborough.gov.uk

Scarborough North Cliff North Cliff Ave, Burniston Rd, NW : 2 m. by A 165, ✆ (01723) 355 397

Scarborough South Cliff Deepdale Ave, S : 1 m. by A 165, off Filey Rd, ✆ (01723) 374 737

Robin Hood's Bay★, N : 16 m. on A 171 and minor rd to the right (signposted) – Whitby Abbey★, N : 21 m. on A 171 – Sledmere House★, S : 21 m. on A 645, B 1249 and B 1253 (right)

Plan on next page

Beiderbecke's

1-3 The Crescent ✉ YO11 2PW – ✆ (01723) 365 766 – www.beiderbeckes.com – info@beiderbeckes.com – Fax (01723) 367 433 Zs

26 rm – £ 65/105 £ 130/150 – 1 suite

Rest – (dinner only) Carte £ 25/35

◆ Named after the jazz musician. Although housed in a restored Georgian building, the rooms' décor is balanced between period style and contemporary feel with bright colours. Themed restaurant with nightclub feel.

The Royal

St Nicholas St ✉ YO11 2HE – ✆ (01723) 364 333 – www.englishrosehotels.co.uk – royalhotel@englishrosehotels.co.uk – Fax (01723) 500 618 Za

118 rm – £ 65/95 £ 100/160

Rest – Menu £ 15/30 – Carte (dinner) £ 37/45 **s**

◆ Make-up recently re-applied to one of the town's grand old ladies; 1830s elegance exemplified by unforgettable main staircase. Mix of original or contemporary bedroom styles. Formal ambience in grand dining room.

The Crown Spa H.

7-11 Esplanade ✉ YO11 2AG – ✆ (01723) 357 400 – www.crownspahotel.com – info@crownspahotel.com – Fax (01723) 357 404 Zi

90 rm – £ 39/115 £ 84/250, £ 14.95 – 1 suite

Rest *Taste* – (dinner only) Menu £ 25 – Carte £ 20/35 **s**

Rest *Taste Café Bar* – Carte £ 18/30 **s**

◆ 19C landmark - the town's first resort hotel, on the esplanade overlooking the bay. Spacious lounges in the classic style. Large bedrooms, many with fine sea views. Popular Taste serves family favourites. Informal dining in Taste Café Bar.

Ox Pasture Hall

Lady Edith's Drive, Raincliffe Woods, West : 3 ¼ m. by A 171 following signs for Raincliffe Woods ✉ YO12 5TD – ✆ (01723) 365 295 – www.oxpasturehall.com – oxpasture.hall@btconnect.com – Fax (01723) 355 156

21 rm – £ 89/140 £ 119/160

Rest – (bar lunch) Menu £ 19/30 – Carte £ 33/40 **s**

◆ Deep in the countryside, yet close to the sea. A charming part-17C farmhouse: most bedrooms offer pleasant views, some around an attractive wisteria-clad courtyard. Dining room has uniform feel.

Alexander

33 Burniston Rd ✉ YO12 6PG – ✆ (01723) 363 178 – www.alexanderhotelscarborough.co.uk – enquiries@alexanderhotelscarborough.co.uk – March-October Ya

10 rm – £ 42/48 £ 72/74

Rest – (closed Sunday) (dinner only) (residents only) Menu £ 18 **s**

◆ Red-brick 1930s house situated close to North Bay attractions. Smartly furnished lounge. Bedrooms vary in size and are all pleasantly decorated and comfortable.

ENGLAND

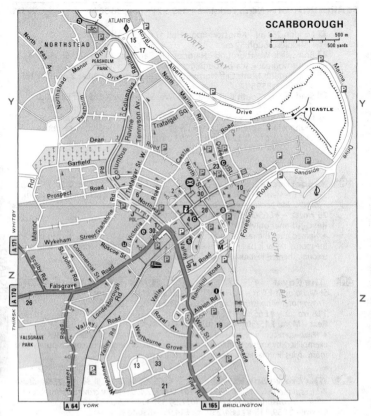

SCARBOROUGH

0   500 m
0   500 yards

⌂ **Windmill** without rest   🌿 **P** VISA ⬤⬤
Mill St, by Victoria Rd ⊠ YO11 1SZ – 𝒞 (01723) 372 735
– www.windmill-hotel.co.uk – info@windmill-hotel.co.uk – Fax (01723) 377 190
– Closed 25 December   Z**u**
11 rm � – **†**£25/65 **††**£96/100
♦ For a unique place to stay, look no further than this restored 18C windmill with
fascinating 3000 piece toy museum. All rooms built round courtyard; some with
direct access.

XX **Lanterna**   VISA ⬤⬤ ①
33 Queen St ⊠ YO11 1HQ – 𝒞 (01723) 363 616 – www.lanterna-ristorante.co.uk
– ralessio@lanterna-ristorante.co.uk – Fax (01723) 363 616 – Closed last 2 weeks
October, 2 weeks January, 25-26 December, 1 January and Sunday   Y**c**
Rest – Italian – (dinner only) Carte £28/96
♦ Scarborough's best known restaurant: a landmark for decades. Endearing trattoria
style "clutter". Classic Italian menu, plus a renowned selection of truffle dishes.

✗ **Pepper's**   *VISA* *MO* *AE* *O*
11 York Place ✉ *YO11 2NP –* ℰ *(01723) 500642 – www.peppersrestaurant.co.uk*
– peppers.restaurant@virgin.net
– Closed 25-26 December, 1-7 January and Sunday dinner   **Zc**
Rest – (dinner only and lunch Friday-Sunday) Carte £ 27/34
♦ Smart, personally run restaurant. Good cooking and extremely passionate sourcing
– owner visits farms to assess animal's welfare, as well as butchering techniques.

✗ **The Green Room**   *VISA* *MO* *AE*
138 Victoria Rd ✉ *YO11 1SL –* ℰ *(01723) 501801*   **Ze**
Rest – (Closed Monday) (dinner only) Carte £ 27/37
♦ Pleasant family run bistro; son cooks and mum is out front serving. Great care is
taken to use only locally sourced produce and ingredients. Cooking is modern and
imaginative.

at Sawdon Southwest : 9 ¾ m. by A 170 - Z – ✉ **Scarborough**

🏠 **The Anvil Inn**   🚗 ⅍ **P** *VISA* *MO*
Main St ✉ *YO13 9DY –* ℰ *(01723) 859896 – www.theanvilinnsawdon.co.uk*
– theanvilinnsawdon@btinternet.com
– Closed 26 December, 1 January and 2 weeks in January
Rest – (Closed Sunday dinner and Monday) Carte £ 18/28
♦ Locally renowned pub, an ex-forge with old furnace, bellows and tools providing a
sense of place. Intimate restaurant serves serious, hearty Yorkshire fare in good
portions.

Good food and accommodation at moderate prices?
Look for the Bib symbols:
red Bib Gourmand 🍽 for food, blue Bib Hotel 🏨 for hotels

SCAWTON – N. Yorks. – **502** Q 21 – see **Helmsley**

SCILLY (Isles of) – Cornwall – **503** A/B 34   **1 A3**
Access Helicopter service from St Mary's and Tresco to Penzance : ℰ (01736)
363871
🛫 St Mary's Airport : ℰ (01720) 422677, E : 1 ½ m. from Hugh Town
🚢 from Hugh Town to Penzance (Isles of Scilly Steamship Co. Ltd) (summer
only) (2 h 40 mn)
🛈 Hugh Street, St Mary's ℰ (01720) 424031, tic@scilly.gov.uk
🏝 Islands★ - The Archipelago (≤★★★)
🏝 St Agnes : Horsepoint★

Bryher – Cornwall – pop. 78 – ✉   **1 A3**
🏝 Watch Hill (≤★) – Hell Bay★

🏨 **Hell Bay** ⌖   ≤ 🚗 ⌖ ⅉ 🏊 🐾 👶 *VISA* *MO*
✉ *TR23 0PR –* ℰ *(01720) 422947 – www.hellbay.co.uk*
– contactus@hellbay.co.uk – Fax (01720) 423004 – April-October
11 rm ⌁ – †£ 162/600 ††£ 260/600 – 14 suites – ††£ 280/580
Rest – (bar lunch) (booking essential for non-residents) Menu £ 35
♦ Totally renovated, with a charming style that's relaxed, modern, comfy and colourful. Courtyard terraces, a vast lounge/bar and clean-lined rooms add to an idyllic
appeal. Dining room with garden views and daily changing menu.

🏠 **Bank Cottage** without rest ⌖   ≤ 🚗 ⅍
✉ *TR23 0PR –* ℰ *(01720) 422612 – www.bank-cottage.com*
– macmace@homecall.co.uk – Fax (01720) 422612 – April-October
4 rm ⌁ – †£ 48/49 ††£ 90/100
♦ A modern guesthouse in lush sub-tropical gardens, complete with koi fish pond. A
peaceful haven with floral bedrooms and a cosy little boxroom where you can buy
seafood.

ENGLAND

Tresco – Cornwall – pop. 167 – ⊠   1 **A3**

　　Island★ - Abbey Gardens★★ **AC** (Lighthouse Way ⩻★★)

The Island ⩘   ⩻ 🚗 🕭 🏊 🛠 ⧜ **VISA** **MO**
Old Grimsby ⊠ *TR24 0PU* – *ℰ (01720) 422 883* – *www.islandhotel.co.uk*
– islandhotel@tresco.co.uk – *Fax (01720) 423 008* – *March-October*
45 rm (dinner included) ⊊ – **†**£ 210/338 **††**£ 280/450 – 2 suites
Rest – (bar lunch) Menu £ 39 – Carte £ 19/32
♦ A heated pool, sub-tropical gardens, panoramic views to be had at this luxurious
hotel. Enthusiastic owners collect art for interiors. Well appointed garden rooms.
Light, welcoming dining room boasts sea vistas and friendly staff.

New Inn ⩻ 🏠 🛠 ⧜ **VISA** **MO**
⊠ *TR24 0QQ* – *ℰ (01720) 423 006* – *www.tresco.co.uk* – *newinn@tresco.co.uk*
– Fax (01720) 423 200
16 rm ⊊ – **†**£ 70/150 **††**£ 140/230
Rest – (booking essential for non-residents) Carte £ 18/30
♦ This stone built former inn makes a hospitable stopping off point. Friendly, bus-
tling ambience in lounges and bars; very pleasant garden terrace. Comfortable bed-
rooms. Same menu can be taken in the restaurant or the bar.

St Martin's – Cornwall – pop. 113   1 **A3**

　　St Martin's Head (⩻★★)

St Martin's on the Isle ⩘   ⩻ 🚗 🏠 🔲 🛠 ⛷ ⚶ **VISA** **MO** **AE** **O**
⊠ *TR25 0QW* – *ℰ (01720) 422 092* – *www.stmartinshotel.co.uk*
– stay@stmartinshotel.co.uk – *Fax (01720) 422 298* – *Mid March-late October*
27 rm ⊊ – **†**£ 140/204 **††**£ 280/370 – 3 suites
Rest Teän – see restaurant listing
Rest *Bistro* – (closed Monday dinner) Carte £ 25/32
♦ Set on the quayside with unrivalled views of white beaches and blue sea; a truly
idyllic island setting. Snooze peacefully in snug bedrooms. Bistro, with terrace and
eclectic menu, is perfect for lunch.

Teän – at St Martin's on the Isle Hotel   ⩻ 🚗 🏠 🛠 **VISA** **MO** **AE** **O**
⊠ *TR25 0QW* – *ℰ (01720) 422 092* – *www.stmartinshotel.co.uk*
– stay@stmartinshotel.co.uk – *Fax (01720) 422 298* – *Late March-late October*
Rest – (dinner only) (booking essential) Menu £ 45 **s**
♦ The restaurant offers fantastic views. The kitchen focuses on carefully-prepared,
seasonal dishes which make the best of local produce, including home grown vegetables and herbs.

St Mary's – Cornwall – pop. 1 607   1 **A3**

　　Carn Morval, *ℰ (01720) 422 692*
　　Gig racing★★ - Garrison Walk★ (⩻★★) – Peninnis Head★ – Hugh Town -
　　Museum★

Star Castle ⩘   ⩻ 🚗 🏠 🔲 🛠 **VISA** **MO** **AE**
The Garrison ⊠ *TR21 0JA* – *ℰ (01720) 422 317* – *www.star-castle.co.uk*
– info@star-castle.co.uk – *Fax (01720) 422 343*
– Closed 1-22 December and 2 January - 10 February
34 rm ⊊ – **†**£ 96/225 **††**£ 170/260 – 4 suites
Rest *Castle Dining Room* – (dinner only) Menu £ 29 **s** – Carte £ 10/24
Rest *Conservatory* – Seafood – (April-October) Menu £ 29
♦ Elizabethan castle built in 1593 in the shape of an eight pointed star, surrounded by
dry moat. There are harbour views; palms, echiums in garden. Airy rooms; subtle colours.
Medieval wall tapestry highlight of Castle Dining Room. Seafood menus in Conservatory.

Atlantic ⩻ ⅋ rm, ⓘ **VISA** **MO**
Hugh St, Hugh Town ⊠ *TR21 0PL* – *ℰ (01720) 422 417*
– www.atlantichotelscilly.co.uk – *atlantichotel@staustellbrewery.co.uk*
– Fax (01720) 423 009 – *Closed 2 January-12 February*
25 rm ⊊ – **†**£ 115/160 **††**£ 180/260   **Rest** – (dinner only) Carte £ 21/26
♦ A traditional white, comfortable hotel with views of St Mary's harbour and bobbing
boats. Some bedrooms in extension but all rooms now have a more contemporary
feel. Traditional dinner menu.

ENGLAND

⌂ **Evergreen Cottage** without rest
Parade, Hugh Town ⊠ TR21 0LP – ℰ (01720) 422711
– www.evergreencottageguesthouse.co.uk – evergreen.scilly@btinternet.com
– Closed Christmas-New Year and 2 weeks February
5 rm � – ♦£30/65 ♦♦£60/78
♦ A 300-year old captain's cottage; very pleasant, with window boxes, a few minutes walk from the quay. Plenty of local literature in low beamed lounge. Compact, tidy rooms.

SEAHAM – Durham – **501** P/Q 19 – pop. 21 153   24 **B2**
> ▣ London 284 mi – Carlisle 77 mi – Leeds 84 mi – Middlesbrough 24 mi
> – Newcastle upon Tyne 17 mi

🏨 **Seaham Hall** ⬩ ⟨ ⟫ 🏊 🔄 🔥 ⚷ rm, ℳ ⚘ ⟪ 🅿 ₩ ⑳ ⒶⒺ
✿ *Lord Byron's Walk, North : 1¼ m. by B 1287 ⊠ SR7 7AG – ℰ (0191) 516 1400*
– www.seaham-hall.co.uk – info@seaham-hall.com – Fax (0191) 516 1410
16 rm � – ♦£250/595 ♦♦£250/595 – 3 suites
Rest *The White Room* – (booking essential for non-residents) Carte £24/85
Spec. Seared scallops, celeriac, truffle, apple and lovage. Roast venison, chorizo, shallots and watercress. Saffron panna cotta, apricot sorbet.
♦ Imposing 17C and 19C mansion with ultra-modern technology in spacious rooms. Contemporary sculpture and décor. Unique Oriental spa has relaxing, Far Eastern ambience. Crisp linen and fine china define restaurant. Accomplished modern cooking uses luxury ingredients.

SEAHOUSES – Northumberland – **501** P 17 ▮ *Great Britain*   24 **B1**
> ▣ London 328 mi – Edinburgh 80 mi – Newcastle upon Tyne 46 mi
> 🄸 Car Park, Seafield Rd ℰ (01665) 720884,
> seahousesTIC@berwick-upon-tweed.gov.uk
> 🄸🄸 Beadnell Rd, ℰ (01665) 720 794
> 🄶 Farne Islands★ (by boat from harbour)

🏠 **Olde Ship** ⚘ ⟪ 🅿 ₩ ⑳
9 Main St ⊠ NE68 7RD – ℰ (01665) 720 200 – www.seahouses.co.uk
– theoldeship@seahouses.co.uk – Fax (01665) 721 383 – February-November
13 rm � – ♦£50/116 ♦♦£100/116 – 5 suites
Rest – (bar lunch Monday-Saturday) Carte £20/23
♦ Built in 1745 as a farmhouse but has left origins far behind, proudly proclaiming nautical links. Harbour views and marine artefacts throughout. Cosy, comfortable rooms. Dine in characterful bar at lunch or classic dining room for dinner.

SEASALTER – Kent – **504** X 29 – **see Whitstable**

SEAVIEW – I.O.W. – **503** Q 31 – **see Wight (Isle of)**

SEDLESCOMBE – East Sussex – **504** V 31 – ⊠ Battle   8 **B3**
> ▣ London 56 mi – Hastings 7 mi – Lewes 26 mi – Maidstone 27 mi

🏨 **Brickwall** 🚿 🏡 🏊 ⚘ ⟪ 🅿 ₩ ⑳ ⒶⒺ ①
The Green ⊠ TN33 0QA – ℰ (01424) 870 253 – www.brickwallhotel.com
– info@brickwallhotel.com – Fax (01424) 870 785
25 rm � – ♦£60/100 ♦♦£85/140
Rest – Menu £30 (dinner) – Carte lunch £22/27
♦ Part Tudor mansion at top of village green, built for local ironmaster in 1597. Well placed for beauty spots. Range of rooms include family, four-poster and ground floor. Dining room boasts characterful low beamed ceiling.

SEMINGTON – Wilts. – **503** N 29 – **see Trowbridge**

ENGLAND

SETTLE – North Yorkshire – **502** N 21 – pop. 3 621   22 **A2**

D London 238 mi – Bradford 34 mi – Kendal 30 mi – Leeds 41 mi
i Town Hall, Cheapside ℰ (01729) 825192, settle@ytbtic.co.uk
6 Giggleswick, ℰ (01729) 825 288

X **Little House**   *VISA* **@O**

*17 Duke St ⊠ BD24 9DJ – ℰ (01729) 823 963 – www.littlehouserestaurant.co.uk
– Closed 1 week January, 1 week September, Sunday except May to September,
Monday and Tuesday*
Rest – (dinner only) (booking essential) Carte £ 21/29
◆ Former 19C gate house, a 'little house' of stone that was once a cobblers. Well-kept, rustic style within a compact space. Traditional and classic styles of cooking prevail.

SEVENOAKS – Kent – **504** U 30 – pop. 26 699 📗 *Great Britain*   8 **B1**

D London 26 mi – Guildford 40 mi – Maidstone 17 mi
i Buckhurst Lane ℰ (01732) 450305, tic@sevenoakstown.gov.uk
18 Woodlands Manor Tinkerpot Lane, ℰ (01959) 523 806
18 Darenth Valley Shoreham Station Rd, ℰ (01959) 522 944
G Knole★★ **AC**, SE : ½ m. – Ightham Mote★★ **AC**, E : 5 m. by A 25

XX **Sun Do**   *AK* *VISA* **@O** *AE*

*61 High St ⊠ TN13 1JF – ℰ (01732) 453 299 – Fax (01732) 454 860 – Closed
25-26 December*
Rest – Chinese – Carte £ 18/36
◆ Meaning "Happiness", with attentive staff and oriental setting, you can expect authentic Chinese food here. Extensive choice, including various set menus.

at Ightham Common Southeast : 5 m. by A 25 on Common Rd – ⊠ Sevenoaks

🍴 **Harrow Inn**   🕸 🖑 **P** *VISA* **@O**

*Common Rd ⊠ TN15 9EB – ℰ (01732) 885 912 – Fax (01732) 885 912 – Closed
25-26 December*
Rest – (Closed Sunday dinner and Monday) Carte £ 21/35
◆ 17C stone and brick pub with welcoming fire and candles on every table. Hearty, rustic dishes served in traditional bar and more formal restaurant. Small back terrace.

SHAFTESBURY – Dorset – **503** N 30 – pop. 6 665   4 **C3**

D London 115 mi – Bournemouth 31 mi – Bristol 47 mi – Dorchester 29 mi
– Salisbury 20 mi
i 8 Bell St ℰ (01747) 853514, tourism@shaftesburydorset.com
G Gold Hill★ (≤★) – Local History Museum★ **AC**
G Wardour Castle★ **AC**, NE : 5 m

⌂ **The Retreat** without rest   🕭 🖑 🖑 **P** *VISA* **@O**

*47 Bell St ⊠ SP7 8AE – ℰ (01747) 850 372 – www.the-retreat.org.uk
– info@the-retreat.org.uk – Closed 3 weeks January*
10 rm ⊋ – ♦£ 50/68 ♦♦£ 80/85
◆ Georgian townhouse in good location - central but not noisy. Spotlessly clean throughout. Individually decorated bedrooms; several overlook the rear, so particularly quiet.

XX **La Fleur de Lys** with rm   ㄟ rm, 🖑 **P** *VISA* **@O** *AE*

*Bleke St ⊠ SP7 8AW – ℰ (01747) 853 717 – www.lafleurdelys.co.uk
– info@lafleurdelys.co.uk – Fax (01747) 853 130 – Closed Sunday dinner, Monday,
2 weeks in January and Tuesday lunch*
7 rm ⊋ – ♦£ 85/95 ♦♦£ 145/175   **Rest** – Menu £ 29 (dinner) – Carte £ 30/43
◆ Owners relocated to this address in 2003: smart restaurant in an 1870s ivy-covered house. Comfy bar with plenty of sofas. Well-kept bedrooms, named after grape varieties.

XX **Le Chanterelle**   🗟 **P** *VISA* **@O**

*Sherborne Causeway, West : 3 m. on A 30 ⊠ SP7 9PX – ℰ (01747) 852 821
– Fax (01747) 852 821 – Closed Monday and Tuesday*
Rest – Menu £ 18 (lunch) – Carte £ 35/40
◆ Whitewashed wisteria clad building just off the A30, with the occasional beam and large inglenook. French based menu boasts good ingredients and some unusual combinations; good value lunch.

SHALDON – Devon – 503 J 32 – pop. 1 628

▶ London 188 mi – Exeter 16 mi – Torquay 7 mi – Paignton 13 mi

ODE
VISA MO

21 Fore St ⊠ TQ14 0DE – ℰ (01626) 873 977 – www.odetruefood.co.uk
– info@odetruefood.co.uk – Closed 2 weeks October, Monday, Tuesday, Sunday
dinner and Bank Holidays
Rest – Organic – (dinner only and lunch Saturday and Sunday and lunch
Thursday and Friday in summer) (booking essential) Menu £ 20 (lunch)
– Carte £ 33/41

♦ Intimate restaurant in glass-fronted Georgian house. Menus use good quality, local organic produce; dishes have some innovative twists and Asian influences.
Charming service.

SHANKLIN – I.O.W. – 503 Q 32 – see Wight (Isle of)

SHEDFIELD – Hampshire – 503 Q 31 – pop. 3 558 – ⊠ Southampton

▶ London 75 mi – Portsmouth 13 mi – Southampton 10 mi
Meon Valley Shedfield Sandy Lane, off A 334, ℰ (01329) 833 455

Vatika
← 🏡 AC *VISA* MO AE

Botley Rd, Wickham Vineyard, on A334 ⊠ SO32 2HL – ℰ (01329) 830 405
– www.vatikarestaurant.co.uk – info@vatikarestaurant.co.uk
– Closed 1-15 January, Sunday dinner and Monday
Rest – (booking advisable at dinner) Menu £ 35

♦ Owned by Atul Kochhar of Benares restaurant in London. Stylish surroundings
overlook the vineyard. Indian flavours at the heart of the cooking, which is refined,
delicate and original.

SHEFFIELD – South Yorkshire – 502 P 23 – pop. 439 866 ▮ *Great Britain*

▶ London 174 mi – Leeds 36 mi – Liverpool 80 mi – Manchester 41 mi
– Nottingham 44 mi
🖪 14 Norfolk Row ℰ (0114) 221 1900, visitor@sheffield.gov.uk
Tinsley Park Darnall High Hazel Park, ℰ (0114) 203 7435
Beauchief Abbey Lane, ℰ (0114) 236 7274
Birley Wood Birley Lane, ℰ (0114) 264 7262
Concord Park Shiregreen Lane, ℰ (0114) 257 7378
Abbeydale Dore Twentywell Lane, ℰ (0114) 236 0763
Lees Hall Norton Hemsworth Rd, ℰ (0114) 255 4402
◎ Cutlers' Hall ★ CZ **A** – Cathedral Church of SS. Peter and Paul CZ **B** :
Shrewsbury Chapel (Tomb★)
Ⓖ Magna★ **AC**, NE : 3 m. by A 6178 - BY - and Bessemer Way

Plan on next page

Mercure St Paul's H & Spa
🖵 ⊛ 🐾 ƒ5 🛋 ♿ rm, AC 🖤 🛁

119 Norfolk St ⊠ S1 2JE – ℰ (0870) 122 65 85
VISA MO AE ①
– www.mercure.com – h6628@accor.com – Fax (0870) 122 65 86
CZ**a**
159 rm – ♦£ 185 ♦♦£ 185, ⊃ £15.95 – 2 suites
Rest *The Yard* – Carte £ 20/30

♦ Modern city centre hotel with spacious guest areas and marble flooring. Bedrooms
– some with floor to ceiling windows – boast first rate facilities and stylish bathrooms.
Excellent leisure/wellness centre. Bright, spacious restaurant looks to Winter Garden;
traditional menu.

Leopold
🛋 ♿ AC ⅍ 🕻 🛁 *VISA* MO AE

Leopold Sq ⊠ S1 1GZ – ℰ (0114) 252 40 00 – www.leopoldhotel.co.uk
– reservations@leopoldhotel.co.uk – Fax (0114) 252 40 01
– Closed 24 December-5 January
CZ**a**
76 rm – ♦£ 169/189 ♦♦£ 169/189, ⊃ £10.50 – 14 suites
Rest *1880* – (meals in bar) Carte £ 18/27

♦ Former Boys Grammar School, now an elegant boutique townhouse with stylish,
contemporary bedrooms, state-of-the-art facilities and old school photos on the
walls. Light meals served in the bar.

ENGLAND

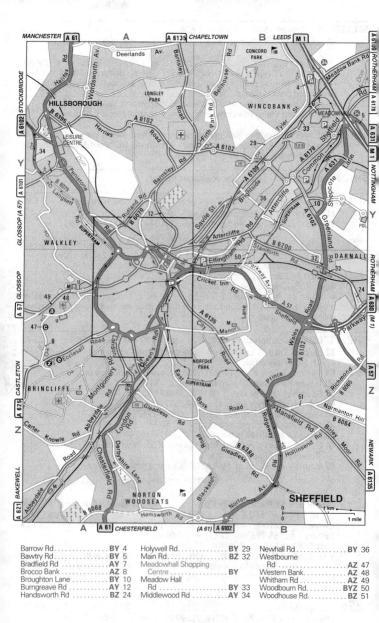

Good food without spending a fortune?
Look out for the Bib Gourmand 😊

718

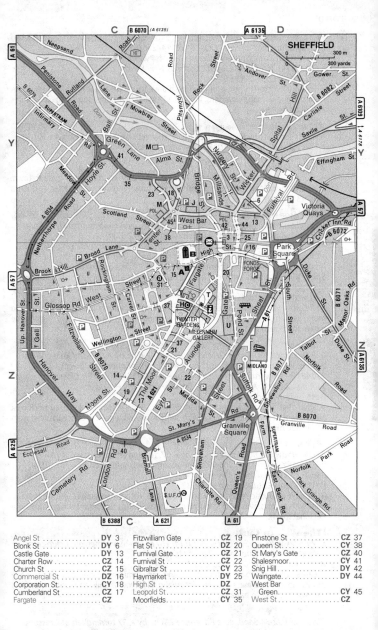

SHEFFIELD

300 m
300 yards

Angel St	**DY** 3	Fitzwilliam Gate	**CZ** 19	Pinstone St	**CZ** 37
Blonk St	**DY** 6	Flat St	**DZ** 20	Queen St	**CY** 38
Castle Gate	**DY** 13	Furnival Gate	**CZ** 21	St Mary's Gate	**CZ** 40
Charter Row	**CZ** 14	Furnival St	**CZ** 22	Shalesmoor	**CY** 41
Church St	**CZ** 15	Gibraltar St	**CY** 23	Snig Hill	**DY** 42
Commercial St	**DZ** 16	Haymarket	**DY** 25	Waingate	**DY** 44
Corporation St	**CY** 18	High St	**DZ**	West Bar	
Cumberland St	**CZ** 17	Leopold St	**CZ** 31	Green	**CY** 45
Fargate	**CZ**	Moorfields	**CY** 35	West St	**CZ**

A good night's sleep without spending a fortune?
Look for a Bib Hotel

The Westbourne without rest   🚗 ⚙ 🛰 **P** VISA ⓜ
25 Westbourne Rd ⊠ S10 2QQ – ℰ (0114) 2660109
– www.westbournehousehotel.com – guests@westbournehousehotel.com
– Fax (0114) 2667778 – Closed Christmas-New Year   AZc
8 rm ⌑ – †£55/72 ††£85
◆ Red brick Victorian house in residential area; lovely breakfast room and rear bedrooms overlook mature gardens. Individually styled bedrooms boast original features and good facilities.

Quarry House without rest   🚗 🛰 **P**
Rivelin Glen Quarry, Rivelin Valley Rd, Northwest : 4½ m. by A 61 on A 6101
⊠ S6 5SE – ℰ (0114) 2340382 – www.quarryhouse.org.uk
– penelopeslack@aol.com
3 rm ⌑ – †£45 ††£80
◆ Stone built, former Quarry Master's house in a pretty wooded valley close to town. Bright, contemporary bedrooms with quality furnishings, good facilities and extra touches. Homely lounge.

Old Vicarage (Tessa Bramley)   🚗 **P** VISA ⓜ
ⅇ₃
Marsh Lane, Ridgeway Moor, Southeast : 6¾ m. by A 6135 (signed Hyde Park)
and B 6054 turning right at Ridgeway Arms ⊠ S12 3XW
– ℰ (0114) 2475814 – www.theoldvicarage.co.uk – eat@theoldvicarage.co.uk
– Closed first two weeks August, Christmas, Sunday, Monday and Bank Holidays
Rest – (lunch by arrangement) Menu £40/55 – Carte approx. £60 ⅛
Spec. King scallops with confit chicken, celeriac and horseradish. Gloucester old spot with black pudding and caramelised apples. Blackberry sorbet and jelly with honeycomb parfait.
◆ Victorian vicarage in mature gardens. Traditional, homely lounge; abstract art in more modern dining room. Innovative cooking makes vibrant use of local/home grown ingredients.

Rafters   AC VISA ⓜ AE
220 Oakbrook Rd, Nether Green, Southwest : 2½ m. by A 625 and Fulwood rd,
turning left at mini roundabout, on right at traffic lights ⊠ S20 7ED – ℰ (0114)
2304819 – www.raftersrestaurant.co.uk – Fax (0114) 2304819 – Closed 1 week
January, 2 weeks August, Sunday, Tuesday and Bank Holidays.
Rest – (dinner only) Menu £35
◆ Small first floor restaurant above residential shops, displaying exposed brickwork and vibrant decor. Classical menu with some Asian influences; produce sourced from within 100 miles.

Artisan   VISA ⓜ AE
(☺)
32-34 Sandygate Rd, West : 2¼ m. by A 57, turning left at Crosspool Tavern
⊠ S10 5RY – ℰ (0114) 2666096 – www.artisanofsheffield.co.uk – Fax (0114)
2660279 – Closed 25-26 December
Rest – Menu £16/26 – Carte £22/32
◆ Refined yet rustic restaurant with terrace, red leather banquettes and walls crammed with mirrors, wine racks and menus. Classic British brasserie cooking displays a personal touch.

The Walnut Club   VISA ⓜ
557 Ecclesall Rd ⊠ S11 8PR – ℰ (0114) 2676566 – www.thewalnutclub.com
– rich@thewalnutclub.com – Closed Mondays   AZz
Rest – Menu £16/20 – Carte £20/33
◆ Large open plan room with central island bar, vibrant atmosphere and regular live music. Good value menu displays international flavours, grills and platters. Fri and Sat, over 25s only in bar area.

Catch   AC VISA ⓜ AE
(first floor) 32-34 Sandygate Rd, West : 2¾ m. by A 57 turning left at Crosspool
Tavern ⊠ S10 5RY – ℰ (0114) 2666096 – www.catchofsheffield.co.uk – Closed
25-26 December and Sunday
Rest – Seafood – (booking essential) Menu £16 – Carte £21/32
◆ Popular seafood restaurant. Blackboard menu offers carefully sourced fish from the market/fishmongers. Cooking is robust yet refined; relying on quality produce and good flavours.

ENGLAND

X **Thyme Cafe**   🕸 VISA ⓿ⓞ
490-492 Glossop Rd ⊠ S10 2QA – ℰ (0114) 267 0735 – www.thymecafe.co.uk
– Fax (0114) 267 67 58 – Closed 25-26 December and Bank Holidays   AZ**a**
Rest – (bookings not accepted) Carte £ 22/28
♦ Busy café in city suburbs with simple, rustic style. Large menus display classic British dishes in generous portions, with influences from Asia/the Med. Coffee and cakes 3-5pm.

X **Nonna's**   🚃 VISA ⓿ⓞ AE
535-541 Ecclesall Rd ⊠ S11 8PR – ℰ (0114) 268 6166 – www.nonnas.co.uk
– info@nonnas.co.uk – Closed 25 December and 1 January   AZ**e**
Rest – Italian – Carte £ 18/35
♦ Popular eatery with bar, deli and wine shop. Food ranges from pastries to the full 3 courses. Extensive Italian menus offer classic, homemade, flavoursome dishes; themed monthly specials.

at Chapeltown North : 6 m. on A 6135 - AY – ⊠ Sheffield

XX **Greenhead House**   🚃 P VISA ⓿ⓞ AE
84 Burncross Rd ⊠ S35 1SF – ℰ (0114) 246 9004 – Fax (0114) 246 9004 – Closed 2 weeks Easter, 2 weeks August, Christmas-New Year and Sunday-Tuesday
Rest – (dinner only and lunch Friday) (booking essential) Carte £ 40/44
♦ Traditional suburban house with homely, velvet furnished lounge displaying ornaments/antiques. Simple dining room; friendly service. Concise menu of home-cooked, largely classical dishes.

ENGLAND

at Totley Southwest : 5½ m. on A 621 - AZ

🏠 **The Cricket Inn**   🕸 P VISA ⓿ⓞ
Penny Lane ⊠ S17 3AZ – ℰ (0114) 236 52 56 – simon@cricketinn.co.uk
Rest – Menu £ 18 – Carte £ 20/35
♦ Popular village pub with extensive Yorkshire-based menu covering bar snacks through to grills and roasts. Hearty, robust cooking with local beers recommended for each dish.

SHEFFORD – Bedfordshire – **504** S 27 – pop. 3 319   12 **A1**
🄳 London 48 mi – Bedford 10 mi – Luton 16 mi – Northampton 37 mi

🏠 **The Black Horse** with rm   🚃 🕸 ⚇ P VISA ⓿ⓞ AE
Ireland, Northwest : 1 ¾ m. by Northbridge St and B 658 on Ireland rd
⊠ SG17 5QL – ℰ (01462) 811 398 – www.blackhorseireland.com
– etaverns@aol.com – Fax (01462) 817 238 – Closed 25-26 December, 1 January
2 rm ⌷ – ♯£55 ♯♯£55   **Rest** – (Closed Sunday dinner) Carte £ 19/30
♦ Part 18C brick and timbered pub with garden and chalet-style bedrooms. Confident cooking, interesting menus based round old favourites. Eat in traditional bar or restaurant.

SHELLEY – W. Yorks. – **502** O 23 – see Huddersfield

SHEPSHED – Leicestershire – **503** Q 25 – pop. 12 882   16 **B2**
🄳 London 111 mi – Derby 21 mi – Leicester 15 mi

🏠 **The Grange Courtyard** without rest   🚃 ⚇ P VISA ⓿ⓞ AE
Forest St ⊠ LE12 9DA – ℰ (01509) 600 189 – www.thegrangecourtyard.co.uk
– linda.lawrence@thegrangecourtyard.co.uk – Fax (01509) 603 834
– Closed 22 December-2 January
20 rm ⌷ – ♯£71 ♯♯£82/94
♦ Well-kept, Grade II listed building near to Donnington Park. Tastefully converted courtyard cottages; immaculate bedrooms. Guest lounge with honesty bar. Family style breakfast.

SHEPTON MALLET – Somerset – 503 M 30 – pop. 8 830 4 **C2**

> ▣ London 127 mi – Bristol 20 mi – Southampton 63 mi – Taunton 31 mi
> ▦ The Mendip Gurney Slade, ✆ (01749) 840 570
> ◉ Town★ – SS. Peter and Paul's Church★
> ◎ Downside Abbey★ (Abbey Church★) N : 5½ m. by A 37 and A 367.
> Longleat House★★★ **AC**, E : 15 m. by A 361 and B 3092 – Wells★★ –
> Cathedral★★★, Vicars' Close★, Bishop's Palace★ **AC** (≤★★) W : 6 m. by
> A 371 – Wookey Hole★ (Caves★ **AC**, Papermill★) W : 6½ m. by B 371 –
> Glastonbury★★ – Abbey★★ (Abbot's Kitchen★) **AC**, St John the Baptist★★,
> Somerset Rural Life Museum★ **AC** – Glastonbury Tor★ (≤★★★) SW : 9 m.
> by B 3136 and A 361 – Nunney★, E : 8½ m. by A 361

 Charlton House 🛏 🍴 🛎 ⬚ ☼ ※ ₺ rm, Ⓚ rest, ☏ 🛁 🅿
East : 1 m. on A 361 (Frome rd) ✉ BA4 4PR   **VISA ⬤⬤ AE ①**
– ✆ (01749) 342 008 – www.charltonhouse.com – enquiry@charltonhouse.com
– Fax (01749) 346 362
26 rm ☑ – †£115/327 ††£425/465   **Rest** – Menu £20/53 – Carte £27/53
◆ Grand 17C house owned by founders of Mulberry Company; a smart, boutique
style prevails touched by informality. Antiques in luxury bedrooms: Adam and Eve
carved four-poster. Well used local produce to the fore in conservatory dining room.

SHERBORNE – Dorset – 503 M 31 – pop. 9 350 4 **C3**

> ▣ London 128 mi – Bournemouth 39 mi – Dorchester 19 mi – Salisbury 36 mi
> – Taunton 31 mi
> ▤ 3 Tilton Court, Digby Rd ✆ (01935) 815341,
> sherborne.tic@westdorset-dc.gov.uk
> ▦ Higher Clatcombe, ✆ (01935) 812 274
> ◉ Town★ – Abbey★★ – Castle★ **AC**
> ◎ Sandford Orcas Manor House★ **AC**, NW : 4 m. by B 3148 – Purse Caundle
> Manor★ **AC**, NE : 5 m. by A 30. Cadbury Castle (≤★★) N : 8 m. by A 30 –
> Parish Church★, Crewkerne, W : 14 m. on A 30

🏠 **The Eastbury** 🛏 ☼ 🛁 🅿 **VISA ⬤⬤ AE**
Long St ✉ DT9 3BY – ✆ (01935) 813 131 – www.theeastburyhotel.co.uk
– enquiries@theeastburyhotel.co.uk – Fax (01935) 817 296
23 rm ☑ – †£68/89 ††£125/130
Rest – (Closed Sunday lunch) (bar lunch) Carte approx. £31
◆ Traditional town house, a former gentleman's residence, built in 1740 with peace-
ful walled garden. Well-kept rooms named after country flowers. 15C abbey is nearby.
Bright restaurant looking onto garden.

※※ **The Green** 🍴 ⇄ **VISA ⬤⬤ AE**
On The Green ✉ DT9 3HY – ✆ (01935) 813821 – www.thegreensherborne.co.uk
– Closed 2 weeks winter, 1 week summer, Sunday, Monday and Bank Holidays
Rest – Carte £23/33
◆ Pretty Grade II listing at the top of the hill in town centre with stone floor and
inglenook. A bistro feel predominates; dishes are traditional with a strong seasonal base.

at Oborne Northeast : 2 m. by A 30 – ✉ Sherborne

 The Grange ⌖ 🛏 ₺ rm, ☼ ☏ 🛁 🅿 **VISA ⬤⬤ AE ①**
✉ DT9 4LA – ✆ (01935) 813 463 – www.thegrangeatoborne.co.uk
– reception@thegrange.co.uk – Fax (01935) 817 464
18 rm ☑ – †£90 ††£150
Rest – (Closed Sunday dinner) (light lunch) Menu £33
◆ A 200-year old country house with floodlit gardens. Rooms are a treat: some
modern, some traditional, all large; some have patio access; others have balconies.
Friendly owner. Dorset and Somerset ingredients zealously used in dining room.

at Hermitage South : 7½ m. by A 352 – ✉ Sherborne

⌂ **Almshouse Farm** without rest ⌖ ≤ 🛏 ☼ 🅿
✉ DT9 6HA – ✆ (01963) 210 296 – Fax (01963) 210 296 – February-October
3 rm ☑ – †£35 ††£60
◆ Part 16C former monastery, now a working farm, surrounded by rural landscape.
Original features include inglenook fireplace in cosy breakfast room. Pretty, neat
bedrooms.

at Sandford Orcas North : 4¼ m. by B3148

The Alders without rest

✉ DT9 4SB – ℰ (01963) 220 666 – www.thealdersbb.com
– jonsue@thealdersbb.com
3 rm – †£45/58 ††£55/68
♦ Characterful stone house in attractive walled garden, near to 13C church. Pleasant, traditionally furnished bedrooms. Torches for evening pub visits and aromatherapy treatments available.

at Chetnole Southeast : 7 m. by A 352

The Chetnole Inn with rm

Chetnole ✉ DT9 6NU – ℰ (01935) 872 337 – www.thechetnoleinn.co.uk
– enquiries@thechetnoleinn.co.uk
3 rm ☑ – †£50/60 ††£75/85   **Rest** – Carte £ 20/30
♦ Sofa-furnished locals' bar with jukebox and skittle alley; cosy beamed dining room with wood-burner and understated style. Simple, tasty, value-for-money cooking. Pleasant, pine-furnished bedrooms.

SHERE – Surrey – **504** S 30 – see Guildford

SHERINGHAM – Norfolk – **504** X 25 – pop. 7 143   15 **C1**
🚩 London 136 mi – Cromer 5 mi – Norwich 27 mi

The Dales Country House ⌖

Lodge Hill, Upper Sheringham, Southwest : 1 ¼ m. by A 149 on B 1157
✉ NR26 8TJ – ℰ (01263) 824 555 – www.mackenziehotels.com
– dales@mackenziehotels.com – Fax (01263) 822 647
20 rm ☑ – †£95/150 ††£150/172
Rest *Upchers* – Menu £ 17 (lunch) – Carte £ 26/39
♦ Substantial 19C country house whose rich décor affords much comfort. Famous gardens conveniently adjacent. Original oak staircase in situ. Traditional bedrooms overlook the grounds. Wood-panelled restaurant with superb oak-carved inglenook.

Fairlawns without rest

26 Hooks Hill Rd ✉ NR26 8NL – ℰ (01263) 824 717
– www.fairlawns-sheringham.co.uk – info@fairlawns-sheringham.co.uk – Closed Christmas
5 rm ☑ – †£60 ††£90
♦ Attractive late Victorian house in peaceful area with large, well kept garden, comfy lounge and honesty bar. Spacious, modern bedrooms, some with sea/garden views; excellent bathrooms.

SHERWOOD BUSINESS PARK – Nottingham – see Nottingham

SHILTON – W. Mids. – **503** P 26 – see Coventry

SHINFIELD – Reading – **504** R 29 – see Reading

SHIPSTON-ON-STOUR – Warwickshire – **503** P 27 – pop. 4 456   19 **C3**
🚩 London 85 mi – Oxford 30 mi – Stratford-upon-Avon 12 mi

The George

The High Street ✉ CV36 4AJ – ℰ (01608) 661 453
– www.thefabulousgeorgehotel.com – info@thefabulousgeorgehotel.com
16 rm – †£120/160 ††£120/160   **Rest** – Carte £ 19/33
♦ Pleasantly located coaching inn with snug open fires and rustic feel. Comfy, individually designed bedrooms display a historic focus with a sense of modernity. Casual approach to dining with all day menu of bistro style dishes.

ENGLAND

at Long Compton South : 5 m. on A 3400 – pop. 1 994 – ⊠ Shipston-on-Stour

🍴 **The Red Lion** with rm   🚗 🌳 **P** 𝑽𝑰𝑺𝑨 ⓵ 𝔸𝔼
on A 3400 ⊠ *CV36 5JS* – ℰ *(01608) 684 221* – *www.redlion-longcompton.co.uk*
– *info@redlion-longcompton.co.uk* – *Fax (01608) 684 968*
5 rm ⌷ – †£55 ††£70/90   **Rest** – Carte £ 20/30
♦ 18C coaching inn of golden stone, tastefully madeover, with cosy, intimate feel. Seasonal menu of British favourites. Smiley service and a friendly atmosphere. Comfortable bedrooms stylishly furnished in cool linen shades.

SHIPTON GORGE – Dorset – see Bridport

SHOBDON – County of Herefordshire – **503** L 27 – ⊠ Leominster   18 **A3**
🄳 London 158 mi – Birmingham 55 mi – Hereford 18 mi – Shrewsbury 37 mi – Worcester 33 mi

⭡ **The Paddock** without rest   🌿 **P**
⊠ *HR9 9NQ* – ℰ *(01568) 708 176* – *thepaddock@talk21.com* – *Fax (01568) 708 829* – *March-October*
4 rm ⌷ – †£40 ††£62
♦ Well-priced, ground floor accommodation in this pleasant, village centre bungalow. All rooms are comfy and immaculately kept. Well run by hospitable owner.

SHOCKLACH – Cheshire   20 **A3**
🄳 London 193 mi – Liverpool 42 mi – Stoke-on-Trent 37 mi – Saint Helens 45 mi

🍴 **The Bull**   🌳 **P** 𝑽𝑰𝑺𝑨 ⓵ 𝔸𝔼
Worthenbury Road ⊠ *SY14 7BL* – ℰ *(01829) 250 239*
– *www.thebullshocklach.com* – *info@thebullshocklach.com*
Rest – Carte £ 25/33
♦ Smart village restaurant with large terrace and modern, stylish feel. Gorgeous tiled floor; plenty of antiques and curios. Menu of tasty dishes with a seasonal, traceable base.

SHOTTLE – Derbs. – see Belper

SHREWSBURY – Shropshire – **502** L 25 – pop. 67 126 📗 *Great Britain*   18 **B2**
🄳 London 164 mi – Birmingham 48 mi – Chester 43 mi – Derby 67 mi – Gloucester 93 mi – Manchester 68 mi – Stoke-on-Trent 39 mi
🄸 The Music Hall, The Square ℰ (01743) 281200, tic@shrewsburytourism.co.uk
🄸🄱 Condover, ℰ (01743) 872 977
🄸🄾 Meole Brace, ℰ (01743) 364 050
◉ Abbey★**D**
🄶 Ironbridge Gorge Museum★★ **AC** (The Iron Bridge★★ - Coalport China Museum★★ - Blists Hill Open Air Museum★★ – Museum of the Gorge and Visitor Centre★) SE : 12 m. by A 5 and B 4380

Plan opposite

🏨 **Prince Rupert**   🐾 ℱ♨ 🛗 ♿ rm, 🄰🄲 rest, 🌿 🎵 ♨ **P** 𝑽𝑰𝑺𝑨 ⓵ 𝔸𝔼 ⓪
Butcher Row ⊠ *SY1 1UQ* – ℰ *(01743) 499 955* – *www.prince-rupert-hotel.co.uk*
– *mikematthews@prince-rupert-hotel.co.uk* – *Fax (01743) 357 306*   **n**
68 rm ⌷ – †£75/95 ††£ 105 – 2 suites
Rest *Royalist* – (Closed Sunday dinner and Monday) Carte £ 24/33 **s**
Rest *Chambers* – Carte £ 21/28 **s**
♦ 12C home of Prince Rupert, in the shadow of the cathedral. A collection of old buildings, some 15C, affords tremendous character. Rooms vary in age: the oldest are the best. Baronial style Royalist. Olde Worlde atmosphere of Chambers.

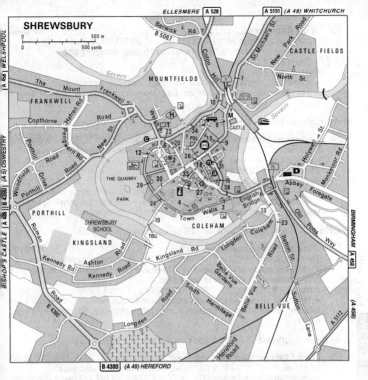

SHREWSBURY

ELLESMERE A 528 / A 5191 (A 49) WHITCHURCH

Pinewood House without rest

Shelton Park, The Mount, Northwest : 1½ m. on A 458 ⊠ SY3 8BL – 𝒞 (01743)
364 200 – Closed 2 weeks February and 24-26 December

3 rm ⊇ – ♛£45/50 ♛♛£58/70

♦ A Regency house surrounded by wooded gardens. A homely, intimate atmosphere
pervades the drawing room with its sofas and fresh flowers, whilst bedrooms are
charmingly decorated.

Tudor House without rest

2 Fish St ⊠ SY1 1UR – 𝒞 (01743) 351 735 – www.tudorhouseshrewsbury.co.uk
– enquire@tudorhouseshrewsbury.co.uk – Fax (01743) 351 735   e

4 rm ⊇ – ♛£69/95 ♛♛£79/120

♦ On a picturesque medieval street in a historic part of Shrewsbury, this compact 15C
house retains its antiquated charm in its cosy sitting room and simple bedrooms.

✗ **Mad Jack's** with rm   VISA 🅒🅞 AE ①

15 St.Mary's St ⊠ SY1 1EQ – 𝒞 (01743) 358 870 – www.madjacks.uk.com
– info@madjacks.uk.com – Fax (01743) 344 422 – Closed 25 December   a

4 rm ⊇ – ♛£65 ♛♛£85   **Rest** – Menu £25 (dinner) – Carte £20/39

♦ Centrally located in the heart of a busy market town. Spacious main dining area,
snug and hidden courtyard, with plain décor and marble tables. Good service, slightly
eclectic menu. Modern, comfy bedrooms.

🍽️ **The Armoury**   VISA ⓒⓞ AE

Victoria Quay, Welsh Bridge ⊠ *SY1 1HH –* ℰ *(01743) 340 525*
– www.brunningandprice.co.uk – armoury@brunningandprice.co.uk
– Closed 25-26 December   c
Rest – Carte £ 15/30

♦ Former 18C riverside warehouse with huge open-plan interior; sturdy brick walls full of old pictures and bookshelves. Daily changing menus offer an wide range of dishes.

at Albrighton North : 3 m. on A 528 – ⊠ **Shrewsbury**

🏨 **Albright Hussey Manor** ⌖   ≤ 🚗 🛜 ⅙ rm, ⁙ 🎿 P VISA ⓒⓞ AE ⓞ

Ellesmere Rd ⊠ *SY4 3AF –* ℰ *(01939) 290 571 – www.albrighthussey.co.uk*
– info@albrighthussey.co.uk – Fax (01939) 291 143
25 rm � – †£ 70/85 ††£ 95/120 – 1 suite
Rest – Menu £ 25 (dinner) – Carte £ 27/35

♦ Most impressive part 16C moated manor house. Fountains, stone walls and bridge in lawned gardens. The five rooms in the original house have oak panelling and huge fireplaces. Hugely characterful, heavily beamed 16C dining room.

at Grinshill North : 7 ¾ m. by A 49 – ⊠ **Shrewsbury**

🍴🍴 **The Inn at Grinshill** with rm   🛜 📶 P VISA ⓒⓞ

The High St ⊠ *SY4 3BL –* ℰ *(01939) 220 410 – www.theinnatgrinshill.co.uk*
– info@theinnatgrinshill.co.uk – Fax (01939) 220 327 – Closed dinner Sunday and Bank Holidays and Monday in low season
6 rm �)⅃ – †£ 90 ††£ 120   **Rest** – Menu £ 15 – Carte £ 23/40

♦ 18C stable block in small village: a cosy bar with sofas awaits, while beyond a light and airy, modern restaurant serves a wide range of menus. Spacious, stylish bedrooms.

at Atcham Southeast : 3 m. by A 5064 on B 4380 – ⊠ **Shrewsbury**

🍽️ **The Mytton and Mermaid** with rm   🚗 🛜 🎿 P VISA ⓒⓞ AE ⓞ

⊠ *SY5 6QG –* ℰ *(01743) 761 220 – www.myttonandmermaid.co.uk*
– admin@myttonandmermaid.co.uk – Fax (01743) 761 297 – Closed 25 December
18 rm ⊲ – †£ 80/85 ††£ 105/165   **Rest** – Menu £ 25 – Carte £ 23/33

♦ Impressive Georgian building beside the river, with neat lawns and terraces. Mix of classic and modern cooking in bar; more substantial seasonal and local fare in restaurant. Comfy, well kept bedrooms – split between house and stables.

at Acton Burnell Southeast : 7 ½ m. by A 458 – ⊠ **Shrewsbury**

🏠 **Acton Pigot** without rest ⌖   🚗 🛜 🟧 💥 ⅗ ⁙ P

Acton Pigot, Northeast : 1 ¾ m. by Kenley rd ⊠ *SY5 7PH –* ℰ *(01694) 731 209*
– www.actonpigot.co.uk – actonpigot@farming.co.uk – Fax (01694) 731 399
– Closed 25 December
3 rm ⊲ – †£ 50 ††£ 75

♦ 17C farmhouse on working farm. Wealth of pursuits includes heated pool, fishing lake and tennis court. Age of house handsomely apparent in guest areas. Pleasant, cosy rooms.

SHURDINGTON – Glos. – **503** N 28 – see Cheltenham

SIBFORD GOWER – Oxon. – see Banbury

SIDFORD – Devon – **503** K 31 – see Sidmouth

SIDLESHAM – West Sussex – see Chicester

SIDMOUTH – Devon – **503** K 31 – pop. 12 066   2 **D2**

🚊 London 176 mi – Exeter 14 mi – Taunton 27 mi – Weymouth 45 mi
ℹ️ Ham Lane ℰ (01395) 516441, sidmouthtic@eclipse.co.uk
🟥 Cotmaton Rd, ℰ (01395) 513 451
🟩 Bicton★ (Gardens★) AC, SW : 5 m

ENGLAND

Riviera

The Esplanade ⌧ *EX10 8AY* – ✆ *(01395) 515 201* – *www.hotelriviera.co.uk*
– enquiries@hotelriviera.co.uk – Fax (01395) 577 775 – Closed 2 January-February
26 rm ⌐ – †£114/170 ††£228/368   **Rest** – Menu £26/37 – Carte £42/50
♦ An established seafront hotel with fine Regency façade and bow fronted windows.
Peach and pink bedrooms with floral touches and friendly staff make for a comfortable stay. Formal dining salon affords views across Lyme Bay.

Belmont

The Esplanade ⌧ *EX10 8RX* – ✆ *(01395) 512 555* – *www.belmont-hotel.co.uk*
– reservations@belmont-hotel.co.uk – Fax (01395) 579 101
50 rm – †£100/210 ††£130/220, ⌐ £16
Rest – Menu £15/35 – Carte approx. £53 **s**
♦ A former 19C family summer residence situated on seafront with attendant views.
Spacious lounge; traditional bedrooms. Guests can use leisure facilities at Victoria
hotel. Stylish dining room with resident pianist.

Old Farmhouse

Hillside Rd, off Salcombe Rd ⌧ *EX10 8JG* – ✆ *(01395) 512 284 – April-October*
6 rm ⌐ – †£45/59 ††£56/70   **Rest** – (by arrangement) Menu £13
♦ Utterly charming 16C ex-cider mill and farmhouse with low ceilings, heavy beams,
numerous inglenooks, cosy lounge and pleasant rooms that boast rafters and sloping
roofs. Dinner served in rustic dining room.

at Sidford North : 2 m. – ⌧ Sidmouth

Salty Monk with rm

Church St, on A 3052 ⌧ *EX10 9QP* – ✆ *(01395) 513 174* – *www.saltymonk.co.uk*
– saltymonk@btconnect.com – Closed 2 weeks November and 2 weeks January
5 rm ⌐ – †£75/100 ††£180/200
Rest – (dinner only and lunch Thursday-Saturday) (booking essential)
Menu £40 (dinner) – Carte lunch £29/42
♦ Former 16C salt house where monks stayed en route to Exeter Cathedral. Fine
lounge with deep leather armchairs. Modern cooking in conservatory restaurant.
Pleasant bedrooms.

at Newton Poppleford Northwest : 4 m. by B 3176 on A 3052 – ⌧ Sidmouth

Moores'

6 Greenbank, High St ⌧ *EX10 0EB* – ✆ *(01395) 568 100*
*– www.mooresrestaurant.co.uk – info.moores@btconnect.com – Closed 3 weeks
January, Sunday dinner and Monday*
Rest – Menu £18/28 **s**
♦ Two pretty 18C cottages set back from the main road are the setting for this busy,
personally run restaurant with conservatory extension. Modern, locally sourced
dishes.

SINNINGTON – N. Yorks. – **502** R 21 – **see Pickering**

SISSINGHURST – Kent – **504** V 30 – **see Cranbrook**

SITTINGBOURNE – Kent – **504** W 29   9 **C1**

▶ London 44 mi – Canterbury 18 mi – Maidstone 15 mi – Sheerness 9 mi

Hempstead House

London Rd, Bapchild, East : 2 m. on A 2 ⌧ *ME9 9PP* – ✆ *(01795) 428 020*
*– www.hempsteadhouse.co.uk – info@hempsteadhouse.co.uk – Fax (01795)
436 362*
27 rm ⌐ – †£80 ††£150
Rest *Lakes* – (residents only Sunday dinner) Menu £18/25 – Carte £27/37
♦ Part Victorian manor, a former estate house for surrounding farmland. Currently
being expanded; new spa added. Cheerful, individually designed, modern bedrooms.
Sunny restaurant with terrace.

ENGLAND

SIX MILE BOTTOM – Cambs. – see Newmarket (Suffolk)

SIZERGH – Cumbria – see Kendal

SKELWITH BRIDGE – Cumbria – **502** K 20 – see Ambleside

SKIPTON – North Yorkshire – **502** N 22 – **pop. 14 313** ▯ *Great Britain*   22 **A2**
> ▶ London 217 mi – Kendal 45 mi – Leeds 26 mi – Preston 36 mi – York 43 mi
> 🛈 35 Coach St ✆ (01756) 792809, skipton@ytbtic.co.uk
> 🖪 Short Lee Lane, off NW Bypass, ✆ (01756) 793 922
> 👁 Castle★ AC

⌂   **Carlton House** without rest   🖉 𝚅𝙸𝚂𝙰 ◍◉
46 Keighley Rd ⊠ BD23 2NB – ✆ (01756) 700 921
– www.carltonhouse.rapidal.co.uk – carltonhouse@rapidial.co.uk – Fax (01756)
700 921
5 rm ⌕ – ♦£30 ♦♦£60
♦ Victorian terraced house near centre of town. Pleasantly furnished in sympathetic style. Attractive dining room serves full English breakfast. Individually decorated bedrooms.

🍴   **The Bull**   🍽 🅿 𝚅𝙸𝚂𝙰 ◍◉ 𝙰𝙴
Broughton, West : 3 m. on A 59 ⊠ BD23 3AE – ✆ (01756) 792 065
– www.thebullatbroughton.co.uk – janeneil@thebullatbroughton.co.uk
– Fax (01756) 792 065
Rest – Menu £13 (weekdays) – Carte £19/31
♦ Set on busy main road, this delightful country pub has open log fire and its own specially brewed beer. Intimate dining room serving varied, tasty menus full of local produce.

at Hetton North : 5 ¾ m. by B 6265 – ⊠ Skipton

✗✗✗   **Angel Inn and Barn Lodgings** with rm   🅰🅲 🖉 🅿 𝚅𝙸𝚂𝙰 ◍◉ 𝙰𝙴
⊠ BD23 6LT – ✆ (01756) 730 263 – www.angelhetton.co.uk
– info@angelhetton.co.uk – Fax (01756) 730 363
– Closed 25 December and 1 week January
5 rm ⌕ – ♦£115/165 ♦♦£130/180
Rest – (Closed Sunday dinner) (dinner only and Sunday lunch) (booking essential) Carte £25/35 ⌘
♦ Well regarded restaurant with stone walls, beams and roaring log fire. Fine quality, locally sourced produce. Bedrooms with antique furniture and modern appointments.

🍴   **The Angel Inn**   🍽 🖉 🅿 𝚅𝙸𝚂𝙰 ◍◉ 𝙰𝙴
😊   *⊠ BD23 6LT – ✆ (01756) 730 263 – www.angelhetton.co.uk*
– info@angelhetton.co.uk – Fax (01756) 730 363
– Closed 25 December and 1 week January
Rest – (booking essential) Menu £23/35 – Carte £25/35 ⌘
♦ Ancient beams and inglenooks in hugely characterful pubby part of renowned 18C inn. Fine modern British cooking. Shares rooms with restaurant in converted farmbuildings.

at Elslack West : 5 m. by A 59 and A 56 – ⊠ Skipton

🏠   **The Tempest Arms**   ⸮ 🏊 🅿 𝚅𝙸𝚂𝙰 ◍◉ 𝙰𝙴 ◍
⊠ BD23 3AY – ✆ (01282) 842 450 – www.tempestarms.co.uk
– info@tempestarms.co.uk – Fax (01282) 843 331
21 rm ⌕ – ♦£60 ♦♦£80/135   **Rest** – (closed 25-26 December) Carte £19/26
♦ Extended 18C stone inn with characterful beams and traditional feel. Smart bedrooms; those in annexed block are best - spacious, most with balconies, two with outdoor hot tubs. Open plan bar and dining room. Huge choice on menus.

SLALEY – Northd. – **501** N 19 – see Hexham

SLAPTON – Devon – **503** J 33   2 **C3**

▶ London 223 mi – Dartmouth 7 mi – Plymouth 29 mi
ⓖ Dartmouth★★, N : 7 m. by A 379 – Kingsbridge★, W : 7 m. by A 379

🏠 **The Tower Inn** with rm   🖫 🕸 **P** **VISA** **⑩** **AE**
Church Rd ⊠ TQ7 2PN – ℰ (01548) 580 216 – www.thetowerinn.com
– towerinn@slapton.org – Closed Sunday dinner
3 rm ⊇ – †£40/55 ††£60/75
Rest – (Closed Monday in winter) Carte £ 21/30
♦ Built in 1347 as cottages for men working on local chantry. Beams, flag floors, stone walls: all very characterful. Surprisingly modern menus. Simple annex bedrooms.

SLOUGH – Slough – **504** S 29 – pop. 126 276   11 **D3**

▶ London 29 mi – Oxford 39 mi – Reading 19 mi

🏨 **Heathrow/Windsor Marriott**   🖾 🕸 ⅃⅂ ✻ 🍽 㕥 & rm, 🔝 ❝ 🔏
Ditton Rd, Langley, Southeast : 2½ m. on A 4 ⊠ SL3   **P** **VISA** **⑩** **AE** **①**
8PT – ℰ (01753) 400 72 44 – www.heathrowwindsormarriott.co.uk
– mhrs.lhrsl.conferenceandevents@marriotthotels.co.uk – Fax (01753) 400 73 44
381 rm – †£169 ††£169, ⊇ £14.95 – 1 suite
Rest – (buffet lunch) Menu £ 18/24 **s** – Carte £ 23/38 **s**
♦ A five-storey hotel, 15 minutes from Heathrow airport, with well-equipped leisure club. Bedrooms are furnished with good quality fabrics; Executive rooms have private lounge. All-day restaurant option.

SNAINTON – North Yorkshire – **502** S 21   23 **C2**

▶ London 241 mi – Pickering 8 mi – Scarborough 10 mi

🏠 **Coachman Inn** with rm   🖫 🕸 **P** **VISA** **⑩** **AE**
Pickering Road West, West : ½ m. by A 170 on B 1258 ⊠ YO13 9PL – ℰ (01723)
859 231 – www.coachmaninn.co.uk – james@coachmaninn.co.uk – Fax (01723)
850 008
5 rm ⊇ – †£50 ††£70
Rest – (Closed Monday and lunch Tuesday) Carte £ 20/30
♦ Georgian former coaching inn, with cosy firelit bar and cloth-clad dining room. Traditional cooking keeps up to date with modern influences and uses seasonal, local produce. Classically-furnished, spacious bedrooms.

SNAPE – Suffolk – **504** Y 27   15 **D3**

▶ London 113 mi – Ipswich 19 mi – Norwich 50 mi

🏠 **The Crown Inn** with rm   🖫 🕸 **P** **VISA** **⑩**
Bridge Rd ⊠ IP17 1SL – ℰ (01728) 688 324 – snapecrown@tiscali.co.uk – Closed
November-March Sunday and Monday dinner
3 rm ⊇ – †£65 ††£75   **Rest** – Carte £ 15/25
♦ 15C inn with antique settle, log fire and exposed beams. Agricultural artefacts and paintings fill the small dining rooms where seasonal dishes are served. Comfortable rooms.

SNETTISHAM – Norfolk – **504** V 25 – pop. 2 145   14 **B1**

▶ London 113 mi – King's Lynn 13 mi – Norwich 44 mi

🏠 **The Rose and Crown** with rm   🖫 🕸 & **P** **VISA** **⑩**
Old Church Rd ⊠ PE31 7NE – ℰ (01485) 541 382
– www.roseandcrownsnettisham.co.uk – info@roseandcrownsnettisham.co.uk
– Fax (01485) 543 172
16 rm ⊇ – †£70/90 ††£90/110   **Rest** – Carte £ 20/25
♦ Large, quirky pub divided into numerous rooms. Fresh local ingredients form a variety of dishes from across the globe; there really is something for everyone. Individually styled and bright bedrooms.

SOAR MILL COVE – Devon – see Salcombe

ENGLAND

SOLIHULL – West Midlands – 503 O 26 – pop. 94 753   19 C2

🚆 London 109 mi – Birmingham 7 mi – Coventry 13 mi – Warwick 13 mi
🖈 Central Library, Homer Rd ℰ (0121) 704 6130

🍴🍴 **The Town House**   AC P VISA ☎ AE
727 Warwick Rd ⊠ B91 3DA – ℰ (0121) 704 1567 – www.thetown-house.com
– reservations@thetown-house.com – Fax (0121) 705 9315 – Closed 1 January
Rest – Menu £ 16 (weekdays) – Carte £ 27/36
♦ Once a salubrious nightclub with town centre location. Stylish open-plan interior
boasts large dining area with leather banquettes. Soundly prepared modern dishes.

🍴 **Metro Bar and Grill**   AC VISA ☎ AE
680-684 Warwick Rd ⊠ B91 3DX – ℰ (0121) 705 9495
– www.metrobarandgrill.co.uk – solihull@metrobarandgrill.co.uk – Fax (0121)
705 4754 – Closed 25-26 December and Sunday
Rest – Menu £ 17 (weekday lunch) – Carte £ 25/35
♦ Locally renowned town centre bar/restaurant that combines buzzy informality with
appealing range of brasserie dishes. Dine alongside busy bar: don't expect a quiet
night out!

at Olton Northwest : 2½ m. on A 41 – ⊠ Solihull

🍴🍴 **Rajnagar**   AC VISA ☎ AE ①
256 Lyndon Rd ⊠ B92 7QW – ℰ (0121) 742 8140 – www.rajnagar.com
– info@rajnagar.com – Fax (0121) 743 3147
Rest – Indian – (dinner only) Menu £ 15 – Carte £ 19/30
♦ A busy, modern neighbourhood favourite, privately owned, offering authentic,
regional specialities of Indian cuisine. Service is flexible and friendly.

Don't confuse 🍴 with ✿!
🍴 defines comfort, while stars are awarded for the best cuisine,
across all categories of comfort.

SOMERLEYTON – Suffolk   15 D2

🚆 London 134 mi – Great Yarmouth 10 mi – Norwich 20 mi

🏠 **The Duke's Head**   ☂ P VISA ☎ ①
Slugg's Lane, West : ¾ m. off B 1074 ⊠ NR32 5QR – ℰ (01502) 730 281
– www.somerleyton.co.uk – dukeshead@somerleyton.co.uk
Rest – Carte £ 20/40
♦ Part of the Somerleyton Estate; boasts a super sundrenched terrace "down by the
river". Appetizing modern dishes employ tasty fresh cooking with ingredients from
the estate.

SOMERTON – Somerset – 503 L 30 – pop. 4 133   3 B2

🚆 London 138 mi – Bristol 32 mi – Taunton 17 mi
🏙 Town★ - Market Place★ (cross★) – St Michael's Church★
🌳 Long Sutton★ (Church★★) SW : 2½ m. by B 3165 – Huish Episcopi
(St Mary's Church Tower★★) SW : 4½ m. by B 3153 – Lytes Cary★,
SE : 3½ m. by B 3151 – Street - The Shoe Museum★, N : 5 m. by B 3151.
Muchelney★★ (Parish Church★★) SW : 6½ m. by B 3153 and A 372 – High
Ham (≤★★, St Andrew's Church★) NW : 9 m. by B 3153, A 372 and minor
rd – Midelney Manor★ AC, SW : 9 m. by B 3153 and A 378

🏠 **Lynch Country House** without rest   ≤ ☂ ⚛ P VISA ☎ AE ①
4 Behind Berry ⊠ TA11 7PD – ℰ (01458) 272 316
– www.thelynchcountryhouse.co.uk – the-lynch@talk21.com – Fax (01458)
272 590
9 rm ⌂ – †£ 60/65 ††£ 100
♦ Stands on a crest overlooking the Cary Valley. The grounds of this Regency house
are equally rich with unusual shrubs, trees and lake. Coach house rooms more modern.

▶ London 87 mi – Bristol 79 mi – Plymouth 161 mi

Access Itchen Bridge (toll) AZ

✈ Southampton/Eastleigh Airport : ✆ (0870) 040 0009, N : 4 m. BY

⛴ to Hythe (White Horse Ferries Ltd) frequent services daily (12 mn) – to the Isle of Wight (Cowes) (Red Funnel Ferries) frequent services daily (approx. 22 mn)

⛴ to the Isle of Wight (East Cowes) (Red Funnel Ferries) frequent services daily (55 mn)

🛈 9 Civic Centre Rd ✆ (023) 8083 3333, tourist.information@southampton.gov.uk

⛳ Southampton Municipal Bassett Golf Course Rd, ✆ (023) 8076 0546

⛳ Stoneham Bassett Monks Wood Close, ✆ (023) 8076 9272

⛳ Chilworth Main Rd, ✆ (023) 8074 0544

👁 Old Southampton AZ : Bargate ★ B - Tudor House Museum ★ M1

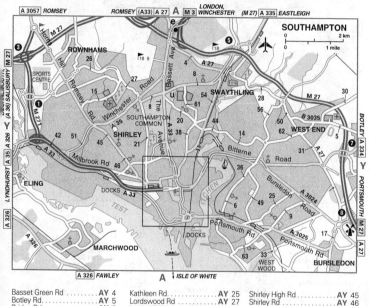

Basset Green Rd	**AY** 4	Kathleen Rd	**AY** 25
Botley Rd	**AY** 5	Lordswood Rd	**AY** 27
Bridge Rd	**AY** 6	Lords Hill Way	**AY** 26
Burgess Rd	**AY** 8	Mansbridge Rd	**AY** 28
Butts Rd	**AY** 9	Moorgreen Rd	**AY** 30
Cobden Ave	**AY** 14	Moor Hill	**AY** 31
Coxford Rd	**AY** 15	Newtown Rd	**AY** 33
Hamble Lane	**AY** 17	Peartree Ave	**AY** 36
Highfield Lane	**AY** 20	Portswood Rd	**AY** 38
Hill Lane	**AY** 21	Redbridge Rd	**AY** 42
Kane's Hill	**AY** 24	St Denys Rd	**AY** 44

Shirley High Rd	**AY** 45
Shirley Rd	**AY** 46
Spring Rd	**AY** 49
Swaything Rd	**AY** 50
Tebourba Way	**AY** 51
Thomas Lewis Way	**AY** 54
Townhill Way	**AY** 56
Welbeck Ave	**AY** 61
Westend Rd	**AY** 62
Weston Lane	**AY** 63

🏨 **De Vere Grand Harbour**   📺 🕸 🏧 🛗 🛁 🛗 🖐 rm, 🅰️🅲 rest, 🍽 📞 🛎

West Quay Rd ⊠ *SO15 1AG* – ✆ *(023) 8063 3033*   🅿 *VISA* 🆎 🆎 ①

– www.devere.co.uk – grandharbour@devere-hotels.com

– Fax (023) 8063 3066   AZ**a**

169 rm ⊑ – 🛏£ 99/240 🛏🛏£ 120/280 – 1 suite

Rest *Allerton's* – (Closed Sunday-Monday) (dinner only) (booking essential) Menu £ 43

Rest *Number 5* – (bar lunch Monday-Saturday) Menu £ 26 – Carte £ 26/28 **s**

♦ Modern and stylish. The split-level pavilion leisure club boasts a Finnish sauna, Turkish steam room and bar. Well furnished rooms; some with balconies and king-size beds. Allerton's is arcaded, with screens. Chic, informal Number 5.

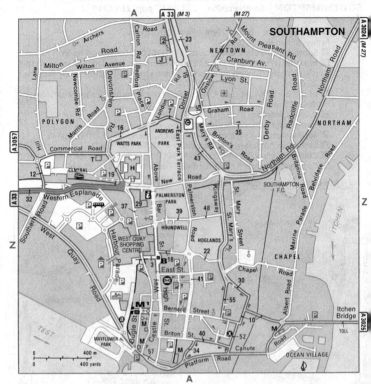

A

Above Bar St.	**AZ**	High St.	**AZ**	Pound Tree Rd.	**AZ** 39

 Hilton Southampton 🔲 🏖 Ló 🗐 & rm, 🕍 ⅍ 🕪 🖚 🅿 VISA ⚬⚬ 🅰🅴 ⓪
Bracken Pl, Chilworth ⊠ *SO16 3RB –* ℰ *(023) 8070 2700*
– www.hilton.co.uk/southampton – Fax (023) 8076 7233   AYe
133 rm – 🛉£ 169 🛉🛉£ 169, ⊊ £16.75 – 2 suites
Rest – Menu £ 23 – Carte £ 22/40
◆ A purpose-built hotel with smart marbled lobby and busy reception. Extensive leisure facilities and good size bedrooms, well furnished to a high standard. Informal, family-oriented restaurant.

 Jurys Inn 🗐 & rm, 🕪 🖚 🅿 VISA ⚬⚬ 🅰🅴 ⓪
1 Charlotte Pl ⊠ *SO14 0TB –* ℰ *(023) 8037 1111 – www.jurysinns.com*
– jurysinnsouthampton@jurysinns.com – Fax (023) 8037 1100
– Closed 24-27 December   AZc
270 rm – 🛉£ 74/115 🛉🛉£ 99/115, ⊊ £ 9.95
Rest *Innfusion* – (bar lunch) Carte approx. £ 20 **s**
◆ Up-to-date hotel, handily placed close to city centre. Well-equipped conference facilities; spacious coffee shop/bar. Good value, ample sized accommodation. Modern dining room with modish menus.

Oxfords
35-36 Oxford St ⊠ SO14 3DS – ✆ (023) 8022 4444
– www.oxfordsrestaurant.com – bookings@oxfordsrestaurant.com
– Fax (023) 8022 2284   AZx
Rest – (Closed Sunday) Menu £16/17 – Carte £21/28
♦ Well-run, modern eatery in lively part of town. Entrance bar has impressively vast wall of wines. Restaurant features bold, fresh brasserie cuisine with extensive choice.

The White Star Tavern, Dining and Rooms with rm
28 Oxford Street ⊠ SO14 3DJ – ✆ (023) 8082 1990
– www.whitestartavern.co.uk – manager@whitestartavern.co.uk – Fax (023) 8090 4982 – Closed 25-26 December
13 rm – †£83 ††£155   **Rest** – Carte £20/29   AZx
♦ Smart corner pub with large windows, eye-catching black exterior and modern, open plan design. Food ranges from sandwiches and pub classics to more contemporary European dishes. Understated, stylish bedrooms with modern bathrooms.

at Hamble-le-Rice Southeast : 5 m. by A 3025 - A - and B 3397 – ⊠ Southampton

The Bugle
High St ⊠ SO31 4HA – ✆ (023) 8045 3000 – www.buglehamble.co.uk
– manager@buglehamble.co.uk – Fax (023) 8045 3051 – Closed 25 December and 1 January
Rest – (booking essential) Carte £18/27 **s**
♦ Part 12C inn on Southampton Water, with exposed beams and brickwork, stone and oak floors and a wood burning stove. Serves a traditional menu and appealing bar bites.

at Netley Marsh West : 6½ m. by A 33 off A 336

Hotel TerraVina
174 Woodlands Rd ⊠ SO40 7GL – ✆ (023) 8029 3784
– www.hotelterravina.co.uk – info@hotelterravina.co.uk – Fax (023) 8029 3627
11 rm – †£150/230 ††£150/230, ⊇ £13.50   **Rest** – Carte £28/40
♦ Attractive Victorian house with extensions beautifully clad in cedar, and friendly, hands-on Anglo-French owners. Comfy, boutique-style bedrooms; some with terraces. Classic British and French dishes; precise, well judged cooking. Superb wine list and cellars. Wonderful colonial style roofed terrace.

SOUTH DALTON – East Riding – see Beverley

SOUTHEND-ON-SEA – Southend-on-Sea – **504** W 29 – pop. 160 257   13 **C3**
▶ London 39 mi – Cambridge 69 mi – Croydon 46 mi – Dover 85 mi
✈ Southend-on-Sea Airport – ✆ (01702) 608100, N : 2 m
🛈 Western Esplanade ✆ (01702) 215120, vic@southend.gov.uk
🏌 Belfairs Leigh-on-Sea Eastwood Road North, ✆ (01702) 525 345
🏌 Ballards Gore G. & C.C. Gore Rd, Canewdon, ✆ (01702) 258 917
🏌 Garon Park Golf Complex Garon Park, Eastern Ave, ✆ (01702) 601 701

Beaches without rest
192 Eastern Esplanade, Thorpe Bay ⊠ SS1 3AA – ✆ (01702) 586 124
– www.beachesguesthouse.co.uk – mark@beachesguesthouse.co.uk
– Closed 31 December and 1 January
7 rm – †£40 ††£75/85
♦ A sunny guesthouse on Thorpe Bay with panorama of Thames Estuary. Continental buffet breakfast. Individually styled rooms: four have sea views; two have balconies.

Pebbles without rest
190 Eastern Esplanade, Thorpe Bay ⊠ SS1 3AA – ✆ (01702) 582 329
– res@mypebbles.co.uk – Fax (01702) 582 329
7 rm ⊇ – †£45 ††£65/85
♦ Friendly guesthouse on the Esplanade overlooking estuary; away from bustle of town but within easy walking distance. Rooftop garden and sea views from most bedrooms.

ENGLAND

⌂ **Atlantis** without rest   ⌘ 📶 **P** VISA ◉◉ AE
63 Alexandra Rd ⊠ SS1 1EY – 𝒞 (01702) 332538
– www.atlantisguesthouse.co.uk – info@atlantisinvestments.co.uk – Fax (01702) 392736
10 rm ⌕ – ♦£45 ♦♦£75
♦ Centrally located Victorian terraced house; pretty cloth-clad dining room with good traditional breakfast choice. Thoughtfully decorated bedrooms are all very well maintained.

SOUTH LEIGH – Oxon. – **503** P 28 – **see Witney**

SOUTH MOLTON – Devon – **503** I 30   2 **C1**
🚆 London 197 mi – Barnstaple 11 mi – Bristol 81 mi

⌂ **Kerscott Farm** ◈   ⇐ 🖭 🕭 ⌘ **P**
Ash Mill, Southeast : 5 m. by A 361 on B 3227 ⊠ EX36 4QG – 𝒞 (01769) 550262
– www.devon-bandb.co.uk – kerscott.farm@virgin.net – Fax (01769) 550910
– Closed Christmas and New Year
3 rm ⌕ – ♦£45/60 ♦♦£60/66   **Rest** – (communal dining) Menu £17
♦ Beautiful, personally run 14C/17C farmhouse with fine views to Exmoor. Watch out for lambs and geese. Bags of internal character: beams and vast inglenooks. Charming rooms. Communal farmhouse dinners using farm's own produce.

at Knowstone Southeast : 9½ m. by A 361 – ⊠ South Molton

⌘ **The Masons Arms** (Mark Dodson)   🖭 🕭 **P** VISA ◉◉ AE
❀   *⊠ EX36 4RY – 𝒞 (01398) 341231 – www.masonsarmsdevon.co.uk*
– dodsonmasonsarms@aol.com
– Closed first two weeks January, Sunday dinner and Monday
Rest – (booking essential) Carte £30/37
Spec. Salad of wood pigeon with pine nuts and blackcurrant sauce. Roulade of pork belly with cabbage and an apple compote. Pineapple and ginger sablé with rum sauce.
♦ Delightful, thatched 13C inn, with beams, vast fireplace and exquisite ceiling mural in restaurant. Superb, flavourful, modern dishes, employing quality seasonal ingredients.

SOUTH NORMANTON – Derbyshire – **502** Q 24 – **pop. 14 114**   16 **B1**
🚆 London 130 mi – Derby 17 mi – Nottingham 15 mi – Sheffield 31 mi

🏨 **The Derbyshire Hotel**   🔳 🕭 ┣ᣠ ⅊ rm, 🖳 rest, 🕻 🖧 **P** VISA ◉◉ AE ①
Carter Lane East, on A 38 ⊠ DE55 2EH – 𝒞 (01773) 812000
– www.renaissancederbynottingham.co.uk – Fax (01773) 580032
157 rm ⌕ – ♦£170 ♦♦£170
Rest – (Closed Sunday lunch) Menu £23 (dinner) **s** – Carte £19/29 **s**
♦ Located close to M1; a modern hotel offering comfortable, well-equipped rooms; those away from motorway are quieter. Usefully, newspapers, toiletries available at reception. Capacious restaurant.

SOUTHPORT – Merseyside – **502** K 23 – **pop. 91 404**   20 **A2**
🚆 London 221 mi – Liverpool 25 mi – Manchester 38 mi – Preston 19 mi
🛈 112 Lord St 𝒞 (01704) 533333, info@visitsouthport.com
⛳ Southport Golf Links Park Road West, 𝒞 (01704) 535286

🏨 **Vincent**   ┣ᣠ 🖃 ⅊ rm, 🖳 🕭 🖧 🖾 VISA ◉◉ AE ①
98 Lord Street ⊠ PR8 1JR – 𝒞 (01704) 883800 – www.thevincenthotel.com
– info@thevincenthotel.com – Fax (01704) 883830
59 rm – ♦£110/180 ♦♦£110/180, ⌕ £12.50 – 1 suite
Rest *V-Deli/Cafe* – Carte £26/31
♦ Striking modern glass, steel and stone boutique hotel, unique to the area. Compact but very stylish with chic lobby and bar. Contemporary bedrooms in dark colours. Informal dining; menu with global influences.

Cambridge House
P VISA

4 Cambridge Rd, Northeast : 1½ m. on A 565 ✉ PR9 9NG – ✆ (01704) 538 372 – www.cambridgehousehotel.co.uk – info@cambridgehousehotel.co.uk – Fax (01704) 547 183

16 rm – †£ 63 ††£ 94/118

Rest – (dinner only and Sunday lunch) (booking essential for non residents.) Menu £ 22 – Carte £ 22/25 **s**

◆ Personally run and sizeable Victorian town house; lavishly furnished lounge and cosy bar. Very comfortably appointed period rooms in main house. Comfortable, Regency-style dining room.

Lynwood House without rest
P VISA

11A Leicester St ✉ PR9 0ER – ✆ (01704) 540 794 – www.lynwoodhotel.com – info@lynwoodhotel.com – Fax (01704) 500 724 – Closed Christmas

10 rm – †£ 40/50 ††£ 70/80

◆ Only a couple of minutes' walk from busy Lord Street, this 19C terraced house retains period style in its lounge and neat breakfast room. Pleasantly individual bedrooms.

Warehouse Brasserie
AK VISA

30 West St ✉ PR8 1QN – ✆ (01704) 544 662 – www.warehouse-brasserie.co.uk – info@warehousebrasserie.co.uk – Fax (01704) 500074 – Closed 25-26 December

Rest – Menu £ 16 (lunch)/18 (weekday dinner) – Carte £ 22/32

◆ Former warehouse, now a sleek modern restaurant with Salvador Dali prints and buzzy atmosphere. The open-plan kitchen offers modern cooking with interesting daily specials.

We try to be as accurate as possible when giving room rates but prices are susceptible to change. Please check rates when booking.

ENGLAND

SOUTHWOLD – Suffolk – 504 Z 27 – pop. 3 858 15 D2

London 108 mi – Great Yarmouth 24 mi – Ipswich 35 mi – Norwich 34 mi

69 High St ✆ (01502) 724729, southwold.tic@waveney.gov.uk

The Common, ✆ (01502) 723 234

Swan
P VISA

Market Pl ✉ IP18 6EG – ✆ (01502) 722 186 – www.adnams.co.uk – swan.hotel@adnams.co.uk – Fax (01502) 724 800

40 rm – †£ 94/139 ††£ 168/178 – 2 suites

Rest – Menu £ 21 (lunch) – Carte £ 30/35 **s**

◆ Restored coaching inn by Adnams Brewery. Antique filled interiors: 17C portrait of local heiress in hallway. Vintage rooms in main house; garden rooms built round the green. Tall windows define elegant restaurant.

The Randolph with rm
P VISA

41 Wangford Rd, Reydon, Northwest : 1 m. by A 1095 on B 1126 ✉ IP18 6PZ – ✆ (01502) 723 603 – www.therandolph.co.uk – reception@therandolph.co.uk – Fax (01502) 722 194

10 rm – †£ 60/75 ††£ 80/100 **Rest** – Carte £ 21/28

◆ Renovated in bright contemporary style, a substantial turn of 20C inn named in honour of Randolph Churchill. Heartwarming, modern food. Spacious rooms with distinctive décor.

The Crown with rm
P VISA

90 High St ✉ IP18 6DP – ✆ (01502) 722 275 – www.adnams.co.uk – crown.hotel@adnams.co.uk – Fax (01502) 727 263

14 rm – †£ 86 ††£ 232 – 1 suite **Rest** – Carte £ 24/33

◆ Smart, elegant restaurant with impressive wine list. Whitewashed inn combines a smart bar with buzzy dining area and locally popular real ale pub. Unfussy rooms are furnished in contemporary style.

SOWERBY BRIDGE – West Yorkshire – **502** O 22 – pop. 9 901   22 **A2**
– ✉ Halifax

▶ London 211 mi – Bradford 10 mi – Burnley 35 mi – Manchester 32 mi – Sheffield 40 mi

⌂ **The Millbank**   📶 VISA ⬤⬤
Mill Bank, Southwest : 2¼ m. by A 58 ⊠ HX6 3DY – ℰ (01422) 825 588 – www.themillbank.com – eat@themillbank.com – Closed first week in January, first 2 weeks in October
Rest – (Closed Monday except bank holidays) (booking essential)
Carte £ 18/31
♦ Contemporary pub, boasting a conservatory with views over the Ryburn Valley. The extensive menu offers sophisticated pub grub and features knowledgably prepared, quality produce.

at Rishworth Southwest : 4 m. by A 58 and A 672 – ⊠ Sowerby Bridge

⌂ **The Old Bore**   📶 P VISA ⬤⬤ AE
Oldham Rd, South :½ m. on A 672 ⊠ HX6 4QU – ℰ (01422) 822 291 – www.oldbore.co.uk – chefhessel@aol.com – Closed first 2 weeks in January
Rest – (Closed Monday-Tuesday) Carte £ 25/35
♦ Inviting pub with busy walls, smart dining rooms and delightful terrace. Monthly-changing menus offer classical and more ambitious British dishes, made from quality ingredients.

SPALDING – Lincolnshire – **502** T 25   17 **C2**
▶ London 108 mi – Peterborough 23 mi – Stamford 19 mi

at Surfleet Seas End North : 5 ¾ m. by A 16 – ⊠ Spalding

⌂ **The Ship Inn** with rm   ⪡ 📶 ⌖ ⌖ P VISA ⬤⬤ AE
154 Reservoir Rd ⊠ PE11 4DH – ℰ (01775) 680 547 – www.shipinnsurfleet.com – info@shipinnsurfleet.com – Fax (01775) 680 541 – Closed 1 January
4 rm ⌷ – †£ 60 ††£ 75
Rest – (Closed Sunday dinner, Monday) Menu £ 9/17 – Carte £ 15/25
♦ Spacious pub with upstairs terrace and excellent jetty views. Menu features timeless British classics and homemade old-school puddings, crafted from quality, local ingredients. Bedrooms are large and simply furnished.

SPALDWICK – Cambs. – **504** S 26 – see Huntingdon

SPARSHOLT – Hants. – **503** P 30 – see Winchester

SPEEN – Buckinghamshire – **504** R 28 – ⊠ Princes Risborough   11 **C2**
▶ London 41 mi – Aylesbury 15 mi – Oxford 33 mi – Reading 25 mi

✕✕ **Old Plow (Restaurant)**   📶 P VISA ⬤⬤ AE
Flowers Bottom, West :½ m. by Chapel Hill and Highwood Bottom ⊠ HP27 0PZ – ℰ (01494) 488 300 – www.yeoldplough.co.uk – info@yeoldplough.co.uk – Fax (01494) 488 702 – Closed 1 week late May, Christmas-New Year, August, Sunday and Monday
Rest – Menu £ 30/34
♦ A fine, oak beamed restaurant at back of the bistro; more formal in style with linen table cover and high-back chairs. Set menus show French influence with classic sauces.

✕ **Bistro** – at Old Plow   📶 P VISA ⬤⬤ AE
Flowers Bottom, West :½ m. by Chapel Hill and Highwood Bottom ⊠ HP27 0PZ – ℰ (01494) 488 300 – www.yeoldplough.co.uk – info@yeoldplough.co.uk – Fax (01494) 488 702 – Closed 1 week late May, Christmas-New Year, August, Sunday and Monday
Rest – (booking essential) Menu £ 15 (lunch and weekday dinner) – Carte £ 24/38
♦ A cosy little bistro: low ceiling, tiled floors; log fire in the lounge. Blackboards announce simple à la carte menus; includes separate Brixham fish board. Affable owners.

SPEKE – Mersey. – **502** L 23 – see Liverpool

SPELDHURST – Kent – **504** U 30 – see Royal Tunbridge Wells

SPENNYMOOR – Durham – **501** P 19 – pop. 17 270 – ✉ Darlington   24 **B3**
▶ London 275 mi – Durham 6 mi – Leeds 75 mi – Newcastle upon Tyne 24 mi

🏨 **Whitworth Hall** ॐ   ⟨ 🚗 ⑩ ⤵ ⚥ ⫴ 🛁 **P** **VISA** **⚫⚫** **AE**
Whitworth Hall Country Park, Northwest : 1½ m. by Middlestone Moor rd on
Brancepeth rd ✉ DL16 7QX – 𝒞 (01388) 811 772 – www.bw-whitworthhall.co.uk
– enquiries@whitworthhall.co.uk – Fax (01388) 818 669
29 rm ⊆ – †£ 128 ††£ 136
Rest *Library* – (Closed Sunday dinner) (dinner only and Sunday lunch)
Carte £ 22/35
Rest *Silver Buckles Brasserie* – (Closed dinner Friday and Saturday and
Sunday lunch) Menu £ 12 (lunch) – Carte £ 19/36
◆ Part 19C country house, sympathetically converted; fine views over deer park and
vineyard. Orangery lounge; larger rooms, in the original house, are in period style.
The Library handsomely set in eponymous room. Conservatory dining in Silver
Buckles Brasserie.

SPRIGG'S ALLEY – Oxon. – see Chinnor

STADDLEBRIDGE – N. Yorks. – see Northallerton

STADHAMPTON – Oxfordshire – **503** Q 28   10 **B2**
▶ London 53 mi – Aylesbury 18 mi – Oxford 10 mi

✗✗ **Crazy Bear** with rm   🚗 🏠 ⚥ 🛁 **P** **VISA** **⚫⚫** **AE**
Bear Lane, off Wallingford rd ✉ OX44 7UR – 𝒞 (01865) 890 714
– www.crazybeargroup.co.uk – enquiries@crazybeargroup.co.uk – Fax (01865)
400 481
17 rm ⊆ – †£ 125/175 ††£ 145/235
Rest – Carte £ 26/49 **s**
Rest *Thai Thai* – (closed Sunday lunch) (booking essential) Carte £ 23/35
◆ Crazy by name, crazy by nature: reception is a red London bus and barside acivities
are overseen by large stuffed bear. Uniquely designed bedrooms are zany and luxurious. Modern British menu served in restaurant with leather walls, huge mirrors and
chandeliers. Alternatively, Thai Thai serves authentic Thai cuisine.

STAFFORD – Staffordshire – **502** N 25 – pop. 63 681   19 **C1**
▶ London 142 mi – Birmingham 26 mi – Derby 32 mi – Shrewsbury 31 mi
  – Stoke-on-Trent 17 mi
🛈 Market St 𝒞 (0871) 7161932
📷 Stafford Castle Newport Rd, 𝒞 (01785) 223 821

🏨 **Moat House**   🚗 ᕼ rm, 🅺 rest, ⚥ 🛁 **P** **VISA** **⚫⚫** **AE**
Lower Penkridge Rd, Acton Trussell, South: 3 ¾ m. by A 449 ✉ ST17 0RJ
– 𝒞 (01785) 712 217 – www.moathouse.co.uk – info@moathouse.co.uk
– Fax (01785) 715 344 – Closed 25 December and 1 January
40 rm ⊆ – †£ 130 ††£ 150 – 1 suite
Rest *The Conservatory* – Menu £ 20 (lunch) – Carte £ 33/42
◆ Timbered 15C moated manor house with modern extensions and lawned gardens,
within sight of the M6. Characterful rustic bar. Colourful rooms with individual style.
Bright, airy conservatory restaurant overlooks canal.

🏨 **The Swan**   📶 ᕼ rm, 🅺 rest, ⚥ 🕭 **P** **VISA** **⚫⚫** **AE**
46-46A Greengate St ✉ ST16 2JA – 𝒞 (01785) 258 142
– www.theswanstafford.co.uk – info@theswanstafford.co.uk – Fax (01785)
225 372 – Closed 25 December
31 rm ⊆ – †£ 80 ††£ 120
Rest *The Brasserie at The Swan* – (closed dinner 24 and 26 December)
Menu £ 11/17 – Carte £ 21/36
◆ Part 17C coaching inn with modern décor throughout. Convenient central location.
Stylish reception. Well-equipped bedrooms with good facilities. Light, airy brasserie is
open all day.

ENGLAND

STAITHES – North Yorkshire – **502** R 20 – ⊠ **Saltburn (Cleveland)**   23 **C1**

◘ London 269 mi – Middlesbrough 22 mi – Scarborough 31 mi

✗ **Endeavour** with rm   **P** VISA 🌑🌑

1 High St ⊠ TS13 5BH – 𝒞 (01947) 840825 – www.endeavour-restaurant.co.uk
– endeavour.restaurant@virgin.net – Closed December- mid April, Sunday and
Monday

4 rm � – ♦♦£ 80/95

Rest – Seafood – (dinner only and lunch Friday-Saturday) Menu £ 24/32

♦ Named after Captain Cook's sailing ship: a compact former fisherman's cottage
serving tasty menus, with emphasis on locally caught fish. Neat, well-appointed
bedrooms.

STAMFORD – Lincolnshire – **502** S 26 – **pop. 19 525** 📗 Great Britain   17 **C2**

◘ London 92 mi – Leicester 31 mi – Lincoln 50 mi – Nottingham 45 mi

🛈 The Arts Centre, 27 St Mary's St 𝒞 (01780) 755611

◎ Town ★★ - St Martin's Church ★ – Lord Burghley's Hospital ★ – Browne's
Hospital ★ **AC**

◎ Burghley House ★★ **AC**, SE : 1 ½ m. by B 1443

🏠🏠🏠 **The George of Stamford**   🚗 ☂ 🍴 🏖 **P** VISA 🌑🌑 AE ⓪

71 St Martin's ⊠ PE9 2LB – 𝒞 (01780) 750750
– www.georgehotelofstamford.com – reservations@georgehotelofstamford.com
– Fax (01780) 750701

46 rm ⊠ – ♦£ 90/105 ♦♦£ 245 – 1 suite

Rest – Menu £ 19 – Carte £ 36/56 **s**

Rest *Garden Lounge* – Carte £ 26/51 **s**

♦ Historic inn, over 900 years old. Crusading knights stayed here en route to Jerusa-
lem. Walled garden and courtyard with 17C mulberry tree. Original bedrooms; designer décor. Oak panelled dining room exudes elegance. Garden Lounge with leafy
courtyard.

✗ **Jim's Yard**   ☂ VISA 🌑🌑
😊
3 Ironmonger St, off Broad St ⊠ PE9 1PL – 𝒞 (01780) 756080
– www.jimsyard.biz – jim@jimsyard.biz
– Closed 20 July-4 August, 23 December-5 January, Sunday and Monday

Rest – Menu £ 17 (lunch) – Carte £ 22/29

♦ Two 18C houses in a courtyard: conservatory or first-floor dining options. Smart
tableware enhances enjoyment of great value menus employing well-executed, classic cooking.

at Collyweston Southwest : 3 ½ m. on A 43 – ⊠ **Stamford**

🏠 **The Collyweston Slater** with rm   ☂ ☂ ☏ **P** VISA 🌑🌑

87-89 Main Road ⊠ PE9 3PQ – 𝒞 (01780) 444288
– www.collywestonslater.co.uk – info@collywestonslater.co.uk
– Closed 25 December

5 rm ⊠ – ♦£ 60 ♦♦£ 85   **Rest** – (Closed Sunday dinner) Carte £ 20/28

♦ Charming stone pub with a modern interior. Cooking is European and displays
local produce, careful preparation and bold flavours: concise main menu is supported
heavily by specials. Bedrooms are comfortable and stylish.

at Clipsham Northwest : 9 ½ m. by B 1081 off A 1 – ⊠ **Stamford**

🏠 **The Olive Branch & Beech House** (Sean Hope) with rm   ☂
🏵
Main St ⊠ LE15 7SH – 𝒞 (01780) 410355   ☕ rm, ☏ **P** VISA 🌑🌑
– www.theolivebranchpub.com – info@theolivebranchpub.com – Fax (01780)
410000 – Closed 26 December, 1 January

6 rm ⊠ – ♦£ 100/110 ♦♦£ 120/200

Rest – (booking essential) Menu £ 20 (lunch) – Carte £ 25/41

Spec. Shallot tatin with stilton and rocket. Seabass with fennel cassoulet
and pesto crème fraîche. Queen of puddings with raspberry ripple ice cream.

♦ Soundly judged, flavoursome cooking, varied and modern, in cosy firelit pub with
simple pews and sepia prints. Rooms, over the road in Georgian house, are sassy and
stylish.

ENGLAND

STANDISH – Greater Manchester – **502** M 23 – pop. 14 350 – ⊠ **Wigan**   20 **A2**
   ▶ London 210 mi – Liverpool 25 mi – Manchester 21 mi – Preston 15 mi

at Wrightington Bar Northwest : 3 ½ m. by A 5209 on B 5250 – ⊠ **Wigan**

🏠 **The Mulberry Tree**   ✸ **P** *VISA* **⬤⬤**
      9 Wood Lane ⊠ WN6 9SE – ℰ (01257) 451 400 – www.themulberrytree.info
      – info@themulberrytree.info – Fax (01257) 451 400
      – Closed 26 December and 1 January
      Rest – Menu £ 17/20 – Carte £ 25/40
      ♦ Hugely spacious roadside pub with open bar and more formal, linen-clad dining area. Range of menus offer extensive choice of generously proportioned dishes. Warm atmosphere.

STANNERSBURN – Northumberland – **501** M 18 – ⊠ **Hexham**   24 **A2**
   ▶ London 363 mi – Carlisle 56 mi – Newcastle upon Tyne 46 mi

🏠 **The Pheasant Inn** with rm ⊗   ✾ ✸ **P** *VISA* **⬤⬤**
      Falstone ⊠ NE48 1DD – ℰ (01434) 240 382 – www.thepheasantinn.com
      – enquiries@thepheasantinn.com – Fax (01434) 240 382 – Closed 25-27 December
      and November-March Monday-Tuesday
      8 rm ⊆ – †£ 50/55 ††£ 85/90   **Rest** – Carte £ 17/25
      ♦ Set in Northumberland National Park, near Kielder reservoir; epitome of a traditional inn. Pine dining room serves homecooked local fare. Cottagey rooms in converted stables.

      Undecided between two equivalent establishments?
      Within each category, establishments are classified
      in our order of preference.

ENGLAND

STANSTED AIRPORT – Essex – **504** U 28 – ⊠ **Stansted Mountfitchet**   12 **B2**
   ▶ London 37 mi – Cambridge 29 mi – Chelmsford 18 mi – Colchester 29 mi
   ✈ Stansted International Airport : ℰ (0870) 0000303

🏨 **Radisson SAS H. London Stansted Airport**   🛬 ⊛ 🀤 🛁
      Waltham Close ⊠ CM24 1PP   📶 & rm, 🆔 ✸ ¶ ⓢ **P** *VISA* **⬤⬤** 🆎 **①**
      – ℰ (01279) 661 012 – www.stansted.radissonsas.com
      – info.stansted@radissonsas.com – Fax (01279) 661 013
      484 rm – †£ 135 ††£ 135, ⊆ £ 14.95 – 16 suites
      Rest *New York Grill Bar* – (Closed lunch Saturday and Sunday) Carte £ 33/58
      Rest *Wine Tower* – Carte £ 22/30
      Rest *Filini* – Italian – Carte (dinner only) £ 22/35
      ♦ Impressive hotel just two minutes from main terminal; vast open atrium housing 40 foot wine cellar. Extensive meeting facilities. Very stylish bedrooms in three themes. Small, formal New York Grill Bar. Impressive Wine Tower. Filini for Italian dishes.

🏨 **Hilton London Stansted Airport**   🖼 🀤 🛁 📶 & rm, 🆔 rest,
      Round Coppice Rd ⊠ CM24 1SF – ℰ (01279)   ⓢ **P** *VISA* **⬤⬤** 🆎 **①**
      680 800 – www.hilton.co.uk – reservations.stansted@hilton.com – Fax (01279)
      680 890
      237 rm – †£ 79/115 ††£ 79/115, ⊆ £ 17.95 – 2 suites
      Rest – (closed lunch Saturday and Bank Holidays) Menu £ 27
      ♦ Bustling hotel whose facilities include leisure club, hairdressers and beauty salon. Modern rooms, with two of executive style. Transport can be arranged to and from terminal. Restaurant/bar has popular menu; sometimes carvery lunch as well.

STANSTED MOUNTFITCHET – Essex – **504** U 28 – **see Bishop's Stortford**
(Herts.)

STANTON – Suffolk – 504 W 27 – pop. 2 073   15 C2

🚗 London 88 mi – Cambridge 38 mi – Ipswich 40 mi – King's Lynn 38 mi
– Norwich 39 mi

XX **The Leaping Hare**   🚗 🅿 VISA ⓒⓔ
🕸 *Wyken Vineyards, South : 1¼ m. by Wyken Rd ⊠ IP31 2DW – ℰ (01359) 250 287*
– www.wykenvineyards.co.uk – Fax (01359) 253 022 – Closed 24 December-5
January
Rest – (lunch only and dinner Friday and Saturday) (booking essential)
Menu £ 20 (lunch) – Carte £ 25/29 ⅜
♦ 17C long barn in working farm and vineyard. Hare-themed pictures and tapestries
decorate a beamed restaurant and café. Tasty dishes underpinned by local, organic
produce.

STANTON ST QUINTIN – Wilts. – 503 N 29 – see Chippenham

STANTON ST JOHN – Oxon. – 503 Q 28 – see Oxford

STANWICK – Northamptonshire   17 C3

🚗 London 83 mi – Northampton 18 mi – Milton Keynes 36 mi
– Peterborough 27 mi

↑ **The Courtyard**   🚗 📶 🅿 VISA ⓒⓔ
West St ⊠ NN9 6QY – ℰ (01933) 622 233 – www.thecourtyard.me.uk
– bookings@thecourtyard.me.uk – Fax (01933) 622 276
12 rm ⊇ – ♦£59 ♦♦£75   **Rest** – (by arrangement) Carte £ 18/37
♦ Cosy, traditional bedrooms in main house; bright, contemporary bedrooms in converted stable block. Lounge opens into pleasant courtyard and neat gardens. Light,
airy conservatory restaurant offers dishes with a Mediterranean slant.

STAPLEFORD – 504 Q 25 – see Nottingham

STATHERN – Leics. – see Melton Mowbray

STAVERTON – Devon – 503 I 32 – pop. 682 – ⊠ Totnes   2 C2

🚗 London 220 mi – Exeter 20 mi – Torquay 33 mi

🏠 **Kingston House** 🌿   ← 🚗 🕭 📶 ⅙ 📶 ♨ 🅿 VISA ⓒⓔ AE ①
Northwest : 1 m. on Kingston rd ⊠ TQ9 6AR – ℰ (01803) 762 235
– www.kingston-estate.com – info@kingston-estate.com – Fax (01803) 762 444
– Closed Christmas and New Year
3 rm ⊇ – ♦£110/120 ♦♦£180/200
Rest – (dinner only) (residents only, set menu only) Menu £ 38 **s**
♦ A spectacular Georgian mansion in sweeping moorland. Unique period details
include painted china closet, marquetry staircase, authentic wallpapers. Variety of
antique beds.

STAVERTON – Northants. – 504 Q 27 – see Daventry

STEDHAM – W. Sussex – 504 R 31 – see Midhurst

STEPPINGLEY – Bedfordshire   12 A1

🚗 London 44 mi – Luton 12 mi – Milton Keynes 13 mi

🍴 **The French Horn**   🚗 ⅌ 🅿 VISA ⓒⓔ AE
Church End ⊠ MK45 5AU – ℰ (01525) 712 051 – www.atouchofnovelli.com
– info@atouchof novelli.com – Fax (01717) 334 305 – Closed 1-12 January and
lunch Monday-Tuesday
Rest – Menu £ 20 (weekday lunch) – Carte £ 28/37
♦ Now part of the Jean-Christophe Novelli bourgeoning chain of pubs. Co-ordinated,
stylish interior; bold, confident cooking. Service is on the ball; terrace backs onto
cricket ground.

STEYNING – West Sussex – 504 T 31 – pop. 8 692   7 D2
D London 52 mi – Brighton 12 mi – Worthing 10 mi

🏠 **Springwells** without rest 　　　　　　　　🚗 ⅀ 🏠 ❛❜ **P** 𝘃𝗶𝘀𝗮 ⓪⑨ 𝗔𝗘
9 High St ⊠ BN44 3GG – ℰ (01903) 812 446 – www.springwells.co.uk
– contact@springwells.co.uk – Fax (01903) 879823 – Closed Christmas-New Year
11 rm ⊇ – †£43/65 ††£98/120
♦ Built in 1772, a picturesque former merchant's house in the heart of town. Tidy accommodation in pretty chintz; four-poster rooms on the first floor face the High Street.

at Ashurst North : 3½ m. on B 2135 – ⊠ Steyning

🍴 **The Fountain Inn** 　　　　　　　　　　　　　　🚗 **P** 𝘃𝗶𝘀𝗮 ⓪⑨
⊠ *BN44 3AP – ℰ (01403) 710 219*
Rest – Carte approx. £ 20
♦ 16C inn overflowing with character in form of beamed ceilings, flagstone floors, open fires, garden pond and skittle alley. Down-to-earth cooking is fresh and full of flavour.

STILTON – Cambridgeshire – 504 T 26 – pop. 2 500 – ⊠ Peterborough   14 A2
D London 76 mi – Cambridge 30 mi – Northampton 43 mi
– Peterborough 6 mi

🏨 **Bell Inn** 　　　　　　　　🚗 ❄ ❛❜ ♿ **P** 𝘃𝗶𝘀𝗮 ⓪⑨ 𝗔𝗘 ⓪
Great North Rd ⊠ PE7 3RA – ℰ (01733) 241 066 – www.thebellstilton.co.uk
– reception@thebellstilton.co.uk – Fax (01733) 245 173 – Closed 25-26 December and 1 January
22 rm ⊇ – †£74 ††£101
Rest *Village Bar* – see restaurant listing
♦ A swinging red bell pub sign hangs outside this part 16C inn with garden. Deluxe bedrooms are individually styled; some retain original rafters and stonework.

🍴 **Village Bar** (at Bell Inn) 　　　　　　　　　　🍽 **P** 𝘃𝗶𝘀𝗮 ⓪⑨ 𝗔𝗘 ⓪
Great North Rd ⊠ PE7 3RA – ℰ (01733) 241 066 – www.thebellstilton.co.uk
– reception@thebellstilton.co.uk – Fax (01733) 245 173 – Closed 25 December, dinner 26 December and 1 January
Rest – Menu £ 27 – Carte £ 19/33
♦ As one would expect, Stilton cheese is used to full effect in this rustic bar, appearing in soups, dumplings, quiche and dressings. Blackboard specials to tickle taste-buds.

STOCKBRIDGE – Hampshire – 503 P 30   6 B2
D London 75 mi – Salisbury 14 mi – Southampton 19 mi – Winchester 9 mi

🍴 **The Greyhound** with rm 　　　　　　　🚗 ❛❜ ❄ ❛❜ **P** 𝘃𝗶𝘀𝗮 ⓪⑨
31 High St ⊠ SO20 6EY – ℰ (01264) 810 833 – www.thegreyhound.info
– enquiries@thegreyhound.info
– Closed 25-26 and 31 December, 1 January and 1 week in January
8 rm ⊇ – †£90 ††£120
Rest – (Closed Sunday dinner) Menu £ 24 – Carte £ 30/40
♦ Pretty pub with relaxing open-fired bar and sophisticated dining area. Classical menu displays satisfying combinations with a modern edge, which arrive appetisingly presented. Bedrooms are modern and stylish, with huge showers.

at Longstock North : 1½ m. on A 3057 – Stockbridge – ⊠ Stockbridge

🍴 **The Peat Spade Inn** with rm 　　　　　　　❛❜ 🍽 ❛❜ **P** 𝘃𝗶𝘀𝗮 ⓪⑨
😊 *Village Street ⊠ SO20 6DR – ℰ (01264) 810 612 – www.peatspadeinn.co.uk*
– info@peatspadeinn.co.uk – Fax (01264) 811 078
– Closed 25 December, 1 January
6 rm ⊇ – †£120 ††£120
Rest – (Closed Sunday dinner) (booking essential) Carte £ 23/30
♦ The ultimate shooting and fishing pub, with country pursuit décor and furnishings. Cooking is proper, proud and local, featuring flavoursome, well-presented British pub classics. Bedrooms are modern and stylish.

STOCKTON-ON-TEES – Stockton-on-Tees – **502** P 20 – pop. 80 060   24 **B3**

- ▶ London 251 mi – Leeds 61 mi – Middlesbrough 4 mi – Newcastle upon Tyne 39 mi
- ✈ Durham Tees Valley Airport : ℰ (08712) 242426, SW : 6 m. by A 1027, A 135 and A 67
- 🛈 Stockton Central Library, Church Road ℰ (01642) 528130, touristinformation@stockton.gov.uk
- 🏌 Eaglescliffe Yarm Rd, ℰ (01642) 780 098
- 🏌 Knotty Hill Golf Centre Sedgefield, ℰ (01740) 620 320
- 🏌 Norton Junction Rd, ℰ (01642) 676 385

at Eaglescliffe South : 3½ m. on A 135 – ✉ Stockton-on-Tees

🏨🏨 **Parkmore**   🖺 🕉 🛌 ⑪ 🆗 🅿 🆚🆂🅰 🐼 🅰🅴 ①
636 Yarm Rd, Eaglescliffe ✉ TS16 0DH – ℰ (01642) 786 815
– www.parkmorehotel.co.uk – enquiries@parkmorehotel.co.uk – Fax (01642) 790 485
54 rm – ♦£79/87 ♦♦£99/110, ☷ £8.95 – 1 suite
Rest J's @ 636 – Menu £14 (lunch) **s** – Carte £20/35 **s**
♦ Built in 1896 for shipbuilding family; combines a sense of the old and new. Rooms are furnished in modern style; leisure and conference facilities also available. Dining room specialises in steak options.

> Your opinions are important to us:
> please write and let us know about your discoveries and experiences – good and bad!

STOKE BY NAYLAND – Suffolk – **504** W 28   15 **C3**

- ▶ London 70 mi – Bury St Edmunds 24 mi – Cambridge 54 mi – Colchester 11 mi – Ipswich 14 mi

🏠 **The Crown**   🚗 🕉 🅿 🆚🆂🅰 🐼
✉ CO6 4SE – ℰ (01206) 262 001 – www.eoinns.co.uk – thecrown@eoinns.co.uk
– Fax (01206) 264 026 – Closed 25-26 December
Rest – Carte £20/34 ⑱
♦ 16C pub with smart terrace, huge garden and 21C style: spacious rooms offer variety of cool dining options. Locally renowned menus: a seasonal, modern take on classic dishes.

STOKE D'ABERNON – Surrey – **504** S 30 – see Cobham

STOKE GABRIEL – Devon – **503** J 32 – see Totnes

STOKE HOLY CROSS – Norfolk – **504** X 26 – see Norwich

STOKENCHURCH – Buckinghamshire – **504** R 29 – pop. 3 949   11 **C2**
- ▶ London 42 mi – High Wycombe 10 mi – Oxford 18 mi

at Radnage Northeast : 1¾ m. by A 40 – ✉ Stokenchurch

🏠 **The Three Horseshoes Inn** with rm   🚗 🕉 🕻 🅿 🆚🆂🅰 🐼
😊 Bennett End, North : 1¼ m. by Town End rd ✉ HP14 4EB – ℰ (01494) 483 273
– www.thethreehorseshoes.net – threehorseshoe@btconnect.com
6 rm ☷ – ♦£85 ♦♦£145
Rest – (Closed Sunday dinner, Monday lunch and Tuesday after Bank Holiday Monday lunch) Carte £24/30
♦ Attractive red brick pub with tiny front bar, rear restaurant and telephone box in duck pond. Good value, precisely cooked British dishes; well presented and locally sourced. Comfortable bedrooms have character beds and modern bathrooms. Molières is best.

ENGLAND

🛡 *Great Britain*

- ▶ London 162 mi – Birmingham 46 mi – Leicester 59 mi – Liverpool 58 mi
  – Manchester 41 mi – Sheffield 53 mi
- 🛈 Quadrant Rd, Hanley ✆ (01782) 236000, stoke.tic@virgin.net
- 🏌 Greenway Hall Stockton Brook, ✆ (01782) 503 158
- 🏌 Parkhall Weston Coyney Hulme Rd, ✆ (01782) 599 584
- ◉ The Potteries Museum and Art Gallery★ Y **M** – Gladstone Pottery
  Museum★ **AC** V
- ◎ The Wedgwood Story★ **AC**, S : 7 m. on A 500, A 34 and minor rd V. Little
  Moreton Hall★★ **AC**, N : 10 m. by A 500 on A 34 U – Biddulph Grange
  Garden★, N : 7 m. by A 52, A 50 and A 527 U

STOKE-ON-TRENT
NEWCASTLE-
UNDER-LYME

Alexandra Rd	**U**	3
Bedford Rd	**U**	4
Brownhills Rd	**U**	12
Church Lane	**U**	19

Cobridge Rd	**U**	21
Davenport St	**U**	23
Elder Rd	**U**	24
Etruria Vale Rd	**U**	27
Grove Rd	**V**	30
Hanley Rd	**U**	31
Heron St	**V**	34
Higherland	**U**	37
High St	**U**	35
Manor St	**V**	44
Mayne St	**V**	45

Moorland Rd	**U**	48
Porthill Rd	**U**	59
Snow Hill	**U**	63
Stoke Rd	**U**	68
Strand (The)	**V**	69
Victoria Park Rd	**V**	75
Victoria Pl. Link	**V**	76
Watlands View	**U**	77
Williamson St	**U**	78
Wolstanton Link Rd	**U**	80

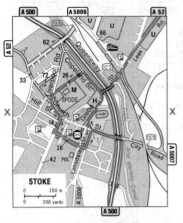

ENGLAND

The Manor at Hanchurch

Newcastle Road ⊠ *ST4 8SD – ℰ (01782) 643 030 – www.hanchurchmanor.co.uk – barbarajames@hathanchurchmanor.co.uk – Fax (01782) 643 714*

7 rm ⊇ – †£85/198 ††£185/275 Vx

Rest The Manor at Hanchurch – (closed Sunday and Monday dinner)
Menu £25 (lunch) – Carte £35/53

♦ Recently refurbished period house. Stylish bedrooms boast thick carpets, quality furnishings and smart modern bathrooms, some with spa baths. Spacious bar displays plush fabrics. Restaurant offers modern menu with a classical base and daring flavour combinations.

STOKE POGES – Buckinghamshire – 504 S 29 – pop. 4 112   11 D3

▶ London 30 mi – Aylesbury 28 mi – Oxford 44 mi
◢ Stoke Park Park Rd, ℰ (01753) 717 171

Stoke Park Club

Park Rd ⊠ *SL2 4PG – ℰ (01753) 717 171*
– www.stokeparkclub.com – info@stokeparkclub.com – Fax (01753) 717 181
– Closed 24-26 December and 3-21 January

49 rm – †£285 ††£285, ⊇ £18

Rest The Dining Room – (dinner only and Sunday lunch) (residents only)
Menu £40

♦ A palatial hotel, all pillars, balconies and cupola with golf course where James Bond played Goldfinger in film. Rooms are impressive: antiques, marble baths, heated floors. Snug, plush chairs in relaxed brasserie with French posters on walls.

Stoke Place

Stoke Green, South : ½ m. by B 416 ⊠ *SL2 4HT – ℰ (01753) 534 790*
– www.stokeplace.co.uk – enquiries@stokeplace.co.uk – Fax (01753) 512 743

29 rm ⊇ – †£225 ††£450

Rest Garden Room – Carte £26/39

♦ 17C extended Queen Anne mansion in 22 acres with lake and geese. Boutique makeover has particularly benefitted Gloucester and Queen Anne rooms with their cool, sleek lines. Chic Garden Room restaurant serves fresh, local modern menus.

STOKE ROW – Oxfordshire
11 **C3**

▶ London 45 mi – Henley-on-Thames 6 mi – Reading 10 mi

The Cherry Tree Inn with rm
✉ RG9 5QA – ℰ (01491) 680 430 – www.thecherrytreeinn.com
– info@thecherrytreeinn.com – Closed 25-26 December
4 rm ⌿ – †£95 ††£95   **Rest** – Carte £25/40
♦ 17C inn with an impressive 21C refurbishment: bags of charm and character typified by low ceiling and beams. Platefuls of good value dishes offering eclectic mix. Plush rooms.

STOKESLEY – North Yorkshire – 502 Q 20 – pop. 4 725
23 **C1**
– ✉ Middlesbrough ▌ Great Britain

▶ London 239 mi – Leeds 59 mi – Middlesbrough 8 mi – Newcastle upon Tyne 49 mi – York 52 mi

⒢ Great Ayton (Captain Cook Birthplace Museum★ AC), NE : 2½ m. on A 173

Chapter's with rm
27 High St ✉ TS9 5AD – ℰ (01642) 711 888 – www.chaptershotel.co.uk
– enquiries@chaptershotel.co.uk – Fax (01642) 713 387 – Closed 1 week January,
1 week September, 25-26 December and 1 January
13 rm ⌿ – †£69/85 ††£95/99
Rest – (Closed Sunday dinner and Monday lunch) Menu £20 (lunch)
– Carte £24/41
♦ Solid, mellow brick Victorian house with colour washed rooms. Bistro style dining with strong Mediterranean colour scheme. Eclectic menu: classics and more modern dishes.

STOKE SUB HAMDON – Somerset – 503 L 31 – see Yeovil

STON EASTON – Somerset – 503 M 30 – ✉ Bath (Bath & North East
4 **C2**
Somerset)

▶ London 131 mi – Bath 12 mi – Bristol 11 mi – Wells 7 mi

Ston Easton Park ⌂
✉ BA3 4DF – ℰ (01761) 241 631 – www.stoneaston.co.uk
– info@stoneaston.co.uk – Fax (01761) 241 377
21 rm – †£170/255 ††£195/285, ⌿ £4.50 – 3 suites
Rest *The Sorrel* – (booking essential for non-residents) Menu £23/45 **s**
♦ Aristocratic Palladian mansion; grounds designed by Humphrey Repton, given subtle contemporary styling. Lavish rooms: Grand Saloon with Kentian plasterwork. Formal restaurant served by a Victorian kitchen garden.

STONESFIELD – Oxfordshire – 504 P 28 – pop. 1 538
10 **B2**

▶ London 70 mi – Oxford 15 mi – Witney 8 mi

The White Horse
The Ridings ✉ OX29 8EA – ℰ (01993) 891 063 – www.thewhitehorse.uk.com
– info@thewhitehorse.uk.com – Closed 25 December
Rest – (Closed Sunday dinner, Monday) Carte £17/25
♦ Modernised dining pub with central bar, smart oak-floored dining room and lounge with leather sofas and open fires. Some ambitiously original dishes served on à la carte.

STORRINGTON – West Sussex – 504 S 31 – pop. 7 727
7 **C2**

▶ London 54 mi – Brighton 20 mi – Portsmouth 36 mi

Old Forge
6 Church St ✉ RH20 4LA – ℰ (01903) 743 402 – www.fine-dining.co.uk
– enquiry@oldforge.co.uk – Fax (01903) 742 540
– Closed Christmas-New Year, 2 weeks Spring, 2 weeks Autumn, Saturday lunch,
Sunday dinner and Monday-Wednesday
Rest – Menu £18/34
♦ Appealing whitewashed and brick cottages with three dining rooms bearing all hallmarks of flavoursome traditional cuisine. Array of cheeses; fine wine from small producers.

ENGLAND

STOURPORT-ON-SEVERN – Worcestershire – 503 N 26   18 B2
– pop. 18 889

> London 137 mi – Birmingham 21 mi – Worcester 12 mi

🏠 **Stourport Manor**   🚗 🔥 🔟 ⚲ Ⅰ₆ ✗ ¶ 𝔾 **P** **VISA** **⦿** **AE** **①**
Hartlebury Rd, East : 1¼ m. on B 4193 ⊠ *DY13 9JA* – ☎ *(01299) 289 955*
– www.menzieshotels.co.uk – stourport@menzieshotels.co.uk
– Fax (01299) 878 520
66 rm ⍁ – †£160 ††£190 – 2 suites
Rest *The Brasserie* – Carte £26/33

♦ Gracious country house, once home to former prime minister, Stanley Baldwin. Lovely, warm-hued lounge; wide-ranging indoor leisure facilities. Bedrooms are nicely spacious. Brasserie overlooks the garden; wide ranging menus.

STOWMARKET – Suffolk – 504 W 27 – pop. 15 059   15 C3

> London 95 mi – Ipswich 14 mi – Colchester 35 mi – Clacton-on-Sea 40 mi

at Buxhall West : 3¾ m. by B 115 – ⊠ Stowmarket

🍴 **The Buxhall Crown**   🕌 **P** **VISA** **⦿** **AE**
Mill Road ⊠ *IP14 3DW* – ☎ *(01449) 736 521 – www.thebuxhallcrown.co.uk*
– Closed for food 25-26 December (open for drinks 12pm-2pm)
Rest – Carte £21/30

♦ Cosy and characterful, with wattle and daub walls, heavy wood beams and an inglenook fireplace. Good use of local produce, including particularly nice beef. Popular terrace.

STOW-ON-THE-WOLD – Gloucestershire – 503 – pop. 2 074   4 D1
🔖 *Great Britain*

> London 86 mi – Birmingham 44 mi – Gloucester 27 mi – Oxford 30 mi
> 🛈 Hollis House, The Square ☎ (01451) 831082, stowvic@cotswold.gov.uk
> 🏰 Chastleton House★★, NE : 6½ m. by A 436 and A 44

🏠 **Grapevine**   🕌 ¶ 𝔾 **P** **VISA** **⦿** **AE** **①**
Sheep St ⊠ *GL54 1AU* – ☎ *(01451) 830 344 – www.vines.co.uk*
– enquiries@vines.co.uk – Fax (01451) 832 278
22 rm ⍁ – †£85 ††£150
Rest *The Conservatory* – Menu £20/33
Rest *Lavigna* – Carte £18/22

♦ Among the antique shops, two extended 17C houses. Rooms in bright, modern décor with a nod to tradition, half with beams and bare stone. Timbered bar; sepia photos of Stow. In Conservatory black grapes hang from spreading vine. Easy-going, informal Lavigna.

🏠 **The Royalist**   ¶ **P** **VISA** **⦿** **AE** **①**
Digbeth St ⊠ *GL56 1BN* – ☎ *(01451) 830 670 – www.theroyalisthotel.com*
– stay@theroyalisthotel.com – Fax (01451) 870 048
14 rm ⍁ – †£65/95 ††£140/180
Rest *Eagle & Child* – Carte £19/29
Rest *947 AD* – Menu £25/35

♦ Historic high street inn - reputedly England's oldest. Comfortable, stylish rooms, individual in shape and décor and quieter at the rear. Two-room bar in exposed stone. Robust cooking in the attached stone pub. Fine dining in the intimate, beamed restaurant with inglenook fireplace.

🏠 **Fosse Manor**   🚗 🕌 ✗ ¶ 𝔾 **P** **VISA** **⦿** **AE** **①**
Fosse Way, South : 1¼ m. on A 429 ⊠ *GL54 1JX* – ☎ *(01451) 830 354*
– www.fossemanor.co.uk – enquiries@fossemanor.co.uk – Fax (01451) 832 486
19 rm ⍁ – †£95 ††£180/225   **Rest** – Menu £17 (lunch) – Carte £20/35

♦ Former coaching inn on the main road. Contemporary public areas with informal feel. Up-to-date bedrooms, some of which are set in the coach house. Lunch available in bar. Classically proportioned dining room with menu of Mediterranean favourites.

ENGLAND

↑ **Number Nine** without rest VISA ◉◉
9 Park St ⊠ *GL54 1AQ* – ℰ *(01451) 870 333* – *www.number-nine.info*
– *enquiries@number-nine.info*
3 rm � – **†**£50/60 **††**£65/75
♦ Ivy-clad 18C Cotswold stone house run by friendly owners on the high street. Winding staircase leads to the large bedrooms which occupy each floor.

✗✗ **The Old Butchers** AC VISA ◉◉ AE ①
Park St ⊠ *GL54 1AQ* – ℰ *(01451) 831 700* – *www.theoldbutchers.com*
– *louise@theoldbutchers.com* – *Fax (01451) 831 388* – *Closed second week May, second week October, Sunday dinner and Monday*
Rest – Carte £21/32
♦ Former butcher's shop of Cotswold stone: closely set tables in a very busy, modern restaurant. Daily changing, affordable, modish menus feature prominent use of local produce.

at Upper Oddington East : 2 m. by A 436 – ⊠ Stow-on-the-Wold

🍴 **Horse & Groom Village Inn** with rm P VISA ◉◉
⊠ *GL56 0XH* – ℰ *(01451) 830 584* – *www.horseandgroom.uk.com*
– *info@horseandgroom.uk.com* – *Closed 2 weeks January*
8 rm � – **†**£85/95 **††**£90/100 **Rest** – Carte £20/30
♦ Popular, welcoming pub, with open fire and characterful beams. Substantial menu displays carefully sourced produce, including venison from nearby estates and veg from the village.

at Daylesford East : 3½ m. by A 436 – ⊠ Stow-on-the-Wold

✗ **The Cafe at Daylesford Organic** P VISA ◉◉ AE ①
⊠ *GL56 0YG* – ℰ *(01608) 731 700* – *www.daylesfordorganic.com*
– *enquiries@daylesfordorganic.com* – *Fax (01608) 731 701* – *Closed 25 December and 1 January*
Rest – Organic – (lunch only) (bookings not accepted) Carte £23/29
♦ Beautifully designed farm shop, spa, yoga centre and two-floor café, which becomes very busy as customers tuck into tasty dishes whose ingredients are all organically sourced.

at Bledington Southeast : 4 m. by A 436 on B 4450 – ⊠ Kingham

🍴 **The Kings Head Inn** with rm rm, P VISA ◉◉
The Green ⊠ *OX7 6XQ* – ℰ *(01608) 658 365* – *www.kingsheadinn.net*
– *kingshead@orr-ewing.com* – *Fax (01608) 658 902* – *Closed 25-26 December*
12 rm ⊠ – **†**£55/65 **††**£70/125 **Rest** – Carte £20/28
♦ 15C stone inn with low-ceilinged, beamed bar and comfortable dining room. Traditional dishes with odd international influence; robust, rustic cooking. Smart bedrooms; those in pub more characterful; those in annex more stylish.

at Lower Oddington East : 3 m. by A 436 – ⊠ Stow-on-the-Wold

🍴 **The Fox Inn** with rm P VISA ◉◉
⊠ *GL56 0UR* – ℰ *(01451) 870 555* – *www.foxinn.net* – *info@foxinn.net*
– *Fax (01451) 870 669* – *Closed 25 December*
3 rm ⊠ – **††**£95 **Rest** – (booking essential) Carte £20/29
♦ 16C ivy dressed pub in a charming village. Flag floors, beams, fireplaces, nooks, crannies, books and candlelight. Hearty English fare. Sumptuously decorated rooms.

at Lower Swell West : 1¼ m. on B 4068 – ⊠ Stow-on-the-Wold

↑ **Rectory Farmhouse** without rest P
by Rectory Barns Rd ⊠ *GL54 1LH* – ℰ *(01451) 832 351*
– *rectory.farmhouse@cw-warwick.co.uk* – *Closed Christmas and New Year*
3 rm ⊠ – **†**£60 **††**£90/95
♦ 17C former farmhouse of Cotswold stone. Bedrooms are very comfortable and decorated in distinctive cottage style. Breakfast in kitchen, conservatory or, in summer, on the terrace.

STRATFORD-UPON-AVON – Warwickshire – **503** P 27 – pop. **22 187**   19 **C3**

🛆 Great Britain

> ▶ London 96 mi – Birmingham 23 mi – Coventry 18 mi – Leicester 44 mi
> – Oxford 40 mi
> 🖪 Bridgefoot 𝒞 (0870) 1607930, stratfordtic@shakespeare-country.co.uk
> 🖬 Tiddington Rd, 𝒞 (01789) 205 749
> 🖬 Menzies Welcombe Hotel & GC Warwick Rd, 𝒞 (01789) 413 800
> 🖬 Stratford Oaks Snitterfield Bearley Rd, 𝒞 (01789) 731 980
> 🌐 Town★★ - Shakespeare's Birthplace★ **AC**, AB
> 🖸 Mary Arden's House★ **AC**, NW : 4 m. by A 3400 A. Ragley Hall★ **AC**, W :
> 9 m. by A 422 A

Plan opposite

🏨🏨🏨 **Ettington Park** 🛆   🚗 💆 🎣 🖾 🏊 ✕ 🖹 ㅎ rm, 📞 😘 **P** **VISA** **⓪** **AE**
Alderminster, Southeast : 6 ¼ m. on A 3400 ⊠ *CV37 8BU –* 𝒞 *(01789) 450 123*
– www.handpicked.co.uk – ettingtonpark@handpicked.co.uk
– Fax (01789) 450 472
42 rm � – †£ 155/170 ††£ 165/180 – 6 suites
Rest – (dinner only) Menu £ 32 – Carte £ 40/48
♦ Imposing, corporate friendly, Gothic mansion with sympathetic extensions in attractive grounds. Ornate ceilings, classic country house feel. Comfy, well-equipped bedrooms. Oak-panelled dining room with medieval feel.

🏨🏨🏨 **Welcombe H. Spa and Golf Club**   ← 🚗 🎣 🖾 ⊛ 🏊 ✕
Warwick Rd, Northeast : 1½ m. on A 439   🖬 📞 😘 **P** **VISA** **⓪** **AE** **①**
⊠ *CV37 0NR –* 𝒞 *(01789) 295 252 – www.menzieshotels.co.uk*
– welcombe@menzieshotels.co.uk – Fax (01789) 414 666
73 rm ⊻ – ††£ 185 – 5 suites
Rest *Trevelyan* – (Closed Saturday lunch) Menu £ 25/35 **s** – Carte £ 36/43 **s**
♦ Jacobean house built 1869; sweeping Italian gardens and gracious, oak panelled interiors. Grand rooms in main house with many antique features. Golf course overlooks Avon. Savour views of gardens, fountain and waterfall from restaurant.

🏨🏨 **The Shakespeare**   🖹 📞 😘 **P** **VISA** **⓪** **AE** **①**
Chapel St ⊠ *CV37 6ER –* 𝒞 *(01789) 294 997 – www.mercure.com*
– h6630-re@accor.com – Fax (01789) 415 411   A**v**
73 rm ⊻ – †£ 150/210 ††£ 190/250 – 1 suite
Rest *David Garrick* – 𝒞 *(0870) 400 8182 (dinner only and Sunday lunch)*
Menu £ 25 – Carte £ 21/31 **s**
♦ Exudes atmosphere with gabled façade, leaded windows; this 18C inn was once a writers' watering hole. Afternoon tea served in vintage lounge; rooms with modern furnishings. Medieval styled restaurant; abundance of tried-and-tested dishes.

↑ **Cherry Trees** without rest   ✕ 📞 **P** **VISA** **⓪**
Swan's Nest Lane ⊠ *CV37 7LS –* 𝒞 *(01789) 292 989*
– www.cherrytrees-stratford.co.uk – gotocherrytrees@aol.com
– Fax (01789) 292 989   B**e**
3 rm ⊻ – †£ 65 ††£ 90/115
♦ Friendly welcome to this chalet style guest house. Luxurious bedrooms with every detail taken care of to include four poster room with own garden. Breakfast cooked to order.

↑ **Victoria Spa Lodge** without rest   🚗 ✕ 📞 **P** **VISA** **⓪**
Bishopton Lane, Northwest : 2 m. by A 3400 on Bishopton Lane turning left at roundabout with A 46 ⊠ *CV37 9QY –* 𝒞 *(01789) 267 985*
– www.stratford-upon-avon.co.uk/victoriaspa.htm
– ptozer@victoriaspalodge.demon.co.uk – Fax (01789) 204 728 – Closed Christmas and New Year
7 rm ⊻ – †£ 50/55 ††£ 65/70
♦ Built as spa, hotel and pump room; Queen Victoria stayed as one of its many guests, testified by the gables which bear her coat of arms. Pristine rooms are among its charms.

ENGLAND

748

STRATFORD-UPON-AVON

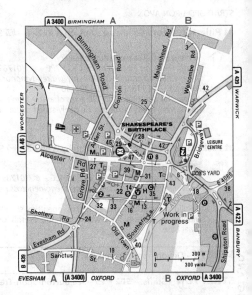

⌂ **Sequoia House** without rest   🛏 📶 P
51 Shipston Rd ⊠ CV37 – ℰ (01789) 268 852 – www.sequoia-house.co.uk
– reservations@sequoia-house.co.uk   B**a**
6 rm � – 🛏£85 🛏🛏£125
♦ Large terraced house close to town, with small garden and river access. Spacious
bedrooms feature character beds, antique furniture and modern bathrooms; no TVs.
Interesting breakfast.

✕ **Malbec**   𝘝𝘐𝘚𝘈 ⓂⓄ
6 Union St ⊠ CV37 6QT – ℰ (01789) 269 106 – www.malbecrestaurant.co.uk
– eatmalbec@aol.com – Fax (01789) 269 106
– Closed one week October, 25 December-2 January, Sunday and Monday   A**n**
Rest – Menu £15 (lunch) – Carte £29/32 **s**
♦ Pleasant modern restaurant with atmospheric barrel ceiling in intimate basement.
Good value set menus: accomplished à la carte with season's larder bolstering a
classic base.

✕ **Lambs**   🍴 𝘝𝘐𝘚𝘈 ⓂⓄ
12 Sheep St ⊠ CV37 6EF – ℰ (01789) 292 554 – www.lambsrestaurant.co.uk
– eat@lambsrestaurant.co.uk – Fax (01789) 293 372
– Closed 25-26 December, Sunday dinner, Monday lunch   B**c**
Rest – Menu £15/26 – Carte £22/32
♦ 16C town house with zesty bistro-style cooking in old-world surrounds of white
wattle walls, rafters and well-spaced wooden tables.

---

at Alveston East : 2 m. by B 4086 - B - ⊠ Stratford-upon-Avon

---

🍴 **The Baraset Barn**   🪑 🗚 ⇔ P 𝘝𝘐𝘚𝘈 ⓂⓄ ①
1 Pimlico Lane, on B 4086 ⊠ CV37 7RJ – ℰ (01789) 295 510
– www.lovelypubs.co.uk – barasetbarn@lovelypubs.co.uk – Fax (01789) 292 961
– Closed 25 December
Rest – (Closed Sunday dinner) Menu £20 – Carte £25/40
♦ Modern, stylish pub with glass-fronted kitchen, hidden inside a traditional exterior.
Cooking is assured and flavoursome and the modern menu offers something for
everyone.

at Pillerton Priors Southeast : 7 m. on A 422 - B – ⊠ Stratford-upon-Avon

⩕ **Fulready Manor** without rest ⌂ ≤ 🚗 ◑ ⅍ **P**
South : ¾ m. on Halford rd ⊠ *CV37 7PE –* ℰ *(01789) 740 152*
– www.fulreadymanor.co.uk – stay@fulreadymanor.co.uk – Fax (01789) 740 247
3 rm ⚏ – ♥£ 115/130 ♥♥£ 130/140
♦ Peaceful guest house in 120 acres of arable farmland. Warm welcome and delightful drawing room. Luxurious, uniquely-styled bedrooms with sumptuous furnishings and comforts.

at Ardens Grafton Southwest : 5 m. by A 46 - A – ⊠ Stratford-upon-Avon

🍴 **The Golden Cross** 🚗 🍴 ⅍ **P** VISA ◍◍ AE ①
Wixford Road, South : ¼ m. ⊠ *B50 4LG –* ℰ *(01789) 772 420*
– www.thegoldencross.net – info@thegoldencross.net – Fax (01798) 491 358
Rest – Menu £ 15 – Carte £ 20/27
♦ Solid stone floor, exposed beams, open fire, scrubbed wooden furnishing: all the winning ingredients for a welcoming pub. Freshly prepared dishes with tasty seasonal base.

STRETE – Devon – see Dartmouth

STRETTON – Staffs. – **502** P 25 – see Burton-upon-Trent

STRETTON – Ches. – **502** M 23 – see Warrington

STROUD – Gloucestershire – **503** N 28 – pop. 32 052   4 **C1**
🚉 London 113 mi – Bristol 30 mi – Gloucester 9 mi
🛈 Subscription Rooms, George St ℰ (01453) 760960, tic@stroud.gov.uk
🖫 Minchinhampton, ℰ (01453) 833 840
🖫 Painswick Golf Course Rd, ℰ (01452) 812 180

at Brimscombe Southeast : 2 ¼ m. on A 419 – ⊠ Stroud

🏨 **Burleigh Court** ⌂ ≤ 🚗 ⅃ ❞ **P** VISA ◍◍ ①
Burleigh Lane, South : ½ m. by Burleigh rd via The Roundabouts ⊠ *GL5 2PF*
– ℰ *(01453) 883 804 – www.burleighcourthotel.co.uk*
– info@burleighcourthotel.co.uk – Fax (01453) 886 870 – Closed 24-26 December
18 rm ⚏ – ♥£ 85/105 ♥♥£ 130/150
Rest – Menu £ 25 (lunch) – Carte (dinner) £ 30/39
♦ Regency house with mature garden, on edge of a steep hill overlooking Golden Valley. Swimming pool and terrace at the rear a real suntrap. Smart bedrooms with views. Comfortable dining room overlooks the gardens.

STUCKTON – Hants. – see Fordingbridge

STUDLAND – Dorset – **503** O 32   4 **C3**
🚉 London 135 mi – Bournemouth 25 mi – Southampton 53 mi
– Weymouth 29 mi

🍴 **Shell Bay** 🍴 VISA ◍◍ AE
Ferry Rd, North : 3 m. or via car ferry from Sandbanks ⊠ *BH19 3BA –* ℰ *(01929)*
450 363 – www.shellbay.co.uk – keith@shellbay.unioffice.co.uk – Fax (01929)
450 570 – April-October
Rest – Seafood – (booking essential at dinner) Carte £ 22/32
♦ Hut-like appearance, but in a spectacular location with views of Poole Harbour and Brownsea Island. Inside, large windows and mirrors make the most of this. Seafood emphasis.

STURMINSTER NEWTON – Dorset – **503** N 31 – **pop. 2 317** 4 **C3**

▶ London 123 mi – Bournemouth 30 mi – Bristol 49 mi – Salisbury 28 mi – Taunton 41 mi

◎ Mill ★ **AC**

Plumber Manor ⌖ 🗄 ◑ ※ ⅏ 🅿 *VISA* ◍ AE ①
Southwest : 1 ¾ m. by A 357 on Hazelbury Bryan rd ⊠ *DT10 2AF* – 🅟 *(01258) 472 507 – www.plumbermanor.com – book@plumbermanor.com – Fax (01258) 473 370 – Closed February*

16 rm ⌑ – ♦£95/115 ♦♦£180

Rest – (dinner only and Sunday lunch) Menu £23/30

♦ Manor house in a peaceful, secluded spot, owned by the same family since it was built in the 17C. The bedrooms are well kept and some have antique furniture. Choice of three dining rooms; traditional cooking.

SUDBURY – Suffolk – **504** W 27 – **pop. 20 188** 15 **C3**

▶ London 70 mi – Ipswich 22 mi – Cambridge 45 mi – Chelmsford 30 mi

Hitchcock's ※ *VISA* ◍ ①
10 Station Rd ⊠ *CO10 2SS* – 🅟 *(01787) 377 037 – www.hitchcocksdining.co.uk – Fax (01787) 377 037 – Closed first week January, 1 week mid July and Monday*

Rest – (lunch only and dinner Thursday-Saturday) Carte £20/28

♦ 150 year old former coal merchants; now a passionately run restaurant with food-store and deli. Cooking is simple and precise and uses only the finest local ingredients.

SUMMERCOURT – Cornwall – **503** F 32 – ⊠ **Newquay** 1 **B2**

▶ London 263 mi – Newquay 9 mi – Plymouth 45 mi

Viners 🏠 ※ ⇔ 🅿 *VISA* ◍
Carvynick, Northwest : 1½ m. off the junction of A 30 and A 3058 ⊠ *TR8 5AF* – 🅟 *(01872) 510 544 – www.vinersrestaurant.co.uk – info@vinersrestaurant.co.uk – Fax (01872) 510 468 – Closed January and Monday in winter*

Rest – Menu £19 – Carte £33/40

♦ Rustic, stone-built inn with informal atmosphere and enthusiastic staff. Old favourites and more ambitious offerings share the menu, and dishes make good use of local produce.

SUNBURY ON THAMES – Surrey – **504** S 29 – **pop. 27 415** 7 **C1**

▶ London 16 mi – Croydon 38 mi – Barnet 44 mi – Ealing 10 mi

Indian Zest 🏠 🅿 *VISA* ◍ AE ①
21 Thames St ⊠ *TW16 5QF* – 🅟 *(01932) 765 000 – www.indianzest.co.uk – info@indianzest.co.uk – Fax (01932) 765 000*

Rest – Indian – Carte £16/25

♦ Original in its decoration and food. 450 year old building; a series of small rooms set around a bar; subtle colonial feel. Interesting mix of modern Indian and traditional regional cuisine.

SUNDERLAND – Tyne and Wear – **501** P 19 – **pop. 177 739** 24 **B2**

▌ *Great Britain*

▶ London 272 mi – Leeds 92 mi – Middlesbrough 29 mi – Newcastle upon Tyne 12 mi

🛈 50 Fawcett St 🅟 (0191) 553 2000, tourist.info@sunderland.gov.uk

🏌 Whitburn South Shields Lizard Lane, 🅟 (0191) 529 2144

◎ National Glass Centre ★ A

Plan on next page

Sunderland Marriott ≪ 🗄 🏠 ⅙ 🗄 ⅗ rm, 🅺 rest, 🎶 ⅏ 🅿
Queens Parade, Seaburn ⊠ *SR6 8DB* – 🅟 *(0870) 400 72 87* *VISA* ◍ AE ①
– www.marriott.co.uk/nclsl – mhrs.nclsl.frontoffice@marriotthotels.com – Fax (0870) 400 73 87 A**e**

82 rm ⌑ – ♦£119/310 ♦♦£119/310 **Rest** – Carte £24/37

♦ Overlooks Whitburn Sands. A smart, contemporary, branded commercial hotel. Equally modern bedrooms with stylish, comfortable facilities. Restaurant and bar dining alternatives.

SUNDERLAND

SUNNINGDALE – Windsor and Maidenhead – **504** S 29   11 **D3**

  ◘ London 33 mi – Croydon 39 mi – Barnet 46 mi – Ealing 22 mi

XXX   **Bluebells**   🌐 AC ⇔ P. VISA ⑳ AE
Shrubbs Hill, London Rd, Northeast : ¾ m. on A 30 ⊠ SL5 0LE – ℰ (01344)
622 722 – www.bluebells-restaurant.com – info@bluebells-restaurant.com
– Fax (01344) 620 990 – Closed 25-30 December, 1-12 January and Monday
  Rest – Menu £ 22 (lunch) – Carte (dinner) £ 34/51
  ♦ Smart, well-manicured façade matched by sophisticated interior of deep green.
Large rear terrace, deck and garden. Modern British cooking with original starting
point.

SUNNINGHILL – Windsor & Maidenhead – **504** S 29 – **see Ascot**

SURFLEET SEAS END – Lincs. – **502** T 25 – **see Spalding**

SUTTON COLDFIELD – West Midlands – **503** O 26 – **pop. 105 452**   19 **C2**

  ◘ London 124 mi – Birmingham 8 mi – Coventry 29 mi – Nottingham 47 mi
    – Stoke-on-Trent 40 mi
  ▥ Pype Hayes Walmley Eachelhurst Rd, ℰ (0121) 351 1014
  ▥ Boldmere Monmouth Dr., ℰ (0121) 354 3379
  ▥ 110 Thornhill Rd, ℰ (0121) 580 7878
  ▥ The Belfry Wishaw Lichfield Rd, ℰ (01675) 470 301

                   Plan : see Birmingham pp. 4 and 5

🏨🏨🏨 **The Belfry**   ⇐ 🛏 🐕 🔲 ⊛ 🏯 ↳ ✕ 🖼 🛗 & rm, AC rest, ✕ ⸙ 🚣
Wishaw, East : 6½ m. by A 453 on A 446 ⊠ B76 9PR   P. VISA ⑳ AE ①
  – ℰ (01675) 470 301 – www.thebelfry.com – enquiries@thebelfry.com
  – Fax (01675) 470 256
  311 rm ⌁ – ♦£ 109/149 ♦♦£ 129/169 – 13 suites
  Rest *French Restaurant* – (dinner only and Sunday lunch) Carte £ 28/50 **s**
  Rest *Atrium* – (light lunch Monday-Saturday) Menu £ 25 **s**
  ♦ Famed for championship golf course, this large hotel has an unashamedly leisure
oriented slant, including a superb AquaSpa. Sizeable rooms; superior variety overlook
courses. Formal French Restaurant has golfing vistas. Atrium dominated by glass
dome ceiling.

🏨🏨🏨 **Moor Hall**   🛏 🔲 🏯 ↳ 🛗 & rm, ✕ ⸙ 🚣 P. VISA ⑳ AE ①
Moor Hall Drive, Northeast : 2 m. by A 453 and Weeford Rd ⊠ B75 6LN
  – ℰ (0121) 308 3751 – www.moorhallhotel.co.uk – mail@moorhallhotel.co.uk
  – Fax (0121) 308 8974   DT**r**
  82 rm ⌁ – ♦£ 98/132 ♦♦£ 98/132
  Rest *Moor Hall* – (closed Saturday lunch and Sunday dinner) (dinner only and
Sunday lunch) Menu £ 13/26 **s** – Carte £ 27/32 **s**
  Rest *Country Kitchen* – (Carvery) Carte approx. £ 16 **s**
  ♦ Imposing, commercially oriented manor house featuring 19C/early 20C fixtures and
fittings, set in quiet parkland. Fine range of rooms: some look over sunken gardens.
Refined Oak Room. Carvery at Country Kitchen.

SUTTON GAULT – Cambs. – **504** U 26 – **see Ely**

SUTTON-ON-THE-FOREST – North Yorkshire – **502** P 21   23 **C2**

  ◘ London 230 mi – Kingston-upon-Hull 50 mi – Leeds 52 mi
    – Scarborough 40 mi – York 12 mi

🏠   **Rose & Crown**   🛏 ✕ P. VISA ⑳ AE ①
☺ *Main St ⊠ YO61 1DP – ℰ (01347) 811 333 – www.rosecrown.co.uk*
   – ben@rosecrown.co.uk – Fax (01347) 811 333
   Rest – (Closed Sunday dinner and Monday) (booking essential) Carte £ 20/30
   ♦ Lovely enclosed rear terrace and garden. Rustic bar ambience made all the warmer
by roaring fires. Modern menu plus blackboard specials with imaginative, stylish
twists.

SUTTON-ON-THE-FOREST

ENGLAND

The Blackwell Ox Inn with rm 　　　　　　　　🛏 ⚒ **P** VISA ⦿
Huby Rd, Sutton-on-the-Forest ⊠ *YO61 1DT* – ℰ *(01347) 810328*
– www.blackwelloxinn.co.uk – enquiries@blackwelloxinn.co.uk – Fax (01347) 812738

7 rm ⊆ – †£95/110 ††£95/110　**Rest** – Menu £14 **s** – Carte £19/28 **s**
♦ Welcoming 19C brick-built pub. Twice-daily menus of hearty, straightforward cooking feature many classics; sourcing, traceability and seasonality are paramount. Bedrooms are furnished to a high standard; some feature four-posters.

SWANAGE – Dorset – **503** O 32 – pop. 11 097　　　　　　　　　　4 **C3**
■ London 130 mi – Bournemouth 22 mi – Dorchester 26 mi
　– Southampton 52 mi
🖪 The White Swan, Shore Rd ℰ (01929) 422885, mail@swanage.gov.uk
🖪 Isle of Purbeck Studland, ℰ (01929) 450 361
◙ Town★
◙ St Aldhelm's Head★★ (≤★★★), SW : 4 m. by B 3069 – Durlston Country
　Park (≤★★), S : 1 m. – Studland (Old Harry Rocks★★, Studland Beach
　(≤★), St Nicholas Church★), N : 3 m. – Worth Matravers (Anvil Point
　Lighthouse ≤★★), S : 2 m. – Great Globe★, S : 1¼ m. Corfe Castle★
　(≤★★) **AC**, NW : 6 m. by A 351 – Blue Pool★, NW : 9 m. by A 351 and
　minor roads – Lulworth Cove★, W : 18 m. by A 351 and B 3070

Cauldron Bistro　　　　　　　　　　　　　　　　　　VISA ⦿
5 High St ⊠ *BH19 2LN* – ℰ *(01929) 422671* – *Closed 2 weeks January, last week November, first week December and Monday-Wednesday*
Rest – (light lunch) Carte £19/38
♦ Quaint and cosy; boothed tables, mix and match furniture. Quality ingredients, local fish, generous portions cooked with care. Unusual vegetarian dishes.

SWAY – Hants. – **503** P 31 – see Brockenhurst

SWINBROOK – Oxon. – **503** P 28 – see Burford

SWINDON – Swindon – **503** O 29 – pop. 155 432　　　　　　　4 **D2**
■ London 83 mi – Bournemouth 69 mi – Bristol 40 mi – Coventry 66 mi
　– Oxford 29 mi – Reading 40 mi – Southampton 65 mi
🖪 37 Regent St ℰ (01793) 530328, infocentre@swindon.gov.uk
🖪 Broome Manor Pipers Way, ℰ (01793) 532 403
🖪 Shrivenham Park Shrivenham Penny Hooks, ℰ (01793) 783 853
🖪 The Wiltshire G & CC Wootton Bassett Vastern, ℰ (01793) 849 999
🖪 Wrag Barn G & C.C. Highworth Shrivenham Rd, ℰ (01793) 861 327
◙ Great Western Railway Museum★ **AC** – Railway Village Museum★ **AC** Y **M**
◙ Lydiard Park (St Mary's★) W : 4 m. U. Ridgeway Path★★, S : 8½ m. by
　A 4361 – Whitehorse (≤★)E : 7½ m. by A 4312, A 420 and B 400 off B 4057

Plan opposite

at Blunsdon North : 4½ m. by A 4311 on A 419 – ⊠ Swindon

Blunsdon House　　🚗 🅿 ▦ ♨ ⛴ ✗ 🖪 ⬟ ♿ rm, 🕴 ᴬᶜ rest, ⚒
⊠ *SN26 7AS* – ℰ *(01793) 721 701*　　　　　　　　📞 ♿ **P** VISA ⦿ AE ①
– www.blunsdonhouse.co.uk – info@blunsdonhouse.co.uk
– Fax (01793) 721 056　　　　　　　　　　　　　　　　　　　　Ua
111 rm ⊆ – †£85/140 ††£105/150 – 3 suites
Rest *Nichols* – (closed Sunday dinner) Menu £30 **s** – Carte £30/38
Rest *Christophers* – (carvery lunch) Menu £15/18 **s**
♦ Built as a farmhouse, this vast family-owned establishment now offers conference rooms and excellent leisure facilities. Large bedrooms with patios or balconies are popular. Nichols is elegant and stylish. Christophers offers lively carvery - and discos!

754

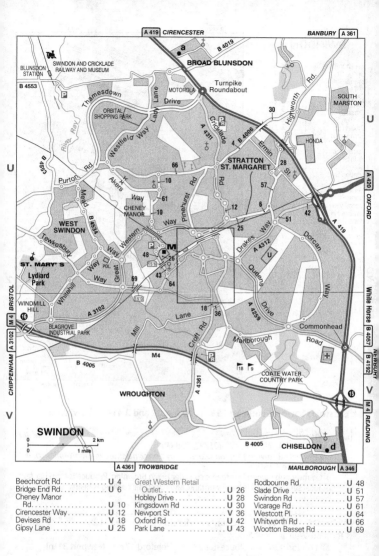

SWINDON

Beechcroft Rd.	**U** 4
Bridge End Rd.	**U** 6
Cheney Manor Rd.	**U** 10
Cirencester Way	**U** 12
Devises Rd.	**V** 18
Gipsy Lane	**U** 25

Great Western Retail Outlet	**U** 26
Hobley Drive	**U** 28
Kingsdown Rd	**U** 30
Newport St	**V** 36
Oxford Rd	**U** 42
Park Lane	**U** 43

Rodbourne Rd.	**U** 48
Slade Drive	**U** 51
Swindon Rd	**U** 57
Vicarage Rd.	**U** 61
Westcott Pl.	**U** 64
Whitworth Rd	**U** 66
Wootton Basset Rd	**U** 69

at Chiseldon South : 6 ¼ m. by A 4259, A 419 and A 346 on B 4005 – ⊠ Swindon

🏠 **Chiseldon House** ⏛ ⅍ ⁽⁾ 🛁 **P** 🆅🅸🆂🅰 **👁** 🅰🅴

New Rd ⊠ SN4 0NE – ✆ (01793) 741 010 – www.chiseldonhousehotel.co.uk
– info@chiseldonhousehotel.co.uk – Fax (01793) 741 059   V**d**
21 rm ⏢ – †£80/110 ††£110/140
Rest Orangery – Menu £ 15/25 – Carte £ 25/33 **s**
♦ The gardens are one of the strongest aspects of this extended Georgian house.
Rooms are a particularly good size with all mod cons. Close to motorway and easily
accessible. Ornate, split-level restaurant decorated with murals.

SWINDON

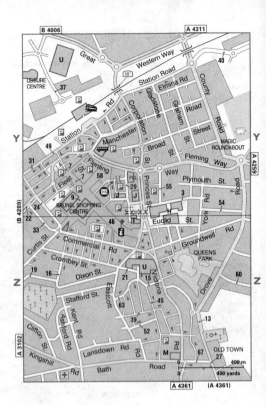

at Bishopstone – Southeast : 5 ¼ m. by A 4312 and A 419 – ⊠ Swindon

The Royal Oak
Cues Lane ⊠ SN6 8PP – ℰ *(01793) 790 481*
– www.helenbrowningorganics.co.uk – royaloak@helenbrowningorganics.co.uk
Rest – Carte £ 18/30
♦ Country pub owned by organic crusader Helen Browning. Produce is from her farm or local suppliers and is largely organic and fair-trade: cooking is hearty, seasonal and creative.

SYMONDS YAT WEST – County of Herefordshire – 503 M 28   18 B3
– ⊠ Ross-on-Wye ▌ *Great Britain*

▶ London 126 mi – Gloucester 23 mi – Hereford 17 mi – Newport 31 mi
◙ Town★ – Yat Rock (≤★)
◙ S : Wye Valley★

Norton House without rest
Whitchurch ⊠ HR9 6DJ – ℰ *(01600) 890 046 – www.norton-house.com*
– enquiries@norton-house.com – Fax (01600) 890 045 – Closed 25-26 December
3 rm ⊠ – ♥£40/45 ♥♥£60/80
♦ Built of local stone, this 18C farmhouse of 15C origins boasts quaint interiors. Rooms with antique beds in patchwork quilts and flowers. Tea, cake on arrival.

If breakfast is included the ⊠ symbol appears after the number of rooms.

756

TADCASTER – North Yorkshire – **502** Q 22 – pop. 6 548   22 **B2**
> ▶ London 206 mi – Harrogate 16 mi – Leeds 14 mi – York 11 mi

🏨🏨🏨 **Hazlewood Castle** ⚭   ⟨ 🚗 🌖 🞥 ☏ 🐾 **P** **VISA** **⚫** **AE** **①**
Paradise Lane, Hazlewood, Southwest : 2 ¾ m. by A 659 off A 64 ✉ *LS24 9NJ*
– ℰ (01937) 535 353 – www.hazlewood-castle.co.uk
– info@hazlewood-castle.co.uk – Fax (01937) 530 630
12 rm � – †£ 155 ††£ 195 – 9 suites
Rest *Restaurant Anise* – Carte £ 25/35
♦ Impressive part 13C fortified manor house in parkland. Panelled entrance hall, ornate lounges. Extensive conference facilities. Spacious rooms, individually styled. Dine in former orangery.

at Colton Northeast : 3 m. by A 659 and A 64 – ✉ Tadcaster

🍴 **Ye Old Sun Inn**   🚗 🕾 **P** **VISA** **⚫**
Main Street ✉ *LS24 8EP – ℰ (01904) 744 261 – www.yeoldsuninn.co.uk*
– kelly.mccarthy@btconnect.com – Closed 26 December, 1-21 January
Rest – (Closed Monday) Menu £ 17 (lunch) – Carte £ 18/25
♦ Homely, rustic pub with solar theme and deli serving homemade goodies. Spacious gardens and decked terrace. Classically-based, seasonal cooking with international flavours.

TALLAND BAY – Cornwall – **503** G 32 – see Looe

TANGMERE – W. Sussex – **504** R 31 – see Chichester

TANWORTH-IN-ARDEN – Warks. – **503** O 26 – see Henley-in-Arden

---

TAPLOW – Buckinghamshire – **504** R 29   11 **C3**
> ▶ London 33 mi – Maidenhead 2 mi – Oxford 36 mi – Reading 12 mi

🏨🏨🏨🏨 **Cliveden** ⚭   ⟨ 🚗 🌖 🞥 🏊 🞣 ⬚ ⓦ 🞧 🛦 🞥 ♨ 🛎 ⓣ 🐾 **P** **VISA** **⚫** **AE** **①**
North : 2 m. by Berry Hill ✉ *SL6 0JF – ℰ (01628) 668 561*
– www.clivedenhouse.co.uk – reservations@clivedenhouse.co.uk – Fax (01628) 661 837
32 rm � – †£ 240/370 ††£ 240/370 – 7 suites – ††£ 400/650
Rest *Waldo's* – (dinner only) (booking essential) Menu £ 75
Rest *Terrace* – Menu £ 35/59
♦ Breathtakingly stunning 19C stately home in National Trust gardens. Ornate, sumptuous public areas, filled with antiques. Exquisitely appointed rooms the last word in luxury. Exquisitely upholstered restaurant, seamlessly weaving into the grand tapestry of Cliveden. Superbly prepared ingredients contribute to seasonal menus served with flair. View parterre and Thames in top class style from Terrace.

TARPORLEY – Cheshire – **502** L/M 24 – pop. 2 634   20 **A3**
> ▶ London 186 mi – Chester 11 mi – Liverpool 27 mi – Shrewsbury 36 mi
> 🔟 Portal G & C.C. Cobblers Cross Lane, ℰ (01829) 733 933
> 🔟 Portal Premier Forest Rd, ℰ (01829) 733 884

at Little Budworth Northeast : 3 ½ m. on A 49 – ✉ Tarporley

✗✗ **Cabbage Hall**   🚗 🞥 **P** **VISA** **⚫**
Forest Road ✉ *CW6 9ES – ℰ (01829) 760 292*
– www.cabbagehallrestaurant.com – information@cabbagehallrestaurant.com
– Fax (01829) 760 292 – Closed Monday except Bank Holidays
Rest – Menu £ 17 (weekday lunch) – Carte £ 29/49
♦ Sleek former pub in 11 acres of land. Beautiful interior with gilded mirrors and startling copies of Picasso and Van Gogh. Impressively comprehensive range of bistro dishes.

at **Bunbury** South : 3 ¼ m. by A 49 – ⊠ Tarporley

🍴📖 **Dysart Arms** 🍺 🏠 **P** **VISA** **⑩** **AE**
Bowes Gate Rd, by Bunbury Mill rd ⊠ CW6 9PH – ☎ (01829) 260 183
– www.dysartarms-bunbury.co.uk – dysart-arms@brunningandprice.co.uk
– Fax (01829) 261 286
Rest – Carte £ 18/28
♦ Traditional red brick pub with French windows, terrace and garden. Daily changing menu displays a mix of fresh, tasty British and Mediterranean dishes, and classical puddings.

at **Willington** Northwest : 3 ½ m. by A 51 – ⊠ Tarporley

🏨 **Willington Hall** 🌿 � 🕭 🦺 **P** **VISA** **⑩** **AE**
⊠ CW6 0NB – ☎ (01829) 752 321 – www.willingtonhall.co.uk
– enquiries@willingtonhall.co.uk – Fax (01829) 752 596 – Closed 25-26 December
10 rm ⌑ – †£ 80 ††£ 130
Rest – (closed Sunday dinner and Bank Holidays) Menu £ 18/30
– Carte (dinner) £ 25/28
♦ Imposing 19C country house with ornate façade in mature grounds; many original features remain, including vast hall and impressive staircase. Most rooms have rural outlook. Intimate dinners served in classically proportioned surroundings.

The ❀ award is the crème de la crème.
This is awarded to restaurants
which are really worth travelling miles for!

TARR STEPS – Somerset – **503** J 30 3 **A2**
🚩 London 191 mi – Taunton 31 mi – Tiverton 20 mi
◎ Tarr Steps ★★ (Clapper Bridge ★★)

🍴📖 **Tarr Farm Inn** with rm 🍺 🕭 🏠 ☏ **P** **VISA** **⑩**
⊠ TA22 9PY – ☎ (01643) 851 507 – www.tarrfarm.co.uk
– enquiries@tarrfarm.co.uk – Fax (01643) 851 111 – Closed 1-13 February
9 rm ⌑ – †£ 75 ††£ 150 **Rest** – Carte £ 15/28
♦ Beside a river, in idyllic countryside, this is a true destination pub. Food ranges from cream teas and sandwiches to three courses at lunch, with more ambitious dishes at dinner. Bedrooms are elegant, luxurious and extremely well-equipped.

TATTENHALL – Cheshire – **502** L 24 – pop. 1 860 20 **A3**
🚩 London 200 mi – Birmingham 71 mi – Chester 10 mi – Liverpool 29 mi
– Manchester 38 mi – Stoke-on-Trent 30 mi

🏠 **Higher Huxley Hall** without rest 🌿 � 🕭 ☏ **P** **VISA** **⑩** **AE**
North : 2 ¼ m. on Huxley rd ⊠ CH3 9BZ – ☎ (01829) 781 484
– www.huxleyhall.co.uk – info@huxleyhall.co.uk
– Closed 25 December - 7 January
5 rm ⌑ – †£ 50/80 ††£ 90/98
♦ This historic manor house, sited on a former farm, dates from 14C and is attractively furnished with antiques. Bedrooms are comfortable and well equipped.

at **Higher Burwardsley** Southeast : 1 m. – ⊠ Tattenhall

🍴📖 **The Pheasant Inn** with rm 🌿 🏠 ☏ **P** **VISA** **⑩** **AE**
⊠ CH3 9PF – ☎ (01829) 770 434 – www.thepheasantinn.co.uk
– info@thepheasantinn.co.uk – Fax (01829) 771 097
12 rm ⌑ – †£ 65 ††£ 130 **Rest** – Carte £ 17/30
♦ Sits on a hill in the flat Cheshire Plains; lovely garden and terrace. Daily changing menu features local produce, ranging from afternoon tea, to deli boards and pub classics. Bedrooms are compact, stylish and comfortable; most have views.

ENGLAND

TAUNTON – Somerset – 503 K 30 – pop. 58 241   3 B3

- **D** London 168 mi – Bournemouth 69 mi – Bristol 50 mi – Exeter 37 mi – Plymouth 78 mi – Southampton 93 mi – Weymouth 50 mi
- **i** The Library, Paul St ℰ (01823) 336344, tauntontic@tauntondeane.gov.uk
- Taunton Vale Creech Heathfield, ℰ (01823) 412 220
- Vivary Vivary Park, ℰ (01823) 289 274
- Taunton and Pickeridge Corfe, ℰ (01823) 421 876
- **◉** Town★ - St Mary Magdalene★ V – Somerset County Museum★ **AC** V **M** – St James'★ U – Hammett St★ V **25** – The Crescent★ V – Bath Place★ V **3**
- **ᴳ** Trull (Church★), S : 2½ m. by A 38 – Hestercombe Gardens★, N : 5 m. by A 3259 BY and minor roads to Cheddon Fitzpaine. Bishops Lydeard★ (Church★), NW : 6 m. – Wellington : Church★, Wellington Monument (⩽★★), SW : 7½ m. by A 38 – Combe Florey★, NW : 8 m. – Gaulden Manor★ **AC**, NW : 10 m. by A 358 and B 3227

Plan on next page

🏨 The Castle   🛏 🛎 📶 🍴 🚲 **P** 🏦 **VISA ⓪ AE ①**

Castle Green ⊠ TA1 1NF – ℰ (01823) 272 671 – www.the-castle-hotel.com
– reception@the-castle-hotel.com – Fax (01823) 336 066   V**a**
44 rm – ♦£140 ♦♦£245, ⊿ £13.50
Rest – (Closed Sunday dinner) Menu £ 29/53 ⅏
♦ Traditionally renowned, family owned British hotel: afternoon tea a speciality. 12C origins with Norman garden. Wisteria-clad and castellated. Individually styled rooms. Classic British cooking uses top quality West Country produce.

🏠 Meryan House   🛏 📶 **P** **VISA ⓪**

Bishop's Hull Rd, West : ¾ m. by A 38 ⊠ TA1 5EG – ℰ (01823) 337 445
– www.meryanhouse.co.uk – meryanhousehotel@yahoo.co.uk
– Fax (01823) 322 355   AZ**c**
12 rm ⊿ – ♦£60/68 ♦♦£95
Rest – (Closed Sunday) (dinner only) (booking essential for non-residents) Menu £25
♦ Privately owned extended house on town outskirts. Comfortable sitting room has adjacent patio garden and small bar with jukebox. Well-kept, individually styled rooms. Intimate dining room with large inglenook.

✗✗ The Willow Tree   🌳 ⇔ **VISA ⓪**

3 Tower Lane ⊠ TA1 4AR – ℰ (01823) 352 835
– www.willowtreerestaurant.co.uk
– Closed January, August, Sunday and Monday   V**c**
Rest – (dinner only) Menu £28/33
♦ Converted 17C town house in central location. Exposed beams and large inglenook fireplaces. Friendly service. Appealing menu of modern seasonal cooking with a classical base.

✗ Brazz   🅰🅲 **P** **VISA ⓪ AE ①**

Castle Bow ⊠ TA1 1NF – ℰ (01823) 252 000 – www.brazz.co.uk
– taunton@brazz.co.uk – Fax (01823) 336 066 – Closed 25 December   V**e**
Rest – Carte £ 26/37
♦ Bright and breezy bistro style eatery to rear of The Castle hotel. Large, bustling bar area. Main restaurant has large aquarium, concave ceiling and brasserie favourites.

at Hatch Beauchamp Southeast : 6 m. by A 358 - BZ – ⊠ Taunton

🏠 Farthings   🛏 **P** **VISA ⓪ AE**

Village Road ⊠ TA3 6SG – ℰ (01823) 480 664 – www.farthingshotel.co.uk
– info@farthingshotel.co.uk – Fax (01823) 481 118
11 rm ⊿ – ♦£125 ♦♦£145   **Rest** – Menu £ 35/39 – Carte dinner £ 32/45
♦ Georgian country house with pleasant, spacious gardens in pretty village. Personally run, with small lounge and well-stocked bar. Sizeable, individually decorated rooms. Smart dining room; local produce to fore.

ENGLAND

TAUNTON

ENGLAND

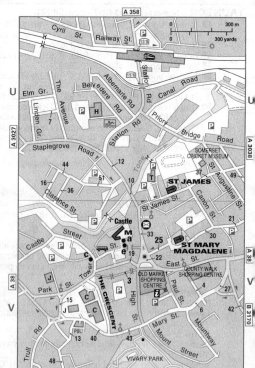

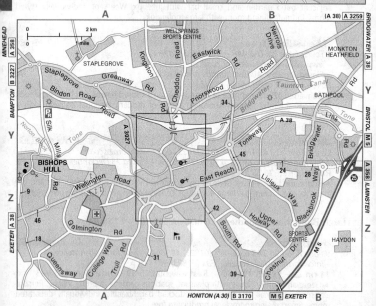

at West Bagborough Northwest : 10½ m. by A 358 - AY – ⊠ Taunton

⌂ **Tilbury Farm** without rest ॐ ≤ 🚗 🕭 ⅏ **P**
East : ¾ m. ⊠ *TA4 3DY –* ℰ *(01823) 432391 – Closed 26-30 December*
3 rm ⊊ – 🛉£40 🛉🛉£60/75
♦ Impressively characterful 18C house with terrific views of Vale of Taunton. Welcoming lounge boasts log fire. Well-kept, spacious bedrooms all with beams and good views.

🏠 **The Rising Sun Inn** with rm 🛜 **VISA ⦁⦁ AE**
⊠ *TA4 3EF –* ℰ *(01823) 432575 – www.therisingsun.info*
– jon@therisingsun.info
2 rm ⊊ – 🛉£55 🛉🛉£85 **Rest** – Carte £14/25
♦ Warm, intimate inn with a 'village pub' atmosphere. Local ingredients contribute to a well-balanced mix of modern and traditional dishes, with plenty of care taken in the kitchen.

at West Hatch Southeast : 5m by A38 – ⊠ Taunton

🏠 **The Farmers Inn** with rm 🚗 🕭 🛜 **P** **VISA ⦁⦁ AE**
Higher West Hatch ⊠ *TA3 5RS –* ℰ *(01823) 480480*
– www.farmersinnwesthatch.co.uk – letsgostay@farmersinnwesthatch.co.uk
– Fax (01823) 481177
5 rm ⊊ – 🛉£70/100 🛉🛉£120/140 **Rest** – Menu £14 (lunch) – Carte £20/29
♦ A soft-stone inn with welcoming owners serving local or home-brewed ales and ciders alongside an ambitious British/European menu. Luxurious bedrooms and bathrooms; most with sitting areas and views.

TAVISTOCK – Devon – **503** H 32 – pop. 11 018 2 **C2**
▶ London 239 mi – Exeter 38 mi – Plymouth 16 mi
🛈 Town Hall, Bedford Sq ℰ (01822) 612938, tavistocktic@westdevon.org.uk
▦ Down Rd, ℰ (01822) 612344
▦ Hurdwick Tavistock Hamlets, ℰ (01822) 612746
◎ Morwellham★ **AC**, SW : 4½ m. E : Dartmoor National Park★★ – Buckland Abbey★★ **AC**, S : 7 m. by A 386 – Lydford★★, N : 8½ m. by A 386

🏨 **Browns** 🚗 ♨ 🛏 ⅏ 🛜 **P** **VISA ⦁⦁ AE**
80 West St ⊠ *PL19 8AQ –* ℰ *(01822) 618686 – www.brownsdevon.co.uk*
– info@brownsdevon.co.uk – Fax (01822) 618646
20 rm – 🛉£79/99 🛉🛉£199/259, ⊊ £8.50 **Rest** – Menu £25/40
♦ Former coaching inn and oldest licensed premises in town; now a stylish and contemporary hotel. The mews rooms have a particularly comfortable feel to them. Busy, friendly, informal brasserie.

⌂ **April Cottage** ⅏ **P** **VISA ⦁⦁**
12 Mount Tavy Rd ⊠ *PL19 9JB –* ℰ *(01822) 613280*
– aprilcottage12@hotmail.co.uk
3 rm ⊊ – 🛉£45/50 🛉🛉£65/70 **Rest** – Menu £18
♦ Compact but homely Victorian cottage. Meals taken in rear conservatory overlooking River Tavy. Curios adorn small lounge. Carefully furnished rooms with varnished pine.

at Gulworthy West : 3 m. on A 390 – ⊠ Tavistock

XXX **The Horn of Plenty** with rm ॐ ≤ 🚗 🕭 **P** **VISA ⦁⦁ AE**
Gulworthy, West : 4 m. by A 390 off Chipshop rd ⊠ *PL19 8JD –* ℰ *(01822)*
832532 – www.thehornofplenty.co.uk – enquiries@thehornofplenty.co.uk
– Fax (01822) 834390 – Closed 24-26 December
10 rm ⊊ – 🛉£150 🛉🛉£250 **Rest** – French – Menu £27/47
♦ Stylish, contemporary restaurant featuring local artwork, in enchanting, creeper-clad country house. Classic cooking uses local ingredients. Polite service. Modern country house style bedrooms; those in annex have terrace.

ENGLAND

at Milton Abbot Northwest : 6 m. on B 3362 – ✉ Tavistock

Hotel Endsleigh ⬧   ≤ 🚗 🦌 🐟 ☆ **P** *VISA* ⚫⚫ **AE**
Southwest : 1 m. ✉ *PL19 0PQ –* ✆ *(01822) 870 000 – www.hotelendsleigh.com*
– mail@hotelendsleigh.com – Fax (01822) 870 578
13 rm ⬚ – †£270 ††£300 – 3 suites   **Rest** – Menu £40 **s**
◆ Painstakingly restored Regency lodge in magnificent Devonian gardens and
grounds. Stylish lounge and refined bedrooms are imbued with an engaging, understated elegance. Interesting, classically based dishes served in two minimalist
dining rooms.

at Chillaton Northwest : 6 ¼ m. by Chillaton rd – ✉ Tavistock

Tor Cottage without rest ⬧   ≤ 🚗 🦌 ♨ ☆ **P** *VISA* ⚫⚫
*Southwest : ¼ m. by Tavistock rd, turning right at bridle path sign, down
unmarked track for ½ m.* ✉ *PL16 0JE –* ✆ *(01822) 860 248*
*– www.torcottage.co.uk – info@torcottage.co.uk – Fax (01822) 860 126 – Closed
mid December to mid January*
5 rm ⬚ – †£94 ††£140/150
◆ Lovely cottage and peaceful gardens in 28 hillside acres. Terrace or conservatory
breakfast. Individual rooms, most spread around garden, with open fires or wood
stoves.

Red = Pleasant. Look for the red 🍴 and 🏠 symbols.

TEFFONT – Wilts. – see Salisbury

TEIGNMOUTH – Devon – **503** J 32 – pop. 14 799   2 **D2**
🔼 London 216 mi – Exeter 16 mi – Torquay 8 mi
🇮 The Den, Sea Front ✆ (01626) 215666

Britannia House without rest   🚗 ♨ 🖥 *VISA* ⚫⚫ **AE**
26 Teign St ✉ *TQ14 8EG –* ✆ *(01626) 770 051 – www.britanniahouse.org
– gillettbritannia@aol.com – Fax (01626) 879 903 – Closed January*
3 rm ⬚ – †£50/60 ††£70/80
◆ Intimate 17C Grade II listed townhouse enhanced by many original features. Tuck
into an organic breakfast and relax in walled garden or cosy upstairs lounge. Homely
rooms.

Thomas Luny House without rest   🚗 ♨ 🖥 **P** *VISA* ⚫⚫
Teign St, follow signs for the Quays, off the A 381 ✉ *TQ14 8EG –* ✆ *(01626)
772 976 – www.thomas-luny-house.co.uk
– alisonandjohn@thomas-luny-house.co.uk*
4 rm ⬚ – †£68/70 ††£85/98
◆ Personally run Georgian house with sheltered walled garden. Smart breakfast room
with antique pieces. Well furnished drawing room. Stylish, individually appointed
bedrooms.

TELFORD – Telford and Wrekin – **502** M 25 – pop. 138 241   18 **B2**
📗 Great Britain
🔼 London 152 mi – Birmingham 33 mi – Shrewsbury 12 mi
   – Stoke-on-Trent 29 mi
🇮 Management Suite, The Telford Centre ✆ (01952) 238008,
tourist-info@telfordshopping.co.uk
🏌 Telford Sutton Heights Great Hay, ✆ (01952) 429 977
🏌 Wrekin Wellington, ✆ (01952) 244 032
🏌 The Shropshire Muxton Muxton Grange, ✆ (01952) 677 800
🏛 Ironbridge Gorge Museum★★ **AC** (The Iron Bridge★★, Coalport China
Museum★★, Blists Hill Open Air Museum★★, Museum of the River and
Visitor Centre★) S : 5 m. by B 4373. Weston Park★★ **AC**, E : 7 m. by A 5

ENGLAND

Dovecote Grange without rest 🛋 ⚄ ⁿ₁ P VISA ⊙⊙ ①

Bratton Rd, Northwest : 6¾ m. by A 442 and B 5063 (following signs for Admaston) off B 4394 ⊠ TF5 0BS – ℰ (01952) 243 739
– www.dovecotegrange.co.uk – mandy@dovecotegrange.co.uk – Fax (01952) 243 739
5 rm ⊂⊃ – †£45/55 ††£70
♦ Attractive guesthouse, garden and terrace enjoying views over the local fields. Combined lounge and breakfast area with modern leather furniture. Large, comfy, modish rooms.

at Norton South : 7 m. on A 442 – ⊠ Shifnal

Hundred House with rm 🛋 🏡 P VISA ⊙⊙ AE ①

Bridgnorth Rd ⊠ TF11 9EE – ℰ (01952) 730 353 – www.hundredhouse.co.uk
– reservations@hundredhouse.co.uk – Fax (01952) 730 355 – Accommodation closed 25-26 December
10 rm ⊂⊃ – †£30/70 ††£60/125   **Rest** – Menu £18/19 – Carte £20/35
♦ Characterful, family run redbrick inn with herb garden. Carefully sourced dishes, robust and original. Sizable rooms in 19C style, some with canopied beds and swings.

TEMPLE SOWERBY – Cumbria – **502** M 20 – see Penrith

TENBURY WELLS – Shropshire – **503** M 27 – pop. 3 316   18 **B2**
   ▷ London 144 mi – Birmingham 36 mi – Hereford 20 mi – Shrewsbury 37 mi
       – Worcester 28 mi

Cadmore Lodge ⤳ ≤ ◑ ⌇ 🖼 🖾 🔟 ⚄ ⁿ₁ 🔬 P VISA ⊙⊙

St Michaels, Southwest : 2¾ m. by A 4112 ⊠ WR15 8TQ – ℰ (01584) 810 044
– www.cadmorelodge.com – reception.cadmore@cadmorelodge.com
– Fax (01584) 810 044
15 rm ⊂⊃ – †£50/60 ††£80/130
Rest – (bar lunch only on Monday) Menu £19/23 – Carte £15/24
♦ Family run hotel in pleasant location. Lakeside setting. Plenty of outdoor activities, including golf and fishing. Well-planned rooms: some larger ones have antique furniture. Restaurant overlooks the lake.

TETBURY – Gloucestershire – **503** N 29 – pop. 5 250 ▌ *Great Britain*   4 **C1**
   ▷ London 113 mi – Bristol 27 mi – Gloucester 19 mi – Swindon 24 mi
   🛈 33 Church St ℰ (01666) 503552, tourism@tetbury.org
   🖥 Westonbirt, ℰ (01666) 880 242
   🄲 Westonbirt Arboretum★ **AC**, SW : 2½ m. by A 433

Calcot Manor 🛋 ◑ 🏡 🔟 🖳 ⊕ 🏊 🖿 🎾 🚴 ⚄ ⁿ₁ 🔬 P

*Calcot, West : 3½ m. on A 4135 ⊠ GL8 8YJ – ℰ (01666)   VISA ⊙⊙ AE ①
890 391 – www.calcotmanor.co.uk – reception@calcotmanor.co.uk – Fax (01666) 890 394*
34 rm ⊂⊃ – †£180 ††£230/285 – 1 suite
Rest *The Gumstool Inn* – see restaurant listing
Rest *Conservatory* – (booking essential) Menu £23 (lunch) – Carte £33/40
♦ Impressive Cotswold farmhouse, gardens and meadows with converted ancient barns and stables. Superb spa. Variety of luxuriously appointed rooms with contemporary flourishes. Stylish Conservatory serves interesting modern dishes.

Snooty Fox 🏡 VISA ⊙⊙ AE

Market Pl ⊠ GL8 8DD – ℰ (01666) 502 436 – www.snooty-fox.co.uk
– res@snooty-fox.co.uk – Fax (01666) 503 479
12 rm ⊂⊃ – †£79/103 ††£103/149   **Rest** – Carte £20/33
♦ Stone built former 17C wool factory, with extensions, opposite Tudor market place. Characterful bar with inglenook. Individualistic rooms with superior drapes and fabrics. Cosy wood panelled bistro with all-day menu.

ENGLAND

The Chef's Table
VISA CO

49 Long St ⊠ GL8 8AA – ℰ (01666) 504 466 – sarah@thechefstable.co.uk
– Closed Sundays
Rest – (lunch only) Carte £27/32

♦ Glass-fronted deli shop with busy, informal restaurant to the rear; mix of tables and high stools. Daily blackboard menu displays rustic, generous dishes of local, organic produce.

The Trouble House
P VISA CO AE

Cirencester Rd, Northeast : 2 m. on A 433 ⊠ GL8 8SG – ℰ (01666) 502 206
– www.thetroublehouse.co.uk – info@troublehouse.co.uk – Closed 25 December,
first week in January and Bank Holidays
Rest – (Closed Sunday dinner, Monday) Menu £20 (weekdays dinner)
– Carte £24/34

♦ Although unremarkable in appearance, this pub conceals a characterful, cosy inner. Cooking is unfussy, using the best ingredients and keeping flavours natural and complementary.

The Gumstool Inn – at Calcot Manor Hotel
P

West : 3½ m. on A 4135 ⊠ GL8 8YJ – ℰ (01666) 890 391   *VISA CO AE ①*
– www.calcotmanor.co.uk – reception@calcotmanor.co.uk – Fax (01666) 890 394
Rest – (booking essential) Carte £25/35

♦ Converted farm out-building on the Calcot Estate, which dates back to the 14C. Cooking is seasonal, rustic and hearty, with a wide-ranging menu and extensive daily specials.

ENGLAND

TEWKESBURY – Gloucestershire – **503** N 28 – pop. **9 978** ▌*Great Britain*   4 **C1**

🚇 London 108 mi – Birmingham 39 mi – Gloucester 11 mi
🛈 100 Church St ℰ (01684) 855040, outofthehat@tewkesbury.gov.uk
🏌 Tewkesbury Park Hotel Lincoln Green Lane, ℰ (01684) 295 405
◎ Town★ – Abbey★★ (Nave★★, vault★)
◐ St Mary's, Deerhurst★, SW : 4 m. by A 38 and B 4213

Alstone Fields Farm without rest
P

Stow Rd, Teddington Hands, East : 5 m. by A 438 and A 46 on B 4077 ⊠ GL20 8NG
– ℰ (01242) 620 592 – janeandrobin@yahoo.co.uk – Closed 25 December
6 rm �: – ♥£45 ♥♥£70

♦ Farmhouse in well-tended garden. Communal breakfast room with view; local ingredients and fruit from the garden. Bright, clean, homely rooms, two on the ground floor.

at Corse Lawn Southwest : 6 m. by A 38 and A 438 on B 4211 – ⊠ Gloucester

Corse Lawn House
P VISA CO AE ①

⊠ GL19 4LZ – ℰ (01452) 780 771 – www.corselawn.com
– enquiries@corselawn.com – Fax (01452) 780 840 – Closed 24-26 December
17 rm ⊒ – ♥£95 ♥♥£150 – 2 suites
Rest *The Restaurant* – Menu £32 – Carte £27/38
Rest *Bistro* – Menu £19/22 – Carte £27/38

♦ Elegant Queen Anne Grade II listed house, set back from village green and fronted by former "coach wash". Two comfortable lounges and classic country house style rooms. Formal restaurant with period décor and framed prints, nicely set overlooking rear garden. Extensive à la carte and set menu. Classic style of dishes; quality wine list. Informal brasserie style eatery in atmospheric bar.

at Eldersfield Southwest : 8½ m. by A38, A438 and B4211

The Butchers Arms
P VISA CO

Lime St, Eldersfield, Southeast : 1 m. ⊠ GL19 4NX – ℰ (01452) 840 381
– www.thebutchersarms.net – Closed first week in January
Rest – (Closed Sunday dinner, Monday, Tuesday lunch) (booking essential)
Carte £25/32

♦ Traditional pub run by a husband and wife team. Concise regularly-changing menu features local or homemade produce and refined cooking, but hurry, only 25 diners can be accommodated.

THAXTED – Essex – **504** V 28 – pop. 2 066   13 **C2**
> ◪ London 44 mi – Cambridge 24 mi – Colchester 31 mi – Chelmsford 20 mi

⌂ **Crossways** without rest   ⛢ ⅏ ⌕
32 Town St ⊠ CM6 2LA – ℰ (01371) 830 348 – www.crosswaysthaxted.co.uk
– info@crosswaysthaxted.co.uk – Restricted opening October-March
3 rm ⌑ – ✝£45 ✝✝£65
♦ 16C house in picturesque, largely timbered village. Breakfast room is tea room during day. Small lounge with fireplace and beams. Rooms in keeping with age of property.

THIRSK – North Yorkshire – **502** P 21 – pop. 9 099   22 **B1**
> ◪ London 227 mi – Leeds 37 mi – Middlesbrough 24 mi – York 24 mi
> ℹ 49 Market Pl ℰ (01845) 522755, thirsktic@hambleton.gov.uk
> ⛳ Thirsk & Northallerton Thornton-Le-Street, ℰ (01845) 522 170

🏨 **Golden Fleece**   ⅏ ⅍ 𝐏 𝘝𝘐𝘚𝘈 ⦿ 𝐀𝐄
42 Market Pl ⊠ YO7 1LL – ℰ (01845) 523 108 – www.goldenfleecehotel.com
– reservations@goldenfleecehotel.com – Fax (01845) 523 996
23 rm ⌑ – ✝£55/70 ✝✝£95
Rest – (bar lunch Monday-Saturday) Carte £19/30
♦ Sizeable Grade II listed 16C coaching inn located in centre of market town. Dick Turpin was a regular visitor. Spacious, comfortable lounge. Well-kept, inviting rooms. Yorkshire flavours are a staple of restaurant.

⌂ **Spital Hill**   ⛢ ⅟ ⅏ 𝐏 𝘝𝘐𝘚𝘈 ⦿
York Rd, Southeast : 1 ¾ m. on A 19, entrance between 2 white posts ⊠ YO7 3AE
– ℰ (01845) 522 273 – www.spitalhill.co.uk – spitalhill@spitalhill.entadsl.com
– Fax (01845) 524 970
3 rm ⌑ – ✝£62/66 ✝✝£90/106
Rest – (by arrangement, communal dining) Menu £32
♦ Expansive early Victorian house surrounded by nearly two acres of secluded gardens. Fully tiled entrance hall and comfortable sitting room. Spacious rooms, warmly furnished. Communal dining at mealtimes.

at Topcliffe Southwest : 4½ m. by A 168 – ⊠ Thirsk

🏠 **Angel Inn**   ⛰ ⅏ ⅍ 𝐏 𝘝𝘐𝘚𝘈 ⦿ ⓞ
Long St ⊠ YO7 3RW – ℰ (01845) 577 237 – www.topccliffeangelinn.co.uk
– res@topcliffeangelinn.co.uk – Fax (01845) 578 000 – Closed 25 December
15 rm ⌑ – ✝£40/55 ✝✝£70   **Rest** – Carte £17/28
♦ Enlarged hostelry dating back to early 17C in tiny village. Spacious lounge and characterful bar. Popular with business travellers. Sizeable bedrooms have pine furniture. Bright décor enlivens dining room.

at Asenby Southwest : 5¼ m. by A 168 – ⊠ Thirsk

🏨 **Crab Manor**   ⛢ ⌂ ⅏ 𝐏 𝘝𝘐𝘚𝘈 ⦿ 𝐀𝐄
Dishforth Rd ⊠ YO7 3QL – ℰ (01845) 577 286 – www.crabandlobster.co.uk
– info@crabandlobster.co.uk – Fax (01845) 577 109
14 rm ⌑ – ✝£90 ✝✝£230 – 2 suites
Rest Crab and Lobster – see restaurant listing
♦ Part Georgian manor filled with quality objects and Victoriana. Highly individual bedrooms, themed around world famous hotels. Some rooms have outdoor hot tubs.

🍴 **Crab and Lobster**   ⛢ ⛰ ⅏ 𝐏 𝘝𝘐𝘚𝘈 ⦿ 𝐀𝐄
Dishforth Rd ⊠ YO7 3QL – ℰ (01845) 577 286 – www.crabandlobster.co.uk
– Fax (01845) 577 109
Rest – Seafood – Menu £18 – Carte £30/40
♦ Atmospheric and individual eating place filled with memorabilia. Choose the informal bar or formal Pavilion restaurant. Seafood oriented menus with blackboard specials.

ENGLAND

THORNBURY – South Gloucestershire – **503** M 29 – pop. 11 969   4 **C1**
– ✉ Bristol

🚗 London 128 mi – Bristol 12 mi – Gloucester 23 mi – Swindon 43 mi

🏰 **Thornbury Castle** ⤳   🍴 🕪 ♨ ✆ 🅿 VISA ◉◉ AE ◑
Castle St ✉ BS35 1HH – ✆ (01454) 281 182 – www.thornburycastle.co.uk
– info@thornburycastle.co.uk – Fax (01454) 416 188
22 rm ☕ – †£90/215 ††£255/360 – 3 suites   **Rest** – Menu £28/48
♦ 16C castle built by Henry VIII with gardens and vineyard. Two lounges boast plenty
of antiques. Rooms of stately comfort; several bathrooms resplendent in marble.
Restaurant exudes formal aura.

THORNHAM MAGNA – Suffolk – **504** X 27 – ✉ Eye   15 **C2**

🚗 London 96 mi – Cambridge 47 mi – Ipswich 20 mi – Norwich 30 mi

🏠 **Thornham Hall** ⤳   ⪡ 🍴 🕪 🔊 ✾ ⅋ 🅿 VISA ◉◉ AE ◑
✉ IP23 8HA – ✆ (01379) 783 314 – www.thornhamhall.com
– thornhamhall@aol.com – Fax (01379) 788 347
3 rm ☕ – †£65/100 ††£100
Rest – (by arrangement, communal dining) Menu £15/25
♦ 20C incarnation of former Tudor, Georgian and Victorian homes. House party
atmosphere. Lovely paintings throughout. Comfortable, welcoming rooms. Dining
room of character in converted coach house.

at Yaxley Northeast : 2¼ m. by Eye rd and A 140 – ✉ Eye

🏠 **The Bull Auberge**   AC 🕪 🅿 VISA ◉◉ AE ◑
Ipswich Rd, on A140 ✉ IP23 8BZ – ✆ (01379) 783 604 – www.the-auberge.co.uk
– aubmail@the-auberge.co.uk – Fax (01379) 788 486 – Closed Saturday lunch,
Sunday and Monday
11 rm ☕ – †£75 ††£200
Rest – (Closed Sunday and Monday) (dinner only) Menu £25
– Carte £25/40
♦ 15C inn by busy road; rustic origins enhanced by brick walls, beams and open fire.
Original, well presented, modern menus prepared with care. Stylish, well appointed
rooms.

THORNTON – Lancs. – **502** K 22 – see Blackpool

THORNTON HOUGH – Merseyside – **502** – ✉ Wirral   20 **A3**

🚗 London 215 mi – Birkenhead 12 mi – Chester 17 mi – Liverpool 12 mi

🏨 **Thornton Hall**   🍴 📺 ♨ 🍸 ⅙ & rm, ✾ 🕪 ⅍ 🅿 VISA ◉◉ AE
on B 5136 ✉ CH63 1JF – ✆ (0151) 336 3938 – www.thorntonhallhotel.com
– reservations@thorntonhallhotel.com – Fax (0151) 336 7864
62 rm – †£75/125 ††£75/125, ☕ £14.50 – 1 suite
Rest The Italian Room – (bar lunch Saturday) Menu £16/29 **s**
– Carte £37/47 **s**
♦ Family owned, extended manor house with lawned gardens in rural location. Atmospheric wood panelled lounges with heavy drapes. Excellent leisure club. Spacious
bedrooms. Rich, warmly decorated dining room with chandelier.

THORPE LANGTON – Leics. – see Market Harborough

THORPE MARKET – Norfolk – **504** X 25 – ✉ North Walsham   15 **D1**

🚗 London 130 mi – Norwich 21 mi

🏠 **Elderton Lodge** ⤳   ⪡ 🍴 🕪 🅿 VISA ◉◉ AE
Gunton Park, South : 1 m. on A 149 ✉ NR11 8TZ – ✆ (01263) 833 547
– www.eldertonlodge.co.uk – enquiries@eldertonlodge.co.uk – Fax (01263)
834673
11 rm ☕ – †£65 ††£100/120
Rest – Menu £18 (lunch) **s** – Carte dinner £26/33 **s**
♦ Late 18C former shooting lodge on large estate and deer park. Tranquil air. Favoured retreat of Lillie Langtry. Bedrooms are individually styled in a country house
theme. Local ingredients used widely in restaurant; particularly good value lunches.

THRELKELD – Cumbria – **502** K 20 – **see Keswick**

THRUSCROSS – North Yorkshire   22 **B2**
> ◘ London 223 mi – Leeds 22 mi – Bradford 23 mi – Huddersfield 37 mi

🏠 **The Stone House Inn**   🍽 **P** *VISA* **◎◎** **AE**
⊠ HG3 4AH – 𝒞 (01943) 880 325 – www.stonehouseinn.co.uk
Rest – (Closed Monday in winter) Carte £ 16/23
◆ 300 year old coaching inn set high in the Yorkshire dales. A real family pub, with a
kids menu designed by the owners' children and a wide-ranging main menu of local, seasonal fare.

THUNDER BRIDGE – W. Yorks. – **see Huddersfield**

THUNDERSLEY – Essex – **504** V 29 – **see Rayleigh**

THURSFORD GREEN – Norfolk   15 **C1**
> ◘ London 120 mi – Fakenham 7 mi – Norwich 29 mi

🏠 **Holly Lodge** ⌂   🍽 ⌗ 🌐 **P** *VISA* **◎◎**
The Street ⊠ NR21 0AS – 𝒞 (01328) 878 465 – www.hollylodgeguesthouse.co.uk
– info@hollylodgeguesthouse.co.uk – *Closed January*
3 rm ⌕ – †£90 ††£110   **Rest** – Menu £ 18
◆ Stylishly furnished 18C house set in delightful garden. Welcome includes Pimms by
the pond or afternoon tea. Excellent breakfast. Well appointed bedrooms in converted stables. Home-cooked evening meals.

ENGLAND

> The red ⌂ symbol?
> This denotes the very essence of peace
> – only the sound of birdsong first thing in the morning…

THWING – East Riding of Yorkshire   23 **D2**
> ◘ London 228 mi – Bridlington 10 mi – York 16 mi

🏠 **The Falling Stone**   **P** *VISA* **◎◎**
Main St ⊠ YO25 3DS – 𝒞 (01262) 470 403
Rest – (Closed Sunday dinner) (dinner only and lunch Saturday-Sunday)
Menu £ 7/18 – Carte £ 15/28
◆ Traditional firelit bar, comfy lounge and smart, linen-clad restaurant. Blackboard
menu of classic pub dishes and fine selection of local ales from the Wold Brewery.
Chatty service.

TICKTON East Riding – **502** S 22 – **see Beverley**

TILSTON Ches – **502** L 24 – **see Malpas**

TITCHWELL – Norfolk – **504** V 25 – **pop. 99**   15 **C1**
> ◘ London 128 mi – King's Lynn 25 mi – Boston 56 mi – Wisbech 36 mi

🏨 **Titchwell Manor**   🍽 🌣 ᴎ **P** *VISA* **◎◎** **AE** **①**
⊠ PE31 8BB – 𝒞 (01485) 210 221 – www.titchwellmanor.com
– margaret@titchwellmanor.com – Fax (01485) 210 104
27 rm ⌕ – †£55/150 ††£110/250   **Rest** – Carte £ 27/36
◆ Victorian, red bricked former farmhouse. Bedrooms in the main house more traditional; those in converted outbuildings more modern and the best look over the
lavender garden. Traditional menus in conservatory restaurant.

TITLEY – Herefordshire – **503** L 27 – see Kington

TIVERTON – Devon – **503** J 31 – pop. 16 772   2 **D2**

🖪 London 191 mi – Bristol 64 mi – Exeter 15 mi – Plymouth 63 mi

⌂ **Hornhill** without rest ⌖   ⪕ ⇋ ◐ ⅀ **P**
Exeter Hill, East :½ m. by A 396 and Butterleigh rd ✉ *EX16 4PL* – ✆ *(01884)*
253 352 – www.hornhill-farmhouse.co.uk – hornhill@tinyworld.co.uk
– Fax (01884) 253 352
3 rm ⌑ – ♦£35/40 ♦♦£60/65
♦ Georgian house on hilltop boasting pleasant views of the Exe Valley. Well-furnished drawing room with real fire. Attractively styled bedrooms with antiques.

TOOT BALDON – Oxon. – see Oxford

TOPCLIFFE – N. Yorks. – **502** P 21 – see Thirsk

TOPSHAM – Devon – **503** J 31 – ✉ **Exeter**   2 **D2**

🖪 London 175 mi – Torbay 26 mi – Exeter 4 mi – Torquay 24 mi

✗ **The Galley**   **VISA** ⬤⬤
41 Fore St ✉ *EX3 0HU* – ✆ *(01392) 876 078 – www.galleyrestaurant.co.uk*
– fish@galleyrestaurant.co.uk – Fax (01392) 876 333 – Closed Sunday and
Monday
Rest – Seafood – Carte £36/47
♦ Idiosyncratic and gloriously eccentric, every nook and cranny filled with bric-a-brac
or foody paraphernalia. Original, tasty, locally sourced piscine dishes.

TORQUAY – Torbay – **503** J 32 – pop. 62 968   2 **C-D2**

🖪 London 223 mi – Exeter 23 mi – Plymouth 32 mi
🛈 Vaughan Parade ✆ (01803) 211211, torquay.tic@torbay.gov.uk
🕍 St Marychurch Petitor Rd, ✆ (01803) 327 471
◉ Torbay★ – Kent's Cavern★ **AC** CX A
🔄 Paignton Zoo★★ **AC**, SE : 3 m. by A 3022 - Cockington★, W : 1 m. AX

Plans on following pages

🏨 **The Imperial**   ⪕ ⇋ ⅀ 🖵 ◉ ∰ *Là* ✗ 🏮 ፌ rm, ⛫ **M** rest, ⅍
Park Hill Rd ✉ *TQ1 2DG* – ✆ *(01803)*   ⁋ ⅍ **P** ⤳ **VISA** ⬤⬤ **AE** ⓪
294 301 – www.paramount-hotels.co.uk – cg.iman@paramount-hotels.co.uk
– Fax (01803) 298 293   CZ**a**
135 rm ⌑ – ♦£67 ♦♦£67 – 17 suites
Rest *Regatta* – (dinner only) Carte approx. £20
♦ Landmark hotel's super clifftop position is part of Torquay skyline. Palm Court
lounge has classic style. Excellent leisure facilities. Rooms provide stunning bay views.
Regatta's style emulates cruise liner luxury.

🏨 **The Palace**   ⇋ ◐ ⅀ 🖵 ∰ *Là* 🖻 🖾 ⅍ ⅍ **P** ⤳ **VISA** ⬤⬤ **AE** ⓪
Babbacombe Rd ✉ *TQ1 3TG* – ✆ *(01803) 200 200 – www.palacetorquay.co.uk*
– info@palacetorquay.co.uk – Fax (01803) 299 899   CX**u**
135 rm ⌑ – ♦£69/94 ♦♦£168 – 6 suites
Rest – (dinner only) Menu £28 – Carte £27/39 **s**
♦ Large, traditional hotel in 25 acres of gardens with sub-tropical woodland and
charming terraces. Well-furnished lounge. Excellent leisure facilities. Comfortable
rooms. Spacious restaurant exudes air of fine dining.

🏨 **The Osborne**   ⪕ ⇋ ⇋ ⅀ 🖵 ∰ *Là* ✗ 🏮 ⅍ ⁋ ⅍ **P** **VISA** ⬤⬤ **AE**
Hesketh Crescent, Meadfoot ✉ *TQ1 2LL* – ✆ *(01803) 213 311*
– www.osborne-torquay.co.uk – enq@osborne-torquay.co.uk
– Fax (01803) 296 788   CX**n**
32 rm ⌑ – ♦£67/110 ♦♦£135/230
Rest *Langtry's* – (dinner only and Sunday lunch October-May) Menu £27 **s**
– Carte approx. £36 **s**
Rest *The Brasserie* – Carte £19/25
♦ Smart hotel situated within elegant Regency crescent. Charming terrace and gar-
den with views over Torbay. Well-appointed rooms: those facing sea have telescope
and balcony. Langtry's has classic deep green décor. Informal Brasserie with terrace.

🏨 **Corbyn Head** ⟨ P VISA ⓜⓞ AE

Seafront ⊠ TQ2 6RH – ℰ (01803) 213 611 – www.corbynhead.com
– info@corbynhead.com – Fax (01803) 296 152 BXa
45 rm ⊇ – †£55/95 ††£140/170
Rest *Orchid* – see restaurant listing
Rest *Harbour View* – British – (booking essential at lunch) Menu £19/25
♦ Boasts sea views across Torbay. Pleasant, enthusiastic staff. Very large, comfy sitting room and cosy bar. Bright, airy bedrooms, prettily created from a pastel palette. A friendly atmosphere pervades the main Harbour View dining room.

🏠 **Marstan** without rest 🚗 🏊 🕸 🕯 P VISA ⓜⓞ AE

Meadfoot Sea Rd ⊠ TQ1 2LQ – ℰ (01803) 292 837 – www.marstanhotel.co.uk
– enquiries@marstanhotel.co.uk – Fax (01803) 299 202
– Closed January and 1-21 December CXa
9 rm ⊇ – †£55/80 ††£120/138
♦ Substantial 19C house in quiet area; given a 21C edge with hot tub, sun deck and pool. Opulent interior with gold coloured furniture and antiques. Room décor of high standard.

🏡 **Colindale** 🕸 🕯 P VISA ⓜⓞ AE
📇 *20 Rathmore Rd, Chelston ⊠ TQ2 6NY – ℰ (01803) 293 947*
– www.colindalehotel.co.uk – rathmore@blueyonder.co.uk BZa
7 rm ⊇ – †£35/60 ††£60/75 **Rest** – (by arrangement) Menu £18
♦ Yellow hued 19C terraced house with pretty front garden. Particularly attractive sitting room with deep sofas and books. Welsh dresser in breakfast room. Immaculate bedrooms. Homecooked dishes have a French accent.

🏡 **Kingston House** without rest 🕯 P VISA ⓜⓞ AE
75 Avenue Rd ⊠ TQ2 5LL – ℰ (01803) 212 760 – www.kingstonhousehotel.co.uk
– stay@kingstonhousehotel.co.uk – Fax (01803) 201 425
– Closed 25-26 December BYn
5 rm ⊇ – †£55/85 ††£68/85
♦ Sunny yellow Victorian house enhanced by vivid summer floral displays; run by friendly husband and wife. Convivial sitting room; bedrooms of individual character.

🏡 **Fairmount House** without rest 🚗 🕯 P VISA ⓜⓞ AE
Herbert Rd, Chelston ⊠ TQ2 6RW – ℰ (01803) 605 446
– www.fairmounthousehotel.co.uk – stay@fairmounthousehotel.co.uk
– Fax (01803) 605 446 AXa
8 rm ⊇ – †£25/40 ††£50/66
♦ Yellow-hued Victorian house above picturesque Cockington Valley. Small bar in conservatory. Spotless, chintz bedrooms: two have doors leading onto secluded rear garden.

🍴🍴🍴 **The Orchid** – at Corbyn Head Hotel ⟨ AK P VISA ⓜⓞ AE
Seafront ⊠ TQ2 6RH – ℰ (01803) 296 366 – www.orchidrestaurant.net
– dine@orchidrestaurant.net
– Closed 2 weeks January and 2 weeks October, Sunday and Monday BXa
Rest – Menu £14/25
♦ On first floor of hotel; benefits from plenty of windows making most of sea view. Immaculate linen cover. Elaborate, modern dishes using top quality ingredients.

🍴🍴 **The Room in the Elephant** ⟳ VISA ⓜⓞ AE
ॐ *3-4 Beacon Terrace ⊠ TQ1 2BH – ℰ (01803) 200 044*
– www.elephantrestaurant.co.uk – info@elephantrestaurant.co.uk – Fax (01803)
202 717 – Closed January-March, Sunday and Monday CZe
Rest – (dinner only) Menu £45/55 **s**
Spec. Crab with warm croquette and a watermelon and pink grapefruit salad. Fillets of brill with parsnip purée and verjus butter. Sweet Cicely panna cotta, pineapple carpaccio, carrot and orange sorbet.
♦ Overlooking the harbour, with bohemian style bar for pre-dinner drinks. Refined, confident cooking makes use of quality local produce; classically based dishes; modern touches.

ENGLAND

Abbey Pl.	CZ 2
Castle Circus	CY 4
Chestnut Ave	BY 6
East St.	BY 13
Fleet St.	CYZ
Goshen Rd	BY 14
Grange Rd.	AZ 15
Hatfield Rd	CY 16
Lucius St.	BY 20
Manor Rd	BX 22
Market St	CY
Pimlico	CY 23
Reddenhill Rd	CX 24
Shedden Hill Rd	CYZ 26
South St	BY 28
Stentiford Hill Rd	CY 32
Strand	CZ 33
Temperance St.	CY 34
Tor Church Rd	BCY 36
Tor Hill Rd	CY 37
Trematon Ave.	CY 38
Union Square Shopping Centre	CY
Union St	CY
Vaughan Parade	CZ 39
Victoria Parade	CZ 41

TORBAY
TORQUAY-PAIGNTON
0 1 km
0 1/2 mile
A
B
C
X
X
A 380 EXETER
A 379 TEIGNMOUTH
A 3022
Riviera Way
RIVIERA WAY RETAIL CENTRE
Hele
HELE
Barton Hill Road
Happaway Rd
St. Marychurch Rd.
BABBACOMBE MODEL VILLAGE
Westhill Rd
B 3198
Teignmouth Road
Babbacombe Road
A 379
BABBACOMBE
T.U.F.C.
Warbro Rd
Lymington Rd
St. Marychurch Rd
Newton Rd
Barton Road
Newton La
Cadewell
Shiphay Lane
Marldon Rd
Nut
Hamelin Way
Higher Edginswell Lane
GALLOWS GATE
Hellevoetsluis Way
A 380
TORRE
COCKINGTON COUNTRY PARK
Sherwell Valley Road
Bush Lane
Cockington
COCKINGTON
Lane
TORQUAY
Road
MARLDON
PRESTON DOWN
Preston Down Road
Totnes Rd
CHURSCOMBE
Torbay
Lincombe Drive
Meadfoot
Sea Road
Ilsham Rd
Ilsham Marine Drive
HOPE'S NOSE
BLACK HEAD
10'6

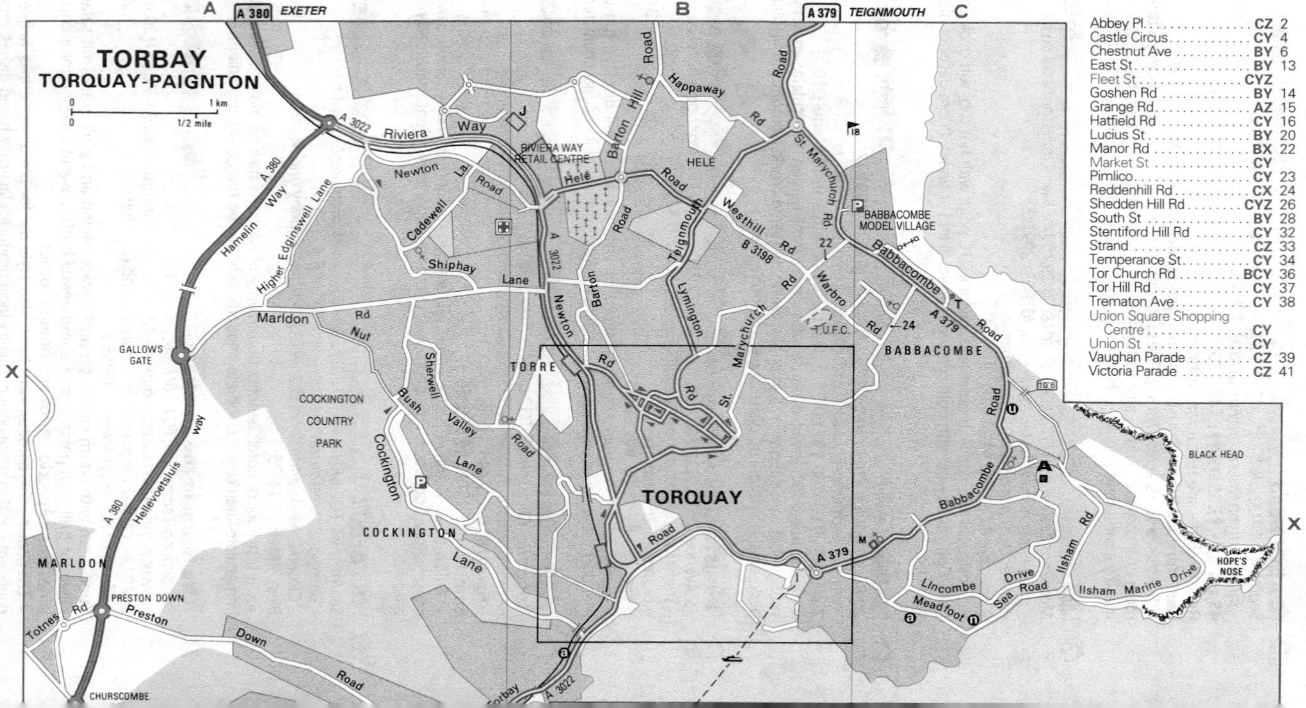

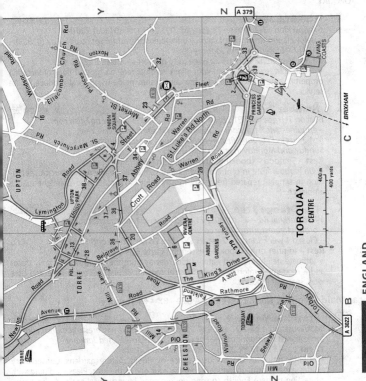

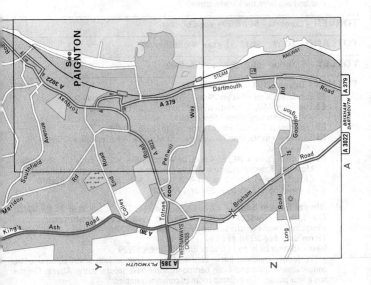

X **The Brasserie** `VISA` `OO` `AE`

Ground Floor, 3-4 Beacon Terrace ⊠ *TQ1 2BH –* ℰ *(01803) 200 044*
– www.elephantrestaurant.co.uk – info@elephantrestaurant.co.uk – Fax (01803)
202 717 – Closed 2 weeks January CZe
Rest – Menu £ 18 (lunch)/22 (weekday dinner) **s** – Carte £ 28/32 **s**

♦ Smart split level restaurant with slight colonial feel, on ground floor of Victorian property. Large choice of classic brasserie dishes made using local produce. Polite service.

X **Number 7** `AC` `VISA` `OO` `AE`

Beacon Terrace ⊠ *TQ1 2BH –* ℰ *(01803) 295 055 – www.no7-fish.com*
– enquiries@no7-fish.com – Closed 2 weeks Christmas-New Year,
first 2 weeks February, first week November, Tuesday lunch,
Sunday and Monday in winter CZe
Rest – Seafood – (booking advisable) Carte £ 27/35

♦ On harbour front in centre of town: modest, friendly, family run restaurant specialising in simply prepared fresh fish, mostly from Brixham. Fishing themes enhance ambience.

X **The Orange Tree** `VISA` `OO`

14-16 Parkhill Rd – ℰ *(01803) 213 936 – www.orangetreerestaurant.co.uk*
– orangetreerestaurant@live.co.uk
– Closed 1 week January, 2 weeks October, 26 December and Sunday CZu
Rest – (dinner only) (booking essential) Carte £ 29/37 **s**

♦ Intimate neighbourhood eatery hidden away from the town, with homely décor and a modern, comfortable feel. Classical cooking displays a French base and uses local, seasonal produce.

at Maidencombe North : 3½ m. by A 379 - BX – ⊠ Torquay

🏠 **Orestone Manor** ⊗ ≤ 🍴 🛋 🌊 ⚌ 🔄 **P** `VISA` `OO` `AE`

Rockhouse Lane ⊠ *TQ1 4SX –* ℰ *(01803) 328 098 – www.orestonemanor.com*
– info@orestonemanor.com – Fax (01803) 328 336 – Closed January
12 rm ⊇ – ♥£ 149 ♥♥£ 225 **Rest** – Menu £ 18/39

♦ Country house in the woods! Terrace overlooks mature gardens. Conservatory exudes exotic charm. Individual rooms; ask for one in the attic. Pleasant dining with interesting modern English cooking underpinned by tasty local seafood plus herbs, fruit and veg from the kitchen garden.

TORVER – Cumbria – **502** K 20 – see Coniston

TOTLAND – I.O.W. – **503** P 31 – see Wight (Isle of)

TOTLEY – S. Yorks. – **502** P 24 – see Sheffield

TOTNES – Devon – **503** I 32 – pop. 7 929 2 **C2**

🚉 London 224 mi - Exeter 24 mi - Plymouth 23 mi - Torquay 9 mi
🛈 The Town Mill, Coronation Rd ℰ (01803) 863168, enquire@totnesinformation.co.uk
🏌 Dartmouth G & C.C. Blackawton, ℰ (01803) 712686
◉ Town★ – Elizabethan Museum★ - St Mary's★ - Butterwalk★ - Castle (≤★★★) AC
◉ Paignton Zoo★★ AC, E : 4½ m. by A 385 and A 3022 – British Photographic Museum, Bowden House★ AC, S : 1 m. by A 381 – Dartington Hall (High Cross House★), NW : 2 m. on A 385 and A 384. Dartmouth★★ (Castle ≤★★★), SE : 12 m. by A 381 and A 3122

🏠 **Royal Seven Stars** 🍴 🔄 **P** `VISA` `OO` `AE`

The Plains ⊠ *TQ9 5DD –* ℰ *(01803) 862 125 – www.royalsevenstars.co.uk*
– enquiry@royalsevenstars.co.uk – Fax (01803) 867 929
18 rm ⊇ – ♥£ 50/110 ♥♥£ 139
Rest – (dinner only and Sunday lunch) Carte £ 17/29

♦ 17C former coaching inn in centre of town. Lounge with smart colonial edge, contemporary, light and fresh bedrooms; some have jacuzzi baths, Agatha Christie has a four poster. TQ9 a dining room in converted stables.

at Stoke Gabriel Southeast : 4 m. by A 385 – ⊠ Totnes

The Steam Packet Inn with rm 　　　　　　　 🛜 **P** *VISA* **©©** **AE**
*St Peter's Quay ⊠ TQ9 5EW – ℰ (01803) 863 880 – www.steampacketinn.co.uk
– steampacket@buccaneer.co.uk – Fax (01803) 862 754 – Closed 25-26 December
dinner, 1 January dinner*
4 rm ⌷ – †£60 ††£80　**Rest** – Carte £17/29
◆ Deservedly popular pub with vast terrace, set on the River Dart, close to the town
centre. Eclectic, wide-ranging menu has something for everyone, with fresh fish a
speciality. Bedrooms are elegant, cosy and snug, with a contemporary feel.

TOWCESTER – Northamptonshire – 503 R 27 – pop. 8 073　　　　　16 **B3**
　　　🚊 London 70 mi – Birmingham 50 mi – Northampton 9 mi – Oxford 36 mi
　　　🏌 Whittelbury Park G. & C.C. Whittelbury, ℰ (01327) 850 000
　　　🏌 Farthingstone Hotel Farthingstone, ℰ (01327) 361 291

at Paulerspury Southeast : 3 ¼ m. by A 5 – ⊠ Towcester

Vine House with rm 　　　　　　　　　　　🛏 🅧 **P** *VISA* **©©**
*100 High St ⊠ NN12 7NA – ℰ (01327) 811 267 – www.vinehousehotel.com
– info@vinehousehotel.com – Fax (01327) 811 309 – Closed 1 week Christmas,
Sunday and Monday lunch*
6 rm – †£65/85 ††£95　**Rest** – Menu £30
◆ Converted 17C stone building with cottage garden in old village. Pleasantly rustic
sitting room, bar with log fire. Quality cooking with traditional base. Modest, in-
divdually styled bedrooms, named after grape vines.

TREBETHERICK – see Rock

TREFONEN – Shrops. – 502 K 25 – see Oswestry

TREGREHAN – Cornwall – 503 F 32 – see St Austell

TRELOWARREN – Cornwall – see Helston

TRESCO – Cornwall – 503 B 34 – see Scilly (Isles of)

TRING – Hertfordshire – 504 S 28 – pop. 11 835　　　　　12 **A2**
　　　🚊 London 38 mi – Aylesbury 7 mi – Luton 14 mi – Oxford 31 mi

Pendley Manor 　　　　　　　　　　*VISA* **©©** **AE** **①**
*Cow Lane, East : 1 ½ m. by B 4635 off B 4251 ⊠ HP23 5QY
– ℰ (01442) 891 891 – www.pendley-manor.co.uk – info@pendley-manor.co.uk
– Fax (01442) 890 687*
73 rm ⌷ – †£90/140 ††£110/140
Rest – (closed Saturday lunch) Menu £31
◆ Attractive manor house in 35 acres of parkland. Good outdoor leisure facilities.
Charming, wicker furnished lounge in the modern conservatory. Spacious, functional
rooms. Smart, comfy air pervades dining room.

TROUTBECK – Cumbria – 502 L 20 – see Windermere

TROWBRIDGE – Wiltshire – 503 N 30 – pop. 34 401　　　　　4 **C2**
　　　🚊 London 115 mi – Bristol 27 mi – Southampton 55 mi – Swindon 32 mi
　　　🛈 St Stephen's Pl ℰ (01225) 710535, tic@trowbridge.gov.uk
　　　🇬 Westwood Manor★, NW : 3 m. by A 363 – Farleigh Hungerford★ (St
　　　Leonard's Chapel★) AC, W : 4 m. Longleat House★★★ AC, SW : 12 m.
　　　by A 363, A 350 and A 362 – Bratton Castle (≤★★) SE : 7 ½ m. by A 363
　　　and B 3098 – Steeple Ashton★ (The Green★) E : 6 m. – Edington (St Mary,
　　　St Katherine and All Saints★) SE : 7 ½ m

ENGLAND

ENGLAND

Old Manor

⊞⊞

🔒 🔌 rm, ※ ⁇ **P** **VISA** ◍ **AE**

Trowle Common, Northwest : 1. m. on A 363 ⊠ BA14 9BL – ℰ (01225) 777 393
– www.oldmanorhotel.com – romanticbeds@oldmanorhotel.com – Fax (01225)
765 443

19 rm � – †£90 ††£165 **Rest** – (dinner only) Carte approx. £25

♦ Attractive Grade II listed Queen Anne house with 15C origins. Lovely gardens and pleasant lounges: wealth of beams adds to charm. Most bedrooms - some four poster - in annex. Spacious restaurant with welcoming ambience.

at Semington Northeast : 2½ m. by A 361 – ⊠ Trowbridge

🏠 ### The Lamb on the Strand

🔒 🔌 **P** **VISA** ◍

99 The Strand, East : 1½ m. on A 361 ⊠ BA14 6LL – ℰ (01380) 870 263
– philip@cbcc.fsworld.co.uk – Fax (01380) 871 203
– Closed 25 December and 1 January

Rest – (Closed Sunday dinner) (booking essential) Carte £19/23

♦ Ivy-clad, red-brick pub with a decked terrace and neat garden. Flavoursome cooking displays honest country foundations and good combinations; excellent homemade puddings.

TRUMPET – Herefordshire – see Ledbury

TRURO – Cornwall – **503** E 33 – pop. 20 920   1 **B3**

▶ London 295 mi – Exeter 87 mi – Penzance 26 mi – Plymouth 52 mi
🚹 Municipal Buildings, Boscawen St ℰ (01872) 274 555, tic@truro.gov.uk
🏌 Treliske, ℰ (01872) 272 640
🏌 Killiow Kea Killiow, ℰ (01872) 270 246
◎ Royal Cornwall Museum★★ **AC**
◉ Trelissick Garden★★ (≤★★) **AC**, S : 4 m. by A 39 – Feock (Church★) S : 5 m. by A 39 and B 3289. Trewithen★★★, NE : 7½ m. by A 39 and A 390 – Probus★ (tower★ - garden★) NE : 9 m. by A 39 and A 390

⊞⊞ ### Mannings

🔌 rm, ※ ⁇ **P** **VISA** ◍ **AE** ◍

Lemon St ⊠ TR1 2QB – ℰ (01872) 270 345 – www.royalhotelcornwall.co.uk
– reception@royalhotelcornwall.co.uk – Fax (01872) 242 453
– Closed 24-28 December

43 rm ⊽ – †£65/99 ††£99/120

Rest *Mannings* – (Closed Sunday lunch) Carte £18/35

♦ The name came after Prince Albert stayed in 1846: the Royal Arms stands proudly above the entrance. Comfortable, stylish lounges; modern bedrooms. Cuisine with global influences.

XX ### Tabb's

VISA ◍ **AE**

85 Kenwyn St ⊠ TR1 3BZ – ℰ (01872) 262 110 – www.tabbs.co.uk
– info@tabbs.co.uk

Rest – (dinner only) Carte £30/38

♦ Stylish restaurant with lilac walls, flint floors and well-spaced, cloth-covered tables. Hearty, well-constructed dishes show good understanding of flavours. Relaxed atmosphere.

X ### Saffron

VISA ◍

5 Quay St ⊠ TR1 2HB – ℰ (01872) 263 771 – www.saffronrestauranttruro.co.uk
– saffronrestaurant@btconnect.com – Closed 25-26 December, Bank Holidays,
and Monday dinner January-May

Rest – Menu £20 (dinner) **s** – Carte £26/33 **s**

♦ Bright exterior with colourful hanging baskets and attractive brightly coloured interior with a rustic tone. Varied Cornish menus to be enjoyed at any hour of the day.

TUNBRIDGE WELLS – Kent – **504** U 30 – see Royal Tunbridge Wells

TUNSTALL – Lancashire – see Kirkby Lonsdale

TURNERS HILL – West Sussex – 504 T 30 – pop. 1 534　　　　7 **D2**
> ❱ London 33 mi – Brighton 24 mi – Crawley 7 mi

🏨🏨🏨 **Alexander House** ⌖　< 🚗 🕭 🏧 🕸 ※ ▤ 🛱 ⁗ 🖄 **P** *VISA* ⓶ **AE** ⓵
East St, East : 1 m. on B 2110 ✉ *RH10 4QD –* ✆ *(01342) 714914*
– www.alexanderhouse.co.uk – admin@alexanderhouse.co.uk – Fax (01342)
859759
36 rm ⌑ – ♦£155/190 ♦♦£380/450 – 2 suites
Rest *Alexanders* – (dinner only and Sunday lunch) Menu £22/35
– Carte £37/53
Rest *Reflections Brasserie* – Carte £24/38
♦ Set in extensive gardens, a stunning, classically comfortable country house, once owned by the family of poet Percy Shelley. Luxuriously appointed, quite modern bedrooms. Sumptuous Alexanders. Informal air at Reflections.

TURVILLE – Buckinghamshire – ✉ Henley-on-Thames　　　11 **C2**
> ❱ London 45 mi – Oxford 22 mi – Reading 17 mi

🍴 **The Bull & Butcher**　　　　🚗 🛱 **P** *VISA* ⓶
✉ *RG9 6QU –* ✆ *(01491) 638283 – www.thebullandbutcher.com*
– info@thebullandbutcher.com
Rest – Carte £20/27
♦ Small pub in charming 'Vicar of Dibley' village. Flagstone flooring, log fires and scrubbed pine. Slightly different modern and traditional menus served in all dining areas.

TWO BRIDGES – Devon – 503 I 32 – ✉ Yelverton　　　2 **C2**
> ❱ London 226 mi – Exeter 25 mi – Plymouth 17 mi
> ⌖ Dartmoor National Park★★

🏠 **Prince Hall** ⌖　　　< 🚗 ⁀ ⁗ **P** *VISA* ⓶ **AE**
East : 1 m. on B 3357 ✉ *PL20 6SA –* ✆ *(01822) 890403 – www.princehall.co.uk*
– info@princehall.co.uk – Fax (01822) 890676 – Closed January
9 rm ⌑ – ♦£60/160 ♦♦£80/160
Rest – (light lunch) (booking essential for non-residents) Menu £35 **s**
♦ Unique 18C country house, traditional in style, set alone in heart of Dartmoor. Magnificent view over West Dart River to rolling hills. Individually styled rooms. Local dishes proudly served in rustic restaurant.

TYLER HILL – at CANTERBURY

TYNEMOUTH – Tyne and Wear – 501 P 18 – pop. 17 056　　　24 **B2**
> ❱ London 290 mi – Newcastle upon Tyne 8 mi – Sunderland 7 mi

🏨 **Grand**　　　　< ▤ ※ ⁗ 🖄 *VISA* ⓶ **AE**
Grand Parade ✉ *NE30 4ER –* ✆ *(0191) 2936666 – www.grandhotel-uk.com*
– info20@grandhotel-uk.com – Fax (0191) 2936665
44 rm ⌑ – ♦£85 ♦♦£95
Rest – (Closed Sunday dinner and Monday dinner) Menu £13/21
– Carte dinner £19/25
♦ Impressive Victorian hotel built as home for Duchess of Northumberland. Commanding views over coastline. Atmospheric lounges and bars. Well-equipped rooms with fine views. Classical dining room with imposing drapes, floral displays and ceiling cornices.

🏠 **Martineau Guest House** without rest　　　🚗 ※ ⁗
57 Front St ✉ *NE30 4BX –* ✆ *(0191) 2960746 – www.martineau-house.co.uk*
– martineau.house@gmail.net
3 rm ⌑ – ♦£55/70 ♦♦£80
♦ 18C Georgian stone terraced house in main street, named after Harriet Martineau. Breakfast in open plan kitchen. Homely spacious individually styled rooms, two with view.

※ **Sidney's**   *VISA* **©©** AE
3-5 Percy Park Rd ⊠ NE30 4LZ – ℰ (0191) 257 8500 – www.sidneys.co.uk
– bookings@sidneys.co.uk – Fax (0191) 257 9800
– Closed 25-26 December, and Sunday
Rest – (booking essential) Menu £15 (lunch) – Carte £25/31
♦ Fine painted, wood floored, busy little restaurant with two dining areas. The modern British cooking is interesting with plenty of variety and choice.

UCKFIELD – East Sussex – **504** U 31 – pop. 15 374   8 **A2**
🄳 London 45 mi – Brighton 17 mi – Eastbourne 20 mi – Maidstone 34 mi

Horsted Place 🏡   ← 🚗 ... ※ 📺 📶 ... 🛁 🍴 P *VISA* **©©** AE ①
Little Horsted, South : 2½ m. by B 2102 and A 22 on A 26 ⊠ TN22 5TS
– ℰ (01825) 750 581 – www.horstedplace.co.uk – hotel@horstedplace.co.uk
– Fax (01825) 750 459 – Closed first week January
15 rm ⊇ – †£130/175 ††£130/175 – 5 suites
Rest – (Closed Saturday lunch) Menu £20 (lunch) – Carte approx. £40
♦ Imposing country house from the height of the Victorian Gothic revival; handsome Pugin-inspired drawing rooms and luxurious bedrooms overlook formal gardens and parkland. Pristine restaurant with tall 19C archways and windows.

Buxted Park 🏡   ← 🚗 ... 🛁 🛗 rm, 🍴 🛁 P *VISA* **©©** AE ①
Buxted, Northeast : 2 m. on A 272 ⊠ TN22 4AY – ℰ (01825) 733 333
– www.handpicked.co.uk/buxtedpark – buxtedpark@handpicked.co.uk
– Fax (01825) 732 770
43 rm ⊇ – †£175/215 ††£175/215 – 1 suite
Rest *Dining Room* – Carte £32/42
♦ 18C Palladian mansion in 300 acres with ornate public areas exuding much charm: spacious, period lounges. Rooms, modern in style, in original house or garden wing. Beautiful all-glass Orangery restaurant with large terrace.

ULLINGSWICK – County of Herefordshire – **503** M 27 – ⊠ Hereford   18 **B3**
🄳 London 134 mi – Hereford 12 mi – Shrewsbury 52 mi – Worcester 19 mi

🄓 **Three Crowns Inn**   🚗 ※ P *VISA* **©©**
Bleak Acre, East : 1¼ m. ⊠ HR1 3JQ – ℰ (01432) 820 279
– www.threecrownsinn.com – info@threecrownsinn.com – Fax (08707) 515 338
– Closed 25 December, 1 January
Rest – (Closed Monday) Menu £15 (lunch) – Carte approx. £26
♦ Pleasant part-timbered pub on a quiet country road: hops hang from the beams. Eclectic assortment of benches and pews. Rustic, robust dishes on daily changing menus.

ULLSWATER – Cumbria – **502** L 20 – ⊠ Penrith   21 **B2**
🄳 London 296 mi – Carlisle 25 mi – Kendal 31 mi – Penrith 6 mi
🄸 Beckside Car Park, Glenridding, Penrith ℰ (017684) 82414,
ullswatertic@lake-district.gov.uk

at Pooley Bridge on B 5320 – ⊠ Penrith

Sharrow Bay Country House 🏡   ← 🚗 🍴 AC rest, ※ P *VISA* **©©** AE
South : 2 m. on Howtown rd ⊠ CA10 2LZ – ℰ (017684) 86 301
– www.sharrowbay.co.uk – info@sharrowbay.co.uk – Fax (017684) 86 349
20 rm ⊇ – †£135/210 ††£350/420 – 4 suites
Rest – (booking essential) Menu £40/65 🕸
Spec. Suissesse soufflé of stilton, spinach and roasted onion. Duckling with black pudding, cabbage, apple and sage sauce. Francis Coulson's icky sticky toffee sponge.
♦ Victorian country house in idyllic spot on shores of Lake Ullswater. Richly appointed, antique-filled interior. Traditional bedrooms blend luxury and old-fashioned charm. Richly flavoured, classical cooking. Personable service.

at Watermillock on A 592 – ✉ Penrith

⌂⌂⌂ **Rampsbeck Country House** ⌂   ≤ 🚗 🏕 **P** **VISA** **①①**
✉ CA11 0LP – ☏ (017684) 86442 – www.rampsbeck.co.uk
– enquiries@rampsbeck.co.uk – Fax (017684) 86688
– Closed 4 January - 25 January
18 rm ⌷ – ♦£80/120 ♦♦£260 – 1 suite
Rest *The Restaurant* – see restaurant listing
♦ Personally run country house with peaceful gardens and homely guest areas. Very comfortable deluxe bedrooms, some with balconies; standard rooms more traditionally furnished.

⌂⌂⌂ **Leeming House** ⌂   ≤ 🚗 🏕 ❀ 🍴 ⚓ ⅃ **P** **VISA** **①①** **AE** **①**
on A 592 ✉ CA11 0JJ – ☏ (0870) 400 81 31 – www.macdonald-hotels.co.uk
– leeminghouse@macdonald-hotels.co.uk – Fax (017684) 86443
40 rm ⌷ – ♦£115/200 ♦♦£125/200
Rest *Regency* – (dinner only) Menu £40
♦ Built as private residence in 19C for local family; in stepped gardens leading down to Lake Ullswater. A rural retreat with croquet lawn; appropriately styled country rooms. Georgian dining room brightened by mirrors and chandelier.

✗✗✗ **The Restaurant** – at Rampsbeck Country House Hotel   ≤ 🚗 🏕 **P** **VISA** **①①**
✉ CA11 0LP – ☏ (017684) 86442 – Fax (017684) 86688
– Closed 4 January-9 February
Rest – (booking essential) (lunch by arrangement Monday-Saturday)
Menu £45 s
♦ Refurbished house retains traditional character, with polished silver, fresh flowers and lake views. Seasonal menu combines modern with more traditional. Unobtrusive service.

ULVERSTON – Cumbria – **502** K 21 – pop. 11 210   21 **A3**
◘ London 278 mi – Kendal 25 mi – Lancaster 36 mi
🇮 Coronation Hall, County Sq ☏ (01229) 587120,
ulverstontic@southlakeland.gov.uk

⌂ **The Bay Horse** with rm ⌂   ≤ 🍴 **P** **VISA** **①①** **AE**
Canal Foot, East : 2¼ m. by A 5087, turning left at Morecambe Rd and beyond
Industrial area, on the coast ✉ LA12 9EL – ☏ (01229) 583 972
– www.thebayhorsehotel.co.uk – reservations@thebayhorsehotel.co.uk
– Fax (01229) 580 502
9 rm ⌷ – ♦£80 ♦♦£95/120
Rest – (Closed Monday lunch) (booking essential) Carte £22/45
♦ Well-established inn by Ulverston Sands. Smart conservatory, flavourful seasonal menu and friendly staff. Cosy rooms, some equipped with binoculars and birdwatching guides.

UPPER ODDINGTON – Glos. – see Stow-on-the-Wold

UPPER SLAUGHTER – Glos. – **503** O 28 – see Bourton-on-the-Water

---

UPPINGHAM – Rutland – **504** R 26 – pop. 3 947   17 **C2**
◘ London 101 mi – Leicester 19 mi – Northampton 28 mi – Nottingham 35 mi

✗ **Lake Isle** with rm   **AC** rest, 🍴 **P** **VISA** **①①** **AE**
16 High St East ✉ LE15 9PZ – ☏ (01572) 822 951 – www.lakeisle.co.uk
– info@lakeisle.co.uk – Fax (01572) 824 400
12 rm ⌷ – ♦£55/65 ♦♦£75/100
Rest – (Closed Sunday dinner and Monday lunch) (light lunch)
Carte £22/35
♦ Named from a Yeats ballad, this is a pleasant, simply furnished restaurant with enthusiastic owners who know their wines. Traditional and honest cooking, full of flavour. Pine decorated rooms; good breakfasts.

at Lyddington South : 2 m. by A 6003 – ⊠ Uppingham

🗋 **Old White Hart** with rm   🖼 ⚡ **P** *VISA* ⚫⚫
51 Main Street ⊠ *LE15 9LR* – ℰ *(01572) 821 703* – *www.oldwhitehart.co.uk*
– *mail@oldwhitehart.co.uk* – *Fax (01572) 821 965* – *Closed 25 December*
9 rm ⌂ – ♦£60 ♦♦£90
Rest – (Closed Sunday dinner in winter) Menu £ 13 – Carte £ 21/34
♦ Very pleasant 17C pub in pretty village; rural memorabilia within and huge petan-
que court without. Tasty, carefully prepared dishes. Welcoming rooms with a country
feel.

UPTON SCUDAMORE – **Wilts.** – **503** N 30 – **see Warminster**

UPTON-UPON-SEVERN – **Worcestershire** – **503** N 27 – **pop. 1 789**   18 **B3**
🛣 London 116 mi – Hereford 25 mi – Stratford-upon-Avon 29 mi
– Worcester 11 mi
🅸 4 High St ℰ (01684) 594200, upton.tic@malvernhills.gov.uk

↑ **Tiltridge Farm and Vineyard** without rest ⬥   🖼 📶 **P** *VISA* ⚫⚫
Upper Hook Rd, West : 1½ m. by A 4104 and Greenfields Rd following B&B signs
⊠ *WR8 0SA* – ℰ *(01684) 592 906* – *www.tiltridge.com* – *info@tiltridge.com*
– *Fax (01684) 594 142* – *Closed Christmas-New Year*
3 rm ⌂ – ♦£40 ♦♦£70
♦ Extended 17C farmhouse at the entrance to a small vineyard. Homely lounge,
dominated by a broad inglenook fireplace, and spacious bedrooms, one with original
timbers.

at Hanley Swan Northwest : 3 m. by B 4211 on B 4209 – ⊠ Upton-upon-Severn

↑ **Yew Tree House** without rest   🖼 ⚡ 📶 **P** *VISA* ⚫⚫
🏥 ⊠ *WR8 0DN* – ℰ *(01684) 310 736* – *www.yewtreehouse.co.uk*
– *info@yewtreehouse.co.uk* – *Fax (01684) 311 709*
– *Closed 25 December-1 January*
3 rm ⌂ – ♦£45 ♦♦£75
♦ Imposing cream coloured Georgian guesthouse, built in 1780, in centre of pleasant
village. One mile from Three Counties Showground. Cosy lounge; individually styled
rooms.

URMSTON – **Greater Manchester** – **502** M 23   20 **B2**
🛣 London 204 mi – Manchester 9 mi – Sale 4 mi

✕ **Isinglass**   *VISA* ⚫⚫ **AE**
46 Flixton Rd ⊠ *M40 1AB* – ℰ *(0161) 749 8400* – *www.isinglassrestaurant.co.uk*
– *isinglass@btconnect.com* – *Closed 26-30 December, 1 January and Monday*
Rest – Menu £ 14 (weekdays) – Carte £ 17/29
♦ Hidden away in Manchester suburb, this is a neighbourhood favourite. Very personally run, with warm rustic interior. Unusual dishes underpinned by a strong Lancastrian base.

UTTOXETER – **Staffordshire** – **503** O 25 – **pop. 12 023**   19 **C1**
🛣 London 150 mi – Birmingham 41 mi – Stafford 16 mi

at Beamhurst Northwest : 3 m. on A 522 – ⊠ Uttoxeter

✕✕ **Gilmore at Strine's Farm**   🖼 **P** *VISA* ⚫⚫
⊠ *ST14 5DZ* – ℰ *(01889) 507 100* – *www.restaurantgilmore.com*
– *paul@restaurantgilmore.com* – *Fax (01889) 507 238*
– *Closed 1 week January, 1 week Easter, 1 week August, 1 week November,*
Monday, Tuesday, Sunday dinner and lunch Saturday and Wednesday
Rest – (booking essential) Menu £ 28/40
♦ Personally run converted farmhouse in classic rural setting. Three separate,
beamed, cottage style dining rooms. New approach to classic dishes: fine local in-
gredients used.

VAZON BAY – **503** P 33 – **see Channel Islands (Guernsey)**

VENTNOR – **I.O.W.** – **503** Q 32 – **see Wight (Isle of)**

ENGLAND

VERYAN – Cornwall – **503** F 33 – ⊠ Truro   1 **B3**

🚗 London 291 mi – St Austell 13 mi – Truro 13 mi
👁 Village ★

 Nare 🌊   ⟨ 🔥 ⌂ ⌂ 🏊 🏊 🖥 Ⅰ🟰 ⚙ 🏛 rest, 🍴 **P** **VISA** **◯◯** **AE**
Carne Beach, Southwest : 1¼ m. ⊠ *TR2 5PF* – 𝒞 *(01872) 501 111*
– www.narehotel.co.uk – office@narehotel.co.uk – Fax (01872) 501 856
35 rm ⟄ – †£189/240 ††£358/440 – 4 suites
Rest *The Dining Room* – (dinner only and Sunday lunch) Menu £45
Rest *Quarterdeck* – 𝒞 (01872) 500 000 – Carte £23/54
♦ On the curve of Carne Bay, surrounded by National Trust land; superb beach. Inside, owner's Cornish art collection in evidence. Most rooms have patios and balconies. The Dining Room boasts high windows and sea views; dinner dress code. Informal Quarterdeck.

at Ruan High Lanes West : 1¼ m. on A 3078 – ⊠ Truro

🏠 **The Hundred House**   🔥 ⚙ 🍴 **P** **VISA** **◯◯** **AE**
⊠ *TR2 5JR* – 𝒞 *(01872) 501 336 – www.hundredhousehotel.co.uk*
– enquiries@hundredhousehotel.co.uk – Fax (01872) 501 151
10 rm ⟄ – †£85/143 ††£170/190
Rest *Fish in the Fountain* – (dinner only) (booking essential for non-residents) Menu £30 **s**
♦ Personally run small hotel: its period furnished hallway with fine staircase, ornate wallpaper sets tone of care and attention to detail. Mirrors, flowers, fine china abound. Comfortable dining room serves West Country fare.

VIRGINSTOW – Devon – **503** H 31   2 **C2**

🚗 London 227 mi – Bideford 25 mi – Exeter 41 mi – Launceston 11 mi
– Plymouth 33 mi

🏠 **Percy's**   ⟨ 🔥 🌙 🍴 **P** **VISA** **◯◯**
Coombeshead Estate, Southwest : 1¼ m. on Tower Hill rd ⊠ *EX21 5EA*
– 𝒞 (01409) 211 236 – www.percys.co.uk – info@percys.co.uk – Fax (01409) 211 460
7 rm ⟄ – †£150/190 ††£215/290
Rest *Percy's* – see restaurant listing
♦ Rural location surrounded by 130 acres of woodland and forest which include woodland trails and animals. Airy, modern rooms in granary or bungalow boast range of charming extras.

🍴🍴 **Percy's**   ⌂ 🍴 **P** **VISA** **◯◯**
Coombeshead Estate, Southwest : 1¼ m. on Tower Hill rd ⊠ *EX21 5EA*
– 𝒞 (01409) 211 236 – www.percys.co.uk – info@percys.co.uk – Fax (01409) 211 460
Rest – (dinner only) Menu £40
♦ Modern rear extension with deep sofas alongside chic ash and zinc bar. Restaurant has an understated style. Locally sourced, organic produce and homegrown vegetables.

WADDESDON – Buckinghamshire – **504** R 28 – pop. 1 865   11 **C2**
– ⊠ **Aylesbury** ▌ *Great Britain*

🚗 London 51 mi – Aylesbury 5 mi – Northampton 32 mi – Oxford 31 mi
👁 Chiltern Hills ★
👁 Waddesdon Manor ★★, S : ½ m. by a 41 and minor rd – Claydon House ★, N : by minor rd

🍴🍴 **The Five Arrows** with rm   🔥 ⌂ 🍴 **P** **VISA** **◯◯** **AE**
High St ⊠ *HP18 0JE* – 𝒞 *(01296) 651 727 – www.waddesdon.org.uk*
– five.arrows@nationaltrust.org.uk – Fax (01296) 658 596
11 rm – †£70/110 ††£150, ⟄ £7.50 – 1 suite
Rest – Menu £20 (lunch) – Carte £29/36
♦ Beautiful 19C inn on Rothschild estate, an influence apparent in pub crest and wine cellar. Striking architecture, stylish dining, relaxed ambience, Anglo-Mediterranean menu. Individually decorated bedrooms - some four posters - divided between main house and courtyard, the latter being smaller but quieter.

ENGLAND

779

WALBERSWICK – Suffolk – 504 Y 27 – pop. 1 648   15 D2

> London 115 mi – Norwich 31 mi – Ipswich 31 mi – Lowestoft 16 mi

The Anchor   🔲 🎍 🌳 P VISA ⚫ AE ⓪
Main St ⊠ IP18 6UA – ℘ (01502) 722 112 – www.anchoratwalberswick.com
– info@anchoratwalberswick.com – Fax (01502) 724 464
Rest – Carte £16/25 🌿

♦ Large pub with a sizeable garden and seaward views. Hearty, flavoursome cooking
uses local or homemade produce where possible; seafood features highly. Excellent
beer and wine.

WALBERTON – W. Sussex – see Arundel

WALCOTT – Norfolk – ⊠ Norwich   15 D1

> London 134 mi – Cromer 12 mi – Norwich 23 mi

Holly Tree Cottage without rest 🌿   🔲 🌾 P
Walcott Green, South : 2 m. by B 1159 and Stalham rd taking 2nd left after
Lighthouse Inn ⊠ NR12 0NS – ℘ (01692) 650 721 – May-September
3 rm 🍴 – ♦£40 ♦♦£60

♦ A hospitable couple keep this traditional Norfolk flint cottage in excellent order.
Snug lounge with wood-fired stove and neat rooms overlooking fields. Good breakfasts.

WALLASEY – Merseyside – 502 K 23 – pop. 58 710 – ⊠ Wirral   20 A2

> London 222 mi – Birkenhead 3 mi – Liverpool 4 mi
🏌 Wallasey Bayswater Rd, ℘ (0151) 691 1024

Grove House   🔲 AK rest, 🌾 ⁕ 🍴 P VISA ⚫ AE ⓪
Grove Rd ⊠ CH45 3HF – ℘ (0151) 639 3947 – www.thegrovehouse.co.uk
– reception@thegrovehouse.co.uk – Fax (0151) 639 0028
14 rm – ♦£70/90 ♦♦£80/90, 🍴 £8.95
Rest – (Closed Bank Holidays) (dinner only and Sunday lunch) Menu £21 **s**
– Carte £27/32 **s**

♦ Part Victorian house in a residential street. Meeting room with conservatory. Bedrooms in different shapes and sizes: quieter rear accommodation overlooks garden.
Oak-panelled dining room.

WALLINGFORD – Oxfordshire – 503 Q 29 – pop. 8 019 📗 Great Britain   10 B3

> London 54 mi – Oxford 12 mi – Reading 16 mi
🛈 Town Hall, Market Pl ℘ (01491) 826972, ticwallingford@freenet.co.uk
🗺 Ridgeway Path ★★

North Moreton House without rest   🔲 🌊 ⁕ 🌾 🍴 P
North Moreton, West : 4 m. by A 4130 ⊠ OX11 9AT – ℘ (01235) 813 283
– www.northmoretonhouse.co.uk – katie@northmoretonhouse.co.uk
– Fax (01235) 511 305
3 rm 🍴 – ♦£48/50 ♦♦£70/72

♦ Grade II listed house in mature lawned gardens with fine 17C barn. Spacious, individually decorated bedrooms. Breakfast on local organic produce at vast antique
table.

WALTON – W. Yorks. – 502 Q 22 – see Wetherby

WANTAGE – Oxfordshire – 503 – pop. 9 452   10 B3

> London 71 mi – Oxford 16 mi – Reading 24 mi – Swindon 21 mi
🛈 Vale and Downland Museum, 19 Church St ℘ (01235) 760176,
wantagetic@btconnect.com

The Boar's Head with rm   🔲 🌾 ⁕ ⓣ P VISA ⚫ AE
Church St, Ardington, East : 2½ m. by A 417 ⊠ OX12 8QA – ℘ (01235) 833 254
– www.boarsheadardington.co.uk – info@boarsheadardington.co.uk
3 rm 🍴 – ♦£80 ♦♦£150   **Rest** – Menu £24 (lunch) – Carte £23/40

♦ Pretty, timbered pub: pine tables, hunting curios and rural magazines. Locally-
grown salad, modern British dishes, good wine and ale draw the locals. Bright modern bedrooms.

■ London 24 mi – Cambridge 30 mi – Luton 22 mi
🏌18 Whitehill Dane End, 𝒫 (01920) 438 495

Marriott Hanbury Manor H. & Country Club   ⇐ 🛏 🕭 🐴 🖥
⑱ 🕭 ⅃₅ 🏊 🖥18 🕭 & rm, 🏌⬆ ⓀC rest, ¶¹ 🕭 🅿 🆅🆂🅰 ⓂⓈ 🅰🅴 ⓞ
Thundridge, North : 1 ¾ m. by A 1170 on A 10 ⊠ SG12 0SD – 𝒫 (01920) 487 722
– www.marriotthanburymanor.co.uk – Fax (01920) 487 682
156 rm – ♥£ 189 ♥♥£ 189, ⊇ £19.50 – 5 suites
Rest *Zodiac* – (Closed Sunday dinner and Monday) Menu £ 49
Rest *Oakes* – Carte £ 30/43
♦ 1890s neo-Jacobean mansion, a former convent, in 220 acres. Tea in firelit, oak-beamed hall. Classically luxurious rooms; many overlook golf course and lake. Walled garden. Formal, fine dining Zodiac. Mediterranean menus in spacious Oakes.

Jacoby's   🕭 ⓀC 🕭 🆅🆂🅰 ⓂⓈ 🅰🅴
Churchgate House, 15 West St ⊠ SG12 9EE – 𝒫 (01920) 469 181
– www.jacobys.co.uk – info@jacobys.co.uk – Fax (01920) 469 182
Rest – Menu £ 10/13 – Carte £ 20/30
♦ 16C Grade II listed building, with a continental style pavement terrace. Bar menu offers light snacks, while the restaurant provides a more substantial, wide-ranging selection.

■ London 123 mi – Bournemouth 13 mi – Weymouth 19 mi
🅸 Holy Trinity Church, South St 𝒫 (01929) 552740, tic@purbeck-dc.gov.uk
◎ Town★ – St Martin's★
🅶 Blue Pool★ **AC**, S : 3 ½ m. by A 351 – Bovington Tank Museum★ **AC**,
Woolbridge Manor★, W : 5 m. by A 352. Moreton Church★★, W : 9 ½ m. by
A 352 – Corfe Castle★ (⇐★★) **AC**, SE : 6 m. by A 351 – Lulworth Cove★,
SW : 10 m. by A 352 and B 3070 – Bere Regis★ (St John the Baptist
Church★), NW : 6 ½ m. by minor rd

The Priory ♨   ⇐ 🛏 🐴 🕭 🏊 ¶¹ 🅿 🆅🆂🅰 ⓂⓈ 🅰🅴 ⓞ
Church Green ⊠ BH20 4ND – 𝒫 (01929) 551 666 – www.theprioryhotel.co.uk
– reservations@theprioryhotel.co.uk – Fax (01929) 554 519
16 rm ⊇ – ♥£ 180 ♥♥£ 270 – 2 suites
Rest – Menu £ 40 (dinner) – Carte lunch £ 28/33
♦ Charming, privately run part 16C priory, friendly and discreetly cosy. Well-equipped rooms. Manicured four-acre gardens lead down to River Frome: luxury suites in boathouse. Charming restaurant beneath stone vaults of undercroft.

Gold Court House ✓   🛏 🏊 ¶¹ 🅿
St John's Hill ⊠ BH20 4LZ – 𝒫 (01929) 553 320 – www.goldcourthouse.co.uk
– info@goldcourthouse.co.uk – Fax (01929) 553 320
3 rm ⊇ – ♥£ 45/50 ♥♥£ 75
Rest – (winter only) (by arrangement, communal dining) Menu £ 17
♦ Affable hosts are justly proud of this pretty 1760s house on a quiet square. Classically charming sitting room and bedrooms; well-chosen books and antiques. Dine communally while viewing delightful courtyard garden.

at Kimmeridge South : 4 ½ m. by A 351

Kimmeridge Farmhouse without rest   🛏 🕭 ¶¹
⊠ BH20 5PE – 𝒫 (01929) 480 990 – www.kimmeridgefarmhouse.co.uk
– kimmeridgefarmhouse@hotmail.com – Fax (01929) 481 503
3 rm ⊇ – ♥£ 55/65 ♥♥£ 70/80
♦ 14C stone farmhouse in attractive hamlet with farmland touching the Jurassic coast. Traditionally decorated bedrooms with modern bathrooms. Farm eggs and local produce at breakfast.

WAREN MILL – Northd. – **501** O 17 – see Bamburgh

ENGLAND

WARKWORTH – Northumberland – **502** P 17

24 **B2**

▶ London 316 mi – Alnwick 7 mi – Morpeth 24 mi

Roxbro House without rest · ※ ⧉ ⧉ **P** ₩₴₳ ₥₢

5 Castle Terrace ⊠ *NE65 0UP – ℰ (01665) 711 416 – www.roxbrohouse.co.uk*
– info@roxbrohouse.co.uk – Closed 24-26 December
3 rm – ♦£40/85 ♦♦£85

♦ A discreet style enhances this 19C stone house in the shadow of Warkworth castle. Stylish lounge in harmony with very smart boutique bedrooms, two of which face the castle.

WARMINSTER – Wiltshire – **503** N 30 – pop. 17 486

4 **C2**

▶ London 111 mi – Bristol 29 mi – Exeter 74 mi – Southampton 47 mi
ℹ Central Car Park ℰ (01985) 218548, visitwarminster@btconnect.com
ⓖ Longleat House★★★ AC, SW : 3 m. Stonehenge★★★ AC, E : 18 m. by A 36 and A 303 – Bratton Castle (≤★★) NE : 6 m. by A 350 and B 3098

at Upton Scudamore North : 2½ m. by A 350 – ⊠ Warminster

The Angel Inn with rm · ⧉ **P** ₩₴₳ ₥₢

⊠ *BA12 0AG – ℰ (01985) 213 225 – www.theangelinn.co.uk*
– mail@theangelinn.co.uk – Fax (01985) 218 182
– Closed 25-26 December, 1 January
10 rm ⊇ – ♦£80 ♦♦£88   **Rest** – Menu £15 (lunch) – Carte £15/25

♦ Village pub with a country-cottage interior and decked terrace. Hearty à la carte menu with blackboard specials, daily fresh fish dishes, homemade bread and ice creams. Comfortable, modern rooms with individually co-ordinated furnishings.

at Heytesbury Southeast : 3¾ m. by B 3414 – ⊠ Warminster

The Resting Post without rest

67 High St ⊠ *BA12 0ED – ℰ (01985) 840 204 – www.therestingpost.co.uk*
– enquiries@therestingpost.co.uk
3 rm ⊇ – ♦£60 ♦♦£70

♦ Immaculately kept Grade II listed building dating back to 17C – originally a post office and general store run by the same couple. Individually styled bedrooms, one with a 6ft bed.

The Angel Inn · ⧉ **P** ₩₴₳ ₥₢

High St ⊠ *BA12 0ED – ℰ (01985) 840 330 – www.theangelheytesbury.co.uk*
– admin@theangelheytesbury.co.uk – Fax (01985) 840 931 – Closed 25 December
Rest – (Closed Monday) Carte £25/45

♦ Exposed beams and brickwork combined with bold, modern styling. Concise menu features big dishes and local produce, including legendary well-hung steaks and generous sharing boards.

at Horningsham Southwest : 5 m. by A 362 – ⊠ Warminster

The Bath Arms with rm · ⧉ ⧉ **P** ₩₴₳ ₥₢

Longleat, ⊠ *BA12 7LY – ℰ (01985) 844 308 – www.batharms.co.uk*
– enquiries@batharms.co.uk – Fax (01985) 845 187
15 rm ⊇ – ♦£70/130 ♦♦£80/145   **Rest** – Menu £16/30 – Carte £14/30

♦ Stylish creeper-clad pub next to the Longleat Estate. Modern, honest British menu uses produce sourced from within 50 miles; dishes are presented in a straightforward manner. Unique bedrooms with eccentric design themes.

WARTLING – E. Sussex – **504** V 31 – see Herstmonceux

Good food and accommodation at moderate prices?
Look for the Bib symbols:
red Bib Gourmand ⊕ for food, blue Bib Hotel ⊠ for hotels

▶ London 96 mi – Birmingham 20 mi – Coventry 11 mi – Leicester 34 mi
   – Oxford 43 mi

🔼 The Court House, Jury St 𝒞 (01926) 492212, touristinfo@warwick-uk.co.uk

🏇 Warwick Racecourse, 𝒞 (01926) 494 316

◉ Town★ – Castle★★ **AC** Y – Leycester Hospital★ **AC** Y **B** – Collegiate Church
   of St Mary★ (Tomb★) Y **A**

WARWICK-ROYAL
LEAMINGTON SPA

Birmingham Rd	**Z** 7
Bowling Green St	**Y** 9
Brook St	**Y** 12
Butts (The)	**Y** 13
Castle Hill	**Y** 15
Church St	**Y** 17
High St	**Y** 23
Jury St	**Y**
Lakin Rd	**Y** 25
Linen St	**Y** 26
Market Pl.	**Y** 29
Old Square	**Y** 35
Old Warwick Rd	**Z** 36
Radford Rd.	**Y** 39
Rock (The)	**Y** 32
St John's Rd	**Y** 42
St Nicholas Church St.	**Y** 43
Shires Retail Park	**Z**
Smith St	**Y**
Swan St.	**Y** 46
Theatre St	**Y** 48
West St	**Y** 50

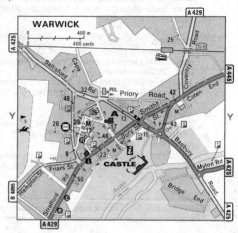

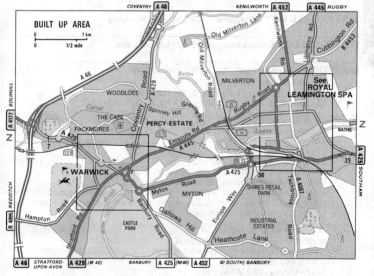

🏠   **Charter House** without rest   🍴 AC ⚡ 👖 **P** *VISA* **◎ ①**

87 West St ✉ CV34 6AH – 𝒞 (01926) 496 965
– www.charterhouseguesthouse.com – sheila@penon.gotadsl.co.uk
– Closed Christmas   **Y**c

3 rm 🍽 – 🛏£65/70 🛏🛏£95/105

♦ Timbered 15C house not far from the castle. Comfortable, delicately ordered rooms
with a personal touch: pretty counterpanes and posies of dried flowers. Tasty breakfasts.

⛩ Park Cottage without rest ✿ ⁽ᵖ⁾ P VISA ◉◉ AE
113 West St ⊠ CV34 6AH – ℰ (01926) 410319
– www.parkcottagewarwick.co.uk – janet@parkcottagewarwick.co.uk
– Fax (01926) 497994   Y**e**
7 rm ⌂ – †£50/65 ††£70/90
♦ Between the shops and restaurants of West Street and the River Avon, a listed part
Tudor house offering a homely lounge and sizeable, traditionally appointed bedrooms.

✕✕ Saffron ᴬᶜ VISA ◉◉ AE ◉
Unit 1, Westgate House, Market St ⊠ CV34 4DE – ℰ (01926) 402061
– www.saffronwarwick.co.uk – Closed 25 December   Y**n**
Rest – Indian – (dinner only) Carte £14/31
♦ Split-level dining room hung with sitars and prints from the subcontinent. Piquant
seafood and Goan dishes are the specialities of a freshly prepared Indian repertoire.

✕ Art Kitchen ᴬᶜ VISA ◉◉ AE
7 Swan St ⊠ CV34 4BJ – ℰ (01926) 494303 – www.theartkitchen.com
– reservations@theartkitchen.com – Fax (01926) 494304   Y**r**
Rest – Thai – Menu £13/20 **s** – Carte £16/24 **s**
♦ Unpretentious town centre restaurant with upstairs dining area featuring artwork
for sale by owners' daughter. Authentic Thai cooking with attention paid to originality.

> Look out for red symbols, indicating particularly pleasant establishments.

WATERGATE BAY – Cornwall – **503** E 32 – see Newquay

WATERMILLOCK – Cumbria – **502** L 20 – see Ullswater

WATFORD – Hertfordshire – **504** S 29 – pop. 120 960   12 **A2**
▱ London 21 mi – Aylesbury 23 mi
▥ West Herts. Cassiobury Park, ℰ (01923) 236484
▦ Oxhey Park South Oxhey Prestwick Rd, ℰ (01923) 248213

🏨🏨🏨 The Grove ➰ 🅙 🌊 📺 ⑩ ⓦ ᵣ🌡 ✕ 🔟 🏢 ㅎ rm, 🏃🏇 ᴬᶜ ✿ ⁽ᵖ⁾ 🎿 P VISA ◉◉ AE ◉
Chandler's Cross, Northwest : 2 m. on A 411 ⊠ WD3
4TG – ℰ (01923) 807807 – www.thegrove.co.uk – info@thegrove.co.uk
– Fax (01923) 221008
215 rm ⌂ – †£290 ††£290 – 12 suites
Rest Colette's and **Stables** – see restaurant listing
Rest Glasshouse – (buffet) Menu £30/45
♦ Converted country house with large gardens and golf course. Modern décor in
public rooms. Impressive spa facility. Hi-tech bedrooms and suites in modern ex-
tension. Glasshouse for buffet meals.

✕✕✕ Colette's – at The Grove Hotel ᴬᶜ P VISA ◉◉ AE ◉
Northwest : 2 m. on A 411 ⊠ WD3 4TG – ℰ (01923) 296010
– www.thegrove.co.uk – info@thegrove.co.uk – Fax (01923) 221008 – Closed
Sunday and Monday
Rest – (dinner only) Menu £58
♦ Formal restaurant with an adjacent bar and lounge. Divided into two rooms
and decorated with original artwork. Elaborately presented and ambitious cooking.

✕✕ Stables – at The Grove Hotel ᴬᶜ P
Chandler's Cross, Northwest : 2 m. on A 411 ⊠ WD3 4TG – ℰ (01923) 296015
– www.thegrove.co.uk – info@thegrove.co.uk
Rest – Carte £35/48
♦ Next to the golf course, this converted 19C stable block retains rustic style and
original exposed beams. Menu features classics, comfort food and assorted snacks.

ENGLAND

WATTON – Norfolk – 504 W 26

15 **C2**

▶ London 95 mi – Norwich 22 mi – Swaffham 10 mi

XX **The Café at Brovey Lair** with rm 🗲   🗲 🗲 🗲 🖪 rest, 🗲 🗲 🗲 **P**
Carbrooke Rd, Ovington, Northeast : 1¾ mi. by A 1075   VISA **@0** AE
⊠ *IP25 6SD – ℰ (01953) 882 706 – www.broveylair.com*
– thecafe@broveylair.com – Fax (01953) 882 706 – Closed 25 December
2 rm ⌑ – ♦£110 ♦♦£125
Rest – Seafood – (dinner only) (booking essential 2 days in advance) (set
menu only) Menu £48
♦ Unique dining experience, within chef's own house: you're encouraged to watch
her cook an accomplished four-course, no choice set seafood menu with a hint of
fusion. Smart rooms; healthy and exotic breakfasts.

WELFORD-ON-AVON – Warwickshire

19 **C3**

▶ London 109 mi – Alcester 9 mi – Stratford-upon-Avon 4 mi

🏠 **The Bell Inn**   🗲 🗲 🗲 **P** VISA **@0** AE
Binton Rd ⊠ *CV37 8EB – ℰ (01789) 750 353 – www.thebellwelford.co.uk*
– info@thebellwelford.co.uk – Fax (01789) 750 893
Rest – Carte £20/29
♦ Part 17C inn in neat village near Stratford. Attractive dining terrace. Flagged and
beamed bar with open fire. Eclectic mix of dishes: local suppliers printed on back of
menu.

WELLINGHAM – Norfolk

15 **C1**

▶ London 120 mi – King's Lynn 29 mi – Norwich 28 mi

🏠 **Manor House Farm** without rest 🗲   🗲 🗲 🗲 **P**
⊠ *PE32 2TH – ℰ (01328) 838 227 – www.manor-house-farm.co.uk*
– libby.ellis@btconnect.com – Fax (01328) 838 348
4 rm ⌑ – ♦£50/80 ♦♦£80/100
♦ Idyllic setting beside church, surrounded by gardens and working farm. Family
style breakfast; home grown bacon and sausage. Charming rooms in the house or
comfortable annexe.

WELLINGTON – Herefordshire – 503 L 27

18 **B3**

▶ London 161 mi – Gloucester 38 mi – Worcester 31 mi – Hereford 6 mi

🏠 **The Wellington**   🗲 🗲 **P** **@0** AE
⊠ *HR4 8AT – ℰ (01432) 830 367 – www.wellingtonpub.co.uk*
– thewellington@hotmail.com – Closed 25 December
Rest – (Closed Monday lunch) Carte £23/30
♦ An extremely popular, much-loved neighbourhood pub. In line with their highly
seasonal ethos, menus change daily and feature classic combinations of local, traceable produce.

WELLS – Somerset – 503 M 30 – pop. 10 406

4 **C2**

▶ London 132 mi – Bristol 20 mi – Southampton 68 mi – Taunton 28 mi
🖥 Town Hall, Market Pl ℰ (01749) 672552, touristinfo@wells.gov.uk
🖼 East Horrington Rd, ℰ (01749) 675 005
◉ City★★ – Cathedral★★★ (≼★★) **AC** – St Cuthbert★
◎ Glastonbury★★ – Abbey★★ (Abbot's Kitchen★) **AC**, St John the Baptist★★,
Somerset Rural Life Museum★ **AC**, Glastonbury Tor★ (≼★★★), SW : 5½ m.
by A 39 – Wookey Hole★ (Caves★ **AC**, Papermill★), NW : 2 m. Cheddar
Gorge★★ (Gorge★★, Caves★, Jacob's Ladder ❋★), - St Andrew's Church★,
NW : 7 m. by A 371 – Axbridge★★ (King John's Hunting Lodge★, St John
the Baptist Church★), NW : 8½ m. by A 371

🏨 **The Swan**   🗲 🗲 rm, 🗲 🗲 🗲 **P** VISA **@0** AE **①**
11 Sadler St ⊠ *BA5 2RX – ℰ (01749) 836 300 – www.swanhotelwells.co.uk*
– info@swanhotelwells.co.uk – Fax (01749) 836 301
50 rm ⌑ – ♦£90/102 ♦♦£114/170 – 1 suite   **Rest** – Carte £25/32
♦ Refurbished to a very good standard, this friendly former posting inn faces the
Cathedral's west front. Two firelit lounges; stylish, individually decorated rooms. Stunning Cathedral suite. Restaurant boasts framed antique clothing and oak panelling.

⌂ **Beryl** without rest ⇔   ← ⊞ ⬭ ⊐ ⬝ **P** VISA ⬤⬤
East : 1¼ m. by B 3139 off Hawkers Lane ⊠ *BA5 3JP* – ℰ *(01749) 678738*
*– www.beryl-wells.co.uk – stay@beryl-wells.co.uk – Fax (01749) 670508 – Closed
24-25 December*
10 rm ⌇ – **†**£65/85 **††**£100/130
♦ Neo-gothic former hunting lodge in formal gardens run in idiosyncratic style. Impeccable antique-filled drawing room. Traditional rooms, larger on first floor. Charming hosts.

✗ **The Old Spot**   VISA ⬤⬤ AE
⊕ *12 Sadler St* ⊠ *BA5 2SE* – ℰ *(01749) 689099 – Closed 1 week Christmas,
Monday, Sunday dinner and Tuesday lunch*
Rest – Menu £15/28
♦ Restaurant's rear leads straight onto stunning Cathedral grounds. Relaxing interior
"spot on" for enjoying gloriously unfussy, mouth-wateringly tasty dishes. Good value,
too.

at Wookey Hole Northwest : 1¾ m. by A 371 – ⊠ Wells

⌂ **Miller's at Glencot House** ⇔   ⊞ ⬝ ⬭ ⬶ ⬝ ⬝ ⬝ **P** VISA ⬤⬤ AE ⬤
Glencot Lane ⊠ *BA5 1BH* – ℰ *(01749) 677160 – www.glencothouse.co.uk
– relax@glencothouse.co.uk – Fax (01749) 670210*
15 rm ⌇ – **†**£165 **††**£165/295
Rest – (booking essential for non-residents) Menu £18/33
♦ 19C mansion in Jacobean style, bursting with personality and now owned by Martin Miller who has filled the house with antiques. Rooms all refurbished; relaxed atmosphere throughout. French inspired menu with good local produce.

at Easton Northwest : 3 m. on A 371 – ⊠ Wells

⌂ **Beaconsfield Farm** without rest   ⊞ ⬝ ⬝ **P**
⊕ *on A 371* ⊠ *BA5 1DU* – ℰ *(01749) 870308 – www.beaconsfieldfarm.co.uk
– carol@beaconsfieldfarm.co.uk – Closed 23 December-2 January*
3 rm ⌇ – **†**£60/70 **††**£70/85
♦ In the foothills of the Mendips, a renovated farmhouse offering well-fitted, cottage-style rooms. Generous breakfasts in the parlour overlooking the four-acre grounds.

WELLS-NEXT-THE-SEA – Norfolk – **504** W 25 – **pop. 2 451**   **15 C1**
◨ London 122 mi – Cromer 22 mi – Norwich 38 mi

⌂ **The Crown**   ⬝ ⬝ VISA ⬤⬤
The Buttlands ⊠ *NR23 1EX* – ℰ *(01328) 710209 – www.thecrownhotelwells.co.uk
– reception@thecrownhotelwells.co.uk – Fax (01328) 711432*
12 rm ⌇ – **†**£70/135 **††**£90/155
Rest Restaurant – (dinner only) Menu £30 – Carte £30/35
Rest Bar – (bookings not accepted) Carte £17/38
♦ 16C coaching inn with smart Georgian façade, overlooking the village green. Bedrooms are contemporary in style; service is informal and friendly. Light, airy Restaurant with bright décor. Modern conservatory Bar with terrace.

⌂ **Machrimore** without rest   ⊞ ⬝ **P**
Burnt St, on A149 ⊠ *NR23 1HS* – ℰ *(01328) 711653 – www.machrimore.co.uk
– enquiries@machrimore.co.uk*
4 rm ⌇ – **†**£41 **††**£72/76
♦ Converted farm buildings with delightful gardens and illuminated water features.
Accessed via the garden, bedrooms have quality furniture, good facilities, their own
patio and seating.

at Wighton Southeast : 2½ m. by A149

⌂ **Meadowview** without rest   ⊞ ⬝ **P** VISA ⬤⬤ AE ⬤
53 High St ⊠ *NR23 1PF* – ℰ *(01328) 821527 – www.meadow-view.net
– bookings@meadow-view.net*
5 rm ⌇ – **†**£60 **††**£100
♦ Set in peaceful village, with neat garden, hot tub, comfy furniture and gazebo
overlooking meadow. Smart, modern interior with comfy furnishings; good facilities.
Breakfast cooked on Aga.

WELWYN – Hertfordshire – 504 T 28 – pop. 10 512   12 B2

▶ London 31 mi – Bedford 31 mi – Cambridge 31 mi

Tewin Bury Farm   🍴 🕐 AC rest, ⚿ 📶 🛏 P VISA ☺ AE ①
Southeast : 3½ m. by A 1000 on B 1000 ⊠ AL6 0JB – ℰ (01438) 717 793
– www.tewinbury.co.uk – reservations@tewinbury.co.uk – Fax (01438) 840 440
39 rm ⊇ – †£140 ††£155   **Rest** – Carte approx. £14
♦ Consisting of a range of converted farm buildings on 400-acre working farm. 17C
tythe barn used as function room located next to river. Individual rooms have
beamed ceilings. Restaurant located in timbered farm building.

White Hart   ⚿ 📶 🛏 P VISA ☺ AE
2 Prospect Place ⊠ AL6 9EN – ℰ (01438) 715 353 – www.thewhitehardhotel.net
– bookings@thewhitehardhotel.net – Fax (01438) 714 448
13 rm ⊇ – †£110 ††£110   **Rest** – (Closed Sunday dinner) Carte £17/34
♦ Family-run converted 17C inn with snug bar filled with photos of yesteryear. Some
contemporary bedrooms, others more traditional; those in courtyard are most spacious. Charming dining room with impressive high ceiling serves traditional English
dishes.

WELWYN GARDEN CITY – Hertfordshire – 504 T 28   12 B2

▶ London 22 mi – Luton 21 mi
🏌 Panshanger Golf Complex Old Herns Lane, ℰ (01707) 333 312

XXX   **Auberge du Lac**   🕐 🍽 AC ⇔ P VISA ☺ AE ①
❀   *Brocket Hall, West : 3 m. by A 6129 on B 653 ⊠ AL8 7XG – ℰ (01707) 368 888*
– www.brocket-hall.co.uk – auberge@brocket-hall.co.uk – Fax (01707) 368 898
– Closed 27 December - 7 January, Sunday dinner and Monday
Rest – Menu £30/55 🌿
Spec. Caramelised scallops, watercress, apple and pickled cockles. Roast duck
with peach, gingerbread and Sichuan pepper. Iced coconut parfait with pineapple caramel, jelly and sorbet.
♦ Part 18C former hunting lodge with lakeside terrace in the grounds of Brocket Hall
- a charming setting for the technically adept cooking, with good understanding of
flavours.

WENDLING – Norfolk – 504 W 25 – see East Dereham

WENTBRIDGE – West Yorkshire – 502 Q 23 – ⊠ Pontefract   22 B3

▶ London 183 mi – Leeds 19 mi – Nottingham 55 mi – Sheffield 28 mi

Wentbridge House   🍴 🕐 📺 ⚿ 📶 🛏 P VISA ☺ AE ①
Old Great North Rd ⊠ WF8 3JJ – ℰ (01977) 620 444
– www.wentbridgehouse.co.uk – info@wentbridgehouse.co.uk – Fax (01977)
620 148 – Closed 25 December
41 rm ⊇ – †£100 ††£170/200
Rest Fleur de Lys – (dinner only and Sunday lunch) Carte £32/50
Rest Wentbridge Brasserie – Carte £24/40
♦ Once owned by the late Queen Mother's family, a part 18C bay-windowed house
decorated in traditional colours. Sizeable rooms, some overlooking the lawned
grounds. Fleur de Lys adjacent to smart firelit bar. Informal Wentbridge Brasserie.

WEOBLEY – County of Herefordshire – 503 L 27 – ⊠ Hereford   18 A3

▶ London 145 mi – Brecon 30 mi – Hereford 12 mi – Leominster 9 mi

Broxwood Court ⑤   ≼ 🍴 🕐 ⋊ ⚿ AC rm, ⚿ P VISA ☺
Broxwood, Northwest : 3¼ m. by A 4112, Broxwood rd on Lyonshall rd
⊠ HR6 9JJ – ℰ (01544) 340 245 – www.broxwoodcourt.co.uk
– mikeanne@broxwood.kc3.co.uk – Fax (01544) 340 573
– Closed 21 December - 6 January
5 rm ⊇ – †£50/65 ††£100
Rest – (by arrangement, communal dining) Menu £30
♦ 1950s house set in wonderfully tranquil location: vast grounds and formally laid-
out gardens. Spacious drawing room, cosy library. Individually styled rooms with
views.

WEST BAGBOROUGH – Somerset – 503 K 30 – see Taunton

WESTBURY – Wiltshire – 503 N 30   4 C2
■ London 111 mi – Trowbridge 5 mi – Warminster 4 mi

Garden House   🚗 🌳 𝔸𝕀ℂ rest, ❝¶❞ 𝕍𝕀𝕊𝔸 ⊚⊚ 𝔸𝔼
*26 Edward St, ✉ BA13 3BD – 𝒞 (01373) 859995
– www.thegardenhotel.co.uk – reception@thegardenhotel.co.uk – Fax (01373)
858586 – Closed 24 December - 4 January*
11 rm ☷ – ♦£65/75 ♦♦£110
Rest – (dinner only and Sunday lunch) Carte £17/31 **s**
♦ Welcoming former town post office with comfy lounge and friendly bar. Spacious
bedrooms blend the classic and the contemporary; 3 annexe rooms nearby. All boast
spa baths. Restaurant uses local produce to create traditional dishes.

WEST DIDSBURY – Gtr Manchester – see Manchester

WEST END – Surrey – 504 S 29 – pop. 4 135 – ✉ Guildford   7 C1
■ London 37 mi – Bracknell 7 mi – Camberley 5 mi – Guildford 8 mi
– Woking 6 mi

The Inn @ West End   ℙ 𝕍𝕀𝕊𝔸 ⊚⊚ 𝔸𝔼
*42 Guildford Road, on A 322 ✉ GU24 9PW – 𝒞 (01276) 858652
– www.the-inn.co.uk – greatfood@the-inn.co.uk*
Rest – Menu £24 (Sunday lunch) – Carte £25/75
♦ Pretty pub with a 'tea shop' atmosphere, lovely garden and terrace. Really fresh
local produce and simple techniques create a wholesome, traditional menu. Good
range of wines.

WESTFIELD – East Sussex – 504 V 31 – pop. 1 509   8 B3
■ London 66 mi – Brighton 38 mi – Folkestone 45 mi – Maidstone 30 mi

ХХ **The Wild Mushroom**   🚗 ℙ 𝕍𝕀𝕊𝔸 ⊚⊚ 𝔸𝔼
*Woodgate House, Westfield Lane, Southwest : ½ m. on A 28 ✉ TN35 4SB
– 𝒞 (01424) 751 137 – www.wildmushroom.co.uk – info@wildmushroom.co.uk
– Fax (01424) 753405 – Closed 2 weeks Christmas, second week August, last week
October, Monday, Saturday lunch and Sunday dinner*
Rest – (booking essential) Menu £19 (lunch) – Carte dinner £29/31
♦ Bustling and hospitable with modern interior and conservatory lounge. Flavourful,
well-priced dishes from a varied, interesting menu. Loyal local following: be sure to book.

WEST HATCH – Somerset – see Taunton

WEST KIRBY – Merseyside – 502 K 23 ▮ Great Britain   20 A3
■ London 219 mi – Chester 19 mi – Liverpool 12 mi
◉ Liverpool★ - Cathedrals★★, The Walker★★, Merseyside Maritime
Museum★ and Albert Dock★, E : 13½ m. by A 553

Hillbark ◈   🚗 ❀ ❝¶❞ ℙ 𝕍𝕀𝕊𝔸 ⊚⊚ 𝔸𝔼 ⓞ
*Royden Park, Frankby, East : 2¾ m. by A 540 and B 5139 off Hillbark Rd
✉ CH48 1NP – 𝒞 (0151) 624 2400 – www.hillbarkhotel.co.uk
– enquiries@hillbarkhotel.co.uk – Fax (0151) 625 4040*
17 rm ☷ – ♦£175 ♦♦£175 – 1 suite
Rest *The Yellow Room* – see restaurant listing
Rest *Hillbark Grill* – Carte £27/38 **s**
♦ Set in mature grounds with westerly views, an impressive Elizabethan/Tudor style
house boasting 13C church doors and stained glass windows. Classical rooms; granite
bathrooms. Informal oak panelled restaurant serves grill menu.

Peel Hey without rest   🚗 �&. ❀ ❝¶❞ ℙ 𝕍𝕀𝕊𝔸 ⊚⊚ 𝔸𝔼
*Frankby Rd, Frankby, East : 2¼ m. by A 540 on B 5139 ✉ CH48 1PP – 𝒞 (0151)
677 9077 – www.peelhey.com – enquiries@peelhey.com – Fax (0151) 625 4115*
9 rm – ♦£65/75 ♦♦£85, ☷ £7.75
♦ Modernised 19C house that offers a good standard of accommodation. Attractive,
comfortable rooms.

XXX **The Yellow Room** – at Hillbark Hotel   🍽 🛇 **P** **VISA** **🅮🅾** **AE** **①**
Royden Park, Frankby, East : 2 ¾ m. by A 540 and B 5139 off Hillbark Rd ⊠ CH48
1NP – ℰ (0151) 624 2400 – www.hillbarkhotel.co.uk
– enquiries@hillbarkhotel.co.uk – Fax (0151) 625 4040
Rest – (Closed Sunday-Monday) Carte £ 55/75 **s**
♦ Yellow walled restaurant with opulent, ornate furnishings, chandeliers and magnificent fireplace. Quality ingredients and well-judged flavours are coupled with intricate presentation.

↑ **42 Caldy Road** without rest   ≤ 🍽 🛇 ⁽ᵗⁱ⁾ **P** **VISA** **🅮🅾** **AE**
42 Caldy Road, Southeast : 1 ¼ m on B 5141 ⊠ CH48 2HQ – ℰ (0151) 625 8740
– www.warrencott.demon.co.uk – office@warrencott.demon.co.uk – Fax (0151)
625 4115 – Closed Christmas and New Year
3 rm – ✚£69/79 ✚✚£89
♦ Creeper-clad guesthouse with attractive garden and estuary views, set on smart residential road. Crisp, white, up to date bedrooms, two with sea views; modern bathrooms.

WEST MALLING – Kent – **504** V 30 – pop. 2 144   8 **B1**
▶ London 35 mi – Maidstone 7 mi – Royal Tunbridge Wells 14 mi
🛈 Addington Maidstone, ℰ (01732) 844 785

↑ **Scott House** without rest   🛇 ⁽ᵗⁱ⁾ **VISA** **🅮🅾** **①**
37 High St ⊠ ME19 6QH – ℰ (01732) 841 380 – www.scott-house.co.uk
– mail@scott-house.co.uk – Fax (01732) 522 367 – Closed Christmas-New Year
4 rm � – ✚£79 ✚✚£89
♦ Comfy rooms in period style and a relaxing first-floor lounge share this part Georgian town house with a fine interior décor shop, run by the same warm husband and wife team.

X **The Swan**   🍴 **AC** ⇄ **VISA** **🅮🅾** **AE**
☺ *35 Swan St ⊠ ME19 6JU – ℰ (01732) 521 910 – www.theswanwestmalling.co.uk*
– info@theswanwestmalling.co.uk – Fax (01732) 522 898 – Closed 26 December
and 1 January
Rest – Carte £ 27/38
♦ Radically renovated 16C pub in modern pine. Stylish lounge: leopard-print carpet, purple cushions. Modish menu at sensible prices; informal, very efficient service.

WEST MEON – Hampshire – **504** Q 30   6 **B2**
▶ London 74 mi – Southampton 27 mi – Portsmouth 21 mi
– Basingstoke 32 mi

🍴 **The Thomas Lord**   🍽 🍴 **P** **VISA** **🅮🅾**
High Street ⊠ GU32 1LN – ℰ (01730) 829 244 – www.thethomaslord.co.uk
– enjoy@thethomaslord.co.uk
Rest – (Closed Sunday dinner) Carte £ 21/29
♦ Named after the founder of Lord's, with a cricketing theme. Constantly evolving menus and a passion for local produce; cooking is generous and robust, British with a hint of Mediterranean.

WESTON-SUPER-MARE – North Somerset – **503** K 29 – pop. 78 044   3 **B2**
▶ London 147 mi – Bristol 24 mi – Taunton 32 mi
🛈 Beach Lawns ℰ (01934) 888800, westontouristinfo@n-somerset.gov.uk
🛈 Worlebury Monks Hill, ℰ (01934) 625 789
◉ Seafront (≤ ★★) BZ
⬡ Axbridge ★★ (King John's Hunting Lodge ★, St John the Baptist Church ★)
SE : 9 m. by A 371 - BY - and A 38 – Cheddar Gorge ★★ (Gorge ★★, Caves ★,
Jacob's Ladder ※ ★) – Clevedon ★ (≤ ★★, Clevedon Court ★), NE : 10 m. by
A 370 and M 5 – St Andrew's Church ★, SE : 10 ½ m. by A 371

Plan on next page

ENGLAND

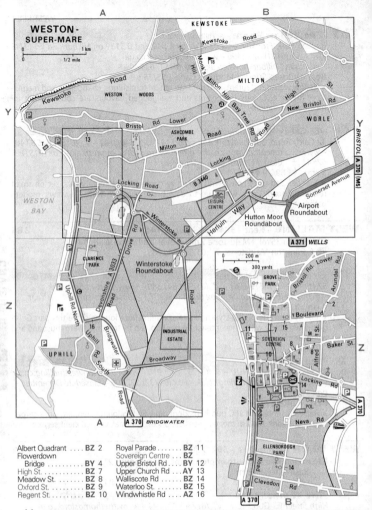

WESTON-SUPER-MARE

Albert Quadrant . . . . **BZ** 2	Royal Parade . . . . **BZ** 11
Flowerdown	Sovereign Centre . . . **BZ**
Bridge . . . . **BY** 4	Upper Bristol Rd . . . **BY** 12
High St. . . . . **BZ** 7	Upper Church Rd . . **AY** 13
Meadow St. . . . . . . **BZ** 8	Walliscote Rd . . . . . **BZ** 14
Oxford St. . . . . **BZ** 9	Waterloo St. . . . . . . **BZ** 15
Regent St. . . . . **BZ** 10	Windwhistle Rd . . . . **AZ** 16

🏨 The Beachlands   🚗 ⚘ 🐾 ᵹ rm, 🛰 ☏ 🕍 🅿 𝑉𝐼𝑆𝐴 🆖 AE ①

17 Uphill Road North ⊠ BS23 4NG – ℰ (01934) 621 401
– www.beachlandshotel.com – info@beachlandshotel.com – Fax (01934) 621 966
– Closed 24 December - 4 January   AZ**c**

23 rm ⊇ – †£65/90 ††£118/125

Rest – (bar lunch Monday-Saturday) Menu £21

◆ Well-established and family run, convenient for beach and golf course. Rooms in traditional prints; some, south-facing, have veranda doors giving on to a secluded garden. Formal dining room overlooks pleasant gardens.

🏠 Queenswood *without rest*   ☏ 𝑉𝐼𝑆𝐴 🆖 AE

Victoria Park, off Upper Church Rd ⊠ BS23 2HZ – ℰ (01934) 416 141
– www.queenswoodhotel.com – stay@queenswoodhotel.com – Fax (01934) 621 759 – Closed 10 December-10 January   BZ**s**

19 rm ⊇ – †£58/70 ††£85/100

◆ Sizeable, 19C-style house, well kept by friendly, long-standing owners. Red velour lounge sofas and neat rooms in the time-honoured tradition of the British seaside holiday.

XX **Duets**   VISA ◑◐
103 Upper Bristol Rd ⊠ BS22 8ND – ℰ (01934) 413 428 – www.duets.co.uk
– Closed 2 weeks summer, 1 week autumn, Monday, Tuesday, Saturday lunch and
Sunday dinner   BYa
Rest – Menu £18/27 – Carte £30/32
♦ Diligent and unfussy service sets the tone in this traditionally styled restaurant,
deservedly a neighbourhood favourite. Ably judged cooking on a tasty classical base.

X **The Cove**   ≤ 🍽 VISA ◑◐
Birnbeck Rd ⊠ BS23 2BX – ℰ (01934) 418 217 – www.the-cove.co.uk
– info@the-cove.co.uk – Closed first 2 weeks January, Sunday dinner and Monday
Rest – Carte £21/31   AYe
♦ Seafront eatery with striking lines, contemporary styling and bay views. Modern,
seasonal menu displays European flair and seafood slant; most produce from within
20 miles. Tapas 3-9pm.

WESTON UNDER WETHERLEY – Warks. – see Royal Leamington Spa

WESTON UNDERWOOD – Derbs. – see Derby

WESTOW – North Yorkshire   23 **C2**
▶ London 224 mi – Malton 8 mi – York 15 mi

🏠 **The Blacksmiths Inn**   🍽 ఉ rm, P VISA ◑◐
Main St ⊠ YO60 7NE – ℰ (01653) 618 365
Rest – (Closed Monday, except Bank Holiday Monday, and lunch Tuesday)
Carte £15/30
♦ Former blacksmiths forge with original brick fire. Menu displays a classical York-
shire base and changes monthly in line with the seasons; snack menu available in the
bar area.

WEST PECKHAM – Kent – see Maidstone

WEST STOKE – W. Sussex – see Chichester

WEST TANFIELD – North Yorkshire – **502** P 21 – ⊠ Ripon   22 **B2**
▶ London 237 mi – Darlington 29 mi – Leeds 32 mi – Middlesbrough 39 mi
– York 36 mi

🏠 **The Old Coach House** without rest   🚗 ⚒ P VISA ◑◐ AE
2 Stable Cottages, Southeast : 1 m. on A 6108 ⊠ HG4 3HT – ℰ (01765) 634 900
– www.oldcoachhouse.info – enquiries@oldcoachhouse.info
8 rm ⊊ – ♥£45/69 ♥♥£89
♦ Nestled between the Dales and the Moors, a smart 18C house with 'country living'
feel. Spacious, modern bedrooms furnished by local, independent suppliers; some
boast beams/wetrooms.

🏠 **The Bruce Arms** with rm   🍽 P VISA ◑◐ AE ◐
Main St ⊠ HG4 5JJ – ℰ (01677) 470 325 – www.bruce-arms.co.uk
– info@bruce-arms.co.uk – Fax (01677) 470 925 – Closed Monday
2 rm ⊊ – ♥£85 ♥♥£80/85
Rest – Menu £24 – Carte £12/27
♦ Stone-built village pub: log fire, local ales, leather sofas. Vine covered, decked
terrace. Well-spaced candlelit pub tables. Satisfying blackboard menu. Rustic bedrooms.

WETHERBY – West Yorkshire – **502** P 22 – **pop. 10 562** ▮ *Great Britain*   22 **B2**
▶ London 208 mi – Harrogate 8 mi – Leeds 13 mi – York 14 mi
🛈 The Library, 17 Westgate ℰ (01937) 582 151,
wetherbytic@leedslearning.net
⛳ Linton Linton Lane, ℰ (01937) 580 089
◉ Harewood House★★ (The Gallery★) **AC**, SW : 5½ m. by A 58 and A 659

ENGLAND

Wood Hall

Trip Lane, Linton, Southwest : 3 m. by A 661 and Linton Rd ⊠ LS22 4JA
– ℎ (01937) 587 271 – www.handpicked.co.uk – enquiries@woodhall.co.uk
– Fax (01937) 584 353
44 rm ⌿ – †£190 ††£220
Rest – (bar lunch Monday-Saturday) Menu £35 – Carte £35/54 **s**
♦ Peacefully set part Jacobean and Georgian manor in 100 acres of woods and gardens. Refurbished contemporary public areas; well-appointed bedrooms. Popular wedding venue. Elegant dining room with candelabras and tall sash windows.

at Walton East : 4 m. by B 1224 – ⊠ Wetherby

The Fox and Hounds

Hall Park Road ⊠ LS23 7DQ – ℎ (01937) 842 192
Rest – (booking essential) Carte £16/25
♦ Characterful, low-beamed stone pub with a cosy snug, home to stuffed fox, Basil. Hearty, robust cooking; classic British dishes. Friendly atmosphere and polite, chatty service.

Don't confuse ✗ with ✿!
✗ defines comfort, while stars are awarded for the best cuisine, across all categories of comfort.

ENGLAND

WEYMOUTH – Dorset – 503 M 32 – pop. 48 279

4 **C3**

◘ London 142 mi – Bournemouth 35 mi – Bristol 68 mi – Exeter 59 mi – Swindon 94 mi
▣ to Guernsey (St Peter Port) and Jersey (St Helier) (Condor Ferries Ltd)
🖪 The King's Statue, The Esplanade ℎ (01305) 785747, tic@weymouth.gov.uk
🖬 Links Rd, ℎ (0844) 980 9909
◉ Town★ – Timewalk★ AC – Nothe Fort (≤★) AC – Boat Trip★ (Weymouth Bay and Portland Harbour) AC
ⓒ Chesil Beach★★ – Portland★ – Portland Bill (❋★★) S : 2½ m. by A 354. Maiden Castle★★ (≤★) N : 6½ m. by A 354 – Sub-Tropical Gardens★ AC, St Catherine's Chapel★) NW : 9 m. by B 3157

Chandlers

4 Westerhall Rd ⊠ DT4 7SZ – ℎ (01305) 771 341 – www.chandlershotel.com
– info@chandlershotel.com – Fax (01305) 830 122 – Closed 2 weeks winter
10 rm ⌿ – †£60/85 ††£160   **Rest** – (by arrangement) Menu £25
♦ Substantial Victorian house with comfy, stylish interior. Every bedroom has a unique focus point – maybe a spa bath or striking colour scheme. Good breakfasts with daily specials; regularly changing home cooked dinners.

Bay View without rest

35 The Esplanade ⊠ DT4 8DH – ℎ (01305) 782 083
– www.bayview-weymouth.co.uk – info@bayview-weymouth.co.uk – Fax (01305) 782 083 – February-November
8 rm – †£35/45 ††£45/50, ⌿ £7.50
♦ Generously sized en suite rooms, many with four-poster beds or broad bay windows, in a sizeable townhouse with views over the bay. Neatly kept basement lounge.

✗✗ Perry's

4 Trinity Rd, The Old Harbour ⊠ DT4 8TJ – ℎ (01305) 785 799
– www.perrysrestaurant.co.uk – perrysrestaurant@hotmail.co.uk – Fax (01305) 787 002 – Closed Monday in winter
Rest – Seafood – Menu £20 (lunch) – Carte £24/34 ⌾
♦ Simple, family-run local favourite by the old harbour. Friendly staff, tasty cooking and plenty of seafood specials: shellfish soup, Portland crab, citrus-dressed bass.

WHALLEY – Lancashire – **502** M 22 – pop. 3 230 – ⊠ Blackburn

- ▶ London 233 mi – Blackpool 32 mi – Burnley 12 mi – Manchester 28 mi – Preston 15 mi
- ▣ Long Leese Barn Clerkhill, ℰ (01254) 822 236

at Mitton Northwest : 2 ½ m. on B 6246 – ⊠ Whalley

The Three Fishes   🍴 **P** **VISA** ⓒ **AE**
Mitton Road ⊠ BB7 9PQ – ℰ (01254) 826 888 – www.thethreefishes.com – enquiries@thethreefishes.com – Fax (01254) 826 026 – Closed 25 December
Rest – (bookings not accepted) Carte £ 17/29
♦ Huge, 140 cover modern dining pub, once a coaching inn. Lancashire and north-west England regional specialities dominate the menu. Perenially busy: remember, you can't book!

WHICKHAM – Tyne and Wear – **501** O/P 19 – see Gateshead

WHITBY – North Yorkshire – **502** S 20 – pop. 13 594 ▮ *Great Britain*

- ▶ London 257 mi – Middlesbrough 31 mi – Scarborough 21 mi – York 45 mi
- ▮ Langborne Rd ℰ (01723) 383637, whitbytic@scarborough.gov.uk
- ▣ Low Straggleton Sandsend Rd, ℰ (01947) 600 660
- ◉ Abbey★

Bagdale Hall   ⚡ **P** **VISA** ⓒ **AE** ⓞ
1 Bagdale ⊠ YO21 1QL – ℰ (01947) 602 958 – www.bagdale.co.uk – Fax (01947) 820 714
14 rm ⌿ – ♦£70 ♦♦£150   **Rest** – (dinner only) Carte £ 12/30
♦ Tudor manor with fine fireplaces in carved wood and 19C Delft tiles; panelled rooms with mullioned windows; four-posters in period style bedrooms. Annex for more modern rooms. Dining room boasts timbered ceiling and massive wooden fireplace.

Cross Butts Stable   🚗 🐴 🍴 ♿ rm, ⚡ 🐾 **P** **VISA** ⓒ
Guisborough Rd, West : 1 ¾ m. on A 171 (Teeside rd) ⊠ YO21 1TL – ℰ (01947) 820 986 – www.cross-butts.co.uk – info@cross-butts.co.uk – Fax (01947) 825 665
9 rm ⌿ – ♦£60 ♦♦£130   **Rest** – Carte £ 16/31 **s**
♦ Extended farmhouse on working farm personally run by a welcoming family. Su-perb bedrooms, set round courtyard with water feature, have flag floors and warm, sumptuous aura. Smart, informal restaurant areas over two floors: a mix of suites, sofas and tables.

Green's   **AC** **VISA** ⓒ
13 Bridge St ⊠ YO22 4BG – ℰ (01947) 600 284 – www.greensofwhitby.com – info@greensofwhitby.com – Closed 25-26 December and 1 January
Rest – Seafood – (dinner only and lunch Friday-Sunday) (booking essential)
Menu £ 40 – Carte £ 25/38
♦ Set in town centre, close to quayside, with a rustic, informal ambience. Constantly changing seafood menus are simply cooked and employ much produce freshly lan-ded at Whitby.

Red Chard Lounge and Grill   **VISA** ⓒ **AE**
22-23 Flowergate ⊠ YO21 3BA – ℰ (01947) 606 660 – www.redchard.com – info@redchard.com – Closed 1-14 January, 25 December, Monday, and lunch Sunday-Tuesday
Rest – Beef specialities – Carte £ 24/34
♦ Modern town centre bar/lounge/dining room in one; funky and relaxing, with art-covered walls. Wide ranging menu with local produce to the fore; quality 21 day hung beef.

WHITBY

at Briggswath Southwest : 3 ½ m. by A 171 (Teesdie rd), A 169 on B 1410 – ⊠ Whitby

⌂ **The Lawns** without rest ≤ 🚗 🌾 **P**
73 Carr Hill Lane ⊠ YO21 1RS – ℰ (01947) 810310
– www.thelawnsbedandbreakfastwhitby.co.uk – lorton@onetel.com
– Fax (01947) 810310 – Closed 15 January - February
3 rm ☐ – ♥♥£70
♦ Sizeable, converted house above a south-facing garden and verge of evergreens. Stripped wooden floors, understated décor. Spotless rooms. Fine views of moors and Esk valley.

at Dunsley West : 3 ¼ m. by A 171 – ⊠ Whitby

🏨 **Dunsley Hall Country House** ᔕ ≤ 🚗 🖼 🕏 ᴌᴓ 🛎 🌾 ♨
⊠ YO21 3TL – ℰ (01947) 893 437 – www.dunsleyhall.com **P** **VISA** **◎◎** **AE**
– reception@dunsleyhall.com – Fax (01947) 893 505
26 rm ☐ – ♥£95/124 ♥♥£149/198
Rest – British – (bar lunch Monday-Saturday) Carte £25/49
♦ Behind pillared gates, a personally run late Victorian house: intricately oak panelled lounge with leather furnished bar. Comfortable, period styled rooms with country views. Dining room boasts Whitby seafood.

at Sandsend Northwest : 3 m. on A 174 – ⊠ Whitby

🍴🍴 **Estbek House** with rm «ᵢᵖ» **VISA** **◎◎**
East Row ⊠ YO21 3SY – ℰ (01947) 893 424 – www.estbekhouse.co.uk
– info@estbekhouse.co.uk – Fax (01947) 893 623 – Closed January
4 rm ☐ – ♥£70/85 ♥♥£100/180
Rest – Seafood – (dinner only) Carte £29/44
♦ This personally run Regency house, adjacent to beach, boasts delightful terrace, basement bar, smart restaurant serving local, wild seafood, and utterly charming rooms.

at Goldsborough Northwest : 6 m. by A 174

🍴 **Fox & Hounds** 🌾 **P** **VISA** **◎◎** **AE**
– ℰ (01947) 893 372 – Closed Christmas, New Year and Bank Holidays
Rest – (Closed Sunday dinner, Monday-Tuesday) Carte £21/34
♦ Cosy pub in a coastal hamlet, run by a team of two. Constantly evolving blackboard menu features local produce and unfussy cooking. Seasonality is paramount and fresh fish a speciality.

WHITCHURCH – Shropshire – 502 L 25 18 B1
🖪 London 168 mi – Nantwich 11 mi – Wrexham 15 mi

at Burleydam East : 4 ¼ m. on A 525 – ⊠ Whitchurch

🍺 **The Combermere Arms** 🚗 🌿 **P** **VISA** **◎◎** **AE**
⊠ SY13 4AT – ℰ (01948) 871 223 – www.combermerearms-burleydam.co.uk
– combermere@brunningandprice.co.uk – Fax (01948) 661 371
Rest – Carte £18/29
♦ Rurally located pub with smart terrace ideal for al fresco refreshment. Interior skylights lend an open, airy feel. Informal, eclectic menus. Some vast tables for big parties.

WHITEHAVEN – Cumbria – 502 J 20 21 A2
🖪 London 332 mi – Carlisle 39 mi – Keswick 28 mi – Penrith 47 mi

🍴🍴 **Zest** **P** **VISA** **◎◎** **①**
Low Rd, South : ½ m. on B 5345 (St Bees) ⊠ CA28 9HS – ℰ (01946) 692 848
– www.zestwhitehaven.com – zestcomments@googlemail.com – Fax (01946)
66 984 – Closed 25 December-3 January and Sunday-Tuesday
Rest – (dinner only) Carte £17/30
♦ Don't be put off by the unprepossessing exterior: inside is a smart, stylish eatery and bar with brown leather sofas. Eclectic range of modern menus with numerous influences.

ENGLAND

WHITEPARISH – Wilts. – **503** P 30 – see Salisbury

WHITEWELL – Lancashire – **502** M 22 – ⊠ Clitheroe   20 **B2**

 ☑ London 281 mi – Lancaster 31 mi – Leeds 55 mi – Manchester 41 mi
 – Preston 13 mi

🏠   **The Inn at Whitewell** with rm   ⩽ 🛋 🔧 **P** _VISA_ ◑◐
Forest of Bowland ⊠ BB7 3AT – ℰ (01200) 448 222 – www.innatwhitewell.com
– reception@innatwhitewell.com – Fax (01200) 448 298
23 rm ⚏ – ♥£70 ♥♥£197 – 1 suite   **Rest** – (bar lunch) Carte £18/40
♦ Dining room overlooks river Hodder and Trough of Bowland and the inn was once home to the Royal Keeper of the Forest. Has its own character and charm. Traditional cooking. Stylish bedrooms.

WHITSTABLE – Kent – **504** X 29 – pop. 30 195   9 **C1**

 ☑ London 68 mi – Dover 24 mi – Maidstone 37 mi – Margate 12 mi
 🛈 7 Oxford St ℰ (01227) 275482, whitstableinformation@canterbury.gov.uk

🏨   **Continental**   ⩽ 🛋 ⅏ ๚ **P** _VISA_ ◑◐
29 Beach Walk, East : ½ m. by Sea St and Harbour St ⊠ CT5 2BP – ℰ (01227)
280 280 – www.hotelcontinental.co.uk – jamie@hotelcontinental.co.uk
– Fax (01227) 284 114
30 rm ⚏ – ♥£63 ♥♥£100/145   **Rest** – (bar lunch) Carte £20/32
♦ Laid-back, privately owned hotel with an unadorned 30s-style façade overlooking the sea; simply furnished, plain-walled rooms - picture windows and warm colours. Split-level bistro with "no frills" approach.

✗   **Whitstable Oyster Fishery Co.**   ⩽ _VISA_ ◑◐ 🅰🄴 ①
Royal Native Oyster Stores, The Horsebridge ⊠ CT5 1BU – ℰ (01227) 276 856
– www.oysterfishery.co.uk – Fax (01227) 770 829 – Closed 25-26 and 31 December
and Monday except Bank Holidays
Rest – Seafood – (booking essential) Carte £30/40
♦ Relaxed and unfussy converted beach warehouse; seafood on display in open kitchen; oysters and moules-frites draw a trendy young set at weekends. Arthouse cinema upstairs.

✗   **Jo Jo's**   🖵
209 Tankerton Rd, East : 1½ m. by Sea St and Harbour St ⊠ CT5 2AT
– ℰ (01227) 274 591 – www.jojosrestaurant.co.uk – Closed mid December - late
January, Monday-Tuesday and Sunday dinner
Rest – (booking essential) Carte approx. £20
♦ Neighbourhood eatery in residential parade. Concise Mediterranean menu of meze/tapas with daily specials; lots of fish and meat. Veg and herbs from kitchen garden. Closed 1 week in 6.

at Seasalter Southwest : 2 m. by B 2205 – ⊠ Whitstable

🏠   **The Sportsman** (Steve Harris)   🛋 **P** _VISA_ ◑◐
🖐   *Faversham Rd, Southwest : 2 m. following coast rd ⊠ CT5 4BP – ℰ (01227)*
273 370 – www.thesportsmanseasalter.co.uk – Closed 25-26 December
Rest – (Closed Sunday dinner and Monday) Carte £23/34
Spec. 'Salmagundi'- seasonal English salad. Turbot with smoked herring sauce. Rhubarb sorbet with burnt cream and shortbread.
♦ Set between shingle and marsh on the coastal road, serving confident, unfussy and fantastically flavoursome cooking, made from ingredients very much rooted in the locality.

We try to be as accurate as possible when giving room rates but prices are susceptible to change.
Please check rates when booking.

ENGLAND

WHITTLESFORD – Cambridgeshire – 504 U 27

14 B3

🚇 London 50 mi – Cambridge 11 mi – Peterborough 46 mi

XX **The Tickell**　　　　　　　　　　　　🚗 🌲 **P** **VISA** **CO**

1 North Rd ⊠ CB2 4NZ – ☎ (01223) 833 128 – www.thetickell.co.uk
– Fax (01223) 835 907
– Closed 1-22 January, 25 December, Monday and Sunday dinner
Rest – Menu £ 31 – Carte (lunch) £ 22/33 ⌘

♦ Richly ornate 300 year-old exterior with conservatory and terrace. Quirky feel pervades: emerald green walls, yellow ceiling. Rich, classic meals from the Gallic repertoire.

WHITWELL-ON-THE-HILL – North Yorkshire – 502 R 21 – ⊠ York

23 C2

🚇 London 240 mi – Kingston-upon-Hull 47 mi – Scarborough 29 mi
– York 13 mi

🏠 **The Stone Trough Inn**　　　　　　　🌲 **P** **VISA** **CO**

Kirkham Abbey, East : 1 ¾ m. by A 64 on Kirkham Priory rd ⊠ YO60 7JS
– ☎ (01653) 618 713 – www.stonetroughinn.co.uk – info@stonetroughinn.co.uk
– Fax (01653) 618 819 – Closed 25 December
Rest – (Closed Monday except Bank Holiday Monday) Carte £ 20/34

♦ Friendly rustic pub, two minutes from the striking ruins of Kirkham Abbey. Wideranging menu on a sound local base: satisfying and full of flavour. Warm, attentive service.

WHORLTON – Durham – see Barnard Castle

WICKFORD – Essex – 504 V 29 – see Basildon

WIGGINTON – Oxon. – see Banbury

WIGHT (Isle of) – Isle of Wight – 503 P/Q 31 – pop. 124 577 📗 Great Britain

🚢 from Ryde to Portsmouth (Hovertravel Ltd) frequent services daily (10 mn)
– from Ryde to Portsmouth (Wightlink Ltd) frequent services daily (15 mn)
– from East Cowes to Southampton (Red Funnel Ferries) frequent services
daily (22 mn)
🚢 from East Cowes to Southampton (Red Funnel Ferries) frequent services
daily (1 h) – from Yarmouth to Lymington (Wightlink Ltd) frequent services
daily (30 mn) – from Fishbourne to Portsmouth (Wightlink Ltd) frequent
services daily (35 mn)
🔵 Island★★
🟢 Osborne House, East Cowes★★ AC – Carisbrooke Castle, Newport★★ AC
(Keep ⩽★) – Brading★ (Roman Villa★ AC, St Mary's Church★, Nunwell
House★ AC) – Shorwell : St Peter's Church★ (wall paintings★)

Bonchurch – Isle of Wight – ⊠ Isle of Wight

6 B3

X **The Pond Café**　　　　　　　　　　🌲 **VISA** **CO**

Bonchurch ⊠ PO38 1RG – ☎ (01983) 855 666 – www.thepondcafe.com
– info@thepondcafe.com – Closed Tuesday and Wednesday lunch
Rest – Carte £ 30/35 **s**

♦ Intimate restaurant, with duck pond, in sleepy hamlet. Cosy sunlit terrace. Island's larder utilised to the full for seasonal dishes in unfussy, halogen lit surroundings.

Brighstone

6 B3

🏠 **The Lodge** without rest ⌘　　　　　🚗 🌲 🌲 **P**

Main Rd ⊠ PO30 4DJ – ☎ (01983) 741 272 – www.thelodgebrighstone.com
– thelodgeb@hotmail.com – Fax (01983) 741 272 – Easter-November
7 rm ⊐ – †£45/75 ††£70/75

♦ Victorian country house set in two and a half acres: quiet location. Real fire centrepiece of large sitting room. Completely co-ordinated rooms of varnished pine.

Niton – Isle of Wight   6 **B3**

🏠 **The Hermitage** without rest ⌁   🚗 🕦 🞲 **P** **VISA** **©©** **AE**
North : 3 m by Newport rd (A3020) – ⌀ *(01983) 730 010*
– www.hermitage-iow.co.uk – enquiries@hermitage.iow.co.uk
10 rm ⚏ – **†**£45/98 **††**£110/150

♦ 19C country house in 12 acres of gardens; flora and fauna abound. Traditional bedrooms, named after their antique furniture. The best boast impressive period beds and luxury bathrooms.

Seaview – Isle of Wight – pop. 2 286 – ⊠ Isle of Wight   6 **B3**

🏠🏠 **Priory Bay** ⌁   🚗 🕦 🞲 🏊 🞲 🞲 **P** **VISA** **©©** **AE**
Priory Drive, Southeast : 1½ m. by B 3330 ⊠ *PO34 5BU –* ⌀ *(01983) 613 146*
– www.priorybay.co.uk – enquiries@priorybay.co.uk – Fax (01983) 616 539
18 rm ⚏ – **†**£115/225 **††**£200/270 – 2 suites
Rest *The Restaurant* – Menu £30 (dinner) – Carte £20/35

♦ Medieval priory with Georgian additions, surrounded by woodland. High ceilinged drawing room and bar area with leaded windows. Characterful rooms. Main Restaurant has views of the garden.

🏠🏠 **Seaview**   ⚿ 🞲 **VISA** **©©** **AE** **①**
High St ⊠ *PO34 5EX –* ⌀ *(01983) 612 711 – www.seaviewhotel.co.uk*
– reception@seaviewhotel.co.uk – Fax (01983) 613 729 – Closed 21-26 December
25 rm ⚏ – **†**£95/165 **††**£165/199 – 3 suites
Rest *The Restaurant and Sunshine Room* – see restaurant listing

♦ Victorian hotel with smart genuine style. Integral part of the community, on street leading to seafront. Bold modern bedrooms and nautically styled, welcoming public areas.

🞲🞲 **The Restaurant and Sunshine Room** – at The Seaview Hotel   🞲 **AK**
High St ⊠ *PO34 5EX –* ⌀ *(01983) 612 711*   **VISA** **©©** **AE** **①**
– www.seaviewhotel.co.uk – reception@seaviewhotel.co.uk – Fax (01983) 613 729
– Closed 21-26 December
Rest – (dinner only and lunch Saturday and Sunday) (in bar Sunday dinner except Bank Holidays) (booking essential) Menu £30

♦ Traditional dining room with contemporary conservatory. Boasts rare model ship collection. Very visual, modern, elaborate dishes make the best use of seasonal Island produce.

Shanklin – Isle of Wight – pop. 8 055 – ⊠ Isle of Wight   6 **B3**

▶ Newport 9 mi
🛈 67 High St ⌀ (01983) 813 818, info@islandbreaks.co.uk
⛳ The Fairway Lake Sandown, ⌀ (01983) 403 217

🏠 **Rylstone Manor** ⌁   🚗 🞲 **P** **VISA** **©©**
Rylstone Gdns ⊠ *PO37 6RG –* ⌀ *(01983) 862 806 – www.rylstone-manor.co.uk*
– rylstone.manor@btinternet.com – Fax (01983) 862 806 – Closed January
9 rm ⚏ – **†**£60/120 **††**£140/164   **Rest** – (dinner only) Menu £28 **s**

♦ Part 19C former gentleman's residence set in the town's cliff-top gardens. Interior has a comfortable period feel. Well furnished, individually styled bedrooms. Characterful Victorian hued dining room.

🏠 **Grange Bank** without rest   🞲 ⚿ **P** **VISA** **©©**
Grange Rd ⊠ *PO37 6NN –* ⌀ *(01983) 862 337 – www.grangebank.co.uk*
– grangebank@btinternet.com – February-November
9 rm ⚏ – **†**£29/45 **††**£58/70

♦ Extended Victorian house near high street. Comfortable, simple and immaculately kept with friendly, domestic ambience. Good value accommodation.

🏠 **Foxhills** without rest   🚗 🞲 ⚿ **P** **VISA** **©©**
30 Victoria Ave ⊠ *PO37 6LS –* ⌀ *(01983) 862 329 – www.foxhillsofshanklin.co.uk*
– info@foxhillsofshanklin.co.uk – Fax (01983) 866 666 – April-October
8 rm ⚏ – **†**£88/108 **††**£88/108

♦ Attractive house in leafy avenue with woodland to the rear. Bright lounge with fireplace. Bedrooms in pastel shades. Unusual jacuzzi, spa and beauty treatments.

ENGLAND

Totland – Isle of Wight – pop. 7 317 – ⊠ Isle of Wight   6 **A3**
> ▶ Newport 13 mi

🏠 **Sentry Mead**   🗝 ⁿⁱ P VISA ⚫⚫
Madeira Rd ⊠ PO39 0BJ – ℰ (01983) 753 212 – www.sentrymead.co.uk
– info@sentrymead.co.uk – Fax (01983) 754 710
12 rm – †£45/60 ††£90/120
Rest – (residents only Monday-Tuesday) (bar lunch Monday-Saturday)
Carte £26/37
♦ Detached Victorian house with quiet garden 100 yards from beach. Traditional interiors include bar area and conservatory lounge. Comfortable rooms furnished with light wood. Popular menus in dining room.

Ventnor – Isle of Wight – pop. 6 257 – ⊠ Isle of Wight   6 **B3**
> ▶ Newport 10 mi
> 🛈 34 High St, ℰ (01983) 813818, info@islandbreaks.co.uk
> 🖻 Steephill Down Rd, ℰ (01983) 853 326

🏘 **Royal**   🗝 ⌧ ⊫ ⚙ P VISA ⚫⚫ AE ⓪
Belgrave Rd ⊠ PO38 1JJ – ℰ (01983) 852 186 – www.royalhoteliow.co.uk
– enquiries@royalhoteliow.co.uk – Fax (01983) 855 395 – Closed 2 weeks January
55 rm – ⊆ – †£131/177 ††£200/221
Rest – (bar lunch Monday-Saturday) Menu £37 **s**
♦ Largest hotel on the island, a Victorian property, in the classic style of English seaside hotels. Traditional décor throughout the public areas and comfortable bedrooms. Light lunches in conservatory; classic meals in capacious dining room.

✗✗ **The Hambrough** with rm   ⩽ 🗝 AE rest, ⁿⁱ VISA ⚫⚫
❀ *Hambrough Rd ⊠ PO38 1SQ – ℰ (01983) 856 333 – www.thehambrough.com*
– info@thehambrough.com – Fax (01983) 857 260
– Closed 2 weeks Christmas, 1 week spring, and 1 week autumn
7 rm – †£80/180 ††£160/200, ⊆ £14
Rest – (Closed Sunday and Monday) Menu £22/45
Spec. Terrine of smoked eel with foie gras and pork belly. Fillet of sea bass, crab and tomato vierge. Blackberry soufflé with Ventnor stout ice cream.
♦ Victorian house with contrastingly modish bar and avant-garde restaurant. Young chef creates accomplished and innovative dishes, underpinned by a sound classical base. State-of-the-art rooms in neutral hues.

Yarmouth – Isle of Wight – ⊠ Isle of Wight   6 **A3**
> ▶ Newport 10 mi

🏘 **The George**   ⩽ 🗝 ⚙ VISA ⚫⚫ AE
Quay St ⊠ PO41 0PE – ℰ (01983) 760 331 – www.thegeorge.co.uk
– res@thegeorge.co.uk – Fax (01983) 760 425
18 rm ⊆ – †£100/138 ††£268
Rest *The Brasserie* – see restaurant listing
♦ 17C quayside hotel in shadow of Yarmouth Castle. Flagged central hall and extensive wood panelling. Traditionally decorated bedrooms; best are 'balcony suites' with views of Solent.

✗ **The Brasserie** – at The George Hotel   ⩽ 🗝 🗝 VISA ⚫⚫ AE
Quay St ⊠ PO41 0PE – ℰ (01983) 760 331 – www.thegeorge.co.uk
– res@thegeorge.co.uk – Fax (01983) 760 425
Rest – Carte £33/48
♦ Informal brasserie restaurant overlooks terrace and garden, with views out to sea. Mediterranean-influenced menu.

St Lawrence – Isle of Wight – ⊠ Isle of Wight   6 **B3**
> ▶ Newport 16 mi

🏠 **Little Orchard** without rest   🗝 ⚙ P
Undercliffe Drive, West : 1 m. on A 3055 ⊠ PO38 1YA – ℰ (01983) 731 106
3 rm ⊆ – †£42 ††£60
♦ A pretty, detached stone cottage with secluded rear garden and some views of the sea. Large, welcoming lounge with piano. Simple, comfortable bedrooms.

WILLESLEY – Wiltshire – **503** N 29   4 **C2**
> ▶ London 115 mi – Bristol 23 mi – Swindon 37 mi – Gloucester 38 mi

⌂   **Beaufort House** without rest   🚗 ⅍ **P**
> ✉ GL8 8QU – ☏ (01666) 880 444 – beauforthouseuk@aol.com
> **4 rm** ☲ – †£75 ††£89
> ◆ Part 17C former inn and staging post with an attractive garden. Much improved
> and modernised by current owner. Smart bedrooms; those at the rear look over
> garden and are quieter.

WILLIAN – Herts. – see Letchworth

WILLINGTON – Ches. – see Tarporley

WILMINGTON – E. Sussex – **504** U 31 – see Eastbourne

WILMINGTON – Kent – **504** V 29 – see Dartford

WILMSLOW – Cheshire – **502** N 24 – **pop. 28 604**   20 **B3**
> ▶ London 189 mi – Liverpool 38 mi – Manchester 12 mi
>   – Stoke-on-Trent 27 mi
> 🖼 Great Warford Mobberley, ☏ (01565) 872 148

🏨   **Stanneylands**   🚗 ⅼ ⅍ ⅋ 👍 **P** **VISA** **◑◐** **AE** **①**
> Stanneylands Rd, North : 1 m. by A 34 ✉ SK9 4EY – ☏ (01625) 525 225
> – www.primahotels.co.uk – enquiries@stanneylandshotel.co.uk – Fax (01625)
> 537 282
> **53 rm** – †£70/165 ††£70/165, ☲ £14.50 – 1 suite
> **Rest** *The Restaurant* – (residents only Sunday dinner) Menu £20/32
> – Carte £31/43
> ◆ Attractive 19C redbrick hotel standing in mature grounds; exudes pleasant, country
> house style. Two characterful lounges and comfortable, traditional bedrooms. Comfy
> oak-panelled surroundings for diners.

⌂   **Marigold House** without rest   🚗 ⅍ **P**
> 132 Knutsford Rd, Southwest : 1 m. on B 5086 ✉ SK9 6JH – ☏ (01625) 584 414
> – Closed Christmas
> **2 rm** ☲ – †£38 ††£55
> ◆ 18C former farmhouse, 10 minutes from Manchester Airport; flagged floors
> throughout with log fires and antiques. Oak beams in bedrooms. Communal break-
> fast at superb oak table.

WIMBORNE MINSTER – Dorset – **503** O 31 – **pop. 14 844**   4 **C3**
> ▶ London 112 mi – Bournemouth 10 mi – Dorchester 23 mi – Salisbury 27 mi
>   – Southampton 30 mi
> 🖼 29 High St ☏ (01202) 886116, wimbornetic@eastdorset.gov.uk
> ◉ Town★ - Minster★ – Priest's House Museum★ **AC**
> 🖼 Kingston Lacy★★ **AC**, NW : 3 m. by B 3082

XXX   **Les Bouviers** with rm   🚗 ⅋ **P** **VISA** **◑◐** **AE**
> Arrowsmith Rd, Canford Magna, South : 2¼ m. by A 349 and A 341 ✉ BH21 3BD
> – ☏ (01202) 889 555 – www.lesbouviers.co.uk – info@lesbouviers.co.uk
> – Fax (01202) 639428
> **6 rm** – †£102 ††£200, ☲ £12.50
> **Rest** – (Closed Sunday dinner) Menu £20/30 – Carte £30/43
> ◆ Plush yet homely restaurant affording views to acres of mature grounds. Formal
> feel lightened by personable service. Complex dishes with modern twists. Stylish
> bedrooms.

WINCHCOMBE – Gloucestershire – 503 O 28 – pop. 3 682   4 D1

▶ London 100 mi – Birmingham 43 mi – Gloucester 26 mi – Oxford 43 mi
🛈 Town Hall, High St ℰ (01242) 602925, winchcombetic@tewkesbury.gov.uk

ENGLAND

⌂ **Isbourne Manor House** without rest
Castle St ⊠ GL54 5JA – ℰ (01242) 602 281 – www.isbourne-manor.co.uk
– felicity@isbourne-manor.co.uk – Fax (01242) 602 281 – Closed Christmas
3 rm ☲ – †£80/85 ††£95/100
♦ Wisteria-clad Georgian and Elizabethan manor. Cosy drawing room: antique furniture and open fire. One room has a four-poster bed, one a roof top terrace. Riverside garden.

⌂ **Westward** without rest
Sudeley Lodge, East : 1½ m. by Castle St on Sudeley Lodge/Parks/Farm rd
⊠ GL54 5JB – ℰ (01242) 604 372 – www.westward-sudeley.co.uk
– jimw@haldon.co.uk – Fax (01242) 604 640 – March-November
3 rm ☲ – ††£65/85
♦ Secluded, personally run 18C farmhouse: elegant, wood-floored drawing room and charming sitting room, bedrooms share fine views of 550-acre estate and mature gardens.

XX **Wesley House** with rm
High St ⊠ GL54 5LJ – ℰ (01242) 602 366 – www.wesleyhouse.co.uk
– enquiries@wesleyhouse.co.uk – Fax (01242) 609 046
5 rm ☲ – †£65 ††£80
Rest – (Closed Sunday dinner) Menu £38 (dinner) – Carte lunch approx. £22 **s**
♦ Hugely characterful part 15C house: dine amongst the beams or in the stylish glass-roofed extension. Tasty modern British cooking with original twists. Smilingly quaint rooms.

XX **5 North St** (Marcus Ashenford)
✿
5 North St ⊠ GL54 5LH – ℰ (01242) 604 566 – marcusashenford@yahoo.co.uk
– Fax (01242) 603 788 – Closed 2 weeks January, 1 week August, Sunday dinner,
Tuesday lunch and Monday
Rest – Menu £24/40 – Carte (dinner) £34/44
Spec. Shallot tart tatin with pigeon and coffee sauce, Turbot, asparagus, sorrel and lobster vinaigrette. Salted caramel mousse with peanut praline.
♦ Personally run, cosy, 17C timbered restaurant with low-beamed ceiling and a pleasantly relaxed, friendly atmosphere. Good value menus offer flavoursome and refined cooking.

X **Wesley House Bar & Grill**
20 High St ⊠ GL54 5LJ – ℰ (01242) 602 366 – www.wesleyhouse.co.uk
– enquiries@wesleyhouse.co.uk – Fax (01242) 609 046 – Closed Sunday and
Monday
Rest – Carte £15/20 **s**
♦ Located on busy high street, this is a buzzy place to be, with trendy bar, comfy lounge, and wood-floored dining area serving authentic Spanish tapas beneath the big mirrors.

🍴 **The White Hart Inn** with rm
High St ⊠ GL54 5LJ – ℰ (01242) 602 359 – www.wineandsausage.com
– info@wineandsausage.com – Fax (01242) 602 703
8 rm ☲ – †£45/95 ††£85/115   **Rest** – Menu £18 (lunch) – Carte £18/35
♦ Whitewashed former coaching inn with rustic feel. Hearty homemade dishes; sausages have their own menu. Friendly, chatty atmosphere and service. Well-stocked wine shop. Comfortable bedrooms have a traditional feel; the rear rooms are quieter.

Undecided between two equivalent establishments?
Within each category, establishments are classified
in our order of preference.

800

WINCHELSEA – East Sussex – 504 W 31 ▮ Great Britain   9 C3
- ◻ London 64 mi – Brighton 46 mi – Folkestone 30 mi
- ◙ Town★ – St Thomas Church (effigies★)

⌂ **Strand House**   ⇗ ⌁ 🗟 **P** _VISA_ ⓂⓄ AE
Tanyard's Lane, East :¼ m. on A 259 ⊠ *TN36 4JT* – ℰ *(01797) 226 276*
– www.thestrandhouse.co.uk – info@thestrandhouse.co.uk – Fax (01797) 224 806
10 rm � – †£60/70 ††£110/125
Rest – (booking essential) (by arrangement) Menu £30
♦ 14C and 15C half-timbered house of low beams and inglenook fireplaces: carefully tended rear garden shaded by tall trees, snug lounge; well-kept rooms in traditional style. Simple homecooking.

WINCHESTER – Hampshire – 503 P 30 – pop. 41 420 ▮ Great Britain   6 B2
- ◻ London 72 mi – Bristol 76 mi – Oxford 52 mi – Southampton 12 mi
- ℹ Guildhall, High Street ℰ (01962) 840500, tourism@winchester.gov.uk
- ◙ City★★ - Cathedral★★★ **AC** B – Winchester College★ **AC** B **B** – Castle Great Hall★B **D** – God Begot House★B **A**
- ◙ St Cross Hospital★★ **AC** A

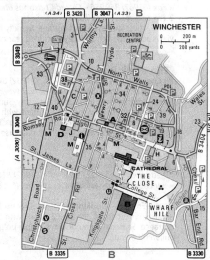

Alresford Rd .... A 2	Eastgate St .... B 16	St George's St .... B 32
Andover Rd .... B 3	Easton Lane .... A 18	St Paul's Hill .... B 33
Bereweeke Rd .... A 5	East Hill .... B 15	St Peter's St .... B 34
Bridge St .... B 6	Friarsgate .... B 19	Southgate St .... B 35
Broadway (The) .... B 7	High St .... B	Stockbridge Rd .... B 37
Brooks Shopping Centre ... B 8	Kingsgate Rd............. A 22	Stoney Lane .... A 36
Chilbolton Ave............. A 9	Magdalen Hill............. B 23	Sussex St............. B 38
City Rd............. B 10	Middle Brook St .... B 24	Union St............. B 39
Clifton Terrace............. B 12	Park Rd .... A 26	Upper High St .... B 40

🏨 **Hotel du Vin**   ⇗ 🅺 ⌁ ⚙ **P** _VISA_ ⓂⓄ AE ⓪
14 Southgate St ⊠ *SO23 9EF* – ℰ *(01962) 841 414 – www.hotelduvin.com*
– info.winchester@hotelduvin.com – Fax (01962) 842 458   B**i**
24 rm – †£145/215 ††£145/215, ⊻ £13.50
Rest *Bistro* – see restaurant listing
♦ Elegant bedrooms, each with CD player, mini bar and distinct décor reflecting its wine house sponsors, in a 1715 redbrick house. Smart Champagne bar with inviting sofas.

🏠 **Giffard House** without rest ⬜ ❄ 🗝 **P** 🚗 **VISA** ⓒ **AE**
50 Christchurch Rd ⊠ SO23 9SU – 𝒞 (01962) 852628 – www.giffardhotel.co.uk
– giffardhotel@aol.com – Fax (01962) 856722
– Closed 24 December-1January **Bs**
13 rm ⬜ – †£69/83 ††£125
♦ Imposing part Victorian, part Edwardian house. Well-furnished throughout; comfortable sitting room with large fireplace. Immaculate rooms with good facilities.

↑ **29 Christchurch Road** without rest ❄ 🗝
29 Christchurch Road – 𝒞 (01962) 868661 – www.fetherstondilke.com
– dilke@waitrose.com – Fax (01962) 868661 **Bv**
3 rm ⬜ – †£50/70 ††£75/90
♦ 21C Regency style guesthouse in attractive residential area. Tastefully furnished guest areas display classical artwork. 3 comfy bedrooms; 2 with shower, 1 with private bathroom.

↑ **Dawn Cottage** without rest ≼ ⬜ ❄ **P**
Romsey Rd ⊠ SO22 5PQ – 𝒞 (01962) 869956 – dawncottage@hotmail.com
– Fax (01962) 869956 – Closed Christmas and New Year **Ac**
3 rm ⬜ – †£55 ††£70
♦ Attractive, spotlessly kept cottage; friendly hosts. Comfortable bedrooms; all have views across the Itchen Valley. Secluded rear garden flanked by tall trees.

🍴 **The Black Rat** ⟷ **VISA** ⓒ ⓪
88 Chesil Street ⊠ SO23 0HX – 𝒞 (01962) 844465 – www.theblackrat.co.uk
– Closed late December- mid January, 2 weeks October and 1 week April **Ba**
Rest – (dinner only and lunch Saturday-Sunday) Carte £29/35
♦ Hugely atmospheric, rustic restaurant with busy walls and unique garden huts. Nightly changing modern British menu boasts produce from within 50 miles and veg/herbs from allotment. Generous, flavoursome cooking.

🍴 **Brasserie Blanc** 🗝 🅰🅺 ⟷ 🚗 **AE**
19-20 Jewry St ⊠ SO23 8RZ – 𝒞 (01962) 810870 – www.brasserieblanc.com
– winchester@brasserieblanc.com – Fax (01962) 810871
– Closed 25 December **Bx**
Rest – French – (booking advisable) Menu £15/18 – Carte £18/38
♦ Bustling restaurant set over 2 floors, with terrace on each level and chic bar at entrance. Seasonal menu displays simply prepared classical French cooking; special children's menu.

🍴 **Bistro** – at Hotel du Vin ⬜ 🗝 **P** **VISA** ⓒ **AE**
14 Southgate St ⊠ SO23 9EF – 𝒞 (01962) 841414 – Fax (01962) 842458 **Bi**
Rest – (booking essential) Carte £25/35 ⌘
♦ Oenophile memorabilia covers panelled cream walls; hops crown tall sash windows. Terrace under broad sunshades. Classic modern flavours set off the carefully chosen wines.

🍺 **The Wykeham Arms** with rm ⬜ 🗝 **P** **VISA** ⓒ **AE**
75 Kingsgate St ⊠ SO23 9PE – 𝒞 (01962) 853834
– www.accommodating-inns.co.uk/wykeham
– wykehamarms@accommodating-inns.co.uk – Fax (01962) 854411
– Closed 25 December **Bu**
14 rm ⬜ – †£62 ††£150
Rest – (Closed Sunday dinner) (booking essential) Carte £20/26
♦ Characterful, curio-crammed 18C inn, hidden away betwixt cathedral and college. Traditional lunch menu; more elaborate evening à la carte. Individually-styled bedrooms, those in annex are quieter, with their own terrace garden.

at Easton Northeast : 4 m. by A 3090 - A - off B 3047 – ⊠ Winchester

🏠 **The Chestnut Horse**   🍴 **P** 𝘝𝘐𝘚𝘈 ⊙⊙
⊠ SO21 1EG – ℰ (01962) 779257 – www.thechestnuthorse.com
– info@thechestnuthorse.com – Fax (01962) 779037
Rest – Carte £ 16/30
♦ 16C pub with colourful décor; choose from the red room, green room or pretty terrace. Extensive menu displays pub classics alongside more modern dishes and interesting specials.

at Ovington East : 5¾ m. by B 3404 - A - and A 31 – ⊠ Winchester

🏠 **The Bush Inn**   🖿 🍴 **P** 𝘝𝘐𝘚𝘈 ⊙⊙ 𝘈𝘌
⊠ SO24 0RE – ℰ (01962) 732764 – thebushinn@wadworth.co.uk – Fax (01962)
735130 – Closed 25 December
Rest – (Closed Sunday dinner) Carte £ 21/35
♦ Friendly, family-run 18C inn hidden away in idyllic spot on banks of River Itchen, its walls cluttered with curios and taxidermy. Wholesome, unfussy dishes on blackboard menus.

at Pitt Southwest : 3 m by B 3040 off A 3090 – ⊠ Winchester

🏠 **Enmill Barn** without rest ⌂   🖿 🍴 🕸 (ⁱ)
Enmill lane ⊠ SO22 5QR – ℰ (01962) 856740 – www.enmill-barn.co.uk
– jennywas21@hotmail.com – Fax (01962) 854219 – Closed Christmas-New Year
3 rm ⌂ – †£40/45 ††£70
♦ 19C cottage with unusual chalk barn and lovely gardens. Sitting room with open fire, countryside views and wooden cider press. Pleasant bedrooms, 2 with shower, 1 with private bathroom. Fresh, organic breakfast.

at Sparsholt Northwest : 3½ m. by B 3049 - A – ⊠ Winchester

🏘 **Lainston House** ⌂   ≤ 🔟 🕸 🍴 𝟦 🕸 (ⁱ) 𝐬𝐚 **P** 𝘝𝘐𝘚𝘈 ⊙⊙ 𝘈𝘌 ⊙
⊠ SO21 2LT – ℰ (01962) 776088 – www.exclusivehotels.co.uk
– enquiries@lainstonhouse.com – Fax (01962) 776672
48 rm ⌂ – †£ 125/235 ††£ 235 – 2 suites
Rest *Avenue* – Menu £ 32/45 – Carte £ 47/60
♦ Charming 17C manor with pretty grounds, parks and old herb garden. Traditionally styled lounge, cedar-panelled bar and up-to-date gym. Rooms, some more modern, vary in size. Dark wood dining room overlooks lawn.

🏠 **Plough Inn**   🖿 🍴 **P** 𝘝𝘐𝘚𝘈 ⊙⊙
Main Road ⊠ SO21 2NW – ℰ (01962) 776353 – Fax (01962) 776400
– Closed 25 December
Rest – (booking essential) Carte £ 20/30
♦ Traditionally styled, open plan inn serving good old pub favourites as well as more elaborate dishes. Delightful lawned garden with countryside views and children's play area.

WINDERMERE – Cumbria – **502** L 20 – pop. 7 941 📗 Great Britain   21 **A2**
🖸 London 274 mi – Blackpool 55 mi – Carlisle 46 mi – Kendal 10 mi
🖪 Victoria St ℰ (015394) 46499, windermeretic@southlakeland.gov.uk
🖾 Lake Windermere★★ – Brockhole National Park Centre★ **AC**, NW : 2 m. by A 591

Plan on next page

🏘 **Langdale Chase**   ≤ 🖿 𝐀𝐂 rest, **P** 𝘝𝘐𝘚𝘈 ⊙⊙ 𝘈𝘌 ⊙
Northwest : 3 m. on A 591 ⊠ LA23 1LW – ℰ (015394) 32201
– www.langdalechase.co.uk – sales@langdalechase.co.uk – Fax (015394) 32604
28 rm ⌂ – †£80/110 ††£90/210 – 1 suite   **Rest** – Menu £ 19/34
♦ Substantial 19C house with beautiful gardens and wonderful lakeside setting boasting a wealth of ornate Victoriana and superbly preserved carvings. Pleasantly styled rooms. Formal dining in a classic room; sweeping views across the lake.

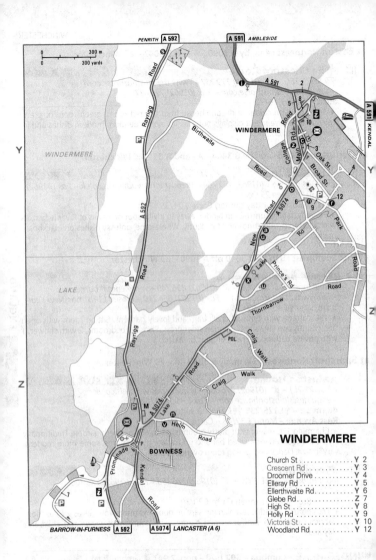

WINDERMERE

Holbeck Ghyll ⊗ ≤ 록 ⌂ ⇗ ℡ ❀ 🛜 ♨ P VISA ◑ AE
*Holbeck Lane, Northwest : 3¼ m. by A 591 ⊠ LA23 1LU – ℘ (015394) 32375
– www.holbeckghyll.com – stay@holbeckghyll.com – Fax (015394) 34743
– Closed first 2 weeks January*
21 rm ⌑ – ♦£175/375 ♦♦£320/450 – 5 suites
Rest – (booking essential at lunch) Menu £30/36 – Carte (lunch) £33/55⊛
Spec. West coast scallops with celeriac and balsamic dressing. Best end of
lamb with puy lentils, swede and haggis beignets. Raspberry millefeuille, sorbet, vanilla cream.
♦ Charming Victorian hunting lodge with pleasant gardens and stunning views.
Individually decorated bedrooms combine country house style with a contemporary
edge. Cooking is confident and precise; appealing menus are complemented by an
exceptional wine list.

Cedar Manor
🏠 🚭 📶 P VISA ⓪ AE

Ambleside Rd ⊠ LA23 1AX – ℰ *(015394) 43 192 – www.cedarmanor.co.uk*
– info@cedarmanor.co.uk – Fax (015394) 45 970 – Closed 24-26 December   **Yi**
10 rm ☲ – **♦**£63/90 **♦♦**£150/170 – 1 suite
Rest – (dinner only) Menu £28 – Carte £25/33
♦ 1860s house, its mature garden shaded by an ancient cedar. Sizeable bedrooms, including the Coniston Room with views of Langdale Pike and lounge with ornate stained glass. Locally sourced menus.

Glenburn
🏠 🚿 📶 P VISA ⓪

New Rd ⊠ LA23 2EE – ℰ *(015394) 42 649 – www.glenburn.uk.com*
– glen.burn@virgin.net – Fax (015394) 88 998   **Yu**
16 rm ☲ – **♦**£70 **♦♦**£78/92
Rest – (dinner only) (booking essential) Menu £22 – Carte £16/27
♦ Well-placed for exploring the central Lakes, a privately run hotel offering homely rooms in soft-toned décor plus a small bar and lounge with an open fire. Neatly set dining room with peach and white linen.

Newstead without rest
🚿 P

New Rd ⊠ LA23 2EE – ℰ *(015394) 44 485 – www.newstead-guesthouse.co.uk*
– info@newstead-guesthouse.co.uk – Fax (015394) 88 904
– Closed 1 week Christmas   **Ya**
9 rm ☲ – **♦**£45/70 **♦♦**£55/105
♦ A warm welcome is assured at this restored Victorian residence. Original features aplenty; fireplaces in all the cosy, spotless bedrooms. Hearty breakfasts a speciality.

Fir Trees without rest
🏠 🚿 📶 P VISA ⓪ AE ①

Lake Rd ⊠ LA23 2EQ – ℰ *(015394) 42 272 – www.fir-trees.com*
– enquiries@fir-trees.com – Fax (015394) 42 512   **Zx**
9 rm ☲ – **♦**£54/62 **♦♦**£64/72
♦ Built in 1888 as gentleman's residence and retains original pine staircase. Contrastingly modern, stylish and individually decorated bedrooms. Broad-windowed breakfast room.

The Howbeck
🚿 📶 P VISA ⓪

New Rd ⊠ LA23 2LA – ℰ *(015394) 44 739 – www.howbeck.co.uk*
– relax@howbeck.co.uk – Closed 24-25 December   **Yo**
11 rm ☲ – **♦**£71/119 **♦♦**£95/158   **Rest** – (by arrangement) Menu £29 **s**
♦ Victorian slate house on the outskirts. Well appointed lounge with maritime theme. Spacious bedrooms, some boasting four-posters, stylishly painted in up-to-date palette. Attractive dining room with well-laid tables: home-cooked, daily changing dinners.

1 Park Rd
🚿 📶 P VISA ⓪ AE ①

1 Park Rd ⊠ LA23 2AN – ℰ *(015394) 42 107 – www.1parkroad.com*
– enquiries@1parkroad.com – Fax (015394) 48 997
– Closed 25-26 December   **Yr**
6 rm – **♦**£72/86 **♦♦**£92/98   **Rest** – Menu £22 (by arrangement)
♦ Large lakeland property built in 1883, with relaxing guest lounge and piano; resident dog, Maggie, and well-equipped bedrooms (those on the top floor are the best). Fresh cooking served in modern dining room.

Beaumont House without rest
🚿 📶 P VISA ⓪

Holly Rd ⊠ LA23 2AF – ℰ *(015394) 47 075 – www.lakesbeaumont.co.uk*
– thebeaumonthotel@btinternet.com – Fax (015394) 88 311
– Closed 3 weeks January   **Yn**
10 rm ☲ – **♦**£45/80 **♦♦**£75/136
♦ Substantial Victorian house, its period stained glass and tiling still intact. Good-sized en suite bedrooms, comfortably furnished with a traditional feel.

ENGLAND

ENGLAND

⌂ Glencree without rest
Lake Rd ⊠ LA23 2EQ – ℰ (015394) 45 822 – www.glencreelakes.co.uk
– h.butterworth@btinternet.com   Zs
6 rm ⌨ – ♦£45/60 ♦♦£70
♦ Personally managed, detached guesthouse built of local slate. Spotless, individually decorated - and affordable - rooms in co-ordinated fabrics offer a good level of comfort.

⌂ Braemount House without rest
Sunny Bank Rd, by Queens Drive ⊠ LA23 2EN – ℰ (015394) 45 967
– www.braemount-house.co.uk – enquiries@braemount-house.co.uk
– Fax (015394) 88 154 – Closed Christmas   Zu
8 rm ⌨ – ♦£40/45 ♦♦£70/80
♦ Extended 1870s bay-windowed house: original tiles and decorative glasswork add period character. Homely bedrooms; simple breakfast room with slate fireplace.

✗✗ Miller Howe with rm
Rayrigg Rd ⊠ LA23 1EY – ℰ (015394) 42 536 – www.millerhowe.com
– info@millerhowe.com – Fax (015394) 45 664 – Closed 2 weeks January   Ys
13 rm ⌨ – ♦£150/180 ♦♦£240/300 – 2 suites
Rest – (booking essential) Menu £22/40 – Carte £26/39
♦ Renowned, elegantly furnished lakeside villa with handsomely fitted rooms. Modern Italianate restaurant; distinct Northern character to classic, seasonal dishes. Smart bedrooms.

✗✗ Jerichos
College Rd ⊠ LA23 1EG – ℰ (015394) 42 522 – www.jerichos.co.uk
– enquiries@jerichos.co.uk – Fax (015394) 42 522 – Closed 2 weeks spring,
24-26 December and Thursday   Yz
Rest – (dinner only) Carte £26/37
♦ Personally run restaurant with open kitchen; well-spaced tables, elegant glassware and framed Beryl Cook prints. Local produce enhances rich, complex blend of modern flavours.

✗ Francine's
27 Main Rd ⊠ LA23 1DX – ℰ (015394) 44 088
– www.francinesrestaurantwindermere.co.uk – Fax (015394) 44 088 – Closed
25-26 December, 2 weeks January, 1 week June, last week November and dinner
Sunday-Tuesday   Yc
Rest – (booking essential at dinner) Carte £28/48
♦ Unpretentious bistro/coffee house with light décor, well-spaced tables and an informal feel, offers traditional French-influenced cooking. Eponymous owner bakes the cakes.

at Bowness-on-Windermere South : 1 m. - Z – ⊠ Windermere

⌂⌂ Gilpin Lodge ⅏
Crook Rd, Southeast : 2½ m. by A 5074 on B 5284 ⊠ LA23 3NE – ℰ (015394)
88 818 – www.gilpinlodge.co.uk – hotel@gilpinlodge.co.uk – Fax (015394) 88 058
20 rm (dinner included) ⌨ – ♦£200/220 ♦♦£310/380
Rest – (booking essential for non-residents) Menu £28/50 – Carte lunch
£20/33
♦ Extended country house with comfortable, very English sitting room and delightful Oriental bar and terrace. Most bedrooms have contemporary décor; private hot tubs in Garden suites. Four individually styled dining rooms. Cooking combines classic technique and modern influences.

⌂⌂ Storrs Hall ⅏
South : 2 m. on A 592 ⊠ LA23 3LG – ℰ (015394) 47 111 – www.elh.co.uk
– storrshall@elhmail.co.uk – Fax (015394) 47 555
29 rm ⌨ – ♦£113 ♦♦£304 – 1 suite
Rest The Terrace – Menu £20/40 s
♦ Oils, antiques and fine fabrics fill an elegant Georgian mansion. Traditional orangery, 19C bar in dark wood and stained glass and comfortable, individually decorated rooms. Ornate dining room overlooks lawns and lake.

Linthwaite House ⚜ ≤ 🚗 🔟 🔇 🕯 P VISA ◑◐ AE
Crook Rd, South : ¾ m. by A 5074 on B 5284 ⊠ LA23 3JA – 𝒞 *(015394) 88 600*
– www.linthwaite.com – stay@linthwaite.com – Fax (015394) 88 601
32 rm (dinner included) ⊴ – ♦£145/195 ♦♦£310/365
Rest – (light lunch Monday-Saturday) Menu £18/50 **s**
♦ Set in superb elevated position with stunning views of Lake Windermere. Chic, modern rooms. Cane chairs and louvred blinds give conservatory teas an almost colonial feel. Refined modern cooking in restaurant boasting vast mirror collection!

 Lindeth Howe ⚜ ≤ 🚗 📺 🔇 & rm, 🕯 P VISA ◑◐ AE
Storrs Park, South : 1 ¼ m. by A 592 off B 5284 ⊠ LA23 3JF – 𝒞 *(015394) 45 759*
– www.lindeth-howe.co.uk – hotel@lindeth-howe.co.uk – Fax (015394) 46 368
– Closed 2 weeks January
36 rm ⊴ – ♦£85 ♦♦£180
Rest *The Dining Room* – (light lunch Monday-Saturday) Menu £16/38
♦ Once owned by Beatrix Potter, this extended and updated house surveys a broad sweep of Lakeland scenery. Smart, spacious rooms in traditional style, some with useful extras. Spacious dining room with wonderful fell views.

 Fayrer Garden House ⚜ ≤ 🚗 AC rest, P VISA ◑◐
Lyth Valley Rd, South : 1 m. on A 5074 ⊠ LA23 3JP – 𝒞 *(015394) 88 195*
– www.fayrergarden.com – lakescene@fayrergarden.com – Fax (015394) 45 986
– Closed 2-19 January
29 rm ⊴ – ♦£75/142 ♦♦£254/300
Rest *The Terrace* – (dinner only) (booking essential for non-residents)
Menu £38
♦ Extensive house with five acres of grounds and beautiful gardens. Clubby bar and pleasantly homely lounge. Cosy rooms show the owners' feel for thoughtful detail. Wonderful views to be gained from The Terrace.

 Lindeth Fell ⚜ ≤ 🚗 🔇 🕯 P VISA ◑◐
Lyth Valley Rd, South : 1 m. on A 5074 ⊠ LA23 3JP – 𝒞 *(015394) 43 286*
– www.lindethfell.co.uk – kennedy@lindethfell.co.uk – Fax (015394) 47 455
– Closed 2-26 January
14 rm ⊴ – ♦£50/95 ♦♦£130/180 **Rest** – Menu £17/38
♦ In landscaped gardens with bowls and croquet lawns, a privately owned 1907 house with neat, bright rooms, oak-panelled hall and curios and watercolours in the drawing room. Elegantly set dining room with superb Lakeland views.

Angel Inn 🚗 🕯 AC rest, 🕯 P VISA ◑◐ AE ◑
Helm Rd ⊠ LA23 3BU – 𝒞 *(015394) 44 080 – www.the-angelinn.com*
– rooms@the-angelinn.com – Fax (015394) 46 003 Z**v**
14 rm ⊴ – ♦£60/65 ♦♦£150/170 **Rest** – Carte £18/30
♦ Homely, good-sized rooms in an enlarged early 18C cottage, set in a secluded spot yet close to town. Cosy, unpretentious bar, its armchairs centred on an open fire. Dining room has columned archway and landscape murals.

Oakbank House without rest ≤ 🕯 P VISA ◑◐ AE
Helm Rd ⊠ LA23 3BU – 𝒞 *(015394) 43 386 – www.oakbankhousehotel.co.uk*
– enquiries@oakbankhousehotel.co.uk – Fax (015394) 47 965
– Closed 24-27 December Z**n**
12 rm ⊴ – ♦£55 ♦♦£110
♦ Privately run house off the main street. Affordable bedrooms, stylish and individually decorated. Ferns and chandeliers lend grandeur to substantial Cumbrian breakfasts.

 Low House ≤ 🚗 🕯 P VISA ◑◐ ◑
South : 1 m. by A 5074 and B 5284 on Heathwaite rd ⊠ LA23 3NA – 𝒞 *(015394)*
43 156 – www.lowhouse.co.uk – info@lowhouse.co.uk
3 rm ⊴ – ♦£60/90 ♦♦£75/140
Rest – (dinner only) (by arrangement) Menu £25
♦ Charming 17C country house with fine furnishings, log burner, organic breakfasts and welcoming feel. Bedrooms boast top comforts and one can borrow the boat or the Bentley.

ENGLAND

↑ **Fair Rigg** without rest   ≤ ⅍ **P** 𝘝𝘐𝘚𝘈 ⓪

Ferry View, South : ½ m. on A 5074 ⊠ *LA23 3JB –* ✆ *(015394) 43 941*
– www.fairrigg.co.uk – stay@fairrigg.co.uk – Closed 1 week Christmas
6 rm ⌐ – ♦£40/50 ♦♦£68/88

♦ 19C property with pleasing views over the lake to the hills. Hearty Cumbrian breakfasts guaranteed, accompanied by the fine vista. Original fireplaces enhance comfy rooms.

at Troutbeck North : 4 m. by A 592 - Y – ⊠ Windermere

🏨 **Broadoaks** ⌂   ≤ 🚲 🐾 **P** 𝘝𝘐𝘚𝘈 ⓪

Bridge Lane, South : 1 m. on Windermere rd ⊠ *LA23 1LA –* ✆ *(015394) 45 566*
– www.broadoakscountryhouse.co.uk – enquiries@broadoakscountryhouse.co.uk
– Fax (015394) 88 766
15 rm ⌐ – ♦£95/145 ♦♦£95/350   **Rest** – Menu £16/38 **s** – Carte £18/36 **s**

♦ Extended 19C manor in mature 10-acre garden. Victoriana fills the panelled hall and a handsome Music Room with Bechstein piano. Individual rooms, many with four-poster beds. Imposing period fireplace is dining room's focal point.

🍺 **The Queen's Head** with rm   ≤ 🚲 🐾 **P** 𝘝𝘐𝘚𝘈 ⓪

North : ¾ m. on A 592 ⊠ *LA23 1PW –* ✆ *(01539) 432 174*
– www.queensheadhotel.com – feast@queensheadhotel.com – Fax (01539)
431 398
14 rm (dinner included) ⌐ – ♦£76/95 ♦♦£151
Rest – Menu £19 – Carte £19/36

♦ Atmospheric pub with Elizabethan details, set amongst Lakeland scenery. Wide ranging menu features traditional, wholesome cooking and a delicious assortment of homemade bread. Two bedrooms have great fell views.

at Winster South : 4 m. on A 5074 – ⊠ Windermere

🍺 **Brown Horse Inn** with rm   🚲 ⍍ **P** 𝘝𝘐𝘚𝘈 ⓪

on A 5074 ⊠ *LA23 3NR –* ✆ *(01539) 443 443 – www.thebrownhorseinn.co.uk*
– steve@thebrownhorseinn.co.uk
9 rm ⌐ – ♦£50/65 ♦♦£75/90   **Rest** – Carte £18/25

♦ Traditional 1850s coaching inn with real fires and candlelit tables. Robust, flavourful dishes classically prepared with prime local produce. Wine tastings and race nights. Light modern bedrooms are simply decorated yet comfortable.

WINDLESHAM – Surrey – 504 S 29 – pop. 4 103   7 **C1**

🔲 London 40 mi – Reading 18 mi – Southampton 53 mi

🍺 **The Brickmakers**   🚲 **P** 𝘝𝘐𝘚𝘈 ⓪ 𝘈𝘌

Chertsey Rd, East : 1 m. on B 386 ⊠ *GU20 6HT –* ✆ *(01276) 472 267*
– www.4cinns.co.uk – thebrickmakers@4cinns.co.uk – Fax (01276) 451 014
Rest – Menu £24 – Carte £22/30

♦ Red-brick pub with restaurant, conservatory and sizeable garden. Straightforward bar dishes or more substantial à la carte; all well-cooked and full of flavour.

WINDSOR – Windsor and Maidenhead – 504 S 29 – pop. 30 568   11 **D3**

📗 *Great Britain*

🔲 London 28 mi – Reading 19 mi – Southampton 59 mi
🚢 to Marlow, Maidenhead and Cookham (Salter Bros. Ltd) (summer only)
🛈 The Old Booking Hall, Central Station, Thames St ✆ (01753) 743900, windsor.tic@rbwm.gov.uk
◎ Town★ – Castle★★★ : St George's Chapel★★★ AC (stalls★★★), State Apartments★★ AC, North Terrace (≤★★) Z – Eton College★★ AC (College Chapel★★, Wall paintings★) Z
◎ Windsor Park★ AC Y

Plan opposite

ENGLAND

WINDSOR

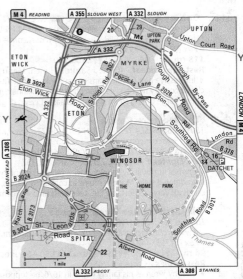

ENGLAND

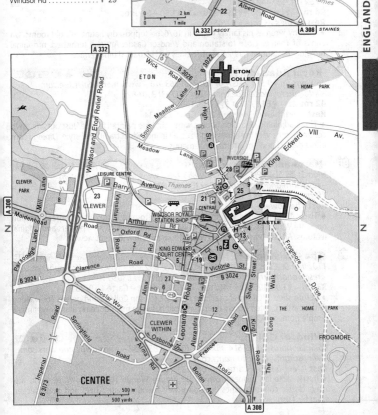

CENTRE

809

ENGLAND

Oakley Court
≤ 🛏 🐕 📺 🐕 🕹 ✕ 🔟 ₰ rm, 🖽 🕸 ₰ 🏠 ₱
Windsor Rd, Water Oakley, West : 3 m. on A 308 ⊠ *SL4*   VISA ⓸ AE ①
5UR – ℰ *(01753) 609 988 – www.oakleycourt.com – info@oakleycourt.com*
– Fax (01753) 609 939
118 rm � – **†**£100/190 **††**£100/300
Rest *The Oakleaf* – (Closed Saturday lunch) Menu £19/33 – Carte £38/50
♦ Impressive part Gothic mansion on banks of river Thames. Spacious public areas in
classic country house style. Many bedrooms in annex, most characterful ones in main
house. Large dining room provides pleasant views of gardens and river.

The Mercure Castle
🏢 🖽 🕸 🕹 🏠 ₱ VISA ⓸
18 High St ⊠ *SL4 1LJ –* ℰ *(01753) 851 577 – www.mercure-uk.com*
– h6618@accor.com – Fax (01753) 856 930 – Closed 25 and 31 December   Zc
104 rm – **†**£150/290 **††**£150/290 – 4 suites
Rest *Eighteen* – Menu £22/35 – Carte £27/37
♦ Former inn built by monks, now a terraced property with Georgian façade. Décor
in traditional style. Modern rooms in converted stables, more characterful ones in old
building. Very comfortable Eighteen with modern menus.

Sir Christopher Wren's House
🐕 🐕 🕹 🖽 rest, 🕸 🕹 🏠
Thames St ⊠ *SL4 1PX –* ℰ *(01753) 861 354*   VISA ⓸ AE ①
– www.sirchristopherwren.co.uk – reservations@windsor.wrensgroup.com
– Fax (01753) 442 490   Ze
90 rm – **†**£85/230 **††**£97/230, � £11.50 – 5 suites
Rest *Strok's* – Carte £32/45
♦ Built by Wren as his family home in 1676, he supposedly haunts his old rooms. On
banks of Thames close to station and Windsor Castle. Antique furnished in original
building. Restaurant has views of Thames and elegant dining terrace.

Royal Adelaide
🖽 🕹 🏠 ₱ VISA ⓸ AE
46 Kings Rd ⊠ *SL4 2AG –* ℰ *(01753) 863 916 – www.meridianleisure.com*
– info@theroyaladelaide.com – Fax (01753) 830 682   Zv
42 rm � – **†**£115/160 **††**£135/160
Rest – (light lunch) Menu £25 – Carte £24/34
♦ Three adjoining Georgian houses with light blue painted façade. Just outside town
centre. Rooms vary in shapes and sizes, all in individual traditional style. Dining room
offers daily changing, international menus.

Harte and Garter
🕸 🏢 ₰ 🕹 VISA ⓸ AE ①
High St ⊠ *SL4 1PH –* ℰ *(01753) 863 426 – www.harteandgarter.com*
– res@harteandgarter.com – Fax (01753) 830 527   Zn
79 rm – **†**£175 **††**£175, � £20
Rest *The Tower* – Carte £30/40
♦ Two 14C inns joined together in the 19C to form a hotel; set in a great location
opposite Windsor Castle. Modern, stylish bedrooms, some with 4 posters and original
features. All day brasserie offers wide ranging menu and great views.

The Christopher
🕹 ₱ VISA ⓸ AE
110 High St, Eton ⊠ *SL4 6AN –* ℰ *(01753) 852 359 – www.thechristopher.co.uk*
– reservations@thechristopher.co.uk – Fax (01753) 830 914   Za
33 rm – **†**£98/125 **††**£148/165, � £10   **Rest** – Carte £19/26
♦ Refurbished 17C former coaching inn close to Eton College and perfect for walking
to the castle. Contemporary bedrooms split between main building and mews annex.
Simple homecooking.

Windsor Grill
⇔ VISA ⓸ AE
65 St Leonards Rd ⊠ *SL4 3BX –* ℰ *(01753) 859 658 – www.awtrestaurants.com*
– windsorgrill@awrestaurants.com   Zx
Rest – Menu £15 – Carte approx. £31
♦ Rustic Victorian property owned by Antony Worrall Thompson. Wide menu displays classic comfort dishes, including well flavoured hung beef and pork/chicken
from his farm.

WINEHAM – W. Sussex – **504** T 31 – see Henfield

WINFORTON – Herefordshire – **503** K 27 – **see Hereford**

WINGHAM – Kent – **504** X 30 – **pop. 1 618**   9 **D2**
> ◻ London 67 mi – Canterbury 7 mi – Dover 16 mi

at Goodnestone South : 2 m. by B 2046 – ⊠ Wingham

🏠 **The Fitzwalter Arms**   *VISA* **◍**
The Street ⊠ *CT3 1PJ* – ℰ *(01304) 840 303* – *Closed 25 December and 1 January*
Rest – (Closed Sunday dinner and Tuesday) Carte £21/28
♦ Striking brick pub with castellated exterior and mullioned windows. Darts, billiards and open fire in characterful beamed bar create feel of village local. Large beer garden.

WINSFORD – Somerset – **503** J 30 – ⊠ **Minehead**   3 **A2**
> ◻ London 194 mi – Exeter 31 mi – Minehead 10 mi – Taunton 32 mi
> ◉ Village ★
> ◉ Exmoor National Park ★★

🏠 **Karslake House**   📶 **P** *VISA* **◍**
Halse Lane ⊠ *TA24 7JE* – ℰ *(01643) 851 242* – *www.karslakehouse.co.uk*
– enquiries@karslakehouse.co.uk – *Fax (01643) 851 242* – *Closed February-March and 1 week Christmas*
6 rm � – †£70 ††£120
Rest – (Closed Sunday-Monday) (dinner only) Menu £30
♦ Personally run 15C malthouse with lovely gardens. Good home-cooked fare on varied menus with fine use of local produce. Welcoming accommodation including four-poster comfort.

🏠 **The Royal Oak Inn** with rm   🚗 🛜 **P** *VISA* **◍** **AE**
Exmoor National Park ⊠ *TA24 7JE* – ℰ *(01643) 851 455*
– www.royaloakexmoor.co.uk – *enquiries@royaloakexmoor.co.uk* – *Fax (01643) 851009*
8 rm ⊒ – †£80/116 ††£130
Rest – (in bar Monday-Saturday lunch and Sunday dinner) Menu £25 (dinner) – Carte £19/25
♦ Out-and-out English cooking prevails. Attractive part 12C thatched inn overlooking the village green. Quaint cottage atmosphere, especially in those rooms in the main house; annex rooms of more recent vintage.

> Your opinions are important to us:
> please write and let us know about your discoveries and experiences – good and bad!

WINSTER – Cumbria – **502** L 20 – **see Windermere**

WINSTER – Derbyshire – **502** P 24 – **pop. 1 787**   16 **A1**
> ◻ London 153 mi – Derby 25 mi – Matlock 4 mi

🏠 **The Dower House** without rest   🚗 🍽 **P**
Main St ⊠ *DE4 2DH* – ℰ *(01629) 650 931* – *www.thedowerhousewinster.com*
– fosterbig@aol.com – *Fax (01629) 650 391*
– Closed 25-26 December and 1 January
3 rm ⊒ – †£75 ††£95
♦ Attractive stone house dating from 16C, with lovely walled garden, cosy lounge and spacious, well-kept bedrooms; choose the four poster for its view of the historic village.

WINTERBOURNE STEEPLETON – Dorset – **503** M 31 – **see Dorchester**

ENGLAND

WINTERINGHAM – North Lincolnshire – **502** S 22 – ✉ **Scunthorpe**   23 **C3**
🅳 London 176 mi – Kingston-upon-Hull 16 mi – Sheffield 67 mi

XXXX   **Winteringham Fields** with rm   🅿 VISA ⓪⓪
1 Silver St ✉ DN15 9ND – ℰ (01724) 733 096 – www.winteringhamfields.com
– wintfields@aol.com – Fax (01724) 733 898 – Closed 1 week April, 3 weeks
August, 1 week October and 2 weeks Christmas-New Year
8 rm – †£160 ††£120, ☲ £20 – 2 suites
Rest – (Closed Sunday-Monday) (booking essential for non-residents)
Menu £40/75 – Carte approx. £75 🕮
♦ 16C house with beamed ceilings, and original range with fire. Cosy, cottagey
atmosphere. Carefully executed menu, served in choice of dining rooms. Characterful
bedrooms.

WITNEY – Oxfordshire – **503** P 28 – **pop. 22 765**   10 **B2**
🅳 London 69 mi – Gloucester 39 mi – Oxford 13 mi
🅸 26A Market Sq ℰ (01993) 775802, witney.vic@westoxon.gov.uk

🏠   **The Fleece** with rm   🈂 🕾 🅿 VISA ⓪⓪ AE
11 Church Green ✉ OX28 4AZ – ℰ (01993) 892 270 – www.fleecewitney.co.uk
– fleece@peachpubs.com – Closed 25 December
10 rm ☲ – †£80/110 ††£90/120   **Rest** – Carte £18/32
♦ Modernised dining pub in pretty setting. Front room has leather sofas. Open plan
rear restaurant serves flavourful dishes from classic menu. Polite, efficient service.
Comfortable bedrooms boast eye-catching decor; those at front overlook village
green.

at South Leigh Southeast : 3 m. by A 40 – ✉ Witney

XX   **Mason Arms**   🚘 🕉 🅿 AE
✉ OX29 6XN – ℰ (01993) 702 485 – Closed 1 week Christmas, 1 week Spring,
August, Sunday dinner and Monday
Rest – Carte £30/65
♦ Privately owned 15C thatched inn with unique style and much individuality. Dimly
lit, with intimate atmosphere. French influenced traditional cooking and extensive
wine list.

at Barnard Gate East : 3 ¼ m. by A 40 – ✉ Eynsham

🏠   **The Boot Inn**   🈂 🕉 🅿 VISA ⓪⓪
✉ OX29 6XE – ℰ (01865) 881 231 – www.theboot-inn.com
– info@theboot-inn.com
Rest – Carte £20/35
♦ Friendly pub in Cotswold stone. Snug interior with memorabilia and boot collection, including footwear from Bee Gees and Stanley Matthews. Traditional menu,
informal service.

A good night's sleep without spending a fortune?
Look for a Bib Hotel 🛏

WIVETON – Norfolk – see Blakeney

WIX – Essex – **504** X 28 – ✉ **Manningtree**   13 **D2**
🅳 London 70 mi – Colchester 10 mi – Harwich 7 mi – Ipswich 16 mi

⌂   **Dairy House Farm** without rest ॐ   ≼ 🚘 🅘 🕉 🕪 🅿
Bradfield Rd, Northwest : 1 m. ✉ CO11 2SR – ℰ (01255) 870 322
– www.dairyhousefarm.info – bridgetwhitworth@btinternet.com
3 rm ☲ – †£40/45 ††£62/66
♦ Victorian farmhouse, delightfully secluded in 700 acres of working arable and fruit
farmland. Friendly and welcoming. Simple, comfortable style and well-kept throughout.

WOBURN – Bedfordshire – **504** S 28 – ✉ **Milton Keynes** ▮ *Great Britain* 12 **A2**
  ▶ London 49 mi – Bedford 13 mi – Luton 13 mi – Northampton 24 mi
  – Oxford 47 mi
  ◙ Woburn Abbey ★★

🏠 **Inn at Woburn** &rm, 🗚 rest, 🔊 🅿 VISA ◍ AE ◑
George St ✉ MK17 9PX – ℰ (01525) 290441 – www.theinnatwoburn.com
– re@theinnatwoburn.com – Fax (01525) 290432
52 rm – ♦£115/135 ♦♦£135/145, � £11 – 5 suites
Rest – Menu £13 (lunch) – Carte £19/32
♦ 18C coaching inn, part of Woburn Estate with its abbey and 3000 acre park.
Pleasant modern furnishings and interior décor. Tastefully decorated rooms: book a
Cottage suite. Brasserie open throughout the day.

XXX **Paris House** 🖼 🕩 ⇔ 🅿 VISA ◍ AE
Woburn Park, Southeast : 2¼ m. on A 4012 ✉ MK17 9QP – ℰ (01525) 290692
– www.parishouse.co.uk – info@parishouse.co.uk – Fax (01525) 290471 – Closed
2 weeks January, 25-27 December, Sunday dinner and Monday
Rest – Menu £25 (weekday lunch)/60
♦ Built 1878 for Paris Exhibition, dismantled and rebuilt on Woburn Estate, this
striking timbered house provides an august setting for classic French-inspired cuisine.

🍺 **The Birch** 🏤 🗚 🕉 🅿 VISA ◍ AE
20 Newport Rd, North :½ m. on A 5130 ✉ MK17 9HX – ℰ (01525) 290295
– www.birchwoburn.com – etaverns@aol.com – Fax (01525) 290899 – Closed
25-26 December, 1 January
Rest – (Closed Sunday dinner) (booking essential) Carte £19/30
♦ Established modern dining pub. Stylish décor in the smart restaurant and bar.
Modern menu specialising in meat and fish from an open grill. Attentive service.

at Milton Bryan Southeast : 2½ m. by A 4012 – ✉ **Woburn**

🍺 **The Red Lion** 🏤 🕉 🅿 VISA ◍
Toddington Rd ✉ MK17 9HS – ℰ (01525) 210044
– www.redlion-miltonbryan.co.uk – paul@redlion-miltonbryan.co.uk – Closed
25-26 and 31 December, 1 January
Rest – (Closed Sunday dinner and Monday, except Bank Holiday Mondays)
Carte £20/33
♦ Open fires and exposed beams define the lovely old world charm of this tastefully
furnished pub. Carefully sourced ingredients underpin tasty, home cooked dishes.

Good food without spending a fortune?
Look out for the Bib Gourmand 🅐

WOLD NEWTON – East Riding of Yorkshire 23 **D2**
  ▶ London 229 mi – Bridlington 25 mi – Scarborough 13 mi

🏠 **Wold Cottage** without rest ♠ ⇐ 🖼 🕩 🕉 🌐 🅿 VISA ◍
South :½ m. on Thwing rd ✉ YO25 3HL – ℰ (01262) 470696
– www.woldcottage.com – katrina@woldcottage.com – Fax (01262) 470696
5 rm � – ♦£50/70 ♦♦£90
♦ Georgian former farmhouse set in many rural acres; a country house style prevails
with antique furniture in all areas. Spacious, individually named rooms: two in barn
annex.

WOLVERCOTE – Oxfordshire – **504** Q 28 – **see Oxford**

▶ London 132 mi – Birmingham 15 mi – Liverpool 89 mi – Shrewsbury 30 mi

🛈 18 Queen Sq ✆ (01902) 312051, wolverhampton.tic@dial.pipex.com

Plan of Enlarged Area : see Birmingham pp. 4 and 5

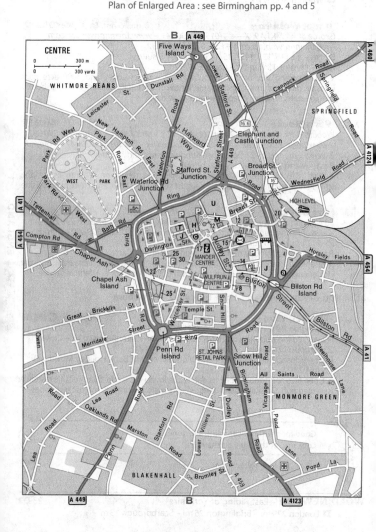

Novotel

Union St ✉ WV1 3JN – ✆ (01902) 871 100 – www.novotel.com
– h1188@accor.com – Fax (01902) 870 054   B**a**

132 rm ⌿ – ♦£59 ♦♦£59/139

Rest *Elements* – (dinner only) Carte approx. £ 18

♦ Conveniently located in the centre of town near to train station. Purpose-built lodge hotel with well fitted modern furnishings. Suitable for business and leisure stopovers. Large windows give bright feel to restaurant.

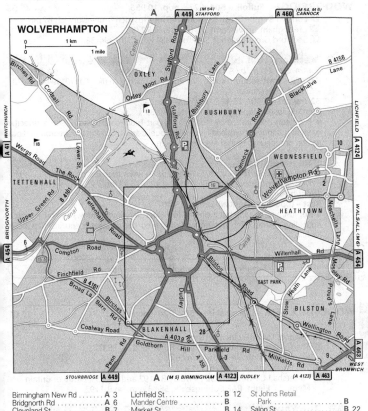

WOLVERHAMPTON

0 — 1 km
0 — 1 mile

A 449 (M 54) STAFFORD
A 460 (M 54, M 6) CANNOCK

B 4156 Lane

A 41 WHITCHURCH
A 454 BRIDGNORTH

OXLEY
BUSHBURY
WEDNESFIELD
HEATHTOWN
TETTENHALL
EAST PARK
BILSTON
BLAKENHALL

LICHFIELD A 4124
WALSALL (M 6) A 454
WEST BROMWICH A 463

STOURBRIDGE A 449
(M 5) BIRMINGHAM A 4123 DUDLEY
(A 4123)

Bilash

No 2 Cheapside ⊠ WV1 1TU – 𝒞 (01902) 427 762 – www.thebilash@co.uk
– table@thebilash.co.uk – Fax (01902) 311 991 – Closed Sunday

Bc

AC ✷ ⇔ VISA ⓪ AE ①

Rest – Indian – Menu £12/20 – Carte £30/50
♦ In a pleasant square, and easily identified by its bright yellow façade and modish interior. Family owned; well established, locally renowned Indian/Bangladeshi cooking.

WOOBURN COMMON – Bucks. – see Beaconsfield

Good food and accommodation at moderate prices?
Look for the Bib symbols:
red Bib Gourmand 🏠 for food, blue Bib Hotel 🛏 for hotels

WOODBRIDGE – Suffolk – **504** X 27 – **pop. 10 956**   15 **D3**

▶ London 81 mi – Great Yarmouth 45 mi – Ipswich 8 mi – Norwich 47 mi
🖪 Cretingham Grove Farm, ℰ (01728) 685 275
🖫 Seckford Great Bealings Seckford Hall Rd, ℰ (01394) 388 000

⛨ Seckford Hall ⚘   ← 🚗 🕭 ⚘ ▨ ⅙ 🖫 �& rm, 🖾 rest, ℱ ᯤ 🅿

Southwest : 1¼ m. by A 12 ⊠ IP13 6NU – ℰ (01394)   🆅🆂🅰 ⚫ 🅰🅴 ⓪
385 678 – www.seckford.co.uk – reception@seckford.co.uk – Fax (01394) 380 610
– Closed 25 December
32 rm ⊊ – ♥£90/125 ♥♥£140/160 – 7 suites
Rest – (Closed Monday lunch) Carte £30/39 **s**
♦ Reputedly once visited by Elizabeth I, a part Tudor country house set in attractive gardens. Charming traditionally panelled public areas. Comfortable bedrooms. Local lobster proudly served in smart dining room.

✗ The Riverside   🍴 🖾 🆅🆂🅰 ⚫ 🅰🅴

Quayside ⊠ IP12 1BH – ℰ (01394) 382 587 – www.theriverside.co.uk
– riversidetheatre@aol.com – Fax (01394) 382 656 – Closed 25 December,
1 January and Sunday dinner
Rest – (booking essential) Carte £25/40
♦ Not just a restaurant, but a cinema too! Floor to ceiling windows and busy terrace. Appealing menus offer modern, well-presented cooking. Set menu includes ticket for film.

> If breakfast is included the ⊊ symbol appears after the number of rooms.

WOODHALL SPA – Lincolnshire – **502** T 24 – **pop. 4 133**   17 **C1**

📙 *Great Britain*

▶ London 138 mi – Lincoln 18 mi
🛈 The Cottage Museum, Iddesleigh Rd ℰ (01526) 353 775,
  woodhallspainfo@e-lindsey.gov.uk
🖫 Woodhall Spa, ℰ (01526) 351 835
◎ Tattershall Castle★ **AC**, SE : 4 m. by B 1192 and A 153 – Battle of Britain
  Memorial Flight, RAF Coningsby★, SE : 3½ m. on B 1192

⛨ The Petwood ⚘   ← 🚗 🕭 🖫 📶 �& rm, ℱ ᯤ 🅿 🆅🆂🅰 ⚫ 🅰🅴 ⓪

Stixwould Rd ⊠ LN10 6QG – ℰ (01526) 352 411 – www.petwood.co.uk
– reception@petwood.co.uk – Fax (01526) 353 473
52 rm ⊊ – ♥£99/123 ♥♥£122 – 1 suite
Rest – (bar lunch Monday-Saturday) Menu £24
♦ Wartime officers' mess for 617 "Dambusters" Squadron - memorabilia fills the bar. Traditional interiors include panelled reception. Lovely gardens. Comfortable bedrooms. Dining room with strong traditional feel.

WOODHOUSE EAVES – Leics. – **503** Q 25 – see Loughborough

WOODSTOCK – Oxfordshire – **503** P 28 – **pop. 2 389** 📙 *Great Britain*   10 **B2**

▶ London 65 mi – Gloucester 47 mi – Oxford 8 mi
🛈 Oxfordshire Museum, Park St ℰ (01993) 813 276,
  woodstock.vic@westoxon.gov.uk
◎ Blenheim Palace★★★ (Park★★★) **AC**

⛨ Bear   �& rm, ℱ 🅿 🆅🆂🅰 ⚫ 🅰🅴 ⓪

Park St ⊠ OX20 1SZ – ℰ (0870) 400 82 02 – www.macdonald-hotels.co.uk/bear
– bear@macdonald-hotels.co.uk – Fax (01993) 810 968
47 rm – ♥£164/230 ♥♥£164/230, ⊊ £17.50 – 7 suites
Rest – Menu £22/30 – Carte £32/41
♦ Characterful part 16C inn. Original personality and charm; oak beams, open fires and stone walls. Particularly comfortable contemporary furnished rooms. Dining room exudes an elegant air.

ENGLAND

Feathers 🛎 📶 VISA 👁️ AE 👁️

Market St ⊠ OX20 1SX – ℰ (01993) 812 291 – www.feathers.co.uk
– enquiries@feathers.co.uk – Fax (01993) 813 158
16 rm ⊑ – †£79/179 ††£ 169/297 – 4 suites
Rest – (Closed Sunday dinner) (booking essential) Menu £ 25/29
– Carte approx. £46
♦ Restored 17C houses in centre of charming town. Much traditional allure with highly individual, antique furnished bedrooms. High levels of comfort and style throughout. Stylish restaurant offers formal dining experience.

The Kings Arms 🍴 📶 VISA 👁️ AE

19 Market St ⊠ OX20 1SU – ℰ (01993) 813 636
– www.kings-hotel-woodstock.co.uk – stay@kingshotelwoodstock.co.uk
– Fax (01993) 813 737
15 rm ⊑ – †£75 ††£150   **Rest** – Carte £18/28
♦ Centrally located, modernised hotel with an informal feel and café style bar with leather bucket seats. Contemporary bedrooms are named after kings. Restaurant with glass roof serves brasserie style dishes.

The Laurels without rest 🍴 VISA 👁️

40 Hensington Rd ⊠ OX20 1JL – ℰ (01993) 812 583
– www.laurelsguesthouse.co.uk – stay@laurelsguesthouse.co.uk – Fax (01993)
810041 – Closed December - mid January
3 rm ⊑ – †£60/70 ††£70/85
♦ Fine Victorian house just off the town centre. Personally run home with pretty guest rooms and private room facilities.

WOOFFERTON – Shrops. – see Ludlow

WOOKEY HOLE – Somerset – **503** L 30 – see Wells

WOOLACOMBE – Devon – **503** H 30   2 **C1**
  ▶ London 237 mi – Barnstaple 15 mi – Exeter 55 mi
  ℹ️ The Esplanade ℰ (01271) 870553, info@woolacombetourism.co.uk
  ◎ Exmoor National Park★★ - Mortehoe★★ (St Mary's Church★, Morte Point - vantage point★) N : ½ m. – Ilfracombe : Hillsborough (≤★★) **AC**, Capstone Hill★ (≤★), St Nicholas' Chapel (≤★) **AC**, NE : 5 ½ m. by B 3343 and A 361. Braunton★ (St Brannock's Church★, Braunton Burrows★), S : 8 m. by B 3343 and A 361

Woolacombe Bay ≤ 🚣 ⅃ 📺 ♨ 🛁 🍴 🛎 🏊 Ⓜ rest, 🍴 🎿

South St ⊠ EX34 7BN – ℰ (01271) 870 388   P. VISA 👁️
– www.woolacombe-bay-hotel.co.uk – woolacombe.bayhotel@btinternet.com
– Fax (01271) 870613 – Closed 2 January-8 February
63 rm ⊑ – †£75/102 ††£150/204 – 5 suites
Rest Doyles – (dinner only) Menu £ 32
Rest Bay Brasserie – (lunch only and dinner during summer and school holidays) Carte approx. £ 15
♦ Large, traditional, family oriented Victorian seaside hotel with gardens and beach access. Activities from board games to health suite. Well-kept, bright bedrooms. Classic Doyles dining room. Informal brasserie.

at Mortehoe North : ½ m. – ⊠ **Woolacombe**

Watersmeet ≤ 🚣 ⅃ 📺 ⬡ ⬡ rm, 🍴 🎿 P. VISA 👁️ 👁️

The Esplanade ⊠ EX34 7EB – ℰ (01271) 870 333 – www.watersmeethotel.co.uk
– info@watersmeethotel.co.uk – Fax (01271) 870890
30 rm ⊑ – †£ 120/201 ††£150/296   **Rest** – Menu £ 17/37 **s**
♦ Edwardian house on the National Trust's rugged North Atlantic coastline. Superb views of Morte Bay. Smart country house style, large lounges and steps to the beach. Stylish restaurant offers tremendous sea views.

ENGLAND

⚐ Ё rm, ⌖ P. VISA ✆

Cleeve House
✉ EX34 7ED – ☎ (01271) 870 719 – www.cleevehouse.co.uk
– info@cleevehouse.co.uk – Fax (01271) 870 719 – April-October
6 rm ☲ – ♦£57/59 ♦♦£84/88
Rest – (by arrangement) Menu £ 22 – Carte £ 25/33
♦ Bright and welcoming feel in décor and atmosphere. Very comfortable lounge and individually styled bedrooms with co-ordinated fabrics. Rear rooms with great country views. Neat dining room; walls hung with local artwork.

WOOLAVINGTON – Somerset – **503** L 30 – see Bridgwater

WOOLER – Northumberland – **502** N 17   24 **A1**
🚘 London 330 mi – Alnwick 17 mi – Berwick-on-Tweed 17 mi

⚐ ⌖ P. VISA ✆

Firwood without rest ♨
Middleton Hall, South : 1 ¾ m. by Earle rd on Middleton Hall rd ✉ NE71 6RD
– ☎ (01668) 283 699 – www.firwoodhouse.co.uk – welcome@firwoodhouse.co.uk
– Restricted opening in winter
3 rm ☲ – ♦£60 ♦♦£80
♦ Victorian former hunting lodge in the Cheviot. Homely lounge and open-fired breakfast rooms boast bay windows with country views. Good sized rooms with individual style.

WOOLHAMPTON – West Berkshire – **503** Q 29 ▌ Great Britain   10 **B3**
🚘 London 56 mi – Newbury 8 mi – Thatcham 4 mi
🖾 Basildon Park★, NE : 10 m. by A 4, A 340 and A 417

🏠 **The Angel**   ⌂ ⌖ P. VISA ✆
Bath Rd ✉ RG7 5RT – ☎ (0118) 971 3307 – www.thea4angel.com
– mail@thea4angel.com
Rest – Carte £ 19/30
♦ Ivy-covered pub with distinctive interior of hanging hops, rows of jars and a ceiling lined with wine bottles. Hearty cooking; lunchtime sandwiches; more varied à la carte.

WOOLSTHORPE-BY-BELVOIR – Lincs. – **502** R 25 – see Grantham

---

WORCESTER – Worcestershire – **503** N 27 – pop. 94 029 ▌ Great Britain   18 **B3**
🚘 London 124 mi – Birmingham 26 mi – Bristol 61 mi – Cardiff 74 mi
🛈 The Guildhall, High St ☎ (01905) 726311,
touristinfo@cityofworcester.gov.uk
⛳ Perdiswell Park Bilford Rd, ☎ (01905) 754 668
◉ City★ – Cathedral★★ – Royal Worcester Porcelain Works★ (Museum of Worcester Porcelain★) **M**
🖾 The Elgar Trail★

Plan opposite

🏨 **Diglis House**   ⟨ ⚐ ⌂ ⌖ ⚃ P. VISA ✆ AE ⓪
Severn St ✉ WR1 2NF – ☎ (01905) 353 518 – www.diglishousehotel.co.uk
– diglishouse@yahoo.com – Fax (01905) 767 772   o
28 rm ☲ – ♦£85/90 ♦♦£110/130 – 1 suite
Rest – (bar lunch Monday-Saturday) Carte £ 22/35
♦ Georgian house on banks of river Severn. Close to Royal Worcester factory. Attractive bar terrace. Characterful rooms in main house, those in annex more modern. Conservatory dining room with river outlook.

❌❌ **Glasshouse**   ⌂ AC VISA ✆ AE
Sidbury ✉ WR1 2HU – ☎ (01905) 611 120 – www.theglasshouse.co.uk
– eat@theglasshouse.co.uk
– Closed 25 December, Bank Holidays and Sunday dinner   c
Rest – Carte £ 25/40
♦ Leather furnished lounge. Stylish chocolate and blue hued dining areas; the first floor has glass wall and views of city. Brasserie style menu offers modern British dishes.

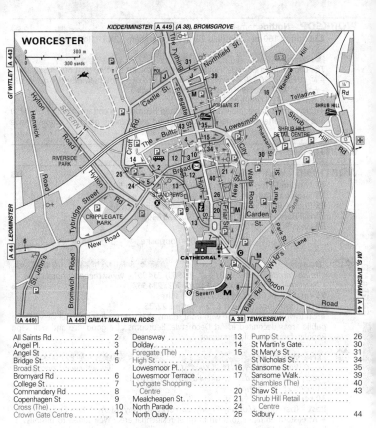

WORCESTER

XX **Brown's**   VISA ◐ AE

24 Quay St ⊠ WR1 2JJ – ℰ (01905) 26 263 – www.brownsrestaurant.co.uk
– enquiries@brownsrestaurant.co.uk – Fax (01905) 25 768
– Closed 25 December and 1 January   x
Rest – Menu £25 (lunch) **s** – Carte £27/58 **s**
♦ Converted riverside corn mill. Spacious, open interior as befits the building's origins. Impressive collection of modern artwork. Mainly British dishes are renowned locally.

at Bransford West : 4 m. by A 44 on A 4103 – ⊠ Worcester

🏠 **Bear and Ragged Staff**   🚗 🛋 ⅏ **P** VISA ◐ AE ①

Station Rd, Southeast :½ m. on Powick rd ⊠ WR6 5JH – ℰ (01886) 833 399
– www.bear.uk.com – mail@bear.uk.com – Fax (01886) 833 106 – Closed dinner
25 December and 1 January
Rest – Carte £20/30
♦ Two oak trees dominate the front of this traditional pub in quiet country lane. Huge blackboard menus offer plenty of interest: vegetables travel from rear garden to kitchen.

WORFIELD – Shrops. – see Bridgnorth

WORKSOP – Nottinghamshire – **502** Q 24 – **pop. 39 072**   16 **B1**

  ◘ London 160 mi – Sheffield 20 mi – Nottingham 37 mi – Rotherham 17 mi

⚐ **Browns** without rest   ▱ **P**
The Old Orchard Cottage, Holbeck Lane, Southwest : 4½ m. by A 60 ⊠ S80 3NF
– 𝒞 (01909) 720659 – www.brownsholbeck.co.uk – browns@holbeck.fsnet.co.uk
– Fax (01909) 720659 – Closed 1 week Christmas
3 rm ⏦ – †£57/65 ††£74/84

  ♦ Cosy, comfortable, individually-decorated bedrooms in cottage dating from 1730
  and named after the owners. Mature orchard and tranquil garden. Comprehensive
  breakfast.

WORTH – Kent – **504** Y 30 – **see Deal**

WORTHING – West Sussex – **504** S 31 – **pop. 96 964**   7 **D3**

  ◘ London 59 mi – Brighton 11 mi – Southampton 50 mi
  ◪ Shoreham Airport : 𝒞 (01273) 467373, E : 4 m. by A 27 BY
  🛈 Chapel Rd 𝒞 (01903) 221066, tic@worthing.gov.uk
  🖽 Hill Barn Hill Barn Lane, 𝒞 (01903) 237301
  🖽 Links Rd, 𝒞 (01903) 260801

                          Plan opposite

🏛 **Beach**   ≤ 🖼 ₺ rm, ℅ ⸲° 🖾 **P** **VISA** **©©** **AE** **①**
Marine Parade ⊠ BN11 3QJ – 𝒞 (01903) 234001 – www.thebeachhotel.co.uk
– info@thebeachhotel.co.uk – Fax (01903) 234567   AZ**e**
75 rm ⏦ – †£52/92 ††£86/130 – 4 suites
Rest – (light lunch) Menu £22 – Carte £22/35

  ♦ On town's marine parade with front rooms all boasting clear Channel views. Large
  public areas decorated in Art Deco style. Bedrooms of a good size and well kept.
  Popular, family-friendly restaurant.

🏨 **The Windsor**   ▱ ₺ 🖾 ℅ ⸲° 🖾 **P** **VISA** **©©** **AE** **①**
14-20 Windsor Rd ⊠ BN11 2LX – 𝒞 (01903) 239655 – www.thewindsor.co.uk
– reception@thewindsor.co.uk – Fax (01903) 210763
– Closed 23-31 December   BY**i**
30 rm ⏦ – †£95 ††£130
Rest – (bar lunch Monday-Friday, carvery Saturday) Menu £17 – Carte £19/28

  ♦ At eastern entrance to town in quiet residential area. Well suited to business or
  leisure traveller with a wide range of rooms. Front rooms particularly spacious and
  bright. Large dining room with welcoming atmosphere.

🏨 **Chatsworth**   🖼 ₺ rm, 🖾 rest, ⸲° 🖾 **VISA** **©©** **AE**
Steyne ⊠ BN11 3DU – 𝒞 (01903) 236103 – www.chatsworthworthing.co.uk
– hotel@chatsworthworthing.co.uk – Fax (01903) 823726   BZ**x**
98 rm ⏦ – †£75/115 ††£99/140   **Rest** – (dinner only) Menu £19 **s**

  ♦ In a Georgian terrace overlooking Steyne Gardens and ideally located for a range
  of the town's resort activities. Attentive service and good sized bedrooms. Simple,
  uncluttered dining room.

⚐ **Beacons** without rest   ℅ ⸲° **P** **VISA** **©©**
18 Shelley Rd ⊠ BN11 1TU – 𝒞 (01903) 230948
– thebeacons@btconnect.com   BZ**e**
8 rm ⏦ – †£40/45 ††£70/76

  ♦ Friendly traditional home providing classic English seaside accommodation. In the
  centre of town close to parks. Ideal base for visiting historic Arundel and Chichester.

🍴 **The Parsonage**   ⇔ **VISA** **©©** **AE**
6-10 High St, Tarring ⊠ BN14 7NN – 𝒞 (01903) 820140
– www.theparsonage.co.uk – parsonage.bookings@ntlworld.com – Fax (01903)
523233 – Closed 26 December-4 January, Sunday and Monday   AY**c**
Rest – Carte £22/33

  ♦ Within one of Tarring high street's original 15C cottages. Exposed beams and
  framed photographs. Good international cuisine and a friendly, comfortable atmosphere.

ENGLAND

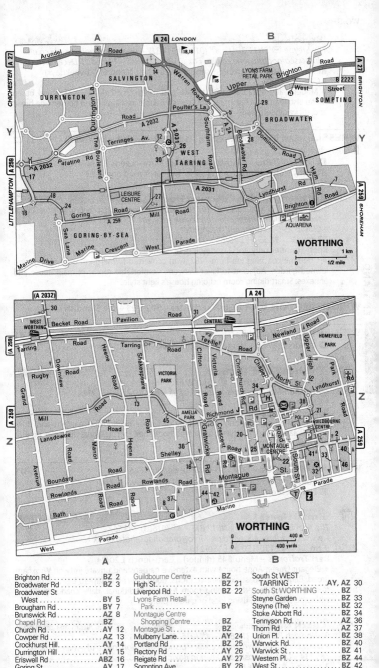

WORTHING

✗ **Bryce's** 🛆 VISA ◍◍

The Steyne ✉ BN11 3DU – ☏ *(01903) 214 317* – *www.seafoodbrasserie.co.uk*
– *info@seafoodbrasserie.co.uk* – *Fax (01903) 213 842* – *Closed 25 December*
Rest – Seafood – (booking essential in summer) Menu £ 15 (weekdays)
– Carte £ 24/29   BZ**x**
♦ Modern, airy restaurant with terrace and pier/promenade views. Seafood based
menu also features a few grills. All starters available as mains. Good homemade bread
and sticky gingerbread.

WRESSLE – East Riding of Yorkshire – **502** R 22 – ✉ **Selby (N. Yorks.)**   23 **C2**
📗 *Great Britain*

▶ London 208 mi – Kingston-upon-Hull 31 mi – Leeds 31 mi – York 19 mi
◉ Selby (Abbey Church★), W : 5 m. by minor road and A 63

🏨 **Loftsome Bridge Coaching House**   🚗 🎟 rest, ✗ 🅿 VISA ◍◍ AE

South :½ m. ✉ YO8 6EN – ☏ *(01757) 630 070* – *www.loftsomebridge-hotel.co.uk*
– *reception@loftsomebridge-hotel.co.uk* – *Fax (01757) 638 437*
– *Closed 25 December and 1 January*
17 rm ☕ – †£ 55 ††£ 75/88 – 1 suite
Rest – (dinner only and Sunday lunch) Menu £ 28 **s**
♦ One-time coaching inn from 1782, with converted former farm outbuildings and
lawned garden. Adjacent to River Derwent. Comfortable rooms in main house and
annexes. Smart dining room echoing house's light style.

WRIGHTINGTON BAR – Gtr Manchester – **502** L 23 – **see Standish**

WRINEHILL – Staffordshire   18 **B1**
▶ London 167 mi – Nantwich 10 mi – Stoke-on-Trent 10 mi

🍴 **The Hand and Trumpet**   🚗 🏠 🅿 VISA ◍◍

Main Road ✉ CW3 9BJ – ☏ *(01270) 820 048*
– *www.hand-and-trumpet-wrinehill.co.uk* – *Fax (01270) 821 911*
– *Closed 25 December*
Rest – Carte £ 22/30
♦ Refurbished country pub with delightful terrace overlooking gardens and duck
pond. Relaxing country style interior with book shelves. Traditional dishes recognisable to all.

WROXHAM – Norfolk – **504** Y 25 📗 *Great Britain*   15 **D1**
▶ London 118 mi – Great Yarmouth 21 mi – Norwich 7 mi
◉ Norfolk Broads★

🏨 **Broad House** ⏳   ＜ 🚗 ⏳ 🐾 🛥 🅿 VISA ◍◍ AE ◍

The Avenue, off a1151 ✉ NR12 8TS – ☏ *(01603) 783 567*
– *www.broadhousehotel.co.uk* – *info@broadhousehotel.co.uk*
9 rm ☕ – †£ 130/150 ††£ 150/210 – 1 suite
Rest *Trafford's* – Menu £ 45 (dinner) – Carte lunch £ 20/24
♦ Elegant Queen Anne house with extensive gardens and private jetty on Wroxham
Broad. Bedrooms boast excellent comforts, good views and superb bathrooms; attic
rooms most charkerful. Dining room features traditional, daily changing menus
with a personal twist, using local or garden produce.

🏠 **Coach House** without rest   ✗ ⏳ 🅿 VISA ◍◍ AE ◍

96 Norwich Rd ✉ NR12 8RY – ☏ *(01603) 784 376*
– *www.coachhousewroxham.co.uk* – *bishop@worldonline.co.uk* – *Fax (01603)
783 734 – Closed Christmas Day and Boxing Day*
3 rm ☕ – †£ 40 ††£ 60
♦ Converted Georgian coach house. Interior décor retains an English country feel
with a snug lounge and good-sized, well-kept bedrooms.

WYCH CROSS – E. Sussex – **504** U 30 – see Forest Row

WYE – Kent – **504** W 30 – pop. 2 066 – ⊠ Ashford   9 **C2**
▸ London 60 mi – Canterbury 10 mi – Dover 28 mi – Hastings 34 mi

XX   **Wife of Bath** with rm   ⌿ ⁺⁺ **P** _VISA_ **CO AE**
       4 Upper Bridge St ⊠ TN25 5AF – ℰ (01233) 812 232 – www.thewifeofbath.com
       – relax@thewifeofbath.com – Closed 25-26 and 31 December
       5 rm ⌷ – ♥£70 ♥♥£95
       Rest – (Closed Monday, Tuesday lunch and Sunday dinner) Menu £19
       (weekday lunch) – Carte £25/33
       ♦ A lovely timber-framed house built in 1760. Fine cloth tables. Well chosen menu of
       satisfying dishes. Full or Continental breakfast after staying in comfy, soft-toned
       rooms.

WYMONDHAM – Norfolk – **504** X 26   15 **C2**
▸ London 102 mi – Cambridge 55 mi – King's Lynn 49 mi – Norwich 12 mi

⌂   **Old Thorn Barn** without rest   ⅍ ⅘ ⁺⁺ **P** _VISA_ **CO**
      Corporation Farm, Wymondham Rd, Hethel, Southeast : 3½ m. on B 1135
      (following signs to Mulbarton) ⊠ NR14 8EU – ℰ (01953) 607 785
      – www.oldthornbarn.co.uk – enquiries@oldthornbarn.co.uk – Fax (01953) 601 909
      10 rm ⌷ – ♥£34/38 ♥♥£56/60
      ♦ Simple, rural guesthouse sited on farm and utilising former outbuildings as bed-
      rooms with hand-built wood furniture. Rustic lounge and breakfast area with wood-
      burning stove.

Red = Pleasant. Look for the red X and ⌂ symbols.

ENGLAND

WYTHAM – Oxon. – see Oxford

YANWATH – Cumbria – see Penrith

YARCOMBE – Devon – **503** K 31 – see Honiton

YARM – Stockton-on-Tees – **502** P 20 – pop. 8 929   24 **B3**
▸ London 242 mi – Middlesbrough 8 mi – Newcastle upon Tyne 47 mi

🏠🏠   **Judges Country House** ⌂   ≼ ⌿ ⅃ ⅃⌅ ⅘ ⁺⁺ ⅍ **P** _VISA_ **CO AE ①**
      Kirklevington Hall, Kirklevington, South : 1½ m. on A 67 ⊠ TS15 9LW
      – ℰ (01642) 789 000 – www.judgeshotel.co.uk – enquiries@judgeshotel.co.uk
      – Fax (01642) 787 692
      21 rm – ♥£150/160 ♥♥£190/205, ⌷ £13.50
      Rest – Menu £18/44 – Carte £44/56
      ♦ Former Victorian judge's residence surrounded by gardens. Welcoming panelled
      bar and spacious lounge filled with antiques and curios. Attractive rooms with a host
      of extras. Conservatory dining room overlooks the gardens.

YARMOUTH – I.O.W. – **503** P 31 – see Wight (Isle of)

YARPOLE – County of Herefordshire   18 **B2**
▸ London 166 mi – Worcester 31 mi – Shrewsbury 38 mi – Hereford 18 mi

🏠   **The Bell Inn**   ⌿ ⌂ **P** _VISA_ **CO ①**
😊   *Green Lane ⊠ HR6 0BD – ℰ (01568) 780 359 – www.thebellinnyarpole.co.uk*
     Rest – (Closed Sunday dinner in winter, Monday) Carte £19/24
     ♦ Characterful black and white timbered inn with a real sense of identity. Cooking
     mixes French and British, featuring classic bar dishes alongside those of a more
     ambitious nature.

YATTENDON – West Berkshire – **503** Q 29 – ✉ Newbury

▶ London 61 mi – Oxford 23 mi – Reading 12 mi

at Frilsham South : 1 m. by Frilsham rd on Bucklebury rd – ✉ Yattendon

🍴 **The Pot Kiln** 〒 🏠 **P** VISA ⓿ AE ⓪
✉ RG18 0XX – 𝒞 (01635) 201 366 – www.potkiln.org – info@potkiln.org – Closed
25 December
Rest – Menu £ 15 (lunch) – Carte £ 27/34🏚

♦ 17C red brick pub country pub. Food is fresh, local and homemade; 90% of game
and all river fish are caught by the owner. Dishes range from pub favourites with a
modern/local twist to more restaurant style.

YAXLEY – Suffolk – see Thornham Magna

YEOVIL – Somerset – **503** M 31 – pop. 41 871

▶ London 136 mi – Exeter 48 mi – Southampton 72 mi – Taunton 26 mi
🛈 Hendford 𝒞 (01935) 845946, yeoviltic@southsomerset.gov.uk
Cart Gate Picnic Site, stoke sub-hamdon 𝒞 (01935) 829333,
cartgate.tic@southsomerset.gov.uk
🏌 Sherborne Rd, 𝒞 (01935) 422 965
◉ St John the Baptist★
🄲 Monacute House★★ **AC**, W : 4 m. on A 3088 – Fleet Air Arm Museum,
Yeovilton★★ **AC**, NW : 5 m. by A 37 – Tintinhull House Garden★ **AC**,
NW : 5½ m. – Ham Hill (≤★★) W : 5½ m. by A 3088 – Stoke sub Hamdon
(parish church★) W : 5¼ m. by A 3088. Muchelney★★ (parish church★★)
NW : 14 m. by A 3088, A 303 and B 3165 – Lytes Cary★, N : 7½ m. by A 37,
B 3151 and A 372 – Sandford Orcas Manor House★, NW : 8 m. by A 359 –
Cadbury Castle (≤★★) NE : 10½ m. by A 359 – East Lambrook Manor★ **AC**,
W : 12 m. by A 3088 and A 303

🏨 **Lanes** 〒 🏠 🏊 **Få** 🛏 ⅙ rm, 🕭 🕭 ⚒ **P** VISA ⓿ AE
West Coker, Southwest : 3 m. on A 30 ✉ BA22 9AJ – 𝒞 (01935) 862 555
– www.laneshotel.net – stay@laneshotel.net – Fax (01935) 864 260
29 rm ☂ – †£90 ††£110   **Rest** – (Closed Saturday lunch) Carte £ 17/26

♦ 18C stone former rectory in walled grounds. Stylish modern interior with chocolate
and red leather predominant. Stretch out in relaxed lounge. Airy, modish bedrooms.
Modern classics and lots of glass in the Brasserie.

at Barwick South : 2 m. by A 30 off A 37 – ✉ Yeovil

XX **Little Barwick House** with rm �></ 〒 🄺 rest, **P** VISA ⓿ AE
✉ BA22 9TD – 𝒞 (01935) 423 902 – www.littlebarwickhouse.co.uk
– reservations@barwick7.fsnet.co.uk – Fax (01935) 420 908 – Closed 2 weeks
Christmas
6 rm ☂ – †£80/126 ††£138/154
Rest – (Closed Sunday dinner, Monday and Tuesday lunch) (booking
essential) Menu £ 25/38

♦ Charming Georgian dower house in a secluded spot, run by a delightful and hospitable couple. The cooking is robust, gutsy and visually bold but without gimmicks.
Comfortable, stylish and immaculately kept bedrooms.

at Stoke sub Hamdon Northwest : 5½ m. by A 3088 – ✉ Yeovil

XX **The Priory House** VISA ⓿ AE
1 High St ✉ TA14 6PP – 𝒞 (01935) 822 826
– www.theprioryhouserestaurant.co.uk
– reservations@theprioryhouserestaurant.co.uk – Fax (01935) 825 822 – Closed
last 2 weeks May, first 2 weeks November, Sunday, Monday and Bank Holidays
Rest – (dinner only and Saturday lunch) (booking essential) Menu £ 23 (lunch)
– Carte dinner £ 34/40

♦ Village centre restaurant that sticks firmly to traditions with tried and tested classics to the fore: a quiet and relaxing experience. Swallow a cider brandy after dinner!

ENGLAND

🖪 London 203 mi – Kingston-upon-Hull 38 mi – Leeds 26 mi
 – Middlesbrough 51 mi – Nottingham 88 mi – Sheffield 62 mi
🚺 The De Grey Rooms, Exhibition Sq ℰ (01904) 550099, info@visityork.org.
🖩 Strensall Lords Moor Lane, ℰ (01904) 491 840
🖩 Heworth Muncastergate Muncaster House, ℰ (01904) 424 618
👁 City★★★ – Minster★★★ (Stained Glass★★★, Chapter House★★, Choir
Screen★★) CDY – National Railway Museum★★★ CY – The Walls★★CDXYZ
– Castle Museum★ **AC** DZ **M2** – Jorvik Viking Centre★ **AC** DY **M1** – Fairfax
House★ **AC** DY **A** – The Shambles★DY **54**

Plan on next page

🏨 **Middlethorpe Hall**   ⟪ 🛏 🐾 🔲 🕭 🐾 🛋 🖻 🐱 rm, 🛞 ⁽⁾ 🏊 🅿
Bishopthorpe Rd, South : 1¾ *m.* ⊠ *YO23 2GB* – ℰ *(01904)* 🆅🅸🆂🅰 ⓂⓄ 🅰🅴
641 241 – *www.middlethorpe.com* – *info@middlethorpe.com* – *Fax (01904)*
620 176
21 rm – ♥£130/185 ♥♥£190/350, ⊆ £6.95 – 8 suites
Rest – (booking essential for non-residents) Menu £23 (lunch) **s**
 – Carte (dinner) £36/47 **s**
♦ Impressive William and Mary country house dating from 1699. Elegantly and carefully restored; abundantly furnished with antiques. Most characterful rooms in main house. Wood-panelled, three-roomed restaurant with period feel.

🏨 **The Grange**   ⁽⁾ 🏊 🅿 🆅🅸🆂🅰 ⓂⓄ 🅰🅴
Clifton ⊠ *YO30 6AA* – ℰ *(01904) 644 744* – *www.grangehotel.co.uk*
 – *info@grangehotel.co.uk* – *Fax (01904) 612 453*   CX**u**
35 rm ⊆ – ♥£117/195 ♥♥£160/235 – 1 suite
Rest *The Ivy Brasserie* – (Closed Sunday dinner) (dinner only and Sunday
lunch) Carte £26/36
Rest *The Cellar Bar* – (lunch only and dinner Friday-Saturday) Carte £23/36
♦ Elegant Regency town house with stylish period furniture throughout. Comfortable lounges and marble columned entrance hall. Excellently kept rooms vary in shapes and sizes. Ivy Brasserie boasts grand ceiling mural. Cellar Bar exudes much character.

🏨 **Hotel du Vin**   🛏 🖻 ⁽⁾ 🏊 🅿 🆅🅸🆂🅰 ⓂⓄ 🅰🅴
89 The Mount ⊠ *YO24 1AX* – ℰ *(01904) 557 350* – *www.hotelduvin.com*
 – *info.york@hotelduvin.com* – *Fax (01904) 567 361*   CZ**a**
44 rm – ♥£150 ♥♥£150, ⊆ £13.50
Rest *Bistro* – see restaurant listing
♦ Georgian house close to Knavesmire racecourse and just outside of city centre. As part of a 'wine-orientated' group, the contemporary bedrooms boast smart, wine-coloured themes.

🏨 **York Pavilion**   🐾 🛞 ⁽⁾ 🏊 🅿 🆅🅸🆂🅰 ⓂⓄ 🅰🅴 ⓪
45 Main St, Fulford, South : 1½ *m. on A 19* ⊠ *YO10 4PJ* – ℰ *(01904) 622 099*
 – *www.yorkpavilionhotel.com* – *help@yorkpavilionhotel.com* – *Fax (01904)*
626 939
63 rm ⊆ – ♥£89/125 ♥♥£99/130
Rest *Langtons Brasserie* – Menu £17 (lunch) – Carte £21/34
♦ Georgian house on main road in suburbs. Wood panelled reception and period-style lounge. Older, more individual rooms in main house and uniform, chintzy style in extension. Informal dining.

🏨 **Dean Court**   🛗 🅰🅲 rest, 🛞 ⁽⁾ 🏊 🅿 🆅🅸🆂🅰 ⓂⓄ 🅰🅴 ⓪
Duncombe Pl ⊠ *YO1 7EF* – ℰ *(01904) 625 082* – *www.deancourt-york.co.uk*
 – *info@deancourt-york.co.uk* – *Fax (01904) 620 305*   CY**c**
36 rm ⊆ – ♥£85/160 ♥♥£135/225 – 1 suite
Rest *DCH* – Menu £18 (lunch) – Carte (dinner) £29/35
♦ Built in the 1850s to house clerics visiting the Minster, visible from most rooms. Now a very modern feel pervades the public areas. Aforementioned rooms more traditional. Minster outlook from smart restaurant.

ENGLAND

ENGLAND

YORK

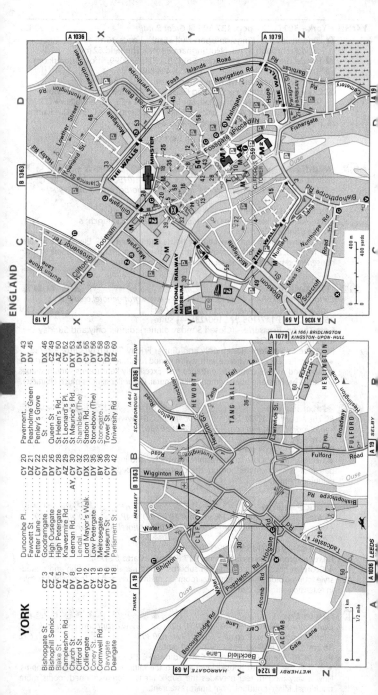

Monkbar
🏨 📶 ♿ 🅿 VISA ⦿ AE ①

St Maurice's Rd ✉ *YO31 7JA –* ℰ *(01904) 638 086 –* www.monkbarhotel.co.uk
– sales@monkbarhotel.co.uk – Fax (01904) 629 195 DX**a**
99 rm ☲ – †£90/115 ††£110/175
Rest – Menu £15 (lunch) – Carte (dinner) £21/31

♦ Purpose-built and close to impressive Monkbar Gate. Modern décor throughout. Two room types: traditional, cottage-style in annex and uniform, modern rooms in main building. Restaurant exudes medieval atmosphere.

Holmwood House without rest
🏠 ℅ 📶 🅿 VISA ⦿

114 Holgate Rd ✉ *YO24 4BB –* ℰ *(01904) 626 183*
– www.holmwoodhousehotel.co.uk *– holmwood.house@dial.pipex.com*
– Fax (01904) 670899 – Closed 24-26 December AZ**x**
14 rm ☲ – †£60/70 ††£80/120

♦ Informal atmosphere in well-kept terraced Victorian property. Individually decorated bedrooms include William Morris styling. Bright basement breakfast room.

Alexander House without rest
℅ 🅿 VISA ⦿

94 Bishopthorpe Rd ✉ *YO23 1JS –* ℰ *(01904) 625 016*
– www.alexanderhouseyork.co.uk *– info@alexanderhouseyork.co.uk*
– Closed mid-December-mid-January CZ**v**
4 rm ☲ – ††£75/85

♦ Classic Victorian terraced house, immaculately refurbished by experienced owners. Delightful sitting room with porcelain and artworks. Hearty breakfasts. Attractive bedrooms.

The Hazelwood without rest
℅ 📶 🅿 VISA ⦿

24-25 Portland St ✉ *YO31 7EH –* ℰ *(01904) 626 548*
– www.thehazelwoodyork.com *– reservations@thehazelwoodyork.com*
– Fax (01904) 628 032 CX**c**
14 rm ☲ – †£50/105 ††£110

♦ Two 19C town houses with characterful basement sitting room featuring original cooking range. Welcoming breakfast room in blue. Individual bedrooms, some with four posters.

Crook Lodge without rest
℅ 📶 🅿 VISA ⦿

26 St Mary's, Bootham ✉ *YO30 7DD –* ℰ *(01904) 655 614*
– www.crooklodge.co.uk *– crooklodge@hotmail.com*
– Fax (01904) 625 915 CX**z**
6 rm ☲ – †£45/75 ††£70/80

♦ Privately owned, attractive Victorian redbrick house in quiet location. Basement breakfast room with original cooking range. Some rooms compact, all pleasantly decorated.

Acer without rest
℅ VISA ⦿

52 Scarcroft Hill ✉ *YO24 1DE –* ℰ *(01904) 653 839 –* www.acerhotel.co.uk
– info@acerhotel.co.uk – Fax (01904) 677 017 – Closed 25 December CZ**x**
5 rm ☲ – †£55 ††£90

♦ Terraced Victorian house with a creeper covered exterior. Warm welcome into homely and immaculately kept surroundings. Individually styled, traditionally appointed rooms.

Apple House without rest
📶 🅿 VISA ⦿

74-76 Holgate Rd ✉ *YO24 4AB –* ℰ *(01904) 625 081*
– www.applehouseyork.co.uk *– pamelageorge1@yahoo.co.uk – Fax (01904) 628918 – Closed 20 December- 8 January* AZ**c**
10 rm ☲ – †£40/70 ††£70/100

♦ 19C terraced house that's been refurbished to a neat and tidy standard. Rooms vary in shape and size; all have good modern facilities. A friendly address to lay your head.

ENGLAND

⌂ **Bronte** without rest ❄ ⁽ᵗᵖ⁾ VISA ⍟⍟
22 Grosvenor Terrace ⊠ YO30 7AG – ℰ (01904) 621066
– www.bronte-guesthouse.com – enquiries@bronte-guesthouse.com
– Fax (01904) 653434   CXn
6 rm ⌸ – ♦£40/50 ♦♦£80
♦ Cosy little Victorian terraced house with pretty exterior, decorated in keeping with
period nature of property. Charming breakfast room has antique furnishings. Comfy
rooms.

⌂ **The Heathers** without rest 🛏 ❄ ⁽ᵗᵖ⁾ P VISA ⍟⍟ AE
54 Shipton Rd, Clifton-Without, Northwest : 1½ m. on A 19 ⊠ YO30 5RQ
– ℰ (01904) 640989 – www.heathers-guest-house.co.uk
– mich@heathers-guest-house.co.uk – Fax (01904) 640989
– Closed 24-26 December   AYn
6 rm ⌸ – ♦£60/86 ♦♦£76/120
♦ A personally run guesthouse in an extended 1930s property overlooking meadowland. Bedrooms, which vary in size, are colourfully decorated and well furnished.

✗✗ **Melton's** AK ⇔ VISA ⍟⍟
7 Scarcroft Rd ⊠ YO23 1ND – ℰ (01904) 634341 – www.meltonrestaurant.co.uk
– Fax (01904) 635115
– Closed 2 weeks Christmas, Monday lunch and Sunday   CZc
Rest – (booking essential) Menu £21 (lunch) – Carte £27/33
♦ Glass fronted restaurant with mural decorated walls and neighbourhood feel.
Smart, crisp tone in both service and table cover. Good modern British food with
some originality.

✗✗ **J. Baker's** AK VISA ⍟⍟ AE ①
🍽 7 Fossgate ⊠ YO1 9TA – ℰ (01904) 622688 – www.jbakers.co.uk
– info@jbakers.co.uk – Fax (01904) 671931
– Closed 1-9 January, Sunday and Monday   DYc
Rest – (light lunch) Menu £28 (dinner) **s** – Carte (lunch) £20/25 **s**
♦ Contemporary restaurant in city centre. Spacious first floor 'chocolate' lounge for
coffee and truffles. Modern dining room matched by good value, funky, cutting edge
dishes.

✗✗ **Bistro** – at Hotel du Vin VISA ⍟⍟ AE ①
89 The Mount ⊠ YO24 1AX – ℰ (01904) 567350 – www.hotelduvin.com
– info.york@hotelduvin.com – Fax (01904) 567361   CZa
Rest – French – Carte £25/38
♦ Typical bustling Bistro offering modern French dishes as well as all the old favourites. Set in Hotel du Vin, it offers a good selection of wines by the glass.

✗ **Blue Bicycle** with rm VISA ⍟⍟
34 Fossgate ⊠ YO1 9TA – ℰ (01904) 673990 – www.thebluebicycle.com
– info@thebluebicycle.com – Fax (01904) 677688   DYe
5 rm ⌸ – ♦£150 ♦♦£150   **Rest** – (booking essential) Carte £34/47
♦ Delightfully cluttered, atmospheric restaurant full of objets d'art, ornaments and
pictures. Wood floors and heavy, old, pine tables. Bustling and busy; British cuisine.
Spacious modern bedrooms, luxuriously appointed.

✗ **31 Castlegate** VISA ⍟⍟ AE
31 Castlegate ⊠ YO1 9RN – ℰ (01904) 621404 – www.31castlegate.co.uk
– Closed 25-26 December, 1 January and Monday   DYr
Rest – Menu £13 – Carte dinner £21/27
♦ Superbly located former home of Georgian architect. Impressive period décor in
situ. First floor, high ceilinged dining room for well-priced, tasty dishes on eclectic
menus.

✗ **Melton's Too** ⬛ ⬛ ⬛
25 Walmgate ⊠ YO1 9TX – ℰ (01904) 629 222 – www.meltonstoo.co.uk
– greatfood@meltonstoo.co.uk – Fax (01904) 636 677 – Closed 25-26 December
and 1 January DY**a**
Rest – Carte £19/25
♦ Café-bistro 'descendant' of Melton's restaurant. Located in former saddlers shop with oak beams and exposed brick walls. Good value eclectic dishes, with tapas a speciality.

at Escrick South : 5¾ m. on A 19 - BZ – ⊠ York

🏠 **Parsonage Country House** ⬛ ⬛ ⬛ ⬛ ⬛ ⬛ ⬛ ⬛ ⬛ ⬛
Main St ⊠ YO19 6LF – ℰ (01904) 728 111 – www.parsonagehotel.co.uk
– reservations@parsonagehotel.co.uk – Fax (01904) 728 151
50 rm ⊊ – †£95 ††£140
Rest – Menu £16 (lunch) **s** – Carte dinner £28/36 **s**
♦ Ivy-clad former parsonage with gardens; dating from 1848 and located adjacent to the parish church of St. Helen. Main house rooms most characterful, all are well appointed. Dining room with palpable country house feel.

at Newton-on-Ouse Northwest : 8 m. by A 19

🍴 **The Dawnay Arms** ⬛ ⬛ ⬛ ⬛ ⬛ ⬛
Newton-on-Ouse ⊠ YO32 2BR – ℰ (01347) 848 345
– www.thedawnayatnewton.co.uk – dine@thedawnayarms.co.uk
– Closed 2 weeks in January
Rest – (Closed Sunday dinner and Monday) Carte £20/35
♦ Spacious 18C inn boasting handsome rustic style, with beamed ceilings and roaring fires. Tasty, good value dishes on seasonal menus. Dining room looks out over River Ouse.

ZENNOR – Cornwall – 503 D 33 1 **A3**
🚩 London 305 mi – Penzance 11 mi – St Ives 5 mi

🍴 **The Gurnard's Head** with rm ⬛ ⬛ ⬛
Treen, West : 1½ m. on B 3306 ⊠ TR26 3DE – ℰ (01736) 796 928
– www.gurnardshead.co.uk – enquiries@gurnardshead.co.uk
– Closed 24-25 December
7 rm ⊊ – †£60/75 ††£83/140
Rest – (restricted lunch Monday) Carte £16/25
♦ Roughly textured, mustard hued pub. Shelves of books give it a shabby chic edge. Eat in restaurant or bar: clever, satisfying, carefully balanced combinations. Smart rooms.

ENGLAND

© Foti/MICHELIN

Towns
from A to Z

Villes
de A à Z

Città
de A a Z

Städte
von A bis Z

Scotland

▶ Edinburgh 130 mi – Dundee 67 mi
✈ Aberdeen Airport, Dyce : *℘* (0870) 0400006, NW : 7 m. by A 96 X
⛴ to Shetland Islands (Lerwick) and via Orkney Islands (Stromness) (P and O Scottish Ferries) 1-2 daily
🛈 23 Union St (01224) 288828, aberdeen@visitscotland.com
🖪 Hazelhead Hazelhead Park, *℘* (01224) 321 830
🖪 Royal Aberdeen Bridge of Don Links Rd, *℘* (01224) 702 571
🖪 Balnagask St Fitticks Rd, *℘* (01224) 871 286
🖪 King's Links Golf Rd, *℘* (01224) 632 269
🖪 Portlethen Badentoy Rd, *℘* (01224) 781 090
🖾 Murcar Links Bridge of Don, *℘* (01224) 704 354
🖪 Auchmill West Heatheryfold Bonnyview Rd, *℘* (01224) 715 214
◎ City★★ - Old Aberdeen★★ X – St Machar's Cathedral★★ (West Front★★★, Heraldic Ceiling★★★) X **A** – Art Gallery★★ (Macdonald Collection★★) Y **M** – Mercat Cross★★ Y **B** – King's College Chapel★ (Crown Spire★★★, medieval fittings★★★) X **D** – Provost Skene's House★ (painted ceilings★★) Y **E** – Maritime Museum★ Y **M1** – Marischal College★ Y **U**
◎ Brig o' Balgownie★, by Don St X. SW : Deeside★★ - Crathes Castle★★ (Gardens★★★) **AC**, SW : 16 m. by A 93 X – Dunnottar Castle★★ **AC** (site★★★), S : 18 m. by A 90 X – Pitmedden Garden★★, N : 14 m. by A 90 on B 999 X – Castle Fraser★ (exterior★★) **AC**, W : 16 m. by A 944 X - Fyvie Castle★, NW : 26½ m. on A 947

Plan opposite

SCOTLAND

The Marcliffe H. and Spa   🚗 🗲 *Lₒ* 🛗 & rm, 🕭 rest, ⁇ 🕸 **P**
North Deeside Rd ⊠ AB15 9YA – *℘* (01224) 861 000   **VISA** **◎◎** **AE** **①**
– www.marcliffe.com – enquiries@marcliffe.com – Fax (01224) 868 860   X**r**
40 rm ⊇ – ♦£ 160/220 ♦♦£ 180/260 – 2 suites
Rest *Conservatory* – Carte £ 32/46 s ⅏
♦ Family owned and professionally run modern country house set amidst 8 acres of pleasant grounds. Spacious, individually decorated rooms with antique furniture. Light, airy conservatory dining.

Mercure Ardoe House H. and Spa   ← 🚗 🖉 🗈 🎝 *Lₒ* 🏋 🖾
South Deeside Rd, Blairs, Southwest : 5 m.   & rm, ⁇ 🕸 **P** **VISA** **◎◎** **AE** **①**
on B 9077 ⊠ AB12 5YP – *℘* (01224) 860 600 – www.accorhotels.com
– H6626@accor.com – Fax (01224) 860 644
107 rm – ♦£ 180 ♦♦£ 210, ⊇ £15.95 – 2 suites
Rest *Blairs* – Menu £ 33 – Carte £ 33/45
♦ Imposing 18C Scottish baronial style mansion with annexes. Country house character aligned to excellent leisure facilities. Modern bedrooms, many overlooking the grounds. Formal, wood-panelled Blairs.

Simpson's   🖾 🕻 **P** **VISA** **◎◎** **AE** **①**
59 Queen's Rd ⊠ AB15 4YP – *℘* (01224) 327 777 – www.simpsonshotel.co.uk
– reservations@simpsonshotel.co.uk – Fax (01224) 327 700
– Closed 25-26 December and 1-2 January   X**o**
48 rm ⊇ – ♦£ 170/180 ♦♦£ 205 – 2 suites
Rest *Brasserie* – Menu £ 24/33
♦ Period granite façade belies vibrantly decorated and contemporary interior. Family owned and relaxed "boutique" hotel. Stylish and modern bedrooms with business facilities. Roman bath house styled brasserie.

Skene House Holburn without rest   🎇 🕻 **P** **VISA** **◎◎** **AE** **①**
6 Union Grove ⊠ AB10 6SY – *℘* (01224) 580 000 – www.skene-house.co.uk
– holburn@skene-house.co.uk – Fax (01224) 585 193   Z**v**
39 suites – ♦♦£ 195/214, ⊇ £8
♦ Row of five granite former tenements. Not your conventional hotel, but a number of serviced apartments. Each suite benefits from its own kitchen. Ideal for long stays.

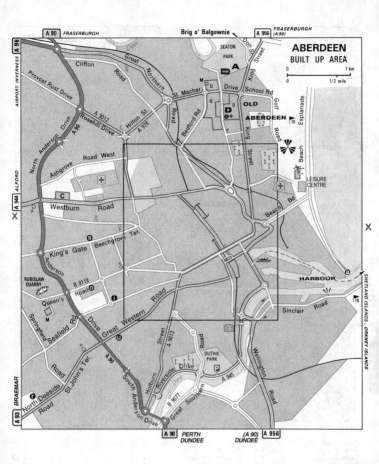

The Mariner
&. rm, 🌿 ⟨ℙ⟩ 🛜 📶 ℙ VISA ⓜⓞ AE ①

349 Great Western Rd ⊠ *AB10 6NW –* ℰ *(01224) 588 901*
– www.themarinerhotel.co.uk – info@themarinerhotel.co.uk – Fax (01224)
571621 – Closed 26 December   X**u**
25 rm ⊊ – †£ 100 ††£ 125
Rest *Atlantis* – Seafood – *(Closed Saturday lunch)* Menu £ 21 *(lunch)*
– Carte £ 24/44

♦ A nautical theme prevails through the ground floor of this commercial hotel.
Spacious, colourfully decorated bedrooms with extensive facilities. More seclusion in
annex rooms. Long established restaurant with wood panelling and maritime themed
décor.

Atholl
&. rm, 🌿 ⟨ℙ⟩ 🛁 ℙ VISA ⓜⓞ AE ①

54 King's Gate ⊠ *AB15 4YN –* ℰ *(01224) 323 505 – www.atholl-aberdeen.com*
– info@atholl-aberdeen.co.uk – Fax (01224) 321 555 – Closed 1 January   X**s**
34 rm ⊊ – †£ 90/105 ††£ 135/140   **Rest** – Carte £ 17/36

♦ Baronial style hotel set in leafy suburbs; well run by friendly staff. Traditional
lounge bar; well-priced, up-to-date rooms. A useful address for visitors to the city.
Dining room specialises in tried-and-tested Scottish cooking.

833

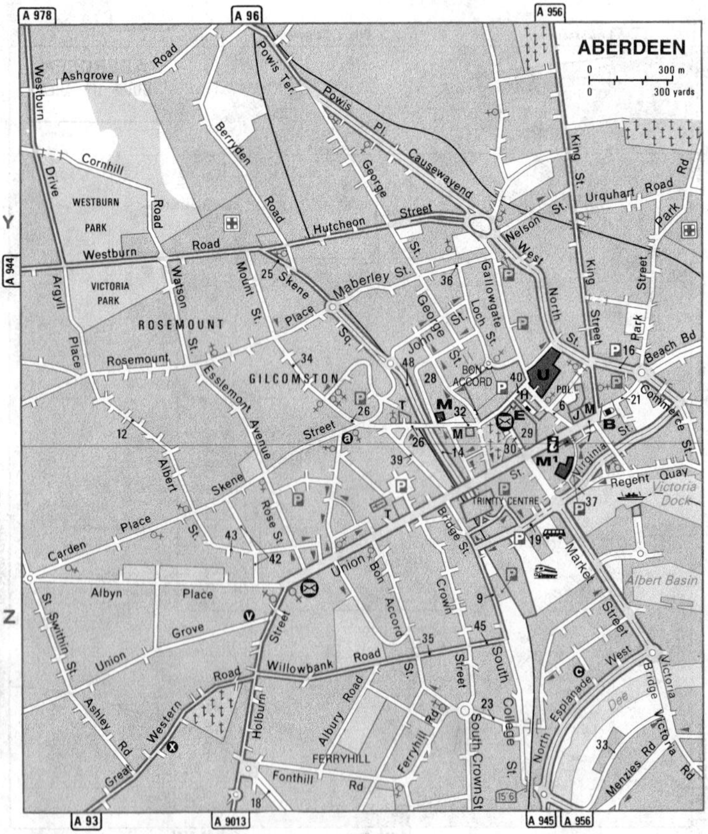

Carmelite

Stirling St – ✆ (01224) 589 101 – www.carmelitehotels.com
– info@carmelitehotel.com – Fax (01224) 574 288 Zc

50 rm – 🚹£45/135 🚹🚹£65/325 **Rest** – Carte £22/29

◆ Boutique hotel on site of former monastery. Refurbished first floor bedrooms have contemporary style; top two floors are more traditional, while luxury suites are the largest. Traditional restaurant serving simple, flavoursome food.

Penny Meadow without rest

189 Great Western Rd ✉ AB10 6PS – ✆ (01224) 588 037
– frances@pennymeadow.freeserve.co.uk – Fax (01224) 573 639 Zx

3 rm – 🚹£55 🚹🚹£75

◆ Attractive Victorian house built of local granite. Welcoming service by owners. Light and airy bedrooms have some thoughtful touches and are well-appointed.

XX Silver Darling   ← 🛜 VISA ⓒⓄ AE ⓞ

Pocra Quay, North Pier ⊠ AB11 5DQ – ℰ (01224) 576 229
– www.silverdarlingrestaurant.co.uk – Fax (01224) 588 119 – Closed 2 weeks
Christmas-New Year, Saturday lunch and Sunday   X**a**
Rest – Seafood – Carte £ 40/49
♦ Former customs house attractively set at port entrance; panoramic views across harbour and coastline. Attentive service of superb quality seafood prepared in imaginative ways.

XX Nargile   AC 🍴 VISA ⓒⓄ AE ⓞ

77-79 Skene St ⊠ AB10 1QD – ℰ (01224) 636 093 – tayfur.kaplan@homecall.co.uk
– Fax (01224) 636 202 – Closed 25-26 December, 1-2 January and Sunday lunch   Y**a**
Rest – Turkish – Menu £ 23 (dinner) – Carte £ 22/28
♦ Traditionally decorated Turkish restaurant with subdued lighting from Turkish lamps. Open-plan kitchen allows the diner to watch the chefs prepare the authentic dishes.

X Rendezvous at Nargile   AC VISA ⓒⓄ AE

106-108 Forest Ave ⊠ AB15 4UP – ℰ (01224) 323 700
– www.rendezvousatnargile.co.uk – kiridag@hotmail.com
– Fax (01224) 312 202   X**i**
Rest – Turkish – Menu £ 20/26 – Carte £ 25/37
♦ Corner restaurant with contemporary décor. Mediterranean - predominantly Turkish - menu from snacks to a full a la carte meal; fixed price menu between 5-7pm.

ABERFELDY – Perth and Kinross – 501 I 14   28 C2
◗ Edinburgh 75 mi – Dunkeld 17 mi – Pitlochry 14 mi

at Fortingall West : 8 m. by B 846 and Fortingall rd

⌂ Fortingall Hotel   ← 🚗 🔌 P. VISA ⓒⓄ

⊠ PH15 2NQ – ℰ (01887) 830 367 – www.fortingallhotel.com
– hotel@fortingallhotel.com – Closed 2 weeks in February
10 rm ⊇ – †£ 99 ††£ 148   **Rest** – Carte £ 22/39 **s**
♦ Refurbished arts and crafts style house on private estate. Bedrooms, named after local estates, have a contemporary style with a touch of tweed; those at front boasting views. Daily-changing menu served in antique-furnished restaurant.

ABERLADY East Lothian – 501 L 15 – see GULLANE

ABERLOUR – Moray – 501 K 11 ▌ Scotland   28 C1
◗ Edinburgh 192 mi – Aberdeen 60 mi – Elgin 15 mi – Inverness 55 mi
▣ Rothes Blackhall, ℰ (01340) 831 443
◉ Dufftown (Glenfiddich Distillery★), SE : 6 m. by A 95 and A 941

⌂⌂ Dowans   🚗 🔌 ⁽ᵖ⁾ P. VISA ⓒⓄ

Southwest : ¾ m. by A 95 ⊠ AB38 9LS – ℰ (01340) 871 488
– www.dowanshotel.com – enquiries@dowanshotel.com – Fax (01340) 871 038
19 rm ⊇ – †£ 55/68 ††£ 140   **Rest** – Carte £ 20/37
♦ Welcoming, informal establishment with classic Scottish country house style. Inviting public areas. Comfortably smart rooms, refurbished in 2006; best views from the front. Two roomed restaurant.

ABOYNE – Aberdeenshire – 501 L 12 – pop. 2 202 ▌ Scotland   28 D1
◗ Edinburgh 131 mi – Aberdeen 30 mi – Dundee 68 mi
▣ Formanston Park, ℰ (013398) 86 328
◉ Craigievar Castle★ AC, NE : 12 m. by B 9094, B 9119 and A 980

⌂ Struan Hall without rest   🚗 🌿 P. VISA ⓒⓄ

Ballater Rd ⊠ AB34 5HY – ℰ (013398) 87 241 – www.struanhall.co.uk
– struanhall@zetnet.co.uk – Fax (013398) 87 241 – 6 April- 20 September
3 rm ⊇ – †£ 36/47 ††£ 72/80
♦ An agreeable and welcoming guesthouse with attractive garden. Well kept throughout. Large sitting room and antique breakfast table. Simple, comfy bedrooms.

SCOTLAND

ACHILTIBUIE – Highland – 501 D 9

30 **C1**

▶ Edinburgh 243 mi – Inverness 84 mi – Ullapool 25 mi

Summer Isles 🐾
≤ 🖨 🗴 **P** VISA ⓒⓞ

✉ IV26 2YG – ℰ (01854) 622 282 – www.summerisleshotel.co.uk
– info@summerisleshotel.co.uk – Fax (01854) 622 251 – 8 April - 31 October
10 rm ☷ – ☝£170 ☝☝£200 – 3 suites
Rest – (booking essential)(set menu only at dinner)(light seafood lunch)
Carte £25/55 **s**

Rest *Summer Isles Bar* – see restaurant listing

Spec. Quail with wilted spinach and mushroom purée. Seared scallops with champ, caviar and Greek basil. Iced hazelnut terrine with raspberry sauce.
♦ Exceedingly well run with a fine setting and superb views of Summer Isles. Very comfy lounges and real fire. Superb duplex suite and cosy log cabin rooms. Pleasant restaurant boasts exacting cooking to a very high standard; local seafood to the fore.

Summer Isles (Bar) – at Summer Isles Hotel
🖨 🕯 **P** VISA ⓒⓞ

✉ IV26 2YG – ℰ (01854) 622 282 – www.summerisleshotel.co.uk
– info@summerisleshotel.co.uk – Fax (01854) 622 251 – 8 April - 31 October
Rest – Seafood – (bookings not accepted) Carte £25/45 **s**
♦ Simple, informal bar with outside seating for sunny days and snug interior for more bracing weather. Seafood oriented blackboard menu and puddings from the restaurant.

ALLOWAY – South Ayrshire – 501 G 17 – see Ayr

ALYTH – Perth and Kinross – 501 J 14 – pop. 2 301

28 **C2**

▶ Edinburgh 63 mi – Aberdeen 69 mi – Dundee 16 mi – Perth 21 mi
🖼 Pitcrocknie, ℰ (01828) 632 268

Tigh Na Leigh
🖨 🕯 **P** VISA ⓒⓞ AE

22-24 Airlie St ✉ PH11 8AJ – ℰ (01828) 632 372 – www.tighnaleigh.co.uk
– bandcblack@yahoo.co.uk – Fax (01828) 632 279
– Closed 23 December- 14 February
5 rm ☷ – ☝£43/70 ☝☝£115
Rest – (dinner only) (booking essential) Menu £24 **s**
♦ Extremely spacious, modern bedrooms in this comfortable and contemporary conversion, which retains many original features. Look out for Tom and Eddie, the cats. Dining room overlooks kitchen garden, church and carp pond. Daily-changing dinner menu and small wine list.

ANNBANK – South Ayrshire – 501 G 17

25 **B2**

▶ Edinburgh 84 mi – Ayr 6 mi – Dumfries 54 mi – Dumfries 38 mi

Enterkine 🐾
≤ 🖨 🗴 🕯 🕯 🛁 **P** VISA ⓒⓞ AE

Southeast : ½ m. on B 742 (Coylton rd) ✉ KA6 5AL – ℰ (01292) 520 580
– www.enterkine.com – mail@enterkine.com – Fax (01292) 521 582
6 rm ☷ – ☝£80/100 ☝☝£160/200 – 1 suite
Rest – (booking essential) Menu £18/45
♦ 1930s country house surrounded by extensive gardens and woodlands. Spacious, comfortable lounges. Luxurious bedrooms; one with large roof terrace. Charming library. Formal restaurant with views over River Ayr serves modern cooking; popular with non-residents.

ANSTRUTHER – Fife – 501 L 15 – pop. 3 442 📗 Scotland

28 **D2**

▶ Edinburgh 46 mi – Dundee 23 mi – Dunfermline 34 mi
🗓 Scottish Fisheries Museum, Harbourhead ℰ (01333) 311073
(April-October), anstruther@visitfife.com
🖼 Marsfield Shore Rd, ℰ (01333) 310956
◎ Scottish Fisheries Museum★★ **AC**
◎ The East Neuk★★ – Crail★★ (Old Centre★★, Upper Crail★) NE : 4 m. by A 917. Kellie Castle★ **AC**, NW : 7 m. by B 9171, B 942 and A 917

⛰ **The Spindrift**   📶 **P** 🆅🅸🆂🅰 ⓿ 🅰🅴

Pittenweem Rd ⊠ KY10 3DT – ℰ (01333) 310573 – www.thespindrift.co.uk
– info@thespindrift.co.uk – Fax (01333) 310573 – Closed January and Christmas
8 rm ⊆ – †£40/50 ††£64/76   **Rest** – (by arrangement) Menu £21
♦ Victorian house originally owned by tea clipper captain whose bedroom replicates
a master's cabin. Comfortable period style throughout and local kippers for breakfast.
19C style dining room reflects house's age.

⛰ **The Grange** without rest   🚗 🕉 **P**

45 Pittenweem Rd ⊠ KY10 3DT – ℰ (01333) 310842
– www.thegrangeanstruther.com – pamelarae@hotmail.com – Fax (01333)
310842 – Closed January and February
4 rm ⊆ – †£30/70 ††£70/75
♦ Spacious Edwardian house on main road into this delightful coastal village. Snug
lounges including charming sun room. Neatly kept, traditional bedrooms.

✕✕ **Cellar**   🆅🅸🆂🅰 ⓿ 🅰🅴 ⓪

24 East Green ⊠ KY10 3AA – ℰ (01333) 310378 – Fax (01333) 312544 – Closed
Christmas, Sunday, Monday in Winter and lunch mid week except in Summer
Rest – Seafood – (booking essential) Menu £24/38
♦ Located through an archway on quiet back streets. Warm ambience with fires and
exposed brick and stone. Bold, original cooking, more elaborate at dinner.

APPLECROSS – Highland – **501** C 11   29 **B2**

🇩 Edinburgh 234 mi – Gairloch 56 mi – Portree 76 mi

✕ **The Potting Shed**   🚗 🕉 **P** 🆅🅸🆂🅰 ⓿ 🅰🅴 ⓪

Applecross Walled Garden, Northeast : ½ m. ⊠ IV54 8ND – ℰ (01520) 744440
– www.eatinthewalledgarden.co.uk – jonglover@hotmail.com
– Restricted opening in winter
Rest – (Closed Sunday dinner) Carte £17/29
♦ Lovely 17C walled kitchen garden whose restaurant has grown from a tearoom. Its
simple structure belies its tasty dishes, fresh from owner's fishing boat or the garden
itself.

🏠 **Applecross Inn** with rm   ⪡ 🚗 🕉 & rm, **P** 🆅🅸🆂🅰 ⓿

Shore St ⊠ IV54 8LR – ℰ (01520) 744262 – www.applecross.uk.com
– applecrossinn@globalnet.co.uk – Fax (01520) 744400
– Closed 25 December, 1 January
7 rm ⊆ – †£70 ††£100   **Rest** – (booking essential) Carte £15/30
♦ An unforgettable coastal road journey of 24 miles ends at this cosy row of stone
fishermen's cottages with lots of windows to enjoy the stupendous views. Blackboard
menus feature local seafood. Smart, comfy rooms.

ARBROATH – Angus – **501** M 14   28 **D2**

🇩 Edinburgh 72 mi – Dundee 17 mi – Montrose 12 mi

⛰ **The Old Vicarage** without rest   🚗 🕉 📶 **P** 🆅🅸🆂🅰 ⓿ 🅰🅴

2 Seaton Rd, Northeast : ¾ m. by A 92 and Hayshead Rd ⊠ DD11 5DX
– ℰ (01241) 430475 – www.theoldvicaragebandb.co.uk
– loris@theoldvicaragebandb.co.uk
3 rm ⊆ – †£50/55 ††£65/75
♦ Detached 19C house, of large proportions, clothed in Victorian style throughout. Antique furnished bedrooms: ask for view of Arbroath Abbey.

ARCHIESTOWN – Moray – **501** K 11 – ⊠ Aberlour (Aberdeenshire)   28 **C1**

🇩 Edinburgh 194 mi – Aberdeen 62 mi – Inverness 49 mi

🏠 **Archiestown**   🚗 🕙 🕉 📶 **P** 🆅🅸🆂🅰 ⓿

The Square ⊠ AB38 7QL – ℰ (01340) 810218 – www.archiestownhotel.co.uk
– jah@archiestownhotel.co.uk – Fax (01340) 810239 – Closed 23-29 December
11 rm ⊆ – †£45/80 ††£100/130
Rest *Bistro* – Carte £27/37
♦ Privately owned little hotel appealing to all with its characterful, comfortable
lounges and nearby golf and distilleries. Comfy, individual rooms, prettily decorated.
Informal bistro with daily changing menu.

SCOTLAND

ARDEONAIG – Perth and Kinross – **501** H 14 – see Killin (Stirling)

ARDHASAIG – Western Isles Outer Hebrides – **501** Z 10 – see Lewis and Harris (Isle of)

ARDRISHAIG – Argyll and Bute – **501** D 15 – ⊠ **Lochgilphead**   27 **B2**
  ▶ Edinburgh 132 mi – Glasgow 86 mi – Oban 40 mi

⌂   **Allt-na-Craig**   ≼ ⬚ ⁽ⁱ⁾ **P** 𝘝𝘐𝘚𝘈 ◍
Tarbert Rd, on A 83 ⊠ *PA30 8EP –* ℰ *(01546) 603 245 – www.allt-na-craig.co.uk*
– information@allt-na-craig.co.uk – Fax (01546) 603 255
– Closed Christmas-New Year
5 rm ⌷ **–** ♦£45/65 ♦♦£ 90   **Rest** – (by arrangement) Menu £ 25
♦ Spacious, modernised Victorian house with lovely gardens, once the childhood home of author Kenneth Grahame. Front bedrooms have good views over loch. Simple, traditional dining room where breakfasts and evening meals are served.

ARDUAINE – Argyll and Bute – **501** D 15 – ⊠ **Oban** ▌ *Scotland*   27 **B2**
  ▶ Edinburgh 142 mi – Oban 20 mi
  ◔ Loch Awe★★, E : 12 m. by A 816 and B 840

🏠   **Loch Melfort** ⚶   ≼ ⬚ ◍ ♨ **P** 𝘝𝘐𝘚𝘈 ◍ 𝗔𝗘
⊠ *PA34 4XG –* ℰ *(01852) 200 233 – www.lochmelfort.co.uk*
– reception@lochmelfort.co.uk – Fax (01852) 200 214
– Closed 2 January-mid February
25 rm ⌷ **–** ♦£50/89 ♦♦£100/138   **Rest** – Seafood – (bar lunch) Menu £ 30
♦ Next to Arduaine Gardens and with glorious, captivating views of the Sound of Jura, the hotel has spacious public areas including a bistro bar. Largest rooms in main house. Formal atmosphere in the main restaurant with a focus on quality local seafood.

ARRAN (Isle of) – North Ayrshire – **501** E 17 ▌ *Scotland*   25 **A2**
  ⛴ from Brodick to Ardrossan (Caledonian MacBrayne Ltd) 4-6 daily (55 mn) – from Lochranza to Kintyre Peninsula (Claonaig) (Caledonian MacBrayne Ltd) frequent services daily (30 mn) – from Brodick to Isle of Bute (Rothesay) (Caledonian MacBrayne Ltd) 3 weekly (2 h 5 mn)
  ◎ Island★★ - Brodick Castle★★ **AC**

Brodick – North Ayrshire – pop. 621   25 **A2**
  🛈 The Pier ℰ (01770) 303776, arran@ayreshire-arran.com
  ▦ Brodick, ℰ (01770) 302 349
  ▦ Machrie Bay, ℰ (01770) 850 232

🏠   **Kilmichael Country House** ⚶   ⬚ **P** 𝘝𝘐𝘚𝘈 ◍ ◍
Glen Cloy, West : 1 m. by Shore Rd, taking left turn opposite Golf Club
⊠ *KA27 8BY –* ℰ *(01770) 302 219 – www.kilmichael.com*
– enquiries@kilmichael.com – Fax (01770) 302 068 – Easter-October
5 rm ⌷ **–** ♦£95 ♦♦£ 120/190 **– 3 suites**
Rest – (Closed Tuesday) (dinner only) (booking essential) Menu £ 42 **s**
♦ Reputedly the oldest house on the Isle of Arran, in peaceful location with immaculate lawned grounds. Comfortable country house style and individually decorated bedrooms. Welcoming owners. Restaurant housed in extension. Daily-changing menus.

⌂   **Alltan** without rest   ⬚ ⁝⁝ ⁽ⁱ⁾ **P**
Knowe Rd, West : ½ m. by Shore Rd taking left at Golf Club ⊠ *KA27 8BY*
– ℰ *(01770) 302 937 – www.alltanarran.co.uk – alltanarran@yahoo.co.uk*
– Closed December
3 rm ⌷ **–** ♦£65/76 ♦♦£ 76
♦ Friendly, modern guest house outside village. Comfortable rear lounge with wood-burning stove overlooks garden and river. Raised decked balcony with wrought iron furniture.

SCOTLAND

↑ **Dunvegan House** ≤ 🚗 🅿
*Shore Rd ⊠ KA27 8AJ – ℰ (01770) 302811 – www.dunveganhouse.co.uk
– dunveganhouse1@hotmail.com – Fax (01770) 302811 – Closed Christmas and
New Year*
9 rm ⊡ – ♦♦£80   **Rest** – Menu £21
♦ Close to ferry terminal on Brodick seafront with view out over bay. Small lawned garden, comfortable lounge and simple, homely bedrooms with pastel décor. Dining room to front.

Kilmory – North Ayrshire – pop. 65   25 **A2**
🚇 Edinburgh 105 mi – Ayr 38 mi – Troon 32 mi

🏠 **Lagg** 🚗 🕪 🌙 🅿 VISA ☒☺
*Lagg, on A 841 ⊠ KA27 8PQ – ℰ (01770) 870255 – www.lagghotel.com
– info@lagghotel.com – Fax (01770) 870250 – 19 March-3 November*
13 rm ⊡ – ♦£65 ♦♦£90/100   **Rest** – (bar lunch) Carte £20/34 **s**
♦ Extended 18C inn with acres of grounds and a river. Traditional lounges with open fires and a characterful, beamed bar. Antique furnished bedrooms. Smartly refurbished restaurant with brushed purple velvet walls.

Lochranza – North Ayrshire   25 **A2**
🛈 The Pier ℰ (01770) 830320 (summer only)

↑ **Apple Lodge** ≤ 🚗 🌂 🅿
*⊠ KA27 8HJ – ℰ (01770) 830229 – Fax (01770) 830229 – Closed Christmas and
New Year, minimum 3 night stay*
4 rm ⊡ – ♦£52/54 ♦♦£76/88   **Rest** – (by arrangement) Menu £25
♦ Extended period house with small garden and pleasing views, in centre of quiet village. Homely cottage-style decor with antique furniture and a welcoming atmosphere. Food is home-cooked and uses island and home produce in good, hearty, varied dishes.

Whiting Bay – North Ayrshire   25 **A2**
🛈 Whiting Bay Golf Course Rd, ℰ (01770) 700487

↑ **Royal Arran** without rest ≤ 🚗 🌂 🅿 VISA ☒☺
*Shore Rd ⊠ KA27 8PZ – ℰ (01770) 700286 – www.royalarran.co.uk
– royalarran@btinternet.com – March-October*
4 rm ⊡ – ♦£50/89 ♦♦£99
♦ Large, late Victorian house revitalised by owners. Comfy lounge and breakfast room with homely touches and ornaments. Nicely-sized bedrooms - front one has excellent view.

ASCOG – Argyll and Bute – 501 E 16 – see Bute (Isle of)

AUCHENCAIRN – Dumfries and Galloway – 501 I 19 – ⊠ Castle   25 **B3**
Douglas
🚇 Edinburgh 94 mi – Dumfries 21 mi – Stranraer 60 mi

🏠🏠 **Balcary Bay** ⊛ ≤ 🚗 ᴋ rm, 🅿 VISA ☒☺
*Southeast : 2 m. on Balcary rd ⊠ DG7 1QZ – ℰ (01556) 640217
– www.balcary-bay-hotel.co.uk – reservations@balcary-bay-hotel.co.uk
– Fax (01556) 640272 – Closed December and January*
20 rm ⊡ – ♦£67/90 ♦♦£160
Rest – (lunch by arrangement) Menu £36 – Carte £28/39
♦ Perched on the eponymous bay with magnificent views of Auchencairn Bay and Solway Firth. Comfortable, family run hotel. Bedrooms have bay or garden views. Restaurant decorated in keeping with the hotel's traditional style; window tables much in request.

SCOTLAND

AUCHENCAIRN

⌂ **Balcary Mews** without rest ⌕　　　　　　　≤ 🛋 ✗ **P**
🍴 *Balcary Bay, Southwest : 2 m. on Balcary rd* ✉ *DG7 1QZ –* ✆ *(01556) 640 276*
– www.balcarymews.co.uk – pamelavaughan@yahoo.com – Fax (01556) 640 276
– Closed Christmas-New Year
3 rm ⌷ – **†**£45/50 **††**£80
♦ Well-priced, smuggler-built 18C property with lovely views. Warm welcome enhances overall homely feel, typified by comfy lounge overlooking pretty garden. Quality rooms.

AUCHTERARDER – Perth and Kinross – 501 I 15 – pop. 3 945　　28 **C2**
🔳 *Scotland*

　▶ Edinburgh 55 mi – Glasgow 45 mi – Perth 14 mi
　🅱 90 High St ✆ (0845) 2255121, auchterarder@visitscotland.com
　🔟 Ochil Rd, ✆ (01764) 662 804
　📷 Dunning Rollo Park, ✆ (01764) 684 747
　🅖 Tullibardine Chapel★, NW : 2 m

🏨 **Gleneagles**　≤ 🛋 🕐 🐎 🎣 🔲 🅷 🛝 *Iₒ* ✗ 🚗 🅘 ♿ rm, 🏃 👥
Southwest : 2 m. by A 824 on A 823 ✉ *PH3 1NF*　**P** **VISA** **GO** **AE** **①**
– ✆ *(01764) 662 231 – www.gleneagles.com – resort.sales@gleneagles.com*
– Fax (01764) 662 134
216 rm ⌷ – **†††**£440/560 – 16 suites
Rest *Andrew Fairlie at Gleneagles* – see restaurant listing
Rest *Strathearn* – (dinner only and Sunday lunch) Menu £ 53
Rest *Deseo* – Carte £ 27/45
♦ World famous for its championship golf courses and extensive leisure facilities. Graceful art deco and constant reinvestment ensure the impressive grandeur of this early 20C mansion remains. Strathearn is elegant art deco dining room. Deseo offers Mediterranean dishes in informal atmosphere.

XXX **Andrew Fairlie at Gleneagles**　🅰🅲 **P** **VISA** **GO** **AE** **①**
❀❀ *Southwest : 2 m. by A 824 on A 823* ✉ *PH3 1NF –* ✆ *(01764) 694 267*
– www.andrew.fairlie.com – andrew.fairlie@gleneagles.com – Fax (01764)
694 163 – Closed Christmas, January and Sunday
Rest – (dinner only) Menu £ 75 **s**
Spec. Home smoked lobster, lime and herb butter. Peelham grass fed veal loin, shin and sweetbreads. Warm raspberry shortcake and fromage blanc.
♦ Discreet, minimalist restaurant, decorated with still life, food themed oil paintings. Precise, well-presented cooking utilises prime Scottish ingredients. Welcoming staff.

AULTBEA – Highland – 501 D 10　　29 **B2**
　▶ Edinburgh 231 mi – Gairloch 13 mi – Ullapool 45 mi

⌂ **Mellondale**　　　　　　　≤ 🛋 ✗ **P** **VISA** **GO**
🍴 *47 Mellon Charles, Northwest : 3 m. on Mellon Charles rd* ✉ *IV22 2JL*
– ✆ *(01445) 731 326 – www.mellondale.co.uk – mellondale@lineone.net*
– Fax (01445) 731 326 – March-October
4 rm ⌷ – **†**£40/42 **††**£60/70　**Rest** – ((by arrangement)) Menu £ 18
♦ Remotely located whitewashed house with neat garden. Immaculately kept dining room and homely lounge look to Loch Ewe. Smart, modern bedrooms with bright décor, two with views. Concise dinner menu of local, home cooked produce.

AVIEMORE – Highland – 501 I 12 – pop. 2 397 🔳 *Scotland*　30 **D3**
　▶ Edinburgh 129 mi – Inverness 29 mi – Perth 85 mi
　🅱 Grampian Rd ✆ (0845) 2255121, info@visitscotland.com
　◎ Town★
　🅖 The Cairngorms★★ (≤★★★) – ❋★★★ from Cairn Gorm, SE : 11 m. by
　B 970 – Landmark Visitor Centre (The Highlander★) **AC**, N : 7 m. by A 9 –
　Highland Wildlife Park★ **AC**, SW : 7 m. by A 9

840

Corrour House without rest ⟨ ⫘ ⸙ **P.** *VISA* ⦾

Rothiemurchus, Southeast : 1 m. on B 970 ⊠ PH22 1QH – ℰ (01479) 810 220
– www.corrourhouse.co.uk – enquiries@corrourhouse.co.uk – Fax (01479) 811 500
– Restricted opening in winter

8 rm ⊇ – †£55 ††£84/96

♦ Victorian dower house in charming setting surrounded by neat lawned garden. Rooms are comfortably furnished with reproduction furniture - those on top floor have best views.

The Old Minister's Guest House without rest ⫘ ⸙ ⸙ **P.** *VISA* ⦾ **AE**

Rothiemurchus, Southeast : 1 m. on B 970 ⊠ PH22 1QH – ℰ (01479) 812 181
– www.theoldministershouse.co.uk – kate@theoldministershouse.co.uk
– Fax (0871) 661 9324 – Closed mid December - mid January

4 rm ⊇ – †£50 ††£80/94

♦ Early 20C house on outskirts of town, recently vacated by minister. River at bottom of pretty garden. Nicely-laid breakfast room. Spacious bedrooms, finished to high standard.

AYR – South Ayrshire – **501** G 17 – pop. 46 431 ▌ *Scotland* 25 **A2**

▶ Edinburgh 81 mi – Glasgow 35 mi
🛈 22 Sandgate ℰ (01292) 290300, info@visitscotland.com
🏌 Seafield Doonfoot Rd, Belleisle Park, ℰ (01292) 441 258
🏌 Dalmilling Westwood Ave, ℰ (01292) 263 893
🏌 Doon Valley Patna Hillside, ℰ (01292) 531 607
◉ Alloway★ (Burns Cottage and Museum★ **AC**) S : 3 m. by B 7024 BZ.
Culzean Castle★ **AC** (setting★★★, Oval Staircase★★) SW : 13 m. by A 719 BZ

SCOTLAND

Plan on next page

Western House ⫘ 🖨 & rm, ⸙ ⸙ ⸙ **P.** *VISA* ⦾ **AE**

Ayr Racecourse, 2 Craigie Rd ⊠ KA8 0HA – ℰ (0870) 055 55 10
– www.westernhousehotel.co.uk – info@westernhousehotel.co.uk
– Fax (0870) 055 55 15 BZ**a**

48 rm ⊇ – †£80/190 ††£80/190 – 1 suite

Rest *The Jockey Club* – Carte £ 22/32

♦ Built in 1920 and designed by Lutyens on Ayr racecourse. Contemporary bedrooms named after racecourses - those in main house the most spacious; some overlook the golf course. Modern restaurant with horseracing theme offers classically based dishes.

Fairfield House ⫯ 🔲 ⸙ ƒ🔥 🖨 & rm, 🖾 rest, ⸙ ⸙ ⸙ **P.** *VISA* ⦾ **AE** ⓪

12 Fairfield Rd ⊠ KA7 2AS – ℰ (01292) 267 461 – www.fairfieldhotel.co.uk
– manager@fairfieldhotel.co.uk – Fax (01292) 261 456 AY**a**

44 rm ⊇ – †£89/109 ††£109/129

Rest *Martins Bar & Grill* – Carte £ 17/47

♦ Former holiday retreat for Glasgow tea merchant, refurbished in contemporary browns and beiges. Bedrooms in main house have sea view. Those in extension well-equipped but smaller. Restaurant offers traditional cooking, popular with locals.

Ellisland ⫘ ⫯ ⸙ **P.** *VISA* ⦾ **AE**

19 Racecourse Rd ⊠ KA7 2TD – ℰ (01292) 260 111 – www.costley-hotels.co.uk
– ellisland@costley-hotels.co.uk – Fax (01292) 260 124 BZ**e**

7 rm ⊇ – †£85 ††£145 – 2 suites **Rest** – Carte £ 18/22

♦ Victorian house furnished in reds and greens and hung with modern art; tartan carpet lines the corridors. Terrace with fountain and manicured lawns. Smart, spacious bedrooms. Traditional menu served in restaurant and conservatory. Lighter snacks in lounge.

Carrick Lodge ⫘ ⸙ ⫯ **P.** *VISA* ⦾

46 Carrick Rd ⊠ KA7 2RE – ℰ (01292) 262 846 – www.murdochhospitality.co.uk
– reservations@murdochhospitality.co.uk – Fax (01292) 611 101 BZ**n**

7 rm ⊇ – †£60 ††£90 **Rest** – Carte £ 21/37

♦ Victorian building close to town centre, refurbished to a high standard. Family-run; warm, welcoming feel and smiley staff. Contemporary bedrooms named after local areas. Traditional Scottish dishes on menu.

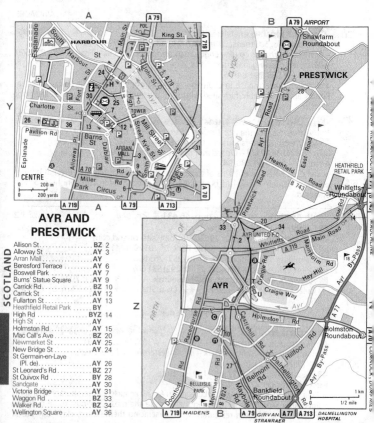

AYR AND PRESTWICK

⌂ **No.26 The Crescent** without rest 🛇 📶 **P** **VISA** **CO** **AE**

26 Bellevue Crescent ⊠ KA7 2DR – ℰ (01292) 287 329 – www.26crescent.co.uk
– joyce&mike@26crescent.co.uk – Closed Christmas and New Year BZ**c**
5 rm ⌧ – †£45/65 ††£60/70

♦ Superior, well-priced guest house with mix of traditional and modern décor. Comfortable and well-run, with individually-furnished bedrooms – best one at front has four poster.

⌂ **Coila** without rest 🛇 📶 **P** **VISA** **CO**

10 Holmston Rd ⊠ KA7 3BB – ℰ (01292) 262 642 – www.coila.co.uk
– hazel@coila.co.uk – Closed Christmas and New Year AY**u**
4 rm ⌧ – †£40/50 ††£55/80

♦ Spotlessly-kept house proudly decorated with owners' personal ornaments and family photos. Warm, homely lounge. Good-sized bedrooms with king-size beds and modern facilities.

at Alloway South : 3 m. on B 7024 - BZ - ⊠ Ayr

🏠 **Brig O'Doon House** 🍴 🔄 🛇 📞 🔧 **VISA** **CO** **AE**

⊠ KA7 4PQ – ℰ (01292) 442 466 – www.costleyhotels.co.uk
– brigodoon@costleyhotels.co.uk – Fax (01292) 441 999
5 rm ⌧ – †£85 ††£120 **Rest** – Carte £17/31

♦ Busy inn whose name refers to bridge behind hotel – as in Burns' Tam O'Shanter. Beamed bar, tartan carpets, pretty garden. Refurbished bedrooms with state-of-the-art facilities. Brasserie-style dining room offers extensive menus.

at Dunfoot/Doonfoot Southwest : 2½ m. on A 719 - BZ – ⊠ Ayr

⌂ **Greenan Lodge** without rest   🌿 P
39 Dunure Rd, on A 719 ⊠ KA7 4HR – ℰ (01292) 443939
– www.greenanlodge.com – helen@greenanlodge.com
3 rm ☑ – †£45/50 ††£60/65
♦ Modern and Mediterranean in style with friendly owner. Roomy lounge; guests welcome to have a tinkle on the ivories. Light bedrooms with flat screen TVs. Good base for golf.

BADACHRO – Highland – **501** C 10 – pop. 58 – ⊠ Gairloch   29 **B2**
 🖿 Edinburgh 224 mi – Inverness 71 mi – Ullapool 61 mi

🏠 **Badachro Inn**   P VISA ⓪ AE ⓪
⊠ IV21 2AA – ℰ (01445) 741255 – www.badachroinn.com
– lesley@badachroinn.com – Fax (01445) 741319 – Closed 25 December
Rest – Carte approx. £20
♦ Nestled in secluded inlet on South shore of Loch Gairloch. Cosily rustic atmosphere with beamed bar, open fire and maritime charts on walls. Menus make good use of local catch.

BALLACHULISH – Highland – **501** E 13 ▌*Scotland*   30 **C3**
 🖿 Edinburgh 117 mi – Inverness 80 mi – Kyle of Lochalsh 90 mi – Oban 38 mi
 🖪 Loan sern ℰ (01855) 811866, info@glencoetourism.co.uk
 🖸 Glen Coe★★, E : 6 m. by A 82

🏠 **Ballachulish House** ⌂   ← 🚗 🖾 🌿 P VISA ⓪ AE
❀ *West : 2½ m. by A 82 off A 828 ⊠ PH49 4JX – ℰ (01855) 811266*
– www.ballachulishhouse.com – mclaughlins@btconnect.com – Fax (01855) 811498
8 rm ☑ – †£95 ††£147/221
Rest – (booking essential for non-residents) Menu £26/48
Spec. Ballottine of foie gras, apple purée and butter brioche. Assiette of west coast fish with crab ravioli and saffron sauce. Raspberry soufflé with lemon verbena sorbet.
♦ Cosy, whitewashed 17C house with walled garden, country house style and colourful history that inspired Stevenson's 'Kidnapped.' Comfortable bedrooms with loch views. Precise, well presented, flavourful cooking served in formal dining room at 8 p.m.

⌂ **Ardno House** without rest   ← 🚗 🌿 P
Lettermore, Glencoe, West : 3½ m. by A 82 on A 828 ⊠ PH49 4JD – ℰ (01855) 811830 – www.ardnohouse.co.uk – pam@ardnohouse.co.uk
3 rm ☑ – ††£60/66
♦ Purpose-built guesthouse with fine view of Loch Linnhe and the Morven Hills. Personally run and providing good value, comfortable accommodation. Spacious bedrooms.

BALLANTRAE – South Ayrshire – **501** E 18 – ⊠ Girvan   25 **A2**
 🖿 Edinburgh 115 mi – Ayr 33 mi – Stranraer 18 mi

🏰 **Glenapp Castle** ⌂   ← 🚗 🐾 🎐 🌿 ⎚ 🍴 P VISA ⓪ AE
South : 1 m. by A 77 taking first right turn after bridge ⊠ KA26 0NZ – ℰ (01465) 831212 – www.glenappcastle.com – enquiries@glenappcastle.com – Fax (01465) 831000 – Closed 3 January-20 March and Christmas
14 rm ☑ – †£255/275 ††£375/575 – 3 suites
Rest – (light lunch) (booking essential for non-residents) (set menu only) Menu £55
♦ Magnificent Baronial castle in extensive grounds; built as home for Deputy Lord Lieutenant of Ayrshire. Spacious, antique-furnished bedrooms with tall Victorian windows. Much local produce is used by the kitchen. Professional service.

↑ **Cosses Country House** ⌘ 　　　　　　🗄 🔊 📶 **P** _VISA_ ⚅⚅
East : 2¼ m. by A 77 (South) taking first turn left after bridge ⊠ *KA26 0LR*
– ℰ (01465) 831 363 – www.cossescountryhouse.com
– staying@cossescountryhouse.com – Fax (01465) 831 598
– Restricted opening in winter
3 rm ⌧ – 🛇£58 🛇🛇£85/100
Rest – (by arrangement, communal dining) Menu £ 26/30
◆ Very well run former shooting lodge, dating from 1670. Warm lounge with log fire;
afternoon tea and homemade cakes served on arrival. Thoughtful extras provided in
bedrooms. Set three course menu uses home grown produce.

BALLATER – Aberdeenshire – **501** K 12 – **pop. 1 446**　　　　　　28 **C1**
　　D Edinburgh 111 mi – Aberdeen 41 mi – Inverness 70 mi – Perth 67 mi
　　i Station Square ℰ (013397) 55306, ballater@agtb.org
　　Is Victoria Rd, ℰ (013397) 55 567

🏨 **Darroch Learg**　　　　　　　　　　🔇 🗄 **P** _VISA_ ⚅⚅ ①
Braemar Rd ⊠ *AB35 5UX – ℰ (013397) 55 443 – www.darrochlearg.co.uk*
– enquiries@darrochlearg.co.uk – Fax (013397) 55 252 – Closed last 3 weeks
January and Christmas
12 rm ⌧ – 🛇£140/155 🛇🛇£300/330
Rest *The Conservatory* – see restaurant listing
◆ Country house hotel: enjoy superb views from its elevated position. Plush lounges
with soft suites, open fires and antiques. Enticing bedrooms: upper floors have best
outlook.

🏠 **The Auld Kirk**　　　　　　　　　　　　　**P** _VISA_ ⚅⚅
Braemar Rd ⊠ *AB35 5RQ – ℰ (01339) 755 762 – www.theauldkirk.com*
– info@theauldkirk.com – Closed first 2 weeks January and 25-26 December
6 rm ⌧ – 🛇£65 🛇🛇£100/100
Rest – (Closed Sunday and lunch in winter) Menu £ 33
◆ Hotel in former church with bar, lounge and breakfast room refurbished in contemporary style. Well equipped bedrooms currently being redecorated to similar
standard. Restaurant in former side chapel has vaulted ceiling and chandeliers and
serves traditional menu.

↑ **Moorside House** without rest　　　　　　🗄 ⌘ **P** _VISA_ ⚅⚅
 26 Braemar Rd ⊠ *AB35 5RL – ℰ (013397) 55 492 – www.moorsidehouse.co.uk*
– info@moorsidehouse.co.uk – Fax (013397) 55 492
– April-October
9 rm ⌧ – 🛇£45 🛇🛇£60
◆ Detached Victorian pink stone guesthouse on main road just outside town centre.
Neat garden. Vividly coloured breakfast room. Sizeable, well-furnished rooms.

↑ **Morvada House** without rest　　　　　　　⌘ **P** _VISA_ ⚅⚅
28 Braemar Rd ⊠ *AB35 5RL – ℰ (013397) 56 334 – www.morvada.com*
– morvada@aol.com – Fax (013397) 56 092
– February-October
5 rm ⌧ – 🛇£40/60 🛇🛇£55/60
◆ Attractive stone built house. Personally run. Notable for its collection of Russel
Flint pictures. Immaculately kept, individually decorated rooms, some with mountain
views.

XX **The Conservatory** – at Darroch Learg Hotel　　
Braemar Rd ⊠ *AB35 5UX – ℰ (013397) 55 443 – www.darrochlearg.co.uk*
– enquiries@darrochlearg.co.uk – Fax (013397) 55 252 – Closed Christmas and
last 3 weeks January
Rest – (dinner only and Sunday lunch) Menu £ 48⌘
◆ Attractive conservatory restaurant with a fine view from its garden location: comfortable dining enhanced by attentive service. Notably impressive wine list.

SCOTLAND

XX **The Green Inn** with rm · VISA ®®
9 Victoria Rd ⊠ AB35 5QQ – ℰ (013397) 55 701 – www.green-inn.com
– info@green-inn.com – Closed January
3 rm – ♦£50 ♦♦£70, � £10
Rest – (Closed Sunday-Monday) (dinner only) Menu £39
♦ Former temperance hall, opposite the green, boasting comfy lounges and pleasant
conservatory. Interesting, well sourced and accomplished modern British cooking.
Cosy rooms.

BALLOCH – West Dunbartonshire – **501** G 15 – ⊠ Alexandria ▮ Scotland   25 **B1**
🛈 Edinburgh 72 mi – Glasgow 20 mi – Stirling 30 mi
🛈 The Old Station Building, Balloch Rd ℰ (08707) 200607 (April-October),
info@balloch.visitscotland.com
🛈 N : Loch Lomond★★

🏨🏨 **De Vere Deluxe Cameron House** ⟨...⟩
Loch Lomond,   ⟨...⟩ rm, ⟨...⟩ rest, ⟨...⟩ VISA ®® AE ①
Northwest : 1½ m. by A 811 on A 82 ⊠ G83 8QZ – ℰ (01389) 755 565
– www.devere.co.uk – reservations@cameronhouse.co.uk – Fax (01389) 759 522
128 rm ⊇ – ♦£99/419 ♦♦£119/419 – 12 suites
Rest Lomonds – see restaurant listing
Rest Camerons Grill – (dinner only) Carte £30/58
♦ Extensive Victorian house superbly situated on shores of Loch Lomond. Impressive
leisure facilities. Luxurious rooms with four posters and panoramic views. Camerons
Grill has a contemporary feel.

XXX **Lomonds** – at De Vere Deluxe Cameron House Hotel   ⟨...⟩ AE P. VISA ®® AE ①
Loch Lomond, Northwest : 1½ m. by A 811 on A 82
⊠ G83 8QZ – ℰ (01389) 755 565 – www.devere.co.uk
– reservations@cameronhouse.co.uk – Fax (01389) 759 522
Rest – (Closed 31 December, Sunday and Monday) (dinner only) Menu £55
– Carte £35/53
♦ Intimate restaurant with views of the mountains and loch; plush, contemporary
styling, comfy central banquettes, formal service and well-presented, modern cook-
ing.

BALLYGRANT – Argyll and Bute – **501** B 16 – see Islay (Isle of)

BALMEDIE – Aberdeenshire – **501** N 12   28 **D1**
🛈 Edinburgh 137 mi – Aberdeen 7 mi – Peterhead 24 mi

🍴 **Cock and Bull**   P. VISA ®® AE
Ellon Rd, Blairton, North : 1 m. on A 90 ⊠ AB23 8XY – ℰ (01358) 743 249
– www.thecockandbull.co.uk – info@thecockandbull.co.uk – Fax (01358) 742 466
– Closed 25-26 December and 1-2 January
Rest – Carte £12/25
♦ Whitewashed 19C pub and conservatory with North Sea views. Bar and restaurant
have bags of atmosphere, courtesy of characterful artefacts. Hearty dishes cover wide
range.

BALQUHIDDER – Stirling – **501** H 14 – see Lochearnhead – ⊠ Stirling

---

BALTASOUND – Shetland Islands – **501** R 1 – see Shetland Islands (Island of
Unst)

BANAVIE – Highland – **501** E 13 – see Fort William

BANCHORY – Aberdeenshire – **501** M 12 – pop. 6 034 ▮ Scotland   28 **D2**
🛈 Edinburgh 118 mi – Aberdeen 17 mi – Dundee 55 mi – Inverness 94 mi
🛈 Bridge St ℰ (01330) 822000 (Easter-October)
🛈 Kinneskie Kinneskie Rd, ℰ (01330) 822 365
🛈 Torphins Bog Rd, ℰ (013398) 82 115
🛈 Crathes Castle★★ (Gardens★★★) **AC**, E : 3 m. by A 93 – Cairn o'Mount
Road★ (⩽★★), S : by B 974. Dunnottar Castle★★ (site★★★) **AC**, SW :
15½ m. by A 93 and A 957 – Aberdeen★★, NE : 17 m. by A 93

Raemoir House 🦢
≤ 🚗 �🌡 ❄ 🕴 🏄 **P** **VISA** **◑◐** **AE**

North : 2½ m. on A 980 ⊠ *AB31 4ED* – ℰ *(01330) 824 884 – www.raemoir.com*
– hotel@raemoir.com – Fax (01330) 822 171 – Closed 25-29 December
20 rm ⊈ – †£95/125 ††£180/225
Rest – Menu £35 (dinner) – Carte lunch £19/28
♦ Enviably located 18C Highland mansion with 17C "ha-hoose" (hall house) as popular alternative to main house. Country house ambience: antiques abound. Very comfortable rooms. The "Oval" dining room luxuriates with Victorian tapestry walls.

Banchory Lodge 🦢
≤ 🚗 ⤳ ❄ 🏄 **P** **VISA** **◑◐** **AE** **①**

Dee St ⊠ *AB31 5HS* – ℰ *(01330) 822 625 – www.banchorylodge.co.uk*
– enquiries@banchorylodge.co.uk – Fax (01330) 825 019
22 rm ⊈ – †£95/105 ††£170/190
Rest – Menu £21 (dinner) – Carte £18/35
♦ Part 16C former coaching inn delightfully situated on River Dee. Country house style accentuated by antiques and china. Individually decorated bedrooms. Dee views and floral displays enhance the attraction of the dining room.

The Old West Manse without rest
🚗 ❄ **P** **VISA** **◑◐** **AE** **①**

71 Station Rd, on A 93 ⊠ *AB31 5YD* – ℰ *(01330) 822 202*
– www.deeside-bed-and-breakfast.com – westmanse@btinternet.com
– Fax (01330) 822 202
3 rm ⊈ – †£50 ††£70
♦ Immaculately distinctive guesthouse just outside village. Bright yellow exterior, lovely gardens and homely lounge with warm décor. Spotlessly kept, bright bedrooms.

> Look out for red symbols, indicating particularly pleasant establishments.

BARRA (Isle of) – Western Isles – 501 X 12/13 – ⊠ Castlebay   29 A3

Castlebay – Western Isles   29 A3

Castlebay
≤ ❄ **P** **VISA** **◑◐** **①**

⊠ *HS9 5XD* – ℰ *(01871) 810 223 – www.castlebayhotel.com*
– info@castlebayhotel.com – Fax (01871) 810 455 – Closed 25 December
15 rm ⊈ – †£49/89 ††£120/140   **Rest** – (bar lunch) Carte £16/29
♦ Personally run, early 20C hotel situated in prominent position overlooking Kisimul Castle and Isle of Vatersay. Cosy sitting room and spacious bar. Homely, well-kept rooms. Linen-clad dining room with excellent bay view and traditional fare.

Grianamul without rest
≤ 🚗 ❄ **P** **VISA** **◑◐**

⊠ *HS9 5XD* – ℰ *(01871) 810 416 – www.members.aol.com/macneilronnie*
– macneilronnie@aol.com
3 rm ⊈ – †£35 ††£56
♦ Purpose-built guesthouse, convenient for local amenities; adjacent to heritage centre. Comfortable, homely lounge. Very sunny breakfast room. Sizeable, well-kept rooms.

North Bay – Western Isles   29 A3

Heathbank
≤ 🚗 🚗 ❄ **P** **VISA** **◑◐** **①**

⊠ *HS9 5YQ* – ℰ *(01871) 890 266 – www.barrahotel.co.uk*
– info@barrahotel.co.uk – Fax (01871) 890 266
5 rm ⊈ – †£55/90 ††£80/90
Rest – (bar lunch) (booking essential) Carte £14/29 **s**
♦ Former 19C schoolhouse on a quiet road. Relax in ample space, including a terrace to admire the landscape. Airy bedrooms, in light lemon hues with DVDs, are the strong point. Home-cooked menus in bar and intimate dining room.

BEAULY – Highland – **501** G 11 – pop. 1 164

30 **C2**

▶ Edinburgh 169 mi – Inverness 13 mi – Wick 125 mi

  Lovat Arms ⏻ 🗻 **P** **VISA** **◑◐**
High St ✉ *IV4 7BS* – ☎ *(01463) 782 313* – *www.lovatarms.com*
– info@lovatarms.com – Fax (01463) 782 862
34 rm – ♦£40/90 ♦♦£60/99
Rest – (bar lunch Monday-Saturday) Carte £16/29
♦ Stylish, family owned hotel in village centre with distinctive Scottish feel: full tartan décor abounds. Spacious sitting room, busy bar. Smart rooms with clan influence. All-enveloping tartan curtains dominate warmly hued dining room.

BELLANOCH – Argyll and Bute – **501** D 15 ▯ *Scotland*   27 **B2**

▶ Edinburgh 134 mi – Arduaine 16 mi – Oban 34 mi
◙ Crinan★, W : 2 m. by B 841. Auchindrain Township Open Air Museum★, E : 25 m. by B 841 and A 83

⌂ **Bellanoch House**   ≤ 🚗 🖉 🕸 📞 **P**
Bellanoch Bay, Crinan Canal ✉ *PA31 8SN* – ☎ *(01546) 830 149*
– www.bellanochhouse.co.uk – stay@bellanochhouse.co.uk
4 rm ☷ – ♦£40/55 ♦♦£80/90   **Rest** – (by arrangement) Menu £30
♦ Former church and school-house with gardens. Stylish lounge boasts stone fireplace from Italy. Owners' family paintings on walls. Airy rooms; front two with good views. Home-cooked food served in dining area.

BENDERLOCH – Argyll and Bute – **501** D 14 – see Connel

BISHOPTON – Renfrewshire – **501** G 16   25 **B1**

▶ Edinburgh 59 mi – Dumbarton 9 mi – Glasgow 13 mi

🏰 **Mar Hall** ⌖   ≤ 🚗 🖉 🐾 🖼 ⊕ 🕸 ℔ ♨ ᐧ rm, 🖉 🗻 **P** **VISA** **◑◐** **AE**
Earl of Mar Estate, Northeast : 1 m. on B 815 ✉ *PA7 5NW* – ☎ *(0141) 812 9999*
– www.marhall.com – sales@marhall.com – Fax (0141) 812 9997
50 rm – ♦£125/135 ♦♦£350/500, ☷ £15.50 – 3 suites
Rest *Cristal* – (dinner only and Sunday lunch) Menu £40
♦ 19C Gothic mansion set in parkland. Spacious and stylish; ideal weekend break location. Impressive Aveda spa with well-equipped gym. Contemporary bedrooms. Elaborate fine dining with exceptional levels of service in The Cristal.

BLAIRGOWRIE – Perth and Kinross – **501** J 14 – pop. 7 965 ▯ *Scotland*   28 **C2**

▶ Edinburgh 60 mi – Dundee 19 mi – Perth 16 mi
🛈 26 Wellmeadow ☎ (01250) 872960, blairgowrietic@perthshire.co.uk
◙ Scone Palace★★ **AC**, S : 12 m. by A 93

⌂🏠 **Kinloch House** ⌖   ≤ 🚗 🖉 🖼 🕸 ℔ **P** **VISA** **◑◐** **AE**
West : 3 m. on A 923 ✉ *PH10 6SG* – ☎ *(01250) 884 237*
– www.kinlochhouse.com – reception@kinlochhouse.com – Fax (01250) 884 333
– Closed 2 weeks Christmas
17 rm ☷ – ♦£100/185 ♦♦£225/300 – 1 suite   **Rest** – Menu £28/52
♦ Wonderfully tranquil, ivy-clad 19C country house set in its own grounds. Appealingly traditional lounges. Conservatory and leisure centre. Large, smart, well-furnished rooms. Restaurant with bright yellow décor and Scottish influenced cooking.

⌂ **Heathpark House** without rest   🚗 🖉 **P** **VISA** **◑◐**
Coupar Angus Rd, Rosemount, Southeast : ¾ m. on A 923 ✉ *PH10 6JT*
– ☎ (01250) 870 700 – www.heathparkhouse.com
– lori@forsyth12.freeserve.co.uk – Fax (01250) 870 700 – Closed Christmas-New Year and 2 weeks October
3 rm ☷ – ♦£45 ♦♦£75
♦ Substantial Victorian guesthouse in a quiet residential spot with mature gardens. Spacious lounge; breakfasts taken in welcoming dining room. Large, individually styled rooms.

SCOTLAND

847

⌂ **Gilmore House** without rest   �📶 P VISA ◉◉
Perth Rd, Southwest : ½ m. on A 93 ⊠ *PH10 6EJ* – ℰ *(01250) 872 791*
– www.gilmorehouse.co.uk – jill@gilmorehouse.co.uk – Closed Christmas
3 rm ⊡ – ♥♥£64
   ◆ Traditional stone-built guesthouse only a few minutes' walk from town, well run by owners. Comfortable front lounge and breakfast room. Cosy and keenly priced accommodation.

BOAT OF GARTEN – Highland – 501 I 12   30 D2
🚩 Edinburgh 133 mi – Inverness 28 mi – Perth 89 mi
🚉 Boat of Garten, ℰ (01479) 831 282

🏨 **The Boat**   🚃 📶 ♨ P VISA ◉◉ AE
⊠ *PH24 3BH* – ℰ *(01479) 831 258 – www.boathotel.co.uk*
– info@boathotel.co.uk – Fax (01479) 831 414
24 rm ⊡ – ♥£35/45 ♥♥£70/110 – 1 suite
Rest *Capercaillie* – (dinner only) Menu £35 **s**
Rest *The Osprey Bar* – Carte £20/40 **s**
   ◆ An evocative hiss of steam from adjacent Strathspey railway line adds character to this 19C hotel, run by keen, friendly young team. Pleasant traditional or modern rooms. Vivid artwork in comfy Capercaillie. Busy Osprey bar/bistro overlooks the trains.

BONNYRIGG – Midlothian – 501 K 16   26 C1
🚩 Edinburgh 8 mi – Galashiels 27 mi – Glasgow 50 mi

🏨 **Dalhousie Castle** ⬧   ⟨ 🚃 🏇 ⌇ ⊕ ⌣ 📶 ♨ P VISA ◉◉ AE ⓪
Southeast : 1 ¼ m. on B 704 ⊠ *EH19 3JB* – ℰ *(01875) 820 153*
– www.dalhousiecastle.co.uk – info@dalhousiecastle.co.uk – Fax (01875) 823 365
36 rm ⊡ – ♥£150/160 ♥♥£195/220
Rest *Dungeon* – (dinner only) (booking essential for non-residents)
Menu £43 **s**
Rest *The Orangery* – Carte £26/32
   ◆ 13C castle on the banks of the South Esk with spacious, medieval style rooms and historically-themed bedrooms. Popular venue for weddings, with falconry centre in grounds. Barrel-vaulted Dungeon restaurant features suits of armour. The Orangery overlooks river and parkland, and offers a less formal menu.

BRAEMAR – Aberdeenshire – 501 J 12 ▌Scotland   28 C2
🚩 Edinburgh 85 mi – Aberdeen 58 mi – Dundee 51 mi – Perth 51 mi
ℹ️ The Mews, Mar Rd ℰ (013397) 41600
🚉 Cluniebank Rd, ℰ (013397) 41618
🅖 Lin O'Dee★, W : 5 m

⌂ **Callater Lodge** without rest   🚃 ✍ P VISA ◉◉ AE
9 Glenshee Rd ⊠ *AB35 5YQ* – ℰ *(013397) 41 275 – www.hotel-braemar.co.uk*
– info@hotel-braemar.co.uk – Closed 23-28 December
6 rm ⊡ – ♥£38/70 ♥♥£70
   ◆ Stone house in large garden on the road to Glenshee. Lounge with leather chairs and library with inglenook. Pleasant spacious bedrooms, some with view across the valley.

BREASCLETE – Western Isles Outer Hebrides – 501 Z 9 – see Lewis and Harris (Isle of)

BRIDGEND OF LINTRATHEN – Angus – 501 K 13 – ⊠ Kirriemuir   28 C2
🚩 Edinburgh 70 – Dundee 20 – Pitlochry 37

✕✕ **Lochside Lodge** with rm   ⌇ P VISA ◉◉
– ℰ *(01575) 560 340 – www.lochsidelodge.com – enquiries@lochsidelodge.com*
– Fax (01575) 560 251 – Closed 25-26 December, 1-31 January , 2 weeks October, Sunday and Monday
6 rm ⊡ – ♥£70 ♥♥£120   **Rest** – (dinner only) Menu £35
   ◆ The Roundhouse restaurant offers more formal dining than The Steading. Smart, linen-clad tables and a menu showing ambition and some imagination. Well-kept bedrooms are divided between the converted hayloft and the courtyard.

The Steading
(at Lochside Lodge) ⊠ DD8 5JJ – ℰ *(01575) 560 340 – www.lochsidelodge.com*
– enquiries@lochsidelodge.com
– Fax (01575) 560 251
– Closed 25-26 December, January, 2 weeks October, Sunday and Monday
Rest – Carte £ 18/20
◆ More informal part of Lochside, decorated with farm tools, tartan and whisky boxes. Cooking has a traditional, local base with good breads and desserts; home-made jams for sale.

BROADFORD – Highland – **501** C 12 – **see Skye (Isle of)**

BRODICK – North Ayrshire – **501** E 17 – **see Arran (Isle of)**

BRORA – Highland – **501** I 9 – **pop. 1 140**   30 **D2**
▶ Edinburgh 234 mi – Inverness 78 mi – Wick 49 mi
▣ Golf Rd, ℰ (01408) 621 417

Royal Marine
Golf Rd ⊠ KW9 6QS – ℰ *(01408) 621 252 – www.royalmarinebrora.com*
– info@royalmarinebrora.com – Fax (01408) 621 181
22 rm – †£ 110 ††£ 130/190   **Rest** – Carte £ 17/33
◆ Originally a laird's home. Traditional lounge with log fire. Good leisure facilities plus snooker room and unlimited golf. Refurbished, modern bedrooms. Cuisine reflects Highland location.

Glenaveron without rest
Golf Rd ⊠ KW9 6QS – ℰ *(01408) 621 601 – www.glenaveron.co.uk*
– glenaveron@hotmail.com – Closed Christmas, New Year and 2 weeks October
3 rm ⊆ – †£ 45/55 ††£ 68/72
◆ Agreeable looking, detached, stone guesthouse with gardens. Spick and span lounge. Pleasant communal breakfast room. Very spacious rooms with superior pine furnishings.

BROUGHTY FERRY – Dundee – **501** L 14 – **see Dundee**

BUNCHREW – Highland – **see Inverness**

BUNESSAN – Argyll and Bute – **501** B 15 – **see Mull (Isle of)**

BURRAY – Orkney Islands – **501** L 7 – **see Orkney Islands**

BUTE (Isle of) – Argyll and Bute – **501** E 16 – **pop. 7 354**   27 **B3**
⛴ from Rothesay to Wemyss Bay (Mainland) (Caledonian MacBrayne Ltd) frequent services daily (35 mn) – from Rhubodach to Colintraive (Mainland) (Caledonian MacBrayne Ltd) frequent services daily (5 mn)

Ascog – Argyll and Bute   27 **B3**

Balmory Hall without rest
Balmory Rd ⊠ PA20 9LL – ℰ *(01700) 500 669 – www.balmoryhall.com*
– enquiries@balmoryhall.com – Fax (01700) 500 669 – February - October
4 rm ⊆ – †£ 87 ††£ 160
◆ Impressive, carefully restored mid 19C Italianate mansion. Columned hall and well-furnished lounge. Tastefully furnished bedrooms. Breakfast at an antique table.

CADBOLL – Highland – **see Tain**

CAIRNBAAN – Argyll and Bute – **501** D 15 – **see Lochgilphead**

SCOTLAND

CALLANDER – Stirling – 501 H 15 – pop. 2 754 ▯ Scotland 28 C2

🖸 Edinburgh 52 mi – Glasgow 43 mi – Oban 71 mi – Perth 41 mi
🛈 Rob Roy and Trossachs Visitor Centre, Ancaster Sq (08707) 200628, info@callander.visitscotland.com
🖪 Aveland Rd, ℰ (01877) 330 090
☑ Town ★
🖸 The Trossachs ★★★ (Loch Katrine ★★) – Hilltop Viewpoint ★★★ (❊ ★★★)
W : 10 m. by A 821

🏛 Roman Camp ⟡ 　　　　 ← 🖼 🕪 ⬧ & ⬥ 🅿 𝑉𝐼𝑆𝐴 ⓜⓞ 𝔸𝔼 ⓞ
Main St ✉ FK17 8BG – ℰ (01877) 330 003 – www.romancamphotel.co.uk
– mail@romancamphotel.co.uk – Fax (01877) 331 533
11 rm ⊇ – ♦£85/125 ♦♦£135/170 – 4 suites
Rest *The Restaurant* – see restaurant listing
♦ Part 17C hunting lodge set in extensive gardens. Traditionally and charmingly decorated rooms with open fires, floral prints and antiques. Individually decorated bedrooms.

🏠 Lubnaig without rest 　　　　　　　 🖼 ⬧ 🅿 𝑉𝐼𝑆𝐴 ⓜⓞ
Leny Feus ✉ FK17 8AS – ℰ (01877) 330 376 – www.lubnaighouse.co.uk
– info@lubnaighouse.co.uk – Fax (01877) 330 376 – May-October
8 rm ⊇ – ♦£47/57 ♦♦£64/84
♦ Built in 1864, a characterful Victorian house on the outskirts of town. Well-kept mature gardens visible from communal rooms. Homely bedrooms, two in converted stables.

🏠 Brook Linn without rest ⟡ 　　　　　 ← 🖼 🅿 𝑉𝐼𝑆𝐴 ⓜⓞ
Leny Feus ✉ FK17 8AU – ℰ (01877) 330 103 – www.brooklinn-scotland.co.uk
– derek@blinn.freeserve.co.uk – Fax (01877) 330 103 – Easter-October
4 rm ⊇ – ♦♦£70/80
♦ Victorian house in a fairly secluded rural location. Homely style lounge and wood furnished dining room for breakfast. Traditional, well-kept bedrooms.

✕✕✕ The Restaurant – at Roman Camp Hotel 　　　　 🅿 𝑉𝐼𝑆𝐴 ⓜⓞ 𝔸𝔼 ⓞ
Main St ✉ FK19 8BG – ℰ (01877) 330 003 – mail@romancamphotel.co.uk
– Fax (01877) 331 533
Rest – Menu £25/50 – Carte £50/60
♦ Spacious, formal restaurant set with crisp, linen-covered tables bedecked with lillies. Modern Scottish cooking proudly made with locally sourced produce.

CAMPBELTOWN – Argyll and Bute – 501 D 17 – see Kintyre (Peninsula)

CARDROSS – Argyll and Bute – 501 G 16 ▯ Scotland 25 A-B1

🖸 Edinburgh 63 mi – Glasgow 17 mi – Helensburgh 5 mi
🖸 The Clyde Estuary ★

🏠 Kirkton House without rest ⟡ 　　　 ← 🖼 ⬧ 🅿 𝑉𝐼𝑆𝐴 ⓜⓞ 𝔸𝔼 ⓞ
Darleith Rd ✉ G82 5EZ – ℰ (01389) 841 951 – www.kirktonhouse.co.uk
– mich@kirktonhouse.co.uk – Fax (01389) 841 868 – February-October
6 rm ⊇ – ♦£45 ♦♦£70
♦ Former farmhouse with origins in 18C; quiet, elevated spot overlooking North Clyde. Ideal stop-off between Glasgow airport and Highlands. Bedrooms all have country views.

CARINISH – Western Isles – 501 Y 11 – see Uist (Isles of)

CARNOUSTIE – Angus – 501 L 14 – pop. 10 561 28 D2

🖸 Edinburgh 68 mi – Aberdeen 59 mi – Dundee 12 mi
🛈 Carnoustie Library, 21 High St ℰ (01241) 859620, enquiries@angusanddundee.co.uk
🖪 Monifieth Golf Links Princes St, Medal Starter's Box, ℰ (01382) 532 767
🖪 Burnside Links Par, ℰ (01241) 802 290
🖪 Panmure Barry, ℰ (01241) 855 120
🖪 Buddon Links Links Par, ℰ (01241) 802 280

SCOTLAND

↑ **The Old Manor** without rest ⌂   ⟨ 🖥 🐾 📶 P VISA ©©
Panbride, Northeast : 1 ¼ m. by A 930 on Panbride Rd ⊠ *DD7 6JP –* ℰ *(01241)*
854 804 – www.oldmanorcarnoustie.com – stay@oldmanorcarnoustie.com
– Fax (01241) 855 327 – Closed 25 December-4 January
5 rm ⌓ *–* ♦£60 ♦♦£80
♦ Substantial 18C house five minutes' drive from championship golf course. Good
views of Tay Estuary. Hearty Scottish breakfast guaranteed. Smart rooms, some with
brass beds.

CARRADALE – Argyll and Bute – **501** D 17 – **see Kintyre Peninsula**

CASTLEBAY – Western Isles – **501** X 12/1 – **see Barra (Isle of)**

CASTLE DOUGLAS – Dumfries and Galloway – **501** I 19 – pop. 3 671   25 **B3**

📗 *Scotland*

> 🚾 Edinburgh 98 mi – Ayr 49 mi – Dumfries 18 mi – Stranraer 57 mi
> 🛈 Market Hill ℰ (01556) 502611 (Easter-October),
> castledouglas@dgtb.visitscotland.com
> 🖥 Abercromby Rd, ℰ (01556) 502 801
> 🄶 Threave Garden ★★ AC, SW : 2 ½ m. by A 75 – Threave Castle ★ AC, W : 1 m

↑ **Douglas House** without rest   🐾 📶 VISA ©©
63 Queen St ⊠ *DG7 1HS –* ℰ *(01556) 503 262 – www.douglas-house.com*
– info@douglas-house.com – Restricted opening in winter
4 rm ⌓ *–* ♦£38/65 ♦♦£80/85
♦ Attractive stone built house (1880) with some original features near the high street.
Communal breakfast table in guest lounge. Comfortable individually decorated bedrooms.

↑ **Smithy House** without rest   🖥 🐾 📶 P
The Buchan, Southwest : ¾ m on A 75 (Stranraer rd) ⊠ *DG7 1TH –* ℰ *(01556)*
503 841 – www.smithyhouse.co.uk – enquiries@smithyhouse.co.uk
3 rm ⌓ *–* ♦£60/70 ♦♦£70/75
♦ Converted 14C smithy in large garden 10 minutes walk from town. Communal
breakfast table. Guests' lounge featuring original forge. Pleasant bedrooms facing
garden or loch.

at Kirkpatrick Durham Northeast : 5 ½ m. by A 75 and B 794 – ⊠ **Castle**
Douglas

↑ **Chipperkyle** without rest ⌂   🖥 🐾 📶 P VISA ©©
⊠ *DG7 3EY –* ℰ *(01556) 650 223 – www.chipperkyle.co.uk*
– Closed Christmas-New Year
3 rm ⌓ *–* ♦£60 ♦♦£92
♦ Georgian manor house in rural location. Charming country house atmosphere in a
family style environment. Comfortable, spacious rooms.

CAWDOR – Highland – **501** I 11 – ⊠ **Inverness**   30 **D2**
> 🚾 Edinburgh 170 mi – Aberdeen 100 mi – Inverness 14 mi

🍺 **Cawdor Tavern**   🖥 P VISA ©© AE
The Lane ⊠ *IV12 5XP –* ℰ *(01667) 404 777 – www.cawdortavern.info*
– enquiries@cawdortavern.info – Fax (01667) 404 777
– Closed 25 December, 1 January
Rest – (booking essential) Carte £ 13/26
♦ Country inn within stone's throw of castle. Well run with an emphasis on the food.
Friendly staff serve dishes from large menu offering traditional or more adventurous
fare.

If breakfast is included the ⌓ symbol appears after the number of rooms.

SCOTLAND

CHIRNSIDE – Scottish Borders – **501** N 16 – **pop. 1 204** – ⊠ **Duns**   26 **D1**

▶ Edinburgh 52 mi – Berwick-upon-Tweed 8 mi – Glasgow 95 mi – Newcastle upon Tyne 70 mi

🛏️ **Chirnside Hall** 🐾   ⟨ 🍴 🔄 ↳ 🎾 📶 **P** **VISA** **⦿⦿** **AE**
East : 1¼ m. on A 6105 ⊠ *TD11 3LD –* ℰ *(01890) 818219*
– www.chirnsidehallhotel.com – reception@chirnsidehallhotel.com – Fax (01890) 818231 – Closed March
10 rm ⌂ – 🛏️£85 🛏️🛏️£165
Rest – (dinner only) (booking essential for non-residents) Menu £30
♦ Large, imposing, Victorian country house in a rural location. Well appointed interiors with good quality period atmosphere. Individually decorated bedrooms. Smart place settings in a traditionally appointed dining room.

CLACHAN SEIL – Argyll and Bute – **501** D 15 – see Seil (Isle of)

CLEAT – **501** KL 6/7 – see Orkney Islands (Island of Westray) – ⊠ **Orkney Islands**

CLYDEBANK – West Dunbartonshire – **501** G 16 – **pop. 29 858**   25 **B1**

▶ Edinburgh 52 mi – Glasgow 6 mi
🏌️ Clydebank Overtoun Dalmuir Overtoun Rd, ℰ (0141) 952 2070

🏨 **The Beardmore**   🍴 🖥️ 🐾 ↳ 🏊 ఉ rm, 🎮 🎾 📶 🏋️ **P** **VISA** **⦿⦿** **AE** **①**
Beardmore St, off A 814 ⊠ *G81 4SA –* ℰ *(0141) 951 6000*
– www.thebeardmore.co.uk – info@beardmore.scot.nhs.uk – Fax (0141) 951 6019 – Closed 25 December
160 rm – 🛏️£99/109 🛏️🛏️£99/109, ⌂ £14.50 – 6 suites
Rest Arcoona – (dinner only) Carte £17/36
Rest B bar cafe – (lunch only) Carte £16/23
♦ Hotel on banks of River Clyde known for its conference facilities and its attachment to an NHS hospital. Well-equipped bedrooms, some with views over the river. Formal Arcoona restaurant offers globally-influenced menu. Bright, open-plan B Bar café serves light snacks.

COLONSAY (Isle of) – Argyll and Bute – **501** B 15   27 **A2**

🚢 from Scalasaig to Oban (Caledonian MacBrayne Ltd) 3 weekly (2 h) – from Scalasaig to Kintyre Peninsula (Kennacraig) via Isle of Islay (Port Askaig) (Caledonian MacBrayne Ltd) weekly
🏌️ Colonsay, ℰ (01951) 200 290

Scalasaig – Argyll and Bute – ⊠ **Colonsay**   27 **A2**

🏠 **The Colonsay** 🐾   ⟨ 🍴 📶 **P** **⦿⦿** **AE**
⊠ *PA61 7YP –* ℰ *(01951) 200 316 – www.thecolonsay.com*
– reception@thecolonsay.com – Fax (01951) 200 353 – Closed February-2 March
9 rm – 🛏️£60/100 🛏️🛏️£145, ⌂ £7.50   **Rest** – (bar lunch) Carte £18/29
♦ Listed building from mid-18C; a thoroughly rural, remote setting. Public areas include excellent photos of local scenes and the only bar on the island. Bright, modern rooms. Welcoming, informal dining room.

COMRIE – Perth and Kinross – **501** I 14 – **pop. 1 926**   28 **C2**

▶ Edinburgh 66 mi – Glasgow 56 mi – Oban 70 mi – Perth 24 mi
🏌️ Comrie Laggan Braes, ℰ (01764) 670 055

🛏️ **The Royal**   🍴 🐾 📶 **P** **VISA** **⦿⦿** **AE** **①**
Melville Sq ⊠ *PH6 2DN –* ℰ *(01764) 679 200 – www.royalhotel.co.uk*
– reception@royalhotel.co.uk – Fax (01764) 679 219 – Closed 25-26 December
11 rm ⌂ – 🛏️£85 🛏️🛏️£140
Rest Royal – Menu £28 (dinner) **s** – Carte £19/33 **s**
♦ 18C coaching inn in centre of town: Queen Victoria once stayed here. Stylish, contemporary feel, especially individually decorated bedrooms, with four posters and antiques. Restaurant with two rooms: conservatory brasserie or intimate dining room.

SCOTLAND

CONNEL – Argyll and Bute – 501 D 14 – ⊠ Oban   27 **B2**
> ◘ Edinburgh 118 mi – Glasgow 88 mi – Inverness 113 mi – Oban 5 mi

↑ **Ards House** without rest   ≤ ➪ ♔ ☂ **P** **VISA** **⚫⚫** **①**
on A 85 ⊠ PA37 1PT – ℰ (01631) 710 255 – www.ardshouse.com
– info@ardshouse.com – Fax (01631) 710857 – Closed Christmas and New Year
4 rm � – ♦£50/60 ♦♦£76/90
♦ Victorian house overlooking Loch Etive. Well run with a smart and elegant atmosphere. Traditional décor and appointments throughout communal areas and bedrooms.

↑ **Ronebhal** without rest   ≤ ➪ ♔ **P** **VISA** **⚫⚫**
on A 85 ⊠ PA37 1PJ – ℰ (01631) 710310 – www.ronebhal.co.uk
– info@ronebhal.co.uk – Fax (01631) 710310 – April-September
6 rm ⊑ – ♦£27/70 ♦♦£55/76
♦ Victorian house built in granite, with fine views over Loch Etive. Attractive guests' lounge with plenty of local information. Individually decorated bedrooms.

🏠 **The Oyster Inn** with rm   ♔ **P** **VISA** **⚫⚫** **AE** **①**
⊠ PA37 1PJ – ℰ (01631) 710666 – www.oysterinn.co.uk – stay@oysterinn.co.uk
– Fax (01631) 710042
11 rm ⊑ – ♦£52/67 ♦♦£84/114   **Rest** – Seafood – Carte £18/28 **s**
♦ Three in one: a modern restaurant with loch view; adjacent bar/pub, The Ferryman's; comfy, modish bedrooms. Fresh, home-made dishes throughout: seafood specials prevail. Comfortable, modern bedrooms, with bunk-style budget rooms also available for groups.

at Benderloch North : 2 ½ m. by A 828 – ⊠ Connel

↑ **Dun Ma Mara** without rest   ≤ ➪ ♔ **P** **VISA** **⚫⚫**
⊠ PA37 1RT – ℰ (01631) 720233 – www.dunnamara.com
– stay@dunnamara.com – February-November
7 rm ⊑ – ♦£50/65 ♦♦£90/110
♦ Fully restored Edwardian home with fine views. Minimalistic, intimate interior. Pleasant gardens lead to idyllic private beach. Individual, modish rooms boast clean lines.

CONON BRIDGE – Highland – 501 G 11   30 **C2**
> ◘ Edinburgh 168 mi – Inverness 12 mi

🏠 **Kinkell House** ॐ   ≤ ➪ ᴪ rm, **P** **VISA** **⚫⚫** **①**
Easter Kinkell, Southeast : 3 m. by B 9163 and A 835 on B 9169 ⊠ IV7 8HY
– ℰ (01349) 861 270 – www.kinkellhousehotel.com
– info@kinkellhousehotel.com – Fax (01349) 867 240
9 rm ⊑ – ♦£60/80 ♦♦£100/150
Rest – (lunch by arrangement Monday-Saturday) Menu £15/25
♦ Peacefully located house in a rural location makes for a welcoming country house atmosphere, keenly overseen by a young team. Homely bedrooms. Traditional dining room overlooks the garden.

CRAIGHOUSE – Argyll and Bute – 501 C 16 – see Jura (Isle of)

CRAIGNURE – Argyll and Bute – 501 C 14 – see Mull (Isle of)

CRAILING – Borders – 501 M 17 – see Jedburgh

CRIEFF – Perth and Kinross – 501 I 14 – pop. 6 579 ▤ Scotland   28 **C2**
> ◘ Edinburgh 60 mi – Glasgow 50 mi – Oban 76 mi – Perth 18 mi
> ▤ Town Hall, High St ℰ (01764) 652578, crieffttic@perthshire.co.uk
> 🏌 Perth Rd, ℰ (01764) 652 909
> 🏌 Muthill Peat Rd, ℰ (01764) 681 523
> ◙ Town ★
> ◙ Drummond Castle Gardens ★ **AC**, S : 2 m. by A 822. Scone Palace ★★ **AC**, E : 16 m. by A 85 and A 93

Merlindale 🏠 🛏️

Perth Rd, on A 85 ✉ PH7 3EQ – ☎ (01764) 655 205 – www.merlindale.co.uk
– merlin.dale@virgin.net – Fax (01764) 655 205 – Closed December-mid January
3 rm ⌷ – ♦£50/70 ♦♦£75/85
Rest – (by arrangement, communal dining) Menu £ 30
♦ Traditional, stone-built house close to the town. Well-equipped bedrooms are individually decorated and very comfortable. Accomplished evening meals at a communal table.

The Bank 🍴

32 High St ✉ PH7 3BS – ☎ (01764) 656 575 – www.thebankrestaurant.co.uk
– mail@thebankrestaurant.co.uk – Fax (01764) 656 575 – Closed 2 weeks
January, 2 week July, 25-26 December, Sunday and Monday
Rest – (dinner only and Saturday lunch) Carte £ 20/28
♦ Impressive, Gothic, former bank dating from 1901 which dominates the high street. Traditional, good value cooking using fine ingredients and an informal, friendly atmosphere.

CRINAN – Argyll and Bute – **501** D 15 – ✉ **Lochgilphead** 🏴 *Scotland*   27 **B2**
▶ Edinburgh 137 mi – Glasgow 91 mi – Oban 36 mi
◉ Hamlet★
◎ Kilmory Knap (Macmillan's Cross★) SW : 14 m

SCOTLAND

Crinan 🏨

✉ PA31 8SR – ☎ (01546) 830 261 – www.crinanhotel.com
– reservations@crinanhotel.com – Fax (01546) 830 292
20 rm (dinner included) ⌷ – ♦£120/140 ♦♦£250/310
Rest – (bar lunch) Menu £ 50
♦ Superbly located in a commanding setting with exceptional views of Loch Crinan and Sound of Jura. Cosy, wood panelled, nautically themed bar. Bright, pleasant bedrooms. Restaurant provides wonderful views and interesting cuisine with seafood predominance.

CROCKETFORD – Dumfries and Galloway – **501** I 18 – ✉ **Castle**   25 **B3**
Douglas 🏴 *Scotland*
▶ Edinburgh 89 mi – Dumfries 9 mi – Kirkcudbright 18 mi
◎ Sweetheart Abbey★, SE : 10 m. by minor rd – Threave Garden★★ and Threave Castle★, S : 10 m. by A 75

Craigadam 🏠 🌿

West : 2 m. on A 712 ✉ DG7 3HU – ☎ (01556) 650 233 – www.craigadam.com
– inquiry@craigadam.com – Fax (01556) 650 233
– Closed 23 December-4 January
10 rm ⌷ – ♦£55/90 ♦♦£90
Rest – (dinner only) (communal dining) Menu £ 26
♦ 18C country house on working farm. Comfortable, spacious rooms, some with south-facing view. Communal meals. Distinctively themed bedrooms in house or rear courtyard.

CROSSFORD – Fife – **501** J 15 – **see Dunfermline**

CULLODEN – Highland – **501** H 11 – **see Inverness**

CUPAR – Fife – **501** K 15 – **pop. 8 506**   28 **C2**
▶ Edinburgh 45 mi – Dundee 15 mi – Perth 23 mi

Ostler's Close 🍴

25 Bonnygate ✉ KY15 4BU – ☎ (01334) 655 574 – www.ostlerclose.co.uk
– Fax (01334) 654 036 – Closed 1-2 January, 2 weeks April, 2 weeks October,
25-26 December, Sunday, Monday and lunch Tuesday-Friday
Rest – Carte £ 25/41
♦ Welcoming restaurant with snug atmosphere and low ceilings. Very personally run, with cottage feel throughout. Particular attention to prime Scottish meat and local fish.

DALRY – North Ayrshire – **501** F 16

25 **A1**

🚂 Edinburgh 70 mi – Ayr 21 mi – Glasgow 25 mi

⌂ **Lochwood Farm Steading** without rest ♨   ⟨ ✗ P VISA ⬤⬤

Southwest : 5 m. by A 737 and the Saltcoats rd ✉ KA21 6NG
– ✆ (01294) 552 529 – www.lochwoodfarm.co.uk – info@lochwoodfarm.co.uk
– Closed Christmas-New Year
5 rm ⌸ – ♦£45/55 ♦♦£75/120
♦ Excellent hospitality at a good value farmhouse on one hundred acres of dairy farm. Fine views of country and coast from outside hot tub. Pleasant, well-kept little bedrooms.

✗✗ **Braidwoods** (Keith Braidwood)   P VISA ⬤⬤ AE ⬤
❀
Drumastle Mill Cottage, Southwest : 1½ m. by A 737 on Saltcoats rd
✉ KA24 4LN – ✆ (01294) 833 544 – www.braidwoods.co.uk
– keithbraidwood@btconnect.com – Fax (01294) 833 553
– Closed first 3 weeks January, first 2 weeks September, 25-26 December, Monday, Tuesday lunch and Sunday except lunch mid-September - April
Rest – (booking essential) Menu £ 25/38
Spec. Scallops, cardamom, lentil and coriander dhal. Loin and confit of lamb with ragoût of aubergine, courgette and tomato. Vanilla panna cotta with strawberry soup.
♦ Rurally-set restaurant in whitewashed cottage, keenly run by husband and wife team. Weekly-changing menus feature fresh, seasonal, local produce, simply cooked and presented.

DINGWALL – Highland – **501** G 11 – **pop. 5 026**

30 **C2**

🚂 Edinburgh 172 mi – Inverness 14 mi

✗✗ **Cafe India Brasserie**   AC VISA ⬤⬤ AE

Lockhart House, Tulloch St ✉ IV15 9JZ – ✆ (01349) 862 552
– Closed 25 December
Rest – Indian – Carte £ 21/36
♦ Bustling, locally regarded Indian restaurant, handily located in town centre. Updated décor is fresh and modern. Authentically prepared, tasty regional Indian food.

DOONFOOT – South Ayrshire – **501** G 17 – **see Ayr**

DORNOCH – Highland – **501** H 10 – **pop. 1 206** 📗 *Scotland*

30 **D2**

🚂 Edinburgh 219 mi – Inverness 63 mi – Wick 65 mi
🛈 The Coffee Shop, The Square ✆ (0845) 2255121, info@visitscotland.com
🏌 Royal Dornoch Golf Rd, ✆ (01862) 810 219
◉ Town ★

⌂ **Highfield House** without rest   ⟨ 🚗 ⸙ P

Evelix Rd ✉ IV25 3HR – ✆ (01862) 810 909 – www.highfieldhouse.co.uk
– enquiries@highfieldhouse.co.uk – Closed Christmas, New Year and January
3 rm ⌸ – ♦£53 ♦♦£73
♦ Purpose-built guesthouse with garden and fine Highland views. Small, spruce lounge; neat and tidy breakfast room. Bedrooms offer ample comforts: one has whirlpool bath.

✗✗ **2 Quail** with rm   ⸙ VISA ⬤⬤ AE

Castle St ✉ IV25 3SN – ✆ (01862) 811 811 – www.2quail.com
– bookings@2quail.com – Closed 2 weeks Spring and 1 week Christmas
3 rm ⌸ – ♦£110/120 ♦♦£120/140
Rest – (closed Sunday-Monday) (dinner only) (set menu only) Menu £ 38
♦ Personally and proudly run, book-lined little restaurant in townhouse. Interesting and traditionally based dishes, using good quality ingredients. Homely bedrooms.

DOUNBY – Orkney Islands – **501** K 6 – **see Orkney Islands**

DRUMNADROCHIT – Highland – **501** G 11 – ✉ **Milton** ▯ *Scotland* 30 **C2**

▶ Edinburgh 172 mi – Inverness 16 mi – Kyle of Lochalsh 66 mi
▯ Loch Ness★★ – Loch Ness Monster Exhibition★ **AC** – The Great Glen★

⌂ **Drumbuie Farm** without rest ◁ ◊ ⅌ **P** VISA ◑◑
Drumbuie, East : ¾ m. by A 82 ✉ IV63 6XP – ℰ *(01456) 450634*
– www.loch-ness-farm.co.uk – drumbuie@loch-ness-farm.bandb.co.uk
– Fax (01456) 450459
3 rm ⌷ – **†**£35 **††**£60
♦ Immaculate purpose-built guesthouse on working farm with Highland cattle. Conservatory breakfast room has Loch Ness views. Good collection of malt whiskies. Spacious bedrooms.

DUFFUS – Moray – **501** K 11 – see Elgin

DULNAIN BRIDGE – Highland – **501** J 12 – see Grantown-on-Spey

Good food without spending a fortune?
Look out for the Bib Gourmand ⓘ

DUMFRIES – Dumfries and Galloway – **501** J 18 – pop. 31 146 26 **C3**
▯ *Scotland*

▶ Edinburgh 80 mi – Ayr 59 mi – Carlisle 34 mi – Glasgow 79 mi
– Manchester 155 mi – Newcastle upon Tyne 91 mi
🅩 64 Whitesands ℰ (01387) 253862, info@dgtb.visitscotland.com A
🅟 Dumfries & Galloway Maxwelltown 2 Laurieston Ave, ℰ (01387) 253 582
🅟 Dumfries & County Edinburgh Rd, Nunfield, ℰ (01387) 253 585
🅟 Crichton Bankend Rd, ℰ (01387) 247 894
◉ Town★ – Midsteeple★ A **A**
▯ Lincluden College (Tomb★) **AC**, N : 1½ m. by College St A. Drumlanrig Castle★★ (cabinets★) **AC**, NW : 16½ m. by A 76 A – Shambellie House Museum of Costume (Costume Collection★) S : 7¼ m. by A 710 A – Sweetheart Abbey★ **AC**, S : 8 m. by A 710 A – Caerlaverock Castle★ (Renaissance fa½ade★★) **AC**, SE : 9 m. by B 725 B – Glenkiln (Sculptures★) W : 9 m. by A 780 - A - and A 75

Plan opposite

⌂ **Hazeldean House** without rest 🚗 ⅌ **P** VISA ◑◑
4 Moffat Rd ✉ DG1 1NJ – ℰ *(01387) 266 178 – www.hazeldeanhouse.com*
– Fax (01387) 266 178 **B**u
7 rm ⌷ – **†**£33/40 **††**£58
♦ Interestingly furnished 19C villa. Entrance door has original stained glass. Characterful antiques and Victoriana in lounge. Conservatory breakfast room. Spacious bedrooms.

⌂ **Rivendell** without rest 🚗 ⅌ 🕪 **P**
105 Edinburgh Rd ✉ DG1 1JX – ℰ *(01387) 252 251 – www.rivendellbnb.co.uk*
– info@rivendellbnb.co.uk – Fax (01387) 263 084 **B**i
7 rm ⌷ – **†**£30/45 **††**£58
♦ Attractive Rennie Mackintosh style villa with parquet floors, decorative woodwork and brass fittings. Comfortable, pleasant bedrooms with view of large garden.

✕✕ **The Linen Room** VISA ◑◑ AE
53 St Michael St ✉ DG1 2QB – ℰ *(01387) 255 689 – www.linenroom.com*
– enquiries@linenroom.com – Fax (01387) 253 387 – Closed Christmas-New Year,
6-21 January, Monday and Tuesday **B**c
Rest – Menu £17 (lunch) – Carte £31/36
♦ Don't be put off by unprepossessing exterior: a young team run a serious restaurant where tasting menus are prominent and original dishes use good quality local produce.

DUMFRIES

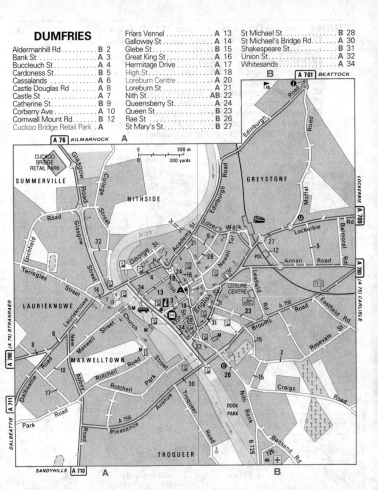

DUNAIN PARK – Highland – see Inverness

DUNBLANE – Stirling – **501** I 15 – **pop. 7 911** 🏴 *Scotland*   28 **C2**

▶ Edinburgh 42 mi – Glasgow 33 mi – Perth 29 mi

🛈 Stirling Rd 𝒞 (08707) 200613 (May-September),
info@dunblane.visitscotland.com

◎ Town★ – Cathedral★★ (west front★★)

◎ Doune★ (castle★ **AC**) W : 4½ m. by A 820

🏠 **Cromlix House** 🦆

Kinbuck, North : 3½ m. on B 8033 ✉ *FK15 9JT* – 𝒞 *(01786) 822125*
– www.cromlixhouse.com – reservations@cromlixhouse.com – Fax (01786)
825450

6 rm 🍽 – †£130/160 ††£180/210 – 8 suites

Rest – (booking essential) Menu £28/48

♦ Effortlessly relaxing 19C mansion in extensive grounds with ornate private chapel.
Charming morning room; spacious conservatory with plants. Definitive country house
rooms. Two elegant, richly furnished dining rooms.

DUNDEE – Dundee City – **501** L 14 – pop. 154 674 ▮ *Scotland* 28 **C2**

▶ Edinburgh 63 mi – Aberdeen 67 mi – Glasgow 83 mi
Access Tay Road Bridge (toll) Y
🛫 Dundee Airport : ☏ (01382) 662200, SW : 1½ m. Z
ℹ Discovery Point, Discovery Quay ☏ (01382) 527527,
dundee@visitscotland.com
🏌 Caird Park Mains Loan, ☏ (01382) 453 606
🏌 Camperdown Camperdown Park, ☏ (01382) 623 398
🏌 Downfield Turnberry Ave, ☏ (01382) 825 595
◉ Town★ - The Frigate Unicorn★ **AC** Y **A** – Discovery Point★ **AC** Y **B** –
Verdant Works★ Z **D** – McManus Galleries★ Y **M**

Albert St	Z	2
Bell St	Y	6
City Quay	Y	
City Square	Y	7
Commercial St	Y	8
Coupar Angus Rd	Z	9
Douglas Rd	Z	10
Drumgeith Rd	Z	12
Dudhope Terrace	Z	13
East Dock St	Y	14
East Marketgait	Y	15
Greendykes Rd	Z	16
High St	Y	17
Kingsway East Shopping Centre	Z	
Kingsway West Shopping Centre	Z	
Logie St	Z	18
Mains Rd	Z	21
Meadowside	Y	23
Moncur Crescent	Y	24
Murraygate	Y	25
Nethergate	Y	26
Old Glamis Rd	Z	32
Overgate Centre	Y	
Provost Rd	Z	34
Reform St	Y	35
St Andrews St	Y	36
Strathmartine Rd	Z	40
Trades Lane	Y	41
Ward Rd	Y	42
Wellgate Centre	Y	
West Bell St	Y	43
West Marketgait	Y	44
West Port	Z	46

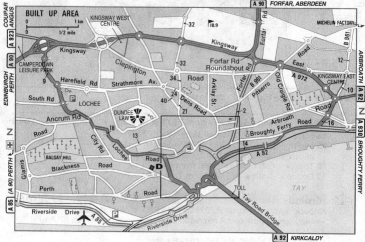

If breakfast is included the ⌑ symbol appears after the number of rooms.

858

Apex City Quay ← 🔲 ⊕ ⋒ Là 🎗 ⤓ rm, 🅺 rest, ⁽ᵞ⁾ 🖑 🅿 VISA ⓪ AE ⓪
1 West Victoria Dock Rd ⊠ DD1 3JP – ℰ (01382) 202404
– www.apexhotels.co.uk – dundee.reservations@apexhotels.co.uk
– Fax (01382) 201401   Y**a**
150 rm – 🛉£75/120 🛉🛉£75/120, ⊆ £12.50 – 2 suites
Rest *Metro Brasserie* – Menu £13/20 – Carte £21/30
Rest *Alchemy* – (dinner only Thursday-Saturday) Menu £28 – Carte £16/30
♦ Modern hotel on the waterfront. Business and leisure facilities to the fore, the smart spa offering plenty of treatments. Airy, up-to-date rooms all with views. Fine dining in Alchemy. Informal feel suffuses Metro: both restaurants look out over dockside.

at Broughty Ferry East : 4½ m. by A 930 - Z - ⊠ **Dundee**

Broughty Ferry 🔲 ⋒ Là 🎗 ⁽ᵞ⁾ 🅿 VISA ⓪ AE
16 West Queen St ⊠ DD5 1AR – ℰ (01382) 480027
– www.hotelbroughtyferry.co.uk – enquiries@hotelbroughtyferry.co.uk
– Fax (01382) 739426
16 rm ⊆ – 🛉£68/80 🛉🛉£88
Rest *Bombay Brasserie* – Indian – Carte £19/32 s
♦ Family owned and friendly modern hotel beside the main road. The spacious, individually decorated bedrooms are furnished to a high standard. Brasserie serves elaborate, authentic Indian menus.

Invermark House 🖨 🎗 ⁽ᵞ⁾ 🅿 VISA ⓪ AE ⓪
23 Monifieth Rd ⊠ DD5 2RN – ℰ (01382) 739430 – www.invermarkhouse.com
– enquiries@invermarkhotel.co.uk – Fax (01382) 220834
6 rm – 🛉£30 🛉🛉£50   **Rest** – (by arrangement) Menu £12
♦ Imposing, detached Victorian house retains a period charm. Welcoming owners and relaxed atmosphere. Individually decorated rooms with thoughtful touches. Contemporary dining room offering homemade fayre.

DUNFERMLINE – Fife – **501** J 15 – **pop. 39 229** ▌*Scotland*   28 **C3**
🚆 Edinburgh 16 mi – Dundee 48 mi – Motherwell 39 mi
🛈 1 High St ℰ (01383) 720999 (April-September), dunfermline@visitfife.com
🏌 Canmore Venturefair Ave, ℰ (01383) 724969
🏌 Pitreavie Queensferry Rd, ℰ (01383) 722591
🏌 Pitfirrane Crossford, ℰ (01383) 723534
🏌 Saline Kinneddar Hill, ℰ (01383) 852591
👁 Town★ - Abbey★ (Abbey Church★★) **AC**
🅖 Forth Bridges★★, S : 5 m. by A 823 and B 980. Culross★★ (Village★★★, Palace★★ **AC**, Study★ **AC**), W : 7 m. by A 994 and B 9037

Garvock House 🖨 ⁽ᵞ⁾ 🖑 🅿 VISA ⓪ AE
St John's Drive, Transy, East : ¾ m. by A 907 off Garvock Hill ⊠ KY12 7TU
– ℰ (01383) 621067 – www.garvock.co.uk – sales@garvock.co.uk – Fax (01383) 621168
26 rm ⊆ – 🛉£70/93 🛉🛉£90/148   **Rest** – Menu £19 (lunch) – Carte £21/37
♦ Privately owned Victorian house in woodland setting with classically decorated public areas. Contrastingly, most of the attractive, modish rooms are in a modern extension. Comfortable, smartly decorated dining room.

at Crossford Southwest : 1¾ m. on A 994 - ⊠ **Dunfermline**

Keavil House 🖨 🔲 ⋒ Là ⤓ rm, 🎗 ⁽ᵞ⁾ 🖑 🅿 VISA ⓪ AE ⓪
Main St ⊠ KY12 8QW – ℰ (01383) 736258 – www.keavilhouse.co.uk
– sales@keavilhouse.co.uk – Fax (01383) 621600
– Accommodation closed 25-26 December
72 rm ⊆ – 🛉£85/125 🛉🛉£110/160
Rest *Cardoon* – Menu £25 – Carte £18/25 s
♦ Busy, part 16C country house in woods and gardens on edge of estate. Useful for business traveller. Small bar, extensive leisure facilities. Well-equipped rooms. Elegant, linen-clad conservatory restaurant offering verdant surroundings in which to dine.

SCOTLAND

DUNFOOT – South Ayrshire – **501** G 17 – see Ayr

DUNKELD – Perth and Kinross – **501** J 14 – **pop. 1 005** ▯ *Scotland*   28 **C2**

▶ Edinburgh 58 mi – Aberdeen 88 mi – Inverness 98 mi – Perth 14 mi

🖼 The Cross ℰ (01350) 727688 (April-October), dunkeldtic@perthshire.co.uk

🖼 Dunkeld & Birnam Fungarth, ℰ (01350) 727 524

◎ Village★ - Cathedral Street★

 Kinnaird ⌂   ⋖ ⟍ 🖰 ⟍ ※ 📱 🛜 📱 🅿️ VISA ⓸ AE

Northwest : 6 ¾ m. by A 9 on B 898 ⊠ *PH8 0LB* – ℰ (01796) 482 440
– *www.kinnairdestate.com* – *enquiry@kinnairdestate.com* – *Fax (01796) 482 289*
8 rm (dinner included) ⌸ – ♦£ 300/425 ♦♦£ 350/475 – 1 suite
Rest – Menu £ 30/59

♦ Imposing Georgian mansion with superb Tay Valley views and sprawling gardens. Antiques, framed oils and country house drapes throughout. Immaculately kept, luxurious rooms. Formal restaurant with hand painted frescoes and ornate ceilings.

↑ **Letter Farm** without rest ⌂   📧 ☆ 🅿️ VISA ⓸
🖼 *Loch of the Lowes, Northeast : 3 . m. by A 923 on Loch of Lowes rd* ⊠ *PH8 0HH*
– ℰ (01350) 724 254 – *www.letterfarm.co.uk* – *letterfarm@btconnect.com*
– *Fax (01350) 724 254* – *mid May-November*
3 rm ⌸ – ♦£ 35/45 ♦♦£ 60/80

♦ Attractive, traditional farm house close to the Loch of the Lowes Nature Reserve. Welcoming, homely atmosphere and comfortable bedrooms.

> A good night's sleep without spending a fortune?
> Look for a Bib Hotel 🖾

DUNOON – Argyll and Bute – **501** F 16 – **pop. 8 251** ▯ *Scotland*   27 **B3**

▶ Edinburgh 73 mi – Glasgow 27 mi – Oban 77 mi

🚢 from Dunoon Pier to Gourock Railway Pier (Caledonian MacBrayne Ltd) frequent services daily (20 mn) – from Hunters Quay to McInroy's Point, Gourock (Western Ferries (Clyde) Ltd) frequent services daily (20 mn)

🖼 7 Alexandra Parade ℰ (08707) 200629, info@dunoon.visitscotland.com

🖼 Cowal Ardenslate Rd, ℰ (01369) 705 673

🖼 Innellan Knockamillie Rd, ℰ (01369) 830 242

◎ The Clyde Estuary★

🏠 **Dhailling Lodge**   📧 🖿 ఉ rm, ☆ 🛜 🅿️ VISA ⓸ AE
155 Alexandra Parade, North : ¾ m. on A 815 ⊠ *PA23 8AW* – ℰ (01369) 701 253
– *www.dhaillinglodge.com* – *james@dhaillinglodge.com* – *Restricted opening in winter*
7 rm ⌸ – ♦£ 42 ♦♦£ 79   **Rest** – (dinner only) Menu £ 20 **s**

♦ Victorian villa with neat and tidy gardens, overlooking Firth of Clyde. Homely lounge boasts books and local guides. Individually decorated rooms with welcoming extra touches. Smart dining room with good views from all tables.

DUNVEGAN – Highland – **501** A 11 – see Skye (Isle of)

DURNESS – Highland – **501** F 8   30 **C1**

▶ Edinburgh 259 mi – Tongue 30 mi

🏠 **Mackay's**   ⟍ 🅿️ VISA ⓸
⊠ *IV27 4PN* – ℰ (01971) 511 202 – *www.visitmackays.com*
– *fiona@visitmackays.com* – *Easter-October*
7 rm ⌸ – ♦£ 90/100 ♦♦£ 100/120   **Rest** – Carte £ 20/33

♦ Smart grey house in most North Westerly village of the British Isles. Modern, comfortable bedrooms, pleasant bathrooms and good facilities. Small, cosy guest lounge. Rustic dining room serves concise menu of traditionally based dishes with a Scottish base.

DUROR – Highland – 501 E 14   29 B3
▶ Edinburgh 131 mi – Ballachulish 7 mi – Oban 26 mi

Bealach House ⌖   ⌸ ⌧ P VISA ⓪

Salachan Glen, Southeast : 4½ m. by A 828 ⊠ PA38 4BW – ℰ (01631) 740 298
– www.bealach-house.co.uk – info@bealach-house.co.uk – Closed December and
January

3 rm ⌴ – ♦£55/65 ♦♦£80/100

Rest – (by arrangement, communal dining) Menu £28

♦ Down a one-and-a-half mile rural track for total privacy. This former crofter's house,
set in eight acres, is immaculate, with snug conservatory and smart, well-kept rooms.
Communal dining: daily changing menus have strong local base.

DYKE – Moray – 501 J 11 – see Forres

EDDLESTON – Scottish Borders – 501 K 16 – see Peebles
▶ Edinburgh 20 – Galashiels 22 – Peebles 4

EDINBANE – Highland – 501 A 11 – see Skye (Isle of)

M.P. Renier/MICHELIN

EDINBURGH

County: City of Edinburgh
Michelin REGIONAL map: n° 501 K 16
▶ Glasgow 46 mi – Newcastle upon Tyne 105 mi

Population: 430 082   26 **C1**
▮ *Scotland*

PRACTICAL INFORMATION

🛈 Tourist Information

Edinburgh & Scotland Information Centre, 3 Princes St ℘ (0131) 4733800, info@visitscotland.co.uk

Edinburgh Airport, Tourist Information Desk ℘ (0845) 2255121

Airport

🛧 Edinburgh Airport: ℘ (0870) 040 0007, W: 6 m. by A 8 AV

Golf Courses

🏌 Braid Hills Braid Hills Rd, ℘ (0131) 447 6666
🏌 Carrick Knowe Glendevon Park, ℘ (0131) 337 10 96
🏌 Duddingston Duddingston Road West, ℘ (0131) 661 7688
🏌 Silverknowes Parkway, ℘ (0131) 336 3843
🏌 Liberton 297 Gilmerton Rd, Kingston Grange, ℘ (0131) 664 3009
🏌 Marriott Dalmahoy Hotel & C.C. Kriknewton, ℘ (0131) 335 80 10
🏌 Portobello Stanley St, ℘ (0131) 669 4361

◉ SIGHTS

IN TOWN

City★★★ - Edinburgh International Festival★★★ (August) - Royal Museum of Scotland★★★ EZ **M2** – National Gallery of Scotland★★ DY **M4** - Royal Botanic Garden★★★ AV – The Castle★★ **AC** DYZ : Site★★★ - Palace Block (Honours of Scotland★★★) - St Margaret's Chapel (❄ ★★★) - Great Hall (Hammerbeam Roof★★) – ≤ ★★ from Argyle and Mill's Mount DZ – Abbey and Palace of Holyroodhouse★★ **AC** (Plasterwork Ceilings★★★, ❄ ★★ from Arthur's Seat) BV – Royal Mile★★ : St Giles' Cathedral★★ (Crown Spire★★★) EYZ - Gladstone's Land★ **AC** EYZ **A** - Canongate Talbooth★ EY **B** – New Town★★ (Charlotte Square★★★ CY **14** - The Georgian House★ **AC** CY **D** – Scottish National Portrait Gallery★ EY **M6** - Dundas House★ EY **E**) – Scottish National Gallery of Modern Art★ **M1** - Victoria Street★ EZ **84** – Scott Monument★ (≤ ★) **AC** EY **F** - Craigmillar Castle★ **AC**, SE: 3 m.

by A 7 BX – Calton Hill (❄ ★★★ **AC** from Nelson's Monument) EY – Dean Gallery★ AV opposite **M1** - Royal Yacht Britannia★ BV

ON THE OUTSKIRTS

Edinburgh Zoo★★ **AC** AV – Hill End Ski Centre (❄ ★★) **AC**, S: 5 ½ m. by A 702 BX – The Royal Observatory (West Tower ≤ ★) **AC** BX – Ingleston, Scottish Agricultural Museum★, W: 6 ½ m. by A 8 AV

IN THE SURROUNDING AREA

Rosslyn Chapel★★ **AC** (Apprentice Pillar★★★) S: 7 ½ m. by A 701 - BX - and B 7006 – Forth Bridges★★ , NW: 9 ½ m. by A 90 AV – Hopetoun House★★ **AC**, NW: 11 ½ m. by A 90 - AV - and A 904 – Dalmeny★ - Dalmeny House★ **AC**, St Cuthbert's Church★ (Norman South Doorway★★) NW: 7 m. by A 90 AV – Crichton Castle (Italianate courtyard range★) **AC**, SE: 10 m. by A 7 - X - and B 6372

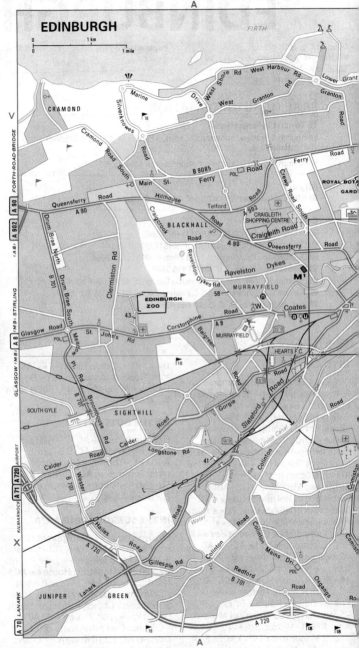

EDINBURGH

0 ——— 1 km
0 ——— 1 mile

FIRTH

SCOTLAND

CRAMOND

Marine   Drive   West Shore Rd   West Harbour Rd   Lower Grant

West   Granton   Rd   Granton   Road

Silverknowes

Cramond   Road South   Road

FORTH-ROAD-BRIDGE

Ferry   Road

Main   St.   Ferry   POL   Road

B 9085   Road   Crewe Road South

ROYAL BOTA
GARD

Queensferry   Road   Hillhouse   Telford   A 902   CRAIGLEITH
SHOPPING CENTRE

A 90   Craigcrook   Road   Craigleith Road

Drum Brae North   BLACKHALL   A 90   Queensferry   Road

Clermiston Rd   Road   Ravelston   Dykes

Drum Brae South   Ravelston Dykes Rd   58   MURRAYFIELD   M¹

B 701   EDINBURGH   43   W   Coates   a u

ZOO   Road   Corstorphine   A 8   Balgreen   MURRAYFIELD   12·9

Glasgow   Road   St.   John's   Rd   18   HEARTS F.C.   Road   15·6

POL   Mebzow   Pl.   Rd   Road   Road

SOUTH GYLE   B 701   Broomhouse   SIGHTHILL   Road   Gorgie   Road

Calder   Road   Longstone Rd   14·9   Union Canal   Slateford

Calder   B 701   Wester   41   Colinton   Road   Comiste

Hailes   Road   Colinton   Road   Comis

A 720   Water   Colinton Mains Dri.   POL

Gillespie Rd   Colinton   Redford   Organgs   Ro.

JUNIPER   GREEN   Lanark   B 701   Road

A 720   18   18   18

Lanark

SCOTLAND   (A8)   A 902   A 90   GLASGOW (M8)   A 8   (M9) STIRLING   KILMARNOCK   A 71   A 720   AIRPORT   A 70   LANARK

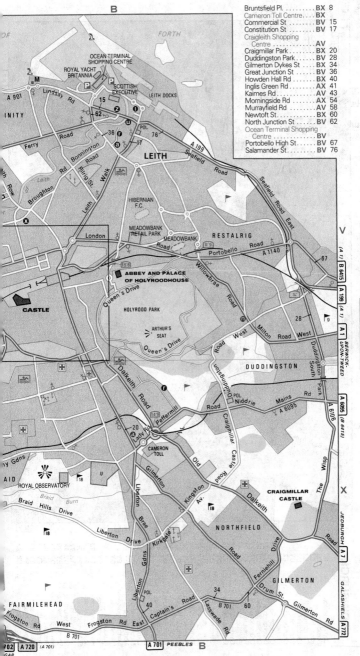

SCOTLAND

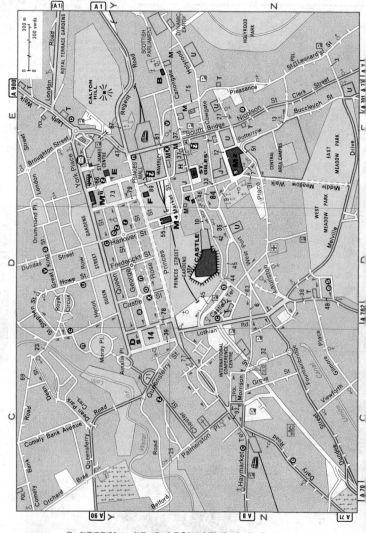

EDINBURGH

The Balmoral
1 Princes St ✉ *EH2 2EQ* – ✆ *(0131) 556 2414* – *www.roccofortecollection.com*
– *reservations.balmoral@roccofortecollection.com* – *Fax (0131) 557 8740* EY**n**
167 rm – †£ 305/320 ††£ 535/555, ☕ £18.50 – 21 suites
Rest Number One and **Hadrian's** – see restaurant listing
◆ Richly furnished rooms in grand baronial style complemented by contemporary furnishings in the Palm Court exemplify this de luxe Edwardian railway hotel and city landmark.

Sheraton Grand H. & Spa
1 Festival Sq ✉ *EH3 9SR* – ✆ *(0131) 229 9131*
– *www.sheraton.com/grandedinburgh*
– *grandedinburgh.sheraton@sheraton.com* – *Fax (0131) 221 6254* CDZ**v**
244 rm – †£ 293/334 ††£ 323/364, ☕ £19 – 16 suites
Rest Santini – see restaurant listing
Rest *Terrace* – (buffet) Menu £ 21/22 – Carte £ 23/33
◆ A modern, centrally located and smartly run hotel. A popular choice for the working traveller, as it boasts Europe's most advanced urban spa. Comfy, well-kept rooms. Glass expanse of Terrace restaurant overlooks Festival Square.

The George
19-21 George St ✉ *EH2 2PB* – ✆ *(0131) 225 1251* – *www.principal-hayley.com*
– *george.reservations@principal-hayley.com* – *Fax (0131) 226 5644* DY**z**
247 rm – †£ 99/299 ††£ 99/299, ☕ £16.50 – 1 suite
Rest *The Tempus* – Carte £ 25/40
◆ Grade II listed Georgian classic in the heart of the city's most chic street; makes the most of Robert Adam's listed design. Modern decor allied to smartly refurbished rooms. Interesting modern menus at The Tempus.

SCOTLAND

Prestonfield
Priestfield Rd ✉ *EH16 5UT* – ✆ *(0131) 225 7800* – *www.prestonfield.com*
– *mail@prestonfield.com* – *Fax (0131) 220 4392* BX**r**
20 rm ☕ – †£ 225/275 ††£ 225/275 – 2 suites
Rest *Rhubarb* – Menu £ 17/25 – Carte £ 39/51
◆ Superbly preserved interior, tapestries and paintings in the main part of this elegant country house, built in 1687 with modern additions. Set in parkland below Arthur's Seat. Two-roomed, period-furnished 18C dining room with fine views of the grounds.

The Howard
34 Great King St ✉ *EH3 6QH* – ✆ *(0131) 274 7402* – *www.thehoward.com*
– *reserve@thehoward.com* – *Fax (0131) 274 7405* DY**s**
14 rm ☕ – †£ 100/275 ††£ 190/275 – 4 suites
Rest *The Atholl* – (booking essential for non-residents) Carte £ 33/43
◆ Crystal chandeliers, antiques, richly furnished rooms and the relaxing opulence of the drawing room set off a fine Georgian interior. An inviting "boutique" hotel. Elegant, linen-clad tables for sumptuous dining.

The Scotsman
20 North Bridge ✉ *EH1 1YT* – ✆ *(0131) 556 5565* – *www.theetoncollection.com*
– *reservations@tshg.com* – *Fax (0131) 652 3652* EY**x**
69 rm – †£ 350/500 ††£ 350/500, ☕ £18.50 – 2 suites
Rest *North Bridge Brasserie* – Carte £ 24/35
◆ Imposing former offices of "The Scotsman" newspaper, with marble reception hall and historic prints. Notably impressive leisure facilities. Well-equipped modern bedrooms. North Bridge Brasserie serves seasonal, modern Scottish dishes.

Channings
15 South Learmonth Gdns ✉ *EH4 1EZ* – ✆ *(0131) 274 7401*
– *www.channings.co.uk* – *reserve@channings.co.uk* – *Fax (0131) 274 7405* CY**e**
38 rm – †£ 100/200 ††£ 140/200, ☕ £11.50 – 3 suites
Rest – Menu £ 17 (lunch) – Carte £ 28/36 **s**
◆ Sensitively refurbished rooms and fire-lit lounges blend an easy country house elegance with original Edwardian character. Individually appointed bedrooms. A warm, contemporary design doesn't detract from the formal ambience pervading this basement restaurant in which classic Gallic flavours hold sway.

The Bonham
🛋 & rm, ⚑ ℅ ⓦ 🖵 P̄ VISA ⬤ AE

35 Drumsheugh Gdns ⊠ EH3 7RN – ℘ (0131) 274 7400 – www.thebonham.com
– reserve@thebonham.com – Fax (0131) 274 7405   CYz
46 rm – †£ 110/185 ††£ 175/215, ⌧ £11.50 – 2 suites
Rest – Menu £ 16 – Carte £ 27/44 s
♦ A striking synthesis of Victorian architecture, eclectic fittings and bold, rich colours
of a contemporary décor. Numerous pictures by "up-and-coming" local artists. Chic
dining room with massive mirrors and "catwalk" in spotlights.

The Glasshouse *without rest*
≤ 🚄 🛋 & rm, ⚑ ℅ ⓦ VISA ⬤ AE ①

2 Greenside Pl ⊠ EH1 3AA – ℘ (0131) 525 8200 – www.theetoncollection.com
– resglasshouse@theetoncollection.com – Fax (0131) 525 8205
– Closed Christmas   EYo
65 rm – †£ 160/355 ††£ 200/510, ⌧ £16.50
♦ Glass themes dominate the discreet style. Modern bedrooms, with floor to ceiling
windows, have views of spacious roof garden or the city below. Breakfast room to the
rear.

Tigerlily
🛋 & rm, 🄰🄲 ⓦ VISA ⬤ AE

125 George St ⊠ EH2 4JN – ℘ (0131) 225 5005 – www.tigerlilyedinburgh.co.uk
– info@tigerlilyedinburgh.co.uk – Fax (0131) 225 7046
– Closed 25 December   DYa
33 rm – †£ 195 ††£ 195   **Rest** – Carte £ 25/34
♦ Coverted Georgian townhouse boasting hip interior, including pink furnished bar,
buzzy basement nightclub and glamourous, well-appointed bedrooms. Busy dining
room offers wide choice of dishes, with Asian tendencies.

Le Monde
🛋 & rm, 🄰🄲 ⚑ ℅ ⓦ VISA ⬤ AE ①

16 George St ⊠ EH2 2PF – ℘ (0131) 270 3900 – www.lemondehotel.co.uk
– info@lemondehotel.co.uk – Fax (0131) 270 3901
– Closed 24-26 December   DYr
18 rm ⌧ – †£ 125/195 ††£ 145/295
Rest *Paris* – Carte £ 18/32 s
♦ Smartly appointed hotel in city centre, with two trendy bars and a nightclub. Contemporary bedrooms are themed on cities from around the world, even down to
the DVDs. First floor restaurant offers simple menu.

Edinburgh Marriott
📺 ☕ ♨ ℔ 🛋 🄰🄲 ⓦ ⚓ P̄ VISA ⬤ AE ①

111 Glasgow Rd, West : 4½ m. on A 8 ⊠ EH12 8NF – ℘ (0131) 334 9191
– www.edinburghmarriott.co.uk – mhrs.edieb.frontdesk@marriotthotels.com
– Fax (0131) 316 4507
241 rm ⌧ – †£ 130/150 ††£ 140/160 – 4 suites
Rest *Mediterrano* – Menu £ 16 (lunch) – Carte (dinner) £ 19/28
♦ Excellent road connections for the airport and Glasgow and well-equipped rooms
make this large, group-operated hotel a practical choice for business travel. Modern
restaurant with Mediterranean twist.

The Roxburghe
📺 ♨ ℔ 🛋 & rm, 🄰🄲 rest, ⚑ ℅ ⚓ VISA ⬤ AE ①

38 Charlotte Sq ⊠ EH2 4HQ – ℘ (0844) 879 9063
– www.macdonaldhotels.co.uk/roxburghe – roxburghe@macdonald-hotels.co.uk
– Fax (0131) 240 5555   DYi
196 rm ⌧ – †£ 95/200 ††£ 95/255 – 1 suite
Rest *The Melrose* – Carte £ 17/43 s
♦ Attentive service, understated period-inspired charm and individuality in the British style. Part modern, part Georgian but roomy throughout; welcoming bar. Restaurant reflects the grandeur of architect Robert Adam's exterior.

Number Ten *without rest*
⚑ ℅ ⓦ VISA ⬤ AE ①

10 Gloucester Place ⊠ EH3 6EF – ℘ (0131) 225 2720
– www.hotelnumberten.co.uk – reservations@hotelnumberten.co.uk
– Fax (0131) 220 4706   CYc
28 rm ⌧ – †£ 98/158 ††£ 118/248
♦ Georgian house on cobbled street in quiet residential area; a chintzy feel overlays
the contemporary interior. Eclectically styled bedrooms feature homely extra
touches.

SCOTLAND

Ten Hill Place without rest 　　　　　　🛎 �🚹 🅰 ℀ 🕻 VISA ⓪ AE
10 Hill Place ⊠ EH8 9DS – ℰ (0131) 662 2080 – www.tenhillplacehotel.com
– reservations@tenhillplace.com – Fax (0131) 662 2082
– Closed Christmas　　　　　　　　　　　　　　　　　　　EZ**a**
78 rm � – ♦£110/150 ♦♦£110/150
♦ Brand new hotel owned by Royal College of Surgeons and next to main college. Contemporary bedrooms boast state-of-the-art facilities; views from Skyline rooms worth extra cost.

Edinburgh Lodge without rest 　　　　　🚗 ℀ 🕻 P VISA ⓪ AE
6 Hampton Terrace, West Coates ⊠ EH12 5JD – ℰ (0131) 337 3682
– www.thelodgehotel.co.uk – info@thelodgehotel.co.uk
– Fax (0131) 313 1700　　　　　　　　　　　　　　　　　　AV**u**
12 rm ⊂ – ♦£50/70 ♦♦£80/135
♦ A converted Georgian manse, family owned and immaculately kept. Individually designed bedrooms and lounge decorated with taste and care; close to Murrayfield rugby stadium.

Kildonan Lodge 　　　　　　　　　℀ 🕻 P VISA ⓪ AE ①
27 Craigmillar Park ⊠ EH16 5PE – ℰ (0131) 667 2793
– www.kildonanlodgehotel.co.uk – info@kildonanlodgehotel.co.uk – Fax (0131)
667 9777 – Closed 1 week Christmas　　　　　　　　　　　　BX**a**
12 rm ⊂ – ♦£65/98 ♦♦£78/149
Rest – (dinner only, booking essential) Menu £20 – Carte £18/31 s
♦ Privately managed, with a cosy, firelit drawing room which feels true to the Lodge's origins as a 19C family house. One room has a four-poster bed and a fine bay window.

Davenport House without rest 　　　　　　℀ 🕻 VISA ⓪ ①
58 Great King St ⊠ EH3 6QY – ℰ (0131) 558 8495 – www.davenport-house.com
– davenporthouse@btinternet.com – Fax (0131) 558 8496
– Closed Christmas　　　　　　　　　　　　　　　　　　　DY**v**
6 rm ⊂ – ♦£65/110 ♦♦£75/110
♦ Three-storey Georgian townhouse on cobbled street. Welcoming period style lounge; chintzy breakfast room. The bedrooms are of varying styles and sizes; all are well equipped.

Kew House without rest 　　　　　　　℀ 🕻 P VISA ⓪ AE
1 Kew Terrace, Murrayfield ⊠ EH12 5JE – ℰ (0131) 313 0700
– www.kewhouse.com – info@kewhouse.com
– Fax (0131) 313 0747　　　　　　　　　　　　　　　　　AV**a**
8 rm ⊂ – ♦£83/125 ♦♦£90/161
♦ Secure private parking and good road access for the city or Murrayfield Stadium. Neat, carefully kept rooms which are modern and well-proportioned.

Elmview without rest 　　　　　　　　　　℀ 🕻 VISA ⓪
15 Glengyle Terrace ⊠ EH3 9LN – ℰ (0131) 228 1973 – www.elmview.co.uk
– nici@elmview.co.uk – 19 March-October　　　　　　　　　DZ**e**
5 rm ⊂ – ♦£70/100 ♦♦£90/120
♦ Basement of a Victorian house in pretty terrace overlooking The Meadows. Bedrooms are spotlessly kept and feature a host of extras: videos, fridges, sherry and more.

The Glenora without rest 　　　　　　　℀ 🕻 VISA ⓪ ①
14 Rosebery Crescent – ℰ (0131) 337 1186 – www.theglenorahotel.co.uk
– enquiries@glenorahotel.co.uk – Fax (0131) 337 1119　　　CZ**c**
11 rm ⊂ – ♦£58/75 ♦♦£90/140
♦ Capacious Georgian house split over three floors with modern, stylish décor and generously sized bedrooms. Exclusively organic produce served at breakfast.

SCOTLAND

SCOTLAND

⌂ **The Beverley** without rest · 📶 🛜 VISA ⓪ AE
40 Murrayfield Ave ⊠ EH12 6AY – 𝒞 (0131) 337 1128 – www.thebeverley.com
– enquiries@thebeverley.com – Fax (0131) 313 3275 – Closed Christmas · AV**n**
8 rm ⌣ – †£40/80 ††£70/100
♦ Elegant 19C bay windowed house in quiet, tree-lined avenue close to the rugby stadium. Good value, individually appointed rooms with modern facilties and thoughtful extras.

⌂ **Castle View** without rest · 📶 VISA ⓪
30 Castle St ⊠ EH2 3HT – 𝒞 (0131) 226 5784 – www.castleviewgh.co.uk
– booking@castleviewgh.co.uk – Fax (0131) 226 1603 · DY**x**
8 rm ⌣ – †£45/100 ††£110
♦ As name implies, set in great position for tourists. Lounge with comfy sofas. Well-kept, individual rooms in a terraced house; those at front have castle views.

XXXX **Number One** – at The Balmoral Hotel · AC VISA ⓪ AE ①
❀ 1 Princes St ⊠ EH2 2EQ – 𝒞 (0131) 622 8831 – www.roccofortecollection.com
– numberone@roccofortecollection.com – Fax (0131) 557 8740
– Closed first 2 weeks January · EY**n**
Rest – Modern – (dinner only) Menu £55 ⌘
Spec. Citrus scallops with braised artichokes and lentils. Lamb with lettuce and niçoise garnish. Prune soufflé and armagnac ice cream.
♦ Opulently-appointed basement restaurant offering fine dining in grand railway hotel. Luxurious feel. Complex and elaborate cooking showcases Scottish produce.

XXX **Oloroso** · ⪜ 🏠 AC ⇔ VISA ⓪ AE
33 Castle St ⊠ EH2 3DN – 𝒞 (0131) 226 7614 – www.oloroso.co.uk
– info@oloroso.co.uk – Fax (0131) 226 7608
– Closed first 3 weeks January and 25-26 December · DY**o**
Rest – Innovative – Carte £33/52
♦ Modish third floor restaurant in heart of city. Busy, atmospheric bar. Lovely terrace with good castle views to the west. Stylish, modern cooking with Asian influence.

XXX **Abstract** · VISA ⓪ AE ①
33-35 Castle Terrace ⊠ EH1 2EL – 𝒞 (0131) 229 1222
– www.abstractrestaurant.com – reservations@abstractrestaurant.com
– Fax (0131) 228 2398 – Closed Sunday and Monday · DZ**a**
Rest – French – Menu £17 (weekday lunch) – Carte £32/45
♦ Tucked away behind the castle, all mock snakeskin furniture and vibrant wallpaper. Seasonal French cooking is balanced and thoughtful; formal service by a well-versed team.

XX **Santini** – at Sheraton Grand H. & Spa. · AC P VISA ⓪ AE ①
8 Conference Sq ⊠ EH3 8AN – 𝒞 (0131) 221 7788
– www.sheraton.com/grandedinburgh
– grandeedinburgh.sheraton@sheraton.com – Fax (0131) 221 7789 · CDZ**v**
Rest – Italian – Menu £10/19 – Carte £16/44 **s**
♦ The personal touch is predominant in this stylish restaurant appealingly situated under a superb spa. Charming service heightens the enjoyment of tasty, modern Italian food.

XX **Atrium** · AC VISA ⓪ AE ①
☺ 10 Cambridge St ⊠ EH1 2ED – 𝒞 (0131) 228 8882
– www.atriumrestaurant.co.uk – eat@atriumrestaurant.co.uk – Fax (0131)
228 8808 – Closed 24-26 December, 1 January, Sunday and Saturday lunch except during Edinburgh Festival and Rugby matches · DZ**c**
Rest – Modern – Menu £20/27 – Carte £35/46 ⌘
♦ Located inside the Traverse Theatre, an adventurous repertoire enjoyed on tables made of wooden railway sleepers. Twisted copper lamps subtly light the ultra-modern interior.

XX **Hadrian's** – at The Balmoral Hotel   AC 🍴 VISA ⓪ AE ①
2 North Bridge ⊠ EH1 1TR – ℰ (0131) 557 5000
– hadrians@roccofortecollection.com – Fax (0131) 557 3747   EY**n**
Rest – Modern – Menu £ 22 (lunch) – Carte £ 25/41
♦ Drawing on light, clean-lined styling, reminiscent of Art Deco, and a "British new wave" approach; an extensive range of contemporary brasserie classics and smart service.

XX **Forth Floor - Restaurant (at Harvey Nichols)**   ≤ 😤 AC
30-34 St Andrew Sq ⊠ EH2 2AD – ℰ (0131) 524 8350   🍴 VISA ⓪ AE ①
– www.harveynichols.com – forthfloorreservations@harveynichols.com
– Fax (0131) 524 8351   EY**z**
Rest – Modern – (closed Sunday dinner and Monday) Menu £ 24 (lunch)
– Carte £ 31/40
♦ Stylish restaurant with delightful outside terrace affording views over the city. Half the room in informal brasserie-style and the other more formal. Modern, Scottish menus.

XX **The Stockbridge**   VISA ⓪ AE
54 St Stephens St ⊠ EH3 5AL – ℰ (0131) 226 6766
– www.thestockbridgerestaurant.com – Closed first 2 weeks January,
25, 31 December, Monday and lunch Tuesday   CY**n**
Rest – Modern – Menu £ 22 (dinner) – Carte £ 28/41
♦ Intimate neighbourhood restaurant, its black walls hung with colourful Scottish art. Professional staff serve a mix of classical and more modern dishes, precisely prepared.

XX **Duck's at Le Marche Noir**   🖨 VISA ⓪ AE ①
😊 14 Eyre Pl ⊠ EH3 5EP – ℰ (0131) 558 1608 – www.ducks.co.uk
– enquiries@ducks.co.uk – Fax (0131) 556 0798
– Closed 25-26 December, Sunday and Monday   BV**x**
Rest – Innovative – Menu £ 16 – Carte £ 24/39
♦ Confident, inventive cuisine with a modern, discreetly French character, served with friendly efficiency in bistro-style surroundings - intimate and very personally run.

XX **The Tower**   ≤ 😤 AC VISA ⓪ AE ①
Museum of Scotland (5th floor), Chambers St ⊠ EH1 1JF – ℰ (0131) 225 3003
– www.tower-restaurant.com – mail@tower-restaurant.com – Fax (0131)
220 4392 – Closed 25-26 December   EZ**s**
Rest – Carte £ 26/43
♦ Game, grills and seafood feature in a popular, contemporary brasserie style menu. On the fifth floor of the Museum of Scotland - ask for a terrace table and admire the view.

XX **La Garrigue**   VISA ⓪ AE
31 Jeffrey St ⊠ EH1 1DH – ℰ (0131) 557 3032 – www.lagarrigue.co.uk
– lagarrigue@btconnect.com – Fax (0131) 557 30 32
– Closed 25-26 December, first week January and Sunday   EY**v**
Rest – French – Menu £ 16/30
♦ Very pleasant restaurant near the Royal Mile: beautiful handmade wood tables add warmth to rustic décor. Authentic French regional cooking with classical touches.

XX **Roti**   VISA ⓪ AE
73 Morrison St ⊠ EH3 8BU – ℰ (0131) 221 9998 – www.roti.uk.com
– info@roti.uk.com – Fax (0131) 225 5374 – Closed Sunday   CZ**z**
Rest – Indian – Carte £ 23/27
♦ Modern Indian restaurant in central location; traditional carved wood meets funky new fittings. Accomplished kitchen serves authentic dishes; tasting menus a highlight.

SCOTLAND

X **First Coast**   AC 🏧 VISA ◑◐ AE
97-101 Dalry Rd ⊠ EH11 2AB – ℰ (0131) 313 4404 – www.first-coast.co.uk
– info@first-coast.co.uk – Fax (0131) 346 7811
– Closed 25-26 December, 1-2 January and Sunday   CZ**e**
Rest – Carte £ 20/30
♦ Informal restaurant near Haymarket station. The exposed stone walls in one of the rooms lend a rustic aspect. Sizeable menus boast a classic base with modern twists.

X **Nargile**   VISA ◑◐ AE
73 Hanover St ⊠ EH2 1EE – ℰ (0131) 225 5755 – www.nargile.co.uk
– info@nargile.co.uk
– Closed 24-26 December, 1-2 January, Monday lunch and Sunday   DY**e**
Rest – Turkish – Menu £ 24 (dinner) – Carte £ 18/27
♦ Unpretentious and welcoming restaurant with simple décor and enthusiastic service. A la carte, set menus and lunch time mezes of tasty, well-prepared Turkish cuisine.

X **Blue**   AC 🏧 VISA ◑◐ AE ①
10 Cambridge St ⊠ EH1 2ED – ℰ (0131) 221 1222 – www.bluescotland.com
– eat@bluescotland.com – Fax (0131) 228 8808 – Closed 25-26 December   DZ**c**
Rest – Carte £ 26/34
♦ Strikes a modern note with bright, curving walls, glass and simple settings. A café-bar with a light, concise and affordable menu drawing a young clientele. Bustling feel.

X **The Dogs**   VISA ◑◐
⊛ 110 Hanover St. ⊠ EH2 1DR – ℰ (0131) 220 1208 – www.thedogsonline.co.uk
– info@thedogsonline.co.uk – Closed 25 December-1 January   DY**e**
Rest – Carte £ 16/20
♦ Set on the first floor of a classic Georgian mid-terrace; impressive staircase, simple décor, high-ceilings. Robust, good value comfort food crafted from local, seasonal produce.

🍴 **Iglu**   🍸 VISA ◑◐ AE
2B Jamaica Street ⊠ EH3 6HH – ℰ (0131) 476 5333 – www.theiglu.com
– mail@theiglu.com
– Closed 25 December dinner, 26 December, 1-2 January   DY**u**
Rest – Modern – (booking essential) Menu £ 12 (lunch) – Carte £ 22/32
♦ Vivid blue façade. Plasma screens, low tub chairs and funky music; fish tanks and potted plants upstairs. Their ethos is ethical eating; their motto 'wild, organic and local.'

at Leith

🏨 **Malmaison**   🚣 📶 ⑁ 🔥 rm, 🍸 🐾 🧖 P. VISA ◑◐ AE ①
1 Tower Pl ⊠ EH6 7DB – ℰ (0131) 468 5000 – www.malmaison.com
– edinburgh@malmaison.com – Fax (0131) 468 5002   BV**i**
95 rm – ♦£ 150 ♦♦£ 150, ⊊ £ 13.95 – 5 suites
Rest Brasserie – Menu £ 14/15 – Carte £ 26/41
♦ Imposing quayside sailors' mission converted in strikingly elegant style. Good-sized rooms, thoughtfully appointed, combine more traditional comfort with up-to-date overtones. Sophisticated brasserie with finely wrought iron.

XXX **Martin Wishart**   VISA ◑◐ AE
❀ 54 The Shore ⊠ EH6 6RA – ℰ (0131) 553 3557 – www.martin-wishart.co.uk
– info@martin-wishart.co.uk – Fax (0131) 467 7091 – Closed first 2 weeks
January, last week July, 25 December, Sunday and Monday   BV**u**
Rest – Innovative – (booking essential) Menu £ 25/55 **s** – Carte approx. £ 55 **s**
Spec. Ceviche of halibut with mango, passion fruit and coriander. Shin of beef with pumpkin purée and wild mushroom risotto. St. Felicien and apple cannelloni, blueberry brûlée and apple sorbet.
♦ Simply decorated dockside conversion with a fully formed reputation. Modern French-accented menus characterised by clear, intelligently combined flavours. Formal service.

XX **The Kitchin** (Tom Kitchin)   🍴 `VISA` `OO` `AE`
❀ 78 Commercial Quay ⊠ EH6 6LX – ✆ (0131) 555 1755 – www.thekitchin.com
– info@thekitchin.com – Fax (0131) 553 0608 – Closed Christmas - 7 January,
Sunday and Monday   BV**z**

Rest – Contemporary – Menu £ 25 (lunch) – Carte £ 44/59

Spec. Roast langoustine with pig's head and crispy ear salad. Roast duck with
endive, roasted fig and orange sauce. Orange tuille with lemon mousse, citrus
marmalade and Earl Grey sorbet.

♦ Former dockside warehouse, the industrial feel enhanced by original metal supports and battleship grey décor. Well-priced menus offering skilful, accomplished,
modern cooking.

XX **Plumed Horse** (Tony Borthwick)   ⇔ `VISA` `OO` `AE`
❀ 50-54 Henderson St ⊠ EH6 6DE – ✆ (0131) 554 5556 – www.plumedhorse.co.uk
– plumedhorse@aol.com – Closed 2 weeks July, 2 weeks November,
25-26 December, 1 January, Sunday and Monday   BV**a**

Rest – Modern – Menu £ 21/39

Spec. Foie gras terrine with water melon, Sauternes and golden raisin vinaigrette. Scallop and langoustine lasagne, sea bass and champagne sauce. Fudge
and ginger parfait, vanilla, lime and 'Sailor Jerry' granita.

♦ Stylish, personally run restaurant with ornate ceiling, vivid paintings, an intimate
feel and formal service. Precise, well-crafted cooking makes good use of Scottish ingredients.

XX **The Vintners Rooms**   `VISA` `OO` `AE`
The Vaults, 87 Giles St ⊠ EH6 6BZ – ✆ (0131) 554 6767
– www.thevintnersrooms.com – enquiries@thevintnersrooms.com – Fax (0131)
555 5653 – Closed 23 December-9 January, Sunday and Monday   BV**r**

Rest – Mediterranean – Carte £ 37/48

♦ Atmospheric 18C bonded spirits warehouse with high ceilings, stone floor, rug-
covered walls and candlelit side-room with ornate plasterwork. French/Mediterra-
nean cooking.

🍺 **The Kings Wark**   `VISA` `OO`
36 The Shore ⊠ EH6 6QU – ✆ (0131) 554 9260
– Closed 25-26 December and 1 January   BV**u**

Rest – Modern – Carte £ 13/29

♦ Distinctive blue façade and cosy, characterful interior with exposed stone and
beams. Hearty, unpretentious Scottish cooking. Well known for its all day weekend
breakfasts.

---

at Kirknewton Southwest : 7 m. on A 71 - AX – ⊠ **Edinburgh**

🏨🏨 **Dalmahoy H. & Country Club** 🌿   ≤ 🚗 🕐 📺 ☕ ⌘ 🏋 ✗
⊠ EH27 8EB – ✆ (0131)   🔞 🛗 & rm, Ⓚ rest, ✗ ⁿ 🛁 🅿 `VISA` `OO` `AE` `①`
333 1845 – www.marriottdalmahoy.co.uk
– mhrs.edigs.frontdesk@marriotthotels.com – Fax (0131) 333 1433

212 rm ⊆ – ♛£ 135/175 ♛♛£ 135/175 – 3 suites

Rest *Pentland* – (dinner only) Menu £ 32 – Carte £ 27/42

Rest *The Long Weekend* – Carte £ 18/27 **s**

♦ Extended Georgian mansion in 1000 acres with 2 Championship golf courses.
Comprehensive leisure club, smart rooms and a clubby cocktail lounge. Tranquil
atmosphere with elegant comfort in Pentland restaurant. Informal modern dining at
The Long Weekend.

EDNAM – Borders – see Kelso

Look out for red symbols, indicating particularly pleasant establishments.

SCOTLAND

🅳 Edinburgh 94 mi – Aberdeen 36 mi – Dundee 31 mi
🅖 Castle★ **AC** (The Pleasance★★★) W : 2 m. Glen Esk★, NW : 7 m

🏨 **Glenesk**   🛏 🔲 🐾 ⅃ś ⚒ 🐾 🛁 🅿 📶 ⓌⓈⒶ ⒸⒸ 🄰🄴
High St ⊠ DD9 7TF – ℰ (01356) 648 319 – www.gleneskhotel.co.uk
– gleneskhotel@btconnect.com – Fax (01356) 647 333 – Closed 2-15 January
23 rm ⌷ – †£70/85 ††£120/135
Rest – (bar lunch) Menu £28 **s** – Carte £20/33 **s**
♦ Well run and family owned, a substantial 19C hotel with the pleasant village on its doorstep. Friendly atmosphere prevails. The good sized bedrooms are being refurbished. Restaurant overlooks golf course and gardens.

🅳 Edinburgh 198 mi – Aberdeen 68 mi – Fraserburgh 61 mi – Inverness 39 mi
🅸 17 High St ℰ (01343) 542666, elgin@visitscotland.com
🅸🅱 Moray Lossiemouth Stotfield Rd, ℰ (01343) 812 018
🅸🅱 Hardhillock Birnie Rd, ℰ (01343) 542 338
🅸🅱 Hopeman Moray, ℰ (01343) 830 578
🔘 Town★ - Cathedral★ (Chapter house★★) **AC**
🅖 Glenfiddich Distillery★, SE : 10 m. by A 941

🏨 **Mansion House**   🛏 🔲 🐾 ⅃ś ⚒ 🐾 🛁 🅿 ⓌⓈⒶ ⒸⒸ 🄰🄴
The Haugh, via Haugh Rd ⊠ IV30 1AW – ℰ (01343) 548811
– www.mansionhousehotel.co.uk – reception@mhelgin.co.uk – Fax (01343)
547916 – Closed January
23 rm ⌷ – †£89/100 ††£175/185
Rest – Menu £20 (lunch) – Carte (dinner) £19/38
♦ 19C Baronial mansion surrounded by lawned gardens. Country house-style interior. Rooms in main house most characterful, those in purpose-built annex more modern. The formal restaurant is decorated in warm yellows and blues.

🏠 **The Pines** without rest   🛏 ⚒ 🐾 🅿 ⓌⓈⒶ ⒸⒸ
East Rd, East :½ m. on A 96 ⊠ IV30 1XG – ℰ (01343) 552 495
– www.thepinesguesthouse.com – enquiries@thepinesguesthouse.com
– Fax (01343) 552 495
5 rm ⌷ – †£45/50 ††£60/66
♦ Detached Victorian house with a friendly and warm ambience amidst comfy, homely décor. Bedrooms are of a good size and furnished with colourful, modern fabrics.

🏠 **The Croft** without rest   🛏 ⚒ 🅿
10 Institution Rd, via Duff Ave ⊠ IV30 1QX – ℰ (01343) 546 004
– www.thecroftelgin.co.uk – thecroftelgin@hotmail.com – Fax (01343) 546 004
– Closed December and January
3 rm ⌷ – †£36/60 ††£66/70
♦ Victorian family home with delightful garden. Large, comfortable, library-style lounge and a breakfast room with fine dining suite. Comfy, pine furnished rooms.

🏠 **The Lodge**   🛏 ⚒ 🐾 🅿 ⓌⓈⒶ ⒸⒸ
20 Duff Ave ⊠ IV30 1QS – ℰ (01343) 549 981 – www.thelodge-elgin.com
– info@thelodge-elgin.com – Fax (01343) 540 527
8 rm ⌷ – †£38/50 ††£58/68   **Rest** – (by arrangement) Carte £16/24
♦ Victorian house with a distinctive facade. Antique furnished hall and homely lounge with open fires. Comfortable bedrooms with dark wood furniture. Tasty home-cooked meals.

at Urquhart East : 5 m. by A 96 – ⊠ Elgin

🏠 **Parrandier** ⑧   ⟨ 🛏 🅿 ⓌⓈⒶ ⒸⒸ
The Old Church of Urquhart, Meft Rd, Northwest :¼ m. by Main St and Meft Rd
⊠ *IV30 8NH – ℰ (01343) 843 063 – www.oldchurch.eu – info@oldchurch.eu*
– Fax (01343) 843 063 – Easter-October
7 rm ⌷ – †£38 ††£58/68
Rest – (by arrangement, communal dining) Menu £12
♦ Former 19C church in quiet rural location converted to provide open plan lounge and split level dining area. Comfortable bedrooms with original church features.

SCOTLAND

at Duffus Northwest : 5 ½ m. by A 941 on B 9012 – ✉ Elgin

⛫ **Burnside House** without rest   ⪕ 🚗 🎏 **P**
Northwest : 1 ¾ m. by B 9012 on B 9040 ✉ IV30 5QS – ℰ (01343) 835 165
– www.burnsidehouse.net – burnsidehouse@hotmail.com – Fax (01343) 835 165
4 rm ⌂ – ♦£36 ♦♦£60
♦ 19C house with garden; the residence of the founder of Gordonstoun School nearby. Attractive rooms with view; snooker table. Large bedrooms with tartan themes.

ELIE – Fife – 501 L 15   28 D2
🚇 Edinburgh 44 mi – Dundee 24 mi – St Andrews 13 mi

✗✗ **Sangster's** (Bruce Sangster)   **VISA 🟠 ①**
ॐ *51 High St ✉ KY9 1BZ – ℰ (01333) 331 001 – www.sangsters.co.uk*
– bruce@sangsters.co.uk – Fax (01333) 331 001
– Closed January, first week November, 25-26 December, Monday, Tuesday, dinner Sunday and lunch Saturday
Rest – (booking essential) Menu £21/36
Spec. Seared scallops with chilli, ginger and galangal dressing. Fillet and featherblade of beef with girolles, asparagus and broad beans. Raspberry soufflé and yoghurt ice cream.
♦ Husband and wife team run this homely, modern restaurant with local artwork for sale on the walls. Detailed, finely tuned cooking employs notable use of good, local produce.

ERISKA (Isle of) – Argyll and Bute – 501 D 14 – ✉ Oban   27 B2
🚇 Edinburgh 127 mi – Glasgow 104 mi – Oban 12 mi

🏨 **Isle of Eriska** ॐ   ⪕ 🚗 ⓚ 🖥 🛜 🎏 ⅃ₛ ✗ 🔲 ₢ rm, Ⓐ rest, ¶¶ ♨
Benderloch ✉ PA37 1SD – ℰ (01631) 720 371   **P VISA 🟠 AE**
– www.eriska-hotel.co.uk – office@eriska-hotel.co.uk – Fax (01631) 720 531
– Closed January
23 rm ⌂ – ♦£155/230 ♦♦£310/430 – 7 suites
Rest – (light lunch residents only) (booking essential) Menu £40
♦ On a private island, a wonderfully secluded 19C Scottish Baronial mansion with dramatic views of Lismore and mountains. Highest levels of country house comfort and style. Elegant dining.

EUROCENTRAL – Glasgow – see Glasgow

FAIRLIE – North Ayrshire – 501 F 16   25 A1
🚇 Edinburgh 75 mi – Ayr 50 mi – Glasgow 36 mi

✗ **Fins**   **P VISA 🟠**
Fencebay Fisheries, Fencefoot Farm, South : 1 ½ m. on A 78 ✉ KA29 0EG
– ℰ (01475) 568 989 – www.fencebay.co.uk – fencebay@aol.com – Fax (01475) 568 921 – Closed 25-26 December, 1 January, Sunday dinner and Monday
Rest – Seafood – (booking essential) Carte £28/46
♦ Converted farm buildings house a simple, flag-floored restaurant, craft shops and a traditional beech smokery. Friendly service and fresh seasonal seafood.

FASNACLOICH – Argyll and Bute – ✉ Appin   27 B2
🚇 Edinburgh 133 mi – Fort William 34 mi – Oban 19 mi

⛫ **Lochside Cottage** ॐ   ⪕ 🚗 **P**
✉ PA38 4BJ – ℰ (01631) 730 216 – www.lochsidecottage.net
– broadbent@lochsidecottage.net – Fax (01631) 730 216 – Closed Christmas and New Year
3 rm ⌂ – ♦£57 ♦♦£76
Rest – (by arrangement, communal dining) Menu £29
♦ Captivating views of surrounding mountains and Loch Baile Mhic Chailen, on whose shore it stands in idyllic seclusion. Log fires in the lounge and inviting, cosy bedrooms. Dinners take place with a house party atmosphere as guests dine together at one table.

SCOTLAND

FLODIGARRY – Highland – **501** B 11 – **see Skye (Isle of)**

FORGANDENNY – Perth. and Kinross – **501** J 14 – **see Perth**

FORRES – Moray – **501** J 11 – **pop. 8 967** ▯ Scotland   28 **C1**
- Edinburgh 165 mi – Aberdeen 80 mi – Inverness 27 mi
- 116 High St ℰ (01309) 672938 (Easter-October), forres@visitscotland.com
- Muiryshade, ℰ (01309) 672 949
- Sueno's Stone★★, N : ½ m. by A 940 on A 96 – Brodie Castle★ **AC**, W : 3 m. by A 96. Elgin★ (Cathedral★, chapter house★★ **AC**), E : 10 ¼ m. by A 96

🏨 **Knockomie** ⚐   ⌂ 🕏 &. rm, ☝ ⚐ 🅿 𝚅𝙸𝚂𝙰 ⓐ 𝔸𝔼 ⓞ
Grantown Rd, South : 1 ½ m. on A 940 ⊠ IV36 2SG – ℰ (01309) 673 146
– www.knockomie.co.uk – stay@knockomie.co.uk – Fax (01309) 673 290
– Closed 24-26 December
15 rm ⌂ – ♦£115 ♦♦£210
Rest *The Grill Room* – Menu £38 (dinner) – Carte £27/37
♦ Extended Arts and Crafts house in comfortable seclusion off a country road. Country house atmosphere. Bedrooms in main house older and more characterful. The Grill baronial style restaurant specializes in Scottish beef.

🏨 **Ramnee**   ⌂ ☝ &. 🅿 𝚅𝙸𝚂𝙰 ⓐ 𝔸𝔼 ⓞ
Victoria Rd ⊠ IV36 3BN – ℰ (01309) 672 410 – www.ramneehotel.com
– info@ramneehotel.com – Fax (01309) 673 392
– Closed 25 December and 1-3 January
19 rm ⌂ – ♦£99 ♦♦£160 – 1 suite
Rest *Hamlyns* – Carte £23/36
♦ Family owned Edwardian building in town centre with extensive lawned grounds. Welcoming public areas include panelled reception and pubby bar. Warmly traditional bedrooms. Formal dining room in traditional style.

🏠 **Cluny Bank**   ⌂ ☝ 🅿 𝚅𝙸𝚂𝙰 ⓐ 𝔸𝔼
St Leonard's Rd, South : ½ m. by Tolbooth St ⊠ IV36 1DW – ℰ (01309) 674 304
– www.clunybankhotel.co.uk – admin@clunybankhotel.co.uk – Fax (01309)
671 400 – Closed 2 weeks January
8 rm ⌂ – ♦£75/85 ♦♦£140   **Rest** – (dinner only) Carte £24/34 **s**
♦ Personally run 19C listed house, nestling beneath Cluny Hill. Extended in 1910, it boasts antiques, oak staircase, original floor tiling and simple, pleasant, airy bedrooms. Dining room features much work by local artist.

at Dyke West : 3 ¾ m. by A 96 – ⊠ Forres

🏠 **The Old Kirk** without rest ⚐   ⁒ 🅿 𝚅𝙸𝚂𝙰 ⓐ
Northeast : ½ m. ⊠ IV36 2TL – ℰ (01309) 641 414 – www.oldkirk.co.uk
– enquiries@oldkirk.com – Restricted opening in winter
3 rm ⌂ – ♦£45 ♦♦£65
♦ Former 19C church in country location. Stained glass window in first floor lounge; wood furnished breakfast room. Pleasantly furnished bedrooms with original stonework.

FORT AUGUSTUS   30 **C3**
- Edinburgh 159 mi – Inverness 34 mi – Fort William 32 mi

🏨 **Lovat Arms**   ⌂ 🛗 &. rm, ☝ 🅿 𝚅𝙸𝚂𝙰 ⓐ 𝔸𝔼
⊠ PH32 4DU – ℰ (01456) 459 250 – www.lovatarms-hotel.com
– info@lovatarms-hotel.com – Fax (01320) 366 677
29 rm ⌂ – ♦£60/105 ♦♦£180/250
Rest – (Closed Sunday-Monday) Menu £35 (dinner) – Carte £20/38
♦ Professionally run, refurbished 19C hotel at southern end of Loch Ness. Superb bedrooms; the largest have traditional furnishings; those on 2nd floor more contemporary in style. Simple dishes, created using quality ingredients.

FORTINGALL Perth. and Kinross – **501** H 14 – **see ABERFELDY**

FORTROSE Highland – Highland – 501 H 11 – pop. 1 174

▶ Edinburgh 168 mi – Inverness 14 mi – Nairn 27 mi

↑ **Water's Edge** without rest   🔒 🍴 🌐 🛏 **P** **VISA** ⚫ ①
Canonbury Terrace, on A 832 ✉ *IV10 8TT –* ✆ *(01381) 621 202*
– www.watersedge.uk.com – gill@watersedge.uk.com – Fax (08704) 296 806
– Christmas-New Year
3 rm ⚏ – **♦**£80 **♦♦**£90
♦ Charming guest house in fishing village boasts excellent comforts. Bedrooms have French windows onto terrace. Lounge with brick fire, large oak table and stunning views.

FORT WILLIAM – Highland – 501 E 13 – pop. 9 908 ▌ *Scotland*

▶ Edinburgh 133 mi – Glasgow 104 mi – Inverness 68 mi – Oban 50 mi
🅩 Cameron Sq ✆ (0845) 2255121, info@visitscotland.com
🄱 North Rd, ✆ (01397) 704 464
⊙ Town★
⊙ The Road to the Isles★★ (Neptune's Staircase (≤★★), Glenfinnan★ ≤★, Arisaig★, Silver Sands of Morar★, Mallaig★), NW : 46 m. by A 830 – Ardnamurchan Peninsula★★ - Ardnamurchan Point (≤★★), NW : 65 m. by A 830, A 861 and B 8007 - SE : Ben Nevis★★ (≤★★) - Glen Nevis★

🏨🏨 **Inverlochy Castle** ❧   ≤ 🍴 🕙 🎣 ℀ ✌ **P** **VISA** ⚫ **AE**
✿ *Torlundy, Northeast : 3 m. on A 82* ✉ *PH33 6SN –* ✆ *(01397) 702 177*
– www.inverlochycastlehotel.com – info@inverlochy.co.uk – Fax (01397) 702 953
17 rm ⚏ – **♦**£300/410 **♦♦**£410/510 – 1 suite
Rest – (booking essential for non-residents) Menu £35/65 ⅋
Spec. Lobster ravioli with artichoke and gazpacho. Canon of lamb with kidney, rosemary and garlic. Bloomed panna cotta with gooseberry compote, biscotti.
♦ Victorian castle in extensive parkland with beautiful gardens, panoramic views and luxurious, antique-filled interior. Great Hall sets the tone. Sumptuous bedrooms. Cooking has classical roots with original, modern touches and uses top quality, Scottish produce.

🏠 **Distillery House** without rest   🍴 ℀ **P** **VISA** ⚫ **AE**
Nevis Bridge, North Rd ✉ *PH33 6LR –* ✆ *(01397) 700 103*
– www.stayinfortwilliam.co.uk – disthouse@aol.com
10 rm ⚏ – **♦**£40/70 **♦♦**£70/104
♦ Conveniently located a short walk from the centre of town, formerly part of Glenlochy distillery. Cosy guests' lounge and comfortable rooms, some with views of Ben Nevis.

↑ **The Grange** without rest ❧   ≤ 🍴 ℀ ✌ **P** **VISA**
Grange Rd, South : ¾ m. by A 82 and Ashburn Lane ✉ *PH33 6JF –* ✆ *(01397) 705 516 – www.thegrange-scotland.co.uk – info@grangefortwilliam.com*
– March-September
4 rm ⚏ – **♦**£98/99 **♦♦**£110
♦ Large Victorian house with attractive garden, in an elevated position in a quiet residential part of town. Very comfortable and tastefully furnished with many antiques.

↑ **Crolinnhe** without rest ❧   ≤ 🍴 ℀ ✌ **P** **VISA**
Grange Rd, South : ¾ m. by A 82 and Ashburn Lane ✉ *PH33 6JF –* ✆ *(01397) 702 709 – www.crolinnhe.co.uk – crolinnhe@yahoo.com – April-October*
3 rm ⚏ – **♦**£125 **♦♦**£125
♦ Very comfortably and attractively furnished Victorian house, run with a real personal touch. Relaxing guests' sitting room and well furnished bedrooms.

↑ **Lochan Cottage** without rest   🍴 ℀ **P** **VISA** ⚫
Lochyside, North : 2½ m. by A 82, A 830 on B 8006 ✉ *PH33 7NX –* ✆ *(01397) 702 695 – www.fortwilliam-guesthouse.co.uk – lochanco@btopenworld.com*
– February-October
6 rm ⚏ – **♦♦**£54/66
♦ Spotlessly kept, whitewashed cottage with homely public areas. Breakfast taken in conservatory overlooking delightfully landscaped gardens. Neat, well-kept rooms.

SCOTLAND

⌂ **Ashburn House** without rest   🖼 ♨ ⁿⁱ **P** **VISA** ◉◉
18 Achintore Rd, South : ½ m. on A 82 ⊠ PH33 6RQ – ℰ (01397) 706 000
– www.highland5star.co.uk – christine@no-1.fsworld.co.uk – Fax (01397) 702 024
– Closed 25 December
7 rm ⌇ – ♦£55 ♦♦£110
♦ Attractive Victorian house overlooking Loch Linnhe, on the main road into town
which is a short walk away. Well furnished bedrooms and a comfortable conservatory
lounge.

⌂ **Lawriestone** without rest   ← 🖼 ♨ ⁿⁱ **P** **VISA** ◉◉
Achintore Rd, South : ½ m. on A 82 ⊠ PH33 6RQ – ℰ (01397) 700 777
– www.lawriestone.co.uk – susan@lawriestone.co.uk – Fax (01397) 700 777
– Closed 25-26 December and 1-2 January
5 rm ⌇ – ♦♦£60/80
♦ Victorian house overlooking Loch Linnhe; not far from town centre, ideal for touring Western Highlands. Especially proud of Scottish breakfasts. Airy rooms; some with
views.

⌂ **The Gantocks** without rest   ← 🖼 ♨ ⁿⁱ **P** **VISA** ◉◉
Achintore Rd, South 1 m. on A 82 – ℰ (01397) 702 050
– www.scotland2000.com/thegantocks – thegantocks@hotmal.co.uk
– March-November
3 rm ⌇ – ♦£80 ♦♦£80/100
♦ Spacious whitewashed bungalow with Loch views. Modern bedrooms have king
size beds and large baths; 1 overlooks the Loch. Handmade shortbread on arrival.
Unusual homemade breakfasts.

✗ **Lime Tree An Ealdhain** with rm   ← 🖼 ☂ ⁿⁱ **P** **VISA** ◉◉
Achintore Rd ⊠ PH33 6RQ – ℰ (01397) 701 806 – www.limetreefortwilliam.co.uk
– info@limetreefortwilliam.co.uk – Fax (01397) 701 806
9 rm ⌇ – ♦£60/100 ♦♦£80/100   **Rest** – Menu £10 (lunch) – Carte £22/28
♦ Restaurant, art gallery and hotel in one, with comfy, contemporary lounges, popular decked terrace and rustic dining area. Seasonally-changing menu; Scottish/Medi-
terranean dishes. Stylish bedrooms; some with Loch views.

✗ **Crannog**   ← ♨ **VISA** ◉◉
Town Pier ⊠ PH33 6DB – ℰ (01397) 705 589 – www.crannog.net
– olivia@crannog.net – Fax (01397) 708 666
– Closed dinner 24 December, 25 December and 1 January
Rest – Seafood – (booking essential) Carte £29/40
♦ Lochside dining on Fort William town pier; choose a window table for the view.
Interior of bright reds and yellows with some Celtic artwork. Locally sourced sea-
food dishes.

at Banavie North : 3 m. by A 82 and A 830 on B 8004 – ⊠ **Fort William**

🏠 **Moorings**   ← 🖼 ⚜ **P** **VISA** ◉◉ **AE**
⊠ PH33 7LY – ℰ (01397) 772 797 – www.moorings-fortwilliam.co.uk
– reservations@moorings-fortwilliam.co.uk – Fax (01397) 772 441
27 rm ⌇ – ♦£94/108 ♦♦£114/146   **Rest** – (bar lunch) Carte £24/36 **s**
♦ Modern accommodation in traditional style. Adjacent to Caledonian Canal and at
start of "Road to the Isles". Most rooms boast views of mountains and Neptune's
Staircase. Meals served in panelled lounge bar with views of Ben Nevis.

GALSON – Western Isles Outer Hebrides – **501** A 8 – see Lewis and Harris (Isle of)

If breakfast is included the ⌇ symbol appears after the number of rooms.

GATEHOUSE OF FLEET – Dumfries and Galloway – **501** H 19   25 **B3**
– pop. 892

> ▶ Edinburgh 113 mi – Dumfries 33 mi – Stranraer 42 mi
> 🖬 Car Park ℰ (01557) 814212 (Easter-October),
>   gatehouseoffleettic@visitscotland.com
> 🖸 Gatehouse Innisfree Lauriston Rd, Castle Douglas, ℰ (01557) 814 766

🏨🏨🏨 **Cally Palace** ⤳   ← 🛋 🛰 🔺 🕓 ⊕ 🎏 ⅃♂ ✕ 📷 ➡ 🛗 📔 VISA ⑩ AE
East : ½ m. on B 727 ⊠ *DG7 2DL – ℰ (01557) 814341 – www.callypalace.co.uk*
– info@callypalace.co.uk – Fax (01557) 814522
50 rm (dinner included) � – ♦£101/139 ♦♦£248/260 – 5 suites
Rest – Menu £30 (dinner) – Carte lunch £20/23 **s**
 ♦ Highly impressive 18C mansion with golf course. Sitting room with fantastically
ornate ceiling of original gilding. Small leisure centre. Large rooms with delightful
views. Elegant dining room serving Galloway produce. Pianist in attendance.

GATTONSIDE – Borders – see Melrose

GIGHA (Isle of) – Argyll and Bute – **501** C 16   27 **A3**

> ▶ Edinburgh 168 mi
> ⛴ to Tayinloan (Caledonian MacBrayne Ltd) 8-10 daily (20 mn)

🏨 **Gigha** ⤳   ← 🛋 🛰 📔 VISA ⑩ ⓪
⊠ *PA41 7AA – ℰ (01583) 505 254 – www.gigha.org.uk – hotel@gigha.org.uk*
– Fax (01583) 505 244 – Closed 25 December
13 rm ⊒ – ♦£35/57 ♦♦£70/95 – 1 suite
Rest – (bar lunch) (booking essential for non-residents) Carte £15/29
 ♦ 18C whitewashed house on island owned by residents; views over Ardminish Bay
to Kintyre. Cosy pine-panelled bar. Elegant lounge. Simple, clean and tidy rooms.
Inviting restaurant with exposed stone walls and pine tables.

GLAMIS – Angus – **501** K/L 14 – ⊠ Forfar   28 **C2**

> ▶ Edinburgh 69 mi – Dundee 13 mi – Forfar 7 mi
> 🅾 Town ★ – Castle ★★
> 🖸 Meigle Museum ★ **AC** W : 7 m. by A 94

🏨 **Castleton House**   🛋 ◑ 👘 📔 VISA ⑩ AE
West : 3 ¼ m. on A 94 ⊠ *DD8 1SJ – ℰ (01307) 840 340*
– www.castletonglamis.co.uk – hotel@castletonglamis.co.uk – Fax (01307)
840 506
6 rm ⊒ – ♦£140/160 ♦♦£210
Rest *The Conservatory* – Menu £35 (dinner) **s** – Carte lunch approx. £28 **s**
 ♦ Moat still visible in gardens of this 20C country house built on site of medieval
fortress. Appealing lounges, cosy bar. Individually designed, attractively appointed
rooms. Stylish conservatory restaurant looks out to garden.

O. Forir/MICHELIN

GLASGOW

County: Glasgow City
Michelin REGIONAL map: n° **501** H 16
▶ Edinburgh 46 mi – Manchester 221 mi

Population: 629 501   25 **B1**
▌*Scotland*

PRACTICAL INFORMATION

🛈 Tourist Information

11 George Sq ✆ (0141) 204 4400, enquiries@seeglasgow.com

Glasgow Airport, Tourist Information Desk ✆ (0141) 848 4440, glasgowairport@ visitscotland.com

Airports

✈ Glasgow Airport: ✆ (0870) 0400008, W: 8 m. by M 8, AV

Access to Oban by helicopter

Golf courses

🏌 Littlehill Auchinairn Rd, ✆ (0141) 772 1916

🏌 Rouken Glen Thornlibank Stewarton Rd, ✆ (0141) 638 7044

🏌 Linn Park Simshill Rd, ✆ (0141) 633 0377

Lethamhill Cumbernauld Rd, ✆ (0141) 770 6220

🏌 Alexandra Park Dennistoun, ✆ (0141) 556 1294

🏌 King's Park Croftfoot 150a Croftpark Ave, ✆ (0141) 630 1597

🏌 Knightswood Lincoln Ave, ✆ (0141) 959 6358

🏌 Ruchill Park Brassey St, ✆ (0141) 946 7676

📷 SIGHTS

IN TOWN

City★★★ – Cathedral★★★ (≤ ★)
DZ - The Burrell Collection★★★
AX M1 – Hunterian Art Gallery★★
(Whistler Collection★★★ - Mackintosh
Wing★★★) AC CY M4 – Museum of
Transport★★ (Scottish Built Cars★★★,
The Clyde Room of Ship Models★★★)
AV M6 – Art Gallery and Museum
Kelvingrove★★ CY – Pollok House★
(The Paintings★★) AX D – Tolbooth
Steeple★ DZ - Hunterian Museum
(Coin and Medal Collection★) CY M5
– City Chambers★ DZ C – Glasgow
School of Art★ AC CY M3 – Necropolis
(≤ ★ of Cathedral) DYZ – Gallery of
Modern Art★ – Glasgow (National)
Science Centre★, Pacific Quay AV

ON THE OUTSKIRTS

Paisley Museum and Art Gallery
(Paisley Shawl Section★), W: 4 m. by
M 8 AV

IN THE SURROUNDING AREA

The Trossachs★★★, N: 31 m. by
A 879 - BV -, A 81 and A 821 – Loch
Lomond★★, NW: 19 m. by A 82 AV
– New Lanark★★, SE: 20 m. by M 74
and A 72 BX

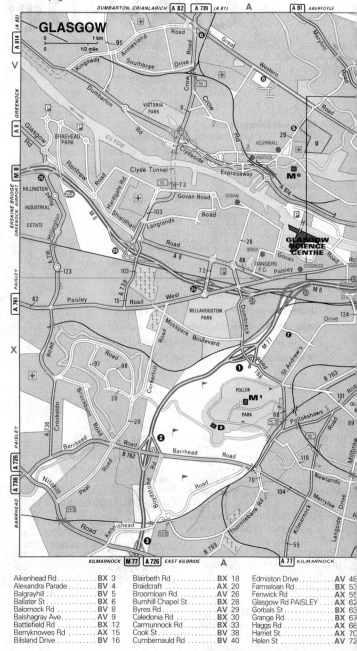

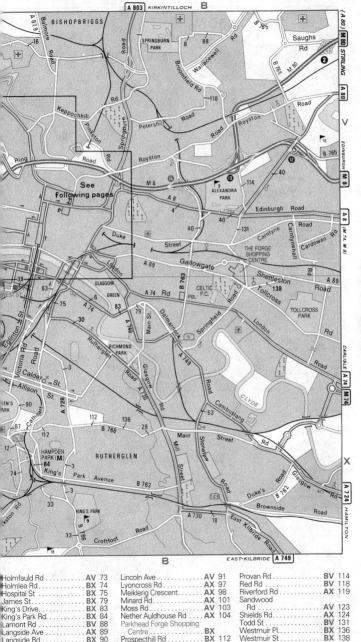

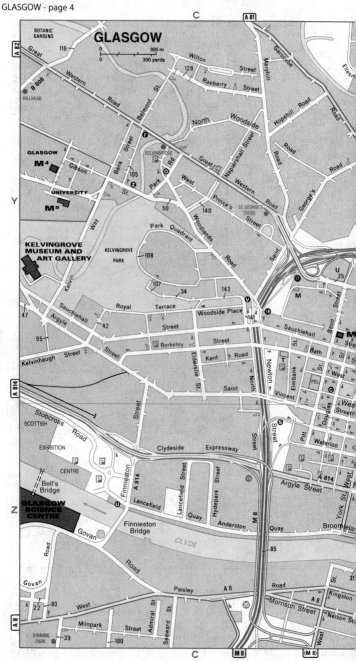

GLASGOW

SCOTLAND

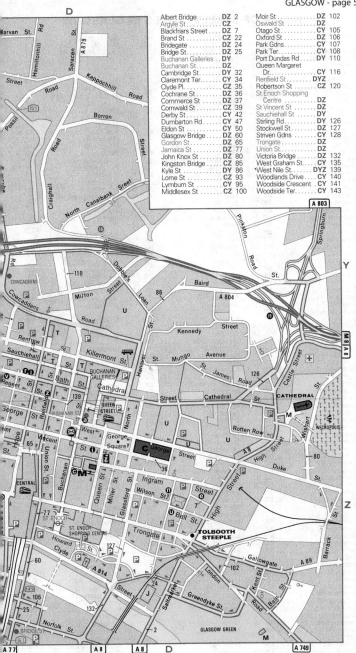

INDEX OF STREET NAMES IN GLASGOW

SCOTLAND

Hotel du Vin at One Devonshire Gardens 🛜 🖴 ᚦ rm, ⁇

1 Devonshire Gardens ⊠ G12 OUX – ℰ (0141) 339 2001   **⅍A** **VISA OO AE**
– www.onedevonshiregardens.com – Fax (0141) 337 1663   AV**a**
45 rm – †£145 ††£145/395, ⊊ £17 – 4 suites
Rest *Bistro* – (Closed Saturday lunch) Menu £18/21 – Carte £33/56
♦ Collection of adjoining 19C houses in terrace, refurbished with attention to detail. Warm, intimate and comfortable bedrooms are named after wines. High levels of service. Smart Bistro offers classic grill menu as well as more innovative carte.

Radisson SAS 🔲 🕉 🖴 🛗 ᚦ rm, 🕮 ⁇ ⁇ ⅍A 🅿 VISA OO AE ⓞ

301 Argyle St ⊠ G2 8DL – ℰ (0141) 204 3333 – www.glasgow.radissonsas.com
– reservations.glasgow@radissonsas.com – Fax (0141) 204 3344   DZ**o**
246 rm – †£220 ††£220, ⊊ £15.50 – 1 suite
Rest *Collage* – Mediterranean – Carte £15/55 **s**
Rest *TaPaell'Ya* – (Closed Sunday-Monday) Carte £15/35 **s**
♦ A stunning, angular, modish exterior greets visitors to this consummate, modern commercial hotel. Large, stylish, eclectically furnished bedrooms. Collage is a bright modern restaurant. Ta Paell'Ya serves tapas.

Hilton Glasgow ≤ 🔲 🕉 🖴 ᚦ rm, 🕮 ⁇ ⁇ ⅍A 🗢 VISA OO AE ⓞ

1 William St ⊠ G3 8HT – ℰ (0141) 204 5555 – www.hilton.com/glasgow
– reservations.glasgow@hilton.com – Fax (0141) 204 5004   CZ**s**
317 rm – †£90/250 ††£90/250, ⊊ £17.95 – 2 suites
Rest *Camerons* – (Closed Saturday lunch and Sunday) Carte approx. £40
Rest *Minsky's* – Buffet – Menu £15/25
♦ A city centre tower with impressive views on every side. Comfortable, comprehensively fitted rooms. Extensive leisure and conference facilities. Spacious, modern Minsky's has the style of a New York deli. Contemporary cuisine served in formal Camerons.

Malmaison 🖴 🛗 ᚦ rm, 🕻 ⅍A VISA OO AE ⓞ

278 West George St ⊠ G2 4LL – ℰ (0141) 572 1000 – www.malmaison.com
– glasgow@malmaison.com – Fax (0141) 572 1002   CY**c**
68 rm – †£170/220 ††£170/250, ⊊ £13.95 – 4 suites
Rest *The Brasserie* – Menu £16 – Carte £26/41
♦ Visually arresting former Masonic chapel. Comfortable, well-proportioned rooms seem effortlessly stylish with bold patterns and colours and thoughtful extra attentions. Informal Brasserie with French themed menu and Champagne bar.

Abode Glasgow 🛗 ᚦ rm, 🕮 ⁇ ⁇ ⅍A VISA OO AE ⓞ

129 Bath St ⊠ G2 2SZ – ℰ (0141) 221 6789 – www.abodehotels.co.uk
– reservationsglasgow@abodehotels.co.uk – Fax (0141) 221 6777   DY**v**
60 rm ⊊ – †£99/245 ††£99/245
Rest *Michael Caines* – see restaurant listing
Rest *Cafe Bar* – Carte £16/31
♦ Near Mackintosh's School of Art, an early 20C building decorated with a daring modern palette: striking colour schemes and lighting in the spacious, elegantly fitted rooms. All-day dining in stylish Café Bar.

Carlton George 🛗 ᚦ rm, 🕮 ⁇ ⁇ VISA OO AE ⓞ

44 West George St ⊠ G2 1DH – ℰ (0141) 353 6373 – www.carltonhotels.co.uk
– resgeorge@carltonhotels.co.uk – Fax (0141) 353 6263
– Closed 24-26 December and 1-2 January   DZ**a**
64 rm – ††£130/220, ⊊ £14
Rest *Windows* – Menu £19 (lunch) **s** – Carte £27/35 **s**
♦ A quiet oasis away from the city bustle. Attractive tartan decorated bedrooms bestow warm tidings. Comfortable 7th floor business lounge. An overall traditional ambience. Ask for restaurant table with excellent view across city's rooftops.

SCOTLAND

SCOTLAND

Sherbrooke Castle   🚗   ₺ rm, 🅰🅲 rest, % 🎵 ⚓ 🅿 𝒱𝐼𝒮𝒜 ⓜⓞ 🄰🄴 ①
11 Sherbrooke Ave, Pollokshields ✉ *G41 4PG –* ℰ *(0141) 427 4227*
– www.sherbrooke.co.uk – mail@sherbrooke.co.uk – Fax (0141) 427 5685   AX**r**
16 rm ⊇ – ✝£105 ✝✝£155 – 2 suites
Rest *Morrisons* – Carte £18/32
♦ Late 19C baronial Romanticism given free rein inside and out. The hall is richly furnished and imposing; rooms in the old castle have a comfortable country house refinement. Panelled Victorian dining room with open fire.

City Inn   ≤ 🚗 📶 ₺ rm, 🅰🅲 🎵 ⚓ 🅿 𝒱𝐼𝒮𝒜 ⓜⓞ 🄰🄴 ①
Finnieston Quay ✉ *G3 8HN –* ℰ *(0141) 240 1002 – www.cityinn.com*
– glasgow.reservations@cityinn.com – Fax (0141) 248 2754
– Closed 24-25 December   CZ**u**
164 rm – ✝£79/179 ✝✝£89/189, ⊇ £12.50
Rest – Menu £15/17 – Carte £22/36
♦ Quayside location and views of the Clyde. Well priced hotel with a "business-friendly" ethos; neatly maintained modern rooms with sofas and en suite power showers. Restaurant fronts waterside terrace.

Marks   📶 ₺ rm, 🅰🅲 rest, % 🎵 𝒱𝐼𝒮𝒜 ⓜⓞ 🄰🄴 ①
110 Bath St ✉ *G2 2EN –* ℰ *(0141) 353 0800 – www.markshotels.com*
– info@markshotels.com – Fax (0141) 353 0900 – Closed 25 December   DY**r**
102 rm – ✝£149 ✝✝£149, ⊇ £12.50 – 1 suite
Rest *One Ten Bar & Grill* – Carte £16/22 **s**
♦ In the middle of Glasgow's shopping streets, with fashionable front bar. Modern bedrooms have bold fushia print wallpaper; mezzanine suites are worth the upgrade. Contemporary dining room with booth seating.

Rococo   🅰🅲 🍴 𝒱𝐼𝒮𝒜 ⓜⓞ 🄰🄴 ①
48 West Regent St ✉ *G2 1LP –* ℰ *(0141) 221 5004 – www.rococoglasgow.co.uk*
– info@rococoglasgow.co.uk – Fax (0141) 221 5006   DY**z**
Rest – Contemporary – Menu £20/42 – Carte lunch approx. £42
♦ In style, more like studied avant-garde: stark, white-walled cellar with vibrant modern art and high-backed leather chairs. Accomplished, fully flavoured contemporary menu.

Lux   🅰🅲 🅿 𝒱𝐼𝒮𝒜 ⓜⓞ 🄰🄴
1051 Great Western Rd ✉ *G12 0XP –* ℰ *(0141) 576 7576*
– www.luxstazione.co.uk – enquiries@luxstazione.co.uk – Fax (0141) 576 0162
– Closed 25-26 December, 1-2 January, Sunday and Monday   AV**e**
Rest – Modern – (dinner only) Menu £34
♦ 19C railway station converted with clean-lined elegance: dark wood, subtle lighting and vivid blue banquettes. Fine service and flavourful, well-prepared modern menus.

Brian Maule at Chardon d'Or   🍴 𝒱𝐼𝒮𝒜 ⓜⓞ 🄰🄴
176 West Regent St ✉ *G2 4RL –* ℰ *(0141) 248 3801 – www.brianmaule.com*
– info@brianmaule.com – Fax (0141) 248 3901 – Closed 2 weeks January,
25-26 December, Saturday lunch, Sunday and Bank Holidays   CY**i**
Rest – Modern – Menu £20 (lunch) – Carte £36/54
♦ Large pillared Georgian building. Airy refurbished interior with ornate carved ceiling. Classical French cooking made with fine Scottish produce. Function rooms in basement.

Rogano   🚗 🅰🅲 🍴 𝒱𝐼𝒮𝒜 ⓜⓞ 🄰🄴
11 Exchange Place ✉ *G1 3AN –* ℰ *(0141) 248 4055 – www.roganoglasgow.com*
– rogano@btconnect.com – Closed 25 December and 1 January   DZ**c**
Rest – Seafood – Menu £15 (lunch) – Carte £31/56
♦ Long-standing Glasgow institution; art deco, with original panelling, stained glass windows and etched mirrors. Classic menus lean towards local seafood. Table 16 most popular.

XX **Michael Caines** – at Abode Glasgow Hotel 🛅 ⚡ 𝘝𝘐𝘚𝘈 ⓪⓪ 🅰🅴 ⓪
129 Bath St ✉ *G2 2SZ* – ✆ *(0141) 5726011* **DYv**
Rest – Modern – (closed Sunday and Monday) Menu £10 (lunch)
– Carte £30/45
♦ Smart, stylish restaurant in boutique hotel, a mirrored wall creating impression of size. Quality décor matched by clean, unfussy cooking prepared with finesse and skill.

XX **Urban** 🛅 ⇔ 𝘝𝘐𝘚𝘈 ⓪⓪ 🅰🅴
23-25 St Vincent Place ✉ *G1 2DT* – ✆ *(0141) 248 5720*
– *www.urbanbrasserie.co.uk* – *info@urbanbrasserie.co.uk*
– *Closed 1-2 January and 25-26 December* **DZi**
Rest – Modern – Menu £18 (lunch) – Carte £24/36
♦ Imposing 19C building in heart of city centre. Stylish, modern interior with individual booths and illuminated glass ceiling. Modern English cooking. Live piano at weekends.

XX **Manna** 🍴 𝘝𝘐𝘚𝘈 ⓪⓪ 🅰🅴
104 Bath St ✉ *G2 2EN* – ✆ *(0141) 3326678* – *www.mannarestaurant.co.uk*
– *info@mannarestaurant.co.uk* – *Fax (0141) 3326549*
– *Closed 25-26 December, 1-2 January and Sunday lunch* **DYi**
Rest – Menu £15 (lunch) – Carte £24/42
♦ Parrot motifs recur everywhere, even on the door handles! Well-spaced tables and mirrored walls add a sense of space to the basement. A free-ranging fusion style prevails.

XX **Gamba** 🍴 𝘝𝘐𝘚𝘈 ⓪⓪ 🅰🅴
225a West George St ✉ *G2 2ND* – ✆ *(0141) 5720899* – *www.gamba.co.uk*
– *info@gamba.co.uk* – *Fax (0141) 5720896*
– *Closed 25-26 December, 1-2 January and Sunday* **DZx**
Rest – Seafood – Menu £19 (lunch) – Carte £27/45
♦ Seafood specialists: an enterprising diversity of influences and well-priced lunches. Compact, brightly decorated basement in hot terracotta with a pleasant cosy bar.

XX **La Parmigiana** 🛅 🍴 𝘝𝘐𝘚𝘈 ⓪⓪ 🅰🅴 ⓪
447 Great Western Rd, Kelvinbridge ✉ *G12 8HH* – ✆ *(0141) 3340686*
– *www.laparmigiana.co.uk* – *s.giovanazzi@btclick.com* – *Fax (0141) 3575595*
– *Closed 25-26 December, 1 January and Sunday* **CYr**
Rest – Italian – (booking essential) Menu £13 (lunch) – Carte £31/46 **s**
♦ Compact, pleasantly decorated traditional eatery with a lively atmosphere and good local reputation. Obliging, professional service and a sound, authentic Italian repertoire.

XX **Shish Mahal** 🛅 𝘝𝘐𝘚𝘈 ⓪⓪ 🅰🅴
60-68 Park Rd ✉ *G4 9JF* – ✆ *(0141) 3398256* – *www.shishmahal.co.uk*
– *reservations@shishmahal.co.uk* – *Fax (0141) 5720800*
– *Closed 25 December and Sunday lunch* **CYo**
Rest – Indian – Carte £12/17
♦ Tandoori specialities in a varied pan-Indian menu, attentive service and an evocative modern interior of etched glass, oak and Moorish tiles have won city-wide recognition.

X **The Dhabba** 𝘝𝘐𝘚𝘈 ⓪⓪ 🅰🅴
44 Candleriggs ✉ *G1 1LE* – ✆ *(0141) 553 1249* – *www.thedhabba.com*
– *info@thedhabba.com* – *Fax (0141) 553 1730*
– *Closed 25 December and 1 January* **DZu**
Rest – Indian – Menu £10 (lunch) – Carte £25/36
♦ In the heart of the Merchant City, this large, modern restaurant boasts bold colours and huge wall photos. Concentrates on authentic, accomplished North Indian cooking.

SCOTLAND

SCOTLAND

✗ Stravaigin
🖭 ☜ VISA ⓜ AE ①

28 Gibson St, (basement) ⊠ G12 8NX – ℰ (0141) 334 2665
– www.stravaigin.com – stravaigin@btinternet.com – Fax (0141) 334 4099
– Closed 25 December, 1 January and lunch Monday-Thursday CYz
Rest – Menu £ 14 (lunch) – Carte £ 29/42

♦ Basement restaurant with bright murals. A refined instinct for genuinely global cuisine produces surprising but well-prepared combinations - ask about pre-theatre menus.

✗ Stravaigin 2
🖭 ☜ VISA ⓜ AE ①

8 Ruthven Lane, off Byres Rd ⊠ G12 9BG – ℰ (0141) 334 7165
– www.stravaigin.com – stravaiginl.@btinternet.com – Fax (0141) 357 4785
– Closed 25 December and 1 January AVs
Rest – Carte £ 25/34

♦ Lilac painted cottage tucked away in an alley off Byres Road. Simple, unfussy, modern bistro-style interior. Contemporary menu offering eclectic range of original dishes.

✗ Dakhin
VISA ⓜ AE ①

First Floor, 89 Candleriggs ⊠ G1 1NP – ℰ (0141) 553 2585 – www.dakhin.com
– info@dakhin.com – Fax (0141) 553 2492
– Closed 25 December and 1 January DZn
Rest – South Indian – Menu £ 10 (lunch) – Carte £ 22/35

♦ Large open plan first floor restaurant in redeveloped area of city serving authentic, flavoursome South Indian cooking. Friendly, informal atmosphere; knowledgable service.

🛏 Babbity Bowster
☜ ⅍ VISA ⓜ AE

16-18 Blackfriars St ⊠ G1 1PE – ℰ (0141) 552 5055 – Fax (0141) 552 7774
– Closed 25 December DZe
Rest – Traditional – Carte £ 16/26

♦ Well regarded pub of Georgian origins with columned façade. Paradoxically simple ambience: gingham-clothed tables, hearty Scottish dishes, slightly more formal in evenings.

at Eurocentral East : 12 m. by M 8 off A 8 – ⊠ Glasgow

🏨 Dakota
ₔ 🖣 ₕ rm, 🖭 🕪 🔏 🅿 VISA ⓜ AE

⊠ ML1 4WJ – ℰ (0870) 220 82 81 – www.dakotaeurocentral.co.uk
– info@dakotaeurocentral.co.uk – Fax (01698) 835 445
– Closed 25-26, 31 December and 1-2 January
90 rm ⌧ – ♦£ 95 ♦♦£ 95
Rest *Grill* – Carte £ 30/34

♦ Stylish, modern hotel with sleek, masculine feel. Well-thought out bedrooms have king-sized beds and plasma TVs. Comfortable lounge popular for afternoon tea. Open plan bar and grill offers good selection of modern cooking.

GLENDALE – Highland – see Skye (Isle of)

GLENDEVON – Perth and Kinross – 501 I/J 15
28 **C2**

🖪 Edinburgh 37 mi – Perth 26 mi – Stirling 19 mi

🛏 An Lochan Country Inn with rm
☜ 🏠 🅿 VISA ⓜ

⊠ FK14 7JY – ℰ (01259) 781 252 – www.anlochan.co.uk
– tormaukin@anlochan.co.uk – Fax (01259) 781 526 – Closed 24-25 December
12 rm ⌧ – ♦£ 85 ♦♦£ 100 **Rest** – Menu £ 13/25 – Carte £ 20/60

♦ Extended 18C drovers' inn tucked away in this picturesque glen. Traditional Scottish fare is served in the atmospheric bar or in the cosy restaurant. Comfortable bedrooms.

 Red = Pleasant. Look for the red ✗ and 🛏 symbols.

> ◨ Edinburgh 33 mi – Dundee 25 mi – Stirling 36 mi
> ◨ Thornton Station Rd, ℰ (01592) 771 173
> ◨ Golf Course Rd, ℰ (01592) 758 686
> ◨ Balbirnie Park Markinch, ℰ (01592) 612 095
> ◨ Auchterderran Cardenden Woodend Rd, ℰ (01592) 721 579
> ◨ Leslie Balsillie Laws, ℰ (01592) 620 040
> ◨ Falkland★ (Palace of Falkland★ **AC**, Gardens★ **AC**) N : 5½ m. by A 92 and A 912

Balbirnie House ⌖   ◨ ◨ ◨ ◨ ◨ ◨ ◨ **VISA** **MO** **AE** ◨

Markinch, Northeast : 1¾ m. by A 911 and A 92 on B 9130 ✉ *KY7 6NE – ℰ (01592) 610 066 – www.balbirnie.co.uk – info@balbirnie.co.uk – Fax (01592) 610 529*

28 rm ⌂ – ♦£85 ♦♦£150 – 2 suites
Rest *Orangery* – (closed Monday and Tuesday) Menu £16/33 – Carte £19/27
Rest *Bistro* – Menu £12 – Carte £17/25

♦ Highly imposing part Georgian mansion in Capability Brown-styled grounds. Several lounges and library bar with period style and individually furnished country house rooms. Glass-roofed restaurant; friendly service from kilted staff. Informal dining in the Bistro.

> ◨ Edinburgh 143 mi – Inverness 34 mi – Perth 99 mi
> ◨ 54 High St ℰ (01479) 872 773 (April-October), grantown@host.co.uk
> ◨ Golf Course Rd, ℰ (01479) 872 079
> ◨ Abernethy Nethy Bridge, ℰ (01479) 821 305

Culdearn House   ◨ ◨ ◨ **P** **VISA** **MO**

Woodlands Terrace ✉ *PH26 3JU – ℰ (01479) 872 106 – www.culdearn.com – enquiries@culdearn.com – Fax (01479) 873 641*

6 rm (dinner included) ⌂ – ♦£90/100 ♦♦£190/200
Rest – (dinner only) (booking essential for non-residents) Menu £32 **s**

♦ Personally run Victorian granite stone hotel offering a high degree of luxury, including beautifully furnished drawing room and very tastefully furnished bedrooms. Formally attired dining room; good Scottish home cooking.

The Pines   ◨ ◨ **P** **VISA** **MO**

Woodside Ave ✉ *PH26 3JR – ℰ (01479) 872 092 – www.thepinesgrantown.co.uk – info@thepinesgrantown.co.uk – March-October*

5 rm ⌂ – ♦£98 ♦♦£196
Rest – (dinner only) (residents only, set menu only) Menu £35

♦ Top level hospitality in an attractive 19C house with lovely rear garden leading onto woods and Spey. Elegant lounges display fine pieces of art. Individually appointed rooms. Candlelit dinners, full of Scottish flavours, are a special event!

Ravenscourt House   ◨ ◨ **P** **VISA** **MO** ◨

Seafield Ave ✉ *PH26 3JG – ℰ (01479) 872 286 – www.ravenscourthouse.co.uk – info@ravenscourthouse.co.uk – Fax (05601) 162 846 – Closed 2 weeks in winter*

8 rm ⌂ – ♦£45/50 ♦♦£75/90
Rest – (dinner only) (booking essential for non-residents) Carte dinner £17/28 **s**

♦ 19C former manse. Solid stone exterior. Interiors designed to enhance original house. Two comfortable drawing rooms; very welcoming, spacious bedrooms. Huge conservatory dining room with menu of locally sourced produce.

The Glass House   ◨ **P** **VISA** **MO** **AE**

Grant Rd ✉ *PH26 3LD – ℰ (01479) 872 980 – www.theglasshouse.grantown.co.uk – info@theglasshouse-grantown.co.uk – Fax (01479) 872 980 – Closed 25-26 December, 1-2 January, 2 weeks November, Sunday dinner, Monday and Tuesday lunch*

Rest – Menu £14 (lunch) – Carte dinner £31/38

♦ Conservatory style dining in a house extension near the high street. Light-filled interior overlooks the garden. Amiable owner serves tasty, seasonal modern British dishes.

at Dulnain Bridge Southwest : 3 m. by A 95 on A 938 – ⊠ Grantown-on-Spey

🏠 **Muckrach Lodge** ॐ　　≤ 🚗 ⚕ & rm, ⁕ �· P VISA ⚫ AE
West : ½ m. on A 938 ⊠ PH26 3LY – ℰ *(01479) 851 257 – www.muckrach.com*
– info@muckrach.com – Fax (01479) 851 325
10 rm � – ♦£60/110 ♦♦£100/175 – 2 suites
Rest *Conservatory* – (bar lunch) Carte £ 28/38
◆ 19C country house whose name translates as "haunt of the wild boar". Log fires and soft sofas in lounges. Bedrooms with fresh flowers and old books. Modern, original dining in Conservatory.

GRETNA GREEN – Dumfries and Galloway – **501** K 19　　　　25 **B2**
🔼 Edinburgh 88 mi – Annan 10 mi – Carlisle 11 mi

🏠 **Smiths**　　🖼 & rm, ⓀⒸ ⁕ �· P VISA ⚫ AE
⊠ DG16 5EA – ℰ *(01461) 337 007 – www.smithsgretnagreen.co.uk*
– info@smithsgretnagreen.com – Fax (01461) 336 000
49 rm � – ♦£115 ♦♦£155 – 1 suite　　**Rest** – Carte £ 25/35
◆ Family owned hotel near famous Blacksmiths Shop. Airy, open-plan lounge/bar. Rooms and suites are the strength - all are modern and well equipped: revolving bed in penthouse. Brasserie dishes in bright, spacious restaurant.

GRULINE – Argyll and Bute – see Mull (Isle of)

GUILDTOWN – Perth and Kinross – **501** J 14 – see Perth

GULLANE – East Lothian – **501** L 15 – pop. 2 172 ▌ *Scotland*　　26 **C1**
🔼 Edinburgh 19 mi – North Berwick 5 mi
ⓒ Dirleton★ (Castle★) NE : 2 m. by A 198

at Aberlady Southwest : 1 ½ m. on A 198 – pop. 873

🏠 **Kilspindie House**　　⁕ �· P VISA ⚫ AE ⓪
Main St ⊠ EH32 0RE – ℰ *(01875) 870 682 – www.ducks.co.uk*
– kilspindie@ducks.co.uk – Fax (01875) 870 504
26 rm � – ♦£55/75 ♦♦£80/98
Rest *Duck's at Kilspindie House* – see restaurant listing
◆ Converted late 17C house and neighbouring school; close to many excellent golf courses. Smart, comfortable bedrooms with pleasant bathrooms. Casual bar offering good whisky collection.

🍴 **Duck's at Kilspindie House**　　☕ P VISA ⚫ AE ⓪
Main St ⊠ EH32 0RE – ℰ *(01875) 870 682 – www.ducks.co.uk*
– kilspindie@ducks.co.uk – Fax (01875) 870 504
Rest – Menu £ 18 (lunch) – Carte £ 28/36
◆ Warm and welcoming restaurant offering al fresco dining. Menu boasts carefully prepared, satisfying dishes crafted from fresh, local produce. Seasonality plays a key role.

HARRAY – Orkney Islands – **501** K 6 – see Orkney Islands (Mainland)

HARRIS (Isle of) – Western Isles Outer Hebrides – **501** Z 10 – see Lewis and Harris (Isle of)

HAWICK – Scottish Borders – **501** – pop. 14 573 ▌ *Scotland*　　26 **C2**
🔼 Edinburgh 51 mi – Galashiels 18 mi – Jedburgh 12 mi
ⓒ Jedburgh★ - Abbey★★, Mary Queen of Scots Visitor Centre★, NE : 11 m. by A 698 and B 6358 – Bowhill★★, N : 15 m. by A 7, B 7009 and B 7039

🏠 **Glenteviot Park** ॐ　　≤ 🚗 🦢 ⁕ P VISA ⚫
Hassendeanburn, Northeast : 3 ¾ m. by A 698 ⊠ TD9 8RU – ℰ *(01450) 870 660*
– www.glenteviotpark.com – enquiries@glenteviotpark.com – Fax (01450) 870 154
5 rm � – ♦£85 ♦♦£110　　**Rest** – (dinner only) (residents only) Menu £ 30
◆ Purpose-built hotel idyllically sited overlooking River Teviot and surrounding hills. Rustic bar/lounge, sauna and snooker room. Individually furnished, well-equipped rooms. Cosy dining room offering homecooked menus.

SCOTLAND

INVERGARRY – Highland – **501** F 12 – ✉ **Inverness** Scotland 30 **C3**

■ Edinburgh 159 mi – Fort William 25 mi – Inverness 43 mi – Kyle of Lochalsh 50 mi
© The Great Glen ★

Glengarry Castle ⌖ ≤ 🚗 🐾 🥂 🍴 ⁴ **P** **VISA** **⚫**
on A 82 ⊠ PH35 4HW – ✆ (01809) 501 254 – www.glengarry.net
– castle@glengarry.net – Fax (01809) 501 207 – 20 March- 9 November
26 rm ☐ – †£62/97 ††£146/166
Rest – (light lunch Monday-Saturday) Menu £29
◆ On shores of Loch Oich, and named after eponymous Victorian castle whose ruin stands in grounds. Warm country house feel throughout; many bedrooms retain original fittings. Dining room shares the warm, country house style of the hotel.

INVERGORDON – Highland – **501** H 10 30 **C2**

■ Edinburgh 178 mi – Inverness 25 mi – Forres 49 mi

Kincraig House ≤ 🚗 ⅗ rm, 🥂 ⁴ 🏊 **P** **VISA** **⚫** **AE**
on A 9 ⊠ IV18 0LF – ✆ (01349) 852 587 – www.kincraig-house-hotel.co.uk
– info@kincraig-house-hotel.co.uk – Fax (01349) 852 193
15 rm ☐ – †£95/180 ††£150/220
Rest – (bar lunch) Menu £17/33 – Carte £15/31
◆ In an enviably elevated position, this Georgian house has been restored with style, retaining wood panelling and Adams fireplaces. Some of the comfy rooms are four-postered. Smart restaurant serves locally sourced, traditional dishes.

INVERKEILOR – Angus – **501** M 14 – ✉ **Arbroath** 28 **D2**

■ Edinburgh 85 mi – Aberdeen 32 mi – Dundee 22 mi

Gordon's with rm 🚗 **P** **VISA** **⚫**
32 Main St ⊠ DD11 5RN – ✆ (01241) 830 364 – www.gordonsrestaurant.co.uk
– gordonsrest@aol.com – Restricted opening in winter
4 rm ☐ – †£65 ††£100/150
Rest – (Closed Monday, lunch Tuesday and Sunday dinner to non-residents) (booking essential) Menu £28/45
◆ Family owned restaurant in small village. Welcoming atmosphere, beams, open fires and rugs on the wood floors. Good cooking with some innovative touches. Well-kept bedrooms.

INVERMORISTON – Highland – **501** G 12 30 **C2**

■ Edinburgh 166 mi – Inverness 28 mi – Dingwall 42 mi

Tigh na Bruach without rest 🚗 🐾 🥂 ⁴ **P** **VISA** **⚫** **①**
Southwest : ½ m. on A 82 ⊠ IV63 7YE – ✆ (01320) 351 349
– www.tighnabruach.com – tighnabruach@btconnect.com
3 rm ☐ – †£65/90 ††£90/110
◆ Don't be put off by rather unprepossessing exterior: located by Loch Ness, it has beautiful gardens, and very comfy rooms with pleasant little terraces overlooking a lake.

INVERNESS – Highland – **501** H 11 – pop. 40 949 Scotland 30 **C2**

■ Edinburgh 156 mi – Aberdeen 107 mi – Dundee 134 mi
✈ Inverness Airport, Dalcross : ✆ (01667) 464000, NE : 8 m. by A 96 Y
🚢 Castle Wynd ✆ (01463) 234353 Y, invernesstic@host.co.uk
🏌 Culcabock Rd, ✆ (01463) 239 882
🏌 Torvean Glenurquhart Rd, ✆ (01463) 711 434
◎ Town ★ – Museum and Art Gallery ★ Y **M**
© Loch Ness ★★, SW : by A 82 Z – Clava Cairns ★, E : 9 m. by Culcabock Rd, B 9006 and B 851 Z – Cawdor Castle ★ **AC**, NE : 14 m. by A 96 and B 9090 Y

Plan on next page

SCOTLAND

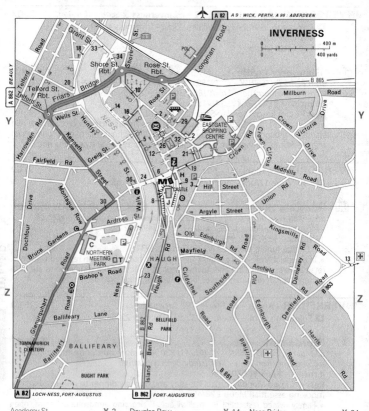

INVERNESS

A 9 : WICK, PERTH, A 96 : ABERDEEN

A 82 LOCH-NESS, FORT-AUGUSTUS

B 862 FORT-AUGUSTUS

🛏️ **Rocpool Reserve**   🌳 ⅙ rm, 🆔 ⅙ ⅋ 👘 **P** **VISA** **◍◍** **AE**

Culduthel Rd ⊠ IV2 4AG – 𝒞 (01463) 240 089 – www.rocpool.com
– info@rocpool.com – Fax (01463) 248 431   Z**r**
11 rm ⊑ – ⅋£ 140/160 ⅋⅋£ 170/365
Rest *Reserve* – Menu £ 20 (lunch) – Carte £ 32/35

◆ 19C house reborn as a boutique hotel - the talk of the city! Look cool in sexy, stylish bar and sleep in rooms the ultimate in chic design, with breathtaking bathrooms. Italian twists enhance accomplished modern dishes in sleek restaurant.

🛏️ **Glenmoriston Town House**   ⅋ 👘 **P** **VISA** **◍◍** **AE** **①**

20 Ness Bank ⊠ IV2 4SF – 𝒞 (01463) 223 777 – www.glenmoristontownhouse.com
– reception@glenmoristontownhouse.com – Fax (01463) 712 378   Z**x**
30 rm ⊑ – ⅋⅋£ 170/185
Rest *Abstract* – see restaurant listing
Rest *Contrast* – Carte £ 16/27

◆ Chic, stylish town house. Modern cocktail bar a trendy meeting point. Bedrooms are individualistic, those on the front enjoying river views; those at the rear are quieter. Locally sourced cooking at Contrast.

⌂ **Ballifeary House** without rest   𝒮⅍ ⸙ 🅿 VISA ⓪⓪

10 Ballifeary Rd ⊠ IV3 5PJ – ℰ (01463) 235 572
– www.ballifearyguesthouse.co.uk – info@ballifearyguesthouse.co.uk
– Fax (01463) 717583 – Closed 24-27 December   Z**n**
7 rm ⊊ – ∤£35/70 ∤∤£70/76
♦ Immaculately kept Victorian house with a pretty rear garden. Peaceful and relaxing feel as no children under 15 years are taken. A wholly non-smoking establishment.

⌂ **Moyness House** without rest   🚗 𝒮⅍ ⸙ 🅿 VISA ⓪⓪

6 Bruce Gdns ⊠ IV3 5EN – ℰ (01463) 233 836 – www.moyness.co.uk
– stay@moyness.co.uk – Fax (01463) 233 836
– Closed 25-26 December   Z**c**
6 rm ⊊ – ∤£55/75 ∤∤£76/96
♦ Immaculately clipped hedges frame this attractive Victorian villa. Bedrooms vary in shape and size but all are comfortable, individually decorated and fully en suite.

⌂ **Eden House** without rest   𝒮⅍ 🅿 VISA ⓪⓪ ⓪

8 Ballifeary Rd ⊠ IV3 5PJ – ℰ (01463) 230 278
– www.edenhouse.btinternet.co.uk – edenhouse@btinternet.com – Fax (01463)
230 278 – March-Christmas   Z**o**
4 rm ⊊ – ∤£40/65 ∤∤£66/74
♦ Pleasant ten minute walk into the city centre. Friendly proprietors run a neat and spotless house. Pretty little conservatory and good sized bedrooms.

𝈓𝈓𝈓 **Abstract** – at Glenmoriston Town House Hotel   🅿 VISA ⓪⓪ AE ⓪

20 Ness Bank ⊠ IV2 4SF – ℰ (01463) 223 777 – www.abstractrestaurant.com
– reception@abstractrestaurant.com – Fax (01463) 712 378
– Closed Sunday-Monday   Z**x**
Rest – (dinner only) Carte £30/47 **s**
♦ Restaurant, bar and conservatory with considerable style. Vast wall mirror offsets abstract ink pictures. Accomplished cooking with Gallic accent is impressively original.

𝈓𝈓 **Rocpool**   🔤 VISA ⓪⓪ AE

1 Ness Walk ⊠ IV3 5NE – ℰ (01463) 717 274 – www.rocpoolrestaurant.com
– info@rocpoolrestaurant/com – Closed 25-26 December, 1-2 January, Sunday
lunch and Sunday dinner October-March   Y**i**
Rest – Carte £22/34
♦ On the banks of the river Ness, this modern, cosmopolitan restaurant has a stylish ambience, popular with business diners. Modern cooking with a British/Mediterranean axis.

𝈓 **Café 1**   VISA ⓪⓪ AE

Castle St ⊠ IV2 3EA – ℰ (01463) 226 200 – www.cafe1.net – info@cafe1.net
– Fax (01463) 716 363 – Closed 25-26 December, 1 January and Sunday   Y**e**
Rest – Carte £17/32
♦ Personally run bistro opposite the castle with an informal touch, enhanced by tiled flooring and modish chairs. Local ingredients feature in regularly changing modern menus.

at Culloden East : 3 m. by A 96 - Y – ⊠ **Inverness**

🏛🏛 **Culloden House** ⑊   ⩽ 🚗 🕭 🕥 ⸙ 🅿 VISA ⓪⓪ AE

⊠ IV2 7BZ – ℰ (01463) 790 461 – www.cullodenhouse.co.uk
– info@cullodenhouse.co.uk – Fax (01463) 792 181 – Closed 1 week Christmas
25 rm ⊊ – ∤£100/240 ∤∤£180/300 – 3 suites
Rest Adams Dining Room – Carte £28/48
♦ Imposing Georgian country house in 40 acres, requisitioned by Bonnie Prince Charlie in 1746. Drawing rooms boast ornate wall-hung plaster friezes. Antique-furnished rooms. Adam's plaster reliefs adorn walls and ceiling of grand dining room; traditional menu.

at Dunain Park Southwest : 2½ m. on A 82 - Z – ⊠ Inverness

Dunain Park ⤳   ⟨ 🚗 📶 P VISA ⓪ AE

⊠ IV3 8JN – ℰ (01463) 230 512 – www.dunainparkhotel.co.uk
– info@dunainparkhotel.co.uk – Fax (01463) 224 532
5 rm ⊇ – ✝£100/250 ✝✝£150/270 – 8 suites   **Rest** – Carte approx. £37
♦ Secluded Georgian country house, surrounded by gardens and woodland. Nicely furnished sitting rooms. Marbled bathrooms and spacious bedrooms, some with four-poster beds. Dining room is warmly decorated and the tables highly polished.

at Bunchrew West : 3 m. on A 862 - Y – ⊠ Inverness

Bunchrew House ⤳   ⟨ 🚗 🕪 & rm, ℅ P VISA ⓪ AE

⊠ IV3 8TA – ℰ (01463) 234 917 – www.bunchrew-inverness.co.uk
– welcome@bunchrew-inverness.co.uk – Fax (01463) 710 620
– Closed 5 days Christmas
16 rm ⊇ – ✝£105/145 ✝✝£180/260   **Rest** – Menu £26/40 – Carte £26/42
♦ Unhurried relaxation is assured at this 17C Scottish mansion nestling in a tranquil spot on the shores of Bealy Firth. Drawing room is wood panelled; bedrooms restful. Gardens seen through the windows provide a pleasant backdrop to spacious dining room.

INVERURIE – Aberdeenshire – **501** M 12 – pop. 10 882 ▪ Scotland   28 **D1**

▶ Edinburgh 147 mi – Aberdeen 17 mi – Inverness 90 mi
🖪 18 High St ℰ (01467) 625 800
🖪 Davah Wood, ℰ (01467) 624 080
🖪 Kintore Balbithan Rd, ℰ (01467) 632 631
🖪 Kemnay Monymusk Rd, ℰ (01467) 642 060
⊙ Castle Fraser★ (exterior★★) AC, SW : 6 m. by B 993 – Pitmedden Gardens★★, NE : 10 m. by B 9170 and A 920 – Haddo House★, N : 14 m. by B 9170 and B 9005 – Fyvie Castle★, N : 13 m. by B 9170 and A 947

Strathburn   🚗 AC rest, 🕪 P VISA ⓪ AE ⓪

Burghmuir Drive, Northwest : 1¼ m. by Inverness rd (A 96) ⊠ AB51 4GY
– ℰ (01467) 624 422 – www.strathburn-hotel.co.uk – strathburn@btconnect.com
– Fax (01467) 625 133 – Closed 24-26 December and 1-2 January
27 rm ⊇ – ✝£65/90 ✝✝£100/120
Rest – (Closed lunch Saturday and Sunday) Carte £18/36
♦ Uncluttered purpose-built hotel in a residential area of town and conveniently located for A96. Well-planned modern interiors. Rooms in uniform fitted style. Dining available in the comfortable lounge-bar area or the adjacent dining room.

ISLAY (Isle of) – Argyll and Bute – **501** B 16   27 **A3**

🛫 Port Ellen Airport : ℰ (01496) 302 022
⛴ from Port Askaig to Isle of Jura (Feolin) (Caledonian MacBrayne Ltd) frequent services daily (approx. 4 mn) – from Port Ellen or Port Askaig to Kintyre Peninsula (Kennacraig) (Caledonian MacBrayne Ltd) 1-2 daily – from Port Askaig to Oban via Isle of Colonsay (Scalasaig) (Caledonian MacBrayne Ltd) weekly – from Port Askaig to Isle of Colonsay (Scalasaig) and Kintyre Peninsula (Kennacraig) (Caledonian MacBrayne Ltd) weekly
🖪 The Square, Main St, Bowmore ℰ (01496) 810 254, bowmore@visitscotland.com
🖪 Port Ellen 25 Charlotte St, ℰ (01496) 300 094

Ballygrant – Argyll and Bute   27 **A3**

Kilmeny ⤳   ⟨ 🚗 🕪 ℅ 📶 P

Southwest :½ m. on A 846 ⊠ PA45 7QW – ℰ (01496) 840 668
– www.kilmeny.co.uk – info@kilmeny.co.uk – Fax (01496) 840 668 – Closed Christmas and New Year
5 rm ⊇ – ✝£90 ✝✝£110/136
Rest – (by arrangement, communal dining) Menu £34
♦ 19C converted farmhouse on a working farm. Its elevated position affords far reaching countryside views. Best of Scottish hospitality, home-cooking and comfort.

Bowmore – Argyll and Bute   27 **A3**

XX **Harbour Inn** with rm   < % VISA ©©
The Square ⊠ *PA43 7JR –* ℰ *(01496) 810 330 – www.harbour-inn.com*
– info@harbour-inn.com – Fax (01496) 810 990
7 rm ⌂ – †£99/149 ††£119/199   **Rest** – Carte £26/45
♦ Attractive whitewashed inn in busy little town, short walk from distillery. Panelled bar and a dining room with bay views. Menus centre on Islay produce. Bright bedrooms.

Port Charlotte – Argyll and Bute   27 **A3**

🏠 **Port Charlotte**   < 🛏 📶 P VISA ©© ①
Main St ⊠ *PA48 7TU –* ℰ *(01496) 850 360 – www.portcharlotte.co.uk*
– info@portcharlottehotel.co.uk – Fax (01496) 850 361 – Closed 24-26 December
10 rm ⌂ – †£95 ††£150   **Rest** – (bar lunch) Carte £24/35
♦ Simple, well-modernised, Victorian building in attractive conservation village. Pine panelled bar and relaxing lounge with open fires. Rooms furnished with fine old pieces. Attractive wood furnished restaurant with stone walls and views over the bay.

Port Ellen – Argyll and Bute   27 **A3**

🏠 **Glenegedale House**   🛏 P
Northwest : 4¾ m. on A 846 ⊠ *PA42 7AR –* ℰ *(01496) 300 400*
– www.glenegedalehouse.com – info@glenegedalehouse.com
8 rm ⌂ – †£85 ††£100   **Rest** – (by arrangement) Menu £35
♦ Refurbished in elegantly sympathetic style, this stalwart house proffers neutral tones with quality soft furnishings. Antiques abound. Well-equipped rooms. Handy for airport. Spacious dining room with homely cooked fare.

🏠 **Glenmachrie Farmhouse** without rest   🛏 🌣 📶 P
Northwest : 4½ m. on A 846 ⊠ *PA42 7AQ –* ℰ *(01496) 302 560*
– www.glenmachrie.com – glenmachrie@lineone.net – Fax (01496) 302 560
5 rm ⌂ – †£75 ††£90
♦ Modern farmhouse on a working farm a short drive from a number of Islay's distilleries and Duich Nature Reserve. Run on "green" low-impact policies. Warm welcoming rooms.

JEDBURGH – Scottish Borders – 501 M 17 – pop. 4 090 📖 *Scotland*   26 **D2**
▶ Edinburgh 48 mi – Carlisle 54 mi – Newcastle upon Tyne 57 mi
🛈 Murray's Green ℰ (01835) 863170, bordersinfo@visitscotland.com
📷 Jedburgh Dunion Rd, ℰ (01835) 863 587
◉ Town★ - Abbey★★ **AC** – Mary Queen of Scots House Visitor Centre★ **AC** – The Canongate Bridge★
◎ Waterloo Monument (❋★★) N : 4 m. by A 68 and B 6400

🏠 **Jedforest** 🦢   🛏 🌣 & rm, 📞 P VISA ©© AE
Camptown, South : 4 m. on A 68 ⊠ *TD8 6PJ –* ℰ *(01835) 840 222*
– www.jedforesthotel.com – info@jedforesthotel.com – Fax (01835) 840 226
12 rm ⌂ – †£75 ††£100/140   **Rest** – (dinner only) Carte £25/30
♦ Extended country house with outbuildings and attractive views. Public areas include spacious and comfortable drawing room. Bedrooms in varying co-ordinated styles and sizes. Formal dining room decorated to have an intimate feel with alcoves and low lighting.

🏠 **The Spinney** without rest   🛏 % P VISA ©© AE
Langlee, South : 2 m. on A 68 ⊠ *TD8 6PB –* ℰ *(01835) 863 525*
– www.thespinney-jedburgh.co.uk – thespinney@btinternet.com – March-October
3 rm ⌂ – †£40/60 ††£60/64
♦ Good value accommodation with homely atmosphere and ambience. Traditional feel from the gardens to the lounge. Bedrooms of a good size overlooking the attractive gardens.

SCOTLAND

⌂ **Hundalee House** without rest ⚇   ⟨ 🚗 🕪 ⚗ ♘ **P**
South : 1½ m. by A 68 ⊠ TD8 6PA – ℰ (01835) 863011
– www.accommodation-scotland.org – sheila.whittaker@btinternet.com
– Fax (01835) 863011 – March-October
5 rm ⬚ – †£30/45 ††£52/60
♦ 18C country lodge in a rural location, with good gardens featuring mature topiary.
County house feel and a warm welcome. Distinctive period décor and some antiques.

at Crailing Northeast : 4 m. by A 68 on A 698 – ⊠ Jedburgh

⌂ **Crailing Old School**   🚗 ₰ rm, ♘ **P** 🆅🆂🅰 ⓪⓪ 🅰🅴
on B 6400 ⊠ TD8 6TL – ℰ (01835) 850382 – www.crailingoldschool.co.uk
– info@crailingoldschool.co.uk – Closed Christmas-New Year and 2 weeks
October-November
4 rm ⬚ – †£35/50 ††£60/80
Rest – (by arrangement, communal dining) Menu £28
♦ Former village school well sited for touring and golfing. Attractive guests' lounge
also used for communal breakfast. Comfortable bedrooms in the house and the
garden lodge. Home-cooked dinners.

JOHN O'GROATS – Highland – 501 K 8

✉ - Shipping Services : see Orkney Islands

KELSO – Scottish Borders – 501 M 17 – pop. 5 116 ▌ Scotland   26 D2

▶ Edinburgh 44 mi – Hawick 21 mi – Newcastle upon Tyne 68 mi
ℹ Town House, The Square ℰ (01835) 863170 (mornings only in winter),
bordersinfo@visitscotland.com
🅱 Golf Course Rd, ℰ (01573) 223009
◉ Town ★ - The Square ★★ – ⟨★ from Kelso Bridge
🄶 Tweed Valley ★★ - Floors Castle ★ **AC**, NW : 1½ m. by A 6089.
Mellerstain ★★ (Ceilings ★★★, Library ★★★) **AC**, NW : 6 m. by A 6089 –
Waterloo Monument (❋★★), SW : 7 m. by A 698 and B 6400 – Jedburgh
Abbey ★★ **AC**, SW : 8½ m. by A 698 – Dryburgh Abbey ★★ **AC**
(setting ★★★), SW : 10½ m. by A 6089, B 6397 and B 6404 – Scott's
View ★★, W : 11 m. by A 6089, B 6397, B 6404 and B 6356 – Smailholm
Tower ★ (❋★★), NW : 6 m. by A 6089 and B 6397 – Lady Kirk (Kirk
o'Steil ★), NE : 16 m. by A 698, A 697, A 6112 and B 6437

🏤 **The Roxburghe** ⚇   ⟨ 🚗 🕪 🦢 🈸 🅸 🅰 **P** 🆅🆂🅰 ⓪⓪ 🅰🅴
Heiton, Southwest : 3½ m. by A 698 ⊠ TD5 8JZ – ℰ (01573) 450331
– www.roxburghe.net – hotel@roxburghe.net – Fax (01573) 450611
20 rm ⬚ – †£147 ††£147 – 2 suites   **Rest** – (light lunch) Menu £40
♦ Wonderfully characterful Jacobean style mansion built in 1853. Sitting rooms with
log fires and fresh flowers. Lovely conservatory, attractive library bar. Luxurious
rooms. Warmly hued, formal restaurant with collection of horse racing pictures.

🏤 **Ednam House**   ⟨ 🚗 ⚇ ♘ 🅰 **P** 🆅🆂🅰 ⓪⓪
Bridge St ⊠ TD5 7HT – ℰ (01573) 224168 – www.ednamhouse.com – contact@
ednamhouse.com – Fax (01573) 226319 – Closed Christmas and New Year
32 rm ⬚ – †£67/115 ††£115/142
Rest – (bar lunch Monday-Saturday) Carte £17/28
♦ Dominant Georgian mansion on Tweed. Distinctive décor exudes period appeal.
Three impressively ornate lounges. Bar with fishing theme. Traditional rooms. Spa-
cious dining room with relaxed atmosphere, overlooking gardens and river.

at Ednam North : 2¼ m. on B 6461 – ⊠ Kelso

🏠 **Edenwater House** ⚇   ⟨ 🚗 ⚗ ♘ **P** 🆅🆂🅰 ⓪⓪
off Stichill rd ⊠ TD5 7QL – ℰ (01573) 224070 – www.edenwaterhouse.co.uk
– jeffnjax@hotmail.com – Fax (01573) 226615 – Closed December and January
4 rm ⬚ – †£65 ††£100
Rest – (Closed Sunday- Monday) (dinner only) (booking essential) Menu £36
♦ Charming house in rural location next to 17C kirk. Beautiful gardens with stream
and meadows beyond. Antique filled lounges. Rooms boast fine quality furnishings.
Elegant dining room serving traditionally based meals using local produce.

KENMORE – Perth and Kinross – **501** I 14 ▯ *Scotland* 28 **C2**

- ▶ Edinburgh 82 mi – Dundee 60 mi – Oban 71 mi – Perth 38 mi
- 🏛 Taymouth Castle Aberfeldy, 𝒸 (01887) 830 228
- 🔝 Mains of Taymouth, 𝒸 (01887) 830 226
- 🔵 Village ★
- 🔲 Loch Tay ★★. Ben Lawers ★★, SW : 8 m. by A 827

BA **Kenmore** ⌨ 🔌 🏛 ♨ AC rest, ⁏₁ 🔱 P. VISA ⚫ AE
The Square ✉ PH15 2NU – 𝒸 (01887) 830 205 – www.kenmorehotel.com
– *reception@kenmorehotel.co.uk* – *Fax* (01887) 830 262
40 rm (dinner included) ⌷ – †£95/105 ††£159/179
Rest *Taymouth* – Carte £ 21/36 **s**
♦ Scotland's oldest inn. Standing on the Tay, it is now a smart, white-fronted hotel with Poet's Parlour featuring original pencilled verse by Burns. Cosy, well-kept rooms. Restaurant with panoramic river views.

KILBERRY – Argyll and Bute – **501** D 16 – **see Kintyre (Peninsula)**

KILCHRENAN – Argyll and Bute – **501** E 14 – ✉ **Taynuilt** ▯ *Scotland* 27 **B2**

- ▶ Edinburgh 117 mi – Glasgow 87 mi – Oban 18 mi
- 🔲 Loch Awe ★★, E : 1 ¼ m

fff **Ardanaiseig** 🌿 ≤ ⌨ 🔌 🔌 ✗ ⁏₁ P. VISA ⚫ AE ⓪
Northeast : 4 m. ✉ PA35 1HE – 𝒸 (01866) 833 333 – www.ardanaiseig.com
– *ardanaiseig@clara.net* – *Fax* (01866) 833 222 – *Closed 2 January- mid February*
17 rm ⌷ – †£91/160 ††£122/342 – 1 suite
Rest – (light lunch) (booking essential for non-residents) Menu £ 50
♦ Substantial country house in extensive informal gardens beside Loch Awe. Undisturbed peace. Impressively elegant interior; antiques to the fore. Tasteful bedrooms. Dining room boasts views to loch; classic country house cooking.

↑ **Roineabhal** 🌿 ⌨ 🅖 rm, ⁏₁ P. VISA ⚫
✉ PA35 1HD – 𝒸 (01866) 833 207 – www.roineabhal.com
– *maria@roineabhal.com* – *Fax* (01866) 833 477
3 rm ⌷ – †£65 ††£90 **Rest** – (by arrangement) Menu £ 40
♦ Large stone house, built by the owners, enviably located by rushing stream and close to Loch Awe. Rusticity prevails in welcoming interior; spacious rooms with homely extras. By arrangement five-course communal dinner, home-cooked using local produce.

KILDRUMMY – Aberdeenshire – **501** L 12 – ✉ **Alford** ▯ *Scotland* 28 **D1**

- ▶ Edinburgh 137 mi – Aberdeen 35 mi
- 🔵 Castle ★ **AC**
- 🔲 Huntly Castle (Heraldic carvings ★★★) N : 15 m. by A 97 – Craigievar Castle ★, SE : 13 m. by A 97, A 944 and A 980

fff **Kildrummy Castle** 🌿 ≤ ⌨ 🔌 🔌 P. VISA ⚫ AE
South : 1 ¼ m. on A 97 ✉ AB33 8RA – 𝒸 (019755) 71 288
– *www.kildrummycastlehotel.co.uk* – *bookings@kildrummycastlehotel.co.uk*
– *Fax* (019755) 71 345 – *Closed January*
16 rm ⌷ – †£90/120 ††£213
Rest *The Dining Room* – Menu £ 33 (dinner) – Carte (lunch) approx. £ 19
♦ Imposing, stone built 19C mansion in superb grounds with fine view of original 13C castle. Baronial, country house style abounds: lounges flaunt antiques. Variable rooms. Delightfully wood-panelled dining room; homely Scottish cooking.

KILLIECRANKIE – Perth and Kinross – **501** I 13 – **see Pitlochry**

KILLIN – Stirling – **501** H 14 – **pop. 666** ▯ *Scotland* 27 **B2**

- ▶ Edinburgh 72 mi – Dundee 65 mi – Oban 54 mi – Perth 43 mi
- 🅘 The Old Mill, Falls of Dochart 𝒸 (08707) 200627, killin@vs.net
- 🔝 Killin, 𝒸 (01567) 820 312
- 🔲 Loch Tay ★★, Ben Lawers ★★, NE : 8 m. by A 827

🏠 **Dall Lodge Country House** without rest 🚪 📶 **P** VISA 𝐎𝐎
Main St ⊠ FK21 8TN – ℰ (01567) 820 217 – www.dalllodge.co.uk
– connor@dalllodge.co.uk – Fax (01567) 820 726 – April-September
9 rm ⌷ – **†**£35/45 **††**£50/76
♦ Victorian hotel of stone, proudly overlooking river Lochay. Walls adorned by foreign artefacts and local oils. Conservatory with exotic plants. Stylish, halogen lit rooms.

🏠 **Breadalbane House** 🕉 **P** VISA 𝐎𝐎
Main St ⊠ FK21 8UT – ℰ (01567) 820 134 – www.breadalbanehouse.com
– info@breadalbanehouse.com
5 rm ⌷ – **†**£30/45 **††**£52/65 **Rest** – (by arrangement) Menu £15
♦ Surrounded by Ben Lawers, Loch Tay, Glen Lochay and the Falls of Dochart, this cosy guesthouse offers simple, homely comforts. Clean, well-kept rooms with good views. Evening meals available by prior arrangement in the simple, pine furnished dining room.

at Ardeonaig Northeast : 6 ¾ m. – ⊠ Killin (Stirling)

🏠 **Ardeonaig** ⌂ ⟨ 🚪 🕉 📶 **P** VISA 𝐎𝐎
South Road, Loch Tay ⊠ FK21 8SU – ℰ (01567) 820 400
– www.ardeonaighotel.co.uk – info@ardeonaighotel.co.uk – Fax (01567) 820 282
26 rm (dinner included) ⌷ – **†**£95/125 **††**£180/300
Rest The Restaurant – see restaurant listing
♦ 17C inn and super, modern, airy lochside suite, in wooded meadows on shore of Loch Tay. Cheery, well-stocked bar. Cosy sitting room. Library with fine views. Smart rooms.

🍴🍴 **The Restaurant** – at Ardeonaig Hotel 🚪 🕉 🍽 **P** VISA 𝐎𝐎
South Road, Loch Tay ⊠ FK21 8SU – ℰ (01567) 820 400
– www.ardeonaighotel.co.uk – info@ardeonaighotel.co.uk – Fax (01567) 820 282
Rest – Menu £27 (dinner) – Carte £27/44
♦ Located in Ardeonaig hotel extension. Rennie Mackintosh style chairs, white linen-clad tables. Good value dishes: South African influences merge well with local ingredients.

KILMARNOCK – East Ayrshire – **501** G 17 ▯ *Scotland* 25 **B2**
🚹 Edinburgh 64 mi – Ayr 13 mi – Glasgow 25 mi
◉ Dean Castle (arms and armour ★, musical instruments ★)

🏨 **The Park** 🛁 🕼 ⅙ rm, 🕉 📶 🔌 **P** VISA 𝐎𝐎 AE 𝐎
Kilmarnock Football Club, Rugby Park, off Dundonald Rd ⊠ KA1 2DP
– ℰ (01563) 545 999 – www.theparkhotel.uk.com
– enquiries@theparkhotel.uk.com – Fax (01563) 545 322
50 rm ⌷ – **†**£130 **††**£150
Rest Blues – Menu £12 (lunch) – Carte £23/44
♦ Adjacent to Kilmarnock Football Club, who are its owners, this stylish, glass structured hotel offers up-to-date facilities. Spacious, well-equipped and comfortable bedrooms. Mezzanine-level restaurant boasts tables with views of the pitch.

KILMORY – North Ayrshire – **501** E 17 – see Arran (Isle of)

KINCLAVEN – Perth and Kinross – **501** J 14 – pop. 394 – ⊠ Stanley 28 **C2**
🚹 Edinburgh 56 mi – Perth 12 mi

🏨 **Ballathie House** ⌂ ⟨ 🚪 🕉 ⅙ rm, 🕼 🔌 **P** VISA 𝐎𝐎 AE 𝐎
Stanley ⊠ PH1 4QN – ℰ (01250) 883 268 – www.ballathiehousehotel.com
– email@ballathiehousehotel.com – Fax (01250) 883 396
39 rm ⌷ – **†**£95/130 **††**£190/210 – 3 suites **Rest** – Menu £22/42
♦ Imposing mid 19C former shooting lodge on banks of Tay, imbued with tranquil, charming atmosphere. Elegant, individually furnished bedrooms with a floral theme. Richly alluring restaurant overlooking river.

KINGUSSIE – Highland – **501** H 12 – **pop. 1 410** 🏴 *Scotland* 30 **C3**

▶ Edinburgh 117 mi – Inverness 41 mi – Perth 73 mi

🔗 Gynack Rd, 𝒞 (01540) 661 600

🄖 Highland Wildlife Park★ **AC**, NE : 4 m. by A 9. Aviemore★, NE : 11 m. by A 9 – The Cairngorms★★ (≤★★★) - ❅★★★ from Cairn Gorm, NE : 18 m. by B 970

⌂ **Hermitage**   ⎘ ⅋ **P** ₻ ⚫

🏵 *Spey St ⊠ PH21 1HN – 𝒞 (01540) 662 137 – www.thehermitage-scotland.com – thehermitage@clara.net – Fax (01540) 662 177 – Closed 25-26 December*

5 rm – ⌕ – ♦£35/50 ♦♦£60/80   **Rest** – (by arrangement) Menu £ 18

♦ Pleasant Victorian detached house with views of Cairngorms. Attractive lawned garden. Homely, welcoming lounge with log fire. Colourful, floral rooms. Garden views from conservatory style dining room.

⌂ **Homewood Lodge** without rest ॐ   ≤ ⎘ ⅋ **P**

Newtonmore Rd ⊠ PH21 1HD – 𝒞 (01540) 661 507 – www.homewood-lodge-kingussie.co.uk – jenniferander5@hotmail.com – March - October

3 rm ⌕ – ♦£30/35 ♦♦£60

♦ An immaculate whitewashed exterior and a prominent hilltop position attract the visitor's eye to this Victorian villa guesthouse with its uncluttered feel and simple rooms.

✕✕ **The Cross at Kingussie** with rm ॐ   ⅋ ⁽ᵗᵗ⁾ **P** ₻ ⚫ ᴀᴇ

Tweed Mill Brae, Ardbroilach Rd ⊠ PH21 1LB – 𝒞 (01540) 661 166 – www.thecross.co.uk – relax@thecross.co.uk – Fax (01540) 661 080 – Closed 2 weeks January, 2 weeks February, Christmas, Sunday and Monday

8 rm (dinner included) ⌕ – ♦£170/205 ♦♦£240/280

Rest – (dinner only) (booking essential) Menu £ 50 **s**🕮

♦ Personally run converted tweed mill restaurant in four acres of waterside grounds with beamed ceilings and modern artwork. Modish Scottish cuisine. Comfortable rooms.

 Look out for red symbols, indicating particularly pleasant establishments.

KINLOCH LODGE – Highland – see Skye (Isle of)

KINROSS – Perth and Kinross – **501** J 15 – **pop. 4 681**   28 **C2**

▶ Edinburgh 28 mi – Dunfermline 13 mi – Perth 18 mi – Stirling 25 mi

🄳 Heart of Scotland Visitor Centre, junction 6, M 90 𝒞 (01577) 863680 (closed weekends October-April), kinrosstic@perthshire.co.uk

🔗 Green Hotel 2 The Muirs, 𝒞 (01577) 863 407

🄖 Milnathort South St, 𝒞 (01577) 864 069

🄖 Bishopshire Kinnesswood Woodmarch

🏠 **The Green**   ⎘ ⚲ ✕ 🔗 ⁽ᵗᵗ⁾ ꜱ **P** ₻ ⚫ ᴀᴇ ⓞ

2 Muirs ⊠ KY13 8AS – 𝒞 (01577) 863 467 – www.green-hotel.com – reservations@green-hotel.com – Fax (01577) 863 180 – Closed 24-27 December

46 rm ⌕ – ♦£68/110 ♦♦£95/175

Rest *Basil's* – (dinner only) Menu £ 30

♦ 18C former coaching inn in neat grounds off village high street. Spacious, welcoming lounge. Try your hand at curling. Comfortable, modern rooms. Bright, airy modern restaurant with modish menus to match.

⌂ **Burnbank** without rest   ⎘ ⅋ ⁽ᵗᵗ⁾ **P** ₻ ⚫

79 Muirs, North : ¾ m. on A 922 ⊠ KY13 8AZ – 𝒞 (01577) 861 931 – www.burnbank-kinross.co.uk – bandb@burnbank-kinross.co.uk

3 rm ⌕ – ♦£40/45 ♦♦£75/80

♦ Well-kept guesthouse with a cosy reception room full of maps and local info. Good breakfasts. Lomond Hills vistas from comfortable and co-ordinated bedrooms.

SCOTLAND

KINTYRE (Peninsula) – Argyll and Bute – 501 D 16 ▮ Scotland   27 B3

🛬 Campbeltown Airport : ☎ (01586) 553797
🚢 from Claonaig to Isle of Arran (Lochranza) (Caledonian MacBrayne Ltd)
frequent services daily (30 mn) – from Kennacraig to Isle of Islay (Port Ellen
or Port Askaig) (Caledonian MacBrayne Ltd) 1-3 daily – from Kennacraig to
Oban via Isle of Colonsay (Scalasaig) and Isle of Islay (Port Askaig) 3 weekly
🏌 Machrihanish Campbeltown, ☎ (01586) 810 213
🏌 Dunaverty Campbeltown Southend, ☎ (01586) 830 677
🏌 Gigha Isle of Gigha, ☎ (01583) 505 242
◎ Carradale★ – Saddell (Collection of grave slabs★)

Carradale – Argyll and Bute   27 B3

🏠 **Dunvalanree** ⌂   ≤ 🚗 ७. rm, ⑪ 🅿 VISA ⑳ AE
Port Righ Bay ⌂ PA28 6SE – ☎ (01583) 431 226 – www.dunvalanree.com
– eat@dunvalanree.com – Closed Christmas
5 rm ⌂ – †£110 ††£170   **Rest** – (dinner only) Menu £28
♦ 1930s house on the bay facing Arran and Kilbrannan Sound. Comfortable firelit
lounge, "Arts and Crafts" stained glass entrance and well-fitted rooms, one in Mackintosh style. Intimate dining room takes up the period style.

Kilberry – Argyll and Bute   27 A3

▶ Edinburgh 165 mi – Glasgow 121 mi – Oban 75 mi

✗ **The Kilberry Inn** with rm ⌂   🅿 VISA ⑳
⌂ PA29 6YD – ☎ (01880) 770 223 – www.kilberryinn.com
– relax@kilberryinn.com – Closed January - mid March
4 rm ⌂ – ††£95
Rest – (Closed Monday) (booking essential at dinner) Carte £20/31
♦ Characterful, cosy, red tin-roofed cottage incorporating open fires, beams, exposed
stone. Walls hung with local artists' work. Well-priced dishes. Stylish, modern bedrooms.

KIRKBEAN – Dumfries and Galloway – 501 ▮ Scotland   26 C3

▶ Edinburgh 92 mi – Dumfries 13 mi – Kirkcudbright 29 mi
◎ Sweetheart Abbey★, N : 5 m. by A 710. Threave Garden★★ and Threave
Castle★, W : 20 m. by A 710 and A 745

🏠 **Cavens** ⌂   ≤ 🚗 🅿 VISA ⑳ ①
⌂ DG2 8AA – ☎ (01387) 880 234 – www.cavens.com – enquiries@cavens.com
– Fax (01387) 880 467 – Closed January-March
8 rm ⌂ – †£120/150 ††£130/190   **Rest** – (dinner only) Menu £30 **s**
♦ 18C house with extensions set in mature gardens. Very comfortable lounges opening onto terrace. Spacious well furnished bedrooms. Simple refreshing meals using
local produce.

KIRKCOLM – Dumfries and Galloway – 501 E 19 – see Stranraer

KIRKCUDBRIGHT – Dumfries and Galloway – 501 H 19 – pop. 3 447   25 B3
▮ Scotland

▶ Edinburgh 108 mi – Dumfries 28 mi – Stranraer 50 mi
🛈 Harbour Sq ☎ (01557) 330494 (Easter-October),
kirkcudbright@dgtb.visitscotland.com
🏌 Stirling Crescent, ☎ (01557) 330 314
◎ Town★
◎ Dundrennan Abbey★ AC, SE : 5 m. by A 711

🏨 **Selkirk Arms**   🚗 ⑪ 🅿 VISA ⑳ AE
High St ⌂ DG6 4JG – ☎ (01557) 330 402 – www.selkirkarmshotel.co.uk
– reception@selkirkarmshotel.co.uk – Fax (01557) 331 639 – Closed 26 December
16 rm ⌂ – †£68/93 ††£98/110
Rest – Menu £26 (dinner) – Carte (lunch) £19/32
♦ Traditional coaching inn in centre of quaint town; Burns reputedly wrote "The
Selkirk Grace" here. Rustic interior. Large bar serving simple food. Good sized rooms.
Comfortable dining room with seasonal, classically based menu.

SCOTLAND

↑ Gladstone House 🛏 ⚡ VISA 💳

48 High St ⊠ DG6 4JX – 𝒞 (01557) 331 734 – www.kirkcudbrightgladstone.co.uk
– hilarygladstone@aol.com – Fax (01557) 331 734
3 rm ⊑ – ✦£43 ✦✦£63 **Rest** – (by arrangement) Menu £ 21
♦ Attractive Georgian house. Spacious, comfortably furnished sitting room and breakfast room. Evening meals offered. Traditional rooms with stripped wooden furnishings.

KIRKMICHAEL – Perth and Kinross – **501** J 13   28 **C2**
▶ Edinburgh 73 mi – Aberdeen 85 mi – Inverness 102 mi – Perth 29 mi

↑ Cruachan Country Cottage without rest 🛏 P

on A 924 ⊠ PH10 7NZ – 𝒞 (01250) 881 226 – www.kirkmichael.net
– cruachan@strathardle.co.uk – Closed 25-26 December
3 rm ⊑ – ✦£35/37 ✦✦£58/62
♦ Extended stone cottage with neat garden, overlooking River Ardle. Homely lounge with open fire and interesting, local prints. Individually decorated bedrooms.

KIRKNEWTON – Edinburgh – **501** J 16 – **see Edinburgh**

KIRKPATRICK DURHAM – Dumfries and Galloway – **501** I 18 – **see Castle Douglas**

KIRKTON OF GLENISLA – Angus – **501** K 13 – ⊠ Blairgowrie   28 **C2**
▶ Edinburgh 73 mi – Forfar 19 mi – Pitlochry 24 mi

↑ Glenmarkie Health Spa and Riding Centre 🐾 ≤ 🛏 🐕 ⚡ P

East : 3 ¾ m. by B 951 ⊠ PH11 8QB – 𝒞 (01575) 582 295
– www.glenmarkie.co.uk – holidays@glenmarkie.freeserve.co.uk – Fax (01575) 582 295
4 rm ⊑ – ✦£40 ✦✦£56 **Rest** – (by arrangement) Menu £ 25
♦ Stunningly located, cosy little farmhouse in beautiful glen. Horse riding and massages available, not necessarily in that order. Simple, individually decorated bedrooms.

KIRKWALL – Orkney Islands – **501** L 7 – **see Orkney Islands**

KIRK YETHOLM – Scottish Borders   26 **D2**
▶ London 346 mi – Edinburgh 57 mi – Hawick 26 mi – Galashiels 27 mi

↑ Mill House without rest 🛏 ⚡ ((₁)) P

Main St ⊠ TD5 8PE – 𝒞 (01573) 420 604 – www.millhouseyetholm.co.uk
– millhousebb@tiscali.co.uk – Fax (01573) 420 644
3 rm ⊑ – ✦£55/90 ✦✦£70/90
♦ Converted grain mill with a spacious and immaculately presented interior, full of homely, warm touches. Well appointed bedrooms add the final touch to a most appealing house.

KIRRIEMUIR – Angus – **501** K 13 – pop. 5 963   28 **C2**
▶ Edinburgh 65 mi – Aberdeen 50 mi – Dundee 16 mi – Perth 30 mi

↑ Purgavie Farm 🐾 ≤ 🛏 ((₁)) P VISA 💳

Lintrathen, West : 5 ½ m. on B 951 ⊠ DD8 5HZ – 𝒞 (01575) 560 213
– www.purgavie.co.uk – purgavie@aol.com – Fax (01575) 560 213
3 rm ⊑ – ✦£35 ✦✦£60
Rest – (by arrangement, communal dining) Menu £ 15
♦ Farmhouse on working farm at foot of Glen Isla, part of lovely Glens of Angus. Homely lounge with open fire. Large, comfortable rooms with panoramic views. Meals are taken communally in the comfortable dining room.

SCOTLAND

KYLESKU – Highland – 501 E 9 ▮ Scotland
30 **C1**

    🚘 Edinburgh 256 mi – Inverness 100 mi – Ullapool 34 mi
    ◙ Loch Assynt★★, S : 6 m. by A 894

🏠 **Kylesku**   ≤ ⌦ ⅍ _VISA_ 🞓
  ✉ IV27 4HW – ℰ (01971) 502 231 – www.kyleskuhotel.co.uk
  – info@kyleskuhotel.co.uk – Fax (01971) 502 313
  – Closed mid-October to end February
  8 rm ⌕ – †£60 ††£94
  Rest _Kylesku (Bar)_ – see restaurant listing
  Rest – (dinner only) Menu £29 – Carte £18/27
  ♦ Delightfully located 17C coaching inn, set beside 2 sea-lochs in a peaceful village. Spectacular panoramic views from cosy lounge, restaurant and most of the homely bedrooms. Cooking centres around fresh Highland game and locally landed seafood.

🏠 **Newton Lodge** without rest 🍃   ≤ 🚗 ⅍ 🅿 _VISA_ 🞓
  South : 1½ m. on A 894 ✉ IV27 4HW – ℰ (01971) 502 070
  – www.newtonlodge.co.uk – info@newtonlodge.co.uk – Fax (01971) 502 070
  – May-September
  7 rm ⌕ – †£67 ††£84
  ♦ Spacious hotel on a hillside in the Global Geopark. Exceptional loch and mountain views, with Glencoul fault escarpment directly opposite. Floral themed bedrooms, most with views.

🍽 **Kylesku (Bar)** – at Kylesku Hotel   _VISA_ 🞓
  ✉ IV27 4HW – ℰ (01971) 502 231 – www.kyleskuhotel.co.uk
  – info@kyleskuhotel.co.uk – Fax (01971) 502 313 – March-mid October
  Rest – (dinner only) Menu £29 – Carte £18/27
  ♦ Wonderfully located beside two-sea lochs, with outside seating and spectacular mountain views. Wide menu offers fresh Highland meats, and seafood landed daily on the neighbouring slipway.

LADYBANK – Fife – 501 K 15 – pop. 1 373 ▮ Scotland
28 **C2**

    🚘 Edinburgh 38 mi – Dundee 20 mi – Stirling 40 mi
    🏌 Ladybank Annsmuir, ℰ (01337) 830 814
    ◙ Falkland★ – Palace of Falkland★ – Gardens★ – Village★, S : ½ m. by A 914
    on A 912

🏠 **Redlands Country Lodge** without rest 🍃   🚗 🛈⁰ 🅿 _VISA_ 🞓
  Pitlessie Rd, East : ¾ m. by Kingskettle rd taking first left after railway bridge
  ✉ KY15 7SH – ℰ (01337) 831 091 – www.redlandslodge.com
  – info@redlandslodge.com
  4 rm ⌕ – †£45/70 ††£65/70
  ♦ Detached cottage on a quiet country lane in a rural location. Bedrooms, which have a simple snug air, are located in an adjacent pine lodge.

LAIRG – Highland – 501 G9 – pop. 857
30 **C2**

    🚘 Edinburgh 218 mi – Inverness 61 mi – Wick 72 mi
    🖪 Ferrycroft Countryside Centre, Sutherland ℰ (01549) 402 160
    (April-October), ferrycroft@croftersrestaurant.fsnet.co.uk

🏠 **Park House**   ≤ 🚗 ⌦ 🅿 _VISA_ 🞓
  ✉ IV27 4AU – ℰ (01549) 402 208 – www.parkhousesporting.com
  – david-walker@park-house.freeserve.co.uk – Fax (01549) 402 693 – Closed
  Christmas and New Year
  4 rm ⌕ – †£35/55 ††£70/84   **Rest** – (by arrangement) Menu £22
  ♦ Victorian house, just set back from Loch Shin, comfortable and well furnished with high ceilings and views of the loch. Good spacious bedrooms. Country pursuits organised. Hunting and fishing activities of the establishment reflected in the home-cooked menus.

LANGASS – Western Isles – see Uist (Isles of)

LAUDER – Scottish Borders – **501** L 16 – pop. 1 081   26 **D2**

> ☑ Edinburgh 27 mi – Berwick-upon-Tweed 34 mi – Carlisle 74 mi – Newcastle upon Tyne 77 mi
>
> 🖬 Galashiels Rd, ℰ (01578) 722 526

🏠   **The Lodge**   ☞ 🕅 🐭 ⚓ **P** *VISA* **⦿** **AE**

Carfraemill, Northwest : 4 m. by A 68 on A 697 ☒ *TD2 6RA –* ℰ *(01578) 750 750*
– www.carfraemill.co.uk – enquiries@carfraemill.co.uk – Fax (01578) 750 751
10 rm ⊠ – ✝£60 ✝✝£90
Rest *Jo's Kitchen* – Carte £ 20/28

♦ Family run hotel, once a coaching inn, just off the Newcastle-Edinburgh road. Warmly traditional style of décor and a welcoming ambience. Well-equipped bedrooms. A choice of informal eating areas with a traditional farmhouse feel.

🛏   **Black Bull** with rm   🌂 **P** *VISA* **⦿**

13-15 Market Place ☒ *TD2 6SR –* ℰ *(01578) 722 208*
– www.blackbull-lauder.com – enquiries@blackbull-lauder.com – Fax (01578) 722 419
8 rm ⊠ – ✝£68 ✝✝£100   **Rest** – Carte £ 18/30 **s**

♦ Hanging baskets catch the eye outside this former coaching inn. Various snugs provide a cosy welcome. Extensive menus of popular, home-cooked dishes. Clean, well-kept rooms.

LEITH – Edinburgh – **501** K 16 – see Edinburgh

LERWICK – Shetland Islands – **501** Q 3 – see Shetland Islands (Mainland)

LEVERBURGH – Western Isles Outer Hebrides – **501** Y 10 – see Lewis and Harris (Isle of)

LEWIS and HARRIS (Isle of) – **501** A 9 🔲 Scotland

> 🚢 from Stornoway to Ullapool (Mainland) (Caledonian MacBrayne Ltd) 2/3 daily (2 h 40 mn) – from Kyles Scalpay to the Isle of Scalpay (Caledonian MacBrayne Ltd) (10 mn) – from Tarbert to Isle of Skye (Uig) (Caledonian MacBrayne Ltd) 1-2 daily (1 h 45 mn) – from Tarbert to Portavadie (Caledonian MacBrayne Ltd) (summer only) frequent services daily (25 mn) – from Leverburgh to North Uist (Otternish) (Caledonian MacBrayne Ltd) (3-4 daily) (1 h 10 mn)
>
> ◎ Callanish Standing Stones★★ – Carloway Broch★ – St Clement's Church, Rodel (tomb★)

LEWIS – Western Isles

Breasclete   29 **B1**

🏠   **Eshcol** ⏿   ⪜ 🛋 🕅 **P**

21 Breasclete ☒ *HS2 9ED –* ℰ *(01851) 621 357 – www.eshcol.com*
– neil@eshcol.com – Fax (01851) 621 357 – March-October
3 rm ⊠ – ✝£50 ✝✝£80   **Rest** – (by arrangement) Menu £ 22

♦ Friendly, family run house in rural location, set against a backdrop of delightful scenery. Immaculately kept throughout with a homely atmosphere and views from most rooms. Dinners served at Loch Roag next door.

🏠   **Loch Roag** ⏿   🛋 🕅 🗝 **P**

22A Breasclete ☒ *HS2 9EF –* ℰ *(01851) 621 357 – www.lochroag.com*
– donald@lochroag.com – Fax (01851) 621 357
4 rm ⊠ – ✝£35/65 ✝✝£70/80   **Rest** – (by arrangement) Menu £ 22

♦ Charming rural location with super views. Run by same family as Eshcol! Bedrooms are decorated in traditional style and the house as a whole has a snug welcoming atmosphere. Simple uncluttered dining room with lovely loch view.

SCOTLAND

Galson – Western Isles   29 **B1**

⚰ **Galson Farm** ⌂   ⪬ 🚗 ◑ **P** 𝘝𝘐𝘚𝘈 ⊕⊕
South Galson ✉ *HS2 0SH* – ℰ *(01851) 850 492* – *www.glasonfarm.co.uk*
– galsonfarm@yahoo.com – Fax (01851) 850 492
4 rm ⌂ – ⱐ£ 45 ⱐⱐ£ 100
Rest – (by arrangement, communal dining) Menu £ 23
♦ Characterful working farm in a very remote location. Close to the ocean and ideally placed for exploring the north of the island. Cosy, comfortable, well-kept bedrooms. Traditionally styled dining room where meals are taken communally at a large central table.

Stornoway – Western Isles   29 **B1**

🖪 26 Cromwell St ℰ (01851) 703 088, stornaway@visitthebrides.com
🖼 Lady Lever Park, ℰ (01851) 702 240

🏨 **Cabarfeidh**   🚗 📶 ᴀᴄ rest, "¶" ♨ **P** 𝘝𝘐𝘚𝘈 ⊕⊕ ᴀᴇ
Manor Park, North : ½ m. on A 859 ✉ *HS1 2EU* – ℰ *(01851) 702 604*
– www.calahotels.com – cabarfeidh@calahotels.com
– Fax (01851) 705 572
46 rm ⌂ – ⱐ£ 109 ⱐⱐ£ 149
Rest – Menu £ 14 (lunch) – Carte dinner £ 28/35 **s**
♦ Modern purpose-built hotel surrounded by gardens and close to golf course. Up-to-date, well-equipped bedrooms. Range of banqueting and conference facilities. Restaurant is divided into four areas including conservatory, bistro and garden rooms.

⚰ **Braighe House** without rest   🚗 ℅ "¶" **P** 𝘝𝘐𝘚𝘈 ⊕⊕ ⓪
20 Braighe Rd, Southeast : 3 m. on A 866 ✉ *HS2 0BQ* – ℰ *(01851) 705 287*
– www.braighehouse.co.uk – alison@braighehouse.co.uk
– Closed 2 weeks Christmas - New Year
5 rm ⌂ – ⱐ£ 70/80 ⱐⱐ£ 110
♦ Spacious proportions allied to enviable coastal outlook. Style and taste predominate in the large, comfy lounge and airy bedrooms. Hearty breakfasts set you up for the day.

HARRIS – Western Isles

Ardhasaig – Western Isles   29 **A1**

🍴🍴 **Ardhasaig House** with rm ⌂   ⪬ **P** 𝘝𝘐𝘚𝘈 ⊕⊕ ᴀᴇ
✉ *HS3 3AJ* – ℰ *(01859) 502 500* – *www.ardhasaig.co.uk*
– accommodation@ardhasaig.co.uk – Fax (01859) 502 077 – March-October
6 rm ⌂ – ⱐ£ 55/65 ⱐⱐ£ 53/80
Rest – (dinner only) (booking essential for non-residents) (set menu only)
Menu £ 48 **s**
♦ Purpose built house with wild, dramatic views. Smart dining room with daily changing menu; accomplished dishes feature seasonal island produce. Well-kept bedrooms.

Leverburgh – Western Isles   29 **A2**

⚰ **Carminish** ⌂   ⪬ 🚗 "¶" **P**
1a Strond, South : 1 m. on Srandda rd ✉ *HS5 3UD* – ℰ *(01859) 520 400*
– www.carminish.com – info@carminish.com
– Restricted opening in winter
3 rm ⌂ – ⱐ£ 28/50 ⱐⱐ£ 56/66
Rest – (by arrangement, communal dining) Menu £ 20 **s**
♦ Idyllically located guesthouse with spectacular views of the Carminish Islands and Sound of Harris. Comfortable lounge. Well-kept rooms. Hearty meals in communal setting.

SCOTLAND

Scalpay – Western Isles   29 B2

Hirta House without rest ≤ ✒ ⁽ᵗ⁾ P. VISA ⓞⓞ AE
⊠ HS4 3XZ – ℰ (01859) 540 394 – www.hirtahouse.co.uk
– m.mackenzie@tiscali.co.uk – Fax (01859) 540 394
3 rm ☲ – †£50/60 ††£60/70
◆ Enter Scalpay by impressive modern bridge and admire the hills of Harris from this stylish guesthouse with its bold wall colours, vivid artwork and nautically inspired rooms.

Scarista – Western Isles – pop. 2 363   29 A2

Scarista House ⑤ ≤ ⎙ P. VISA ⓞⓞ
⊠ HS3 3HX – ℰ (01859) 550 238 – www.scaristahouse.com
– timandpatricia@scaristahouse.com – Fax (01859) 550 277 – Closed Christmas, January and February
5 rm ☲ – †£140 ††£190/195
Rest – (dinner only) (booking essential for non-residents) (set menu only) Menu £ 40
◆ Sympathetically restored part 18C former manse, commanding position affords delightful views of Scarista Bay. Elegant library and inviting antique furnished bedrooms. Strong local flavour to the daily changing menu.

Tarbert – Western Isles – pop. 1 338 – ⊠ Harris   29 A2

Ceol na Mara without rest ⑤ ⎙ ✒ ⁽ᵗ⁾ P. VISA ⓞⓞ AE
7 Direcleit ⊠ HS3 3DP – ℰ (01859) 502 464 – www.ceolnamara.com
– midgie@madasafish.com
4 rm ☲ – †£50 ††£90
◆ Wonderful views and a loch's edge setting enhance the allure of this idyllically set house with smart decking area, peaceful garden, lovely lounge and simple, spacious rooms.

Hillcrest without rest ≤ ⎙ ✒ P. VISA ⓞⓞ AE ⓞ
Northwest : 1 ¾ m. on A 859 ⊠ HS3 3AH – ℰ (01859) 502 119
– angusahillcrest@tiscali.co.uk – Fax (01859) 502 119
3 rm ☲ – †£40 ††£50
◆ A private house, family run, in a commanding position overlooking Loch Tarbert. Small cosy sitting room and spacious bedrooms, most enjoying sea views.

If breakfast is included the ☲ symbol appears after the number of rooms.

LEWISTON – Highland – 501 G 12 ▌Scotland   30 C2
▶ Edinburgh 173 mi – Inverness 17 mi
◉ Loch Ness★★ – The Great Glen★

Woodlands without rest ⎙ & ✒ ⁽ᵗ⁾ P. VISA ⓞⓞ
East Lewiston ⊠ IV63 6UJ – ℰ (01456) 450 356
– www.woodlands-lochness.co.uk – stay@woodlands-lochness.co.uk
– Fax (01456) 450 927 – Closed December-February
4 rm ☲ – †£37/40 ††£54/66
◆ Spacious, purpose-built guesthouse with large garden and decked terrace situated just away from the town. Airy, immaculately kept and comfortable bedrooms.

Glen Rowan without rest ⎙ ✒ ⁽ᵗ⁾ P. VISA ⓞⓞ
West Lewiston ⊠ IV63 6UW – ℰ (01456) 450 235 – www.glenrowan.co.uk
– info@glenrowan.co.uk
3 rm ☲ – †£35/40 ††£44/60
◆ Purpose-built house in a quiet spot with pleasant garden bordering a mountain stream. Tea served to arriving guests. Compact but charming and well-kept bedrooms.

LINLITHGOW – West Lothian – **501** J 16 – pop. **13 370** ▮ *Scotland*   26 **C1**

▶ Edinburgh 19 mi – Falkirk 9 mi – Glasgow 35 mi

ℹ Burgh Hall, The Cross ℰ (08452) 255121 (April-October)

▦ Braehead, ℰ (01506) 842 585

▦ West Lothian Airngath Hill, ℰ (01506) 826 049

◉ Town★★ – Palace★★ **AC** : Courtyard (fountain★★), Great Hall (Hooded Fireplace★★), Gateway★ – Old Town★ – St Michaels★

ⓒ Cairnpapple Hill★ **AC**, SW : 5 m. by A 706 – House of the Binns (plasterwork ceilings★) **AC**, NE : 4½ m. by A 803 and A 904. Hopetoun House★★ **AC**, E : 7 m. by A 706 and A 904 – Abercorn Parish Church (Hopetoun Loft★★) NE : 7 m. by A 803 and A 904

⛧ **Arden House** without rest 🈂   📇 ⇘ ⑨⓪ **P** **VISA** **⊕⊕** **AE**
🈯 *Belsyde, Southwest : 2¼ m. on A 706 ✉ EH49 6QE – ℰ (01506) 670 172
– www.ardencountryhouse.com – info@ardencountryhouse.com – Fax (01506) 670 172 – Closed 25 December*
3 rm 🍽 – ♦£50/100 ♦♦£78/100
♦ Charmingly run guesthouse set in peaceful location with lovely rural views. Thoughtful extras include scones and shortbread on arrival. Rooms boast a luxurious style.

✗✗✗ **Champany Inn** with rm   📇 ⑨⓪ **P** **VISA** **⊕⊕** **AE** **①**
☆ *Champany, Northeast : 2 m. on A 803 at junction with A 904 ✉ EH49 7LU
– ℰ (01506) 834 532 – www.champany.com – reception@champany.com
– Fax (01506) 834 302
– Closed 25-26 December, 1-2 January, Saturday lunch and Sunday*
16 rm 🍽 – ♦£115 ♦♦£135
Rest – Beef specialities – Menu £20 (lunch) – Carte £51/72 🈝
Spec. Langoustine with smoked cod ravioli. Sirloin of Aberdeen Angus beef. Champany cheesecake with pineapple salsa.
♦ Personally run restaurant offers precise cooking, specialising in succulently-flavoured prime Scotch beef, with a superb South African wine list. Formal service from 'wenches.' Handsomely equipped bedrooms are themed around tartan colour schemes.

✗✗ **Livingston's**   📇 🈝 **VISA** **⊕⊕** **AE** **①**
*52 High St ✉ EH49 7AE – ℰ (01506) 846 565 – www.livingstons-restaurant.co.uk
– contact@livingstons-restaurant.co.uk – Closed first two weeks January, one week June, third week October, Sunday and Monday*
Rest – Menu £20/37
♦ Friendly restaurant tucked away off high street. Menus offer good value meals using fresh regional produce; comfortable dining room, conservatory and summer terrace.

🍴 **The Chop and Ale House** – at Champany Inn   **P** **VISA** **⊕⊕** **AE** **①**
*Champany, Northeast : 2 m. on A 803 at junction with A 904 ✉ EH49 7LU
– ℰ (01506) 834 532 – www.champany.com – reception@champany.com
– Fax (01506) 834 302 – Closed 25-26 December, 1 January*
Rest – Carte £23/35
♦ Former bar of Champany Inn: a more relaxed alternative to its restaurant. Stone walls filled with shotguns and animal heads. Meat is all-important; try the homemade burgers.

LOANS – South Ayrshire – **501** G 17 – **see Troon**

LOCHALINE – Highland – **501** C 14   29 **B3**

▶ Edinburgh 162 mi – Craignure 6 mi – Oban 7 mi

✗ **Whitehouse**   **P** **VISA**
*✉ PA34 5XT – ℰ (01967) 421 777 – www.thewhitehouserestaurant.co.uk
– info@whitehouserestaurant.co.uk – Fax (01967) 421 220 – Easter-October and restricted opening in winter*
Rest – (Closed Sunday dinner and Monday) Carte £24/31
♦ Remote setting adds to welcoming feel endorsed by hands-on owners. Two lovely, cosy, wood-lined dining rooms where the ethos of seasonal and local cooking shines through.

LOCHEARNHEAD – Stirling – 501 H 14 ■ Scotland 28 C2

▶ Edinburgh 65 mi – Glasgow 56 mi – Oban 57 mi – Perth 36 mi

Mansewood Country House 🛋 ❧ ⒴ P̲ VISA ◍

South : ½ m. on A 84 ⊠ FK19 8NS – ℰ (01567) 830 213
– www.mansewoodcountryhouse.co.uk – stay@mansewoodcountryhouse.co.uk
– Restricted opening in winter
5 rm ☲ – ♦£43/45 ♦♦£66/70
Rest – (dinner only) (residents only) Menu £ 20 **s**
♦ An attractive stone building, once a toll house and later a manse. Comfortable lounge and a bar area, well stocked with whiskies. Bedrooms have a cosy snug feel.

at Balquhidder West : 4m. by A84 – ⊠ Stirling

XX **Monachyle Mhor** with rm 🌿 ≤ 🛋 🕭 ⒴ ℰ⒴ P̲ VISA ◍

West : 4 m ⊠ FK19 8PQ – ℰ (01877) 384 622 – www.mhor.net
– monachyle@mhor.net – Fax (01877) 384 305
– Closed 3 weeks January-February
14 rm (dinner included) ☲ – ♦£143 ♦♦£197
Rest – (booking essential) Menu £48 (dinner) – Carte £ 29/34
♦ Single track winds past Lochs to this enchanting location. Chef is passionate about the area's produce. Meat from their 1,000 sheep and 200 cattle; home grown veg. Dinner to be savoured. Contemporary rooms contrast with rural surroundings; breakfast taken seriously.

LOCHGILPHEAD – Argyll and Bute – 501 D 15 – pop. 2 326 ■ Scotland 27 B2

▶ Edinburgh 130 mi – Glasgow 84 mi – Oban 38 mi
🛈 Lochnell St ℰ (08707) 200 618 (April-October),
   info@lochgilphead.visitscotland.org
🖼 Blarbuie Rd, ℰ (01546) 602 340
◐ Loch Fyne★★, E : 3½ m. by A 83

Empire Travel Lodge without rest ✆ ⒴ P̲ VISA ◍ ⓞ

Union St ⊠ PA31 8JS – ℰ (01546) 602 381 – www.empirelodge.co.uk
– enquiries@empirelodge.co.uk – Fax (01546) 606 606
– Closed Christmas-New Year
9 rm ☲ – ♦£35 ♦♦£65
♦ Former cinema whose interior walls are decorated with classic posters of screen stars. Provides simple, spacious, good value accommodation.

at Cairnbaan Northwest : 2¼ m. by A 816 on B 841 – ⊠ Lochgilphead

🎏 **Cairnbaan** 🎏 ⒴ Ⓕ P̲ VISA ◍

⊠ PA31 8SJ – ℰ (01546) 603 668 – www.cairnbaan.com – info@cairnbaan.com
– Fax (01546) 606 045
12 rm ☲ – ♦£80 ♦♦£132 **Rest** – (bar lunch) Carte £ 19/30
♦ 18C former coaching inn overlooking the Crinan Canal. Comfortable lounges and panelled bar. Well-equipped, individually decorated rooms, some in attractive contemporary style. Light, airy restaurant with modern art decorating the walls.

LOCHINVER – Highland – 501 E 9 – ⊠ Lairg ■ Scotland 30 C1

▶ Edinburgh 251 mi – Inverness 95 mi – Wick 105 mi
🛈 Assynt Visitor Centre, Main St ℰ (01845) 2255121 (April-October),
   info@visitscotland.com
◉ Village★
◐ Loch Assynt★★, E : 6 m. by A 837

Inver Lodge ≤ 🛋 ⒴ 🕭 ⒴ P̲ VISA ◍ AE ⓞ

Iolaire Rd ⊠ IV27 4LU – ℰ (01571) 844 496 – www.inverlodge.com
– stay@inverlodge.com – Fax (01571) 844 395 – April-October
20 rm ☲ – ♦£100 ♦♦£200 **Rest** – (bar lunch) Menu £ 48
♦ Family owned hotel set in hillside above the village, surrounded by unspoilt wilderness. Choice of spacious lounges. All the bedrooms have good views. Restaurant boasts wonderful outlook.

SCOTLAND

SCOTLAND

⌂ **Ruddyglow Park Country House** ⏚ ≪ 🚗 🤚 🛁 📶 📶 **P** VISA ⓪ AE
Assynt, Northeast : 6 ¾ m. on A 837 ⊠ *IV27 4HB –* ☏ *(01571) 822216*
– www.ruddyglowpark.com – info@ruddyglowpark.com
– Fax (01571) 822216
3 rm ⌷ – †£100/120 ††£140/160
Rest – (by arrangement) Menu £45
♦ Honey yellow house in superb location; excellent Loch and mountain views. Two
traditional bedrooms and one – in a log cabin – more modern. Good facilities and
extra touches. Communal dining; home cooked dishes with a Scottish base.

⌂ **Veyatie** without rest ⏚ ≪ 🚗 🛁 📶 **P**
66 Baddidarroch, West : 1 ¼ m. by Baddidarroch rd ⊠ *IV27 4LP –* ☏ *(01571)*
844424 – www.veyatie-scotland.co.uk – veyatie-lochinver@tiscali.co.uk
– Fax (01571) 844424 – April-December
3 rm ⌷ – †£50/55 ††£60/70
♦ An idyllic secluded haven with stunning views of Loch Inver Bay and mountains.
Lovely conservatory. Friendly welcome, relaxing gardens and simple bedrooms.

⌂ **Davar** without rest ≪ 🚗 🛁 **P**
Baddidarroch Rd, West : ½ m. on Baddidarroch rd ⊠ *IV27 4LJ –* ☏ *(01571)*
844501 – jean@davar36.fsnet.co.uk – March-November
3 rm ⌷ – †£35/40 ††£60
♦ Purpose-built guesthouse in an excellent position which affords wonderful views
of Loch Inver Bay and Suilven. Homely and simple with well-kept bedrooms and
communal breakfast.

XX **The Albannach** (Colin Craig & Lesley Crosfield) with rm ⏚ ≪ 🚗 🛁
☸ *Baddidarroch, West : 1 m. by Baddidarroch rd* 📶 **P** VISA ⓪
⊠ *IV27 4LP –* ☏ *(01571) 844407 – info@thealbannach.co.uk – Fax (01571)*
844285 – Closed January-February
5 rm (dinner included) ⌷ – †£175/200 ††£234/260
Rest – (closed Monday and Tuesday-Wednesday November-December and
March) (dinner only) (booking essential for non-residents) (set menu)
Menu £50
Spec. Ragoût of langoustine with lobster and ginger. Roast saddle of roe deer,
truffled squash, potato galette and port sauce. Citrus soufflé with bitter chocolate ice cream.
♦ Pleasant restaurant and conservatory set on the hillside; exceptional views. The
very best Scottish ingredients are impressively showcased on the traditional 5 course
menu. Stylish, contemporary bedrooms with modern bathrooms.

> If breakfast is included the ⌷ symbol appears after the number of rooms.

LOCHMADDY – Western Isles Outer Hebrides – **501** Y 11 – **see Uist (Isles of)**

LOCHRANZA – North Ayrshire – **501** E 16 – **see Arran (Isle of)**

LOCKERBIE – Dumfries and Galloway – **501** – pop. 4 009   26 **C3**
🚉 Edinburgh 74 mi – Carlisle 27 mi – Dumfries 13 mi – Glasgow 73 mi
🛈 Corrie Rd, ☏ (01576) 203 363
🛈 Lochmaben Castlehill Gate, ☏ (01387) 810 552

🏨 **Dryfesdale Country House** ≪ 🚗 🛁 rm, 📶 🛗 **P** VISA ⓪ AE
Northwest : 1 m. by Glasgow rd off B 7076 ⊠ *DG11 2SF –* ☏ *(01576) 202427*
– www.dryfesdalehotel.co.uk – reception@dryfesdalehotel.co.uk – Fax (01576)
204187
28 rm ⌷ – †£75/85 ††£110   **Rest** – Carte £23/33
♦ Extended, commercially oriented 17C house in a rural setting with pleasant countryside views. Lounge bar with fine selection of malts. Refurbished rooms are modish
and smart. Enjoy the vistas from renovated dining room.

LUSS – Argyll and Bute – **501** G 15 – pop. 402 📗 *Scotland*   27 **B2**

- ▶ Edinburgh 89 mi – Glasgow 26 mi – Oban 65 mi
- ◎ Village ★
- ◎ E : Loch Lomond ★★

🏨 **Lodge on the Loch**   < 🗔 🕸 ⅗ rm, 🕿 ⚄ **P** *VISA* ⚫ ⒶⒺ ⓪
⊠ G83 8PA – ℰ (01436) 860 201 – www.loch-lomond.co.uk
– res@loch-lomond.co.uk – Fax (01436) 860 203
46 rm (dinner included) ⌑ – ♦£ 188 ♦♦£ 189/208 – 1 suite
Rest *Colquhoun's* – (light lunch Monday-Saturday) Menu £ 30 **s**
– Carte £ 17/22 **s**
♦ Busy family run establishment in a superb spot on the shores of Loch Lomond.
Most of the cosy pine panelled rooms have balconies; some of them can boast a
sauna. Restaurant and bar lounge carefully designed on two levels, opening the view
to every table.

MAIDENS – South Ayrshire – **501** F 18   25 **A2**

- ▶ Edinburgh 99 mi – Glasgow 53 mi – Maybole 7 mi

🏠 **Wildings**   < 🎟 rest, ⅗ **P** *VISA* ⚫
21 Harbour Rd ⊠ KA26 9NR – ℰ (01655) 331 401
– bookings@wildingsrestaurant.co.uk – Fax (01655) 331 330 – Closed Christmas
and New Year
12 rm ⌑ – ♦£ 50 ♦♦£ 90   **Rest** – Seafood – Carte £ 15/23
♦ Don't be put off by dated exterior. Popular, bustling hotel adjacent to harbour in
coastal hamlet. Refurbished bedrooms; those at front overlook sea. Ground floor
restaurant; window tables popular. Seafood orientated menus with plenty of daily
specials.

MAYBOLE – South Ayrshire – **501** 402 – pop. 4 552 📗 *Scotland*   25 **A2**

- ▶ Edinburgh 93 mi – Ayr 10 mi – New Galloway 35 mi – Stranraer 42 mi
- 🄵 Memorial Park, ℰ (01655) 889 770
- ◎ Culzean Castle ★ **AC** (setting ★★★, Oval Staircase ★★) W : 5 m. by B 7023
  and A 719

🏠 **Ladyburn** ⌂   < 🚗 🐎 ⅗ **P** *VISA* ⚫
South : 5½ m. by B 7023 and B 741 (Girvan rd) on Walled Garden rd
⊠ KA19 7SG – ℰ (01655) 740 585 – www.ladyburn.co.uk – jh@ladyburn.co.uk
– Closed Christmas-New Year
5 rm ⌑ – ♦£ 60/80 ♦♦£ 120/140
Rest – (by arrangement) (residents only set menu only) Menu £ 27
♦ Friendly and relaxed family run dower house in beautiful rose gardens. Elegant,
bay windowed drawing room, firelit library, charming rooms with antique furniture
and prints. Richly flavoured Scottish or Gallic dishes served at candlelit tables.

MELROSE – Scottish Borders – **501** L 17 – pop. 1 656 📗 *Scotland*   26 **D2**

- ▶ Edinburgh 38 mi – Hawick 19 mi – Newcastle upon Tyne 70 mi
- 🄸 Abbey House, Abbey St ℰ (01835) 863170, melrose@visitscotland.com
- 🄵 Melrose Dingleton Dingleton Rd, ℰ (01896) 822 855
- ◎ Town ★ - Abbey ★★ (decorative sculpture ★★★) **AC**
- ◎ Eildon Hills (⁂ ★★★) – Scott's View ★★ – Abbotsford ★★ **AC**, W : 4½ m. by
  A 6091 and B 6360 – Dryburgh Abbey ★★ **AC** (setting ★★★), SE : 4 m. by
  A 6091 – Tweed Valley ★★. Bowhill ★★ **AC**, SW : 11½ m. by A 6091, A 7
  and A 708 – Thirlestane Castle (plasterwork ceilings ★★) **AC**, NE : 21 m. by
  A 6091 and A 68

🏨 **Burts**   🚗 🐎 ⚄ **P** *VISA* ⚫
Market Square ⊠ TD6 9PL – ℰ (01896) 822 285 – www.burtshotel.co.uk
– burtshotel@aol.com – Fax (01896) 822 870
– Closed 26 December and 2-3 January
20 rm ⌑ – ♦£ 60/85 ♦♦£ 120   **Rest** – Carte £ 20/30
♦ One-time coaching inn on main square - traditionally appointed and family run.
Unpretentious rooms behind a neat black and white façade, brightened by pretty
window boxes. Cosy, clubby restaurant.

The Townhouse
Market Sq ⊠ TD6 9PQ – ℰ (01896) 822 645 – www.thetownhousemelrose.co.uk
– enquiries@thetownhousemelrose.co.uk – Fax (01896) 823 474 – Closed 1 week
January
11 rm � – †£85/114 ††£114/130
Rest – Menu £23/29
Rest *Brasserie* – Menu £23/30 – Carte £19/33
♦ Refreshed and refurbished, this 17C townhouse has a spruce, clean-lined appeal throughout. The bedrooms continue the theme of simple, well-kept attention to detail. Warm and intimate restaurant or informal brasserie options.

at Gattonside North : 2 m. by B 6374 on B 6360 – ⊠ Melrose

Fauhope House *without rest* ⏚
East : ¼ m. by B 6360 taking unmarked lane to the right of Monkswood Rd at edge of village ⊠ TD6 9LU – ℰ (01896) 823 184 – info@fauhopehouse.com – Fax (01896) 823 184
3 rm ⊡ – †£65/70 ††£90/100
♦ Melrose Abbey just visible through the trees of this charming 19C country house with its antiques and fine furniture. Valley views at breakfast. Flower strewn, stylish rooms.

Red = Pleasant. Look for the red ※ and 🏠 symbols.

METHVEN – Perth and Kinross – **501** J 14 – **see Perth**

MOFFAT – Dumfries and Galloway – **501** J 17 – pop. **2 135** ▐ *Scotland*   **26 C2**
🛣 Edinburgh 61 mi – Carlisle 43 mi – Dumfries 22 mi – Glasgow 60 mi
🛈 Churchgate ℰ (01683) 220620 (Easter-October),
moffat@dgtb.visitscotland.com
🏌 Coatshill, ℰ (01683) 220020
◎ Grey Mare's Tail★★, NE : 9 m. by A 708

Hartfell House
Hartfell Crescent ⊠ DG10 9AL – ℰ (01683) 220 153 – www.hartfellhouse.co.uk
– enquires@hartfellhouse.co.uk – Closed 10 days October and Christmas
7 rm ⊡ – †£40/50 ††£70
Rest *The Lime Tree* – (closed Sunday dinner and Monday) (dinner only and Sunday lunch) Menu £28
♦ Welcoming house with immense charm. Plenty of original fittings on display, including ornate cornicing and marquetry on the doors. Good sized bedrooms have a homely feel. Large dining room with huge windows and wood panelling serves appealing, brasserie menu.

Bridge House
Well Rd, East : ¾ m. by Selkirk rd (A 708) taking left hand turn before bridge
⊠ DG10 9JT – ℰ (01683) 220 558 – www.bridgehousemoffat.co.uk
– info@bridgehousemoffat.co.uk – Closed Christmas-mid Feburary
7 rm ⊡ – †£50 ††£70/105   **Rest** – (by arrangement) Menu £28
♦ Personally run early Victorian guesthouse. Lots of room to stretch out in comfy, modish lounge overlooking garden. Front two bedrooms have best views, one boasts four poster. Local, seasonal menus in linen-laid dining room.

Well View
Ballplay Rd, East : ¾ m. by Selkirk rd (A 708) ⊠ DG10 9JU – ℰ (01683) 220 184
– www.wellview.co.uk – info@wellview.co.uk – Fax (01683) 220 088
3 rm ⊡ – †£65/80 ††£90/120
Rest – (by arrangement, communal dining) Menu £38
♦ Well established, family run 19C house. The bedrooms are the strong point: traditionally furnished, they're of a good size and most comfortable.

SCOTLAND

MONTROSE – Angus – **501** M 13 – **pop. 10 845** ▊ *Scotland* 28 **D2**

▶ Edinburgh 92 mi – Aberdeen 39 mi – Dundee 29 mi

🛈 Bridge St ✆ (01674) 673232 (Easter-September),
enquiries@angusanddundee.co.uk

▦ Traill Drive, ✆ (01674) 672932

☖ Edzell Castle★ (The Pleasance★★★) **AC**, NW : 17 m. by A 935 and B 966 –
Cairn O'Mount Road★ (≤★★) N : 17 m. by B 966 and B 974 – Brechin
(Round Tower★) W : 7 m. by A 935 – Aberlemno (Aberlemno Stones★,
Pictish sculptured stones★) W : 13 m. by A 935 and B 9134

⌂ **36 The Mall** without rest   🚗 ⅏ 🎙️ *VISA* ⓪ AE

▥ *36 The Mall, North : ½ m. by A 92 at junction with North Esk Road ⊠ DD10 8SS
– ✆ (01674) 673646 – www.36themall.co.uk – enquiries@36themall.co.uk
– Fax (01674) 673646*
3 rm � ⊆ – †£45/55 ††£56/70
♦ Bay windowed 19C former manse with pleasant conservatory lounge. Impressive
plate collection the talking point of communal breakfast room. Well-kept rooms with
high ceilings.

MOTHERWELL – North Lanarkshire – **501** I 16   25 **B1**

▶ Edinburgh 38 mi – Glasgow 12 mi

🏨 **Alona**   🛗 ⅙ rm, 🅐🅒 rest, 🎙️ 🔥 🅿 *VISA* ⓪ AE

*Strathclyde Country Park, Northwest : 4½ m. by A 721 and B 7070 off A 725
⊠ ML1 3RT – ✆ (01698) 333888 – www.alonahotel.co.uk
– reservations@alonahotel.co.uk – Fax (01698) 338720*
51 rm ⊆ – †£128 ††£128   **Rest** – Menu £8/17 – Carte £16/27
♦ Attractively set modern hotel in 1500 acres of Strathclyde Country Park. Conservatory atrium with open-plan lounge and bar. Good-sized bedrooms exuding
contemporary taste. Restaurant affords pleasant lakeside views.

MUIR OF ORD – Highland – **501** G 11 – **pop. 1 812**   30 **C2**

▶ Edinburgh 173 mi – Inverness 10 mi – Wick 121 mi

▦ Great North Rd, ✆ (01463) 870825

⌂ **Dower House** ⌂   🚗 🎙️ 🅿 *VISA* ⓪

*Highfield, North : 1 m. on A 862 ⊠ IV6 7XN – ✆ (01463) 870090
– www.thedowerhouse.co.uk – enquiries@thedowerhouse.co.uk – Fax (01463)
870090 – Closed 25 December*
3 rm ⊆ – †£75/120 ††£90/140 – 1 suite
Rest – (booking essential for non-residents) (set menu only, lunch by
arrangement) Menu 40 **s**
♦ Personally run, part 17C house in mature garden. Stacked bookshelves, soft fireside
armchairs, cosy bedrooms and fresh flowers: a relaxed but well-ordered country
home. Dining room offers careful cooking of fine fresh ingredients.

MULL (Isle of) – Argyll and Bute – **501** B/C – **pop. 1 841** ▊ *Scotland* 27 **A2**

⛴ from Fionnphort to Isle of Iona (Caledonian MacBrayne Ltd) frequent
services daily (10 mn) – from Pierowall to Papa Westray (Orkney Ferries
Ltd) (summer only) (25 mn)

⛴ from Craignure to Oban (Caledonian MacBrayne Ltd) frequent services
daily (45 mn) – from Fishnish to Lochaline (Mainland) (Caledonian
MacBrayne Ltd) frequent services daily (15 mn) – from Tobermory to Isle of
Tiree (Scarinish) via Isle of Coll (Arinagour) (Caledonian MacBrayne Ltd)
3 weekly (2 h 30 mn) – from Tobermory to Kilchoan (Caledonian MacBrayne
Ltd) 4 daily (summer only) (35 mn)

🛈 The Pier, Craignure ✆ (08707) 200610, info@mull.visitscotland.com - Main
Street, Tobermory ✆ (01688) 302182 (April-October),
info@tobermory.visitscotland.com

▣ Craignure Scallastle, ✆ (01688) 302517

◉ Island★ - Calgary Bay★★ – Torosay Castle **AC** (Gardens★ ≤★)

☖ Isle of Iona★ (Maclean's Cross★, St Oran's Chapel★, St Martin's High
Cross★, Infirmary Museum★ **AC** (Cross of St John★))

MULL (Isle of)

Bunessan – Argyll and Bute 27 **A2**

✗ **Reef** *VISA* ❶❷
Main St ✉ PA67 6DG – ☎ (01681) 700 291 – Fax (01681) 700 534 – Closed November-April, Saturday lunch and Sunday
Rest – Seafood – Carte £ 16/33
♦ Don't be put off by simple tea-room façade and standard menu. Come here to enjoy the supremely fresh, excellent value daily blackboard seafood specials - owner is a fisherman.

Craignure – Argyll and Bute 27 **B2**

⌂ **Birchgrove** without rest ☜ ＜ 🚗 ♒ ⁿⁱ **P** *VISA* ❶❷
Lochdon, Southeast : 3 m. on A 849 ✉ PA64 6AP – ☎ (01680) 812 364
– www.birchgrovebandb.co.uk – birchgrove.mull@btinternet.com
– 21 March-October
3 rm ⌑ – †£ 45/56 ††£ 60/68
♦ Modern guesthouse with landscaped gardens in peaceful setting with good views. Close to ferry pier. Clean, well-kept rooms, all boasting pleasant island outlook.

Gruline – Argyll and Bute 27 **A2**

⌂ **Gruline Home Farm** ☜ ＜ 🚗 **P** *VISA* ❶❷
✉ PA71 6HR – ☎ (01680) 300 581 – www.gruline.com – boo@gruline.com
– April-November
3 rm ⌑ – †£ 158 ††£ 200
Rest – (by arrangement, communal dining) Menu £ 38
♦ Spot deer, eagles and buzzards in utter tranquillity at this delightful farm, located off the beaten track with fine views over nearby mountains. Beautifully appointed rooms. Creative cooking brings out true flavour of island produce.

Tiroran – Argyll and Bute 27 **A2**

🏠 **Tiroran House** ☜ ＜ 🚗 ♪ ⁿ ⁿⁱ **P** *VISA* ❶❷
✉ PA69 6ES – ☎ (01681) 705 232 – www.tiroran.com – info@tiroran.com
– Fax (01681) 705 240
7 rm ⌑ – †£ 135 ††£ 190
Rest – (dinner only) (booking essential) (residents only) Menu £ 40
♦ Attractive whitewashed hotel sited in remote location with superb views across Loch Scridain. Well-decorated lounges with country house style. Individually appointed rooms. Home-cooked dinners in vine-covered dining room or conservatory.

Tobermory – Argyll and Bute – pop. 980 27 **A2**
🛈 Erray Rd, ☎ (01688) 302 387

🏠 **Tobermory** ＜ ♿ rm, ⁿⁱ *VISA* ❶❷
53 Main St ✉ PA75 6NT – ☎ (01688) 302 091 – www.thetobermoryhotel.com
– tobhotel@tinyworld.co.uk – Fax (01688) 302 254 – Closed 13 January-9 February and 1 week Christmas
16 rm ⌑ – †£ 45/49 ††£ 90/122
Rest *Waters Edge* – (dinner only) (booking essential for non-residents) Menu £ 32
♦ Pink-painted, converted fishing cottages - cosy, well-run and informal - on the pretty quayside. Soft toned bedrooms in cottage style, most overlooking the bay. Intimate setting: linen-clad tables and subtly nautical décor.

⌂ **Brockville** without rest ＜ 🚗 ♒ ⁿⁱ **P**
Raeric Rd, by Back Brae ✉ PA75 6RS – ☎ (01688) 302 741
– www.brockville-tobermory.co.uk – helen@brockville-tobermory.co.uk
– Fax (01688) 302 741
3 rm ⌑ – †£ 40/70 ††£ 60/70
♦ Modern guesthouse in the residential part of town. The communal breakfast room has good views over the sea. Cottagey rooms have extra touches including videos and CDs.

XX **Highland Cottage** with rm   📶 P VISA ⬤⬤

Breadalbane St, via B 8073 ⊠ PA75 6PD – ℰ (01688) 302 030
– www.highlandcottage.co.uk – davidandjo@highlandcottage.co.uk – Closed
January-15 March
6 rm � – †£120/140 ††£165/185
Rest – (dinner only) (booking essential for non-residents) Menu £45
♦ Modern cottage near the harbour. Prettily set dining room shows the same care
and attention as the locally sourced menu. Individually styled rooms with good views.

NAIRN – Highland – **501** I 11 – **pop. 8 418** ▮ *Scotland*   30 **D2**

▶ Edinburgh 172 mi – Aberdeen 91 mi – Inverness 16 mi
🚏 Seabank Rd, ℰ (01667) 453 208
🏌 Nairn Dunbar Lochloy Rd, ℰ (01667) 452 741
◉ Forres (Sueno's Stone★★) E : 11 m. by A 96 and B 9011 – Cawdor Castle★
AC, S : 5½ m. by B 9090 – Brodie Castle★ **AC**, E : 6 m. by A 96. Fort
George★, W : 8 m. by A 96, B 9092 and B 9006

🏨 **Golf View**   ← 🛏 ▦ ♨ ᴸᵅ ※ 🛗 ⇄ 🅐🅒 rest, ⚒ P VISA ⬤⬤ AE

The Seafront ⊠ IV12 4HD – ℰ (01667) 452 301 – www.swallowhotels.com
– gm.golfview@crerarmgmt.com – Fax (01667) 455 267
41 rm � – †£85/170 ††£140/220 – 1 suite
Rest Restaurant – (dinner only) Menu £33 – Carte £32/42
Rest Conservatory – Carte £16/31
♦ Non-golfers may prefer the vista of the Moray Firth from one of the sea-view rooms
or a poolside lounger. Smart, traditional accommodation, up-to-date gym and beauty
salon. Half-panelled dining room. Stylish, spacious conservatory restaurant.

🏠 **Claymore House**   🛏 & rm, 📶 P VISA ⬤⬤ AE

45 Seabank Rd ⊠ IV12 4EY – ℰ (01667) 453 731
– www.claymorehousehotel.com – claymorehouse@btconnect.com – Fax (01667)
455 290 – Closed 2-9 January
13 rm – †£50/80 ††£95/120 – 2 suites   **Rest** – (bar lunch) Carte £16/31
♦ A privately-run, extended 19C house in a residential area. Comfortable lounge and
conservatory. Modern rooms in warm colours are quieter at the rear. Neatly laid-out
dining room: choose from a range of traditional Scottish favourites.

🏠 **Boath House**   ← 🛏 🐾 ♨ & rm, 📶 P VISA ⬤⬤ AE
🕃
Auldearn, East : 2 m. on A 96 ⊠ IV12 5TE – ℰ (01667) 454 896
– www.boath-house.com – info@boath-house.com – Fax (01667) 455 469
– Closed 1 week Christmas
8 rm (dinner included) � – †£310 ††£370
Rest – (closed for non-residents Monday-Wednesday lunch) (booking
essential) Carte £30/65
Spec. Confit of salmon with beetroot jelly and quail's egg. Red deer with peas,
chanterelles and garlic. Rhubarb spiced bread with sorbet and jelly.
♦ 1820s neo-classical mansion, owned by a charming couple, hosts modern Highland
art collections. Intimate, elegant rooms may have half-tester beds or views of the
trout lake. Dining room with 18C garden views: precise, accomplished cooking in a
modern style.

🏠 **Sunny Brae**   ← 🛏 🏠 📶 P VISA ⬤⬤

Marine Rd ⊠ IV12 4EA – ℰ (01667) 452 309 – www.sunnybraehotel.com
– reservations@sunnybraehotel.com – Fax (01667) 454 860
– Closed 21 December-January
8 rm – †£69/118 ††£90/140
Rest – (dinner only and lunch Thursday-Friday) Carte approx. £28
♦ Behind an unassuming façade, this family-owned hotel offers sizeable, neatly kept
bedrooms in cheerful patterns - many, like the terrace, have views of the shore. Light,
summery dining room; traditional Scottish menus.

⌂ **Bracadale House** without rest   ⌐ ⅏ **P** _VISA_ ⚏
⌘ Albert St ⊠ IV12 4HF – ℰ (01667) 452 547 – www.bracadalehouse.com
– hannah@bracadalehouse.com – mid March - September
3 rm ⌗ – ♦£50/60 ♦♦£55/60

♦ This elegant Victorian house, near the beach, is enthusiastically run by a friendly owner. There's an attractive first floor lounge and rooms finished with a tasteful palette.

✕ **The Classroom**   _VISA_ ⚏ AE
1 Cawdor St ⊠ IV12 4QD – ℰ (01667) 455 999 – www.theclassroombistro.co.uk
– enquiries@cawdortavern.info – Fax (01667) 455 999 – Closed 25 December and 1 January
Rest – Carte £18/28

♦ Extended former school house in town centre. Split level modern brasserie style with L-shaped bar and pictures of pupils on the walls. Extensive menu with daily specials.

NETHERLEY – Aberdeenshire – 501 N 13 – **see Stonehaven**

NEW LANARK – South Lanarkshire – 501 I 17 ▌ Scotland   25 **B2**
▶ Edinburgh 44 mi – Dumfries 55 mi – Glasgow 31 mi
◉ Town ★★

🏢 **New Lanark Mill**   ≼ ▦ ☞ ♨ 👙 ⅙ rm, 🔐 **P** _VISA_ ⚏ AE ⓪
Mill One, New Lanark Mills ⊠ ML11 9DB – ℰ (01555) 667 200
– www.newlanark.org – hotel@newlanark.org – Fax (01555) 667 222
38 rm ⌗ – ♦£85 ♦♦£129
Rest _Mill One_ – (carvery lunch Sunday, bar lunch Monday-Saturday) Menu £28 **s**

♦ Converted Clydeside cotton mill on the riverside in this superbly restored Georgian village, a World Heritage site. Usefully equipped, modern accommodation. Formal restaurant overlooking the river.

NEWTON STEWART – Dumfries and Galloway – 501 G 19   25 **B3**
– **pop. 3 573** ▌ Scotland
▶ Edinburgh 131 mi – Dumfries 51 mi – Glasgow 87 mi – Stranraer 24 mi
🛈 Dashwood Sq ℰ (01671) 402431 (Easter-October), newtonstewart@dgtb.visitscotland.com
⛳ Minnigaff Kirroughtree Ave, ℰ (01671) 402 172
⛳ Wigtownshire County Glenluce Mains of Park, ℰ (01581) 300 420
◎ Galloway Forest Park★, Queen's Way★ (Newton Stewart to New Galloway) N : 19 m. by A 712

🏠 **Kirroughtree House** ⌖   ≼ ⌐ ⅏ 🛎 ⅋ **P** _VISA_ ⚏ AE
Northeast : 1½ m. by A 75 on A 712 ⊠ DG8 6AN – ℰ (01671) 402 141
– www.kirroughtreehouse.co.uk – info@kirroughtreehouse.co.uk – Fax (01671) 402425 – Closed 2 January-mid February
15 rm ⌗ – ♦£105/145 ♦♦£190/240 – 2 suites
Rest – (booking essential for non-residents) Menu £35 (dinner) **s** – Carte lunch £21/28 **s**

♦ Grand 1719 mansion dominates acres of sculpted garden. Well-proportioned bedrooms; firelit lounge with antiques, period oils and French windows leading to the croquet lawn. Elegant fine dining, in keeping with formal grandeur of the house.

⌂ **Rowallan**   ⌐ ⅏ ⅋ **P**
Corsbie Rd, via Jubilee Rd off Dashwood Sq ⊠ DG8 6JB – ℰ (01671) 402 520
– www.rowallan.co.uk – enquiries@rowallan.co.uk – Fax (01671) 402 520
6 rm ⌗ – ♦£40/45 ♦♦£66/70   **Rest** – (by arrangement) Menu £18

♦ Victorian house in attractive large garden not far from town centre. Large lounge with bar; meals served in conservatory. Brightly decorated bedrooms.

NORTH BAY – Western Isles – **see Barra (Isle of)**

SCOTLAND

NORTH BERWICK – East Lothian – **501** L 15 – pop. 6 223 ▯ *Scotland*   26 **D1**

> ▷ Edinburgh 24 mi – Newcastle upon Tyne 102 mi
> 🛈 Quality St 𝒸 (01620) 892197
> 🔟 North Berwick Beach Rd, West Links, 𝒸 (01620) 890 312
> 🔟 Glen East Links, Tantallon Terrace, 𝒸 (01620) 892 726
> ◎ North Berwick Law (※★★★) S : 1 m. - Tantallon Castle★★ (clifftop site★★★) **AC**, E : 3½ m. by A 198 – Dirleton★ (Castle★ **AC**) SW : 2½ m. by A 198. Museum of Flight★, S : 6 m. by B 1347 – Preston Mill★, S : 8½ m. by A 198 and B 1047 – Tyningham★, S : 7 m. by A 198 – Coastal road from North Berwick to Portseton★, SW : 13 m. by A 198 and B 1348

⌂   **Glebe House** without rest ⅏   🖼 🕸 **P**
Law Rd ⊠ EH39 4PL – 𝒸 (01620) 892 608 – www.glebehouse-nb.co.uk
– gwenscott@glebehouse-nb.co.uk – Closed 25-26 December
3 rm ☷ – ✝£70 ✝✝£100
♦ Owned by a likeable couple, a classically charming 1780s manse in secluded gardens. En suite rooms are pleasantly unfussy and well-kept. Breakfasts at a long communal table.

⌂   **Beach Lodge** without rest   ≼ 🕸
🖭 *5 Beach Rd ⊠ EH39 4AB – 𝒸 (01620) 892 257 – www.beachlodge.co.uk*
– william@beachlodge.co.uk
5 rm ☷ – ✝£40/60 ✝✝£80/85
♦ Friendly and well-run: breakfast room and compact, modern bedrooms share an appealing, clean-lined style. All rooms have fridges and videos, one overlooks the sea.

NORTH QUEENSFERRY – Fife – **501** J 15 – pop. 1 102   28 **C3**

> ▷ Edinburgh 13 mi – Dunfermline 6 mi – Glasgow 45 mi

✗   **The Wee Restaurant**   𝚅𝙸𝚂𝙰 ◍◎ 𝙰𝙴
🈂 *17 Main St ⊠ KY11 1JG – 𝒸 (01383) 616 263 – www.theweerestaurant.co.uk*
– Closed 25 December, 1 January and Monday
Rest – Menu £16 (lunch) **s** – Carte (dinner) £28/31 **s**
♦ Small, intimate restaurant, as suggested by its name. Simple wooden tables. Delightful local photos. Tasty, carefully prepared food with a French flavour. Chatty service.

NORTH UIST – Western Isles Outer Hebrides – **501** X/Y – see Uist (Isles of)

OBAN – Argyll and Bute – **501** D 14 – pop. 8 120 ▯ *Scotland*   27 **B2**

> ▷ Edinburgh 123 mi – Dundee 116 mi – Glasgow 93 mi – Inverness 118 mi
> **Access** Access to Glasgow by helicopter
> ⛴ to Isle of Mull (Craignure) (Caledonian MacBrayne Ltd) (45 mn) – to Isle of Tiree (Scarinish) via Isle of Mull (Tobermory) and Isle of Coll (Arinagour) (Caledonian MacBrayne Ltd) – to Isle of Islay (Port Askaig) and Kintyre Peninsula (Kennacraig) via Isle of Colonsay (Scalasaig) (Caledonian MacBrayne Ltd) (summer only) – to Isle of Lismore (Achnacroish) (Caledonian MacBrayne Ltd) 2-3 daily (except Sunday) (55 mn) – to Isle of Colonsay (Scalasaig) (Caledonian MacBrayne Ltd) 3 weekly (2 h)
> 🛈 Church Building, Argyll Sq 𝒸 (08707) 200630, info@oban.org.uk
> 🔟 Glencruitten Glencruitten Rd, 𝒸 (01631) 562 868
> ◎ Loch Awe★★, SE : 17 m. by A 85 – Bonawe Furnace★, E : 12 m. by A 85 – Cruachan Power Station★ **AC**, E : 16 m. by A 85 – Seal and Marine Centre★ **AC**, N : 14 m. by A 828

🏯   **Manor House**   ≼ 🖼 🛜 **P** 𝚅𝙸𝚂𝙰 ◍◎ 𝙰𝙴
Gallanach Rd ⊠ PA34 4LS – 𝒸 (01631) 562 087 – www.manorhouseoban.com
– info@manorhouseoban.com – Fax (01631) 563 053 – Closed 25-26 December
11 rm ☷ – ✝£114/172 ✝✝£186/239
Rest – (lunch by arrangement) Menu £36
♦ Period furniture and colour schemes bring out the character of this 18C dower house, once part of the Argyll ducal estate. Individual rooms, most with fine views of the bay. Green and tartan restaurant warmed by an ancient range.

SCOTLAND

OBAN

The Barriemore without rest

Corran Esplanade ⊠ PA34 5AQ – ℰ (01631) 566 356
– www.barriemore-hotel.co.uk – reception@barriemore-hotel.co.uk – Fax (01631)
571 084 – Closed January
11 rm ⊆ – †£45/70 ††£75/96

♦ Gabled 1890s house overlooking town and islands. A comfortable blend of modern
and period styling - front bedrooms are larger and look towards Oban Bay, Kerrera
and Mull.

Glenburnie House without rest

Corran Esplanade ⊠ PA34 5AQ – ℰ (01631) 562 089 – www.glenburnie.co.uk
– graeme.strachan@btinternet.com – Fax (01631) 562 089 – March-November
12 rm ⊆ – †£45/80 ††£78/100

♦ Bay-windowed Victorian house has enviable views over the bay. Pleasant lounge
with a hint of homely informality and usefully equipped rooms, one with a four-
poster bed.

Alltavona without rest

Corran Esplanade ⊠ PA34 5AQ – ℰ (01631) 565 067 – www.alltavona.co.uk
– carol@alltavona.co.uk – Fax (01631) 565 067 – Closed 2 weeks Christmas
10 rm ⊆ – †£25/90 ††£75/90

♦ 19C villa on smart esplanade with fine views of Oban Bay. Attractively furnished
interiors in keeping with the house's age. Fine oak staircase and individually styled
rooms.

Coast

104 George St ⊠ PA34 5NT – ℰ (01631) 569 900 – www.coastoban.com
– coastoban@yahoo.co.uk – Closed 25 December, 2 weeks January, Sunday lunch
and Sunday dinner in winter
Rest – Menu £15 (lunch) **s** – Carte dinner £27/37 **s**

♦ Former bank building in town centre. Contemporary interior of stripped wood
floors and khaki coloured walls. Appealing modern menus including plenty of fish
and shellfish.

The Waterfront

No 1, The Pier ⊠ PA34 4LW – ℰ (01631) 563 110 – www.waterfrontoban.co.uk
– waterfrontrestaurant@live.co.uk – Fax (01631) 562 853 – Closed 25 December
Rest – Seafood – Carte £19/34

♦ Converted quayside mission with fine views of harbour and bay; airy, open-plan
interior. Flavourful but simple seafood: blackboard specials feature the day's fresh
catch.

Ee-usk at The North Pier

The North Pier ⊠ PA34 5DQ – ℰ (01631) 565 666 – www.eeusk.com
– eeusk.fishcafe@virgin.net – Fax (01631) 570 282 – Closed 25 December and
1 January
Rest – Seafood – Carte £21/35

♦ A smart addition to the pier with its harbour proximity; excellent views of the bay
add a relaxing charm. Fresh seafood menus with daily specials.

OLDMELDRUM – Aberdeenshire – 501 N 11 ▊ Scotland

28 **D1**

▪ Edinburgh 140 mi – Aberdeen 17 mi – Inverness 87 mi
▪ Oldmeldrum Kirkbrae, ℰ (01651) 872 648
▪ Haddo House★, NE : 9 m. by B 9170 on B 9005

Cromlet Hill without rest

South Rd ⊠ AB51 0AB – ℰ (01651) 872 315 – www.cromlethill.co.uk
– johnpage@cromlethill.co.uk – Fax (01651) 872 164
3 rm ⊆ – †£45/50 ††£70/80

♦ Half Georgian, half Victorian house with attractive front garden. Characterful sitting
room; smart, airy, well-equipped rooms. Communal breakfast at antique dining table.

918

ONICH – Highland – **501** E 13 – ✉ Fort William

29 **B3**

▶ Edinburgh 123 mi – Glasgow 93 mi – Inverness 79 mi – Oban 39 mi

Lodge on the Loch

≤ 🚗 ⓘ **P** 𝗩𝗜𝗦𝗔 ⓥ⓪

on A 82 ✉ PH33 6RY – ✆ (01855) 821 238 – www.lodgeontheloch.com
– info@lodgeontheloch.com – Fax (01855) 821 190
14 rm ⌷ – **♦**£ 86/118 **♦♦**£ 108/133 – 1 suite
Rest – (dinner only) Carte approx. £ 30
♦ Steam shower or sleigh bed, Shaker or Art Nouveau styling: carefully composed bijou rooms in a Victorian hotel above Loch Linnhe - classically cosy lounges have fine views. Formally set tables in the dining room and a great view south across the water.

Lochleven Seafood Café

≤ 🍽 **P** 𝗩𝗜𝗦𝗔 ⓥ⓪

Lockleven, Southeast 6½ m. by A82 on B863 ✉ PH33 6SA – ✆ (01855) 821 048
– www.lochlevenseafoodcafe.co.uk – alison@lochlevenseafoodcentre.co.uk
– Closed 2 weeks mid November, 2 weeks mid January, Sunday dinner and
Wednesday lunch in winter
Rest – Seafood – (booking advisable at dinner) Carte £ 15/30
♦ Stunning Lochside location looking toward Glencoe Mountains. Extremely fresh, simply prepared seafood; shellfish platter and razor clams a speciality. Themed evenings in winter.

ORKNEY ISLANDS – **501** KL 6/7 – **pop. 19 800** ▮ Scotland

⛴ see Kirkwall
🚢 from Burwick (South Ronaldsay) to John O'Groats (John O'Groats Ferries)
2-4 daily (40 mn) (summer only)
🚢 service between Isle of Hoy (Longhope), Isle of Hoy (Lyness), Isle of Flotta
and Houton (Orkney Ferries Ltd) – from Stromness to Scrabster (P & O
Scottish Ferries) (1-3 daily) (2 h) – from Stromness to Shetland Islands
(Lerwick) and Aberdeen (Northlink Ferries) 1-2 daily – from Kirkwall to
Westray, Stronsay via Eday and Sanday (Orkney Ferries Ltd) – from
Tingwall to Wyre via Egilsay and Rousay (Orkney Ferries Ltd) – from
Kirkwall to Shapinsay (Orkney Ferries Ltd) (25 mn) – from Stromness to Isle
of Hoy (Moness) and Graemsay (Orkney Ferries Ltd) – from Kirkwall to
North Ronaldsay (Orkney Ferries Ltd) weekly (2 h 40 mn) - from Kirkwall to
Invergordon (Orcargo Ltd) daily (8 h 30 mn) – from Houton to Isle of Hoy
(Lyness), Flotta and Longhope (Orkney Ferries Ltd)
◉ Old Man of Hoy★★★ – Islands★★ – Maes Howe★★ **AC** – Skara Brae★★ **AC**
– Kirkbuster Museum and Corrigal Farm Museum★ **AC** – Brough of Birsay★
AC – Birsay (≤★) – Ring of Brodgar★ – Unstan Cairn★

MAINLAND – Orkney Islands

Burray – Orkney Islands

31 **A3**

Sands

≤ 🛁 ⓘ **P** 𝗩𝗜𝗦𝗔 ⓥ⓪ 𝗔𝗘

✉ KW17 2SS – ✆ (01856) 731 298 – www.thesandshotel.co.uk
– info@thesandshotel.co.uk – Fax (01856) 731 303
– Accommodation closed 24-26 December
8 rm ⌷ – **♦**£ 75/85 **♦♦**£ 95/110 – 2 suites   **Rest** – (bar lunch) Carte £ 15/24
♦ Harbourside hotel – previously a fish store – in small coastal hamlet overlooking the Scapa Flow. Modern in style, with pleasant bedrooms, smart bathrooms and harbour/bay views. Nautical themed restaurant features fresh Orkney produce; plenty of local fish.

Dounby – Orkney Islands

31 **A3**

Ashleigh without rest ⚘

≤ 🚗 🛁 ⓘ **P**

Howaback Rd, South : ¾ m. by A986 ✉ KW17 2JA – ✆ (01856) 771 378
– audreypoke@hotmail.com – Fax (01856) 771 378
4 rm ⌷ – **♦**£ 34/72 **♦♦**£ 68/72
♦ Purpose built guesthouse in rural central Island location. Smart bedrooms with warm fabrics, good facilities and modern bathrooms. Lounge has pleasant loch and mountain views; neat garden.

Harray – Orkney Islands
31 **A3**

🏨 **Merkister** ⊗   ⇐ 🚗 🔍 ढ़ (¹) **P** **VISA** **⑩** **AE**
off A 986 ⊠ KW17 2LF – ℰ (01856) 771 366 – www.merkister.com
– merkister-hotel@ecosse.net – Fax (01856) 771 515
– Closed 23 December-5 January
16 rm ⊆ – †£33/75 ††£85/130
Rest – (bar lunch Monday-Saturday) (booking essential) Menu £24
– Carte £21/39
♦ Cream washed hotel in rural location, overlooking Loch Harray. Comfy lounge with leather sofas, small library and honesty bar. Spacious bedrooms with good facilities and views. Lounge bar offers snacks, more formal restaurant offers traditional menu and plenty of seafood.

⌂ **Holland House** *without rest* ⊗   ⇐ 🚗 (¹) **P** **VISA** **⑩** **AE** **①**
on St Michael's Church rd ⊠ KW17 2LQ – ℰ (01856) 771 400
– www.hollandhouseorkney.co.uk – info@hollandhouseorkney.co.uk
– Closed Christmas and New Year
3 rm ⊆ – †£48/55 ††£96
♦ Smart, very comfy late Victorian guesthouse, formerly a manse. Modern bedrooms – named after local Lochs – display warm hues and good front views. Good facilities, quality extra touches.

Kirkwall – Orkney Islands – pop. 6 206 📙 *Scotland*
31 **A3**

🛪 Kirkwall Airport : ℰ (01856) 886210, S : 3½ m
🛈 West Castle St ℰ (01856) 872856, info@visitorkney.com
🏌 Grainbank, ℰ (01856) 872 457
◎ Kirkwall★★ - St Magnus Cathedral★★ – Western Mainland★★, Eastern Mainland (Italian Chapel★) - Earl's Palace★ **AC** – Tankerness House Museum★ **AC** – Orkney Farm and Folk Museum★

🏨 **Ayre**   ♨ **P** **VISA** **⑩** **AE**
Ayre Rd ⊠ KW15 1QX – ℰ (01856) 873 001 – www.ayrehotel.co.uk
– enquiries@ayrehotel.co.uk – Fax (01856) 876 289
– Closed 25 December and 1 January
33 rm ⊆ – †£75/90 ††£110/120   **Rest** – Carte £17/32
♦ Originally 3 Victorian houses, now a traditionally styled town centre hotel. Individually designed bedrooms display co-ordinating décor and fabrics; front rooms have sea/harbour views. Traditional restaurant; menu split between steak, chicken and seafood.

🏠 **The Albert**   📱 ढ़ ⅗ (¹) **VISA** **⑩** **AE**
Mounthoolie St ⊠ KW15 1JZ – ℰ (01856) 876 000 – www.alberthotel.co.uk
– enquiries@alberthotel.co.uk – Fax (01856) 875 397
18 rm ⊆ – †£90/110 ††£110/130   **Rest** – (light lunch) Carte £18/33
♦ Recently refurbished hotel located in the centre of town. Spacious, contemporary bedrooms boast stylish furnishings, modern bathrooms and good facilities. Guest areas include a pub, small lounge bar and restaurant.

⌂ **Avalon House** *without rest*   🚗 ⅗ (¹) **P** **VISA** **⑩**
Carness Rd, Northeast : 1½ m. by Shore Street ⊠ KW15 1UE – ℰ (01856) 876 665 – www.avalon-house.co.uk – jane@avalon-house.co.uk – Closed Christmas
5 rm ⊆ – †£40/50 ††£64/74
♦ Purpose built guesthouse in small residential area just out of town. Spacious bedrooms boast modern décor and quality furniture; showers only (bath in family room). Pleasant breakfast room.

⌂ **Polrudden** *without rest*   ⅗ (¹) **P** **VISA** **⑩**
Peerie Sea Loan, West : 1 m. by Pickaquoy Rd ⊠ KW15 1UH – ℰ (01856) 874 761 – www.polrudden.com – linda@polrudden.com – Closed Christmas and New Year
7 rm ⊆ – †£40/50 ††£50/60
♦ Pebble dashed house with small lawned garden, just outside town centre. Modern bedrooms have plain décor offset by colour co-ordinated fabrics and curtains. Traditional breakfast room.

XX **Foveran** with rm ⚶   ⌂ ⌗ 🛜 📶 **P** *VISA* **㏇**
St Ola, Southwest : 3 m. on A 964 ✉ KW15 1SF – ☏ *(01856) 872 389*
– www.foveranhotel.co.uk – foveranhotel@aol.com – Fax (01856) 876 430
– Restricted opening in winter
8 rm ⌸ – †£70/85 ††£110   **Rest** – (dinner only) Carte £22/33
♦ Pleasant hotel overlooking the Scapa Flow, in quiet, out of town location. Smart,
immaculately kept bedrooms boast homely décor, simple colour schemes and good
bathrooms. Large restaurant boasts excellent views and traditional menu of local
produce; daily seafood specials.

Stromness – Orkney Islands ▊ *Scotland*   31 **A3**

📷 Town★ - Pier Gallery (collection of abstract art★)

X **Hamnavoe**   *VISA* **㏇** **AE**
35 Graham Pl, off Victoria St ✉ KW16 3BY – ☏ *(01856) 850 606*
– thehamnavoe@tiscali.co.uk – (dinner only and lunch Friday and Saturday in
summer) closed Monday
Rest – (booking essential) Carte £26/35
♦ Set on a narrow street in a small harbourside town, with welcoming coal fire and
walls filled with oil paintings of local scenes. Local Orkadian produce informs the
traditional menus.

St Margaret's Hope – Orkney Islands   31 **A3**

XX **Creel** with rm   ⌂ **P** *VISA* **㏇**
Front Rd ✉ KW17 2SL – ☏ *(01856) 831 311 – www.thecreel.co.uk*
– alan@thecreel.freeserve.co.uk – Closed mid October - Easter
4 rm ⌸ – †£105 ††£110
Rest – Seafood – (closed Monday) (dinner only) Menu £35
♦ Neat yellow washed building in seafront village. Restaurant boasts colourful artwork, nautical ornaments and sea views. Daily changing, seafood based menus feature fresh, tasty produce and some unusual fish. Modern bedrooms with good bathrooms and views over St Margaret's Hope Bay.

SCOTLAND

 Look out for red symbols, indicating particularly pleasant establishments.

ISLE OF WESTRAY – Orkney Islands   31 **A2**

Cleat – ✉ Orkney Islands   31 **A2**

🏠 **Cleaton House** ⚶   ⌂ ⌗ 🖐 ☕ **P** *VISA* **㏇**
✉ KW17 2DB – ☏ *(01857) 677 508 – www.cleatonhouse.com*
– info@cleatonhouse.co.uk – Fax (01857) 677 442
6 rm ⌸ – †£50/65 ††£80/95
Rest – (bar lunch) (booking essential for non-residents) Menu £35
♦ Mid Victorian former Lairds mansion; set on a peninsula, with panoramic views.
Comfy, classical guest areas boast heavy fabrics and antique furniture – a style echoed in the bedrooms. Rear lounge bar offers informal dining with a concise, seafood
based menu.

Pierowall – Orkney Islands – 501 L 6   31 **A2**

⌂ **No 1 Broughton** ⚶   ⌂ ⌗ 🛜 📶 **P** *VISA* **㏇**
✉ KW17 2DA – ☏ *(01857) 677 726 – www.no1broughton.co.uk*
– no1broughton@hotmail.com – Closed 17 December - 6 January
3 rm ⌸ – †£35/40 ††£60   **Rest** – (by arrangement) Menu £17
♦ Pleasant whitewashed house overlooking Pierowall Bay. Comfy lounge; dining
room with views. Bedrooms boast good facilities and modern bathrooms. Home
cooked breakfast of Island produce.

PEAT INN – Fife

28 **D2**

▶ London 462 mi – Edinburgh 45 mi – Dundee 17 mi – Kirkcaldy 19 mi

XXX **The Peat Inn** with rm   P VISA ©© AE

✉ KY15 5LH – ℰ (01334) 840 206 – www.thepeatinn.co.uk
– stay@thepeatinn.co.uk – Fax (01334) 840 530 – Closed 1-14 January, 1 week
mid November, 25-26 December and Sunday-Monday
8 rm – ♦£115/135 ♦♦£155/175
Rest – (booking essential) Menu £34 – Carte £26/45
♦ Former coaching inn with a homely country house style.Three dining rooms serve
tasty, traditional dishes. Annex bedrooms are very strong and full of charming extra
touches.

PEEBLES – Scottish Borders – **501** K 17 – **pop. 8 065** Scotland

26 **C2**

▶ Edinburgh 24 mi – Glasgow 53 mi – Hawick 31 mi
ℹ High St ℰ (01835) 863170, bordersinfo@visitscotland.com
▥ Kirkland St, ℰ (01721) 720 197
◎ Tweed Valley★★. Traquair House★★ **AC**, SE : 7 m. by B 7062 – Rosslyn
Chapel★★ **AC**, N : 16½ m. by A 703, A 6094, B 7026 and B 7003

SCOTLAND

🏨 **Cringletie House** ⟨ ⟩   ≤ 🞥 🝙 🛏 ☏ P VISA ©© AE

Edinburgh Rd, North : 3 m. on A 703 ✉ EH45 8PL – ℰ (01721) 725 750
– www.cringletie.com – enquiries@cringletie.com – Fax (01721) 725 751
13 rm ⌑ – ♦£140/175 ♦♦£260/310
Rest – Menu £43 – Carte lunch approx. £20
♦ Smoothly run and handsomely furnished Victorian hotel in country house style
with contemporary edge. Rooms are modern, well-equipped and peaceful. Spacious,
formal restaurant with a trompe l'oeil ceiling.

🏨 **Park**   🞥 🛏 ☏ P VISA ©© AE ①

Innerleithen Rd ✉ EH45 8BA – ℰ (01721) 720 451 – www.parkhotelpeebles.co.uk
– reserve@parkhotelpeebles.co.uk – Fax (01721) 723 510
– Closed 2 weeks January
24 rm ⌑ – ♦£88/111 ♦♦£192/214   **Rest** – Menu £26
♦ Extended town-centre hotel - tidy and unpretentious - overlooks a well-tended
lawn. Simple bar with tartan sofas, neatly kept rooms: a good address for the mature
traveller. Wood-panelled restaurant continues the traditional décor and atmosphere
of the hotel.

🏠 **Rowanbrae** without rest   ⅍

103 Northgate ✉ EH45 8BU – ℰ (01721) 721 630
– john@rowanbrae.freeserve.co.uk – Fax (01721) 723 324 – Closed Christmas-New
Year
3 rm ⌑ – ♦£40/55 ♦♦£55/60
♦ Built for the manager of a 19C woollen mill. Pleasant, affordable rooms, well kept
by a cheerful couple. Fortifying breakfasts with posies of garden flowers on each
table.

at Eddleston North : 4 1/2 m. on A 703

XX **The Horseshoe Inn** with rm   ☏ P VISA ©©

✉ EH45 8QP – ℰ (01721) 730 225 – www.horseshoeinn.co.uk
– reservations@horseshoe.inn.co.uk – Fax (01721) 730 268 – Closed 1 week
January, 1 week October, 25 December and dinner Sunday-Monday
8 rm ⌑ – ♦£75 ♦♦£95
Rest – Menu £20 (lunch) – Carte dinner £17/46
Rest *Bistro* – (Closed Monday) Menu £20 (lunch) – Carte (dinner) £17/32
♦ It's easy to drive past this roadside former pub but stop off for serious cooking
from experienced French chef or lighter dishes in adjacent bistro. Simple, comfy
bedrooms.

If breakfast is included the ⌑ symbol appears after the number of rooms.

▶ Edinburgh 44 mi – Aberdeen 86 mi – Dundee 22 mi – Dunfermline 29 mi – Glasgow 64 mi – Inverness 112 mi – Oban 94 mi

🅹 Lower City Mills, West Mill St ℰ (01738) 450600, perthtic@perthshire.co.uk

🏳 Craigie Hill Cherrybank, ℰ (01738) 620 829

🏳 King James VI Moncreiffe Island, ℰ (01738) 625 170

🏳 Murrayshall New Scone, ℰ (01738) 554 804

🏳 North Inch, c/o Perth & Kinross Council 35 Kinncoll St, ℰ (01738) 636 481

◎ City★ – Black Watch Regimental Museum★ Y **M1** – Georgian Terraces★ Y – Museum and Art Gallery★ Y **M2**

🅖 Scone Palace★★ **AC**, N : 2 m. by A 93 Y – Branklyn Garden★ **AC**, SE : 1 m. by A 85 Z – Kinnoull Hill (≼★) SE : 1¼ m. by A 85 Z – Huntingtower Castle★ **AC**, NW : 3 m. by A 85 Y – Elcho Castle★ **AC**, SE : 4 m. by A 912 - Z - and Rhynd rd. Abernethy (11C Round Tower★), SE : 8 m. by A 912 - Z - and A 913

Plan on next page

🏨 **Huntingtower** 🌿   🍴 🛋 🐾 & rm, 🛜 🐾 **P** VISA ❻ AE ❶

Crieff Rd, West : 3½ m. by A 85 ✉ *PH1 3JT –* ℰ *(01738) 583 771*
– www.huntingtowerhotel.co.uk – reservations@huntingtowerhotel.co.uk
– Fax (01738) 583 777

34 rm ⌂ – ♦£65/105 ♦♦£75/149

Rest *Oak Room* – (bar lunch) Menu £17/30 **s** – Carte £21/50 **s**

♦ Late Victorian half-timbered country house named after nearby castle. Choose bedrooms in the more traditional old house or modern, executive rooms. Restaurant with views towards lawn and stream.

🏨 **Parklands**   🍴 🛜 **P** VISA ❻

2 St Leonard's Bank ✉ *PH2 8EB –* ℰ *(01738) 622 451*
– www.theparklandshotel.com – info@theparklandshotel.com
– Fax (01738) 622 046   **Z**n

15 rm ⌂ – ♦£109/149 ♦♦£129/169

Rest *No. 1 The Bank* – see restaurant listing

♦ Modern hotel set opposite the railway station. Contemporary bedrooms – some overlooking the garden – boast spacious bathrooms and good facilities; great for businesspeople.

🏠 **Beechgrove** without rest   🍴 ❀ **P**

Dundee Rd ✉ *PH2 7AQ –* ℰ *(01738) 636 147 – the-beechgrove@btconnect.com*
– Fax (01738) 636 147   **Z**s

8 rm ⌂ – ♦£30/60 ♦♦£70/80

♦ Virginia creeper clad Georgian manse, immaculately kept. Bedrooms are spacious and boast mahogany furniture and added extras; comfy firelit lounge in traditional décor.

🏠 **Taythorpe** without rest   ❀ **P**

Isla Rd, North : 1 m. on A 93 ✉ *PH2 7HQ –* ℰ *(01738) 447 994*
– www.taythorpe.co.uk – stay@taythorpe.co.uk
– Fax (01738) 447 994   **Y**a

3 rm ⌂ – ♦£42 ♦♦£70

♦ Immaculately kept, modern guesthouse close to Scone Palace. Good value accommodation. Welcoming, homely lounge. Cosy, communal breakfasts. Warmly inviting, well-kept bedrooms.

🏠 **Kinnaird** without rest   🍴 ❀ 🛜 **P** VISA ❻

5 Marshall Pl ✉ *PH2 8AH –* ℰ *(01738) 628 021*
– www.kinnaird-guesthouse.co.uk – info@kinnaird-guesthouse.co.uk   **Z**c

7 rm ⌂ – ♦£40/60 ♦♦£60/70

♦ Neatly kept Georgian town house behind a tidy front lawn edged with flowers. Traditional sitting room with a touch of period style. Individual rooms, thoughtfully appointed.

SCOTLAND

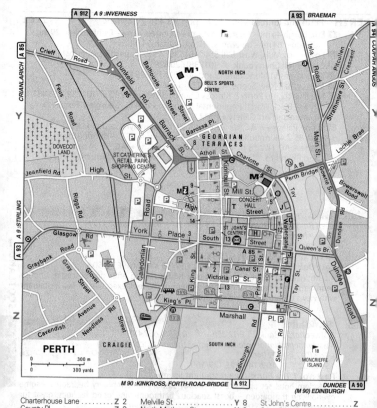

𝖃𝖃 63 Tay Street

VISA 𝐌𝐎 AE

63 Tay St ⊠ PH2 8NN – 𝒞 (01738) 441 451 – www.63taystreet.co.uk
– Fax (01738) 441 461

– Closed 3 weeks late December, 1 week July, Sunday and Monday   Z**r**

Rest – Menu £ 20/30 – Carte £ 30/38

◆ Contemporary style restaurant close to the riverside. Subtle décor with bright sea-blue chairs. Well-priced modern cuisine with penchant for seasonal ingredients.

𝖃𝖃 No.1 The Bank – at Parklands Hotel

🛏 🏡 P VISA 𝐌𝐎

2 St Leonard's Bank ⊠ PH2 8EB – 𝒞 (01738) 622 451
– www.theparklandshotel.com – enquiries@no1thebank.com
– Fax (01738) 622 046   Z**n**

Rest – Carte £ 24/33

◆ Set close to the station within a contemporary hotel. Cooking combines the best local and seasonal produce with modern techniques and artistic flair. Confident flavours.

𝖃𝖃 Deans @ Let's Eat

VISA 𝐌𝐎

77-79 Kinnoull St ⊠ PH1 5EZ – 𝒞 (01738) 643 377 – www.letseatperth.co.uk
– deans@letseatperth.co.uk – Fax (01738) 621 464

– Closed 2 weeks January, Sunday and Monday   Y**c**

Rest – Menu £ 17 (lunch) – Carte £ 22/38

◆ Polite, unflustered service and relaxed, warm-toned setting combine in a strong neighbourhood favourite. Robust, varied modern dishes at a good price.

X **Duncan's**   AC   VISA
33 George St ⊠ PH1 5LA – ℰ (01738) 626 016 – www.duncansinperth.com
– Closed Sunday   Y**e**
Rest – Menu £15/23 – Carte £16/25
♦ Honest, good value restaurant in centre of town; popular with the locals. Well structured monthly menus of homely bistro cooking displays unfussy, confidently flavoured dishes.

at Guildtown North : 5 m. on A 93 - Y – ⊠ Perth

▥ **The Anglers Inn** with rm   P   VISA   AE
Main Road, ⊠ PH2 6BS – ℰ (01821) 640 329 – www.theanglersinn.co.uk
– info@theanglersinn.co.uk – Closed 25-26 December and first 2 weeks January
5 rm ⊑ – †£40/50 ††£80/100   **Rest** – Menu £18 (lunch) – Carte £19/29
♦ Whitewashed roadside inn in a tiny hamlet, with plain décor and restaurant styling. Good value à la carte menu with a classical French base uses careful cooking and fresh ingredients. Clean simple rooms.

at Forgandenny Southwest : 6½ m. by A 912 - Z - on B 935 – ⊠ Perth

⌂ **Battledown** without rest ⌂   &   P   VISA   AE
by Station Rd on Church and School rd ⊠ PH2 9EL – ℰ (01738) 812 471
– www.battledown.net – dunsire9@aol.com – Fax (01738) 812 471
3 rm ⊑ – †£35/40 ††£65/75
♦ Immaculately whitewashed, part 18C cottage in quiet village. Lovely garden; owner's paintings on show. Cosy, pine-furnished breakfast room. Neat, tidy rooms, all on ground level.

SCOTLAND

at Methven West : 6½ m. on A 85 - Y – ⊠ Perth

X **Hamish's**   VISA   ①
Main St ⊠ PH1 3PU – ℰ (01738) 840 505 – www.hamishs.co.uk
– info@hamishs.co.uk – Closed 2 weeks January, 1 week May, 1 week October, Monday and Tuesday
Rest – Carte £18/31 **s**
♦ Former Victorian school-house with smart, modish interior accentuated by striking red leather chairs. Accomplished modern cooking with classical base and Scottish bias.

PIEROWALL – Orkney Islands – 501 K 6 – see Orkney Islands (Isle of Westray)

PITLOCHRY – Perth and Kinross – 501 I 13 – pop. 2 564 ▯ *Scotland*   28 **C2**
   ▶ Edinburgh 71 mi – Inverness 85 mi – Perth 27 mi
   🛈 22 Atholl Rd ℰ (01796) 472215, pitlochrytic@perthshire.co.uk
   ▥ Pitlochry Estate Office, ℰ (01796) 472 792
   ◎ Town★
   ◪ Blair Castle★★ AC, NW : 7 m. by A 9 A – Queen's View★★, W : 7 m. by B 8019 A – Falls of Bruar★, NW : 11 m. by A 9 A

Plan on next page

▥▥ **Green Park**   ≤   ▦   ☎   & rm, ℱ   P   VISA
Clunie Bridge Rd ⊠ PH16 5JY – ℰ (01796) 473 248 – www.thegreenpark.co.uk
– bookings@thegreenpark.co.uk – Fax (01796) 473 520   A**a**
51 rm (dinner included) ⊑ – †£69/94 ††£138/188
Rest – (light lunch residents only) (booking essential for non-residents) Menu £25 **s**
♦ Family run 1860s summer retreat on Loch Faskally. Rooms in the old house are decorated in floral patterns; impressive up-to-date wing has good, contemporary facilities. Unhurried dinners at lochside setting.

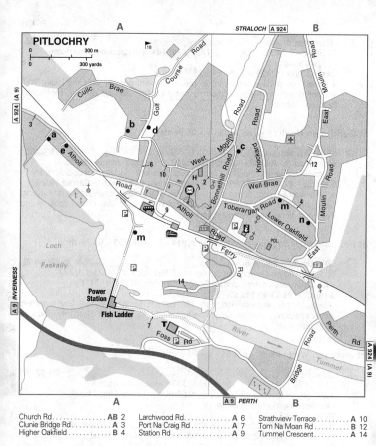

PITLOCHRY

STRALOCH A 924

A 924 (A 9)

A 9 INVERNESS

A 9 PERTH

A 924 (A 9)

 Pine Trees ⚲ ← 🍴 AC rm, P VISA ☺☺ AE

Strathview Terrace ⊠ *PH16 5QR –* ℰ *(01796) 472 121*
– www.pinetreeshotel.co.uk – info@pinetreeshotel.co.uk
– Fax (01796) 472 460 **Ab**
20 rm ⊇ *–* †£55/124 ††£104/124
Rest *– Menu £26 – Carte (lunch) £17/26* s

♦ Extended 1892 mansion: superb wood-panelled hall with open fire, period prints and antiques. Modern rooms in warm décor; those at front have best views of 8-acre gardens. Two eating alternatives: dining room or bistro area.

 Craigatin House and Courtyard *without rest* 🍴 ₰ 🌱 P VISA ☺☺

165 Atholl Rd ⊠ *PH16 5QL –* ℰ *(01796) 472 478*
– www.craigatinhouse.co.uk
– enquiries@craigatinhouse.co.uk
– Closed 3 days Christmas **Ae**
12 rm ⊇ *–* †£70/80 ††£75/85 *– 1 suite*

♦ 19C detached house with converted stables. Smart, stylish décor, including comfy conservatory lounge and breakfast room. Eye-catchingly inviting rooms, some in the annexe.

🏠 Knockendarroch House
2 Higher Oakfield ✉ *PH16 5HT –* ✆ *(01796) 473 473*
– www.knockendarroch.co.uk – bookings@knockendarroch.co.uk – Fax (01796)
474 068 – Closed Christmas and 5-23 January   **Bm**
12 rm (dinner included) ☲ – †£85/115 ††£130/180
Rest – (dinner only) Menu £30 **s**
♦ A handsome late Victorian house in a neat garden. Most of the large, light bedrooms have good views; comfortably furnished, bright, airy, two-room lounge. Cosy, homely dining room.

🏠 Beinn Bhracaigh without rest
Higher Oakfield ✉ *PH16 5HT –* ✆ *(01796) 470 355 – www.beinnbhracaigh.com*
– info@beinnbhracaigh.com
– Closed Chirstmas and 2 weeks mid-November   **Bn**
10 rm ☲ – †£45/80 ††£75/90
♦ Affordable, spacious, refurbished bedrooms - with good town views from front - in a local stone house of late 19C origin. Impressive range of whiskies in residents' bar.

🏠 The Moulin Inn
Kirkmichael Road, East : 1 m. by West Moulin Rd ✉ *PH16 5EH –* ✆ *(01796)*
472 196 – www.moulinhotel.co.uk – enquiries@moulinhotel.co.uk – Fax (01796)
474 098
15 rm ☲ – †£45/60 ††£75/90
Rest *Moulin Inn* – see restaurant listing
♦ Whitewashed 300 year old inn in pleasant conservation village, away from centre of town. Traditional Scottish feel. Cosy residential bar. Comfortable bedrooms.

🏠 Torrdarach House without rest
Golf Course Rd ✉ *PH16 5AU –* ✆ *(01796) 472 136 – torrdarach@.msn.com*
– Restricted opening in winter   **Ad**
7 rm ☲ – †£26/50 ††£52/68
♦ New owners. Pleasant bedrooms in bright colours and cosy, traditional sitting room behind the deep red façade of this Edwardian country house. Nicely kept, ornate gardens.

🏠 Dunmurray Lodge without rest
72 Bonnethill Rd ✉ *PH16 5ED –* ✆ *(01796) 473 624 – www.dunmurray.co.uk*
– tony@dunmurray.co.uk – Fax (01796) 473 624
– Restricted opening in winter   **Bc**
4 rm ☲ – †£35/60 ††£50/70
♦ Pretty, immaculately kept 19C cottage, once a doctor's surgery. Relax in homely sitting room's squashy sofas. Bedrooms are small and cosy with soothing cream colour scheme.

XX Old Armoury
Armoury Rd ✉ *PH16 5AP –* ✆ *(01796) 474 281*
– www.theoldarmouryrestaurant.com – info@theoldarmouryrestaurant.com
– Fax (01796) 473 157 – Closed 3 weeks January, 24-29 December and
Monday-Wednesday November-March   **Am**
Rest – Menu £21 (lunch) – Carte £18/43
♦ 18C former Black Watch armoury. Smart al fresco dining area and wishing well. Inside: a bright lounge, three dining rooms and traditional menus with distinct Scottish accent.

🍴 Moulin Inn – at The Moulin Hotel
11-13 Kirkmichael Rd, East : 1 m. by West Moulin Rd ✉ *PH16 5EH –* ✆ *(01796)*
472 196 – www.pitlochryhotels.co.uk – enquiries@moulinhotel.co.uk
– Fax (01796) 474 098 – Restaurant closed 25 December
Rest – Menu £24 (dinner) – Carte £16/26
♦ Popular pub with open fires, exposed stone walls and large tables, serving real ales and hearty cooking made with Perthshire produce. Pleasant terrace.

SCOTLAND

at Killiecrankie Northwest : 4 m. by A 924 - A - and B 8019 on B 8079
– ⊠ Pitlochry

Killiecrankie House ◎ ← ⊟ **P** VISA ◎◎ AE
⊠ PH16 5LG – ℰ (01796) 473 220 – www.killiecrankiehotel.co.uk
– enquiries@killiecrankiehotel.co.uk – Fax (01796) 472 451 – 3 January-8 March
9 rm ⊠ – †£ 75/140 ††£ 150/170 – 1 suite   **Rest** – (bar lunch) Menu £ 38
♦ Quiet and privately run, a converted 1840 vicarage with a distinct rural feel.
The sizeable bedrooms come in co-ordinated patterns and overlook pleasant countryside. Warm, red dining room; garden produce prominent on menus.

PLOCKTON – Highland – **501** D 11 ▐ Scotland   29 **B2**
▶ Edinburgh 210 mi – Inverness 88 mi
◎ Village★
◎ Wester Ross★★★

Plockton Inn with rm   ⊟ ⌂ & rm, **P** VISA ◎◎
Innes Street ⊠ IV52 8TW – ℰ (01599) 544 222 – www.plocktoninn.co.uk
– info@plocktoninn.co.uk – Fax (01599) 544 487
14 rm ⊠ – †£ 40/45 ††£ 80/90   **Rest** – Seafood – Carte £ 15/26
♦ Family run converted manse, with a cosy locals bar refreshingly short on airs and
graces. Welcoming lounges for dining on local fish and shellfish. Trim, cheerful bedrooms.

Plockton with rm   ← ⊟ ⌂ & rm, � ⌖ VISA ◎◎ AE
41 Harbour St ⊠ IV52 8TN – ℰ (01599) 544 274 – www.plocktonhotel.co.uk
– info@plocktonhotel.co.uk – Fax (01599) 544 475
– Closed 25 December and 1 January
15 rm ⊠ – †£ 45 ††£ 110   **Rest** – Carte £ 14/40
♦ Popular menu served in the spacious modern restaurant. Enlarged traditional inn
commands fine views of the mountains and Loch Carron. Convivial, half-panelled bar;
local ale. New rooms in particular have a simple, stylish feel.

PORT APPIN – Argyll and Bute – **501** D 14 – ⊠ Appin   27 **B2**
▶ Edinburgh 136 mi – Ballachulish 20 mi – Oban 24 mi

Airds ◎   ← ⊟ ⌇ ⌖ **P** VISA ◎◎ AE
⊠ PA38 4DF – ℰ (01631) 730 236 – www.airds-hotel.com
– airds@airds-hotel.com – Fax (01631) 730 535
11 rm ⊠ – †£ 230/295 ††£ 295/360
Rest – (booking essential for non-residents) Menu £ 50 – Carte lunch £ 26/33
♦ Former ferry inn with superb views of Loch Linnhe and mountains. Charming
rooms - antiques and floral fabrics. Firelit, old-world sitting rooms hung with landscapes. Smartly set tables, picture windows looking across the water in the restaurant.

PORT CHARLOTTE – Argyll and Bute – **501** A 16 – see Islay (Isle of)

PORT ELLEN – Argyll and Bute – **501** B 17 – see Islay (Isle of)

PORTMAHOMACK – Highland – **501** I 10   30 **D2**
▶ Edinburgh 194 mi – Dornoch 21 mi – Tain 12 mi

XX **The Oystercatcher** with rm   ⌂ **P** VISA ◎◎ AE
Main St ⊠ IV20 1YB – ℰ (01862) 871 560 – www.the-oystercatcher.co.uk
– s.robertson5@btconnect.com – Fax (01862) 871 777
– Restricted opening in winter
3 rm ⊠ – †£ 43 ††£ 98
Rest – Seafood – (closed Monday-Tuesday) (booking essential) Carte £ 28/66 **s**
♦ Personally run bistro and piscatorially themed main dining room in a lovely setting.
Numerous seafood menus, offering a vast choice and some unusual combinations.
Simple bedrooms.

PORTPATRICK – Dumfries and Galloway – 501 E 19 – pop. 585   25 A3
– ⊠ Stranraer

> ▶ Edinburgh 141 mi – Ayr 60 mi – Dumfries 80 mi – Stranraer 9 mi
> 🏌 Golf Course Rd, ℰ (01776) 810 273

Knockinaam Lodge ⌖   ← 🚗 🐾 🐕 🄿 VISA ⓪ AE
Southeast : 5 m. by A 77 off B 7042 ⊠ DG9 9AD – ℰ (01776) 810 471
– www.knockinaamlodge.com – reservations@knockinaamlodge.com
– Fax (01776) 810 435
10 rm (dinner included) ⌖ – ♟£ 150/300 ♟♟£ 250/410
Rest – (booking essential for non-residents) (set menu only) Menu £ 39/55 ⅋
Spec. Scallops, vine tomato consommé, basil and ginger. Steamed sea bass, spinach, chive butter sauce. Calvados soufflé, apple sorbet and tuiles.
♦ Idyllically-situated in its own private cove, this family-run Victorian house exudes a warm, friendly feel. Country house style bedrooms; most with sea view. Fine selection of malt whiskies. Daily-changing set 4 course menu uses fine local produce: carefully-prepared and accomplished modern dishes.

Fernhill ⌖   ← 🚗 ৬ rm, ⑨ 🄿 VISA ⓪ AE
Heugh Rd ⊠ DG9 8TD – ℰ (01776) 810 220 – www.fernhillhotel.co.uk
– info@fernhillhotel.co.uk – Fax (01776) 810 596 – Closed 2 January - 13 February
36 rm (dinner included) ⌖ – ♟£ 63/83 ♟♟£ 188/228   **Rest** – Menu £ 16/33
♦ Family owned hotel in an elevated position; comfortable lounge and bar with fine view of the harbour and sea. Rooms vary in size; the more luxurious have balconies. Unpretentious restaurant and conservatory with menu which changes with the seasons.

Campbells ⌖   ← 🚗 VISA ⓪ ①
1 South Crescent ⊠ DG9 8JR – ℰ (01776) 810 314
– www.campbellsrestaurant.co.uk
– dianecampbell@campbellsrestaurant.wanadoo.co.uk – Fax (01776) 810 361
– Closed 2 weeks January-February, 1 week November, 25 December, and Monday
Rest – Seafood – Carte £ 18/31
♦ Personally run attractive harbourside restaurant with modern rustic feel throughout. Tasty, appealing menus, full of seafood specialities and Scottish ingredients.

PORTREE – Highland – 501 B 11 – see Skye (Isle of)

QUOTHQUAN – South Lanarkshire – 501 J 27 – ⊠ Biggar ▌ Scotland   26 C2

> ▶ Edinburgh 32 mi – Dumfries 50 mi – Glasgow 36 mi
> 🄖 Biggar★ (Gladstone Court Museum★ AC – Greenhill Covenanting Museum★ AC) SE : 4 ½ m. by B 7016

Shieldhill Castle ⌖   ← 🚗 ⑨ 🄚 🄿 VISA ⓪ AE
Northeast : ¾ m. ⊠ ML12 6NA – ℰ (01899) 220 035 – www.shieldhill.co.uk
– enquiries@shieldhill.co.uk – Fax (01899) 221 092
26 rm ⌖ – ♟£ 85/90 ♟♟£ 248
Rest *Chancellors* – Carte £ 31/43 ⅋
♦ Part 12C fortified manor with 16C additions and invitingly comfortable panelled lounge. Large rooms, individually furnished, some with vast sunken baths. Popular for weddings. Accomplished cooking in 16C dining room with high carved ceilings.

RANNOCH STATION – Perth and Kinross – 501 G 13   27 B2

> ▶ Edinburgh 108 mi – Kinloch Rannoch 17 mi – Pitlochry 36 mi

Moor of Rannoch ⌖   ← 🚗 🄿 VISA ⓪
⊠ PH17 2QA – ℰ (01882) 633 238 – www.moorofrannoch.co.uk
– bookings@moorofrannoch.co.uk – 14 February-14 November
5 rm ⌖ – ♟£ 52 ♟♟£ 88
Rest – (dinner only) (booking essential for non-residents) Carte £ 18/34 **s**
♦ Immaculately whitewashed 19C property "in the middle of nowhere", next to railway station with link to London! Comfy, sofa-strewn lounges. Rustic rooms with antiques. Home-cooked menus in characterful dining room with conservatory.

SCOTLAND

ST ANDREWS – Fife – **501** L 14 – **pop. 14 209** ▮ *Scotland*   28 **D2**

▶ Edinburgh 51 mi – Dundee 14 mi – Stirling 51 mi

🛈 70 Market St ✆ (01334) 472021, standrews@visitfife.com

🖥 Duke's Craigtoun Park, ✆ (01334) 474 371

◉ City★★ - Cathedral★ (※★★) **AC** B – West Port★A

◎ Leuchars (parish church★), NW : 6 m. by A 91 and A 919. The East
Neuk★★, SE : 9 m. by A 917 and B 9131 B – Crail★★ (Old Centre★★, Upper
Crail★) SE : 9 m. by A 917 B – Kellie Castle★ **AC**, S : 9 m. by B 9131 and
B 9171 B – Ceres★, SW : 9 m. by B 939 - E : Inland Fife★A

ST ANDREWS

		Church St	**AB** 13	Murray Park	**A** 28
		Ellice Pl	**A** 15	Murray Pl	**A** 29
Abbey St	**B** 2	Gibson Pl	**A** 17	Pilmour Links	**A** 31
Abbey Walk	**B** 3	Gillespie Terrace	**A** 18	Pilmour Pl	**A** 32
Alexandra Pl	**A** 5	Greenside Pl	**B** 20	Playfair Terrace	**A** 34
Alfred Pl	**A** 6	Gregory Lane	**B** 21	Queen's Gardens	**A** 35
Bridge St	**A** 7	Gregory Pl	**B** 22	Queen's Terrace	**B** 36
Butts Wynd	**B** 9	Greyfriars Garden	**A** 24	St Mary's	
Castle St	**B** 10	Hepburn Gardens	**A** 25	Pl	**A** 37
		Link Crescent	**A** 27	Union St	**B** 38

A   **B**

🏰🏰🏰🏰 **Old Course H. Golf Resort and Spa**   ⟨ 🔲 ⊛ 🕸 🛴 🖼 🛗

Old Station Rd ⊠ KY16 9SP   🛠 rm, ⚒ 📶 🛠 **P** 🗺 🚾 🅰🅴 ①
– ✆ (01334) 474 371 – www.oldcoursehotel.co.uk
– reservations@oldcoursehotel.co.uk – Fax (01334) 477 668   A**b**
116 rm ⊇ – ♦£ 175/390 ♦♦£ 205/390 – 28 suites – ♦♦£ 680
Rest *Road Hole Grill* – (dinner only) Carte £ 45/55 **s**
Rest *Sands* – Carte £ 27/70 **s**
◆ Relax into richly composed formal interiors and comprehensive luxury with a fine malt
or a spa mudpack. Bright, stylish rooms. Unrivalled views of the bay and Old Course.
Road Hole Grill has a fine view of the 17th hole. Worldwide flavours at Sands brasserie.

🏰🏰🏰 **Fairmont St Andrews**   ⟨ 🚗 🔲 ⊛ 🕸 🛴 🖼 🛗 🛠 rm, 🅰 ⚒

Southeast : 3 m. on A 917 ⊠ KY16 8PN   🛠 **P** 🗺 🚾 🅰🅴 ①
– ✆ (01334) 837 000 – www.fairmont.com/standrews
– standrews.scotland@fairmont.com – Fax (01334) 471 115
192 rm ⊇ – ♦£ 169/310 ♦♦£ 169/310 – 17 suites
Rest *The Squire* – Carte £ 32/44
Rest *Esperante* – (closed Monday-Tuesday) (dinner only) Carte £ 65/85
◆ Golf oriented modern, purpose-built hotel on clifftop site with wonderful Tayside
views and pristine fairways. Extensive conference facilities. Stylish, modern rooms.
Golf chat to the "fore" in informal Squire. Mediterranean influenced Esperante.

Rufflets Country House 🕸   ≤ 🚗 🞕 & rm, 🞖 ¶ 🍷 **P**
Strathkinness Low Rd, West : 1½ m. on B 939 ✉ *KY16 9TX*   VISA ◉◉ AE ◉
– ℰ *(01334) 472 594 – www.rufflets.co.uk – reservations@rufflets.co.uk*
– Fax (01334) 478 703
22 rm ⌷ – †£125/155 ††£195/245 – 2 suites
Rest *Terrace* – (dinner only and Sunday lunch) Carte £31/46
Rest *Music Room* – (lunch only Monday-Saturday) Menu £14
♦ Handsome 1920s house set in ornamental gardens. Traditional drawing room with cosy fireside sofas, thoughtfully appointed rooms are pristine and characterful. Terrace restaurant offers fine vantage point to view the lawns. Informal Music Room for lunch.

 The Scores   ≤ 🚗 🞖 🞖 ¶ 🍷 **P** VISA ◉◉ AE ◉
76 The Scores ✉ *KY16 9BB* – ℰ *(01334) 472 451 – www.scoreshotel.co.uk*
– reception@scoreshotel.co.uk – Fax (01334) 473 947   **An**
29 rm ⌷ – †£86/133 ††£152/239 – 1 suite
Rest *Alexanders* – (dinner only Thursday-Saturday) Menu £27
♦ Practically equipped rooms in a handsome 1880s terrace by the Old Course and facing the bay. Bar celebrates Scots heroes and the filming of "Chariots of Fire" on the beach. Formal, classic restaurant; views out to sea.

Albany without rest   🚗 🞖 ¶ VISA ◉◉ AE ◉
56-58 North St ✉ *KY16 9AH* – ℰ *(01334) 477 737 – www.standrewsalbany.co.uk*
– enq@standrewsalbany.co.uk – Fax (01334) 477 742
– Closed 2 weeks Christmas and New Year   **Ba**
22 rm ⌷ – †£57/82 ††£83/133
♦ Well-kept, pleasingly unfussy rooms - quieter at the rear - in a family run 1790s house. Homely, firelit lounge with stacked bookshelves, antique sideboards and deep sofas.

Aslar House without rest   🚗 🞖 ¶ VISA ◉◉
120 North St ✉ *KY16 9AF* – ℰ *(01334) 473 460 – www.aslar.com*
– enquiries@aslar.com – Fax (01334) 477 540
– Closed first 2 weeks December and Christmas   **Ar**
6 rm ⌷ – †£42/80 ††£84/90
♦ Victorian house, privately run in a welcoming spirit. Homely, pine furnished rooms, all en suite, are larger on the top floor; most overlook a quiet rear garden. Good value.

18 Queens Terrace without rest   🚗 🞖 ¶ VISA ◉◉ AE
18 Queens Terrace, by Queens Gardens ✉ *KY16 9QF* – ℰ *(01334) 478 849*
– stay@18queensterrace.com – Fax (01334) 470 283
– Closed Christmas and New Year
4 rm ⌷ – †£70/75 ††£90/95
♦ Characterful Victorian guesthouse in smart street next to one of the colleges. Very well-furnished lounge with antiques. Stunning rooms in period and sympathetic style.

Deveron House without rest   🞖 ¶ VISA ◉◉
64 North St ✉ *KY16 9AH* – ℰ *(01334) 473 513 – www.deveronhouse.com*
– bookings@deveronhouse.com – Closed 14 December-7 February   **Bb**
6 rm ⌷ – †£58/78 ††£95
♦ Centrally located Victorian guesthouse. Cosy, clean lounge. Sunny, bright and modern breakfast room with smart wicker chairs. Flowery bedrooms with varnished pine.

XXX **The Seafood**   ≤ 🚗 AC VISA ◉◉ AE ◉
The Scores ✉ *KY16 9AB* – ℰ *(01334) 479 475 – www.theseafoodrestaurant.com*
– info@theseafoodrestaurant.com – Fax (01334) 479 476
– Closed 25-26 December and 1 January   **Ac**
Rest – Seafood – (booking essential) Menu £26/45
♦ Super views as restaurant's four sides are of glass. A very pleasant attitude and attention to detail accompanies agreeable, top quality, regularly changing seafood menus.

SCOTLAND

ST BOSWELLS – Scottish Borders – 501 L 17 – pop. 1 199 – ✉ Melrose 26 D2

Scotland

Edinburgh 39 mi – Glasgow 79 mi – Hawick 17 mi – Newcastle upon Tyne 66 mi

St Boswells, ✆ (01835) 823 527

Dryburgh Abbey★★ AC (setting★★★), NW : 4 m. by B 6404 and B 6356 – Tweed Valley★★. Bowhill★★ AC, SW : 11½ m. by A 699 and A 708

Dryburgh Abbey

North : 3½ m. by B 6404 on B 6356 ✉ TD6 0RQ – ✆ (01835) 822 261 – www.dryburgh.co.uk – enquiries@dryburgh.co.uk – Fax (01835) 823 945

36 rm (dinner included) – †£ 63/220 ††£ 226/256 – 2 suites

Rest *Tweed* – (bar lunch Monday-Saturday) Menu £ 35 – Carte £ 18/39

♦ With the dramatic ruins of the abbey in its grounds, a restored country house near the river Tweed. Comfortable, well-equipped bedrooms, named after salmon-fishing flies. Spacious, soft-toned setting for armchair dining.

Whitehouse

Northeast : 3 m. on B 6404 ✉ TD6 0ED – ✆ (01573) 460 343 – www.whitehousecountryhouse.com – whitehouse.tyrer@tiscali.co.uk

3 rm – †£ 75/85 ††£ 100/110 **Rest** – (by arrangement) Menu £ 30

♦ Appreciate the good rural views from enticingly comfortable country house style lounge in this 19C former dower house. Nourishing breakfast specials. Airy, welcoming rooms. Home-cooked meals in dining room overlooking the fields.

Clint Lodge

North : 2¼ m. by B 6404 on B 6356 ✉ TD6 0DZ – ✆ (01835) 822 027 – www.clintlodge.co.uk – clintlodge@aol.com – Fax (01835) 822 656

5 rm – †£ 50/75 ††£ 110 **Rest** – (dinner only) Menu £ 30

♦ Personally run Victorian shooting lodge with sweeping prospects of the Tweed Valley and Cheviots. Antiques, open fires, fishing memorabilia and comfortable, classic rooms. A choice of tables allows for private or communal dining.

Undecided between two equivalent establishments? Within each category, establishments are classified in our order of preference.

ST FILLANS – Perth and Kinross – 501 H 14 28 C2

Edinburgh 65 mi – Lochearnhead 8 mi – Perth 29 mi

Achray House

✉ PH6 2NF – ✆ (01764) 685 231 – www.achray-house.co.uk – info@achray-house.co.uk – Fax (01764) 685 320 – Closed 3-28 January

8 rm (dinner included) – †£ 90/105 ††£ 130/160 **Rest** – Carte £ 20/32

♦ Well run, former Edwardian villa with a stunning Loch Earn view. A homely warmth pervades all areas. Bedrooms are clean and simple; some are suitable for families. Freshly prepared seafood a feature of dining room menus.

The Four Seasons

✉ PH6 2NF – ✆ (01764) 685 333 – www.thefourseasonshotel.co.uk – info@thefourseasonshotel.co.uk – Fax (01764) 685 444 – Closed January, February and midweek November, December and March

12 rm – †£ 55/90 ††£ 110/130 **Rest** – Menu £ 35 (dinner) – Carte £ 19/29

♦ Small hotel in enviable location beside Loch Earn, with welcoming atmosphere, neat bedrooms and slightly retro edge; front facing rooms have Loch views. Cosy bar and lounge. Bistro open for lunch, restaurant for 4 course dinner.

ST MARGARET'S HOPE – Orkney Islands – 501 L 7 – see Orkney Islands

ST MONANS – Fife – 501 L 15 – pop. 3 965   28 **D2**
▶ Edinburgh 47 mi – Dundee 26 mi – Perth 40 mi – Stirling 56 mi

XX **The Seafood**   ≤ 🏠 *VISA* **⚫** **AE**
16 West End ⊠ KY10 2BX – ℰ (01333) 730 327
– www.theseafoodrestaurant.com – info@theseafoodrestaurant.com
– Fax (01333) 730 508 – Closed 25-26 December, 2 weeks January, Monday and
Tuesday except June-August
Rest – Seafood – (booking essential) Menu £ 25/38
♦ Informal former pub in a quiet fishing village; nautical memorabilia abounds. Smart
lounge bar leads into a neatly set restaurant with sea views. Tasty, locally caught
dishes.

SANQUHAR – Dumfries and Galloway – 501 I 17 – pop. 2 028   25 **B2**
▶ London 368 mi – Edinburgh 58 mi – East Kilbride 51 mi – Hamilton 43 mi

XX **Blackaddie House** with rm   *VISA* **⚫** **AE**
Blackaddie Road ⊠ DG4 6JJ – ℰ (01659) 50 270 – www.blackaddiehotel.co.uk
– ian&jane@blackaddiehotel.co.uk – Fax (01659) 50 900
9 rm � – ♦£ 50/60 ♦♦£ 100   **Rest** – Carte £ 25/38
♦ Manor house, with homely feel, on banks of River Nith. Classical cooking with
seasonal base, plenty of choice and strong seafood element. Bedrooms named after
whisky distilleries.

SCALASAIG – Argyll and Bute – 501 B 15 – see Colonsay (Isle of)

SCALPAY – Western Isles – 501 A 10 – see Lewis and Harris (Isle of)

SCOURIE – Highland – 501 E 8 – ⊠ Lairg ▌ Scotland   30 **C1**
▶ Edinburgh 263 mi – Inverness 107 mi
🄶 Cape Wrath ★★★ (≤ ★★) **AC**, N : 31 m. (including ferry crossing) by A 894
and A 838 – Loch Assynt ★★, S : 17 m. by A 894

🏠 **Eddrachilles** ⬙   ≤ 🚗 ⤴ 🍴 ⦿ **P** *VISA* **⚫** **AE**
Badcall Bay, South : 2½ m. on A 894 ⊠ IV27 4TH – ℰ (01971) 502 080
– www.eddrachilles.com – enq@eddrachilles.com – Fax (01971) 502 477
– Mid March-mid October
11 rm (dinner included) � – ♦£ 82/85 ♦♦£ 124/130
Rest – (bar lunch) Menu £ 25 **s**
♦ Isolated hotel, converted from small part 18C former manse, magnificently set at
the head of Badcall Bay and its islands. Conservatory lounge. Traditional, well-kept
rooms. Dining room room with stone walls and flagstone floors.

SCRABSTER – Highland – 501 J 8 – see Thurso

SEIL (Isle of) – Argyll and Bute – 501 D 15 – ⊠ Oban   27 **B2**

Clachan Seil – Argyll and Bute – ⊠ Oban   27 **B2**

🏠 **Willowburn** ⬙   ≤ 🚗 ⦿ **P** *VISA* **⚫**
⊠ PA34 4TJ – ℰ (01852) 300 276 – www.willowburn.co.uk
– willowburn.hotel@virgin.net – Mid March-mid November
7 rm (dinner included) � – ♦£ 95/140 ♦♦£ 190
Rest – (dinner only) (booking essential for non-residents) Menu £ 45 **s**
♦ Simple, white-painted hotel overlooking Clachan Sound. Comfortable lounge with
birdwatching telescope. Cosy bedrooms show an individual, personal touch. Airy
dining room overlooks the water.

SCOTLAND

SELKIRK – Scottish Borders – **501** L 17 – **pop. 5 742** 🏴 *Scotland*

> ▶ Edinburgh 48 mi – Hawick 11 mi – Newcastle upon Tyne 77 mi
> ℹ Halliwell's House 𝒞 (01835) 863170 (Easter-October),
> bordersinfo@visitscotland.com
> 🏴 The Hill, 𝒞 (01750) 20 621
> ☞ Bowhill★★ **AC**, W : 3½ m. by A 708 – Abbotsford★★ **AC**, NE : 5½ m. by A 7
> and B 6360 – Tweed Valley★★. Melrose Abbey★★ (decorative
> sculpture★★★) **AC**, NE : 8½ m. by A 7 and A 6091 – Eildon Hills (⁂★★★)
> NE : 7½ m. by A 699 and B 6359

🛏 **Philipburn Country House** 🐾   🍴 🏊 🛁 P. ᴠɪѕᴀ ◍

West : 1 m. by A 707 at junction with A 708 ✉ *TD7 5LS* – 𝒞 *(01750) 20 747*
– *www.philipburnhousehotel.co.uk* – *info@philipburnhousehotel.co.uk*
– *Fax (01750) 721 690* – *Closed 11-25 January*
12 rm ⌹ – 🛏£ 110 🛏🛏£ 165
Rest *1745* – (dinner only and Sunday lunch) Menu £ 31 – Carte £ 31/34
Rest *Charlie's Bistro* – Carte £ 18/20
◆ Extended 18C house along private driveway with smart gardens. Eclectic variety of
rooms, most having pleasant rural outlook, two overlooking outdoor pool. Linen-laid
1745 has fine dining menu. Informal Charlie's for bistro favourites.

SCOTLAND

SHETLAND ISLANDS – **501** P/Q 3 – **pop. 21 988** 🏴 *Scotland*

> 🛬 Tingwall Airport : 𝒞 (01595) 840306, NW : 6½ m. of Lerwick by A 971
> 🚢 from Foula to Walls (Shetland Islands Council) 1-2 weekly (2 h 30 mn) –
> from Fair Isle to Sumburgh (Shetland Islands Council) 1-2 weekly
> (2 h 40 mn)
> 🚢 from Lerwick (Mainland) to Aberdeen and via Orkney Islands (Stromness)
> (P and O Scottish Ferries) – from Vidlin to Skerries (Shetland Islands
> Council) booking essential 3-4 weekly (1 h 30 mn) – from Lerwick
> (Mainland) to Skerries (Shetland Islands Council) 2 weekly (booking
> essential) (2 h 30 mn) – from Lerwick (Mainland) to Bressay (Shetland
> Islands Council) frequent services daily (7 mn) – from Laxo (Mainland) to
> Isle of Whalsay (Symbister) (Shetland Islands Council) frequent services
> daily (30 mn) – from Toft (Mainland) to Isle of Yell (Ulsta) (Shetland Islands
> Council) frequent services daily (20 mn) – from Isle of Yell (Gutcher) to Isle
> of Fetlar (Oddsta) and via Isle of Unst (Belmont) (Shetland Islands Council)
> – from Fair Isle to Sumburgh (Mainland) (Shetland Islands Council)
> 3 weekly (2 h 40 mn)
> ☞ Islands★ - Up Helly Aa (last Tuesday in January) – Mousa Broch★★★ **AC**
> (Mousa Island) – Jarlshof★★ - Lerwick to Jarlshof★ (≤★) – Shetland Croft
> House Museum★ **AC**

MAINLAND – Shetland Islands   31 **B2**

Lerwick – Shetland Islands – **pop. 6 830** 🏴 *Scotland*   31 **B2**

> ℹ The Market Cross, Lerwick 𝒞 (08701) 999440, info@visitshetland.com
> 🏴 Shetland Gott Dale, 𝒞 (01595) 840 369
> ☞ Clickhimin Broch★
> ☞ Gulber Wick (≤★), S : 2 m. by A 970

🛏 **Kveldsro House**   🐾 📶 P. ᴠɪѕᴀ ◍ ᴀᴇ ❶

Greenfield Pl ✉ *ZE1 0AQ* – 𝒞 *(01595) 692 195* – *www.shetlandhotels.com*
– *reception@kveldsrohotel.co.uk* – *Fax (01595) 696 595* – *Closed 25-26 December
and 1-2 January*
17 rm ⌹ – 🛏£ 95 🛏🛏£ 118
Rest – (bar lunch Monday-Saturday, carvery lunch Sunday) Carte £ 20/34 **s**
◆ Neat, modern style in evidence throughout this smoothly run hotel - its name
comes from the Norse for "evening peace". Tidy rooms, well-equipped and furnished
in pale wood. Classically smart and formally set restaurant.

Grand   🌿 📶 *VISA* 🟠 AE ①
149 Commercial St ✉ ZE1 0EX – ℰ *(01595) 692 826 – www.kgqhotels.co.uk*
– info@kgqhotels.co.uk – Fax (01595) 694 048 – Closed 24 December-4 January
24 rm ⌷ – 💵£77/89 💵💵£100   **Rest** – (bar lunch) Carte £ 18/30
♦ Handsome period hotel with turret and stepped gables. Above the row of ground-floor shops are neatly kept rooms with modern fittings, a simple lounge bar and a night-club. Comfortably furnished dining room with a formal atmosphere.

Shetland   ⟨ 📺 ⟨& rm, 🌿 📶 ⟨& 🅿 *VISA* 🟠 AE ①
Holmsgarth Rd ✉ ZE1 0PW – ℰ *(01595) 695 515 – www.shetlandhotels.com*
– reception@shetlandhotel.co.uk – Fax (01595) 695 828
63 rm ⌷ – 💵£85/110 💵💵£110 – 1 suite   **Rest** – (bar lunch) Carte £ 18/28 **s**
♦ Purpose-built hotel near the harbourside. Mahogany furnished bar, a choice of modern conference rooms and usefully fitted rooms in co-ordinated fabrics. Simply but formally arranged dining room.

Glen Orchy House   ⟨& rm, 🅿 *VISA* 🟠
20 Knab Rd ✉ ZE1 0AX – ℰ *(01595) 692 031 – www.guesthouselerwick.com*
– glenorchy.house@virgin.net – Fax (01595) 692 031
23 rm ⌷ – 💵£55 💵💵£80
Rest – Thai – (dinner only) (booking essential) (residents only) Carte £ 15/17 **s**
♦ Built as a convent in the 1900s and sympathetically extended. Colourful public areas. Bright honesty bar. Spotless bedrooms with neat modern fabrics and fittings. Restaurant offers authentic Thai menus.

Veensgarth – Shetland Islands   31 **B2**

Herrislea House   ⟨ 📶 🅿 *VISA* 🟠 ①
✉ ZE2 9SB – ℰ *(01595) 840 208 – www.herrisleahouse.co.uk*
– hotel@herrisleahouse.co.uk – Fax (01595) 840 630 – Closed Christmas, New Year and 3 weeks January
13 rm ⌷ – 💵£70 💵💵£110
Rest – (dinner only) (booking essential for non-residents) Carte £ 17/30 **s**
♦ Purpose-built hotel run by native islanders; a homely hall, with mounted antlers, leads to tidy bedrooms, pleasantly furnished in solid pine, and an angling themed bar. Neatly laid out but fairly informal restaurant.

ISLAND OF UNST – Shetland Islands   31 **B1**

Baltasound – Shetland Islands

Buness House ⟨≫⟩   ⟨ 🚗 ⟨ 🅿 *VISA* 🟠
East :½ m. by A 968 and Springpark Rd ✉ ZE2 9DS – ℰ *(01957) 711 315*
– www.users.zetnet.co.uk/buness-house – buness-house@zetnet.co.uk
– Fax (01957) 711 815 – Restricted opening December-February
3 rm ⌷ – 💵£70 💵💵£120
Rest – (by arrangement, communal dining) Menu £ 40 **s**
♦ Whitewashed house of 16C origin. Cosy, well-stocked library. Comfortable rooms facing Balta Sound, one decorated with Victorian prints and découpages. Nearby nature reserve. Willow-pattern china and sea views from the conservatory dining room.

SHIELDAIG – Highland – **501** D 11 – ✉ Strathcarron ▌ *Scotland*   29 **B2**
🄳 Edinburgh 226 mi – Inverness 70 mi – Kyle of Lochalsh 36 mi
🄶 Wester Ross ★★★

Tigh An Eilean   ⟨ 📶 *VISA* 🟠 AE
✉ IV54 8XN – ℰ *(01520) 755 251 – tighaneilea@keme.co.uk – Fax (01520) 755 321 – Mid March-October*
11 rm ⌷ – 💵£75 💵💵£160
Rest – (bar lunch) (booking essential for non-residents) Menu £ 40
♦ In a sleepy lochside village, an attractive, personally run 19C inn with fine views of the Shieldaig Islands. Cosy, well-kept bedrooms and a comfy lounge with a homely feel. Linen-clad dining room showing eclectic variety of art; Scottish produce to the fore.

SCOTLAND

SKEABOST – Highland – **501** B 11 – see Skye (Isle of)

SKIRLING – Scottish Borders – **501** – ✉ **Biggar** ▌ *Scotland*   26 **C2**

> ◻ Edinburgh 29 mi – Glasgow 45 mi – Peebles 16 mi
> ◙ Biggar★ - Gladstone Court Museum★, Greenhill Covenanting Museum★,
> S : 3 m. by A 72 and A 702. New Lanark★★, NW : 16 m. by A 72 and A 73

⟑ **Skirling House**   ⌷ ◑ ✕ ⟦ **P** **VISA** **◑◐**

✉ ML12 6HD – ℘ (01899) 860 274 – www.skirlinghouse.com
– enquiry@skirlinghouse.com – Fax (01899) 860 255 – Closed January, February
and 1 week autumn
5 rm ⌷ – ♥£80 ♥♥£120   **Rest** – (by arrangement) Menu £30 **s**
♦ Attractive Arts and Crafts house (1908). 16C Florentine carved ceiling in drawing
room. Comfortable bedrooms with modern conveniences. Daily dinner menu using
fresh produce.

SKYE (Isle of) – Highland – **501** B 11 – pop. 9 232 ▌ *Scotland*   29 **B2**

> ▤ from Mallaig to Isles of Eigg, Muck, Rhum and Canna (Caledonian
> MacBrayne Ltd) (summer only) – from Mallaig to Armadale (Caledonian
> MacBrayne Ltd) (summer only) 1-2 weekly (30 mn)
> ▤ from Mallaig to Armadale (Caledonian MacBrayne Ltd) 1-5 daily (30 mn) –
> from Uig to North Uist (Lochmaddy) or Isle of Harris (Tarbert) (Caledonian
> MacBrayne Ltd) 1-3 daily (1 h 50 mn) – from Sconser to Isle of Raasay
> (Caledonian MacBrayne Ltd) 9-10 daily (except Sunday) (15 mn)
> ◙ Island★★ - The Cuillins★★★ – Skye Museum of Island Life★ **AC**
> ◙ N : Trotternish Peninsula★★ – W : Duirinish Peninsula★ – Portree★

Broadford – Highland   29 **B2**

⟑ **Tigh an Dochais** without rest   ≤ ⌷ ✕ ⟦ **P** **VISA** **◑◐** **AE**

⟦◉⟧ 13 Harrapool, on A 87 ✉ IV49 9AQ – ℘ (01471) 820 022
– www.skyebedandbreakfast.co.uk – hopeskye@btinternet.com – April -
December
3 rm ⌷ – ♥£60 ♥♥£80
♦ Stylish, award-winning architecture; this is a striking house, full of glass, in a fabulous setting. Superb views at breakfast and stark, clean-lined surroundings at night.

Dunvegan – Highland   29 **B2**

⟑ **Roskhill House**   ⌷ **P** **VISA** **◑◐**

Roskhill, Southeast : 2½ m. by A 863 ✉ IV55 8ZD – ℘ (01470) 521 317
– www.roskhillhouse.co.uk – stay@roskhillhouse.co.uk – March-October
5 rm ⌷ – ♥£45/50 ♥♥£70   **Rest** – (by arrangement) Menu £20
♦ In friendly personal ownership, an extended, traditional 19C croft house which
preserves its exposed brick walls and peat fires. Bedrooms are homely and unpretentious. Once a post office, the dining room offers homely cooking at simple
wooden tables.

✕✕ **The Three Chimneys & The House Over-By** with rm ✎   ≤

Colbost, Northwest : 5¾ m. by A 863 on B 884   ⌷ ⅋ rm, **P** **VISA** **◑◐** **AE**
(Glendale) ✉ IV55 8ZT – ℘ (01470) 511 258 – www.threechimneys.co.uk
– eatandstay@threechimneys.co.uk – Fax (01470) 511 358 – Closed 5-30 January
6 rm ⌷ – ♥£159/265 ♥♥£238/265
Rest – Seafood – (Closed Sunday lunch) (dinner only in winter) (booking
essential) Menu £35/52
♦ Internationally renowned crofter's cottage restaurant on Loch Dunvegan shores.
Accomplished Skye seafood dishes, plus Highland lamb, beef and game. Sumptuous
bedrooms.

Edinbane – Highland
29 **B2**

Greshornish House ⤢ ≪ 🛏 🍴 ♨ P VISA ◎ AE
North : 3 ¾ m. by A 850 in direction of Dunvegan ✉ IV51 9PN – ℰ (01470)
582266 – www.greshornishhouse.com – info@greshornishhouse.com
– Fax (01470) 582345 – Restricted opening in winter
8 rm (dinner included) ⌑ – †£150/200 ††£190/248
Rest – (booking essential at lunch) Menu £38 – Carte £22/41
♦ Utter tranquillity: a beautifully sited hotel in 10 acres of grounds, with cluttered
sitting rooms, snooker room, smart bedrooms with a view - and Skye's only tennis
court! Conservatory breakfasts; Western Isle ingredients to fore in the dining room.

Flodigarry – Highland – ✉ Staffin
29 **B2**

Flodigarry Country House ⤢ ≪ 🛏 🍴 㐬 rm, P VISA ◎
✉ IV51 9HZ – ℰ (01470) 552203 – www.flodigarry.co.uk – info@flodigarry.co.uk
– Fax (01470) 552301 – Closed January and November
18 rm ⌑ – †£90/120 ††£180/200
Rest – (bar lunch Monday-Saturday) Carte £30/42
♦ With views of Staffin and the coast, a curio-filled country house once home to Flora
Macdonald. Traditional down to its old-world rooms, peat fire and 19C conservatory.
Semi-panelled candlelit restaurant.

Glendale – Highland
29 **A2**

Clach Ghlas without rest ⤢ ≪ 🛏 ♨ P
Lower Milovaig ✉ IV55 8WR – ℰ (01470) 511205 – www.clachghlas.com
– info@clachghlas.com – Fax (01470) 511205 – April-December
3 rm ⌑ – †£100 ††£140
♦ Modern house commanding superb hillside spot and vistas to lochs and head-
lands. Attractive breakfast conservatory; relaxing sitting room. Quiet bedrooms and
super Jacuzzis.

SCOTLAND

Portree – Highland – pop. 1 917
29 **B2**

🄸 Bayfield House, Bayfield Rd ℰ (08452) 255121

Cuillin Hills ⤢ ≪ 🛏 ♨ 㐬 rm, ⁙ 🛁 P VISA ◎ AE
Northeast : ¾ m. by A 855 ✉ IV51 9QU – ℰ (01478) 612003
– www.cuillinhills-hotel-skye.co.uk – info@cuillinhills-hotel-skye.co.uk
– Fax (01478) 613092
26 rm ⌑ – †£100/200 ††£300
Rest – (bar lunch Monday-Saturday, buffet lunch Sunday) Menu £40
– Carte £24/32
♦ Enlarged 19C hunting lodge in 15-acre grounds above lochside with fine views.
Well-proportioned drawing room with broad Chesterfields; usefully equipped rooms
vary in size. Smart and spacious dining room with views of Portree Bay.

Bosville ≪ 🛏 ⁙ VISA ◎ AE
Bosville Terrace ✉ IV51 9DG – ℰ (01478) 612846
– www.macleodhotels.co.uk/bosville – bosville@macleodhotels.co.uk
– Fax (01478) 613434
19 rm ⌑ – †£69/120 ††£88/128
Rest *Chandlery* – see restaurant listing
Rest *Bistro* – Carte £17/31
♦ Well-established, busy hotel overlooking harbour and hills. First-floor sitting room
and tidy, modern accommodation in co-ordinated décor. Buzzy ground floor bistro.

Rosedale ≪ 🛏 P VISA ◎
Beaumont Crescent ✉ IV51 9DB – ℰ (01478) 613131
– www.rosedalehotelskye.co.uk – rosedalehotelsky@aol.com – Fax (01478)
612531 – 20 March-October
18 rm ⌑ – †£40/60 ††£100/140   **Rest** – (dinner only) Menu £29
♦ Converted quayside terrace of fishermen's houses with fine views over the water.
Neat and cosy lounge and compact but immaculately kept bedrooms in floral prints.
First-floor, linen-clad restaurant with a traditionally based, seasonal menu.

SKYE (Isle of)

↑ **Almondbank** without rest   ⇔ 🚗 📶 🅿 _VISA_ ⓪
Viewfield Rd, Southwest : ¾ m. on A 87 ⊠ *IV51 9EU –* ℰ *(01478) 612 696*
– j.n.almondbank@btconnect.com – Fax (01478) 613 114
4 rm ⊿ – †£55/65 ††£65/75
♦ Situated away from the town centre, a converted modern house, well maintained
by the friendly owner. Spotless bedrooms; superb views across Portree Bay.

XX **The Chandlery** – at Bosville Hotel   _VISA_ ⓪ 𝔸𝔼
Bosville Terrace ⊠ *IV51 9DG –* ℰ *(01478) 612 846 – www.macleodhotels.co.uk*
– bosville@macleodhotels.co.uk – Fax (01478) 613 434
Rest – Seafood – (dinner only) (booking essential) Menu £40
♦ Purple colour scheme distinguishes this formal but relaxed restaurant from adjacent bistro. Skilfully executed seafood dishes display a proven touch of orginality and
flair.

Skeabost – ⊠ Skeabost Bridge

🏠 **Toravaig House**   ⇔ 🚗 ⅌ 📶 🅿 _VISA_ ⓪
Knock Bay, on A 851 ⊠ *IV44 8RE –* ℰ *(01471) 820 200 – www.skyehotel.co.uk*
– info@skyehotel.co.uk – Fax (01471) 833 231
9 rm ⊿ – †£70/150 ††£120/160
Rest – (booking essential for non-residents) Menu £22/39 **s**
♦ Quality range of fabrics and furniture in a whitewashed house on road to Mallaig
ferry. Small but perfectly formed lounge. Rooms designed to a high standard. Hearty
sea views. Dine on best Skye produce in attractive surroundings.

Sleat – Highland   30 **C1**

🏠🏠 **Kinloch Lodge** ⌖   ⇔ 🚗 🐎 📶 🅿 _VISA_ ⓪
⊠ *IV43 8QY –* ℰ *(01471) 833 214 – www.kinloch-lodge.co.uk*
– reservations@kinloch-lodge.co.uk – Fax (01471) 833 277
13 rm ⊿ – †£200/275 ††£225/275 – 1 suite
Rest – (booking essential for non-residents) Menu £25/49 – Carte lunch
£40/53 ⅋
♦ An historic 17C hunting lodge on Loch Na Dal. Antiques abound, with a very
handsome and comfortable drawing room. The bedrooms are spacious and reflect
the age of the house. Atmospheric candlelit dining.

Struan – Highland   29 **B2**

🏠 **Ullinish Country Lodge** ⌖   ⇔ 🚗 ⅌ 🅿 _VISA_ ⓪
West : 1½ m. by A 863 ⊠ *IV56 8FD –* ℰ *(01470) 572 214*
– www.theisleofskye.co.uk – ullinish@theisleofskye.co.uk – Fax (01470) 572 341
– Closed January and 1 week November
6 rm ⊿ – †£120 ††£160
Rest – (light lunch) (booking essential for non-residents) Menu £48
♦ Country lodge comforts in superb windswept spot with fine views. Chilled sitting
room; each bedroom has a distinct style with luxury fabrics and character beds built
of wood. Skye ingredients put to compelling, highly original use on creative modern
dishes.

Waternish – Highland   29 **A2**

X **Loch Bay Seafood**   ⅌ 🅿 _VISA_ ⓪ 𝔸𝔼
1 MacLeod Terrace, Stein ⊠ *IV55 8GA –* ℰ *(01470) 592 235*
– www.lochbay-seafood-restaurant.co.uk
– reservations@lochbay-seafood-restaurant.co.uk – Fax (01470) 592 235
– Easter-October and New Year
Rest – Seafood – (closed Sunday and Monday) (booking essential)
Carte £19/29
♦ Cottage restaurant with simple wooden tables and benches. Tiny, atmospheric
room where the freshest local seafood, including halibut, sole and turbot, is prepared
faultlessly.

SCOTLAND

⏸ **Stein Inn** with rm ⬙   ⬍ ⬈ **P** *VISA* ⓶
MacLeod Terr, Stein ⊠ IV55 8GA – ℰ (01470) 592 362 – www.stein-inn.co.uk
– angus.teresa@steininn.co.uk – Closed 25 December, 1 January
5 rm ⌑ – †£40 ††£50
Rest – Seafood – (residents only Monday dinner except Bank Holidays)
Carte £16/25
♦ Solid traditional fare in the dining room. The oldest inn on Skye with dramatic
waterfront views. Charming friendly place serving locally brewed ale and over 90 malt
whiskies. Comfy well-kept rooms with seaview.

SLEAT – Highland – see Skye (Isle of)

SORN – East Ayrshire – **501** H 17   25 **B2**
▶ Edinburgh 67 mi – Ayr 15 mi – Glasgow 35 mi

⏸ **The Sorn Inn** with rm   **P** *VISA* ⓶
🏡 *35 Main St ⊠ KA5 6HU – ℰ (01290) 551 305 – www.sorninn.com*
– craig@sorninn.com – Fax (01290) 553 470
– Closed 2 weeks in January and Monday
4 rm ⌑ – †£40/45 ††£70/75   **Rest** – Menu £15 (lunch) – Carte £19/28
♦ Family run, traditional pub in small village. Its hub is the dining room, where good
value, locally sourced modern dishes are cooked in an accomplished way. Comfy
rooms.

SOUTH QUEENSFERRY – City of Edinburgh – **501** J 15 – pop. **9 370**   26 **C1**
▶ Edinburgh 9 mi – Dunfermline 8 mi – Glasgow 41 mi

🏨 **Dakota**   🖥 ⬥ ⬙ ⬗ **P** *VISA* ⓶ **AE** ⓪
Ferrymuir Retail Park ⊠ EH30 9QZ – ℰ (0870) 423 42 93
– www.dakotahotels.co.uk – info@dakotahotels.co.uk – Fax (0131) 319 3699
132 rm – †£99/149 ††£99/149, ⌑ £10.95
Rest *Bar & Grill* – Carte £21/45 **s**
♦ Vast, vibrant black block on retail park; has modern, minimalistic décor and eponymous aeroplane memorabilia. Comfortable, spacious bedrooms with contempory,
quality feel. Spacious Bar and Grill serves something to suit all tastes.

SOUTH UIST – Western Isles Outer Hebrides – **501** XY 12 – see Uist (Isles of)

SPEAN BRIDGE – Highland – **501** F 13   30 **C3**
▶ Edinburgh 143 mi – Fort William 10 mi – Glasgow 94 mi – Inverness 58 mi
– Oban 60 mi
ℹ The Kingdom of Scotland, by Fort William, Inverness-shire v (0845)
2255121 (April-October), info@visitscotland.com
⬡ , ℰ (01397) 703 907

🏠 **Corriegour Lodge**   ⬍ ⬚ ⬙ **P** *VISA* ⓶ **AE** ⓪
Loch Lochy, North : 8¾ m. on A 82 ⊠ PH34 4EA – ℰ (01397) 712 685
– www.corriegour-lodge-hotel.com – info@corriegour-lodge-hotel.com
– Fax (01397) 712 696 – March-October and New Year
11 rm ⌑ – †£80/90 ††£159/179
Rest – (booking essential for non-residents) Carte £40/48
♦ Enthusiastically run 19C hunting lodge in woods and gardens above Loch Lochy.
Bright, individually decorated rooms and a cosy bar and lounge share a warm, tradi-
tional feel. Formally set dining room with wide picture windows.

🏠 **Spean Lodge** without rest   ⬚ ⬙ **P** *VISA* ⓶
⊠ *PH34 4EP – ℰ (01397) 712 004 – www.speanlodge.co.uk*
– welcome@speanlodge.co.uk – Closed 24-26 December
3 rm ⌑ – †£50/60 ††£70/80
♦ 19C former shooting lodge whose gardens are filled with mature trees. Antiques
and period furnishings abound. Utterly restful sitting room. Pleasantly individual
rooms.

SCOTLAND

SCOTLAND

↑ **Corriechoille Lodge** ⊗ ← ⇔ ₺ rm, ⚿ 🛜 **P.** 𝘝𝘐𝘚𝘈 𝗺𝗼
East : 2¾ m. on Corriechoille rd ⊠ *PH34 4EY –* ☏ *(01397) 712 002*
– www.corriechoille.com – April-October
4 rm ☷ – ♦£46 ♦♦£72 **Rest** – (by arrangement) Menu £25
♦ Off the beaten track in quiet estate land, a part 18C lodge: stylishly modern lounge, spacious en suite rooms: those facing south have fine views of the Grey Corries.

↑ **Distant Hills** without rest ⇔ ⚿ 🛜 **P.** 𝘝𝘐𝘚𝘈 𝗺𝗼
Roybridge Road, East ½ m. on A86 ⊠ *PH34 4EU –* ☏ *(01397) 712 452*
– www.distanthills.com – enquiry@distanthills.com – Closed January
7 rm – ♦£65 ♦♦£78
♦ Welcoming guesthouse with comfy, contemporary furnishings. Lounge boasts French windows onto terrace and colourful garden; small stream nearby. Tea on arrival. Wide ranging breakfast.

✕✕ **Russel's at Smiddy House** with rm **P.** 𝘝𝘐𝘚𝘈 𝗺𝗼
Roybridge Road ⊠ *PH34 4EU –* ☏ *(01397) 712 335 – www.smiddyhouse.co.uk*
– enquiry@smiddyhouse.co.uk – Fax (01397) 712 043 – Closed Monday except June-August and Tuesday April-May and September
4 rm – ♦£60/75 ♦♦£75/85
Rest – (dinner only) (booking essential) Menu £30 **s**
♦ Spacious Victorian house in small Highland village with intimate, candlelit dining rooms and attentive service. Weekly-changing menu with strong, locally sourced seafood base. Immaculately-kept, individually decorated bedrooms.

✕ **Old Pines** with rm ⊗ ← 🕭 ₺ rm, 🛜 **P.** 𝘝𝘐𝘚𝘈 𝗺𝗼 𝗔𝗘 ①
Northwest : 1½ m. by A 82 on B 8004 ⊠ *PH34 4EG –* ☏ *(01397) 712 324*
– www.oldpines.co.uk – enquiries@oldpines.co.uk
7 rm ☷ – ♦£45/70 ♦♦£90/110
Rest – (booking essential for non-residents) Menu £35 (dinner) – Carte lunch £25/38
♦ There's almost a dinner party atmosphere at this warm, simple restaurant. The emphasis is firmly on the seasonal and the organic. The staff are very friendly. The bedrooms are well-kept.

Red = Pleasant. Look for the red ✕ and 🏠 symbols.

SPITTAL OF GLENSHEE – Perth and Kinross – **501** J 13 **28 C2**
– ⊠ **Blairgowrie** ▌ *Scotland*
▶ Edinburgh 69 mi – Aberdeen 74 mi – Dundee 35 mi
🎿 Glenshee (❄ ★★) (chairlift **AC**)

🏠 **Dalmunzie Castle** ⊗ ← ⇔ 🕭 🔌 ✕ 🎞 🛁 ⚿ **P.** 𝘝𝘐𝘚𝘈 𝗺𝗼
⊠ *PH10 7QG –* ☏ *(01250) 885 224 – www.dalmunzie.com*
– reservations@dalmunzie.com – Fax (01250) 885 225 – Closed 1-29 December
17 rm ☷ – ♦£95/155 ♦♦£160/250 **Rest** – (bar lunch) Menu £42 **s**
♦ Edwardian hunting lodge in a magnificent spot, encircled by mountains. Traditional rooms mix antique and pine furniture. Bar with cosy panelled alcove and leather chairs. Modern dining room with views down the valley.

STEVENSTON – North Ayrshire – **501** F 17 – pop. 9 129 **25 A2**
▶ Edinburgh 82 mi – Ayr 19 mi – Glasgow 36 mi

↑ **Ardeer Farm Steading** without rest ⚿ 🛜 **P.** 𝘝𝘐𝘚𝘈 𝗺𝗼
Ardeer Mains Farm, East : ¾ m. by A 738 and B 752, on no through rd
⊠ *KA20 3DD –* ☏ *(01294) 465 438 – www.ardeersteading.co.uk*
– info@ardeersteading.co.uk
6 rm ☷ – ♦£35 ♦♦£45/48
♦ Comfortable family-owned guest house has contemporary furnishings, with bright cushions and bed throws. Pleasant breakfast room and modern lounge with cream leather sofas.

▶ Edinburgh 37 mi – Dunfermline 23 mi – Falkirk 14 mi – Glasgow 28 mi – Greenock 52 mi – Motherwell 30 mi – Oban 87 mi – Perth 35 mi

🛈 Dumbarton Rd ℰ (08707) 200620, stirlingtic@aillst.ossian.net -Stirling Royal Burgh, Castle Esplanade ℰ (08707) 200622, info@rbsvc.visitscotland.com - Pirnhall, Motorway Service Area, junction 9, M 9/ M80 ℰ (08707) 200621 (April-October), info@pirnhall.visitscotland.com

◉ Town★★ – Castle★★ **AC** (Site★★★, external elevations★★★, Stirling Heads★★, Argyll and Sutherland Highlanders Regimental Museum★) B – Argyll's Lodging★ (Renaissance decoration★) B **A** – Church of the Holy Rude★B **B**

◉ Wallace Monument (⁂★★) NE : 2½ m. by A 9 - A - and B 998. Dunblane★ (Cathedral★★, West Front★★), N : 6½ m. by A 9 A

STIRLING

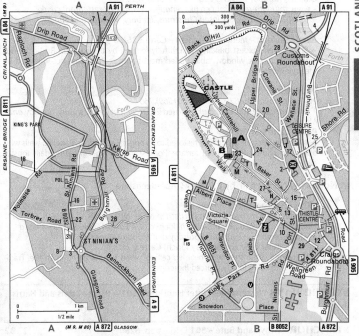

SCOTLAND

Park Lodge
32 Park Terrace ✉ *FK8 2JS –* ℰ *(01786) 474 862 – www.parklodge.net – info@parklodge.net – Fax (01786) 449 748 – Closed Christmas and New Year*　　　　B**a**

9 rm ☲ – †£65/85 ††£110/115　　**Rest** – (Closed Sunday) Menu £ 15/28 **s**
♦ Creeper-clad Georgian and Victorian house, still in private hands and furnished with an enviable collection of antiques. Compact but well-equipped rooms with a stylish feel. Intimate dining room overlooking a pretty garden.

↑ **Number 10** without rest   🗔 🕸
Gladstone Pl ⊠ *FK8 2NN* – *𝒞 (01786) 472 681* – *www.cameron-10.co.uk*
– cameron-10@tinyonline.co.uk – *Fax (01786) 472 681*   B**v**
3 rm ⊡ – †£ 50/60 ††£ 60
♦ Surprisingly spacious 19C terrace house in a pleasant suburb. Pine furnished en suite bedrooms are characteristically well kept and comfortable. Friendly owner.

↑ **West Plean House** without rest ⊗   🗔 🕭 🕸 **P** 𝗩𝗜𝗦𝗔 ⓶⓪
South : 3½ m. on A 872 (Denny rd) ⊠ *FK7 8HA* – *𝒞 (01786) 812 208*
– www.westpleanhouse.com – *moira@westpleanhouse.com* – *Fax (01786)*
480 550 – *Closed mid December-mid January*
3 rm ⊡ – †£ 42/45 ††£ 64/70
♦ Dating back to the 1800s, a homely and traditional house under pleasant personal ownership. Simple en suite accommodation. Neat gardens, duckpond and working farm close by.

STONEHAVEN – **Aberdeenshire** – **501** N 13 ▌ *Scotland*   28 **D2**
   ▶ Edinburgh 109 mi – Aberdeen 16 mi – Montrose 22 mi
   ⓖ Dunnottar Castle★★, S : 1½ m. by A 92

XX **Tolbooth**   𝗩𝗜𝗦𝗔 ⓶⓪
Old Pier, Harbour ⊠ *AB39 2JU* – *𝒞 (01569) 762 287*
– www.tolbooth-restaurant.co.uk – *enquiries@tolbooth-restaurant.co.uk*
– Fax (01569) 762 287 – *Closed Christmas, January, Monday and Sunday*
October-April
Rest – Seafood – Menu £ 16 (lunch) – Carte £ 26/30
♦ Stonehaven's oldest building, delightfully located by the harbour. Rustic interior with lovely picture window table. Varied menus with seafood base accompanied by great views.

XX **Carron**   🕭 𝗩𝗜𝗦𝗔 ⓶⓪
20 Cameron St ⊠ *AB39 2HS* – *𝒞 (01569) 760 460*
– www.carron-restaurant.co.uk – *Closed 24 December- mid January, Sunday and*
Monday
Rest – Carte £ 21/30
♦ 1930s Art Deco elegance fully restored to its original splendor. Panelled walls with old mono photos. Sunny front terrace. Popular menus highlighted by daily lobster dishes.

at Netherley North : 6 m. by B 979 – ⊠ Aberdeenshire

XX **The Crynoch** – at Lairhillock Inn   **P** 𝗩𝗜𝗦𝗔 ⓶⓪ 𝗔𝗘
Northeast : 1½ m. by B 979 on Portlethen rd ⊠ *AB39 3QS* – *𝒞 (01569) 730 001*
– www.lairhillock.co.uk – *info@lairhillock.co.uk* – *Fax (01569) 731 175* – *Closed*
25-26 December, 1-2 January, Sunday and Monday dinner
Rest – (dinner only and Sunday lunch) Carte £ 24/35
♦ Converted cattle shed with beamed ceiling, wood panelling and open fire. Traditional dishes using locally sourced ingredients.

STORNOWAY – **Western Isles Outer Hebrides** – **501** A 9 – **see Lewis and Harris**
(Isle of)

STRACHUR – **Argyll and Bute** – **501** E 15 – **pop. 628**   27 **B2**
   ▶ Edinburgh 112 mi – Glasgow 66 mi – Inverness 162 mi – Perth 101 mi

🔠 **The Creggans Inn**   ⩽ 🗔 🕆 **P** 𝗩𝗜𝗦𝗔 ⓶⓪
⊠ *PA27 8BX* – *𝒞 (01369) 860 279* – *www.creggans-inn.co.uk*
– info@creggans-inn.co.uk
14 rm ⊡ – †£ 65/85 ††£ 90/150 – 1 suite   **Rest** – Carte £ 20/30
♦ Locally renowned inn, with splendid views over Loch Fyne. Cosy bar with busy pub dining trade and two lounges, one with fine outlook. Individually styled, comfy rooms. Large dining room with wood floor and warm colour scheme.

✗ **Inver Cottage**   ← 🏠 ⇔ P VISA 🐱
Strathlaclan, Southwest : 6½ m. by A 886 on B 8000 ⌧ *PA27 8BU –* ✆ *(01369) 860 537 – www.invercottage.co.uk*
– Closed 23 December-early April, Monday and Tuesday
Rest – Carte £ 17/32
♦ Wonderfully located former crofters' cottage with fine views over loch and mountains. The simple little restaurant, with its own craft shop, serves tasty Scottish based menus.

STRANRAER – Dumfries and Galloway – **501** E 19 – pop. 10 851   25 **A3**
 📖 *Scotland*

> ▶ Edinburgh 132 mi – Ayr 51 mi – Dumfries 75 mi
> ⛴ to Northern Ireland (Belfast) (Stena Line) (1 h 45 mn) – to Northern Ireland (Belfast) (Stena Line) 4-5 daily (1 h 45 mn/3 h 15 mn)
> 🛈 28 Harbour St ✆ (01776) 702595, stranraer@dgtb.visitscotland.com
> 🏌 Creachmore Leswalt, ✆ (01776) 870 245
> ◉ Logan Botanic Garden★ **AC**, S : 11 m. by A 77, A 716 and B 7065

⛫ **Glenotter** without rest   🚗 🕸 P
Leswalt Rd, Northwest : 1 m. on A 718 ⌧ *DG9 0EP –* ✆ *(01776) 703 199*
– www.glenotter.co.uk – enquiries@glenotter.co.uk – Closed 25-26 December and 1 January
3 rm ⌂ – ♦£ 40/42 ♦♦£ 55/60
♦ Homely guesthouse run by a husband and wife team, on main road just out of town, convenient for ferry. Well-kept rooms in co-ordinated colours are simple and sensibly priced.

at Kirkcolm Northwest : 6 m. by A 718 – ⌧ Stranraer

🏠 **Corsewall Lighthouse** ⌖   ← 🔔 ᠙ rm, P VISA 🐱 AE ①
Corsewall Point, Northwest : 4¼ m. by B 738 ⌧ *DG9 0QG –* ✆ *(01776) 853 220*
– www.lighthousehotel.co.uk – info@lighthousehotel.co.uk – Fax (01776) 854 231
5 rm ⌂ – ♦£ 130/150 ♦♦£ 200/250 – 3 suites
Rest – Menu £ 33 (dinner) – Carte £ 28/31
♦ Sensitively converted and family run, a 19C working lighthouse at the mouth of Loch Ryan. Snug bedrooms in traditional fabrics - views of the sea or the windswept promontory. Simple, characterful restaurant with seascapes and old black beams.

> Your opinions are important to us:
> please write and let us know about your discoveries and experiences – good and bad!

STRATHPEFFER – Highland – **501** G 11 – pop. 918   30 **C2**
> ▶ Edinburgh 174 mi – Inverness 18 mi
> 🛈 The Square ✆ (01997) 421415, (0845) 2255121 (April-October), info@visitscotland.com
> 🏌 Strathpeffer Spa Golf Course Rd, ✆ (01997) 421 219

⛫ **Craigvar** without rest   🚗 🕸 📶 P VISA 🐱
The Square ⌧ *IV14 9DL –* ✆ *(01997) 421 622 – www.craigvar.com*
– craigvar@talk21.com – Closed Christmas and New Year
3 rm ⌂ – ♦£ 37/40 ♦♦£ 68/72
♦ Georgian house overlooking main square of pleasant former spa town. Charming owner guarantees an agreeable stay. Bedrooms are crammed with antiques and original fittings.

SCOTLAND

STRATHYRE – Stirling – **501** H 15 – ⊠ **Callander** 🏴 *Scotland*   27 **B2**

> ◐ Edinburgh 62 mi – Glasgow 53 mi – Perth 42 mi
> 🅖 The Trossachs ★★★ (Loch Katrine ★★) SW : 14 m. by A 84 and A 821 –
> Hilltop viewpoint ★★★ (❄ ★★★) SW : 16½ m. by A 84 and A 821

XX   **Creagan House** with rm   ⇐ **P** 𝘝𝘐𝘚𝘈 ◍◍ 𝖠𝖤
on A 84 ⊠ *FK18 8ND* – *℃ (01877) 384 638* – *www.creaganhouse.co.uk*
– *eatandstay@creaganhouse.co.uk* – *Fax (01877) 384 319*
– *Closed February, 1-19 November and 24-26 December*
5 rm � – **†**£70 **††**£120
Rest – (Closed Wednesday and Thursday) (dinner only) (booking essential)
Menu £30
♦ Surrounded by hills which inspired Sir Walter Scott; a feast for the eye to be enjoyed in baronial style dining room. French classics with Scottish overtones. Cosy rooms.

STROMNESS – Orkney Islands – **501** K 7 – see **Orkney Islands**

> The ✿ award is the crème de la crème.
> This is awarded to restaurants
> which are really worth travelling miles for!

STRONTIAN – Highland – **501** D 13   29 **B3**

> ◐ Edinburgh 139 mi – Fort William 23 mi – Oban 66 mi
> 🅑 Acharacle ℃ (01967) 402131 (April-October)

🏠   **Kilcamb Lodge** ⌂   ⇐ 🛋 ⏏ ⤳ ⛲ **P** 𝘝𝘐𝘚𝘈 ◍◍ 𝖠𝖤
⊠ *PH36 4HY* – *℃ (01967) 402 257* – *www.kilcamblodge.co.uk*
– *enquiries@kilcamblodge.co.uk* – *Fax (01967) 402 041* – *Closed January*
10 rm � – **†**£95/148 **††**£188/198
Rest – (booking essential for non-residents at dinner) Menu £ 18/48
♦ A spectacular location in 19 acres of lawn and woodland, leading down to a private shore on Loch Sunart. The idyll continues indoors: immaculate bedrooms; thoughtful extras. Savour views from large windows and tuck into roast grouse.

STRUAN – Highland – see **Skye (Isle of)**

STRUY – Highland – **501** F 11   30 **C2**

> ◐ Edinburgh 180 mi – Inverness 19 mi – Kyle of Lochalsh 82 mi

X   **The Glass at the Struy Inn**   **P** 𝘝𝘐𝘚𝘈 ◍◍ ◍
⊠ *IV4 7JS* – *℃ (01463) 761 219* – *www.glassrestaurant.supanet.com*
– *glassrest@supanet.com* – *20 March - 20 October*
Rest – (dinner only and Sunday lunch) (booking essential) Menu £ 23
– Carte £ 20/27
♦ Converted inn retains a traditional, almost homely feel. Wide-ranging menu of wholesome, satisfying dishes, plus a blackboard listing daily specials and fresh seafood.

SWINTON – Scottish Borders – **501** N 16 – pop. 472 – ⊠ **Duns**   26 **D2**

> ◐ Edinburgh 49 mi – Berwick-upon-Tweed 13 mi – Glasgow 93 mi – Newcastle upon Tyne 66 mi

🏠   **The Wheatsheaf** with rm   🛋 🛋 ⓖ rm, ⅍ **P** 𝘝𝘐𝘚𝘈 ◍◍
Main Street ⊠ *TD11 3JJ* – *℃ (01890) 860 257* – *www.wheatsheaf-swinton.co.uk*
– *reception@wheatsheaf-swinton.co.uk* – *Fax (01890) 860 688*
– *Closed 25-26 December and 2 January*
10 rm ⌑ – **†**£75 **††**£112   **Rest** – Carte £ 19/39
♦ A village inn with firelit real ale bar and comfortable, well-furnished rooms. Classic, unfussy seasonal dishes bring out the distinctive flavour of local produce.

TAIN – Highland – **501** H 10   30 **D2**
▶ Edinburgh 191 mi – Inverness 35 mi – Wick 91 mi
🏨 Tain Chapel Rd, ℰ (01862) 892 314
🏌 Tarbat Portmahomack, ℰ (01862) 871 278

↑ **Golf View House** without rest   ⪕ 🚗 ⌘ **P** **VISA** **CO**
13 Knockbreck Rd ⌂ IV19 1BN – ℰ (01862) 892 856 – www.golf-view.co.uk
– golfview@hotmail.co.uk – Fax (01862) 892 856 – 15 March-October
5 rm ⌂ – ♦£40/60 ♦♦£60/66
♦ Built as a manse, a local sandstone house overlooking the Firth and the fairways.
Bright rooms are well kept and tidy. Lawn and flowers shaded by beech trees.

at Cadboll Southeast : 8½ m. by A 9 and B 9165 (Portmahomack rd) off Hilton rd
– ⌂ Tain

🏠 **Glenmorangie House** ⌖   ⪕ 🚗 🕭 🌾 ⅋ **P** **VISA** **CO** **AE**
Fearn ⌂ IV20 1XP – ℰ (01862) 871 671 – www.theglenmorangiehouse.com
– relax@glenmorangieplc.co.uk – Fax (01862) 871 625 – Closed January
9 rm (dinner included) ⌂ – ♦£190 ♦♦£380 – 3 suites
Rest – (dinner only) (booking essential for non-residents) (communal dining,
set menu only) Menu £45
♦ Restored part 17C house owned by the famous distillery. Tasteful, old-world morning room and more informal firelit lounge; house party ambience prevails. Smart,
comfy rooms. Imposing communal dining room: gilt-framed portraits, eastern rugs
and a long table.

TALMINE – Highland – **501** G 8 – ⌂ Lairg   30 **C1**
▶ Edinburgh 245 mi – Inverness 86 mi – Thurso 48 mi

↑ **Cloisters** without rest ⌖   ⪕ 🚗 ⅋ **P**
Church Holme ⌂ IV27 4YP – ℰ (01847) 601 286 – www.cloistertal.demon.co.uk
– reception@cloistertal.demon.co.uk – Fax (01847) 601 286 – Closed Christmas
and New Year
3 rm ⌂ – ♦£28/33 ♦♦£50/55
♦ Pleasantly located guesthouse, with guest areas in converted church. Simple but
trim and spotless rooms in annexe; superb views of Rabbit Islands and Tongue Bay.

TARBERT – Western Isles Outer Hebrides – **501** Z 10 – see Lewis and Harris (Isle of)

TARBET – Argyll and Bute – **501** F 15 – ⌂ Arrochar   27 **B2**
▶ Edinburgh 88 mi – Glasgow 42 mi – Inverness 138 mi – Perth 78 mi

↑ **Lomond View** without rest   ⪕ 🚗 ⅋ 🕪 **P** **VISA** **CO**
on A 82 ⌂ G83 7DG – ℰ (01301) 702 477 – www.lomondview.co.uk
– lomondviewhouse@aol.com – Fax (01301) 702 477
3 rm ⌂ – ♦£60/70 ♦♦£75/80
♦ Purpose-built guesthouse which lives up to its name: there are stunning loch
views. Spacious sitting room. Light and airy breakfast room. Sizeable, modern bedrooms.

TAYVALLICH – Argyll and Bute – **501** D 15 – ⌂ Lochgilphead   27 **B2**
▶ Edinburgh 148 mi – Glasgow 103 mi – Inverness 157 mi

🍴 **Tayvallich Inn**   ⪕ 🏠 **P** **VISA** **CO**
⌂ PA31 8PL – ℰ (01546) 870 282 – www.tayvallichinn.co.uk
– glen@tayvallichinn.co.uk – Closed 25-26 December
Rest – (Closed in winter Monday-Tuesday) Carte £16/32
♦ Well-regarded pub in little coastal hamlet close to the shores of Loch Sween.
Interior of pine panelling and log fires. Simple or creative seafood dishes are the
speciality.

SCOTLAND

945

THORNHILL – Dumfries and Galloway – **501** I 18 – pop. 1 633   25 **B2**

■ Scotland

▶ Edinburgh 64 mi – Ayr 44 mi – Dumfries 15 mi – Glasgow 63 mi
◉ Drumlanrig Castle ★★ (cabinets ★) **AC**, NW : 4 m. by A 76

Trigony House   🚄 🛰 ⁽ᵞ⁾ P̱ VISA ◍

Closeburn, South : 1½ m. on A 76 ⊠ DG3 5EZ – ℰ (01848) 331 211
– www.countryhousehotelscotland.com – info@trigonyhotel.co.uk
– Closed 25-26 December

10 rm � – †£ 70 ††£ 160   **Rest** – (closed Monday lunch) Carte £ 19/31
♦ Ivy-clad Victorian shooting lodge, family owned, mixes period décor and modern
art. Cosy bar with an open fire. Traditional rooms overlook four acres of woodland
and garden. Tasty, locally inspired dishes.

Gillbank House without rest   🚄 ⁄⁄ P̱ VISA ◍

8 East Morton St ⊠ DG3 5LZ – ℰ (01848) 330 597 – www.gillbank.co.uk
– hanne@gillbank.co.uk – Fax (01848) 331 713

6 rm ⊆ – †£ 45 ††£ 65
♦ Victorian stone built personally run house just off town square. Guests' sitting
room and airy breakfast room. Spacious, well-furnished bedrooms with bright décor.

THURSO – Highland – **501** J 8 – pop. 7 737 ■ Scotland   30 **D1**

▶ Edinburgh 289 mi – Inverness 133 mi – Wick 21 mi
⛴ from Scrabster to Stromness (Orkney Islands) (P and O Scottish Ferries) (2 h)
🛈 Riverside ℰ (0845) 2255121 (April-October)
⛳ Newlands of Geise, ℰ (01847) 893 807
◉ Strathy Point ★ (≤ ★★★) W : 22 m. by A 836

Forss House ⌂   🚄 ◍ 🛰 P̱ VISA ◍ AE ⓪

Forss, West : 5½ m. on A 836 ⊠ KW14 7XY – ℰ (01847) 861 201
– www.forsshousehotel.co.uk – anne@forsshousehotel.co.uk – Fax (01847)
861 301 – Closed 23 December-6 January

14 rm ⊆ – †£ 105 ††£ 155   **Rest** – (dinner only) Carte £ 28/36
♦ Traditional décor sets off the interior of this 19C house, smoothly run in a friendly
style. Peaceful location. Annexed rooms are the more contemporary. Vast choice of
malts in restaurant bar.

Murray House   ⁄⁄ ⁽ᵞ⁾ P̱

1 Campbell St ⊠ KW14 7HD – ℰ (01847) 895 759 – www.murrayhousebb.com
– enquiries@murrayhousebb.com – Closed Christmas and New Year

5 rm ⊆ – †£ 30/35 ††£ 50/70   **Rest** – (by arrangement) Menu £ 16
♦ A centrally located and family owned Victorian town house. Pine furnished bedrooms are colourfully decorated and carefully maintained. Modern dining room with
home-cooked evening meals.

at Scrabster Northwest : 2¼ m. on A9

The Captain's Galley   VISA ◍ ⓪

The Harbour ⊠ KW14 7UJ – ℰ (01847) 894 999 – www.captainsgalley.co.uk
reservations@captainsgalley – Closed 25 December, 1 January, Sunday and Monday
Rest – Seafood – (booking essential) (dinner only and lunch June-September)
Menu £ 25/40 **s**
♦ Former ice house and salmon station, boasting a concise menu of unfussy, flavoursome, largely seafood dishes. Landed in the harbour, fish is strictly seasonal and
sustainable.

TIGHNABRUAICH – Argyll and Bute – **501** E 16   27 **B3**

▶ Edinburgh 113 mi – Glasgow 63 mi – Oban 66 mi

An Lochan   ≤ ⁽ᵞ⁾ P̱ VISA ◍

⊠ PA21 2BE – ℰ (01700) 811 239 – www.anlochan.co.uk – info@anlochan.co.uk
– Fax (01700) 811 300 – Closed Christmas

12 rm ⊆ – †£ 190 ††£ 190   **Rest** – Carte £ 25/35
♦ Privately owned 19C hotel with firelit shinty bar, in an unspoilt village overlooking
the Kyles of Bute. Deep burgundy walls, vivid landscapes and modernised bedrooms.
Formal restaurant with fine loch views. Innovative cooking from a dynamic young team.

TILLICOULTRY – Clackmannanshire – **501** I 15 – pop. 5 400   28 **C2**

▶ Edinburgh 35 mi – Dundee 43 mi – Glasgow 38 mi
◩ Alva Rd, ☏ (01259) 750 124

🛏 **Harviestoun Country Inn**   ⏚ ⚘ ♫ ⚗ **P** **VISA** **⓪⓪**
Dollar Rd, East : ¼ *m. by A 91* ✉ *FK13 6PQ* – ☏ *(01259) 752 522*
– www.harviestouncountryhotel.com – info@harviestouncountryhotel.com
– Fax (01259) 752 523
10 rm ☲ – ✝£60 ✝✝£80   **Rest** – Carte £15/25 **s**
♦ Converted Georgian stable block, now a smoothly run modern hotel. Neat, unfussy,
pine furnished bedrooms, half facing the Ochil hills; coffees and home baking in the
lounge. Beams and flagstones hint at the restaurant's rustic past.

TIRORAN – Argyll and Bute – **501** B 14 – see Mull (Isle of)

TOBERMORY – Argyll and Bute – **501** B 14 – see Mull (Isle of)

TONGUE – Highland – **501** G 8 – ✉ Lairg ▌ *Scotland*   30 **C1**

▶ Edinburgh 257 mi – Inverness 101 mi – Thurso 43 mi
◉ Cape Wrath★★★ (≤★★) W : 44 m. (including ferry crossing) by A 838 –
Ben Loyal★★, S : 8 m. by A 836 – Ben Hope★ (≤★★★) SW : 15 m. by A 838
– Strathy Point★ (≤★★★) E : 22 m. by A 836 – Torrisdale Bay★ (≤★★) NE :
8 m. by A 836

🛏🛏 **Tongue**   ≤ ⏚ ⚘ ♫ **P** **VISA** **⓪⓪** **AE**
Main St ✉ *IV27 4XD* – ☏ *(01847) 611 206 – www.tonguehotel.co.uk*
– info@tonguehotel.co.uk – Fax (01847) 611 345 – Closed 1 week Christmas
19 rm ☲ – ✝£60/65 ✝✝£100/120 – 1 suite   **Rest** – (bar lunch) Carte £20/38
♦ Former hunting lodge of the Duke of Sutherland overlooking Kyle of Tongue.
Smart interiors include intimate bar and beamed lounge. Bedrooms are more contemporary in style. Restaurant with fireplace and antique dressers.

🛏 **Ben Loyal**   ≤ **P** **VISA** **⓪⓪**
Main St ✉ *IV27 4XE* – ☏ *(01847) 611 216 – www.benloyal.co.uk*
– stay@btinternet.com – Fax (01847) 611 212 – March-November
11 rm ☲ – ✝£45/65 ✝✝£90   **Rest** – Carte £17/35
♦ Unassuming hotel in the village centre enjoys excellent views of Ben Loyal and the
Kyle of Tongue - a useful hiking or fishing base. Rooms are unfussy, modern and well
kept. Pine furnished restaurant overlooks the hills and sea.

TORRIDON – Highland – **501** D 11 – ✉ Achnasheen ▌ *Scotland*   29 **B2**

▶ Edinburgh 234 mi – Inverness 62 mi – Kyle of Lochalsh 44 mi
◉ Wester Ross★★★

🛏🛏🛏 **The Torridon** ॐ   ≤ ⏚ ♫ ⚘ ⚗ ☰ & rm, ♫ **P** **VISA** **⓪⓪** **AE**
South : 1½ *m. on A 896* ✉ *IV22 2EY* – ☏ *(01445) 791 242*
– www.thetorridon.com – info@thetorridon.com – Fax (01445) 712 253
– Closed 2 January - 4 February, Monday and Tuesday from November-March
18 rm ☲ – ✝£140/275 ✝✝£220/275 – 1 suite
Rest – (bar lunch) (booking essential) Menu £45
♦ 19C hunting lodge; idyllic view of Loch Torridon and mountains. Ornate ceilings,
peat fires and Highland curios add to a calm period feel shared by the more luxurious
rooms. Formal, pine-panelled restaurant uses fine local produce, some from the
grounds.

🛏 **The Torridon Inn** ॐ   ⏚ ♫ ⚘ ⚗ & rm, **P** **VISA** **⓪⓪** **AE**
South : 1½ *m. on A 896* ✉ *IV22 2EY* – ☏ *(01445) 791 242*
– www.thetorridon.com – inn@thetorridon.com – Fax (01445) 712 253 – Closed
November - mid March
12 rm – ✝£80 ✝✝£80   **Rest** – Carte £20/27
♦ Simple, modern, affordable rooms - some sleeping up to six - in a converted stable
block, set in a quiet rural spot and named after the mountain nearby. Spacious pubby
bar. Traditionally styled and informal restaurant.

TROON – South Ayrshire – **501** G 17 – **pop. 14 766**   25 **A2**
- ☐ Edinburgh 77 mi – Ayr 7 mi – Glasgow 31 mi
- ☐ to Northern Ireland (Larne) (P and O Irish Sea) 2 daily
- ☐ Troon Municipal Harling Drive, ✆ (01292) 312 464

🏰 **Lochgreen House** ॐ   ✏ ※ 🍴 ᴅ ᵡ 🐾 ⚚ 🅿 VISA ◉◉ AE
Monktonhill Rd, Southwood, Southeast : 2 m. on B 749 ⊠ *KA10 7EN*
– ✆ (01292) 313 343 – www.costley-hotels.co.uk
– lochgreen@costley-hotels.co.uk – Fax (01292) 318 661
37 rm ☲ – **†**£ 125 **††**£ 180 – 1 suite
Rest *Tapestry* – see restaurant listing
♦ Attractive, coastal Edwardian house in mature grounds. Lounges exude luxurious country house feel. Large rooms, modern or traditional, have a good eye for welcoming detail.

XXX **Tapestry** – at Lochgreen House Hotel   ✏ AK 🅿 VISA ◉◉ AE
Monktonhill Rd, Southwood, Southeast : 2 m. on B 749 ⊠ *KA10 7EN*
– ✆ (01292) 313 343 – Fax (01292) 318 661
Rest – Carte £ 25/40
♦ Spacious dining room with baronial feel. Elegant chandeliers; large pottery cockerels. Classical, modern cooking, with a strong Scottish base.

at Loans East : 2 m. on A 759 – ⊠ Troon

🏨 **Highgrove House**   ⇐ ✏ ※ 🅿 VISA ◉◉ AE
Old Loans Rd, East : ¼ m. on Dundonald rd ⊠ *KA10 7HL* – ✆ *(01292) 312 511*
– www.costleyhotels.co.uk – highgrove@costley-hotels.co.uk – Fax (01292) 318 228
9 rm ☲ – **†**£ 69 **††**£ 110   **Rest** – Carte £ 20/35
♦ Immaculate whitewashed hotel in elevated position, offering superb coastal panorama. Comfy floral bedrooms; 1 and 2 have the best views. Tartan carpets remind you where you are. Large restaurant with floor to ceiling windows and granite coloumns. Popular, long-established menus.

UIST (Isles of) – **501** X/Y 10 – **pop. 3 510**
- ☒ see Liniclate
- ☐ from Lochmaddy to Isle of Skye (Uig) (Caledonian MacBrayne Ltd) 1-3 daily (1 h 50 mn) – from Otternish to Isle of Harris (Leverburgh) (Caledonian MacBrayne Ltd) (1 h 10 mn)

NORTH UIST – Western Isles   29 **A2**

Carinish – Western Isles   29 **A2**

🏠 **Temple View**   ⇐ ✏ ᵡ 🅿 VISA ◉◉
⊠ *HS6 5EJ* – ✆ *(01876) 580 676 – www.templeviewhotel.co.uk*
– templeviewhotel@aol.com – Fax (01876) 580 682
10 rm ☲ – **†**£ 55/75 **††**£ 95/105
Rest – (bar lunch) Menu £ 24 **s** – Carte £ 20/27 **s**
♦ Extended Victorian house on main route from north to south. Pleasantly refurbished, it offers a smart sitting room, cosy bar with conservatory, and up-to-date bedrooms. Extensive local specialities the highlight of small dining room.

Langass – Western Isles   29 **A2**

🏨 **Langass Lodge** ॐ   ⇐ ✏ ◻ ⚲ ᴅ rm, ᵡ 🅿 VISA ◉◉
⊠ *HS6 5HA* – ✆ *(01876) 580 285 – www.langasslodge.co.uk*
– langasslodge@btconnect.com – Fax (01876) 580 385
11 rm ☲ – **†**£ 60/85 **††**£ 130
Rest – (dinner only and Sunday lunch) Carte £ 24/34 **s**
♦ Former Victorian shooting lodge boasting superb views, classical comforts, a modish conservatory extension, and bedrooms styled from traditional to clean-lined modernity. Superior cooking of fine Hebridean produce from land and sea.

Lochmaddy – Western Isles 29 **A2**

Tigh Dearg 🔒 🎾 🕰 🔥 &️ rm, ☆ 🅿 VISA ◑◐
✉ HS6 5AE – ✆ (01876) 500700 – www.tighdearghotel.co.uk
– info@tighdearghotel.co.uk – Fax (01876) 500701
8 rm ☲ – ♦£79/90 ♦♦£89/139 **Rest** – Carte £15/28 **s**
♦ 'The Red House', visible from a long distance, is an outpost of utterly stylish chic. Modish bar matched by well-equipped gym, sauna and steam room, and sleek 21C bedrooms. Hebridean produce well sourced in designer-style restaurant.

ULLAPOOL – Highland – 501 E 10 – pop. 1 308 ▮ Scotland 30 **C2**

🚩 Edinburgh 215 mi – Inverness 59 mi
🚢 to Isle of Lewis (Stornoway) (Caledonian MacBrayne Ltd) (2 h 40 mn)
🄸 Argyle St ✆ (0845) 2255121
◎ Town ★
🄶 Wester Ross ★★★ - Loch Broom ★★. Falls of Measach ★★, S : 11 m. by A 835 and A 832 - Corrieshalloch Gorge ★, SE : 10 m. by A 835 – Northwards to Lochinver ★★, Morefield (≤ ★★ of Ullapool), ≤ ★ Loch Broom

Point Cottage without rest ≤ 🚗 ☆ 🅿
West Shore St ✉ IV26 2UR – ✆ (01854) 612494 – www.pointcottage.co.uk
– macrae@pointcottage.co.uk – March-October
3 rm ☲ – ♦£25/50 ♦♦£50/65
♦ Converted fisherman's cottage of 18C origin. Rooms in bright modern fabrics enjoy beautiful views across Loch Broom to the hills. Substantial breakfasts. Convenient for ferry.

Ardvreck without rest ⊱ ≤ 🚗 ☆ 🍸 🅿 VISA ◑◐
Morefield Brae, Northwest : 2 m. by A 835 ✉ IV26 2TH – ✆ (01854) 612028
– www.smoothhound.co.uk/hotels – ardvreck@btinternet.com – Fax (01854) 613000 – March-October
10 rm ☲ – ♦£35/65 ♦♦£65/75
♦ Peacefully located house boasting fine views of loch and mountains. Well appointed breakfast room with splendid vistas. Spacious rooms: some with particularly fine outlooks.

Tanglewood House ⊱ ≤ 🚗 ☆ 🅿
on A 835 ✉ IV26 2TB – ✆ (01854) 612059 – www.tanglewoodhouse.co.uk
– info@tanglewoodhouse.co.uk – Closed Christmas, New Year and Easter
3 rm ☲ – ♦£69 ♦♦£102
Rest – (by arrangement, communal dining) Menu £36
♦ Blissfully located guesthouse on heather covered headland. Drawing room has a 20 foot window overlooking loch. Homely, traditional rooms, all with vistas. Meals taken at communal table.

The Sheiling without rest ≤ 🚗 🦢 🎾 ☆ 🅿 VISA ◑◐
Garve Rd ✉ IV26 2SX – ✆ (01854) 612947 – www.thesheilingullapool.co.uk
– mail@thesheilingullapool.co.uk – Fax (0870) 1236165 – Closed Christmas and 2 weeks in winter
6 rm ☲ – ♦£55/80 ♦♦£60/85
♦ Welcoming guesthouse by the shores of Loch Broom. Renowned breakfasts, with views to the loch. Homely lounge and comfortable bedrooms.

Dromnan without rest ≤ 🚗 ☆ 🍸 🅿 VISA ◑◐ ①
Garve Rd ✉ IV26 2SX – ✆ (01854) 612333 – www.dromnan.com
– info@dromnan.com – Closed Christmas and New Year
7 rm ☲ – ♦£30/40 ♦♦£60/70
♦ Family run, modern house overlooking Loch Broom. Lovely conservatory breakfast room. Practically equipped rooms vary in décor from patterned pastels to dark tartan.

UNST (Island of) – Shetland Islands – 501 R 1 – see Shetland Islands

URQUHART – Moray – see Elgin

SCOTLAND

VEENSGARTH – Shetland Islands – see Shetland Islands (Mainland)

WALKERBURN – Scottish Borders   26 **C2**
   ◧ Edinburgh 30 mi – Galashiels 23 mi – Peebles 8 mi

   Windlestraw Lodge ⟪   ⟨ 🛋 ⬚ **P** _VISA_ ⓭
Tweed Valley, on A 72 ⊠ EH43 6AA – ℰ *(01896) 870636*
– www.windlestraw.co.uk – reception@windlestraw.co.uk – Fax (01896) 870639
– Closed 2 weeks spring,1 week autumn, 23 December-4 January
6 rm ⌕ – †£85/90 ††£150/180
Rest – (dinner only) (booking essential for non-residents) Menu £42
♦ Edwardian country house in picturesque Tweed Valley: lovely views guaranteed.
Period style lounges serviced by well-stocked bar. Half the good-sized rooms enjoy
the vista. Linen-clad dining room.

WATERNISH – Highland – **501** A 11 – see Skye (Isle of)

WESTRAY (Isle of) – Orkney Islands – **501** KL 6/7 – see Orkney Islands

---

WHITING BAY – North Ayrshire – **501** E 17 – see Arran (Isle of)

WICK – Highland – **501** K 8 – pop. 9 713 ▐ *Scotland*   30 **D1**
   ◧ Edinburgh 282 mi – Inverness 126 mi
   ✈ Wick Airport : ℰ (01955) 602215, N : 1 m
   🛈 Whitechapel Rd ℰ (0845) 2255121
   🛈 Reiss, ℰ (01955) 602726
   ◙ Duncansby Head★ (Stacks of Duncansby★★) N : 14 m. by A 9 – Grey
     Cairns of Camster★ (Long Cairn★★) S : 17 m. by A 9 – The Hill O'Many
     Stanes★, S : 10 m. by A 9

↑   **The Clachan** without rest   🛋 ℀ "ŷ"
South Rd, South : ¾ m. on A 99 ⊠ KW1 5NJ – ℰ *(01955) 605384*
– www.theclachan.co.uk – enquiry@theclachan.co.uk – Closed Christmas and
New Year
3 rm ⌕ – †£40/45 ††£50/52
♦ This detached 1930s house on the town's southern outskirts provides homely en
suite accommodation in pastels and floral patterns. Charming owner.

✗   **Bord De L'Eau**   _VISA_ ⓭
2 Market St (Riverside) ⊠ KW1 4AR – ℰ *(01955) 604400 – Closed first 3 weeks*
January, 25-26 December, Sunday lunch and Monday
Rest – French – Carte £23/32
♦ Totally relaxed little riverside eatery with French owner. Friendly, attentive service
of an often-changing, distinctly Gallic repertoire. Keenly priced dishes.

Y. Duhamel/MICHELIN

Towns
from A to Z

Villes
de A à Z

Città
de A a Z

Städte
von A bis Z

Wales

ABERAERON – Ceredigion – 503 H 27 33 B3
> ▶ Cardiff 90 mi – Aberystwyth 16 mi – Fishguard 41 mi

Ty Mawr Mansion Country House 🏠   🚗 🔥 ⚓ 🐾 📶 **P** VISA ☺ AE
Cilcennin, East : 4½ m. by A 482 ✉ *SA48 8DB –* ☎ *(01570) 470 033*
– www.tymawrmansion.co.uk – info@tymawrmansion.co.uk
– Closed 27 December-10 January
8 rm 🍽 – ♦£ 120/160 ♦♦£ 160/240 – 1 suite
Rest – (Closed Sunday) (dinner only) Menu £ 25 (weekdays) – Carte £ 32/45
♦ Grade II listed Georgian stone mansion in 12 acres of grounds. Three sumptuous reception rooms matched by luxurious bedrooms, which are oversized and full of top facilities. Chefs rear pigs for locally renowned restaurant boasting bold edge to cooking.

Llys Aeron without rest   🚗 ⚓ 📶 **P** VISA ☺
Lampeter Rd, on A 482 ✉ *SA46 0ED –* ☎ *(01545) 570 276 – www.llysaeron.co.uk*
– enquiries@llysaeron.co.uk
3 rm 🍽 – ♦£ 45/55 ♦♦£ 70/90
♦ Imposing Georgian house on main road. Hearty Aga cooked breakfasts overlooking well established rear walled garden. Comfy lounge; light, airy rooms in clean pastel shades.

Harbourmaster with rm   ≤ 📶 **P** VISA ☺
Quay Parade ✉ *SA46 0BA –* ☎ *(01545) 570 755 – www.harbour-master.com*
– info@harbour-master.com – Closed 25 December
13 rm 🍽 – ♦£ 55/60 ♦♦£ 90/250   **Rest** – Carte £ 20/35
♦ Refurbished and enlarged through the acquisition of the adjacent aquarium. New restaurant with Welsh black beef and seafood a feature; more informal bar. Comfortable and brightly decorated new bedrooms.

ABERDOVEY (Aberdyfi) – Gwynedd – 503 H 26 32 B2
> ▶ London 230 mi – Dolgellau 25 mi – Shrewsbury 66 mi
> ⓖ Snowdonia National Park ★★★

Llety Bodfor without rest   ≤ ⚓ 📶 **P** VISA ☺ AE
Bodfor Terrace ✉ *LL35 0EA –* ☎ *(01654) 767 475 – www.lletybodfor.co.uk*
– info@lletybodfor.co.uk – Fax (01654) 767 836 – Closed 23-29 December
9 rm 🍽 – ♦£ 40/50 ♦♦£ 100/125
♦ Two 19C seafront terraces painted pale mauve with modish interior featuring sitting/breakfast room with piano and hi-fi; luxurious bedrooms have blue/white seaside theme.

at Pennal Northeast : 6½ m. on A 493 – ✉ **Aberdovey**

Penmaendyfi without rest 🏠   ≤ 🚗 🔥 🏊 ⚓ ♿ 📶 **P** VISA ☺
Cwrt, Southwest : 1¼ m. by A 493 ✉ *SY20 9LD –* ☎ *(01654) 791 246*
– www.penmaendyfi.co.uk – shana@penmaendyfi.co.uk
– Closed December-January
6 rm 🍽 – ♦£ 55/60 ♦♦£ 80/100
♦ Impressive late 16C mansion with elegant sweeping grounds and ancient trees: a peaceful location. Sumptuous lounge. Spacious, smartly appointed rooms with fine country views.

ABERGAVENNY (Y-Fenni) – Monmouthshire – 503 L 28 – pop. 14 055 33 C4
> ▶ London 163 mi – Cardiff 31 mi – Gloucester 43 mi – Newport 19 mi
>   – Swansea 49 mi
> 🅭 Swan Meadow, Monmouth Rd ☎ (01873) 853 254,
>   abergavennyic@breconbeacons.org
> 🅱 Monmouthshire Llanfoist, ☎ (01873) 852 606
> ⓞ Town ★ - St Mary's Church ★ (Monuments ★★)
> ⓖ Brecon Beacons National Park ★★ – Blaenavon Ironworks ★, SW : 5 m. by
>   A 465 and B 4246. Raglan Castle ★ **AC**, SE : 9 m. by A 40

🏨 Llansantffraed Court   ≤ 🚗 ⏰ 📶 🍴 💬 P VISA ©® AE ①

Llanvihangel Gobion, Southeast : 6½ m. by A 40 and B 4598 off old Raglan rd
✉ NP7 9BA – ℰ (01873) 840 678 – www.llch.co.uk – reception@llch.co.uk
– Fax (01873) 840 674
21 rm ⊡ – ♦£86/97 ♦♦£150/175   **Rest** – Menu £20/30 – Carte £24/40
♦ 12C hotel, set in 19 acres of land with ornamental trout lake; built in country house style of William and Mary; popular for weddings. Magnolia rooms with mahogany furniture. Welsh seasonal fare in chintz dining room.

🏨 The Angel   🍴 📶 💬 ⚓ P VISA ©® AE

15 Cross St ✉ NP7 5EN – ℰ (01873) 857 121
– www.angelhotelabergavenny.com – mail@angelhotelabergavenny.com
– Fax (01873) 858 059 – Closed 25 December
32 rm ⊡ – ♦£65/70 ♦♦£130   **Rest** – Carte £25/33
♦ Updated Georgian building with a warm and cosy bar lit by real fire. Impressive public areas; locally renowned afternoon tea. Cocktails taken before dinner. Functional rooms. Stylish restaurant offers classic French and British blend.

🏚 The Hardwick   🚗 P VISA ©®

Old Raglan Rd, Southeast : 2 m. by A 40 on B 4598 ✉ NP7 9AA – ℰ (01873)
854 220 – www.thehardwick.co.uk – stephen@thehardwick.co.uk – Fax (01873)
854 623 – Closed 25-26 December and 2-3 January*
Rest – (Closed Sunday dinner and Monday) Menu £21 (lunch) – Carte £25/36
♦ Simple, unassuming, whitewashed pub with mountain views. Simplicity and the use of local produce are paramount here and lengthy menus feature influences from Britain and the Med.

at Llanddewi Skirrid Northeast : 3¼ m. on B4521 – ✉ Abergavenny

🍴 The Walnut Tree   P VISA ©® AE

✉ NP7 8AW – ℰ (01873) 852 797 – www.thewalnuttreeinn.co.uk
– Closed 1 week Christmas, Sunday and Monday
Rest – (booking essential) Menu £20 (lunch) – Carte £32/39
♦ Bustling eatery set in a valley; simply furnished with welcoming staff. Good sized, seasonal menu of homely, flavoursome cooking. Dishes arrive as described, with offal a speciality.

at Nant Derry Southeast : 6½ m. by A 40 off A 4042 – ✉ Abergavenny

🏚 The Foxhunter   P VISA ©®

✉ NP7 9DD – ℰ (01873) 881 101 – www.thefoxhunter.com
– info@thefoxhunter.com – Closed 25-26 December
Rest – (Closed Sunday dinner and Monday) Menu £22 (lunch) – Carte £20/35
♦ Bright, contemporary feel within flint-stone former 19C station master's house. Light and airy in summer and cosy in winter. Modern menus using fine local ingredients.

at Llanwenarth Northwest : 3 m. on A 40 – ✉ Abergavenny

🏠 Llanwenarth   ≤ 🔾 🚗 ㅊ rm, ⅍ 📶 P VISA ©® AE

Brecon Rd ✉ NP8 1EP – ℰ (01873) 810 550 – www.llanwenarthhotel.com
– info@llanwenarthhotel.com – Fax (01873) 811 880
17 rm ⊡ – ♦£63 ♦♦£85
Rest – (Closed 26 December and 1 January) Menu £14 (lunch) – Carte £25/30
♦ Part 16C inn; perches on banks of river Usk, famed for salmon, trout fishing. Most bedrooms have balconies from which to enjoy panoramas of Blorenge Mountain and Usk Valley. Tall-windowed dining room with fine valley views and varied menus.

ABERSOCH – Gwynedd – **502** G 25 – ✉ Pwllheli   32 **B2**

▶ London 265 mi – Caernarfon 28 mi – Shrewsbury 101 mi
📛 Golf Rd, ℰ (01758) 712 636
◐ Lleyn Peninsula★★ – Plas-yn-Rhiw★ **AC**, W : 6 m. by minor roads. Bardsey Island★, SW : 15 m. by A 499 and B 4413 – Mynydd Mawr★, SW : 17 m. by A 499, B 4413 and minor roads

WALES

ABERSOCH

Neigwl
Lon Sarn Bach ⊠ LL53 7DY – ℰ (01758) 712 363 – www.neigwl.com
– relax@neigwl.com – Fax (01758) 712 544 – Closed January
9 rm ⊇ – ♦£70/110 ♦♦£140
Rest – (dinner only) (booking essential) Menu £29
♦ A comfortable, family owned hotel close to town yet with fine sea vistas. Rooms are perfectly neat and individually decorated whilst the lounge is the ideal place to relax. The restaurant overlooks sea and mountains.

at Bwlchtocyn South : 2 m. – ⊠ Pwllheli

Porth Tocyn ⟡
⊠ LL53 7BU – ℰ (01758) 713 303 – www.porth-tocyn-hotel.co.uk
– bookings@porthtocyn.fsnet.co.uk – Fax (01758) 713 538 – Easter-October
17 rm – ♦£65/90 ♦♦£125/170, ⊇ £6
Rest – (bar lunch Monday-Saturday) (buffet lunch Sunday) Menu £39
♦ Originally a row of miners' cottages; family run for three generations and family orientated. A pleasant headland location: panoramas of bay and mountains. Pretty bedrooms. Sunday buffet lunch, described as a family event. Interesting, varied menus.

Look out for red symbols, indicating particularly pleasant establishments.

WALES

ABERYSTWYTH – Ceredigion – **503** H 26 – pop. 15 935   32 **B2**
◻ London 238 mi – Chester 98 mi – Fishguard 58 mi – Shrewsbury 74 mi
🛈 Terrace Rd ℰ (01970) 612125, aberystwythtic@ceredigion.gov.uk
🛏 Bryn-y-Mor, ℰ (01970) 615 104
◉ Town★★ - The Seafront★ – National Library of Wales (Permanent Exhibition★)
◉ Vale of Rheidol★★ (Railway★★ AC) - St Padarn's Church★, SE : 1 m. by A 44. Devil's Bridge (Pontarfynach)★, E : 12 m. by A 4120 – Strata Florida Abbey★ AC (West Door★), SE : 15 m. by B 4340 and minor rd

Bodalwyn without rest
Queen's Ave ⊠ SY23 2EG – ℰ (01970) 612 578 – www.bodalwyn.co.uk
– enquiries@bodalwyn.co.uk – Fax (01970) 639 261
– Closed 23 December-2 January
8 rm ⊇ – ♦£35/50 ♦♦£55/70
♦ Victorian house, run enthusiastically and to a very good standard by a young owner. Rooms blend modern and traditional, numbers 3 and 5 being particularly enticing.

Gwesty Cymru
19 Marine Terrace ⊠ SY23 2AZ – ℰ (01970) 612 252 – www.gwestycymru.com
– info@gwestycymru.com – Closed 24-26 December and restricted opening in January
8 rm ⊇ – ♦£65/115 ♦♦£85/125   **Rest** – Carte £26/32
♦ Georgian Grade II listed building on promenade, with front terrace and sea views. Thoughtfully designed bedrooms are colour themed in décor and furnishings; impressive bathrooms. Small dining room serves traditional dishes made from local produce.

at Chancery (Rhydgaled) South : 4 m. on A 487 – ⊠ Aberystwyth

Conrah ⟡
⊠ SY23 4DF – ℰ (01970) 617 941 – www.conrah.co.uk – enquiries@conrah.co.uk
– Fax (01970) 624 546
14 rm ⊇ – ♦£85/95 ♦♦£130   **Rest** – Carte £24/31
♦ Part 18C mansion, elegant inside and out. Lovely grounds, kitchen garden, pleasant views. Airy country house rooms include three very smart new ones in converted outbuildings. Scenic vistas greet restaurant diners.

BARMOUTH (Abermaw) – Gwynedd – **502** H 25 – pop. 2 306   32 **B2**

- London 231 mi – Chester 74 mi – Dolgellau 10 mi – Shrewsbury 67 mi
- The Station, Station Rd ℰ (01341) 280787, (summer only) barmouth.tic@gwynedd.gov.uk
- Town★ - Bridge★ **AC**
- Snowdonia National Park★★★

Bae Abermaw   ≤ 🚗 💥 🐾 **P** VISA ⓪⓪

Panorama Rd ⊠ LL42 1DQ – ℰ (01341) 280 550 – www.baeabermaw.com – enquiries@baeabermaw.com – Fax (01341) 280 346

14 rm ⊇ – †£90/107 ††£132/158

Rest – (dinner only and Sunday lunch) Carte £ 30/37

♦ Victorian house with inspiring views over Cardigan Bay. Classic façade allied to minimalist interior, typified by an uncluttered, airy lounge. Brilliant white bedrooms. Pleasant, comfy restaurant with appealing modern menus.

at Llanaber Northwest : 1 ½ m. on A 496 – ⊠ Barmouth

Llwyndu Farmhouse ⊗   🚗 **P** VISA ⓪⓪

Northwest : 2 ¼ m. on A 496 ⊠ LL42 1RR – ℰ (01341) 280 144 – www.llwyndu-farmhouse.co.uk – intouch@llwyndu-farmhouse.co.uk – Closed 24-26 December

7 rm ⊇ – †£50/65 ††£80

Rest – (Closed Sunday) (dinner only) (by arrangement) Menu £ 28

♦ Grade II listed 16C farmhouse below the Rhinog Mountains, overlooking Cardigan Bay. Traditional beams, inglenooks and quirky, characterful features abound. Using quality Welsh produce, candlelit dinners combine the traditional with the modern.

WALES

> If breakfast is included the ⊇ symbol appears after the number of rooms.

BARRY (Barri) – The Vale of Glamorgan – **503** K 29 – pop. 50 661   33 **C4**

- London 167 mi – Cardiff 10 mi – Swansea 39 mi
- The Promenade, The Triangle, Barry Island ℰ (01446) 747171, barrytic@valeofglamorgan.gov.uk
- RAF St Athan St Athan Clive Rd, ℰ (01446) 751 043

Egerton Grey Country House ⊗   ≤ 🚗 🐾 **P** VISA ⓪⓪ AE

Southwest : 4 ½ m. by B 4226 and A 4226 and Porthkerry rd via Cardiff Airport ⊠ CF62 3BZ – ℰ (01446) 711 666 – www.egertongrey.co.uk – info@egertongrey.co.uk – Fax (01446) 711 690

10 rm ⊇ – †£90/110 ††£170   **Rest** – Menu £ 17/32 **s**

♦ A secluded country house with a restful library and drawing room. Part Victorian rectory. Bedrooms overlook gardens with views down to Porthkerry Park and the sea. Intimate dining room with paintings and antiques.

BEAUMARIS – Isle of Anglesey – **502** H 24 – pop. 1 513   32 **B1**

- London 253 mi – Birkenhead 74 mi – Holyhead 25 mi
- Baron Hill, ℰ (01248) 810 231
- Town★ - Castle★ **AC**
- Anglesey★★ – Penmon Priory★, NE : 4 m. by B 5109 and minor roads. Plas Newydd★ **AC**, SW : 7 m. by A 545 and A 4080

Ye Olde Bull's Head Inn   💥 🕍 **P** VISA ⓪⓪ AE

Castle St ⊠ LL58 8AP – ℰ (01248) 810 329 – www.bullsheadinn.co.uk – info@bullsheadinn.co.uk – Fax (01248) 811 294 – Closed 25 -26 December, 1 January, Sunday dinner and Monday

13 rm ⊇ – †£80/85 ††£105/110

Rest *The Loft and Ye Olde Bull's Head Inn* – see restaurant listing

♦ Brightly painted coaching inn, where bedrooms of all shapes and sizes mix the contemporary with existing period features. More, spacious, state-of-the-art rooms are to be added.

WALES

🏠 Bishopsgate House
P VISA ◉◉ AE

54 Castle St ⊠ LL58 8BB – 𝒞 (01248) 810 302 – www.bishopsgatehotels.co.uk
– hazel@bishopsgatehotel.co.uk – Fax (01248) 810 166
9 rm ⊑ – ✝£55/65 ✝✝£100
Rest – (dinner only and Sunday lunch) (booking essential for non-residents)
Menu £18 **s** – Carte £25/30 **s**

♦ Georgian townhouse on the high street. Chesterfields in the lounge, a rare Chinese Chippendale staircase and a small bar area. Individually decorated bedrooms. Neatly decorated dining room in keeping with the character of the establishment.

↑ Cleifiog without rest
⇐ 🚗 ⅍ VISA ◉◉

Townsend ⊠ LL58 8BH – 𝒞 (01248) 811 507 – www.cleifiogbandb.co.uk
– liz@cleifiogbandb.com – Closed Christmas-New Year
3 rm ⊑ – ✝£65 ✝✝£95

♦ Lovely views from this seafront part Georgian house with 16C origins. Comfy, relaxing period style lounge. Bedrooms mix Arts and Crafts with up-to-date style and facilities.

✕✕ The Loft – at Ye Olde Bull's Head Inn Hotel
VISA ◉◉ AE P

Castle St ⊠ LL58 8AP – 𝒞 (01248) 810329 – www.bullsheadinn.co.uk
– info@bullsheadinn.co.uk – Fax (01248) 811 294 – Closed 25 -26 December,
1 January and Sunday
Rest – (dinner only) Menu £40

♦ In contrast to the inn, The Loft has a contemporary style engendered by its bold decoration. The cooking is modern and imaginative.

🏠 Ye Olde Bull's Head Inn
VISA ◉◉ AE P

Castle St ⊠ LL58 8AP – 𝒞 (01248) 810329 – www.bullsheadinn.co.uk
– info@bullsheadinn.co.uk – Fax (01248) 811 294
– Closed 25-26 December and 1 January
Rest – (bookings not accepted) Carte £16/22

♦ Welcoming inn with traditional bar, contemporary lounge and airy brasserie. Menu displays a mix of homely classics and more adventurous international dishes; good puddings.

> Your opinions are important to us:
> please write and let us know about your discoveries and experiences –
> good and bad!

BEDDGELERT – Gwynedd – **502** H 24 – pop. 535
32 **B1**

🚗 London 249 mi – Caernarfon 13 mi – Chester 73 mi
ⓖ Snowdonia National Park★★★ - Aberglaslyn Pass★, S : 1½ m. on A 498

🏠 Sygun Fawr Country House ⌖
⇐ 🚗 ⅍ P VISA ◉◉

Northeast : ¾ m. by A 498 ⊠ LL55 4NE – 𝒞 (01766) 890 258
– www.sygunfawr.co.uk – sygunfawr@aol.com – Closed January
11 rm ⊑ – ✝£59 ✝✝£78/105
Rest – (dinner only) (booking essential for non-residents) Menu £24 **s**
♦ Part 16C stone built house in Gwynant Valley. Superbly located, an elevated spot which affords exceptional views of Snowdon, particularly from double deluxe rooms. Dine in new conservatory extension or traditional room in house.

BENLLECH – Isle of Anglesey – **502** H 24
32 **B1**

🚗 London 277 mi – Caernarfon 17 mi – Chester 76 mi – Holyhead 29 mi

↑ Hafod without rest
🚗 ⅍ P

Amlwch Rd ⊠ LL74 8SR – 𝒞 (01248) 853 092 – Closed 25 December
3 rm ⊑ – ✝£50 ✝✝£64/68
♦ Sensitively renovated 19C house with lawned garden and views of sea and bays. Comfortably finished bedrooms, well maintained by the charming owner.

BETWS GARMON – Gwynedd

32 **B1**

🚹 Cardiff 194 mi – Betws-y-Coed 25 mi – Caernarfon 5 mi

Betws Inn 🍴 ❄ **P** _VISA_ ⓴
Northwest : 1 m. on A 4085 ✉ *LL54 7YY* – ☎ *(01286) 650 324*
– www.betws-inn.co.uk – stay@betws-inn.co.uk
3 rm ☐ – †£50/60 ††£70/80   **Rest** – (by arrangement) Menu £ 25
♦ Former village coaching inn with characterful beamed lounge. After a day's trek-
king, sleep in well-priced, good sized rooms with quality wood furniture and smart
fabrics. Home-cooked local produce proudly served in rustic dining room.

BETWS-Y-COED – Conwy – 502 I 24 – pop. 848

32 **B1**

🚹 London 226 mi – Holyhead 44 mi – Shrewsbury 62 mi
ℹ Royal Oak Stables ☎ (01690) 710 426, tic.byc@eryri-npa.gov.uk
🏌 Clubhouse, ☎ (01690) 710 556
◎ Town ★
◉ Snowdonia National Park ★★★. Blaenau Ffestiniog ★ (Llechwedd Slate
Caverns ★ **AC**), SW : 10 ½ m. by A 470 – The Glyders and Nant Ffrancon
(Cwm Idwal ★), W : 14 m. by A 5

Tan-y-Foel Country House 🐾 ⬅ 🍴 ❄ **P** _VISA_ ⓴
East : 2 ½ m. by A 5, A 470 and Capel Garmon rd on Llanwrst rd ✉ *LL26 ORE*
– ☎ (01690) 710 507 – www.tyfhotel.co.uk – enquiries@tyfhotel.co.uk
– Fax (01690) 710 681 – Closed 24-26, 31 December and 1 January
6 rm ☐ – †£120/160 ††£155/185
Rest – (dinner only) (booking essential) Menu £ 45
♦ Part 16C country house, stylishly decorated in modern vein. Stunning views of Vale
of Conwy and Snowdonia. Lovely rooms revel in the quality and elegance of the
establishment. Contemporary rear room makes up the restaurant.

Henllys The Old Courthouse without rest 🍴 ❄ 📶 **P** _VISA_ ⓴
Old Church Rd ✉ *LL24 0AL* – ☎ *(01690) 710 534*
– www.guesthouse-snowdonia.co.uk – welcome@guesthouse-snowdonia.co.uk
– Fax (01690) 710 884 – March-October
4 rm ☐ – †£55/75 ††£70/90
♦ Former Victorian magistrates' court and police station overlooking the River
Conwy. Comfortable rooms with homely feel. Police memorabilia all around.

Bryn Bella without rest ⬅ ❄ 📶 **P** _VISA_ ⓴
Lôn Muriau, Llanrwst Rd, Northeast : 1 m. by A 5 on A 470 ✉ *LL24 0HD*
– ☎ (01690) 710 627 – www.bryn-bella.co.uk – welcome@bryn-bella.co.uk
5 rm ☐ – †£60/65 ††£75/80
♦ Smart guesthouse in an elevated position with splendid views of the Vale of
Conwy. Affordable accommodation; modern colours. Convenient base for touring the
Snowdonia region.

Pengwern without rest 🍴 ❄ 📶 **P** _VISA_ ⓴
Allt Dinas, Southeast : 1 ½ m. on A 5 ✉ *LL24 0HF* – ☎ *(01690) 710 480*
– gwawr.pengwern@btopenworld.co.uk – Closed 24 December-3 January
3 rm ☐ – †£55/65 ††£70/80
♦ Former Victorian artist 'colony' with a comfy, homely and stylish lounge, warmly
decorated breakfast room and individually appointed bedrooms, two with superb
valley vistas.

Llannerch Goch without rest 🐾 ⬅ 🍴 ❄ **P**
Capel Garmon, East : 2 m. by A 5 and A 470 on Capel Gorman rd ✉ *LL26 0RL*
– ☎ (01690) 710 261 – www.betwsycoed.co.uk – eirian@betwsycoed.co.uk
– Easter-September
3 rm ☐ – †£45/50 ††£68/70
♦ Very peaceful 17C country house with original features. Pleasant sun lounge overlooking the garden. Set in four idyllic acres. Cosy sitting room, smart bedrooms.

WALES

959

WALES

↑ **Glyntwrog House** without rest ⚄ ✻ 🛜 **P** VISA ⬤⬤
Southeast : ¾ m. on A 5 ⊠ LL24 0SG – ℰ (01690) 710 930
– www.glyntwrogsnowdonia.co.uk – welcome@glyntwrogsnowdonia.co.uk
4 rm ⌑ – †£40/45 ††£60/70
♦ Victorian stone house set just off the road and surrounded by woodland. Pleasantly renovated to a homely and attractive standard. Comfortable bedrooms in varying sizes.

at Penmachno Southwest : 4 ¾ m. by A 5 on B 4406 – ⊠ Betws-y-Coed

↑ **Penmachno Hall** 🐾 ≤ ⚄ ✻ ⒤ **P** VISA ⬤⬤
on Ty Mawr rd ⊠ LL24 0PU – ℰ (01690) 760 410 – www.penmachnohall.co.uk
– stay@penmachnohall.co.uk – Fax (01690) 760 410 – Closed Christmas-New Year
3 rm ⌑ – †£90 ††£90
Rest – (by arrangement, communal dining) Menu £35
♦ Former rectory built in 1862 with neat garden; super country setting. Sunny morning room where breakfast is served. Modern, bright bedrooms personally styled by the owners. Tasty home-cooking in deep burgundy communal dining room.

BODUAN – Gwynedd – see Pwllheli

BONVILSTON (Tresimwn) – The Vale of Glamorgan – **503** J 29   33 **C4**
🚘 London 164 mi – Cardiff 9 mi – Swansea 25 mi

↑ **The Great Barn** without rest 🐾 ≤ ⚄ ⒤ **P** VISA ⬤⬤
Lillypot, Northwest : 1 m. by A 48 off Tre-Dodridge rd ⊠ CF5 6TR – ℰ (01446)
781 010 – www.greatbarn.com – nina@greatbarn.com – Fax (01446) 781 185
6 rm ⌑ – †£40/50 ††£70/80
♦ Converted corn barn, personally run in simple country home style. Pleasant antiques, pine and white furniture in rooms. Great traditional breakfasts; relax in conservatory.

BRECON – Powys – **503** J 28 – pop. 7 901   33 **C3**
🚘 London 171 mi – Cardiff 40 mi – Carmarthen 31 mi – Gloucester 65 mi
🛈 Cattle Market Car Park ℰ (01874) 622485, brectic@powys.gov.uk
🏌 CradocPenoyre Park, ℰ (01874) 623 658
🏌 Newton Park Llanfaes, ℰ (01874) 622 004
◎ Town★ - Cathedral★ **AC** – Penyclawdd Court★
🅶 Brecon Beacons National Park★★. Llanthony Priory★★, S : 8 m. of
Hay-on-Wye by B 4423 - Dan-yr-Ogof Showcaves★ **AC**, SW : 20 m. by A 40
and A 4067 – Pen-y-Fan★★, SW : by A 470

↑ **Canal Bank** without rest ⚄ ✻ ⒤ **P**
 off B 4601 over bridge on unmarked rd ⊠ LD3 7HG – ℰ (01874) 623 464
– www.accommodation-breconbeacons.co.uk
– enquiries@accommodation-breconbeacons.co.uk – Closed Christmas
3 rm ⌑ – †£60/65 ††£80/90
♦ Delightfully stylish and peaceful 18C canalside cottage. Charming garden with pergola and access to Usk. Organic breakfasts. Immaculate rooms with extra attention to detail.

↑ **Cantre Selyf** without rest ⚄ ✻ **P**
5 Lion St ⊠ LD3 7AU – ℰ (01874) 622 904 – www.cantreselyf.co.uk
– enquiries@cantreselyf.co.uk – Fax (01874) 622 315
– Closed Christmas and New Year
3 rm ⌑ – †£50 ††£78
♦ An engaging 18C townhouse in town centre. Georgian fireplaces and beamed ceilings. Lovely quiet rooms with period feel. Attractive rear walled garden with sun house.

⟰ Felin Glais ⌂   🖨 📶 **P**
Aberyscir, West : 4 m. by Upper Chapel rd off Cradoc Golf Course rd turning right immediately after bridge ✉ LD3 9NP – ℰ (01874) 623 107
– www.felinglais.co.uk – felinglais@keme.co.uk – Fax (01874) 623 107
4 rm ⌂ – †£80 ††£80
Rest – (by arrangement, communal dining) Menu £32
♦ Mid-17C house in a tranquil hamlet with a wonderfully relaxing sitting room and comfy rooms which boast many thoughtful extras, such as cosy seating areas with magazines. Seriously considered menus: fresh, country cooking on large-choice menus.

⟰ Coach House   🖨 ✎ 📶 **P** **VISA** ⬤⬤
Orchard St ✉ LD3 8AN – ℰ (0844) 357 1304 – www.coachhousebrecon.com
– info@coachhousebrecon.com – Fax (01874) 622 454
6 rm ⌂ – †£50/70 ††£69/110
Rest – (by arrangement) Menu £25 – Carte £21/35
♦ 17C building just over Usk Bridge a short walk from town. Rear garden and terrace. The bedrooms are modern, co-ordinated and well-equipped, with stylish fabrics and Wi-Fi. Dining room offers best local produce on a classic Welsh base.

🛏 The Felin Fach Griffin with rm   🖨 ☆ **P** **VISA** ⬤⬤
Felin Fach, Northeast : 4¾ m. by B 4602 off A 470 ✉ LD3 0UB – ℰ (01874) 620 111 – www.felinfachgriffin.co.uk – enquiries@eatdrinksleep.ltd.uk
– Closed 24-25 December and 4 days in January
7 rm ⌂ – †£60/70 ††£100/110
Rest – (Closed Monday lunch except Bank Holidays) Menu £19/27
– Carte £21/35
♦ Terracotta hued traditional pub, once a farmhouse. Characterful interior boasts log fire with sofas, antiques and reclaimed furniture. Modern menus and smart bedrooms.

WALES

BRIDGEND (Pen-y-Bont) – **Bridgend** – **503** J 29 – pop. 39 429   33 **B4**
🇩 London 177 mi – Cardiff 20 mi – Swansea 23 mi
🇮 McArthur Glen Design Outlet Village, The Derwen, junction 36, M 4
ℰ (01656) 654906, bridgendtic@bridgend.gov.uk

at Southerndown Southwest : 5½ m. by A 4265 on B 4524 – ✉ Bridgend

❌ La Plie   **P** **VISA** ⬤⬤ **AE**
Beach Rd ✉ CF32 0RP – ℰ (01656) 880 127 – Fax (01656) 724 282 – *Closed first 2 weeks January, last week November, 26 December, Sunday dinner, Tuesday lunch and Monday*
Rest – Menu £18/34
♦ Meaning 'The Plaice'; simple restaurant perched above the cliffs in tiny hamlet. Set course menus display modern, well presented dishes. Seafood, game and offal feature highly.

at Laleston West : 2 m. on A 473 – ✉ Bridgend

🅷 Great House   🖨 ♨ ℔ ✎ 📶 **P** **VISA** ⬤⬤ **AE** ⓪
High St, on A 473 ✉ CF32 0HP – ℰ (01656) 657 644
– www.great-house-laleston.co.uk – enquiries@great-house-laleston.co.uk
– Fax (01656) 668 892 – Closed Christmas
12 rm ⌂ – †£80/110 ††£125/150
Rest *Leicester's* – see restaurant listing
♦ 15C Grade II listed building, believed to have been a gift from Elizabeth I to the Earl of Leicester. Personally run - attention to detail particularly evident in the rooms.

❌❌ Leicester's – at Great House Hotel   🖨 ✎ **P** **VISA** ⬤⬤ **AE** ⓪
High St, on A 473 ✉ CF32 0HP – ℰ (01656) 657 644
– www.great-house-laleston.co.uk – enquiries@great-house-laleston.co.uk
– Fax (01656) 668 892 – Closed Sunday dinner and Bank Holidays
Rest – Menu £15/20 – Carte £21/42
♦ Comfortable dining courtesy of exposed beams, original windows and owner's personal touches and nuances. Imaginative, seasonal menus using finest local and Welsh produce.

CAERNARFON – Gwynedd – **502** H 24 – pop. 9 726   32 **B1**

> ◨ London 249 mi – Birkenhead 76 mi – Chester 68 mi – Holyhead 30 mi
>   – Shrewsbury 85 mi
>
> ◨ Oriel Pendeitsh, Castle St. ℘ (01286) 672232,
>   caernarfon.tic@gwynedd.gov.uk
>
> ◨ Aberforeshore Llanfaglan, ℘ (01286) 673 783
>
> ◉ Town ★★ - Castle ★★★ **AC**
>
> ◙ Snowdonia National Park ★★★

WALES

🏨 **Celtic Royal**   🖥 🕅 ♠ 🖢 ♿ rm, ⅍ 🚿 **P** **VISA** **⚫** **AE**
Bangor St ⊠ *LL55 1AY – ℘ (01286) 674 477 – www.celtic-royal.co.uk*
– reservations@celtic-royal.co.uk – Fax (01286) 674 139
110 rm � – ♦£88 ♦♦£120   **Rest** – (bar lunch) Carte £17/25 **s**
♦ Updated Victorian hotel which now caters primarily for the corporate market. Good
access to Holyhead and Bangor. Strong leisure and conference facilities. Modern
rooms. Comfortable, split-level restaurant with classic style.

---

at Seion Northeast : 5 ½ m. by A4086 and B4366 on Seion Rd – ⊠ **Caernarfon**

🍴🍴 **Ty'n Rhos Country House** with rm   ← 🛏 ♿ ⅍ **P** **VISA** **⚫** **AE** **①**
Southwest : ¼ m. ⊠ *LL55 3AE – ℘ (01248) 670 489 – www.tynrhos.co.uk*
– enquiries@tynrhos.co.uk – Fax (01248) 671 772
14 rm ⊠ – ♦£75/90 ♦♦£130/150   **Rest** – Menu £25/40
♦ Formal restaurant with contemporary furnishings, French windows and views over
Anglesey. Classic country house cooking uses local, seasonal produce to create hearty
old favourites. Modern bedrooms, some with views/terraces.

---

at Llanrug East : 3 m. on A 4086 – ⊠ **Caernarfon**

🏠 **Plas Tirion Farm** without rest 🦢   🛏 🕅 ⅍ **P**
South : 1 m. by Ffordd Glanmoelyn Rd on Waenfawr rd ⊠ *LL55 4PY – ℘ (01286)*
673 190 – www.plas-tirion.co.uk – cerid@plastirion.plus.com – Fax (01286)
671 883 – April-October
3 rm ⊠ – ♦£40 ♦♦£60
♦ Stone built farmhouse on dairy farm surrounded by 300 acres. Relaxing, homely
sitting room. Generous portions served in airy breakfast room with log burner. Cottagey rooms.

---

at Groeslon South : 3 m. by A 487 – ⊠ **Caernarfon**

🏠 **Y Goeden Eirin**   🛏 ⅍ **P**
Dolydd, North : ½ m. ⊠ *LL54 7EF – ℘ (01286) 830 942*
– www.ygoedeneirin.co.uk – john_rowlands@tiscali.co.uk
3 rm ⊠ – ♦£60/65 ♦♦£90/95   **Rest** – (by arrangement) Menu £30
♦ Charming stone guest house – originally a cow shed – with pastoral views, crammed bookcases and plenty of curios. One bedroom upstairs, two across the garden.
Concise menu of local or garden grown produce.

---

at Saron Southwest : 3 ¼ m. by A 487 on Saron rd – ⊠ **Caernarfon**

🏠 **Pengwern** 🦢   🛏 🕅 ⅍ **P** **VISA** **⚫** **AE** **①**
Southwest : ¼ m. ⊠ *LL54 5UH – ℘ (01286) 831 500 – www.pengwern.net*
– janepengwern@aol.com – Fax (01286) 830 741 – May-September
3 rm ⊠ – ♦£55 ♦♦£60/90   **Rest** – (by arrangement) Menu £25
♦ Charming farmhouse on working farm, picturesquely situated between mountains
and sea. Snowdonia views. Neat and tidy guest areas. Bedrooms of traditional quality.
Owner serves fresh, robust farmhouse cuisine including home-reared beef and lamb.

If breakfast is included the ⊠ symbol appears after the number of rooms.

▶ London 194 mi – Aberystwyth 39 mi – Chester 63 mi – Shrewsbury 42 mi

at Pontdolgoch Northwest : 1 ½ m. on A 470 – ✉ Newtown

The Talkhouse with rm   ⊟ ⌂ ⅍ **P** *VISA* ⓪ ①
✉ *SY17 5JE* – ☏ *(01686) 688 919* – *www.talkhouse.co.uk* – *info@talkhouse.co.uk*
– *Closed 25-26 December and first 2 weeks January*
3 rm ⊠ – ♦£70 ♦♦£125
Rest – (Closed Sunday dinner and Monday) (dinner only and Sunday lunch)
(booking essential) Carte £ 22/32

♦ Owner-run 17C coaching inn on Aberystwyth-Shrewsbury road. Ornate rustic bar.
Dining room opening onto terrace and gardens. Locally-based blackboard menu.
Stylish bedrooms.

WALES

WALES

Y. Duhamel/MICHELIN

CARDIFF

County: Cardiff
Michelin REGIONAL map: n° **503** K 29
▶ London 155 mi – Birmingham 110 mi
– Bristol 46 mi – Coventry 124 mi

Population: 292 150   33 **C4**
🏴 Wales

PRACTICAL INFORMATION

🖪 Tourist Information
The Old Library, The Hayes, Working St ℘ (0870) 1211258, visitor@cardiff.gov.uk

Airport
✈ Cardiff (Wales) Airport: ℘ (01446) 711111, SW: 8 m. by A 48 AX

Golf Courses
⛳ Dinas Powis Old Highwalls, ℘ (029) 5105 2727

👁 SIGHTS

IN TOWN

City★★★ - National Museum and
Gallery★★★ **AC** (Evolution of Wales★★,
Picture galleries★★) BY – Castle★ **AC** BZ
– Llandaff Cathedral★ AV **B** – Cardiff
Bay★ (Techniquest★ **AC**) AX

ON THE OUTSKIRTS

Museum of Welsh Life★★ **AC**, St
Fagan's, W: 5 m. by A 4161 AV – Castell
Coch★★ **AC**, NW: 5 m. by A 470 AV

IN THE SURROUNDING AREA

Caerphilly Castle★★ **AC**, N: 7 m. by
A 469 AV – Dyffryn Gardens★ **AC**,
W: 8 m. by A 48 AX

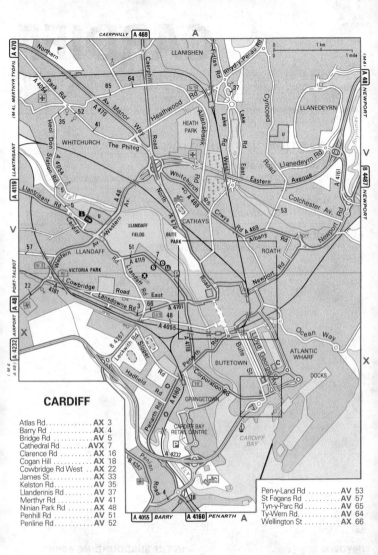

CARDIFF

The St David's H. & Spa

Havannah St, Cardiff Bay, South : 1 ¾ m. by Bute St

✉ CF10 5SD – ☎ (029) 2045 4045 – www.principalhotels.com

– reservations.stdavids@principalhotels.com – Fax (029) 2031 3075

CUa

120 rm ☲ – †£ 115/325 ††£ 125/325

– 12 suites

Rest *Tides Grill* – Carte £ 28/46

Rest *Waves* – (buffet lunch) (booking essential) Menu £ 17/26

◆ Striking modern hotel with panoramic views across waterfront. High-tech meeting rooms and fitness club. Well-proportioned rooms, all with balconies, in minimalist style. Informal Tides Grill. Welsh sourced menus at Waves.

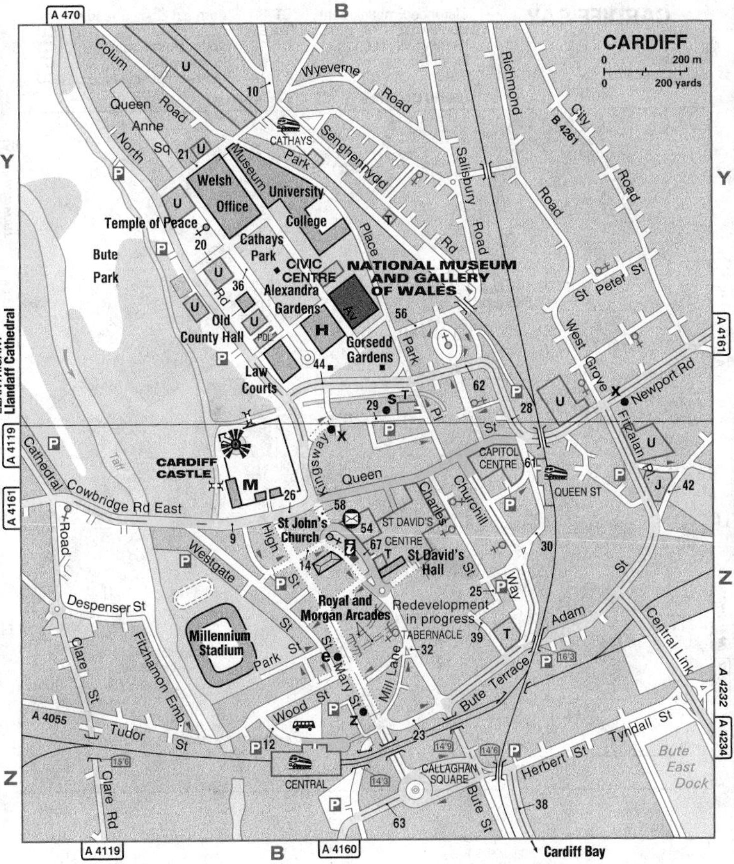

Capitol Centre	BZ		Dumfries Pl.	BY	28	Queens Arcade Shopping Centre	BZ	54
Castle St	BZ	9	Greyfriars Rd	BY	29	Queen St	BZ	
Cathays Terrace	BY	10	Guilford St	BZ	30	St Andrews Pl.	BY	56
Central Square	BZ	12	Hayes (The)	BZ	32	St David's Centre	BZ	
Church St	BZ	14	High St	BZ		St John St	BZ	58
City Hall Rd	BY	15	King Edward VII Ave	BY	36	St Mary St	BZ	
College Rd	BY	20	Lloyd George Ave	BZ	38	Station Terrace	BZ	61
Corbett Rd	BY	21	Mary Ann St	BZ	39	Stuttgarter Strasse	BY	62
Customhouse St	BZ	23	Moira Terrace	BZ	42	Tresillian Way	BZ	63
David St	BZ	25	Nantes (Boulevard de)	BY	44	Working St	BZ	67
Duke St	BZ	26						

Hilton Cardiff

Kingsway ✉ *CF10 3HH – ✆ (029) 2064 6300 – www.hilton.co.uk*
– Fax (029) 2064 6333 BZ**x**

193 rm – †£ 90/350 ††£ 90/350, ☕ £ 17.95
– 4 suites

Rest – Menu £ 19/27 **s** – Carte £ 27/38

♦ State-of-the-art meeting rooms and leisure facilities feature in this imposingly modern corporate hotel. Spacious, comfy bedrooms boast fine views of castle or City Hall. Popular menu in conservatory-style restaurant.

CARDIFF BAY

Britannia Quay . . . . CU 2
Bute Crescent . . . . CT 4
Clarence Embankment . . . CT 8
Dudley St. . . . . CU 9
Hemingway Rd. . . . . CT 12
Lloyd George Ave . . . . CT 14
Mermaid Quay Shopping Centre. . . . . CU
Mount Stuart Square . . . . CT 15
Pomeroy St. . . . . CT 17
Windsor Esplanade . . . . . CU 19

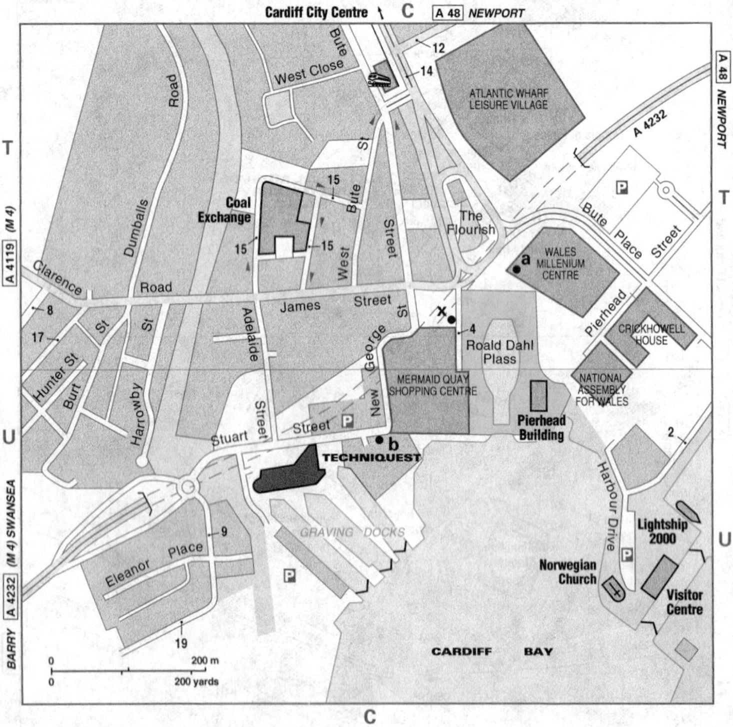

Park Plaza

Greyfriars Rd ✉ CF10 3AL – ✆ (029) 2011 1111
– www.parkplazacardiff.com
– ppcres@parkplazahotels.co.uk
– Fax (029) 2011 1112 BY**s**

129 rm – £ 90/260 £ 110/320

Rest ***Laguna Kitchen and Bar*** – see restaurant listing

◆ Central hotel, opened early 2005. Vast leisure centre boasts stainless steel pool. Impressive meeting rooms. Spacious, contemporary bedrooms, with good, up-to-date amenities.

Mercure Holland House H & Spa

rm,

24-26 Newport Rd ✉ CF24 0DD
– ✆ (029) 2043 5000 – www.mercure.com – h6622@accor.com
– Fax (029) 2048 8894 BY**x**

160 rm – £ 230/280 £ 230/280, £ 13.95
– 5 suites

Rest – Menu £ 22 (dinner) – Carte £ 21/38

◆ 14-storey converted office block that opened as an hotel in 2004. Large marbled lobby; spacious busy bar. State-of-the-art gym and therapy rooms. Airy, well-equipped rooms. Modern menus with local produce to fore in informal restaurant.

Royal without rest
10 St Mary St ⊠ CF10 5DW – ℰ (029) 2055 0750
– www.theroyalhotelcardiff.com – enquiries@theroyalhotelcardiff.com
– Fax (029) 2055 0760   BZe
64 rm – †£55/85 ††£65/95, ☐ £4
♦ Don't be put off by stark entrance. This central hotel has an extensive continental breakfast buffet and sleek rooms with bold fabrics, crisp Egyptian bedding and DVD library.

Jolyon's without rest
5 Bute Crescent, Cardiff Bay ⊠ CF10 5AN – ℰ (029) 2048 8775
– www.jolyons.co.uk – info@jolyons.co.uk – Fax (029) 2048 8775   CTx
6 rm ☐ – †£99/145 ††£99/145
♦ Georgian townhouse within Cardiff Bay's oldest terrace. Boutique style prevails. Rustic, slate-floored bar with log stove, red leather sofas. Light, modern, stylish bedrooms.

Lincoln House without rest
118-120 Cathedral Rd ⊠ CF11 9LQ – ℰ (029) 2039 5558
– www.lincolnhotel.co.uk – reservations@lincolnhotel.co.uk
– Fax (029) 2023 0537   AVe
23 rm ☐ – †£60/80 ††£85/120
♦ Sympathetically restored Victorian house close to the attractive Bute Gardens. Friendly service by eager-to-please owners. Four-poster room in period style most comfortable.

The Town House without rest
70 Cathedral Rd ⊠ CF11 9LL – ℰ (029) 2023 9399
– www.thetownhousecardiff.co.uk – thetownhouse@msn.com
– Fax (029) 2022 3214   AVu
8 rm ☐ – †£50/60 ††£70/90
♦ Carefully restored Victorian house, hospitably run by owners. Light and airy bedrooms have some thoughtful touches and are well appointed: ones at front are the most spacious.

Annedd Lon without rest
157 Cathedral Rd ⊠ CF11 9PL – ℰ (029) 2022 3349 – www.annedd.co.uk
– Closed 22-30 December   AVs
6 rm ☐ – †£45/55 ††£80
♦ Victorian house with Gothic influences located within a conservation area. Genuine hospitality in a friendly house. Portmeirion China at breakfast. Comfortable bedrooms.

Le Gallois
6-10 Romilly Cres ⊠ CF11 9NR – ℰ (029) 2034 1264
– www.legallois-ycymro.com – info@legallois-ycymro.com – Fax (029) 2023 7911
– Closed Christmas-New Year, Sunday dinner and Monday   AXx
Rest – Menu £16 (lunch) – Carte £28/56
♦ Bright and relaxed restaurant where keen owners provide both the friendly service and the assured modern European cooking. Gallic and Welsh combinations with inventive edge.

Laguna Kitchen and Bar – at Park Plaza Hotel
Greyfriars Rd ⊠ CF10 3AL – ℰ (029) 2011 1103
– www.lagunakitchenandbar.com – ppc-lkb@parkplazahotels.co.uk   BYs
Rest – Menu £15 (lunch) – Carte £24/32
♦ On ground floor of hotel, this smart, modern restaurant serves an intriguing mix of local or international dishes. There's a bar, too, with an area of booths for casual dining.

WALES

Ⅹ **Woods Brasserie**   AC 🕽 VISA ◑◉ AE ⓪
The Pilotage Building, Stuart St, Cardiff Bay, South : 1½ m. by Bute St ⊠ CF10 5BW – ℰ (029) 2049 2400 – www.woods-brasserie.com – serge@woodsbrasserie.com – Fax (029) 2048 1998   CU**b**
Rest – (booking essential at dinner) Menu £ 17/35 – Carte dinner £ 25/38
♦ Modern brasserie dishes and European influences from an open kitchen. Bay view from the first-floor terrace. Popular for business lunches and bay visitors in the evening.

at Thornhill North : 5¼ m. by A 470 - AV - on A 469

🏠 **Manor Parc**   🕭 Ⅹ ⅍ ⅏ ⅍ P VISA ◑◉ AE
Thornhill Rd, on A 469 ⊠ CF14 9UA – ℰ (029) 2069 3723 – www.manorparc.com – enquiry@manorparc.com – Fax (029) 2061 4624 – Closed 25 December-2 January
21 rm ⊇ – ♥£ 70/80 ♥♥£ 100
Rest – (Closed Sunday dinner) Menu £ 20 (weekdays) – Carte £ 23/27
♦ Personally run country house set in attractive terraced gardens. Some of the well-appointed rooms have south facing balconies and views over the Bristol Channel. Bright, airy orangery restaurant with Continental menu.

at Penarth South : 3 m. by A 4160 - AX - ⊠ Cardiff

🏠 **Holm House**   🕭 ⅍ ⅏ P VISA ◑◉ AE ⓪
Marine Parade – ℰ (029) 2070 1572 – www.holmhouse.com – info@holmhouse.co.uk – Fax (029) 2070 9875
12 rm ⊇ – ♥£ 145 ♥♥£ 305   **Rest** – Carte £ 20/42
♦ Built in 1920s for son of local shipbuilder. Part Art Deco, part modern styling, displaying flock wallpapers and bold colours; some bedrooms boast feature baths and oversized windows. Restaurant with views to distant Holm Islands; weekly menus of simple, wholesome combinations.

ⅩⅩ **The Olive Tree**   🕽 VISA ◑◉ AE
21 Glebe St ⊠ CF64 1EE – ℰ (029) 2070 7077 – www.the-olive-tree.net – Closed Sunday dinner and Monday
Rest – (dinner only and Sunday lunch) Menu £ 28 (weekdays) – Carte Saturday £ 24/39
♦ Rewarding discovery tucked away in the centre of town. Relaxing feel augmented by vivid artwork. Warm, friendly service of good value, seasonal, frequently changing dishes.

at Pentyrch Northwest : 7 m. by A 4119 - AV – ⊠ Cardiff

ⅩⅩⅩⅩ **De Courcey's**   🕭 ⇔ P VISA ◑◉ AE
Tyla Morris Ave (off Church Rd), South : 1 m. ⊠ CF15 9QN – ℰ (029) 2089 2232 – www.decourceys.co.uk – dinedecourceys@aol.com – Fax (029) 2089 1949 – Closed 25 December, January-March, Monday and Tuesday
Rest – (dinner only and Sunday lunch) Menu £ 20/30 – Carte £ 32/40
♦ Long-standing restaurant in an ornately decorated neo-Georgian house. Formal yet homely atmosphere. Accomplished traditional cuisine, served by smartly attired staff.

CARDIGAN – Ceredigion – 503 G 27 – pop. 4 082   33 **A3**
🚗 London 250 mi – Carmarthen 30 mi – Fishguard 19 mi
🛈 Theatr Mwldan, Bath House Rd ℰ (01239) 613230, cardigan.tic@ceridigion.gov.uk
🏌 Gwbert-on-Sea, ℰ (01239) 612035
🎖 Pembrokeshire Coast National Park★★

at Gwbert on Sea Northwest : 3 m. on B 4548 – ⊠ Cardigan

🏠 **Gwbert**   ≤ 🕭 🕾 ⅙ ⅟ AC rest, ⅏ P VISA ◑◉ AE ⓪
on B 4548 ⊠ SA43 1PP – ℰ (01239) 612 638 – www.gwberthotel.net – gwbert@enterprise.net – Fax (01239) 621 474
17 rm ⊇ – ♥£ 40/49 ♥♥£ 80/97   **Rest** – Carte £ 17/28
♦ Traditional seaside hotel on banks of Teifi with inspiring views of Cardigan Bay. Contemporary public areas and smart bar. Well-kept rooms with co-ordinated neutral scheme. Bistro/brasserie with panoramic views of Pembroke National Park coastline.

WALES

CARMARTHEN – Carmarthenshire – **503** H 28 – **pop. 14 648**   33 **B3**

  London 219 mi – Fishguard 47 mi – Haverfordwest 32 mi – Swansea 27 mi
  113 Lammas St ℰ (01267) 231557, carmarthentic@carmarthenshire.gov.uk
  Kidwelly Castle ★ – National Botanic Garden ★

at Felingwm Uchaf Northeast : 8 m. by A 40 on B 4310 – ⊠ Carmarthen

⌂ **Allt y Golau Uchaf** without rest   ⇲ ⅌ **P**
   North : ½ m. on B 4310 ⊠ SA32 7BB – ℰ (01267) 290 455 – www.alltygolau.com
   – alltygolau@btinternet.com – Fax (01267) 290 743 – Closed Christmas
   3 rm ⊡ – †£45 ††£65
   ♦ Georgian farmhouse in uplifting elevated position, perfect for walkers. Tranquil
   garden bursts to life in spring. Home-baked breakfasts of repute. Neat, pretty, compact rooms.

at Nantgaredig East : 5 m. on A 40 – ⊠ Carmarthen

🍴 **Y Polyn**   ⇲ ⇱ **P** **VISA** **◑◐**
   South : 1 m. by B4310 on B4300 ⊠ SA32 7LH – ℰ (01267) 290 000
   – www.ypolynrestaurant.co.uk – ypolyn@hotmail.com
   Rest – (Closed Sunday dinner and Monday) Menu 28 – Carte £ 18/25
   ♦ Relaxed dining pub by a stream; set in great rural location. Cooking is classically
   based but displays a modern vein. Dishes are hearty, tasty and wholesome. Choise
   expands at dinner.

CEMAES (Cemais) – Isle of Anglesey – **502** G 23   32 **B1**

  London 272 mi – Bangor 25 mi – Caernarfon 32 mi – Holyhead 16 mi
  Anglesey ★★

⌂ **Hafod Country House** without rest   ≤ ⇲ ⅌ **P** **VISA** **◑◐**
   South : ½ m. on Llanfechell rd ⊠ LL67 0DS – ℰ (01407) 711 645
   – hbr1946@aol.com – April-September
   3 rm ⊡ – †£40 ††£65
   ♦ Pleasant Edwardian guesthouse with very welcoming owner on outskirts of picturesque fishing village. Comfortable sitting room. The bedrooms are in immaculately
   kept order.

CHANCERY = Rhydgaled – **Ceredigion** – **503** H 26 – **see Aberystwyth**

CHEPSTOW (Cas-gwent) – Monmouthshire – **503** M 29 – **pop. 10 821**   33 **C4**

  London 131 mi – Bristol 17 mi – Cardiff 28 mi – Gloucester 34 mi
  Castle Car Park, Bridge St ℰ (01291) 623772,
    chepstow.tic@monmouthshire.gov.uk
  Town ★ – Castle ★★ **AC**
  Wynd Cliff ★, N : 2½ m. by A 466 – Caerwent ★ (Roman Walls ★), SW : 4 m.
    by A 48

at Shirenewton East : 5 m. by B 4293 off B 4235 – ⊠ Chepstow

⌂ **Coalpits Farm** without rest   ⇲ ⇱ ⅌ **P** **VISA** **◑◐**
   South : 1 m. on Crick rd ⊠ NP16 6LS – ℰ (01291) 641 820 – Fax (01291) 641 820
   3 rm ⊡ – †£40/45 ††£70
   ♦ Extended stone farmhouse, extraordinarily welcoming owner, horses at the window, woodland walks, charming garden, fine breakfasts, immaculate rooms...what
   more can we add?

CLYNNOG-FAWR – Gwynedd – **503** G 24   32 **B1**

  London 273 mi – Caerdydd / Cardiff 179 mi – Bangor 19 mi – Caergybi /
    Holyhead 39 mi

🏠 **Bryn Eisteddfod** ⅏   ≤ ⇲ ⅌ ⋔ **P** **VISA** **◑◐**
   ⊠ LL54 5DA – ℰ (01286) 660 431 – www.bryneisteddfod.com
   – info@bryneisteddfod.com
   7 rm ⊡ – †£53 ††£70   **Rest** – (dinner only) (residents only) Carte £ 18/29
   ♦ Owner of this 19C former rectory is local guide, full of useful info. Enjoy breakfast in
   the conservatory, and relax in homely lounge. Front rooms look to bay and mountains.
   Dining room has views through conservatory and offers tasty home-cooked dishes.

WALES

COLWYN BAY (Bae Colwyn) – **Conwy** – **502** I 24 – **pop. 30 269**   32 **B1**

▶ London 237 mi – Birkenhead 50 mi – Chester 42 mi – Holyhead 41 mi

🖪 Imperial Buildings, Station Sq, Princes Drive ✆ (01492) 530478, colwynbaytic@conwy.gov.uk - Cayley Promenade, Rhos-on-Sea ✆ (01492) 548778 (summer only)

🏌 Abergele Tan-y-Goppa Rd, ✆ (01745) 824 034

🏌 Old Colwyn Woodland Ave, ✆ (01492) 515 581

◉ Welsh Mountain Zoo★ **AC** (⇐★)

◉ Bodnant Garden★★ **AC**, SW : 6 m. by A 55 and A 470

⌂ **Rathlin Country House** without rest   🗇 🔟 ⅏ ⅍ ℡ **P** **VISA** **⦵⦵**
48 Kings Rd, Southwest : 1/4 m. on B 5113 ⊠ *LL29 7YH* – ✆ *(01492) 532 173*
– www.rathlincountryhouse.co.uk – enquiries@rathlincountryhouse.co.uk
– Fax (0871) 661 9887 – Closed Christmas
3 rm ⌿ – ⍮£65/85 ⍮⍮£85
♦ Surrounded by almost an acre of mature gardens, this personally run guesthouse has a large summer pool, inglenook fireplace, oak panelling and slightly modish rooms of style.

🍽 **Pen-y-Bryn**   🗇 ⅍ **P** **VISA** **⦵⦵** **AE**
Pen-y-Bryn Rd, Upper Colwyn Bay, Southwest : 1 m. by B 5113 ⊠ *LL29 6DD*
– ✆ (01492) 533 360 – www.penybryn-colwynbay.co.uk – Fax (01492) 536 127
– Closed dinner 25-26 December and 1 January
Rest – Carte £ 18/28
♦ Built in the 1970s, with lawned garden and bay view. Spacious interior with large, polished wood tables. Extensive menus feature Welsh dishes with eclectic influences.

at Rhos-on-Sea Northwest : 1 m. – ⊠ Colwyn Bay

⌂ **Plas Rhos** without rest   ⇐ 🗇 ⅍ ⅍ ℡ **P** **VISA** **⦵⦵** **AE**
Cayley Promenade ⊠ *LL28 4EP* – ✆ *(01492) 543 698 – www.plasrhos.co.uk*
– info@plasrhos.co.uk – Fax (01492) 540 088 – Closed 20 December-February
8 rm ⌿ – ⍮£48 ⍮⍮£60/70
♦ 19C house on first promenade from Colwyn Bay. Homely front lounge with bay view. Breakfasts feature local butcher's produce. Immaculately kept rooms: superior ones to front.

CONWY – **Conwy** – **502** I 24 – **pop. 3 847**   32 **B1**

▶ London 241 mi – Caernarfon 22 mi – Chester 46 mi – Holyhead 37 mi

🖪 Conwy Castle Visitor Centre ✆ (01492) 592248, conwytic@conwy.gov.uk

🏌 Penmaenmawr Conway Old Rd, ✆ (01492) 623 330

◉ Town★★ - Castle★★ **AC** - Town Walls★★ - Plas Mawr★★

◉ Snowdonia National Park★★★ - Bodnant Garden★★ **AC**, S : 8 m. by A 55 and A 470 - Conwy Crossing (suspension bridge★)

🏠 **Sychnant Pass House** ⏩   ⇐ 🗇 🔟 ⅍ ﯿ6 **P** **VISA** **⦵⦵**
Sychnant Pass Rd, Southwest : 2 m. by A 547 and Sychnant rd, turning right at T junction ⊠ *LL32 8BJ* – ✆ *(01492) 596 868 – www.sychnant-pass-house.co.uk*
– bre@sychnant-pass-house.co.uk – Fax (01492) 585 486 – Closed 23-26 December and January
12 rm ⌿ – ⍮£90 ⍮⍮£130/180 – 1 suite
Rest – (dinner only) (booking essential for non-residents) Menu £ 30
♦ Country house with Snowdonia National Park providing utterly peaceful backdrop. Charming sitting room with attractive décor. Comfy rooms, named after cats from T.S. Elliott. Informal dining room with rustic style and seasonal menus.

🏠 **Castle**   ⅍ ﯿ **P** **VISA** **⦵⦵** **AE**
High St ⊠ *LL32 8DB* – ✆ *(01492) 582 800 – www.castlewales.co.uk*
– mail@castlewales.co.uk – Fax (01492) 582 300 – Closed 26 December
27 rm ⌿ – ⍮£87/90 ⍮⍮£140/179 – 1 suite
Rest *Dawson's* – Menu £ 23 – Carte £ 24/33
♦ Two eye-catching ex-coaching inns on site of former Cistercian abbey. Characterful interior with original features in situ. Refurbished rooms have a stylish period feel. Dining room serves seasonal brasserie style menu.

WALES

at Llansanffraid Glan Conwy Southeast : 2½ m. by A 547 on A 470 – ⌂ Conwy

🏠 **Old Rectory Country House** without rest 🌦   ⬅ 🚗 **P** **VISA** **◐◐**
Llanrwst Rd, on A 470 ⌂ *LL28 5LF –* 🕾 *(01492) 580611*
– www.oldrectorycountryhouse.co.uk – info@oldrectorycountryhouse.co.uk
– Closed 15 December-15 January
6 rm ☷ – †£99/119 ††£139/159
♦ Enjoys fine position on estuary; once home to parish rectors, renovated in Georgian style. House motto: "beautiful haven of peace"; antiques throughout, watercolours abound.

at Tyn-y-Groes South : 4 m. on B 5106 – ⌂ Conwy

🏠 **The Groes Inn** with rm   ⬅ 🚗 ☞ ⅍ **P** **VISA** **◐◐** **AE** **①**
North : 1½ m. on B5106 ⌂ *LL32 8TN –* 🕾 *(01492) 650545 – www.groesinn.com*
– reception@groesinn.com – Fax (01492) 650855
14 rm ☷ – †£85/157 ††£103/189
Rest – Menu £30 (dinner) – Carte £23/30
♦ Georgian-style dining room. Part 16C inn, Wales' first licensed house. Beamed ceilings, log fires and historic bric-a-brac. Immaculately sumptuous bedrooms, some with super rural views.

COWBRIDGE (Y Bont Faen) – **The Vale of Glamorgan** – **503** J 29   33 **B4**
– pop. 3 616
🚇 London 170 mi – Cardiff 15 mi – Swansea 30 mi

✗✗ **Huddarts**   **VISA** **◐◐**
69 High St ⌂ *CF71 7AF –* 🕾 *(01446) 774645 – www.huddartsrestaurant.co.uk*
– Fax (01446) 772215 – Closed 1 week spring, 1 week autumn,
26 December-8 January, Sunday dinner and Monday
Rest – Menu £25 (weekdays) – Carte £23/34
♦ Intimate, family run restaurant located on high street of this ancient market town. Welsh tapestries on wall. Skilfully executed traditional dishes with modern influences.

CRICCIETH – **Gwynedd** – **502** H 25 – pop. 1 826   32 **B2**
🚇 London 249 mi – Caernarfon 17 mi – Shrewsbury 85 mi
🛈 Ednyfed Hill, 🕾 (01766) 522154
🖾 Lleyn Peninsula★★ – Ffestiniog Railway★★

🏠 **Mynydd Ednyfed Country House** 🌦   ⬅ 🚗 ⅍ **P** **VISA** **◐◐**
Caernarfon Rd, Northwest : ¾ m. on B 4411 ⌂ *LL52 0PH –* 🕾 *(01766) 523269*
– www.criccieth.net – mynydd-ednyfed@criccieth.net – Fax (01766) 522929
– Closed 22 December-4 January
9 rm ☷ – †£75 ††£125   **Rest** – (closed Sunday) (dinner only) Carte £20/30
♦ Idyllically located 17C country house in eight acres of gardens and woods overlooking Tremadog Bay. Refurbished lounge bar. Airy conservatory for breakfasts. Homely rooms. Small, cosy, comfortable dining room.

CRICKHOWELL (Crucywel) – **Powys** – **503** K 28   33 **C4**
🚇 London 169 mi – Abergavenny 6 mi – Brecon 14 mi – Cardiff 40 mi
– Newport 25 mi
🛈 Resource and Information Centre, Beaufort St 🕾 (01873) 811970
🖾 Brecon Beacons National Park★★. Llanthony Priory★★, NE : 10 m. by minor roads

🏠🏠 **Gliffaes Country House** 🌦   ⬅ ◖ ☞ ⅍ ⚒ **P** **VISA** **◐◐** **AE** **①**
West : 3¾ m. by A 40 ⌂ *NP8 1RH –* 🕾 *(01874) 730371 – www.gliffaeshotel.com*
– calls@gliffaeshotel.com – Fax (01874) 730463 – Closed 2-31 January
23 rm ☷ – †£96/110 ††£230
Rest – (light lunch Monday-Saturday) Menu £36 **s**
♦ 19C country house and gardens on banks of Usk, offering great tranquillity. Welcoming bar, lounge and conservatory. Popular for outdoor pursuits. Luxuriously individual rooms. Bold, country house dining room has pleasant garden views.

WALES

The Bear

High St ✉ NP8 1BW – ✆ (01873) 810408 – www.bearhotel.co.uk – bearhotel@aol.com – Fax (01873) 811696 – Closed 25 December
34 rm – †£70/117 ††£153 – 2 suites
Rest *The Restaurant and The Bear* – see restaurant listing
◆ Imposing, part 15C former coaching inn with maze of public areas. Bustling bar and lounges. Good conference facilities. Plush, spacious bedrooms with individual furnishings.

Ty Croeso

The Dardy, West : 1½ m. by A 4077 off Llangynidr rd ✉ NP8 1PU – ✆ (01873) 810573 – www.ty-croeso.co.uk – tycroeso@gmail.com – Fax (01873) 810573
8 rm – †£50/59 ††£72/75
Rest – (dinner only) Menu £20 – Carte £20/23
◆ Small hotel of Welsh stone, originally part of a Victorian workhouse. Personally run by pleasant owners. Large bar with log fire. Neatly designed rooms have rewarding views. Interesting menus feature well-sourced ingredients.

Glangrwyney Court

South : 2 m. on A 40 ✉ NP8 1ES – ✆ (01873) 811288 – www.glancourt.co.uk – info@glancourt.co.uk – Fax (01873) 810317
8 rm – †£50/85 ††£95/120 **Rest** – (by arrangement) Menu £25
◆ Spacious Georgian house with sizeable garden and warm welcome. Large front lounge in chintz with antiques and trinkets. Pleasantly cluttered, well-kept rooms.

WALES

The Restaurant – at The Bear Hotel

High St ✉ NP8 1BW – ✆ (01873) 810408 – www.bearhotel.co.uk – bearhotel@aol.com – Fax (01873) 811696 – Closed Sunday-Monday
Rest – (dinner only) Carte £22/30
◆ Charming dining rooms - with polite service, wide-ranging menus employing classical base underpinned by Welsh ingredients - are a sedate option to the ever busy bar.

Nantyffin Cider Mill Inn

Brecon Rd, West : 1½ m. on A 40 ✉ NP8 1SG – ✆ (01873) 810775 – www.cidermill.co.uk – info@cidermill.co.uk – Fax (01873) 810986 – Closed Monday October to March
Rest – Carte £22/30
◆ Converted 16C cider mill, its working parts still in situ. Choose between bars or Mill Room. Local farm meat, fish and - yes - cider on offer on Drovers menu or blackboard.

The Bear

High St ✉ NP8 1BW – ✆ (01873) 810408 – www.bearhotel.co.uk – bearhotel@aol.com – Fax (01873) 811696 – Closed 25 December dinner
Rest – Carte £18/29
◆ Bustling 15C former coaching inn, with a characterful open-fired bar, warm welcome, friendly atmosphere and antiques aplenty. Menu ranges from light meals to hearty, wholesome dishes.

CROSSGATES – Powys – 503 J 27 – see Llandrindod Wells

CWMBRAN (Cwmbrân) – Torfaen – 503 K 29 – pop. 47 254 — 33 C4

London 149 mi – Bristol 35 mi – Cardiff 17 mi – Newport 5 mi

Parkway

rm, rest,

Cwmbran Drive, South : 1 m. by A 4051 ✉ NP44 3UW – ✆ (01633) 871199 – www.bwparkwayhotel.co.uk – enquiries@parkwayhotel.co.uk – Fax (01633) 869160 – Closed 26-30 December
69 rm – †£70/115 ††£85/125 – 1 suite
Rest *Ravello's* – (dinner only and Sunday lunch) Carte £21/31 **s**
◆ Purpose-built hotel aimed at the business traveller with extensive conference facilities. Spacious lounge. Smart, well-kept bedrooms benefit from refurbishment. Small, comfortable restaurant with formal chairs and water fountain in centre.

DEGANWY – Conwy – 502 I 24 – see Llandudno

DOLFOR Powys – Powys – 503 K 26

▶ London 199 – Cardiff 93 – Oswestry 34 – Ludlow 39

32 **C2**

⌂ **Old Vicarage**   ≤ 🛋 ⚙ 🐾 **P** VISA ⚫⚫
North : ½ m. off A 483 – 🕿 *(01686) 629 051 – www.theoldvicaragedolfor.co.uk*
– tim@theoldvicaragedolfor.co.uk
3 rm 🍽 – ♦£65 ♦♦£95   **Rest** – (by arrangement) Menu £28
♦ 19C former vicarage with pleasant garden and homely lounge with fire-place. Comfy bedrooms; the green room is the largest, with an equally big bathroom. Polished antique tables and candles in attractive dining room. Most of the produce is local or from the garden.

DOLGELLAU – Gwynedd – 502 I 25 – pop. 2 407

32 **B2**

▶ London 221 mi – Birkenhead 72 mi – Chester 64 mi – Shrewsbury 57 mi
🛈 Ty Meirion, Eldon Sq 🕿 (01341) 422888, tic.dolgellau@eryri-npa.gov.uk
⛳ Hengwrt Estate Pencefn Rd, 🕿 (01341) 422 603
◉ Town★
ⓒ Snowdonia National Park★★★ – Cadair Idris★★★ - Precipice Walk★, NE :
   3 m. on minor roads

🏰 **Penmaenuchaf Hall** 🌿   ≤ 🛋 🐬 🐾 🏠 **P** VISA ⚫⚫ ⓘ
Penmaenpool, West : 1 ¾ m. on A 493 (Tywyn Rd) ✉ *LL40 1YB –* 🕿 *(01341)*
422 129 – www.penhall.co.uk – relax@penhall.co.uk – Fax (01341) 422 787
14 rm 🍽 – ♦£95/140 ♦♦£150/230   **Rest** – Menu £40 – Carte dinner £39/45
♦ From a handsome drawing room, enjoy the enviable position of this Victorian mansion with its Rhinog Mountain and Mawddach Estuary vistas. Bedrooms are tastefully furnished. Dine in smart garden room with outside terrace.

⌂ **Tyddyn Mawr** without rest 🌿   ≤ 🛋 🐬 🐾 ⚙ **P**
🔲 *Islawdref, Cader Rd, Southwest : 2 ½ m. by Tywyn rd on Cader Idris rd* ✉ *LL40 1TL*
– 🕿 *(01341) 422 331 – February-November*
3 rm 🍽 – ♦£60 ♦♦£68
♦ Part 18C farmhouse with sympathetic extension: boasts spectacular views from breathtaking position. Timbered breakfast room. Superb rooms: one with patio, one with balcony.

WALES

Red = Pleasant. Look for the red ✗ and 🏠 symbols.

EAST ABERTHAW (Aberddawan) – The Vale of Glamorgan – 503 J 29   33 **B-C4**
– ✉ Barry

▶ London 180 mi – Cardiff 20 mi – Swansea 33 mi

🏠 **The Blue Anchor Inn**   **P** VISA ⚫⚫
✉ *CF62 3DD –* 🕿 *(01446) 750 329 – www.blueanchoraberthaw.com*
Rest – (Closed Sunday dinner) Carte £15/25
♦ Characterful thatched inn dating back to 1380. Bar menu offer sandwiches and pub classics; formal restaurant menu is more substantial. Produce is local and desserts are homemade.

ERWOOD Powys – Powys – 503 K 27 – pop. 1 815

33 **C3**

▶ London 183 mi – Cardiff 56 mi – Merthyr Tydfil 35 mi – Hereford 34 mi

⌂ **Trericket Mill**   🛋 ⚙ 🐾 **P**
South : ¾ m. off A 470 ✉ *LD2 3TQ –* 🕿 *(01982) 560 312 – www.trericket.co.uk*
– mail@trericket.co.uk – Closed Christmas and 3 weeks January
3 rm 🍽 – ♦£40/44 ♦♦£68   **Rest** – Vegetarian – Menu £18
♦ Red brick, grade II listed water corn mill with a comfy, rustic feel, log fires and riverside garden. Simple bedrooms; the Mill Room has its own little balcony. Vegetarian menu served in dining room, which also houses the mill machinery.

FELINGWM UCHAF – Carmarthenshire – see Carmarthen

FISHGUARD – Pembrokeshire – **503** F 28 – **pop. 3 193**   33 **A3**

▶ London 265 mi – Cardiff 114 mi – Gloucester 176 mi – Holyhead 169 mi
– Shrewsbury 136 mi – Swansea 76 mi

⛴ to Republic of Ireland (Rosslare) (Stena Line) 2-4 daily (1 h 50 mn/3 h 30 mn)

🛈 Town Hall, The Square ℘ (01437) 776636,
fishguard.tic@pembrokeshire.gov.uk - Ocean Lab, The Parrog, Goodwick
℘ (01348) 872037, fishguardharbour.tic@pembrokshire.gov.uk

🖸 Pembrokeshire Coast National Park★★

⌂   **Manor Town House** without rest   ≤ 🚗 🍳 📶 **VISA** **◉◉**
11 Main St ⊠ SA65 9HG – ℘ (01348) 873 260 – www.manortownhouse.com
– enquiries@manortownhouse.com – Fax (01348) 873 260
6 rm �◻ – ✝£40/65 ✝✝£75/85
♦ Georgian Grade II listed house. Bedrooms are individually styled and furnished with
antiques, choose from Victorian and Art Deco; some with harbour and sea views.

at Welsh Hook Southwest : 7 ½ m. by A 40 – ⊠ Haverfordwest

✗✗   **Stone Hall** with rm ⌂   🚗 🍳 **P.** **VISA** **◉◉** **AE** **①**
⊠ SA62 5NS – ℘ (01348) 840212 – www.stonehall-mansion.co.uk – Fax (01348)
840815 – Closed 25-26 December, 2 weeks autumn, Sunday and Monday
5 rm �◻ – ✝£85 ✝✝£100
Rest – (dinner only) (booking essential) Menu £30 – Carte £30/36
♦ Charming part-14C manor house with 17C additions. Tranquil setting and personal
hospitality. Home-cooked, French-style dishes using prime seasonal produce. Comfy
rooms.

> Luxury pad or humble abode?
> 🏨🏨 and ⌂ denote categories of comfort.

GRESFORD = Groes-ffordd – Wrexham – **502** L 24 – see Wrexham

GROESLON – Gwynedd – see Caernarfon

GWBERT ON SEA – Ceredigion – **503** F 27 – see Cardigan

HARLECH – Gwynedd – **502** H 25 – **pop. 1 233**   32 **B2**

▶ London 241 mi – Chester 72 mi – Dolgellau 21 mi
🛈 High St ℘ (01766) 780658, tic.harlech@aryri-npa.gov.uk
🏌 Royal St David's, ℘ (01766) 780 203
◉ Castle★★ **AC**
🖸 Snowdonia National Park★★★

⌂   **Gwrach Ynys** without rest   🚗 🍳 📶 **P.**
North : 2 ¼ m. on A 496 ⊠ LL47 6TS – ℘ (01766) 780 742
– www.gwrachynys.co.uk – info@gwrachynys.co.uk – Fax (01766) 781 199
– February-October
7 rm �◻ – ✝£30/55 ✝✝£60/70
♦ Edwardian house in good location for exploring Snowdonia and Cardigan Bay.
Welcoming owners. Traditional bedrooms, two of which are ideal for families.

✗✗   **Castle Cottage** with rm   **VISA** **◉◉**
Pen Llech, off B 4573 ⊠ LL46 2YL – ℘ (01766) 780479
– www.castlecottageharlech.co.uk – glyn@castlecottageharlech.co.uk
– Closed 3 weeks November
7 rm �◻ – ✝£80 ✝✝£160   **Rest** – (dinner only) (booking essential) Menu £35
♦ A little cottage just a short distance from the imposing Harlech Castle. Stylish,
modern restaurant where Welsh food with a modern twist is served. Smart contemporary rooms.

HAVERFORDWEST (Hwlffordd) – Pembrokeshire – **503** F 28

– pop. 13 367

- ▶ London 250 mi – Fishguard 15 mi – Swansea 57 mi
- ℹ Old Bridge ℰ (01437) 763110, haverfordwest.tic@pembrokeshire.gov.uk
- 🏌 Arnolds Down, ℰ (01437) 763 565
- ◎ Scolton Museum and Country Park★
- ◎ Pembrokeshire Coast National Park★★. Skomer Island and Skokholm Island★, SW : 14 m. by B 4327 and minor roads

⌂ Lower Haythog Farm 🐾   🚲 ⌖ ℙ

Spittal, Northeast : 5 m. on B 4329 ⊠ SA62 5QL – ℰ (01437) 731 279
– www.lowerhaythogfarm.co.uk – nesta@lowerhaythogfarm.co.uk – Fax (01437) 731 279

6 rm �''' – †£40/50 ††£75/85   **Rest** – (by arrangement) Menu £23
♦ Friendly atmosphere, traditional comforts and a warm welcome at this 250 acre working dairy farm with accessible woodland walks. Well kept and comfortable throughout. Dining room in homely, country style reflected in hearty, home-cooked food.

HAWARDEN (Penarlâg) – Flintshire – **502** K 24

- ▶ London 205 mi – Chester 9 mi – Liverpool 17 mi – Shrewsbury 45 mi

✗ The Hawarden Brasserie   🆉 VISA ◉ 🆎

68 The Highway ⊠ CH5 3DH – ℰ (01244) 536 353
– www.thehawardenbrasserie.com – Fax (01244) 520 888
– Closed Saturday lunch

Rest – (booking essential) Carte £20/27
♦ Neutral walls, wood floors and spot lighting contribute to the busy, modern ambience in this good value, small restaurant; well reputed locally. Cuisine with a Welsh tone.

HAY-ON-WYE (Y Gelli) – Powys – **503** K 27 – pop. 1 846

- ▶ London 154 mi – Brecon 16 mi – Cardiff 59 mi – Hereford 21 mi
  – Newport 62 mi
- ℹ Craft Centre, Oxford Rd ℰ (01497) 820144
- 🏌 Rhosgoch Builth Wells, ℰ (01497) 851 251
- ◎ Town★
- ◎ Brecon Beacons National Park★★. Llanthony Priory★★, SE : 12 m. by minor roads

🏠 The Swan at Hay   🚲 🆖 ℙ VISA ◉ 🆎 ◐

Church St ⊠ HR3 5DQ – ℰ (01497) 821 188 – www.swanathay.co.uk
– info@swanathay.co.uk – Fax (01497) 821 424 – Closed 2 weeks January

18 rm ☷ – †£75/89 ††£125   **Rest** – (bar lunch) Menu £28 – Carte £19/33
♦ Constantly evolving 18C former coaching inn bordered by neat book-lovers' garden. Restyled front bar is light, airy and inviting. Guest lounge with 21C makeover. Spruce rooms. French influenced modern menus in the restaurant.

🏠 Old Black Lion with rm   🆉 ℙ VISA ◉

26 Lion St ⊠ HR3 5AD – ℰ (01497) 820 841 – www.oldblacklion.co.uk
– info@oldblacklion.co.uk – Fax (01497) 822 960 – Closed 25 December

10 rm ☷ – †£48 ††£95   **Rest** – Carte £21/31
♦ Inn with parts dating back to 13C and 17C when it reputedly hosted Oliver Cromwell. A friendly place with a traditional atmosphere, popular menu and comfortable bedrooms.

at Llanigon Southwest : 2½ m. by B 4350 – ⊠ Hay-on-Wye

⌂ Old Post Office without rest   ℙ

⊠ HR3 5QA – ℰ (01497) 820 008 – www.oldpost-office.co.uk – March-November

3 rm ☷ – †£35/70 ††£70/80
♦ Dating from 17C, a converted inn. Near the "book town" of Hay-on-Wye. Smart modern ambience blends with characterful charm. Pine furnished rooms with polished floors.

HENSOL – The Vale of Glamorgan
33 **C4**

- ▶ London 161 mi – Bridgend 10 mi – Cardiff 8 mi – Cowbridge 7 mi
- ⓒ Museum of Welsh Life★★, E : 8 m. by minor rd north to Miskin, A 4119 and minor rd south

※※ **Calon** with rm 🛜 ⑨ ⑪ VISA ⑩ AE P.
- ✉ CF72 8GG – ℰ (01443) 225 877 – www.llanerch-vineyard.co.uk
- enquiries@llanerch-vineyard.co.uk – Fax (01443) 225 546 – Closed Sunday dinner and Monday
- **8 rm** ⌂ – †£50/55 ††£70/75
- **Rest** – Menu £18/26 (lunch) – Carte £30/45
- ◆ Spacious restaurant set in a vineyard, with airy conservatory and pleasant terrace. Concise menu of simple, unfussy cooking uses local, seasonal ingredients and veg from the garden. Immaculately kept bedrooms boast good facilities.

HOLYHEAD (Caergybi) – Isle of Anglesey – **502** G 24 – pop. 11 237
32 **B1**

- ▶ London 269 mi – Birkenhead 94 mi – Cardiff 215 mi – Chester 88 mi – Shrewsbury 105 mi – Swansea 190 mi
- ⛴ to Republic of Ireland (Dun Laoghaire) (Stena Line) 4-5 daily (1 h 40 mn) – to Republic of Ireland (Dublin) (Irish Ferries) 2 daily (3 h 15 mn) – to Republic of Ireland (Dublin) (Stena Line) 1-2 daily (3 h 45 mn)
- 𝒊 Terminal 1, Stena Line ℰ (01407) 762622
- ⓒ South Stack Cliffs★, W : 3 m. by minor roads

WALES

↑ **Yr Hendre** without rest 🚗 ⑨ ⑪ P.
Porth-y-Felin Rd, Northwest : ½ m. turning left at war memorial and by Thomas St
- ✉ LL65 1AH – ℰ (01407) 762 929 – www.yr-hendre.co.uk
- rita@yr-hendre.freeserve.co.uk – Fax (01407) 762 929
- **3 rm** ⌂ – †£40 ††£65
- ◆ Detached house dating from the 1920s in a pleasant, residential area of town and ideally located for the ferry terminus. Comfortable and well-furnished bedrooms.

> Good food and accommodation at moderate prices?
> Look for the Bib symbols:
> red Bib Gourmand ⓐ for food, blue Bib Hotel 🏨 for hotels

HOWEY – Powys – see Llandrindod Wells

KNIGHTON (Trefyclawdd) – Powys – **503** K 26 – pop. 2 851
33 **C3**

- ▶ London 162 mi – Birmingham 59 mi – Hereford 31 mi – Shrewsbury 35 mi
- 𝒊 Offa's Dyke Centre, West St ℰ (01547) 529424, oda@offasdyke.demon.co.uk
- 🏌 Ffrydd Wood, ℰ (01547) 528 646
- ⓞ Town★
- ⓒ Offa's Dyke★, NW : 9½ m

🏠 **Milebrook House** 🚗 ↘ ⑨ ⑪ P. VISA ⑩
Ludlow Rd, Milebrook, East : 2 m. on A 4113 ✉ LD7 1LT – ℰ (01547) 528 632
- www.milebrookhouse.co.uk – hotel@milebrook.kc3ltd.co.uk – Fax (01547) 520 509
- **10 rm** ⌂ – †£59 ††£148
- **Rest** – (closed Monday lunch) Menu £15/34 **s** – Carte £22/34 **s**
- ◆ Located in the Teme Valley; good for exploring the Welsh Marches. Possesses a fine, formal garden well stocked with exotic plants. Rooms are large and pleasingly decorated. The kitchen garden provides most of the vegetables which appear in the restaurant.

LAKE VYRNWY – Powys – 502 J 25 – ⊠ Llanwddyn

🚊 London 204 mi – Chester 52 mi – Llanfyllin 10 mi – Shrewsbury 40 mi
🛈 Unit 2, Vyrnwy Craft Workshops ℰ (01691) 870346, laktic@powys.gov.uk
◎ Lake ★

🏠 **Lake Vyrnwy** 🔌 ⟨ 🚗 🦆 🦢 ⊛ 🌲 ↕ ✗ 🖼 ♿ rm, 🎿 P VISA ⓒⓞ AE
⊠ SY10 0LY – ℰ (01691) 870692 – www.lakevyrnwyhotel.co.uk
– info@lakevyrnwyhotel.co.uk – Fax (01691) 870259
51 rm ⌁ – ✝£180/190 ✝✝£205/215 – 1 suite
Rest – Menu £18/38 – Carte lunch £18/21
♦ Victorian country house built from locally quarried stone overlooking the lake; an
RSPB sanctuary and sporting estate, ideal for game enthusiasts. Rooms have timeless
chic. Spectacular lakeside views from the restaurant are matched by accomplished
cooking.

LALESTON – Bridgend – 503 J 29 – see Bridgend

LAMPHEY = Llandyfai – Pembrokeshire – 503 F 28 – see Pembroke

LLANABER Gwynedd – 502 H25 – see Barmouth

LLANARMON DYFFRYN CEIRIOG – Wrexham – 502 K 25
– ⊠ Llangollen (Denbighshire)

🚊 London 196 mi – Chester 33 mi – Shrewsbury 32 mi

🏠 **West Arms** 🚗 🦆 🎿 P VISA ⓒⓞ
⊠ LL20 7LD – ℰ (01691) 600665 – www.thewestarms.co.uk
– gowestarms@aol.com – Fax (01691) 600622
13 rm ⌁ – ✝£119 ✝✝£225 – 2 suites
Rest – (bar lunch Monday-Saturday) Menu £33 – Carte £24/32
♦ Set in Ceiriog Valley; enjoys many original fixtures associated with a part 16C
country inn - slate-flagged floors, inglenooks, timberwork. Bedrooms with matching
ambience. A concise but well-balanced menu offered in atmospheric dining room.

LLANDDEWI SKIRRID – Monmouthshire – see Abergavenny

LLANDEILO – Carmarthenshire – 503 I 28 – pop. 1 731

🚊 London 218 mi – Brecon 34 mi – Carmarthen 15 mi – Swansea 25 mi
◎ Town ★ - Dinefwr Park ★ AC
Ⓖ Brecon Beacons National Park ★★ – Black Mountain ★, SE : by minor roads –
Carreg Cennen Castle ★ AC, SE : 4 m. by A 483 and minor roads

🏠 **Plough Inn** ⟨ 🚗 🌲 ↕ ♿ rm, ✗ 🦑 🎿 P VISA ⓒⓞ AE
Rhosmaen, North : 1 m. on A 40 ⊠ SA19 6NP – ℰ (01558) 823431
– www.ploughrhosmaen.com – info@ploughrhosmaen.com – Fax (01558)
823969 – Closed 26 and 31 December
15 rm ⌁ – ✝£65 ✝✝£90/120 **Rest** – Carte £20/28
♦ Once a farmhouse, the perfect base for country pursuits. Rooms, named after characters from Mabinogion, are well-kept and co-ordinated; large windows for views.
Wholesome favourites to fore in light, airy and relaxed modern dining room.

at Salem North : 3 m. by A 40 off Pen y banc rd – ⊠ Llandeilo

🏠 **The Angel Inn** 🦆 ✗ P VISA ⓒⓞ
⊠ SA19 7LY – ℰ (01558) 823394 – www.angelsalem.co.uk
– eat@angelsalem.co.uk – Closed Sunday dinner, Monday (except Bank Holiday
Monday), Tuesday lunch
Rest – Carte £20/32
♦ Cream coloured pub next to chapel in small village. Inviting bar lounge with chair
and sofa assortment. Edwardian style dining room: elaborate cooking utilising local
fare.

WALES

LLANDENNY – Monmouthshire – **503** L 28 – see Usk

LLANDOVERY Carmarthenshire – Carmarthenshire – **503** I 28   33 **B3**
– pop. 2 235

▶ London 207 mi – Cardiff 61 mi – Swansea 37 mi – Merthyr Tydfil 34 mi

🏠 **New White Lion**   &. rm, ⁄⁄ 🅟 ▨ ⑩
43 Stone St ✉ SA20 0BZ – ℰ (01550) 720 685 – www.newwhitelion.co.uk
– info@newwhitelion.co.uk – Closed 24-26 December
6 rm ⌑ – †£70/80 ††£125
Rest – (dinner only) (booking essential residents only) Menu £22 **s**
◆ Stylish grade II listed hotel with individually designed bedrooms named after characters from local folklore, and cool sitting room with honesty bar. Cosy dining room;
homemade dishes make good use made of local, seasonal produce.

LLANDRILLO – Denbighshire – **502** J 25 – ✉ Corwen   32 **C2**
▶ London 210 mi – Chester 40 mi – Dolgellau 26 mi – Shrewsbury 46 mi

XXX **Tyddyn Llan** with rm ⤳   ⬚ 🅟 ▨ ⑩
✉ LL21 0ST – ℰ (01490) 440 264 – www.tyddynllan.co.uk
– tyddynllan@compuserve.com – Fax (01490) 440 414 – Closed 3 weeks January
13 rm (dinner included) ⌑ – †£100/120 ††£200/260
Rest – (dinner only and lunch Friday-Sunday) (booking essential)
Menu £28/45 ❀
◆ Charming sitting areas for pre-dinner drinks. Two dining rooms with blue painted
wood panels. Classic menus employing local produce. Fine selection of country
house rooms.

Look out for red symbols, indicating particularly pleasant establishments.

LLANDRINDOD WELLS – Powys – **503** J 27 – pop. 5 024   33 **C3**
▶ London 204 mi – Brecon 29 mi – Carmarthen 60 mi – Shrewsbury 58 mi
🄸 Old Town Hall, Memorial Gardens ℰ (01597) 822 600,
llandtic@powys.gov.uk
⛳ Llandrindod Wells The Clubhouse, ℰ (01597) 823 873
🄶 Elan Valley★★ (Dol-y-Mynach and Claerwen Dam and Reservoir★★, Caban
Coch Dam and Reservoir★, Garreg-ddu Viaduct★, Pen-y-Garreg Reservoir
and Dam★, Craig Goch Dam and Reservoir★), NW : 12 m. by A 4081, A 470
and B 4518

🏨 **Metropole**   ⬚ 🄳 ⋒ 🕮 &. rm, ⋒ ⚙ 🅟 ▨ ⑩ 🄰🄴
Temple St ✉ LD1 5DY – ℰ (01597) 823 700 – www.metropole.co.uk
– info@metropole.co.uk – Fax (01597) 824 828
120 rm ⌑ – †£85/120 ††£120/140 – 2 suites
Rest – (bar lunch) Menu £26 – Carte £22/27
◆ Run by Baird-Murray family for 100 years and popular for hosting vintage car rallies.
Leisure complex is in 19C style conservatory. Eight "Tower" rooms with adjoining
lounge. Expect to find cuisine committed to using local ingredients.

at Crossgates Northeast : 3 ½ m. on A 483 – ✉ Llandrindod Wells

⌂ **Guidfa House**   ⬚ ⁄⁄ ⋒ 🅟 ▨ ⑩
✉ LD1 6RF – ℰ (01597) 851 241 – www.guidfahouse.co.uk
– guidfa@globalnet.co.uk – Fax (01597) 851 875 – Closed Christmas and New
Year
6 rm ⌑ – †£50/60 ††£80/85   **Rest** – (by arrangement) Menu £30
◆ Georgian house with white painted façade and pleasant garden to relax in. Indoors,
find spacious, bright bedrooms. A friendly welcome is given with tips on local activities. Seasonally changing menu of zesty home cooking in traditionally decorated
dining room.

at Howey South : 1½ m. by A 483 – ⊠ Llandrindod Wells

↑ **Acorn Court Country House** without rest ⊗ 🗚 🕭 🛇 **P**
Chapel Rd, Northeast :½ m. ⊠ *LD1 5PB –* ℰ *(01597) 823 543*
– www.acorncourt.co.uk – info@acorncourt.co.uk – Fax (01597) 823 543
4 rm ⌲ – ♦£35/48 ♦♦£68/75
♦ Chalet-style house in lovely countryside; guests can fish in the lake. Bedrooms are
large with many extra touches: hairdryers, stationery, soft toys - homely and welcoming.

LLANDUDNO – Conwy – **502** I 24 – pop. **14 872**   32 **B1**
 🚃 London 243 mi – Birkenhead 55 mi – Chester 47 mi – Holyhead 43 mi
 🖪 Library Building, Mostyn St ℰ (01492) 876413, llandudnotic@conwy.gov.uk
 🔞 Rhos-on-Sea Penrhyn Bay, ℰ (01492) 549 641
 🔞 72 Bryniau Rd West Shore, ℰ (01492) 875 325
 🔞 Hospital Rd, ℰ (01492) 876 450
 ⊙ Town★ - Pier★ B – The Great Orme★ (panorama★★, Tramway★, Ancient
    Copper Mines★ **AC**) AB
 🅶 Bodnant Garden★★ **AC**, S : 7 m. by A 470 B

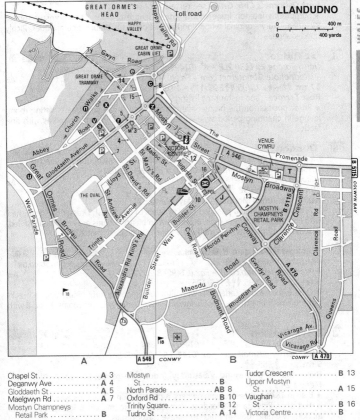

Bodysgallen Hall

Southeast : 2 m. on A 470 ✉ LL30 1RS – ☎ (01492) 584 466 – www.bodysgallen.com – info@bodysgallen.com – Fax (01492) 582 519

18 rm – †£ 150 ††£ 185, ☕ £6.95 – 20 suites – ††£ 215/405

Rest – (booking essential) Menu £ 23/43 **s** – Carte dinner £ 36/52 **s**

◆ Majestic and rare sums up this part 17C-18C hall with tower, once a soldier's lookout, now a place to take in views of mountains and terraced gardens. Antique filled rooms. Formal dining room with tall windows; serves fine and distinctive dishes.

The Empire

73 Church Walks ✉ LL30 2HE – ☎ (01492) 860 555 – www.empirehotel.co.uk – reservations@empirehotel.co.uk – Fax (01492) 860 791 – Closed 20-30 December A**e**

46 rm ☕ – †£ 60/95 ††£ 105/130 – 7 suites

Rest *Watkins and Co.* – (dinner only and Sunday lunch) Menu £ 15/21

◆ A porticoed façade sets the Victorian tone found in bedrooms with original cast iron beds, antiques and Russell Flint prints on walls. 21C mod cons bring them bang up-to-date. Fine menus with a mix and match of the Celtic and the Continental.

Osborne House

17 North Parade ✉ LL30 2LP – ☎ (01492) 860 330 – www.osbornehouse.co.uk – sales@osbornehouse.com – Fax (01492) 860 791 – Closed 20-30 December A**c**

6 rm – †£ 145/210 ††£ 145/210

Rest *Osborne's Cafe Grill* – see restaurant listing

◆ Sumptuous interior: huge rooms extend length of house; bedrooms epitomise Victorian luxury - original wood flooring, elaborate silk drapes, fine antiques. Richly hued lounge.

WALES

St Tudno

North Parade ✉ LL30 2LP – ☎ (01492) 874 411 – www.st-tudno.co.uk – sttudnohotel@btinternet.com – Fax (01492) 860 407 A**c**

17 rm ☕ – †£ 75/95 ††£ 95/115 – 1 suite

Rest *Terrace* – see restaurant listing

◆ Prime position on the promenade opposite a Victorian pier; boasts sitting room, lounge in charming period style with seafront vistas. Comfortable rooms with fine fabrics.

Dunoon

Gloddaeth St ✉ LL30 2DW – ☎ (01492) 860 787 – www.dunoonhotel.co.uk – reservations@dunoonhotel.co.uk – Fax (01492) 860 031 – Closed mid December - mid March A**r**

49 rm ☕ – †£ 69/98 ††£ 138

Rest – (bar lunch Monday-Saturday) Menu £ 21

◆ A hospitable hotel; a panelled hallway leads to the "Welsh Dresser Bar" furnished with an antique cooking range. Bygone era ambience. Rooms are individually styled. Restaurant, modernised in a traditional style, with menu to match.

Escape Boutique B & B without rest

48 Church Walks ✉ LL30 2HL – ☎ (01492) 877 776 – www.escapebandb.co.uk – info@escapebandb.co.uk – Fax (01492) 878 777 A**n**

9 rm ☕ – †£ 70/95 ††£ 115/125

◆ Ornate, elevated Victorian villa with ultra contemporary furnishings. Modish breakfast room with fine choice. Cool beige/brown or 'French boudoir' rooms. B and B with style.

Bryn Derwen

34 Abbey Rd ✉ LL30 2EE – ☎ (01492) 876 804 – www.bryn-derwen.co.uk – brynderwen@fsmail.net – Fax (01492) 876 804 – February-November A**v**

9 rm ☕ – †£ 55 ††£ 92

Rest – (dinner only Monday-Saturday) (booking essential for non-residents) Menu £ 24 **s**

◆ Built in 1878 with welcoming owners. A beauty salon offering range of treatments is next door. Pine staircase leads to immaculate bedrooms. Quiet lounge to unwind in. Homely dining room in which to sample classic dishes.

Tan Lan
🄷   🅿 VISA ⓴

14 Great Orme's Rd, West Shore ⊠ LL30 2AR – ℰ (01492) 860 221
– www.tanlanhotel.co.uk – info@tanlanhotel.co.uk – Fax (01492) 870 219
– 3 March-27 November and 24-26 December   Au
17 rm ⊆ – ♥£50 ♥♥£80   **Rest** – (dinner only) Menu £18 **s**
♦ Detached, neat and tidy house, personally run and located in quiet part of town. A sunny lounge in yellow and comfortable rooms, two with balconies, make for a pleasant stay. A bright dining room delivers varied set meals.

The Wilton without rest
🄷   🅿 VISA ⓴ AE

14 South Parade ⊠ LL30 2LN – ℰ (01492) 878 343 – www.wiltonhotel.com
– info@wiltonhotel.com – Fax (01492) 878 343 – Mid March - 23 December   ABz
14 rm ⊆ – ♥£30/43 ♥♥£60/146
♦ Situated adjacent to the beach and pier. Lounge bar with interesting Victorian prints; the bedrooms, some of which have four-posters, are in bright, warm colour schemes.

Abbey Lodge without rest
🏠   ✍ ⌘ 🕯 🅿

14 Abbey Rd ⊠ LL30 2EA – ℰ (01492) 878 042 – www.abbeylodgeuk.com
– enquiries@abbeylodgeuk.com – Restricted opening in winter   Ax
4 rm ⊆ – ♥£38/45 ♥♥£70/75
♦ Built as a gentlemen's residence in early 1850s; a pretty, gabled house with terraced garden where you're made to feel at home. Smart drawing room and cosy, comfy bedrooms.

Epperstone
🏠   🅿 VISA ⓴ AE ⓞ

15 Abbey Rd ⊠ LL30 2EE – ℰ (01492) 878 746 – www.epperstone-hotel.co.uk
– epperstonehotel@btconnect.com – Fax (01492) 871 223   As
8 rm (dinner included) ⊆ – ♥£51/55 ♥♥£102/110
Rest – (by arrangement) Menu £23
♦ A period house, evident in the fixtures: stained glass, ornate fireplace, mahogany staircase. Other attractions include a marine aquarium in conservatory and neat bedrooms. Intimate dining room serving varied dishes using fresh, local ingredients.

Sefton Court without rest
🏠   ✍ ⌘ 🅿 VISA ⓴ ⓞ

49 Church Walks ⊠ LL30 2HL – ℰ (01492) 875 235
– www.seftoncourt-hotel.co.uk – seftoncourt@aol.com – Fax (01492) 879 560
– Easter-October   An
10 rm ⊆ – ♥£35/40 ♥♥£66/70
♦ Imposing Victorian house, fully refurbished in 2006, perched on quiet hillside. Large, comfy lounge; spacious breakfast room. Smart, homely rooms. Near Great Orme Tramway.

Lympley Lodge without rest
🏠   ✍ ⌘ 🅿

Colwyn Road, East 2½ m. on B5115 ⊠ LL30 3AL – ℰ (01492) 549 304
– www.lympleylodge.co.uk – patricia@lympleylodge.co.uk – Closed mid
December - mid January
3 rm ⊆ – ♥£50/55 ♥♥£80
♦ Charming Victorian house built in 1870. Traditional, homely feel, with antique furniture, wrought iron beds and thoughtful extras – including every toiletry imaginable. Hearty breakfast.

Terrace – at St Tudno Hotel
XXX   AC VISA ⓴ AE ⓞ

North Parade ⊠ LL30 2LP – ℰ (01492) 874 411
– Fax (01492) 860 407   Ac
Rest – Menu £22 (lunch) – Carte £28/35
♦ Smart and formal dining room incorporating blown-up photograph of Lake Como and, on a smaller scale, a neat little water feature. Accomplished and precise modern cooking.

XX **Osborne's Cafe Grill** – at Osborne House Hotel ← AC 🐾 P VISA ⓿ AE ⓪
17 North Parade ⊠ *LL30 2LP* – ℰ *(01492) 860 330* – *www.osbornehouse.co.uk*
– *sales@osbornehouse.com* – *Fax (01492) 860 791* – *Closed 20-30 December*   A**c**
Rest – Carte £ 22/37
♦ Impressive, ornate main dining room with velvet drapes and ornate gold lighting. Eclectic, modern menus, and the bustling informal style of a bistro; enthusiastic service.

at Deganwy South : 2 ¾ m. on A 546 – A – ⊠ Llandudno

🏨 **Quay H. & Spa** ← 🚗 🔲 ⬛ 🀫 🎴 ⬛ 🍴 🎴 🛄 P VISA ⓿ AE ⓪
Deganwy Quay ⊠ *LL31 9DJ* – ℰ *(01492) 564 100* – *www.quayhotel.com*
– *info@quayhotel.com* – *Fax (01492) 564 115*
55 rm – ✝£ 125/285 ✝✝£ 180/285, ⊇ £ 12.95 – 19 suites   **Rest** – Carte £ 25/40
♦ Stylish hotel with harbour and Castle views, good facilities and seven room spa. Spacious, contemporary bedrooms range from standard, to penthouse and three private 'towers'. Restaurant boasts classical menu, good views and a pianist at weekends.

X **Nikki Ip's** AC VISA ⓿
57 Station Rd ⊠ *LL31 9DF* – ℰ *(01492) 596 611* – *Fax (01492) 596 600* – *Closed 25 December, 1 January*
Rest – Chinese – (dinner only) (booking essential) Menu £ 27 – Carte £ 20/36
♦ Good value, stylish and unconventional, but beware: no signage outside. Particularly welcoming owners. Coral interior; Cantonese, Peking and Szechuan specialities are served.

LLANDYRNOG – Denbighshire – **503** J/K 24 32 **C1**
🔼 Cardiff 158 mi – Denbigh 7 mi – Ruthin 6 mi

⬆ **Pentre Mawr** ⬇ ← 🚗 🐾 ⬛ ⬛ 🏹 🍴 🐾 P VISA ⓿
North : 1 ¼ m. by B 5429 taking left hand fork after ¾ m. ⊠ *LL16 4LA*
– ℰ *(01824) 790 732* – *www.pentremawrcountryhouse.co.uk*
– *info@pentremawrcountryhouse.co.uk* – *March-October*
7 rm ⊇ – ✝£ 75/130 ✝✝£ 95/150   **Rest** – (by arrangement) Menu £ 28
♦ Spacious, rebuilt 17C former farmhouse in nearly 200 acres. Very comfortable, with period style lounges, morning room, pool, terrace and tastefully individualistic rooms. Communal dining room offers classic décor and homely touches.

LLANELLI – Carmarthenshire – **503** H 28 33 **B4**
🔼 London 202 mi – Cardiff 54 mi – Swansea 12 mi

🏠 **Llwyn Hall** 🚗 🐾 🍴 P VISA ⓿ AE ⓪
Llwynhendy, East : 3 ½ m. by A 484 ⊠ *SA14 9LD* – ℰ *(01554) 777 754*
– *www.llwynhall.co.uk* – *info@llwynhall.co.uk*
6 rm ⊇ – ✝£ 65/70 ✝✝£ 90/120   **Rest** – (booking essential) Carte £ 25/29
♦ Pretty yellow-and-white 19C gabled house with extension. Country style soft furnishings. Chintzy rooms of pleasant individuality: those at front face garden and North Gower.

LLANERCHYMEDD – Isle of Anglesey – **502** G 24 32 **B1**
🔼 London 262 mi – Bangor 18 mi – Caernarfon 23 mi – Holyhead 15 mi
◉ Anglesey ★★

⬆ **Llwydiarth Fawr** without rest ⬇ ← 🚗 🐾 ⬛ 🏹 🐾 P VISA ⓿
North : 1 m. on B 5111 ⊠ *LL71 8DF* – ℰ *(01248) 470 321*
– *www.llwydiarthfawr.com* – *llwydiarth@hotmail.com*
4 rm ⊇ – ✝£ 55/65 ✝✝£ 85
♦ Part of an 800-acre cattle and sheep farm, Georgian in style with picturesque vistas. Guests can enjoy nature walks, fishing on lake; welcoming owner. Airy, well-kept rooms.

↑ **Drws-Y-Coed** without rest ⤳ ⟨ 🚗 🌾 ♨ P. VISA ⊚⊚
East : 1½ m. by B 5111 on Benllech rd ⊠ *LL71 8AD –* ℰ *(01248) 470 473*
– drwsycoed2@hotmail.com – Closed Christmas
3 rm ⌑ – ∮£40/45 ∮∮£70/75
♦ Meaning "Door of the Wood"; 1960s house, run by Welsh speaking family in 550-acre farm of cattle and cereal crops. Countryside views add to enjoyment of neat and tidy rooms.

LLAN FFESTINIOG – Gwynedd 32 B2

🗗 London 234 mi – Bangor 35 mi – Wrexham 52 mi
🄶 Llechwedd Slate Caverns★ **AC** N : 4 m. by A 470

↑ **Cae'r Blaidd Country House** ⤳ ⟨ 🚗 ♨ ⏻ P. VISA ⊚⊚
North : ¾ m. by A 470 on Blaenau Rd ⊠ *LL41 4PH –* ℰ *(01766) 762 765*
– www.caerblaidd.fsnet.co.uk – info@caerblaidd.fsnet.co.uk – Fax (01766) 762 765
– Closed January
3 rm ⌑ – ∮£45 ∮∮£75 **Rest** – (communal dining) Menu £ 18
♦ Spacious Victorian country house in wooded gardens; spectacular views of Ffestiniog and Moelwyn Mountains. Smart, uncluttered rooms. Guided tours and courses are organised. A huge dining room; large refectory table where communal dinners are served.

LLANFIHANGEL – Powys – 502 J 25 – see Llanfyllin

LLANFYLLIN – Powys – 502 K 25 32 C2

🗗 London 188 mi – Chester 42 mi – Shrewsbury 24 mi – Welshpool 11 mi
🄶 Pistyll Rhaeadr★, NW : 8 m. by A 490, B 4391, B 4580 and minor roads

※ **Seeds** VISA ⊚⊚
5 Penybryn Cottages, High St ⊠ *SY22 5AP –* ℰ *(01691) 648 604 – Closed 2 weeks June, 1 week October, 25 December, Monday - Wednesday and Sunday dinner*
Rest – (restricted opening in winter) Menu £ 26 (dinner) – Carte lunch £ 19/31
♦ Converted 16C rustic cottages with eclectic décor: souvenirs from owner's travels. Blackboard menu offers modern or traditional dishes. Local seasonal ingredients to the fore.

at Llanfihangel Southwest : 5 m. by A 490 and B 4393 on B 4382 – ⊠ Llanfyllin

↑ **Cyfie Farm** ⤳ ⟨ 🚗 🕭 🕸 ♨ ⏻ P. VISA ⊚⊚ AE ⊙
South : 1½ m. by B 4382 ⊠ *SY22 5JE –* ℰ *(01691) 648 451*
– www.cyfiefarm.co.uk – info@cyfiefarm.co.uk – Fax (01691) 648 363 – Mid February - mid November
4 suites ⌑ – ∮∮£95/110
Rest – (by arrangement, communal dining) Menu £ 28
♦ 17C longhouse, now a sheep farm, with super views of Meifod Valley. One room has distinctly quaint feel. Luxurious new cottages: outdoor hot tub affords great vistas. Cordon Bleu trained owners serve at communal table.

LLANGAMMARCH WELLS – Powys – 503 J 27 33 B3

🗗 London 200 mi – Brecon 17 mi – Builth Wells 8 mi – Cardiff 58 mi

🏛 **Lake Country House and Spa** ⤳ ⟨ 🚗 🕭 🎣 🖼 ⊚ ⅄ ※
East : ¾ m. ⊠ *LD4 4BS –* ℰ *(01591)* 🚗 ⅙ rm, 🕪 🛁 P. VISA ⊚⊚ AE ⊙
620 202 – www.lakecountryhouse.co.uk – info@lakecountryhouse.co.uk
– Fax (01591) 620 457
19 rm ⌑ – ∮£140 ∮∮£250 – 11 suites
Rest – (booking essential) Menu £19/39 🍽
♦ 19C country house in mature grounds. Welsh teas a speciality. Rooms in house or lodge full of antiques, flowers and extravagant fabrics. Tranquil spa adds to the experience. Candlelit dining; super wine list.

LLANGOLLEN – Denbighshire – **502** K 25 – pop. 2 930   32 **C2**

> ▷ London 194 mi – Chester 23 mi – Holyhead 76 mi – Shrewsbury 30 mi
> ℹ️ Y Chapel, Castle St 𝒞 (01978) 860828, llangollen@nwtic.com
> 🞮 Vale of Llangollen Holyhead Rd, 𝒞 (01978) 860906
> ◉ Town★ - Railway★ **AC** - Plas Newydd★ **AC**
> ⓒ Pontcysyllte Aqueduct★★, E : 4 m. by A 539 - Castell Dinas Bran★, N : by
> footpath – Valle Crucis Abbey★ **AC**, N : 2 m. by A 542. Chirk Castle★★ **AC**
> (wrought iron gates★), SE : 7½ m. by A 5 – Rug Chapel★ **AC**, W : 11 m. by
> A 5 and A 494

🏠🏠 **Bryn Howel** 🌿   ← 🚗 🕸 🛗 🔧 **P** 🆅🆂🅰 🐾 🅰🅴

East : 2¾ m. by A 539 ✉ *LL20 7UW* – 𝒞 *(01978) 860 331 – www.brynhowel.com*
– hotel@brynhowel.com – Fax (01978) 860 119
35 rm ⊆ – ♦£70 ♦♦£100/120 – 1 suite
Rest *Cedar Tree* – Menu 20 **s** – Carte £ 24/33 **s**

♦ Built 1896 for owner of Ruabon brick company, mock Jacobean in style with Vale
of Llangollen views. Bar has unique "Anthem Fireplace". Rooms in main house and
modern wing. Admire panoramas and dine on classic Welsh cuisine.

🏠 **Gales**   🏡 🍽 📶 🔧 **P** 🆅🆂🅰 🐾 🅰🅴 🅾

18 Bridge St ✉ *LL20 8PF* – 𝒞 *(01978) 860 089 – www.galesoflangollen.co.uk*
– richard@galesoflangollen.co.uk – Fax (01978) 861 313 – Closed Christmas and
New Year
13 rm – ♦£70 ♦♦£90, ⊆£5 – 2 suites
Rest – (closed Sunday dinner) Carte £ 17/26

♦ Part 17C and 18C town house; rooms are divided between two buildings and
display many historic features: wattle and daub walls, brass and walnut beds, beams
and inglenooks. A wooden floored dining room and bar with inn-like ambience.

🏠 **Oakmere** without rest   🚗 🍽 📶 **P**

Regent St, on A 5 ✉ *LL20 8HS* – 𝒞 *(01978) 861 126*
– www.oakmere.llangollen.co.uk – oakmeregh@aol.com
6 rm ⊆ – ♦£60 ♦♦£65/70

♦ A restored Victorian house with an immaculate garden. Indoors are polished pitch
pine furnishings, a breakfast room with conservatory area and tidy bedrooms.

🏠 **Hillcrest** without rest   🚗 **P** 🆅🆂🅰 🐾

Hill St, on Plas Newydd rd ✉ *LL20 8EU* – 𝒞 *(01978) 860 208*
– www.hillcrest-guesthouse.com – d_rayment@btconnect.com – Fax (01978)
860 208
7 rm ⊆ – ♦£35/38 ♦♦£60/75

♦ A semi-detached house with large garden, close to the town centre. Homely and
tidy inside with nicely decorated bedrooms and some original features: a slate fireplace.

LLANGRANNOG – Ceredigion – **503** G 27   33 **B3**

> ▷ London 241 mi – Caerdydd / Cardiff 96 mi – Aberystwyth /
> Aberyswyth 30 mi – Caerfyrddin / Carmarthen 28 mi

🏠 **The Grange** 🌿   🚗 **P**

Pentregat, Southeast : 3 m. by B 4321 on A 487 ✉ *SA44 6HW* – 𝒞 *(01239)*
654 121 – www.grangecountryhouse.co.uk – theresesexton@madasafish.com
– Fax (01239) 654 121
4 rm ⊆ – ♦£55/60 ♦♦£80/85   **Rest** – (by arrangement) Menu £ 20

♦ Pink washed Georgian house with most welcoming owner. Afternoon tea trolley in
real silver. Immaculate room décor in keeping with house age. Very handy for coast
and country. Breakfast and country dinner proudly served: honest, fresh home cooking.

LLANIGON – Powys – **503** K 27 – see Hay-on-Wye

LLANRHIDIAN – Swansea – **503** H 29 – see Swansea

LLANRUG – Gwynedd – **502** H 24 – see Caernarfon

LLANSANFFRAID GLAN CONWY – Conwy – **502** I 24 – see Conwy

LLANTWIT MAJOR (Llanilltud Fawr) – The Vale of Glamorgan   33 **B4**
– **503** J 29 – pop. 13 366
> ▶ London 175 mi – Cardiff 18 mi – Swansea 33 mi

 West House Country   🚗 🍸 **P. VISA ©© AE**
West St ✉ *CF61 1SP* – ✆ *(01446) 792 406* – *www.westhouse-hotel.co.uk*
– *enq@westhouse-hotel.co.uk* – *Fax (01446) 796 147*
21 rm ☲ – ♦£57/70 ♦♦£75/85   **Rest** – (closed 26 December)
Carte £19/39 **s**
♦ 16C hotel in Vale of Glamorgan. After a bracing cliff top walk, relax in the welcoming bar. Rooms vary in style; traditional dominates. Conservatory used for small weddings. Light, clean Heritage restaurant with seasonal, local produce to fore.

LLANUWCHLLYN – Gwynedd – **503** I/J 25   32 **B2**
> ▶ Cardiff 147 mi – Dolgellau 13 mi – Llangollen 27 mi

⌂ **Eifionydd** without rest ॐ   ≼ 🚗 🛇 🍸 **P.**
✉ *LL23 7UB* – ✆ *(01678) 540 622* – *stay@eifionydd.com* – *March-October*
3 rm ☲ – ♦£34/45 ♦♦£70/80
♦ Good value guesthouse with lovely gardens and inspiring mountain views. Comfy lounge; linen-clad breakfast room; relaxing conservatory. Individual rooms with homely touches.

LLANWENARTH – Monmouthshire – see Abergavenny

LLANWRTYD WELLS – Powys – **503** J 27 – pop. 649   33 **B3**
> ▶ London 214 mi – Brecon 32 mi – Cardiff 68 mi – Carmarthen 39 mi
> 🛈 Ty Barcud, The Square ✆ (01591) 610666
> ◉ Abergwesyn-Tregaron Mountain Road★, NW : 19 m. on minor roads

⌂ **Lasswade Country House**   ≼ 🚗 🛇 🛇 **P. VISA ©© AE ①**
Station Rd ✉ *LD5 4RW* – ✆ *(01591) 610 515* – *www.lasswadehotel.co.uk*
– *info@lasswadehotel.co.uk* – *Fax (01591) 610 611*
8 rm ☲ – ♦£58/70 ♦♦£105   **Rest** – (dinner only) Menu £30
♦ Personally run Edwardian country house, with fine views of mid-Wales countryside from the breakfast conservatory; cosy lounge. Bedrooms in traditional style. Proudly pro-organic meals on the daily menu.

XX **Carlton Riverside** with rm   **VISA ©© AE**
Irfon Crescent ✉ *LD5 4ST* – ✆ *(01591) 610 248* – *www.carltonrestaurant.co.uk*
– *info@carltonrestaurant.co.uk* – *Closed 22-30 December*
4 rm ☲ – ♦£45/80 ♦♦£100/110
Rest – (dinner only and Sunday lunch) (booking essential) Menu £23
– Carte £25/44
♦ 400 yards from the old premises, overlooking the River Irfon. Skilled cooking based on traditional combinations uses quality ingredients. Two comfy lounges and courteous host. Simple, well-priced bedrooms.

LLYSWEN – Powys – **503** K 27 – ✉ Brecon   33 **C3**
> ▶ London 188 mi – Brecon 8 mi – Cardiff 48 mi – Worcester 53 mi
> ◉ Brecon Beacons National Park★★

🏨 **Llangoed Hall** ॐ   ≼ 🚗 🖉 🛇 🍸 **P. VISA ©© AE ①**
Northwest : 1¼ m. on A 470 ✉ *LD3 0YP* – ✆ *(01874) 754 525*
– *www.llangoedhall.com* – *enquiries@llangoedhall.com* – *Fax (01874) 754 545*
20 rm ☲ – ♦£175/350 ♦♦£210/400 – 3 suites
Rest – (booking essential for non-residents) Menu £25/40
♦ Set up by Sir Bernard Ashley of Laura Ashley group: rooms furnished accordingly. River Wye to rear. Pleasant gardens, carved staircase; guests can arrive by helicopter. Dining room menu has classic Welsh roots; Rex Whistler etchings in adjoining room.

WALES

MACHYNLLETH – Powys – 502 – pop. 2 147
32 **B2**

- London 220 mi – Shrewsbury 56 mi – Welshpool 37 mi
- Royal House, Penrallt St *&* (01654) 702401, mactic@powys.gov.uk
- Felingerrig, *&* (01654) 702 000
- Town★ - Celtica★ **AC**
- Snowdonia National Park★★★ - Centre for Alternative Technology★★ **AC**, N : 3 m. by A 487

Ynyshir Hall ⬩   ⟵ 🚗 🕭 ⑩ 🛈 **P** _VISA_ ⓪ AE ①
Eglwysfach, Southwest : 6 m. on A 487 ☒ SY20 8TA – & (01654) 781 209
– www.ynyshir-hall.co.uk – info@ynyshir-hall.co.uk – Fax (01654) 781 366
– Closed first two weeks January
6 rm ⊆ – ✝£120/275 ✝✝£250/285 – 3 suites
Rest – (booking essential) Menu £ 32/65 **s**
◆ Part Georgian house set within 1000 acre RSPB reserve; bright, individually appointed bedrooms, classically cosy drawing room with art, antiques and Welsh pottery. Modern cooking with a refined style.

MENAI BRIDGE (Porthaethwy) – Isle of Anglesey – 502 H 24
32 **B1**

- London 270 mi – Caernarfon 10 mi – Chester 69 mi – Holyhead 22 mi

Neuadd Lwyd ⬩   ⟵ 🚗 ⑩ ℀ ⑨ **P** _VISA_ ⓪
Penmynydd, Northwest : 4 ¾ m. by B 5420 on Eglwys St Gredifael Church rd
☒ LL61 5BX – & (01248) 715 005 – *www.neuaddlwyd.co.uk*
– post@neuaddlwyd.co.uk – Closed December-21 January
4 rm ⊆ – ✝£95/145 ✝✝£100/160   **Rest** – (by arrangement) Menu £ 38
◆ This fine 19C rectory, set in a beautiful rural location, has had a sleek and stylish refit, lending it a luxurious air. Elegant interiors are matched by stunning bedrooms. Freshest Welsh ingredients incorporated into tasty evening meals.

Wern Farm without rest ⬩   ⟵ 🚗 ⑩ ℀ ⑨ **P** _VISA_ ⓪
Pentraeth Rd, North : 2 ¼ m. by B 5420 off A 5025 ☒ LL59 5RR – & (01248)
712 421 – www.angleseyfarms.com/wern.htm – wernfarmanglesey@onetel.com
– Fax (01248) 715 421 – March-October
3 rm ⊆ – ✝£50/75 ✝✝£75/85
◆ Attractive Georgian farmhouse run by a friendly couple. Bedrooms are spacious and comfortable. Enjoy countryside views in conservatory where vast breakfast is offered.

Ruby   AC _VISA_ ⓪
Dale St ☒ LL59 5AW – & (01248) 714 999 – *www.rubymenai.com – Fax* (01248)
717 888 – Closed Saturday lunch and Sunday
Rest – Menu £ 11/18 – Carte dinner £ 25/31
◆ Former firestation and council offices; now a lively, bustling eatery on two floors with good local reputation. Eclectic, global menus employing flavoursome, vibrant cooking.

MOLD (Yr Wyddgrug) – Flintshire – 502 K 24 – pop. 9 568
32 **C1**

- London 211 mi – Chester 12 mi – Liverpool 22 mi – Shrewsbury 45 mi
- Library, Museum and Art Gallery, Earl Rd *&* (01352) 759331, mold@nwtic.com
- Pantmywyn Clicain Rd, *&* (01352) 740 318
- Old Padeswood Station Rd, Old Padeswood, *&* (01244) 547 701
- Padeswood & Buckley Station Lane, The Caia, *&* (01244) 550 537
- Caerwys, *&* (01352) 721 222
- St Mary's Church★

Tower without rest ⬩   ⟵ 🚗 ℀ ⓦ **P** _VISA_ ⓪
Nercwys, South : 1 m. by B 5444, Nercwys rd on Treuddyn rd ☒ CH7 4EW
– & (01352) 700 220 – *www.towerwales.co.uk – Closed 20 December-20 January*
3 rm ⊆ – ✝£50 ✝✝£80
◆ Last of the Welsh fortified border houses, owned by the same family for 500 years. Combined lounge/breakfast room. Spacious, simply furnished rooms overlook private parkland.

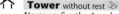

🛏 **Glas Fryn**   🍴 🍴 **P** **VISA** **⚫⚫** **AE**
Raikes Lane, Sychdyn, North : 1 m. by A 5119 on Civic Centre rd (Theatr Clwyd)
✉ *CH7 6LR* – ℰ *(01352) 750500* – *www.glasfryn-mold.co.uk*
– *glasfryn@brunningandprice.co.uk* – *Fax (01352) 751923*
– *Closed 25-26 December*
Rest – Carte £18/28
♦ Informal and open-plan; sepia prints, crammed bookshelves and rows of old bottles surround wooden tables. Varied brasserie menu draws a lively young set.

🛏 **The Stables**   🍴 🍴 🍽 rm, **P** **VISA** **⚫⚫** **AE**
Soughton Hall, North : 2½ m. by A 5119 and Alltami Rd ✉ *CH7 6AB*
– ℰ *(01352) 840577* – *www.soughtonhall.co.uk* – *info@soughtonhall.co.uk*
– *Fax (01352) 840872*
Rest – (booking essential) Carte £24/31
♦ 17C stable block in grounds of wedding venue hotel; bar and first-floor brasserie in bare brick and scrubbed pine. Tasty classics from open kitchen. Terrace for summer lunch.

MONMOUTH (Trefynwy) – *Monmouthshire* – **503** L 28 – pop. 8 547   33 **C4**
   ◘ London 135 mi – Abergavenny 19 mi – Cardiff 40 mi
   ◉ Town ★

at Whitebrook South : 8¼ m. by A 466 – ✉ **Monmouth**

WALES

🍴🍴🍴 **The Crown at Whitebrook** with rm 🏡   🍴 **P** **VISA** **⚫⚫**
✿ ✉ *NP25 4TX* – ℰ *(01600) 860254* – *www.crownatwhitebrook.co.uk*
   – *info@crownatwhitebrook.co.uk* – *Fax (01600) 860607*
   – *Closed 23 December-7 January*
   8 rm ☲ – †£80/100 ††£115/140
   Rest – (closed Sunday, Monday and Tuesday lunch) (booking essential)
   Menu £28/48
   Spec. Foie gras with toffee and smoked sweetcorn sorbet. Fillet of rabbit with leg meat cannelloni, carrot, fennel, and confit garlic. Pineapple carpaccio with white chocolate, hibiscus and jasmine.
   ♦ Attentively run, with modern feel; lounge bar with deep leather sofas and immaculately laid dining room. Well-presented dishes are elaborate, original and flavoursome. Smart bedrooms in contemporary colours.

at Rockfield Northwest : 2½ m. on B 4233 – ✉ **Monmouth**

🍴 **Stonemill**   🍴 **P** **VISA** **⚫⚫**
West : 1 m. on B 4233 ✉ *NP25 5SW* – ℰ *(01600) 716273*
– *www.thestonemill.co.uk* – *Fax (01600) 715257*
– *Closed 25-26 December, 2 weeks January, Sunday dinner and Monday*
Rest – Menu £15/19 – Carte £34/40
♦ Converted 16C stone cider mill with exposed timbers; leather sofa in sitting area/bar. Attentive service. Well sourced modern seasonal dishes using small local suppliers.

MONTGOMERY (Trefaldwyn) – *Powys* – **503** K 26   32 **C2**
   ◘ London 194 mi – Birmingham 71 mi – Chester 53 mi – Shrewsbury 30 mi
   ◉ Town ★

🏠 **Little Brompton Farm** without rest 🏡   🖐 🍽 **P**
Southeast : 2 m. on B 4385 ✉ *SY15 6HY* – ℰ *(01686) 668371*
– *www.littlebromptonfarm.co.uk* – *gaynor.brompton@virgin.net*
3 rm ☲ – †£35 ††£60
♦ Part 17C cottage on working farm, run by friendly couple: husband's lived here all his life! Cosy beamed lounge and inglenook. Hearty breakfast. Traditionally appointed rooms.

MUMBLES (The) – *Swansea* – **503** I 29 – **see Swansea**

NANNERCH – Flintshire – **502** K 24 – ⊠ **Mold**
32 **C1**

▶ London 218 mi – Chester 19 mi – Liverpool 29 mi – Shrewsbury 52 mi

⚐ **Old Mill** without rest 🚗 ⚙ 🐾 **P** **VISA** **①** **AE** **①**
Melin-y-Wern, Denbigh Rd, Northwest : ¾ m. on A 541 ⊠ *CH7 5RH* – ✆ *(01352)*
741542 – *www.old-mill.co.uk* – *mail@old-mill.co.uk* – *Closed November*
6 rm ⌂ – ♦£47/53 ♦♦£68/81
♦ Renovated stone-built Victorian stables set in well-kept gardens on a busy road.
The beamed bedrooms are comfortable, modern and pine-fitted.

NANT DERRY – Monmouthshire – see Abergavenny

NANTGAREDIG – Carmarthenshire – **503** H 28 – see Carmarthen

---

NEWPORT – Newport – **503** L 29 – pop. 116 143
33 **C4**

▶ London 145 mi – Bristol 31 mi – Cardiff 12 mi – Gloucester 48 mi
🛈 Museum and Art Gallery, John Frost Sq ✆ (01633) 842962,
newport.tic@newport.gov.uk
🏌 Caerleon Broadway, ✆ (01633) 420342
🏌 Parc Coedkernew Church Lane, ✆ (01633) 680933
◉ Museum and Art Gallery★ AX **M** - Transporter Bridge★ **AC** AY - Civic Centre
(murals★) AX
ⓖ Caerleon Roman Fortress★★ **AC** (Fortress Baths★ - Legionary Museum★ -
Amphitheatre★), NE : 2½ m. by B 4596 AX - Tredegar House★★
(Grounds★ - Stables★), SW : 2½ m. by A 48 AY. Penhow Castle★, E : 8 m.
by A 48 AX

Plan opposite

🏨🏨🏨🏨 **Celtic Manor Resort** 🕭 🔲 🐾 🏊 🎱 ⚙ 🏓 📶 🍴 🖥 ⚙ 🛏, 🧖 🧴 🗚 ⚙
Coldra Woods, East : 3 m. on A 48 🍴 🗚 **P** 🛋 **VISA** **①** **AE** **①**
⊠ *NP18 1HQ* – ✆ *(01633) 413 000* – *www.celtic-manor.com*
– *bookings@celtic-manor.com* – *Fax (01633) 412 910*
298 rm – ♦£240/310 ♦♦£240/310, ⌂£16.95 – **32 suites** – ♦♦£410/1750
Rest *The Crown at Celtic Manor* – (closed Sunday and Monday) (dinner only)
Menu £28/48 – Carte £38/48
Rest *Rafters* – Menu £21 (lunch) – Carte £21/43
Rest *The Olive Tree* – (dinner only and Sunday lunch) Menu £30
♦ Classical, Celtic and country house motifs on a grand modern scale. Smart con-
temporary rooms boast hi-tech mod cons. State-of-the-art gym, golf academy and
spa. Modern cuisine in The Crown. Rafters in the club house. Simple Olive Tree.

🍴 **The Chandlery** 🗚 **VISA** **①** **AE**
⊛ *77-78 Lower Dock St* ⊠ *NP20 1EH* – ✆ *(01633) 256 622*
– *www.thechandleryrestaurant.com* – *food@thechandleryrestaurant.com*
– *Fax (01633) 256 633* – *Closed 1 week Christmas, Sunday and Monday* AY**a**
Rest – Menu £15 (lunch) – Carte £21/32
♦ Converted 18C chandler's store by the Usk. Spacious split-level restaurant. Polite
service. Wide-ranging menu of freshly prepared dishes: confident, good-value modern cooking.

at Tredunnock Northeast : 8 ¾ m. by A 4042 - AX -, B 4596 and B 4236, off Usk rd,
turning right at Cwrt Bleddyn Hotel – ⊠ **Newport**

🏠 **The Newbridge** with rm ⬳ 🐾 🌳 ⚙ **P** **VISA** **①** **AE**
East : ¼ m. ⊠ *NP15 1LY* – ✆ *(01633) 451 000* – *www.evanspubs.co.uk*
– *newbridge@evanspubs.co.uk* – *Fax (01633) 451 001*
6 rm ⌂ – ♦£90 ♦♦£110/135 **Rest** – Carte £18/25
♦ Country pub boasting a spiral staircase, river views and fishing rights. The kitchen's
experience at the smarter end of the hospitality business is evident on the menu and
dishes arrive neatly presented. Bedrooms are comfortably furnished.

WALES

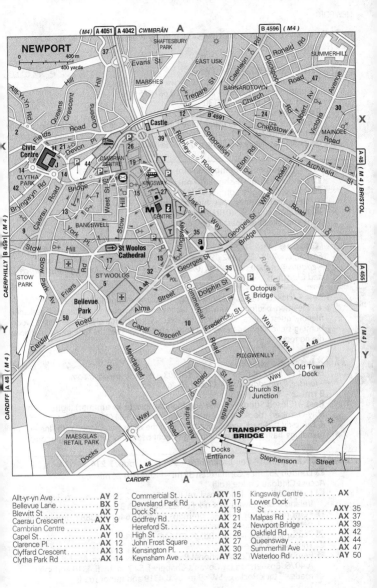

NEWPORT

0 — 400 m
0 — 400 yards

at Redwick Southeast : 9 ½ m. by M 4 - AY - off B 4245 – ⊠ Magor

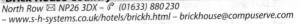

⚐ **Brick House Country** without rest ॐ   🍽 ⅏ P VISA ⓪⓪
North Row ⊠ *NP26 3DX* – ℰ *(01633) 880 230*
– www.s-h-systems.co.uk/hotels/brickh.html – brickhouse@compuserve.com
– Fax (01633) 882 441
7 rm ⚏ – ♦£40/50 ♦♦£65
♦ Ivy-covered Georgian house on edge of peaceful village boasts faultlessly neat
bedrooms with traditional floral décor and a spacious front lounge and bar.

at St Brides Wentlooge Southwest : 4½ m. by A 48 - AY - on B 4239
– ✉ Newport

The Inn at The Elm Tree
✉ NP10 8SQ – ☎ (01633) 680225 – www.the-elm-tree.co.uk
– inn@the-elm-tree.co.uk – Fax (01633) 681035
10 rm ☑ – ♦£80 ♦♦£90/130
Rest – Menu £10 (lunch) – Carte £22/38
♦ Converted 19C barn. Pristine, pine-furnished rooms in bright fabrics thoughtfully supplied with 21C mod cons; all individually styled. Lounge bar serves Champagne on ice. Immaculately set dining room; wide-ranging, Welsh-based dishes.

NEWPORT (Trefdraeth) – **Pembrokeshire** – **503** F 27 – **pop. 1 162**   33 **A3**
🚗 London 258 mi – Fishguard 7 mi
🛈 2 Bank Cottages, Long St ☎ (01239) 820912 (summer only),
NewportTIC@pembrokeshirecoast.org.uk
⛳ Newport Links, ☎ (01239) 820244
🅖 Pembrokeshire Coast National Park★★

Cnapan
East St, on A 487 ✉ SA42 0SY – ☎ (01239) 820575 – www.cnapan.co.uk
– enquiry@cnapan.co.uk – Fax (01239) 820878 – Closed 7 January - mid March and Christmas
5 rm ☑ – ♦£44/54 ♦♦£88
Rest – (closed Tuesday) (dinner only) (booking essential) Menu £30
♦ Pine-fitted bedrooms with floral fabrics and individual character in a genuinely friendly guest house, family run for over 15 years. Homely lounge has a wood-burning stove. Clothed tables and family photographs set the tone in the traditional dining room.

Llysmeddyg with rm
East St ✉ SA42 0SY – ☎ (01239) 820008 – www.llysmeddyg.com
– louise@llysmeddyg.com – Closed 25-26 December
8 rm ☑ – ♦£75 ♦♦£150
Rest – (Closed Sunday dinner and Monday except in summer) (light lunch May-October) (booking essential at lunch) Carte £31/37
♦ Earnestly laid-back style; lunch offered in the cellar bar. Dinner, with fine art surroundings, has more of a modern edge. Bright bedrooms with good bathrooms.

PEMBROKE (Penfro) – **Pembrokeshire** – **503** F 28 – **pop. 7 214**   33 **A4**
🚗 London 252 mi – Carmarthen 32 mi – Fishguard 26 mi
Access Cleddau Bridge (toll)
⛴ to Republic of Ireland (Rosslare) (Irish Ferries) 2 daily (4 h) – to Republic of Ireland (Cork) (Swansea Cork Ferries) daily (8 h 30 mn)
🛈 Pembroke Visitor Centre, Commons Rd ☎ (01646) 622388 (summer only),
pembroke.tic@pembrokeshire.gov.uk
⛳ Pembroke Dock Military Rd, ☎ (01646) 621453
◎ Town★★ - Castle★★ **AC**
🅖 Pembrokeshire Coast National Park★★ - Carew Castle★ **AC**, NE : 4 m. by A 4075. Bosherston (St Govan's Chapel★), S : 7 m. by B 4319 and minor roads – Stack Rocks★, SW : 9 m. by B 4319 and minor roads

at Lamphey East : 1¾ m. on A 4139 – ✉ Pembroke

Lamphey Court ⚜
✉ SA71 5NT – ☎ (01646) 672273 – www.lampheycourt.co.uk
– info@lampheycourt.co.uk – Fax (01646) 672480
38 rm ☑ – ♦£92/115 ♦♦£110/165   **Rest** – Carte £27/39 s
♦ Large Georgian mansion surrounded by parkland, built by Charles Mathias in an idyllic location. Well furnished throughout with fine mahogany in the co-ordinated bedrooms. Formal restaurant with a good country house-style menu.

Lamphey Hall
SA71 5NR – (01646) 672394 – www.lampheyhallhotel.co.uk – Fax (01646) 672369
11 rm – £50/65 £90   **Rest** – Carte £20/35
♦ Small country house with a neat garden and a rich style of décor throughout. Bedrooms are a mix of shapes and sizes and all are individually styled. The restaurant or bar offers spacious, comfortable surroundings in which to enjoy Welsh produce.

PENALLY = Penalun – **Pembrokeshire** – **503** F 29 – **see Tenby**

PENARTH – **Cardiff** – **503** K 29 – **see Cardiff**

PENMACHNO – **Conwy** – **502** I 24 – **see Betws-y-Coed**

PENNAL – **Gwynedd** – **503** I 26 – **see Aberdovey**

PENTYRCH – **Cardiff** – **503** K 29 – **see Cardiff**

PONTDOLGOCH – **Powys** – **see Caersws**

PONTYPRIDD – **Rhondda, Cynon, Taff** – **503** K 29 – pop. 29 781   33 **C4**
■ London 164 mi – Cardiff 9 mi – Swansea 40 mi
🖪 Pontypridd Museum, Bridge St (01443) 490748, tourism@pontypriddmuseum.org.uk
◪ Rhondda Heritage Park★ **AC**, NW : 4 m. by A 4058. Caerphilly Castle★★ **AC**, SE : 7 m. by A 470 and A 468 – Llancaiach Fawr Manor★ **AC**, NE : 6½ m. by A 4054, A 472, B 4255 and B 4254

Llechwen Hall
Llanfabon, Northeast : 4¼ m. by A 4223 off A 4054 ⊠ CF37 4HP – (01443) 742050 – www.llechwen.com – steph@llechwenhall.co.uk – Fax (01443) 742189 – Closed 24-29 December
20 rm – £70 £95   **Rest** – Menu £13 (lunch) **s** – Carte £23/32 **s**
♦ 17C house with Victorian frontage, overlooks the Aberdare and Merthyr Valleys. Smart country house style and comforts. Spotless bedrooms in either the main or coach house. Two dining options, both decorated in similar traditional style.

PORTH – **Rhondda, Cynon, Taff** – **503** J 29 – pop. 6 225 – ⊠ Pontypridd   33 **C4**
■ London 168 mi – Cardiff 13 mi – Swansea 45 mi
◪ Trehafod (Rhondda Heritage Park★), E : 1½ m. by A 4058

Heritage Park
Coed Cae Rd, Trehafod, on A 4058 ⊠ CF37 2NP – (01443) 687057 – www.heritageparkhotel.co.uk – reservations@heritageparkhotel.co.uk – Fax (01443) 687060 – Closed 24-26 December and 1 January
44 rm – £89 £113
Rest *The Loft* – Menu £18 (dinner) – Carte £15/20
♦ Brick-built hotel in Rhondda Valley, adjacent to Heritage Park Centre; Museum of Mining close by. Countryside location, yet not far from Cardiff. Co-ordinated, classic rooms. Loft dining with verandah or conservatory options.

PORTHCAWL – **Bridgend** – **503** I 29 – pop. 15 640   33 **B4**
■ London 183 mi – Cardiff 28 mi – Swansea 18 mi
🖪 The Old Police Station, John St (01656) 786639, porthcawltic@bridgend.gov.uk
◪ Glamorgan Heritage Coast★

WALES

Fairways
≤ ⓘ ⊠ ⑨ ⑨ 🄿 VISA ⓪ AE

West Drive ⊠ *CF36 3LS –* ℰ *(01656) 782 085 – www.thefairwayshotel.co.uk*
– info@thefairwayshotel.co.uk – Fax (01656) 785 351
19 rm � – †£80 ††£110 **Rest** – Menu £9/10 – Carte £16/29
♦ Traditionally attired 18C seafront hotel. Relaxed, easy-going public areas. Half the
rooms have sea views: check out Room 1, which is particularly airy and boasts Jacuzzi.
'Safe' classics in cloth-clad dining room.

Foam Edge without rest
≤ ⑨ 🄿

9 West Drive ⊠ *CF36 3LS –* ℰ *(01656) 782 866 – hywelandhelen@aol.com*
– Closed Christmas
3 rm � – †£35/55 ††£55/80
♦ Enjoy original breakfast dishes and Bristol Channel views. Impressive front bedrooms:
one's a four poster with sun lounge, other's nicely co-ordinated in neutral shades.

✗✗ Coast
VISA ⓪ ⓪

2-4 Dock St ⊠ *CF36 3BL –* ℰ *(01656) 782 025 – www.coastrestaurants.co.uk*
– chris@coastrestaurants.co.uk – Closed 1-8 January, 26-31 December, Sunday
dinner and Monday except July and December
Rest – Carte £18/38
♦ Locally renowned, this airy, up-to-date restaurant has a front lounge and rear
dining room, where you can choose between the tried-and-tested or dishes with an
original edge.

PORTHGAIN – Pembrokeshire – see St Davids

PORTHMADOG – Gwynedd – 503 H 25
32 **B2**

🄳 Cardiff 162 mi – Blanau Ffestiniog 12 mi – Caernarfon 19 mi

Plas Tan-yr-Allt ⌂
≤ 🚗 ⑨ ⑨ 🄿 VISA ⓪ AE

Tremadog, North : 1½ m. by A 487 on A 498 ⊠ *LL49 9RG –* ℰ *(01766) 514 545*
– www.tanyrallt.co.uk – info@tanyrallt.co.uk – Closed Christmas, restricted
opening in winter
6 rm ⊡ – †£140 ††£175
Rest – (closed Monday-Tuesday) (dinner only) (booking essential) (communal
dining) Menu £39 **s**
♦ Fully refurbished, this former home of Shelley, built into wooded cliffside, has an
airy, stylish and comfy feel bordering on the luxurious. Charming, individualistic
rooms. Dine en-famille style: a Welsh country house menu prevails.

PORTMEIRION – Gwynedd – 502 H 25
32 **B2**

🄳 London 245 mi – Caernarfon 23 mi – Colwyn Bay 40 mi – Dolgellau 24 mi
◉ Village★★★ AC
ⓖ Snowdonia National Park★★★ - Lleyn Peninsula★★ – Ffestiniog
Railway★★ AC

Portmeirion ⌂
≤ 🚗 🚗 ⌷ ⑨ ⓦ ⚓ 🄿 VISA ⓪ AE ⓪

⊠ *LL48 6ET –* ℰ *(01766) 770 000 – www.portmerion-village.com*
– hotel@portmeirion-village.com – Fax (01766) 771 331 – Closed 1 week January
28 rm ⊡ – †£135/265 ††£170/300 – 14 suites
Rest – (booking essential for non-residents) Menu £21/37 **s** – Carte £28/54 **s**
♦ Set in private Italianate village in extensive gardens and woodland designed by Sir
Clough Williams-Ellis. Delightful views of village and woodland. Antique furnished
rooms. Restaurant offers lovely views of the estuary and an open and light style of
décor.

Castell Deudraeth
≤ 🚗 🚗 ⓘ 🄰🄲 rest, ⑨ ⓦ ⚓ 🄿 VISA ⓪ AE

⊠ *LL48 6EN –* ℰ *(01766) 772 400 – www.portmeirion-village.com*
– hotel@portmeirion-village.com – Fax (01766) 771 771 – Closed 25-30 January
9 rm ⊡ – †£265 ††£190/300 – 2 suites
Rest *Grill* – Menu £23 – Carte £23/45
♦ Crenellated 19C manor, its modern decor in harmony with the original Welsh oak,
slate and stone. Superbly stylish rooms in blues, greys and pale wood. Restored
walled garden. Victorian solarium, converted into a modish minimalist restaurant.

PWLLHELI – Gwynedd – **502** G 25 – pop. 3 861   32 **B2**

- ◘ London 261 mi – Aberystwyth 73 mi – Caernarfon 21 mi
- **ℹ** MinyDon, Station Sq ℰ (01758) 613000, pwllheli.tic@gwynedd.gov.uk
- 🏌 Golf Rd, ℰ (01758) 701 644
- ◎ Lleyn Peninsula★★

XX **Plas Bodegroes** with rm ⌂   🚗 **P** **VISA ⬤⬤**
Northwest : 1 ¾ m. on A 497 ✉ LL53 5TH – ℰ (01758) 612 363
– www.bodegroes.co.uk – gunna@bodegroes.co.uk – Fax (01758) 701 247
– 10 March- 22 November
11 rm ⌂ – ♦£50/80 ♦♦£170
Rest – (closed Sunday-Monday, except Bank Holidays) (dinner only and
Sunday lunch) (booking essential) Menu £42 ⌘
♦ Delightful Grade II listed Georgian house in secluded gardens. Local art decorates
the pale green dining room. Classically based cooking, using good quality local ingredients. Contemporary, Scandinavian style bedrooms.

at Boduan Northwest : 3 ¾ m. on A 497 – ✉ Pwllheli

⌂ **The Old Rectory** without rest   🚗 **P**
✉ LL53 6DT – ℰ (01758) 721 519 – www.theoldrectory.net
– thepollards@theoldrectory.net – Fax (01758) 721 519 – Closed 1 week Christmas
3 rm – ♦£75/90 ♦♦£90/95
♦ Part Georgian house with garden and paddock, adjacent to church. Well restored
providing comfortable, individually decorated bedrooms and attractive sitting room.

 Red = Pleasant. Look for the red X and 🏠 symbols.

WALES

RAGLAN – Monmouthshire – **503** L 28 – ✉ Abergavenny   33 **C4**

- ◘ London 154 mi – Cardiff 32 mi – Gloucester 34 mi – Newport 18 mi
  – Swansea 58 mi
- ◎ Castle★ **AC**

🏠 **The Clytha Arms** with rm   🚗 **P** **VISA ⬤⬤ AE ①**
West : 3 m. on Clytha rd (old Abergavenny Rd) ✉ NP7 9BW – ℰ (01873) 840 206
– clythaarms@tiscali.co.uk – Closed 25 December
4 rm ⌂ – ♦£60/80 ♦♦£80/100
Rest – (Closed Sunday dinner and Monday lunch except Bank Holiday Monday)
Menu £25 – Carte £28/38
♦ Personally run converted dower house. Welcoming, open fires; traditional games
sprinkled around tapas-serving bar. Generous, eclectic menus utilise the best of
Welsh produce. Individually styled bedrooms include one four poster.

REDWICK – Newport – **503** L 29 – see Newport (Newport)

RHAYADER – Powys – **503** J 27 – pop. 1 783   33 **B3**

- ◘ London 195 mi – Aberystwyth 39 mi – Carmarthen 67 mi
  – Shrewsbury 60 mi
- **ℹ** The Leisure Centre, North Street ℰ (01597) 810591,
  rhayader.tic@powys.gov.uk

⌂ **Beili Neuadd** without rest ⌂   ≤ 🚗 ⏸ **P**
Northeast : 2 m. by A 44 off Abbey-cwm-hir rd ✉ LD6 5NS – ℰ (01597) 810 211
– www.midwalesfarmstay.co.uk – rhayaderbreaks@yahoo.co.uk – March-October
3 rm ⌂ – ♦£30/32 ♦♦£56/60
♦ Part 16C stone-built farmhouse in a secluded rural setting with countryside views.
Personally run with comfortable bedrooms. Close to Rhayader and the "Lakeland of
Wales".

RHOS-ON-SEA = Llandrillo-yn-Rhos – Conwy – **502** I 24 – see Colwyn Bay

RHYL – Denbighshire – **502** J 24 – **pop. 24 889**   32 **C1**
- Cardiff 182 mi – Chester 34 mi – Llandudno 18 mi
- Rhuddlan Castle★★, S : 3 m. by A 525 – Bodelwyddan★★, S : 5 m. by A 525 and minor rd – St Asaph Cathedral★, S : 5 m. by A 525. Llandudno★, W : 16 m. by A 548, A 55 and B 5115

XX **Barratt's at Ty'n Rhyl** with rm   🚗 ⚒ ⁾⁾ P VISA ⚫⚫
167 Vale Rd, South : ½ m. on A 525 ⊠ LL18 2PH – ℰ (01745) 344 138
– ebarratt5@aol.com – Fax (01745) 344 138 – Closed Monday and Tuesday
3 rm ⊊ – †£67 ††£90
Rest – (dinner only and lunch Saturday-Sunday) (booking essential)
Carte approx. £ 34
♦ Rhyl's oldest house boasts comfortable lounges with rich oak panelling. Dine in either new conservatory or original house. Ambitious cooking on classic base. Individual rooms.

ROCKFIELD – Monmouthshire – **503** L 28 – **see Monmouth**

RUTHIN (Rhuthun) – Denbighshire – **502** K 24 – **pop. 5 218**   32 **C1**
- London 210 mi – Birkenhead 31 mi – Chester 23 mi – Liverpool 34 mi – Shrewsbury 46 mi
- ℹ Ruthin Craft Centre, Park Rd ℰ (01824) 703992
- ⛳ Ruthin-Pwllglas, ℰ (01824) 702 296
- Llandyrnog (St Dyfnog's Church★), Llanrhaeder-yng-Nghinmeirch (Jesse Window★★), N : 5½ m. by A 494 and B 5429. Denbigh★, NW : 7 m. on A 525

↑ **Firgrove**   🚗 ⚒ ⁾⁾ P VISA ⚫⚫
Llanfwrog, West : 1¼ m. by A 494 on B 5105 ⊠ LL15 2LL – ℰ (01824) 702 677
– www.firgrovecountryhouse.co.uk – meadway@firgrovecountryhouse.co.uk
– Fax (01824) 702677 – March-November
3 rm ⊊ – †£55 ††£80
Rest – (by arrangement, communal dining) Menu £ 30
♦ Well-furnished house with tasteful interiors set within attractive gardens. Bedrooms are comfortable; one is a self-contained cottage with a small kitchen. Close to the town. Traditionally furnished dining room with meals taken at a communal table.

↑ **Eyarth Station** 🐾   ← 🚗 ⌔ P VISA ⚫⚫
Llanfair Dyffryn Clwyd, South : 1¾ m. by A 525 ⊠ LL15 2EE – ℰ (01824) 703 643
– www.eyarthstation.co.uk – stay@eyarthstation.com – Fax (01824) 707 464
6 rm ⊊ – †£50 ††£72/80   **Rest** – (by arrangement) Menu £ 18
♦ Former railway station with a fine collection of photographs of its previous life. Pleasant country location. Traditional décor in bedrooms, sitting room and a small bar. Views over the countryside and hearty home-cooked food in the dining room.

ST BRIDES WENTLOOGE – Newport – **503** K 29 – **see Newport (Newport)**

ST CLEARS – Carmarthenshire – **503** G 28   33 **B3**
- London 221 mi – Caerdydd / Cardiff 76 mi – Abertawe / Swansea 37 mi – Llanelli 33 mi

↑ **Coedllys Country House** without rest 🐾   ← 🚗 ⌔ ⁾⁾ P VISA ⚫⚫
Llangynin, Northwest : 3½ m. by A 40 turning first left after 30 mph sign on entering village. ⊠ SA33 4JY – ℰ (01994) 231 455
– www.coedllyscountryhouse.co.uk – coedlly@btinternet.com – Fax (01944) 231441 – Closed 22-27 December
3 rm ⊊ – †£53/58 ††£80/90
♦ Idyllic country house and animal sanctuary with picture-perfect façade. Delightful owner keeps everything immaculate. Superb breakfasts. Rooms with unerring eye for detail.

ST DAVIDS (Tyddewi) – **Pembrokeshire** – **503** E 28 – **pop. 1 959**
– ✉ **Haverfordwest**

> ◻ London 266 mi – Carmarthen 46 mi – Fishguard 16 mi
> 🚹 National Park Visitor Centre ✆ (01437) 720392,
>   enquiries@stdavids.pembrokeshirecoast.org.uk
> 🏌 St Davids City Whitesands Bay, ✆ (01437) 721 751
> ◉ Town★ – Cathedral★★ - Bishop's Palace★ **AC**
> ◗ Pembrokeshire Coast National Park★★

🗓🗓 **Warpool Court** ❧   ≼ 🚗 ◻ ※ **P** VISA ◕◕ AE
Southwest : ½ m. by Porth Clais rd ✉ *SA62 6BN* – ✆ *(01437) 720 300*
– www.warpoolcourthotel.com – info@warpoolcourthotel.com – Fax (01437)
720 676 – Closed January and 2 weeks November
25 rm ☐ – †£115/185 ††£180/300
Rest – Menu £45 (dinner) **s** – Carte (lunch) £19/28 **s**
♦ Over 3000 hand-painted tiles of Celtic or heraldic design decorate the interior of
this 19C house. Modern bedrooms, some with views over neat lawned gardens to the
sea. Daily changing classic menus accompanied by fine views.

🏠 **Old Cross**   🚗 **P** VISA ◕◕
Cross Sq ✉ *SA62 6SP* – ✆ *(01437) 720 387* – *www.oldcrosshotel.co.uk*
– enquiries@oldcrosshotel.co.uk – Fax (01437) 720 394 – Closed January
16 rm ☐ – †£40/85 ††£70/110   **Rest** – (bar lunch) Carte £20/27
♦ Overlooking the old market square, a long-established, ivy-clad hotel: rooms are
modern and simply decorated. Beamed lounge - club chairs grouped around a brick
fireplace. Wheelback chairs and yellow linen-clad tables in an unassuming, traditional
restaurant.

🏠 **Crug-Glas** ❧   🚗 🕭 **P** VISA ◕◕ AE
Abereiddy, Northeast : 5½ m. on A 487 ✉ *SA62 6XX* – ✆ *(01348) 831 302*
– www.crug-glas.co.uk – janet@crugglas.wanadoo.co.uk – Fax (01348) 831 302
– Closed Christmas
5 rm ☐ – †£60 ††£100/130   **Rest** – (by arrangement) Carte £19/30
♦ Imposing family run Georgian house on a farm believed to have been worked since
12/13C. Partake of honesty bar then retire to one of the luxurious bedrooms: ask for
no. 5. Good local choice on tried-and-tested evening menu.

🏠 **Ramsey House**   ≼ 🚗 ※ 🍴 **P**
Lower Moor ✉ *SA62 6RP* – ✆ *(01437) 720 321* – *www.ramseyhouse.co.uk*
– info@ramseyhouse.co.uk – Closed 24-26 December
6 rm ☐ – †£50/85 ††£80/85   **Rest** – (by arrangement) Menu £25
♦ Detached house just outside town centre. Spotlessly kept, homely interior with
small bar overlooking gardens. Compact, neat and tidy rooms. Dinners cooked using
fresh Pembrokeshire produce. Fine breakfasts employ tasty home baking.

🏠 **The Waterings** without rest ❧   🚗 ※ **P**
Anchor Drive, High St, East : ¼ m. on A 487 ✉ *SA62 6QH* – ✆ *(01437) 720 876*
– www.waterings.co.uk – enquiries@waterings.co.uk – Fax (01437) 720 876
5 rm ☐ – †£50/80 ††£75/80
♦ Set in peaceful landscaped gardens and named after a sheltered cove on Ramsey
Island. Spacious rooms, furnished in solid pine, around a central courtyard. Likeable
hosts.

🏠 **Y-Gorlan** without rest   ※ **P** VISA ◕◕
77 Nun St ✉ *SA62 6NU* – ✆ *(01437) 720 837* – *www.stdavids.co.uk/gorlan*
– mikebohlen@aol.com – Closed 2 weeks February and Christmas
5 rm ☐ – †£35/40 ††£70/76
♦ Run by a friendly couple, Y-Gorlan - "the fold" - offers comfortable, spotless modern
rooms, all en suite. Homely lounge looks towards Whitesands Bay. Good breakfasts.

WALES

⚒ Cwtch   VISA ◉◉ AE
– ℰ *(01437) 720 491 – www.cwtchrestaurant.co.uk – info@cwtchrestaurant.co.uk*
– *Closed Christmas, 6-18 January and Monday-Tuesday November-March*
Rest – (dinner only and Sunday lunch) Menu £ 28
♦ Simple, friendly restaurant. Daily menu features hearty portions of honest British classics, crafted from local produce and arriving with large side of veg; old school desserts.

at Porthgain Northeast : 7 ¾ m. by A 487 – ✉ Haverfordwest

⚒ The Shed   ☆ P VISA ◉◉
*The Quay ✉ SA62 5BN – ℰ (01348) 831 518 – www.theshedporthgain.co.uk
– caroline@theshedporthgain.co.uk – Restricted opening in winter*
Rest – Seafood – (booking essential) Carte £ 27/40
♦ At the tip of the harbour in a charming spot, this locally renowned rustic eatery started life as a lobster pot store and now serves simply prepared, tasty seafood dishes.

SALEM – Carmarthenshire – see Llandeilo

SARON – Gwynedd – see Caernarfon

SAUNDERSFOOT – Pembrokeshire – **503** F 28   33 **A4**
▶ London 241 mi – Cardiff 90 mi – Pembroke 12 mi

🏨 St Brides Spa Hotel   ⟨ ☆ ◉ ☆ & rm, ⚒ ☆ ⚙ P VISA ◉◉ AE
*St Brides Hill ✉ SA69 9NH – ℰ (01834) 812 304 – www.stbridesspahotel.com
– reservations@stbridesspahotel.com – Fax (01834) 811 766*
35 rm ☲ – †£ 180 ††£ 280
Rest *Cliff* – Carte £ 36/44 **s**
♦ Occupying a great position over Carmarthen Bay, with breathtaking spa equipped to the highest spec. Fabulous terraces and outdoor infinity pool. Superbly designed bedrooms. Modern European cooking in fine dining restaurant with informal style.

🏨 Gower   ⇄ ☆ P VISA ◉◉
*Milford Terrace ✉ SA69 9EL – ℰ (01834) 813 452 – www.gower-hotel.com
– enquiries@gower-hotel.com – Fax (01834) 813 452*
20 rm ☲ – †£ 65 ††£ 94
Rest – (dinner only and Sunday lunch) Menu £ 20 – Carte £ 21/31
♦ Four-storey yellow hued hotel, refurbished in 2004, close to the beach. Leather chesterfields enhance wood-floored bar. Immaculate bedrooms in a uniform style. Bright, spacious dining room with conservatory extension; good choice of fish.

SEION – Gwynedd – see Caernarfon

SHIRENEWTON – Monmouthshire – **503** L 29 – see Chepstow

SKENFRITH – Monmouthshire   33 **C4**
▶ London 135 mi – Hereford 16 mi – Ross-on-Wye 11 mi

🍴 The Bell at Skenfrith with rm   ☆ ☆ ☆ P VISA ◉◉
✉ *NP7 8UH – ℰ (01600) 750 235 – www.skenfrith.co.uk
– enquiries@skenfrith.co.uk – Fax (01600) 750 525 – Closed 2 weeks late January
to early February, Monday from November to Easter*
11 rm ☲ – †£ 75 ††£ 220
Rest – (booking essential) Menu £ 19 (lunch) – Carte £ 26/32 ☷
♦ Michelin's 2007 Pub of the Year is a charming 17C coaching inn with antiques, curios, open fires and tasty modern menus. Very comfy rooms have state-of-the-art appointments.

SOUTHERNDOWN – Bridgend – **503** J 29 – see Bridgend

▶ London 191 mi – Birmingham 136 mi – Bristol 82 mi – Cardiff 40 mi – Liverpool 187 mi – Stoke-on-Trent 175 mi

🛈 Plymouth St ✆ (01792) 468321, tourism@swansea.gov.uk

🏌 Morriston 160 Clasemont Rd, ✆ (01792) 796 528

🏌 Clyne Mayals 120 Owls Lodge Lane, ✆ (01792) 401 989

🏌 Langland Bay, ✆ (01792) 366 023

🏌 Fairwood Park Fairwood Blackhills Lane, ✆ (01792) 297 849

🏌 Inco Clydach, ✆ (01792) 841 257

🏌 Allt-y-Graban Pontlliw Allt-y-Graban Rd, ✆ (01792) 885 757

🏌 Palleg Swansea Valley Lower Cwmtwrch, ✆ (01639) 842 193

◎ Town★ - Maritime Quarter★ B – Maritime and Industrial Museum★ B – Glynn Vivian Art Gallery★ B – Guildhall (British Empire Panels★ A **H**)

🗗 Gower Peninsula★★ (Rhossili★★), W : by A 4067 A. The Wildfowl and Wetlands Trust★, Llanelli, NW : 6½ m. by A 483 and A 484 A

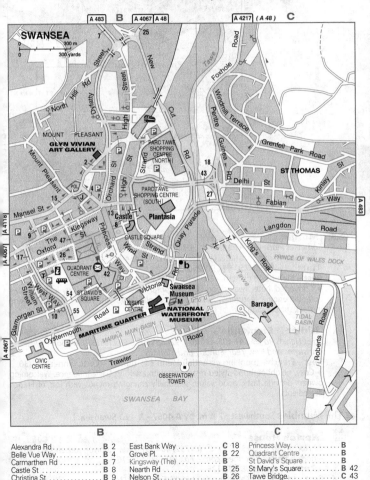

SWANSEA

WALES

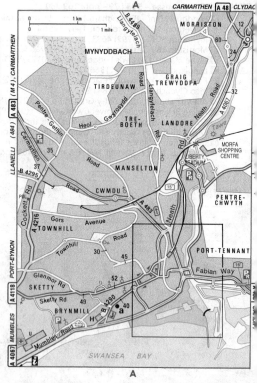

Morgans ⚐ 🖹 🛇 rm, 𝐀𝐂 ⚒ ⸙ 🛁 🅿 𝘝𝘐𝘚𝘈 𝕮𝕺 𝐀𝐄

Somerset Place ⊠ SA1 1RR – ℰ (01792) 484 848 – www.morganshotel.co.uk
– reception@morganshotel.co.uk – Fax (01792) 484 849 B**b**

41 rm ⚏ – ♦£90/250 ♦♦£90/250

Rest – Menu £18 (lunch) – Carte dinner £25/38 **s**

◆ Converted hotel near docks. Contemporary feel: neutral colours, leather sofas. Splendid original features include soaring cupola. Very stylish rooms. Modish cooking in sleek surroundings.

Didier & Stephanie's 𝐀𝐂 𝘝𝘐𝘚𝘈 𝕮𝕺

56 St Helens Rd ⊠ SA1 4BE – ℰ (01792) 655 603 – Fax (01792) 470 563 – Closed
Christmas and New Year, Sunday and Monday A**a**

Rest – French – (booking essential) Menu £17 (lunch) – Carte dinner £27/30

◆ Cosy, neighbourhood-styled restaurant with a strong Gallic influence. Welcoming owners provide tasty, good value, seasonally changing menus with lots of French ingredients.

---

at The Mumbles Southwest : 7 ¾ m. by A 4067 - A – ⊠ Swansea

Norton House 🚏 ⸙ 🛁 🅿 𝘝𝘐𝘚𝘈 𝕮𝕺 𝐀𝐄 ⓪

17 Norton Rd ⊠ SA3 5QT – ℰ (01792) 404 891 – www.nortonhousehotel.co.uk
– nortonhouse@btconnect.com – Fax (01792) 403 210

15 rm ⚏ – ♦£86/98 ♦♦£125

Rest – (dinner only and Sunday lunch) Carte £26/34

◆ Georgian former master mariner's house in peaceful grounds. Tidy rooms in traditional fabrics and furnishings - some have four-poster beds. Elegant, classically proportioned dining room, offset by French etched glassware.

at Llanrhidian West : 10 ½ m. by A 4118 - A - and B 4271 – ⊠ Reynoldston

🏠 **Fairyhill** 🌿   🛋 ◑ 🌲 ⅋ ⁿ 🚁 **P** *VISA* ◍
Reynoldston, West : 2 ½ m. by Llangennith Rd ⊠ *SA3 1BS* – ℰ *(01792) 390 139*
– www.fairyhill.net – postbox@fairyhill.net – Fax (01792) 391 358
– Closed 1-27 January and Christmas
8 rm � – ♦£ 145 ♦♦£ 275   **Rest** – Menu £ 20/40 – Carte lunch £ 26/43 🍴
◆ Georgian country house in extensive parkland and gardens. Mix includes sleek lounge, eclectic bedrooms, treatment and meeting rooms, all set within general modish ambience. Gower produce dominates seasonal menus.

✗✗ **The Welcome To Town**   **P** *VISA* ◍
⊠ *SA3 1EH* – ℰ *(01792) 390 015 – www.thewelcometotown.co.uk*
– enquiries@thewelcometotown.co.uk – Fax (01792) 390 015 – Closed last
2 weeks February, 25-26 December, 1 January, Sunday dinner and Monday.
Rest – (booking essential) Menu £ 22/35 **s** – Carte £ 16/41
◆ Converted pub set on picturesque peninsula. Cosy, traditional interior with good service of seasonal dishes cooked with real quality from wide choice menu.

TALSARNAU – Gwynedd – **502** H 25 – **pop. 647** – ⊠ Harlech   32 **B2**
▣ London 236 mi – Caernafon 33 mi – Chester 67 mi – Dolgellau 25 mi
◙ Snowdonia National Park ★★★

🏠 **Maes-y-Neuadd** 🌿   ≤ 🛋 **P** *VISA* ◍
South : 1 ½ m. by A 496 off B 4573 ⊠ *LL47 6YA* – ℰ *(01766) 780 200*
– www.neuadd.com – maes@neuadd.com – Fax (01766) 780 211
14 rm (dinner included) ⊠ – ♦£ 75/90 ♦♦£ 99/270 – 1 suite
Rest – Menu £ 35 – Carte lunch £ 18/29
◆ Part 14C country house with pleasant gardens in delightful rural seclusion. Furnished throughout with antiques and curios. Charming service. Individually styled bedrooms. Traditional dining room with linen-clad tables.

TAL-Y-LLYN – Conwy – **502** I 25 – ⊠ Tywyn   32 **B1**
▣ London 224 mi – Dolgellau 9 mi – Shrewsbury 60 mi
◙ Snowdonia National Park ★★★ - Cadair Idris ★★★

🏠 **Tynycornel**   ≤ 🛋 🌲 ⅋ **P** *VISA* ◍
on B 4405 ⊠ *LL36 9AJ* – ℰ *(01654) 782 282 – www.tynycornel.co.uk*
– reception@tynycornel.co.uk – Fax (01654) 782 679
21 rm ⊠ – ♦£ 65/75 ♦♦£ 150/170 – 1 suite
Rest – (bar lunch Monday-Saturday) Menu £ 28 – Carte approx. £ 17
◆ Extended former inn with fine views of Tal-y-Llyn Lake, renowned for its fishing, and Cadair Idris. Comfortable rooms with good facilities, some in converted outbuildings. Purpose-built extension houses modern restaurant.

TENBY – Pembrokeshire – **503** F 28 – **pop. 4 934**   33 **A4**
▣ London 247 mi – Carmarthen 27 mi – Fishguard 36 mi
🛈 Unit 2, the Gateway Complex ℰ (01834) 842 404,
    tenby.tic@pembrokeshire.gov.uk
🏳 The Burrows, ℰ (01834) 842 978
◉ Town ★★ – Harbour and seafront ★★
◙ Pembrokeshire Coast National Park ★★ - Caldey Island ★, S : by boat

🏠 **Broadmead**   🛋 ⅋ **P** *VISA* ◍ **AE**
Heywood Lane, Northwest : ¾ m. ⊠ *SA70 8DA* – ℰ *(01834) 842 641*
– www.broadmeadhoteltenby.com – broadmead-tenby@googlemail.com
– Fax (01834) 845 757 – Closed Christmas-March
20 rm ⊠ – ♦£ 33/56 ♦♦£ 80/92   **Rest** – (dinner only) Menu £ 20 **s**
◆ Privately owned country house hotel. Traditionally styled public rooms include conservatory overlooking gardens. Individually decorated rooms with modern amenities. Dining room in the traditional style common to the other parts of the house.

Fourcroft ⟨ 🚗 🏊 🏠 📶 🛎 ⚡ ♨ 🏊 *VISA* ⓪ AE ⓪

North Beach ✉ *SA70 8AP* – 🕿 *(01834) 842 886* – *www.fourcroft-hotel.co.uk*
– *staying@fourcroft-hotel.co.uk* – *Fax (01834) 842 888*
40 rm ☌ – ✝£70/150 ✝✝£140/160
Rest – (bar lunch) Menu £25 – Carte £26/33
♦ Well-established, family owned hotel forming part of a Georgian terrace. Sea facing rooms benefit from large original windows. Attractions and water activities nearby. The dining room overlooks the sea and is decorated in traditional style.

at Penally (Penalun) Southwest : 2. m. by A 4139 – ✉ Tenby

 Penally Abbey ⟨ 🚗 🛎 ♨ P *VISA* ⓪ AE

✉ *SA70 7PY* – 🕿 *(01834) 843 033* – *www.penally-abbey.com*
– *penally.abbey@btinternet.com* – *Fax (01834) 844 714*
17 rm ☌ – ✝£138 ✝✝£190 **Rest** – (booking essential at lunch)
Carte £36/39
♦ Gothic style, stone built house with good views of Carmarthen Bay and surrounded by woodland. Calm, country house décor and atmosphere. Lodge rooms are particularly pleasant. Candlelit dining room, decorated in the country style of the establishment.

⌂ **Wychwood House** 🚗 🛎 ♨ P *VISA* ⓪

✉ *SA70 7PE* – 🕿 *(01834) 844 387* – *www.wychwoodhousebb.co.uk*
– *wychwoodbb@aol.com*
3 rm ☌ – ✝£45/60 ✝✝£45/60 **Rest** – (by arrangement) Menu £28
♦ Large 1940s house with a comfy, friendly ambience. Well-appointed guest drawing room. Individually styled bedrooms exude a winningly retro 'Noel Coward' feel. Serious dining: far eastern and modern European dominate owner's repertoire.

 Look out for red symbols, indicating particularly pleasant establishments.

THORNHILL – Cardiff – **503** K 29 – **see Cardiff**

TINTERN (Tyndyrn) – **Monmouthshire** – **503** L 28 – ✉ **Chepstow**   33 **C4**
🚩 London 137 mi – Bristol 23 mi – Gloucester 40 mi – Newport 22 mi
◎ Abbey★★ AC

🏠 **Parva Farmhouse** ♨ P *VISA* ⓪

on A 466 ✉ *NP16 6SQ* – 🕿 *(01291) 689 411* – *www.parvafarmhouse.co.uk*
– *parvahoteltintern@fsmail.net* – *Fax (01291) 689 941*
8 rm ☌ – ✝£45/60 ✝✝£70/80 **Rest** – (dinner only) Carte £18/23
♦ Mid 17C stone farmhouse adjacent to River Wye; refurbished to country standard. Traditional cooking, warm hospitality and a pleasant ambience. Comfortable rooms.

TREARDDUR BAY – Isle of Anglesey – **502** G 24 – ✉ **Holyhead**   32 **B1**
🚩 London 269 mi – Bangor 25 mi – Caernarfon 29 mi – Holyhead 3 mi
◎ Anglesey★★. Barclodiad y Gawres Burial Chamber★, SE : 10 m. by B 4545, A 5 and A 4080

 Trearddur Bay ⟨ 🚗 🏊 🛎 ♨ 🏊 P *VISA* ⓪ AE ⓪

✉ *LL65 2UN* – 🕿 *(01407) 860 301* – *www.trearddurbayhotel.co.uk*
– *enquiries@trearddurbayhotel.co.uk* – *Fax (01407) 861 181*
40 rm ☌ – ✝£99 ✝✝£153/175
Rest – (dinner only and Sunday lunch) Carte £17/28
♦ Situated next to "Blue Flag" beach. Well run with good facilities, including pool and spacious, comfortable rooms: go for balcony rooms with bay window seating. Modern dining room; drinks in cocktail lounge before dining.

TREDUNNOCK – Newport – **503** L 29 – **see Newport (Newport)**

WALES

TREMEIRCHION – Denbighshire – **502** J 24 – ⊠ St Asaph · · · · · · · · · · · · · · · · 32 **C1**

🚇 London 225 mi – Chester 29 mi – Shrewsbury 59 mi

⚑ **Bach-Y-Graig** without rest 🍃 · · · · · · · · · · 🗐 🔃 🔈 🏦 **P** **VISA** **◍◍**
Southwest : 2 m. by B 5429 off Denbigh rd ⊠ LL17 0UH – ℰ (01745) 730 627
– www.bachygraig.co.uk – anwen@bachygraig.co.uk
– Closed Christmas and New Year
3 rm ⊇ – ✦£45/56 ✦✦£70/75
◆ Attractive brick-built farmhouse dating from 16C, on working farm. In quiet spot
with woodland trails nearby. Large open fires and wood furnished rooms with cast
iron beds.

TYN-Y-GROES – Gwynedd – see Conwy (Aberconwy and Colwyn)

USK – Monmouthshire – **503** L 28 – pop. 2 318 · 33 **C4**

🚇 London 144 mi – Bristol 30 mi – Cardiff 26 mi – Gloucester 39 mi
– Newport 10 mi
🔢 Alice Springs Usk Kemeys Commander, ℰ (01873) 880 708
🄖 Raglan Castle★ **AC**, NE : 7 m. by A 472, A 449 and A 40

🏨 **Glen-yr-Afon House** · · · · · · · · · 🗐 🏣 🕭 rm, 🄰🄲 rest, 🍽 🏦 **P** **VISA** **◍◍** **AE**
Pontypool Rd ⊠ NP15 1SY – ℰ (01291) 672 302 – www.glen-yr-afon.co.uk
– enquiries@glen-yr-afon.co.uk – Fax (01291) 672 597
27 rm ⊇ – ✦£96 ✦✦£138 **Rest** – Menu £15 (lunch) – Carte £24/31
◆ Across bridge from town is this warmly run 19C villa with relaxing country house
ambience. Several welcoming lounges and comfy, warm, well-kept bedrooms.
Friendly welcome. Stylish restaurant.

at Llandenny Northeast : 4 ¼ m. by A 472 off B 4235 – ⊠ Usk

🍴 **Raglan Arms** · 🔝 **P** **VISA** **◍◍** **AE**
⊠ NP15 1DL – ℰ (01291) 690 800 – www.raglanarms.com
– raglanarms@aol.com – Fax (01291) 690 155 – Closed 26-27 December
Rest – (Closed Sunday dinner and Monday) Carte £20/24
◆ Stone-faced pub in the middle of small village. Busy central bar: eating area includes big leather sofas in front of the fire, and good value dishes enhanced by sharp
cooking.

> Don't confuse 🍴 with 🏵!
> 🍴 defines comfort, while stars are awarded for the best cuisine,
> across all categories of comfort.

WELSH HOOK – Pembrokeshire – **503** F 28 – see Fishguard

WHITEBROOK – Monmouthshire – see Monmouth

WOLF'S CASTLE (Cas-Blaidd) – Pembrokeshire – **503** F 28 · · · · · · · · 33 **A3**
– ⊠ Haverfordwest

🚇 London 258 mi – Fishguard 7 mi – Haverfordwest 8 mi
🄖 Pembrokeshire Coast National Park★★

🏨 **Wolfscastle Country H.** · · · · · · · · · · · · · · 🗐 🍽 🏦 **P** **VISA** **◍◍** **AE**
⊠ SA62 5LZ – ℰ (01437) 741 225 – www.wolfscastle.com
– enquiries@wolfscastle.com – Fax (01437) 741 383 – Closed 24-26 December
20 rm ⊇ – ✦£70 ✦✦£100/135
Rest – (lunch by arrangement Monday-Saturday) Carte £19/33
◆ Spacious, family run country house; tidy rooms in traditional soft chintz, modern
conference room and simply styled bar with a mix of cushioned settles and old
wooden chairs. Dining room with neatly laid tables in pink linens.

WALES

WREXHAM (Wrecsam) – **Wrexham** – **502** L 24 – **pop. 42 576**

- ▣ London 192 mi – Chester 12 mi – Liverpool 35 mi – Shrewsbury 28 mi
- 🛈 Lambpit St ℰ (01978) 292015, tic@wrexham.gov.uk
- 🔁 Chirk, ℰ (01691) 774407
- 🔟 Clays Golf Centre Bryn Estyn Rd, ℰ (01978) 661406
- 🔟 Moss Valley Moss Rd, ℰ (01978) 720518
- 🔟 Pen-y-Cae Ruabon Rd, ℰ (01978) 810108
- 🔟 Plassey Oaks Golf Complex Eyton, ℰ (01978) 780020
- ◉ St Giles Church ★
- ◉ Erddig ★★ **AC** (Gardens ★★), SW : 2 m – Gresford (All Saints Church ★), N : 4 m. by A 5152 and B 5445

at Gresford Northeast : 3 m. by A 483 on B 5445

🏠 **Pant-yr-Ochain**　　　　　🍴 🕯 ⌑ **P** VISA ◐ AE
Old Wrexham Rd, South : 1 m. ✉ LL12 8TY – ℰ (01978) 853525
– www.brunningandprice.co.uk – pant.yr.ochain@brunningandprice.co.uk
– Fax (01978) 853505 – Closed 25-26 December
Rest – (booking essential) Carte £ 19/28

♦ Bustling part 16C inn overlooking a lake with pleasant gardens and terrace. Open-plan dining rooms, bar and library. Blackboard menu and real ales.

O. Fonir/MICHELIN

Ireland

O. Forir/MICHELIN

Towns
from A to Z

Villes
de A à Z

Città
de A a Z

Städte
von A bis Z

Northern Ireland

ARMAGH – **Armagh** – **712** M 4   35 **C3**

> ▣ Belfast 39 mi – Dungannon 13 mi – Portadown 11 mi
>
> ◉ St Patrick's Cathedral★ (Anglican) - St Patrick's Cathedral★ (Roman Catholic) - The Mall★ : Armagh County Museum★ **AC**, Royal Irish Fusiliers Museum★ **AC**
>
> ◉ Navan Fort★ **AC** W : 2 m. by A 28. The Argory★ **AC** N : 10 m. by A 29 and minor road right

Armagh City H.   🔲 🏊 ⅙ 📶 ⅙ rm, ♠ 🐎 ⚥ ⁽ᵗⁱᵖ⁾ ⚙ **P** VISA ◉◉ AE
2 Friary Rd ✉ *BT60 4FR* – ✆ *(028) 37518888 – www.armaghcityhotel.com – info@armaghcityhotel.com – Fax (028) 37512777 – Closed 24-25 December*
82 rm ☑ – 🍴£89 🍴🍴£102
Rest – (dinner only and Sunday lunch) Carte £21/27
♦ Modern purpose-built hotel well geared-up to the business traveller. Stylish, wood furnished bedrooms, the city's two cathedrals visible from those to the front. Large, split-level restaurant serving traditional dishes.

> Look out for red symbols, indicating particularly pleasant establishments.

BALLYCLARE – **Newtownabbey** – **712** N/O 3   35 **D2**

> ▣ Belfast 14 mi – Newtownabbey 6 mi – Lisburn 23 mi

Oregano   AK ⟷ **P** VISA ◉◉
29 Ballyrobert Rd, South : 3 ¼ m. by A 57 on B 56 ✉ *BT39 9RY* – ✆ *(028) 9084 0099 – www.oreganorestaurant.co.uk – info@oreganorestaurant.co.uk – Fax (028) 9084 0033*
– Closed 12-20 July, Christmas, Monday and Saturday lunch
Rest – Menu £13 (lunch) – Carte £26/37
♦ Traditional facade contrasts with modish interior. Light, bright dining room is spacious and contemporary, in keeping with the flavoursome, modern European dishes on offer.

BALLYMENA (An Baile Meánach) – **Ballymena** – **712** N 3 – pop. 28 717   35 **C2**
▌ *Ireland*

> ▣ Belfast 27 mi – Dundalk 78 mi – Larne 21 mi – Londonderry 51 mi – Omagh 53 mi
>
> 🛈 1-29 Bridge St ✆ (028) 2563 5900, tourist.information@ballymena.gov.uk
>
> 🏌 128 Raceview Rd, ✆ (028) 2586 1207
>
> ◉ Antrim Glens★★★ - Murlough Bay★★★ (Fair Head ≤★★★), NE : 32 m. by A 26, A 44, A 2 and minor road - Glengariff Forest Park★★ **AC** (Waterfall★★), NW : 13 m. by A 43 – Glengariff★, NE : 18 m. by A 43 – Glendun★, NE : 19 m. by A 43, B 14 and A2 – Antrim (Round Tower★) S : 9½ m. by A 26

Rosspark   🚐 ⅙ ⅙ rm, AK rest, 🐎 ⁽ᵗⁱᵖ⁾ ⚙ **P** VISA ◉◉ AE
20 Doagh Rd, Southeast : 6 m. by A 36 on B 59 ✉ *BT42 3LZ* – ✆ *(028) 2589 1663 – www.rosspark.com – info@rosspark.com – Fax (028) 2589 1477*
– Closed 24-25 December
39 rm ☑ – 🍴£65/80 🍴🍴£80/95 – 3 suites
Rest – Menu £25 (dinner) – Carte £20/25
♦ Off the beaten track, yet fully equipped with all mod cons. Rooms are smart and contemporary styled, some with sofas. Executive rooms have large working areas. Restaurant in the heart of the hotel decorated in terracotta colours.

Marlagh Lodge   🚐 🐎 ⁽ᵗⁱᵖ⁾ **P** VISA ◉◉
71 Moorfields Rd, Southeast : 2 ¼ m. on A 36 ✉ *BT42 3BU* – ✆ *(028) 2563 1505 – www.marlaghlodge.com – info@marlaghlodge.com – Fax (028) 2564 1590*
3 rm ☑ – 🍴£45 🍴🍴£90   **Rest** – (by arrangement) Menu £33
♦ Substantial 19C house with immediate, if busy, road connection. Many original features restored; stained glass in front door and hall. Tasteful, individually furnished rooms. Guests treated to seasonally changing five course dinner, upon arrangement.

NORTHERN IRELAND

at Galgorm West : 4 m. by A 42 on Fenaby rd – ✉

Galgorm Resort and Spa ॐ
136 Fenaghy Rd ✉ BT42 1EA – ℰ (028)
2588 1001 – www.galgorm.com – sales@galgorm.com – Fax (028) 2588 0080
75 rm ☟ – †£145 ††£365
Rest *Gillies* – Carte approx. £22
Rest *River Room* – (closed Monday-Tuesday) (dinner only) Carte approx. £50
♦ Former manor house with extensions; a delightful mix of the modern and the more traditional. Bedrooms are furnished in a contemporary style; the best are in the new buildings. The all day restaurant opens out onto gardens, an outdoor bar and games area.

BANGOR (Beannchar) – **North Down** – 712 O/P 4 ▌ Ireland   35 **D2**

🚘 Belfast 15 mi – Newtownards 5 mi
🛈 34 Quay St ℰ (028) 9127 0069, tic@northdown.gov.uk
◉ North Down Heritage Centre★
◉ Ulster Folk and Transport Museum★★ **AC**, W : 8 m. by A 2. Newtownards : Movilla Priory (Cross Slabs★) S : 4 m. by A 21 - Mount Stewart★★★ **AC**, SE : 90 m. by A 21 and A 20 – Scrabo Tower (≤★★) S : 6½ m. by A 21 – Ballycopeland Windmill★, SE : 10 m. by B 21 and A 2, turning right at Millisle – Strangford Lough★ (Castle Espie Centre★ **AC** - Nerndum Monastery★) - Grey Abbey★ **AC**, SE : 20 m. by A 2, A 21 and A 20

Clandeboye Lodge
10 Estate Rd, Clandeboye, Southwest : 3 m. by A 2 and Dundonald rd following signs for Blackwood Golf Centre ✉ BT19 1UR – ℰ (028) 9185 2500
– www.clandeboyelodge.com – info@clandeboyelodge.co.uk – Fax (028) 9185 2712 – Closed 25-26 December
43 rm ☟ – †£85/125 ††£100/140
Rest *Lodge* – (bar lunch Monday-Saturday) Carte £20/33 **s**
♦ On site of former estate school house, surrounded by 4 acres of woodland. Well placed for country and coast. Meetings and weddings in separate extension. Contemporary rooms. Restaurant boasts minimal, stylish décor. Modish menus.

Cairn Bay Lodge
278 Seacliffe Rd, East : 1¼ m. by Quay St ✉ BT20 5HS – ℰ (028) 9146 7636
– www.cairnbaylodge.com – info@cairnbaylodge.com – Fax (028) 9145 7728
3 rm ☟ – †£60/70 ††£70/80   **Rest** – (by arrangement) Menu £15
♦ Built in 1913; retains lots of period charm: Dutch fireplaces, stained glass, panelling. Beach views; individually styled rooms. Attractive garden. Health/beauty treatments.

Hebron House without rest
68 Princetown Rd ✉ BT20 3TD – ℰ (028) 9146 3126 – www.hebron-house.com
– reception@hebron-house.com – Fax (028) 9146 3126
– Closed 22 December-1 January
3 rm ☟ – †£50/80 ††£80/85
♦ Redbrick double fronted 19C property in elevated location. Immaculate styling, yet in keeping with age of house. Ultra stylish rooms offer every conceivable facility.

Shelleven House
59-61 Princetown Rd ✉ BT20 3TA – ℰ (028) 9127 1777
– www.shellevenhouse.com – shellevenhouse@aol.com – Fax (028) 9127 1777
– Restricted opening in winter
11 rm ☟ – †£36/60 ††£80/85   **Rest** – (by arrangement) Menu £40
♦ Personally run, end of terrace, double front Victorian house; short stroll to marina. Large, uniformly appointed rooms: ask for a large one at the front. Homely, good value.

Coyle's
44 High St ✉ BT20 5AZ – ℰ (028) 9127 0362 – www.coylesbistro.co.uk
– Fax (028) 9127 0362 – Closed 25 December
Rest – (Closed Monday) Carte £15/28
♦ Black exterior advertising real music and hard liquor! Also serves super dishes in an Art Deco upstairs restaurant: safe steaks meet ambitious, well executed surprises.

O. Fonir/MICHELIN

BELFAST
(Béal Feirste)

County: Belfast
Michelin REGIONAL map: n° 712 O 4
▶ Dublin 103 mi – Londonderry 70 mi

Population: 276 459   35 **D2**
▮ *Ireland*

PRACTICAL INFORMATION

🛈 Tourist Information

47 Donegal Pl ✆ (028) 9024 6609, info@belfastvisitor.com

Belfast International Airport, Information desk ✆ (028) 9448 4677

Belfast City Airport, Sydenham Bypass ✆ (028) 9093 5372

Airports

✈ Belfast International Airport, Aldergrove: ✆ (028) 9448 4848, W: 15 ½ m. by A 52 AY

George Best Belfast City Airport: ✆ (028) 9093 9093

Ferries and Shipping Lines

⛴ to Isle of Man (Douglas) (Isle of Man Steam Packet Co. Ltd) (summer only) (2 h 45 mn)
– to Stranraer (Stena Line) 4-5 daily (1 h 30 mn/3 h 15 mn), (Seacat Scotland) March-
January (90 mn) – to Liverpool (Norfolkline Irish Sea) daily (8 h 30 mn)

Golf Courses

🏌 Balmoral 518 Lisburn Rd, ✆ (028) 9038 1514

🏌 Belvoir Park Newtonbreda 73 Church Rd, ✆ (028) 9049 1693

🏌 Fortwilliam Downview Ave, ✆ (028) 9037 0770

🏌 The Nock Club Dundonald Summerfield, ✆ (028) 9048 2249

🏌 Shandon Park 73 Shandon Park, ✆ (028) 9080 5030

🏌 Cliftonville Westland Rd, ✆ (028) 9074 4158

🏌 Ormeau 50 Park Road, ✆ (028) 9064 1069

👁 SIGHTS

IN TOWN

City★ - Ulster Museum★★ (Spanish
Armada Treasure★★, Shrine of
St Patrick's Hand★) AZ **M1** – City
Hall★ – BY – Donegall Square★ BY **20**
– Botanic Gardens (Palm House★) AZ
– St Anne's Cathedral★ BX – Crown
Liquor Saloon★ BY – Sinclair Seamen's
Church★ BX – St Malachy's Church★
BY

ON THE OUTSKIRTS

Belfast Zoological Gardens★★ **AC**,
N: 5 m. by A 6 AY

IN THE SUROUNDING AREA

Carrickfergus (Castle★★ **AC**,
St Nicholas' Church★) NE: 9 ½ m.
by A 2 – Talnotry Cottage Bird Garden,
Crumlin★ **AC**, W: 13 ½ m. by A 52

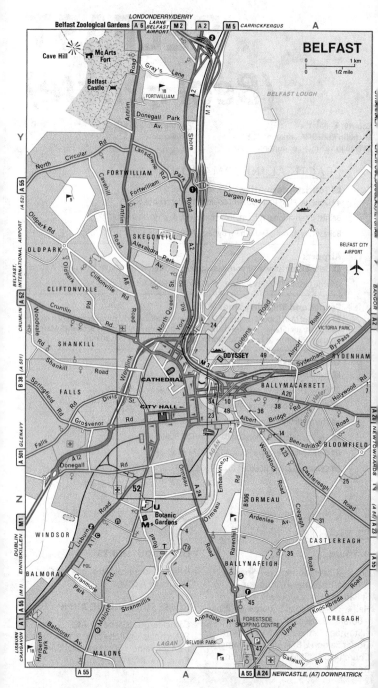

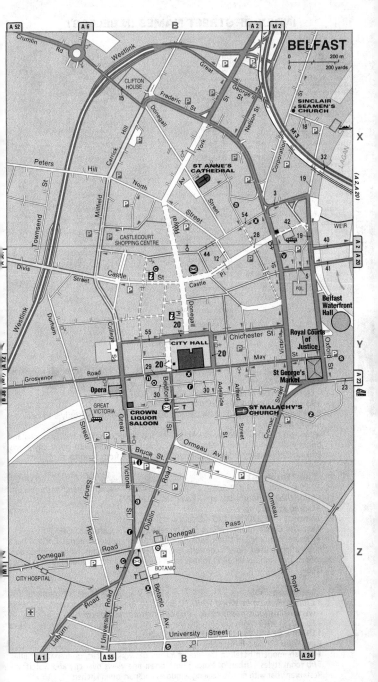

INDEX OF STREET NAMES IN BELFAST

NORTHERN IRELAND

 Hilton Belfast　　　　　📻 🈁 & rm, 🅰🅲 🈷 🛜 🛠 🅿 VISA 🆎 🆎 ⓪

4 Lanyon Pl ⊠ *BT1 3LP –* 𝒸 *(028) 9027 7000 – www.hilton.co.uk/belfast*
– reservation.belfast@hilton.com – Fax (028) 9027 7277　　　　　　　**BYs**
193 rm – ♦†£89/184 ♦†♦†£99/194, ☞ £10 – 4 suites
Rest *Sonoma* – (Closed lunch Saturday and Sunday) (dinner only and bar
lunch) Menu £ 26
♦ Modern branded hotel overlooking river and close to concert hall. Spacious and
brightly decorated rooms with all mod cons. Upper floors with good city views.
Striking California-style décor and good choice menus from Sonoma.

 The Merchant　　　　　🈁 & rm, 🅰🅲 🈷 🛜 🅿 VISA 🆎 🆎

35-39 Waring St ⊠ *BT1 2DY –* 𝒸 *(028) 9023 4888 – www.themerchanthotel.com*
– info@themerchanthotel.com – Fax (028) 9024 7775
– Closed 25 December　　　　　　　　　　　　　　　　　　　**BXx**
24 rm ☞ – ♦†£220 ♦†♦†£220 – 2 suites
Rest *The Great Room* – Menu £ 22 (weekdays)/27 – Carte £ 31/50
♦ Ornate former HQ of Ulster Bank imbued with rich, opulent interior. Cocktail bar a
destination in itself. Hotel's comforts exemplified by sumptuous, highly original bedrooms. Tremendous detail in former main banking hall dining room.; French based
dishes.

 Radisson SAS　　　　　≤ 🈁 & rm, 🅰🅲 🈷 🤳 🛠 🅿 VISA 🆎 🆎 ⓪

3 Cromac Pl, Cromac Wood ⊠ *BT7 2JB –* 𝒸 *(028) 9043 4065*
– www.belfastradissonsas.co.uk – info.belfast@radissonsas.com
– Fax (028) 9043 4066　　　　　　　　　　　　　　　　　　**BYz**
119 rm – ♦†£160 ♦†♦†£170, ☞ £14.95 – 1 suite
Rest *Filini* – Italian influences – Carte approx. £ 33
♦ Stylish, modern hotel on the site of former gasworks. Smart, up-to-date facilities.
Two room styles - Urban or Nordic; both boast fine views over city and waterfront.
Restaurant/bar with floor-to-ceiling windows and part-open kitchen.

Malmaison
f_8 🛋 🍴 rm, AC rest, 🕻 VISA ◑ AE

34-38 Victoria St ✉ *BT1 3GH –* 𝒞 *(028) 9022 0200 – www.malmaison.com*
– belfast@malmaison.com – Fax (028) 9022 0220   BYv
62 rm – ✝£160 ✝✝£160, ☑ £13.95 – 2 suites
Rest *Brasserie* – Carte £24/38

♦ An unstuffy, centrally located hotel hides behind its intricate Victorian façade. Originally two warehouses, many original features remain. Modern, comfortable rooms. Stylish, comfortable, modern dining in Brasserie.

Ten Square
🛋 🍴 rm, AC 🎾 🕯 $\hat{sa}$ VISA ◑ AE

10 Donegall Square South ✉ *BT1 5JD –* 𝒞 *(028) 9024 1001*
– www.tensquare.co.uk – reservations@tensquare.co.uk
– Fax (028) 9024 3210   BYx
23 rm ☑ – ✝£170/265 ✝✝£170/265
Rest *Grill Room* – Carte £19/29 s

♦ Victorian mill building in heart of city renovated to a thoroughly contemporary standard. Notably spacious deluxe bedrooms. Access to private bar for guests. Smart, stylish Grill Room.

Malone Lodge
🏠 f_8 🛋 🍴 rm, AC rest, 🎾 🕯 $\hat{sa}$ P VISA ◑ AE ①

60 Eglantine Ave ✉ *BT9 6DY –* 𝒞 *(028) 9038 8000*
– www.malonelodgehotelbelfast.com – info@malonelodgehotel.com
– Fax (028) 9038 8088   AZn
51 rm ☑ – ✝£85/120 ✝✝£85/160
Rest *The Green Door* – (Closed Sunday dinner) Menu £15/23 s – Carte dinner £19/28 s

♦ Imposing hotel in 19C terrace in quiet residential area. Elegant lobby lounge and smart bar. Conference facilities. Basement gym. Stylish, modern rooms with good comforts. Restaurant provides a comfortable, contemporary environment.

The Crescent Townhouse
🍴 rm, AC rest, 🎾 🕯 $\hat{sa}$ VISA ◑ AE

13 Lower Crescent ✉ *BT1 1NR –* 𝒞 *(028) 9032 3349*
– www.crescenttownhouse.com – info@crescenttownhouse.com
– Fax (028) 9032 0646 – Closed 25 December and 1 January   BZx
17 rm ☑ – ✝£90/150 ✝✝£150
Rest *Metro Brasserie* – (Closed Sunday lunch) Menu £14/20
– Carte £19/28

♦ Intimate Regency house that blends original features with modern amenities. Relaxed, discreet atmosphere. Spacious and luxurious rooms with interior designed period feel. Modern classic brasserie with a lively and relaxed ambience.

Benedicts
🍴 rm, AC rest, 🎾 🕯 VISA ◑ AE ①

7-21 Bradbury Pl, Shaftesbury Sq ✉ *BT7 1RQ –* 𝒞 *(028) 9059 1999*
– www.benedictshotel.co.uk – info@benedictshotel.co.uk – Fax (028) 9059 1990
– Closed 24-25 December and 11-12 July   BZc
32 rm ☑ – ✝£70 ✝✝£80/90
Rest *Benedicts Restaurant* – Menu £13/25 – Carte £17/26

♦ A lively, strikingly designed bar with nightly entertainment can be found at the heart of this busy commercial hotel. Well-appointed bedrooms above offer modern facilities. Relaxed, popular restaurant.

Ravenhill House
without rest   🎾 🕯 P VISA ◑

690 Ravenhill Rd ✉ *BT6 0BZ –* 𝒞 *(028) 9020 7444 – www.ravenhillhouse.com*
– olive@ravenhillhouse.com – Fax (028) 9028 2590
– Closed 20 December -4 January and 30 June - 20 July   AZs
5 rm ☑ – ✝£50/55 ✝✝£75

♦ Personally run detached 19C house, attractively furnished in keeping with its age. The largely organic breakfast is a highlight. Good sized rooms with bold shades predominant.

NORTHERN IRELAND

↑ **Ash Rowan Town House** without rest   🔲 ⌘ **P** _VISA_ ⚫⚫
12 Windsor Ave ⊠ *BT9 6EE* – ℰ *(028) 9066 1758 – Fax (028) 9066 3227*
– Closed 20 December-1 January   AZ**c**
5 rm ⌐ – ♥£59/69 ♥♥£110
♦ Late 19C house in quiet tree-lined avenue. Personally run; interestingly "cluttered" interior. Comfy conservatory sitting room. Well-judged bedrooms with thoughtful touches.

↑ **The Old Rectory** without rest   🔲 ⌘ **P**
148 Malone Rd ⊠ *BT9 5LH* – ℰ *(028) 9066 7882 – www.anoldrectory.co.uk*
– info@anoldrectory.co.uk – Fax (028) 9068 3759
– Closed Christmas-New Year and 1 week Easter   AZ**e**
7 rm ⌐ – ♥£40/50 ♥♥£79
♦ Former 19C rectory in residential area; period charm retained. Attractive drawing room. Traditionally furnished rooms. Super breakfasts: speciality sausages, organic produce.

↑ **Roseleigh House** without rest   ⌘ 📶 **P** _VISA_ ⚫⚫
19 Rosetta Park, South : 1½ m. by A 24 (Ormeau Rd) ⊠ *BT6 0DL* – ℰ *(028)*
9064 4414 – www.roseleighhouse.co.uk – info@roseleighhouse.co.uk
– Closed Christmas and New Year   AZ**r**
9 rm ⌐ – ♥£45/50 ♥♥£65
♦ Imposing Victorian house close to the Belvoir Park golf course and in a fairly quiet residential suburb. Brightly decorated and well-kept bedrooms with modern amenities.

✕✕ **Deanes**   🅰️🅲 _VISA_ ⚫⚫ 🅰🅴
✧ *34-40 Howard St* ⊠ *BT1 6PF* – ℰ *(028) 9033 1134 – www.michaeldeane.co.uk*
– info@michaeldeane.co.uk – Fax (028) 9056 0001
– Closed 25-26 December, Bank Holidays and Sunday   BY**n**
Rest – Menu £22 (lunch) – Carte £33/48 🌢
Spec. Scallops with pickled carrot and orange salad. Rabbit with smoked bacon, cèpes, macaroni gratin and salsify. Custard cake with blueberry jelly.
♦ Refurbished ground floor restaurant with bar and lounge. Polished service by approachable team. Menu of refined, classically based modern Irish dishes; lunch is a simpler affair.

✕✕ **Roscoff Brasserie**   🅰️🅲 _VISA_ ⚫⚫ 🅰🅴
7-11 Linenhall St ⊠ *BT2 8AA* – ℰ *(028) 9031 1150 – www.rankingroup.co.uk*
– Fax (028) 9031 1151
– Closed 25-26 December, 1 January and Sunday dinner   BY**r**
Rest – Menu £20 (weekdays)/25 – Carte dinner £26/40
♦ Not your typical brasserie - more formal and a little quieter than most, but stylish and modern. Confidently prepared modish cooking with classic base. Good value lunches.

✕✕ **James Street South**   🅰️🅲 ⌘ _VISA_ ⚫⚫ 🅰🅴
21 James Street South ⊠ *BT2 7GA* – ℰ *(028) 9043 4310*
– www.jamesstreetsouth.co.uk – info@jamesstreetsouth.co.uk – Fax (028)
9043 4310 – Closed 1 January, 12 July, 25-26 December and Sunday lunch   BY**o**
Rest – Menu £17 (lunch) – Carte £26/45
♦ Tucked away down back alley in heart of the city. 19C façade hides distinctly modish interior. Good value menus; modern cooking based upon well-sourced, fine quality produce.

✕✕ **Cayenne**   🅰️🅲 ⌘ ⇄ _VISA_ ⚫⚫ 🅰🅴 ⓪
☺ *7 Ascot House, Shaftesbury Sq* ⊠ *BT2 7DB* – ℰ *(028) 9033 1532*
– www.rankingroup.co.uk – reservations@cayennerestaurant.com – Fax (028)
9026 1575 – Closed 25-26 December, 1 January and Monday lunch   BZ**r**
Rest – (booking essential) Menu £20 (dinner) – Carte £15/38
♦ Striking modern artwork and a lively atmosphere feature in this busy, relaxed and stylish restaurant. Carefully prepared selection of creative Asian influenced dishes.

XX **Shu**   AC ⇔ VISA ◉◎ AE
253 Lisburn Rd ⊠ BT9 7EN – ℰ (028) 9038 1655 – www.shu-restaurant.com
– eat@shu-restaurant.com – Fax (028) 9068 1632
– Closed 1 January, 11-13 July, 24-26 December and Sunday   AZz
Rest – Menu £ 15/26 – Carte £ 23/35
♦ Trendy, modern restaurant on the Lisburn Road. Converted from terraced houses,
it is spacious and uncluttered with neutral and black décor. Eclectic, contemporary
dishes.

XX **Aldens**   AC VISA ◉◎ AE ◐
229 Upper Newtownards Rd, East : 2 m. on A 20 ⊠ BT4 3JF – ℰ (028) 9065 0079
– www.aldensrestaurant.com – info@aldensrestaurant.com – Fax (028) 9065 0032
– Closed Sunday dinner and Bank Holidays
Rest – (booking essential) Menu £ 22 – Carte £ 24/30
♦ Well established, spacious and contemporary restaurant in "up-and-coming" area.
Extensive menus of classic and modern dishes. Moderately priced midweek menu,
friendly service.

XX **The Wok**   AC VISA ◉◎
126 Great Victoria St ⊠ BT2 7BG – ℰ (028) 9023 3828
– Closed 25-26 December and lunch Saturday-Sunday   BZa
Rest – Chinese – Menu £ 19/23 – Carte £ 13/26
♦ Smart, modern Chinese restaurant with pleasant ambience. Menus feature classic
interpretations and less well-known authentic dishes: most regions of China are
represented.

X **Nick's Warehouse**   AC VISA ◉◎ AE ◐
35-39 Hill St ⊠ BT1 2LB – ℰ (028) 9043 9690 – www.nickswarehouse.co.uk
– info@nickswarehouse.co.uk – Fax (028) 9023 0514
– Closed 1 January, 12 July, 25-26 December, Monday dinner and Sunday BXa
Rest – Carte £ 27/36
♦ Built in 1832 as a bonded whiskey store. On two floors, the ground floor Anix is
relaxed and buzzy. Upstairs more formal. Well informed service of an eclectic menu.

X **The Ginger Tree**   AC VISA ◉◎
23 Donegall Pass ⊠ BT7 1DQ – ℰ (028) 9032 7151 – www.ni.gingertree.co.uk
– Closed 12-13 July, 24-25 December and Sunday lunch   BZe
Rest – Japanese – Menu £ 10/15 – Carte £ 21/29
♦ Cosy Japanese eatery boasting distinctive black tables and chairs with red cushions. One wall highlighted by striking Japanese dress. Endearing service of authentic
dishes.

X **Ginger Bistro**   ⊛ VISA ◉◎ ◐
7-8 Hope St ⊠ BT12 5EE – ℰ (028) 9024 4421 – www.gingerbistro.com
– info@gingerbistro.com
– Closed 25, 26 and 31 December, Sunday and lunch Monday   BYZi
Rest – Carte £ 23/31
♦ Simple, intimate neighbourhood diner with chocolate ceiling and aluminium duct
pipes; modern art for sale. Local produce to fore on eclectic menus with distinct
global twists.

X **Molly's Yard**   ⊛ VISA ◉◎
1 College Green Mews, Botanic Ave ⊠ BT7 1LW – ℰ (028) 9032 2600
– www.mollysyard.com – mollys-yard@yahoo.co.uk
– Closed 11 July, 25-26 December and Sunday   BZs
Rest – (booking essential) Menu £ 27 (dinner) – Carte £ 20/27
♦ Converted stables and coach house with popular summer courtyard. Downstairs a
cosy bistro; upstairs a casual restaurant. Both serve fresh, earthy and robust seasonal
dishes.

NORTHERN IRELAND

❌ **Mourne Seafood Bar**   AC VISA ⓜ
34 Bank St ⊠ BT1 1HJ – ℰ (028) 9024 8544 – www.mourneseafood.com
– belfast@mourneseafood.com
– Closed 24-26 December and dinner Sunday and Monday   BY**c**
Rest – Seafood – (booking essential at dinner) Carte £ 18/24
◆ Classic seafood menu supplemented by daily specials; mussels are a speciality, served in black enamel pots. Gets very busy, so arrive early, or be prepared to wait.

at Belfast International Airport West : 15½ m. by A 52 - AY – ⊠ Belfast

🏨 **Park Plaza Belfast**   📶 ⅏ rm, AC ⑰ ⅍ P VISA ⓜ AE ⓞ
⊠ BT29 4ZY – ℰ (028) 9445 7000 – www.parkplazabelfast.com
– reception@parkplazabelfast.com – Fax (028) 9442 3500
106 rm – †£ 145 ††£ 165, � £ 12 – 2 suites
Rest *Circles* – (dinner only) (booking essential) Carte £ 20/30 **s**
◆ Imposingly up-to-date hotel with sun-filled lobby, 50 metres from terminal entrance. Terrace, secluded garden, cocktail bar; conference facilities. Distinctively modern rooms. Formal restaurant with smart, cosmopolitan ambience.

BELFAST INTERNATIONAL AIRPORT = Aerphort Béal Feirste – **Antrim**
– 712 N 4 – **see Belfast**

BELLEEK (Béal Leice) – **Fermanagh** – **712** H 4 ▌ *Ireland*   34 **A2**
🚗 Belfast 117 mi – Londonderry 56 mi
◉ Belleek Pottery **AC**

🏨 **Carlton**   📶 ⅏ rm, ⅍ ⑰ ⅍ P VISA ⓜ AE
Main St ⊠ BT93 2FX – ℰ (028) 6865 8282 – www.hotelcarlton.co.uk
– reception@hotelcarlton.co.uk – Fax (028) 6865 9005
34 rm ⊃ – †£ 48 ††£ 90   **Rest** – Menu £ 15 (lunch) – Carte £ 15/30
◆ Located in the heart of Ireland's Lake District, bordering the river Erne and ideal for fishing enthusiasts. Bedrooms are in soft pastel colours and most have river views. Classic styled daily menu in contemporary restaurant.

BUSHMILLS (Muileann na Buaise) – **Moyle** – **712** M 2 – ⊠ **Bushmills**   35 **C1**
▌ *Ireland*
🚗 Belfast 57 mi – Ballycastle 12 mi – Coleraine 10 mi
📷 Bushfoot Portballintrae 50 Bushfoot Rd, ℰ (028) 2073 1317
◉ Giant's Causeway★★★ (Hamilton's Seat ≼★★) N : 2 m. by A 2 and minor road - Dunluce Castle★★ **AC** W : 3 m. by A 2 – Carrick-a-rede Rope Bridge★★★ **AC**, E : 8 m. by A 2 – Magilligan Strand★★, W : 18 m. by A 2, A 29 and A 2 - Gortmore Viewpoint★★, SW : 23 m. by A 2, A 29, A 23 and minor road from Downhill – Downhill★ (Mussenden Temple★), W : 15 m. by A 2, A 29 and A 2

🏨 **Bushmills Inn**   ⅍ ⑰ ⅍ P VISA ⓜ AE
9 Dunluce Rd ⊠ BT57 8QG – ℰ (028) 2073 3000 – www.bushmillsinn.com
– mail@bushmillsinn.com – Fax (028) 2073 2048 – Closed 24-26 December
32 rm ⊃ – †£ 98/118 ††£ 148/268
Rest *The Restaurant* – (carvery lunch Sunday) Carte £ 20/47
◆ Very characterful part 18C inn near famous whiskey distillery. Period features include turf fires, oil lamps, grand staircase and circular library. Rooms in house and mill. Try Irish coffee with Bushmills in restaurant overlooking courtyard.

🍴 **The Distillers Arms**   P VISA ⓜ
140 Main St ⊠ BT57 8QE – ℰ (028) 2073 1044 – www.distillersarms.com
– simon@distillersarms.com – Fax (028) 2073 2843
Rest – (Closed 25-26 December, Mondays and Tuesdays in winter)
Carte £ 20/25
◆ Modern rusticity in village centre. Sit in squashy sofas in peat fired sitting area. Eat tasty dishes from frequently changing menus with a seasonal Irish base.

CARRICKFERGUS (Carraig Fhearghais) – Carrickfergus – 712 O 3   35 D2

▣ Ireland

▸ Belfast 11 mi – Ballymena 25 mi
🛈 Heritage Plaza, Antrim Street ✆ (028) 9335 8049 (April-September), touristinfo@carrickfergus.org
🖼 35 North Rd, ✆ (028) 9336 3713
◎ Castle★ **AC** - St Nicholas' Church★ **AC**

Clarion   📶 🕭 rm, 🄺 rest, 🛠 🎧 ⑁ 🅿 🚾 ⑩ 🕮 ⓞ

75 Belfast Rd, on A 2 ⊠ BT38 8PH – ✆ (028) 9336 4556
– www.clarioncarrick.com – reservations1@clarioncarrick.com – Fax (028)
9335 1620 – Closed 24-25 December
68 rm � – ✝£110 ✝✝£130 – 2 suites
Rest *Red Pepper* – (Closed Sunday) (dinner only) Carte £ 20/33
♦ A large, purpose-built hotel with trim, neatly furnished bedrooms; some suites have jacuzzis and views of Belfast Lough; the Scottish coastline can be seen on a clear day. Expect modern French 'prestige' and à la carte menu.

CASTLEDAWSON – Magherafelt – 712 M 3   35 C2

▸ Belfast 34 mi – Antrim 17 mi – Ballymena 23 mi

XX   The Inn at Castledawson with rm   ⬮ 🕭 rm, 🅿 🚾 ⑩

47 Main St ⊠ BT45 8AA – ✆ (028) 7946 9777
– www.theinnatcastledawson.co.uk – info@theinnatcastledawson.co.uk
– Fax (028) 7946 9888 – Closed 25-26 December
12 rm ⊆ – ✝£59 ✝✝£79   **Rest** – Carte £ 16/25
♦ Stylishly updated restaurant, with pine rafters, in 200 year-old inn. Accomplished cooking blends classic and modern styles with finesse. Sleek rooms; fine views from rear.

CASTLEWELLAN – Down – 712 O 5 – pop. 2 392 ▣ Ireland   35 D3

▸ Belfast 32 mi – Downpatrick 12 mi – Newcastle 4 mi
◎ Castlewellan Forest Park★★ **AC**
◱ Mourne Mountains★★ (Silent Valley Reservoir★), SW : 15 m. by A 50, B 180 and B 27 – Dundrum Castle★ **AC** E : 6 m. by A 50 and A 180

Slieve Croob Inn 🌄   ≤ 🚗 ⑁ 🛠 ⑁ 🅿 🚾 ⑩ 🕮

119 Clanvaraghan Rd, North : 5½ m. by A 25 off B 175 ⊠ BT31 9LA – ✆ (028)
4377 1412 – www.slievecroobinn.com – info@slievecroobinn.com
– Fax (028) 4377 1162
7 rm ⊆ – ✝£60 ✝✝£75   **Rest** – Carte £ 17/25 s
♦ Pleasant inn in stunningly attractive mountainous area with panoramic sea views. Modern, rustic style. Bedooms with simple comforts. Peace and quiet aplenty. Roof timbers and fine views in open, buzzy dining room: same menu also in bar.

COLERAINE (Cúil Raithin) – Coleraine – 712 L 2 – pop. 24 089 ▣ Ireland   35 C1

▸ Belfast 53 mi – Ballymena 25 mi – Londonderry 31 mi – Omagh 65 mi
🛈 Railway Rd ✆ (028) 7034 4723, info@northcoastni.com
🖼 Castlerock 65 Circular Rd, ✆ (028) 7084 8314
🖼 Brown Trout 209 Agivey Rd, Aghadowey, ✆ (028) 7086 8209
◱ Giant's Causeway★★★ (Hamilton's Seat ≤★★), NE : 14 m. by A 29 and A2 - Dunluce Castle★★ **AC**, NE : 8 m. by A 29 and A 2 – Carrick-a-rede-Rope Bridge★★★ **AC**, NE : 18 m. by A 29 and A 2 – Benvarden★ **AC** E : 5 m. by B 67 – Magilligan Strand★★, NW : 8 m. by A 2 - Gortmore Viewpoint★★, NW : 12 m. by A 2 and minor road from Downhill - Downhill★ **AC** (Mussenden Temple★), NE : 7 m. by A 2

Bushtown House   🚗 🖳 🌀 𝄞 🛠 🎧 ⑁ 🅿 🚾 ⑩

283 Drumcroone Rd, South : 2½ m. on A 29 ⊠ BT51 3QT – ✆ (028) 7035 8367
– www.bushtownhotel.com – reception@bushtownhotel.com
– Fax (028) 7032 0909
39 rm ⊆ – ✝£70 ✝✝£100   **Rest** – (Carvery lunch) Carte £ 16/22 s
♦ Set in mature gardens on outskirts of university town. Indoors, comfortable and homely with various rooms to relax in. Traditional, co-ordinated bedrooms in muted colours. Intimately lit, cosy restaurant with wide variety of simple menus.

NORTHERN IRELAND

Brown Trout Golf and Country Inn 🕪 🥢 ⅙ 🖻 ⅙ rm, ⑪
209 Agivey Rd, Aghadowey, 🕰 **P** **VISA** **◍◍** **AE** **①**
Southeast : 9 m. on A 54 ⊠ *BT51 4AD –* ℰ *(028) 7086 8209*
– www.browntroutinn.com – bill@browntroutinn.com – Fax (028) 7086 8878
15 rm � – ☗£60/70 ☗☗£80/110   **Rest** – Carte £18/25
♦ A farm and blacksmith's forge was here in 1600s; now an inn well set up for those
with an active disposition - fishing, golf, shooting are on hand. Simple rooms in
annexe. Traditionally styled restaurant offers fresh home-cooked meals.

Greenhill House without rest ⅔ 🚗 🕪 ⅗ ⑪ **P** **VISA** **◍◍** **AE**
24 Greenhill Rd, Aghadowey, South : 9 m. by A 29 on B 66 ⊠ *BT51 4EU*
– ℰ *(028) 7086 8241 – www.greenhill-house.co.uk – info@greenhill-house.co.uk*
– Fax (028) 7086 8365 – March-October
6 rm ⊑ – ☗£40 ☗☗£60
♦ An agreeably clean-lined Georgian house with large windows overlooking fields.
Game and course fishing available locally. Neat bedrooms replete with extra touches.

COMBER – Ards – 712 O 4   35 D2
🚊 Belfast 10 mi – Newtownards 5 mi – Lisburn 17 mi

Anna's House without rest ⅔ ≤ 🚗 🕪 ⅙ ⅗ ⑪ **P** **VISA** **◍◍**
Tullynagee, 35 Lisbarnett Rd, Southeast : 3½ m. by A 22 ⊠ *BT23 6AW –* ℰ *(028)*
9754 1566 – www.annashouse.com – anna@annashouse.com – Closed
Christmas-New Year
4 rm ⊑ – ☗£50/60 ☗☗£80/95
♦ Farmhouse with cosy lounge and comfy bedrooms with lovely vistas. Glass-walled
extension has geo-thermal heating and lake views. Organic breakfasts utilise produce
from garden.

CRUMLIN (Cromghlinn) – Antrim – 712 N 4 – pop. 4 259   35 C2
🚊 Belfast 14 mi – Ballymena 20 mi

Caldhame Lodge without rest 🚗 ⅙ ⅗ ⑪ **P** **VISA** **◍◍**
102 Moira Rd, Nutts Corner, Southeast : 1¼ m. on A 26 ⊠ *BT29 4HG –* ℰ *(028)*
9442 3099 – www.caldhamelodge.co.uk – info@caldhamelodge.co.uk
– Fax (028) 9442 3313
8 rm ⊑ – ☗£40/50 ☗☗£60/80
♦ Spic and span, with thoroughly polished, wood furnished hall, complete with
grandfather clock. Immaculate, co-ordinated, individualistic rooms; bridal suite with
whirlpool.

DONAGHADEE (Domhnach Daoi) – Ards – 712 P 4 ▮ *Ireland*   35 D2
🚊 Belfast 18 mi – Ballymena 44 mi
🏬 Warren Rd, ℰ (028) 9188 3624
🄶 Ballycopeland Windmill★ **AC** S : 4 m. by A 2 and B 172. Mount
Stewart★★★ **AC**, SW : 10 m. by A 2 and minor road SW – Movilla (cross
slabs★), Newtownards, SW : 7 m. by B 172

Grace Neill's 🍴 **P** **VISA** **◍◍** **AE**
33 High St ⊠ *BT21 0AH –* ℰ *(028) 9188 4595 – www.graceneills.com*
– info@graceneills.com – Fax (028) 9188 9631 – Closed 25 December
Rest – Carte £14/26
♦ Reputedly Ireland's oldest pub; dates from 1611. Thoroughly traditional bar; contemporary restaurant. Modern dishes full of freshness. Good value early evening
meals for two.

Pier 36 with rm 🍴 ⅗ **P** **VISA** **◍◍** **AE**
36 The Parade ⊠ *BT21 0HE –* ℰ *(028) 9188 4466 – www.pier36.co.uk*
– info@pier36.co.uk – Fax (028) 9188 4636
5 rm ⊑ – ☗£50 ☗☗£70/90   **Rest** – Carte £20/35
♦ Personally run spacious pub by the harbour. Appealing rustic feel with stone
flooring, curios and wood panelling. Extensive menus with an global range. Modern,
comfy bedrooms.

DOWNPATRICK (Dún Pádraig) – Down – 712 O 4/5 🏛 *Ireland*   35 **D3**

- 🔼 Belfast 23 mi – Newry 31 mi – Newtownards 22 mi
- ◎ Cathedral★ **AC** - Down County Museum★ **AC**
- ⊙ Struell Wells★ **AC**, SE : 2 m. by B 1 - Ardglass★ (Jordan's Castle **AC**),
  SE : 7 m. by B 1 - Inch Abbey★ **AC**, NW : 2 m. by A 7 – Quoile Countryside
  Centre★ **AC**, E : 2 m. by A 25 – Castle Ward★★ **AC** (Audley's Castle★),
  E : 8 m. by A 25

Pheasants' Hill Farm *without rest*   🛋 🐾 ♨ 🅿 VISA ◎◎

37 Killyleagh Rd, North : 3 m. on A 22 ⊠ BT30 9BL – ℰ (028) 4461 7246
– www.pheasantshill.com – info@pheasantshill.com – Fax (028) 4461 7246
– Closed 1 December-4 January

3 rm ⌂ – †£50 ††£75

♦ Purpose-built house surrounded by an organic smallholding with livestock which provides many ingredients for hearty breakfasts. Homely, pine furnished bedrooms.

DUNDRUM – Down – 712 O 5 🏛 *Ireland*   35 **D3**

- 🔼 Belfast 29 mi – Downpatrick 9 mi – Newcastle 4 mi
- ◎ Castle★ **AC**
- ⊙ Castlewellan Forest Park★★ **AC**, W : 4 m. by B 180 and A 50 - Tollymore
  Forest Park★ **AC**, W : 3 m. by B 180 - Drumena Cashel and Souterrain★, W :
  4 m. by B 180

The Carriage House *without rest*   🛋 ♨ ⁋ 🅿

71 Main St ⊠ BT33 0LU – ℰ (028) 4375 1635
– www.carriagehousedundrum.com – inbox@carriagehousedundrum.com

3 rm ⌂ – †£40/50 ††£70

♦ Charming owner runs super, comfy guesthouse: lilac exterior, very well-appointed guest areas. Breakfast sources local organic ingredients. Warm bedrooms with personal touches.

Buck's Head Inn   🛋 ♨ ♨ VISA ◎◎ AE

77-79 Main St ⊠ BT33 0LU – ℰ (028) 4375 1868
– www.thebucksheaddundrum.co.uk – buckshead1@aol.com – Fax (028)
4481 1033 – Closed 24-25 December and Monday October-April

Rest – Seafood – Carte £ 20/29

♦ Traditional high street bar. Interesting, well-cooked dishes with strong seafood base served in conservatory or cosy front room. Early evening high tea popular with walkers.

Mourne Seafood Bar   🛋 VISA ◎◎ AE ◎

10 Main St ⊠ BT33 0LU – ℰ (028) 4375 1377 – www.mourneseafood.com
– bob@mourneseafood.com – Fax (028) 4375 1161 – Closed Thursday to Sunday
in winter

Rest – Seafood – (booking essential in summer) Carte £ 19/30

♦ Simple, casual seafood pub featuring the day's local catch. Tasty, out-of-ordinary menus based on fish with healthy stocks, rather than threatened species. Reasonably priced.

DUNGANNON (Dún Geanainn) – Dungannon – 712 L 4 🏛 *Ireland*   35 **C2**

- 🔼 Belfast 42 mi – Ballymena 37 mi – Dundalk 47 mi – Londonderry 60 mi
- ⊙ The Argory★, S : 5 m. by A 29 and east by minor rd. Ardboe Cross★, NW :
  17 m. by A 45, B 161 and B 73 – Springhill★ **AC**, NE : 24 m. by A 29 –
  Sperrin Mountains★ : Wellbrook Beetling Mill★ **AC**, NW : 22 m. by A 29
  and A 505 - Beaghmore Stone Circles★, NW : 24 m. by A 29 and A 505

Grange Lodge ☜   🛋 ♨ ⁋ 🅿 VISA ◎◎

7 Grange Rd, Moy, Southeast : 3½ m. by A 29 ⊠ BT71 7EJ – ℰ (028) 8778 4212
– www.grangelodgecountryhouse.com – stay@grangelodgecountryhouse.com
– Fax (028) 8778 4313 – Closed 20 December-1 February

5 rm ⌂ – †£60/69 ††£85/89   **Rest** – (by arrangement) Carte £ 32/39

♦ Attractive Georgian country house surrounded by well-kept mature gardens with a peaceful ambience. Fine hospitality and period furnishings. Tastefully decorated bedrooms. Large dining room furnished with elegant antiques and fine tableware.

ENNISKILLEN (Inis Ceithleann) – **Fermanagh** – **712** J 4 – **pop. 13 599**　　34 **A2**

 Ireland

- ▶ Belfast 87 mi – Londonderry 59 mi
- 🖪 Wellington Rd ℰ (028) 6632 3110, tic@fermanagh.gov.uk
- 🖪 Castlecoole, ℰ (028) 6632 5250
- 🖪 Castle Coole★★★ **AC**, SE : 1 m – Florence Court★★ **AC**, SW : 8 m. by A 4 and A 32 – Marble Arch Caves and Forest Nature Reserve★ **AC**, SW : 10 m. by A 4 and A 32. NW by A 26 : Lough Erne★★ : Cliffs of Magho Viewpoint★★★ **AC**- Tully Castle★ **AC** – N by A 32, B 72, A 35 and A 47 : Devenish Island★ **AC** - Castle Archdale Forest Park★ **AC** - White Island★ - Janus Figure★

　Manor House ⊗　

Killadeas, North : 7½ m. by A 32 on B 82 ⊠ BT94 1NY – ℰ (028) 6862 2200
– www.manor-house-hotel.com – info@manor-house-hotel.com
– Fax (028) 6862 1545
81 rm ⊡ – ♚£105 ♚♚£130/155　　**Rest** – Menu £18/28

♦ In a commanding position overlooking Lough Erne. Noted for fine Italian plaster-work evident in guest areas. Relaxing conservatory lounge. Spacious, comfortable bedrooms. Classically appointed dining room featuring chandeliers and ornate plas-terwork.

🏠　**Cedars**　　　　　　　　　　　　　　　　　　　　　　　

North : 10 m. by A 32 on B 82 ⊠ BT94 1PG – ℰ (028) 6862 1493
– www.cedarsguesthouse.com – info@cedarsguesthouse.com – Fax (028)
6862 8335 – Closed Christmas
10 rm ⊡ – ♚£40/75 ♚♚£90/100

Rest *Rectory Bistro* – (closed Monday-Tuesday in winter) (dinner only and Sunday lunch) Carte £22/31

♦ Good value, converted 19C former rectory with pleasant gardens. Exudes impres-sion of spaciousness; country style décor. Individually styled bedrooms: ask for num-bers 2 or 5. Country style bistro serves hearty cuisine.

GALGORM Antrim – 712 N 3 – see Ballymena

HILLSBOROUGH (Cromghlinn) – **Lisburn** – **712** N 4 *Ireland*　　35 **C2**

- ▶ Belfast 12 mi
- 🖪 TThe Courthouse, he Square ℰ (028) 9268 9717, tic.hillsborough@lisburn.gov.uk
- ◻ Town★ – Fort★
- 🖪 Rowallane Gardens★ **AC**, Saintfield, E : 10 m. by B 178 and B 6. The Argory★, W : 25 m. by A 1 and M 1

🍺　**The Plough Inn**　　　　　　　　　　　　　　　　

3 The Square ⊠ BT26 6AG – ℰ (028) 9268 2985 – www.barretro.com
– pattersonderek@hotmail.co.uk – Fax (028) 9268 2472
Rest – Carte £18/30
Rest *Bar Retro* – Carte £18/30

♦ Well-established, family run inn. The traditional bar is popular with older diners; youngsters tend to head upstairs to the trendy bistro, while families tend towards the café. A mix of traditional and more modern dishes come in generous portions.

at Annahilt Southeast : 4 m. on B 177 – ⊠ Hillsborough

🏠　**Fortwilliam** without rest　　　　　　　　　　　　

210 Ballynahinch Rd, Northwest : ¼ m. on B 177 ⊠ BT26 6BH – ℰ (028)
9268 2255 – www.fortwilliamcountryhouse.com
– info@fortwilliamcountryhouse.com – Fax (028) 9268 9608
4 rm ⊡ – ♚£50 ♚♚£70

♦ Large house on a working farm with attractive gardens. Charming hospitality amidst traditional farmhouse surroundings. Characterful bedrooms with a range of extras.

NORTHERN IRELAND

🏠 The Pheasant 🟥 🛜 **P** _VISA_ ⓒⓔ **AE** ⓞ
410 Upper Ballynahinch Rd, North : 1 m. on Lisburn rd ⊠ BT26 6NR – ℰ (028)
9263 8056 – www.barretro.com/pheasant – pheasantinn@aol.com – Fax (028)
9263 8026 – Closed 25-26 December and 12-13 July
Rest – Menu £ 15 (lunch) – Carte £ 15/30
♦ Modern rustic feel with peat fires and wood floors. Extensive menu offers hearty portions of classic country dishes. Live music on Fridays. A local favourite.

HOLYWOOD (Ard Mhic Nasca) – **North Down** – 712 O 4 – **pop. 12 037**   35 **D2**

📗 Ireland

> 🔁 Belfast 7 mi – Bangor 6 mi
> 🔁 Holywood Demesne Rd, Nuns Walk, ℰ (028) 9042 2138
> 🔁 Cultra : Ulster Folk and Transport Museum★★ **AC**, NE : 1 m. by A 2

🏨 Culluden ≤ 🛜 🅿 🗋 ⊕ 🎁 🎐 📶 rest, 🌾 🎙️ 🔥 **P** _VISA_ ⓒⓔ **AE** ⓞ
142 Bangor Rd, East : 1½ m. on A 2 ⊠ BT18 0EX – ℰ (028) 9042 1066
– www.hastingshotels.com – res@cull.hastingshotel.com – Fax (028) 9042 6777
102 rm – †£ 190/215 ††£ 240/390 – 3 suites
Rest Mitre – (dinner only) Menu £ 40
Rest Cultra Inn – Carte £ 24/28
♦ Part Victorian Gothic manor, originally built as an official residence for the Bishops of Down. Top class comfort amid characterful interiors. Smart, comfortable bedrooms. The Mitre has a smart and well-kept air. Timbered, flagged Cultra Inn.

🏠 Rayanne House ≤ 🛜 🚻 🌾 🎙️ **P** _VISA_ ⓒⓔ
60 Demesne Rd, by My Lady's Mile Rd ⊠ BT18 9EX – ℰ (028) 9042 5859
– www.rayannehouse.com – rayannehouse@hotmail.com – Fax (028) 9042 5859
11 rm ⌧ – †£ 80/95 ††£ 110
Rest – (booking essential) (by arrangement only) Menu £ 35/48
♦ Redbrick house with attractive views of town. Very personally run with smart, alluring interiors. Individually styled rooms feature hand-painted murals and personal trinkets. Warm, attentive service and fine choice menu.

🏠 Beech Hill without rest 🍃 ≤ 🛜 🎙️ **P** _VISA_ ⓒⓔ **AE**
23 Ballymoney Rd, Craigantlet, Southeast : 4½ m. by A 2 on Craigantlet rd
⊠ BT23 4TG – ℰ (028) 9042 5892 – www.beech-hill.net – info@beech-hill.net
– Fax (028) 9042 5892
3 rm ⌧ – †£ 55/65 ††£ 45/50
♦ Country house in rural location. Pleasant clutter of trinkets and antiques in guest areas which include a conservatory. Neat, traditionally styled bedrooms: a very fine home.

🍴 Fontana _VISA_ ⓒⓔ
61A High St ⊠ BT18 9AE – ℰ (028) 9080 9908
– fontanarestaurant@btinternet.com – Closed 25-27 December, 1-2 January,
Monday, Sunday dinner and Saturday lunch
Rest – (Sunday brunch) (booking essential) Menu £ 15/18 – Carte £ 22/32
♦ Modish dining room. Friendly staff. Tasty, unfussy, modern Irish food with refreshing Californian and Mediterranean influences. Choose between main or 'mini' good value menus.

KIRCUBBIN (Cill Ghobáin) – **Ards** – 712 P 4   35 **D2**

> 🔁 Belfast 20 mi – Donaghadee 12 mi – Newtownards 10 mi

🍴🍴 Paul Arthurs with rm 🛜 _VISA_ ⓒⓔ ⓞ
66 Main St ⊠ BT22 2SP – ℰ (028) 4273 8192 – www.paularthurs.com
– info@paularthurs.com – Closed January, Christmas, Sunday dinner and Monday
7 rm ⌧ – †£ 60 ††£ 80   **Rest** – (dinner only and Sunday lunch)
Carte £ 24/37
♦ Distinctive salmon/coral façade. Cosy ground floor lounge. Upstairs dining room flaunts modern Belfast art. Confident, unfussy menus exude bold, classic flavours. Comfy rooms.

NORTHERN IRELAND

LARNE (Latharna) – **Larne** – 712 O 3 – **pop. 18 228** 🗋 *Ireland*   35 **D2**

- ◗ Belfast 23 mi – Ballymena 20 mi
- ⛴ to Fleetwood (Stena Line) daily (8 h) – to Cairnryan (P & O Irish Sea) 3-5 daily (1 h/2 h 15 mn)
- 🄩 Narrow Gauge Rd ℰ (028) 2826 0088, larnetourism@btconnect.com
- 🖫 Cairndhu Ballygally 192 Coast Rd, ℰ (028) 2858 3954
- 🄶 SE : Island Magee (Ballylumford Dolmen★), by ferry and 2 m. by B 90 or 18 m. by A 2 and B 90. NW : Antrim Glens★★★ - Murlough Bay★★★ (Fair Head ≤★★★), N : 46 m by A 2 and minor road – Glenariff Forest Park★★ **AC** (Waterfall★★), N : 30 m. by A 2 and A 43 - Glenariff★, N : 25 m. by A 2 - Glendun★, N : 30 m. by A 2 – Carrickfergus (Castle★★ - St Nicholas' Church★), SW : 15 m. by A 2

⛫ **Manor House** without rest   🖭 🎎 **P** **VISA** **MO**
23 Olderfleet Rd, Harbour Highway ✉ *BT40 1AS* – ℰ *(028) 2827 3305*
– www.themanorguesthouse.com – welcome@themanorguesthouse.com
– Fax (028) 2826 0505 – Closed 25-26 December
8 rm 🍽 – ♦£30/35 ♦♦£55/60
♦ Spacious Victorian terraced house two minutes from ferry terminal. Well-furnished lounge with beautifully varnished wood floors. Small breakfast room. Cosy, homely bedrooms.

Your opinions are important to us:
please write and let us know about your discoveries and experiences – good and bad!

LIMAVADY (Léim an Mhadaidh) – **Limavady** – 712 L 2 🗋 *Ireland*   34 **B1**

- ◗ Belfast 62 mi – Ballymena 39 mi – Coleraine 13 mi – Londonderry 17 mi – Omagh 50 mi
- 🄩 Council Offices, 7 Connell St ℰ (028) 7776 0307, tourism@limavady.gov.uk
- 🖫 Benone Par Three Benone 53 Benone Ave, ℰ (028) 7775 0555
- 🄶 Sperrin Mountains★ : Roe Valley Country Park★ **AC**, S : 2 m. by B 68 - Glenshane Pass★, S : 15 m. by B 68 and A 6

 Radisson SAS Roe Park H. & Golf Resort ⛳ 🏌 🖫 🛗 🐾 rm, 🏃 **AC** rest, 🖭 🎎 🛎 **P** **VISA** **MO** **AE** **①**
Roe Park, West : ½ m. on A 2 ✉ *BT49 9LB* – ℰ *(028) 7772 2222*
– www.radissonroepark.com – limavady.reservations@radissonsas.com
– Fax (028) 7772 2313
117 rm 🍽 – ♦£125 ♦♦£160/200 – 1 suite
Rest *Greens* – (Closed Sunday dinner and Monday) (dinner only and Sunday lunch) Carte £20/33
Rest *The Coach House* – Carte £15/30
♦ A golfer's idyll with academy and driving range in the grounds of Roe Park. Good leisure centre. Spacious modern bedrooms. Complimentary broadband. Greens is formal in character with menu to match. Brasserie Coach House with open fire and all day service.

✕ **Lime Tree**   **VISA** **MO** **AE**
60 Catherine St ✉ *BT49 9DB* – ℰ *(028) 7776 4300* – *www.limetreerest.com*
– info@limetreerest.com – Closed third week July, 25-26 December, Sunday and Monday
Rest – (dinner only) Carte £24/37
♦ Well regarded, contemporary neighbourhood restaurant, personally run by friendly husband and wife team. Seasonal produce often includes seafood and a Mediterranean influence.

LONDONDERRY/DERRY (Doire) – Derry – 712 K 2/3 – pop. 83 699 34 B1

Ireland

Belfast 70 mi – Dublin 146 mi
City of Derry Airport : (028) 7181 0784, E : 6 m. by A 2
44 Foyle St (028) 7126 7284, info@derryvisitor.com
City of Derry 49 Victoria Rd, (028) 7134 6369
Town★ - City Walls and Gates★★ – Guildhall★ **AC** – Long Tower Church★ – St Columb's Cathedral★ **AC** – Tower Museum★ **AC**
Grianan of Aileach★★ (≤★★) (Republic of Ireland) NW : 5 m. by A 2 and N 13. Ulster-American Folk Park★★, S : 33 m. by A 5 - Ulster History Park★ **AC**, S : 32 m. by A 5 and minor road – Sperrin Mountains★ : Glenshane Pass★ (≤★★), SE : 24 m. by A 6 - Sawel Mountain Drive★ (≤★★), S : 22 m. by A 5 and minor roads via Park – Roe Valley Country Park★ **AC**, E : 15 m. by A 2 and B 68 – Beaghmore Stone Circles★, S : 52 m. by A 5, A 505 and minor road

City
rm, AC rest, P VISA MC AE

Queens Quay BT48 7AS – (028) 7136 5800 – www.cityhotelderry.com – reservations@cityhotelderry.com – Fax (028) 7136 5801 – Closed 25-26 December
144 rm – £ 150 £ 150 – 1 suite
Rest *Thompson's on the River* – (bar lunch Monday-Saturday) Menu £ 20 **s** – Carte £ 22/27 **s**

◆ Hotel in purpose-built modern style. Well located, close to the city centre and the quay. Smart rooms ordered for the business traveller. Useful conference facilities. Modern restaurant overlooks water.

Beech Hill Country House
rm, P VISA MC AE

32 Ardmore Rd, Southeast : 3½ m. by A 6 BT47 3QP – (028) 7134 9279 – www.beech-hill.com – info@beech-hill.com – Fax (028) 7134 5366 – Closed 24-25 December
25 rm – £ 100 £ 120 – 2 suites
Rest *The Ardmore* – Menu £ 20/33 **s** – Carte £ 30/41 **s**

◆ 18C country house, now personally run but once a US marine camp; one lounge is filled with memorabilia. Accommodation varies from vast rooms to more traditional, rural ones. Restaurant housed within conservatory and old billiard room. Fine garden.

Ramada H. Da Vinci's
rm, AC rest, P VISA MC AE D

15 Culmore Rd, North : 1 m. following signs for Foyle Bridge BT48 8JB – (028) 7127 9111 – www.davincishotel.com – info@davincishotel.com – Fax (028) 7127 9222 – Closed 24-25 December
70 rm – £ 75/100 £ 75/100, £9.50
Rest *The Grill Room* – (dinner only and Sunday lunch) Menu £ 22 – Carte £ 18/28

◆ Modern purpose-built hotel at northern end of city's quayside close to major through routes. Stylish lobby area. Large, atmospheric bar. Good sized, well-equipped bedrooms. Spacious restaurant has an elegant ambience.

Mandarin Palace
AC VISA MC AE D

Lower Clarendon St BT48 7AW – (028) 7137 3656 – www.mandarinpalace.net – info@mandarinpalace.net – Fax (028) 7136 8924 – Closed 25-26 December and Saturday lunch
Rest – Chinese – Carte £ 20/26 **s**

◆ Oriental restaurant, with good views of Foyle river and bridge. Smart staff oversee the service of unfussy, well-executed Chinese cuisine, featuring good value set menus.

MAGHERA (Machaire Rátha) – Magherafelt – 712 L 3 35 C2

Belfast 40 mi – Ballymena 19 mi – Coleraine 21 mi – Londonderry 32 mi

Ardtara Country House
rm, P VISA MC AE

8 Gorteade Rd, Upperlands, North : 3¼ m. by A 29 off B 75 BT46 5SA – (028) 7964 4490 – www.ardtara.com – Fax (028) 7964 5080
9 rm – £ 85/90 £ 130/150
Rest – (booking essential for non-residents) (lunch by arrangement) Carte £ 20/30

◆ 19C house with a charming atmosphere. The interior features "objets trouvés" collected from owner's travels; original fireplaces set off the individually styled bedrooms. Restaurant set in former billiard room with hunting mural and panelled walls.

NEWCASTLE (An Caisleán Nua) – **Down** – 712 O 5 – **pop. 7 444** ⬛ *Ireland*   35 **D3**
> ▣ Belfast 32 mi – Londonderry 101 mi
> 🛈 10-14 Central Promenade ℰ (028) 4372 2222,
>   newcastle.tic@downdc.gov.uk
> ◎ Castlewellan Forest Park★★ **AC**, NW : 4 m. by A 50 – Tolymore Forest
>   Park★ **AC**, W : 3 m. by B 180 – Dundrum Castle★ **AC**, NE : 4 m. by A 2.
>   Silent Valley Reservoir★ (≤★) - Spelga Pass and Dam★ - Kilbroney
>   ForestPark (viewpoint★) – Annalong Marine Park and Cornmill★ **AC**, S :
>   8 m. by A 2 – Downpatrick : Cathedral★ **AC**, Down Country Museum★ **AC**,
>   NE : 20 m. by A 2 and A 25

🏨 **Slieve Donard**   ≤ 🚗 🖼 🕓 🏊 ⅙ 🖣 🖕 rm, 🍴 🎾 🅿 *VISA* 🐵 🃏 ①
Downs Rd ⋈ BT33 0AH – ℰ (028) 4372 1066 – www.hastingshotels.com
– gm@sdh.hastingshotels.com – Fax (028) 4372 1166
178 rm – ♦£ 140/180 ♦♦£ 160/200, ⊆ £ 16
Rest *Oak* – Menu £ 30/40
Rest *Percy French* – Carte £ 19/26
♦ Victorian grand old lady with sea views. Domed lobby with open fire. Highly
impressive spa and leisure. Chaplins bar named after Charlie, who stayed here. Modern rooms. Grand style dining in semi-panelled Oak. Percy French bar-restaurant has
easy-going menu.

🏨 **Burrendale H. & Country Club**   🚗 🖼 🕓 🏊 ⅙ 🖣 🖕 rm,
51 Castlewellan Rd, North : 1 m. on A 50   🆎 rest, 🎾 🎾 🅿 *VISA* 🐵 🃏 ①
⋈ BT33 0JY – ℰ (028) 4372 2599 – www.burrendale.com
– reservations@burrendale.com – Fax (028) 4372 2328
67 rm ⊆ – ♦£ 80 ♦♦£ 120 – 1 suite
Rest *Vine* – (dinner only and Sunday lunch) Carte £ 17/29 **s**
Rest *Cottage Kitchen* – Menu £ 15/20 **s** - Carte £ 17/24 **s**
♦ Set between the Mourne Mountains and Irish Sea, with the Royal Country Down
Golf Course nearby. Leisure oriented. Range of rooms from small to very spacious.
Linen-clad Vine for traditional dining. Homely cooking to the fore at Cottage Kitchen.

> If breakfast is included the ⊆ symbol appears after the number of rooms.

NEWTOWNARDS (Baile Nua na hArda) – **Ards** – 712 O 4   35 **D2**
> ▣ Belfast 10 mi – Bangor 144 mi – Downpatrick 22 mi

🏠 **Edenvale House** without rest ⌂   ≤ 🚗 🍴 🅿 *VISA* 🐵
130 Portaferry Rd, Southeast : 2 ¾ m. on A 20 ⋈ BT22 2AH – ℰ (028) 9181 4881
– www.edenvalehouse.com – info@edenvalehouse.com
– Closed 1 week Christmas
3 rm ⊆ – ♦£ 55/60 ♦♦£ 85/90
♦ Attractive Georgian house with fine views of the Mourne Mountains. Elegant sitting room. Communal breakfasts featuring home-made bread and jams. Individually
styled rooms.

PORTAFERRY (Port an Pheire) – **Ards** – 712 P 4 ⬛ *Ireland*   35 **D3**
> ▣ Belfast 29 mi – Bangor 24 mi
> 🛈 The Stables, Castle St ℰ (028) 4272 9882 (Easter-September),
>   tourism.portaferry@ards-council.gov.uk
> ◎ Exploris★ **AC**
> ◎ Castle Ward★★ **AC** (Audley's Castle★), W : 4 m. by ferry and A 25

🏨 **Portaferry**   ≤ 🎾 🍴 *VISA* 🐵 🃏
10 The Strand ⋈ BT22 1PE – ℰ (028) 4272 8231 – www.portaferryhotel.com
– info@portaferryhotel.com – Fax (028) 4272 8999 – Closed 24-25 December
14 rm ⊆ – ♦£ 40/55 ♦♦£ 40/55
Rest – (bar lunch Monday-Saturday) Menu £ 30 – Carte £ 24/32
♦ Formerly private dwellings, this hotel dates from 18C. Located on Strangford
Lough, most rooms have waterside views. Lounge features Irish paintings. Crisp and
fresh dining room with strong emphasis on local produce.

NORTHERN IRELAND

🚗 Belfast 58 mi – Coleraine 4 mi – Londonderry 35 mi
🛈 Sandhill Drive ℰ (028) 7082 3333 (March-October),
portrushtic@btconnect.com
🏌 Royal Portrush Dunluce Rd, ℰ (028) 7082 2311
🄶 Giant's Causeway ★★★ (Hamilton's Seat ≤ ★★, E: 9 m by A 2) - Carrick-
a-rede Rope Bridge ★★★, E: 14 m. by A 2 and B 15 - Dunluce Castle ★★ **AC**,
E: 3 m. by A 2 - Gortmore Viewpoint ★★, E: 14 m. by A 29, A 2 and minor
road - Magilligan Strand ★★, E: 13 m. by A 29 and A 2 - Downhill ★
(Mussenden Temple ★), E: 12 m. by A 29 and A 2

⌂ **Beulah** without rest   🛇 🄿 VISA ⓪ ①
16 Causeway St ⊠ BT56 8AB – ℰ (028) 7082 2413
– www.beulahguesthouse.com – stay@beulahguesthouse.com
10 rm ⊊ – †£30/60 ††£60/65
♦ Terraced Victorian house in perfect central location. Sound Irish breakfasts. Homely
guest lounge. Colourful, co-ordinated and immaculately kept modern bedrooms.

✗ **The Harbour Bistro**   VISA ⓪
6 Harbour St ⊠ BT56 8DF – ℰ (028) 7082 2430 – www.portrushharbour.co.uk
– Fax (028) 7082 3194 – Closed 24-26 December
Rest – (dinner only) (bookings not accepted) Carte £18/27
♦ Buzzy bistro in the old part of town near to popular beach. Modern décor. Wide
ranging menus providing generous servings. Expect to order and carry your own
drinks from bar.

– ⊠ **Ballyclare**

🚗 Belfast 13 mi – Ballymena 16 mi – Dundalk 65 mi – Larne 16 mi

---

🏨 **Templeton**   🖨 ⅋ rm, 🛇 ⌘ 🏊 🄿 VISA ⓪ AE ①
882 Antrim Rd ⊠ BT39 0AH – ℰ (028) 9443 2984 – www.templetonhotel.com
– reception@templetonhotel.com – Fax (028) 9443 3406 – Closed 25-26 December
24 rm ⊊ – †£75/97 ††£95/125
Rest *Raffles* – (closed Monday-Tuesday) (dinner only and Sunday lunch)
Menu £29 – Carte £23/35 **s**
Rest *Upton Grill* – Carte £13/30 **s**
♦ Large and distinctive pine "chalet" appearance. Inside, a swish atrium leads you to
a pillared lounge; bedrooms are warm and light. Very popular for weddings. Peaceful
library themed Raffles for fine dining. Buzzy Upton Grill with popular menu.

🚗 Belfast 44 mi – Newry 7 mi – Lisburn 37 mi

✗✗ **Copper**   AC VISA ⓪ AE
4 Duke St ⊠ BT34 3JY – ℰ (028) 4175 3047 – www.copperrestaurant.co.uk
*– info@copperrestaurant.co.uk – Closed 24-26 December, Tuesday lunch and
Monday*
Rest – Menu £16/24 – Carte £19/32
♦ Modish restaurant with an eye-catching blood red interior and high ceiling. Chatty,
attentive service. Interestingly balanced menus: classic repertoire with ambitious
touches.

✗ **Restaurant 23**   VISA ⓪ AE ①
☺ *23 Church St ⊠ BT34 3HN – ℰ (028) 4175 3222 – www.restaurant-23.co.uk*
– restaurant23@btconnect.com – Fax (028) 4177 4323
*– Closed 24-25 December, last week January, Monday and Tuesday, except Bank
Holidays when open Monday*
Rest – Menu £18 (dinner) **s** – Carte £23/29 **s**
♦ A very stylish interior makes most of intimate space. Easy-going, good value bras-
serie style lunches; evening dishes - adopting a more original slant - are more serious.

O. Forir/MICHELIN

Towns
from A to Z

Villes
de A à Z

Città
de A a Z

Städte
von A bis Z

Republic
of
Ireland

ABBEYLEIX (Mainistir Laoise) – **Laois** – 712 J 9 🏛 *Ireland* 39 **C2**
- ▶ Dublin 96 km – Kilkenny 35 km – Limerick 108 km
- 🏌 Abbeyleix Rathmoyle, ℰ (0502) 31 450
- 🎫 Emo Court★★ **AC**, N : 17 km by R 425 and R 419 – Rock of Dunamase★, NE : 10 km by R 425 and N 80 – Stradbally Steam Museum★ **AC**, NE : 19 km by R 425 and R 427 – Timahoe Round Tower★, NE : 15 km by R 430 and a minor road

🏠 **Abbeyleix Manor** ♿ rm, 🖾 ✕ ⁽ᵖ⁾ 🔥 **P** 𝓥𝓘𝓢𝓐 ⓒⓒ 🅰🅴 ⓞ
Cork Rd, Southwest : ¾ km on N 8 – ℰ (05787) 30 111
– www.abbeyleixmanorhotel.com – info@abbeyleixmanorhotel.com
– Fax (05787) 30 220 – Closed 25 December
46 rm ⌑ – ♦€ 75/85 ♦♦€ 125/135
Rest – (carvery lunch Monday-Friday, bar lunch Saturday) Carte € 26/36 **s**
♦ Modern purpose-built hotel painted a distinctive yellow. Mural decorated public areas. Well-kept bar and a games room. Uniform bedrooms with simple, comfortable style. Restaurant has a bright modern feel.

> Look out for red symbols, indicating particularly pleasant establishments.

ACHILL ISLAND (Acaill) – **Mayo** – 712 B 5/6 🏛 *Ireland* 36 **A2**
- 🚺 Achill ℰ (098) 47 353 (July-August), info@achilltourism.com
- 🏌 Achill Island Keel, ℰ (098) 43 456
- 🎫 Island★

Doogort (Dumha Goirt) – **Mayo** – ✉ **Achill Island**

🏠 **Gray's** 🛋 **P**
– ℰ (098) 43 244 – Closed Christmas
14 rm ⌑ – ♦€ 50/55 ♦♦€ 61 **Rest** – (by arrangement) Menu € 32
♦ A row of tranquil whitewashed cottages with a homely atmosphere; popular with artists. Cosy sitting rooms with fireplaces and simple but spotless bedrooms. Local scene paintings adorn dining room walls.

Keel – **Mayo** – ✉ **Achill Island**

🏠 **Achill Cliff House** ≤ ⋒ ✕ ⁽ᵖ⁾ **P** 𝓥𝓘𝓢𝓐 ⓒⓒ 🅰🅴
– ℰ (098) 43 400 – www.achillcliff.com – info@achillcliff.com – Fax (098) 43 007
– Closed 23-27 December
10 rm ⌑ – ♦€ 55/120 ♦♦€ 80/160
Rest – (dinner only and Sunday dinner) Menu € 18/27 – Carte € 29/41
♦ Whitewashed modern building against a backdrop of countryside and ocean. Within walking distance of Keel beach. Well-kept, spacious bedrooms with modern furnishings. Spacious restaurant with sea views.

ADARE (Áth Dara) – **Limerick** – 712 F 10 🏛 *Ireland* 38 **B2**
- ▶ Dublin 210 km – Killarney 95 km – Limerick 16 km
- 🚺 Heritage Centre, Mains St ℰ (061) 396 255
- 🎫 Town★ – Adare Friary★ – Adare Parish Church★
- 🎫 Rathkeale (Castle Matrix★ **AC** - Irish Palatine Heritage Centre★) W : 12 km by N 21 – Newcastle West★, W : 26 km by N 21 – Glin Castle★ **AC**, W : 46½ km by N 21, R 518 and N 69

🏰 **Adare Manor H. and Golf Resort** ⊛ ≤ 🛋 🏊 🎾 🏞 🖾 🔞
– ℰ (061) 396 566 🔁 ✕ ⁽ᵖ⁾ 🔥 **P** 𝓥𝓘𝓢𝓐 ⓒⓒ 🅰🅴 ⓞ
– www.adaremanor.com – reservations@adaremanor.com – Fax (061) 396 124
62 rm – ♦€ 240/443 ♦♦€ 360/505, ⌑ € 25
Rest *The Oakroom* – (dinner only) Carte € 42/69
Rest *The Carraigehouse* – Carte € 32/51
♦ Part 19C Gothic mansion on banks of River Maigue in extensive parkland. Impressively elaborate interiors and capacious lounges. Most distinctive rooms in the oldest parts. Oak-panelled dining room overlooks river. Informal Carraigehouse.

Dunraven Arms 🖨 🔟 🖪 🛋 ⛽ ⟨ᵀ⟩ 🚿 🅿 VISA ⑩ AE ①

Main St – ℰ (061) 605 900 – www.dunravenhotel.com
– reservations@dunravenhotel.com – Fax (061) 396 541
86 rm – ♦♦€ 135/200, � €25
Rest *Maigue Restaurant* – ℰ (061) 396 633 (dinner only and Sunday lunch)
Carte € 33/41
♦ Considerably extended 18C building opposite town's charming thatched cottages. Understated country house style. Comfortable bedrooms in bright magnolia. Well-equipped gym. Burgundy décor, antique chairs and historical paintings create a classic traditional air. Menus offer some eclectic choice on an Irish backbone. Formal yet friendly service.

Berkeley Lodge without rest 🚿 ⟨ᵀ⟩ 🅿 VISA ⑩

Station Rd – ℰ (061) 396 857 – www.adare.org – berlodge@iol.ie – Fax (061) 396857
6 rm ⊆ – ♦€ 55/60 ♦♦€ 80/95
♦ Good value accommodation with a friendly and well-run ambience. Hearty breakfast choices include pancakes and smoked salmon. Simply furnished traditional bedrooms.

The Wild Geese 🗙🗙 VISA ⑩ AE ①

Rose Cottage – ℰ (061) 396 451 – www.thewild-geese.com
– wildgeese@indigo.ie – Closed 24 December - 13 January, Sunday in winter and Monday
Rest – (dinner only) (booking essential) Carte € 35/53
♦ Traditional 18C cottage on main street. Friendly service and cosy welcoming atmosphere. Varied menu with classic and international influences uses much fresh local produce.

ARAN ISLANDS (Oileáin Árann) – Galway – 712 CD 8 📖 *Ireland* 38 **B1**

Access Access by boat or aeroplane from Galway city or by boat from Kilkieran, Rossaveel or Fisherstreet (Clare) and by aeroplane from Inverin
🚺 Cill Ronain, Inis Mor ℰ (099) 61355, info@visitaranislands.com
◎ Islands★ – Inishmore (Dún Aonghasa★★★)

Inishmore – Galway – ⊠ Aran Islands 38 **A1**

Óstán Árann ≼ 🖨 🖭 🖪 & rm, 🚿 ⟨ᵀ⟩ 🅿 VISA ⑩ AE ①

Kilronan – ℰ (099) 61 104 – www.aranislandshotel.com
– info@aranislandshotel.com – Fax (099) 61 225 – Closed 21-29 December
22 rm – ♦€ 74/84 ♦♦€ 160/190, ⊆ €13.50
Rest – Menu € 25/35 – Carte dinner € 36/48
♦ Comfortable, family-owned hotel with great view of harbour. Bustling bar with live music every night in the season. Spacious, up-to-date bedrooms decorated in bright colours. Traditional dishes served in wood-floored restaurant.

Pier House ≼ 🖨 🚿 🅿 VISA ⑩

Kilronan – ℰ (099) 61 417 – www.pierhousearan.com – pierh@iol.ie – Fax (099) 61 122 – March-October
12 rm ⊆ – ♦€ 55/100 ♦♦€ 80/130
Rest *The Restaurant* – see restaurant listing
♦ Purpose-built at the end of the pier with an attractive outlook. Spacious, planned interiors and spotlessly kept bedrooms furnished in a comfortable modern style.

Ard Einne Guesthouse 🕸 ≼ 🖨 🚿 🅿 VISA ⑩

Killeany – ℰ (099) 61 126 – www.ardeinne.com – ardeinne@eircom.net
– Fax (099) 61 388 – March-early November
8 rm ⊆ – ♦€ 60/90 ♦♦€ 90/120   Rest – (by arrangement) Menu € 27
♦ Purpose-built chalet-style establishment in isolated spot with superb views of Killeany Bay. Homely atmosphere amidst traditional appointments. Simple, comfortable bedrooms. Spacious dining room provides home-cooked meals.

⌂ **Kilmurvey House** ⊜　　　　　　　≤ ⃝ ⅌ ⁜ VISA Ⓜⓒ
Kilmurvey – ℰ (099) 61 218 – www.kilmurveyhouse.com
– kilmurveyhouse@eircom.net – Fax (099) 61 397 – April-October
12 rm ⌂ – †€60/110 ††€95/110　**Rest** – (by arrangement) Menu €30 **s**
◆ Extended stone-built house in tranquil, secluded location with the remains of an ancient fort in grounds. Well-kept traditional style throughout. Simply decorated bedrooms. Traditional dining room. Good use of fresh island produce.

✗ **The Restaurant** – at Pier House Hotel　　　　≤ ⌂ VISA Ⓜⓒ
Kilronan – ℰ (099) 61 417 – www.pierhouserestaurant.com – pierh@iol.ie
– Fax (099) 61 811 – March-October
Rest – (light lunch) Menu €34 – Carte €30/45
◆ Cosy, snug, cottagey restaurant, typified by its rustic, wooden tables. Light lunches are replaced by more serious dinner menus with strong selection of local fish dishes.

ARDFINNAN (Ard Fhíonáin) – 712 I 11　　　　　　　　39 **C2**
　▯ Dublin 185 km – Caher 9 km – Waterford 63 km

⌂ **Kilmaneen Farmhouse** ⊜　　　　　 ⃞ ⃝ ⃠ P VISA Ⓜⓒ
East : 4¼ km by Goatenbridge rd – ℰ (052) 36 231 – www.kilmaneen.com
– kilmaneen@eircom.net – Fax (052) 36 231 – April-October
5 rm ⌂ – †€50 ††€90　**Rest** – (by arrangement) Menu €30
◆ Traditional farmhouse on dairy farm hidden away in the countryside. Cosy and neat, with a welcoming lounge. Comfortable bedrooms are well kept and individually furnished. Tasty menus with a rural heart.

ARDMORE – Waterford – 712 I 12　　　　　　　　　39 **C3**
　▯ Dublin 147 km – Waterford 44 km – Clonmel 41 km – Cobh 34 km

🏨 **Cliff House** 　≤ ⌂ ⃞ ⃠ ⃘ ⃐ ⃑ ⃒ ⅌ ⃝ ⃙ P VISA Ⓜⓒ AE Ⓞ
– ℰ (024) 87 800 – www.thecliffhousehotel.com – info@thecliffhousehotel.com
– Fax (024) 87 820
36 rm ⌂ – ††€200/250 – 3 suites
Rest – (dinner only and Sunday lunch in Summer) Menu €63
◆ No expense was spared with this ground-breaking hotel, built into the cliff. Contemporary in style, but using local materials. All the well-equipped bedrooms have views and great bathrooms. Innovative and imaginative cooking using modern techniques.

ARTHURSTOWN (Colmán) – Wexford – 712 L 11　　　　39 **D2**
　▯ Dublin 166 km – Cork 159 km – Limerick 162 km – Waterford 42 km

🏨 **Dunbrody Country House** ⊜　 ≤ ⃞ ⃝ ⃠ ⌂ ⅍ rm, ⅌ ⁜ P VISA Ⓜⓒ AE Ⓞ
– ℰ (051) 389 600 – www.dunbrodyhouse.com
– dunbrody@indigo.ie – Fax (051) 389 601 – Closed 21-26 December
17 rm ⌂ – †€140/170 ††€275/360 – 5 suites
Rest – (bar lunch Monday-Saturday) (booking essential for non-residents) (residents only Sunday dinner) Menu €65 – Carte €40/65
◆ A fine country house hotel with a pristine elegant style set within a part Georgian former hunting lodge, affording much peace. Smart comfortable bedrooms. Elegant dining room in green damask and burgundy.

ASHBOURNE (Cill Dhéagláin) – Meath – 712 M 7　　　37 **D3**
　▯ Dublin 21 km – Drogheda 26 km – Navan 27 km

🏨 **Ashbourne Marriott** 　 ⃞ ⃙ ⅍ ⌂ ⅍ rm, AC ⅌ ⁜ ⃙ P VISA Ⓜⓒ AE
The Rath, North : 2 km by R 135 at junction with N 2 motorway – ℰ (01) 835 0800 – www.marriottashbourne.com – info@marriottashbourne.com
– Fax (01) 801 0301 – Closed 24-26 December
144 rm – †€89/199 ††€89/199, ⌂ €15.50 – 4 suites
Rest – (closed Sunday dinner) (bar lunch Monday-Saturday) Menu €45 – Carte €28/55
◆ Modern hotel with striking glass front. Trendy bar furnished in red with karaoke room. Well equipped leisure club. Bedrooms are stylish, with bright decor and smart bathrooms. Restaurant specialises in steak and seafood.

⛫ **Broadmeadow Country House** without rest ⑤   🛋 🔥 ✗ ⑨
Bullstown, Southeast : 4 km by R 135 on R 125 (Swords rd)   📶 **P.** 🚗 **OO**
– 𝒞 *(01) 835 2823 – www.irishcountryhouse.com – info@irishcountryhouse.com*
– *Fax (01) 835 2819 – Closed 23 December-2 January*
8 rm ⌂ – ♦€ 60/80 ♦♦€ 100/120
♦ Substantial ivy-clad guesthouse and equestrian centre in rural area yet close to airport. Light and airy breakfast room overlooks garden. Spacious rooms have country views.

ASHFORD – Wicklow – 712 N 8 – pop. 1 349   39 **D2**
▶ Dublin 43 km – Rathdrum 17 km – Wicklow 6 km

⛫ **Ballyknocken House**   🛋 🔥 ✗ ⑨ **P.** 🚗 **OO**
Glenealy, South : 4¾ km on L 1096 – 𝒞 (0404) 44 627 – www.ballyknocken.com
– *cfulvio@ballyknocken.com – Fax (0404) 44 696 – February-November*
7 rm ⌂ – ♦€ 69/95 ♦♦€ 118/138   **Rest** – (by arrangement) Menu € 47
♦ Part Victorian guesthouse on a working farm: the comfy bedrooms are furnished with antiques, and some have claw foot baths: most are in the new wing. Charming owner proud of home cooking.

ATHLONE (Baile Átha Luain) – Westmeath – 712 I 7 – pop. 17 544   37 **C3**
▮ *Ireland*

▶ Dublin 120 km – Galway 92 km – Limerick 120 km – Roscommon 32 km – Tullamore 38 km
🅳 Athlone Castle, St Peter's Sq 𝒞 (090) 647 2107 (April-October), jwalsh@athlonetc.ie
🅗 Hodson Bay, 𝒞 (090) 649 20 73
🅒 Clonmacnois★★★ (Grave Slabs★, Cross of the Scriptures★) S : 21 km by N 6 and N 62 – N : Lough Ree (Ballykeeran Viewpoint★)

🏨 **Radisson SAS** ≼ 📺 📶 🏋 📶 ⅙ rm, ⅛ rest, ✗ 📶 🛁 **P.** 🚗 **OO** 🅰🅴 ⓪
Northgate St – 𝒞 (090) 644 26 00 – www.athlone.radissonsas.com
– *info.athlone@radissonsas.com – Fax (090) 644 26 55*
127 rm ⌂ – ♦€ 129/179 ♦♦€ 139/299
Rest – (closed Sunday and dinner Monday) (buffet lunch Monday-Saturday) Menu € 38 – Carte € 31/52
♦ Overlooks River Shannon, cathedral and marina. Quayside bar with super terrace. Impressive leisure and meeting facilities. Very modern rooms with hi-tech mod cons. Modish restaurant serving buffet or à la carte.

🏨 **Sheraton Athlone** 📺 ⊕ 📶 🏋 📶 ⅙ 📶 📶 🛁 **P.** 🚗 **OO** 🅰🅴 ⓪
Gleeson St – 𝒞 (090) 645 1000 – www.sheraton.com/athlone
– *info@sheratonathlonehotel.com – Fax (090) 645 1001*
164 rm ⌂ – ♦€ 69/159 ♦♦€ 138/318 – 3 suites
Rest – (dinner only and Sunday lunch) Menu € 35 – Carte € 29/46
♦ Contemporary international hotel masked by unspectacular exterior. Impressive leisure and spa facilities. Good-sized bedrooms: the higher the floor, the bigger the room. Traditional menu of classics.

⛫ **Shelmalier House** without rest   🛋 📶 ✗ **P.** 🚗 **OO**
Retreat Rd, Cartrontroy, East : 2½ km by Dublin rd (N 6) – 𝒞 (090) 647 22 45
– *www.shelmalierhouse.com – shelmalier@eircom.net – Fax (090) 647 31 90*
– *April-October*
7 rm ⌂ – ♦€ 50 ♦♦€ 72
♦ Modern house with large garden in a quiet residential area of town. Homely décor throughout, including comfortable bedrooms which are well kept.

⛫ **Cooson Cottage** without rest   🛋 ⅙ 📶 **P.** 🚗 **OO** 🅰🅴 ⓪
Cooson Point Rd, North : 3¾ km by Northgate St and following signs to Cooson Point – 𝒞 (090) 647 34 68 – www.ecoguesthouse.com – info@ecoguesthouse.com
10 rm ⌂ – ♦€ 50 ♦♦€ 100
♦ First eco-guest house in Ireland; keenly run with friendly, welcoming owners. Comfy lounge, good-sized bedrooms and bright breakfast room with decked area overlooking garden.

REPUBLIC OF IRELAND

ATHLONE

↑ **Riverview House** without rest 🖼 �% P. VISA ⓪ AE
*Summerhill, Galway Rd, West : 4 km on N 6 – ℰ (090) 649 45 32
– www.riverviewhousebandb.com – riverviewhouse@hotmail.com – Fax (090)
649 45 32 – March-18 December*
4 rm ⬜ – ♦€48/51 ♦♦€70/75
♦ Modern house with well-kept garden. Homely, comfortable lounge and wood furnished dining room. Uniformly styled fitted bedrooms. Good welcome.

✗ **Left Bank Bistro** AC VISA ⓪
*Fry Pl – ℰ (090) 649 44 46 – www.leftbankbistro.com – info@leftbankbistro.com
– Fax (090) 649 45 09 – Closed 25 December-8 January, Sunday and Monday*
Rest – (light lunch) Menu €28 – Carte €35/47
♦ Glass-fronted with open-plan wine store and bright, modern bistro buzzing with regulars. Salads and foccacias, plus modern Irish dishes and fish specials in the evening.

at Glassan Northeast : 8 km on N 55 – ✉ Athlone

🏨 **Wineport Lodge** ≤ 🖼 ⧉ 🗐 & rm, AC ⁗ P. VISA ⓪ AE
*Southwest : 1½ km – ℰ (090) 643 90 10 – www.wineport.ie – lodge@wineport.ie
– Fax (090) 643 90 33 – Closed 24-26 December*
28 rm ⬜ – ♦€145/195 ♦♦€195/330 – 1 suite
Rest – (dinner only) Menu €75 – Carte €59/76
♦ Beautifully located by Lough Ree. Come in from the delightful terrace and sip champagne in stylish bar. Superb rooms of limed oak and ash boast balconies and lough views. Smart restaurant with separate galleried area for private parties.

🏨 **Glasson Golf H. & Country Club** ≤ 🖼 ᴖ ⫟ 🕲 ↳ 🖼
West : 2¾ km – ℰ (090) 🗐 & rm, AC rm, ⚖ ⁗ ↳ P. VISA ⓪ AE ⓪
*648 51 20 – www.glassongolf.ie – info@glassongolf.ie – Fax (090) 648 54 44
– Closed 25 December*
63 rm ⬜ – ♦€130/170 ♦♦€200/240 – 2 suites
Rest – (bar lunch) Menu €40 **s**
♦ Family owned hotel commands fine views of Lough Ree and its attractive golf course. Modern bedrooms are spacious with superior rooms making most of view. Original Georgian house restaurant with wonderful outlook.

↑ **Glasson Stone Lodge** without rest 🖼 ⚑ P. VISA ⓪
*– ℰ (090) 648 50 04 – www.glassonstonelodge.com
– glassonstonelodge@eircom.net – April-November*
6 rm ⬜ – ♦€50/55 ♦♦€72/84
♦ A warm welcome and notable breakfasts with home-baked breads and locally sourced organic bacon. Bedrooms and communal areas are airy and tastefully furnished.

↑ **Harbour House** without rest 🖼 ⚑ P. VISA ⓪
*Southwest : 2 km – ℰ (090) 648 50 63 – www.harbourhouse.ie
– ameade@indigo.ie – April-October*
6 rm ⬜ – ♦€50 ♦♦€74/80
♦ Sited in quiet rural spot a stone's throw from Lough Ree. Traditionally styled lounge with stone chimney breast; adjoining breakfast room. Comfy bedrooms overlook garden.

ATHY (Baile Átha Í) – **Kildare** – **712** L 9 – **pop. 8 218** ▌ *Ireland* **39 D2**
▶ Dublin 64 km – Kilkenny 46 km – Wexford 95 km
🔟 Athy Geraldine, ℰ (059) 863 1729
🔘 Emo Court★★, N : 32 km by R 417 (L 18), west by N 7 (T 5) and north by R 422 – Stradbally Steam Museum★ **AC**, W : 13 km by R 428 - Castledermot High Crosses★, SE : 15¼ km by R 418 – Moone High Cross★, E : 19¼ km by Ballitore minor rd and south by N9 - Rock of Dunamase★ (≤★), NW : 19¼ km by R 428 (L109) and N80 (T16) – Timahoe Round Tower★, W : 16 km by R 428 (L 109) and N 80 (T 16)

Clanard Court   🚗 📶 & rm, 🏧 rest, ⚡ ☎ 🅿 📶 🚿 AE ①
Dublin Rd, Northeast : 2 km on N 78 – ☎ *(059) 864 06 66 – www.clanardcourt.ie
– sales@clanardcourt.ie – Fax (059) 864 08 88 – Closed 24-26 December*
38 rm � – 🛏€ 79/130 🛏🛏€ 99/189
Rest *Courtyard Bistro* – (closed Sunday-Wednesday dinner) (carvery lunch)
Carte € 25/45
♦ Commercially oriented modern hotel in bright yellow which opened in 2005. Well-equipped meeting rooms. Large bar to snack, sup and unwind. Comfy, smart bedrooms. Restaurant offers Mediterranean/North African style and menus.

AUGHRIM (Eachroim) – **Wicklow** – **712** N 9   39 **D2**
▶ Dublin 74 km – Waterford 124 km – Wexford 96 km
ℹ The Battle of Aughrim Visitors Centre, Ballinasloe ☎ (0909) 742604
(summer only)

Brooklodge H & Wells Spa ⊗   🚗 🔌 🖥 ⊗ 📶 🔥 📷 📶 📶 ♨
Macreddin Village, North : 3 ¼ km – ☎ *(0402) 36 444*   🔥 🅿 📶 🚿 AE
– www.brooklodge.com – brooklodge@macreddin.ie – Fax (0402) 36 580
77 rm ⊘ – 🛏€ 160/180 🛏🛏€ 230/270 – 13 suites
Rest *Orchard Cafe* – Carte € 18/20
Rest *Strawberry Tree* – (dinner only and Sunday lunch) Menu € 65
♦ Very individual hotel in idyllic parkland setting. Self-contained microbrewery, smokehouse and bakery. Well-appointed bedrooms and a friendly comfortable style throughout. Orchard Cafe is relaxed, informal eatery. Organic ingredients in Strawberry Tree.

AVOCA (Abhóca) – **Wicklow** – **712** N 9 📖 *Ireland*   39 **D2**
▶ Dublin 75 km – Waterford 116 km – Wexford 88 km
🟢 Avondale★, N : by R 752 – Meeting of the Waters★, N : by R 752

Keppel's Farmhouse without rest ⊗   ⬅ 🚗 🔌 ⚡ 🅿 📶 📶
Ballanagh, South : 3 ¼ km by unmarked rd – ☎ *(0402) 35 168
– www.keppelsfarmhouse.com – keppelsfarmhouse@eircom.net – Fax (0402)
30 950 – May-October*
5 rm ⊘ – 🛏€ 60 🛏🛏€ 90
♦ Farmhouse set in seclusion at end of long drive on working dairy farm. Attractively simple modern and traditional bedrooms; those in front have far-reaching rural views.

BAGENALSTOWN (Muine Bheag) – **Carlow** – **712** L 9   39 **D2**
▶ Dublin 101 km – Carlow 16 km – Kilkenny 21 km – Wexford 59 km

Kilgraney Country House ⊗   ⬅ 🚗 ⊗ 📶 ⚡ 🅿 📶 📶 AE
South : 6 ½ km by R 705 (Borris Rd) – ☎ *(059) 977 52 83
– www.kilgraneyhouse.com – info@kilgraneyhouse.com – Fax (059) 977 55 95
– March-November*
8 rm ⊘ – 🛏€ 110 🛏🛏€ 280
Rest – (closed Monday-Tuesday) (dinner only) (booking essential) (Communal dining) Menu € 52 **s**
♦ 18C house with individual interiors featuring Far Eastern artefacts from owners' travels. Sitting room in dramatic colours, paintings resting against wall. Stylish rooms. Communal dining in smart surroundings.

BALLINA (Béal an Átha) – **Mayo** – **712** E 5 – **pop. 10 490** 📖 *Ireland*   36 **B2**
▶ Dublin 241 km – Galway 117 km – Roscommon 103 km – Sligo 59 km
ℹ Cathedral Rd ☎ (096) 70848 (April-October), ballina@irelandwest.ie
⛳ Mossgrove Shanaghy, ☎ (096) 21 050
🟢 Rosserk Abbey★, N : 6 ½ km by R 314. Moyne Abbey★, N : 11 ¼ km by R 314 - Pontoon Bridge View (≤★), S : 19 ¼ km by N 26 and R 310 – Downpatrick Head★, N : 32 km by R 314

REPUBLIC OF IRELAND

REPUBLIC OF IRELAND

Mount Falcon ⊛   ⟨ 🚗 🅿 🐟 🏊 👗 🛁 🎒 ⅙ rm, ⅔ 🍸 ⛳ 🅿

Faxford Rd, South : 6 ¼ km on N 26 – ℰ (096) 74472   VISA ⓜⓞ AE
– www.mountfalcon.com – info@mountfalcon.com – Fax (096) 74473 – Closed 24-25 December

31 rm ⌶ – ♥€ 135 ♥♥€ 160/200 – 1 suite
Rest *The Kitchen* – (bar lunch) Menu € 64 **s** – Carte € 53/62 **s**

♦ Classic Victorian style country house in 100 acres of mature grounds. Most bedrooms are in the new extension; comfortable and furnished in keeping with character of the house. High-ceilinged, formal restaurant, in what was the original kitchen and pantry.

Ramada   🖼 🐟 🏊 🎒 ⅙ rm, 🛗 rest, ⅔ 🍸 ⛳ 🅿 VISA ⓜⓞ AE ①

Dublin Rd, South : 3 km by N 26 – ℰ (096) 23600 – www.ramadaballina.ie
– stay@ramadaballina.ie – Fax (096) 23623 – Closed 24-26 December

87 rm ⌶ – ♥€ 100/140 ♥♥€ 180/240
Rest – (bar lunch) Menu € 38 – Carte € 31/44

♦ Very spacious and modern purpose built hotel, with huge bar, well-equipped leisure facilities and comfortable, contemporary bedrooms of generous proportions. Formal dining in restaurant.

The Ice House   ⟨ 🍴 🐟 🎒 ⅔ 🍸 ⛳ 🅿 VISA ⓜⓞ AE

The Quay Village, Northeast : 2½ km by N 59 – ℰ (096) 23500
– www.theicehouse.ie – chill@theicehouse.ie – Fax (096) 23598
– Closed 25-26 December

32 rm ⌶ – ♥€ 175/195 ♥♥€ 295/395 – 5 suites
Rest – (dinner only and light lunch) Carte € 45/75

♦ A former ice vault for local fishermen with two modern extensions. Terrific river views. The bedrooms a quirky mix of the old and the new; some with full-length windows. Modern menus in restaurant.

Crockets on the Quay with rm   🍴 ⅔ 🅿 VISA ⓜⓞ AE

The Quay Village, Northeast : 2½ km by N 59 – ℰ (096) 75930
– www.crocketsonthequay.ie – info@crocketsonthequay.ie – Fax (096) 70069
– Closed 25 December and Good Friday

8 rm ⌶ – ♥€ 45 ♥♥€ 80   **Rest** – Menu € 30 (dinner) – Carte € 27/45

♦ Friendly, atmospheric Irish pub on the river, with plasma screens, terrace and dining area in beamed former boat house. Hearty, fresh cooking uses quality ingredients. Modest bedrooms; 6, 7 and 8 are the quietest.

BALLINADEE (Baile na Daidhche) – **Cork** – **712** G 12 – **see Kinsale**

BALLINASLOE (Béal Átha na Sluaighe) – **Galway** – **712** H 8 – **pop. 6 303**   36 **B3**

📗 *Ireland*

🛣 Dublin 146 km – Galway 66 km – Limerick 106 km – Roscommon 58 km – Tullamore 55 km

🖼 ℰ (0909) 642604 (July-August), ballinasloe@failteireland.ie

🖼 Rossgloss, ℰ (0905) 42126

🖼 Mountbellew, ℰ (090) 9679259

🖼 Clonfert Cathedral★ (west doorway★★), SW : by R 355 and minor roads. Turoe Stone, Bullaun★, SW : 29 km by R 348 and R 350 – Loughrea (St Brendan's Cathedral★), SW : 29 km by N 6 – Clonmacnoise★★★ (grave slabs★, Cross of the Scriptures★) E : 21 km by R 357 and R 444

Carlton Shearwater   🖼 🐟 🏊 🎒 ⅙ rm, 🛗 🍸 ⛳ 🅿 🚗 VISA ⓜⓞ AE

Marina Point – ℰ (090) 9630400 – www.carltonshearwater.com
– info.shearwater@carlton.ie – Fax (090) 9630401

84 rm ⌶ – ♥€ 70/150 ♥♥€ 130/280 – 20 suites
Rest – Menu € 45 – Carte approx. € 41

♦ Striking building on edge of town centre, with huge lobby and lounge and two stylish bars. State-of-the-art leisure facilities; large, modern bedrooms. Irish and European menu served in spacious restaurant.

Moycarn Lodge 〔icons〕 rm, P VISA ⓒ AE

Shannonbridge Rd, Southeast : 2½ km by N 6 off R 357 – ℰ *(090) 964 5050*
– www.moycarnlodge.ie – info@moycarnlodge.ie – Fax (090) 964 4760
15 rm ⌂ – †€ 59 ††€ 99   **Rest** – Menu € 13 (lunch) – Carte € 19/49
♦ Pleasant rural spot next to River Suck, with berthing available for boats and family cruisers for hire. Light, simply furnished bedrooms; some with river view. Hospitable owners. Rustically-styled restaurant.

BALLINCOLLIG Cork – **712** D 12   38 **B3**
   ▶ Dublin 168 km – Cork 6 km – Carrigaline 17 km – Cobh 20 km

Oriel House 〔icons〕 rm, AC ⅍ 🕊 ♨ P VISA ⓒ AE

West : 1 km on A 608 – ℰ *(021) 420 84 00 – www.corkluxuryhotels.com*
– info@orielhousehotel.ie – Fax (021) 487 58 80 – Closed 25-26 December
76 rm ⌂ – †€ 150 ††€ 200 – 2 suites
Rest – Menu € 24 (lunch) **s** – Carte dinner € 32/61 **s**
♦ Former manor house with modern extensions boasts smart spa, conference suite and contemporary bar. Most bedrooms are in the new wings; those at the rear are quieter. Simple menu served in smart, airy restaurant.

BALLINGARRY (Baile an Gharraí) – **Limerick** – **712** F 10 ▌Ireland   38 **B2**
   ▶ Dublin 227 km – Killarney 90 km – Limerick 29 km
   ⓖ Kilmallock★ (Kilmallock Abbey★, Collegiate Church★), SE : 24 km by R 518
      – Lough Gur Interpretive Centre★ **AC**, NE : 29 km by R 519, minor road to
      Croom, R 516 and R 512 – Monasteranenagh Abbey★, NE : 24 km by R 519
      and minor road to Croom

Mustard Seed at Echo Lodge 🍃 〔icons〕 ⅍ rm, ♨ P VISA ⓒ AE

– ℰ *(069) 68 508 – www.mustardseed.ie – mustard@indigo.ie – Fax (069) 68 511*
– Closed 17 January - 6 February, and 24-26 December
14 rm ⌂ – †€ 130/170 ††€ 240 – 2 suites
Rest – (dinner only) (booking essential for non-residents) Menu € 64
♦ Converted convent with very neat gardens and peaceful appeal. Cosy lounge with fireplace and beautiful fresh flowers. Individually furnished rooms with mix of antiques. Meals enlivened by home-grown herbs and organic farm produce.

BALLINROBE Mayo – **Mayo** – **712** E 7 – pop. 2 098   36 **B3**
   ▶ Dublin 163 km – Castlebar 18 km – Galway 31 km – Westport 20 km

JJ Gannons with rm 〔icons〕 rm, AC ⅍ 🕊 ♨ P VISA ⓒ

Main St – ℰ *(094) 954 1008 – www.jjgannons.com – info@jjgannons.com*
– Fax (094) 952 0018 – Closed 25 December and Good Friday
10 rm ⌂ – †€ 65/100 ††€ 130/150   **Rest** – Menu € 23/45 – Carte € 23/45
♦ Traditionally-fronted town centre pub run by third generation of Gannons, with stylish, seductively-lit bar and smart, spacious restaurant. Interesting menu of modern classics. Bright, modern bedrooms.

BALLINTOGHER Sligo – **Sligo** – **712** G 5 – pop. 182   36 **B2**
   ▶ Dublin 135 km – Sligo 11 km – Carrick-on-Shannon 32 km – Castlerea 42 km

Kingsfort Country House without rest 〔icons〕 P VISA ⓒ AE

– ℰ *(071) 911 5111 – www.kingsfortcountryhouse.com*
– info@kingsfortcountryhouse.com – Fax (071) 911 5979
– 15 March - 5 November
8 rm ⌂ – †€ 70/130 ††€ 140/190
♦ Relaxed French bohemian feel to converted 18C courthouse in centre of rural village; bedrooms in main house are larger; those in outbuilding are cosy and characterful.

BALLSBRIDGE (Droichead na Dothra) – **Dublin** – **712** N 8 – **see Dublin**

🖭 Dublin 238 km – Londonderry 48 km – Sligo 93 km
🖼 Ballybofey & Stranorlar The Glebe, 𝒞 (074) 31 093

🏨 **Kee's**   🔲 📶 🕭 🛉 🌡 ✂ 🏋 ᰍ 🅟 🚗 **VISA ⦾ AE ①**

Main St, Stranorlar, Northeast : ¾ km on N 15 – 𝒞 (074) 913 10 18
– www.keeshotel.ie – info@keeshotel.ie – Fax (074) 913 19 17
53 rm ⚌ – ♦€ 96/106 ♦♦€ 158/178   **Rest** – Carte € 25/50 **s**
♦ Very comfortable hotel established over 150 years ago. Smart lobby with plush sofas. Atmospheric bar and raised lounge area. Comfortable rooms. Popular favourites served in the restaurant.

🏨 **Villa Rose**   🛗 �& rm, ᰍ rest, ✂ **VISA ⦾ AE ①**

Main St – 𝒞 (074) 913 22 66 – www.villarose.net – info@villarose.net – Fax (074) 913 06 66
55 rm ⚌ – ♦€ 65/99 ♦♦€ 138/188   **Rest** – Menu € 12/25 – Carte € 27/35
♦ Under private ownership, a modern hotel in the centre of the town. Neat, well-appointed accommodation, furnished in co-ordinated colours and fabrics. Bright, airy dining room with contemporary style and wide international choice.

🖭 Dublin 283 km – Limerick 90 km – Tralee 42 km
🖼 Ballybunnion Sandhill Rd, 𝒞 (068) 27 146
🅖 Rattoo Round Tower★, S : 10 km by R 551. Ardfert★, S : 29 km by R 551, R 556 and minor road W – Banna Strand★, S : 28 km by R 551 – Carrigafoyle Castle★, NE : 21 km by R 551 – Glin Castle★ **AC**, E : 30½ km by R 551 and N 69

🏠 **Harty Costello Townhouse**   ✂ **VISA ⦾ AE**

Main St – 𝒞 (068) 27 129 – www.hartycostello.com – hartycostello@eircom.net – Fax (068) 27 489 – 2 April-15 October
8 rm ⚌ – ♦€ 70/110 ♦♦€ 120/180
Rest – (closed Sunday and Monday) (dinner only) Carte € 27/53 **s**
♦ This personally run hotel, set around and above the pub downstairs, is smart, stylish and contemporary. A popular choice for visitors to this golfing town. Local fish in spruce, welcoming restaurant.

🏠 **Teach de Broc Country House**   🛗 �& rm, ✂ 🛉 🅟 **VISA ⦾ AE**

Link Rd, South : 2½ km on Golf Club rd – 𝒞 (068) 27 581
– www.ballybuniongolf.com – info@ballybuniongolf.com – Fax (068) 27 919 – Mid March - October
14 rm ⚌ – ♦€ 85/135 ♦♦€ 145/170
Rest – (closed Monday) (dinner only) Carte € 29/51
♦ Clean, tidy guesthouse with coastal proximity and great appeal to golfers as it's adjacent to the famous Ballybunion golf course. Home cooked meals. Neat, spacious rooms.

⛾ **The 19th Lodge** without rest   🚗 �& ᰍ ✂ 🛉 🅟 **VISA ⦾**

Golf Links Rd, South : 2¾ km by Golf Club rd – 𝒞 (068) 27 592
– www.the19thlodgeballybunion.com – the19thlodge@eircom.net – Fax (068) 27 830 – Closed 20 December - 10 January
14 rm ⚌ – ♦€ 70/150 ♦♦€ 100/180
♦ Orange washed house aimed at golfers playing at adjacent course. First floor lounge with honesty bar and comfy sofas. Linen-clad breakfast room. Luxurious rooms.

⛾ **Cashen Course House** without rest   🚗 �& ᰍ ✂ 🛉 🅟 **VISA ⦾ AE**

Golf Links Rd, South : 2¾ km by Golf Club rd – 𝒞 (068) 27 351
– www.playballybunion.com – golfstay@eircom.net – Fax (068) 28 934 – March-October
9 rm ⚌ – ♦€ 80/110 ♦♦€ 120/150
♦ Overlooks first hole at the Cashen Course: clubhouse just one minute away. Bright, breezy breakfast room; quality furnishings in comfy lounge. Spacious, colourful rooms.

REPUBLIC OF IRELAND

BALLYCASTLE (Baile an Chaisil) – Mayo – 712 D 5 🏛 Ireland   36 B2
▶ Dublin 267 km – Galway 140 km – Sligo 88 km
🄲 Cáide Fields ★, **AC**, NE : 8 km by R 314

🏨 **Stella Maris** ॐ   ≤ 🚗 ⅙ rm, ⌁ 🛰 **P** **VISA** 🔞
Northwest : 3 km by R 314 – ℰ (096) 43 322 – www.stellamarisireland.com
– info@stellamarisireland.com – Fax (096) 43 965 – April-September
12 rm ⌂ – †€ 170 ††€ 260   **Rest** – (dinner only) Carte € 35/50
◆ Former coastguard station and fort in a great spot overlooking the bay. Public areas include a long conservatory. Attractive rooms with antique and contemporary furnishings. Modern menus in stylish dining room.

BALLYCONNELL (Báal Atha Conaill) – Cavan – 712 J 5   37 C2
▶ Dublin 143 km – Drogheda 122 km – Enniskillen 37 km
🄵🄰 Slieve Russell, ℰ (049) 952 6458

🏨 **Slieve Russell**   ≤ 🏊 🔲 🌀 🎿 ♨ ℐ𝒮 ⅙ 🄵🄰 ⑆ ⅙ rm, 🏃 ⌁ 🛰 ♨
Southeast : 2 ¾ km on N 87 – ℰ (049) 952 6444   **P** **VISA** 🔞 **AE** ①
– www.quinnhotels.com – slieve-russell@quinn-hotels.com – Fax (049) 952 6474
218 rm ⌂ – †€ 150 ††€ 270 – 4 suites
Rest *Conall Cearnach* – (dinner only and Sunday lunch) Menu € 50
Rest *Setanta* – (closed Sunday lunch) Menu € 19 (lunch) **s** – Carte € 30/52
◆ Purpose-built hotel set in extensive gardens and golf course. Marbled entrance, large lounges, leisure and conference facilities. Spacious, modern rooms. Conall Cearnach has sophisticated appeal. Modern, informal, Mediterranean menu in Setanta.

🏠 **Carnagh House** without rest   🚗 ⅙ **P**
Clinty, West : 3 km on N 87 – ℰ (049) 952 3300 – www.carnaghhouse.com
– caraghhouse@eircom.net – Fax (049) 952 3300
10 rm ⌂ – †€ 50 ††€ 80
◆ Modern guesthouse with pleasant rural aspect. Warmly run by owners: tea and sandwiches await guests on arrival. Comfortable lounge with views. Good-sized bedrooms.

BALLYCOTTON (Baile Choitín) – Cork – 712 H 12 🏛 Ireland   39 C3
▶ Dublin 265 km – Cork 43 km – Waterford 106 km
🄲 Cloyne Cathedral ★, NW : by R 629

🏨 **Bayview**   ≤ 🚗 ⑆ ⅙ **P** **VISA** 🔞 **AE** ①
– ℰ (021) 464 67 46 – www.thebayviewhotel.com – res@thebayviewhotel.com
– Fax (021) 464 60 75 – April-October
33 rm ⌂ – †€ 117/142 ††€ 170/220 – 2 suites
Rest – (bar lunch Monday-Saturday) Menu € 35 (lunch) – Carte dinner € 39/55
◆ A series of cottages in an elevated position with fine views of bay, harbour and island. Bar and lounge in library style with sofas. Spacious, comfy rooms with ocean views. Warm, inviting dining room.

BALLYDAVID (Baile na nGall) – Kerry – 712 A 11 – ⌷ Dingle   38 A2
▶ Dublin 362 km – Dingle 11 km – Tralee 58 km

🏠 **Gorman's Clifftop House** ॐ   ≤ 🚗 ⅙ 🛰 **P** **VISA** 🔞
Glaise Bheag, North : 2 km on Feomanagh rd. – ℰ (066) 915 5162
– www.gormans-clifftophouse.com – info@gormans-clifftophouse.com
– Fax (066) 915 5003 – Closed 24-26 December and 12 January-12 February
9 rm ⌂ – †€ 85/125 ††€ 120/180   **Rest** – Carte € 33/52 **s**
◆ Fine views of Ballydavid Head and the Three Sisters from this peaceful modern house. Cosy sitting room with log fire; stylish, spacious rooms in vibrant colours and old pine. Bright restaurant invites diners to look out over the water.

🏠 **Old Pier** ॐ   ≤ 🚗 **P** **VISA** 🔞
An Fheothanach, North : 3 km on Feomanagh rd – ℰ (066) 915 5242
– www.oldpier.com – info@oldpier.com
5 rm ⌂ – †€ 45/55 ††€ 80/90   **Rest** – (by arrangement) Carte € 24/63
◆ Run by the charming owner, a pretty clifftop house surveying the harbour and the Three Sisters. Immaculate rooms with bright bedspreads and cherrywood floors.

BALLYFARNAN – Roscommon – 712 H 5   37 C2

▶ Dublin 111 km – Roscommon 42 km – Sligo 21 km – Longford 38 km

Kilronan Castle
South East 3½ km on Keadew rd – *Ƥ* (071) 964 7771 – www.kilronancastle.ie
– enquiries@kilronancastle.ie – Fax (071) 964 7772
84 rm ☷ – ♥€ 99/299 ♥♥€ 129/399
Rest Douglas Hyde – Carte € 29/56
♦ Restored and rebuilt castle with lots of wood panelling, antiques and portraits. Bedrooms in the main castle more characterful; those in extension more contemporary. Grand dining room; traditional menu uses local produce.

BALLYFERRITER – Kerry – 712 A 11 – ⊠ Dingle ▌Ireland   38 A2

▶ Dublin 363 km – Killarney 85 km – Limerick 167 km
🏌 Ceann Sibéal, *Ƥ* (066) 915 62 55
🖭 Corca Dhuibhne Regional Museum★ AC
🖭 Gallarus Oratory★★, E : 4 km by F 559 – Kilmalkedar★, E : 8 km by R 559 –
Slea Head★★ (beehive huts★), S : 14 km by R 559. Blasket Islands★,
S : 8 km by R 559 and by boat from Dunquin – Connor Pass★★,
NE : 24 km by R 559 and minor road

Smerwick Harbour
East : 4½ km on R 559 – *Ƥ* (066) 915 64 70 – www.smerwickhotel.ie
– info@smerwickhotel.ie – Fax (066) 915 64 73 – April-October
33 rm ☷ – ♥€ 60/110 ♥♥€ 180   **Rest** – (dinner only) Carte € 25/41
♦ Purpose-built hotel in dramatic Dingle Peninsula, Ireland's most westerly point. Large, atmospheric oak tavern with local artefacts. Sizeable rooms have spectacular views. Inviting dining room has fire with large brick surround.

BALLYGAWLEY Sligo – Sligo – 712 G 5 – pop. 186   36 B2

▶ Dublin 131 km – Sligo 10 km – Ballina 38 km – Carrick-on-Shannon 29 km

Castle Dargan
East : ½ km on R 290 – *Ƥ* (071) 911 8080 – www.castledargan.com
– sales@castledargan.com – Fax (071) 911 8090 – Closed 24-26 December
48 rm ☷ – ♥€ 150 ♥♥€ 360   **Rest** – Menu € 35/45 – Carte € 36/57
♦ Modern, annexed hotel with castle ruins in its extensive grounds. Contemporary bar and outside terrace with views over golf course. Well-equipped bedrooms. Dining room serves popular menus.

BALLYLICKEY (Béal Átha Leice) – Cork – 712 D 12 – ⊠ Bantry ▌Ireland   38 A3

▶ Dublin 347 km – Cork 88 km – Killarney 72 km
🏌 Bantry Bay Donemark, *Ƥ* (027) 50 579
🖭 Bantry Bay★ - Bantry House★ AC, S : 5 km by R 584. Glengarriff★
(Ilnacullin★★, access by boat) NW : 13 km by N 71 - Healy Pass★★ (≤★★)
W : 37 km by N 71, R 572 and R 574 – Slieve Miskish Mountains (≤★★) W :
46¾ km by N 71 and R 572 – Lauragh (Derreen Gardens★ AC) NW : 44 km
by N 71, R 572 and R 574 – Allihies (copper mines★) W : 66¾ km by N 71,
R 572 and R 575 – Garnish Island (≤★) W : 70¾ km by N 71 and R 572

Seaview House
– *Ƥ* (027) 50 462 – www.seaviewhousehotel.com – info@seaviewhousehotel.com
– Fax (027) 51 555 – Mid March-mid November
25 rm ☷ – ♥€ 85/125 ♥♥€ 140/185
Rest – (dinner only and Sunday lunch) Menu € 45
♦ Tall, well-run, whitewashed Victorian house set amidst lush gardens which tumble down to Bantry Bay. Traditional lounges with bar and spacious, individually designed rooms. Warmly decorated dining room.

Ballylickey House without rest
– *Ƥ* (027) 50 071 – www.ballylickeymanorhouse.com – ballymh@eircom.net
– Mid April-October
6 rm ☷ – ♥€ 80/95 ♥♥€ 110/175
♦ Impressive hotel with attractive gardens set amongst Bantry Bay's ragged inlets. Spacious, cosy bedrooms, named after flowers and birds. Breakfast room with fireside armchairs.

BALLYLIFFIN – Donegal – 712 J 2

37 **C1**

▶ Dublin 174 km – Lifford 46 km – Letterkenny 39 km

⌂ Ballyliffin Lodge 🔲 🏵 🗠 Ⅰ⅄ 📶 ᗶ 🕭 rm, 🕅 rest, ※ ¶¶ ᔑᴧ 🅿 VISA ⚈ AE ⬤
Shore Rd – 𝒞 (074) 9378200 – www.ballyliffinlodge.com
– info@ballyliffinlodge.com – Fax (074) 9378985 – Closed 25 December
40 rm 🖙 – ♦€105/120 ♦♦€190/240
Rest – (bar lunch Monday-Saturday) Menu €45 – Carte €37/53
♦ Nick Faldo part-designed golf course set close to this new hotel with rural/beach
views. Well-appointed lounge and good quality spa. Well-equipped rooms, some
with sea vistas. Fine dining restaurant inspired by classical cuisine.

BALLYMACARBRY (Baile Mhac Cairbre) – Waterford – 712 I 11

39 **C2**

– ⊠ Clonmel ▮ *Ireland*

▶ Dublin 190 km – Cork 79 km – Waterford 63 km

◩ Clonmel★ (St Mary's Church★, County Museum★ **AC**), N : 16 km by R 671
– Lismore★ (Castle Gardens★ **AC**, St Carthage's Cathedral★), SW : 26 km
by R 671and N 72 – W : Nier Valley Scenic Route★★

⌂ Hanora's Cottage ॐ ⪕ 🚄 ※ 🅿 VISA ⚈
Nire Valley, East : 6½ km by Nire Drive rd and Nire Valley Lakes rd – 𝒞 (052)
6136134 – www.hanorascottage.com – hanorascottage@eircom.net – Fax (052)
6136540 – Closed 1 week Christmas
10 rm 🖙 – ♦€95/120 ♦♦€170/190
Rest – (closed Sunday) (dinner only) (booking essential for non-residents)
Carte approx. €50
♦ Pleasant 19C farmhouse with purpose-built extensions in quiet location at foot of
mountains. Very extensive and impressive breakfast buffet. Stylish rooms, all with
jacuzzis. Locally renowned menus, brimming with fresh produce.

⌂ Glasha Farmhouse ॐ ⪕ 🚄 ※ 🅿 VISA ⚈
Northwest : 4 km by R 671 – 𝒞 (052) 36108 – www.glashafarmhouse.com
– glasha@eircom.net – Fax (052) 36108 – Closed 1-28 December
6 rm 🖙 – ♦€60/65 ♦♦€100/120   **Rest** – (by arrangement) Carte €25/45
♦ Immaculate farmhouse rurally set on working farm. Garden water feature is focal
point. Spacious conservatory. Wonderful breakfasts with huge choice. Neat, tidy
rooms.

⌂ Cnoc-na-Ri without rest ॐ ⪕ 🚄 ※ 🅿
Nire Valley, East : 6 km on Nire Drive rd – 𝒞 (052) 36239
– richardharte@eircom.net – February-October
4 rm 🖙 – ♦€55 ♦♦€90
♦ Purpose-built guesthouse situated in the heart of the unspoilt Nire Valley, a perfect
location for walking holidays. Immaculately kept, clean and spacious bedrooms.

Your opinions are important to us:
please write and let us know about your discoveries and experiences –
good and bad!

BALLYMOTE – Sligo – 712 G 5 – ⊠ Sligo

36 **B2**

▶ Dublin 199 km – Longford 77 km – Sligo 24 km

◪ Ballymote Ballinascarrow, 𝒞 (071) 83504

⌂ Mill House without rest 🚄 ※ ※ 🅿
Keenaghan – 𝒞 (071) 9183449 – millhousebb@eircom.net – April-September
6 rm 🖙 – ♦€35/47 ♦♦€70/79
♦ Simple guesthouse situated on edge of busy market town. Very friendly welcome.
Small, comfortable sitting room. Light, airy breakfast room. Spacious, immaculate
bedrooms.

BALLYNAHINCH (Baile na hInse) – **Galway** – **712** C 7 – ⊠ **Recess**   36 **A3**

📔 *Ireland*

> 🔼 Dublin 225 km – Galway 66 km – Westport 79 km
>
> ◻ Connemara★★★ – Roundstone★, S : by R 341 – Cashel★, SE : by R 341 and R 340

⌂⌂⌂   **Ballynahinch Castle**   ⑤   ↙ ⌂ ◊ ↖ ⅍ ⑨ **P** **VISA** **⓪** **AE** ⓪

– ℰ (095) 31 006 – www.ballynahinch-castle.com – bhinch@iol.ie – Fax (095) 31 085 – Closed 1 week Christmas

37 rm ⌔ – 🛇€170/180 🛇🛇€260/420 – 3 suites

Rest – (bar lunch) (booking essential for non-residents) Menu €60 **s**

♦ Grey stone, part 17C castle in magnificent grounds with fine river views. Two large sitting rooms, characterful bar frequented by fishermen. Spacious rooms with antiques. Inviting dining room with stunning river views.

BALLYNAMULT (Béal na Molt) – **Waterford**   39 **C2**

> 🔼 Dublin 194 km – Clonmel 21 km – Waterford 63 km

⌂   **Sliabh gCua Farmhouse** without rest   ↙ ⌂ **P**

Tooraneena, Southeast : 2 km – ℰ (058) 47 120 – www.sliabhgcua.com – breedacullinan@sliabhgcua.com – April-October

4 rm ⌔ – 🛇€50 🛇🛇€90

♦ Creeper clad early 19C house in quiet hamlet with rural views. Tea and scones on arrival. Comfy lounge with real fire. Individually decorated rooms boast period furniture.

BALLYSHANNON (Béal Atha Seanaidh) – **Kildare** – **712** H 4   39 **D2**
– pop. 1 627

> 🔼 Dublin 53 km – Donegal 272 km – Letterkenny 283 km – Sligo 215 km

⌂   **Heron's Cove**   ⅍ ↖ **P** **VISA** **⓪**

Creevy, Northwest : 3 km on R 231 – ℰ (071) 982 20 70 – www.heronscove.ie – info@heronscove.ie – Fax (071) 982 20 75 – Closed January and Monday-Tuesday in winter

10 rm ⌔ – 🛇€55/75 🛇🛇€90/110

Rest – (dinner only and Sunday lunch) Carte €37/45 **s**

♦ A well priced, friendly and informal destination on the road to Rossnowlagh. Identical bedrooms are clean and light with contemporary soft furnishings. An informal dining room offers a good choice menu with local seafood specialities.

BALLYVAUGHAN (Baile Uí Bheacháin) – **Clare** – **712** E 8 – pop. 224   38 **B1**

📔 *Ireland*

> 🔼 Dublin 240 km – Ennis 55 km – Galway 46 km
>
> ◻ The Burren★★ (Scenic Route★★, Aillwee Cave★ **AC** (Waterfall★★), Corcomroe Abbey★, Poulnabrone Portal Tomb★) – Kilfenora (Crosses★, Burren Centre★ **AC**), S : 25 km N 67 and R 476. Cliffs of Moher★★★, S : 32 km by N 67 and R 478

⌂⌂⌂   **Gregans Castle**   ⑤   ↙ ⌂ ◊ ⅍ ↖ **P** **VISA** **⓪** **AE**

Southwest : 6 km on N 67 – ℰ (065) 707 7005 – www.gregans.ie – stay@gregans.ie – Fax (065) 707 7111 – 12 February- November

17 rm ⌔ – 🛇€152/192 🛇🛇€195/235 – 4 suites

Rest – (bar lunch) Carte €39/60 **s**

♦ Idyllically positioned, family owned hotel with fine views to The Burren and Galway Bay. Relaxing sitting room, cosy bar lounge, country house-style bedrooms. Sizeable conservatory dining room specialising in seasonal, regional dishes.

⌂⌂   **Burren Coast**   ⌂ ⌸ ⌖ rm, ⅍ ↖ ⅍ **P** **VISA** **⓪** **AE**

Old Coast Rd – ℰ (065) 708 3000 – www.burrencoast.ie – info@burrencoast.ie – Fax (065) 708 3001

20 rm ⌔ – 🛇€75/85 🛇🛇€100/130   **Rest** – Carte €26/37

♦ Tucked away on western side of village, this modern hotel boasts comfortable, stylish bedrooms, a traditional beamed bar and garden terrace which looks onto pretty quay. Restaurant with mezzanine floor offers traditional menu.

REPUBLIC OF IRELAND

Drumcreehy House without rest ≤ 🗐 �, 🖭 P VISA ⚙
*Northeast : 2 km on N 67 – 𝒞 (065) 707 73 77 – www.drumcreehyhouse.com
– info@drumcreehyhouse.com – Fax (065) 707 73 79 – Booking essential in winter*
12 rm ⊅ – ♦€ 80/100 ♦♦€ 80/100
♦ Pristine house overlooking Galway Bay. Bedrooms are excellent value: spacious, comfortable and furnished in German stripped oak.

Rusheen Lodge without rest 🗐 ⅙ 🖭 P VISA ⚙
*Southwest : 1 km on N 67 – 𝒞 (065) 707 70 92 – www.rusheenlodge.com
– rusheen@iol.ie – Fax (065) 707 71 52 – Mid February-mid November*
8 rm ⊅ – ♦€ 65/75 ♦♦€ 100/110 – 1 suite
♦ Cheery yellow façade decked with flowers, lounge with fine sofas and rooms in pale woods and floral patterns. Pretty gardens complete the picture. Charming, welcoming area.

Ballyvaughan Lodge without rest ⅙ P VISA ⚙
– 𝒞 (065) 707 72 92 – www.ballyvaughanlodge.com – ballyvau@iol.ie – Fax (065) 707 72 87 – Closed Christmas - January
11 rm ⊅ – ♦€ 50/70 ♦♦€ 80/95
♦ Red hued guesthouse, attractively furnished throughout. Light and airy sitting room with large windows. Home-made bread and jams for breakfast. Clean, tidy bedrooms.

Cappabhaile House without rest ≤ 🗐 ⅙ 🖭 P VISA ⚙ AE
*Southwest : 1½ km on N 67 – 𝒞 (065) 707 72 60 – www.cappabhaile.com
– cappabhaile@gmail.com – March-October*
10 rm ⊅ – ♦€ 50/79 ♦♦€ 80/104
♦ Stone clad bungalow with pleasant gardens and good views across the Burren. Spacious open-plan lounge-cum-breakfast room with central fireplace. Very large, spotless rooms.

BALTIMORE (Dún na Séad) – **Cork** – 712 D 13 ▌ *Ireland* 38 **A3**
🔼 Dublin 344 km – Cork 95 km – Killarney 124 km
🄖 Sherkin Island ★ (by ferry) – Castletownshend ★, E : 20 km by R 595 and R 596 – Glandore ★, E : 26 km by R 595, N 71 and R 597

Casey's of Baltimore ≤ 🖭 rest, ⅙ 🖲 🕹 P VISA ⚙ AE ①
*East : ¾ km on R 595 – 𝒞 (028) 20 197 – www.caseysofbaltimore.com
– info@caseysofbaltimore.com – Fax (028) 20 509 – Closed 20-27 December*
14 rm ⊅ – ♦€ 103 ♦♦€ 158 **Rest** – Carte € 33/52 s
♦ Popular hotel near sea-shore. Cosy bar with open fires and traditional music at weekends, with beer garden overlooking bay. Large, well-decorated rooms with pine furniture. Great sea views from dining room.

Baltimore Townhouse without rest 🖲 P VISA ⚙ AE ①
*– 𝒞 (028) 20 197 – www.baltimoretownhouse.com
– info@baltimoretownhouse.com – Fax (028) 20 509 – Closed 20-27 December*
6 rm ⊅ – ♦€ 120/160 ♦♦€ 120/160
♦ Six open plan suites comprising bedroom, living area, small kitchen and bathroom. Check in at Casey's on your way into the village; breakfast is also served here.

Slipway without rest 🕊 ≤ 🗐 ⅙ 🖲 P
*The Cove, East : ¾ km – 𝒞 (028) 20 134 – www.theslipway.com
– theslipway@hotmail.com – Fax (028) 20 134 – April-October*
4 rm ⊅ – ♦€ 60/70 ♦♦€ 74/80
♦ Relaxed, informal guesthouse with yellow façade and lovely views of local harbour, particularly from veranda outside breakfast room. Simple, individualistic, well-kept rooms.

Customs House
*Main St – 𝒞 (028) 20 200 – www.thecustomshouse.com – gillian@
thecustomshouse.com – May - mid September (weekends only May and September)*
Rest – (closed Tuesday in June and Monday) (dinner only) (booking essential)
Menu € 38/48
♦ Converted customs house, consisting of three small rooms with a painted wood floor, decorated with modern art. Good value menu: all dishes are tasty and carefully prepared.

BANDON Cork – Cork – 712 F 12 – pop. 5 822   38 B3
▷ Dublin 181 km – Cork 20 km – Carrigaline 28 km – Cobh 33 km

Poacher's Inn   AC ⅏ P VISA ◉◉
Clonakilty Rd , Southwest : 1½ km on N 71 – ℰ *(023) 41 159*
Rest – Carte € 30/40
♦ Busy refurbished pub with downstairs bar, sofas and wood burning stove; simple menu served all day. Small restaurant upstairs offers larger selection, including lots of fish.

BANGOR (Baingear) – Mayo – 712 C 5 ▯ *Ireland*   36 A2
▷ Dublin 281 km – Ballina 42 km – Westport 63 km
◱ Cáide Fields★ AC, NE : 30 km by minor road and R 314

Teach Iorrais   ≼ ₺ rm, AC rest, ⅏ ₷ P VISA ◉◉ AE
Geesala, Southwest : 12 km on Geesala rd – ℰ *(097) 86 888*
– www.teachiorrais.com – teachlor@iol.ie – Fax (097) 86 855
31 rm ⌂ – †€ 42/52 ††€ 84/104
Rest – (dinner only and weekends only in winter) Carte € 33/46
♦ Purpose-built hotel with views of Neifin mountains. Public bar with live music at weekends and quieter residents lounge. Bright bedrooms, those to the front with best views. Charming views from window tables of Gothic styled restaurant.

BANTRY Cork – 712 D 12 – pop. 3 309   38 A3
▷ Dublin 215 km – Cork 53 km – Killarney 49 km – Macroom 34 km

The Maritime   ≼ ▯ ⅏ ₤₆ ▤ ₺ rm, AC ⅋ ₷ P VISA ◉◉ AE
The Quay – ℰ *(027) 54 700 – www.themaritime.ie – info@themaritime.ie*
– Fax (027) 54 701
114 rm ⌂ – †€ 120/180 ††€ 150/280
Rest *Ocean* – Carte € 33/47
♦ Situated on the quayside, with a modern style and spacious feel. Smart, comfortable bedrooms; the best at the front have a bay view, and 4th floor suites have a roof terrace. Ocean restaurant offers traditional fare.

BARNA (Bearna) – Galway – 712 E 8   36 B3
▷ Dublin 227 km – Galway 9 km

The Twelve   ▤ ₺ rm, AC ⅋ ₷ P VISA ◉◉ AE ①
Barna Crossroads – ℰ *(091) 597 000 – www.thetwelvehotel.ie*
– enquire@thetwelvehotel.ie – Fax (091) 597 003
38 rm ⌂ – †€ 112/220 ††€ 120/220 – 10 suites
Rest *West* – (Closed Sunday dinner and Monday) (dinner only and Sunday lunch) Menu € 25/35 **s** – Carte € 43/48 **s**
Rest *The Pins* – Menu € 25 (lunch) – Carte € 25/40 **s**
♦ Boutique hotel whose bedrooms are stylish and modern with quality furniture, up-to-date technology and designer toiletries. Original menu offered in elegant West restaurant. The Pins offers an interesting menu of European dishes in an informal atmosphere.

O'Grady's on the Pier   ≼ AC VISA ◉◉ AE
– ℰ *(091) 592 223 – www.ogradysonthepier.com – Fax (091) 590 677 – Closed 24-26 December*
Rest – Seafood – (booking essential) Carte € 25/55
♦ Converted quayside pub on two floors with great views of Galway Bay. Cheerful, attentive staff and daily menus of simple, flavourful seafood have earned good local reputation.

BARRELLS CROSS – Cork – 712 G 12 – see Kinsale

BEAUFORT (Lios an Phúca) – Kerry – 712 D 11 – see Killarney

BELMULLET Mayo – **Mayo** 36 **A2**

> ▶ Dublin 200 km – Castlebar 47 km – Crossmolina 32 km

⊞⊞   **Broadhaven Bay**   ≤ ⌧ ⋒ ♨ ⌸ & rm, ⅍ ⍣ ⓢ ₧ VISA ⚌

– ℰ (097) 20 600 – www.broadhavenbay.com – info@broadhavenbay.com
– Fax (097) 20 610
88 rm ⌑ – †€ 80/140 ††€ 120/190
Rest – (bar lunch Monday-Saturday) Menu € 35 – Carte € 30/45
♦ Smart hotel on the eastern side of town with good view over sea, towards mountains. Spacious lobby, quality bedrooms and modern bar/lounge popular with locals. Linen-clad restaurant with coastal aspect.

BETTYSTOWN (Baile an Bhiataigh) – **Meath** – 712 N 6 – **pop. 8 978** 37 **D3**

> ▶ Dublin 46 km – Drogheda 10 km – Dundalk 59 km

⊞⊞⊞   **Bettystown Court**   ⌧ ⋒ ♨ ⌸ & rm, ⓐⓒ rest, ⅍ ⍤ ⓢ ₧ VISA ⚌ ⚎ ⓪

– ℰ (041) 981 2900 – www.bettystowncourt.com
– info@bettystowncourthotel.com – Fax (041) 981 2989
116 rm ⌑ – †€ 120/140 ††€ 180/220 – 4 suites
Rest – (bar lunch Monday-Saturday) Menu € 35 **s** – Carte € 23/43 **s**
♦ Unimposing façade belies light, airy interior featuring stylish conference and leisure facilities. Spacious bedrooms continue contemporary theme; those at back have sea view. Restaurant serves traditional Irish dishes with a modern twist. Carvery at Sunday lunch.

The ✿ award is the crème de la crème.
This is awarded to restaurants
which are really worth travelling miles for!

BIRR – **Offaly** – 712 I 8 – **pop. 5 081** ▮ Ireland 39 **C1**

> ▶ Dublin 140 km – Athlone 45 km – Kilkenny 79 km – Limerick 79 km
> ❖ Brendan St ℰ (0509) 20110
> ⛳ The Glenns, ℰ (057) 912 00 82
> ◎ Town★ – Birr Castle Demesne★★ AC (Telescope★★)
> ⓒ Clonfert Cathedral★ (West doorway★★), NW : 24 km by R 439, R 356 and minor roads – Portumna★ (Castle★ AC), W : 24 km by R 489 – Roscrea★ (Damer House★ AC) S : 19¼ km by N 62 – Slieve Bloom Mountinas★, E : 21 km by R 440

⊞   **The Maltings** without rest   ⅍ ⍣ ₧ VISA ⚌

Castle St – ℰ (057) 91 21 345 – themaltingsbirr@eircom.net – Fax (057) 91 22 073
10 rm ⌑ – †€ 55 ††€ 80/90
♦ Characterful 19C hotel on riverside near Birr Castle, originally built to store malt for Guinness. Cosy bar and lounge. Bedrooms enriched by flowery fabrics and drapes.

BLACKLION (An Blaic) – **Cavan** – 712 I 5 34 **A3**

> ▶ Dublin 194 km – Drogheda 170 km – Enniskillen 19 km
> ⛳ Blacklion Toam, ℰ (072) 53 024

✗✗✗   **Mac Nean House** with rm   VISA ⚌ ⚎

Main St – ℰ (071) 985 30 22 – www.macneanrestaurant.com
– info@macneanrestaurant.com – Fax (071) 985 34 04 – Closed 21-28 December,
1 January-13 February
10 rm ⌑ – †€ 80 ††€ 140
Rest – (Closed Wednesday except June-September, Monday and Tuesday) (dinner only and Sunday lunch) (booking essential) Menu € 35/70
♦ Family run, contemporary restaurant with stylish lounge in the heart of border town. Local produce to the fore in high quality, original menus. Refurbished bedrooms.

BLARNEY (An Bhlarna) – **Cork** – **712** G 12 – **pop. 2 400** – ⊠ **Cork**   38 **B3**

📗 *Ireland*

> 🚗 Dublin 268 km – Cork 9 km
> 🏛 ℰ (021) 4381624
> 👁 Blarney Castle★★ **AC** – Blarney Castle House★ **AC**

↑ **Killarney House** without rest   🚗 ❄ **P**
Station Rd, Northeast : 1½ km – ℰ (021) 438 18 41
*– www.killarneyhouseblarney.com – info@killarneyhouseblarney.com – Fax (021)
438 18 41*
6 rm ⊆ – ♦€ 47/55 ♦♦€ 70/80

♦ Spacious, modern guesthouse set above attractive village. Very comfortable
lounge. Breakfast room equipped to high standard. Sizeable, immaculately kept
rooms.

---

at Tower West : 3 ¼ km on R 617 – ⊠ **Cork**

🏛🏛 **Blarney Golf Resort** ⌲   ≤ 🐾 🔲 🍸 ♪₅ 🍴🅗 🛗 ₤ rm, 🎚 ⁽¹⁾ ⚒ **P**
– ℰ (021) 438 4477 – www.blarneygolfresort.com   **VISA** **◎◎** **AE** **①**
– reservations@blarneygolfresort.com – Fax (021) 451 6453
60 rm ⊆ – ♦€ 85/110 ♦♦€ 95/120 – 4 suites
Rest – Menu € 25/40 – Carte € 36/46

♦ Two storey, purpose built hotel set around John Daly designed 18 hole golf
course. Traditional bedrooms all have views; the more popular executive-style rooms
have balconies. Traditional Irish fare served in restaurant.

🏛 **Ashlee Lodge**   🍸 ₤ rm, 🎚 ⁽¹⁾ **P** **VISA** **◎◎** **AE** **①**
*– ℰ (021) 438 53 46 – www.ashleelodge.com – info@ashleelodge.com – Fax (021)
438 57 26*
10 rm ⊆ – ♦€ 85/95 ♦♦€ 99/140
Rest – (closed Sunday-Monday) (dinner only) Carte approx. € 40 **s**

♦ Relaxing modern house, ideally located for Blarney Castle. Breakfast room with
extensive menu. Outdoor Canadian hot tub. Very well-equipped rooms, some with
whirlpool baths.

↑ **Maranatha Country House** without rest ⌲   🚗 🐾 ❄ ⁽¹⁾ **P** **VISA** **◎◎**
East : ¾ km on R 617 – ℰ (021) 438 51 02 – www.maranathacountryhouse.com
– douglasvenn@eircom.net – Fax (021) 438 29 78 – March-15 November
6 rm ⊆ – ♦€ 45/90 ♦♦€ 70/120

♦ Charming Victorian house in acres of peaceful grounds. Antique furnished drawing
room. Relaxing, individual bedrooms, one lined with books, another with a large
circular bath.

> Luxury pad or humble abode?
> 🏛🏛 and ↑↑ denote categories of comfort.

BOYLE (Mainistir na Búille) – **Roscommon** – **712** H 6 – **pop. 2 522**   36 **B2**

📗 *Ireland*

> 🚗 Dublin 175 km – Longford 53 km – Sligo 45 km
> 👁 King House★ **AC**
> 🏛 Boyle Abbey★ **AC**, E : 2 km by N 4 – Lough Key Forest Park★ **AC**,
> E : 3 ¼ km by N 4. Arigna Scenic Drive★ (≤★), NE : 20 km by N 4, R 280
> and R 207 – Curlew Mountains (≤★), NW : 3 ½ km by N 4

↑ **Rosdarrig House** without rest   🚗 ⁽¹⁾ **P** **VISA**
Carrick Rd – ℰ (071) 966 20 40 – www.rosdarrig.com – rosdarrig@yahoo.co.uk
5 rm ⊆ – ♦€ 45/50 ♦♦€ 70/75

♦ Comfortable, well-kept guesthouse with friendly owners. Attractive lounge and
appealing wood-floored breakfast room. Good sized, smartly decorated rooms overlooking garden.

BRAY (Bré) – Wicklow – **712** N 8 – **pop. 31 901** ▮ *Ireland*　　　　　39 **D1**
> ▸ Dublin 21 km – Wicklow 32 km
> ▦ Woodbrook Dublin Rd, ℰ (01) 282 4799
> ▦ Old Conna Ferndale Rd, ℰ (01) 282 6055
> ▦ Greystones Rd, ℰ (01) 276 3200
> ◉ Powerscourt★★ (Waterfall★★ **AC**) W : 6½ km - Killruddery House and Gardens★ **AC**, S : 3¼ km by R 761. Wicklow Mountains★★

🏨　**Ramada Woodland Court**　　🔲 ⅄ rm, 🆔 rest, ⅍ ⅍ **P.** 💳 ⦿ 🆎 ⓪
Southern Cross Rd, South : 4 km by R 761 on Greystones rd – ℰ (01) 276 0258
– *www.ramadawoodlandcourt.com* – *info@ramadawoodlandcourt.com*
– *Fax (01) 276 0298* – *Closed 25 December*
88 rm – ♦€ 85 ♦♦€ 85, ⴲ €10
Rest – (bar lunch) Menu € 25 – Carte approx. € 25 **s**
♦ Bright, yellow painted hotel and smart garden. Warm lounge and bar boasts burgundy and dark green sofas and chairs. Comfortable rooms with thick carpeting and rich décor. Afternoon tea a staple of airy restaurant.

BUNBEG – Donegal – **712** H 2 ▮ *Ireland*　　　　　37 **C1**
> ▸ Dublin 314 km – Donegal 106 km – Londonderry 88 km
> ◉ The Rosses★, S : by R 257

🏨　**Ostan Gweedore** ⧖　　　⧠ ⟁ 🔲 ⅍ 𝄫 ⅍ ⅍ **P.** 💳 ⦿ 🆎
– ℰ (074) 953 11 77 – *www.ostangweedore.com*
– *reservations@ostangweedore.com* – *Fax (074) 953 17 26* – *Easter-November*
31 rm ⴲ – ♦€ 95/105 ♦♦€ 160/185 – 3 suites
Rest *Restaurant* – (dinner only) Carte € 47/71 **s**
Rest *Sundowner* – Tapas – (dinner only) Carte € 20/28 **s**
♦ Traditional hotel in a prominent position commanding spectacular views over Gweedore Bay. Large bar and pleasant sitting room. Treatment room. Classic, spacious bedrooms. Fresh, local produce to fore in Restaurant. Tapas menus in informal Sundowner.

BUNCLODY – Wexford – **712** M 10　　　　　39 **D2**
> ▸ Dublin 73 km – Wexford 27 km – Kilkenny 39 km – Carlow 20 km

🏨　**The Carlton Millrace**　　🔲 𝄫 ⅍ 🔲 ⅄ rm, ⅍ ⅍ **P.** 💳 ⦿ 🆎
Carrigduff – ℰ (053) 937 51 00 – *www.carltonmillracehotel.ie*
– *reservations.millrace@carlton.ie* – *Fax (053) 937 51 24* – *Closed 23-26 December*
56 rm ⴲ – ♦€ 80/130 ♦♦€ 100/250 – 16 suites
Rest *Lady Lucys* – (dinner only) Menu € 39 – Carte € 30/50
Rest *Bistro* – Carte € 23/44
♦ A family friendly hotel of vivid hues which also incorporates meeting facilties and sizable leisure centre. Spacious family apartments and suites are in adjacent block. Panoramic views from fourth floor Lady Lucys; formal menus. All-day, popular Bistro.

BUNDORAN – Donegal – **712** H 4 – **pop. 1 964** ▮ *Ireland*　　　　　37 **C2**
> ▸ Dublin 259 km – Donegal 27 km – Sligo 37 km
> 🅸 The Bridge, Main St ℰ (071) 9842539 (April-October)
> ◉ Creevykeel Court Cairn★, S : 5 km by N 15 - Rossnowlagh Strand★★, N : 8½ km by N 15 and R 231

🏨　**Fitzgerald's**　　　　　⧠ 🔲 ⅍ ⅍ **P.** 💳 ⦿
– ℰ (071) 984 13 36 – *www.fitzgeraldshotel.com* – *info@fitzgeraldshotel.com*
– *Fax (071) 984 21 21* – *Restricted opening in winter*
16 rm ⴲ – ♦€ 65/85 ♦♦€ 100/150
Rest *The Bistro* – (closed Monday-Tuesday to non-residents July-August) (dinner only) Carte € 27/38 **s**
♦ Family owned hotel in centre of popular seaside town overlooking Donegal Bay. Reception rooms warmed by wood-burning stove. Sumptuous sofas abound. Sea-facing front bedrooms. Linen-clad, informal Bistro with carefully compiled menu.

REPUBLIC OF IRELAND

BUNRATTY (Bun Raite) – Clare – 712 F 9 ▮ *Ireland*   38 B2

◨ Dublin 207 km – Ennis 24 km – Limerick 13 km
◉ Town★★ – Bunratty Castle★★

⌂ **Bunratty Manor**   ⟨ icons ⟩ 🍴 ⟨ ⟩ 👫 rm, ✄ 🍴 **P** *VISA* **⦿⦿** **AE ①**
– *℘* (061) 707 984 – www.bunrattymanor.net – bunrattymanor@eircom.net
– Fax (061) 360 588 – Closed 1 week Christmas
23 rm ☲ – ♦€ 95/115 ♦♦€ 135/165
Rest – (dinner only) Menu € 45 – Carte approx. € 50
♦ Purpose-built, tourist-oriented hotel in village centre. Comfy lounge with chintz suites; Neat, modern rooms in colourful fabrics and drapes. Smart terrace fringed by pleasant garden. Popular menus.

⌂ **Bunratty Grove** without rest   ⟨ icons ⟩ ✄ 🍴 **P** *VISA* **⦿⦿**
Castle Rd, North : 2½ km – *℘* (061) 369 579 – www.bunrattygrove.com
– *bunrattygrove@eircom.net – Fax (061) 369 561*
– *Closed 15 December - 1 February*
6 rm ☲ – ♦€ 40/70 ♦♦€ 70/80
♦ Pink painted guesthouse on country road with peaceful ambience. Large lounge-cum-library and pleasant, cottagey breakfast room. Immaculate rooms with polished wood floors.

⌂ **Bunratty Woods** without rest   ⟨ icons ⟩ ✄ **P** *VISA* **⦿⦿**
Low Rd, North : 1½ km – *℘* (061) 369 689 – www.bunrattywoods.com
– *bunratty@iol.ie – Fax (061) 369 454 – March-October*
14 rm ☲ – ♦€ 45/55 ♦♦€ 70/90
♦ Characterful guesthouse with large front garden. Owner collects and restores assorted items to decorate rooms, such as farmyard tools and old food tins. Sizeable bedrooms.

BUTLERSTOWN = Baile an Bhuitléaraigh – Waterford – see Waterford

CAHERDANIEL (Cathair Dónall) – Kerry – 712 B 12 – ✉ Killarney   38 A3
▮ *Ireland*

◨ Dublin 383 km – Killarney 77 km
◉ Ring of Kerry★★ – Derrynane National Historic Park★★ – Skellig Islands★★
AC, by boat – Sneem★, E : 19 km by N 70 – Staigue Fort★, E : 8 km by N 70 and minor road

⌂ **Iskeroon** without rest ⟨ ⟩   ⟨ icons ⟩ ⇐ ✄ 🍴 **P** *VISA* **⦿⦿**
West : 8 m. by N 70, Bunavalla Pier rd taking left turn at junction then turning left onto track immediately before pier – *℘* (066) 947 51 19 – www.iskeroon.com
– *info@iskeroon.com – Fax (066) 947 54 88*
– *May-September, minimum stay 2 nights*
3 rm ☲ – ♦♦€ 170
♦ A "design icon", this low-lying house looking out to Derrynane Harbour was built in 1930s by the Earl of Dunraven. Lush gardens; boldly designed, vividly coloured bedrooms.

⌂ **Derrynane Bay House** without rest   ⟨ icons ⟩ ⇐ ✄ **P** *VISA* **⦿⦿**
West : ¾ km on N 70 – *℘* (066) 947 54 04 – www.ringofkerry.net
– *derrynanebayhouse@eircom.net – Fax (066) 947 54 36 – April-October*
6 rm ☲ – ♦€ 50/60 ♦♦€ 76/80
♦ Purpose-built house on the Ring of Kerry with vast views over namesake bay. Stone Age monuments in the surrounding hills. Family-friendly; spacious bedrooms.

CAHERLISTRANE (Cathair Loistreáin) – Galway – 712 E 7   36 B3
◨ Dublin 256 km – Ballina 74 km – Galway 42 km

⌂ **Lisdonagh House** ⟨ ⟩   ⟨ icons ⟩ ⇐ ✄ 🍴 🍴 ✄ **P** *VISA* **⦿⦿** **AE**
Northwest : 2½ km by Shrule rd – *℘* (093) 31 163 – www.lisdonagh.com
– *cooke@lisdonagh.com – Fax (093) 31 528 – May-November*
10 rm ☲ – ♦€ 120/150 ♦♦€ 140/280 – 4 suites **Rest** – Carte € 39/49 **s**
♦ Georgian house overlooking Lough Hacket; row across to island in the middle. A grand entrance hall with fine murals leads to antique filled rooms named after Irish artists. Locally caught fish predominant in dining room.

CAHERSIVEEN (Cathair Saidhbhín) – **Kerry** – **712** B 12 ▮ *Ireland*   38 **A2**

▶ Dublin 355 km – Killarney 64 km
🖸 Ring of Kerry★★

🏠 **O'Neill's (The Point) Seafood Bar**   ← 🏠 🖾 ⅍ **P**
Renard Point, Southwest : 2¾ km by N 70 – ℰ *(066) 9472165*
– oneillsthepoint@eircom.net – Fax (087) 2595345 – March-October
Rest – (bookings not accepted) Carte € 32/50
♦ A warm welcome and freshly prepared seafood await at this simply furnished pub,
situated on the western edge of the Iveragh Peninsula. Concise menu. Maritime
décor.

CAMPILE (Ceann Poill) – **Wexford** – **712** L 11 ▮ *Ireland*   39 **D2**

▶ Dublin 154 km – Waterford 35 km – Wexford 37 km
🖸 Dunbrody Abbey★, S : 3¼ km by R 733 – J F Kennedy Arboretum★,
N : 3¼ km by R 733. Tintern Abbey★, SE : 12¾ km by R 733 – Duncannon
Fort★, S : 12¾ km by R 733

🏠 **Kilmokea Country Manor** 🌿   ← 🚴 🖾 🖾 🏊 *fá* ⅍ 🕭 rm, ¶
West : 8 km by R 733 and Great Island rd – ℰ *(051)*   **P**, **VISA** **◍◍** **AE**
388 109 – www.kilmokea.com – kilmokea@eircom.net – Fax (051) 388 776
– Restricted opening in winter
6 rm ⌂ – ♦€ 75/120 ♦♦€ 300
Rest – (booking essential for non-residents) Menu € 55 (dinner) **s**
– Carte (lunch) € 26/32 **s**
♦ Former Georgian rectory in large public gardens. Elegantly furnished. Games room,
tennis and fishing. Comfortable bedrooms in house and converted stable block.
Formal dining room with polished tables and period style; breakfast in conservatory.

CAPPOQUIN (Ceapach Choinn) – **Waterford** – **712** I 11 ▮ *Ireland*   39 **C2**

▶ Dublin 219 km – Cork 56 km – Waterford 64 km
🖸 Lismore★ (Lismore Castle Gardens★ **AC**, St Carthage's Cathedral★),
W : 6½ km by N 72. The Gap★ (←★) NW : 14½ km by R 669

🍴🍴 **Richmond House** with rm   🚴 🕭 **P**, **VISA** **◍◍** **AE** **①**
Southeast :¾ km on N 72 – ℰ *(058) 54278* – www.richmondhouse.net
– info@richmondhouse.net – Fax (058) 54988 – Closed 22 December-20 January
and Monday
9 rm ⌂ – ♦♦€ 160/240   **Rest** – (closed Sunday) (dinner only) Menu € 60
♦ Built for Earl of Cork and Burlington in 1704; retains Georgian style with stately,
cove-ceilinged dining room: local produce to the fore. Individually decorated period
rooms.

at Millstreet East : 11¼ km by N 72 on R 671 – ✉ Cappoquin

🏠 **Castle Country House** without rest 🌿   🚴 🕭 ⅍ **P**, **VISA** **◍◍** **AE** **①**
– ℰ *(058) 68049* – www.castlecountryhouse.com – castlefm@iol.ie
– April-October
5 rm ⌂ – ♦€ 50/55 ♦♦€ 100
♦ Extended farmhouse on working dairy and beef farm with 15C origins. Rural loca-
tion and lovely gardens. Individual bedrooms with cottage style decor.

CARAGH LAKE (Loch Cárthaí) – **Kerry** – **712** C 11 ▮ *Ireland*   38 **A2**

▶ Dublin 341 km – Killarney 35 km – Tralee 40 km
🏌 Dooks Glenbeigh, ℰ *(066) 976 82 05*
◎ Lough Caragh★
🖸 Iveragh Peninsula★★ (Ring of Kerry★★)

🏨 **Ard-Na-Sidhe** 🌿   🚴 🕭 🖾 ⅍ **P**, **VISA** **◍◍** **AE**
– ℰ *(066) 976 91 05* – www.killarneyhotels.ie – hotelsales@liebherr.com
– Fax (066) 976 92 82 – May-15 October
18 rm ⌂ – ♦€ 150/270 ♦♦€ 170/300
Rest – (dinner only) (booking essential for non-residents) Carte € 41/53
♦ Built 1880 by an English Lady who called it "House of Fairies". Elizabethan in style;
gardens lead down to lake. Possesses atmosphere of private home. Antique filled
rooms. Tasteful dining room with intimate feel.

Carrig Country House ⟩ ≤ ⌂ ⤳ 🛇 P VISA ⓪ ①
– 𝒞 (066) 976 91 00 – www.carrighouse.com – info@carrighouse.com – Fax (066) 976 91 66 – March-November

17 rm ⊇ – ♦€ 125/140 ♦♦€ 150/250

Rest – (dinner only) (booking essential for non-residents) Carte € 30/47

♦ Down a wooded drive, the yellow ochre façade of the house immediately strikes you. Its loughside setting assures good views. Ground floor rooms have their own private patio. Caragh Lough outlook from dining room windows.

CARLINGFORD (Cairlinn) – Louth – 712 N 5 ▮ Ireland   37 **D2**
🚩 Dublin 106 km – Dundalk 21 km
◎ Town★
◎ Windy Gap★, NW : 12 ¾ km by R 173 – Proleek Dolmen★, SW : 14½ km by R 173

Four Seasons   ≤ ⌂ 🖥 ⋙ ▮₆ 🛉 ⅙ rm, Ⓐ rest, 🛇 ⸱📶 ⅚ P VISA ⓪
– 𝒞 (042) 937 35 30 – www.4seasonshotel.ie – info@fshc.ie – Fax (042) 937 35 31

59 rm ⊇ – ♦€ 129/135 ♦♦€ 198/210

Rest – (bar lunch Monday-Saturday) Menu € 42 – Carte € 32/45

♦ Impressive purpose-built hotel on outskirts of scenic market town. Extensive conference facilities; smart leisure centre. Spacious and well-equipped bedrooms. Popular bar leading to intimate dining room with Irish menus.

Beaufort House without rest ⟩   ≤ ⌂ ⅙ P VISA ⓪
– 𝒞 (042) 937 38 79 – www.beauforthouse.net
– michaelcaine@beauforthouse.net – Fax (042) 937 38 78 – Closed 25 December

6 rm ⊇ – ♦€ 70/100 ♦♦€ 90/120

♦ Modern house attractively sited on shores of Carlingford Lough. Very comfortable, spacious rooms with sea or mountain views. Substantial breakfasts served overlooking lough.

CARLOW (Ceatharlach) – Carlow – 712 L 9 – pop. 20 724   39 **D2**
🚩 Dublin 80 km – Kilkenny 37 km – Wexford 75 km
🏛 College St 𝒞 (059) 913 1554, carlowtouristoffice@failteireland.ie
🏌 Carlow Dublin Rd, Deer Park, 𝒞 (059) 913 1695

Seven Oaks   ⌂ 🖥 ⋙ ▮₆ 🛉 ⅙ ⸱📶 ⅚ P VISA ⓪ AE ①
Athy Rd – 𝒞 (059) 913 13 08 – www.sevenoakshotel.com
– info@sevenoakshotel.com – Fax (059) 913 21 55 – Closed 25-26 December

89 rm ⊇ – ♦€ 80/100 ♦♦€ 160

Rest – (carvery lunch Saturday) Menu € 25/38 – Carte dinner € 26/37

♦ Close to the sights of the River Barrow walk, this neat hotel in a residential area makes a good resting place. Well-kept rooms: ask for those on first or second floor. Intimate booths in tranquil dining room.

Barrowville Town House without rest   ⌂ ⅙ ⸱📶 P VISA ⓪ AE
Kilkenny Rd, South : ¾ km on N 9 – 𝒞 (059) 914 33 24 – www.barrowville.com
– barrowvilletownhouse@eircom.net – Fax (059) 914 19 53
– Closed 24-28 December

7 rm ⊇ – ♦€ 60/95 ♦♦€ 110/140

♦ Regency townhouse professionally managed. Its conservatory breakfast room looks out over the garden containing ancient grape producing vine. Orthopaedic beds in all rooms.

CARNAROSS – Meath – 712 L 6 – ⊠ Kells   37 **D3**
🚩 Dublin 69 km – Cavan 43 km – Drogheda 48 km

✗✗ The Forge   ⟳ P VISA ⓪
Pottlereagh, Northwest : 5½ km by N 3 on Oldcastle rd – 𝒞 (046) 924 50 03
– theforgerest@eircom.net – Fax (046) 924 59 17
– Closed 24 December-2 January, Sunday dinner and Monday

Rest – (dinner only and Sunday lunch) Menu € 45 – Carte € 43/56

♦ Former forge tucked away in rural isolation. Family run, traditionally styled restaurant serving tried-and-tested dishes with modern twist: ample, good value choice.

REPUBLIC OF IRELAND

CARNE – Wexford – 712 M 11 — 39 D3

> ▶ Dublin 169 km – Waterford 82 km – Wexford 21 km

🍴 The Lobster Pot — AC P VISA ⓿

– ✆ (053) 913 1110 – Fax (053) 913 1401 – Closed 25-26 December, January, first week February and Monday except Bank Holidays when closed Tuesday

Rest – Seafood – Carte € 25/50

♦ Long-standing, popular pub quirkily cluttered with nautical knick-knacks. Wide-ranging seafood menu offers the freshest fish available; precisely cooked and simply served.

CARRICKMACROSS – Monaghan – 712 L 6 – pop. 4 387 📖 Ireland — 37 D2

> ▶ Dublin 92 km – Dundalk 22 km
> 🏨 Nuremore Hotel & CC, ✆ (042) 966 14 38
> 🅖 Dún a' Rí Forest Park★, SW : 8 km by R 179 – St Mochta's House★, E : 7 km by R 178 and minor road S

🏨 Nuremore ﹩ — ⟨ 🚗 🐕 🏊 🎱 🌐 🐎 📶 Ⅰ6 ※ 🏨 🛗 ㅎ 🌿 🎾 ㏈ P — VISA ⓿ AE ⓪

South : 1½ km on N 2 – ✆ (042) 966 14 38
– www.nuremore.com – info@nuremore.com – Fax (042) 966 18 53

72 rm � 立 – ♦€ 135/160 ♦♦€ 195/230

Rest *The Restaurant* – see restaurant listing

♦ Much extended Victorian house in attractive grounds; a rural retreat in which to swim, ride or practice golf. Comfortable rooms, most with views over countryside.

🍴🍴🍴 The Restaurant – at Nuremore Hotel — AC P VISA ⓿ AE ⓪

South : 1½ km on N 2 – ✆ (042) 966 14 38 – Fax (042) 966 18 53 – Closed Saturday lunch

Rest – Menu € 28/52 **s**

♦ Split-level dining room; tables laid with white linen, bone china and stylish glassware. Menu of seasonal dishes influenced by French fine dining. Attentive service.

CARRICK-ON-SHANNON – Leitrim – 712 H 6 – pop. 3 163 📖 Ireland — 37 C2

> ▶ Dublin 156 km – Ballina 80 km – Galway 119 km – Roscommon 42 km – Sligo 55 km
> 🚊 Old Barrel Store, The Marina ✆ (0719) 620170 (April-October), leitrim@failteireland.ie
> 🏌 Carrick-on-Shannon Woodbrook, ✆ (079) 67 015
> 🔲 Town★
> 🅖 Lough Rynn Demesne★

🏨 The Landmark — ⟨ 🛗 ㅎ rm, AC rest, ※ 🌿 📶 P VISA ⓿ AE

on N 4 – ✆ (071) 962 22 22 – www.thelandmarkhotel.com
– reservations@thelandmarkhotel.com – Fax (071) 962 22 33
– Closed 24-25 December

60 rm ☰ 立 – ♦€ 98/134 ♦♦€ 150/208

Rest CJ's – Carte € 27/36 **s**

♦ Overlooks the Shannon; some areas reminiscent of a luxury liner: wooden floors, panelled ceiling. Marble fountain in lobby. Richly furnished rooms; water scenes on walls. CJ's boasts pleasant river views.

🏠 Hollywell without rest ﹩ — ⟨ 🚗 ※ P VISA ⓿ AE

Liberty Hill, off N 4, taking first left over bridge – ✆ (071) 962 11 24
– hollywell@esatbiz.com – Fax (071) 962 11 24 – March-October

4 rm 立 – ♦€ 75/85 ♦♦€ 130/150

♦ A charming part 18C house in a peaceful spot by the river. Read up on area in a well-appointed lounge, take breakfast in dining room run by hospitable owner. Neat rooms.

🍴 The Oarsman — 🐕 ※ VISA ⓿

Bridge St – ✆ (071) 962 17 33 – www.theoarsman.com – info@theoarsman.com
– Fax (071) 962 17 34 – Closed 25 December and Good Friday

Rest – (Closed Sunday-Monday) Carte € 19/40

♦ Friendly, family-run pub with lively, local feel, set on busy, town centre street. Eclectic menus offer wide range; from snacks and salads through to restaurant-style dishes.

CARRIGALINE (Carraig Uí Leighin) – Cork – **712** G 12 – pop. 12 835   38 **B3**

D Dublin 262 km – Cork 14 km

F8 Fernhill, *&* (021) 437 2226

🏠🏠🏠 **Carrigaline Court**   🈀 🖂 🕸 *I₆* 🗐 🕭 rm, 🅰🄲 rest, 🛇 🍸 🕸 **P**

Cork Rd – *&* (021) 485 21 00 – www.carrigcourt.com   VISA ⓶ AE ①
– reception@carrigcourt.com – Fax (021) 437 11 03 – Closed 25-26 December
89 rm ⌴ – ♦€ 150 ♦♦€ 200 – 2 suites
Rest *The Bistro* – (carvery lunch) Carte €38/50 **s**

♦ Modern hotel with airy interiors; rooms are spacious, with all mod cons, whilst leisure centre boasts a 20m pool, steam room, sauna. Corporate friendly with large ballroom. Local products to the fore in stylish restaurant.

🏠 **Raffeen Lodge** without rest   🚗 🕸 **P** VISA ⓶

Ringaskiddy Rd, Monkstown, Northeast : 4 km by R 611 and N 28 off R 610
– *&* (021) 437 16 32 – www.raffeenlodge.com – info@raffeenlodge.com
– Fax (021) 437 16 32 – Closed 20 December-7 January
6 rm ⌴ – ♦€ 45/50 ♦♦€ 70/76

♦ A short drive from the fishing village of Ringaskiddy and Cork airport. A neat and tidy, good value house; rooms are uniformly decorated in pastel shades, simple in style.

🏠 **Shannonpark House** without rest   🚗 🕸 🕭 **P**

Cork Rd, North : 1½ km on R 611 – *&* (021) 437 2091
– Closed 23-28 December
4 rm ⌴ – ♦€ 45/55 ♦♦€ 80/90

♦ Breakfasts at the lace-topped communal table in this simple, homely guesthouse. Cosy little sitting room; bedrooms, always immaculate, furnished in dark wood.

CARRIGANS (An Carraigáin) – Donegal – **712** J 3   37 **C1**

D Dublin 225 km – Donegal 66 km – Letterkenny 230 km – Sligo 124 km

🏠 **Mount Royd** without rest   🚗 🕸 **P**

– *&* (074) 914 01 63 – www.mountroyd.com – jmartin@mountroyd.com
– Fax (074) 914 04 00 – March-October
4 rm ⌴ – ♦€ 40 ♦♦€ 70/80

♦ Genuinely hospitable owners keep this creeper-clad period house in excellent order. En suite rooms are cosy and individually styled. Traditional, pleasantly cluttered lounge.

CASHEL – Galway – **712** C 7 ▌*Ireland*   36 **A3**

D Dublin 278 km – Galway 66 km

🔘 Town ★

🄲 Connemara ★★★

🏠🏠🏠 **Cashel House** 🕸   🚗 🕭 🔾 🛇 **P** VISA ⓶ AE

– *&* (095) 31 001 – www.cashel-house-hotel.com – res@cashel-house-hotel.com
– Fax (095) 31 077 – Closed 4-31 January
29 rm ⌴ – ♦€ 107/270 ♦♦€ 214/304
Rest – (booking essential for non-residents) Menu €34/68 **s** – Carte €56/60 **s**

♦ Built 1840; a very comfortable and restful country house, warmly decorated with delightful gardens. General de Gaulle stayed in one of the luxurious country house rooms. Dining room, with Queen Anne style chairs, opens into elegant conservatory.

🏠 **Zetland Country House** 🕸   ≤ 🚗 🔾 🛇 🔾 **P** VISA ⓶ AE ①

– *&* (095) 31 111 – www.zetland.com – zetland@iol.ie – Fax (095) 31 117
22 rm ⌴ – ♦€ 122 ♦♦€ 240/320   **Rest** – (bar lunch) Menu €60 **s**

♦ Lord Zetland's sporting lodge in 1800s; a splendid position in gardens sweeping down to Cashel Bay. Snooker, scuba diving, hunting organised. Pastel rooms. Dining room with silver cutlery, peerless views.

CASHEL – Tipperary – 712 I 10 – **pop. 2 936** 📖 *Ireland*   39 **C2**

- ▶ Dublin 162 km – Cork 96 km – Kilkenny 55 km – Limerick 58 km – Waterford 71 km
- 🛈 Heritage Centre, Town Hall, Main St ℰ (062) 62511, cashelhc@iol.ie
- 👁 Town★★★ – Rock of Cashel★★★ **AC** – Cormac's Chapel★★ – Round Tower★ – Museum★ – Cashel Palace Gardens★ – GPA Bolton Library★ **AC**
- 🄶 Holy Cross Abbey★★, N : 14½ km by R 660 – Athassel Priory★, W : 8 km by N 74. Caher (Castle★★, Swiss Cottage★), S : 18 km by N 8 – Glen of Aherlow★, W : 21 km by N 74 and R 664

🏛 **Cashel Palace**   🚗 🕭 📶 🛁 🖳 **VISA** 🞉 **AE** ①

Main St – ℰ (062) 62 707 – www.cashel-palace.ie – reception@cashel-palace.ie – Fax (062) 61 521 – Closed 24-27 December

23 rm ⊡ – †€ 175/205 ††€ 260/430

Rest – (carvery lunch Monday-Saturday) Menu € 60 – Carte € 38/55

♦ A stately Queen Anne house, once home to an Archbishop, in walled gardens with path leading up to Cashel Rock. Inside, an extensive, pillared lounge and capacious rooms. Harmonious dining room: vaulted ceilings, open fire and light, bright colours.

🏛 **Baileys of Cashel**   📺 🕭 ℒ6 📶 🛁 rm, 🄰🄲 📶 🖳 **VISA** 🞉 **AE**

Main St – ℰ (062) 61 937 – www.baileys-ireland.com – info@baileys-ireland.com – Fax (062) 63 957 – Closed 25-26 December and 1 January

20 rm ⊡ – †€ 95 ††€ 150/180   **Rest** – Carte € 21/41

♦ Extended Georgian townhouse, used as grain store during Irish famine. Contemporary bedrooms are furnished to a high standard. Small lounge with library; bar area in basement. Restaurant with open plan kitchen serves modern European cooking.

🏠 **Aulber House** without rest   🚗 🛁 📶 🖳 **VISA** 🞉

Deerpark, Golden Rd, West : ¾ km on N 74 – ℰ (062) 63 713 – www.aulberhouse.com – info@aulberhouse.com – Fax (062) 63 715 – Closed 21 December - 20 January

12 rm ⊡ – †€ 50/80 ††€ 100

♦ Modern house in Georgian style with lawned gardens; five minutes from town centre. Comfy, leather furnished lounge. Smart, individually styled rooms.

🏠 **Hill House** without rest   ← 🚗 🛁 📶 🖳 **VISA** 🞉

Palmershill – ℰ (062) 61 277 – www.hillhousecashel.com – hillhouse1@eircom.net – April-October

5 rm ⊡ – †€ 60/70 ††€ 100/120

♦ Historic, family run 18C guest house with charming garden and well appointed lounge. Bedrooms 3, 4 and 5 have views of famous Rock of Cashel; 4 and 5 also have four posters.

XXX **Chez Hans**   🖳 **VISA** 🞉 ①

Rockside, Moor Lane St – ℰ (062) 61 177 – www.chezhans.net – Fax (062) 61 177 – Closed 2 weeks January, 1 week September, Sunday and Monday

Rest – (dinner only) (booking essential) Carte € 59/70

♦ A converted synod hall with stained glass windows, near Cashel Rock: an unusual setting for a restaurant. Carefully prepared and cooked meals, using local ingredients.

X **Cafe Hans**   🄰🄲 🖳

😊 Rockside, Moore Lane St – ℰ (062) 63 660 – Closed last 2 weeks January, 2 weeks mid September, Sunday and Monday

Rest – (lunch only) (bookings not accepted) Carte € 23/36

♦ Next door to Chez Hans; white emulsioned walls, open kitchen and glass roof. Simple, tasty dishes are prepared with good, local ingredients. Come early as you can't book.

Good food and accommodation at moderate prices?
Look for the Bib symbols:
red Bib Gourmand 😊 for food, blue Bib Hotel 🔲 for hotels

REPUBLIC OF IRELAND

CASTLEBALDWIN (Béal Átha na gCarraigíní) – Sligo – 712 G 5   36 **B2**
– ✉ Boyle (Roscommon) 📗 *Ireland*

▶ Dublin 190 km – Longford 67 km – Sligo 24 km
🎏 Carrowkeel Megalithic Cemetery (≤ ★★), S : 4 ¾ km. Arigna Scenic Drive★,
N : 3 ¼ km by N 4 - Lough Key Forest Park★ **AC**, SE : 16 km by N 4
– View of Lough Allen★, N : 14 ½ km by N 4 on R 280 – Mountain Drive★,
N : 9 ½ km on N 4 – Boyle Abbey★ **AC**, SE : 12 ¾ km by N 4 - King House★,
SE : 12 ¾ km by N 4

🏨 **Cromleach Lodge** 🌿   ≤ 🚗 🐾 🦌 🛁 🏠 🕯️ 🎿 **P** 🚫 **VISA ⬤ AE ①**
Ballindoon, Southeast : 5 ½ km – 𝒞 (071) 916 51 55 – www.cromleach.com
– info@cromleach.com – Fax (071) 916 54 55 – Closed 23-27 December
68 rm ⌓ – 🛏️€65/149 🛏️🛏️€130/198
Rest – Menu €30/55 – Carte dinner approx. €53
♦ Has gone from 9 to now 68 rooms, built into the hillside overlooking the Lough
and linked to the hotel via walkway. Contemporary new bedrooms, with all mod
cons, can be adapted into 'cottages'. Open plan restaurant uses much local produce.

> Red = Pleasant. Look for the red 🍴 and 🏠 symbols.

CASTLEGREGORY (Caisleán Ghriaire) – Kerry – 712 B 11   38 **A2**
▶ Dublin 330 km – Dingle 24 km – Killarney 54 km

↑ **The Shores Country House** without rest   ≤ 🚗 🎿 **P** 🚫 **VISA ⬤**
Conor Pass Rd, Kilcummin, Southwest : 6 km on Brandon rd – 𝒞 (066) 713 91 95
– www.shorescountryhouse.com – theshores@eircom.net – Fax (066) 713 91 96
– March-15 November
6 rm ⌓ – 🛏️€45/90 🛏️🛏️€90
♦ Between Stradbally Mountain and a long sandy beach, a modern guest house run
by the friendly longstanding owner. Immaculate, comfortable rooms, some with
antique beds.

CASTLEKNOCK (Caisleán Cnucha) – Dublin – see Dublin

CASTLELYONS (Caisleán Ó Liatháin) – Cork – 712 H 11 – pop. 203   38 **B2**
▶ Dublin 219 km – Cork 30 km – Killarney 104 km – Limerick 64 km

↑ **Ballyvolane House** 🌿   ≤ 🚗 🐾 🦌 🕯️ **P** 🚫 **VISA ⬤ AE**
Southeast : 5 ½ km by Midleton rd on Britway rd – 𝒞 (025) 36 349
– www.ballyvolanehouse.ie – info@ballyvolanehouse.ie – Fax (025) 36 781
– Closed Christmas-New Year
6 rm ⌓ – 🛏️€140/160 🛏️🛏️€230/270
Rest – (by arrangement, communal dining) Menu €65
♦ Stately 18C Italianate mansion mentioned in local legend, with lakes in parkland.
Name means "place of springing heifers". Antique-filled rooms, some with Victorian
baths. Dining room with silver candlesticks and balanced dishes.

CASTLEMARTYR Cork – 712 H 12   39 **C3**
▶ Dublin 174 km – Cork 20 km – Ballincollig 25 km – Carrigaline 24 km

🏨 **Capella**   🚗 🐾 🦌 📺 🍴 📶 📡 🛁 🛁 🛀 rm, 🔳 🕯️ 🎿 **P** 🚫 **VISA ⬤ AE**
– 𝒞 (021) 464 4050 – www.capellacastlemartyr.com
– info.castlemartyr@capellahotels.com – Fax (021) 464 4051
83 rm ⌓ – 🛏️€175/400 🛏️🛏️€175/400 – 26 suites
Rest *Bell Tower* – Carte €43/70 **s**
Rest *Garden Room* – Carte €34/52 **s**
♦ Grand 17C manor house in 220 acres, with river, castle ruins, golf course and
spa. Maximum luxury; from the meeting room and lounge to the contemporary bed-
rooms and suites. Traditional fine dining in the Bell Tower. Breakfast or lunch in the
Garden Room, overlooking the formal gardens and fountain.

REPUBLIC OF IRELAND

CASTLEPOLLARD – Westmeath – 712 K 6   37 C3

> ▪ Dublin 63 km – Mullingar 13 km – Tullamore 37 km – Édenderry 36 km

⌂ **Lough Bishop House** ⊗   🖼 🕪 ❄ P

*Derrynagarra, Collinstown, Southeast : 6 km by R 394 taking left turn on
unmarked rd opposite church and school after 4 km* – ℰ *(044) 966 13 13*
– www.loughbishophouse.com – chkelly@eircom.net – Fax (044) 966 13 13
– Closed Christmas-New Year

3 rm � – †€ 55/65 ††€ 110

Rest – (by arrangement, communal dining) Menu € 30

♦ Renovated 19C farmhouse on south-facing hillside. Well-kept, with homely lounge
and simple, antique-furnished bedrooms; the two larger with countryside views.
Home cooked dishes made with local produce, including meat and eggs from the
farm and fruit from the orchard.

CASTLEREA – Roscommon – 712 G 6   36 B2

> ▪ Dublin 115 km – Roscommon 19 km – Newbridge 33 km
> – Carrick-on-Shannon 24 km

⌂ **Fallons** without rest   🖼 ❄ P

Knock Rd, West : 2 km on N 60 – ℰ *(094) 962 11 83 – www.fallonsbb@eircom.net*

5 rm ⊗ – †€ 50 ††€ 64/75

♦ Modern guest house on main road on outskirts of town - popular with those
travelling to Knock - with simple, neat bedrooms and homely, wood-furnished breakfast room.

CASTLETOWNBERE (Baile Chaisleáin Bhéarra) – Cork – 712 C 13   38 A3
– pop. 868 ▯ *Ireland*

> ▪ Dublin 360 km – Cork 130 km – Killarney 93 km
> ⛴ Berehaven Millcove, ℰ (027) 70 700
> ⌨ Ring of Beara★, W : by R 572 (Allihies, mines★ - Garnish Bay ≤★) – Slieve
> Miskish Mountains (≤★)

⌂ **Rodeen** without rest ⊗   ≤ 🖼 ❄ P VISA ◐◐ Æ

East : 3¼ km by R 572 – ℰ *(027) 70 158 – www.rodeencountryhouse.com*
– rodeen@iolfree.ie – March - October

6 rm ⊗ – †€ 40/80 ††€ 80/90

♦ Owner used to run a horticulture business and this is evident in the variety of
shrubs in the garden. Rooms are compact but nicely decorated; some look out to
Bantry Bay.

CASTLETOWNSHEND (Baile an Chaisleáin) – Cork – 712 E 13 ▯ *Ireland*   38 B3

> ▪ Dublin 346 km – Cork 95 km – Killarney 116 km
> ⌨ Glandore★, NE : 10 km R 596 – Sherkin Island★ AC, W : 15 km by R 596
> and R 595 and ferry

🍽 **Mary Ann's**   🖼 VISA ◐◐

*– ℰ (028) 36 146 – www.westcorkweek.com/maryanns – maryanns@eircom.net
– Fax (028) 36 920 – Closed 24-26 December and 3 weeks January*

Rest – (Closed Monday and lunch Tuesday November-March) (bookings not
accepted) Carte € 20/45

♦ A pleasant 19C pub in pretty village. Tempting dishes are distinguished by the fact
that almost everything is homemade. Sunny terrace is popular for lunch.

CAVAN – Cavan – 712 J 6 – pop. 7 883 ▯ *Ireland*   37 C2

> ▪ Dublin 114 km – Drogheda 93 km – Enniskillen 64 km
> 🛈 Central Library,Farnham St ℰ (049) 4331942 (April-September),
> cavan@failteireland.com
> ⌨ Killykeen Forest Park★, W : 9½ km by R 198

Radisson SAS Farnham Estate ≤ 🚗 🕭 🤚 ⛱ 🎾 ⚓ ⬜ 🏊 🗑 🕸

Farnham Estate, 🛏 🕭 🕭 rm, Ⅸ rest, 🎾 🕸 🚿 **P** 🏊 *VISA* **⬤⬤** AE ⬤
Northwest : 3 ¾ km on R 198 – ℰ (049) 437 77 00 – www.farnhamestatecom
– info@farnhamestate.com – Fax (049) 437 77 01
152 rm � – †€ 225 ††€ 250 – 6 suites
Rest *Botanica* – Carte € 41/54 **s**

♦ Period charm and acres of mature parkland in this renovated 400-year old mansion, offset by 21C hotel with meeting facilities, wellness centre and snazzy, well-equipped rooms. Universal menus at Botanica.

Cavan Crystal 🗑 🕸 🛏 🕭 🕭 rm, Ⅸ rest, 🎾 🕸 🏊 **P** *VISA* **⬤⬤** AE

Dublin Rd, East : 1½ km on N 3 – ℰ (049) 436 0600 – www.cavancrystalhotel.com
– info@cavancrystalhotel.com – Fax (049) 436 0699 – Closed 24-26 December
85 rm ⊷ – †€ 110/130 ††€ 160/195
Rest *Opus One* – Carte € 30/45

♦ Modern hotel next to Cavan Crystal factory. Vast atrium is distinctive and stylish. Extensive meeting and leisure facilities. Comfy, well-equipped, modish bedrooms. Dining room serves menus true to Irish roots with stylish twists.

at Cloverhill North : 12 km by N 3 on N 54 – ✉ Belturbet

⌂ Rockwood House without rest 🌿 🚗 🎾 **P**

– ℰ (047) 55 351 – jbmac@eircom.net – Fax (047) 55 373
– Closed 10 December-1 February
4 rm ⊷ – †€ 43 ††€ 64

♦ Stone-faced house with a charming garden located in a woodland clearing. Comfortable guests' lounge and a conservatory for breakfast. Simply appointed, comfortable bedrooms.

🍴🍴 The Olde Post Inn with rm 🚗 **P** *VISA* **⬤⬤** AE

– ℰ (047) 55 555 – www.theoldepostinn.com – gearoidlynch@eircom.net
– Fax (047) 55 111 – Closed 24-26 December and Monday
6 rm ⊷ – †€ 75 ††€ 130
Rest – (dinner only and Sunday lunch) Menu € 33/56 **s** – Carte € 35/54 **s**

♦ Former village post office; now a restaurant with much character: exposed stone and brick, large rafters. A feel of genuine hospitality prevails. Fine dining with Gallic edge.

CLAREMORRIS Mayo – Mayo – **712** E/F 6 – pop. 2 595 36 **B2**
🄳 Dublin 149 km – Castlebar 18 km – Galway 39 km – Newbridge 41 km

McWilliam Park 🗑 🕸 🛏 🕭 🕭 rm, Ⅸ rest, 🎾 🕸 🏊 **P** *VISA* **⬤⬤** AE

Knock Rd, East : 2 km on N 60 – ℰ (094) 937 8000 – www.mcwilliamparkhotel.ie
– info@mcwilliamparkhotel.ie – Fax (094) 937 8001
101 rm ⊷ – †€ 110/130 ††€ 170/260 – 2 suites
Rest – (bar lunch) Carte € 30/45 **s**

♦ Named after a local 18C landowner, this busy, purpose built hotel is located on the outskirts of town, convenient for the N17, Knock and the airport. Modern bedrooms. Stylish restaurant offers dishes made using local produce.

CLIFDEN – Galway – **712** B 7 🔲 *Ireland* 36 **A3**
🄳 Dublin 291 km – Ballina 124 km – Galway 79 km
🄸 Galway Rd ℰ (095) 21163 (March-October),
clifdentouristoffice@failteireland.ie
🄲 Connemara★★★, NE : by N 59 – Sky Road★★ (≤★★), NE : by N 59 –
Connemara National Park★, NE : 1½ km by N 59 – Killary Harbour★, NE :
35 km by N 59 – Kylemore Abbey★ **AC**, N : 18 km by N 59

Clifden Station House 🗑 🕸 🕸 🛏 🕭 🕭 rm, 🏃 🎾 🕸 🏊 **P**

– ℰ (095) 21 699 – www.clifdenstationhouse.com *VISA* **⬤⬤** AE ⬤
– info@clifdenstationhouse.com – Fax (095) 21 667 – Closed 24-25 December
78 rm ⊷ – †€ 80/140 ††€ 100/280
Rest – (bar lunch) Menu € 40 – Carte € 30/45

♦ A modern hotel on site of the Galway-Clifden railway line closed in 1935. Now forms part of a complex which includes a museum. Good sized rooms in cheerful colours. Traditional fare offered in restaurant.

⛟ **Ardagh** ⟨ ⇘ 📶 **P** **VISA** **MO** **AE** **⓪**

Ballyconneely Rd, South : 2¾ km on R 341 – ℰ (095) 21384
– www.ardaghhotel.com – ardaghhotel@eircom.net – Fax (095) 21314
– Easter-November
14 rm ⊆ – †€95/195 ††€179/195 – 3 suites
Rest – (dinner only) Menu €55 – Carte €45/62
♦ Family run hotel on edge of Ardbear Bay. A welcoming, domestically furnished interior with turf fires, piano, pictures and plants. Bedrooms are large, especially superiors. Fresh, pine dining room with views.

⛫ **Dolphin Beach Country House** ⟨ ⇘ 📶 **P** **VISA** **MO**

Lower Sky Rd, West : 5½ km by Sky Rd – ℰ (095) 21204
– www.dolphinbeachhouse.com – stay@dolphinbeachhouse.com – Fax (095)
22935 – Mid February-mid November
9 rm ⊆ – †€70/100 ††€160/185   **Rest** – (residents only) Menu €42 **s**
♦ Terracotta coloured former farmhouse, perched on side of hill with stunning views of bay. Delightful sitting room with huge windows to accommodate vista. Attractive rooms. Tasty, home-cooked meals.

⛫ **The Quay House** without rest ⟨ 📶 **VISA** **MO**

Beach Rd – ℰ (095) 21369 – www.thequayhouse.com – thequay@iol.ie
– Fax (095) 21608 – Mid March-November
14 rm ⊆ – †€75/120 ††€140/180
♦ Once a harbour master's residence, then a Franciscan monastery. Rooms are divided between the main house: bohemian in style, and new annex: spacious with kitchenettes.

⛫ **Byrne Mal Dua House** without rest 📶 **P** **VISA** **MO** **AE** **⓪**

Galway Rd, East : 1¼ km on N 59 – ℰ (095) 21171 – www.maldua.com
– info@maldua.com – Fax (095) 21739 – Closed 22-26 December
14 rm ⊆ – †€40/99 ††€80
♦ A white, detached house in well-tended gardens. Deep colours and subdued lighting indoors. Bedrooms are immaculately kept with fitted furniture.

⛰ **Sea Mist House** without rest 📶 **P** **VISA** **MO** **AE**

– ℰ (095) 21441 – www.seamisthouse.com – sgriffin@eircom.net – Restricted opening in winter
6 rm ⊆ – †€55/80 ††€100/130
♦ 20C terraced stone house with sloping garden in town centre. Good choice at breakfast in cheerful room. Lounge at front and in conservatory. Spacious, modern bedrooms.

⛰ **Buttermilk Lodge** without rest ⟨ 📶 **P** **VISA** **MO** **AE**

Westport Rd – ℰ (095) 21951 – www.buttermilklodge.com
– buttermilklodge@eircom.net – Fax (095) 21953 – Closed January-February
11 rm ⊆ – †€50/75 ††€80/100
♦ Yellow painted, name refers to nearby lough, a theme which is continued indoors as each room bears the name of a lough. Daily breakfast specials; maps provided for exploring.

⛰ **Connemara Country Lodge** without rest 📶 **P** **VISA** **MO**

Westport Rd – ℰ (095) 21122 – www.connemaracountrylodge.com
– connemara@unison.ie – Fax (095) 21122
10 rm ⊆ – †€50/100 ††€80/110
♦ Affordable accommodation in a personally run guest house. Breakfasts include home-baked raisin bread and scones: owner has tendency to break into song at this point!

⛰ **Benbaun House** without rest 📶 **P** **VISA** **MO**

Westport Rd – ℰ (095) 21462 – www.benbaunhouse.com
– benbaunhouse@eircom.net – Fax (095) 21462 – Late May-October
12 rm ⊆ – †€50/60 ††€70/90
♦ Family owned house to the north of the town: modern bedrooms - simple, spacious and decorated in cheerful patterned fabrics - represent very good value for money.

REPUBLIC OF IRELAND

▶ Dublin 122 km – Tipperary 23 km – Clonmel 21 km – Dungarvan 28 km

XX **Old Convent** with rm   ≤ 🚗 🕪 **P** **VISA** **©©**

Mount Anglesby, Southeast : ½ km on R 668 (Lismore rd) – ℰ (052) 65 565
– www.theoldconvent.ie – info@theoldconvent.ie – Closed 24 December-February
and Monday-Wednesday

7 rm ☲ – ❙€ 110/150 ❙❙€ 150/200

Rest – (dinner only) (booking essential) (set menu only) Menu € 65

♦ Home to the Sisters of Mercy for over 100 years, this converted convent retains
a serene feel. Dine in the candlelit former chapel on seasonal 8 course tasting menu.
Comfortable bedrooms, decorated in calming colours.

▶ Dublin 310 km – Cork 51 km

🖪 25 Ashe St ℰ (023) 33226, clonakiltytio@aircom.net

🛍 Dunmore Muckross, ℰ (023) 34 644

◎ West Cork Regional Museum★ **AC**

🅖 Courtmacsherry★, E : 12 km by R 600 and R 601 – Timoleague Friary★, E :
8 km by R 600. Carbery Coast★ (Drombeg Stone Circle★, Glandore★,
Castletownshend★) by N 71 and R 597

🏨🏨 **Inchydoney Island Lodge & Spa**   ≤ 🍴 🖥 ☺ 🖘 £6 🛉 ₰ rm,

South : 5 ¼ km by N 71 following 🖈 **AC** rest, ⅍ 🕪 🔄 **P** **VISA** **©©** **AE** **①**
signs for Inchydoney Beach – ℰ (023) 33 143 – www.inchydoneyisland.com
– reservations@inchydoneyisland.com – Fax (023) 35 229 – Closed 23-27 December

67 rm ☲ – ❙€ 225/240 ❙❙€ 330/360 – 4 suites

Rest *The Gulfstream* – (dinner only) Menu € 62

Rest *Dunes Bistro* – Carte € 26/47

♦ Set on a headland looking out to sea. Range of leisure facilities; treatments - aqua-
marine spa, underwater massages - are especially good. Big, bright bedrooms with
extras. The Gulfstream has fine sea views. The Dunes Bistro has a hearty, nautical theme.

🏨 **Quality**   🖥 🖘 £6 🛉 ₰ rm, 🖈 **AC** rest, ⅍ 🔄 **P** **VISA** **©©** **AE**

Clogheen, West : ¾ km by N 71 (Skibbereen rd) – ℰ (023) 36 400
– www.qualityhotelclonakilty.com – info.clonakilty@qualityhotels.ie – Fax (023)
35 404 – Closed 23-26 December

77 rm ☲ – ❙€ 65/134 ❙❙€ 78/218 – 20 suites

Rest – (carvery lunch Monday-Saturday) Menu € 26 – Carte € 22/34

♦ Modern hotel; rooms are uniformly decorated with matching fabrics. What distinguishes it is the three screen multiplex cinema, the "KidKamp" in summer, and
leisure complex. Menus feature popular favourites.

🏠 **An Garrán Coir**   🚗 🍴 ⅍ 🕪 **P** **VISA**

Castlefreke, Rathbarry, West : 6 ½ km by N 71 – ℰ (023) 48 236
– www.angarrancoir.com – angarrancoir@eircom.net – Fax (023) 48 236

5 rm ☲ – ❙€ 60 ❙❙€ 85   **Rest** – (by arrangement) Menu € 30 **s**

♦ Working farm overlooking rolling countryside: organic garden supplies ingredients
for dinner. Homely lounge, well-kept rooms in bright, cheery colours. Good base for
walking.

XX **Gleeson's**   **VISA** **©©** **AE**

3-4 Connolly St – ℰ (023) 21 834 – www.gleesons.ie – reservations@gleeson.ie
– Fax (023) 33 166 – Closed Sunday and Monday

Rest – (dinner only) Menu € 35 – Carte € 37/57

♦ Town centre restaurant with wood blinds. Low beamed interior with wood burning
stove. Classically based menus; dishes have individual twist and local produce is to
the fore.

🍸 **An Súgán**   **VISA** **©©**

41 Wolfe Tone St – ℰ (023) 33 498 – www.ansugan.com – ansugan4@eircom.net
– Fax (023) 33 825 – Closed 25-26 December and Good Friday

Rest – Carte € 28/40

♦ Situated in the old quays area of town. Homely wooden bar leads upstairs to
restaurant hung with old photographs. Known for lobster, baked crab and black
pudding terrine.

REPUBLIC OF IRELAND

CLONBUR – Galway – **712** D 7

36 **A3**

▶ Dublin 260 km – Ballina 79 km – Galway 46 km

🛏 **John J Burke** with rm 🔆 VISA ⓪⓪
Mount Gable House – ℰ (094) 954 6175 – www.burkes-clonbur.com
– tibhurca@eircom.net – Closed 25 December
4 rm ⌧ – †€40 ††€80 **Rest** – Carte €25/47
♦ Traditional pub, owned by the Burke family since 1922. Friendly, buzzy bar; restaurant and terrace look to Mount Gable. Light meals at lunch; more hearty fare in the evening. Simple bedrooms.

CLONDALKIN – Dublin – **712** M 8 – see Dublin

CLONEGALL Carlow – **712** M 9

39 **D2**

▶ Dublin 73 km – Carlow 20 km – Kilkenny 39 km – Wexford 30 km

🍴 **Sha Roe Bistro** VISA ⓪⓪
Main St – ℰ (053) 937 56 36 – sha-roebistro@hotmail.com – Closed January,
1 week April, 1 week September, Sunday dinner, Monday and Tuesday
Rest – (booking essential) Menu €32 (lunch) – Carte dinner €31/45
♦ Spacious sitting room, comfy sofas, rustic artwork and candles help create relaxing feel. Simple dining room with inglenook fireplace; seasonal cooking uses local ingredients.

CLONMEL (Cluain Meala) – **712** I 10 – pop. 17 008 📖 *Ireland*

39 **C2**

▶ Dublin 174 km – Cork 95 km – Kilkenny 50 km – Limerick 77 km
– Waterford 46 km
🖪 Mary St ℰ (052) 22960, clonmeltouristoffice@aircom.net
🏧 Lyreanearla Mountain Rd, ℰ (052) 24050
◎ Town★ - County Museum★, St Mary's Church★
⊙ Fethard★, N : 13 km by R 689. Nier Valley Scenic Route★★ - Ahenny High
Crosses★, E : 30½ km by N 24 and R 697 - Ormond Castle★, E : 33¾ km by
N 24

🏨 **Minella** 🕸 🕭 🞇 🞷 🖷 🞗 Ⅰ♨ 🕿 🍴 rm, 🎢 rest, 🞊 🕨 🛁 🅿 VISA ⓪⓪ 🅐🅔 🅞
Coleville Rd, Southeast : ½ km – ℰ (052) 22388 – www.hotelminella.ie
– frontdesk@hotelminella.ie – Fax (052) 24381
90 rm ⌧ – †€116 ††€180 **Rest** – Menu €28/40 s
♦ Heavily extended Georgian house on banks of River Suir. Excellent leisure facility. Bedrooms decorated in soft pinks and blues; garden rooms have pleasant views. Basement restaurant has river vistas.

CLONTARF (Cluain Tarbh) – Dublin – **712** N 7 – see Dublin

CLOVERHILL – Cavan – **712** J 5 – see Cavan

COBH – Cork – **712** H 12 – pop. 11 303 📖 *Ireland*

38 **B3**

▶ Dublin 264 km – Cork 24 km – Waterford 104 km
🖻 Ballywilliam, ℰ (021) 812 399
◎ Town★ – St Colman's Cathedral★ – Lusitania Memorial★
⊙ Fota Island★ (Fota House★★ **AC**, Fota Wildlife Park★ **AC**), N : 6½ km by
R 624 – Cloyne Cathedral★, SE : 24 km by R 624/5, N 25, R 630 and R 629

🏨 **WatersEdge** ≤ 🕿 🍴 rm, 🎢 rest, 🞊 🞟 🅿 VISA ⓪⓪ 🅐🅔
– ℰ (021) 481 5566 – www.watersedgehotel.ie – info@watersedgehotel.ie
– Fax (021) 481 2011 – Closed 25-26 December
18 rm ⌧ – †€70/110 ††€100/220 – 1 suite
Rest *Jacob's Ladder* – (light lunch) Carte €36/47 s
♦ Next to the Heritage Centre, a converted salvage yard office overlooking Cork harbour. Some of the spacious, soft-toned rooms have French windows opening on to the veranda. Stylish restaurant with waterside setting.

Knockeven House *without rest*

Rushbrooke, West : 2 km off R 624 – ℰ (021) 481 17 78
– www.knockevenhouse.com – info@knockevenhouse.com – Fax (021) 481 17 19
– Closed 15-28 December
4 rm ☲ – †€ 75/120 ††€ 120
♦ Characterful house with friendly owners and tea and scones on arrival. Comfy lounge with fireplace and flowers, antique-furnished bedrooms; two largest overlook front garden.

CONG (Conga) – Mayo – 712 E 7 🛇 *Ireland* 36 **A3**

🄳 Dublin 257 km – Ballina 79 km – Galway 45 km
🄸 ℰ (094) 9546542 (March-October)
◎ Town★
🄶 Lough Corrib★★. Ross Errilly Abbey★ (Tower ≼★) – Joyce Country★★
(Lough Nafooey★) W : by R 345

Ashford Castle ⌂

– ℰ (094) 954 60 03 – www.ashford.ie
– ashford@ashford.ie – Fax (094) 954 62 60
78 rm – †€ 244/452 ††€ 244/452, ☲ €24 – 5 suites
Rest *Connaught Room* – ℰ (094) 954 43 21 (Closed late October-mid March, Monday and Tuesday) (dinner only) Menu € 90 – Carte € 72/93
Rest *George V Room* – (dinner only) (residents only) Menu € 75
Rest *Cullens* – (closed Tuesday-Wednesday except July and August and weekends only in winter) Carte € 29/49 **s**
♦ Hugely imposing restored castle in formal grounds on Lough Corrib. Suits of armour and period antiques in a clubby lounge. Handsomely furnished country house rooms. Smart fine dining in Connaught Room. George V imbued with air of genteel formality. Cullens serves bistro-style menu in informal atmosphere.

Lisloughrey Lodge ⌂

The Quay, Southeast : 2 km by R 346 – ℰ (094) 954 54 00 – www.lisloughrey.ie
– lodge@lisloughrey.ie – Fax (094) 954 54 24 – Closed 24-26 December
41 rm ☲ – †€ 200/250 ††€ 225/275 – 9 suites
Rest *Salt* – Menu € 73 (dinner) – Carte € 28/65
♦ Traditional exterior belies modernity of this stylish boutique hotel, with its sexy black and red lounge. Bedrooms set around courtyard; 'Duplex', the most comfortable. First floor restaurant boasts Lough view; modern menus use local produce and offer some unusual combinations.

Michaeleen's Manor *without rest*

Quay Rd, Southeast : 1½ km by R 346 – ℰ (094) 954 60 89
– www.quietman-cong.com – info@quietman-cong.com – Fax (094) 954 64 48
11 rm ☲ – †€ 55/70 ††€ 75/85
♦ Named after the lead character in the film 'The Quiet Man,' filmed in the village; comfortable, brightly decorated bedrooms follow suit. Homely lounges; airy breakfast room.

Ballywarren House

East : 3½ km on R 346 – ℰ (094) 954 69 89 – www.ballywarrenhouse.com
– ballywarrenhouse@gmail.com – Fax (094) 954 69 89 – Closed 2 weeks spring and 2 weeks autumn
3 rm ☲ – †€ 98/136 ††€ 148 **Rest** – (by arrangement) Menu € 42
♦ Modern but 18C in style - open fires, galleried landing, oak staircase. Fresh colours: mint green, pink contrast pleasingly with woodwork. Carved pine beds; one four poster. Meals include own vegetables and daughter's farm eggs.

Don't confuse 𝕏 with ۞!
𝕏 defines comfort, while stars are awarded for the best cuisine, across all categories of comfort.

▶ Dublin 248 km

✈ Cork Airport : 𝒞 (021) 4313131, S : 6 ½ km by L 42 X

⛴ to France (Roscoff) (Brittany Ferries) weekly (14 h/16 h) – to Pembroke (Swansea Cork Ferries) 2-6 weekly (8 h 30 mn)

🛈 Cork City, Grand Parade 𝒞 (021) 4255100, corktio@failteireland.ie

🏌 Douglas, 𝒞 (021) 489 10 86

🏌 Mahon Blackrock Cloverhill, 𝒞 (021) 429 25 43

🏌 Monkstown Parkgarriffe, 𝒞 (021) 484 13 76

🏌 Little Island, 𝒞 (021) 435 34 51

◉ City ★★ – Shandon Bells ★★ Y, St Fin Barre's Cathedral ★★ **AC** Z, Cork Public Museum ★ X **M** – Grand Parade ★ Z , South Mall ★ Z , St Patrick Street ★ Z , Crawford Art Gallery ★ Y – Elizabethan Fort ★ Z

◔ Dunkathel House ★ **AC**, E : 9 ¼ km by N 8 and N 25 X. Fota Island ★ (Fota House ★★ **AC**, Fota Wildlife Park ★ **AC**), E : 13 km by N 8 and N 25 X – Cobh ★ (St Colman's Cathedral ★, Lusitania Memorial ★) SE : 24 km by N 8, N 25 and R 624 X

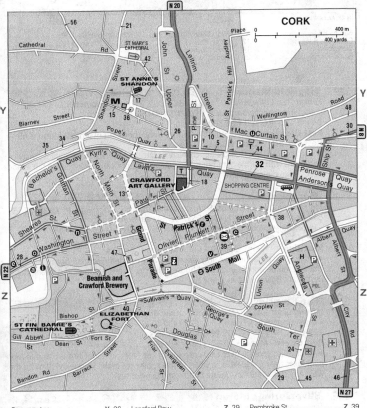

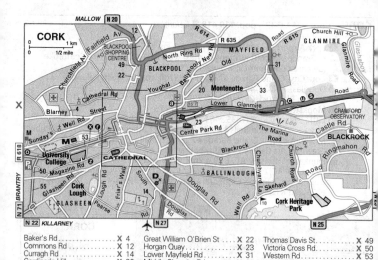

⚞⚟⚞ Hayfield Manor

🏊 🖥 ⅃ 🎱 ⅋ ♿ rm, 🅰🅲 ⁘ ⌦ 🈂 🅿 💳 ⚫ 🅰🅴 ⓪

Perrott Ave, College Rd – ℰ (021) 484 59 00 – www.hayfieldmanor.ie
– enquiries@hayfieldmanor.ie – Fax (021) 431 68 39   Xz
84 rm ⚍ – ♦€ 380 ♦♦€ 380 – 4 suites
Rest *Orchids* – (closed Sunday) (dinner only) (booking essential) Menu € 69
Rest *Perrotts* – Carte € 33/55

♦ Purpose-built yet Georgian in character. Stately interiors and harmoniously styled bedrooms with marble bathrooms and quality furniture - armchairs, coffee tables and desks. Twin dining options to suit all tastes.

⚞⚟⚞ Maryborough ⚘

🏊 ⅄ 🖥 ⅃ 🎱 🈂 ⅃ ♨ ⌦ ⅋ ♿ rm, 🅰🅲 rest, ⁘ ⌦
🈂 🅿 💳 ⚫ 🅰🅴 ⓪

Maryborough Hill, Douglas, Southeast : 4¾ km by R
609 and R 610 – ℰ (021) 436 55 55 – www.maryborough.ie
– info@maryborough.ie – Fax (021) 436 56 62 – Closed 24-26 December
88 rm ⚍ – ♦€ 145/185 ♦♦€ 198/250 – 5 suites
Rest *Zing's* – Menu € 30/50 – Carte (dinner) € 41/52 **s**

♦ Built as a home for a wealthy merchant, an extended Georgian house. Five very characterful bedrooms in original house; others are sleek, stylish and contemporary. Restaurant boasts walk-in wine cellar.

⚟⚞⚟ The Kingsley

⚟ 🏊 🖥 🎱 🈂 ⅃ 🎱 ♿ rm, 🅰🅲 ⁘ 🈂 🅿 💳 ⚫ 🅰🅴

Victoria Cross – ℰ (021) 480 05 55 – www.kingsleyhotel.com
– resv@kingsleyhotel.com – Fax (021) 480 05 26   Xo
129 rm ⚍ – ♦€ 139/200 ♦♦€ 175/280 – 2 suites
Rest *Otters* – Menu € 30/50 – Carte € 45/78

♦ An inviting spot by river Lee, once site of Lee baths: outdoor hot tub and indoor pool takes their place. Relax in smart rooms or take tea in the lounge overlooking the weir. Airy restaurant has private booths and banquettes.

⚟⚞⚟ Silversprings Moran H.

🏊 ⅄ 🖥 🎱 ⅃ ♨ ⌦ 🎱 🅰🅲 rest, ⁘ ⌦
🈂 🅿 💳 ⚫ 🅰🅴 ⓪

Tivoli, East : 4 km by N 8 – ℰ (021) 450 75 33
– www.silverspringshotel.ie – silverspringsres@moranhotels.com – Fax (021)
450 76 41 – Closed 24-26 December   Xc
109 rm ⚍ – ♦€ 100/205 ♦♦€ 140/300
Rest – Menu € 25/40 **s** – Carte € 35/41 **s**

♦ Conference oriented hotel surrounded by gardens and grounds. Smartly furnished public areas includes business and leisure centres. Comfortably appointed bedrooms. After dining, relax in smart, contemporary lounge.

Jurys 🔲 ⥥ ⼚ 🎽 & rm, 📶 🕱 ⅋ 🚱 P. VISA ⓸⓸ AE ①

Western Rd – ℰ (021) 425 27 00 – www.jurysdoyle.com – cork@jurysdoyle.com
– Fax (021) 427 44 77 – Closed 25-26 December   Za
182 rm – †€ 140/330 ††€ 220/340, ⣁ €16
Rest – Menu € 24/40 **s** – Carte dinner € 33/55 **s**
♦ Contemporary city hotel by River Lee with light, spacious feel and complementary health club. Good-sized, modern bedrooms; the higher you go, the better the view. Weir bar and restaurant has terrace overlooking river.

The Ambassador ⪕ ⥥ ⼚ 🎽 & rm, ⅋ 🚱 P. VISA ⓸⓸ AE ①

Military Hill – ℰ (021) 453 90 00 – www.ambassadorhotel.ie
– info@ambassadorhotel.ie – Fax (021) 455 19 97 – Closed 24-26 December   Xa
69 rm ⣁ – †€ 125/155 ††€ 150/185 – 1 suite
Rest – Menu € 28/40 **s** – Carte € 35/45 **s**
♦ Built as a military hospital; its high position affords city views from which most rooms benefit. All are furnished to a comfortable standard and most have a balcony. Home-made treats adorn dining room menus.

Isaacs 🎽 & rm, ⅋ 🕱 🚱 VISA ⓸⓸ AE ①

48 MacCurtain St – ℰ (021) 450 00 11 – www.isaacscork.com – cork@isaacs.ie
– Fax (021) 450 63 55   Yu
47 rm ⣁ – †€ 90/120 ††€ 110/150
Rest *Greenes* – ℰ (021) 455 22 79 (dinner only and Sunday lunch)
Carte € 40/50 **s**
♦ Refurbished hotel across from the theatre in city centre. Bedrooms are modern and comfortable; most of them situated around a small courtyard. Two-roomed restaurant overlooks waterfall; one room is traditional in style, the other modern and bright. French chef cooks dishes with global influences. Friendly staff.

Lancaster Lodge without rest 🎽 & ⅋ 🕱 🚱 P. VISA ⓸⓸ AE ①

Lancaster Quay, Western Rd – ℰ (021) 425 11 25 – www.lancasterlodge.com
– info@lancasterlodge.com – Fax (021) 425 11 26 – Closed 24-28 December   Zi
48 rm ⣁ – †€ 95/135 ††€ 125/165
♦ Purpose-built hotel with crisp, modern interior. Bedrooms are chintz-free, pleasingly and sparingly decorated. Largest rooms on the fourth floor; rear rooms are quieter.

Lotamore House without rest ⪕ ⤢ ⅋ 🕱 P. VISA ⓸⓸ AE

Tivoli, East : 4¾ km on N 8 – ℰ (021) 482 23 44 – www.lotamorehouse.com
– lotamore@iol.ie – Fax (021) 482 22 19
– Closed mid-December to mid-January   Xs
18 rm ⣁ – †€ 75/85 ††€ 89/149
♦ Georgian house perched on hill with fine view over river and harbour. Country house style lounge with antiques. Individually styled rooms; relish vista from one at the front.

Crawford House without rest ⅋ P. VISA ⓸⓸ AE ①

Western Rd – ℰ (021) 427 90 00 – www.crawfordguesthouse.com
– info@crawfordguesthouse.com – Fax (021) 427 99 27
– Closed mid December- mid January   Xx
12 rm ⣁ – †€ 70/90 ††€ 100/110
♦ Victorian-style building offering bright, airy and comfortable guesthouse accommodation. Modern interiors with a choice of wood floors or carpeting in guest rooms.

Garnish House without rest ⅋ P. VISA ⓸⓸ AE ①

Western Rd – ℰ (021) 427 51 11 – www.garnish.ie – garnish@iol.ie
– Fax (021) 427 38 72   Xr
21 rm ⣁ – †€ 70/120 ††€ 90/110
♦ Justifiably proud of gourmet breakfast: 30 options include pancakes and porridge. Guests are welcomed with home-made scones in cosy rooms; those at the rear have quiet aspect.

⌂ **Achill House** without rest ✂ ((VISA ☺☺
Western Rd – ℰ (021) 427 94 47 – www.achillhouse.com – info@achillhouse.com
– Fax (021) 427 94 47 Z**e**
9 rm ⌁ – ✝€60/80 ✝✝€90/120
♦ Immaculate accommodation in a well run terrace house, five minutes from the centre; the two attic rooms, decorated in warm pastel tones, are the most cosy and characterful.

𝕏𝕏𝕏 **Flemings** with rm ⎙ ✂ ⓒ P. VISA ☺☺ AE ①
Silver Grange House, Tivoli, East : 4½ km on N 8 – ℰ (021) 482 16 21
– www.flemingsrestaurant.ie – info@flemingsrestaurant.ie – Fax (021) 482 18 00
– Closed 24-27 December and Sunday dinner-Monday lunch
June-September X**u**
3 rm ⌁ – ✝€90 ✝✝€110 **Rest** – Carte €45/55
♦ Classical cuisine, French bias; uses local produce, organically home-grown vegetables, herbs. Two dining rooms in keeping with Georgian character of house. Period furnished bedrooms.

𝕏𝕏 **Jacobs on the Mall** AC ⇕ VISA ☺☺ AE ①
30A South Mall – ℰ (021) 425 15 30 – www.jacobsonthemall.com
– info@jacobsonthemall.com – Fax (021) 425 15 31
– Closed Christmas Day, Good Friday and Sundays Z**s**
Rest – (booking essential) Menu €35/48 – Carte €26/36
♦ 19C former Turkish bath has retained its old steam windows and added contemporary Irish art. Modern dishes reveal a taste for bold, original combinations.

𝕏𝕏 **Ambassador** AC VISA ☺☺ AE ①
3 Cook St – ℰ (021) 427 32 61 – www.ambassadorrestaurant.ie
– info@ambassadorrestaurant.ie – Fax (021) 427 23 57
– Closed 25-26 December and Good Friday Z**r**
Rest – Chinese – (dinner only and lunch in December) Menu €26/33
– Carte €37/46
♦ Richly hued oak panelling and smoothly professional service add to the enjoyment of dishes prepared with care and fine ingredients in a long-established Chinese favourite.

𝕏𝕏 **Jacques** AC VISA ☺☺ AE
Phoenix St – ℰ (021) 427 73 87 – www.jacquesrestaurant.ie
– jacquesrestaurant@eircom.net – Closed Sundays and Bank Holidays Z**c**
Rest – (dinner only) Carte €25/51
♦ A long, warmly decorated room with modern tables on which old Irish classics are delivered. Farm ducks, wild game, fresh fish and organic vegetables are used in the cooking.

𝕏𝕏 **Les Gourmandises** VISA ☺☺ AE ①
17 Cook St – ℰ (021) 425 19 59 – www.lesgourmandises.ie
– info@lesgourmandises.ie – Fax (021) 489 90 05
– Closed 2 weeks March, 2 weeks August, Sunday and Monday Z**v**
Rest – French – (dinner only) (booking essential) Menu €45 s
– Carte €42/57 s
♦ Relaxed city centre restaurant boasting stained glass door, skylight and comfy lounge bar with red banquettes and modern art. Irish produce employed on classic French menus.

𝕏 **Isaacs Restaurant** VISA ☺☺ AE ①
48 MacCurtain St – ℰ (021) 450 38 05 – isaacs@iol.ie – Fax (021) 455 13 48
– Closed 1 week Christmas, lunch Sunday and Bank Holidays Y**u**
Rest – (booking essential) Carte €27/50 s
♦ Tall brick arches and modern art in converted warehouse: buzzy, friendly and informal. Modern and traditional brasserie dishes plus home-made desserts and blackboard specials.

REPUBLIC OF IRELAND

REPUBLIC OF IRELAND

X **Cafe Paradiso** with rm ((¶)) VISA ⓪ AE
16 Lancaster Quay, Western Rd – ℰ (021) 427 79 39 – www.cafeparadiso.ie
– info@cafeparadiso.ie – Closed 1 week Christmas, Sunday and Monday Zo
3 rm ⌑ – ♥€ 160 ♥♥€ 160
Rest – Vegetarian – (booking essential) Carte € 29/48
♦ A growing following means booking is essential at this relaxed vegetarian restaurant. Colourful and inventive international combinations; blackboard list of organic wines. Spacious bedrooms in bright colours; the back one is the quietest.

X **Fenn's Quay** AC VISA ⓪ AE
5 Sheares St – ℰ (021) 427 95 27 – www.fennsquay.ie – polary@eircom.net
– Fax (021) 427 95 26 Zn
Rest – Carte € 29/47
♦ In a renovated 18C terrace in historic part of the city, this informal café-restaurant boasts modern art on display. Popular for mid-morning coffees and, light lunches.

at Cork Airport South : 6½ km by N 27 - X – ⌂ Cork

🏨 **International Airport** 📶 & rm, AC ℀ ℡ 🕍 P VISA ⓪ AE
– ℰ (021) 454 9800 – www.corkinternationalairporthotel.com
– info@corkairporthotel.com – Fax (021) 454 9999 – Closed 25 December
146 rm ⌑ – ♥€ 120/170 ♥♥€ 130/400 **Rest** – (carvery lunch) Carte € 33/48
♦ Quirky hotel with aviation theme and various eateries. Decently-sized bedrooms come in Economy, Business and First Class. The superb Pullman lounge resembles cabin of a plane. Modern restaurant with interesting smoking terrace.

at Little Island East : 8½ km by N 25 - X - and R 623 – ⌂ Cork

🏨 **Radisson SAS** 🚃 🛋 🖼 🌐 🐎 ℔ 🕍 & rm, AC rest, ℀ ℡ 🕍 P
Ditchley House – ℰ (021) 429 70 00 VISA ⓪ AE ①
– www.cork.radissonsas.com – info@cork.radissonsas.com – Fax (021) 429 71 01
120 rm ⌑ – ♥€ 130/165 ♥♥€ 140/185 – 9 suites
Rest *The Island Grill Room* – (closed Saturday lunch) (buffet lunch)
Menu € 22/45 – Carte € 35/53
♦ Opened in 2005 around the core of an 18C house: stylish and open-plan. Superbly equipped spa. Modish rooms in two themes: choose from Urban or highly individual Ocean! Island Grill Room serves an eclectic range of dishes.

CORK AIRPORT Cork – 712 G 12 – see Cork

CORROFIN – Clare – 712 E 9 38 **B1**
▶ Dublin 228 km – Gort 24 km – Limerick 51 km

🏠 **Fergus View** without rest ≤ 🚃 ℀ P
Kilnaboy, North : 3¼ km on R 476 – ℰ (065) 683 76 06 – www.fergusview.com
– deckell@indigo.ie – Fax (065) 683 70 83 – March-October
6 rm ⌑ – ♥€ 54 ♥♥€ 156
♦ Originally built for the owner's grandfather as a schoolhouse, with good countryside views. Conservatory entrance into cosy lounge with piles of books. Pristine bedrooms.

CROOKHAVEN (An Cruachán) – Cork – 712 C 13 38 **A3**
▶ Dublin 373 km – Bantry 40 km – Cork 120 km

🏠 **Galley Cove House** without rest ℀ ≤ 🚃 ℀ P VISA ⓪
West : ¾ km on R 591 – ℰ (028) 35 137 – www.galleycovehouse.com
– info@galleycovehouse.com – Fax (028) 35 137 – 14 March- 1 November
4 rm ⌑ – ♥€ 45/60 ♥♥€ 80/100
♦ Perched overlooking eponymous bay and its pleasant harbour. Conservatory breakfast room has bamboo seating. Rooms are neat and tidy, and enhanced by colourful fabrics.

CROSSMOLINA (Crois Mhaoilíona) – Mayo – 712 E 5 – pop. 930   36 B2

Ireland

> ▶ Dublin 252 km – Ballina 10 km
>
> ◙ Errew Abbey★, SE : 9½ km by R 315. Cáide Fields★ AC, N : 24 km by R 315 and R 314 W – Killala★, NE : 16 km by R 315 and minor road – Moyne Abbey★, NE : 18 km by R 115, minor road to Killala, R 314 and minor road – Rosserk Abbey★, NE : 18 km by R 115, minor road to Killala, R 314 and minor road

⌂ Enniscoe House ⌂   ← 🚗 ⌂ 🔑 🌳 **P** 𝘃𝘪𝘴𝘢 ⓜⓒ

Castlehill, South : 3¼ km on R 315 – ℰ (096) 31 112 – www.enniscoe.com
– mail@enniscoe.com – Fax (096) 31 773 – Closed 7 January - 31 March
6 rm ⚏ – †€ 128/140 ††€ 216/240
Rest – (dinner only) (booking essential for non-residents) Menu € 40/50
♦ Georgian manor, overlooking Lough Conn, on Enniscoe estate with walled garden and heritage centre. Hallway boasts original family tree; antique beds in flower-filled rooms. Home cooked country dishes served in the dining room.

DALKEY (Deilginis) – Dún Laoghaire-Rathdown – 712 N 8 ▌Ireland   39 D1

> ▶ Dublin 13 km – Bray 9 km
>
> ◙ Killiney Bay (←★★), S : by coast road

✗✗ Jaipur   🄰🄺 𝘃𝘪𝘴𝘢 ⓜⓒ 🄰🄴

21 Castle St – ℰ (01) 285 0552 – www.jaipur.ie – dalkey@jaipur.ie – Fax (01)
284 0900 – Closed 25 December
Rest – Indian – (dinner only) Carte € 28/56
♦ Central location and smart, lively, brightly coloured, modern décor. Well-spaced, linen-clad tables. Warm, friendly ambience. Contemporary Indian dishes.

DINGLE – Kerry – 712 B 11 – pop. 1 772 ▌Ireland   38 A2

> ▶ Dublin 347 km – Killarney 82 km – Limerick 153 km
>
> 𝒊 The Quay ℰ (066) 9151188, dingletio@eircom.net
>
> ◙ Town★ – St Mary's Church★ – Diseart (stained glass★ AC)
>
> ◙ Gallarus Oratory★★, NW : 8 km by R 559 – NE : Connor Pass★★ – Kilmalkedar★, NW : 9 km by R 559. Dingle Peninsula★★ – Connor Pass★★, NE : 8 km by minor road – Stradbally Strand★★, NE : 17 km via Connor Pass – Corca Dhuibhne Regional Museum★ AC, NW : 13 km by R 559 – Blasket Islands★, W : 21 km by R 559 and ferry from Dunquin

Plan opposite

🏨🏨 Dingle Skellig ⌂   ← 🚗 🔲 ◉ ≋ 🛁 🛌 & rm, 🏃 ⅀ 🎾 🏌 **P**

– ℰ (066) 915 02 00 – www.dingleskellig.com   𝘃𝘪𝘴𝘢 ⓜⓒ 🄰🄴 ⓞ
– reservations@dingleskellig.com – Fax (066) 915 15 01
– Closed 21-27 December   Y**e**
111 rm ⚏ – †€ 90/155 ††€ 150/250 – 2 suites
Rest – (bar lunch) Menu € 45
♦ Large purpose-built hotel with views of Dingle Bay. Interior decorated in a modern style with good levels of comfort: the smartest executive rooms are on the third floor. Restaurant makes most of sea and harbour view.

🏨 Benners without rest   🛌 ⅀ **P** 𝘃𝘪𝘴𝘢 ⓜⓒ 🄰🄴 ⓞ

Main St – ℰ (066) 915 16 38 – www.dinglebenners.com
– info@dinglebenners.com – Fax (066) 915 14 12 – Closed Christmas   Z**b**
52 rm ⚏ – †€ 85/127 ††€ 120/210
♦ Traditional-style property located on town's main street. Comfortable public areas include lounge bar and guest's sitting room. Rooms in extension have a more modern feel.

⌂ Emlagh Country House without rest   ← 🚗 🛌 & 🄺 ⅀ 🕙 **P**

– ℰ (066) 915 23 45 – www.emlaghhouse.com   𝘃𝘪𝘴𝘢 ⓜⓒ 🄰🄴
– info@emlaghhouse.com – Fax (066) 915 23 69 – 15 March-October   Y**d**
10 rm ⚏ – †€ 125/185 ††€ 190/380
♦ Modern hotel in Georgian style. Inviting lounge with a log fire and well-fitted, antique furnished bedrooms: the colours and artwork of each are inspired by a local flower.

REPUBLIC OF IRELAND

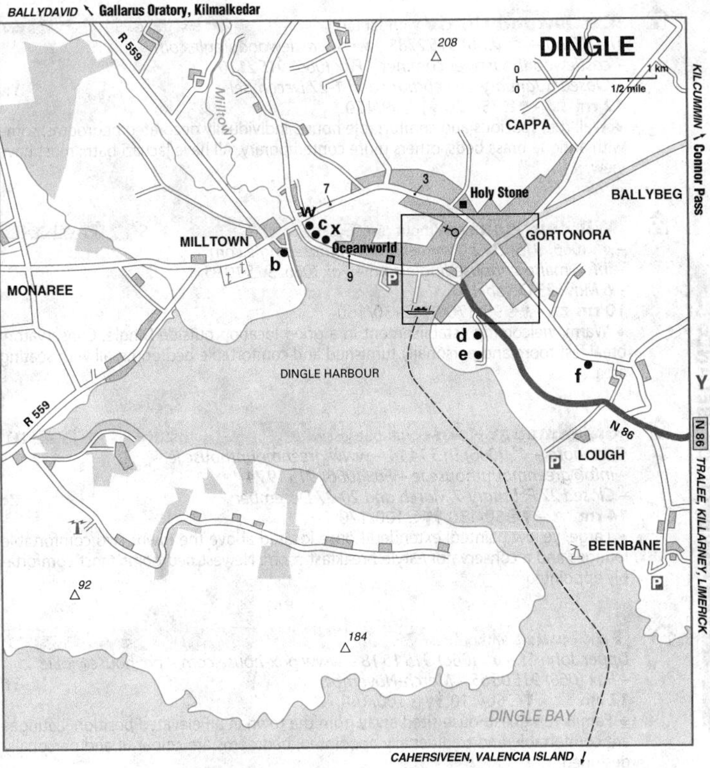

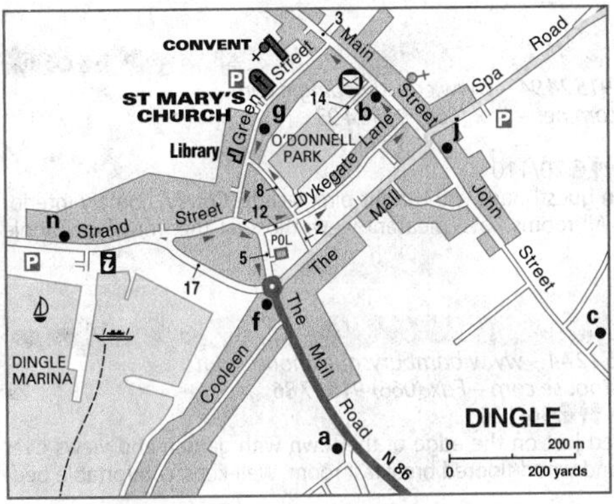

Z

Avondale St	Z 2
Bridge St	Z 5
Goat St	Y, Z 3
Grey's Lane	Z 8
High Road (The)	Y 7
Holy Ground	Z 12
Orchard Lane	Z 14
Tracks (The)	Z 17
Wood (The)	Y 9

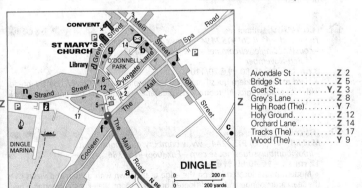

Heatons without rest

The Wood, West : ¾ km on R 559 – ✆ (066) 915 22 88 – www.heatonsdingle.com – heatons@iol.ie – Fax (066) 915 23 24 – Closed 29 November-26 December Y**c**

16 rm – †€ 58/99 ††€ 80/138

◆ Carefully planned and recently built house with a spacious, modern look: comfortably furnished lounge area and bedrooms take up the contemporary style.

🏠 **Castlewood House** without rest ≤ 🚗 📶 ⅃ 🛁 ⅌ ☂ **P** **VISA** **⦿**
The Wood – ☎ *(066) 915 2788 – www.castlewooddingle.com*
– castlewoodhouse@eircom.net – Fax (066) 915 2110
– Closed 6 January-10 February and 1-27 December   Y**w**
12 rm ⊇ – 🛏€ 75/120 🛏🛏€ 99/170
♦ Well run, spacious and comfortable house. Individually decorated bedrooms; some with antique brass beds, others more contemporary. All have jacuzzi bath; most have view.

🏠 **Milltown House** without rest ॐ ≤ 🚗 ⅌ ☂ **P** **VISA** **⦿** **AE**
– ☎ *(066) 915 13 72 – www.milltownhousedingle.com*
– info@milltownhousedingle.com – Fax (066) 915 10 95
– 6 May -23 October   Y**b**
10 rm ⊇ – 🛏€ 95/170 🛏🛏€ 130/160
♦ Warm, welcoming establishment in a good location outside Dingle. Conservatory breakfast room and personally furnished and comfortable bedrooms, all with seating area.

🏠 **Greenmount House** without rest ≤ 🚗 ⅌ ☂ **P** **VISA** **⦿**
Gortonora – ☎ *(066) 915 14 14 – www.greenmounthouse.ie*
– info@greenmounthouse.ie – Fax (066) 915 19 74
– Closed 27 February-7 March and 20-27 December   Z**c**
14 rm ⊇ – 🛏€ 50/130 🛏🛏€ 100/170
♦ Large, yellow painted, extended house located above the town. Two comfortable lounges and a conservatory-style breakfast room. Newest bedrooms most comfortably appointed.

🏡 **Pax House** without rest ॐ ≤ 🚗 **P** **VISA** **⦿**
Upper John St – ☎ *(066) 915 15 18 – www.pax-house.com – paxhouse@iol.ie*
– Fax (066) 915 08 65 – March-November   Y**f**
12 rm ⊇ – 🛏€ 50/110 🛏🛏€ 100/160
♦ Family run guesthouse sited away from the town in an elevated position. Lounges are comfortable and traditionally appointed; bedrooms are colourful and personally designed.

🏡 **Coastline** without rest ≤ 🚗 ⅌ ☂ **P** **VISA** **⦿** **①**
The Wood – ☎ *(066) 915 24 94 – www.coastlinedingle.com*
– coastlinedingle@eircom.net – Fax (066) 915 24 93
– March-November   Y**x**
8 rm ⊇ – 🛏€ 45/80 🛏🛏€ 70/110
♦ Hard to miss modern guesthouse with bright pink façade. Comfy, homely interior with lots of local info. All rooms have pleasant view; those at the front face Dingle harbour.

🏡 **Bambury's** without rest ≤ ⅌ ☂ **P** **VISA** **⦿**
Mail Rd – ☎ *(066) 915 12 44 – www.bamburysguesthouse.com*
– info@bamburysguesthouse.com – Fax (066) 915 17 86   Z**a**
12 rm ⊇ – 🛏€ 40/80 🛏🛏€ 90/120
♦ Modern house located just on the edge of the town with garden and views over the sea. Large lounge and wood-floored breakfast room. Well-kept, comfortable bedrooms.

🍴 **The Chart House** A/C **VISA** **⦿**
☺ *The Mall –* ☎ *(066) 915 22 55 – www.thecharthousedingle.com – charthse@iol.ie*
– Fax (066) 915 22 55 – Closed 7 January-7 February   Z**f**
Rest – (dinner only) Menu € 35 – Carte € 38/44
♦ Attractive cottage close to a main route into town. Snug interior with exposed flint walls and wooden ceiling. Modern flourish applied to local ingredients.

REPUBLIC OF IRELAND

✗ The Half Door ⬛ VISA ◉◉ AE

3 John St – ℰ (066) 915 16 00 – halfdoor@iol.ie – Fax (066) 915 18 83
– Closed 20 December-14 February   Z**j**
Rest – Seafood – Menu € 32/40 – Carte € 32/55

♦ A cosy atmosphere amid beams, wood and stone flooring. Menus offer a mix of dishes though the emphasis is on seafood in the classic French style. Lobsters from the tank.

✗ Out of the Blue 🔊 VISA ◉◉

Waterside – ℰ (066) 915 08 11 – www.outoftheblue.ie – info@outoftheblue.ie
– Closed November-mid March and Wednesday   Z**n**
Rest – Seafood – (dinner only and lunch weekends) (booking essential)
Carte € 31/48

♦ Pleasingly unpretentious, this brightly painted shack with corrugated iron roof has fish on display at the front, and tasty seafood menus in the rustic restaurant to the rear.

DONABATE Dublin – Fingal – 712 N 7 – pop. 5 499   39 **D1**

🄳 Dublin 14 km – Swords 5 km – Dún Laoghaire 22 km – Bray 34 km

🏨 The Waterside House ≤ ⬛ ✗ 🛜 🍴 P VISA ◉◉ AE ◐

East : 2 km – ℰ (01) 843 6155 – www.watersidehousehotel.ie
– info@watersidehousehotel.ie – Fax (01) 843 6111
35 rm – †€ 60 ††€ 260, ⬜ € 10.95
Rest *Signal* – Menu € 30/40 **s** – Carte € 20/60 **s**

♦ Hidden away, yet close to city; set on a pretty beach and surrounded by golf courses, with large open bar and lovely decked area. Worth paying more for a front facing bedroom. Small formal ground floor dining room has good views.

DONEGAL (Dún na nGall) – Donegal – 712 H 4 – pop. 2 339 📗 Ireland   37 **C1**

🄳 Dublin 264 km – Londonderry 77 km – Sligo 64 km
🄰 Donegal Airport ℰ (074) 9548284
🄸 The Quay ℰ (074) 9721148
◎ Donegal Castle★ AC
🄶 Donegal Coast★★ - Cliffs of Bunglass★★, W : 48 ¼ km by N 56 and R 263 –
Glencolmcille Folk Village★★ AC, W : 53 km by N 56 and R 263 -
Rossnowlagh Strand★★, S : 35 ½ km by N 15 and R 231 – Trabane Strand★,
W : 58 km by N 56 and R 263

🏨 Solis Lough Eske Castle ⬛ 🔊 📺 ⊕ ♨ 🍴 🛜 ✗ 🍴 P VISA ◉◉ AE ◐

Northeast : 6 ½ km by N15 (Killybegs rd) – ℰ (074) 9725 100
– www.solisloughheskecastle.com – andrew.turner@solishotels.com
– Fax (074) 9723 762
95 rm ⬜ – †€ 175/350 ††€ 175/350 – 1 suite
Rest – (Closed lunch Monday-Friday) Carte € 50/55

♦ Rebuilt 17C castle with a driveway that skirts the lough. The many extensions detract somewhat from the character but the bedrooms are comfortable and contemporary in style. Floor to ceiling windows in restaurant; traditional menu.

🏨 Harvey's Point ⬛ ≤ ⬛ 🔊 🔦 📺 ⬛ ✗ 🍴 ✗ P VISA ◉◉ AE

Lough Eske, Northeast : 7 ¼ km by T 27 (Killybegs rd) – ℰ (074) 972 22 08
– www.harveyspoint.com – sales@harveyspoint.com
– Fax (074) 972 23 52
55 rm ⬜ – †€ 129/195 ††€ 198/290 – 4 suites
Rest *The Restaurant* – see restaurant listing

♦ Large hotel in tranquil setting on shores of Lough Eske and at foot of Blue Stack Mountains. Large, luxury bedrooms, some with Lough views.

REPUBLIC OF IRELAND

REPUBLIC OF IRELAND

🏛️🏛️🏛️ Mill Park

The Mullins, Northwest : ¾ km by N 56 on Letterbarrow rd – ℰ (074) 972 28 80
– www.millparkhotel.com – info@millparkhotel.com – Fax (074) 972 26 40
– Closed 25-27 December
105 rm ⌂ – †€ 150/200 ††€ 250
Rest – Menu € 24/40 – Carte € 19/43
♦ Open-plan lounge in timber and stone leads to a well-equipped gym and large, comfortable bedrooms generously provided with mod cons - a useful family option. Spacious mezzanine restaurant; its tall pine trusses lend a rustic feel.

🏠 Ardeevin without rest 🌿

Lough Eske, Barnesmore, Northeast : 9 km by N 15 following signs for Lough Eske Drive – ℰ (074) 972 17 90 – www.members.tripod.com/ardeevin
– seanmcginty@eircom.net – Fax (074) 972 17 90
– March-November
6 rm ⌂ – †€ 50 ††€ 70/80
♦ Inviting, individual rooms, almost all with superb views of Lough Eske and the quiet countryside. Hearty Irish breakfasts with fresh bread baked by the long-standing owners.

🏠 Island View House without rest

Ballyshannon Rd, Southwest : 1 ¼ km on R 267 – ℰ (074) 972 24 11
– www.eirbyte.com/islandview – dowds@indigo.ie
– Closed 15 December-January
4 rm ⌂ – †€ 55/60 ††€ 70
♦ Simple, homely establishment overlooking Donegal Bay. Though a modern building, it has a traditional appearance and style. Neatly kept bedrooms.

🍴🍴 The Restaurant – at Harvey's Point Hotel

Lough Eske, Northeast : 7 ¼ km by T 27 (Killybegs rd) – ℰ (074) 972 22 08
– www.harveyspoint.com – sales@harveyspoint.com – Fax (074) 972 23 52
– Closed Sunday dinner and Wednesday November-Easter
Rest – Menu € 35 (lunch) **s** – Carte € 45/55 **s**
♦ Wonderful views in a loughside setting. Very comfy, spacious cocktail lounge and bar. Huge restaurant: appealing menu uses regional ingredients and international elements.

at Laghy South : 5 ½ km on N 15 – ✉ **Donegal**

🏛️🏛️ Coxtown Manor 🌿

South : 3 km. on Ballintra rd – ℰ (074) 973 45 75 – www.coxtownmanor.com
– coxtownmanor@oddpost.com – Fax (074) 973 45 76
– February-October
9 rm ⌂ – †€ 55/75 ††€ 130/170
Rest – (closed Monday) (dinner only) (booking essential)
Carte € 45/55 **s**
♦ Serenely located, this attractive, creeper-clad Georgian house boasts a comfy, country-house style sitting room and bedrooms which have a warm aura of luxury about them. Affable Belgian owner guarantees top-notch desserts using chocolate from his homeland!

We try to be as accurate as possible when giving room rates but prices are susceptible to change.
Please check rates when booking.

DONNYBROOK (Domhnach Broc) – **Dublin** – **712** N 8 – **see Dublin**

DOOGORT (Dumha Goirt) – **Mayo** – **712** B 5/6 – **see Achill Island**

> Undecided between two equivalent establishments?
> Within each category, establishments are classified
> in our order of preference.

DOOLIN (Dúlainn) – **Clare** – **712** D 8 ▮ *Ireland*   38 **B1**

▷ Dublin 275 km – Galway 69 km – Limerick 80 km

◪ The Burren★★ (Cliffs of Moher★★★, Scenic Route★★, Aillwee Cave★ **AC**
(Waterfall★★), Poulnabrone Portal Tomb★, Corcomroe Abbey★, Kilfenora
Crosses★, Burren Centre★ **AC**)

REPUBLIC OF IRELAND

Tír Gan Éan   🛎 �& rm, 🔣 🕉 **P** 🆚 ⦾ 🄰🄴
– ℘ (065) 707 57 26 – www.atlantisholidaygroup.ie – info@tirganean.ie
– Fax (065) 707 57 34
12 rm ⬚ – †€ 140/160 ††€ 140/160
Rest – (dinner only and Sunday lunch) Carte € 30/38
♦ Stylish boutique hotel on main through road, with contemporary open plan bar.
Bedrooms come in creams and browns, with flat screens, fridges and modern art.
Accessible menu; local produce.

Hotel Doolin   🚃 🛎 �& rm, 🕉 ⦿ 🔾 **P** 🆚 ⦾
Fitz's Cross – ℘ (065) 707 41 11 – www.hoteldoolin.ie
– info@hoteldoolin.ie
– Fax (065) 707 57 72
– Closed 25 December
17 rm ⬚ – †€ 85/110 ††€ 130/170
Rest South Sound – (dinner only and Sunday lunch) Menu € 22/38 **s**
– Carte € 31/40 **s**
♦ Boutique hotel, integrating a parade of shops and a tourist information cen-
tre. Contemporary, cream coloured bedrooms come with flat screen TVs and vivid
artwork. Spacious South Sound restaurant offers modern menu.

Aran View House   ⩽ 🚃 ⦿ **P** 🆚 ⦾ ⦿
Coast Rd, Northeast : ¾ km – ℘ (065) 707 44 20 – www.aranview.com
– aranview@eircom.net – Fax (065) 707 45 40
– Closed 27 October - 10 April
19 rm ⬚ – †€ 80/120 ††€ 130/150
Rest – (Closed Sunday) (bar lunch) Carte € 33/43
♦ Georgian house set in 100 acres of working farmland, located on the main coastal
road. Well-kept public areas and bedrooms, some in adjacent converted barn. Simply
styled restaurant with a snug feel and traditional furnishings.

Ballyvara House without rest ⌂   ⩽ 🚃 ✕ �& 🕉 **P** 🆚 ⦾ 🄰🄴
Southeast : 1 km – ℘ (065) 707 44 67 – www.ballyvarahouse.ie
– info@ballyvarahouse.ie – Fax (065) 707 48 68
– April-September
11 rm ⬚ – †€ 60 ††€ 100/150 – 2 suites
♦ Pleasant rural views from this 19C former farm cottage, close to tourist village.
Comfy lounge with squashy sofas; outside a smart decked courtyard. Bright, im-
pressive rooms.

1073

✗✗ Cullinan's with rm   🍴 📶 P VISA ⚫⚫
– 𝒞 (065) 707 41 83 – www.cullinansdoolin.com
– cullinans@eircom.net
– Fax (065) 707 42 39
– Accommodation closed mid December-mid February
10 rm ⌣ – ♦€ 60/80 ♦♦€ 70/100
Rest – (Closed November-April, Sunday and Wednesday) (dinner only)
(booking essential) Carte € 36/49
♦ Simple wood-floored restaurant serving contemporary dishes which make good
use of local produce. Friendly service and charming setting with garden views and
fresh flowers. Immaculate, pine-furnished bedrooms; some overlooking a little
river.

DROGHEDA (Droichead Átha) – Louth – 712 M 6 – pop. 35 090 🔖 Ireland   37 D3

REPUBLIC OF IRELAND

▷ Dublin 46 km – Dundalk 35 km
🛈 Mayoralty St 𝒞 (041) 9837070 (May-September), tourism@drogheda.ie
🖥 Seapoint Termonfeckin, 𝒞 (041) 982 23 33
🖥 Towneley Hall Tullyallen, 𝒞 (041) 984 2229
◎ Town★ – Drogheda Museum★ – St Laurence Gate★
🄲 Monasterboice★★, N : 10½ km by N 1 – Boyne Valley★★, on N 51 –
Termonfeckin★, NE : 8 km by R 166. Newgrange★★★, W : 5 km by N 51 on
N 2 – Mellifont Old Abbey★ **AC** - Knowth★

⌂⌂⌂ The D   ⅄ 🛗 🔿 rm, AC rest, 🛁 📞 🛗 P VISA ⚫⚫ AE ⚪
Scotch Hall – 𝒞 (041) 987 77 00 – www.thed.ie
– reservethed@monogramhotels.ie – Fax (041) 987 77 02
– Closed 24-30 December
104 rm ⌣ – ♦€ 110/130 ♦♦€ 150/180
Rest – Menu € 35 – Carte € 39/47
♦ Stylish hotel adjacent to shopping centre on banks of the Boyne. Modish, minimalistic interiors include two comfy bars and spacious bedrooms with a cool, clinical
appeal. Popular menus in the airy dining room.

⌂⌂ Boyne Valley H. and Country Club   🍴 🔿 🔿 🐾 ⅄ ✗ 🛗
Southeast : 2 km on N 1   🔿 rm, 🐾 AC rest, 🛁 📶 🛗 P VISA ⚫⚫ AE ⚪
– 𝒞 (041) 983 77 37 – www.boyne-valley-hotel.ie
– reservations@boyne-valley-hotel.ie – Fax (041) 983 91 88
72 rm ⌣ – ♦€ 70/85 ♦♦€ 120/160
Rest – Menu € 27/33 **s** – Carte € 34/49 **s**
♦ Extended, ivy-clad house dating from the 1840s, with some character and set in
pretty grounds. Well run and kept with well-proportioned bedrooms, the best have
garden views. Basement bistro with original cast-iron range; intimate booths.

⌂⌂ Scholars Townhouse   🍴 🛗 🔿 rm, ✗ 📶 P VISA ⚫⚫ AE
King St, by West St and Lawrence St turning left at Lawrence's Gate
– 𝒞 (041) 983 54 10 – www.scholarshotel.com
– info@scholarshotel.com – Fax (041) 987 77 52
– Closed 25-26 December and Good Friday
18 rm ⌣ – ♦€ 75/90 ♦♦€ 120/130
Rest – Menu € 34 (lunch) – Carte € 47/59
♦ Wood panelling and ornate coving reflect Victorian style of this tastefully refurbished 19C townhouse. Some bedrooms have original stained glass windows; good
level of facilities. Formal restaurant serves classically-based menus. Dine under ceiling
murals commemorating the Battle of the Boyne.

Good food without spending a fortune?
Look out for the Bib Gourmand 🍴

DRUMSHANBO (Droim Seanbhó) – **Leitrim** – **712** H 5 ▊ *Ireland*　　37 **C2**

▶ Dublin 166 km – Carrick-on-Shannon 14 km – Sligo 48 km

 Arigna Scenic Drive★ (≤★), N : 8 km by R 280

🏠🏠 **Ramada H. and Suites at Lough Allen**　　≤ 🏛 ⤢ 🖥 ♨ 🏋

Carrig Na Brac , on Keadew rd　　🛗 ⅙ rm, 🅰🅲 rest, 🏊 🌙 ⚙ 🅿 *VISA* ⊕⊚ 🅐🅔

– ℰ (071) 964 01 00 – www.loughallenhotel.com

– info@loughallenhotel.com

– Fax (071) 964 01 01

– Closed 25-27 December

72 rm 🍽 – 🛇€ 99/170 🛇🛇€ 149/245

Rest *Rushes* – (bar lunch) Menu € 35 **s**

◆ Purpose-built hotel, beside Lough Allen, with part-stone exterior. Airy, up-to-the-minute bar. Pleasant terrace includes hot tub. Well-equipped spa. Minimalist, modern rooms. Dining room boasts stylish blond wood and seasonal menus.

O. Forir/MICHELIN

DUBLIN
(Dublin)

County: Dublin
Michelin REGIONAL map: n° **712** N 7
▶ Belfast 166 km – Cork 248 km – London-derry 235 km

Population: 1 045 769   39 **D1**
▌ *Ireland*

PRACTICAL INFORMATION

🛈 Tourist Information
Bord Failte Offices, Baggot Street Bridge ✆ (01) 602 4000, - Suffolk St, (01) 605 7700, information@dublintourism.ie

Airport
🛧 Dublin Airport: ✆ (01) 814 1111, N: 9 km by N 1 BS

Ferries
⛴ to Holyhead (Irish Ferries) 4 daily (3 h 15 mn) – to Holyhead (Stena Line) 1-2 daily (3 h 45 mn) – to the Isle of Man (Douglas) (Isle of Man Steam Packet Co. Ltd) (2 h 45 mn/4 h 45 mn) – to Liverpool (P & O Irish Sea) (8 h)

Golf Courses
🏌 Elm Park DonnybrookNutley House, ✆ (01) 269 3438
🏌 Milltown Lower Churchtown Rd, ✆ (01) 497 6090
🏌 Royal Dublin Dollymount North Bull Island, ✆ (01) 833 6346
🏌 Forrest Little Cloghran, ✆ (01) 840 17 63
🏌 Lucan Celbridge Rd, ✆ (01) 628 2106
🏌 Edmondstown, ✆ (01) 493 24 61
🏌 Coldwinters St Margaret'sNewtown house, ✆ (01) 864 0324

◎ SIGHTS

IN TOWN

Suffolk St - Arrivals Hall, Dublin Airport - The Square Shopping Centre, TallaghtCity★★★ - Trinity College★★ JY - Old Library★★★ (Treasury★★★, Long Room★★) – Dublin Castle★ (Chester Beatty Library★★★) HY - Christ Church Cathedral★★ HY - St Patrick's Cathedral★★ HZ - Marsh's Library★★ HZ – National Museum★★ (The Treasury★★) KZ - National Gallery★★ KZ - Newman House★★ JZ - Bank of Ireland★★ JY – Custom House★★ KX - Kilmainham Gaol Museum★★ AT **M6** - Kilmainham Hospital★★ AT – Phoenix Park★★ AS - National Botanic Gardens★★ BS - Marino Casino★★ CS – Tailors' Hall★ HY - City Hall★ HY - Temple Bar★ HJY - Liffey Bridge★ JY – Merrion Square★ KZ -

Number Twenty-Nine★ KZ **D** - Grafton Street★ JYZ - Powerscourt Centre★ JY – Rotunda Hospital Chapel★ JX - O'Connell Street★ (GPO Building★) JX - Hugh Lane Municipal Gallery of Modern Art★ JX **M4** – Pro-Cathedral★ JX - Bluecoat School★ BS **F** - Guinness Museum★ BT **M7** - Rathfarnham Castle★ AT – Zoological Gardens★ AS – Ceol★ BS **n**

ON THE OUTSKIRTS

The Ben of Howth★ (≼ ★), NE: 9 ½ km by R 105 CS

IN THE SURROUNDING AREA

Powerscourt★★ (Waterfall★★ **AC**), S: 22 ½ km by N 11 and R 117 EV – Russborough House★★★, SW: 35 ½ km by N 81 BT

DUBLIN

🏠🏠🏠🏠 The Shelbourne

🛗 ⚙ AK 🌡 🛁 VISA ⬤⬤ AE

27 St Stephen's Green – ✆ (01) 663 4500 – www.theshelbourne.ie
– info@renaissancehotels.com – Fax (01) 661 6006

JZ**c**

265 rm – ♦€ 219/289 ♦♦€ 219/289, ⊇ €29
– 19 suites

Rest *The Saddle Room* – see restaurant listing

◆ A delightful refit of a grand old hotel, with elegant meeting rooms and sumptuous bedrooms offering a host of extras. The historic Horseshoe Bar and Lord Mayor's Room remain.

🏠🏠🏠 The Merrion

🚗 📺 🕰 🛗 AK 🌀 🌡 🛁 🐾 VISA ⬤⬤ AE ⬤

Upper Merrion St – ✆ (01) 603 0600 – www.merrionhotel.com
– info@merrionhotel.com – Fax (01) 603 0700

KZ**e**

133 rm – ♦€ 480 ♦♦€ 510, ⊇ €29
– 10 suites

Rest The Cellar and **The Cellar Bar** – see restaurant listing

◆ Classic hotel in series of elegantly restored Georgian town houses; many of the individually designed grand rooms overlook pleasant gardens. Irish art in opulent lounges.

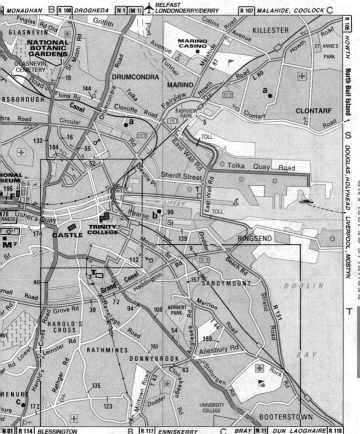

The Westin

College Green, Westmoreland St – ℰ (01) 645 1000 – www.westin.com/dublin
– reservations.dublin@westin.com – Fax (01) 645 1234   JYn
150 rm – †€ 179/489 ††€ 179/489, ☲ €28 – 13 suites
Rest The Exchange – (Closed Sunday dinner and Monday)
Menu €26 (lunch) – Carte dinner €34/59
Rest The Mint – Carte approx. €30

♦ Immaculately kept and consummately run hotel in a useful central location. Smart, uniform interiors and an ornate period banking hall. Excellent bedrooms with marvellous beds. Elegant, Art Deco 1920s-style dining in Exchange. More informal fare at The Mint.

The Westbury

Grafton St – ℰ (01) 679 1122 – www.jurysdoyle.com – westbury@jurysdoyle.com
– Fax (01) 679 7078   JYb
179 rm – †€ 209/309 ††€ 209/309, ☲ €28 – 8 suites
Rest The Wilde – Menu €35/50 – Carte €51/83
Rest Café Novo – Carte €32/47 **s**

♦ Imposing marble foyer and stairs lead to lounge famous for afternoon teas. Stylish Mandarin bar. Luxurious bedrooms offer every conceivable facility. Modern grill restaurant serves carefully sourced produce; Black Angus steak a speciality. Café Novo offers more international brasserie menu.

1079

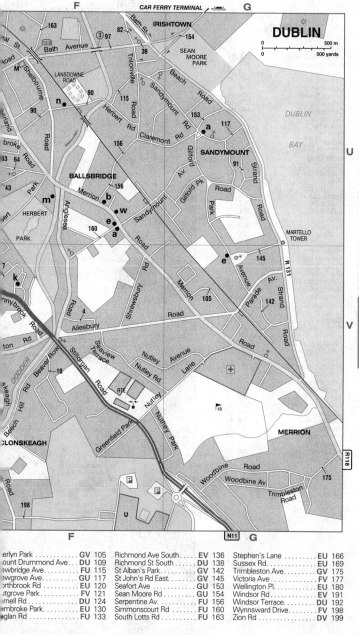

DUBLIN

REPUBLIC OF IRELAND

DUBLIN

REPUBLIC OF IRELAND

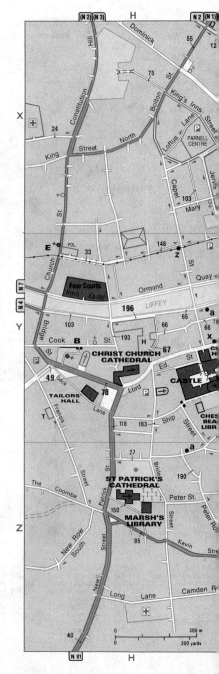

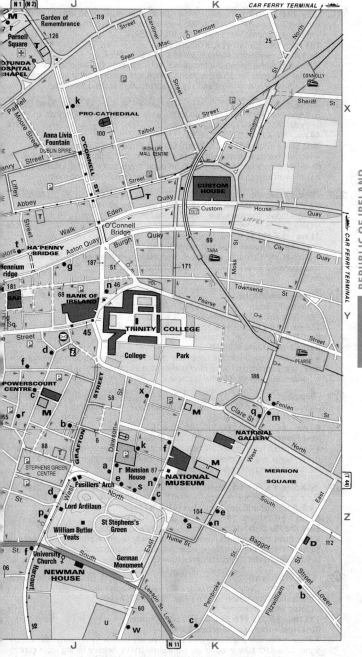

REPUBLIC OF IRELAND

REPUBLIC OF IRELAND

Conrad Dublin 🛏️ 🎩 ⚄ rm, 🔳 ⚅ 🕭 🏌️ 🚗 VISA ⓪ AE ①

Earlsfort Terrace – ℰ (01) 602 8900 – www.conradhotels.com/dublin
– dubhc_rs@conradhotels.com – Fax (01) 676 5424 JZ**w**
191 rm – †€ 185/380 ††€ 200/380, � €15
Rest *Alex* – Seafood – Menu € 30/40 **s** – Carte € 38/68 **s**
♦ Smart, business oriented international hotel opposite the National Concert Hall. Popular, pub-style bar. Spacious rooms with bright, modern décor and comprehensive facilities. Modern, bright and airy restaurant offers seafood specialities.

Dylan 🎩 ⚄ rm, 🔳 ⚅ 🕯️ VISA ⓪ AE ①

Eastmoreland Place – ℰ (01) 660 3000 – www.dylan.ie – justask@dylan.ie
– Fax (01) 660 3005 – Closed Christmas EU**a**
44 rm – †€ 395 ††€ 395, ⊇ €30
Rest *Still* – (Closed Saturday lunch) Carte € 45/74
♦ Modern boutique hotel with vibrant use of colour. Supremely comfortable, individually decorated bedrooms boast an opulent feel and a host of unexpected extras. Modern Irish cooking served in elegant, white-furnished dining room.

The Clarence 🦽 🛏️ ⚄ ⚅ 🕭 🅿️ VISA ⓪ AE ①

6-8 Wellington Quay – ℰ (01) 407 0800 – www.theclarence.ie
– reservations@theclarence.ie – Fax (01) 407 0820
– Closed 24-26 December HY**a**
44 rm – †€ 390 ††€ 390, ⊇ €28 – 5 suites
Rest *The Tea Room* – see restaurant listing
♦ Discreet, stylish former warehouse overlooking river boasting 21C interior design. Small panelled library. Modern, distinctive rooms: quietest face courtyard on fourth floor.

The Fitzwilliam 🦽 🛏️ 🎩 🔳 ⚅ 🕯️ 🏌️ 🚗 VISA ⓪ AE ①

St Stephen's Green – ℰ (01) 478 7000 – www.fitzwilliamhotel.com
– enq@fitzwilliamhotel.com – Fax (01) 478 7878 JZ**d**
136 rm – †€ 220/380 ††€ 220/380, ⊇ €24 – 3 suites
Rest *Thornton's* – see restaurant listing
Rest *Citron* – Carte € 28/50
♦ Rewardingly overlooks the Green and boasts a bright contemporary interior. Spacious, finely appointed rooms offer understated elegance. Largest hotel roof garden in Europe. Very trendy, informal brasserie.

Brooks 🕭 🦽 🎩 🔳 ⚅ 🕯️ 🏌️ VISA ⓪ AE

Drury St – ℰ (01) 670 4000 – www.brookshotel.ie – reservations@brookshotel.ie
– Fax (01) 670 4455 JY**r**
98 rm – †€ 170/200 ††€ 200/240, ⊇ €20
Rest *Francesca's* – (dinner only) Carte € 19/44
♦ Commercial hotel in modish, boutique, Irish town house style. Smart lounges and stylish rooms exude contemporary panache. Extras in top range rooms, at a supplement. Fine dining with open kitchen for chef-watching.

Stephen's Green 🦽 🎩 🔳 ⚅ 🕯️ 🏌️ 🚗 VISA ⓪ AE

Cuffe St, off St Stephen's Green – ℰ (01) 607 3600 – www.ocallaghanhotels.com
– info@ocallaghanhotels.com – Fax (01) 478 1444 JZ**f**
67 rm – †€ 150/480 ††€ 150/480, ⊇ €17 – 11 suites
Rest *The Pie Dish* – (Closed lunch Saturday and Sunday) Carte € 35/60
♦ This smart modern hotel housed in an originally Georgian property frequented by business clients; popular Magic Glass bar. Bright bedrooms offer a good range of facilities. Bright and breezy bistro restaurant.

The Morrison 🎩 🔳 ⚅ 🕭 🏌️ VISA ⓪ AE ①

Lower Ormond Quay – ℰ (01) 887 2400 – www.morrisonhotel.ie
– reservations@morrisonhotel.ie – Fax (01) 874 4039
– Closed 24-26 December HY**r**
135 rm – †€ 355 ††€ 355, ⊇ €21.50 – 3 suites
Rest *Halo* – (bar lunch) Carte € 33/46
♦ Modern riverside hotel with ultra-contemporary interior by acclaimed fashion designer John Rocha. New rooms are particularly stylish. Relaxed dining room concentrates on Irish produce in modish and home-cooked blend of dishes.

The Gresham
23 Upper O'Connell St – ✆ (01) 874 6881 – www.gresham-hotels.com
– info@thegresham.com – Fax (01) 878 7175 JX**k**
282 rm – †€ 150/600 ††€ 150/600, ☕ €23 – 6 suites
Rest 23 – (dinner only) Carte € 40/50
Rest *The Gallery* – Menu € 30 – Carte € 40/50
◆ Long-established restored 19C property in a famous street offers elegance tinged with luxury. Some penthouse suites. Well-equipped business centre, lounge and Toddy's bar. 23 is named after available wines by glass. The Gallery boasts formal ambience.

Jurys Croke Park
Jones's Rd – ✆ (01) 871 4444 – www.jurysdoyle.com – crokepark@jurysdoyle.com – Fax (01) 871 4400 – Closed 24-26 December BS**a**
230 rm ☕ – †€ 450 ††€ 450 – 2 suites **Rest** – (bar lunch) Carte € 38/56
◆ Corporate styled hotel opposite Croke Park Stadium. Stylish 'Side Line' bar with terrace. Rooms are a strong point: spacious with good business amenities. Bistro boasts the Canal terrace and modern/Mediterranean influenced menus.

O'Callaghan Alexander
Fienian St, Merrion Sq – ✆ (01) 607 3700 – www.ocallaghanhotels.com – info@ocallaghanhotels.com – Fax (01) 661 5663 KY**f**
98 rm – †€ 150/480 ††€ 150/480, ☕ €17 – 4 suites
Rest *Caravaggio's* – (bar lunch Saturday and Sunday) Carte € 38/45
◆ This bright corporate hotel, well placed for museums and Trinity College, has a stylish contemporary interior. Spacious comfortable rooms and suites with good facilities. Stylish contemporary restaurant with wide-ranging menus.

O'Callaghan Davenport
Lower Merrion St, off Merrion Sq – ✆ (01) 607 3500 – www.ocallaghanhotels.com – info@ocallaghanhotels.com – Fax (01) 661 5663 KY**m**
113 rm – †€ 150/480 ††€ 150/480, ☕ €17 – 2 suites
Rest *Lanyons* – Carte € 40/47
◆ Sumptuous Victorian gospel hall façade heralds elegant hotel popular with business clientele. Tastefully furnished, well-fitted rooms. Presidents bar honours past leaders. Dining room with fine choice menu.

Radisson SAS Royal
Golden Lane – ✆ (01) 898 2900 – www.dublin.radissonsas.com – info.royal.dublin@radissonsas.com – Fax (01) 898 2901 HZ**a**
146 rm – †€ 170/180 ††€ 170/180, ☕ €22 – 4 suites
Rest *Verres en Vers* – French – Menu € 20 (lunch) – Carte € 36/58
◆ Modern, purpose-built hotel in the heart of the city, geared to the corporate market. Bedrooms get bigger, the higher the floor - Executive rooms have lots of extras; some with balconies. Classic French brasserie cooking.

La Stampa
35-36 Dawson St – ✆ (01) 677 4444 – www.lastampa.ie – hotel@lastampa.ie – Fax (01) 677 4411 – Closed 25-27 December and Good Friday JZ**a**
27 rm – †€ 200/300 ††€ 220/300, ☕ €14.95 – 1 suite
Rest Balzac – see restaurant listing
Rest *Tiger Becs* – Thai – (dinner only) Carte approx. € 40
◆ Silks and oriental furnishings give an Eastern feel to this substantial Georgian house. Elegant bar, beautiful spa and individually appointed, well-equipped bedrooms. Basement restaurant Tiger Becs serves an authentic Thai menu.

O'Callaghan Mont Clare without rest
Lower Merrion St, off Merrion Sq – ✆ (01) 607 3800 – www.ocallaghanhotels.com – info@ocallaghanhotels.com – Fax (01) 661 5663 – Closed 23-28 December KY**q**
74 rm – †€ 130/300 ††€ 130/300, ☕ €17
◆ Classic property with elegant panelled reception and tasteful comfortable rooms at heart of Georgian Dublin. Corporate suites available. Traditional pub style Gallery bar.

DUBLIN

REPUBLIC OF IRELAND

Buswells
fitness icons 🛗 📶 🅿 VISA ⑩ AE ①
23-25 Molesworth St – ℰ (01) 614 6500 – www.quinnhotels.com
– buswells@quinn-hotels.com – Fax (01) 676 2090 – Closed Christmas — KZ**f**
65 rm ☐ – †€ 245 ††€ 288 – 2 suites
Rest *Trumans* – (carvery lunch) Menu € 49 **s**
◆ Elegant little hotel in quiet central location offering modern amenities while retaining its Georgian charm. Relax in cushioned lounge or cosy, pleasingly furnished rooms. Smart Trumans for formal dining.

Maldon
🖼 🕸 ↕ 🄰 rest, 🎦 📞 🛗 VISA ⑩ AE ①
Sir John Rogerson's Quay, Cardiff Lane – ℰ (01) 643 9500
– www.maldonhotels.com – info.cardifflane@maldonhotels.com
– Fax (01) 643 9510 — BS**b**
213 rm – †€ 99/359 ††€ 99/359, ☐ € 15
Rest – (bar lunch) Menu € 35 **s** – Carte € 30/46 **s**
◆ Based in 'new generation' quayside area. Sleek Vertigo bar named after U2 song. Impressive health club with large pool. Spacious, modern rooms, 48 boasting balconies. Irish and European mix of dishes in open plan restaurant.

Trinity Lodge
🄰 🎦 ↕ VISA ⑩ AE ①
12 South Frederick St – ℰ (01) 617 0900 – www.trinitylodge.com
– trinitylodge@eircom.net – Fax (01) 617 0999 – Closed Christmas — JY**x**
23 rm ☐ – †€ 140/195 ††€ 250
Rest *George's wine bar* – (closed Sunday) Menu € 13 (lunch) **s**
– Carte € 31/44 **s**
◆ Elegant, centrally located Georgian town houses near local landmarks. Airy, well-furnished bedrooms with good level of comfort: the modern deluxe rooms are worth asking for. Warm, welcoming wine bar.

Eliza Lodge without rest
◁ 🖼 🄰 🎦 VISA ⑩ AE
23-24 Wellington Quay – ℰ (01) 671 8044 – www.elizalodge.com
– info@dublinlodge.com – Fax (01) 671 8362 – Closed Christmas — JY**u**
18 rm ☐ – †€ 130/150 ††€ 300/340
◆ Ideally placed for Temple Bar nightlife. Small and friendly hotel with comfortable, practical rooms: the balconied penthouse floor has fine river views.

Kilronan House without rest
🎦 VISA ⑩ AE
70 Adelaide Rd – ℰ (01) 475 5266 – www.kilronanhouse.com
– info@kilronanhouse.com – Fax (01) 478 2841 – Closed Christmas — DU**c**
12 rm ☐ – †€ 55/170 ††€ 89/170
◆ In the heart of Georgian Dublin, a good value, well-kept town house run by knowledgeable, friendly couple. Individually styled rooms; sustaining breakfasts.

Patrick Guilbaud (Guillaume Lebrun)
🄰 ↔ VISA ⑩ AE ①
☆☆ 21 Upper Merrion St – ℰ (01) 676 4192 – www.restaurantpatrickguilbaud.ie
– restaurantpatrickguilbaud@eircom.net – Fax (01) 661 0052
– Closed 25-26 December, 17 March, Good Friday, Sunday and Monday — KZ**e**
Rest – French – Menu € 50 (lunch) – Carte € 93/135 ⌂
Spec. Crubeen with crispy pork, quail egg, cream and Meaux mustard. Turbot with sweet onion, white asparagus and tomato caramel. Lime soufflé with honey and Yuzu lemon.
◆ Run by consummate professional offering accomplished and acclaimed Irish-influenced dishes in redesigned Georgian town house. Contemporary Irish art; glass-roofed terrace.

Thornton's – at The Fitzwilliam Hotel
🄰 VISA ⑩ AE ①
☆ 128 St Stephen's Green – ℰ (01) 478 7008 – www.thorntonsrestaurant.com
– thorntonsrestaurant@eircom.net – Fax (01) 478 7009
– Closed Sunday and Monday — JZ**d**
Rest – Modern – Menu € 55 (lunch) – Carte € 104/108 ⌂
Spec. Bacon and cabbage terrine, celeriac purée and pea sorbet. Fillet of turbot, white onion and samphire. Prune and armagnac soufflé with pear sorbet.
◆ Sample canapés in spacious lounge; dine at linen-clad tables in restaurant, hung with the chef's striking photos. Luxury ingredients are prepared with balance and knowledge.

XXXX **Shanahan's on the Green**   AC VISA ◎◎ AE ①
119 St Stephen's Green – ℰ (01) 407 0939 – www.shanahans.ie
– sales@shanahans.ie – Fax (01) 407 0940
– Closed Christmas and Good Friday   JZ**p**
Rest – Beef specialities – (dinner only and lunch Friday and Sunday) (booking essential) Menu € 45 (lunch) – Carte € 76/122
♦ Sumptuous Georgian town house; upper floor window tables survey the Green. Supreme comfort enhances your enjoyment of strong seafood dishes and choice cuts of Irish beef.

XXX **L'Ecrivain** (Derry Clarke)   AC ⇔ VISA ◎◎ AE
✿ *109A Lower Baggot St – ℰ (01) 661 1919 – www.lecrivain.com*
– enquiries@lecrivain.com – Fax (01) 661 0617
– Closed 10 days Christmas, Easter, Saturday lunch and Sunday   KZ**b**
Rest – Contemporary – (booking essential) Menu € 50/85 – Carte dinner € 86/100
Spec. Scallops with frog's leg beignet, morels and garlic foam. Suckling pig with tortellini and baby vegetable salad. Lemon tart, raspberry granite, raspberry and basil mascarpone.
♦ Well-established restaurant serving well prepared, modern Irish menus with emphasis on fish and game. Attentive service from well-versed team. Delightful private dining room.

XXX **Chapter One** (Ross Lewis)   AC ⇔ VISA ◎◎
✿ *The Dublin Writers Museum, 18-19 Parnell Sq – ℰ (01) 873 2266*
– www.chapteronerestaurant.com – info@chapteronerestaurant.com
– Fax (01) 873 2330 – Closed first 2 weeks August, 24 December-8 January, Sunday, Monday and Saturday Lunch   JX**r**
Rest – Modern – Menu € 38 (lunch) – Carte dinner € 62/74
Spec. White pudding with horseradish, lentils, and poached egg hollandaise. Sea bream with fennel, squid, tomato and shellfish sauce. Hazelnut parfait, citrus jelly and espresso sauce.
♦ Stylish restaurant in basement of historic building; rustic walls filled with contemporary art. Seasonal, classically-based cooking demonstrates skill and understanding.

XXX **The Saddle Room** – at The Shelbourne Hotel   AC ⇔ VISA ◎◎ AE ①
27 St Stephen's Green – ℰ (01) 663 4500 – www.theshelbourne.ie
– info@renaissancehotels.com – Fax (01) 651 6066   JZ**c**
Rest – Grills – Menu € 30/55 – Carte € 51/69
♦ Smart restaurant in heart of hotel with delightful seafood bar. Grill/seafood menu offers quality Irish produce including superior 21 day hung steaks. Two private dining rooms.

XXX **Bentley's Oyster Bar & Grill**   AC VISA ◎◎ AE ①
22 St. Stephen's Green – ℰ (01) 638 39 39 – www.bentleysdublin.com
– info@bentleysdublin.com – Fax (01) 638 39 00 – Closed 25-27 December   JZ**s**
Rest – Seafood – (booking advisable) Carte € 39/80
♦ Imposing Georgian house in main city square. Large formally laid dining room and marble topped oyster bar with stools. Menus display tasty dishes crafted from quality produce.

XX **Balzac** – at La Stampa Hotel   VISA ◎◎ AE
35-36 Dawson St – ℰ (01) 677 8611 – hotel@lastampa.ie – Fax (01) 677 4411
– Closed 25-26 December, Good Friday and Sunday   JZ**a**
Rest – French – (closed Sunday lunch) Carte € 34/65
♦ Elegant yet spacious restaurant with high ceiling, blond wood bar, mirrors, banquette seating and a real bistro feel. Tasty, classical French cooking from an appealing menu.

REPUBLIC OF IRELAND

XX **Locks** ⟺ 𝘝𝘐𝘚𝘈 ⓸ 𝗔𝗘
Number 1, Windsor Terrace – ℰ (01) 454 3391 – www.locksrestaurant.ie
– info@locksrestaurant.ie – Fax (01) 453 8352
– Closed 25, 26 and 31 December, 1 January and Sunday dinner DU**a**
Rest – French – Carte € 35/59
♦ Quirky modern restaurant by the canal boasting stylish inner with wooden floor, comfy leather seating and dining split over 2 floors. French menu includes some regional dishes.

XX **The Tea Room** – at The Clarence Hotel 𝘝𝘐𝘚𝘈 ⓸ 𝗔𝗘 ⓞ
6-8 Wellington Quay – ℰ (01) 407 0813 – tearoom@theclarence.ie – Fax (01)
407 0826 – Closed 24-26 December and Saturday lunch HY**a**
Rest – Modern – (booking essential) Menu € 31/39 – Carte € 44/74
♦ Spacious elegant ground floor room with soaring coved ceiling and stylish contemporary décor offers interesting modern Irish dishes with hint of continental influence.

XX **Dax** 𝘝𝘐𝘚𝘈 ⓸ 𝗔𝗘
23 Pembroke Street Upper – ℰ (01) 676 1494 – www.dax.ie – olivier@dax.ie
– Closed Christmas and New Year, Easter, Saturday lunch,
Sunday and Monday KZ**c**
Rest – French – (booking essential) Menu € 29 (lunch) – Carte € 52/91
♦ Hidden away in basement of Georgian terrace, with rustic inner, immaculately laid tables, wine cellar and bar serving tapas. Knowledgeable staff serve French influenced menus.

XX **Fallon & Byrne** 𝘝𝘐𝘚𝘈 ⓸ 𝗔𝗘
First Floor, 11-17 Exchequer St – ℰ (01) 472 1000 – www.fallonandbyrne.com
– Fax (01) 472 1016 – Closed 25-26 December,1 January and Good Friday JY**f**
Rest – French – Menu € 23 (lunch) – Carte € 33/57
♦ Food emporium boasting vast basement wine cellar, ground floor full of fresh quality produce, and first floor French style bistro with banquettes, mirrors and tasty bistro food.

XX **One Pico** 𝗔𝗖 ⓺ ⟺ 𝘝𝘐𝘚𝘈 ⓸ 𝗔𝗘 ⓞ
5-6 Molesworth Pl – ℰ (01) 676 0300 – www.onepico.com
– eamonnoreilly@ireland.com – Fax (01) 676 0411
– Closed 25 December-February, Sunday and Bank Holidays JZ**k**
Rest – Modern – Menu € 37 (lunch) – Carte dinner € 57/67
♦ Wide-ranging cuisine, classic and traditional by turns, always with an original, eclectic edge. Décor and service share a pleasant formality, crisp, modern and stylish.

XX **Rhodes D7** ⌂ 𝗔𝗖 𝘝𝘐𝘚𝘈 ⓸ 𝗔𝗘 ⓞ
The Capel Buildings, Mary's Abbey – ℰ (01) 804 4444 – www.rhodesd7.com
– info@rhodesd7.com – Fax (01) 804 4445 – Closed Sunday and Monday HY**z**
Rest – Modern – Menu € 18 (lunch) – Carte € 36/47
♦ Cavernous restaurant: take your pick from four dining areas. Bright, warm décor incorporating bold, colourful paintings accompanies classic Rhodes menus given an Irish twist.

XX **Les Frères Jacques** 𝗔𝗖 𝘝𝘐𝘚𝘈 ⓸ 𝗔𝗘
74 Dame St – ℰ (01) 679 4555 – www.lesfreresjacques.com
– info@lesfreresjacques.com – Fax (01) 679 4725 – Closed 24 December-2 January,
Saturday lunch, Sunday and Bank Holidays HY**x**
Rest – French – Menu € 38 – Carte € 34/65
♦ Smart and well established, offering well prepared, classic French cuisine with fresh fish and seafood a speciality, served by efficient French staff. Warm, modern décor.

XX **Peploe's**   AC VISA ☤ AE

16 St Stephen's Green – ℰ (01) 676 3144 – www.peploes.com
– reception@peploes.com – Fax (01) 676 3154
– Closed 25-29 December and Good Friday   JZ**e**
Rest – Mediterranean – Carte € 40/56
♦ Fashionable restaurant - a former bank vault - by the Green. Irish wall mural, Italian leather chairs, suede banquettes. Original dishes with pronounced Mediterranean accents.

XX **Town Bar and Grill**   AC ☤ VISA ☤ AE

21 Kildare St – ℰ (01) 662 4800 – www.townbarandgrill.com
– reservations@townbarandgrill.com – Fax (01) 662 3857
– Closed 25-26 December, 1 January and Good Friday   JZ**n**
Rest – Italian influences – Menu € 30 (lunch) – Carte dinner € 45/58
♦ Located in wine merchant's old cellars: brick pillars divide a large space; fresh flowers and candles add a personal touch. Italian flair in bold cooking with innovative edge.

XX **Dobbin's**   🍴 AC ⇨ P VISA ☤ AE ⓪

15 Stephen's Lane, (off Stephen's Place) off Lower Mount St – ℰ (01) 661 9536
– www.dobbins.ie – dobbinsbistro@g.mail.com – Fax (01) 661 3331
– Closed 1 week Christmas-New Year, Good Friday, Saturday lunch,
Sunday dinner and Bank Holidays   EU**s**
Rest – Traditional – (booking essential) Menu € 24 (lunch) – Carte € 53/81
♦ In the unlikely setting of a former Nissen hut, and now with contemporary styling, this popular restaurant, something of a local landmark, offers good food to suit all tastes.

XX **Siam Thai**   AC VISA ☤ AE

14-15 Andrew St – ℰ (01) 677 3363 – www.siamthai.ie – siam@eircom.net
– Fax (01) 670 7644
– Closed 25 December, Good Friday and lunch Saturday and Sunday   JY**d**
Rest – Thai – Menu € 18/36 – Carte € 28/37
♦ Invariably popular, centrally located restaurant with a warm, homely feel, embodied by woven Thai prints. Daily specials enhance Thai menus full of choice and originality.

XX **Jaipur**   VISA ☤ AE ⓪

41 South Great George's St – ℰ (01) 677 0999 – www.jaipur.ie – dublin@jaipur.ie
– Fax (01) 677 0919   JY**a**
Rest – Indian – (dinner only and lunch in December) Menu € 50
– Carte € 35/45
♦ Vivid modernity in the city centre; run by knowledgeable team. Immaculately laid, linen-clad tables. Interesting, freshly prepared Indian dishes using unique variations.

XX **Bang Café**   🍴 AC VISA ☤ ⓪

11 Merrion Row – ℰ (01) 676 0898 – www.bangrestaurant.com
– bangcafe@eircom.net – Fax (01) 676 0899 – Closed 2 weeks late December-early
January, Sunday and Bank Holidays   KZ**a**
Rest – Modern – (booking essential) Menu € 30 (lunch) – Carte € 28/43
♦ Stylish feel, closely set tables and an open kitchen lend a lively, contemporary air to this established three-tier favourite. Menus balance the classical and the creative.

XX **The Cellar** – at The Merrion Hotel   AC VISA ☤ AE ⓪

Upper Merrion St – ℰ (01) 603 0630 – www.merrionhotel.com
– info@merrionhotel.com – Fax (01) 603 0700 – Closed Saturday lunch   KZ**e**
Rest – Mediterranean – Menu € 27 (lunch) – Carte dinner € 40/58
♦ Smart open-plan basement restaurant with informal ambience offering well-prepared formal style fare crossing Irish with Mediterranean influences. Good value lunch menu.

REPUBLIC OF IRELAND

REPUBLIC OF IRELAND

✗ **The Winding Stair** `VISA` `MO`
40 Lower Ormond Quay – ℰ (01) 872 7320 – www.winding-stair.com
– Closed 25 December - 4 January JYt
Rest – Modern – (booking essential) Carte € 39/47
♦ Delightfully rustic restaurant on banks of River Liffey, unusually set above a book-shop. Open dining room with wooden tables; frequently-changing menu has strong organic base.

✗ **Pearl Brasserie** `AC` `VISA` `MO` `AE`
20 Merrion St Upper – ℰ (01) 661 3572 – www.pearl-brasserie.com
– info@pearl-brasserie.com – Fax (01) 661 3629
– Closed 25 December and Sunday KZn
Rest – French – Carte € 31/59 s
♦ A metal staircase leads down to this intimate, newly refurbished, vaulted brasserie where Franco-Irish dishes are served at smart, linen-laid tables. Amiable, helpful service.

✗ **Eden** `AC` `VISA` `MO` `AE`
Meeting House Sq, Temple Bar – ℰ (01) 670 5372 – www.edenrestaurant.ie
– eden@edenrestaurant.ie – Fax (01) 670 3330
– Closed 25 December-4 January HYe
Rest – Modern – Menu € 27 (lunch) – Carte dinner € 36/51
♦ Modern minimalist restaurant with open plan kitchen serves good robust food. Terrace overlooks theatre square, at the heart of a busy arty district. The place for pre-theatre.

✗ **Mermaid Café** `AC` `VISA` `MO` `AE`
69-70 Dame St – ℰ (01) 670 8236 – www.mermaid.ie – info@mermaid.ie
– Fax (01) 670 8205 – Closed 24-26 December, 1 January and Good Friday HYd
Rest – Modern – (Sunday brunch) (booking essential) Carte € 34/52
♦ This informal restaurant with unfussy décor and bustling atmosphere offers an interesting and well cooked selection of robust modern dishes. Efficient service.

✗ **L'Gueleton** `VISA` `MO`
1 Fade St – ℰ (01) 675 3708 – Closed 25-26 and 31 December, 1 January JYc
Rest – French – (bookings not accepted) Carte € 30/49
♦ Busy, highly renowned recent arrival. Rustic style: mish-mash of roughed-up chairs and tables with candles or Parisian lamps. Authentic French country dishes full of flavour.

✗ **Bleu** `AC` `VISA` `MO` `AE`
Joshua House, Dawson St – ℰ (01) 676 7015 – www.bleu.ie – Fax (01) 676 7027
– Closed 25-26 December, Sunday and Bank Holidays JZr
Rest – Modern – Menu € 25 (lunch) – Carte € 30/49
♦ Black leather and polished wood provide a modern feel to this friendly all-day restaurant. The appealing, varied menu is well executed and very tasty. Good wine selection.

✗ **La Maison des Gourmets** `VISA` `MO` `AE` `O`
15 Castlemarket – ℰ (01) 672 7258 – info@la-maison.ie – Fax (01) 672 7238
– Closed 25-27 December and Bank Holidays JYc
Rest – French – (lunch only) (bookings not accepted) Carte € 19/26
♦ Neat, refurbished eatery on first floor above an excellent French bakery. Extremely good value Gallic meals with simplicity the key. Get there early or be prepared to wait!

🛏 **The Cellar Bar** – at The Merrion H. `VISA` `MO` `AE` `O`
Upper Merrion St – ℰ (01) 603 0600 – www.merrionhotel.com
– info@merrionhotel.com – Fax (01) 603 0700 – Closed 25 December KZe
Rest – Traditional – (Closed Sunday) (carvery lunch) Carte € 29/43
♦ Characterful stone and brick bar-restaurant in the original vaulted cellars with large wood bar. Popular with Dublin's social set. Offers wholesome Irish pub lunch fare.

at Sandymount – Dublin

❌ **Itsa 4**   A/C VISA ⓪
6A Sandymount Green – ✆ (01) 219 4676 – www.itsabagel.com
– itsa4@itsabagel.com – Fax (01) 219 4654 – Closed 1 week Christmas, Good
Friday and Monday except Bank Holidays   GU**a**
Rest – (booking essential) Carte € 33/60
♦ Dark wood and bright lime green chairs seduce the eye in this smart contemporary restaurant in smart suburb. Traceability of ingredients key to tasty, easy-going menu.

at Ballsbridge – Dublin

 Four Seasons   ☁ 🅃 ⊕ 🐾 ℞ 📶 ⅋ rm, A/C ⁇ ⅏ P ⌂ VISA ⓪ AE ⓪
Simmonscourt Rd – ✆ (01) 665 4000 – www.fourseasons.com/dublin
– reservations.dublin@fourseasons.com – Fax (01) 665 4099   FU**e**
157 rm – †€ 225/610 ††€ 225/610, � € 32 – 40 suites
Rest *Seasons* – Menu € 40 (lunch) – Carte dinner € 62/84
Rest *The Cafe* – (lunch only) Carte € 38/75
♦ Every inch the epitome of international style - supremely comfortable rooms with every facility; richly furnished lounge; a warm mix of antiques, oils and soft piano études. Dining in Seasons guarantees luxury ingredients. Good choice menu in The Café.

 Herbert Park   ☁ ℞ ⅋ A/C ⁇ ⁇ ⅏ P VISA ⓪ AE ⓪
– ✆ (01) 667 2200 – www.herbertparkhotel.ie – reservations@herbertparkhotel.ie
– Fax (01) 667 2595   FU**m**
151 rm – †€ 135/300 ††€ 150/385, �cup € 23.50 – 2 suites
Rest *The Pavilion* – Menu € 26 – Carte € 36/72
♦ Stylish contemporary hotel. Open, modern lobby and lounges. Excellent, well-designed rooms with tasteful décor: fifth floor Executive rooms boast several upgraded extras. French-windowed restaurant with alfresco potential; oyster/lobster specialities.

 Merrion Hall without rest   ☁ ⅋ ⁇ P VISA ⓪ AE ⓪
54-56 Merrion Rd – ✆ (01) 668 1426 – www.halpinsprivatehotels.com
– merrionhall@iol.ie – Fax (01) 668 4280   FU**b**
34 rm ⊂ – †€ 99/119 ††€ 139/169 – 2 suites
♦ Manor house hotel has comfy sitting rooms with Georgian feel and some original features plus rear breakfast room with conservatory. Minimalist bedrooms boast quality feel.

 The Schoolhouse   ☁ ⅏ A/C ⅋ ⁇ P VISA ⓪ AE ⓪
2-8 Northumberland Rd – ✆ (01) 667 5014 – www.schoolhousehotel.com
– reservations@schoolhousehotel.com – Fax (01) 667 5015
– Closed 24-27 December   EU**a**
31 rm ⊂ – †€ 169/500 ††€ 199/500
Rest – (brunch Saturday and Sunday) Menu € 31 (lunch) – Carte € 28/48
♦ Spacious converted 19C schoolhouse, close to canal, boasts modernity and charm. Inkwell bar exudes a convivial atmosphere. Rooms contain locally crafted furniture. Old classroom now a large restaurant with beamed ceilings.

Ariel House without rest   ⅋ P VISA ⓪
50-54 Lansdowne Rd – ✆ (01) 668 5512 – www.ariel-house.net
– reservations@ariel-house.net – Fax (01) 668 5845
– Closed 23-28 December   FU**n**
37 rm ⊂ – †€ 99/130 ††€ 130/180
♦ Restored, listed Victorian mansion in smart suburb houses personally run, traditional small hotel. Rooms feature period décor and some antiques; comfy four poster rooms.

REPUBLIC OF IRELAND

REPUBLIC OF IRELAND

Bewley's 🛎 ᵹ rm, 🖾 rest, 🕸 🕪 🏄 🛥 ᵥᵢₛₐ ⚫ 🅰 ⓘ

Merrion Rd – ℰ (01) 668 1111 – www.bewleyshotels.com
– ballsbridge@bewleyshotels.com – Fax (01) 668 1999
– Closed 24-26 December   FU**a**

304 rm – ♥€ 119/199 ♥♥€ 119/199, � €12

Rest *The Brasserie* – (carvery lunch) Menu € 28 – Carte € 27/37

♦ Huge hotel offers stylish modern accommodation behind sumptuous Victorian façade of former Masonic school. Location, facilities and value for money make this a good choice. Carvery lunch served in The Brasserie.

Aberdeen Lodge 🚗 🕸 🕪 🅿 ᵥᵢₛₐ ⚫ 🅰 ⓘ

53-55 Park Ave – ℰ (01) 283 8155 – www.halpinsprivatehotels.com
– aberdeen@iol.ie – Fax (01) 283 7877   GV**e**

17 rm ⊑ – ♥€ 99/119 ♥♥€ 139/169

Rest – (residents only, light meals) Carte € 25/34 **s**

♦ Neat red brick house in smart residential suburb. Comfortable rooms with Edwardian style décor in neutral tones, wood furniture and modern facilities. Some garden views. Comfortable, traditionally decorated dining room.

Pembroke Townhouse without rest 🖾 🕸 🕪 🅿 ᵥᵢₛₐ ⚫ 🅰 ⓘ

90 Pembroke Rd – ℰ (01) 660 0277 – www.pembroketownhouse.ie
– info@pembroketownhouse.ie – Fax (01) 660 0291
– Closed 21 December- 4 January   FU**d**

48 rm – ♥€ 145/190 ♥♥€ 190/220, ⊑ €14

♦ Period-inspired décor adds to the appeal of a sensitively modernised Georgian terrace town house in the smart suburbs. Neat, simple accommodation.

Glenogra House without rest 🕸 🕪 🅿 ᵥᵢₛₐ ⚫ 🅰 ⓘ

64 Merrion Rd – ℰ (01) 668 3661 – www.glenogra.com – info@glenogra.com
– Fax (01) 668 3698 – Closed 23 December-10 January   FU**w**

13 rm ⊑ – ♥€ 79/109 ♥♥€ 120/190

♦ Neat and tidy bay-windowed house in smart suburb. Personally-run to good standard with bedrooms attractively decorated in keeping with a period property. Modern facilities.

Roly's Bistro 🖾 😊 🔄 ᵥᵢₛₐ ⚫ 🅰 ⓘ

7 Ballsbridge Terrace – ℰ (01) 668 2611 – www.rolysbistro.ie
– ireland@rolysbistro.ie – Fax (01) 660 3342 – Closed Christmas   FU**r**

Rest – Traditional – (booking essential) Menu € 22/42 – Carte € 41/54

♦ A Dublin institution: this roadside bistro is very busy and well run with a buzzy, fun atmosphere. Its two floors offer traditional Irish dishes and a very good value lunch.

at Donnybrook – Dublin

Marble Hall without rest 🕸 🅿

81 Marlborough Rd – ℰ (01) 497 7350 – www.marblehall.net
– marblehall@eircom.net – Closed December - 15 January   EV**a**

3 rm ⊑ – ♥€ 55/65 ♥♥€ 90/100

♦ Georgian townhouse with effusive welcome guaranteed. Individually styled throughout, with plenty of antiques and quality soft furnishings. Stylish, warmly decorated bedrooms.

Poulot's 🖾 ᵥᵢₛₐ ⚫ 🅰

Mulberry Gardens, off Morehampton Rd – ℰ (01) 269 3300 – www.poulots.ie
– Fax (01) 269 3260 – Closed 25 December-5 January, Sunday and Monday   FV**k**

Rest – Menu € 35 (lunch) – Carte dinner € 50/72

♦ A light, airy ambience is enhanced by garden views from all tables. Vivid oils and prints liven up white walls. Modern, complex dishes with distinctive French starting point.

at Ranelagh – Dublin

XX
&
Mint (Dylan McGrath)   🔲 *VISA* 🔵 **AE**
47 Ranelagh – ℰ (01) 497 8655 – www.mintrestaurant.ie
– info@mintrestaurant.ie – Fax (01) 497 9035
– Closed 23 December-6 January, 6-17 April, Sunday, Monday
and Saturday lunch   EV**e**
Rest – Inventive – Menu € 30/75 – Carte € 37/75 🕮
Spec. Salmon, beetroot, lemon and avocado mousse. Smoked loin and belly of
pork, sweetcorn, polenta and pearl barley. Pear and chocolate frangipan, chocolate sorbet.
♦ Intimate, pastel-hued restaurant in up and coming area of the city. Ambitious,
confident kitchen serving uncompromisingly rich and elaborate dishes with French
influences.

at Rathmines – Dublin

🏠
Uppercross House   📶 ⁝⁚ **P** *VISA* 🔵 **AE** ⓪
26-30 Upper Rathmines Rd – ℰ (01) 497 5486 – www.uppercrosshousehotel.com
– reservations@uppercrosshousehotel.com – Fax (01) 497 5361
– Closed 24-28 December   DV**d**
49 rm � – ♦€ 69/109 ♦♦€ 99/158
Rest – (dinner only and lunch Friday-Sunday) Carte € 20/37 **s**
♦ Privately run suburban hotel in three adjacent town houses with modern extension wing. Good size rooms and standard facilities. Live music midweek in traditional
Irish bar. Restaurant offers a mellow and friendly setting with welcoming wood
décor.

XX
Zen   🔲 *VISA* 🔵 **AE** ⓪
89 Upper Rathmines Rd – ℰ (01) 497 94 28
– Fax (01) 491 17 28   DV**t**
Rest – Chinese – (dinner only and lunch Friday) Menu € 16 **s**
*– Carte € 25/36 **s***
♦ Renowned family run Chinese restaurant in the unusual setting of an old church
hall. Imaginative, authentic oriental cuisine with particular emphasis on spicy Sze-
chuan dishes.

at Terenure South : 9½ km by N 81

XX
Vermilion   *VISA* 🔵 **AE** ⓪
1st Floor above Terenure Inn, 94-96 Terenure Road North – ℰ (01) 499 1400
– www.vermilion.ie – mail@vermilion.ie – Fax (01) 499 1300
– Closed 25-26 December   BT**c**
Rest – Indian – (dinner only and Sunday lunch) Carte € 26/43
♦ Smart restaurant above a busy pub in a residential part of town. Vividly coloured
dining room and efficient service. Well-balanced, modern Indian food with a Keralan
base.

at Dublin Airport North : 10½ km by N 1 - BS - and M 1 – ⊠ Dublin

🏨🏨
Hilton Dublin Airport   🔧 📶 ⅙ rm, 🔲 ⅙ ⁝⁚ 🖧 **P** *VISA* 🔵 **AE** ⓪
Northern Cross, Malahide Rd, East : 3 km by A 32 – ℰ (01) 866 18 00
– www.hilton.com/dublinairport – reservations.dublinairport@hilton.com
– Fax (01) 866 18 66 – Closed 24-29 December
162 rm – ♦€ 100/240 ♦♦€ 100/260, � €21.50 – 4 suites
Rest *Barnell Bar and Grill* – Menu € 22 (lunch) **s** – Carte € 31/51 **s**
♦ Opened in 2005, just five minutes from the airport, adjacent to busy shopping
centre. Modish feel throughout. State-of-the-art meeting facilities. Airy, well-equipped rooms. Spacious bar and grill serve modern dishes with Irish and international
flavours.

REPUBLIC OF IRELAND

 Carlton H. Dublin Airport ⇐ 🛏️ 🔥 rm, AC 🕸️ 📶 🔐 **P** VISA ⓜⓞ AE

Old Airport Rd, Cloughran, on R 132 Santry rd – 𝒞 (01) 866 7500
– www.carlton.ie/dublinairport – info@carltondublinairport.com – Fax (01)
862 3114 – Closed 24-26 December
117 rm – 🛉 € 165 🛉🛉 € 330, ⇌ € 16.50 – 1 suite
Rest *Kilty Hawks* – (dinner only and Sunday lunch) Carte € 22/42 **s**
♦ Purpose-built hotel on edge of airport. State-of-the-art conference rooms. Impressive bedrooms, though many a touch compact, in warm colours with high level of facilities. Fine dining restaurant: worldwide cooking accompanied by excellent views.

 Bewleys 🛗 🔥 rm, AC 🕸️ 📶 **P** 🚗 VISA ⓜⓞ AE ⓞ

Baskin Lane, East : 1½ km on A 32 – 𝒞 (01) 871 1000
– www.bewleyshotels.com – dublinairport@bewleyshotels.com – Fax (01)
871 1001 – Closed 24-25 December
466 rm – 🛉 € 99 🛉🛉 € 99, ⇌ € 12
Rest *The Brasserie* – Menu € 27 (dinner) **s** – Carte € 24/36 **s**
♦ Immense eight floor hotel, ten minutes from the airport, with selection of small meeting rooms. Immaculately kept bedrooms; good value for money. Wide-ranging menu served in The Brasserie.

at Clontarf Northeast : 5½ km by R 105 – ✉ Dublin

 Clontarf Castle 🔥 🛗 🔥 rm, 🕸️ ☎️ 🔐 **P** VISA ⓜⓞ AE ⓞ

Castle Ave – 𝒞 (01) 833 2321 – www.clontarfcastle.ie – info@clontarfcastle.ie
– Fax (01) 833 0418 – Closed 25 December CS**a**
108 rm ⇌ – 🛉 € 400 🛉🛉 € 400 – 3 suites
Rest *Fahrenheit Grill* – (carvery lunch Monday-Friday) Carte € 45/66
♦ Set in an historic castle, partly dating back to 1172. Striking medieval style entrance lobby. Modern rooms and characterful luxury suites, all with cutting edge facilities. Restaurant boasts grand medieval style décor reminiscent of a knights' banqueting hall; fresh local meats and seafood feature.

at Dundrum Southeast : 8 km by N 11 - CT – ✉ Dublin

XXX **Harvey Nichols First Floor Restaurant** AC ⇔ VISA ⓜⓞ AE

Harvey Nichols, Town Square, Sandyford Rd – 𝒞 (01) 291 0488
– www.harveynichols.com – michael.andrews@harveynichols.com – Fax (01)
291 0489 – Closed 25 December and Easter, dinner Sunday and Monday
Rest – Menu € 25/30 – Carte dinner € 47/57
♦ Up the lift to ultra-stylish bar and plush, designer-led restaurant. Attentive, professional service. Dishes are modern, seasonal and confident with a fine dining feel.

XX **Ananda** AC VISA ⓜⓞ AE

Town Square – 𝒞 (01 296) 0099 – www.anandarestarant.ie
– info@anandarestaurant.ie – Fax (01 296) 0033
– Closed 25-26 December
Rest – (booking advisable) Menu € 30 (lunch) – Carte € 40/58
♦ Meaning 'bliss' in ancient Sanskrit. Stylish restaurant located in city centre arcade. Beautiful décor, attractive fretwork and gorgeous lighting. Extremely tasty modern Indian cuisine.

X **Cafe Mao** 🌇 AC VISA ⓜⓞ

Town Square, Sandyford Rd – 𝒞 (01) 296 2802 – www.cafemao.com
– dundrum@cafemao.com – Fax (01) 296 2813 – Closed 25-26 December and Easter Sunday
Rest – South East Asian – (bookings not accepted) Carte € 29/40
♦ Situated in an upmarket 21C shopping centre, this café has a smart terrace and balconies from which you can watch the elegant dancing fountains. Wide-ranging, Asian menus.

REPUBLIC OF IRELAND

at Stillorgan Southeast : 8 km on N 11 - CT - ✉ Dublin

🏛️🏛️🏛️ Radisson SAS St Helen's   🚗 ⅃ᴁ 🏧 ᴁ & rm, 🆎 ⅗ 🛜 🧳 🅿 🆅🆂🅰 ⓒⓞ 🅰🅴 ①

Stillorgan Rd – ℰ (01) 218 6000 – www.sthelens.dublin.radissonsas.com
– info.dublin@radissonsas.com – Fax (01) 218 6010
130 rm – �|€ 167/360 ♦♦€ 167/360, ☑ €25 – 21 suites
Rest *Talavera* – Italian – (dinner only) Carte € 33/63
♦ Imposing part 18C mansion with substantial extensions and well laid out gardens. Well run with good level of services. Smart modern rooms with warm feel and all facilities. Delicious antipasti table at basement Talavera.

🏛️🏛️ Stillorgan Park   🆂 ⅃ᴁ 🏧 & rm, 🆎 ⅗ 🛜 🧳 🅿 🆅🆂🅰 ⓒⓞ 🅰🅴

Stillorgan Rd – ℰ (01) 200 1800 – www.stillorganpark.com
– sales@stillorganpark.com – Fax (01) 283 1610 – Closed 25 December
150 rm – ♦€ 329 ♦♦€ 330/380, ☑ €14.95
Rest *Purple Sage* – (closed Saturday lunch and Sunday dinner) (carvery lunch) Menu € 29/43 – Carte € 33/47
♦ Modern commercial hotel in southside city suburb. Spacious rooms with modern facilities. Interesting horse theme décor in large stone floored bar with buffet. Mosaics, frescoes and hidden alcoves add spice to popular Irish dishes in Purple Sage.

at Sandyford Southeast : 9 km by N 11 - CT - off Leopardstown Rd – ✉ Dublin

🏛️🏛️ The Beacon   🆂 🏧 🆎 rest, ⅗ 🛜 🧳 🚗 🆅🆂🅰 ⓒⓞ 🅰🅴

Beacon Court, Sandyford Business Region – ℰ (01) 291 5000
– www.thebeacon.com – sales@thebeacon.com – Fax (01) 291 5005
– Closed 25 December
88 rm – ♦€ 120 ♦♦€ 300, ☑ €20
Rest *My Thai* – Thai – Menu € 25/45 – Carte € 34/46
♦ Ultra-stylish hotel with uniquely quirky entrance lobby featuring a chandelier on the floor and bed with central seating! Modish bar, low-key meeting rooms, sleek bedrooms. Funky, relaxed restaurant serving authentic Asian dishes.

at Foxrock Southeast : 13 km by N 11 - CT – ✉ Dublin

🍴🍴 Bistro One   🆅🆂🅰 ⓒⓞ

3 Brighton Rd – ℰ (01) 289 7711 – www.bistro-one.ie – bistroone@eircom.net
– Fax (01) 207 0742 – Closed 25 December-3 January, Sunday and Monday
Rest – (booking essential) Menu € 24 (lunch) – Carte € 34/55
♦ Pleasantly set and homely, with beams and walls of wine racks. Simple menu offers well-prepared, distinctively seasonal Irish, Asian or Italian classics. Passionate owner.

at Leopardstown Southeast : 12 km by N 11 - CT – ✉ Dublin

🏛️🏛️ Bewleys   🏧 & rm, 🆎 rest, ⅗ 🕻 🧳 🚗 🆅🆂🅰 ⓒⓞ 🅰🅴 ①

Central Park – ℰ (01) 293 5000 – www.bewleyshotels.com
– leopardstown@bewleyshotels.com – Fax (01) 293 5099
352 rm – ♦€ 89 ♦♦€ 89, ☑ €11
Rest *Brasserie* – (carvery lunch) Carte € 22/30
♦ Handily placed next to racecourse, this modern hotel boasts smart bar with leather armchairs, decked terrace, and comfy, uniform bedrooms with good facilities. Informal brasserie with neutral, stylish tones.

at Clondalkin Southwest : 12 km by N 7 on R 113 - AT – ✉ Dublin

🏛️🏛️ Red Cow Moran   🏧 & rm, 🆎 ⅗ 🛜 🧳 🅿 🆅🆂🅰 ⓒⓞ 🅰🅴 ①

Naas Rd, Southeast : 3¼ km on N 7 at junction with M 50 – ℰ (01) 459 3650
– www.redcowhotel.com – redcowres@moranhotels.com – Fax (01) 459 1588
– Closed 24-26 December
120 rm ☑ – ♦€ 130/380 ♦♦€ 130/380 – 3 suites
Rest *The Winter Garden* – Menu € 29/35 – Carte € 34/53
♦ Sweeping lobby staircase gives a foretaste of this smart commercial hotel's mix of traditional elegance and modern design. Landmark Red Cow inn and Diva nightclub. Large characterful Winter Garden restaurant with bare brick walls and warm wood floor.

Bewley's H. Newlands Cross   � — rm, 🅰️ rest, ♨ ☝ 🅿️

Newlands Rd, Naas Rd (N 7) – ℰ *(01) 464 0140*   𝖵𝖨𝖲𝖠 ◐◐ 🅰️🅴 ①
– *www.bewleyshotels.com* – *newlandscross@bewleyshotels.com* – *Fax (01) 464 0900*
299 rm – 🛉€ 89 🛉🛉€ 89, ⌷ € 8   **Rest** – (carvery lunch) Carte € 28/38
♦ Well run, busy, commercial hotel popular with business people. Spacious rooms with modern facilities can also accommodate families. Represents good value for money. Large, busy café-restaurant with traditional dark wood fittings and colourful décor.

at Lucan West : 12 km by N 4 - AT – ⊠ Dublin

Clarion H. Dublin Liffey Valley   🔲 🐾 🛁 🖃 & rm, 🅰️ rest, ♨

Liffey Valley, off N 4 at M 50 junction   ☝ ♨ 🅿️ 🚗 𝖵𝖨𝖲𝖠 ◐◐ 🅰️🅴 ①
– ℰ *(01) 625 80 00* – *www.clarionhotelliffeyvalley.com*
– *info@clarionhotelliffeyvalley.com* – *Fax (01) 625 80 01* – *Closed 23-27 December*
284 rm – 🛉€ 79/265 🛉🛉€ 265/475, ⌷ € 16 – 68 suites
Rest *Sinergie* – (dinner only and Sunday lunch) Menu € 30/45 – Carte € 30/41
Rest *Kudos* – Carte € 19/25
♦ U-shaped hotel opened in 2005; bright, open public areas. Well equipped conference facilities; smart leisure club. Sizable, up-to-date rooms with high quality furnishings. Irish dishes with a twist at Sinergie. Asian themed Kudos with on-view wok kitchen.

at Castleknock Northwest : 13 km by N 3 (Caven Rd) - AS - and Auburn Ave – **712** M 7 – ⊠ Dublin

Castleknock H. & Country Club   🚗 🕭 🌐 🐾 🛁 📺 🖃 & rm,

Porterstown Rd, Southwest : 1½ km by   🅰️ rest, ♨ ☏ ♨ 🅿️ 𝖵𝖨𝖲𝖠 ◐◐ 🅰️🅴 ①
Castleknock Rd and Porterstown Rd – ℰ *(01) 640 63 00*
– *www.castleknockhotel.com* – *info@chcc.ie* – *Fax (01) 640 63 03*
– *Closed 23-26 December*
140 rm ⌷ – 🛉€ 109/300 🛉🛉€ 119/340 – 4 suites
Rest *The Park* – (carvery lunch) Carte € 37/45
♦ Impressive corporate hotel incorporating golf course and 160 acres of grounds. Stylish, contemporary design; extensive business and leisure facilities; well equipped rooms. Formal Park restaurant with golf course views.

> Look out for red symbols, indicating particularly pleasant establishments.

DUBLIN AIRPORT – Dublin – **712** N 7 – **see Dublin**

DUNBOYNE – Meath – **712** M 7   37 **D3**
🔁 Dublin 17 km – Drogheda 45 km – Newbridge 54 km

Dunboyne Castle   🚗 🕭 🌐 ♨ 🛁 🖃 & rm, 🅰️ ♨ ☝ ♨ 🅿️ 𝖵𝖨𝖲𝖠 ◐◐ 🅰️🅴 ①
– ℰ *(01) 801 35 00* – *www.dunboynecastlehotel.com*
– *info@dunboynecastlehotel.com* – *Fax (01) 436 68 01*
141 rm ⌷ – 🛉€ 280 🛉🛉€ 340 – 4 suites
Rest – (bar lunch Monday-Saturday) Menu € 29/40 – Carte € 28/52
♦ Extended Georgian house in 26 acres. Ornate ceilings typify style in original house. Some bedrooms have balconies; most overlook grounds. Popular choice for conferences. Discreet, stylish spa. Large, formal restaurant serves classic Irish dishes.

DUNCANNON (Dún Canann) – Wexford – **712** L 11 – **pop. 291** 🔲 *Ireland*   39 **D2**
🔁 Dublin 167 km – New Ross 26 km – Waterford 48 km
🔳 Fort★ **AC**
🔳 Dunbrody Abbey★ **AC**, N : 9 km by R 733 – Kilmokea Gardens★ **AC**, N : 11 km by R 733 – Tintern Abbey★ **AC**, E : 8 km by R 737 and R 733. Kennedy Arboretum★ **AC**, N : 21 km by R 733

✗✗ Aldridge Lodge with rm   🚗 **P** VISA 🐵

South : 1 km by Hook Head Rd – ℰ (051) 389 116 – www.aldridgelodge.com – info@aldridgelodge.com – Fax (051) 389 116 – Closed 2 weeks January, 1 week May, 1 week September, Monday and Tuesday

3 rm ⌂ – †€50 ††€100

Rest – (dinner only and Sunday lunch) (booking essential) Menu €40 **s**

♦ Close to the beach, a smart, cheery restaurant with gardens serving good value, quality local menus: lobster a speciality as owner's dad's a lobster fisherman! Cosy rooms.

✗ Sqigl   VISA 🐵

Quay Rd – ℰ (051) 389 700 – www.sqiglrestaurant.com – info@sqiglrestaurant.com – Closed 25 December, Good Friday, 3-4 weeks in January, Sunday, Monday and Tuesday in winter

Rest – (dinner only) (booking essential) Menu €28 (weekdays) – Carte €32/49

♦ Stone-built restaurant; a converted barn standing behind a popular bar in this coastal village. Faux leopard skin banquettes. Modern European cuisine with amiable service.

DUNDALK – Louth – 712 M 5/6 – pop. 35 085 ▌ *Ireland*   37 **D2**

▶ Dublin 82 km – Drogheda 35 km

🏠 Killinbeg Killin Park, ℰ (042) 933 93 03

◉ Dún a' Rí Forest Park★, W : 34 km by R 178 and R 179 – Proleek Dolmen★, N : 8 km by N 1 R 173

🏠 Ballymascanlon ⌖   🚗 🌀 🖾 🀄 ⅃ఠ ✗ 🖼 🛎 ᵬ rm, ✗ 🐦 🕍 **P**

Northeast : 5 ¾ km by R 132, N 52 on R 173 – ℰ (042)   VISA 🐵 AE ①
935 82 00 – www.ballymascanlon.com – info@ballymascanlon.com – Fax (042) 937 15 98

90 rm ⌂ – †€115/120 ††€185 – 3 suites   **Rest** – Menu €34/49

♦ Victorian house with modern extensions, surrounded by gardens and golf course. Good size leisure club. Bedrooms and various lounges are in a modern style. Bright restaurant with stylish terrace bar.

🏠 Rosemount without rest   🚗 🐦 **P**

Dublin Rd, South : 2½ km on R 132 – ℰ (042) 933 58 78 – www.rosemountireland.com – maisieb7@eircom.net – Fax (042) 933 58 78

9 rm – †€40/50 ††€70/75

♦ A modern house a short drive from the town with good access to the M1. Well-appointed guests' lounge and attractive breakfast room. Comfortably furnished bedrooms.

✗✗ Rosso   AC ⟷ VISA 🐵

5 Roden Pl – ℰ (042) 935 6502 – www.rossorestaurant.com – enquiries@rossorestaurant.com – Fax (042) 935 6503 – Closed 25-26 December and Monday

Rest – Carte €31/45

♦ Traditional on the outside, contemporary on the inside, with stylish furnishings and banquette seating. Front windows overlook cathedral. Classic cooking with a modern twist.

DUNDRUM – Dublin – 712 N 8 – see Dublin

DUNFANAGHY (Dún Fionnachaidh) – Donegal – 712 I 2 – pop. 316   37 **C1**
– ✉ Letterkenny ▌ *Ireland*

▶ Dublin 277 km – Donegal 87 km – Londonderry 69 km

🏠 Dunfanaghy Letterkenny, ℰ (074) 913 6335

◉ Horn Head Scenic Route★, N : 4 km. Doe Castle★, SE : 11¼ km by N 56 – The Rosses★, SW : 40¼ km by N 56 and R 259

🏠 Arnolds ⟨ 🚗 ⚡ 🐕 P VISA ⓪ AE ①

Main St – ℰ (074) 913 62 08 – www.arnoldshotel.ie
– enquiries@arnoldshotel.com – Fax (074) 913 63 52 – 10 April-8 November
30 rm ☲ – ♦€ 75/115 ♦♦€ 150/170
Rest *Sea Scapes* – (light lunch) Carte € 29/42

♦ Pleasant traditional coaching inn with a variety of extensions. Spacious lounge area and a charming bar with open fires. Family run with traditional bedrooms. Informal Sea Scapes serves wide-ranging menus.

✗✗ The Mill with rm ⟨ 🚗 ⚡ P VISA ⓪

Southwest : ¾ km on N 56 – ℰ (074) 913 69 85 – www.themillrestaurant.com
– themillrestaurant@oceanfree.net – Fax (074) 913 69 85 – Closed January,
February and midweek March, November and December
6 rm ☲ – ♦€ 75 ♦♦€ 105   **Rest** – (Closed Monday) (dinner only) Menu € 45

♦ Flax mill on New Lake with Mount Muckish view. Locally renowned and warmly run; enhanced by personally decorated ambience. Well-judged modern Irish menu. Pleasant rooms.

DUNGARVAN – Waterford – **712** J 11 – pop. 8 362 📗 *Ireland*   39 **C3**

　🚹 Dublin 190 km – Cork 71 km – Waterford 48 km
　🅇 The Courthouse ℰ (058) 41741
　🅇 Knocknagrannagh, ℰ (058) 41 605
　🅇 Gold Coast Ballinacourty, ℰ (058) 42 249
　◉ East Bank (Augustinian priory, ≤★)
　🅖 Ringville (≤★), S : 13 km by N 25 and R 674 – Helvick Head★ (≤★),
　SE : 13 km by N 25 and R 674

🏠 An Bohreen 🐦 ⟨ 🚗 ⚡ P VISA ⓪

Killineen West, East : 8 km by N 25 – ℰ (051) 291 010 – www.anbohreen.com
– mulligans@anbohreen.com – Fax (051) 291 010 – 15 March - October
4 rm ☲ – ♦€ 60/65 ♦♦€ 90   **Rest** – (by arrangement) Menu € 40

♦ Very personally run bungalow with fine views over countryside and bay. Cosy sofa area within large open plan layout. Individually designed rooms are tastefully furnished. Dinner menu employs best local ingredients and is cooked with some passion.

🏠 Powersfield House 🚗 ⚡ P VISA ⓪ AE

Ballinamuck West, Northwest : 2½ km on R 672 – ℰ (058) 45 594
– www.powersfield.com – eunice@powersfield.com – Fax (058) 45 550
4 rm ☲ – ♦€ 60/75 ♦♦€ 100/120   **Rest** – (by arrangement) Menu € 30

♦ Set on main road just out of town. Georgian style exterior welcomes guests into a cosy lounge. All bedrooms have individual style with warm feel and some antique furniture.

🏠 Gortnadiha Lodge without rest 🐦 ⟨ 🚗 🐕 P VISA

South : 6½ km by N 25 off R 674 – ℰ (058) 46 142 – www.gortnadihalodge.com
– gortnadihalodge@eircom.net – February-November
3 rm ☲ – ♦€ 55 ♦♦€ 90

♦ Friendly guesthouse set in its own glen with fine bay views, a first floor terrace for afternoon tea, homemade jams and breads for breakfast, and antique furnished bedrooms.

✗✗ Tannery with rm   🅰🅲 rest, 📞 VISA ⓪ AE ①

10 Quay St, via Parnell St – ℰ (058) 45 420 – www.tannery.ie
– tannery@cablesurf.com – Fax (058) 45 814 – Closed 25 December, 10 days
January, 10 days September, Good Friday and Monday
7 rm – ♦€ 70 ♦♦€ 120/160
Rest – (dinner only and lunch Friday and Sunday) Menu € 28 (lunch)
– Carte approx. € 50

♦ Characterful 19C former tannery. Informal ambience and contemporary styling with high ceilings and wood floors. Imaginative modern menus. Stylish rooms in adjacent townhouse.

REPUBLIC OF IRELAND

   ▶ Dublin 156 km – Lifford 42 km – Sligo 53 km – Ballybofey 28 km

XX   **Castle Murray House** with rm ⌂   ⟨ **P** *VISA* **⊙⊙**
– ℰ (074) 973 70 22 – www.castlemurray.com – info@castlemurray.com
– Fax (074) 973 73 30 – Closed mid January–mid February
10 rm ⌂ – †€ 80/95 ††€ 130/150
Rest – Seafood – (dinner only and Sunday lunch, light lunch June–September)
Menu € 53/69
♦ In delightful, picturesque position with view of sea and sunsets from the con-
servatory. Pleasant dining room. Good local seafood. Comfortable, individually
themed bedrooms.

   ▶ Dublin 14 km
   ⛴ to Holyhead (Stena Line) 4-5 daily (1 h 40 mn)
   ℹ Ferry Terminal, Dun Laoghaire Harbour ℰ (01) 602 4000
   ⛳ Dun Laoghaire Eglinton Park, ℰ (01) 280 3916
   ◎ ⟨ ★★ of Killiney Bay from coast road south of Sorrento Point

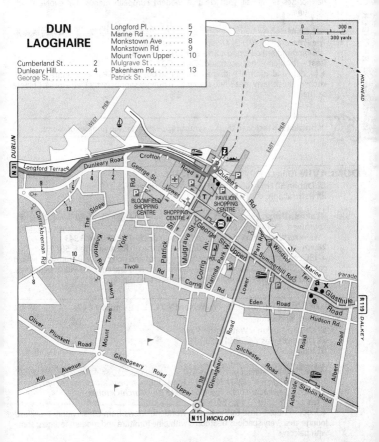

※※ Rasam
`VISA` `MC`

1st Floor (above Eagle House pub), 18-19 Glasthule Rd – ℰ (01) 230 0600
– www.rasam.ie – info@rasam.ie – Fax (01) 230 1000
– Closed 25-26 December and Good Friday   **e**
Rest – Indian – (dinner only) Menu € 50 – Carte € 41/53
♦ Located above Eagle House pub, this airy, modern, stylish restaurant shimmers with silky green wallpaper. Interesting, authentic dishes covering all regions of India.

※ Cavistons
`VISA` `MC` `AE` `①`

58-59 Glasthule Rd – ℰ (01) 280 9120 – www.cavistons.com
– info@cavistons.com – Fax (01) 284 4054
– Closed 23-29 December, Sunday and Monday   **a**
Rest – (lunch only) (booking essential) Carte € 30/48
♦ Simple, informal restaurant attached to the well-established seafood shop which specialises in finest piscine produce. Mermaid friezes and quality crustacean cuisine.

※ Tribes
`AC` `VISA` `MC` `AE` `①`

57a Glasthule Rd – ℰ (01) 236 5971 – tribesrestaurant@yahoo.com
– Closed 25-26 December and Good Friday   **x**
Rest – (dinner only and Sunday lunch) Carte € 34/46
♦ Personally run neighbourhood restaurant next to Cavistons. Smart, original interior harmonises seamlessly with creative modern European menus that evolve slowly over time.

※ Café Mao
`AC` `VISA` `MC` `①`

The Pavilion – ℰ (01) 214 8090 – www.cafemao.com
– dunlaoghaire@cafemao.com – Fax (01) 214 7064   **r**
Rest – (bookings not accepted) Carte € 24/32
♦ Modern and informal with the background bustle of the Pavillion Centre and open kitchen. Quick, tasty meals find favour with hungry shoppers: try Vietnamese, Chinese or Thai.

If breakfast is included the ⬜ symbol appears after the number of rooms.

DUNLAVIN (Dún Luáin) – **Wicklow** – **712** L 8   **39 D2**
    ◗ Dublin 50 km – Kilkenny 71 km – Wexford 98 km
    ⓚ Rathsallagh, ℰ (045) 403 316

🏠 Rathsallagh House ⬚
≤ 🚗 ♨ ⌁ ※ ⓚ 👌 rm, 📞 🏋 P
Southwest : 3¼ km on Grangecon Rd – ℰ (045) 403 112   `VISA` `MC` `AE` `①`
– www.rathsallagh.com – info@rathsallagh.com – Fax (045) 403 343
28 rm ⬜ – †€ 195/275 ††€ 200/330 – 1 suite   **Rest** – Carte € 55/75
♦ 18C converted stables set in extensive grounds and golf course. Picturesque walled garden. Characterful, country house-style public areas and cosy, individual bedrooms. Kitchen garden provides ingredients for welcoming dining room.

DUNMORE EAST (Dún Mór) – **Waterford** – **712** L 11 – **pop. 1 547**   **39 C2**
– ✉ Waterford ▮ *Ireland*
    ◗ Dublin 174 km – Waterford 19 km
    ⓚ Dunmore East, ℰ (051) 383 151
    ◉ Village★

🏠 The Beach *without rest*
≤ 👌 ⚡ 📶 P `VISA` `MC` `AE`
1 Lower Village – ℰ (051) 383 316 – www.dunmorebeachguesthouse.com
– beachouse@eircom.net – Fax (051) 383 319 – March-October
7 rm ⬜ – †€ 50/70 ††€ 80/100
♦ Modern house close to the beach. Wonderful views from conservatory breakfast/lounge area. Very spacious bedrooms with pine furniture and modern facilities; some with balcony.

REPUBLIC OF IRELAND

DUNSANY (Dún Samhnaí) – Meath – 712 M 7

37 **D3**

▶ Dublin 42 km – Dunboyne 23 km – Navan 17 km

🏠 **Dunsany Lodge** 🛏 ♿ rm, ℿ 🅿 VISA ✱✱ ①

*Butterjohn Cross, Dublin Rd, Southwest : 3½ km, at junction with R 154
– 𝒞 (046) 902 63 39 – www.dunsanylodge.ie – info@dunsanylodge.ie – Fax (046)
902 63 42 – Closed 25 December*
10 rm ⊥ – †€ 55/65 ††€ 100/110   **Rest** – Menu € 19/30 **s** – Carte € 28/40 **s**
◆ Modern lounge and bar with red and cream leather seats. Uniformly-sized bedrooms with up-to-date facilities; the rear rooms are the quietest. Lawned garden.
Smart formal restaurant with decked terrace serves tried-and-tested dishes.

DURROW (Darú) – Laois – 712 J 9

39 **C2**

▶ Dublin 108 km – Cork 141 km – Kilkenny 27 km

🏛 **Castle Durrow** ⟡ ⟨ 🛏 ♨ ⟍ 🏕 ⚲ ♨ 🅿 VISA ✱✱ AE

*– 𝒞 (057) 87 36 555 – www.castledurrow.com – info@castledurrow.com
– Fax (057) 87 36 552 – Closed 24 December-16 January*
41 rm (dinner included) ⊥ – †€ 165 ††€ 250/310
Rest – (bar lunch) Menu € 55
◆ Imposing greystone early 18C country mansion set in carefully manicured gardens
and 30 acres of parkland. Eye-catching stained glass. Modern, understated bedrooms.
High, ornate ceilings and views across gardens from the dining room.

DURRUS (Dúras) – Cork – 712 D 13

38 **A3**

▶ Dublin 338 km – Cork 90 km – Killarney 85 km

🏠 **Blairs Cove House** ⟡ ⟨ 🛏 ♨ 🅿 VISA ✱✱ AE ①

*Southwest : 1½ km on R 591 – 𝒞 (027) 61 127 – www.blairscove.ie
– blairscove@eircom.net – Fax (027) 61 487 – Restricted opening in winter*
5 rm ⊥ – ††€ 150/270
Rest *Blairs Cove* – see restaurant listing
◆ Fine Georgian house with outbuildings and sea views, set around a courtyard.
Spacious, modern suites come with own kitchens and dining areas.

✗✗ **Blairs Cove** at Blairs Cove House ⟨ 🛏 ♨ 🅿 VISA ✱✱ ①

*Southwest : 1½ km on R 591 – 𝒞 (027) 62 913 – www.blairscove.ie
– blairscove@eircom.net – Fax (027) 61 487*
Rest – (closed Sunday dinner) (dinner only and Sunday lunch) (booking
essential) Menu € 32/55 **s**
◆ Cosy bar with roaring fire leads to converted 17C barn. Imposing chandelier and
candelabras; grand piano doubles as sweet trolley. Meats are a speciality, cooked in
open grill.

✗ **Good Things Cafe** 🛏 ⟍ 🅿 VISA ✱✱

*Ahakista Rd, West : ¾ km on Ahakista rd – 𝒞 (027) 61 426
– www.goodthingscafe.net – info@thegoodthingscafe.com – Fax (027) 62 896
– Mid June - mid September and Easter*
Rest – (closed Tuesday and booking essential Wednesday) Carte € 27/45 **s**
◆ Simple and unpretentious. Walls filled with shelves full of books and foods of all kinds
for sale. Open-plan kitchen serves accomplished dishes full of quality local produce.

ENNIS (Inis) – Clare – 712 F 9 – pop. 24 253 📘 *Ireland*

38 **B2**

▶ Dublin 228 km – Galway 67 km – Limerick 35 km – Roscommon 148 km
– Tullamore 149 km
🛈 Arthurs Row 𝒞 (065) 6828366, touristofficeennis@shannondevelopment.ie
🏌 Drumbiggle Rd, 𝒞 (065) 682 40 74
◉ Ennis Friary★ AC
◉ Dysert O'Dea★, N : 9 ¾ km by N 85 and R 476, turning left after 6 ½ km and
right after 1 ½ km - Quin Franciscan Friary★, SE : 10 ½ km by R 469 –
Knappogue Castle★ AC, SE : 12 ¾ km by R 469 – Corrofin (Clare Heritage
Centre★ AC), N : 13 ¾ km by N 85 and R 476 – Craggaunowen Centre★
AC, SE : 17 ¾ km by R 469 - Kilmacduagh Churches and Round Tower★,
NE : 17 ¾ km by N 18 - Kilrush★ (Scattery Island★ by boat) SW : 43 ½ km
by N 68 - Bridge of Ross, Kilkee★, SW : 57 km by N 68 and N 67

🏢 Temple Gate
🛗 ⚙ ⅋ ♨ ♨ P VISA ◉◉ AE ①

The Square – ℰ *(065) 682 33 00 – www.templegatehotel.com*
– info@templegatehotel.com – Fax (065) 682 33 22 – Closed 25-26 December
68 rm ⌑ – †€ 105/145 ††€ 150/220 – 2 suites
Rest *Legends* – (carvery lunch Monday-Saturday) Menu € 38 – Carte € 34/47
♦ A professional yet friendly mood prevails at this privately run hotel in modern, subtly neo-Gothic style. Panelled library and well-fitted rooms in traditional patterns. Legends serves carefully presented modern dishes in informal surroundings.

🏢 Old Ground
🚗 🛗 ⅋ rm, ⚙ ♨ ♨ P VISA ◉◉ AE ①

O'Connell St – ℰ *(065) 682 81 27 – www.flynnhotels.com*
– reservations@oldgroundhotel.ie – Fax (065) 682 81 12 – Closed 25 December
105 rm ⌑ – †€ 95/160 ††€ 125/190
Rest *O'Brien's* – Menu € 21/35 **s** – Carte € 31/45 **s**
Rest *Town Hall* – Carte € 30/44 **s**
♦ Handsome ivy-clad hotel. Firelit lounge and inviting panelled bar with paintings, curios and book-lined snugs. Traditional rooms in cream, burgundy and dark wood. Gilt-framed mirrors and white linen lend a formal aspect to O'Brien's. Informal Town Hall.

> Red = Pleasant. Look for the red 🏺 and 🏠 symbols.

ENNISCORTHY (Inis Córthaidh) – Wexford – 🗺 712 M 10 – pop. 9 538   39 D2
🔲 *Ireland*

- 🚉 Dublin 122 km – Kilkenny 74 km – Waterford 54 km – Wexford 24 km
- 🎫 Castle Museum ℰ (0539) 234699
- 🏌 Knockmarshal, ℰ (053) 923 31 91
- ⊙ Enniscorthy Castle★ (County Museum★)
- 🖼 Ferns★, NE : 13 km by N 11 – Mount Leinster★, N : 27 ¼ km by N 11

🏨 Monart
🚗 🐾 🔲 ◉ 🐕 🏋 🛗 🔟 AC rest, ⚙ P VISA ◉◉ AE

The Still, Northwest : 3 km by N 11 (Dublin rd) – ℰ *(053) 923 8999*
– www.monart.ie – info@monart.ie – Closed 24-27 December
68 rm ⌑ – †€ 285/300 ††€ 400/700 – 2 suites
Rest *The Restaurant* – (dinner only and Sunday lunch) Carte € 59/73 **s**
Rest *Garden Lounge* – Carte € 26/46 **s**
♦ Spa resort in 100 acres; enter via the elegant Georgian house and experience various therapies in state-of-the-art treatment rooms. Bedrooms all have views; many have balconies. Formal dining in The Restaurant. Enjoy lighter dishes in the Garden Lounge or out on the terrace.

🏢 Riverside Park
🔲 🐕 🏋 🛗 ⅋ rm, AC rest, ⚙ ℡ ♨ P VISA ◉◉ AE ①

The Promenade – ℰ *(053) 923 7800 – www.riversideparkhotel.com*
– info@riversideparkhotel.com – Fax (053) 923 7900 – Closed 24-26 December
59 rm ⌑ – †€ 115/135 ††€ 190/210 – 1 suite
Rest *The Moorings* – (closed Monday-Wednesday in winter) (carvery lunch Monday-Saturday) Carte € 40/66
♦ Purpose-built hotel just outside the town: a high, airy lobby leads into smart bedrooms in matching patterns, modern meeting rooms and a rustic, "no-frills" wood-fitted bar. Spacious, modern Moorings restaurant with light, soft tones.

🏠 Ballinkeele House ⌑
≼ 🚗 🐾 ⚙ ♨ P VISA ◉◉

Ballymurn, Southeast : 10½ km by unmarked road on Curracloe rd – ℰ *(053) 91 38 105 – www.ballinkeele.com – john@ballinkeele.com – Fax (053) 91 38 468 – February-November*
5 rm ⌑ – †€ 95/105 ††€ 170
Rest – (by arrangement, communal dining) Menu € 45
♦ High ceilinged, firelit lounge plus sizeable rooms with period-style furniture and countryside views add to the charm of a quiet 1840 manor, well run by experienced owners. Dining room enriched by candlelight and period oils.

ENNISKERRY (Áth an Sceire) – **Wicklow** – **712** N 8 – pop. 1 881 ▮ *Ireland*   39 **D1**

- ▶ Dublin 25 km – Wicklow 32 km
- 🏠 Powerscourt Powerscourt Estate, 𝒞 (01) 204 6033
- ◉ Powerscourt ★★ **AC** (Waterfall ★★, **AC**)

🏨🏨🏨 **Ritz Carlton**   ⟨ 🛏 🅿 ⚡ 🏊 🎣 📺 ⊕ 🏥 ⯑ 🛗 🅫 ⛱ ⛷ 📶 🅿
West : 2 km. by Powerscourt rd – 𝒞 (01) 274 8888   ⬛ 🆅🅸🆂🅰 ⊕ 🅰🅴 ⓞ
– www.ritzcarlton.com – powerscourtenquiries@ritzcarlton.com
– Fax (01) 274 9999
200 rm ⌑ – ♦♦€ 250/390 – 124 suites – ♦♦€ 280/410
Rest *Gordon Ramsay at Powerscourt* – Carte € 79/90 **s**
Rest *The Sugar Loaf* – (dinner only Thursday-Saturday) Carte € 49/60 **s**
♦ Opened in 2008 within the Powerscourt House Estate, a vast and impressive structure with lots of leisure activities. Many rooms are suites; bathrooms are luxurious. Formal restaurant with mountain views and mix of Gordon Ramsay dishes and re-interpreted Irish classics. Relaxed Sugar Loaf.

ENNISTIMON (Inis Díomáin) – **Clare** – **712** E 9 – pop. 813 ▮ *Ireland*   38 **B1**

- ▶ Dublin 254 km – Galway 83 km – Limerick 63 km
- 🄶 The Burren ★★ : Cliffs of Moher ★★★, Scenic Route ★★, Aillwee Cave ★ **AC** (waterfall ★★), Corcomroe Abbey ★, Kilfenora High Crosses ★, Burren Centre ★ **AC**

⛰ **Grovemount House** without rest   🛏 ⚡ 📶 🅿 🆅🅸🆂🅰 ⊕
Lahinch Rd, West : ¾ km on N 67 – 𝒞 (065) 707 1431 – www.grovemount-
ennistymon.com – grovmnt@eircom.net – Fax (065) 707 1823 – May-October
6 rm ⌑ – ♦€ 45/55 ♦♦€ 70/84
♦ Spotless bedrooms in warm oak and a homely lounge in this modern guesthouse, run by the friendly owner. A short drive to the sandy beach at Lahinch and the Cliffs of Moher.

FETHARD (Fiodh Ard) – **712** I 10 ▮ *Ireland*   39 **C2**

- ▶ Dublin 161 km – Cashel 16 km – Clonmel 13 km
- 🄶 Cashel ★★★ : Rock of Cashel ★★★ **AC** (Cormac's Chapel ★★, Round Tower ★), Museum ★ **AC**, Cashel Palace Gardens ★, GPA Bolton Library ★ **AC**, NW : 15 km by R 692 – Clonmel ★ : County Museum ★ **AC**, St Mary's Church ★, S : 13 km by R 689

⛰ **Mobarnane House** ⊚   ⟨ 🛏 ⚡ ⚙ 📶 🅿 🆅🅸🆂🅰 ⊕
North : 8 km by Cashel rd on Ballinure rd – 𝒞 (052) 31 962
– www.mobarnanehouse.com – info@mobarnanehouse.com – Fax (052) 31 962
– March-October
4 rm ⌑ – ♦€ 105 ♦♦€ 150/190
Rest – (by arrangement, communal dining) Menu € 45 **s**
♦ Very personally run classic Georgian house with mature gardens in quiet rural setting, tastefully restored to reflect its age. Ask for a bedroom with its own sitting room. Beautiful dining room for menus agreed in advance.

⛰ **An-Teach**   🛏 ⚙ ⚙ 📞 🅿 🆅🅸🆂🅰 ⊕ 🅰🅴 ⓞ
Killusty, Southeast : 8 km by R 706 (Kilsheelan rd) – 𝒞 (052) 32 088
– www.an-teach.com – anteach@anteach.com – Fax (052) 32 462
10 rm ⌑ – ♦€ 50 ♦♦€ 90   **Rest** – (by arrangement) Menu € 35 **s**
♦ Extended family home against the backdrop of the Sliabh na Mban mountains. Airy en suite rooms in solid pine, two facing the hills. Carefully prepared wholesome meals.

FOTA ISLAND – **Cork** – **712** H 12   38 **B3**

🏨🏨🏨 **Sheraton Fota Island**   🛏 ⚡ 📺 ⊕ 🏥 🛗 📶 🅫 ⛱ & rm, 🅰🆄 ⯑ ⛷
– 𝒞 (021) 467 3000 – www.sheraton.com   🅿 🆅🅸🆂🅰 ⊕ 🅰🅴 ⓞ
– reservations.fota@sheraton.com – Fax (021) 488 3713
123 rm – ♦€ 109/330 ♦♦€ 330/700, ⌑ €22 – 8 suites
Rest *The Cove* – (Closed Sunday-Wednesday) (dinner only) Carte € 40/80
Rest *Fota* – (bar lunch) Carte € 25/70
♦ All-encompassing resort location within Ireland's only wildlife park boasting Wellness Centre with 'walking river' and 18 hole golf course. Stylish rooms from the top drawer. The Cove is a very formal place to dine. Fota's appealing menus suit all tastes.

FURBOGH/FURBO (Na Forbacha) – **Galway** – **712** E 8   36 **A3**
> ▶ Dublin 228 km – Galway 11 km

🏠 **Connemara Coast** ≤ 🚗 🔲 🕸 ※ 🏃 ℉ & rm, 🏕 ℉ ⁇ 🛁 **P** VISA ⓒⓞ AE
– 𝒞 (091) 592 108 – www.sinnotthotels.com – info@connemaracoast.ie
– Fax (091) 592 065
141 rm ⌷ – ♦€ 130/200 ♦♦€ 178/350 – 1 suite
Rest *The Gallery* – (bar lunch) Menu € 40
♦ Sprawling hotel with super views of Galway Bay, The Burren and Aran from the well-kept bedrooms. Marbled reception area. Characterful Players bar. Good leisure facilities. Two informal dining areas overlooking the bay.

GALWAY – **Galway** – **712** E 8 – pop. 72 414 ▓ *Ireland*   36 **B3**
> ▶ Dublin 217 km – Limerick 103 km – Sligo 145 km
> ✈ Carnmore Airport : 𝒞 (091) 755569, NE : 6½ km
> 🛈 Galway City Aras Failte, Forster St 𝒞 (091) 537700,
> irelandwestinfo@failteireland.ieSalthill Promenade 𝒞 (091) 520500
> (May-August)
> 🖸 Galway Salthill Blackrock, 𝒞 (091) 522 033
> ◎ City★★ – St Nicholas' Church★BY - Roman Catholic Cathedral★AY – Eyre
> Square : Bank of Ireland Building (sword and mace★) BY
> ◪ NW : Lough Corrib★★. W : by boat, Aran Islands (Inishmore - Dun
> Aenghus★★★) BZ - Thoor Ballylee★, SE : 33 ¾ km by N 6 and N 18 D –
> Dunguaire Castle, Kinvarra★ **AC**, S : 25 ¾ km by N 6, N 18 and N 67 D –
> Aughnanure Castle★, NW : 25 ¾ km by N 59 - Oughterard★ (≤★★), NW :
> 29 km by N 59 - Knockmoy Abbey★, NE : 30½ km by N 17 and N 63 D –
> Coole Park (Autograph Tree★), SE : 33 ¾ km by N 6 and N 18 D - St Mary's
> Cathedral, Tuam★, NE : 33 ¾ km by N 17 D – Loughrea (St Brendan's
> Cathedral★), SE : 35½ km by N 6 D - Turoe Stone★, SE : 35½ km by N 6
> and north by R 350

Plan opposite

🏠 **Glenlo Abbey** ♨ ≤ 🚗 🔄 🔌 🖸 🍴 & rm, ℉ ⁇ 🛁 **P** VISA ⓒⓞ AE ⓪
*Bushypark, Northwest : 5 ¼ km on N 59 – 𝒞 (091) 526 666 – www.glenlo.com
– info@glenloabbey.ie – Fax (091) 527 800 – Closed 24-27 December*
42 rm – ♦€ 190/315 ♦♦€ 250/400, ⌷€ 20 – 4 suites
Rest *River Room* – (dinner only) Carte € 44/56
Rest *Pullman* – (dinner only) Carte € 38/57
♦ Imposing 18C greystone country house with adjacent church and bay views. Formal service. Very comfortable lounge, leading into chapel. Spacious, smart rooms. River Room boasts golfcourse views. Pullman, a converted railway carriage offers modern dishes with an Asian base.

🏠 **Radisson SAS** ≤ 🕌 🔲 🕮 🕸 🍴 🖸 & rm, 🗚 ℉ ⁇ 🛁 ☁ VISA ⓒⓞ AE ⓪
*Lough Atalia Rd – 𝒞 (091) 538 300 – www.radissonhotelgalway.com
– reservations.galway@radissonsas.com – Fax (091) 538 380*   D**a**
259 rm ⌷ – ♦€ 175/195 ♦♦€ 550/600 – 2 suites
Rest *Marinas* – (bar lunch Monday-Saturday) Carte € 38/50 **s**
♦ Striking atrium leads to ultra-modern meeting facilities and very comfortable accommodation: sumptuous 5th floor rooms have private glass balconies. Superb penthouse suite. Split-level dining in dark walnut wood.

🏠 **The G** ≤ 🕮 🔄 🖢 & rm, 🗚 ⁇ 🛁 ☁ VISA ⓒⓞ AE
*Wellpark – 𝒞 (091) 865 200 – www.theghotel.ie
– reservetheg@monogramhotels.ie – Fax (091) 865 203
– Closed 23-27 December*   D**g**
100 rm ⌷ – ♦€ 450 ♦♦€ 450/550 – 1 suite
Rest *Riva at the G* – Italian influences – (dinner only and Sunday lunch)
Menu € 45/60 – Carte € 59/68
♦ Uber-hip hotel cutting edge design from renowned milliner Philip Treacy. Vividly assured sitting room styles; décor imbued with fashion shoot portraits. Cool, slinky bedrooms. Sexy purple restaurant. Understated cooking with Italian influences.

REPUBLIC OF IRELAND

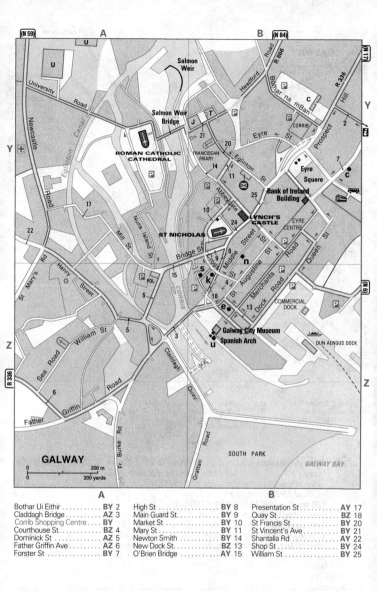

GALWAY

0 ____ 200 m
0 ____ 200 yards

A

Bothar Ui Eithir		**BY** 2
Claddagh Bridge		**AZ** 3
Corrib Shopping Centre		**BY**
Courthouse St		**BZ** 4
Dominick St		**AZ** 5
Father Griffin Ave		**AZ** 6
Forster St		**BY** 7

High St		**BY** 8
Main Guard St		**BY** 9
Market St		**BY** 10
Mary St		**BY** 11
Newton Smith		**BY** 14
New Dock St		**BZ** 13
O'Brien Bridge		**AY** 15

Presentation St		**AY** 17
Quay St		**BZ** 18
St Francis St		**BY** 20
St Vincent's Ave		**BY** 21
Shantalla Rd		**AY** 22
Shop St		**BY** 24
William St		**BY** 25

Clayton 🔲 ⅍ Ŀở 🀫 ᕃ rm, 🄰🄲 📞 🕭 🅿 🆅🅸🆂🅰 🆎 🄰🄴 ①

Ballybrit, East : 4 km on N 6 – 𝒞 (091) 721 900 – www.clayton.ie
– info@clayton.ie – Fax (091) 721 901
– Closed 21-28 December
196 rm – 🛆€ 140/180 🛆🛆€ 190/380, ☁ €14
Rest – (closed Sunday) (bar lunch) Menu € 45 – Carte € 29/54

♦ Striking angular building on edge of city, with stylish, modern interior and bar with buffet carvery. Smart white bedrooms have a minimalistic feel, with dark wood furniture. Large first floor restaurant offers traditional menu.

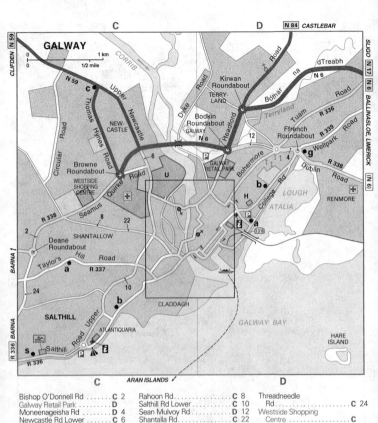

GALWAY

The Ardilaun 🚗 🛏 📺 ⚙ ⌘ 🏋 🍴 ⚙ &. rm, 🆎 rest, ⚙ 🏊 **P** 𝗩𝗜𝗦𝗔 ⓶⓷ 𝗔𝗘 ①

Taylor's Hill – 𝒞 *(091) 521 433 – www.theardilaunhotel.ie*
– info@theardilaunhotel.ie – Fax (091) 521 546
– Closed 23-27 December   C**a**
120 rm ⊇ – 🛉€ 105/380 🛉🛉€ 150/380 – 5 suites
Rest – (bar lunch Saturday) Carte € 25/30
Rest *Camilaun* – Menu € 24/43 – Carte dinner € 36/45
♦ Georgian style country house hotel in five acres of gardens and ancient trees.
Informal bar. Extensive leisure facilities. Spacious rooms in dark woods with quilted
fabrics. Seafood, including oysters, feature strongly in restaurant. Stylish, formal Cami-
laun.

The Westwood 🛏 &. rm, 🆎 ⚙ 📞 🏊 **P** 𝗩𝗜𝗦𝗔 ⓶⓷ 𝗔𝗘 ①

Dangan, Upper Newcastle – 𝒞 *(091) 521 442 – www.westwoodhousehotel.com*
– info@westwoodhousehotel.com – Fax (091) 521 400
– Closed 24-25 December   C**c**
58 rm ⊇ – 🛉€ 179/339 🛉🛉€ 229/339
Rest *The Meridian* – (dinner only and Sunday lunch) Menu € 25
– Carte € 30/47
♦ Striking hotel with pastel orange painted exterior on outskirts of town. Impressive
reception area and huge bar on two levels. Small conservatory. Modern, comfy
rooms. Appealing carvery restaurant.

Park House 🛗 ⅓ rm, 🅰🅒 rest, ⚒ 📶 🅿 VISA 🆎

Forster St, Eyre Sq – ℰ (091) 564924 – www.parkhousehotel.ie
– parkhousehotel@eircom.net – Fax (091) 569219
– Closed 24-26 December   BY**c**
84 rm ⫱ – †€ 109/450 ††€ 140/450   **Rest** – Carte € 32/56
♦ Popular greystone hotel in city centre. Marble reception and comfy seating areas. Boss Doyle's Bar is busy and spacious. Dark wood bedrooms with rich, soft fabrics. Strong international flavours define restaurant menus.

The House 🗼 🛗 ⅓ rm, 🅰🅒 ⚒ 🕻 VISA 🆎

Spanish Parade – ℰ (091) 538900 – www.thehousehotel.ie
– info@thehousehotel.ie – Fax (091) 568262 – Closed 24-27 December   BZ**e**
39 rm ⫱ – †€ 220/425 ††€ 220/425 – 1 suite
Rest – (bar lunch) Carte € 26/43
♦ Luxury boutique hotel, blending contemporary design with a cosy, relaxed style. Bedrooms are divided between cosy, classy and swanky. Modern menus take on a global reach; try to get a seat on the outdoor deck.

Ardawn House without rest ⚒ 📶 🅿 VISA 🆎

College Rd – ℰ (091) 568833 – www.ardawnhouse.com – ardawn@iol.ie
– Fax (091) 563454 – Closed 22-27 December   D**b**
8 rm ⫱ – †€ 50/120 ††€ 90/180
♦ Sample Irish hospitality at this family-run guest house. Individually decorated bedrooms and comfy lounge. Extensive breakfast menu served at linen-clad tables.

XX **Kirwan's Lane** 🗼 🅰🅒 VISA 🆎

Kirwan's Lane – ℰ (091) 568266 – Fax (091) 561645
– Closed 24-30 December and Sunday lunch   BZ**s**
Rest – Carte € 40/48
♦ Modern restaurant in warm, autumnal shades. Adventurous menus. Welcoming atmosphere and a genuine neighbourhood feel.

XX **Vina Mara** 🅰🅒 VISA 🆎

19 Middle St – ℰ (091) 561610 – www.vinamara.com – vinamara@hotmail.com
– Fax (091) 562607 – Closed 24-26 December and Sunday   BY**n**
Rest – Menu € 24/49 – Carte € 28/49
♦ Spacious restaurant in warm welcoming colours - smart yet informal; attentive service. Mediterranean style dishes with Irish and other touches.

X **Ard Bia at Nimmos** VISA 🆎

Spanish Arch – ℰ (091) 561114 – www.ardbia.com – ardbia@gmail.com
– Closed 25-26 December and 1 January   BZ**u**
Rest – (dinner only) (booking essential) Carte € 31/51
♦ Simple restaurant in two-storey building with buzzy, bohemain feel. Generous, full-flavoured, rustic dishes have Mediterranean and Irish influences and are simply presented.

at Salthill Southwest : 3 ¼ km

Galway Bay ⬅ 🛎 🖾 🏊 ⅙ 🛗 ⅓ rm, 🅰🅒 rest, ⚒ 🕻 🔱 🅿 VISA 🆎 ①

The Promenade – ℰ (091) 520520 – www.galwaybayhotel.com
– info@galwaybayhotel.com
– Fax (091) 520530   C**s**
149 rm ⫱ – †€ 140/225 ††€ 205/290 – 4 suites
Rest *Lobster Pot* – (bar lunch Monday-Friday) Menu € 40 – Carte € 34/62 **s**
♦ Imposing, yellow painted hotel on promenade with super views of the Aran Isles. Characterful public bar. Good leisure facilities. Very large rooms with armchairs and sofas. Dining room has bay views and floral displays.

⌂ **West Winds** without rest 🎇 **P** **VISA** **◐**
5 Ocean Wave, Dr Colohan Rd – ℰ (091) 520 223
– www.travelaccommodation.co.uk/westwind.htm – westwinds@eircom.net
– Fax (091) 520 223 – May-August ⊂**b**
8 rm � – †€ 45/80 ††€ 75/100
♦ Detached guesthouse in an ideal spot for holiday makers: right on the seafront. Cosy sitting room; breakfast room has conservatory extension. Simple, spotlessly kept bedrooms.

GARRYKENNEDY 39 C2
D Dublin 176 km – Killaloe 14 km – Youghal 2 km

🍴 **Larkins** 🚲 🎇 **P** **VISA** **◐**
– ℰ (067) 23 232 – www.larkinspub.com – info@larkinspub.com – Fax (067) 23 933 – Closed 25 December, Good Friday and lunch midweek November to April
Rest – Carte € 20/35
♦ Thatched whitewashed inn - bigger inside than it looks from the outside - sparks nostalgia with classic adverts and tins of food. Honest hearty cooking comes in generous portions.

GARRYVOE (Garraí Uí Bhuaigh) – Cork – 712 H 12 – ⊠ Castlemartyr 39 C3
D Dublin 259 km – Cork 37 km – Waterford 100 km

🏨 **Garryvoe** ≤ 📱 & rm, 🎇 🎝 🚿 **P** **VISA** **◐** **AE** **◑**
– ℰ (021) 464 67 18 – www.garryvoehotel.com – res@garryvoehotel.com
– Fax (021) 464 68 24 – Closed 24-25 December
65 rm � – †€ 75/120 ††€ 170/190 – 1 suite
Rest – (bar lunch Monday-Saturday) Carte € 39/41
♦ Traditionally styled hotel adjacent to the beach with good sea views, to be enjoyed in characterful locals bar. A purpose-built, up-to-date wing features smart, modern rooms. Bright, colourful, contemporary restaurant.

GLASLOUGH (Glasloch) – Monaghan – 712 L 5 – see Monaghan

GLASSAN (Glasán) – Westmeath – 712 I 7 – see Athlone

GLIN (An Gleann) – Limerick – 712 E 10 📖 Ireland 38 B2
D Dublin 244 km – Limerick 51 km – Tralee 51 km
🔲 Glin Castle ★ AC

🏨 **Glin Castle** ⟨⟩ ≤ 🚲 🎲 🎇 🎝 **P** **VISA** **◐** **AE** **◑**
– ℰ (068) 34 173 – www.glincastle.com – knight@iol.ie – Fax (068) 34 364
– Closed December, January and February
15 rm � – †€ 495 ††€ 495 **Rest** – (dinner only) (residents only) Menu € 60
♦ Crenellated Georgian country house, overlooking the Shannon estuary, with superb collection of antique furnishings, paintings and porcelain. Beautifully appointed rooms. Home cooked meals full of local produce.

GOREY (Guaire) – Wexford – 712 N 9 – pop. 7 193 📖 Ireland 39 D2
D Dublin 93 km – Waterford 88 km – Wexford 61 km
🅸 Main St ℰ (055) 942 1248, info@northwexford.com
🅱 Courtown Kiltennel, ℰ (055) 25 166
🔲 Ferns ★, SW : 17 ¾ km by N 11

🏨 **Seafield Golf H. and Spa** 🔲 ⊕ 🎐 ⅃♨ 🎰 📱 🎝 AC 🎇 ✆ 🎲 **P**
Ballymoney, East : 8 km by R 742 – ℰ (053) 942 4000 **VISA** **◐** **AE**
– www.seafieldhotel.com – sales@seafieldhotel.com – Fax (053) 942 4050
– Closed 22-27 December
101 rm – †€ 110/140 ††€ 170/230 **Rest** – (bar lunch) Carte € 35/64
♦ New build hotel on what was originally a farm, with extensive gardens, fringed by an immaculate golf course. Elegant, contemporary décor; spacious bedrooms with balconies. Traditional Irish menu served in high-ceilinged, formal dining room.

🏠 Marlfield House ✿   ⟨ 🚗 🐕 🛖 ✂ 🌐 **P.** **VISA** **CO** **AE** **O**
Courtown Rd, Southeast : 1½ km on R 742 – ☏ (053) 942 11 24
– www.marlfieldhouse.com – info@marlfieldhouse.ie – Fax (053) 942 15 72
– Closed January
19 rm ⌖ – ♦€ 120/145 ♦♦€ 210/550 – 1 suite
Rest – (dinner only and Sunday lunch) (booking essential for non-residents)
Menu €67
♦ Luxuriously comfortable Regency mansion, with extensive gardens and woods. Utterly charming public areas with fine antiques and splendid fabrics. Thoughtfully furnished rooms. Very comfortable conservatory restaurant utilising produce from the garden.

GRAIGUENAMANAGH (Gráig na Manach) – **Kilkenny** – **712** L 10   **39 D2**
🟩 *Ireland*

    🅳 Dublin 125 km – Kilkenny 34 km – Waterford 42 km – Wexford 26 km
    ◎ Duiske Abbey★★ **AC**
    🅖 Jerpoint Abbey★★ **AC**, W : 15 km by R 703 and N 9 – Inistioge★, SW : 8 km by minor road – Kilfane Glen and Waterfall★ **AC**, SW : 17 km by R 703 and N 9

✗ Waterside with rm   ⟨ ✂ **VISA** **CO** **AE**
The Quay – ☏ (059) 972 42 46 – www.watersideguesthouse.com
– info@watersideguesthouse.com – Fax (059) 972 47 33 – Closed 25 December
and January
10 rm ⌖ – ♦€ 65/69 ♦♦€ 110/118
Rest – (restricted opening in winter, dinner only and Sunday lunch)
Carte € 32/44
♦ Converted 19C cornstore on banks of river Barrow, at foot of Brandon Hill. Base for hillwalkers. Modern cooking with Mediterranean flourishes. Beamed rooms with river views.

> The 🕸 award is the crème de la crème.
> This is awarded to restaurants
> which are really worth travelling miles for!

GREYSTONES (Na Clocha Liatha) – **Wicklow** – **712** N 8 – **pop. 14 569**   **39 D1**
🟩 *Ireland*

    🅳 Dublin 35 km
    🅸🅱 Greystones, ☏ (01) 287 6624
    🅖 Killruddery House and Gardens★ **AC**, N : 5 km by R 761 – Powerscourt★★ (Waterfall★★) **AC**, NW : 10 km by R 761, minor road, M 11 and minor road via Enniskerry. Wicklow Mountains★★

✗✗✗ Chakra by Jaipur   **AC** **VISA** **CO** **AE**
First Floor, Meridan Point Centre, Church Rd – ☏ (01) 201 7222 – info@chakra.ie
– Fax (01) 201 7220 – Closed 25 December
Rest – Indian – (dinner only) Carte € 38/45
♦ Red and ochre restaurant overlooked by elephant god, Ganesh, on 1st floor of modern shopping centre. Vibrant Indian cooking represents all regions; a blend of old and new.

✗ Hungry Monk   **AC** **VISA** **CO** **AE**
Church Rd – ☏ (01) 287 5759 – www.thehungrymonk.ie
– info@thehungrymonk.ie – Fax (01) 287 7183 – Closed 24-26 December, Good
Friday, Monday, Tuesday and Sunday dinner
Rest – (dinner only and Sunday lunch) Carte € 40/59
♦ Busy, long-established, candlelit restaurant above a wine bar. Pictures of monks in all areas. Robust, traditional cooking including blackboard seafood specials.

REPUBLIC OF IRELAND

GWEEDORE (Gaoth Dobhair) – Donegal – 712 H 2   37 C1
D Dublin 278 km – Donegal 72 km – Letterkenny 43 km – Sligo 135 km

Gweedore Court   ⪦ 🕾 🖃 🕹 rm, 🛠 🕾 🚣 **P** *VISA* 🌑 **AE**
on N 56 – ℰ (074) 953 2900 – www.anchuirt-hotel.ie
– info@gweedorecourthotel.com – Fax (074) 953 2929 – Closed January-March and November
69 rm ☑ – ♦€ 100/120 ♦♦€ 140/160
Rest – (bar lunch Monday-Saturday) Menu € 48 – Carte € 32/42
♦ Rebuilt 19C house sharing grounds with a Gaelic heritage centre. Spacious accommodation in classic patterns; east-facing rooms enjoy superb views of Glenreagh National Park. Classic menu matched by traditional surroundings and period-inspired décor.

HORSE AND JOCKEY (An Marcach) – Tipperary – 712 I 10   39 C2
D Dublin 146 km – Cashel 14 km – Thurles 9 km

Horse and Jockey   🔲 ⑨ 🏊 🗓 🖃 🕹 rm, 🚴 🛠 🕾 🚣 **P**
– ℰ (0504) 44 192 – www.horseandjockeyhotel.com   *VISA* 🌑 **AE** ①
– info@horseandjockeyhotel.com – Fax (0504) 44 747 – Closed 25 December
65 rm ☑ – ♦€ 80/100 ♦♦€ 140/180 – 1 suite   **Rest** – Carte € 25/40
♦ Much extended hotel with stylish, state-of-the-art meeting rooms, superb spa and great gift shop. Bar full of horse racing pictures on walls. Spacious, contemporary bedrooms. Easy going dining room with traditional menus.

HOWTH – Fingal – 712 N 7 – ⊠ Dublin ▌ *Ireland*   39 D1
D Dublin 16 km
🖼 Deer Park Hotel Howth Castle, ℰ (01) 832 6039
◎ The Cliffs★ (⪦★)

Inisradharc without rest   ⪦ 🚗 🛠 **P** *VISA* 🌑 **AE**
Balkill Rd, North : ¾ km – ℰ (01) 832 23 06 – harbour-view@msn.com
– Closed 19 December - 7 January
3 rm ☑ – ♦€ 69/79 ♦♦€ 80/90
♦ High above the pretty fishing village with views of the harbour and Eye Island. Conservatory breakfast room and spacious en suite bedrooms share a homely style.

Aqua   ⪦ **AC** *VISA* 🌑 **AE**
1 West Pier – ℰ (01) 832 0690 – www.aqua.ie – dine@aqua.ie – Fax (01)
832 0687 – Closed 25 December and Monday except Bank Holidays
Rest – Seafood – Menu € 30 (lunch) – Carte € 44/73
♦ Glass sided, first floor restaurant affording super bay views. Intimate bar filled with local photos, whetting the appetite for accomplished dishes of freshly caught seafood.

King Sitric with rm   ⪦ **AC** rest, ⁽¹⁾ *VISA* 🌑 **AE**
East Pier – ℰ (01) 832 5235 – www.kingsitric.ie – info@kingsitric.ie – Fax (01)
839 2442 – Closed Christmas
8 rm ☑ – ♦€ 110/145 ♦♦€ 205
Rest – Seafood – (Closed Tuesday) (dinner only and Sunday lunch)
Menu € 58 – Carte € 50/67
♦ Well established for 50 years; one of Ireland's original seafood restaurants. Enjoy locally caught produce in first floor dining room with bay views. Modern, comfy bedrooms.

Deep   *VISA* 🌑
12 West Pier – ℰ (01) 806 39 21 – www.deep.ie – info@deep.ie – Fax (01)
806 39 21 – Closed 25-26 December, 1 January and Monday
Rest – Carte € 36/50
♦ Personally run, intimate restaurant on busy pier. Deep brown leather banquettes accentuate stylish feel. Wide-ranging, freshly prepared menus underpinned by local seafood.

INISHCRONE (Inis Crabhann) – **Sligo** – **712** E 5 🏠 *Ireland*   36 **B2**
> 🚗 Dublin 257 km – Ballina 13 km – Galway 127 km – Sligo 55 km
> 🏛 Rosserk Abbey★, W : 16 km by R 297, N 59 and R 314 – Moyne Abbey★,
> W : 19 km by R 297, N 59 and R 314. Killala★, W : 21 km by R 297, N 59 and
> R 314

⌂   **Ceol na Mara** without rest   ⩽ 🛇 ⌾ P̄ VISA ❻
     Main St – ℰ (096) 36 351 – www.ceol-na-mara.com – ceolnamara@eircom.net
     – Closed 20-27 December
     9 rm ⊿ – ♥€ 50 ♥♥€ 90
     ♦ At the centre of town, a sizeable guest house kept spotless by the friendly long-standing owners. Simply appointed bedrooms are all en suite, with sea views to the rear.

INISHMORE – **Galway** – **712** C/D 8 – **see Aran Islands**

INISTIOGE (Inis Tíog) – **Kilkenny** – **712** K 10   39 **C2**
> 🚗 Dublin 82 km – Kilkenny 16 km – Waterford 19 km – Wexford 33 km

✗   **Bassetts at Woodstock**   🌅 P̄ VISA ❻
     Woodstock Gardens, Northwest : 3 km – ℰ (056) 775 8820 – www.bassetts.ie
     – info@bassetts.ie – Closed 3 weeks January and February, Monday, Tuesday,
     and Sunday dinner - except Bank Holidays
     Rest – (light lunch) Carte € 39/57
     ♦ Personally run restaurant at entrance to Woodstock gardens. Homely inner with delightful terrace. Food is ethical, seasonal and traceable, and the owner rears his own pigs.

KANTURK – **Cork** – **712** F 11 – **pop. 1 915** 🏠 *Ireland*   38 **B2**
> 🚗 Dublin 259 km – Cork 53 km – Killarney 50 km – Limerick 71 km
> 🏌 Fairy Hill, ℰ (029) 50 534
> ◎ Town★ - Castle★

⌂   **Glenlohane** without rest 🌲   ⩽ 🚗 🐾 🛇 P̄ VISA ❻ AE
     East : 4 km by R 576 and Charlville rd on Cecilstown rd – ℰ (029) 50 014
     – www.glenlohane.com – glenlohane@iol.ie
     3 rm ⊿ – ♥€ 100 ♥♥€ 200
     ♦ In the family for over 250 years, a Georgian country house at the centre of wooded parkland and a working farm. Library and cosy, en suite rooms overlooking the fields.

KEEL (An Caol) – **Mayo** – **712** B 5/6 – **see Achill Island**

KENMARE (Neidín) – **Kerry** – **712** D 12 – **pop. 1 701** 🏠 *Ireland*   38 **A3**
> 🚗 Dublin 338 km – Cork 93 km – Killarney 32 km
> 🛈 Heritage Centre ℰ (064) 41 233 (April-October),
>   kenmare@corkkerrytourism.ie AY
> 🏌 Kenmare, ℰ (064) 41 291
> ◎ Town★
> 🏛 Ring of Kerry★★ - Healy Pass★★ (⩽★★), SW : 30½ km by R 571 and R 574
>   AY – Mountain Road to Glengarriff (⩽★★) S : by N 71 AY - Slieve Miskish
>   Mountains (⩽★★), SW : 48¼ km by R 571 AY – Gougane Barra Forest
>   Park★★, SE : 16 km AY - Lauragh (Derreen Gardens★ **AC**), SW : 23½ km by
>   R 571 AY – Allihies (Copper Mines★), SW : 57 km by R 571 and R 575 AY –
>   Garnish Island (⩽★), SW : 68½ km by R 571, R 575 and R 572 AY

Plan on next page

🏨   **Park** 🌲   ⩽ 🚗 🐾 ⌾ ⊗ ⌂ 👄 ⅙ ✗ 🏌 🍴 ⌔ rm, 🛇 ⌾ P̄ VISA ❻ AE ⓪
     – ℰ (064) 41 200 – www.parkkenmare.com – info@parkkenmare.com – Fax (064)
     41 402 – April-October, weekends mid February - April, November and Christmas
     46 rm ⊿ – ♥€ 220/344 ♥♥€ 440/550   BY**k**
     Rest – (dinner only) Menu € 76
     ♦ Privately run country house boasts many paintings and antiques. Superb spa facilities. Inviting, classically tasteful rooms; many offer superb views of Kenmare Bay and hills. Grand, bay-windowed dining room; local produce to fore.

REPUBLIC OF IRELAND

KENMARE

Back Lane . . . . BY 2
Cromwell's Bridge . . . . . . AY
Davitt's Place. . . . . AY
Downing's Row . . . . BY 5
East Park St. . . . . AY 7
Finnihy Bridge . . . . AY
Henry St . . . . AY
Henry's Lane . . . . ABY 8
Killarney Rd . . . . AY
Main St . . . . BY
Market St . . . . AY
New St . . . . AY
Old Bridge St. . . . . AY 12
Railway Rd . . . . BY
Rock St . . . . BY 14
Shelborne St. . . . . BY
The Square . . . . AY

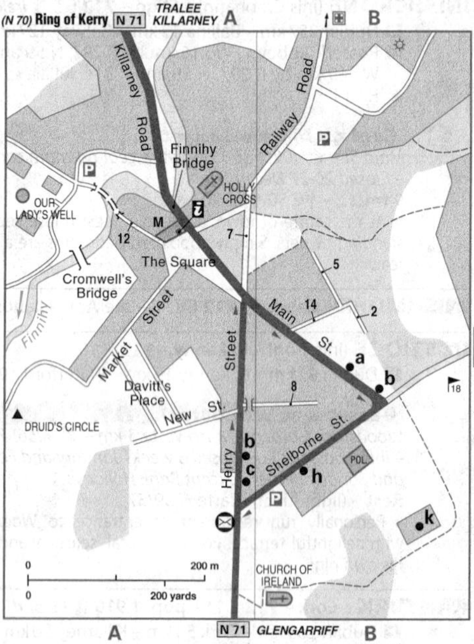

Sheen Falls Lodge

Southeast : 2 km by N 71 – ✆ (064) 41 600
– www.sheenfallslodge.ie – info@sheenfallslodge.ie – Fax (064) 41 386
– Closed 2 January - 6 February
57 rm – 🚹€ 310/455 🚹🚹€ 310/455, ☕ €24 – 9 suites – 🚹🚹€ 465/1870
Rest *La Cascade* – (dinner only) Carte € 60/86
Rest *Oscar's* – (dinner only and Sunday lunch in summer) Carte € 31/55
◆ On the banks of the Sheen; modern but classically inspired. Spacious rooms with stunning extras. Extensive spa, gym and stables. Attentive, formal service. Floodlit river views at La Cascade. Oscars, more informal, also overlooks the falls.

Brook Lane

rm,

Gortamullen, North : 1 km by N 71 on N 70 – ✆ (064) 42 077
– www.brooklanehotel.com – info@brooklanehotel.com – Fax (064) 40 869
– Closed 24-26 December
20 rm ☕ – 🚹€ 75/110 🚹🚹€ 130/210
Rest *Casey's Bistro* – Carte € 20/33
◆ Modern hotel meets country house resulting in homely charms with a designer edge. Main strength here is the airy bedrooms, which are delightfully comfy with a host of extras.

Shelburne Lodge without rest

East : ¾ km on R 569 (Cork Rd) – ✆ (064) 41 013 – www.shelburnelodge.com
– shelburnekenmare@eircom.net – Fax (064) 42 135
– Mid March- mid November
9 rm ☕ – 🚹€ 75/120 🚹🚹€ 110/170
◆ Georgian farmhouse with pleasant lawns and herb garden. Antiques stylishly combined with contemporary colours and modern art. Firelit lounge and cosy rooms. Affable hosts.

↑ **Sallyport House** without rest   ⬱ 🚗 🌴 📶 **P**
South : ½ km on N 71 – ℰ (064) 664 20 66 – www.sallyporthouse.com
– port@iol.ie – Fax (064) 664 20 67 – April-October
5 rm ☲ – ♦€ 110 ♦♦€ 170
♦ 1930s house in garden and orchard. Wood floored hall, full of books and local information, leads to pristine, antique furnished bedrooms and a pretty front sitting room.

↑ **Sea Shore Farm** without rest ⬲   ⬱ 🚗 🌴 & 🌴 📶 **P** **VISA** **⬤⬤**
Tubrid, West : 1½ km by N 70 (Sneem rd) – ℰ (064) 41 270
– www.seashorekenmare.com – seashore@eircom.net – Fax (064) 41 270
– 1 March - 10 November
6 rm ☲ – ♦€ 65/90 ♦♦€ 100/130
♦ Guesthouse set in 32 acres of working farmland and park with lovely views. All of the individually decorated bedrooms have full length windows which make the most of the view.

XX **The Lime Tree**   **AC** **P** **VISA** **⬤⬤**
Shelbourne St – ℰ (064) 41 225 – www.limetreerestaurant.com
– limetree@limetreerestaurant.com – Fax (064) 41 839
– April-October, Christmas and New Year   BY**h**
Rest – (dinner only) Carte € 38/48
♦ Tasty, unelaborate modern Irish cooking in a 19C former schoolhouse: stone walls, modern art on walls and in first-floor gallery. Busy, affordable and unfailingly friendly.

XX **Mulcahys**   **AC** **VISA** **⬤⬤** **AE** **①**
36 Henry St – ℰ (064) 42 383 – Fax (064) 42 383
– Closed 24-27 December, 10-26 January, Tuesday and Wednesday January-June
and October-December   AY**c**
Rest – (dinner only) Menu € 35 – Carte € 33/51
♦ Stylish wine racks, high-backed chairs, polished tables and friendly, attentive service set the tone here. Modern dishes appeal to the eye and palate alike.

XX **D'Arcy's Oyster Bar and Grill**   **VISA** **⬤⬤** **AE**
Main St – ℰ (064) 41 589 – keatingrestaurants@ownmail.net
– Restricted opening in winter   BY**b**
Rest – (dinner only) (booking essential) Carte € 32/48 **s**
♦ Restaurant set in striking, green-painted former bank. Pop in for oysters or fresh Kerry seafood at Oyster Bar or modern Irish menu in restaurant, with open fire and candles.

X **Leath Phingin Eile**   **AC** **VISA** **⬤⬤**
35 Main St – ℰ (064) 41 559 – Closed 25 December, Monday and Tuesday except
Bank Holidays. Restricted opening in winter.   BY**a**
Rest – (dinner only) (booking essential) Carte € 29/47
♦ Simply styled restaurant set over two floors serving classical dishes which follow the seasons. Excellent breads and tapenade. Popular with locals, its name means 'halfpenny'.

X **Packies**   **VISA** **⬤⬤**
Henry St – ℰ (064) 41 508 – www.kenmarerestaurants.com – Closed 25
December, 1 week January, 1 week February and Sunday   AY**b**
Rest – (dinner only) (booking essential) Carte € 31/50
♦ Locally popular, personally run little place with understated rustic feel. Handwritten menu of fresh modern Irish dishes prepared with care and simplicity. Personable staff.

KILBRITTAIN – Cork – **712** F 12   38 **B3**
🅳 Dublin 289 km – Cork 38 km – Killarney 96 km

↑ **The Glen** without rest ⬲   🚗 🌴 🌴 📶 **P** **VISA** **⬤⬤** **①**
Southwest : 6½ km by un-marked rd off R 600 – ℰ (023) 884 98 62
– www.glencountryhouse.com – info@glencountryhouse.com – Fax (023)
884 98 62 – Easter - October
6 rm ☲ – ♦€ 75/85 ♦♦€ 130/140
♦ 130 year-old family house, part of working farm close to beach. Delicious organic farmhouse breakfasts. Lovingly restored bedrooms elegantly furnished to a high standard.

REPUBLIC OF IRELAND

Casino House 🍴🍴 🚗 P VISA ⓜ AE
😊 Coolmain Bay, Southeast : 3½ km by unmarked rd on R 600 – ℰ (023) 88 49 944
– chouse@eircom.net – Fax (023) 88 49 945 – Closed January-17 March and
Wednesday
Rest – (dinner only and Sunday lunch) Carte € 34/53 **s**
♦ Whitewashed walls, Shaker style furniture and art on a culinary theme in this
converted farmhouse run by a husband and wife. Locally sourced menu is balanced
and flavourful.

KILCOLGAN (Cill Cholgáin) – **Galway** – **712** F 8 – ⊠ **Oranmore**   36 **B3**
▶ Dublin 220 km – Galway 17 km

Moran's Oyster Cottage 🍴 VISA ⓜ AE ⓞ
The Weir, Northwest : 2 km by N 18 – ℰ (091) 796 113
– moranstheweir@eircom.net – Closed 24-26 December and Good Friday
Rest – Seafood – Carte € 26/40
♦ Likeable thatched pub in sleepy village. Settle down in one of the beamed snugs
and parlours to enjoy prime local seafood - simple and fresh - or soups, salads and
sandwiches.

The red 🖎 symbol?
This denotes the very essence of peace
– only the sound of birdsong first thing in the morning...

KILKEE – **Clare** – **712** D 9 – **pop. 1 325** 📖 Ireland   38 **A-B2**
▶ Dublin 285 km – Galway 124 km – Limerick 93 km
🛈 The Square (065) 9056112 (June-early September),
tourisminfo@shannondevelopments.ie
🏞 Kilkee East End, ℰ (065) 905 60 48
⛴ Kilrush★ (Scattery Island★ by boat), SE : 16 m. by N 67 – SW : Loop Head
Peninsula (Bridge of Ross★)

Stella Maris 🍴 ⓦ VISA ⓜ AE
– ℰ (065) 905 64 55 – www.stellamarishotel.com – info@stellamarishotel.com
– Fax (065) 906 00 06
20 rm � – †€ 80/130 ††€ 110/180   **Rest** – Carte € 22/43
♦ Family-run hotel in centre of bustling seaside town, whose refurbished bedrooms
offer a surprising amount of space. Terrace, with view of bay, is popular spot from
which to people-watch. Enjoy traditional fare in the atmospheric bar or on the veranda.

Halpin's Townhouse ⓦ P VISA ⓜ AE ⓞ
Erin St – ℰ (065) 905 60 32 – www.halpinsprivatehotels.com
– halpinshotel@iol.ie – Fax (065) 905 63 17 – 15 March-October
12 rm ⊡ – †€ 75/85 ††€ 90/130
Rest – (bar lunch Monday-Saturday) Menu € 26 – Carte € 22/37
♦ Attractive terraced house offering good value accommodation and a warm wel-
come. Pub-style bar in the basement and uniform bedrooms with fitted furniture.
Traditionally appointed ground floor restaurant.

Kilkee Thalassotherapy Centre and Guest House without rest Spa
Grattan St – ℰ (065) 905 67 42   ⓦ P VISA ⓜ
– www.kilkeethalasso.com – info@kilkeethalasso.com – Fax (065) 905 67 62
5 rm ⊡ – †€ 50/90 ††€ 100/140
♦ Modern guest house with combined breakfast room and sitting room. Spacious
well-equipped bedrooms. Preferential booking for guests in the adjoining thalasso-
therapy centre.

▶ Dublin 114 km – Cork 138 km – Killarney 185 km – Limerick 111 km
– Tullamore 83 km – Waterford 46 km

🅸 Shee Alms House 𝄐 (056) 7751500, kilkennytouristoffice@failteireland.ie

🆗 Glendine, 𝄐 (056) 776 5400

🆗 Callan Geraldine, 𝄐 (056) 772 5136

🆖 Castlecomer Drumgoole, 𝄐 (056) 444 1139

👁 Town ★★ – St Canice's Cathedral ★★ – Kilkenny Castle and Park ★★ **AC** –
Black Abbey ★ – Rothe House ★

🅶 Jerpoint Abbey ★★ **AC**, S : 19 ¼ km by R 700 and N 9 – Kilfane Glen and
Waterfall ★ **AC**, S : 21 km by R 700 and N 9 – Kells Priory ★, S : 12 ½ km by
R 697 – Dunmore Cave ★ **AC**, N : 11 ¼ km by N 77 and N 78

🏩 **Kilkenny**   🚗 🖥 ⅍ 🐟 🔥 ⅙ rm, 🏃 AC rest, ⅗ ⒱ 🆚 🅿 VISA ⊕⊙ AE ①
College Rd, Southwest : 1 ¼ km at junction with N 76 – 𝄐 (056) 776 20 00
– www.hotelkilkenny.ie – experience@hotelkilkenny.ie
– Fax (056) 776 59 84
138 rm ⌷ – ♥€ 90/140 ♥♥€ 180/290
Rest *Taste* – Menu € 25/38 – Carte € 30/42
◆ Well run, refurbished hotel boasts contemporary interior with silver finishes and
black wallpaper, spacious meeting rooms, well equipped leisure centre and comfy
bedrooms. Italian menu served in split level dining room.

🏠 **The Hibernian**   🖥 🔥 rm, AC rest, ⅗ ⒱ 🆚 🅿 VISA ⊕⊙ AE ①
1 Ormonde St – 𝄐 (056) 777 18 88 – www.kilkennyhibernianhotel.com
– info@kilkennyhibernianhotel.com – Fax (056) 777 18 77
– Closed 24-25 December
43 rm ⌷ – ♥€ 145/190 ♥♥€ 220/240 – 3 suites
Rest – (bar lunch Monday-Friday) Menu € 20/32 **s** – Carte € 25/45 **s**
◆ Part Georgian hotel, set in former bank, in sight of Kilkenny Castle: classically
proportioned, understated modern bedrooms, spacious bar in dark wood with long
tan sofas. Comfortable restaurant with traditional appeal.

🏠 **Butler House** without rest   🚗 ⅗ ⒱ 🆚 🅿 VISA ⊕⊙ AE ①
15-16 Patrick St – 𝄐 (056) 776 57 07 – www.butler.ie – res@butler.ie – Fax (056)
776 56 26 – Closed 23-29 December
12 rm ⌷ – ♥€ 80/155 ♥♥€ 120/250 – 1 suite
◆ Substantial part Georgian house. Spacious accommodation with 1970s-style furnishings - superior bow-fronted bedrooms to the rear overlook neat, geometric
lawned gardens.

🏠 **Blanchville House** ☜   ⬳ 🚗 🕭 ⅗ ⅗ 🅿 VISA ⊕⊙ AE
Dunbell, Maddoxtown, Southeast : 10 ½ km by N 10 turning right ¾ km
after the Pike Inn – 𝄐 (056) 772 71 97 – www.blanchville.ie
– mail@blanchville.ie
– Fax (056) 772 76 36
– March-October
6 rm ⌷ – ♥€ 70/75 ♥♥€ 120/130
Rest – (by arrangement) Menu € 30
◆ Follow the tree-lined drive to this restored Georgian country house in quiet farmland. Firelit drawing room. Charming bedrooms furnished with antiques and family
heirlooms.

🏠 **Fanad House** without rest   🚗 🔥 ⅗ ⒱ 🅿 VISA ⊕⊙
Castle Rd, South : ¾ km on R 700 – 𝄐 (056) 776 41 26
– www.fanadhouse.com
– fanadhouse@hotmail.com
– Fax (056) 775 60 01
8 rm ⌷ – ♥€ 60/110 ♥♥€ 90/120
◆ Modern, purpose-built, green painted house within the castle walls. A warm welcome and bright, well-appointed bedrooms await the visitor.

REPUBLIC OF IRELAND

XXX **Campagne**   AC ℅ VISA ❿
5 The Arches – ℰ (056) 772 2858 – www.campagne.ie – info@campagne.ie
– Fax (056) 772 2875 – Closed 25-26 December and 1 January
Rest – (closed Monday and Tuesday) (dinner only and Sunday lunch)
(booking advisable) Menu € 28 – Carte € 43/52
♦ Hidden close to the railway arches, away from the city centre. Crescent shaped
dining room with bright contemporary art. Modern French and Irish cooking; tasty,
unfussy dishes.

XX **Zuni** with rm   ☎ ⑤ ⑤ rm, AC ℅ ⑤ P VISA ❿ AE
26 Patrick St – ℰ (056) 772 39 99 – www.zuni.ie – info@zuni.ie – Fax (056)
775 64 00 – Closed 23-27 December
13 rm ☑ – ♦€ 65/110 ♦♦€ 90/150
Rest – Menu € 38 (dinner) – Carte € 34/44
♦ Chic modern design in leather and dark wood draws the smart set to this former theatre. Friendly service; bold, generous and eclectic cooking. Stylish, good-value rooms.

XX **Ristorante Rinuccini**   AC ℅ ⑤ VISA ❿ AE ①
1 The Parade – ℰ (056) 776 15 75 – www.rinuccini.com – info@rinuccini.com
– Fax (056) 775 12 88 – Closed 25-26 December
Rest – Italian – Menu € 28 (dinner) – Carte € 33/53
♦ Named after the 17C archbishop, "bon viveur" and papal nuncio to Ireland, a family
owned restaurant with basement dining room: Italian classics served at closely set tables.

KILLALOE – Clare – 712 G 9 ∥ *Ireland*   38 **B2**
🗗 Dublin 175 km – Ennis 51 km – Limerick 21 km – Tullamore 93 km
🖊 The Bridge – ℰ (061) 376866, tourisminfo@shannon-dev.ie
◎ Town★ – St Flannan's Cathedral★
🄲 Graves of the Leinstermen (≤★), N : 7 ¼ km by R 494 – Castleconnell★, S :
16 km by R 494 and R 466 – Clare Glens★, S : 24 km by R 494, R 504 and
R 503. Nenagh (Castle★), NE : 19 ¼ km by R 496 and N 7 – Holy Island★ **AC**,
N : 25 ¾ km by R 463 and boat from Tuamgraney

XX **Cherry Tree**   ≤ ⇔ P VISA ❿ AE
Lakeside, Ballina, following signs for Lakeside H. – ℰ (061) 375 688
– www.cherrytreerestaurant.ie – cherrytreerestaurant@gmail.com – Fax (061)
375 689 – Closed 25-26 December, first two weeks January, Good Friday, and
Monday
Rest – (dinner only and Sunday lunch) Menu € 32/48 – Carte € 48/55
♦ Contemporary, relaxing interior, polite staff and a wide range of original, well-
sourced modern Irish dishes on offer from an open kitchen. Seasonal produce of the
essence.

KILLARNEY – Kerry – 712 D 11 – pop. 14 603 ∥ *Ireland*   38 **A2**
🗗 Dublin 304 km – Cork 87 km – Limerick 111 km – Waterford 180 km
✈ Kerry (Farranfore) Airport : ℰ (066) 976 4644, N : 15 ¼ km by N 22
🖊 Beech Rd ℰ (064) 31633, tioinfo@killarney.corkkerrytourism.ie
🏕 Mahoney's Point, ℰ (064) 31 034
◎ Town★★ – St Mary's Cathedral★ CX
🄲 Killarney National Park★★★ (Muckross Friary★, Muckross House and
Farms★) AZ - Gap of Dunloe★★, SW : 9 ½ km by R 562 AZ – Ross Castle★
AC, S : 1 ½ km by N 71 and minor rd – Torc Waterfall★, S : 8 km by N 71 BZ.
Ring of Kerry★★ – Ladies View★★, SW : 19 ¼ km by N 71 BZ – Moll's Gap★,
SW : 25 km by N 71 BZ

Plan opposite

🏠🏠🏠 **Killarney Park**   ⟿ ▢ 🕺 ⑤ 🏕 ℅ ⑤ ⑤ rm, AC ℅ ⑤ ⓼ P VISA ❿ AE
– ℰ (064) 35 555 – www.killarneyparkhotel.ie – info@killarneyparkhotel.ie
– Fax (064) 35 266 – Closed 24-26 December   DX**k**
67 rm ☑ – ♦€ 275/400 ♦♦€ 275/400 – 3 suites
Rest *Park* – (bar lunch) Carte € 50/61
♦ Smart modern hotel. Firelit library, panelled billiard room and the bedrooms' décor
and fine details balance old-world styling and contemporary convenience. Armchair
dining beneath sparkling chandeliers and Corinthian capitals.

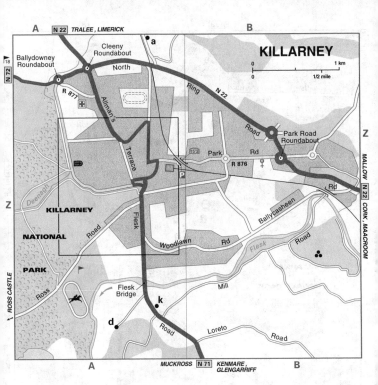

KILLARNEY

A22 *TRALEE, LIMERICK*

Cleeny Roundabout

Ballydowney Roundabout

North

Ring

N 22

Road

Park Road Roundabout

R 877

Allman's

Park

Rd

R 876

Terrace

KILLARNEY

NATIONAL

Deenagh

Flesk

PARK

Road

Ballycasheen

Woodlawn Rd

Flesk

Road

Road

Ross

Flesk Bridge

Mill

k

d

Road

Loreto

Road

ROSS CASTLE

MUCKROSS N 71 *KENMARE, GLENGARRIFF*

MALLOW N 22 CORK, MAACROOM

🏨 Aghadoe Heights H. and Spa 🦢 ≤ ⊞ 🕭 🔲 ⊞ 🐾 ⅓ ✕
Northwest : 4½ km by N 22 — 📶 ♿ rm, 🔟 ❄ 📶 🔲 ⊞ 🐾 ⅓ ✕
– 𝒞 (064) 31 766 – www.aghadoeheights.com – info@aghadoeheights.com
– Fax (064) 31 345
72 rm – †€ 250/370 ††€ 315/435, ⊋ €22 – 2 suites
Rest *Lake Room* – (bar lunch Monday-Saturday) Menu €60
♦ Striking glass-fronted hotel: stylish bar, modern health and fitness centre and contemporary rooms, many with sumptuous sofas. Balconied front rooms offer views of the lough. Picture-windowed restaurant with rural views.

🏨 Europe 🦢 ≤ ⊞ 🕭 🔲 ⊞ 🐾 ⅓ 📶 ♿ rm, ❄ ⅍ 📶 🔲 ⊞ 🐾
Fossa, West : 4¾ km by R 562 on N 72 – 𝒞 (064) 71 300 – www.killarneyhotels.ie
– hotelsales@liebherr.com – Fax (064) 37 900 – 1 February -15 December
139 rm ⊋ – †€ 250/300 ††€ 290/350 – 49 suites – ††€ 350/1750
Rest – (light lunch) Carte €42/56 **s**
♦ Spacious lounges and bedrooms plus excellent prospects of Macgillicuddy's Reeks and Lough Leane. Fully equipped modern comfort, even luxury, on a vast but well managed scale. Restaurant offers Lough views.

🏨 The Brehon 🔲 ⊞ 🐾 ✕ 📶 ♿ rm, 🔟 ❄ 📶 🔲 ⊞ 🐾
Muckross Rd – 𝒞 (064) 66 30 700 – www.thebrehon.com – info@thebrehon.com
– Fax (064) 66 30 701
AZ**k**
120 rm ⊋ – †€ 155/195 ††€ 190/280 – 5 suites
Rest *The Brehon* – (bar lunch) Carte €40/50
♦ Spacious hotel near Muckross Park with views to mountains. High standards of comfort. Basement Wellness Centre. Airy bedrooms are well equipped with latest mod cons. Stylish restaurant for formal, original dining.

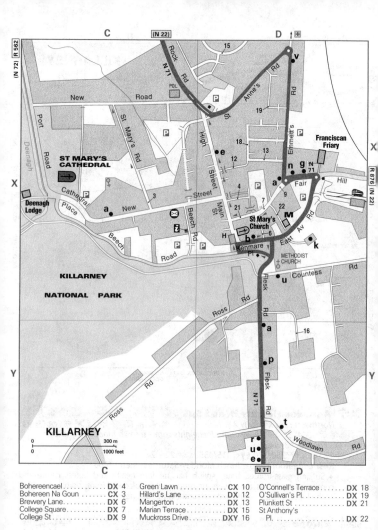

KILLARNEY

Muckross Park

🍴 🔍 ⊕ ↳ 🛄 AK ☆ 🄿 VISA ⑳ AE ①

South : 5½ km on N 71 – ✆ (064) 23 400 – www.muckrosspark.com
– info@muckrosspark.com – Fax (064) 31 965 – Closed January - 14 February and
Thursday-Sunday 14 February - 15 March

62 rm � – †€ 200 ††€ 300 – 6 suites

Rest *Blue Pool* – (dinner only) Menu €60

Rest *G. B. Shaw* – (June-October) (dinner only) Carte €45/65

◆ Extended, refurbished 18C hotel boasts high levels of comfort. Includes spa with
outdoor hot tub and yoga terrace. Comfortable bedrooms; those in extension more
contemporary. Modern main restaurant offers traditional menus. Seafood served in
G. B. Shaw.

The Ross

📱 ⅋ rm, 🅰🅲 ⚡ 🕻 📘 🆅🅸🆂🅰 ⓩ 🅰🅴

– ℰ (064) 31 855 – www.theross.ie – info@theross.ie – Fax (064) 27 633
– Closed 24 December-10 January   DX**b**
29 rm ⊇ – †€ 170/245 ††€ 170/245   **Rest** – (bar lunch) Carte approx. € 50
♦ Boutique hotel boasting extreme comfort and style, with trendy pink bar, friendly staff and quality bedrooms with enormous beds; the best at the front overlooking the street. Ultra modern pink and lime green restaurant - accessed down winding metal staircase - serves modern international food to match.

Cahernane House

≤ 🚗 🕽 📱 🕻 📘 🆅🅸🆂🅰 ⓩ 🅰🅴 ⓞ

Muckross Rd – ℰ (064) 31 895 – www.cahernane.com
– reservations@cahernane.com – Fax (064) 34 340
– Closed mid December-1 February   AZ**d**
37 rm ⊇ – †€ 140/200 ††€ 210/264 – 1 suite
Rest The Herbert Room – (bar lunch) Carte € 50/70
♦ Peacefully located 19C house with pleasant mountain outlook. Array of lounges in sympathetic style. Rooms in main house or modern wing: all are large, comfy and well equipped. Restaurant offers formal dining with inspiring views.

Randles Court

🔲 🕽 🏋 📱 🅰🅲 rest, 🕻 🏊 📘 🆅🅸🆂🅰 ⓩ 🅰🅴

Muckross Rd – ℰ (064) 35 333 – www.randlescourt.com – info@randlescourt.com
– Fax (064) 35 206 – Closed 24-28 December   DY**p**
72 rm ⊇ – †€ 80/160 ††€ 100/198
Rest Checkers – (bar lunch) Menu € 45 – Carte € 31/47
♦ Family run hotel, centred on a rectory built in 1906. Good leisure facilities. Rooms, at their best in the modern extension, and comfy lounge subtly reflect the period style. Good choice of local produce in chequerboard floored restaurant.

Dromhall

🔲 🕽 📱 📶 rm, 🅰🅲 rest, 🕻 🏊 📘 🆅🅸🆂🅰 ⓩ 🅰🅴 ⓞ

Muckross Rd – ℰ (064) 39 300 – www.dromhall.com – info@dromhall.com
– Fax (064) 39 301 – Closed 24-28 December   DY**p**
72 rm ⊇ – †€ 70/150 ††€ 90/190
Rest Abbey – (dinner only) Menu € 30 **s** – Carte € 26/37 **s**
Rest Kayne's Bistro – (dinner only) Menu € 35 **s** – Carte € 28/40 **s**
♦ Modern, marble-tiled lobby leads to sizeable rooms with reproduction furnishings and an unexpectedly homely lounge: ideal for business travel. Abbey restaurant offers a classic repertory. Kayne's bistro serves a wide-ranging modern menu.

Killarney Royal

📱 🅰🅲 🕻 🆅🅸🆂🅰 ⓩ 🅰🅴 ⓞ

College St – ℰ (064) 31 853 – www.killarneyroyal.ie – info@killarneyroyal.ie
– Fax (064) 34 001 – Closed 23-26 December   DX**g**
29 rm ⊇ – †€ 160/205 ††€ 240/320
Rest – (Closed Monday -Tuesday November and January) (bar lunch)
Menu € 28/39 – Carte € 28/54
♦ Smart yet cosy lounge with an open fire, spacious, individually decorated rooms and a traditional bar in a town house hotel, built at the turn of the 20th century. Classic, candlelit dining room with flowing white linen.

Fairview

📱 rm, 🅰🅲 rest, 🕽 🕻 🆅🅸🆂🅰 ⓩ 🅰🅴 ⓞ

College St – ℰ (064) 34 164 – www.fairviewkillarney.com
– info@fairview.killarney.com – Fax (064) 71 777 – Closed 24-25 December   DX**a**
29 rm ⊇ – †€ 75/195 ††€ 100/250
Rest – (dinner only) Menu € 30 – Carte € 34/46
♦ Stylish townhouse with smart, leather furnished lounge. Bright, up-to-date bedrooms exude distinctively individualistic flourishes; penthouse has whirlpool bath and roof terrace. Modern restaurant serves traditional menu of local meat and fish.

McSweeney Arms

📱 rm, 🅰🅲 rest, 🕽 🕻 🆅🅸🆂🅰 ⓩ 🅰🅴

College St – ℰ (064) 31 211 – www.mcsweeneyarms.com – mcsweeney@
eircom.net – Fax (065) 34 553 – Closed January and February   DX**n**
26 rm ⊇ – †€ 75/150 ††€ 130/200   **Rest** – Menu € 25/32 – Carte € 33/48
♦ The hotel's unusual corner tower provides extra seating areas in some rooms; the characterful bar has been family run for over 50 years. Well-fitted rooms in modern tones. Long-standing owner lends a hand in the bar and restaurant.

REPUBLIC OF IRELAND

Foley's Townhouse   🛏 AC rest, ⚿ P. VISA ◯◯ AE ◯

23 High St – ℰ (064) 31 217 – www.foleystownhouse.com
– info@foleystownhouse.com – Fax (064) 34 683 – Closed 1-27 December   DXe
28 rm ⚌ – †€ 70/95 ††€ 95/130   **Rest** – (bar lunch) Carte € 37/52

♦ Formerly a posting inn, now a likeable town-centre hotel, still personally owned and run; spacious modern accommodation is individually styled with a good range of mod cons. Appetising range of seafood in restaurant.

Killarney Lodge without rest   🚗 AC ⚿ �"ŵ P. VISA ◯◯ AE

Countess Rd – ℰ (064) 36 499 – www.killarneylodge.net – klylodge@iol.ie
– Fax (064) 31 070 – March - 27 October   DXu
16 rm ⚌ – †€ 85/105 ††€ 120/140

♦ Run by a likeable couple, a purpose-built hotel offering comfortable, thoughtfully furnished rooms. Within easy walking distance of the town centre.

Earls Court House without rest   🚗 🛏 ఈ ⚿ P. VISA ◯◯ AE

Woodlawn Junction, Muckross Rd – ℰ (064) 66 34 009
– www.killarney-earlscourt.ie – info@killarney-earlscourt.ie – Fax (064) 66 34 366
– March-15 November   DYt
36 rm ⚌ – †€ 80/120 ††€ 100/180

♦ Behind an unassuming façade, reproduction furniture combines well with modern facilities in spotlessly kept rooms. Tasty breakfasts served at antique dining tables.

Old Weir Lodge without rest   🛏 ⚿ P. VISA ◯◯ AE

Muckross Rd – ℰ (064) 35 593 – www.oldweirlodge.com
– oldweirlodge@eircom.net – Fax (064) 35 583 – Closed 24-26 December   DYr
30 rm ⚌ – †€ 55/95 ††€ 90/140

♦ Just south of the centre, a sizeable modern hotel owned and run by a welcoming couple. Neat rooms - particularly spacious on the second floor - and hearty breakfasts.

Fuchsia House without rest   🚗 ⚿ "ŵ P. VISA ◯◯

Muckross Rd – ℰ (064) 663 37 43 – www.fuchsiahouse.com
– fuchsiahouse@eircom.net – Fax (064) 663 65 88
– 14 March - 1 November   DYu
10 rm ⚌ – †€ 45/90 ††€ 95/130

♦ Inviting bedrooms, firelit lounge and a leafy conservatory in carefully chosen fabrics and patterns; homely without a trace of preciousness or fuss. Personally run.

Kathleens Country House without rest   🚗 ⚿ "ŵ P. VISA ◯◯

Madams Height, Tralee Rd, North : 3 ¼ km on N 22 – ℰ (064) 32 810
– www.kathleens.net – info@kathleens.net – Fax (064) 32 340
– 1 April -10 October
17 rm ⚌ – †€ 70/120 ††€ 120/150

♦ Cosy lounge with broad, pine-backed armchairs facing an open fire and neat bedrooms in traditional patterns - an extended house run by the eponymous owner for over 20 years.

Abbey Lodge without rest   ⚿ "ŵ P. VISA ◯◯

Muckross Rd – ℰ (064) 34 193 – www.abbey-lodge.com
– abbeylodgekly@eircom.net – Fax (064) 35 877 – Closed 20-28 December   DYa
15 rm ⚌ – †€ 70/90 ††€ 100/130

♦ Smart accommodation not far from the centre of town. Cosy lounge in cheerful yellows. Spotless, well-equipped rooms with Queen size beds and CD players.

Gleann Fia Country House without rest ॐ   🚗 P. VISA ◯◯

Old Deerpark, North : 2 km by Emmett's Rd – ℰ (064) 35 035
– www.gleannfia.com – info@gleannfia.com – Fax (064) 35 000   AZa
20 rm ⚌ – †€ 45/100 ††€ 70/150

♦ Meaning "Glen of the Deer", a substantial, purpose-built hotel in country house style, ringed by woods. Smartly kept bedrooms are usefully supplied with modern facilities.

↑ **Kingfisher Lodge** without rest ⌲ ✧ ⑨ **P** ⦸ ⦵

Lewis Rd – ℰ (064) 663 71 31 – www.kingfisherkillarney.com
– kingfisherguesthouse@eircom.net – Fax (064) 663 98 71
– 12 February-December DXv
10 rm ⊆ – ❖€ 50/75 ❖❖€ 80/120

♦ Friendly owners, a mine of local information, keep this modern guesthouse in immaculate order. Affordable accommodation in pastel shades; rear rooms face a quiet garden.

↑ **Rivermere** without rest ⌲ ✧ **P** ⦸ ⦵ ⦰ ⦱

Muckross Rd, South : ¾ km on N 71 – ℰ (064) 37 933
– www.killarney-rivermere.com – info@killarney-rivermere.com
– Fax (064) 37 944 DYe
9 rm ⊆ – ❖€ 60/70 ❖❖€ 110/130

♦ Well-maintained house; large bedrooms simply furnished in dark wood; those at the rear are quieter. Breakfast room overlooks walled garden. Hearty breakfast at clothed tables.

✗✗ **Chapter Forty** ⦸ ⦵ ⦰ ⦱

40 New St – ℰ (064) 66 71 833 – www.chapter40.ie – info@chapter40.ie
– Closed Sunday CXa
Rest – (dinner only) Menu € 50 – Carte € 34/45

♦ Refurbished restaurant in contemporary browns and creams with small bar area and window looking into kitchen. Large menu includes some eclectic combinations. Great soda bread.

at Beaufort West : 9 ¾ km by R 562 - **AZ** - off N 72 - ✉ **Killarney**

🏠 **Dunloe Castle** ⌾ ≤ ⌲ ⦿ ⦵ ⌹ ⩔ ✧ ⩚ **P** ⦸ ⦵ ⦰ ⦱

Southeast : 1 ½ km on Dunloe Golf Course rd – ℰ (064) 71 350
– www.killarneyhotels.ie – hotelsales@liebherr.com – Fax (064) 44 583
– 15 April - 15 October
100 rm ⊆ – ❖€ 170 ❖❖€ 290 – 2 suites **Rest** – (light lunch) Carte € 48/61

♦ Creeper-clad modern hotel offers sizeable, well-equipped rooms and smart conference suites, not forgetting an impressive view of the Gap of Dunloe and Macgillicuddy's Reeks. Restaurant serves Irish classic dishes.

> Look out for red symbols, indicating particularly pleasant establishments.

KILLASHANDRA (Cill na Seanrátha) – **Cavan** – **712** J 5 37 **C2**
🔁 Dublin 133 km – Belturbet 14 km – Cavan 19 km

↑ **Eonish Lodge** without rest ⌾ ≤ ⌲ ⦿ ✧ **P**

Eonish, Northeast : 4 ¾ km by Belturbet rd – ℰ (049) 433 44 87
– www.eonishlodge.com – info@eonishlodge.com – Closed January and February
4 rm ⊆ – ❖€ 60 ❖❖€ 100

♦ Just a stone's throw from Lough Oughter, in Killykeen Forest Park. Perfect for fishermen and walkers. Simple, neatly furnished bedrooms; front two have best views over lough.

KILLEAGH (Cill Ia) – **Cork** – **712** H 12 – **pop. 521** 39 **C3**
🔁 Dublin 243 km – Cork 37 km – Waterford 85 km

↑ **Ballymakeigh House** ⌾ ⌲ ⦿ ✗ ✧ **P** ⦸ ⦵

North : 1 ½ km – ℰ (024) 95 184 – www.ballymakeighhouse.com
– ballymakeigh@eircom.net – Fax (024) 95 523 – March-October
5 rm ⊆ – ❖€ 65 ❖❖€ 130 **Rest** – (by arrangement) Menu € 50

♦ Smoothly run modern country house on a working dairy farm. Attractive conservatory lounge and en suite rooms simply but thoughtfully decorated without starchiness or fuss.

REPUBLIC OF IRELAND

KILLENARD Laois – Laois
39 **C-D1**

▶ Dublin 48 km – Portlaoise 19 km – Naas 25 km – Carlow 36 km

The Heritage   ⛳ 🏊 🖥 🌐 🐾 ⅃🏐 ✗ 🖼 🎽 & rm, 🏃 AC ✗ 🎙️ 🕸️   P VISA ⓪ AE ①
– ☎ (057) 864 55 00 – www.theheritage.com
– info@theheritage.com – Fax (057) 864 23 50 – Closed 22-28 December
94 rm ⌂ – ☗€ 325 ☗☗€ 325 – 25 suites – ☗☗€ 450/750
Rest *The Arlington* – Menu € 65 – Carte (dinner) € 52/72
Rest *Greens* – (dinner only Monday, Tuesday, Friday and Saturday)
Carte € 31/46
Rest *Sol Oriens* – (dinner only Wednesday-Sunday) Carte € 22/39
♦ Stunning hotel surrounded by extensive gardens and golf course. State-of-the-art meeting facilities and superb spa. Capacious, elegant bedrooms offer supreme comforts. Formal dining in The Arlington. More of a brasserie feel to Greens, in the leisure centre. Pizza, pasta, salad and steaks in informal Sol Oriens.

KILLORGLIN – Kerry – **712** C 11 🔖 *Ireland*
38 **A2**

▶ Dublin 333 km – Killarney 19 km – Tralee 26 km
🏭 Killorglin Stealroe, ☎ (669) 761 979
◉ Lough Caragh★, SW : 9 km by N 70 and minor road S. Ring of Kerry★★

Bianconi without rest   ↘ ✗ 🎙️ VISA ⓪ AE ①
Annadale Rd – ☎ (066) 976 11 46 – www.bianconi.ie – bianconi@iol.ie
– Fax (066) 976 19 50 – Closed 24-29 December
14 rm ⌂ – ☗€ 65/85 ☗☗€ 100/120
♦ Classic street-corner pub; tiled lounge bar with stools and banquettes and likeable mis-match of paintings, old photos and vintage Guinness posters. Trim, soft-toned bedrooms.

Grove Lodge without rest   🖥 ↘ ✗ 🎙️ P VISA ⓪ AE
Killarney Rd, East : ¾ km on N 72 – ☎ (066) 976 11 57 – www.grovelodge.com
– info@grovelodge.com – Fax (066) 976 27 26 – February-November
10 rm ⌂ – ☗€ 55/65 ☗☗€ 100/120
♦ Comfortable, well-fitted rooms - one with four-poster bed and private patio - in a smoothly run riverside house. Try smoked salmon or eggs or a full Irish breakfast.

KILLYBEGS (Na Cealla Beaga) – Donegal – **712** G 4 🔖 *Ireland*
36 **B1**

▶ Dublin 291 km – Donegal 27 km – Londonderry 103 km – Sligo 92 km
◉ Cliffs of Bunglass★★, W : 27 km by N 56, R 263 and minor road –
Glencolmcille Folk Village★★ **AC**, W : 25 km by R 263 – Glengesh Pass★★,
SW : 24 km by N 56 and R 263 – Donegal Castle★ **AC**, E : 29 km by N 56 –
Gweebarra Estuary★, NE : 31 km by R 262 and R 252 - Trabane Strand★,
W : 32 km by R263 and minor road

Tara   ≤ 🐾 ⅃🏐 🎽 & rm, 🌡️ rest, ✗ 🕻 🛁 VISA ⓪ AE
– ☎ (074) 974 17 00 – www.tarahotel.ie – info@tarahotel.ie – Fax (074) 974 17 10
31 rm ⌂ – ☗€ 68/88 ☗☗€ 145/165 **Rest** – (bar lunch) Carte € 20/46
♦ Town centre hotel, its bright, commercial style typified by sleek bar with plasma TVs. Light, co-ordinated rooms: ask for one on first floor with balcony overlooking harbour. International menus in contemporary dining room.

KILMALLOCK – Limerick – **712** G 10 🔖 *Ireland*
38 **B2**

▶ Dublin 212 km – Limerick 34 km – Tipperary 32 km
◉ Abbey★ - Collegiate Church★
◉ Lough Gur Interpretive Centre★ **AC**, N : 16 km by R 512 and minor road –
Monasteranenagh Abbey★, N : 24 km by R 512 to Holycross and minor
road W

Flemingstown House 🌾   ≤ 🍴 ✗ P VISA ⓪
Southeast : 4 km on R 512 – ☎ (063) 98 093 – www.flemingstown.com
– info@flemingstown.com – Fax (063) 98 546 – March-October
5 rm ⌂ – ☗€ 70 ☗☗€ 120 **Rest** – (by arrangement) Menu € 45
♦ Creeper clad, extended 19C house in centre of 200 acre working farm. The attractively decorated bedrooms boast countryside vistas and pieces of antique furniture. Satisfying homemade fare served in comfy dining room.

KILMESSAN – Meath – 712 L/M 7   37 **D3**
🚉 Dublin 38 km – Navan 16 km – Trim 11 km

🏨 **The Station House**   🚗 ⓘ ⌨ ⁞ 🛌 🅿 VISA 💳 AE ①
– ℰ (046) 902 52 39 – www.thestationhousehotel.com
– info@thestationhousehotel.com – Fax (046) 902 55 88
20 rm ☷ – ♦ € 76/95 ♦♦ € 120/190   **Rest** – Menu € 20/45 – Carte € 22/60
♦ Former 19C railway station. Bedrooms spread around between station house and converted engine shed! The Signal Suite, the original signal box, now offers four poster comforts. Appealing restaurant using local ingredients.

KILTIMAGH Mayo – Mayo – pop. 1 096   36 **B2**
🚉 Dublin 150 km – Castlebar 17 km – Ballina 22 km – Westport 26 km

🏨 **Park**   🏊 Ⓕ ⌨ 🖐 & rm, 🆔 rest, ⁞ 🛌 🅿 VISA 💳 AE
Swinford Rd, Northeast : 1 km on R 320 – ℰ (094) 937 49 22
– www.parkhotelmayo.com – info@parkhotelmayo.com – Fax (094) 937 49 24
– Closed 25 December
42 rm ☷ – ♦ € 55/90 ♦♦ € 100/150
Rest – Menu € 23/35 – Carte approx. € 47
♦ Spacious hotel – near Marian shrine – boasts contemporary design, from its stylish lounge and bar to its up-to-date bedrooms. Well-equipped gym; hot tubs outside on balcony. Bright elegant restaurant.

KINLOUGH (Cionn Locha) – Leitrim – 712 H 4   37 **C2**
🚉 Dublin 220 km – Ballyshannon 11 km – Sligo 34 km

🍴 **Courthouse** with rm   VISA 💳
Main St – ℰ (071) 984 23 91 – www.thecourthouserest.com
– thecourthouserest@eircom.net – Fax (071) 984 28 24 – Weekends only in winter
4 rm ☷ – ♦ € 45/50 ♦♦ € 80/100
Rest – Italian influences – (dinner only and Sunday lunch) Carte € 27/45
♦ Simple, unassuming, pink-painted former courthouse has terracotta palette and wall-mounted gargoyles. Prominent Italian menus include home-made breads, pasta, desserts.

KINNEGAD (Cionn Átha Gad) – Westmeath – 712 K 7   37 **C3**
🚉 Dublin 61 km – Mullingar 20 km – Tullamore 41 km

🏨 **Hilamar**   ⏏ & rm, 🆔 rest, ⌨ ⁞ 🛌 🅿 VISA 💳 AE ①
Main St – ℰ (044) 939 17 19 – www.hilamarhotel.com – info@hilamarhotel.com
– Fax (044) 939 17 18 – Closed 25 December
45 rm ☷ – ♦ € 79/110 ♦♦ € 99/160   **Rest** – (carvery lunch) Carte € 36
♦ Trendy hotel with relaxed feel. Stylish bedrooms decorated in bright, modern colours, with quality furniture and up-to-date facilities. Flat screens in bar. Pavement terrace. Modern restaurant.

KINSALE – Cork – 712 G 12 – pop. 4 099 📖 Ireland   38 **B3**
🚉 Dublin 286 km – Cork 27 km
🄸 Pier Rd ℰ (021) 4772234, kinsaletio@eircom.ie
🄾 Town ★★ – St Multose Church ★ Y – Kinsale Regional Museum ★ AC Y M1
🄶 Kinsale Harbour ★ (≤ ★ from St Catherine's Anglican Church, Charles
Fort ★). Carbery Coast ★, W : 61 km by R 600

Plan on next page

🏨 **Carlton** ॐ   ≤ 🔥 🚗 🖥 ⊛ 🏊 Ⓕ ⌨ 🖐 & rm, 🆔 ⌨ ⁞ 🛌 🅿 VISA 💳 AE ①
Rathmore Rd, East : 5 km off R 600 – ℰ (021) 470 60 00
– www.carltonkinsalehotel.ie – reservations.kinsale@carlton.ie – Fax (021)
470 60 01 – Closed 23-27 December
89 rm ☷ – ♦ € 210/250 ♦♦ € 270/350
Rest – (dinner only) Carte approx. € 47 **s**
♦ Hotel built partially into side of cliff with well run spa complex and Captain's bar. Contemporary bedrooms; some in main hotel, others linked by covered walkway. Traditional menu served in modern restaurant.

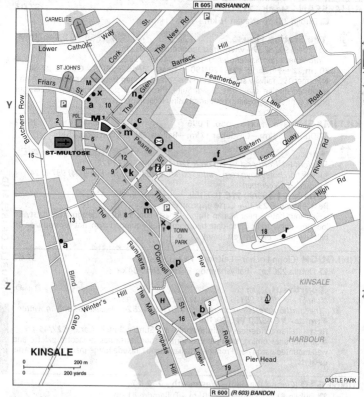

R 605 *INISHANNON*

CARMELITE

Lower Catholic Way

Cork St.

The New Rd

Barrack Hill

Featherbed

ST JOHN'S

Friars St.

Y

M

x

a

n Glen

The

10

c

P

POL.

M 1

m

Pearse

d

6

ST-MULTOSE

f

Eastern

Long Quay

River Rd

15

12

8

k

9

5

The

8

13

m

P

a

Ramparts

Z

O'Connell

m

x

TOWN PARK

p

Pier

KINSALE

Winter's Hill

Gale

Blind

The Mall

H

Compass

St.

16

b 3

HARBOUR

Road

Lower

KINSALE

0   200 m

0   200 yards

Pier Head

19

CASTLE PARK

18

r

High Rd

R 600 *(R 603) BANDON*

 Actons ≤ 🚗 🗄 🖭 ᓀ Ƙ₀ ⑤ 🔟 rest, ℀ ⑲ 🖧 🅿 𝖵𝖨𝖲𝖠 ⓸ 🄰🄴 ⓸

Pier Rd – ℰ *(021) 477 99 00 – www.actonshotelkinsale.com*
– res@actonshotelkinsale.com – Fax (021) 477 22 31
– Closed 4 January - 8 February   Z**p**
73 rm ⌲ – ✦€ 105/130 ✦✦€ 150/200
Rest – (bar lunch Monday-Saturday) Carte € 36/48 **s**

♦ Group owned and business oriented. Smart modern lounge, panelled in warm wood, and well-appointed bedrooms in a classic palette, at their best in two newer wings. Stylish dining room.

Perryville House without rest   ℀ ⑲ 🅿 𝖵𝖨𝖲𝖠 ⓸

Long Quay – ℰ *(021) 477 27 31 – www.perryvillehouse.com*
– sales@perryville.iol.ie – Fax (021) 477 22 98 – 15 April-30 November   Y**f**
26 rm ⌲ – ✦€ 250 ✦✦€ 250/300

♦ Imposing Georgian house facing the harbour. Antiques and lavish bouquets fill the hall and two period lounges. Rooms are spacious and stylish, the service keen and friendly.

1124

Trident ≤ 🏖 🎲 🖼 🕭 rm, ⁇ 🏊 **P** **VISA** **OO** **AE**

World's End, South : ¾ km on R 600 – ℰ (021) 477 9300
– www.tridenthotel.com – info@tridenthotel.com – Fax (021) 474 4173
74 rm – †€ 90/120 ††€ 130/190 – 1 suite
Rest Pier One – Menu € 35 – Carte approx. € 45
Rest Wharf – Carte approx. € 15
♦ At end of the harbour, right by the water's edge. Good-sized bedrooms all have sea view; some have balconies. Executive rooms most recently refurbished, with large bathrooms. Upstairs is the formal Pier One restaurant. Lunchtime carvery and traditional evening menu in nautical but nice Wharf bar.

Blue Haven 🎲 **AC** rest, ⁇ ⁇ **VISA** **OO** **AE** ①

3 Pearse St – ℰ (021) 477 22 09 – www.bluehavenkinsale.com
– info@bluehavenkinsale.com – Fax (021) 477 42 68
– Closed 24-25 December   Yc
17 rm � – †€ 90/140 ††€ 160/230
Rest Blu – (Closed Monday and Tuesday October-February) (dinner only)
Menu € 45 – Carte € 29/48
Rest Blue Haven – Carte € 19/33
♦ Well established hotel in centre of town boasts refurbished public areas and floral bedrooms of varying size, named after wine estates; the largest at the front. Blu serves a traditional British menu. Wood panelled Blue Haven looks like the interior of a yacht, and has small terrace.

Old Bank House without rest 🖼 ⁇ ⁇ **VISA** **OO** **AE**

11 Pearse St – ℰ (021) 477 40 75 – www.oldbankhousekinsale.com
– info@oldbankhousekinsale.com – Fax (021) 477 42 96
– Closed 24-25 December   Yd
18 rm ⊆ – †€ 160/180 ††€ 180/230
♦ Personally and enthusiastically run town house: cosy lounge and comfortable, neatly kept accommodation - bedrooms above the post office are slightly larger.

Harbour Lodge ≤ ⁇ **P** **VISA** **OO** **AE**

Scilly – ℰ (021) 477 23 76 – www.harbourlodge.com – relax@harbourlodge.com
– Fax (021) 477 26 75 – Closed December - 15 January   Zr
9 rm ⊆ – †€ 110/150 ††€ 198/240   **Rest** – Menu € 38 – Carte € 23/38
♦ Modern waterfront house; well kept, with fresh white walls and light carpets. Spacious conservatory and five of the comfortable bedrooms overlook the yachts in Kinsale harbour. Traditional menu offered.

The Old Presbytery without rest ⁇ ⁇ **P** **VISA** **OO**

43 Cork St – ℰ (021) 477 20 27 – www.oldpres.com – info@oldpres.com
– Fax (021) 477 21 66 – February-November   Ya
9 rm ⊆ – †€ 70/120 ††€ 90/170
♦ Tucked away down a side street, a Georgian house run by a husband and wife team. Comfortable, thoughtfully furnished bedrooms in old Irish pine.

Blindgate House without rest 🗂 ⁇ ⁇ **VISA** **OO** **AE**

Blindgate – ℰ (021) 477 78 58 – www.blindgatehouse.com
– info@blindgatehouse.com – Fax (021) 477 78 68
– March-December   Za
11 rm ⊆ – †€ 145/180 ††€ 145/180
♦ Friendly and modern: stylish, clean-lined bedrooms in crisp, light colours, a little front sitting room and smart, wood-floored breakfast room with high backed chairs.

Chart House without rest ⁇ ⁇ **VISA** **OO** **AE** ①

6 Denis Quay – ℰ (021) 477 45 68 – www.charthouse-kinsale.com
– charthouse@eircom.net – Fax (021) 477 79 07   Zb
4 rm ⊆ – †€ 40/50 ††€ 140/170
♦ Elegant, cream-painted Georgian guesthouse with cosy, quaint ambience. William IV dining suite for breakfast. Bedrooms boast antique beds with crisp white linen.

⌂ **Desmond House** without rest   ⚄ ⁽ᵖ⁾ *VISA* ⓪⑩
42 Cork St – ℰ (021) 477 35 35 – www.desmondhousekinsale.com
– desmondhouse@gmail.com   **Yx**
4 rm ⌿ – ♦€70/110 ♦♦€100/140
♦ Small guest house with comfortable lounge and breakfast room. Traditional bed-rooms have period furniture and jacuzzi baths and are named after castles. Friendly owners.

✗✗ **Toddies**   ⌂ *VISA* ⓪⑩ AE
Kinsale Brew Co., The Glen – ℰ (021) 477 77 69 – www.toddies.ie
– toddies@eircom.net – Closed 15 January-16 February and Monday   **Yn**
Rest – (booking essential) Carte €34/53
♦ Delightful terrace leading to lively restaurant set over two floors, with lots modern artwork. Traditional menus; fish dishes are particularly popular. Charming service.

✗✗ **Oz-Haven**   ⌂ P *VISA* ⓪⑩ AE
– ℰ (021) 4700 007 – www.ozhaven.com – info@ozhavon.com
– Closed 25 December, and lunch Monday-Friday   **Yk**
Rest – (dinner only and Sunday lunch) Carte €40/48
♦ Smart modern restaurant boasting bold colours and distinctive lighting – relocated from Ballinclashet. As before, detailed menu displays highly original dishes.

✗ **Max's**   AC *VISA* ⓪⑩ AE
Main St – ℰ (021) 477 24 43
– Closed mid December - 1 March and Tuesday   **Zm**
Rest – Menu €24 (lunch) – Carte €38/54
♦ Unadorned yet intimate restaurant: try light lunches, early evening meal or full à la carte menu. Keenly devised wine list. Friendly service.

✗ **Fishy Fishy Cafe**   ⌂
⊕ *Pier Road – ℰ (021) 4700 04 15 – www.fishyfishy.ie – fishyfishycafe@eircom.net*
– Closed 23-27 December   **Zx**
Rest – Seafood – (lunch only except Tuesday-Friday April-October) (bookings not accepted) Carte €37/42
♦ Friendly, informal and busy: arrive early, be prepared to queue (or the original little 'Fishy' is a 5 minute walk). Good-value seafood, with daily catch on view in display fridges.

🍴 **Dalton's**   P
3 Market St – ℰ (021) 477 8025 – www.kinsalecookingschool.com
– fedalton@eircom.net   **Ym**
Rest – (Closed Sunday; also dinner) (lunch only) Carte €15/25
♦ Brightly-painted town centre pub with cosy, traditional feel, run by eponymous husband and wife team. Mostly seafood menu of wholesome fare attracts loyal local following.

at Barrells Cross Southwest : 5 ¾ km on R 600 - Z – ✉ Kinsale

⌂ **Rivermount House** without rest ⌂   ≤ 🚗 ⚄ ⁽ᵖ⁾ P *VISA* ⓪⑩
Northeast : ¾ km – ℰ (021) 477 80 33 – www.rivermount.com
– info@rivermount.com – Fax (021) 477 82 25 – 15 March -1 November
6 rm ⌿ – ♦€50/90 ♦♦€80/90
♦ A friendly and conscientious couple keep this purpose-built guesthouse in good order. Well-appointed en suite rooms in flowery fabrics overlook the quiet fields.

at Ballinadee West : 12 km by R 600 - Z – ✉ Kinsale

⌂ **Glebe Country House** without rest ⌂   🚗 P *VISA* ⓪⑩
– ℰ (021) 477 82 94 – www.glebecountryhouse.com
– info@glebecountryhouse.com – Fax (021) 477 84 56 – Closed Christmas and New Year
4 rm ⌿ – ♦€60/70 ♦♦€90/110
♦ Creeper-clad Georgian rectory. Handsomely furnished drawing room; well-chosen fabrics and fine wooden beds in pretty rooms, one with french windows on to the garden.

REPUBLIC OF IRELAND

KINVARRA (Cinn Mhara) – **Galway** – **712** F 8

▶ Dublin 228 km – Galway 27 km – Limerick 59 km

Keogh's Bar   🛋 📶 💱 **P** **VISA** **◯◯** **AE**
*Main St – 𝒞 (091) 637 145 – www.kinvara.com/keoghs – keoghsbar@eircom.net
– Fax (091) 637 028 – Closed 25 December*
Rest – Carte € 17/30
◆ Red-hued traditional Irish pub in rural fishing village, with small front lounge, locals' bar and more formal rear dining area. Hearty classics and seafood dominate the menu.

KNIGHTS TOWN – **Kerry** – **712** B 12 – see Valencia Island

---

KNOCK (An Cnoc) – **Mayo** – **712** F 6 📗 *Ireland*

▶ Dublin 212 – Galway 74 – Westport 51
✈ Knock (Connaught) Airport : 𝒞 (094) 9368100, NE : 14½ km by N 17
🛈 Knock Village 𝒞 (094) 9388193 (May-September)
◉ Basilica of our Lady, Queen of Ireland★
◉ Museum of Country Life★★ **AC**, NW : 26 km by R 323, R 321 and N 5
Hotels see : Cong SW : 58 km by N 17, R 331 R 334 and R 345

LAGHY (An Lathaigh) – **Donegal** – **712** H 4 – see Donegal

---

LAHINCH – **Clare** – **712** D 9 📗 *Ireland*

▶ Dublin 260 km – Galway 79 km – Limerick 66 km
🏌 Lahinch, 𝒞 (065) 708 10 03
🏌 Spanish Point Miltown Malbay, 𝒞 (065) 708 42 19
◉ Cliffs of Moher★★★ – Kilfenora (Burren Centre★ **AC**, High Crosses★), NE : 11 km by N 85 and R 481

Vaughan Lodge   🛋 🛗 & rm, 💱 🍴 **P** **VISA** **◯◯** **AE**
*Ennistymon Rd – 𝒞 (065) 708 11 11 – www.vaughanlodge.ie
– info@vaughanlodge.ie – Fax (065) 708 10 11 – April - November*
22 rm 🍽 – †€ 135/175 ††€ 170/300
Rest – (closed Monday) (dinner only) Menu € 47 – Carte € 41/58
◆ Stylish reception area and comfortable lounge and bar offering large array of malts and satellite TV to keep abreast of the golf. Modern bedrooms of a good size; one balcony. Contemporary restaurant decorated with photos of local coastline.

Moy House 🦢   ← 🛋 🐾 💱 **P** **VISA** **◯◯** **AE** **◯**
*Southwest : 4 km on N 67 (Milltown Malbay rd) – 𝒞 (065) 708 28 00
– www.moyhouse.com – moyhouse@eircom.net – Fax (065) 708 25 00 – Closed
January- 13 February*
8 rm 🍽 – †€ 150/270 ††€ 255/295 – 1 suite
Rest – (closed Sunday) (dinner only) (residents only) Menu € 55
◆ Early 19C country house in lovely spot away from town and with delightful views of Lahinch Bay. Genuine country house atmosphere with antiques and curios; charming bedrooms. Stylishly understated dining room.

Greenbrier Inn without rest   & 💱 🍴 **P** **VISA** **◯◯**
*Ennistymon Rd – 𝒞 (065) 708 12 42 – www.greenbrierinn.com – gbrier@indigo.ie
– Fax (065) 708 12 47 – March-November*
14 rm 🍽 – †€ 55/115 ††€ 120/170
◆ Smartly appointed guesthouse with a modern feel. Conservatory-style breakfast room overlooking Lahinch golf course. Well-kept pine furnished bedrooms.

Dough Mor Lodge without rest   🛋 💱 **P** **VISA** **◯◯**
*Station Rd – 𝒞 (065) 708 20 63 – www.doughmorlodge.com
– dough@gofree.indigo.ie – Fax (065) 707 13 84 – March-October*
6 rm 🍽 – †€ 65/75 ††€ 90/130
◆ Attractive, well-kept guesthouse with large front garden, a minute's walk from the town centre. Cosy lounge; Gingham-clad breakfast room. Spacious bedrooms in white or cream.

LEENANE (An Líonán) – **Galway** – **712** C 7 – ⊠ **Clifden** 🏊 *Ireland*　　36 **A3**
- 🄳 Dublin 278 km – Ballina 90 km – Galway 66 km
- ◎ Killary Harbour★
- 🄶 Joyce Country★★ – Lough Nafooey★, SE : 10½ km by R 336 – Aasleagh Falls★, NE : 4 km. Connemara★★★ – Lough Corrib★★, SE : 16 km by R 336 and R 345 – Doo Lough Pass★, NW : 14½ km by N 59 and R 335

🏠　**Delphi Lodge** ⌖　　⟨ 🚗 🌡 🕸 🕸 ⟨🎣 💪 **P** **VISA**
Northwest : 13¼ km by N 59 on Louisburgh rd – ℰ (095) 42 222
– www.delphilodge.ie – stay@delphilodge.ie – Fax (095) 42 296
– Closed 20 December-6 January
12 rm ⊏⊐ – 🛉€ 133 🛉🛉€ 266
Rest (dinner only) (residents only, communal dining, set menu only) Menu € 50
♦ Georgian sporting lodge in a stunning loughside setting with extensive gardens and grounds. Haven for fishermen. Country house feel and simple bedrooms. Communal dining table: fisherman with the day's best catch sits at its head.

LEIGHLINBRIDGE – **Carlow** – **712** L 9 – **pop. 674**　　39 **D2**
- 🄳 Dublin 63 km – Carlow 8 km – Kilkenny 16 km – Athy 22 km

🏘　**Lord Bagenal**　　🖭 🛏 rm, 🕸 🕸 💪 **P** **VISA** **◎◎** **AE** **①**
Main St – ℰ (059) 977 40 00 – www.lordbagenal.com – info@lordbagenal.com
– Fax (059) 972 26 29 – Closed 25-26 December
40 rm ⊏⊐ – 🛉€ 65/120 🛉🛉€ 110/199
Rest *Waterfront* – (Closed Sunday-Tuesday) (dinner only) Menu € 45
Rest *Lord Bagenal* – (carving lunch) Menu € 38 – Carte € 21/48
♦ Impressive hotel on banks of River Barrow; originally a coaching inn, now with vast new extension. Characterful bar with excellent collection of Irish art. Spacious bedrooms. Appealingly formal cooking in the elegant, Roman style Waterside. More informal Lord Bagenal bar and restaurant.

LEIXLIP (Léim an Bhradáin) – **Kildare** – **712** M 7 – **pop. 14 676**　　39 **D1**
- 🄳 Dublin 22 km – Drogheda 63 km – Galway 201 km – Kilkenny 117 km

🏨　**Leixlip House**　　🕸 🕸 💪 **P** **VISA** **◎◎** **AE** **①**
Captain's Hill – ℰ (01) 624 2268 – www.leixliphouse.com
– info@leixliphouse.com – Fax (01) 624 4177 – Closed 25-27 December
19 rm ⊏⊐ – 🛉€ 95/140 🛉🛉€ 130/170
Rest *The Bradaun* – see restaurant listing
♦ Georgian house on town's main street. Well-geared up to banquets. Luxurious soft furnishings and antiques in bedrooms; front-facing rooms with particularly large windows.

🍴🍴　**The Bradaun** – at Leixlip House Hotel　　**P** **VISA** **◎◎** **AE** **①**
Captain's Hill – ℰ (01) 624 2268 – Fax (01) 624 4177 – Closed 24-27 December
Rest – (closed Monday and Bank Holidays) (dinner only and Saturday-Sunday lunch) Menu € 33 – Carte € 39/54
♦ Good size room with high ceilings and large windows commensurate with the age of the property. Simple, fresh décor. Classic dishes with modern and Irish influences.

LEOPARDSTOWN – **Dublin** – **712** N 7 – **see Dublin**

LETTERFRACK (Leitir Fraic) – **Galway** – **712** C 7 🏊 *Ireland*　　36 **A3**
- 🄳 Dublin 304 km – Ballina 111 km – Galway 91 km
- 🄶 Connemara★★★ - Sky Road★★ (⟨★★⟩) – Connemara National Park★ – Kylemore Abbey★, E : 4¾ km by N 59

🏨　**Rosleague Manor** ⌖　　⟨ 🚗 🌡 🕸 🕸 **P** **VISA** **◎◎** **AE**
West : 2½ km on N 59 – ℰ (095) 41 101 – www.rosleague.com
– info@rosleague.com – Fax (095) 41 168 – March - November
20 rm ⊏⊐ – 🛉€ 95/145 🛉🛉€ 85/110
Rest – (dinner only) Menu € 50 **s** – Carte € 38/45 **s**
♦ Imposing, part 19C manor in a secluded, elevated position affording delightful views of Ballynakill harbour and mountains. Antique furnished, old fashioned comfort. Country house-style dining room: distinctive artwork on walls.

LETTERKENNY – Donegal – 712 I 3 – pop. 17 586 ▯ Ireland

- ▶ Dublin 241 km – Londonderry 34 km – Sligo 116 km
- ℹ Neil T Blaney Rd ℰ (074) 9121160, donegaltourism@eircom.net
- ▦ Dunfanaghy, ℰ (074) 913 6335
- ▣ Glenveagh National Park★★ (Gardens★★), NW : 19 ¼ km by R 250, R 251 and R 254 – Grianan of Aileach★★ (≤★★) NE : 28 km by N 13 – Church Hill (Glebe House and Gallery★ **AC**) NW : 16 km by R 250

▭ Radisson SAS   ▥ ⋔ ⬚ ⬚ & rm, Ⓐ rest, ⅍ ☙ ⅍ Ⓟ Ⓥ Ⓜ Ⓐ Ⓞ
Paddy Harte Rd – ℰ (074) 919 44 44 – www.radissonsas.com
– info.letterkenny@radissonsas.com – Fax (074) 919 44 55 – Closed 25 December
114 rm ⌐ – †€ 109/129 ††€ 149/199
Rest – (bar lunch) Menu € 35 – Carte € 32/51
♦ Corporate accommodation in town centre. Bar serves a daily changing menu; rooms are identically appointed: all are clean, modern and spacious. Business class has extras. Dinner in restaurant offers modern international choice.

⌂ Pennsylvania House without rest ⌂   ≤ ⬚ ⋔ ☙ Ⓟ Ⓥ Ⓜ
Curraghleas, Mountain Top, North : 3 ½ km by N 56 – ℰ (074) 912 68 08
– www.accommodationdonegal.com – info@accommodationdonegal.com
– Fax (074) 912 89 05 – Closed 20-27 December
6 rm ⌐ – †€ 55/70 ††€ 110
♦ Comfortable house run by a welcoming couple: rooms in floral fabrics, comfortable lounge decorated with Eastern artefacts, hilltop views towards the Derryveagh Mountains.

⌂ Ballyraine Guesthouse without rest   ⅍ ⬚ Ⓟ Ⓥ Ⓜ
Ramelton Rd, East : 2 ¾ km by N 14 on R 245 – ℰ (074) 912 44 60
– www.homepage.eircom.net/+ballyraineguesthouse
– ballyraineguesthouse@eircom.net – Fax (074) 912 08 51
8 rm ⌐ – †€ 35/50 ††€ 70/85
♦ Purpose-built guest house in the suburbs of this busy market town. Wood floored breakfast room in warm pine. En suite bedrooms are spacious and usefully equipped.

LIMERICK (Luimneach) – Limerick – 712 G 9 – pop. 90 757 ▯ Ireland

- ▶ Dublin 193 km – Cork 93 km
- ✈ Shannon Airport : ℰ (061) 712000, W : 25 ¾ km by N 18 Z
- ℹ Arthur's Quay ℰ (061) 317522 Y, limericktouristoffice@shannondev.ie
- ◉ City★★ - St Mary's Cathedral★ Y – Hunt Museum★★ **AC** Y - Georgian House★ **AC** Z – King John's Castle★ **AC** Y - Limerick Museum★ Z **M2** – John Square★ Z **20** – St John's Cathedral★ Z
- ▣ Bunratty Castle★★ **AC**, W : 12 km by N 18 – Cratloe Wood (≤★) NW : 8 km by N 18 Z. Castleconnell★, E : 11 ¼ km by N 7 - Lough Gur Interpretive Centre★ **AC**, S : 17 ¾ km by R 512 and R 514 Z – Clare Glens★, E : 21 km by N 7 and R 503 Y – Monasteranenagh Abbey★, S : 21 km by N 20 Z

Plan on next page

▭ The Strand   ▥ ⋔ ℒⅰ ⬚ & rm, Ⓐ ⅍ ☙ ⅍ ⌂ Ⓥ Ⓜ Ⓐ Ⓞ
Ennis Rd – ℰ (061) 421 800 – www.strandlimerick.ie – hello@strandlimerick.ie
– Fax (061) 421 866   Y**z**
184 rm ⌐ – †€ 184/224 ††€ 194/234
Rest River Restaurant – (bar lunch) Menu € 45 – Carte € 45/60
♦ Extensive function and leisure facilities. Modern bedrooms come in dark wood and autumnal browns and oranges; Junior suites have balconies. Terrace bar overlooks River Shannon. River restaurant serves mix of traditional and more modern dishes.

▭ Limerick Marriott   ▥ ⋔ ℒⅰ ⬚ & rm, Ⓐ ⅍ ☙ ⅍ Ⓥ Ⓜ Ⓐ
– ℰ (061) 448 700 – www.limerickmarriott.ie – reservations@limerickmarriott.ie
– Fax (061) 448 701 – Closed 25 December   Z**c**
94 rm ⌐ – †€ 170 ††€ 195
Rest – (closed Monday and Tuesday lunch, Sunday and Monday dinner)
Menu € 33 (lunch) – Carte € 43/59
♦ In heart of city centre; bedrooms are modern and stylish, some with balconies. Liszt lounge and Savoy bar reflect the history of the old Savoy Theatre. Contemporary restaurant.

REPUBLIC OF IRELAND

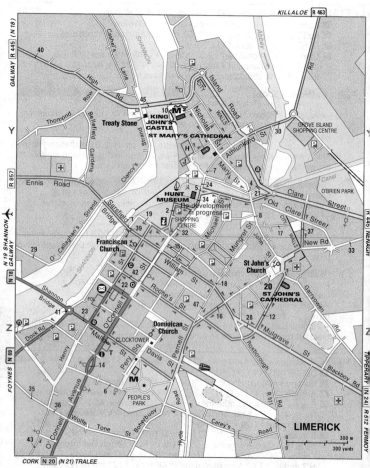

KILLALOE R 463

GALWAY R 445 (N 18)

R 857

N 19 SHANNON GALWAY / N 18

FOYNES N 69

GROVE ISLAND SHOPPING CENTRE

O'BRIEN PARK

H 445 / NENAGH

TIPPERARY (N 24) / R 512 FERMOY

Y

Z

Treaty Stone

KING JOHN'S CASTLE

ST MARY'S CATHEDRAL

HUNT MUSEUM

Re-development in progress

SHOPPING CENTRE

Franciscan Church

St John's Church

ST JOHN'S CATHEDRAL

Dominican Church

CLOCKTOWER

PEOPLE'S PARK

LIMERICK

300 m

300 yards

CORK N 20 (N 21) TRALEE

Arthur Quay	**Y** 2	Grove Island Shopping	Roches St	**Z**
Arthur Quay Shopping		Centre	**Y**	Rutland St	**Y** 34
Centre	**Y**	High St	**Y** 18	St Alphonsus St	**Z** 35
Baal's Bridge	**Y** 4	Honan's Quay	**Y** 19	St Gerard St	**Z** 36
Bank Pl.	**Y** 5	John Square	**Z** 20	St Lelia St	**YZ** 37
Barrington St	**Z** 6	Lock Quay	**Y** 21	Sarfield St	**Y** 39
Bridge St	**Y** 7	Lower Cecil St	**Z** 22	Sexton St North	**Y** 40
Broad St	**Y** 8	Lower Mallow St	**Z** 23	Shannonside
Castle St	**Y** 10	Mathew Bridge	**Y** 24	Roundabout	**Z** 41
Cathedral Pl.	**Z** 12	Newtown Mahon	**Z** 28	Shannon St	**Z** 42
Charlotte's Quay	**Y** 13	North Circular Rd	**Z** 29	South Circular Rd	**Z** 43
Cruises St	**Z** 15	O'Connell St	**Z**	The Crescent	**Z** 14
Gerald Griffen		O'Dwyer Bridge	**Y** 30	Thomond Bridge	**Y** 45
St	**Z** 16	Patrick St	**YZ** 32	Wickham St	**Z** 47
Grattan St	**Y** 17	Penniwell Rd	**Z** 33	William St	**Z**

Absolutehotel.com   ⬡ ⬢ 🌐 📶 🛗 AC ✂ rm, 📡 🚿 🅿 🚗 _VISA_ ⑩⓪ AE

Sir Harry's Mall – ℰ (061) 463 600 – www.absolutehotel.com
– info@absolutehotel.com – Fax (061) 463 601   Y**a**

99 rm – 🛏€ 95 🛏🛏€ 189, ⌷ €12.50   **Rest** – Carte € 33/49 **s**

♦ Stylish, modern hotel and spa on outskirts of city centre; designed like an old mill
to reflect the area's industrial heritage. Clever use of space in light-coloured bedrooms. Restaurant serves traditional menu and overlooks river.

🏨 Radisson SAS
☒ 🏢 🛋 🍸 🍽 👥 ☒ rm, 🅰 rest, 🍸 📶 🚿 ᴘ

Ennis Rd, Northwest : 6½ km on N 18 – ℰ *(061) 456 200* 💳 🆚 🆎 ⓪
– www.limerick.radissonsas.com – sales.limerick@radissonsas.com
– Fax (061) 327 418
152 rm ☕ *–* †€ 115/125 ††€ 135/165 *– 2 suites*
Rest *Porters* – (carvery lunch) Menu € 30 **s** – Carte € 31/48 **s**
♦ Modern hotel with tastefully used chrome and wood interiors. Well-equipped conference rooms and a leisure centre which includes tennis court. Smart, state-of-the-art bedrooms. Informal Porters restaurant with traditional menus.

🏨 The Clarion
≪ ☒ 🏢 🛋 🏋 ☒ rm, 🅰 🍸 📞 🚿 ᴘ 💳 🆚 🆎

Steamboat Quay – ℰ *(061) 444 100 – www.clarionlimerick.com*
– info@clarionhotellimerick.com – Fax (061) 444 101
– Closed 24-26 December Zn
155 rm ☕ *–* †€ 130/170 ††€ 145/185 *– 3 suites*
Rest *Sinergie* – Menu € 27/45 **s** – Carte € 35/48 **s**
♦ Impressive newly built hotel by the River Shannon with excellent views of the city. Contemporary décor throughout and great views from the pool. Well-appointed, modern rooms. Formal dining room with modern menu.

🏨 The George
👥 ☒ rm, 🍸 📶 💳 🆚 🆎

O'Connell St – ℰ *(061) 460 400 – www.thegeorgeboutiquehotel.com*
– thegeorgeboutique@lynchhotels.com – Fax (061) 460 410 Zo
125 rm *–* †€ 99/179 ††€ 149/179, ☕ € 10
Rest – (light lunch) Menu € 20 – Carte € 21/43
♦ Boutique hotel with modern low lit reception and spacious, contemporary bedrooms in greens and pinks, with light wood furniture. Restaurant has floor to ceiling windows overlooking the street. Tasty Italian cooking.

🍴🍴 Brûlées
💳 🆚 🆎

Corner Mallow/Henry St – ℰ *(061) 319 931 – brulees@eircom.net – Closed*
Sunday and Monday, and lunch Tuesday, Wednesday and Saturday Ze
Rest – Carte € 35/48
♦ Situated on the ground floor of a Georgian building. Three seating levels give spacious feel. Modern Irish cooking with classic base: good emphasis on local produce.

🍴🍴 Market Square Brasserie
🔅 💳 🆚 🆎

74 O'Connel St – ℰ *(061) 316 311 – abranigan@eircom.net*
– Closed 24 December-3 January, Sunday and Monday Zi
Rest – (dinner only) (booking essential) Menu € 50 – Carte € 35/50
♦ Atmospheric restaurant with cosy, clothed tables, candles and flowers. Extensive, seasonally-changing menu; beef is popular and desserts particularly good. Hearty portions.

LISCANNOR (Lios Ceannúir) – **Clare** – **712** D 9 ▌ *Ireland* 38 **B1**
  ◨ Dublin 272 km – Ennistimmon 9 km – Limerick 72 km
  ⬚ Cliffs of Moher★★★, NW : 8 km by R 478 – Kilfenora (Burren Centre★ AC, High Crosses★), NE : 18 km by R 478, N 67 and R 481

🏠 Vaughan's Anchor Inn
🍸 ᴘ 💳 🆚

Main Street – ℰ *(065) 708 1548 – www.vaughans.ie – Fax (065) 706 8977*
– Closed 25 December
Rest – Seafood – Carte € 24/39
♦ Lively, characterful family-run pub in picturesque fishing village near Cliffs of Moher. Emphasis on seafood, with pub favourites at lunch; more elaborate meals in the evenings.

LISDOONVARNA – **Clare** – **712** E 8 ▌ *Ireland* 38 **B1**
  ◨ Dublin 268 km – Galway 63 km – Limerick 75 km
  ⬚ The Burren★★ (Cliffs of Moher★★★, Scenic Route★★, Aillwee Cave★ AC (Waterfall★★), Corcomroe Abbey★, Kilfenora Crosses★)

Ballinalacken Castle Country House

Coast Rd, Northwest : 4 ¾ km by N 67 (Doolin rd) on R 477
– ℰ (065) 707 40 25 – www.ballinalackencastle.com
– ballinalackencastle@eircom.net – Fax (065) 707 40 25 – 19 April-October
11 rm ☑ – ♦€ 150/200 ♦♦€ 150/200 – 1 suite
Rest – (closed Tuesday) (dinner only) Carte € 37/48
♦ 1840's house with purpose-built extension overlooked by imposing ruin of a 15C castle. Characterful communal areas in traditional style. Large, antique furnished bedrooms. Diners greeted by open fireplace and linen-clad tables.

Sheedy's Country House

Sulphir Hill – ℰ (065) 707 40 26 – www.sheedys.com – info@sheedys.com
– Fax (065) 707 45 55 – Easter-October
11 rm ☑ – ♦€ 105/150 ♦♦€ 150/200
Rest The Restaurant – see restaurant listing
♦ Classic late 19C mustard painted property in an elevated position. Public areas centre around the bright, wicker furnished sun lounge. Neat, well-equipped bedrooms.

Kincora House

– ℰ (065) 707 43 00 – www.kincorahotel.ie – kincorahotel@eircom.net
– Fax (065) 707 44 90 – April-October
14 rm ☑ – ♦€ 50/100 ♦♦€ 90/130
Rest – (closed Tuesday dinner) Carte € 28/36 **s**
♦ Charming hotel; oldest part dating back to 1860. Attractive walled garden to the rear. Comfy sitting room with plenty of local books. Light, airy bedrooms. Spacious rustic bar with open fires and bar menu.

Woodhaven without rest

Doolin Coast Rd, West : 1½ km by N 67 (Doolin rd) off R 478 – ℰ (065) 707 40 17
– woodhavenbb@eircom.net – Closed Christmas week
5 rm ☑ – ♦€ 47/51 ♦♦€ 64/70
♦ Whitewashed house on a country lane with pretty gardens. Traditionally styled interior decoration to the lounge and breakfast room. Simple bedrooms with a homely feel.

XX The Restaurant – at Sheedy's Country House Hotel

Sulphir Hill – ℰ (065) 707 40 26 – www.sheedys.com – info@sheedys.com
– Fax (065) 707 45 55 – Easter-October
Rest – (dinner only) (booking essential for non-residents) Carte € 36/52 **s**
♦ Attractive, comfortable restaurant at the front of the building. Linen covered tables and smart place settings. Interesting menus using freshest, local produce.

LISMORE (Lios Mór) – Waterford – 712 I 11   39 **C2**

▶ Dublin 227 km – Cork 56 km – Fermoy 26 km

Lismore House

Main St – ℰ (058) 72 966 – www.lismorehousehotel.com
– info@lismorehousehotel.com – Fax (058) 53 068 – Closed 25-26 December
29 rm – ♦€ 140/160 ♦♦€ 150/160, ☑ € 12.50
Rest – (bar lunch) Carte € 28/47
♦ Georgian house with purpose built rear. Bedrooms are all brand new with up-to-date facilities including plasmas and playstations; several overlook the Millennium Gardens. Intimate dining room.

Northgrove without rest

Tourtane, West : 1½ km by N 72 on Ballyduff rd – ℰ (058) 54 325
– www.lismorebedandbreakfast.com – johnhoward1@eircom.net
– March-October
3 rm ☑ – ♦€ 45/55 ♦♦€ 70/80
♦ Modern guesthouse providing a keenly priced and accessible resting place for visitors to this historic town. Good sized, pine furnished bedrooms with colourful décor.

▶ Dublin 270 km – Killarney 54 km – Limerick 75 km – Tralee 27 km
🛈 St John's Church ✆ (068) 22590 (June-September),
tourisminfo@shannon-dev.ie
◉ Ardfert★ **AC**, SW : 32 km by N 69 and minor roads via Abbeydorney –
Banna Strand★, SW : 35 km by N 69 and minor roads via Abbeydorney –
Carrigafoyle Castle★, N : 17 km by R 552 and minor road – Glin Castle★
AC, N : 24 km by N 69 – Rattoo Round Tower★, W : 19 km by R 553, R 554
and R 551

🏠 **Allo's Bar** with rm   🍴 😤 **VISA 🆀 AE**
41 Church St, Listowel – ✆ (068) 22 880 – allos@eircom.net – Fax (068) 22 803
– Closed Sunday-Monday
3 rm – †€ 50/60 **††**€ 80/100   **Rest** – (booking essential) Carte € 17/45
♦ Brightly-painted pub with covered terrace and cosy, citrus snug; once a handy
hidey-hole for the local priest to sup a swift drink. Classic menu has international
touches. Comfortable, antique-furnished bedrooms - but no breakfast served.

LITTLE ISLAND (An tOileán Beag) – **Cork** – 712 G/H 12 – see Cork

LONGFORD – Longford – 712 I 6   37 **C3**

▶ Dublin 124 km – Drogheda 120 km – Galway 112 km – Limerick 175 km
🛈 Market Square ✆ (043) 42577, info@longfordtourism.com

🏠 **Viewmount House** ⟡   🍴 😤 **P. VISA 🆀 AE**
Dublin Rd, Southeast : 1½ km by R 393 – ✆ (043) 41 919
– www.viewmounthouse.com – info@viewmounthouse.com – Fax (043) 42 906
13 rm ⌂ – **†**€ 70/85 **††**€ 120/150
Rest – (dinner only and Sunday lunch) Menu € 53
♦ Impressive Georgian house in four acres; breakfast room has attractive vaulted ceiling, lounge reached by fine staircase. Rooms boast antique beds and period furniture.

LUCAN (Leamhcán) – **Dublin** – 712 M 7 – see Dublin

MACROOM (Maigh Chromtha) – **Cork** – 712 F 12 – pop. 3 553   38 **B3**

▶ Dublin 299 km – Cork 40 km – Killarney 48 km
🏌 Lackaduve, ✆ (026) 41 072

🏨 **Castle**   🍴 **Ƒδ 🍸 &. rm, 🎖 😤 🎶 ⚗ P. VISA 🆀 AE**
Main St – ✆ (026) 41 074 – www.castlehotel.ie – castlehotel@eircom.net
– Fax (026) 41 505 – Closed 24-28 December
58 rm ⌂ – **†**€ 90/115 **††**€ 160/190
Rest B's – Menu € 27/47
♦ A traditional hotel with gabled windows located in the town centre. Boasts a stylish
leisure complex and neat, comfortable bedrooms. Informal B's.

MALAHIDE (Mullach Íde) – **Fingal** – 712 N 7 – pop. 14 937 📖 *Ireland*   39 **D1**

▶ Dublin 14 km – Drogheda 38 km
🏌 Beechwood The Grange, ✆ (01) 846 1611
◉ Castle★★
◉ Newbridge House★ **AC**, N : 8 km by R 106, M1 and minor road

🍴🍴🍴 **Bon Appétit** (Oliver Dunne)   **🎖 VISA 🆀 AE ⓞ**
ℰℬ *(First Floor) No.9 St James Terrace – ✆ (01) 845 0314 – www.bonappetit.ie*
– info@bonappetit.ie – Fax (01) 845 5365
– Closed 24-26 December, Sunday and Monday
Rest – French – (dinner only and Friday lunch) – (booking essential)
Menu € 38/75
Spec. Breast and confit of quail, red onion, ventrèche and balsamic. Halibut
with fennel purée, leeks and crab velouté. Chocolate tart with vanilla ice
cream.
♦ Set in delightful converted Georgian terrace. Sumptuous bar; formally set dining
room with fine china and linen. Cooking uses classic combinations and has a French
accent.

REPUBLIC OF IRELAND

REPUBLIC OF IRELAND

XX **Cruzzo** ← 🏛 AK P. VISA 🐵 AE
Marina Village – ℰ (01) 845 0599 – www.cruzzo.ie – info@cruzzo.ie – Fax (01) 845 0602 – Closed 25-26 December, 1 January, Good Friday and Monday lunch except Bank Holidays
Rest – Menu € 29 (lunch) – Carte € 43/60
♦ Modern glass and designer furnishings in a striking marina restaurant above the water. Pleasantly distinctive ground-floor bar for lighter dishes. Tasty, modern cuisine.

XX **Siam Thai** AK VISA 🐵 AE
1 The Green, off Strand St – ℰ (01) 845 4698 – www.siamthai.ie – siammalahide@eircom.net – Fax (01) 845 4489 – Closed 25-26 December and Good Friday
Rest – Thai – (booking essential) Menu € 15/35 – Carte € 29/44
♦ Centrally located restaurant with piano bar providing a light feel. Immaculately set tables and ornate, carved chairs. Richly authentic Thai cuisine, freshly prepared.

XX **Jaipur** AK VISA 🐵 AE
5 St James Terrace – ℰ (01) 845 5455 – www.jaipur.ie – info@jaipur.ie – Fax (01) 845 5456 – Closed 25 December
Rest – Indian – (dinner only) Carte approx. € 30
♦ Friendly basement restaurant in impressive Georgian terraced parade. Well-run by efficient, welcoming staff. Simple but lively modern décor. Contemporary Indian dishes.

XX **Cafe Bon** AK VISA 🐵 AE ①
(basement) No.9 St James Terrace – ℰ (01) 845 0314 – www.bonappetit.ie – info@bonappetit.ie – Fax (01) 835 5365 – Closed 24-26 December
Rest – Bistro – (dinner only and Sunday lunch) (booking essential) Menu € 29 **s** – Carte € 29/46 **s**
♦ In basement of Georgian terraced house - a popular alternative to the more formal 'Bon Appetit' upstairs - serving classical bistro dishes such as moules or steak frites.

MALLOW – Cork – 712 F 11 – pop. 10 241 ▌ *Ireland*   38 **B2**
🔁 Dublin 240 km – Cork 34 km – Killarney 64 km – Limerick 66 km
🏌 Ballyellis, ℰ (022) 21 145
◎ Town ★ – St James' Church ★
🟢 Annes Grove Gardens ★, E : 17 ¾ km by N 72 and minor rd – Buttevant Friary ★, N : 11 ¼ km by N 20 – Doneraile Wildlife Park ★ AC, NE : 9 ½ km by N 20 and R 581 – Kanturk ★ (Castle ★), W : 16 km by N 72 and R 576

🏛🏛 **Longueville House** 🕭 ← 🚗 🕭 ⚲ 🞉 🔥 P. VISA 🐵 AE
West : 5 ½ km by N 72 – ℰ (022) 47 156 – www.longuevillehouse.ie – info@longuevillehouse.ie – Fax (022) 47 459 – Closed 4 January-10 March
20 rm ☑ – †€ 110/200 ††€ 235/260
Rest Presidents – (dinner only) (booking essential) Menu € 65
♦ Part Georgian manor; exudes history from oak trees planted in formation of battle lines at Waterloo and views of Dromineen Castle to richly ornate, antique-filled bedrooms. Restaurant offers gourmet cuisine.

MAYNOOTH – Kildare – 712 M 7 – pop. 10 715 ▌ *Ireland*   39 **D1**
🔁 Dublin 24 km
🟢 Castletown House ★★ AC, SE : 6 ½ km by R 405

🏛🏛 **Glenroyal** 🔲 🕭 ℆ 🖃 🕭 rm, AK rest, 🞉 🔥 P. VISA 🐵 AE ①
Straffan Rd – ℰ (01) 629 0909 – www.glenroyal.ie – info@glenroyal.ie – Fax (01) 629 0919 – Closed 25 December
113 rm ☑ – †€ 79/115 ††€ 89/125
Rest Bistro – (dinner only carvery lunch) Carte € 28/42
Rest Lemongrass – Asian – Carte € 21/39
♦ Adjacent to shopping centre, ideal for conferences and weddings. Rooms are furnished in smart fabrics with good quality furniture. Informal bistro. Authentic Asian menus at Lemongrass.

MILLSTREET – Waterford – **712** I 11 – see Cappoquin

MOHILL – Leitrim – **712** I 6
39 C2

▶ Dublin 98 km – Carrick-on-Shannon 11 km – Cavan 41 km – Castlerea 44 km

🏠 **Lough Rynn Castle** ⊗   🚗 🕭 ㅎ rm, 🔟 🖋 🙌 🐆 🄿 VISA ⚙ AE
East : 4 km by R 201 and Drumlish rd – ℰ *(071) 963 27 00 – www.loughrynn.ie*
– enquiries@loughrynn.ie – Fax (071) 963 27 10
40 rm – †€ 155/255 ††€ 195/255, ⊡ €14 – 2 suites
Rest *The Sandstone* – (dinner only and Sunday lunch) Menu € 42
– Carte € 46/68
♦ Extended 18C house on large estate. Bedrooms in main house and converted stables have warm décor and a high level of facilities. Baronial Hall features huge original fireplace. French influenced menus served in formal, intimate dining room.

MONAGHAN – Monaghan – **712** L 5 – pop. 6 710
37 D2

▶ Dublin 133 km – Belfast 69 km – Drogheda 87 km – Dundalk 35 km
– Londonderry 120 km
🄸 Clones Rd ℰ *(047) 81122 (April-October)*

🏠 **Four Seasons**   🚗 🔟 🕭 *L*ᵟ ㅎ rm, 🔟 rest, 🖋 🙌 🐆 🄿 VISA ⚙ AE
Coolshannagh, North : 1½ km on N 2 – ℰ *(047) 81 888 – www.4seasonshotel.ie*
– info@4seasonshotel.ie – Fax (047) 83 131 – Closed 25 December
59 rm ⊡ – †€ 65/165 ††€ 130/198
Rest *Avenue* – (Closed Friday, Saturday and lunch Sunday) Menu € 30/40 **s**
– Carte € 27/44 **s**
Rest *The Range* – Menu € 30/35 **s** – Carte € 24/42 **s**
♦ A hotel which offers a blend of the traditional and the modern. Bedrooms are in uniform style and there is an atmospheric pub. Avenue offers modern dining. The Range has a farmhouse feel with beams and dressers.

at Glaslough Northeast : 9½ km by N 12 on R 185 – ⊠ Monaghan

🏠 **The Hunting Lodge at Castle Leslie**   🚗 🕭 🤏 🚲 🐎 🗣 🖋
– ℰ *(047) 88 100 – www.castleleslie.com*   🐆 🄿 VISA ⚙ AE
– info@castleleslie.com – Fax (047) 88 256
29 rm – †€ 145/165 ††€ 200/240 – 1 suite
Rest *Snaffles* – Menu € 47 (dinner) – Carte € 31/55
♦ Estate set in 1000 acres, with 55 horses and a large indoor arena; contemporary bedrooms have balconies which overlook equestrian centre. The Castle now operates a member's club. Snaffles mezzanine brasserie has open kitchen and serves Mediterranean meets Irish cooking.

MONKSTOWN (Baile na Mhanaigh) – Cork – **712** G/H 12
38 B3

▶ Dublin 257 km – Cork 14 km – Waterford 120 km
🄸 Parkgarriffe, ℰ *(021) 484 1376*

🏠 **The Bosun**   ⬕ 🕭 🗣 🔟 rest, 🖋 🙌 VISA ⚙ AE ①
The Pier – ℰ *(021) 484 21 72 – www.thebosun.ie – info@thebosun.ie – Fax (021)*
484 20 08 – Closed 24-26 December and Good Friday
15 rm ⊡ – †€ 73 ††€ 125   **Rest** – Menu € 35/55 – Carte € 26/50
♦ After a walk along the waterway, unwind in the cosy environment of this quayside hotel. There is a private entrance for the bedrooms which are neatly and simply furnished. Seaside location reflected in restaurant menus.

MULLINGAR – Westmeath – **712** J/K 7 – pop. 18 416 🛈 *Ireland*
37 C3

▶ Dublin 79 km – Drogheda 58 km
🄸 Dublin Rd ℰ *(0449) 348650*
🄶 Belvedere House and Gardens★ **AC**, S : 5½ km by N 52. Fore Abbey★, NE : 27¼ km by R 394 – Multyfarnham Franciscan Friary★, N : 12¾ km by N 4 – Tullynally★ **AC**, N : 21 km by N 4 and R 394

REPUBLIC OF IRELAND

Mullingar Park
🔲 ⊛ 🏠 ⅃♠ 🍴 ⅃ rm, AC rest, ⅍ ⁇ 🏊 P VISA ⁇ AE
Dublin Rd, East : 2½ km on Dublin Rd (N 4) – ℘ (044) 933 7500
– www.mullingarparkhotel.com – info@mullingarparkhotel.com – Fax (044)
933 5937 – Closed 25-26 December
94 rm ⊇ – ♦€ 90/150 ♦♦€ 140/180 – 1 suite
Rest – (buffet lunch) Menu € 35 – Carte € 34/47 **s**
♦ Spacious modern hotel with a strong appeal to business and leisure travellers: there's a hydrotherapy pool and host of treatment rooms. Airy, light bedrooms with mod cons. Smart, airy restaurant with international menus.

Marlinstown Court without rest
🛏 ⅍ ⁇ P VISA ⁇
Dublin Rd, East : 2½ km on Dublin Rd (N 4) – ℘ (044) 934 00 53
– www.marlinstowncourt.com – marlinstownct@eircom.net – Fax (044) 934 00 57
– Closed 23-28 December
5 rm ⊇ – ♦€ 45/50 ♦♦€ 75/85
♦ Clean, tidy guesthouse close to junction with N4. Modern rear extension. Light and airy pine-floored lounge and breakfast room overlooking garden. Brightly furnished bedrooms.

Hilltop Country House without rest
🛏 ⅍ P
Delvin Rd, Rathconnell, Northeast : 4 km by N 52 – ℘ (044) 9348 958
– www.hilltopcountryhouse.com – hilltopcountryhouse@eircom.net
– March-November
4 rm ⊇ – ♦€ 50 ♦♦€ 80
♦ Chalet styled house with attractive gardens. Reception and lounge areas cheered by paintings. Good Irish breakfast served. Snug, homely rooms with pleasant views.

MULRANNY – Mayo – 712 C 6
36 **A2**
▣ Dublin 270 km – Castlebar 35 km – Westport 29 km

Park Inn
⩘ 🚗 🔲 🏠 ⅃♠ 🍴 ⅃ rm, 🚶 AC rest, ⅍ P VISA ⁇
on N 59 – ℘ (098) 36 000 – www.parkinnmulranny.ie – info@parkinnmulranny.ie
– Fax (098) 36 899 – Closed 4-30 January
39 rm ⊇ – ♦€ 75/120 ♦♦€ 150/240 – 21 suites
Rest Nephin – see restaurant listing
Rest Waterfront Bistro – (bar lunch Monday-Saturday) Carte € 25/36
♦ Purpose-built business oriented hotel behind 19C façade: lovely Clew Bay views. Impressive leisure and conference facilities. Airy rooms with slightly minimalist interiors. Waterfront Bistro has informal, relaxing ambience.

Nephin – at Park Inn Hotel
⩘ AC ⅍ P
on N 59 – ℘ (098) 36 000 – www.parkinnmulranny.ie – info@parkinnmulranny.ie
– Fax (098) 36 899 – Closed 4-30 January
Rest – (dinner only) Menu € 49 – Carte € 47/70
♦ Large, lively restaurant with fine southerly views. Modern, intricately presented cooking offers interesting combinations based around well sourced, quality ingredients.

NAAS – Kildare – 712 L/M 8 – pop. 20 044 🔲 Ireland
39 **D1**
▣ Dublin 30 km – Kilkenny 83 km – Tullamore 85 km
🏌 Kerdiffstown Naas, ℘ (045) 874 644
🔲 Russborough ★★★ **AC**, S : 16 km by R 410 and minor road – Castletown House ★★ **AC**, NE : 24 km by R 407 and R 403

Killashee House H. & Villa Spa ♨
🛏 🔲 ⊛ 🏠 ⅃♠ 🍴
South : 1½ km on R 448 (Kilcullen ⅃ rm, AC rest, ⅍ ⁇ 🏊 P VISA ⁇ AE
Rd) – ℘ (045) 879 277 – www.killasheehouse.com
– reservations@killasheehouse.com – Fax (045) 879 266 – Closed 24-26 December
129 rm ⊇ – ♦€ 150/250 ♦♦€ 160/325 – 12 suites
Rest Turners – (dinner only and Sunday lunch) Menu € 60
Rest Nun's Kitchen – Carte € 22/35
♦ Imposing part 1860s hunting lodge in acres of parkland. Rooms in the original house are most characterful: French antique furniture, original panelling and fireplaces. Elegant Turners overlooking garden. Informal Nun's Kitchen.

NAVAN – Meath – 712 L 7 – pop. 24 851 ▮ *Ireland* 37 **D3**

D Dublin 48 km – Drogheda 26 km – Dundalk 51 km
🏌 Moor Park Mooretown, 𝒞 (046) 27 661
🏇 Royal Tara Bellinter, 𝒞 (046) 902 5244
🔘 Brú na Bóinne : Newgrange★★★ **AC**, Knowth★, E : 16 km by minor road to Donore – Bective Abbey★, S : 6½ km by R 161 – Tara★ **AC**, S : 8 km by N 3. Kells★ (Round Tower and High Crosses★★, St Columba's House★), NW : by N 3 – Trim★ (castle★★), SW : 12¾ km by R 161

🏨 **Newgrange** 🏮 &. rm, 🔲 rest, 𝒮 ⟨👤⟩ 🔏 **P** 𝗩𝗜𝗦𝗔 ⓶ ⒶⒺ
Bridge St – 𝒞 (046) 907 41 00 – www.newgrangehotel.ie
– info@newgrangehotel.ie – Fax (046) 907 39 77 – Closed 25 December
62 rm 🖙 – ♦€ 110 ♦♦€ 160
Rest – (carvery lunch) Menu € 25 – Carte € 22/42 **s**
♦ Warm-toned, well-fitted modern rooms and an inviting, traditionally styled bar, plus ample meeting space, make this town centre hotel a popular function venue. Smart, bright brasserie

🏠 **Ma Dwyers** without rest 𝒮 ⟨👤⟩ **P** 𝗩𝗜𝗦𝗔 ⓶ ⒶⒺ ⓞ
Dublin Rd, South : 1¼ km on N 3 – 𝒞 (046) 907 79 92 – Fax (046) 907 79 95
9 rm 🖙 – ♦€ 60 ♦♦€ 100
♦ Yellow-painted, mock-Georgian house; comfortable guest lounge, modern breakfast room. Hospitality trays in equally bright, simple bedrooms.

🏠 **Killyon** without rest 𝒮 ⟨👤⟩ **P** 𝗩𝗜𝗦𝗔 ⓶ ⒶⒺ ⓞ
Dublin Rd, South : 1½ km on N 3 – 𝒞 (046) 907 12 24
– www.killyonguesthouse.ie – info@killyonguesthouse.ie – Fax (046) 907 27 66
– Closed 24-26 December
6 rm 🖙 – ♦€ 45/55 ♦♦€ 80
♦ Very good value, comfortable guesthouse, overlooking the river Boyne, run by husband and wife team. Bedrooms are individually decorated. Home baking and good breakfast choice.

> If breakfast is included the 🖙 symbol appears after the number of rooms.

NENAGH – 712 H 9 – pop. 7 751 ▮ *Ireland* 39 **C2**

D Dublin 154 km – Galway 101 km – Limerick 42 km
🛈 Pearse St 𝒞 (067) 31610 (mid May-Nov),
touristofficenenagh@shannondevelopments.ie
🏌 Nenagh Beechwood, 𝒞 (067) 31 476
◎ Castle★

🏨 **Abbey Court** 🔲 〰 🛁 🏮 &. rm, 𝒮 ⟨👤⟩ 🔏 **P** 𝗩𝗜𝗦𝗔 ⓶ ⒶⒺ ⓞ
Dublin Rd, East :½ km – 𝒞 (067) 41 111 – www.abbeycourt.ie
– info@abbeycourt.ie – Fax (067) 41 022 – Closed 23-27 December
82 rm 🖙 – ♦€ 105/115 ♦♦€ 180/240
Rest – (carvery lunch) Menu € 43 – Carte approx. € 53 **s**
♦ A castellated façade, clock tower and arched windows add a historical theme to a modern hotel. Fitness club offers all amenities including hair salon. Modern bedrooms. Wooden statue of monk distinguishes beamed dining room.

NEWCASTLE – 712 M 8 39 **D1**

D Dublin 16 km – Tallaght 9 km – Rathmines 14 km

🍽🍽 **La Serre** 🔲 🔲 **P** 𝗩𝗜𝗦𝗔 ⓶ ⒶⒺ
The Village at Lyons, Northwest : 3½ km by Athgoe Rd – 𝒞 (01) 630 3500
– www.villageatlyons.com – info@villageatlyons.com – Fax (01) 630 35 05
– Closed Monday and Tuesday
Rest – Menu € 35 (lunch) – Carte € 58/76
♦ Delightful restaurant in 17C Turner designed conservatory, with rustic courtyard for outdoor dining. Emphasis is on simplicity, with fish pies, steak and chips or oysters.

NEWMARKET-ON-FERGUS (Cora Chaitlín) – **Clare** – **712** F 7   38 **B2**
– pop. 1 542 ▯ *Ireland*
> ▣ Dublin 219 km – Ennis 13 km – Limerick 24 km
> ▤ Dromoland Castle, ℰ (061) 368 444
> ▣ Bunratty Castle★★ **AC**, S : 10 km by N 18 – Craggaunowen Centre★ **AC**,
> NE : 15 km by minor road towards Moymore – Knappogue Castle★ **AC**,
> NE : 12 km N 18 and minor roads via Quin – Quin Friary★ **AC**, N : 10 km by
> N 18 and minor road to Quin

▮▮▮ **Dromoland Castle** ⌖   ≤ 𝄢 ⵀ ⵄ ☞ ⊡ ⓪ ⍟ ⑤ ⚖ 𝄢 ⚷ 🅟
Northwest : 2½ km – ℰ *(061) 368 144 – www.dromoland.ie*   𝗩𝗜𝗦𝗔 ⓶⓪ 𝗔𝗘 ⓪
– sales@dromoland.ie – Fax (061) 363 355 – Closed 25-26 December
93 rm – ♥€ 238/442 ♥♥€ 238/442, ⌐ €25 – 5 suites
Rest *Earl of Thomond* – (dinner only and Sunday lunch) Menu € 68
– Carte € 61/73
Rest *Fig Tree* – (bar lunch) Carte € 26/53
♦ Restored 16C castle with 375 acres of woodland and golf course. Sumptuous rooms
with plenty of thoughtful extras. Waterford crystal chandeliers and gilded mirrors in the
Earl of Thormond restaurant. More informal style in the Fig Tree, popular with golfers.

NEWPORT – **Mayo** – **712** D 6 ▯ *Ireland*   36 **A2**
> ▣ Dublin 264 km – Ballina 59 km – Galway 96 km
> ▤ James St, Westport ℰ (098) 25711, westport@failteireland.ie
> ▣ Burrishoole Abbey★, NW : 3 ¼ km by N 59 – Furnace Lough★, NW : 4 ¾ km
> by N 59. Achill Island★, W : 35 km by N 59 and R 319

▮▮ **Newport House** ⌖   𝄢 ⵀ ⵄ ⍟ 🅟 𝗩𝗜𝗦𝗔 ⓶⓪ 𝗔𝗘
– ℰ *(098) 41 222 – www.newporthouse.ie – info@newporthouse.ie – Fax (098)*
41613 – 18 March-October
16 rm ⌐ – ♥€ 181/190 ♥♥€ 310/328
Rest – (dinner only) Menu € 68 **s** – Carte approx. € 54 **s**
♦ Mellow ivy-clad Georgian mansion; grand staircase up to gallery and drawing
room. Bedrooms in main house or courtyard; some in self-contained units ideal for
families. Enjoy the fresh Newport estate produce used in the dishes served in the
elegant dining room.

NEWTOWNMOUNTKENNEDY (Baile An Chinnéidieh) – **Wicklow**   39 **D2**
– **712** N 8
> ▣ Dublin 35 km – Glendalough 22 km – Wicklow 16 km

▮▮▮ **Marriott Druids Glen H. & Country Club** ⌖   ⍟ ⌂ ⊡ ⓪
⍟ ⚖ 𝄢 ⍞ & rm, ⒶⒸ ⚷ ⓰ ⚖ 🅟 𝗩𝗜𝗦𝗔 ⓶⓪ 𝗔𝗘 ⓪
East : 2 ¾ km off Kilcoole rd – ℰ *(01) 287 0800 – www.marriottdruidsglen.com*
– mhrs.dubgs.reservations@marriotthotels.com – Fax (01) 287 0801
134 rm ⌐ – ♥€ 105/165 ♥♥€ 290 – 11 suites
Rest *Druids Brasserie* – (dinner only) Carte € 38/56
♦ Modern hotel in 400 acres, next to golf course. Spacious marble and granite atrium;
leisure, conference facilities. Very comfortable rooms, with every conceivable facility.
Druids offers a popular buffet.

OUGHTERARD (Uachtar Ard) – **Galway** – **712** E 7 ▯ *Ireland*   36 **A3**
> ▣ Dublin 240 km – Galway 27 km
> ▤ Main Street ℰ (091) 552808
> ▤ Gortreevagh, ℰ (091) 552 131
> ▣ Town★
> ▣ Lough Corrib★★ (Shore road - NW - ≤★★) – Aughnanure Castle★ **AC**, SE :
> 3 ¼ km by N 59

▮▮ **Ross Lake House** ⌖   𝄢 ⚷ ⚷ ⓰ 🅟 𝗩𝗜𝗦𝗔 ⓶⓪ 𝗔𝗘
Rosscahill, Southeast : 7 ¼ km by N 59 – ℰ *(091) 550 109*
– www.rosslakehotel.com – rosslake@iol.ie – Fax (091) 550 184 – 14 March-October
12 rm ⌐ – ♥€ 105/140 ♥♥€ 150/220 – 1 suite
Rest – (dinner only) (booking essential to non-residents) Menu € 50
♦ Georgian country house set in its own estate of woods and attractive gardens. The
period theme is carried right through interiors. Bright bedrooms with antiques. Spacious, comfortable dining room with smartly set polished tables.

Currarevagh House ⟡ ≤ 🚲 🍷 🍴 **P.** *VISA* **⚫**
Northwest : 6½ km on Glann rd – ☏ (091) 552 312 – www.currarevagh.com
– rooms@currarevagh.com – Fax (091) 552 731 – 11 March-26 October
12 rm ☒ – ♦€ 99/150 ♦♦€ 198/230
Rest – (dinner only) (booking essential to non-residents) (set menu only)
Menu € 50 **s**
♦ Victorian manor on Lough Corrib, set in 170 acres. Period décor throughout plus much fishing memorabilia. Two lovely sitting rooms. Comfortable, well-kept rooms. Country house style dining room, popular with fishing parties.

Railway Lodge without rest ⟡ ≤ 🚲 📶 **P.** *VISA* **⚫**
West : ¾ km by Costello rd taking first right onto unmarked road – ☏ (091)
552 945 – www.railwaylodge.net – railwaylodge@eircom.net
4 rm ☒ – ♦€ 70/80 ♦♦€ 100/110
♦ Elegantly furnished modern guest house in remote farm location. Communal breakfast with plenty of choice. Open fires, books and magazine but no TV. Beautifully kept bedrooms.

Waterfall Lodge without rest 🚲 🍷 🍴 **P.**
West : ¾ km on N 59 – ☏ (091) 552 168 – www.waterfalllodge.net
– kdolly@eircom.net
6 rm ☒ – ♦€ 50 ♦♦€ 80
♦ Two minutes from the centre, a well-priced guesthouse rebuilt with gleaming wood and original Victorian fittings. A good fishing river flows through the charming gardens.

PARKNASILLA (Páirc na Saileach) – **Kerry** – 712 C 12 ▯ *Ireland* 38 **A3**
🔲 Dublin 360 km – Cork 116 km – Killarney 55 km
🔲 Sneem★, NW : 4 km by N 70. Ring of Kerry★★ : Derrynane National Historic Park★★, W : 25 ¾ km by N 70 – Staigue Fort★, W : 21 km by N 70

Parknasilla ≤ 🚲 🍷 🎿 🏊 ✈ ♨ ♨ 🎿 🍴 📺 🅰 rest, **P.** *VISA* **⚫** **AE** **①**
– ☏ (064) 45 122 – www.parknasillahotel.ie – info@parknasillahotel.ie
– Fax (064) 45 323 – Closed January and February
69 rm ☒ – ♦€ 129/249 ♦♦€ 129/249 – 9 suites
Rest *Pigmaylion* – (booking essential for non residents) Menu € 60 (dinner)
– Carte € 41/63
♦ Set in 500 acres and built by the railway. Huge sums have been spent, with state-of-the-art spa and leisure facilities. Bedrooms kept fairly light; bigger ones in main house. Traditionally formal restaurant; lighter lunches in bar.

PASSAGE EAST – **Waterford** – 712 L 11 39 **C2**

Parkswood ⟡ ≤ 🚲 🍴 **P.**
on R 683 – ☏ (051) 380 863 – www.parkswood.com – info@parkswood.com
– Closed Christmas-New Year
4 rm ☒ – ♦€ 95 ♦♦€ 160 **Rest** – (by arrangement) Menu € 30
♦ Delightful hosts give a friendly welcome, with tea and scones, to their 17C house, with super views and charming garden. Immaculate bedrooms are colour themed, with balconies. Tasty homecooking; the choice depends on the latest catch and what's available locally.

PORTLAOISE (Port Laoise) – **Laois** – 712 K 8 39 **C2**
🔲 Dublin 88 km – Carlow 40 km – Waterford 101 km

Ivyleigh House without rest 🚲 🍴 **P.** *VISA* **⚫**
Bank Pl, Church St – ☏ (057) 862 20 81 – www.ivyleigh.com – info@ivyleigh.com
– Fax (057) 866 33 43 – Closed January
6 rm ☒ – ♦€ 65/80 ♦♦€ 110/150
♦ Attractive Georgian listed house with gardens. Breakfast a feature: owner makes it all herself from fresh produce. Charming period drawing room. Airy bedrooms with antiques.

REPUBLIC OF IRELAND

PORTMAGEE (An Caladh) – **Kerry** – **712** A 12 ▮ *Ireland* 38 **A2**
- ▶ Dublin 365 km – Killarney 72 km – Tralee 82 km
- 🖼 Ring of Kerry★★

🏠 **Moorings** ≼ 🏧 rest, ⅏ 🅿 🆚 ⓾ 🅰🅴
- ℰ (066) 947 71 08 – www.moorings.ie – moorings@iol.ie – Fax (066) 947 72 20
- Closed 19 December- 2 January
16 rm ⊆ – †€ 60/70 ††€ 90/100
Rest – (closed Monday dinner except Bank Holidays) (bar lunch) Menu € 40
– Carte € 34/61
♦ Pub-style hotel in the high street of this attractive village. Spacious, nautical themed bar and trim upstairs lounge. Bedrooms with views over harbour and its fishing boats. Stone-walled, candlelit dining room with seafaring curios.

PORTMARNOCK (Port Mearnóg) – **Fingal** – **712** N 7 – **pop. 8 979** 39 **D1**
▮ *Ireland*
- ▶ Dublin 8 km – Drogheda 45 km
- 🖼 Malahide Castle★★ **AC**, N: 4 km by R 124 – Ben of Howth★, S: 8 km by R 124
  – Newbridge House★ **AC**, N: 16 km by R 124, M 1 and minor road east

🏛 **Portmarnock H. and Golf Links** ≼ 🚗 🕥 🌫 ᴌ₆ 🖼 🕭 ᕼ
Strand Rd – ℰ (01) 846 0611 🏧 rest, ⅏ ⑼ ⅍ 🅿 🆚 ⓾ 🅰🅴 ⓪
– www.portmarnock.com – reservations@portmarnock.com – Fax (01) 846 2442
138 rm – †€ 99 ††€ 129/169, ⊆ €16.95
Rest *The Osborne* – see restaurant listing
♦ Large golf-oriented hotel with challenging 18-hole course. Original fittings embellish characterful, semi-panelled Jamesons Bar. Very comfortable, individually styled rooms.

XXX **The Osborne** – at Portmarnock Hotel and Golf Links 🏧 ⅏ 🅿 🆚 ⓾ 🅰🅴 ⓪
– ℰ (01) 846 0611 – www.portmarnock.com – osborne@portmarnock.com
– Fax (01) 846 2442
Rest – (closed Sunday) (dinner only) Menu € 45 – Carte € 32/52
♦ Distinctively formal restaurant named after artist Walter Osborne. Regularly changing menus balance the modern and traditional. Professionally run with good golf course views.

RANELAGH (Raghnallach) – **Dublin** – **712** N 7 – **see Dublin**

RATHMELTON (Ráth Mealtain) – **Donegal** – **712** J 2 ▮ *Ireland* 37 **C1**
- ▶ Dublin 248 km – Donegal 59 km – Londonerry 43 km – Sligo 122 km
- 🖼 Town★

⋔ **Ardeen** without rest ⌖ 🚗 ⅏ ⅏ ⑼ 🅿 🆚 ⓾
turning by the Town Hall – ℰ (074) 915 12 43 – www.ardeenhouse.com
– ardeenbandb@eircom.net – Fax (074) 915 12 43 – Easter-October
5 rm ⊆ – †€ 45/50 ††€ 90
♦ Simple Victorian house, with very welcoming owner, on edge of village. Homely ambience in lounge and breakfast room. Immaculately kept bedrooms.

RATHMINES (Ráth Maonais) – **Dublin** – **712** N 8 – **see Dublin**

RATHMULLAN (Ráth Maoláin) – **Donegal** – **712** J 2 – **pop. 469** 37 **C1**
– ✉ Letterkenny ▮ *Ireland*
- ▶ Dublin 265 km – Londonderry 58 km – Sligo 140 km
- 🖼 Otway Saltpans, ℰ (074) 915 1665
- 🖼 Knockalla Viewpoint★, N: 12 ¾ km by R 247 – Rathmelton★, SW: 11 ¼ km
  by R 247

🏛 **Rathmullan House** ⌖ ≼ 🚗 🕥 🍃 🔲 ⅏ 🅿 🆚 ⓾ 🅰🅴
North: ½ m. on R 247 – ℰ (074) 915 81 88 – www.rathmullanhouse.com – info@
rathmullanhouse.com – Fax (074) 915 82 00 – Closed 10 January- 5 February
34 rm ⊆ – †€ 85/205 ††€ 170/320
Rest – (bar lunch) Menu € 55 – Carte € 60/69
♦ Part 19C country house with fine gardens in secluded site on Lough Swilly. Choose a lounge as pleasant spot for lunch. Stylish, individualistic rooms: newer ones very comfy. Restaurant boasts serious dinner menus at linen-clad tables.

🏨 **Fort Royal** ⬧   ⟜ 🚗 🕭 🗙 **P** **VISA** **◑◐** **AE** **①**
North : 1½ km by R 247 – ℰ *(074) 9158100 – www.fortroyalhotel.com
– fortroyal@eircom.net – Fax (074) 9158103 – April - October*
15 rm ⬚ – **†**€ 100/110 **††**€ 130/150
Rest – (Closed Sunday) (bar lunch) Menu € 45
♦ Early 19C house in a very quiet location with attractive gardens that run down to
the beach. Two comfortable lounges and a spacious bar. Characterful, homely bedrooms. Lunchtime sandwiches in the bar; main evening meal in comfy restaurant.

RATHNEW (Ráth Naoi) – **Wicklow** – **712** N 8 – **see Wicklow**

RIVERSTOWN (Baile idir Dhá Abhainn) – **Sligo** – **712** G 5   36 **B2**
▶ Dublin 198 km – Sligo 21 km

🏠 **Coopershill** ⬧   ⟜ 🚗 🕭 ⚲ 🗙 ⍟ 📶 **P** **VISA** **◑◐** **AE** **①**
– ℰ *(071) 9165108 – www.coopershill.com – ohara@coopershill.com – Fax (071)*
9165466 – April-October
8 rm ⬚ – **†**€ 153/171 **††**€ 236/272
Rest – (dinner only) (booking essential for non-residents) Menu € 59
♦ Magnificent Georgian country house set within 500 acre estate. Home to six generations of one family. Antique furnished communal areas and rooms exude charm
and character. Family portraits, antique silver adorn dining room.

ROSCOMMON – **Roscommon** – **712** H7 – **pop. 5 017** 📘 *Ireland*   36 **B3**
▶ Dublin 151 km – Galway 92 km – Limerick 151 km
🛈 Harrison Hall ℰ *(090) 6626342 (June-August)*
🏘 Moate Park, ℰ *(09066) 26382*
◉ Castle★
🅖 Castlestrange Stone★, SW : 11¼ km by N 63 and R 362 – Strokestown★
(Famine Museum★ **AC**, Strokestown Park House★ **AC**), N : 19¼ km by
N 61 and R 368 – Castlerea : Clonalis House★ **AC**, NW : 30½ km by N 60

🏨 **Abbey**   🚗 🖳 🏯 ⛨ 🗗 & rm, ⍟ 📶 ⚱ **P** **VISA** **◑◐** **AE** **①**
on N 63 (Galway rd) – ℰ *(090) 6662640 – www.abbeyhotel.ie*
– info@abbeyhotel.ie – Fax (090) 6626021 – Closed 24-26 December
50 rm ⬚ – **†**€ 160/180 **††**€ 280/300   **Rest** – Menu € 50 – Carte € 37/43
♦ Part 19C house with modern extensions, convenient central location and surrounded by attractive gardens. Excellent leisure facilities. Comfortable bedrooms. Spacious restaurant overlooks ruins of Abbey.

🏠 **Gleeson's Townhouse**   🚗 **AC** rest, ⍟ ⚱ **P** **VISA** **◑◐** **AE** **①**
Market Sq – ℰ *(090) 6626954 – www.gleesonstownhouse.com*
– info@gleesonstownhouse.com – Fax (090) 6627425 – Closed 25-26 December
21 rm ⬚ – **†**€ 65/95 **††**€ 120/140 – 2 suites
Rest – Menu € 35 – Carte € 27/40 **s**
♦ 19C former manse with courtyard overlooking the market square. This substantial
stone-built edifice was once a minister's residence. Comfortable, well-equipped bedrooms. Meals available in the farmhouse-style restaurant.

↰ **Westway** without rest   🚗 ⍟ 📶 **P** **VISA** **◑◐**
Galway Rd, Southwest : 1¼ km on N 63 – ℰ *(090) 6626927*
– www.westwayguests.com – westwayguests@eircom.net – March-October
5 rm ⬚ – **†**€ 45 **††**€ 70
♦ Modern guesthouse with friendly welcome near town centre. Comfy, traditional
residents' lounge. Breakfast room with conservatory extension. Brightly decorated
rooms.

ROSCREA – **712** I 9 📘 *Ireland*   39 **C2**
▶ Dublin 125 km – Birr 19 km – Nenagh 34 km
◉ Town★ – Damer House★ **AC**

Racket Hall 🖼️ 🛏️ 🍽️ rm, 🅰️ rest, ⚙️ 🎧 🏊 🅿️ 𝚅𝙸𝚂𝙰 ⦿ 𝖠𝖤 ⓘ

Dublin Rd, East : 2 ¾ km on N 7 – ℰ (0505) 21 748 – www.rackethallhotel.com
– info@rackethall.ie – Fax (0505) 23 701
40 rm ⌑ – ∱€ 69/99 ∱∱€ 119/149
Rest – (carvery lunch) Menu € 33 – Carte € 24/40
♦ Bright yellow, creeper-clad, extended roadside inn. Huge rustic pubby area with sofas and shelves of books. Bedrooms offer good levels of comfort and modern facilities. Formal dining to the rear.

ROSSLARE – Wexford – **712** M 11 🔖 *Ireland*   39 **D2**

▶ Dublin 167 km – Waterford 80 km – Wexford 19 km
ℹ️ Kilrane ℰ (053) 33232 (April-September)
🗓️ Rosslare Strand, ℰ (053) 913 2203
◉ Irish Agricultural Museum, Johnstown Castle★★ **AC**, NW : 12 km by R 740, N 25 and minor road. Kilmore Quay★, SW : 24 km by R 736 and R 739 – Saltee Islands★, SW : 24 km by R 736, R 739 and ferry

REPUBLIC OF IRELAND

Kelly's Resort ≪ 🖼️ 🖼️ 🌐 ♨️ 🛁 🍽️ rm, 🏃 🅰️ rest, ⚙️ 🎧 🅿️ 𝚅𝙸𝚂𝙰 ⦿ 𝖠𝖤

– ℰ (053) 91 32 114 – www.kellys.ie – info@kellys.ie
– Fax (053) 91 32 222 – Closed mid December - mid February
121 rm ⌑ – ∱€ 127/220 ∱∱€ 254/330
Rest Beaches – Menu € 25/48
Rest La Marine – (closed Good Friday) Carte € 34/42
♦ Large, purpose-built hotel on the beachfront of this popular holiday town. Good range of leisure facilities; well-appointed rooms. Kelly's dining room offers a classic popular menu. La Marine is a French inspired, bistro-style restaurant.

ROSSLARE HARBOUR (Calafort Ros Láir) – Wexford – **712** N 11   39 **D2**

▶ Dublin 169 km – Waterford 82 km – Wexford 21 km
🚢 to France (Cherbourg and Roscoff) (Irish Ferries) (17 h/15 h) – to Fishguard (Stena Line) 1-4 daily (1 h 40 mn/3 h 30 mn) – to Pembroke (Irish Ferries) 2 daily (3 h 45 mn)
ℹ️ Kilrane ℰ (053) 33232 (April-October)

Ferryport House ⚙️ 🅿️ 𝚅𝙸𝚂𝙰 ⦿

on N 25 – ℰ (053) 91 33 933 – www.ferryporthouse.com
– info@ferryporthouse.com – Fax (053) 91 61 707 – Closed 25-26 December
16 rm ⌑ – ∱€ 45/65 ∱∱€ 59/90
Rest Fusion – Chinese – (dinner only) Carte € 25/35
♦ Contemporary hotel conveniently located for the ferry terminus. Simple communal areas include a pine furnished breakfast room. Comfortable bedrooms with fitted wood furniture. Seafood and Chinese cuisine in Fusion.

at Tagoat West : 4 km on N 25 – ✉ Rosslare

Churchtown House ॐ 🖼️ & rm, ⚙️ 🅿️ 𝚅𝙸𝚂𝙰 ⦿

North : ¾ km on Rosslare rd – ℰ (053) 913 2555 – www.churchtownhouse.com
– info@churchtownhouse.com – Fax (053) 913 2577 – 15 March-October
12 rm ⌑ – ∱€ 85/120 ∱∱€ 170/200   **Rest** – (closed Sunday and Monday) (dinner only) (booking essential) (residents only) Menu € 45
♦ Part 18C house with extension, set in spacious, well-kept garden. Traditional country house-style lounge and wood furnished dining room. Individually decorated rooms. Fresh country cooking in the Irish tradition.

ROSSNOWLAGH (Ros Neamhlach) – Donegal – **712** H 4 🔖 *Ireland*   37 **C2**

▶ Dublin 246 km – Donegal 22 km – Sligo 50 km
◉ Rossnowlagh Strand★★

Sand House ॐ ≪ 🐟 🌐 ⚙️ 🍽️ & rm, 🎧 🏊 🅿️ 𝚅𝙸𝚂𝙰 ⦿ 𝖠𝖤

– ℰ (071) 985 1777 – www.sandhouse.ie – info@sandhouse.ie – Fax (071) 985 2100 – Closed December-January
50 rm ⌑ – ∱€ 110/150 ∱∱€ 250/310
Rest – (dinner only and Sunday lunch) Menu € 55
♦ Victorian sandstone hotel in coastal location with superb views of bay, beach and mountains. Real fire in the hall. Spacious, individual rooms with modern styling. Attractive dining room with a comfortable atmosphere and classic traditional feel.

SALTHILL (Bóthar na Trá) – **Galway** – **712** E 8 – **see Galway**

SANDYFORD – **Dublin** – **712** N 8 – **see Dublin**

SANDYMOUNT – **Dublin** – **see Dublin**

SHANAGARRY (An Seangharraí) – **Cork** – **712** H 12 – ⊠ **Midleton**   39 **C3**

 Ireland

> ▶ Dublin 262 km – Cork 40 km – Waterford 103 km
> ◉ Cloyne Cathedral★, NW : 6½ km by R 629

  Ballymaloe House ﴾   ⬩ ⬩ ⬩ ⬩ ⬩ ⬩ ⬩ ⬩ P VISA ☜ AE ⓪
Northwest : 2¾ km on L 35 – ℰ *(021) 465 25 31* – *www.ballymaloe.ie*
– res@ballymaloe.ie – Fax (021) 465 20 21
– Closed 24-26 December and 2 weeks January
33 rm ⊒ – †€ 150/195 ††€ 280/320
Rest – (buffet dinner Sunday) (booking essential) Menu € 40/75 **s**
♦ Hugely welcoming part 16C, part Georgian country house surrounded by 400 acres of farmland. Characterful sitting room with cavernous ceiling. Warm, comfortable bedrooms. Characterful dining room divided into assorted areas.

> Red = Pleasant. Look for the red 🍴 and 🏠 symbols.

SHANNON (Sionainn) – **Clare** – **712** F 9 – **pop. 9 222** *Ireland*   38 **B2**

> ▶ Dublin 219 km – Ennis 26 km – Limerick 24 km
> ✈ Shannon Airport : ℰ (061) 712000
> 🛈 Shannon Airport, Arrivals Hall ℰ (061) 471664, info@shannondev.ie
> 🛈 Shannon, ℰ (061) 471849
> ◉ Bunratty Castle★★ **AC**, E : 11 km by N 19 and N 18 – Cratloe Wood (≼★), E : 14 km by N 19 and N 18. Craggaunowen Centre★ **AC**, NE : 20 km by N 19, N 18 S, R 471 and R 462 – Knappogue Castle★ **AC**, N : 26 km by N 19, N 18 and minor road via Quin – Quin Friary★ **AC**, N :22 km by N 19, N18 N and minor road to Quin

🏨🏨🏨 **Oak Wood Arms**   ⬩ ﯼ ⬩ rm, ﭏ rest, ⬩ ⬩ ⬩ P VISA ☜ AE ⓪
– ℰ (061) 361 500 – www.oakwoodarms.com – reservations@oakwoodarms.com
– Fax (061) 361 414 – Closed 24-25 December
98 rm ⊒ – †€ 90/130 ††€ 120/160 – 2 suites
Rest *Palm Court* – (carvery lunch Monday-Saturday) Carte € 32/45 **s**
♦ Low rise hotel with good access to Shannon International airport. Large bar with carvery. Lots of small lounges. Good conference facilities. Spacious rooms with fresh décor. Dining room decorated with aeronautical memorabilia.

SKERRIES – **Fingal** – **712** N 7 – **pop. 9 535** *Ireland*   39 **D1**

> ▶ Dublin 30 km – Drogheda 24 km
> 🛈 Skerries Mills ℰ (01) 849 5208, skerriesmills@indigo.ie
> 🛈 Skerries Hacketstown, ℰ (01) 849 1576
> ◉ Malahide Castle★★ **AC**, S : 23 km by R 127, M 1 and R 106 – Ben of Howth (≼★), S : 23 km by R 127, M 1 and R 106 – Newbridge House★ **AC**, S : 16 km by R 217 and minor road

🍴🍴 **Redbank House** with rm   ⬩ rm, ⬩ VISA ☜ AE ⓪
5-7 Church St – ℰ *(01) 849 1005* – *www.redbank.ie* – *info@redbank.ie* – *Fax (01) 849 1598 – Closed 24-26 December*
18 rm ⊒ – †€ 75 ††€ 80/120
Rest – Seafood – (Closed Sunday dinner) (dinner only and Sunday lunch) Menu € 33/50 – Carte € 43/72
♦ One of Ireland's most well-renowned and long-standing restaurants. Fresh seafood from Skerries harbour is served simply or in more elaborate fashion. Smart, comfy bedrooms.

REPUBLIC OF IRELAND

SLIGO – Sligo – 712 G 5 – pop. 19 402 ▌Ireland 36 **B2**

▸ Dublin 214 km – Belfast 203 km – Dundalk 170 km – Londonderry 138 km
✈ Sligo Airport, Strandhill : ℰ (071) 9168280
🛈 Aras Reddan, Temple St ℰ (071) 9161201, northwestinfo@failteireland.ie
🖼 Rosses Point, ℰ (071) 9177134
◉ Town★★ – Abbey★ **AC** – Model Arts and the Niland Gallery★ **AC**
◔ SE : Lough Gill★★ – Carrowmore Megalithic Cemetery★ **AC**, SW : 4 ¾ km –
Knocknarea★ (≤★★) SW : 9 ½ km by R 292. Drumcliff★, N : by N 15 -
Parke's Castle★ **AC**, E : 14 ½ km by R 286 – Glencar Waterfall★, NE :
14 ½ km by N 16 – Creevykeel Court Cairn★, N : 25 ¾ km by N 15

🏨 Clarion   🛋 🖼 🌐 🛜 Là 🖹 🕭 rm, 🏃 🔟 🍴 rest, ⅋ 🛁 **P** 🈁 **VISA ⅏ AE ①**

Clarion Rd, Northeast : 3 km by N 16 – ℰ (071) 911 9000
– www.clarionhotelsligo.com – info@clarionhotelsligo.com – Fax (071) 911 9001
– Closed Christmas
163 rm – †€ 250 ††€ 250, ⯌ €16 – 149 suites
Rest *Kudos* – Carte € 26/37 **s**
Rest *Sinergie* – (dinner only) Menu € 35 – Carte € 34/49
♦ Extensive Victorian building with granite façade: now the height of modernity with excellent leisure club, and impressive, spacious bedrooms, many being plush suites. Informal Asian inspired Kudos. Modern European menus at Sinergie.

⭫ Tree Tops without rest   🛋 ⅋ 🛜 **P** 🈁 **VISA ⅏ AE**

Cleveragh Rd, South : 1 ¼ km by Dublin rd – ℰ (071) 916 0160
– www.sligobandb.com – treetops@iol.ie – Fax (071) 916 2301 – Closed Christmas
and New Year
5 rm ⯌ – †€ 50/53 ††€ 70/78
♦ Pleasant guesthouse in residential area. Stunning collection of Irish art. Cosy public areas include small lounge and simple breakfast room. Neat, comfortable rooms.

⅋⅋ Montmartre   🔟 ⅋ **VISA ⅏ AE**

Market Yard – ℰ (071) 916 9901 – edelmckeon@eircom.net – Fax (071) 919 2232
– Closed 24-26 December and 6 January-3 February, Sunday and Monday
Rest – (dinner only) Carte € 38/53
♦ Smart, modern restaurant near cathedral with small bar at entrance and plenty of light from windows. Efficient, formal staff serve broadly influenced classic French food.

SNEEM – Kerry – 712 C 12 – pop. 279 38 **A3**

▸ Dublin 228 km – Tralee 56 km – Cill Airne / Killarney 37 km – Bantry 45 km

🏨 Sneem Hotel 🌲   ≤ 🛋 🐕 🛜 Là 🖹 🕭 rm, 🔟 ⅋ 🛁 **P** 🈁 **VISA ⅏ ①**

Goldens Cove, East : ½ km on N 70 – ℰ (064) 75 100 – www.sneemhotel.com
– information@sneemhotel.com – Fax (064) 75 199 – Closed 23-27 December
69 rm – †€ 95/135 ††€ 110/190
Rest – (bar lunch) – Carte € 22/44
♦ Modern hotel overlooking tidal cove and mountains. Lounge with fireplace for a drink or afternoon tea; comfy bedrooms - the largest have balconies, and 221 is the best. Traditional Irish fare served in restaurant with terrace.

SPANISH POINT (Rinn na Spáinneach) – Clare – 712 D 9 – ✉ Milltown 38 **B2**
Malbay

▸ Dublin 275 km – Galway 104 km – Limerick 83 km

🏨 Admiralty Lodge   🛋 🕭 🔟 **P** 🈁 **VISA ⅏ AE**

– ℰ (065) 708 5007 – www.admiralty.ie – info@admiralty.ie – Fax (065) 708 5030
– April-October
11 rm ⯌ – †€ 145/165 ††€ 160/230
Rest Piano Room – see restaurant listing
♦ Purpose-built coastal hotel built around a former 19C seamans lodge. Three warm, comfy lounges bring out period character. Individually stylish rooms a notably strong point.

REPUBLIC OF IRELAND

XXX **The Piano Room** – at Admiralty Lodge Hotel 🚗 AC P VISA ◑ AE
– ℰ (065) 708 50 07 – www.admiralty.ie – info@admiralty.ie – Fax (065) 708 50 30
– April-October
Rest (dinner only) (booking essential to non-residents) Menu €49 Carte €39/47
♦ Keen young French chef produces well presented, sophisticated cooking; a mix of classic and more modern dishes. Piano playing at weekends.

STILLORGAN – Dublin – 712 N 8 – see Dublin

STRAFFAN (Teach Srafáin) – Kildare – 712 M 8 – pop. 439 📗 Ireland　　39 **D1**
 🚗 Dublin 24 km – Mullingar 75 km
 🏠 Naas Kerdiffstown, ℰ (045) 874 644
 🄶 Castletown House, Celbridge★ **AC**, NW : 7 km by R 406 and R 403

🏨🏨🏨 **The K Club** 🦅 　🚗 🕊 🐟 🚣 🖼 🐕 📶 ᵣ₆ 🖼 📶 🍴 🎿 🏌 🏊 P
– ℰ (01) 601 7200 – www.kclub.ie – resortsales@kclub.ie 　VISA ◑ AE ◐
– Fax (01) 601 7297 – Closed January
79 rm ⌂ – ♥€380/565 ♥♥€380/565 – 13 suites
Rest Byerley Turk – (Closed Sunday-Monday and Tuesday-Friday in winter)
(booking essential for non-residents) Carte €89/106
Rest Legends – (dinner only and Sunday lunch) Carte €52/82
Rest River Room – (closed Monday-Wednesday in winter) Menu €35
– Carte €49/80
♦ Part early 19C country house overlooking River Liffey, with gardens, arboretum and championship golf course. Huge leisure centre. Exquisitely sumptuous rooms. Opulent food in the formal Byerley Turk. Informal Legends has views of the golf course. Accessible menu offered in The River Room.

🏨🏨 **Barberstown Castle** 🦅 🚗 🖼 ᵩ rm, 🎿 🏌 🏊 P VISA ◑ AE
North : ¾ km – ℰ (01) 628 8157 – www.barberstowncastle.ie – info@barberstown
castle.ie – Fax (01) 627 7027 – Closed January, Easter and 24-26 December
59 rm ⌂ – ♥€160/210 ♥♥€290
Rest – (Closed Sunday-Tuesday) (dinner only) (booking essential) Menu €65
– Carte €24/36
♦ Whitewashed Elizabethan and Victorian house with 13C castle keep and gardens. Country house style lounges exude style. Individually decorated, very comfortable bedrooms. Dine in characterful, stone-clad keep.

SWORDS – Fingal – 712 N 7 – pop. 33 998 📗 Ireland　　39 **D1**
 🚗 Dublin 13 km – Drogheda 35 km
 🏠 Balheary Ave, ℰ (01) 840 9819
 🄶 Fingal★ – Newbridge House★, N : by N 1 and east by R 126. Malahide
Castle★★, SE : by N 1 and R 106

🏨 **Kettle's Country House** 📶 AC 🎿 🏌 🏊 P VISA ◑ AE
Lispopple, Northwest : 6 km on R 125 – ℰ (01) 813 8511 – www.kettleshotel.ie
– Info@kettleshotel.ie – Fax (01) 813 8510 – Closed 25 December
24 rm ⌂ – ♥€149/229 ♥♥€200/350 – 1 suite　**Rest** – Carte €29/44
♦ Built on the site of a former pub, this stylish hotel has very well kept bedrooms with flat screen TVs. Pristine bar with carvery.

TAGOAT (Teach Gót) – Wexford – 712 M 11 – see Rosslare Harbour

---

TAHILLA (Tathuile) – Kerry – 712 C 12 📗 Ireland　　38 **A3**
 🚗 Dublin 357 km – Cork 112 km – Killarney 51 km
 🄶 Ring of Kerry★★ – Sneem★, NW : 6½ km by N 70

🏨 **Tahilla Cove** without rest 🦅 🚗 🕊 🐟 P VISA ◑ AE
– ℰ (064) 66 45 204 – www.tahillacove.com – tahillacove@eircom.net – Fax (064)
66 45 104 – May - 15 October
9 rm ⌂ – ♥€105 ♥♥€150
♦ Two houses surrounded by oak forest, with Caha Mountains as a backdrop and garden sweeping down to Coongar harbour. Some bedrooms have balconies from which to savour views.

TERENURE – Dublin – 712 N 8 – see Dublin

REPUBLIC OF IRELAND

TERMONBARRY – Roscommon – **712** I 6 ▯ *Ireland* 37 **C3**

> ◘ Dublin 130 km – Galway 137 km – Roscommon 35 km – Sligo 100 km
> ◙ Strokestown★ (Famine Museum★ **AC**, Strokestown Park House★ **AC**),
> NW : by N 5

⌂ **Shannonside House** without rest 🛇 **P** 🚗 🏧 🎴 ⓪
– ℰ *(043) 26 052* – *www.keenans.ie* – *info@keenans.ie* – *Fax (043) 26 198*
– *Closed 25-26 December*
7 rm ⌻ – ♦€48/55 ♦♦€90
♦ Hospitable owner and well-proportioned bedrooms are among the guesthouse's
chief attractions. Good value and comfortable. Located close to the Shannon River.

THOMASTOWN – Kilkenny – **712** K 10 – pop. 1 837 – ⊠ **Kilkenny** 39 **C2**
▯ *Ireland*

> ◘ Dublin 124 km – Kilkenny 17 km – Waterford 48 km – Wexford 61 km
> ◙ Jerpoint Abbey★★, SW : 3 km by N9 – Graiguenamanagh★ (Duiske
> Abbey★★ **AC**), E : 16 km by R 703 – Inistioge★, SE : 8 km by R 700 – Kilfane
> Glen and Waterfall★ **AC**, SE : 5 km by N 9

⌂ **Abbey House** without rest 🚗 ☎ **P** 🏧 🎴 🅰🅴
Jerpoint Abbey, Southwest : 2 km on N 9 – ℰ *(056) 772 41 66*
– *www.abbeyhousejerpoint.com* – *abbeyhousejerpoint@eircom.net* – *Fax (056)
772 41 92* – *Closed 20 December - 30 January*
7 rm ⌻ – ♦€55/80 ♦♦€85/110
♦ Neat inside and out, this whitewashed house in well-kept gardens offers simple
but spacious rooms and pretty wood furnished breakfast room. Read up on area in
lounge.

⌂ **Carrickmourne House** without rest 🛇 ≤ 🚗 🛇 **P** 🏧 🎴
New Ross Rd, Southeast : 3¼ km by R 700 – ℰ *(056) 772 41 24*
– *carrickmournehouse@eircom.net* – *Fax (056) 772 41 24*
– *Closed 15 December-15 January*
5 rm ⌻ – ♦€50/60 ♦♦€75/80
♦ Modern, split-level house looks down on peaceful countryside. Agreeably simple,
traditional décor and gleaming wood floors in pristine rooms: homely and well
priced.

THURLES – **712** I9 – pop. 7 682 ▯ *Ireland* 39 **C2**

> ◘ Dublin 148 km – Cork 114 km – Kilkenny 48 km – Limerick 75 km
> – Waterford 93 km
> 🏌 Turtulla, ℰ *(0504) 21 983*
> ◙ Holy Cross Abbey★★ **AC**, SW : 8 km by R 660

🏠 **Inch House** 🛇 ≤ 🚗 🔊 🔟 rest, 🛇 ⁿ🎴 **P** 🏧 🎴
Northwest : 6½ km on R 498 – ℰ *(0504) 51 348* – *www.inchhouse.ie*
– *mairin@inchhouse.ie* – *Fax (0504) 51 754*
– *Closed 2 weeks Christmas and 1 week Easter*
5 rm ⌻ – ♦€90 ♦♦€150
Rest – (closed Sunday-Monday) (dinner only) (booking essential for
non-residents) Menu €70
♦ 1720s country house on a working farm; lovely rural views. Handsomely restored
with a fine eye for decorative period detail. Individually styled en suite bedrooms.
Classically proportioned yet intimate dining room.

at Twomileborris East : 6¾ km on N 75 – ⊠ Thurles

⌂ **The Castle** 🚗 🛇 ⁿ🎴 **P** 🏧 🎴
Two Mile Borris – ℰ *(0504) 44 324* – *www.thecastletmb.com*
– *info@thecastletmb.com* – *Fax (0504) 44 352*
4 rm ⌻ – ♦€55/65 ♦♦€90/110 **Rest** – (by arrangement) Menu €55
♦ Charming 17C house adjacent to partly ruined tower of the local castle which runs
close to back door. Furnished with numerous period pieces. Pleasantly decorated
rooms. Traditionally furnished dining room.

TIPPERARY (Tiobraid Árann) – **712** H 10   39 **C2**

  ▶ Dublin 116 km – Limerick 26 km – Clonmel 25 km – Thurles 28 km

Ballykisteen   🔄 🦢 ⅃₆ 🖼 🕮 🖳 ఉ rm, 🕮 rest, 🕭 🚿 **P.** **VISA** **⬤⬤** **AE**
Limerick Junction, Northwest : 4 km on N 24 – 𝒞 (062) 33 333
– www.ballykisteenhotel.com – info@ballykisteenhotel.com – Fax (062) 31 555
– Closed 25 December
40 rm – ♦€ 119/149 ♦♦€ 119/149
Rest – (dinner only and Sunday lunch) Menu € 25/23 – Carte € 29/40
♦ Handy for the gee gees as it's situated opposite the racecourse, this small, modern hotel is also surrounded by an 18 hole golf course. Comfortable bedrooms with views. Informal restaurant.

TOORMORE (An Tuar Mór) – **Cork** – **712** D 13 – ⊠ **Goleen**   38 **A3**

  ▶ Dublin 355 km – Cork 109 km – Killarney 104 km

Fortview House without rest   🚗 **P.**
Gurtyowen, Northeast : 2½ km on Durrus rd (R 591) – 𝒞 (028) 35 324
– www.fortviewhousegoleen.com – fortviewhousegoleen@eircom.net
– March-October
5 rm ⌂ – ♦€ 50 ♦♦€ 100
♦ Stone built farmhouse; antique country pine furniture in coir carpeted rooms and brass, iron bedsteads. Fresh vegetable juice, home-made museli, potato cake for breakfast.

Rock Cottage 🦢   🚗 🕭 🕅 **P.** **VISA** **⬤⬤**
Barnatonicane, Northeast : 3¼ km on Durrus rd (R 591) – 𝒞 (028) 35 538
– www.rockcottage.ie – rockcottage@eircom.net – Fax (028) 35 538
3 rm ⌂ – ♦€ 100 ♦♦€ 140   **Rest** – (by arrangement) Menu € 50
♦ Georgian former hunting lodge idyllically set in 17 acres of parkland. Very well appointed lounge: modern art on walls. Immaculate, light and airy bedrooms.

TOWER – **Cork** – **712** G 12 – see Blarney

TRALEE – **Kerry** – **712** C 11 – pop. 22 744 📗 *Ireland*   38 **A2**

  ▶ Dublin 297 km – Killarney 32 km – Limerick 103 km
  🖪 Ashe Memorial Hall, Denny St 𝒞 (066) 7121288,
      tourisminfo@shannon-dev.ie
  ◉ Kerry - The Kingdom★ **AC**
  🖸 Blennerville Windmill★ **AC**, SW : 3¼ km by N 86 – Ardfert★, NW : 8 km by
      R 551. Banna Strand★, NW : 12¾ km by R 551 - Crag Cave★ **AC**, W : 21 km
      by N 21 – Rattoo Round Tower★, N : 19¼ km by R 556

Fels Point   🔄 ⅃₆ 🚭 ఉ 🕮 🚿 🕭 🐾 **P.** **VISA** **⬤⬤** **AE**
Fels Point, East: 2 Km. on N70 – 𝒞 (066) 7199100 – www.felspointhotel.ie
– info@felspointhotel.ie – Fax (066) 711 9987 – Closed 24-26 December
166 rm – ♦€ 150/200 ♦♦€ 150/200, ⌂ € 15.95
Rest *Morels* – 𝒞 (066) 711 9986 (Closed Sunday lunch)
Menu € 40 (dinner) – Carte € 41/50
♦ Corporate hotel on outskirts of city centre with contemporary style throughout. Bedrooms come in three grades; all are a good size, Executive come with a balcony and view. Traditional dishes served in Morels restaurant.

Manor West   🔄 🔄 ⅃₆ 🚭 ఉ 🕮 🐾 🕭 **P.** **VISA** **⬤⬤** **AE**
Killarney Rd, Southwest: 2½ km. on N21 – 𝒞 (066) 719 4500
– www.manorwesthotel.ie – info@manorwesthotel.ie – Fax (066) 719 4545
– Closed 24-25 December
77 rm – ♦€ 85/135 ♦♦€ 120/240
Rest *Mercantile* – Traditional – (dinner only) Carte approx. € 20
Rest *Walnut* – (dinner only) Menu € 29 – Carte € 32/42
♦ New build hotel next to large retail park of same name. Bedrooms are spacious, with modern furnishings and good level of facilities; marble-floored lobby features piano. Modern, airy Mercantile for informal dining. Walnut for buffet style breakfast and traditional dinner menus.

REPUBLIC OF IRELAND

The Meadowlands
Oakpark, Northeast : 1¼ km on N 69 – ℰ *(066) 718 04 44*
– www.meadowlandshotel.com – info@meadowlandshotel.com – Fax (066)
718 09 64 – Closed 24-25 December
56 rm ⌑ – †€ 75/100 ††€ 120/250 – 2 suites
Rest – (closed Sunday dinner) (bar lunch) Menu € 39 – Carte € 37/54
♦ Smart, terracotta hotel, a good base for exploring area. Inside are warmly decorated, air conditioned rooms and mellow library lounge with open fire and grandfather clock. Proprietor owns fishing boats, so seafood takes centre stage in dining room.

The Grand
Denny St – ℰ *(066) 712 14 99 – www.grandhoteltralee.com*
– info@grandhoteltralee.com – Fax (066) 712 28 77
44 rm ⌑ – †€ 65/95 ††€ 65/90   **Rest** – Menu € 25/30 **s** – Carte € 22/40 **s**
♦ Established 1928; enjoys a central position in town. Rooms are decorated with mahogany furniture whilst the popular bar, once a post office, bears hallmarks of bygone era. Appetising dinners in restaurant with historic ambience.

Brook Manor Lodge *without rest*
Fenit Rd, Spa, Northwest : 3½ km by R 551 on R 558 – ℰ *(066) 712 04 06*
– www.brookmanorlodge.com – brookmanor@eircom.net – Fax (066) 712 75 52
– February-October
8 rm ⌑ – †€ 65/95 ††€ 100/145
♦ Modern purpose-built manor in meadowland looking across to the Slieve Mish mountains: good for walks and angling. Breakfast in conservatory. Immaculate bedrooms.

The Forge *without rest*
Upper Oakpark, Northeast : 2½ km on N 69 – ℰ *(066) 712 52 45*
– www.theforgebandb.com – theforgebnb@gmail.com – Fax (066) 712 52 45
– Closed Christmas and January
6 rm ⌑ – †€ 50/60 ††€ 70/80
♦ Comfortable, family-run house; sporting activities and scenic spots on doorstep. Hallway with hexagonal light leads upstairs to cosy rooms. Complimentary drinks on arrival.

David Norris
Ivy Terrace – ℰ *(066) 718 56 54 – www.restaurantdavidnorris.com*
– restaurantdavidnorris@eircom.net – Fax (066) 712 66 00 – Closed 1 week
February, 1 week August, 1 week November, Sunday and Monday
Rest – (dinner only) Carte € 30/46
♦ Pleasant restaurant on first floor of unprepossessing modern building, featuring Rennie Macintosh style chairs. Good blend of cuisine: exotic hints and popular favourites.

TRAMORE (Trá Mhór) – **Waterford** – **712** K 11 – **pop. 9 634** ⓘ *Ireland*   39 **C2**
  ◻ Dublin 170 km – Waterford 9 km
  ⓘ ℰ (051) 381572 (June-August)
  ◉ Dunmore East★, E : 18 km by R 675, R 685 and R 684

Glenorney *without rest*
Newtown, Southwest : 1½ km by R 675 – ℰ *(051) 381 056 – www.glenorney.com*
– info@glenorney.com – Fax (051) 381 103 – March-November
6 rm ⌑ – †€ 50/90 ††€ 80
♦ On a hill overlooking Tramore Bay. Inside are personally decorated rooms: family photographs and curios; sun lounge with plenty of books. Rear rooms have lovely bay views.

TRIM – **Meath** – **712** L 7 – **pop. 6 870** ⓘ *Ireland*   37 **D3**
  ◻ Dublin 43 km – Drogheda 42 km – Tullamore 69 km
  ⓘ Old Town Hall, Castle St ℰ (046) 9437227, trimvisitorcentre@eircom.net
  ▥ County Meath Newtownmoynagh, ℰ (046) 943 1463
  ◎ Trim Castle★★ – Town★
  ◉ Bective Abbey★, NE : 6½ km by R 161

Trim Castle
🛎 🛆 rm, 🅰🅲 rest, ⅌ ᵞᵖ 🕍 🅿 🆅🅸🆂🅰 ⓪⓪ 🅰🅴 ⓪

Castle St – ℰ (046) 948 3000 – www.trimcastlehotel.com
– info@trimcastlehotel.com – Fax (046) 948 3077 – Closed 25 December
68 rm ⊇ – ♦€ 135/155 ♦♦€ 145/200
Rest *Jules* – (closed Sunday-Tuesday) (dinner only) Menu € 35 **s**
– Carte € 23/51 **s**
♦ Newly-built hotel. Decently-sized, contemporary bedrooms; those at the front overlook Trim Castle, as does the third floor roof terrace. Ideal venue for wedding receptions. All-day café serves light dishes. More formal dining in first floor restaurant.

Highfield House without rest
🚗 ᵞᵖ 🅿 🆅🅸🆂🅰 🅰🅴

Maudlins Rd – ℰ (046) 943 63 86 – www.highfieldguesthouse.com
– highfieldhouseaccom@eircom.net – Fax (046) 943 81 82
8 rm ⊇ – ♦€ 55 ♦♦€ 82/84
♦ 19C former maternity home in lawned gardens overlooking Trim Castle and River Boyne. Sizeable bedrooms in cheerful colours offer a welcome respite after sightseeing.

Crannmór without rest ॐ
🚗 ⌇ 🛆 ⅌ ᵞᵖ 🅿 🆅🅸🆂🅰 ⓪⓪

Dunderry Rd, North : 2 km – ℰ (046) 943 16 35 – www.crannmor.com
– cranmor@eircom.net – Fax (046) 943 80 87 – March-October
5 rm ⊇ – ♦€ 55 ♦♦€ 80
♦ Particularly friendly owners run this creeper-clad Georgian farmhouse in a rural location, offering bright and comfortable bedrooms and a cosy atmosphere.

TUBBERCURRY Sligo
36 **B2**

🇩 Dublin 131 km – Sligo 22 km – Castlebar 33 km – Ballina 20 km

Murphy's
🛎 🛆 rm, 🅰🅲 rest, ⅌ ᵞᵖ 🕍 🅿 🆅🅸🆂🅰 ⓪⓪ 🅰🅴

Teeling St – ℰ (071) 918 55 98 – www.murphyshotel.ie – info@murphyshotel.ie
– Fax (071) 918 50 34 – Closed 25-27 December
17 rm ⊇ – ♦€ 50/65 ♦♦€ 90/120   **Rest** – Carte € 17/40
♦ Family owned hotel on main road of rural market town. Decently-sized rooms are simply decorated with a good level of facilities; those to the rear are quieter. Tried and tested menu offered in smart cream dining room.

TULLAMORE (Tulach Mhór) – **Offaly** – **712** J 8 – **pop. 12 927**
39 **C1**

🇩 Dublin 104 km – Kilkenny 83 km – Limerick 129 km
🇮 Bury Quay Tullamore ℰ (057) 9352617, tullamoredhc@eircom.net
🇮🅱 Tullamore Brookfield, ℰ (057) 93 21 439

Bridge House
🏡 🖼 🎴 ᴸ🅱 🛎 🛆 rm, 🅰🅲 rest, ⅌ ᵞᵖ 🕍 🅿 🆅🅸🆂🅰 ⓪⓪ 🅰🅴 ⓪

off Main St – ℰ (057) 93 22 000 – www.bridgehouse.com
– emma@bridgehouse.com – Fax (057) 93 25 690 – Closed 24-25 December
70 rm ⊇ – ♦€ 60/200 ♦♦€ 110/300   **Rest** – (bar lunch) Carte € 35/41
♦ The grand, pillared entrance with steps leading to an ornate reception with crystal chandelier sums up rarified ambience. Polished library bar and impressive bedrooms. Dining options with restaurant or bar carvery.

TULLY CROSS – Galway – **712** C 7
36 **A3**

🇩 Dublin 301 km – Galway 85 km – Letterfrack 3 km

Maol Reidh
🛎 🛆 rm, ⅌ ᵞᵖ 🅿 🆅🅸🆂🅰 ⓪⓪ 🅰🅴

– ℰ (095) 43 844 – www.maolreidhhotel.com – maolreidhhotel@eircom.net
– Fax (095) 43 784 – March-October
12 rm ⊇ – ♦€ 75/95 ♦♦€ 130/220
Rest – (bar lunch) Menu € 29 – Carte € 27/39
♦ This good value, personally run hotel was built with local stone and a noteworthy attention to detail. Cosy rear bar and sitting room. Good sized bedrooms. Stylish restaurant with modern menus.

TWOMILEBORRIS (Buiríos Léith) – **Tipperary** – **712** I 9 – **see Thurles**

VALENCIA ISLAND (Dairbhre) – **Kerry** – **712** A/B 12   38 **A2**
    ▶ Dublin 381 km – Killarney 88 km – Tralee 92 km

Knights Town – **Kerry**   38 **A2**

    Glanleam House ♨   ⟨ 🚗 🕭 🐾 ⅋ 🄿 🆅🆂🅰 ⓸ 🄰🄴
Glanleam, West : 2 km taking right fork at top of Market St – ℰ *(066) 947 61 76*
– www.glanleam.com – info@glanleam.com – Mid March-October
5 rm ⊒ – ♦€ 70/150 ♦♦€ 140/300 – 1 suite
Rest – (dinner only) (booking essential for non-residents) (communal dining)
Menu € 50 **s**
♦ Part 17C and 18C country house in extensive sub-tropical gardens, superbly located off West Kerry coast. Art Deco interiors. Spacious drawing room. Individually
styled rooms. Communal dining; produce grown in hotel's 19C walled gardens.

WATERFORD – **Waterford** – **712** K 11 – **pop. 49 213** 📖 *Ireland*   39 **C2**
    ▶ Dublin 154 km – Cork 117 km – Limerick 124 km
    🛧 Waterford Airport, Killowen : ℰ (051) 846600
    🖬 41 The Quay ℰ (051) 875823 Y, info@southeasttourism.ie Waterford
    Crystal Visitor Centre ℰ (051) 358397 (Jan-Oct),
    WaterfordCrystal@failteireland.ie
    🖬 Newrath, ℰ (051) 876 748
    ◎ Town★ - City Walls★ – Waterford Treasures★ **AC** Y
    🄶 Waterford Crystal★, SW : 2½ km by N 25 Y. Duncannon★, E : 19¼ km by
    R 683, ferry from Passage East and R 374 (south) Z – Dunmore East★,
    SE : 19¼ km by R 684 Z – Tintern Abbey★, E : 21 km by R 683, ferry from
    Passage East, R 733 and R 734 (south) Z

Plan opposite

    Waterford Castle H. and Golf Club ♨   ⟨ 🚗 🕭 ⅋ 🎞 🕼
The Island, Ballinakill, East : 4 km by R 683,   ⅋ 🄿 🆅🆂🅰 ⓸ 🄰🄴 ⓿
Ballinakill Rd and private ferry – ℰ *(051) 878 203 – www.waterfordcastle.com*
*– gm@waterfordcastle.com – Fax (051) 879 316 – Closed 4 January - 6 February
and 24-26 December*
14 rm – ♦€ 160/245 ♦♦€ 195/335, ⊒ €20 – 5 suites
Rest *The Munster Dining Room* – (bar lunch Monday-Saturday) Menu € 65
– Carte € 41/55
♦ Part 15C and 19C castle in charmingly secluded, historic river island setting. Classic
country house ambience amid antiques and period features. Comfortable, elegant
rooms. Oak panelled dining room with ornate ceilings and evening pianist.

    Granville   🕼 ♿ rm, 🄺 rest, ⅋ 🕼 🅂 🆅🆂🅰 ⓸ 🄰🄴 ⓿
Meagher Quay – ℰ *(051) 305 555 – www.granville-hotel.ie*
– stay@granville-hotel.ie – Fax (051) 305 566 – Closed 25-26 December   Y**a**
98 rm ⊒ – ♦€ 80/135 ♦♦€ 100/200
Rest *Bianconi Room* – (carvery lunch Monday-Saturday) Menu € 28
– Carte € 26/45
♦ Early 19C hotel that reputedly once hosted Charles Stewart Parnell. Individually
styled bedrooms with a consistent traditional standard of décor. Some views of river
Suir. Etched glass, drapes and panelling enhance gravitas of classic dining room.

    🗗🄷   **Athenaeum House**   🚗 🖼 🕼 🄺 rest, ⅋ 🕼 🅂 🄿 🆅🆂🅰 ⓸ 🄰🄴
Christendom, Ferrybank, Northeast : 1½ km by N 25 – ℰ *(051) 833 999*
– www.athenaeumhousehotel.com – info@athenaeumhousehotel.com
– Fax (051) 833 977 – Closed 25-26 December   Z**n**
29 rm ⊒ – ♦€ 120/150 ♦♦€ 150/180
Rest *Zak's* – (light lunch) Carte € 31/56
♦ In a quiet residential area, this extended Georgian house has retained some original features; elsewhere distinctly modern and stylish. Well equipped rooms exude
modish charm. Eclectic mix of dishes in restaurant overlooking garden.

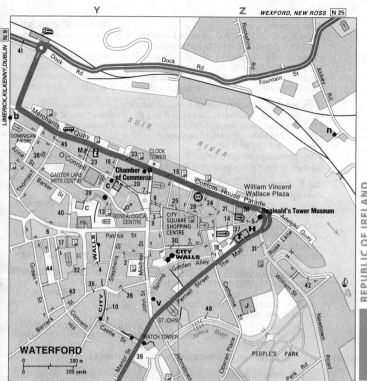

REPUBLIC OF IRELAND

Arlington Lodge

🛏 💷 🖥 📶 🚭 🅿️ 🅥🅘🅢🅐 ⓜⓞ 🅐🅔

Johns Hill, South : 1¼ km by N 25, John St and Johnstown Rd
– 𝒞 (051) 878 584
– www.arlingtonlodge.com
– info@arlingtonlodge.com – Fax (051) 878 127
– Closed 24-31 December
20 rm 🖵 – †€130/150 ††€150/230
Rest *Robert Paul* – (closed Sunday) (dinner only) Menu €35 – Carte €36/51
♦ Stylish, personally run Georgian former bishop's residence: period style precision. Antiques, gas fires in most of the very comfy and spacious individually styled rooms. Local produce richly employed in tasty menus.

1151

🔒 Fitzwilton 📶 👤 rm, 🛇 👑 𝑉𝐼𝑆𝐴 ◉◉ 𝐴𝐸
Bridge St – ☏ (051) 846 900 – www.dghotels.com – info@thefitzwiltonhotel.com
– Fax (051) 878650 – Closed 24-26 December Y**b**
91 rm ☲ – †€79/109 ††€99/245 **Rest** – Menu €26 – Carte €32/39
♦ Central hotel featuring glass façade and trendy bar. Bedrooms are modern, with a
good finish: some are more spacious than others; those at the back are much quieter.
Contemporary restaurant offers international dishes made with Irish ingredients.

Foxmount Country House without rest ⅌ 🚗 🕭 🛇 🛇 **P**
Passage East Rd, Southeast : 7¼ km by R 683, off Cheekpoint rd – ☏ (051)
874 308 – www.foxmountcountryhouse.com – info@foxmountcountryhouse.com
– Fax (051) 854 906 – Mid March-November
4 rm ☲ – †€130 ††€180
♦ Ivy-clad house, dating from the 17C, on a working farm. Wonderfully secluded and
quiet yet within striking distance of Waterford. Neat, cottage-style bedrooms.

XX La Bohème 🎬 ⇄ 𝑉𝐼𝑆𝐴 ◉◉ 𝐴𝐸
2 George's St – ☏ (051) 875 645 – www.labohemerestaurant.ie
– labohemerestaurant@eircom.net – Fax (051) 875 645 – Closed 24-27 December,
Sunday and Monday except Bank Holidays Y**c**
Rest – French – (dinner only) (booking essential) Menu €29 (weekdays)
– Carte €41/60
♦ Careful restoration of this historic building has created an atmospheric, candlelit din-
ing room. Classic French cooking, traditionally prepared, includes daily market specials.

X Bodéga 𝐴𝐶 𝑉𝐼𝑆𝐴 ◉◉ 𝐴𝐸
54 John's St – ☏ (051) 844 177 – www.bodegawaterford.com
– info@bodegawaterford.com – Fax (051) 844 177 – Closed 25-26 December,
1 January, Good Friday, Sunday and lunch Saturday Y**v**
Rest – Carte €29/47
♦ Tucked away in the heart of the city. Purple exterior; orange interior, augmented by
mosaics and wall murals. Classic rustic French menus or warming lunchtime dishes.

at Butlerstown Southwest : 8½ km by N 25 - Y – ✉ Waterford

Coach House without rest ⅌ ⇐ 🚗 🕭 🛇 👑 **P** 𝑉𝐼𝑆𝐴 ◉◉ 𝐴𝐸
Butlerstown Castle, Cork Rd – ☏ (051) 384 656 – www.butlerstowncastle.com
– coachhse@iol.ie – Fax (051) 384 751 – Easter-October
7 rm ☲ – †€70/85 ††€100/125
♦ Victorian house in grounds of Butlerstown Castle. Smart traditional communal areas
with warmly decorated breakfast room. Tasteful bedrooms offering good comforts.

WATERVILLE – Kerry – **712** B 12 📗 Ireland **38 A3**
 ☑ Dublin 383 km – Killarney 77 km
 🛈 ☏ (066) 9474646 (June-September)
 🏌 Ring of Kerry Golf Links Rd, ☏ (066) 947 41 02
 ◩ Ring of Kerry★★ – Skellig Islands★★, W: 12¾ km by N 70, R 567 and ferry
   from Ballinskelligs – Derrynane National Historic Park★★ AC, S: 14½ km by
   N70 – Leacanabuaile Fort (≤★★), N: 21 km by N 70

🔒 Butler Arms ≤ 🚗 🔽 📶 👑 **P** 𝑉𝐼𝑆𝐴 ◉◉ 𝐴𝐸
– ☏ (066) 947 41 44 – www.butlerarms.com – reservations@butlerarms.com
– Fax (066) 947 45 20 – March-October
36 rm ☲ – †€90/110 ††€160/350 **Rest** – (bar lunch) Carte €36/59
♦ Built 1862; Charlie Chaplin's holiday retreat. Family owned for three generations.
Sea views from most bedrooms: spacious junior suites particularly comfortable and
luxurious. Unstinting devotion to locally sourced cuisine.

Brookhaven House without rest 🚗 🛇 👑 **P** 𝑉𝐼𝑆𝐴 ◉◉ ◉
New Line Rd, North : 1¼ km on N 70 – ☏ (066) 947 44 31
– www.brrokhavenhouse.com – brookhaven@esatclear.ie – Fax (066) 947 47 24
– March-November
6 rm ☲ – †€75/120 ††€135
♦ Spacious modern guesthouse overlooking Waterville golf course; large and neat,
with restful lounge and cottage style bedrooms. Proud of its home-baked breakfasts.

🖪 Dublin 262 km – Galway 80 km – Sligo 104 km

🛈 James St ℰ (098) 25711, westport@failteireland.ie

◙ Town★★ (Centre★) – Westport House★★ **AC**

◙ Ballintubber Abbey★, SE : 21 km by R 330. SW : Murrisk Peninsula★★ – Croagh Patrick★, W : 9½ km by R 335 – Bunlahinch Clapper Bridge★, W : 25 ¾ km by R 335 - Doo Lough Pass★, W : 38½ km by R 335 – Aasleagh Falls★, S : 35½ km by N 59

🏠🏠 **Westport Plaza**   🕭 🖳 🖄 *ʃ₅* 📶 🖶 🔥 rm, 🖾 ⚡ ᐟᐟ 🕸 🚗 🚘 **VISA ⦿ AE ①**

Castlebar St – ℰ (098) 51 166 – www.westportplazahotel.ie
– info@westportplazahotel.ie – Fax (098) 51 133
85 rm 🖵 – 🛉€ 95/210 🛉🛉€ 130/250 – 3 suites
Rest *Merlot* – (dinner only) Menu € 43 – Carte € 16/43
♦ Contemporary lobby sets tone for this hotel, with deep leather sofas and marble floors. Trendy bar and terrace; well-equipped, spacious bedrooms boast flat screens and jacuzzis. Formal dining in stylish Merlot.

🏠🏠 **Carlton Atlantic Coast**   ≤ 🖳 ⦿ 📶 *ʃ₅* 🖶 🔥 rm, ⚡ 🕸 **P.**

The Quay, West : 1½ km by R 335 – ℰ (098) 29 000   **VISA ⦿ AE**
– www.carltonatlanticcoasthotel.com – reservations@atlanticcoasthotel.com
– Fax (098) 29 111 – Closed 16-27 December
84 rm 🖵 – 🛉€ 135/160 🛉🛉€ 220/270 – 1 suite
Rest *Blue Wave* – (bar lunch Monday-Saturday) Menu € 42
♦ Striking 18C mill conversion on shores of Clew Bay. Enjoy a seaweed treatment in the hydrotherapy jet bath or a drink in the lively Harbourmaster bar. Well-kept bedrooms. Top-floor restaurant with harbour and bay views.

🏠🏠 **Hotel Westport**   🖃 🖳 ⦿ 📶 *ʃ₅* 🖶 🔥 rm, 🏃 ⚡ ᐟᐟ 🕸 **P.**

Newport Rd – ℰ (098) 25 122 – www.hotelwestport.ie   **VISA ⦿ AE ①**
– reservations@hotelwestport.ie – Fax (098) 26 739
129 rm 🖵 – 🛉€ 140/160 🛉🛉€ 240/280
Rest – (dinner only and Sunday lunch) Menu € 31 – Carte € 31/46
♦ In attractive grounds running down to Carrowbeg river, a modern hotel appealing to families and conferences alike."Panda Club" and leisure centre will keep the kids busy. Sample traditional Irish fare on the daily changing menu.

🏠 **Ardmore Country House**   ≤ 🖃 ⚡ ᐟᐟ **P. VISA ⦿ AE**

The Quay, West : 2½ km on R 335 – ℰ (098) 25 994
– www.ardmorecountryhouse.com – ardmorehotel@eircom.net – Fax (098)
27795 – March-October, Sunday and Monday in low season.
13 rm 🖵 – 🛉€ 100/150 🛉🛉€ 200/250
Rest – (dinner only) Menu € 50 – Carte € 37/54
♦ Attractive family-run hotel in commanding setting with views across gardens and Clew Bay. Bedrooms are stylishly appointed with a country house feel. Chef owner proudly promotes organic produce.

🏠 **The Wyatt**   🖶 🔥 rm, ⚡ 🕸 **P. VISA ⦿ AE**

The Octagon – ℰ (098) 25 027 – www.wyatthotel.com – info@wyatthotel.com
– Fax (098) 26 316 – Closed 24-26 December
52 rm 🖵 – 🛉€ 65/130 🛉🛉€ 110/210
Rest – (dinner only and Sunday lunch) Menu € 36 – Carte € 25/47
♦ Refurbished hotel with some style located in the very centre of town. Comfortable furniture and décor from the spacious bar to the deeply carpeted bedrooms. Contemporary menus served in warmly painted dining room.

🏠 **Augusta Lodge** without rest   🖃 ⚡ ᐟᐟ **P. VISA ⦿**

Golf Links Rd, North : ¾ km off N 59 – ℰ (098) 28 900 – www.augustalodge.ie
– info@augustalodge.ie – Fax (098) 28 995 – Closed 22-27 December
10 rm 🖵 – 🛉€ 45/60 🛉🛉€ 70/90
♦ Family run, purpose-built guesthouse, convenient for Westport Golf Club; the owner has a collection of golfing memorabilia. Spacious, brightly decorated rooms.

REPUBLIC OF IRELAND

⌂ **Ashville House** without rest   🔌 ℀ ℘ ⑴ **P** *VISA* ⓪⓪

Castlebar Rd, East : 3¼ km on N 5 – ℰ (098) 27 060
– www.ashvilleguesthouse.net – ashvilleguesthouse@eircom.net – Fax (098)
27 060 – 16 March- 7 November

9 rm – ♦€70/100 ♦♦€100/110

♦ Set back from the main road two miles outside town with sun-trap patio to the side of the house. Comfortable appointments throughout and countryside views from the lounge.

⌂ **Quay West** without rest   ℀ ⑴ **P** *VISA* ⓪⓪

Quay Rd, West : ¾ km – ℰ (098) 27 863 – www.quaywestport.com
– quaywest@eircom.net – Fax (098) 28 379

6 rm ⌷ – ♦€40/55 ♦♦€74/80

♦ Purpose-built guesthouse located within walking distance of the town centre. Simply appointed throughout providing sensibly priced, well kept rooms.

🍴 **Sheebeen**   🔌 **P** *VISA* ⓪⓪

Rosbeg, Westport., West : 3 km on R 335 – ℰ (098) 26 528
– www.croninssheebeen.com – info@croninssheebeen.com – Fax (098) 24 396

Rest – Carte € 25/38

♦ Thatched roadside pub to west of town. Cosy front bar has some tables but main dining is upstairs. Fresh, accurate cooking; go for the fresh local fish and seafood specials.

Good food and accommodation at moderate prices?
Look for the Bib symbols:
red Bib Gourmand ⑬ for food, blue Bib Hotel 🛏 for hotels

REPUBLIC OF IRELAND

WEXFORD – Wexford – 712 M 10 – pop. 18 163 📖 Ireland   39 **D2**

� Dublin 141 km – Kilkenny 79 km – Waterford 61 km

ℹ Crescent Quay ℰ (053) 23111

🏌 Mulgannon, ℰ (053) 42 238

◎ Town★ - Main Street★YZ - Franciscan Friary★Z – St Iberius' Church★Y **D** - Twin Churches★Z

◩ Irish Agricultural Museum, Johnstown Castle★★ **AC**, SW : 7¼ km X – Irish National Heritage Park, Ferrycarrig★ **AC**, NW : 4 km by N 11 V – Curracloe★, NE : 8 km by R 741 and R 743 V. Kilmore Quay★, SW : 24 km by N 25 and R 739 (Saltee Islands★ - access by boat) X – Enniscorthy Castle★ (County Museum★ **AC**) N : 24 km by N 11 V

Plan opposite

🏨 **Whites**   🔲 ⑳ 🎵 ♨ 📶 ⬚ ♿ rm, 🅰🅲 ℀ ⑴ 🧖 **P** 🚗 *VISA* ⓪⓪ *AE*

Abbey St – ℰ (053) 912 2311 – www.whitesofwexford.ie
– info@whitesofwexford.ie – Fax (053) 914 5000 – Closed 23-26 December   Y**a**

152 rm ⌷ – ♦€85/120 ♦♦€150/200 – 5 suites

Rest – (dinner only) Menu € 45

♦ Smart new hotel built around a paved central courtyard. Spacious and modern, with a busy bar, popular meeting rooms, superb leisure facilities and very comfortable bedrooms. Traditional menu served in formal dining room.

🏨 **Ferrycarrig**   ≤ 🔌 🔲 ⑳ 🎵 📶 🏌 ⬚ ♿ rm, 🅰🅲 rest, ℀ 🧖 **P** *VISA* ⓪⓪ *AE* ⓪

Ferrycarrig, Northwest : 4½ km on N 11 – ℰ (053) 91 20 999
– www.ferrycarrighotel.ie – reservations@ferrycarrighotel.com – Fax (053) 91 20 982   V**a**

98 rm ⌷ – ♦€120/200 ♦♦€190/450 – 4 suites

Rest *Reeds* – (dinner only and Sunday lunch) Carte € 31/51

♦ Imposing hotel idyllically set on River Slaney and estuary. Public areas on enchanting waterfront curve. Good leisure facilities. Modern rooms with super views and balconies. Lively, informal Reeds.

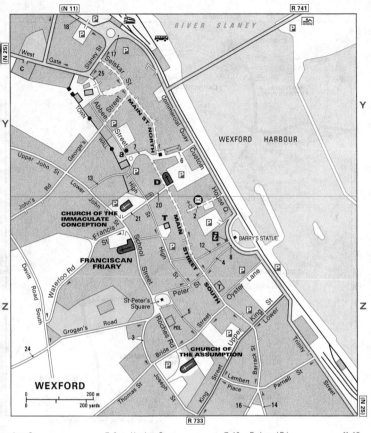

Whitford House   rest,

New Line Rd, West : 3½ km on R 733 – & *(053) 91 43 444 – www.whitford.ie*
– info@whitford.ie – Fax (053) 91 46 399 – Closed 25-27 December   **V d**
36 rm ⌂ – †€ 68/144 ††€ 110/238

Rest – (closed dinner Sunday-Wednesday in low season) (carvery lunch Monday-Saturday) Menu € 22/29 – Carte € 22/42

♦ Late 20C hotel with bright yellow exterior. Lounge bar has traditional food and nightly entertainment. Conference facilities. Spacious, well-kept rooms, some with patios. Dining room has eye-catching lemon interior.

Rathaspeck Manor without rest

Rathaspeck, Southwest : 6½ km by Rosslare Rd off Bridgetown rd – & *(053)*
914 16 72 – www.rathaspeckmanor.com – info@rathaspeckmanor.com
– June-November   **X k**
4 rm ⌂ – †€ 60/70 ††€ 120/140

♦ Georgian country house with 18-hole golf course half a mile from Johnstone Castle. Period furnishings adorn the public rooms. Comfortable, spacious bedrooms.

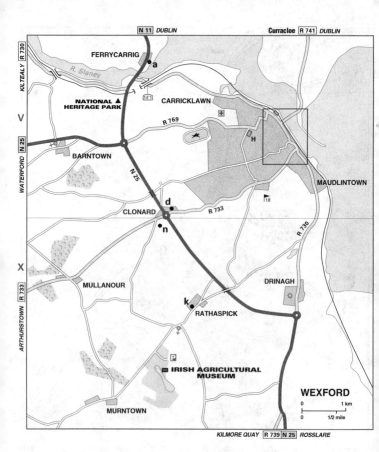

WICKLOW – Wicklow – **712** N 9 – **pop. 10 071** 🟦 *Ireland*   39 **D2**

  🅳 Dublin 53 km – Waterford 135 km – Wexford 108 km

  🛈 Fitzwilliam Sq 𝒞 (0404) 69117, wicklow@failteireland.ie

  🅶 Mount Usher Gardens, Ashford ★ **AC**, NW : 6½ km by R 750 and N 11 –
    Devil's Glen★, NW : 12¾ km by R 750 and N 11. Glendalough★★★ (Lower
    Lake★★★, Upper Lake★★, Cathedral★★, Round Tower★★, St Kevin's
    Church★★, St Saviour's Priory★) – W : 22½ km by R 750, N 11, R 763, R 755
    and R 756 – Wicklow Mountains★★ (Wicklow Gap★★, Sally Gap★★,
    Avondale★, Meeting of the Waters★, Glenmacnass Waterfall★,
    Glenmalur★, – Loughs Tay and Dan★)

at Rathnew Northwest : 3¼ km on R 750 – ⊠ Wicklow

🏠🏠🏠   **Tinakilly House** 🕭   ← ⛵ ᴋ₆ 🕭 ₆ rm, 🅰 rest, ⅏ ⑴ 🛦 🅿
    on R 750 – 𝒞 (0404) 69 274 – www.tinakilly.ie   𝗩𝗜𝗦𝗔 ⑩⑤ 🅐🅔 ⑪
    – reservations@tinakilly.ie – Fax (0404) 67 806
    – Closed 24-27 December
    50 rm � – †€ 150/200 ††€ 200/250 – 1 suite
    Rest *The Brunel Room* – (bar lunch) Carte € 45/57
    ♦ Part Victorian country house with views of sea and mountains. Grand entrance hall
    hung with paintings. Mix of comfortable room styles, those in main house most
    characterful. Large dining room with rich drapes, formal service.

Hunter's ⌖ 🍴 ∿ P VISA ⚫

Newrath Bridge, North : 1¼ km by N 11 on R 761 – ℰ (0404) 40 106
– www.hunters.ie – reception@hunters.ie – Fax (0404) 40 338
– Closed 24-26 December
16 rm ⌷ – †€ 100 ††€ 200 **Rest** – Menu € 30/50 – Carte approx. € 24
♦ Converted 18C coaching inn set in 2 acres of attractive gardens. Characterful, antique furnished accommodation. Elegant, traditionally appointed communal areas. Dining room in hotel's welcoming country style.

WOODENBRIDGE – Wicklow – **712** N 9   39 **D2**
  ▶ Dublin 74 km – Waterford 109 km – Wexford 66 km
  ⛳ Woodenbridge Arklow Vale of Avoca, ℰ (0402) 35 202

Woodenbridge ⪅ ⌖ & rm, 🍴 ⁴⁴ ∿ P VISA ⚫ AE ①
Vale of Avoca – ℰ (0402) 35 146 – www.woodenbridgehotel.com
– reservations@woodenbridgehotel.com – Fax (0402) 35 573
22 rm ⌷ – †€ 60/90 ††€ 100/140
Rest – (dinner only and Sunday lunch) Menu € 40 **s** – Carte € 20/30 **s**
♦ Reputedly the oldest hotel in Ireland, dating from about 1608. Situated in the picturesque Vale of Avoca. Period furnishings abound. Well-appointed rooms, some with balconies. Dining room has warm, friendly ambience.

Woodenbridge Lodge ⌖ ⤳ 🛏 & rm, 🍴 ⁴⁴ P VISA ⚫ AE ①
Vale of Avoca – ℰ (0402) 35 146 – www.woodenbridgehotel.com
– reservations@woodenbridgehotel.com – Fax (0402) 35 573
40 rm ⌷ – †€ 60/90 ††€ 100/140
Rest – (dinner only Friday-Sunday) Carte € 27/45 **s**
♦ Sister hotel to Woodenbridge, sympathetically built to blend into local hills. Bedrooms in yellow or pink: ask for one overlooking the lyrical Avoca River. Bright dining room with large windows and high ceilings.

YOUGHAL – Cork – **712** I 12 – pop. 6 785 *Ireland*   39 **C3**
  ▶ Dublin 235 km – Cork 48 km – Waterford 75 km
  🛈 Market Sq ℰ (024) 20170, info@youghalchamber.ie
  ⛳ Knockaverry, ℰ (024) 92 787
  ◎ Town★ – St Mary's Collegiate Church★★ – Town Walls★ - Clock Gate★
  ⊙ Helvick Head★ (⪅★), NE : 35½ km by N 25 and R 674 – Ringville (⪅★),
  NE : 32¼ km by N 25 and R 674 – Ardmore★ - Round Tower★ - Cathedral★
  (arcade★), N : 16 km by N 25 and R 674 – Whiting Bay★, SE : 19¼ km by
  N 25, R 673 and the coast road

Aherne's with rm & rm, ⁴⁴ ∿ P VISA ⚫ AE ①
163 North Main St – ℰ (024) 92 424 – www.ahernes.com – ahernes@eircom.net
– Fax (024) 93 633 – Closed 23-28 December
12 rm ⌷ – †€ 125/130 ††€ 170/210
Rest – Seafood – (bar lunch) Menu € 45 – Carte € 27/53
♦ Comfy sofas, books and sitting room fire announce this pleasant restaurant, which has modern art on walls and elegant linen-clad tables. Renowned seafood menus. Smart rooms.

REPUBLIC OF IRELAND

- *Discover the best restaurant ?*
- *Find the nearest hotel ?*
- *Find your bearings using our maps and guides ?*
- *Understand the symbols used in the guide...*

ℓ *Follow the red Bibs !*

Advice on restaurants from **Chef Bib**.

Tips and advice from **Clever Bib** on finding your way around the guide and on the road.

Advice on hotels from **Bellboy Bib**.

The MICHELIN Guide

A collection to savor!

Belgique & Luxembourg
Deutschland
España & Portugal
France
Great Britain & Ireland
Italia
Nederland
Österreich
Portugal
Suisse-Schweiz-Svizzera
Main Cities of Europe

Also:

Hong Kong Macau
Las Vegas
London
Los Angeles
New York City
Paris
San Francisco
Tokyo

Major hotel groups
Central reservation telephone numbers

Principales chaînes hôtelières
Centraux téléphoniques de réservation

Principali catene alberghiere
Centrali telefoniche di prenotazione

Die wichtigsten Hotelketten
Zentrale für telefonische Reservierung

ACCOR HOTELS (MERCURE & NOVOTEL)	0208 2834500
CHOICE HOTELS	0800 444444 *(Freephone)*
DE VERE HOTELS PLC	0870 6063606
HILTON HOTELS	08705 515151
HOLIDAY INN WORLDWIDE	0800 897121 *(Freephone)*
HYATT HOTELS WORLDWIDE	0845 8881234
INTERCONTINENTAL HOTELS	0800 0289387 *(Freephone)*
JURYS/DOYLE HOTELS	0870 9072222
MACDONALD HOTELS PLC	08457 585593
MARRIOTT HOTELS	0800 221222 *(Freephone)*
MILLENNIUM & COPTHORNE HOTELS PLC	0845 3020001
RADISSON HOTELS WORLDWIDE	0800 374411 *(Freephone)*
SHERATON HOTELS & RESORTS WORLDWIDE	0800 353535 *(Freephone)*

International Dialling Codes

Note: When making an international call, do not dial the first (0) of the city codes (except for calls to Italy).

Indicatifs téléphoniques internationaux

Important : pour les communications internationales, le zéro (0) initial de l'indicatif interurbain n'est pas à composer (excepté pour les appels vers l'Italie).

from \ to	A	B	CH	CZ	D	DK	E	FIN	F	GB	GR
A Austria		0032	0041	00420	0049	0045	0034	00358	0033	0044	0030
B Belgium	0043		0041	00420	0049	0045	0034	00358	0033	0044	0030
CH Switzerland	0043	0032		00420	0049	0045	0034	00358	0033	0044	0030
CZ Czech Republic	0043	0032	0041		0049	0045	0034	00358	0033	0044	0030
D Germany	0043	0032	0041	00420		0045	0034	00358	0033	0044	0030
DK Denmark	0043	0032	0041	00420	0049		0034	00358	0033	0044	0030
E Spain	0043	0032	0041	00420	0049	0045		00358	0033	0044	0030
FIN Finland	0043	0032	0041	00420	0049	0045	0034		0033	0044	0030
F France	0043	0032	0041	00420	0049	0045	0034	00358		0044	0030
GB United Kingdom	0043	0032	0041	00420	0049	0045	0034	00358	0033		0030
GR Greece	0043	0032	0041	00420	0049	0045	0034	00358	0033	0044	
H Hungary	0043	0032	0041	00420	0049	0045	0034	00358	0033	0044	0030
I Italy	0043	0032	0041	00420	0049	0045	0034	00358	0033	0044	0030
IRL Ireland	0043	0032	0041	00420	0049	0045	0034	00358	0033	0044	0030
J Japan	00143	00132	00141	001420	00149	00145	00134	001358	00133	00144	00130
L Luxembourg	0043	0032	0041	00420	0049	0045	0034	00358	0033	0044	0030
N Norway	0043	0032	0041	00420	0049	0045	0034	00358	0033	0044	0030
NL Netherlands	0043	0032	0041	00420	0049	0045	0034	00358	0033	0044	0030
PL Poland	0043	0032	0041	00420	0049	0045	0034	00358	0033	0044	0030
P Portugal	0043	0032	0041	00420	0049	0045	0034	00358	0033	0044	0030
RUS Russia	81043	81032	81041	6420	81049	81045	*	810358	81033	81044	*
S Sweden	0043	0032	0041	00420	0049	0045	0034	00358	0033	0044	0030
USA	01143	01132	01141	001420	01149	01145	01134	01358	01133	01144	01130

*Direct dialling not possible   *Pas de sélection automatique

Indicativi Telefonici Internazionali

Importante: per le comunicazioni internazionali, non bisogna comporre lo zero (0) iniziale del prefisso interurbano (escluse le chiamate per l'Italia).

Telefon-Vorwahlnummern International

Wichtig: bei Auslandsgesprächen darf die Null (0) der Ortsnetzkennzahl nicht gewählt werden (außer bei Gesprächen nach Italien).

(H)	(I)	(IRL)	(J)	(L)	(N)	(NL)	(PL)	(P)	(RUS)	(S)	(USA)	
0036	0039	00353	0081	00352	0047	0031	0048	00351	007	0046	001	**A Austria**
0036	0039	00353	0081	00352	0047	0031	0048	00351	007	0046	001	**B Belgium**
0036	0039	00353	0081	00352	0047	0031	0048	00351	007	0046	001	**CH Switzerland**
0036	0039	00353	0081	00352	0047	0031	0048	00351	007	0046	001	**CZ Czech Republic**
0036	0039	00353	0081	00352	0047	0031	0048	00351	007	0046	001	**D Germany**
0036	0039	00353	0081	00352	0047	0031	0048	00351	007	0046	001	**DK Denmark**
0036	0039	00353	0081	00352	0047	0031	0048	00351	007	0046	001	**E Spain**
0036	0039	00353	0081	00352	0047	0031	0048	00351	007	0046	001	**FIN Finland**
0036	0039	00353	0081	00352	0047	0031	0048	00351	007	0046	001	**F France**
0036	0039	00353	0081	00352	0047	0031	0048	00351	007	0046	001	**GB United Kingdom**
0036	0039	00353	0081	00352	0047	0031	0048	00351	007	0046	001	**GR Greece**
	0039	00353	0081	00352	0047	0031	0048	00351	007	0046	001	**H Hungary**
0036		00353	0081	00352	0047	0031	0048	00351	*	0046	001	**I Italy**
0036	0039		0081	00352	0047	0031	0048	00351	007	0046	001	**IRL Ireland**
00136	00139	001353		001352	00147	00131	00148	001351	*	001146	0011	**J Japan**
0036	0039	00353	0081		0047	0031	0048	00351	007	0046	001	**L Luxembourg**
0036	0039	00353	0081	00352		0031	0048	00351	007	0046	001	**N Norway**
0036	0039	00353	0081	00352	0047		0048	00351	007	0046	001	**NL Netherlands**
0036	0039	00353	0081	00352	0047	0031		00351	007	0046	001	**PL Poland**
0036	0039	00353	0081	00352	0047	0031	048		007	0046	001	**P Portugal**
81036	*	*	*	*	*	81031	1048	*		*	*	**RUS Russia**
0036	0039	00353	0081	00352	0047	0031	0048	00351	007		001	**S Sweden**
01136	01139	011353	01181	011352	01147	01131	01148	011351	*	011146		**USA**

Selezione automatica impossibile   *Automatische Vorwahl nicht möglich*

Index of towns

Index des localités

Indice delle località

Ortsverzeichnis

Place with at least

- ● a hotel or a restaurant
- ✿ a starred establishment
- 🔴 a « Bib Gourmand » restaurant
- 🔲 a « Bib Hotel »
- ✗ a particularly pleasant restaurant
- 🍺 a traditional pub serving good food
- 🏠 a particularly pleasant hotel
- 个 a particularly pleasant guesthouse
- 🖐 a particularly quiet hotel

Localité possédant au moins

- ● un hôtel ou un restaurant
- ✿ une table étoilée
- 🔴 un restaurant « Bib Gourmand »
- 🔲 un hôtel « Bib Hôtel »
- ✗ un restaurant agréable
- 🍺 un pub traditionnel servant des repas
- 🏠 un hôtel agréable
- 个 une maison d'hôte agréable
- 🖐 un hôtel très tranquille

La località possiede come minimo

- ● un albergo o un ristorante
- ✿ una delle migliori tavole dell'anno
- 🔴 un ristorante « Bib Gourmand »
- 🔲 un albergo « Bib Hotel »
- ✗ un ristorante molto piacevole
- 🍺 un pub tradizionali con cucina
- 🏠 un albergo molto piacevole
- 个 locande e affittacamere ameni
- 🖐 un esercizio molto tranquillo

Ort mit mindestens

- ● einem Hotel oder Restaurant
- ✿ einem der besten Restaurants des Jahres
- 🔴 einem Restaurant « Bib Gourmand »
- 🔲 einem Hotel « Bib Hotel »
- ✗ einem sehr angenehmen Restaurant
- 🍺 einem traditionelle Pubs, die Speisen anbieten
- 🏠 einem sehr angenehmen Hotel
- 个 einem Privatzimmer
- 🖐 einem sehr ruhigen Haus

Maps
Regional maps of listed towns

Cartes
Cartes régionales des localités citées

Carta
Carta regionale delle località citate

Regionalkarten
Regionalkarten der erwähnten Orte

Distances in miles

(except for the Republic of Ireland: km). The distance is given from each town to other nearby towns and to the capital of each region as grouped in the guide. To avoid excessive repetition some distances have only been quoted once – you may therefore have to look under both town headings.
The distances quoted are not necessarily the shortest but have been based on the roads which afford the best driving conditions and are therefore the most practical.

Distances en miles

Pour chaque région traitée, vous trouverez au texte de chacune des localités sa distance par rapport à la capitale et aux villes environnantes. La distance d'une localité à une autre n'est pas toujours répétée aux deux villes intéressées : voyez au texte de l'une ou de l'autre. Ces distances ne sont pas nécessairement comptées par la route la plus courte mais par la plus pratique, c'est-à-dire celle offrant les meilleures conditions de roulage.

Belfast	Cork	Dublin	Dundalk	Galway	Killarney	Limerick	Londonderry	Omagh	Sligo	Tullamore	Waterford
265											
105	163										
53	212	53									
213	126	133	183								
294	57	192	242	134							
228	63	125	175	64	70						
72	301	147	103	172	296	227					
70	266	113	69	157	295	228	36				
126	204	129	124	87	211	142	86	70			
165	129	62	112	85	138	71	162	136	106		
206	76	103	153	143	131	79	242	207	222	84	

129 Miles

Dublin - Sligo

Distanze in miglia

Per ciascuna delle regioni trattate, troverete nel testo di ogni località la sua distanza dalla capitale e dalle città circostanti. Le distanza da una località all'altra non è sempre ripetuta nelle due città interessate : vedere nel testo dell'una o dell'altra. Le distanze non sono necessariamente calcolate seguendo il percorso più breve, ma vengono stabilite secondo l'itinerario più pratico, che offre cioè le migliori condizioni di viaggio.

Entfernungsangaben in Meilen

Die Entfernungen der einzelnen Orte zur Landeshauptstadt und zu den nächstgrößeren Städten in der Umgebung sind im allgemeinen Ortstext angegeben. Die Entfernung zweier Städte voneinander können Sie aus den Angaben im Ortstext der einen oder der anderen Stadt ersehen. Die Entfernungsangaben gelten nicht immer für der kürzesten, sondern für den günstigsten Weg.

Distances between major towns
Distances entre principales villes
Distanze tra le principali città
Entfernungen zwischen den größeren Stäten

Edinburgh - Southampton: 433 Miles

	Aberdeen	Ayr	Birmingham	Blackpool	Brighton	Bristol	Cambridge	Cardiff	Carlisle	Coventry	Dover	Dumfries	Dundee	Edinburgh	Glasgow	Inverness	Ipswich	Kingston-upon-Hull	Leeds	Leicester	Liverpool	London	Manchester	Middlesbrough	Newcastle	Norwich	Nottingham	Oban	Oxford	Plymouth	Portsmouth	Sheffield	Southampton	Stoke-on-Trent	Swansea
Ayr	182																																		
Birmingham	425	327																																	
Blackpool	330	232	127																																
Brighton	596	498	177	299																															
Bristol	506	408	92	209	158																														
Cambridge	486	388	98	220	121	173																													
Cardiff	527	429	113	230	191	46	204																												
Carlisle	230	132	196	101	367	277	258	298																											
Coventry	443	345	24	146	157	95	85	125	214																										
Dover	604	506	201	323	104	203	122	236	376	180																									
Dumfries	212	59	230	135	401	312	292	332	36	249	427																								
Dundee	68	123	359	265	531	441	412	462	165	378	530	147																							
Edinburgh	127	86	293	198	465	375	351	395	99	312	470	80	56																						
Glasgow	149	36	293	198	464	375	355	396	99	312	490	80	90	49																					
Inverness	105	206	449	354	620	531	511	552	255	468	646	236	142	157	173																				
Ipswich	540	442	152	274	127	210	58	243	311	138	130	345	465	404	408	565																			
Kingston-upon-Hull	399	301	138	139	276	227	141	248	170	142	260	205	324	264	267	424	194																		
Leeds	354	256	119	86	257	209	148	229	125	123	267	159	279	218	222	379	202	61																	
Leicester	443	345	43	146	163	118	82	150	215	29	185	249	378	307	312	468	135	117	98																
Liverpool	355	257	99	58	271	181	193	202	126	118	296	160	289	223	223	380	246	127	74	118															
London	538	440	119	241	71	122	60	156	310	98	76	344	473	405	407	563	81	196	196	103	213														
Manchester	350	252	96	52	267	178	189	198	121	115	292	155	284	218	218	375	243	97	44	115	34	210													
Middlesbrough	290	226	176	133	313	265	199	286	95	179	318	130	219	159	192	321	253	112	72	155	143	253	122												
Newcastle	253	191	208	157	345	297	231	318	60	211	350	94	182	122	157	284	285	144	105	187	175	285	154	43											
Norwich	537	439	163	285	177	244	69	270	308	149	179	343	462	402	406	562	46	157	198	146	257	115	252	249	281										
Nottingham	416	318	53	137	190	142	89	163	188	56	212	222	341	281	285	441	142	91	72	28	109	130	82	129	161	140									
Oban	181	123	387	293	559	469	449	490	193	406	584	174	120	124	97	110	503	362	323	406	318	501	313	287	251	500	379								
Oxford	498	400	79	201	108	74	99	107	270	60	146	304	433	366	367	523	142	190	170	78	173	65	168	227	259	164	104	461							
Plymouth	620	522	206	323	217	120	286	154	392	209	287	426	555	489	489	645	307	341	322	232	295	220	291	379	411	342	256	583	194						
Portsmouth	581	483	162	284	52	124	154	157	352	142	140	387	516	449	450	606	162	272	253	160	256	88	251	310	342	210	187	544	87	174					
Sheffield	391	293	91	104	228	180	131	201	162	94	250	196	316	255	259	415	184	65	41	70	90	168	50	103	135	181	44	354	142	294	225				
Southampton	565	467	145	267	64	107	151	140	336	126	152	370	499	433	433	589	172	256	237	144	239	85	235	294	326	207	170	527	71	154	20	209			
Stoke-on-Trent	383	285	46	86	218	128	140	149	154	65	243	189	318	251	251	408	193	128	93	63	58	161	53	162	194	205	54	346	120	242	203	81	186		
Swansea	532	434	152	234	230	85	243	46	303	164	267	337	466	400	400	556	281	287	268	190	186	195	202	325	357	308	202	495	146	192	195	240	179	189	
Wick	206	307	550	455	721	632	612	652	356	569	747	337	243	258	274	104	666	525	485	569	481	664	476	422	385	663	542	213	624	745	706	516	690	508	657

For distances refer to the colour key in the table
Les distances sont indiquées dans la couleur du point de passage
Le distanze sono indicate con il colore del punto di passaggio
Die Entfernungen sind angegeben in der Farbe des betroffenen Passagepinktes

● FOLKESTONE
(CHANNEL TUNNEL
● SOUTHAMPTON
● TYNEMOUTH

Glasgow - Barcelona   1305 Miles

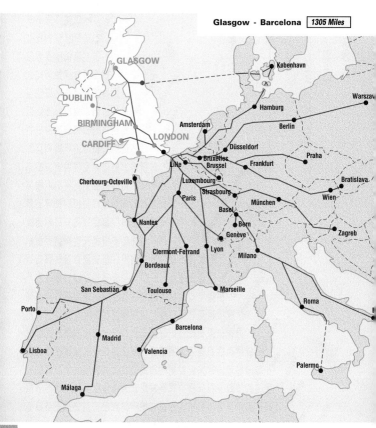

Birmingham	Cardiff	Dublin	Glasgow	London	
230	449	397	336	133	**Amsterdam**
1017	1043	1185	1305	891	**Barcelona**
652	678	820	939	526	**Basel**
774	800	943	726	649	**Berlin**
725	751	893	996	600	**Bern**
723	749	892	1011	598	**Bordeaux**
1060	1086	1229	1348	935	**Bratislava**
1493	1519	1661	1781	1368	**Brindisi**
319	345	488	607	194	**Bruxelles-Brussel**
162	158	331	451	80	**Cherbourg**
637	663	806	925	512	**Clermont-Ferrand**
446	472	614	734	320	**Düsseldorf**
567	593	735	855	442	**Frankfurt am Main**
663	689	832	951	538	**Genève**
510	692	678	607	541	**Hamburg**
701	883	869	797	731	**København**
265	291	433	553	139	**Lille**
1446	1472	1614	1734	1320	**Lisboa**
453	479	621	741	327	**Luxembourg**

Birmingham	Cardiff	Dublin	Glasgow	London	
668	694	836	956	542	**Lyon**
1154	1180	1322	1442	1028	**Madrid**
1488	1514	1656	1776	1362	**Málaga**
861	887	1029	1149	736	**Marseille**
874	900	1043	1162	749	**Milano**
801	827	970	1089	676	**München**
565	591	732	852	439	**Nantes**
1788	1814	1957	2076	1663	**Palermo**
370	396	537	658	245	**Paris**
1349	1375	1518	1637	1224	**Porto**
895	921	1063	1183	769	**Praha**
1235	1261	1404	1523	1110	**Roma**
871	897	1039	1159	745	**San Sebastián**
580	606	749	868	455	**Strasbourg**
796	822	965	1084	671	**Toulouse**
1232	1258	1400	1519	1106	**Valencia**
1123	1149	1291	1074	997	**Warszawa**
1006	1032	1175	1294	881	**Wien**
1117	1143	1285	1405	991	**Zagreb**

Great Britain & Ireland in 39 maps

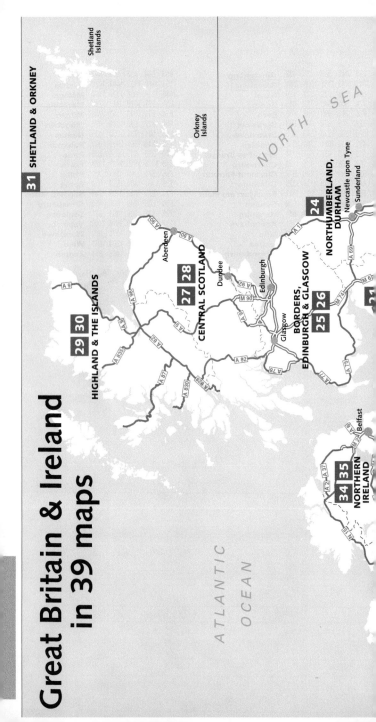

ATLANTIC
OCEAN

NORTH SEA

31 SHETLAND & ORKNEY

Shetland
Islands

Orkney
Islands

Aberdeen

29 **30** HIGHLAND & THE ISLANDS

27 **28** CENTRAL SCOTLAND

Dundee

Edinburgh

Glasgow

25 **26** BORDERS, EDINBURGH & GLASGOW

24 NORTHUMBERLAND, DURHAM

Newcastle upon Tyne
Sunderland

34 **35** NORTHERN IRELAND

Belfast

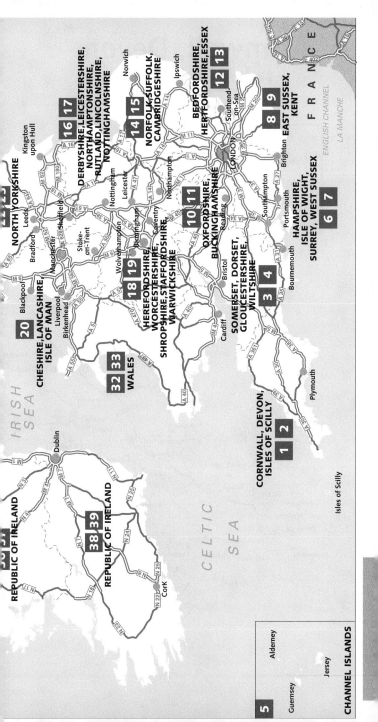

1 Cornwall, Devon, Isles of Scilly

BR

A

1

Bryher

St. Martin's

Tresco

St. Mary's

Isles of Scilly

B

Clo

Hartland

Bude

Crackington Haven

Boscastle

Launces

2

C O R N W A L

Rock

A 30

Padstow

Helland

A 30

Newquay

Bodmin

Liskeard

Summercourt

Mitchell

St. Blazey

St. Agnes

Tregrehan

Golant

Loo

Ladock

St. Austell

Fowey

Polperro

Illogan

Truro

Mevagissey

Zennor

St. Ives

Veryan

Portloe

St. Just

Marazion

Portscatho

Penzance

St. Hilary

St. Mawes

Perranuthnoe

Falmouth

Mousehole

Porthleven

Helston

Mawnan Smith

St. Keverne

Mullion

Coverack

3

Lizard

A

B

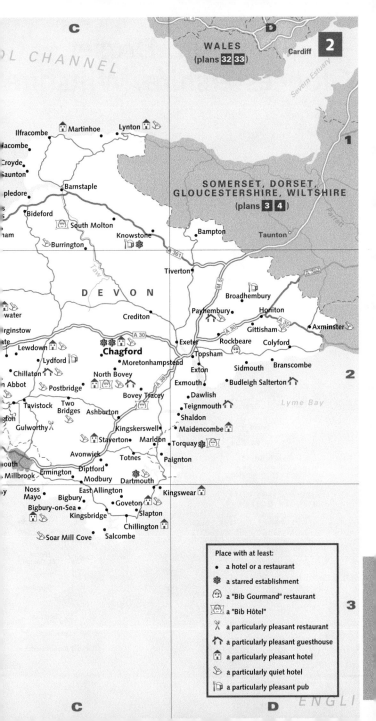

C

BRISTOL CHANNEL

D

WALES
(plans 32 33)

Cardiff

2

Ilfracombe • Martinhoe • Lynton

Combe Martin •

Croyde •
Saunton •

Appledore •

Bideford •

South Molton •

Burrington •

Knowstone •

Bampton •

Taunton •

**SOMERSET, DORSET,
GLOUCESTERSHIRE, WILTSHIRE**
(plans 3 4)

Tiverton •

D E V O N

Broadhembury •

water

Georginstow •

Lewdown • **Chagford**

Lydford •

Chillaton •

n Abbot • Postbridge •

Crediton •

Payhembury •

Honiton •

Gittisham •

Axminster

Exeter •

Rockbeare

Colyford •

Moretonhampstead •

Topsham •

North Bovey

Exton •

Sidmouth •

Branscombe •

Bovey Tracey •

Exmouth •

Budleigh Salterton •

Tavistock •

Two
Bridges

Dawlish •

Teignmouth •

Ashburton •

Gulworthy •

Kingskerswell •

Shaldon •

Maidencombe •

Staverton •

Marldon •

Torquay •

Avonwick •

Totnes •

Paignton •

outh

Millbrook •

Ermington •

Diptford •

Modbury •

Dartmouth •

Kingswear •

Noss
Mayo •

East Allington •

Bigbury •

Goveton •

Bigbury-on-Sea •

Kingsbridge •

Slapton •

Chillington •

Soar Mill Cove •

Salcombe •

Lyme Bay

2

Place with at least:

- • a hotel or a restaurant
- ❀ a starred establishment
- 😊 a "Bib Gourmand" restaurant
- 🏨 a "Bib Hôtel"
- ✕ a particularly pleasant restaurant
- ⌂ a particularly pleasant guesthouse
- 🏠 a particularly pleasant hotel
- ➿ a particularly quiet hotel
- 🍺 a particularly pleasant pub

3

C

D

ENGLI

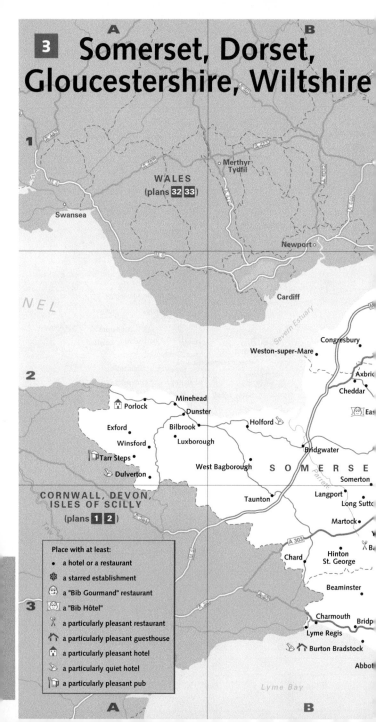

3 Somerset, Dorset, Gloucestershire, Wiltshire

A   B

WALES
(plans 32 33)

Swansea

Merthyr
Tydfil

NEL

Cardiff

Newport

Severn Estuary

Congresbury

Weston-super-Mare

Axbrid

Cheddar

Eas

Porlock

Minehead
Dunster

Holford

Exford

Bilbrook

Winsford

Luxborough

Tarr Steps

Bridgwater

Dulverton

West Bagborough

S O M E R S E

Somerton

CORNWALL, DEVON,
ISLES OF SCILLY
(plans 1 2)

Taunton

Langport

Long Sutto

Martock

Ba

Chard

Hinton
St. George

Place with at least:
• a hotel or a restaurant
❀ a starred establishment
☺ a "Bib Gourmand" restaurant
🏠 a "Bib Hôtel"
✕ a particularly pleasant restaurant
🏠 a particularly pleasant guesthouse
🏠 a particularly pleasant hotel
🌿 a particularly quiet hotel
🍺 a particularly pleasant pub

Beaminster

Charmouth   Bridp

Lyme Regis

Burton Bradstock

Abbot

Lyme Bay

A   B

A B

1

ENGLISH CHANNEL

LA MANCHE

Alderney

Braye

St. Anne

Cherbourg-
Octeville

Guernsey

Catel

Vazon Bay

Herm

Kings Mills

St. Peter Port

St. Saviour

Fermain Bay

Forest

Sark

St. Martin

FRANCE

2

St. Lawrence

Bouley Bay

Rozel Bay

St. Peter

St. Saviour

La Pulente

Gorey

St. Brelade's Bay

Grouville

St. Aubin

La Rocque

Beaumont

Green Island

Jersey

La Haule

St. Helier

3

A B

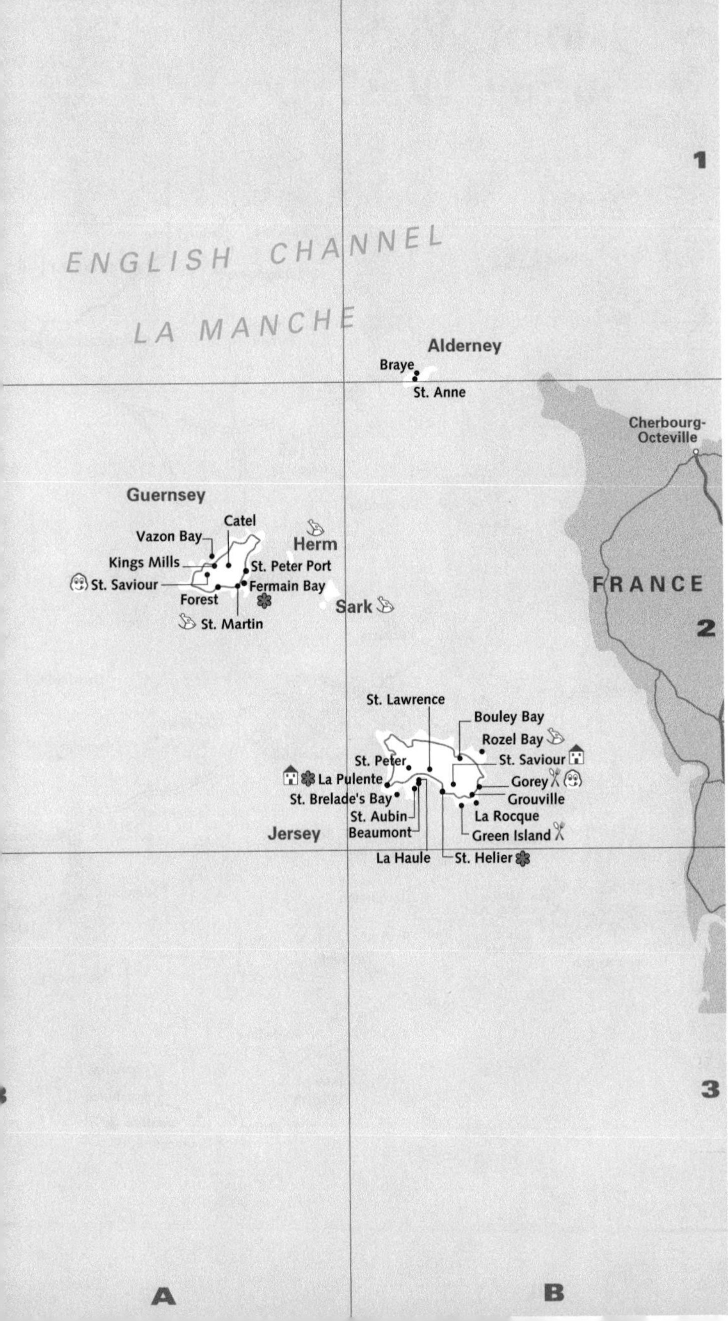

A   **B**

OXFORDSHIRE, BUCKINGHAMSHIRE
(plans 10 11)

Rea

1

SOMERSET, DORSET, GLOUCESTERSHIRE, WILTSHIRE
(plans 3 4)

Newbury

Highclere   • Burghclere

Old Burghclere •   • Baughurst

Hurstbourne Tarrant   Basingstoke•

Longstock

Stockbridge

Salisbury   Sparsholt •

Winchester   H A M P S H I R E

Romsey•   West Meon •

Fordingbridge   Droxford

Brook •

Netley Marsh   Shedfield •

Southampton   Denmead •

Ringwood

Brockenhurst •   Fareham•

New Milton   Beaulieu   Emsw

Lymington   Portsmouth   Hayli

Barton-on-Sea   Milford-on-Sea   Isla

Bournemouth   Yarmouth   Seaview

Totland

Brighstone   Shanklin

Isle of Wight   Bonchurch

Niton   Ventnor
St Lawrence

A   **B**

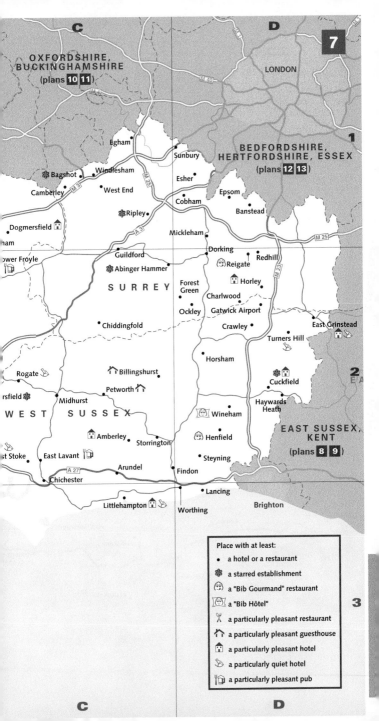

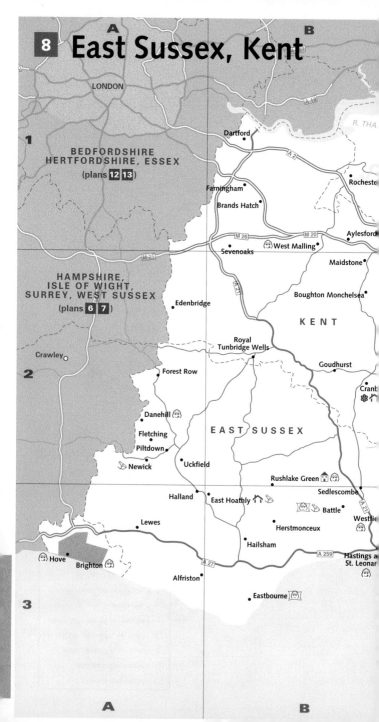

LONDON

BEDFORDSHIRE
HERTFORDSHIRE, ESSEX
(plans 12 13)

HAMPSHIRE,
ISLE OF WIGHT,
SURREY, WEST SUSSEX
(plans 6 7)

Crawley

Dartford

Farningham
Brands Hatch

Rochester

West Malling

Aylesford

Sevenoaks

Maidstone

Edenbridge

Boughton Monchelsea

KENT

Royal
Tunbridge Wells

Forest Row

Goudhurst

Cranb

Danehill

EAST SUSSEX

Fletching
Piltdown

Uckfield

Newick

Rushlake Green

Sedlescombe

Halland

East Hoathly

Battle

Westfie

Lewes

Herstmonceux

Hove

Brighton

Hailsham

Hastings a
St. Leonar

Alfriston

A 259

Eastbourne

R. THA

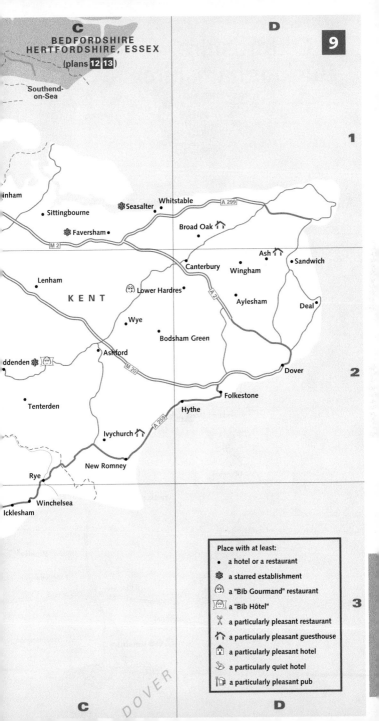

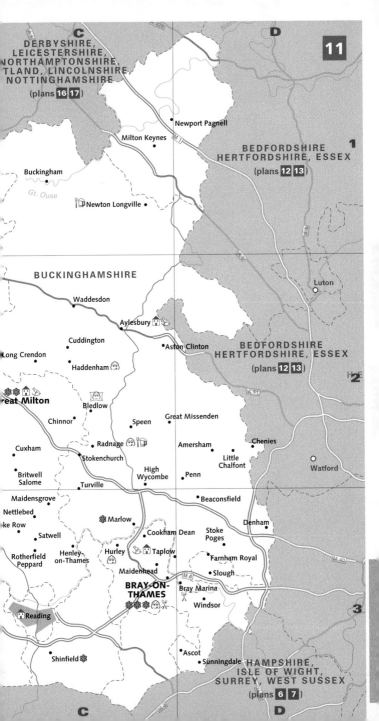

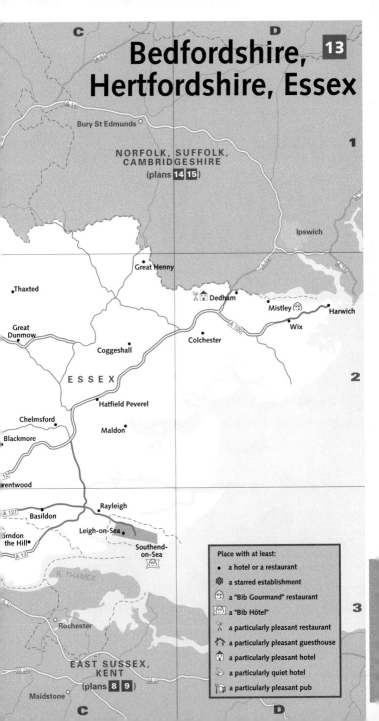

Bedfordshire, Hertfordshire, Essex

13

C

D

Bury St Edmunds

NORFOLK, SUFFOLK, CAMBRIDGESHIRE
(plans **14** **15**)

1

Ipswich

Great Henny

Thaxted

Dedham

Mistley

Harwich

Wix

Great Dunmow

Coggeshall

Colchester

2

ESSEX

Hatfield Peverel

Chelmsford

Maldon

Blackmore

Brentwood

A 127

Rayleigh

Basildon

Leigh-on-Sea

Orndon the Hill

A 13

Southend-on-Sea

R. THAMES

Rochester

3

EAST SUSSEX, KENT
(plans **8** **9**)

Maidstone

C

D

Place with at least:
- • a hotel or a restaurant
- ✿ a starred establishment
- 😊 a "Bib Gourmand" restaurant
- 🍴 a "Bib Hôtel"
- ✗ a particularly pleasant restaurant
- 🏠 a particularly pleasant guesthouse
- 🏠 a particularly pleasant hotel
- 🌜 a particularly quiet hotel
- 🍺 a particularly pleasant pub

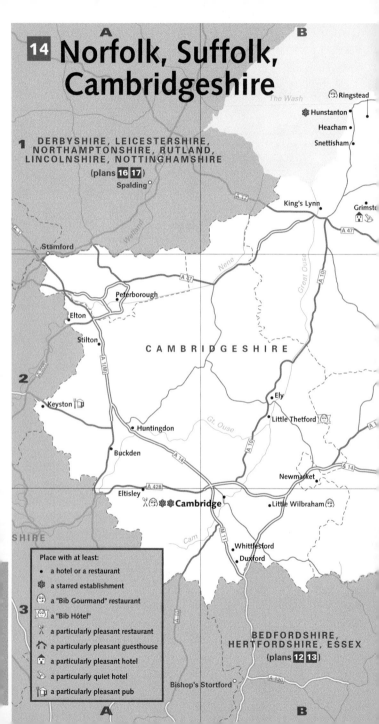

14 Norfolk, Suffolk, Cambridgeshire

The Wash

Ringstead
Hunstanton
Heacham
Snettisham

1 DERBYSHIRE, LEICESTERSHIRE, NORTHAMPTONSHIRE, RUTLAND, LINCOLNSHIRE, NOTTINGHAMSHIRE
(plans **16 17**)

Spalding

King's Lynn

Grimsto

Stamford

Nene

Great Ouse

Peterborough

Elton

Stilton

CAMBRIDGESHIRE

2

Keyston

Ely

Little Thetford

Gt. Ouse

Huntingdon

Buckden

Newmarket

Eltisley

Cambridge

Little Wilbraham

Cam

Whittlesford

Duxford

SHIRE

Place with at least:

- • a hotel or a restaurant
- ✿ a starred establishment
- ☺ a "Bib Gourmand" restaurant
- ▣ a "Bib Hôtel"
- ✗ a particularly pleasant restaurant
- ↑ a particularly pleasant guesthouse
- ▥ a particularly pleasant hotel
- ⌣ a particularly quiet hotel
- ▯ a particularly pleasant pub

3

BEDFORDSHIRE, HERTFORDSHIRE, ESSEX
(plans **12 13**)

Bishop's Stortford

caster
aithe   Holkham   Wells-next-the-Sea
well   Blakeney   Sheringham
        Burnham   Morston   Cromer
        Market   Aylmerton
                  Hindringham   Holt   Thorpe Market
t   Walcott
am   Thursford   Hunworth
                     Green   North Walsham
                          Itteringham   Erpingham

        Wellingham

                N O R F O L K   Coltishall
                                                Wroxham
            East Dereham

                                        Norwich   Bure
                                              Brundall   Great
        Watton   Wymondham   Yarmouth
                                   Stoke Holy Cross   Yare
                                                      Fritton
                                                    Somerleyton
                                                        Lowestoft
                          Pulham Market   2
            North Lopham   Bungay
                          Diss   Waveney
                                                            Southwold
        Stanton   Fressingfield
                  Thornham Magna   Bramfield   Walberswick
    Bury
    St Edmunds
            Beyton   Kelsale
        Stowmarket   Earl Stonham   Framlingham   Saxmundham
        Buxhall   S U F F O L K   Snape   Aldeburgh
    Lavenham   Bildeston
            Monks Eleigh   Orford
    Long Melford   Hadleigh   Ipswich   Woodbridge
    Sudbury
        Stoke-by-Nayland   3
    Nayland   Levington
                                    Harwich

        Colchester

C   D

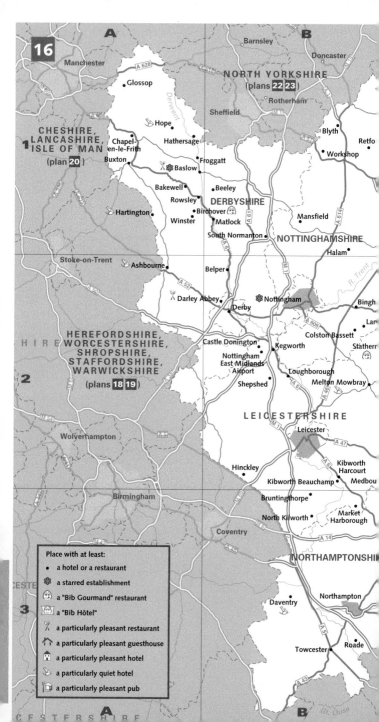

C Scunthorpe

D

17

1

• Louth

• Belchford

• Lincoln

Horncastle •

• Woodhall Spa

L I N C O L N S H I R E

vark-on-Trent

• Hough-on-the-Hill

• Great Gonerby

antham •

ripton

Spalding •

Holbeach

The Wash

• King's Lynn

2

• Clipsham

T L A N D

Oakham

Stamford

Hambleton

• Barrowden

pingham

• Oundle

Peterborough

NORFOLK, SUFFOLK, CAMBRIDGESHIRE
(plans **14 15**)

• Kettering

• Stanwick

Bedford

BEDFORDSHIRE, HERTFORDSHIRE, ESSEX
(plans **12 13**)

C

Derbyshire, Leicestershire, Northamptonshire, Rutland, Lincolnshire, Nottinghamshire

3

D

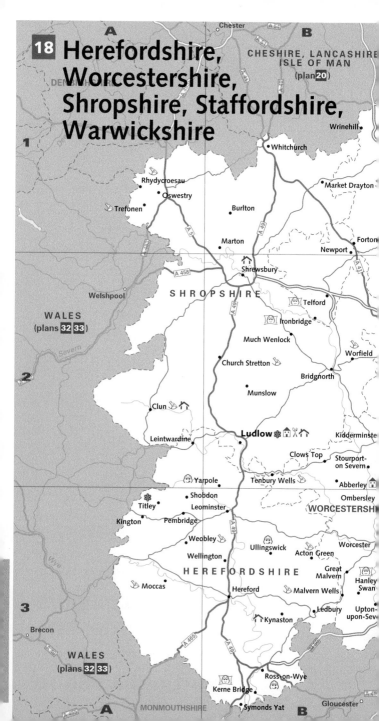

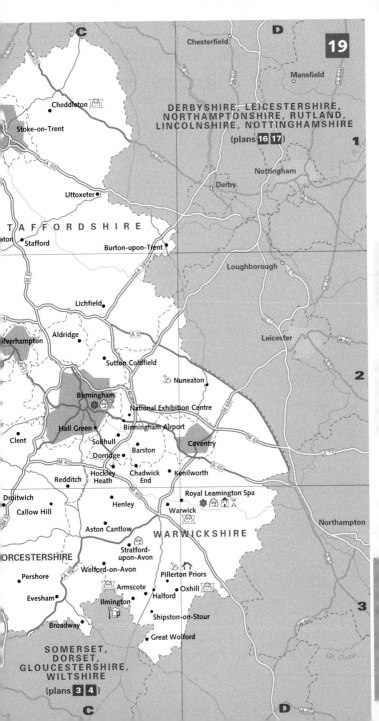

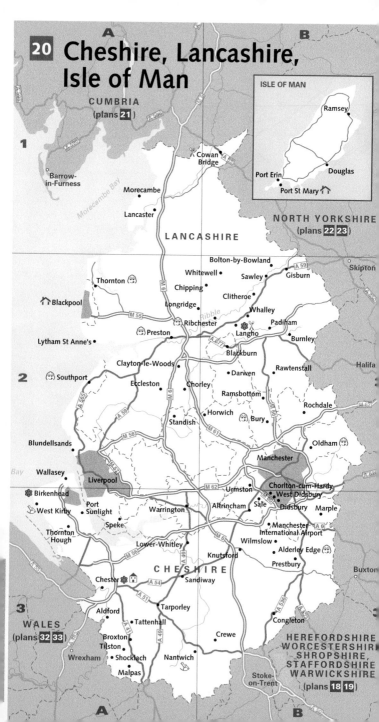

20 Cheshire, Lancashire, Isle of Man

ISLE OF MAN

Ramsey

Port Erin • Douglas

Port St Mary

CUMBRIA (plans 21)

Barrow-in-Furness

Morecambe

Lancaster

Cowan Bridge

LANCASHIRE

NORTH YORKSHIRE (plans 22 23)

Skipton

Thornton

Blackpool

Whitewell

Chipping

Bolton-by-Bowland

Sawley

Clitheroe

Gisburn

Longridge

Whalley

Ribchester

Langho

Padiham

Preston

Blackburn

Burnley

Lytham St Anne's

Clayton-le-Woods

Darwen

Rawtenstall

Southport

Eccleston

Chorley

Ramsbottom

Rochdale

Horwich

Bury

Halifax

Standish

Oldham

Blundellsands

Manchester

Wallasey

Liverpool

Urmston

Chorlton-cum-Hardy

West Didsbury

Birkenhead

Port Sunlight

Altrincham

Sale

Didsbury

Marple

West Kirby

Warrington

Speke

Thornton Hough

Lower-Whitley

Wilmslow

Manchester International Airport

Alderley Edge

Knutsford

Prestbury

Buxton

CHESHIRE

Chester

Sandiway

WALES (plans 32 33)

Aldford

Tarporley

Tattenhall

Congleton

HEREFORDSHIRE WORCESTERSHIRE SHROPSHIRE STAFFORDSHIRE WARWICKSHIRE (plans 18 19)

Broxton

Crewe

Tilston

Shocklach

Nantwich

Wrexham

Malpas

Stoke-on-Trent

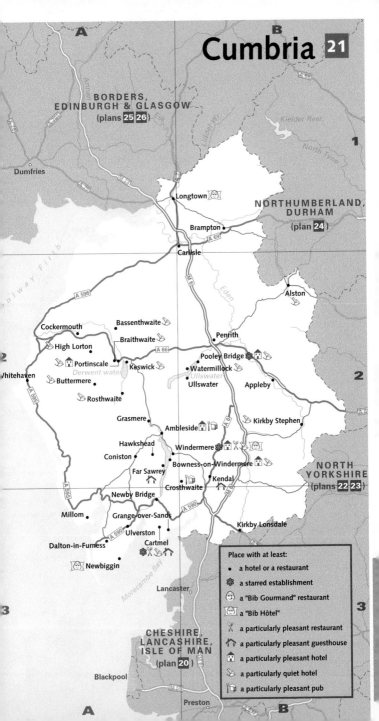

Cumbria 21

BORDERS,
EDINBURGH & GLASGOW
(plans 25 26)

Dumfries

Longtown

NORTHUMBERLAND,
DURHAM
(plan 24)

Brampton

Carlisle

Alston

Cockermouth   Bassenthwaite

High Lorton   Braithwaite   Penrith

Portinscale   Pooley Bridge

Whitehaven   Keswick   Watermillock

Derwent water   Ullswater

Buttermere   Ullswater   Appleby

Rosthwaite

Grasmere   Kirkby Stephen

Ambleside

Hawkshead   Windermere

Coniston   Bowness-on-Windermere   NORTH
YORKSHIRE
(plans 22 23)

Far Sawrey   Kendal

Newby Bridge   Crosthwaite

Millom   Grange-over-Sands

Ulverston   Kirkby Lonsdale

Dalton-in-Furness   Cartmel

Newbiggin

Lancaster

CHESHIRE,
LANCASHIRE,
ISLE OF MAN
(plan 20)

Blackpool

Preston

Place with at least:

- • a hotel or a restaurant
- ❀ a starred establishment
- 😊 a "Bib Gourmand" restaurant
- 🏠 a "Bib Hôtel"
- ✗ a particularly pleasant restaurant
- ⛺ a particularly pleasant guesthouse
- 🏠 a particularly pleasant hotel
- 🌲 a particularly quiet hotel
- 🍺 a particularly pleasant pub

BORDERS,
DINBURGH & GLASGOW
(plans 25 26)

Berwick-upon-Tweed

Cornhill-on-Tweed

Belford

Bamburgh Castle
Seahouses
Beadnell

Wooler

Jedburgh

Alnwick

Rothbury

Warkworth

Eshott

Longhorsley

Kirkwhelpington

Morpeth

Kielder Resr.

Stannersburn

North Tyne

NORTHUMBERLAND

Matfen

Seaton Burn

Ponteland

Cobalt Business Park

Gilsland

Gosforth

Tynemouth

Hexham

Heddon on the Wall

Newcastle-upon-Tyne

Haltwhistle

Corbridge

Gateshead

Hedley on the Hill

Derwent

Sunderland

Carterway Heads

Chester-le-Street

DURHAM

Seaham

Cowshill

Eastgate

Wear

Durham

Middleton-in-Teesdale

Spennymoor

CUMBRIA
(plan 21)

Romaldkirk

Headlam

Barnard Castle

Stockton-on-Tees

Middlesbrough

Hutton Magna

Yarm

Guisborough

NORTH YORKSHIRE
(plans 22 23)

Swale

Thirsk

Ripon

A1

A68

A69

A66

A19

of Forth

Teviot

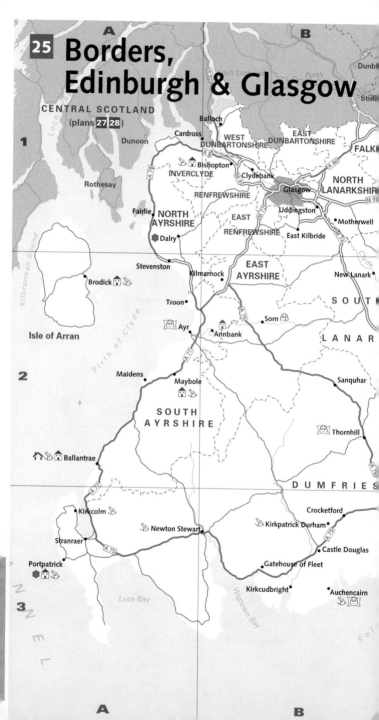

CENTRAL SCOTLAND
(plans **27 28**)

Loch Lomond

Dunoon

Balloch

Cardross

WEST
DUNBARTONSHIRE

EAST
DUNBARTONSHIRE

Dunb

Forth

Stirli

FALK

Rothesay

Bishopton

INVERCLYDE

Clydebank

RENFREWSHIRE

Glasgow

Uddingston

NORTH
LANARKSHIRE

M 9

Fairlie

NORTH
AYRSHIRE

EAST
RENFREWSHIRE

East Kilbride

Motherwell

Dalry

Stevenston

Kilmarnock

EAST
AYRSHIRE

New Lanark

SOUT

Isle of Arran

Brodick

Troon

Ayr

Annbank

Sorn

LANAR

Kilbrannan Sound

Firth of Clyde

Maidens

Maybole

SOUTH
AYRSHIRE

Sanquhar

Thornhill

Ballantrae

DUMFRIES

Kirkcolm

Newton Stewart

Crocketford

Kirkpatrick Durham

Stranraer

A 75

Castle Douglas

Portpatrick

Gatehouse of Fleet

Luce Bay

Kirkcudbright

Auchencairn

Wigtown Bay

Sol

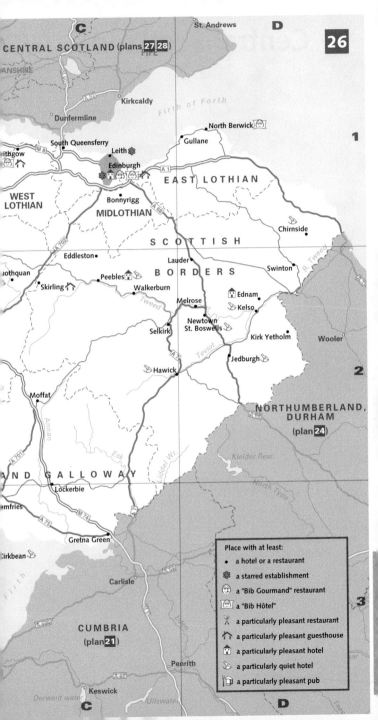

St. Andrews

26

CENTRAL SCOTLAND (plans 27 28)

ANSHIRE

FIFE

Kirkcaldy

Firth of Forth

Dunfermline

North Berwick

South Queensferry

Gullane

Leith

ithgow

Edinburgh

EAST LOTHIAN

M 8

WEST
LOTHIAN

Bonnyrigg

A 1

MIDLOTHIAN

A 68

Chirnside

Eddleston

S C O T T I S H

Lauder

R. Tweed

othquan

A 702

Peebles

B O R D E R S

Swinton

Skirling

Walkerburn

Tweed

Melrose

Ednam

Kelso

Selkirk

Newtown
St. Boswells

Teviot

Kirk Yetholm

Wooler

Hawick

Jedburgh

2

Moffat

NORTHUMBERLAND,
DURHAM
(plan 24)

A 7

Esk

Liddel Wr.

Kielder Resr.

A 68

North Tyne

AND G A L L O W A Y

Lockerbie

A 701

mfries

Annan

A 75

Gretna Green

M 74

irkbean

Firth

Carlisle

A 69

3

CUMBRIA
(plan 21)

M 6

Penrith

A 66

Keswick

Derwent water

Ullswater

C

D

Place with at least:

•	a hotel or a restaurant
✿	a starred establishment
😊	a "Bib Gourmand" restaurant
🏨	a "Bib Hôtel"
🗡	a particularly pleasant restaurant
🏠	a particularly pleasant guesthouse
🏨	a particularly pleasant hotel
🛏	a particularly quiet hotel
🍺	a particularly pleasant pub

A
B

Sgurr
Snizort
The Little
Loch Maree
Loch Fannich

HIGHLAND & THE ISLANDS
(plans 29 30)

1

SEA OF
THE HEBRIDES

Isle of Skye

Kyle of
Lochalsh

Loch Bracadale
Cuillin Sound
Sound of Raasay
Loch Torridon
Sound of Sleat

Loch Quoich
Loch Arkaig
Loch Lochy
Loch Morar
Sound of Arisaig

Loch Shiel
Fort William
Caledonian

Backwater Resr

Tobermory

Sound of Mull
Isle of Mull

Port Appin
Eriska
Fasnacloich
Rann
Stati

2

Gruline
Craignure
Connel
Loch Etive

Tiroran
Oban
Ki

Bunessan
Clacham-Seil
Kilchrenan
ARGYLL
AND
BUTE
Balquhidd

Isle of Seil
Loch Awe
Strathy

Arduaine
STIRLIN

Scalasaig
Colonsay
Crinan
Strachur
Tarbet

Bellanoch
Lochgilphead
Loch Lom

Tayvallich
Ardrishaig
Luss

Isle of Jura
Tighnabruaich
Dunoon
Killearr

Ballygrant
Greenock

Port Charlotte
Kilberry
Ascog

Bowmore
Isle
of Bute

Isle of Islay
Gigha
Peninsula

Port Ellen
of

Carradale

Kintyre

Kilmarnock

EAS

3

Isle
of Arran

Firth of Clyde

Ayr

NORTHERN
IRELAND
(plans 34 35)

BORDERS,
EDINBURGH
& GLASGOW
(plans 25 26)

Coleraine

A
B

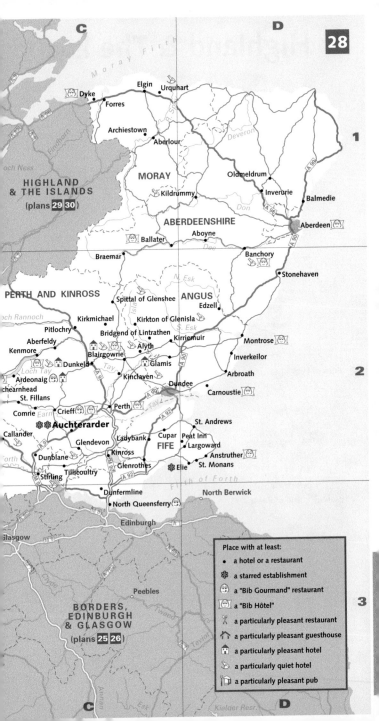

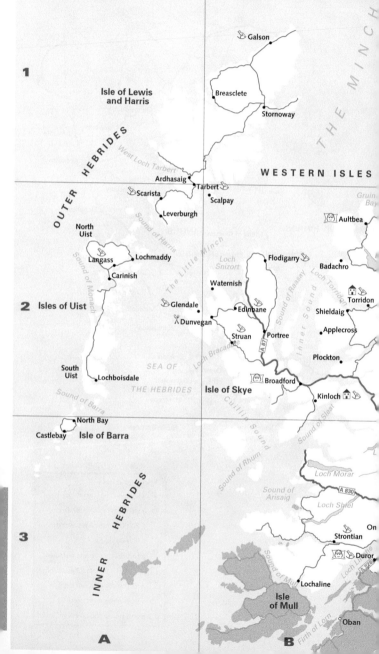

Isle of Lewis and Harris

Galson

Breasclete

Stornoway

THE MINCH

WESTERN ISLES

OUTER HEBRIDES

West Loch Tarbert

Ardhasaig

Tarbert

Scarista

Scalpay

Leverburgh

Sound of Harris

North Uist

Langass

Lochmaddy

Carinish

Isles of Uist

Sound of Monach

The Little Minch

Glendale

Waternish

Loch Snizort

Flodigarry

Gruin Bay

Aultbea

Badachro

Torridon

Loch Torridon

Sound of Raasay

Edinbane

Dunvegan

Struan

Portree

A 87

Shieldaig

Applecross

Inner Sound

Loch Bracadale

SEA OF

South Uist

Lochboisdale

THE HEBRIDES

Isle of Skye

Broadford

Plockton

Kinloch

Cuillin Sound

Sound of Barra

North Bay

Castlebay

Isle of Barra

Sound of Sleat

Sound of Rhum

Loch Morar

A 830

INNER HEBRIDES

Sound of Arisaig

Loch Shiel

Strontian

Duror

Sound of Mull

Lochaline

Isle of Mull

Oban

Firth of Lorn

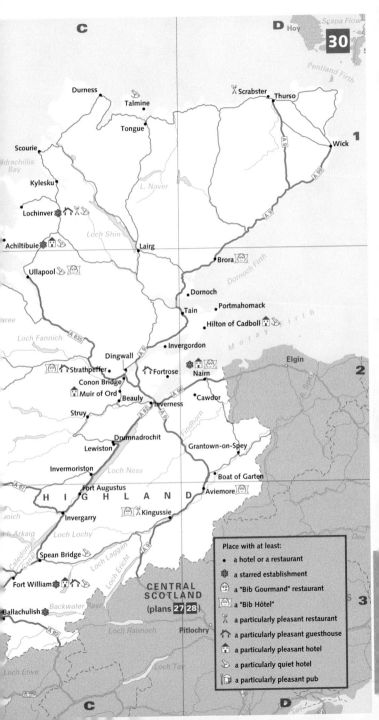

Shetland & Orkney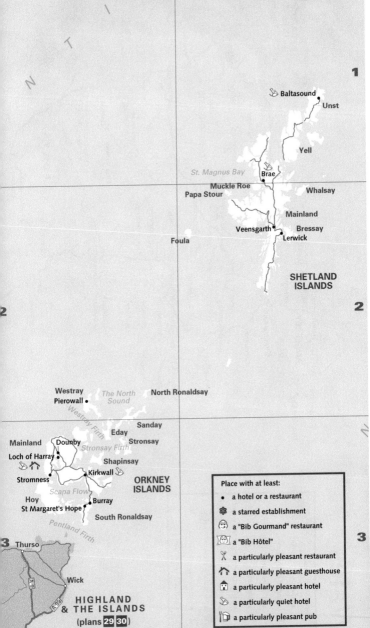

A **B**

1

🐦 Baltasound

Unst

Yell

St. Magnus Bay

🐦 Brae

Muckle Roe   Whalsay
Papa Stour

Mainland

Veensgarth •   Bressay
Lerwick

Foula

**SHETLAND
ISLANDS**

2 **2**

Westray   *The North*   North Ronaldsay
Pierowall •   *Sound*

Westray Firth

Sanday
Eday
Mainland   Dounby   Stronsay
Loch of Harray   *Stronsay Firth*
🐦 ⌂
Shapinsay
Stromness   Kirkwall 🐦

**ORKNEY
ISLANDS**

Hoy   *Scapa Flow*
St Margaret's Hope •   • Burray

Pentland Firth   South Ronaldsay

Place with at least:

•	a hotel or a restaurant
❋	a starred establishment
😊	a "Bib Gourmand" restaurant
🛏	a "Bib Hôtel"
✕	a particularly pleasant restaurant
⌂	a particularly pleasant guesthouse
🏠	a particularly pleasant hotel
🐦	a particularly quiet hotel
🍺	a particularly pleasant pub

3   Thurso

• Wick

**HIGHLAND
& THE ISLANDS**
(plans **29** **30**)

A   **B**

Wales

Place with at least:

- a hotel or a restaurant
- ❀ a starred establishment
- 🖼 a "Bib Gourmand" restaurant
- 🏨 a "Bib Hôtel"
- ✕ a particularly pleasant restaurant
- ⛌ a particularly pleasant guesthouse
- 🏯 a particularly pleasant hotel
- 🍃 a particularly quiet hotel
- 🍺 a particularly pleasant pub

32

CHESHIRE, LANCASHIRE, ISLE OF MAN (plan 20)

Liverpool
Birkenhead
Liverpool Bay

C

Chester
Hawarden
Wrexham

FLINTSHIRE
Mold
Nannerch
Ruthin
Tremeirchion
Llandyrnog
Rhyl

DENBIGHSHIRE
Colwyn Bay
Llansanffraid Glan Conwy
Conwy
Llandudno
Betws-y-Coed
Tal y Llyn

B

Cemaes
Holyhead
Trearddur Bay
Llanerchymedd
Benllech
Beaumaris

ANGLESEY

Menai Bridge
Caernarfon
Betws Garmon
Clynnog-Fawr
Boduan
Pwllheli
Abersoch
Bwlchtocyn

Beddgelert
Criccieth
Portmeirion
Porthmadog
Harlech
Llanbedr
Llanaber
Abermaw
Aberdovey

CONWY
Penmachno
Llan Ffestiniog

GWYNEDD
Talsarnau
Llanuwchllyn
Dolgellau
Machynlleth

Llangollen
Llandrillo
Llanarmon Dyffryn Ceiriog
Llanfyllin
Lake Vyrnwy
Llanfihangel-yng-Ngwynfa

POWYS
Pontdolgoch
Caersws
Dolfor

HEREFORDSHIRE, WORCESTERSHIRE, SHROPSHIRE, STAFFORDSHIRE, WARWICKSHIRE (plans 18, 19)

Shrewsbury
Montgomery

Caernarfon Bay

CHANNEL

A

1

2

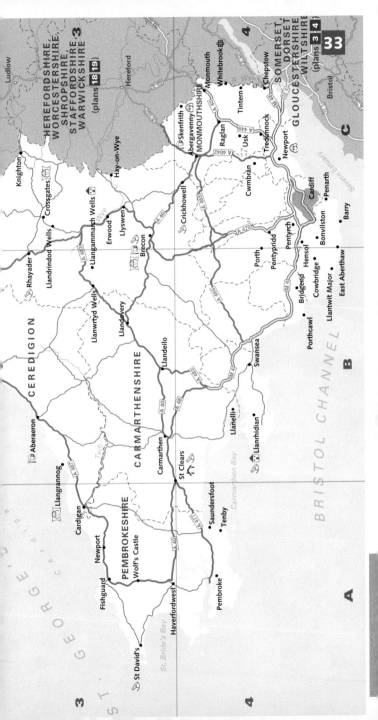

33

HEREFORDSHIRE,
WORCESTERSHIRE,
SHROPSHIRE,
STAFFORDSHIRE,
WARWICKSHIRE **3**
(plans **18 19**)

SOMERSET,
DORSET,
WILTSHIRE **3 4**
(plans **3 4**)

GLOUCESTERSHIRE

Ludlow

Knighton

Crossgates

Rhayader

Llandrindod Wells

Llangammarch Wells

Llanwrtyd Wells

Erwood

Llyswen

Hay-on-Wye

Hereford

Brecon

Crickhowell

Abergavenny

Skenfrith

Monmouth

Whitebrook

Tintern

Raglan

Chepstow

Bristol

Usk

Tredunnock

Newport

Cwmbrân

Cardiff

Penarth

Barry

Bonvilston

East Aberthaw

Llantwit Major

Cowbridge

Bridgend

Hensol

Pentyrch

Pontypridd

Porth

Porthcawl

Swansea

Llanelli

Llanrhidian

Llandeilo

Llandovery

Llandrindod Wells

CARMARTHENSHIRE

CEREDIGION

Aberaeron

Llangrannog

Cardigan

Newport

Fishguard

St David's

Haverfordwest

Pembroke

Tenby

Saundersfoot

St Clears

Carmarthen

Wolf's Castle

PEMBROKESHIRE

MONMOUTHSHIRE

ST. GEORGE'S CHANNEL

St. Bride's Bay

Carmarthen Bay

BRISTOL CHANNEL

Severn Estuary

A 40

A 483

A 470

A 465

M 4

A 48

A 477

A 40

A 449

A 4042

3 **C**

B

4 **A**

34 Northern Ireland

Place with at least:
- • a hotel or a restaurant
- ✿ a starred establishment
- 😊 a "Bib Gourmand" restaurant
- 🏨 a "Bib Hôtel"
- ✕ a particularly pleasant restaurant
- ↑ a particularly pleasant guesthouse
- 🏠 a particularly pleasant hotel
- ⑤ a particularly quiet hotel
- 📱 a particularly pleasant pub

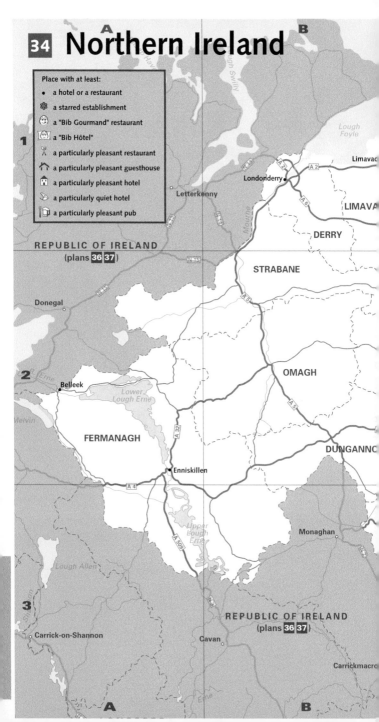

Lough Foyle

Limavac

Londonderry

Letterkenny

LIMAVA

DERRY

STRABANE

REPUBLIC OF IRELAND
(plans 36 37)

Donegal

OMAGH

Belleek

Lower Lough Erne

FERMANAGH

DUNGANNC

Enniskillen

Upper Lough Erne

Monaghan

Lough Allen

Carrick-on-Shannon

REPUBLIC OF IRELAND
(plans 36 37)

Cavan

Carrickmacro

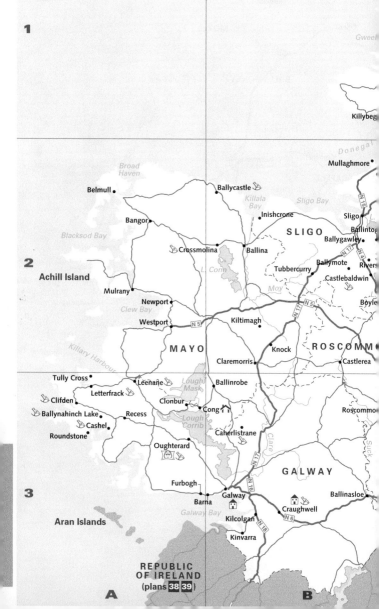

REPUBLIC
OF IRELAND
(plans 38 39)

37

Place with at least:
- • a hotel or a restaurant
- ✿ a starred establishment
- 🙂 a "Bib Gourmand" restaurant
- 🙂 a "Bib Hôtel"
- ✗ a particularly pleasant restaurant
- ⋔ a particularly pleasant guesthouse
- 🏠 a particularly pleasant hotel
- ⌂ a particularly quiet hotel
- ▯ a particularly pleasant pub

Dunfanaghy
Gweedore
eg
Redcastle
Rathmullan
Ballyliffin
Lough Swilly
Sneep Haven
Rathmelton
Letterkenny
Londonderry
Lough Foyle
Carrigans
Mourne
DONEGAL
Ballybofey
Donegal
kineely
Rossnowlagh
ndoran
nlough
Lower Lough Erne
Melvin
NORTHERN IRELAND
(plans 34 35)
Blacklion
Enniskillen
Upper Lough Erne
Armagh
yfarnan
Lough Allen
Drumshanbo
Ballyconnell
Keshcarrigan
Killashandra
Carrick-on-Shannon
Cavan
LEITRIM
MONAGHAN
Monaghan
Carrickmacross
Carlingford Lough
Carlingford
Dundalk
Dundalk bay
CAVAN
Erne
L. Sheelin
onbarry
Longford
LONGFORD
Castlepollard
Carnaross
LOUTH
Lough Ree
L. Derravaragh
Drogheda
Bettystown
Royal Canal
Navan
Boyne
Athlone
Moate
Mullingar
WEST MEATH
Kinnegad
MEATH
Trim
Kilmessan
Dunsany
Ashbourne
Dunboyne
Tullamore
Dublin
REPUBLIC OF IRELAND
(plans 38 39)
Grand Canal
Grand
Naas
Poulaphouca Resr

REPUBLIC
OF IRELAND
(plans **36 37**)

A

B

Killa

Clifden

Lough
Mask

Lough
Corrib

Clare

Galway

Galway Bay

Inishmore

Aran Islands

Ballyvaughan

Doolin

Lisdoonvarna

Liscannor

Ennistimon

Lahinch

Corrofin

Spanish Point

Milltown Malbay

Ennis

CLARE

Kilkee

Newmarket on Fergus

Killal

Shannon

Bunratty

River Shannon

Limeri

N 18

Mouth of
the Shannon

Ballybunnion

Glin

Adare

N 20

N 21

Listowel

LIMERICK

Tralee
Bay

Ballingarry

Castlegregory

Ballydavid

Charleville

Kilmallo

Ballyferriter

Tralee

N 21

N 22

Dingle

Killorglin

N 23

**Valencia
Island**

Caragh
Lake

Killarney

Kanturk

Mallow

Knight's Town

Cahersiveen

KERRY

CORK

Blackwate

Castle

Portmagee

Sneem

Kenmare

Macroom

Tower

Blarney

Waterville

Parknasila

Tahilla

Cork

Caherdaniel

Lee

Ballincollig

N 22

N 20

N 2

Castletownbere

Ballylickey

Bantry

Bandon

Carrigaline

Bantry Bay

Durrus

Bandon

Kilbrittain

Kinsale

Dunmanus Bay

Toormore

Clonakilty

Monks

Crookhaven

Baltimore

Castletownshend

Roaringwater Bay

C

E

L

T

A

B

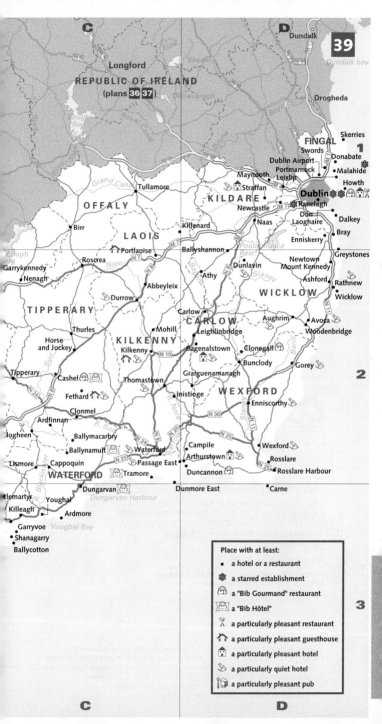

Great Britain : Based on the Ordnance Survey of Great Britain with the permission of the Controller of Her Majesty's Stationery's Office © Crown Copyright 100000247

Northern Ireland : Reproduced from the OSNI map with the permission of the Controller of HMSO © Crown Copyright 2009 Permit Number 80161

Ireland : Based on Ordnance Survey Ireland Permit No. 8509 © Ordnance Survey Ireland / Government of Ireland

Cover photographs :
HAUSER / Jupiterimages and Ludovic Maisant / Hemis / Corbis (interior designer : Stephen Ryan)

Manufacture française des pneumatiques Michelin

Société en commandite par actions au capital de 304 000 000 EUR.
Place des Carmes-Déchaux – 63 Clermont-Ferrand (France)
R.C.S. Clermont-Fd B 855 200 507

© 2009 Michelin, Propriétaires-Éditeurs
Dépôt légal Janvier 2009

Printed in Belgium 12-08

No part of of this publication may be reproduced in any form without the prior permission of the publisher.

Compogravure : A.P.S.-Chromostyle, 37000 TOURS

Impression : CASTERMAN, Tournai (Belgique)

Reliure : S.I.R.C., Marigny-le-Châtel

Our editorial team has taken the greatest care in writing this guide and checking the information in it. However, practical information (prices, addresses, telephone numbers, internet addresses, etc) is subject to frequent change and such information should therefore be used for guidance only. It is possible that some of the information in this guide may not be accurate or exhaustive as at the date of publication. We therefore accept no liability in regard to such information.

CROSSMOLINA (Crois Mhaoilíona) – **Mayo** – **712** E 5 – **pop. 930**   36 **B2**

Ireland

> ▶ Dublin 252 km – Ballina 10 km
>
> ◉ Errew Abbey★, SE : 9½ km by R 315. Cáide Fields★ **AC**, N : 24 km by R 315 and R 314 W – Killala★, NE : 16 km by R 315 and minor road – Moyne Abbey★, NE : 18 km by R 115, minor road to Killala, R 314 and minor road – Rosserk Abbey★, NE : 18 km by R 115, minor road to Killala, R 314 and minor road

🏠 **Enniscoe House** ⌇   ⟨ 🚘 🌐 ⌇ **P** 𝘝𝘐𝘚𝘈 ◍

Castlehill, South : 3¼ km on R 315 – 𝒞 (096) 31 112 – www.enniscoe.com – mail@enniscoe.com – Fax (096) 31 773 – Closed 7 January - 31 March
6 rm ⌂ – †€ 128/140 ††€ 216/240
Rest – (dinner only) (booking essential for non-residents) Menu € 40/50
♦ Georgian manor, overlooking Lough Conn, on Enniscoe estate with walled garden and heritage centre. Hallway boasts original family tree; antique beds in flower-filled rooms. Home cooked country dishes served in the dining room.

DALKEY (Deilginis) – **Dún Laoghaire-Rathdown** – **712** N 8 *Ireland*   39 **D1**

> ▶ Dublin 13 km – Bray 9 km
>
> ◉ Killiney Bay (⟨★★), S : by coast road

✗✗ **Jaipur**   **AC** 𝘝𝘐𝘚𝘈 ◍ **AE**

21 Castle St – 𝒞 (01) 285 0552 – www.jaipur.ie – dalkey@jaipur.ie – Fax (01) 284 0900 – Closed 25 December
Rest – Indian – (dinner only) Carte € 28/56
♦ Central location and smart, lively, brightly coloured, modern décor. Well-spaced, linen-clad tables. Warm, friendly ambience. Contemporary Indian dishes.

DINGLE – **Kerry** – **712** B 11 – **pop. 1 772** *Ireland*   38 **A2**

> ▶ Dublin 347 km – Killarney 82 km – Limerick 153 km
>
> 🛈 The Quay 𝒞 (066) 9151188, dingletio@eircom.net
>
> ◎ Town★ – St Mary's Church★ – Diseart (stained glass★ **AC**)
>
> ◉ Gallarus Oratory★★, NW : 8 km by R 559 – NE : Connor Pass★★ – Kilmalkedar★, NW : 9 km by R 559. Dingle Peninsula★★ – Connor Pass★★, NE : 8 km by minor road – Stradbally Strand★★, NE : 17 km via Connor Pass – Corca Dhuibhne Regional Museum★ **AC**, NW : 13 km by R 559 – Blasket Islands★, W : 21 km by R 559 and ferry from Dunquin

Plan opposite

🏯 **Dingle Skellig** ⌇   ⟨ 🚘 🌐 ◍ 🛠 𝕝♨ 🏊 ᕻ rm, 🚶 ❊ (¹) 🎿 **P**
– 𝒞 (066) 915 02 00 – www.dingleskellig.com   𝘝𝘐𝘚𝘈 ◍ **AE** ⓪
– reservations@dingleskellig.com – Fax (066) 915 15 01
– Closed 21-27 December   Y**e**
111 rm ⌂ – †€ 90/155 ††€ 150/250 – 2 suites
Rest – (bar lunch) Menu € 45
♦ Large purpose-built hotel with views of Dingle Bay. Interior decorated in a modern style with good levels of comfort: the smartest executive rooms are on the third floor. Restaurant makes most of sea and harbour view.

🏨 **Benners** without rest   🛗 ❊ **P** 𝘝𝘐𝘚𝘈 ◍ **AE** ⓪
Main St – 𝒞 (066) 915 16 38 – www.dinglebenners.com
– info@dinglebenners.com – Fax (066) 915 14 12 – Closed Christmas   Z**b**
52 rm ⌂ – †€ 85/127 ††€ 120/210
♦ Traditional-style property located on town's main street. Comfortable public areas include lounge bar and guest's sitting room. Rooms in extension have a more modern feel.

🏠 **Emlagh Country House** without rest   ⟨ 🚘 🛗 ᕻ **AC** ❊ (¹) **P**
– 𝒞 (066) 915 23 45 – www.emlaghhouse.com   𝘝𝘐𝘚𝘈 ◍ **AE**
– info@emlaghhouse.com – Fax (066) 915 23 69 – 15 March-October   Y**d**
10 rm ⌂ – †€ 125/185 ††€ 190/380
♦ Modern hotel in Georgian style. Inviting lounge with a log fire and well-fitted, antique furnished bedrooms: the colours and artwork of each are inspired by a local flower.

X **Cafe Paradiso** with rm   📶 VISA ⓜⓞ AE
16 Lancaster Quay, Western Rd – 𝒞 (021) 427 79 39 – www.cafeparadiso.ie
– info@cafeparadiso.ie – Closed 1 week Christmas, Sunday and Monday   Z**o**
3 rm ⌑ – ♦€160 ♦♦€160
Rest – Vegetarian – (booking essential) Carte €29/48
♦ A growing following means booking is essential at this relaxed vegetarian restaurant. Colourful and inventive international combinations; blackboard list of organic wines. Spacious bedrooms in bright colours; the back one is the quietest.

X **Fenn's Quay**   AC VISA ⓜⓞ AE
5 Sheares St – 𝒞 (021) 427 95 27 – www.fennsquay.ie – polary@eircom.net
– Fax (021) 427 95 26   Z**n**
Rest – Carte €29/47
♦ In a renovated 18C terrace in historic part of the city, this informal café-restaurant boasts modern art on display. Popular for mid-morning coffees and, light lunches.

at Cork Airport South : 6½ km by N 27 - X - ✉ Cork

🏨 **International Airport**   📶 ⓖ rm, AC ⚑ ☏ 🛗 P VISA ⓜⓞ AE
– 𝒞 (021) 454 9800 – www.corkinternationalairporthotel.com
– info@corkairporthotel.com – Fax (021) 454 9999 – Closed 25 December
146 rm ⌑ – ♦€120/170 ♦♦€130/400   **Rest** – (carvery lunch) Carte €33/48
♦ Quirky hotel with aviation theme and various eateries. Decently-sized bedrooms come in Economy, Business and First Class. The superb Pullman lounge resembles cabin of a plane. Modern restaurant with interesting smoking terrace.

at Little Island East : 8½ km by N 25 - X - and R 623 – ✉ Cork

🏨 **Radisson SAS**   🛋 ☂ 📺 ⊕ 🛁 🏊 🛗 ⓖ rm, AC rest, ⚑ 📶 🛗 P
Ditchley House – 𝒞 (021) 429 70 00   VISA ⓜⓞ AE ①
– www.cork.radissonsas.com – info.cork@radissonsas.com – Fax (021) 429 71 01
120 rm ⌑ – ♦€130/165 ♦♦€140/185 – 9 suites
Rest *The Island Grill Room* – (closed Saturday lunch) (buffet lunch)
Menu €22/45 – Carte €35/53
♦ Opened in 2005 around the core of an 18C house: stylish and open-plan. Superbly equipped spa. Modish rooms in two themes: choose from Urban or highly individual Ocean! Island Grill Room serves an eclectic range of dishes.

CORK AIRPORT Cork – 712 G 12 – see Cork

CORROFIN – Clare – 712 E 9   38 **B1**
▶ Dublin 228 km – Gort 24 km – Limerick 51 km

🏠 **Fergus View** without rest   ≤ 🛋 ⚑ P
Kilnaboy, North : 3¼ km on R 476 – 𝒞 (065) 683 76 06 – www.fergusview.com
– deckell@indigo.ie – Fax (065) 683 70 83 – March-October
6 rm ⌑ – ♦€54 ♦♦€156
♦ Originally built for the owner's grandfather as a schoolhouse, with good countryside views. Conservatory entrance into cosy lounge with piles of books. Pristine bedrooms.

CROOKHAVEN (An Cruachán) – Cork – 712 C 13   38 **A3**
▶ Dublin 373 km – Bantry 40 km – Cork 120 km

🏠 **Galley Cove House** without rest ⚓   ≤ 🛋 ⚑ P VISA ⓜⓞ
West : ¾ km on R 591 – 𝒞 (028) 35 137 – www.galleycovehouse.com
– info@galleycovehouse.com – Fax (028) 35 137 – 14 March- 1 November
4 rm ⌑ – ♦€45/60 ♦♦€80/100
♦ Perched overlooking eponymous bay and its pleasant harbour. Conservatory breakfast room has bamboo seating. Rooms are neat and tidy, and enhanced by colourful fabrics.

REPUBLIC OF IRELAND